The Sloane-Dorland Annotated Medical-Legal Dictionary

The Sloane-Dorland Annotated Medical-Legal Dictionary

Richard Sloane
Professor of Law Emeritus
University of Pennsylvania Law School
Member of the New York Bar

West Publishing Company
St. Paul   New York   Los Angeles   San Francisco

COPYRIGHT © 1987   By WEST PUBLISHING COMPANY
50 West Kellogg Boulevard
P.O. Box 64526
St. Paul, MN 55164–1003

Library of Congress Cataloging-in-Publication Data
Sloane, Richard, 1916–
    The Sloane-Dorland annotated medical-legal
dictionary.

    1. Medical jurisprudence—Dictionaries.   2. Medicine
—Dictionaries.   I. Title.

RA1017.S56   1987   614'.1'0321   86–28245
ISBN   0–314–93512–6

Preface

The unique feature of this dictionary is that it combines established definitions of medical terms with judicial interpretations of the same terms. These are drawn from court opinions, the testimony of medical experts, and extracts of lawyers' briefs found in those opinions.

Definitional Levels

This dictionary provides three levels of legal definitions:

- *First Level:* A straightforward definition, viz., *diuresis,* "the washing of salt and water out of the body by urinary excretion."
- *Second Level:* An explanation of a term by showing how a process works, viz., *diuretic,* "the use of a *diuretic,* such as Enduron, which causes the body to lose fluids, may also cause an imbalance."
- *Third Level:* The use of a term in context, viz., *cancerphobia,* "She had an overwhelming *cancerphobia* and in view of her limited life expectancy I see no reason to burden her with this further fear."

Value to Lawyers

Legal research is a matter of matching the facts in an existing problem with the solutions arrived at in similar problems. Through definitions of terms, this book shows how lawyers have handled a myriad of diverse matters. Lawyers should look particularly for the following language that judges tend to use when they are about to reach a decision: "The evidence shows . . ." or "The expert testimony establishes. . ."

The kind of evidence that persuades a judge may be the most valuable feature of this book for lawyers.

Value to Doctors, Dentists, and Members of Allied Professions

Nothing is more useful—and comforting—than to find other doctors and dentists in identical or near identical situations. It is useful to learn that courts appreciate the difficulty of diagnosing appendicitis, how often an impacted wisdom tooth extraction results in a fractured jaw, and how rarely they will decide a medical issue without listening to a medical expert.

Value to the General Public

The fascination that medicine holds for everyone is evidenced by the popularity of medical programs that one sees on television. That prime time is given to the birth of a baby or the implantation of a heart is evidence enough of the grip that those subjects have on many people. Prospective patients may want to learn more about a particular operation, medical procedure, or new drug before submitting to treatment. This dictionary describes the making and fitting of contact lenses. It takes the reader through a hip replacement operation. It provides simple answers to a host of basic medical questions.

Standard of Care

Most medical cases turn on whether or not a doctor met the medical standard of his community, similar community, state, or specialty. A section of this dictionary under the heading, *care, standard of,* contains extracts from decisions that spell out the particular standards for doctors, specialists, dentists, anesthesiologists, nurses, and hospitals in a variety of situations.

Informed Consent

Similarly, it is essential to know in many cases whether or not a patient was "informed" and "consented" to a particular form of treatment or surgery. Cases on this subject are collected under the heading, *consent, informed.* The definition of "informed consent" varies widely and the dictionary provides a broad range of definitions for jurisdictions across the country.

Use of Full Opinions

The dictionary includes extracts from cases that most clearly explain the use of particular medical terms. Copies of the full opinions can be found in most court, county, bar association, and law school libraries as well as in the larger law offices.

Use of Briefs

Trial and appellate briefs are on file in the courts where cases were decided and can usually be obtained from court clerks for the cost of copying. In addition, the lawyers who appear for either plaintiffs or defendants usually keep duplicate files of their own briefs. Their names are listed in the court reports directly after the headnotes of the West reporters and above the judge's name in each case. A brief will often contain fuller treatment of a medical term than is found in the court's opinion.

Cross-References

Many hundreds of cross-references tie together seemingly unrelated terms and help clarify the meaning of each.

Bibliographies

Short bibliographical notes complement the definitions of a few hundred terms in the dictionary. They include additional court decisions and the writings of authorities. Some examples: *obesity, death, euthanasia, life-sustaining equipment, marijuana.*

Experts

The testimony of experts appears throughout the book. It is used to amplify the meaning of medical terms and not infrequently the cases turn on their testimony. The effectiveness of an expert on the witness stand is crucial, and the selection of an expert is often made both on his paper credentials and how well he "stood up" under hostile cross-examination. This book contains numerous examples.

New Terms

Medicine is a rapidly changing profession. New diseases are being discovered and cured, new terms coined. The most recent disease awaiting a cure appears to be AIDS. The most recently coined term that I know of is in space medicine: *extraterrestrial exposure.* Both terms have a place in the dictionary. As other terms are coined, a supplement will collect them.

Reversed or Remanded Cases

A number of lower court decisions that are cited in the dictionary have been reversed or remanded on appeal. The lower court definitions have been retained wherever the appellate rulings do not touch on those definitions, but deal with unrelated issues.

Spelling

The court opinions have been quoted verbatim. Retained are the occasional misspellings that are found in the court reports.

Summary

This dictionary is based on reading some 20,000 medical cases in the various federal and state jurisdictions of the United States during the past ten years.

Selected for inclusion are the problem cases. One comes away from reading them, not with a lopsided view of the medical profession because something went wrong, but with a wholesome regard for those who tried and for the many who succeeded.

That other doctors fail and some are careless are facts for which the law may have a remedy. Part of each remedy is the judge's decision. In the course of his deliberations a judge often gives new insights into the meaning of medical terms. Whenever he does, extracts from his opinions have been quoted. They provide the annotations that form the heart of this book.

This dictionary is more than a compendium of words. It is a dramatic record of medical and legal lexicography set in a courtroom rather than on a stage.

Richard Sloane
Philadelphia, Pennsylvania
January 1, 1987

Acknowledgments

It was Robert B. Rowan, then acting head of W. B. Saunders Company in Philadelphia, with whom I first discussed my idea for an annotated medical legal dictionary. It was he too who helped provide the medical basis for it—*Dorland's Illustrated Medical Dictionary*—and who briefed me on the rudiments of medical lexicography.

Librarians in five libraries were tireless in helping to locate source materials:

- *Biddle Law Library at the University of Pennsylvania Law School in Philadelphia*— Nancy Irvin Arnold, then reference librarian, gave constant help, support, and encouragement. Ronald E. Day, former documents librarian and now reference librarian, kept watch for congressional documents and regulatory papers. Cynthia R. Arkin, associate librarian, gave support at all times. Kenneth Funderburk, Barbara English-Scott, and Harvey Sudler cooperated to the full. To my successor as library director, Professor Elizabeth Slusser Kelly, and her entire staff, I am indebted for continued support and assistance.

- *Van Pelt Library, the University's main library*—Warm thanks are due Jane G. Bryan, reference librarian, and Carl Jankiewicz at circulation, for their unstinting help.

- *Biomedical Library, the University's Medical School Library*—Eleanor Y. Goodchild, then librarian and now at Stanford University, together with her entire staff cooperated at each stage of the work. I am particularly grateful to Dr. Mary C. Berwick, Holly Lucas, Judie Malamud, and Linda Rosenstein.

- *Academy of Medicine Library and New York Public Library Reference Department, both in New York*—Their staffs gave valuable assistance, particularly in helping to locate official publications relating to asbestos and asbestosis.

My personal assistant, Edwin C. Clark, worked closely with me during his four undergraduate years at Penn and after graduation. His command of medical terminology and his work on the final manuscript were of enormous help. He is now engaged in enzyme research at the University. Kimberly Funderburk, now on the library staff at Thomas Jefferson University Hospital in Philadelphia, worked skillfully with me on the dictionary for two years, as did Cindy Marshall, my former secretary.

I am grateful to many people at West Publishing Company for their help and cooperation. My editor, Theresa J. Lippert, gave wise counsel and provided many thoughtful suggestions. Her encouragement has been constant. I have drawn on the skills of Laura J. Carlson in her capacity as production editor on numerous occasions during the past year. To Mary Jo Bjork and Melanie Vogel I owe thanks for manuscript preparation work, as well as to Rolin Graphics for skillful art contributions. To the many other careful hands and eyes at West who participated in this work I express my gratitude.

I want also to thank Harold Cramer and Alan C. Kessler of Philadelphia for their keen advice and generous support.

To my closest friends, whom the dictionary work has often seemed to supplant during the past ten years, I am grateful for their forbearance.

The Sloane-Dorland Annotated Medical-Legal Dictionary

A

abandonment (anesthesiologist) See *anesthesiologist* (Medvecz case).

abdomen (ab-do'men) [L., possibly from *abdere* to hide] that portion of the body which lies between the thorax and the pelvis; called also *venter*. It contains a cavity (*abdominal cavity*) separated by the diaphragm from the thoracic cavity, and lined with a serous membrane, the peritoneum. This cavity contains the viscera (see illustration accompanying *viscera*) and is enclosed by a wall (*abdominal wall* or *parietes*) formed by the abdominal muscles, vertebral column, and the ilia. It is divided into nine regions by four imaginary lines, of which two pass horizontally around the body (the upper at the level of the cartilages of the ninth ribs, the lower at the tops of the crests of the ilia), and two extend vertically on each side of the body from the cartilage of the eighth rib to the center of the inguinal ligament, as in A. The regions are: three upper—right hypochondriac, epigastric, left hypochondriac; three middle—right lateral, umbilical, left lateral; and three lower—right inguinal, pubic, left inguinal. Called also *belly*.

abdomen, acute an abdominal condition of abrupt onset usually associated with abdominal pain due to inflammation, perforation, obstruction, infarction, or rupture of intra-abdominal organs. Emergency surgical intervention is usually required. Examples are acute cholecystitis or appendicitis, perforated peptic ulcer, strangulated hernia, superior mesenteric artery thrombosis, and splenic rupture. Called also *surgical a.*

Dr. Abramson felt at the time that the patient now had a "surgical abdomen," which is an **acute condition of the abdomen** in which there is tenderness, pain and muscle rigidity. Babin v. St. Paul Fire and Marine Ins. Co., 385 So.2d 849, 853 (Ct. App.La.1980).

abduct (ab-dukt') [*ab-* + L. *ducere* to draw] to draw away from the median plane or (in the digits) from the axial line of a limb.

By November, 1977, he had shown some improvement but had marked limitation of motion of the left upper extremity demonstrated by his inability to **abduct** beyond 45° as compared to normal **abduction** of above 90°. When Dr. Horn next saw plaintiff in June, 1978, his range of motion was still limited in the left shoulder. Brown v. Celotex Corp., 420 So.2d 205, 207 (Ct.App.La.1982).

He stated that "the brace had his leg **abducted** or pulled away from the body so that the femoral head would be seated in the socket. Arrendale v. U.S., 469 F.Supp. 883, 890 (N.D. Tex.1979).

She also had vertical nystagmus, ... It was greater in the **abducting** eye, the eye looking away from the body. McSwain v. Chicago Trans. Authority, 362 N.E.2d 1264, 1272 (App.Ct.Ill. 1977).

abducting [eye] See *abduct.*

abduction (ab-duk'shun) the act of abducting or state of being abducted. See also *abduct.*

At that time her hip was put through a full range of motion by Dr. Richards in the presence of Dr. Duncan. Some pain was

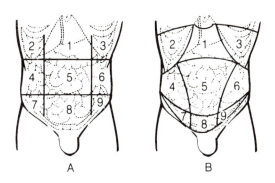

Regions of abdomen bounded according to (A) the standard and (B) a variant system: 1, epigastric; 2, right hypochondriac; 3, left hypochondriac; 4, right lateral (or lumbar); 5, umbilical; 6, left lateral (or lumbar); 7, right inguinal (or iliac); 8, pubic (hypogastric); 9, left inguinal (or iliac).

elicited on quick **abduction** in the region of the abductor muscles. Leavell v. Alton Ochsner Medical Foundation, 201 F.Supp. 805, 807 (E.D.La.1962).

The recurrent laryngeal nerves control the motion of **abduction**, that is, the movement of the vocal chords away from each other. Roberts v. Wood, 206 F.Supp. 579, 582 (S.D.Ala. 1962).

The motion of the shoulder was good except for **abduction**, the motion of bringing the arm out to the side and overhead, which was limited by about 30 degrees. This limitation means that Nelson was not able to bring his arm much beyond the right angle in the sideways position. Texas Employers' Ins. Ass'n v. Nelson, 534 S.W.2d 150, 152 (Ct.Civ.App.Tex. 1976).

abductor (ab-duk'tor) [L.] that which abducts. See *Table of Musculi.*

abiruana

Several months prior to September 1972, the plant began using a foreign wood named **abiruana**. It developed that the dust from this wood is highly dangerous and causes chronic pulmonary obstruction and disease. Mid-South Insulation Co. v. Buckley, 396 So.2d 7, 10 (Miss.1981).

abnormality (ab"nor-mal'ĭ-te) a malformation or deformity. See also *abnormity*; and *anomaly.*

abnormity (ab-nor'mĭ-te) abnormality; deformity.

abortifacient (ah-bor"tĭ-fa'shent) [L. *abortio* abortion + *facere* to make] 1. causing abortion. 2. an agent which causes abortion; called also *abortient* and *aborticide.*

(6) **Distribution of Abortifacients.** A person who sells, offers to sell, possesses with intent to sell, advertises, or displays for sale anything specially designed to terminate a pregnancy, or held out by the actor as useful for that purpose, commits a misdemeanor, unless:

(a) the sale, offer or display is to a physician or druggist or to an intermediary in a chain of distribution to physicians or druggists; or

(b) the sale is made upon prescription or order of a physician; or

(c) the possession is with intent to sell as authorized in paragraphs (a) and (b); or

(d) the advertising is addressed to persons named in paragraph (a) and confined to trade or professional channels not likely to reach the general public.

(7) **Section Inapplicable to Prevention of Pregnancy.** Nothing in this Section shall be deemed applicable to the prescription, administration or distribution of drugs or other substances for avoiding pregnancy, whether by preventing implantation of a fertilized ovum or by any other method that operates before, at or immediately after fertilization. [ALI Model Penal Code, Section 230.3 Abortion.] Doe v. Bolton, 410 U.S. 179, 207, 93 S.Ct. 739, 35 L.Ed.2d 201 (1973).

abortion (ah-bor'shun) [L. *abortio*] 1. the premature expulsion from the uterus of the products of conception—of the embryo, or of a nonviable fetus. The four classic symptoms, usually present in each type of abortion, are uterine contractions, uterine hemorrhage, softening and dilatation of the cervix, and presentation or expulsion of all or part of the products of conception. 2. premature stoppage of a natural or a morbid process. See also *amniocentesis, saline; curet* (Koehler case); *D and C; hysterectomy*; and *prostaglandin.*

In addition to a D & E an **abortion** may be performed by a saline amniocentesis, prostaglodin installation, hysterectomy and hysterotomy. These involve serious surgical procedures. American College of Obstetricians, etc. v. Thornburgh, 552 F.Supp. 791, 705 (E.D.Pa.1982).

An **abortion** undertaken to prevent birth of a genetically defective child is termed ''eugenic'' while one to prevent harm to the mother-to-be is termed ''therapeutic.'' (Speck v. Finegold (1979) 268 Pa.Super. 342, 408 A.2d 496, 499, fn. 4.) Curlender v. Bio-Science Laboratories, 165 Cal.Rptr. 477, 480 (Ct.App.1980).

With respect to the State's important and legitimate interest in the health of the mother, the ''compelling'' point, in the light of present medical knowledge, is at approximately the end of the first trimester. This is so because of the now-established medical fact, referred to above at 149, that until the end of the first trimester mortality in **abortion** may be less than mortality in normal childbirth. It follows that, from and after this point, a State may regulate the **abortion** procedure to the extent that the regulation reasonably relates to the preservation and protection of maternal health. Examples of permissible state regulation in this area are requirements as to the qualifications of the person who is to perform the **abortion**; as to the licensure of that person; as to the facility in which the procedure is to be performed, that is, whether it must be a hospital or may be a clinic or some other place of less-than-hospital status; as to the licensing of the facility; and the like.

This means, on the other hand, that, for the period of pregnancy prior to this ''compelling'' point, the attending physician, in consultation with his patient, is free to determine, without regulation by the State, that, in his medical judgment, the patient's pregnancy should be terminated. If that decision is reached, the judgment may be effectuated by an **abortion** free of interference by the State. Roe v. Wade, 410 U.S. 113, 159, 93 S.Ct. 705, 731, 35 L.Ed.2d 147 (1973).

abortion, eugenic See *eugenics*; and *eugenics, negative* and *positive.*

At that time eugenic abortions (to prevent the birth of a defective child) were prohibited in Texas; the only justification for abortion was the preservation of the mother's life.[1] [[1] In 1959 the commissioners of the American Law Institute tentatively proposed that the grounds for justifiable abortion include not only the protection of the health and life of the mother but also the avoidance of birth of a child with grave physical or mental defect and, additionally, those cases where the pregnancy resulted from either rape or incest. Art. 207.11, Model Penal Code, Tentative Draft No. 9, May 8, 1959.] Jacobs v. Theimer, 519 S.W.2d 846, 847 (Tex.1975).

Here there was no threat to the health or life of the mother. The abortion contemplated by the plaintiffs might better be described as a ''eugenic abortion'' intended to prevent the birth of a defective child. Dumer v. St. Michael's Hospital, 233 N.W.2d 372, 375 (Wis.1975).

abortion, incomplete abortion in which the uterus is not entirely rid of its contents.

An **incomplete abortion** is one in which the uterus has already begun to evacuate itself naturally and spontaneously and the fetus or a portion has already passed. Schenck v. Government of Guam, 609 F.2d 387, 388 (9th Cir. 1979).

abortion, induced abortion brought on intentionally; called also *artificial* or *therapeutic a.*

. . . he diagnosed it as **induced septic abortion**, meaning that some external force was used on the uterus. Russo v. Commonwealth, 148 S.W.2d 820, 824 (Va.1966).

abortion, prostaglandin See *prostaglandin.*

abortion, saline See *amniocentesis, saline.*

abortion, septic abortion associated with serious infection of the uterus, leading to generalized infection; more common after criminal abortion.

abortion, spontaneous abortion occurring naturally.

A **spontaneous abortion** is one that terminates as the result of an abnormal, natural cause rather than one that is induced by an individual either therapeutically or criminally. Russo v. Commonwealth, 148 S.E.2d 820, 823 (Va.1966).

abortion, suction D & C

She consulted Dr. Hall about the performance of an abortion and was scheduled for an **abortion** by **suction dilation and curettage** at Lutheran Hospital on August 31, 1970. She was then at the end of her first trimester of pregnancy. **Suction D & C** is a procedure whereby the contents of the uterus are evacuated by means of a suction cannula. A cannula is a clear plastic tube which is attached to a vacuum machine. The procedure is done by dilating the cervix (gradually opening the mouth of the uterus by inserting increasingly larger instruments) and then inserting the suction cannula and vacuuming the walls of the uterus. If the patient is pregnant, the products of conception are removed by this process. During the course of the procedure, after the appellee had vacuumed the wall of the uterus, he discovered that some of the products of conception were too large to fit through the suction cannula. Because this tissue had to be removed, he inserted a sponge stick, also called a sponge forceps (a plier type device) into the uterus to remove the debris. On his second attempt, the appellee felt the forceps go deeper than on the first attempt. He realized then that the appellant's uterus had been perforated. Hitch v. Hall, 399 A.2d 953, 955 (Ct.Spec.App.Md.1979).

abortion, therapeutic abortion induced to save the life or health (physical or mental) of a pregnant woman; sometimes performed after rape or incest.

The complaint uses the term "therapeutic abortion." A therapeutic abortion as we understand it, generally means the termination of a pregnancy that was a serious threat to the health or life of the mother. Dumer v. St. Michael's Hospital, 233 N.W.2d 372, 375 (Wis.1975).

Dr. Elswick explained that a therapeutic abortion is the termination of a pregnancy to preserve the health of the mother. Russo v. Commonwealth, 148 S.E.2d 820, 823 (Va.1966).

Other Authorities: Schenck v. Government of Guam, 609 F.2d 387, 388 (9th Cir. 1979).

abrasion (ah-bra'zhun) [L. *abrasio*] 1. the wearing away of a substance or structure (such as the skin or the teeth) through some unusual or abnormal mechanical process. See also *planing*. 2. an area of body surface denuded of skin or mucous membrane by some unusual or abnormal mechanical process.

Over the right frontal region of the forehead, the right of the midline, there was a superficial contused abrasion. In laymen's terms a bruise crease, which was one inch in greatest diameter. State v. Mendell, 523 P.2d 79, 81 (Ariz.1974).

abruptio (ab-rup'she-o) [L.] a rending asunder.

abruptio placentae premature detachment of a placenta, often attended by maternal systemic reactions in the form of shock, oliguria, and fibrinogenopenia.

His colleague, Dr. Karl Pizzolato, examined Mrs. Juge at Woman's Hospital and his records indicated he found no evidence of fetal distress. Further, there was no evidence of abruptio placenta (separation of the afterbirth) or of any uterine damage. Juge v. Cunningham, 422 So.2d 1253, 1255 (Ct.App.La. 1982).

. . . or it could be an obstetrical complication, such as a separation of the uterus, called an abruptio placentae. Spike v. Sellett, 430 N.E.2d 597, 600 (App.Ct.Ill.1981).

The final diagnosis was that Betty Friel had suffered an abruptio placenta. . . .

. . . Dr. Nathanson concludes that plaintiff probably began suffering abruptio placenta with consequent blood loss on April 30, 1978, and that if the condition prevails for a significant period of time, fetal hypoxia with brain damage may result. Friel v. Vineland Obstetrical, Etc., 400 A.2d 147, 149–50 (Super.Ct.N.J.1979).

Other Authorities: Vecchione v. Carlin, 168 Cal.Rptr. 571, 573 (Ct.App.1980).

abscess (ab'ses) [L. *abscessus*, from *ab* away + *cedere* to go] a localized collection of pus in a cavity formed by the disintegration of tissues.

Dr. Lieberman, a board certified internist, testified: "Yes. I reviewed the records, and according to Dr. Abarbanel's notes,

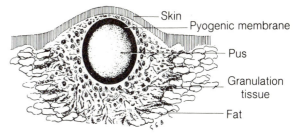
Diagram of cross-section of abscess.

there was a clear-cut inflammatory process in a mass, which, by definition—or at least my definition—is an abscess, and in his own words, he said there was a ruptured diverticulosis as the cause of it." Jines v. Abarbanel, 143 Cal.Rptr. 818, 822 (Ct.App.Cal.1978).

. . . we learned in Vietnam in treating dirty wounds you don't close them up again because that causes abscessing and the thing we want to guard against, so her abdomen was left open and treated in this very advanced way so as to reduce the possibility that she may develop an abscess. Raitt v. Johns Hopkins Hospital, 322 A.2d 548, 562 (Ct.Spec.App.Md. 1974), reversed 336 A.2d 90 (1975).

Dr. Shapiro testified that an abscess requires immediate treatment inasmuch as bacteria invade the pulp and cause the eventual death of the pulp. Dr. Nall confirmed the necessity for immediate root canal therapy when any symptom of an abscess appears (such as a fistula), and that failure to refer plaintiff to a root canal therapist after discovering the closed fistula would constitute a breach of good practice. Evans v. Ohanesian, 112 Cal.Rptr. 236, 241 (Ct.App.1974).

Other Authorities: Jeanes v. Milner, 428 F.2d 598, 600 (8th Cir. 1970).

abscess, brain one affecting the brain as a result of extension of an infection (e.g., otitis media) from an adjacent area or through bloodborne infection.

Even among experts little is known about the causation of brain abscesses. Their nature is such that they are difficult to study. Since most brain abscesses originate in areas other than the throat (sinus passages, middle ear and lungs being the most common sources), and over a longer time, it is not even a common knowledge that the abscess was probably caused by the tonsillectomy, let alone that the abscess was probably caused by a negligently performed tonsillectomy. [Folk v. Kilk, 126 Cal.Rptr. 172 at 178 (1975)]. Barton v. Owen, 139 Cal.Rptr. 494, 500 (Ct.App.1977).

abscess, perirectal one in the areolar tissue around the rectum.

Plaintiff testified that four attempts were made to insert the tube, that each time he felt a "cutting," "scratching," or "tearing" sensation which was painful, and that his rectum "kept stinging and burning" all night. . . .

. . . Dr. Wood testified that 90 per cent or more of all perirectal abscesses result from a bacterial infection, that the mucous membrane, which lines the rectum, prevents such infection, that so far as he knew the only way the infection in plaintiff's rectum could have started would have been from a break in the mucous membrance, and that in his opinion the insertion of the enema tube caused the break. He stated that a properly given enema is not painful. *Davis v. Memorial Hospital,* 376 P.2d 561–2 (Cal.1962).

abscess, Pott's one associated with tuberculosis of the spine.

abscess, subhepatic one situated beneath the liver.

A **subhepatic abscess** developed, and on November 9, 1964, the doctors performed a further operation to drain the resulting phlegma. *Kelly v. U.S.,* 554 F.Supp. 1001, 1002 (E.D.N.Y. 1983).

absorption (ab-sorp'shun) [L. *absorptio*] the uptake of substances into or across tissues, e.g., skin, intestine, and kidney tubules.

abuse (ah-būs') misuse or wrong use, particularly excessive use of anything.

abuse, drug

When it speaks of "**drug abuse**," it is referring to the broader problem which includes also those drugs which create only psychological dependency. We will use the term "**drug abuse**" in this report as existing when an individual takes psychotoxic drugs under any of the following circumstances: (a) in amounts sufficient to create a hazard to his own health or to the safety of the community; or (b) when he obtains drugs through illicit channels; or (c) when he takes drugs on his own initiative rather than on the basis of professional advice. **Drug abuse** today involves not only the narcotic drugs and marihuana, but to an increasingly alarming extent other drugs such as the barbiturates, the amphetamines and even certain of the "tranquilizers." This latter group will be referred to in this report as the "dangerous drugs." *Hoffmann-La Roche, Inc. v. Kleindienst,* 478 F.2d 1, 4 (3d Cir. 1973).

accelerate See *disk, slipped* (Abernathy case).

accessory nerve See *nervus, accessorius.*

accident (ak'sĭ-dent) an unforeseen occurrence, especially one of an injurious character; an unexpected complicating occurrence in the regular course of a disease. See also *aspiration* (Jones case); *heart failure*; and *injury.*

The Court said, in *Schemmel v. T. B. Gatch & Sons Contracting and Building Co.,* 164 Md. 671, 680, 166 A. 39 (1933), that:

The word "**accident**" in its ordinary and usual implications is associated with ideas of trauma, and involves to a degree at least elements of force, violence and surprise. But in Workmen's Compensation Law its meaning has been expanded to include any mischance resulting in physical injury to the bodily tissues produced by some unusual and extraordinary condition or happening in the employment. It has therefore been interpreted to include such untoward occurrences as the rupture of an aneurism, pulmonary and cerebral hemorrhages, hernia, infection, and heart dilation, arising out of some unusual or extraordinary condition in the employment, even where the injury was due in part to pre-existing disease or physical abnormality in the claimant. (Emphasis added.)

... Whenever a person engages in an occupation requiring violent physical contact with others similarly inclined, he must expect that injury may arise therefrom. The injury is neither unusual nor extraordinary. Therefore, we hold that an injury sustained by a professional football player as the result of legitimate and usual physical contact with other players, whether under actual or simulated game conditions, cannot be said to be an "**accidental** injury" within the meaning of the Maryland Workmen's Compensation Law.[6] [[6] We do not herein decide whether injury caused to the player as the direct result of extraordinary violence is compensable. That decision must await another day.] See *Palmer v. Kansas City Chiefs Football Club,* 621 S.W.2d 350 (Mo.App.1981). *Rowe v. Baltimore Colts,* 454 A.2d 872, 877–8 (Ct.Spec.App.Md.1983).

On the question of whether the plaintiff sustained his burden of proof, we consider LSA–R.S. 23:1021(1), which defines

"**accident**" as "... an unexpected or unforeseen event happening suddenly or violently, with or without human fault and producing at the time objective symptoms of an injury." *Byrer v. Southern Baptist Hospital, Inc.,* 350 So.2d 1233 (La. App.4th Cir. 1977).

If there is a suddenness either in the precipitating incident or in the manifestation of disability, the requirement of "**accident**" is satisfied. *Self v. Riverside Companies, Inc.,* 382 So.2d 1037 (La.App.2d Cir. 1980), writ denied 385 So.2d 793 (La.1980); *Francis v. Kaiser Aluminum & Chemical Corporation,* 225 So. 2d 756 (La.App.4th Cir. 1969).

... Insect bites or stings are compensable as "**accidents**" under the workers' compensation law. *Cohrs v. Meadows,* 342 So.2d 1172 (La.App.1st Cir. 1977). We hold that the flea bites constituted an accident within the intendment of the workers' compensation law.... *Oalmann v. Brock and Blevins Co., Inc.,* 428 So.2d 892, 894, 896 (Ct.App.La.1983).

In *Hinkle v. H. J. Heinz Co.,* 7 Pa.Cmwlth. 216, 298 A.2d 632, 635 (1972), we found that the cases disclose at least four basic categories of **accidents**: (1) a sudden, unexpected traumatic event such as a fall or blow; (2) unusual exertion in the course of work causing an unexpected and sudden injury; (3) an unusual pathological result of an ordinary condition of work; and (4) sudden and unexpected injury caused by the failure of an employer to furnish medical care to an employee.[4] [[4] An additional category might include falls from a pre-existing disease as in *Miller v. Schiffner & Sons,* 196 Pa.Super. 84, 173 A.2d 707 (1961), and in *Allen v. Patterson-Emerson-Comstock, Inc.,* 180 Pa.Super. 286, 119 A.2d 832 (1956).]

As we recently stated in *Collins v. U.S. Steel Corp.,* 7 Pa. Cmwlth. 333, 298 A.2d 637, 638–639 (1972):

In this case, because it was acknowledged that the claimant, when injured, was performing his usual work in the usual manner, only the first and third classifications mentioned above could be applicable. It is our opinion, however, that the claimant has failed to carry the burden to show that his injury was caused by an "**accident**", as defined by either of these remaining classifications.

To prove an **accident** under the first classification requires a showing of more than a feeling of pain. There must be a specific occurrence causally related to the onset of the pain. *A.P. Green Refractories Co. v. Workmen's Comp.App.Bd.,* 301 A.2d 914, 917–18 (Commonwealth Ct.Pa.1973).

Other Authorities: *Wynn v. J. R. Simplot Co.,* 666 P.2d 629, 632 (Idaho 1983). *Bahr v. Iowa Beef Processors, Inc.,* 663 P.2d 1144, 1147 (Ct.App.Kan.1983). *Prestige Homes, Inc. v.*

Legouffe, 658 P.2d 850, 855 (Colo.1983); Martin Industries, Inc. v. Dement, 435 So.2d 85, 87 (Ct.Civ.App.Ala.1983); Shatoska v. Intern. Grain Transfer, Inc., 430 So.2d 1255, 1259 (Ct.App.La.1983); Cabe v. Union Carbide Corp., 644 S.W.2d 397, 399 (Tenn.1983); Yeend v. United Parcel Service, Inc., 659 P.2d 87, 89 (Idaho 1982); Bingham v. Smith's Transfer Corp., 286 S.E.2d 570, 574 (Ct.App.N.Car.1982); Naquin v. Texaco, Inc., 423 So.2d 31, 34 (Ct.App.La.1982); Wheat v. Ford, Bacon and Davis Const. Corp., 424 So.2d 293, 298 (Ct.App.La.1982); Daney v. Argonaut Ins. Co., 421 So.2d 331, 336–7 (Ct.App.La.1982); Guillory v. U.S. Fidelity & Guar. Ins. Co., 420 So.2d 119, 122 (La.1982); Lovely v. Cooper Indus. Products, Inc., 429 N.E.2d 274, 277 (Ct.App. Ind.1981); Harris v. Rainsoft of Allen Cty., Inc., 416 N.E.2d 1320, 1322–3 (Ct.App.Ind.1981); Johnston v. Sel-Mor Garment Co., 571 S.W.2d 691, 693 (Ct.App.Mo.1978); Warshaw v. Trans World Airlines, Inc., 442 F.Supp. 400, 407, 413 (E.D.Pa.1977); DeMarines v. KLM Royal Dutch Airlines, 433 F.Supp. 1047, 1052 (E.D.Pa.1977); Haycraft v. Corhart Refractories Co., 544 S.W.2d 222, 224–5 (Ky.1976); Bethlehem Steel Corp. v. Yuhas, 303 A.2d 266, 268 (Commonwealth Ct.Pa.1973); International Harvester Co. v. Industrial Com'n, 305 N.E.2d 529, 532 (Ill.1973); Hartford Accident & Indemnity Co. v. Contreras, 498 S.W.2d 419, 424 (Ct.Civ.App.Tex. 1973); Watkins v. Underwriters at Lloyd's, London, 473 P.2d 464, 470 (Ct.App.Ariz.1970); Barber v. Fleming-Raugh, Inc., 222 A.2d 423, 427 (Super.Ct.Pa.1966).

accident and disease distinguished See *disease* (Froust case).

accidental

The statute defines "**accidental**" as follows:
Bodily injury is **accidental** as to a person claiming personal protection insurance benefits unless suffered intentionally by the injured person or caused intentionally by the claimant. Even though a person knows that bodily injury is substantially certain to be caused by his act or omission, he does not cause or suffer injury intentionally if he acts or refrains from acting for the purpose of averting injury to property or to any person including himself. M.C.L. § 500.3105(4); M.S.A. § 24.13105(4). Wheeler v. Tucker Freight Lines Co., Inc., 336 N.W.2d 14, 16 (Ct.App.Mich.1983).

The parties agree that a heart attack or disorder induced by a strain or exertion in the course and scope of employment is an **accidental** injury to the physical structure of the body and compensable under the workmen compensation laws. Commercial Standard Fire & Marine Co. v. Thornton, 540 S.W.2d 521, 522 (Ct.Civ.App.Tex.1976).

However, the issue is foreclosed by the Mississippi Supreme Court's determination in Britt v. All American Assurance Co. of Louisiana, 333 So.2d 629 (Miss.1976) that **accidental** bodily injury does include death by exposure. Britt v. Travelers Ins. Co., 556 F.2d 336, 340 (5th Cir. 1977).

Other Authorities: Cobb v. Aetna Life Ins. Co., 274 N.W.2d 911, 914–15 (Minn.1979); Lee v. Fidelity & Cas. Co. of New York, 567 F.2d 1340, 1342 (5th Cir. 1978); Liberty National Life Ins. Co. v. Morris, 208 S.E.2d 637, 638 (Ct.App.Ga. 1974); Jones v. Aetna Life Ins. Co., 439 S.W.2d 721, 725, 727 (Ct.Civ.App.Tex.1969).

accommodation (ah-kom"o-da'shun) [L. *accommodere* to fit to] adjustment, especially that of the eye for various distances (see illustration).

accommodative (ah-kom'o-da"tiv) pertaining to, of the nature of, or affecting accommodation.

There was expert testimony that after the accident Brian had a temporary problem with his eyesight ("marked **accommodative** insufficiency") which was a condition caused in children of Brian's age only by concussion from injuries to the head. Healy v. White, 378 A.2d 540, 544–5 (Conn.1977).

acetabulum (as"ĕ-tab'u-lum), pl. *acetab'ula* [L. "vinegar-cruet," from *acetum* vinegar] [NA] the large cup-shaped cavity on the lateral surface of the os coxae in which the head of the femur articulates; called also *acetabular bone*, *cotyloid cavity*, and *os acetabulum*.

The **acetabulum** is the socket located in the hips into which the ball-like head of the femur fits. Fractures were sustained in both sockets. Collins v. Hand, 246 A.2d 398, 400 (Pa.1968).

Dr. Shaughnessy examined the X-rays ordered by Dr. Fetzer and determined that Reeg had a comminuted left tibia and a displaced fractured **acetabulum** (the cup that holds the femur in place), but that there was no evidence of a dislocation of the femur ("thigh bone"). Reeg v. Shaughnessy, 570 F.2d 309, 312 (10th Cir. 1978).

Petitioner's injury has necessitated the deepening and expansion of the **acetabulum** (pelvic socket) to approximately two inches in diameter to receive the replacement plastic socket. Roeder v. Industrial Com'n, 556 P.2d 1148, 1152 (Ct.App. Ariz.1976).

Other Authorities: Fontenot v. American Fidelity Fire Ins. Co., 386 So.2d 165, 169 (Ct.App.La.1980); Rosario v. Amer. Export-Isbrandtsen Lines, Inc., 395 F.Supp. 1192, 1204 (E.D.Pa. 1975); Ins. Co. of North America v. Stroburg, 456 S.W.2d 402, 408 (Ct.Civ.App.Tex.1970); Quilter v. Elgin, Joliet and Eastern Ry. Co., 409 F.2d 338, 339 (7th Cir. 1969).

acetazolamide

Diamox stops the production of fluid within the eye and also softens the eye. Lazenby v. Beisel, 425 So.2d 84, 85 (D.Ct. App.Fla.1982).

In fact, by the druggist's error, she had been given Diamox, a diuretic, instead of Dymelor, when she had her prescription filled. Brown v. Crews, 363 So.2d 1121, 1122 (Dist.Ct.App. Fla.1978).

Changes during accommodation: Contraction of ciliary muscle; approximation of ciliary muscle to lens; relaxation of suspensory ligament; increased curvature of anterior surface of lens. (Helmholtz.)

acetohexamide (as″ĕ-to-heks′ah-mīd) [USP] chemical name: 4-acetyl-*N*-[[cyclohexylamino]carbonyl]benzenesulfonamide. An oral hypoglycemic agent, $C_{15}H_{20}O_4S$, occurring as a white, crystalline powder.

Dymelor, described as an oral hypoglycemic designed to reduce the amount of sugar in the blood. Brown v. Crews, 363 So.2d 1121, 1122 (Dist.Ct.App.Fla.1978).

achalasia (ak″ah-la′ze-ah) [*a* neg + Gr. *chalasis* relaxation + *-ia*] failure to relax of the smooth muscle fibers of the gastrointestinal tract at any point of junction of one part with another. Especially the failure of the esophagogastric sphincter to relax with swallowing, due to degeneration of ganglion cells in the wall of the organ. The thoracic esophagus also loses its normal peristaltic activity and becomes dilated (megaesophagus). Called also *cardiospasm.*

. . . **achalasia** (a constriction of the lower esophagus). James H. Boyle & Son, Inc. v. Prudential Ins. Co., 268 N.E.2d 651, 652 (Sup.Jud.Ct.Mass.1971).

Achilles bursa, jerk (reflex), tendon (ah-kil′ēz) [Gr. *Achilleus* Greek hero, whose mother held him by the ankle to dip him in the Styx] See *bursa tendinis calcanei [Achillis]; triceps surae jerk,* under *jerk;* and *tendo calcaneus.*

achlorhydria (ah″klor-hi′dre-ah) [*a* neg. + *chlorhydria*] absence of hydrochloric acid from maximally stimulated gastric secretions; a result of gastric mucosal atrophy. Called also *gastric anacidity.*

acicular (ah-sik′u-lar) [L. *acicularis*] shaped like a needle or needle point.

The most abundant variety of cummingtonite-grunerite, although not as abundant in the eastern end of the range as it is in the western, is the typically fine to medium grained, prismatic to **acicular** grunerite. [Footnote omitted.] U.S. v. Reserve Mining Co., 380 F.Supp. 11, 31 (D.Minn.1974), remanded 498 F.2d 1073 (8th Cir. 1974).

acid (as′id) 1. [L. *acidus,* from *acere* to be sour] sour; having properties opposed to those of the alkalis. 2. [L. *acidum*] any compound of an electronegative element with one or more hydrogen atoms that are readily replaceable by electropositive atoms; a compound which, in aqueous solution, undergoes dissociation with the formation of hydrogen ions (protons) a substance whose molecule or ion can give up a proton (to a base); a substance capable of accepting a pair of electrons to form a coordinate covalent bond. Acids have a sour taste, turn blue litmus red, and unite with bases to form salts. Acids are distinguished as *binary* or *hydracids,* and *ternary* or *oxacids:* the former contain no oxygen; in the latter hydrogen is united to the electronegative element by oxygen. The hydracids are distinguished by the prefix *hydro-.* The names of acids end in "ic," except in the case in which there are two degrees of oxygenation. The acid containing the greater amount of oxygen has the termination *-ic,* the one having the lesser amount, the termination *-ous.* Acids ending in *-ic* form the salts with the termination *-ate;* those ending in *-ous* form the salts ending in *-ite.* The salts of hydracids end in *-ide.* Acids are called *monobasic, dibasic, tribasic,* and *tetrabasic,* respec-

tively, when they contain one, two, three, or four replaceable hydrogen atoms.

acid, aminosalicylic [USP], chemical name: 4-amino-2-hydroxybenzoic acid. An antibacterial, $C_7H_7NO_3$, occurring as a white, or nearly white, bulky powder; used orally as a tuberculostatic. Called also *para-aminosalicylic* acid (*PAS* or *PASA*).

The county contends that benzine fumes could not cause cirrhosis of the liver, and argues that his illness was caused either by his practice of drinking one can of beer daily or by his prior use of a drug called P.A.S. (**para-aminosalicylic acid**) for treatment of a condition of pulmonary tuberculosis. County of Cook v. Industrial Com'n, 310 N.E.2d 6, 7 (Ill.1974).

acid, barbituric chemical name: 2,4,6,-trioxohexahydropyrimidine. A crystalline substance, $CO(NHCO)_2CH_2$, known in medicine chiefly because of its derivatives, such as barbital and phenobarbital, and from which the term applied to the class of drugs, barbiturates, is derived. Called also *malonyl urea.*

acid, carbolic See *phenol.*

acid, dehydrocholic [USP], a white bitter powder, $C_{24}H_{34}O_5$, formed by the oxidation of cholic acid and derived from natural bile acids; used as a choleretic.

He believes that the consumption of Decholin by an individual who has an obstruction would lead to an increase in the accumulation of bile ahead of the intestine, and because of the blockage, the fluid could not pass into the intestine as it normally would during the course of digestion. Furthermore, according to Dr. Sklar, the accumulated bile will eventually become absorbed into the bloodstream, leading to the likelihood of serious harm. U.S. v. Article of Drug Labeled Decholin, 264 F.Supp. 473, 477 (E.D.Mich.1967).

acid, deoxyribonucleic a nucleic acid originally isolated from fish sperm and thymus gland, but later found in all living cells; on hydrolysis it yields adenine, guanine, cytosine, thymine, deoxyribose, and phosphoric acid. It is the carrier of genetic information for all organisms except the RNA viruses. See also *Watson-Crick helix* (and illustration), under *helix.* Abbreviated DNA.

Plaintiff seeks a preliminary injunction to prevent an experiment testing the biological properties of polyoma DNA (deoxyribonucleic acid) cloned in bacterial cells. . . .

The research involves dividing and then rejoining the hereditycarrying material of various organisms—**deoxyribonucleic acid**, or DNA—to make recombinant hybrids that carry some of the traits of two unrelated forms. It is contended that the value of such work is that it may create new medicines, vaccines, industrial chemicals or crops. The risk, some scientists claim, is that it could create unexpectedly dangerous new ailments or epidemics. Many scientists are of the opinion that exaggerations of the hypothetical hazards have gone far beyond any reasoned assessment. Mack v. Califano, 447 F.Supp. 668, 670 (D.D.C.1978).

acid, fatty, essential an unsaturated fatty acid that cannot be formed in the body and therefore must be provided by the diet; the most important are linoleic acid, linolenic acid, and arachidonic acid.

acid, diatrizoic [USP], chemical name: 3,5-bis(ace-tylamino)-2,4,6-tri-iodobenzoic acid. A white powder, $C_{11}H_9I_3N_2O_4$, used in the preparation of certain radiopaque media. See also *diatrizoate meglumine*; and *diatrizoate sodium*.

Natural linoleic and other higher polyunsaturates are referred to in the patent in suit as "**essential fatty acids**" because they are required for control of plasma cholesterol levels in the human body. The patent states the object of the invention is to provide a margarine "of a high **essential fatty acid** content" in which there will be "a high ratio of **essential fatty acid** to saturated fatty acid content," with "a fatty acid pattern approximating that of the liquid unhydrogenated domestic vegetable oils." Corn Products Co. v. Standard Brands, Inc., 359 F.2d 739, 741 (7th Cir. 1966).

acid, folic chemical name: N-{p-{[(2-amino-4-hydroxy-6-pteridinyl)methyl]-amino}benzoyl}glatamic acid. A widely distributed water-soluble vitamin, $C_{19}H_{19}N_7O_6$, existing in a number of natural products in free form or in various conjugates, which have been designated by various names, including *pteroylglutamic acid, fermentation Lactobacillus casei factor, liver L. casei factor, Norit eluate factor, factor R, Streptococcus lactis R* (or *SLR*) *factor, factor U, yeast L. casei factor, vitamin B_c, vitamin B_c conjugate,* and *vitamin M*. It is an essential growth factor for many animals and microorganisms. Folic acid serves as a coenzyme in the transfer of one-carbon units, and its deficiency in man inhibits the synthesis of DNA, which first becomes obvious clinically in hematopoietic cells, resulting in certain types of macrocytic anemias. Synthetic folic acid is pteroylglutamic acid, $COOH \cdot (CH_2)_2 \cdot CH \cdot (COOH) \cdot NH \cdot CO \cdot C_6HN_4 \cdot (NH_3) \cdot OH$.

Dr. Glover testified that prenatal supplements had not been included on CMADL which contain certain vital elements, notably **pholic acid**, the absence of which might cause central nervous deficiencies in the new born child. Dodson v. Parham, 427 F.Supp. 97, 106 (N.D.Ga.1977).

acid, para-aminosalicylic aminosalicylic a. Often abbreviated PAS or PASA.

acid, pholic See *acid, folic.*

acid, sorbic 1. chemical name: 2,4-hexadienoic acid. An acid $CH_3(CH)_4COOH$, found in berries of mountain ash, *Sorbus aucuparia*. 2. [NF] a preparation occurring as a free-flowing, white, crystalline powder, containing 99 to 101 per cent to the labeled amount of sorbic acid; used as an antimicrobial preservative.

The Secretary of Agriculture in promulgating Regulation 9 C.F.R. 318.7(d)(2), made a finding to that effect in the following stated "considerations:"

"Mold and bacterial slime develop on the surface of cooked sausages and similar products held for long periods under good refrigeration or for shorter periods at higher temperatures. The appearance of mold and other surface growth serves to alert consumers to the condition of the product. **Sorbates** are most effective moldicides and bactericides for products with high acidity, i.e., a pH of 5 or below. These chemicals are not effective in products such as cooked sau-

sages since their pH ranges from 5.9 to 6.2. The presence of **sorbates** in subsurface sausage tissues results in changes in bacterial flora of the products. **Sorbates** have been demonstrated to inhibit selectively the development of aerobic bacteria and "simultaneously permit the luxuriant growth of clostridium perfringes and clostridium botulinum which are organisms associated with serious health hazards. The use of **sorbates** for such products therefore conceals damage and inferiority because of bacterial action, and makes the products appeal better and of greater value than they are in view of their decomposing condition." (35 Fed.Reg. No. 193, pt. II at p. 15553 (Oct. 3, 1970))

. . . it appears that there is no genuine issue as to the following material fact, i.e., that **sorbic acid** and **sorbates** prevent the growth of mold and other surface growths in meat products, such as cooked sausages, while not inhibiting certain bacterial subsurface spoilage and thus make meat products appear better than they actually are, thereby misleading the consumer. Chip Steak Co. v. Hardin, 332 F.Supp. 1084, 1090–1 (N.D. Cal.1971).

acid, sulfuric an oily, highly caustic, and poisonous acid, H_2SO_4, used widely in chemistry, industry, and the arts, and formerly used as a topical caustic and in serous diarrhea and gastric hypoacidity. The concentrated acid, formerly called oil of vitriol, causes severe skin burns by dehydration; explosive spattering occurs when water is added.

Sulphuric acid in the plant is also a hazard. It is irritating to the skin and can cause severe burns. When the acid contacts clothing, it causes disintegration or rapid deterioration. Moreover, the effects of **sulphuric acid** make the employee more susceptible than he would otherwise be to contamination by particles of lead and lead compounds. Steiner v. Mitchell, 350 U.S. 247, 250, 76 S.Ct. 330, 100 L.Ed. 267 (1956).

A vast majority (97 per cent) of **sulfuric acid** plants in the United States produce **sulfuric acid** by means of a "contact" process, involving these three steps:

(1) Elemental sulfur or other sulfur-bearing raw material is burned to obtain sulfur dioxide gas [SO(2)];

(2) Sulfur dioxide gas is converted into sulfur trioxide [SO(3)], upon contact with a catalyst, generally vanadium pentoxide;

(3) Sulfur trioxide gas is then absorbed in **sulfuric acid** [H(2)SO(4)], through combination with the water in a 98 to 99 percent **sulfuric acid** solution with which it is circulated in an absorption tower. Essex Chemical Corp. v. Ruckelshaus, 486 F.2d 427, 434 (D.C.Cir.1973).

acid, sulfuric, fuming a heavy, colorless, oily liquid compounded of sulfuric acid, H_2SO_4, and sulfur trioxide, SO_3, which gives off suffocating fumes; it is widely used in industry for sulfonations and nitrations. Called also *pyrosulfuric a.*

acid, trichloroacetic [USP], a poisonous, extremely caustic acid, $C_2HCl_3O_2$, occurring as colorless, deliquescent crystals; used as a topical caustic for local destruction of lesions and for treatment of dermatological diseases.

Then Mrs. Wilson applied to Mrs. Rosenblum's face a 5% solution of **trichloroacetic acid** (called "TCA") with two cotton swabs. . . .

... Mrs. Wilson took a cotton swab and began to apply 100% **TCA** to Mrs. Rosenblum's right cheek, whereupon Mrs. Rosenblum complained out loud that "it's burning",....

It is undisputed that 100% **TCA** is a very strong substance and is damaging to human skin when applied as it was to Mrs. Rosenblum's cheek. The affected area of Mrs. Rosenblum's right cheek scabbed over for a few weeks, after which the scabbing came off and left some scar tissue on her right cheek. Rosenblum v. Bloom, 492 S.W.2d 321, 322–3 (Ct.Civ.App. Tex.1973).

acid, trichlorophenoxyacetic

It began back in 1970 (before the creation of the Environmental Protection Agency when the Department of Agriculture suspended immediately the registration of 2,4,5 **trichlorophenoxyacetic acid** (a substance which will hereinafter be referred to as "**2,4,5–T**") for some uses and issued cancellation notices respecting others....

The Secretary's actions were taken because of evidence indicating "that **2,4,5–T**, as well as its contaminant, dioxins, may produce abnormal development in unborn animals. Nearly pure **2,4,5–T** was reported to cause birth defects when injected at high doses into experimental pregnant mice but not in rats. Dow Chemical Co. v. Ruckelshaus, 477 F.2d 1317, 1318–19 (8th Cir. 1973).

acid mist See *acid, sulfuric fuming.*

"Acid mist" is defined as "**sulfuric acid mist**, as measured by test methods set forth in this part," 40 C.F.R. § 60.81(b). Essex Chemical Corp. v. Ruckelshaus, 486 F.2d 427, 432 (D.C.Cir. 1973).

acidosis (as"ĭ-do'sis) a pathologic condition resulting from accumulation of acid or depletion of the alkaline reserve (bicarbonate content) in the blood and body tissues, and characterized by an increase in hydrogen ion concentration (decrease in pH). Cf. *alkalosis.*

Plaintiff alleges that she was in a state of **acidosis** at the time she entered surgery and that her condition contributed to cause the cardiac arrest and affected respiratory control.

Dr. O'Donoghue testified that based on his physical examination of the patient at 10 p.m. the indications were such to proceed to surgery, and it was his opinion that the 40 milliequivalents of potassium chloride added to the 9 p.m. I.V. solution would bring the patient into metabolic balance. Burrow v. Widder, 368 N.E.2d 443, 448 (App.Ct. of Ill.1977).

Other expert witnesses testified that an **acidosis** (high blood sugar) condition was developing over the days prior to the boy's death. Maltempo v. Cuthbert, 504 F.2d 325, 328 (5th Cir. 1974).

acinitis (as"ĭ-ni'tis) inflammation of the acini of a gland.

acinus (as'ĭ-nus), pl. *ac'ini* [L. "grape"] a general term used in anatomical nomenclature to designate a small saclike dilatation, particularly one found in various glands. See also *alveolus.*

acinus, liver a functional unit of the liver, smaller than a portal lobule, being a diamond-shaped mass of liver parenchyma that is supplied by a terminal branch of the portal vein and of the hepatic artery and drained by a terminal branch of the bile duct.

acne (ak'ne) [possibly a corruption of Greek *akmē* a point or of *achnē* chaff] an inflammatory disease of the pilosebaceous unit, the specific type usually being indicated by a modifying term; frequently used alone to designate common acne, or *acne vulgaris.*

acne conglobata a form of acne characterized by the presence of numerous comedones, marked suppuration, the formation of cysts and sinuses, and severe scarring.

The course of **acne conglobata** is chronic, and the prognosis is poor. Severe and disfiguring scars as well as the chronicity of the process often cripple patients with this condition both physically and mentally. [Quoting **Dermatology** by Maschella, Pillsbury and Hurley.] Dupuy v. Tilley, 380 So.2d 634, 635 (Ct. App.La.1979).

acromioclavicular (ah-kro"me-o-klah-vik'u-lar) pertaining to the acromion and clavicle, especially to the articulation between the acromion and clavicle. See also *articulatio acromioclavicularis.*

After her fall Mrs. Hamm frequently experienced pain in her right shoulder, and in April of 1973 she underwent surgery for the purpose of removing the distal clavicle. The surgery resulted in permanent impairment to the right shoulder, and Mrs. Hamm's condition was diagnosed as **acromioclavicular** arthritis on the right side with some cystic degeneration. Hamm v. Univ. of Maine, 423 A.2d 548, 549 (Me.1980).

He suffered severe injuries to his chest and shoulder causing him to be hospitalized for surgery for repair of his shoulder. The shoulder surgery was unsuccessful, leaving him with a chronic "**acromioclavicular** separation". Eggleston v. Industrial Com'n, 539 P.2d 918 (Ct.App.Ariz.1975).

... at this point it was noted that he had a right shoulder injury (right **acromioclavicular** separation, traumatic). Hyatt v. Sierra Boat Co., 145 Cal.Rptr. 47, 58 (Ct.App.1978).

Other Authorities: Mortimer v. Harry C. Crooker & Sons, Inc., 404 A.2d 228, 229 (Sup.Jud.Ct.Me.1979).

acromion (ah-kro'me-on) [*acro-* + Gr. *ōmos* shoulder] [NA] the lateral extension of the spine of the scapula, projecting over the shoulder joint and forming the highest point of the shoulder; called also *acromial process* and *acromion scapulae.*

He testified that the fracture line went through the base of the **acromion** and the whole thing became somewhat depressed. This means that the shoulder blade was tilted downward. He testified that the boney prominence on Nelson's right shoulder seemed to be larger than a similar boney prominence on the left shoulder. He said that that was because the shoulder was lower. The prominence was in the correct place, but the rest was not. Texas Employers' Ins. Ass'n v. Nelson, 534 S.W.2d 150, 151 (Ct.Civ.App.Tex.1976).

... she underwent a resection of the outer end of the **acromin** [sic]. Claussell v. Secretary of Health, Education & Welf., 337 F.Supp. 717, 719 (S.D.1972).

Dr. Pepe performed an **acromioplasty** and a transfer of the long head of the bicep tendon to the humerus. Hamm v. Univ. of Maine, 423 A.2d 548, 549 (Me.1980).

acromioplasty See *acromion* and *-plasty.*

acrylic (ah-kril'ik) an acrylic resin. See under *resin*.

ACTH adrenocorticotropic hormone. See *corticotropin*.

action (ak'shun) [L. *actio*] any performance of function or movement either of any part or organ or of the whole body.

action, reflex a response resulting from the passage of excitation potential from a receptor to a muscle or gland, over a system of neurons without the necessity of volition.

acuity (ah-ku'ĭ-te) [L. *acuitas* sharpness] clarity or clearness, especially of the vision.

acuity, central visual

The Hearing Examiner's finding that claimant's "poor vision is correctable with glasses to $^{20}/_{20}$ in the right and $^{20}/_{30}$ in the left" means only that "her **Central Visual Acuity**" is correctable with glasses. **Central visual acuity** results in the ability to distinguish detail and to read and do fine work; and loss of **central visual acuity** may be caused by impaired distant vision or impaired near vision. It has nothing to do with vertical deviation resulting in double vision. Jenkins v. Gardner, 430 F.2d 243, 294 (6th Cir. 1970).

acupuncture (ak"u-pungk'chŭr) [*acu-* + L. *punctura* a prick] the Chinese practice of piercing specific peripheral nerves with needles to relieve the discomfort associated with painful disorders, to induce surgical anesthesia, and for therapeutic purposes. See also *medicine* (Mirsa case).

Before proceeding to the merits of this action, it may prove useful to review the theory and practice of **acupuncture**. **Acupuncture**, one branch of traditional Chinese medicine, has been practiced for 2,000 to 5,000 years. It consists of the insertion and manipulation of very fine needles at specific points on or near the surface of the skin. The needles, solid in construction, are usually one to three inches in length, although needles ranging from one-third of an inch to eight inches may be used. They are generally made of stainless steel, although other metals are often employed, and are sterilized before insertion. They may be used to affect the perception of pain (**acupuncture** analgesia) or to treat certain diseases or dysfunctions (**acupuncture** therapy).

The traditional Chinese explanation of how **acupuncture** works relies heavily on concepts unfamiliar to the Western scientific community. According to traditional Chinese theory, the basic energy or force of life, which flows through all living things, is called "Ch'i." When this force flows through the human body, it travels along twelve primary and two secondary channels or meridians. It is along these channels that the **acupuncture** points lie. Ch'i, traditional Chinese theory teaches, has two aspects to it: Yin, the negative aspect, and Yang, the positive aspect. The twelve primary channels through which Ch'i flows are divided accordingly into six Yin and six Yang channels and paired. For each Yin channel, there is a Yang channel.

Despite the reference to them as "negative" and "positive," as Yin and Yang are two aspects of the same force, one is no more desirable than the other. In fact, it is a basic tenet of traditional Chinese theory that Yin and Yang must be in balance for Ch'i to flow freely and for all living things, therefore, to function properly. Thus, the theory teaches that it is when Yin and Yang are out of balance that the body is susceptible to pain and illness. **Acupuncture** treatment is designed to correct this imbalance. The skilled **acupuncturist**, by placing and manipulating the needles in the proper points, brings Yin and Yang back into balance. This allows Ch'i to flow freely and the body's natural defenses to combat disease and pain. Andrews v. Ballard, 498 F.Supp. 1038, 1042, 1043, 1055, 1057 (S.D. Tex.1980).

Courts from several jurisdictions have ruled that a general license to practice medicine is required before one may engage in the practice of **acupuncture**. State v. Rich, 44 Ohio St.2d 195, 73 Ohio Op.2d 487, 339 N.E.2d 630 (1975); Louisiana State Board of Medical Examiners v. Moran, 290 So.2d 383 (La.App.1974); State v. Won, 19 Or.App. 580, 528 P.2d 594 (1974); Commonwealth v. Schatzberg, 29 Pa.Cmwlth. 426, 371 A.2d 544 (1977). Risks involved in the practice of **acupuncture** by nonphysicians have been identified as improper use of needles leading to infection, bruising, needles breaking in the body, delay in diagnosis and serious illnesses. The penetration of the skin with needles is a surgical act. Note, Regulating the Practice of Acupuncture: Recent Developments in California, 7 U.C.D.L.Rev. 385, 391–392, 396 (1974). Further, the majority of state licensing boards addressing the question consider **acupuncture** as the practice of medicine or osteopathy. Two states, Indiana and Kansas, forbid the use of **acupuncture** by licensed physicians. Pisani, Acupuncture: The Practice of Medicine? 38 Albany Law Rev. 633 (1974).

The issue of the right of a chiropractor to perform **acupuncture** has been addressed in several states. All decisions have denied the right. State v. Won, supra; Commonwealth v. Schatzberg, supra; State v. Rich, supra. The Pennsylvania decision is particularly pertinent since that state's statutory definition of chiropractic, like Michigan's, includes "preparatory to" language. Defendant's excellent and comprehensive brief does not cite nor have we discovered any authority to the contrary. We thus conclude that as a matter of law a chiropractor is not authorized to perform **acupuncture** in this State. Kelley v. Raguckas, 270 N.W.2d 665, 669 (Ct.App.Mich. 1978).

As commonly understood and as stated by appellee in his brief to this court, **acupuncture** consists of the insertion of needles to various nerves below the skin, thus stimulating reactions to alleviate pain and other conditions of ill health. According to appellee's testimony before the trial court, the needles are inserted approximately one-quarter inch to one inch beneath the skin, depending on the weight of the patient and the area of the body involved. State v. Rich, 339 N.E.2d 630, 632 (Ohio 1975).

Other Authorities: Andrews v. Ballard, 498 F.Supp. 1038, 1042–3, 1055, 1057 (S.D.Tex.1980); State v. Rich, 339 N.E.2d 630, 632 (Ohio 1975). People v. Amber, 349 N.Y.S.2d 604, 609 (Sup.Ct. Queens Cty.N.Y.1973).

acupuncture, galvanic

Defendant also argues that he should be allowed to engage in **galvanic acupuncture**, since it is a form of electrotherapy, and drugless healers are permitted by statute to practice electrotherapy. We are not informed by the record whether or not electrotherapy involves skin penetration. We assume that it does not because of the prohibition mentioned above. We are, however, informed by the record that **galvanic acupunc-**

ture involves the insertion of needles into various portions of the body and the application of electric current. This process is even more involved than acupuncture, which is now only in the experimental stage by the medical profession in this country. If we were to allow the extension of permissible electrotherapy in this manner, we would involve the judiciary in a medical matter which, according to the constitution, belongs with the legislature. Since **galvanic acupuncture** does involve the penetration of human tissue, we hold that it is not an authorized practice for chiropractors and drugless healers. Griffith v. Dep't of Motor Vehicles, 598 P.2d 1377, 1382 (Ct.App. Wash.1979).

acute (ah-kūt') [L. *acutus* sharp] 1. sharp; poignant. 2. having a short and relatively severe course.

By "acute" he meant something of sudden onset rather than something of long term standing. Hartford Accident & Indemnity Co. v. Contreras, 498 S.W.2d 419, 421 (Ct.Civ.App.Tex. 1973).

Acute is something what takes place within hours, let's say, after some given injurious event. An **acute** response to some process going on means a response within hours or maybe days. Woodall Industries, Inc. v. Massachusetts Mutual Life Insurance Co., 483 F.2d 986, 1000 (6th Cir. 1973).

adaptation (ad"ap-ta'shun) [L. *adaptare* to fit] the normal ability of the eye to adjust itself to variations in the intensity of light; the adjustment to such variations. See also *lens, adaptation of*.

The statute, however, is aimed at correcting "defects or abnormal conditions" by use of lenses. The use of the word "**adaptation**" must be construed in connection with the intent of the statute. In this light, "**adaptation**" does not refer to the fitting process, but to the correction of refractive errors caused by "defects or abnormal conditions." These are the responsibility of the physician. The defendants do not "**adapt**" the lenses by determining that certain optical qualities are needed to correct refractive error. State ex rel. Londerholm v. Doolin, 497 P.2d 138, 151–2 (Kan.1972).

addict (ad'ikt) a person who cannot resist a habit, especially the use of drugs or alcohol, for physiological or psychological reasons.

addict, narcotic

Where **narcotic addiction** has progressed beyond the incipient, volitional stage, California provides for commitment of three months to two years in a state hospital. California Welfare and Institutions Code § 5355. For the purposes of this provision, a **narcotic addict** is defined as

any person who habitually takes or otherwise uses to the extent of having lost the power of self-control any opium, morphine, cocaine, or other narcotic drug as defined in Article 1 of Chapter 1 of Division 10 of the Health and Safety Code. California Welfare and Institutions Code § 5350. Robinson v. California, 370 U.S. 660, 680–1, 82 S.Ct. 1417, 8 L.Ed.2d 758 (1962).

addiction (ah-dik'shun) the state of being given up to some habit, especially strong dependence on a drug. See also *abuse; dependence; drug, habit-forming*; and *opium*.

The term **addiction** refers to the physical, rather than a psychological dependence on the drug. People v. McCabe, 275 N.E.2d 407, 410 (Ill.1971).

Very relevant to that history is the Final Report of the President's Advisory Commission on Narcotics and Drug Abuse, at 2 (1963), which states: "When this report speaks of 'drug **addiction**' it is using the term in its full technical sense to include both the psychological and the physical dependence. When it speaks of 'drug abuse' it is referring to the broader problem which includes also those drugs which create only psychological dependency. We will use the term 'drug abuse' in this report as existing when an individual takes psychotoxic drugs under any of the following circumstances: (a) in amounts sufficient to create a hazard to his own health or to the safety of the community; or (b) when he obtains drugs through illicit channels; or (c) when he takes drugs on his own initiative rather than on the basis of professional advice." Hoffmann-La Roche, Inc. v. Kleindienst, 478 F.2d 1, 4 (3d Cir. 1973).

addiction, drug a state of periodic or chronic intoxication produced by the repeated consumption of a drug, characterized by (1) an overwhelming desire or need (compulsion) to continue use of the drug and to obtain it by any means, (2) a tendency to increase the dosage, (3) a psychological and usually a physical dependence on its effects, and (4) a detrimental effect on the individual and on society. Cf. *habituation*.

The trial court defined "**addicted** to narcotics" as used in § 11721 [Cal. Health and Safety Code] in the following charge to the jury:

The word "**addicted**" means, strongly disposed to some taste or practice or habituated, especially to drugs. In order to inquire as to whether a person is **addicted** to the use of narcotics is in effect an inquiry as to his habit in that regard. Does he use them habitually. To use them often or daily is, according to the ordinary acceptance of those words, to use them habitually. Robinson v. California, 370 U.S. 660, 680, 82 S.Ct. 1417, 8 L.Ed.2d 758 (1962).

Addiction is a broad word used to refer to dependencies caused by a variety of factors. A dependency may develop from a chemical change in the body, usually coupled with a growing tolerance for the drug requiring larger and larger doses and severe physical reactions such as tremors, nausea, hallucinations or even death when the drug is withheld. The opiates are the drugs best known to produce this type of dependency, but barbiturates and amphetamines also produce it. The authorities reviewed by this court have found marijuana users do not develop this sort of dependency. Bourassa v. State, 366 So.2d 12, 17 (Fla.1978).

The legislative history of the Act must be referred to. Very relevant to that history is the Final Report of the President's Advisory Commission on Narcotics and Drug Abuse, at 2 (1963), which states: "When this report speaks of "**drug addiction**" it is using the term in its full technical sense to include both the psychological and the physical dependence. Hoffmann-La Roche, Inc. v. Kleindienst, 478 F.2d 1, 4 (3d Cir. 1973).

addiction, heroin

The most widely accepted and authoritative definition of **heroin addiction** is that promulgated by the World Health Organization, which lists the characteristics of the disease as follows:

(1) an overpowering desire or need to continue taking the drug and to obtain it by any means; the need can be satisfied by the drug taken initially or by another with morphine-like properties;

(2) a tendency to increase the dose owing to the development of tolerance;

(3) a psychic dependence on the effects of the drug related to a subjective and individual appreciation of those effects; and

(4) a physical dependence on the effects of the drug requiring its presence for maintenance of homeostasis and resulting in a definite, characteristic, and self-limited abstinence syndrome when the drug is withdrawn.

Development of such an **addiction** is, of course, a gradual process, and it is the purpose of this section to explore briefly the nature of this process and the effects of the disease upon the addict. U.S. v. Moore, 486 F.2d 1139, 1229–30 (D.C.Cir. 1973).

Addison's planes, point (ad'ĭ-sonz) [Christopher *Addison*, English anatomist, 1869–1951] See under *plane* and *point*.

adductus, metatarsus See *metatarsus adductus*.

adductor muscles See *musculus, adductor brevis; musculus, adductor longis; musculus, adductor magnus; and musculus, adductor minimus*.

adductor (ah-duk'tor) [L.] that which adducts. See *Table of Musculi*.

adduction (ah-duk'shun) the act of adducting or the state of being adducted.

The superior laryngeal nerves control the motion of **adduction**, that is, the movement of the vocal chords toward each other. Roberts v. Wood, 206 F.Supp. 579, 582 (S.D.Ala.1962).

additive (ad'ĭ-tiv) 1. characterized by addition. See also under *effect*. 2. a substance, as a flavoring agent, preservative, or vitamin, added to another substance to improve its appearance, increase its nutritional value, etc.

additive, food

21 U.S.C. § 321(s) provides: The term "**food additive**" means any substance the intended use of which results or may reasonably be expected to result, directly or indirectly, in its becoming a component or otherwise affecting the characteristics of any food . . . , if such substance is not generally recognized, among experts qualified by scientific training and experience to evaluate its safety, as having been adequately shown through scientific procedures (or, in the case of a substance used in food prior to January 1, 1958, through either scientific procedures or experience based on common use in food) to be safe under the conditions of its intended use. . . . U.S. v. Naremco, Inc., 553 F.2d 1138, 1141–2 (8th Cir. 1977).

21 U.S.C. § 348(a) a **food additive** shall, with respect to any particular use or intended use of such **additives**, be deemed to be unsafe for the purposes of the application of clause (2)(C) of § 342(a) of this title, unless—

(1) It and its intended use conform to the terms of an exemption which is in effect pursuant to subsection (i) of this section; or

(2) There is in effect, and it and its use or intended use are in conformity with, a regulation issued under this section prescribing the conditions under which such **additive** may be safely used.

While such a regulation relating to a **food additive** is in effect, a food shall not, by reason of bearing or containing such an **additive** in accordance with the regulation, be considered adulterated within the meaning of clause (1) of § 342(a) of this title. U.S. v. 41 Cases, More or Less, 420 F.2d 1126, 1128 (5th Cir. 1970).

The Delaney clause, 21 U.S.C. § 348(c)(3)(A), provides that no **additive** "shall be deemed to be safe if it is found to induce cancer when ingested by man or animal," and is generally intended to prohibit the use of any additives which under any conditions induce cancer in any strain of test animal. Bell v. Goddard, 366 F.2d 177, 181 (7th Cir. 1966).

Other Authorities: Nutrilab, Inc. v. Schweiker, 713 F.2d 335, 337 (7th Cir. 1983); National Nutritional Foods Ass'n v. Kennedy, 572 F.2d 377, 390–1 (2d Cir. 1978); U.S. v. Nova Scotia Food Products Corp., 568 F.2d 240, 246 (2d Cir. 1977).

ADEM See *encephalomyelitis, acute disseminated*.

adenitis (ad"ĕ-ni'tis) inflammation of a gland. Cf. *acinitis*.

adenitis, mesenteric mesenteric lymphadenitis.

On the latter occasion he noted a "complicating abdominal pain, possibly **mesenteric adenitis**" (an infection of the mesentery glands of the stomach). He considered her condition to be caused by a staphylococcus aureus coagulose positive infection. On both occasions he prescribed Chloromycetin, and the child responded well. . . .

. . . he also gave the opinion that **mesenteric adenitis** is a common condition, that it cannot be ascertained by external palpation; and that in any case it requires no treatment. Incollingo v. Ewing, 282 A.2d 206, 211, 213 (Pa.1971).

"The next most common would be **mesenteric adenitis**, which is swelling of the glands with throat infections or colds. These are the most common in childhood." Tonsillitis is one of the diseases included in the term **mesenteric adenitis**. Sinkey v. Surgical Associates, 186 N.W.2d 658, 660 (Iowa 1971).

adenocarcinoma (ad"ĕ-no-kar"sĭ-no'mah) carcinoma derived from glandular tissue or in which the tumor cells form recognizable glandular structures; adenocarcinomas may be classified according to the predominant pattern of cell arrangement, as papillary, alveolar, etc., or according to a particular product of the cells, as mucinous adenocarcinoma.

Plaintiff, apparently healthy at birth, began hemorrhaging at age 19. Examinations disclosed a condition known as clear-cell **adenocarcinoma**, cancer of the vagina and cervix. She immediately underwent surgery followed by radiation therapy. Four years later, a recurrence of the cancer was diagnosed, and she underwent radical surgery, removing all tissue in her pelvis, including her bladder, rectum, and the remainder of her vagina.

Expert testimony was introduced concerning the relationship between the ingestion of DES by mothers and the tragically commonplace incidence of **adenocarcinoma** in their daughters. Mertan v. E. R. Squibb & Sons, Inc., 190 Cal.Rptr. 349, 351 (Ct. of App.1983).

In the past decade the link between prenatal DES exposure and the later development in female offspring of clear cell cervical or vaginal **adenocarcinoma**, a hitherto rare disease involving cancerous growth in glandular tissue, has been unquestionably confirmed (see L.1978, ch. 715, § 1; Note, Market Share Liability: An Answer to the DES Causation Problem, 94 Harv.L.Rev. 668, 669, n.8, and authorities cited therein). Bichler v. Eli Lilly & Co., 436 N.E.2d 182, 184 (N.Y.1982).

. . . upon testing he discovered enlarged, exterior hemorrhoids and a mass in the area of internal hemorrhoids; he then referred plaintiff to a specialist who discovered "a moderately well-differentiated **adenocarcinoma**"; plaintiff was told that to save his life a complete colostomy would have to be performed by a specialist; . . . Bennett v. Raag, 431 N.E.2d 48, 50 (App.Ct.Ill.1982).

Other Authorities: Sindell v. Abbott Laboratories, 607 P.2d 924, 925 (Cal.1980); Lyons v. Premo Pharmaceutical Labs, Inc., 406 A.2d 185, 188 (Super.Ct.N.J.1979); Joynt v. Barnes, 388 N.E.2d 1298, 1304 (App.Ct.Ill.1979); Helmrich v. Eli Lilly & Co., 455 N.Y.S.2d 460, 461 (4th Dep't 1982); Needham v. White Laboratories, Inc., 639 F.2d 394, 396 (7th Cir. 1981); Parsons v. Wood, 584 P.2d 1332, 1334–5 (Okl.1978).

adenofibroma (ad"ĕ-no-fi-bro'mah) a tumor composed of connective tissue containing glandular structures.

. . . plaintiff was admitted to the Medical College of Virginia Hospital (MCV) for excision of a benign **adenofibroma** (tumor composed of connective tissue with glandular structures) of the right breast. Hurst v. Mathews, 426 F.Supp. 245, 246 (E.D.Va. 1976).

adenoma (ad"ĕ-no'mah) [*adeno-* + *-oma*] a benign epithelial tumor in which the cells form recognizable glandular structures or in which the cells are clearly derived from glandular epithelium.

The defendant examined the plaintiff on May 17, 1966, and diagnosed her condition as an **adenoma** ("nontoxic" tumor) occupying most of the left lobe of the thyroid gland, and enlarging. . . .

. . . In his opinion the operation to remove the **adenoma** carried some risk of injury to the vocal cords by reason of possible damage to the recurrent laryngeal nerve, but it was not a high risk. In about 150 similar operations performed by him, there had been no such casualty. Schroeder v. Lawrence, 359 N.E.2d 1301, 1302 (Sup.Jud.Ct.Mass.1977).

adenoma, villous a large soft papillary polyp on the mucosa of the large intestine.

adenomyosis (ad"ĕ-no-mi-o'sis) a benign condition characterized by ingrowth of the endometrium into the uterine musculature, sometimes associated with an overgrowth of the latter. If the lesion forms a circumscribed tumorlike nodule, it is called *adenomyoma*. Called also *endometriosis interna or uterina, adenomyosis uteri,* and *adenomyometritis*.

Post-surgical pathological examination also revealed evidence of **adenomyosis**, a disease necessitating surgical removal via hysterectomy, required irrespective of whether fibroid tumors existed. Gayle v. Neyman, 457 N.Y.S.2d 499, 501 (1st Dep't 1983).

The medical expert also testified that the operation uncovered the fact that Mrs. Hammock had endometriosis or **ademyosis** (in layman's terms from Dorland's Illustrated Medical Dictionary, 24th Edition—the uterine mucous membrane occurring aberrantly in various locations in the pelvic cavity. **Ademyosis**— in the ovarian tissue as small superficial islands or in the form of endometrial cysts), which probably had a lot to do with her discomfort, excessive bleeding, pressure and pain. Hammock v. Allstate Insurance Co., 186 S.E.2d 353, 354–5 (Ct.App.Ga. 1971).

There was also a condition, not unusual, called **adenomyosis** which is inclined to cause the uterus to have "a little less tone and be a little more prone to bleeding." This condition predated the accident, and could have caused the heavier bleeding during the menstrual periods previous to the accident. Ketcham v. Thomas, 283 S.W.2d 642, 649 (Mo.1955).

Other Authorities: Smithers v. Collins, 278 S.E.2d 286, 287 (Ct.App.N.Car.1981).

adenosis (ad"ĕ-no'sis) 1. any disease of the glands. 2. the abnormal development or formation of gland tissue.

Since the initial study and FDA banning order, maternal ingestion [of DES and DEN] has been associated with **adenosis** (abnormal presence of glandular epithelial cells or tissue in the vagina or cervix), structural abnormalities of the cervix and vagina, surgical interventions such as vaginectomies, and a host of other afflictions (infertility, anxiety, embarrassment, mental anguish, and other psychological sequela). Schering Corp. v. Home Ins. Co., 712 F.2d 4, 7 (2d Cir. 1983).

In addition, the FDA estimated in 1975 that 30 to 90% of these offspring develop vaginal **adenosis**, a noncancerous condition in which glandular tissue normally found only in the cervix is also found in the vagina (Sheiner, DES and a Proposed Theory of Enterprise Liability, 46 Ford L.Rev. 963, 965, n.10). Bichler v. Eli Lilly and Co., 450 N.Y.S.2d 776, 778 (N.Y.1982).

DES also causes **adenosis**, precancerous vaginal and cervical growths which may spread to other areas of the body. The treatment for **adenosis** is cauterization, surgery, or cryosurgery. Women who suffer from this condition must be monitored by biopsy or colposcopic examination twice a year, a painful and expensive procedure. Sindell v. Abbott Laboratories, 607 P.2d 924, 925 (Cal.1980).

adenosis, vaginae the presence in the vagina of multiple ectopic areas of folded endocervical mucosa.

In addition, the FDA estimated in 1975 that 30 to 90% of these offspring develop **vaginal adenosis**, a noncancerous condition in which glandular tissue normally found only in the cervix is also found in the vagina (Sheiner, DES and a Proposed Theory of Enterprise Liability, 46 Ford L.Rev. 963, 965, n.10). Because of the "paramount public importance" of identifying, screening, diagnosing, caring for and treating the estimated more than 100,000 New York women whose health has been endangered by prenatal exposure to DES (L.1978, ch. 715, § 1), the Legislature has enacted section 2500–c of the Public Health Law aimed at locating, monitoring and establishing special programs for these young women. Bichler v. Eli Lilly & Co., 436 N.E.2d 182, 184 (N.Y.1982).

adhesion (ad-he'zhun) [L. *adhaesio,* from *adhaerere* to stick to] 1. the property of remaining in close proximity, as that resulting from the physical attraction of molecules to a substance, or the molecular attraction existing between the surfaces of contacting bodies. 2. the stable joining of parts to each other, which may occur abnormally. 3. a fibrous band or structure by which parts abnormally adhere.

Dr. Collins discovered that, as a result of the previous surgery (the uterine suspension operation), plaintiff had developed **adhesions**—tissue bands which form during the healing process following surgery—involving the uterus, the space behind the uterus, and the tubes and ovaries on each side....

... Dr. Collins testified that **adhesions** develop in the first several days following surgery as a normal part of the healing process and that **adhesions** that do not disappear spontaneously develop into stronger fibrous **adhesions** within five to ten days. These fibrous **adhesions** sometimes "bind down the organ that's involved in the area" of the surgery. The distal small bowel, or ileum, is often the organ involved, and its normal function may be affected, though many people live a full and normal life with a partial bowel obstruction following surgery. Smithers v. Collins, 278 S.E.2d 286, 287 (Ct.App.N.Car. 1981).

In brief, the evidence is that the pressure on the ureter was caused by a build up of **adhesions** and swelling, edema, and reaction to the ligatures necessarily placed within approximately one and one half centimeters of the ureter. Dr. Howard tells us the **adhesions** are "... little tissue bands, that are a little bit tougher than the ordinary tissue around it and those occur due to Nature's way of reacting to irritation, inflammation or infection." Cronin v. Hagan, 221 N.W.2d 748, 752–3 (Iowa 1974).

adhesion, tubo-ovarian

It was also noted that both tubes and ovaries were adhered by some very fine, very fine **tubo-ovarian adhesions**. This means that both tubes and ovaries were kind of stuck together and stuck to the pelvic side wall or abdominal wall by piano string, just like strings of mucus across in a spider web fashion. Baker v. Beebe, 367 So.2d 102, 105–6 (Ct.App.La.1979).

adjustment (ad-just′ment) in chiropractic, manipulation of the spine, said to restore normal nerve function and cure disease.

adjustment, specific

Here, the testimony of two State's witnesses, Dr. Weis and Dr. Kaye, gave a definition of the term "specific adjustment" upon which the jury could make a proper decision of what "specific adjustment" was, which was "when a person is presented with a localized condition involving one or two or three vertebrae and intentionally brings about a movement of these vertebrae to relieve that condition, he or she has performed a **specific adjustment**." State v. Blinzler, 599 P.2d 349, 353–4 (Mont.1979).

adrenal (ah-dre′nal) [L. *ad* near + *ren* kidney] an adrenal gland.

administer

The word "**administer**" is defined in 21 U.S.C. § 802(2) as follows:

The term "**administer**" refers to the direct application of a controlled substance to the body of a patient ... by—

(A) a practitioner (or, in his presence, by his authorized agent), or

(B) the patient ... at the direction and in the presence of the practitioner,

whether such application be by injection, inhalation, ingestion, or any other means. U.S. v. Bartee, 479 F.2d 484, 487 (10th Cir. 1973).

adsorb (ad-sorb′) to attract and retain other material on the surface. See also *adsorption*.

The resin, usually a polystyrene, has sulphonic acid or carboxyl functional groups for **adsorbing** basic drugs such as ephedrine or amphetamine, or the resin may have quaternary ammonium or primary amino functional groups for **adsorbing** acidic drugs such as barbituric acid derivatives. The rate of release of the drugs may be varied by factors including the percent of cross-linkage and particle size of the resin or varying the amount of drug chemically combined with the resin. Clinical Products Ltd. v. Brenner, 255 F.Supp. 131, 134 (D.D.C.1966).

adsorption (ad-sorp′shun) [L. *ad* to + *sorbere* to suck] the attachment of one substance to the surface of another; the concentration of a gas or a substance in solution in a liquid on a surface in contact with the gas or liquid, resulting in a relatively high concentration of the gas or solution at the surface. Cf. *absorption*.

adulterated See *adulteration*.

adulteration (ah-dul″ter-a′shun) addition of an impure, cheap, or unnecessary ingredient to cheat, cheapen, or falsify a preparation; in legal terminology, incorrect labeling, including dosage not in accordance with the label.

Adulteration is defined by Section 7 of the Act, 35 P.S. § 780–107, which provides in part as follows:

A controlled substance, other drug, device or cosmetic shall be deemed to be **adulterated**:

(1)(i) If it consists, in whole or in part, of any filthy, putrid or decomposed substance; (ii) if it has been prepared, packed or held under unsanitary conditions whereby it may have been contaminated with filth, or whereby it may have been rendered injurious to health;.... DeMarco v. Com. Dep't of Health, 397 A.2d 61, 62–63 (Cmwlth.Ct.Pa.1979).

Oysters packed and shipped in their natural unopened state which were found to harbor bacteria making them unfit for consumption were held to be "**adulterated**" within the meaning of the Act [21 U.S.C. § 342]. The Court said (208 F. at 422)

The ordinary use of "**adulteration**" implies an actual addition to the original substance, through human agency. But the word as used in the section does not restrict this to addition by the hand of man, and if the **adulteration** of filthy, decomposed, or putrid substance has been added by nature, and is contained in the article to be shipped, it is **adulterated** in the eyes of the law. U.S. v. Nova Scotia Food Products Corp., 417 F.Supp. 1364, 1369–70 (E.D.N.Y.1976), reversed 568 F.2d 240 (2d Cir. 1977).

21 U.S.C. § 601(m)(1) states that a product is **adulterated** "if it bears or contains any poisonous or deleterious substance which may render it injurious to health." Schuck v. Butz, 500 F.2d 810, 811 (D.C.Cir.1974).

Proceeding under the statute, the government contends that the lots were "**adulterated**" in one or more of the definitions prescribed by Congress in 21 U.S.C. § 342, which provides in part:

A food shall be deemed to be **adulterated**—

(a)(1) If it bears or contains any poisonous or deleterious substance which may render it injurious to health;...

(3) If it consists in whole or in part of any filthy, putrid, or decomposed substance, or....

(4) If it has been prepared, packed, or held under insanitary conditions whereby it may have become contaminated with filth, or whereby it may have been rendered injurious to health;... U.S. v. 1,200 Cans, Pasteurized Whole Eggs, 339 F. Supp. 131, 134 (N.D.Ga.1972).

Other Authorities: U.S. v. General Foods Corp., 446 F.Supp. 740, 743 (N.D.N.Y.1978); U.S. v. 41 Cases, More or Less, 420 F.2d 1126, 1128 (5th Cir. 1970).

adverse reaction report

The "**adverse reaction**" **reports** are completed by a physician or hospital personnel and forwarded to the drug manufacturer, informing the manufacturer that a patient has suffered from a reaction of side effects which is not detailed on the package insert. Mauldin v. Upjohn Co., 697 F.2d 644, 648 (5th Cir. 1983).

Aerobacter (a″er-o-bak′ter) [aero- + Gr. *baktērion* little rod] a genus of bacteria of the tribe Escherichieae, family Enterobacteriaceae, order Eubacteriales, made up of short, motile or nonmotile, gram-negative rods, which ferment glucose and lactose to produce acid and gas. It includes two species, A. (*Bacterium*) *aero'genes* and A. (*Bacterium*) *cloa'cae*.

On Saturday, June 10th, defendant received the results from the culture and sensitivity tests which indicated that plaintiff had an **aerobacter** aerogenes bacteria that was gram-negative. Casey v. Penn, 360 N.E.2d 93, 97 (App.Ct.Ill.1977), supplemented 362 N.E.2d 1373 (1977).

aerosol (a′er-o-sol″) 1. a colloid system in which the continuous phase (dispersion medium) is a gas, e.g., fog.

The terms "**aerosol**" and pressurized container are apparently used interchangeably. Commercial ingredients such as insecticides, hair sprays, cleaning fluids, shoe polishes, and many others are packaged in a container together with a gas propellant. When the valve on the container is depressed, a mist consisting of a mixture of the components is expelled. The commercial substance or the propellant or both may be flammable. Fluorocarbon gases which are considered to be nonflammable and hydrocarbon gases which are considered to be flammable are frequently used in combination as a propellant. As a result, use of a pressurized container in conjunction with heat may have a blowtorch effect. Moreover, regardless of the flammability of the components, pressurized containers always have an explosive potential if subjected to heat. Chemical Specialties Mfrs. Ass'n, Inc. v. Lowery, 452 F.2d 431, 432 (2d Cir. 1971).

afebrile (a-feb′ril) without fever.

At the time of discharge he was **afebrile** and was requiring only a small dressing and wrap of the stump. Office follow-up is planned. Alexander v. Weinberger, 536 F.2d 779, 781 (8th Cir. 1976).

affect (af′fekt) a freudian term for the feeling of pleasantness or unpleasantness evoked by a stimulus; also the emotional complex associated with a mental state; the feeling experienced in connection with an emotion.

Therefore, I want to amplify on this term, "upset." From what she told me, and also from the nature of the situation to which she had an emotional reaction, it is obvious that the disturbance of **affect**—which is the professional term that we use instead of upset—the disturbance of **affect** which she manifested was one of tremendous anger because of her feeling that any implications regarding her handling of this particular situation were unjust; regardless of what was intended in the writing of the letter, her reaction to it was such that it evoked this type of disturbance of **affect**. Bowes v. Inter-Community Action, Inc., 411 A.2d 1279, 1281 (Cmwlth.Ct.Pa.1980).

affect, flat

Dr. Merideth explained some of these terms as follows: A "**flat affect**" refers to a noncommittal facial expression. Johnson v. U.S., 409 F.Supp. 1283, 1286 (M.D.Fla.1976), reversed 576 F.2d 606 (5th Cir. 1978).

Afrodex See *methyltesterone* (U.S. v. 1,048,000 Capsule case).

agaric (ah-gar′ik) [Gr. *agarikon* a sort of tree fungus] any mushroom, more especially any species of *Agaricus*.

Agaricus (ah-gar′ĭ-kus) a genus of mushrooms. See also *agaric*.

agent (a′jent) [L. *agens* acting] any power, principle, or substance capable of producing an effect, whether physical, chemical, or biological.

Agent Orange a herbicide containing 2,4,5-trichlorophenoxyacetic acid and 2,4-dichlorophenoxyacetic acid and used to kill broadleaf plants by overstimulating their phototropic response; it also contains the contaminant dioxin. The compound is suspected of having oncogenic and teratogenic properties.

All herbicides derived from 2,4,5-trichlorophenol—including 2,4,5-T and silvex (but not 2,4-D)—contain a chemical contaminant formed in the manufacturing process known as 2,3,7,8-tetrachlorodibenzo-p-dioxin (TCDD). TCDD is one of the most toxic chemicals known to man. Its presence and significance in phenoxy herbicides have become known only in recent years, although the herbicides themselves have been in use since the late 1940s. TCDD cannot be eliminated entirely from the products of 2,4,5-trichlorophenol. However, refinements in production methods have succeeded in reducing the level of TCDD from up to 80 parts per million (ppm) to less than 0.1 ppm....

The concern over TCDD and the phenoxy herbicides has reached its current level, however, only since the late 1960s. Two significant events took place at that time. First, a mixture of 2,4-D and 2,4,5-T known as **Agent Orange** was used extensively in South Vietnam as a defoliant. Charges of resulting damage to human, animal, and plant life lead to a number of scientific studies of the effects of **Agent Orange**....

... A contaminant of 2,4,5-T—tetrachlorodibenzoparadioxin (TCDD, or dioxin)—is one of the most teratogenic chemicals known. The registrants have not established that 1 part per million of this contaminant—or even 0.1 ppm—in 2,4,5-T does not pose a danger to the public health and safety.

2. There is a substantial possibility that even "pure" 2,4,5-T is itself a hazard to man and the environment.

3. The dose-response curves for 2,4,5-T and dioxin have not been determined, and the possibility of "no effect" levels for these chemicals is only a matter of conjecture at this time....

... Professor Virgil C. Boekelheide, Professor of Organic Chemistry and Acting Head of the Department of Chemistry of the University of Oregon, testified that TCDD

is fantastically toxic and is commonly quoted as being the most toxic simple organic molecule known to man. Its acute oral lethal toxicity (LD_{50}) in guinea pigs is 0.0000006g/kg. At sublethal dose levels it still has highly toxic effects on thymus, liver and other organs, as well as being extremely teratogenic....

If one considers the human LD_{50} to be similar to the LD_{50} of the most sensitive animal thus far tested (the guinea pig) the LD_{50} for humans would be 30 μg (based on the guinea pig LD_{50} of 0.6 μg per kg body weight and a human weight of 50 kg (110 lb). An ounce of pure dioxin would therefore contain about 800,000 lethal doses for humans. Citizens Against Toxic Sprays, Inc. v. Bergland, 428 F.Supp. 908, 914–15, 927–8 (D.Ore.1977). .

Agents, progestational a group of hormones secreted by the corpus luteum and placenta and, in small amounts, by the adrenal cortex, including progesterone, Δ^4-3-ketopregnene-20(α)-ol, and Δ^4-3-ketopregnene-20(β)-ol. Agents having progestational activity are also produced synthetically. Called also *gestogens, progestins, progestational hormones*, and *progestogens*.

agglutination (ah-gloo″tǐ-na′shun) [L. *agglutinatio*] the clumping together in suspension of antigen-bearing cells, microorganisms, or particles in the presence of specific antibodies (agglutinins). Called also *clumping*.

Blood groups refer to the properties of red blood corpuscles which cause them to clump together when in contact with appropriate anti-sera, the process being known as "agglutination." Anonymous v. Anonymous, 460 P.2d 32, 34 (Ct.App. Ariz.1969).

agglutinin (ah-gloo′tǐ-nin) antibody which aggregates a particulate antigen, e.g., bacteria, following combination with the homologous antigen in vivo or in vitro. Also, any substance other than antibody, e.g., lectin, that is capable of agglutinating particles.

The substance in the anti-sera which causes agglutination is designated as an **agglutinin**. Anonymous v. Anonymous, 460 P.2d 32, 34 (Ct.App.Ariz.1969).

agglutinogen (ag″loo-tin′o-jen) any substance which, acting as an antigen, stimulates the production of agglutinin.

A substance in the blood cells which is capable of producing an element having the power of agglutination is designated as one of the **agglutinogens**. Anonymous v. Anonymous, 460 P.2d 32, 34 (Ct.App.Ariz.1969).

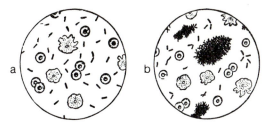

Agglutination: *a.* bacilli unagglutinated; *b.* bacilli agglutinated.

aggravate See *aggravation.*

aggravation See *osteoarthritis* (Lumbermen's case); and *preexisting.*

In Dressler v. Grand Rapids Die Casting Corp., 402 Mich. 243, 253–254, 262 N.W.2d 629 (1978), the Court considered an **aggravation** of an injury which involved successive employers:

" ' "The Massachusetts-Michigan rule in successive-injury cases is to place full liability upon the carrier covering the risk at the time of the most recent injury that bears a causal relation to the disability.

" ' "If the second injury takes the form merely of a recurrence of the first, and if the second incident does not contribute even slightly to the causation of the disabling condition, the insurer on the risk at the time of the original injury remains liable for the second. In this class would fall most of the cases discussed in the section on range of consequences in which a second injury occurred as the direct result of the first, as when claimant falls because of his crutches which his first injury requires him to use. This group also includes the kind of case in which a man has suffered a back strain, followed by a period of work with continuing symptoms indicating that the original condition persists, and culminating in a second period of disability precipitated by some lift or exertion.

" ' "On the other hand, if the second incident contributes independently to the injury, the second insurer is solely liable, even if the injury would have been much less severe in the absence of the prior condition, and even if the prior injury contributed the major part to the final condition. This is consistent with the general principle of the compensability of the **aggravation** of a preexisting condition." 3 Larson, Workmen's Compensation Law, § 95.12, pp 508.130–508.133.' Mullins v. Dura Corp., supra, 46 Mich.App. 52, 55–56, 207 N.W.2d 404 (1973), lv. den. 392 Mich. 792 (1974). (Emphasis changed.)" McManus v. Copper & Brass Sales, 327 N.W.2d 379, 381–2 (Ct.App.Mich.1982).

In sum, Dr. Mitchell's overall testimony was consistent with at least two theories of work-related **aggravation**, namely, that pustular lesions appeared initially as a response to the physical trauma of driving, or that driving **aggravated** existing lesions to the point that they cracked, bled and made driving impossible. It is possible both things happened. In either case, work-related **aggravation** of an underlying psoriatic condition is clearly established on this record. Hensley v. Washington Metro. Area Transit Auth., 655 F.2d 264, 275 (D.C.Cir.1981).

Labor Code section 4663 governs apportionment of disability resulting from **aggravation** of a prior disease. It provides: "In case of **aggravation** of any disease existing prior to a compensable injury, compensation shall be allowed only for the proportion of the disability due to the **aggravation** of such prior disease which is reasonably attributed to the injury''. . . .

. . . Numerous commentators on California and American law have also written explanations of this apportionment statute based on their interpretations of case law concerning section 4663. (Comment, Injury to the Deceased or Disabled Employee Under the California Workmen's Compensation Laws (1956) 44 Cal.L.Rev. 548; Hanna, Apportionment of Permanent Disability: A Review of Recent California Court Opinions (1970) 21 Hastings L.J. 623; 2 Witkin, Summary of Cal.Law (8th ed.) §§ 180–181, pp. 1000–1002; 2 Hanna, California Law of Employee Injuries and Workmen's Compensation (2d ed.) § 14.04[2][f]; 1 Herlick, California Workers' Compensation Law Handbook (2d ed.) § 7.45, pp. 262–263; Swezey, California Workmen's Compensation Practice 1973, §§ 14.23–14.24; 2 Larson, Law of Workmen's Compensation, § 59.20.) Duthie v. Worker's Compensation Appeals Bd., 150 Cal.Rptr. 530, 533–4 (Ct.App.Cal.1978).

Other Authorities: Bearden Lumber Co. v. Bond, 644 S.W.2d 321, 324 (Ct.App.Ark.1983); Berry v. Workmen's Compensation Appeals Board, 441 P.2d 908, 910 (Cal.1968).

aggression (ah-gresh'un) [L. *aggressus*, from *ad*to + *gradi*to step] a form of behavior which leads to self-assertion; it may arise from innate drives and/or a response to frustration; it may be manifested by destructive and attacking behavior, by covert attitudes of hostility and obstructionism, or by a healthy self-expressive drive to mastery.

Unsocialized, **aggressive** reaction of childhood 308.40. . . .

. . . This nomenclature is derived from the Diagnostic and Statistical Manual of Mental Disorders published by the American Psychiatric Association. J.L. v. Parham, 412 F.Supp. 112, 117 (M.D.Ga.1976).

aggressive See *aggression.*

aging (āj'ing) the gradual changes in the structure of any organism that occur with the passage of time, that do not result from disease or other gross accidents, and that eventually lead to the increased probability of death as the individual grows older. Cf. *senescence.* See also *senescence*; and *synergistic* (U.S. Equal Employ. Opp. case).

The **aging** process affects all human beings and cannot be avoided. It manifests itself in virtually all physical and mental aspects of the human body. As a person **ages**, many physiological changes occur. Visual perception decreases. Older persons experience difficulty in color discrimination, depth perception, the ability to adapt to darkness, the ability to focus, and have reduced depth perception. Auditory perception also declines with **age**. Cognitive functions are adversely affected with advancing **age** due to structural and chemical changes that occur in the neuroendocrinal and central nervous systems. Some loss of memory, particularly short term memory, is common with advancing **age**.

In addition to these effects on a person's sensory and cognitive abilities, **aging** also affects physical motor skills. Strength declines because of a decrease in muscle mass that accompanies **aging**. Speed and agility decline with **age** due to stiffening of the joints. Stamina and endurance decline with **age. Aging** also results in decreased ability to maintain homeostatic

balance, such as in a decline in the body's ability to adjust to temperature changes. Moreover, health problems affect a substantial number of persons over the age of 65. About 10 to 15 percent of all 65 year olds show soft signs of some form of dementia, such as Alzheimer's disease. . . .

Despite these general effects of **aging** on the human body, individuals vary greatly in the way they are affected by **age**. Many individuals in their sixties or seventies can physically outperform persons in their twenties. Lifestyle factors such as regular exercise, refraining from smoking, and eating a balanced diet have a substantial effect on the functional capacity of persons as they **age**. Moreover, the changes that accompany **age** occur on a continuum, and some of the changes are significant in many individuals by age 50, while others may become significant much later. U.S. Equal Employ. Oppor. Com'n. v. City of Minneapolis, 537 F.Supp. 750, 754–5 (D.Minn.1982).

agrammatism (ah-gram'ah-tizm") [Gr. *agrammatos* unlettered] inability to speak grammatically because of brain injury or disease.

agraphia (ah-graf'e-ah) [*a* neg. + Gr. *graphein* to write + *-ia*] inability to express thoughts in writing, due to a lesion of the cerebral cortex.

In Matter of Kirkpatrick, 77 Misc.2d 646, 354 N.Y.S.2d 499, congenital learning disabilities of dyslexia and **disagraphia** [sic] were intertwined with an emotional problem;. . . . In Matter of Jessup, 379 N.Y.S.2d 626, 633 (Fam.Ct., City of N.Y., N.Y. Cty.1975).

aid (ād) help or assistance; by extension, applied to any device by which a function can be improved or augmented, as a hearing aid.

aid, hearing a device which amplifies sound to help persons with hearing loss; audiphone; otophone.

Concern over allegations of consumer abuses in the sale of **hearing aids** prompted the Legislature to pass the Hearing Aid Dispensers Act, L.1973, c. 19, N.J.S.A. 45:9A–1 et seq. ("the Act"), which became law on January 31, 1973. This enactment created a Hearing Aid Dispensers Examining Committee ("the Committee") under the State Board of Medical Examiners in the Division of Consumer Affairs of the Department of Law and Public Safety. N.J.S.A. 45:9A–1, 3.

We note that the FDA has formally stated its view that trade regulations proposed by the Federal Trade Commission governing **hearing aid** industry sales practices, see 40 Fed.Reg. 26646–51 (June 24, 1975), portions of which are substantially identical to several provisions of the Committee regulations, ". . . complement, rather than conflict with [the] FDA regulations relating to labeling and conditions of sale of **hearing aids**." See 42 Fed.Reg. 9286 (February 15, 1977) (comment to proposed 21 **C.F.R.** § 801.420, 421). New Jersey Guild of Hearing Aid D. v. Long, 384 A.2d 795, 798, 811 (N.J.1978).

A.I.D. donor insemination.

AIDS acquired immune deficiency syndrome See under *syndrome.*

airway (ār'wa) a tubular device for securing unobstructed passage of air into and out of the lungs during general anesthesia or on occasions when the patient is not ventilating properly.

It should be noted that in its opinion the district court stated that the only testimony as to the standard of care was that an **airway** must be established in four minutes for a patient to survive. Marek v. U.S., 639 F.2d 1164, 1165 (5th Cir. 1981).

akathisia (ak"ah-the'ze-ah) [*a* neg. + Gr. *kathisis* a sitting down + *-ia*] a condition of motor restlessness, ranging from a feeling of inner disquiet to inability to sit or lie quietly or to sleep; seen in toxic reactions to the phenothiazines. Called also *acathisia* and *kathisophobia*.

Akathesia [sic] is a subjective state and refers to an inability to be still; a motor restlessness which may produce a shaking of the hands or arms or feet or an irresistable desire to keep walking or tapping the feet. Rennie v. Klein, 462 F.Supp. 1131, 1138 (D.N.J.1978).

akinesia (ah"ki-ne'ze-ah) [*a* neg. + Gr. *kinēsis* motion + *-ia*] absence or poverty of movements.

Akinesia refers to a state of diminished spontaneity, and feeling of weakness and muscle fatigue.... Patients with severe cases of **akinesia** had to be dropped from the Rifkin study of prolixin. Rennie v. Klein, 462 F.Supp. 1131, 1138 (D.N.J. 1978).

akinesis (ah"ki-ne'sis) akinesia.

... "left ventricular **akinesis** of the inferior basilar constrictor muscle." This shows that part of his cardiac muscle has lost it's [sic] ability to contract effectively. **Akinesis** means absence, loss or weakness of muscle function. Icenhour v. Weinberger, 375 F.Supp. 312, 315 (E.D.Tenn.1973).

albumin (al-bu'min) a protein found in nearly every animal and in many vegetable tissues, and characterized by being soluble in water and coagulable by heat; it contains carbon, hydrogen, nitrogen, oxygen, and sulfur. The formula for crystallized albumin has been given as $C_{720}H_{1134}N_{218}S_5O_{248}$.

In reading from that report, Dr. Adonizio quoted Dr. Myers as stating that appellee was " 'first noted at least ten years ago to have **albumin** in his urine and to have high blood pressure a year ago,' ..." (N.T. 90). Dr. Adonizio then continued to explain that traces of **albumin** do not necessarily evidence the presence of nephritis. Ranieli v. Mutual Life Ins. Co. of America, 413 A.2d 396, 399 (Super.Ct.Pa.1979).

alcohol (al'ko-hol) [Arabic *al-koh'l* something subtle] 1. chemical name: ethanol. A transparent, colorless, mobile, volatile liquid, C_2H_5OH, miscible with water, ether, and chloroform, obtained by fermentation of carbohydrates with yeast. Called also *ethyl alcohol*. 2. [USP] a preparation containing not less than 92.3 per cent and not more than 93.8 per cent by weight, corresponding to not less than 94.9 per cent and not more than 96.0 per cent by volume, at 15.56°C., of C_2H_5OH; used as a topical anti-infective and solvent. See also *barbiturate* (Met. Life Ins. Co. case); *synergism* (Met. Life Ins. Co. case); and *chlorpromazine hydrochloride* (In re Cameron case).

Alcohol is the only powerful self-administered intoxicant used in the United States with social approval and without fear of criminal sanctions. The subjective effects of **alcohol** are well-known but the physical and psychological effects of the use of this drug have long been neglected or ignored. **Alcohol** operates in the body as a central nervous system depressant: its effects are very similar to

those produced by the barbiturates. Tolerance develops from continued use, and discontinued use precipitates a severe withdrawal syndrome similar to that of barbiturate withdrawal and marked by hallucinations and delirium tremens which may lead to death. What is commonly called "alcoholism" is actually physical addiction to the drug **alcohol**. **Alcohol** abuse causes cirrhosis of the liver, which ranks seventh nationally as a cause of death. It also leads to kidney dysfunction, Korsakoff's psychosis, and hyperthyroid. Because **alcohol** supplies calories to the body, thus depressing the appetite without supplying needed vitamins and amino acids, **alcohol** abuse engenders nutritional deficiencies not common to other types of drug abuse. These nutritional deficiencies in turn make it more difficult for the alcoholic to withstand the stresses of the withdrawal syndrome. Perhaps the most dangerous characteristic of **alcohol** is the effect it produces on the user in his relations to the outside world. The feisty pugnaciousness of the tippler may be a joke; the hostile aggressiveness of the **alcohol** abuser is not. It has been estimated that of 120,000 American deaths in accidents each year, **alcohol** is a major factor in up to 70 percent. About 55 percent of all arrests involve **alcohol**-related offenses such as drunkenness, drunk driving, and violations of alcoholic beverage control statutes; more than half of those arrested for crimes of violence, such as murder and rape, acted under the influence of **alcohol**. [Soler Of Canabis and the Courts 6 Conn.L.Rev. 601, 617–19 (1974)] [DISSENT] State v. Mitchell, 563 S.W.2d 18, 32 (Mo.1978).

The toxicologist also stated that 0.12 percent blood **alcoholic** content causes "an impairment of coordination, especially fine coordination [and] there is a slowing of the reflex time." Arnold v. Reynolds, 211 S.E.2d 46, 47 (Va.1975).

Under § 561.01, F.S., its definitive construction of the words "**alcoholic** beverages" is termed to mean "all beverages containing more than one per cent of **alcohol** by weight",.... Castlewood International Corp. v. Wynne, 305 So.2d 773, 776 (Fla.1974).

Other Authorities: Germann v. Matriss, 260 A.2d 825, 830 (N.J.1970).

alcohol, isopropyl [USP], chemical name: 2-propanol. A clear colorless liquid, $CH_3CH(OH)CH_3$, an isomer of propyl alcohol and a homologue of ethyl alcohol. It is miscible with water, alcohol, ether, and chloroform; used as a solvent and as a basis for isopropyl rubbing alcohol (q.v.). Called also *avantin* and *dimethyl carbinol*, and *isopropanol*.

Methyl alcohol and **isopropyl** alcohol are intoxicants of a much more toxic nature than ethyl alcohol. Those who have ingested such liquids tend to become ill or comatose and unlikely to drive a motor vehicle, before they would register significantly on a breath testing instrument. Intoximeters, Inc. v. Younger, 125 Cal.Rptr. 864, 868 (Ct.App.Cal.1975).

alcoholic (al"ko-hol'ik) [L. *alcoholicus*] a person suffering from alcoholism (q.v.). See also *alcoholism*.

The term has been variously defined. The National Council on Alcoholism has defined "**alcoholic**" as "a person who is powerless to stop drinking and whose drinking seriously alters his normal living pattern." The American Medical Association has defined **alcoholics** as "those excessive drinkers whose dependence on alcohol has attained such a degree that it shows a noticeable disturbance or interference with their bodily or mental health, their interpersonal relations, and their satisfactory social and economic functioning."

For other common definitions of **alcoholism**, see Keller, Alcoholism: Nature and Extent of the Problem, in Understanding Alcoholism, 315 Annals 1, 2 (1958); O. Diethelm, Etiology of Chronic Alcoholism 4 (1955); T. Plaut, Alcohol Problems—A Report to the Nation by the Cooperative Commission on the Study of Alcoholism 39 (1967) (hereafter cited as Plaut); Aspects of Alcoholism 9 (1963) (published by Roche Laboratories); The Treatment of Alcoholism—A Study of Programs and Problems 8 (1967) (published by the Joint Information Service of the American Psychiatric Association and the National Association for Mental Health) (hereafter cited as The Treatment of Alcoholism); 2 R. Cecil & R. Loeb, A Textbook of Medicine 1620, 1625 (1959). [DISSENT] Powell v. Texas, 392 U.S. 514, 560, 88 S.Ct. 2145, 20 L.Ed.2d 1254 (1968).

alcoholism (al'ko-hol-izm) a chronic behavioral disorder manifested by repeated drinking of alcoholic beverages in excess of the dietary and social uses of the community and to an extent that interferes with the drinker's health or his social or economic functioning; some degree of habituation, dependence, or addiction is implied. See also *dependence, chemical*.

Dr. Wade sketched the outlines of the "disease" concept of **alcoholism**; noted that there is no generally accepted definition of "**alcoholism**"; alluded to the ongoing debate within the medical profession over whether alcohol is actually physically "addicting" or merely psychologically "habituating"; and concluded that in either case a "chronic alcoholic" is an "involuntary drinker," who is "powerless not to drink," and who "loses his self-control over his drinking." . . . .

Furthermore, the inescapable fact is that there is no agreement among members of the medical profession about what it means to say that "**alcoholism**" is a "disease." One of the principal works in this field states that the major difficulty in articulating a "disease concept of **alcoholism**" is that "**alcoholism** has too many definitions and disease has practically none." [2] This same author concludes that "a disease is what the medical profession recognizes as such." [3] In other words, there is widespread agreement today that "**alcoholism**" is a "disease," for the simple reason that the medical profession has concluded that it should attempt to treat those who have drinking problems. There the agreement stops. Debate rages within the medical profession as to whether "**alcoholism**" is a separate "disease" in any meaningful biochemical, physiological or psychological sense, or whether it represents one peculiar manifestation in some individuals of underlying psychiatric disorders.[4] [[2] E. Jellinek, The Disease Concept of Alcoholism 11 (1960). [3] Id., at 12 (emphasis in original). [4] See, e.g., Joint Information Serv. of the Am. Psychiatric Assn. & the Nat. Assn. for Mental Health, The Treatment of Alcoholism—A Study of Programs and Problems 6–8 (1967) (hereafter cited as Treatment of Alcoholism).] Powell v. Texas, 392 U.S. 514, 522, 88 S.Ct. 2145, 20 L.Ed.2d 1254 (1968).

alcoholism, delta

A "delta" **alcoholic**, on the other hand, "shows the first three characteristics of gamma alcoholism as well as a less marked form of the fourth characteristic—that is, instead of loss of control there is inability to abstain." [9] [[9] Jellinek at 38.] Powell

v. Texas, 392 U.S. 514, 523–4, 88 S.Ct. 2145, 20 L.Ed.2d 1254 (1968).

alcoholism, gamma

He applies the label "**gamma alcoholism**" to "that species of alcoholism in which (1) acquired increased tissue tolerance to alcohol, (2) adaptive cell metabolism . . . , (3) withdrawal symptoms and 'craving,' i.e., physical dependence, and (4) loss of control are involved." [8] [[8] Jellinek, supra, n. 2, at 37.] Powell v. Texas, 392 U.S. 514, 523, 88 S.Ct. 2145, 20 L.Ed.2d 1254 (1968).

aldecarb

The active ingredient in Temik is the organophosphate pesticide "**aldecarb**." Aldecarb is combined with an inert ingredient to form a granular substance which is placed on the soil at the base of the plant. Upon watering, the pesticide is leached into the soil surrounding the roots and is internally absorbed by the plant; the plant pest is destroyed as a result of eating some portion of the plant.

Expert testimony established that the action of Temik's active ingredient **aldecarb** is to reduce the body's cholinesterase level, thus interfering with the parasympathetic nervous system which controls the involuntary body functions. In humans, exposure to **aldecarb** results in the victim losing control over his body functions, with symptoms that include headache, nausea, abdominal cramps, tightness in the chest, pinpoint pupils and blurred vision, vomiting, excessive salivation and tearing, sweating, diarrhea, incontinence, weakness, muscle twitching pulmonary edema, convulsions and, if the cholinesterase level is sufficiently reduced, coma and death. It is a unique feature of this pesticide that a minimal exposure, that is an exposure which does not result in a significant lowering of the cholinesterase level, is asymptomatic and is without physical consequences or residual effects. On the other hand, an exposure sufficient to produce a significant lowering of the cholinesterase level will typically cause the entire complex of symptoms to appear. Polk Nursery Co., Inc. v. Riley, 433 So.2d 1233, 1234 (Dist.Ct.App.Fla.1983).

aldosterone (al'do-ster-ōn″, al-dos'ter-ōn) the main mineralocorticoid hormone secreted by the adrenal cortex, the principal biological activity of which is the regulation of electrolyte and water balance by promoting the retention of sodium (and therefore of water) and the excretion of potassium; the retention of water induces an increase in plasma volume and an increase in blood pressure. The secretion of aldosterone is stimulated by angiotensin II.

aldosteronism (al″do-ster′ōn-izm″) an abnormality of electrolyte metabolism caused by excessive secretion of aldosterone; called also *hyperaldosteronism*.

aldosteronism, secondary that due to extra-adrenal stimulation of aldosterone secretion; it is commonly associated with edematous states, as in nephrotic syndrome, hepatic cirrhosis, heart failure, and accelerated phase hypertension.

The jury's second finding was that Dr. Varon was not negligent in prescribing treatment for **secondary aldosteronism** (excessive hormonal secretion by the adrenal gland in response to another disorder). . . .

On the other hand, Dr. Varon testified that he diagnosed **secondary aldosteronism** on Andrea's initial visit, and based his diagnosis upon a finding of edema (excess fluid retention in the body). Dr. Varon noted the presence of "swelling" on his progress reports, and testified that he indicated the presence of edema by this notation. He testified that frequently no cause can be isolated for **secondary aldosteronism**, and that this was especially true for women with fluid retention problems in association with obesity. . . .

Dr. Mahaney testified that a finding of edema and Andrea's historical condition of tiredness were both consistent with a diagnosis of **secondary aldosteronism**, and that Dr. Varon's diagnosis was reasonable under local standards. He further stated that Andrea's weight loss of seventeen pounds in one week would confirm Dr. Varon's initial impression of edema, and that the extraordinary loss would also be consistent with a diagnosis of **secondary aldosteronism**. Mendoza v. Varon, 563 S.W.2d 646, 651 (Ct.Civ.App.Tex.1978).

Alevaire

Alevaire is an aerosol prescription drug administered to patients with chronic respiratory diseases, to aid in the evacuation of mucous from the lungs. **Alevaire** is a solution of 0.125% tyloxapol, 2% sodium bicarbonate, 5% glycerine, and 92.875% water. Tyloxapol is described as the "active" mucoevacuant agent, while glycerine is a "stabilizer" and sodium bicarbonate acts to adjust the "pH factor" (alkalinity and acidity) in the lungs. Sterling Drug, Inc. v. Weinberger, 503 F.2d 675, 676 (2d Cir. 1974).

algae (al'je) [L., pl., "seaweeds"] a group of cryptogamous plants, in which the body is unicellular or consists of a thallus; it includes the seaweed and many unicellular fresh-water plants, most of which contain chlorophyll. Algae account for about 90 per cent of the earth's photosynthetic activity.

Expert testimony brought out by the County revealed that on some waterways in Dade County the amount of **algae** growth is so heavy that solid objects that would ordinarily sink below the surface of the water are unable to do so and rest on top of the **algae** growth. In turn, this same blanket of **algae** covering the water blocks out sunlight normally available and necessary to the growth of aquatic plant life whose principal function is to produce oxygen, and thus deprives the water of the oxygen level essential to the life-support of many freshwater game fish. Soap and Detergent Ass'n v. Clark, 330 F.Supp. 1218, 1220 (S.D.Fla.1971).

alimentary canal See *canalis alimentarius*.

alkalosis (al"kah-lo'sis) a pathologic condition resulting from accumulation of base, or from loss of acid without comparable loss of base in the body fluids, and characterized by decrease in hydrogen ion concentration (increase in pH). Cf. *acidosis*.

alkene (al'kēn) an unsaturated aliphatic hydrocarbon containing one double bond; olefin.

Alkene: A straight or branched chain hydrocarbon characterized by the presence of two carbon atoms with a double bond between them (C = C). **Alkenes** have a deficiency of hydrogen in their structures and are therefore said to be unsaturated. **Alkenes** are a member of the olefin series. Ritter v. Rohm &

Haas Co., 271 F.Supp. 313, 154 U.S.P.Q. 518, 554 (S.D.N.Y. 1967).

alkyl mercury poisoning See *poisoning, mercury*.

allantiasis (al"an-ti'ah-sis) [*allanto-* + *-iasis*] sausage poisoning; poisoning from sausages containing the toxins of *Clostridium botulinum*. See also *botulism*.

allergen (al'er-jen) [*allergy* + Gr. *gennan* to produce] 1. a substance capable of inducing allergy or specific hypersensitivity; such a substance may be a protein or a nonprotein. 2. any of the extracts of certain foods, bacteria, or pollen, for example, the proteins of milk, egg, or wheat; they are used in the treatment of or testing for hypersensitivity to specific substances.

Allergic reactions are caused by an inherent weakness or inability in certain people to tolerate exposure to substances known as **allergens**. Often this inherent weakness remains hidden for years but a sufficiently prolonged or unusual exposure will cause a sensitization to a particular **allergen** and an allergic reaction will develop. This allergic reaction will not develop, however, in other individuals equally exposed to the same substance unless they too are affected with the inherent inability to withstand such exposure. Princess Mfg. Co. v. Jarrell, 465 S.W.2d 45, 47 (Ct.App.Ky.1971).

On October 8, 1973, Dr. Salzmann conducted allergy tests and determined that claimant was allergic to inhalant **allergins** [sic], i.e., weeds, trees, molds, dust, and dog dander. United Airlines, Inc. v. Industrial Com'n, 405 N.E.2d 789, 791 (Ill. 1980).

allergenic (al"er-jen'ik) acting as an allergen; inducing allergy.

allergic (ah-ler'jik) pertaining to, caused by, affected with, or of the nature of allergy.

allergic purpura See *purpura, Schonlein-Henoch*.

allergy (al'er-je) [Gr. *allos* other + *ergon* work] a hypersensitive state acquired through exposure to a particular allergen, reexposure bringing to light an altered capacity to react. Originally, the term denoted any altered reactivity, whether decreased or increased, but is now usually used to denote a hypersensitive state. Allergies may be classified as immediate and delayed, and include atopy, serum sickness, allergic drug reactions, contact dermatitis, and anaphylactic shock. The allergies are principally manifested in the gastrointestinal tract, the skin, and the respiratory tract. Cf. *anaphylaxis* and *hypersensitivity*. See also *allergen*; and *disease, occupational* (both Princess Mfg. Co. case).

Dr. Weiss explained that there must be exposure to an offending substance over a period of time before the **allergy** will develop. He made a comparison with poison oak, a type of dermatitis:

Certain individuals can work in the woods and be exposed to poison oak for years and years and never have any problems, and then all of a sudden, for reasons not clear to us, they become **allergic** and develop an **allergy** to it. Subsequent exposures, though, they always break out. . . . Matter of Compensation of Baer, 652 P.2d 873, 874 (Ct.App.Ore. 1982).

Once an individual becomes sensitized he'll maintain that sensitivity [permanently]. The sensitivity is an **allergic** reaction caused by the individual's immunological makeup that will permit him to become sensitized to the material. If his immunological status is such that he reacts to the antigen, which is the material, the chromate, then he develops antibodies to that material and he'll have a reaction. That reaction can be in the skin, in the mucous membrane, wherever. That's how the **allergy** develops. Some people have the capacity to develop this type of reaction and some people do not. . . . Once the sensitivity develops, subsequent exposures to these materials could bring on a more severe type reaction. . . . It is plaintiff's skin [that is **allergic** to the chromate]. It could be his hands, feet, body area . . . wherever the chromate material contacts the skin. . . . This sensitivity has affected all the skin of his whole body. . . . He cannot work in an area where he'll be exposed to chromates or chromium salt because he's likely to break out again all over if he gets exposed to it. . . . [I] would classify [his] contact dermatitis as an occupational disease. Texas Employers' Ins. Ass'n v. Turner, 634 S.W.2d 364, 365 (Ct.App. Tex.1982).

The transcript of evidence in this case does not reveal an extensive inquiry as to whether allergic reactions properly may be regarded as diseases. It is noted, however, that Doctor Maurice Kaufmann, an **allergy** specialist, testified as follows:

"... **Allergy** can be defined as a disease of hypersensitivity and about fifteen-percent of the population have a tendency to develop **allergies**, what we call major **allergies**, which takes the form of hives, eczema, hay fever or asthma. . . ." Princess Mfg. Co. v. Jarrell, 465 S.W.2d 45, 46 (Ct.App.Ky.1971).

Other Authorities: Haynes v. Hoffman, 296 S.E.2d 216 (Ct. App.Ga.1982); Hill v. Squibb & Sons, E.R., 592 P.2d 1383, 1385 (Mont.1979); Reyes v. Wyeth Laboratories, 498 F.2d 1264, 1279 (5th Cir. 1974).

allograft (al'o-graft) a graft of tissue between individuals of the same species but of disparate genotype; called also *allogeneic graft* and *homograft.*

After the disk and osteophyte had been removed we made an incision over his right ilium, as I recall, and we were going to get some bone from his ilium to perform the fusion, what we call a **homograft.** Insurance Company of North America v. Chinowith, 393 F.2d 916, 919 (5th Cir. 1968).

. . . a skin graft transplant, technically termed a "**homograft**" from the person of the plaintiff-mother to her seriously injured minor daughter;. . . . Fleming v. Michigan Mutual Liability Co., 363 F.2d 186 (5th Cir. 1966).

allopathy (al-lop'ah-the) [*allo-* + Gr. *pathos* disease] a term applied to that system of therapeutics in which diseases are treated by producing a condition incompatible with or antagonistic to the condition to be cured or alleviated. Called also *heteropathy.* Cf. *homeopathy.*

Allopathy is defined as the treatment of disease by remedies that produce effects different from or opposite to those produced by the disease. People v. Amber, 76 Misc.2d 267, 273 (Sup.Ct.Queens Cty.N.Y.1973).

alopecia (al"o-pe'she-ah) [Gr. *alōpekia* a disease in which the hair falls out] baldness; absence of the hair from skin areas where it normally is present. See also *baldness.*

alopecia areata a microscopically inflammatory, usually reversible, patchy loss of hair, occurring in sharply defined areas and usually involving the beard or scalp; called also *a. circumscripta* and *area celsi.*

Dr. Ida Walton testified to the following: She is a dermatologist by profession, and a licensed medical doctor; that plaintiff suffered from **alopecia areata**, which resulted in his hair loss. His problem was a postinflammation alopecia, with destruction and atrophy of the underlying hair follicles, resulting from the intense dermatitis and subsequent infection which followed the use of the hair dye;. . . . [DISSENT] Revlon, Inc. v. Hampton, 551 S.W.2d 121, 124 (Ct.Civ.App.Tex.1977).

alopecia, senile; alopecia senilis loss of hair accompanying old age.

. . . appellee suffered from **senile-type alopecia**, i.e., normal hair loss attendant upon old age. Appellee was seventy one years old at the time of trial. Hussey v. May Department Stores, Inc., 357 A.2d 635, 636–7 (Super.Ct.Pa.1976).

alpha-amylose (al"fah-am'ĭ-lōs) the linear component of starch, usually amylose.

. . . **alpha-amylase** [sic] is an enzyme produced by the body which is utilized in digesting starch. When starch blockers are ingested during a meal, the protein acts to prevent the **alpha-amylase** enzyme from acting, thus allowing the undigested starch to pass through the body and avoiding the calories that would be realized from its digestion. Nutrilab, Inc. v. Schweiker, 713 F.2d 335, 336 (7th Cir. 1983).

alpha-olefin See *olefin, alpha.*

alpha wave See *wave, alpha.*

ALS See *sclerosis, amyotrophic lateral.*

aluminosis (ah-loo"mĭ-no'sis) a form of pneumoconiosis due to the presence of aluminum-bearing dust in the lungs; called also *a. pulmonum.*

aluminum (ah-loo'mĭ-num) an extremely light, whitish, lustrous, metallic element, obtainable from bauxite or clay: specific gravity, 2.699; atomic weight, 26.982; atomic number, 13; symbol, Al. It is very malleable and ductile, and is used for the manufacture of instruments and as a base for artificial dentures. The aluminum of the pharmacopeia is a fine, free-flowing, silvery powder, free from gritty or discolored particles. Aluminum compounds are used chiefly for their antacid and astringent properties.

aluminum sulfate an odorless white, crystalline powder, with a sweet taste, $Al_2(SO_4)_3 + 18H_2O$, that is astringent and antiperspirant. Incorrectly called *concentrated alum.*

The principal active ingredient of Arrid is **aluminum sulphate**, an astringent. When applied to the skin it tends to cause a swelling which contracts or closes the mouths of the sweat glands, and thus reduces the flow of such glands. Later the swelling gradually decreases, permitting sweat to flow again from the glands.

The Commission found that the extent of the reduction of the flow of sweat depends upon the temperature, the humidity, the physical activity of the individual, and the degree of tendency to perspire peculiar to the particular individual. The Commission further specifically found, "The use of 'Arrid' will not terminate or bring to an end the flow of underarm perspiration." Carter Products v. F.T.C., 186 F.2d 821 (7th Cir. 1951).

aluminum sulphate See *aluminum sulfate.*

alveolar (al-ve'o-lar) [L. *alveolaris*] pertaining to an alveolus.

alveolar nerve, inferior See *nervus alveolaris inferior* in Table of Nervi.

alveolus (al-ve'o-lus), pl. *alve'oli* [L., dim. of *alveus* hollow] a general term used in anatomical nomenclature to designate a small saclike dilatation. See also *acinus.*

alveolus, dental the bony cavities or sockets in the mandible or maxilla in which the roots of the teeth are attached. See also *alveoli dentales mandibulae* and *alveoli dentales maxillae.*

Additional diagnosis by Dr. T. related to degenerating fractured teeth and **alveolar** bone, which necessitated further oral surgery. Sears, Roebuck & Co. v. Tatum, 586 P.2d 734, 736 (Okla.1978).

alveolus, dental mandible [NA], dental alveoli of the mandible: the cavities or sockets in the alveolar process of the mandible in which the roots of the teeth are held by the periodontal ligament; called also *alveolar cavities.*

alveolus, dental maxilla [NA], dental alveoli of the maxilla: the cavities or sockets in the alveolar process of the maxilla in which the roots of the teeth are held by the periodontal ligament; called also *alveolar cavities.*

Alzheimer's disease See *dementia, presenile.*

amaurosis (am"aw-ro'sis) [L. from Gr. *amaurōsis* darkening] blindness (Hippocrates), especially blindness occurring without apparent lesion of the eye, as from disease of the optic nerve, spine, or brain. Cf. *amblyopia.*

ambivalence (am-biv'ah-lens) [*ambi-* + L. *valentia* strength, power] the simultaneous existence of conflicting attitudes, as of love and hate, toward the same object.

"Q.   Doctor, with reference to your examination of Miss Loughran, would you describe how conversion symptoms and secondary gain elements apply to her case?
"A.   I think that she has great **ambivalence**—'ambivalence' means mixed emotions—about testifying. Part of her does not want to testify, and perhaps part would like to cooperate or is being forced to cooperate. This causes a conflict. The conflict winds up being converted into some symptom. Now, the symptom, as I say, is the result of the conflict. The secondary gain features are, if the symptom is severe enough, it will get her out of this undesirable situation...." In re Loughran, 276 F.Supp. 393, 410 (Centr.D.Cal.1967).

amblyopia (am"ble-o'pe-ah) [*ambly-* + Gr. *ōps* eye + *-ia*] dimness of vision without detectable organic lesion of the eye. Cf. *amaurosis.*

ambubag

An "**ambu bag**" is a football shaped device into which oxygen can be directed and which can be manually squeezed to force oxygen into a patient's lungs. Battles v. Aderhold, 430 So.2d 307, 309 (Ct.App.La.1983).

He hurried into the recovery room and began assisted respiration with a device known as an **ambubag**, which is a hand operated contrivance designed to force room air into a patient. Chapman v. Argonaut-Southwest Insurance Co., 290 So. 2d 779, 781 (Ct.App.La.1974).

ambulant (am'bu-lant) [L. *ambulans* walking] walking or able to walk.

ambulatory (am'bu-lah-to"re) ambulant.

Nurse Virginia Agcayab stated the chart revealed plaintiff was "**ambulatory**" on December 22. This meant plaintiff had been able to sit up and stand. Ziegert v. South Chicago Community Hospital, 425 N.E.2d 450, 454 (App.Ct.Ill.1981).

amenorrhea (ah-men"o-re'ah) [*a* neg. + Gr. *mēn* month + *rhoia* flow] absence or abnormal stoppage of the menses; called also *amenia.*

Mrs. Dorothea M. Hammock, the plaintiff, had been under the care of a gynecologist for a number of years for **amenorrhea** (absence or suppression of menstrual period); and had developed menometrorrhagia from time to time;.... Hammock v. Allstate Insurance Co., 124 Ga.App. 854, 186 S.E.2d 353 (App.Ct.Ga.1971).

amenorrhea, primary failure of menstruation to occur at puberty.

He failed to inform her that because **primary amenorrhea** generally indicates infertility, the chances of her becoming pregnant were slight. He failed to inform her that the birth control pill he prescribed for her was not a treatment for the underlying cause of her **primary amenorrhea**. He failed to inform her that the longer the underlying cause of the **primary amenorrhea** remained undiagnosed and untreated, her chances of ever becoming pregnant were reduced. Klink v. G. D. Searle & Co., 614 P.2d 701, 703 (Ct.App.Wash.1980).

Ames test See *test, Ames.*

amide (am'īd) [*ammonia* + *-ide*] an organic compound derived from ammonia by substituting an acyl radical for hydrogen, or from an acid by replacing the —OH group by —NH_2.

Amide: An organic compound characterized by a carbon atom doubly bonded to an oxygen atom and singly bonded to a nitrogen atom (N—C=O). Ritter v. Rohm & Haas Co., 271 F.Supp. 313, 154 U.S.P.Q. 518, 554 (S.D.N.Y.1967).

amine (ah-mēn'; am'in) an organic compound containing nitrogen; any member of a group of chemical compounds formed from ammonia by replacement of one or more of the hydrogen atoms by organic (hydrocarbon) radicals. The **amines** are distinguished as *primary, secondary,* and *tertiary,* according to whether one, two, or three hydrogen atoms are replaced. The **amines** include allylamine, amylamine, ethylamine, methylamine, phenylamine, propylamine, and many other compounds.

Amine: An organic compound structurally similar to amonia (NH_3); in an **amine**, one hydrogen atom of the amonia molecule has been replaced by one or more hydrocarbon radicals. Ritter v. Rohm & Haas Co., 271 F.Supp. 313, 154 U.S.P.Q. 518, 554 (S.D.N.Y.1967).

aminoglycoside (am′ĭ-no-gli-ko′sīd) any of a group of bacterial antibiotics (e.g., streptomycin and gentamycin), derived from various species of *Streptomyces*, which interfere with the function of bacterial ribosomes. These compounds contain an inositol substituted with two amino or guanidino groups and with one or more sugars and aminosugars.

aminophylline (ah-me″no-fil′in) [USP] chemical name: 3,7-dihydro-1,3-dimethyl-1H-purine-2,6-dione compound with 1,2-ethanediamine. A salt of theophylline, $C_{16}H_{24}N_{10}O_4$, occurring as white or slightly yellowish granules or powder. Aminophylline is a smooth muscle relaxant and is used chiefly for its bronchodilator effect in such diseases as asthma, bronchitis, and emphysema; administered orally, rectally, or intravenously. It also may be used for its myocardial stimulant and coronary vasodilator actions, diuretic action, and respiratory center stimulant effect. Called also *theophylline ethylenediamide.*

The issue [as to safety] is whether in a case where a particular drug will not alleviate the cause of an ailment it will, nevertheless, effect a disappearance of the indicative symptoms with the result that a user may have every reason to feel that he has been cured when, in fact, he has not been.[12] [[12] During House Committee hearings on the proposed amendment, George P. Larrick, Associate Commissioner of Food and Drugs, used the drug **aminophylline** as an example of this point. He commented: "It is not a poison. It is an effective diuretic and will reduce swelling of the ankles other than that caused by insect bites and the like. A layman cannot effectively treat himself with the diuretic because the underlying cause of the swelling is heart or kidney disease and the use of the diuretic to control the symptoms does not affect the progress of the underlying cause.] U.S. v. Article of Drug Labeled Decholin, 264 F.Supp. 473, 483 (E.D.Mich.1967).

aminotransferase (ah-me″no-, am″ĭ-no-trans′fer-ās) transaminase.

ammonia (ah-mo′ne-ah) [named from Jupiter *Ammon*, near whose temple in Libya it was formerly obtained] a colorless alkaline gas, NH_3, of a penetrating odor and soluble in water, forming ammonia water; called also *volatile alkali.*

ammonia hydroxide

Upon trial a chemist testified that when ammonia comes in contact with goods such as those the appellee had in the storage room, the ammonia and the water in the goods chemically react to form **ammonia hydroxide**, a caustic substance which is highly dangerous if consumed. American Casualty Co. of Reading, Pa. v. Myrick, 304 F.2d 179, 183 (5th Cir. 1962).

ammonia thioglycolate

His explanation indicated that the permanent wave solution used on appellee's head contained **ammonia thioglycolate**, a chemical capable of penetrating the keratin composing the hair. (N.T. 102) (This information had been introduced into evidence by Arthur W. Forbriger, a vice-president of Revlon Realistic Professional Products, the manufacturer of the permanent waving solution (N.T. 74 et seq.).) Dr. Krugh stated that, assuming the truth of Mr. Forbriger's testimony, the acid concentration in the curling lotion was such that "[i]t is considered to be a primary irritant and it does have the capability of producing the chemical burn if it is allowed to stay on say too long" (N.T. 106). Hussey v. May Department Stores, Inc., 357 A.2d 635, 639 (Super.Ct.Pa.1976).

amnesia (am-ne′ze-ah) [Gr. *amnēsia* forgetfulness] lack or loss of memory, especially inability to remember past experiences.

All three defense psychiatrists Dr. Catton, Dr. Adams, and Dr. Burbridge, and both prosecution psychiatrists, Dr. Jackson and Dr. Tipton, agreed that Cameron was suffering true **amnesia** at the time of the trial. They disagreed, however, as to whether his **amnesia** was primary or secondary. The defense psychiatrists opined that it was primary **amnesia**; i.e., that his memory never recorded the occurrences because he was in a dissociative state due to pathological intoxication at the time of the killing. The prosecution psychiatrists opined that he suffered secondary **amnesia**; i.e., that he was not dissociative when the killing occurred (although they agreed he was pathologically intoxicated at the time) and his memory recorded the events, but subsequently blocked out the memory because it was too painful. In re Cameron, 439 P.2d 633, 642 (Cal.1968).

amnesia, hysterical See *fugue.*

amnesia, primary

The defense psychiatrists opined that it was **primary amnesia**; i.e., that his memory never recorded the occurrences because he was in a dissociative state due to pathological intoxication at the time of the killing. In re Cameron, 439 P.2d 633, 642 (Cal.1968).

amnesia, retrograde amnesia for events which occurred before the trauma or disease causing the condition.

Mrs. Droddy sustained severe, painful and permanent injuries in the accident. She received cerebral concussion with hematoma about both eyes; bruising of the anterior chest wall and abdomen, hematoma of the anterior wall, headache and lacerations and abrasions of the left forearm and both knees. As a result, she had **retrograde amnesia** and was unable to remember anything for some days after the accident. The headaches continued for almost one year, her thinking was "fuzzy" and she was unable to keep her mind on anything. She was still on prescribed medication and suffering from mental lapses on the day of the trial. Bush v. State, Through Dep't of Highways, 395 So.2d 916, 922 (Ct.App.La.1981).

The claimant sustained a **retrograde traumatic amnesia** and has no recollection of what occurred between the time he talked to Jansco at the J and J Ranch on the night of May 31 and two and one half weeks later, when he was a patient in St. Luke's Hospital in St. Louis. Bradford Supply Co. v. Industrial Com'n, 277 N.E.2d 854, 856 (Ill.1971).

amnesia, secondary

The prosecution psychiatrists opined that he suffered **secondary amnesia**; i.e., that he was not dissociative when the killing occurred (although they agreed he was pathologically intoxicated at the time) and his memory recorded the events, but subsequently blocked out the memory because it was too painful. In re Cameron, 439 P.2d 633, 642 (Cal.1968).

amniocentesis (am″ne-o-sen-te′sis) surgical transabdominal perforation of the uterus, to obtain amniotic fluid. See also *idiocy, amaurotic familial* (Curlender case).

. . . they did not discover the negligence until an attorney advised them that Down's Syndrome (also called Mongolism) can be discovered through **amniocentesis**. . . .

. . . Plaintiff alleges that defendant did not cause the mongolism (the injury) but that he failed to detect the connection through the procedure of **amniocentesis** thereby precluding the parents from having an abortion performed. Call v. Kezirian, 185 Cal.Rptr. 103, 105 (Ct.App.Cal.1982).

The **amniocentesis**, an operation in which amniotic fluid is withdrawn for genetic testing, was performed by Dr. Kessler on February 26, 1974 at the Thomas Jefferson University Hospital.

Dr. Kessler explicitly guaranteed that the results of the **amniocentesis** would categorically determine whether or not the fetus would have Tay-Sachs disease. . . .

Society has an interest in insuring that genetic testing is properly performed and interpreted. The failure to properly perform or interpret an **amniocentesis** could cause either the abortion of a healthy fetus, or the unwanted birth of a child afflicted with Tay-Sachs disease. Either of these occurrences is contrary to the public policy of Pennsylvania. The recognition of a cause of action for negligence in the performance of genetic testing would encourage the accurate performance of such testing by penalizing physicians who fail to observe customary standards of good medical practice. Gildiner v. Thomas Jefferson Univ. Hosp., 451 F.Supp. 692, 694, 696 (E.D.Pa.1978).

. . . an **amniocentesis**, a diagnostic procedure which the plaintiffs assert would have revealed that the child the mother was bearing was afflicted with a chromosomal defect which preordained its abnormality. . . . Johnson v. Yeshiva Univ., 364 N.E.2d 1340, 1341 (N.Y.1977).

Other Authorities: Phillips v. U.S., 566 F.Supp. 1, 3 (D.S.Car. 1981); Becker v. Schwartz, 413 N.Y.S.2d 895, 896 (N.Y. 1978).

amniocentesis, saline See *abortion.*

To analyze this argument, it is necessary to review some of the uncontested facts about **saline amniocentesis**. According to the report submitted by plaintiffs, National Academy of Sciences, Legalized Abortion and the Public Health (1975), saline abortions are usually performed after the 15th week of pregnancy. Some amniotic fluid is withdrawn from the uterine cavity by a needle inserted through the abdominal wall and this fluid is replaced with a concentrated salt solution. This process induces labor and the fetus is expelled from the uterus, usually dead, 24 to 48 hours after the injection. Id. at 139. Saline abortions expose the woman to the risk of complications. Placental tissue may be retained in the uterus. Infection and hemorrhage may result. Id. at 54. The blood clotting mechanism may be disturbed. It is also possible that the saline solution will enter the blood stream, damaging the central nervous system or causing convulsions. Wynn v. Scott, 449 F.Supp. 1302, 1324 (N.D.III.1978).

Section 9 of the statute prohibits the use of **saline amniocentesis**, as a method or technique of abortion, after the first 12 weeks of pregnancy. It describes the method as one whereby the amniotic fluid is withdrawn and ''a saline or other fluid'' is inserted into the amniotic sac. Planned Parenthood of Missouri v. Danforth, 428 U.S. 52, 75–76, 96 S.Ct. 2831, 49 L.Ed.2d 788 (1976).

amnion (am′ne-on) [Gr. "bowl"; "membrane enveloping the fetus"] the thin but tough extraembryonic membrane of reptiles, birds, and mammals that lines the chorion and contains the fetus and the amniotic fluid around it; in mammals it is derived from trophoblast by folding or splitting.

. . . that plaintiff's prolonged recovery and pain might have been caused by amnionitis, which he described as an infection of the **amnion** or membrane lining of the pregnant womb;. . . . Lindsey v. Clinic for Women, 253 S.E.2d 304, 306 (Ct.App.N. Car.1979).

Appellee stated that it is very common to be unable to ascertain whether a child is in a vertex or breech presentation until after the amniotic sac bursts.[4] [[4] The child, while in the uterus lives in a sac of fluid known as the amniotic sac. This sac bursts just prior to birth.] Freed v. Priore, 372 A.2d 895, 897 (Super. Ct.Pa.1977).

amniotic sac See *amnion.*

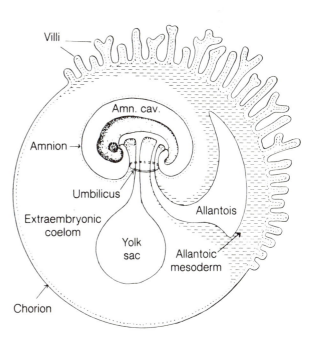

Amnion, chorion, and other embryonic membranes surrounding the embryo of a placental mammal; *amn. cav.* = amniotic cavity. (Balinsky.)

amnionitis (am″ne-o-ni′tis) inflammation of the amnion.

amobarbital (am″o-bar′bĭ-tal) [USP] chemical name: 5-ethyl-5-(methylbutyl)-2,4,6(1H,3H,5H)-pyrimidine-trione. An intermediate-acting barbiturate, $C_{11}H_{18}N_2O_3$, occurring as a white, crystalline powder; used orally as a sedative and hypnotic. Called also amylobarbitone and *isoamylethylbarbituric acid.*

To anesthetize the patient, defendant injected either **amobarbital** or surital into the vein, using the familiar syringe and needle. State v. Weiner, 41 N.J. 21, 26, 194 A.2d 467, 470 (N.J.1963).

amobarbital sodium [USP], the monosodium salt of amobarbital, $C_{11}H_{17}N_2NaO_3$, occurring as a white, friable, granular powder; administered orally, intravenously, and intramuscularly as a hypnotic and sedative.

The "Orders" sheet indicates the administration of a dose of **amytal sodium**, a barbiturate used in narcotherapy (U.S. Dispensatory 65–66).... Miranda v. U.S., 325 F.Supp. 217, 221 (S.D.N.Y.1970).

Sodium amytal is a hypnotic sedative. It puts people to sleep. Had Cameron been under the influence of the sedative the doctors thought he had been given, he would have been incoherent or asleep. Accordingly, when they interviewed him, they thought all of the sedation was out of his system. They attributed the mental and physical retardation noted in him to a hangover. In re Cameron, 439 P.2d 633, 637 (Cal.1968).

amosite

Amosite too, is a trade name and a non-mineralogical term, for certain fibrous minerals in the cummingtonite-grunerite range that have commercial importance. The name was derived from a certain mine in South Africa. Amosite does not indicate a specific mineral composition; it is a range of mineral compositions with a range in bulk chemistry. (U.S. Exhibit 169) U.S. v. Reserve Mining Co., 380 F.Supp. 11, 31–2 (D.Minn. 1974), remanded 498 F.2d 1073 (8th Cir. 1974).

amotivational syndrome See under *syndrome.*

amphetamine (am-fet′ah-min) 1. chemical name: $(\pm)$-α-methylbenzeneethannine. Racemic amphetamine; a sympathomimetic amine, $C_9H_{13}N$, occurring as a colorless mobile liquid, has a stimulating effect on both the central and peripheral nervous systems. It relaxes both systolic and diastolic blood pressure and bronchial muscle, contracts the sphincter of the urinary bladder, and depresses the appetite. Abuse of this drug and its salts may lead to dependence, characterized by strong psychic dependence, to marked tolerance, and to mild physical dependence associated with tachycardia, increased blood pressure, restlessness, irritability, insomnia, personality changes, and in the severe form of chronic intoxication, psychosis similar to schizophrenia. Abrupt withdrawal can cause severe fatigue, mental depression, and abnormalities in the electroencephalogram. 2. [pl.] a group of closely related compounds having similar actions, including both racemic amphetamine and its salts, dextroamphetamine, and methamphetamine. See also *flashback;* and *methamphetamine.*

[21 C.F.R.] § 310.504 Amphetamines (amphetamine, dextroamphetamine, and their salts and levamfetamine and its salts) for human use.

(a) **Amphetamine** and dextroamphetamine and their salts. (1) Pursuant to the drug efficacy requirements of the Federal Food, Drug, and Cosmetic Act, the National Academy of Sciences-National Research Council, Drug Efficacy Study Group, has evaluated certain dosage forms of **amphetamines** and other sympathomimetic stimulant drugs intended for use in the treatment of obesity and for other uses. The Academy found that such drugs as a class have been shown to have a generally short-term anorectic action. They further commented that clinical opinion on the contribution of the sympathomimetic stimulants in a weight reduction program varies widely, the anorectic effect of these drugs often plateaus or diminishes after a few weeks, most studies of them are for short periods, no available evidence shows that use of anorectic alters the natural history of obesity, some evidence indicates that anorectic effects may be strongly influenced by the suggestibility of the patient, and reservations exist about the adequacy of the controls in some of the clinical studies. Their significant potential for drug abuse was also cited. U.S. v. Zwick, 413 F.Supp. 113, 117–18 (N.D.Ohio 1976).

The consensus of the **amphetimines** [sic] (stimulants) is that, unlike the barbiturates, their abuse does not lead to a physical dependence, but the development of a high tolerance and a strong psychological dependence are common. Occasional dosage use under medical supervision causes only an elevation in mood and a state of well-being. Long term dependence, however, leads to serious mental and physical problems. Malnutrition and debilitation due to self-neglect will appear. A well known complication of **amphetamine** abuse is paranoid schizophrenia. The user may react violently to his persecutive delusions. Visual and auditory hallucinations occur and can persist long after use is discontinued. Although true withdrawal symptoms do not occur, the latter stages of excitement and mental disarrangement are difficult to endure. To take the edge off this tense euphoria, the user will sometimes turn to barbiturates or the opiates. People v. McCabe, 275 N.E.2d 407, 411 (Ill. 1971).

amphetamine sulfate [USP], a white, crystalline powder, $C_{18}N_{28}N_2H_2O_4S$, having the same actions as the base, used chiefly for its central stimulant effects in the treatment of mental depression, psychopathic states, narcolepsy, hyperkinetic behavior disorders in children, and exogenous obesity; administered orally.

The latter appeared to the officers to be benzedrine, a form of **amphetamine**, possession of which is a felony under Health and Safety Code section 11910. People v. Gavin, 98 Cal. Rptr. 518, 520 (Ct.App.Cal.1971).

amphiboles

... witnesses identified **amphiboles** [11] in the cummingtonite-grunerite series.... [[11] A group of minerals with essentially alike crystal structures involving a silicate chain $[OH(Si_4O_{11})N]$ and generally containing three groups of metal ions: sodium or calcium, iron or magnesium or manganese, and silicon or aluminum. The general formula being $A_2B_5(SiA1)_8O_{22}(OH)_2$.] U.S. v. Reserve Mining Co., 380 F.Supp. 11, 31 (D.Minn.1974).

amphoteric (am-fo-ter'ik) [Gr. *amphoteros* pertaining to both] having opposite characters; capable of acting either as an acid or as a base; combining with both acids and bases; affecting both red and blue litmus.

Appellant defines an **amphoteric** detergent as:

A detergent which can be either an anionic detergent, a cationic detergent or a zwitterionic detergent depending on the pH. An amphoteric detergent can only be a zwitterionic detergent at a specific pH. Under the normal conditions of use in a built detergent system an amphoteric detergent bears only an anionic (negative) charge on the hydrophobic portion of the molecule. Application of Smith, 398 F.2d 849, 850 (U.S.Ct.Cust. & Pat.App.1968).

ampoule See *ampule.*

ampule (am'pūl) [Fr. *ampoule*] a small glass or plastic container capable of being sealed so as to preserve its contents in a sterile condition; used principally for containing sterile parenteral solutions.

Ampoules are sealed vessels containing a solution of potassium dichromate, which are replaced for each operation of the breathalyzer apparatus. People v. Godbout, 356 N.E.2d 865, 869 (App.Ct.Ill.1976).

amputation (am"pu-ta'shun) [L. *amputare* to cut off, or to prune] the removal of a limb or other appendage or outgrowth of the body; called also *apocope.* See also *forearm* (Lykouras case); and *severance.*

While the Act [77 P.S. Sect. 513(24)] may foreclose loss of use benefits where the only impairment to the arm is the **amputation**, it does not preclude an award of such benefits based on additional impairment. Lykouras v. W.C.A.B. (Lyk-Math Inc.), 463 A.2d 1203, 1205 (Commonwealth Ct.Pa.1983).

After making surgical incisions, Dr. Barron found the infection to be so extensive in the leg that he decided **amputation** above the knee was necessary. On February 29, Murphy was returned to surgery for revision of the stump, and an additional four (4) inches of the leg was removed, together with a portion of his buttock. King v. Murphy, 424 So.2d 547, 549 (Miss. 1982).

Other orthopedic surgeons were consulted and another debridement was done by the defendant. During the operation on the 26th the defendant discovered that there was no longer a blood supply to the arm and the forearm was a mass of necrotic tissue with nothing salvageable. Thereafter the left forearm was **amputated** below the elbow by the defendant on June 30th. Casey v. Penn, 360 N.E.2d 93, 97 (App.Ct.Ill.1977), supplemented 362 N.E.2d 1373 (1977).

Other Authorities: Dobbs v. Villa Capri Restaurant, 329 N.W.2d 503, 506 (Ct.App.Mich.1982); Brown v. Arlen Management Corp., 663 F.2d 575, 577 (5th Cir. 1981); Voegeli v. Lewis, 568 F.2d 89, 91 (8th Cir. 1977).

amputation, closed one in which flaps are made from the skin and subcutaneous tissue and sutured over the end of the bone; called also *flap a.*

... **amputation** of left ring finger at level of P/P joint with removal of proximal phalanx, left ring finger, construction of fillet flap graft from ring finger with suture of flap into palm of left hand. Trovatten v. U.S., 342 F.Supp. 866, 869–70 (E.D.Pa. 1972).

amputation, forequarter interscapulothoracic amputation.

amputation, guillotine rapid amputation of a limb by a circular sweep of the knife and a cut of the saw, the entire cross-section being left open for dressing; done when primary closure of the stump is contraindicated, owing to the possibility of recurrent or developing infection. Called also *flapless a.* and *open a.*

... and finally a modified **guillotine amputation** of the lower left extremity at the mid-thigh level. LaRive v. U.S., 318 F.Supp. 119, 121 (D.S.Dak.1970).

amputation, interscapulothoracic amputation of the upper extremity, including the scapula and the clavicle; called also *forequarter a.*

Gaal stated that in his judgment it would be inadvisable to simply re-excise a tumor which had already twice recurred, which was growing rapidly, and which, on clinical grounds, appeared to be quite malignant. He told appellant of the availability of the **forequarter amputation**, the removal of the arm and shoulder, and of the alternative technique of the isolation perfusion. Gaal told appellant that the forequarter amputation was an extremely incapacitating, mutilating procedure that he would recommend if there were no alternative. Clemens v. Regents of University of California, 87 Cal.Rptr. 108, 111 (Ct.App.Cal.1970).

amputation, root the removal of one or more roots from a multirooted tooth, leaving at least one root to support the crown; when only the apical portion of a root is involved, it is called *apicoectomy.*

amputation, Symes amputation of the foot at the ankle joint with removal of both malleoli; called also *Syme's operation.* See also *Dopamine* (Erickson case).

On August 26, 1976, Dr. Assimacopoulous performed bilateral modified **Symes' amputations**, i.e., ankle level amputation, on Erickson. Dr. Assimacopoulous testified that although the level was not ideal for the fitting of prosthetic devices, he felt it was necessary to amputate where the least amount of blood loss would occur in light of the prior myocardial infarction. Erickson v. U.S., 504 F.Supp. 646, 650 (D.S.Dak.1980).

amputee (am"pu-te') a person who has one or more of his limbs amputated. See also *prosthesis.*

Amputees are prone to excessive perspiration since they have lost a substantial portion of the entire body surface. As a result the **amputee** is subject to various skin disorders of the residual limb, such as oozing and maceration of the skin with a true dermatitis and a red reaction. There can also be fungus and bacterial infections. Daw Industries, Inc. v. U.S., 561 F.Supp. 433, 436 (U.S.Ct.Int.Trade 1983), reversed 714 F.2d 1140 (Fed.Cir. 1983).

amygdalin (ah-mig'dah-lin) chemical name: (R)-α-[(6-O-β-glucopyranosyl-β-D-glucopyranosyl)oxy]benzeneacetonitrile. A cyanogenetic glycoside, $C_6H_5CH(CN) \cdot O \cdot C_{12}H_{21}O_{10}$, characteristically found in seeds and other plant parts of members of the Rosaceae family, e.g., almonds. It is split by the enzyme emulsin into glucose, benzaldehyde, and hydrocyanic acid. The term is sometimes used interchangeably with *Laetrile.*

Plaintiffs' medical expert by deposition testified that **laetrile** is a plant chemical containing cyanide, six percent by weight (one gram of oral **laetrile** containing "60 milligrams of cyanide"), and that in taking **laetrile** orally along with certain plant enzymes eaten with it (a vegetarian diet) the cyanide is released by the plant enzymes causing "cyanide poisoning." Deponent testified that "what you get from oral **Laetrile** is cyanide poisoning in proportion to how much of your diet with it is a vegetarian diet, and what you get from injected **Laetrile** is infection with bacteria and fungus released cyanide from the deteriorated **Laetrile** in insect parts." Sullivan v. Henry, 287 S.E.2d 652, 656 (Ct.App.Ga.1982).

Amygdalin is commonly known as **Laetrile** and also as "Vitamin B–17" (Article entitled "The Vitamin Fraud in Cancer Therapy" by David M. Greenberg, Ph.D., p. 346, attached to affidavit of Dr. Greenberg, Exhibit 18 [hereafter referred to as "Greenberg article"]....

The **amygdalin** produced and sold by defendants is intended for use in the cure, mitigation, palliation, treatment, and prevention of various forms of human cancer....

There has been widespread publicity generated by proponents of **Laetrile** which has encouraged cancer victims to rely on **amygdalin** instead of surgery, radiation, and chemotherapy, and other forms of treatment that have established value in cancer management. Misleading claims that **amygdalin** has some established value have appeared in newspapers, magazines, popular books, promotional films, and the news media. (Defendants' Exhibits 1016 & 1024; Exhibits 71 & 90;...

Amygdalin is a cyanogenic glucoside which reacts with Beta-glucosidase, an enzyme found in a number of commonly eaten foods, to form hydrogen cyanide, a highly toxic substance. (Affidavits of Thomas H. Jukes, Ph.D., Exhibit 15; Carl M. Leventhal, M.D., Exhibit 16; the American Medical Association by James H. Sammons, M.D., Exhibit 17;...

Due to the presence therein of cyanide, a poisonous and deleterious substance, **amygdalin** is potentially harmful and ordinarily injurious to health (See references to finding 25; also: Death Certificate of Elizabeth Hankin, Exhibits 11 and 79;...

The danger in the use of **amygdalin** by the public, and in particular by cancer victims, is in delaying and foregoing diagnosis and treatment known to be beneficial and effective. U.S. v. Articles of Food & Drug, 444 F.Supp. 266, 270 (E.D.Wis.1977).

The Government charges that the kernels are poisonous because **amygdalin** contains cyanide which, if exposed to enzymes, releases a toxic gas known as hydrocyanic acid....

... **Laetrile**, which is derived from apricot kernels, contains a highly concentrated dosage of **amygdalin**, the same substance that occurs naturally in apricot kernels, and is generally administered intravenously or in tablet form to cancer patients who believe in its efficacy. Millet, Pit & Seed Co., Inc. v. U.S., 436 F.Supp. 84, 87, 90 (E.D.Tenn.1977), vacated and remanded [without opinion] 627 F.2d 1093 (6th Cir. 1980).

Other Authorities: People v. Privitera, 153 Cal.Rptr. 431, 436 (Cal.1979); U.S. v. General Research Laboratories, 397 F.Supp. 197, 199–200 (C.D.Cal.1975).

amygdalotomy, stereotactic

Dr. Keller performed brain surgery known as a **stereotactic amygdalotomy** on Marcella. This is an operation in which electrodes or probes are inserted under x-ray observation through holes drilled in the skull, for the specific purpose of locating and destroying certain brain tissue which controls affected areas of the body....

... Dr. Brown testified that surgeons had been performing stereotactic surgery for about 28–30 years. He testified that the **amygdalotomy** was a well-recognized surgical procedure; that the surgery ordinarily produced few side effects, and that paresis and loss of voice were not usual or customary results of this surgery....

... The parents knew that the surgery involved inserting a probe through the skull to create a brain lesion, i.e., to destroy certain brain tissue which controlled the area of the brain responsible for the behavioral problems their daughter had. Ritz v. Florida Patient's Compensation Fund, 436 So.2d 987, 988, 990–1 (Dist.Ct.App.Fla.1983).

amyloidosis (am"ĭ-loi-do'sis) the accumulation of amyloid in various body tissues, which, when advanced, engulfs and obliterates parenchymal cells and thus injures the affected organ. The disorder is divided, mainly for descriptive purposes, into the following categories: (1) primary, (2) secondary, (3) familial, (4) associated with multiple myeloma, and (5) associated with familial Mediterranean fever.

Allingham died on April 11, 1969, of primary **amyloidosis**, a rare disease which had been diagnosed in the fall of 1968. Farmers & Bankers Life Ins. Co. v. Allingham, 457 F.2d 21, 22 (10th Cir. 1972).

amyotrophic lateral sclerosis See under *sclerosis*.

amyotrophy (ah"mi-ot'ro-fe) atrophy of muscle tissue.

amyotrophy, neuralgic a condition characterized by pain across the shoulder and upper arm, with atrophy and paralysis of the muscles of the shoulder girdle.

... she complains of pain in the right upper extremity from the shoulder to the fingers which is diagnosed as probably bilateral brachial neuritis which has resisted all attempts at therapy. Longo v. Weinberger, 369 F.Supp. 250, 254 (E.D.Pa.1974).

Dr. Gregg, defendant's expert witness, indicated that medical knowledge does not reveal why extremely few people who exercise their muscles too strenuously suffer paralysis while almost all others develop only soreness. He termed this rare condition "paralytic brachial neuritis." [3] [[3] See generally Evans, Paralytic Brachial Neuritis (1965) 65 New York State Journal of Medicine 2926; Kennedy & Resch, Paralytic Brachial Neuritis (1966) 86 Journal-Lancet 459.] Bardessono v. Michels, 478 P.2d 480, 484 (Cal.1970).

Amytal (am'ĭ-tal) trademark for amobarbital. See *amobarbital*.

anacephalic

Modern techniques can preserve the lives of infants born with little or no brain (**anacephalic**) or digestive tract for weeks or even months. American Academy of Pediatrics v. Heckler, 561 F.Supp. 395, 396 (D.D.C.1983).

Anacin

Each **Anacin** tablet, he explained, consists of 400 milligrams of aspirin and 32 milligrams of caffeine, the aspirin components being, in weight, some one-third greater than a plain aspirin tablet, which typically contains 300 milligrams of aspirin. Torsiello v. Whitehall Laboratories, 398 A.2d 132, 135 (Super.Ct. N.J.1979).

anaerobic (an″a-er-o′bik) growing in the absence of molecular oxygen.

. . . it is **anaerobic**, meaning that it dies on exposure to oxygen and only can grow in the absence of air. King v. Murphy, 424 So.2d 547, 549 (Miss.1982).

An **anaerobic** culture of an abscess taken as soon as the abdomen was opened, revealed no **anaerobic** growth in 48 hours. A culture taken from tubo-ovarian abscesses revealed the presence of four types of bacteria. Spike v. Sellett, 430 N.E.2d 597, 599 (App.Ct.Ill.1981).

analgesia (an″al-je′ze-ah) [*an* neg. + Gr. *algēsis* pain + -*ia*] absence of sensibility to pain; absence of pain on noxious stimulation; designating particularly the relief of pain without loss of consciousness; called also *alganesthesia*.

analgesia, algera spontaneous pain in a denervated part; pain in an area or region which is anesthetic; called also *a. dolorosa*.

analgesic (an″al-je′zik) 1. relieving pain. 2. not sensitive as to pain. 3. an agent that alleviates pain without causing loss of consciousness. See also *analgesia*.

"Q.   What is an analgesic?
"A.   To subdue or kill pain." (Record, page 154.) Conway v. State Horse Racing Com'n, 276 A.2d 840, 842 (Commonwealth Ct.Pa.1971).

analogous (ah-nal′o-gus) [Gr. *analogos* according to a due ratio, conformable, proportionate] resembling or similar in some respects, as in function or appearance, but not in origin or development; cf. *homologous*.

A product was said to be **analogous** "to a serum, if prepared from some protein constituent of the blood and intended for parenteral administration." 42 C.F.R. § 22.11 (Supp.1940); see 42 C.F.R. § 22.11 (1938). . . .
. . . Regulations in force at the present time state that a product is **analogous** "to a therapeutic serum, if composed of whole blood or plasma or containing some organic constituent or product other than a hormone or an amino acid, derived from whole blood, plasma, or serum, and not intended for ingestion." 42 C.F.R. § 73.1(i)(5)(ii) (1968). . . .
. . . Blood is a common source of numerous products but that fact sheds little light on whether the products, in the primary sense of **analogy**, have attributes or effects that resemble one another, or in the broader sense of **analogy** the products are similar or corresponding. Many serums, some fertilizers, beef extracts for human consumption, and blood sausage all have their source in blood, but this does not make them **analogous**. [Footnotes omitted.] Blank v. U.S., 400 F.2d 302, 303–4 (5th Cir. 1968).

analogue (an′ah-log) a chemical compound with a structure similar to that of another but differing from it in respect to a certain component; it may have a similar or opposite action metabolically. Cf. *homologue*.

Analogs are related compounds that are neither isomers nor homologs. GAF Corp. v. Amchem Products, Inc., 399 F.Supp. 647, 651 (E.D.Pa.1975), reversed 570 F.2d 457 (3d Cir. 1978).

. . . **analogue**—one of a series of slightly varied molecules which all have a similar basic structure of atoms. Eli Lilly & Co. v. Generix Drug Sales, Inc., 460 F.2d 1096, 1100 (5th Cir. 1972).

anamnestic response See *response, anamnestic*.

anaphylactic reaction See *anaphylaxis*.

anaphylactic shock See *anaphylaxis*; and *shock, anaphylactic*.

anaphylaxis (an″ah-fĭ-lak′sis) [*ana*- + Gr. *phylaxis* protection] an unusual or exaggerated allergic reaction of an organism to foreign protein or other substances. Use of the term was originally restricted to a condition of sensitization in laboratory animals produced by the injection of foreign matter, such as horse serum, but has since been extended to human reactions. Such an injection renders the individual hypersusceptible to a subsequent injection. This is termed *active a.* Anaphylaxis produced in an animal by injecting the blood serum of a sensitized animal is termed *passive a.* The reaction results from the release of histamine, serotonin, and other vasoactive substances when antigen combines with antibody on cell surfaces. Cf. *allergy* and *hypersensitivity*. Called also *hypersensitization, Theobald Smith phenomenon, hypersusceptibility*, and *protein sensitization*. See also *shock, anaphylactic*.

Having pointed out that an **anaphylactic** type reaction to oral penicillin is extremely rare, Dr. Clay stated that most reactions to the drug occur from injectable penicillin usually within fifteen minutes of the injection and usually in a situation where the patient is fairly accessible to a doctor. In such a case, he agrees that immediate drug therapy is mandatory. Furthermore, he states that as a rule of thumb Epinephrine is the drug of first choice where the acute situation of **anaphylactic** reaction is accompanied by laryngeal edema. Wright v. U.S., 507 F.Supp. 147, 153 (E.D.La.1980).

In describing **anaphylactic** shock, Dr. Hardy testified: "I believe the classical definition of **anaphylactic** shock would be something like a hypersensitivity resulting from previous exposure to a foreign protein, usually by injection". All veterinarians testifying agreed **anaphylactic** shock could also be caused by contact with a fungus through the skin, through injection, or eating, usually some plant that might synthetize animals. However, Dr. Hardy testified **anaphylactic** shock "is not a well understood thing". An examination of the defendant's expert witnesses seemed to confirm this conclusion. O. M. Franklin Serum Co. v. C. A. Hoover & Son, 437 S.W.2d 613, 616 (Ct. Civ.App.Tex.1969).

It was defendant's contention that the calves had somehow become sensitized to penicillin in the serum and reacted abnormally to its injection. There was evidence that the animals suffered **anaphylactic** shock, and this indicated a reaction to the drug contents of the serum. C. A. Hoover and Son v. O. M. Franklin Serum Co., 444 S.W.2d 596, 597 (Tex.1969).

The defendants also urge that Moore's seizure could have resulted from **anaphylatic** reaction to penicillin injected intramuscularly. There are two reasons why this theory should not foreclose the jury from consideration of Moore's case. First, Moore's doctor testified that an **anaphylatic** reaction could not result from one injection of penicillin. It could result from a second injection, but in his opinion an interval of about ten days between the first injection and a following injection was required to allow the production of antibodies leading to a reaction. . . .

. . . Secondly, the **anaphylatic** reaction from successive intramuscular injections would not be instantaneous. If the penicillin were given intramuscularly, at least five or ten minutes, and possibly as long as one to three hours, would be required for absorption and reaction. On the basis of this testimony, a reasonable inference can be drawn that Moore's seizure was not caused by successive intramuscular injections of penicillin. Moore v. Guthrie Hospital, Inc., 403 F.2d 366, 370 (4th Cir. 1968).

Other Authorities: Daniels v. Hadley Memorial Hospital, 566 F.2d 749, 752 (D.C.Cir.1977).

anaplasia (an"ah-pla'ze-ah) [Gr. *ana* backward + *plassein* to form] a loss of differentiation of cells (dedifferentiation) and of their orientation to one another and to their axial framework and blood vessels, a characteristic of tumor tissue.

This point is driven home by the testimony of plaintiffs' witnesses that in 1976 the tumor may have been far less, and perhaps not at all undifferentiated (i.e., virulent). . . .

Inasmuch as the degree of undifferentiation of a tumor may increase over time, the government's attempt to apply survival statistics retroactively from a time when James's undiagnosed tumor may have been far less virulent is an unconvincing exercise. James v. U.S., 483 F.Supp. 581, 587 (N.D.Cal.1980).

Anaplasma (an"ah-plaz'mah) [Gr. *anaplasma* something formed] a genus of microorganisms of the family Anaplasmataceae (q.v.), including three species, *A. centra'le, A. margina'le* (the causative agent of anaplasmosis), and *A. ovis.*

anaplasmosis (an"ah-plaz-mo'sis) a disease of cattle and related ruminants marked by high temperature, anemia, and icterus, and caused by *Anaplasma marginale*, which is transmitted by ticks and other blood-sucking arthropods. Called also *gallsickness*. See also *Anaplasma.*

. . . there was at least some uncertainty as to the hazardous nature of Anaplaz. It said in part: "Vaccinating brood cows with **anaplasmosis** vaccine sometimes may cause fatal side effect in calves." Haste v. American Home Products Corp., 577 F.2d 1122, 1123 (10th Cir. 1978).

The disease, **anaplasmosis**, is a disease which infects mature cattle primarily in the humid and warm areas of the United States. It is caused by a tiny parasitic microorganism, the anaplasma marginale, which is transmitted primarily by flying insects. It attacks the red blood cells of the cow and will frequently produce death in older cattle by destruction of the red blood cells, producing an extremely anemic condition. . . .

. . . The calves exhibited uniform symptoms, appearing very jaundiced, languid, and extremely weak, and with the membranes and skin taking on a very yellow and jaundice appearance. Waller v. Fort Dodge Laboratories, 356 F.Supp. 413, 414 (E.D.Mo.1972).

Anaplaz See *anaplasmosis*; and *isoerythrolysis, neonatal.*

. . . a patented vaccine which is called **Anaplaz** and which prevents the symptoms of a common bovine disease called anaplasmosis. . . .

Dr. Dahlgren testified that the vaccine in question was made from the whole blood of cattle infected with anaplasmosis. He testified that the patent called for centrifuging the blood cells at 20,000 r.p.m. to obtain release and sedimentation of the anaplasma marginale, the microorganism which produces anaplasmosis. He further testified that when operating the centrifuge at that speed red blood cell antigens would also be caused to sedimentate and be removed along with the anaplasma marginale matter. He further testified that the patent did not provide for removing the red blood cell antigens from the vaccine at any time during the manufacturing process. Dr. Searl, for defendant, testified each dose of **Anaplaz** contained 1 mg. of red cell stroma. Waller v. Fort Dodge Laboratories, 356 F.Supp. 413, 414–16 (E.D.Mo.1972).

anasarca (an"ah-sar'kah) [*ana-* + Gr. *sarx* flesh] generalized massive edema.

He believed that plaintiff's shortness of breath, edema of her ankles, and **anasarca** (general accumulation of fluid in the abdomen and lower extremities) were the products of the enlarged liver. Warner v. Schweiker, 551 F.Supp. 789, 792 (E.D. Mo.1982), reversed 722 F.2d 428 (8th Cir. 1983).

anastomose (ah-nas'to-mōs) 1. to communicate with one another by anastomosis, as arteries and veins. 2. to create a communication between two formerly separate structures. See also *anastomosis.*

anastomosis (ah-nas"to-mo'sis), pl. *anastomo'ses* [Gr. *anastomōsis* opening, outlet] 1. a communication between two vessels by collateral channels. 2. an opening created by surgical, traumatic, or pathological means between two normally distinct spaces or organs.

An intensive search revealed that Mrs. Williams' common bile duct had been severed during the first operation, allowing the bile to drain into her abdominal cavity. The doctor performed an **anastomosis** by inserting twenty-four inches of Mrs. Williams' intestine where the common duct, which normally is three to four inches in length, had been cut. Bronwell v. Williams, 597 S.W.2d 542, 543 (Ct.Civ.App.Tex.1980).

Dr. McClenathan discovered that a major leg vein, the common femoral, had been severed. Although this vein is normally much further below the surface of the leg than the superficial ones that are stripped, Dr. Raffaelly had apparently mistaken it for one which was to be removed. To remedy the error, Dr. McClenathan immediately joined the remaining portion of the severed femoral vein to an intact portion of the greater saphenous vein. This surgical procedure, known as an **anastomosis**, restored the drainage of blood from Bridgford's leg. Bridgford v. U.S., 550 F.2d 978, 980 (4th Cir. 1977).

. . . he underwent an ileal loop operation consisting of the urethra being **anastomosed** to a loop of intestine and the urinary bladder bypassed. Warner v. City of Bay St. Louis, 408 F.Supp. 375, 380 (S.D.Miss.1975).

Other Authorities: Sindler v. Goldman, 389 A.2d 1192, 1194 (Super.Ct.Pa.1978). DaRoca v. St. Bernard General Hospital, 347 So.2d 933, 934 (Ct.App.La.1977); Matthews v. Matthews, 415 F.Supp. 201, 202 (E.D.Va.1976); Raitt v. Johns

Hopkins Hospital, 322 A.2d 548, 562 (Ct.Spec.App.Md. 1974).

anastomosis, intestinal the establishment of a communication between two portions of the intestinal tract; see illustration.

A. I found about a one to two inch mass, round mass, in his colon, in his large intestine, that looked like it was hard, firm, and almost appeared to be breaking through the bowel at that point."

Dr. Abramson feared that this mass might represent a carcinoma, and thus performed resection of the colon with an end to end **anastomosis**. Babin v. St. Paul Fire and Marine Ins. Co., 385 So.2d 849, 854 (Ct.App.La.1980).

anatomist (ah-nat'o-mist) a person skilled or learned in anatomy; a specialist in the field of anatomy.

anatomy (ah-nat'o-me) [*ana-* + Gr. *temnein* to cut] 1. the science of the structure of the animal body and the relation of its parts; it is largely based on dissection, from which it obtains its name. 2. dissection of an organized body.

Anectine (an-ek'tin) trademark for preparations of succinylcholine chloride. See also *succinylcholine chloride.*

anemia (ah-ne'me-ah) [Gr. *an* neg. + *haima* blood + *-ia*] a reduction below normal in the number of erythrocytes per cu. mm., in the quantity of hemoglobin, or in the volume of packed red cells per 100 ml. of blood which occurs when the equilibrium between blood loss (through bleeding or destruction) and blood production is disturbed. See also *benzene* (Am. Petroleum Inst. case); and *thalossemia.*

Anemia, which can be caused by lead-induced deformation and destruction of erythrocytes (red blood cells) and decreased hemoglobin synthesis, is often the earliest clinical manifestation of lead intoxication. CD 11–7, 11–8, 11–13, JA 1229–1230, 1235. Symptoms of **anemia** include pallor of the skin, shortness of breath, palpitations of the heart, and fatigability. The Criteria Document concluded, after a review of various studies, that in "children, a threshold level for **anemia** is about 40 u[g] Pb/dl, whereas the corresponding value for adults is about 50 ug Pb/dl." CD 11–13, JA 1235. (The concentration of lead in the blood is measured in micrograms of lead per deciliter of blood—ug Pb/dl.) [Footnotes omitted.] Lead Industries Ass'n, Inc. v. Environmental Protection Agency, 647 F.2d 1130, 1138 (D.C.Cir.1980).

[Attributed to benzene]: A decline in the red blood cell count **(anemia)** results in a decreased capacity of the blood to carry oxygen to various parts of the body and is characterized by fatigue. American Pet. Institute v. Occupational Safety, 581 F.2d 493, 498 (5th Cir. 1978).

The diagnosis is that the gangrene is caused by arteriosclerosis (a thickening and hardening of arteries and other vessels leading to acute diminishment of blood flow) inducing high fever, dehydration and profound **anemia** (number of red blood cells being less than normal). Matter of Quackenbush, 383 A.2d 785, 787 (Morris Ct.Ct.Prob.Div.1978).

anemia, aplastic a form of anemia generally unresponsive to specific antianemia therapy, often accompanied by granulocytopenia and thrombocytopenia, in which the

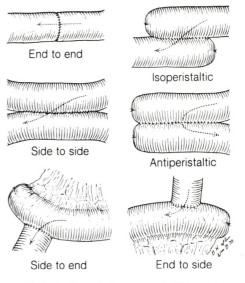

End to end

Isoperistaltic

Side to side

Antiperistaltic

Side to end

End to side

Methods of intestinal anastomosis (Babcock).

bone marrow may not necessarily be acellular or hypoplastic but fails to produce adequate numbers of peripheral blood elements. The term actually is all-inclusive and most probably encompasses several clinical syndromes. Called also *aregenerative a.* and *refractory a.* See also *chloramphenicol.*

From her use of the penicillamine Mrs. Reinhardt developed **aplastic anemia**, which is a disease which suppresses one's ability to product blood....

... During this vacation, she experienced bleeding of the gums and cuticles, unusual bruising, and heavy menses....

... On August 22 she noticed bruising on her hands that was "not a regular type of bruising." At the urging of a co-worker, she called Dr. Colton, saw him in his office, and was immediately admitted to the hospital. She had developed **aplastic anemia** as a result of taking the drug penicillamine. Reinhardt v. Colton, 337 N.W.2d 88, 89, 91 (Minn.1983).

In January, 1974, appellant consulted Dr. Herbert Lipkin, complaining of fatigue, sore throat, swollen glands and bruising. These symptoms are consistent with developing **aplastic anemia** which can be caused by Butazolidin treatment. [The Appeal Court noted]: ... Mrs. Baldino was diagnosed as suffering from **aplastic anemia**: a serious blood disorder which has resulted in a shortened life expectancy, an inability to have children, and general physical malaise; requiring her to take blood transfusions every two months, and take male hormones which have deepened her voice and caused abnormal growths of body hair. Baldino v. Castagna, 454 A.2d 1012, 1014 (Super.Ct.Pa.1982), reversed 478 A.2d 807, 809 (Pa.1984).

In May 1968, when Timothy was two years old, a physician prescribed chloromycetin for an injury to his palate, and again in December for bronchitis. He soon developed **aplastic anemia**, which results from the failure of bone marrow to produce blood cells. The disease is generally irreversible and apparently has left Timothy permanently and seriously disabled. Salmon v. Parke, Davis and Co., 520 F.2d 1359, 1361 (4th Cir. 1975).

Other Authorities: Stevens v. Parke, Davis & Co., 507 P.2d 653, 655 (Cal.1973); Incollingo v. Ewing, 282 A.2d 206, 212, 218 (Pa.1971); Love v. Wolf, 58 Cal.Rptr. 42, 46 (Ct.App.Cal. 1967); Stottlemire v. Cawood, 213 F.Supp. 897, 898 (D.D.C. 1963).

anemia, hemolytic anemia due to shortened *in vivo* survival of mature red blood cells and inability of the bone marrow to compensate completely for their decreased life span. See also *isoerythrolysis, neonatal.*

anemia, iron deficiency anemia characterized by low or absent iron stores, low serum iron concentration, low transferrin saturation, elevated transferrin, low serum ferritin, low hemoglobin concentration or hematocrit, and hypochromic microcytic red blood cells. Symptoms may include pallor, angular stomatitis and other oral lesions, gastrointestinal complaints, and thinning and brittleness of the nails, occasionally leading to spoon nails (koilonychia). See also *hemoglobin.*

The loss of iron results in **iron deficiency anemia** when the hemoglobin level is below the acceptable range for a particular individual. Thus **iron deficiency anemia** results when there is a lack of sufficient iron for the synthesis of hemoglobin....

... Not all **iron deficiency anemia** is hypochromic and microcytic; when the anemia is mild, there may be no change in color of the blood or the cell size. Since the red blood cells are mass-produced in bone marrow, the most reliable test is to extract a sample of the bone marrow and examine it for iron content....

"Q. ... Doctor, in your observation, what are the symptoms of anemia, **iron-deficiency anemia**, I should say?

"A. Well, **iron-deficiency anemia** results in a deficiency of hemoglobin and hemoglobin has, as its main purpose, the transportation of oxygen to the tissues. So the symptoms would depend on what we call anoxia, or deficiency of oxygen. A patient showing anoxia would usually be short of breath, with the exertion that would previously not bother him. His pulse rate would be increased. His blood pressure would usually be decreased compared to his normal blood pressure. He would feel weak with exertion. He might have a light fever. Most patients with that condition do. It is not very marked, and it usually doesn't cause the patient any discomfort." J. B. Williams Co. v. F.T.C., 381 F.2d 884, 887–8 (6th Cir. 1967).

anemia, normocytic anemia characterized by a proportionate decrease in the hemoglobin content, the packed red cell volume, and the number of erythrocytes per cubic millimeter of blood.

When hospitalized in March, 1967, she was diagnosed as having **anemia normocytic** due to hypothyroidism. Coleman v. Weinberger, 538 F.2d 1045, 1046 (4th Cir. 1976).

anemia, pernicious a megaloblastic anemia occurring in children but more commonly in later life, characterized by histamine-fast achlorhydria, in which the laboratory and clinical manifestations are based on malabsorption of vitamin B_{12} due to a failure of the gastric mucosa to secrete adequate and potent intrinsic factor. Called also *Addison's* or *addisonian a., Addison-Biermer a., cytogenic a.,* and *malignant a.* See also *cyanocobalamin.*

In 1926 it was found that **pernicious anemia** patients were benefited by the addition to their diets of substantial amounts of the liver of cattle....

Relative to the work of the patentees in this case, the production of amphetamine sulphate from amphetamine with sulphuric acid would seem comparatively simple. No one, before Alles, had produced it, however, and the product was of such value....

... A short time thereafter, other employees of Merck, who had continued to work with liver, succeeded in isolating a pure, red, crystalline material which, upon analysis, was found to be identical in chemical structure and function to that obtained from fermentates. Clinical tests proved the material derived from both sources to be the anti-pernicious anemia factor [Vitamin B–12].

... The patentees have given us for the first time a medicine which can be used successfully in the treatment of **pernicious anemia**, a medicine which avoids the dangers and disadvantages of the liver extracts, the only remedies available prior to this invention, a medicine subject to accurate standardization and which can be produced in large quantities and inexpensively, a medicine which is valuable for other purposes, as well as for the treatment of pernicious anemia. It did not exist in nature in the form in which the patentees produced it and was produced by them only after lengthy experiments. Merck & Co. v. Olin Mathieson Chemical Corp., 253 F.2d 156, 158, 164 (4th Cir. 1958).

anemia, sickle cell a hereditary, genetically determined hemolytic anemia, one of the hemoglobinopathies, occurring almost exclusively in Negroes, characterized by arthralgia, acute attacks of abdominal pain, ulcerations of the lower extremities, sickle-shaped erythrocytes in the blood, and, for full clinical expression, the homozygous presence of S hemoglobin in the red blood cells, as defined by hemoglobin electrophoresis. Called also *sicklemia,* and *Herrick's a.* See also *sickle cell-thalassemia disease,* under *disease.*

Sickle cell anemia (a definite form of cell that is found in the anemic person, a red cell that looks like a sickle). Glover v. Bruce, 265 S.W.2d 346, 351 (Mo.1954).

anesthesia (an"es-the'ze-ah) [*an* neg. + Gr. *aisthēsis* sensation] loss of feeling or sensation. Although the term is used for loss of tactile sensibility, or of any of the other senses, it is applied especially to loss of the sensation of pain, as it is induced to permit performance of surgery or other painful procedures.

Dr. Greene also stated his opinion as to deviations from reasonable standards of **anesthesia** which caused or contributed to cause the condition which led to the cardiac arrest and subsequent condition. Among these were: administration of a muscle paralyzing drug and muscle relaxant with insufficient ventilation; use of a mask instead of an endotracheal tube; and administration of gasses under positive pressure without a tube, resulting in aspiration and irritation of the lungs. Burrow v. Widder, 368 N.E.2d 443, 450–1 (App.Ct.Ill.1977).

The trial court excluded from evidence on the grounds of materiality and relevancy a publication of the Joint Commission on Accreditation of Hospitals entitled "Accreditation Manual for Hospitals—1970," which was in force at Miller Hospital at the time of Mrs. Cornfeldt's operation. The rationale for the court's ruling was that the manual was immaterial to the applicable standard of care, Dr. Tongen and Dr. Beals both testified that they had no familiarity with the manual. Plaintiff attempted to introduce the manual into evidence because it set forth standards to be followed by the hospital in supplying **anesthesia** care.[16] [[16] Standard IV provides: "Practices employed in the delivery of **anesthesia** care shall be consistent with the policies of the medical staff. Interpretation. Because individuals with varying backgrounds may properly administer **anesthetic** agents the medical staff must approve policies relative to **anesthesia** procedures, including the delineation of pre- and post-anesthetic responsibilities. Written policies of the medical staff relative to **anesthesia** care would include provision for at least: The **preanesthesia** evaluation of the patient by a physician, with appropriate documentation of pertinent information relative to the choice of **anesthesia** and the surgical or obstetrical procedure anticipated. This evaluation should include the patient's previous drug history, other **anesthetic** experiences and any potential **anesthetic** problems. The review of the patient's condition immediately prior to induction of **anesthesia**. This should include a review of the chart, with regard to completeness, pertinent laboratory data, time of administration and the dosage of **preanesthesia** medications, together with an appraisal of any changes in the patient's condition, as compared with that noted on previous visits."] Cornfeldt v. Tongen, 262 N.W.2d 684, 703 (Minn.1977), modified on appeal after remand 295 N.W.2d 638.

[A] great amount of discretion [is] necessary in the administration of that ether through the tube ... Unless the proper amount is given the child would not stay in the proper stage of **anesthesia**, and if it bubbles too slowly he will probably awake and be turning, and if it is given too fast, if he breathes it too fast it is apt to stop his heart ... [T]here is a grave danger which may well occur if the ether is sent too rapidly in the form of bubbles through that tube"; the witness further stated that ether "is a relatively safe **anesthetic**, and ... is one ... entrusted to the less experienced, in fact, that is what you train them on in giving **anesthetics**, [in] a tonsillectomy." Cavero v. Franklin General Benev. Soc., 223 P.2d 471, 473 (Cal.1950). **Other Authorities:** McCarthy v. Hauck, 447 N.E.2d 22, 24 (App.Ct.Mass.1983); King v. Retz, 454 N.Y.S.2d 594, 595–6 (Sup.Ct.Onondaga Ct.1982). Dill Products v. Workmen's Comp. App. Bd., 401 A.2d 409, 410 (Commonwealth Ct.Pa. 1979); Carter v. Phillips, 365 So.2d 48, 49 (Ct.App.La.1978); Burrow v. Widder, 368 N.E.2d 443, 446 (App. Ct. of Ill.1977); Harvey v. Kellin, 566 P.2d 297, 301 (Ariz.1977); Whitfield v. Whittaker Memorial Hospital, 169 S.E.2d 563, 565 (Sup.Ct. App.Va.1969).

anesthesia, caudal anesthesia produced by injection of a local anesthetic into the caudal or sacral canal.

In a **caudal anesthetic** the anesthetic solution is not placed within the spinal column or subarachnoid space. Funke v. Fieldman, 512 P.2d 539, 542 (Kan.1973).

anesthesia, dolorosa pain in an area or region that is anesthetic.

Appellant was not permitted to introduce evidence of Dr. Pittman's previous experience with phenol injections. Prior to the operation on Hales, Dr. Pittman had utilized the same procedure on four patients. Two of these patients, but not Hales, developed a complication known as **anesthesia dolorosa**. This

is a constant pain which is sometimes worse than the tic douloureux which the operation is designed to eliminate. Hales v. Pittman, 576 P.2d 493, 498 (Ariz.1978).

anesthesia, general a state of unconsciousness, produced by anesthetic agents, with absence of pain sensation over the entire body and a greater or lesser degree of muscular relaxation; the drugs producing this state can be administered by inhalation, intravenously, intramuscularly, rectally, or via the gastrointestinal tract.

Unfortunately, **general anesthesia**, by its very nature as a trespass on a person's normal physiology, carries with it an inherent risk of loss of cerebral function and even death. Such tragic results can and do occur in a certain number of cases even where **general anesthesia** is administered with all due care, in full accord with accepted medical standards, and without any negligence whatsoever. **General anesthesia** has a morbidity and mortality rate approximately four or five times that for spinal anesthesia. Haas v. U.S., 492 F.Supp. 755, 758 (D.Mass. 1980).

anesthesia, inhalation anesthesia produced by the inhalation of vapors of a volatile liquid or gaseous anesthetic agent.

... and that defendant Duker, the anesthesiologist, negligently ordered the administration of an **inhalation type of anesthesia** without examining the decedent. Vogan v. Byers, 447 F.2d 543, 544–5 (3d Cir. 1971).

anesthesia, regional the production of insensibility of a part by interrupting the sensory nerve conductivity from that region of the body. It may be produced by (1) *field block*, that is, the creation of walls of anesthesia encircling the operative field by means of injections of a local anesthetic; or (2) *nerve block*, that is, injection of the anesthetic agent close to the nerves whose conductivity is to be cut off. Called also *blocking a., conduction a.*, and *block*.

He stated further that prior to the rhizotomy, Linda had undergone two nerve blocks in the lumbar area.[1] [[1] These nerve blocks were described as the induction by injection, after local anesthetic, of an anti-inflammatory agent for the purpose of relieving pain.] Brown v. Fidelity & Cas. Co. of New York, 385 So.2d 572, 574 (Ct.App.La.1980).

It is agreed that assisted respiration must be furnished following administration of Anectine because the patient either ceases to breathe spontaneously or suffers impaired breathing until the initial effects of Anectine, known as a Phase I Block wear off. The initial effects are characterized as a depolarizing block meaning the drug produces its results by blocking the muscle fibers by preventing further build up of the process of muscular contraction.... This mechanism is said to differ from the curare mechanism which operates on the nerve receptor endings of the muscles to produce blockage.

... So long as a Phase I Block continues, the patient must be kept on assisted respiration, and should not be given Tensilon as it will prolong the Phase I Block produced by Anectine. During a Phase II Block, a patient may experience either the loss or impairment of spontaneous breathing that has returned after the Phase I Block has ended. There is considerable dispute concerning the use of Tensilon either as a diagnostic aid to determine the existence of a Phase II Block or as a curative agent to restore spontaneous breathing interrupted or impaired during a Phase II Block.

... [A Phase I Block may turn into a Phase II Block which differs mechanically from a Phase I Block in that a Phase II Block is a nondepolarizing or desensitizing Block. Although different mechanically from a Phase I Block, a Phase II Block produces effects similar to those of a Phase I Block. A Phase II Block may result in a cessation or impairment of spontaneous breathing resumed following termination of a Phase I Block. It is agreed that between a Phase I and Phase II Block a "gray zone" may occur, meaning a transitional period in which some effects of the Phase I Block will linger. It is also conceded that, in exceptional cases, the effects of Anectine may linger indefinitely, perhaps for hours, depending upon the degree of deficiency of cholinesterase. So long as a Phase I Block continues, the patient must be kept on assisted respiration, and should not be given Tensilon as it will prolong the Phase I Block produced by Anectine. During a Phase II Block, a patient may experience either the loss or impairment of spontaneous breathing that has returned after the Phase I Block has ended.] Chapman v. Argonaut-Southwest Insurance Co., 290 So.2d 779, 782 (Ct.App.La.1974).

anesthesia, saddle block the production of anesthesia in a region corresponding roughly with the areas of the buttocks, perineum, and inner aspects of the thighs which impinge on the saddle in riding, by introducing the anesthetic agent low in the dural sac.

Plaintiff's counsel asked the question which included details relating to a technique of administering a "saddle block". The technique as first described omitted any reference to the insertion of the spinal needle through an introducer and the withdrawal of the stylette to show a clear spinal fluid (called aspirating) before injecting the anesthetic. On defendant's objection, the trial judge required the plaintiff to restate the question including these two features to accord with the technique as described by Dr. Dyer on cross-examination. In his discovery deposition, Dr. Dyer omitted any reference to these features but added them at trial. We think the required correction was error and counsel should have been allowed to ask his question in accord with his theory of the case, i.e. that Dr. Dyer did not use the introducer or aspirate, leaving the integrity of the question to cross-examination. 2 Wigmore on Evidence, (3rd Ed.) § 682(b). Murphy v. Dyer, 409 F.2d 747, 749 (10th Cir. 1969).

anesthesia, spinal 1. anesthesia produced by injection of a local anesthetic into the subarachnoid space around the spinal cord; called also *Corning's a.* or *method, intraspinal a.*, and *subarachnoid a.* 2. loss of sensation due to a spinal lesion. See also *canalis sacralis*; and *detoxification* (Clark case).

The negligent act for which liability was sought to be imposed is the surgeon's deviation from acceptable medical practice by his invasion of the anesthesiologist's province in prescribing pre-medication (Demerol) for the **spinal block**.

... P, another medical expert for the plaintiff, noted on the patient's hospital chart that the cause of the respiratory failure was "block and Demerol, most likely". This was based on Dr. P's initial assessment that the **spinal block** extended too high and that it paralyzed the patient's ability to breathe which was then depressed by the superimposition of the Demerol....

Repressed breathing of a patient during surgery can be caused by a spinal block that extends too high, particularly when combined with Demerol as the premedication anesthetic. Proper monitoring of the patient's vital signs by the anesthesiologist would facilitate early detection of the onset of breathing difficulties. Thompson v. Presbyterian Hosp., Inc., 652 P.2d 260, 263, 265–6 (Okla.1982).

Because the natural tendency of the **spinal anesthesia** administered to Mrs. Reichman was to paralyze the sympathetic nerves and dilate the vessels, thus lowering the patient's blood pressure, her blood pressure was artificially elevated during and following surgery by the use of neo-synephrine. Reichman v. Wallach, 452 A.2d 501, 503 (Super.Ct.Pa.1982).

... while in a **spinal anesthetic** the solution is placed within the subarachnoid space. There is a lateral approach or method of giving a **spinal anesthetic** which consists of the insertion of the needle through the skin lateral to the midline of the patient's back. The aim in the performance of the **spinal anesthetic** using the lateral approach is to place the needle within the midline or the center of the intervertebral canal.

... Dr. William H. L. Dornette, called as a witness upon behalf of the defendant, testified the purpose of **spinal anesthesia** is to produce a block of the spinal nerves which will relieve pain and will produce muscular relaxation. Funke v. Fieldman, 512 P.2d 539, 542–3 (Kan.1973).

anesthesiological chart See *chart, anesthesiological.*

anesthesiologist (an"es-the"ze-ol'o-jist) a physician specializing in anesthesiology. Cf. *anesthetist.*

During surgery it is the **anesthesiologist's** job to monitor breathing which can be done by watching the drape over the patient or watching an electrocardiogram monitor....

... She testified that his custom was to secure tubing from the anesthesia machine to the patient's chest so that the patient could breathe. He would watch the patient's respiration and tell him to breathe. He would also place his hand on the patient's chest to see if he was breathing. Vuletich v. Bolgla, 407 N.E.2d 566, 569 (App.Ct.Ill.1980).

One major risk that arises from the abandonment of a patient by an **anesthesiologist** is manifest: if there is no qualified **anesthesiologist** in attendance during an operation, the administration of anesthesia itself may be faulty, and it thus may create a danger to the patient's health and safety.

Yet, that was not the only substantial risk arising from the operation here, in which a drug known to have neurotoxic properties was injected into the patient's blood stream. In this case, the patient's blood pressure, which was monitored by the **anesthesiologist**, dropped drastically during the operation. There is an indication that by 1:30 p.m., when Dr. Choi conceded that he had left the operating room, the patient's blood pressure had fallen to 70 over 0. In such circumstances, given that the **anesthesiologist** is responsible for recording blood pressure and for administering medications in response to falling blood pressure, an abandonment by the **anesthesiologist** creates a serious danger that improper steps may be taken to counteract the patient's lowered blood pressure. Also, without a qualified **anesthesiologist** in the operating room, there would be no trained person to inform the surgeon during the radiography procedure of the radical change in the patient's condition. [Footnote omitted.] Medvecz v. Choi, 569 F.2d 1221, 1229 (3d Cir. 1977).

Dr. Collins further stated that the responsibilities of the **anesthesiologist** include: the method of giving anesthesia; the choice of inducing and maintaining agents; the use or non-use of a relaxant drug; whether or not to use an endotracheal tube; and whether or not to use a cardiac monitor.

Dr. Ginsberg, an **anesthesiologist**, testified that in his opinion the choice of method of anesthesia administration, the agent of administration, and the decision whether or not to intubate were the responsibilities of the **anesthesiologist**. Burrow v. Widder, 368 N.E.2d 443, 450 (App.Ct.Ill.1977).

anesthesiology (an"es-the"ze-ol'o-je) [*anesthesia* + *-logy*] that branch of medicine which studies anesthesia and anesthetics. See also *care, standard of* (anesthesiologist); and *hospital* [rules] (Weeks case).

anesthetic (an"es-thet'ik) 1. pertaining to, characterized by, or producing anesthesia. 2. a drug or agent that is used to abolish the sensation of pain. See also *methoxyflurane*; and *anesthesia*.

According to the medical testimony there is always the danger of cardiac arrest (the heart stops beating) with the use of **anesthetic** agents such as were used in this procedure. This always present danger requires careful observation and monitoring of the gases used, pulse, blood pressure and use of a "bag" to ventilate, all of this is the responsibility of the anesthesiologist. Seaton v. Rosenberg, 573 S.W.2d 333, 335 (Ky.1978).

... the child was taken to surgery and anesthesized by Dr. Wyly, who used a mixture of Fluothane and oxygen as an **anesthetic** which he administered through a face mask. Chapman v. Argonaut-Southwest Ins. Co., 290 So.2d 779, 781 (Ct.App. La.1974).

Mrs. Adams received injections of sodium brevital, a general **anesthetic**, and xylocaine, a local anesthetic. Barnes v. Tenin, 429 F.2d 117 (2d Cir. 1970).

anesthetic, general an agent that produces general anesthesia.

A second **general anesthetic**, a mixture of nitrous oxide and oxygen, was administered throughout the operation by means of a nosepiece connected to an anesthesia machine. Dr. Tenin apparently made no detailed examination to ensure this machine was in proper functioning order before commencing the oral surgery. Holding the nosepiece, making appropriate adjustments in the settings on the anesthesia machine, and administering additional sodium brevital during the extraction were the responsibilities of Mrs. Barlow, whose formal training in anesthetics was extremely limited. Barnes v. Tenin, 429 F.2d 117–118 (2d Cir. 1970).

anesthetic, halogenated

All **halogenated anesthetics** contain halogens which are a group of elements consisting primarily of fluorine and bromine. Carlsen v. Javurek, 526 F.2d 202, 204 (8th Cir. 1975).

anesthetic, local an agent whose anesthetic action is limited to an area of the body determined by the site of its application; it produces its effect by blocking nerve conduction.

A buccal fat pad covered by the lining or mucous membrane of the mouth lies in a depression near the foramen. The hypodermic needle is inserted through the mucous membrane into the

tissue of the pad until it reaches the jawbone, small amounts of the **anesthetic** being ejected as the needle is inserted. When the needle reaches the bone it is withdrawn slightly and the remaining anesthetic injected into the area of the foramen or nerve center. Surabian v. Lorenz, 40 Cal.Rptr. 410, 411 (Dist. Ct.App.1964).

anesthetist (ah-nes'thĕ-tist) a person, such as a nurse or technician, trained in the administration of anesthetics. Cf. *anesthesiologist*.

[W]hile an anesthetic is being administered ... through the tube ... the **anesthetist** [must] ... Watch the color, the patient's pulse, respiration and reflexes, especially the eye reflexes ... it is her duty ... [T]he reflexes should [not] return at all during the course of surgery to a person who is supposedly in the proper state of anesthesia.... Cavero v. Franklin General Benev. Soc., 223 P.2d 471, 473 (Cal.1950).

aneurysm (an'u-rizm) [Gr. *aneurysma* a widening] a sac formed by the dilatation of the wall of an artery, a vein, or the heart. The chief signs of arterial aneurysm are the formation of a pulsating tumor, and often a bruit (*aneurysmal bruit*) heard over the swelling. Sometimes there are symptoms from pressure on contiguous parts. See also *arch, aortic* (Griffin case).

An arteriogram, however, showed the **aneurysm** to be located in another blood vessel in the area. When the operation was performed, the **aneurysm** was found to be in the blood vessel within the sciatic nerve—a condition of extreme rarity. Spitzer v. Ciprut, 437 N.Y.S.2d 27, 28 (2d Dep't 1981).

Dr. Glenn Barnett likened an **aneurysm** to a weak spot on an inner tube, which when extra pressure is placed upon it, may rupture and leak....

... He related that a common time for the **aneurysm** to bleed is during sexual intercourse or after having a bowel movement. At the same time he noted that there are many people who wake up with them in the morning, who have a headache or who are simply walking down a street or driving a car, so it is impossible to say what actually happens except that the vessel gets weak enough and the blood comes out. Cunningham v. Am. Mut. Ins. Co., 390 So.2d 1372, 1375 (Ct. App.La.1980).

None of the witnesses excluded the possibility that the fall could have caused the **aneurysm** to burst. It showed that an unruptured **aneurysm** does not cause symptoms, but that upon the rupture the principal initial symptoms are headaches, stiff neck, dizziness, nausea, difficulty in thinking, and loss of muscular control. Dr. Minster was asked if it were possible that the rupture originally could have occurred as a leak causing a momentary imbalance resulting in the fall. He responded that it was possible, but that he assumed otherwise because the symptoms followed the fall and because it was unusual for loss of balance to precede the symptoms of a headache and stiff neck. Simon v. Lumbermens Mut. Cas. Co., 368 N.E.2d 344, 348 (App.Ct.Ill.1977).

Other Authorities: Karp v. Cooley, 493 F.2d 408, 412 (5th Cir. 1974). Woodall Ind., Inc. v. Mass. Mut. Life Ins. Co., 483 F.2d 986, 995 (6th Cir. 1973); H. P. Foley Elec. Co. v. Industrial Com'n, 501 P.2d 960, 962 (Ct.App.Ariz.1972); York v. Daniels, 259 S.W.2d 109, 111 (Springfield Ct.App.Mo.1953).

aneurysm, abdominal an aneurysm of the abdominal aorta.

Abdominal Aortic Aneurysm: Sac formed by the filation of the walls of an artery or vein and filled with blood, in the aorta. McClaflin v. Califano, 448 F.Supp. 69, 73 (D.Kan.1978).

aneurysm, aortic aneurysm of the aorta.

The ALJ acknowledges the **aortic aneurysm** as one of plaintiff's several medical conditions but he does not address it specifically. The medical evidence indicates that since discovery in August 1979, it has increased in size from five cm. to eight cm. in May, 1981. According to treating physician McKee's evaluation, surgical correction, is inadvisable because of intervening problems. (Tr. 167). Dr. McKee stated that the **aneurysm** will have to be repaired before it spontaneously ruptures. (Tr. 167). However, there is no indication of when it will be advisable relative to his other medical problems. The undisputed evidence shows that the plaintiff's **aneurysm** to be equal to an Appendix I impairment.

The impairments listed in Appendix I have been legislatively determined to be severe enough in themselves to prevent a person from doing any gainful activity. 20 C.F.R. § 404–1525....

... Section 4.11(A) of Appendix I states: **Aneurysm of aorta** or major branches (demonstrated by roentgenographic evidence). With: (A) Acute or chronic dissection not controlled by prescribed medical or surgical treatment.

The **aneurysm** meets the Appendix I requirement since it cannot be surgically repaired because of plaintiff's other medical conditions. The medical reports indicate that it should be repaired in the future (at least before it ruptures). Thus, the record shows that death is almost certain if the **aneurysm** is not repaired; yet surgery cannot be scheduled during the foreseeable future. Wilson v. Schweiker, 553 F.Supp. 728, 735 (E.D. Wash.1982).

In January of 1976, the plaintiff developed an **aortic aneurysm** which was secondary to the valve transplant. It is alleged that the **aneurysm** has drastically affected the Plaintiff's life; has rendered him totally incapacitated; severely restricts his activities and has significantly shortened his life expectancy. Shadle v. Pearce, 430 A.2d 683, 684 (Super.Ct.Pa.1981).

aneurysm, berry a small saccular aneurysm of a cerebral artery, usually at the junction of vessels in the circle of Willis, having a narrow opening into the artery; such aneurysms frequently rupture, causing subarachnoid hemorrhage. Called also *cerebral a.*

A **berry aneurysm** is an outpouching or ballooning of the wall of a cerebral artery....

... The proof to support this claim of medical malpractice came from Dr. Charles Salamone, a qualified neurologist, who testified that **berry aneurysms** are treatable, that a severe headache, along with associated stiffness and neck pain and possibly vomiting, are the symptoms of a hemorrhaging **aneurysm**, and that the condition does not usually cause a neurological deficit....

... Dr. Salamone testified that surgery or conservative treatment such as bed rest and sedation are the two possible methods of treating a **berry aneurysm**. According to Dr. Salamone, Larkin's aneurysm could have been treated and cured anytime prior to the "blowout" on January 3. He said that the aneurysm was accessible and that with surgical treatment there was "at least a 75 per cent chance of survival...." Larkin v. State, 446 N.Y.S.2d 818, 819 (4th Dep't 1982).

This cause is before us on petition for writ of certiorari to review the decision of the Industrial Relations Commission which affirms an order of the Judge of Industrial Claims awarding compensation for a ruptured **cerebral aneurysm** sustained by the claimant, Richard Mosca. In deciding this case, we must determine whether Victor Wine & Liquor, Inc. v. Beasley, 141 So.2d 581 (Fla.1962), which heretofore has been applied only in cases involving heart attacks, should be extended to other internal failures of the cardiovascular system. We conclude that it should, and applying the doctrine of Victor Wine to the facts of this case, we hold that claimant's ruptured **cerebral aneurysm** was not a compensable injury.[1] [[1] In Victor Wine, we adopted the following rule: When disabling heart attacks are involved and where such heart conditions are precipitated by work-connected exertion affecting a pre-existing non-disabling heart disease, said injuries are compensable only if the employee was at the time subject to unusual strain or overexertion not routine to the type of work he was accustomed to performing.]

... This means that, before a ruptured aneurysm can qualify as an accident arising out of employment, the rupture must be shown to have been caused by an unusual strain or overexertion by the claimant resulting from a specifically identifiable effort by him not routine to the type of work he is accustomed to performing.[2] [[2] We recede from Tracy v. Americana Hotel, 234 So.2d 641 (Fla.1970), insofar as it is inconsistent with our present decision.] Richard E. Mosca & Co., Inc. v. Mosca, 362 So.2d 1340, 1341–2 (Fla.1978).

The Court finds that the hemorrhage was the result of the bursting of a **berry aneurysm**—an abnormal weakness in the wall of the blood vessel—which **aneurysm** had existed for some time prior to the day of Zorn's death. The Court further finds that the unusual physical exertion engaged in by Zorn on the morning of his death caused an extraordinary strain to be placed on the walls of the blood vessel at the site of the **aneurysm** which, in turn, caused the **aneurysm** to burst or rupture. Zorn v. Aetna Life Insurance Co., 260 F.Supp. 730, 731–2 (E.D.Tex.1965).

aneurysm, fusiform a spindle-shaped arterial aneurysm in which the stretching process affects the entire circumference of the artery; called also *Richet's a.* Cf. *saccular a.*

aneurysm, saccular an eccentric localized distended sac affecting only a part of the circumference of the arterial wall. Cf. *fusiform a.*

Plaintiffs contend that the insured either struck his head on the transom of a staircase or fell from the staircase while descending the stairs and ruptured a perhaps congenital and certainly undetected **saccular aneurysm** of the right middle cerebral artery, resulting in hemorrhage in the right temporal lobe of the brain, causing death; the rupture, it is argued, resulted from the head injury or from a surge of blood occasioned by the fall. Defendant contends that the evidence shows no accident and that even if an accident ruptured the **aneurysm**, the insured's injury was not effected solely through accidental means and did not result directly from the injury independently of any other cause but resulted directly or indirectly, wholly or partly, from a disease or infirmity, that is, the preexisting **aneurysm**. . . .

. . . How long the insured's **aneurysm** antedated his death is unknown; it was developmental and its final state a function of time measured in years. Such an **aneurysm** as the insured's can be symptomatized by headache, double vision, nausea, fainting, and unsteadiness of gait; but an **aneurysm** can also go wholly undetected for a very long time and then produce sudden death by entirely spontaneous rupture. An **aneurysm** may be ruptured by a blow to the head or by an activity of the body that increases intracranial pressure. Discovery of such an **aneurysm** as the insured's (and such discovery would be unlikely in the extreme in the absence of manifest symptoms) would result in immediate medical treatment, either a straitened regimen of activity calculated to prevent occasions of increased intracranial pressure, or immediate brain surgery. The **aneurysm** in its final state was a grossly abnormal condition in the affected artery. . . .

. . . The **aneurysm** was not dormant or inactive nor was it a static condition. It was, on the evidence, a developmental abnormality and capable, unaided of any external stimulus, of producing death though not, even in extended time, certain to do so. The **aneurysm** had not produced recognizable sensible effects, but it was an unrelenting threat to life. Sugarman v. New England Mutual Life Ins. Co., 201 F.Supp. 759, 760–1 (E.D.N.Y.1962).

angiitis (an″je-i′tis), pl. *angii′tides* [*angi-* + *-itis*] inflammation of a vessel, chiefly of a blood or a lymph vessel; called also *vasculitis*.

angina (an-ji′nah, an′jĭ-nah) [L.] spasmodic, choking, or suffocative pain; now used almost exclusively to denote angina pectoris. See also *angia pectoris*.

"Angina" is defined not as a disease but as a symptom of the underlying disease. The **angina** is the pain resulting from the underlying disease. In appellee's case it was a symptom of his arteriosclerosis or hardening of the arteries. . . .

. . . Obviously, **angina** represents a warning that impending damage exists and is the warning which tells a person to stop this activity. It should be noted that 25% of patients who sustain a myocardial infarction have had no **angina** whatsoever. Kempner's and Dodson Ins. Co. v. Hall, 646 S.W.2d 31, 32 (Ct.App.Ark.1983).

Dr. Patrick testified that in his opinion the working conditions produced the symptoms of **angina**, which is the pain message to the heart, but that no damage is done by the **angina** in the sense of death of cells. Dr. Patrick was of the opinion that Mr. Black's working conditions neither aggravated nor accelerated his two pre-existing heart conditions, but would rather aggravate the symptomatology. . . .

. . . Mr. Black had two pre-existing heart conditions. His work aggravated the symptoms of those conditions, consisting of chest pains which is called **angina pectoris**. Black v. Riverside Furniture Co., 642 S.W.2d 338, 340–1 (Ct.App.Ark. 1982).

By way of explanation, Dr. Gabatin stated that arteriosclerotic heart disease reduces the supply of oxygen to the heart muscles, which in turn causes some pain in the chest area. This is the pain syndrome commonly referred to as **anginal** pain. As to the symptomatology which one would look for in diagnosing **anginal** pain associated with heart disease, Dr. Gabatin

testified that typical symptoms are chest pains which come after exertion or meals, shortness of breath, and pain to the extremities on the left side of the body. Bishop v. Capitol Life Insurance Co., 545 P.2d 1125, 1127 (Kan.1976).

Other Authorities: Fain v. St. Paul. Ins. Co., 602 S.W.2d 577, 580 (Ct.App.Tex.1980); Kelley-Rickman, Inc. v. Hartford Life Ins., 557 F.2d 639, 641 (8th Cir. 1977); Great American Reserve Ins. Co. v. Britton, 406 S.W.2d 901, 905 (Tex.1966).

angina, Ludwig's diffuse purulent inflammation of the floor of the mouth, its fascial spaces, muscles, and glands, and spreading to the soft tissues of the upper neck; edema may cause airway obstruction. Called also *Gensoul's disease*. See also *tracheotomy* (Spadaccini case).

In diagnosing the condition as **Ludwig's Angina**, Dr. Sherman noted a severe infection, evidenced by marked swelling under the chin and marked edema of the floor of the mouth. The condition is usually caused by a dental infection which can spread from the bottom front of the mouth in toward the back of the tongue and, if not treated, can cause swelling on the outside of the neck. Primary treatment is administration of antibiotics and/or surgery. Spadaccini v. Dolan, 407 N.Y.S.2d 840, 842 (1st Dep't 1978).

angina, pectoris a paroxysmal thoracic pain, with a feeling of suffocation and impending death, due, most often, to anoxia of the myocardium and precipitated by effort or excitement; has been called *a. cordis, angor pectoris, Elsner's asthma, Heberden's asthma or disease, Rougnon-Heberden disease*, and *stenocardia*.

Before complete blockage and a heart attack occurs, symptomatic chest pain associated with coronary artery disease called **angina pectoris** can occur. In effect, **angina** is a warning signal indicating that the blood and oxygen supply to the heart at that time is not sufficient. Immediate rest and/or medication is indicated or else a heart attack which could permanently destroy part of the heart muscle tissue, or even cause death, might occur. Pierce v. Kentucky Galvanizing Co., Inc., 606 S.W.2d 165, 167 (Ct.App.Ky.1980).

In 1972, three tests existed which were used to diagnose **angina pectoris**: nitroglycerin, treadmill EKG, and an angiogram. Keogan v. Holy Family Hosp., 589 P.2d 310, 313 (Ct.App. Wash.1979), judgment reversed 622 P.2d 1246, 1255 [including a discussion of the tests] (1980).

In 1966 Pastor suffered a heart attack and in 1968, 1972 and 1974 he was hospitalized for varying periods suffering from **angina pectoris**, which refers to chest pains often due to coronary disease. . . .

. . . While it is undisputed that Pastor suffered from arteriosclerosis, hardening of the arteries, both the government physician and Pastor's own physician characterized his attack on May 18 as **angina pectoris**, which is chest pain resulting from inadequate blood flow to the heart due to reduced artery capacity. Necessarily, the key symptom of such an attack is the patient's subjective statement that he is feeling pain. . . .

. . . Physical activity, which taxes the reduced capacity of the arteries, is known to cause **angina pectoris**, and Pastor's "mild" congestive heart failure of February 17, characterized by coughing and the presence of fluid in the lungs, can be self-induced in a patient suffering from arteriosclerosis by ingestion of large amounts of liquids. U.S. v. Pastor, 557 F.2d 930, 934, 937–8 (2d Cir. 1977).

Other Authorities: Adams v. New Orleans Public Serv., Inc., 395 So.2d 470, 471 (Ct.App.La.1981); Chenoweth v. Weinberger, 421 F.Supp. 955, 959 (W.D.Mo.1976); Bewley v. American Home Assur. Co., 450 F.2d 1079, 1080 (10th Cir. 1971); Great American Reserve Ins. Co. v. Britton, 406 S.W.2d 901, 908 (Tex.1966).

anginal (an-ji'nal, an'ji̇-nal) pertaining to or characteristic of angina.

angiogram (an'je-o-gram") a roentgenogram of blood vessels filled with a contrast medium.

While hospitalized, a four vessel **angiogram** was performed on Mr. Lemke. The results of this test were interpreted by the doctors at the VA Hospital as indicating that Mr. Lemke was suffering from occlusive disease of the left and right carotid arteries....

... The **angiogram** revealed 85% narrowing of the left carotid artery and approximately 70% narrowing on the right. Lemke v. U.S., 557 F.Supp. 1205, 1207 (D.N.Dak.1983).

This contemplated procedure involved the following risks for Salis: (1) adverse reaction to the dye, (2) injury from insertion of the catheter, and (3) creation of a clot caused by the breaking off of plaque that had collected along the vessel walls.

The risk of significant complications in the case of an average **angiogram** is in the vicinity of 1 to 2 per cent....

... The radiologist who performed the **angiogram** inserted the catheter into Salis's left femoral artery. This action was taken even though the purpose of the procedure was to take x-rays of Salis's right leg....

... The **angiogram** procedure dislodged plaque from the walls of Salis's blood vessels.

These plaques showered into Salis's left leg and left foot, thereby causing massive clotting.

The **angiogram** procedure also caused an acute renal shutdown, or kidney failure, because of either the shower of plaque or a reaction of the kidneys to toxic substances in the dye. Salis v. U.S., 522 F.Supp. 989, 993 (M.D.Pa.1981).

Dr. Reitt's initial diagnosis was uncertain, and he recommended conducting an **angiogram** upon Gragg at Crawford W. Long Hospital. The procedure entails insertion of a catheter into each of the two carotid arteries, which supply blood to the brain. The catheter first is inserted into the femoral artery, located in the groin region, and then is carefully moved up through the vascular system to the left carotid artery. A contrast material is injected into the left artery, and later into the right, and X-rays are obtained which would indicate whether there is any blockage or occlusion present....

... Testimony was given by Dr. James C. Hoffman, Jr., an associate professor of radiology and a director of neuroradiology at Emory University School of Medicine, concerning the importance of monitoring a patient's condition during an **angiogram** so as to avoid delay in treating possible complications. Dr. Hoffman expressed the opinion that it "would be relevant to know" if the patient, "after an injection in a vessel, was unconscious," and that there were certain "specifications" that should be taken in immediate response to loss of consciousness. Dr. Hoffman explained that when an **angiogram** was completed, the physician would normally "pull the cathe-

ter out, hold pressure, talk to the patient and say, 'How do you feel?' And if they are feeling okay, we move them out on a stretcher. You can see when you are moving them on a stretcher if they are moving everything. So it is pretty obvious to you that they have no side effects at that time." If evidence of side effects is apparent, we immediately take their blood pressure. We [may] start intravenous fluids on them and we will ask for a neurology or a neurosurgery consult....

... In Dr. Hoffman's opinion, it was "not normal" for a patient to leave the room unconscious after this procedure. "Certainly that could be a complication from the **angiogram**. The patient could have gotten hypotensive from the studies which they do.... If the patient was not talking to me and came into the room talking, I would be very concerned ... [and] would look into it and wouldn't just leave...." Gragg v. Spenser, 284 S.E.2d 40, 41 (Ct.App.Ga.1981).

Other Authorities: Zeck v. U.S., 559 F.Supp. 1345, 1347 (D.S. Dak.1983); Fain v. St. Paul Ins. Co., 602 S.W.2d 577, 580 (Ct. App.Tex.1980).

angiography (an"je-og'rah-fe) [*angio-* + Gr. *graphein* to record] the roentgenographic visualization of blood vessels following introduction of contrast material; used as a diagnostic aid in such conditions as cerebrovascular attacks (strokes) and myocardial infarctions.

Angiography is a medical procedure in which a catheter is inserted into a blood vessel and an iodine-based dye is introduced into the circulatory system. The dye then outlines the vessels which are photographed by x-rays. Cardiac catheterization involves the same procedure with insertion of the catheter in the area near the heart....

... **Angiography** is strictly diagnostic and has no purpose other than to provide physicians with information to assist them in deciding if a patient should undergo an operation. Salis v. U.S., 522 F.Supp. 989, 991, 994 (M.D.Pa.1981).

angiography, coronary radiographic visualization of the coronary arteries after the introduction of contrast material.

A coronary **angiography** performed while Mr. Lemke was a patient at Overlake Hospital revealed a 95% obstruction of the right coronary artery with minimal disease in the anterior descending and circumflex coronary arteries. Left ventricular function was normal. Lemke v. U.S., 557 F.Supp. 1205, 1207 (D.N.Dak.1983).

His—he also had **coronary cenoangiography** with left ventriculography, which simply means the dye in the left ventricle or the main pumping chamber of the heart. Fain v. St. Paul Ins. Co., 602 S.W.2d 577, 581 (Ct.App.Tex.1980).

angioma (an"je-o'mah) [*angio-* + *-oma*] a tumor whose cells tend to form blood vessels (*hemangioma*) or lymph vessels (*lymphangioma*); a tumor made up of blood vessels or lymph vessels.

angioma, arteriovenus congenital angioma of the brain composed of arterial and venous channels with many arteriovenous shunts, and characterized by frequent focal epileptic seizures and progressive impairment of the blood supply, which gives rise to increasing hemiparesis. It is distinguished by an intracranial bruit.

After taking tests, including a myelogram, the diagnosis was made that there existed a space-taking lesion of the thoracic area of the spinal cord, known as an **arteriovenus angioma** (AVA), extra-medullary in nature, that is outside the substance of the spinal cord. Tyminski v. U.S., 481 F.2d 257, 260 (3d Cir. 1973).

angioplasty (an'je-o-plas"te) [*angio-* + Gr. *plassein* to form] surgical reconstruction of blood vessels.

angioplasty, patch graft See *graft, patch.*

Dr. Lillehei found a small obstruction of the artery at the site of the incision made by Dr. Murray for the catheterization, which Dr. Lillehei rectified by taking a little piece of vein and patching the artery so as to widen it at that point (a **patch graft angioplasty**). Walstad v. University of Minnesota Hospitals, 442 F.2d 634, 637 (8th Cir. 1971).

angiosarcoma (an"je-o-sar-ko'mah) [*angio-* + *sarcoma*] a hemangiosarcoma.

... after an exploratory laparotomy and biopsy was carried out, he was found to have **angiosarcoma** of the liver, an exceptionally rare and irreversible cancer which strikes only 1 person in some 50,000, no more than 20–30 persons a year. Eighteen months later, on March 3, 1973, another former employee of the Lousiville plant died, and a third died on December 19, 1973, again of **angiosarcoma** of the liver. Recognizing the rarity of the tumor and learning that all three had worked in the Goodrich PVC plant, Dr. Creech brought the matter to the attention of Goodrich, and then on January 22, 1974, to the attention of the National Institute of Occupational Safety and Health (NIOSH).

News of other deaths followed swiftly. On January 29, 1974, Goodrich reported the death of a fourth former employee from **angiosarcoma**; a report of the death of a fifth employee followed on February 15th. Six days later, Union Carbide advised NIOSH of the death of one of its PVC workers from liver **angiosarcoma**. Goodyear Tire and Rubber Company announced a vinyl chloride worker fatality from liver **angiosarcoma** on March 1, 1974, and reported two more such deaths from the same cause on March 22nd. Goodrich reported cases of liver **angiosarcoma** in two of its living employees. On April 16, 1974, Firestone Plastics announced the death of one of its employees from the same disease. Finally, on May 10, 1974, the National Cancer Institute diagnosed another Union Carbide VCM worker as a victim of the same disease. In all, the deaths of 13 workers in the PVC and fabricating industries were reported. Society of Plastics Indus., Inc. v. Occupational S. & H.A., 509 F.2d 1301, 1306 (2d Cir. 1975).

angle (ang'g'l) [L. *angulus*] the area or point of junction of two intersecting borders or surfaces. See also *angulus.*

angle, cerebellopontile that between the cerebellum and the pons. Called also *cerebellopontine.*

This epidermoid tumor, according to all experts testifying, apparently originated in the **cerebella pontine angle**. Swanson v. U.S. By and Through Veterans Admin., 557 F.Supp. 1041, 1044 (D.Idaho 1983).

angle, costophrenic the angle formed at the junction of the costal and diaphragmatic pleurae.

Dr. Rosenstein noted a thickened pleura of the right **costophrenic angle**, but found the film to be negative for evidence of pneumoconiosis. Hash v. Califano, 451 F.Supp. 383, 386 (S.D.Ill.1978).

angle, lumbosacral See *angle, sacrovertebral.*

angle, sacrovertebral the angle formed at the junction of the sacrum with the lowest lumbar vertebra; called also *lumbosacral a.*

... increased **lumbosacral angle** producing chronic strain.... Gotschall v. Weinberger, 391 F.Supp. 73, 74 (D.Neb.1975).

anguish

The term "**anguish**" is defined in Webster's Third New International Dictionary as "extreme pain" and "excruciating distress". Therefore, in common usage, the term "**mental anguish**" means extreme pain or excruciating distress of the mind....

... In our opinion, the proper inquiry to determine whether there is sufficient evidence of the **mental anguish** element is whether the victim suffered any significant degree of mental distress greater than that normally attendant to criminal sexual assaults accomplished by force or coercion....

... Another witness described her behavior as being on the verge of hysteria. The doctor who examined complainant shortly following the incident testified that she was shaking and quivering. Two days after the incident the doctor prescribed Valium to relieve the victim's anxiety, and 12 days after the attack he discontinued the Valium and prescribed another medicine in the treatment of her insomnia.

In our view, there was sufficient evidence that complainant suffered a degree of mental distress significantly higher than that normally suffered by a sexual assault victim. The trial court did not err in submitting the **mental anguish** theory to the jury. People v. Jenkins, 328 N.W.2d 403, 406 (Ct.App.Mich.1982).

angulation (ang"gu-la'shun) [L. *angula'tus* bent] deviation from a straight line, as in a badly set bone.

With regard to how much deformity she had on June 2, she had some **angulation** at that point and approximately about 20% apposition at that time. I did not tell her that only 20% of the bones in the radius of her arm were touching and meeting each other. Powell v. Shull, 293 S.E.2d 259, 263 (Ct.App. N.Car.1982).

Dr. R. R. Raub, full-time specialist in orthopedic surgery, examined plaintiff July 31, 1957, and found him to have a healed fracture of the lower right leg with extreme **angulation** that probably was not acceptable from a functional standpoint. Dr. Raub felt that an osteotomy should be performed since he thought that otherwise plaintiff would eventually have arthritis in his knee or ankle. Abshire v. Gardner, 271 F.Supp. 927, 931 (S.D.W.Va.1967).

X-ray pictures taken April 22 showed that the **angulation** in the tibia fracture had been completely reduced but with a slight override, the lower fragment being only slightly to the side and back in relation to the upper fragment allowing eighty percent contact between them. Odom v. Celebrezze, 230 F.Supp. 732, 733 (E.D.S.Car.1964).

angulus (ang'gu-lus), pl. *an'guli* [L.] an angle; used as a general term in anatomical nomenclature to designate a triangular area or the angle of a particular structure or part of the body.

anileridine (an"ĭ-ler'ĭ-dēn) [USP] chemical name: 1–[2–(4-aminophenyl)ethyl]-4-phenyl-4-piperidinecarboxylic acid. A synthetic narcotic analgesic, $C_{22}H_{28}N_2O_2$, occurring as a white, crystalline powder, used as the phosphate salt for premedication for general anesthesia in surgery, as a postoperative sedative, and obstetric analgesic; administered subcutaneously or intramuscularly. Abuse of this drug may lead to dependence.

anileridine

Following the spinal induction and with the surgery coming up, **anileridine** was administered as a sedative to potentiate the sedative effect of the diazepam. **Anileridine** is a narcotic which depresses the respiratory system. Siegel v. Mt. Sinai Hospital of Cleveland, 403 N.E.2d 202, 205 (Ct.App.Ohio 1978).

animal (an'ĭ-mal) [L. *animalis*, from *anima* life, breath] a living organism having sensation and the power of voluntary movement and requiring for its existence oxygen and organic food.

animal, spinal an animal whose spinal cord has been severed, thus cutting off communication with the brain.

anion (an'i-on) [Gr. *ana* up + *ion* going] an ion carrying a negative charge owing to the gain of one or more electrons. Hence, because unlike forms of electricity attract each other, it is attracted by, and travels to, the anode or positive pole. See also *ion*. The anions include all the nonmetals, the acid radicals, and the hydroxyl ion. They are indicated by a minus sign, as Cl– (formerly by an accent mark, as Cl').

anionotropy (an"e-on-ot'ro-pe) [*anion* + Gr. *tropos* a turning] a type of tautomerism in which the migrating group is a negative ion rather than the more usual hydrogen ion. Cf. *prototropy*.

ankle (ang'k'l) 1. the part of the leg just above the foot. 2. the joint between the foot and the leg; ankle joint (articulatio talocruralis [NA]). See also *fracture, trimalleolar*; and *malleolus*.

It was Dr. Materson's opinion that the **ankle** symptoms were enhanced by the amputation of the right great toe, whether or not there was direct injury to the ankle. This is because the gait pattern of the great toe along with the fractures of the second and third toes is dramatically changed from normal. The result is a dramatic change in the weight bearing relationship between the **ankle** joint and the hind foot, which causes the advancement of degenerative changes post-fracture and increased **ankle** symptoms. Johnson v. Alexander, 424 So.2d 1269, 1273 (Ct.App.La.1982).

In April 1979 he suffered a fracture to his right **ankle**; this injury did not arise out of or in the course of his employment. The fracture was reduced by Dr. Dewey Jones, an orthopedic surgeon, who placed a pin and screw in the joint to hold the bones together. Brown v. Pullman, Inc., 423 So.2d 250, 251 (Ct.Civ.App.Ala.1982).

X-rays of his **ankles** taken with various attempts at strain submitted from Dr. J. Hussussion, dated 9/27/71 were reviewed. These films do show a very slight tilt of the talus in the **ankle** mortise on a strain film. There is an exostosis on the dorsum of the talus at the site of the attachment of the **ankle** joint. This is characteristic for repeated strain of the **ankle** capsule and represents a response to this type of injury. Ballard v. Commanding General, Fort Leonard Wood, Mo., 355 F.Supp. 143, 148 (W.D.Mo.1973).

ankylosing See *spondylitis.*

ankylosis (ang"kĭ-lo'sis), pl. *ankylo'ses* [Gr. *ankylōsis*] immobility and consolidation of a joint due to disease, injury, or surgical procedure.

He made a final diagnosis of a post-operative partial **ankylosis** of the right hip with flexion contractures and herniation of the nucleus pulposus with severe degenerative changes between L–5 and S–1. He stated further that Mrs. Rodenski, without further surgery, was a "total invalid." Ray v. Industrial Com'n, 284 N.E.2d 272, 274 (Ill.1972).

The report also noted "partial **ankylosis** of [plaintiff's] left knee (with) about 30% limitation of motion in flexion" and "progressive weakness of grip (with) obvious deformity of both wrists." Sellars v. Secretary of Dep't of Health, Ed. & Welf., 331 F.Supp. 1103, 1106 (E.D.Mo.1971), judgment reversed 453 F.2d 984 (8th Cir. 1972).

In explaining the difference between multiple calcification in the bursa of the left hip and **ankylosis** of the left hip, Dr. Snyder said that "**Ankylosis** and calcium in the bursa are two different pathologic conditions. Now the **ankylosis** is the deposit of calcium which ties the head of the femur to the acetabulum, [and that] deposit of calcium in the bursa, which is the tissue that surrounds the hip joint and holds in the fluid is spotty, in other words, it's not a continuous sheet—it's spotty, all over that there's multiple areas," and is not a part of **ankylosis**, but there definitely was some **ankylosis** at the time of the hearing. Colwell v. Gardner, 386 F.2d 56, 62 (6th Cir. 1967).

anomaly (ah-nom'ah-le) [Gr. *anōmalia*] marked deviation from the normal standard, especially as a result of congenital or hereditary defects.

Explanatorily, Dr. Bronwell said there was an abnormality in that Mrs. Williams' common duct went into her gall bladder and not into her duodenum. He never had seen the **anomaly** before in any of the patients undergoing gall bladder surgery....

... Later in his trial testimony, the doctor said that in all of his approximately four thousand gall bladder operations, he never had seen the **anomaly** he found in Mrs. Williams, he never had read of it in literature at any time, and he never heard it presented during his attendance at many seminar and medical society talks on gall bladder surgery, including **anomalies** that might be found in the human body. Bronwell v. Williams, 597 S.W.2d 542, 545, 549 (Ct.Civ.App.Tex.1980).

Dr. Kelley testified that from his examination of Plaintiff and the X-rays made and interpreted by Dr. Wybourn Plaintiff had an anterior arthritic spur on his fifth lumbar vertebra, as well as a congenital **anomaly**, to wit, the transverse process on the right side was incorporated into the sacrum (tailbone), so that Plaintiff has only four lumbar vertebrae on the right side, but five lumbar vertebrae on the left side. Robinson v. Charter Oak Fire Ins. Co., 551 S.W.2d 794, 797 (Ct.Civ.App.Tex.1977).

anomia (ah-no′me-ah) [*an* neg. + Gr. *anoma* name + *-ia*] loss of the power of naming objects or of recognizing and recalling their names; cf. *nominal aphasia* and *dysnomia.*

anorectic (an″o-rek′tik) [Gr. *anorektos* without appetite for] a substance that diminishes the appetite.

The diethylproprion hydrochloride put out by plaintiff purports to be a ''me-too'' of Tenuate Dospan which is marketed by Merrell. The medication is a sustained release **anorectic**, designed for use in control of obesity. It is related to the amphetamines.... Pharmadyne Laboratories, Inc. v. Kennedy, 466 F.Supp. 100, 106 (D.N.J.1979).

The Court finds that a legal issue exists as to the circumstances under which it may become unlawful for a physician under Title 21, United States Code, to dispense or prescribe **anorectic** controlled drugs described therein in the treatment of obesity to a large number of patients.... U.S. v. Zwick, 413 F.Supp. 113, 115 (N.D.Ohio 1976).

Prior to June, 1973, Pastor and Weiner, pharmacists in the Philadelphia area, had been dealing in large quantities of **anoretic** drugs known as phendimetrazine and phentermine. These drugs are often prescribed for use in weight reduction programs, but are also in demand for illicit purposes because they have qualities similar to amphetamines (''speed''). U.S. v. Pastor, 557 F.2d 930, 932 (2d Cir. 1977).

anoretic See *anorectic.*

anorexia (an″o-rek′se-ah) [Gr. "want of appetite"] lack or loss of the appetite for food.

anorexia nervosa a psychophysiologic condition, usually seen in girls and young women, characterized by severe and prolonged inability or refusal to eat, sometimes accompanied by spontaneous or induced vomiting, extreme emaciation, amenorrhea (impotence in males), and other biological changes. See also *depression* (Warfield case).

Finding that her weight had dropped to 93 pounds and realizing that she had a psychiatric problem, Dr. Holmes suggested that Nancy be admitted to the rehabilitation department of Wyandotte General Hospital, where she could be taken care of both physically and emotionally....

... Dr. Hughett saw Nancy late in the afternoon of March 7th. His working diagnosis was **anorexia nervosa**. He prescribed for Nancy three types of drugs and a program of recreational therapy such as attendance at ice shows and going on walks. The recreational therapy program was designed to get a patient out of his or her depression. Warfield v. City of Wyandotte, 323 N.W.2d 603, 605 (Ct.App.Mich.1982).

The staff at Children's Hospital finally diagnosed Mary's condition as **anorexia nervosa**, a psychiatric condition. Whitfield v. Roth, 519 P.2d 588, 591 (Cal.1974).

anosmia (an-oz′me-ah) [*an* neg. + Gr. *osmē* smell + *-ia*] absence of the sense of smell; called also *anosphrasia* and *olfactory anesthesia.*

... anosmia (loss of sense of smell).... U.S. Auto Stores v. Workmen's Compensation App. Bd., 482 P.2d 199, 201 (Cal. 1971).

anoxia (ah-nok′se-ah) absence of oxygen supply to tissue despite adequate perfusion of the tissue by blood; the term is often used interchangeably with *hypoxia*, to indicate a reduced oxygen supply. See also *brain damage* (Pederson case).

Dr. Kelly believed that the coma had been induced by ''**anoxia**'', lack of oxygen to the brain, following cardiac arrest and consequential brain damage. Eichner v. Dillon, 426 N.Y.S.2d 517, 527 (2d Dep't 1980), order modified 438 N.Y.S.2d 266 (1981).

He testified that deprivation of oxygen causes cerebral **anoxia**; that cerebral **anoxia** in turn produces brain damage and then brain death in a short time;... Daniels v. Hadley Memorial Hospital, 566 F.2d 749, 758 (D.C.Cir.1977).

... he was of opinion that death was caused by ''**anoxia**, probably secondary to aspiration and regurgitation of foreign material,'' that **anoxia** is the lack of oxygen, that food eaten such as he described as being present at the scene of death, and the coffee-like grounds, could have caused regurgitation, could have been the material that was aspirated into the lungs, and could have caused the death. Liberty National Life Insurance Co. v. Morris, 208 S.E.2d 637, 639 (Ct.App.Ga.1974).

Other Authorities: Bergstreser v. Mitchell, 577 F.2d 22, 24 (8th Cir. 1978); Matter of Quinlan, 348 A.2d 801, 806 (Super. Ct.N.J.1975); Buie v. Birtell, 516 P.2d 963–4 (Kan.1973).

anoxia, acute

The lungs showed evidence of **acute anoxia**, or sudden lack of oxygen. This is represented by a swelling of the lungs and typical signs of particular hemorrhages which are small hemorrhages over the surfaces of the lungs all as a result of the sudden lack of oxygen (**acute anoxia**)....

... Had the subject survived the aspiration it may have produced inflammatory action or a pneumonic state which is the interpretation of aspiration. Aspiration causes a lack of oxygen (**acute anoxia**) which in turn produces acute edema which produces the hemorrhages over the surface of the lungs. Jones v. Aetna Life Insurance Co., 439 S.W.2d 721, 723–4 (Ct.Civ. App.Tex.1969).

anoxia, cerebral

After examining infant plaintiff Dr. Rizzoli stated in his consultation note that it was his impression that infant plaintiff had experienced **cerebral anoxia** but that he believed he would recover. He recommended that hypothermia be continued. At trial Dr. Rizzoli explained his note ''will recover'' meant infant plaintiff would survive in terms of life and death....

... During the ten minutes that the respirator was malfunctioning on February 22, 1968, in the intensive care unit because of the kink in the tube, plaintiff's brain was deprived of needed oxygen which resulted in increased **anoxia**. Rose v. Hakim, 335 F.Supp. 1221, 1224–5, 1227 (D.D.C.1971).

These [resuscitating] procedures, to be effective, must be initiated with a minimum of delay as **cerebral anoxia**, due to a cutoff of oxygen to the brain, will normally produce irreversible brain damage within three to five minutes and total brain death within fifteen minutes. Matter of Dinnerstein, 380 N.E.2d 134, 135 (App.Ct.Mass.1978).

That the **cerebral anoxia** was caused by either of the following accidental causes of means:

a) An obstruction in the airway (endotracheal tube) that was then being used to introduce, artificially, both the anesthetic gases, nitrous oxide and cyclopropane, as well as the oxygen necessary to sustain the viability of the brain at a time when the patient lacked capacity for spontaneous respiration.

or

b) From an overdose of cyclopropane anesthetic gas which caused the patient's heart to stop and thereby making it impossible for the oxygen then being introduced through a clear airway (endotracheal tube) from reaching the brain through the normal blood flow emanating from the patient's heart to the brain. Latragna v. Colonial Life Ins. Co. of America, 357 N.Y.S.2d 795, 797–8 (Monroe Cty.Ct.1974).

anoxic (ah-nok'sik) pertaining to or characterized by anoxia.

Most importantly, all vital signs are normal during the entire anesthetic and surgical period, which flatly contradicts the possibility of an **anoxic** episode having occurred to deprive Mr. Haas of sufficient oxygen during this period. A deprivation of the necessary amount of oxygen would have to be reflected in blood pressure, pulse, respiration, and/or EKG, all of which were normal during this entire period. Additionally, all signs point to Mr. Haas responding normally and being on the road to normal recovery from anesthesia until about 12 noon, 1½ hours after completion of surgery....

... In a supplemental affidavit of February 15, 1980, Dr. Roaf adds:

I have read those portions of plaintiff's Memorandum in Opposition to Defendant's Motion for Summary Judgment in which plaintiff's attorney alleges that plaintiff suffered brain damage as a result of an **anoxic** episode whereby his brain was deprived of oxygen while he was under general anesthesia (see plaintiff's Memorandum, pp. 4, 7, 13, 14, 16). As indicated in my first Affidavit (p. 4, ¶6) this possibility is flatly contradicted by the normalcy of all vital signs revealed by the close monitoring which took place during the entire anesthetic and surgical period. While it is true that ordinarily in circumstances like this an **anoxic** episode would be suspected initially, that tentative suspicion must be categorically rejected in light of a review of the carefully monitored and recorded vital signs during the entire relevant period. Haas v. U.S., 492 F.Supp. 755, 758 (D.Mass.1980).

antabuse See *disulfiram.*

antecubital (an"te-ku'bĭ-tal) situated in front of the cubitus, or elbow.

... He also defined the **antecubital** area as the elbow. The affected area was about 32 square inches, being basically four inches by eight inches and running from above the elbow to below the elbow. Ohligschlager v. Proctor Community Hospital, 303 N.E.2d 392, 395 (Ill.1973).

antenatal (an"te-na'tal) [*ante-* + L. *natus* born] occurring or formed before birth; prenatal. Cf. *antepartal.*

antepartal (an"te-par'tal) occurring before parturition, or childbirth, with reference to the mother. Cf. *antenatal.*

anterior cervical excision See *surgery, anterior cervical.*

anterior tibial compartment syndrome See under *syndrome.*

anterolateral (an"ter-o-lat'er-al) situated in front and to one side.

Shatoska was admitted to the coronary intensive care unit of the Slidell Memorial Hospital suffering with what was diagnosed as an acute **anterolateral** myocardial infarction (heart attack). Shatoska v. Intern. Grain Transfer, Inc., 430 So.2d 1255, 1258 (Ct.App.La.1983).

Dr. L. M. Heinz performed a lumbar myelogram on Daney and determined that he had an extradural defect L4–5 on the left **anterolaterally** and that these findings were "compatible" with herniated nucleus pulposis. Daney v. Argonaut Ins. Co., 421 So.2d 331, 333 (Ct.App.La.1982).

Subsequent diagnosis revealed an acute **anterolateral** myocardial infarct, with which was coupled a considerable degree of congestive heart failure, resulting in total disability. J. V. Vozzolo, Inc. v. Britton, 377 F.2d 144, 146 (D.C.Cir.1967).

anteroseptal (an"ter-o-sep'tal) situated in front of the atrioventricular septum.

The strain of lifting the transmission from his body, superimposed upon preexisting coronary arteriosclerosis from which he suffered, produced an acute **anteroseptal** myocardial infarct. J. V. Vozzolo, Inc. v. Britton, 377 F.2d 144, 146 (D.C. Cir.1967).

anteversion (an"te-ver'zhun) [*ante-* + L. *versio* a turning] the forward tipping or tilting of an organ; displacement in which the organ is tipped forward, but is not bent at an angle, as occurs in anteflexion.

... the patient suffered of coccygodynia and described her as a "well developed, well nourished, adult, female of the stated age [34 years old] in no distress" (Tr. p. 248). The neurological examination was normal. X-rays revealed an anteverted coccyx with no evidence of fracture or dislocation....

... An earlier examination performed upon claimant on June 2, 1966 by Dr. Karl Horn, orthopedic surgeon, also revealed that the coccyx was **anteverted**, in a horizontal position and freely movable. Santiago v. Finch, 314 F.Supp. 326, 327 (D.Puerto Rico 1970).

anthelmintic (ant"hel-min'tik) [*ant-* + Gr. *helmins* worm] an agent that is destructive to worms. See also *vermicide.*

anthophyllite See *tremolite* [fiber] (R. T. Vanderbilt Co. case).

anthracosilicosis (an"thrah-ko-sil"ĭ-ko'sis) [*anthraco-* + *silicon*] a mixed condition of anthracosis and silicosis. See also *fibrosis, idiopathic pulmonary* (Consolidation Coal case).

... it is extremely doubtful, with an admitted second stage **anthracosilicotic** condition, accompanied by emphysema, coughing and expectoration, that he could possibly obtain the required health certificate with which to obtain such a job. Indeed, it would be hoped that he could not because the eating public should not be exposed to the high probability of accompanying tuberculosis so highly prevalent in silicotics and anthracosilicotics....

... It is evident that anthracite, as such, exists and has been mined and recovered only in a small area consisting of not more than approximately five counties located in northeastern Pennsylvania. **Anthracosilicosis** is peculiar to that area. While the condition bears similarity to silicosis contracted in the bituminous and soft-coal fields of Pennsylvania and elsewhere, it is, nonetheless, not identical and its results peculiar....

... Thus far, the medical profession has accomplished little or nothing by way of arresting the progress of this insidious disease.

Exhibit 21 (p. 79 et seq.) discloses that the plaintiff suffers, as previously indicated, shortness of breath, constant cough and weakness, all the result of a second stage **anthracosilicosis** with emphysema. Dr. Weaver, noting dyspnea, "barrelchestedness", and a decrease in vital capacity, concludes that plaintiff is totally and permanently disabled and, after labeling the condition as "progressive", concludes "no exertion allowed"....

... He found "ventilatory difficulty". (p. 90) He likewise found pulmonary insufficiency, and "hyperventilation syndrome", all obviously related to **anthracosilicosis**....

... The difference as we understand it in the language of a layman is that "**anthracosilicosis**" is contracted by reason of the inhalation of coal dust and rock dust (free silica) whereas pneumoconiosis is contracted by reason of the inhalation of coal dust only.[4] [[4] Because seams of anthracite, unlike bituminous coal, are always overlaid and underlaid with sandrock, it appears evident that anthracite miners will, in all probability, always suffer "silicosis" whereas bituminous miners, operating in areas where there is no rock, will inhale coal dust only and therefore contract what is known as "pneumoconiosis" as opposed to "silicosis" or what is here and otherwise described in the anthracite region as "**anthracosilicosis**".] Dabravalskie v. Gardner, 281 F.Supp. 919, 923–4,926 (E.D.Pa.1968).

anthracosis (an-thrah-ko'sis) [*anthraco- + -osis*] a usually asymptomatic form of pneumoconiosis caused by deposition of coal dust in the lungs; it is present in most urban dwellers. When the coal dust accumulates in large amounts, it may result in pneumoconiosis of coal workers.

Anthracosilicosis is a different situation from **anthracosis**. However, the microscopic findings make me wonder whether the description of the **anthracosis** was accurate.... [T]he description of **anthracosis** alone was accurate because, you are quite right when you say that **anthracosis** is carbon particles, per se, and are not indicative of the disease process. But then, quite the contrary, the pathology described here is that of anthracosilicosis or **anthracosis** combined with some other pneumoconiosis. Crucible Steel v. Workmen's Comp. App. Bd., 425 A.2d 1108, 1112 (Commonwlth.Ct.Pa.1980).

anthropophobia (an"thro-po-fo'be-ah) [*anthropo- + Gr. phobein* to be affrighted by + *-ia*] (*obs.*) morbid dread of human society. See also *anthropo-*; and *phobia*.

... **anthropophobia** wherein he suffers a morbid fear of engaging anyone in conversation or other type of social relationship, believed to be lifelong but aggravated by accident.... Phillips v. Celebrezze, 330 F.2d 687, 690 (6th Cir. 1964).

anthroum See *antrum*.

antiadrenergic (an"tĭ-ah-dren-er'jik) 1. opposing the effects of impulses conveyed by adrenergic postganglionic fibers of the sympathetic nervous system. 2. an agent that so acts. Called also *sympatholytic*. Cf. *anticholinergic*.

anti-aldosterone See *aldosterone*.

antibiotic (an"tĭ-bi-ot'ik) [*anti- +* Gr. *bios* life] a chemical substance produced by a microorganism which has the capacity, in dilute solutions, to inhibit the growth of or to kill other microorganisms. Antibiotics that are sufficiently nontoxic to the host are used as chemotherapeutic agents in the treatment of infectious diseases of man, animals, and plants.

Various **antibiotics**, known more commonly as "wonder drugs" under such familiar names as penicillin, aureomycin, terramycin, tetracycline, and streptomycin, have proved very useful since World War II in treating numerous infectious diseases.[1] Produced biologically, however, these drugs tend to vary greatly in their quality and potency unless developed, and thereafter tested, under very carefully controlled conditions. [[1] See generally L. Goodman & A. Gilman, The Pharmacological Basis of Therapeutics (3d ed., 1965).] U.S. v. Bacto-Unidisk, 394 U.S. 784, 785–6, 89 S.Ct. 1410, 22 L.Ed.2d 726 (1969).

Broad Spectrum **Antibiotics** are **antibiotics** which are effective against a wide range of harmful micro-organisms, including gram positive and gram negative patheogenic micro-organisms, rickettsiae, viruses, spirochetes and protozoa. In re Coordinated Pretrial Proceedings, etc., 410 F.Supp. 659, 664 (D.Minn.1974).

antibiotic sensitivity disk See *disk, antibiotic sensitivity*.

antibody (an"tĭ-bod"e) an immunoglobulin molecule that has a specific amino acid sequence by virtue of which it interacts only with the antigen that induced its synthesis in cells of the lymphoid series (especially plasma cells), or with antigen closely related to it. Antibodies are classified according to their mode of action as agglutinins, bacteriolysins, hemolysins, opsonins, precipitins, etc. See also *immunoglobulin*.

Appellant Garber's blood has substantial commercial value due to the presence of an extremely rare **antibody** known to be possessed by only two or three other persons in the world. This **antibody** is used in the production of diagnostic reagents for blood typing serums. U.S. v. Garber, 589 F.2d 843, 845 (5th Cir. 1979), rejected by 782 F.2d 593 (6th Cir. 1986).

anticholinergic (an"tĭ-ko"lin-er'jik) [*anti- + cholinergic*] an agent that blocks the parasympathetic nerves. Called also *parasympatholytic*. Cf. *antiadrenergic*.

Treatment has been a bland diet and **anticholinergic** medication which has helped to control the symptoms of the hiatus hernia, namely indigestion and occasionally vague chest discomfort. Landess v. Weinberger, 361 F.Supp. 247, 250 (E.D. Mo.1973), judgment reversed 490 F.2d 1187 (8th Cir. 1974).

anticoagulant (an"tĭ-ko-ag'u-lant) any substance that, *in vivo* or *in vitro*, suppresses, delays, or nullifies coagulation of the blood.

With all candor, Dr. Halsey stated that early treatment with **anticoagulants** is a controversial area prior to arteriography being run on the patient, but that, nevertheless, the possibility of worsening the patient's condition (if there is an incorrect diagnosis) by administering **anticoagulants** is extremely slight compared with the very great benefits to those patients, correctly diagnosed, who are so treated. Riddlesperger v. U.S., 406 F.Supp. 617, 622 (N.D.Ala.1976).

antifungal (an″tĭ-fung′gal) an agent that is destructive to fungi, suppresses the growth or reproduction of fungi, or is effective against fungal infections.

Pharmacraft had been marketing two products sold as nonprescription ethical drugs, that is, to physicians rather than to consumers. One was Desenex, an **anti-fungal** agent primarily offered for athlete's foot and general fungus infections; and Caldesene, a powder to treat diaper rash in babies.

In 1961 marketing of these items as proprietary products over the counter to consumers was begun. The **anti-fungal** agent in Desenex was undecylenic acid, and in Caldesene it was calcium undecylenate. Pennwalt Corp. v. Becton, Dickinson & Co., 434 F.Supp. 758, 759 (D.N.J.1977).

antigen (an′tĭ-jen) [*antibody* + Gr. *gennan* to produce] any substance which is capable, under appropriate conditions, of inducing a specific immune response and of reacting with the products of that response, that is, with specific antibody or specifically sensitized T-lymphocytes, or both. Antigens may be soluble substances, such as toxins and foreign proteins, or particulate, such as bacteria and tissue cells; however, only the portion of the protein or polysaccharide molecule known as the antigenic determinant (q.v.) combines with antibody or a specific receptor on a lymphocyte. Abbreviated Ag.

Dr. Lewis testified that plaintiff presented nine serum samples for testing. The nine samples were taken prior to, during, and after plaintiff's episode of GBS. In the samples taken at the height of the disease, there were immune complexes in which there was a cross-reactive antibody against both nerve and **antigen** (the **antigen** being the catalyst in the vaccine that incites the antibody). The significance of this positive cross-reactivity, according to Dr. Lewis, is that it indicates a relationship between the vaccine and the GBS. Lima v. U.S., 708 F.2d 502, 504 (10th Cir. 1983).

Dr. Dines said that it [Goodpasture's syndrome] is an immunologic disease in which it is thought that the victim develops antibodies to some **antigen** (a substance to which he is hypersensitive) and that these antibodies react against the kidneys and lungs. He also said that the **antigen** to which a victim reacts "can probably be different for different people" and that it is not known whether the reaction results from one exposure to an **antigen** or from multiple exposures. Boldt v. Jostens, Inc., 261 N.W.2d 92, 93 (Minn.1977).

It is an established fact that bovine bone contains a high degree of protein known as **antigens**. When the bone containing such **antigens** is implanted in another animal or a human being, the body produces antibodies which cause a rejection reaction resulting in an incapsulation of the implant bone and its resorption by the bodily processes of the host tissue. Such reaction which normally occurs as a result of the protein-containing **antigens** present in the implant bone causes the graft to fail. E. R. Squibb & Sons, Inc. v. Stickney, 274 So.2d 898, 901 (Dist.Ct.App.Fla.1973).

Other Authorities: Varga v. U.S., 566 F.Supp. 987, 1011 (N.D.Ohio 1983).

antigen, Australia See *antigen, hepatitis B surface.*

antigen, hepatitis B surface (HB$_s$Ag) an antigen present in the serum of those infected with viral hepatitis type B, consisting of the outer lipoprotein coat (surface) of the Dane particle. Originally called *Australia (Au) antigen* because it was first found in an Australian aborigine, it is also known as *hepatitis-associated a. (HAA)* and *serum-hepatitis (SH) a.*

Both experts testified, however, that no test will detect the presence of the Type A virus in the donor's blood. The experts also agreed that an **antigen** test had been developed which discloses the presence of hepatitis Type B, but it is not totally accurate. Appellant's medical expert placed the test's accuracy as to Type B hepatitis at 70%, and at 35% overall accuracy as to carriers of both types. According to appellee's expert, the **antigen** test picks up about 30% of hepatitis carriers. Fisher v. Sibley Memorial Hospital, 403 A.2d 1130, 1131–2 (D.C.Cir.1979).

antihypertensive (an″tĭ-hi″per-ten′siv) an agent that reduces high blood pressure.

"Antihypertensive" means a chemical substance which reduces blood pressure and is used for the treatment of hypertension. U.S. v. Ciba Geigy Corp., 508 F.Supp. 1118, 1122 (D.N.J.1976).

anti-inflammatory (an″tĭ-in-flam′ah-to″re) an agent that counteracts or suppresses the inflammatory process.

Trypsin and Chymotrypsin had been previously isolated and identified as compounds found in pancreatin, but it was Innerfield who first saw their unique therapeutic value as **anti-inflammatory** agents. Armour Pharmaceutical Co. v. Richardson-Merrell, Inc., 396 F.2d 70, 71 (3d Cir. 1968).

antineoplastic (an″tĭ-ne″o-plas′tik) 1. inhibiting or preventing the development of neoplasms; checking the maturation and proliferation of malignant cells. 2. an agent having such properties.

antiperspirant (an″tĭ-per′spĭ-rant″) an agent that inhibits or prevents perspiration. See also *aluminum sulfate.*

antiseptic (an″tĭ-sep′tik) a substance that will inhibit the growth and development of microorganisms without necessarily destroying them. Cf. *disinfectant.*

The word "antiseptic" refers to similar agents [See **disinfect** (Poncy case)] or methods used to clean surfaces of the human body itself, such as the swabbing of the skin with alcohol, before inserting a hypodermic needle. This, too, falls short of sterilization since what would be needed to sterilize would also destroy human tissue. Poncy v. Johnson & Johnson, 460 F.Supp. 795, 800 (D.N.J.1978).

antithrombin (an″tĭ-throm′bin) [*anti-* + *thrombin*] a general term for a naturally occurring or therapeutically administered substance (e.g., heparin) that neutralizes the action of thrombin and thus limits or restricts blood coagulation. Six naturally occurring antithrombins have been designated by Roman numerals (I to VI); of these, antithrombins I and III appear to be of major importance.

Following 1967 it was discovered that oral contraceptive hormones also decrease the level of **antithrombin III**, a blood factor which inhibits the clotting processes. Mahr v. G. D. Searle & Co., 390 N.E.2d 1214, 1226 (App.Ct.Ill.1979).

antitoxin (an″tĭ-tok′sin) [*anti-* + Gr. *toxicon* poison] antibody to the toxin of a microorganism (usually the bacterial exotoxins), to a zootoxin (e.g., spider or bee venom), or to a phytotoxin (e.g., ricin of the castor bean), which combines specifically with the toxin, in vivo and in vitro, with neutralization of toxicity.

antitoxin, tetanus [USP], a sterile solution of refined and concentrated antibody globulins obtained from the blood serum or plasma of a healthy animal, usually the horse, immunized against tetanus toxin or toxoid; used as a passive immunizing agent, administered intramuscularly, subcutaneously, or intravenously.

In addition to cleansing the wound and applying a dressing, he concluded that the best treatment would consist of giving her an injection of **tetanus antitoxin**. The administration of the **antitoxin** involved known medical dangers, such as a local reaction and necrosis of the skin. Proper medical procedure required that a test be given to the patient before administering the **antitoxin**. Defendant further testified that he performed a common test, the injection of a microscopic amount of serum beneath the superficial layer of the skin. If a wheal formed on the skin, it would indicate a positive reaction. A positive reaction would show that the patient was sensitive to the serum and should either be given a lesser dosage of **antitoxin** or none at all. Anderson v. Martzke, 266 N.E.2d 137, 139 (App.Ct.Ill. 1970).

antivenin (an″tĭ-ven′in) [*anti-* + L. *venenum* poison] a proteinaceous material used in the treatment of poisoning by animal venom. See also *antivenomous serum*, under *serum*.

That the physicians, Koontz and Martone, having elected to use a recognized and proper form of treatment for the snakebite by the use of **antivenin**, it appears that there was clear negligence in the failure of such physicians to adequately follow the instructions contained with such medication. Buck v. U.S., 433 F.Supp. 896, 900 (M.D.Fla.1977).

antrectomy (an-trek′to-me) [*antrum* + Gr. *ektome* excision] surgical excision of an antrum, as resection of the pyloric antrum of the stomach.

At surgery on April 23, 1973, no definite ulcer was found, but a bilateral truncal vagotomy and **antrectomy** with gastrojejunostomy was performed. Matthews v. Matthews, 415 F.Supp. 201, 202 (E.D.Va.1976).

antrum (an′trum), pl. *an′trums* or *an′tra* [L.; Gr. *antron* cave] a cavity or chamber; used as a general term in anatomical nomenclature, especially to designate a cavity or chamber within a bone.

According to the dentist's office records he made the extraction on 14 May, at which time he noted an oral **anthroum** opening. Appellee testified: ''I told him he had an **anthroum** communication and I told him sometimes you get trouble from

it and sometimes you have a problem from it.'' Graham v. Roberts, 441 F.2d 995, 996 (D.C.Cir.1970).

antrum, maxillare; maxillary See *sinus, maxillaris.*

Anturane (an′choo-rān) trademark for a preparation of sulfinpyrazone. See also *sulfinpyrazone.*

anulus (an′u-lus), pl. *an′uli* [L. dim. of *anus*] [NA] a term used to designate a ringlike anatomical structure; called also *annulus.*

anulus inguinalis profundus [NA], deep inguinal ring: an aperture in the fascia transversalis for the spermatic cord or for the round ligament; called also *annulus abdominalis abdominis, annulus inguinalis abdominalis, deep* or *internal abdominal ring*, and *internal inguinal ring.*

anulus inguinalis superficialis [NA], superficial abdominal ring: an opening in the aponeurosis of the external oblique muscle for the spermatic cord or for the round ligament; called also *annulus inguinalis subcutaneus, external abdominal ring*, and *superficial* or *external inguinal ring.*

The **external inguinal ring** was definitely enlarged in comparison with the left side and a definite more marked impulse could be felt within the ring on coughing or straining. Hurlburt v. Fidelity Window Cleaning Co., 160 A.2d 251, 255 (Super.Ct. Pa.1960).

aorta (a-or′tah), pl. *aor′tas, aor′tae* [L.; Gr. *aorte*] the main trunk from which the systemic arterial system proceeds [NA]. It arises from the left ventricle of the heart; passes upward (*a. ascen′dens*), bends over (*arcus aortae*), passes down through the thorax (*a. thoraca′lis*) and through the abdomen to about the level of the fourth lumbar vertebra (*a. abdomina′lis*), where it divides into the two common iliac arteries. Called also *arteria a.* and *arteria maxima Galeni.* See *Table of Arteriae.*

On September 28, the insured died from the affects of a ruptured **aorta**, which is the main artery that distributes blood to the body organs. The pathologist who conducted a post mortem had no opinion as to how long the deceased had a degenerated condition of the **aorta**. He was of the opinion that high blood pressure was a contributing factor in his death. Medical proof further showed that **aortic** ruptures are known to occur when there is no high blood pressure. Life Insurance Co. of Virginia v. Shifflet, 359 F.2d 501, 503 (5th Cir. 1966).

aorta-femoral by-pass See *by-pass, aorta-femoral.*

aortic arch See *arch, aortic.*

aortic arch study See *study, aortic arch.*

aortic valve See *valva, aortae.*

aortogram (a-or′to-gram″) the roentgenographic record resulting from aortography. See also *aortography.*

In this case, Dr. Randolph performed a highly sophisticated transfemoral **aortogram**, which is the procedure of ''injecting radio-opaque media into the renal artery by means of a catheter inserted into the femoral artery through an incision in the thigh near the groin, and moving it upwards to the renal artery, in order to visualize by x-rays the kidneys and surrounding areas.'' Brief for Appellee Randolph at 5 n. 1. Haven v. Randolph, 494 F.2d 1069 (D.C.Cir.1974).

To further diagnose the cause of the blood clotting, defendant requested that the staff urologist, Dr. Miles, who had previously performed over 300 **aortograms**,[2] perform one on the plaintiff. [[2] Defined as a diagnostic surgical procedure in which (while the patient is under general anesthetic) a long, hollow, 18 gauge needle, 14 centimeters long, is inserted in the back until it touches the tip of the twelfth vertebra; it is then partially withdrawn and its direction changed, and reinserted so that it enters the aorta itself, at which time dye is injected and x-rays of the area are made.] Dill v. Scuka, 279 F.2d 145, 146 (3d Cir. 1960).

aortography (a"or-tog'rah-fe) [*aorta* + Gr. *graphein* to write] roentgenography of the aorta after the intravascular injection of an opaque medium.

aortography, translumbar roentgenography of the aorta after injection of a radiopaque medium into it through a needle inserted into the lumbar area at about the level of the 12th thoracic vertebra.

During his hospitalization in June 1977, Salis underwent a **translumbar aortogram**, a type of angiogram in which the dye is inserted through the aorta....

... The results of the **translumbar aortogram** were not completely satisfactory, because the x-rays did not yield pictures of many small blood vessels. This problem arose because the dye became too diluted to outline these vessels. Salis v. U.S., 522 F.Supp. 989, 992 (M.D.Pa.1981).

In Salgo v. Leland Stanford etc. Bd. of Trustees, supra, 154 Cal.App.2d 560, 565–568, 317 P.2d 170, the defendant doctor performed a **translumbar aortography** in which the aorta was punctured and radioopaque substance injected to determine the location of a suspected block in plaintiff's circulatory system. The next morning plaintiff awoke and found that his lower extremities were permanently paralyzed. The court observed, ''There can be little question but that **aortography** and its results, because it is a relatively new diagnostic procedure, is not a matter of common knowledge among laymen. Bardessono v. Michels, 478 P.2d 480, 487 (Cal.1970).

Mrs. Lorene Ball brought suit against Dr. Jesse Adams, a vascular surgeon, charging malpractice in the performance of a test known as **translumbar aortogram** by the injection of Urokon 70, manufactured and sold by the defendant Mallinkrodt Chemical Works....

... At that time Dr. McCallie advised her that it might be possible to determine by means of the diagnostic procedure known as **translumbar aortogram** whether, as is sometimes the case, her high blood pressure was being caused by a partial blocking of the renal arteries leading to the kidneys....

... As we understand, this procedure consists of passing a flexible tube syringe through the patient's back and against the wall of the aorta, the large artery leading off in an upward direction from the heart. A long needle is then inserted within the tube and forced through the lumen or outer wall of the aorta. The contrast agent is then forced through the needle into the aorta and passes very rapidly into the renal arteries leading down to the kidneys, permitting the taking of X-ray pictures of these arteries to show any existing obstructions.

Ball v. Mallinkrodt Chemical Works, 381 S.W.2d 563, 565 (Ct.App.Tenn.1964).

Apgar rating See *score, Apgar.*

aphacic See *aphakic.*

aphakia (ah-fa'ke-ah) [*a* neg. + Gr. *phakos* lentil + *-ia*] absence of the lens of the eye; it may occur congenitally or from trauma, but is most commonly caused by extraction of a cataract.

Petitioner seeks annulment of the award of permanent disability, contending: (1) the records of Dr. Richards compel a finding that the natural lens of the enucleated eye had been extracted in the cataract surgery, leaving the left eye with the condition of abnormal vision known as ''**aphakia**'';... State Compensation Ins. Fund v. Workmen's Comp. App. Bd., 88 Cal.Rptr. 469, 471 (Ct.App.1970).

aphakic (ah-fa'kik) pertaining to aphakia; having no lens in the eye. See also *presbyopia* (Piper case).

The operation on both eyes was for the removal of cataracts, and resulted in what is known as ''**aphacic**'' eyes. That is, eyes without lens. Piper v. Kansas Turnpike Authority, 436 P.2d 396, 397 (Kan.1968).

aphasia (ah-fa'ze-ah) [*a* neg. + Gr. *phasis* speech] defect or loss of the power of expression by speech, writing, or signs, or of comprehending spoken or written language, due to injury or disease of the brain centers. For types of aphasia not given below, see *agrammatism, anomia, paragrammatism,* and *paraphasia.*

Stephen had trouble with his language remembering the right word to use. He had impaired recent and past memory....

... While there he received physical therapy to strengthen the muscles and improve his walking; occupational therapy to work on the arms; intellectual activity; perceptional activity; and speech therapy because of his **aphasia** or language disturbance. Kinsey v. Kolber, 431 N.E.2d 1316, 1323 (App.Ct. Ill.1982).

William B. Breedon, the subject of this appeal, is a young man with **aphasia**, a disorder which renders it exceedingly difficult for him to communicate with the world because language is something which he cannot readily comprehend....

... Mrs. Breedon diligently sought out an educational program for William but found that **aphasic** children were in a virtual no man's land, as she explained to the Hearing Review Board:

If you want to find the gaps in the educational system have an **aphasic** child.

The retarded didn't want him because he wasn't retarded. The deaf didn't want him because he wasn't deaf. He didn't belong with the emotionally disturbed. Breedon v. Maryland State Dep't of Ed., 411 A.2d 1073, 1074 (Ct.Spec.App.Md. 1980).

Other Authorities: Simmons v. Inman, 471 S.W.2d 203, 204 (Mo.1971).

aphasia, expressive aphasia in which there is impairment of the ability to speak and write, due to a lesion of the cortical center. The patient understands written and spoken words, and knows what he wants to say, but cannot utter the words. Called also *ataxic a., Broca's a., motor a., frontocortical a.*, and *verbal a.*

Dr. Cushman indicated that he had seen Lashley on "numerous occasions" and "believed that he [was] totally disabled." He summarized his findings as follows: "The patient has an **expressive aphasia** which alternates quite a bit. This patient's symptoms have fluctuated quite a bit with severe cerebral vascular disease and difficulty talking." Lashley v. Secretary of Health and Human Services, 708 F.2d 1048, 1050 (6th Cir. 1983).

aphasia, nominal aphasia marked by the defective use of names of objects; cf. *anomia* and *dysnomia.*

apical resorption See *resorption, apical.*

apicoectomy (a″pē-ko-ek′to-me) [*apex* + Gr. *ektomē* excision] excision of the apical portion of a tooth root through an opening made in the overlying labial, buccal, or palatal alveolar bone. See also *root amputation.*

Dr. Karam advised Mrs. Wiley that since the root canal therapy was unsuccessful, only two alternatives were available which were to either extract the tooth and replace it with a false tooth or undergo a surgical procedure called an **apicoectomy** with retrograde filling. Dr. Karam indicated that the latter procedure was not appropriate in her case because of the trauma involved and her loss of bone structure. Wiley v. Karam, 421 So.2d 294, 295 (Ct.App.La.1982).

Dr. Mahan testified at trial that he had performed some 100 **apicoectomies**, a procedure for cleaning out granulation areas of an abscessed tooth. Thornton v. Mahan, 423 So.2d 181, 182 (Ala.1982).

apnea (ap-ne′ah) [*a* neg. + Gr. *pnoia* breath] cessation of breathing. See also *succinylcholine chloride* (Coppolino case).

At 11:30, the baby was still experiencing labored respiration and periodic **apnea** (stopped breathing). Vecchione v. Carlin, 168 Cal.Rptr. 571, 573 (Ct.App.Cal.1980).

Other Authorities: Fraijo v. Hartland Hospital, 160 Cal.Rptr. 246, 249 (Ct.App.Cal.1979).

apnea, late cessation of respiration in an infant for more than 60 seconds after spontaneous breathing has been established and sustained.

However, on March 15, 1979, Roderick suffered his first "**apneic** episode" in which he quit breathing, and once again had to be given emergency resuscitation. A second such episode occurred two days later after which the child was finally transferred to Charity Hospital in New Orleans for more sophisticated testing and treatment....

... Furthermore, Dr. Boothby felt that the prolonged delivery of the head was probably related to the child's later "**apneic** episodes" described elsewhere as a "seizure disorder."

Another pediatrician who treated the child while at Lallie Kemp Charity Hospital and a witness presented on behalf of the State, Dr. Arthur C. Watts, likewise testified that he believed that the child's condition was caused by brain injury in turn caused by oxygen deprivation which occurred either during the prolonged delivery of the head of the child or in one or both of the **apneic** episodes which occurred several days after

the child's birth. Williams v. Lallie Kemp Charity Hosp., 428 So.2d 1000, 1003–4 (Ct.App.La.1983).

apomorphine (ap″o-mor′fin) [*apo-* + *morphine*] a crystalline alkaloid, $C_{17}H_{17}NO_2$, derived from morphine by the abstraction of a molecule of water; it is administered intravenously to induce instantaneous vomiting and was formerly used as an expectorant. See also *stimulus, aversive.*

The summary of the evidence contained in the report of the magistrate showed that **apomorphine** had been administered at ISMF for some time prior to the hearing as "aversive stimuli" in the treatment of inmates with behavior problems. The drug was administered by intra-muscular injection by a nurse after an inmate had violated the behavior protocol established for him by the staff....

... When it was determined to administer the drug, the inmate was taken to a room near the nurses' station which contained only a water closet and there given the injection. He was then exercised and within about fifteen minutes he began vomiting. The vomiting lasted from fifteen minutes to an hour. There is also a temporary cardiovascular effect which involves some change in blood pressure and "in the heart." Knecht v. Gillman, 488 F.2d 1136, 1137 (8th Cir. 1973).

aponeurosis (ap″o-nu-ro′sis), pl. *aponeuro′ses* [Gr. *aponeurōsis*] [NA] 1. a white, flattened or ribbon-like tendinous expansion, serving mainly to connect a muscle with the parts that it moves. 2. a term formerly applied to certain fasciae.

aponeurosis, plantar; aponeurosis plantaris [NA], bands of fibrous tissue radiating toward the bases of the toes from the medial process of the tuber calcanei; called also *plantar fascia.*

apothecary See *pharmacist.*

apparatus (ap″ah-ra′tus), pl. *apparatus* or *apparatuses* [L., from *ad* to + *parare* to make ready] an arrangement of a number of parts acting together in the performance of some special function; used in anatomical nomenclature to designate a number of structures or organs which act together in serving some particular function.

apparatus, underwater drainage

19. The patented one-piece unitary **underwater drainage apparatus** includes a water seal chamber which is constructed in such a way that it is virtually impossible to lose the underwater seal even while a patient is being transported or due to the tipping of the unit from the vertical position.

20. The water seal chamber provides the surgeon with diagnostic tools that he did not have available with the old two and three-bottle systems. The water levels within both arms of the U-shaped chamber are readily readable through the transparent plastic and the doctor can immediately ascertain the relative pressure conditions within the pleural cavity by a rapid glance at the underwater seal.

21. In an **underwater drainage apparatus** a U-shaped chamber in which gases flow in a U-shaped path is not the equivalent of a large jar with a small tube projecting down into the same as in the classic three-bottle system, or to a miniaturized tube within a tube arrangement such as in the Hannon apparatus, in both of which the gas follows an inverted "um-

brella'' shaped path down the small tube and upwardly all around the small tube.

22. The one-piece unitary **underwater drainage apparatus** here involved includes an enlarged chamber adjacent the upper end of one arm of the underwater seal which prevents loss of the underwater seal during conditions of high negativity within the patient's pleural cavity.

High negativity within the pleural cavity is a not infrequent occurrence which may be caused by a number of conditions such as blockage of the bronchial tubes so that the lung does not fill with air when the chest is expanded, thus leaving the patient gasping for air and creating very high levels of negativity within the pleural cavity. Under such circumstances the higher pressure on that side of the water seal remote from the collection chamber will force the water seal up the arm of the U-tube toward the collection chamber where it will collect within the enlarged chamber at the upper end of this arm.

The water seal will return to its normal position when the high negativity is reduced. Deknatel, Inc. v. Bentley Sales, Inc., 173 U.S.P.Q. 129, 131 (U.S.D.C., Central D.Cal.1971).

appendicitis (ah-pen"dĭ-si'tis) inflammation of the vermiform appendix.

As to proof of the standard of medical care in diagnosing **appendicitis**, we first review the responses of Dr. Bacon when he was asked about a classic picture of appendicitis, ''the textbook teachings'': The first indication of **appendicitis** is pain, possibly around the navel, later shifting to the right lower quadrant of the abdomen. Temperature may be normal or low grade. Rebound tenderness can be, but is not always, related to **appendicitis**. One would expect the white blood cell count to be elevated. If deep palpation over the left side of the abdomen does not elicit severe pain but palpation over the appendix area does produce severe pain, this should be suggestive of **appendicitis**—or of peritoneal irritation. Rigidity of the muscles in the abdomen does not necessarily mean that the patient has **appendicitis**.

Dr. Bacon testified further that in 1973 a physician in this community exercising ordinary care in diagnosing **appendicitis** in a hypothetical 39 year old male with a history of some abdominal pain would take the following steps: 1) get a comprehensive patient history, 2) physically examine the patient, 3) feel or palpate and listen to the entire abdomen, 4) order a routine blood count to determine whether the white blood cell count is elevated, 5) order a urinalysis to determine whether there is any evidence of pus, blood, or urinary tract infection (which can mimic **appendicitis**), 6) order a flat plate abdominal x-ray to rule out the possibility of gall stones or kidney stones, and 7) if there was a history of prostatitis or if **appendicitis** was suspected, perform a rectal examination....

... Dr. Grummon, the surgeon who repaired appellant's incisional hernia, was in practice in Harris County, Texas, in 1973 and has performed approximately 200 appendectomies. He said that in 1973 the treatment and diagnosis of **appendicitis** was no different in Harris County than anywhere else. He testified that if he found pain around the navel area, pain upon pressing the stomach area, and a history of nausea in a 270 pound male patient with no prior history of abdominal complaints, and if the patient had begun experiencing those pains over the two or three day period prior to the consultation, he would have to consider the possibility of **appendicitis**. Dr.

Grummon testified that as a medical doctor with knowledge and skills of the average practitioner in 1973, he would have to consider **appendicitis** as one of the differential diagnoses in a patient who had had low grade temperature and pain around the navel area, becoming increasingly worse for two or three days, had the general appearance of being ill, complained of pain upon palpation of the abdomen, generally felt sick, and was slightly nauseous. He later testified that although anything is medically possible, it is ''pretty risky'' to assume that a patient exhibiting the so-called classic symptoms does not have **appendicitis**....

... Dr. Harold testified that as diagnosed and reviewed by doctors in Houston and other places, the symptoms related by a patient with **appendicitis** are very vague. He may just say he doesn't feel good, that he hurts in the Xiphoid area, that he feels a little hot and cold and woozy, that he hurts on the right side, that he has diarrhea, or that he is sick at his stomach and vomiting; he may have all of these symptoms or only one. One of the early symptoms of **appendicitis** can be pain around the navel which tends to localize in the lower right quadrant as the disease progresses. Dr. Harold said that he would have to consider **appendicitis** if he pressed on the lower right area of a patient's abdomen and elicited severe pain while similar pressure on the left side did not elicit the same response....

... Concerning the wound infection, Dr. Harold testified that ''there is nothing you can do'' to prevent it from occurring; by definition, **appendicitis** is an infection, and an appendectomy wound is infected with millions of microscopic bacteria and germs. Emanuel v. Bacon, 615 S.W.2d 847, 849–50, 852 (Ct. Civ.App.Tex.1981).

... every expert to testify on the subject agreed that in one of every five cases of **appendicitis** in pregnant women, the diagnosis cannot be made until after the organ has ruptured. Defendant's expert Dr. John Long, a board-certified obstetrician and Professor of Obstetrics and Gynecology at Rush Medical College, characterized the diagnosis of **appendicitis** in pregnant women as ''the hardest diagnosis to make in the practice of obstetrics.'' It is fortunate that the illness only occurs once in every 1,200 to 2,000 pregnancies because pregnancy masks its symptoms. Spike v. Sellett, 430 N.E.2d 597, 600 (App.Ct. III.1981).

With acute **appendicitis** the white blood count usually rises ''quite remarkably''. Normally, with a child of Joy's age the blood count will be from six to ten thousand and with acute **appendicitis** it can be expected to rise to twelve thousand five hundred to eighteen thousand. Dr. Sorenson testified, however, that Joy's count was even lower than the usual and that this is ''ordinarily constant with a viral infection such as tonsillitis''. Sinkey v. Surgical Associates, 186 N.W.2d 658, 659–660 (Iowa 1971).

Other Authorities: Parsons v. Wood, 584 P.2d 1332, 1334 (Okl.1978); Burrow v. Widder, 368 N.E.2d 443 (App.Ct. of III. 1977); Bruno v. Clements, 326 So.2d 562, 563–4 (Ct.App.La. 1976); Hawkins v. Ozborn, 383 F.Supp. 1389, 1391–3 (N.D. Miss.1974); Rogers v. U.S., 334 F.2d 931, 932 (6th Cir. 1964).

appendicitis, acute appendicitis of acute onset requiring surgical intervention and usually characterized by pain in the right lower abdominal quadrant with local and referred rebound tenderness, overlying muscle spasm, and cutaneous hyperesthesia. Periumbilical, colicky pain at the onset may be due to obstruction of the appendix by a fecalith. Fever and polymorphonuclear leukocytosis result from the localized infection. Symptoms and signs may be modified by the location of the appendix, by adhesive bands, or by kinking.

Dr. Harold, the surgeon who removed Mr. Emanuel's appendix, testified that the longer **acute appendicitis** is undiagnosed and the surgery is delayed, the more difficulty is encountered in later managing the peritoneal cavity area infection. Emanuel v. Bacon, 615 S.W.2d 847, 850–1 (Ct.Civ.App.Tex.1981).

The initial diagnosis after X-ray examination was an acute intestinal obstruction due to a ruptured appendix....

... Dr. Monge, who performed the operation, testified that he encountered large amounts of pus upon opening the peritoneal cavity. The appendix had ruptured and infected the entire peritoneal cavity, the pelvis and upper abdomen. The small intestine was dilated, abscessed, and due to fibronous adhesions was kinked. There were already signs of liver dysfunction and jaundice. Dr. Monge removed the appendix and irrigated the peritoneal cavity. Koch survived the surgery but his condition did not improve; liver and renal failure followed. He died on June 12, 1970....

Dr. Gorrilla tacitly admitted the potential danger in prescribing an enema and heat pack for a patient with a possible **appendicitis**, but he stated that the decision to pursue this course of treatment had to be made by the treating physician, in light of the particular circumstances of the individual case....

... Drs. Gertz and Santini testified that a patient with an already ruptured appendix need not undergo surgery immediately and that where the patient's condition is poor, conservative treatment is the more proper course. Dr. Gorrilla concurred, stating that the decision to treat conservatively or to operate in such a case depends upon a number of factors, including whether the patient is in shock, whether his fluid balances are sufficient for surgery, and whether his heart, kidneys and other vital organs are functioning properly. All three doctors admitted the dangers inherent in not excising a ruptured appendix, but all agreed that the course of treatment in such a case is a matter for the sound discretion of the treating physician. Koch v. Gorrilla, 552 F.2d 1170, 1172, 1175–76 (6th Cir. 1977).

appendix (ah-pen′diks), pl. *appendixes, appen′dices* [L. from *appendere* to hang upon] a general term used in anatomical nomenclature to designate a supplementary, accessory, or dependent part attached to a main structure; called also *appendage*. Frequently used alone to refer to the *appendix vermiformis* [NA], or *vermiform appendix*. See also *appendix, vermiformis*; and *tract, gastro-intestinal* (Goss case).

Dr. Haygood indeed stated that ''gastro-intestinal'' could mean merely the stomach and the intestine. However, he went on to state that ''the **appendix** rises with the cecum, which is the right portion of the large intestine, and it communicates with and is a part of the gastro-intestinal tract.'' Mid-Western Life Ins. Co. of Tex. v. Goss, 552 S.W.2d 430, 432 (Tex. 1977).

appendix vermiformis [NA], vermiform appendix; a wormlike diverticulum of the cecum, varying in length

from 3 to 6 inches, and measuring about $\frac{1}{3}$ inch in diameter.

Dr. Haygood indeed stated that ''gastro-intestinal'' could mean merely the stomach and the intestine. However, he went on to state that ''the **appendix** rises with the cecum, which is the right portion of the large intestine, and it communicates with and is a part of the gastro-intestinal tract.'' This testimony is contradictory of the contention made by Ann and Larry Goss and would not be such as to allow a jury to reasonably conclude that the **appendix** was not part of the ''gastro-intestinal tract.'' Mid-Western Life Ins. Co. of Tex. v. Goss, 552 S.W.2d 430, 432 (Tex.1977).

apposition (ap″o-zish′un) [L. *appositio*] the placing of things in juxtaposition or proximity; specifically, the deposition of successive layers upon those already present, as in cell walls. Called also *juxtaposition*.

Although defendant Shull concluded on 1 July 1977 that plaintiff ''only had 10% **apposition**'' remaining, that the radius had not aligned properly, and that ''there was an increase of angulation at the fracture site,'' Dr. Shull did not inform plaintiff about these matters....

... In the course of Dr. Shull's treatment of plaintiff, there was a progressive slippage and an increase in displacement of the fracture; by 1 July 1977, according to the radiologist, the displacement was probably 100%, and the ends of the fracture were not touching at the site of the fracture.[3] [3 The radiologist testified: As to the degree of displacement illustrated by plaintiff's Exhibit No. 23, well, it's somewhat more than it was before. I think, probably, it's 100%. I think there's some overriding there. There is no **apposition**, I don't think there's any **apposition** between the actual fracture ends. I mean that the ends of the fracture are not touching. Now the bones are touching but in a different position than where the actual fracture site is. It could go ahead and heal in that position.] Powell v. Shull, 293 S.E.2d 259, 260, 264 (Ct.App.N.Car.1982).

Dr. Shalgos was then shown People's Exhibit 30 a color photograph of the head after **apposition** (placing together) of the skin margins. People v. Garrett, 339 N.E.2d 753, 757 (Ill. 1976).

Aprikern

The article **Aprikern** contains hydrogen cyanide in the amount of 1.5 mg. to 2.7 mg. per gram of ground and defatted apricot kernel and 1.09 mg. to 1.60 mg. hydrogen cyanide per capsule of **aprikern**....

... Acute oral toxicity tests conducted by the University of Arizona Department of Pharmacology and Toxicology determined the minimum lethal dose of **Aprikern** (50% of or more of the subject animals died) to be 2g/kg of body weight in rats. U.S. v. General Research Laboratories, 397 F.Supp. 197, 198–9 (C.D.Calif.1975).

Aquamatic K-Pad See *pad, heating*.

Aquamatic K-Thermia machine See *machine, Aquamatic K-Thermia*.

aqueduct of Silvius See *aqueductus, cerebri*.

aqueductus (ak″we-duk′tus) [L., from *aqua* water + *ductus* canal] [NA] a passage or channel in a body structure or organ, especially a channel for the conduction of fluid; called also *aqueduct* and *aquaeductus*.

aqueductus cerebri [NA], cerebral aqueduct: the narrow channel in the midbrain, about 1 cm. long, that connects the third and fourth ventricles; called also *aqueduct* or *iter of Sylvius*, and *mesocele*.

In surgery Dr. Pisarello found that there was no brain tumor but that plaintiff's **Aqueduct of Sylvius**, the passageway between the third and fourth ventricles of the brain, was blocked by a web. This was removed and the spinal fluid flowed freely through the aqueduct. Gendusa v. St.Paul Fire & Marine Ins. Co., 435 So.2d 479, 481 (Ct.App.La.1983).

arachnoid See *arachnoidea*.

arachnoid of brain; arachnoid cranial See *arachnoidea encephali*.

arachnoid spinal; arachnoid of spinal cord See *arachnoidea spinalis*.

arachnoidea (ar″ak-noi′de-ah), pl. *arachnoi′deae* [Gr. *arachnoeidēs* like a cobweb] [NA] a delicate membrane interposed between the dura mater and the pia mater, being separated from the pia mater by the subarachnoid space.

arachnoidea encephali [NA], the arachnoidea covering the brain; called also *arachnoid of brain* and *cranial arachnoid*.

Arachnoid is the membrane between the dural and the innermost (pia) membrane covering the brain and spinal cord. Larkin v. State, 446 N.Y.S.2d 818, 819 (4th Dep't 1982).

arachnoidea spinalis [NA], spinal arachnoid: the arachnoidea covering the spinal cord; called also *arachnoid of spinal cord*.

arachnoiditis (ah-rak″noid-i′tis) [*arachnoid* + *-itis*] inflammation of the arachnoidea; called also *arachnitis*. See also *arachnoidea; myelography* (Wasem case).

... that the third problem was found to be of mild arachnoditis [sic] from previous surgery....

... Because complaints of posterior thigh pain and sacral pain increased during his hospitalization, particularly during times when he was confined to bed as after his myelogram, the day of his discharge, an epidural injection through the sacral hiatus with 80 mg of Depo-Medrol was done to try to relieve any pain in his legs from the **arachnoiditis**. Jimison v. North Dakota Workmen's Comp. Bur., 331 N.W.2d 822, 824–5 (N.Dak.1983).

He noted that because of the extended period of plaintiff's condition, there was a possibility of **arachnoiditis**, which involves an inflammation of the covering of the brain. Marbury v. Matthews, 433 F.Supp. 1081, 1085 (W.D.N.Y.1977).

If plaintiff is suffering from a herniated disc, a spinal operation would have a 60 to 70% chance of relieving his pain and disability. (N.T. 76, 241, 280)

If plaintiff is suffering from **arachnoiditis**, an inflammation of the covering of the spinal cord, such an operation would not improve his condition. (N.T. 243)

Further surgery could worsen plaintiff's condition. (N.T. 51, 104). McGinley v. U.S., 329 F.Supp. 62, 64 (E.D.Pa.1971).

Other Authorities: Bearden Lumber Co. v. Bond, 644 S.W.2d 321, 324 (Ct.App.Ark.1983).

arachnoiditis, adhesive See *arachnoiditis, chronic adhesive*.

arachnoiditis, chronic adhesive thickening and adhesions of the leptomeninges in the brain or spinal cord, resulting from previous meningitis, other disease processes, or trauma; the signs and symptoms vary with extent and location.

Wasem contended that, when conducted properly, a Pantopaque myelogram is a harmless test and that removal of the dye is the only way to properly conduct the test. He further contended that **adhesive arachnoiditis** resulted from a toxic reaction to the dye and that the paralysis resulted therefrom. He further contended that, even though the results may have been extremely rare, the doctors failed to fulfill their obligation to inform him of the abnormal condition. Wasem v. Laskowski, 274 N.W.2d 219, 221 (N.Dak.1979).

Aralen (ār′ah-len) trademark for a preparation of chloroquine. See also *chloroquine phosphate*.

Aramine (ār′ah-min) trademark for a preparation of metaraminol. See also *metaraminol*.

arc (ark) [L. *arcus* bow] a structure or projected path having a curved or bowlike outline; by extension, a visible electrical discharge generally taking the outline of an arc. In neurophysiology, the pathway of neural reactions.

arc, reflex the neural arc utilized in a reflex action; an impulse travels centrally over afferent fibers to a nerve center, and the response outward to an effector organ or part over efferent fibers.

arch (arch) [L. *arcus* bow] a structure with a curved or bowlike outline. See also *arcus*.

arch, aortic paired vessels arching from the ventral to the dorsal aorta through the branchial arches of fishes and amniote embryos. In mammalian development, arches 1 and 2 disappear; arch 3 joins the common to the internal carotid; the left arch 4 remains as the arch of the definitive aorta while the right arch 4 joins the aorta to the subclavian artery; arch 5 disappears; and the ventral halves of arch 6 form the pulmonary arteries while the connections to the dorsal aorta are lost, although the left half, or ductus arteriosus, serves until birth.

While bathing, decedent stopped breathing due to a tear in the **aortic arch**, caused by the accident. Some motion of dece-

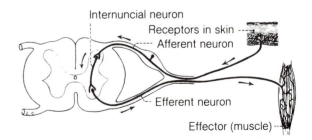

Three-neuron reflex arc (King and Showers).

dent's arm apparently pulled open the tear in the **aortic arch**, resulting in his immediate death. Other injuries found by the medical examiner were massive contusions of the anterior chest wall and multiple rib fractures. Watson v. Storie, 300 S.E.2d 55, 56 (Ct.App.N.Car.1983).

However, it was his opinion that if deceased had died of a rupture of the thoracic aneurysm as the death certificate stated,

> ... then I would not attribute death in any way to his coronary disease because the resection of **aortic arch** aneurysms is largely experimental and very high risk and would not be attempted probably in a man of 65 with chronic obstructive pulmonary disease, even if his heart were of average health. Griffin v. Time, DC, Inc., 661 P.2d 579, 580 (Ct.App.Ore. 1983).

The procedure of an **aortic arch** study entails the passing of a catheter to the orifice of each of the brain vessels in turn and similar pictures taken. Although different kinds of catheters are used in each of these two procedures, both go through the same hole in the artery. If the amount of dye used for the coronary arteriogram, which has first priority, is too much, ... "it may not be safe for the patient to do at the same sitting the other study"; ... Morgenroth v. Pacific Medical Center, Inc., 126 Cal.Rptr. 681, 684 (Ct.App.1976).

arch, dental the curving structure formed by the teeth in their normal position; called also *arcus dentalis*. The *inferior dental arch* (*arcus dentalis inferior* or *arch of the mandible*) is formed by the mandibular teeth, and the *superior dental arch* (*arcus dentalis superior* or *maxillary arch*) is formed by the maxillary teeth. See also *wire, arch*.

arcing See *shock, electric* (Thomas case).

arcus (ar'kus), pl. *ar'cus* [L. "a bow"] an arch; a general term used in anatomical nomenclature to designate any structure having a curved or bowlike outline.

arcus aortae [NA], arch of the aorta: the continuation of the ascending aorta, giving rise to the brachiocephalic trunk, and the left common carotid and left subclavian arteries; it continues as the thoracic aorta (aorta thoracica).

arcus vertebrae [NA], vertebral arch: the bony arch composed of the laminae and pedicles of a vertebra; called also *arch of vertebra* and *neural arch of vertebra*.

The congenital abnormalities in claimant's back made it easier for him to sustain injuries to his back and—"the fact of the matter is that when you have mechanical abnormalities, structural abnormalities, you don't have the normal strength of a normal back". The irregular formation of the fifth lumbar **neural arch** did not come about as a result of any specific trauma, but is something that a person is born and grows with. It is a mechanical alteration and associated with mechanical deficiencies. Hardwick v. General Motors Corp., 476 P.2d 244, 247 (Kan.1970).

arcus zygomaticus [NA], zygomatic arch: the arch formed by the articulation of the broad temporal process of the zygomatic bone and the slender zygomatic process of the temporal bone, giving attachment to the masseter muscle

and serving as a line of demarcation between the temporal and infratemporal fossae; called also *malar arch*.

> ... a fracture of the left **zygomatic arch** (a combination of two bones that gives contour to the cheekbone).... Yarrow v. U.S., 309 F.Supp. 922, 924 (S.D.N.Y.1970).

area (a're-ah), pl. *a'reae* or *areas* [L.] a limited space; a general term used in anatomical nomenclature to designate a specific surface or functional region. See also *region*.

area, septal the area on either cerebral hemisphere comprising the parolfactory area of Broca (area subcallosa) and the corresponding half of the septum pellucidum; the area has olfactory, hypothalamic, and hippocampal connections.

area subcallosa [NA]; **area, subcallosal** a small area of cortex on the medial surface of each cerebral hemisphere, immediately in front of the gyrus subcallosus; called also *a. parolfactoria [Brocae], parolfactory a. of Broca*, and *gyrus olfactorius medialis (of Retzius)*.

areflexia (ah"re-flek'se-ah) [*a* neg. + *reflex* + *-ia*] absence of the reflexes.

Areflexia, the second required finding in GBS, is the absence or depression of deep tendon reflexes ("DTRs"). The type of reflex loss finding required to substantiate a diagnosis of GBS is a value less than one-plus or two-plus, which are considered to be in the normal range. This loss of DTRs must occur within days or, at most, a few weeks of the onset of the illness....

> ... The second criterion under the NINCDS "Features Required for Diagnosis" is **Areflexia**, or loss of tendon jerks. Stich v. U.S., 565 F.Supp. 1096, 1101 (D.N.J. 1983).

Other Authorities: O'Gara v. U.S., 560 F.Supp. 786, 788 (E.D. Pa.1983).

areola (ah-re'o-lah), pl. *are'olae* [L., dim. of *area* space] a circular area of a different color, surrounding a central point, as such an area surrounding a pustule or vesicle, or the part of the iris surrounding the pupil of the eye, or surrounding the nipple of the breast.

Dr. Burkons' records indicate that he examined appellant's breast and diagnosed the presence of cysts with a slightly more prominent mass under the **areola** (nipple area). Shapiro v. Burkons, 404 N.E.2d 778, 779 (Ct.App.Ohio 1978).

argon laser photocoagulation See *photocoagulation*.

Aristospan (ah-ris'to-span) trademark for preparations of triamcinolone hexacetonide. See also *triamcinolone hexacetonide*; and *cortisone*.

arm (arm) [L. *armus*] the part of the upper extremity between the shoulder and elbow, as distinguished from the forearm; popularly the upper extremity from shoulder to hand. See also *brachium; forearm*; and *hand* (Dobbs case).

In 1927, the Legislature amended the act to provide the following guidelines:

> An amputation between the elbow and wrist six or more inches below the elbow shall be considered a hand, above this point an **arm**;... Dobbs v. Villa Capri Restaurant, 329 N.W.2d 503, 504–6 (Ct.App.Mich.1982).

The only argument raised on this appeal is that, although claimant and all four doctors testified that the pain and situs of the injury are in the shoulder, for purposes of workmen's compensation law anything located on the "**arm** side" of the junction which connects **arm** to body must be denominated an "**arm**", and therefore compensated as a scheduled injury....

... This argument is based on language in the recent case of Eggleston v. Industrial Commission, 24 Ariz.App. 444, 539 P.2d 918 (1975) which, quoting from the Arizona Supreme Court's decision in Ujevich v. Inspiration Consolidated Copper Co., 44 Ariz. 16, 33 P.2d 599 (1934), set out the legal definition of an **arm** as "a complete **arm**, in common parlance, extends from where it connects to the shoulder blade to the hand." Eggleston, supra, 24 Ariz.App. at 445, 539 P.2d at 919....

... In Ujevich v. Inspiration Consol. Copper Co., 44 Ariz. 16, 33 P.2d 599, 600, in identifying the meaning of the word "limb" as used in the Arizona Compensation Law, the court said:

The human body has two arms and two legs, or four limbs. A complete **arm**, in common parlance, extends from where it connects with the shoulder blade to the hand;...

... Other jurisdictions which have considered the question here presented have determined that:

... the shoulder is not part of the **arm** and where the injury is to the shoulder it is not proper to base the award on the proportionate loss to the use of the **arm**."

M. R. Thomason & Assoc. v. Jones, 48 Ala.App. 67, 261 So. 2d 899, 902 (1972)....

... All the cases therein discussed recognize that the shoulder is a distinct anatomical entity, not part of the **arm**. Safeway Stores, Inc. v. Industrial Com'n, 558 P.2d 971, 972, 974 (Ct. App.Ariz.1976).

arrest (ah-rest) stoppage; the act of stopping.

arrest, cardiac sudden cessation of cardiac function, with disappearance of arterial blood pressure, connoting either ventricular fibrillation or ventricular standstill. See also *"code blue"* (Rose case).

The medical testimony in this record establishes that **cardiac arrest** can occur at any time, under any circumstances, in otherwise healthy persons and under the care of the most experienced and skillful physicians. The testimony of the expert witnesses clearly establishes that the causes for **cardiac arrest** during surgery can be varied and that, when an arrest does occur, it does not indicate that someone was at fault or negligent. Further, it is expected that in a certain number of cases where **cardiac arrest** occurs, the patient will suffer irreversible brain damage despite resuscitative efforts and under the best professional care. On this point, the testimony herein is the same as we found in the case of McAdams v. Holden, 349 So. 2d 900 (La.App.1st Cir. 1977), writ refused 351 So.2d 176 (La. 1977). Ewen v. Baton Rouge General Hospital, 378 So.2d 172, 174 (Ct.App.La.1979).

Following a **cardiac arrest** it is good medical practice to reduce and maintain the body temperature of the patient. Reduced temperature diminishes the demand of body tissues for oxygen, particularly the tissues of the brain and the myocardium of the heart. Increasing body temperature increases the brain's demand for oxygen and unless corrected will result in seizures or convulsions. It was to give the infant plaintiff's brain

and heart the rest needed after the **cardiac arrest** that Hakim in his first orders in the recovery room ordered hypothermia at 90° Fahrenheit....

... Dr. Jenkins testified that many people have **cardiac arrests** without suffering permanent brain damage; that the fact of a **cardiac arrest** does not automatically mean permanent brain damage; that a **cardiac arrest** may cause a neurological injury or insult which is reversible....

... Typical of their testimony is that of Dr. Manchester, a cardiologist. He stated that one would have to look elsewhere for the cause of permanent brain damage if the **cardiac arrest** was only two and one-half minutes in duration. Rose v. Hakim, 335 F.Supp. 1221, 1224–5, 1227, 1229 (D.D.C.1971).

"Q. ... What is a reflex arrest?
"A. A reflex arrest is usually due to a sudden discharge of nerves, impulses consequent upon a sudden insult that's inflicted on the body.

"For example, if I were to go up to one of you ladies and gentlemen and push two fingers in your eyeballs, there is a well-known reflex that causes a discharge to the heart and causes it to stop instantly and this can also apply to a patient who has a blow in the upper abdomen or a sudden physical insult or an alternative electric shock can do the same thing....

... Dr. Gravenstein explained the reflex **cardiac arrest** in this way (upon cross-examination):

"A. The heart is supplied with two different types of nerves and a strong stimulation coming down to the heart via these nerves, a stimulation triggered by another event in the body is called a reflex and sometimes such reflexes can cause cardiac standstill."

"Q. Now, what would initiate such a reflex?
"A. A strong stimulation of these nerves. The stimulus can be a variety, pressure on the eyeballs, for instances, or pressure on the neck. This sort of thing.
"Q. A heavy blow to the chest?
"A. Yes.
"Q. An extremely frightening occurrence?
"Q. Yes." Siegel v. Mt. Sinai Hospital of Cleveland, 403 N.E.2d 202, 211–12 (Ct.App.Ohio 1978).

Other Authorities: Eichner v. Dillon, 426 N.Y.S.2d 517, 527 (2d Dep't 1980); Seaton v. Rosenberg, 573 S.W.2d 333, 335–6 (Ky.1978); U.S. v. Narciso, 446 F.Supp. 252, 262 (E.D.Mich. 1977).

arrest, reflex See *arrest, cardiac.*

arrhythmia (ah-rith'me-ah) [*a* neg. + Gr. *rhythmos* rhythm] any variation from the normal rhythm of the heart beat, including sinus arrhythmia, premature beat, heart block, atrial fibrillation, atrial flutter, pulsus alternans, and paroxysmal tachycardia. See also *fibrillation, ventricular*; and *tachycardia, ventricular.*

The experts further agreed, however, that arteriosclerotic and hypertensive heart disease can result in an **arrhythmia**, which is a disturbance of the rhythm of the heart caused by a malfunction of the heart's electrical system. They agreed that an **arrhythmia** is a fatal condition that causes the heart to cease pumping blood to the body effectively and can result in unconsciousness in ten to fifteen seconds. They also agreed that an **arrhythmia** cannot be observed after death because it is an electrical event which does not cause any structural change in the heart. Van Hook v. Aetna Life Ins. Co., 550 F.Supp. 888, 892 (E.D.Mich.1982).

Dr. Hamilton stated that the cause of death was an **arrhythmia** pattern of auricular fibrillation resulting in cardiac arrest. In his opinion it had been precipitated by the emotional stress of the evening fire. Dr. Nay, while conceding the real possibility of such stress precipitating the fatal **arrhythmia**, was of the opinion that such causal relationship was not predictable with any certainty. Harris v. Rainsoft of Allen Cty., Inc., 416 N.E.2d 1320, 1322 (Ct.App.Ind.1981).

The types of **arrhythmias** range from those which cause no great threat to the patient's life to those like ventricular tachycardia, which is extremely dangerous. There are two phases in correcting a cardiac **arrhythmia**: One, conversion of the abnormally beating heart to a normally beating heart or a normal sinus rhythm; and two, maintenance of the normal heart rhythm after conversion. Quinidine is helpful in both phases. U.S. v. Article of Drug, etc., 268 F.Supp. 245, 246 (E.D.Mo.1967).

Other Authorities: Dunn v. Vic Mfg. Co., 327 N.W.2d 572, 574 (Minn.1982); Henderson v. Travelers Ins. Co., 544 S.W. 2d 649, 652 (Tex.1976); Vander Veer v. Continental Cas. Co., 346 N.Y.S.2d 655, 658, 661 (3d Dep't 1973).

arrhythmia, sinus the physiologic cyclic variation in heart rate related to vagal impulses to the sinoatrial node; it occurs commonly in children (juvenile a.) and in the aged, and requires no treatment. Called also *phasic a.* and *respiratory a.*

Dr. Hirsch's examination revealed the child's heart and lungs to be in good condition, but disclosed a marked **sinus arrhythmia** or irregular heartbeat upon inspiration, a condition normal to small children. Chapman v. Argonaut-Southwest Ins. Co., 290 So.2d 779, 780 (Ct.App.La.1974).

arsenic (ar′sĕ-nik) [L. *arsenicum, arsenium,* or *arsenum;* from Gr. *arsēn* strong] 1. a medicinal and poisonous element; it is a brittle, lustrous, grayish solid, with a garlicky odor. Symbol, As; atomic number, 33; atomic weight, 74.922; specific gravity, 5.73. See also under *poisoning.* 2. arsenic trioxide. See also *poisoning, arsenic.*

When **arsenic** is ingested by cattle, it travels through the liver and kidneys and is excreted in the urine; very little **arsenic** remains in the body of the cow but severe damage to the liver, kidneys, and renal tubes usually results. Gaar v. State Through Dep't of Highways, 389 So.2d 426, 427 (Ct.App.La.1980).

The doctor further testified that **arsenic** is not a part of dairy feed and is a severe poison to dairy cattle; that there are organic and inorganic sources of **arsenic**; that the effect of **arsenic** differs on various animals; that a certain level of organic **arsenic** may not kill one animal while only one fourth of that same amount may be fatal to another; that four parts per million of **arsenic** in the liver of a cow might possibly be enough to kill a cow, depending on the form of the **arsenic**; that it is difficult to diagnose the effects of toxic **arsenic** on cows because the symptoms are obscure; you may get a poor hair coat, loss of appetite, emaciation, production affected; that there should be no **arsenic** in feed for dairy cows; that there is absolutely no tolerance for **arsenic** in dairy feed and that he suspected the feed at the time....

... that the first sign of **arsenic** poisoning in a dairy cow is a decrease in milk production and a lack of appetite; that within twenty-four hours or so the animal has loose diarrhea and there may be blood involved; that if a lethal dose is involved the fourth stomach of the cow would be fiery red and the intestines the same way; that the intestinal contents will be high in **arsenic** and if the animal has lived long enough the liver and kidneys will contain considerable **arsenic**; that the animal will be depressed and give very little milk; and that she may drink considerable water but the next thing is diarrhea and that either clears up or the cow dies....

... Over 2 P.P.M. [parts per million] of **arsenic** in tissues are considered toxic. Marian v. Lena Pellet Co., 256 N.E.2d 93, 95–96 (App.Ct.Ill.1970).

arsenic trioxide white arsenic, a white or glassy compound, As_2O_3, with a sweetish taste and erythropoietic effect; taken in repeated small doses in Alpine countries to increase hemoglobin, resulting in increased working capacity and a ruddy complexion. Formerly used in treatment of skin and hematologic disorders. Called also *arsenous acid, arsenous anhydride,* and *flowers of arsenic.*

Arsenic trioxide has an LD50 toxicity of 385. **Arsenic trioxide** is not a product highly toxic to man, under USDA standards. Pax Company of Utah v. U.S., 324 F.Supp. 1335, 1341 (D.Utah 1970), judgment reversed 454 F.2d 93 (10th Cir. 1972).

arteria (ar-te′re-ah), pl. *arte′riae* [L.; Gr. *artēria*] a general term used in anatomical nomenclature to designate any vessel carrying blood away from the heart. For names and description of specific vessels. See *Table of Arteriae.* See also *artery.*

TABLE OF ARTERIAE

arteria aorta aorta.

arteria carotis communis [NA], common carotid artery: *origin,* brachiocephalic trunk (right), aortic arch (left); *branches,* external and internal carotids; *distribution.* Called also *cephalic artery.* See also *arteria carotis externa;* and *arteria carotis interna.*

The **carotid arteries** are the principal vessels supplying blood to the head and neck. It was believed by the doctors at the VA Hospital that this narrowing of the **carotid arteries** was caus-ing Mr. Lemke's blurred vision, headaches, numbness and weakness. Lemke v. U.S., 557 F.Supp. 1205, 1207 (D.N.Dak. 1983).

Within a week of the last of these prescriptions written for the undercover agents, Dr. Carroll was suddenly stricken by a very dangerous vascular attack, which consisted of the plugging of the **carotid artery** which arises from the arch of the aorta and which supplies blood to the brain— producing the effect of a stroke. U.S. v. Carroll, 518 F.2d 187, 197 (6th Cir. 1975).

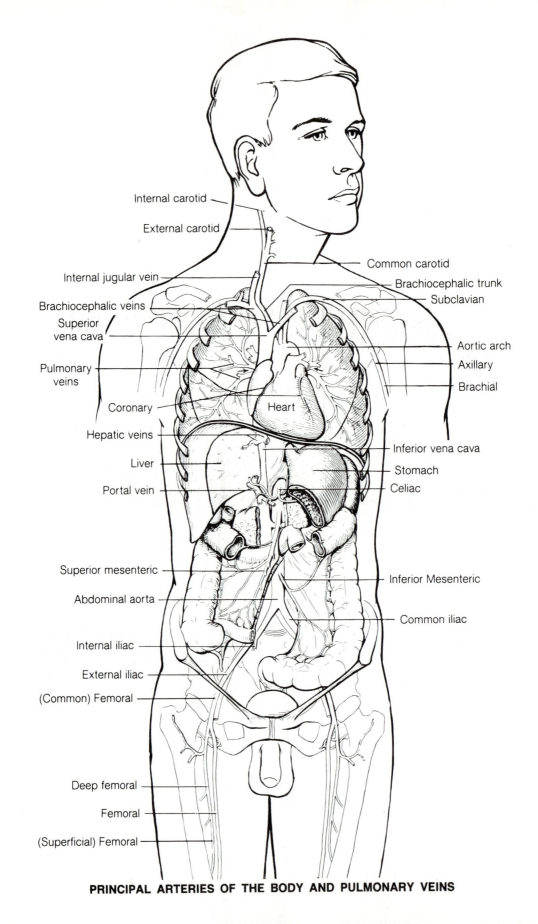

Internal carotid

External carotid

Common carotid

Internal jugular vein

Brachiocephalic trunk

Subclavian

Brachiocephalic veins

Superior vena cava

Aortic arch

Axillary

Pulmonary veins

Brachial

Coronary

Heart

Hepatic veins

Inferior vena cava

Liver

Stomach

Portal vein

Celiac

Superior mesenteric

Inferior Mesenteric

Abdominal aorta

Common iliac

Internal iliac

External iliac

(Common) Femoral

Deep femoral

Femoral

(Superficial) Femoral

PRINCIPAL ARTERIES OF THE BODY AND PULMONARY VEINS

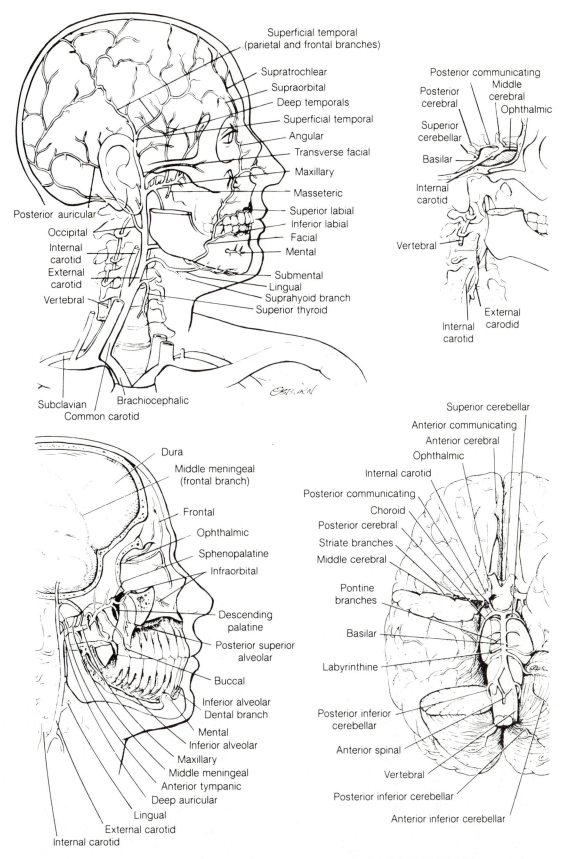

ARTERIES OF THE HEAD, NECK, AND BASE OF THE BRAIN

54

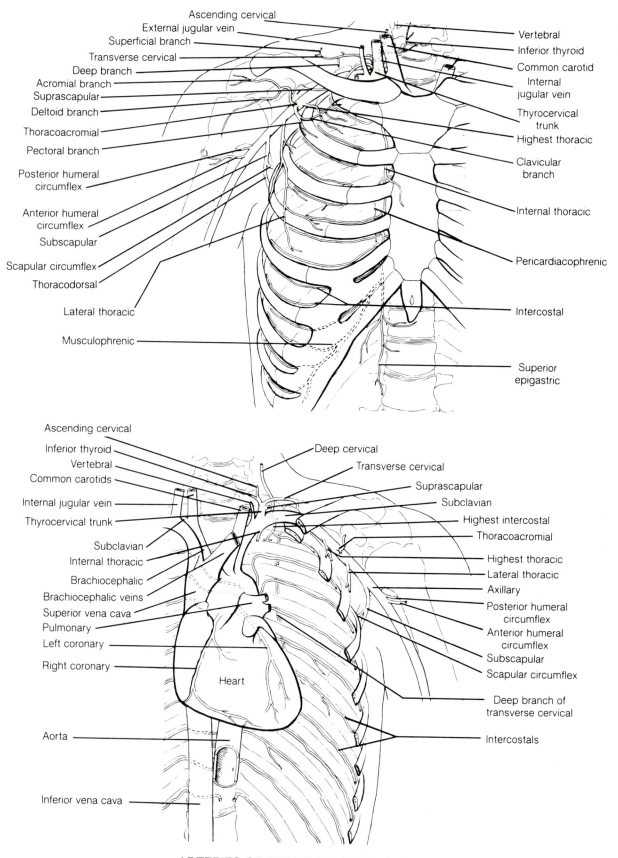

ARTERIES OF THE THORAX AND AXILLA

Ascending cervical
External jugular vein
Superficial branch
Transverse cervical
Deep branch
Acromial branch
Suprascapular
Deltoid branch
Thoracoacromial
Pectoral branch
Posterior humeral circumflex
Anterior humeral circumflex
Subscapular
Scapular circumflex
Thoracodorsal
Lateral thoracic
Musculophrenic

Vertebral
Inferior thyroid
Common carotid
Internal jugular vein
Thyrocervical trunk
Highest thoracic
Clavicular branch
Internal thoracic
Pericardiacophrenic
Intercostal
Superior epigastric

Ascending cervical
Inferior thyroid
Vertebral
Common carotids
Internal jugular vein
Thyrocervical trunk
Subclavian
Internal thoracic
Brachiocephalic
Brachiocephalic veins
Superior vena cava
Pulmonary
Left coronary
Right coronary
Aorta
Inferior vena cava

Deep cervical
Transverse cervical
Suprascapular
Subclavian
Highest intercostal
Thoracoacromial
Highest thoracic
Lateral thoracic
Axillary
Posterior humeral circumflex
Anterior humeral circumflex
Subscapular
Scapular circumflex
Deep branch of transverse cervical
Intercostals

Heart

55

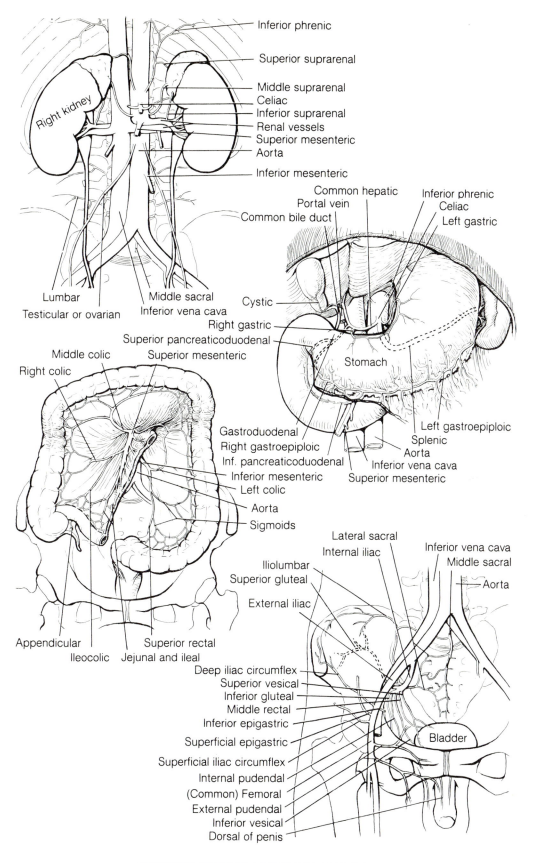

Inferior phrenic

Superior suprarenal

Middle suprarenal
Celiac
Inferior suprarenal
Renal vessels
Superior mesenteric
Aorta

Inferior mesenteric

Right kidney

Lumbar

Testicular or ovarian

Middle sacral
Inferior vena cava

Common hepatic
Portal vein
Common bile duct
Inferior phrenic
Celiac
Left gastric

Cystic

Right gastric

Superior pancreaticoduodenal   Superior mesenteric

Stomach

Middle colic
Right colic

Gastroduodenal
Right gastroepiploic
Inf. pancreaticoduodenal

Left gastroepiploic
Splenic
Aorta
Inferior vena cava
Superior mesenteric

Superior mesenteric

Inferior mesenteric
Left colic
Aorta
Sigmoids

Appendicular
Ileocolic   Jejunal and ileal

Superior rectal

Lateral sacral
Internal iliac
Inferior vena cava
Middle sacral
Iliolumbar   Aorta
Superior gluteal

External iliac

Deep iliac circumflex
Superior vesical
Inferior gluteal
Middle rectal
Inferior epigastric

Superficial epigastric

Superficial iliac circumflex

Internal pudendal

(Common) Femoral

External pudendal

Inferior vesical

Dorsal of penis

Bladder

ARTERIES OF THE ABDOMEN AND PELVIS

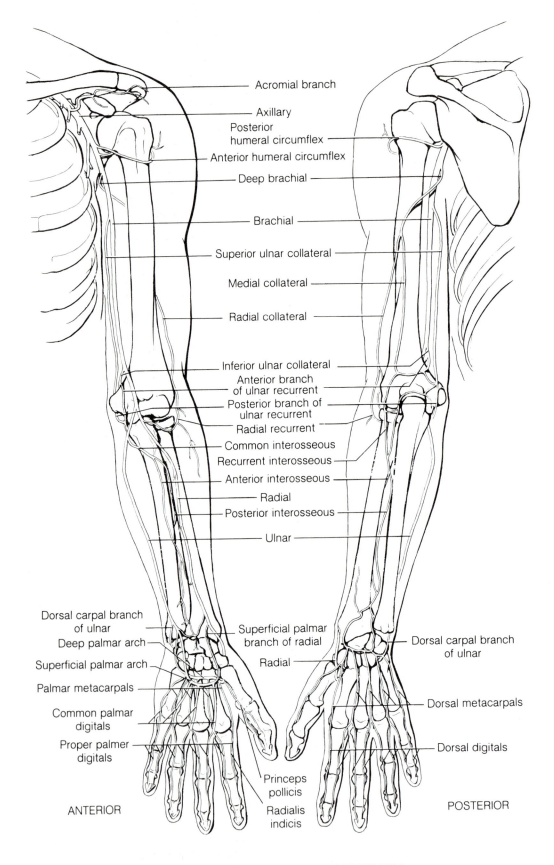

Acromial branch

Axillary

Posterior
humeral circumflex

Anterior humeral circumflex

Deep brachial

Brachial

Superior ulnar collateral

Medial collateral

Radial collateral

Inferior ulnar collateral

Anterior branch
of ulnar recurrent

Posterior branch of
ulnar recurrent

Radial recurrent

Common interosseous

Recurrent interosseous

Anterior interosseous

Radial

Posterior interosseous

Ulnar

Dorsal carpal branch
of ulnar

Deep palmar arch

Superficial palmar arch

Palmar metacarpals

Common palmar
digitals

Proper palmer
digitals

Superficial palmar
branch of radial

Radial

Dorsal carpal branch
of ulnar

Dorsal metacarpals

Dorsal digitals

Princeps
pollicis

Radialis
indicis

ANTERIOR

POSTERIOR

ARTERIES OF THE UPPER EXTREMITY

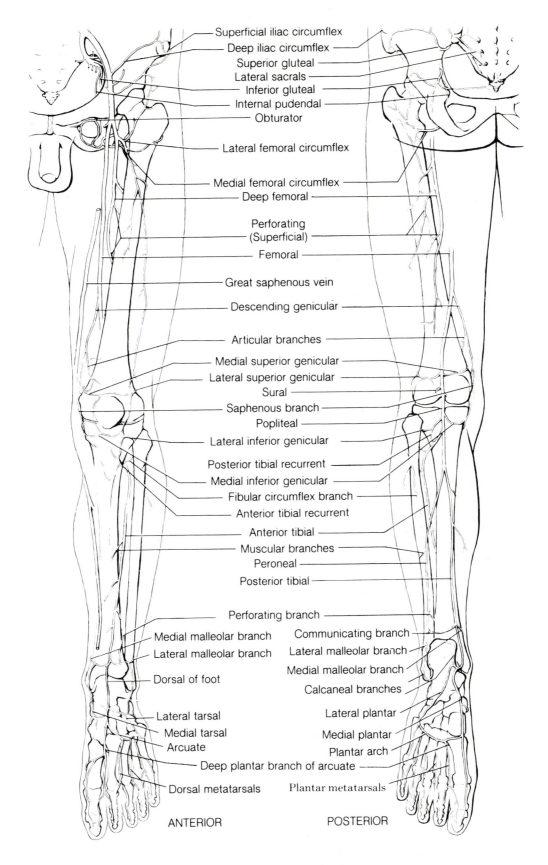

ARTERIES OF THE LOWER EXTREMITY

arteria carotis externa [NA], external carotid artery: *origin*, common carotid; *branches*, superior thyroid, ascending pharyngeal, lingual, facial, sternocleidomastoid, occipital, posterior auricular, superficial temporal, maxillary; *distribution*, neck, face, skull. Called also *facial artery*.

arteria carotis interna [NA], internal carotid artery: *origin*, common carotid; *branches*, caroticotympanic rami, and ophthalmic, posterior communicating, anterior choroid, anterior cerebral, and middle cerebral arteries; *distribution*, middle ear, brain, pituitary gland, orbit, choroid plexus.

His review of the arteriograms disclosed an almost complete occlusion in the left **internal carotid artery**. This occlusion led to the patient's stroke and the resulting paralysis as well as the convulsions that had been experienced....

... He testified that the **internal carotid artery** furnished blood to the left side of the brain and that surgery was ruled out in Sandra's case because of the location of the occlusion. Mahr v. G. D. Searle & Co., 390 N.E.2d 1214, 1222 (App.Ct. Ill.1979).

arteria femoralis [NA], femoral artery: *origin*, continuation of external iliac; *branches*, superficial epigastric, superficial circumflex iliac, external pudendal, deep femoral, descending geniculate; *distribution*, lower abdominal wall, external genitalia, lower extremity. NOTE: Vascular surgeons refer to the portion of the femoral artery proximal to the branching of the deep femoral as the *common femoral a.*, and to its continuation as the *superficial femoral a.* In this classification, the descending geniculate artery is a branch of the superficial femoral artery.

Dr. Blazek, Dr. Parsa's expert and a specialist in cardiology, testified that, to locate a **femoral artery** in performing a renal arteriography, a physician should palpate the arterial pulse to act as a guideline to insertion of the needle....

... She explained that the proper procedure in locating the **femoral artery** is to extend the thigh and palpate the blood vessel. The artery is distinguished from the vein because the blood from it is red rather than blue. If a vein is hit before the artery is found, the procedure is not stopped but rather pressure is applied for a minute or two to the vein and then another attempt to hit the artery is made. After completing the procedure, pressure should be applied for between five to ten minutes depending upon the individual patient. Hirn v. Edgewater Hospital, 408 N.E.2d 970, 974 (App.Ct.Ill.1980).

About 2:00 the surgery began and Dr. McDowell discovered that Mrs. Lea had a blockage of the **femoral artery**. This is the large artery in the upper part of the leg. Dr. McDowell testified that in his opinion the clot did not occlude or block the artery more than twelve to eighteen hours before he saw her, ... Lea v. Family Physicians, P.A., 517 F.2d 797, 800 (5th Cir. 1975).

arteria iliaca externa [NA], external iliac artery: *origin*, common iliac; *branches*, inferior epigastric, deep circumflex iliac; *distribution*, abdominal wall, external genitalia, lower limb. Called also *anterior iliac artery*.

The plaintiff claimed the defendant negligently severed the right **external iliac artery** during surgery to remove kidney stones from the ureter. Perry v. Langstaff, 383 So.2d 1104, 1105 (Dist.Ct.App.Fla.1980).

arteria iliaca interna [NA], internal iliac artery: *origin*, continuation of common iliac; *branches*, iliolumbar, obturator, superior gluteal, inferior gluteal, umbilical, inferior vesical, uterine, middle rectal, and internal pudendal arteries; *distribution*, wall and viscera of pelvis, buttock, reproductive organs, medial aspect of thigh. Called also *a. hypogastrica, hypogastric artery*, and *posterior pelvic artery*.

In order to stop the bleeding, the common iliac artery and the common iliac vein were repaired, and the **internal iliac artery**, also known as the hypogastric artery, was ligated. There was a significant factual dispute concerning the external iliac artery, which is a major source of blood to the right leg....

... Amputation of the leg became necessary at a subsequent date, however, because of diminished blood supply. There was evidence, if believed, that the amputation of the leg had been made necessary by a complete occlusion of the right, common iliac artery occurring during surgery and not timely diagnosed. Hoeke v. Mercy Hospital of Pittsburgh, 445 A.2d 140, 146 (Super.Ct.Pa.1982).

arteria mesenterica superior [NA], superior mesenteric artery: *origin*, abdominal aorta; *branches*, inferior pancreaticoduodenal, jejunal, ileal, ileocolic, right colic, and middle colic arteries; *distribution*, small intestine, proximal half of colon.

Dr. Zarins operated on Norma in October of 1976 to remove an occlusion at the juncture of her **superior mesentery artery** and her aorta. However, because of the advanced state of her bowel's deterioration, the operation did not prevent her death on October 14, 1976. Weinstock v. Ott, 444 N.E.2d 1227, 1232 (Ct.App.Ind.1983).

Autopsy revealed arteriosclerotic occlusion of the **superior mesentery artery** with infarction of virtually the entire small bowel and most of the large bowel. Arteriosclerosis of the **superior mesenteric artery** in other areas was evidenced. Allstate Insurance Co. v. Holcombe, 207 S.E.2d 537, 540 (Ct. App.Ga.1974).

arteria poplitea [NA], popliteal artery: *origin*, continuation of femoral artery; *branches*, lateral and medial superior genicular, middle genicular, sural, lateral and medial inferior genicular, anterior and posterior tibial arteries, and the genicular articular and the patellar rete; *distribution*, knee, calf. See also *occlusion* (Lewin case).

Plaintiff was referred to the defendant surgeon for the removal of an aneurysm in the right leg. The initial clinical diagnosis placed the aneurysm in the **popliteal artery** (behind the right knee). Spitzer v. Ciprut, 437 N.Y.S.2d 27, 28 (2d Dep't 1981).

According to Dr. Lewis' testimony, he inspected the leg at 7:05 p.m., following a telephone report by Nurse Preston that the leg appeared mottled and cold and Voegeli could not move his toes. Lewis did not take a pulse at that time....

... According to Dr. Lewis' testimony, when he was recording the cold feeling Voegeli was still experiencing in his right foot, and his cold but not blanched skin, it occurred to him that "probably there was some embarrassment of the **popliteal vessels** and its function."...

... He conceded that a plateau fracture and swelling should alert a doctor to the possibility of a laceration of the **popliteal artery** and that taking a pulse is one way to find out if an artery has been injured. He also agreed that pain is a symptom of lack of circulation, and that if a foot is numb or cold there is reason to suspect lack of circulation...

... He testified that if a **popliteal artery** and vein are lacerated, the area should be pale or white, not mottled. All of the experts testified to the contrary. Voegeli v. Lewis, 568 F.2d 89, 92–3 (8th Cir. 1977).

Donna was returned to the operating room later the same day when it became apparent that circulation in her lower left leg was still inadequate. Dr. Lillehei opened the **popliteal artery** behind her knee and again used the Fogarty catheter procedure up and down the femoral artery. Walstad v. Univ. of Minnesota Hospitals, 442 F.2d 634, 638 (8th Cir. 1971).

---

arteriograft

Appellant contends first that the lower court erred in permitting appellee's expert to testify to the success rates of **arteriografts** generally and in cases of arteriosclerotic blockage. One of appellant's theories of appellee's negligence was the failure to perform an arteriogram, a test that would have indicated damage to the arteries and the need for an **arteriograft** to restore the blood flow to the lower leg. In response to that contention, appellee's expert testified to reasons why **arteriografts** are not always successful and opined that under the circumstances of this case, there was no chance for a successful graft. Brozana v. Flanigan, 454 A.2d 1125, 1126 (Super.Ct. Pa.1983).

arteriogram (ar-te're-o-gram") [*artery* + Gr. *gramma* a writing] a roentgenogram of an artery after injection of a radiopaque medium.

Most importantly, Doctor Kairys testified that he was the physician who ultimately ordered the **arteriogram**, a vascular procedure, for Mrs. Hoeke which was a crucial issue insofar as the postoperative liability aspect of this case was concerned. Hoeke v. Mercy Hospital of Pittsburgh, 445 A.2d 140, 145 (Super.Ct.Pa.1982).

He advised her that an **arteriogram** is a special x-ray for examining blood vessels. A contrast material is introduced into the blood vessels through a catheter placed in an artery in the groin area and the blood vessels are studied by television monitor in an adjoining room.

Dr. Ellis warned her that the **arteriogram** involved the risk of a blood clot at the site of the catheter entry and the possibility of severe headaches following the operation. Dr. Ellis testified that he advised Ms. McPherson that there was a 1 in 500 chance of "severe complication or permanent neurologic deficit" (meaning blindness or paralysis); Ms. McPherson testified that he did not so advise her. McPherson v. Ellis, 287 S.E.2d 892, 893 (N.Car.1982).

An **arteriogram** is a test whereby a large needle filled with dye is inserted into one of the patient's major arteries. A dye-type solution is injected and an xray is then taken of the patient to see if any bullet passed through any artery. Normally, this test causes heat to the patient. This heat sensation can be painful as there is a definite burning sensation....

Other Authorities: Borowski v. Von Solbrig, 328 N.E.2d 301, 304 (Ill.1975); Lewin v. Metropolitan Life Ins. Co., 394 F.2d 608, 613 (3d Cir. 1968).

arteria subclavia [NA], subclavian artery: *origin*, brachiocephalic trunk (right), arch of aorta (left); *branches*, vertebral, internal thoracic arteries, thyrocervical and costocervical trunks; *distribution*, neck, thoracic wall, spinal cord, brain, meninges, upper limb.

During the surgical intervention of his arm ... the **subclavian** and inominate **arteries** of decedent's right arm were damaged. Stites v. Rex Bar, 198 A.2d 615, 616 (Super.Ct.Pa.1964).

arteria uterina [NA], uterine artery: *origin*, internal iliac artery; *branches*, ovarian and tubal rami, vaginal artery; *distribution*, uterus, vagina, round ligament of uterus, uterine tube, ovary. Called also *fallopian artery*.

... The procedure for this examination was to place Mr. Choice under local Xylocaine anesthesia in the right groin, and then place an 18 gauge Seldinger needle in the common femoral artery using the Seldinger technique and a guide wire followed by a polyethylene catheter advanced to the lower abdominal aorta. This procedure was done in the xray department and it was concluded that there was no evidence of arterial injuries or bleeding. However, there is a suggestion of minimal spasm at the take-off of the left profunda femoral artery. U.S. v. Choice, 392 F.Supp. 460, 463 (E.D.Pa.1975).

Other Authorities: Beins v. U.S., 695 F.2d 591, 595 (D.C.Cir. 1982); Flamm v. Ball, 476 S.W.2d 710, 712 (Ct.Civ.App.Tex. 1972); Walstad v. Univ. of Minn. Hospitals, 442 F.2d 634, 637 (8th Cir. 1971).

arteriogram, carotid

A **carotid arteriogram** was performed, the results of which indicated a "beading appearance" in the left internal carotid artery. Dr. Prewitt tentatively diagnosed a spasm within the artery causing a blockage in the flow of blood to the left side of the brain. Mahr v. G. D. Searle & Co., 390 N.E.2d 1214, 1221 (App.Ct.Ill.1979).

arteriogram, coronary

The procedure of the **coronary arteriogram** entails the passing of a catheter into a hole in an artery and the tip of the catheter is guided up to the aortic arch and then into the orifice of a coronary artery, dye is injected and an X-ray moving picture is then taken. The catheter is then repositioned into the orifice of the other coronary artery and X-ray moving pictures are similarly taken. Morgenroth v. Pacific Medical Center, Inc., 126 Cal.Rptr. 681, 684 (Ct.App.Cal.1976).

arteriography (ar"te-re-og'rah-fe) [*artery* + Gr. *graphein* to write] roentgenography of arteries after injection of radiopaque material into the blood stream.

Violet Medvecz underwent elective renal **arteriography** at the Altoona Hospital, Altoona, Pennsylvania, on December 27, 1972. The procedure required the injection of a radiopaque dye, angio-conray, into her blood vessels for the purpose of taking x-rays of her right kidney.[1] [1 The aim of the procedure, which was entirely elective and could have been postponed, was to determine whether Ms. Medvecz suffered from any tumors in her right kidney. As a result of the operation, it was ascertained that she did not suffer from such a condition.] Medvecz v. Choi, 569 F.2d 1221, 1222 (3d Cir. 1977).

arterionephrosclerosis

Severe **arterionephrosclerosis** (hardening of the arteries of the kidneys). Glover v. Bruce, 265 S.W.2d 346, 351 (Mo.1954).

arteriosclerosis (ar-te"re-o-sklĕ-ro'sis) [*artery* + Gr. *sklēros* hard] a group of diseases characterized by thickening and loss of elasticity of arterial walls; it comprises three distinct forms: atherosclerosis, Mönckeberg's arteriosclerosis, and arteriolosclerosis. See also *chelation* (Rogers case); and *drop-attack* (Frazier case).

Defendant argues that all that changed as a result of the ischemic attacks on August 14 is that afterwards plaintiff and the doctors knew that he had diffused **arteriosclerosis** in the vessels leading to the brain, whereas before the episode they did not know he suffered from that condition. In other words, defendant argues that a transient ischemic attack is but a symptom of the pre-existing **arteriosclerosis** and that a symptom cannot of itself be the cause of disability. Daily v. Bechtel Power Corp., 420 So.2d 1337, 1341 (Ct.App.La.1982).

Arteriosclerosis is by legal definition an ordinary disease of life; it follows, therefore, that **arteriosclerosis** is not compensable heart damage.

However, even though **arteriosclerosis** alone does not justify compensation, neither does it bar compensation. Heart damage, such as would result from a heart attack, is compensable if linked by sufficient evidence to the workplace. Miklik v. Michigan Special Mach. Co., 329 N.W.2d 713, 715 (Mich. 1982).

He was, however, diagnosed as having **arteriosclerotic** heart disease ("hardening of the arteries of the coronary vessels") which can cause pain on exertion. The medical restrictions placed on plaintiff were no heavy exertion or heavy stress.

The medical testimony is that coronary **arteriosclerosis** "requires many years to develop, particularly to a point where it produces symptoms or complaints; perhaps even longer to produce findings." "In the absence of a thrombosis or infarction occurring, there is no detectable difference" in the coronary arteries as the result of a single incident of the chest pains called angina pectoris. Adams v. New Orleans Public Serv., Inc., 395 So.2d 470, 471 (Ct.App.La.1981).

Arteriosclerosis is hardening of the arteries. An **arteriosclerotic** heart does not manifest at once but is a condition which develops over a period of time. The condition did not and would not disappear after the 1975 myocardial infarction, but was an ongoing disease which inexorably continues. While the damaged heart muscle will heal, the hardening process in the arteries continues and it is to be expected that episodes of either infarction or of pain in the heart, called angina pectoris or weakening of the heart muscle, may occur in the future. Harris v. Rainsoft of Allen Cty., Inc., 416 N.E.2d 1320, 1322 (Ct. App.Ind.1981).

Other Authorities: Cook v. Marshall Bros. Lincoln-Mercury, Inc., 427 So.2d 655, 658 (Ct.App.La.1983); Salis v. U.S., 522 F.Supp. 989, 992 (M.D.Pa.1981); Matter of Quackenbush, 383 A.2d 785, 787 (Morris Ct.Ct.Prob.Div.1978); Kelley-Rickman, Inc. v. Hartford Life Ins. Co., 557 F.2d 639, 641 (8th Cir.

1977); Stogsdill v. Manor Convalescent Home, Inc., 343 N.E.2d 589, 598 (App.Ct.Ill.1976); Muznik v. Workers' Comp. App. Bd. of Cty. of Los Angeles, 124 Cal.Rptr. 407, 411 (Ct. App.Cal.1975); Thompson v. Occidental Life Ins. Co. of Cal., 513 P.2d 353, 365 (Cal.1973); Community Life & Health Ins. Co. v. McCall, 497 S.W.2d 358, 363 (Ct.App.Tex.1973); Watkins v. Underwriters at Lloyd's, London, 473 P.2d 464, 467 (Ct.App.Ariz.1970); Glover v. Bruce, 265 S.W.2d 346, 351 (Mo.1954).

arteriosclerosis, cerebral arteriosclerosis of the arteries of the brain.

Cerebral **arteriosclerosis** (hardening of the blood vessels of the brain). Glover v. Bruce, 265 S.W.2d 346, 351 (Mo.1954).

arteriosclerosis, coronary arteriosclerosis (atherosclerosis) of the coronary arteries.

On August 9, 1978, the Medical Board issued its report and findings on the medical questions involved in the claim and concluded as follows:

It is medically accepted that the underlying basis for most myocardial infarctions is **arteriosclerotic cardiovascular disease**, a long term process which progresses slowly to the point where it becomes clinically manifested....

... It is the opinion of the Medical Board that the disability of the claimant is attributable to **arteriosclerotic cardiovascular disease**, resulting in a myocardial infarction and subsequent episodes of angina. Multiple "risk factors" are recognized in the claimant. Montgomery Cty. Fire Bd. v. Fisher, 454 A.2d 394, 396 (Ct.Spec.App.Md.1983).

arteriosclerotic (ar-te"re-o-sklĕ-rot'ik) pertaining to or affected with arteriosclerosis. See also *arteriosclerosis*.

Evidence was introduced, however, which indicated that appellant had a preexisting **arteriosclerotic** heart disease (a narrowing of the arteries in and around the heart).... Kirnan v. Dakota Midland Hosp., 331 N.W.2d 72, 73 (S.Dak.1983).

Plaintiff was kept in the hospital for three days. During that time further tests were run and an arteriogram revealed diffused **arteriosclerotic** changes (diffused hardening of the arteries) in the arteries on the right side of the brain supplying the area of the brain which controls the functions of the left side of the body. The formal name for this condition is **arteriosclerotic** cerebral vascular disease. The tests also determined that he had suffered no permanent damage from the two events at work and in the hospital. The doctors described these events as transient ischemic attacks, in lay terms called light strokes or mini-strokes. Daily v. Bechtel Power Corp., 420 So.2d 1337, 1339 (Ct.App.La.1982).

arteriosclerotic cardiovascular disease See *arteriosclerosis, coronary.*

arteriovenous malformation See *malformation, arteriovenous.*

arteritis (ar"tĕ-ri'tis), pl. *arterit'ides* [*artery* + *-itis*] inflammation of an artery; cf. *endarteritis* and *periarteritis*.

artery (ar'ter-e) [L. *arteria;* Gr. *artēria,* from *aēr* air + *tērein* to keep, because the arteries were supposed by the ancients to contain air, or from Gr. *aeirein* to lift or attach] a vessel through which the blood passes away from the heart to the various parts of the body; called also *arteria* [NA]. The wall of an artery consists typically of an outer coat (tunica adventitia), a middle coat (tunica media), and an inner coat (tunica intima).

arthralgia (ar-thral'je-ah) [*arthr-* + *-algia*] pain in a joint.

Dr. Rubinowitz administered a neurological as well as a sensory examination and concluded that the claimant was suffering from "Spinal **Arthralgia**—moderate to severe" and that the prognosis was "fair with intensive physiotherapy." Rosa v. Weinberger, 381 F.Supp. 377, 379 (E.D.N.Y.1974).

Other Authorities: Ghazibayat v. Schweiker, 554 F.Supp. 1005, 1015 (S.D.N.Y.1983).

arthritis (ar-thri'tis), pl. *arthrit'ides* [Gr. *arthron* joint + *-itis*] rheumatism in which the inflammatory lesions are confined to the joints. See also *osteoarthritis*.

Arthritis: He has a long history of low back pain with intermittent radiation down his right lateral leg which, since latter August, has progressed to the point where he is unable to walk more than four or five blocks without having a great deal of discomfort and is unable to work even a half a day without having much discomfort in his leg and back. As a component of this, he has hyperesthesia involving the right anterior thigh. He has had no history of back injury and we have documented **arthritis** in his back by x-ray for some time. Wilson v. Schweiker, 553 F.Supp. 728, 731–2 (E.D.Wash.1982).

She testified that she had ceased working on September 15, 1973 because she could not stand on her feet or even sit because of the **arthritis** in her hips and legs, and because three doctors who had examined her, Dr. Harris, Dr. Irby and Dr. Owen advised her to stop working. Her medication consisted of ascriptin, indocin, and hydrodiuril. The plaintiff testified that the pain was constant, mostly in her hips and knees but also in her hands and elbows. In the morning she is very stiff and it may take several hours before she can get any mobility, although on what she describes as bad days she cannot acquire mobility at all. Flippen v. Mathews, 423 F.Supp. 135, 136 (E.D. Va.1976).

... [I]t was discovered that X rays of appellant's left hip showed multiple areas of calcification, diminished functional use, and that he actually had severe **arthritis** of the left hip joint, due to trauma, of which he had been complaining and vainly telling the doctors for fifteen years, and concerning which they had continually reported that the X rays showed no **arthritis** and that he was suffering only from psychoneurosis....

... As hereafter set forth, this seemingly inexplicable situation was explained by Dr. C. Dana Snyder, an expert orthopedic surgeon, who testified without contradiction, that such severe **arthritis** develops over a long period of time, with no subjective or objective symptoms discernible, and that appellant in all probability had been suffering from this **arthritis** for twenty years, at the end of which period it could finally be proved by X-ray examinations, and at a time when appellant was totally and permanently disabled because of this condition. Colwell v. Gardner, 386 F.2d 56, 60–61 (6th Cir. 1967).

Other Authorities: Dolcin Corp. v. Reader's Digest Ass'n, 7 A.D.2d 449, 451, 183 N.Y.S.2d 342 (1st Dep't 1959).

arthritis, acromioclavicular See *acromioclavicular*.

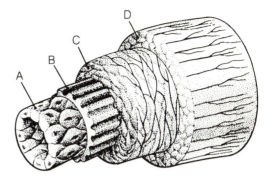

Artery; representation of arterial coats; *A.* tunica intima; *B.* internal elastic lamina; *C.* tunica media; *D.* tunica adventitia.

arthritis, degenerative See *osteoarthritis*.

arthritis, hypertrophic See *osteoarthritis*.

arthritis, patellofemoral

Dr. Schreiber also stated that chondromalacia patella is the first stage of **patellofemoral arthritis** and becomes **patellofemoral arthritis** as the condition progresses. No indication is given, however, that the condition inevitably will progress to the later stage in the absence of kneeling work which brought about the chondromalacia patella. Kern v. Industrial Commission, 588 P.2d 353, 354 (Ct.App.Ariz.1978).

arthritis, rheumatoid a chronic systemic disease primarily of the joints, usually polyarticular, marked by inflammatory changes in the synovial membranes and articular structures and by atrophy and rarefaction of the bones. In late stages deformity and ankylosis develop. The cause is unknown, but autoimmune mechanisms and virus infection have been postulated. Called also *atrophic a., a. deformans, a. nodosa, a. pauperum, chronic inflammatory a., proliferative a., arthronosos deformans, arthrosis deformans*, and *rheumatic gout*.

On cross-examination, Dr. Rentschler testified that **rheumatoid arthritis** is not caused by trauma or injury, but denied that an injury to the area could not aggravate it. According to Dr. Rentschler, a blow to the area could "precipitate" the **rheumatoid arthritis** in that it could make the condition apparent, i.e., bring it from a subclinical to a clinical phase. Caterpillar Tractor Co. v. Industrial Com'n, 440 N.E.2d 861, 864 (Ill. 1982).

The first document, a brief report prepared for submission to the Veterans Administration and dated May 22, 1968, stated that plaintiff had chronic **rheumatoid arthritis** with early deformity of arms, hands and elbows, concluding that he was then totally disabled. Dr. Cosby also submitted an HEW medical report form dated April 15, 1969, showing that he had treated plaintiff at irregular intervals from December 1968 to late February 1969 for pain, swelling, enlargement and deformity of the joints in plaintiff's back, hip, knees, ankles, arms and hands due to arthritis, for which he was given darvon, valium, indocin and other like drugs, with disappointing results. Hamm v. Richardson, 324 F.Supp. 328, 330 (N.D.Miss.1971).

Dr. Snyder replied to the Hearing Examiner as follows:

This **arthritis** develops in any individual, particularly the **rheumatoid** type, which this man evidently has from the examination now, develops over a long period of time with subjective symptoms that first are not discernible by X-ray examination and physical examination as long as the joints are freely movable, makes it difficult to diagnose except subjectively. This man has progressed now to the point where there are objective findings in support of the symptoms which he complains of. I don't doubt but what this man has had this trouble for twenty years, as his record shows, but you couldn't prove it up until very recently....

... Q. Now in the record of this case, Dr. Snyder, the complaint first was left leg and then right leg?

A. That is characteristic of arthritis in its beginning stages; they have first one hip, one knee, one elbow, one shoulder; it spreads then to the other joints and in this **rheumatoid** pattern, which this man has, it usually affects very severely one or sometimes multiple joints, nearly always one joint. With this man it seems to affect him mostly in the left hip; but it's a progressive thing.

Q. Now from your examination of the claimant and from your inspection of the X-ray, do you diagnose the claimant's condition as **rheumatoid arthritis**?

A. I do.

... ATTORNEY: What is the distinction between degenerative arthritis and **rheumatoid arthritis**?

A. You know there's all kinds of classifications for arthritis, but degenerative arthritis and **rheumatoid arthritis** in general are the same thing.... Colwell v. Gardner, 386 F.2d 56, 63–64 (6th Cir. 1967).

Other Authorities: Martin Industries, Inc. v. Dement, 435 So. 2d 85, 86–7 (Ct.Civ.App.Ala.1983); Reinhardt v. Colton, 337 N.W.2d 88, 90 (Minn.1983).

arthro-, arthr- [Gr. *arthron* joint] a combining form denoting some relationship to a joint or joints.

arthrocentesis (ar″thro-sen-te′sis) puncture and aspiration of a joint.

Arthrocentesis, which is the injection of a steroid or other substance into a joint, was described in the reports as being applied variously to either shoulder, as well as both hips and ankles....

... He described the time involved in preparing a patient for these procedures and the various locations where penetration is usually made. [He testified that normally an injection of penicillin takes place farther down the arm than an **arthrocentesis** or aspiration of a shoulder. He said that **arthrocentesis** involves an actual puncturing of a joint with a needle and this requires insertion directly into the joint.] He also testified that he knew of no causal relationship between the common cold and a condition requiring **arthrocentesis** or an aspiration. It was his testimony that it would be impossible to perform an **arthrocentesis** of a shoulder joint by inserting a needle in the fleshy or muscular part of the arm. U.S. v. Russo, 480 F.2d 1228, 1233, 1237 (6th Cir. 1973).

arthrodesis (ar″thro-de′sis) [*arthro-* + Gr. *desis* binding] the surgical fixation of a joint by a procedure designed to accomplish fusion of the joint surfaces by promoting the proliferation of bone cells; called also *artificial ankylosis*.

Nevertheless, the pain continued and Musial underwent a triple **arthrodesis**, a fusion procedure, which doctors hoped would reduce the pain. Unfortunately, the surgery resulted in increased pain and a second triple **arthrodesis** was recommended by a surgeon who expressly concluded that Musial's complaints of pain were sincere. The second surgery was performed but the pain remained and an infection developed in the injured area of the lower right leg. Musial v. A & A Boats, Inc., 696 F.2d 1149, 1151 (5th Cir. 1983).

The surgical procedure—known as **Arthrodesis**—was performed the next day at St. John's Hospital. Briefly, this surgical procedure fuses the joints by removing bone and stabilizes the toes with a Kirschner Wire which goes through the center of the bone and connects the phalanges. To be able, post-operatively, to test for circulation, the tips of the toes are exposed to facilitate observation. Brown v. St. John's Hospital, 367 N.E.2d 155 (App.Ct. of Ill.1977).

Lily May Moore has, as a result of a removal of an internal medial meniscus a series of unfortunate events took place that resulted in an **arthrodesis** of her left knee joint, making it a fixed joint. After the treatment and after the joint was arthrodesed and the immediate postoperative surgical course had reached a level it was founded [sic] that she ended up with a stiff knee plus an inversion of her foot. Moore v. Industrial Com'n, 492 P.2d 1222, 1223 (Ct.App.Ariz.1972).

Other Authorities: Minney v. Sec. of Health, Ed. & Welfare, 439 F.Supp. 706–7 (W.D.Ark.1977); South Texas Natural Gas Gathering Co. v. Guerra, 469 S.W.2d 899, 915 (Ct.Civ.App. Tex.1971); Torrez v. Industrial Com'n, 467 P.2d 245 (Ct.App. Ariz.1970).

arthrogenesis See *arthro-*; and *genesis*.

He has hardening of the arteries and then the coronary arteries. The work certainly would aggravate it, but that is not really a—it is a cause, but it is not the actual cause. The actual cause is his aging process and the **arthrogenesis** of his coronary arteries causing an occlusion, lack of blood supply to a particular area of his heart. The heart muscle dies and an infarction occurs. This is a heart attack. It can be precipitated by exertion, it can be precipitated by stress of any sort. Shatoska v. Intern. Grain Transfer, Inc., 430 So.2d 1255, 1260 (Ct.App. La.1983).

arthrogram (ar′thro-gram) a roentgenographic record after introduction of opaque contrast material into a joint.

It was also reported: "There is full flexion and extension of the right knee with tenderness over the lateral meniscus. Pain is also present on manipulation." The doctor recommended an **arthrogram** of the right knee, continued petitioner on restricted duty and prescribed darvon for the pain....

... On October 11, 1978 petitioner underwent an **arthrogram** conducted by a police physician who reported "an incomplete tear of the floor of the [medial] meniscus." His impression was that there were "adhesions involving the inferior surface of the posterior horn of the medial meniscus with a suspected incomplete tear." An arthroscopy was recommended based upon the "conclusive findings on **arthrogram**." Carey v. McGuire, 450 N.Y.S.2d 24, 26 (1st Dep't 1982).

Dr. J. J. Diaz, made an **arthrogram** study of claimant's knee which revealed an abnormality. Dr. Diaz opined that it was either a lipoma (fatty accumulation) above the knee-cap or a hypertrophy (enlargement) of the villi of the joint, something that can be caused by trauma." Eller and Co. v. Golden, 620 F.2d 71, 73 (5th Cir. 1980).

An **arthrogram** conducted during this period revealed a flattening of the superior lateral aspect of the femur head with total head involvement and the appearance of the regenerative stage of the disease. X-rays taken during this period revealed a complete involvement of the femur head with minimal deformity. Arrendale v. U.S., 469 F.Supp. 883, 886 (N.D.Tex. 1979).

arthroplasty (ar'thro-plas"te) [*arthro-* + Gr. *plassein* to form] plastic surgery of a joint or of joints; the formation of movable joints.

He further alleged that thereafter he had to undergo **arthroplasty**, an operation in which one's hip joint and socket are replaced. Reeg v. Shaughnessy, 570 F.2d 309, 311 (10th Cir. 1978).

arthroplasty, Bankart

In 1959 plaintiff was admitted to the VA Hospital in Houston, Texas, where he underwent a closed manipulation of his left shoulder and a surgical procedure known as a **Bankart arthroplasty**[4] for correction of frequent shoulder dislocation. [4 The Bankart procedure is described in Orr's Operations of General Surgery (4th ed. 1968), 648–649; The Craft of Surgery (2d ed.), 1831–1836; Operative Surgery (2d ed.), Vol. 8, 145; and Lewis' Practice of Surgery (rev.ed.1975), Orthopedics, Vol. 2, ch. 8, 21–23. The object is to re-attach the subcapularis muscle capsule (membrane encasing the muscle below the shoulder blade) and the glenoid labrum (fibrocartilage in the shoulder blade socket) to the bony anterior glenoid margin (the forward part of the rim of the shoulder blade socket). The operation involves the drilling of 3 or 4 suture holes in the anterior glenoid margin. Ibid.] Exnicious v. U.S., 563 F.2d 418, 420 (10th Cir. 1977).

arthroplasty, cup

... and that reconstructive surgery known as "**cup arthroplasty**" was required and, if successful, would probably result in only an ultimate 30% disability. Cleere v. Humphreys, 280 So.2d 23, 24 (Dist.Ct.App.Fla.1973).

arthroplasty, hip

On the morning of July 3, 1975, Dr. David Lipton assisted by Dr. Harold Massoff performed a total **Hip Arthroplasty** on a consenting patient. The procedure is described as follows:

They opened up the patient's right hip in this case and they removed the neck of the femur. They reset the greater trochanter, reamed out the acetabulum cavity. They take methacrylate bone cement, implant that in the acetabulum, put a cup into the cement then they broach out the femur canal, put in the methacrylate cement there, take the Charnley prosthesis, insert that down into the cavity, reapproximate the greater trochanter and sew him up. People v.

Smithtown General Hospital, 402 N.Y.S.2d 318, 321 (Sup. Ct.Suffolk Cty.1978).

arthroscopy (ar-thros'ko-pe) examination of the interior of a joint with an arthroscope.

On August 10, 1979 petitioner underwent an **arthroscopy**. The doctor concluded "a small tear was noted in the posterior horn." Carey v. McGuire, 450 N.Y.S.2d 24, 26 (1st Dep't 1982).

Another **arthroscopy** revealed "gross problems and changes within the knee ... secondary to tuberculosis which [was felt to be] the reason for [claimant's] slow postoperative progress following the meniscectomy." Matter of Compensation of Aquillon, 653 P.2d 264, 265 (Ct.App.Ore.1982).

Two surgical procedures were performed: (1) an **anthroscopy** (sic)—the insertion of an optical instrument into the knee for observation purposes; and (2) an arthrotomy—the excising of torn cartilage. There were no complications. Normal recovery involves a recuperative period of eight to ten weeks. Liner v. City of Houma, 423 So.2d 93, 97 (Ct.App.La.1982).

arthrotomy (ar-throt'o-me) [*arthro-* + Gr. *tomē* cut] surgical incision of a joint.

... an arthrotomy—the excising of torn cartilage. There were no complications. Normal recovery involves a recuperative period of eight to ten weeks. Liner v. City of Houma, 423 So. 2d 93, 97 (Ct.App.La.1982).

... [H]e underwent an **arthrotomy** (surgical incision of a joint) for excision of the left medial meniscus (internal semilunar cartilage of the knee joint). He was discharged on August 4, 1970, with diagnoses of degenerative osteoarthritis of the left knee, and tear of the left medial meniscus. Pruchniewski v. Weinberger, 415 F.Supp. 112, 113 (D.Md.1976).

Dr. Wolf, who was called as the State's witness, testified that if the primary operation (the **arthrotomy**) had been skillfully and properly done a transection of the peroneal nerve would not have been expected. Welsh v. State of N.Y., 51 A.D.2d 602, 603, 377 N.Y.S.2d 790, 791 (3d Dep't 1976).

articular (ar-tik'u-lar) [L. *articularis*] of or pertaining to a joint.

articulatio (ar-tik"u-la'she-o), pl. *articulatio'nes* [L.] an articulation: a place of junction between two discrete objects; used in anatomical nomenclature to designate the place of union or junction between two or more bones of the skeleton, indicated by the modifying term. Also used in the plural as a general term to indicate such joints. Called also *joint, junctura ossium* [NA alternative], and *osseous junction*.

articulatio, acromioclavicularis [NA], acromioclavicular articulation: the joint formed by the acromion of the scapula and the acromial extremity of the clavicle; called also *scapuloclavicular articulation* or *joint*.

articulatio genu; articulatio genus [NA], articulation of knee: the compound joint formed between the articular surface of the patella, the condyles and patellar surface of the femur, and the superior articular surface of the tibia; called also *knee joint*.

articulation (ar-tik″u-la′shun) [L. *articulatio*] the place of union or junction between two or more bones of the skeleton. See also *articulatio; junctura;* and *joint.*

articulator (ar-tik′u-la″tor) 1. a device for effecting a joint-like union. See also *dental articulator.* 2. See cases below.

The **articulators** include the lips, teeth, tongue, soft palate, and jaw muscles. People v. Rogers, 385 N.Y.S.2d 228, 233 (Sup.Ct.Kings Cty.1976).

Another function which controls the production of intelligible speech is the use of the muscles of speech. These are called **articulators** and they consist, principally, of the lips and the tongue and soft palate and muscles in the jaw.

According to Kersta, the manner in which a person uses his speech **articulators** causes a dynamic interplay. The size of the cavities used for a particular utterance depends upon the utterance which the speaker is making and there is a continual change in the movement of the **articulators**. The size of a person's vocal tract, size of his cavities and the method by which he operates his **articulators** are uniquely his. People v. King, 72 Cal.Rptr. 478, 486 (Ct.App.1968).

An individual's speech is created by a complex physiological and mechanical operation. The waves generated by the vocal cords are modified by vocal cavities (throat, nose, and cavities formed in the mouth by positioning the tongue), and by **articulators** (lips, teeth, tongue, palate and jaw muscles). The vocal cavities act as resonators which cause sound energy to be reinforced in specific sound spectrum areas, dependent upon the size, shape and interrelationship of the cavities. The **articulators** cooperate in a controlled dynamic interplay in the production of intelligible speech. The manner in which each of us manipulates his articulators when speaking has been developed by a process of imitation and trial and error.

Voice analysis thus rests on the non-likelihood that two individuals would have identical vocal cavities and identical dynamic patterns of **articulator** manipulation, and on the inability of an individual to change or disguise the particular voice characteristics created by his unique combination of cavities and **articulator** manipulative patterns.... U.S. v. Williams, 583 F.2d 1194, 1196–97 (2d Cir. 1978).

articulator, dental a mechanical device by which movements of the temporomandibular joints or mandible can be simulated; used in matching upper and lower dentures and for mounting artificial teeth in order to obtain proper relations of occlusion and articulation.

artificial limb See *prosthesis.*

asbestos (as-bes′tos) [Gr. *asbestos* unquenchable] a fibrous, incombustible, magnesium and calcium silicate, used as thermal insulation; its dust causes asbestosis. See also *asbestosis; mesothelioma;* and *carcinoma, bronchogenic* (Ins. Co. of No. Am. case esp.).

Asbestos is a generic term that describes a variety of naturally occurring fibrous, incombustible silicate minerals. Although tremendously valuable to industry, these minerals have been closely linked to lung cancer and asbestosis, a degenerative lung-scarring disease. See generally Notice of Proposed Rulemaking, "Occupational Exposure to Asbestos," 40 Fed.Reg. 47652 at 47653–56 (Oct. 9, 1975). The Occupational Safety and Health Administration

(OSHA) therefore has regulated employee exposure to **asbestos** since shortly after the agency's inception. OSHA has defined asbestos, established standards for its use, and set permissible exposure limits.[1] 29 C.F.R. § 1910.1001. [[1] On May 29, 1971, pursuant to 29 U.S.C.A. § 655(a), the Secretary of Labor published a table setting threshold limit values for a number of airborne contaminants, including tremolite, **asbestos** and talc. 29 C.F.R. § 1910.93, Table G–3; 36 Fed.Reg. 10503–06. On December 7, 1971, pursuant to 29 U.S.C.A. § 655(c), OSHA issued a temporary emergency standard revising Table G–3. 36 Fed.Reg. 23267. The emergency standard deleted the table's reference to **asbestos** and tremolite, adding a new section entitled "**asbestos** dust." The Secretary then published a notice of proposed rulemaking along with a proposed permanent **asbestos** standard which paralleled the emergency standard. Interested parties were invited to comment or object. 37 Fed.Reg. 466. A five-member Advisory Committee was formed to assist in developing the final standard and the National Institute for Occupational Safety and Health (NIOSH) also submitted recommendations. A public hearing was conducted from March 14–17, 1972, at which various representatives and experts appeared on behalf of interested parties, and on June 7, 1972, the Secretary published a final Standard for Exposure to Asbestos Dust. 37 Fed.Reg. 11318–22. The standard included a new subsection which defined "**asbestos**" and "**asbestos** fibers." As defined, " 'Asbestos' includes chrysotile, amosite, crocidolite, tremolite, anthophyllite, and actinolite." 29 C.F.R. § 1910.1001(a)(1).] R. T. Vanderbilt Co. v. Occ. Saf. & H. Rev. Com'n, 708 F.2d 570, 572 (11th Cir. 1983).

Asbestos is a mineral easily separable into long flexible fibers. Its particles are not of uniform shape or size. The Occupational Safety and Health Administration classifies **asbestos** fibers by six different types. Each type has a different length, texture, strength, acid resistance, and flexibility.[1A] The number of small **asbestos** fibers that will pass through the filter of a respirator, therefore, may be dependent on the particular types of **asbestos** particles present in the atmosphere of employment.[2] [[1A] During cross-examination, Dr. Bruce Held, an expert witness offered by defendants, admitted that there were different types of **asbestos** particles. He specifically named two types, crocidolite and amianthus, but could not recall all the types. The attorney for the plaintiff discussed three additional types—cross fibers, slip fibers, and mass fibers—listed in a publication called "**Asbestos**" put out by the Bureau of Mines of the United States Department of Interior. [[2] The size, shape, strength, texture, and flexibility of various **asbestos** fibers may affect the ability of the fibers to pass through a filter. Fibers which have a smooth surface and high flexibility are more likely to pass through a filter. Those with a rough surface and hard texture are more likely to be trapped by a filter screen.] Porter v. American Optical Corp., 641 F.2d 1128, 1132 (5th Cir. 1981).

It must be noted that **asbestos** is a commercial term that has no independent mineralogical or geological significance....

... As was noted previously [at page 31], **asbestos** is a generic term for a number of hydrated silicates that, when crushed or processed, separate into flexible fibers made up of fibrils. A serpentine mineral, chrysotile and the amphiboles, amosite, crocidolite, are used commercially as **asbestos.** Actinolite, tremolite and anthophyllite have additional commercial uses. Exposure to each of the minerals listed above can produce cancer in man. The cancers appear in various areas of the body, including the larynx, lung, pleura, peritoneum, and gastro-intestinal tract. Exposure to **asbestos** can result in mesothelioma, a diffuse, invariably fatal cancer of the linings of the pleura and the abdomen. It may be that no human tissue is immune to disease caused by exposure to **asbestos** fibers. Inhalation of **asbestos** has been shown to cause pathological changes in the chest including diffuse interstitial scarring (fibrosis) of the lung, pleural plaques, and pleural calcification....

... Optical examination is of limited value in the detection of **asbestos** particles in that many particles are so small as to be undetectable under optical microscopy. U.S. v. Reserve Mining Co., 380 F.Supp. 11, 31, 41, 52 (D.Minn.1974), cause remanded 498 F.2d 1073 (8th Cir. 1974).

Other Authorities: Public Citizen Health Research Group v. Auchter, 702 F.2d 1150, 1158 (D.C.Cir.1983); Lundy v. Union Carbide Corp., 695 F.2d 394, 395 (9th Cir. 1982); Moran v. Johns-Manville Sales Corp., 691 F.2d 811, 814–15 (6th Cir. 1982); Borel v. Fibreboard Paper Products Corp., 493 F.2d 1076, 1083, 1093 (5th Cir. 1973). Asten Hill Mfg. Co. v. Bambrick, 291 A.2d 354, 358–59 (Commonwealth Ct.Pa.1972).

asbestos, amosite See *cummingtonite-grunerite.*

The suggestion that particles of the cummingtonite-grunerite in Reserve's discharges are the equivalent of **amosite asbestos** raised an immediate health issue, since inhalation of **amosite asbestos** at occupational levels of exposure is a demonstrated health hazard resulting in asbestosis and various forms of cancer. However, the proof of a health hazard requires more than the mere fact of discharge,....

... A study by Dr. Selikoff of workers at a New Jersey asbestos manufacturing plant demonstrated that occupational exposure to **amosite asbestos** poses a hazard of increased incidence of asbestosis and various forms of cancer. Similar studies in other occupational contexts leave no doubt that asbestos, at sufficiently high dosages, is injurious to health.[5] However, in order to draw the conclusion that environmental exposure to Reserve's discharges presents a health threat in the instant case, it must be shown either that the circumstances of exposure are at least comparable to those in occupational settings, or, alternatively, that the occupational studies establish certain principles of asbestos-disease pathology which may be applied to predicting the occurrence of such disease in altered circumstances. [5 See Industrial Union Department, AFL–CIO, et al. v. Hodgson, No. 72–1713, 499 F.2d 467 at 471, n. 7 (D.C.Cir., filed April 15, 1974), where the following appears as a quotation from the Secretary of Labor: No one has disputed that exposure to asbestos of high enough intensity and long enough duration is causally related to asbestosis and cancers. The dispute is as to the determination of a specific level below which exposure is safe.] Reserve Mining Co. v. U.S., 498 F.2d 1073, 1076, 1078 (8th Cir. 1974).

Many of these [cummingtonite-grunerite] fibers are morphologically and chemically identical to **amosite asbestos** and an even larger number are similar to **amosite asbestos.**

Exposure to these fibers can produce asbestosis, mesothelioma, and cancer of the lung, gastrointestinal tract and larynx.

Most of the studies dealing with this problem are concerned with the inhalation of fibers; however, the available evidence indicates that the fibers pose a risk when ingested as well as when inhaled. U.S. v. Reserve Mining Co., 380 F.Supp. 11, 36 (D.Minn.1974), cause remanded 498 F.2d 1073 (8th Cir. 1974).

asbestosis (as"bĕ-sto'sis) [*asbestos* + *-osis*] a form of lung disease (pneumoconiosis) caused by inhaling fibers of asbestos and marked by interstitial fibrosis of the lung varying in extent from minor involvement of the basal areas to extensive scarring; it is associated with pleural mesothelioma and bronchogenic carcinoma. Called also *amianthosis.* See also *asbestos, amosite* (Reserve Mining Co. case); *cummingtonite-grunerite* (Reserve Mining Co. case); *fibrothorax* (Nelson case); *injury* (Keene Corp. case); *mesothelioma; pancreas*; and *cancer; pancreatic.*

In an affidavit, Dr. Russell S. Fisher, Chief Medical Examiner for the State of Maryland, said:

The disease of **asbestosis** is one which affects the lungs of individuals exposed to the mineral asbestos. The main feature of the disease is that the lungs of the affected individual become scarred and that the normal lung tissue is converted into fibrotic tissue which prevents the lungs from functioning normally. A major effect of this action is to seriously impair an individual's ability to breathe normally. The disease in a particular individual can become progressively worse, even though that individual may no longer be exposed to the causative agent, asbestos.

Nevertheless, if the **asbestosis** of a particular individual is not seriously advanced, that individual may continue to survive with a relatively normal life. Even in a more advanced stage, though an individual may not be able to continue to do active physical work, the individual can nevertheless survive to an age which is close to a normal life expectancy.

We note that **asbestosis** generally has a latent period of 10 to 25 years between initial exposure and apparent effect. Wilson v. Johns-Manville Sales Corp., 684 F.2d 111, 115 n. 21 (D.C.Cir.1982); Keene Corp. v. Insurance Co. of N. Am., 667 F.2d 1034, 1040 n. 9 (D.C.Cir.1981); cert. denied, 455 U.S. 1007, 102 S.Ct. 1644, 71 L.Ed.2d 875 (1982); Borel v. Fibreboard Paper Prods. Corp., 493 F.2d 1076, 1083 (5th Cir. 1973), cert. denied, 419 U.S. 869, 95 S.Ct. 127, 42 L.Ed.2d 107 (1974). See I. Selikoff & D. Lee, Asbestos and Disease 205 (1978); Selikoff, Churg, & Hammond, The Occurrence of Asbestosis Among Insulation Workers, 132 Ann.New York Acad.Sci. 139 (1965). Pierce v. Johns-Manville Sales Corp., 464 A.2d 1020, 1022 (Ct.App.Md.1983).

With a large concentration of the fibers lodged in the lung cavities, scar tissue eventually replaces most of the healthy lung tissue, disrupting the intake of air into lung air sacs and causing a shortness of breath. A sufficiently high concentration and buildup of the condition will cause death. This process, called **asbestosis**, can also be a precipitating cause of other illnesses such as emphysema, bronchitis, and pneumonia.

Asbestosis is a cumulative and progressive disease. It does not occur overnight after breathing in a substantial number of asbestos particles during the day. Rather, the disease is a culmination of body reaction to the particles inhaled during years of exposure. The disease is slow in nature and may require from ten to twenty years from onset to fully manifest itself. Persons may develop **asbestosis** long after they have left contact with an asbestos environment. Continuous exposure to asbestos particles, however, prods the disease at a greater rate. Even though the body has begun a reaction to the fibers, inhalation of new fibers adds to the lung inflammation and accelerates injury. Porter v. American Optical Corp., 641 F.2d 1128, 1133 (5th Cir. 1981).

Asbestosis is a non-malignant disease resulting from the inhalation of asbestos fibers of a certain length over a considerable period of time causing a bodily reaction that may eventually impair the function of the lungs. The body has several defense mechanisms that exclude from the functional areas of the lungs most of the foreign matter inhaled. It also has a mechanism for removing such matter that passes these defenses. Asbestos fibers of a certain length, however, cannot be removed and become embedded in the lung tissue in the areas where the alveoli are found and where the transfer of gases in and out of the blood takes place. Being unable to remove these minute particles of foreign matter, the body copes by walling off the particles. The walling off is done by a proliferation of fibrous cells that eventually produce a dense scar-like material in the functional area of the lungs. This process takes about six (6) months and is irreversible. Each repetition of inhalation and reaction adds a tiny deposit of scar-like tissue in this critical area....

The accumulation of scar-like tissue decreases the functional volume of the lungs, stiffens the passage ways, and impedes the transfer of gases in and out of the blood. If the process continues, the functional capacity of the lungs becomes inadequate to support normal activities and may eventually be unable to support life....

... **Asbestosis** progresses slowly as a disease. Damage begins with the initial insult, and scar-like tissue builds up over many years before symptoms become noticeable or a diagnosis can be made. In the majority of cases symptoms do not appear until more than twenty (20) years after initial exposure. The intensity and duration of each insult as well as the frequency of repetition combine with numerous individual characteristics to determine which persons who are exposed sustain noticeable lung damage, when functional impairment becomes noticeable, and what symptoms such a person finally demonstrates. Even if after a period of exposure, no additional asbestos fibers are inhaled, tissue change may nonetheless continue and be unnoticed for decades. Since the effects of tissue changes are cumulative, an exposed person's condition is the product of an unknowable sequence of insults arranged randomly or in groups along a continuum that stretches from as long as 50 years to less than six months prior to manifestation. Additional factors such as variations in ventilation, moisture in the air, and an exposed person's health at the time of any exposure combine to make it impossible to determine which exposure to asbestos caused injury or to determine when such a person becomes "diseased." [3] [[3] For a discussion of **asbestosis** and its effects on the body see Selikoff, Bader, Bader, Churg, and Hammond, "Asbestosis and Neoplasis," 42 Am.J.

Med. 487 (1967); Selikoff, Churg, and Hammond, "The Occurrence of Asbestosis Among Insulation Workers," 132 Ann. New York Acad.Sc. 139 (1965).] Ins. Co. of No.Am. v. Forty-Eight Insulations, 451 F.Supp. 1230, 1237 (E.D.Mich.1978).

Other Authorities: Indus. Indem. Co. v. Workers' Comp. App. Bd., 193 Cal.Rptr. 471, 473 (Ct.App.Cal.1983); Neubauer v. Owens-Corning Fiberglas Corp., 686 F.2d 570, 571 (7th Cir. 1982); Wilson v. Johns-Manville Sales Corp., 684 F.2d 111, 113, 115 (D.C.Cir.1982); Schultz v. L. B. Smith, Inc., 456 N.Y.S.2d 191–2 (3d Dep't 1982); Nelson v. Industrial Comn of Ariz., 656 P.2d 1230, 1232 (Ariz.1982); Howard v. Johns-Manville Sales Corp., 420 So.2d 1190, 1192 (Ct.App.La. 1982); Keene Corp. v. Ins. Co. of North America, 667 F.2d 1034, 1038 (D.C.Cir.1981); Mid-South Insulation Co. v. Buckley, 396 So.2d 7, 9 (Miss.1981); Eagle-Picher Industries, Inc. v. Liberty Mut. Ins. Co., 523 F.Supp. 110, 114–17 (D.Mass. 1981); Nelson v. Industrial Commission of Arizona, 585 P.2d 887, 889 (Ct.App.Ariz.1978); U.S. v. Reserve Mining Co., 380 F.Supp. 11, 39 (D.Minn.1974); Borel v. Fibreboard Paper Products Corp., 493 F.2d 1076, 1082–5 (5th Cir. 1973); Utter v. Asten-Hill Mfg. Co., 309 A.2d 583–5 (Pa.1973); Asten-Hill Mfg. Co. v. Bambrick, 291 A.2d 354, 357–9 (Commonwealth Ct.Pa.1972).

ASHD (arteriosclerotic heart disease) See *arteriosclerosis*.

The myocardial infarction was listed as due to, or as a consequence of "ASHD" [5] with the approximate period between onset and death listed as seven years. [[5] Although "ASHD" is not defined, presumably it stands for "arteriosclerotic heart disease." (Tr. 130).] Poore v. Mathews, 406 F.Supp. 47, 50 (E.D.Tenn.1975).

aspartame (ah-spar'tām) chemical name: N-L-α-aspartyl-L-phenylalanine methyl ester. An artificial sweetener, $C_{14}H_{18}N_2O_5$, which is about 200 times as sweet as sucrose and has potential as a low-calorie sweetener.

Aspergillus (as"per-jil'us) [L. *aspergere* to scatter] a genus of imperfect fungi of the family Moniliaceae. When found, the perfect, or sexual, stage is classified with the ascomycetous fungi in the family Eurotiaceae, order Eurotiales. It includes several of the common molds and some that are opportunistic pathogens. It is characterized by elongated conidiophores thickly set with chains of basipetally formed conidia. See illustration under *mold*.

Employer-appellee's doctor testified that claimant-appellant's present illness was not tuberculosis, but rather that he was suffering from a secondary fungus infection known as **aspergillus**. Hollingsworth v. Commonwealth Dep't of Health, 301 A.2d 123, 125 (Commonwealth Ct.Pa.1973).

Aspergillus (de Rivas).

asphyxia (as-fik′se-ah) [Gr. "a stopping of the pulse"] a condition due to lack of oxygen in respired air, resulting in impending or actual cessation of apparent life.

The referee concluded:

"FIRST: On October 7, 1974, the decedent, Walter H. Pollard, III, died during the course of his employment on premises of the employer due to **asphyxia** caused by the aspiration of gastric contents into the respiratory tract produced by vomiting following the ingestion of ethanol and drugs and medications which severely depressed his Central Nervous System setting in motion the events which caused death,...." Westinghouse Elec. Corp. v. Workmen's Comp., 400 A.2d 1324, 1326 (Commonwealth Ct.Pa.1979), judgment reversed 414 A.2d 625 (1980).

asphyxia, neonatorum respiratory failure in the newborn. See also *respiratory distress syndrome*, under *syndrome*.

asphyxia, perinatal See *asphyxia, neonatorum*; and *syndrome, respiratory distress of newborn*.

A neonatologist at Fort Worth Children's Hospital diagnosed the baby as suffering from severe **perinatal asphyxia**—that is, a severe deprivation of oxygen before, during, or after birth—and from meconium aspiration syndrome—the distress caused by inhalation of meconium into the lungs. Haught v. Maceluch, 681 F.2d 291, 295 (5th Cir. 1982).

asphyxiation (as-fik″se-a′shun) suffocation.

The lung tissue was extremely swollen from stomach fluids, and severely burned by the acid. This condition prevented the deceased from inhaling sufficient amounts of oxygen, and resulted in his death by **asphyxiation**. Lee v. Fidelity & Cas. Co. of New York, 567 F.2d 1340, 1341 (5th Cir. 1978).

Asphyxiation means that the air or oxygen supply to the body is cut off. Jones v. Aetna Life Insurance Co., 439 S.W.2d 721, 724 (Ct.Civ.App.Tex.1969).

aspirate (as′pĭ-rāt) 1. to treat by aspiration. 2. the substance or material obtained by aspiration. See also *aspiration* (Landeche case).

aspiration (as″pĭ-ra′shun) [L. *ad* to + *spirare* to breathe] the removal of fluids or gases from a cavity by the application of suction.

When he returned on the morning of the 19th his elbow was swollen. Rowe was sent to the team's physician, where the elbow was **aspirated**. Rowe then returned to the practice field and joined the scrimmage. During that scrimmage, Rowe says he received the injury that led to this litigation. [Footnote omitted.] Rowe v. Baltimore Colts, 454 A.2d 872, 874 (Ct.Spec. App.Md.1983).

Prior to her discharge on November 1, her right knee and left knee were aspirated,[1] each on one occasion. [[1] Injecting local anesthetic beneath the skin and slipping a needle behind the kneecap he withdrew 4 cc's of fluid....] Landeche v. Weaver, 384 So.2d 540, 541 (Ct.App.La.1980).

The **aspiration** of the bursa was usually described in the DSR's as being applied to one of the shoulders or one of the hips. This procedure involves withdrawal of a fluid from the bursa or hematoma by means of either one or two needles....

... He stated that in **aspiration** of a bursa or hematoma the purpose is to extract fluid and that often two needles are used,

one to inject an anesthetic and another larger bored needle to withdraw the fluid. U.S. v. Russo, 480 F.2d 1228, 1233 (6th Cir. 1973).

The term **aspiration**, according to Dr. Gwozdz, "means lodging of any material into the windpipe and into the parts of the dividing tubes of the lung, which material follows the act of general inspiration, well, the inhaling, the act of inhaling; in other words, foreign particles of material, a fluid, or a solid material that follows the process of inhaling and lodges into the tubular structures is called, in our terminology, **aspiration**."....

... **Aspiration** is not the natural and usual effect of vomiting. It was an independent cause or agency which intervened to produce the injury to the lungs of Mr. Jones. Vomiting in itself produced no injury. The **aspiration** which was unusual, unexpected, and so extraordinary and rare in persons of the age and physical condition of Mr. Jones clearly makes his death an accidental one. Jones v. Aetna Life Insurance Co., 439 S.W.2d 721, 724, 727 (Ct.Civ.App.Tex.1969).

Other Authorities: Cobb v. Aetna Life Ins. Co., 274 N.W.2d 911, 914–15 (Minn.1979); Funke v. Fieldman, 512 P.2d 539, 543 (Kan.1973).

aspiration, vacuum removal of the uterine contents by application of a vacuum through a hollow curet or a cannula introduced into the uterus. Called also *vacuum extraction*.

At sometime before 11:25 a.m. Dr. Zearfoss attached an instrument known as a **vacuum extractor** to Matthew's head and brought him down into his mother's vagina. Dr. Zearfoss then removed the **vacuum extractor**, applied forceps to the head, and delivered Matthew. Rutherford v. Zearfoss, 272 S.E.2d 225, 226 (Va.1980).

aspirator (as′pĭ-ra′tor) an apparatus used for removal by suction of fluids or gases contained within a cavity.

In response to the poor ventilation, he connected the insured to an "**aspirator-resuscitator inhalater**" a machine designed to clear out the mouth and throat area with suction and then blow air into the lungs. Cobb v. Aetna Life Ins. Co., 274 N.W.2d 911, 913 (Minn.1979).

aspirin (as′pĭ-rin) chemical name: 2-(acetyloxy) benzoic acid. A compound, $C_9H_8O_4$, occurring as white crystals that are commonly tabular or needle-like, or as a white, crystalline powder; used as an analgesic, antipyretic, and antirheumatic. Called also *acetylsalicylic acid*.

He further explained that the salicylate compound which is the analgesic component of **aspirin** is, as a matter of medical and pharmaceutical knowledge, recognized as a gastrointestinal irritant and despite the inclusion of an anti-irritant component in **aspirin**, a significant number of people using **aspirin** over a long period of time develop gastrointestinal bleeding as the result of the continuing direct irritating effect of the salicylate compound on the membranes lining the stomach and intestinal tract. Torsiello v. Whitehall Laboratories, 398 A.2d 132, 135 (Super.Ct.N.J.1979).

Joann Rewis drew her last labored breath—the result of acute salicylate (**aspirin**) poisoning. This tragic story has been thrice told and little purpose would be served in reciting the facts of that fateful event. A concise statement of the pertinent facts, together with the history of two previous trials and one appeal, appear in this court's opinion in Rewis v. United States, 369 F.2d 595 (5th Cir. 1966), and the lower court's judgment from which the instant appeal is taken. Rewis v. United States, 304 F.Supp. 410 (S.D.Ga., 1969)....

... "Q. Doctor, is there any one single feature which is critically important in the diagnosis of **aspirin** poisoning?

"A. Clinical finding. I would say one single feature of greatest importance, if I had to pick one, would probably be deep rapid breathing." Rewis v. U.S., 445 F.2d 1303, 1305 (5th Cir. 1971).

astereognosis (ah-ster"e-og-no'sis) [*a* neg. + Gr. *stereos* solid + *gnōsis* recognition] loss of power to recognize objects or to appreciate their form by touching or feeling them; called also *tactile amnesia*.

Because of brain damage the claimant suffered from **astereognosis**, which is an inability to identify objects or forms by touch. He cannot hold an object in his left hand, he said unless he looks at the object and concentrates on grasping it....

... There was definite immunization to pin prick in his left side, the physician related, and he had difficulty in recognizing objects placed in the left hand. A patient with **astereognosis** has to look at his hand and use his vision to identify objects in the hand and to observe the position of the hand. He found the claimant had a diminished sensitivity to pain and could not measure with what force he might be gripping an object. The doctor said he was thus subject to injury in that he would be unable to tell the position of his hand and might not be aware of the presence of a flame or his nearness to machinery....

... Dr. John Hetherington, a neurosurgeon who examined the claimant and testified on behalf of the employer, also found a condition of **astereognosis**. He acknowledged that if the claimant were not looking at his hand he could injure himself by pressing too forcefully on a sharp object. Bradford Supply Co. v. Industrial Com'n, 277 N.E.2d 854, 856–7 (Ill. 1971).

asthenia (as-the'ne-ah) [Gr. *asthenēs* without strength + *-ia*] lack or loss of strength and energy; weakness.

asthenia, neurocirculatory a symptom-complex characterized by the occurrence of breathlessness, giddiness, a sense of fatigue, pain in the chest in the region of the precordium, and palpitation. It occurs chiefly in soldiers in active war service, though it is seen in civilians also. Called also *effort syndrome, cardiac neurosis, DaCosta's disease or syndrome, anxiety neurosis, neurasthenia, cardiasthenia, cardiac neurasthenia*, and *cardioneurosis*.

Allen opined Chester had a "cardiac type of neurosis." By that phrase Allen said he meant that Chester was overreacting to the lack of evidence that his heart is abnormal and that is what is incapacitating him....

... by definition a cardiac neurosis is a **neurocirculatory asthenia**, that is, a loss of strength resulting from anxiety of psychic origin. What Allen really had in mind probably was an accident neurosis—a psychoneurosis caused by an accident. Chester v. Oklahoma Natural Gas Co., 619 P.2d 1266, 1268 (Ct.App.Okl.1980).

asthma (az'mah) [Gr. *asthma* panting] a condition marked by recurrent attacks of paroxysmal dyspnea, with wheezing due to spasmodic contraction of the bronchi. Some cases of asthma are allergic manifestations in sensitized persons (*bronchial allergy*); others are provoked by a variety of factors, including vigorous exercise, irritant particles, psychologic stresses, etc. See also *bronchospasm*; and *toluene diisocyanate*.

Claimant gave a further history of being frequently fatigued on Mondays when she first went to work and of developing sneezing and lacrimation shortly after exposure to dust and of being very tired and weak at the end of the work week and of shortness of breath which became more prominent toward the end of her employment.

On the basis of the claimant's history and his examination including laboratory tests and pulmonary function studies, Dr. Hayes was of the opinion that claimant had mild **asthma** by history;...

... This patient by history has mild **asthma**. I expect that any dusty environment or exposure to various irritating fumes could trigger an asthmatic attack. In such cases, it is frequently impossible to discern a direct cause and effect relationship between cotton dust exposure and symptoms. Thompson v. Burlington Industries, 297 S.E.2d 122, 123–4 (Ct.App.N.Car. 1982).

McHale filed a claim petition describing his disease as acute **asthma** aggravated by the conditions of his employment. The petition specifically cited the claimants' inhalation of smoke, dust, metal particles and asbestos in the course of his work as a sheet metal welder and grinder. McHale v. Workmen's Compensation Appeal Bd., 425 A.2d 34, 35 (Cmwlth.Ct.Pa. 1981).

Patient is rehospitalized at this time for recurrent bronchial **asthma** precipitated primarily by extreme emotional stress due to marital problems at home. Patient is considering divorce in that her husband reportedly becomes drunk and beats the patient up. Extensive pulmonary evaluation was done by Dr. Lim with considerable improvement in the patient's status while she was in the hospital. Emotional agitation, however, has been directly observed to reproduce attacks.... Palik v. Mathews, 422 F.Supp. 547, 549–50 (D.Neb.1976).

Other Authorities: Fraijo v. Hartland Hospital, 160 Cal.Rptr. 246, 248 (Ct.App.Cal.1979); Siegel v. Mt. Sianai Hospital of Cleveland, 403 N.E.2d 202, 204 (Ct.App.Ohio 1978). Baker v. Industrial Accident Com'n, 52 Cal.Rptr. 276, 278–9 (Dist.Ct. App.Cal.1966).

asthma, isocyanate bronchial asthma caused by allergy to toluene diisocyanate and similiar materials.

... the employee, claimed a disablement and personal injury by reason of an occupational disease—chronic obstructive lung disease and **isocyanate asthma**—caused by exposure to chemicals, dust and fumes in his work as a spray painter....

... About October 1, 1980, Abram had an episode of breathing difficulty so severe that he then stopped applying paint and took a lower paying job sanding vehicles and applying primer and sealer. He testified that even though the medications have helped, his general vitality has decreased and he becomes so fatigued that he has cut his work week to 4 days and at times leaves work early on those days. Abram v. Art Goebel Ford, 327 N.W.2d 88, 89–90 (Minn.1982), overruled by 336 N.W.2d 255 (1983).

Asthmador

She believed the minor to be under the influence of a drug which she called "**Azmidor**."[2] He was described as being "incoherent." [2 This unquestionably refers to "**Asthmador**." That is a proprietary product. Its active ingredients are stramonium and belladonna.] In re H.L.R., 75 Cal.Rptr. 308, 310 (Ct.App. Cal.1969).

astigmatism (ah-stig′mah-tizm) [*a* neg. + Gr. *stigma* point] unequal curvature of the refractive surfaces of the eye as a result of which a ray of light is not sharply focused on the retina but is spread over a more or less diffuse area. This results from the radius of curvature in one plane being longer or shorter than that of the radius at right angles to it (Airy, 1827).

She had a refractive area consisting of myopia, combined with some **astigmatism** (faulty vision caused by an abnormal curvature in the eye),... Ortiz v. Allergan Pharmaceuticals, 489 S.W.2d 135, 137 (Ct.Civ.App.Tex.1972).

astroblastoma (as″tro-blas-to′mah) an astrocytoma of Grade II, composed of cells with abundant cytoplasm and two or three nuclei.

astrocyte (as′tro-sīt) [*astro-* + Gr. *kytos* hollow vessel] a neuroglial cell of ectodermal origin, characterized by fibrous, protoplasmic, or plasmatofibrous processes. Collectively, such cells are called *astroglia*.

astrocytoma (as″tro-si-to′mah) a tumor composed of astrocytes; such tumors have been classified in order of increasing malignancy as: *Grade I*, consisting of fibrillary or protoplasmic astrocytes; *Grade II* (see *astroblastoma*); and *Grades III* and *IV* (see *glioblastoma multiforme*).

astroglia (as-trog′le-ah) [*astro-* + *neuroglia*] the astrocytes considered as tissue; formerly called *microglia*.

asymmetric See under *asymmetry*.

asymmetry (a-sim′ĕ-tre) [*a* neg. + Gr. *symmetria* symmetry] lack or absence of symmetry; dissimilarity in corresponding parts or organs on opposite sides of the body which are normally alike. In chemistry, lack of symmetry in the special arrangements of the atoms and radicals within the molecule or crystal.

By convention, the various positions (**asymmetric centers**) on the basic molecule common to the compounds of the tetracycline family have been assigned numbers.... One can distinguish a particular compound by referring to its stereochemical configuration at one or more individually numbered positions on the molecule. Pfizer, Inc. v. International Rectifier Corp., 538 F.2d 180, 187 (8th Cir. 1976).

asymptomatic (a″simp″to-mat′ik) showing or causing no symptoms.

Q. What does he mean by discogenic disease of the cervical spine, by history, relatively **asymptomatic**? First explain **asymptomatic** to me.
A. **Asymptomatic** means without symptoms.
Q. In other words, there are no symptoms there?
A. He uses the word "relatively" **asymptomatic**, so I would think he meant with few symptoms. Floyd v. Finch, 441 F.2d 73, 91 (6th Cir. 1971).

Astigmatism: the appearance of lines as seen by (*a*) the normal eye and (*b*) the astigmatic eye.

A. When I saw Mr. Britton he was always **asystematic** [sic].
Q. Meaning what?
A. Meaning that he was not having any difficulty at all when I saw him;... Great American Reserve Ins. Co. v. Britton, 389 S.W.2d 320, 323 (Ct.Civ.App.Tex.1965).

Atabrine (ah′tah-brin) trademark for a preparation of quinacrine hydrochloride. See also *quinacrine hydrochloride*.

ataxia (ah-tak′se-ah) [Gr., from *a* negative + *taxis* order] failure of muscular coordination; irregularity of muscular action. See also *sign, Romberg's*; and *rombergism*.

... (difficulty in walking characterized by stumbling, wobbling, falling);... McSwain v. Chicago Transit Authority, 362 N.E.2d 1264, 1265 (App.Ct.Ill.1977).

... she had mild gait **ataxia** or imbalance with inability to stand with one foot in front of the other and to balance in that way suggesting a fourth lesion in the area of the cerebellum. McSwain v. Chicago Transit Authority, 362 N.E.2d 1264, 1272–3 (App.Ct.Ill.1977).

atelectasis (at″e-lek′tah-sis) [Gr. *atelēs* imperfect + *ektasis* expansion] 1. airlessness of a lung that had once been expanded. 2. collapse of a lung.

A chest x-ray revealed the existence of discoid **atelectasis** (airlessness of the lungs) of the right mid-lung. Brissette v. Schweiker, 566 F.Supp. 626, 628 (E.D.Mo.1983), judgment affirmed in part, reversed in part 784 F.2d 864 (1986).

Dr. Borders on September 6, 1970, entered a statement on the patient's history sheet to the effect that there was no evidence of infection of the knee and that the temperature "yesterday" was 100.4, probably due to "postoperative **atelectasis** which would not occur in more cooperative patient." Contreras v. St. Luke's Hosp., 144 Cal.Rptr. 647, 650 (Ct.App.Cal.1978).

The surgery revealed extensive fibrous tissue in the left thorax together with marked thickening of the surface of the lung and the membrane lining the thorax as well as a total **atelectasis** of the lower lobe of the left lung. Nelson v. Industrial Commission, 585 P.2d 887, 888 (Ct.App.Ariz.1978).

Other Authorities: Hogan v. Almand, 205 S.E.2d 440, 442 (Ct. App.Ga.1974).

atelectasis, absorption that produced by any factor, e.g., secretions, foreign body, tumor, abnormal external pressure, etc., which completely obstructs the airway, preventing intake of air into the alveolar sacs and permitting absorption of air into the bloodstream. Called also *obstructive a., reabsorption a.*, and *secondary a.*

The left lung was **atelectatic** due to a thick pleural coat of metastatic tumor and dense fibrous tissue....

... That the direct cause of death was acute bronchopneumonia developing in an **atelectatic** and fibrotic left lung.... Consolidation Coal Co. v. Workmen's Compensation, 391 A.2d 14, 17–18 (Cmwlth.Ct.Pa.1978), affirmed 460 A.2d 237 (1983).

atelectasis, pulmonary

Pulmonary **atelectasis** (collapsing of the blood vessels of the spaces in the lungs)....

... that, when she came to the hospital the second time, she had **pulmonary atelectasis**, a hemorrhage of the lungs which is almost always fatal;.... Glover v. Bruce, 265 S.W.2d 346, 351 (Mo.1954).

atelectatic See *atelectasis.*

atheroma (ath"er-o'mah) [Gr. *athērē* gruel + *-oma*] a mass of plaque of degenerated, thickened arterial intima occurring in atherosclerosis.

... that Mr. Chenoweth's "extensive **atheramatous** [sic] disease demonstrated clinically and by arteriography and findings suggest long standing arteriosclerotic disease [Ex. 50, Tr. 251]. Chenoweth v. Weinberger, 421 F.Supp. 955, 959 (W.D. Mo.1976).

However, the superior mesenteric artery appears totally occluded, as if possibly by an **atheromatous** embolus. Allstate Insurance Co. v. Holcombe, 207 S.E.2d 537, 540 (Ct.App.Ga. 1974).

atheromatous See *atheroma.*

atherosclerosis (ath"er-o"skle-ro'sis) an extremely common form of arteriosclerosis in which deposits of yellowish plaques (atheromas) containing cholesterol, lipoid material, and lipophages are formed within the intima and inner media of large and medium-sized arteries. See also *disease, triple vessel.*

Coronary artery disease is an **atherosclerosis** of all the coronary arteries with varying degree of involvement in different parts of the arterial system. Bypassing the obstruction merely provides more oxygen to that part of the heart supplied by that artery but the artery **distal** to the obstruction is also involved and can respond to exertion and/or emotion or other factors ... which cause chest pain and coronary insufficiency. Icenhour v. Weinberger, 375 F.Supp. 312, 315–16 (E.D.Tenn. 1973).

The experts also agree that Mr. Van Hook had, in addition to arteriosclerosis and hypertension, **atherosclerosis** which is the most common cause of sudden death in adults of Mr. Van Hook's age [50 years] and race. They agreed that one of the left coronary arteries was ninety percent obstructed, the other left coronary artery was fifty percent obstructed, and the right coronary artery was smaller than usual. Van Hook v. Aetna Life Ins. Co., 550 F.Supp. 888, 892 (E.D.Mich.1982).

Coronary atherosclerosis is an insidious, slowly developing condition unrelated to trauma or strain.

"Now the question as to whether the 'slight' exertion of lifting the board to the scaffold had any relation to the heart condition and the subsequent heart attack I would say first that it had no etiological relationship to the heart, condition,

which, despite his denial of symptoms, undoubtedly existed before the strain occurred. The next question to be answered is: Can a strain precipitate thrombosis in a coronary vessel that is already atherosclerotic? In answer to this I quote directly from a chapter on Trauma and Heart Disease by Dr. Paul D. White and myself from Trauma and Disease edited by Brahdy and Kahn ... 'Probably yes, in infrequent cases. Certainly in the large majority of instances sudden occlusion of a coronary artery takes place when the patient is at rest, often at night, when the slowing of the blood stream may play a role. Occasionally, however, there appears to be a direct relationship between trauma and coronary thrombosis. A few minutes, a few hours, or a day or two after some fall or blow, or other physical strain typical coronary occlusion may set in." Williams v. Fuqua, 101 S.E.2d 562, 564 (Sup.Ct.App.Va.1958).

Other Authorities: Zeck v. U.S., 559 F.Supp. 1345, 1348–9 (D.S.Dak.1983); Pierce v. Kentucky Galvanizing Co., Inc., 606 S.W.2d 165–7 (Ct.App.Ky.1980); Fain v. St. Paul Ins. Co., 602 S.W.2d 577, 580 (Ct.App.Tex.1980); Community Life & Health Ins. Co. v. McCall, 497 S.W.2d 358 (Ct.App.Tex. 1973); Watkins v. Underwriters at Lloyd's London, 481 P.2d 849, 852 (Ariz.1971).

athetosis (ath"ĕ-to'sis) [Gr. *athetos* not fixed + *-osis*] a derangement marked by ceaseless occurrence of slow, sinuous, writhing movements, especially severe in the hands, and performed involuntarily; it may occur after hemiplegia, and is then known as *posthemiplegic chorea.* Called also *mobile spasm.*

A profound **athetosis** (a nervous disorder marked by continual slow movements);... Schnebly v. Baker, 217 N.W.2d 708, 716 (Iowa 1974).

atlas (at'las) [Gr. *Atlas* the Greek god who bears up the pillars of Heaven] [NA], the first cervical vertebra, which articulates above with the occipital bone and below with the axis. See also *vertebrae, cervical.*

atrial septal defect See *defect, atrial septal.*

atrophic skin See *atrophy.*

atrophy (at'ro-fe) [L., Gr. *atrophia*] a wasting away; a diminution in the size of a cell, tissue, organ, or part.

Q. Why would the condition of the skin be important?
A. **Atrophic** skin, a devitalized skin means a lessened amount of blood is getting to the skin of the extremities. Isgett v. Seaboard Coast Line Ry. Co., 332 F.Supp. 1127, 1134 (D.S.Car. 1971).

atrophy, bilateral optic

The principal factual issue at trial in this negligence action was whether the defendant's product, Parnon, was the cause of the plaintiff's blindness, more specifically, his condition of **bilateral optic atrophy**. While working for a commercial rose grower, the plaintiff had sprayed roses with Parnon, and he claimed that his loss of vision was caused by toxic agents in that product. The jury found for the defendant. Diaz v. Eli Lilly & Co., 440 N.E.2d 518, 519 (App.Ct.Mass.1982).

atrophy, Leber's optic a hereditary disorder of males characterized by bilateral progressive optic atrophy, with onset usually at about the age of twenty. It is thought to be an X-linked trait.

Leber's Optic Atrophy is a rare disease of unknown etiology which attacks the optic nerves. The disease is thought to be attributable in part to hereditary factors. However, there is no history of the disease in Gunter's family....

... **Leber's Optic Atrophy** is not well understood by the medical profession, and consequently, petitioners' expert could not say that the chemicals to which Gunter was exposed did not trigger or accelerate the disease. In fact, petitioners produced no evidence of any cause of the impairment of Gunter's eyesight other than the suggestion that the blindness may have occurred spontaneously....

... Gunter showed conclusively that: (1) he worked for over a year in an environment containing toxic chemicals known to have inflammatory effects on nerve fibers; (2) the temperature of his work environment and the amount of chemicals present were such that the chemicals could have had the effect of causing the disability; (3) he is older than the usual victim of **Leber's Optic Atrophy**; (4) although the disease is thought to be in part a result of hereditary factors, there is no incidence of the disease in his family; (5) there is no evidence that he was not in good health, with normal eyesight, before his employment, and; (6) there is evidence that at least one of the chemicals to which he was exposed is a cause of or a precipitating factor in the onset of retrobulbar neuritis, a condition associated with the onset of **Leber's Optic Atrophy**. Parsons Corp. of Cal. v. Director, Office of Wkrs., 619 F.2d 38, 40, 42 (9th Cir. 1980).

atrophy, optic atrophy of the optic disk resulting from degeneration of the nerve fibers of the optic nerve and optic tract.

He diagnosed arteriosclerosis of the retinal vessels in both eyes, and **optic atrophy** in the left eye.... Gudlis v. Califano, 452 F.Supp. 401, 404 (N.D.Ill.1978).

atrophy, peroneal neuromuscular See *atrophy, progressive neuropathic (peroneal) muscular.*

atrophy, progressive neuropathic (peroneal) muscular a hereditary form of muscular atrophy, beginning in the muscles supplied by the peroneal nerves, progressing slowly to involve the muscles of the hands and arms. Called also *peroneal a., Charcot-Marie-Tooth a.* or *disease, Charcot-Marie type, Tooth type,* and *progressive neural muscular (neuromuscular) a.*

Dr. Griffin testified that he had never heard of anyone breaking such a heavy addiction himself, and that **Charcot-Marie-Tooth disease** is a rare, progressive, neurological illness which is not always continuously painful and that treatment must be symptomatic. Although the illness itself could not be treated, the pain should be carefully controlled. Plaintiff, once he withdrew from drugs, suffered only such pain as could easily be controlled by empirin, and treatment with narcotics was not necessary. Ballenger v. Crowell, 247 S.E.2d 287, 289–90 (Ct. App.N.Car.1978).

Dr. Tyler gave as his diagnosis "Liver disease of undetermined etiology, and possible **Charcot-Marie-Tooth disease**." The latter is a chronic nerve tissue disease which leads to muscular paralysis and atrophy. At the time of his discharge, claimant was totally disabled, diagnosis was not positive, and it had not

been determined whether the disease was caused by the injury. Benites v. Industrial Com'n, 467 P.2d 911–12 (Ariz.1970).

Crawford has been afflicted with a rare neurological disorder known as **peroneal neuromuscular atrophy**, also referred to as **Charcot-Marie-Tooth disease** (CMT), for approximately 30 years prior to the Potomac disaster.[53] [[53] The disease in question is a slowly developing degenerative condition which affects the nerves and muscles below the knee, resulting finally in the disappearance of muscle tissue through atrophy thus leaving only skin and bones. By the time of the trial, approximately 90% of the muscles in both legs were absent in Crawford's case.] Petition of U.S., 303 F.Supp. 1282, 1320 (E.D.N.Car. 1969).

atrophy, Sudeck's See *dystrophy, reflex sympathetic*; and *osteoporosis, posttraumatic.*

... **Sudeck's atrophy**, the loss of calcium in the ankle bones, causing brittleness. Fancher v. Overhead Doors, Inc., 425 So. 2d 965, 966 (Ct.App.La.1983).

The Doctor also stated that his clinical examination of the right ankle disclosed no sign of "**Sudeck's atrophy**", a neurovascular problem which can develop from trauma. Jones v. Workmen's Comp. Appeal Bd., 412 A.2d 686, 687 (Commonwealth Ct.Pa.1980).

atropine (at'ro-pēn) [USP] chemical name: *endo-*($+$)-*a*-(hydroxymethyl) benzeneacetic acid 8-methyl-8-azabicyclo[3.2.1]oct-3-yl ester. An alkaloid, $C_{17}H_{23}NO_3$, derived from species of belladonna, hyoscyamus, or strammonium, or produced synthetically, and occurring as white crystals, usually needle-like, or as a white, crystalline powder. Atropine is an anticholinergic and is used chiefly as an antispasmodic to relax smooth muscles; to relieve the tremor and rigidity of parkinsonism; to increase the heart rate by blocking the vagus nerve; as an antidote for various toxic and anticholinesterase agents; and as an antisecretory, mydriatic, and cycloplegic.

While **atropine** helps cure iritis by dilating the pupil, isoptocarpine constricts the pupil. For this reason, isopto-carpine should not be used by a patient with iritis. Harris v. Robert C. Groth, M.D., Inc., 663 P.2d 113, 114 (Wash.1983).

Dr. O'Donoghue prescribed **atropine** as premedication in preparation for surgery. Burrow v. Widder, 368 N.E.2d 443, 446 (App.Ct.Ill.1977).

This court was unfamiliar with its characteristics until we resorted to the United States Dispensatory and Physicians' Pharmacology (26th ed.) (Library of Congress Catalog Card Number 67–17443). There we learn that stramonium and belladonna, the active ingredients of Asthmador, are among the sources of **atropine**, the racemic form of an alkaloid, 1-hyoscyamine. The central effects of **atropine** may be attributed to central stimulation of the vagus nerve and of the respiratory center. There is also a primary depressant action on certain motor mechanisms. Toxic doses, however, after causing restlessness, disorientation, and delirium, ultimately will produce paralysis of the medulla. Under reference to "Actions and Uses" and a subhead "Respiratory Effects" it is noted that it is used to check hay fever and for bronchial asthma. The effect of overdoses is outlined under "Toxicology," where it is stated: "**Atropine** poisoning may occur from the ingestion of any of the numerous plants of which it is the active principle, most frequently however, from either belladonna or stramonium.... The most striking symptom is the delirium. In the early stages this manifests itself simply by profuse and incoherent talkativeness; later there is complete confusion, often with hallucinations, sometimes maniacal in character." [4] [[4] Taking overdoses of the drug is said not usually to be fatal. It is sold over the counter in drug stores.] In re H.L.R., 75 Cal.Rptr. 308, 310–11 (Ct.App.Cal.1969).

attenuation (ah-ten"u-a'shun) [L. *attenuatio*, from *ad* to + *tenuis* thin] the alteration of the virulence of a pathogenic microorganism by passage through another host species, decreasing the virulence of the organism for the native host and increasing it for the new host.

An **attenuated** polio virus is one which laboratory processes have rendered incapable of producing disease (to the extent of **attenuation**), but which ratains sufficient strength to cause the production of antibodies to resist and destroy an attacking wild or virulent polio virus in the vaccinee's alimentary tract. Reyes v. Wyeth Laboratories, 498 F.2d 1264, 1278, 1296 (5th Cir. 1974).

audiogram (aw'de-o-gram") [L. *audire* to hear + Gr. *gramma* a writing] a record of the thresholds of hearing of an individual for various sound frequencies. See also *test, bone conduction.*

The analysis of the relevant **audiograms** further established that, in the opinion of those testifying, the hearing aids sold to Vanderhaeven and Dill were either unnecessary or inadequate. Milligan v. Hearing Aid Dispensers Exam. Comm., 191 Cal.Rptr. 490, 493 (Ct.App.Cal.1983).

Dr. Guttman examined petitioner on July 18, 1978, at which time he performed various tests, including an **audiogram**. Dr. Guttman's diagnosis was that petitioner had a bilateral sensorineural hearing impairment. According to Dr. Guttman, the results of the tests performed on petitioner were inconsistent with a finding that petitioner's hearing impairment was caused by noise exposure. Dr. Guttman gave the following bases for this opinion, first, the **audiogram** did not show the presence of an acoustic notch, a unique characteristic of noise-induced hearing impairment; second, there was no evidence of recruitment, a condition peculiar to two causes of hearing loss, one cause being exposure to acoustic trauma; third, petitioner had a markedly depressed discrimination score, uncharacteristic of noise-induced hearing impairment; and fourth, petitioner's complaints of tinnitus postdated his hearing loss. United Elec. Coal Co. v. Industrial Com'n, 444 N.E.2d 115, 117 (Ill.1982).

audiological screening test See *test, audiological screening.*

audiologist (aw"de-ol'o-jist) a person skilled in audiology, including the rehabilitation of those whose impaired hearing cannot be improved by medical or surgical means.

... the "**audiologist**," a trained specialist in the evaluation and rehabilitation of persons with hearing disorders (21 C.F.R. § 801.420(a)(4)). New Jersey Guild of Hearing Aid D. v. Long, 384 A.2d 795, 801 (N.J.1978).

audiology (aw"de-ol'o-je) [L. *audire* to hear + *-logy*] the science of hearing, particularly the study of impaired hearing that cannot be improved by medication or surgical therapy.

T.C.A. § 63–1703(f) defines "audiologist" as:
"One who practices **audiology**;..." Subsection (g) establishes:
"The practice of **audiology**" means the application of nonmedical principles, methods, and procedures of measurement, testing, appraisal, prediction, consultation, counseling, and instruction relat[ing] to hearing and disorders of hearing for the purpose of modifying communicative disorders involving speech, language, auditory function, or other aberrant behavior related to hearing loss.... Levy v. State Bd. of Examiners for Speech Path., 578 S.W.2d 646, 648–9 (Ct. App.Tenn.1978)
... Pursuant to the hearing, the Board determined that to be licensed as an audiologist or to have been so engaged for the statutory time requisite, one should be capable of applying:
A wide variety of testing techniques utilizing, in some instances, sophisticated equipment to determine the "site of lesion" or cause of hearing disfunction. Working in this capacity as audiologists would have the capability of utilizing, where appropriate, such tests as the pure-tone audiometry test, the impedience audiometry test, the Bekesy audiometry test, the loudness balance test, and the tone decay test.
Further:
Once the site of lesion or cause of a hearing disfunction is determined, the audiologists, again in conjunction with a doctor of medicine, has the capability of utilizing a number of rehabilitative or habilitative techniques aimed at the hearing disfunction. Such techniques include drill work to develop lipreading abilities or sound differentation, counseling on the social and psychological aspects of a hearing disfunction, use of amplification devices, including hearing aids and auditory training.

auditory nerve See *nervus vestibulocochlearis.*

augmentation, mammary See *implant* (Henderson case); *auxesis*; and *auxetic.*

auris (aw'ris), pl. *au'res* [L.] [NA] the ear; the organ of hearing. See also *ear.*

auris externa [NA], external ear: the portion of the auditory organ comprising the auricle and the external acoustic meatus.

auris interna [NA], internal ear: the labyrinth, comprising the vestibule, cochlea, and semicircular canals; called also *inner ear.*

auris media [NA], middle ear: it includes the space medial to the tympanic membrane (mesotympanum), the epitympanum, and the hypotympanum, and it contains the auditory ossicles and connects with the mastoid cells and auditory tube. Called also *cavum tympani* [NA alternative], *eardrum, tympanic cavity,* and *tympanum.*

auscultation (aws"kul-ta'shun) the act of listening for sounds within the body, chiefly for ascertaining the condition of the lungs, heart, pleura, abdomen and other organs, and for the detection of pregnancy.

autoclave (aw'to-klāv) [*auto-* + L. *clavis* key] an apparatus for effecting sterilization by steam under pressure; it is fitted with a gauge that automatically regulates the pressure, and therefore the degree of heat to which the contents are subjected.

The package, as thus wrapped and taped, thereafter would be taken from the Minor Surgery Department to Central Supply for sterilization by a device known as an "Autoclave." That device subjected the item to procedures that assured elimination of germs, bacteria or other contaminants. In the course of sterilization in the **autoclave**, the special cream colored tape that was used to seal the package containing the item underwent a change to a wholly different appearance. Black diagonal lines, measuring a couple of millimeters in diameter became visible upon the tape. Those markings upon the tape gave assurance of the sterility of the contents of the package. The package was marked with the Doctor's name and dated 14 days ahead, the period the item would remain sterile. Suburban Hospital Ass'n v. Hadary, 322 A.2d 258, 262 (Ct.Spec. App.Md.1974).

Boiling or **autoclaving** the denture after fabrication would warp it and change its shape. Germann v. Matriss, 260 A.2d 825, 830 (N.J.1970).

autogenous (aw-toj'ĕ-nus) [*auto-* + *genesis*] self-generated; originated within the body. As applied to bacterial vaccines, the term denotes those vaccines which are made from the patient's own bacteria, as opposed to stock vaccines which are made from standard cultures. In transplantation immunology, denoting tissue arising, transferred, or transplanted within an individual.

The most desirable bone implant as a grafting material is what is known medically as **autogenous** bone taken from one part of the patient's body and implanted in another part of the body where the defect exists. The advantages of this type of bone implant is that it normally will not produce an antigen-antibody reaction in the implant site and possesses an osteogenic or bone-making capacity of its own which complements that of the host bone in producing a successful graft. The procedure for utilizing **autogenous** bone has marked disadvantages, however, in that it requires two operations simultaneously at different sites in the patient's body; such second operation presents possibilities of infection, discomfort, morbidity, and other harmful effects. E. R. Squibb & Sons, Inc. v. Stickney, 274 So. 2d 898, 900 (Dist.Ct.App.Fla.1973).

. . . autogenous bone—bone coming from the patient's own body;. . . . E. R. Squibb & Sons, Inc. v. Jordan, 254 So.2d 17, 19 (Dist.Ct.App.Fla.1971).

autograft (aw'to-graft) a graft of tissue derived from another site in or on the body of the organism receiving it; called also *autologous* or *autochthonous graft*, and *autoplast.*

A "homograft" is distinguished from an "**autograft**" in that the latter procedure involves a skin transplant from another portion of the patient's own body, whereas the former involves a skin transplant to the patient from a separate donor. Fleming v. Michigan Mutual Liability Co., 363 F.2d 186, 187 (5th Cir. 1966).

automatic (aw"to-mat'ik) [Gr. *automatos* self-acting] spontaneous or involuntary; done by no act of the will.

Q. When you say "**automatic** behavior" what type of behavior do you consider to be **automatic** behavior?

A. Well, it's **automatic** in the sense that it is not voluntarily motivated by the brain. It is **automatic** in the sense that he is unconscious, that the patient is unconscious of what he is do-

ing. He may continue to walk. He may drive an automobile. He may do anything. People v. Williams, 99 Cal.Rptr. 103, 120 (Ct.App.Cal.1971).

automatism (aw-tom'ah-tizm) [Gr. *automatismos* self-action] the performance of nonreflex acts without conscious volition; called also *automatic behavior.*

autopsy (aw'top-se) [*auto-* + Gr. *opsis* view] the postmortem examination of a body, including the internal organs and structures after dissection, so as to determine the cause of death or the nature of pathological changes. Called also *necropsy.*

I am not familiar with the rules in [New Jersey] but certainly in New York City all maternal deaths are immediate medical examiner's case and an **autopsy** is required in every case. It has been shown again and again that this is the only way that one can learn and profit by previous poor results. Without the information obtained at an **autopsy**, all we can state for certain is that it is not clear as to why Mrs. Maslonka died. . . .

. . . Under the statute the decision to perform an **autopsy** rests with the county medical examiner, not the treating physician, although the State Medical Examiner, the assignment judge, the prosecutor or the Attorney General may also authorize an **autopsy**. N.J.S.A. 52:17B–88. Maslonka v. Hermann, 414 A.2d 1350, 1353, 1357 (Super.Ct. N.J.1980).

Dr. Andrews made a thorough and complete **autopsy** on the body of Main. He examined the body cavities for abnormal accumulations of fluid and checked to be sure that the lungs were not filled with air. He examined all of the vital organs, including the abdominal organs and major blood vessels. He examined the heart, liver, gall bladder, pancreas, spleen, both kidneys, bladder, prostate, adrenal glands, stomach, esophagus, small intestine and large intestine. He examined the body to determine whether there were any lymph nodes. He checked the thyroid gland. He examined the brain and took samples of the blood, the spinal fluid, and the urine. Chemical tests were made of the blood, the spinal fluid, and urine. He made a thorough and complete examination of all of Main's vital organs for every possible cause of death. He took blocks of tissue from all the vital organs, subjected them to a preservative solution, mounted portions of the tissue taken from each of such blocks on microscopic slides, and stained and examined them under the microscope. The blocks of tissue were embedded in paraffin and they and the microscopic slides were preserved for further examination. He found no evidence of injury, infirmity, or disease in any of the organs. Metropolitan Life Ins. Co. v. Main, 383 F.2d 952, 955–6 (5th Cir. 1967).

auxesis (awk-se'sis) [Gr. *auxēsis*] increase in the size of an organism; often used specifically to designate increase in volume of an organism as a result of growth of its individual cells, without increase in their number.

auxetic (awk-set'ik) [Gr. *auxētikos* growing] 1. pertaining to auxesis. 2. a substance that stimulates auxesis.

AVA See *angioma, arteriovenus.*

aversive stimuli See *stimulus, aversive.*

avulsion (ah-vul'shun) [L. *avulsio*, from *a*-away + *vellere* to pull] the tearing away of a part of structure.

... a one and one-half inch avulsion on his left cheek,... Blanchard v. City of Bridgeport, 463 A.2d 553, 556 (Conn. 1983).

He suffered scalp **avulsion** (a hole the size of a nickel in his scalp), cervical strain, numbness of the left hand and multiple contusions. Landry v. Aetna Ins. Co., 422 So.2d 1287, 1289 (Ct.App.La.1982), remanded 429 So.2d 150 (1983).

axilla (ak-sil'ah), pl. *axil'lae* [L.] [NA] a small pyramidal space between the upper lateral part of the chest and the medial side of the arm, and including, in addition to the armpit, axillary vessels, the brachial plexus of nerves, a large number of lymph nodes, and fat and loose areolar tissue; called also *armpit, fossa axillaris*, and *axillary space*. See also *node, lymph* (Lopez case).

At that time, I advised him to have an **axillary** dissection and a skin graft in the area of his original melanoma. That was performed May 1, 1972, and it revealed that the malignancy had spread from the original site into the lymph nodes and that two of the twenty nodes in his armpit were positive for malignancy. Cox v. Ulysses Cooperative Oil and Supply Co., 544 P.2d 363, 368 (Kan.1975).

When malignancy was discovered, a radical mastectomy was performed. Metastasis was suspected during surgery, as a result of which "all lymph glands that they could find in the **axilla** ... everyone in sight" were also removed. Metastasis was

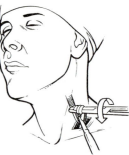

Avulsion of a phrenic nerve.

confirmed on pathologic report the following day. Lopez v. Swyer, 279 A.2d 116, 119 (Super.Ct.N.J.1971).

axillary See *axilla*.

axis (ak'sis), pl. *ax'es* [L.; Gr. *axōn* axle] [NA] the second cervical vertebra; called also *epistropheus, odontoid vertebra*, and *vertebra dentata*. See also *vertebrae, cervical*.

azotemia (az"o-te'me-ah) [*azote* + Gr. *haima* blood + *-ia*] an excess of urea or other nitrogenous bodies in the blood.

The warning stated that "[i]n patients with impaired kidney function or with prerenal **azotemia**, systemic use of neomycin sulfate may result in irreversible deafness...." Richards v. Upjohn Co., 625 P.2d 1192, 1194 (Ct.App. New Mex.1980).

B

Babcock clamp See *clamp, Babcock*.

Babcock-Bacon "pull-through" operation See *proctosigmoidectomy*.

Babinski's reflex, response, sign and test See under *reflex*; and *sign*.

baby (ba'be) an infant; a child not yet able to walk.

baby, intrauterine growth retarded

An **IUGR baby** is one which has been carried in the uterus the full gestational period or longer, yet which has a relatively low birth weight. Characteristically, an **IUGR baby** has wasted, flaccid buttocks but a normal sized head. Studies indicate that they have a fairly high mortality rate and, in those that survive, there is an increased risk of neurological abnormalities. Freed v. Priore, 372 A.2d 895, 898 (Super.Ct.Pa.1977).

Bacillus (bah-sil'lus) [L. "little rod"] a genus of microorganisms of the family Bacillaceae, order Eubacteriales, including large gram-positive, aerobic, spore-forming bacteria separated into 33 species, of which three are pathogenic, or potentially pathogenic, and the remainder are saprophytic soil forms. Many organisms historically called *Bacillus* are now classified in other genera.

Bacillus subtilis a common saprophytic soil and water form, often occurring as a laboratory contaminant, and

in rare instances found in apparently causal relation to pathologic processes, such as conjunctivitis.

... the Claimant was exposed to silica, **bacillus subtilis**, and other ingredients used in the manufacture of the soap products and other products mentioned above.

Solely as a result of the exposure mentioned above, the Claimant contracted chronic obstructive restrictive pulmonary disease, from which he became totally disabled.... Purex, Inc. v. W.C.A.B. (Oden), 454 A.2d 203, 205 (Commonwealth Ct.Pa.1982).

back (bak) the posterior part of the trunk from the neck to the pelvis; called also *dorsum* [NA]. See also *spine*; and *vertebra*.

Back disabilities in particular shout loudly for expert advice. No human ailment has produced more medicolegal headaches than the aching **back**. This delicately articulated structure of nodulated bones, cushioned by cartilaginous bodies and gelatinous material, interlaced by the complex and sensitive fibers of the cerebrospinal nervous system and held in array by strands and cords of muscular and ligamentous tissue, is vulnerable to a vast and bewildering variety of traumatic, pathological, deteriorative ailments and neurotic manifestations, singly and in diverse combinations. Precise diagnosis often baffles neurologists and orthopedists. In assessing the respective roles of trauma and predisposing conditions and of objective and subjective complaints, subtle value judgments may be unavoidable. In the face of this anatomical, physiological and psychological intricacy, semantically dubious, pseudomedical jargon infiltrates the conflux of medicine and jurisprudence. Whiplash, traumatic arthritis, traumatic neurasthenia and railroad spine are solecisms in current or past fashion. These verbal conveniences tempt the medically untrained into complacent substitution of simplicity for complexity. In a field which forces the experts into hypothesis, unaided lay judgment amounts to nothing more than speculation. [Footnote omitted.] Peter Kiewit Sons v. Industrial Accident Com'n, 44 Cal.Rptr. 813, 818–19 (Dist Ct.App.Cal.1965).

back strain See *strain, back.*

Bacteria (bak-te´re-ah) in some systems of classification, a division of the kingdom Procaryotae, including all prokaryotic organisms that are not blue-green algae. See also *Cyanophyceae.* In other systems, prokaryotic organisms without a true cell wall are considered to be unrelated to the Bacteria and are placed in a separate class—the Mollicutes.

bacteria Aerobacter See *Aerobacter.*

bactericide (bak-ter´ĭ-sīd) an agent that destroys bacteria. See also *moldicide* (Chip Steak Co. case).

The method of combating bacterial infections of a plant growing in soil infested at the ground surface thereof with harmful bacteria, which comprises applying to the surface of the plant and to the soil surrounding the base of the plant, a halogen-containing organic **bactericide** in bactericidal percentages. Nationwide Chemical Corp. v. Wright, 458 F.Supp. 828, 833 (M.D.Fla.1976).

bacterium (bak-te´re-um), pl. *bacte´ria* [L.; Gr. *baktērion* little rod] in general, any of the unicellular prokaryotic microorganisms that commonly multiply by cell division (fission) and whose cell is typically contained within a cell wall. They may be aerobic or anaerobic, motile or nonmotile, and may be free-living, saprophytic, parasitic, or even pathogenic, the last causing disease in plants or animals. See also *Bacteria.*

Bacteria are commonly classified in accordance with whether they take or reject a so-called Gram stain, named after the scientist who discovered the classification test. Those which take stain are termed gram-positive; those which reject it, gram-negative. Zenith Laboratories, Inc. v. Eli Lilly and Co., 460 F.Supp. 812, 814–15 (D.N.J.1978).

bacterium coliform See *Escherichia coli.*

Bacteroides (bak˝te-roi´dez) a genus of nonsporulating obligate anaerobic filamentous bacteria occurring as normal flora in the mouth and large bowel; often found in necrotic tissue, probably as secondary invaders. Thirty species have been described.

Ten days after the boy's removal to Children's Hospital, the hospital laboratory expert bacteriologist was able to culture and identify the pathogenic organism-**bacteroides**—as the principal agent in the child's infection. This organism is generally found in the human intestinal tract and usually, as a result of an appendectomy, invades the peritoneal cavity. This does not, except on very rare occasions, cause trouble, as the body is normally able to handle the organism. Cases of peritonitis

and resulting septicemia, wherein **bacteroides** is the causative agent, are rare in medical literature,... Rogers v. U.S., 334 F.2d 931, 933 (6th Cir. 1964).

bacteroides (bak˝te-roi´dez) 1. a general term for highly pleomorphic rod-shaped bacteria. 2. a microorganism of the genus *Bacteroides.*

bag (bag) a sac or pouch.

bag, colostomy a receptacle worn over the stoma to receive the fecal discharge from a colostomy.

The hole through the skin of the abdomen gradually enlarged and a **colostomy** bag became necessary. Chester v. U.S., 403 F.Supp. 458, 460 (W.D.Pa.1975).

bagasse See *bagassosis.*

bagassosis (bag˝ah-so´sis) a respiratory disorder due to the inhalation of the dust of bagasse, the waste of sugar cane after the sugar has been extracted.

Bagasse is a pulpy residue obtained from crushing cane in the sugar industry; **bagasse** is ordinarily used as the primary fuel to fire the boilers in the steam generating plant. Hodgson v. Sugar Cane Growers Coop. of Florida, 346 F.Supp. 132, 135 (S.D.Fla.1972), judgment affirmed in part, reversed in part 486 F.2d 1006 (5th Cir. 1973).

Appellants alleged that while working for Grace in 1959 each of them, with the exception of the above three, contracted and sustained permanent disability from "bagassosis", a compensable occupational disease under the Workmen's Accident Compensation Act (Act), 11 L.P.R.A. § 1 et seq. [Footnote omitted.] Bussati v. Grace & Compania, Puerto Rico, 396 F.2d 233, 234 (1st Cir. 1968).

baldness (bawld´nes) alopecia, especially absence of hair from the scalp. See also *alopecia.*

Joel Singer, a plastic surgeon, testified regarding the hereditary nature of **baldness** and that, if a person's father has a certain pattern of **baldness**, his son has a great likelihood of having the same pattern of **baldness**. Blanchard v. City of Bridgeport, 463 A.2d 553, 557–8 (Conn.1983).

By the time he was thirty-three years old, plaintiff David Dixon had male pattern **baldness** and was bald approximately halfway back from the top of his head. Dixon v. Peters, 306 S.E.2d 477, 478 (Ct.App.N.Car.1983).

band (band) in dentistry, a thin strip of metal formed to encircle horizontally the crown of a natural tooth or its root.

Dr. Bernard Bender, a dentist, examined Deep and ordered and installed for him orthodontic appliances. They consisted of eight **bands** and two **arch** wires. Four teeth in his upper jaw and four in his lower were **banded**; the arch wires were attached to and passed through loops in these **bands**. There were no small wires, which actually supply the tension to the appliances, available in Dr. Bender's office at that time....
   ... The doctor stated:
   If the **bands** were left on too long, there is a very good possibility of decay and things like this happening underneath the **bands**. So even during full treatment that takes two years we like to take the **bands** off periodically to clean the patient's teeth, to take X-rays to make sure the teeth are in a

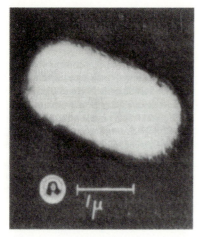

Escherichia coli. (Hedén and Wyckoff, S.A.B. LS-290.)

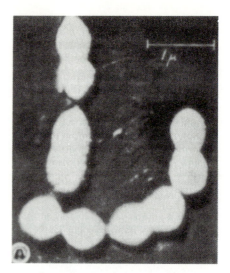

Streptococcus pneumoniae, type 2. (Williams, S.A.B. LS-162.)

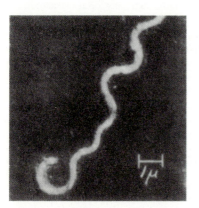

Borrelia vincentii. (Hampp, Scott, and Wyckoff, S.A.B. LS-248.)

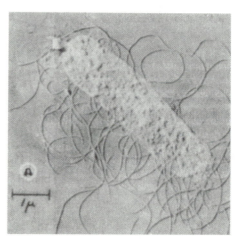

Proteus vulgaris. (Robinow and van Iterson. S.A.B. LS-260.)

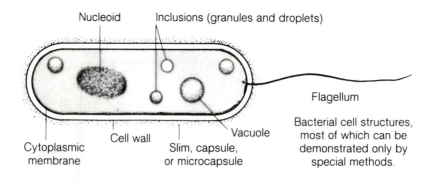

ELECTRON MICROGRAPHS OF VARIOUS MICROORGANISMS, AND DIAGRAM SHOWING VARIOUS STRUCTURES OF TYPICAL BACTERIAL CELL

healthy condition during orthodontic treatment. U.S. v. Deep, 497 F.2d 1316, 1318, 1320 (9th Cir. 1974).

bandage (ban'dij) a strip or roll of gauze or other material for wrapping or binding any part of the body.

bandage, compression a bandage by which pressure is applied to a limb to prevent edema.

The defendant testified that when he placed the **compressive type bandage** on plaintiff's arm he did so with full realization that additional swelling could follow post-operatively and that swelling alone could have the capacity to interfere or embarrass the circulation in the extremity. He testified if the **compressive bandage** were applied too tightly, it could interfere in even a greater way with the circulation of the arm. Casey v. Penn, 360 N.E.2d 93, 95–96 (App.Ct.Ill.1977), opinion supplemented 362 N.E.2d 1373 (1977).

bandage, spica a figure-of-8 bandage with turns that cross one another regularly like the letter V, usually applied to anatomical areas of quite different dimensions, as the pelvis and thigh or the thorax and arm. See illustration.

Bandl's ring See *ring, retraction.*

bar (bahr) in orthodontics, a connector which may consist of a heavy wire or a wrought or cast metal segment, longer than it is wide, which connects different parts of a removable partial denture.

bar, arch a heavy wire shaped to the outer circumference of the dental arch and extending from one side to the other so that intervening teeth may be attached to it; usually used for fixation in jaw fractures.

The maxilla was refractured and a Steinman pin and Jelenko **arch bars** were inserted to treat the jaw fractures. Castellanos v. Industrial Com'n, 488 P.2d 675, 676 (Ct.App.Ariz.1971).

barber's itch See *pseudofolliculitis.*

barbiturate (bar-bit'u-rāt) a salt or derivative of barbituric acid.

It specifically defined the term "**barbiturate**" as meaning "the salts and derivatives of barbituric acid, also known as malonyl urea, having hypnotic or somnifacient actions, and compounds, preparations and mixtures thereof." At that time, Article 726b, V.A.P.C., since repealed, provided that an amphetamine was "commonly called" a **barbiturate**. Lapp v. State, 519 S.W.2d 443, 447 (Ct.Crim.App.Tex.1975).

Frequent use of the **barbiturates** at high dosage levels leads invariably to the development of physical dependence, tolerance and severe withdrawal symptoms, similar to those associated with heroin use. The effects of **barbiturate** intoxication resemble those of alcoholic intoxication. There is a general sluggishness, difficulty in concentrating and thinking, speech impairment, memory lapse, faulty judgment and exaggeration of basic personality traits. Irritability and quarrelsomeness are common. Hostile and paranoid ideas as well as suicidal tendencies can occur. **Barbiturates** are said to be the most frequently used chemical in suicides in the United States. Accidental death from an overdose also can occur. There is a clear association between **barbituric** intoxication and accidents and traffic fatalities. The drug can depress a wide range of func-

tions, including the nerves, skeletal muscles and the cardiac muscle. **Barbiturates** are frequently used by heroin addicts to boost the effect of weak heroin. People v. McCabe, 275 N.E. 2d 407, 411 (Ill.1971).

Both alcohol and **barbiturates** depress the brain center that controls breathing and also controls blood pressure and circulation. When either alcohol or a barbiturate is ingested by a person in sufficient quantity to depress such brain center to the point where the blood will not supply the body with its minimum requirement of oxygen, body tissue dies and death ensues. Metropolitan Life Ins. Co. v. Main, 383 F.2d 952, 956 (5th Cir. 1967).

bariatric See *bariatrics.*

bariatrics (bar″e-at′riks) [Gr. *baros* weight + *iatrikē* medicine, surgery] a field of medicine encompassing the study of overweight, its causes, prevention, and treatment.

The board listed six charges against Zwick: (1) dispensing 3,403,503 dosage units of anorectic controlled substance (mostly amphetamine compounds) to **bariatric** patients (**bariatric** medicine deals with the treatment of obesity) on or about October 1, 1972, through July 27, 1975;.... Ohio State Medical Bd. v. Zwick, 392 N.E.2d 1276, 1277 (Ct.App.Ohio 1978).

The Court further finds that the Defendants by means of order forms issued under Title 21, United States Code, Section 828 obtained anorectic controlled substances through interstate commerce in the amount of 3,886,634 dosage units from October, 1972 through October, 1975 for the purpose of dispensing in the conduct of his medical **bariatric** practice [See Standards appended at page 117 this case] which involved a substantial number of patients who were being treated for obesity. U.S. v. Zwick, 413 F.Supp. 113, 114 (N.D.Ohio 1976).

Barr body test See *chromatin-positive.*

bartholin cyst See *glandula, vestibularis major.*

basal metabolism See *metabolism, basal.*

basilar fracture of the skull See *basilaris cranii.*

basilaris (bas″ĭ-la′ris) [L.] situated at the base.

basilaris cranii a composite of the numerous bones which serve the brain as a supportive floor and form the axis of the whole skull.

A diagnosis of **basilar fracture of the skull** was made and she was transported in a comatose condition to, and hospitalized at, the Medical University of South Carolina Hospital, in Charleston, South Carolina, for treatment of a concussion, laceration of the right mastoid area, right basilar skull fracture, draining blood from her right ear, and a fracture of the left index finger. Doyle v. U.S., 441 F.Supp. 701, 706 (D.S.Car. 1977).

basophil (ba′so-fil) [Gr. *basis* base + *philein* to love] a granular leukocyte with an irregularly shaped, relatively pale-staining nucleus that is partially constricted into two lobes, and with cytoplasm that contains coarse bluish

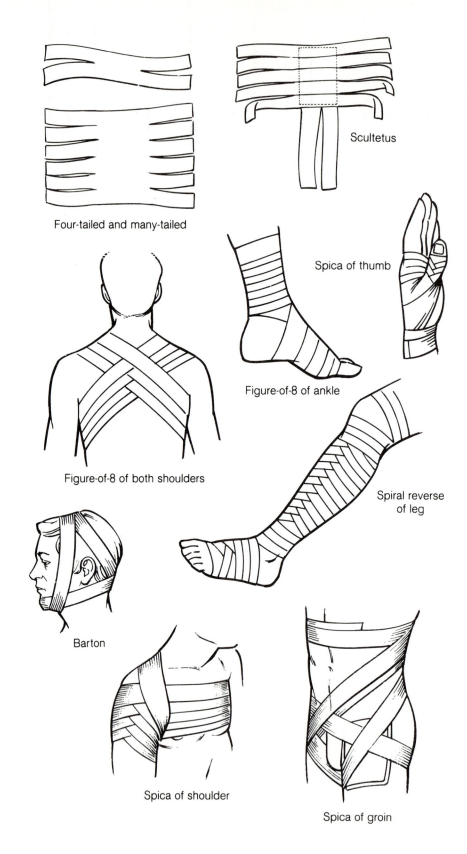

Four-tailed and many-tailed

Scultetus

Spica of thumb

Figure-of-8 of ankle

Figure-of-8 of both shoulders

Spiral reverse of leg

Barton

Spica of shoulder

Spica of groin

VARIOUS TYPES OF BANDAGE

black granules of variable size. Basophils contain vasoactive amines, e.g., histamine and serotonin, which are released on appropriate stimulation. Called also *basophilic leukocytes*.

bath (bath) 1. a conductive or convective medium, as water, vapor, sand, or mud, with which the body is laved or in which the body is wholly or partly immersed for therapeutic or cleansing purposes; called also *balneum*. 2. the application of a conductive or convective medium to the body for therapeutic or cleansing purposes. 3. a piece of equipment or scientific apparatus in which a body or object may be immersed.

bath, whirlpool a variously sized tank in which the body or an extremity can be submerged as the heated water is mechanically agitated.

Although Dr. Perrine stated in his affidavit of February 24, 1981, that the **whirlpool baths** "aggravated and inflamed the infected left kidney causing its surgical removal," the testimony given by deposition on March 9, 1981, is far less positive. There he states only that in his opinion the baths "could have allowed" the incursion of additional bacteria but that any aggravation could equally well have come from another source and, moreover, that it was unlikely that the baths could have caused the kidney stone to form. Wade v. Thomasville Orthopedic Clinic, 306 S.E.2d 366, 370 (Ct.App.Ga.1983).

battered child See *syndrome, battering parent*.

battered-child syndrome See under *syndrome*.

battering parent See *syndrome, battering parent*.

bead (bēd) a small spherical structure or mass.

At the time of the trial, plaintiff had developed numerous small "**beads**" underneath the left eyelid which were causing her pain and discomfort. Obviously plaintiff will have to seek further medical attention in regard to this condition. Hukill v. U.S. Fidelity and Guaranty Co., 386 So.2d 172, 174 (Ct.App.La. 1980).

beam (bēm) a unidirectional or approximately unidirectional emission of electromagnetic radiation or particles.

"Q.   What is a straight AP port?
"A.   I started out with two converging **beams** AP, meaning anterior-posterior, then using the time dose relationship, it is of critical importance in radiotherapy, having used these converging anterior fields, I would then treat a lateral area directed at the deep pelvic nodes and then a posterior area, that then would allow a long interval of time for the skin on the front of her pelvis to recover normally and possibly tolerate additional radiation if the other portals didn't permit delivery of this critical 4,000 R tumor dose." Hecht v. First National Bank & Trust Co., 490 P.2d 649, 652 (Kan.1971).

beat (bēt) a throb or pulsation, as of the heart or of an artery. See also *pulse*.

beat, ectopic a heart beat originating at some point other than the sinus node.

A.   Well, in order to explain these things, I have previously mentioned, I would just say that back to the heart, an **ectopic beat** just means a beat that comes in out of time. There are

numerous types of these. Fain v. St. Paul Ins. Co., 602 S.W.2d 577, 580 (Ct.App.Tex.1980).

bedsore See *ulcer, decubitus*.

beer (bēr) the fermented infusion of malted barley and hops.

Under § 563.01, F.S., relative to "**beer**", as well as malt beverages, it is defined to mean all brewed beverages containing malt,.... Castlewood International Corp. v. Wynne, 305 So. 2d 773, 776 (Fla.1974).

beetle See *Lasioderma serricorne; Carpophilus hemipterus;* and *Tribolium*.

behavior, automatic See *automatic;* and *automatism*.

belief See *knowledge*.

bel (bel) the common logarithm of the ratio of two powers, usually electric or acoustic powers; such ratios are usually expressed in decibels (q.v.). An increase of one bel in intensity approximately doubles the loudness of most sounds.

belladonna (bel"ah-don'ah) [Ital. "fair lady"] the *Atropa belladonna* L. (Solanaceae), or deadly nightshade, a perennial plant indigenous to central and southern Europe and cultivated in North America, containing various anticholinergic alkaloids (e.g., atropine, hyoscyamine, belladonnine, scopolamine, etc.), some of which are produced during the extraction process. Called also *banewort, death's herb,* and *dwale. Belladonna leaf* [USP], consisting of the dried leaves and fruiting tops of *A. belladonna* or *A. belladonna* var. *acuminata*, is used in the preparation of standardized dosage forms; see under *extract* and *tincture*. The root has also been used. See also *atropine*.

... tincture of **belladonna**, a toxic and bad-tasting drug which, if misued, may cause heart disorders,.... Dodson v. Parham, 427 F.Supp. 97, 106–7 (N.D.Ga.1977).

Bender-Gestalt test See *test, Bender gestalt*.

Bendectin (ben-dek'tin) trademark for tablets containing a combination of dicyclomine hydrochloride, doxylamine succinate, and pyridoxine hydrochloride; used in management of nausea and vomiting during pregnancy.

The child suffered from a combination of birth defects, which included malformed and missing fingers and a missing pectoral muscle. Thereafter, she extensively investigated the possible origin of her son's injury and became convinced that a drug she had ingested for nausea during the pregnancy was the cause. That drug, **Bendectin**, is manufactured by the defendant. Mekdeci by and through Mekdeci v. Merrell Nat. Labs., 711 F.2d 1510, 1512 (11th Cir. 1983).

benign (be-nīn') [L. *benignus*] not malignant; not recurrent; favorable for recovery. See also *tumor, benign*.

"Q.   Doctor, when cancerous tissue is removed, the pathologist sees some **benign** tissue around the entire mass, generally isn't that true?

"A.   Almost always.

"Q.   And **benign** is what for the jury's benefit?

''A. **Benign** is non-cancerous tissue. Shapiro v. Burkons, 404 N.E.2d 778, 783 (Ct.App.Ohio 1978).

benthic

Benthic organisms include mussels and fiddler crabs. Conservation Council of North Carolina v. Constanzo, 398 F.Supp. 653, 661 (E.D.N.Car.1975).

benzalkonium chloride (ben"zal-ko'ne-um) [NF] a mixture of alkylbenzyl dimethylammonium chlorides of the general formula, $[C_6H_5CH_2N(CH_3)_2 \ R]CL$. A rapidly acting surface disinfectant and detergent, occurring as a white or yellowish white, thick gel or gelatinous pieces, which is active against both gram-negative and gram-positive bacteria and certain viruses, fungi, yeasts, and protozoa; applied topically to the skin and mucous membranes. It is also used as an antimicrobial preservative in ophthalmic solution.

Sterilization of the menghini needles after use was undertaken by the Hospital. This was commenced by the washing and soaking of the used needle in **Zephiran** and its subsequent placement within a sealed test tube. Suburban Hospital Ass'n v. Hadary, 322 A.2d 258, 262 (Ct.Spec.App.Md.1974).

Immediately thereafter, it was placed in a plastic, self-sealing bag holding **zephiran chloride**, a disinfectant also compatible with the composition of acrylic dentures. Germann v. Matriss, 55 N.J. 193, 198, 260 A.2d 825, 827 (1970).

Benzedrine (ben'zĕ-drēn) trademark for preparations of amphetamine sulfate. See also *amphetamine sulfate*.

benzene (ben'zēn) a colorless volatile liquid hydrocarbon, C_6H_6, obtained mainly as a by-product in the destructive distillation of coal, along with coal tar, etc. It has an aromatic odor, and burns with a light-giving flame. It dissolves sulfur, phosphorus, iodine, and organic compounds. The fumes may cause fatal poisoning. It was formerly used as a pulmonary antiseptic in influenza, etc., as a teniacide, externally as a parasiticide, and has been suggested in leukemias. Called also *benzol*. See also *dripolene* (Martinez case).

Benzene is a ubiquitous hydrocarbon compound (C_6H_6) that is manufactured for a wide variety of industrial uses.[8] . . . [[8] Although **benzene** does occur naturally in small quantities (a few parts per billion) in certain substances, including the ambient air, it is produced in substantial quantities by the petroleum and steel industries. The production of **benzene** is rapidly expanding, and at present only eleven other chemicals and only one other hydrocarbon are produced in greater tonnage in the United States. See 43 Fed.Reg. 5918] . . . .

. . . **Benzene** has been recognized since 1900 as a toxic substance capable of producing acute and chronic nonmalignant effects in humans. When **benzene** vapors are inhaled, the **benzene** diffuses rapidly through the lungs and is quickly absorbed into the blood. Acute circulatory failure resulting in death within minutes often accompanies exposure to **benzene** concentrations as high as 20,000 ppm. Other acute effects of exposure to milder, though still high (250–500 ppm), concentrations of **benzene** include vertigo, nervous excitation, headache, nausea, and breathlessness. When exposure is stopped, rapid recovery from these symptoms usually occurs.

The most common nonmalignant effects of chronic exposure to low **benzene** concentration levels are a non-functioning bone marrow and deficiencies in the formed elements of the blood. The degree of severity of such disorders ranges from mild and transient episodes to severe and fatal effects. Chromosomal aberrations have also been associated with chronic **benzene** exposure, and dermatitis or other dermal infections can be caused by direct bodily contact with liquid **benzene** . . . .

. . . [During the 1970's several additional studies reported a statistically significant increased risk of leukemia among workers occupationally exposed to high levels of **benzene** and concluded **benzene** was a leukemogen.] [Footnote omitted.] American Pet. Institute v. Occupational Safety, 581 F.2d 493, 497–8 (5th Cir. 1978).

In this case, after having determined that there is a causal connection between **benzene** and leukemia (a cancer of the white blood cells), the Secretary set an exposure limit on airborne concentrations of **benzene** of one part benzene per million parts of air (1 ppm), regulated dermal and eye contact with solutions containing **benzene**, and imposed complex monitoring and medical testing requirements on employers whose workplaces contain 0.5 ppm or more of benzene. 29 CFR §§ 1910.1028(c), (e) (1979) . . . .

. . . **Benzene** is a familiar and important commodity. It is a colorless, aromatic liquid that evaporates rapidly under ordinary atmospheric conditions . . . .

. . . **Benzene** is used in manufacturing a variety of products including motor fuels (which may contain as much as 2% **benzene**), solvents, detergents, pesticides, and other organic chemicals. 43 Fed.Reg. 5918 (1978) . . . .

. . . The entire population of the United States is exposed to small quantities of **benzene**, ranging from a few parts per billion to 0.5 ppm, in the ambient air. Tr. 1029–1032. Over one million workers are subject to additional low-level exposures as a consequence of their employment . . . .

. . . **Benzene** is a toxic substance. Although it could conceivably cause harm to a person who swallowed or touched it, the principal risk of harm comes from inhalation of **benzene** vapors. When these vapors are inhaled, the **benzene** diffuses through the lungs and is quickly absorbed into the blood. Exposure to high concentrations produces an almost immediate effect on the central nervous system. Inhalation of concentrations of 20,000 ppm can be fatal within minutes; exposures in the range of 250 to 500 ppm can cause vertigo, nausea, and other symptoms of mild poisoning. 43 Fed.Reg. 5921 (1978). Persistent exposures at levels above 25–40 ppm may lead to blood deficiencies and diseases of the blood-forming organs, including aplastic anemia, which is generally fatal. Industrial Union v. American Petroleum, 448 U.S. 607, 100 S.Ct. 2844, 2849–51, 65 L.Ed.2d 1010 (1980).

However, a reading of the testimony of Dr. Sultani, the treating physician, clearly shows that in describing the effect of continued inhalation of fumes of hydrocarbons he was not limiting his testimony solely to the effect of **benzene** fumes. His testimony refers as well to other hydrocarbons which produce toxic fumes. County of Cook v. Industrial Com'n, 310 N.E.2d 6, 8 (Ill.1974).

Other Authorities: Martinez v. Dixie Carriers, Inc., 529 F.2d 457, 463 (5th Cir. 1976).

benzethonium chloride (ben″zĕ-tho′ne-um) [USP] chemical name: *N,N*-dimethyl-*N*-[2-[2-[4-(1,1,3,3-tetramethylbutyl)phenoxy]ethoxy]ethyl]benzene-methanaminium chloride. A synthetic quartenary ammonium compound, $C_{27}H_{42}CINO_2$, occurring as white crystals; used as a local anti-infective applied topically as a solution, and as a preservative in pharmaceutical preparations. It is also used in various concentrations for cleaning eating and cooking utensils, as a disinfectant in laundering, to control algal growth in swimming pools, and as an environmental deodorant.

Parke-Davis selected a different preservative for use in Quadrigen. This preservative was **benzethonium chloride**, or Phemerol, which was Parke-Davis' trade name for this product. Later research, however, indicated that use of Phemerol caused certain endotoxins in the pertussis vaccine to leak out from the bacterial cell into the fluid which was injected.... Ezagui v. Dow Chemical Corp., 598 F.2d 727, 731 (2d Cir. 1979).

benzidine (ben′zĭ-din) a colorless, crystalline compound, paradiaminodiphenyl, $(NH_2 \cdot C_6H_4 \cdot C_6H_4 \cdot NH_2)$, formed by the action of acids on hydrazobenzene; used as a test for blood.

benzidine test See *test, benzidine.*

benzin, benzine (ben′zin) [L. *benzinum*] petroleum benzin.

benzine, petroleum a purified distillate from petroleum consisting of hydrocarbons chiefly of the methane series (mainly pentanes and hexanes), which occurs as a clear, colorless, volatile liquid with a strong ethereal odor; it is highly flammable and may be explosive if the vapors mix with air and are ignited. It is used as a solvent for organic compounds. Called also *benzin* or *benzine, petroleum ether,* and *naphtha.*

In the course of his work he was continually exposed to the fumes of a toxic paint thinner, which he identified as benzene, but which was later established to be **benzine**, a less toxic substance than benzene. He contends that his continued exposure to the toxic paint-thinner fumes in this poorly ventilated work area caused the damage to his liver....

... The county introduced into evidence county purchase orders which showed that the paint thinner used by the county was **benzine** (also known as VMP Naphtha) rather than benzene. A chemist testified that **benzine** was much less toxic than benzene, but conceded that even this milder substance could cause a toxic reaction when used over a long period of time....

... In addition to the testimony of Dr. Sultani, the testimony of the county's chemist established that **benzine**, though less toxic than benzene, is nonetheless capable of producing a toxic reaction upon continued exposure. Taken together, the testimony of Dr. Sultani and of the county's chemist established the causal relationship between the exposure to the toxic fumes of **benzine** and the claimant's condition. Furthermore, the claimant's physical improvement after discontinuing his painting activities and exposure to these fumes is also strongly indicative of a causal relationship between his illness and his prior employment. County of Cook v. Industrial Com'n, 310 N.E.2d 6, 7–8 (Ill.1974).

benzocaine (ben′zo-kān) [USP] chemical name: 4-aminobenzoic acid ethyl ester. A local anesthetic, $C_9H_{11}NO_2$, occurring as small, white crystals or as a white crystalline powder; applied topically to the skin and mucous membranes.

Considering the evidence as a whole, I find that **benzocaine** in the quantity here involved would not appreciably affect the users' appetite or hunger.... [Postal Service Decision at p. 8]. Institute for Weight Control, Inc. v. Klassen, 348 F.Supp. 1304, 1309 (D.N.J.1972).

benzodiazepine (ben′zo-di-az′ĕ-pēn) any of a group of minor tranquilizers, including chlordiazepoxide, clorazepate, diazepam, flurazepam, oxazepam, etc., having a common molecular structure and similar pharmacological activities, such as antianxiety, muscle relaxing, and sedative and hypnotic effects. See also *diazepam.*

It is believed that the primary site of action of these drugs [benzodiazepines] is in the subcortical structures of the brain. The precise site of action cannot be determined with certitude. Dr. Gerhard Zbinden of Roche Laboratories stated that their tests showed it to be in the hippocampus (Tr. 2187–88). However, Dr. Harold Himwich, another Respondent witness, testified that his tests showed that the area most sensitive to low doses of Librium and Valium, was in the transmission from the amygdala to the hippocampus (Tr. 2677). Moreover a doubling of the dose in these tests done at Roche Laboratories resulted in the drug effect spreading to the cortex, the area of the brain associated with judgmental functions. Hoffmann-La Roche, Inc. v. Kleindienst, 478 F.2d 1, 8 (3d Cir. 1973).

benzothiadiazide, benzothiadiazine (ben″zo-thi″ah-di′ahzīd; ben″zo-thi″ah-di′ah-zēn) thiazide. See *cyclothiazide; hydrochlorothiazide;* and *chlorothiazide.*

benztropine mesylate (benz′tro-pēn) [USP] chemical name: *endo*-3-(diphenylmethoxy)-8-azabicyclo[3.2.1]octane methanesulfonate. A drug, $C_{21}H_{25}NO \cdot CH_4O_3S$, occurring as a white, crystalline powder, having anticholinergic, antihistaminic, and local anesthetic actions; used as an antiparkinsonian agent, administered intramuscularly, intravenously, and orally. See also *psychotic* (Guillory case).

... it was well known that some of the drugs given Guillory would cause sweat inhibition and a high body temperature. Thereafter, noting Guillory's extremely high temperature prior to death, the district court concluded: "Having found by a preponderance of the evidence that the decedent's death was caused by heat stroke, the court has no difficulty in finding that but for the drugs in the decedent's system, the heat stroke probably would not have occurred." This finding led the district court to the ultimate conclusion that "it was negligence on the part of the hospital and its employees in failing to advise the decedent's family that he should not be exposed to warm temperatures while under the medications prescribed, particularly **Cogentin**." Guillory on Behalf of Guillory v. U.S., 699 F.2d 781, 783 (5th Cir. 1983).

Dr. Philibert prescribed **cogentin** for this condition **and** the spasms and seizures stopped. Circello saw Dr. Philibert on January 9, 1980, and complained of blurring of his vision which was a side effect of the **cogentin**. Circello v. Government Employees Ins. Co., 425 So.2d 239, 244 (Ct.App.La. 1982).

With the realization that Mr. Chabert was not merely having spasms in the back but in actuality was having drug induced extraparamidal seizures he was placed immediately with an injection of **Cojentin** [. . .] and placed then on **Conjentin** tablets twice a day and the extraparamidal seizures and spasms in the back have completely subsided with the onset of this medication. Chabert v. City of Westwego Police Pension, 423 So. 2d 1190, 1195 (Ct. of App.La.1982).

berylliosis (ber"il-le-o'sis) beryllium poisoning, a morbid condition, usually of the lungs, more rarely of the skin, subcutaneous tissue, lymph nodes, liver, and other structures, characterized by formation of granulomas. Fumes of beryllium salts or finely divided dust may be inhaled or the substance may be accidentally implanted in the skin or subcutaneous tissue by laceration or puncture.

The referee awarded claimant workmen's compensation benefits for total disability caused by **berylliosis**, as the result of claimant's exposure to the dust and fumes from beryllium in his employment. Murhon v. Workmen's Compensation App.Bd., 414 A.2d 161–2 (Commonwealth Ct.Pa.1980).

biceps (bi'seps) [bi- + L. *caput* head] a muscle having two heads.

biceps brachii See *Table of Musculi.*

bilateral thoracic outlet compression syndrome See *syndrome, thoracic outlet.*

bile (bīl) [L. *bilis*] a fluid secreted by the liver and poured into the small intestine via the bile ducts. Important constituents are conjugated bile salts, cholesterol, phospholipid, bilirubin diglucuronide, and electrolytes. Bile is alkaline due to its bicarbonate content, golden brown to greenish yellow in color, and has a bitter taste. Hepatic bile (see *A b.*) secreted by the liver, is concentrated in the gallbladder. Its formation depends on active secretion by liver cells into the bile canaliculi. Excretion of bile salts by liver cells and secretion of bicarbonate rich fluid by ductular cells in response to secretin are the major factors which normally determine the volume of secretion. Conjugated bile salts and phospholipid normally dissolve cholesterol in a mixed micellar solution. In the upper small intestine, bile is in part responsible for alkalinizing the intestinal content, and conjugated bile salts play an essential role in fat absorption by dissolving the products of fat digestion (fatty acids and monoglyceride) in water soluble micelles. Called also *gall.*

The presence of mucus, the greenish fluid, is due to **bile**. Bile is refluxed into the stomach to assist in solution of fat material prior to absorption, so this accounts for the greenish color that was present in both. And also the fact that it was green indicates that you have had **bile** come down from the gall bladder down into the duodenum back into the stomach, and it has had to come all the way up. There is no other way for **bile** to get into the trachea except to be carried up through with the gastric contents, which further establishes the nature of the material as vomitus rather than incompletely chewed food, in which case it would not be a green color. Jones v. Liberty Nat. Life Ins. Co., 357 So.2d 976, 977–8 (Ala.1978).

The operation took place on January 17. On the second day thereafter plaintiff observed a large quantum of **bile**, which was staining, saturating and seeping through the padding which covered her surgical incision, and accompanied by pain in the right side of her back. The heavy drainage persisted throughout her stay in the hospital. Yerzy v. Levine, 260 A.2d 533–4 (Super.Ct.N.J.1970).

bile, A bile from the common bile duct; samples are obtained by use of a duodenal tube before gallbladder stimulation. It usually contains 20–200 mg. of bilirubin per 100 ml.

bile duct, common See *ductus, choledochus.*

bilirubin (bil"i-roo'bin) [bili- + L. *ruber* red] a bile pigment; it is a breakdown product of heme mainly formed from the degradation of erythrocyte hemoglobin in reticuloendothelial cells, but also formed by breakdown of other heme pigments, e.g., cytochromes. Bilirubin normally circulates in plasma as a complex with albumin, and is taken up by the liver cells and conjugated to form bilirubin diglucuronide, which is the water-soluble pigment excreted in bile. In patients with cholestasis conjugated bilirubin (bilirubin diglucuronide) accumulates in the blood and tissues and is excreted in the urine; unconjugated bilirubin is not excreted in the urine. High concentrations of bilirubin may result in jaundice.

Bilirubin is normally handled by the liver and is excreted in the urine or by way of the gall bladder. But during the first 72 hours of life, an infant's liver may not yet be able to handle **bilirubin**. The critical level of **bilirubin** is 20 milligrams per 100 milliliters of blood (20 mgs %), at which point brain irritation begins to occur with possible brain cell damage. The rate of rise of **bilirubin** in the newborn is predictable. The "indirect" **bilirubin** reading is the one used. . . .

. . . Blood tests for **bilirubin** are not invariably accurate; hence the physician also regularly observes the child for signs of heightened **bilirubin** levels. These signs include jaundice, lessened suck reflex and Moro's reaction (instinctive embracing grasp when jarred), lethargy, irritability, shrill cry, rigidity, and enlargement of liver and spleen. Treatment, when indicated, usually consists of one or more exchange transfusions of blood and is successful in a high proportion of cases. Blood transfusions in small infants are attended with moderate—although not negligible—risks. Schnebly v. Baker, 217 N.W.2d 708, 712 (Iowa 1974).

bilirubin test See *test, van den Bergh's.*

Billroth II procedure See *operation, Billroth's.*

bimalleolar See *malleolus.*

bioavailability (bi"o-ah-vāl"ah-bil'ĭ-te) the degree to which a drug or other substance becomes available to the target tissue after administration.

The **bio-availability** of a drug product is the time within which the active ingredient reaches the site of its intended action in the body, together with the amount of the active ingredient that reaches that site. See 21 C.F.R. § 320.1(a). **Bio-availability** is measured clinically by administering the drug to a subject and measuring periodically thereafter the amount of the active ingredient present at the site of its intended action (or, if measurements cannot be taken at that site, then by measuring the amount of the active ingredient present in the bloodstream). The results of these measurements can be displayed on a graph in which the time since the drug was taken is shown on the horizontal axis and the measured amount of active ingredient shown on the vertical axis. If the results of each measurement are plotted on the graph, they will form a curve that begins where the two axes intersect (representing the time when the subject first took the drug and had none of the active ingredient in his bloodstream), then rises to a peak (representing the time when the subject had the greatest amount of the active ingredient in his bloodstream), and ultimately falls back to the horizontal axis (representing the time when the subject had eliminated all of the active ingredient from his bloodstream).

When such a curve is drawn it is possible to determine the three values by which the **bio-availability** of a drug product is measured, namely, C-max, T-max, and the area under the curve. The area under the curve is the area enclosed by the curve and the horizontal axis and is a measure of the total amount of the active ingredient that was present in the body from the time when the drug was taken through the time when all of the active ingredient was eliminated. Premo Pharmaceutical Laboratories, Inc. v. U.S., 475 F.Supp. 52, 54 (S.D.N.Y. 1979), judgment reversed 629 F.2d 795 (2d Cir. 1980).

First, **bioavailability** of a drug means the "rate and extent to which the active drug ingredient or therapeutic moiety is absorbed from a drug product and becomes available at the site of drug action," 21 C.F.R. § 320.1(a) (1978), that is, the degree to which a drug or other substance becomes available to the target tissue after administration. Dorland's Illustrated Medical Dictionary 200 (25th ed. 1974). Pharmadyne Laboratories, Inc. v. Kennedy, 466 F.Supp.100, 102 (D.N.J.1979).

bioequivalence (bi″o-e-kwiv′ah-lens) the quality of being bioequivalent.

Bioequivalence speaks of pharmaceutical equivalents, whose rate and extent of absorption do not show a significant difference when administered at the same molar dose of therapeutic moiety under similar experimental conditions. See 21 C.F.R. § 320.1(e) (1978)....

... In addition, when analyzing **bioequivalence** criteria, the Commissioner must consider a number of factors to identify specific pharmaceutical equivalents that may not be bioequivalent drug products. Such factors include physiochemical evidence that specific inactive ingredients may be required for absorption of the active drug ingredient. 21 C.F.R. § 320.52(e)(6) (1978).

Secondly, quality control and the likely potential for differing manufacturing processes are also of significance. **Bioequivalence** criteria mandates that the active drug ingredients have a low solubility in water, a certain particle size and/or surface area, certain physical structural characteristics, a specific degree of absorption, protections thereto to assure adequate absorption, and indicia that there will be absorption in large part in a particular segment of the gastrointestinal tract or from a localized site. 21 C.F.R. § 320.52(e), (f) (1978). In addition, changes in manufacturing processes, including a change in product formulation or dosage strength, require FDA scrutiny before a drug product is marketed. See 21 C.F.R. § 320.21(b) (1978). Pharmadyne Laboratories, Inc. v. Kennedy, 466 F.Supp.100, 102 (D.N.J.1979).

bioequivalent (bi″o-e-kwiv′ah-lent) having the same strength and similar bioavailability in the same dosage form as another specimen of a given drug substance.

Drug products are said to be **bioequivalent** [or equally bioavailable] when their active ingredients are absorbed from the gastrointestinal tract at substantially the same rate and to the same extent as indicated by the time-course of their concentration in the blood. They are said to be therapeutic equivalents when they produce the same therapeutic effect with no difference in toxicity or side-effects.[31] [[31] Hearings Before the Subcommittee on Monopoly of the Select Committee on Small Business of the U.S. Senate, 94th Cong., 1st Sess., pt. 26, p. 11656 (1975) [hereinafter cited as Monopoly Committee Hearings]. These hearings were not in the administrative record but they echo similar testimony before a different Senate committee by Dr. Berliner. That testimony was placed in the record, 40 Fed.Reg. 32285. See Hearings on the Examination of the Office of Technology Assessment Report of the Drug Bioequivalence Study Panel Before the Subcommittee on Health of the Senate Committee on Labor and Public Welfare, 93d Cong., 2d Sess., 81–82 (1974) [hereinafter cited as OTA Report Hearings]. American Medical Ass'n v. Mathews, 429 F.Supp. 1179, 1186 (N.D.Ill.1977).

bioflavonoid (bi″o-fla′vo-noid) a generic term for a group of compounds that are widely distributed in plants and that are concerned with maintenance of a normal state of walls of small blood vessels. See also *flavonoid*.

CVP is the trade name under which the petitioner markets drugs containing citrus flavonoid compound, a derivative of citrus fruit pulp and peel, and vitamin C, with and without vitamin K. CVP is a **bioflavonoid**, a generic term which may refer not only to citrus flavonoid compounds but also to any of its separate components. These drugs are recommended by the petitioner for the control of abnormal capillary permeability and a number of serious blood disorders....

... The National Academy of Science-National Research Council reported that there is no evidence that **bioflavonoids** are effective for use in man for any condition. USV Pharmaceutical Corp. v. Secretary of Health, E. & W., 466 F.2d 455–6, 459 (D.C.Cir.1972).

biopsy (bi′ŏp-se) [bio- + Gr. *opsis* vision] the removal and examination, usually microscopic, of tissue from the living body, performed to establish precise diagnosis. See also *smear, cytological* (O'Brien case).

The plastic surgeons and the pathologist who testified for Mrs. Wilkinson made it quite clear that a **biopsy** supplies conclusive proof of whether or not a tumor is or is not malignant. Wilkinson v. Vesey, 295 A.2d 676, 683 (R.I.1972).

He did not order a tissue **biopsy** which probably would have revealed the presence of a tissue cancer, poorly differentiated epidermoid carcinoma of the oral cavity, which was the ultimate cause of her death....

... Here a distinction between a cytological smear and a tissue **biopsy** is necessary. Both are tests done to discover a tissue cancer. A cytological smear consists of scraping cells from the surface of the affected area for microscopic examination. A tissue **biopsy** consists of making an incision in the affected area and taking a section of the tissue for microscopic examination. O'Brien v. Stover, 443 F.2d 1013–15 (8th Cir. 1971).

In performing a **biopsy** through the tube to obtain a piece of tissue for microscopic examination the doctor severed a blood vessel. Profuse bleeding resulted which caused defendant's death in spite of emergency procedures instituted. McKay v. Bankers Life Co., 187 N.W.2d 736–7 (Iowa 1971).

Other Authorities: Davis v. Caldwell, 445 N.Y.S.2d 63, 65 (N.Y.1981); Taylor v. Dirico, 606 P.2d 3, 4 (Ariz.1980).

biopsy, aspiration biopsy in which the tissue is obtained by the application of suction through a needle attached to a syringe.

In June 1975 an **aspiration biopsy** of the liver was positive for malignant melanoma, a fatal complication. Silverman v. Lathrop, 403 A.2d 18, 20 (Super.Ct.N.J.1979).

biopsy, liver

Since it appeared to him that some of the patient's symptoms were consistent with hepatitis, Dr. Best suggested that the attending physicians consider a **liver biopsy**. (Expert testimony at trial established that a **liver biopsy** is not an inconsequential surgical procedure; it is contra-indicated if the patient demonstrates any problem with the blood, i.e., bleeding or clotting, because the danger of hemorrhage is present.) Cade v. Mid-City Hospital Corp., 119 Cal.Rptr. 571, 573 (Ct.App.Cal. 1975).

biopsy, lymph node See *nervus accessorius* (Peterson case).

biopsy, needle biopsy in which tissue is obtained by the puncture of a tumor, the tissue within the lumen of the needle being detached by rotation and withdrawal of the needle. See also *aspiration biopsy*.

In October, 1972, he advised her to undergo a kidney biopsy to determine the extent of lupus involvement in her kidneys. He explained that the biopsy was a simple procedure, which would be carried out under a local anesthetic, that she might suffer some bleeding and discomfort, but that she would be able to leave the hospital in a day or two if there were no complications. Newberg described the operation in a general way as consisting of the insertion of a surgical needle into her back in order to obtain a specimen of kidney tissue....

After the plaintiff had been placed upon the table, Bogdan injected a local anesthetic into the kidney region by using a small gauge anesthesia needle. He then inserted the **biopsy needle** and, using the fluoroscopic screen between six and eight times, he located the kidney and extracted a tissue specimen. Logan v. Greenwich Hosp. Ass'n, 465 A.2d 294, 297 (Conn.1983).

A Craig **needle biopsy** is a procedure by which instruments are inserted into the body of a patient and a sample is extracted from a vertebra. In this case, the instruments were inserted from a posterior position of the patient so that they would not perforate a major artery or organ. As a part of the procedure, a fluoroscope was used which provided an X-ray picture of the area in which the instruments were inserted so that the person performing the biopsy could properly place the instrument on the vertebra to draw a sample. An image intensifier was used with the fluoroscope in order to get a better image of the area in which the instruments were inserted. Brigham v. Hicks, 260 S.E.2d 435–6 (Ct.App.N.Car.1979).

A **needle or section biopsy** may be performed. Some doctors are concerned about performing a biopsy of the pancreas because pancreatic juices could escape or malignant cells could be disseminated. It is standard practice to do a biopsy where a laparotomy is performed and cancer is suspected, unless the cancer is obvious. Conrad v. Christ Community Hospital, 395 N.E.2d 1158, 1159 (App.Ct.Ill.1979).

biopsy, open See *biopsy, surgical.*

biopsy, surgical biopsy of tissue obtained by surgical excision.

He did not discuss the alternative of an **open biopsy**, which would require an incision and would be conducted under general anesthesia, because he did not consider that procedure advisable. Logan v. Greenwich Hosp. Ass'n, 465 A.2d 294, 297 (Conn.1983).

biopsy, tissue

He did not order a **tissue biopsy** which probably would have revealed the presence of a tissue cancer, poorly differentiated epidermoid carcinoma of the oral cavity, which was the ultimate cause of her death....

... A **tissue biopsy** consists of making an incision in the affected area and taking a section of the tissue for microscopic examination. The cytological smear is not a very good diagnostic device. It is a good screening device—i.e., a good method of discovering unsuspected cancers in the general population, as is commonly done with cervical cancers in women. But where there are other symptoms leading one to suspect a cancer is present, it is not a good method of getting a definitive diagnosis because of the danger of getting a "false negative"—i.e., as compared to a tissue biopsy, a cytological smear has a much greater chance of failing to indicate a cancer which is actually present. Therefore, in order to get a definite diagnosis, a **tissue biopsy** should be done. O'Brien v. Stover, 443 F.2d 1013–15 (8th Cir. 1971).

biopsy distinguished from operation See *operation* (Farmers case).

biphenyl (bi-fe′nil) diphenyl.

biphenyl, polychlorinated (PCB) Any of a group of substances in which chlorine replaces hydrogen in biphenyl and which are toxic and accumulate in animal tissues; it is used as a heat-transfer agent and as an insulator in electrical equipment.

Mr. Retallick testified that materials containing **PCB's** in excess of 50 ppm are considered to be a toxic substance. As to the effect of **PCB's**, Mr. Retallick stated that **PCB** causes liver cancer in test animals, such as mice and rats. When humans come into contact with **PCB's**, they are susceptible to a skin reaction much like acne, dizziness, jaundice, loss of appetite, sterility and nausea. Also, **PCB's** are not biodegradable and remain in the environment for approximately the same length of time as the insecticide DDT. The soil can absorb **PCB's**. In waterways, **PCB's** sink to the bottom and rest in the sediment where it can be consumed by fish and other acquatic [sic] species. If these fish are in turn eaten by others along the food chain, the **PCB's** are passed along, resting in the fatty tissue of the recipient. Anne Arundel Cty. v. Governor, 413 A.2d 281, 285 (Ct.Spec. App.Md.1980).

birth (birth) the act or process of being born.

birth, wrongful See *life, wrongful.*

The courts in the majority of States that have considered "wrongful pregnancy" or "**wrongful birth**" actions have recognized a cause of action against a physician where it is alleged that because of the doctor's negligence the plaintiff conceived or gave birth. (See Annot., Tort Liability for Wrongfully Causing One to be Born, 83 A.L.R.3d 15, 29 (1978).) These courts have generally held that in such actions the infant's parents may recover for the expenses of the unsuccessful operation, the pain and suffering involved, any medical complications caused by the pregnancy, the costs of delivery, lost wages, and loss of consortium. (83 A.L.R.3d 15, 29–30.) There is sharp disagreement, however, on the question involved here: whether plaintiffs may recover as damages the costs of rearing a healthy child....

This court today has come to the conclusion that child-rearing costs are not recoverable in a **wrongful birth** action in Illinois. Cockrum v. Baumgartner, 447 N.E.2d 385, 387, 389 (Ill. 1983).

In order to determine the parents' compensatory damages herein, a court would have to evaluate the denial to them of the intangible, unmeasurable and complex human benefits of motherhood and fatherhood and weigh these against the alleged emotional injuries....

In addition, recognition of the claim for emotional harm herein would, in my opinion, constitute an unwarranted and dangerous extension of malpractice liability. Under the plaintiffs' theory as to what the law should be, an obstetrician in our ever-expanding heterogeneous and pluralistic society would have an absolute duty to conduct an exhaustive genealogical profile of both parents in order for him to counsel them as to the wisdom of the wife obtaining an abortion....

Unavoidably, the claim for damages for emotional harm in this case raises questions of public policy. In my opinion allowance of recovery would place an unreasonable burden upon physicians and obstetricians....

... An illustration of the lengths to which causes of action arising out of "**wrongful birth**" may reach if such theory is ever adopted by the courts is set forth in Cox v. Stretton, 77 Misc. 2d 155, 156, 352 N.Y.S.2d 834, 837. In Cox the wife became pregnant and bore a child subsequent to the performance by the defendant physician of a vasectomy upon her husband. In the action charging the physician with malpractice, a cause of action was interposed on behalf of the two other children of the marriage. It was alleged therein that, as a result of the physician's malpractice, each of the two other children had been and would be deprived "of a portion of the care, affection, training and financial support each would have received except for the birth of their unplanned brother". Howard v. Lecher, 386 N.Y.S.2d 460, 462–3 (2d Dep't 1976).

The cause of action for **wrongful birth**, which is brought by the parents of an unwanted child, must be distinguished from that for "wrongful life," which is brought on behalf of the child himself for injuries suffered from a negligent failure to prevent his birth. Every jurisdiction that has considered actions for wrongful life, except for California, has held that no such cause of action exists. See, e.g., Elliott v. Brown, Ala., 361 So. 2d 546 (1978); Becker v. Schwartz, 46 N.Y.2d 401, 413 N.Y.S.2d 895, 386 N.E.2d 807 (1978); Dumer v. St. Michael's

Hospital, 69 Wis.2d 766, 233 N.W.2d 372 (1975); Jacobs v. Theimer, Tex., 519 S.W.2d 846 (1975). But see Curlender v. Bio-Science Laboratories, 106 Cal.App.3d 811, 165 Cal.Rptr. 477 (1980). Despite the Government's argument to the contrary, a child's ability to recover for its injury should not in any way affect the parents' right to recover for the same negligence. Courts that have rejected actions for wrongful life have done so largely because of a reluctance to hold that the child is more injured from having been born than it would have been never having been born in the first place. See, e.g., Dumer v. St. Michael's Hospital, supra, 69 Wis.2d at 771–773, 233 N.W.2d 372. An action for **wrongful birth**, on the other hand, involves different considerations of policy and of perspective....

Cases recognizing a cause of action for **wrongful birth** have involved a number of prenatal conditions. In addition to the two rubella syndrome cases described above (Jacobs and Dumer), they are Karlsons v. Guerinot, 57 A.D.2d 73, 394 N.Y.S.2d 933 (1977) (failure to advise of available amniocentesis test); Berman v. Allen, supra, (Mongolism); Becker v. Schwartz, supra, (Mongolism); Park v. Chessin, supra, (Polycystic Kidney Disease); Speck v. Finegold, 268 Pa.Super. 342, 408 A.2d 496 (1979) (Congenital neurofibromatosis); Gildiner v. Thomas Jefferson Univ. Hospital, 451 F.Supp. 692 (E.D.Pa. 1978) (Tay-Sachs Disease).

A second line of **wrongful birth** cases has recognized a cause of action for the parents of children born after a negligently performed sterilization operation. Cockrum v. Baumgartner, 50 U.S.L.W. 2050, 99 Ill.App.3d 271, 425 N.E.2d 968, 54 Ill.Dec. 751 (Ill.App.1st Dist.1981); Sorkin v. Lee, 78 A.D.2d 180, 434 N.Y.S.2d 300 (N.Y.Sup.Ct., App.Div., December 23, 1980); Public Health Trust v. Brown, 388 So.2d 1084 (Fla.Ct.App., 1980); Mason v. Western Pennsylvania Hospital, 286 Pa.Super. 354, 428 A.2d 1366, 1367 (1981) (en banc); Custodio v. Bauer, 251 Cal.App.2d 303, 59 Cal.Rptr. 463 (1967) (negligent sterilization); Stills v. Gratton, 55 Cal. App.3d 698, 127 Cal.Rptr. 652 (1976) (failure to diagnose pregnancy); Anonymous v. Hospital, et al., 33 Conn.Sup. 125, 366 A.2d 204 (1976) (negligent sterilization); Troppi v. Scarf, 31 Mich.App. 240, 187 N.W.2d 511 (1971) (negligent supplying of contraceptives); Bushman v. Burns Clinic Medical Center, 83 Mich.App. 453, 268 N.W.2d 683 (1978) (negligent sterilization); Sherlock v. Stillwater Clinic, 260 N.W.2d 169 (Minn.1977) (negligent vasectomy); Betancourt v. Gaylor, 136 N.J.Super. 69, 344 A.2d 336 (1975) (negligent sterilization); Bowman v. Davis, 48 Ohio St.2d 41, 356 N.E.2d 496 (1976) (negligent sterilization); Bishop v. Byrne, 265 F.Supp. 460 (S.D.W.Va.1967) (negligent sterilization). See also, "Tort Liability for Wrongful Birth," 83 ALR3d 15. Robak v. U.S., 658 F.Supp. 471, 474–6 (7th Cir. 1981).

Other Authorities: Ochs v. Borrelli, 445 A.2d 883, 884–5 (Conn.1982); Phillips v. U.S., 508 F.Supp. 544, 545 (D.S.Car. 1981); Sherlock v. Stillwater Clinic, 260 N.W.2d 169, 172, 174–5 (Minn.1977); LaPoint v. Shirley, 409 F.Supp. 118–20 (W.D.Tex.1976).

birth control pill See *contraceptive, oral.*

bishydroxycoumarin (bis"hi-drok"se-koo'mah-rin) [USP] dicumarol.

bite See *occlusion.*

bite, insect See *accident.*

bite, open a condition marked by failure of certain opposing teeth to establish occlusal contact when the jaws are closed, usually confined to the anterior teeth; called also *apertognathia.*

He testified that the top portion of the left condyle was stuck. He removed the left condyle and clipped it. This, he testified, shortened the condyle and would cause a cross bite. He testified that in order to effect a balance between the condyles, he operated and clipped the healthy right condyle so that both condyles would be of the same length. The trouble with this latter procedure is that it resulted in an **open bite**. She now has occlusion on only four teeth in the back of her mouth, i.e., on the rear two teeth on each side; there is no contact whatsoever with the front teeth. She is unable to close her mouth and it remains open. This condition is permanent. She continues to suffer pain. She can open her mouth only about $^{11}/_{16}$ of an inch. The normal opening is one and one-half to two inches. She can eat only soft food. Campbell v. Oliva, 424 F.2d 1244, 1247 (6th Cir. 1970).

bite, rattlesnake

The Court finds and acknowledges that a **rattlesnake bite** in and of itself is a serious occurrence and that it is a potentially lethal event; . . . Buck v. U.S., 433 F.Supp. 896, 900 (M.D.Fla. 1977).

bite, underhung a characteristic of mandibular prognathism in which the incisal edges of the mandibular anterior teeth extend labially to the incisal edges of the maxillary anterior teeth when the jaws are in habitual occlusion.

The facts show that as early as 1970 or 1971 appellee's wife, Mrs. Crowe, suffered from a fairly severe **underbite**. She complained of difficulty in properly masticating her food which occasionally prevented her from retaining all the food in her mouth while chewing because of the jut of her lower jaw beyond the upper row of teeth. There was some evidence that such a physical defect may be congenital although it may also be caused by a medically determinable disease or by trauma. . . .

. . . In February, 1975, Mrs. Crowe went to a dental surgeon who for the first time informed her that the appropriate corrective procedure was to remove a portion of the lower jaw thereby retracting or shortening the lower jaw into alignment with the upper jaw. Life & Cas. Ins. Co. of Tennessee v. Crowe, 249 S.E.2d 682–3 (Ct.App.Ga.1978).

bite-wing (bīt'wing) a wing or fin attached along the center of the tooth side of a dental x-ray film and bitten on by the patient; used for making radiographic projections showing simultaneously the corona of the teeth in both dental arches and their contiguous periodontal tissues.

A "bitewing" radiograph generally depicts the crown portion of the tooth; several teeth in both the mandibular and maxillary jaws are shown in each X-ray. **Bitewing** radiographs are most commonly used to diagnose caries or cavities caused by decay on the interproximal surfaces of the teeth and to determine the crestal level of the jaw bone. . . .

. . . **Bitewing** radiographs are generally considered to be an inadequate tool to determine that root canal therapy is appro-

priate since these X-rays do not depict the root portion of the teeth. U.S. v. Talbott, 460 F.Supp. 253, 256–7 (S.D.Ohio 1978).

bivalence (biv'ah-lens) [*bi-* + L. *valens* powerful] the property of an atom of certain chemical elements of forming chemical bonds with two other atoms or groups.

bivalent (bi-va'lent, biv'ah-lent) 1. having a valence of two; characterized by bivalence. 2. denoting homologous chromosomes associated in pairs, during the zygotene stage of the first meiotic prophase, each of which splits (pachytene stage) into two sister chromatids to form a tetrad. Called also *divalent.* See also *monovalent.*

Bjork-Shiley prosthetic valve See *valve, Bjork-Shiley prosthetic.*

black See *black mollie.*

black mollie

"Blacks" or "**Black Mollies**" are "uppers" or central nervous stimulants. The evidence shows both to be dangerous drugs as same were defined in Article 726d, Vernon's Ann.P.C., at the time of this offense. . . .

George Taft, a duly qualified chemist with the Department of Public Safety, testified that, on chemical analysis, the "blacks" or black capsules contained amphetamines. Lapp v. State, 519 S.W.2d 443, 445–6 (Ct.Crim.App.Tex.1975).

blackout (blak'owt) a condition characterized by failure of vision and momentary unconsciousness, due to diminished circulation to the brain.

blackout, alcoholic

It was his opinion however, that after the first drink, Leeper had gone on a drinking spree and had blacked out. Such an **alcoholic blackout**, though permitting the person to perform physical acts, would produce an amnesia concerning them. He concluded that Leeper was probably not conscious of the nature of the acts which he had committed. U.S. v. Leeper, 413 F.2d 123, 125 (8th Cir. 1969).

bladder (blad'der) [L. *vesica, cystis;* Gr. *kystis*] a membranous sac, such as one serving as receptacle for a secretion; often used alone to designate the urinary bladder. Called also *vesica.*

The trial judge erred in not finding that the fistula caused a loss of function of the **bladder**. The function of the **bladder** is to act as a reservoir for urine until it is voided. A **bladder** which leaks no longer performs this function. LaCaze v. Collier, 434 So.2d 1039, 1047 (La.1983).

Skinner's testimony is that Dr. Coleman had forgotten about the catheter left in his body and same had migrated to the **bladder** causing him damage as established. Skinner v. Coleman-Nincic Urology Clinic, 300 S.E.2d 319, 321 (Ct.App.Ga. 1983).

biological oxygen demand See under *demand.*

bladder, automatic neurogenic bladder due to complete transection of the spinal cord above the sacral segments, marked by complete loss of micturition reflexes and bladder sensation, violent involuntary voiding, and an abnormal amount of residual urine. Called also *cord b.*, *reflex b.*, and *spastic b.*

In August of 1982, Dr. Rhamy performed urodynamic studies on the Plaintiff. He testified that a **spastic bladder**, one which has a small capacity and increased tone, is characteristic of a spinal cord lesion or TM, while a flaccid bladder, one with a large volume and decreased muscle tone, is classically evidence of peripheral nerve damage or GBS. McDonald v. U.S., 555 F.Supp. 935, 947 (M.D.Pa.1983).

Dr. Mori found from the cystometrogram that plaintiff had a **spastic reflex bladder**, which is a bladder that contracts and expels urine without voluntary control from the brain, but through motor reaction of the spinal cord. Harrigan v. U.S., 408 F.Supp. 177, 179 (E.D.Pa.1976).

bladder, autonomic See *bladder, autonomous.*

bladder, autonomous neurogenic bladder due to a lesion in the sacral portion of the spinal cord that interrupts the reflex arc which controls the bladder. The lesion may be in the cauda equina, conus medullaris, sacral roots, or pelvic nerve. It is marked by loss of normal bladder sensation and reflex activity, inability to initiate urination normally, and incontinence. Called also *denervated b.* and *nonreflex b.*

Autonomic means contractions of the bladder occurred without plaintiff's control. Harrigan v. U.S., 408 F.Supp. 177, 180 (E.D.Pa.1976).

bladder flap See *flap, bladder.*

bladder, neurogenic any condition of dysfunction of the urinary bladder caused by a lesion of the central or peripheral nervous system, as *atonic neurogenic b., automatic b., autonomous b., motor paralytic b.,* and *uninhibited neurogenic b.*

... Anne was hospitalized for treatment of a **neurogenic bladder**. She developed a 105° fever on April 21 (on her own check), had a deep rattling in her chest and body aches, especially in the area of her kidneys. Sanders v. U.S., etc., 551 F.2d 458, 459 (D.C.Cir.1977).

A **neurogenic bladder** is one not having normal nerve control because of disruption either in supply or exit of nerves to the bladder. Since damage to the plaintiff's spinal cord prevented nerve signals from reaching the brain, the muscles of the bladder would not work synchronously, and the bladder would not empty completely or at all....

... A **neurogenic bladder** is dangerous, because failure of the bladder to empty allows infected urine to collect and spread infection to the ureters and kidneys. Doctors Malloy and Murphy stated that infection can spread to the kidneys from the bladder through the ureters, the lymphatics, or the blood stream. Harrigan v. U.S., 408 F.Supp. 177, 180 (E.D.Pa. 1976).

Dr. Robert Carter, the well qualified and impressive urologist who testified as a witness for the plaintiff and whose operation resulted in the permanent removal of the catheter and the dramatic improvement of the plaintiff thereafter, was of the opinion that Vistaril probably caused the bladder damage characterized as a distended or flaccid **neurogenic bladder**, that is, one paralyzed so that it has poor tone and ability to

contract because of interference with its nerve supply. Miller v. U.S., 431 F.Supp. 988, 992 (S.D.Miss.1976).

Other Authorities: Langton v. Brown, 591 S.W.2d 84–5 (Ct. App.Mo.1979); Miller v. U.S., 431 F.Supp. 988, 992 (S.D. Miss.1976).

bladder, spastic See *bladder, automatic.*

bladder, spastic reflex See *bladder, automatic.*

bladder, urethral See *bladder, urinary.*

bladder, urinary the musculomembranous sac, situated in the anterior part of the pelvic cavity, that serves as a reservoir for urine, which it receives through the ureters and discharges through the urethra. Called also *vesica urinaria* [NA].

In October 1976, Albert Nahmias was found to have cancer of the bladder. Treatment was planned in three stages: (1) diversion of urine from the **bladder**, (2) radiation of the pelvic area to destroy as much of the tumor as possible, and (3) surgical removal of the **bladder**, prostate, seminal vesicles, and most of the fat and lymph nodes in that area.

On October 27, 1976, the urinary diversion was performed by Dr. Frankel, Albert's urologist. This was accomplished by means of an ileal loop, whereby the ureters were severed and connected to a loop of bowel which was then severed from the bowel, closed at one end, and drained through Albert's side. Nahmias v. Trustees of Indiana University, 444 N.E.2d 1204, 1205 (Ct.App.Ind.1983).

According to the witness, standard practice in the type of exploratory operation performed on plaintiff requires the surgeon to be "particularly careful" that an underlying vital structure not be injured. "In this particular instance," he said, "there were adhesions and fibrous tissue because she had a number of operations at that particular site. The **urinary bladder** lies in that area so that when one does a dissection in that particular area, they have to be very careful that they don't injure an underlying vital structure."...

... but I am assuming that in this instance, because of her prior surgery and the extent of the scar tissue there that the bladder was not in its usual anatomical position behind the pubic bone. Buckelew v. Grossbard, 435 A.2d 1150, 1154–5 (N.J.1981).

Dr. Welling's initial examination revealed a 1½ centimeter hole near the neck of the **urethral bladder** down into the vagina. Although it is unclear as to whether he explained the specific origin of the condition to appellant, Dr. Welling did tell her that it was not uncommon for this condition to develop following the birth of a woman's first child. When, on direct examination as a defense witness, Dr. Welling was asked if he though that appellant was aware of the origin of her problem, he replied,

"A. Just from her initial history, she stated that she had a 'traumatic child birth' the quote being mine, and that she had stitches and could not empty her **bladder** and then by forcing and straining some 'X' number of hours later was able to empty her **bladder** and it leaked continuously, since that time. I would assume through association with her that the patient had had such a labor and repair and then a leakage following that. I think anybody with normal intelligence would assume that something happened, during the delivery, to have caused such a thing." See also system, urogenital. Hall v. Musgrave, 517 F.2d 1163–65 (6th Cir. 1975).

Blalock-Taussig shunt See *operation, Blalock-Taussig.*

bleb (bleb) a large flaccid vesicle, usually at least 1 cm. in diameter.

He noted that she had a tremendously swollen left leg with hemorrhagic **blebs** and that her leg was cyanotic and cold. Harris v. State, Through Huey P. Long Hospital, 371 So.2d 1221, 1223 (Ct.App.La.1979).

... x-rays were taken at the Baton Rouge General Hospital which revealed a two by two cm. cystic cavity which it was concluded may be due to an emphysematous **bleb** or water filled blister, without any active infiltration. Claborn v. Cohen, 303 F.Supp. 167, 168 (E.D.La.1969).

Dr. Gibbons testified that, when he made the decision to terminate, he expected to complete the operation later, but did not do so because **blebs**, infected blisters of the skin, developed; that it was very common for **blebs** to accompany an injury of this nature, that plaintiff's **blebs** healed at the normal rate, but that healing of **blebs** at the normal rate did not permit a second operation within the time when a second operation would have been of any value. Clark v. Gibbons, 426 P.2d 525, 529 (Cal.1967).

bleeding (blēd'ing) the escape of blood from an injured vessel.

The District Court found that the proximate cause of Tyminski's injuries was the existence of post-operative **bleeding** within the operative site resulting in the formation of an epidural hematoma which put pressure on the spinal cord. Tyminski v. U.S., 481 F.2d 257, 263 (3d Cir. 1973).

bleeding, fetal-maternal

... (premature separation of the placenta from the uterus before the baby was born), which, according to medical experts, could produce serious consequences including a **fetal-maternal bleed** (the baby will bleed backward through the placenta). Vecchione v. Carlin, 168 Cal.Rptr. 571, 573 (Ct.App.Cal. 1980).

bleeding, internal

He testified without objection that decedent would have been monitored and tested for **internal bleeding** and that **internal bleeding** could be determined by the use of dyes or exploratory surgery if necessary. Watson v. Storie, 300 S.E.2d 55, 57 (Ct.App.N.Car.1983).

Because her failure to respond adequately to drugs, plasma, fluids and whole blood intended to stabilize her blood pressure suggested the possibility of **internal bleeding**, Drs. Viner and Wallach caused her to be placed in an intensive care unit. After Mrs. Reichman had spent a restless night in intensive care, surgery was performed to correct what was then believed to be **internal bleeding**. The source of the bleeding was determined to be a branch of the ovarian artery, approximately two inches above the site of the original dissection of the ovarian bundle, and it was doubly ligated to arrest the bleeding. Reichman v. Wallach, 452 A.2d 501, 504 (Super.Ct.Pa. 1982).

bleeding, vaginal

That day or shortly thereafter Mrs. Juge experienced slight **vaginal bleeding** (referred to in the medical profession as "spotting") and was told by her doctor (Dr. Roy Rabalais) or his nurses she should stay in bed until the bleeding stopped. The spotting continued off and on for several weeks....

... Dr. Rabalais could not say for sure whether or not the accident had caused the bleeding at all. He noted any bleeding brought on by the accident would have likely occurred immediately and that it was not extremely uncommon for women to experience spotting in the late stages of pregnancy. Juge v. Cunningham, 422 So.2d 1253, 1255 (Ct.App.La.1982).

blepharoconjunctivitis (blef"ah-ro-kon-junk"tĭ-vi'tis) inflammation of the eyelids and conjunctiva.

Appellant complained that "both eyes were tearing but it was more marked on the right". Dr. Wilson's diagnosis was chronic **blepharoconjunctivitis** (inflammation of the eyelids and conjunctiva). McMullen v. Celebrezze, 335 F.2d 811, 815 (9th Cir. 1964).

blind (blīnd) not having the sense of sight. See also *blindness.*

... he found his vision to be ¹⁰⁄₂₀₀ in each eye, which rendered him **legally blind** under Pennsylvania law. Hoffman v. Sterling Drug, Inc., 485 F.2d 132, 135 (3d Cir. 1973).

blinded See *effect, placebo.*

blindness (blīnd'nes) lack or loss of ability to see; lack of perception of visual stimuli, due to disorder of the organs of sight or to lesions in certain areas of the brain. See also *amaurosis; fibroplasia, retrolental; pressure, intracranial* (Gendusa case); *sinus, cavernous* (Speed case); and *thrombosis, cavernous sinus* (Speed case).

"Blindness" means "central visual acuity of ²⁰⁄₂₀₀ or less in the better eye with the use of a correcting lens," 42 U.S.C. § 416(i)(1)(B), though limitation in the fields of vision so that the visual field at its widest diameter is no more than 20° also constitutes **blindness**, id.[1] [[1] Under New York law an individual is legally blind if his vision is no better than ²⁰⁄₂₀₀ with correction. N.Y.Unconsol.Laws § 8704(b) (McKinney 1974).] McBrayer v. Secretary of Health and Human Serv., 712 F.2d 795, 797 (2d Cir. 1983).

Dr. Delavasio also stated that Mr. Naylor's injuries have caused a functional **blindness** in his right eye, in which the optic nerves have simply ceased to operate. Naylor v. La. Dep't of Public Highways, 423 So.2d 674, 685 (Ct.App.La.1982).

Rusty Spears was blinded at birth and will be **blind** for his entire life. Loss of sight is loss of the most substantial part of an individual's perception of the world. In a visually oriented world simple tasks for the sighted become major obstacles for the **blind**—dressing, eating, moving about in public, catching a bus, distinguishing objects. **Blind** persons earn substantially less than sighted persons. Of the 20,000 to 30,000 jobs available, the **blind** person is qualified for only about 200 of them. There is evidence Rusty would have a future loss of earning capacity of $1,939,546. Air Shields, Inc. v. Spears, 590 S.W.2d 574, 579 (Ct.Civ.App.Tex.1979).

block See *anesthesia, regional.*

block, brachial See *anesthesia, regional.*

Dr. Woods and Dr. Wideman described the **brachial block** procedure. In it the anesthetist deadens the entire arm by injecting the anesthetic into the brachial complex of nerves, lying next to the first rib. The needle is inserted at the base of the neck, near the collarbone. The lung often extends above the first rib, behind it. It is impossible to tell, even by an x-ray, just how deep the brachial complex and the lung lie below the surface, because the thickness of the overlying soft tissue varies. Dr. Woods testified that there is no way to prevent an occasional puncture of the lung if enough **brachial blocks** are performed. Dr. Wideman testified that as a surgeon he has seen probably more than 500 **brachial blocks** and that in more than one but less than five of them a pneumothorax developed as a result of the anesthesia. Napier v. Northrum, 572 S.W.2d 153, 155 (Ark.1978).

block, epidural anesthesia produced by injection of the anesthetic agent between the vertebral spines and beneath the ligamentum flavum into the extradural space.

The patient states that he was treated by **epidural block** at one time in February of 1975 but this did not offer specific relief. He is having more pains in the left side than the right and has recently experienced intermittent numbness of both feet. He says that this reaction seems to come and go. Chabert v. City of Westwego police pension, 423 So.2d 1190, 1192 (Ct. App.La.1982).

block, nerve regional anesthesia secured by making extraneural or paraneural injections of anesthetics in close proximity to the nerve whose conductivity is to be cut off.

A phrenic **nerve block** was employed as a palliative for the intense pain. Lopez v. Swyer, 279 A.2d 116, 119 (Super.Ct. N.J.1971).

block, paracervical

Anesthesia of the inferior hypogastric plexus and ganglia produced by injection of the local anesthetic into the lateral fornices of the vagina; called also **uterosacral b.**

The plaintiff was hospitalized at Greenville Hospital from July 10, 1977 through July 17, 1977 for a chronic cervical sprain (R. 105–110, 144–145). At that time a **paracervical block** was performed and he improved and was discharged. Vanderslice v. Harris, 487 F.Supp. 475, 480 (W.D.Pa.1980).

block, pudendal anesthesia produced by blocking the pudendal nerves, accomplished by injection of the local anesthetic into the tuberosity of the ischium.

"This patient has a nerve root irritation secondary to a **pudendal block**. I feel that she should be seen by a neurologist, being referred to same." Rothman v. Silber, 216 A.2d 18, 20 (Super.Ct.N.J.1966).

block, sympathetic blocking of the sympathetic trunk by paravertebral infiltration with an anesthetic agent.

Because of her perceived condition, an operation which Dr. Smith termed a "regional **sympathetic block**" was performed. Zick v. Industrial Com'n, 444 N.E.2d 164, 166 (Ill.1982).

He referred plaintiff to Dr. William F. Yost, Jr., an anesthesiologist, to perform a lumbar **sympathetic block** which is the injection of an anesthetic into the area of the sympathetic

nerves. It was successful, but relief was only temporary. Aretz v. U.S., 456 F.Supp. 397, 404 (S.D.Ga.1978).

block, ventricular obstruction to the flow of cerebrospinal fluid within the ventricular system or through the exit foramina (foramina of Magendie and Luschka) by which the ventricles communicate with the subarachnoid space; it results in obstructive hydrocephalus.

blockade (blok-ād') the prevention of the effects of certain drugs by an agent, as the effect of nalorphine on heroin action.

blockade, narcotic inhibition of the euphoric effects of narcotic drugs by the use of other drugs, such as methadone, in the treatment of addition.

blockage (blok'ij) the process of blocking or obstructing; the condition of being blocked or obstructed.

Plaintiff's expert, Dr. Roy Dickman, testified in detail concerning the manner in which the inner surface of the arteries in Mrs. Lamke's knees were likely to have been damaged in the accident. This damage would have produced internal blood clotting which in turn would lead to the ultimate blood flow **blockage** in plaintiff's legs. Lamke v. Louden, 269 N.W.2d 53, 56 (Minn.1978).

blocker (blok'er) something that blocks or obstructs passage, activity, etc.

blocker, starch

Plaintiffs manufacture and market a product known as "**starch blockers**" which "block" the human body's digestion of starch as an aid in controlling weight. On July 1, 1982, the Food and Drug Administration ("FDA") classified **starch blockers** as "drugs" and requested that all such products be removed from the market until FDA approval was received....

The only issue on appeal is whether **starch blockers** are foods or drugs under the Federal Food, Drug, and Cosmetic Act, 21 U.S.C. § 301 et seq. **Starch blocker** tablets and capsules consist of a protein which is extracted from a certain type of raw kidney bean. That particular protein functions as an alpha-amylase inhibitor; ...

... alpha-amylase is an enzyme produced by the body which is utilized in digesting starch. When **starch blockers** are ingested during a meal, the protein acts to prevent the alpha-amylase enzyme from acting, thus allowing the undigested starch to pass through the body and avoiding the calories that would be realized from its digestion.

Kidney beans, from which alpha-amylase inhibitor is derived, are dangerous if eaten raw. By August 1982, FDA had received seventy-five reports of adverse effects on people who had taken **starch blockers**, including complaints of gastro-intestinal distress such as bloating, nausea, abdominal pain, constipation and vomiting....

... The tablets and pills at issue are not consumed primarily for taste, aroma, or nutritive value under Section 321(f)(1); in fact, as noted earlier, they are taken for their ability to block the digestion of food and aid in weight loss.... To qualify as a drug under Section 321(g)(1)(C), the articles must not only be articles "other than food," but must also be "intended to affect the structure or any function of the body of man or other animals." **Starch blockers** indisputably satisfy this requirement for they are intended to affect digestion in the people who take them. Therefore, **starch blockers** are drugs under Section 321(g)(1)(C) of the Food, Drug, and Cosmetic Act. Nutrilab, Inc. v. Schweiker, 713 F.2d 335–6, 338–9 (7th Cir. 1983).

blood (blud) [L. *sanguis, cruor;* Gr. *haima*] the fluid that circulates through the heart, arteries, capillaries, and veins, carrying nutriment and oxygen to the body cells; called also *sangius* [NA]. It consists of a pale yellow liquid, the *plasma*, containing the microscopically visible formed elements of the blood: the erythrocytes, or red blood corpuscles; the leukocytes, or white blood corpuscles; and the thrombocytes, or blood platelets. See also *transfusion*.

Throughout this litigation, appellant has placed considerable emphasis on the fact that the IRS has, for certain purposes, classified the donation of **blood** as a personal service [6] while the Food and Drug Administration has classified **blood** as a product.[7] [[6] See Rev.Rul. 162, 1953–2 C.B. 127–28. In this ruling the IRS decided that the value of **blood** donated to a charitable institution was not deductible as a charitable contribution because the donation of **blood** was characterized as a personal service. [7] FDA regulations dealing with the collection, processing and storage of human **blood** have treated **blood** as a product even while it remains in the donor. See, e.g., 40 Fed.Reg. 53,532 (Nov. 18, 1975); 21 C.F.R. parts 606 & 640 (1977).] U.S. v. Garber, 589 F.2d 843, 848 (5th Cir. 1979).

W.Va.Code, 16–23–1 [1971]: "The procuring, furnishing, donating, processing, distributing or the using of human whole **blood, blood** plasma, **blood** products, **blood** derivatives, corneas, bones or organs or other human tissue for the purpose of injecting, transfusing or transplanting any of them in the human body, is declared for all purposes to be the rendition of a service by every person, firm or corporation participating therein, whether or not any remuneration is paid therefor, and is declared not to be a sale of any such items and no warranties of any kind or description shall be applicable thereto." [Acts of the Legislature, 1971 Regular Session, Ch. 75, p. 371.] Foster v. Memorial Hosp. Ass'n of Charleston, W.Va., 219 S.E.2d 916 (Sup.Ct.App.W.Va.1975).

blood, aerated that which carries oxygen to the tissues through the systemic arteries.

blood, arterial See *aerated*.

There was disputed expert opinion evidence whether the blood was arterial or venous and, therefore, whether it derived from the aorta or the vena cava, the aorta having received greater manipulation during the operation. Fiorentino v. Wenger, 227 N.E.2d 296, 298 (N.Y.1967).

blood, venous blood that has given up its oxygen to the tissues and carries carbon dioxide back through the systemic veins for gas-exchange in the lungs. See also *blood, arterial*.

blood, whole blood from which none of the elements have been removed. *Whole blood* [USP] or *whole human blood* is blood that has been drawn from a selected donor under strict aseptic conditions, containing citrate ion or heparin as an anticoagulant, and used as a blood replenisher. See also *hepatitis, viral, type A*.

Health and Safety Code section 1606 reads:
"The procurement, processing, distribution, or use of **whole blood**, plasma, blood products, and blood derivatives for the purpose of injecting or transfusing the same, or any of them, into the human body shall be construed to be, and is declared to be, for all purposes whatsoever, the rendition of a service by each and every person, firm, or corporation participating therein, and shall not be construed to be, and is declared not to be, a sale of such **whole blood**, plasma, blood products, or blood derivatives, for any purpose or purposes whatsoever." Fogo v. Cutter Laboratories, Inc., 137 Cal.Rptr. 417, 420 (Ct.App.Cal.1977).

... citrated **whole blood** (human)[2].... [[2] **Whole human blood** to which a chemical has been added to prevent clotting.] Blank v. U.S., 400 F.2d 302 (5th Cir. 1968).

blood alcohol test See *test, blood alcohol*.

blood clot See *clot, blood*.

blood count See *count, blood*.

blood gas, arterial (studies)

Dr. O'Neill reported that **arterial blood gas studies** showed evidence of mild arterial hypoxemia and that the breath sounds were coarsely bronchovesicular with rhonchi and wheezing occurring. His diagnosis was chronic obstructive airway disease—mild to moderate, chronic bronchitis, and coal worker's pneumoconiosis state 1/1 (p and q). Haywood v. Secretary of Health & Human Services, 699 F.2d 277, 286 (6th Cir. 1983).

blood group (blud' grōōp) 1. an erythrocytic allotype (or phenotype) defined by one or more cellular antigenic structural groupings under the control of allelic genes. Erythrocytic antigenic determinants irregularly incite allotypic and sometimes xenotypic immune responses. Blood groups, especially for man, are identified by agglutination supported by specific human or animal antisera and by lectins extracted from certain plants. Bovine blood group reactions, however, are usually lytic. An abbreviated classification of human blood groups is given in the accompanying table. 2. any characteristic, function, or trait of a cellular or fluid component of blood, considered as the expression (phenotype or allotype) of the actions and interactions of dominant genes, and useful in medicolegal and other studies of human inheritance. Such characteristics include the antigenic groupings of erythrocytes, leukocytes, platelets, and plasma proteins. Called also *blood type*.

These substances—agglutinogens and agglutinins—are capable of identification through their reaction to one another. By classifying these reactions, scientists have established systems of **blood groupings** to include all human beings. The most familiar of these types are the ABO group, the MN type and the Rh type. (See K. B. Brilhart, M.D., Medical Evidence to Exclude Paternity, 1 Ariz. Bar Journal 19 [June, 1965].) Anonymous v. Anonymous, 460 P.2d 32, 34 (Ct.App.Ariz.1969).

blood group, ABO the major human blood type system, which depends on the presence or absence of two antigenic structures, A and B. The gene for A is responsible for

91

HUMAN BLOOD GROUP SYSTEMS AND ERYTHROCYTIC ANTIGENIC DETERMINANTS

Antigenic determinants are systematized according to observed and assumed independent assortment of their responsible genes. Within many systems, alleles are responsible for differing combinations of antigenic determinants.

BLOOD GROUP SYSTEM	ANTIGENIC DETERMINANTS [*]
ABO	A, A_1, B
H	H
I	I, i, I^T, I^D, I^F
MN	M, N, S, s, U, Cl^a, Far, He, Hill, Hu, M^A, M^C, M^e, M^g, M_1, Mi^a, Mt^a, Mur, M^V, Ny^a, Ri^a, S^B, Sj, St^a, Sul, Tm, U^B, Vr, Vw, N^A, Z
P	P1, P2 (Tj^a), P3 (P^K)
Rh	Rh1 (D, Rh_o), Rh2 (C, rh′), Rh3 (E, rh″), Rh4 (c, hr′), Rh5 (e, hr″), Rh6 (f, ce, hr), Rh7 (Ce, rh_i), Rh8 (C^w, rh^{w1}), Rh9 (C^x, rh^x), Rh10 (V, ce^s, hr^v), Rh11 (E^w, rh^{w2}), Rh12 (G, rh^C), Rh13 (Rh^A), Rh14 (Rh^B), Rh15 (Rh^C), Rh16 (Rh^D), Rh17 (Hr_o), Rh18 (Hr), Rh19 (hr^s), Rh20 (VS, e^s), Rh21 (C^G), Rh22 (CE), Rh23 (D^w), Rh24 (E^T), Rh26, Rh27 (cE), Rh28 (hr^H), Rh29 (RH), Rh30 (Go^a), Rh31 (hr^B), Rh32, Rh33
Lutheran	Lu^a (Lu1), Lu^b (Lu2), Lu^{ab} (Lu3), Lu4, Lu5, Lu6, Lu7, Lu8, Lu9, Lu10, Lu11, Lu12, Lu13, Lu14 (Sw^a)
Kell	K1 (K), K2 (k), K3 (Kp^a), K4 (Kp^b), K5 (Ku), K6 (Js^a), K7 (Js^b), K8 (kw), K9 (KL), K10 ($U1^a$), K11, K12, K13, K14, K15, K16
Lewis	Le^a (Le1), Le^b (Le2), Le^x (Le^{ab}, Le3), Mag (Le4), Le^c (Le5), Le^d
Duffy	Fy^a (Fy1), Fy^b (Fy2), Fy^{ab} (Fy3), Fy4
Kidd	Jk^a (Jk1), Jk^b (Jk2), Jk^{ab} (Jk3)
Cartwright	Yt^a, Yt^b
Xg	Xg^a
Dombrock	Do^a, Do^b
Auberger	Au^a
Cost-Sterling	Cs^a, Yk^a
Wright	Wr^a, Wr^b
Diego	Di^a, Di^b
Vel	Vel 1, Vel 2
Sciana	Sm, Bu^a
Bg	Bg^a, Bg^b, Bg^c, Ho, Ho-like, Ot, Sto, DBG (similar to HL–A7 of lymphocytes)
Gerbich	Ge1, Ge2, Ge3 (anti-Gel = M.Y.; anti-Ge1,2 = Ge; anti-Ge1,2,3 = Yus)
Coltan	Co^a, Co^b
Stoltzfus	Sf^a

Low-incidence antigenic determinants not thus far associated with a blood group system:
Be^a, Bec, Bi, Big Charles, Bp^a, Bx^a, By, Cad, Chr^a, Coates, Craig, Dahl, Donaviesky, Driver, Duch, Evans, Evelyn, Fin, Fuerhart, Gf^a, Gilbraith, Good, Green, Hands, Heibel, Hil, Ht^a, Je^a, Jn^a, Job, Kam, Ken, Kosis, Lev, Lw^a, McCall, Man, Mar, Mo^a, Nij, Orr, Pt^a, Rd^a, Reid, Rm, Skjelbred, Th^a, To^a, Tr^a, Ven, Wb, Weeks, Wu, Yh^a, Za, 754

High-incidence antigenic determinants not thus far associated with a blood group system:
An^a, At^a, Bou, Bra, Car, Chido (Gursha), Cip, Dp, El, En^a, Fuj, Gn^a Go^b, Gy^a, Hen, Hy, Jo^a, Jr, Kelly, Knops, Lan, MZ443, Ola, Pea, Savior, Sch, Sd^a, Simon, Ters, Todd, Vennera, Wil, Winbourne

Antigenic determinants that depend on gene interactions:	
ABO/I	IH, IA, IB, iH
P/I	IP1, IP2 (IT_j^a), I^TP1, iP1
Lewis/I	ILe^{bh}
Lewis/ABO	A_1Le^b
P/ABO	Luke
Xor/Duffy	Fy5
Rh/LW	Rh25 (LW)

[*] Symbols within parentheses are those of alternative nomenclatures.

(Compiled by Dr. Fred H. Allen, Jr.)

synthesis N-acetyl-α-D-galactosaminyl transferase, whereas that for B is responsible for α-D-galactosyl transferase. Either A or B is created when one of these hexasaccharides is positioned by a specific transferase in $1 \rightarrow 3$ linkage to the β-D-galactose of an H-active oligosaccharide. Type O occurs when neither transferase is present or, very rarely (Bombay type), when H does not exist. When both transferases are present, type AB results. Differences in degree of transferase activity are determined at the same locus: weak transferase gives rise to weak antigens (A_2, A_3 A_x, B_3 B_x). Similar oligosaccharides, especially in bacterial cell walls, immunize persons lacking A or B so that their serum contains anti-A or anti-B activity. A and B antigens are on the mucopolysaccharides of secretors; persons with dominant genes have H-active mucoids. A and B are largely glycolipids in the red cell membrane.

Similarly, the trial court did not abuse its discretion in allowing the chemist to testify that only 12 or 14 percent of the population has international **blood group B**. Redd v. State, 243 S.E.2d 16, 18 (Ga.1978).

Blood samples taken from the house indicated that in addition to the blood of the victim, there also were present stains of blood type B, rh positive, configuration c,c,D,e,e. Expert testimony indicates that on the average thirteen persons in ten thousand have blood of this type and configuration. Mitchell v. State, 238 S.E.2d 100, 102 (Ga.1977).

blood group B See *blood group ABO*.

blood group, Rh the most complex of all human blood groups because the genes differ by determining a different number of the 33 antigens thus far described, and do so with remarkably different quality. Negroes show the greatest degree of diversity, Orientals the least. The major antigen, Rh1 (Rh_o,D), is highly immunogenic and, before the development of passive immunization prophylaxis, was responsible for serious hemolytic disease of the newborn. Two other pairs of alternative antigens are inherited with or without Rh1; these are Rh21 (rh^G, C^G) and Rh4 (hr′, c), and Rh3 (rh″, E) and Rh5 (hr″, e). The commonest groups of antigens are $R^{-1,-3,-21}$ (in Caucasians), $R^{1,-3,-21}$ (in Negroes), $R^{1,-3,21}$ (in Orientals and Caucasians), and $R^{1,3,-21}$ (in Orientals and Caucasians). Another antigen Rh10 (hr^v, V) is common in Negroes. See also *sensitization, Rh*.

Garber's blood has a very rare **Rh factor** and she produces the antibody as an immunological response to the introduction of blood with a different **Rh factor** into her bloodstream. U.S. v. Garber, 589 F.2d 843, 845 (5th Cir. 1979).

Plaintiff's six-count complaint for negligence and willful and wanton misconduct alleges that in October of 1965, when her mother was 13 years of age, the defendants, on two occasions, negligently transfused her mother with 500 cubic centimeters of **Rh-positive blood**. The mother's **Rh-negative blood** was incompatible with, and was sensitized by, the **Rh-positive blood**. Her mother had no knowledge of an adverse reaction from the transfusions and did not know she had been improperly transfused or that her blood had been sensitized. Renslow v. Mennonite Hosp., 367 N.E.2d 1250, 1251 (Ill.1977).

The **Rh, or Rhesus, factor** in blood is present in about 85 per cent of the population, who are accordingly classified as having Rh positive blood. The other 15 per cent of the population, without the **Rh factor**, are classified as Rh negative. A person whose **Rh factor** is strongly positive is said to be Rh positive homozygous. A child born of an Rh positive homozygous father and an Rh negative mother will have Rh positive blood....

The testimony of various doctors established that a child of an Rh positive homozygous father and a sensitized Rh negative mother would be Rh positive and, in all probability, would suffer from erythroblastosis fetalis at birth. Price v. Neyland, 320 F.2d 674, 675–6 (D.C.Cir.1963).

Other Authorities: Ortho Pharmaceutical Corp. v. American Cyanamid Co., 361 F.Supp. 1032, 1035 (D.N.J.1973).

blood group Rh negative and Rh positive See *sensitization*.

blood-letting device See *device, blood-letting*.

blood plasma (blud plaz′mah) the liquid portion of the blood in which the particulate components are suspended. See also *blood*.

blood pressure See *pressure, blood*.

blood sugar See *sugar, blood*.

blood serum (blud se′rum) the clear liquid that separates from the blood when it is allowed to clot completely. It is therefore blood plasma from which fibrinogen has been removed in the process of clotting.

blood type See *blood group*.

blowout, stump See *gastrectomy* (Reams case).

blue baby See *tetralogy of Fallot* (Johnson case).

BOD See *biochemical oxygen demand*, under *demand*.

bodily injury [Warsaw Convention] See under *injury, bodily*.

body (bod′e) any mass or collection of material.

body (as a whole)

The question presented is whether plaintiff's impairment is to her right arm or to her **body** as a whole. In one sense an impairment of any part of the **body** is necessarily, to some extent, an impairment of the whole **body**. The statute, (Neb.Rev. Stat.) § 48–121, however, requires that we distinguish between scheduled member impairments and nonscheduled **body** as a whole impairments....

... See, also, Scamperino v. Federal Envelope Co., (205 Neb. 508, 288 N.W.2d 477 [1980]), wherein we held the evidence supported a finding that a fracture to the right leg which healed with such a deformity as to affect the hip and rest of the **body** produced a disability of the **body** as a whole. In this case there is no finding of the development of such unusual and extraordinary conditions which affected the **body** as a whole. Nordby v. Gould, Inc., 329 N.W.2d 118–20 (Neb. 1983).

body, carotid a small neurovascular structure lying in the bifurcation of the right and left carotid arteries; it contains chemoreceptors that monitor the oxygen content of the blood and help to regulate respiration. Called also *glomus caroticum*.

Paul Guidry, appellant, sued appellee Dr. John R. Phillips alleging malpractice, negligence, fraud, and breach of warranty in the performance of alleged unnecessary surgery to remove appellant's **carotid body** from his neck in an effort to cure his asthma.[1] . . .

. . . Clearly Dr. Petty is expressing his opinion of this type of surgery as of 1972:

The removal of the **carotid body** is not an accepted procedure for the cure or treatment of emphysema or asthma or chronic bronchitis. The reason that it is not accepted is as follows: The **carotid body** is important in the respiration, and its removal robs the body of one of the regulatory mechanisms of breathing. Nonetheless, the procedure has been proposed really without much scientific rationale, tried by a number of physicians worldwide; found ineffectual and abandoned. In my own judgment, the procedure is not only not beneficial, but potentially harmful.

The concluding portion of this testimony indicates that Dr. Petty's opinion as to the treatment for asthma is expressed of the year in which his deposition was taken. The record shows that the operation on appellant was performed during the time in which the **carotid body** surgery was being proposed and performed by a number of physicians worldwide. It was only subsequent to 1963 that it was generally found to be ineffectual and was abandoned. [1 For an explanation of carotid body surgery see Hood v. Phillips, 554 S.W.2d 160 (Tex.1977), especially footnote 2, at 162.] Guidry v. Phillips, 580 S.W.2d 883, 885, 887 (Ct.Civ.App.Tex.1979).

Attempting to reduce Mr. Hood's suffering, Dr. Phillips removed one of the **carotid bodies** from his neck.[2] . . .

Dr. Thomas Petty, a physician employed by the University of Colorado Medical Center as an associate professor of medicine in charge of the pulmonary disease division, testified upon deposition by written questions that **carotid surgery** is not an accepted procedure for the cure or treatment of emphysema. [2 As described by Dr. Phillips, this surgical procedure involved the removal of the **carotid body** and the nerves surrounding it. The **carotid body** is a receptor for chemical stimuli "sensitive to the concentration of carbon dioxide in the blood, and assist[s] in reflex control of respiration." Henry Gray, F.R.S., Anatomy of the Human Body, at 895 (29th Am. ed. 1973). At trial, Dr. Phillips explained the surgical removal of the **carotid body** as an attempt to improve the airflow to the lungs by lessening the spasms of the involuntary muscles in the bronchial tubes.] Hood v. Phillips, 554 S.W.2d 160, 162–3 (Tex.1977).

As described by Dr. Phillips, this surgical procedure involved the removal of the **carotid body** and the nerves surrounding it. The **carotid body** is a receptor for chemical stimuli "sensitive to the concentration of carbon dioxide in the blood, and assist[s] in reflex control of respiration." Henry Gray, F.R.S., Anatomy of the Human Body, at 895 (29th Am. ed. 1973). At trial, Dr. Phillips explained the surgical removal of the **carotid body** as an attempt to improve the airflow to the lungs by lessening the spasms of the involuntary muscles in the bronchial tubes. Hood v. Phillips, 554 S.W.2d 160, 162 (Tex.1977).

body, ketone the substances acetone, acetoacetic acid, and β-hydroxybutyric acid. Except for acetone (which may arise spontaneously from acetoacetic acid), they are normal metabolic products of lipid (and pyruvate) metabolism via acetyl-CoA within the liver, and are oxidized by the muscles. Acetoacetic acid is convertible to fatty acids and to steroids. Excessive production leads to urinary excretion of these bodies, as in diabetes mellitus. Called also *acetone b's.*

body, pineal a small, somewhat flattened, cone-shaped body in the epithalamus, lying above the superior colliculi and below the splenium of the corpus callosum. Arising embryologically from the ependyma of the third ventricle of the brain and consisting of cords of pinealocytes supported by interstitial cells, it is the site of synthesis of melatonin, which inhibits gonad development and influences estrus in mammals and produces marked lightening of the dermal pigmentation in amphibians by stimulating the aggregation of melanosomes into melanophores. Melatonin secretion is diminished during exposure to environmental light; the pineal body synthesizes and releases melatonin in response to norepinephrine, whose rate of release, in turn, declines when light activates retinal photoreceptors. Called also *corpus pineale* [NA], *conarium, epiphysis cerebri,* and *pineal gland.*

Dr. Price performed a series of tests consisting of ordinary skull X-ray, brain scan, spinal tap and an echoencephologram. The skull X-ray indicated a **pineal** shift of five millimeters, ordinarily symptomatic of a growth in the brain or a malformation of blood vessels. Stinnett v. Price, 446 S.W.2d 893, 894 (Ct.Civ. App.Tex.1969).

Boeck's sarcoid See *sarcoidosis.*

Bogen's method See *test, Bogen's.*

boilermakers' deafness See *tinnitus* (Marsh case).

bone (bōn) [L. *os;* Gr. *osteon*] 1. the hard form of connective tissue that constitutes the majority of the skeleton of most vertebrates; it consists of an organic component (the cells and matrix) and an inorganic, or mineral, component; the matrix contains a framework of collagenous fibers and is impregnated with the mineral component, chiefly calcium phosphate (85 per cent) and calcium carbonate (10 per cent), which imparts the quality of rigidity to bone. Called also *osseous tissue.* 2. any distinct piece of the osseous framework, or skeleton, of the body; called also *os.* See illustration accompanying *skeleton.* See also *autogenous; graft, bone; heterogenous; homogenous; os;* and *xenograft.*

bone, carpal the eight bones of the wrist. See also *ossa carpi.* [NA].

bone, coffin the third or distal phalanx of the foot of a horse; called also *pedal b.* and *os pedis.*

In this case, drugs did not halt the inflammation and the laminae began to separate. This in turn caused the **coffin bone**, which is the bone inside the hoof, to rotate and penetrate the sole of the hoof. Because of the severe pain from the exposure of this bone, the horse had to be destroyed. Campbell v. C.I.R., 504 F.2d 1158, 1163 (6th Cir. 1974).

bone, cranial the bones that constitute the cranial part of the skull, including the occipital, sphenoid, temporal, parietal, frontal, ethmoid, lacrimal and nasal bones, the inferior nasal concha, and vomer; called also *ossa cranii.* [NA]. See also *facial bones.*

bone, cuneiform, internal See *os cuneiforme media.*

bone, cuneiform, medial See *os cuneiforme mediale.*

bone, facial the bones that constitute the facial part of the skull, including the hyoid, palatine, and zygomatic bones, the mandible, and the maxilla; called also *ossa faciei* [NA]. The facial bones are considered by many to include the lacrimal and nasal bones, the inferior nasal concha, and the vomer, but not the hyoid bone.

bone, lubinate See *os lunatum.*

bone, metacarpal the five cylindrical bones of the hand. See also *ossa metacarpalia I–V.*

He was taken to the hospital where X-rays revealed a fracture of the **metacarpal bone** in his right foot. He was fitted with a walking cast and he returned to work with the cast in place. Giant Food, Inc. v. Coffey, 451 A.2d 151, 153 (Ct.Spec.App. Md.1982).

bone, navicular [of hand] See *os scaphoideum.*

bone, occipital a single trapezoidal-shaped bone situated at the posterior and inferior part of the cranium. See also *os occipitale* [NA].

bone, parietal one of the two quadrilateral bones forming part of the superior and lateral surfaces of the skull, and joining each other in the midline at the sagittal suture; called also *os parietale* [NA] and *bregmatic b.*

He received a laceration of the scalp over the **parietal** area and was bruised over his left shoulder and upper chest. Fillwock v. Brown & Root, Inc., 422 So.2d 458–9 (Ct.App.La. 1982).

bone, scaphoid See *os scaphoideum.*

bone, sesamoid a type of short bone occurring mainly in the hands and feet, and found embedded in tendons or joint capsules; called also *ossa sesamoidea* [NA].

Her **sesamoid bones**, which are small bones located in the tendons, were removed, and a metal pin was inserted in her left great toe. Following her release from the hospital, she continued to see Dr. Smith approximately once each week. However, claimant's condition failed to improve, and she was required to undergo surgery on two further occasions. Claimant testified that she still suffers extreme pain, and that her foot swells, runs a fever, and is subject to a discoloration which extends to her knee. Zick v. Industrial Com'n, 444 N.E.2d 164–5 (Ill.1982).

bone, temporal one of the two irregular bones forming part of the lateral surfaces and base of the skull, and containing the organs of hearing; called also *os temporale* [NA].

bone, zygomatic the triangular bone of the cheek. See also *os zygomaticum.*

bone screw See *bur*; and *drill.*

Bon-ecine See *cholera, hog* (Denman case).

Under a government license Armour manufactured the **Bon-Ecine** product, which is a modified live virus vaccine of homologous tissue culture origin. Denman v. Armour Pharmaceutical Co., 322 F.Supp. 1370, 1372 (N.D.Miss.1970).

Bo-plant See *graft, bone* (E. R. Squibb & Sons, Inc. case); and *hetogenous.*

botulinum See *Clostridium botulinum.*

botulism (boch'oo-lizm) [L. *botulus* sausage] a type of food poisoning caused by a neurotoxin (botulin) produced by the growth of *Clostridium botulinum* in improperly canned or preserved foods. It is characterized by vomiting, abdominal pain, difficulty of vision, nervous symptoms of central origin, disturbances of secretion, motor disturbances, dryness of the mouth and pharynx, dyspepsia, a barking cough, mydriasis, ptosis, etc. *Botulism* is the broader term; *allantiasis* refers only to sausage poisoning. See also *Clostridium botulinum.*

The history of **botulism** occurrence in whitefish, as established in the trial record, which we must assume was available to the FDA in 1970, is as follows. Between 1899 and 1964 there were only eight cases of **botulism** reported as attributable to hot-smoked whitefish. In all eight instances, vacuum-packed whitefish was involved. All of the eight cases occurred in 1960 and 1963. The industry has abandoned vacuum-packing, and there has not been a single case of **botulism** associated with commercially prepared whitefish since 1963, though 2,750,000 pounds of whitefish are processed annually.

[But on appeal the court noted]: . . . There has not been a single case of **botulism** associated with commercially prepared whitefish since 1963, though 2,750,000 pounds of whitefish are processed annually. U.S. v. Nova Scotia Food Products Corp., 568 F.2d 240, 250 (2d Cir. 1977), judgment reversed 568 A.2d 240, 250 (2d Cir. 1977).

The same witness testified that since 1899 there had been ten outbreaks of **botulism** traced to C. botulinum Type E and that the toxin produced by the C. botulinum Type E spore development is a lethal toxin. It is common knowledge that **botulism** is an acute food poisoning marked by a high rate of mortality. (See, generally Exhibits P, P–1.) U.S. v. Nova Scotia Food Products Corp., 417 F.Supp. 1364, 1371 (E.D.N.Y.1976).

He also pointed to evidence that the addition of nitrites may reduce the dangers of **botulism** in meat products, and suggested that a ban on nitrites would eliminate this benefit, perhaps unnecessarily. Schuck v. Butz, 500 F.2d 810, 811 (D.C.Cir. 1974).

bougie (boo-zhe') [Fr. "wax candle"] a slender, flexible, hollow or solid, cylindrical instrument for introduction into the urethra or other tubular organ, usually for the purpose of calibrating or dilating constricted areas. See illustration.

In making this [Nissen] repair, a **bougie**, which is a dilator, is pushed down like a tube through the esophagus, so the repair will not be made too tight and the surgeon will have something to stabilize the esophagus enabling him to wrap the stomach around it. Stringer v. Zacheis, 434 N.E.2d 50, 52 (App.Ct.Ill. 1982).

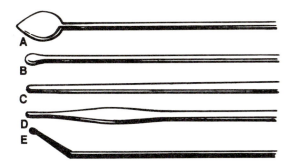

Bougies: *A*, Otis bougie à boule; *B*, olive-tipped bougie; *C*, Garceau bougie; *D*, Braasch bulbous bougie; *E*, filiform bougie.

Bovie machine See *machine, Bovie; electrosurgery*; and *resectoscope* (Thomas case).

bowel (bow'el) [Fr. *boyau*] the intestine. See also *disease, ischemic bowel; infarction* (Allstate case); and *"run the bowel"* (Hitch case).

bowel, inflammatory, disease See *disease, inflammatory bowel*.

bowel sound See *sound, bowel*.

Bowen's lesion See *disease, Bowen's*.

BPH (benign prostatic hypertrophy) See under *hypertrophy*.

brace (brās) an orthopedic appliance or apparatus (an orthosis) used to support, align, or hold parts of the body in correct position; also, usually in the plural, an orthodontic appliance for the correction of malaligned teeth. See also *arch, band*; and *wire, arch* (both U.S. v. Deep case).

Q. Did you experience any problems as a result of wearing that **hinged knee brace** for approximately a year?

A. Yes. I would have to lace it so tight in order to keep my left knee in place that I would cut off the circulation off of my leg and my leg would swell above the **brace** and also below the **brace**. And my toes would discolor, and three to four times a night I would have to open it up and massage my leg in order to get circulation back. The pain was terrible.... If I slacked off a little bit on the **brace**, [the left knee] would not stay in place. I'd go to step down, and I would fall because there was nothing there. Shepard v. Midland Foods, Inc., 666 P.2d 758, 760 (Mont.1983).

A supportive **brace** enables Ms. Storey to walk without dragging the disabled foot. The device is attached at the calf and extends into her shoe where a thin piece of plastic supports her foot from underneath. In this way the foot is kept at a right angle to her leg. Storey v. Lambert's Limbs & Braces, Inc., 426 So.2d 676–8 (Ct.App.La.1982).

brace, four poster neck

Upon her release, she was required to wear a full body cast until some time in October 1968. After that was removed, she was fitted with a "**four poster neck brace**," which she wore continuously through December of that year. Modave v. Long

Island Jewish Medical Center, 501 F.2d 1065, 1068 (2d Cir. 1974).

brace, halo

The **halo brace** is a device wherein the head is held in a rigid position with reference to the neck, by screws which are surgically inserted into the skull from a steel frame above the head, supported by a collar around the neck and chest. Mrs. Rue wore this type brace for a period of three months during which time she was totally disabled. She had complaints of neck, shoulder, and head pains consistently during this three-month period of agonizing neck tension and was heavily sedated the first nineteen days of its application. Rue v. State, Dept. of Highways, 376 So.2d 525–6 (Ct.App.La.1979).

brace, Jewitt

Thereafter, Worthington was required to wear a **Jewitt brace**, a padded metal device that immobilizes the spine. Worthington v. Bynum, 281 S.E.2d 166, 170 (Ct.App.N.Car.1981), reversed 290 S.E.2d 599 (N.C.1982).

brachial block See *block, brachial*.

brachial neuritis See *amyotrophy, neuralgic*.

brachial plexus See *plexus, brachial*.

brachial plexus palsy See *brachial paralysis; Erb-Duchenne paralysis*; and *Klumpke-Dejerine paralysis* under *paralysis*.

brachium (bra'ke-um), pl. *bra'chia* [L.; Gr. *brachiōn*] [NA] the arm; specifically the arm from shoulder to elbow.

bradycardia (brad"e-kar'de-ah) [*brady-* + Gr. *kardia* heart] slowness of the heart beat, as evidenced by slowing of the pulse rate to less than 60.

bradycardia, vasovagal

Petitioner, David M. Ramonett, had been employed three months as an electrician's helper underground when he accidentally pricked his finger on some wires, fainted, and went into convulsions. He recovered with seemingly nothing more major than a slightly cut finger and a minor head laceration which he sustained when he fell, but because of the fainting and convulsions he embarked on a series of medical tests. It was feared he might have epilepsy. The tests eventually led to a diagnosis of "**vasovagal bradycardia**", a condition which would cause slowing of petitioner's heartbeat, fainting, and seizures, if he sustained even a minor injury. The exact medical etiology of **vasovagal bradycardia** is unknown; painful physical or mental stimuli seem to bring on the attacks. There is no contention that the condition itself is in any way work related. Ramonett v. Industrial Com'n, 558 P.2d 923–4 (Ct.App.Ariz. 1976).

brain (brān) [Anglo-Saxon *braegen*] that part of the central nervous system contained within the cranium, comprising the prosencephalon; mesencephalon, and rhombencephalon; it is derived (developed) from the anterior part of the embryonic neural tube. Called also *encephalon*. See also *cerebrum*; and *infection, fungal*. See illustrations.

96

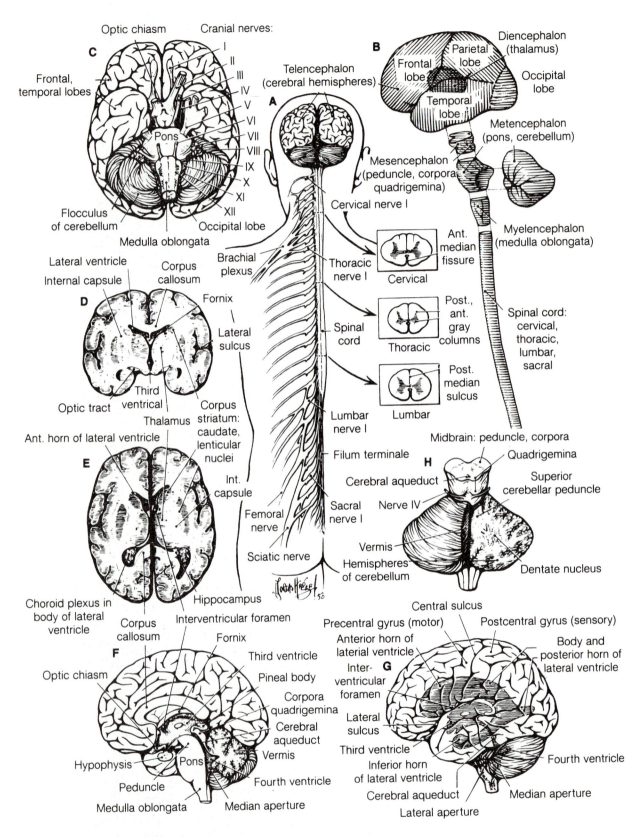

C

Optic chiasm

Cranial nerves:
I
II
III
IV
V
VI
VII
VIII
IX
X
XI
XII

Frontal,
temporal lobes

Pons

Flocculus
of cerebellum

Medulla oblongata

Occipital lobe

Telencephalon
(cerebral hemispheres)

A

B

Diencephalon
(thalamus)

Frontal
lobe

Parietal
lobe

Occipital
lobe

Temporal
lobe

Mesencephalon
(peduncle, corpora
quadrigemina)

Metencephalon
(pons, cerebellum)

Cervical nerve I

Myelencephalon
(medulla oblongata)

Brachial
plexus

Thoracic
nerve I

Ant.
median
fissure

Cervical

Post.,
ant.
gray
columns

Thoracic

Spinal cord:
cervical,
thoracic,
lumbar,
sacral

Spinal
cord

Lateral ventricle

Corpus
callosum

Internal capsule

D

Fornix

Lateral
sulcus

Post.
median
sulcus

Lumbar

Lumbar
nerve I

Optic tract

Third
ventrical

Thalamus

Corpus
striatum:
caudate,
lenticular
nuclei

Ant. horn of lateral ventricle

E

Int.
capsule

Filum terminale

Femoral
nerve

Sacral
nerve I

Sciatic nerve

Midbrain: peduncle, corpora

H

Quadrigemina

Cerebral aqueduct

Superior
cerebellar peduncle

Nerve IV

Vermis

Hemispheres
of cerebellum

Dentate nucleus

Choroid plexus in
body of lateral
ventricle

Corpus
callosum

Interventricular foramen

Fornix

Hippocampus

Central sulcus

Precentral gyrus (motor)

Postcentral gyrus (sensory)

Anterior horn of
lateral ventricle

Body and
posterior horn of
lateral ventricle

F

Third ventricle

Inter-
ventricular
foramen

G

Optic chiasm

Pineal body

Corpora
quadrigemina

Lateral
sulcus

Cerebral
aqueduct

Third ventricle

Vermis

Inferior horn
of lateral ventricle

Fourth ventricle

Hypophysis

Pons

Peduncle

Fourth ventricle

Cerebral aqueduct

Median aperture

Medulla oblongata

Median aperture

Lateral aperture

VARIOUS ASPECTS AND SECTIONS OF BRAIN AND SPINAL CORD

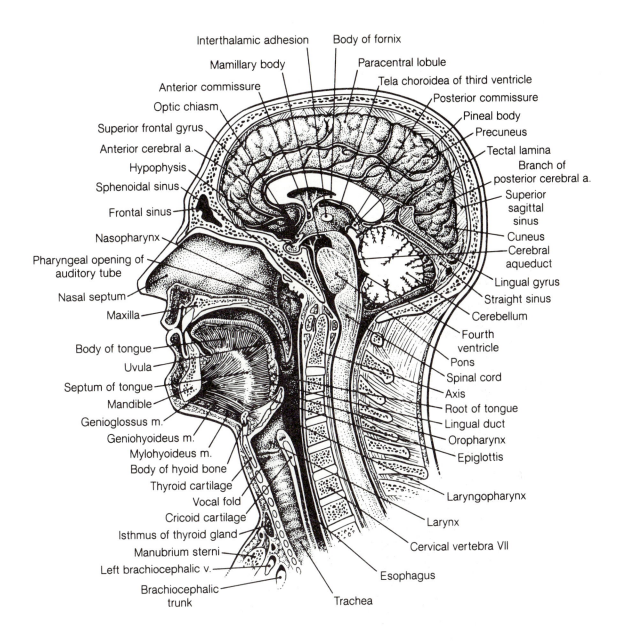

Interthalamic adhesion
Mamillary body
Anterior commissure
Optic chiasm
Superior frontal gyrus
Anterior cerebral a.
Hypophysis
Sphenoidal sinus
Frontal sinus
Nasopharynx
Pharyngeal opening of auditory tube
Nasal septum
Maxilla
Body of tongue
Uvula
Septum of tongue
Mandible
Genioglossus m.
Geniohyoideus m.
Mylohyoideus m.
Body of hyoid bone
Thyroid cartilage
Vocal fold
Cricoid cartilage
Isthmus of thyroid gland
Manubrium sterni
Left brachiocephalic v.
Brachiocephalic trunk

Body of fornix
Paracentral lobule
Tela choroidea of third ventricle
Posterior commissure
Pineal body
Precuneus
Tectal lamina
Branch of posterior cerebral a.
Superior sagittal sinus
Cuneus
Cerebral aqueduct
Lingual gyrus
Straight sinus
Cerebellum
Fourth ventricle
Pons
Spinal cord
Axis
Root of tongue
Lingual duct
Oropharynx
Epiglottis
Laryngopharynx
Larynx
Cervical vertebra VII
Esophagus
Trachea

HEMISECTION OF HEAD AND NECK, SHOWING VARIOUS PARTS OF BRAIN AND OTHER STRUCTURES
(Anson)

The contusions to the **brain** suffered by Mr. Naylor involved the **brain** stem, an area important to respiration, heart function, and other automatic functions. Additionally, Dr. Kirgis stated that Mr. Naylor received damage to both hemispheres of the **brain**, causing dysfunction to both sides of the body. The accident caused interruptions in the connections from the **brain** stem to the cerebral cortex, involved in the thinking process. Thus, Dr. Kirgis testified that it is impossible for Mr. Nay-

lor to tend to himself, since his injuries have caused a loss of motor coordination. Damage to the **brain** stem itself causes Mr. Naylor to have problems breathing and in relieving his bladder and bowels, which he cannot control. Naylor v. La. Dep't of Public Highways, 423 So.2d 674, 685 (Ct.App.La. 1982).

The fungal infection invaded his **brain** and he was required to undergo three operations on his skull and **brain**. A portion of the frontal lobe of his **brain** was removed together with a large portion of his skull. Although the hair does to some extent hide the crater left by the removal of the skull, it can be seen and is a tragically disfiguring annoyance to the plaintiff. McLean v. U.S., 446 F.Supp. 9, 13 (E.D.La.1977).

There is substantial medical evidence as to the effect of the destruction of a portion of the plaintiff's **brain**. The neurosurgeon who treated minor plaintiff following the accident testified to the condition of Ronald Masters upon admission to the Lower Bucks County Hospital:

''. . . At that time he had sustained a deep laceration of the right side of his head in the front which . . . had penetrated through the bone, through the covering of the **brain**, and into the **brain** itself. He also had **brain** tissue oozing out of the opening which this injury had made, and fluid which normally covers the **brain** was also oozing out in large, rather large amounts at that time.''

He further testified that:

''The **brain** itself, which was mascerated by the injury was removed—that portion of it which was protruding through the hole.''. . .

The minor plaintiff also sustained severe permanent disfigurement due to this accident. For instance, in testifying as to his examination in May of 1961, Dr. Sagan said:

''On that occasion Ronald had a large defect in the frontal part of the head where the bone had been removed . . . This area here was devoid of any bone, was an open area. You could see his **brain** pulsating underneath it, jumping and beating as it normally does. What I did was to put a plate in there to cover that area so that the pulsation of the **brain** would not be visible, and also so he would have some protection over the front part of his **brain** from any further injury.'' Masters v. Alexander, 225 A.2d 905, 911–12 (Pa. 1967).

brain, cortical motor system of See *system, cortical motor, of the brain*.

brain, tumor

Prior to discharge from the army 12/2/70 and thereafter, the deceased presented with behavior classical for an intercranial lesion but the V.A. failed to diagnose a **brain tumor** until or about 8/18/75. They kept treating him for a psychiatric disorder; by the time they finally worked him up for a **brain tumor**, five years had elapsed from when it should have been diagnosed until the time it was diagnosed. Dundon v. U.S., 559 F.Supp. 469, 476 (E.D.N.Y.1983).

brain, wet an edematous condition of the brain. See also *brain edema*, under *edema*.

brain damage See *abruptio placentae* (Friel case); *arrest, cardiac* (Rose case); *homorrhage, pial*; and *syndrome, postconcussional*.

Dr. Rosenberg testified that Evelyn Seaton's **brain damage** resulted from a lack of oxygen due to the cardiac arrest and that according to medical literature if the brain is deprived of oxygen for a period of four to six minutes **brain damage** results. The surgeon declined to be unequivocal on this point, testifying that depending on the individual a shorter or longer period of time would be required. Seaton v. Rosenberg, 573 S.W.2d 333, 335 (Ky.1978).

Infant plaintiff has suffered permanent **brain damage**. As a result, although he can see some light, he is cortically blind and will remain so for the rest of his life. He will never be able to read nor will he ever be able to learn through the Braille system. The nerves in his right hand have been so affected that he does not have the sense of touch in that hand required to utilize the Braille system. His mind is functioning well and he must learn whatever he can through listening. . . .

. . . I find that the permanent **brain damage** which the infant plaintiff suffered was not caused by the cardiac arrest in the operating room. At most that arrest resulted in a neurological injury or insult which was reversible and Hakim, Associated Anesthesiologists and Dr. Ho were in no way at fault for that arrest or injury.

The permanent **brain damage** with which infant plaintiff must live for the rest of his life was proximately caused by Hospital through the negligent acts and omissions of its employees and the defective equipment utilized in the care of the infant plaintiff in the intensive care unit. Rose v. Hakim, 335 F.Supp. 1221, 1228 (D.C.Cir.1971).

. . . plaintiff suffered severe and permanent **brain damage** from cerebral anoxia or hypoxia (complete or partial deprivation of oxygen to the brain) while he was anesthetized during surgery, and that cerebral anoxia or hypoxia was due to inadequate ventilation of the patient during the anesthesia or postoperative period. Pederson v. Dumouchel, 431 P.2d 973, 976 (Wash.1967).

Other Authorities: Vallot v. Camco, Inc., 396 So.2d 980, 985 (Ct.App.La.1981); Healy v. White, 378 A.2d 540, 544 (Conn. 1977); Rose v. Hakim, 335 F.Supp. 1221, 1228 (D.D.C.1971).

brain damage, asphyxial

The evidence at trial conflicted as to the cause of plaintiff's resulting condition. Dr. Harris, an anesthesiologist, testified that after reviewing plaintiff's hospital records, Dr. Bolgla's anesthesiology records of plaintiff and others, and depositions of certain people, it was his opinion that a respiratory depression had occurred during plaintiff's operation. He stated that plaintiff's symptoms were the result of **asphyxial** (characterized by suffocation) **brain damage** which probably occurred over a five to twelve minute period. Vuletich v. Bolgla, 407 N.E.2d 566, 568 (App.Ct.Ill.1980).

brain disease See *disease, brain*.

brain scanner See *roentgenograph*, and *tomograph*.

brain stem (brān'stem) the stemlike portion of the brain connecting the cerebral hemispheres with the spinal cord and comprising the pons, medulla oblongata, and mesencephalon; the diencephalon is considered part of the brain stem by some. See also *stroke*.

She found an abnormal jerking-type movement of plaintiff's eyes on the gaze to the right and a marked right side weakness in examination of the motor system. Cerebral function was normal on the left side, but impaired on the right, which caused plaintiff to walk with a limp. She concluded plaintiff had a **brainstem** infarction or stroke, but had no opinion as to the cause. Cook v. Marshall Bros. Lincoln-Mercury, Inc., 427 So. 2d 655, 657 (Ct.App.La.1983).

The notes and summaries then indicate that, between fifteen minutes and an hour after the needle was removed, Mr. Mc-

Clain developed a severe headache, nausea and vomiting, high blood pressure, and lowered pulse and respiratory rates. Immediately after demerol was administered for the plaintiff's headache, Mr. McClain became rigid and unresponsive, or "decerebrate," and remained in this state over the next twenty-four to forty-eight hours.

Both of the plaintiff's medical experts testified that these symptoms demonstrated that Mr. McClain sustained a **brain stem** injury sometime during the procedure [Cisternal Puncture, Q.V.]. Both testified that the respiratory and cardiac symptomatology indicated an injury to the medulla obligata, the lower portion of the **brain stem**, and that the decerebrate rigidity showed an injury to the pons, the middle portion of the **brain stem**, located just above the medulla. McClain v. U.S., 490 F.Supp. 485, 486 (E.D.Wis.1980).

Further testing showed Anunti's dizziness to result from **brain stem** damage rather than damage to the inner ear. Anunti v. Payette, 268 N.W.2d 52, 54 (Minn.1978).

Other Authorities: Matter of Quinlan, 348 A.2d 801, 809–10 (Super.Ct.N.J.1975).

brain surgery See under *stereoencephalotomy.*

brain wave See *wave, brain.*

breathalyzer test See *test, breathalyzer.*

breathing (brēth'ing) the alternate inspiration and expiration of air into and out of the lungs. See also **pleura**; and *respiration.*

breathing, intermittent positive pressure the active inflation of the lungs during inspiration under positive pressure from a cycling valve; abbreviated IPPB.

Dr. Savonen ordered an **Intermittent Positive Pressure Breathing** (IPPB), a machine that keeps the lungs expanded. Erickson v. U.S., 504 F.Supp. 646, 648 (D.S.Dak.1980).

On these occasions, she had received medication and had received assistance with breathing from an inhalation machine known as an **IPPB** device. Fraijo v. Hartland Hospital, 160 Cal. Rptr. 246, 248 (Ct.App.Cal.1979).

breech delivery See *delivery, breech.*

breech, frank See *presentation, breech, frank.*

breech position, frank See *presentation, breech, frank.*

bridge See *denture.*

broach (brōch) a fine instrument used by dentists for assisting in the instrumental cleansing of a root canal or for extirpating the pulp.

broach, root canal a broach for use in removing the contents of a root canal of a tooth.

Thereafter, the defendant proceeded to prepare the tooth for a possible root canal filling using a tiny instrument known as an endodontic broach or **root canal broach**. This device is approximately 1¼ inches long and has tiny barbs along one end of it. It is used to extract tissue from within the root canal of the tooth. In size and shape, it somewhat resembles a common straight pin.

During the course of the dental work, the plaintiff swallowed this small instrument. Major abdominal surgery was ultimately required for its removal and this suit followed. Bean v. Stephens, 534 P.2d 1047–48 (Ct.App.Wash.1975).

bronchial See *bronchus.*

bronchiectasis (brong"ke-ek'tah-sis) [*bronchus* + Gr. *ektasis* dilatation] chronic dilatation of the bronchi marked by fetid breath and paroxysmal coughing, with the expectoration of mucopurulent matter. It may affect the tube uniformly (*cylindric b.*), or occur in irregular pockets (*sacculated b.*), or the dilated tubes may have terminal bulbous enlargements (*fusiform b.*).

He now weighs 105 pounds; when he was hired at the foundry he weighed 145 pounds. He had no breathing problems when hired; he now has chest pains, cough, dizziness and weakness. He has difficulty climbing stairs, carrying anything or breathing in a supine position.

On cross-examination, claimant testified that at Louise Burg Hospital in 1962 or 1963 his condition was diagnosed as **bronchiectasis**. Gray v. Industrial Commission, 394 N.E.2d 1153–54 (Ill.1979).

However, X-rays confirmed that she was suffering from a lung condition diagnosed as bilateral **bronchiectasis**, an anatomical derangement in the bronchial tree that increases the susceptibility to lung infection. Stevens v. Parke, Davis & Co., 507 P.2d 653, 655 (Cal.1973).

... he concluded that tuberculosis was ruled out and that plaintiff probably suffered from **bronchiectasis**, a lung condition causing cough and expectoration. Claborn v. Cohen, 303 F.Supp. 167, 168 (E.D.La.1969).

Other Authorities: Black v. Richardson, 356 F.Supp. 861, 866 (D.S.Car.1973).

bronchitis (brong-ki'tis) [*bronchus* + *-itis*] inflammation of one or more bronchi. See also *asthma.*

He entered the shed and was overcome by a high concentration of grain dust produced by an unloading operation which was taking place below. He could hardly see but he made his way to the man-lift and descended to the main floor. As he proceeded down, he experienced extreme breathing difficulties. The claimant was immediately taken to a physician. The treating physician prescribed epinephrine to relieve bronchial spasm, and diagnosed Ridenour's condition as acute asthmatic **bronchitis**. Ridenour v. Equity Supply Co., 665 P.2d 783–84 (Mont.1983).

On January 19, 1981, the appellant again consulted with Dr. Allain and for the first time referred to her history of creosote related problems. She complained of coughing, congestion and sputum production. Dr. Allain's examination revealed thick postnasal drainage, a flushed appearance over the maxillary sinus area, and coarse breath sounds throughout the chest. Dr. Allain assumed that the congestion and sputum production was caused by a streptococcal infection. Dr. Allain gave the appellant a broad spectrum antibiotic, a decongestant and an expectorant and recommended that she continue to use a bronchial dilater. He diagnosed this condition as **bronchitis**. Sellers v. Breaux, 422 So.2d 1231, 1235 (Ct.App.La.1982).

According to Doctor Levinson the claimant's symptoms were related to recurrent **bronchitis** that is triggered by repeated respiratory infections and a history of multiple episodes of pneumonia, hypertension and sinus tachycardia. According to

Doctor Levinson the claimant's condition was also aggravated by a history of heavy cigarette smoking. In the opinion of Doctor Levinson, the claimant's condition was not work related or occupational in nature. McHale v. Workmen's Compensation Appeal Bd., 425 A.2d 34, 35 (Cmwlth.Ct.Pa.1981).

Other Authorities: Young v. Marsillett, 473 S.W.2d 128–29 (Ct.App.Ky.1971).

He diagnosed the appellant's condition as recurrent **asthmatic bronchitis** associated with previous chemical inhalation with residual chronic bronchial inflammation, coupled with chronic rhinitis and sinusitis resulting from the previous chemical inhalation. Dr. Perret was of the opinion that the appellant was disabled from the point of view that irritating fumes, vapors and smoke would cause her to have attacks. Sellers v. Breaux, 422 So.2d 1231, 1235 (Ct.App.La.1982).

... he had continually experienced coughing spells, shortness of breath, dizziness, wheezing and congestion. His condition was diagnosed as **asthmatic bronchitis** and was concluded to be a manifestation of an organic problem due to the exposure to various fumigants and corn husking fumes. Duquesne Brewing Co. v. Workmen's Comp. App. Bd., 303 A.2d 541, 542 (Cmwlth.Ct.Pa.1973).

Dr. Metz diagnosed appellant's condition as a moderately severe **chemical bronchitis** secondary to allergy with contact dermatitis. He treated her primarily with cortisone and determined that she was disabled at this point in time. Sellers v. Breaux, 422 So.2d 1231–32 (Ct.App.La.1982).

bronchitis, chronic a long-continued form, often with a more or less marked tendency to recurrence after stages of quiescence. It is due to repeated attacks of acute bronchitis or to chronic general diseases; characterized by attacks of coughing, by expectoration, either scanty or profuse, and secondary changes in the lung tissue.

Dr. Spotnitz, a specialist in chest conditions, diagnosed petitioner's condition as **chronic asthmatic bronchitis** which he defined as:

"... a term that is defined as a history of a cough almost everyday of the year for at least three months for two consecutive years. And what this means generally is that the patient does have overgrowth or enlargement of the mucous secreting glands of the bronchial tubes, which is usually due to chronic irritation from some cause or other."

"In my mind I am not satisfied that we know enough as to why people get this. But certainly smoking is usually a very significant part of the history in those patients that develop this type of problem."

On cross-examination, Dr. Spotnitz specifically excluded petitioner's employment as a cause of the preexisting **chronic asthmatic bronchitis:**

"Q. Is it your opinion then—let me put it in a question—that you don't think that working around the flour caused this asthmatic bronchitis, the chronic asthmatic bronchitis condition?

"A. Right." Sutton v. Industrial Com'n, 509 P.2d 234, 236 (Ct.App.Ariz.1973).

bronchitis, chronic asthmatic See *bronchitis, chronic*; and *asthma.*

bronchogenic carcinoma See *carcinoma, bronchogenic*; and *bronchus.*

bronchography (brong-kog'rah-fe) [*bronchus* + Gr. *graphein* to write] roentgenography of the lung after the instillation of an opaque medium in a bronchus.

My new compounds are useful as X-ray contrast agents and are particularly valuable for visualizing the bronchial tree (**bronchography**).... Application of Papesch, 315 F.2d 381, 389 (U.S.Ct.Cust. & Pat.App.1963).

bronchopneumonia (brong"ko-nu-mo'ne-ah) [*bronchus* + *pneumonia*] a name given to an inflammation of the lungs which usually begins in the terminal bronchioles. These become clogged with a mucopurulent exudate forming consolidated patches in adjacent lobules. The disease is frequently secondary in character, following infections of the upper respiratory tract, specific infectious fevers, and debilitating diseases. In infants and debilitated persons of any age it may occur as a primary affection. Called also *bronchial pneumonia, bronchiolitis, bronchoalveolitis, bronchopneumonitis, catarrhal pneumonia, lobular pneumonia, capillary bronchitis* and *vesicular bronchiolitis.*

On August 8, 1973, Decedent was suddenly inflicted by a severe headache followed in the next days by a rash and a high fever, among other symptoms of an illness....

... Thereafter, Decedent's condition quickly deteriorated; he fell into unconsciousness and died on August 29, 1973. On the official death certificate filed August 30, 1973, the cause of Decedent's death was listed as "Bi-lateral Confluent **Bronchopneumonia**." Novak v. Workmen's Compensation Appeal Bd., 430 A.2d 703, 705 (Commonwealth.Ct.Pa.1981).

That the direct cause of death was acute **bronchopneumonia** developing in an atelectatic and fibrotic left lung secondary to pleural carcinomatosis and that bilaterial anthracosilicosis of moderate severity contributed to the demise of the decedent."...

... There was also an acute and organizing necrotizing **bronchopneumonia**.... Consolidation Coal Co. v. Workmen's Compensation, 391 A.2d 14, 17 (Cmwlth.Ct.Pa.1978).

bronchoscope (brong'ko-skōp) an instrument for inspecting the interior of the tracheobronchial tree and carrying out endobronchial diagnostic and thereapeutic maneuvers, such as taking specimens for culture and biopsy and removing foreign bodies.

bronchoscopy (brong-kos'ko-pe) [*bronchus* + Gr. *skopein* to examine] examination of the bronchi through a bronchoscope.

From the evidence it appears that the most effective diagnostic tool in detecting tracheal tumors of any kind is a **bronchoscopy** examination, which was the procedure used when Joynt's tumor was finally discovered. A **bronchoscopy** involves placing an instrument called the bronchoscope down the patient's throat. This tube-like instrument is equipped with fiber optics which permit the administering physician to conduct a visual examination of the trachea and the main bronchial tubes. The bronchoscope can also be fitted with surgical instruments which can be used to obtain tissue samples for biopsies. The procedure involves some risk and at least a day in the hospital as an out-patient. Joynt v. Barnes, 388 N.E.2d 1298, 1304 (App.Ct.Ill.1979).

... she underwent **bronchoscopy** and a bronchogram. These tests disclosed that the entire lower lobe and middle lobe of her right lung were essentially completely destroyed by bronchiectatic disease. Black v. Richardson, 356 F.Supp. 861, 866 (D.S.Car.1973).

A **bronchoscopy** report indicates a tumor mass displacing the lower trachea, corona, and left main bronchial branch downward and to the right. Smith left the hospital on November 11, with a final diagnosis of bronchogenic carcinoma of the left lung, and it was recommended that he return in ten days for exploratory surgery. Petition of U.S., 303 F.Supp. 1282, 1310 (E.D.N.Car.1969).

Other Authorities: ZeBarth v. Swedish Hospital Medical Center, 499 P.2d 1, 4 (Wash.1972); McKay v. Bankers Life Co., 187 N.W.2d 736–7 (Iowa 1971).

bronchospasm (brong'ko-spazm) spasmodic contraction of the smooth muscle of the bronchi, as occurs in asthma.

When the smooth type muscles encircling the bronchial tubes constrict, they close down the tubes so that less and less air passes through them. This constriction of the bronchial tubes is known as bronchial spasm or **bronchospasm**. During a severe bronchial spasm there is a complete closing of the bronchial tubes, blocking any air from reaching the lungs. A bronchial spasm is part and parcel of an asthmatic attack. Siegel v. Mt. Sinai Hospital of Cleveland, 403 N.E.2d 202, 204–5 (Ct.App. Ohio 1978).

The anesthesiologist's report stated that Smith had experienced a "**broncho spasm**" which, Di Maio explained, could have blocked the air passage making it impossible for the anesthesiologist to ventilate the patient. The surgeons' report on the other hand stated that when they noticed the patient's color change they asked the anesthesiologist about the status of the patient, [and] he said he had difficulty ventilating the patient....

... If the anesthesiologist is correct, and I have to assume so, there was a **bronchial spasm**, the diaphragm couldn't move because he couldn't get the air beyond the obstruction. People v. Stewart, 358 N.E.2d 487, 490 (N.Y.1976).

Dr. Martin J. Sokoloff testified on Cuevas' behalf that he was suffering from severe chemical bronchitis with marked **bronchospasm**. He testified that this condition rendered Cuevas totally disabled and unable to pursue gainful employment which required physical exertion. Cuevas v. Platers & Coaters, Inc., 346 A.2d 6, 7 (Pa.1975).

bronchus (brong'kus), pl. *bron'chi* [L.; Gr. *bronchos* windpipe] any of the larger air passages of the lungs, having an outer fibrous coat with irregularly placed plates of hyaline cartilage, an interlacing network of smooth muscle, and a mucous membrane of columnar ciliated epithelial cells.

Dr. Norton, the examining physician, referred Smith to Dr. Williams, a thoracic surgeon, who noted the progressive consolidation and retraction of the left upper lobe, probably occasioned by the tumor compressing the **bronchus** "rather than being related to the accident two months previous." Petition of U.S., 303 F.Supp. 1282, 1310 (E.D.N.Car.1969).

"Brown Lung" disease See *byssinosis.*

Brucella (broo-sel'lah) [Sir David *Bruce*] a genus of microorganisms of the family Brucellaceae, order Eubacteriales, made up of nonmotile short, rod-shaped to coccoid, gram-negative encapsulated cells. It includes three species which may be differentiated on the basis of (1) the relative content of two antigens, A and M, (2) sensitivity to thionine and basic fuchsin, (3) production of hydrogen sulfide, and (4) the requirement for carbon dioxide on primary isolation.

... **brucella** produces brucellosis.... U.S. v. City of Asbury Park, 340 F.Supp. 555, 566 (D.N.J.1972).

brucellosis (broo"sel-lo'sis) a generalized infection of man involving primarily the reticuloendothelial system, caused by species of *Brucella*, namely, *B. melitensis, B. abortus, B. suis,* and *B. canis,* derived from contact respectively with goats, cattle, pigs, and dogs. Its incubation is an average of three weeks, and symptoms include fever of verying pattern, malaise, and headache. It has been variously called *undulant fever, abortus fever, Malta or Maltese fever, Mediterranean fever* or *phthisis, Cyprus fever, goat fever, goat's milk fever, Gibraltar fever, mountain fever, Neapolitan fever, rock fever, febris melitensis, febris sudoralis, febris undulans, fièvre caprine, Bruce's septicemia, brucellemia, brucelliasis, melitensis septicemia,* and *melitensis.*

Bruce-Protocol See *protocol, stress test.*

bruit (brwe, broot) [Fr.] a sound or murmur heard in auscultation, especially an abnormal one.

The examination further revealed a **bruit** which indicates blood going through a compressed artery, over the left collarbone when Cress' arm was elevated. Cress v. Mayer, 626 S.W.2d 430, 432–3 (Ct.App.Mo.1981).

bruxism (bruk'sizm) [Gr. *brychein* to gnash the teeth] rhythmic or spasmodic grinding of the teeth in other than chewing movements of the mandible, especially such movements performed during sleep. Dental malocclusion and tension-release factors are the usual inciting causes. Cf. *bruxomania* and *clenching.*

Plaintiff complained to him that defendant had ground off an excessive amount of her upper left lateral incisor (No. 10). His examination revealed that most of plaintiff's teeth exhibited excessive wear. Such wear is usually the result of **bruxism, i.e.,** the unconscious grinding or clenching of the teeth, usually done while sleeping. He attributed plaintiff's wear and fractured enamel to **bruxism**. Also, plaintiff stated to him that she bit her fingernails; that can result in wear on the teeth. Normal chewing results in a force on the teeth of between 2 to 12 pounds per square inch. On the other hand, **bruxism** can result in a force of over 300 pounds per square inch. Sullivan v. Russell, 338 N.W.2d 181, 185 (Mich.1983).

bruxomania (bruk"so-ma'ne-ah) grinding of the teeth occurring as a tension-release habit in the waking state; called also *brychomania.* Cf. *bruxism.*

Bryant's traction See *line, Bryant's.*

buccal (buk'al) [L. *buccalis,* from *bucca* cheek] pertaining to or directed toward the cheek.

Subsequently, other methods of administration were developed, notably the **buccal** method, which comprises putting a tablet in the pouch of the cheek.... Armour Pharmaceutical Co. v. Richardson-Merrell, Inc., 396 F.2d 70, 71 (3d Cir. 1968).

buccally (buk'al-le) toward the cheek.

... **buccally** (by holding the material in the mouth against the cheek wall through which it can be absorbed). Armour Pharmaceutical Co. v. Richardson-Merrell, Inc., 396 F.2d 70, 72 (3d Cir. 1968).

bucking

"Bucking" is the manifestation of the "gag reflex" which is a reaction of the body to prevent foreign material from entering the trachea, e.g. the characteristic gagging that occurs when a physician places a tongue depressor into the back of the throat. Battles v. Aderhold, 430 So.2d 307, 310 (Ct.App.La. 1983).

bulla (bul'ah), pl. *bul'lae* [L.] a large vesicle, usually 2 cm. or more in diameter.

Dr. Goyer examined him around 8:30 a.m., and detected increased swelling, eccymosis (spots of blood in the skin) and hemorrhagic **bullae** (blisters filled with blood). King v. Murphy, 424 So.2d 547, 548 (Miss.1982), modified 466 So.2d 856 (1985).

BUN blood urea nitrogen. See *urea nitrogen.*

Dr. Purpura noted that he left the hospital "in poor condition with an elevated blood sugar and a **BUN**." Ressegiue v. Secretary of H.E.W. of United States, 425 F.Supp. 160, 162 (E.D. N.Y.1977).

A blood test, called a **BUN**, for amounts of blood, urea, and nitrogen in the blood also indicated that plaintiff had infection. Harrigan v. U.S., 408 F.Supp. 177, 180 (E.D.Pa.1976).

bunion (bun'yun) [L. *bunio;* Gr. *bounion* turnip] abnormal prominence of the inner aspect of the first metatarsal head, accompanied by bursal formation and resulting in a lateral or valgus displacement of the great toe.

She worked alone in six-hour and nine-hour shifts without scheduled breaks or lunch hours, and her duties required her to be constantly on her feet. As part of her uniform, Bean was required to buy and wear "closed shoes" with hard soles. In November, she began having pain in her left foot, and in February she consulted Dr. Bruce Vogel, a podiatrist. Dr. Vogel diagnosed her condition as "chronic bursitis secondary to hallux valgus, metatarsus primus varus, inflamed metatarsal-phalangeal joint (**bunion**) [secondary] to repeated trauma." Ashland Oil Co. v. Bean, 300 S.E.2d 739 (Va.1983).

bunionectomy (bun-yun-ek'to-me) [*bunion* + Gr. *ektomē* excision] excision of an abnormal prominence on the mesial aspect of the first metatarsal head.

Bean underwent surgery ("**Bunionectomy** left foot" and "Wedge osteotomy 1st metatarsal") on March 4, 1981, and thereafter was unable to return to work. Ashland Oil Co. v. Bean, 300 S.E.2d 739 (Va.1983).

bur (ber) a form of drill used for creating openings in bone or similar hard substances. Such an instrument is used in dentistry, in the hand piece of a dental engine, for opening and preparing tooth cavities; called also *bur drill.*

One picture ... revealed an opaque area in the corner of the picture. Reynolds stated that, in his opinion, the image was produced by a broken dental **burr** left in plaintiff's jaw after oral surgery. He said the x-ray taken by the defendant ... had been cut to exclude the showing of the opaque area. Lugo v. Joy, 205 S.E.2d 658–59 (Va.1974).

In bone surgery, a surgical bone screw, said screw made of metal suitable for bone surgery, a cruciate head on said screw, said screw comprising a threaded portion and a cylindrical pilot portion, said pilot portion adapted to fit snugly in a cylindrical hole drilled in the bone cortex, and one or more recesses or pockets provided in the screw and extending from a point in the pilot portion to a point in the threaded portion to provide a self-tapping screw and to receive the bone chips. Collison Engineering Co. v. Murray-Baumgartner Co., 230 F.Supp. 572–3 (D.Md.1964).

During the course of the extraction, it was necessary for defendant to use a drill, called a **burr**, in order to cut the tooth to permit its removal. In removing the tooth small portions of the **burr** broke off, but defendant did not know whether these small pieces remained in the gum or not. In view of the fact that the pieces might be lodged in the patient's gum (although defendant couldn't locate them after an examination) and because plaintiff was exhausted and tired, defendant instructed plaintiff to go home and to return the next day for a further examination. Percifield v. Foutz, 285 P.2d 130–1 (Nev.1955).

burn (bern) a lesion caused by the contact of heat or fire. Burns of the first degree show redness; of the second degree, vesication; of the third degree, necrosis through the entire skin. Burns of the first and second degree are known as partial thickness burns, those of the third degree as full-thickness burns.

He received first and second degree **burns** of both hands and forearms to a point above the elbow, with some third degree **burns** on the arm, hands, and fingers being confined to small areas, such areas being so small that skin grafting was not required. The left hand was more severely **burned** and has resulted in arthritis, with a 20% permanent loss of function of the lower portion of this arm. The only permanent scarring was some depigmentation of the arms and hands. For several years following the injury his skin would be more sensitive to sunlight. Petition of U.S., 303 F.Supp. 1282, 1312 (E.D.N.Car.1969).

... her lower left gums became very sore and painful, and had all the evidences of an extreme **burn**....

... The left side of the lower jaw was red, with a grayish white membrane, and an inflammation of the soft tissues in that region. Mrs. Newport was running a fever. There were lymph nodes on the left side, below the jaw and down the neck, which were enlarged and tender....

... The grayish white membrane on the lower left jaw later sloughed off and the jawbone was exposed. She gave him a history of having received the **burn** when Dr. Hyde took an impression for a partial plate. The condition he found was consistent with that **burn** stated in her history. Dr. Foster knew of nothing else which could have caused that type of **burn** on the gums, localized to the lower left side. It could not be attributable to hot coffee or other hot liquid, because it was localized;

the tongue and right side were not **burned**. Newport v. Hyde, 147 So.2d 113–14 (Miss.1962).

When the chemical gushed out of the bottle, it ran over the palmar surfaces of the middle, ring and small fingers of the left hand, between the fingers and around and onto the dorsum or back of the fingers. It produced third degree **burns** of the backs of the fingers, which involved the deepest layers of the skin. They were painful and required treatment for a long period of time. Crumbled areas of dead tissue appeared and all of the skin sloughed off. Eventually "some little islands of skin" developed and they grew so as to cover the **burned** areas. Lorenc v. Chemirad Corp., 37 N.J. 56, 73, 179 A.2d 401, 410 (1962).

Other Authorities: Piso v. Weirton Steel Co., Div. of Nat. Steel Corp., 345 A.2d 728, 730 (Super.Ct.Pa.1975); Young v. Caribbean Assoc., Inc., 358 F.Supp. 1220, 1223 (D.V.I.1973); Hill v. Gonzalez, 454 F.2d 1201–2 (8th Cir. 1972); Larive v. U.S., 318 F.Supp. 119–21 (D.S.Dak.1970).

burn, brush a wound caused by violent rubbing or friction, as by a rope pulled through the hands; called also *friction b.*

He said Landry "had sustained a **brush burn**", third degree, through the entire skin, considered severe. There were no broken bones, no dislocation of the ankle. He removed all the dead tissue down to a good viable tissue. Landry v. Offshore Logistics, Inc., 544 F.2d 757, 759 (5th Cir. 1977).

burn, cement a corrosive destruction of tissue caused by contact with cement or concrete.

His testimony shows that **cement and concrete burns** occur when there is excessive exposure of the cement juices to the skin. Cement solutions will dissolve the skin and produce a severe burn depending on the time of the exposure and the sensitivity of the skin of the user. Jowers v. Commercial Union Ins. Co., 435 So.2d 575, 577 (Ct.App.La.1983).

burn, first degree

Asked to describe first- and second-degree burns, he testified: "A **first-degree burn** is one which merely produces a redness of the skin, similar to sunburn." Johnson v. Havener, 534 F.2d 1232–33 (6th Cir. 1976).

burn, second degree

A **second-degree burn** produces some destruction of the superficial layers of the skin, like blistering; what is commonly known as blistering.... Johnson v. Havener, 534 F.2d 1232–33 (6th Cir. 1976).

burn, third degree

A **third-degree burn** [w]ould be total destruction of the skin and underlying tissue. Johnson v. Havener, 534 F.2d 1232–33 (6th Cir. 1976).

"The patient was scheduled for surgery, however, prior to surgery he developed **third degree burns** of the buttocks as a result of Aqua Pad malfunctioning." The day after Hale was admitted, Dr. Sciarretta prescribed medication and instructed that the patient be kept "off the burns at all times." One day after that he examined the burned area and noticed that "on both buttocks there were open areas which were nasty looking: Red, with blisters and seepage, sort of a protein-type

seep." Hale v. Holy Cross Hospital, Inc., 513 F.2d 315, 318 (5th Cir. 1975).

It alleged: the Plaintiff sustained first, second and **third degree burns** on her body when the merthiolate and alcohol, with which the Plaintiff had been prepared, was ignited by the negligent use of a hot cautery, which resulted in a flash blaze. Holloway v. Hauver, 322 A.2d 890–91 (Ct.Spec.App.Md. 1974).

burr See *bur.*

bursa (ber'sah), pl. *bur'sae* [L.; Gr. "a wine skin"] a sac or sac-like cavity filled with a viscid fluid and situated at places in the tissues at which friction would otherwise develop. Cited in Langsam v. Minitz, 346 F.Supp. 1340, 1342 (E.D.Pa.1972).

bursa tendinis calcanei [NA], bursa of calcaneal tendon: a bursa between the calcaneal tendon and the back of the calcaneus; called also *b. of Achilles (tendon), calcaneal b., deep postcalcaneal b., subachilleal b.,* and *b. tendinis Achillis* [NA alternative].

bursa trochanterica subcutanea [NA], subcutaneous trochanteric bursa: a bursa between the greater trochanter of the femur and the skin.

bursitis (ber-si'tis) inflammation of a bursa, occasionally accompanied by a calcific deposit in the underlying supraspinatus tendon; the most common site is the subdeltoid bursa. See also *bursa.*

Plaintiff's expert, Dr. Raymond Lipton, testified that plaintiff was suffering from chronic **bursitis** of the hips with a calcific deposit on her right side. Selk v. Detroit Plastic Products, 328 N.W.2d 15, 23 (Ct.App.Mich.1982).

Dr. Woodward deposed that Mattingly has had satisfactory recovery from the surgical procedures, but now suffers from osteoarthritis and trochanteric **bursitis**. Dr. Woodward explained that the **bursitis** was occasioned by Mattingly's being required to lie on his side after the surgery, resulting in irritation of the bursa in his thigh. Pennsylvania Life Ins. Co. v. Mattingly, 464 S.W.2d 632, 634 (Ct.App.Ky.1970).

Other Authorities: Langsam v. Minitz, 346 F.Supp. 1340, 1342 (E.D.Pa.1972).

bursitis, olecranon inflammation and enlargement of the bursa over the olecranon; called also *miners' elbow.*

He had a permanent painful injury consisting of a chronic **olecranon bursitis**; a life expectancy of 13 years; and as symptoms of the injury restricted motion, lack of strength, tenderness and swelling in his elbow. The award here may properly be upheld as one for disability, pain and suffering. Williamson v. Compania Anonima Venezolana de Navigacion, 446 F.2d 1339 (2d Cir. 1971).

bursitis, subscapular See *bursitis;* and *subscapular.*

Schmuck was later diagnosed as having subcoracoid and **subscapular bursitis** in the left shoulder as a result of the accident. This condition produced persistent pain and persistent limitation of motion, such that the claimant had to undergo surgery to remove the bursa, medical procedures for a dislocated shoulder, and the implantation of staples to stabilize the shoulder joint. City of Williamsport v. W.C.A.B., 423 A.2d 817–18 (Commonwealth Ct.Pa.1980).

busulfan (bu-sul'fan) [USP] chemical name: 1,4-butanediol dimethanesulfonate. An alkylating agent, $C_6H_{14}O_6S_2$, occurring as a white, crystalline powder; used as an antineoplastic, chiefly in the treatment of granulocytic (myelocytic) leukemia, administered orally.

Park concluded that his patient was suffering from primary polycythemia. Accordingly, the doctor prescribed a course of treatment which called for the daily consumption of a drug called **Myleran**. During direct examination, Park edified the jury when he pointed out that bone marrow is an essential part of the process that manufactures red blood cells and that **Myleran** "suppresses the activity" of the bone marrow, thereby reducing the blood-cell production....

... Park testified that he had told Young that his use of **Myleran** carried with it the risk of anemia. Young v. Park, 417 A.2d 889, 892–3 (R.I.1980).

butadiene See *ethylene*.

butane (bu'tān) *n*-butane; an aliphatic hydrocarbon of the methane series, C_4H_{10}, from petroleum, occurring as a colorless flammable gas with a characteristic odor.

butazide

They continued her on medicine previously prescribed by Dr. Cuza except that they changed the high blood pressure medicine from butazerpizide to **butazide**. The latter contained a combination of two of the three drugs making up the former....

Dr. Leyden, who treated Mrs. Stanley at the University of Pennsylvania Hospital, said that the best way to ascertain what drug was causing the rash was to cease all medication and then reinstitute them one at a time to see which one was causing the reaction. He thought **butazide** was the most likely culprit and that is why he ordered Mrs. Stanley off it. Stevens v. Barnhart, 412 A.2d 1292–93 (Ct.Spec.App.Md.1980).

Butazolidin (bu"tah-zol'ĭ-din) trademark for preparations of phenylbutazone. See also *phenylbutazone*; and *syndrome, Stevens-Johnson*.

bypass (bi'pas) an auxiliary flow; a shunt.

bypass, aortocoronary a section of saphenous vein or suitable substitute grafted between the aorta and a coronary artery distal to an obstructive lesion in the latter. Called also *coronary artery b.* See also *atherosclerosis* (Icenhour case).

Petitioner was again hospitalized on May 6, 1975. Dr. T. S. Shay's "Final Summary" states that because petitioner had recently developed more symptoms of congestive heart failure, it was determined that he should have a **triple coronary bypass** operation. During the operation it was discovered that the left anterior descending coronary artery was too thin and thus unsuitable for grafting, but two other coronary arteries were grafted. Extensive deterioration due to atherosclerosis was noted. Riley v. Industrial Com'n, 447 N.E.2d 799, 800 (Ill. 1983).

It was determined that Thurmond was suffering from severe occlusive disease of both the major systems of arteries in the heart. A **coronary bypass** operation was recommended by Dr.

Howell. Hartford Acc. & Indem. Co. v. Thurmond, 527 S.W.2d 180, 185 (Ct.Civ.App.Tex.1975).

The operation did not in any way change the condition of his arteries. It only bypassed the obstruction....

... About twenty percent of the venous bypass operations close up again....

... It is my observation after forty years of practice in cardiology that these bypass operations do not cure the underlying disease. Icenhour v. Weinberger, 375 F.Supp. 312, 315 (E.D. Tenn.1973).

by-pass, aorta-femoral

An "**aorta-femoral by-pass**" is a lengthy surgical procedure designed to alleviate poor circulation to the lower extremities of the body. Battles v. Aderhold, 430 So.2d 307, 312 (Ct. App.La.1983).

bypass, coronary See *bypass, aortocoronary*.

bypass, femoropopliteal insertion of a vascular prosthesis from the femoral to the popliteal artery to bypass occluded segments.

Because circulation in Donna's leg was still unsatisfactory on April 10, Dr. Lillehei reopened the area of the previous incisions and, using part of the saphenous vein, constructed a bypass graft in the femoral artery around the site of the previous incisions. Walstad v. University of Minnesota Hospitals, 442 F.2d 634, 637–8 (8th Cir. 1971).

bypass, gastric gastrojejunostomy in which the stomach is transected high on the body, the proximal remnant being joined to a loop of jejunum in end-to-side anastomosis.

Carol, weighing almost 250 pounds, also consulted with Thornton, a board certified abdominal surgeon, concerning a surgical technique for treatment of obesity known as a **gastric bypass**. This technique consists of implanting a row of staples across the upper part of the stomach, segmenting that portion from the rest of the stomach, thus limiting the area available for ingested food. Mercer v. Thornton, 646 S.W.2d 375, 377 (Mo.Ct.App.1983).

bypass, jejuno; bypass, jejunoileal surgical anastomosis of the proximal part of the jejunum to the distal part of the ileum so as to bypass much of the small intestine and reduce intestinal absorption.

... this person underwent an operation for a **jejunoileal bypass** in order to help her reduce her weight which at the time was over two hundred pounds. The operation procedure was a success and the patient has responded favorably to weight reduction type diet. Dean v. Califano, 439 F.Supp. 730, 732 (W.D.Ark.1977).

by-product (bi-prod'ukt) a secondary product obtained during the manufacture of a primary product.

by-product material

The term "**byproduct material**" means any radioactive material (except special nuclear material) yielded in or made radioactive by exposure to the radiation incident to the process of producing or utilizing special nuclear material. 42 U.S.C. § 2014(e). Train v. Colorado Pub. Int. Research Group, 426 U.S. 1, 6, 96 S.Ct. 1938, 48 L.Ed.2d 434 (1976).

byssinosis (bis'ĭ-no'sis) [Gr. *byssos* flax + *-osis*] a pulmonary disease occurring among cotton textile workers and preparers of flax and soft hemp, due to inhalation of textile dust. The acute form is marked by tightness of the chest, wheezing, and cough on return to work after a brief absence (Monday dyspnea). The chronic form, occurring after years of exposure, is marked by permanent dyspnea. It is probably due to smooth muscle contraction resulting from histamine release induced by chemicals in the dust. Called also *brown lung, cotton-dust* or *stripper's asthma, cotton-mill fever,* and *Monday fever.*

Plaintiff's claim is one for **byssinosis** and/or chronic obstructive lung disease both of which are characterized by cough, chest tightness, shortness of breath, fatigue, and sometimes wheezing. Classically, it is worse on Monday when an employee returns to work after having been out on a weekend and his or her condition improves either on days off or on vacation. As the disease progresses, however, the employee continues to worsen throughout the workweek and eventually sees no improvement when he leaves his work environment.

Byssinosis and/or chronic obstructive lung disease is due to chronic exposure to respirable cotton dust. It is, therefore, characteristic of and peculiar to the employment in the textile trade. The general public is not equally exposed outside the employment. Swink v. Cone Mills, Inc., 300 S.E.2d 848, 850 (Ct.App.N.Car.1983), opinion withdrawn 309 S.E.2d 271 (N.C.App.1983). [But see Rutledge v. Tultex Corp., 301 S.E.2d 359 (N.Car.1983).]

For several years preceding Marquard's death, he experienced symptoms of **byssinosis**,[2] i.e., difficulty in breathing, tightness in his chest, and coughing fits. The hearing commissioner determined that the unusual stress placed upon Mar-

quard's heart by **byssinosis** caused his fatal heart attack and that his death was due to accidental injury. [[2] Byssinosis is an obstructive lung disease caused by exposure to cotton dust.] Marquard v. Pacific Columbia Mills, 295 S.E.2d 870 (S.Car. 1982).

The referee made the following finding:
5. On March 5, 1975, the claimant became totally disabled due to chronic obstructive pulmonary disease, mainly of a chronic bronchial asthmatic type. This disease is the result of exacerbation in claimant's occupation involving direct contact with, handling of, or exposure to cotton dust cotton materials, or cotton fibers....

... The claimant's application indicated that benefits were being sought under Sections 108(n) and 108(p) of the Act, 77 P.S. §§ 27.1(n), 27.1(p), and Section 108(p) defines as an occupational disease:
(p) **Byssinosis** in any occupation involving direct contact with, handling of, or exposure to cotton dust, cotton materials, or cotton fibers.

Although, therefore, the finding states that the claimant was exposed to the hazard indicated in Section 108(p), it does not say that the claimant has **byssinosis**. Scranton Garment Co. v. Workmen's Compensation, 381 A.2d 210–11 (Commwlth.Ct. Pa.1977).

Other Authorities: Rutledge v. Tultex Corp. Kings Yarn, 301 S.E.2d 359, 380, 382 (N.Car.1983); Donnell v. Cone Mills Corp., 299 S.E.2d 436–37 (Ct.App.N.Car.1983); Thompson v. Burlington Ind., 297 S.E.2d 122, 124 (Ct.App.N.Car.1982); Taylor v. Cone Mills Corp., 289 S.E.2d 60, 62–66 (Ct.App.N. Car.1982); Walston v. Burlington Ind., 285 S.E.2d 822, 824 (N.Car.1982); Reilly v. Industrial Com'n, 398 P.2d 920–21 (Ct. App.Ariz.1965).

C

c. contact; curie.

cachexia (kah-kek'se-ah) [*cac-* + Gr. *hexis* habit + *-ia*] a profound and marked state of constitutional disorder; general ill health and malnutrition.

Dr. Privitera contends many conceded cancer victims, competent and responsible adults, seek and use amygdalin as a food substance to ameliorate the horrifying physical wasting away of the body (**cachexia**) which accompanies cancer. People v. Privitera, 153 Cal.Rptr. 431, 441 (Cal.1979).

calamine (kal'ah-mīn) [USP] a mild astringent and protectant, consisting of zinc oxide with a small proportion of ferric oxide, and occurring as a fine, pink powder; applied topically in the treatment of skin diseases.

It is without dispute that **calamine** is composed largely of zinc oxide, which when placed on the skin has a drying action, combined with an antiseptic and antipruritic (relief from itching) action, and is pink in color.... Folds v. Federal Trade Commission, 187 F.2d 658–9 (7th Cir. 1951).

calcaneus (kal-ka'ne-us), pl. *calca'nei* [L.] 1. [NA] the irregular quadrangular bone at the back of the tarsus;

called also *calcaneal bone, calcaneum, heel bone, os calcis,* and *os tarsi fibulare.* 2. *talipes calcaneus.*

According to two orthopedic surgeons who examined Musial, Dr. Daniel Kingsley and Dr. James Etheredge, the blow to Musial's heel crushed the **calcenus** [sic] (heel bone) and drove it up into the talus (the shaft of the ankle). Musial v. A & A Boats, Inc., 696 F.2d 1149, 1151 (5th Cir. 1983).

The plaintiff's injuries consisted of a bilateral comminuted fracture of the **os calci** (heel bone) and injuries to the soft tissues of the left foot. Scittarelli v. Manson, 447 F.Supp. 279, 281 (D.Conn.1978).

Other Authorities: Keen v. Prisinzano, 100 Cal.Rptr. 82, 83–4 (Ct.App.Cal.1972); Sharpe v. Grindstaff, 329 F.Supp. 405, 410 (M.D.N.Car.1970).

calcification (kal″sĭ-fĭ-ka'shun) [*calcium* + L. *facere* to make] the process by which organic tissue becomes hardened by a deposit of calcium salts within its substance. See also *ankylosis.*

The **calcification** was the result of an aortic valve disease which may have been congenital or may have been caused by other disease such as rheumatic fever, syphilis or bacterial infections at some earlier time in his life. Guillory v. U.S. Fidelity & Guar. Ins. Co., 420 So.2d 119, 121 (La. 1982).

Calcification is a calcium deposit in tissue which may be indicative of a cancerous process. Davis v. Caldwell, 445 N.Y.S.2d 63, 65 (N.Y.1981).

calcium (kal′se-um), gen. *cal′cii* [L. *calx* lime] a silvery yellow metal, the basic element of lime. Symbol, Ca; atomic number, 20; atomic weight, 40.08. It is found in nearly all organized tissues, being the most abundant mineral in the body. In combination with phosphorus it forms calcium phosphate, the dense, hard material of the teeth and bones. It is an essential dietary element, a constant blood calcium level being essential for the maintenance of the normal heartbeat, and for the normal functioning of nerves and muscles. It also plays a role in multiple phases of blood coagulation (in which it is called *coagulation factor IV*) and in many enzymatic processes.

calcium carbide grayish black lumps or crystals, CaC_2, which yields acetylene on decomposition by water.

Dr. Eads testified that **calcium carbide** when mixed with water produces a compound known as acetylene, which is principally used in this country for cutting steel along with pure oxygen. It has also been used to ripen fruit, i.e. "certain fruit is ripened, or turns yellow, whether it actually ripens or not, it's questionable, but the color of the fruit turns yellow." Dr. Eads stated that bananas are one of the fruits that so react. Eddleman v. Scalco, 484 S.W.2d 122, 125 (Ct.Civ.App.Tex.1972).

calcium hydroxide [USP], a salt, $Ca(OH)_2$, occurring as a white powder; used in solution as a topical astringent.

He then went on to say that when calcium carbide is mixed with water, along with the production of acetylene, **calcium hydroxide** is produced which is very sensitive to volume changes by which he meant that "if you have a mixture of this gas with air, let's say, and you release the pressure at least a tenth to three-tenths of an atmosphere, the gas will decompose and explode. ... It doesn't require a spark, due to its high heat of formation or low heat of formation a minus 50.4 kilograms calories per mole. It's a tricky molecule .... Eddleman v. Scalco, 484 S.W.2d 122, 125 (Ct.Civ.App.Tex. 1972).

calcium sorbate See *acid, sorbic* (Chip Steak Co. case).

calculus (kal′ku-lus), pl. *cal′culi* [L. "pebble"] an abnormal concretion occurring within the animal body and usually composed of mineral salts.

calculus, renal a calculus occurring in the kidney; called also *nephritic c.*

The stone was located in the ureter near its entrance into the bladder. The surgeon first sought to remove the stone by use of a cystascope and a "basket." This procedure was unsuccessful. Major surgery was indicated.

Hart was taken to the operating room and given a general anesthetic. The surgeon opened his abdomen and exposed the ureter and bladder. In order to remove the stone it was necessary for the surgeon to incise both the ureter and bladder. After the stone was removed, the surgeon closed. City of Somerset v. Hart, 549 S.W.2d 814–15 (Ky.1977).

Caldesene See *antifungal* (Pennwalt case).

Caldwell-Luc procedure See *operation, Caldwell-Luc.*

callus (kal′us) [L.] an unorganized meshwork of woven bone developed on the pattern of the original fibrin clot, which is formed following fracture of a bone and is normally ultimately replaced by hard adult bone; called also *bony c.*

There was a fairly large amount of **callus** on the ribs which had been broken, and the rib cage was tender to the touch. Bray v. Yellow Freight System, Inc., 483 F.2d 500, 507 (10th Cir. 1973).

camphor, spirits of See *spirit, camphor.*

camptocormia (kamp″to-kor′me-ah) [Gr. *kamptos* bent + *kormos* trunk + *-ia*] a static deformity consisting of forward flexion of the trunk; called also *camptospasm.*

She walks with a good deal of difficulty, holding her trunk forward 15 degrees, and tilted ten degrees to the right....
... Her peculiar posture is known as "**camptocormia**". Weinstein v. Levy, 18 A.D.2d 398–400 (2d Dep't 1963).

canal (kah-nal′) a relatively narrow tubular passage or channel. See also *canalis.*

canal, root (of tooth) that portion of the pulp cavity in the root of a tooth extending from the pulp chamber to the apical foramen; more than one canal may be present in a root, two commonly being present in the mesial root of the mandibular first molar. Called also *canalis radicis dentis* [NA] and *pulp c.*

We hold that the evidence is insufficient to support the Board's finding and conclusion that "[t]he standard of practice on or about October 1977, among members of the health care profession of general dentistry with similar training and experience as the respondent and situated in the New Bern, North Carolina community or similar communities was that when a **root canal** is performed, the canal of the root is filled with filling material." Dailey v. N.C. State Bd. of Dental Examiners, 299 S.E.2d 473, 479 (Ct.App.N.Car.1983).

Examination revealed that the infection had substantially subsided and that her mouth pain was isolated to her upper right central incisor tooth (number eight). After percussion testing of this tooth, Dr. Karam determined that it did not have a viable blood supply and that the nerve was dead. X-rays of this tooth showed a small **root canal**, pulp stones in the canal and root chamber and infection at the tip of the root....
... Dr. Karam advised Mrs. Wiley that her alternatives were to either remove the tooth or remove the dead material from the **root canal** of the tooth. Mrs. Wiley elected the **root canal** therapy. Dr. Karam then drilled into the tip of the root through the back of the tooth and found pulp stones in the **root canal** which he drilled out with a Pisso reamer. Dr. Karam then attempted to clean out the **root canal** with a root canal reamer, but encountered great difficulty because of the decreased size of the **root canal** caused by calcification. Dr. Karam tried for approximately one hour to complete the **root canal** procedure, but was unsuccessful. During the course of this attempt, a portion of the root canal reamer broke off and lodged in Mrs. Wiley's **root canal**. Wiley v. Karam, 421 So.2d 294–5 (Ct. App.La.1982).

Two, three or possibly four injections of a standard local anesthetic were administered, after which Dr. Faget isolated the tooth with cotton rolls and installed a saliva ejector and began the procedure, which involves the insertion of the reamer into the **root canal** of the tooth. This instrument is held between the thumb and forefinger and is manipulated with a vertical circular motion, the purpose of which is to extract the infected pulp. Dr. Faget had almost completed this process when the reamer slipped from his grasp and fell laterally over the top of the patient's tongue. Dufrene v. Faget, 260 So.2d 76, 78 (Ct.App. La.1972).

canal, verterbral See *canalis vertebralis.*

canalis (kah-na′lis), pl. *cana′les* [L.] [NA] a general term for a relatively narrow tubular passage or channel; called also *canal.*

canalis alimentarius [NA], alimentary canal: that part of the digestive tract formed by the esophagus, stomach, and small and large intestines; called also *alimentary tract, digestive canal, tract,* or *tube,* and *tubus digestorius.*

... when one speaks of the gastro-intestinal tract or GI tract, this generally refers to the entire **alimentary canal,** which starts with the mouth, the pharynx, the esophagus, the stomach, the entire small intestine, the entire large intestine, the rectum and ending at the anus. Mid-Western Life Ins. Co. of Texas v. Goss, 552 S.W.2d 430, 432 (Tex.1977).

canalis facialis [NA]; **canalis fascialis** [Fallo′pii] facial canal: a canal in the temporal bone for the facial nerve, beginning in the internal acoustic meatus and passing anterolaterally dorsal to the vestibule of the inner ear for about 2 mm. Turning sharply backward at the genu of the facial canal, it runs along the medial wall of the tympanic cavity, then turns inferiorly and reaches the exterior of the petrous part of the bone at the stylomastoid foramen. Called also *canal for facial nerve, fallopian aqueduct* or *canal, aqueduct of Fallopius,* and *spiroid canal.*

canalis inguinalis [NA], inguinal canal: the passage superficial to the deep inguinal ring for transmission of the spermatic cord in the male and the round ligament in the female; called also *abdominal canal.*

At that time Dr. Dorman "found an increase in the size of the external **inguinal canal** and the probability of an inguinal hernia" .... Hurlburt v. Fidelity Window Cleaning Co., 160 A.2d 251, 254 (Super.Ct.Pa.1960).

canalis sacralis [NA], sacral canal: the continuation of the vertebral canal through the sacrum.

canalis vertebralis [NA], vertebral canal: the canal formed by the foramina in the successive vertebrae, which encloses the spinal cord and meninges; called also *c. spinalis, medullary canal, neural canal,* and *spinal canal.*

Examination of the **vertebral canal** which is the hole in the center of the vertebrae from the upper aspects. York v. Daniels, 259 S.W.2d 109, 116 (Springfield Ct.App.Mo.1953).

cancellous (kan′sĕ-lus) of a reticular, spongy, or lattice-like structure; said mainly of bony tissue.

When we got into the **cancellous** bone of the ilium, the bone looked abnormal. [In this case the bone was apparently both "cancellous" or spongy and "cancerous"—Ed.] Insurance Company of North America v. Chinowith, 393 F.2d 916, 919 (5th Cir. 1968).

cancer (kan′ser) [L. "crab"] a cellular tumor the natural course of which is fatal. Cancer cells, unlike benign tumor cells, exhibit the properties of invasion and metastasis and are highly anaplastic. Cancers are divided into two broad categories of carcinoma and sarcoma. See also *asbestosis; carcinoma, epidermoid* (Utter case) *echography* (Wild case); *histology, pathologic; invasion; metastasis* (Env. Defense Fund, Inc. case); *mesothelioma; radiation* (Greenberg case); and *sarcoma;* as well as additional terms referred to under these headings.

The plaintiff presented expert testimony that during that month the decedent's **cancer** had progressed from Stage 1 to Stage 2. Testimony also indicated that patients whose **cancer** is diagnosed at Stage 1 have a statistical survival rate of 35 percent; patients at Stage 2 have a survival rate of 24 percent. Herskovits v. Group Health Co-op., 664 P.2d 474, 483 (Wash.1983).

The policy contains the following provisions: ...
Part 2 CANCER DEFINED—POSITIVE PATHOLOGY REQUIRED
   A. **Cancer** is defined as a disease manifested by the presence of a malignant tumor characterized by the uncontrolled growth and spread of malignant cells, the invasion of tissue, or leukemia.
   Such **cancer** as above defined must be positively so diagnosed by a legally licensed doctor of medicine certified by the American Board of Pathology to practice Pathologic Anatomy or by an Osteopathic Pathologist, upon the basis of a microscopic examination of fixed tissue, or preparations from the hemic system (either during the life or post-mortem). The pathologist establishing the diagnosis shall base his judgment solely on the criteria of malignancy as accepted by the American Board of Pathology or the Osteopathic Board of Pathology after a study of the histocytologic architecture or pattern of the suspect tumor, tissue, or specimen. Clinical diagnosis does not meet this standard. Mathis v. American Family Life Assur. Co., 614 S.W.2d 800–2 (Ct.App.Tenn. 1981).

The next expert appearing for the plaintiff was Dr. Johnson, a noted **cancer** specialist. He stated the normal **cancer** growth rate is that it will double in four to six months. He testified that given the average growth rate for **cancer,** if the one by one centimeter cyst in 1971 was the same as the tumor removed in 1972, the growth would have been in excess of six centimeters in October, 1972. He added that the **cancer** growth rate is increased during pregnancy since estrogen receptive **cancer** cells feed upon and grow more rapidly because of the greater hormone secretions caused by pregnancy. Dettmann v. Flanary, 273 N.W.2d 348, 352–3 (Wis.1979).

Other Authorities: Ins. Co. of North America v. Chinowith, 393 F.2d 916, 920 (5th Cir. 1968).

cancer, breast

The collective testimony of the medical experts appearing at the trial indicates that in 1971 the diagnostic procedures available for **breast cancer** were palpation, aspiration, a pap smear, xerography or mammography, biopsy and mastectomy.

Dr. Johnson's own testimony dismisses palpation and aspiration as viable diagnostic procedures in this case. . . . Dr. Hurley stated a mammogram was ill-advised for a pregnant woman. Dettmann v. Flanary, 273 N.W.2d 348, 354 (Wisc.1979).

cancer, cervical

Dr. Thomas knew that the potential harm of failing to detect the disease at an early stage was death.[4] [[4] Expert testimony established that if **cervical cancer** is detected in the early stages of its development, there is a very high probability that the progress of this disease can be permanently arrested.] Truman v. Thomas, 165 Cal.Rptr. 308, 313 (Cal.1980).

cancer, epidermal malignant epithelioma of the skin.

cancer, epidermoid See *cyst, epidermoid*; and *cholesteatoma*.

He did not order a tissue biopsy which probably would have revealed the presence of a tissue cancer, poorly differentiated **epidermoid carcinoma** of the oral cavity, which was the ultimate cause of her death. . . .

. . . They also testified that there is an overall 30 per cent survival rate from this type of cancer and that chance is considerably improved the earlier the cancer is discovered. O'Brien v. Stover, 443 F.2d 1013–14, 1018 (8th Cir. 1971).

. . . at this point Dr. Stover observed what was likely a cancerous tumor on her gum. . . .

. . . There she was immediately diagnosed as suffering from poorly differentiated **epidermoid cancer**. The remaining medical history is not material to this opinion. She underwent massive surgery, radiology treatments, &c., which were unsuccessful, and ultimately died of the cancer. O'Brien v. Stover, 443 F.2d 1013, 1015 (8th Cir. 1971).

cancer, lung See *carcinoma, bronchogenic*; and *carcinoma, epidermoid*.

In his affidavit, Dr. Fisher [Russell S. Fisher Chief Medical Examiner State of Maryland] further stated:

"The diseases of mesothelioma and lung cancer are also associated with prior exposure to asbestos by inhalation. **Lung cancer** is a malignant disease that involves the cells found within the substance of the lung and the airways of the lung. It is a progressive disease which nearly always kills the victim within a year of its diagnosis, in the inoperable state. The duration of the developmental process of **lung cancer** from inception to gross clinical manifestation cannot be stated with absolute certainty but modern medical opinion indicates this time lag to be of the order of months to a year or two at the extreme.

"This kind of disease process is entirely different from the disease process involved with asbestosis, though they both may be associated with an individual's exposure to the mineral asbestos.

"It is a medically accepted fact that an individual who has been diagnosed with the disease of asbestosis will not inevitably contract either of the cancers mentioned above. It is also true that individuals who have been exposed to asbestos and who develop **lung cancer** or mesothelioma, as a result of such exposure, may well not have significant asbestosis. These two situations are possible because, although all

three diseases are associated with the inhalation of asbestos fibers, there is at the present time no medically accepted link between the development of malignant diseases and the development of asbestosis." (Emphasis added.) Pierce v. Johns-Manville Sales Corp., 464 A.2d 1020, 1023 (Ct.App.Md. 1983).

The testimony indicates that only five percent of all **lung cancer** cases survive as long as five years from diagnosis, nearly all of these being operable cases. A typical patient with inoperable **lung cancer** has an eight percent chance of surviving fifteen months with radiation treatments. Once **lung cancer** has penetrated into the mediastinum, the chances of survival are less than two percent. James v. U.S., 483 F.Supp. 581, 586–7 (N.D.Cal.1980).

Dr. Selikoff, expert witness for the claimants:

Lung cancer in general has certain characteristics and I don't refer to the cell type which can be any one of a number including adeno carcinoma, aquamous cell carcinoma, eat cell carcinoma, undifferentiated carcinoma etc., plus its tendency to metastasize in many parts of the body, plus its invasive and often fatal nature, plus its clinical symptoms such as coughing blood etc., but it has the characteristic in general of occurring in the large bronchi, the trachea, the main bronchus and the bronchi near the main bronchus on either side. It is generally a main bronchus tumor.

Q. Excuse me doctor, just to clear my own thinking here. You're talking about cancer in general?

A. In general not related to asbestos, in general. And that's one of the reasons why it's so frequently fatal as you know on the overall I don't think we cure more than 5% because when it's in the main bronchi you just can't go far enough to remove it completely in many cases and when it hits the trachea or the carina you just can't remove two lungs. There is a peculiarity about **lung cancer** associated with asbestos exposure however, in that it occurs typically peripherally in the outer part of the lung. Utter v. Asten-Hill Mfg. Co., 309 A.2d 583, 586–7 (Pa.1973).

cancer, oat cell See *carcinoma, oat cell*; and *cell, oat*.

cancer, pancreatic See *laparotomy* (Conrad case); and *Fluorouracil* (Rizzo case).

At the compensation hearing, Dr. Bristow expressed his conclusion that the pneumonia was "entirely related" to debilitation caused by **cancer of the pancreas**, which he thought itself "very likely a direct complication of Baptist's pulmonary asbestosis." Baptist v. W.C.A.B. of State of Cal., 187 Cal.Rptr. 270 (Ct.App.1982).

cancer, stomach See *gastrectomy* (Cornfeldt case).

cancer, tracheal

An important factor in this case is that **tracheal cancer** is a relatively rare disease—only 400 cases have been reported in world medical literature. The type of cancer cell and the location of Joynt's tumor made his malady even more rare. Another factor making the situation in this case even rarer is the fact that he was only 28 years old at the time the lesion was discovered. Most other reported victims of **tracheal cancer** were in at least their forties when the disease struck. Joynt v. Barnes, 388 N.E.2d 1298, 1304 (App.Ct.Ill.1979).

cancerous See *cancer*.

cancerophobia See *cancerphobia*.

cancerphobia (kan"ser-fo'be-ah) morbid dread of becoming affected with cancer. Called also *carcinophobia*.

She had an overwhelming **cancerophobia** [sic] and in view of her limited life expectancy, I see no reason to burden her with this further fear. Lewis v. U.S., 75–2 Tax Cases Par. 13,087 at 88,830, 88,833 (N.D.Ga.1975).

Candida (kan'dĭ-dah) [L. *candidus* glowing white] a genus of yeastlike imperfect fungi of the family Cryptococcaceae, order Moniliales, characterized by producing yeast cells, mycelia, pseudomycelia, and blastospores. It is commonly part of the normal flora of the skin, mouth, intestinal tract, and vagina, but can cause a variety of infections, including candidiasis, onychomycosis, tinea corporis, tinea pedis, vaginitis, and thrush. *C. albicans* is the usual pathogen, but *C. tropicalis* may also cause infection. Other species are *C. guilliermondi* and *C. krusei*. Called also *Monilia* and *Oidium*, and, formerly, *Blastodendrion*, and *Castellania*.

The purpose of the assembly is to detect **Monilia** within the vaginal tract, and in use the insert device is removed from the container and a specimen is taken from the vaginal tract by direct contact with the culture medium. The applicator is then returned to the container, the cap replaced and the specimen is incubated at room temperature or in an incubator. If **Monilia** is present, a black or brown colony growth appears on the culture medium. Fink v. SmithKline Corp., 186 U.S.P.Q. 262, 267 (N.D.Cal.1975).

Candida parapsilosis a species of limited pathogenicity but particularly associated with endocarditis, paronychia, and otitis externa. See also *candidiasis*; and *candidiasis, endocardial*.

The evidence of adulteration presented at the hearings was expert testimony that one of Dr. DeMarco's syringes containing Procaine-PVP was found to contain **candida parapsylosis** [sic], a yeast-like organism associated with the disease of endocarditis in humans. This evidence sufficiently established adulteration. DeMarco v. Com. Dep't of Health, 397 A.2d 61, 63 (Cmwlth.Ct.Pa.1979).

candidiasis (kan"dĭ-di'ah-sis) infection with a fungus of the genus *Candida*. It is usually a superficial infection of the moist cutaneous areas of the body, and is generally caused by *C. albicans;* it most commonly involves the skin (dermatocandidiasis), oral mucous membranes (thrush, def. 1), respiratory tract (bronchocandidiasis), and vagina (vaginitis). Rarely there is a systemic infection or endocarditis. Called also *moniliasis, candidosis, oidomycosis*, and, formerly, *blastodendriosis*.

candidiasis, endocardial mycotic endocarditis caused by various species of *Candida*.

cannabis (kan'ah-bis) [Gr. *kannabis* hemp] the dried flowering tops of hemp plants, *Cannabis sativa* L. (Cannabaceae), which contains the euphoric principles Δ^1-3,4-*trans* and Δ^6-3,4-*trans* tetrahydrocannabinol, as well as cannabinol and cannabidiol. It is classified as a hallucinogenic and is prepared as bhang, ganja, hashish, and marihuana. See also *cannabism*; and *tetrahydrocannabinol*.

In contrast to the CSA, the Single Convention prescribes different controls for various parts of the **cannabis** plant, as defined in Article 1, ¶1:

(b) "**Cannabis**" means the flowering or fruiting tops of the cannabis plant (excluding the seeds and leaves when not accompanied by the tops) from which the resin has not been extracted, by whatever name they may be designated.

(c) "**Cannabis** plant" means any plant of the genus cannabis.

(d) "**Cannabis** resin" means the separated resin, whether crude or purified, obtained from the **cannabis** plant.

The United States ratified the Single Convention in 1967. For a discussion of the events surrounding that ratification, *see* Cohrssen & Hoover, The International Control of Dangerous Drugs, 9 J. Int'l L. & Econ. 81, 84–87 (1974).

For a history of the Single Convention and its predecessor treaties, *see* Cohrssen & Hoover, supra, at 81–87; Lande, The International Drug·Control System, reprinted in National Commission on Marihuana and Drug Abuse, Second Report, Drug Use in America: Problem in Perspective, Vol. III, at 11–35 (1973); Lande, The Single Convention on Narcotic Drugs, 1961, 16 Int'l Org. 776 (1962). [Footnote Omitted.] Nat. Organization for Reform, etc. v. Drug Enforcement, 559 F.2d 735, 737, 739 (D.C.Cir.1977).

The existence of two species of **Cannabis**, namely **Cannabis sativa** L. and **Cannabis indica Lam.**, has been known and published since about 1783, and the probable existence of the third species, **Cannabis ruderalis Jan.**, has been published since about 1924....

I am also aware that the Courts of Appeals in at least three circuits have accepted the proposition that when Congress used the term "**Cannabis sativa** L." in 1938 and in 1970, it intended to include all plants within the genus **Cannabis**, whether the genus **Cannabis** is considered polytypic or monotypic. United States v. Moore, 446 F.2d 448 (3d Cir. 1971); United States v. Rothberg, 480 F.2d 534 (2d Cir. 1973); United States v. Gaines, 489 F.2d 690 (5th Cir. 1974). Rather, the critical factor is whether in fact the distinctions between **Cannabis sativa** L. and **Cannabis indica Lam.** (and perhaps **Cannabis ruderalis Jan.**) are so insignificant that they are not to be treated as distinct species within the genus **Cannabis**. On the basis of this record, the distinctions are not in fact so insignificant. That penal statutes are to be strictly construed requires no citation of authority....

... This statute is not vague; it applies to **Cannabis sativa** L. and to nothing else. U.S. v. Lewallen, 385 F.Supp. 1140–2 (W.D.Wis.1974).

In RCW 69.33.220(13, 14), of the Uniform Narcotic Drug Act (before the 1969 amendment), it was designated as a narcotic through both its scientific and common names, as follows:

(13) "**Cannabis**" includes all parts of the plant **Cannabis Sativa** L., whether growing or not; the seeds thereof; the resin extracted from any part of such plant; and every compound, manufacture, salt, derivative, mixture, or preparation of such plant, its seeds, or resin; but shall not include the mature stalks of such plant, fiber produced from such stalks, oil or cake made from the seeds of such plant, any other compound, manufacture, salt derivative, mixture or preparation of such mature stalks (except the resin extracted therefrom), fiber, oil, or cake, or the sterilized seed of such plant which is

incapable of germination. State v. Zornes, 475 P.2d 109, 122 (Wash.1970).

cannabism (kan'ah-bizm) a morbid state produced by misuse of cannabis; it is usually responsive to simple reassurance in its acute stage. The occurrence of a chronic brain syndrome as a result of frequent and prolonged use is unsubstantiated.

cannula (kan'u-lah) [L. dim of *canna* "reed"] a tube for insertion into a duct or cavity; during insertion its lumen is usually occupied by a trocar. See also *abortion, suction D & C* (Hitch case); and *trocar*.

William Signorini, an experienced physician's assistant, was causally negligent. He placed a **cannula** on the aortic line [of the heart-lung machine], which should have been left without one. The improper connection caused him to arrange the lines improperly on the operating table, thus setting the stage for what followed. Without Mr. Signorini's initial acts of negligence, the line reversal would not have occurred. Green v. U.S., 530 F.Supp. 633, 643 (E.D.Wis.1982).

You did willfully fail to use medically proper sterilization techniques in the performance of abortions by (1) reusing unsterilized disposable **cannulae** not meant for reuse, (2) using unsterilized tenaculums, sounds and forceps. Sherman v. Com'n on Licensure to Practice, 407 A.2d 595, 598 (D.C.Ct.App. 1979).

A **cannula** is a small needle-like tube, in this case metallic, which may be inserted into a patient's blood vessels for collection purposes. Becton, Dickinson & Co. v. Sherwood Medical Ind. Inc., 516 F.2d 514–15 (5th Cir. 1975).

Other Authorities: Hitch v. Hall, 399 A.2d 953, 955 (Ct.Spec. App.Md.1979).

cannula, nasal

Nasal **cannulas** are devices which release oxygen into the nostrils for the purpose of making pure oxygen available to the patient if he is breathing voluntarily. They are not a means of oxygenating a patient whose respiration has become seriously impaired or ceased altogether. See, e.g., Tr. 117, 246–7. Daniels v. Hadley Memorial Hospital, 566 F.2d 749, 755 (D.C.Cir.1977).

cannulate (kan'u-lāt) to introduce a cannula, which may be left in place.

He was responsible for **cannulating** Mrs. Green. He had been instructed as to how it should be done. He was told to use two safety procedures, either one of which would have prevented the reversal of the lines. He performed neither one. Furthermore, by his own admission, it was his responsibility to watch the directional flow of the liquid in the line when the machine was turned on. He failed to do so. Green v. U.S., 530 F.Supp. 633, 642 (E.D.Wis.1982).

canthotomy (kan-thot'o-me) [*cantho-* + Gr. *temnein* to cut] surgical division of the outer canthus.

However, Mr. Beisel's expert witness, Dr. Soloway, testified that in the treatment of the hemorrhage, Dr. Lazenby should have either performed a lateral **canthotomy** or given Mr. Beisel Malatal or intravenous Diamox. A **canthotomy** consists of splitting the small triangle formed by the eyelids which allows the lids to open wider and the eye to move forward, thereby relieving the pressure ....

On cross-examination, Dr. Soloway admitted that he could not state whether Mr. Beisel's eye would have been saved if Dr. Lazenby had performed a lateral **canthotomy** or administered either Malatal or Diamox. On redirect examination, counsel asked Dr. Soloway whether it was reasonably probable that one of the three methods of treatment he recommended would have saved the eye. Rather than directly responding to the question, Dr. Soloway stated that he had had three patients with severe retrobulbar hemorrhages whose sight had been saved after he performed a **canthotomy**. Two other ophthalmologists testified that Dr. Lazenby's treatment met accepted standards of care and that none of the treatments advocated by Dr. Soloway would have reduced the pressure in the amount necessary to save Mr. Beisel's sight. The jury awarded Mr. Beisel $40,000 and his wife $10,000 for loss of consortium. Lazenby v. Beisel, 425 So.2d 84–5 (D.Ct.App. Fla.1982).

canthus (kan'thus), pl. *can'thi* [L.; Gr. *kanthos*] the angle at either end of the fissure between the eyelids; the canthi are distinguished as outer or temporal, inner or nasal.

cap, duodenal See *pars superior duodeni*.

capacity (kah-pas'i-te) [L. *capacitas*, from *capere* to take] 1. power or ability to hold, retain, or contain, or the ability to absorb. 2. an expression of the measurement of material that may be held or contained. 3. mental ability to receive, accomplish, endure, or understand.

capacity, functional (Class III)

She would have early **Class III functional capacity** [2] of the American Heart Association classification as far as the heart is concerned. [[2] A **Class III functional capacity** is defined as follows:

Class III. Patients with cardiac disease resulting in marked limitation of physical activity. They are comfortable at rest. Less than ordinary physical activity causes fatigue, palpitation, dyspnea, or anginal pain.

See Diseases of the Heart and Blood Vessels—Nomenclature and Criteria for Diagnosis, (6th ed. 1964) cited in Appellant's Br. at 8.] Jackson v. Schweiker, 696 F.2d 630–2 (8th Cir. 1983).

capacity, functional residual the amount of air remaining at the end of normal quiet respiration; abbreviated FRC. See accompanying illustration.

Residual functional capacity consists of two aspects: (1) exertional limitations (i.e., ability to do sedentary, light, medium, heavy or very heavy work), and (2) nonexertional limitations (i.e., mental, sensory, or skin impairments).

The tables of Appendix II consider only the physical exertion aspect of **residual functional capacity**. If the findings in a particular case deal only with exertional limitations, then the applicable rule in the tables of Appendix II is conclusive. However, where non-exertional limitations are involved, the rule serves as a guideline along with the principles and definitions in the regulations, and full consideration must be given to all relevant facts in the case. [26 C.F.R. PART 404] App. II § 200.00(e). Hilliard v. Schweiker, 563 F.Supp. 99, 100 (D.Mont.1983).

Residual functional capacity is defined as:

Your **residual functional capacity** is what you can still do despite your limitations. If you have more than one impairment, we will consider all of your impairments of which we are aware. We consider your capacity for various functions as described in the following paragraphs; (b) physical abilities; (c) mental impairments, and (d) other impairments. **Residual functional capacity** is a medical assessment. However, it may include descriptions (even your own) of limitations that go beyond the symptoms that are important in the diagnosis and treatment of your medical condition. Observations of your work limitations in addition to those usually made during formal medical examinations may also be used. These descriptions and observations, when used, must be considered along with the rest of your medical record to enable us to decide to what extent your impairment keeps you from performing particular work activities. This assessment of your remaining capacity for work is not a decision on whether you are disabled, but is used as the basis for determining the particular types of work you may be able to do despite your impairment.
20 C.F.R. § 404.1545 (1982) (emphasis added). . . .

. . . **Residual functional capacity** is the degree to which an individual can function limited by the physical or mental impairment. § 404.1505(a). Rivers v. Schweiker, 684 F.2d 1144, 1147, 1151 (5th Cir. 1982).

capacity, mental

"The test of **mental capacity** is whether a person is capable of understanding in a reasonable manner, the nature and effect of the act in which the person is engaged." Matter of Estate of Head, In connection with the assertion or non-assertion of legal rights, Annot., 9 A.L.R.2d 964 at 965 (1950), states the disability must be such that the person is "unable to manage his business affairs or estate, or to comprehend his legal rights or liabilities." See also, Adkins v. Nabors Alaska Drilling, Inc., 609 P.2d 15 (Alaska 1980). Lent v. Employment Sec. Com'n of State of New Mex., 658 P.2d 1134, 1137 (Ct.App.N.M. 1982), certiorari quashed 656 P.2d 889 (1983).

capacity, residual functional See *capacity, functional residual*.

caponette

A "caponette" is defined by the Department of Agriculture regulations as:

. . . a young, tender-meated bird (usually under 8 months of age) with a soft, pliable smooth-textured skin, which has been treated with diethylstilbestrol or its equivalent. 7 C.F.R. § 81.131(f)(v) (1960). Bell v. Goddard, 366 F.2d 177–8 (7th Cir. 1966).

capsula (kap'su-lah), pl. *cap'sulae* [L. "a small box"] [NA] a general term for a cartilaginous, fatty, fibrous, or membranous structure enveloping another structure, organ, or part; called also *capsule*.

He diagnosed plaintiff's malady as a **capsular** formation, or scar tissue buildup around the left prosthesis, which should be surgically released. Simons v. Georgiade, 286 S.E.2d 596, 598 (Ct. of App.N.C.1982).

capsula articularis coxae [NA], capsule of hip joint: a large, strong ligamentous sac surrounding the hip joint.

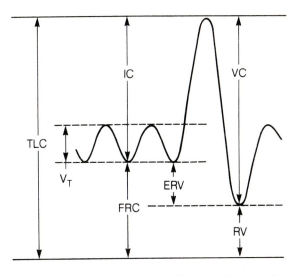

Subdivisions of total lung capacity: *TLC* = total lung capacity; V_T = tidal volume; *IC* = inspiratory capacity; *FRC* = functional residual capacity; *ERV* = expiratory reserve volume; *VC* = vital capacity; *RV* = residual volume. (Bates, Macklem, and Christie.)

Such stretch of the **capsula of the hip joint** interferes with the blood supply to the femoral head. (N.T. 248, 249). Rosario v. American Export—Isbrandtsen Lines, Inc., 395 F.Supp. 1192, 1202 (E.D.Pa.1975).

capsula of the hip joint See *capsula articularis coxae*.

capsular See *capsula*.

capsule (kap'sūl) [L. *capsula* a little box] an anatomical structure enclosing an organ or body part. See also *capsula*.

. . . there was a fracture of the neck of the femur within the **capsule**, the cartilaginous socket for the head of the femur. . . . Agnew v. City of Los Angeles, 286 P.2d 556 (Dist.Ct. App.Cal.1955).

capsule, Gerota's the fascia surrounding the kidney.

Attention was then directed to the renal area. **Gerota's fascia** was opened posteriorly and the perirenal fascia was stripped free from the kidney capsule where there was evidence of a fairly large stellate injury to the midportion of the kidney. Wolff v. Coast Engine Products, Inc., 432 P.2d 562, 567 (Wash.1967).

capsule, joint See *capsula, articularis coxae*.

capsulitis (kap"su-li'tis) the inflammation of a capsule, as that of the lens.

capsulitis, adhesive adhesive inflammation between the joint capsule and the peripheral articular cartilage of the shoulder with obliteration of the subdeltoid bursa, characterized by painful shoulder of gradual onset, with increasing pain, stiffness, and limitation of motion. Called also *adhesive bursitis, peritendinitis,* or *tendinitis, frozen shoulder,* and *periarthritis of shoulder*.

Approximately thirty-six hours after receiving the Swine Flu vaccine Ms. Freeman began to experience extreme pain in her right shoulder and arm, the arm in which the vaccine was administered. Her condition was diagnosed as **adhesive capsulitis** of the right shoulder, an inflammation of the protective sheath that surrounds the joint. The pain restricted the mobility of Ms. Freeman's right arm, which inhibited her ability to perform her duties as a waitress. It also prevented her from sleeping comfortably. According to Ms. Freeman, the pain in her right arm and shoulder continued, in gradually diminishing degrees of severity, through the time of trial in May 1981. Freeman v. U.S., 704 F.2d 154, 159–60 (5th Cir. 1983).

. . . a closed manipulation under general anesthesia was performed on July 14 in order to free an **adhesive capulitis** [sic] or frozen shoulder which had developed . . . .

. . . plaintiff had complaints of pain in his neck on the left side as well as his right shoulder and low back. An orthopedic examination revealed no explanation for these complaints and when given tests for his left shoulder he reached a maximum elevation of 45° in abduction and maximum of 80° in anterior flexion. However, Dr. Grunsten explained that these tests are subjective with the patient being required to raise his arm to the extent he can. However, Dr. Grunsten noted that as plaintiff disrobed he pulled off an undershirt overhead and elevated his left shoulder well above 90° to approximately 110°. Brown v. Celotex Corp., 420 So.2d 205, 207 (Ct.App.La.1982).

Plaintiff was having trouble flexing his middle and ring fingers on his left hand, though he had a full range of motion in his left thumb, index and little fingers. Dr. Morgan diagnosed the problem as **adhesive capsilidus** [sic] (a thickening of the joint capsules caused by the formation of scar tissue along the tendons) in plaintiff's middle and ring fingers. Parnell v. Reed & Sims, Inc., 428 So.2d 899, 902 (Ct.App.La.1983).

Other Authorities: City of Williamsport v. W.C.A.B., 423 A.2d 817, 819 (Commonwealth Ct.Pa.1980). Slater v. Kehoe, 113 Cal.Rptr. 790, 793 (Ct.App.Cal.1974); Hartford Accident & Indemnity Co. v. Helms, 467 S.W.2d 656, 660 (Ct.Civ.App. Tex.1971); Bardessono v. Michels, 478 P.2d 480, 482 (Cal. 1970).

capsulotomy (kap"su-lot'o-me) [*capsule* + Gr. *temnein* to cut] the incision of a capsule, especially of that of the eye, as in cataract operation; or that of a joint. See also *capsule*.

According to Dr. Greenfield, in the performance of a **capsulotomy** the surgical site may be approached from the top or the underside of the toe. An incision is made into the capsule of a toe joint to allow a bent toe to straighten out; blood will necessarily appear and generally a small scar will remain. A true hammertoe cannot be corrected by merely taping the bent toe to its neighbor.

According to appellant, in performing a **capsulotomy** he uses a block anesthesia and a very thin blade to cut the capsule. The next toe is used as a splint, and gauzetex is used to keep the toes together. Matter of Silberman, 404 A.2d 1164, 1167 (Super.Ct.N.J.1979).

"Captain of the Ship" doctrine See *doctrine, "Captain of the Ship"*.

carbamide (kar-bam'īd) urea in anhydrous, lyophilized, sterile powder form; it is injected intravenously in dextrose or invert sugar solution to induce diuresis.

Carbocaine See *mepivacaine hydrochloride*.

carbolic acid See *phenol*.

carbon (kar'bon) [L. *carbo*, coal, charcoal] a nonmetallic tetrad element, found nearly pure in the diamond, and approximately pure in charcoal, graphite, and anthracite; symbol, C; atomic number, 6; atomic weight, 12.011.

carbon chloroform extract test See *test, carbon chloroform extract*.

carbon dioxide an odorless, colorless gas, CO_2, resulting from the oxidation of carbon. It is formed in the tissues and eliminated by the lungs. CO_2 and the carbonates assist in maintaining the neutrality of the tissues and fluids of the body. Inhalations of carbon dioxide, containing not less than 99 percent by volume of CO_2 [USP], mixed with air or oxygen, are used to stimulate respiration. Solid carbon dioxide (*Dry Ice* or *carbon dioxide snow*) has been used as an escharotic to destroy certain skin lesions.

Dr. James T. Weston, chief medical examiner for the State of Utah, testified as to the effects of **carbon dioxide** upon the human body. Dr. Weston's testimony was that lack of oxygen causes dizziness and lightheadedness, and eventually causes a person to pass out. A concentration of **carbon dioxide**, on the other hand, associated with a decrease in oxygen, presents a more hazardous situation since the **carbon dioxide** in the blood returning to the lungs is not released but returns to the body and brain. This situation causes a person to pass out without any warning in as little as three or four breaths. Smith v. Clayton and Lambert Mfg. Co., 488 F.2d 1345, 1347 (10th Cir. 1973).

carbon disulfide a colorless, flammable, poisonous liquid, CS_2, used as a solvent; it is a counterirritant and has local anesthetic properties but is not used as such.

Union Carbide's unique knowledge of the neurotoxicity of CS_2 through its operation since 1971 of the Toxicological Information Response Center at Oak Ridge, Tennessee, and its publication there of Toxicity and Analysis of Carbon Disulfide, an annotated bibliography of 369 references on the analytical methods, toxic effects on humans and animals, and other environmental effects of **carbon disulfide**. Vann v. Dow Chemical Co., 561 F.Supp. 141, 143–4 (W.D.Ark.1983).

carbonium ion See *ion, carbonium*.

carboxypridine disulphide

"CPDS", or **carboxypridine disulphide**, according to plaintiff, retards the growth or spread of cancer by reacting with cancer cells in such manner as to form a stable compound on the surface of such cell. In a sense, then, the theory of the anti-metastatic (or anti-growth or spread) mechanism of **CPDS** is that it forms a hard wall around cancer cells, which does not admit of further growth. Grassetti v. Weinberger, 408 F.Supp. 142, 144 (N.D.Cal.1976).

carcass (kar'kas) [Fr. *carcasse*] a dead body; generally applied to other than a human body.

A **carcass** is "the commercially prepared or dressed body of any cattle, sheep or swine." M.S.A. § 12.964(1)(g), M.C.L.A. § 289.581(g)....

... **Carcass** is defined as "all parts, including viscera, of any slaughtered livestock." 9 C.F.R. § 301.2(ss). However, 9 C.F.R. § 318.6 prohibits as ingredients in meat food products intestines and certain other named internal organs. Armour & Co. v. Ball, 468 F.2d 76, 86 (6th Cir. 1972).

carcina

The examination revealed a tumor at the lower end of the trachea, or windpipe, at the point where the trachea splits off to form the two main bronchial tubes to each lung. This point is called the **carcina**. Joynt v. Barnes, 388 N.E.2d 1298, 1303–4 (App.Ct.Ill.1979).

carcinogen (kar-sin′o-jen) any cancer-producing substance. See also *diethylstilbestrol*.

On the basis of animal tests and clinical experience, experts have concluded that DES is a **carcinogen** to man. Prolonged exposure to small amounts of **carcinogenic** substances has been shown to be more dangerous than single or short term exposure to the same or larger quantities. Bell v. Goddard, 366 F.2d 177, 180 (7th Cir. 1966).

carcinogenesis (kar″sĭ-no-jen′ĕ-sis) [Gr. *karkinos* cancer + *genesis* production] the production of carcinoma.

... **carcinogenesis** [cancer generating].... Dow Chemical Co. v. Ruckelshaus, 477 F.2d 1317, 1320 (8th Cir. 1973).

carcinogenic (kar″sĭ-no-jen′ik) producing carcinoma.

The Department also quotes from a scientific article as follows: "A chemical that is reliably and definitely **carcinogenic** in one or two species very likely will be so in other species, including man." Weisburger & Weisburger, "Chemicals As Causes of Cancer," Chemical Eng. News 44:124 (1966) at p. 127. Dry Color Mfrs. Ass'n Inc. v. Dep't of Labor, 486 F.2d 98, 104 (3d Cir. 1973).

carcinogenicity (kar″sĭ-no-jĕ-nis′ĭ-te) the power, ability, or tendency to produce carcinoma. Cited in Citizens Against Toxic Sprays, Inc. v. Bergland, 428 F.Supp. 908, 916 (D.Or.1977).

carcinoid (kar′sĭ-noid) a yellow circumscribed tumor occurring in the small inntestine, appendix, stomach, or colon; argentaffinoma (q.v.). See also under *syndrome*.

The most probable [cause of death], he said, was a serotonin hormone produced by a **carcinoid** in the appendix. He based that hypothesis upon the fact that 14 years earlier the decedent had undergone surgery for the removal of the right half of the colon for a growth involving the tip of the appendix. This, the doctor said, suggested a **carcinoid**. According to that hypothesis, "this serotonin producing **carcinoid** resulted in a pulmonary hypertension, increased pressure on the right side of the heart, ultimately resulting in a failure of the right side of the heart and the patient's death in the automobile prior to the time that the automobile left the road...." The doctor stated that about two-thirds to three-fourths of the **carcinoids** in the appendix are serotonin producing. Interlake, Inc. v. Industrial Com'n, 447 N.E.2d 339, 342 (Ill.1983).

carcinoma (kar″sĭ-no′mah), pl. *carcinomas* or *carcino'mata* [Gr. *karkinōma* from *karkinos* crab, cancer] a malignant new growth made up of epithelial cells tending to infiltrate the surrounding tissues and give rise to metastases. See also *cancer*; and *esophagus* (Chester case).

As early as June 12, 1972 he was exhibiting symptoms consistent with **carcinoma** of the esophagus. From June on he experienced a steady decline in health. He weighed 232 pounds, he had very high cholesterol, he complained of loss of energy, fatigue, decreasing exercise tolerance, suffered pain intermittently under his rib on his left side which radiated into his left arm, his liver was enlarged, and his appearance changed radically. In August his pains were more frequent and severe, he could not swallow well and regurgitated several times a week, he experienced pain on swallowing and pain on eating. His eating habits changed; from being a hearty, fast eater he changed to eating slowly, eating soft foods and drinking liquids to get the food down; he became pale and lost considerable weight. Chester v. U.S. 403 F.Supp. 458–9 (W.D.Pa. 1975).

According to the hospital records, the final diagnosis was:
Carcinoma of the abdomen either from the sigmoid or from the pancreas with multiple metastases throughout the peritoneal surfaces including obstructive lesions in the small bowel and in the distal ileum and obstructing lesions in the area of the cecum and ascending colon. Disposable Services, Inc. v. ITT Life Ins. Co. of New York, 453 F.2d 218, 220 (5th Cir. 1971).

Other Authorities: Davis v. Caldwell, 445 N.Y.S.2d 63, 65 (N.Y.1981).

carcinoma, anaplastic

It was determined in March 1969 that Joe had **anaplastic carcinoma**, commonly referred to as lung cancer....

... It would be my opinion that the exposure to radiation in uranium mines was probably the cause of his lung cancer. State Compensation Fund v. Joe, 543 P.2d 790–2 (Ct.App.Ariz. 1975).

carcinoma, basal cell; carcinoma bascellulare an epithelial tumor that seldom metastasizes but has potentialities for local invasion and destruction. Clinically, it is divided into types: nodular, cicatricial, morphaic, and erythematoid (pagetoid). Called also *basaloma* or *basiloma*, and *hair matrix c.*

... a growth on the left side of her nose diagnosed as **basal cell carcinoma**. Defendant removed the growth surgically and apparently there was no recurrence at the site until late in 1966. A second operation was performed in February or March of 1967. This was followed by further recurrences and additional surgery performed by defendant. One operation may have been performed in February 1968 according to information attributed to defendant. Another operation was performed in August 1970 which included removal of a growth and plastic reconstruction, including skin grafting, involving the eyelid, cheek and nose....

... A "massive tumor" was discovered, requiring the removal of plaintiff's left eye and a portion of her nose. Radiation therapy was commenced, but plaintiff's condition deteriorated and she was readmitted to Memorial Hospital in 1978 for "excision of **basal cell carcinoma** of nose with total amputation of nose," according to the discharge summary of May 13, 1978. Vasily v. Cole, 413 A.2d 954, 956 (Super.Ct.N.J.1980).

carcinoma, bronchogenic carcinoma of the lung, so called because it arises from the epithelium of the bronchial tree.

Lung cancer, or **bronchogenic carcinoma**, is also generally thought to be caused by prolonged inhalation of asbestos. It too can develop and manifest itself long after inhalation ceases. Keene Corp. v. Ins. Co. of North America, 667 F.2d 1034, 1038 (D.C.Cir.1981).

Bronchogenic carcinoma (lung cancer) is another malignant disease that has been associated with asbestos, at least in persons who smoke cigarettes. It also has a latent period following inhalation averaging approximately 15 to 20 years. It also progresses slowly, but can and often is diagnosed within a few years of its initial appearance. Ins. Co. of No. Am. v. Forty-Eight Insulations, 451 F.Supp. 1230, 1237 (E.D.Mich. 1978).

In November 1964 Mr. Meeks had a slight cold and in December he complained of laryngitis. He then developed a cough, with difficulty in speech and breathing. In February he was admitted to the hospital. Diagnosis of **bronchogenic carcinoma** was made which after a steady downhill course resulted in his death on June 1, 1965. . . .

"... There is no evidence of pulmonary fibrosis reactive elsewhere in the lung, which usually we associate with dust, whether there is silica or otherwise produced. . . .

"A My findings were fundamentally a **bronchogenic carcinoma** of the left lung with extensive invasions of the pleura, mediastinum, and pericardium by tumor; mestastases to lymph nodes, liver, and right adrenal; there was wasting of the body which we see in these cancer cases; there was a pleural effusion, in other words, a release of fluid into the pleural space, which was related to the carcinoma invading the pleura. There was some necrotizing bronchopneumonia. . . .

"... In statistical analysis, in other words, in reviewing the case reports of **bronchogenic carcinoma**—and I looked for them when I found out I was coming—I found none of the literature that indicated that dust exposure, per se, was specifically related to carcinoma of the lungs." Meeks v. Industrial Com'n, 436 P.2d 928–9, 931 (Ct.App.Ariz.1968).

Other Authorities: Petition of U.S., 303 F.Supp. 1282, 1310 (E.D.N.Car.1969).

carcinoma, comedo-type See *comedocarcinoma.*

carcinoma, embryonal 1. a highly malignant, primitive form of carcinoma, probably of germinal cell or teratomatous derivation, usually arising in a gonad and rarely in other sites. 2. (*obs.*) seminoma.

The testicle was sent to the M. D. Anderson Hospital and Tumor Institute, Houston, Texas, for study. The diagnosis was mixed **embryonal carcinoma** and seminoma of the testicle. Sawyer v. Sigler, 320 F.Supp. 690, 694 (D.Neb.1970).

carcinoma, epidermoid carcinoma in which the cells tend to differentiate in the same way that the cells of the epidermis do; that is, they tend to form prickle cells and undergo cornification. See also *carcinoma, squamous.*

He talks about the fact that it's an **epidermoid carcinoma** which is another way of saying **aquamus** [Sic. squamous] **carcinoma** [Sic. But] he was struck by its peripheral location [Sic. He] says the peripheral location in the lung parenchyma is somewhat atypical for a primary carcinoma of the lung however, on the assumption that no other **epidermoid carcinoma** has been identified in other parts of the body the primary pulmonary nature of this lesion may be assumed. In other words what Dr. Fite is saying that there is an awfully unusual place for a lung cancer. Could it have been coming from somewhere else, this is very unusual for an ordinary lung cancer and it is. Most of the usual lung cancers are central in location, the asbestos lung cancers are usually peripheral in location although they may assume different forms that location is significant." Utter v. Asten-Hill Mfg. Co., 309 A.2d 583, 587 (Pa.1973).

Dissection was made over the nodule tumor found at the periphery of the superior segment of the left lower lobe [of the left lung] and this tumor mass was sent for frozen section which appeared to be **epidermoid carcinoma,** Campbell v. U.S., 325 F.Supp. 207–8 (M.D.Fla.1971).

He did not order a tissue biopsy which probably would have revealed the presence of a tissue cancer, poorly differentiated **epidermoid carcinoma** of the oral cavity, which was the ultimate cause of her death. O'Brien v. Stover, 443 F.2d 1013–14 (8th Cir. 1971).

carcinoma, oat cell a small-cell carcinoma.

He smoked very little and he had 1,280 work level months of exposure and the cell type of his cancer was **oat cell**, so considering all those things I would state that most probably his lung cancer was caused by radiation exposure which he received in uranium mines. State Compensation Fund v. Joe, 543 P.2d 790, 792 (Ct.App.Ariz.1975).

carcinoma, scirrhous carcinoma with a hard structure owing to the formation of dense connective tissue in the stroma.

In her application, plaintiff alleged that she became disabled on June 15, 1965, at the age of 45, by reason of "**scirrhous carcinoma,** mastectomy," that is, surgical removal of a breast due to a hard malignant tumor. Sellars v. Secretary of Dep't of Health, Ed. & Welf., 331 F.Supp. 1103–4 (E.D.Mo.1971).

carcinoma, small cell a radiosensitive tumor composed of small, oval, undifferentiated cells that are intensely hematoxyphilic and typically bronchogenic. Called also *oat-cell c.*

carcinoma, squamous; carcinoma, squamous cell carcinoma developed from squamous epithelium, and having cuboid cells.

A short time later, doctors in California confirmed the diagnosis of **squamous cell carcinoma,** for which they performed a radical hysterectomy and lymph node dissection. After the surgery, her attending physicians informed her that they believed her cancer was related to her mother's ingestion of DES. Renfroe v. Eli Lilly & Co., 686 F.2d 642, 644 (8th Cir. 1982).

... a biopsy was taken from the lower lobe of the left lung, which was found to be nonresectable, and which was interpreted by two pathologists as **squamous cell carcinoma.** These biopsy slides were subsequently referred to Dr. William

G. Battaile, a highly qualified pathologist who is also a Clinical Associate Professor [of] Pathology at the Georgetown University School of Medicine in Washington, D.C. Dr. Battaile concurred in the hospital diagnosis of **squamous cell carcinoma** and found "no evidence of complicated or uncomplicated coal miner's pneumoconiosis." Hash v. Califano, 451 F.Supp. 383, 386 (S.D.Ill.1978).

In the fall of that year, Phelps noticed a change in the appearance of the lesion and thought it was finally "breaking up." However, after becoming concerned when he noticed a dark brown spot, Phelps returned to the Clinic on March 5, 1974, where he saw Dr. VanDeRiet. Dr. VanDeRiet immediately recommended that a new biopsy be taken and an excision was performed. Within a few days Phelps received a telephone call from Dr. VanDeRiet informing him that the lesion was malignant and had been diagnosed as **squamous cell carcinoma**. Phelps v. Blomberg Roseville Clinic, 253 N.W.2d 390, 392 (Minn.1977).

Other Authorities: Schwartz v. U.S., 230 F.Supp. 536, 538–9 (E.D.Pa.1964).

cardiac arrest See *arrest, cardiac.*

cardiac pacing See *pacing, cardiac.*

cardiogram (kar'de-o-gram") [*cardio-* + Gr. *gramma* a writing] a tracing of a cardiac event made by means of the cardiograph. See also *electrocardiogram*; and *electrocardiograph.*

cardiomegaly (kar"de-o-meg'ah-le) [*cardio-* + Gr. *megas* large] cardiac hypertrophy.

X-ray examination revealed normal lungs and a heart condition of "borderline **cardiomegaly**," defined as "the morbid enlargement or overgrowth of an organ or part due to an increase in size of its constituent cells." Bolton v. Sec. of Health & Human Services, 504 F.Supp. 288, 291 (E.D.N.Y.1980).

Dr. Dickstein found that petitioner suffered from **cardiomegaly** brought on by hypertension and hypertensive cardiovascular disease. His opinion was that petitioner's condition stemmed from aggravation of his hypertension by the stress and harassment of his job. Duthie v. Workmen's Compensation Appeals Bd., 150 Cal.Rptr. 530, 532 (Ct.App.Cal.1978).

Cardiomegaly, a morbid condition characterized by enlargement of the heart, with localized deposits of glycogen in the heart muscle was also detected. This latter diagnosis was supported by an X-ray and an electrocardiogram (Def.Ex.T; Bloomfield). Nye was described by one attending physician as a grossly obese white male diabetic (Def.Ex.T at p. J). Nye v. A/S D/S Svendborg, 358 F.Supp. 145, 149 (S.D.N.Y.1973), judgment affirmed in part, reversed in part 501 F.2d 376 (2d Cir. 1974).

Other Authorities: Poore v. Mathews, 406 F.Supp. 47, 49 (E.D.Tenn.1975); Prudential Ins. Co. of America v. Beaty, 456 S.W.2d 164, 170 (Ct.Civ.App.Tex.1970).

cardiomyopathy (kar"de-o-mi-op'ah-the) [*cardio-* + Gr. *mys* muscle + *pathos* disease] a general diagnostic term designating primary myocardial disease, often of obscure or unknown etiology.

After conducting tests on the plaintiff, Dr. Beazley diagnosed the cause of plaintiff's CHF as **cardiomyopathy** which is a dis-

ease of the heart. Bonsack v. Keystone Shipping Co., 425 So. 2d 869–70 (Ct.App.La.1982).

An autopsy disclosed the cause of death to be "acute pulmonary congestion and edema due to idiopathic [unknown] **cardiomyopathy**." The medical examiner reported that "This is a natural cause of death and persons with this type of heart disease [3] are subject to sudden death under a wide variety of circumstances, it appears likely that the vigorous exertion which Mr. Iannelli was subjected in performing his duties on that day played a role in precipitating his death." [[3] The autopsy report disclosed "no occlusions or marked narrowing" of the coronary arteries. Although the aorta displayed "moderately severe atherosclerosis," there was no "definite evidence of an infarct grossly." The pulmonary arteries displayed "minimal atherosclerosis in their approximal branches but no evidence of emboli."] Matter of Iannelli, 384 A.2d 1104, 1106 (Super.Ct.N.J.1978).

cardiomyotomy See esophagogastromyotomy.

cardiopulmonary (kar"de-o-pul'mo-ner-e) pertaining to the heart and lungs.

During the months of July and August, 1975, 35 patients at the Ann Arbor Veterans Administration Hospital suffered a total of 51 **cardiopulmonary** arrests. U.S. v. Narciso, 446 F.Supp. 252, 262 (E.D.Mich.1977).

cardiosphygmograph (kar"de-o-sfig'mŏ-graf) a combination of the cardiograph and sphygmograph for recording the movements of the heart and an arterial pulse.

The polygraph machine is an electromechanical instrument which measures and records these physiological fluctuations that are detected with the aid of three basic components:... (2) the **cardiosphygmograph** which gauges blood pressure and pulse rate.... U.S. v. Alexander, 526 F.2d 161, 163 (8th Cir. 1975).

carditis (kar-di'tis) [*cardio-* + *-itis*] inflammation of the heart.

"Myo" means muscle and "**carditis**" refers to the inflammation of that muscle. State Reserve Life Ins. Co. v. Ives, 535 S.W.2d 400, 403 (Ct.Civ.App.Tex.1976).

care, custodial

"**Custodial care**," however is not statutorily defined.

In contrast, in the area of extended care services, the regulations define **custodial care** as "any care which does not meet the definition of extended care in Sec. 405.126–405.128." 20 C.F.R. Sec. 405.310(g)....

... In addition, the statute does not define the exclusionary category of "**custodial care**," while the regulations define "**custodial care**" as that care which does not consist of "skilled nursing services" provided on a continuing basis.

Although the distinction the courts have made between the "services received" and the "condition of the patient" standards has not always been clear, the significance of the distinction is suggested by the definition which the Courts have given for the term "**custodial care**":

Indeed, it appears to this Court that the purpose of the custodial care disqualification in § 1395y(a)(9) was not to disentitle old, chronically ill and basically helpless, bewildered and confused people ... from the broad remedy which

Congress intended to provide for our senior citizens. Rather, the provision was intended to stop cold-blooded thoughtless relatives from relegating an oldster who could care for him or herself to the care of an ECF merely so that that oldster would have a place to eat, sleep, or watch television. But when a person is sick, especially a helpless old person, and when those who love that person are not skilled enough to take care of that person, Congress has provided a remedy in the Medicare Act, and that remedy should not be eclipsed by an application of the law and findings of fact which are blinded by bureaucratic economics to the purpose of the Congress. Ridgely v. Secretary of Department of Health, Education and Welfare, 345 F.Supp. 983, 993 (D.Md.1972), aff'd 475 F.2d 1222 (4th Cir. 1973).

This seems to be a common sense view of what "**custodial care**" is. It is care that could be administered by a layman, without any possible harm to the health of the one in custody. That is the simple reason why payment for it is not covered in a law the purpose of which is to pay medical benefits to the aged. This view of "**custodial care**" is also in agreement with the definition of "custodial" as found in Webster's Third New International Dictionary (1967 ed.) i.e., "relating to or marked by guardianship or maintaining safely." Thus mere "**custodial care**" refers quite simply to guardianship for convenience that has no significant relation to medical care of any type. Samuels v. Weinberger, 379 F.Supp. 120, 123 (S.D.Ohio 1973).

On the basis of the regulations, the Secretary has limited compensable post-hospital extended care services to "skilled nursing services," and has characterized services falling outside that definition as excluded "**custodial care**." The Court has concluded that the latter standard is the appropriate standard to be applied to the instant case. Klofta v. Mathews, 418 F.Supp. 1139, 1142–3 (E.D.Wis.1976).

care, extended

Extended care services consist of certain items and services furnished to an inpatient of a skilled nursing facility and by such skilled nursing facility, including, inter alia, "(1) nursing care provided by or under the supervision of a registered professional nurse; (2) bed and board in connection with the furnishing of such nursing care; (3) physical ... therapy.... (5) ... drugs ...; and (7) such other services necessary to the health of the patients as are generally provided by skilled nursing facilities...." 42 U.S.C. Sec. 1395x(h). Klofta v. Mathews, 418 F.Supp. 1139, 1142 (E.D.Wis.1976).

care, post-hospital extended

Post-hospital extended care is defined as "that level of care provided after a period of intensive hospital care for a patient who continues to require skilled nursing services (as defined in Sec. 405.127) on a continuing basis (see Sec. 405.128)" 20 C.F.R. Sec. 405.126. Klofta v. Mathews, 418 F.Supp. 1139, 1142 (E.D.Wis.1976).

care, standard of See *malpractice*.

We think the time has come to broaden the geographical limitation we have previously imposed to include the entire nation. Under contemporary conditions there is little reason to retain this vestige of former times when there was a substantial basis for believing "that the rural doctor should not be held to the **standards** of the urban doctor, since the latter had greater

access to new theories and had more opportunity to refine his method of practice." Fitzmaurice v. Flynn, supra, 167 Conn. at 617, 356 A.2d 887. We are not aware of any differences in the educational background and training of physicians practicing in Connecticut compared with those in other states. Medical literature of significance is normally disseminated throughout this country and not confined to a particular state. We align ourselves with many other jurisdictions which have in recent years abandoned similar geographical restrictions in medical malpractice cases. May v. Moore, 424 So.2d 596, 601 (Ala.1982); Fain v. Moore, 155 Ga.App. 209, 270 S.E.2d 375 (1980); Speed v. State, 240 N.W.2d 901, 908 (Iowa 1976); Blair v. Eblen, 461 S.W.2d 370, 372–73 (Ky.1970); Shilkret v. Annapolis Emergency Hospital Assn., 276 Md. 187, 200–201, 349 A.2d 245 (1975); Brune v. Belinkoff, 354 Mass. 102, 109, 235 N.E.2d 793 (1968); Pharmaseal Laboratories, Inc. v. Goffe , 90 N.M. 753, 758, 568 P.2d 589 (1977); King v. Williams , 276 S.C. 478, 279 S.E.2d 618, 620 (1981); Pederson v. Dumouchel, 72 Wash.2d 73, 79, 431 P.2d 973 (1967); Shier v. Freedman, 58 Wis.2d 269, 283–84, 206 N.W.2d 166 (1973). Logan v. Greenwich Hosp. Ass'n, 465 A.2d 294, 304–5 (Conn.1983).

The Alabama Code, § 6–5–484, prescribes the duty of care owed to patients by physicians, surgeons, dentists, and hospitals, and is as follows:

(a) In performing professional services for a patient, a physician's, surgeon's or dentist's duty to the patient shall be to exercise such reasonable care, diligence and skill as physicians, surgeons, and dentists in the same general neighborhood, and in the same general line of practice, ordinarily have and exercise in a like case. In the case of a hospital rendering services to a patient, the hospital must use that degree of care, skill and diligence used by hospitals generally in the community.

This section appears to be a codification of the case law of this state. Watterson v. Conwell, 258 Ala. 180, 61 So.2d 690; Orange v. Shannon, 284 Ala. 202, 224 So.2d 236. Brazil v. U.S., 484 F.Supp. 986, 989 (N.D.Ala.1979).

The **standard of care** in malpractice cases is also well known. With unimportant variations in phrasing, we have consistently held that a physician is required to possess and exercise, in both diagnosis and treatment, that reasonable degree of knowledge and skill which is ordinarily possessed and exercised by other members of his profession in similar circumstances. (Brown v. Colm (1974) 11 Cal.3d 639, 642–643, 114 Cal.Rptr. 128, 522 P.2d 688; Bardessono v. Michels (1970) 3 Cal.3d 780, 788, 91 Cal.Rptr. 760, 478 P.2d 480; Lawless v. Calaway (1944) 24 Cal.2d 81, 86, 147 P.2d 604; Hesler v. California Hospital Co. (1918) 178 Cal. 764, 766–767, 174 P. 654.) Landeros v. Flood, 551 P.2d 389, 392–3 (Cal.1976).

Other Authorities: Lea v. Family Physicians, P.A., 517 F.2d 797, 800 (5th Cir. 1975); Riddlesperger v. U.S., 406 F.Supp. 617, 620 (N.D.Ala.1976); Watkins v. U.S., 589 F.2d 214, 217 (5th Cir. 1979); Baker v. Chastain, 389 So.2d 932, 934–5 (Ala. 1980); Overstreet v. U.S., 528 F.Supp. 838, 841, 844 (M.D. Ala.1981); Moses v. Gaba, 435 So.2d 58, 60–61 (Ala.1983); Taylor v. Dirico, 606 P.2d 3, 8 (Ariz.1980); Keen v. Prisinzano, 100 Cal.Rptr. 82, 84 (Ct.App.1972); Brown v. Colm, 522 P.2d 688, 690–1 (Cal.1974); Jines v. Abarbanel, 143 Cal.Rptr. 818, 821–2 (Ct.App.Cal.1978); Katsetos (Estate of Katsetos)

v. Nolan, 368 A.2d 172, 177, 178 (Conn.1976); Rotan v. Greenbaum, 273 F.2d 830, 831 (D.C.Cir.1959); Stottlemire v. Cawood, 213 F.Supp. 897, 898 (D.D.C.1963); Robbins v. Footer, 553 F.2d 123, 126 (D.C.Cir.1977); Morrison v. MacNamara, 407 A.2d 555 (D.C.Cir.1979); Washington Hospital Center v. Martin, 454 A.2d 306, 309 (D.C.Ct.App. 1982); Skinner v. Coleman-Nincic Urology Clinic, 300 S.E.2d 319, 321 (Ct.App.Ga.1983); Swanson v. U.S. By and Through Veterans Admin., 557 F.Supp. 1041, 1043 (D.Idaho 1983); Borowski v. Von Solbrig, 328 N.E.2d 301, 304 (Ill.1975); Wynn v. Scott, 449 F.Supp. 1302, 1320 (N.D.Ill.1978); Chamness v. Odum, 399 N.E.2d 238, 246 (App.Ct.Ill.1974); Stanley v. Fisher, 417 N.E.2d 932, 937 (Ct.App.Ind.1981); Bryant v. Rankin, 332 F.Supp. 319, 322 (S.D.Iowa 1971); Sinkey v. Surgical Associates, 186 N.W.2d 658, 660 (Iowa 1971); O'Brien v. Stover, 443 F.2d 1013, 1017 (8th Cir. 1971); Clites v. State, 322 N.W.2d 917, 919 (Ct.App.Iowa 1982); Downs v. American Employers Ins. Co., 423 F.2d 1160, 1163 (5th Cir. 1970); Bruno v. Clements, 326 So.2d 562, 564 (Ct.App.La.1976); Samuels v. Doctors Hospital, Inc., 414 F.Supp. 1124, 1128 (W.D.La.1976); Hankel v. Hartford Fire Ins. Co., 366 So.2d 1031, 1033 (Ct.App.La.1978); Richard v. Southwest Louisiana Hospital Ass'n., 383 So.2d 83, 88 (Ct.App.La.1980); Steinbach v. Barfield, 428 So.2d 915, 923 (Ct.App.La.1983); Hemingway v. Ochsner Clinic, 722 F.2d 1220, 1225 (5th Cir. 1984); Betesh v. U.S., 400 F.Supp. 238, 245, 247 (D.D.C.1974); Holloway v. Hauver, 322 A.2d 890, 898 (Ct. Spec.App.Md.1974); Raitt v. Johns Hopkins Hospital, 322 A.2d 548, 551, 553 (Ct.Spec.App.Md.1974); Bridgeford v. U.S., 550 F.2d 978, 980 (4th Cir. 1977); McCarthy v. Boston City Hospital, 266 N.E.2d 292, 295 (Mass.1971); Koch v. Gorrilla, 552 F.2d 1170, 1173–4 (6th Cir. 1977); Reinhardt v. Colton, 337 N.W.2d 88, 94–95 (Minn.1983); Larsen v. Yelle, 246 N.W.2d 841, 844–5 (Minn.1976); Fisher v. Wilkinson, 382 S.W.2d 627, 630 (Mo.1964); Brown v. U.S., 419 F.2d 337, 341 (8th Cir. 1969); Payne v. U.S., 711 F.2d 73, 75 (7th Cir. 1983); Cebula v. Benoit, 652 S.W.2d 304, 307, 309 (Mo. Ct.App.1983); Eichelberger v. Barnes Hosp., 655 S.W.2d 699, 703 (Mo.Ct.App.1983); Hawkins v. Ozborn, 383 F.Supp. 1389, 1395 (N.D.Miss.1974); Anderson v. Moore, 275 N.W. 2d 842, 847, 849–50 (Neb.1979); Stumper v. Kimel, 260 A.2d 526, 528 (Super.Ct.N.J.1970); Marek v. Professional Health Services, Inc., 432 A.2d 538, 541 (Super.Ct.N.J.1981); Bucke- lew v. Grossbard, 435 A.2d 1150, 1154–5 (N.J.1981); Barnes v. Tenin, 429 F.2d 117, 120 (2d Cir. 1970); Ketchum v. Ward, 422 F.Supp. 934 (W.D.N.Y.1976); Spadaccini v. Dolan, 407 N.Y.S.2d 840, 843–5 (1st Dep't 1978); Davis v. Caldwell, 429 N.E.2d 741, 744 (N.Y.1981); Littlejohn v. State, 451 N.Y.S.2d 225, 226 (3d Dep't 1982); Lipsius v. White, 458 N.Y.S.2d 928, 930–1 (2d Dep't 1983); Hazelwood v. Adams, 95 S.E.2d 917, 919 (N.Car.1957); Cozart v. Chapin, 251 S.E.2d 682, 685 (Ct.App.N.Car.1979); Lowery v. Newton, 278 S.E.2d 566, 570 (Ct.App.N.Car.1981); Simons v. Georgiade, 286 S.E.2d 596, 602 (Ct.App.N.Car.1982); Tice v. Hall, 303 S.E.2d 832, 834 (Ct.App.N.Car.1983); Warren v. Canal Industries, Inc., 300 S.E.2d 557, 559–60 (Ct.App.N. Car.1983); Shapiro v. Burkons, 404 N.E.2d 778, 781 (Ct.App. Ohio 1978); Phillips v. Good Samaritan Hospital, 416 N.E.2d 646, 650 (Ct.App.Ohio 1979); Reeg v. Shaughnessy, 570 F.2d 309, 314 (10th Cir. 1978); Incollingo v. Ewing, 282 A.2d 206, 214, 217, 224–5 (Pa.1971); McPhee v. Reichel, 461 F.2d 947,

951 (3d Cir. 1972); U.S. ex rel. Fear v. Rundle, 506 F.2d 331, 332 (3d Cir. 1974); Foskey v. U.S., 490 F.Supp. 1047, 1057 (D.R.I.1979); Brannan v. Lankenau Hospital, 417 A.2d 196, 200 (Pa.1980); Polischeck v. U.S., 535 F.Supp. 1261 (E.D.Pa. 1982); Denardo v. Carneval, 444 A.2d 135, 137–8 (Super.Ct. Pa.1982); Wilkinson v. Vesey, 295 A.2d 676, 682 (R.I.1972); Young v. Park, 417 A.2d 889, 893 (R.I.1980); McNeill v. U.S., 519 F.Supp. 283, 288 (D.S.Car.1981); Erickson v. U.S., 504 F.Supp. 646, 651 (D.S.Dak.1980); Perkins v. Park View Hospital, Inc., 456 S.W.2d 276, 288 (Ct.App.Tenn. 1970); Richardson v. Holmes, 525 S.W.2d 293, 297–8 (Ct. Civ.App.Tex.1975); Hood v. Phillips, 554 S.W.2d 160, 165 (Tex.1977); Sebree v. U.S., 567 F.2d 292, 295 (5th Cir. 1978); Guidry v. Phillips, 580 S.W.2d 883, 887–8 (Ct.Civ.App.Tex. 1979); Stanton v. Westbrook, 598 S.W.2d 331, 333 (Ct.Civ. App.Tex.1980); Garza v. Keillor, 623 S.W.2d 669, 671 (Ct. Civ.App.Tex.1981); Hersh v. Hendley, 626 S.W.2d 151, 154– 5 (Ct.App.Tex.1981); Swan v. Lamb, 584 P.2d 814, 817, 820 (Utah 1978); Dietze v. King, 184 F.Supp. 944, 948 (E.D.Va. 1960); Price v. Neyland, 320 F.2d 674, 678 (D.C.Cir.1963); Whitfield v. Whittaker Memorial Hospital, 169 S.E.2d 563, 568 (Sup.Ct.App.Va.1969); Noll v. Rahal, 250 S.E.2d 741, 745 (Va.1979); Fitzgerald v. Manning, 679 F.2d 341, 346 (4th Cir. 1982); Largess v. Tatem, 291 A.2d 398, 403 (Vt.1972); Pederson v. Dumouchel, 431 P.2d 973, 978 (Wash.1967); Harris v. Robert C. Groth, M.D., Inc., 663 P.2d 113, 120 (Wash.1983); Nimmer v. Purtell, 230 N.W.2d 258, 264 (Wis. 1975).

care, standard of (anesthesiologist) See *anesthesiologist* (Burrow case).

Dr. Greene also stated his opinion as to deviations from reasonable **standards of anesthesia** which caused or contributed to cause the condition which led to the cardiac arrest and subsequent condition. Among these were: administration of a muscle paralyzing drug and muscle relaxant with insufficient ventilation; use of a mask instead of an endotracheal tube; and administration of gasses under positive pressure without a tube, resulting in aspiration and irritation of the lungs....

Dr. Kessler, a surgeon called by plaintiff as an expert witness, testified as follows:

Now, it is also the surgeon's duty to request or see to it that the patient is going to be given the appropriate type of anesthetic. He may not decide specifically the agent to be used, but in 1969, there were very few surgeons who would not make a fuss about the failure to provide endotracheal anesthesia in a diabetic 15-year old who is in electrolyte imbalance.

We find that Dr. Kessler's statement that "there were very few surgeons who would not make a fuss ..." is insufficient to establish the **standard of care** against which a surgeon's conduct may be measured in a malpractice case. Burrow v. Widder, 368 N.E.2d 443, 450–1 (App.Ct. of Ill.1977).

According to Dr. Nicholas Greene, a certified anesthesiologist and a professor of anesthesiology at Yale Medical School who testified for the plaintiff, Dr. Tenin's departures from the applicable **standard of care** were legion: the pre-operatory examination of the patient was perfunctory; both the Doctor's knowledge of his anesthesia machine and his examination of it prior to beginning the extraction were deficient; his assistants were insufficiently trained; the operation should have been terminated as soon as signs of serious cyanosis appeared; the attempts at resuscitation were both inadequate and ineptly performed; Dr. Tenin's failure to accompany Mrs. Adams to the hospital was a departure from accepted medical practice. Dr. Saul Bahn, another oral surgeon who testified for the plaintiff, corroborated most of Dr. Greene's opinions. Even Dr. George Montano, Dr. Tenin's only expert witness, testified that administering sodium brevital to a patient throughout an operation which lasted an hour and forty-five minutes coupled with failure to halt the operation as soon as indications of a serious cyanotic condition became apparent represented deviations from the accepted **standard of care**. Barnes v. Tenin, 429 F.2d 117, 120 (2d Cir. 1970).

care, standard of (appendicitis) See *appendicitis* (Emanuel case).

care, standard of (chiropodist)

As a **chiropodist**, licensed pursuant to N.J.S.A. 45:5–1 et seq., defendant was required to possess that degree of knowledge and skill usually pertaining to other members of his profession. Cf. Hull v. Plume, 131 N.J.L. 511, 37 A.2d 53 (E. & A.1944). See Annotation, "Liability of Chiropodist for Malpractice," 80 A.L.R.2d 1278 (1961). In the rendition of his professional services, he was required to exercise that degree of care, knowledge, and skill ordinarily possessed and exercised in similar situations by the members of his profession. Cf. Fernandez v. Baruch, 52 N.J. 127, 244 A.2d 109 (1968). Jones v. Stess, 268 A.2d 292, 294 (Super.Ct.N.J.1970).

care, standard of (dentist)

Dr. Downs reviewed Dr. Matriss' procedure in making, sterilizing and inserting the acrylic denture in Mrs. Germann's mouth and testified that it was standard procedure. He described it as the "optimum standard," "the highest **standard** that we know of," and as the practice that was then taught in dental schools. He opined that nothing more could have been done by defendant. The doctor said that it was impossible to completely sterilize an acrylic denture against a tetanus spore and that tetanus was extremely rare in oral surgery....

... Dr. Lane has written approximately 40 articles for medical journals on surgery of the head, neck, oral cavity and related areas. He was familiar with and had used immediate acrylic dentures in his work. In his opinion the use of such dentures was **standard** in the profession in New York and New Jersey. Germann v. Matriss, 260 A.2d 825, 828, 830 (N.J.1970).

What is the legal duty that defendant owed plaintiff in the instant case? A dentist who undertakes to treat a patient assumes a duty to that patient to exercise such reasonable **care** and skill as is usually exercised by a dentist in good standing in the community in which he resides. Donathan v. McConnell, 121 Mont. 230, 193 P.2d 819. If a dentist possesses and uses that degree of **care** and skill in ministering to a patient in a given case, he is not liable to his patient even though a bad result occurs causing injury to the patient. Negaard v. Estate of Feda, 446 P.2d 436, 440 (Mont.1968).

Other Authorities: Dailey v. N.C. State Bd. of Dental Examiners, 299 S.E.2d 473, 478 (Ct.App.N.Car.1983); Wiley v. Karam, 421 So.2d 294, 296 (Ct.App.La.1982); LeBeuf v. Atkins, 594 P.2d 923, 926 (Ct.App.Wash.1979); Bean v. Stephens, 534 P.2d 1047, 1049 (Ct.App.Wash.1975); Sanderson v. Moline, 499 P.2d 1281, 1284 (Ct.App.Wash.1972); LaRoc-

que v. LaMarche, 292 A.2d 259, 261 (Vt.1972); Summerour v. Lee, 121 S.E.2d 80–1 (Ct.App.Ga.1961); Simone v. Sabo, 231 P.2d 19, 21–2 (Cal.1951).

care, standard of (hospital)

"A hospital is bound to exercise a requisite amount of **care** toward a patient that the particular patient's condition may require. It is the hospital's duty to protect a patient from dangers that may result from the patient's physical and mental incapacities as well as from external circumstances peculiarly within the hospital's control. A determination of whether a hospital has breached the duty of **care** it owes to a particular patient depends upon the circumstances and facts of the case.

"The hospital, like all other employers in our society, may be held liable for the acts of negligence committed by its employees during the exercise of the functions for which they are employed. A patient is admitted to a hospital under an obligation, owed to him by the hospital and its employees, to provide such reasonable **care** and attention for his safety as his mental and physical condition, as known to the defendant or its nurses or other employees, may require.

"However, a hospital is not an insurer of a patient's safety, and the rules as to the **care** required are limited by the rule that no one is required to guard against or to take measures to avert that which a reasonable person under the circumstances would not anticipate as likely to happen. The hospital is obligated to use reasonable **care** in the light of the requirements of the patient's known condition.

"Therefore, to recover against East Ascension Parish General Hospital, the plaintiff must prove by a preponderance of the evidence:

"1. The degree of **care** ordinarily provided by hospitals in the area to patients having the same known medical condition as the plaintiff;

"2. That one or more employees or the defendant East Ascension General Hospital failed to provide such **care**."

We find these charges are in substantial compliance with those developed by the jurisprudence. Bryant v. St. Paul Fire & Marine Insurance Company, 365 So.2d 537 (La.App. 3 Cir. 1978), writ denied, 367 So.2d 1184 (La.1979). The judge did not indicate a "community-standard" should be used to determine lack of proper **care** by the hospital. Babin v. St. Paul Fire and Marine Ins. Co., 385 So.2d 849, 857 (Ct.App.La.1980).

The **standard of care** required of hospitals in Alabama is one of "ordinary care" as defined in South Highlands Infirmary v. Galloway, 233 Ala. 276, 171 So. 250, 253 (1936):

"... that **care** which persons of common prudence exercise under like conditions.... This implies a **care** having regard to the conditions of the particular case, and to the fact that the subjects of ministry are sick people. It implies an obligation to have such training and possess such skill as will enable the nurse to give reasonable and ordinary **care** to the patient....

"It is not to be construed as imposing a greater 'degree of **care**, skill, and diligence' than that 'used by hospitals generally in that community'...."

... The standard is not broadened by the patient's illness where, as in Mobile Infirmary v. Eberlein, 270 Ala. 360, 119 So.2d 8 (1960), the patient was under psychiatric **care**; there the **standard of care** required was expressed in this manner at 270 Ala. 367, 119 So.2d 15:

The **care** required of the hospital is not that care which persons of prudence exercise under like conditions, but that **care** which persons of common prudence, engaged in the hospital business, exercise under like conditions.
A hospital is not an insurer of its patients' safety. Riddlesperger v. U.S., 406 F.Supp. 617, 622–3 (N.D.Ala.1976).
Other Authorities: Belmon v. St. Frances Cabrini Hospital, 427 So.2d 541, 544 (Ct.App.La.1983); Polischeck v. U.S., 535 F.Supp. 1261, 1270 (E.D.Pa.1982); Clites v. State, 322 N.W.2d 917, 919 (Ct.App.Iowa 1982); Brannan v. LanKenau Hospital, 417 A.2d 196, 201 (Pa.1980); Schenck v. Government of Guam, 609 F.2d 387, 390 (9th Cir. 1979); Harris v. State Through Huey P. Long Hosp., 371 So.2d 1221, 1224 (Ct.App.La.1979); Spadaccini v. Dolan, 407 N.Y.S.2d 840, 843 (1st Dep't 1978); Garfield Park Community Hospital v. Vitacco, 327 N.E.2d 408, 411–12 (App.Ct.Ill.1975); Dumer v. St. Michael's Hospital, 233 N.W.2d 372, 374 (Wis.1975); Cline v. Lund, 107 Cal.Rptr. 629, 635 (Ct.App.Cal.1973); Perkins v. Park View Hospital, Inc., 456 S.W.2d 276, 288 (Ct.App.Tenn.1970); Toth v. Community Hospital at Glen Cove, 239 N.E.2d 368, 374 (N.Y.1968); Pederson v. Dumanchel, 431 P.2d 973, 978 (Wash.1967); Leonard v. Watsonville Community Hospital, 305 P.2d 36, 39, 42 (Cal.1956).

care, standard of (national standard)

We are in general agreement with those courts which have adopted a **national standard of care**. Varying geographical standards of care are no longer valid in view of the uniform standards of proficiency established by national board certification. Moreover, the tremendous resources available in the District for medical professionals keep them abreast of advances in the care and treatment of patients that occur in all parts of the country. More importantly, residents of the District desirous of medical treatment do not rely upon a medical professional's conforming to the standard of care practiced in the District or in a similar locality. Rather, they rely upon his training, certification, and proficiency. "Negligence cannot be excused on the ground that others in the same [or similar locality] practice the same kind of negligence." Pederson v. Dumanchel, supra, 72 Wash.2d at 78, 431 P.2d at 977. Substandard practice is substandard whether it is followed in the same or in a similar community....

... Thus we hold that at least as to board certified physicians, hospitals, medical laboratories, and other health care providers, the standard of care is to be measured by the national standard. It follows that an instruction which compares a nationally certified medical professional's conduct exclusively with the standard of care in the District or a similar community is erroneous. Morrison v. MacNamara, 407 A.2d 555, 565 (D.C.Cir.1979).

care, standard of (nurse)

That instruction reads as follows:
"It is the duty of one who undertakes to perform the service of a trained or graduate nurse to have the knowledge and skill ordinarily possessed, and to exercise the care and skill ordinarily used in like cases, by trained and skilled members of the nursing profession practicing their profession in the same or a similar locality and under similar circumstances. Failure to fulfil either of those duties is negligence."
BAJI No. 6.02, as modified and given, reads as follows:

"A physician or nurse is not negligent simply because their efforts prove unsuccessful. It is possible for a physician or nurse to err in judgment, or to be unsuccessful in their treatment without being negligent. [¶] However, if a physician or nurse does not possess that degree of learning and skill ordinarily possessed by physicians and nurses of good standing practicing in the same or a similar locality and under similar circumstances, or if they fail to exercise the care ordinarily exercised by reputable members of their professions in the same or a similar locality and under similar circumstances, it is no defense to a charge of negligence that they did the best they could and their efforts simply proved unsuccessful." (BAJI No. 6.02 has been shortened considerably in the 1977 Revision (see Calif. Jury Instructions—Civil—6th ed.), but in essence remains the same.)
BAJI No. 6.03, as modified and given, reads as follows:
"Where there is more than one recognized method of diagnosis or treatment, and no one of them is used exclusively and uniformly by all practitioners of good standing, a physician or nurse is not negligent if, in exercising their best judgment, they select one of the approved methods, which later turns out to be a wrong selection, or one not favored by certain other practitioners." Fraijo v. Hartland Hospital, 160 Cal.Rptr. 246, 251 (Ct.App.Cal.1979).

The principal case relied upon in Thompson for this proposition, Norton v. Argonaut Ins. Co., 144 So.2d 249 (La.App. 1st Cir.1962), clearly holds that nurses are held to exercise that degree of skill ordinarily employed under similar circumstances by members of the nursing profession in good standing in the same community or locality. See also Powell v. Fidelity & Casualty Co. of New York, 185 So.2d 324 (La.App. 1st Cir. 1966) and Favalora v. Aetna Casualty & Surety Co., 144 So.2d 544 (La.App. 1st Cir. 1962). Thompson v. U.S., 368 F.Supp. 466, 468 (W.D.La.1973).
Other Authorities: Belmon v. St. Frances Cabrini Hospital, 427 So.2d 541, 544 (Ct.App.La.1983); Friel v. Vineland Obstetrical, etc., 400 A.2d 147, 149 (Super.Ct.N.J.1979); Peeples v. Sargent, 253 N.W.2d 459, 465 (Wis.1977); Stogsdill v. Manor Convalescent Home, Inc., 343 N.E.2d 589, 600 (App.Ct.Ill. 1976); Lhotka v. Larson, 238 N.W.2d 870, 876 (Minn.1976); Garfield Park Community Hospital v. Vitacco, 327 N.E.2d 408, 411 (App.Ct.Ill.1975); Hiatt v. Groce, 523 P.2d 320, 324 (Kan.1974).

care, standard of (nursing home)

The witness agreed that there is a significant difference between a nursing home and a hospital in the level of care. The hospital has the lab, a higher standard of treatment and follow-up, capacity of testing and evaluating in detail. Stogsdill v. Manor Convalescent Home, Inc., 343 N.E.2d 589, 600 (App. Ct.Ill.1976).

care, standard of (obesity)

It is further declared that the minimum medical standards of practice for physicians treating obesity by dispensing and prescribing large quantities of controlled anorectic drugs is not met where they are dispensed and prescribed to a large number of patients as a standard treatment, nor are they met by only taking the pulse, blood pressure, weight, stethoscopic examination of the patient, a five minute personal interview with the physician, a casual concern as to possible dependency or addiction of the patient to anorectic drugs, and the delivery of a recommended diet to the patient on any office visit. . . .

. . . The Court declares that the standards of medical practice and other modalities of care and treatment of obesity and the use of anorectic drugs is set forth, including but not limited to, the following publications:

Obesity in Perspective, by The Fogarty Conference, sponsored by the John E. Fogarty National Center for Advanced Study in Health Sciences, edited by George A. Bray, M.D., National Institutes of Health, October 1–3, 1973, Bethesda, Maryland, DHEW publication NIH 75–708, Superintendent of Documents, U.S. Government Printing Office, Washington, D.C. 20402.

Influence of Obesity on Health, by George V. Mann, M.D., Vanderbilt University School of Medicine, Nashville, Tennessee, appeared in the July 25, 1974 New England Journal of Medicine, pages 178–185, and the New England Journal of Medicine, August 1, 1974, pages 226–232. The Management of Obesity, by Thaddeus S. Danowski, University of Pittsburgh, appeared in the April, 1976 issue of Hospital Practice, Volume 11, Number 4.

Textbook of Medicine, Volume II, edited by Paul B. Beeson and Walsh McDermott, W. B. Saunders Co., publisher, 1975. The article on obesity is by Professor M. J. Albrink of the W. Va. School of Medicine in Morgantown, W. Va.

Harrison's Principles of Internal Medicine, 7th edition, edited by Maxwell Wintrobe and 5 others. McGraw-Hill, publishers, 1974. The article on obesity is by one of the editors, Professor George W. Thorne, of Harvard Medical School, Boston, Massachusetts. U.S. v. Zwick, 413 F.Supp. 113, 115–16 (N.D.Ohio 1976).

care, standard of (obstetrician)

"Dr. Charles D. Alford, Jr., a Hammond physician specializing in OB-GYN and called as an expert witness on behalf of the State, agreed that the fetal heart rate should be taken and recorded at least every thirty minutes in the first stage of labor and every five minutes in the second stage, citing the 'Standard for Obstetric-Gynecologic Services' published by the American College of Obstetricians and Gynecologists. The record shows that this simply was not done, but rather, that the fetal heart tones were taken only twice during the three and one-half hours between the time she was admitted to the hospital and the time she was taken to the delivery room. Furthermore, while it appears that the electronic fetal heart monitoring device was available for use on Ms. Williams after 5:30 a.m., this was likewise not utilized. It is likely that this child suffered at least some degree of oxygen deprivation during labor which went unrecognized because of the failure of the staff at Lallie Kemp to adequately monitor this child, either manually or mechanically, in accordance with the clearly recognized **standard of care** . . . ." Williams v. Lallie Kemp Charity Hosp., 428 So.2d 1000, 1005 (Ct.App.La.1983).

care, standard of (ophthalmologist)

For the guidance of the trial judge upon retrial of this matter, we suggest that the following language be included in the charge:

An ophthalmologist acting within his specialty owes to his patient a higher standard of skill, learning and care than a general practitioner. He is expected to exercise that degree of skill, learning, and care normally possessed and exercised by the average physician who devotes special study and attention to the diagnosis and treatment of eye diseases. Due regard must of course be shown to the advanced state of the profession at the time of the diagnosis or treatment.

This charge conforms with the Pennsylvania practice of alerting the jury to the fact that a defendant who is a specialist should be held to a higher degree of care than a general practitioner. The case law and scholarly comment also support this instruction. Laub's Pennsylvania Trial Guide, Physicians and Surgeons, Chapter 2, § 21, Pp. 258–9.[11] [[11] See also 1939–1940 Op.Atty.Gen. of Pennsylvania 321, p. 325; "Physicians & Surgeons—Standard of Skill and Care Required of Specialist," Ann. 21 ALR3d 953; 61 Am.Jur.2d § 119, p. 244 (1972); Restatement Torts 2d, § 299A, Comment'd. Cf. Smith v. Yohe, 412 Pa. 94, 194 A.2d 167, p. 170 (1963); Donaldson v. Mafucci, 397 Pa. 548, 156 A.2d 835, p. 838 (1959); Wohlert v. Seibert, 23 Pa.Super. 213, pp. 215, 218 (1903); Hodgson v. Bigelow, 335 Pa. 497, p. 508, 7 A.2d 338 (1939).] [Footnote omitted.] McPhee v. Reichel, 461 F.2d 947, 951 (3d Cir. 1972).

care, standard of (optometrist)

Additional evidence of the breach of the **standard of care** is found in the established text The Optometric Profession. That authoritative work explicitly states that an optometrist is bound not to try to differentiate between pathologies such as hemorrhages. Instead, an optometrist must refer the patient to a medical practitioner for prompt examination.

I conclude that competent optometric practice required that Timothy's parents be notified and that the child be referred. The failure to inform and refer was not a "judgment call" but a violation of the governing principles of professional standards.[9] [[9] The Alaska Supreme Court has recently recognized that there are certain minimum levels of professional competence which must be adhered to in negligence actions, Priest v. Lindig, 583 P.2d 173, 179 (1978). The facts of the instant case indicate that base line principles of optometry were not followed.] Steele v. U.S., 463 F.Supp. 321, 330 (D.Alas.1978).

care, standard of (plastic surgeon)

Dr. McDowell, plaintiff's expert, testified that in his opinion the services were not rendered in a manner consistent with the care and skill usually employed by qualified plastic surgeons in this community. He gave as his reasons for his opinion that too much tissue was removed from the nose, uneven implants had been placed in the chin, and scars placed in improper directions and locations and he stated: "The results I feel are certainly below the results that you ordinarily expect from a capable plastic surgeon." He further testified that further surgery would be recommended, but that good results could not be assured because the condition of plaintiff's nostrils was such that normal passage of air through them could not be guaranteed. Kellogg v. Gaynor, 285 P.2d 288–9 (Dist.Ct.App.Cal. 1955).

care, standard of (prosthetist)

Much like members of the medical profession, prosthetists should exercise the degree of skill ". . . ordinarily employed, under similar circumstances, by the members of his profession in good standing in the same community or locality, and to use reasonable care and diligence along with his best judgment in the application of his skill to the case." Butler v. Louisiana

State Board of Education, 331 So.2d 192 (La.App.3d Cir. 1976), writ refused, 334 So.2d 230. Storey v. Lambert's Limbs & Braces, Inc., 426 So.2d 676, 679 (Ct.App.La.1982).

care, standard of (psychiatrist)

A psychiatrist who becomes sexually involved with a relative of a patient is not exercising the requisite amount of skill, learning, and ability that a psychiatrist in any community in the United States ought to exercise. All the aforementioned standards and duties of physicians and psychiatrists are applicable in Chapel Hill.

There is ample evidence in the present case that the relevant **standard of care** applicable to Chapel Hill psychiatrists included the negative imperative that they not have sexual relations with their patients' spouses. The expert testimony tended to establish an obligation on the part of psychiatrists, as a part of their duties within the patient-psychiatrist relationship, to conduct themselves in a certain way and this obligation applies even beyond the office, clinic, hospital, or laboratory. Mazza v. Huffaker, 300 S.E.2d 833, 838 (Ct.App.N.Car.1983).

With reference to the **standard of care** observed by the attending physician, the trial court made these observations:

" . . . Undoubtedly a psychiatrist who discharges from hospitalization a patient with a history of excessive use of alcohol and medications never knows when the patient may harm himself through improper use of alcohol and medications. It would seem to the Court, however, that a psychiatrist under such circumstances is obligated to take such reasonable precautions as are customarily taken by other psychiatrists in this community to obviate or minimize the patient suffering harm after discharge because he was not prepared or competent to care for himself or because suitable arrangements had not been made to provide proper continued care for him. That in substance is the reason given by Dr. Zeller for his opinion that Dr. Cranston failed to meet the standard of customary practice of psychiatrists in the area when he discharged the plaintiff by telephone order without having first evaluated his fitness for discharge.

"When asked what precautions a psychiatrist ordinarily would take in discharging a patient from hospitalization and sending him home with habit-forming drugs, Dr. Caplan replied:

" 'A.   Well, he ordinarily would prescribe a small amount of a dangerous drug, but that's not very much of a safeguard. The patient that is determined to misuse it can accumulate them or he can usually get drugs elsewhere, as in this case— he had other sources—or you turn the medications over to the mate, in this case the wife, and ask her to watch that he doesn't take them excessively and you keep a good record to make sure you yourself are not prescribing too many medications.

" 'Q.   And warn the wife about the possibility?

" 'A.   Yes.

" 'Q.   Of addiction?

" 'A.   Or suicide, yes. That's always a threat in the practice of psychiatry' . . . . "

. . . From the evidence the jury could properly conclude, as they did, that in prescribing medications for a discharged psychiatric patient with a complaint and history comparable to those of the plaintiff, a psychiatrist practicing in this area at the time would (1) instruct the patient and his wife about the proper use of the medication, (2) warn them of the dangers inherent in excessive use of those medications, and (3) in the case of a patient with a history of taking alcohol and medications to excess cause the patient's wife to assume custody of the medications prescribed and control over dispensing them. Christy v. Saliterman, 179 N.W.2d 288, 298–9 (Minn.1970).

care, standard of (specialist)

We therefore hold that at least with respect to nationally certified medical specialists like Dr. Footer the "same or similar locality" rule no longer applies. Specialists are required to exercise that degree of care and skill expected of a reasonably competent practitioner in his specialty acting in the same or similar circumstances. . . .

. . . Under this **national standard for specialists**, it is of course improper to exclude the testimony of a witness who has established his familiarity with the national standards of the specialty. Similarly, a national standard does not permit instructions to the jury to indicate that the defendant's conduct be compared only to the practice within his own geographic community or that of a similar locality. Robbins v. Footer, 553 F.2d 123, 129–30 (D.C.Cir.1977).

It is the generally accepted rule that a physician or surgeon or dentist who holds himself out to be a specialist is bound to bring to the discharge of his professional duties as a specialist that degree of skill, care and learning ordinarily possessed by specialists of a similar class, having regard to the existing state of knowledge in medicine, surgery and dentistry, that is, a higher degree of skill, care and learning than that of the average practitioner. (Rule in Cheeseman, Executrix, 181 Kan. 957, 965, 317 P.2d 472; 61 Am.Jur.2d, Physicians, Surgeons, Etc., § 119, p. 244; 70 C.J.S. Physicians and Surgeons § 41, p. 949; and W. Morris, Dental Litigation, 76 W.Va.L.Rev. 153, 153–154 [1974].) Simpson v. Davis, 549 P.2d 950, 954 (Kan. 1976).

Other Authorities: Wright v. U.S., 507 F.Supp. 147, 151 (E.D. La.1980); Baker v. Story, 621 S.W.2d 639, 642–3 (Ct.Civ. App.Tex.1981); Moore v. St. Paul Fire and Marine Ins. Co., 395 So.2d 838, 840 (Ct.App.La.1981); Villetto v. Weilbaecher, 377 So.2d 132, 134 (Ct.App.La.1979); Harris v. State, Through Huey P. Long Hosp., 371 So.2d 1221, 1224 (Ct.App.La.1979); Spadaccini v. Dolan, 407 N.Y.S.2d 840, 845–6 (1st Dep't 1978); Sears v. Cooper, 574 S.W.2d 612, 615 (Ct.Civ.App.Tex.1978); Gaston v. Hunter, 588 P.2d 326, 346 (Ct.App.Ariz.1978); Swan v. Lamb, 584 P.2d 814, 820–1 (Utah 1978); Bly v. Rhoads, 222 S.E.2d 783, 788–9 (Va.1976), Cline v. Lund, 107 Cal.Rptr. 629, 638 (Ct.App.Cal.1973); Toth v. Community Hospital at Glen Cove, 239 N.E.2d 368, 372–3 (N.Y.1968).

carisoprodol (kar"i-so-pro'dol) chemical name: (1-methylethyl)carbamic acid-2-[[aminocarbonyl)oxy] methyl]-2-methylpentyl ester. A centrally acting skeletal muscle relaxant, $C_{12}H_{24}N_2O_4$, occurring as a white, crystalline powder; used for the symptomatic management of acute, painful musculoskeletal disorders, administered orally. Called also *isopropyl meprobamate*.

The experience reported in the article involved an adverse skin reaction from use of the drug **carisoprodol**, after which the drug was discontinued and meprobamate was administered with the same skin reaction. The only inference to be drawn from this article is that if a patient displays an allergy to **carisoprodol**, then the same patient would probably also display an allergy to meprobamate. Perkins v. Park View Hospital, Inc., 456 S.W.2d 276, 281 (Ct.App.Tenn.1970).

carotid (kah-rot′id) [Gr. *karōtis* from *karos* deep sleep] relating to the principal artery of the neck (arteria carotis communis). See also under *body*; and *sinus*, etc.

Carotid occlusive disease is a condition where plaque builds up on the walls of the **carotid** arteries, reducing the amount of blood flowing through them. Lemke v. U.S., 557 F.Supp. 1205, 1207 (D.N.Dak.1983).

carotid artery See *arteria carotis interna*; *arteria carotis communis*; and *arteria carotis externa*.

carotid body See *body, carotid*; and *carotid*.

carpal (kar′pal) [L. *carpalis*] of or pertaining to the carpus, or wrist. See also *carpus*.

carpal lunate See *os lunatum*.

carpal tunnel release See *tunnel, carpal*; and *decompression*.

carpal tunnel syndrome See *syndrome, carpal tunnel*.

Carpophilus hemipterus

Carpophilus hemipterus (L.) is sometimes called the dried fruit beetle....
... The dried fruit beetle is attracted to decaying materials. U.S. v. Central Gulf Steamship Corp., 321 F.Supp. 945, 951 (E.D.La.1970).

carpus (kar′pus) [L.; Gr. *karpos*] [NA] the joint between the arm and hand, the wrist, made up of eight bones; see *ossa carpi*, and names of specific bones. Also, the part of the hand between the forearm and metacarpus. The term is also applied to the corresponding forelimb joint in quadrupeds.

carrier (kar′e-er) an individual who harbors in his body the specific organisms of a disease without manifest symptoms and thus acts as a carrier or distributor of the infection; the condition of such an individual is known as *carrier state*.

Evidently, after infection with hepatitis B, one of two things can happen. In one case, if the patient has built up enough antibody, the hepatitis B virus or "antigen" will be eliminated. The antibodies will remain, and the patient will be immune for an indefinite period of time. Immunity, therefore, implies past experience with the disease. In the other case, the patient does not create antibodies, or sufficient antibodies, to eliminate the hepatitis B antigen. Under these conditions, an equilibrium is reached where the patient appears clinically to be healthy, and yet, upon examination, will be found to have the antigen in his blood. Such persons are known as **carriers**. Thus, one **carrier** can transmit the hepatitis B antigen to another, who may also become a **carrier**, without either having passed through the acute stage of the illness. New York State Ass'n, etc., v. Carey, 466 F.Supp. 479, 482–3 (E.D.N.Y.1978).

cart (kart) a wheeled vehicle for conveying patients or equipment and supplies in a hospital.

cart, resuscitation one containing all the equipment necessary for initiating emergency resuscitation.

At about the same time Nurse Curry rushed a "**crash cart**" to the scene. The **crash cart** carried the medical equipment and drugs necessary for emergency resuscitation. Notably, the cart contained equipment for positive pressure oxygen, including an ambu bag unit, oxygen tanks, tubing, masks, and airways. There is some evidence that the **crash cart** contained needles of various sizes, including the "medi-cut" needle eventually used in establishing an intravenous route. Daniels v. Hadley Memorial Hospital, 566 F.2d 749, 755 (D.C.Cir. 1977).

cartilage (kar′tĭ-lij) [L. *cartilago*] a specialized, fibrous connective tissue, forming most of the temporary skeleton of the embryo, providing a model in which most of the bones develop, and constituting an important part of the growth mechanism of the organism. It exists in several types, the most important of which are hyaline cartilage, elastic cartilage, and fibrocartilage. Also used as a general term to designate a mass of such tissue in a particular site in the body. See also *cartilago*.

Since these surgical procedures involved the removal of **cartilage** which provides a cushion for the kneecap, Dr. Kilroy told Mrs. Perry that she should refrain from any excessive kneeling. Dodd v. Nicolon Corp., 422 So.2d 398, 400 (La.1982).

Dr. John G. Caden, orthopedic surgeon, operated on Cash and removed the medial knee **cartilage** which was torn in the accident. Cash v. Illinois Cent. Gulf R. Co., 388 So.2d 871, 876 (Miss.1980).

cartilago (kar-tĭ-lah′go), pl. *cartilag′ines* [L.] a specialized, fibrous brous connective tissue. Used in anatomical nomenclature to designate a mass of such tissue in a particular site in the body. See also *cartilage*.

casein (ka′se-in, ka′sēn, ka-sēn′) [L. *caseus* cheese] a phosphoprotein, the principal protein of milk, the basis of curd and of cheese. It is precipitated from milk as a white amorphous substance by dilute acids, and redissolves on the addition of alkalis or of excess acid. Rennin (and other milk-clotting enzymes) influence the hydrolysis of casein to soluble paracasein, which in the presence of calcium (Ca^{++}) is converted to an insoluble curd (insoluble paracasein or calcium paracaseinate). Casein, usually in the form of its calcium, potassium, or sodium salts, is added to other ingredients of the diet to increase its protein content. NOTE: In British nomenclature, casein is called *caseinogen*, and paracasein is called *casein*.

casein-sodium a nutrient preparation of casein and sodium hydroxide.

Sodium caseinate is derived by the chemical process of precipitating the casein in skim milk with an acid making an acid-curd and the liquefication of the acid-curd by neutralization with an alkali such as sodium bicarbonate or sodium hydroxide. M & R Dietetic Laboratories, Inc. v. Dean Milk Co., 203 F.Supp. 130, 132 (N.D.Ill.1961).

cast (kast) 1. to form an object in a mold. 2. a stiff dressing or casing made of bandage impregnated with plaster of Paris or other hardening material, used for immobilization of various parts of the body, in cases of fractures, dislocations, and infected wounds. See also *circulation, impaired.*

... the leg was placed in a stockinette, wrapped with sheet wadding and covered with a plaster of Paris **Cast** [4] from the instep to the groin, with the knee at an angle at 70° and admitted Mr. Mitchell to the hospital. [[4] Gauze or bandage impregnated with a solution consisting of fine powder (calcium sulfate) and water and wrapped around a fractured bone; when the solution dries the bandage becomes stiff and, therefore, immobilizes the part involved.] White v. Mitchell, 568 S.W.2d 216–17 (Ark.1978).

In response to a question as to his opinion of the standard of care in Mohave County in a situation where the tibia is fractured and a long leg **cast** from the upper thigh region to the bottom of the foot is applied, Dr. Arnold testified:

The standard would require—first of all, I would like to say the case [sic] should be applied properly.

From then on the advice to the patient is extremely important and probably more important is the observation of the doctor as to the progress of such fracture, which would include the looks of the foot or toes, the part that was left visible, whether it was cyanotic, whether it was high cyanotic, I mean bluish in coloration, whether it was swelling, whether it was white and blanched.

I will explain in a minute why these are important. Whether the sensation is missing, both by pin pricking and by the individual sensation, and other vasomotor, for instance, sweating of the extremity. These are factors that must be watched for, and perhaps I missed the most important of all, pain, excruciating pain after a **cast** is put on is by far the most important one thing a patient must be warned of, and usually they will tell you about that.

Dr. Harvey testified that he knew when he treated Kellin that a **casted** extremity had to be watched carefully and that a physician should be careful about problems of circulation, excessive swelling, numbness, tingling, pain, and loss of motor function in any casted extremity. He agreed that this knowledge was basic and fundamental. In referring to a medical treatise, "The Management of Fractures and Dislocations", written by Dr. DePalma, Dr. Harvey stated it was one of the most authoritative texts on the subject matter and that he agreed with the following excerpt:

Persistent pain under a plaster **cast** is always indicative of trouble. Always give the patient the benefit of the doubt and uncover the area. Harvey v. Kellin, 566 P.2d 297, 300–1 (Ariz.1977).

He stated that a **cast** applied too tightly interferes with the blood supply, giving rise to severe pain, blue discoloration, swelling and some blanching. Flamm v. Ball, 476 S.W.2d 710, 713 (Ct.Civ.App.Tex.1972).
Other Authorities: Keen v. Prisinzano, 100 Cal.Rptr. 82, 86 (Ct.App.Cal.1972).

cast, bent leg

She underwent surgery for the third time. From her left tibia, bone was removed and fused into the left ankle joint and a bone screw inserted. Following this operation plaintiff spent more than 13 months in a **bent leg cast.** [13] When this cast was removed, the leg was swollen, scarred and painful, and there

was substantial atrophy of the left leg, loss of strength and traumatic arthritis. The bone had knit but her ankle was left stiff and inflexible. [[13] The purpose of the **bent leg cast** was explained by a physician as follows: The muscles which go from the foot and ankle up to the knee and hook on to the big bone above the knee ... are very strong and they try to pull that bone out of place. To try to counteract that, we bent the knee ... to relax the strong muscles in the back of the leg. Joint Appendix, p. 120.] Williams v. Steuart Motor Co., 494 F.2d 1074, 1086 (D.C.Cir.1974).

cast brace

On July 14, 1980, Coleman was taken out of traction, the pin was surgically removed and he was placed in a **cast brace.** Such a cast consists of a solid fiberglass cast from the toes up to the knee. At the knee end of this cast two hinges extended to just above the knee connecting to a plastic sleeve. This plastic sleeve extended up to the groin area. Coleman v. Jackson, 422 So.2d 179, 184 (Ct.App.La.1982).

cast, circular

Dr. Florence did, however, unequivocally testify that orthopedic surgeons do not employ **circular casts** in the treatment of these [Colles] fractures because of the anticipated swelling. Larsen v. Yelle, 246 N.W.2d 841 (Minn.1976).

cast, pressure of

Dr. Denko reported, based on his experience and his examination of the amputated leg, that his examination revealed blood had been released in the tissue which cannot be attributable to **pressure of a tight cast** which would confine the necrosis to the skin; that the muscle was dead; and that, although it is possible that a cast could impinge upon the right pressure point and cause circulatory embarrassment, he was of the opinion that the gangrenous condition was not brought about by the **pressure of the cast.**

Dr. Brown's testimony is based upon his experience and interpretation of the hospital records. He stated that a cast applied too tightly interferes with the blood supply, giving rise to severe pain, blue discoloration, swelling and some blanching. It was his opinion that the cast should have been cut no later than 12:30 p.m. on January 18, 1969, and good medical practice would have been to cut it sooner. Had the cast been cut sooner, Dr. Brown opined that the foot would have been maintained, and that the failure to cut the cast resulted in necessitating amputation of the leg. Flamm v. Ball, 476 S.W.2d 710, 713 (Ct.Civ.App.1972).

cast, spica See *bandage, spica.*

The nail was removed from her femur and she was placed in a **spica cast** with the hope that a voluntary bony fusion could then be procured. Bryant v. Rankin, 332 F.Supp. 319, 321 (S.D. Iowa 1971), judgment affirmed 468 F.2d 510 (8th Cir. 1972).

CAT (computerized axial tomography) See *roentgenography, body section.*

CAT scan See *roentgenography, body section*; and *scintiscan.*

catalysis (kah-tal′ĭ-sis) [Gr. *katalysis* dissolution] increase in the velocity of a chemical reaction or process produced by the presence of a substance that is not consumed in the net chemical reaction or process; *negative catalysis* denotes the slowing down or inhibition of a reaction or process by the presence of such a substance.

catalyst (kat'ah-list) any substance that brings about catalysis; called also *accelerant*. See also *catalysis*.

A chemical **catalyst** is a substance which affects the rate and course of a given chemical reaction (e.g., a polymerization) in some manner without becoming a significant part of the reaction product (e.g., polymer). Thus, the use of a chemical **catalyst** is an integral part of the definition of that particular **catalyst**. **Catalyst** activity is unpredictable, and modest changes in **catalyst** composition can have profound and unpredictable effects on the results obtained. Studiengesellschaft Kohle v. Eastman Kodak Co., 450 F.Supp. 1211, 1214 (E.D.Tex.1977), judgment affirmed in part, reversed in part 616 F.2d 1315 (5th Cir. 1980).

Catalysts are chemical substances that affect the rate or course of a given chemical reaction in some manner without becoming a significant part of the resulting product....

A **catalyst** is defined as a substance which affects the rate or course of a given chemical reaction in some manner without becoming a significant part of the reaction product. Normally, **catalysts** are used in relatively small amounts as compared with the reactants. Ziegler v. Phillips Petroleum Co., 483 F.2d 858, 861–2 (5th Cir. 1973).

Catalysts are substances which affect the rate or course of a given chemical reaction in some manner without becoming a significant part of the reaction products and, hence, are normally used in relatively small amounts as compared to the reactants. Materials designated as **catalysts** are sometimes designated in connection with the general type of reaction or reactions in which they exhibit catalytic activity. Ziegler v. Phillips Petroleum Co., 171 U.S.P.Q. 44–5 (N.D.Tex.1971).

Other Authorities: Continental Oil Co. v. Witco Chemical Corp., 484 F.2d 777, 784 (7th Cir. 1973).

cataract (kat'ah-rakt) [L. *cataracta*, from Gr. *katarrhēgnynai* to break down] an opacity of the crystalline lens of the eye. See also *chalazion* (Frisneggar case).

The surgical procedure utilized by Dr. Padfield to remove the **cataract** from the husband's right eye was described as a "standard cryophake delivery". In layman's language a **cataract** is a clouding of the lens of the eye and its eradication is accomplished by removing the lens of the affected eye. Miller v. Scholl, 594 S.W.2d 324, 326–7 (Mo.Ct. App.1980).

About six weeks after the accident the defendant underwent an operation for the removal of a **cataract** on his right eye. The eye examination which was made just before the operation revealed "both lenses are foggy and cloudy." The examining doctor said that, because of this condition, he could not see into the eye. It is only logical to conclude that if the doctor could not see into the eye, the patient could not see out of it. Masters v. Alexander, 225 A.2d 905, 908 (Pa.1967).

cataract, heat-ray cataract due to long-continued exposure to high temperatures, e.g., glassblowers' cataract.

This claim was made because of cataracts which developed in the claimant's eyes....

... Claimant was required to look into the furnaces every day and was approximately two feet away from them. They were small laboratory furnaces and the heat would not burn claimant's body. On a Saturday, claimant noticed that he could no longer use a microscope as a "filmy-kind of light web structure" obscured whatever he looked through in the microscope....

At the hearing, Dr. Baum testified that within reasonable medical probability, both cataracts were caused by the infrared radiation to which claimant was exposed on his job with the respondent Pratt and Whitney Aircraft. In the doctor's opinion any cataract which would have developed from exposure to infrared radiation would have developed over a period of years from repeated exposure....

... He was exposed to molten glass at regular five-second intervals and the heat of the molten glass was approximately 2000 degrees Fahrenheit. At times he would be as close as one foot to the molten glass. Claimant's vision became poor and an ophthalmologist found a cataract in each eye. The Judge found that the cataracts were the result of his exposure to radiation and heat from molten glass in the course of his employment and that this exposure and risk was different and greater than that to which the general public is exposed. The Judge also found that the cataracts resulted from repeated accidents sustained by the claimant arising out of and in the course of his employment which culminated in the formation of the cataracts as a result of exposure to infrared radiation and heat. The Judge found that this was an injury by accident....

In Ingalls Shipbuilding Corporation v. King, 229 Miss. 871, 92 So.2d 196 (1957), the Supreme Court of Mississippi held that claimant was entitled to workmen's compensation benefits for cataracts which were caused and aggravated by the absorption of radiant energy. The Court pointed out in its opinion that infrared rays, such as given off by a burning torch, may cause cataracts to form and, if one has incipient cataracts, the absorption of radiant energy and infrared rays is calculated to aggravate the cataracts and accelerate the loss of eyesight. Worden v. Pratt and Whitney Aircraft, 256 So.2d 209–11 (Fla. 1971).

catgut (kat'gut) an absorbable sterile strand obtained from collagen derived from healthy mammals, originally prepared from the submucous layer of the intestines of sheep; used as a surgical ligature.

Since no leakage or other sign of damage was noticeable until two or three weeks later, the cause of the injury was probably a suture. It takes **catgut** sutures two or three weeks to dissolve. Rainer v. Buena Community Memorial Hospital, 95 Cal.Rptr. 901, 906 (Ct.App.Cal.1971).

catheter (kath'ĕ-ter) [Gr. *kathetēr*] a tubular, flexible, surgical instrument for withdrawing fluids from (or introducing fluids into) a cavity of the body, especially one for introduction into the bladder through the urethra for the withdrawal of urine. See also *catheterization*.

catheter, central venous a long, fine catheter introduced into a large (jugular, subclavian, etc.) vein for the purposes of administering parenteral fluids (as in hyperalimentation) or medications or for measurement of central venous pressure.

catheter, CVP

Dr. Butts explained that such perforation of the atrium wall by a CVP catheter is a medically recognized, but uncommon, complication in the use of CVP lines. Warren v. Canal Industries, Inc., 300 S.E.2d 557, 559 (Ct.App.N.Car.1983).

catheter, Foley an indwelling catheter retained in the bladder by a balloon which may be inflated with air or liquid. See also Catheter, indwelling.

The compound fracture of one leg required the use of traction and a body cast, and during the entire 54–day hospitalization period there was a ''Foley'' catheter inserted in appellant's urethra. There was testimony that the use of a Foley catheter over so long a period of time almost invariably produces infection in the urinary tract. Wade v. Thomasville Orthopedic Clinic, 306 S.E.2d 366–7 (Ct.App.Ga.1983).

The Foley catheter is inserted through the urethra into the bladder. It has a small balloon on its forward end which is inflated with a sterile liquid after entering the bladder. The catheter is then pulled back until the balloon is seated in a position in the bladder which completely blocks the flow of urine through the urethra and thereafter the urine drains from the bladder through the catheter. Richard v. Southwest Louisiana Hospital Ass'n, 383 So.2d 83, 85 (Ct.App.La.1980).

A Foley [catheter] was inserted into Mr. Choice's penis. A Foley [catheter] is a soft, latex tube with a balloon-type mechanism on the end. Once inserted into the penis, the balloon is blown up. The [catheter] monitors the rate of urinary flow which tells whether or not an individual is going into shock. It is also used to see if there is blood in the urine which would be an indication of internal damage, or damage to the liver. U.S. v. Choice, 392 F.Supp. 460–2 (E.D.Pa.1975).
Other Authorities: Miller v. U.S., 431 F.Supp. 988, 990 (S.D. Miss.1976).

catheter fragment See *feeding, intravenous* (Smothers case).

catheter, French

A red Number 8 French Catheter was inserted in the epidural space all the way to T–1, and the space thoroughly was irrigated with Bacitracin solution. Samuels v. Doctors Hospital, Inc., 414 F.Supp. 1124, 1126 (W.D.La.1976), overruled by evoking the locality rule 360 So.2d 1331 (La.1978).

catheter, indwelling a catheter that is held in position in the urethra.

catheter, splinting

. . . normally a catheter of this type [a splinting catheter] is best removed when ''it was straight up and down in the ureter so that you just grasp the end of it and pull it out than it would be to try and grasp it curled up in the bladder'' (the splinting catheter having descended in this case to the bladder requiring that it be removed therefrom after its migration from the ureter). Skinner v. Coleman-Nincic Urology Clinic, 300 S.E.2d 319, 321 (Ct.App.Ga.1983).

catheter, Swan-Ganz a soft, flow-directed catheter with a balloon at the tip for measuring pulmonary arterial pres-

sures; it is introduced into the basilic vein and is guided by blood flow into the subclavian vein, the superior vena cava, through the right atrium and ventricle, into the pulmonary artery. See also *hypovolemia* (Erickson case).

catheter, Texas

After I/C has been followed a Texas catheter, which is comparable to a condom with a drainage tube, is fitted over the end of the penis. . . .
. . . Texas catheter—was rejected because sphincter muscle was spastic and bladder was infected and not emptying. The elastic band of the Texas catheter could cause gangrene of the penis. Harrigan v. U.S., 408 F.Supp. 177, 181 (E.D.Pa. 1976).

catheterization (kath″ĕ-ter-i-za′shun) the employment or passage of a catheter.

catheterization, cardiac passage of a small catheter through a vein in an arm or leg or the neck and into the heart, permitting the securing of blood samples, determination of intracardiac pressure, and detection of cardiac anomalies.

Based on his examination and the various other information before him, he decided to perform cardiac catheterization studies, which are a series of invasive diagnostic tests of the cardiac function through the use of radiopaque dyes and X-ray. In particular, he decided to perform a right heart catheterization, which requires the placing and passing of a catheter through a vein either in the antecubital fossa of the arm or through the femoral vein of the groin, a left heart catheterization, which requires the placing and passing of a catheter through the brachial artery in the arm or the femoral artery in the groin, and a coronary angiography, which requires injecting a radiopaque substance into an artery. Dr. Steiner chose the right heart catheterization, which constitutes a right heart study, and the left heart catheterization and coronary angiography, which constitutes a left heart study, because the information which he had on plaintiff's condition suggested right and left heart disease. Bergen v. Shah-Mirany, 404 N.E.2d 863, 865 (App.Ct.Ill.1980).

On July 2, 1973, defendant performed the cardiac catheterization on plaintiff. An incision was made in plaintiff's right arm above the elbow, and a hollow, wirelike, tubular instrument called a catheter was inserted up plaintiff's right brachial artery to her heart. Dye was then injected into the catheter which entered the coronary arteries providing visualization of the arteries and heart chambers. During the catheterization, plaintiff's right brachial artery began to contract spasmodically. Defendant testified that although infrequent, this does occur. Crawford v. Anagnostopoulos, 387 N.E.2d 1064, 1066 (App.Ct.Ill.1979).

As part of the evaluation process, a heart catheterization was thought necessary.[2] . . .
. . . Dr. Charles Murray, a cardiovascular surgical resident working and studying under Dr. Lillehei, discussed this procedure at length with Donna Walstad and explained in detail the likelihood of some pain and discomfort and in general what might be expected in the way of side effects, though he did not inform her that complications arose in about 4 per cent of the cases. . . .

... It is necessary that the patient be awake and alert during this type of operation and Donna did not object to Dr. Murray proceeding. She testified she experienced several severe pains in the lower left abdominal region as the catheter was advanced toward her heart. [² In order to perform this diagnostic study an incision must be made in the groin and a catheter is inserted into the left femoral artery. The catheter, a plastic tube slightly smaller than the diameter of the artery, is then pushed upward into the left common iliac artery and from there into the abdominal aorta and then into the heart. The progress of the catheter as it passes through the vessels is simultaneously observed by the surgeon on a television screen as motion picture X-ray cameras record visually the procedure. Once the catheter is in the heart, a contrast medium is rapidly injected through the catheter into the heart which enables diagnostic motion picture X-rays of the heart action to be taken.] Walsted v. University of Minnesota Hospitals, 442 F.2d 634, 636–7 (8th Cir. 1971).

Other Authorities: Loomis v. McLucas, 553 F.2d 634–5 (10th Cir. 1977). Morgenroth v. Pacific Medical Center, Inc., 126 Cal.Rptr. 681, 683 (Ct.App.Cal.1976).

catheterization, clean intermittent

Because of her bladder condition, Amber is unable to void voluntarily, and must be catheterized several times each day. The method of choice is **Clean Intermittent Catheterization** ("CIC"). Tatro v. State of Tex., 516 F.Supp. 968, 970–1, 988 (N.D.Tex.1981).

catheterization, heart See *catheterization, cardiac.*

catheterization, intermittent

An alternative form of treatment to the ileostomy was a procedure called **intermittent catheterization (I/C)**. I/C involves insertion of a catheter into the bladder at time intervals in order to establish regular, periodic voiding....

... **Intermittent catheterization**—was rejected because continuous or straight drainage with Foley catheter was resulting in fever and infection and I/C would cause more urine to be retained in bladder....

... **Intermittent catheterization**—This procedure was not widely accepted in Philadelphia area in 1967. It required introduction of a catheter into the body 3 or 4 times a day, so that damage to the urethera was possible. Harrigan v. U.S., 408 F.Supp. 177, 181, 183 (E.D.Pa.1976).

cation (kat'i-on) [Gr. *kata* down + *iōn* going] an ion having a positive charge owing to the loss of one or more electrons, and hence being attracted by and traveling to the cathode, or negative pole under the influence of an applied electric field.

cationoid See *cation.*

Cationoid: A proton donator (usually an acid). Ritter v. Rohm & Haas Co., 271 F.Supp. 313 (S.D.N.Y.1967).

cauda (kaw'dah), pl. *cau'dae* [L.] [NA] a tail, or tail-like appendage; in anatomical nomenclature, a general term for a structure resembling such an appendage.

cauda equina [NA], the collection of spinal roots that descend from the lower part of the spinal cord and occupy the vertebral canal below the cord; their appearance resembles the tail of a horse.

Below that area [bottom of the spine] the nerves flare out into what is termed the **cauda equina** (horse's tail)....

The nerves that form the **cauda equina** are approximately one to two millimeters in diameter, which is approximately the diameter of the lead in an old fashioned lead pencil. The nerves that formulate the **cauda equina** are within the subarachnoid space and are surrounded by and float within the spinal fluid. Funke v. Fieldman, 512 P.2d 539, 542–3 (Kan. 1973).

Beginning at approximately the first lumbar vertebra, the sacral nerves pass through the spinal column in what is called the **cauda equina**. At each lumbar vertebra the **cauda equina** is found to be located between the lamina of the vertebra and the intervertebral disc (the posterior section of the intervertebral disc would, therefore, be nearest to the **cauda equina**). The first, second, third, fourth and fifth sacral nerves pass through the spinal column in the **cauda equina** at the L4 L5 and the L5 S1 level. At each intervertebral space following the first lumbar vertebra, a nerve root extends from the **cauda equina** to the right and left of the intervertebral disc. Hart v. Van Zandt, 399 S.W.2d 791, 794 (Tex.1965).

causalgic See *causalgia.*

causalgia (kaw-zal'je-ah) [Gr. *kausos* heat + -*algia*] a burning pain, often accompanied by trophic skin changes, due to injury of a peripheral nerve.

The nerve in the left leg was destroyed resulting in **causalgia** (a condition accompanied by burning pain due to injury to a peripheral nerve)....

... He treated him for **causalgia**, "a sort of reflex situation where the sympathetic nerves are overactive, and severe burning pain is mediated via these nerves." (Dep. p. 8). Aretz v. U.S., 456 F.Supp. 397, 402–3 (S.D.Ga.1978).

He was referred to a physician who diagnosed the trouble as a condition known as **causalgia**, the symptoms of which are pain and trophic skin changes attributable to injury of the sympathetic peripheral nerve and a resulting hyperactivity of the nervous system. Harrelson v. U.S., 420 F.Supp. 788, 791 (S.D. Ga.1976).

Other Authorities: Gretchen v. U.S., 618 F.2d 177, 180 (2d Cir. 1980); Grubb v. Jurgens, 373 N.E.2d 1082–3 (App.Ct.Ill. 1978); Baker v. Story, 621 S.W.2d 639, 640 (Ct.Civ.App.Tex. 1981).

causation, medical

We have recently recognized the distinction between legal causation and **medical causation** of an accidental injury in workmen's compensation cases. New Hampshire Supply Co. v. Steinberg, 119 N.H. ___, 400 A.2d 1163 (1979). We said there that the claimant, in addition to proving legal causation, that is, that the injury is work-connected, must also prove **medical causation**. Id. Although RSA 281:2 V–a relieves a claimant firefighter of his usual burden of proving legal causation, that is, that his heart (or lung) disease is causally related to his employment, it does not relieve him of his obligation to prove medically that he in fact has heart or lung disease and that he is disabled by the disease. Nor is it sufficient that a claimant merely testify that he is suffering from some unspecified kind of lung or heart condition. We have acknowledged that medical testimony is sometimes unnecessary "because the matters involved fall within the realm of common knowledge." Bentley v. Adams, 100 N.H. 377, 379, 128 A.2d 202, 204 (1956). We have also recognized, however, that there are "situations where the questions are such that only an expert may be expected to know about them, and in such cases expert testimony is required." Id. City of Rochester v. Smith, 119 N.H. 495, 403 A.2d 421 (N.H.1979).

causation of disease See *disease, causation of.*

cause (kawz) [L. *causa*] that which brings about any condition or produces any effect.

"Again quoting from the same Surgeon General's report on page 280: 'Chronic bronchitis and emphysema probably represent disorders of multiple **causality**.' "

"Since 1963, The Surgeon General's Office has published a book on 'Smoking and Health.' " Baker v. Industrial Accident Com'n, 52 Cal.Rptr. 276, 280 (Dist.Ct.App.1966).

Examples might be multiplied. They condense into the general proposition that the medical **cause** of an ailment is usually a scientific question, requiring a judgment based upon scientific knowledge and inaccessible to the unguided rudimentary capacities of lay arbiters. (See 2 Wigmore on Evidence [3d ed.] secs. 558–568, pp. 638–665; 20 Am.Jur., Evidence, sec. 867, pp. 730–732.) Peter Kiewit Sons v. Industrial Accident Com'n, 44 Cal.Rptr. 813, 818 (Dist.Ct.App.1965).

cauterization (kaw"ter-i-za'shun) the destruction of tissue with a hot instrument, an electric current, or a caustic substance.

cauterization, bilateral tubal

The Rajas alleged that Dr. Tulsky negligently performed a **bilateral tubal cauterization** upon Edna Raja, which operation was designed to make her sterile. They alleged that about five years after the operation Edna Raja began to experience signs of pregnancy. She was examined at Michael Reese's gynecology clinic and advised, however, that she was not pregnant. Later, after the time in which the plaintiffs say it was medically safe to have an abortion, she learned that she was in fact pregnant. Cockrum v. Baumgartner, 447 N.E.2d 385, 387 (Ill. 1983).

cauterization, laparoscopic tubal

Her usual doctor recommended a hysterectomy, the complete removal of the uterus. Hartke, then 33, thought this a rather drastic procedure, so she approached the defendant, Dr. William McKelway, for a second opinion. Dr. McKelway recommended a procedure known as **laparoscopic tubal cauterization**, which involves blocking the Fallopian tubes by burning them with instruments inserted through one or two small incisions in the abdomen. Hartke v. McKelway, 707 F.2d 1544, 1547 (D.C.Cir.1983).

cautery (kaw'ter-e) [L. *cauterium*; Gr. *kautērion*] 1. the application of a caustic substance, a hot instrument, an electric current, or other agent to destroy tissue. 2. a caustic substance or hot instrument used in cauterization.

On the day of admission, the patient had hymenotomy. This operation was complicated by burns to the buttocks resulting from a flash blaze started by the hot **cautery** as it was used to cut the hymen, the blaze being caused by ignition of the merthiolate containing alcohol with which the patient had been prepped. Holloway v. Hauver, 322 A.2d 890–1 (Ct. Spec.App.Md.1974).

cavitas (kav'ĭ-tas), pl. *cavita'tes* [L. from *cavus* hollow] a hollow space or depression; called also *cavity*. See also *cavum.*

cavitas glenoidalis [NA], glenoid cavity: a depression in the lateral angle of the scapula for articulation with the humerus; called also *glenoid fossa of scapula.*

Dr. Citron testified that his examination revealed a healed fracture involving the shoulder bone or scapula with some distortion of the parts and some tilting of the **glenoid fossa**, a part of the shoulder bone that articulates with the arm bone. Texas Employers' Ins. Ass'n v. Nelson, 534 S.W.2d 150–1 (Ct.Civ. App.Tex.1976).

Well, the [biceps] tendon attaches to the **glenoid** process of the shoulder joint so, I mean it is part of the injury. Hartford Accident and Indemnity Co. v. Helms, 467 S.W.2d 656, 658 (Ct.Civ.App.Tex.1971).

Dr. Richard B. Herrick, the expert medical witness offered by Petitioner, described the place of injury as "a slight evulsion or a small chip fracture of bone on the interior surface of the **glenoid socket** of the shoulder." Aetna Casualty and Surety Co. v. Moore, 361 S.W.2d 183–4 (Tex.1962).

cavity (kav'ĭ-te) [L. *cavitas*] a hollow place or space, or a potential space, within the body or in one of its organs; it may be normal or pathological. See also *cavitas*; and *cavum.*

cavity, pleural See *cavum, pleurae.*

cavity, vocal

The **vocal cavities** are the throat, nose, and the two oral cavities formed in the mouth by the positioning of the tongue. People v. Rogers, 385 N.Y.S.2d 228, 233 (Sup.Ct. Kings Cty. 1976).

cavum (ka'vum), pl. *ca'va* [L.] [NA] a general term used to designate a cavity or space. See also *cavitas*; and *cavity.*

cavum epidurale [NA], epidural cavity: the space between the dura mater and the walls of the vertebral canal, containing venous plexuses and fibrous and alveolar tissue; called also *epidural space.*

He was taken to the x-ray room where a lumbar puncture was performed. Pus exudate was found in the subdural space, and a tap of the **epidural space** revealed the presence of still more exudates. Samuels v. Doctors Hospital, Inc., 414 F.Supp. 1124, 1126 (W.D.La.1976).

cavum peritonaei; cavum peritonei [NA], peritoneal cavity: the potential space between the parietal and visceral layers of the peritoneum; called also *greater peritoneal cavity*. See also *peritoneum.*

... that contamination of the **peritoneal cavity** by bacteria increases each hour that surgery is delayed, and that the period of hospitalization is lessened by diagnosis before complete perforation has caused peritoneal contamination. Emanuel v. Bacon, 615 S.W.2d 847, 850–1 (Ct.Civ.App.Tex.1981).

cavum plurae [NA], pleural cavity: the potential space between the parietal and visceral pleurae. See also *apparatus, underwater drainage*.

In the normal person the **pleural cavity** is at a low pressure so the lung which is highly elastic, having a higher pressure within, due to the connection with atmosphere through the bronchial tubes, is expanded to fill the **pleural cavity**. Thus, the parietal pleura and the visceral pleura are in contact and there is in effect no **pleural cavity** since the lung entirely fills the space. During breathing when the rib cage is expanded and the diaphragm lowered, the parietal pleura moves outwardly to enlarge the **pleural cavity** and thus to reduce the pressure therein. The lung then expands against its elasticity to fill the cavity. Similarly, when the rib cage is compressed and the diaphragm raised the natural elasticity of the lung permits it to decrease in size and force air therefrom...

... Any external invasion of the **pleural cavity** which causes the cavity to be connected with atmosphere will permit the pressure within the cavity to reach atmospheric and under these conditions the pressure within and outside the lung will be the same and the lung, being elastic like a balloon, will collapse. No amount of breathing effort on the part of the individual will reinflate the lung as the pressure within the **pleural cavity** will tend to remain at substantially atmospheric. For example, a stab wound in the chest will permit air to enter the pleural region thereby permitting the equalization of pressures inside and outside the lung so that the lung will collapse. Furthermore, blood and liquid will accumulate in the **pleural cavity** to physically block expansion of the lung. Deknatel, Inc. v. Bentley Sales, Inc., 173 U.S.P.Q. 129–30 (U.S.D.C., Central D.Cal.1971).

cavum, subarachnoideale [NA], subarachnoid cavity: the space between the arachnoidea and the pia mater, containing cerebrospinal fluid and bridged by delicate tradeculae; called also *subarachnoid space*.

Dr. Dornette explained the **subarachnoid space** is occupied by the spinal cord and other nerves and is filled with spinal fluid which is a watery like substance. The nerves leave the spinal cord and transverse varying lengths of the **subarachnoid space**....

"To advance or put the needle through an individual's back into the **subarachnoid space** in the spinal anesthetic procedure, it would be necessary for the needle to pass through the subcutaneous tissue, supraspinous ligament between the spinous processes, through the interspinous ligament and through the epidural space, the dura and into the arachnoid membrane which fuses together and forms the **subarachnoid space**." Funke v. Fieldman, 512 P.2d 539, 543 (Kan.1973).

CCE test See *test, carbon chloroform extract*.

CDC Center for Disease Control.

cecal See *cecum*.

cecum (se'kum) [L. *caecum* blind, blind gut] the first part of the large intestine, forming a dilated pouch into which open the ileum, the colon, and the appendix vermiformis; called also *blindgut, caput coli, head of blind colon, blind intestine*, and *intestinum caecum*.

Dr. Claude J. Pumilia, Jr. diagnosed a space-occupying lesion within the **cecal** region of the colon (cancer). This area is locat-

ed in the right lower quadrant of the abdomen. Steinbach v. Barfield, 428 So.2d 915, 919 (Ct.App.La.1983).

Dr. Haygood indeed stated that "gastro-intestinal" could mean merely the stomach and the intestine. However, he went on to state that "the appendix rises with the **cecum**, which is the right portion of the large intestine, and it communicates with and is a part of the gastro-intestinal tract." [Emphasis added.] Mid-Western Life Ins. Co. of Texas v. Goss, 552 S.W.2d 430, 432 (Tex.1977).

celiac disease See under *disease*.

cell (sel) [L. *cella* compartment] any one of the minute protoplasmic masses that make up organized tissue, consisting of a nucleus which is surrounded by cytoplasm which contains the various organelles and is enclosed in the cell or plasma membrane. A cell is the fundamental, structural, and functional unit of living organisms. See illustrations. In some of the lower forms of life, e.g., bacteria, a morphological nucleus is absent, although nucleoproteins (and genes) are present.

cells, epithelial cells that cover the surface of the body and line its cavities.

cells, oat; cells, oat-shaped cells shaped like oat grains, seen in some kinds of carcinoma; also a characteristic of erythrocytes in sickle cell anemia.

cells, packed human blood [USP]; **cells, packed red blood (human)** whole blood from which plasma has been removed; used therapeutically in blood transfusions.

... packed red blood cells (human) [3] .... [[3] Red cells extracted from human blood and packed by centrifugal force.] Blank v. U.S., 400 F.2d 302, 302 (5th Cir. 1968).

cell, squamous a flat, scalelike epithelial cell.

In 1978 James's tumor was diagnosed as being a large or **squamous cell** type, and not a small cell tumor. In all probability, it would have been of the same type in 1976. Unlike small cell tumors, large or **squamous cell** tumors, depending on their location, are operable. Thus, resection could not have been ruled out by reason of the cell type involved. James v. U.S., 483 F.Supp. 581, 585 (N.D.Cal.1980).

cell-mediated reaction See *response, immune*.

cellulitis (sel"u-li'tis) diffuse inflammation of the soft or connective tissue due to infection, in which a thin, watery exudate spreads through the cleavage planes of interstitial and tissue spaces; it may lead to ulceration and abscess. Called also *phlegmon*.

"DIAGNOSIS: Epidural tissue:
1. Acute **cellulitis** of fibrofatty tissue with associated bacteria of micrococcal morphology. Hemolytic coagulase positive Staphylococcus aureus cultured."
In laymen's terms, this simply means that plaintiff suffered an epidural tissue abscess caused by a Staphylococcus infection.
Plaintiff contends that the infection has rendered him a lifelong paraplegic. Samuels v. Doctors Hospital, Inc., 414 F.Supp. 1124, 1126 (W.D.La.1976).

A. If the leg is cool, you have pretty good reason to believe that a lessened amount of blood is getting to the foot. Now, if the temperature is hot, it means that it is infected. There is a

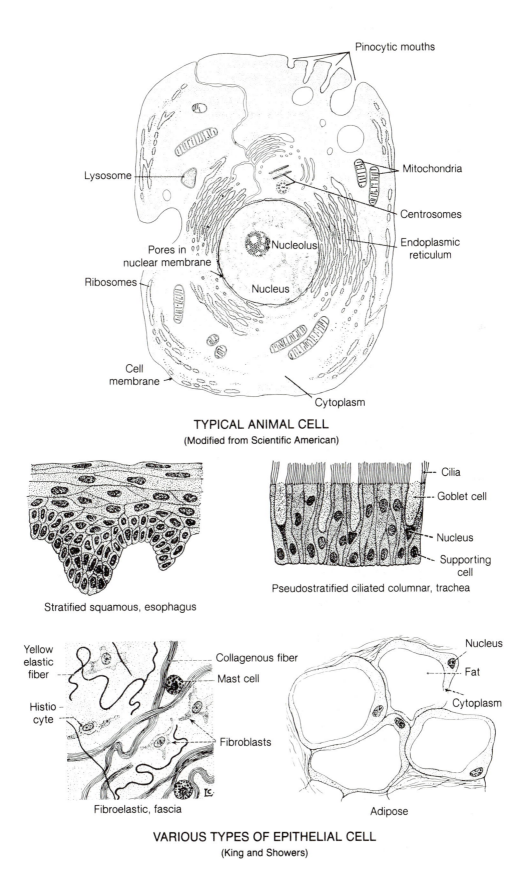

Pinocytic mouths

Lysosome

Mitochondria

Centrosomes

Endoplasmic
reticulum

Pores in
nuclear membrane

Nucleolus

Nucleus

Ribosomes

Cell
membrane

Cytoplasm

TYPICAL ANIMAL CELL
(Modified from Scientific American)

Stratified squamous, esophagus

Cilia

Goblet cell

Nucleus

Supporting
cell

Pseudostratified ciliated columnar, trachea

Yellow
elastic
fiber

Collagenous fiber

Mast cell

Histio-
cyte

Fibroblasts

Fibroelastic, fascia

Nucleus

Fat

Cytoplasm

Adipose

VARIOUS TYPES OF EPITHELIAL CELL
(King and Showers)

130

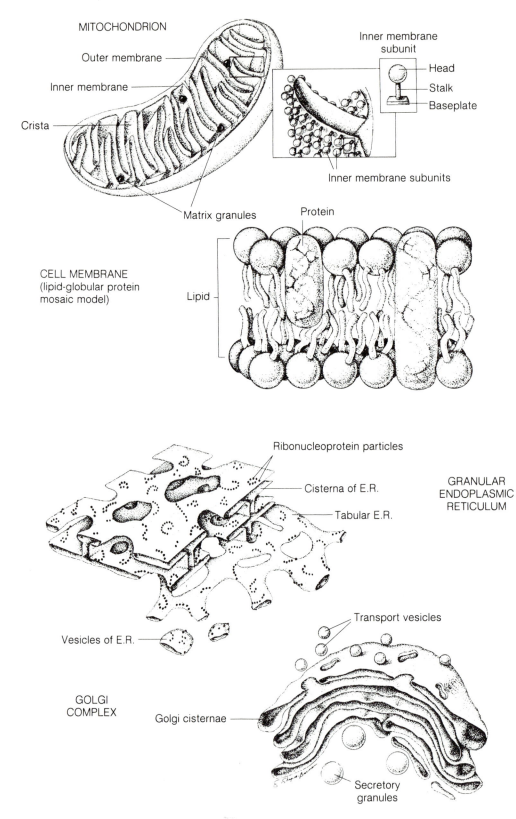

MITOCHONDRION

Outer membrane

Inner membrane

Crista

Matrix granules

Inner membrane subunit

Head

Stalk

Baseplate

Inner membrane subunits

CELL MEMBRANE
(lipid-globular protein
mosaic model)

Protein

Lipid

Ribonucleoprotein particles

Cisterna of E.R.

Tabular E.R.

GRANULAR
ENDOPLASMIC
RETICULUM

Vesicles of E.R.

Transport vesicles

GOLGI
COMPLEX

Golgi cisternae

Secretory
granules

CELL ORGANELLES AND CELL MEMBRANE

cellulitis there. Usually, there is a redness that goes with that. Isgett v. Seaboard Coast Line RR Co., 332 F.Supp. 1127, 1134 (D.S.Car.1971).

Dr. Foster said plaintiff had **cellulitis** of the left mandibular area, a soft tissue infection. Newport v. Hyde, 147 So.2d 113–14 (Miss.1962).

Other Authorities: McNeill v. U.S., 519 F.Supp. 283, 285 (D.S.Car.1981).

cellulitis, orbital inflammation of the cellular tissue within the orbit.

On admission, plaintiff's symptoms included a 104.2° fever, lethargy, marked swelling of the left upper and lower eyelids, swelling and proptosis of the left eyeball, dilation of the left pupil and diminished left corneal reflex, restricted motion of the left eye, swelling on the left and right sides of the head, and hemiparesis (weakness) on the right side of his body.... Expert medical testimony was introduced at trial. Dr. Ronald Hoekstra, a pediatrician who had had training at the Mayo Clinic, testified for plaintiff that, based upon hospital records and the facts, when Dr. Wente saw plaintiff on March 3, 1973, plaintiff had **orbital cellulitis** and that plaintiff should have been hospitalized at that time for head X-rays, blood cultures, culture of the sinus drainage, and immediate institution of aggressive parenteral antibiotic therapy. Weiby v. Wente, 264 N.W.2d 624, 626–7 (Minn.1978).

cement (se-ment') [L. *cemen'tum*] a substance that serves to produce solid union between two surfaces.

The deposition of William Hime, a chemist with expertise in the chemistry of portland **cement** and concrete was offered by plaintiff. His testimony shows that **cement** and concrete burns occur when there is excessive exposure of the **cement** juices to the skin. **Cement** solutions will dissolve the skin and produce a severe burn depending on the time of the exposure and the sensitivity of the skin of the user. Jowers v. Commercial Union Ins. Co., 435 So.2d 575, 577 (Ct.App.La.1983).

cemetery

A ''columbarium'' and a ''**cemetery**'' have different definitions. See Tex.Rev.Civ.Stat.Ann. art. 912a–1 (1963).[1] [[1] ''**Cemetery**'' is . . . a place dedicated to and used and intended to be used for the permanent interment of the human dead. It may be either a burial park for earth interments; a mausoleum for vault or crypt interments, a crematory, or crematory and columbarium for cinerary interments, or a combination of one or more thereof.] City of Beaumont v. Jones, 560 S.W.2d 710, 712 (Ct.Civ.App.Tex.1977).

cenoangiography, coronary See *angiography, coronary.*

center (sen'ter) [Gr. *kentron;* L. *centrum*] the middle point of a body.

Center for Disease Control (CDC), an agency of the U.S. Department of Health and Human Services which serves as a center for the control, prevention, and investigation of diseases.

cephalalgia (sef"ah-lal'je-ah) [Gr. *kephalalgia*] pain in the head; headache. Called also *cephalgia* and *cephalodynia.*

He completely examined Mr. Fillwock in December 1979 and after x-rays were taken diagnosed Mr. Fillwock as suffering from post trauma **cephalagia,** a bruise on the left shoulder, a laceration of the scalp, anxiety and tinnitus in the left ear. Fillwock v. Brown & Root, Inc., 422 So.2d 458–9 (Ct.App.La. 1982).

Cephalalgia [pain in head], probably associated with a post concussion like syndrome, and probably also, in part, of cervical origin. Ascough v. Workmen's Comp. Appeals Board, 98 Cal.Rptr. 357, 359 (Ct.App.Cal.1971).

This witness stated that Matamala's symptoms indicated ''**Cephalgia**, which means pain in the head, buzzing about the left ear....

The medical evidence is far from satisfactory. Despite Matamala's assertion to the contrary, Dr. Markewich found no evidence of any ruptured ear drum, the drums and ossicles were normal, with no symptoms of trauma or concussion. There was, however, an infection in both ears which the doctor could not attribute to the explosion but which he suggested could have been caused by a sudden pulling of the drums. Petition of U.S., 303 F.Supp. 1282, 1326 (E.D.N.Car.1969).

cephalgia See *cephalalgia.*

cephalosporin (sef"ah-lo-spor'in) any of a group of broad-spectrum, relatively penicillinase-resistant antibiotics derived from the fungus *Cephalosporium*, which share the nucleus 7–aminocephalosporanic acid and are structurally related to the penicillins. The cephalosporins available for medicinal use are semisynthetic derivatives of the natural antibiotic *cephalosporin C.*

The **cephalosporins** are a family of antibiotic drugs derived from material produced by the fungus Cephalosporium acremonium. **Cephalosporin-C**, the parent compound from which the drug family was developed, was first isolated by British scientists in the 1950s. As a group the **cephalosporins** possess a number of properties which make them unusually effective as antibiotics....

... While penicillin, a comparable antibiotic, is active against only gram-positive bacteria, the **cephalosporins** are effective against both gram-positive and gram-negative strains. **Cephalosporins** also have low toxicity and allergenicity, producing relatively few adverse side effects and allergic reactions. One consequence of this is that **cephalosporins** may sometimes be used to treat penicillin-allergic individuals. (Abraham Affidavit 1–3; Flynn Affidavit 3–4)....

In terms of chemical structure, the members of the **cephalosporin** family have in common a central structural nucleus formed of a 6–membered ring of 7–aminocephalosporanic acid (7–ACA). The various **cephalosporins** differ from one another in the number and type of side chains attached to the nucleus. While the family members have approximately the same range of antibiotic activity and toxicity, their structural differences result in variant pharmacological properties, that is, differing chemical behavior in the body. Zenith Laboratories, Inc. v. Eli Lilly and Co., 460 F.Supp. 812, 814–15 (D.N.J.1978).

cerebella pontine angle See *angle, cerebello pontile.*

cerebellar dysfunction See *dysfunction, cerebellar.*

cerebral aneurysm See *aneurysm, berry.*

cerebrovascular accident See *syndrome, stroke.*

Certigen See *cholera, hog* (Denman case).

He recommended that all pigs be revaccinated with **Certigen**, a modified live virus vaccine manufactured by another manufacturer. Denman v. Armour Pharmaceutical Co., 322 F.Supp. 1370, 1372 (N.D.Miss.1970).

cerumen (sĕ-roo'men) [L. from *cera* wax] the waxlike secretion found within the external meatus of the ear; called also *earwax*.

The right ear revealed a modified mastoid cavity, which was filled with **cerumen** and squamous debris, with a remnant of middle ear space behind a thin membrane. Adams v. Schweiker, 557 F.Supp. 1373, 1376 (S.D.Tex.1983).

cervical (ser'vĭ-kal) [L. *cervicalis*, from *cervix* neck] pertaining to the neck, or to the neck of any organ or structure. See also *fusion, cervical*.

He determined that Kelly had a straining injury involving the muscles and ligaments of the neck which could be described as a **cervical** strain. Kelly v. International Union, etc., 386 So.2d 1060, 1062 (Ct.App.La.1980).

cervical excision See *surgery, anterior cervical*.

cervical neurological syndrome See *syndrome, cervical*.

cervical spine See *vertebra, cervical*.

cervical spondylosis See *spondylosis, cervical*.

cervical vertebra See *vertebra, cervical*.

cervicitis (ser"vĭ-si'tis) inflammation of the cervix uteri; called also *trachelitis*. See also *cervix uteri*.

She subsequently developed **cervicitis** (infection of the cervix) and underwent surgery for removal of the remainder of the cervix in October, 1981. Trichel v. Caire, 427 So.2d 1227, 1229–30 (Ct.App.La.1983).

Other Authorities: Capaldi v. Weinberger, 391 F.Supp. 502, 505 (E.D.Pa.1975).

cervix (ser'viks), pl. *cer'vices* [L.] neck; [NA] a term denoting the front portion of the collum, or neck (the part connecting the head and trunk), or a constricted part of an organ (e.g., cervix uteri).

cervix uteri neck of uterus: the lower and narrow end of the uterus, between the isthmus and the ostium uteri. See also *dilation of the cervix* (Storrs case).

... It was discovered that part of her **cervix**, which is the neck of the uterus, and some endometrial cells of the uterus had not been removed....

... The **cervix** is normally much smaller and thicker than the body of the uterus, but becomes stretched and very thin during the vaginal delivery of a baby. Therefore, it is difficult to distinguish from the fundus and the vagina. Removal of the **cervix** is further complicated by the fact that it is not visible during abdominal surgery. Trichel v. Caire, 427 So.2d 1227, 1229, 1231 (Ct.App.La.1983).

chain (chān) a collection of objects linked together in linear fashion, or end to end, as the assemblage of atoms or radicals in a chemical compound, or an assemblage of individual bacterial cells.

chain, long

Long chain (adjective): Describes a linear polymer wherein the molecular chains are composed of approximately 100 or more units. Shaw v. E.B. & A.C. Whiting Co., 157 U.S.P.Q. 405, 410 (D.Vt.1967).

chair, geriatric

A **geriatric chair** was described as "a wheel chair with a table on top of it," similar in design to a child's high chair. Washington Hospital Center v. Martin, 454 A.2d 306–7 (D.C.Ct.App. 1982).

chalazion (kah-la'ze-on), pl. *chala'zia* or *chalazions* [Gr. "small lump"] an eyelid mass that results from chronic inflammation of a meibomian gland and shows a granulomatous reaction to liberated fat when subjected to histopathological examination; sometimes called *meibomian* or *tarsal cyst*.

On October 16, 1975, Frisnegger had a **chalazion**, a small growth, in the middle of his left upper eyelid....

Dr. Gibson applied an anesthetic to his left eye area but the first administration of the anesthetic seemed ineffective. On his second attempt to administer an anesthetic with a needle and syringe, the doctor inserted the needle directly into Frisnegger's eye and lens. The **chalazion** was removed....

Before the incident, Frisnegger had $^{20}/_{20}$ vision. When examined by Dr. Gibson a few days after the incident, he had a cataract caused when the needle pierced the lens. Frisnegger's vision is now very blurry. He can see only light and has "tracers" in his eye. The cataract appears to have destroyed its useful vision. Frisnegger v. Gibson, 598 P.2d 574, 576 (Mont.1979).

character (kar'ak-ter) a quality or attribute indicative of the nature of an object or an organism. In genetics, the expression of a gene or group of genes as seen in a phenotype.

characters, mendelian in genetics, the separate and distinct traits that are exhibited by an animal or plant, and are dependent on the genetic constitution of the organism; they may be recessive or dominant. See also *Mendel's law*, under *law*.

Charcot-Marie-Tooth disease See *atrophy, progressive* neuropathic (peroneal) muscular.

Charnley-Mueller total hip replacement See *total hip, replacement, Charnley-Mueller*.

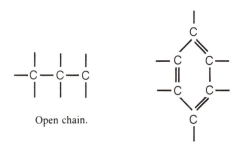

Open chain.

Closed chain.

chart (chart) a simplified graphic representation of the fluctuation of some variable, as of pulse, temperature, and respiration, or a record of all the clinical data of a particular case.

chart, anesthesiological

He further testified that as a part of his regular duties he kept a chart checking blood pressure and pulse as taken and there were no signs that Evelyn Seaton was experiencing any difficulty until he failed to detect a pulse. . . .

Some ten months later, Dr. Rosenberg was notified that Evelyn Seaton's lawyer desired to examine the hospital records of the operation. He then proceeded to the hospital record room and began adding to the chart he kept during the operation until advised by a record room clerk that this was improper. When questioned about the chart as added to and introduced into evidence, Dr. Rosenberg testified in part:

Some of these marks are accurate and were put on the day of the procedure. I don't know which ones they were . . .

Q. How far had you gotten along, Doctor, when the nurse stopped you or the record personnel stopped you?

A. I don't know. I was so flustered. I thought maybe Charlie, or Mr. Williams will misunderstand me. I was so, for a better word, shook I didn't know where I quit and I handed it to them. I have no idea. If I had known, I would have erased them. No, I wouldn't have done that. I will say this. I would not have erased this because that is immoral.

This **anesthesiologist chart**, which, when checked, shows the patient's blood pressure and pulse as noted during the course of the operation, precipitated the difficulty in the trial of this case. . . .

. . . He further testified that the **anesthesiological chart** kept by Dr. Rosenberg was too regular to be believable in that up to the point of the cardiac arrest it showed no change in blood pressure and that by the very nature of the procedures followed there would be changes. Seaton v. Rosenberg, 573 S.W.2d 333, 335–6 (Ky.1978).

cheekbone See *os zygomaticum.*

cheilosis (ki-lo'sis) [*cheilo-* + *-osis*] a condition marked by fissuring and dry scaling of the vermilion surface of the lips and angles of the mouth (perlèche); it is characteristic of riboflavin deficiency.

Bilateral **cheilosis** (fissuring and scaling of lips due to riboflavin deficiency) suggested possible malnutrition. Matthews v. Matthews, 415 F.Supp. 201, 204 (E.D.Va.1976).

chelation (ke-la'shun) combination with a metal in complexes in which the metal is part of a ring.

The record reveals that **chelation therapy** consists of a series of intravenous injections of a chelating drug, usually disodium ethylenediamine tetraacetic acid (hereafter disodium EDTA, Na_2 EDTA, or EDTA). Each injection takes approximately three to four hours to administer, and a normal course of treatment usually involves twenty such injections. The treatments are specifically intended to treat arteriosclerosis (hardening of the arteries), therosclerosis (deposits on the inner lining of the arteries), and other generalized circulatory deficiencies caused by excess calcium in the circulatory vessels. . . .

Chelation therapy is, then, infusion of a chelating agent (generally Na_2 EDTA) into the blood stream over several hours, a treatment which is repeated about 20 times, generally over a period of a month or more. Rogers v. State Bd. of Med. Examiners, 371 So.2d 1037–9 (Dist.Ct.App.Fla.1979).

Chelation involves intravenous injections in the patient of chemicals which tend to react chemically with the harmful metals which accumulate in and deter passage of blood within the blood vessels. Upon dissolution of these harmful substances by the chemical reaction to the chelating drug, the harmful metals are dissolved and pass out of the body through the kidneys. The danger involved is that too many of such substances may be passed into the kidneys too rapidly and, on occasion, renal poisoning sets in, and kidney failure results in the death of the patient. U.S. v. Evers, 453 F.Supp. 1141, 1143 (M.D.Ala. 1978).

chelation therapy See *chelation*; and *therapy, chelation.*

Chemical Abstracts

The **Chemical Abstracts Index** discloses the names and structural formulas of various chemical compounds without any indication as to their properties or utilities. Deutsche Gold-und Silber-Scheid v. Comm. of Patents, 251 F.Supp. 624, 626 (D.D.C.1966).

chemonucleolysis (ke"mo-nu"kle-ol'ĭ-sis) [*chemo-* + *nucleo* nucleus + *lysis*] dissolution of the nucleus pulposus of an intervertebral disk by injection of a chemolytic agent, e.g., the enzyme chymopapain; used especially in the treatment of herniation of a disk.

. . . the defendant doctors treated plaintiff's back by means of a relatively novel procedure known as "**chemonucleolysis**", which involved an injection of chymopapain, an investigational drug manufactured by the defendant drug companies.

The appellant Katherine Gaston, plaintiff in the trial court, had a history of intermittent back pain. . . .

. . . **Chemonucleolysis** is a procedure whereby chymopapain is injected into a bulging disk. The theory was that the drug would dissolve some of the center part of the disk (i.e., the nucleus pulposus), the pressure would be relieved, and the bulging or herniated disk would contract and no longer press upon nerve roots. Gaston v. Hunter, 588 P.2d 326, 330 (Ct. App.Ariz.1978).

chemoprophylaxis (ke"mo-pro"fi-lak'sis) [*chemo-* + Gr. *prophylax* an advanced guard] use of a chemotherapeutic agent as a means of preventing development of a specific disease.

. . . we note that there was no direct evidence at trial that Mario Santoni knew of the risks of taking INH. No informed consent form was ever signed by him nor was there any notation on his chemoprophylaxis register sheet that he was advised of the risk of hepatitis. Santoni v. Moodie, 452 A.2d 1223, 1229 (Ct.Spec.App.Md.1982).

Testimony was also before the court that established procedures called for noting at each visit on the City's own record, called a "**Chemoprophylaxis Register Sheet**," any adverse reactions. That sheet also is a part of the record. It contains reference to each of the visits by Santoni, including a comment as to how many "tablets [were] left" from the previous visit, but it indicates no adverse reactions. Moodie v. Santoni, 441 A.2d 323, 325 (Ct.App.Md.1982).

chemosurgery (ke″mo-sur′jer-e) the destruction of tissue by chemical agents; originally applied to chemical fixation of malignant, gangrenous, or infected tissue, with the use of frozen sections to facilitate systematic microscopic control of the extent of ablation.

... to be followed later by **chemosurgery**, or a "chemical face peel". He testified that the scar on her right cheek was lighter or whiter than the rest of her face; however, in his medical record he made an entry wherein he described Mrs. Rosenblum's scar as "an unobtrusive superficial right facial scar"....

... The **chemosurgery** consists of putting a chemical on the face, which in Mrs. Rosenblum's case will remove some of the pigment from the skin and at the same time increase the tissue tension of the skin other than the scar tissue, and thereby achieve a "cosmetic blend" or uniformity of color over all of her face. "**Chemosurgery**" is a controlled second degree burn. Rosenblum v. Bloom, 492 S.W.2d 321, 323-4 (Ct.Civ. App.Tex.1973).

chemotherapy (ke″mo-ther′ah-pe) the treatment of disease by chemical agents; first applied to use of chemicals that affect the causative organism unfavorably but do not harm the patient.

According to uncontroverted medical evidence in this record, the only known medically effective treatment for acute lymphocytic leukemia is **chemotherapy**, an aggressive three-year treatment program administered in three distinct phases. The first phase is of four weeks' duration, and focuses on killing leukemia cells in the body. In this phase, different anti-leukemia drugs are administered in combination: first, so that the leukemia cells may be attacked at different points in the cell division cycle, and, second, so that the leukemia cells do not develop a resistance to any one drug. The patient in this phase receives two different types of anti-leukemia drugs, one in the form of weekly injections, and another in the form of daily oral dosages.

The second phase of **chemotherapy** treatment is six weeks long. In this phase, new anti-leukemia drugs are introduced: During the first ten days, a drug called L-Asparaginise is administered intravenously each day; on the eleventh day, and for each successive day during the three-year treatment, a drug called 6–Mercaptopurine is taken orally.

This second phase of **chemotherapy** also focuses on attacking leukemia cells which may have migrated into the spinal fluid and which, therefore, may be outside the reach of the anti-leukemia drugs which are administered intravenously or by injection. In some treatment programs, cranial radiation is used to attack leukemia cells that may have invaded the central nervous system. In other treatment plans, a drug called Methotrexate is injected directly into the spinal fluid each week. Thereafter, the drug is taken weekly in pill form until the conclusion of the three-year treatment.

The third phase of **chemotherapy** is a maintenance period, which continues until the three years have elapsed. Once during each month of this phase, the patient visits the hospital and receives another combination of anti-leukemia drugs, one in the form of an intravenous injection, and one in the form of an oral dosage taken each day for one week. Custody of a Minor, 379 N.E.2d 1053, 1056-7 (Sup.Jud.Ct.Mass.1978).

Chemotherapy, as was testified to at the hearing in the Probate Court, involves the administration of drugs over several weeks, the purpose of which is to kill the leukemia cells. This treatment unfortunately affects normal cells as well. One expert testified that the end result, in effect, is to destroy the living vitality of the bone marrow. Because of this effect, the patient becomes very anemic and may bleed or suffer infections—a condition which requires a number of blood transfusions. In this sense, the patient immediately becomes much "sicker" with the commencement of **chemotherapy**, and there is a possibility that infections during the initial period of **severe anemia** will prove fatal....

... According to the medical testimony before the court below, persons over age sixty have more difficulty tolerating **chemotherapy** and the treatment is likely to be less successful than in younger patients.[4] ...

An important facet of the **chemotherapy** process, to which the judge below directed careful attention, is the problem of serious adverse side effects caused by the treating drugs. Among these side effects are severe nausea, bladder irritation, numbness and tingling of the extremities, and loss of hair. The bladder irritation can be avoided, however, if the patient drinks fluids, and the nausea can be treated by drugs. It was the opinion of the guardian ad litem, as well as the doctors who testified before the probate judge, that most people elect to suffer the side effects of **chemotherapy** rather than to allow their leukemia to run its natural course. [4 On appeal, the petitioners have collected in their brief a number of recent empirical studies which cast doubt on the view that patients over sixty are less successfully treated by **chemotherapy**. E.g., Bloomfield & Theologides, Acute Granulocytic Leukemia in Elderly Patients, 226 J.A.M.A. 1190, 1192 (1973); Grann and others, The Therapy of Acute Granulocytic Leukemia in Patients More Than Fifty Years Old, 80 Annals Internal Med. 15, 16 (1974). (Acute myeloblastic monocytic leukemia is a subcategory of acute granulocytic leukemia.) Other experts maintain that older patients have lower remission rates and are more vulnerable to the toxic effects of the administered drugs. E.g., Crosby, Grounds for Optimism in Treating Acute Granulocytic Leukemia, 134 Archives Internal Med. 177 (1974).] Superintendent of Belchertown v. Saikewicz, 370 N.E.2d 417, 420-1 (Sup.Jud.Ct.Mass.1977).

CHF See *heart failure, congestive.*

chickenpox (chik′en-poks) a highly contagious disease caused by the herpes zoster virus and characterized by crops of vesicular eruptions confined mainly to the face and trunk, appearing over a period of a few days to a week, after an incubation period of 17–21 days. The lesions begin as macules, develop quickly into vesicles, and then become crusted. The disease is usually benign in children, but may be serious in infants, children with underlying malignancy, and adults; varicella pneumonia may occur, particularly in adults. Called also *varicella.* See also *herpes zoster.*

She testified that during the period alleged in her claim she came in contact with some 18 to 20 students at six different schools who had skin eruptions which in her opinion were symptoms of **chickenpox**. She testified to the identifying characteristics of **chickenpox** and distinguished them from those of other conditions such as hives, flea bites, bedbug bites, impetigo, and poison ivy and poison oak....

... There was also competent medical opinion, based on the history of exposures given by applicant, that she did, in fact, contract **herpes zoster** as a result of the exposures. There is no evidence to the contrary. Wilhelm v. Workmen's Compensation Appeals Bd., 62 Cal.Rptr. 829–31 (Ct.App.Cal. 1967).

child (chīld) the human young, from infancy to puberty.

child abuse syndrome See *syndrome, battered-child.*

childbirth See *labor.*

chiropody See *podiatry.*

chiropractic (ki"ro-prak'tik) [*chiro-* + Gr. *prattein* to do] a system of therapeutics based upon the claim that disease is caused by abnormal function of the nerve system. It attempts to restore normal function of the nerve system by manipulation and treatment of the structures of the human body, especially those of the spinal column. Called also *chiropraxis.* See also *physician* (Rastetter case).

At the conclusion of the Study, the conclusions and recommendations were made regarding chiropractors:

"1. There is a body of basic scientific knowledge related to health, disease, and health care. **Chiropractic** practitioners ignore or take exception to much of this knowledge despite the fact that they have not undertaken adequate scientific research.

"2. There is no valid evidence that subluxation, if it exists, is a significant factor in disease processes. Therefore, the broad application to health care of a diagnostic procedure such as spinal adjustment is not justified.

"3. The inadequacies of **chiropractic** education, coupled with a theory that de-emphasizes proven causative factors in disease processes, proven methods of treatment, and differential diagnosis, make it unlikely that a chiropractor can make an adequate diagnosis and know the appropriate treatment and subsequently provide the indicated treatment, or refer the patient. Lack of these capabilities in independent practitioners is undesirable because: appropriate treatment could be delayed or prevented entirely; appropriate treatment might be interrupted or stopped completely; the treatment offered could be contraindicated; all treatments have some risk involved with their administration, and inappropriate treatment exposes the patient to this risk unnecessarily.

"4. Manipulation (including chiropractic manipulation) may be a valuable technique for relief of pain due to loss of mobility of joints. Research in this area is inadequate; therefore, it is suggested that research that is based upon the scientific method be undertaken with respect to manipulation." HEW Report at 196–97.

The Study makes the following recommendation for chiropractic:

"**Chiropractic** theory and practice are not based upon the body of basic knowledge related to health, disease, and health care that has been widely accepted by the scientific community. Moreover, irrespective of its theory, the scope and quality of **chiropractic** education do not prepare the practitioner to make an adequate diagnosis and provide ap-

propriate treatment. Therefore, it is recommended that **chiropractic** service not be covered in the Medicare program." HEW Independent Practitioners Under Medicare: A Report to Congress at 197 (1968). Rastetter v. Weinberger, 379 F.Supp. 170, 174 (D.Ariz.1974).

The theory of **chiropractic** is that various ailments and pathological conditions can be cured or allayed through manipulation of the joints and particularly the spinal column. An adjunct of that theory is that drugs and medication interfere with the natural healing processes of the body. It is no secret that the validity of the theory is generally questioned if not rejected by the medical profession. The State of California, however, has licensed the practice of **chiropractic** and a practitioner in the field is no more a guarantor of success than is a medical doctor. People v. Cabral, 190 Cal.Rptr. 194–7 (Ct.App.Cal. 1983).

Other Authorities: Bilbrey v. Industrial Commission, 556 P.2d 27, 29 (Ct.App.Ariz.1976); Rosenthal v. State Bd. of Chiropractic Examiners, 413 A.2d 882, 883 (Del.1980); Kelley v. Raguckas, 270 N.W.2d 665, 668–9 (Ct.App.Mich.1978); Badke v. Barnett, 316 N.Y.S.2d 177, 179 (2d Dep't 1970); Vidra v. Shoman, 59 A.D.2d 714, 715, 398 N.Y.S.2d 377 (2d Dep't [N.Y.] 1977); State v. Blinzler, 599 P.2d 349, 352–3 (Mont.1979); Norville v. Miss. State Medical Ass'n., 364 So. 2d 1084, 1086 (Miss.1978) U.S. v. Article Consisting of 2 Devices, Etc., 255 F.Supp. 374, 378 (W.D.Ark.1966); Chalupa v. Industrial Com'n, 498 P.2d 228, 232 (Ct.App.Ariz.1972).

chiropractic, mixer school

The **mixer view** has a "chiropractic-physician" philosophy which is defined in Board Rule 17, as follows:

Chiropractic is that branch of the healing arts which deals with the diagnosis, treatment and prevention of disease; correction and maintenance of the structural and functional integrity of the neuromusculo-skeletal system and the effects thereof or the interference therewith, by the utilization of all recognized and accepted diagnostic procedures, and the employment of all therapeutic measures as taught in approved chiropractic colleges. [Footnote omitted.] Rosenthal v. State Bd. of Chiropractic Examiners, 413 A.2d 882–4 (Del. 1980).

chiropractic, straight school

The **straight school**, which plaintiff follows, defines chiropractic practice along the traditional lines specified in § 701, that is, as the "science of locating and removing any interference with the transmission of nerve energy." Rosenthal v. State Bd. of Chiropractic Examiners, 413 A.2d 882–3 (Del.1980).

chloracne (klor-ak'ne) an acneiform eruption caused by exposure to chlorine compounds. See also *dioxin* (Citizens Against Toxic Sprays, Inc. case).

The phenoxy herbicides have been the subject of scientific research for many years. From time to time attention has been focused on them because of outbreaks of skin eruptions known as **chloracne** among workers involved in their production. Citizens Against Toxic Sprays, Inc. v. Bergland, 428 F.Supp. 908, 914 (D.Or.1977).

chloral (klo'ral) [*chlor*ine + *-al*] 1. chemical name: trichloroacetaldehyde. A colorless, oily liquid, $Cl_3C\cdot CHO$, having a pungent, irritating odor, and prepared by the mutual action of alcohol and chlorine. It is used in the manufacture of chloral hydrate and DDT. 2. chloral hydrate.

chloral hydrate [USP], chemical name: 2,2,2-trichloro-1,1-ethanediol. A hypnotic and sedative, $C_2H_3Cl_3O_2$, occurring as colorless, transparent, or white crystals; administered orally.

(Count 3) and unlawfully and knowingly possessing **chloral hydrate**, a "depressant or stimulant drug" within the meaning of 21 U.S.C. § 321(v)(3), 21 C.F.R. 166.3 and 26 U.S.C. § 4744(a)(1). U.S. v. Moore, 452 F.2d 569, 571 (6th Cir. 1971).

chloramphenicol (klo"ram-fen'ĭ-kol) [USP] chemical name: [R-(R*,R*)]-2, 2-dichloro-N-[2-hydroxy-1-(hydroxymethy)-2-(4-nitrophenyl)ethyl]acetamide. A broad-spectrum antibiotic, $C_{11}H_{12}Cl_2N_2O_5$, originally derived for *Streptomyces venezuelae* and later shown to be elaborated by other spirochetes, and produced synthetically. It occurs as fine, white to grayish white or yellowish white, needle-like crystals or elongated plates, and is effective against rickettsiae, gram-positive and gram-negative bacteria, and certain spirochetes, being used especially in the treatment of typhus and other rickettsial infections and in typhoid, shigellosis, and related enteric diseases; used as an antibacterial, administered orally or applied topically to the conjunctiva, or as an antirickettsial, administered orally. See also *anemia, aplastic*.

Chloromycetin, Parke, Davis' trade name for **chloramphenicol**, is a potent, broad-spectrum antibiotic. Properly administered, it is a valuable, life-saving drug that can effectively treat stubborn infections. But it can be injurious—even fatal—if its use is not carefully monitored. According to the Food and Drug Administration, its most common, serious toxic effect is the development of anemia. Parke, Davis' package inserts have always mentioned the drug's potential danger, and in 1961 the company revised its warnings, emphasizing precautions that should be observed.

In 1968 Parke, Davis again modified its warning, but apparently this revision was not in effect at the time Timothy was treated ....

... The [earlier] package insert read in part as follows:
"Warning—Serious and even fatal blood dyscrasias (aplastic anemia, hypoplastic anemia, thrombocytopenia, granulocytopenia) are known to occur after the administration of **chloramphenicol**. Blood dyscrasias have occurred after both short-term and prolonged therapy with this drug. Bearing in mind the possibility that such reactions may occur, **chloramphenicol** should be used only for serious infections caused by organisms that are susceptible to its antibacterial effects.

"**Chloramphenicol** should not be used when other less potentially dangerous agents will be effective; or in the treatment of trivial infections such as colds, influenza, or viral infections of the throat; or as a prophylactic agent.

"Precautions—It is essential that adequate blood studies be made during treatment with the drug. While blood studies may detect early peripheral blood changes, such as leukopenia or granulocytopenia, before they become irreversible, such studies cannot be relied on to detect bone marrow repression prior to development of aplastic anemia." Salmon

v. Parke, Davis and Co., 520 F.2d 1359, 1361 (4th Cir. 1975).

Other Authorities: Pratt v. Stein, 444 A.2d 674, 683 (Super.Ct. Pa.1982); Casey v. Penn, 360 N.E.2d 93, 97 (App.Ct.Ill.1977); Love v. Wolf, 58 Cal.Rptr. 42, 45–46 (Ct.App.1967); Stevens v. Parke, Davis & Co., 507 P.2d 653, 655 (Cal.1973); Incollingo v. Ewing, 282 A.2d 206, 210, 212 (Pa.1971); Stottlemire v. Cawood, 213 F.Supp. 897, 898 (D.D.C.1963).

chlordane (klōr'dān) a poisonous substance of the chlorinated hydrocarbon group, used as an insecticide; human poisoning may occur by percutaneous absorption, ingestion, or inhalation.

Technical **chlordane** was arbitrarily named, and actually is made up of 13–15% alphachlordane, 13–15% gammachlordane, and 5–8% heptachlor. ALJ Recommended Decision at 7 ....

... Histological review of the IRDC CD–1 Mouse Study, using a hardy non-inbred strain of mice with low incidence of spontaneous tumors, resulted in the finding of "a highly statistically significant incidence of hepatocellular carcinomas" for those mice fed heptachlor/heptachlor epoxide, and basically the same finding for mice fed **chlordane** ....

... None of the tests yielded negative results; **chlordane** was shown to be independently carcinogenic, as well as to contain a carcinogenic component (heptachlor/heptachlor epoxide). [Footnote omitted.] Environmental Defense Fund, Inc. v. E.P.A., 548 F.2d 998, 1007–8 (D.C.Cir.1977).

chlordiazepoxide (klōr"di-az"ē-pok'sīd) [USP] chemical name: 7-chloro-N-methyl-5-phenyl-3H-1,4-benzodiazepin-2-amine-4-oxide. One of the benzodiazepine tranquilizers, $C_{16}H_{14}ClN_3O$, occurring as a yellow, crystalline powder; administered orally in the treatment of conditions in which anxiety, tension, and apprehension are prominent symptoms, in acute anxiety, and in chronic alcoholism or alcohol withdrawal.

Chlordiazepoxide (Librium) is a benzodiazepine compound with the following chemical formula: 7-chloro-2-methylamino-5-phenyl-3H-1, 4-benzodiazepine 4-oxide hydrochloride. It is a colorless crystalline substance; is soluble in water and its molecular weight is 336.22 (R–119) ....

... Librium and Valium are widely used in the treatment of anxiety and tension, as muscle relaxants, as anticonvulsants, and as anti-depressants.

Librium has been in general medical use since 1960. More than 6 billion capsules of the drug have been commercially distributed, and millions of patients have taken Librium since its approval by the Food and Drug Administration (Bennett, Tr. 4135–36; R–222).

Librium is indicated whenever fear, anxiety and tension are significant components of the clinical profile. Hoffman-La Roche, Inc. v. Kleindienst, 478 F.2d 1, 7–9 (3d Cir. 1973).

chlordiazepoxide hydrochloride [USP], the monohydrochloride salt of chlordiazepoxide, $C_{18}H_{21}ClN_2 \cdot HCl$, occurring as a white, or almost white, crystalline powder; used for the same purposes as the base, administered orally, intravenously, or intramuscularly.

He prescribed **librium** for the epilepsy, which had a tendency to level out the brain waves. Ex Parte Hagans, 558 S.W.2d 457, 459 (Ct.Crim.App.Tex.1977).

chloride (klo'rīd) a salt of hydrochloric acid; any binary compound of chlorine in which the latter is the negative element. Formerly called *muriate*.

chloride, zephiran

Immediately thereafter, it was placed in a plastic, self-sealing bag holding **zephiran chloride**, a disinfectant also compatible with the composition of acrylic dentures. Germann v. Matriss, 260 A.2d 825, 827 (N.J.1970).

chlorofluorocarbon

Chlorofluorocarbons are used as propellants in self-pressurized containers of a variety of products subject to the Commission's jurisdiction. Scientific research has indicated that **chlorofluorocarbons** may pose a risk of depletion of ozone in the stratosphere....

... The stratospheric ozone shield is of great importance in protecting life on earth from shortwave ultra-violet rays of the sun. Ozone depletion allows more of these rays to reach the earth, and the consequences include a possibility of a significant increase in human skin cancer and other effects of unknown magnitude on man, animals, and plants. **Chlorofluorocarbon** release may also cause climatic change, both by reducing stratospheric ozone and by increasing infrared absorption in the atmosphere....

For the purposes of this Part 1401:
(a) "**Chlorofluorocarbon**" means any fully halogenated chlorofluoroalkane. 16 C.F.R.Sec. 1401.2 and 1401.3(a) (1982).

chloroform (klo'ro-form) [L. *chloroformum*; from *chlorine* + *formyl*] [NF] a clear, colorless, volatile liquid, $CHCl_3$, with a strong ethereal smell and a sweetish, burning taste used as a solvent. It was once widely used as an inhalation anesthetic and analgesic, and as an antitussive, carminative, and counterirritant. Called also *trichlormethane*.

The presence of **chloroform** in drinking water has been of particular concern because of its demonstrated carcinogenicity in laboratory animals and widespread presence in municipal water systems. Environmental Defense Fund, Inc. v. Castle, 578 F.2d 337, 350 (D.C.Cir.1978).

Chloromycetin See *chloramphenicol*.

chloroquine (klo'ro-kwin) [USP] chemical name: N^4-(7-chloro-4-quinolinyl)-N^1,N^1-diethyl 1,4-pentanediamine. A compound, $C_{18}H_{26}ClN_3$, occurring as a white or slightly yellow, crystalline powder; used as antimalarial in certain forms of malaria and as an antiamebic in extraintestinal amebiasis, administered intramuscularly. See also *quinacrine hydrochloride* (Cross case).

After examining her, Dr. Fields concluded the "most likely cause" of her hearing loss was **chloroquine** toxicity (Fields deposition, 27). He told her to stop taking the **chloroquine** and advised her there was "a possibility" that it was the cause of her hearing loss. (Fields deposition, 10; Grigsby deposition, 45–6). Grigsby v. Sterling Drug Co., 428 F.Supp. 242, 244 (D.D.C.1975).

In this diversity action Hoffman, plaintiff-appellee cross-appellant, sought to recover damges for serious and permanent injuries allegedly sustained as the result of ingesting the drug

chloroquine phosphate, which was manufactured by Sterling Drug, Inc. and Winthrop Laboratories, Inc., and marketed under the trade name of Aralen....

Suspicion that **chloroquine** use might permanently damage the retina began to arise circa 1957. An article by Dr. Goldman and Dr. Preston, entitled "Reactions to Chloroquine Observed During Treatment of Various Dermatologic Disorders," [12] stated that **chloroquine** was suspected of severe fundal (retinal) changes but this could not be proved....

... Numerous letters were also received by defendants from physicians during this period (1956–1960) reporting loss of vision, field changes, and fundus changes in patients being treated with Aralen and inquiring into the possibility that Aralen might be the cause. [[12] American Journal of Tropical Medicine and Hygiene, Vol. 6, pages 654–657 (1957); Plaintiff's Exhibit 57–1.] Hoffman v. Sterling Drug, Inc., 485 F.2d 132, 136, 147, 149–50 (3d Cir. 1973).

chloroquine phosphate [USP], the phosphate salt of chloroquine, $C_{18}H_{26}ClN_3 \cdot 2H_3PO_4$, occurring as a white, crystalline powder; used as an antimalarial for the suppression and treatment of certain forms of malaria, as an antiamebic in extraintestinal amebiasis, and as a lupus erythematosus suppressant, administered orally.

The accused drug in this case is **chloroquine phosphate** which was marketed by appellant, under the registered trademark names "Aralen Phosphate" and "Aralen". Its chemical structure is described as follows: "7-chloro-4 (4 diethylamino-1-methylbotylamino) quinoline diphosphate." It is also known as one of the "4-aminoquinolines." Sterling Drug, Inc. v. Yarrow, 408 F.2d 978, 983–4 (8th Cir. 1969).

chlorothiazide (klo"ro-thi'ah-zīd) [USP] chemical name: 6-chloro-2*H*-1,2,4-benzothiadiazine-7-sulfonamide-1,1-dioxide. An orally effective diuretic, $C_7H_6ClN_3O_4S_2$, occurring as a white or practically white, crystalline powder; used in the treatment of renal, hepatic, and drug-induced edema, edema and toxemia of pregnancy, and fluid retention associated with various conditions, and in hypertension. Cited in U.S. v. Cika Geigy Corp., 508 F.Supp. 1118, 1122 (D.N.J.1976).

chlorpromazine (klōr-pro'mah-zēn) [USP] chemical name: 2-chloro-*N*,*N*-dimethyl-10*H*-phenothiazine-10-propanamine. A phenothiazine derivative, $C_{17}H_{19}ClN_2S$, occurring as a white, crystalline solid; used as an antiemetic and tranquilizer, administered by rectal suppository. See also *lobotomy* (Cameron case).

Cameron was sedated by an injection of 300 milligrams of **Thorazine (chlorpromazine)** at approximately 3:30 a.m. on December 23. The normal initial dose is 25 to 50 milligrams, and **Thorazine** is contraindicated for persons who are under the influence of alcohol because of the potentiating interaction between alcohol and **Thorazine**....

... an expert on the interaction between **Thorazine** and alcohol, testified that the drug was originally developed as a preanesthetic medication to be given to patients to destroy any anxiety they might feel about oncoming surgery. The drug affects a person mentally by reducing the normal anxiety reactions to a point where he is no longer disturbed by what normally would be upsetting factors in his environment....

Dr. Burbridge described the physical symptoms of a person heavily under the influence of **Thorazine** as slowed speech and short answers. "He won't slur his speech, as when he is drunk, but whereas without **Thorazine** he would not only answer a question but amplify on it, with the **Thorazine** the words will come slowly and he would make his answers as short as possible." [Footnote omitted] In Re Cameron, 439 P.2d 633, 640–2 (Cal.1968).

chlorpromazine hydrochloride [USP], the hydrochloride of chlorpromazine, occurring as a white, crystalline powder, used orally, muscularly, or intravenously as a major tranquilizer.

Certainly the drug was of need apparently in the early stages of his treatment to elievate [sic] the anxiety and emotional trauma that is associated with back injury. However, in the process of treatment of this continuous use of **Thiozides** cause a perputation [sic] of the extraparamidal seizures which in turn complicated the initial injury he sustained to begin with....

... It is not to be implied here however that **Thioziade drugs** should not have been used on Mr. Chabert. It is to be emphasized that certainly these drugs quite often are of great value in relieving patients with back injuries insofar as they increase the tolerance for pain and also at times are of a beneficial nature to the neuralgia reaction that occurs associated with back pain. Chabert v. City of Westwego Police Pension, 423 So.2d 1190, 1195–6 (Ct.App.La.1982).

The jury could reach this conclusion from the plaintiff's testimony and that of her expert witness: that she had been taking orange pills from a bottle labelled "**Thorazine M–65**" obtained by prescription from a doctor at Bellevue and from the hospital pharmacy; that she had the symptoms of jaundice on admission; that Thorazine-induced jaundice is caused by intrahepatic obstruction and is "usually promptly reversible on withdrawal of the medication".... Brown v. City of N.Y., 405 N.Y.S.2d 253, 254 (1st Dep't 1978).

Dr. Schulman testified that in his expert opinion the cause of death was the consecutive administration of **thorazine** (a tranquilizer) and electroshock therapy to someone in decedent's weak condition. Kosberg v. Washington Hospital Center, Inc., 394 F.2d 947, 949 (D.C.Cir.1968).

Other Authorities: In re Cameron, 439 P.2d 633, 640–2 (Cal. 1968).

chlorpropamide (klōr-pro′pah-mīd) [USP] chemical name: 4-chloro-*N*-[(propylamino)carbonyl]benzenesulfonamide. An orally effective hypoglycemic agent, $C_{10}H_{13}ClN_2O_3S$, occurring as a white, crystalline powder.

The plaintiff manufactures a tablet known as "Insulase," which is intended for use in the treatment of adults with mild to moderate chronic diabetes. The active ingredient in Insulase is the chemical **chlorpropamide** ("**CPA**" hereafter). **CPA** is also the active ingredient in a tablet manufactured by Pfizer Laboratories, Inc., "Diabinese," which is likewise used to treat diabetes. The inactive ingredients in Diabinese and Insulase, however, are not the same. Premo Pharmaceutical Laboratories, Inc. v. U.S., 475 F.Supp. 52–3 (S.D.N.Y.1979).

cholangiogram (ko-lan′je-o-gram″) a roentgenogram of the gallbladder and bile ducts.

Dr. DeMeester testified that a **cholangiogram** is the best method for determining the presence of strictures. **Cholangiograms** done post-operatively showed a good flow through the repaired bile duct with no evidence of stricture. Overstreet v. U.S., 528 F.Supp. 838, 843 (M.D.Ala.1981).

By January 27, when the time for Mrs. Yerzy's discharge was at hand and the drainage had not stopped, he ordered X-rays (an intravenous **cholangiogram**) for the asserted purpose of effectuating a visualization of the common bile duct. Because the dye used had not been properly absorbed so as to permit visualization, the X-rays were negative. Yerzy v. Levine, 260 A.2d 533–4 (Super.Ct.N.J.1970).

Other Authorities: McClaflin v. Califano, 448 F.Supp. 69, 74 (D.Ken.1978).

cholangitis (ko″lan-ji′tis) [*chol-* + Gr. *angeion* vessel + *-itis*] inflammation of a bile duct.

... although plaintiff underwent numerous tests to try to uncover the cause of his recurrent episodes of ascending **cholangitis**, the first objective evidence that its cause was the strictures from the severance of the bile duct was not revealed until December 1977 and the conclusive evidence of the stricture causing plaintiff's recurrent problem was not known until March 1980. Overstreet v. U.S., 528 F.Supp. 838, 841 (M.D. Ala.1981).

Dr. Fanaipour examined the plaintiff and made an initial diagnosis of **cholangitis** associated with pancreatitis. Conrad v. Christ Community Hospital, 395 N.E.2d 1158–9 (App.Ct.Ill. 1979).

cholecystectomy (ko″le-sis-tek′to-me) [*cholecyst* + Gr. *ektomē* excision] surgical removal of the gallbladder.

On 24 May 1973, Dr. Bronwell, a Lubbock surgeon, undertook to perform a **cholecystectomy**—the removal of the gall bladder—on Mrs. Williams. In her abdomen, the doctor saw a small duct which he traced to the point it entered a duct he "assumed ... was the common bile duct." He traced the duct back up to and into the gall bladder. It was normal. Once he identified the two points, the duct was cut flush with the duct into which it entered. [Footnote omitted.]

Within thirty minutes after the surgery, Dr. Bronwell dictated his medical notes on the operation for the hospital records. He reported that he palpated, i.e., sensed by touch, the common bile duct which, he twice noted, was normal to palpation. Relating that the "common duct was not explored," the doctor gave this account: "The gallbladder was removed, by dissecting free the cystic duct and artery and clamping and dividing and ligating them separately and gallbladder was removed by sharp dissection and the bed was closed...."

... I would like for you to tell us just exactly what you did from the time you made the first incision on down to the end of the surgery, please? [The question refers to the **cholecystectomy**]....

... We made a subcostal incision, which is an incision underneath the ribs, we opened the peritoneal cavity and the first thing we did was to check the gall bladder and found its walls to be thickened and to contain the stones that we previously mentioned. We looked at the liver and found it to be of normal consistency. We reached down into an area that we call the foramen of Winslow or the porta hepatis and felt along the porta hepatis, which we anticipate would have three structures, the portal vein, the hepatic artery and the common bile duct. As I have testified before, we were feeling for evidence of stones in this area and not feeling any, we considered it to be normal. Bronwell v. Williams, 597 S.W.2d 542–3, 551–2 (Ct.Civ.App.Tex.1980).

... an elective **cholecystectomy** (gall bladder removal)....

... She had earlier complained of chronic epigastric distress which Dr. Javurek had determined was resulting from a malfunctioning gall bladder. Carlsen v. Javurek, 526 F.2d 202, 204–5 (8th Cir. 1975).

Other Authorities: Zanos v. Marine Transport Lines, Inc., 315 F.Supp. 321–2 (E.D.Pa.1970).

cholecystitis (ko"le-sis-ti'tis) [*cholecyst* + *-itis*] inflammation of the gallbladder.

... a cholecystectomy (removal of the gallbladder) was performed due to severe **cholecptitis** [sic]. Byrd v. Richardson, 362 F.Supp. 957, 962 (D.S.Car.1973).

... chronic **cholecystitis**, [inflammation of the gallbladder]. Swihel v. Richardson, 346 F.Supp. 930, 933 (D.Neb.1972).

Other Authorities: McClaflin v. Califano, 448 F.Supp. 69, 74 (D.Kan.1978); Glover v. Bruce, 265 S.W.2d 346, 351 (Mo. 1954).

cholecystogram (ko"le-sis'to-gram) a roentgenogram of the gallbladder.

The first gallbladder x-ray or **cholecystogram** did not visualize. Two days later a second **cholecystogram** was run, and the resulting impression was a normal **cholecystogram**. Harwell v. Pittman, 428 So.2d 1049, 1051 (Ct.App.La.1983).

cholelithiasis (ko"le-lĭ-thi'ah-sis) [*chole-* + *lithiasis*] the presence or formation of gallstones.

The cause of death as discerned by autopsy was hemorrhagic pancreatis resulting from **cholelithiasis**, i.e., gallstone(s) blocking a pancreatic duct. The autopsy revealed the presence of at least 50 gallstones in Kandlbinder's gall bladder. Payne v. U.S., 711 F.2d 73, 75 (7th Cir. 1983).

She had previously suffered several gall bladder attacks and defendant diagnosed her condition as chronic **cholelithiasis** (chronically inflamed gall bladder with stones). On his recommendation plaintiff consented to surgery for removal of the gall bladder. Yerzy v. Levine, 260 A.2d 533 (Super.Ct.N.J. 1970).

Other Authorities: McClaflin v. Califano, 448 F.Supp. 69, 74 (D.Kan.1978); Glover v. Bruce, 265 S.W.2d 346, 351 (Mo. 1954).

cholepoiesis (ko"le-poi-e'sis) the manufacture and secretion by the liver of bile constituents other than water.

cholera (kol'er-ah) [Gr., from *cholē* bile] an acute infectious disease caused by *Vibrio cholerae* and characterized by severe diarrhea with extreme fluid and electrolyte depletion, metabolic acidosis, and by vomiting, muscle cramps, and prostration. A specific toxin of the cholera vibrio blocks sodium absorption and promotes excretion of water and electrolytes. The resultant severe dehydration may lead to shock or renal failure. The disease, most commonly disseminated by contaminated drinking water, is endemic and epidemic in Asia. Called also *Asiatic c.*

cholera, hog an infectious communicable disease of swine occurring in epizootics and caused by a virus; marked by fever, loss of appetite, emaciation, ulceration of the intestines, diarrhea, and ecchymoses in the kidney and on the skin of the ventral surface of the body; called also *swine fever.*

... plaintiff's herd of swine suffered an outbreak of **hog cholera** after being vaccinated with a modified live virus vaccine for the immunization of hogs against that disease. Plaintiff asserts that the vaccine, which Armour manufactured and marketed under the brand name "Bon-Ecine" and which Mosher distributed to the trade, was defective in that it failed to immunize hogs vaccinated with the product against **hog cholera**....

... On July 4, the disease, then reaching epidemic proportions, was diagnosed as **hog cholera** by Dr. Stuart Denman, Jr., a licensed veterinarian and son of the plaintiff. This diagnosis was promptly confirmed by findings from the State Testing Laboratory at Jackson, where tissue samples and autopsies revealed internal lesions typical of **hog cholera**....

The undisputed evidence shows that **hog cholera** is a highly contagious disease, easily passed to pigs without immunity; and that the onset of the disease is insidious, as cholera symptoms do not appear until three weeks following the start of the virus incubation. Furthermore, a pig infected with the virus for as much as five days before vacination will likely die from a fully virulent strain of **hog cholera**, described by the witnesses as a lethal virus capable of exterminating 95% of a susceptible herd. Denman v. Armour Pharmaceutical Co., 322 F.Supp. 1370–1, 1373 (N.D.Miss.1970).

choleretic (ko"ler-et'ik) 1. stimulating the production of bile by the liver by either cholepoiesis or hydrocholeresis. 2. a choleretic agent. See also *acid, dehydrocholic.*

The root of Dr. Sklar's hypothesis is possibly a belief that Decholin serves as a whole bile-producing medicine or, in his words, as a "**choleretic**." This view appears to be shared by the other Government authorities, who seem to consider Decholin as the equivalent of a bile salt. U.S. v. Article of Drug Labeled Decholin, 264 F.Supp. 473, 477 (E.D.Mich.1967).

cholesteatoma (ko"le-ste"ah-to'mah) [*chole-* + *steatoma*] a cystlike mass, with a lining of stratified squamous epithelium, usually of keratinizing type, filled with desquamating debris frequently including cholesterol. Cholesteatomas occur in the meninges, central nervous system, and bones of the skull, but are most common in the middle ear and mastoid region.

The medical evidence reveals that plaintiff was seen by Dr. Barnette Hyman as early as 1968 for stopped up ears. At that time, a granuloma of the right ear canal was removed....

... In August, 1974, plaintiff returned to Dr. Hyman who found an additional polyp on the left tympanic membrane, which was removed. Plaintiff was treated periodically for polypi in the left ear from August, 1977, through May, 1979....

In December, 1979, plaintiff's condition was diagnosed as **cholesteatoma** in both ears. Edwards v. Schweiker, 539 F.Supp. 650–2 (E.D.Tex.1982).

An x-ray revealed extensive infection and disease in the left mastoid area and the possibility of **cholesteatoma**, a tumor of skin which develops in the middle ear after there is a hole in the ear drum....

Dr. Austin stated that although he thought the surgery was necessary for the plaintiff's welfare, it was risky procedure to remove skin with a curette from the region of the facial nerve, especially without the use of a surgical microscope. He noted it is a standard operation to leave **cholesteatoma** in the area of the nerve and the end state of the surgery would be the same whether or not the skin is removed. Livengood v. Howard, 295 N.E.2d 736, 738–9 (App.Ct.Ill.1973).

cholinesteras (ko″lin-es′ter-ās) an enzyme that catalyzes the hydrolysis of acetylcholine to choline and an anion; called also *pseudocholinesterase*.

Fenthion and other organic phosphates cause inhibition of **cholinesterase**, an enzyme the presence of which is vital to the transmission of nerve impulses. Excessive exposure to organic phosphates results in organic phosphate poisoning, which may cause death. Diamond Laboratories, Inc. v. Richardson, 452 F.2d 803, 805 (8th Cir. 1972).

According to the evidence, the enzyme **cholinesterase** is found in all men and animals. It plays a vital role in the conduction of nervous impulses. If the biological action of the enzyme is interfered with or inhibited, serious consequences can result, causing irreparable damage to the central nervous system. Skogen v. Dow Chemical Co., 375 F.2d 692, 697 (8th Cir. 1967).

chondrectomy (kon-drek′to-me) [*chondr-* + Gr. *ektomē* excision] surgical removal of a cartilage.

After examining plaintiff, Dr. Schneider felt that plaintiff's pain was a result of an internal derangement in his left knee caused by a spraining injury. On March 18, 1977, Dr. Schneider performed a lateral meniscectomy and a **chondrectomy** of the left knee cap. Plaintiff contends he is disabled as a result of his knee injury. Istre v. Hudson Engineering Corp., 386 So.2d 366–7 (Ct.App.La.1980).

chondritis (kon-dri′tis) [*chondr-* + *-itis*] inflammation of cartilage.

chondritis, costal See *syndrome, Tietze's*.

chondrocalcinosis (kon″dro-kal″sĭ-no′sis) [*chondro-* + L. *calx* lime + *-osis*] the presence of calcium salts, especially calcium pyrophosphate, in the cartilaginous structures of one or more joints; when accompanied by attacks of goutlike symptoms, it is known as *pseudogout*.

The doctors described **chondrocalcinosis** as the existence of calcium crystal deposits in the joints. The deposits sometimes break free and cause episodes of severe pain and swelling known as "pseudogout." Pseudogout is treatable with anti-inflammatory drugs. **Chondrocalcinosis** and pseudogout do not cause instability or degenerative changes in the bone. They are neither caused nor aggravated by heavy lifting. In fact, pseudogout may flare up during periods of inactivity, as the record shows it did for Dee Shepard. Shepard v. Midland Foods, Inc., 666 P.2d 758, 760 (Mont.1983).

chondromalacia (kon″dro-mah-la′she-ah) [*chondro-* + Gr. *malakia* softness] softening of the articular cartilage, most frequently in the patella.

He further testified that the **chondromalacia** he later diagnosed was not related to the accident in question. Stoltz v. Stonecypher, 336 N.W.2d 654, 656 (S.Dak.1983).

Dr. Euliano, who recommended an operation after he examined x-rays showing evidence of patella alta, i.e. a raised kneecap. The doctor, as Claimant's witness, testified that this condition resulted from the development of **chondromalacia**, a condition aggravated by walking, bicycling or any other activity which would make the knee bend or flex. He said such a condition would be aggravated by a direct blow to the knee but that there would be no aggravation from a sprain or twisting injury to the knee. Noel v. W.C.A.B. (Jones & Laughlin Steel), 453 A.2d 724 (Commonwealth Ct.Pa.1982).

He agreed with Saer's conclusion that the complaints were referable to **chondromalacia**, which is a roughening of the cartilage surface of the back of the kneecap....

... She had symptoms and findings of cracking in the knee with motion which indicated a **chondromalacia** which is a mild form of arthritic change not seen on the x-ray. He was of the opinion there was some degree of fissuring, cracking, or fraying of the joint surface. Typical symptoms of **chondromalacia** are some discomfort with squatting or weight bearing when the knee is bent going up or down steps. Pain would be a nuisance type....

... **Chondromalacia** most commonly occurs with the aging process but can be produced by injury. Treatment is to avoid squatting, stooping and climbing and the use of aspirin or bufferin. Landeche v. Weaver, 384 So.2d 540–1 (Ct.App.La. 1980).

Other Authorities: Dodd v. Nicolon Corp., 422 So.2d 398–9 (La.1982); Cash v. Illinois Cent. Gulf R. Co., 388 So.2d 871, 876 (Miss.1980); Muller v. Lykes Bros. Steamship Co., 337 F.Supp. 700, 707 (E.D.La.1972).

Chondromalacia patellae premature degeneration of the patellar cartilage, the patellar margins being tender so that pain is produced when the patella is pressed against the femur. See also *arthritis, patellofemoral*.

The hearing officer found from the evidence that petitioner "sustained synovitis of the knees ... secondary to **chondromalacia patella**" produced by long hours of kneeling while setting tiles....

The only medical testimony was offered by Saul N. Schreiber, M.D., an orthopedic surgeon and petitioner's treating physician. He explained that years of working on his knees caused in petitioner a condition known as **chondromalacia patella**, which is a permanent change to the cartilaginous undersurface of the kneecap. By reason of this, pain is produced by rubbing or pressure between the kneecap and the lower end of the thighbone or femur. When the kneecap is irritated the lining of the knee joint (synovium) becomes irritated and produces a fluid (synovial fluid) which leads to swelling in the knee joint area. The latter condition is called synovitis. Dr. Schreiber indicated that **chondromalacia patella** and synovitis "go together" and the effects would become worse unless petitioner changed to a job where he was not required to work on his knees. Kern v. Industrial Commission, 588 P.2d 353–4 (Ct.App. Ariz.1978).

chondromalacosis patella See *chondromalacia patellae*; and *patella*.

With respect to the right knee, the diagnosis was **chondromalacosis patella** which the doctor said means that the cartilage on the underside of the patella is no longer of normal quantity and is highly suggestive of a cartilage tear. House v. Stocker, 340 N.E.2d 563, 566 (App.Ct.Ill.1975).

chondrosarcoma (kon″dro-sar-ko′mah) [*chondro-* + *sarcoma*] a malignant tumor derived from cartilage cells or their precursors; called also *chondroma sarcomatosum.*

chorda (kor′dah), pl. *chor′dae* [L.; Gr. *chordē* + cord] [NA] any cord or sinew.

chorda tym′pani [NA], a nerve originating from the facial nerve (nervus intermedius) and distributed to the submandibular, sublingual, and lingual glands and the anterior two-thirds of the tongue; modality: parasympathetic and special sensory.

Upon physical examination, Dr. Pegues discovered that there was injury to the **chorda tympani nerve**, which resulted in loss of taste and numbness to the anterior two-thirds portion of the left side of the tongue. Barshady v. Schlosser, 313 A.2d 296–7 (Super.Ct.Pa.1973).

On the tongue side of the lower gum area (the lingual periosteum) are two nerves, the **chorda tympani**, which supply the sense of taste to the tongue and the lingual nerve, which supplies the sense of feeling. Cassano v. Hagstrom, 159 N.E.2d 348, 350 (N.Y.1959).

chordotomy See *cordotomy.*

chorea (ko-re′ah) [L.; Gr. *choreia* dance] the ceaseless occurrence of a wide variety of rapid, highly complex, jerky movements that appear to be well coordinated but are performed involuntarily.

chorea, acute See *chorea, Sydenham's.*

chorea, hereditary See *chorea, Huntington's.*

chorea, Huntington's a rare hereditary disease characterized by chronic progressive chorea and mental deterioration terminating in dementia; the age of onset is variable but usually occurs in the fourth decade of life. Death usually follows within 15 years. It is transmitted as an autosomal dominant trait. Called also *chronic (progressive hereditary) c., degenerative c.,* and *hereditary c.*

The Cecil-Loeb Textbook of Medicine identifies three types of **choreas** (an involuntary movement disorder): acute chorea, **hereditary chorea**, and senile chorea. Acute chorea is encountered primarily during childhood and "is a self-limited disease, recovery occurring in two to six months. Recurrence, with as many as two or three attacks over a period of years, appears in almost one third of the cases." Cecil and Loeb, Textbook of Medicine 184 (13th ed. 1971)....

. . . **Hereditary chorea** is not a likely possibility as there is no indication that her parents were affected by chorea. . . . Lieberman v. Califano, 592 F.2d 986, 990 (7th Cir. 1979).

chorea, senile a benign, usually mild disorder of the elderly, marked by choreiform movements unassociated with mental disturbance. See also *chorea, Sydenham's* (Lieberman case).

chorea, Sydenham's an acute, usually self-limited disorder of early life, usually between the ages of five and fifteen, or during pregnancy, and closely linked with rheumatic fever. It is characterized by involuntary movements that gradually become severe, affecting all motor activities including gait, arm movements, and speech. A mild psychic component is usually present. The disorder may be limited to one side of the body (hemichorea) or may take the form of muscular rigidity (paralytic chorea). Called also *St. Vitus' dance.*

The Cecil-Loeb Textbook of Medicine identifies three types of choreas (an involuntary movement disorder): **acute chorea,** hereditary chorea, and senile chorea. **Acute chorea** is encountered primarily during childhood and "is a self-limited disease, recovery occurring in two to six months. Recurrence, with as many as two or three attacks over a period of years, appears in almost one third of the cases." Cecil and Loeb, Textbook of Medicine 184 (13th ed. 1971)....

. . . Furthermore, **acute chorea** "may be very mild and may minimally affect normal function or may be so forceful and frequent as to be totally disabling." Textbook of Medicine, supra at 184. The neurologist gave no indication as to how severe Ms. Lieberman's condition was. Nor does the record show that Ms. Lieberman dropped objects, which would have been a manifestation of severe chorea. Id. Lieberman v. Califano, 592 F.2d 986, 990 (7th Cir. 1979).

chorioadenoma (ko″re-o-ad″ĕ-no′mah) adenomatous tumor of the chorion.

chorioadenoma destruens a form of hydatidiform mole in which molar chorionic villi penetrate into the myometrium and/or parametrium or, rarely, are transported to distant sites, most often the lungs; called also *invasive, metastasizing,* or *malignant mole.*

Mr. Cox had had a dark mole on his back below the left scapula for a number of years. In October 1971, Mr. Cox scratched the **mole** on a nail while at work. Claimant testified that prior to this incident the mole was "real dark brown", about the size of a large pea, and that the decedent had had no previous problem with it because it was flat. After the mole was scratched there was a change in its appearance "It was raised up and had gotten bigger around.". . .

. . . Dr. Williams found a "4 cm by 4 cm lesion" which appeared to be a malignant melanoma. On January 19, 1972, Dr. Williams surgically removed the growth and submitted it to a pathologist, who reported "malignant melanoma, adequately excised.". . .

. . . On an examination in May 1972 Dr. Williams found that the malignancy had spread from the original site in the decedent's lymph nodes; and that two nodes in his armpit were positive for malignancy. Cox v. Ulysses Cooperative Oil and Supply Co., 544 P.2d 363, 365 (Kan.1975).

choriomeningitis (ko″re-o-men″in-ji′tis) cerebral meningitis with lymphocytic infiltration of the choriod plexuses.

In June 1975, she contracted **choriomeningitis** and a urinary infection which evolved into psychotic symptomatology. Pisel v. Stamford Hospital, 430 A.2d 1, 5 (Conn.1980).

chorioretinitis (ko″re-o-ret″ĭ-ni′tis) inflammation of the choroid and retina.

Subsequent to the discovery of this injury by claimant's physician, a posterior eye condition developed, described variously as **chorioretinitis**, posterior uveitis or macular edema, which resulted in claimant's loss of vision of the right eye. State ex rel. Goodyear T. & R. Co. v. Industrial Com'n, 310 N.E.2d 240, 242 (Ohio 1974).

Christmas disease See *factor, coagulation (Factor IX).*

chromatin (kro'mah-tin) [Gr. *chrōma* color] the more readily stainable portion of the cell nucleus, forming a network of nuclear fibrils within the achromatin of a cell. It is a deoxyribonucleic acid attached to a protein (primarily histone) structure base and is the carrier of the genes in inheritance. It occurs in two interchangeable states, euchromatin and heterochromatin, and during cell division it coils and folds to form the chromosomes. Called also *chromoplasm.*

chromatin-positive (kro"mah-tin-poz'ĭ-tiv) having sex chromatin (Barr body) in the nuclei of autosomal cells, a characteristic of the normal female.

Dr. Richards says that she is prevented from qualifying and/or participating in the U.S. Open as a woman in the Women's Division since defendants require that she take a **sex-chromatin test** (aka the **Barr body test**) to determine whether she is a female, "which test," she says, "is recognized to be insufficient, grossly unfair, inaccurate, faulty and inequitable by the medical community in the United States for purposes of excluding individuals from sports events on the basis of gender." . . .

The **Barr body test** or **sex-chromatin test**, determines the presence of a second x chromosome in the normal female; a male has a y chromosome instead, as set forth in detail below. . . .

The **Barr body test** is generally administered by having the individual rinse the mouth and obtaining a sample of cells by scraping the inner lining of the cheek. The sample is then transferred to a slide. Dye is applied and the smear is examined under a miscroscope. Dr. Federman describes the procedure:

The examiner typically counts 100 or 200 cells and records the percentage of the cells which show an oval concentration of dye next to the surrounding border of the nucleus of the cell. This heavy concentration of dye reveals the presence of a second x-chromosome.

However, Dr. Federman points out, the **Barr body test** does not determine the presence or absence of a y chromosome. Individuals with chromosomal defects may not therefore be definitively classified by the **Barr body test** alone. Richards v. U.S. Tennis Ass'n, 400 N.Y.S.2d 267–8, 270 (Sup.Ct.N.Y.Cty. 1977).

chromatograph See *chromatography.*

chromatography (kro"mah-tog'rah-fe) [*chromato-* + Gr. *graphein* to write] a method of separating and identifying the components of a complex mixture by differential movement through a two-phase system, in which the movement is effected by a flow of a liquid or a gas (mobile phase) which percolates through an adsorbent (stationary phase) or a second liquid phase, based on the physicochemical principles of adsorption, partition, ion exchange, or exclusion, or a combination of these principles. Chromatographic techniques may be classified according to the nature of the adsorbent employed, the physical characteristics of the mobile and stationary phases, or the type of technique employed.

She testified that she conducted a color test using Erlic's reagent and a series of 3 thin-layer chromatographs (TLC's) upon the substance delivered by defendant. The color test using Erlic's reagent, a more sophisticated test than the Voltex test, also indicated the presence of LSD. . . .

Thin-layer **chromatography** is a comparative test which requires the use of a standard, a substance that has been positively identified, with which the unknown substance can be compared. In the TLC procedure, small amounts of the test substance are taken up in a solvent, and spotted near the bottom of a glass plate coated with an inert material. The solvent dissolves, leaving the test substance as a residue. The glass plate is then dipped in another solvent, and the solvent is allowed to run up the plate. Since different compounds, or test substances, have different relative affinities for the absorbent coating on the glass plate, the solvent will carry different compounds to different heights on the plate. After the solvent evaporates, the height to which the solvent carried the compound is visible as a spot when the plate is viewed under ultraviolet light. This procedure is performed for a known substance, or standard, and for the test substance. The test results are then compared to determine whether the test substance ran to the same height as the standard. People v. Bertram, 358 N.E.2d 1357–9 (App.Ct.Ill.1977).

chromosomal See *chromosome.*

chromosome (kro'mo-sōm) [*chromo-* + Gr. *sōma* body] 1. in animal cells, a structure in the nucleus containing a linear thread of DNA, which transmits genetic information and is associated with RNA and histones; during cell division, the material (chromatin) composing the chromosome is compactly coiled, making it visible with appropriate staining and permitting its movement in the cell with minimal entanglement. Each organism of a species is normally characterized by the same number of chromosomes in its somatic cells, 46 being the number normally present in man, including the two (XX or XY) which determine the sex of the organism. See *illustration.* 2. in bacterial genetics, a closed circle of double-stranded DNA that contains the genetic material of the cell and is attached to the cell membrane; the bulk of the material forms a compact bacterial nucleus (called also *chromatinic body*).

"Q. . . . I would like to ask you what chromosomes are— A. Chromosomes are—

"Q. —and I am speaking now of the reproductive cells particularly. A. Fundamentally **chromosomes** are the part of the cell which contains the inherent characteristics of the individual who may result from that cell.

"Q. How many **chromosomes** are there? A. It varies somewhat; forty-six in most individuals; some exhibiting as many as forty-eight. There are cases where there are fewer.

"Q. Am I correct that in the mating process when conception occurs we have a union of, let us say, twenty-four **chromosomes** of one with twenty-four **chromosomes** of the other? A. That is correct.

"Q. Twenty-four **chromosomes** of the male and twenty-four **chromosomes** of the female? A. This is true, and perhaps

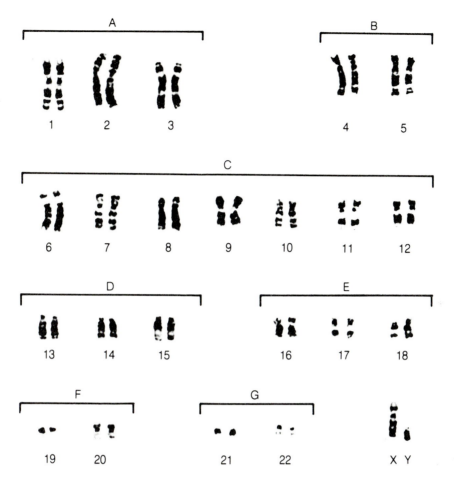

Human male chromosomes with Giemsa banding (Type G banding), arranged as a karyotype. (Courtesy of R. G. Worton in Thompson & Thompson)

if there is one abnormal in the female or in the male, then the resulting fertilized cell contains that abnormality. In other words, there is no opportunity for the corresponding partner to correct the defect?

"Q. (By the Attorney-General): What I am endeavoring to elicit is a physical description of the cellular set-up by way of genes and **chromosomes**, &c. A. Yes. I have already stated that the hereditary material is located within **chromosomes** which are found in the nucleus of each cell. In the human cell there are characteristically forty-six of these **chromosomes**; in the reproductive cells only twenty-three of the forty-six which are present in the body cells, and in the immature germ cells twenty-three are transferred to the original fertilized egg from which all the other cells come, through the maternal parent, and twenty-three derived through the paternal parent, one set through the ovum, the other set through the spermatozoa; so that for every **chromosome** derived from the mother there is a corresponding **chromosome** derived from the father.

"Q. So that out of the pool it isn't just the one **chromosome**, there are forty-eight of them, to make the fertilized—

A. The sum of the male and female sets of **chromosomes** are needed to make a viable fertilized ova.

"Q. And when there is any one or more of those damaged or fractured **chromosomes**, as you said, that cannot be cured by the opposite number, that is when the visible or the genetic effect will result? A. That's right.

"Q. Now, will you state in a little greater detail what happens to that **chromosome** when it is fractured by a photon? The **chromosome**—I am talking now of the reproductive organs. A. The influence of radiation absorbed within a reproductive cell, or other cell, for that matter, and specifically the radiation absorbed by the **chromosome** material of the cell may affect the **chromosome** in a number of ways.

"One way is the manner in which you have just asked the question, that is to cause an actual break of the **chromosome** material, the release of energy being so great and the destructiveness so great that a fracture will actually take place.

"Now, in addition to this sort of action, radiation also may not cause a mechanical destruction of a structure such as a **chromosome**, but may by the release of energy within it disturb the biochemical mechanism. That is a disturbance of the structure now at the macro-molecular level rather than at the gross level, to the extent that mutations will result from that action of radiation. Chiropractic Ass'n of New York, Inc. v. Hilleboe, 227 N.Y.S.2d 309, 355, 363–4 (Sup.Ct.Albany Cty.1961).

chromosome, X the female sex chromosome, being the differential sex chromosome carried by half the male gametes and all female gametes in man and other male-heterogametic species.

chromosome, Y the male sex chromosome, being the differential sex chromosome carried by half the male gametes and none of the female gametes in man and in some other male-heterogametic species in which the homologue of the X chromosome has been retained.

Dr. Federman says that the y chromosome is related to physical characteristics in the normal male that affect an individual's competitive athletic ability. The y chromosome controls the development of the testes, the source of the larger amounts of androgen (the male sex hormone) produced by the male relative to the female:

At puberty, the presence in the male of the y chromosome plus the much higher ratio of androgens to estrogens [the female sex hormone] results, on the average, in greater height, different body proportions, and a higher muscle mass than in the female. In the adult male beyond puberty, neither the removal of the testes by sex reassignment surgery, nor any subsequent treatment with estrogen can affect the individuals achieved height or skeletal structure. Removal of the testes plus ingestion of estrogens can reduce male strength, but any such effect is partial and depends upon continued ingestion of estrogen to be sustained. Richards v. U.S. Tennis Ass'n, 400 N.Y.S.2d 267, 269 (Sup.Ct.N.Y.Cty.1977).

Appellant introduced expert testimony and studies suggesting that males who possess this extra Y chromosome, referred to as "47 XYY individuals" are likely to exhibit certain aggressive behavioral traits. . . .

According to a note published last year in the Georgetown Law Journal (57 Geo.L.J. 892) entitled, "The XYY Chromosome Defense," an XYY criminal defendant in Australia was acquitted by reason of insanity and a French murderer possessing the same abnormality had his sentence reduced.

Apparently this is the first case in California reaching the appellate level that involves this version of the insanity defense and we are unaware of other cases raising this defense elsewhere in the United States. In other words, the genetic criminal is presently legally unrecognized.

The lead paragraph of an article appearing in the Los Angeles Daily Journal of December 16, 1970, is as follows:

"Genetic Scientists attending a convention of the British Society for Social Responsibility in Science here recently have emphasized that the so-called XYY 'criminal gene' theory has been thoroughly discredited." . . .

On the primary issue, the behavioral effects of this abnormal condition, the testimony of appellant's expert witnesses suggests only that aggressive behavior may be one manifestation of the XYY Syndrome. The evidence collected by these experts does not suggest that all XYY individuals are by nature involuntarily aggressive. Some identified XYY individuals have not exhibited such behavior. People v. Tanner, 91 Cal.Rptr. 656–9 (Ct.App.Cal.1970).

chronic (kron'ik) [L. *chronicus,* from Gr. *chronos* time] persisting over a long period of time.

Chronic, in other words, [as opposed to acute. q.v.] on the other side, is a response which goes on over a long period of time. Woodall Industries, Inc. v. Massachusetts Mutual Life Insurance Co., 483 F.2d 986, 1000 (6th Cir. 1973).

chronic asthmatic bronchitis See *bronchitis, chronic;* and *asthma.*

chronic brain syndrome See *syndrome, chronic brain.*

chronic obstructive pulmonary disease See *disease, chronic obstructive pulmonary.*

chronic organic brain syndrome See *syndrome, chronic brain;* and *syndrome, organic brain.*

Chron's disease See *ileitis, regional.*

chyle (kīl) [L. *chylus* juice] the milky fluid taken up by the lacteals from the food in the intestine during digestion. It consists of lymph and droplets of triglyceride fat (chylomicrons) in a stable emulsion. It passes into the veins by the thoracic duct, becoming mixed with the blood; called also *chylus* [NA].

. . . plaintiff was diagnosed by the treating physicians to have a thorium granuloma with chylus peritonitis, a condition which plaintiff alleges was proximately caused by the injection of Thorotrast. Thrift v. Tenneco Chemicals, Inc., Heyden Div., 381 F.Supp. 543–4 (N.D.Tex.1974).

chylus See *chyle.*

Chymar See *chymotrypsin.*

chymopapain (ki"mo-pah-pa'in) a proteolytic enzyme (a sulfhydryl proteinase) from the latex of a chiefly tropical tree, *Carica papaya,* that curdles milk and breaks down the mucopolysaccharide-protein complexes in the nucleus pulposus; used in chemonucleolysis.

When an intervertebral disk is bulging outward, it may press against some of the many nerves in the area of the spine and cause pain. If the situation is severe, a normal medical response is surgery: a laminectomy with excision of the offending disk. The drug chymopapain was designed to provide an alternative to back surgery. Chymopapain is an enzyme derived from the papaya. It was manufactured by Travenol Laboratories, a subsidiary of Baxter Laboratories, under the trade name "Discase". . . .

. . . Dr. Bernard Sussman, a professor of neurosurgery, was not allowed to testify that chymopapain by its injurious effects on tissue, would keep open the pathway made by the needle when the drug was injected into the disk. Gaston v. Hunter, 588 P.2d 326, 330, 336 (Ct.App.Ariz.1978).

chymotrypsin (ki"mo-trip'sin) [USP] a proteolytic enzyme preparation crystallized from an extract of the pancreas of the ox, *Bos taurus.* It is a white to yellowish white, crystalline powder; used for enzymatic zonulolysis in intracapsular lens extraction, applied by irrigation to the posterior chamber of the eye, under the iris. It has also been used to débride necrotic lesions and to reduce inflammation and edema, administered orally, buccally, and intramuscularly. See also *enzyme, proteolytic* (Armour case).

Moore introduced evidence that an intravenous injection of **chymar** could bring on an immediate reaction or seizure but that an intramuscular injection would not cause a reaction for five or ten minutes. Another of his expert witnesses testified the reaction from an intramuscular injection would take from one to three hours. Moore v. Gutherie Hospital, Inc., 403 F.2d 366, 369 (4th Cir. 1968).

Ci symbol for *curie* recommended by the International Commission on Radiological Units and Measurements.

CIC See *catheterization, clean intermittent.*

cilia See *cilium.*

ciliary nerves See *nervi cilares longi.*

cilium (sil'e-um), pl. *cil'ia* [L.] a minute vibratile, hairlike process projecting from the free surface of a cell; composed of nine pairs of microtubules arrayed around a central pair, cilia are extensions of basal bodies. They beat rhythmically to move the cell about in its environment or to move fluid or mucous films over its surface. Ciliary movement consists of an *effective stroke*, in which the cilium stiffens and moves forward rapidly, and a *recovery stroke*, in which the cilium becomes flexible and bends. Cilia may all beat simultaneously (*isochronal rhythm*) or successive cilia in each row may start their beat sequentially producing a wavelike movement (*metachronal rhythm*). Cf. *flagellum.*

[He stated smoke inhalation damages the **cilia** in the bronchial tubes which help the lungs cleanse themselves.] Smoke inhalation, combined with the effect of anesthesia on the lungs, could have made the lungs vulnerable to complications. Bruney v. City of Lake Charles, 386 So.2d 950, 952 (Ct.App.La. 1980).

cingulumotomy (sing"gu-lum-ot'o-me) the creation of precisely placed lesions in the cingulum of the frontal lobe, for relief of intractable pain; called also *cingulotomy.* See also *surgery, stereotactic/stereotaxic.*

The plaintiff's allegations concern electroconvulsive (electric shock) therapy administered to her, and a brain operation performed upon her, in 1974. The operation was a **stereotactic cingulotomy,** commonly referred to as a type of experimental "psychosurgery." The plaintiff had suffered for at least five years prior to 1974 from severe mental depression and severe physical pain in her head, neck, and shoulders. She had a history of suicidal tendencies. Kapp v. Ballantine, 402 N.E.2d 463, 466 (Sup.Jud.Ct.Mass.1980).

circle of Willis See *circulus arteriosus cerebri.*

circularize

An X-ray taken after the cast was applied showed an improper alignment of the bones, so Dr. Brown "**circularized**" the cast (cut the cast open around the leg).... DeWitt v. Brown, 669 F.2d 516, 518 (8th Cir. 1982).

circulation (ser"ku-la'shun) [L. *circulatio*] movement in a regular or circuitous course, as the movement of the blood through the heart and blood vessels.

He also agreed that pain is a symptom of lack of **circulation,** and that if a foot is numb or cold there is reason to suspect lack of **circulation....**

Notwithstanding his awareness of swelling and the fact that swelling in a cast can dangerously impair **circulation,** Dr. Lewis applied a cast to Voegeli's leg. Dr. Lewis testified that for the first five days he thought he was only dealing with a fracture of the medial condyle of the right tibia and hemarthrosis of the right knee. He became fully alerted to the circulatory problem on June 1, when the cast was removed....

... There is no doubt that Dr. Lewis should have known and did know that the injury to the knee could have been accompanied by circulatory damage. Symptoms of such damage were immediately apparent: pain, coldness, and an inability to move ankle or toes. Progressive symptoms were similarly apparent. Yet in the entire five-day period Lewis took, at most, one distal pulse, made no tests, such as an artereogram, ignored x-ray indications of circulatory trouble, and did not call in a vascular consultant until it was no longer possible to repair the artery. Voegeli v. Lewis, 568 F.2d 89, 93–4 (8th Cir. 1977).

During the next two days, the nurses' notes reveal that the patient complained of severe pains in both legs and swelling of the right foot. However, the notes stated that **circulation** remained "good". The initial change in the temperature of the patient's foot, also indicating circulatory problems, occurs in the nurse's notes for the 3 P.M. to 11 A.M. shift on July 12: "Rt. foot sl. swollen and cool to touch." Garfield Park Community Hospital v. Vitacco, 327 N.E.2d 408, 410 (App.Ct.Ill. 1975).

Ball's toes were more swollen and blue, and he complained of numbness. Dr. Flamm, upon being notified of this condition, ordered the cast split its entire length because it was then too tight. A cast restricts venous return, and the purpose in splitting the cast is to assist in venous return to reduce the swelling in the area. At 11:00 a.m., at 3:30 p.m. and at 10:30 p.m., Dr. Flamm saw Ball and on each occasion checked the toes by pressing the nail against the nailbed, and was of the opinion that Ball had some **circulation....**

... Patient states he has no feeling right foot; can barely move toes. All five toes have bluish appearance." Dr. Flamm apparently was not notified of this condition, but later stated the notation is significant in that it indicates that **circulation** is definitely worsening....

... Dr. Flamm testified that he knew on January 18 that the limb was in difficulty because there was some **circulation** interference, the degree of which was not known. He knew that the loss of blood **circulation** in the leg will cause necrosis, which he defined as gangrene, and that the complete loss of **circulation** will cause the limb to die. Flamm v. Ball, 476 S.W.2d 710, 712 (Ct.Civ.App.Tex.1972).

circulation, impaired

Without a dissenting voice, their testimony was that the symptoms of **impaired circulation** are coldness of the limb, pain, and change of color or cyanosis. All of them agreed that the detection of these symptoms was a comparatively simple task for registered nurses. They were uniform in expressing the opinion that presence of these symptoms made prompt action imperative and that the nurses should immediately have notified the doctor of their occurrence. Garfield Park Community Hospital v. Vitacco, 327 N.E.2d 408, 413 (App.Ct.Ill.1975).

Dr. A. E. Minyard, also an orthopedic surgeon, of Galveston, and being qualified as such, testified by deposition that the **impaired circulation** which resulted in the amputation of the boy's leg was the result of edema or swelling which was caused by the injury and which did not have room to expand because of the constricting plaster of paris cast resulting in blockage of the venous return and increased pressure, resulting in no arterial blood supply, and then death of the tissue. Early recognition of **impaired circulation** is of paramount importance to the orthopedic surgeon. When recognized early, many cases which would otherwise go to paralysis, gangrene and amputation can be avoided. Leong v. Wright, 478 S.W.2d 839, 842 (Ct.Civ.App.Tex.1972).

circulatory See *circulation.*

circulus (ser′ku-lus), pl. *cir′culi* [L. "a ring"] a circle or circuit, used in anatomical nomenclature to designate such an arrangement, usually of arteries or veins.

circulus arteriosus cerebri [NA], the important polygonal anastomosis formed by the internal carotid, the anterior and posterior cerebral arteries, the anterior communicating artery, and the posterior communicating arteries; called also *c. arteriosus [Willisi], circle of Willis,* and *c. Willisii.*

If there had been a ruptured aneurysm in the **Circle of Willis,** the embalming fluid would not have removed the blood that had gone out into the tissues from the blood vessels....

... He thought that there had been a rupture of one of the blood vessels of the **Circle of Willis,** which is located at the base of the brain and it was his opinion that if there was a rupture at that place, it would be seen by one conducting a proper post mortem examination. He observed no other injury to patient's nervous system except what he diagnosed as a congenital aneurysm ruptured. Part of the blood vessels emanating from the **Circle of Willis** goes into the brain and part of it around the brain on the outside. York v. Daniels, 259 S.W.2d 109, 115, 117 (Springfield Ct.App.Mo.1953).

circumstantiality (ser″kum-stan″she-al′ĭ-te) a disturbance in the flow of thought in which the patient's conversation is characterized by unnecessary elaboration of many trivial details.

Circumstantiality exists when "a person goes into great detail describing the circumstances of something but never really answering the question. Johnson v. U.S., 409 F.Supp. 1283, 1286 (M.D.Fla.1976), judgment reversed 576 F.2d 606 (5th Cir. 1978).

cirrhosis (sir-ro′sis) [Gr. *kirrhos* orange yellow] liver disease characterized pathologically by loss of the normal microscopic lobular architecture, with fibrosis and nodular regeneration. The term is sometimes used to refer to chronic interstitial inflammation of any organ. See also *cirrhosis of liver.*

cirrhosis of liver a group of chronic diseases of the liver characterized by loss of normal hepatic lobular architecture with fibrosis, and by destruction of parenchymal cells and their regeneration to form nodules. The disease has a lengthy latent period, usually followed by the sudden appearance of abdominal swelling and pain, hematemesis, dependent edema, or jaundice. In advanced

stages, ascites, jaundice, portal hypertension, and central nervous system disorders, which may end in hepatic coma, become prominent. Called also *chronic interstitial hepatitis.*

In fact, shortly before he gave that answer the deceased had been hospitalized for some six days during which he had been diagnosed as suffering from **cirrhosis of the liver.**...

... Mr. Blair again required hospitalization for his cirrhotic liver, which at this point was producing symptoms—bleeding esophageal varices—suggestive of a rapidly deteriorating condition....

Decedent's **cirrhosis** was not in fact caused by diabetes but by excessive consumption of alcohol. Blair v. Inter-Ocean Ins. Co., 589 F.2d 730–1 (D.C.Cir.1978).

Toussaint experienced nausea and dizziness. Several days later he was admitted to the hospital to have his gall bladder removed. During the operation the surgeon, Dr. Sultani, discovered that Toussaint's liver was twice its normal size and was discolored. He diagnosed the condition as **cirrhosis of the liver,** which was confirmed by a subsequent biopsy. Since that time Toussaint has been under continuous treatment for his liver condition. He was advised by his doctor not to return to his job as a painter, and is currently employed in a substantially lower paying position. County of Cook v. Industrial Com'n, 310 N.E.2d 6, 7 (Ill.1974).

Dr. Warden then decribed the process whereby the liver becomes **cirrhosised** which means "scarred". Alcohol has a direct metabolic effect on the liver cells together with the non-nourishment which people using excessive alcohol undergo....

... He then testified that liver damage of the type which Rivas had sustained occurs slowly over many, many years, "the wearing away of a rock by water, this type of damage which occurs in **cirrhosis.**"...

...In summary, his findings were that the liver was granular, like eggnog, characteristic of **cirrhosis.** Rivas v. United States Fire Insurance Co., 470 S.W.2d 249, 251–3 (Ct.Civ.App.Tex. 1971).

cirrhosis, portal

Dr. Sultani, the treating physician, and the only physician who visually observed the diseased liver, stated that in his opinion the condition was caused by continuous exposure to toxic fumes. He stated that Toussaint suffered from **portal cirrhosis** rather than the nutritional cirrhosis usually associated with alcoholism. County of Cook v. Industrial Com'n, 310 N.E.2d 6–7 (Ill.1974).

cirrhosis, primary biliary a rare form of biliary cirrhosis of unknown etiology, occurring without obstruction or infection of the major bile ducts, sometimes developing after the administration of such drugs as chlorpromazine and arsenicals. Affecting chiefly middle-aged women, it is characterized by chronic cholestasis with pruritus, jaundice, and hypercholesterolemia, with xanthomas, and malabsorption. Called also *Charcot's c., Hanot's c., disease,* or *syndrome, hypertrophic c., Todd's c.,* and *unilobular c.*

Dr. Dickson diagnosed her condition as **primary biliary cirrhosis,** the cause of which is unknown. This disease attacks the bile ductular epithelial cells, which carry off bile and waste products from the liver, while hepatitis attacks the liver cells, which metabolize foods taken into the body....

... It is true that the cause of **primary biliary cirrhosis** is unknown. Dr. Gutzmann and Dr. Dickson agreed, however, that a leading theory is that the disease is an immunologic one in which a defense mechanism in the victim's body reacts inappropriately to an injury to the liver. Dr. Gutzmann based his opinion that hepatitis had been a causative factor in employee's contracting **primary biliary cirrhosis** on this theory and on employee's medical history, which he said offered no other explanation for her contracting **primary biliary cirrhosis**. Pommeranz v. State, Dep't of Public Welfare, 261 N.W.2d 90–1 (Minn.1977).

cistron (sis′tron) [L. *cis* on this side + trans on the other side + Gr. *on* neuter ending] the smallest unit of genetic material that must be intact to function as a transmitter of genetic information, i.e., to determine the sequence of amino acids of one polypeptide chain. The cistron is identified by the *cis-trans* test. The gene as traditionally conceived is identical to the cistron. Cf. *muton* and *recon*.

Citrus (sit′rus) [L.] a genus of rutaceous trees: *C. aurantifolia*, the lime; *C. aurantium*, the orange; *C. bergamia*, the bergamot; *C. limonum*, the lemon; *C. medica*, the citron; *C. sinensis*, the sweet orange.

citrus biflavonoid

Petitioner sells a line of drugs containing, as a principal active ingredient, **citrus bioflavonoid**, which is an extract from fruit skins. USV Pharmaceutical Corp. v. Weinberger, 412 U.S. 655, 657, 93 S.Ct. 2498, 37 L.Ed.2d 244 (1973).

Claggett's procedure See *procedure, Claggett's*.

clairvoyance (klăr-voi′ans) [Fr.] a form of extrasensory perception in which knowledge of objective events is acquired without the use of the senses; called also *clairsentience*. Cf. *telepathy*.

clamp (klamp) a surgical instrument for effecting compression.

clamp, Babcock

The operation report read, in relevant part: The left tube was then identified . . . and it was decided at this time to perform a omeroy [sic] tubal ligation on that side. The tube was grasped with a **Babcock clamp** and ligated with O chrom [sic] suture. The distal nub of the tube was excised. McNeal v. U.S., 689 F.2d 1200–1 (4th Cir. 1982).

clamp, Kelly

A scissors-shaped metal instrument about six inches long, called a **Kelly clamp**, was left in plaintiff's abdomen when an operation was performed on her at defendant hospital....

... During the operation Lacy and Slegal used about 18 **Kelly clamps** which are uncurved scissors-shaped instruments. Eiskamp did not use anything but curved clamps. Leonard v. Watsonville Community Hospital, 305 P.2d 36–8 (Cal.1956).

classification (klas″sĭ-fĭ-ka′shun) the systematic arrangement of similar entities on the basis of certain differing characteristics.

classification, functional

Functional Class III is defined as "Patients with cardiac disease resulting in marked limitation of physical activity. They are comfortable at rest. Less than ordinary physical activity causes fatigue, palpitation, dyspnea, or anginal pain." (New York Heart Association, Inc., Diseases of the Heart and Blood Vessels—Nomenclature and Criteria for Diagnosis (6th ed. 1964) p. 114, Boston, Little Brown and Company.) Therapeutic Class B is defined as: "Patients with cardiac disease whose ordinary physical activity need not be restricted, but who should be advised against severe or competitive efforts." (Id.) "The **functional classification** is an estimate of what the patient's heart will allow him to do...." Franklin v. Workers' Comp. Appeals Bd., 145 Cal.Rptr. 22, 27 (Ct.App.Cal.1978).

classification, Lancefield a serologic classification of the hemolytic streptococci based on the precipitin test, depending on the presence of group-specific cell-wall antigens (carbohydrates), and giving a strong indication of their predilections. They are grouped as follows: *group A*, primarily pathogenic for man; *group B*, almost exclusively found in bovine mastitis; *group C*, primarily pathogenic for lower animals; *group D*, isolated from cheese; *group E*, isolated from milk; *group F*, isolated from human throats; *group G*, isolated from man, dogs, and monkeys; *groups H, K, and O*, nonpathogenic from the respiratory tract of man.

claudication (klaw″dĭ-ka′shun) [L. *claudicatio*] limping or lameness.

Dr. Evans saw Morgenroth again and noted: "His legs are still his biggest disability. He cannot walk without **claudication**," and that he was quite free of chest pain. Morgenroth v. Pacific Medical Center, Inc., 126 Cal.Rptr. 681, 685 (Ct.App.Cal. 1976).

In May, 1966, Mr. Bower complained of **claudication** [2] and it was at this time that evaluation and consultation revealed evidence of involvement of both legs with diminishing right femoral pulses and absent posterior tibial pulsation, bilaterally. [[2] The meaning of "**claudication**" is as follows: "**claudication** . . . Limping or lameness, intermittent c., a complex of symptoms characterized by absence of pain or discomfort in a limb when at rest, the commencement of pain, tension, and weakness, after walking is begun, intensification of the condition until walking becomes impossible, and the disappearance of the symptoms after a period of rest. The condition is seen in occlusive arterial diseases of the limbs, such as thrombo-angiitis obliterans." (Dorlands' Illustrated Medical Dictionary (24th ed. 1965) p. 313.)] Bower v. Roy-Al Corp., 109 Cal.Rptr. 612, 614 (Ct.App.Cal.1973).

claudication, intermittent a complex of symptoms characterized by absence of pain or discomfort in a limb when at rest, the commencement of pain, tension, and weakness, after walking is begun, intensification of the condition until walking becomes impossible, and the disappearance of the symptoms after a period of rest. The condition is seen in occlusive arterial diseases of the limbs, such as thromboangiitis obliterans, and in compression of the cauda equina. Called also *Charcot's syndrome* and *angina cruris*.

These pains were caused by "**intermittent claudication**," or pain caused by decreased circulation, which arises when the patient is either exercising or walking. The symptoms are relieved by sitting down or resting. The decreased circulation giving rise to the claudication was caused by Salis's arteriosclerosis....

In January 1978, the patient suffered from **intermittent claudication**. In other words, the blood circulation in his extremities had decreased to the point that when he walked several blocks he felt pain in his right leg and the condition was only relieved by rest.[7] The testimony of the various physicians who appeared at the trial establishes two important facts about this disease. First, surgery is not the ordinary course of treatment for claudicants. In a large majority of cases, the condition will stabilize or improve with a program of "conservative" treatment, e.g., drugs, physical therapy.[8] Second, there are exceptions to the general rule. In such instances, the decision to undergo an operation to relieve the claudication is a highly personal one. The considerations to be weighed include: (1) the patient's life style, (2) the extent to which the disease has developed, (3) the inherent risks, and (4) the likelihood that the problems can be remedied through conservative methods. The appropriateness of surgery depends on the relative weight of these items. [[7] **Intermittent claudication** is a form of arteriosclerosis, a disease with several degrees of severity. Rest pain, the next most serious stage, occurs when the patient experiences aches and soreness while relaxing. Finally, there is gangrene, the point at which all circulation ceases and the tissue of the affected area actually dies. [8] At the trial of the instant case, Dr. Lynch agreed with a scholarly article quoted by counsel which stated that sixty-six percent of claudicants were stabilized without surgery.] Salis v. U.S., 522 F.Supp. 989, 992, 996 (M.D.Pa.1981).

This lameness resulted from "**intermittent claudication**," a condition created by the stoppage of the flow of blood through the arteries.

Intermittent claudication is a result of a thrombosis or blockage of the arteries supplying fresh blood to an area.

The **intermittent claudication** in Tarport Conaway resulted from a thrombosis of the left and right iliac arteries which provide the main blood supply to the hind limbs. Sessa v. Riegle, 427 F.Supp. 760, 763 (E.D.Pa.1977).

Dr. Samuels concluded, on the basis of the tests, plus the history, that ... [plaintiff], for about 18 months to two years prior to the time that he (Dr. Samuels) saw him, had been suffering from "**intermittent claudication**" caused by vascular insufficiency to the lower extremities, particularly on the left side. **Intermittent claudication** was a cramping of the muscles in the lower extremities of a patient when the vascular system was incapable of supplying sufficient amounts of blood to the lower extremities. **Intermittent claudication**, according to Dr. Samuels, was diagnostic of vascular insufficiency in the legs. Bower v. Roy-Al Corp., 109 Cal.Rptr. 612, 614 (Ct.App.Cal.1973).

Other Authorities: Thompson v. Occidental Life Ins. Co. of Cal., 513 P.2d 353, 365 (Cal.1973).

clavicle See *clavicula*.

clavicula (klah-vik′u-lah) [L. dim. of *clavis* key] [NA] the clavicle: a bone, curved like the letter *f*, that articulates with the sternum and scapula, forming the anterior por-

tion of the shoulder girdle on either side; called also *collar bone*.

He was taken by ambulance to the emergency room of Baptist Memorial Hospital where Dr. Hamel, of Drs. Hamel and James, orthopedic specialists, was on duty. Examination revealed that plaintiff had suffered a separation of his **clavicle** (collarbone) at its joint with his scapula (shoulder blade). Vest v. City National Bank and Trust Co., 470 S.W.2d 518–19 (Mo. 1971).

I don't believe it had any impairment of the function of the **clavicle**, which is an expanding mechanism from the chest bone to the shoulder blade. Once it's healed it still carries out that function....

"Q. And the **clavicle**, does that have any separate function?

"A. Basically not, it serves as some attachment for the muscles from the neck, and that's about it." Heredia v. Industrial Com'n, 460 P.2d 43–4 (Ct.App.Ariz.1969).

clavus (kla′vus), pl. *cla′vi* [L. "nail"] a corn.

clavus hystericus a sensation as if a nail were being driven into the head.

"Her headaches, located about the vertex, constant in nature, of boring type, like a 'plate on the head'—is the '**clavus hystericus**' (so typical that it has been given a special name)." Weinstein v. Levy, 18 A.D.2d 398, 400, 293 N.Y.S.2d 752 (2d Dep't 1963).

cleft (kleft) a fissure or elongated opening, especially one occurring in the embryo or derived from a failure of parts to fuse during embryonic development.

cleft, water

Dr. Azar found a "**water cleft**"—a droplet of water in the lense—in the left eye indicating cataract formation when he first examined plaintiff in January 1971. Powell v. Hellenic Lines, Ltd., 347 F.Supp. 855, 861 (E.D.La.1972).

clenching (klench′ing) a frequent oral neuromuscular response during sleep or occurring subconsciously when awake, the jaws being forcibly closed, and the teeth firmly in contact, with continuous pulsating contraction of the temporalis and pterygomassetric muscles. It is often associated with bruxism, and as with bruxism, nervous excitability and dental malocclusion are etiologic factors.

Cleocin See *clindamycin*.

climacteric (kli-mak′ter-ik, kli″mak-ter′ik) [Gr. *klimaktēr* rung of ladder, critical point in human life] the syndrome of endocrine, somatic, and psychic changes occurring at the termination of the reproductive period in the female (menopause); it may also accompany the normal diminution of sexual activity in the male. Called also *climacterium*.

Male **climacteric** is a somewhat outdated, decidedly controversial term used variously to describe (1) an organically caused condition in the male analogous to menopause in the female brought about by a sudden drop of androgen production, or (2) a condition systemic or psychogenic in origin characterized by hot flashes, irritability and impotence. In this sense, the term male **climacteric** does not indicate a decrease in androgen production. U.S. v. 1,048,000 Capsules, More or Less, 347 F.Supp. 768, 772 (S.D.Tex.1972).

clindamycin (klin″dah-mi′sin) chemical name: 2 *S-trans*-methyl-7-chloro-6,7, 8-trideoxy-6-[[(1-methyl-4-propyl-2-pyrrolidinyl)carbonyl]amino]-1-thio-L-*a*-D-*galacto*-octopyranoside. A semisynthetic analogue of the natural antibiotic lincomycin from which it is produced by chlorination, $C_{18}H_{33}ClN_2O_5S$; it is effective primarily against gram-positive bacteria. See also *enterocolitis*.

When Dr. Walker released Mauldin from the hospital, he prescribed **Cleocin** as a continuing prophylaxis against infection. Mauldin v. Upjohn Co., 697 F.2d 644–5 (5th Cir. 1983).

Upjohn defended the case on the proposition that the plaintiff has Crohn's disease and although **Cleocin** has been linked to antibiotic associated colitis, there is no causal relationship between **Cleocin** and either Crohn's disease or ulcerative colitis. Bluestein v. Upjohn Co., 430 N.E.2d 580, 582 (App.Ct.Ill. 1981).

clinical (klin′e-k′l) pertaining to a clinic or to the bedside; pertaining to or founded on actual observation and treatment of patients, as distinguished from theoretical or basic sciences.

"Clinical" is defined as: "Pertaining to or founded on actual observation and treatment of patients, as distinguished from theoretical or experimental." Dorland's Illustrated Medical Dictionary, 23rd Edition, Reprinted August 1960, W. B. Saunders Company, Philadelphia and London. It is obvious, then, that the statement of the Hearing Examiner that where a patient goes to a doctor for treatment, "**clinical** verification" might "be expensive and of little practical use in treatment," is meaningless since, as above stated, the word, "**clinical**," means pertaining to, or founded on treatment of a patient. [Dissent] Jenkins v. Gardner, 430 F.2d 243, 264 (6th Cir. 1970).

clinical evidence See *evidence, clinical*.

clinical test See *test, drug*.

clivogram See *clivography; clivus;* and *fossa cranii posterior*.

clivography (kli-vog′rah-fe) radiographic visualization of the clivus, or posterior cranial fossa.

Dr. Butler decided to do a cervical myelogram, or **clivogram**, primarily to look for a tumor or aneurism, but also to look for evidence of multiple sclerosis or of a reaction to the Pantopaque contrast medium from a previous myelogram. As a result of the **clivogram**, Dr. Butler concluded that the cause of appellant's pain was not "mechanically definable" and that, among possible causes, the presence of Pantopaque in appellant's brain stem had "dropped down" as a possibility. Fidler v. Eastman Kodak Co., 714 F.2d 192, 194 (1st Cir. 1983).

clivus (kli′vus) [L. "slope"] [NA] a bony surface in the posterior cranial fossa, sloping upward from the foramen magnum to the dorsum sellae, the lower part being formed by a portion of the basilar part of the occipital bone (c. ossis occipitalis) and the upper part by a surface of the body of the sphenoid bone (c. ossis sphenoidalis). Called also *c. blumenbachii*.

clonus (klo′nus) [Gr. *klonos* turmoil] alternate muscular contraction and relaxation in rapid succession.

. . . (extreme weakness in the legs). . . .

. . . Dr. Klawans found no **clonus**, which is a manifestation of extreme hyperflexia in the legs. McSwain v. Chicago Trans Authority, 362 N.E.2d 1264–5 (App.Ct.Ill.1977).

clostridial See *Clostridium*.

Clostridium (klo-strid′e-um) [Gr. *klōstēr* spindle] a genus of Schizomycetes, family Bacillaceae, order Eubacteriales, made up of obligate anaerobic or microaerophilic, gram-positive, spore-forming, rod-shaped bacteria, with spores of greater diameter than the vegetative cells. The spores may be central, terminal, or subterminal. Two hundred and five species have been differentiated on the basis of physiology, morphology, and toxin formation. See also *gangrene, gas* (Bell case).

The results of one of the tests taken on the 18th was returned on the 22nd and revealed that **clostridia**, commonly known as gangrene, was present in the wound. Continuing problems with the gangrene resulted in a series of operations to remove infected tissue, amputation of the little finger, amputation of the right arm below the elbow, and finally infected portions of the bone. . . .

. . . Dr. Garza further testified that **clostridia** would have been detected if the gram stain had been done and that this violation of the standard of care caused clostridial destruction of the arm, which was the cause of the amputation. Garza v. Keillor, 623 S.W.2d 669–70 (Ct.Civ.App.Tex.1981).

It merely challenges another, separate ground upon which the regulation was based, i.e., that sorbates are also a medium for the growth in meats of **clostridia**—a cause of food poisoning. Chip Steak Co. v. Hardin, 332 F.Supp. 1084, 1090 (N.D.Cal. 1971).

Clostridium botulinum the agent causing botulism in man, wild ducks, and other waterfowl, limberneck of fowl, certain forms of forage poisoning in cattle and horses in Australia, and lamziekte of cattle in South Africa. It produces a powerful exotoxin that is resistant to proteolytic digestion, and is divided into types A, B, C alpha and beta, D, and E on the basis of the immunological specificity of the toxin. Formerly called *Bacillus botulinus*. See also *acid, sorbic* (Chip Steak Co. case).

The hazard which the FDA sought to minimize was the outgrowth and toxin formation of **Clostridium botulinum Type E** spores of the bacteria which sometimes inhabit fish. There had been an occurrence of several cases of botulism traced to consumption of fish from inland waters in 1960 and 1963 which stimulated considerable bacteriological research. These bacteria can be present in the soil and water of various regions. They can invade fish in their natural habitat and can be further disseminated in the course of evisceration and preparation of the fish for cooking. A failure to destroy such spores through an adequate brining, thermal, and refrigeration process was found to be dangerous to public health. . . .

The Commissioner of Food and Drugs ("Commissioner"), employing informal "notice-and-comment" procedures under 21 U.S.C. § 371(a), issued a proposal for the control of **C. botulinum bacteria Type E** in fish. 34 F.R. 17,176 (Oct. 23, 1969). U.S. v. Nova Scotia Food Products Corp., 568 F.2d 240, 243–4 (2d Cir. 1977).

Clostridium botulinum.

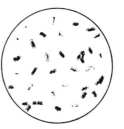

Clostridium perfringens.

Clostridium tetani.

It is argued that the regulations were put forward as the safest known processing parameters for preventing, through thermal destruction of spores of the bacteria, the outgrowth and toxin formation of **Clostridium botulinum Type E.** See Proposal of Part 128a for 21 C.F.R., 34 F.R 17,176 (October 16, 1969). Included were observations of human response to botulinum intrusions and to botulism itself and studies on the temperature sensitivity of the various types of **C. botulinum.** Broadly, those studies indicated that **Type E** was more temperature sensitive than **Types A and B**, particularly in a range in the neighborhood of 176–180°F. U.S. v. Nova Scotia Food Products Corp., 417 F.Supp. 1364, 1368, 1370, 1379 (E.D.N.Y.1976).

Clostridium perfringens most common etiologic agent of gas gangrene, variously reported as occurring in 39 to 83 per cent of cases; differentiable, on the basis of the distribution of nine different toxins and three other substances, which are enzymes, into several different types: type A (the cause of classic gas gangrene in man), B (lamb dysentery), C (struck in sheep), D (enterotoxemia in sheep), E (enterotoxemia in lambs and calves), F (enteritis necroticans in man). It has also been shown to cause a form of food poisoning. Called also *C. welchii* and, formerly, *Bacillus capsulatum* or *welchii.* See also *gangrene, gas*; and *poisoning, food, clostridial.*

A pathologist, Dr. Joseph Young, examined specimens of tissue taken from Murphy's leg wound, and found marked swelling of the tissues, various forms of bacteria and microscopic particles of wood. In particular, he found a type of bacteria, **clostridial perfringens**, commonly known as "gas gangrene." Such bacteria has two unusual characteristics: (1) it is ubiquitous, i.e., seemingly it can be found everywhere in everything, and (2) it is anaerobic, meaning that it dies on exposure to oxygen and only can grow in the absence of air. King v. Murphy, 424 So.2d 547, 549 (Miss.1982).

All physicians who were questioned on the subject testified that the gas gangrene is a rare condition that is seldom seen by doctors in the Alexandria or any other area in this country. Although the bacteria, **clostridium perfringens**, which causes same can be found in most open wounds it will not survive in the presence of oxygen and gas gangrene seldom results. When it does, the infection attacks with suddenness and violence causing fatalities in most cases. Penicillin in massive doses is the only antibiotic that is considered to be effective. This is not generally given until there is good reason to believe this type of infection is present and most often when such a diagnosis is made it is then too late to save the patient with such medication. Harris v. State, Through Huey P. Long Hospital, 371 So.2d 1221, 1223 (Ct.App.La.1979).

Clostridium tetani a common inhabitant of soil and human and horse intestines, and the cause of tetanus in man and domestic animals; its potent exotoxin is made up of two components, a neurotoxin, or tetanospasmin, and a hemolytic toxin, or tetanolysin. It is variously reported as associated with gangrene in 4 to 13 per cent of cases. Formerly called *Bacillus tetani.*

The sole claim is that the acrylic denture had not been properly sterilized before it was inserted in the patient's mouth and that because of that fact the denture carried a **tetanus spore** which somehow entered one of the open wounds left by the extractions and thus produced the disease and the resulting death....

There is no dispute that the **tetanus spore** is a minute organism common to our environment. It is everywhere around us, in the air, dust, soil, water, food and human and animal feces. It may exist in the human mouth, being introduced there through many of the environmental exposures, including of course, ordinary food and drink. The mouth is regarded as a harbor for an immense number of pathogenic organisms including the **tetanus spore.** See, e.g., Mournet v. Sumner, 19 La.App. 346, 139 So. 728 (1932); Freche v. Mary, 16 So.2d 213 (La.Ct. App.1944); Morris v. Weene, 258 Mass. 178, 154 N.E. 860 (1927); Nevinger v. Haun, 197 Mo.App. 416, 196 S.W. 39 (1917). The spore, so long as it retains that form, can remain in the human body for years in a virile but harmless state. Only when it encounters very special conditions which convert it into a **tetanus bacillus** or toxin and which permit it to multiply does it result in the tetanus disease. The bacillus is an anaerobic organism and consequently will not grow in the presence of oxygen. Thus if a spore finds a portal of entry, usually a wound of some kind, into the human body, where the supply of oxygen is cut off, it becomes a bacillus and continues to grow, pouring toxin into other areas of the body and ultimately producing the dread disease. The experts in the case agree that even if a spore enters a wound, converts to a bacillus and begins to spread toxin, growth will cease upon the reappearance of oxygen and will revert to the innocent spore-form....

... Also he testified that the spore is very resistant to heat and chemical disinfectants, including carbolic acid, and that he did not know of any way an acrylic denture could be sterilized against it. Germann v. Matriss, 260 A.2d 825, 829–30 (N.J.1970).

closure (klo'shur) the act of shutting, or of bringing together two parts, one or both of which may be movable.

closure, plastic

When she recovered from phlebitis, Dr. Kilroy performed a **plastic closure** to reduce the size of the scars on Linda Perry's legs. The plaintiff developed suture abscesses as a result of this operation. Dodd v. Nicolon Corp., 422 So.2d 398, 400 (La.1982).

clot (klot) a semisolidified mass, as of blood or lymph; called also *coagulum.*

Blood **clotting** is an ancient art. By about 1860 the notion that it was motion that prevented blood from **clotting** was dispelled by experiments which proved that blood would not **clot** as long as it remained inside a vein or artery, contact with some foreign substance was established as the thing that caused blood to **clot.** Contact with air was early but mistakenly, believed to cause **clotting.** Calcium was identified in 1875 to be necessary in the **clotting** of blood. By about 1900 it had been established that plasma, the watery, liquid part of blood, placed in a glass test tube would **clot** but if the glass tube was lined with paraffin the plasma would not **clot.** Thus, glass was early identified as a foreign substance that would promote **clotting** in blood **clotting** tests. Ortho Pharmaceutical Corp. v. Amer. Hospital Supply Corp., 186 U.S.P.Q. 501, 504 (S.D.Ind. 1975).

clot, blood a coagulum formed of blood, either in or out of the body. See also *blockage;* and *mass.*

"... The **clot** formed gradually, and then finally, if you will excuse the expression, blew off, and went up and blocked the blood supply to the ophthalmic artery of the eye, and of the major portion of the left—of the right side of the brain."...

... the doctor was stating that it was probable the **clot** developed in the neck. The redirect testimony is less clear yet, but "developing thrombosis" apparently refers to the **clot** originating in the neck. Poertner v. Swearingen, 695 F.2d 435–7 (10th Cir. 1982).

The next day, Dr. Brougham operated and removed a large, previously undetected tumor around the third and fourth vertebrae. The tumor contained several **blood clots.** According to Dr. Brougham, these **clots** resulted from prior episodes of hemorrhaging caused by twisting, straining, or some other trauma of the tumor. Corbett v. Riley-Stoker, Corp., 425 A.2d 1335–6 (Sup.Jud.Ct.Me.1981).

clot, intracordical blood

Dr. John Kendig, M.D., a neurosurgeon, operated on McMillian on March 19, 1980 to remove the **intracordical blood clot** that caused McMillian's stroke. The blood clot was located in the right parietal cortex, in the area of McMillian's tumor surgery in 1975. McMillian v. Schweiker, 697 F.2d 215, 218 (8th Cir. 1983).

clotrimazole (klo-trim′ah-zōl) [USP] chemical name: 1-[(2-chlorophenyl)diphenylmethyl]-1*H*-imidazole. A broad-spectrum anti-fungal agent, $C_{22}H_{17}CIN_2$, applied topically to the skin in the treatment of candidiasis and various forms of tinea, and administered intravaginally in the treatment of vulvovaginal candidiasis. See also *processus lenticularis incudis;* and *dermatophyte.*

... a prescription drug, **Lotrimin.** Lotrimin is a synthetic antifungal agent which inhibits the growth of pathogenic der-matophytes, yeasts and Malassezia furfur. **Lotrimin** is available in both cream and solution form....

... **Lotrimin** cream contains spermaceti, a waxy substance derived from the sperm whale. Delbay Pharmaceuticals v. Department of Commerce, 409 F.Supp. 637, 640 (D.D.C.1976).

clotting See *clot,* and *thromboplastin* (Ortho Pharmaceutical Corp. case).

clubbing (klub′ing) a proliferative change in the soft tissues about the terminal phalanges of the fingers or toes, with no constant osseous changes.

clubbing, digital

He further testified that "**digital clubbing**", clubbing of the fingers, exhibited by the plaintiff in 1974 revealed that the plaintiff's disease [interstitial fibrosis] had then progressed to the chronic stage. Harrison v. Flota Mercante Grancolombiana, S.A., 557 F.2d 968, 976 (5th Cir. 1978).

C-max

C-max (which stands for maximum concentration) is the greatest amount of the active ingredient found to be present in the bloodstream during any one measurement. It is represented by the peak of the [bioavailability q.v.] curve. Premo Pharmaceutical Laboratories, Inc. v. U.S., 475 F.Supp. 52, 54 (S.D.N.Y. 1979).

C.N.M. (Certified Nurse-Midwife) See *nurse-midwife.*

CNS See *system, central nervous.*

coagulase (ko-ag′u-lās) an antigenic substance of bacterial origin, produced chiefly by the staphylococci, that may be causally related to thrombus formation. See also under *tests.*

It developed that the cheese causing illness was contaminated by the presence of "**coagulase positive Staphylococci aureus.**" These are microscopic plants, or bacteria, some of which contain an enzyme termed "**coagulase**" which acts as a catalyst. Those that are "**coagulase positive**" may, under certain conditions, produce an "enterotoxin" which is poisonous to the human consumer. L. D. Schreiber Cheese Co. v. Standard Milk Co., 457 F.2d 962–3 (8th Cir. 1972).

coagulation (ko-ag″u-la′shun) [L. *coagulatio*] 1. the process of clot formation. See also *clot, blood.* 2. in surgery, the disruption of tissue by physical means to form an amorphous residuum, as in electrocoagulation and photocoagulation.

coagulation, blood the sequential process by which the multiple coagulation factors of the blood interact, ultimately resulting in the formation of an insoluble fibrin clot; it may be divided into three stages: stage 1, the formation of intrinsic and extrinsic prothrombin converting principle; stage 2, the formation of thrombin; stage 3, the formation of stable fibrin polymers.

coagulation, disseminated intravascular

He said blood clotting studies he conducted at Children's Hospital ruled out the probability of **disseminated intravascular coagulation (DIC).**[2]....

... She testified **DIC** is an intravascular disease of abnormal blood coagulation not uncommon in newborn children.

[² Widely scattered process of the blood changing from a liquid into a semisolid mass (i.e., clotting) within the arteries and veins.] Vecchione v. Carlin, 168 Cal.Rptr. 571, 574 (Ct.App. Cal.1980).

coagulation, radio frequency

Finally, **radio frequency coagulation** [for relief of trigeminal neuralgia] involves a needlelike cathode which is injected into the Gasserian ganglion through an opening in the base of the skull. The nerve fibers are then selectively destroyed by the use of controlled heat developed from radio frequency current. Hales v. Pittman, 576 P.2d 493, 496 (Ariz.1978).

coagulopathy (ko-ag"u-lop'ah-the) any disorder of blood coagulation.

Some of his doctors were concerned about possible **coagulopathy**, that is that the blood's clotting mechanism was diseased. Zeck v. U.S., 559 F.Supp. 1345, 1347 (D.S.Dak. 1983).

coat (kōt) [L. cot'ta a tunic] a membrane or other structure covering or lining a part or organ. See also *tunic*; and *tunica*.

coating See *enteric-coated* (Armour case).

cobalt treatment See *radiation*.

cocaine (ko'kān) [USP] chemical name: [1R-(exo, exo)]-3-(benzoyloxy)-8-methyl-8-azabicyclo[3.2.1]octane-2-carboxylic acid methyl ester. A crystalline alkaloid, $C_{17}H_{21}NO_4$, obtained from leaves of *Erythroxylon coca* (coca leaves) and other species of *Erythroxylon*, or by synthesis from ecgonine or its derivatives; used as a local narcotic anesthetic applied topically to mucous membranes. See also *isomer* (U.S. v. Kolenda case).

Under federal narcotics law, **cocaine** is defined as:
Coca leaves (9040) and any salt, compound, derivative, or preparation of coca leaves, and any salt, compound, derivative, or preparation thereof which is chemically equivalent or identical with any of these substances, except that the substances shall not include decocainized coca leaves or extraction of coca leaves, which extractions do not contain cocaine (9041) or ecgonine (9180).
21 C.F.R. § 1308.12, Schedule II(b)(4); see 21 U.S.C. § 812(a) and (c), Schedule II(a)(4). Thus it was necessary for the government to prove that the substance which Hall sold was either "natural" **cocaine**, derived from coca leaves, or a chemical equivalent thereof. U.S. v. Hall, 552 F.2d 273, 274 (9th Cir. 1977).

"**Cocaine** is not related to the opium poppy but is a substance derived from coca leaves. Unlike the narcotics which are depressants, **cocaine** is a central nervous system stimulant. Its short-term physiological effects include increase in heart rate and blood pressure and eye pupil dilation. To the user it produces a euphoric state and reduces fatigue and hunger. It is not physically addictive in that it does not produce tolerance or withdrawal. Both experts were of the opinion that it does not cause hallucinations or psychosis but may cause a perceptual disorder in which a user experiences the sensation of insects crawling in·or on the skin. Both experts agreed that **cocaine** can be psychologically addictive but felt that such dependency is seen in only 1% of users labeled 'compulsive.'

"**Cocaine** is taken into the body by most users nasally by 'snorting' or 'sniffing.' A small percentage of users (1%) inject **cocaine** intravenously. Both experts were of the opinion that cocaine is not generally harmful in that it is quickly and cleanly eliminated from the body. Nasal ingestion may, however, cause chronic nasal irritation, which can result in the perforation of the nasal septum. Other common side effects are irritability, insomnia and weight loss. Death can occur from a large overdose but is rare in recreational use. **Cocaine** has a recognized medical use as a local anesthetic.

"Although both experts were of the opinion that cocaine has no causal connection to criminal behavior, both conceded that criminal activity, including violent crime, is associated with the illegal trafficking of **cocaine**. Dr. Fort testified that there is some divergence of opinion among experts, especially between human researchers and animal researchers, as to the dangerousness of **cocaine** to users. Although both experts were of the opinion that the danger of **cocaine** had been exaggerated, neither felt that the drug was harmless or advocated its legalization." 86 Ill.2d 251–252, 56 Ill.Dec. 67, 69–70, 427 N.E.2d 149–150. . . .

. . . Moreover, our research has revealed that all courts which have dealt with the identical issue, with the exception of one trial court in the State of Michigan, have upheld the classification of **cocaine** as a 'narcotic' for penalty purposes. (Citations omitted.) 86 Ill.2d 258, 56 Ill.Dec. 67, 72, 427 N.E.2d 152. People v. Key, 328 N.W.2d 609, 613 (Mich.Ct.App. 1982).

In support of his misclassification argument, the defendant has submitted numerous affidavits from medical experts, excerpts from pharmacological texts, and articles from medical journals. These materials appear to confirm, and even the government tends to agree, that **cocaine** is not a narcotic in a strict medical sense. . . .

. . . Cocaine, on the other hand, does not resemble the opiates in any pharmacological sense, but is universally identified with amphetamines. Far from being a depressant, **cocaine** is generally considered as an anti-fatigue, anti-soporific stimulant often used to stimulate alertness or euphoria. Its effects upon respiration, the central nervous system, and the gastrointestinal tract, are different from those of narcotics. **Cocaine** in not addictive, but may be habituating much as marijuana, cigarette smoking, etc. Heavy users do not build up tolerances requiring greater dosages or more frequent usage. Nor does termination appear to cause withdrawal symptoms, although some older pharmacological texts and government affiants suggest possible psychological dependence stemming from the so-called **cocaine** psychosis with formication and paranoia in addition to depression. Defense experts, however, have discounted such reactions as either highly unusual, or the unsubstantiated product of drug mythology. . . .

. . . Even though the available body of knowledge will not permit us to draw conclusions as to the impact of **cocaine** on a person's health, it is clear that the effects are vastly different from those generally associated with true narcotics. Based on the foregoing, it is clear, from a medical standpoint, that Congress has erroneously classified cocaine with heroin and other opiates for penalty purposes. . . .

. . . In light of this medical misclassification, the issue before us, as aptly framed by Judge Lacey in the consolidated cases of United States v. Brookins and United States v. Gueches,

383 F.Supp. 1212 (D.N.J.1974), decided during the pendency of this case on precisely the same claims, is "whether Congress can rationally classify cocaine, a non-narcotic central nervous system stimulant, as a narcotic for penalty and regulatory purposes. In other words, must the legal or congressional classification of **cocaine** as a narcotic mirror its medical classification?"...

... Whether Congress retained the narcotic classification because of the paucity of scientific data on **cocaine**, or because it is allegedly used by drug abusers alone or in combination with heroin, or in furtherance of treaty obligations, Judge Lacey held that there are a number of rational bases which would sustain the statute.

Accepting the realities of the rational basis test, and that Congress need not act wisely or scientifically, only constitutionally, we find Judge Lacey's reasoning and conclusions to be controlling here. U.S. v. Castro, 401 F.Supp. 120, 123–4, 126 (N.D.Ill.1975).

Other Authorities: People v. McCabe, 275 N.E.2d 407, 410 (Ill.1971); Hearing before the Sen. Comm. on Labor and Human Resources on Health Promotion and Disease Prevention Amend. on S. 771, 98th Cong., 1st Sess. 1, 302 (1983).

cocaine, d-cocaine See *cocaine, l-cocaine.*

cocaine hydrochloride [USP], the hydrochloride salt of cocaine, $C_{17}H_{21}NO_4 \cdot HCl$, occurring as colorless crystals or a white crystalline powder; used as an anesthetic, applied topically to mucous membranes.

A chemist from the Drug Enforcement Administration testified as part of the Government's case-in-chief that **cocaine hydrochloride** is a salt of cocaine, and that it is a controlled substance. The expert testified further that **cocaine hydrochloride** of the levo rotary isomer type is a controlled substance. U.S. v. Kolenda, 697 F.2d 149–50 (6th Cir. 1983).

cocaine, l-cocaine

Medina testified that he had not tested the substance to determine whether it consisted of the "levo" isomer of cocaine (**l-cocaine**) or the "dextro" isomer (d-cocaine). **L-cocaine** is "natural" cocaine, a drug derived from the coca leaf, whereas d-cocaine is a chemically synthesized compound. U.S. v. Hall, 552 F.2d 273–4 (9th Cir. 1977).

coccidioidomycosis (kok-sid″e-oi″do-mi-ko′sis) a fungous disease caused by infection with *Coccidioides immitis*, occurring in a primary and a secondary form. Called also *coccidioidal granuloma, Posada's mycosis, Posada-Wernicke disease, California disease,* and *desert fever.* The *primary* form is an acute, benign, self-limited respiratory infection due to inhalation of spores, and varying in severity from that of a common cold to symptoms resembling those accompanying influenza, with pneumonia, cavitation, high fever, and, rarely, erythema nodosum (bumps). Called also *desert rheumatism, San Joaquin Valley fever,* and *valley fever.* The *secondary* form (or *progressive c.*) is a virulent and severe, chronic, progressive, granulomatous disease resulting in involvement of the cutaneous and subcutaneous tissues, viscera, central nervous system, and lungs, with anemia, phlebitis, and various allergic responses. This form may be caused by a new infection or by reactivation of arrested primary disease.

Tommie P. Crawford (Crawford), while working as an operator of a rock crusher for W. R. Skousen Contractor, Inc. (Skousen), at Tonopah, Arizona, exhibited symptoms which were later diagnosed as **coccidioidomycosis (valley fever)**....

... **Valley Fever** is acquired by inhalation of spores, fungus spores. These spores are found in southwestern United States predominantly in the area of Arizona, predominantly in Arizona and southern California. With reasonable medical certainty I would be of the opinion that any man exposed to a dusty environment would have a greater likelihood of acquiring **Valley Fever**.

"I would feel that the most likely source of his **Valley Fever** infection would be related—with reasonable medical certainty would be related to his working conditions. **Valley Fever** is acquired by inhalation. The initial infection is pulmonary....

"... At first people didn't know what this disease was, and then it became evident that it was a fungus-type disease. Because the disease was originally described in the San Joaquin Valley of California it became known as **Valley Fever**. It has no reference to Valley of the Sun, the reference was to the San Joaquin Valley of California....

"During the early 1940's because of the military bases in this area and also in the southern California area, soil that had been undisturbed for centuries was now disturbed by bulldozers and other devices, and so the spores that had been left undisturbed for centuries now were breathed in through the air, and many of the young people, young service personnel, Army and Marine Corps, Air Force, developed **Valley Fever** during that time....

"So the nick name for the disease is **Valley Fever**, the medical term is **coccidioidomycosis**. Now the fungus can infect almost any organ of the body. However, the most likely source of acquiring this disease is through inhalation of the spore." Crawford v. Industrial Commission, 534 P.2d 1077–8, 1082 (Ct.App.Ariz.1975).

It was not until April 1965 this his illness was diagnosed as disseminated **coccidioidomycosis**, a fungus disease endemic to the San Joaquin Valley. It is contracted by the inhalation of tiny spores; these infected Berry's lungs and spread through his bloodstream to various portions of his anatomy. In its disseminated form the disease is deemed to be very serious.

The undisputed evidence established that Berry had contracted **coccidioidomycosis** prior to his knee injury and its dissemination was not caused by the injury. However, two experts, including one who specialized in the study of this uncommon ailment, testified that the trauma to Berry's knee caused the infection to lodge there. That is, prior to the injury the disease had disseminated through Berry's body but it had been dormant; the injury precipitated the localization of the fungus, resulting in "advancement" of the disease. Berry v. Workmen's Compensation Appeals Board, 441 P.2d 908–9 (Cal.1968).

coccimeningitis See *coccidioidomycosis* (Crawford case).

coccydynia See *coccygodynia.*

coccygectomy (kok″se-jek′to-me) [*coccyx* + Gr. *ektomē* excision] excision of the coccyx.

As a result of this occurrence, a partial **coccygectomy** was performed several months later, involving the partial excision of that skeletal part. Examinations of the coccyx showed that it had sustained a fracture. Potts v. Industrial Commission, 413 N.E.2d 1285–6 (Ill.1980).

In the 1966 report, Dr. Johnson states that a **coccygectomy** was performed, following which the petitioner stated she was experiencing considerable relief. He concludes, "It is my opinion that the patient's residual symptomatology in the coccygeal area may have been related to the injury of July 27, 1963." The second report contains the following statement....

> "The patient was seen by me recently, on August 14, 1968, at which time she complained of some difficulty with the rectum protruding through the area of the **coccygectomy**. Apparently she was having herniation at that area." Seeley v. Industrial Com'n, 472 P.2d 485–6 (Ct.App.Ariz.1970).

Other Authorities: Rainer v. Buena Community Memorial Hospital, 95 Cal.Rptr. 901, 904 (Ct.App.Cal.1971).

coccygodynia (kok"se-go-din'e-ah) [*coccyx* + Gr. *odynē* pain] pain in the coccyx and neighboring region; called also *coccygalia*.

He found that she had two recurrent episodes of **coccydynia**, pain at the tip of the sacrum in the region of her sacrococcygeal joint, both of which were responsive to medication.... Range v. Weinberger, 361 F.Supp. 685, 687 (E.D. Tenn.1973).

Dr. Ulises Ferrer after noting that the plaintiff alleged she has been suffering from persistent pain in the coccygeal and cervical regions diagnosed: 1) Post traumatic **coccygodynia**.... Carrero v. U.S. Secretary of Health, Education & Welf., 372 F.Supp. 474–5 (D. Puerto Rico 1973).

In July of 1964, the petitioner was seen in consultation by Dr. William B. McGrath, M.D., a psychiatrist. He commented as follows:

> Comment: This kind of **coccygodynia** is not uncommonly refractory to treatment. And, arising in circumstances of emotional conflict, it is undoubtedly psychogenic, as presumably is also the chronic digestive disorder which she currently presents. Seeley v. Industrial Com'n 472 P.2d 485, 486 (Ct. App.Ariz.1970).

Other Authorities: Santiago v. Finch, 314 F.Supp. 326–7 (D. Puerto Rico 1970); Santiago v. Gardner, 288 F.Supp. 156, 158 (D. Puerto Rico 1968).

coccyx (kok'siks) [Gr. *kokkyx* cuckoo, whose bill it is said to resemble] the small bone caudad to the sacrum in man, formed by union of four (sometimes five or three) rudimentary vertebrae, and forming the caudal extremity of the vertebral column. Called also *os coccygis* [NA], and *coccygeal, cuckoo,* or *pelvic bone.*

Dr. Ulises Ferrer recommended the best chance of rehabilitation for this plaintiff consisted in removal of the last two vertabrae of the **coccyx**, "where, according to X-Rays, there appears to be some arthritic changes." Carrero v. U.S. Secretary of Health, Education & Welf., 372 F.Supp. 474–5 (D. Puerto Rico 1973).

He reported tenderness to palpation over the **coccyx**, and sharp pain when the distal coccygeal segment was moved

through a combined rectal and external examination. Santiago v. Gardner, 288 F.Supp. 156, 158 (D.Puerto Rico 1968).

Other Authorities: Rainer v. Buena Community Memorial Hospital, 95 Cal.Rptr. 901, 904 (Ct.App.Cal.1971); Potts v. Industrial Commission, 413 N.E.2d 1285–8 (Ill.1980).

code (kōd) [L. *codex* something written] a system by which information can be communicated. See also *code blue; Code Fifty-Four;* and *"no code"* order.

code blue

Nurse Wilson signalled "**Code Blue**," which indicated a cardiac arrest was taking place.... Fraijo v. Hartland Hospital, 160 Cal.Rptr. 246, 250 (Ct.App.Cal.1979).

As one might suspect, the action during an emergency resuscitation attempt, or "**Code Blue**" in hospital parlance, is fast and furious. However, the District Court was able to reconstruct the approximate sequence of events on the basis of hospital records. Chief Nurse Curry, in charge of the emergency room, was present during the whole course of the **Code Blue** and one of her duties included a minute-by-minute recordation of what was done. The hospital records also include the notes of Dr. Hassan Vaziri, the emergency room physician who had originally ordered the penicillin injection. [both records appear in full at pages 753–4 of this opinion.] Daniels v. Hadley Memorial Hospital, 566 F.2d 749, 753 (D.C.Cir.1977).

External cardiac pressure, pure oxygen by positive pressure squeeze bag and various drugs were immediately administered to resuscitate infant plaintiff. At the same time Hospital's emergency signal—"**code blue**"—was given. In response to that signal a number of other physicians went immediately to the operating room. Additional drugs were administered and a cardiac monitor was attached to infant plaintiff. Two and one-half minutes after nurse Bowman reported there was no pulse the infant plaintiff's heart beat resumed....

> ... While cardiac arrests fortunately are not every day happenings they are not so rare that they are unheard of in hospitals. Defendant Hospital has an alarm system to meet such emergencies during surgery. It is known in the Hospital as the "**code blue**" signal which when sounded calls all available doctors to the operating room to render assistance. Rose v. Hakim, 335 F.Supp. 1221, 1224 (D.D.C.1971).

Code Fifty-Four

Code Fifty-Four is an emergency code indicating that a patient is in immediate danger of death. It indicates that the patient is in distress and needs immediate resuscitation and emergency treatment. The evidence was sufficient for a finding that there was a delay of some fifteen minutes between the time the **Code Fifty-Four** was issued and the time a doctor responded thereto. Spadaccini v. Dolan, 407 N.Y.S.2d 840, 843 (1st Dep't 1978).

codeine (ko'dēn) [L. *codeina*] [USP] chemical name: 7,8-didehydro - 4,5 α - epoxy - 3 - methoxy - 17 - methyl - morphinan-6 α-ol monohydrate. A narcotic alkaloid obtained from opium or prepared by methylating morphine, $C_{18}H_{21}NO_3 \cdot H_2O$, occurring as colorless or white crystals or as a white, crystalline powder; used as an analgesic and antitussive, administered orally. Called also *methylmorphine.* See also *Spectrophotometer;* and *spectrofluormeter.*

Coecal

Dr. Gonzalez decided to first make an impression of the fingers on her left hand as a guide. He used a substance known as **Coecal**, a dental stone, produced by Coe Laboratories in order to make an impression. The process necessitated the placing of Mrs. Hill's fingers into the **Coecal** contained within an ice cream carton. Since **Coecal** is self-heating as it hardens the plaintiff was requested to tell the doctor when it started getting warm....

... Testing of **Coecal** demonstrated that it can run from an initial 63°F. to 151°F. in fifteen minutes at which point it is in a hardened state. Dr. Hursel O. Kallestad testified for the plaintiffs. He had considerable experience as a prosthetic dentist and testified that **Coecal** would not be suitable as an impression material on the human body because it would be too hard to remove and too dangerous. Hill v. Gonzalez, 454 F.2d 1201–2 (8th Cir. 1972).

cofactor (ko'fak-tor) an element or principle, as a coenzyme, with which another must unite in order to function.

cofactor I, platelet, Factor VIII See *coagulation factors* under *factor*.

cofactor II, platelet, Factor IX See *coagulation factors* under *factor*.

coffin bone See *bone, coffin.*

Cogentin (ko-jen'tin) trademark for preparations of benztropine mesylate. See also benztropine mesylate.

cognition (kog-nish'un) [L. *cognitio*, from *cognoscere* to know] that operation of the mind by which we become aware of objects of thought or perception; it includes all aspects of perceiving, thinking, and remembering.

Dr. Morse states Karen Quinlan will not return to a level of **cognitive** function (i.e., that she will be able to say "Mr. Coburn I'm glad you are my guardian.") Matter of Quinlan, 348 A.2d 801, 811 (Super.Ct.N.J.1975).

cognitive See *cognition.*

coke

Coke is the almost pure carbon residue that remains when most of the volatile matter in coal is removed by destructive thermal distillation .... (Resp.Br. at p. 43.) National Steel Corp., Great Lakes Steel v. Gorsuch, 700 F.2d 314, 319 (6th Cir. 1983).

colchicine (kol'chĭ-sin) [USP] chemical name: (*S*)-*N*-(5,6,7,9-tetrahydro-1,2,3,10-tetramethoxy-9-oxobenzo[*a*]heptalen-7-yl) acetamide. An alkaloid, $C_{22}H_{25}NO_6$, obtained from various species of *Colchicum*, occurring as pale yellow amorphous scales or powder; used as a gout suppressant, usually administered orally.

Colchicine is a poison sometimes prescribed for the control of inflammation due to gout (the tablets swallowed in this case had been prescribed for Miss Webb's father in order to control such inflammation) and the tablets were in a bottle plainly marked "poison". The approximately fifty (50) tablets were equivalent to about 30 milligrams. The drug is highly toxic and

as little as seven milligrams has been known to be lethal. Webb v. U.S., 446 F.2d 760–1 (5th Cir. 1971).

colectomy (ko-lek'to-me) [*colon* + Gr. *ektomē* excision] excision of a portion of the colon (*partial c.*) or of the whole colon (*complete or total c.*).

A **colectomy** is the excision of part or all of the colon. Paris v. Schweiker, 674 F.2d 707, 708 (8th Cir. 1982).

Colectomy: "Excision of a portion of the colon or of the whole colon." Rainer v. Buena Community Memorial Hospital, 95 Cal.Rptr. 901, 903 (Ct.App.1971).

coliform (ko'lĭ-form) [L. *colum* a sieve] 1. a collective term denoting enteric, fermentative gram-negative rods, and sometimes restricted to the lactose-fermenting, gram-negative enteric bacilli, i.e., *Escherichia, Klebsiella, Enterobacter*, and *Citrobacter*. 2. any organism of that group.

coliform, fecal

Fecal **coliforms** are bacteriae originating in the intestinal tract of warm-blooded animals. The presence of **fecal coliforms** in wastewater has a high correlation with increased numbers of both pathogenic viruses and bacteriae. An example of these is Salmonella. Tanners' Council of America, Inc. v. Train, 540 F.2d 1188, 1191 (4th Cir. 1976).

colitis (ko-li'tis) inflammation of the colon.

colitis, pseudomembranous See *enterocolitis.*

colitis, ulcerativa, ulcerative cronic recurrent ulceration in the colon, chiefly of the mucosa and submucosa, of unknown cause; it is manifested clinically by cramping abdominal pain, rectal bleeding, and loose discharges of blood, pus, and mucus with scanty fecal particles. Complications include hemorrhoids, abscesses, fistulas, perforation of the colon, pseudopolyps and carcinoma.

While not uncommon, **ulcerative colitis** is a condition the cause of which remains unknown to modern medicine. See Record, vol. 1, at 193. A condition manifested by ulcers in the colon, **ulcerative colitis** appears more frequently in individuals involved in high stress occupations. Carlton v. Shelton, 722 F.2d 203–4 (5th Cir. 1984).

... a sigmoidoscopic examination disclosed the presence of **ulcerative colitis**, a chronic, debilitating disease of the large intestine. Dr. Zimmerman and Dr. Rieger, an expert witness employed on Mrs. Reichman's behalf, testified that there is no cure for **ulcerative colitis**, that persons suffering from the disease require medical care for the remainder of their lives, and that in some cases a colostomy is required during the later stages of the disease....

... Dr. Zimmerman, appellee's gastroenterologist, testified that although medical science is uncertain of the exact etiology of **ulcerative colitis**, in his opinion the formation of the hematoma, the length of time that she had been under close and prolonged monitoring, and the stresses resulting from the surgical procedures and during the post-operative periods were the factors which caused her to develop **ulcerative colitis**....

... Dr. Wolfgram Reiger, a psychiatrist who had been treating Mrs. Reichman since October 17, 1977, testified that Mrs. Reichman was suffering from marked depression, anxiety and traumatic neuroses, as well as **ulcerative colitis**, and said: "The post-operative course, and specifically the complications, represent the very trauma that caused these many neuroses that I have described and also directly caused the **ulcerative colitis.**" Reichman v. Wallach, 452 A.2d 501, 504, 506 (Super.Ct. Pa.1982).

Claimant testified that in 1977 he had diarrhea 15–20 times a day and his weight dropped from about 195 pounds to about 160 pounds. . . .

. . . He testified that Dr. McKee treated him with Lomotil and diagnosed **ulcerative colitis.** Wilson v. Schweiker, 553 F.Supp. 728, 730 (E.D.Wash.1982).

Other Authorities: Parsons v. Wood, 584 P.2d 1332–3 (Okl. 1978); Rainer v. Buena Community Memorial Hospital, 95 Cal. Rptr. 901, 904 (Ct.App.Cal.1971).

collagen (kol'ah-jen) [Gr. *kolla* glue + *gennan* to produce] the protein substance of the white fibers (collagenous fibers) of skin, tendon, bone, cartilage, and all other connective tissue; composed of molecules of tropocollagen (q.v.), it is converted into gelatin by boiling. See also under *disease.*

collagen disease See *disease, collagen.*

collagen, fibrous long-spacing (FLS) a form of collagen having a periodicity of about 240 nm. instead of the 64 nm. characteristic of the native fibers; found in the trabecular network of the eye and in aging collagen.

collagen, segment long-spacing (SLS) collagen occurring in segments about 240 nm. long instead of in fibers.

collar (kol'ler) an encircling band, generally around the neck.

collar, Thomas

"A **Thomas collar** would be somewhat similar to taking a turkish towel and wrapping it around your neck. It is about the same thickness, but the **Thomas collar** is much stiffer. As a result of this, it keeps the neck at rest." Testimony of Doctor Terrien, Transcript of Trial at 60. West v. Jutras, 456 F.2d 1222, 1224 (2d Cir. 1972).

collar bone See *clavicula.*

collum (kol'lum), pl. *col'la* [L.] [NA] 1. the neck: the portion of the body connecting the head and trunk; the lower front portion of the collum is called the cervix, and the back is called the nucha. 2. a general term applied to any necklike part of a body structure or organ.

collum femoris [NA], neck of femur: the heavy column of bone connecting the head of the femur and the shaft. Cited in Leavell v. Alton Ochsner Medical Foundation, 201 F.Supp. 805–6 (E.D.La.1962).

colon (ko'lon) [L.; Gr. *kolon*] [NA] that part of the large intestine which extends from the cecum to the rectum; sometimes used inaccurately as a synonym for the entire large intestine. See also *megacolon; colitis;* and *transposition, colon.*

The **colon** was adhered to this infection and was infected itself. Dr. Sheid removed approximately two feet of the **colon** and attempted to clean out all the remaining infection. Seeley v. Eaton, 506 S.W.2d 719, 721 (Ct.Civ.App.Tex.1974).

. . . aside from being under the treatment of a psychiatrist or psychologist, she was under the treatment of an internist for an internal condition of her **colon** that was, I think, diagnosed and is usually regarded as a psychosomatic condition, so that it stands to reason to at least suspect that emotional strain may cause physical reactions of one sort or another.

"Q. Do you recall the medical term for that, Doctor?

"A. I believe the diagnosis was given either as megacolon or ulcerative colitis." In re Loughran, 276 F.Supp. 393, 421 (Centr.D.Cal.1967).

colon, resection

Because **colon resection** (removal of a section of bowel and union of the two ends, as opposed to rerouting by colostomy) involved unavoidable leakage of fecal matter in the peritoneal cavity and consequent danger of peritonitis, Dr. Thian ordered that neomycin be administered orally for bowel preparation prior to the surgery. DaRoca v. St. Bernard General Hospital, 347 So.2d 933–4 (Ct.App.La.1977).

colon, sigmoid; colon sigmoideum [NA], the S-shaped part of the colon which lies in the pelvis, extending from the pelvic brim to the third segment of the sacrum, and continuous above with the descending (or iliac) colon and below with the rectum; called also *pelvic c.* and *sigmoid flexure.*

The **sigmoid** is the part of the colon preceding the rectum. Both parts are continuous and represent arbitrary divisions of the large bowel, mainly for convenience of reference. Purcell v. Zimbelman, 500 P.2d 335, 339 (Ct.App.Ariz.1972).

According to the hospital records, the final diagnosis was: "Carcinoma of the abdomen either from the **sigmoid** or from the pancreas with multiple metastases throughout the peritoneal surfaces including obstructive lesions in the small bowel and in the distal ileum and obstructing lesions in the area of the cecum and ascending colon." Disposable Services, Inc. v. ITT Life Ins. Co. of New York, 453 F.2d 218, 220 (5th Cir. 1971).

colon, transverse; colon transversum [NA], the portion of the colon that runs transversely across the upper part of the abdomen, from the right to the left colic flexure.

The **transverse colon** is immediately under the stomach, and the weight of the solid food would cause the stomach to go down on the anastomosis. Lenger v. Physician's General Hospital, Inc., 455 S.W.2d 703, 707 (Tex.1970).

colonoscopy (ko"lon-os'ko-pe) 1. endoscopic examination of the colon during laparotomy by insertion of a sigmoidoscope proximally and distally through a colotomy. 2. examination by means of the colonoscope. Called also *coloscopy.* See also *polypectomy.*

The record reveals that defendant examined plaintiff Alice T. Ogden at his office and concluded she had a polyp in the sigmoid colon which had to be removed; that the best available procedure for its removal was by a **colonoscopy** and polypectomy; that plaintiff was given Valium and Demerol to sedate her and the polyp was removed while she was an outpatient at St. Mary's Hospital in Troy. . . . Ogden v. Bhatti, 460 N.Y.S.2d 166–7 (3d Dep't 1983).

color (kul'or) [L. *color, colos*] 1. a property of a surface or substance resulting from absorption of certain of the incident light rays and reflection of others falling within the range of wavelengths (roughly 370–760 mμ) adequate to excite the retinal receptors. 2. radiant energy within the range of adequate chromatic stimuli of the retina, that is, between the infrared and ultraviolet. 3. a sensory impression of one of the rainbow hues, excited by stimulation of the retinal receptors, notably the cones, by radiant energy of the appropriate wavelength.

Color is a sensation involving complex processes in the human eye and brain. Visual identification depends on many factors, such as the composition of the light falling on the object, and the juxtaposition or not of the objects. Colors may be "additive" or "subtractive". When separate beams of light are superimposed on one target (or fluoresced as separate, tiny dots on a TV screen), the additive primary colors are red, green and blue. When pigments are mixed, as for paints and inks, the subtractive colors are magenta, yellow and cyan. White and black are also used to affect value (brightness) and chroma (saturation). . . .

For useful background information on "additive colors" (separate beams of light integrated on one target as in color TV for which the primary colors are red, green and blue), and on "subtractive colors" (pigments viewed by reflection, for which the primary colors are magenta, yellow and cyan), see "Light and Vision" (Life Science Library, 1966), and "Color", (Encyclopedia Americana, 1957 Edition). The Munsell Color Tree is evidently the most widely used standard for identifying the hue, value and chroma of any color.

These fundamentals have been known since the publication of Newton's "Opticks", which was first printed in 1704. Pennwalt Corp. v. Becton, Dickinson & Co., 434 F.Supp. 758, 762 (D.N.J.1977).

colostomy (ko-los′to-me) [*colon* + Gr. *stomoun* to provide with an opening, or mouth] the surgical creation of an opening between the colon and the surface of the body; also used to refer to the opening, or stoma, so created.

Carlton's physicians recommended a complete colostomy, a process requiring surgical removal of the entire colon and construction of an external opening allowing the collection of the patient's excrement in a small plastic bag. Carlton v. Shelton, 722 F.2d 203–4 (5th Cir. 1984).

At St. Luke's, Dr. Roseman, a surgeon, performed a temporary colostomy which diverted the fecal matter from the rectum to promote the healing of the fistula. Kranda v. Houser-Norborg Medical Corp., 419 N.E.2d 1024, 1032 (Ct.App.Ind.1981).

Purcell did not first institute a temporary colostomy [6] because he did not think it was necessary, even though there had been contamination of this proximal end before he pulled it through into the rectal area and attached it to the anal outlet and even though he knew there had been an infectious process in the abdomen. [[6] The formation of an artificial outlet for discharging the contents of the colon through the wall of the abdomen.] Purcell v. Zimbelman, 500 P.2d 335, 339 (Ct.App.Ariz. 1972).

Other Authorities: Morgan v. Schlanger, 374 F.2d 235, 237 (4th Cir. 1967).

colostomy, ileotransverse surgical anastomosis between the ileum and the transverse colon. See also *hemicolectomy* (Babin case).

colostomy bag See *bag, colostomy.*

colostrum (kŏ-los′trum) [L.] the thin, yellow, milky fluid secreted by the mammary gland a few days before or after parturition. It contains up to 20 per cent protein, predominant among which are immunoglobulins, representing the antibodies found in maternal blood. It contains more minerals and less fat and carbohydrate than does milk. It also contains many colostrum corpuscles and usually will coagulate on boiling due to a large amount of lactalbumin.

The parties agree that NI results from the destruction of red blood cells caused by antibodies to those cells which the calf obtains from the first milk, or colostrum, of the mother cow. Waller v. Fort Dodge Laboratories, 356 F.Supp. 413, 415 (E.D.Mo.1972).

colotomy (ko-lot′o-me) [*colo-* + Gr. *tomē* a cutting] incision into the colon for removal of a foreign body, polyp, or other benign tumor. Cf. *colostomy.*

colpoperineorrhaphy (kol″po-per″ĭ-ne-or′ah-fe) [*colpo-* + Gr. *perinaion* perineum + *rhaphē* suture] suture of the ruptured vagina and perineum; vaginoperineorrhaphy.

He testified that during the Heaney hysterectomy process a colpoperineorrhaphy completes the operation. This is where a wall of the vagina is repaired and "the muscles of the perineum, that is, the bundle of muscles between the vagina and the rectum, are strengthened and shortened as need be". Harris v. Campbell, 409 P.2d 67, 69 (Ct.App.Ariz.1965).

colporrhaphy (kol-por′ah-fe) [*colpo-* + Gr. *rhaphē* suture] 1. the operation of suturing the vagina. 2. the operation of denuding and suturing the vaginal wall for the purpose of narrowing the vagina.

"Columbarium" is defined by the same article [Tex.Rev.Civ. Stat.Ann. Act 912a–1 (1963)] as: . . . a structure or room or other space in a building or structure of most durable and lasting fireproof construction or a plot of earth, containing niches, used, or intended to be used, to contain cremated human remains. City of Beaumont v. Jones 560 S.W.2d 710, 712 (Ct. Civ.App.Tex.1977).

columna (ko-lum′nah), pl. *colum′nae* [L.] [NA] column: a pillar-like structure; in anatomical nomenclature, used to designate a pillar-like structure or part.

columna vertebralis [NA], the columnar assemblage of the vertebrae from the cranium through the coccyx; called also *axon, vertebral, dorsal,* or *spinal column, backbone,* and *spine.*

. . . on his X rays of his dorsal spine—that's the spine between the shoulder blades—his X rays have begun to show the typical early changes of a degenerative joint disease. Micucci v. Industrial Com'n, 492 P.2d 23, 26 (Ct.App.Ariz.1972), decision vacated 494 P.2d 1324 (Ariz.1972).

coma (ko′mah) [L.; Gr. *kōma*] a state of unconsciousness from which the patient cannot be aroused, even by powerful stimulation; called also *exanimation.* See also *comatose.*

coma, diabetic the coma of severe diabetic acidosis.

If **diabetic coma** is suspected, immediate medical attention is mandatory; without treatment, **diabetic coma** results in death. U.S. v. Dunavan, 464 F.2d 1166, 1178 (6th Cir. 1972).

coma, hepatic See *encephalopathy, hepatic.*

comatose (ko′mah-tōs) pertaining to or affected with coma. See also *terminal* (John F. Kennedy Mem. Hosp. case).

Shortly after the "shunt" operations were performed in November of 1975, the decedent lapsed into a **coma** from which he never recovered. During the **comatose** period, the decedent clearly was incapable of comprehending the elements of possible malpractice or of pursuing a remedy for the injuries sustained. More significantly, the very tort that allegedly forms the basis of this suit caused that incapacity. The effect of the operations was to take away the decedent's mental functions entirely. . . .

. . . Having decided earlier that the claim accrued on or about August 18, 1975 when the decedent was informed of the presence of an organic brain lesion, we have the following situation: the statute ran for approximately five months prior to decedent's lapse into a **coma**, was tolled for the following twenty months while decedent was in a coma, and commenced running once again on September 30, 1977, continuing for some sixteen months until plaintiffs filed their claim on January 18, 1979. Therefore, a total of approximately twenty-one months elapsed prior to plaintiffs' filing suit. For the foregoing reasons, plaintiffs' action pursuant to the Federal Tort Claims Act was timely filed under section 2401(b). Dundon v. U.S., 559 F.Supp. 469, 474–5 (E.D.N.Y.1983).

. . . the affidavit of one of the attending physicians asserted that the child's profound **comatose** condition is evidenced by abnormal electroencephalography; failure of head growth; abnormal cranial ultrasound, indicating progressive cerebral atrophy; spastic quadriplegia, including inappropriate response to stimuli; inability to suck and feed except by tube feedings; inability to breathe, necessitating an infant ventilator, heart rate dependent on ventilator therapy; and absence of other appropriate signs of consciousness to indicate spontaneous response to environmental or social stimuli. In Re P.V.W., 424 So.2d 1015, 1017 (La.1982).

comedocarcinoma (kŏ-me″do-kar-sĭ-no′mah) an intraductal carcinoma of the breast, the central cells of which are degenerated and easily expressed from the cut surface of the tumor.

Dr. Tweeddale, another expert witness for appellants, testified that appellant's cancer was a **comedo-type carcinoma**, which is a slow growing type. Shapiro v. Burkons, 404 N.E.2d 778, 780 (Ct.App.Ohio 1978).

commissura (kom″mĭ-su′rah), pl. *commissurae* [L. "a joining together"] [NA] commissure: a site of union of corresponding parts; a general term used to designate such a junction of corresponding anatomical structures, frequently, but not always, across the midplane of the body.

commissure (kom′ĭ-shūr) a site of union of corresponding parts. See also *commissura*. Used also with specific reference to the sites of junction between adjacent cusps of the valves of the heart.

commissurotomy (kom″ĭ-shŭr-ot′o-me) [*commissure* + Gr. *tome* cutting] surgical incision or digital disruption of the component parts of a commissure to increase the size of the orifice; commonly utilized to separate the adherent, thickened leaflets of a stenotic mitral valve. See also *commissura*; and *commissure*.

He had had a **mitro-commissurotomy** performed in the spring of 1967 at the Mayo Clinic in Rochester, Minnesota. Tschohl v. Nationwide Mut. Ins. Co., 418 F.Supp. 1124–5 (D.Minn. 1976).

communications program, total

The Beechwood program utilizes a method known as the "**total communications program.**" This method is the prodominant method of training deaf children in the United States, and there is no indication of inadequacy of the Beechwood program. This program centers around the use of hand signs as a means of communication. Eberle v. Board of Public Ed. of Sch. Dist., 444 F.Supp. 41–2 (D.Pa.1977).

Compazine (kom′pha-zēn) trademark for preparations of prochlorperazine maleate. See also *prochlorperazine maleate*.

complication (kom″plĭ-ka′shun) [L. *complicatio* from *cum* together + *plicare* to fold] a disease or diseases concurrent with another disease.

complication, permanent

On direct examination, plaintiff's expert witness, Doctor Woodruff testified that hypoxia with memory loss was a **permanent complication** suffered by plaintiff as a result of the lung puncture. By definition, **permanent complications** are damages which will be suffered in the future. Mrs. Eichelberger will forever be stricken with memory loss. Eichelberger v. Barnes Hosp., 655 S.W.2d 699, 707 (Mo.Ct.App.1983).

compression (kom-presh′un) [L. *compressio* from *comprimere* to squeeze together] the act of pressing together; an action exerted upon a body by an external force which tends to diminish its volume and augment its density.

compression, nerve

. . . he concludes with the opinion that plaintiff is suffering from a **nerve compression** of the L3–4 on the left side, consistent with his complaints of numbness and pain in the left leg. Jackson v. Maloney Trucking & Storage, Inc., 424 So.2d 1037–9 (Ct.App.La.1982).

compression, nerve root See *decompression, nerve.*

compression, spinal a condition in which pressure is exerted on the spinal cord, as by a tumor, spinal fracture, etc.; its manifestations, which vary with location and degree of pressure, may include pain, paresthesias, and sensory and motor disturbances. See also *neuritis*.

Dr. White testified as a witness for Stark. He stated that in his opinion Stark's pain was caused by **nerve root compression** resulting from scar tissue which had formed in and about the spinal canal after the accident. Dr. White testified that such a condition could not be remedied by surgery, that Stark was his patient, and that he had advised Stark not to submit to any further surgery of the back. Stark v. Shell Oil Co., 450 F.2d 994, 997 (5th Cir. 1971).

When Dr. Powell first saw Mrs. Fritsche on September 12, she told him she was unable to do any work and had cramps in the neck and headaches; she had occasionally dragged her left foot and exhibited other neurological symptoms on her left side. He diagnosed her condition as ''a neuritis or . . . **compression of the cord**, following post cervical laminectomy, . . . a residual type of disease.'' Fritsche v. Westinghouse Electric Corp., 261 A.2d 657, 660 (N.J.1970).

compression of the cord See *compression, spinal.*

compression type bandage See *bandage, compression.*

conception (kon-sep'shun) [L. *conceptio*] the onset of pregnancy, marked by implantation of the blastocyst; the formation of a visable zygote. See also *embryo* (Renslow case); and *life, intrauterine* (Abele case).

conception, wrongful See *pregnancy, wrongful.*

To be distinguished from the cases before us are those in which recovery is sought for what may perhaps be most appropriately labeled ''**wrongful conception**'', wherein parents, one of whom has undergone an unsuccessful surgical birth control procedure, have sought damages for the birth of an unplanned child. There, damages have not been sought on behalf of the child—a healthy and normal infant—but by the parents for expenses attributable to the birth, including the pecuniary expense of rearing the child. Judicial reaction to the ''**wrongful conception**'' cause of action has been mixed.[5] [[5] (See, e.g., La Point v. Shirley, D.C., 409 F.Supp. 118 [unsuccessful tubal ligation]; Clegg v. Chase, 89 Misc.2d 510, 391 N.Y.S.2d 966 [unsuccessful sterilization]; Coleman v. Garrison, 349 A.2d 8 [Del.] [unsuccessful sterilization]; Christensen v. Thornby, 192 Minn. 123, 255 N.W. 620 [unsuccessful sterilization]; Shaheen v. Knight, 11 Pa.D. & C.2d 41 [unsuccessful sterilization]; Terrell v. Garcia, 496 S.W.2d 124 [Tex.Civ.App.], cert. den. 415 U.S. 927, 94 S.Ct. 1434, 39 L.Ed.2d 484 [unsuccessful tubal ligation] [rejecting ''**wrongful conception**'' cause of action]; contra, e.g., Bishop v. Byrne, D.C., 265 F.Supp. 460 [unsuccessful sterilization]; Custodio v. Bauer, 251 Cal.App.2d 303, 59 Cal.Rptr. 463 [unsuccessful sterilization]; Anonymous v. Hospital, 33 Conn.Sup. 125, 366 A.2d 204 [unsuccessful tubal ligation]; Betancourt v. Gaylor, 136 N.J.Super. 69, 344 A.2d 336 [unsuccessful sterilization]; Bowman v. Davis, 48 Ohio St.2d 41, 356 N.E.2d 496 [unsuccessful tubal ligation]; cf. Troppi v. Scarf, 31 Mich.App. 240, 187 N.W.2d 511 [negligent filling of birth control prescription] [recognizing cause of action for ''**wrongful conception**''].] Becker v. Schwartz, 386 N.E.2d 807, 810–11 (N.Y.1978).

conceptus (kon-sep'tus) [L.] the sum of derivatives of a fertilized ovum at any stage of development from fertilization until birth, including extraembryonic membranes as well as the embryo or fetus.

concretism (kon-krēt'izm) thinking and behaving at simple and concrete (as contrasted with abstract) levels which are related to sensation.

In analytical psychology **concretism** is defined as ''a definite peculiarity of thought and feeling which represents the antithesis of abstraction. The actual meaning of concrete is 'grown together.' A concretely-thought concept is one that has grown together or coalesced with other concepts. Such a concept is not abstract, not isolated, and independently thought, but always impure and related. It is not a differentiated concept, but is still embedded in the sense-conveyed material of perception. **Concretistic** thinking moves among exclusively concrete concepts and views; it is constantly related to sensation.'' (Jung, C.G. Psychological Types, tr. by Baynes, H. G., Harcourt, Brace, New York and London, 1923). U.S. v. Currens, 290 F.2d 751, 755 (3d Cir. 1961).

concussion (kon-kush'un) [L. *concussio*] a violent jar or shock, or the condition which results from such an injury. See also *accommodation*; and *syndrome, postconcussion.*

concussion, cerebral See *concussion of the brain.*

concussion of the brain loss of consciousness as the result of a blow to the head. In *mild* concussion there is transient loss of consciousness with possible impairment of the higher mental functions, such as retrograde amnesia and emotional lability. In *severe* concussion there is prolonged unconsciousness with impairment of the functions of the brain stem, such as transient loss of respiratory reflex, vasomotor activity, and dilatation of the pupils. Concussion is sometimes differentiated from contusion in that in the former the injury is functional, whereas in the latter it is organic.

There are three basic methods for diagnosing **concussion**: (1) direct observation, (2) reports of reliable witnesses; (3) close interview of the patient to uncover memory gaps at the time of the accident (Dr. Derby, 372). . . .

In order to permit a diagnosis of **concussion**, it is necessary to have a loss of consciousness (Derby, 404, 407). A basic symptom in **concussion** is loss of consciousness (plaintiff's witness, Dr. Henry Wigderson, 194). A clear memory of all of the events surrounding an accident rules out **concussion** (Wigderson, 196, 202). Yarrow v. U.S., 309 F.Supp. 922, 925 (S.D. N.Y.1970).

Her doctor diagnosed her head injury as a cerebral **concussion** with ''severe injury to the brain or its appendages.'' By June of 1969 the doctor found plaintiff practically asymptomatic and her mother testified that by April plaintiff had no complaints and the mother noticed nothing unusual or abnormal thereafter. . . .

. . . Additionally, present here are headaches, impairment of balance, increased intracranial pressure and edema of the brain. Although the doctor was unable to tell how much scarring of brain tissue had occurred in plaintiff, we think a reasonable reading of his testimony indicates that some had occurred and this scarring would produce fibrous tissue not regenerated brain cells. Stimage v. Union Electric Co., 465 S.W.2d 23, 27–28 (St.Louis Ct.App.Mo.1971).

Other Authorities: Vallot v. Camco, Inc., 396 So.2d 980, 985 (Ct.App.La.1981); Buccery v. General Motors Corp., 132 Cal. Rptr. 605, 608 (Ct.App.1976).

concussion of the spinal cord transient spinal cord dysfunction due to mechanical injury.

''In the absence of pathological changes in any of the viscera and due to the fact that an immediate violent reaction which began at the moment of manipulation and was continuous to the time of death, I would conclude that the cause of death was **spinal concussion**. This is substantiated by the finding of hemorrhage into the pia.'' . . .

. . . He testified that the jerking of the head and neck of the deceased ''could'' have caused the rupture of the coverings of the spinal cord (meninges) and her consequent death. York v. Daniels, 259 S.W.2d 109, 114 (Springfield Ct.App.Mo.1953).

conditioning, Pavlovian See *method, Pavlov's.*

conditioning (kon-dish'un-ing) learning in which a response is elicited by a neutral stimulus which previously has been repeatedly presented in conjunction with the stimulus that originally elicited the response. Called also *classical* or *respondent c.*

conduction (kon-duk'shun) [L. *conductio*] the transfer of sound waves, heat, nervous impulses, or electricity. See also under *system.*

conduction, air the conduction of sound to the inner ear through the auditory canal and middle ear to the inner ear.

conduction deafness See *hearing loss.*

conductivity (kon"duk-tiv'i-te) the capacity of a body to conduct a current; when expressed in figures conductivity is the reciprocal of resistance. Gold, silver, and copper are good conductors.

conduit (kon'doo-it) a channel for the passage of fluids.

conduit, ileal the surgical anastomsis of the ureters to one end of a detached segment of ileum, the other end being used to form a stoma on the abdominal wall.

conduit, urethroileo See *ileostomy* (Rodriguez case).

condylar fracture See *fracture, condylar.*

condyle (kon'dil) [L. *condylus;* Gr. *kondylos* knuckle] a rounded projection on a bone. See also *bite, open* (Campbell case); and *condylus.*

The jaw bone is called the mandible; the ball at the upper extremity of the mandible, which fits into the socket in the skull is called the **condyle**. Rosario v. New York City Health & Hospitals, 450 N.Y.S.2d 805–6 (1st Dep't 1982).

condyle, lateral femoral See *condylus lateralis femoris.*

condyle, medial of tibia See *condylus, medialis tibiae.*

condylectomy (kon"dil-ek'to-me) [*condyle* + Gr. *ektomē* excision] excision of a condyle.

But on his own office record, Oliva made a notation on October 16 that if her condition did not improve he ''will resort to a bilateral **condylectomy**.'' . . . .

''. . . Through a curved incision in the right temporal, the condyle was exposed and the condyle was removed in routine manner. Following adequate repair, the capsule was closed, and routine plastic closure carried out utilizing 4–0 plain and 6–0 nylon. Sterile dressing was applied. The patient tolerated the procedure well and was sent to the recovery room in good condition. This was done bilaterally.'' (App. at 248.) . . .

. . . Sammarco testified that he had never heard of doing a **condylectomy** on a normally functioning joint. Campbell v. Oliva, 424 F.2d 1244, 1246–7 (6th Cir. 1970).

condylus (kon'di-lus), pl. *con'dyli* [L.; Gr. *kondylos* knuckle] [NA] condyle: a rounded projection on a bone, usually for articulation with another.

condylus lateralis femoris [NA], lateral condyle of femur: the lateral of the two surfaces at the distal end of the femur that articulate with the superior surfaces of the head of the tibia; called also *external* or *fibular condyle of femur.*

The x-rays were taken that day and the plaintiff was told they revealed a small defect in the **lateral femoral condyle** of the knee. Arrendale v. U.S., 469 F.Supp. 883, 885 (N.D.Tex. 1979).

condylus medialis tibiae [NA], medial condyle of tibia: the medial articular eminence on the proximal end of the tibia; called also *internal condyle of tibia.*

The physician's report, prepared by Dr. Lewis, indicated that Voegeli had suffered a fracture of the **medial condyle of the right tibia**. Voegeli v. Lewis, 568 F.2d 89, 91 (8th Cir. 1977).

confabulation (kon"fab-u-la'shun) the recitation of imaginary experiences to fill gaps in the memory, especially seen in organic psychoses, such as Korsakoff's psychosis; called also *fabrication.*

Confabulation is defined as: ''In psychiatry, [as] the act of replacing memory loss by phantasy or by reality that is not true for the occasion. The term implies also lack of insight, in the sense that the subject fully believes his answers to be correct. **Confabulation** is not uncommon in organic brain diseases in which intellectual impairment is a prominent feature. For example, the patient with a Korsakoff syndrome often fills in the memory gaps with incorrect details. A patient, bedridden in the hospital for months, said that he had just returned from a European journey and gave many details of the trip, believing thoroughly in his account. U.S. v. Currens, 290 F.2d 751, 754 (3d Cir. 1961).

configuration (kon-fig"u-ra'shun) 1. the general form of a body. 2. in gestalt psychology, an organized whole with interdependent parts so that the whole is more than the sum of its parts. See also *stereochemistry.*

congenital (kon-jen'i-tal) [L. *congenitus* born together] existing at, and usually before, birth; referring to conditions that are present at birth, regardless of their causation. Cf. *hereditary.*

According to defendant's expert witness Dr. Marano (whose particular expertise was in the field of cystic fibrosis) a sickness achieves the characteristic of being ''inherited'' by virtue of its being ''transmitted through the genes of the parents.'' Asked to define ''**congenital disease**'' (the inquiry was made of no other witness) he termed it one which is ''present at birth.'' That distinguishing feature of cystic fibrosis is important in light of plaintiff's attorney's attempt to argue from the clearly imperfect analogy to muscular dystrophy and diabetes, both of which are inherited but neither of which is **congenital** and thus not ''contracted and commencing'' at birth. Kissil v. Beneficial National Life Ins. Co., 319 A.2d 67, 71 (N.J.1974).

Other Authorities: York v. Daniels, 259 S.W.2d 109, 111 (Springfield Ct.App.Mo.1953).

congestive heart disease See *disease, congestive heart.*

conization (kon″ĭ-za′shun) the removal of a cone of tissue, as in partial excision of the cervix uteri.

... performed a **conization** of the cervix on her. The sample of tissue so obtained was found to indicate that she was suffering from cancer of the cervix. Morgan v. Schlanger, 374 F.2d 235, 237 (4th Cir. 1967).

conization, cold that done with a cold knife, as opposed to electrocautery, to better preserve the histologic elements. Cited in Steele v. St. Paul Fire & Marine Ins. Co., 371 So. 2d 843, 845–6 (Ct.App.La.1979).

conjunctiva (kon″junk-tívah), pl. *conjunctívae* [L.] the delicate membrane that lines the eyelids (*palpebral conjunctiva*) and covers the exposed surface of the sclera (*bulbar* or *ocular conjunctiva*); called also *tunica conjunctiva* [NA].

... he considered that an inverted **conjunctiva**, noted in appellant's record, should have put Dr. Saydjari on notice that the eye needed special attention. Bevevino v. Saydjari, 574 F.2d 676, 680–1 (2d Cir. 1978).

Dr. Wallace, an ophthalmologist who testified by deposition, examined appellee with a slit lamp and an ophthalmoscope, and found no foreign bodies in either of her eyes or in the **conjunctiva** (the skin of the inside of the eyelids), and no marks on the cornea to indicate presence of foreign objects....

... Dr. Curry saw her some 64 times up to June 19, 1965, during which time he found marked photophobia, lacrimation, and removed additional microscopic foreign bodies embedded in the palpebral and orbital **conjunctiva** of the upper and lower lids of both eyes. Maryland Casualty Co. v. Davis, 464 S.W.2d 433, 436 (Ct.Civ.App.Tex.1971).

conjunctivitis (kon-junk″tĭ-vi′tis) inflammation of the conjunctiva, generally consisting of conjunctival hyperemia associated with a discharge.

... an inflammatory condition of the eye called **conjunctivitis**. Ortiz v. Allergan Pharmaceuticals, 489 S.W.2d 135, 137 (Ct. Civ.App.Tex.1972).

Doctor Yap, a physician of unspecified qualifications, who diagnosed the injury as "acute traumatic **conjunctivitis**" (injury to outer coating of eye resulting from a blow), washed out the eye with a boric acid wash, and applied yellow oxide and an eye pad. DeZon v. American President Lines, Ltd., 318 U.S. 660, 661–2, 63 S.Ct. 814, 87 L.Ed. 1065 (1943).

Dr. Klein, an ophthalmologist, examined plaintiff on September 4, 1979, and diagnosed her as having chronic **conjunctivitis** of both eyes. This diagnosis was apparently based on a finding that both conjunctivas were "infected with dilated blood vessels." He found a 10% permanent partial total disability. Franklin v. Heckler, 598 F.Supp. 784, 786 (D.N.J.1984).

Janice was suffering from **conjunctivitis**, an inflammation of the mucous membrane which lines the eyelids and the front portion of the eyeball. On that occasion, the doctor prescribed Neodecadron ointment, to be applied topically to the inside of the eyelid. Aetna Casualty & Surety Co. of Illinois v. The Medical Protective Co. of Fort Wayne, Ind., Slip Opinion (No. 82 C 1741 U.S.D.C.N.D.Ill.1983).

Other Authorities: Bates v. U.S., Slip Opinion (No. 245–77 U.S. Ct. of Claims, 1980).

consent, informed See *surgery, ghost* (Perna case).

The root premise is the concept, fundamental in American jurisprudence, that "[e]very human being of adult years and sound mind has a right to determine what shall be done with his own body...." True consent to what happens to one's self is the informed exercise of a choice, and that entails an opportunity to evaluate knowledgeably the options available and the risks attendant upon each. The average patient has little or no understanding of the medical arts, and ordinarily has only his physician to whom he can look for enlightenment with which to reach an intelligent decision. From these almost axiomatic considerations springs the need, and in turn the requirement, of a reasonable divulgence by physician to patient to make such a decision possible....

... A physician is under a duty to treat his patient skillfully but proficiency in diagnosis and therapy is not the full measure of his responsibility. The cases demonstrate that the physician is under an obligation to communicate specific information to the patient when the exigencies of reasonable care call for it. Due care may require a physician perceiving symptoms of bodily abnormality to alert the patient to the condition. It may call upon the physician confronting an ailment which does not respond to his ministrations to inform the patient thereof. It may command the physician to instruct the patient as to any limitations to be presently observed for his own welfare, and as to any precautionary therapy he should seek in the future. It may oblige the physician to advise the patient of the need for or desirability of any alternative treatment promising greater benefit than that being pursued. Just as plainly, due care normally demands that the physician warn the patient of any risks to his well-being which contemplated therapy may involve.

The context in which the duty of risk-disclosure arises is invariably the occasion for decision as to whether a particular treatment procedure is to be undertaken. To the physician, whose training enables a self-satisfying evaluation, the answer may seem clear, but it is the prerogative of the patient, not the physician, to determine for himself the direction in which his interests seem to lie. To enable the patient to chart his course understandably, some familiarity with the therapeutic alternatives and their hazards becomes essential....

... A reasonable revelation in these respects is not only a necessity but, as we see it, is as much a matter of the physician's duty. It is a duty to warn of the dangers lurking in the proposed treatment, and that is surely a facet of due care. It is, too, a duty to impart information which the patient has every right to expect. The patient's reliance upon the physician is a trust of the kind which traditionally has exacted obligations beyond those associated with arms-length transactions. His dependence upon the physician for information affecting his well-being, in terms of contemplated treatment, is well-nigh abject. As earlier noted, long before the instant litigation arose, courts had recognized that the physician had the responsibility of satisfying the vital informational needs of the patient. More recently, we ourselves have found "in the fiducial qualities of [the physician-patient] relationship the physician's duty to reveal to the patient that which in his best interests it is important that he should know." We now find, as a part of the physician's overall obligation to the patient, a similar duty of reasonable disclosure of the choices with respect to proposed therapy and the dangers inherently and potentially involved.

This disclosure requirement, on analysis, reflects much more of a change in doctrinal emphasis than a substantive addition to malpractice law. It is well established that the physician must seek and secure his patient's consent before commencing an operation or other course of treatment. It is also clear that the consent, to be efficacious, must be free from imposition upon the patient. It is the settled rule that therapy not authorized by the patient may amount to a tort—a common law battery—by the physician. And it is evident that it is normally impossible to obtain a consent worthy of the name unless the physician first elucidates the options and the perils for the patient's edification. Thus the physician has long borne a duty, on pain of liability for unauthorized treatment, to make adequate disclosure to the patient. The evolution of the obligation to communicate for the patient's benefit as well as the physician's protection has hardly involved an extraordinary restructuring of the law. [[27] Footnotes omitted. This is the most frequently cited case on the subject. Ed.] Canterbury v. Spence, 464 F.2d 772, 780–3 (D.C.Cir.1972).

Other Authorities: Daniels v. U.S., 704 F.2d 587, 591–2 (11th Cir. 1983); Hales v. Pittman, 576 P.2d 493, 500 (Ariz.1978); Keogan v. Holy Family Hosp., 589 P.2d 310, 312 (Ct.App. Wash.1979); Niblack v. U.S., 438 F.Supp. 383, 388 (D.Col. 1977); Logan v. Greenwich Hosp. Ass'n., 465 A.2d 294, 298, 302 (Conn.1983); Crain v. Allison, 443 A.2d 558, 562 (D.C. Ct.App.1982); Henderson v. Milobsky, 595 F.2d 654, 659 (D.C.Cir.1978); Truman v. Thomas, 165 Cal.Rptr. 308, 311–312 (Cal.1980); Morgenroth v. Pacific Medical Center, Inc., 126 Cal.Rptr. 681, 687 (Ct.App.1976); Ritz v. Florida Patient's Compensation Fund, 436 So.2d 987, 991–2 (Dist.Ct.App.Fla. 1983); Ziegert v. South Chicago Community Hospital, 425 N.E.2d 450 (App.Ct.Ill.1981); Wynn v. Scott, 449 F.Supp. 1302, 1316 (N.D.Ill.1978); Casey v. Penn, 360 N.E.2d 93, 101 (App.Ct.Ill.1977); Funke v. Fieldman, 512 P.2d 539, 548, 550 (Kan.1973); Karl J. Pizzalotto, M.D., Ltd. v. Wilson, 437 So.2d 859, 862–4 (La.1983); La Caze v. Collier, 434 So.2d 1039, 1040–1 (La.1983); Harwell v. Pittman, 428 So.2d 1049, 1053–4 (Ct.App.La.1983); Williams v. Lallie Kemp Charity Hosp., 428 So.2d 1000, 1006–7 (Ct.App.La.1983); Steinbach v. Barfield, 428 So.2d 915, 921 (Ct.App.La.1983); Wiley v. Karam, 421 So.2d 294, 297 (Ct.App.La.1982); Sard v. Hardy, 379 A.2d 1014, 1019–20 (Ct.App.Md.1977); Schroeder v. Lawrence, 359 N.E.2d 1301, 1303 (Sup.Jud.Ct.Mass.1977); Cornfeldt v. Tongen, 262 N.W.2d 684 (Minn.1977); Walstad v. University of Minnesota Hospitals, 442 F.2d 634, 640 (8th Cir. 1971); Cress v. Mayer, 626 S.W.2d 430, 434, 436–7 (Mo.Ct.App.1981); Perna v. Pirozzi, 457 A.2d 431, 438, 440 (N.J.1983); Perna v. Pirozzi, 442 A.2d 1016, 1019–20 (Super. Ct.N.J.1982); P. v. Portadin, 432 A.2d 556, 560 (Super.Ct. N.J.1981); Lipsius v. White, 458 N.Y.S.2d 928, 934–5 (2d Dep't 1983); Ogden v. Bhatti, 460 N.Y.S.2d 166, 167 (3d Dep't 1983); Burton v. Brooklyn Doctors Hosp., 452 N.Y.S.2d 875, 881 (1st Dep't 1982); Davis v. Caldwell, 429 N.E.2d 741, 745 (N.Y.1981); Wilkinson v. Vesey, 295 A.2d 676, 685 (R.I.1975); Fiorentino v. Wenger, 227 N.E.2d 296 (N.Y.1967); Dixon v. Peters, 306 S.E.2d 477, 479 (Ct.App.N.Car.1983); Simons v. Georgiade, 286 S.E.2d 596, 604 (Ct.App.N.Car. 1982); Winkjer v. Herr, 277 N.W.2d 579, 587 (N.Dak.1979); Wasem v. Luskowski, 274 N.W.2d 219, 226 (N.Dak.1979); Siegel v. Mt. Sinai Hospital of Cleveland, 403 N.E.2d 202, 208–9 (Ct.App.Ohio 1978); Lambert v. Park, 597 F.2d 236,

238–9 (10th Cir. 1979); Salis v. U.S., 522 F.Supp. 989, 997–8 (M.D.Pa.1981); DeFulvio v. Holst, 414 A.2d 1087, 1089 (Super.Ct.Pa.1979); Sauro v. Shea, 390 A.2d 259, 261–3 (Super.Ct.Pa.1978); Jeffries v. McCague, 363 A.2d 1167, 1171–2 (Super.Ct.Pa.1976); Barshady v. Schlosser, 313 A.2d 296, 299 (Super.Ct.Pa.1973); Cooper v. Roberts, 286 A.2d 647, 649–50 (Super.Ct.Pa.1971); Dunham v. Wright, 423 F.2d 940, 943–4 (3d Cir. 1970); Kelly v. Gershkoff, 312 A.2d 211, 214 (R.I.1973); Wilkinson v. Vesey, 295 A.2d 676, 690 (R.I.1972); Campbell v. Oliva, 424 F.2d 1244, 1250–1 (6th Cir. 1970); Ball v. Mallinkrodt Chemical Works, 381 S.W.2d 563, 567–8 (Ct.App.Tenn.1964); Menefee v. Guehring, 665 S.W.2d 811 (Ct.App.Tex.1983); Nevauex v. Park Place Hosp., Inc., 656 S.W.2d 923 (Ct.App.Tex.1983); Peterson v. Shields, 652 S.W.2d 929, 930–1 (Tex.1983); Johnson v. Whitehurst, 652 S.W.2d 441, 444–5, 448 (Ct.App.Tex.1983); Roark v. Aven, 633 S.W.2d 804, 808–9 (Tex.1982); Sherrill v. McBride, 603 S.W.2d 365, 367 (Ct.Civ.App.Tex.1980); Hood v. Phillips, 554 S.W.2d 160 (Tex.1977); Karp v. Cooley, 493 F.2d 408, 419–20 (5th Cir. 1974); Dessi v. U.S., 489 F.Supp. 722, 727 (E.D.Va.1980); Pugsley v. Privette, 263 S.E.2d 69, 72 (Va. 1980); Bly v. Rhoads, 222 S.E.2d 783, 786–7 (Va.1976); Smith v. Shannon, 666 P.2d 351 (Wash.1983); Gates v. Jensen, 595 P.2d 919, 922–3 (Wash.1979); ZeBarth v. Swedish Hospital Medical Center, 499 P.2d 1, 11–12 (Wash.1972); Cross v. Trapp, 294 S.E.2d 446, 448, 450–3, 455 (Sup.Ct.App.W.Va. 1982); Simone v. Sabo, 231 P.2d 19, 21 (Calif.1951); Cowman v. Hornaday, 329 N.W.2d 422, 425–6 (Iowa 1983); Scott v. Bradford, 606 P.2d 554, 559 (Okla.1979); Negaard v. Estate of Feda, 446 P.2d 436, 441 (Mont.1968); Buckner v. Allergan Pharmaceuticals, 400 So.2d 820, 824 (Dist.Ct.App. Fla.1981).

consortium

A cause of action for damages for loss of "**consortium**" is for loss of conjugal fellowship and sexual relations. This cause of action is now recognized in California by virtue of plaintiff Mary Anne's prior appeal from a judgment of dismissal of her cause of action following the sustaining of general demurrers without leave to amend. (Rodriguez v. Bethlehem Steel Corp. (1974) 12 Cal.3d 382, 115 Cal.Rptr. 765, 525 P.2d 669.) Rodriguez v. McDonnell Douglas Corp., 151 Cal.Rptr. 399, 402 (Ct.App.Cal.1979).

constant (kon'stant) [L. *constans* standing together] not failing; remaining unaltered.

constant, Michaelis a constant representing the substrate concentration at which the velocity of an enzyme reaction is half the maximal velocity; symbol K_m.

The affinity of an enzyme for any given "substrate"—i.e., material to be chemically converted—may be represented by a number called the "**Michaelis constant**;" the greater the affinity of the enzyme for any given substrate, the smaller is its **Michaelis constant** for that substrate (T. 366–368). CPC International, Inc. v. Standard Brands Inc., 385 F.Supp. 1057, 1063 (D.Del.1974).

constipation (kon"stĭ-pa'shun) [L. *constipatio* a crowding together] infrequent or difficult evacuation of the feces.

Dr. Collins testified: "**Constipation**, however, is a very, very common finding after surgery, and probably fifty percent of patients do not have bowel movement on their own by the time they leave the hospital." Smithers v. Collins, 278 S.E.2d 286–7 (Ct.App.N.Car.1981).

constitution (kon″stĭ-tu'shun) [L. *constitutio*] the make-up or functional habit of the body, determined by the genetic, biochemical, and physiologic endowment of the individual, and modified in great measure by environmental factors. Cf. *diathesis* and *type*.

contaminant (kon-tam′ĭ-nant) something that causes contamination.

The National Academy of Sciences has submitted to Congress a report of its study of **contaminants** in drinking water,[30] undertaken pursuant to section 1412(e) of the Act.[31] [[30] Drinking Water and Health, Report to Congress of Recommendations of the National Academy of Sciences (June 20, 1977), summarized in 42 F.R. 35764 (July 11, 1977). The report lists 20 organic substances found in drinking water that are known to have, or are suspected of having, carcinogenic properties in man or animals. 42 F.R. at 35776, Table 1. Of these, only two (Lindane and Endrin) are controlled under the interim regulations. [31] 42 U.S.C. § 300g–1(e).] Environmental Defense Fund, Inc. v. Costle, 578 F.2d 337, 345–6 (D.C.Cir.1978).

contamination (kon-tam″ĭ-na′shun) [L. *contaminatio,* from *con* together + *tangere* to touch] the soiling or making inferior by contact or mixture as by the introduction of organisms in a wound, or sewage in a stream.

"Contamination" connotes a condition of impurity resulting from mixture or contact with a foreign substance. In its charge, the trial court defined the term as meaning the ". . . state of being **contaminated**; an impurity; that which **contaminates**; to make inferior or impure by mixture; an impairment of purity; loss of purity resulting from mixture or contact." This definition is consistent with common understanding, see Webster's New International Dictionary, **contamination, contaminate**, which is the proper criterion for construing words in an insurance policy. Hall v. Great National Lloyds, 154 Tex. 200, 275 S.W.2d 88; Continental Casualty Co. v. Warren, 152 Tex. 164, 254 S.W.2d 762. [Footnote omitted.] American Casualty Co. of Reading, Pa. v. Myrick, 304 F.2d 179, 183 (5th Cir. 1962).

contraception (kon″trah-sep′shun) the prevention of conception or impregnation.

contraceptive (kon″trah-sep′tiv) an agent that diminishes the likelihood of or prevents conception.

contraceptive, oral a hormonal compound taken orally in order to block ovulation and prevent the occurrence of pregnancy. See also *Enovid* (Lawson case); *syndrome, stroke* (Klink case); and *thrombophlebitis* (Witherell case, e.g.).

By 1970 studies had determined not only significant changes in the clotting factors, but also the fact that **oral contraceptives** induce blood clots in the circulating blood system. Dr. Bachmann stated, "It is my firm opinion that Enovid and other [birth control] pills do contribute to increased coagulation, that there is a positive relationship between clotting and the usage of the pill." Mahr v. G. D. Searle & Co., 390 N.E.2d 1214, 1226 (App.Ct.Ill.1979).

contract (kon-tract′) [L. *contractus,* from *contrahere* to draw together] 1. to shorten, or reduce in size, as a muscle. See also *contraction*. 2. to acquire or incur.

The language of the statute as amended in 1949 remains the same today. At a glance, the distinction between "**contracted**" and "last exposure" does not appear significant. But in Yaeger v. Delano Granite Works [52 N.W.2d 116 (1952)], which was decided in accord with the 1943 statute because the 1949 amendment was approved after the employee's disability, this court recognized the surfacing malignancy of silicosis and ruled that this disease is "**contracted**" when the clinical symptoms appear and not when silica is deposited in the lungs, and that **contracting** is a process which does not cease until physical impairment manifests itself. In essence, the employee urges that this same rationale in construing "**contracted**" should be applied to the present statute so that the 3-year limitation would not begin to run against him until the silicosis was manifested at his examination in November 1968 as opposed to his date of last exposure to silica dust in March 1964. . . .

. . . Nevertheless, to now hold that the "date of . . . last exposure" is synonymous with "**contracted**" would be to blatantly tamper with statutory language and render the 1949 amendment a nullity. . . .

. . . See, Fink v. Cold Spring Granite Co., 262 Minn. 393, 115 N.W.2d 22 (1962); Kress v. Minneapolis-Moline Co., 258 Minn. 1, 102 N.W.2d 497 (1960) (when disability caused by silicosis takes place); Kalmes v. Kahler Corp., 258 Minn. 105, 103 N.W.2d 203 (1960) (contraction of tuberculosis); Anderson v. City of Minneapolis, 258 Minn. 221, 225, note 4, 103 N.W.2d 397, 400 (1960) (presumption of a fireman's **contracting** coronary sclerosis 12 months before the date of disablement. Graber v. Peter Lametti Construction Co., 197 N.W.2d 443, 446–7 (Minn.1972).

We review the evidence within the framework of the trial court's instruction to the jury:

. . . [A] sickness or disease is deemed to have its inception [i.e., **contracted**] at the time that it first manifested itself or became active, or became reasonably apparent, or when sufficient symptoms existed to allow a reasonably accurate diagnosis of the sickness or disease. Keller v. Orion Ins. Co., 422 F.2d 1152–3 (8th Cir. 1970).

contraction (kon-trak′shun) [L. *contractus* drawn together] a shortening or reduction in size; in connection with muscles contraction implies shortening and/or development of tension.

Q. Now, do you have an opinion as to whether the patient was trying to **contract** when you asked her to? A. Well, yes. I concluded that she was not trying, because I had taken a neurological history and performed a neurological examination and looked for any diseases, neurological diseases, as we always do, and I found nothing to indicate that there were other reasons that she couldn't **contract** when I asked her, that is, no brain damage or spinal cord lesions, et cetera.

Q. So you concluded, when you asked her to **contract**, the **contraction** didn't come because she wasn't trying; is that correct? A. Yes. Sanden v. Mayo Clinic, 495 F.2d 221, 224 (8th Cir. 1974).

contraction, clonic contraction of a muscle alternating with periods of relaxation.

contraction, tetanic sustained contraction of a muscle without intervals of relaxation; called also *tonic c.* Symbol ADTe.

contraction, tonic See *contraction, tetanic*.

contraction, tonic-clonic

... after his wife, noticing that he was perspiring heavily and shivering, was unable to wake him. Appellant remained in the hospital for five days. The examining neurologist described appellant as having a **tonic-clonic contraction**. The treating physician wrote in appellant's discharge summary that the patient had suffered a "syncopal episode of excessive muscle contractions; amnesia; stridulous breathing; etiology undetermined." Beins v. U.S., 695 F.2d 591, 595 (D.C.Cir.1982).

contracture (kon-trak′tūr) [L. *contractura*] a condition of fixed high resistance to passive stretch of a muscle, resulting from fibrosis of the tissues supporting the muscles or the joints, or from disorders of the muscle fibers.

Surgery performed by defendant was to correct a **contracture** of Mr. Smith's left hand caused by scars from a severe childhood burn. Plaintiffs' contention was that after the operation the condition of the hand was worse than before. Smith v. Mogelvang, 432 So.2d 119–20 (Dist.Ct. of App.Fla.1983).

contracture, flexion

Plaintiff also has no use of his left hand as a result of **flexion contractures** in the palmar muscles associated with his syringomyelia. Kernall v. U.S., 558 F.Supp. 280, 285 (E.D.N.Y.1982).

Both his knees developed **flexion contractures** (lack of extension) which defendant described as "fixed flexion deformit[ies] of the knee[s] precluding or obviating full extension". According to plaintiff his "knee would go all the way back, but it wouldn't go forward all the way". Monahan v. Weichert, 442 N.Y.S.2d 295–6 (4th Dep't 1981).

Another obstacle to fitting the plaintiff with a prosthesis was the **flexion contracture** he suffered, a condition in which the hip is drawn upwards towards the abdomen. Raines v. New York Railroad Co., 283 N.E.2d 230, 238 (Ill.1972).

contracture, Volkmann's a contraction of the fingers and sometimes of the wrist, with loss of power, developing rapidly after a severe injury in the region of the elbow joint or improper use of a tourniquet. A similar phenomenon may develop in the distal extremity and involve the foot when similar vascular damage is sustained to the muscles of the leg; called also *ischemic muscular atrophy* and *Volkmann's syndrome.*

The negligence alleged in the amended complaint was that the doctor (a) "pre-operatively" failed to obtain Mr. Smith's properly informed consent prior to surgery; (b) "pre-operatively" recommended unnecessary and unreasonable surgery; (c) "post-operatively" failed to diagnose, care for and treat a condition called **Volkmann's ischemic contracture** that allegedly caused further injury to the hand; and (d) "post-operatively" allowed that condition to occur. Smith v. Mogelvang, 432 So.2d 119–20 (Dist.Ct. of App.Fla.1983).

We conclude as regards **Volkmann's ischemic contracture syndrome** the standard of care is the same for both an orthopedic surgeon and one further skilled in hand surgery. It is true the hand surgeon sees more cases of disability resulting from this insidious vascular condition than does a regular orthopedic surgeon, but this "after the fact" experience does not qualify the hand surgeon to more readily recognize the symptoms and make an accurate diagnosis. It is the regular orthopedic surgeon who is found at the threshold of impending **Volkmann's ischemic contracture**. This extremely rare condition affords neither medical discipline the opportunity to gain much experience in diagnosis. As noted by the trial judge, many orthopedic surgeons will not see a single case of **Volkmann's** during their entire medical career. Moore v. St. Paul Fire and Marine Ins. Co., 395 So.2d 838–9 (Ct.App.La. 1981).

In that case [Atkins v. Humes, 110 So.2d 663 (Fla.1959)] we dealt with a situation where a physician applied a cast to a child's arm so tightly that the child's hand became swollen, cold, and discolored. Although notified of these conditions by the child's parents, the physician failed to take any action to relieve the pressure and the child contracted **Volkmann's contracture.** Sims v. Helms, 345 So.2d 721, 723 (Fla.1977).

Other Authorities: Atkins v. Humes, 110 So.2d 663–4, 667–8 (Fla.1959).

contraindication (kon″trah-in″dĭ-ka′shun) any condition, especially any condition of disease, which renders some particular line of treatment improper or undesirable.

In contrast, [to a warning] a "**contraindication**" refers to a circumstance under which the drug must never be given. It is absolute and admits of no exceptions. Baker v. St. Agnes Hospital, 421 N.Y.S.2d 81, 83 (2d Dep't 1979).

contrecoup (kon-tr-koo′) [Fr. "counterblow"] injury resulting from a blow on another site, such as a fracture of the skull caused by a blow on the opposite side.

His examination also revealed a **contrecoup** injury to the brain which could have been caused by a blow to the head. Such an injury occurs when a blow to one side of the head causes the brain to strike the side of the skull directly opposite from the original point of external impact. The injury to the left side of decedent's brain could have been caused by an injury to the head or by the surgery which decedent had undergone prior to his death. People v. Drake, 236 N.W.2d 537, 540 (Ct.App. Mich.1975).

control (kon-trōl′) [Fr. *contrôle* a register] 1. the governing or limitation of certain objects or events. 2. a standard against which experimental observations may be evaluated, as a procedure identical in all respects to the experimental procedure except for absence of the one factor that is being studied.

By the regulations, a study must have some kind of **controls** if it is to constitute more than merely corroborative support for a claim of effectiveness. 21 C.F.R. § 130.12(a)(5)(ii)(c). . . .

... This study is not an adequate and well-controlled study, even though it included six patients who were given saline placebos to which they failed to respond, since, among other reasons, there was no method of selecting patients utilized to insure that subjects were suitable for purposes of the study [21

C.F.R. § 130.12(a)(5)(ii)(a)(2)(i)], subjects were not assigned in such a way as to minimize bias [21 C.F.R. § 130.12(a)(5)(ii)(a)(2)(ii)], and comparability of pertinent variables in test and control groups was not assured [21 C.F.R. § 130.12(a)(5)(ii)(a)(2)(iii)]. . . .

Furthermore, there was neither an explanation of the method of observation and recording of results [21 C.F.R. § 130.12(a)(5)(ii)(a)(3)], nor a comparision of the results of treatment or diagnosis with a **control** in such a fashion as to permit a quantitative evaluation [21 C.F.R. § 130.12(a)(5)(ii)(a)(4)]. Finally, there was no summary of the methods of analysis and evaluation of data derived from the study, including statistical methods [21 C.F.R. § 130.12(a)(5)(ii)(a)(5)]. Final Order, **supra** note 5, 37 Fed.Reg. at 17228–17229. . . .

There is no mention of **controls** in the Xander, Sforzolini and Lehrer studies. Smith uses the word ''**control**,'' but he means by it only that Protamide was tested against two diseases, not that Protamide was tested against an appropriate control substance as required by regulation. 21 C.F.R. § 130.12(a)(5)(ii)(a)(4). Cooper Laboratories, Inc. v. Commissioner, Fed. F.D.A., 501 F.2d 772, 782 (D.C.Cir.1974).

The 1962 amendments clearly demand that efficacy be shown by **controlled** tests—that is, by studies where some diseased persons receive the drug in question while other diseased persons, otherwise comparable, receive nothing, or a ''placebo,'' or some substance of known effect. Cooper Laboratories, Inc. v. Commissioner, Fed.F.D.A., 501 F.2d 772, 778 (D.C.Cir. 1974).

control, executive

He testified that in his opinion Stewart suffered from a ''control problem,'' or loss of ''**executive control**''—that is, a loss of the governing part of his mind in June, 1969. U.S. v. Stewart, 443 F.2d 1129, 1132 (10th Cir. 1971).

Controlled Substances Act a federal law enacted in 1970 that regulates the prescribing and dispensing of psychoactive drugs, including narcotics, according to five schedules based on their abuse potential, medical acceptance, and ability to produce dependence; it also establishes a regulatory system for the manufacture, storage, and transport of the drugs in each schedule. Drugs covered by this Act include opium and its derivatives, opiates, hallucinogens, depressants, and stimulants. [See U.S.C.A. § 801 et seq.]

contusion (kon-tu'zhun) [L. *contusio,* from *contundere* to bruise] a bruise; an injury of a part without a break in the skin.

Circello complained of pain in the small of his back and under his left shoulder blade. Dr. Philibert on examination found evidence of muscle spasms. Dr. Philibert diagnosed this condition as a **contusion** (tear) of the ligaments of the thoracic and lumbar spine. For treatment, Dr. Philibert injected the areas of the fifth lumbar vertebra, first sacral vertebra, and second through sixth thoracic vertebrae with steroids. At this same time, Dr. Philibert also treated Circello for the pain in his right arm stump. Circello v. Government Employees Ins. Co., 425 So.2d 239, 244 (Ct.App.La.1982).

The doctor gave the following diagnosis regarding the plaintiff's injuries. ''**Contusions** to the posterior aspect of the right shoulder with subcutaneous hemorrhage, a **contusion** to the left arm with subcutaneous hemorrhage approximately four inches below the elbow, and a **contusion** of the lateral aspect of the right knee and also over the right patella.'' Fernandez v. Meyers, 396 So.2d 425 (Ct.App.La.1981).

On the 4th of October we explored the left side of the flank, and it was apparent at the time of approaching the kidney that there was not a large accumulation of blood around the kidney, but in examining the kidney it was apparent that the kidney had suffered a severe **contusion** because on the kidney surface there were numerous lacerations, you might say, or **contusions**, measuring from just surface cracks to those measuring perhaps an eighth of an inch in depth. Wolff v. Coast Engine Products, Inc., 432 P.2d 562, 567 (Wash.1967).

Other Authorities: Zorn v. Aetna Life Ins. Co., 260 F.Supp. 730, 733 (E.D.Tex.1965).

contusion, brain contusion with loss of consciousness as a result of direct trauma to the head, usually associated with fracture of the skull. See also *concussion of the brain.*

The plaintiff suffered severe injuries which left him in a coma for three days and caused bizarre behavior after he woke from the coma. He had no memory of the incident. Although the plaintiff is a diabetic, his neurosurgeon testified that his coma and unusual behavior during recovery were the result of and consistent with a bifrontal **cerebral contusion** with swelling and areas of hemorrhage in the brain caused by an automobile accident rather than a diabetic coma. Vanalstyne v. Whalen, 445 N.E.2d 1073, 1075 (App.Ct.Mass.1983).

conus (ko'nus), pl. *co'ni* [L.; Gr. *kōnos*] a cone; [NA] a general term denoting a structure resembling a cone in shape.

conus medullaris [NA], medullary cone: the cone-shaped lower end of the spinal cord, at the level of the upper lumbar vertebrae; called also *c. terminalis* and *terminal cone of spinal cord.*

During the course of this treatment, a doctor, while attempting to perform a spinal tap, punctured her approximately thirteen times at a vertebral interspace substantially above the accepted situs for performing spinal taps. As a result, Mrs. Barriteau sustained traumatic injury to the **conus medullaris**, in the spinal cord, resulting in paralysis of the lower extremities and bodily function organs. District of Columbia v. Barriteau, 399 A.2d 563, 565 (D.C.Ct.App.1979).

The spinal cord which ends in a bulbous mass (**conus medullaris**) normally ends opposite the first lumbar vertebra . . . .

. . . There was also evidence introduced that 1.8 percent of the population, or one in every fifty-five persons, has a low lying **conus medullaris** which extends down to the L2–3 interspace. Funke v. Fieldman, 512 P.2d 539, 542, 544 (Kan.1973).

convergence (kon-ver'jens) inclination toward a common point. In embryology, the movement of cells from the periphery toward the midline during gastrulation. In physiology, the coordinated movement of the two eyes toward fixation of the same near point. In evolution, development of similar structures or organisms in unrelated taxa.

convergence (eyeball)

She had impaired **convergence** of her eyeballs, that is, could not follow my finger, and the eyeballs would not normally converge on the finger in front of her. Talcott v. Holl, 224 So.2d 420, 423 (Dist.Ct.App.Fla.1969).

conversion (kon-ver'zhun) [L. *con* with + *versio* turning] a freudian term for the process by which emotions become transformed into physical (motor or sensory) manifestations. See also *ambivalence* (Loughran case).

We pause to note that the terms "**conversion** hysteria," "**conversion** overlay" and "traumatic neuroses" are used synonymously with reference to a condition following a physical injury. (Barr v. Builders, Inc., [296 P.2d 1106].) Berger v. Hahner, Foreman & Cale, Inc., 506 P.2d 1175, 1179 (Kan.1973).

His diagnosis was that she had sustained a fairly severe sprain of the neck, and that "this was followed by a **conversion** hysteria or another equivalent term would be traumatic neurosis." When the trial judge asked him to explain this in non-technical terms, the witness replied (Tr. 129–130):

"It's a disturbance of the psyche. It's a problem in which an unstable or inadequate or an emotionally disturbed person who has controlled their problems or their conflicts to the degree that they can get along with society and work suddenly something precipitates a breakdown. In this particular case, trauma, traumatic. And as a result, a picture, a clinical picture, a series of activities or actions develops which is fairly characteristic. It results in an exaggeration of the patient's complaints.

"Now, this is all unknowingly, this is not malingering, this is not willingly. A **conversion**, they transform or transfer the emotional problems that they have had into these physical ailments. In this particular case, continued neck pain, severe headaches, partial paralysis of the left arm or great weakness of the left arm.

"These patients also exhibit a great deal of anxiety, which is a form of fear and apprehension. It's also again in an exaggerated form.

"And as a result you get a picture of a person having physical ailments where actually they are manifestations of an emotional disturbance.

"Notoriously they are difficult to treat, very stubborn and very chronic." Bourne v. Washburn, 441 F.2d 1022, 1024 (D.C.Cir.1971).

"Q. Doctor, in your report that has been submitted to the court, you discuss conflict, and you use the term '**conversion** symptoms'; would you describe to the court what you mean by the **conversion** symptoms as it applies to Miss Loughran?

"A. '**Conversion**' means a change. It is a change from some emotional problem into some physical sign. For example whatever the deep conflict might be, it might manifest itself, say, in blindness or something. There would be a transfer. The problem is converted into the physical. Usually that reduces the level of anxiety. Because once a person has a symptom, he can henceforth worry more about the symptom and not about what it was that is really bothering the individual on a deeper level...." In re Loughran, 276 F.Supp. 393, 410 (C.D.Cal.1967).

conversion, hysterical

I would like to clarify the diagnostic impression of the **hysterical conversion** mechanism by reading verbatim from the diagnostic and statistical manual of mental disorders issued by the American Psychiatric Association. Under Hysterical Neurosis, Conversion Type, it says: In the conversion type the special senses or voluntary nervous system are affected causing such symptoms as blindness, deafness, loss of smell, loss of sense of touch, strange feelings in various parts of the body, paralysis, unsteadiness of gait and various bodily pains and aches.

It says furthermore often the patient shows an inappropriate lack of concern about these symptoms which may actually provide secondary gains by winning him sympathy or relieving him of unpleasant responsibilities. Rund v. Cessna Aircraft Co., 518 P.2d 518, 523 (Kan.1974).

conversion, Mantoux a term denoting the change from a tuberculin-negative to a tuberculin-positive state, as determined by the intracutaneous injection of a solution of tuberculin; the opposite of Mantoux reversion.

conversion neurosis See *reaction, conversion.*

conversion reaction See *reaction, conversion.*

converter, recent See *conversion, Mantoux.*

If an individual produces a positive skin test within a two-year period after having had a negative skin test, he is considered a "**recent converter**".

One suffering from an active case of tuberculosis can cause many persons to become "**recent converters**". Plummer v. U.S., 420 F.Supp. 978, 980 (M.D.Pa.1976).

convulsion (con-vul'shun) [L. *convulsio*, from *convellere* to pull together] a violent involuntary contraction or series of contractions of the voluntary muscles.

At 1:45 A.M. on February 22, 1968, the assigned nurse was checking infant plaintiff's vital signs when he had a grand mal **convulsion** and stopped breathing. Rose v. Hakim, 335 F.Supp. 1221, 1226 (D.D.C.1971).

convulsions, febrile those associated with high fever, occurring in infants and children.

Dr. Root, a board certified pathologist and a pathologist for the San Bernardino County Coroner's office, concluded the cause of the child's death was a "**febrile convulsion**," a convulsion respiratory arrest caused by an elevated temperature; a respiratory failure. "The infant stops breathing and the heart continues to pump for a few minutes until death occurs." Cortex v. Macias, 167 Cal.Rptr. 905, 908 (Ct.App.Cal.1980).

COPD See *disease, chronic obstructive pulmonary.*

copolymer (ko-pol'ĭ-mer) a polymer containing monomers of more than one kind.

The claims cover an elastomeric **copolymer** consisting of at least two alpha-olefins together with an unsaturated bridged-ring diene as a third monomer. [Footnotes omitted.] Hercules, Inc. v. Exxon Corp., 434 F.Supp. 136, 141 (D.Del.1977).

... and the word "**copolymer**" describes the polymer made from a mixture of different monomers.

Many **copolymers** which have a relatively large amount of one monomer, and a minor amount of a second monomer are referred to as homopolymers of the dominant monomer of the mixture. Thus the word "polyethylene" could describe a **co-polymer** consisting primarily of ethylene but with minor amounts of another monomer. International Tel. & Tel. Corp. v. Raychem Corp., 538 F.2d 453, 459 (1st Cir. 1976).

cor (kor), gen. *cor'dis* [L.] [NA] the muscular organ that maintains the circulation of the blood. See also *heart.*

cor pulmonale heart disease due to pulmonary hypertension secondary to disease of the lung, or its blood vessels, with hypertrophy of the right ventricle.

The fatal claim petition alleged that decedent died from carcinoma of the right lung, chronic obstructive pulmonary disease, and **cor pulmonale** as a result of his multiple exposure to coal dust, the coking process, and heat. Crucible Steel v. Workmen's Comp. App. Bd., 425 A.2d 1108, 1110 (Commonwlth. Ct.Pa.1980).

The autopsy in Portland, Oregon showed the cause of death as pulmonary emphysema with **cor pulmonale**, indicating that Turner suffered from a severe chronic lung disease which affected his heart, resulting in heart failure. Maritime Overseas Corp. v. U.S., 433 F.Supp. 419, 421 (N.D.Cal.1977), remanded 608 F.2d 1260 (9th Cir. 1979).

Other Authorities: Poore v. Mathews, 406 F.Supp. 47, 49 (E.D.Tenn.1975); Magruder v. Richardson, 332 F.Supp. 1363, 1368 (E.D.Mo.1971).

coracoclavicular (kor"ah-ko-klah-vik'u-lar) pertaining to the coracoid process and the clavicle. See also *processus coracoideus scapulae.*

coracoid (kor'ah-koid) [Gr. *korakoeidēs* crowlike] the coracoid process (processus coracoideus scapulae [NA]).

Coramine (ko'rah-min) trademark for preparations of nikethamide. See also *nikethamide.*

cord (kord) [L. *chorda;* Gr. *chordē* string] any long, rounded, flexible structure. See also *chorda.*

cord, spinal that part of the central nervous system which is lodged in the vertebral canal; it extends from the foramen magnum, where it is continuous with the medulla oblongata, to the upper part of the lumbar region. It ends between the twelfth thoracic and third lumbar vertebrae, often at or adjacent to the disc between the first and second lumbar vertebrae. It is composed of an inner core of gray substance in which nerve cells predominate, and an outer layer of white substance in which myelinated nerve fibers predominate, and is enclosed in three protective membranes, or meninges, the dura mater, the arachnoid, and the pia mater. Thirty-one spinal nerves originate from the spinal cord: 8 cervical, 12 thoracic, 5 lumbar, 5 sacral, and 1 coccygeal. The spinal cord conducts impulses to and from the brain, and controls many automatic muscular activities (reflexes). Called also *chorda spinalis* and *medulla spinalis* [NA]. See also *decompression of spinal cord* (Warner case).

While such a dislocation is not in itself disabling, it can lead to paralysis if not rectified immediately. Any serious disruption in the spinal column poses the danger of injury to the **spinal cord** that runs down the middle of the column. Damage to the sensitive nerve tissues in the **cord** may result in disability in any or all parts of the body below the neck. Since the **cord** tissue is nonregenerative, any disability is likely to be permanent. Abrasion or extended pressure on the **cord** tissue can have such severe results that good medical practice dictates that whenever there is any significant chance of such an injury, the patient's neck must not be manipulated more than is absolutely necessary, and efforts must be made to remedy, or reduce, the dislocation as quickly as possible. Modave v. Long Island Jewish Medical Center, 501 F.2d 1065, 1069 (2d Cir. 1974).

The **spinal cord** runs the length of the back from the brain to approximately the first lumbar vertebra. . . .

The Anatomical Record, volume 88, published April, 1944, (defendant's exhibit No. 6.), states that termination of the **spinal cord** ranges from the level of the lower third of the twelfth thoracic vertebra to that of the middle third of the third lumbar vertebra. . . .

. . . Dr. Dornette continued to testify in detail about this part of the anatomy, stating in part that,

". . . The **spinal cord** ends at the upper part of the small of our back, normally you would not expect it to end lower than the body of the second lumbar vertebra. The cord tapers down gradually and at the very bottom there is a slight enlargement which is called the conus medullaris and the cauda equina extends from the conus medullaris and exits through the lower lumbosacral coccygeal foramen. . . ."

The fetus has a **spinal cord** which extends the entire length of the spinal column. At birth the body is starting to grow much faster than the spinal cord so that the tip of the spinal cord rises within the spinal column until finally in the adult, it is located somewhere in the region of the body of the second lumbar vertebra. Funke v. Fieldman, 512 P.2d 539, 542–3 (Kan.1973).

Other Authorities: McDonald v. U.S., 555 F.Supp. 935, 949 (M.D.Pa.1983); Warner v. City of Bay St. Louis, 408 F.Supp. 375, 379 (S.D.Miss.1975).

cord, umbilical the flexible structure connecting the umbilicus of the embryo and fetus with the placenta and giving passage to the umbilical arteries and vein. In the newborn it measures about 50 cm. in length. First formed during the fifth embryonic week from the allantoic stalk, it contains the omphalomesentric duct and the allantois. Called also *funiculus umbilicalis* [NA] and *chorda umbilicalis.*

Upon delivery, Dr. Maceluch noted that the **umbilical cord** was wrapped three or four times around the baby's neck; he also found gross meconium covering the baby's body and in the baby's throat. These conditions confirmed Dr. Maceluch's preoperative diagnosis of fetal distress. Haught v. Maceluch, 681 F.2d 291, 295 (5th Cir. 1982).

Hanging or extruding from the mouth of the womb was a nonpulsatile cord-like structure, which I suspected was a fetal **umbilical cord**. This was surgically removed with scissors and sent to the laboratory for pathological examination, and was consequently proven to be a fetal **umbilical cord**. Cooper v. State, 447 S.W.2d 179, 184 (Ct.Crim.App.Tex.1969).

cord, vocal, true a fold of mucous membrane covering the vocalis muscle in the larynx forming the inferior boundary of the ventricle. Called also *plica vocalis* [NA], *vocal fold*, and *Ferrein's c.*

The use of the **vocal chords** is controlled by impulses sent from the brain through the nervous system to the muscles attached to the **vocal chords**. There are two sets of nerves which serve as conduits of the impulse in this relay, the superior laryngeal nerves and the recurrent laryngeal nerves, with one of each affecting the use of each **vocal chord**. The superior laryngeal nerves control the motion of adduction, that is, the movement of the **vocal chords** towards each other. The recurrent laryngeal nerves control the motion of abduction, that is, the movement of the **vocal chords** away from each other. The recurrent laryngeal nerve which controls the movement of the right **vocal chord** now fails to function. Roberts v. Wood, 206 F.Supp. 579, 582 (S.D.Ala.1962).

cordotomy (kor-dot'o-me) interruption of the lateral spinothalamic tract of the spinal cord, usually in the anterolateral quadrant, for relief of intractable pain; it may be done by open surgery or percutaneously by sterotaxic surgery. Also spelled *chordotomy*.

A **cordotomy** is a procedure whereby electrodes are inserted into the spinal column and nerves are selectively burned to prevent pain impulses from reaching the brain. Snyder v. U. S., 717 F.2d 1193–4 (8th Cir. 1983).

corium (ko're-um) [L. "hide"] [NA] the dermis: the layer of the skin deep to the epidermis, consisting of a dense bed of vascular connective tissue; called also *cutis vera* and *true skin*.

cornea (kor'ne-ah) [L. *corneus* horny] [NA] the transparent structure forming the anterior part of the fibrous tunic of the eye. It consists of five layers: (1) the anterior corneal epithelium, continuous with that of the conjunctiva, (2) the anterior limiting layer, (Bowman's membrane), (3) the substantia propria, (4) the posterior limiting layer, (Descemet's membrane), and (5) the endothelium of the anterior chamber, called also *keratoderma*. See also *epithelium*; and *substantia propria corneae*.

Plaintiff suffered a **corneal** burn which resulted in significantly impaired vision for several months. Thomas v. American Cystoscope Makers Inc., 414 F.Supp. 255, 258 (E.D.Pa.1976).

. . . it may be helpful to describe the general characteristics of the human **cornea**. First, the normal **cornea** is parabolic in shape, like the end of an egg, although some non-astigmatic **corneas** may be spherical. This means that the radius of normal curvature gradually lengthens as you reach the periphery of the **cornea** or, put another way, the periphery is flatter than the central **cornea**. In addition, it is necessary for the **cornea** to receive a continuous flow of tears or lacrimal fluid to furnish it oxygen and to dispel the carbon dioxide which is normally exuded by the **cornea**. Butterfield v. Oculus Contact Lens Co., 332 F.Supp. 750, 755 (N.D.Ill.1971).

The **cornea** is a thin, transparent membrane which lies over the colored portion of the eye. McDermott v. Manhattan Eye Ear & Throat Hospital, 228 N.Y.S.2d 143, 146 (1st Dep't 1962), judgment modified 203 N.E.2d 469 (N.Y.1964).

corneal See *cornea*.

corneal erosion See *erosion, corneal*.

corneal transplant See *transplant, corneal*.

coronary bypass See *bypass, aortocoronary*.

coronary disease See *disease, coronary*.

corpus (kor'pus), pl. *cor'pora*, gen. *cor'poris* [L. "body"] a discrete mass of material, as of specialized tissue; used in anatomical nomenclature to designate the entire organism, and applied also to the main portion of an anatomical part, structure, or organ.

corpus albicans (pl. *cor'pora albican'tia*) [NA], white fibrous tissue that replaces the regressing corpus luteum in the human ovary in the latter half of pregnancy, or soon after ovulation when pregnancy does not supervene; called also *c. fibrosum*.

corpus femoris [NA], the main part or shaft of the femur.

On November 30, 1975, appellee Raymond R. Bell fractured the distal third of the **femoral shaft** of his left leg in a motorcycle accident. . . . Bell v. Western Pennsylvania Hospital, 437 A.2d 978–9 (Super.Ct.Pa.1981).

corpus luteum (pl. *cor'pora lu'tea*) [L. "yellow body"] [NA], a yellow glandular mass in the ovary formed by an ovarian follicle that has matured and discharged its ovum; if the ovum has been impregnated, the corpus luteum increases in size and persists for several months (*true c. luteum, c. luteum of pregnancy, c. luteum graviditatis);* if impregnation has not taken place, the corpus luteum degenerates and shrinks (*false c. luteum, c. luteum of menstruation, c. luteum menstruationis*). The corpus luteum secretes progesterone. Called also *yellow body of ovary*. Cf. *corpus albicans*.

corpus vitreum [NA], the vitreous body: the transparent substance that fills the part of the eyeball between the lens and the retina; called also *hyaloid body, crystalline* or *vitreous humor*, and *humor cristallinus*.

He was precluded from examining the posterior portion of the eyes because of numerous hemorrhages and **vitreous** material found therein. Excelsior Leather Washer Co. v. Industrial Com'n, 297 N.E.2d 158, 160 (Ill.1973).

The penetrating object had missed the cornea, entered the lens of the eye, and lodged midway in the **vitreous**. About four hours after the accident, the plaintiff was operated on and a steel chip, 5.5 mm × 3.5 mm, was removed from his eye. Hagenbuch v. Snap-on Tools Corp., 339 F.Supp. 676, 684 (D.New Hamp.1972).

corrosive (kŏ-ro'siv) [L. *con* with + rodere to gnaw] a substance that destroys the texture or substance of the tissues. Called also *caustic* and *escharotic*.

cortex (kor'teks), gen. *cor'ticis*, pl. *cor'tices* [L. "bark, rind, shell"] [NA] the outer layer of an organ or other body structure, as distinguished from the internal substance.

In Dorland's **Illustrated Medical Dictionary** (25 ed. 1965), 365, the **cortex** is defined as the outer layer or thin layer of gray matter on the surface of the cerebral hemisphere, and that it reaches its highest development in man, where it is responsible for the higher mental functions, for general movement, for visceral functions, perception, and behavioral reaction, and for the association and integration of these functions. The testimony indicated that white matter is located under the **cortex**. It also reflected a system of nerves commencing with the spine, leading through the brain stem and spreading out in network fashion through the cerebral hemispheres, encompassing the white matter and **cortex**. Matter of Quinlan, 348 A.2d 801, 809 (Super.Ct.N.J.1975).

cortex, cerebral; cortex cerebri; cortex of cerebrum the thin layer of gray matter on the surface of the cerebral hemisphere, folded into gyri with about two-thirds of its area buried in the depths of the fissures. It reaches its highest development in man, where it is responsible for the higher mental functions, for general movement, for visceral functions, perception, and behavioral reactions, and for the association and integration of these functions. Many classifications have been suggested: it has been divided into neopallium, archipallium, paleopallium according to supposed phylogenetic and ontogenetic differences; into areas according to the presence of six cell layers or according to differences in the structure and arrangement of cell and fiber layers; and into functional areas such as motor, sensory, and association areas. Called also *pallium*. See also *neopallium*.

cortical scar See *scar, cortical*.

corticosteroid (kor″tĭ-ko-ste′roid) any of the steroids elaborated by the adrenal cortex (excluding the sex hormones of adrenal origin) in response to the release of corticotropin (adrenocorticotropic hormone) by the pituitary gland, or any of the synthetic equivalents of these steroids. They are divided, according to their predominant biological activity, into two major groups: *glucocorticoids*, chiefly influencing carbohydrate, fat, and protein metabolism, and *mineralocorticoids*, affecting the regulation of electrolyte and water balance. Some corticosteroids exhibit both types of activity in varying degrees, and others exert only one type of effect. The corticosteroids are used clinically for hormonal replacement therapy, for suppression of ACTH secretion by the anterior pituitary, as antineoplastic and anti-inflammatory agents, and to suppress the immune response. Called also *adrenocortical hormone* and *corticoid*.

Appellant, in her complaint, alleged various doctors prescribed **corticosteroids** for eye disorders without warning her of known dangerous side effects; that she took the drugs without knowledge of their danger and that as a result she developed aseptic necrosis of her femoral heads which was one of the known harmful side effects. Buckner v. Allergan Pharmaceuticals, 400 So.2d 820–1 (Dist.Ct.App.Fla.1981).

Since certain steroids were not on the list and, therefore, might not be reimbursed until prior approval could be secured he would be forced to resort to short-term use of **systemic-cortico-steroids**. Systemic steroids are stronger than what he considered medically acceptable in the early stages of treatment, and further have potentially dangerous and undesirable side effects including cataracts and diabetes. Dodson v. Parham, 427 F.Supp. 97, 105 (N.D.Ga.1977).

corticotropin (kor″tĭ-ko-tro′pin) a peptide hormone secreted by the anterior pituitary gland that acts primarily on the adrenal cortex, stimulating its growth and its secretion of corticosteroids. The production of corticotropin is increased during times of stress. A sterile preparation [USP] of the same principle(s) derived from the anterior pituitary of those mammals used for food by man is administered parenterally for diagnostic testing of adrenocortical function and to stimulate the adrenal cortex to release its hormones, especially cortisol (hydrocortisone), in the treatment of several diseases, e.g., allergies, rheumatic disorders, and collagen, dermatologic, ophthalmic, hematologic, and neoplastic diseases, etc. It is used in veterinary medicine in the treatment of ketosis. Called also *adrenocorticotropic hormone (ACTH)* and *adrenocorticotropin*.

Dr. Marks initially treated plaintiff with injections of **ACTH**, a chemical which stimulates natural production of cortisone by the adrenal glands. The **ACTH** was administered in conjunction with topical steroid creams applied directly to the affected areas and prescriptions for steroid pills to be orally ingested. Hill v. Squibb & Sons, E.R., 592 P.2d 1383, 1385 (Mont.1979).

She was placed on therapy with **ACTH** which is the most widely accepted form for her therapy for treatment. It tends to decrease areas of inflammation in the central nervous system and thereby improve function in those areas which are marginally functioning because of the inflammation. McSwain v. Chicago Transit Authority, 362 N.E.2d 1264, 1273 (App.Ct.Ill.1977).

cortisone (kor′tĭ-sōn) chemical name: 17α,21-dihydroxy-4-pregnene-3,11,20-trione. A natural glucocorticoid (q.v.), with significant mineralocorticoid properties, $C_{21}H_{28}O_5$; believed to be both a precursor and a metabolite of cortisol (hydrocortisone). The human adrenal cortex secretes only minute amounts of cortisone; the synthetic hormone exerts its pharmaceutical effects through its metabolic conversion to cortisol. See also *gland*; and *syndrome, Cushing's*.

In January 1977, appellee, Liliane Allison, came under the care of appellants for the treatment of swollen and painful fingers of her right hand. In March 1977, Dr. Crain diagnosed Mrs. Allison's condition as osteoarthritis and started her on a conservative course of treatment. Next, Dr. Crain began a series of injections of Aristospan (**cortisone**) into the affected joints to reduce the inflammation. The right index finger was injected in the distal interphalangeal joint on four occasions and in the proximal interphalangeal joint on five occasions. Dr. Crain agreed that **cortisone** should never be injected into a joint in the presence of infection because it may reduce the body's resistance to infection and the ability to localize the infection; before such an injection, a diagnosis must be established and specific infectious arthritis must be ruled out. [Footnote omitted.] Crain v. Allison, 443 A.2d 558, 560 (D.C.Ct. App.1982).

Expert medical testimony indicates that **cortisone** can have serious side effects on glands and cause osteoporosis, or demineralization of the bone. Dupuy v. Tilley, 380 So.2d 634–5 (Ct.App.La.1979).

cosmetic (koz-met′ik) [Gr. *kosmētikos*] a beautifying substance or preparation. See also *drug* (U.S. v. Article of Drug, etc. case).

Cosmetics are defined as: (1) articles intended to be rubbed, poured, sprinkled, or sprayed on, introduced into, or otherwise applied to the human body or any part thereof, for cleansing, beautifying, promoting attractiveness, or altering the appearance, and (2) articles intended for use as a component of any such articles; except that such term shall not include soap. 21 U.S.C. § 321(i). U.S. v. Article of Drug, etc., 331 F.Supp. 912, 914–15 (D.Md.1971).

cosmetic surgery See *surgery, cosmetic.*

cosmetologist

L.S.A.-R.S. 37:492(2).

"§ 492. Definitions ... (2) 'Cosmetologist,' 'cosmetician,' 'beautician,' 'hairdresser' or 'operator' means any person who, with hands or with mechanical or electrical apparatus or appliances or by use of cosmetic preparations, antiseptics, soaps, detergents, tonics, lotions or creams engages, for compensation, direct or indirect, including tips, in any one or any combination of the following practices: namely, massaging, cleansing, washing, stimulating, manipulating, exercising, beautifying or doing similar work upon the scalp or the face, neck, arms, bust or upper body of any person. This definition shall include the practice of arranging, hair dressing, singeing or shaping, curling, waving, cleansing, shampooing, styling, bleaching, coloring or similar work upon the hair of another person." Pavone v. Louisiana State Board of Barber Examiners, 364 F.Supp. 961–2 (E.D.La. 1973).

cosmetology (koz″mĕ-tol′o-je) the study of the proper care of the body from the point of view of cleanliness and comeliness.

The art of **cosmetology** includes the beautifying of the face, neck, arms, bust or upper part of the human body, by the use of cosmetic preparations, antiseptics, tonics, lotions or creams. People v. Penny, 285 P.2d 926, 929 (Cal.1955).

costoclavicular (kos″to-klah-vik′u-lar) pertaining to the ribs and clavicle.

costophrenic angle See *angle, costophrenic.*

Coumadin (koo-mah-din) trademark for preparations of sodium warfarin. See also *warfarin, sodium.*

count (kownt) [L. *computare* to reckon] a numerical computation or indication.

count, blood determination of the number of formed elements in a measured volume of blood, usually a cubic millimeter (as red blood cell, white blood cell, or platelet count.)

On the same day, January 3, 1980 a **blood count**—the first ordered since December 31, 1979, despite the professed concern that the patient was suffering from osteomyelitis, or infection of the bone, showed an increase of the white blood cell count to 12,800. Kernall v. U.S., 558 F.Supp. 280, 283 (E.D. N.Y.1982).

Koch's white **blood count** was monitored and showed an increase from 12,100 upon admission to 21,000 at the time of his discharge. [after seven days.] Dr. Gorrilla also conceded that a white **blood count** would have been a useful test in diagnosing Koch's appendicitis, but he stated that he had had no opportunity to perform this test on Koch, since Koch never returned after his initial examination....

... Dr. Gertz conceded that Koch's increase in white **blood count** during his stay in Grand View Memorial Hospital could have had medical significance in indicating an increase in infection and toxicity in decedent's system. However, Dr. Gertz offered an alternative explanation for such an increase, stating that a rise in the white **blood count** could also indicate a satisfactory immunological response to infection. Koch v. Gorrilla, 552 F.2d 1170, 1172, 1175–6 (6th Cir. 1977).

count, sponge

When I go into the operating room, by tradition, I know how many sponges are there. I do not count them. There is a traditional number that is put on each lap pack. The sponges are first counted before the operation starts. The instrument nurse and the circulator nurse count them. They frequently do the count in unison. They write the count down on a pad or a note. It is spoken of as the **sponge count**. There are notes kept in the operating room by the nurses....

The next usual **sponge count** is done just prior to the starting of the closure of the wound. This was so in the 1976 and 1979 surgeries of Mrs. Tice. At that point the operation is basically over with. At that point I am ready to close up.

The first count is taken before the peritoneum is closed. As soon as you let the operating room circulator know that you are ready to complete the operation, she then proceeds with the **sponge count**. She tells you the count is correct. The surgeon says, "I am ready to close." It is then she proceeds with this **sponge count**. She says, "I have a correct **sponge count**," or something to that effect. At that point the peritoneum is closed.

The next step is to close the next layer .... At that point, there is another count usually assisted by the instrument nurse, there are two of them doing it. After making the count in the fascia, she says "Dr. Newman, I have another correct count." I close the fascia at that point. There is a third layer which is just in front of or anterior to the fascia. When we get to that third layer there is another sponge count by the instrument nurse and the circulator nurse together. This is done after the surgeon has announced that he is ready for the third closure. After the **sponge count**, the nurse again indicates that they have a correct **sponge count** and the third layer is then closed. The next closing is the skin. There is no **sponge count** related to that. There are three **sponge counts** by two nurses in the employ of the hospital and that terminates the matter unless there is something missing or something wrong. Tice v. Hall, 303 S.E.2d 832, 834–5 (Ct.App.N.Car.1983).

counter (kown′ter) an instrument or apparatus by which numerical value is computed; in radiology, a device for enumerating ionizing events.

Counter, Geiger, counter Geiger-Müller a highly sensitive amplifying device that indicates the presence of ionizing particles.

A gamma radiation monitoring instrument (**geiger counter**) will be placed in the flow line to provide instantaneous monitoring of the gross gamma radiation level. Crowther v. Seaborg, 312 F.Supp. 1205, 1223 (D.Colo.1970).

countertransference (kown″ter-trans-fer′ens) in psychoanalysis, the emotional reaction aroused in the physician by the patient; cf. *transference.*

Counter-transference is a similarly common phenomenon in which the psychiatrist projects onto his patient feelings that the psychiatrist has towards someone else. Mazza v. Huffaker, 300 S.E.2d 833, 840 (Ct.App.N.Car.1983).

CPK See *creatine phosphokinase.*

crack (neck) See *manipulation.*

Craig needle biopsy See *biopsy, needle.*

craniectomy (kra″ne-ek′to-me) [*cranium* + Gr. *ektomē* excision] excision of a part of the skull.

On September 9, 1976, Dr. Wilkins performed a left retromastoid **craniectomy**, at which time the fifth nerve was found to be impinged. The operation was considered a success, and plaintiff was found to be free of his facial pain at the time of his discharge on September 21, 1976. Debolt v. Califano, 445 F.Supp. 893, 900 (S.D.Ill.1978).

... and during that time his doctor performed a right frontotemporal **craniectomy**....

... Since his injury he has reported seizures, severe headaches, dizziness, slurred speech and an inability to concentrate. Lewis v. Weinberger, 515 F.2d 584, 586 (5th Cir. 1975).

craniopharyngioma (kra″ne-o-fah-rin″je-o′mah) a tumor arising from cell rests derived from the hypophyseal stalk or Rathke's pouch, frequently associated with increased intracranial pressure, and showing calcium deposits in the capsule or in the tumor proper. Called also *craniopharyngeal duct tumor, Rathke's (pouch) tumor, suprasella cyst*, and *pituitary adamantinoma* or *ameloblastoma.*

On July 3, 1964, Dr. Bunche examined that X-ray and concluded that Mary had a **craniopharyngioma**, a type of brain tumor. On July 7, 1964, Mary was admitted for the third time, to Children's Hospital where the diagnosis of a **craniopharyngioma** was confirmed. On July 10, Dr. Wyand surgically removed the tumor ....

... On October 19, 1965, pursuant to discovery proceedings plaintiffs obtained Mary's records at the County Hospital and discovered for the first time that Dr. Cramer had tentatively diagnosed a **craniopharyngioma** and had recommended a series of tests in order to determine whether there was a **craniopharyngioma**, that those tests had not been performed, that Dr. Skinner also had thought a brain tumor possible, that none of this had been revealed to Mrs. Chandler, and that the County Hospital had positively represented the absence of any organic disease. Whitfield v. Roth, 519 P.2d 588, 593–4 (Cal.1974).

cranioplasty (kra′ne-o-plas″te) [*cranio-* + Gr. *plassein* to mold] any plastic operation on the skull; surgical correction of defects of the skull.

He suffered from a bone infection, and was required to have plastic surgery on the skull (**cranioplasty** of the right parietal bone) in October of 1951. These operations resulted in several metallic sutures and three metallic clips remaining in the skull. DePaepe v. Richardson, 464 F.2d 92–3 (5th Cir. 1972).

craniotomy (kra″ne-ot′o-me) [*cranio-* + Gr. *tomē* a cut] any operation on the cranium.

During the course of these [shunt] operations, however, the tumor exploded and a **craniotomy** was performed to remove tumor contents from the brain. The tumor contents then spilled into the decedent's spinal fluid. Dundon v. U.S., 559 F.Supp. 469, 471 (E.D.N.Y.1983).

Dr. S. R. Winston performed a **craniotomy** on appellant. He removed a blood clot that was about two and a half inches inside the occipital lobe (located in the left rear of the brain). Dr. Winston also took out a smaller subdural hematoma (a swelling containing blood close to the brain surface) in the same area. Beins v. U.S., 695 F.2d 591, 595 (D.C.Cir.1982).

Soon thereafter the minor plaintiff developed symptoms of neurological disorder leading to the discovery of a brain abscess at the site of the removal of the left rear halo pin. A **craniotomy** was performed, and abscessed brain tissue was removed. This left scar tissue on the brain, resulting in seizures of an epileptic type which (the plaintiffs offered to prove) necessitated repeated hospitalizations and persisted to the time of trial. Harrington v. Cohen, 374 N.E.2d 344–5 (App.Ct. Mass.1978).

Other Authorities: Sears, Roebuck & Co. v. Tatum, 585 P.2d 734, 736 (Okl.1978); Figliomeni v. Bd. of Ed. of City School Dist., 341 N.E.2d 557, 559 (N.Y.1975); Krause v. Milwaukee Mutual Ins. Co., 172 N.W.2d 181, 191 (Wis.1969).

cranium (kra′ne-um), pl. *cra′nia* [L.; Gr. *kranion* the upper part of the head] the skeleton of the head, variously construed as including all of the bones of the head, all of them except the mandible, or the eight bones which form the vault that lodges the brain. See also *cranial bones*, under *bone.*

crash cart See *cart, resuscitation.*

A **crash cart** is a rolling cabinet which contains emergency equipment including a cardiac monitor, defibrillation equipment, emergency drugs, endotracheal tubes which are needed to intubate a patient and an "ambu bag". Battles v. Aderhold, 430 So.2d 307, 309 (Ct.App.La.1983).

creatine (kre′ah-tin) [Gr. *kreas* flesh] N-methyl-guanidinoacetic acid. A crystallizable nitrogenous compound synthesized in the body, phosphorylated creatine being an important storage form of high-energy phosphate. See also *phosphocreatine.*

creatine kinase ATP: creatine phosphotransferase. An enzyme of skeletal muscle and the myocardium and of brain tissue that catalyzes the transfer of a phosphate group from phosphocreatine to ADP, producing creatine and ATP. It occurs as three isoenzymes each having two components labeled M and B: the form in brain tissue is BB, in skeletal muscle MM, and in myocardial tissue both MM and MB. The form normally found in serum is virtually all MM isoenzyme.

creatine phosphokinase

Customary enzyme tests were also done. Three enzymes known as LDH, SGOT, and **CPK** were tested. Their values were elevated—especially the **CPK**-a circumstance that is consistent with damage to the heart muscle, though by no means diagnostic in and of itself. Schales v. U.S., 488 F.Supp. 33, 35 (E.D.Ark.1979).

credate

Donna's mother testified she had to help Donna to **credate** herself, a procedure where the patient pushes on the abdomen to empty the bladder. Zimmerman v. New York City Health & Hospitals, 458 N.Y.S.2d 552, 554 (1st Dep't 1983).

Crede See *method, Credé's.*

cremasteric reflex See *reflex, cremasteric.*

creosote (kre′o-sōt) a mixture of phenols obtained by distilling wood tar, mainly beech *Fagus sylvatica* L. (Fagaceae). The liquid is colorless to yellowish, very refractive and oily, and has an empyreumatic odor. It is used externally as an antiseptic and internally in chronic bronchitis as an expectorant.

Dr. Feske felt that **creosote** was a known respiratory irritant, being made of phenol and aromatic hydrocarbons, but admitted that on occasion it was taken by mouth and by inhalation for respiratory illness. Sellers v. Breaux, 422 So.2d 1231, 1234 (Ct.App.La.1982).

crepitance

His pulse was up, he was jaundiced and a **crepitance** (gas in the tissue) was noticed in the sole of the foot. King v. Murphy, 424 So.2d 547–8 (Miss.1982), modified by 466 So.2d 856 (1985).

crepitant (krep′ĭ-tant) [L. *crepitare* to rattle] rattling or crackling.

crepitation (krep″ĭ-ta′shun) [L. *crepitare* to crackle] the noise made by rubbing together the ends of a fractured bone.

At the present time she has approximately 90° of flexion in the right knee with considerable pain. There is **crepitation** on extension to 180°. Howard v. State Acc. Ins. Fund, 584 P.2d 325–6 (Ct.App.Or.1978).

crepitus See *crepitation.*

Medical examination of Carroll by four doctors in connection with his application to the Workers' Compensation Board for disability benefits revealed that he suffers from severe arthritis, **crepitus** (grating of joint) in both knees.... Carroll v. Secretary of Health & Human Services, 705 F.2d 638, 640 (2d Cir. 1983).

Crepitus describes the sound or rough feeling as a piece of sandpaper moving over an object. It does not necessarily mean there is any discomfort associated with it. Landeche v. Weaver, 384 So.2d 540–1 (Ct.App.La.1980).

crepitus, bony the crackling sound produced by the rubbing together of fragments of fractured bone.

... **crepitance**, that is, movement of the fractured bones of the skull. State v. Durand, 465 A.2d 762–3 (R.I.1983).

Someone stated that they thought they heard **crepitus**, the sound created by bone grating together. Her neck was bruised and she was unconscious; her breathing and pulse rate were normal. Malone v. City of Seattle, 600 P.2d 647–8 (Ct.App. Wash.1979).

crepitus, joint the grating sensation caused by the rubbing together of the dry synovial surfaces of joints; called also *articular c.*

It is significant in that certainly from his injury and the subsequent surgery, one can be certain that there is a significant amount of scar tissue formation or adhesions formed within the knee. This may be contributing to the **crepitus**.

In addition, an injury to the joint may be producing some degenerative changes or wear and tear type of changes to the joint surfaces. This may also be contributing to some of this grinding sound.

Q. Does that mean that he has an increased risk of arthritis in that knee because of this injury that he had?

A. I think it is fair to say that the possibility of his developing degenerative or wear and tear changes is greater having had that type of an injury than it would be without having had that type of an injury.

Q. This clicking and popping, is this an indication that perhaps some of these changes have already started?

A. At best, perhaps. It is quite possible to hear these noises for a long time without noting significant or rapid deterioration of a given situation.

Q. Does a normal, healthy knee have these kind of sounds?

A. No.

(Transcript of videotaped deposition of Dr. William Smulyan, shown to the jury on April 8, 1980, pp. 22–23). Starlings v. Ski Roundtop Corp., 493 F.Supp. 507, 509–10 (M.D.Pa.1980).

cresol (kre′sol) a mixture of isomeric cresols, $CH_3C_6H_4OH$, obtained from coal tar and containing not more than 5 per cent of phenol; it is a poisonous, colorless, or yellowish to brownish yellow, or pinkish liquid, and is more powerful disinfectant and antiseptic than phenol; used chiefly to sterilize instruments, dishes, utensils, and other inanimate objects. Called also *cresylic acid* and *tricresol.*

Cresylic acid is a coal tar product which has a strong pungent odor of creosote or disinfectant. Coca Cola Co., Tenco Division v. S.S. Norholt, 333 F.Supp. 946, 948 (S.D.N.Y.1971).

cresylic acid See *cresol.*

cri du chat See *syndrome, cri du chat.*

cristein See *cyanocobalamin.*

Crohn's disease See *disease, Crohn's.*

crosslinkage

Crosslinkages between individual polymeric chains impart greater form stability to the plastic. **Crosslinkages** are created by bombarding the plastic with electrons, subjecting it to irradiation, or, with some materials, vulcanizing it.

Thus, crosslinked polyolefins are a group of polymers of certain hydrocarbons which have been processed to achieve greater form stability. International Tel. & Tel. Corp. v. Raychem Corp., 538 F.2d 453, 455 (1st Cir. 1976).

crown (krown) [L. *corona*] an artificial crown replacing the natural crown of a tooth. See also *preparation, crown*.

By deposition and personally at trial, Dr. Banowsky testified that to prepare a tooth for a **crown** it was necessary for the enamel to be removed. This is accomplished by grinding the tooth down with a high-speed-rotary instrument. In order to prevent tooth decay at the point where the crown and tooth meet, it is necessary to remove the enamel below the gum line from two to three millimeters. To go below the gum line, a long tapered ''burr'', which would cause less bleeding than the larger instrument used in removing the enamel for the rest of the tooth, was used. Williford v. Banowsky, 563 S.W.2d 702, 704 (Ct.Civ.App.Tex.1978).

crown, artificial a restoration of metal, porcelain, or plastic which reproduces the surface anatomy of the clinical crown of a tooth and which is affixed to the remains of the natural tooth structure.

crude oil See *petroleum*.

Cruex See *antifungal* (Pennwalt case).

crustacea See *shrimp*.

cryophake

The evidence disclosed that a ''**standard cryophake delivery**'' utilizes a small instrument described as ''a cold probe'', which, when placed on the anterior surface of the lens of the eye forms an ''iceball'', thereby securing the lens to the ''cold probe'' and permitting the lens to be ''pulled out of the eye''. . . . Miller v. Scholl, 594 S.W.2d 324, 327 (Mo.Ct.App. 1980).

cryosurgery (kri″o-sur′jer-e) destruction of tissue by the application of extreme cold; utilized in some forms of intracranial and cutaneous surgery.

You did cause, suffer and allow your employee, Helen Overstreet, a person not licensed as a physician or registered as a nurse, to perform **cryosurgery** on your patients. Sherman v. Com'n on Licensure to Practice, 407 A.2d 595, 598 (D.C.Ct. App.1979).

CSA (Controlled Substances Act). See e.g., ''*marihuana*'' (National Organization for Reform, etc. case).

CSF See *fluid, cerebrospinal*.

CST (convulsive shock therapy). See *shock therapy*, under *therapy*.

cuff (kuf) a small bandlike structure encircling a part.

cuff, rotator a musculotendinous structure about the capsule of the shoulder joint, formed by the inserting fibers of the supraspinatus, infraspinatus, teres minor, and subscapularis muscles, blending with the capsule, and providing mobility and strength to the shoulder joint.

Subsequent surgery revealed that the fall caused inflammation and degeneration of the right **rotator cuff** (shoulder muscle), together with fraying and degeneration of the right bicipital tendon. In the orthopedist's opinion these conditions have produced a 15-percent permanent partial disability of plaintiff's right shoulder, a 9-percent permanent partial disability of her body as a whole, secondary to the shoulder problem, limiting plaintiff's ability to use her right arm. Nordby v. Gould, Inc., 329 N.W.2d 118–19 (Neb.1983).

The first is a **rotator cuff tear** which is an injury to the shoulder and arm caused by a tearing of the ligaments and tendons in that area of the body. While it may be treated by cortisone shots to the affected area and anti-inflammatory drugs, it is a permanent injury and cannot be repaired by surgery. Klug v. Keller Industries, Inc., 328 N.W.2d 847–8 (S.Dak.1982).

Appellee diagnosed Appellant's injury as a **rotator cuff** injury and recommended, among other things, exercise of the shoulder and physical therapy. Quinlan v. Brown, 419 A.2d 1274, 1276 (Super.Ct.Pa.1980), order reversed 445 A.2d 715 (Pa. 1980).

Other Authorities: Safeway Stores, Inc. v. Industrial Com'n, 558 P.2d 971–3 (Ct.App.Ariz.1976).

cuff, vaginal

When he opened Mrs. Seeley's abdomen he found an infection of the **vaginal cuff**, which is the place from which the uterus is severed in a vaginal hysterectomy. Seeley v. Eaton, 506 S.W.2d 719, 721 (Ct.Civ.App.Tex.1974).

culture (kul′tūr) [L. *cultura*] 1. the propagation of microorganisms or of living tissue cells in special media conducive to their growth. 2. a growth of microorganisms or other living cells. 3. to induce the propagation of microorganisms or living tissue cells in media conducive to their growth. See also *culture medium*.

A **culture test** consists of taking the submitted specimens and ''incubating'' them in a nutrient medium to see if abnormal bacteria or pathogens are present. U.S. v. Halper, 590 F.2d 422, 425 (2d Cir. 1978).

culture and sensitivity test See *test, culture and sensitivity*.

culture assembly, disposable See *jar, Coplin*; and *dish, Petri*.

culture medium (kul′tūr me′de-um) any substance or preparation used for the cultivation of living cells.

culture test See *culture*.

cummingtonite-grunerite See *acicular*.

Plaintiffs contend that the mineral **cummingtonite-grunerite**,[4] which Reserve admits to be a major component of its taconite wastes and a member of the mineral family known as amphiboles, is substantially identical in morphology (or shape and form and similar in chemistry to amosite asbestos, a fibrous mineral which has been found, in certain occupational settings, to be carcinogenic. [4 **Cummingtonite-grunerite** is a general name for a ''suite'' of minerals which are essentially identical except for the relative quantities of iron and magnesium in them. The iron-rich members are sometimes referred to as grunerites, although the word cummingtonite is used to refer to the entire suite of minerals.] Reserve Mining Co. v. U.S., 498 F.2d 1073, 1075 (8th Cir. 1974).

Dr. Gunderson in his work on the metamorphosed Biwabik Iron Formation of the Eastern Mesabi District, in which Reserve's Peter Mitchell Pit is located, reported that **cummingtonite-grunerite** (Mg$_1$Fe) Si$_8$O$_{22}$(OH)$_2$, is the most abundant silicate which occurs in almost all of the submembers of the metamorphosed iron formation. U.S. v. Reserve Mining Co., 380 F.Supp. 11, 31 (D.Minn.1974), cause remanded 498 F.2d 1073, 1075 (8th Cir. 1974).

cumulative

He said that the chemical had a "**cumulative** effect" meaning "it accumulates in the body" and "(i)t is very rapidly absorbed by the skin." Tripp v. Choate, 415 S.W.2d 808, 812 (Mo. 1967).

cuneiform bone See *os cuneiforme mediale.*

cunnilingus (kun″ĭ-ling′gus) [L. *cunnus* vulva + *lingere* to lick] oral stimulation of the female genitalia.

cupping (kup′ing) the formation of a cup-shaped depression. See also *cupping, pathologic; discus nervi optici;* and *glaucoma* (Thorpe case).

Q. You thought, Doctor, on November 17, 1952 you saw evidence of glaucoma? A. I saw **cupping** of the left optic nerve, that is the eye that I first operated for cataract and that was the first chance that I had to see that optic nerve for quite sometime and it had not been **cupped** before. I interpreted that as early evidence of glaucoma. Thorpe v. Schoenbrun, 195 A.2d 870, 872 (Super.Ct.Pa.1963).

cupula (ku′pu-lah), pl. *cu'pulae* [L.] a small inverted cup or dome-shaped cap over some structure.

cupulolithiasis (ku″pu-lo-lĭ-thi'ah-sis) the presence of calculi in the cupula of the posterior semicircular duct, a cause of benign paroxysmal positional vertigo.

When Anunti continued to complain of dizziness following the surgery, further tests were conducted which resulted in a diagnosis of **cupulomethiasis** [sic]. Further testing showed Anunti's dizziness to result from brain stem damage rather than damage to the inner ear. Anunti v. Payette, 268 N.W.2d 52, 54 (Minn. 1978).

curare (koo-rah′re) [South American] a term applied to a wide variety of highly toxic extracts from numerous botanical sources, including various species of *Strychnos;* used originally as arrow poisons in South America. A form extracted from *Chondodendron tomentosum* has been used for the reduction of spasms in tetanus and in shock treatments, in plastic muscular rigidity, spastic paralysis, and similar conditions, and also as an adjunct to general anesthesia. Cf. *tubocurarine.*

Prior to the operation he was given "a substance which is commonly called **Curare**" which paralyzes the chest muscles making it impossible for the patient to breathe on his own. People v. Stewart, 358 N.E.2d 487, 489 (N.Y.1976).

curative (kūr′ah-tiv) [L. *curare* to take care of] tending to overcome disease and promote recovery.

curet (ku-ret′) [Fr. *curette* scraper] an instrument for removing material from the uterine cavity.

That evidence was presented through the testimony of Dr. Burton Krumholz, called as a witness for defendant, that the purpose of using a sharp **curette** after a suction curettage was "[t]o be assured that the pregnancy termination is not incomplete". . . .

. . . in his affirmative responses to the question "Doctor, when you say scrape, is it intended that the sharp end, by a scraping or cutting process, will loosen and break off any of the contents of the wall of the uterus?" and, following exhibition of the sharp **curette** to the jury, to the question "So that, Doctor, whatever didn't get evacuated by the suction device you would expect would be loosened and scraped out in the manner that you demonstrated with the **curette**; is that right?" . . . [Dissent.] Koehler v. Schwartz, 399 N.E.2d 1140, 1142 (N.Y.1979).

curettage (ku″rĕ-tahzh') [Fr.] the removal of growths or other material from the wall of a cavity or other surface, as with a curet; called also *curettement.*

Mrs. Wiley again returned to see Dr. Karam on September 19, 1979, at which time Dr. Karam performed **curettage** and scaling to scrape her gums and the roots of her teeth to remove dead tissue. Wiley v. Karam, 421 So.2d 294–5 (Ct.App.La. 1982).

curette See *curet.*

curie (ku're) [Marie Sklodowska *Curie,* Polish chemist in Paris, 1867–1934, the discoverer of radium, and Pierre *Curie,* 1859–1906, co-winners, with A. H. Becquerel, of the Nobel prize in physics for 1903, for studies on spontaneous radioactivity; Mme. Curie also received the Nobel prize in chemistry in 1911 for discovery and isolation of radium] a unit of radioactivity, defined as the quantity of any radioactive nuclide in which the number of disintegrations per second is 3.700 × 10^{10}. Abbreviated c and Ci. See also *radioactivity.*

(f) "**Curie**" means that amount of radioactive material which disintegrates at the rate of 37 billion atoms per second. . . . 10 C.F.R. Sec. 30.4(f).

curvature (kur'vah-tūr) [L. *curvatura*] deviation from a rectilinear direction.

curvature, Pott's abnormal posterior curvature of the vertebral column caused by tuberculous caries.

curve (kurv) [L. *curvum*] a nonangular deviation from a straight course in a line or surface.

curve, dose-effect; curve, dose-response a curve indicating the relationship between dose of radiation and the degree of a particular biological effect produced.

A **dose-response curve** shows the relationship between different exposure levels [of Benzene] and the risk of cancer associated with those exposure levels. Generally, exposure to higher levels carries with it a higher risk, and exposure to lower levels is accompanied by a reduced risk. American Pet. Institute v. Occupational Safety, 581 F.2d 493, 504 (5th Cir. 1978).

curve, Lange gold See *test, Lange's.*

curve, lordotic See *lordosis.*

Cushing's syndrome See *syndrome, Cushing's.*

cutaneous nerve See *nervus, cutaneus.*

cutdown (kut′down) creation of a small, incised opening, especially over a vein (venous cutdown), to facilitate venipuncture and permit the passage of a needle or cannula for the withdrawal of blood or administration of fluids.

Doctor Woodruff testified that the "treatment of choice" to administer fluids was a venous **cutdown** which would involve the insertion of an intravenous line into the lower part of the leg. In fact, the venous **cutdown** was the "procedure of choice" at Barnes Hospital when she was on staff there because it enabled physicians to avoid the known risks of a subclavian stick. Eichelberger v. Barnes Hosp., 655 S.W.2d 699, 703 (Mo.Ct.App.1983).

The plaintiff was informed by Dr. Parsa, prior to surgery, that she might have to perform a "**cutdown**" procedure on plaintiff because of her weight. Dr. Parsa testified that she encountered difficulty locating the femoral artery and that she made two or three attempts before hitting it. . . .

. . . Dr. Baker, the plaintiff's expert, testified that a physician, who could not locate the femoral artery due to the obesity of a patient or some other complication, had two alternative techniques to utilize. The physician could use a "**cutdown**" method where an incision is made to clearly expose the artery or, in the alternative, the brachial artery in the arm could be used because it is easier to locate. Hirn v. Edgewater Hospital, 408 N.E.2d 970, 973–4 (App.Ct.Ill.1980).

Dr. Rodriguez, in an attempt to save her life, did an arterial **cut-down** on her left wrist while fluids and other substances were intravenously fed through the right arm. After applying an antiseptic solution to the wrist, Dr. Rodriguez performed the cut-down with a special kit provided by the hospital to introduce blood directly into the wrist artery to increase the pumping of the heart. The procedure involves various risks including gangrene and the loss of the hand because of the necessary binding or ligation of the arteries and because the blood supply to the extremity is temporarily cut off. A special hollow needle is used, then closed with a stylet and left in the artery, with a corner of the wound open, pending further developments. Sanchez v. Rodriguez, 38 Cal.Rptr. 110, 112 (Dist.Ct. App.Cal.1964).

Other Authorities: Daniels v. Hadley Memorial Hospital, 566 F.2d 749, 755 (D.C.Cir.1977).

cutis (ku′tis) [L.] [NA] the skin: the outer protective covering of the body, consisting of the epidermis and the corium, or dermis, and resting upon the subcutaneous tissues.

cutis marmorata a transitory mottling of the skin sometimes occurring on exposure of the skin to cold. Cf. *livedo reticularis.*

The petitioner suffers from a disease known as "**cutis marmorata**", a condition where the hands become mottled and red upon exposure to cold, and he voluntarily terminated his part-time employment at Ender's Food Market (Enders) in December 1974. He was a high school student at the time of this employment and the job required his handling of frozen items and occasionally required him to enter a freezer. Skilton v. Enders Food Market, Inc., 405 A.2d 1381–2 (Commonwealth Ct.Pa.1979).

CVA costovertebral angle; cerebrovascular accident; cardiovascular accident.

CVP central venous pressure. See *bioflavonoid* (USV Pharmaceutical Corp. case).

cyanocobalamin (si″ah-no-ko-bal′ah-min) a water-soluble hematopoietic vitamin (vitamin B_{12}), $C_{63}H_{88}CoN_{14}O_{14}P$, found in the liver, fish meal, eggs, and other natural products, or produced from cultures of *Streptomyces griseus*, which combines with intrinsic factor for intestinal absorption and which is needed for maturation of erythrocytes. Absence of intrinsic factor leads to malabsorption of cyanocobalamin and results in pernicious anemia. The official preparation, prepared in accordance with USP specifications, is used in the prophylaxis and treatment of pernicious anemia and other macrocytic anemias, usually administered intramuscularly or subcutaneously. Called also *antipernicious anemia factor, extrinsic factor*, and *LLD factor*. See also *Castle's factor*, under *factor.*

As other microorganisms, Streptomyces griseus, growing in a nutritional broth, produce elaboration materials. Grisein, a material produced by the growth of Streptomyces griseus, may be adsorbed from the acidified broth upon an activated carbon known as "Norit." After removal, by elution, of the adsorbed grisein, a residue of materials was left in the "spent" Norit. When the "spent" Norit was eluted with ethanol or acetone, residual material was removed from the "spent" Norit, and, in the resulting eluate, there was found the desired activity. . . .

. . . While grisein, itself, contains none of the desired activity, there followed an intensive search of grisein materials and experimental extraction, concentration and fractionization to obtain the desired substance. On October 22, 1947, a fraction having a pinkish color was obtained. This color deepened as further concentration and separation were achieved, until, finally, on December 11, 1947, a pure, red, crystalline material was obtained. . . .

After much additional analysis and investigation, officials of Merck decided the pure material could be classified as a vitamin. Since it was water-soluble [5], it was placed in the "B" group and was assigned the number 12, all lower numbers having been appropriated. [5 The B vitamins differ greatly in chemical structure and function. Water solubility is, perhaps, their only common attribute.] Merck & Co. v. Olin Mathieson Chemical Corp., 253 F.2d 156, 160 (4th Cir. 1958).

cyanoguanidine

The specific poisonous substance involved was a compound in the alkyl mercury group, i.e., a methylmercury compound called **Cyano(methylmercuri)guanidine** or Methylmercury dicyandiamide. . . .

A typical mercury fungicide will contain both active and inert ingredients. The active ingredient is often a methylmercury combined with another chemical compound in such a way that the active ingredient is then water soluble. This facilitates the fungicide's application on seeds during the treatment process. For example, the only active ingredient in Panogen 15 is **Cyano(methylmercuri)guanidine** which is a combination of methylmercury and guanidine. First Nat. Bk. in Albuquerque v. U.S., 552 F.2d 370, 371, 373 (10th Cir. 1977).

Plaintiff Morton International, Inc. manufactures seventeen types of **cyano (methylmercuri) guanadine** known as Panogens. Plaintiff Nor-Am Agricultural Products, Inc. distributes Morton's Panogens. These mercury compounds are used as fungicides in treating seeds intended for planting. They were duly registered as "economic poisons" with the Secretary of Agriculture, as required by Section 4(a) of the Federal Insecticide, Fungicide and Rodenticide Act. 7 U.S.C. § 135b(a)....

... Finally, the letter noted that the ingestion of **cyano (methylmercuri) guanadine** reportedly caused irreversible injury to the central nervous system. Nor-Am Agricultural Products, Inc. v. Hardin, 435 F.2d 1151, 1153, 1157 (7th Cir. 1970).

cyanosis (si"ah-no′sis) [Gr. *kyanos* blue] a bluish discoloration, applied especially to such discoloration of skin and mucous membranes due to excessive concentration of reduced hemoglobin in the blood.

At about 2:00 p.m. or 2:30 p.m. on June 24, Dr. Brown returned to the hospital room of DeWitt, examined DeWitt's leg, saw that DeWitt's left foot and toes were swollen, concluded that DeWitt had severe "**cyanosis**" (a dark blue color) of the toes caused by decreased circulation of oxygenated blood in and to the lower left leg, and attempted to alleviate this condition by splitting and spreading the cast open halfway up the front. DeWitt v. Brown, 669 F.2d 516, 519 (8th Cir. 1982).

Cyanosis according to Dr. Gale, is a discoloration of the skin or color of the patient who takes on a bluish hue. General **cyanosis**, according to Dr. Gale, indicates a problem of bringing oxygen to the body tissue due to either a problem with respiration or circulation. Regional **cyanosis** occurs when the blood is not flowing normally, but rather is "flowing very sluggishly or not flowing at all." Siegel v. Mt. Sinai Hospital of Cleveland, 403 N.E.2d 202, 205 (Ct.App.Ohio 1978).

Dr. O'Donoghue testified that until the crisis occurred during surgery, he was not aware that the patient had not been intubated by means of an endotracheal tube. At the time the crisis was announced, he found that Deborah was receiving anesthesia through a mask and that she had a **cyanotic** or bluish color signifying a lack of oxygenated blood. At that point Dr. Widder removed the mask and oropharyngeal airway, and inserted an endotracheal tube ....

Dr. Greene, an anesthesiologist, testified that based on the observation of **cyanosis** by Dr. O'Donoghue, hypoxia was the precipitating factor of Deborah's cardiac arrest. He stated that for some period of time prior to the cardiac arrest, Deborah was not receiving adequate oxygen, but the heart was still pumping. Burrow v. Widder, 368 N.E.2d 443, 450 (App.Ct. of Ill.1977).

Other Authorities: White v. Mitchell, 568 S.W.2d 216, 218 (Ark.1978); Savage v. Christian Hosp. Northwest, 543 F.2d 44, 46 (8th Cir. 1976); Lhotka v. Larson, 238 N.W.2d 870, 875 (Minn.1976). Garfield Park Community Hosp. v. Vitacco, 327 N.E.2d 408, 410–11 (App.Ct.Ill.1975); Liberty Nat. Life

Ins. Co. v. Morris, 208 S.E.2d 637, 640 (Ct.App.Ga.1974). Barnes v. Tenin, 429 F.2d 117–18 (2d Cir. 1970).

cyanosis, enterogenous a syndrome due to absorption of nitrites and sulfides from the intestine, principally marked by methemoglobinemia and/or sulfhemoglobinemia associated with cyanosis. It is accompanied by severe enteritis, abdominal pain, constipation or diarrhea, headache, dyspnea, dizziness, syncope, anemia, and, occasionally, digital clubbing and indicanuria. Called also *Stokvis' disease, Stokvis-Talma syndrome, van den Bergh's disease*, and *autotoxic cyanosis*.

cyanotic (si-ah-not′ik) pertaining to or characterized by cyanosis. See also *cyanosis*.

By evening of the same day his nailbeds were **cyanotic**. By August 1, 1976, the record reflects that Erickson's feet and lower legs were mottled and more **cyanotic**. No pulse could be heard in those areas. One note entered at 5:00 p.m. on August 1, 1976, indicated that the patient's feet were purple. Nevertheless, the Dopamine was continued. Erickson v. U.S., 504 F.Supp. 646, 649 (D.S.Dak.1980).

Shortly after the Demerol had been given, Ms. Wilson checked Mrs. Boyd and noted that she was **cyanotic**, with lips and fingers turning blue. Fraijo v. Hartland Hospital, 160 Cal. Rptr. 246, 250 (Ct.App.Cal.1979).

"Q. **Cyanotic** is that bluing or ashen turning of the skin, is that correct?
"A. Correct.
"Q. And that is a sign of improper profusion or oxygenation of the body?
"A. That is correct....
"Q. One other question before that, Doctor, when somebody turns **cyanotic** again they turn a bluish or off color?
"A. An off color.
"Q. And that is important, is it not, because it is a sign of poor oxygenation?
"A. Yes.
"Q. And that can lead to cardiac arrest?
"A. It can.
"Q. It can lead to brain damage also, if it continues, is that correct?
"A. It can.
"Q. So that the color that the patient reaches is important, the coloring of the patient is important?
"A. The coloring of the patient is always important." Sauro v. Shea, 390 A.2d 259, 264–5 (Super.Ct.Pa.1978).

Other Authorities: Bellaire General Hosp., Inc. v. Campbell, 510 S.W.2d 94, 96 (Ct.Civ.App.Tex.1974); Vogan v. Byers, 447 F.2d 543–4 (3d Cir. 1971).

cycle (si′kl) [Gr. *kyklos* circle] a round or succession of observable phenomena, recurring usually at regular intervals and in the same sequence.

cycle, menstrual the period of the regularly recurring physiologic changes in the endometrium, occurring during the reproductive period of human females and a few primates, culminating in partial shedding of the endometrium and some bleeding per vagina (menstruation); see illustration.

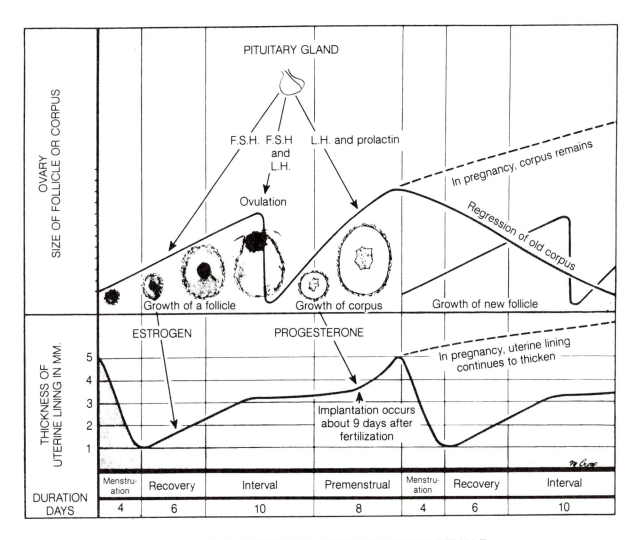

CHANGES IN MENSTRUAL CYCLE IN HUMAN FEMALE

Solid lines indicate course of events when ovum is not fertilized; dotted lines indicate course of events when fertilization occurs. Actions of hormones of pituitary and ovary in regulating the cycle are indicated by arrows. (Villee.)

cycle, urea a cyclic series of reactions that produce urea, a major route for removal of the ammonia produced in the metabolism of amino acids in the liver and kidney: arginine is hydrolyzed (catalyzed by arginase) to ornithine and urea in the soluble cytoplasm, the ornithine then being converted to citrulline in the mitochondria by the addition of the carbamyl group from carbamyl phosphate, and subsequently to arginine by the transfer of nitrogen from aspartate. The arginine is again hydrolyzed to ornithine and urea, and so on. Called also *ornithine c.* and *Krebs-Henseleit c.*

cycloid See *cyclothymic.*

cyclopropane (si″klo-pro′pān) a colorless, inflammable and explosive gas, C_3H_6, with characteristic odor and pungent taste; used by inhalation as a general anesthetic.

That prior to and during the surgical procedure, Mr. Latragna was anesthetized by the introduction of nitrous oxide and **cyclopropane**, both being anesthetic gases and both administered through an endotracheal tube inserted through the patient's mouth by the anesthesiologist. Latragna v. Colonial Life Ins. Co. of America, 357 N.Y.S.2d 795, 797 (Monroe Cty.Ct. 1974).

cycloserine (si″klo-ser′ēn) [USP] chemical name: (*R*)-4-amino-3-isoxazolidinone. A broad-spectrum antibiotic, $C_3H_6N_2O_2$, with tuberculostatic activity, produced by growth of *Streptomyces orchidaceus* or obtained by synthesis, occurring as a white to pale yellow, crystalline powder; effective against many gram-negative and gram-positive bacteria, it is used in the treatment of tuberculosis, pulmonary and extrapulmonary, and sometimes in urinary tract infections due to susceptible pathogens, administered orally.

... a condition which defendant diagnosed as prostatitis; that defendant prescribed a drug called **Seromycin** for treatment of this condition; that **Seromycin** is a powerful anti-tuberculin drug manufactured and marketed by Eli Lilly Company and that said drug is extremely toxic and capable of creating severe adverse effects on the central nervous system.... Moncrief v. Fuqua, 610 S.W.2d 720 (Ct.App.Tenn.1979).

cyclothiazide (si"klo-thi'ah-zīd) [USP] chemical name: 3-bicyclo[2.2.1]hept-5-en-2-yl-6-chloro-3,4-dihydro-2*H*-1,2,4-benzothiadiazone-7-sulfonamide 1,1-dioxide. An orally effective diuretic, $C_{14}H_{16}ClN_3O_4S_2$, occurring as a white to nearly white powder; used in the treatment of edema associated with various conditions and in hypertension.

Another benzothiadiazine which is used as a diuretic and antihypertensive agent is **cyclothiazide**.

... "Cyclothiazide" means, and is the generic name for, the benzothiadiazine with the chemical name 6-chloro-3,4-dihydro-3-(5-nor-boren-2-yl)-7-sulfamoyl-1,2,4,-benzothiadiazin-1,1-dioxide. U.S. v. Ciba Geigy Corp. 508 F.Supp. 1118, 1122–3 (D.N.J.1976).

cyclothymia (si"klo-thīm'e-ah) [cyclo- + Gr. *thymos* spirit] 1. cyclothymic personality. 2. a condition characterized by a predisposition to alternating moods of elation and mild depression.

At that time, he was treated with Lithium Carbonate and diagnosed as having a **cyclothymic** personality and as being addicted to alcohol. Green v. Schweiker, 694 F.2d 108, 111 (5th Cir. 1982).

Stewart testified that he had received some psychiatric treatment in the Army in 1943, in 1956 at Walter Reed Hospital, where he was found to have a "**cyclothymic** personality."... U.S. v. Stewart, 443 F.2d 1129, 1131 (10th Cir. 1971).

cyclothymic (si"klo-thi'mik) 1. of or pertaining to a cyclothymic personality. 2. of, pertaining to, or characterized by cyclothymia. 3. cyclothyme. Called also *cycloid.* See also *cyclothymia.*

cyst (sist) [Gr. *kystis* sac, bladder] any closed cavity or sac, normal or abnormal, lined by epithelium, and especially one that contains a liquid or semisolid material.

Dr. Burkons's records indicate a mass of **cysts**, about 5 × 5 cms., had developed in the lower part of appellant's right breast. Shapiro v. Burkons, 404 N.E.2d 778–9 (Ct.App.Ohio 1978).

cyst, adnexal

Dr. Pizzalotto's clinical examination indicated a potential **adnexal cyst** (a cyst in her tubes and ovaries caused by an outside source).... Karl J. Pizzalotto, M.D., Ltd. v. Wilson, 437 So.2d 859, 861 (La.1983).

cyst, corpus luteum a cyst of the ovary formed by a serous accumulation developed from a corpus luteum. See also *corpus luteum.*

The doctor also noted an oozing surface on the right ovary, indicating a ruptured **corpus luteum cyst**, and sutured the site of the oozing....

... He stated that it was "very common" to see a ruptured **corpus luteum cyst** during an appendectomy.[1] [[1] Dr. Beebe described **corpus luteum cyst** as a normal cyst which develops in one of the ovaries each time a woman ovulates. The cyst ruptures during the menstrual cycle and allows the egg to escape and pass into the fallopian tube. The doctor stated it would not be possible to ovulate without the formation and rupture of **corpus luteum cyst**, noting that the rupture does not indicate anything abnormal.] Baker v. Beebe, 367 So.2d 102, 104 (Ct.App.La.1979).

Corpus luteum: "[A] yellow mass in the ovary formed by a graafian follicle which has matured and discharged its ovum; if the ovum has been impregnated, the **corpus luteum** grows and persists for several months; if impregnation has not taken place, the **corpus luteum** degenerates and shrinks." Carmichael v. Reitz, 95 Cal.Rptr. 381, 388 (Ct.App.Cal.1971).

cyst, dermoid a teratoma, usually benign, representing a disorder of embryologic development, characterized by the presence of mature ectodermal elements, consisting of a fibrous wall lined with stratified epithelium, and containing a keratinous material and hair and sometimes other elements, such as bone, tooth, and nerve tissue; they are most often found in the ovary, but also commonly occur in the skin of the head and neck. Called also *benign cystic teratoma, cystic teratoma, mature teratoma,* and *dermoid.* See also *malignant teratoma.*

Plaintiff returned to Meyer Hospital July 22, 1970 for the surgical removal of a **dermoid cyst** from the left orbit and apparently made a complete recovery from the operation. Marbury v. Matthews, 433 F.Supp. 1081, 1083 (W.D.N.Y.1977).

cyst, endometrial a chocolate cyst, particularly in the ovary, lined with endometrium.

Plaintiff was admitted to Retreat Hospital on April 24, 1974 with a complaint of right lower quadrant pain characterized as mild but persistent. Provisional diagnoses were right pelvic mass and possible polyp of colon. On surgery, **endometrial cysts** (masses of tissue resembling uterine mucous membrane occurring aberrantly in pelvic cavity) of the left ovary and sigmoid colon were found and removed. Hurst v. Mathews, 426 F.Supp. 245–6 (E.D.Va.1976).

cyst, epidermal; cyst, epidermal inclusion; cyst, epidermoid an epithelial cyst of the skin due to proliferation of surface epidermal cells within the corium, arising from occluded pilosebaceous follicles and containing a laminated, cheesy, odoriferous keratinous material. Called also *sebaceous c.* and *wen.* See also *cyst, pilar.*

The gist of this argument is that the cancer Mrs. Cameron was suffering from [epidermoid cyst] is one of the most virulent types of this disease, that even had it been diagnosed June 9, there is a high probability she would not have been cured of it, that ultimately the disease would have taken the same course it did, subjecting her to the same amount of medical expense, pain, suffering, disfigurement, and ultimately death.

Plaintiff's expert witnesses testified that Mrs. Cameron's cancer was probably present on June 9 and that a tissue biopsy would have revealed it. They also testified that there is an overall 30 per cent survival rate from this type of cancer and that chance is considerably improved the earlier the cancer is discovered. O'Brien v. Stover, 443 F.2d 1013, 1018 (8th Cir. 1971).

cyst, ganglionic See *cyst, subchondral.*

cyst, ovarian

At the time of that examination, abdominal pelvic examination revealed fluid in the abdomen. The differential diagnosis of acites versus **ovarian cyst** was made. Subsequent evaluation with SMA–12, CBC, Urine and Liver Package indicated that this was indeed most likely an **ovarian cyst**, and she was advised to have surgical removal. [Dissent]....

... on June 26 she was hospitalized and a 22-pound ovarian tumor subsequently removed. Mutual Life Ins. Co. of New York v. Bishop, 209 S.E.2d 223, 225–6 (Ct.App.Ga.1974).

cyst, parametrial See *parametrium.*

After surgery, the doctor was able to determine that the swelling was a congenital **parametrial cyst**, unrelated to appellant's accident at work. However, the doctor testified that without surgery, he would have been unable to determine the etiology of the cyst. He also testified that the trauma at work aggravated appellant's pelvic inflammatory disease. Barris v. Toppers of Florida, Inc., 382 So.2d 441–2 (Dist.Ct.App.Fla. 1980).

cyst, pilar an epithelial cyst clinically indistinguishable from an epidermal cyst, almost always found on the scalp, and arising from the outer root sheath of the hair follicle. Called also *sebaceous c., tricholemmal c.,* and *wen.*

cyst, piliferous; cyst, pilonidal a hair-containing sacrococcygeal dermoid cyst or sinus which often opens at a postanal dimple. Cf. *coccygeal sinus,* under *sinus.*

An incidental finding is an operative scar at the pilonidal area in the sacral zone about two inches in overall length. This is the residual of an operation in 1960 for a **pilonidal cyst** while he was in the Armed Forces. Chabert v. City of Westwego police pension, 423 So.2d 1190, 1193 (Ct.App.La.1982).

Defendant claims that he suffers from a condition known as a **pilonidal cyst** of the type which is disqualifying under Army Regulation 40–501 of February 2, 1970 which reads in part:
2–35. Skin and Cellular Tissues
   The causes for rejection for appointment, enlistment, and induction are—
   c. Cysts.
   (2) Cysts, pilonidal. **Pilonidal cysts,** if evidenced by the presence of a tumor mass or a discharging sinus....
   ... He testified that a **pilonidal cyst** is a congenital condition formed in the embryo state where in some way the skin overlaps the tailbone forming a sinus or sinuses, sometimes lined with hair. If the cyst becomes infected it requires incision and drainage. U.S. v. Button, 330 F.Supp. 849–51 (D.Minn. 1971).

cyst, solitary bone a pathologic bone space in the metaphyses of long bones of growing children; of disputed origin, it may be either empty or filled with fluid and have a delicate connective tissue lining.

Medical reports described the cyst as a large destructive lesion of the sacrum and indicated that its growth was stretching the bladder and lower bowel. Dr. Wright diagnosed the cyst as a "**benign unicameral bone cyst.**" Furlong Const. Co., Inc. v. Industrial Com'n, 376 N.E.2d 1011, 1013 (Ill.1978).

cyst, subchondral a bone cyst within the fused epiphysis beneath the articular plate; it is lined with a membrane (probably modified synovia) which contains a mucinous material. Called also *ganglionic c.*

cyst, unicameral bone See *cyst, solitary bone.*

cystic duct See *ductus, cysticus.*

cystic fibrosis See *fibrosis, cystic fibrosis of the pancreas.*

cystitis (sis-ti'tis) inflammation of the urinary bladder.

... **cystitis** (inflammation of the bladder). Keflex was administered for the infection. Smith v. U.S., 557 F.Supp. 42, 44 (W.D. Ark.1982).

He also made a urinalysis and found a mild **cystitis**, which meant that claimant perhaps had a mild infection of the bladder. Welker v. MFA Central Co-operative, 380 S.W.2d 481, 483 (St.Louis Ct. of App.1964).

Other Authorities: Capaldi v. Weinberger, 391 F.Supp. 502, 505 (E.D.Pa.1975).

cystitis, interstitial, chronic a condition of the bladder occurring predominantly in women, with an inflammatory lesion, usually in the vertex, and involving the entire thickness of the wall, appearing as a small patch of brownish red mucosa, surrounded by a network of radiating vessels. The lesions, known as Fenwick-Hunner or Hunner ulcers, may heal superficially, and are notoriously difficult to detect. Typically, there is urinary frequency and pain on bladder filling and at the end of micturition. Called also *panmural c., submucous c.,* and *panmural fibrosis of the bladder.* See also *ulcer, Hunner's.*

cystocele (sis'to-sēl) [*cysto-* + Gr. *kēlē* hernia] hernial protrusion of the urinary bladder through the vaginal wall; called also *cystic hernia.* See illustration, next page.

The patient's knee struck her abdomen causing her to involuntarily void urine. The unanimous medical opinion is that she suffered a rectocele and **cystocele** (i.e., hernias in which the rectum and bladder protrude into the vaginal space). The doctors agree that these herniated structures prevent her from heavy lifting. LaMountain v. Alice Hyde Hospital Ass'n, 406 N.Y.S.2d 914–15 (3d Dep't 1978).

An examination revealed a **cystocele**, described by doctors as a protrusion of part of the bladder into the vagina.... Kerbeck v. Suchy, 270 N.E.2d 291–2 (App.Ct.Ill.1971).

... the doctor noted that she was suffering from first degree **cystocele** (hernia of urinary bladder).... Hammock v. Allstate Insurance Co., 186 S.E.2d 353–4 (Ct.App.Ga.1971).

cystometrogram (sis"to-met'ro-gram) the tracing recorded by cystometrography. See also *cystometrography.*

The **cystometrogram** examination undertaken by Dr. Penugonda, a urologist, revealed that the Plaintiff had a "flaccid neurogenic bladder" of the "lower motor neuron" type. McDonald v. U.S., 555 F.Supp. 935, 941 (M.D.Pa.1983).

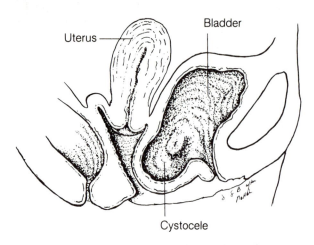

Cystocele

He recommended a **cystometrogram** which is used to determine what the capacity of the plaintiff's bladder was, how well it emptied, and whether reflex contractions were present. Harrigan v. U.S., 408 F.Supp. 177, 179 (E.D.Pa.1976).

cystometrography (sis"to-mĕ-trog'rah-fe) the graphic recording of the pressure exerted at varying degrees of filling of the urinary bladder.

cystoscope (sis'to-skōp") [*cysto-* + Gr. *skopein* to examine] an endoscope for visual examination of the bladder. See also *eyepiece* (Thomas case); and *resectoscope* (Thomas case).

A **cystoscope** is an instrument that permits an interior visualization of the bladder and urethra. Dessi v. U.S., 489 F.Supp. 722, 724 (E.D.Va.1980).

The device in question here is an instrument commonly used in urological surgery. It is part of a complex and highly sophisticated electro-surgical unit and is comprised of several component parts. Chief among them, and relevant for our consideration, is an optical telescope (a **cystoscope**) which permits so called closed surgery by insertion of the instrument directly into the patient's body. The surgeon is able to see and to operate internally by viewing through a monocular eyepiece affixed to the end of the telescope shaft. Thomas v. American Cystoscope Makers, Inc., 414 F.Supp. 255, 258 (E.D.Pa. 1976).

Other Authorities: Langton v. Brown, 591 S.W.2d 84, 86 (Mo. Ct.App.1979).

cystoscopic (sis"to-skop'ik) pertaining to cystoscopy, or performed with the cystoscope. See also *cystoscope*.

cystoscopy (sis-tos'ko-pe) direct visual examination of the urinary tract with a cystoscope.

Guardian argued, however, that the doctor should have disclosed that the diagnosis was based on a reduction in force in his urinary stream which culminated in a complete urinary retention on December 7, 1967. But, at the time the retention occurred, Dr. Urschel had performed a **cystoscopy** (described at trial as a not uncommon diagnostic procedure for determin-

ing the cause of prostatitis) and the condition subsided. Guardian Life Ins. Co. of America v. Robitaille, 495 F.2d 890, 896 (2d Cir. 1974).

Thursday, April 16, defendant ordered X rays of plaintiff's urinary tract; they revealed a partial blockage of the right ureter. A urologist, Dr. Howard, was consulted and he performed a **cystoscopy** the following day. Cronin v. Hagan, 221 N.W.2d 748–9 (Iowa 1974).

... a second **cystoscopy** and retrograde pyelogram to ascertain the continued drainage of urine were also performed (the first cystoscopy and pyelogram had been performed on July 10) and the surgical sponge found and removed. Rainer v. Buena Community Memorial Hospital, 95 Cal.Rptr. 901, 907 (Ct. App.Cal.1971).

Other Authorities: Sanders v. U.S., etc., 551 F.2d 458–9 (D.C. Cir.1977); Ausley v. Johnston, 450 S.W.2d 351, 353 (Ct.App. Tex.1970); Clark v. U.S., 402 F.2d 950, 952 (4th Cir. 1968).

cystostomy (sis-tos'to-me) [*cysto-* + Gr. *stoma* opening] the formation of an opening into the bladder.

cystostomy, tubeless suprapubic *cystostomy* in which a fistula of combined skin and bladder flap is created to enable the collection of urine in a reservoir without using a cystostomy tube. See also *cystotomy, suprapubic*.

cystotomy (sis-tot'o-me) surgical incision of the urinary bladder; vesicotomy.

cystotomy, suprapubic the operation of cutting into the bladder by an incision just above the pubic symphysis.

The first surgery performed to provide an alternative method of disposing of urine was a **suprapubic cystotomy**, which involved placing a tube in the stomach, to which a bag could be attached. The operation was unsuccessful. Rodriguez v. McDonnell Douglas Corp., 151 Cal.Rptr. 399, 413–14 (Ct.App. Cal.1978).

Henderson was admitted into the intensive care unit with blood coming from his Foley catheter. A **suprapubic cystostomy** was performed—opening the bladder through Henderson's lower abdominal wall to relieve the bladder of its urinary content on May 12, 1976. Henderson v. Life and Cas. Ins. Co., 574 S.W.2d 634–5 (Ct.Civ.App.Tex.1979).

Other Authorities: Langton v. Brown, 591 S.W.2d 84, 86 (Mo. Ct.App.1979).

cytological smear See *smear, cytological*.

cytology (si-tol'o-je) [*cyto-* + *-logy*] the study of cells, their origin, structure, function, and pathology.

cytology, exfoliative microscopic examination of cells desquamated from a body surface or lesion as a means of detecting malignancy and microbiologic changes, to measure hormonal levels, etc. Such cells may be obtained by such procedures as aspiration, washing, smear, and scraping, and the technique may be applied to vaginal secretions, sputum, urine, abdominal fluid, prostatic secretion, etc. See also *biopsy* (O'Brien case); and *smear, cytological* (O'Brien case).

D and C *dilation and curettage* (dilation of the cervix and curettage of the uterus).

Dr. Randolph felt that the best medical treatment for his patient was a **D & C** or curetment, a surgical procedure whereby the wall of the uterus is scraped; so he referred Pair Lee to a surgeon. Nevauex v. Park Place Hosp., Inc., 656 S.W.2d 923–4 (Ct.App.Tex.1983).

After reviewing the history she had given and examining her, he performed the abortion by dilatation and curettage (**D&C**), a procedure, according to appellant's brief, ''that involves suctioning out the contents of the uterus through a vacuum tube.'' Tissue obtained from the uterus was compatible with the size of a four to six week's fetus, according to Dr. Thimatariga. Thimatariga v. Chambers, 416 A.2d 1326, 1328 (Ct. Spec.App.Md.1980).

Plaintiff subsequently was admitted to the hospital where Dr. Beebe performed a ''**D and C**'' (dilation and curettage), which consists of an opening of the cervix and a scraping out of the womb. Dr. Beebe concluded that she had not ovulated and had not miscarried. Baker v. Beebe, 367 So.2d 102–3 (Ct. App.La.1979).

Other Authorities: Jones v. Harrisburg Polyclinic Hosp., 410 A.2d 303, 305 (Super.Ct.Pa.1979); Steele v. St. Paul Fire & Marine Ins. Co., 371 So.2d 843, 845 (Ct.App.La.1979); Cline v. Lund, 107 Cal.Rptr. 629, 632 (Ct.App.1973).

D and E (dilation and evacuation) See under *abortion* (American College of Obstetricians case).

Dalkon Shield See *device, intrauterine.*

Dakin's fluid (antiseptic solution) (da'kinz) [Henry Drysdale *Dakin*, New York chemist, 1880–1952] diluted sodium hypochlorite solution. See also *sodium hypochlorite.*

dam (dam) a thin sheet of latex rubber used to isolate teeth from the fluids of the mouth during dental therapy; also used occasionally in surgical procedures to separate certain tissues or structures. Often called *rubber dam.*

A **rubber dam** is a piece of rubber, usually square, which the dentist punches a hole through and then places the tooth or teeth to be worked on through the small hole. The **rubber dam** fits around the tooth to prevent ingress of saliva, moisture from the breath or bacteria, prevent the tongue from getting into the operative area and trap or catch any instrument dropped by the dentist....

''... There are two reasons primarily for the use of a **rubber dam**. The first is that you can keep a tooth dry, free from saliva and sterile. The second reason is that there are fillings, bits of tooth or instruments that are dropped, it would be impossible to go down the patient's throat.... Only occasionally does it take a few seconds to put in a **rubber dam**. Usually a minute or a minute and a half....'' Simpson v. Davis, 549 P.2d 950, 952, 956 (Kan.1976).

But at any rate, when I put the instrument in the canal, she made a, quite a substantial movement and it was; went down the hatch, I guess that is the best way to put it.

Expert testimony pertaining to the recognized standards of dental practice for the procedure in question was presented

by both plaintiffs and defendants. This centered primarily about whether a rubber sheet or ''**dam**'' was necessary to protect against what transpired here. Bean v. Stephens, 534 P.2d 1047, 1049 (Ct.App.Wash.1975).

damage

Damage has been defined as a direct physical injury to a cell, tissue, organ or organ system. Bailey v. American General Insurance Company, 154 Tex. 430, 279 S.W.2d 315 (1955). Hartford Acc. & Indem. Co. v. Thurmond, 527 S.W.2d 180, 188 (Ct.Civ.App.Tex.1975).

dantrolene sodium (dan'tro-lēn) chemical name: 1-[[[5-(4-nitrophenyl)-2-furanyl]methylene]amino]-2,4-imidazolidinedione sodium salt tetrahydrate. A skeletal muscle relaxant, $C_{14}H_9N_4NaO$, used as an antispasmodic in conditions such as stroke, multiple sclerosis, and cerebral palsy.

She further claims that **Dantrolene**, a widely-accepted emergency medicinal treatment for malignant hyperthermia was not available at the hospital. King v. Retz, 454 N.Y.S.2d 594, 595 (Sup.Ct.Onondaga Ct.1982).

Darvon (dar'von) trademark for a preparation of propoxyphene hydrochloride. See *propoxyphene hydrochloride.*

dB, db decibel.

D & C (dilatation and curettage) dilatation of the cervix and curettage of the uterus. See also *D and C.*

DCB See *dichlorobenzedine.*

d-cocaine See *cocaine* (U.S. v. Hall case).

deafness (def'nes) lack of the sense of hearing, or profound hearing loss. Moderate loss of hearing is often called *hearing loss.* See also *hearing loss; communications program, total; Kanamycin* (Marsh case); *neomycin; nervus tympanicus;* and *verbotonal program.*

He stated that, in his opinion, the cause of **deafness** was a traumatic injury to the inner ear nerves, which was caused by the unequalized pressure change displacing the ear drum, attached bones and prosthesis so that the prosthesis penetrated into the inner ear. (N.T. 89–92).

... We find, on the basis of the foregoing medical opinion from a duly qualified medical expert, and on the basis of all the evidence adduced for the purpose of justifying the assumptions of the hypothetical question, that the cabin repressurization as Flight 756 descended to London was a cause of the damage to plaintiff's left ear. We also find, on the basis of Dr. Myers' testimony and the relevant evidentiary facts, that the injury was in part caused by the peculiar condition of plaintiff, who had undergone a stapedectomy, and was suffering from a cold at the time. However, that was not the sole cause, because such an injury could have occurred even had he not suffered from a cold; such an impairment could have occurred to an individual with normally functioning middle ear bones. Warshaw v. Trans World Airlines, Inc., 442 F.Supp. 400, 405 (E.D. Pa.1977).

deafness, boilermakers' that caused by working in places where the noise level is extremely high. See also *tinnitus* (Marsh case).

deafness, conduction See *hearing loss, conductive.*

deafness, nerve; deafness, neural that which is due to a lesion of the auditory nerve or the central neural pathways. See also *chloroquine.*

"A few cases of a **nerve type deafness** have been reported after prolonged therapy [with chloroquine] usually in high doses." Grigsby v. Sterling Drug, Inc., 428 F.Supp. 242, 244 (D.D.C.1975).

"A My observations were that the patient had a moderately severe **nerve-type deafness.** She had some instability of gait and function in walking at this time. An electrony-stagmographic that we perform revealed that the patient had some evidence of dizziness when lying on her left side. This is objective; these are the things I found wrong." . . .

. . . As to causation, Dr. Frerichs testified that the loss of hearing in relation to the explosion and the dizziness in relation to the explosion go together. State Compensation Fund v. Cooke, 495 P.2d 480–2 (Ct.App.Ariz.1972).

Respondent Kubrick, a veteran, was admitted to the Veterans' Administration (VA) hospital in Wilkes-Barre, Pa., in April 1968, for treatment of an infection of the right femur. Following surgery, the infected area was irrigated with neomycin, an antibiotic, until the infection cleared. Approximately six weeks after discharge, Kubrick noticed a ringing sensation in his ears and some loss of hearing. An ear specialist in Scranton, Pa., Dr. Soma, diagnosed the condition as bilateral **nerve deafness**. U.S. v. Kubrick, 444 U.S. 111, 100 S.Ct. 352, 355, 62 L.Ed.2d 259 (1979).

Other Authorities: Ciavarro v. Despatch Shops, Inc., 255 N.Y.S.2d 48, 52 (3d Dep't 1964).

deafness, sensorineural deafness due to a lesion in the sensory mechanism (cochlea) of the ear or to a lesion in the acoustic nerve or the central neural pathways or to a combination of such lesions. See also *Rinne test*, under *tests.*

Dr. Cohen stated that his diagnosis in 1972 was bilateral **sensorineural hearing loss**, and that "[t]he basic loss I feel is his previous noise exposure, the difference in hearing acuity in the ears possibly related to the episode with influenza." . . .

. . . Dr. Cohen stated: "[Petitioner] has bilateral sensory neural hearing loss which is related basically to his previous noise exposure and aggravated [sic] by the passage of time. . . . Just what part the flu had to play in this current situation I cannot state but I doubt if it has any serious and significant contributing factors to the current situation. There is no treatment for this particular problem and I feel there is going to be very slow progression of the hearing loss of both ears due to the age factor. I think that the basic cause of his hearing loss is previous noise exposure." United Elec. Coal Co. v. Industrial Com'n, 444 N.E.2d 115–17 (Ill.1982).

While Nelson has sustained a fairly substantial percentage of hearing loss, it is with respect to high tones. There is no apparent loss at lower tones. We find that Nelson sustained a concussion-type shock from the explosions which, in turn, contrib-

uted appreciably to a perceptive-type hearing loss. Petition of U.S., 303 F.Supp. 1282, 1328 (E.D.N.Car.1969).

death (deth) the cessation of life; permanent cessation of all vital bodily functions. For legal and medical purposes, the following definition of death has been proposed—the irreversible cessation of all of the following: (1) total cerebral function, (2) spontaneous function of the respiratory system, and (3) spontaneous function of the circulatory system.

Health and Safety Code section 7180, subdivision (a), provides: An individual who has sustained either (1) irreversible cessation of circulatory and respiratory functions, or (2) irreversible cessation of all functions of the entire brain, including the brain stem, is dead. A determination of **death** must be made in accordance with accepted medical standards. Dority v. Super. Court of San Bernardino Cty., 193 Cal.Rptr. 288, 290 (Ct.App.Cal.1983).

The advent of life supportive techniques and advanced medical knowledge have raised a controversy over an adequate legal definition of **death**.

Black's Law Dictionary (4 ed. rev. 1968), 488, defines **death** as

The cessation of life; the ceasing to exist; defined by physicians as a total stoppage of the circulation of the blood, and a cessation of the animal and vital functions consequent thereon, such as respiration, pulsation, etc.

The difficulty with a definition which involves blood circulation develops in clinical situations, as present here, where the patient's cardio-respiratory system is mechanically supported, causing the blood to circulate and the related vital functions to continue. There obviously can be no **death** under Black's traditional definition as long as the heart and lungs remain intact. [But see **Black's** 5th Edition under "Death" and "Brain Death"] Yet, all other signs of life as reflected in the Ad Hoc Committee of Harvard Medical School can cease.

In clinical situations, such as the case at bar, the need for adoption of brain **death** as a legal definition is urged by many authorities. The establishment of an appropriate modern-day legal definition of **death** and the criteria to be followed are the subject of a plethora of written material, some of which are: Ad Hoc Committee of the Harvard Medical School to Examine the Definition of Brain Death, Report, "A Definition of 'Irreversible Coma,'" 208 J.A.M.A. 85 (1968); A Statement of the Cerebral Survival Program by The Project Directors, Cerebral Survival Program (performed under contracts with NINDS, Collaborative and Field Research), National Institute of Health, Bethesda, Md.; Task Force on Death and Dying of the Institute of Society, Ethics, and the Life Sciences, Report, "Refinements in the Criteria for the Determination of Death: An Appraisal," 221 J.A.M.A. 48 (1972); Capron and Kass, "A Statutory Definition of the Standard for Determining Human Death: An Appraisal and a Proposal," 121 U.Pa.L.Rev. 87 (1972); Friloux, "Death, When Does It Occur?" 27 Baylor L.Rev. 10 (1975); Halley & Harvey, "Medical vs. Legal Definitions of Death," 204 J.A.M.A. 103 (1968); Hirsh, "Brain Death," 21 Md.Tr.Tech.Q. 377 (1975). Matter of Quinlan, 348 A.2d 801, 817 (Super.Ct.N.J.1975).

. . . it is obvious on reflection that cardiac or respiratory arrest will signal the arrival of death for the overwhelming majority of persons whose lives are terminated by illness or old age; indeed, they are part of the normal [4] act of **death**. [[4] The qualification is necessary because "**death**" is defined for some purposes solely in terms of complete loss of brain function, or "brain death." See Commonwealth v. Golston, ___ Mass. ___, ___ (1977) (Mass.Adv.Sh. [1977] 1778, 1780) 366 N.E.2d 752. Such a definition is of practical importance principally in cases of traumatic injury to the brain where respiration and circulation are maintained artificially.] Matter of Dinnerstein, 380 N.E.2d 134, 136 (App.Ct.Mass.1978).

death, brain irreversible brain damage as manifested by absolute unresponsiveness to all stimuli, absence of all spontaneous muscle activity, including respiration, shivering, etc., and an isoelectric electroencephalogram for 30 minutes, all in the absence of hypothermia or intoxication by central nervous system depressants. Called also *irreversible coma*.

The Loma Linda hospital defines **brain death** as total and irreversible cessation of brain function, although there is no written policy as to how to make that diagnosis. Dority v. Super. Court of San Bernardino Cty., 193 Cal.Rptr. 288–9 (Ct.App. Cal.1983).

Dr. Goldensohn testified as to the varying degrees of coma. "**Brain death**" is that state wherein an individual cannot breathe on his own, has no reflexes other than spinal ones, and has an electroencephalogram (EEG) indicating a complete absence of spontaneous electrical activity in the cortex....

... Thus, while the law has traditionally regarded death as an event, i.e., the cessation of circulatory and respiratory functions, medical science has come to recognize death as a process.[10] Several pre-eminent medical panels—including the previously alluded to Ad Hoc Committee of Harvard Medical School—have attempted to resolve this dilemma by postulating new criteria for the determination of death, commonly referred to as "**brain death**".[11] This solution, however, has not as yet been accepted as legally conclusive of the issue in this State (but see, Matter of New York City Health & Hosps. Corp. v. Sulsona, 81 Misc.2d 1002, 1003, 1005–1007, 367 N.Y.S.2d 686, 687, 689–691 [construing the term "death" under Public Health Law, § 4301, covering anatomical gifts to mean "**brain death**" in accordance with current medical standards]; see, also, the discussion of Sulsona, at Ann. Tests of Death for Organ Transplant Purposes, 76 A.L.R.3d 913). [[10] "Death. The cessation of life; the ceasing to exist; defined by physicians as a total stoppage of the circulation of the blood, and a cessation of the animal and vital functions consequent thereon, such as respiration, pulsation, etc." (Black's Law Dictionary [rev. 4th ed., 1968], p. 488.) (For cases where such definition has been applied to resolve questions involving implications of death, see, e.g., Smith v. Smith, 229 Ark. 579, 586, 317 S.W.2d 275; Thomas v. Anderson, 96 Cal.App.2d 371, 376, 215 P.2d 478.).... (see, also, Collester, Death, Dying and the Law: A Prosecutorial View of the Quinlan Case, 30 Rutgers L.Rev. 304, 307; Note, The Tragic Choice: Termination of Care for Patients in a Permanent Vegetative State, 51 N.Y.U.L.Rev. 285, 287; Note, The Criteria for Determining Death in Vital Organ Transplants—A Medico-Legal Dilemma, 38 Mo.L.Rev. 220, 223, 232; Wasmuth, The Concept of Death, 30 Ohio St.L.J. 33, 36–37; Ann. Tests of Death for Organ Transplant Purposes, 76 A.L.R.3d 913). [11] The proposed criteria for **brain death** recognized by the Ad Hoc

Committee of Harvard Medical School included (1) lack of receptivity and response to externally applied stimuli; (2) no movements or breath; (3) no reflexes; and (4) a flat EEG, indicating a total absence of brain activity (Ad Hoc Committee of the Harvard Medical School to Examine the Definition of Brain Death, A Definition of Irreversible Coma, 205 J.A.M.A. 337, 338).... (See, generally, R. Veatch, Death, Dying and the Biological Revolution, 21–72; Capron & Kass, A Statutory Definition of the Standards for Determining Human Death: An Appraisal and a Proposal, 121 U.Pa.L.Rev. 87.)] Eichner v. Dillon, 426 N.Y.S.2d 517, 529, 531–2 (2d Dep't 1980).

Other Authorities: Matter of Quinlan, 348 A.2d 801, 810 (Super.Ct.N.J.1975).

death, fetal stillbirth; death in utero; failure of the product of conception to show evidence of respiration, heart beat, or definite movement of a voluntary muscle after expulsion from the uterus, with no possibility of resuscitation.

Fetal death is defined as death prior to the complete expulsion or extraction from its mother of a product of human conception, irrespective of the duration of pregnancy. The death is indicated by the fact that after such separation the fetus does not breathe or show any other evidence of life such as beating of the heart, pulsation of the umbilical cord, or definitive movement of voluntary muscles. Ill.Rev.Stat., ch. 111½, § 73–1(6) (1975). Wynn v. Scott, 449 F.Supp. 1302, 1327 (N.D.Ill.1978).

death, wrongful (fetus)

They invoke the "weight of authority," pointing to the fact that 25 states now recognize a cause of action for the **wrongful death** of a fetus, while at most 12 reject it. [Footnote omitted.]...

The United States Supreme Court has said that the development of a cause of action for the **wrongful death** of a fetus is "generally opposed by the commentators...." (Roe v. Wade (1973) 410 U.S. 113, 162, 93 S.Ct. 705, 35 L.Ed.2d 147; see, e.g., 2 Harper & James, The Law of Torts (1956) § 18.3, p. 1031 (see also id., 1968 supp., pp. 71–72); Gordon, The Unborn Plaintiff (1965) 63 Mich.L.Rev. 579, 591–595; Wenger, Developments in the Law of Prenatal Wrongful Death (1965) 69 Dick.L.Rev. 258; but see 1 Speiser, Recovery for Wrongful Death (2d ed. 1975) §§ 4.36–4.38; Del Tufo, Recovery for Prenatal Torts: Actions for Wrongful Death (1960) 15 Rutgers L.Rev. 61, 73–80.) The American Law Institute declines to take a position on the question (Rest.2d Torts (Tent. Draft No. 16, Apr. 24, 1970) § 869, subd. (2)), as does Dean Prosser (Prosser, Torts (4th ed. 1971) p. 338). Justus v. Atchison, 565 P.2d 122, 125–7 (Cal.1977).

débride (da-brēd) to remove foreign material and contaminated or devitalized tissue, usually by sharp dissection.

Dr. Richardson **debrided**, i.e., surgically removed the dead tissue, from her elbow. He then took a four-inch-by-eight-inch graft from her abdomen and applied it to her arm. Ohligschlager v. Proctor Community Hospital, 303 N.E.2d 392, 395 (Ill.1973).

Appellant then **debrided** the wound by cutting away and removing dead and injured tissue. The "standard laceration tray," comprised of surgical instruments, was used by appellant in **debriding** the wound, and it then was sutured in layers. King v. Murphy, 424 So.2d 547–8 (Miss.1982).

Approximately six or seven days following the injury Dr. Aronoff commenced his routine burn treatment. This involved taking Dial twice daily on a cart to a tank of water solution and putting him in the tank. The burnt skin was then washed and "debrided". The **debriding** was done by nurses and consisted of pulling off the dead portions of skin with forceps. Many times this would require sedation by morphine prior to going into the tank because of the pain occasioned in the **debriding** operation. The **debriding** is necessary to prevent infection. Following the **debriding** his burns were covered with a sulfamylon cream. This cream contains acid and burns a great deal. Wry v. Dial, 503 P.2d 979, 983 (Ct.App.Ariz.1972).

débridement (da-brēd′maw) [Fr.] the removal of foreign material and devitalized or contaminated tissue from or adjacent to a traumatic or infected lesion until surrounding healthy tissue is exposed. Cf. *épluchage.*

During this time period, he performed what is referred to as a surgical prep and **debridement** of the left knee. This includes scrubbing some eight to twelve inches both above and below the knee with a betadine solution and betadine scrub, draping the wound with sterile dressing, removal of foreign material, irrigation of the wound, removal of devitalized tissue, and open suturing of the wound to make certain that it would remain open and draining. After this procedure, a dressing was placed over the wound. Harris v. State Through Huey P. Long Mem. Hosp., 378 So.2d 383–5 (La.1979).

Root canal therapy, generally speaking, consists of three steps. The first step is **debridement** or mechanical cleansing of the canal. In this step the pulp tissue is removed from the pulp chamber and the root canal. When there is no vital pulp in the tooth, the authorities in the dental profession are generally agreed that the root canals should be cleansed to the best extent possible. If there is still some vital tissue in the tooth, the authorities agree that the root canal should be cleansed to a point within a few millimeters of the apex, but perhaps not to the furthest extent possible. This point of **debridement**, sometimes referred to as the physiological apex, falls within the last one-third of the root canal short of the anatomical apex. Following the removal of the pulp tissue, the root canal is reamed and shaped to accept a filling material. U.S. v. Talbott, 460 F.Supp. 253, 257 (S.D.Ohio 1978).

During his inpatient treatment at Ochsner, the plaintiff received extensive care for his burns which involved over sixty percent of his body. The treatment for the burns consisted of **debridement,** a painful process in which the skin is removed from the body while the patient is awake and situated in a whirlpool-type tank. McLean v. U.S., 446 F.Supp. 9, 12 (E.D.La.1977).

Other Authorities: Arnold v. Eastern Air Lines, Inc., 681 F.2d 186, 203 (4th Cir. 1982); Piso v. Weirton Steel Co., Div. of National Steel Corp., 345 A.2d 728, 730 (Super.Ct.Pa.1975); Stogsdill v. Manor Convalescent Home, Inc., 343 N.E.2d 589, 594 (App.Ct.Ill.1976).

Decadron (dek′ah-dron) trademark for preparations of dexamethasone. See *dexamethasone.*

decay (de-ka′) [*de-* + L. *cadere* to fall] 1. the gradual decomposition of dead organic matter. 2. the process or stage of decline, as in aging.

decay, dental

Dental decay is the result of a bacterial process in which carbohydrates and sugars are fermented. The bacterial process produces an acid which causes the decalcification of the tooth. Since this bacterial process takes a period of time to cause dental decay, it is found most often in places where bacteria and debris containing carbohydrates and sugars lodge and are not easily dislodged by brushing or by the natural cleansing of the teeth. In other words, **dental decay** is most common in the interproximal areas (the area between teeth) and the biting surfaces of posterior teeth which are irregular. . . .

The surfaces of the anterior teeth are generally smooth and are, therefore, more or less self-cleansing through the normal function of the lips, tongue and eating. The smooth surfaces of the anterior teeth are usually the last areas to be afflicted by **dental decay**. If there is a gross neglect of oral hygiene and rampant caries or cavities exist, the anterior teeth will also likely be affected. In this case, however, the **dental decay** would be most likely to exist at the cervical portion of the tooth where debris would gather close to the soft tissue of the gum.

When decay is found on the smooth surface of the anterior teeth in the coronal region but not in the cervical region, it is generally because there was a pre-existing hypoplastic defect. U.S. v. Talbott, 460 F.Supp. 253, 258 (S.D.Ohio 1978).

deceleration injury See *injury, deceleration.*

decerebrate (de-ser′ĕ-brāt) 1. to eliminate cerebral function by transecting the brain stem between the superior colliculi and the vestibular nuclei or by ligating the common carotid arteries and the basilar artery at the center of the pons. 2. an animal so prepared. 3. a person with brain damage resulting in neurologic signs similar to those of a decerebrated animal. See also *decerebrate rigidity,* under *rigidity.*

As of November 13, 1979, the date prior to his testimony, Dr. Kelly found that the patient had "**decerebrated**".

He has lack of cerebral function. He is in a coma. He has convulsive episodes that need medication for control and has required that since the date of surgery. He does not respond to stimuli, and he has what we call autonomic, vegetative function, that of kidney function, intestinal function which are working, but he has no knowledge. Eichner v. Dillon, 426 N.Y.S.2d 517, 528 (2d Dep't 1980).

Decerebrate movements are neurological signs and should be recorded when observed. . . .

. . . In light of the recognized importance of recording **decerebrate** movements and of preparing to contend with the possible consequences of such signs and the failure to take such precautions I reject as unworthy of belief the testimony of the two nurses that they had observed such movements. Rose v. Hakim, 335 F.Supp. 1221, 1227–8 (D.C.Cir.1971).

decholin See *acid, dehydrocholic.*

decibel (des′ĭ-bel) a unit used to express the ratio of two powers, usually electric or acoustic powers, equal to one-tenth the common logarithm of the ratio of the powers. One decibel is equal approximately to the smallest difference in acoustic power that the human ear can detect. Abbreviated dB and db. See also *bel*.

The proposed ear plugs, according to Dr. McConnell, would reduce the high tone noises 30 to 40 **decibels** (**decibel** is the unit of measurement of sound) and reduce the low tone noises 10 to 15 **decibels**. This type of testimony supports the conclusion of the witness Hadley that it would be dangerous for switchmen to wear ear plugs. Rubley v. Louisville & Nashville Ry.Co., 208 F.Supp. 798, 804 (E.D.Tenn.1962).

decomposition (de"kom-po-zish'un) [*de-* + L. *componere* to put together] the separation of compound bodies into their constituent principles by whatever process. See also *organoleptic* (test).

As precisely as the court recalls, the testimony regarding the meaning of decomposition was as follows:
A condition which has adversely affected the quality of the product and may be injurious to health. (READ)
A substance wherein there is a breakdown due to bacterial conditions which could be harmful or hazardous to health. (DUNIGAN)
An undesirable chemical change in a product from the original form which offends or alarms the consumer or is evidential of a hazard to health. (ATKIN)....
... However, all agree that **decomposition** involves a bacterial separation or breakdown in the elements of the food so as to produce an undesirable disintegration or rot. That in itself is close to the dictionary definition and will have to suffice. Perhaps the term is similar to drunkenness—it is easy to detect, but hard to define. U.S. v. 1,200 Cans, Pasteurized Whole Eggs, 339 F.Supp. 131, 137 (N.D.Ga.1972).

decompression (de"kom-presh'un) the removal of pressure, particularly the slow lessening of pressure on deep-sea divers and caisson workers to prevent the onset of bends, and the reduction of pressure on persons as they ascend to great heights. See also under *sickness*.

Dr. Gol examined Mr. French on November 6, 1968 and diagnosed "multiple nerve root compressions" in the lower lumbar region "probably in the L5–S1 distribution of the right side." Dr. Gol then participated with Dr. Brodsky in the operation describing the procedure as follows:
The **decompression** was carried out at three levels, and the nerve root **decompression** was performed particularly at L5 level nerve root, which was **decompressed**. It was felt at the end of this procedure that a very adequate **decompression** had been carried out, both from the point of view of bony changes and previous scarring. Some further disc material was removed from the L4–5 level at the same time. French v. Brodsky, 521 S.W.2d 670, 684 (Ct.Civ.App.Tex.1975).

decompression, nerve relief of pressure on a nerve by surgical removal of the constricting fibrous or bony tissue.

The post-operative diagnosis was: "Nerve root compression syndrome, left"...
... "There seems to be more tightness of structures particularly of the roots in the dural sac and the lumbar area than one usually encountered. It is felt that this is the situation representing the root compression syndrome, the exact mechanics of which is not apparent. It is felt that for this reason that hemilaminectomy of the left L–5 would afford the patient additional

decompression and this is carried out. After this had been done the dural sac bulges upward in a more normal position. Richardson v. Perales, 402 U.S. 389, 391, 91 S.Ct. 1420, 28 L.Ed.2d 842 (1971).

Dr. James D. Wimpee, a witness for appellant, performed surgery on appellee which Dr. Wimpee described as removing "the pressure that was on the nerves coming out of the back of his leg." This was accomplished "by cutting away the bone and the protruded ruptured bulging disc out of the joint space that had bulged out against this nerve root." Texas Employers' Insurance Ass'n v. Shirey, 391 S.W.2d 75, 77 (Ct.Civ.App.Tex. 1965).

decompression of spinal cord relief of pressure on the spinal cord by means of surgery; the pressure may be due to hematoma, bone fragments, etc.

... he underwent another operative procedure by Dr. Homer Kirgis, a neurosurgeon, which consisted of a **decompression of the spinal cord**, removal of the fifth cervical vertebra and an anterior intrabody fusion at C–4, C–5 and C–6. Warner v. City of Bay St. Louis, 408 F.Supp. 375, 379 (S.D.Miss.1975).

decompression, subtemporal cerebral decompression after removal of a portion of the temporal bone.

decortication (de"kor-tĭ-ka'shun) [*de-* + L. *cortex* bark] removal of portions of the cortical substance of a structure or organ, as of the brain, kidney, lung, etc.

He found her in a state of coma, with evidence of **decortication** indicating altered level of consciousness....
... She did not trigger the respirator, which means that she did not breathe spontaneously nor independently of it at any time during the examination. Due to her **decorticate** posturing, no reflexes could be elicited....
In the **decorticate** posturing the upper arms are drawn into the side of the body. The forearms are drawn in against the chest with the hands generally at right angles to the forearms, pointing towards the waist. The legs are drawn up against the body, knees are up, feet are in near the buttocks and extended in a ballet-type pose. Matter of Quinlan, 348 A.2d 801, 807 (Super.Ct.N.J.1975).
... he had to undergo a "major" tuberculosis operation—a pulmonary **decortication** left. Henning v. U.S., 311 F.Supp. 681, 682 (E.D.Pa.1970).

decubation (de"ku-ba'shun) [*de-* + L. *cubare* to lie down] the period in the course of an infectious disease from the disappearance of the symptoms to complete recovery and the end of the infectious period. Cf. *incubation*.

decubitus (de-ku'bĭ-tus), pl. *decu'bitus* [L. "a lying down"] 1. an act of lying down; also the position assumed in lying down. 2. decubitus ulcer. See also under *ulcer*.

defect (de'fekt) an imperfection, failure, or absence. See also *disease*.

Under the law a product can be in a defective condition if at the time it left the manufacturer's hands it had a **defect** which rendered it dangerous to the user; and so far as the law is concerned, a **defect** can consist of failure to warn the purchaser of that product of any dangers inherent in the product.
In other words, a manufacturer is not required to produce a product which is guaranteed not to cause harm under any cir-

cumstances. Obviously, a vast percentage of the products which are used in our society today do have some potential for harm. [Dissent.] Dougherty v. Hooker Chemical Corp., 540 F.2d 174, 182–3 (3d Cir. 1976).

defects, atrial septal; defects, atrioseptal congenital cardiac anomalies in which there is persistent patency of the atrial septum due to failure of fusion between either the septum secundum or the septum primum and the endocardial cushions. In *ostium secundum defect* there is a rim of septum all around the defect. In *ostium primum defect*, which is an incomplete form of atrioventricularis communis, there is no septum at the base of the defect, between the mitral and tricuspid valves; it is usually associated with a cleft mitral cusp and occasionally with a cleft tricuspid valve.

On February 23, 1981 Dr. Donald Patrick performed surgery on Mr. Black's heart to repair the **atrial septal defect**, which is a hole in the wall of the two upper chambers of the heart, and a double by-pass for the arteriosclerosis. Black v. Riverside Furniture Co., 642 S.W.2d 338, 339 (Ct.App.Ark.1982).

defect, filling any localized defect in the contour of the stomach, duodenum, or intestine, as seen in the roentgenogram after a barium enema, due to a lesion of the wall projecting into the lumen or to an object in the lumen.

... the hospital radiologist concurred that a gastroscopic examination was warranted to investigate a "**filling defect**" within appellant's hernia. Cooper v. Roberts, 286 A.2d 647, 648 (Super.Ct.Pa.1971).

defect, ventricular septal a congenital cardiac anomaly in which there is persistent patency of the ventricular septum in either the muscular or fibrous portions, most often due to failure of the bulbar septum to completely close the interventricular foramen.

Dr. Speilman ran numerous tests on Randy, including an EKG, chest x-ray, and echocardiogram; these tests, in conjunction with the physical examination, led to a diagnosis of the cardiac disorder as a **ventricular septal defect**, which is an abnormal opening in the septum that divides the two lower chambers of the heart. Id. at 78–80, 86–90. See Pl.Ex. 6. [Footnote omitted.] Phillips v. U.S., 566 F.Supp. 1, 9 (D.S.Car.1981).

defibrillation (de-fib″rĭ-la′shun) termination of atrial or ventricular fibrillation, usually by electroshock.

During the respiratory arrest McCrery also suffered a short period of heart arrhythmia and thereafter went into ventricular fibrillation for approximately 15 seconds. Electrical **defibrillation** (shock treatment) was employed to counteract that condition and within a few seconds McCrery's heart pattern returned to normal. U.S. v. Narciso, 446 F.Supp. 252, 287 (E.D. Mich.1977).

defibrillator (de-fib″rĭ-la′tor) [*de-* + *fibrillation*] an electronic apparatus used to counteract atrial or ventricular fibrillation by the application of brief electroshock to the heart, directly or through electrodes placed on the chest wall.

A **defibrillator** may be used, applying electric shock to the heart to induce contractions....

... Many of these procedures are obviously highly intrusive, and some are violent in nature. The **defibrillator**, for example, causes violent (and painful) muscle contractions which, in a patient suffering (as this patient is) from osteoporosis, may cause fracture of vertebrae or other bones. Such fractures, in turn, cause pain, which may be extreme. Matter of Dinnerstein, 380 N.E.2d 134–6 (App.Ct.Mass.1978).

Furthermore, the intensive care unit either did not have, when needed for infant plaintiff, a heart monitor, with a **defibrillator** on it to shock the heart if it started to fail or to beat abnormally, or if it did have such a monitor it was not attached to the infant plaintiff. Rose v. Hakim, 335 F.Supp. 1221, 1225 (D.D.C.1971).

deformity (de-for′mĭ-te) distortion of any part or general disfigurement of the body; malformation.

Any such **deformity** of bone tissue because of the application of external force to bone tissue which has suffered necrosis or death is irreversible. Once the **deformity** occurs, it is permanent....

... The body cannot repair such **deformity**, and the bone will thus retain the deformed character. (N.T. 188, 189). Rosario v. Amer. Export-Isbrandtsen Lines, Inc., 395 F.Supp. 1192, 1202–3 (E.D.Pa.1975), reversed 531 F.2d 1227 (3d Cir. 1976).

deformity, silver fork the peculiar deformity seen in Colles' fracture; see illustration under *fracture*. Called also *Velpeau's deformity*.

Plaintiffs claim that, as a result of failure to reduce the fractures, the fragments of the broken bones were not pushed into proper position and Mrs. Lieder suffered a **silver-fork deformity** of the left wrist, meaning that the wrist, instead of being straight, comes up in a hump and the fingers go down like a fork. Lieder v. Maus, 203 N.W.2d 393–4 (Minn.1973).

degeneration (de-jen″er-a′shun) [L. *degeneratio*] deterioration; change from a higher to a lower form; especially change of tissue to a lower or less functionally active form. When there is chemical change of the tissue itself, it is *true* degeneration; when the change consists in the deposit of abnormal matter in the tissues, it is *infiltration*. Called also *retrogression*.

The doctor concluded that Benny Harrison was probably suffering from cervical osteodegenerative disease, which, in all likelihood, existed before the auto accident. Harrison v. South Central Bell Tel. Co., 390 So.2d 219, 221 (Ct.App.La.1980).

degenerative arthritis See *osteoarthritis*.

degenerative joint disease See *osteoarthritis*.

degloving (de-gluv′ing) intra-oral surgical exposure of the bony mandibular chin; it can be performed in the posterior region if necessary.

She also sustained a **degloving** injury [6] on the right foot. [[6] A **degloving** injury is one in which the skin is peeled off of the underlying tissues for some distance.] Albert v. Alter, 381 A.2d 459, 468 (Super.Ct.Pa.1977).

dehiscence (de-his′ens) [L. *dehiscere* to gape] a splitting open.

It was generally agreed that wound **dehiscence** depends on the healing quality of the patient, not the type of suture used by the surgeon. It was also agreed that the healing quality of the patient may be affected by several different factors. Among those mentioned were prior incision, debilitation of the patient by chronic illness, long-term administration of steroids, old age, nutritional deficiency, obesity, infection, and hematoma (accumulation of blood in the wound). Trichel v. Caire, 427 So.2d 1227, 1231 (Ct.App.La.1983).

Records from the hospital in Beaumont reveal Dr. Miller opened her incision and "immediately voluminous amounts of fecal fluid escaped from the wound, and it became obvious there was a **dehiscence** beneath the skin of the entire abdominal wall...." Richardson v. Holmes, 525 S.W.2d 293, 296 (Ct.Civ.App.Tex.1975).

The record reveals that following a fit of coughing plaintiff suffered a tearing or disruption of the surgical wound. Appellee performed additional surgery for the purpose of correcting such **dehiscence**. Cleveland v. Edwards, 494 S.W.2d 578, 580 (Ct.Civ.App.Tex.1973).

Other Authorities: Richardson v. Holmes, 525 S.W.2d 293, 296 (Ct.Civ.App.Tex.1975).

dehydrocholate (de-hi″dro-ko′lāt) a salt of dehydrocholic acid.

Delalutin (del″ah-lu′tin) trademark for a preparation of hydroxyprogesterone caproate. See *hydroxyprogesterone caproate.*

delivery (de-liv′er-e) expulsion or extraction of the child and the after-birth. See also *labor.*

delivery, breech delivery of an infant in breech presentation. See also *breech extraction*, under *extraction; delivery, partial breech*; and *delivery, total breech*.

In a **breech delivery**, the baby's buttocks are delivered first, the head last; whereas in a normal vertex delivery the head is first. The risk of injury to a child in a **breech delivery** is significantly greater than in a normal vertex delivery. Because the buttocks are smaller than the head, they do not provide a sufficient driving wedge to fully dilate the cervix and allow the head to pass through the cervix. Freed v. Priore, 372 A.2d 895, 897 (Super.Ct.Pa.1977).

delivery, midforceps the application of forceps when the fetal head is engaged, but the conditions for outlet (low) forceps delivery have not been met; any forceps delivery requiring artificial rotation.

At 4:46 a.m., he delivered the baby using a "**midforceps rotation**" delivery. In this procedure, forceps are used to rotate the baby's head to the proper position and then used to extract the baby. In the hospital delivery record, written and signed by defendant, the method of delivery was described as a "**tight midforceps rotation**." At a deposition taken on July 5, 1979, defendant described a tight **midforceps rotation** as being one in which he would have to apply excessive pressure to effect the procedure. Grindstaff v. Tygett, 655 S.W.2d 70, 72 (Mo.Ct.App.1983).

A "moderately difficult **midforceps delivery**" was made in eight or ten minutes during which time the doctor applied compression and traction to the forceps on the baby's face ap-

proximately five times. The Supreme Court (Florida) noted: Tucker-McLane forceps are no longer recognized *as proper* in deliveries involving a molded or elongated head. Wale v. Barnes, 261 So.2d 201–2 (Dist.Ct.App.Fla.1972), quashed 278 So.2d 601, 605 (Fla.1973).

delivery, partial breech

In a **partial breech extraction** the baby's body will have partially emerged through the cervix, the doctor will only have to assist in the extraction of a part of the body, usually the head and arms. Freed v. Priore, 372 A.2d 895, 897 (Super.Ct.Pa. 1977).

delivery, total breech

In a **total breech extraction** no part of the baby's body has emerged through the cervix and the doctor must manually pull the child through the cervix. Freed v. Priore, 372 A.2d 895, 897 (Super.Ct.Pa.1977).

Deltasone (del′tah-sōn) trademark for a preparation of prednisone. See *prednisone.*

delta wave See *wave, delta.*

delusion (de-lu′zhun) [L. *delusio*, from *de* from + *ludus* a game] a false personal belief based on incorrect inference about external reality and firmly maintained in spite of incontrovertible and obvious proof or evidence to the contrary; it is not a belief that is accepted by other members of the person's culture or subculture (i.e., it is not an article of religious faith). Cf. *illusion.*

"There is no such thing as a **delusion** founded upon facts. It is a mental conception in the absence of facts. If the idea entertained has for a basis anything substantial it is not a **delusion**." Wigginton v. Rule, 275 Mo. 412, 205 S.W. 168, 179. An insane **delusion** is insanity, i.e., it is partial insanity in respect to a particular subject....

... An insane **delusion** is defined to be a false and fixed belief not founded on reason and incapable of being removed by reason.... Byars v. Buckley, 461 S.W.2d 817, 820 (Mo. 1970).

demand, biochemical oxygen

Biological oxygen demand (BOD) is a measure of the oxygen consuming capabilities of the organic matter in the wastewater. BOD_5 is BOD measured over a five-day period. Tanners' Council of America, Inc. v. Train, 540 F.2d 1188, 1190 (4th Cir. 1976).

The computation of the surcharge is based upon three factors: the amount of liquid discharged, the "5 day, **Biochemical Oxygen Demand**," or **BOD**, of the sewage and the suspended solid content of the sewage. **Biochemical Oxygen Demand** is defined as "the quantity of dissolved oxygen required for biochemical oxidation of decomposable matter under aerobic conditions in a period of five days at a temperature of 20 degrees centigrade." Chicago Allis Mfg. Corp. v. Metropolitan San. Dist., 288 N.E.2d 436, 438–9 (Ill.1972).

dementia (de-men′she-ah) [*de-* + L. *mens* mind] organic loss of intellectual function; called also *aphrenia, aphronesia,* and *athymia.*

dementia, paralytic; dementia paralytica a chronic syphilitic meningoencephalitis, characterized by degeneration of the cortical neurons, progressive dementia, and a generalized paralysis which, if untreated, is ultimately fatal. Called also *general paresis, general paralysis of the insane, paretic dementia, cerebral tabes,* and *syphilitic meningoencephalitis.*

dementia praecox, paranoid See *schizophrenia, paranoid.*

dementia praesenilis; dementia, presenile dementia of unknown etiology beginning at middle age and characterized by cortical atrophy and secondary ventricular dilatation; called also *Alzheimer's disease, dementia,* or *sclerosis.*

The employer's experts, also eminently qualified, steadfastly maintained that decedent suffered from Alzheimer's disease which caused **pre-senile dementia**, retinitis pigmentosa and generalized arteriosclerosis. Yannon v. New York Telephone Co., 450 N.Y.S.2d 893, 895 (3d Dep't 1982).

The patient is a sixty-seven year old woman who suffers from a condition known as Alzheimer's disease. It is a degenerative disease of the brain of unknown origin, described as **presenile dementia**, and results in destruction of brain tissue and, consequently, deterioration in brain function. The condition is progressive and unremitting, leading in stages to disorientation, loss of memory, personality disorganization, loss of intellectual function, and ultimate loss of all motor function. The disease typically leads to a vegetative or comatose condition and then to death. The course of the disease may be gradual or precipitous, averaging five to seven years. At this time medical science knows of no cure for the disease and no treatment which can slow or arrest its course. No medical breakthrough is anticipated....

... At the present time she is confined to a hospital bed, in an essentially vegetative state, immobile, speechless, unable to swallow without choking, and barely able to cough. Her eyes occasionally open and from time to time appear to fix on or follow an object briefly; otherwise she appears to be unaware of her environment. She is fed through a naso-gastric tube, intravenous feeding having been abandoned because it came to cause her pain. It is probable that she is experiencing some discomfort from the naso-gastric tube, which can cause irritation, ulceration, and infection in her throat and esophageal tract, and which must be removed from time to time, and that procedure itself causes discomfort. She is catheterized and also, of course, requires bowel care. [Footnote omitted.] Matter of Dinnerstein, 380 N.E.2d 134–5 (App.Ct. Mass.1978).

Named plaintiff Juanita Burns suffers from Alzheimer's disease, a chronic neuropsychopathic disorder characterized by impaired intellectual ability and requires skilled nursing home care twenty-four (24) hours per day. Burns v. Vowell, 424 F.Supp. 1135, 1137 (S.D.Tex.1976).

Demerol (dem'er-ol) trademark for preparations of meperidine (pethidine) hydrochloride. See also *meperidine hydrochloride.*

demineralization (de-min″er-al-i-za'shun) excessive elimination of mineral or inorganic salts, as in pulmonary tuberculosis, cancer, and osteomalacia. See also *porotic* (Blackburn case).

There he was told that, because of **demineralization**, his bones resembled those of an 85 or 90 year old man. Coulter v. Weinberger, 527 F.2d 224, 226 (3d Cir. 1975).

demonstrate

The term "**demonstrate**" implies a fairly stringent standard of proof in the empirical sciences. Griffin v. U.S., 351 F.Supp. 10, 27 (E.D.Pa.1972).

demyelinate (de-mi'ĕ-lin-āt) to destroy or remove the myelin sheath of a nerve or nerves.

As defined earlier, GBS is clearly a **demyelinating** peripheral neuropathy. As Dr. Medinets testified, **demyelination** involves the stripping away of the myelin sheath around the nerve, the result being that a **demyelinated** fiber cannot conduct any nerve impulses at all. Despite the interpretation of the EMG reports in this case by plaintiffs, I find that there is insufficient credible evidence of peripheral nerve involvement in Mrs. Stich's upper extremities at any time. Dr. Medinets noted that slowed nerve conduction, or absence of conduction, does not necessarily mean **demyelinating** disease. Stich v. U.S., 565 F.Supp. 1096, 1110 (D.N.J.1983).

demyelinating disease See *disease, demyelinating.*

demyelination (de-mi″ĕ-li-na'shun) destruction, removal, or loss of the myelin sheath of a nerve or nerves.

The resulting "shorting out," or **demyelination**, of the nerves impairs their ability to conduct electrical impulses from the brain that control the reflexes and movement of certain muscles. Padgett v. U.S., 553 F.Supp. 794, 795–6 (W.D.Tex. 1982).

DEN See *dienestrol.*

denervation (de″ner-va'shun) resection of or removal of the nerves to an organ or part.

Dr. Essam Awad, a professor at the University of Minnesota Medical School, specializing in neuromuscular diseases, testified that he had discovered "definite evidence of **denervation** in the inner sphincter." Dr. Joseph Engel, a physician in private practice in Minneapolis, answered in the affirmative when asked whether there was **denervation** of Ms. Sanden's anal sphincter. Sanden v. Mayo Clinic, 495 F.2d 221, 225 (8th Cir. 1974).

denervation, vagal

... abnormal esophageal motility, characterized by lack of peristaltic contraction in distal esophagus, probably secondary to **vagal denervation** (problems with food moving through the esophagus).... Manigan v. Califano, 453 F.Supp. 1080, 1084 (D.Kan.1978).

dental decay See *decay, dental.*

dentin (den'tin) [L. *dens* tooth] the chief substance or tissue of the teeth, which surrounds the tooth pulp and is covered by enamel on the crown and by cementum on the roots of the teeth. Called also *dentinum* [NA] and *substantia eburnea dentis.* Similar to bone, but harder and denser, it consists of a solid organic substratum, infiltrated with lime salts. Dentin is permeated by numerous branching spiral canaliculi or tubules which contain processes of the connective tissue cells (odontoblasts) that line the pulp cavity. Sometimes spelled *dentine*. Called also *substantia dentalis propria, proper substance of tooth, ivory, ebur dentis, membrana eboris of Kölliker*, and *ivory membrane*.

Dentin is calcified tissue which composes the majority of each tooth. It is highly sensitive and extends almost the entire length of each tooth. See generally, Encyclopaedia Britannica, Vol. 21 (1970), pp. 775–779. Sullivan v. Russell, 338 N.W.2d 181, 184 (Mich.1983).

dentistry (den'tis-tre) that department of the healing arts which is concerned with the teeth, oral cavity, and associated structures, including the diagnosis and treatment of their diseases and the restoration of defective and missing tissue.

332.071. Practice of **dentistry** defined.—A person or other entity "practices **dentistry**" within the meaning of this chapter who:

(1) Undertakes to do or perform dental work or dental services or dental operations or oral surgery, by any means or methods, gratuitously or for a salary or fee or other reward, paid directly or indirectly to him or to any other person or entity;

(2) Diagnoses or professes to diagnose, prescribes for or professes to prescribe for, treats or professes to treat, any disease, pain, deformity, deficiency, injury or physical condition of human teeth or adjacent structures or treats or professes to treat any disease or disorder or lesions of the oral regions;

(3) Attempts to or does replace or restore a part or portions of a human tooth;

(4) Attempts to or does extract human teeth or attempts to or does correct malformations of human teeth or jaws;

(5) Attempts to or does adjust an appliance or appliances for use in or used in connection with malposed teeth in the human mouth . . . .

(10) Uses or permits to be used for his benefit or for the benefit of any other person or other entity the following titles or words in connection with his name: 'Doctor', 'Dentist', 'Dr.', 'D.D.S.', or 'D.M.D.', or any other letters, titles, degrees or descriptive matter which directly or indirectly indicate or imply that he is willing or able to perform any type of dental service for any person or persons, or uses or permits the use of for his benefit or for the benefit of any other person or other entity any card, directory, poster, sign or any other means by which he indicates or implies or represents that he is willing or able to perform any type of dental services or operation for any person;

(11) Directly or indirectly owns, leases, operates, maintains, manages or conducts an office or establishment of any kind in which dental services or dental operations of any kind are performed for any purpose: but this section shall not be construed to prevent owners or lessees of real estate from lawfully leasing premises to those who are qualified to practice **dentistry** within the meaning of this chapter;

(12) Constructs, supplies, reproduces or repairs any prosthetic denture, bridge, artificial restoration, appliance or other structure to be used or worn as a substitute for natural teeth, except when one not a registered and licensed dentist does so pursuant to a written uniform laboratory work order, in the form to be prescribed by the board and copies of which shall

be retained by the nondentist for two years, of a dentist registered and currently licensed in Missouri and which said substitute above described is constructed upon or by use of casts or models made from an impression furnished by a dentist registered and currently licensed in Missouri;

(13) Attempts to or does place any substitute described in subdivision (12) above in a human mouth or attempts to or professes to adjust any substitute or delivers any substitute to any person other than the dentist upon whose order the work in producing the substitute was performed;

(14) Advertises, solicits, or offers to or does sell or deliver any substitute described in subdivision (12) above or offers to or does sell his services in constructing, reproducing, supplying or repairing the substitute to any person other than a registered and licensed dentist in Missouri;

(15) Undertakes to do or perform any physical evaluation of a patient in his office or in a hospital, clinic, or other medical or dental facility prior to or incident to the performance of any dental services, dental operations, or dental surgery. Missouri Dental Bd. v. Alexander, 628 S.W.2d 646, 649–50 (Mo. 1982).

The definition of the practice of medicine (Education Law, § 6521) and the definition of the practice of **dentistry** (Education Law, § 6601) are amazingly similar. The practice of dentistry is limited to the human mouth while the practice of medicine involves the entire human body. However, the practice of medicine and use of the title "physician" is limited to those having a degree of doctor of medicine or doctor of osteopathy (Education Law, §§ 6522 and 6524)....

... It seems therefore, that the practice of **dentistry** does not come within the usual and ordinary meaning of the word "medical" and the defendant is not protected by CPLR 3017(c). Donohue v. Martin, 413 N.Y.S.2d 99–100 (Sup.Ct. Rensselaer Cty.1979).

Lastly, we consider whether the Court was correct in holding that the cleaning of dentures constituted the practicing of **dentistry** as it is defined by 59 O.S. § 328.19. Appellant argues that the cleaning of dentures does not constitute the practice of dentistry because subsection (k) of Section 328.19 of Title 59 merely includes the removal of stains, discolorations, or concretions from teeth, and does not include the removal of stains or discolorations from prosthetic dentures (sometimes known as plates) . . . .

... In examining 59 O.S. § 328.19 as a whole, we agree with Appellant's contention. The term "teeth", as used in that Section, clearly refers to human teeth, and not artificial teeth. For example, the practice of **dentistry** is deemed to include the removal of teeth, the repairing or filling of cavities in teeth, attempts to correct malformed teeth, and the taking of impressions of teeth. On the other hand, when the statute is dealing with dentures, it clearly indicates it is doing so by referring to them as "prosthetic dentures (sometimes known as plates), bridges or other substitutes for natural teeth", "appliances, or other structures to be worn in the human mouth." Butler v. Bd. of Gov. of Registered Dentists, 619 P.2d 1262, 1265 (Okla. 1980).

denture (den'chur) [Fr.; L. *dens* tooth] an entire set of natural or artificial teeth; ordinarily used to designate an artificial replacement for missing natural teeth and adjacent tissues. See also *dentistry*; and *tooth* (both Butler case).

It is undisputed that the preparation of such a **denture** and its immediate insertion in the patient's mouth after the extractions is a well-recognized standard practice in the profession of dental oral surgery. The **denture** serves a three-fold purpose: (1) functional—to maintain a constant masticatory apparatus for the patient; (2) cosmetic—to maintain the normal facial expression and the normal relationship of the upper and lower jaws; (3) protective—to supply a bandage or covering for the wounds caused by the removal of the teeth. Germann v. Matriss, 260 A.2d 825, 827 (N.J.1970).

Defendant denies liability on the ground that Dr. Tarver agreed to make the teeth satisfactory to the defendant and that the latter was "honestly dissatisfied" with the **denture** after making a sincere effort to wear them. In this connection the testimony is clear that **dentures** customarily require a number of fittings and adjustments before they can be made to satisfactorily conform to the convenience and comfort of the wearer. Giering v. Lemoine, 106 So.2d 534–5 (Ct.App.La.1958).

denture, acrylic resin a denture made of acrylic resin.

The denture was fabricated from a mold made from the impression taken on December 15. An acrylic material in dough form was placed in the mold, boiled in water, put into a steam bath and cooked for four hours. On removal from the bath it was polished and cleansed by scouring and scrubbing with an antiseptic soap the elements of which were compatible with the composition of **acrylic dentures**. Immediately thereafter, it was placed in a plastic, self-sealing bag holding zephiran chloride, a disinfectant also compatible with the composition of **acrylic dentures**. Then the denture was taken in the sealed bag to the defendant's dental office. It was kept there until shortly before it was to be used, and as the actual time for use neared, it was removed from the plastic bag and immediately placed in a covered stainless steel tray, also containing zephiran chloride, until the moment arrived for insertion in the patient's mouth. The course described is the normal and standard practice utilized by the profession. Germann v. Matriss, 260 A.2d 825, 827 (N.J.1970).

denture, partial removable an appliance for the replacement of one or more natural teeth, so constructed that it may readily be removed and replaced in the mouth; called also *removable bridge*.

Dr. Grogan removed the permanent bridge placed by Dr. Gunter and replaced it with a semi-removable "**Andrews bridge**." The pontics on the remaining teeth were also replaced with a color to blend with the other teeth attached to the "Andrews bridge." Similar work was eventually accomplished by Dr. Grogan on the lower teeth....

... There is no doubt the most beneficial prosthetic device for plaintiff for aesthetic purposes was the so-called "Andrews bridge." This is a **semi-removal bridge** introduced into this area by its inventor some two years prior to 1969. In essence it is a fixed metal rod to which the teeth are clasped onto. The next best device from a cosmetic viewpoint would have been the fully removable partial plate. These devices would have given more support to the upper lip at the gum level. Brock v. Gunter, 292 So.2d 328, 331–2 (Ct.App.La.1974).

denture, permanent a term applied to a denture that is constructed and inserted after the oral tissues have healed and the condition of the alveolar ridges has become fairly stabilized.

Dr. Gunter recommended the removal of these teeth and after treatment of the diseased areas, she be fitted with a **permanent type bridge**, along with crowning and splinting of all other upper teeth to form an arch unit for stabilization of the remaining natural teeth. Brock v. Gunter, 292 So.2d 328–9 (Ct. App.La.1974).

denture, roofless

As heretofore narrated, a **roofless denture** or row of teeth is attached to the posts, but pending completion of a permanent denture a temporary denture is affixed for aesthetic purposes. Kelly v. Gershkoff, 312 A.2d 211, 213 (R.I.1973).

Denver developmental test See under *test*.

deodorant (de-o'der-ant) [L. *de* from + *odorare* to perfume] a substance that masks offensive odors. Called also *antibromic*. See also *aluminum sulfate*.

dependence (de-pend'ens) the psychophysical state of an addict in which the usual or increasing doses of the drug are required to prevent the onset of withdrawal symptoms. See also *opium* (esp. In re Foss case).

Some say the addict has a disease. See Hesse, Narcotics and Drug Addiction (1946), p. 40 et seq. . . .

The addict is under compulsions not capable of management without outside help. As stated by the Council on Mental Health:

"Physical dependence is defined as the development of an altered physiological state which is brought about by the repeated administration of the drug and which necessitates continued administration of the drug to prevent the appearance of the characteristic illness which is termed an abstinence syndrome. When an addict says that he has a habit, he means that he is physically dependent on a drug. When he says that one drug is habit-forming and another is not, he means that the first drug is one on which physical **dependence** can be developed and that the second is a drug on which physical **dependence** cannot be developed. Physical **dependence** is a real physiological disturbance. It is associated with the development of hyperexcitability in reflexes mediated through multineurone arcs. It can be induced in animals, it has been shown to occur in the paralyzed hind limbs of addicted chronic spinal dogs, and also has been produced in dogs whose cerebral cortex has been removed." Report on Narcotic Addiction, 165 A.M.A.J. 1707, 1713. Robinson v. California, 370 U.S. 660, 671, 82 S.Ct. 1417, 8 L.Ed.2d 758 (1962).

Both a psychological and compelling physical **dependence** result from the use of "hard narcotics." The physical **dependence** develops in intensity with continued use and requires the continued administration of the drug to avoid withdrawal symptoms. People v. McCabe, 275 N.E.2d 407, 410 (Ill. 1971).

dependence, chemical See *dependence, chemical*.

Granville presented testimony from eight highly qualified physicians, psychiatrists, and chemical dependency practitioners that **chemical dependency** is a primary disease that should not be viewed as a mental disease for purposes of the Medicaid program....

... Boche stated that the concept of mental disorder is not applied to the treatment of **chemical dependency** in Minnesota, because "the treatment is so very different in this State—between mental illness and **chemical dependency**—that they are literally two different systems." He noted that while there was a clearly established history of recovery in **chemical dependency** treatment, "there is not the same optimism about the successful treatment of mental illness."

... The agency also presented the testimony of Dr. Robert Spitzer, a physician and psychiatrist who is Chief of Psychiatric Research with the Biometrics Research Department, New York State Psychiatric Institute, and Professor of Psychiatry at Columbia University, in support of its classification of **chemical dependency** as a mental disease. Spitzer is a generally recognized expert in disease classification, and he was a consultant to the last revision of the ICD, as well as chairperson of the task force that developed the American Psychiatric Association's DSM–III.

Spitzer testified that the primary reason he believed it was reasonable to classify alcoholism and **chemical dependency** as mental disorders in these references was because that classification "identifies correctly the nature of the symptoms," which are primarily psychological and behavioral. He also noted that this classification "correctly identifies that we don't yet know the entire etiology [or] cause of alcoholism, and ... we generally classify as mental disorders those behavioral or psychological conditions for which the ultimate etiology is still unknown." Finally, he indicated that classifying **chemical dependency** as a mental disorder "suggests that treatment at the present time is probably going to be nonphysical ... that is, drugs are not very effective, and the treatment generally consists of programs and approaches which are essentially psychological." Spitzer's view is that the A.A. model of treatment is "behavioral or psychological rather than physical." Granville House, Inc. v. Dep't of Health & Human Serv., 715 F.2d 1292, 1300–1303 (8th Cir. 1983).

depigmentation (de"pig-men-ta'shun) the removal of pigment, generally of melanin; frequently used to mean hypopigmentation.

This action is novel in that it arises from a total **depigmentation** of the plaintiff, a Negro. Photographs introduced into evidence reflect that prior to the events set forth in plaintiff's complaint, his skin and hair were dark brown in color and he was normal in appearance, and that at the present time, his skin and hair have turned completely white....

Within a few weeks after his discharge from the hospital, the plaintiff experienced another form of skin disorder. His skin coloration began to lighten, and all hair on his head and body fell out. The skin continued to lose its dark color over a period of a few weeks until all pigmentation was gone, and as his hair grew back in, it was white in color. Finley v. U.S., 314 F.Supp. 905–8 (N.D.Ohio 1970).

Stanley received first and second degree burns on his face, neck, hands, arms, and forearms—more extensively on the left hand, arm, and left side of his face. He sustained no third degree burns. The only positive evidence of permanency was **depigmentation** centered over the left dorsal aspect of the left hand and around his ear and nose. **Depigmentation** produces photosensitivity....

... According to medical testimony, the only apparent permanent injury is confined to whitish spots over small areas of the forearm resulting from **depigmentation**. The young man likewise complained that his left arm burned rather easily when exposed to sunlight, and that his face was sensitive to sun. Petition of U.S., 303 F.Supp. 1282, 1313–14 (E.D.N.Car. 1969).

depressant (de-pres'ant) an agent that reduces functional activity and the vital energies in general by producing muscular relaxation and diaphoresis.

The provision of the Code attacked provides: "The term '**depressant** or stimulant drug' means.... 4. Any substance which the State Board shall determine to be habit-forming because of its stimulant effect on the central nervous system or any drug which the State Board shall determine to contain any quantity of a substance having a potential for abuse because of its **depressant** or stimulant effect on the central nervous system or its hallucinogenic effect: Provided, however, no drug shall be considered as a **depressant** or stimulant drug if the State Board shall expressly determine that such drug has no **depressant** or stimulant effect on the central nervous system and has no hallucinogenic effect." Sundberg v. State, 216 S.E.2d 332 (Ga.1975).

V.I.Code Ann. tit. 20 § 493 reads in relevant part: ...

(1) **Depressant** drug. Any drug which contains any quantity of barbituric acid or any of the salts of barbituric acids, or any derivative of barbituric acid which has been designated by the Commissioner of Health as habit forming, or any other drug which contains any quantity of a substance which the Commissioner of Health or the Attorney General of the United States, after investigation, has found to have, and by regulation designates as having, a potential for abuse because of its **depressant** effect on the nervous system. Government of Virgin Islands v. Brown, 571 F.2d 773, 775 (3d Cir. 1978).

The applicable definition of a "**depressant** or stimulant drug," found in 21 U.S.C § 321(v)(2), states: "The term '**depressant** or stimulant drug' means ... (2) Any drug which contains any quantity of (A) amphetamine or any of its optical isomers; (B) any salt of amphetamine or any salt of an optical isomer of amphetamine; or (C) any substance which the Secretary, after investigation, has found to be, and by regulation designated as, habit forming because of its stimulant effect on the central nervous system...." 79 Stat. 227. U.S. v. Schrenzel, 462 F.2d 765, 770 (8th Cir. 1972).

Other Authorities: State v. Pettus, 212 S.E.2d 9, 10–11 (Ct. App.Ga.1974); Hoffman-La Roche, Inc. v. Kleindienst, 478 F.2d 1, 4 (3d Cir. 1973); Carter-Wallace, Inc. v. Gardner, 417 F.2d 1086, 1089 (4th Cir. 1969).

depression (de-presh'un) [L. *depressio; de* down + *premere* to press] 1. a hollow or depressed area; downward or inward displacement. 2. a lowering or decrease of functional activity. 3. a psychiatric syndrome consisting of dejected mood, psychomotor retardation, insomnia, and weight loss, sometimes associated with guilt feelings and somatic preoccupations, often of delusional proportions.

The cause of employee's disability was a severely comminuted **depression** fracture of the lateral tibial plateau of his right leg (the area which is the leg portion of his knee joint). . . . Williamson v. Besco's Services, 270 N.W.2d 297–8 (Minn.1978).

Plaintiff's complaint and theory of the case at the trial was that Nancy was improperly diagnosed as suffering from anorexia nervosa rather than severe **depression** which caused her not to eat or drink; that defendant doctors and the hospital failed to properly treat the patient in accordance with the accepted standard of practice by prescribing the drugs Thorazine, Cogentin and Navana, which were contraindicated and caused depression of the respiratory system; that the hospital and defendant doctors departed from the proper standard of practice by ordering Nancy to go on long walks which caused further injury and damage; that the hospital and defendants departed from the accepted standard of practice by not sufficiently noting the patient's severe malnutrition and emotional problems and by failing to treat her therefor in time; and that Nancy died of malnutrition as a result of the neglect and failure to properly observe and treat the condition and the symptoms for which she was hospitalized. Defendants' theory was that Nancy's condition was properly diagnosed and that she was given the appropriate prescriptions and that she did not die from malnutrition or starvation, although the cause of her death was unknown. Warfield v. City of Wyandotte, 323 N.W.2d 603, 605 (Ct.App.Mich.1982).

Appellee was unable emotionally to adjust to his injury. Prior to the enucleation, appellee was extroverted, conscientious, enjoyed working, and prided himself on his physical appearance. After the accident Bevevino was depressed to the point of crying every day, withdrawn, fearful of people, unable to interact normally even with his family, unable to sleep and incapable of engaging in ordinary daily activities. He no longer could concentrate, had difficulty in verbalizing his thoughts, and was obsessed with feelings of disfigurement, ugliness, self-deprecation and uselessness.

Appellee's **depression** deepened over time. Before Bevevino returned to Brazil in 1974, the psychiatrist diagnosed appellee's mental condition as depressive neurosis. Dr. Kalina was convinced even then that appellee was permanently disabled. The doctor again interviewed Bevevino shortly before trial in 1977. He found that appellee's obsession with his lost eye and his inability to function had exacerbated and that appellee had totally withdrawn from society. In the doctor's opinion, there was even a good chance of suicide. He now characterized appellee's mental condition as psychotic, progressive reaction—a severe type of **depression**. [Footnotes omitted.] Bevevino v. Saydjari, 574 F.2d 676, 682–3 (2d Cir. 1978).

Other Authorities: U.S. v. Allen, 554 F.2d 398, 403 (10th Cir. 1977).

depression, anaclitic impairment of an infant's physical, social, and intellectual development which sometimes follows a sudden separation from the mothering person for long periods of time; called also *hospitalism.*

Jerome Brown, a clinical psychologist, testified that there is a mental defect called **anaclitic depression**. This defect is a sudden depression that can occur in infants between the ages of six months to about two and one-half years old. This depression is caused by a sudden withdrawal of a mother figure to which the infant is extremely attached. One of the results of

anaclitic depression can be that the infant would not eat properly. Dr. Brown was of the opinion that the deceased child was not suffering from mental defect or disease. This opinion was based on appellant's statements that the deceased child had been eating poorly and losing weight, then the baby changed and began eating again and gaining weight, and then the baby stopped eating again and subsequently died. Dr. Brown stated that **anaclitic depression** does not shift back and forth in this manner. Harrington v. State, 547 S.W.2d 616, 619 (Ct. Crim.App.Tex.1977).

depression, reactive depression caused by some external situation, and relieved when that situation is removed.

The defendant-father commenced psychiatric treatment in February of 1977 under the care of Dr. Robert Ancira, Psychiatrist, and was diagnosed as having a "**reactive depression** secondary to break up of his marriage and an underlying narcissistic personality type." . . .

. . . Mrs. Pace commenced treatment in September 1977 under the care of Dr. Francis A. D'Anzi and was diagnosed as undergoing "a **situational depression**". This doctor testified that there were various events in the wife's life, such as a discordant marriage, living alone, and financial difficulties, which sent her into a state of depression and subsequent hospitalization, but that the "precipitating event" was that "she had broken up with her boyfriend." Pace v. Pace, 372 So.2d 775, 776 (Ct.App.La.1979).

depression, respiratory

As the case was submitted to the jury, plaintiff claimed that Dr. Bolgla was negligent in failing to watch and record plaintiff's breathing during the administration of the anesthetics or in allowing a **respiratory depression** to occur to plaintiff as a result of the administration of the combination of anesthetics. Vuletich v. Bolgla, 407 N.E.2d 566, 568 (App.Ct.Ill.1980).

depression, situational See *depression, reactive.*

de Quervain's disease See *disease, de Quervain's.*

DER 599 and DER 331 See *epoxy* (Pereira case).

derangement (de-rānj′ment) disarrangement of a part or organ.

derangement, Hey's internal partial dislocation of the knee, marked by great pain and spasm of the muscles.

Dr. Landry examined McGuire's knee and diagnosed his condition as an **internal derangement** of the knee. McGuire v. National Super Markets, Inc., 425 So.2d 1315–16 (Ct.App. La.1983).

dermabrasion (der-mah-bra′shun) planing of the skin done by mechanical means, e.g., sandpaper, wire brushes, etc. See also *planing.*

She wore a glove, which came midway between the finger and the elbow, for about a year in connection with the injury to her arm, and had **dermabrasion** (a sandpaper like procedure) performed to reduce the scarring. The jury examined plaintiff's arm and noted the scarring and discoloration of which she complained. Camarata v. Benedetto, 420 So.2d 1146, 1148 (Ct.App.La.1982).

In order to restore plaintiff's face as near as possible to its original condition, Dr. Henderson performed a procedure known as a **dermabrasion**. A **dermabrasion** is a surgical procedure wherein a diamond wheel, not unlike a grinding wheel used by a mechanic or carpenter, is used to grind down or bray scar tissue. This is done in an attempt to help the scar tissue to blend into the surrounding tissue. Dr. Henderson, in his deposition, described parts of the operation, stating:

"... she was given sedation through a needle in the vein in her arm, brought to the operating room where her face was washed off and sterilized [sic], as much as possible, needle injections of local anesthetic were carried out in all the areas involving the scars, which was as I said, the lower portions of the—the forehead, just above the eyebrow, the upper eyelid, the lower eyelid and the cheek area, all the places where the scars were. The diamond wheel was then used on a rotating device called a striker dermabrator. ...

"It looked like a sanding machine that you might use in a workshop, except on a minature [sic] fashion, and very much like a carpenter would sand a piece of rough wood and this is done with a sterile machine, it's very small, but it's the same principle. And all of the scarred areas were sanded, with the exception of the areas near where the letter 'c' is." [referring to a photograph]. Hukill v. U.S. Fidelity and Guaranty Co., 386 So.2d 172–4 (Ct.App.La.1980).

dermatitis (der"mah-ti'tis), pl. *dermatit'ides* [*dermato-* + *-itis*] inflammation of the skin. See also *eczema*.

Dermatitis is defined in K.S.A. 44–5a02, subd. 7, as follows:

7. **Dermatitis**, that is, inflammation or infection of the skin due to oils, cutting compounds or lubricants, dust, liquids, fumes, gases, vapors, or solids. Linville v. Steel Fixture Mfg. Co., 469 P.2d 312, 318 (Kan.1970).

Plaintiff's claimed disability stems from a severe **dermatitis** condition. Although the precise irritant or irritants which cause the **dermatitis** have not been isolated, plaintiff's condition is most likely caused by chromates or industrial dust present at his former employer's steel mill. Quintana v. Weinberger, 385 F.Supp. 1102 (D.D.Col.1974).

Dr. Wiener testified that the term "**dermatitis**" used in the brochure was used without the term "exfoliative" and with reference only "to **dermatitis**, meaning essentially a skin irritation" which does not include exfoliative, and the two are distinct conditions, the exfoliative-**dermatitis** being a "much more serious condition than **dermatitis** alone" and also being a "very rare condition." Fisher v. Wilkinson, 382 S.W.2d 627, 629–30 (Mo.1964).

dermatitis, atopic a chronic pruritic eruption occurring in adolescents and adults, of unknown etiology although allergic, hereditary, and psychogenic factors appear to be involved. The lesions occur chiefly on the flexural surfaces of the knees and elbows, but may involve other areas, and are marked by lichenification, excoriations, and crusting. In infants and young children the condition is sometimes called *infantile eczema* or (in Britain) *Besnier's prurigo*. Called also *allergic d., flexural eczema*, and *disseminated neurodermatitis*.

... **atopic dermatitis**—dermatitis triggered by emotional causes. Varady v. D & D Catering Serv., Inc., 450 F.Supp. 182–3 (E.D.La.1978).

... treatment of an **atopical dermatitis**. The summary characterized plaintiff's condition as extensive scaling dermatitis of the face, neck and hands. Plaintiff was found to have responded gradually but progressively to treatment in the hospital, and it was expected that he would progress well outside of the hospital upon the continuation of an allergy diet, application of boric acid ointment and the avoidance of dust and other inhalants. Kupchella v. Finch, 314 F.Supp. 256, 259 (W.D.Pa. 1970).

dermatitis, atopical See *dermatitis, atopic.*

dermatitis, contact an acute allergic inflammation of the skin caused by contact with various substances of a chemical, animal, or vegetable nature to which delayed hypersensitivity has been acquired; when severe, it is called *d. venenata*.

Dr. Lea determined that plaintiff had developed an allergy to chromate salts, a substance found in cement, and that this sensitivity in connection with the contact with the cement on January 10th had produced the blisters and sores on plaintiff's feet and hands. The medical diagnosis was "**contact dermatitis**." ...

... Dr. Lea said, "He [plaintiff] had been working in cement and it was after his traumatic exposure that he developed the eruption, so we patch-tested him to potassium dichromate and he had a positive patch test. ... This would indicate that he is especially allergic to chromates. ... Persons who become allergic to chromate develop a dermatitis, irritation of the skin, that varies from a very mild dermatitis to a very severe dermatitis. It can be very caustic, producing ulcerations. It is a characteristic dermatitis that is slow to heal and is recurrent when the patient is reexposed to that material. Texas Employers' Ins. Ass'n v. Turner, 634 S.W.2d 364–5 (Ct.App.Tex.1982).

Claimant contracted a compensable occupational disease, allergic **contact dermatitis**, from his exposure to a chemical (potassium dichromate) used in his work as a printer, his occupation for 26 years. ...

The medical evidence consists of Dr. Weiss' report and his deposition. He testified that **contact dermatitis**, once acquired, is a condition that remains constant and unchanged, although its symptoms (skin eruptions) may come and go depending upon the extent of the exposure to the offending substance. In sum, once allergic—always allergic. [Footnotes omitted.] Matter of Compensation of Baer, 652 P.2d 873–4 (Ct.App.Or.1982).

Dr. Lorio and Dr. Burks testified at the hearing and they are in agreement that the plaintiff suffers from a **contact dermatitis**, commonly referred to as "dishpan hands" because the principal offending agent is detergent in water. Varady v. D & D Catering Serv., Inc., 450 F.Supp. 182–3 (E.D.La.1978).

Other Authorities: Robbins v. Alberto-Culver Co., 499 P.2d 1080, 1082, 1086 (Kan.1972).

dermatitis, exfoliative a skin disorder evolving from any of several preceding skin disorders, such as drug eruption or psoriasis, and characterized by virtually universal erythema with desquamation, scaling, itching, and loss of hair. See also *erythrodermatitis, exfoliative.*

The hearing officer found—and we do not perceive any serious objection to that finding—that exfoliative erythrodermatitis is not an occupational disease within the definitions and requirements found in A.R.S. §§ 23–901(9)(c) and 23–901.01, supra. According to the medical testimony, it is an idiopathic disease (no known cause). In any event, Slayton had the skin condition for some 20-plus years prior to his employment with KRUX...

"In this type of condition, which we call **exfoliative dermatitis**, the sweat glands are malfunctioning, they are not properly functioning. When heat is applied to the body in any way whatsoever, the response for sweating occurs, because these sweat ductals are blocked to a large degree. The sweat must go somewhere, and we have made assumptions in this condition and other conditions of this kind that the sweat goes through the skin rather than over and outside the skin, which we would call sweating.

"The sweat does carry multiple types of chemicals and metabolic wastes that the body produces, and these can obviously irritate skin when it reaches areas where it is not normally produced."...

Dr. Liebsohn, in answer to a question as to why Slayton's prognosis for recovery was very poor, points us to the ultimate legal resolution of this case:

"A. **Exfoliative dermatitis** is an extremely serious disease. Whatever factors are present that can cause death in this condition, I would equate to a person that was burned with a large portion of his skin denuded, or removed or off, and I would feel that a person with **exfoliative dermatitis** is walking a very fine line, and sudden deaths have occurred in any number of cases, and I would say poor, and with an underlining, underlying it could happen today, tomorrow, or the next day." Slayton v. Industrial Com'n, 550 P.2d 246, 248, 251 (Ct.App.Ariz.1976).

Each of these eminent dermatologists stated, in essence, that in his opinion Mr. Finley initially suffered a drug reaction from the Doriden manifesting itself in the form of a dermatitis condition, that he suffered an **exfoliative dermatitis**, and that thereafter he sustained a total depigmentation of skin and hair. Finley v. U.S., 314 F.Supp. 905, 909 (N.D.Ohio 1970).

On the following Tuesday, May 6, Dr. Reinhardt returned to see plaintiff, and at that time plaintiff was "obviously sick," although not "critically ill," and she "had a redness, a rash, ... over her face and shoulder, ... [and the] upper part of her trunk" which was "an allergic reaction to something."...

... On Thursday, May 8, she re-entered the hospital where her condition was diagnosed as **exfoliative-dermatitis**. Fisher v. Wilkinson, 382 S.W.2d 627, 629 (Mo.1964).

dermatitis medicamentosa drug eruption.

dermatitis, radiation See *radiodermatitis*.

dermatitis, radio See *radiodermatitis*.

dermatitis, seborrheic; dermatitis seborrheica a chronic inflammatory disease of the skin of unknown etiology, characterized by moderate erythema, dry, moist, or greasy scaling, and yellow crusted patches on various areas, including the mid-parts of the face, ears, supraorbital regions, umbilicus, genitalia, and especially the scalp, where it is manifested by small patches of scales that progress to involve the entire scalp, with exfoliation of an excessive amount of dry scales (dandruff). The condition is usually accompanied by itching. Called also *eczema seborrheicum*, *seborrheic eczema*, and *seborrhea*.

Consultation and treatment of **seborrheic dermatitis** (yellowing and flaking of skin).... Aretz v. U.S., 456 F.Supp. 397, 403 (S.D.Ga.1978).

dermatofibroma (der"mah-to-fi-bro'mah) a fibrous tumor-like nodule of the dermis.

Plaintiff alleges that while at the University Hospital the decedent's condition was diagnosed as a malignant fibrous histiocytoma (cancerous tumor) and as treatment for this condition Mr. Hawkins underwent a hemipelvectomy. Hawkins v. Regional Medical Laboratories, 314 N.W.2d 450–1 (Ct.App.Mich. 1979).

dermatome (der'mah-tōm) [*derma-* + Gr. *temnein* to cut] the area of skin supplied with afferent nerve fibers by a single posterior spinal root; called also *dermatomic area*.

Sensory examination reveals decrease in sensation to pin prick in the L 1 **dermatome** on the right side. Bartlett v. Secretary of Dept. of Health, Ed. & Welf., 330 F.Supp. 1273, 1277 (E.D. Ky.1971).

dermatomyositis (der"mah-to-mi"o-si'tis) [*dermato-* + Gr. *mys* muscle + *-itis*] a nonsuppurative inflammation of the skin, subcutaneous tissue, and muscles, with necrosis of muscle fibers; one of the so-called collagen or connective tissue diseases. There is underlying cancer in as many as 50 per cent of adult cases. When the skin lesions are absent, it is known as *polymyositis*.

dermatophyte (der'mah-to-fīt") [*dermato-* + Gr. *phyton* plant] a fungus parasitic upon the skin; the term embraces the imperfect fungi of the genera *Microsporum*, *Epidermophyton*, and *Trichophyton*. Called also *cutaneous fungus* and *dermatomyces*.

DES See *diethylstilbestrol*.

Desenex See *antifungal* (Pennwalt case).

desipramine See *desipramine hydrochloride*.

desipramine hydrochloride (des-ip'rah-mēn) [USP] chemical name: 10,11-dihydro-N-methyl-5H-dibenz[b,f] azepine-5-propanamine monohydrochloride. A metabolite of imipramine, $C_{18}H_{22}N_2 \cdot HCl$, occurring as a white to off-white, crystalline powder; used as an antidepressant, administered orally.

The pathology report indicated that Stuppy died from an overdose of **desipramine** or imipramine, both pharmacologically related drugs which are used as antidepressants. Stuppy v. U.S., 560 F.2d 373, 375 (8th Cir. 1977).

DET See *diethyltryptamine*.

detachment (de-tach'ment) [Fr. *détacher* to unfasten; to separate] the condition of being unfastened, disconnected, or separated.

detachment of retina; detachment, retinal a condition in which the inner layers of the retina (neural retina) are separated from the pigment epithelium.

Subsequently, in June of 1976, Lea was struck by an automobile and received a minor skull fracture. During Lea's examination after this accident an ophthalmologist discovered that Lea's left eye was suffering a **detached retina**. The child was then referred to Dr. Alice McPherson, a retinal specialist. Dr. McPherson determined that the **retinal detachment** most probably was caused by trauma and that it was of long standing, i.e., was not caused by the recent June accident but had occurred at least three months prior to the time she saw Lea in June of 1976. Dr. McPherson performed three operations upon Lea in an attempt to reattach the retina to the wall of her eye but was unsuccessful. As a result, Lea became permanently blind in her left eye. Roth v. Law, 579 S.W.2d 949, 952–3 (Ct. Civ.App.Tex.1979).

The report merely revealed that the **retinal detachment** was caused by bleeding. The doctor explained that pressure from the compresses, eye movement, or even Dr. Adams' surgery could have produced the detachment. Bevevino v. Saydjari, 574 F.2d 676, 681 (2d Cir. 1978).

Holton employed the services of Pfingst for an eye problem which resulted in his performing an operation upon her for a **detached retina**. The operation was successful. Ordinary acceptable medical practice was followed in the operation, including the placement of a hollow polyethylene ring or tubing around the eye as a part of the operative procedure. Holton v. Pfingst, 534 S.W.2d 786–7 (Ct.App.Ky.1975).

Other Authorities: Gleason v. Hall, 555 F.2d 514, 517 (5th Cir. 1977); Langbell v. Industrial Commission, 529 P.2d 227, 228–9 (Ariz.1974).

detachment, tractional

Tractional detachment is the type of detachment related to diabetic retinopathy, and is a different type of detachment from traumatic retinopathy, which may be surgically repaired. Both Doctors Everett and Ashman indicated that a trauma can hasten the occurrence of **tractional detachment**. . . . George v. Workmen's Comp.App.Bd, 437 A.2d 521–2 (Pa.Commonwealth Ct.1981).

detail man

Drug companies employ what are called "**detail men**" whose job it is to visit doctors in a given area to promote the prescription of that company's products. The **detail man** explains the uses for which the drug is intended, attempts to set it apart from any competitive medications and handles any complaints or problems the doctor encounters in using a particular drug. U.S. v. Ciba Geigy Corp., 508 F.Supp. 1118, 1126 (D.N.J.1976).

detergent (de-ter′jent) [L. *detergere* to cleanse] an agent which purifies or cleanses.

"The household synthetic **detergents** presently used embrace a number of different products; however, the bulk of these **detergents** are of the alkyl benezene sulfonate type generally referred to as ABS. This type of **detergent** is made by alkylating benzene with a comparatively highly branched C_{12} and/or C_{15} olefin and then sulfonating the resultant alkylation product. . . .

"In addition to causing foam problems in the sewage plants, the presence of non-decomposable ABS in sewage effluents, including septic tanks effluents, has already resulted in considerable contamination of the available drinking water supply in populous areas. . . ." Continental Oil Co. v. Witco Chemical Corp., 484 F.2d 777, 779–80 (7th Cir. 1973).

However, the plaintiffs now seek a preliminary injunction enjoining the defendants from enforcing Section 24–44(4) of the Code, making it unlawful to sell or use **detergents** containing any phosphorus on or after January 1, 1972, and Section 24–44(2) of the Code, as amended by Ordinance No. 71–61, requiring that all **detergents** sold in Dade County on or after January 1, 1972, be labeled to list all ingredients contained therein and to express the percentages of each ingredient by weight, pending a final hearing and determination of the issues on the merits. . . .

. . . Experts for the **detergent** industry testified that non-phosphate **detergents** are not as effective cleaning agents as their phosphate counterparts, and non-phosphate **detergents** may be more hazardous to children in case of accidental ingestion or contact with their eyes or other sensitive parts of the anatomy. Soap and Detergent Ass'n v. Clark, 330 F.Supp. 1218, 1220 (S.D.Fla.1971).

detoxification (de-tok″sĭ-fi-ka′shun) treatment designed to free an addict from his drug habit.

He was hospitalized on June 3, 1968 by a psychiatrist, Dr. J. Edward Stern, for a process of **detoxification** (to remove the toxic agents in his body) and treatment of his drug dependency. Crocker v. Winthrop Lab. Div. of Sterling Drug, Inc., 514 S.W.2d 429–30 (Tex.1974).

detoxification, metabolic reduction of the toxic properties of a substance by chemical changes induced in the body, producing a compound which is less poisonous or is more readily eliminated.

Dr. Selmants explained that immediately upon the injection of any spinal anesthetizing agent a process of **detoxification** commences within the area of the nerve root blockage which ultimately causes the anesthesia to wear off. The speed of **detoxification** in any individual depends primarily upon the amount of circulation in the nerve area and the amount of myclin covering the nerve itself. Clark v. Gibbons, 426 P.2d 525, 530 (Cal.1967).

deuterium (du-te′re-um) [Gr. *deuteros* second] the mass two isotope of hydrogen, symbol ^2H, or D. It is available as a gas or as heavy water and is used as a tracer or indicator in studying fat and amino acid metabolism; called also *heavy hydrogen*. Cf. *protium* and *tritium*. See also *hydrogen*.

DEV See *vaccine, rabies*.

deviant (de′ve-ant) [L. *deviare* to turn aside] an individual with characteristics varying from what is considered normal, or standard.

deviant, sex an individual exhibiting paraphilia; i.e., one whose sexual behavior varies from that normally considered socially or biologically acceptable. Called also *paraphiliac*.

deviant sexual act See *paraphelia*.

device (dĕ-vīs′) something contrived for a specific purpose.

(h) The term "**device**" . . . means instruments, apparatus, and contrivances, including their components, parts, and accessories, intended (1) for use in the diagnosis, cure mitigation, treatment, or prevention of disease in man or other animals; or (2) to affect the structure or any function of the body of man or other animals. [Fed. Food, Drug and Cosm. Act § 201.] AMP, Inc. v. Gardner, 389 F.2d 825–6 (2d Cir. 1968).

The definition of "**devices**" embraced by the Act [5] is clearly of sufficient breadth and scope to include a surgical nail, which frequently remains in the patient for many months and is designed to and does affect both the "structure and function of the body".[6] [[5] See § 321(h), [21 U.S.C.] [6] Arguably, the intramedullary nail is embraced in clause (1) as well, since a broken bone might reasonably be considered a diseased condition of the body, and the nail is used to assist in the cure, mitigation, and treatment of the diseased condition. An often cited letter containing the Food and Drug Administration's views on this question merits consideration. Trade Correspondence dated March 14, 1940, contains the following: "Visitor at interview submitted a list of questions, the answers to which were furnished in a letter. Are the usual surgical instruments used by surgeons, such as knives, scissors, forceps, saws, mallets, chisels, needles, drills, nails, and screwdrivers, embraced within the definition of '**device**' contained in Section 201(h) of the Federal Food, Drug, and Cosmetic Act? Yes." Quoted in Kleinfeld and Dunn, Federal Food, Drug, and Cosmetic Act 1938–1949, 631 (1949). Although the date of this Trade Correspondence is March 14, 1940, several years before intramedullary nails were first used by Dr. Kuntscher, the ruling would seem logically to cover them within its ambit.] Orthopedic Equipment Co. v. Eutsler, 276 F.2d 455, 459–60 (4th Cir. 1960).

Mr. Justice Douglas, being of the view that an antibiotic sensitivity disc used by physicians to aid them in determining what antibiotic drug, if any, to give to a patient, is a "**device**" as defined in § 201(h) [*] of the Act, not a "drug" as defined in § 201(g), would affirm the judgment. [[*] "The term '**device**' . . . means instruments, apparatus, and contrivances . . . for use in the diagnosis . . . of disease in man . . . ." It would indeed be difficult to write a clearer description of an antibiotic sensitivity disc.] U.S. v. Bacto-Unidisk, 394 U.S. 784–90, 801, 89 S.Ct. 1410, 22 L.Ed.2d 726 (1969).

device, blood-letting

Shortly after World War II, B–D patented a device, the Vacutainer, which partially solved the problem of taking multiple blood samples without risking blood coagulation, or having to puncture the body walls more than once. [Footnote omitted.] Becton, Dickinson & Co. v. Sherwood Medical Ind. Inc., 516 F.2d 514–15 (5th Cir. 1975).

device, intrauterine (IUD) a coil, loop, T, or triangle of plastic or metallic substance inserted into the uterus to prevent conception.

An **intrauterine device** (I.U.D.) is a contraceptive device that fits within the uterus. The body of the **I.U.D.** is made of plastic and is designed to conform to the shape of the uterine cavity. Attached to the body of the **I.U.D.** is a "tail" that extends from the device in the uterus through the cervical canal and into the vagina. Hansen v. A. H. Robins Co., Inc., 715 F.2d 1265–6 (7th Cir. 1983).

In July, 1979, the female plaintiff and her husband commenced this action against her former physician, defendant Bertocchi, to recover damages resulting from the insertion into the female plaintiff of a "Majzlin Spring" intrauterine device (hereinafter

IUD) in 1973. Reyes v. Bertocchi, 459 N.Y.S.2d 834–5 (2d Dep't 1983).

The Dalkon Shield **intrauterine device** is a plastic circle with spokes along the circumference to which is attached a braided string which trails from the uterus in order to let the user know that the shield is in place. It is a fixed device which remains in the uterus, until removal, to serve a continuing function of preventing conception. . . .

The theory of the plaintiffs' claim against defendant Robins is that Joyce Lindsey was caused to sustain the pelvic infection because the braided string or wick attached to the shield constituted an "open highway" inviting invasion by bacteria. Lindsey v. A. H. Robins Co., Inc., 458 N.Y.S.2d 602–4 (2d Dep't 1983).

device, life-sustaining

The pros and cons involved in such tragedies which bedevil contemporary society, mainly because of incredible advancement in scientific medicine, are all exhaustively discussed in Superintendent of Belchertown v. Saikewicz, Mass., 370 N.E.2d 417 (1977). As Saikewicz points out, the right of an individual to refuse medical treatment is tempered by the State's:

1. Interest in the preservation of life.
2. Need to protect innocent third parties.
3. Duty to prevent suicide.
4. Requirement that it help maintain the ethical integrity of medical practice. . . .

. . . Moreover we find no requirement in the law that a competent, but otherwise mortally sick, patient undergo the surgery or treatment which constitutes the only hope for temporary prolongation of his life. This being so, we see little difference between a cancer ridden patient who declines surgery, or chemotherapy, necessary for his temporary survival and the hopeless predicament which tragically afflicts Abe Perlmutter. . . .

. . . It is true that the latter appears more drastic because affirmatively, a mechanical device must be disconnected, as distinct from mere inaction. Notwithstanding, the principle is the same, for in both instances the hapless, but mentally competent, victim is choosing not to avail himself of one of the expensive marvels of modern medical science. . . .

. . . By contrast, we find, and agree with, several cases upholding the right of a competent adult patient to refuse treatment for himself.[3] From this agreement, we reach our conclusion that, because Abe Perlmutter has a right to refuse treatment in the first instance, he has a concomitant right to discontinue it. [[3] Superintendent of Belchertown v. Saikewicz, Mass., 370 N.E.2d 417 (1977). In the Matter of Schiller, 148 N.J.Super. 168, 372 A.2d 360 (1977); In the Matter of Melideo, 88 Misc.2d 974, 390 N.Y.S.2d 523 (Sup.Ct.1976); In re Quinlan, 70 N.J. 10, 355 A.2d 647 (1976); In re Osborne, 294 A.2d 372 (D.C.App.1972). . . .] Satz v. Perlmutter, 362 So.2d 160, 162–3 (Dist.Ct.App.Fla.1978).

dexamethasone (dek"sah-meth'ah-sōn) [USP] chemical name: 9-fluoro-11β,17,21-trihydroxy-16α-methylpregna-1,4-diene-3,20-dione. A synthetic glucocorticoid, $C_{22}H_{29}FO_5$, occurring as a white to practically white, crystalline powder; used primarily as an anti-inflammatory in various conditions, including the collagen diseases and allergic states, administered orally or topically. It is also used in certain neoplastic diseases, soft tissue disorders, and hemolytic anemias, and is the basis of a screening test in the diagnosis of Cushing's syndrome.

Dr. Adriani felt that **Decadron**, the drug which Dr. Lutz did administer, was a drug of third choice, a steroid which is given when someone experiences a prolonged effect from an allergic reaction, an intractable case. By giving **Decadron**, Dr. Adriani felt that Dr. Lutz's medical judgment was improperly exercised because as a steroid it would have taken effect only after an hour or more, with its peak effect occurring two or three hours later. Wright v. U.S., 507 F.Supp. 147, 152 (E.D. La.1981).

According to *Physician's Desk Reference* (PDR), **Decadron** is 25 to 30 times as potent as hydrocortisone. Ex. 10. **Decadron** is a synthetic steroid, which was first sold in the early 1960's by Merck & Co., and is considered to be one of the most important drugs in the field of neurology....

By March 20, 1972, Plaintiff recognized the causal relationship between the aseptic necrosis of his left hip and the **Decadron** treatment. By July 31, 1972, Plaintiff recognized the causal relationship between the aseptic necrosis of his right hip and the **Decadron** treatment....

... At that time I was issued the drug **Decadron** for my eyes which caused the condition in my legs which should be explained later... This drug my orthopedic surgeon concurs has caused me to develop aseptic necrosis....

... Aseptic necrosis is only one of about fifty possible adverse side-effects of **Decadron** listed in PDR....

... Most importantly, aseptic necrosis is not a significant risk of **Decadron**, especially when taken only over a short span of time. Niblack v. U.S., 438 F.Supp. 383–4, 386, 388 (D.Col. 1977).

On that date **decadron** was prescribed to treat swelling of the brain. Dr. Winter testified that swelling of the brain causes additional brain damage. Although Dr. Winter testified that swelling may result from the absence of oxygen in the brain, he did not order **decadron** until July 11 because he fully expected Deborah to come out of the anesthesia after the operation. He weighed the benefits of **decadron** against the fact that the patient was postoperative and diabetic, and the possibility of a peptic ulcer resulting from the use of the drug. His assessment of the risk and possible benefits were based in part upon being told that the patient had been deprived of oxygen for only one minute. Burrow v. Widder, 368 N.E.2d 443, 447 (App.Ct. of Ill.1977).

dextroamphetamine (dek"stro-am-fet'ah-mēn) chemical name: (*S*)-α-methylbenzeneethanamine. The dextrorotatory isomer of amphetamine, which has substantially more central nervous system stimulating effect than the levorotatory form (levamphetamine) or racemic forms of amphetamine. Abuse of this drug may lead to dependence. See also *amphetamine*.

... **dextro amphetamine**, an acknowledged potent anorexigenic agent. U.S. v. 60 28-Capsule Bottles, More or Less, etc., 211 F.Supp. 207, 209 (D.N.J.1962).

dextrocardia (deks"tro-kar'de-ah) location of the heart in the right hemithorax, with the apex pointing to the right, occurring with transposition (situs inversus) of the abdominal viscera, or without such transposition (*isolated dextrocardia*).

... the Stribling infant was born with **dextrocardia**, a condition in which one's heart is farther to the right than is normal. Mason v. Western Pennsylvania Hosp., 428 A.2d 1366, 1369 (Super.Ct.Pa.1981), order vacated 453 A.2d 974 (Pa.1982).

dextrose (deks'trōs) chemical name: *D*-glucose monohydrate. A monosaccharide, $C_6H_{12}O_6H_2O$, known as *glucose* (q.v.) in biochemistry and physiology. The official preparation [USP] is usually obtained by the hydrolysis of starch, and occurs as colorless crystals or as a white, crystalline or granular powder; it is used chiefly as a fluid and nutrient replenisher, usually administered by intravenous infusion. It is also used as a diuretic and alone or in combination with other agents for various other clinical purposes.

The patent-in-suit relates to a process for the enzymatic conversion of **dextrose** (also known as glucose or corn sugar) into levulose (also known as fructose or fruit sugar)—a "sweeter" sugar. CPC International, Inc. v. Standard Brands, Inc., 385 F.Supp. 1057–8 (D.Del.1974).

Dextrose is a chemical substance of the class of carbohydrates. It has a sweet taste and has a high nutritive value. **Dextrose** is sometimes called "corn sugar." Crystalline **dextrose** is manufactured from corn starch or some other plant starch by a crystallized chemical change known as hydrolysis. It is a relatively pure form of **dextrose**. It is to this particular product that the Wallerstein patent relates....

... For commercial purposes, the **dextrose** is recovered from the hydrolyzate in one of three forms. It can be an ingredient of syrup or solidified into so-called "slab sugar", or the crystals of **dextrose** may be recovered apart from the other substances. Baxter Laboratories, Inc. v. Corn Products Co., 394 F.2d 892–3 (7th Cir. 1968).

diabetes (di"ah-be'tēz) [Gr. *diabētēs* a syphon, from *dia* through + *bainein* to go] a general term referring to disorders characterized by excessive urine excretion (polyuria), as in diabetes mellitus and diabetes insipidus. When used alone, the term refers to diabetes mellitus.

diabetes, brittle diabetes that is difficult to control, characterized by unexplained oscillation between hypoglycemia and acidosis.

... it was Dr. Distefano who diagnosed him as having juvenile **brittle diabetes mellitis**, with complications of hyperexia, furunculosis and acute strep throat. When plaintiff left the hospital the prognosis indicated that his blood sugar levels had been over 220 despite treatment, and that he required a daily injection of 70 units of NPH to be supplemented by regular insulin. He was described as susceptible to systemic (sore throat and tonsilitis) as well as skin and feet infections, that at times he would go into hypoglycemic states for which sugar must be given, and that he had muscular atony with early fatigue....

"Brittle" diabetes mellitis is by definition a "more severe" type of diabetes which affects a small group of young people "who are extremely difficult or impossible to maintain on what would appear to be the indicated dosage" of insulin because of the "dangers of producing hypoglycemia in such persons." See The Merck Manual of Diagnosis and Therapy, 1198 (12th ed.). See also Diabetes Mellitus (7th ed., Lilly Research Laboratories), which notes that the brittle diabetic "poses one of the greatest of all therapeutic challenges", and for whom therapy is more difficult to determine. The incidence of such victims ranges from 2 to 10% of the insulin-dependent diabetic population. Id. at 97. Ressegiue v. Secretary of H.E.W. of United States, 425 F.Supp. 160, 162–3 (E.D.N.Y.1977).

He commented as follows:

The patient's diabetes at the present appears under less than optimal control. Some **brittle diabetics**, however, do run wide sugar swings and this does, at times, pose a serious therapeutic difficulty. The patient's greatest disability at the present appears to be her orthostatic hypotension which is significant. Propranolone might be helpful in reducing this orthostatic drop in blood pressure.

Plaintiff responded to Dr. Sisler's report in a written statement dated September 3, 1971, thus:

I feel that I would be unable to do any kind of work, even if I was sitting down all the time, because I get the diabetic symptoms (nausea, vertigo, numbness, sweating, etc.) at any time (regardless of my activity), and I sometimes get them several times a day. When these attacks come on, I have to eat immediately or become extremely ill.

When my condition becomes worse, as it frequently does, my vision becomes impaired, my head feels like it is swelling, and my nervous tension increases to where I am hardly able to stand anyone around me, even my family. Goodwin v. Richardson, 357 F.Supp. 540, 545–6 (E.D.Mo.1973).

"It has been impossible to control the diabetes condition satisfactorily while he does manual labor. He has a **brittle type diabetes**. Have suggested he be relieved of hard manual labor."...

... I can unequivocally say that Tom Simmons is unable to participate in any gainful activity by reason of an unstable diabetic condition, which, in spite of insulin and diabetic therapy, apparently does not remain stable. I feel that he has a very **brittle type of diabetic condition**, which will preclude him from earning a living doing manual labor, which is the only type employment he is capable of performing. Simmons v. Celebrezze, 233 F.Supp. 93, 95–6 (E.D.S.Car.1964).

diabetes, fulminating See *fulminate.*

The result of the blood test was not available until 4 p.m., at which time it indicated that the blood sugar was extremely high and that the patient was suffering from diabetes. Insulin was immediately given to the patient, but he went into a diabetic coma and died at 5:30 p.m. There was no dispute that the cause of death was **fulminating diabetes**....

... He testified that diabetes could have been diagnosed or at the very least suspected as early as the Plaintiff's decedent's office examination with the Defendant, Dr. Raag, on April 22nd. The basis for his opinion was the family history of diabetes and the complaints made of thirst, frequency of urination, and weight loss....

... Dr. Stoker had been called in on April 24, 1971 on Mr. Torrez's case after the tests were in and he diagnosed diabetic acidosis and **fulminating diabetes**. A family history of diabetes was shown in this case. Thirst and extreme urination are classic symptoms of diabetes. Malaise or weakness is found. Torrez v. Raag, 357 N.E.2d 632–3 (App.Ct.Ill.1976).

diabetes, juvenile; diabetes, juvenile-onset severe diabetes mellitus, usually having an abrupt onset before the age of 25 and tending to be difficult to control and unstable ("brittle"); plasma insulin is often deficient and ketoacidosis occurs frequently, and oral hypoglycemics and diet are almost never effective, daily injections of insulin being required in almost all patients. Called also *growth-onset d.* and *ketosis-prone d.*

diabetes, maturity-onset a mild, often asymptomatic, form of diabetes mellitus with onset usually after 40 years of age, most often in overweight persons; although pancreatic insulin reserve is diminished, it is almost always sufficient, except under stressful conditions, to prevent ketoacidosis, and dietary control and/or oral hypoglycemics are usually effective. Called also *adult-onset d.* and *ketosis-resistant d.*

diabetes, mellitus a metabolic disorder in which the ability to oxidize carbohydrates is more or less completely lost, usually due to faulty pancreatic activity, especially of the islets of Langerhans, and consequent disturbance of normal insulin mechanism. This produces hyperglycemia with resulting glycosuria and polyuria giving symptoms of thirst, hunger, emaciation, and weakness and also imperfect combustion of fats with resulting acidosis, sometimes leading to dyspnea, lipemia, ketonuria, and finally coma. It is frequently associated with progressive disease of the small vessels (microangiopathy), particularly by affecting the eye (diabetic retinopathy) and kidney, and atherosclerosis, and there may also be pruritus and lowered resistance to pyogenic infections. Called also *Willis' disease.* See also *juvenile diabetes*; and *maturity-onset diabetes.*

As explained by Dr. Grace, a diabetic is unable to metabolize carbohydrates. As a result, the body accommodates this failing with an alternate chemical reaction which results in a production of ketone bodies which accumulate. This accumulation produces an acidotic condition in the blood stream. Thus, the diabetic having an abnormal ketone level in his blood stream is particularly allergic to ketones. City of Bonifay v. Faulk, 390 So.2d 791–2 (Dist.Ct.App.Fla.1980).

diabetes mellitus See *gangrene, diabetic* (Brown case; Jones case); *hemorrhage, retinal* (Excelsior case); *maceration; Proteus mirabilis*; and *retinopathy, diabetic.*

Diabetes mellitus is a metabolic disorder in which the ability to oxidize carbohydrates is more or less lost, usually resulting from faulty pancreatic activity with consequent disturbance of the normal insulin mechanism. This condition produces hyperglycemia (abnormal increase in the glucose level in the blood) and may result in acidosis and coma. The ravages of this insidious disease may affect other parts and functions of the body and may result in chronic complications, including neuropathy (disorder of the nervous system), retinopathy (degenerative disease of the retina), nephropathy (disease of the kidneys), and generalized changes in large and small blood vessels. Application of Lydia E. Hall Hospital, 455 N.Y.S.2d 706–7 (Sup.Ct. Nassau Cty.1982).

... the Secretary has promulgated comprehensive regulations stating the symptoms which must exist in order to establish disability for the purpose of entitlement to widows' benefits. With respect to diabetes those regulations provide:

DIABETES MELLITUS—

A. When diabetes exists with other physical or mental impairments, evaluate under the criteria for the appropriate body systems; or

B. Diabetes with one of the following (not covered under existing body system listing):

1. Neuropathy with moderate motor deficit in two extremities; or

2. Acidosis occurring at least on the average of once every two months, documented by appropriate blood chemical tests (pH or pCO_2 or bicarbonate levels); or

3. Amputation at, or above, the tarsal region due to diabetic necrosis or peripheral vascular disease; or

4. Ophthalmologic findings of:

a. Retinitis proliferans; or

b. Rubeosis iridis; or

c. Venous distention and capillary pattern distortion with hemorrhages or exudates.

(Appendix to Social Security Administration Reg. #4, Subpart P, Paragraph 9.08). Nickles v. Richardson, 326 F.Supp. 777, 779 (D.S.Car.1971).

Other Authorities: Burrow v. Widder, 368 N.E.2d 443, 444–5 (App.Ct.Ill.1977); Isgett v. Seaboard Coast Line RR Co., 332 F.Supp. 1127, 1133–6 (D.S.Car.1971); Bluebonnet Express, Inc. v. Foreman, 431 S.W.2d 45, 48 (Ct.Civ.App.Tex.1968); U.S. v. McGuire, 381 F.2d 306, 317 (2d Cir. 1967).

diabetic (di″ah-bet′ik) 1. pertaining to or affected with diabetes. 2. a person affected with diabetes. See also under *diabetes* for specific forms.

The only reasonable conclusion to be drawn when a man is found suffering a seizure, and is wearing a **diabetic** emblem around his neck would be that he is a **diabetic** suffering from a **diabetic** seizure. U.S. v. Dunavan, 464 F.2d 1166, 1168 (6th Cir. 1972).

Diabinese (di-ab′ĭ-nēs) trademark for chlorpropamide. See also *chlorpropamide*.

diacetylmorphine (di″ah-se″til-mor′fēn) heroin; a white, bitterish, crystalline powder, $C_{17}H_{17}(O \cdot OC \cdot CH_3)_2 \cdot NO$, the diacetic acid ester of morphine, formerly used as an analgesic and narcotic. Because it is highly addictive, the importation of heroin and its salts into the United States, as well as its use in medicine, is illegal. Called also *acetomorphine* and *dimorphine*. See also *morphine* (People v. Drake case); and *opium*.

Heroin is a narcotic which is generally injected into the bloodstream by a needle. It is a central nervous system depressant. The usual effect is to create a "high"—euphoria, drowsiness—for about thirty minutes, which then tapers off over a period of about three or four hours. At the end of this time the heroin user experiences sickness and discomfort known as "withdrawal symptoms." There is intense craving for another shot of heroin, after which the cycle starts over again. A typical addict will inject **heroin** several times a day.

There are variations in the severity of **heroin** addiction. For instance, it is possible for a **heroin** addict to take moderate amounts of the drug—just enough to avoid the withdrawal symptoms, without producing the euphoric highs. Such a person might function somewhat normally. However, this type of controlled **heroin** addict is very rare. Beazer v. New York City

Transit Authority, 399 F.Supp. 1032, 1038 (S.D.N.Y.1975), opinion supplemented 414 F.Supp. 277 (1976).

Unlike the hallucinogens, **heroin** does not produce a positive euphoric "high" of intensified sensory input. Rather, the drug has a calming, depressant effect which dulls the general sensibilities and allays feelings of pain, insecurity or discomfort. The **heroin** "high" is essentially escape-oriented, and a direct correlation exists between the pleasure one derives from the drug and the user's psychic need to avoid reality. Thus, although the psychologically stable individual may enjoy his experience with **heroin**, his satisfaction generally is not so great as to draw him irresistibly to excessive use. As a result, many such persons are able to administer **heroin** on an occasional basis without ever becoming addicted.

The situation is quite different, however, for those users whose psychological makeup renders them particularly prone to addiction. [Footnotes omitted.] U.S. v. Moore, 486 F.2d 1139, 1231 (D.C.Cir.1973).

Heroin and **morphine** are true narcotic analgesics in the sense that their use produces a marked indifference to pain. In addition, when injected intravenously a warm flushing of the skin and intense pleasurable sensations in the lower abdomen will result. . . .

. . . It appears that the subjective action of the morphine-type drugs also involve changes in mood, an inability to concentrate and the development of apathy. Physical degeneration occurs, arising from drug preoccupation, personal neglect, malnutrition and susceptibility to infections. Overdosage can cause death through excessive respiratory depression. People v. McCabe, 275 N.E.2d 407, 410 (Ill.1971).

Other Authorities: In re Foss, 519 P.2d 1073, 1079 (Cal. 1974); Verdugo v. U.S., 402 F.2d 599, 607 (9th Cir. 1968).

diagnosis (di″ag-no′sis) [*dia-* + Gr. *gnōsis* knowledge] 1. the art of distinguishing one disease from another. 2. the determination of the nature of a case of disease. See also *impression* (Sinkey case); and *treatment, surgical* (McKay case).

At the hearing, Dr. Collier testified that, in his opinion, petitioner continued to suffer emotional consequences from the accident and that there was a direct causal relationship between the petitioner's physical injury and his emotional condition. We think that such an opinion must be considered a "medical **diagnosis**." One Arizona case has defined "**diagnosis**" as the act or art of recognizing the presence of disease from its symptoms. State v. Horn, 4 Ariz.App. 541, 422 P.2d 172 (1967). Dorland's Illustrated Medical Dictionary (25th Ed.) defines "**diagnosis**" as "the art of distinguishing one disease from another." Dorland's also defines it as "the determination of the nature of a case of disease." One of the definitions given for the term "**diagnosis**" in Webster's Third International Dictionary is an "investigation or analysis of the cause or nature of a condition, situation or problem." . . . It seems clear to us that in order to find a causal connection between a mental condition and an industrial accident, it would be necessary to make a "**diagnosis**" of the mental condition, something which is not within the scope of the licensing privilege of a psychologist under Arizona statutes. Bilbrey v. Industrial Commission, 556 P.2d 27–29 (Ct.App.Ariz.1976).

"The term '**diagnosis**' is derived from the Greek prefix 'dia', meaning between, and 'gignoskein', meaning to discern. It is, in modern terminology, a 'sizing up' or a comprehending of the physical or mental status of a patient. It is the conclusion itself rather than the procedures upon which the conclusion is based which constitutes a **diagnosis** per se. No particular language need be used and no disease need be mentioned, for the diagnostician may make or draw his conclusion in his own way." (People v. Zinke, 169 Misc. 573, 578.) People v. Amber, 76 Misc.2d 267, 273–4 (Sup.Ct. Queens Cty.N.Y.1973).

dialysis (di-al′ĭ-sis) [*dia-* + Gr. *lysis* dissolution] the process of separating crystalloids and colloids in solution by the difference in their rates of diffusion through a semipermeable membrane: crystalloids pass through readily, colloids very slowly or not at all. See also *hemodialysis*.

He is in end stage renal disease, and, since 1979, has required hemo **dialysis** in order to live. **Dialysis** is a cleansing procedure of the blood accomplished by way of attachment to a machine. Peter must have **dialysis** three times a week, each procedure taking four hours to accomplish. Application of Lydia E. Hall Hospital, 455 N.Y.S.2d 706, 708 (Sup.Ct.Nassau Cty. 1982).

Renal **dialysis** is a lifesaving procedure for total kidney failure which requires the patient to undergo lengthy treatment sessions on the **dialysis** machine up to three times per week. Testimony of Dr. Diamond, July 23, 1975. Gr. Wash. D.C. Area C. of Sr. Cit. v. D.C. Gov't, 406 F.Supp. 768, 771 (D.D.C.1975).

diameter (di-am′e-ter) the length of a straight line passing through the center of a circle and connecting opposite points on its circumference; hence the distance between two specified opposite points on the periphery of a structure such as the cranium or pelvis.

Diamox (di′ah-moks) trademark for preparations of acetazolamide. See also *acetazolamide*.

diaphoresis (di″ah-fo-re′sis) [Gr. *diaphorēsis*] perspiration, especially profuse perspiration.

. . . a sudden onset of severe chest pain, shortness of breath, and severe **diaphoresis** (profuse perspiration). Savage v. Christian Hospital Northwest, 543 F.2d 44, 46 (8th Cir. 1976).

Her color was generally pale, her skin warm, she was almost constantly suffering from **diaphoresis** (sweating), many times profusely but occasionally moderately or not at all. . . . Matter of Quinlan, 348 A.2d 801, 808 (Super.Ct.N.J.1975).

diastereoisomer (di″ah-ster″e-o-i′so-mer) a compound exhibiting, or capable of exhibiting, diastereoisomerism. See also *diasteroisomerism; stereoisomer;* and *stereoisomerism*.

. . . diastereoisomer—a compound containing more than one set of stereoisomers. In the case at bar we are concerned with a compound in which two such sets are involved. The distinction between the sets of isomers or the stereoisomers in such a compound is based upon a difference in the solubility of each set. The less soluble pair here is designated by the Greek letter alpha, which is written α; and the more soluble pair by the letter beta, written β. Eli Lilly & Co. v. Generix Drug Sales, Inc., 460 F.2d 1096, 1100 (5th Cir. 1972).

diastereoisomerism (di″ah-ster″e-o″i-som′er-izm) a special type of optical isomerism in which the respective molecules of the compounds do not, at any time, exhibit a mirror-image (or enantiomorphic) relationship to one

another. For example, the relationship between either *dextro-* or *levo-*tartaric acid and *meso-*tartaric acid is called diastereoisomeric. Diastereoisomers, in contrast to enantiomorphs, differ in both physical and chemical properties.

diathermy (di′ah-ther″me) [*dia-* + Gr. *thermē* heat] heating of the body tissues due to their resistance to the passage of high-frequency electromagnetic radiation, electric currents, or ultrasonic waves. In *medical d.* (thermopenetration) the tissues are warmed but not damaged; in *surgical d.* (electrocoagulation) tissue is destroyed.

A **diathermy** machine works by sending small electrical impulses through muscle tissue, increasing the healing rate. When the machine was turned on, decedent suffered cardiac arrest due to interference with his pacemaker by the machine. Armstrong v. Stearns-Roger Elec. Contractors, 657 P.2d 131–2 (Ct.App.N.M.1982).

Diathermy [The generation of heat in tissues of the body, as a result of the resistance presented by the tissues to electric currents of high frequency that is forced through them.]. U.S. v. Article Consisting of 2 Devices, etc., 255 F.Supp. 374, 381 (W.D.Ark.1966).

diathermy, microwave See *microwave*.

Dr. Wharton, an orthopedic surgeon and chief of the spinal injury service at Methodist Rehabilitation Center testified that **microwave diathermy** is a form of treatment which concerns the use of radio waves in the microwave spectrum. These microwaves have the capability of developing heat or translating the energy of radio waves deep within the body or at least deeper than the superficial layers of skin. The purpose of **microwave diathermy** according to Dr. Wharton is to produce heat deep within the body and by doing so to increase blood circulation in that particular area. He also testified that if overheating occurs, tissue necrosis (death of the tissue) can occur. He further testified that in his opinion it was possible to cause death with the use of diathermy. Norville v. Miss. State Medical Ass'n, 364 So.2d 1084–5 (Miss.1978).

diathermy, short wave the therapeutic heating of the body tissues by means of an oscillating electromagnetic field of high frequency; the frequency varies from 10 million to 100 million cycles per second and the wavelength from 30 to 3 meters.

diathesis (di-ath′ĕ-sis) [Gr. "arrangement, disposition"] a constitution or condition of the body which makes the tissues react in special ways to certain extrinsic stimuli and thus tends to make the person more than usually susceptible to certain diseases. Cf. *constitution* (def. 1) and *type*. See also *constituting; type;* and *habit*.

diathesis, bleeding See *disease, hemorrhagic diathesis of the newborn*.

diatrizoate (di″ah-tri-zo′āt) any salt of diatrizoic acid.

diatrizoate meglumine [USP], a radiopaque medium, ($C_7H_{17}NO_5 \cdot C_{11}H_9I_3N_2O_4$), available in solution, consisting of diatrizoate meglumine in water for injection or of diatrizoic acid in water for injection, prepared with the aid of meglumine; used intra-arterially in angiocardiography, aortography, cerebral angiography, and peripheral arteriography, intravenously in angiocardiography, excretory urography, and venography, and unilaterally in retrograde pyelography.

diatrizoate sodium [USP], a radiopaque medium, $C_{11}H_8I_3N_2NaO_4$, available in solution, consisting of diatrizoate sodium in water for injection or of diatrizoic acid in water for injection, prepared with the aid of sodium hydroxide; used in cholangiography, intravenously in excretory urography, hysterosalpingography, and unilaterally in retrograde pyelography.

diazepam (di-az′ĕ-pam) [USP] chemical name: 7-chloro-1,3-dihydro-1-methyl-5-phenyl-2H-1,4-benzodiazepin-2-one. One of the benzodiazepine tranquilizers, $C_{16}H_{13}ClN_2O$, occurring as an off-white to yellow, crystalline powder. It is administered orally, intravenously, or intramuscularly as a sedative, and is also used as a skeletal muscle relaxant, to produce anesthesia, as an anticonvulsant, and in the management of alcohol withdrawal symptoms and delirium tremens.

Dr. Daniel Weiss testified that **Valium** is prescribed to tranquilize or relieve nervous distress and that it is not an acceptable medical practice to give a controlled substance to a patient who has no condition requiring medication. Com. v. DeLaCruz, 443 N.E.2d 427, 430 (App.Ct.Mass.1982).

This is an action by plaintiff, an author and television producer against Dr. Peter Janulis, her former psychiatrist, for malpractice in having prescribed excessive amounts of the drug **Valium** and then causing her to discontinue it abruptly causing severe psychological problems and institutionalization, and against Roche Laboratories for product liability in manufacturing and distributing **Valium** without ascertaining its dangers and without warning the public of its harmful side effects....

Plaintiff has written a book about her experiences with **Valium**, entitled "I'm Dancing as Fast as I Can." She spent 13 years under the psychiatric care of Dr. Janulis. During that period, she obviously related to him many of the most intimate details of her life, and dealt with the psychological problems that troubled her. While Dr. Janulis prescribed **Valium**, it was not until after she totally ceased taking it that she was hospitalized. Defendants contend that her extreme reactions were not the result of the cessation of the drug, but rather were caused by her being held captive in her apartment by a lover for 55 days while subjected to sado-masochistic treatment. Gordon v. Roche Lab., Div. of Hoffman-La Roche, 456 N.Y.S.2d 291–2 (Sup.Ct.N.Y.Cty.1981).

He said that **Valium** is not a narcotic drug and is not habit forming; that **Valium** is a tranquilizer and muscle relaxant. He did say that **Valium** is a controlled substance. He stated that when **Valium** and alcohol are combined in the body the alcohol gives an increased effect to the **Valium**. The effects which could be produced by such a combination include slurred speech, difficulty in walking, glassy eyes, and inability to breathe properly. He said appellant's inability to blow into the intoximeter on the night of his arrest was consistent with his ingestion of beer and **Valium** earlier that evening. Leu v. City of Mountain Brook, 386 So.2d 483, 485 (Ct.Crim.App.Ala.1980).

Other Authorities: Watkins v. U.S., 589 F.2d 214, 216–19, 224–5 (5th Cir. 1979); U.S. v. Stegmaier, 397 F.Supp. 611, 615–16 (E.D.Pa.1975); Texas Employers' Ins. Ass'n v. Saun-

ders, 516 S.W.2d 242–3 (Ct.Civ.App.Tex.1974); Hoffman-La Roche, Inc. v. Kleindienst, 478 F.2d 1, 7–9 (3d Cir. 1973).

dichlorobenzedine

Turning first to the finding of carcinogenicity, the independent studies of Pliss, Saffiotti and Stula all support the conclusion that **DCB** causes cancer in rodents (rats and hamsters)....

... Based on this summary of the evidence, we conclude that the most that can be said is that **DCB** and EI pose a "potential" cancer hazard to man. Although the danger of cancer is surely "grave," subsection 6(c)(1) of the Act requires a grave danger of exposure to substances "determined to be toxic or physically harmful." Dry Color Mfrs. Ass'n, Inc. v. Dep't of Labor, 486 F.2d 98, 103–4 (3d Cir. 1973).

dicumarol (di-koo′mah-rol) [USP] chemical name: 3,3′-methyl-enebis[4-hydroxy-2H-1-benzopyran-2-one]. One of the coumarin anticoagulants, $C_{19}H_{12}O_6$, occurring as a white or creamy white, crystalline powder, originally isolated from spoiled sweet clover but now produced synthetically; it acts by inhibiting the hepatic snythesis of vitamin K-dependent coagulation factors (prothrombin, Factors II, VII, IX, and X); administered orally. It is the etiologic agent of the hemorrhagic disease in animals known as *sweet clover disease*. Called also *bishydroxycoumarin* and *dicoumarin*.

The drug involved in this case is **Dicumarol**, an anticoagulant used in the treatment of blood clotting disorders including phlebitis....

... **Dicumarol** has been produced by Lilly since 1944 when its New Drug Application was first approved by the Food and Drug Administration.

By 1963, following substantial controversy, it became generally accepted in the medical community that **Dicumarol** crossed the placental barrier and therefore posed a serious risk to the fetus when given to a pregnant woman....

... In response to the report, Lilly again amended and strengthened the language of its package insert to read:

Dicumarol passes the placental barrier. When pregnant women are treated with the drug, fetal bleeding diathesis may occur and cause fetal death in utero. **Dicumarol** is also secreted in the maternal milk. Therefore, the drug is contraindicated for pregnant patients and for breast-feeding mothers. If anticoagulant therapy is required for such patients, heparin is considered the drug of choice, because it does not pass through the placenta or into the mother's milk....

... The potential danger of **Dicumarol** is extremely grave. It can cause the death of a fetus in utero and can leave a newborn with severe and lifelong injury. Baker v. St. Agnes Hospital, 421 N.Y.S.2d 81, 83, 86 (2d Dep't 1979).

There was also evidence that she knew not only of Stahlin's heart condition but also that he was taking a blood thinner type pill called **Dicumarol** therefor.... Stahlin v. Hilton Hotels Corp., 484 F.2d 580, 583 (7th Cir. 1973).

dicyandiamide, methylmercury See *cyanoguanidine*.

dicyclomine hydrochloride (di-si′klo-mēn) [USP] chemical name: [bicyclohexyl]-1-carboxylic acid 2-(diethylamino)ethyl ester. An anticholinergic, $C_{19}H_{35}NO_2 \cdot HCl$, occurring as a fine, white, crystalline powder; used as an antispasmodic in the treatment of functional gastrointestinal disorders, administered orally or intramuscularly.

-diene a suffix used in chemistry to denote an unsaturated hydrocarbon containing two double bonds.

A **diene** (or diolefin) is a chemically active hydrocarbon containing two carbon-to-carbon double bonds. A bridged-ring (or bicyclic) **diene** is one in which the carbon atoms are arranged in a cyclic, or closed chain structure, and two nonadjacent carbon atoms in a ring are joined by a bridge of one or more carbon atoms. Hercules, Inc. v. Exxon Corp., 434 F.Supp. 136, 141 (D.Del.1977).

dienestrol (di″ĕn-es′trol) [USP] chemical name: 4,4′-(1,2-diethylidene-1,2-ethanediyl)bisphenol. A synthetic estrogen, $C_{18}H_{18}O_2$, occurring as colorless, white, or practically white, needle-like crystals or as a white or practically white, crystalline powder; administered orally in the management of menopausal symptoms, in the treatment of functional uterine bleeding, as a postpartum antigalactagogue, for palliative therapy in certain female breast cancers, and in the management of prostatic carcinoma, and applied locally in the treatment of postmenopausal and senile vulvovaginitis, atrophic vaginitis, pruritus vulvae due to atrophic changes in the vulval epithelium, dyspareunia associated with atrophic vaginal epithelium, and prior to plastic pelvic surgery in menopausal patients. See also *adenosis.*

At stake is Home's potential liability for untold millions of dollars in payment for claims by plaintiffs who assert injury from Schering's synthetic estrogen product, **dienestrol** ("DEN")....

... In particular, **DEN** was widely administered to patients with high-risk pregnancies for the purpose of preventing miscarriages....

In 1971, an association between synthetic estrogens and clear-cell vaginal adenocarcinoma (a cancer of glandular tissues in the vagina) in daughters of women who had taken DES was reported in the medical literature. Herbst, Ulfelder & Poskanzer, Adenocarcinoma of the Vagina, 284 New England J.Med. 878 (1971). Later that year, the Food and Drug Administration (FDA) proscribed the use of **DEN** (as well as DES) in the treatment of pregnant women. Although DES and **DEN** continue to be marketed for purposes other than preventing miscarriages, their deleterious effects on female offspring of women who took the drugs while with child (commonly referred to as "DES daughters") are well documented. Schering Corp. v. Home Ins. Co., 712 F.2d 4, 7 (2d Cir. 1983).

In 1946 the Food and Drug Administration ("FDA") authorized defendant-appellant White Laboratories, Inc. ("White"), to market **dienestrol**, a synthetic estrogen, for the treatment of menopausal symptoms and suppression of lactation.[1] In 1950 the FDA authorized White to market **dienestrol** for treatment of threatened and habitual miscarriages. [[1] In 1941 the FDA had authorized other drug manufacturers to market diethylstilbestrol ("DES"), another synthetic estrogen, for use in the treatment of these two conditions. Although **dienestrol** and DES possess different chemical structures, they are both pharmacologically identical to natural estrogen. In 1947 the FDA authorized drug manufacturers to market DES for treatment of threatened and habitual miscarriages.] Needham v. White Laboratories, Inc., 639 F.2d 394, 396 (7th Cir. 1981).

diet (di′et) [Gr. *diaita* way of living] the customary allowance of food and drink taken by any person from day to day, particularly one especially planned to meet specific requirements of the individual, and including or excluding certain items of food.

diet, Sippy a diet for peptic ulcer and for conditions in which the patient is unable to take bulky foods. It consists of nothing but milk and cream for the first few days, with the addition of crackers, cereals, and eggs on the third day; the amounts increasing gradually until during the later days of the diet puréed vegetables are included. On the twenty-eighth day the patient is placed on the regular ward diet.

The **Sippy diet** is a regimen of frequent feedings and alkalies used in the treatment of peptic ulcer disease. Payne v. U.S., 711 F.2d 73–4 (7th Cir. 1983).

dietary (di′ĕ-ta″re) a regular or systematic scheme of diet.

(3) For purposes of paragraph (1) and of section 403(j) [of the Food, Drug and Cosmetic Act] insofar as that section is applicable to food to which this section applies, the term "special **dietary** use" as applied to food used by man means a particular use for which a food purports or is represented to be used, including but not limited to the following:

(A) Supplying a special **dietary** need that exists by reason of a physical, physiological, pathological, or other condition, including but not limited to the condition of disease, convalescence, pregnancy, lactation, infancy, allergic hypersensitivity to food, underweight, overweight, or the need to control the intake of sodium.

(B) Supplying a vitamin, mineral, or other ingredient for use by man to supplement his diet by increasing the total **dietary** intake.

(C) Supplying a special **dietary** need by reason of being a food for use as the sole item of the diet.... National Nutritional Foods Ass'n v. Kennedy, 572 F.2d 377, 381 (2d Cir. 1978).

diethylstilbestrol (di-eth″il-stil-bes′trol) [USP] chemical name: (*E*)-4,4′-(1,2-diethyl-1,2-ethenediyl)bis-phenol. A synthetic nonsteroidal estrogen, $C_{18}H_{20}O_2$, occurring as a white, crystalline powder, having estrogenic activity similar to but greater than that of estrone. It is used for many purposes, e.g., to relieve menopausal symptoms, to suppress lactation, in amenorrhea, dysmenorrhea, senile vaginitis, and pruritus vulvae, in the palliative treatment of female breast carcinoma, and to relieve the symptoms of prostatic carcinoma; administered orally, intravaginally, or intramuscularly. Formerly used to prevent threatened or habitual abortion and premature labor. Women who have been exposed *in utero* to diethylstilbestrol show characteristic changes in the cervix and vagina and are subject to an increased risk of vaginal or cervical carcinoma. Called also *estrostilben* and *stilbestrol.* See also *adenocarcinoma* (Bichler case); *adenosis; adenosis, vaginae; dienestrol; estrogen* (Bell case); and *endometrium* (Bell case).

... manufactured and marketed the synthetic estrogen **diethylstilbestrol**, commonly known as **DES.** The complaint alleged that those defendants manufactured and distributed the drug for use in the prevention and control of complications of pregnancy. Plaintiff's mother purchased **DES** on prescription of her physician in 1954 and, in 1973, plaintiff contracted cancer of the vagina and cervix. Mertan v. E. R. Squibb and Sons, Inc., 190 Cal.Rptr. 349–50 (Ct. of App.Cal.1983).

DES is the generic name for a medication which duplicates the effects of natural estrogens in the human body. It has been used, and is still being used, to treat a variety of medical conditions. In 1971, however, the Federal Food and Drug Administration banned the use of **DES** for the treatment of problems of pregnancy because of mounting evidence that it was ineffective in preventing miscarriage and dangerous to the unborn children as well....

  Plaintiff was born in 1955 to a mother who ingested **DES** during pregnancy. In 1969 she began to experience a variety of gynecological disorders which persisted after she enrolled as a student at Syracuse University in 1973. Helmrich v. Eli Lilly & Co., 455 N.Y.S.2d 460–1 (4th Dep't 1982).

Nina Diamond, while yet unborn, had administered to her a drug known as **diethylstilbestrol**, produced by the Squibb company under the trademark "stilbetin." They alleged further that in May, 1976, they learned that teenaged girls whose mothers had been treated with stilbetin during pregnancy were developing cancerous or precancerous conditions. Diamond v. E. R. Squibb & Sons, Inc., 397 So.2d 671 (Fla.1981).

Other Authorities: Renfroe v. Eli Lilly & Co., 686 F.2d 642, 644 (8th Cir. 1982); Sindell v. Abbott Laboratories, 607 P.2d 924, 925 (Cal.1980); Bichler v. Eli Lilly & Co., 436 N.E.2d 182, 183–4 (N.Y.1982); Lyons v. Premo Pharmaceutical Labs, Inc., 406 A.2d 185, 187–9, 191–2 (Super.Ct.N.J.1979); Bell v. Goddard, 366 F.2d 177, 179–180 (7th Cir. 1966).

diethyltryptamine (di-eth″il-trip′tah-min) chemical name: N_2N-diethyltryptamine. A hallucinogenic substance closely related to dimethyltryptamine, but prepared synthetically. Abbreviated DET.

  The record contains Government testimony that hallucinogens such as **diethyltryptamine (DET)** and dimethyltryptamine (DMT) can be ingested by smoking parsley cigarettes which have been soaked in or sprayed with the hallucinogen. U.S. v. Moore, 452 F.2d 569, 571 (6th Cir. 1971).

diffusion test See *test, diffusion.*

digestion (di-jest′yun) [L. *digestio,* from *dis-* apart + *gerere* to carry] the process or act of converting food into chemical substances that can be absorbed and assimilated.

digestion, anaerobic

  Decomposition of these removed solids (sludge) is known as **anaerobic digestion**; that is, the oxidation of organic material, with gases as the by-product.[5] [[5] The process of decomposition, or digestion, reduces the removed solids to about 50% of its original content. The remaining solids are not easily degraded biologically; that is, further chemical breakdown is very slow.] U.S. v. City of Asbury Park, 340 F.Supp. 555, 558 (D.N.J.1972).

digitalis (dij″ĭ-tal′is) [USP] the dried leaf of *Digitalis purpurea,* the purple foxglove, the main systemic effects of which are manifested by an increase in the strength of the heart beat while decreasing its rate. When digitalis is

prescribed *powdered digitalis* (see below) is to be dispensed. Called also *d. leaf.*

Dr. Tontiplaphol provided her at time of discharge with a prescription for **Lanoxin**, a form of **digitalis** ....

  ... The witness for the defense was Dr. Joe Milton McCurdy, a Board certified specialist in internal medicine and a former professor at the medical schools of both Tulane and L.S.U....

  ... He testified that from his reading of the records of the **Lanoxin** overdose he would have expected the symptoms to disappear in about two days. As to whether **Lanoxin** produces lasting effects on the heart muscle, he stated that he had personally researched the subject:

  "I have no knowledge of any permanent effects and I have been unable to find any documentation anywhere if there is any permanent effect of **Lanoxin** on the heart muscle." Cazes v. Raisinger, 430 So.2d 104, 106 (Ct. of App.La. 1983).

Does the fact that the child is receiving **Digitalis** have any significance, that is, **Digitalis** within a month-and-a-half or two of his birth. A. Right. **Digitalis** is used to treat only two problems in heart disease: one is an arrhythmia, which is a rhythm problem; and the other is congestive heart failure, and the history was that the child had had congestive heart failure and was receiving **Digitalis** for it. Phillips v. U.S., 566 F.Supp. 1, 11 (D.S.Car.1981).

Digitalis (dij″ĭ-ta′lis) [L. from *digitus* finger, because of the finger-like leaves of the corolla of its flowers] a genus of herbs. *D. purpu′rea* is the purple foxglove whose leaves furnish digitalis. *D. lana′ta* is a Balkan species which yields digoxin and lanatoside.

digoxin (di-goks′in) [USP] chemical name: 3β-[(*O*-2,6-dideoxy-β-D-*ribo*-hexopyranosyl-$(1\rightarrow4)$-*O*-2,6-dideoxy-β-D-*ribo*-hexopyranosyl-$(1\rightarrow4)$-2,6-dideoxy-β-*ribo*-hexopyranosyl)oxy]-12β, 14-dihydroxy-card-5β-20(22)-enolide. A cardiotonic glycoside, $C_{41}H_{64}O_{14}$, obtained from the leaves of *Digitalis lanata,* occurring as clear to white crystals or white crystalline powder. It may be used for the same purposes as digitalis, administered orally, intramuscularly, or intravenously.

dihycon See *phenytoin.*

Dilantin (di-lan′tin) trademark for preparations of phenytoin. See also *phenytoin.*

dilatation (dil-ah-ta′shun) the act of dilating or stretching.

dilatation, esophageal

  As a consequence of the colon transposition, plaintiff must undergo periodic maintenance-type operations on his repaired esophagus, called **esophageal dilatations**. This operation is required on a regular basis, to widen the stricture where the colon and the esophagus were joined, to prevent impairment of the plaintiff's ability to swallow.

  Dr. DeMeules testified that generally either of two procedures can be used to perform the dilatations. The choice depends on the particular type of stricture involved. The first method, referred to as string method, requires that the patient swallow a string several days before the operation to allow the string to anchor itself; then a series of progressively larger rigid dilators are guided into the esophagus over the string until the stricture is dilated to a reasonable size. The second procedure involves the use of a rubber tube filled with mercury and tapered at one end. The tube is inserted through the mouth into the esophagus and into the area of the obstruction. This method is used in cases where the passage from the mouth to the stricture is tortuous and can be performed with or without the aid of a fluoroscope, to provide the surgeon with a continuous x-ray picture of the progress of the operation. Battick v. Stoneman, 421 F.Supp. 213, 217–18 (D.Vt.1976).

dilatation of the stomach distention of the stomach with retained secretions, food, and/or gas due to obstruction, ileus, or denervation; called also *gastric d.*

dilation (di-la'shun) the action of dilating or stretching. See also *dilatation*.

dilation and curettage See *D and C.*

dilation, gastric See *dilatation of the stomach.*

"They can develop acute **gastric dilation** which means that the stomach can dilate to an enormous size . . . they can die with acute **gastric dilation.**" Lenger v. Physician's General Hosp., Inc., 455 S.W.2d 703, 710 (Tex.1970).

dilation of the cervix

In 1972, in a case in which a pregnant woman had a prolapsed umbilical cord which extended outside the vagina, Dr. Storrs attempted manual **dilation of the patient's cervix,** testified to by one witness as an "operation [which] has no place in modern obstetrics," "a deviation from accepted obstetrics procedure" and not really manual dilatation, but "manual laceration of the cervix." Testimony was presented that the procedure created a risk to the woman of an "incompetent cervix," not a risk to the baby being delivered, but a risk to the patient's next baby, were she to become pregnant again. Storrs v. State Medical Bd., 664 P.2d 547, 556 (Alas.1983).

dilator (di-la'tor) an instrument used in enlarging an orifice or canal by stretching.

He advised her to continue to use the bronchial **dilater** [sic] and use inhalation steroids and avoid smoke and nauseous fumes. Sellers v. Breaux, 422 So.2d 1231, 1235–6 (Ct.App.La. 1982).

Dilaudid (di-law'did) trademark for preparations of hydromorphone hydrochloride. See also *hydromorphone hydrochloride.*

dimercaprol (di"mer-kap'rol) [USP] chemical name: 2,3-dimercaptopropanol. A metal complexing agent, $C_3H_8OS_2$, occurring as a colorless or almost colorless liquid; used as an antidote to poisoning by arsenic, gold, and mercury, and sometimes other metals, administered intramuscularly. It has also been used in the treatment of hepatolenticular degeneration.

Dimercaprol is an effective antedote for arsenic trioxide poisoning. Pax Company of Utah v. U.S., 324 F.Supp. 1335, 1342 (D.Utah 1970).

dimethyltryptamine (di-meth"il-trip'tah-mēn) chemical name: *N,N,*dimethyltryptamine. A hallucinogenic substance, $C_{12}H_{16}N_2$, derived from the apocynaceous plant *Prestonia amazonica* (Benth.) Macbride (*Haemadictyon amazonicum* Spruce and Benth.) which is native to parts

of South America and the West Indies. Abbreviated DMT.

DMT is a species of the genus trytamine. U.S. v. Moore, 452 F.2d 569, 571 (6th Cir. 1971).

Dinoflagellata (di"no-flaj"ĕ-la'tah) [Gr. *dinos* whirl + *flagellum* whip] an order of minute, chiefly marine, plant-like protozoa of the class Phytomastigophora, subphylum Mastigophora, with two or more flagella in grooves, transverse and longitudinal, which cause the organism to rotate as it advances. They generally have a cellulose covering and numerous green, yellow, or brown chromatophores. Dinoflagellates may be present in seawater in vast numbers, causing a discoloration known as "red tide" or "red water," which may cause the death of many fish and various invertebrates. It includes the genera *Gonyaulax* and *Gymnodinium.* See also *Gymnodinium.*

The Red Tide is caused by a marine **dinoflagellate,** gymnodium brevis which requires a high degree of phosphates to flourish. Once the Red Tide organism blooms, it secretes a toxin which kills fish and poses other serious health hazards. The only chemical difference between Biscayne Bay and Tampa Bay is that the former has a lower phosphate level than does the latter. Soap and Detergent Ass'n v. Clark, 330 F.Supp. 1218, 1220–1 (S.D.Fla.1971).

dinoflagellate (di-no-flaj'ĕ-lāt) of or pertaining to the order Dinoflagellata.

dinoprost (di'no-prŏst) chemical name: (5 *Z,*9α,11α,13*E,* 15*S*)-9,11,15-trihydroxyprosta-5,13-dien-1-oic acid. A prostaglandin of the F type, $C_{20}H_{34}O_5$, the main action of which is to stimulate the myometrium to contract. Called also *prostaglandin F_{2a}.*

dinoprost tromethamine the tromethamine salt of dinoprost, $C_{20}H_{34}O_5 \cdot C_4H_{11}NO_3$, having the same actions as the base; used as an oxytocic for induction of labor, termination of pregnancy, missed abortion, fetal death, and hydatidiform mole. It is administered intravenously, extra-amniotically, or intra-amniotically. Called also *d. trometanol* and *prostaglandin F_{2a}.*

Prostin F2 alpha is the trademark for Prostaglandin F2 alpha, which is the drug distributed by Upjohn for inducing abortions. Wynn v. Scott, 449 F.Supp. 1302, 1326 (N.D.Ill.1978).

dioxin (di-ok'sin) any of the heterocyclic hydrocarbons present as a trace contaminant in herbicides, especially the chlorinated dioxin 2,3,7,8-tetrachlorodibenzo-para-dioxin, thought to have oncogenic and teratogenic properties. See also *Agent Orange; oncogenic; oncogenicity; teratogenic; tetrachloroparadioxin;* and *tumorigenic.*

All herbicides derived from 2,4,5-trichlorophenol—including 2,4,5-T and silvex (but not 2,4-D)—contain a chemical contaminant formed in the manufacturing process known as 2,3,7,8-tetrachlorodibenzo-p-**dioxin** (TCDD). TCDD is one of the most toxic chemicals known to man. Its presence and significance in phenoxy herbicides have become known only in recent years, although the herbicides have been in use since the late 1940s. TCDD cannot be eliminated entirely from the products of 2,4,5-trichlorophenol. . . .

. . . A contaminant of 2,4,5,-T—tetrachlorodibenzoparadioxin (TCDD, or **dioxin**)—is one of the most teratogenic chemicals known. The registrants have not established that 1 part per million of this contaminant—or even 0.1 ppm—in 2,4,5-T does not pose a danger to the public health and safety....

... There is a substantial possibility that even "pure" 2,4,5-T is itself a hazard to man and the environment....

... The registrants have not established that **dioxin** and 2,4,5-T do not accumulate in body tissues. If one or both does accumulate, even small doses could build up to dangerous levels within man and animals, and possibly in the food chain as well....

... Professor Virgil C. Boekelheide, Professor of Organic Chemistry and Acting Head of the Department of Chemistry of the University of Oregon, testified that TCDD

is fantastically toxic and is commonly quoted as being the most toxic simple organic molecule known to man. Its acute oral lethal toxicity (LD_{50}) in guinea pigs is 0.0000006g/kg. At sublethal dose levels it still has highly toxic effects on thymus, liver and other organs, as well as being extremely teratogenic. Thus, minute quantities of TCDD well below the acute lethal dose level have adverse toxic effects and a threshold limit, below which no toxic effects occur, has never been demonstrated for TCDD. Citizens Against Toxic Sprays, Inc. v. Bergland, 428 F.Supp. 908, 915, 927 (D.Ore.1977).

The new [EPA] order continued with a review of the Advisory Committee report, stated the Administrator's determination that the cancellations of the registrations of 2,4,5-T be continued, made ten findings of fact, set forth in full in the margin hereof [14]... [[14] "1. A contaminant of 2,4,5-T—tetrachlorodibenzoparadioxin (TCDD, or **dioxin**)—is one of the most teratogenic chemicals known. The registrants have not established that 1 part per million of this contaminant—or even 0.1 ppm—in 2,4,5-T does not pose a danger to the public health and safety. "2. There is a substantial possibility that even 'pure' 2,4,5-T is itself a hazard to man and the environment. "3. The dose-response curves for 2,4,5-T and **dioxin** have not been determined, and the possibility of 'no effect' levels for these chemicals is only a matter of conjecture at this time. "4. As with another well-known teratogen, thalidomide, the possibility exists that **dioxin** may be many times more potent in humans than in test animals (thalidomide was 60 times more dangerous to humans than to mice, and 700 times more dangerous than to hamsters; the usual margin of safety for humans is set at one-tenth the teratogenic level in test animals)...".] Dow Chemical Co. v. Ruckelshaus, 477 F.2d 1317, 1321 (8th Cir. 1973).

diphenoxylate hydrochloride (di"fen-ok'sĭ-lāt) [USP] chemical name: 1-(3-cyano-3,3-diphenylpropyl)-4-phenyl-4-piperidinecarboxylic acid ethyl ester monohydrochloride. An antiperistaltic derived from meperidine, $C_{30}H_{32}N_2O_2 \cdot HCl$; used as an antidiarrheal, administered orally.

diphenyl (di-fe'nil) a colorless compound, $C_6H_5C_6H_5$, found in coal tar and used as fungistat in containers for shipping oranges. Called also *biphenyl*.

diphenylhydantoin See *phenytoin*.

diplopia (dĭ-plo'pe-ah) [*diplo-* + Gr. *ōpē* sight + *-ia*] the perception of two images of a single object; called also *ambiopia, double vision*, and *binocular polyopia*. See also *heterotropia, comitant*; and *heterotropia, noncomitant*.

According to Cashwell, the plaintiff has permanent damage to the sixth cranial nerve, resulting in **diplopia**, i.e., double vision, when he exceeds eight degrees to the right and ten degrees to the left. Key v. McLean Trucking, 300 S.E.2d 280 (Ct.App.N. Car.1983).

Any type of ocular imbalance causes **diplopia**, for the reason that images then fall on disparate or non-corresponding parts of the two retinas. After a time, however, the patient learns to suppress the image of one eye. This almost invariably happens early in comcomitant strabismus of congenital nature, and the individual grows up with a weak eye (amyblopia ex anopsia). Principles of Internal Medicine, Harrison, Ed., Fifth Edition, 1966....

From the foregoing, it is seen that while Doctors Azar and Habeeb conceded that concussion can cause **diplopia**, they were of the opinion that Fraley's **diplopia** was not caused by trauma. It was caused by the imbalance in his eyes; it was developmental. Todd Shipyards, Inc. v. Fraley, 592 F.2d 805–6, 809 (5th Cir. 1979).

Diplopia is a condition in which two images of a single object are perceived....

... Mr. Schaffer had undergone multiple reparative operations and that at that time he was suffering from double vision and that he could, therefore, not use both eyes together. Dr. Miller further stated that "this is not helped by, nor have we suggested, patching of the left eye....

... He stated **diplopia** does not affect straight ahead vision, only peripheral....

... With regard to the clarification of Dr. Feldman's report, the claimant took issue with the characterization of his **diplopia** as "only peripheral". He stated that it is true that it does not affect straight ahead vision, but it does affect the upward, downward, and leftward gazes." (Tr. 98). Schaffer v. Califano, 433 F.Supp. 1218, 1221 (D.Md.1977).

Other Authorities: McSwain v. Chicago Transit Authority, 362 N.E.2d 1264, 1272 (App.Ct.Ill.1977); Walker v. North Dakota Eye Clinic, Ltd., 415 F.Supp. 891–2, 894 (D.N.Dak.1976); Perry v. Bertsch, 441 F.2d 939, 942, 944 (8th Cir. 1971); Jenkins v. Gardner, 430 F.2d 243, 286–7 (6th Cir. 1970), Yarrow v. U.S., 309 F.Supp. 922, 925 (S.D.N.Y.1970).

Dipuron

Because Dr. Macias prescribed a temperature-reducing drug, **Dipuron**, which Dr. Root testified should be used only when all other antifebrile medications have failed and only if a convulsion is actually occurring, Dr. Root concluded that Dr. Macias considered the child's condition to be "an extremely emergent situation," a situation requiring absolute immediate attention, "something that the doctor should be there for right now." Cortez v. Macias, 167 Cal.Rptr. 905, 908 (Ct.App.Cal.1980).

diquat

Sometime in the summer of 1977 Cornelius was spraying **diquat**, a strong weed killer, when the nozzle leading from the compressor tank to the hose became clogged. As Cornelius attempted to unclog the nozzle, the spout broke off causing a large quantity of the **diquat** to be sprayed directly into his face, including his nose and mouth....

In the fall of 1977, Cornelius began experiencing both physical and mental problems. He complained of itching, swelling, rash about his body, hair loss, sleep disturbance, and various allergies. In February of 1978 claimant was admitted to Memorial Hospital in Hollywood for psychiatric care and treatment. At that time, claimant was seen by Dr. Akomer who diagnosed Cornelius as a paranoid schizophrenic....

... Although Dr. Israel, the psychologist, believed that Cornelius' psychological problems were attributable to the traumatic effects of the **diquat** spraying incident in 1977, Dr. Taubel, the psychiatrist, believed that heredity was the cause of claimant's disease. Dr. Taubel had previously treated Cornelius' brother who also was diagnosed as a paranoid schizophrenic. Cornelius v. Sunset Golf Course, 423 So.2d 567–8 (Dist.Ct.App.Fla.1982).

disability (dis"ah-bil'ĭ-te) 1. a lack of the ability to function normally, physically or mentally; incapacity. 2. as defined by the federal government: "inability to engage in any substantial gainful activity by reason of any medically determinable physical or mental impairment which can be expected to last or has lasted for a continuous period of not less than 12 months." See also *impairment*.

The statutory definition of a **disability** represents a Congressional decision to provide benefits to those eligible persons whose impairment has a medically ascertainable source.[3] [3 Congress added section 223(d)(3) to the definition of "**disability**" in 1967, Pub.L. No. 90–248, § 158(b), 81 Stat. 821, 868, "to reemphasize the predominant importance of medical factors in the disability determination." H.Rep. No. 544, 90th Cong., 1st Sess. 30 (1967); S.Rep. No. 744, 90th Cong., 1st Sess. 48 (1967), reprinted in 1967 U.S.Code Cong. & Ad. News 2834, 2882.] Gallagher on Behalf of Gallagher v. Schweiker, 697 F.2d 82, 84 (2d Cir. 1983).

However, in passing the Social Security Disability Benefits Reform Act of 1984, Pub.L. No. 98–460, 98 Stat. 1794 (1984), Congress established a temporary statutory standard for evaluating subjective evidence of pain. Section 3(a)(1) of that Act provides that:

Section 223(d)(5) of the Social Security Act is amended by inserting after the first sentence the following new sentences: "An individual's statement as to pain or other symptoms shall not alone be conclusive evidence of **disability** as defined in this section; there must be medical signs and findings, established by medically acceptable clinical or laboratory diagnostic techniques, which show the existence of a medical impairment that results from anatomical, physiological, or psychological abnormalities which could reasonably be expected to produce the pain or other symptoms alleged and which, when considered with all evidence required to be furnished under this paragraph (including statements of the individual or his physician as to the intensity and persistence of such pain or other symptoms which may reasonably be accepted as consistent with the medical signs and findings), would lead to a conclusion that the individual is under a disability. Objective medical evidence of pain or other symptoms established by medically acceptable clinical or laboratory techniques (for example, deteriorating nerve or muscle tissue) must be considered in reaching a conclusion as to whether an individual is under a disability."
Id. at § 3(a)(1), 98 Stat. at 1799 (to be codified at 42 U.S.C. § 423(d)(5)) (emphasis added). This standard applies to all determinations (made by the Secretary or a court on review) to be made prior to January 1, 1987, at which time Congress

intends to set permanent standards for evaluating pain. Id. at § 3(a)(3) and (b); see S.Rep. No. 466, 98th Cong., 2d Sess. 3, 23–24 (1984), U.S.Code Cong. & Admin.News 1984, p. 3038.
Hand v. Heckler, 761 F.2d 1545, 1547–48 (11th Cir. 1985).

Plaintiff has the burden of proving **disability**. Parker v. Harris, 626 F.2d 225, 231 (2d Cir. 1980). Under 42 U.S.C. § 423(d)(1)(A), **disability** is defined[2] as the inability to engage in substantial gainful activity by reason of any medically determinable physical or mental impairment which can be expected to result in death or which has lasted or can be expected to last for a continuous period of not less than 12 months....[2 This definition of disability is virtually identical to the definition used in SSI disability benefit cases under 42 U.S.C. § 1382c(3). In addition the standard for judicial review is also identical, 42 U.S.C. § 1383c(3). As a result, cases under 42 U.S.C. § 423 and 42 U.S.C. § 1382c(3) are cited interchangeably. Hankerson v. Harris, 636 F.2d 893, 897 n. 2 (2d Cir. 1980). Thus, in our case, the discussion is the same for plaintiff's claim to SSI benefits and disability claims.]

Under (d)(2)(A) of the same section, a claimant is not disabled unless his physical or mental impairment or impairments are of such severity that he is not only unable to do his previous work but cannot, considering his age, education, and work experience, engage in any other kind of substantial gainful work which exists in the national economy, regardless of whether such work exists in the immediate area in which he lives, or whether a specific job vacancy exists for him, or whether he should be hired if he applied for work....

In assessing **disability**, four factors are to be considered: (1) the objective medical facts; (2) diagnoses or medical opinions based on such facts; (3) subjective evidence of pain or **disability** testified to by the claimant or others; and (4) the claimant's educational background, age, and work experience. Rivera v. Harris, 623 F.2d 212, 215–16 (2d Cir. 1980); Bastien v. Califano, 572 F.2d 908, 912 (2d Cir. 1978); Gold v. Secretary of H.E.W., 463 F.2d 38, 42 (2d Cir. 1972). Ghazibayat v. Schweiker, 554 F.Supp. 1005, 1013–1014 (S.D.N.Y.1983).

Other Authorities: Bloodsworth v. Heckler, 703 F.2d 1233, 1240 (11th Cir. 1983); Hilliard v. Schweiker, 563 F.Supp. 99, 100 (D.Mont.1983); Rivers v. Schweiker, 684 F.2d 1144, 1150–1 (5th Cir. 1982); Director v. Campbell Industries, Inc., 678 F.2d 836, 840 (9th Cir. 1982); Cornett v. Califano, 590 F.2d 91, 94 (4th Cir. 1978); Knott v. Califano, 559 F.2d 279, 280 (5th Cir. 1977); Spaulding v. Califano, 427 F.Supp. 982, 983 (W.D.Mo.1977); Reese v. Gas Engineering and Construction Co., 548 P.2d 746, 749 (Kan.1976); Rivas v. Weinberger, 475 F.2d 255, 258 (5th Cir. 1973); DePaepe v. Richardson, 464 F.2d 92, 94 (5th Cir. 1972); Torres v. Celebreeze, 349 F.2d 342, 344–5 (1st Cir. 1965).

disability, functional

In Anderson v. Kinsley Sand & Gravel, Inc., 221 Kan. 191, 195, 558 P.2d 146 (1976), the court stated:

Functional disability is the loss of a part of the total physiological capabilities of the human body. Work disability is that portion of the job requirements that a workman is unable to perform by reason of an injury. Work disability generally carries a higher percentage of disability than a functional disability. Bahr v. Iowa Beef Processors, Inc., 663 P.2d 1144, 1150 (Ct.App.Kan.1983).

disability, occupational See *injury.*

disability, permanent

"A **disability** is considered **permanent** after the employee has reached maximum improvement or his condition has been stationary for a reasonable period of time, as may be determined by the Board or a referee. WCAB Rules § 10900." (Swezey, California Workmen's Compensation Practice 1973, § 14.18.). Duthy v. Workers' Compensation Appeals Bd., 150 Cal.Rptr. 530, 534 (Ct.App.Cal.1978).

disability, permanent scheduled

As used in this opinion, the term "scheduled" refers to those **permanent disabilities** for which compensation is provided under the provisions of A.R.S. § 23–1044B. Roeder v. Industrial Com'n, 556 P.2d 1148–9 (Ct.App.Ariz.1976).

disability, permanent unscheduled

The term "unscheduled" refers to those **permanent disabilities** for which compensation is provided under the provisions of A.R.S. § 23–1044C. Roeder v. Industrial Com'n, 556 P.2d 1148–9 (Ct.App.Ariz.1976).

disability, subjective evidence

There are, of course, circumstances where **subjective evidence** alone can be sufficient to prove **disability** or, at least, raise a serious question such that a systematic evaluation thereof is necessary to afford a basis for a finding of nondisability. Ber v. Celebrezze, 332 F.2d 293, 298–300 (2nd Cir. 1964)....

... Of course, we have already explained that subjective medical evidence is not to be discounted solely because of its non-objective nature. This goes far toward meeting counsel's contentions. Nevertheless, at the same time, such evidence will be of a type where credibility will be a significant factor in evaluation, and, consequently, great deference is given to the Hearing Examiner's evaluation and resulting conclusions. Longo v. Weinberger, 369 F.Supp. 250, 257 (E.D.Pa.1974).

disability, total

"Total disability" is defined in terms of the meaning given it by the regulations of the Secretary of HEW, except that the Coal Mine Health and Safety Act of 1969, as amended by the Black Lung Benefits Act of 1972, mandates that such regulations shall provide that a miner shall be considered totally disabled when, as a result of pneumoconiosis, he is unable to engage in gainful employment requiring the skills and abilities comparable to those of any employment in a mine or mines in which the miner previously engaged with some regularity and over a substantial period of time. 30 U.S.C. § 902(f). Collins v. Mathews, 547 F.2d 795, 796 (4th Cir. 1976).

The issue of what constitutes **total disability** has spawned enormous amounts of litigation. See e.g. cases collected in 21 A.L.R.3d 1155, Insurance: "Total Disability or the Like as Referring to Inability to Work a Usual Occupation or Other Occupations." [On appeal the court noted]: Analogous insurance cases consistently agree that the term "**total disability**" does not mean absolute helplessness on the part of the insured. The insured can recover benefits if he is unable to perform all the substantial and material acts necessary to the prosecution of some gainful business or occupation. Helms v. Monsanto Co., 558 F.Supp. 928, 931 (N.D.Ala.1982), reversed and remanded 728 F.2d 1416, 1420 (11th Cir. 1984).

In Texas Employers' Ins. Ass'n v. Mallard, 143 Tex. 77, 79, 182 S.W.2d 1000, 1001 (1944), our Supreme Court determined that:

The term "total incapacity" (or **total disability**), ... does not imply any absolute disability to perform any kind of labor, but a person disqualified from performing the usual tasks of a workman, in such a way as to enable him to procure and retain employment, is regarded as being totally incapacitated, or totally disabled. International Ins. Co. v. Torres, 576 S.W.2d 862, 865 (Ct.Civ.App.Tex.1978).

Under the odd lot doctrine, a claimant is considered **totally disabled** if his injury makes him an odd lot in the labor market, that is, one capable of obtaining employment periodically but one whose services are so limited in quality, dependability or quantity that a reasonably stable market for his services does not exist. An odd lot claimant need not be absolutely helpless to qualify for total disability. If the claimant can prove that his physical condition, mental capacity, education, training age or other factors combine to place him at a substantial disadvantage in the competitive labor market, he has made out a prima facie case for classification in the odd lot category....

... The odd lot doctrine is also applicable to substantial pain cases because a worker who, due to his injury, can function only with substantial pain or with the help of fellow workers may not be considered a particularly desirable employee. Lattin v. HICA Corp., 395 So.2d 690, 693 (La.1981).

disability, total and permanent

The act defines "**total and permanent disability**" as including "permanent and total loss of industrial use of both legs or both hands or both arms or 1 leg and 1 arm." [8] [[8] 1948 C.L. 412.10; M.S.A. § 17.160; now M.C.L.A. § 418.361; M.S.A. § 17.237(361).] Martin v. Ford Motor Co., 258 N.W.2d 465, 467 (Mich.1977).

disability, work See *disability, functional* (Bahr case).

disabled, permanently and totally

§ 233.80. Disability.

(a) State plan requirements. A State plan under title XIV or XVI of the Social Security Act must:

(1) Contain a definition of **permanently and totally disabled**, showing that:

(i) "Permanently" is related to the duration of the impairment or combination of impairments; and

(ii) "Totally" is related to the degree of disability.

The following definition is recommended:

"**Permanently and totally disabled**" means that the individual has some permanent physical or mental impairment, disease, or loss, or combination thereof, this substantially precludes him from engaging in useful occupations within his competence, such as holding a job.

Under this definition:

"Permanently" refers to a condition which is not likely to improve or which will continue throughout the lifetime of the individual; it may be a condition which is not likely to respond to any known therapeutic procedures, or a condition which is likely to remain static or to become worse unless certain therapeutic measures are carried out, where treatment is unavailable, inadvisable, or is refused by the individual on a reasonable basis; "permanently" does not rule out the possibility of vocational rehabilitation or even possible recovery in light of future medical advances or changed prognosis; in this sense the term refers to a condition which continues indefinitely, as distinct from one which is temporary or transient;

"Totally" involves considerations in addition to those verified through the medical findings, such as age, training, skills, and work experience, and the probable functioning of the individual in his particular situation in light of his impairment; an individual's disability would usually be tested in relation to ability to engage in remunerative employment; the ability to keep house or to care for others would be the appropriate test for (and only for) individuals, such as housewives, who were engaged in this occupation prior to the disability and do not have a history of gainful employment; eligibility may continue, even after a period of rehabilitation and readjustment, if the individual's work capacity is still very considerably limited (in comparison with that of a normal person) in terms of such factors as the speed with which he can work, the amount he can produce in a given period of time, and the number of hours he is able to work. 45 C.F.R. § 233.80.

disablement

The applicable statute, Minn.Stat. § 176.66, subd. 1 (1980), requires that the employee prove "disablement" from occupational disease:

The **disablement** of an employee resulting from an occupational disease shall be regarded as a personal injury within the meaning of the workers' compensation law....

... Since the meaning of the term "**disablement**" was well established at the time the statute was amended, we believe that if the legislature had intended to use the term in a different sense in the amended statute, it would have said so. Therefore, to show **disablement** by October 1, 1980, the employee was required to establish that by then he was not able to earn full wages as a paint sprayer. He presented substantial evidence to that effect. Abram v. Art Goebel Ford, 327 N.W.2d 88, 91 (Minn.1982).

K.S.A. 44–5a04 provides:

"Except as hereinafter otherwise provided in this act '**disablement**' means the event of an employee or workman becoming actually incapacitated, partially or totally, because of an occupational disease, from performing his work in the last occupation in which injuriously exposed to the hazards of such disease, and 'disability' means the state of being so incapacitated:..." (Emphasis added.) Linville v. Steel Fixture Mfg. Co., 469 P.2d 312, 318 (Kan.1970).

disagraphia See *agraphia*.

disarthria

"Here [sic] speech was somewhat **disarthic** [sic], that is, not clearly intelligible, as it is now...." Talcott v. Holl, 224 So. 2d 420, 423 (Dist.Ct.App.Fla.1969).

disarticulation (dis"ar-tik"u-la'shun) [L. *dis-* apart + *articulus* joint] amputation or separation at a joint.

This hematoma subsequently became infected and, despite constant treatment, ultimately resulted in the **disarticulation**— or amputation—of her leg at the hip. Sherrill v. McBride, 603 S.W.2d 365–6 (Ct.Civ.App.Tex.1980).

disc (disk) [L. *discus*] disk.

discectomy See *diskectomy*.

discogenic (dis"ko-jen'ik) [*disco-* + Gr. *gennan* to produce] caused by derangement of an intervertebral disk.

Dr. Parker reported that X-rays revealed **discogenic** (relating to the intervertebral discs) disease of the cervical spine.... Bastien v. Califano, 572 F.2d 908, 910 (2d Cir. 1978).

Dr. Raymond O. Stein, the claimant's own physician, stated: "There is definite **discogenic** damage between C–5 and C–6, C–6 and C–7.... City of Philadelphia v. Collins, 320 A.2d 421, 423 (Commonwlth.Ct.Pa.1974).

Q. What does he mean by **discogenic** disease of the cervical spine? What is discogenic, in other words?
A. Yes, sir. Any disease relating to the disc or disc spaces; that is, the intervertebral disc spaces. Floyd v. Finch, 441 F.2d 73, 91 (6th Cir. 1971).

discogram See *diskogram*.

discoidectomy See *diskectomy*.

discontrol, episodic

When questioned as to Dr. Meninger's five common threads in cases of **episodic discontrol** [1] as being present in defendant's case, the doctor gave negative, equivocal or uncertain answers on all five.... [[1] The prosecutor indicated these five common threads were: a) faulty control over aggressive impulses; b) severe degree of sexual inhibition; c) emotional deprivation and parental violence in early life; d) loneliness, having only shallow relationships with others; e) transient moods of depression.] People v. Harrington, 317 N.E.2d 161, 164 (App.Ct.Ill.1974).

discovery

The gravamen of plaintiff's claim is, therefore, that defendant erroneously diagnosed plaintiff's condition and operated on the wrong intervertebral disc....

... For the purposes of application of statutes of limitations, a cause of action generally can be said to accrue at the time when facts come into existence which authorize a claimant to seek a judicial remedy. Williams v. Pure Oil Company, 124 Tex. 341, 78 S.W.2d 929 (1935). In personal injury actions, this means when the wrongful act effects an injury, regardless of when the claimant learned of such injury. An exception to this rule of accrual has been applied by this and many other courts in some situations in which a claimant was unable to know of his injury at the time of actual accrual; the exception is known as the "**discovery**" rule. The issue in this case is whether this "**discovery** rule" will be applied to an action founded upon a misdiagnosis....

... We decline to apply the **discovery** rule to encompass a case of the type involved here....

I respectfully dissent....

As Professor Prosser explains, there has been a "wave of decisions" adopting the "**discovery** rule" for all medical malpractice actions. Prosser, Law of Torts, § 30 (4th ed. 1971).[2] [[2] Courts now more generally applying the **discovery** rule to medical malpractice cases are: Mayer v. Good Samaritan Hospital, 14 Ariz.App. 248, 482 P.2d 497 (1971); Stafford v. Shultz, 42 Cal.2d 767, 270 P.2d 1 (1954); Owens v. Brochner, 172 Colo. 525, 474 P.2d 603 (1970); City of Miami v. Brooks, 70 So.2d 306 (Fla.1954); Yoshizaki v. Hilo Hospital, 50 Haw.

150, 433 P.2d 220 (1967); Renner v. Edwards, 93 Idaho 836, 475 P.2d 530 (1970); Lipsey v. Michael Reese Hospital, 46 Ill. 2d 32, 262 N.E.2d 450 (1970); Baines v. Blenderman, 223 N.W.2d 199 (Iowa 1974); Tomlinson v. Siehl, 459 S.W.2d 166 (Ky.1970); Springer v. Aetna Casualty and Surety Company, 169 So.2d 171 (La.App.1964); Waldman v. Rohrbaugh, 241 Md. 137, 215 A.2d 825 (1966); Johnson v. Caldwell, 371 Mich. 368, 123 N.W.2d 785 (1963); Acker v. Sorensen, 183 Neb. 866, 165 N.W.2d 74 (1969); Iverson v. Lancaster, 158 N.W.2d 507 (N.D.1969); Frohs v. Greene, 253 Or. 1, 452 P.2d 564 (1969); Wilkinson v. Harrington, 104 R.I. 224, 243 A.2d 745 (1968); Teeters v. Currey, 518 S.W.2d 512 (Tenn. 1974); Janisch v. Mullins, 1 Wash.App. 393, 461 P.2d 895 (1969). Six states, including Texas and three of the above jurisdictions, have enacted special statutes of limitation placing a maximum limitation on the time allowed for **discovery**. 7 St. Mary's L.J. 770 (1976).] Robinson v. Weaver, 550 S.W.2d 18– 19, 22–23 (Tex.1977).

discovery of injury See *injury, discovery of.*

discus (dis′kus), pl. *dis′ci* [L.; Gr. *diskos*] a circular or rounded flat plate; used as a general term in anatomical nomenclature to designate such a structure. Called also *disc* or *disk.*

discus nervi optici [NA], the optic disk: the intraocular portion of the optic nerve formed by fibers converging from the retina and appearing as a pink to white disk. Called also *d. opticus, nerve head, optic papilla,* and *papilla nervi optici.*

disease (dĭ-zēz′) [Fr. *dès* from + *aise* ease] any deviation from or interruption of the normal structure or function of any part, organ, or system (or combination thereof) of the body that is manifested by a characteristic set of symptoms and signs and whose etiology, pathology, and prognosis may be known or unknown.

All of the policies of the prior insurers also contain the following provision:

"Bodily Injury by Accident; Bodily Injury by **Disease**.

The contraction of **disease** is not an accident within the meaning of the word 'accident' in the term 'bodily injury by accident' and only such **disease** as results directly from a bodily injury by accident, is included within the term 'bodily injury by accident.' The term 'bodily injury by **disease**' includes only such **disease** as is not included within the term 'bodily injury by accident'." . . .

. . . In the first place, silicosis is generally understood, by laymen as well as by medical men, to be an insidious **disease**. For example, Webster's Third New International Dictionary defines silicosis as a condition of massive fibrosis of the lungs, marked by shortness of breath and resulting from prolonged inhalation of silica dust, and Schmidt's Attorneys Dictionary of Medicine defines silicosis as a **disease** of the lungs caused by the prolonged inhalation of dust derived from sand, stone, etc. In addition, silicosis is listed as an occupational **disease** in workmen's compensation laws, (e.g., La.R.S. 23:1031.1) and a contention that it is the result of bodily injury by accident was rejected by the United States Supreme Court in Urie v. Thompson, 337 U.S. 163, 69 S.Ct. 1018, 93 L.Ed. 1282 (1949). Moreover, in this case, Dr. Morton N. Ziskind, Professor of Medicine in charge of the Pulmo-

nary Diseases Section, Department of Medicine of Tulane University, directly testified that silicosis is a **disease**, that it is an occupational **disease** and that he could not think of a situation in which it would not be an occupational **disease**. Froust v. Coating Specialists, Inc., 364 F.Supp. 1154, 1156 (E.D.La.1973).

Durham did distinguish between "**disease**," as used "in the sense of a condition which is considered capable of either improving or deteriorating," and "defect," as referring to a condition not capable of such change "and which may be either congenital or the result of injury, or the residual effect of a physical or mental **disease**." 94 U.S.App.D.C. at 241, 214 F.2d at 875. U.S. v. Brawner, 471 F.2d 969, 977 (D.C.Cir. 1972).

". . . Under these circumstances, we think we should adopt the definition of the word '**disease**' which would naturally be accepted by the average layman, rather than a highly technical medical definition, if there is a conflict between the two. Webster gives two definitions of '**disease**.' The first is, 'a condition in which bodily health is seriously attacked, deranged or impaired,' and the second—a pathological definition—is 'an alteration of the state of the human body . . . or some of its organs or parts, interrupting or disturbing the performance of the vital functions.'

"We think these definitions represent the sense in which '**disease**' is understood by the layman, and that they imply a condition which either has impaired, or presumably will impair, if it continues in its usual course of progress, the normal working of some of the bodily or mental functions. An example of the last class is a cancer, which even in its earliest stages is a **disease**, for while the victim may not for some time suffer any impairment of the bodily functions, if that cancer continues to develop in its normal manner, sooner or later death ensues." . . . 56 Ariz. at 76–77, 105 P.2d at 519–520.

The above definition of "**disease**" was quoted in the annotation located at 84 A.L.R.2d 176, "Pre-existing Physical Condition as Affecting Liability Under Accident Policy or Accident Feature of Life Policy", in support of the statement that "the terms '**disease**' and 'infirmity' are given their commonly understood meanings and are construed to be practically synonymous." 84 A.L.R.2d at 192–193. Watkins v. Underwriters at Lloyds, London, 481 P.2d 849, 854 (Ariz.1971).

Other Authorities: Princess Mfg. Co. v. Jarrell, 465 S.W.2d 45, 46 (Ct.App.Ky.1971); Giles Industries, Inc. v. Neal, 471 S.W.2d 5–7 (Ct.App.Ky.1971); Appalachian Regional Hospitals, Inc. v. Brown, 463 S.W.2d 323, 325–6 (Ct.App.Ky.1971).

disease, Adams′; disease, Adams-Stokes a condition caused by heart block and characterized by sudden attacks of unconsciousness, with or without convulsions; called also *Adams-Stokes syndrome* or *syncope, Stokes-Adams d., syndrome,* or *syncope, Morgagni-Adams-Stokes syndrome,* and *Stokes′ syndrome.* See also *heart block.*

He noted that Ebarb had a history of heart disease, including a previous myocardial infarction. He had a previous diagnosis of **Stokes-Adams** attack in 1979. Ebarb v. Insurance Co. of North America, 424 So.2d 1266, 1268 (Ct.App.La.1982).

disease, Alzheimer′s See *dementia, presenile.*

disease, arteriosclerotic heart See *arteriosclerosis.*

disease, Bowen's intraepidermal squamous cell carcinoma, often occurring in multiple primary sites; called also *Bowen's precancerous dermatosis* and *precancerous dermatitis.*

In February 1976, petitioner had a growth removed from his right eye. The growth was diagnosed as a "**Bowen's lesion**", which is a localized cancerous growth. Petitioner's treating physicians did not attribute petitioner's eye cancer to his exposure to radioactive materials. Petitioner believed otherwise, and he became severely worried that such cancer would spread throughout his body and cause his death. Martinez v. University of California, 601 P.2d 425–6 (New Mex.1979).

disease, brain

Brain disease, due to trauma, chronic manifested by exaggeration of tendon reflexes in left upper extremity, absent left abdominal reflexes hypoactive left cremasteric reflex, hyperactive patellar and Achilles reflexes, inconsistent ankle clonus on the left, motor weakness and sensory disturbance in left lower extremity; recurrent headache, dizzy spells with occasional "blacking out" and emotional liability....

... On current examination the skull defect which has previously been described was noted. He has **brain disease** due to trauma manifested by exaggeration of tendon reflexes in the left upper extremity and sensory disturbance in the lower extremity; recurrent headaches, dizziness. There was considerable repressed hostility, he was tense, apprehensive, defensive, guarded in his attitude, was having difficulty in accepting and adjusting to his residual disability especially since he has been unable to work and support his family. DePaepe v. Richardson, 464 F.2d 92, 96–7 (5th Cir. 1972).

disease, "Brown Lung" See *byssinosis.*

disease, Buerger's See *thromboangitis obliterans.*

disease, causation of

There are three components in evaluating **causation of disease:** (1) the level of the association between an event and the disease; (2) the biologic credibility of the purported association; and (3) whether there is an alternative explanation for the purported causality that has more credibility than that of causation. In evaluating the first component—the strength of association—chance must be excluded. If the association is not explained by chance alone, then it may be explained by a causal relationship or some other relationship. In evaluating the second component of causality—biologic credibility—the purported association is compared with medical knowledge on the subject. In evaluating the third component of causality—whether there is an alternative explanation for the purported causality—epidemiologists must exclude three alternative explanations: chance, confounding, and bias. Chance has been previously explained. Confounding, not applicable here, would explain a statistically significant relationship between lung cancer and yellow fingers.

Bias is an error in the actually observed rate of a condition that comes about by virtue of the means of counting or the means of establishing the criteria; i.e., an irregularity in the surveillance mechanism. Padgett v. U.S., 553 F.Supp. 794, 800 (W.D.Tex.1982).

disease, celiac a malabsorption syndrome affecting both children and adults, precipitated by the ingestion of gluten-containing foods; its etiology is unknown but a hereditary factor has been implicated. Pathologically, the proximal intestinal mucosa loses its villous structure, surface epithelial cells exhibit degenerative changes, and the absorptive function of these cells is severely impaired. It is characterized by diarrhea in which the stools are bulky, frothy, fatty (steatorrhea), and fetid (occasionally, malabsorption may be associated with the passage of a singly bulky stool without diarrhea); abdominal distention; flatulence; weight loss; asthenia; deficiency of vitamins B, D, and K; and electrolyte depletion. Called also *gluten enteropathy* and *nontropical sprue.* In the *infantile form* the onset is insidious, and is marked by irritability, loss of appetite, weakness, extreme wasting, growth retardation, and celiac crisis. The *adult form* is marked by extreme lassitude, fatigue, difficulty in breathing, clubbing of the fingers, bone pain, cramping of the muscles, tetany, abdominal distention during the day, megacolon, tympanitis, and skin pigmentation. Until recently it was thought that the infantile form and the adult form were different entities, but it is now believed that they are the same.

One of appellants' principal contentions at trial was that Billy's starvation death was caused by **celiac disease** or some other type of "malabsorption syndrome." **Celiac disease** is caused by an intolerance to the gluten found in many grain products and is accompanied by a blunting of the villi or absorbing arms of the small bowel. This and any other form of "malabsorption syndrome" results in an inability to absorb food into the blood stream. State v. Rupp, 586 P.2d 1302, 1306 (Ct.App.Ariz.1978).

disease, Charcot-Marie-Tooth See *atrophy, progressive neuropathic (peroneal) muscular.*

disease, chronic obstructive pulmonary (COPD) any disorder, e.g., asthma, chronic bronchitis, and pulmonary emphysema, marked by persistent obstruction of bronchial air flow.

Sang testified that a chronic obstructive pulmonary disease was a condition that had advanced beyond the stage of asthma and that would cause a patient to be short of breath on exertion, to cough chronically, to be more subject to respiratory infections than the normal individual and to be more sensitive to extremes in temperature, air pollutants, and smoke....

... On re-examination by the ALJ, Dr. Sang further clarified his testimony by pointing to hospital pulmonary function tests that showed Chico's breathing problems did not meet the numerical levels of "forced expired carried volume" and "maximum voluntary ventilation" set forth in § 3.02 of Appendix 1, the "listing" for **chronic obstructive airway diseases**. [20 C.F.R.] Chico v. Schweiker, 710 F.2d 947, 954 (2d Cir. 1983).

Smoking, combined with twelve years of work in a dusty environment had resulted in **Chronic Obstructive Pulmonary Disease (COPD)**. COPD is a medical term describing a spectrum of lung diseases, including asthma, bronchitis, and emphysema. With the **COPD**, claimant was able to perform his job, although at times he experienced shortness of breath. Ridenour v. Equity Supply Co., 665 P.2d 783–4 (Mont.1983).

Plaintiff has chronic pulmonary disease. X-rays indicate that there is a flattening of the diaphram. This is consistent with chronic obstructive lung disease. . . . Swink v. Cone Mills, Inc., 300 S.E.2d 848 (Ct.App.N.Car.1983).

Other Authorities: Rutledge v. Tultex Corp. Kings Yarn, 301 S.E.2d 359, 380–1 (N.Car.1983); Purex, Inc. v. W.C.A.B. (Oden), 454 A.2d 203, 205 (Commonwealth Ct.Pa.1982).

disease, collagen any of a group of diseases that, although clinically distinct and not necessarily related etiologically, have in common widespread pathologic changes in the connective tissue; they include lupus erythematosus, dermatomyositis, scleroderma, polyarteritis nodosa, thrombotic purpura, rheumatic fever, and rheumatoid arthritis.

Q. Would there be any other medical explanation for her symptomatology; in other words, the pain, the numbness, the inability to dorsiflex.

A. I have no explanation other than if she had some systemic disease such as a **collagen disease**, which would be like rheumatoid arthritis or something like that that has not been diagnosed despite the extensive workup. . . . Bardo v. Workmen's Compensation Appeal Bd., 437 A.2d 456–7 (Commonwealth Ct.Pa.1981).

Despite lack of a positive diagnosis by any of the several doctors who expressed an opinion, it was generally conceded that claimant was probably suffering from a **collagen disease**, a loose collective designation for a group of disorders involving increase and proliferation of connective and supportive tissues of several areas of the body, including the lungs and the bones, tendons, skin, et cetera as well, rather than from silicosis, the usual occupational disease associated with sandblasting. **Collagen diseases** are not causally related to inhalation of silica or other foreign matter, so far as is known to medical science. [Footnote omitted.] Aerojet-General Shipyards, Inc. v. O'Keeffe, 442 F.2d 508–10 (5th Cir. 1971).

disease, congestive heart

. . . **congestive heart disease** (deterioration of the blood vessels of the heart and reduced pumping efficiency). Magruder v. Richardson, 332 F.Supp. 1363, 1367 (E.D.Mo.1971).

disease, coronary

He distinguished between instantaneous death, which occurs within thirty seconds of the onset of symptoms, and sudden death, which occurs between thirty seconds and a few hours after the onset of symptoms. He relied on an article that he considered the most thorough study of hearts of persons who die suddenly or instantaneously from **coronary disease**.[4] [4 The article is Friedman, et al., Instantaneous and Sudden Deaths—Clinical and Pathological Differentiation in Coronary Artery Disease, 225 J.A.M.A. 1319–28 (1973), which was admitted into evidence as Defendants' Exhibit 3. Dr. Hirsch testified that the significant points of the study are summarized in the introductory paragraph, which reads in pertinent part: . . . persons dying instantaneously differed from persons dying suddenly of **coronary** artery **disease** in that (1) they rarely experienced acute symptoms or exhibited acute signs before death; (2) more than half died during or immediately after physical exertion; (3) their death appeared to result from a primary arrhythmia; and (4) their hearts rarely showed an acute lesion of any kind and exhibited two old occluded coronary arteries or one old occluded left anterior descending artery. Id. at 1319.] Van

Hook v. Aetna Life Ins. Co., 550 F.Supp. 888, 893 (E.D.Mich. 1982).

Coronary heart disease affects the arteries which supply blood to the heart. U.S. v. DePalma, 466 F.Supp. 920, 925 (S.D.N.Y.1979).

disease, Crohn's a chronic granulomatous inflammatory disease of unknown etiology, involving any part of the gastrointestinal tract from mouth to anus, but commonly involving the terminal ileum with scarring and thickening of the bowel wall; it frequently leads to intestinal obstruction and fistula and abscess formation and has a high rate of recurrence after treatment. Called also *regional enteritis* or *ileitis*. See also *ileitis, regional.*

Rather, it took the position that his injuries were the result of a preexisting bowel condition called **Crohn's disease** and were not related to the ingestion of Cleocin. . . .

. . . However, Dr. Marshall Sparberg stated that data showing a lifelong history of digestive problems was relevant in diagnosing **Crohn's disease** and that liver and spleen problems are also relevant extracolonic manifestations of **Crohn's disease**. Also, there was testimony from Upjohn's experts that aphthous lesions and discharges from the eyes occur characteristically in **Crohn's disease**. Bluestein v. Upjohn Co., 430 N.E.2d 580, 582, 586 (App.Ct.Ill.1981).

Her **Crohn's disease** was first discovered in 1969. **Crohn's disease** is an inflammation of the ileum of the small bowel and large colon. As a result of this disease, Kranda had already had three feet of her intestine in the right colon removed. Kranda v. Houser-Norborg Medical Corp., 419 N.E.2d 1024, 1031 (Ct.App.Ind.1981).

Crohn's disease is another name for regional ileitis. Biopsy reports and X-rays, however, did not reveal the presence of **Crohn's disease**. Anderson v. Moore, 275 N.W.2d 842, 846 (Neb.1979).

disease, cystic disease of the breast a form of mammary dysplasia with formation of cysts of various size containing a semitransparent, turbid fluid that imparts a brown to blue color (blue dome cyst) to the unopened cysts; considered to be due to abnormal hyperplasia of the ductal epithelium and dilatation of the ducts of the mammary gland, occurring as a result of an exaggeration and distortion of the cyclic breast changes that normally occur in the menstrual cycle. Called also *chronic cystic mastitis, fibrocystic disease, fibrocystic disease of breast*, and *Schimmelbusch's disease.*

On 16 April 1975, Georgiade examined plaintiff, diagnosed her condition as due to **fibrocystic disease**, and prescribed treatment by a surgical procedure known as a bilateral subcutaneous mastectomy. Simons v. Georgiade, 286 S.E.2d 596, 598 (App.Ct.N.Car.1982).

disease, degenerative disk

Merck's Manual 1234 (12th ed. 1971) describes the etiology of **degenerative disc disease** as follows:

"The intervertebral disks, especially between the fourth and fifth lumbar vertebrae and between the fifth lumbar and sacrum, are subject to great forces and degenerative changes. When the ligaments surrounding the disk are injured and weakened, disk material begins to extrude. If this happens abruptly, the "acute low back" syndrome appears; if, instead, the disk material produces gradual but persistent pressure, the symptoms are those of the "chronic low back." Both are accompanied by back pain.

"As degenerative changes progress, with disk material protruding posteriorly into the neural canal, the true disk syndrome appears, the result of the pressure on the sciatic nerve root(s). The lesion is usually unilateral, laterally. The amount of nerve pressure may vary, depending on the size of the protrusion, local inflammation, and edema." Ghazibayat v. Schweiker, 554 F.Supp. 1005, 1015 (S.D.N.Y.1983).

disease, demyelinating any condition characterized by destruction of myelin.

Demyelinating disease is characterized by the loss of myelin, a sheath covering the nerves in the body, which impairs transmission of the nerve impulses. It is a major symptom of multiple sclerosis. Giant Food, Inc. v. Coffey, 451 A.2d 151, 154 (Ct. Spec.App.Md.1982).

After the first injection with DEV in May, 1972, Mrs. Hitchcock noted a "tiredness" and "heaviness" in her legs. After the second injection with DEV in June, 1972, she again noticed that her legs felt tired and heavy; she also noticed that she was having difficulty getting up and down stairs. Mrs. Hitchcock began experiencing numbness in her hands in February, 1973; by May, 1973, her legs and waist were numb; the feelings of tiredness progressed....

... She suffers from a progressive **demyelinating disease**,[2] which has caused paralysis, pain, numbness, limitation of physical movement, mental anguish, inability to work or to do housework, and loss of enjoyment of life. She is permanently and totally disabled. [[2] A **demyelinating disease** is a disease which destroys or removes the myelin sheath of a nerve or nerves in a patient. See Dorland's Illustrated Medical Dictionary (1974).] Hitchcock v. U.S., 479 F.Supp. 65, 67 (D.D.C.1979).

He testified that he was convinced—to a reasonable degree of medical certainty—that Mrs. Hitchcock's **demyelinating disease** was produced by the anti-rabies vaccine. Tr. at 168; J.A. at 263. In making this diagnosis, he relied on various articles in the medical literature and on his understanding of Mrs. Hitchcock's medical history. The defendant produced a number of expert witnesses to refute Dr. Herskovits's conclusions....

... Michael Hattwick, also an expert on the rabies vaccine, testified that the course of Mrs. Hitchcock's disease was uncharacteristic of illnesses associated with the rabies vaccine. Tr. at 403–04; J.A. at 499–500. Hitchcock v. U.S., 665 F.2d 354, 358 (D.C.Cir.1981).

disease, de Quervain's painful tenosynovitis due to relative narrowness of the common tendon sheath of the abductor pollicis longus and the extensor pollicis brevis.

Mrs. Jones continued to suffer from two separate conditions causally related to her injury: (1) chronic traumatic adhesive tenosynovitis of the extensor and abductor tendons of the right thumb (**DeQuervain's Disease**)....

... the final diagnosis to be "**DeQuervain's** of the right wrist and early traction inflammatory response of the ulnar

nerve at the elbow." Jones v. W.C.A.B. (First Pa. Bank), 463 A.2d 1266–7 (Commonwealth Ct.Pa.1983).

On April 26, 1977 claimant pulled a tendon in her right wrist in the course of her employment with Kentucky Fried Chicken, Inc.....

... He had diagnosed claimant's condition as **DeQuervains disease**. Surgery to correct this condition had been performed on June 2, 1977....

... but certainly following the natural history of any type of **DeQuervain's**, sixteen to eighteen months of convalescing, her disability is far within the natural history of this disease and now should be resolved.... Bardo v. Workmen's Compensation Appeal Bd., 437 A.2d 456–7 (Commonwealth Ct.Pa. 1981).

He attributed the pain of the wrists and the numbness and lack of sweating of the hands to Mrs. Green's pregnancy. He also considered the possibility that plaintiff was experiencing **de Quervain's disease**, which is another wrist condition, usually developmental not traumatic in origin, but related to pregnancy. Green v. Jee, 224 So.2d 153, 156–7 (Ct.App.La.1969).

Other Authorities: Martin v. Cudahy Foods Co., 646 P.2d 468, 470 (Kan.1982); Jones v. Schweiker, 551 F.Supp. 205, 207 (D.Md.1982); Parlin v. G. H. Bass & Co., 423 A.2d 948, 951 (Me.1980).

disease, end-stage kidney

The ward has "end-stage kidney disease," which is a total, or virtually total, and irreversible loss of kidney function. Dialysis does not cure the underlying disease; it is a substitute for the absent kidney function. Without dialysis the ward would die within a month. In Matter of Spring, 399 N.E.2d 493, 495 (App.Ct.Mass.1979).

disease, fibrocystic disease of breast See *disease, cystic disease of breast.*

disease, Graves' a disorder of the thyroid of unknown etiology, occurring most often in women, and characterized by exophthalmos, enlarged pulsating thyroid gland, marked acceleration of the pulse rate, a tendency to profuse sweats, nervous symptoms (including fine muscular tremors, restlessness, and irritability), psychic disturbances, emaciation, and increased metabolic rate. Called also *Basedow's d., Begbie's d., cachexia exophthalmica, exophthalmic goiter, hyperthyroidism, Parry's d., Stokes' d., thyroid cachexia, thyrotoxicosis, tachycardia strumosa exophthalmica,* and *toxic goiter.* See also *exophthalmos.*

Following the hearing, the Law Judge determined that plaintiff has **Graves Disease**, involving severe exophthalmos, secondary to thyroid disease, hypertension, gout, and occasional double vision....

... Plaintiff testified that, due to the **Graves Disease**, his eyes bulge. He has to tape his eyes shut to sleep at night and is often required to wear a patch over one eye or otherwise he has double vision. Vines v. Califano, 442 F.Supp. 471 (W.D. La.1977).

When hospitalized in June, 1967, the diagnosis was toxic goiter, and she was advised to avoid any strenuous activity. In July, 1967, a physician who examined her gave as his impression probable mild hyperthyroidism—**Graves' disease**—and chronic anxiety reaction. Coleman v. Weinberger, 538 F.2d 1045–6 (4th Cir. 1976).

In 1966 she suffered from **Graves Disease**, a condition caused by an overactive thyroid gland. In an effort to correct this problem, approximately 95% of her thyroid was removed by surgery. The operation left her with a small portion of the gland on each side of her neck. O'Neill v. Kiledjian, 511 F.2d 511–12 (6th Cir. 1975).

disease, heart any organic, mechanical, or functional abnormality of the heart; it may be valvular, myocardial, or neurogenic.

The causes of **heart disease** are not completely known, but several risk factors have been identified. Cigarette smoking, both doctors here agreed, is a major risk factor; Doyle smoked three to four packs a day when his disease was diagnosed and had cut down to one or two packs a day at the time of his attack. Obesity and diabetes are also linked to **heart disease**.... Doyle v. Industrial Com'n, 427 N.E.2d 1223–4 (Ill. 1981).

He was of the opinion that if a physical effort is to induce a heart condition, "the patient should develop signs of cardiac insufficiency within a relatively short span, anywhere from seconds, to possibly a period of twenty-four hours." He stated that the "commonest symptom" of a heart condition is chest pain. He conceded that the "precordial pain" complained of by the petitioner was consistent with "heart trouble". He further stated, "We well know that an initial electrocardiogram may be negative. Even in occlusion, a coronary thrombosis, or even infarct, they are negative many times and, sometimes, as long as ten, fifteen, twenty days later an electrocardiogram may become positive after it is negative." Yeomans v. Jersey City, 143 A.2d 174, 179–81 (N.J.1958).

disease, heart (arteriosclerotic)

Arteriosclerotic heart disease, used interchangeably with the term **atherosclerotic heart disease**, means that the heart is diseased by the hardening of the arteries, or arteriosclerosis; and this disease occurs when there is developed enough hardening of the arteries so that there is not a sufficient blood supply to the heart muscle. Community Life & Health Ins. Co. v. McCall, 497 S.W.2d 358, 363 (Ct.App.Tex.1973).

disease, hemorrhagic disease of the newborn a self-limited hemorrhagic disorder of the first days of life, caused by a deficiency of the vitamin K-dependent blood coagulation factors II, VII, IX, and X.

Consequently, in 1964, Lilly amended its package insert for Dicumarol to include a "warning" that "[w]hen pregnant women are treated with this drug, fetal bleeding diathesis may occur and cause fetal death in utero." Baker v. St. Agnes Hospital, 421 N.Y.S.2d 81, 83 (2d Dep't 1979).

disease, Hodgkin's a malignant condition characterized by painless, progressive enlargement of the lymph nodes, spleen, and general lymphoid tissue; other symptoms may include anorexia, lassitude, weight loss, fever, pruritus, night sweats, and anemia. The characteristic histologic feature is presence of Reed-Sternberg cells. Hodgkin's disease is usually classified as: (1) diffuse, according to the number of lymphocyte and histiocytes (lymphocytes predominant; mixed cellularity; lymphocytes de-

pleted) and (2) nodular sclerosing (marked by birefringent bands of collagen and the presence of the lacunar cells). The condition, which affects twice as many males as females and usually occurs between the ages of 15 and 34 or after 50, is considered by many to be neoplastic in origin, but neither an infectious origin nor an immune response to the development of Reed-Sternberg cells has been excluded.

Six months later Betesh accidentally discovered this notation in the file and promptly saw his doctor who diagnosed **Hodgkin's disease** (cancer of the lymph glands). James v. U.S., 483 F.Supp. 581, 584 (N.D.Cal.1980).

On October 29 his condition was diagnosed as **Hodgkins disease** (cancer of the lymph glands) of the nodular sclerosing type, and he was referred to a therapeutic radiologist for deep x-ray therapy. Treatment was begun November 5, about one week after Mr. Betesh learned of his abnormal x-ray.

When the Selective Service System physicians first observed Mr. Betesh's chest x-ray in April 1964, the abnormal mass was relatively small; by October 1964, the mass had grown more than 6-fold and covered an area that extended to the left chest wall. The delay from April to October in seeking treatment was of critical importance. Tumor size and number of bodily areas affected are major factors in the treatment of **Hodgkins disease**. There is a 95–99% success rate for nodular sclerosing **Hodgkins disease** if treatment is begun in a stage as early as Mr. Betesh's disease appeared to be in April 1964.[3] [3 Specialists in **Hodgkins disease** describe the extent of the disease by placing it in one of four categories, ranging from stage one, with high expectance of cure, to stage four, with virtually no such expectancy. Staging of a patient is frequently a matter of judgment, and competent physicians may reach different conclusions. While there were some differences of medical opinion at trial, the court finds, based on a preponderance of the evidence, that Mr. Betesh's disease was in stage one in April 1964.] Betesh v. U.S., 400 F.Supp. 238, 242 (D.D.C.1974).

Physical and laboratory examination at the public health hospital led to a tentative diagnosis of **Hodgkin's disease**. The doctors there observed a 1½ cm. node in the right supraclavicular fossa and a .6 cm. node in the left. Biopsy of the right node, May 21, proved it to be malignant, and it was identified by the pathologist as Hodgkin's sarcoma. **Hodgkin's disease**, it was agreed, is a generalized malignancy involving the reticuloendothelial system—that is, cells within the lymph system....

... doctors at the public health hospital told plaintiff that he had **Hodgkin's disease**, that it was a form of cancer, and that it would require extensive treatment. The record is not clear whether he was told it was a fatal disease although all experts agree that, if left unimpeded by therapy, it will with extremely rare exception prove fatal. ZeBarth v. Swedish Hospital Medical Center, 499 P.2d 1, 3–4 (Wash.1972).

Other Authorities: Slayton v. Industrial Com'n, 550 P.2d 246, 249 (Ct.App.Ariz.1976); Hecht v. First National Bank & Trust Co., 490 P.2d 649, 651–2 (Kan.1971).

disease, hyaline membrane a disorder affecting newborn infants (usually premature) characterized pathologically by the development of a hyalin-like membrane lining the terminal respiratory passages. Extensive atelectasis is attributed to lack of surfactant. See also *respiratory distress syndrome of newborn*, under *syndrome*.

He was suffering from **hyaline membrane disease** which, he says, happens in premature babies: the air sacs of the lungs collapse. He was of opinion that there was a lack of oxygen in the uterus. Re Wintersgill and Minister of Social Services, 131 D.L.R. 184–5 (Unified Fam.Ct., Sask.1981).

disease, inflammatory bowel a general term for those inflammatory diseases of the bowel of unknown etiology, including Crohn's disease and ulcerative colitis.

Upjohn presented expert testimony to the effect that there are three separate diseases included in the general category of **inflammatory bowel disease**. These are ulcerative colitis, Crohn's disease, and antibiotic associated colitis....

... He then stated that all of the bowel diseases, Crohn's disease, ulcerative colitis, and antibiotic associated colitis have in the past ten years been increasingly categorized under the heading of inflammatory bowel disease because a physician cannot distinguish among them in many cases. Bluestein v. Upjohn Co., 430 N.E.2d 580, 582 (App.Ct.Ill.1981).

disease, ischemic bowel

Dr. Christopher Zarins correctly diagnosed her condition as **Ischemic Bowel disease**, a disorder caused by an inadequate blood supply to the bowel. Ott v. Weinstock, 444 N.E.2d 1227, 1232 (Ct.App.Ind.1983).

disease, Kugelberg-Welander a hereditary juvenile form of muscular atrophy, usually transmitted as an autosomal recessive trait, due to lesions of the anterior horns of the spinal cord. It is marked by onset in the first or second decade, principally between two and seventeen years, atrophy and weakness of the proximal muscles of the lower extremities and pelvic girdle, followed by involvement of the distal muscles and muscular twitchings. Cf. *Werdnig-Hoffman paralysis*.

disease, Meniere's hearing loss, tinnitus, and vertigo resulting from nonsuppurative disease of the labyrinth with the histopathologic feature of endolymphatic hydrops (distention of the membranous labyrinth).

In 1964 she had **Meniere's Syndrome**, a syndrome of the inner ear that causes hearing difficulties and disturbs one's balance. Gates v. U.S., 707 F.2d 1141, 1146 (10th Cir. 1983).

Meniere's Syndrome involves a disorder of the inner ear characterized by symptoms of severe vertigo or dizziness, ear noises, fluctuating hearing loss, nausea and vomiting. According to a medical encyclopedia excerpt submitted to this court for our information by Mrs. Winfield as an appendix to her brief, **Meniere's Syndrome** may in some circumstances be so severe as to be disabling, as for example where attacks of vertigo persist for weeks, rendering even the simplest activities impossible. Clark & Cumley, The Book of Health—A Medical Encyclopedia for Everyone, 588, appellant's Exhibit No. 1 attached to appellant's brief. Winfield v. Mathews, 571 F.2d 164, 169 (3d Cir. 1978).

The district court also found that the stress resulting from this extra work activated a **Meniere's disease syndrome** which Andrews had suffered in the past, which caused Andrews to fall off a ladder aboard ship on June 14, 1962, sustaining crani-

ocerebral injuries which resulted in his death on October 7, 1964....

... Respondents argue that had Andrews not concealed from respondents his several experiences of dizziness, mild deafness and ringing in the ears, which a doctor had diagnosed as "slight **Meniere's disease**" on May 18, 1962, he would not have been even permitted to serve on board the S.S Chemical Transporter, much less perform the work that resulted in his injury and death....

... we reject these arguments advanced by the respondents. Andrews v. Chemical Carriers, Inc., 457 F.2d 636, 639 (3d Cir. 1972).

Other Authorities: Meek v. Califano, 488 F.Supp. 26, 29 (D.Neb.1979).

disease, mental See *disorder, mental*; and *dependence, chemical*.

disease, occupational one due to factors involved in one's employment, e.g., various forms of pneumoconiosis or dermatitis.

The distinction between industrial injury and **occupational disease** has become blurred under the Workers' Compensation Act but it still is important, at least for the purpose of time limitations for claim filing and for application of the last injurious exposure rule. See, e.g., Boise Cascade Corp. v. Starbuck, 61 Or.App. 631, 659 P.2d 424, rev. allowed ___ Or. ___, ___ P.2d ___ (1983). The distinction also assumes some importance in determining the cause of the disability, i.e., whether the disability is related to the work environment. The definition of **occupational disease** devised by the courts is based, in part, on the necessities of applying the dictates of the Act and is not necessarily consonant with the medical definition of disease. In some measure the definition is an attempt to contrast **occupational disease** with accidental injury.

The key case for the appropriate definition of **occupational disease** under the Act is O'Neal v. Sisters of Providence, 22 Or.App. 9, 537 P.2d 580 (1975). In that case we adopted the substance of the definition from 1B Larson's Workmen's Compensation Law § 41:31:

... What set[s] occupational disease apart from accidental injuries [is] both the fact that they [can] not honestly be said to be unexpected, since they [are] recognized as inherent hazards of continued exposure to conditions of the particular employment, and the fact that they [are] gradual rather than sudden in onset....

The facts of O'Neal put the definition in context. The claimant worked as a hospital maid which required her to push a heavy cleaning cart over the carpeted hallways. As a result, she developed strain and muscle spasms in her legs causing her disability. We held that she was suffering from an **occupational disease** because the results were gradual in onset, as they occurred over a period of time and could not honestly be said to be unexpected, i.e., it could be expected that pushing a heavy cart would cause strain and muscle spasms in the worker's legs. One of the principal bases for the distinction between the two types of disability we noted in O'Neal is that an accidental injury results from a distinct identifiable event such as a trauma that a worker can point to as the precipitating cause of the disability. Donald Drake Co. v. Lundmark, 663 P.2d 1303, 1306 (Ct.App.Or.1983).

An **occupational disease**, unlike an accidental-injury disability, is commonly characterized by a long history of injurious exposure without actual disability. Because the date of actual contraction is difficult or not susceptible of positive determination, most state statutes specify that the date of disability is controlling, rather than the actual time of contraction, for fixing the rights and liabilities of the employee and employer. See 4 Larson, The Law of Workmen's Compensation § 95.21, at 17–79 to –82 (1983). Tavares v. A.C. & S. Inc., 462 A.2d 977, 979 (R.I.1983).

The claimant must also demonstrate that the **disease** is causally related to the industry or **occupation** and that the incidence of the disease is substantially greater in the industry or occupation than in the general population. These requirements serve to establish the occupational impact of the disease and to distinguish those diseases which are not occupational in nature. Accordingly, evidence of the conditions in the industry or occupation is necessary; it is not enough to demonstrate that in a particular factory a disease constitutes a hazard. Spartan Abrasive Co., Inc. v. Workmen's Comp., 405 A.2d 594–5 (Commonwealth Ct.Pa.1979).

Other Authorities: Brooks v. State Dep't of Transportation, 255 So.2d 260, 262 (Fla.1971); Norman v. Morrison Food Services, 245 So.2d 234, 236 (Fla.1971); Bahr v. Iowa Beef Processors, Inc., 663 P.2d 1144, 1147 (Ct.App.Kan.1983); Haycraft v. Corhart Refractories Co., 544 S.W.2d 222, 224–5 (Ky.1976); Princess Mfg. Co. v. Jarrell, 465 S.W.2d 45, 47 (Ct.App.Ky.1971); National Stores, Inc. v. Hestel, 393 S.W.2d 603, 604–5 (Ct.App.Ky.1965); Montgomery Cty. Fire Bd. v. Fisher, 454 A.2d 394, 397, 399 (Ct.Spec.App.Md. 1983); Miklik v. Michigan Special Mach. Co., 329 N.W.2d 713, 715 (Mich.1982); Jensen v. Kronick's Floor Covering Serv., 245 N.W.2d 230, 231–2 (Minn.1976); Ridenour v. Equity Supply Co., 665 P.2d 783, 785 (Mont.1983); Estes v. Noranda Aluminum, Inc., 574 S.W.2d 34, 37–38 (Mo.Ct.App. 1978); Martinez v. University of California, 601 P.2d 425, 427 (New Mex.1979); State Ex. Rel. Ohio Bell Telephone Co. v. Krisc, 327 N.E.2d 756, 758, 760 (Ohio 1975); Purex, Inc. v. W.C.A.B. (Oden), 454 A.2d 203, 206 (Commonwealth Ct.Pa. 1982); Utter v. Asten-Hill Mfg. Co., 309 A.2d 583, 586 (Pa. 1973); Asten-Hill Mfg. Co. v. Bambrick, 291 A.2d 354, 360 (Commonwealth Ct.Pa.1972); Transportation Ins. Co. v. Maksyn, 580 S.W.2d 334, 335 (Tex.1979).

disease, pelvic inflammatory

P.I.D. is caused by the presence of bacteria in the uterus. When Dr. Macken saw plaintiff on June 13, he thought that it was unlikely that **P.I.D.** was the cause of plaintiff's illness. Dr. Fabiny, after diagnosing plaintiff as having **P.I.D.**, concluded that the infection probably began in late May, 1978....

... Plaintiff recovered from the **P.I.D.** infection, but the disease left her fallopian tubes blocked, rendering her incapable of bearing children. Hansen v. A. H. Robins Co., Inc., 715 F.2d 1265–6 (7th Cir. 1983).

Dr. Wilson, plaintiff's expert witness who practiced in obstetrics and gynecology, was questioned by plaintiff's counsel concerning surgery for hysterectomy of a patient who has **pelvic inflammatory disease**. The witness stated there were acute stages and chronic stages of the disease. An acute stage would be manifested by an elevated white blood cell count to as much as 20,000 to 25,000, and possibly an elevated tem-

perature. If possible, the witness stated, surgery is ordinarily not performed at that time. It is best to treat the patient with antibiotics until the condition is in the chronic or "smoldering" state. Surgery is preferable at that time. The witness stated that normally the white blood cell count is from 5,000 to 10,000....

... On cross-examination, the witness stated that the laboratory at his hospital considers as a normal range of white blood cell count from 5,000 to 10,000, whereas, some laboratories use the outer limits of the normal range of from 5,000 to 11,000 or 12,000. He also stated that the acute stage would be accompanied by a fever and acute pain. [Concurring and dissenting opinion.] Spidle v. Steward, 402 N.E.2d 216, 225 (Ill.1980).

Appellant had a prior history of **pelvic inflammatory disease**, which was asymptomatic at the time of her injury. She turned from her work area and walked into a steel rod, striking her abdomen on October 18, 1978. She began bleeding vaginally immediately after the trauma....

... Dr. Schiwietz's diagnosis was **pelvic inflammatory disease** and a separate cystic swelling or mass. He felt that the swelling could represent bleeding in the area of the left ligament, possibly caused by the trauma appellant received at work. Barris v. Toppers of Florida, Inc., 382 So.2d 441–2 (Dist. Ct.App.Fla.1980).

Other Authorities: LaCaze v. Collier, 434 So.2d 1039, 1041 (La.1983).

disease, periapical

... severe **periapical disease** (tissues or gum encompassing the apex of teeth including the periodontal membrane and alveolar bone) in four teeth. Jobson v. Dooley, 296 S.E.2d 388, 390 (Ct.App.Ga.1982).

disease, polycystic of kidneys a heritable disorder marked by cysts scattered throughout both kidneys. It occurs in two unrelated forms: The *infantile* form, transmitted as an autosomal recessive trait, may be congenital or appear at any time during childhood. There is a high perinatal mortality rate, and almost all cases lead to hypertension. In older children cystic and fibrotic disease of the liver may be associated. The *adult* form, transmitted as an autosomal dominant trait, is marked by progressive deterioration of renal function. Called also *polycystic kidneys* and *polycystic renal d.*

Polycystic kidney disease is an inherited kidney disorder characterized by the presence of many bilateral cysts which cause enlargement of the kidney, as well as reduced function thereof. It is a disease which progresses slowly over a number of years. Simpson v. Schweiker, 691 F.2d 966, 969–70 (11th Cir. 1982).

In response to plaintiffs' inquiry defendants are alleged to have informed plaintiffs that inasmuch as **polycystic kidney disease** was not hereditary, the chances of their conceiving a second child afflicted with this disease were "practically nil"....

... Alleging that contrary to defendants' advice **polycystic kidney disease** is in fact an inherited condition.... Becker v. Schwartz, 413 N.Y.S.2d 895–6 (N.Y.1978).

In June, 1969 plaintiff Hetty Park gave birth to a baby who lived for only five hours. The cause of death was determined to be **polycystic kidney disease**, a fatal hereditary disease of such nature that there exists a substantial probability that any future baby of the same parents will be born with it....

Plaintiffs contend in their amended complaint and bill of particulars, that, in response to their inquiries, the defendants, in wanton and gross disregard of known medical fact, gave them the medically inaccurate advice that the chances of having any future baby with **polycystic kidney disease** were "practically nil" inasmuch as the disease was not hereditary; that the defendants knew or should have known that the disease was hereditary.... Park v. Chessin, 400 N.Y.S.2d 110–11 (2d Dep't 1977).

disease, Pott's See *tuberculosis, spinal.*

disease, preexisting See *dormant.*

The rule is that when **preexisting diseases** are aggravated by an injury and disabilities result, such disabilities are to be treated and considered as the result of the injury. Gaffney v. Industrial Accident Board (1955), 129 Mont. 394, 403, 287 P.2d 256, 260....

Neither do previous cases suggest such a limited doctrine. We allowed recovery in Gaffney where a fall aggravated **preexisting** Parkinson's **disease** and cerebral arterial sclerosis both of which, like Strandberg's spondylolisthesis, are progressive diseases of a degenerative nature. In Weakley v. Cook (1952), 126 Mont. 332, 249 P.2d 926, a preexisting heart condition was aggravated when the claimant fell backwards. In Moffett v. Bozeman Canning Co. (1933), 95 Mont. 347, 26 P.2d 973, an unexpected back strain triggered **preexisting** Parkinson's **disease** of the nervous system. In both cases compensation was allowed. Strandberg v. Reber Co., 587 P.2d 18–19 (Mont.1978).

disease, Raynaud's a primary or idiopathic vascular disorder characterized by bilateral attacks of Raynaud's phenomenon. The disease affects females more frequently than males. Called also *Raynaud's gangrene.* See also *Raynaud's phenomenon,* under *phenomenon.*

disease, rheumatoid a systemic condition best known by its articular involvement (rheumatoid arthritis) but emphasizing nonarticular changes, e.g., pulmonary interstitial fibrosis, pleural effusion, and lung nodules.

Dr. Dornenberg reported that he examined Camp on May 3, 1977, and that Camp has a 2+ lumbro-sacral area tenderness, a lack of about 25 degrees of complete extension and a lack of perhaps 15 degrees of complete flexion of the right elbow, some narrowing of the L5–S1 disc space, and concluded that Camp "is having a generalized synovitic flare-up compatible with **rheumatoid disease**" and would require surgery in the foreseeable future on his feet and perhaps on his right elbow. Camp v. Schweiker, 643 F.2d 1325, 1328 (8th Cir. 1981).

disease, Sandhoff's a variant of Tay-Sachs disease marked by a progressively more rapid course, due to a defect in the enzymes hexosaminidase A and B. Unlike Tay-Sachs disease, it is not confined to Ashkenazic Jews.

disease, Schimmelbusch's See *disease, cystic d. of breast.*

disease, sickle-cell any of the diseases associated with the presence of hemogloblin S, including sickle cell anemia,

sickle cell-hemoglobin C or D disease, and sickle cell-thalassemia disease.

disease, sickle cell-hemoglobin C a genetically determined anemia in which the red cells contain both hemoglobin S and hemoglobin C.

disease, sickle cell-hemoglobin D a genetically determined anemia characterized by the presence of both hemoglobin S and hemoglobin D in red blood cells.

disease, sickle cell-thalassemia a hereditary anemia involving simultaneous heterozygosity for hemoglobin S and thalassemia. Called also *microdrepanocytosis, microdrepanocytic d., hemoglobin S-thalassemia, sickle cell-thalassemia,* and *thalassemia-sickle cell disease.*

disease, Stokes-Adams See *disease, Adams-Stokes.*

disease, Tay-Sachs the infantile form of cerebral sphingolipidosis in which symptoms become noticeable at about 4 to 6 months of age. A progressive disorder, it is characterized by degeneration of brain cells and the macula (with formation of a cherry-red spot on both retinas) and eventually by dementia, blindness, paralysis, and death. Affecting chiefly Ashkenazic Jewish children, it is inherited as an autosomal recessive trait and is due to an error of lipid metabolism in which a defect in hexosaminidase A results in accumulation of ganglioside GM_2 in the brain. Called also *Sachs'd.* and *GM_2 gangliosidosis.* A variant of Tay-Sachs disease is known as *Sandhoff's disease* (q.v.). See also amniocentesis (Gildiner case); and sphingolipidosis, cerebral.

... her parents, Phillis and Hyam Curlender, retained defendant laboratories to administer certain tests designed to reveal whether either of the parents were carriers of genes which would result in the conception and birth of a child with **Tay-Sachs disease** medically defined as "amaurotic familial idiocy."...

As the result of the disease, plaintiff Shauna suffers from "mental retardation, susceptibility to other diseases, convulsions, sluggishness, apathy, failure to fix objects with her eyes, inability to take an interest in her surroundings, loss of motor reactions, inability to sit up or hold her head up, loss of weight, muscle atrophy, blindness, pseudobulbar palsy, inability to feed orally, decerebrate rigidity and gross physical deformity." It was alleged that Shauna's life expectancy is estimated to be four years. The complaint also contained allegations that plaintiff suffers "pain, physical and emotional distress, fear, anxiety, despair, loss of enjoyment of life, and frustration...." [Footnote omitted.] Curlender v. Bio-Science Laboratories, 165 Cal.Rptr. 477, 480–1 (Ct.App.1980).

Other Authorities: Howard v. Lecher, 386 N.Y.S.2d 460, 463–4 (2d Dep't 1976).

disease, triple vessel

The coronary artery disease was evidenced by the "patchy" narrowing (up to 80%) of all three major coronary vessels, a condition known as "**triple vessel disease.**" Nash v. Prudential Insurance Co. of America, 114 Cal.Rptr. 299, 301 (Ct.App. Cal.1974).

disease, von Recklinghausen's See *neurofibromatosis.*

disfigurement See *scar*.

The nature of Palmer's **disfigurement** and the extent to which his present occupation requires public contact are questions of fact. Whether Palmer's kind of **disfigurement** will ''occasion potential wage loss'' in the carpet laying business is a question of law. See Department of Revenue v. Exxon Corp., 90 Wis.2d 700, 713, 281 N.W.2d 94, 101 (1979). Evans Bros. Co. v. Labor & Industry R. Com'n, 335 N.W.2d 886, 888–9 (Ct.App. Wis.1983).

dish (dish) a shallow vessel of glass or other material for laboratory work.

dish, Petri a shallow glass receptacle for growing bacterial cultures.

''. . . A variant of this [petri dish] technique has shown excellent correlative counts by using an agar-filled spool or an agar-coated microscope slide (41–42). Kass recently employing the latter technique for bacteriuria screening found it to be rapid, simple, accurate and without any false positives or negatives (20).'' Fink v. SmithKline Corp., 186 U.S.P.Q. 262, 268 (N.D.Cal.1975).

disinfect (dis″in-fekt′) [*dis-* + L. *inficere* to corrupt] to free from pathogenic organisms, or to render them inert.

The word ''**disinfect**'' is used in connection with the substantial cleaning or killing of miscroorganisms, but short of sterilization, of the general environment, such as walls, floors, furniture and air ducts. Poncy v. Johnson & Johnson, 460 F.Supp. 795, 800 (D.N.J.1978).

disinfectant (dis″in-fek′tant) an agent that disinfects; applied particularly to agents used on inanimate objects. Cf. *antiseptic*.

disinfection (dis″in-fek′shun) the act of disinfecting.

The second step in root canal therapy is chemical **disinfection**. In this step the crown and root canal where the pulp has been removed are irrigated or various chemicals are placed in the tooth. Regardless of technique, the purpose of this step is to rid the interior of the tooth of bacteria. U.S. v. Talbott, 460 F.Supp. 253, 257 (S.D.Ohio 1978).

disk (disk) [L. *discus;* Gr. *diskos*] a circular or rounded flat plate; also *disc*.

disk, acute, syndrome See *syndrome, acute disk*.

disk, antibiotic sensitivity

The specific item involved in this definitional controversy is a laboratory aid known as an **antibiotic sensitivity disc**, used as a screening test for help in determining the proper antibiotic drug to administer to patients. If the article is a ''drug'' within the general definition of § 201 of the Federal Food, Drug, and Cosmetic Act (52 Stat. 1040, 21 U.S.C. § 321 (1964 ed., Supp. II)), then the Secretary can subject it to pre-market clearance regulations promulgated pursuant to § 507 of the Act (21 U.S.C. § 357). Section 507 authorizes the Secretary to require batch certification of any antibiotic product which also meets the general drug definition of § 201. If, on the other hand, the article is merely a ''device'' under the Act, it is subject only to the misbranding and adulteration proscriptions of the Act and does not have to be pre-tested before marketing; and, of course, if the disc does not fall under either defini-

tion, the Act itself is totally inapplicable. U.S. v. Bacto-Unidisk, 394 U.S. 784–5, 89 S.Ct. 1410, 22 L.Ed.2d 726 (1969).

disk, bulging

At the follow-up visit on March 22, 1982, claimant complained of a symptom which led Dr. Massam to believe she might have a **bulging disc.** Based on this, Dr. Massam, for the first time, ordered a CAT scan done on claimant in an attempt to diagnose the problem. The CAT scan revealed that claimant suffers from a **bulging central disc** which will require surgery. . . .

. . . Since the scar tissue resulting from the injury is not as strong as the original ligament structure, a **bulging disc** can eventually result. Dr. Massam also felt that the disc condition may have been coming on for some lengthy period of time before it was found by the CAT scan. Sun 'N Lake Inn., Inc. v. Folsom, 426 So.2d 1265, 1266 (Dist.Ct.App.Fla.1983).

disk, degenerated

The myelogram disclosed a disc-type defect on the left side of L5 and a smaller defect on the right side of L4. On April 23, 1974, Dr. Jelsma surgically removed an extruded disc with a sequestrated fragment at the left side of the L5 interspace and removed some spurring from the L5–S1 space. . . .

. . . It was Dr. Jelsma's opinion that the claimant's heavy work over the years was an aggravating factor in causing the 1974 incident: ''I think he had an underlying disc disease, and I think that he had a **degenerated disc**, and I think this is the sort of thing that is aggravated by heavy work and that at the particular time he stood up or whatever he was doing was when the disc happened to rupture or actually extruded from this diseased disc space that had been chronically injured over a period of time''. Question: ''I guess what I am really driving at is that you really can't attribute his problems to one specific instance, but rather it is a condition that occurred over a long period of time of heavy work, of a chronic back problem that finally brought forth into the final problem he had on April 15th [sic], but it was the result of many years of problems, a wear and tear on his back?'' Answer: ''Yes. . . . Probably weeks to months.'' Haycraft v. Corhart Refractories Co., 544 S.W.2d 222, 226–7 (Ky.1976).

disk, herniated cervical

Dr. Landry took x-rays which showed a narrowing of the cervical 5–6 disc indicating a **herniated cervical disc** which was pressing on a nerve going into the arm and causing the numbness. Examination verified Naquin's complaints of back pain by muscle spasms and limitation of motion in both neck and lumbar regions. Naquin v. Texaco, Inc., 423 So.2d 31, 33 (Ct. App.La.1982).

In August, 1968 Mrs. Hampton, upon the advice of her attorney, consulted Dr. Joseph Dugas, a general surgeon who recorded complaints of neck pain radiating into the upper extremity as far as the hand, atrophy of the intrinsic muscles of the hand, muscle spasm, and possible loss of reflexes. Dr. Dugas diagnosed a **herniated cervical disc** and recommended a myelogram and possible discogram. . . . Hampton v. Cristina, 362 So.2d 1180, 1181 (Ct.App.La.1978).

disk, herniated lumbar

. . . she gave a history of the fall and related an experience of sudden pain in the lower back, and pain radiating down the posterior aspect of the right leg to her right foot and toes. On this first examination Dr. McCurley found localized tenderness of the left shoulder and localized tenderness of the 4th and 5th lumbar interspaces. He found a reduction of range of motion in the left shoulder and the left lumbar spine. The neurological examination revealed no impairment of tendon reflexes and no loss of sensation. Dr. McCurley concluded that Mrs. Urbina had a **herniated disc** in the lower back and tendonitis in the left shoulder. Urbina v. Alois J. Binder Bakery, Inc., 423 So.2d 765–7 (Ct.App.La.1982).

A **herniated lumbar disc**, on the other hand, is an objective, anatomical deformity which can be detected by diagnostic tests such as a myelogram and an electromyograph. Amie v. General Motors Corp., 429 N.E.2d 1079, 1083 (Ct.App. Ohio 1980).

disk, herniation of intervertebral See under *herniation*.

disk, intervertebral layers of fibrocartilage between the bodies of adjacent vertebrae, consisting of a fibrous ring enclosing a pulpy center; called also *disci intervertebrales* [NA], *intervertebral cartilages, fibrocartilagines intervertebrales*, and *intervertebral fibrocartilages*.

Dr. Parker stated that at that time, he thought claimant suffered from an "L–4 disc attack" (a spinal condition located at the fourth vertebra in the lower part of the back). He prescribed a back support for claimant to wear. Roberts v. Industrial Com'n, 445 N.E.2d 316–17 (Ill.1983).

Each **intervertebral disc** is composed of two parts: (1) the outer part, known as the annulus fibrosis, is a cartilaginious material that holds the disc in place, and (2) the inner part, known as the nucleus pulposus, which is a soft substance that protrudes through the annulus fibrosis when the disc is ruptured. Extra dura pressure may be caused by the nucleus pulposus extruding through the annulus fibrosis and pressing against either the cauda equina or the nerve roots. Hart v. Van Zandt, 399 S.W.2d 791, 795 (Tex.1965).

disk, slipped popular name for herniation of an intervertebral disk, q.v.

On the other hand, the evidence is uncontested that Abernathy was suffering from disc disease ("**slipped disc**") before the accident; his vertebrae were already beginning to disintegrate and press on the nerves. To someone already suffering from disc disease a back injury is a terrible thing; and the fact that a tort victim, because of a preexisting weakness, suffers a worse injury than a normal person would suffer is not in itself a ground for reducing his damage award. See, e.g., Vosburg v. Putney, 80 Wis. 523, 50 N.W. 403 (1891); Johnson v. Bender, 174 Ind.App. 638, 369 N.E.2d 936, 940 (Ind.App.1977). But it is different when the weakness makes it likely that the injury complained of would have occurred anyway, so that the accident merely accelerated it. Abernathy v. Superior Hardwoods, Inc., 704 F.2d 963, 973 (7th Cir. 1983).

diskectomy (dis-kek'to-me) excision of an intervertebral disk.

We know that Dr. Jarrott, who first saw plaintiff in June, 1980, ultimately performed a **discectomy** at C5–C6 in August and in January, 1981, found still another ruptured disc at C4–C–5. Plaintiff had two accidents, on January 17, 1980, and March 18, 1980, both of which caused injuries to her neck and either of which could have caused one or both cervical disc ruptures.

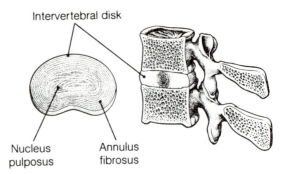

Intervertebral disk

Nucleus pulposus   Annulus fibrosus

The trial court's award was based on his conclusion that both ruptures which already led to one **discectomy** and will probably lead to a second, along with a fusion in order to protect the disc at C6–C7, with all the pain and disability accompanying this condition, were the proximate result of the first accident. Villavaso v. State Farm Mut. Auto Ins. Co., 424 So.2d 536, 540 (Ct.App.La.1982).

A few days later, Dr. Voris informed plaintiff that the myelogram showed possible spinal cord impairment and recommended an anterior interbody **discectomy** and fusion. Dr. Voris informed plaintiff that possible complications from this surgery include infection, quadriplegia and quadriparesis.

The surgery was performed on August 24, 1973, with Drs. Voris and Parameswar making the anterior incision and removing the disc from the patient's spine. Dr. Smith, an orthopedic surgeon, implanted a "plug" of bone into the space left by the removed disc. Kolakowski v. Voris, 415 N.E.2d 397, 399 (Ill. 1980).

Dr. Blitz performed a laminectomy and a **discectomy** on the plaintiff-appellant, Mr. Michel J. Hankel, on May 20, 1975. Three orthopedic surgeons testified, Dr. Roger P. Blitz, the surgeon who performed the operation; Dr. Daniel S. Sinclair, an associate of Dr. Blitz; and Dr. E. J. Dabezies, the plaintiff's current physician. All three testified that the procedure for this type of surgery requires at one point three hands. One hand would hold a nerve root retractor, one hand would hold a sucker (to remove blood), and one hand would hold an instrument for removing a disc or lamina. Hankel v. Hartford Fire Ins. Co., 366 So.2d 1031, 1033 (Ct.App.La.1978).

Other Authorities: Dunn v. St. Francis Hosp., Inc., 401 A.2d 77–8 (Del.1979); Poltorak v. Sandy, 345 A.2d 201, 206, 209–10 (Super.Ct.Pa.1975); Barats v. Weinberger, 383 F.Supp. 276, 279 (E.D.Pa.1974).

diskogram (dis'ko-gram) a roentgenogram of an intervertebral disk.

The neurological examinations and tests performed by Dr. Jackson also proved normal, so he performed a **discogram**, a test designed to detect the presence of a ruptured disc....

Dr. Jackson also testified that it was possible to discover a ruptured disc during the course of surgery even where it had not been diagnosed by a myelogram or **discogram** prior to the operation. He estimated the **discogram** to be 98 percent accurate, but recognized that certain maladies may go undiagnosed no matter how many tests are performed. Martin v. H. B. Zachry Co., 424 So.2d 1002, 1004–5 (La.1982).

The **discogram** has been reported as follows: A needle was inserted into the interspaces of L–3–L4, L4–L5 and L–5–S1. Contrast material was injected into the disc of these spaces. There is no evidence of herniation of the disc from any of the interspaces.

The examination of this patient as of July 23, 1975 does not reveal objective abnormalities of the musculoskeletal system as related to trauma. There are no present findings to indicate operative intervention of the lumbar zone. Chabert v. City of Westwego Police Pension, 423 So.2d 1190, 1194 (Ct.App.La. 1982).

On the morning of the operation Mrs. Grubb was placed under general anesthesia and a **diskogram** was performed. This is a method of X-raying a disc after certain traceable dyes are injected into the neck area. The **diskogram** confirmed the herniated disc diagnosis and the operation was commenced by Dr. Kauffman with Dr. Beller in attendance as explained above. Grubb v. Albert Einstein Medical Center, 387 A.2d 480, 483 (Super.Ct.Pa.1978).

Other Authorities: Perry v. Bertsch, 441 F.2d 939, 942 (8th Cir. 1971).

dislocate See *dislocation.*

dislocation (dis"lo-ka'shun) [*dis-* + L. *locare* to place] the displacement of any part, more especially of a bone; see illustration. Called also *luxation.* See also *subluxation* (Modave case).

After the operation was completed, the patient was x-rayed and it was found that the ''head of the femur popped out of the acetabulum'' or as expressed by a witness ''the joint was **dislocated**''. People v. Smithtown General Hospital, 402 N.Y.S.2d 318, 320 (Sup.Ct.Crim.Term, Suffolk Cty.1978).

The physical therapist wrote a report which stated ''the humerus moved out of joint'' twice. Dr. Sargent was notified and the exercises were terminated. Peeples testified that after moving his arm the therapist stated—''I think it's dislocated.''...

... Dr. James H. Dobyns, an orthopedic surgeon from the Mayo Clinic in Rochester, Minnesota, testified by deposition that an anterior **dislocation** of the humerus is ''a rather obvious deformity'' which he would expect a trained orthopedic nurse to notice. There is no evidence that the **dislocation** was recognized by Nurse Keller or Nurse Boneck, yet Dr. Sargent recognized it immediately upon entering the room.

One or both of the operating room nurses raised Peeples' arm before he regained consciousness. Both nurses were present when Sargent gave the instruction not to raise the arm until Peeples regained consciousness. Peeples v. Sargent, 253 N.W.2d 459, 463–5 (Wis.1977).

A 5 or 6 inch incision was made on the side of the thigh, and the hip **dislocation** was reduced by manipulation. Maguire v. Waukegan Park District, 282 N.E.2d 6, 8 (App.Ct.Ill.1972).

Other Authorities: Santiago v. Gardner, 288 F.Supp. 156, 158 (D. Puerto Rico 1968).

dislocation, metacarpal

Dr. Hillyer, to whom appellant had been referred by his attorney, testified that appellant's injury ''is not sort of rare, it is very rare'' and that as of 1975, only ten cases of this kind of injury of the second and third metacarpals had ever been reported in medical literature worldwide. Dr. Hillyer testified that, in retrospect, the March 9 X-rays show a ''very subtle'' abnormality or misalignment, but that seeing the X-rays without knowing the diagnosis, the very subtle changes on the March 9 X-rays ''could be very easily overlooked.''...

... Dr. Hordurski testified that the injury sustained by the appellant was an extremely rare injury; only eleven are documented in medical literature worldwide and that he had treated only one such injury previously....

... He described the abnormality that he detected in the March 9 X-rays as ''a little bit of discrepancy between the third and fourth metacarpals, but nothing glaring.'' He also stated that in the March 9 X-rays, the bone was out of socket about $3/16$ths of an inch and the fracture was an approximately $3/8$ths inch chip....

... The appellant's own expert medical testimony established that the appellant's injury was very rare and difficult to diagnose. In fact, appellant offered the following statement from a medical text entitled Fractures, Dislocations, and Sprains:

''The obvious clinical deformity that one might expect to see with this injury [carpal, **metacarpal dislocations**] is often obscured by marked swelling of the hand. The fact that many of the **metacarpal dislocations** reported in the literature were missed on initial examination implies that the diagnosis is not always immediately obvious.... Moses v. Gaba, 435 So. 2d 58, 59–61 (Ala.1983).

disorder (dis-or'der) a derangement or abnormality of function; a morbid physical or mental state.

disorder, functional a disorder not associated with clearly defined physical cause or structural change, i.e., having no detectable organic basis. Called also *functional illness.*

disorder, functional nonpsychotic

20 C.F.R. § 12.00(B)(3)(c) of Appendix 1 to Subpart P, at 376 (1979), reads as follows:

''Other **functional nonpsychotic disorders**, including paranoid, cyclothymic, schizoid, explosive, obsessive-compulsive, hysterical, asthenic, antisocial, passive-aggressive, and inadequate personality; sexual deviation; alcohol addiction and drug addiction. These disorders are characterized by deeply ingrained maladaptive patterns of behavior, generally of long duration. Unlike neurotic disorders, conflict in these cases is not primarily within the individual but between the individual and his environment. In many of these conditions, the patient may experience little anxiety and little or no sense of distress, except when anxiety and distress are consequences of maladaptive behavior.''

''**Functional nonpsychotic disorders**'' are further defined as follows in 20 C.F.R. § 12.04 of Appendix 1 to Subpart P, at 377 (1979):

''**Functional nonpsychotic disorders** (psychophysiologic, neurotic, and personality disorders; addictive dependence on alcohol or drugs). With both A and B:

A. Manifested persistence of one or more of the following clinical signs:

1. Demonstrable and persistent structural changes mediated through psychophysiological channels (e.g., duodenal ulcer); or

220

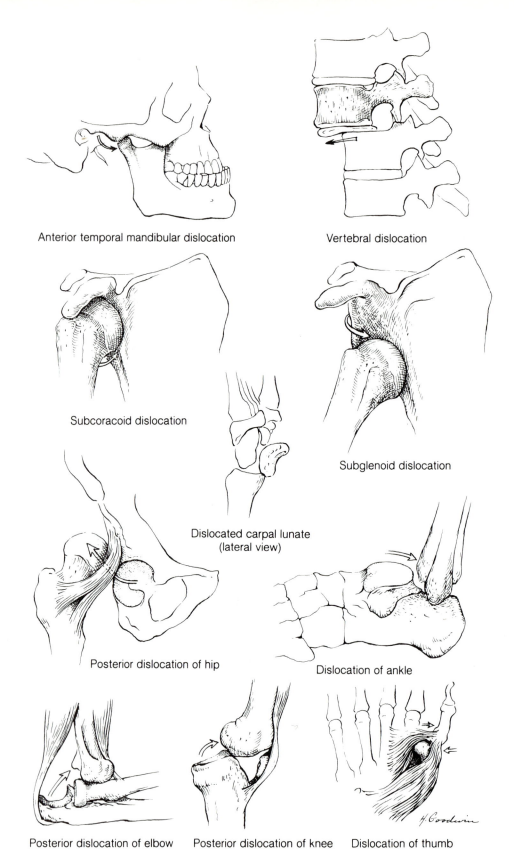

Anterior temporal mandibular dislocation

Vertebral dislocation

Subcoracoid dislocation

Subglenoid dislocation

Dislocated carpal lunate
(lateral view)

Posterior dislocation of hip

Dislocation of ankle

Posterior dislocation of elbow   Posterior dislocation of knee   Dislocation of thumb

VARIOUS TYPES OF DISLOCATION

2. Recurrent and persistent periods of anxiety, with tension, apprehension, and interference with concentration and memory; or

3. Persistent depressive affect with insomnia, loss of weight, and suicidal preoccupation; or

4. Persistent phobic or obsessive ruminations with inappropriate, bizarre, or disruptive behavior; or

5. Persistent compulsive, ritualistic behavior; or

6. Persistent functional disturbance of vision, speech, hearing, or use of a limb with demonstrable structural or trophic changes; or

7. Persistent, deeply ingrained, maladaptive patterns of behavior manifested by either;

   a. Seclusiveness or autistic thinking; or

   b. Pathologically inappropriate suspiciousness or hostility;

   B. Resulting persistence of marked restriction of daily activities and construction of interests and deterioration in personal habits and seriously impaired ability to relate to other people." Crespo v. Harris, 484 F.Supp. 1167, 1171–2 (S.D. N.Y.1980).

disorder, mental any psychiatric illness or disease, whether functional or of organic origin; called also *mental disease or illness* and *emotional illness.*

... Mental diseases are those listed under the heading of **mental disorders** in the eighth revision, International Classification of Diseases, Adapted for Use in the United States ... except that mental retardation is not included for this purpose. Granville House v. Dep't of Health & Human Serv., 715 F.2d 1292, 1295 (8th Cir. 1983).

"**Mental illness**" is defined in 21 D.C.Code § 501 (1967) as "a psychosis or other disease which substantially impairs the mental health of a person." In Re Ballay, 482 F.2d 648, 658 (D.C.Cir.1973).

A "mentally ill person" is defined in section 2 (subd. 8) of the Mental Hygiene Law as "any person afflicted with **mental disease** to such an extent that for his own welfare or the welfare of others, or of the community, he requires care and treatment". Fhagen v. Miller, 278 N.E.2d 615–16 (N.Y.1972).

Other Authorities: People v. Williams, 99 Cal.Rptr. 103, 118 (Ct.App.1971); U.S. v. Currens, 290 F.2d 751 (3d Cir. 1961).

disorder, neurotic See *neurosis.*

disorder, posttraumatic stress

Dr. Butts diagnosed both appellants as having "**post-traumatic stress disorder.**" This is the term used to describe the patient who continues to reexperience a traumatic event, resulting in significant kinds of distress which include recurrent dreams, withdrawal from the outside world, sleep disturbances and difficulty in concentrating. Hoard v. Shawnee Mission Medical Ctr., 662 P.2d 1214, 1218 (Kan.1983).

Serrato withheld information from Dr. Hayes concerning "his continuous difficulty with remembrances of his war trauma, his experiences in Viet Nam, flash-backs and dreams, startled responses, his alienation from the majority of the society that he functioned in prior to the war, and a lot of other symptoms which obviously point to the so-called Vietnamese Syndrome and the **post-traumatic stress disorder.**" ...

... Hayes suspected that Serrato was suffering from **posttraumatic stress disorder** after his examinations, but because Serrato denied any symptoms associated with this disorder, Hayes was unable to make that diagnosis at that time....

... Hayes admitted that "[o]ne of the classic symptoms of this disorder is the denial of its symptoms...."

... Ritter testified that the Veteran's Administration did not recognize **posttraumatic stress disorder** as a treatable disease until October, 1980....

Dr. Ritter stated that Serrato did not possess all of the symptoms associated with **posttraumatic stress disorder**. There was no indication of any "memory impairment or trouble concentrating, avoidance of activities that allow recollection of the traumatic event, [or] intensification of symptoms by exposures to events that symbolize or resemble the traumatic event." State v. Serrato, 424 So.2d 214, 223 (La.1982).

disease, psychophysiologic; disease, psychosomatic a group of disorders characterized by physical symptoms and demonstrable structural and/or physiological changes in which emotional factors are believed to play a major etiologic or pathogenic role. Typically a single organ system is involved, usually under autonomic control.

disorder, skin

He argues that the phrase "**skin disorder**" should be construed to mean an "injury or disease affecting merely the skin" and not involving "the underlying bone, cartilage, tendons and ligaments." Therefore, since his affliction was so severe, in that it affected the blood vessels and bones of the hand, the elimination endorsements should not apply. Also, he argues that the term "**skin disorder**" was ambiguous and should be interpreted in his favor with the result that the elimination endorsements be disregarded. Continental Cas. Co. v. Novy, 437 N.E.2d 1338, 1353 (Ct.App.Ind.1982).

disorientation (dis-o"re-en-ta'shun) the loss of proper bearings, or a state of mental confusion as to time, place, or identity.

"She was **disoriented** in time when I saw her in 1963, and apparently is still in terms of calling this 1965. When I saw her in 1963 she called it 1960 and thought it was December, not September. She also knew that she had three children but could not give their ages accurately...." Talcott v. Holl, 224 So.2d 420, 423 (Dist.Ct.App.Fla.1969).

dispense (dis-pens') [L. *dispensare, dis-* out + *pensare* to weigh] to prepare and distribute medicines to those who are to use them.

[Mass.] General Laws, c. 94C, § 1, as amended by St.1972, c. 806, § 3, defines "**dispense**" as "to deliver a controlled substance to an ultimate user or research subject or to the agent of an ultimate user or research subject by a practitioner or pursuant to the order of a practitioner, including the prescribing and administering of a controlled substance and the packaging, labeling, or compounding necessary for such delivery." Section 1 defines "distribute" as "to deliver other than by administering or dispensing a controlled substance." Com. v. De La Cruz, 443 N.E.2d 427, 430 (App.Ct.Mass.1982).

Section 802(10), 21 U.S.C. defines the word "**dispense**" as follows:

The term "**dispense**" means to deliver a controlled substance to an ultimate user or research subject by, or pursuant to the lawful order of, a practitioner, including the prescribing and administering of a controlled substance and the packaging, labeling, or compounding necessary to prepare the substance for such delivery.... U.S. v. Bartee, 479 F.2d 484, 486–7 (10th Cir. 1973).

dispenser, ophthalmic

KRS Ch. 326 (c. 27, Acts of 1954) defines the practice of **ophthalmic dispensing**, establishes a Board of Ophthalmic Dispensers, and requires the licensing of practitioners. KRS 326.060 provides as follows (emphasis added):

"326.060.   **Dispenser** not to examine or treat eyes—Fitting of contact lenses.—Nothing in this chapter shall be construed to authorize or permit any **opthalmic dispenser** to hold himself out as being able to, or to either offer, undertake or attempt, by any means or method, to examine or exercise eyes, to fit contact lenses, or to diagnose, treat, correct, relieve, operate or prescribe for any human ailment, deficiency, deformity, disease, injury, pain or physical condition except that an **ophthalmic dispenser** holding a license as such issued hereunder may fit contact lenses under the supervision of a physician, osteopath or optometrist." Commonwealth, etc. v. Economy Optical Co., 522 S.W.2d 444–5 (Ct.App.Ky.1975).

displacement (dis-plas′ment) removal from the normal position or place; ectopia.

displacement, bone See *dislocation*.

There was **bone displacement**, that is the bone did not remain in alignment. St. Gregory's Church v. O'Connor, 477 P.2d 540, 542 (Ct.App.Ariz.1970).

dissection, iliac and perfusion See *prophylaxis, chemotherapeutical*.

distal (dis′tal) [L. *distans* distant] remote; farther from any point of reference; opposed to proximal. In dentistry, used to designate a position on the dental arch farther from the median line of the jaw.

The accident happened when a large metal fire door closed on plaintiff's left index finger, amputating it at the **distal** interphalangeal joint. Moazzami v. Bd. of Sup'rs of La. State Univ., 424 So.2d 1112 (Ct.App.La.1982).

This crushing type injury necessitated amputations through the **distal** portion of the middle phalanx of the plaintiff's middle and ring fingers. Thornton v. Deep Sea Boats, Inc., 399 F.Supp. 933–4 (S.D.Ala.1975).

According to Dr. James, the proper surgical procedure for repair of plaintiff's shoulder was a removal of the **distal** (outer) end of the clavicle. Vest v. City National Bank and Trust Co., 470 S.W.2d 518–19 (Mo.1971).

disulfiram (di-sul′fi-ram) [USP] chemical name: tetraethylthioperoxydicarbonic diamide $[(H_2N)C(S)]_2S_2$. An antioxidant, $C_{10}H_{20}N_2S_4$, occurring as a white to off-white, crystalline powder, which inhibits the oxidation of the acetaldehyde metabolized from alcohol, resulting in high concentrations of acetaldehyde in the body. Extremely uncomfortable symptoms occur when alcohol is ingested subsequent to the oral administration of

disulfiram; used to produce an aversion to alcohol in the treatment of chronic alcoholism. Called also *tetraethylthiuram disulfide*. See also *mal rouge*.

Accordingly, appellant was urged by the hospital to accept "**antabuse** therapy," which consists primarily of taking a drug—**antabuse**—"which tends to prevent alcohol intoxication by virtue of making the person ill who takes it while on **antabuse**. U.S. v. McNeil, 434 F.2d 502, 504–5 (D.C.Cir. 1970).

Antabuse is designed to discourage drinking by producing nausea and illness in one who consumes alcohol while having the drug in his system. Leeper understood that while under **Antabuse** therapy, he would become ill if he drank a small quantity of alcohol and that he could die if he consumed a large quantity. U.S. v. Leeper, 413 F.2d 123–4 (8th Cir. 1969).

diuresis (di″u-re′sis), pl. *diure′ses* [Gr. *diourein* to urinate, to pass in urine] increased excretion of urine.

"Diuresis" is the washing of salt and water out of the body by urinary excretion. U.S. v. Ciba Geigy Corp., 508 F.Supp. 1118, 1122 (D.N.J.1976).

diuretic (di″u-ret′ik) [Gr. *diourētikos* promoting urine] an agent that promotes the excretion of urine.

The use of a **diuretic**, such as Enduron, which causes the body to lose fluids, may also cause an imbalance. Laboratory tests performed on a blood sample can determine whether there is a proper concentration of electrolytes in the system. Sears v. Cooper, 574 S.W.2d 612, 614 (Ct.Civ.App.Tex.1978).

"Diuretic" means a chemical substance which produces diuresis. U.S. v. Ciba Geigy Corp., 508 F.Supp. 1118, 1122 (D.N.J. 1976).

diuretic, oral

Prior to 1957, Merck, CIBA and other pharmaceutical companies were engaged in extensive research work to develop an effective **oral diuretic**. At this time, the most prevalent treatment for edema or hypertension was the injection of organic salts of mercury. Understandably, this was not an acceptable form of treatment for people suffering from long-term, asymptomatic hypertension. Patients would not submit to the frequent injection of these salts to treat a disease that caused them no present discomfort. Merck was the first to succeed in discovering such an **oral diuretic**, when in 1956 it isolated and later patented chlorothiazide. Merck marketed this drug in 1957 under the trade name "Diuril," after obtaining the necessary FDA approval. U.S. v. Ciba Geigy Corp., 508 F.Supp. 1118, 1124 (D.N.J.1976).

diverticula (di″ver-tik′u-lah) [L.] plural of *diverticulum*.

diverticulectomy (di″ver-tik″u-lek′to-me) [*diverticulum* + Gr. *ektomē* excision] excision of a diverticulum.

Dr. Scarzella, who had treated Ms. Saxon in the past, confirmed Dr. Ulma's diagnosis and recommended that the diverticulum be removed by means of a surgical operation known as a **diverticulectomy**. Scarzella v. Saxon, 436 A.2d 358–9 (Ct. App.D.C.1981).

diverticulitis (di″ver-tik-u-li′tis) inflammation of a diverticulum, especially inflammation related to colonic diverticula which may undergo perforation with abscess formation. Sometimes called *left-sided* or *L-sided appendicitis*. See also *diverticulosis* (Jines case).

Purcell's initial diagnosis was that Zimbelman had either cancer or **diverticulitis** [1] of the lower large bowel. [[1] Inflammation of the little sacs formed along the large intestine.] Purcell v. Zimbelman, 500 P.2d 335, 339 (Ct.App.Ariz.1972).

diverticulosis (di"ver-tik"u-lo'sis) the presence of diverticula, particularly of colonic diverticula, in the absence of inflamation. Cf. *diverticulitis*.

He emphasizes the difference between **diverticulosis**, which is an outpocketing of the intestine, not a disease as such, and acute diverticulitis, which is an inflamed condition, and chronic diverticulitis, which is characterized by scar tissue resulting from an earlier inflammation. Jines v. Abarbanel, 143 Cal.Rptr. 818, 822 (Ct.App.Cal.1978).

diverticulum (di"ver-tik'u-lum), pl. *divertic'ula* [L. *divertere* to turn aside] a circumscribed pouch or sac of variable size occurring normally or created by herniation of the lining mucous membrane through a defect in the muscular coat of a tubular organ. See also *valva, ileocecalis* (Steinbach case).

... diverticula (pockets in the membrane) in the descending and sigmoid colon. Manigan v. Califano, 453 F.Supp. 1080, 1083 (D.Kan.1978).

diverticulum, urethral

Dr. Ulma diagnosed her problem as a **diverticulum of the urethra**—a cyst on the urethra—and referred Ms. Saxon to a urologist, Dr. Guilio I. Scarzella. Scarzella v. Saxon, 436 A.2d 358–9 (Ct.App.D.C.1981).

dizziness (diz'i-nes) a disturbed sense of relationship to space; a sensation of unsteadiness with a feeling of movement within the head; giddiness; lightheadedness; dysequilibrium. Cf. *vertigo*.

Because of the failure of the first surgery, the greatly diminished hearing in his left ear, and the continuing **dizziness** experienced by the appellant, he was required to undergo a radical operation in which the nerves of the inner ear were severed. LePelley v. Grefenson, 614 P.2d 962, 964 (Idaho 1980).

DMT (dimethyltryptamine) See *dimethyltryptamine*.

DNA (deoxyribonucleic acid) See under *acid*.

DNA, recombinant DNA that has been artificially introduced into a cell so that it alters the genotype and phenotype of the cell and is replicated along with the natural DNA.

doctor (dok'tor) [L. "teacher"] a practitioner of the healing arts, one who has received a degree from a college of medicine, osteopathy, dentistry, or veterinary medicine, licensed to practice by a state.

doctrine (dok'trin) a theory supported by authorities and having general acceptance.

doctrine, "captain of the ship"

Because of the necessity of absolute authority of the operating surgeon in the critical surgical situation it has been held that where the authority of the doctor was complete, as with the surgeon in charge of the operating room, responsibility rests upon the surgeon for all acts of all hospital personnel who assist him or who are responsible for the carrying out of the operative and post-operative procedures. This is also called the "**captain of the ship**" doctrine under the analogy that the surgeon in the operating room

is in the same complete charge of those who are present and assisting him as is the captain of a ship over all on board, and that such supreme control is indeed essential in view of the high degree of protection to which anaesthetized, unconscious patient is entitled ....

McConnell v. Williams, 361 Pa. 355, at p. 362, 65 A.2d 243, at p. 246. This liability has been extended to a surgical patient injured as a result of the negligence of an interne and resident employed by the hospital in the post-surgical treatment of the patient, even though the surgeon was no longer present. Yorston v. Pennell, 397 Pa. 28, 153 A.2d 255, 85 A.L.R.2d 872 (1959). It applies even where the mistake is that of other physicians while the patient is under the direction and control of the surgeon preparatory to surgery. Rockwell v. Kaplan, 404 Pa. 574, 173 A.2d 54 (1961).

There is no question, however, that the "operating room" or "**captain of the ship**" doctrine has not been extended beyond the surgical situation in Pennsylvania.

Shull v. Schwartz, 364 Pa. 554, 73 A.2d 402, 403 (1950), strictly limited this liability to the operating room situation, quoting from McConnell v. Williams, 361 Pa. 355, 65 A.2d 243 (1949):

... [A] surgeon's liability [does not] apply, after the operation is concluded, to treatment administered by floor nurses and internes in the regular course of the services ordinarily furnished by a hospital; as to all such care and attention they would clearly be acting exclusively on behalf of the hospital and not as assistants to the surgeon. 364 Pa. at p. 556, 65 A.2d at p. 247. Honeywell v. Rogers, 251 F.Supp. 841, 847–8 (W.D.Pa.1966).

doll's head phenomenon See *phenomenon, doll's head*.

dominant (dom'i-nant) exerting a ruling or controlling influence; in genetics, capable of expression when carried by only one of a pair of homologous chromosomes.

A. Geneticists speak of what we call **dominant** hereditary defects, examples being dwarfness, misshapen dwarfness, and six-fingerness....

The **dominant** characteristics will be manifested in the immediate generation after the mutation occurs. Chiropractic Ass'n of New York, Inc. v. Hilleboe, 227 N.Y.S.2d 309, 367 (Sup. Ct. Albany Cty.1961).

Donnatol

Dr. Glover testified that he had found **Donnatol** to be an inexpensive drug that was effective in treating stomach and intestinal tract disorders, which is produced by combining twelve drops of tincture of belladona, a toxic and bad-tasting drug which if misused may cause heart disorders, with one drop of elixir phenobarbitol. Dodson v. Parham, 427 F.Supp. 97, 106–7 (N.D.Ga.1977).

donor site See *site, donor*.

dopamine (do′pah-mēn) chemical name: 4-(2-aminoethyl)-1,2-benzenediol. A monoamine, $C_8H_{11}NO_2$, formed in the body by the decarboxylation of dopa; it is an intermediate product in the synthesis of norepinephrine, and acts as a neurotransmitter in the central nervous system.

In the intensive care unit, Erickson was given Heparin for the pulmonary embolism and **Dopamine** for the heart attack. The effect of **Dopamine** is to increase the muscle performance of the heart and the blood flow to the kidneys and the brain, at the expense of peripheral circulation. In lay terms, **Dopamine** increases the blood pressure. It is undisputed that the high dosage amount of **Dopamine** over an 80 hour period caused severe vasoconstriction in the lower extremities resulting in irreversible ischemia or wet gangrene. This led to the bilateral modified Symes' amputations. Defendant argues, however, that the use of **Dopamine** was vital to maintaining Erickson's blood pressure and keeping him alive....

... Dr. Talley, a cardiologist employed by the Veterans Hospital, testified that the recommended dosage of **Dopamine** in the Physician's Desk Reference Book was two to five micrograms, and that the dosage given Erickson was over six times that amount. He continued to maintain, however, that such a dosage was necessary to keep Erickson alive, although he did agree with medical literature that indicates that **Dopamine** should be discontinued in favor of alternative forms of treatment in this case when severe vasoconstriction became apparent in Erickson; nor was Regetine or other means used to counteract the effects of the **Dopamine**. Erickson v. U.S., 504 F.Supp. 646, 649–50 (D.S.Dak.1980).

Doppler effect (phenomenon, principle) (dop′lerz) [Christian Johann *Doppler*, Austrian physicist and mathematician, 1803–1853]. See under *effect*.

Doriden (dor′ĭ-den) trademark for preparations of glutethimide. See also *glutethimide*.

dormant (dor′mant) [L. *dormire* to sleep] sleeping, inactive, quiescent. See also *disease, occupational* (Haycraft case).

"It is difficult to determine the true legislative intent and meaning of the use of the phrase 'a **dormant** non-disabling disease.' The phrase has importance and we must determine that meaning. We conclude that a person who has a disease condition known to him and who is being treated medically for that condition does not have a **dormant** nondisabling disease condition....

"... In Yocom v. Spalding, Ky., 547 S.W.2d 442 at 445, fn. 2 (1977), the Supreme Court stated that a '**dormant**' disease condition was one which had not created any physical impairment in terms of ability to work prior to the subsequent injury. The Pugh opinion notwithstanding whether the pre-existing disease condition was **dormant** does not turn on the employee's knowledge of the condition or whether it was being treated medically prior to the subsequent injury. A pre-existing disease condition is **dormant** if it was non-disabling prior to the subsequent injury ....

"... The case of Young v. Pugh, Ky., 463 S.W.2d 928 (1978) is hereby overruled and should no longer be considered authority....." Yocom v. Loy, 573 S.W.2d 645, 649, 651 (Ky. 1978).

"In the event an insured sustains physical disability resulting from an accidental injury which aggravates or causes a **dormant** disease or ailment to become active, the disability will be regarded as having been caused solely by the injury, so as to render an insurer liable therefor under an accident policy, even though such disability might later have resulted regardless of the accident, and even though the accident might not have affected a normal person to the same extent.

"A **dormant** disease is one which is quiescent, passive, resting or static as opposed to one which is active, lively, or effective." Boring v. Hayes, 496 P.2d 1385, 1392 (Kan.1972).

dorsal spine See *columna, vertebralis*.

dorsiflexion (dor″sĭ-flek′shun) [*dorsi-* + *flexion*] backward flexion or bending, as of the hand or foot.

Dr. Emch found a positive straight leg raising test with some weakness of **dorsiflexion** on the right great toe. Daney v. Argonaut Ins. Co., 421 So.2d 331, 333 (Ct.App.La.1982).

dorsum (dor′sum), pl. *dor′sa* [L.] [NA] the aspect of an anatomical part or structure corresponding in position to the back; posterior, in the human.

dorsum pedis [NA], the upper surface of the foot; the surface opposite the sole.

Dr. David found plaintiff's foot swollen with a burn wound to the **dorsum** (upper surface) of his foot from his toes to about the level of the ankle joint. There was no burn around the ankle or bottom of the foot. Plaintiff Jackson told Dr. David he had burned the foot in water in the tub. Dr. David regarded this explanation skeptically. He testified that if Jackson had sustained the burn he saw by immersing his foot in water hot enough to burn the top of his foot, the bottom of plaintiff's foot would also have been burned. Plaintiff's wound at this time consisted of second and third degree burns to the **dorsum** of the foot which required hospitalization for treatment including skin grafts. Jackson v. City of Alexandria, 424 So.2d 1265, (Ct.App.La.1982).

dose (dōs) [Gr. *dosis* a giving] a quantity to be administered at one time, such as a specified amount of medication, or a given quantity of roentgen ray or other radiation.

dose, absorbed the amount of energy from ionizing radiations absorbed per unit mass of matter, expressed in rads.

"**Dose**," as used in this part, is the quantity of radiation absorbed, per unit of mass, by the body or by any portion of the body. When the regulations in this part specify a dose during a period of time, the dose means the total quantity of radiation absorbed, per unit of mass, by the body or by any portion of the body during such period of time. Several different units of

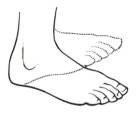

Dorsiflexion of foot (Hauser).

dose are in current use. Definitions of units as used in this part are set forth in paragraphs (b) and (c) of this section. 10 C.F.R. § 20.4(a) (1982).

"Dose", as explained above, is the amount of radiation received and must be distinguished from "dose rate", which is the speed at which a given amount of radiation is received. If a given amount is received very rapidly, in a second for instance, it is received at a higher dose rate than if it is received over a time span of several minutes or hours. Crowther v. Seaborg, 312 F.Supp. 1205, 1232 (D.Colo.1970).

dose, lethal the amount of an agent, such as radiation, which will or may be sufficient to cause death. Called also *fatal d.*

LD$_{50}$ is the **dose** of a chemical which is lethal to 50 percent of the test animals. Dose is usually stated in milligrams of chemical per kilogram of body weight (mg/kg). Citizens Against Toxic Sprays, Inc. v. Bergland, 428 F.Supp. 908, 927–8 (D.Ore. 1977).

dose, lethal, median the amount of pathogenic bacteria, bacterial toxin, or other poisonous substance, required to kill 50 per cent of uniformly susceptible animals inoculated with it. In radiology, the amount of ionizing radiation that will kill, within a specified period, 50 per cent of individuals in a large group or population. Abbreviated L.D.$_{50}$.

dose, occupational (radioactive)

"Occupational dose" includes exposure of an individual to radiation (i) in a restricted area; or (ii) in the course of employment in which the individual's duties involve exposure to radiation, provided, that "occupational dose" shall not be deemed to include any exposure of an individual to radiation for the purpose of medical diagnosis or medical therapy of such individual. 10 C.F.R. § 20.3(a)(10) (1982).

dose, radiation See *dose, absorbed.*

dose, radiation absorbed See *dose, absorbed; rad.*

dose response curve See *curve, dose response.*

dosimeter (do-sim'ĕ-ter) in radiology, an instrument used to detect and measure exposure to radiation, commonly a pencil-sized ionization chamber with a built-in electrometer used in monitoring exposure of personnel. Called also *dosage meter.*

In addition to this testimony, the defendant introduced the readings from each of the plaintiffs' pocket **dosimeters** for the week ending Friday, March 15, 1957. These meters make daily records of the amount of radioactivity to which the wearers are exposed. McVey's total exposure for the week ending March 15 was 270 milliroentgens. Northway's dosimeter recorded 45 milliroentgens for the same week. The maximum permissible weekly accumulation is 300 milliroentgens. These exposure readings were confirmed by weekly reports of exposure to radiation taken from the film badges which appellants wore. McVey v. Phillips Petroleum Co., 288 F.2d 53, 55 (5th Cir. 1961).

He was then given two tubular articles which had been marked plaintiffs' exhibit 19 for identification. He said "they are two small ionization chambers which are to be used for measuring of stray or scattered ionizing radiation, which may be x-radiation or gamma radiation." He said that they were the testing devices which he used in connection with the figures he had given when he was last present at the trial. He said they were a standard testing device "for small amounts of stray and scattered radiation"; that it was common practice to use those instruments for measurement of stray and scattered radiation; that physicists in general would use them either as "pocket **dosimeters** for measuring the amount of radiation that they might receive during this work—"; he was then asked who might receive such amount of radiation and he replied "Anyone working with either isotopes or X or gamma radiation, in order to determine how much radiation they received in the course of their work; that one purpose for which the tubular devices might be used was to determine how much radiation had reached the one who was taking the X-ray picture; he said that another purpose for which they might be used would be, when placed in the room, to determine the amount of stray or scattered radiation at different points in the room. Chiropractic Ass'n of New York, Inc. v. Hilleboe, 227 N.Y.S.2d 309, 339 (Sup.Ct.Albany Cty.1961).

double-blind (dŭ'b'l-blīnd') denoting a study of the effects of a specific agent in which neither the administrator nor the recipient, at the time of administration, knows whether the active or an inert substance is given.

In order to eliminate the bias of the placebo effect in a clinical study, it is common practice to "blind" the participants, i.e., dispense to the control group a placebo which simulates in taste, smell, and appearance the product being tested. Similarly, to neutralize any subconscious bias of the examiner, it is important to blind him, i.e., prevent him from knowing which subjects received the medication and which did not. A study in which both the subjects and the examiner are blinded is referred to as "double-blind." Warner-Lambert Co. v. F.T.C., 562 F.2d 749, 754 (D.C.Cir.1977).

Dr. Thomas Bumbalo conducted a "double blind" study on a group of children having mongolism, the results of which were published in the American Medical Association Journal. Dr. Bumbalo testified that the **double blind** study is the accepted procedure in evaluating any new drug. Under this technique, one-half of the group studied was given the "U" Series Drugs continually for a one year period while the other half (the control group) was given a placebo. The clinical investigators did not know which group was receiving the drug. Ubiotica Corp. v. Food & Drug Administration, 427 F.2d 376, 379 (6th Cir. 1970).

double Master's test See *test, Master "2-step" exercise.*

double Vineberg operation See *operation, Vineberg's.*

double vision See *diplopia.*

Down's syndrome See *syndrome, Down's.*

doxycycline (dok"se-si'klēn) [USP] chemical name: 4αS-(dimethylamino)-1,4,4aα,5,5aα,6,11, 12a-octahydro-3,5α,10,12aα-pentahydroxy-6α-methyl-1,11-dioxo-2-naphthacenecarboxamide monohydrate. A semisynthetic broad-spectrum antibacterial of the tetracycline (q.v.) group, $C_{22}H_{24}N_2O_8 \cdot H_2O$, derived from methacycline, it occurs as a yellow crystalline powder; administered orally.

U.S. Patent No. 3,200,149 was issued on August 10, 1965, for a chemical compound, and the process of producing the compound, called **doxycycline** (Pfizer tradename Vibramycin), a member of the tetracycline family of broad spectrum antibiotic drugs....

... **Doxycycline** is derived by synthesizing a fermentation produced drug called oxytetracycline (Pfizer tradename Terramycin) with a process called hydrogenolysis. A significant concern to Pfizer in patenting **doxycycline** was the prior existence of another compound of nearly identical chemical structure. This prior discovery, referred to as the McCormick compound, was produced in the 1950's by Dr. J. R. D. McCormick for American Cyanamid, and independently by Drs. Stephens and Conover, working for Pfizer, using the same process of hydrogenating oxytetracycline. It was patented by Dr. McCormick in Belgium in 1959.

All three chemical compounds are molecules consisting of component groups of atoms, called substituents, in a configuration unique to each compound. Chemists are able to describe three dimensionally the molecular structure of each compound using the terminology of stereochemistry....

... **Doxycycline** and the McCormick compound are 6-position epimers of each other. That is, the chemical structure of **doxycycline** is identical to that of the McCormick compound except at the 6-position, where their structures are opposite. Pfizer, Inc. v. International Rectifier Corp., 538 F.2d 180, 182, 187 (8th Cir. 1976).

doxylamine succinate (dok-sil'ah-mēn) [USP] chemical name: *N,N*-dimethyl-2-[1-phenyl-1-(2-pyridinyl)ethoxy] ethanamine butanedioate (1:1). An antihistaminic, $C_{17}H_{22}N_2O \cdot C_4H_6O_4$, occurring as a white or creamy white powder; administered orally.

drain (drān) any device by which a channel or open area may be established for the exit of fluids or purulent material from any cavity, wound, or infected area.

Before the inventions of the patents in suit, it had been the practice to **drain** fluids collecting within the pleural cavity by what was known as either the one-bottle system, the two-bottle system, or the three-bottle system. In each of these systems the fluids accumulating within the pleural cavity can **drain** through a thoracotomy tube into a bottle referred to as a collection bottle. Deknatel, Inc. v. Bentley Sales, Inc., 173 U.S. P.Q. 129–30 (C.D.Cal.1971)

drain, cigarette a drain made by drawing a strip of gauze or surgical sponge into a tube of gutta-percha.

On August 12, 1974, defendant respondent, Dr. George T. Cox, performed an abdominal hysterectomy on Susan Reis, the plaintiff appellant. He inserted a **Penrose drain** to prevent the accumulation of fluids which might hinder the healing process. Subsequently, when defendant removed the drain, an edge of the drain appeared uneven and irregular. The defendant's suspicion that a portion of the drain might remain in the plaintiff is evidenced by the following notation made on his progress report: "Drain removed. ? Some remains." Reis v. Cox, 660 P.2d 46, 48 (Idaho 1982).

In the course of performing this corrective surgery, defendant inserted a **Penrose drain** in each of plaintiff's breasts to promote fluid drainage. Greenwell v. Gill, 660 P.2d 1305–6 (Colo.Ct.App.1982).

drain, Penrose See *drain, cigarette.*

drainage (drān'ij) the systematic withdrawal of fluids and discharges from a wound, sore, or cavity. See also *drain.*

drainage, basal withdrawal of the cerebrospinal fluid from the basal subarachnoid space for the relief of intracranial pressure.

A neurosurgeon drilled four holes approximating the size of a penny in Mr. Snell's skull, two on each side, and left a closed continuous **drainage** system to drain the blood so as to permit the brain to re-expand and take up the space occupied by the hematomas. The closed **drainage** system was removed three days later. Wages v. Snell, 360 So.2d 807–8 (Dist.Ct.App.Fla. 1978).

drainage, lymphatic

"The drainage—the normal venous drainage and the **lymphatic drainage**—that is the drainage of the body fluids from the area of the bladder and the vagina and uterus and the rectum go back to a formation of veins and drainage that lies right behind the rectum, between the rectum and the sacrum and the spine.... Rimmele v. Northridge Hosp. Foundation, 120 Cal.Rptr. 39, 47 (Ct.App.Cal.1975).

drape, surgical

She was then draped with a Johnson and Johnson Lithotomy Pack II gynecological disposable **surgical drape** which covered her chest, abdomen, perineum, and legs, and which extended to the floor. The drape contains an opening over the vaginal area through which the surgery is performed. The area of the drape around this opening is reinforced with additional layers of material. The doctor, as an added precaution against infection, also covered Betty's legs with Converter leggings, a stocking-like covering. The purpose of the **surgical drape** is to provide a sterile field and to serve as a barrier to prevent bacteria from reaching the operation site....

... The doctor threw the smoldering sponge at the feet of the circulating nurse for her to extinguish. It landed on, under, or very near the **surgical drape**. As the nurse stepped toward the sponge almost immediately after the doctor threw it, the drape began burning. The nurse threw a pan of water on the drape, but because of the water-repellant characteristics of the drape this had no effect except to possibly intensify the fire....

... The fire, as described by the witnesses, burned at a very nearly explosive rate. Subsequent tests, outside the operating room and in the courtroom, made of the remains of the drape and a drape from the same shipment, also revealed the highly flammable nature of the drape....

... On the record before us we find the **surgical drape** here to be an "unavoidably unsafe" product. It is a highly useful product which affords substantially increased protection against infection during surgical procedures. Its water-repellant attributes increase these protections. In the state of knowledge at the time of the injury no method of making the product fire-resistant was available which did not adversely affect its barrier against infection or create potential injury to the patient from allergy or disease. It is also clear that it is highly flammable. It is designed for gynecological surgery where use of a cautery is not unusual. [footnotes omitted.]

Racer v. Utterman, 629 S.W.2d 387, 391–4 (Mo.Ct.App. 1981).

drill (dril) a rotating cutting instrument for making holes in hard substances, such as bones or teeth. See also *bur;* and "*Stryker plug cutter*" (Grubb case).

dripolene

The B–29 had been used to transport Hytrol-D, a petrochemical mixture containing a substantial concentration of benzene. . . .

. . . the Wilsco employees were advised that it contained a residue of **dripolene**, the generic name in the industry for a common industrial substance that DuPont marketed under the trade name "Hytrol-D." . . .

. . . The benzene warning card was selected because specific Coast Guard instructions required that Hytrol-D be classified and regulated as benzene while in marine transit. . . .

. . . MODERATELY TOXIC ON SHORT EXPOSURE TO HIGH CONCENTRATIONS. SEVERELY TOXIC ON REPEATED EXPOSURE. AFFECTS BLOOD PROPERTIES. CAN BE ABSORBED BY SKIN AND CAUSES IRRITATION TO SKIN. WASH IT OFF WITH COPIOUS QUANTITIES OF WATER & SOAP & GET MEDICAL HELP. HANDLE AS A FLAMMABLE TOXIC MATERIAL. Martinez v. Dixie Carriers, Inc., 529 F.2d 457, 460–1 (5th Cir. 1976).

drop (drop) [L. *gutta*] a minute sphere of liquid as it hangs or falls.

drop, foot See *footdrop.*

drop-attack

On that occasion she had fallen while in downtown Keokuk but was able to drive her car to the hospital where it was determined that she had sustained a fracture of the bone in her right wrist and a severe sprain of her left knee. This incident was attributed to what Dr. Rankin characterized as a "drop-attack" which occurs commonly in patients who have advanced or narrowing arteriosclerosis. Frazier v. State Central Savings Bank, 217 N.W.2d 238, 242 (Iowa 1974).

droperidol (dro-per′ĭ-dol) [USP] chemical name: 1-[1-[4-(4-fluorophenyl)-4-oxobutyl]-1,2,3,6-tetrahydro-4-pyridinyl]-1,3-dihydro-2*H*-benzimidazol-2-one. A drug of the butyrophenone series, $C_{22}H_{22}FN_3O_2$, occurring as a white to light tan, amorphous or microcrystalline powder; used for its antianxiety, sedative, and antiemetic effects as a premedication prior to surgery and during induction and maintenance of anesthesia, administered intravenously or intramuscularly. A combination of droperidol and fentanyl citrate (known as *Innovar*) is administered intramuscularly to produce neuroleptanalgesia.

Because the many doses of valium were not having any effect, **droperidol** was given to calm the patient. According to Dr. Gale, **droperidol** is a tranquilizer and a depressant. Dr. Gravenstein (appellees' expert) classified **droperidol** as one of the more effective major tranquilizers. He believed that anileridine and **droperidol** had a depressant effect on the patient's breathing. Siegel v. Mt. Sinai Hospital of Cleveland, 403 N.E.2d 202, 205 (Ct.App.Ohio 1978).

dropped foot syndrome See *foot, drop.*

drowning (drown′ing) suffocation and death resulting from filling of the lungs with water or other substance or fluid, so that gas exchange becomes impossible.

The two experts agreed that there are no medical tests or findings that can conclusively establish death by drowning. . . .

Dr. Hirsch referred to the chapter on drowning written by Dr. Spitz in the book, Medicological Investigation of Death (2d Ed. W. Spitz and R. Fisher, eds.1980), which was received into evidence as Plaintiff's Exhibit 1. Dr. Spitz wrote:

Only an evaluation of all possible criteria, especially the findings at autopsy and the circumstances in a particular case, together corroborate the diagnosis [of drowning].
Id. at 360. Van Hook v. Aetna Life Ins. Co., 550 F.Supp. 888, 892 (E.D.Mich.1982).

drug (drug) 1. any chemical compound that may be used on or administered to humans or animals as an aid in the diagnosis, treatment, or prevention of disease or other abnormal condition, for the relief of pain or suffering, or to control or improve any physiologic or pathologic condition. 2. a narcotic. See also *drug, safe.*

Drugs are defined as:

(1) articles recognized in the official United States Pharmacopoeia, official Homeopathic Pharmacopoeia of the United States, or official National Formulary, or any supplement to any of them; and (2) articles intended for use in the diagnosis, cure, mitigation, treatment, or prevention of disease in man or other animals; and (3) articles (other than food) intended to affect the structure or any function of the body of man or other animals; and (4) articles intended for use as a component of any article specified in clause (1), (2), or (3) of this paragraph; but does not include devices or their components, parts, or accessories. 21 U.S.C. § 321(g) (1). . . .

. . . The definition of "drug" with which the Court is here concerned is an "article intended to affect the structure or any function of the body of man." If an article which meets the definition for cosmetics also meets that for drugs, it is subject to all of the provisions applying to **drugs**. United States v. An Article Consisting of 36 Boxes etc. "Line Away Temporary Wrinkle Smoother, Coty", 284 F.Supp. 107 (D.Del.1968); 21 U.S.C. § 359. . . . U.S. v. Article of Drug, etc., 331 F.Supp. 912, 914–15 (D.Md.1971).

The plaintiff argues that the word "**drug**" in the terms "new **drug**" denotes only the active ingredient in a **drug** product and, therefore, that if an active ingredient is generally recognized to be safe and effective, then a **drug** product containing that active ingredient is not a "new **drug**". This interpretation of "new **drug**," however, runs afoul of section 201(g)(1)(B) of the Act, 21 U.S.C. § 321(g)(1)(B), which defines "**drug**" as "articles intended for use in the diagnosis, cure, mitigation treatment, or prevention of disease in man . . . ." The word "articles," as used in this definition, is quite broad enough to encompass **drug** products as well as active ingredients. Further, the interpretation advocated by the plaintiff has been rejected by the courts, which have not distinguished between the general recognition of active and inactive ingredients in determining whether a drug product is a "new **drug**." See United States v. X-Otag Plus Tablets, 441 F.Supp. 105, 111 (D.Colo.1977) (citing cases). Furthermore, the evidence shows that differences in excipients may impair the safety or effectiveness of a **drug** product even though its active ingredient is generally recognized as safe and effective. For example, the coating of a tablet used to treat acute conditions may dissolve so slowly that the active ingredient does not reach the site of its intended action in time to do any good. For all these reasons, the Court must reject the view that the term "new **drug**" denotes only active ingredients. Cf. United States v. Articles of Drug (Lannett Co.), 585 F.2d 575, 582–83 (3d Cir. 1978). Premo Pharmaceutical Laboratories, Inc. v. U.S., 475 F.Supp. 52, 54–55 (S.D.N.Y.1979), reversed 629 F.2d 795 (2d Cir. 1980).

In its instructions to the jury, the trial court used the phrase "depressant or stimulant **drug**." The appellant argues that the Comprehensive Drug Abuse and Control Act went into effect on October 27, 1970, approximately three months before the offenses in question here, and that Act used the phrase "depressant or stimulant substance," thus making the trial court's use of the term "**drug**" erroneous. . . .

Upon examining both section 321(v) [of title 21 U.S.C.] and the new Comprehensive Drug Abuse and Control Act, we are convinced that there was no error in the use of the term "**drug**" instead of "substance." Both statutes use the terms interchangeably in various contexts, and the court's use of "**drug**" rather than "substance" was not reversible error. U.S. v. Schrenzel, 462 F.2d 765, 771–2 (8th Cir. 1972).

Other Authorities: Norville v. Miss. State Medical Ass'n, 364 So.2d 1084 (Miss.1978); People v. Privitera, 153 Cal.Rptr. 431, 434–5 (Cal.1979); Palumbere v. Travelers Inc. Co., 404 N.Y.S.2d 939, 940 (Dist.Ct.Suffolk Cty.1976); Hardt v. Board of Naturopathic Examiners, 606 P.2d 1169, 1170 (Ct.App.Or. 1980); Nutrilab, Inc. v. Schweiker, 713 F.2d 335, 336 (7th Cir. 1983); Pharmadyne Laboratories, Inc. v. Kennedy, 466 F.Supp. 100, 103–4 (D.N.J.1979); Millet, Pit & Seed Co., Inc. v. U.S., 436 F.Supp. 84, 89 (E.D.Tenn.1977); U. S. v. Bacto-Unidisk, 394 U.S. 784, 789, 800 (1969).

drug abuse See *abuse; dependence; drug, dangerous; and drug, habit forming.*

drug, dangerous See *drug, habit-forming* (Hoffman-La Roche, Inc. case).

"Sec. 2. For the purposes of this Act:

"(a) The term '**dangerous drug**' means any drug or device unsafe for self-medication, except preparations of drugs defined in Subdivisions (a)(6), (a)(7), (a)(9), and (a)(10) hereof, designed for the purpose of feeding or treating animals (other than man) or poultry, and so labeled, and includes the following:

"(1) Any barbiturate or its compounds, mixtures or preparations. Barbiturate includes barbituric acide derivatives or any salt of a derivative of barbituric acid."

Other than as above shown, the term "barbiturate" was not defined in Article 726d. [V.A.P.C.] Lapp v. State, 519 S.W.2d 443, 446 (Ct.Crim.App.Tex.1975).

Section 220.00(4) of the Penal Law defines a **dangerous drug** as "any narcotic drug, depressant or stimulant drug, or hallucinogenic drug." People v. Einhorn, 346 N.Y.S.2d 986, 991 (Sup.Ct.Spec.Narcotics, N.Y.Cty.1973).

drug, depressant

Section 3371(1) of the Public Health Law defines "**depressant** or stimulant **drugs**", setting forth the qualities the Commission-

er must find present before he can classify the drug pursuant to the authority vested in him by Section 3372 of the Public Health Law. People v. Einhorn, 346 N.Y.S.2d 986, 991 (Sup. Ct.Spec.Narcotics, N.Y.Cty.1973).

drug, ethical

"**Ethical Drug**" means a drug sold on the prescription of a physician. U.S. v. Ciba Geigy Corp., 508 F.Supp. 1118, 1121 (D.N.J.1976).

drug, fixed combination

A **fixed combination drug** is one which combines "two or more drugs . . . in a single dosage form" intended for "concurrent therapy." Sterling Drug. Inc. v. Weinberger, 503 F.2d 675, 680 (2d Cir.1974).

drug, habit-forming any drug, such as alcohol, tobacco, morphine, cocaine, opium, that produces dependence, whether physical or psychic.

Drug abuse today involves not only the narcotic drugs and marihuana, but to an increasingly alarming extent other drugs such as the barbiturates, the amphetamines and even certain of the "tranquilizers." This latter group will be referred to in this report as the "dangerous drugs." Hoffman-La Roche, Inc. v. Kleindienst, 478 F.2d 1, 4 (3d Cir. 1973).

drug, hallucinogenic See *hallucinogen.*

(2) **Hallucinogenic drug.** Any drug which contains any quantity of stramonium, mescaline or peyote, lysergic acid dielhylomide and psilocybin, or any salts or derivative or compounds of any preparations or mixtures thereof. [V.I.Code, Title 20 § 493.] Government of Virgin Islands v. Brown, 571 F.2d 773, 775 (3d Cir. 1978).

drug, hypnotic

Tranquilizers and **hypnotic drugs** operate upon different levels of the brain. A **hypnotic drug** will induce sleep because it operates upon the area of the brain that controls thought process and consciousness. An individual under the influence of a **hypnotic drug** is rendered unconscious. A tranquilizer, on the other hand, does not operate upon the areas of the brain that control consciousness, but upon the areas of the brain that control the reactions of a conscious individual to his environment. Tranquilizers produce sleep by removing the anxiety or worry that is keeping the individual awake. He is then enabled to go to sleep. However, he can be roused from that sleep and will behave in a conscious manner, despite the fact that he is still under the influence of the drug. The drug is still having the effect of removing the normal anxiety or worry reactions the individual would have to his environment. With a **hypnotic drug**, on the other hand, the fact that the individual is conscious indicates that he is no longer under the influence of the drug. In Re Cameron, 439 P.2d 633, 641 (Cal.1968).

drug, investigational See *chymopapain* (Gaston case).

When this operation was discussed with the plaintiff, chymopapain had not been approved for general use by the Food and Drug Administration. However, the drug could be distributed to selected physician investigators as an "**investigational**" drug. Because an **investigational drug** is still in the clinical testing phase, the investigators using the drug had to operate under close supervision of the drug's sponsor (manufacturer) and had to carefully monitor the results experienced in using the drug. Gaston v. Hunter, 588 P.2d 326, 330 (Ct. App.Ariz.1978).

drug, multiple-source

A "multiple-source drug" is a "drug marketed or sold by two or more formulators or labelers or a drug marketed or sold by the same formulator or labeler under two or more different proprietary names or both under a proprietary name and without such a name." 45 C.F.R. § 19.2(d). For example, the antibiotic ampicillin trihydrate is sold under a variety of trademarked brand names, including Amcill and Totacillin. American Medical Ass'n v. Mathews, 429 F.Supp. 1179, 1186 (N.D.Ill. 1977).

drug, narcotic See *narcotic*; and *drug, habit-forming*.

(3) **Narcotic drug.** Any drug which contains any quantity of opium, coca leaves, marihuana (cannabis, sativa), pethidine (isonipecaine, meperidine), and opiates or their compound, manufacture, salt, alkaloid, or derivative, and every substance neither chemically nor physically distinguishable from them and exempted and excepted preparations containing such drugs or their derivatives, by whatever trade name identified and whether produced directly or indirectly by extraction from substances of vegetable origin, or independently by means of chemical synthesis, as the same are designated in the federal narcotic laws and as found by the Commissioner of Health pursuant to the authority vested in him under section 591(10) of Title 19 of the Virgin Islands Code. [VI Code, Title 20, § 493.] Government of Virgin Islands v. Brown, 571 F.2d 773, 775–6 (3d Cir. 1978).

The statutory definition of a **narcotic drug** is contained in 21 U.S.C. § 802(16), which provides in relevant part:

The term "**narcotic drug**" means any of the following, whether produced directly or indirectly by the extraction from substances of vegetable origin, or independently by means of chemical synthesis, or by a combination of extraction and chemical synthesis:

(A) Opium, coca leaves, and opiates.

(B) A compound, manufacture, salt, derivative, or preparation of opium, coca leaves, or opiates.

(C) A substance . . . which is chemically identical with any of the substances referred to in clause (A) or (B).

Such term does not include decocainized coca leaves or extracts of coca leaves, which extracts do not contain cocaine or ecgonine. U.S. v. Castro, 401 F.Supp. 120, 122–3 (N.D.Ill. 1975).

drug, new See *drug* (Premo Pharmaceutical Laboratories, Inc. case).

A "**new drug**" is defined as: "Any drug the composition of which is such that such drug is not generally recognized, among experts qualified by scientific training and experience to evaluate the safety of drugs, as safe for use under the conditions prescribed, recommended, or suggested in the labeling thereof" (Federal Food, Drug, and Cosmetic Act, ch. 675, § 201, subd. [p], par. [1], 52 Stat. 1040, 1041–1042 [current version at U.S.Code, tit. 21, § 321, subd. (p), par. (1)]). Bichler v. Eli Lilly & Co., 436 N.E.2d 182–3 (N.Y.1982).

Before a manufacturer can legally market a **new drug** [1] in interstate commerce, the Food and Drug Administration (FDA) must approve a New Drug Application (NDA) for that drug.[2] An NDA must contain extensive data concerning the drug and its intended use, including full reports of pre-clinical and clinical investigations, adverse reaction reports, and published articles on the use or effectiveness of the drug.[3] [[1] A "**new drug**" is defined, in part, as: Any drug . . . the composition of which is such that such drug is not generally recognized, among experts qualified by scientific training and experience to evaluate the safety and effectiveness of drugs, as safe and effective for use under the conditions prescribed, recommended, or suggested in the labeling thereof. . . . 21 U.S.C. § 321(p)(1) (1976). This includes a drug currently on the market if it is proposed that it be used for a "new" purpose. [2] 21 U.S.C. § 355 (1976). [3] 21 C.F.R. § 314.1 (1982).] Webb v. Dep't of Health and Human Services, 696 F.2d 101–2 (D.C.Cir.1982).

Moreover, pursuant to promulgated regulations the Secretary has declared pursuant to 21 C.F.R. § 310.3(h)(5) that the newness of a drug may arise from "[t]he newness of a dosage, or method or duration of administration or application, or other condition of use prescribed, recommended, or suggested in the labeling of such drug, even though such drug when used in other dosage, or other method or duration of administration or application, or different condition, is not a **new drug**." Here phenytoin in single dosage form is generally recognized as safe and effective. However, phenytoin in time release capsules is not so recognized and under this definition, claimant's drug would have to be classified as a **new drug**. U.S. v. Articles of Drug Labeled Colchicine, 442 F.Supp. 1236, 1243 (S.D.N.Y.1978).

Other Authorities: Premo Pharmaceutical Laboratories, Inc. v. U.S., 475 F.Supp. 52–3, 55–6 (S.D.N.Y.1979); DeMarco v. Com. Dep't of Health, 397 A.2d 61, 63 (Cmwlth.Ct.Pa.1979); USV Pharmaceutical Corp. v. Weinberger, 412 U.S. 655, 660, 93 S.Ct. 2498, 37 L.Ed.2d 244 (1973); U.S. v. 1,048,000 Capsules, More or Less, "Afrodex", 494 F.2d 1158–60 (5th Cir. 1974).

drug, new animal

If a product is a **new animal drug** within the meaning of 21 U.S.C. § 321(w), it may not be sold until a new drug application has been approved. Section 321(w)(1) provides:

The term "**new animal drug**" means any drug intended for use for animals other than man . . . the composition of which is such that such drug is not generally recognized, among experts qualified by scientific training and experience to evaluate the safety and effectiveness of animal drugs, as safe and effective for use under the conditions prescribed, recommended, or suggested in the labeling thereof. U.S. v. Naremco, Inc., 553 F.2d 1138, 1141 (8th Cir. 1977).

drug, non-prescription See *drug, over-the-counter*.

drug, over-the-counter

In our view, the duty of the manufacturer explicitly to warn consumers of the specific risks of **over-the-counter drug** use derives from the basic marketing predicate of the **over-the-counter drug** industry, namely, that nonprescription drugs are purchased by consumers for the purpose of self-medication typically without any intended or actual intervention by a physician. . . .

. . . And in Dunkin v. Syntex Laboratories, Inc., supra, the court again emphasized the prescription/nonprescription dichotomy, observing that the rule relieving the manufacturer of the obligation to warn the consumer "would not apply in a case involving **over-the-counter drugs**." Again, in Pierluisi v. E. R. Squibb & Sons, Inc., 440 F.Supp. 691, 695 (D.Puerto Rico 1977), another prescription drug case, the court noted that "The emphasis of the doctrine [that a manufacturer's duty is to warn the attending physician and not the lay public] is carefully limited to prescription drugs.... An entirely different rule would be applicable in connection with drugs sold over the counter to anyone who asks for them." Torsiello v. Whitehall Laboratories, 398 A.2d 132, 137–9 (Super.Ct.N.J.1979).

But the **over-the-counter (OTC) drugs**, known as the proprietaries, are often made up of old, established ingredients. Such products, coming on the market for the first time between 1938 and 1962, might never have been subject to new drug regulation. If so, they would be entitled to the exemption provided by § 107(c)(4). USV Pharmaceutical Corp. v. Weinberger, 412 U.S. 655, 665, 93 S.Ct. 2498, 37 L.Ed.2d 244 (1973).

drug paraphernalia See *paraphernalia, drug.*

drug, prescribed See *drug, prescription*; and *prescription.*

drug, prescription

Prescription drugs, as defined by § 503(b), 21 U.S.C. § 353(b), include any drug for human use which (A) is habit forming; (B) "because of its toxicity or other potentiality for harmful effect, or the method of its use, or the collateral measures necessary to its use, is not safe for use except under the supervision of a practitioner licensed by law to administer such drug"; or (C) is limited to prescription use in the application under § 505. USV Pharmaceutical Corp. v. Weinberger, 412 U.S. 655, 665, 93 S.Ct. 2498, 37 L.Ed.2d 244 (1973).

Reyes v. Wyeth Laboratories, 498 F.2d 1264 (5th Cir.), cert. denied, 419 U.S. 1096, 95 S.Ct. 687, 42 L.Ed.2d 688 (1974) (characterizing the special standard as an exception to the restatement general rule). The rationale is explained in Reyes as follows

Prescription drugs are likely to be complex medicines, esoteric in formula and varied in effect. As a medical expert, the prescribing physician can take into account the propensities of the drug, as well as the susceptibilities of his patient. His is the task of weighing the benefits of any medication against its potential dangers. The choice he makes is an informed one, an individualized medical judgment bottomed on a knowledge of both patient and palliative. Pharmaceutical companies then, who must warn ultimate purchasers of dangers inherent in patent drugs sold over the counter, in selling **prescription drugs** are required to warn only the prescribing physician, who acts as a "learned intermediary" between manufacturer and consumer.

... Chapters 458, 465 and 500, Florida Statutes, evidences legislated public policy to rely on physicians and pharmacists to protect the consuming public from injury by product use when the product is a **prescription drug**. See, e.g., §§ 500.02(1) and 500.151, Fla.Stat. (1979). Buckner v. Allergan Pharmaceuticals, 400 So.2d 820–2 (Dist.Ct.App.Fla. 1981).

drug product See *product, drug.*

drug, safe

"The word '**safe**,' as used in the definition [in what is now section 503(b)(1)(B)], is intended to have its ordinary [of the Federal Food, Drug and Cosmetic Act] meaning. For example, non-toxic drugs like quinidine sulfate, intended for heart disease, or penicillin, for infections, are not **safe** for self-medication because their unsupervised use may indirectly cause injury or death." S.Rep.No.946, 82d Cong., 1st Sess. 4 (1951), U.S. Code Cong. & Admin. News 1951, p. 2454....

... If, in attempting to evaluate a drug, a court were to consider every contingency and take account of the immaturity or stupidity of every potential user, it would not be paying heed to the Committee's desire that it give to the word "**safe**" the ordinary meaning. U.S. v. Article of Drug Labeled Decholin, 264 F.Supp. 473, 479–80 (E.D.Mich.1967).

drug, stimulant

Stimulant drug. Any drug which contains any quantity of amphetamine or any of its optical isomers; any salt of amphetamine or any salt of an optical isomer of amphetamine; or any substance which the Commissioner of Health, after investigation, has found to be, and by regulation designated as, habit forming because of its stimulant effect of the central nervous system. [V.I.Code, Title 20 § 493.] Government of Virgin Islands v. Brown, 571 F.2d 773, 776 (3d Cir. 1978).

drug, stimulant See *depressant* (Sundberg case).

drug store See *pharmacy.*

drugless practitioner See *naturopathy.*

dry socket See *socket, dry.*

DTR deep tendon reflex See *reflex, deep*; and *reflex, tendon.*

duct (dukt) [L. *ductus*, from *ducere* to draw or lead] a passage with well-defined walls, especially a tube for the passage of excretions or secretions; called also *ductus* [NA].

duct, common bile See *ductus, choledochus.*

duct, cystic See *ductus, cysticus.*

duct, hepatic See *ductus, choledochus.*

ductus (duk'tus), pl. *duc'tus* [L.] [NA] a duct: a general term for a passage with well defined walls, especially such a channel for the passage of excretions or secretions.

ductus arteriosus [NA], arterial duct: a fetal blood vessel connecting the pulmonary artery directly to the descending aorta; called also *arterial canal, Botallo's duct,* and *pulmoaortic canal.*

ductus arteriosus, patent abnormal persistence of an open lumen in the ductus arteriosus after birth, the direction of flow being from the aorta to the pulmonary artery, resulting in recirculation of arterial blood through the lungs.

The possibility of a **patent ductus arteriosis**, a congenital anomaly resulting in the recirculation of arterial blood to the lungs, was apparently never considered. Phillips v. U.S., 566 F.Supp. 1, 9 (D.S.Car.1981).

Although not directly relevant to his "wrongful life" claim, plaintiff's complaint also asserts a distinct cause of action for medical malpractice against defendant's employees at CNRMC based on their alleged failure to diagnose and treat a cardiac disorder in the newborn plaintiff known as "**patent ductus arteriosus**." Phillips v. U.S., 508 F.Supp. 537, 540 (D.S. Car. 1980).

ductus choledochus [NA], choledochous duct: the duct formed by union of the common hepatic and the cystic duct which empties into the duodenum at the major duodenal papilla, along with the pancreatic duct; called also *common bile duct, hepatic funiculus,* and *hepatocystic duct.*

First, plaintiff can undergo further surgery to try to repair the damage from the severance of the **bile duct**, or he can continue on his present course, which entails continuing dosage of antibiotics in an effort to control the abdominal infection caused in large part by bile flowing into the stomach due to the suturing of one end of the severed **bile duct** too close to the stomach. Overstreet v. U.S., 528 F.Supp. 838, 841 (M.D. Ala. 1981).

During the course of the surgery, it was determined that a stone was lodged in the distal part of the **common bile duct**. The stone was removed during the surgery. Bruney v. City of Lake Charles, 386 So.2d 950–1 (Ct.App.La. 1980).

It was explained by Dr. Bronwell that the liver is divided into the right and left lobes from which come the right and left hepatic ducts. These ducts go to join the **common duct** which takes bile generated by the liver to the duodenum. From its juncture with the **common duct**, the cystic duct leads a few centimeters to the gall bladder and exists to carry bile in and out of the gall bladder. It is, the doctor acknowledged, important to identify the common duct in order to perform gall bladder surgery safely....

The evidence shows that an anatomically normal **common bile duct** extends from the left and right hepatic ducts to the duodenum, is in a vertical position and is approximately three to four inches long. The gall bladder is partially embedded into the liver. The cystic duct extends from the neck of the gall bladder to the **common duct**. The cystic duct and the **common duct** join to form a tee, i.e., y-shaped (y) configuration. Bronwell v. Williams, 597 S.W.2d 542, 544, 549 (Ct.Civ.App. Tex. 1980).

Other Authorities: Yerzy v. Levine, 260 A.2d 533–4, 537 (Super.Ct.N.J. 1970).

ductus cysticus [NA], cystic duct: the passage connecting the neck of the gallbladder and the common bile duct; called also *duct of gallbladder.*

During the course of the removal of the gall bladder he "dissected out" the **cystic duct**, i.e., it was ligated in two places and then cut in-between, so as to sever the gall bladder from it. The operation did not call for surgery of the common duct, which was beyond, and at the other end of the **cystic duct**. While Dr. Levine denied severing it, he conceded that "apparently it must have happened" at the time of his operation....

When Mrs. Yerzy questioned defendant he attributed the unusual, heavy bile drainage to a loosening of a suture at the **cystic duct**, and suggested that plaintiff "wait and see, per-

haps nature will take care of it and it will close up by itself." He told her this notwithstanding that he had never seen a suture loosen at the **cystic duct**. Yerzy v. Levine, 260 A.2d 533–4 (Super.Ct.N.J. 1970).

ductus deferens [NA], deferent duct: the excretory duct of the testis, which unites with the excretory duct of the seminal vesicle to form the ejaculatory duct; called also *vas deferens, excretory duct of testis, spermatis duct,* and *testicular duct.*

The ... "Vasectomy General Information" form states that there would be excision of a small piece of each of the sperm tubes. The hospital record noted, "Patient underwent bilateral vasectomy and one of the segments was lost by the laboratory personnel and only one segment of vas was sent for histologic examination." A further hospital note states, "**Vas deferens**— only one **vas deferens** presented.—Two vas sections not presented." Maggard v. McKelvey, 627 S.W.2d 44, 48 (Ct.App. Ky. 1981).

ductus paramesonephricus [NA], paramesonephric duct: either of the paired embryonic ducts arising as a peritoneal pocket, extending caudally to join the urogenital sinus, and developing into uterine tubes, uterus, and vagina in the female and into a vestigial structure (appendix testis) in the male. Called also *d. Muelleri, duct of Müller* or *müllerian duct,* and *gasserian* or *primordial duct.*

From the hospital records, her final diagnosis after surgical removal of her uterus was that she was suffering with a **mullerian tumor** (Carcinosarcoma) with probable vascular invasion. Sullivan v. Henry, 287 S.E.2d 652, 654 (Ct.App.Ga. 1982).

dumping syndrome See *syndrome, dumping.*

duodenal bulb See *pars superior duodeni.*

duodenal cap See *pars superior duodeni.*

duodenal stump blowout See *duodenum* (Franz case).

duodenitis (du"od-ĕ-ni'tis) inflammation of the duodenal mucosa.

A hiatal hernia and **duodenitis** (inflammation of the duodenum) were also diagnosed. McClaflin v. Califano, 448 F.Supp. 69, 71 (D.Kan. 1978).

duodenum (du"o-de'num, du-od'ĕ-num) [L. *duode'ni* twelve at a time] [NA] the first or proximal portion of the small intestine, extending from the pylorus to the jejunum; so called because it is about 12 fingerbreadths in length.

When Olivet arrived he noticed the patient was stuporous and had a distended abdomen. At some point Franz arrived. X-rays were taken. The patient began to complain of left-shoulder pain, a symptom characteristic of rupture of the sutured duodenal stem (a "duodenal stump blowout"). X-rays confirmed that catastrophic diagnosis....

The postoperative report notes that the stump of the **duodenum**, sutured by Ali on October 7, had ripped open, spilling stomach contents into the peritoneum. Olivet resutured the stump but apparently made no thorough effort to drain and sterilize the peritoneal cavity. Franz v. Board of Medical Quality Assur., 181 Cal.Rptr. 732 (Cal. 1982).

Dr. Claude Craighead, the general surgeon who removed the reamer from Mrs. Dufrene's **duodenum** by a 3 to 4 inch surgical incision, testified that her post-operative recovery period was normal and there were no complications from the surgery. Dr. Craighead stated that following such an operation a patient should be able to return to heavy work in about six weeks. Dufrene v. Faget, 260 So.2d 76, 81 (Ct.App.La.1972).

dura See *dura mater.*

dura mater (du'rah ma'ter) [L. "hard mother"] the outermost, toughest, and most fibrous of the three membranes (meninges) covering the brain and spinal cord; called also *pachymeninx.*

It was the radiologist's opinion, based on the tests, that Mr. Dixon had a subdural hematoma—bleeding inside the skull beneath the **dura mater**, the outermost of three membranes covering the brain. Schackow v. Medical-Legal Consulting, etc., 416 A.2d 1303, 1305 (Ct.Spec.App.Md.1980).

In suturing the wound, Dr. Spence attempted to relieve the pressure on the spinal cord by enlarging the **dura**—the outer protective wall of the spinal cord—at the area of swelling. Canterbury v. Spence, 464 F.2d 772, 777 (D.C.Cir.1972).

The pressure resulting from the ruptured disc is called "extra dura pressure" ("**dura**" is the outer covering of the nerve tissues). Hart v. Van Zandt, 399 S.W.2d 791, 795 (Tex.1965). **Other Authorities:** Larkin v. State, 446 N.Y.S.2d 818–19 (4th Dep't 1982).

dural See *dura mater.*

dwarf (dwarf) an abnormally undersized person.

dwarf, psychosocial

Dr. Dorothy Becker, a pediatrician and endocrinologist with a special expertise in **psychosocial dwarfism**, next testified. According to Dr. Becker, **psychosocial dwarfism** is a relatively new diagnosis first identified in 1963 when children presented "what looked like clinical and chemical growth deficiency. These children were tested, were going to be put onto growth hormones and while awaiting therapy in a convalescent home were found to grow faster than any normal child, and it was later confirmed that children with certain specific history, family history, and certain specific physical features fitted this diagnosis which goes by a number of different names [including emotional deprivation].[2] These children have been found to have poor growth physically, and ... mentally in their own home environment, and when they are removed from this home environment have spontaneous improvement in both physical, mental, and emotional development without any intervention medically, frequently without any psychological intervention.... [T]hese children seem to react to their environmental situation which is not necessarily one of deprivation. There is still not a consensus of opinion in the medical world ... whether this syndrome is related to malnutrition....'' Dr. Becker testified that excessive stress on the children appears to cause certain biochemical changes, one of which is that the growth hormone "just switches off." Another classical feature of the syndrome is an abnormally high fat content in the blood. Dr. Becker agreed that a diagnosis of **psychosocial dwarfism** necessarily means that the home environment is unsatisfactory to the child and not adequate for the child's proper care.

Dr. Becker testified that in order to attain "anything near normal growth," either mental or physical, a child must grow faster than normal until he attains at least the minimum limit for normal. This faster growth is called "catch up growth." In her study of 35 children diagnosed **psychosocial dwarves**, Dr. Becker found that only 1 of the 35 attained any degree of catch up growth while in his own home. Of the remaining 34 children, none achieved or maintained catch up growth in the natural home despite psychological and psychiatric intervention. When placed in a foster home or similar setting, 5 children achieved catch up physical growth, and "most" experienced catch up mental growth. While all the children in the study under 10 years old caught up in growth, not all those over 10 years old did. When they reached the lowest limit of normal height for their age, the children returned to their natural home. There they maintained only normal growth despite psychological and other intervention. [[2] See, e.g., Powell, Brasel, and Blizzard, "Emotional Deprivation and Growth Retardation Simulating Idiopathic Hypopituitarism," 276 New Eng.J.Med. 1271 (1967).] In Interest of Parnishek, 408 A.2d 872, 874 (Super.Ct.Pa.1979).

dwarfism (dwarf'izm) the state of being a dwarf; underdevelopment of body.

dye (di) any of various colored substances that contain auxochromes and thus are capable of coloring substances to which they are applied; used for staining and coloring, as test reagents, and as therapeutic agents in medicine. See also *Pantopague.*

Dymelor (di'mĕ-lor) trademark for a preparation of acetohexamide. See also *acetohexamide.*

dynamometer (di"nah-mom'ĕ-ter) [*dynamo-* + Gr. *metron* measure] an instrument for measuring the force of muscular contraction.

They testified that the employee was not making a proper effort with his right hand when being tested on the **dynamometer**, the device used for testing grasping strength. Liberty Mut. Ins. Co. v. Industrial Accident Commission, 199 P.2d 302, 304 (Cal.1948).

dyscrasia (dis-kra'ze-ah) [Gr. *dyskrasia* bad temperament] a term formerly used to indicate a depraved state of the humors, now used generally to indicate a morbid condition, especially one which involves an imbalance of component elements.

dyscrasia, blood any abnormal or pathological condition of the blood.

In 1971, two years before Butazolidin was prescribed for appellant, the FDA required Ciba to modify its prescribing information for the drug and to include a new section on "warnings" which referred, for the first time, to "serious, even fatal **blood dyscrasias**," (aplastic anemia is a form of this disease and added over thirty entries to the list of adverse reactions. Baldino v. Castagna, 454 A.2d 1012, 1015 (Super.Ct.Pa. 1982), order reversed 478 A.2d 807.

"... Warning—Serious and even fatal **blood dyscrasias** (aplastic anemia, hypoplastic anemia, thrombocytopenia, granulocytopenia) are known to occur after the administration of chloramphenicol...." Salmon v. Parke, Davis & Co., 520 F.2d 1359, 1361 (4th Cir. 1975).

Prior to and during the period that Chloromycetin was prescribed for Mary Ann the following language appeared on the immediate container and the outer carton:

"WARNING—**Blood dyscrasias** [disorders] may be associated with intermittent or prolonged use. It is essential that adequate blood studies be made." Incollingo v. Ewing, 282 A.2d 206, 212 (Pa.1971).

Other Authorities: Stevens v. Parke, Davis & Co., 507 P.2d 653, 656 (Cal.1973).

dysesthesia (dis"es-the'ze-ah) [*dys-* + Gr. *aisthēsis* perception] impairment of any sense, especially of that of touch.

Dr. Nicholas Georgiade testified that he examined plaintiff on 8 August 1977 and that in his opinion, plaintiff had a subjective **dysesthesia** consistent with the branches of the nerves of the jawbone. He felt that the plaintiff's delayed perception of the altered sensation was incompatible with the existence of neuroma and that, in his opinion, the incision made by defendant on the left side of plaintiff's mouth could not have damaged the inferior alveolar nerve on that side.

Dr. John Angelillo corroborated the opinion of Dr. Georgiade to the effect that the delay in the onset of the **dysesthesia** is not compatible with nerve injury at the time of plaintiff's injection. Cozart v. Chapin, 251 S.E.2d 682, 684 (Ct. App.N.Car.1979).

dysfunction (dis-funk'shun) disturbance, impairment, or abnormality of the functioning of an organ.

dysfunction, cerebellar

Cerebellar dysfunction refers to a nervous system dysfunction in the cerebellum of the brain characterized by tremor in the upper extremities of the body and ataxia of the lower extremities. Giant Food, Inc. v. Coffey, 451 A.2d 151, 154 (Ct.Spec. App.Md.1982).

dysfunction, cortical See *cortex, cerebral.*

He stated that the second EEG still showed abnormality bilaterally representing "**cortical dysfunction** of a diffuse nature." The neurosurgeon further testified:

[W]hat we are losing here is the higher integrated functions: thinking, mentation, understanding, recognition of a hazardous situation, how long he can hold out, how good your arithmetic is, how well you can balance your checkbook, how much you understand what you read in the paper ... how much mentality is left....

... To me the abnormal EEG suggest that some of the mental changes and reduced capabilities can be attributable to the accident and the subsequent blood clot. Wages v. Snell, 360 So.2d 807–9 (Dist.Ct.App.Fla.1978).

dysfunction, severe cognitive

Social or **cognitive dysfunction** is "severe" if it affects the quality of the worker's personal, nonvocational life in significant activity comparably to the loss of two members or sight of both eyes, and is incurable if it is unlikely that normal functioning can be restored....

... Thus, we must reaffirm the requirement that **severe social or cognitive dysfunction** is that which "affects the quality of

the worker's personal, nonvocational life in significant activity comparably, to the loss of two members or sight of both eyes". Redfern, supra, p. 85, 268 N.W.2d 28. Modreski v. Gen. Motors Corp., Fisher Body, 337 N.W.2d 231, 234, 236–7 (Mich.1983).

dysgenics (dis-jen'iks) [*dys-* + Gr. *gennan* to produce] the study of racial deterioration. Cf. *eugenics.*

dyskinesia (dis"ki-ne'ze-ah) [Gr. *dyskinēsia* difficulty of moving] impairment of the power of voluntary movement, resulting in fragmentary or incomplete movements.

dyskinesia tarda; dyskinesia, tardive a form marked typically by involuntary repetitive movements of the facial, buccal, oral, and cervical musculature, affecting chiefly the elderly; it is induced by long-term administration of neuroleptic (antipsychotic) agents and may persist after withdrawal of the agent.

The one factor which must be considered is the possible irreversible damage that can sometime be caused by the use of extraparamidal drugs. The irreversible damage of the extraparamidal seizures especially that of **tardive dyskinesia** must be considered and must be observed for in the future. Chabert v. City of Westwego Police Pension, 423 So.2d 1190, 1195 (Ct. of App.La.1982).

From 1970 until 1975, Timothy received a myriad of different tranquilizers, administered in various combinations, under the auspices of several different physicians. In 1975, Timothy was diagnosed as suffering from **tardive dyskinesia**, a disease allegedly caused by long-term use of major tranquilizers. Symptoms of **tardive dyskinesia** include grimacing, chewing, tongue moving, blinking and abnormal movements of the limbs. Clites v. State, 322 N.W.2d 917–18 (Ct.App.Iowa 1982).

A potential permanent side effect of prolixin and other antipsychotic medication is **tardive dyskinesia**. **Tardive dyskinesia** is characterized by rhythmical, repetitive, involuntary movements of the tongue, face, mouth, or jaw, sometimes accompanied by other bizarre muscular activity.... The risk of this disorder is greatest in elderly patients, especially women, and is associated with prolonged use. Rennie v. Klein, 462 F.Supp. 1131, 1138 (D.N.J.1978).

dyslexia (dis-lek'se-ah) [*dys-* + Gr. *lexis* diction] an inability to read understandingly, due to a central lesion.

In Matter of Kirkpatrick, 77 Misc.2d 646, 354 N.Y.S.2d 499, congenital learning disabilities of **dislexia** and disagraphia were intertwined with an emotional problem.... In Matter of Jessup, 379 N.Y.S.2d 626, 633 (Fam.Ct.N.Y.Cty.1975).

dysnomia (dis-no'me-ah) [*dys-* + Gr. *onoma* name] partial nominal aphasia; cf. *anomia.*

dysphoria (dis-fo're-ah) [Gr. "excessive pain, anguish, agitation"] disquiet; restlessness; malaise.

dysphoria, gender

It is our finding that [J.D.] suffers from severe **gender dysphoria** and that she will never make an adequate adjustment to life in the male role. J.D. v. Lackner, 145 Cal.Rptr. 570, 571 (Ct.App. Cal.1978).

dysplasia (dis-pla'se-ah) [*dys-* + Gr. *plassein* to form] abnormality of development; in pathology, alteration in size, shape, and organization of adult cells.

dysplasia, fibrous (of bone) a disease of bone marked by thinning of the cortex and replacement of bone marrow by gritty fibrous tissue containing bony spicules, producing pain, disability, and gradually increasing deformity. Only one bone may be involved (*monostotic fibrous d.*), with the process later affecting several or many bones (*polyostotic fibrous d.*). When associated with melanotic pigmentation of the skin and endocrine disorders, it is known as *Albright's syndrome.*

Dr. Blair had X-rays of Mr. Gramlich's left femur and pelvic area taken during the course of treatment. On March 3, 1977, Dr. Egan took X-rays of the areas involved at St. Luke's Hospital. His diagnosis was probable **fibrous dysplasia**. . . .

. . . In addition to the conclusions reached in the former X-rays, Dr. Mell diagnosed additional underlying bony abnormality, presumably **fibrous dysplasia**, with considerable proliferation of callus in the area. Gramlich v. Travelers Ins. Co., 640 S.W.2d 180, 182 (Mo.Ct.App.1982).

dysplasia, spondyloepiphyseal a hereditary dysplasia of the vertebrae and extremities resulting in dwarfism of the short-trunk type, often with shortened limbs due to epiphyseal abnormalities. In the delayed onset form, the principal feature is precocious osteoarthritis. There are several forms, including autosomal dominant, autosomal recessive, and X-linked forms, the dominant form often being associated with such ocular anomalies as myopia and detached retina. See also *syndrome, Morquio's.*

She is only four feet seven inches tall due to a type of dwarfism. . . .

. . . She could walk in a fairly normal manner, but there were limitations of back motions. In the doctor's view she suffered from stunted bone growth (**spondylo-epiphyseal dysplasia** of congenital origin). . . . Reading v. Mathews, 542 F.2d 993, 995 (7th Cir. 1976).

dyspnea (disp'ne-ah) [Gr. *dyspnoia* difficulty of breathing] difficult or labored breathing.

When decedent first went to work at the mill in Erwin, he was experiencing no breathing problems. After a few years of working there he began experiencing chest tightness and developed a cough and breathing difficulties. During the years that he farmed, his breathing problems improved. When he subsequently went to work for defendant employer Cone Mills, his chest tightness with cough recurred; and exertional **dyspnea** became a permanent feature of his health. McCall v. Cone Mills Corp., 300 S.E.2d 245–6 (Ct.App.N.Car.1983).

He found her to be suffering from acute asthma, mild wheezing and increasing exertional **dyspnea** (shortness of breath). Dr. Nilsson found her to be allergic to a number of everyday items including dust, feathers, dog and cattle hair, and a number of molds and plants. Palik v. Mathews, 422 F.Supp. 547, 549 (D.Neb.1976).

He said that it was normal for a post-cardiac patient to experience some **dyspnea**—shortness of breath, and occasional chest pains by exerting oneself too much too soon. Barbato v. Alsan Masonry & Concrete, Inc., 318 A.2d 1, 3 (N.J.1974).

Other Authorities: Savage v. Christian Hospital Northwest, 543 F.2d 44, 46 (8th Cir. 1976). Black v. Richardson, 356 F.Supp. 861, 866 (D.S.Car.1973); Magruder v. Richardson, 332 F.Supp. 1363, 1367 (E.D.Mo.1971); Brown v. U.S., 419 F.2d 337, 341 (8th Cir. 1969).

dyspnea, paroxysmal nocturnal a form of respiratory distress related to posture (especially reclining at night) and usually attributed to congestive heart failure with pulmonary edema.

Paroxysmal nocturnal dyspnea is an acute shortness of breath appearing suddenly at night. Dir., Office of Workers' Comp. Programs v. Rowe, 710 F.2d 251, 254 (6th Cir. 1983).

dyspneic (disp-ne'ik) pertaining to or characterized by dyspnea.

The patient has a long history of heavy cigarette usage and has chronic obstructive pulmonary disease with an FEV–1 of only 53 percent confirmed on pulmonary function studies well over one year ago. He becomes **dyspneic** with moderate activity. Wilson v. Schweiker, 553 F.Supp. 728, 732 (E.D.Wash. 1982).

dysrhythmia (dis-rith'me-ah) [*dys-* + Gr. *rhythmos* any regularly recurring motion + *-ia*] disturbance of rhythm, as abnormality of rhythm in speech: *d. pneumophra'sia* is defective breath grouping; *d. proso'dia* is defective placement of stress; *d. to'nia* is defective inflection.

. . . her main complaint being pain in the left side of the head, temporal regions and dizzy spells. She also claimed to have frequent blackouts. An electroencephalogram performed on October 8, 1971, showed **Dysrhythmia**, Grade II, maximized on the left temporal region, notably where the reported headaches occur. Dr. Saavedra's impression was that she had a convulsive disorder.

In a short statement dated January 17, 1972, Dr. Ross, her family physician, said the claimant had epilepsy with frequent seizures and only mild improvement upon medication. Webb v. Weinberger, 371 F.Supp. 793, 796 (N.D.Ind.1974).

dysthanasia See *euthanasia.*

The question before us is whether, and under what circumstances, a surrogate decision can be made on behalf of the patient when he is incompetent to make it himself, where he has been diagnosed as incurably ill, and where the decision relates to the withholding or withdrawal of extraordinary life support medical procedures. The question poses the problem of judicial involvement in passive euthanasia (sometimes called "dysthanasia")—the deliberate withholding or withdrawal of available clinical means for the prolongation of the life of a patient for whom there is little or no hope of recovery or survival. Matter of Storar, 420 N.E.2d 64, 75 (N.Y.1981).

dystocia (dis-to'se-ah) [*dys-* + Gr. *tokos* birth] abnormal labor or childbirth.

dystocia, fetal that which is due to the shape, size, or position of the fetus. See also *dystocia, head.*

dystocia, head

" . . . One of those complications is '**head dystocia**' or a situation which arises when the head is caught in the birth canal after the rest of the body has already been delivered and is free of the body. During such **head dystocia**, the child may be deprived of oxygen and, accordingly, it is most important that corrective action be taken as quickly as possible to free the head....

"... Dr. Dean T. Yamaguchi, the obstetrician making the delivery, admitted in his deposition that the head did, in fact, become 'hung up' but was not sure as to the amount of time in which it became hung up. He states that he called for the assistance of the senior resident, Dr. Sherrod, to apply 'fundal pressure', to help relieve the situation, a technique used to attempt to correct **head dystocia**." Williams v. Lallie Kemp Charity Hosp., 428 So.2d 1000, 1005–6 (Ct.App.La.1983).

dystocia, shoulder

Plaintiffs' expert testified that defendant had improperly used downward traction on the infant plaintiff's head in an attempt to complete delivery after one of the infant's shoulders had become impacted behind the mother's pubic arch, a condition known as **shoulder dystocia**. Mulligan v. Shuter, 419 N.Y.S.2d 13–14 (2d Dep't 1979).

dystrophia See *dystrophy*

dystrophia epithelialis corneae dystrophy of the epithelium of the cornea marked by erosions; called also *Fuchs' dystrophy*.

Plaintiff's condition was diagnosed as **Fuch's dystrophy**, a disease of the cornea which impairs vision. McDermott v. Manhattan Eye, Ear & Throat Hospital, 228 N.Y.S.2d 143, 146 (1st Dep't 1962), modified 203 N.E.2d 469.

dystrophy (dis'tro-fe) [L. *dystrophia*, from *dys-* + Gr. *trephein* to nourish] any disorder arising from defective or faulty nutrition, especially the muscular dystrophies.

dystrophy, Duchenne type muscular See *dystrophy, pseudohypertrophic muscular*.

dystrophy, Fuchs' See *dystrophia epithelialis corneae*.

dystrophy, pseudohypertrophic muscular a chronic progressive disease affecting the shoulder and pelvic girdles, commencing in early childhood. It is characterized by increasing weakness, pseudohypertrophy of the muscles followed by atrophy, lordosis, and a peculiar swaying gait with the legs kept wide apart. The disorder is transmitted as a sex-linked recessive trait, and affected individuals,

predominantly males, rarely survive to maturity; death is usually due to respiratory weakness or heart failure. Called also *Duchenne's muscular d.* or *type*, *Erb's d.* or *paralysis*, *pseudohypertrophic muscular atrophy* or *paralysis*, and *Zimmerlin's d.* or *type*.

... a podiatrist noted that Mark had tight heel cords bilaterally. The podiatrist referred Mark to Dr. Robert Zeller, a specialist in pediatric neurology. Dr. Zeller examined Mark on February 20, 1980 and concluded the child had **Duchenne Muscular Dystrophy**. According to Dr. Zeller, a child may exhibit some clumsiness by two years of age that in retrospect is consistent with this disease, but it is only when the child gets older while continuing to exhibit clumsiness, not attributable to simply being two years of age or learning to walk, that the disease becomes detectable by a trained eye. Nelson v. Krusen, 635 S.W.2d 582, 584 (Ct.App.Tex.1982).

dystrophy, reflex sympathetic a disturbance of the sympathetic nervous system marked by pallor or rubor, pain, sweating, edema, or skin atrophy following sprain, fracture or injury to nerves or blood vessels.

He determined that she had developed **reflex sympathetic dystrophy**, a condition which is triggered by an injury and results in fibrosis of the muscles, stiffness in the joints, pain, and an atrophy of the bone. Zick v. Industrial Com'n, 444 N.E.2d 164, 166 (Ill.1982).

In Lattin, a maintenance worker who had sustained a severe foot injury requiring surgery and resulting in a disability of twenty to thirty percent thereafter was inactive and constantly complained about the pain and throbbing in his foot. Objective medical findings supported his claim of pain and a pain specialist diagnosed Lattin as having a mild to moderate **reflex dystrophy** complicated by rather severe anxiety.... Lattin v. HICA Corporation, 395 So.2d 690 at 693 (La.1981). Culp v. Belden Corp., 432 So.2d 847, 850 (La.1983).

In addition, plaintiff has been diagnosed as suffering from **reflex sympathetic dystrophy**, which causes a drooping of her right shoulder and restricted mobility in that shoulder. Kosch v. Monroe, 433 N.E.2d 1062, 1070 (App.Ct.Ill.1982).

Other Authorities: Lattin v. HICA Corp., 395 So.2d 690, 693 (La.1981); Gretchen v. U.S., 618 F.2d 177, 180 (2d Cir. 1980); State ex rel. Wallace v. Industrial Com'n, 386 N.E.2d 1109, 1111 (Ohio 1979).

E

E. Coli See *Escherichia coli*.

ear (ēr) [L. *auris;* Gr. *ous*] the organ of hearing and of equilibrium, consisting of the external ear, the middle ear, and the internal ear; called also *auris* [NA]. See illustration.

A normal human **ear** can be described as a mechanism which contains three interrelated systems: (a) the outer **ear**; (b) the middle **ear**; and (c) the inner **ear**. Warshaw v. Trans World Airlines, Inc., 442 F.Supp. 400, 402 (E.D.Pa.1977).

ear, external the pinna and external meatus together (auris externa [NA]).

The **outer ear** includes the auricle (the flaps of skin which we commonly think of as the "ear"), and the ear canal, a passage running into the skull. The ear canal terminates at the ear drum, a piece of skin which vibrates as sound waves, (i.e., pressure variations in the atmosphere) strike it. These vibrations can best be characterized as "in-and-out", the ear drum alternately pushing in and bulging out very slightly. Warshaw v. Trans World Airlines, Inc., 442 F.Supp. 400, 402 (E.D.Pa.1977).

236

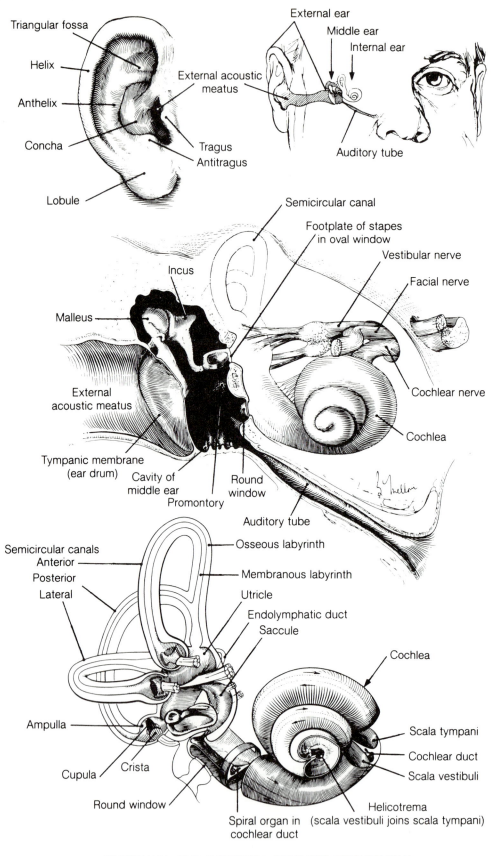

Triangular fossa

Helix

Anthelix

Concha

Lobule

External acoustic meatus

Tragus

Antitragus

External ear

Middle ear

Internal ear

Auditory tube

Semicircular canal

Footplate of stapes in oval window

Vestibular nerve

Facial nerve

Incus

Malleus

External acoustic meatus

Tympanic membrane (ear drum)

Cavity of middle ear

Promontory

Round window

Auditory tube

Cochlear nerve

Cochlea

Semicircular canals
Anterior
Posterior
Lateral

Osseous labyrinth

Membranous labyrinth

Utricle

Endolymphatic duct

Saccule

Cochlea

Ampulla

Cupula

Crista

Round window

Spiral organ in cochlear duct

Scala tympani

Cochlear duct

Scala vestibuli

Helicotrema
(scala vestibuli joins scala tympani)

EXTERNAL AND INTERNAL STRUCTURES OF EAR

ear, inner; ear, internal the labyrinth, comprising the vestibule, cochlea, and semicircular canals (auris interna [NA]).

The **inner ear** contains the cochlea, a fluid-filled labyrinth shaped somewhat like a snail shell, and the endings for the auditory nerves. Movement of the stapes footplate in the oval window sets up pressure waves in the fluid of the **inner ear**. The pressure waves excite the nerve endings, and stimulate electrical currents which the brain recognizes as "sound". Warshaw v. Trans World Airlines, Inc., 442 F.Supp. 400, 402 (E.D.Pa. 1977).

ear, middle the space medial to the tympanic membrane (mesotympanum), the epitympanum, and the hypotympanum; auris media [NA]. It contains the auditory ossicles and connects with the mastoid cells and auditory tubes. Called also *drum, eardrum, tympanic cavity, cavum tympani,* and *tympanum.*

The **middle ear** consists of a chamber in the skull, separated from the outer ear by the ear drum and from the inner ear by two openings called the "oval window" and the "round window". A complex of three tiny bones, the malleus, the incus and the stapes (hammer, anvil, and stirrup), bridge the space between the ear drum and the oval window. Vibrations of the ear drum are multiplied some thirty times in force by the geometry of these tiny bones. The stapes "footplate", a small shaving of bone, sits in the oval window and vibrates in response to the vibrations passed through the three bones from the ear drum to the footplate. The round window is sealed by an elastic membrane that closes off the end of the inner ear (cochlea), which is not sealed by the oval window. The **middle ear** is connected to the pharynx (throat), by the eustachian tube, which permits the pressure inside the ear drum to be equalized to correspond to gross changes in pressure on the outer side of the drum.[2] Ordinarily, swallowing is done four times a minute, at which intervals the eustachian tube permits air to enter into or exit from the **middle ear**, thus equalizing the pressure. Were this not to occur, the ear drum would be pushed either to one side or the other of its normal, centered position, causing pain, possible injury, and perhaps a change in the hearing level. [2 "Gross changes" refer to shifts in pressure which occur, for example, with weather changes, and particularly with variations in altitude or depth. High frequency pressure changes of small magnitude are generally considered to be "sound", and would result in normal vibration of the various parts of the ear which have already been described.] Warshaw v. Trans World Airlines, Inc., 442 F.Supp. 400, 402 (E.D.Pa.1977).

ear, outer See *ear, external.*

ear (specialist) See *otologist;* and *otology.*

The FDA distinguishes between three categories of professionals involved with hearing disabled persons: the "**ear specialist**," a licensed physician specializing in the diagnosis and treatment of ear diseases and hearing loss problems (21 C.F.R. § 801.420(a)(2)).... New Jersey Guild of Hearing Aid D. v. Long, 384 A.2d 795, 801 (N.J.1978).

eardrum (ēr′drum) the middle ear (auris media [NA]).

eardrum, perforated

... that he had great difficulty in hearing, due to a **perforated eardrum**, a condition which eventually necessitated general operations, and that an operation on plaintiff's mastoid cavity left him partially deaf. Chenoweth v. Weinberger, 421 F.Supp. 955, 959 (W.D.Mo.1976).

ecchymosis (ek″ĭ-mo′sis), pl. *ecchymo′ses* [Gr. *ekchymōsis*] a small hemorrhagic spot, larger than a petechia, in the skin or mucous membrane forming a nonelevated, rounded or irregular, blue or purplish patch.

Dr. Goyer examined him around 8:30 a.m., and detected increased swelling, **eccymosis** (spots of blood in the skin) and hemorrhagic bullae (blisters filled with blood). King v. Murphy, 424 So.2d 547–8 (Miss.1982).

Initially his ankles were extremely swollen and **ecchymotic**; consequently immobilization was first applied, with bed rest and elevation of his leg. Scittarelli v. Manson, 447 F.Supp. 279, 281 (D.Conn.1978).

The ankle is diffusely swollen with **ecchymotic** discoloration. Landry v. Offshore Logistics, Inc., 544 F.2d 757, 759 (5th Cir. 1977).

Other Authorities: Bevevino v. Saydjari, 574 F.2d 676, 678 (2d Cir. 1978); McCoy v. McNutt, 227 N.W.2d 219, 220 (Ct. App.Mich.1975).

ecchymotic (ek-ĭ-mot′ik) pertaining to or of the nature of an ecchymosis.

echoencephalogram (ek″o-en-sef′ah-lo-gram″) the record produced by echoencephalography.

echoencephalography (ek″o-en-sef″ah-log′rah-fe) a diagnostic technique in which pulses of ultrasonic waves are beamed through the head from both sides, and echoes from the midline structures of the brain are recorded as graphic tracings; shifts from the midline may indicate a centrally placed mass.

It was on the 10th that the **echoencephalogram** (hereinafter referred to as "echo") was interpreted to show a 4 millimeter shift from left to right of the midline of the brain. The attending physician considered the test results as inconsistent with the clinical findings of Riddlesperger's improvement. Riddlesperger v. U.S., 406 F.Supp. 617, 619 (N.D.Ala.1976).

echogram (ek′o-gram) the record made by echography.

echograph See *echography.*

echography (ĕ-kog′rah-fe) ultrasonography; the use of ultrasound as a diagnostic aid. Ultrasound waves are directed at the tissues, and a record is made, as on an oscilloscope, of the waves reflected back through the tissues, which indicate interfaces of different acoustic densities and thus differentiate between solid and cystic structures.

The results of the gallbladder **echogram** were also normal. Harwell v. Pittman, 428 So.2d 1049, 1051 (Ct.App.La.1983).

Dr. Wild asserted that ... he developed an "**echograph**," a machine with a scanning device that received impulses in much the same way as do radar and sonar pictures, which when properly manipulated translated on a cathode-ray tube (oscilloscope) the presence or absence of cancer in women's breasts. Dr. Wild claimed there is a definite difference between the ultrasonic echo or wave patterns of noncancerous and cancerous tissues. Assuming that early detection is the principal hope to cure cancer, his objective in using "echography" was to discover cancer without the use of surgical procedures and proposed an eventual plan to mass-produce the "echograph" and scan people for cancer throughout the world. Wild v. Rarig, 234 N.W.2d 775, 782 (Minn.1975).

echolalia (ek″o-la′le-ah) [*echo* + Gr. *lalia* speech, babble] the repetition by a patient of words addressed to him; called also *echophrasia*.

"She has a speech disorder which we call perseveration or **echolalia**, that is, she repeats the words she is responding to.... Talcott v. Holl, 224 So.2d 420, 423 (Dist.Ct.App.Fla. 1969).

eclampsia (ĕ-klamp′se-ah) [Gr. *eklampein* to shine forth] convulsions and coma occurring in a pregnant or puerperal woman, associated with preeclampsia, i.e., with hypertension, edema, and/or proteinuria.

... or **even** a death from **eclampsia**. One might consider this in view of the fact that the patient was seen to have a seizure and it is possible from the record that the last blood pressure was indeed quite elevated. Maslonka v. Hermann, 414 A.2d 1350, 1352 (Super.Ct.N.J.1980).

... **eclampsia** of pregnancy (toxemia with convulsions) .... Burwell v. Eastern Air Lines, Inc., 458 F.Supp. 474, 480 (E.D. Va.1978), affirmed in part, reversed in part 633 F.2d 361 (4th Cir. 1980).

Eclampsia is the occurrence of one or more convulsions, not attributable to other cerebral conditions such as epilepsy or cerebral hemorrhage, in a patient with preeclampsia. Sard v. Hardy, 379 A.2d 1014, 1018 (Ct.App.Md.1977).

economic poison See *poison, economic*.

ecotone (ek′o tōn) a transition region where adjacent biomes blend, containing some organisms from each of the adjacent biomes plus some that are characteristic of, and perhaps restricted to, the ecotone; this region tends to have more species and to be more densely populated than either adjacent biome.

Dr. Adams, who conducted the environmental assessment of the proposed development, classifies these wetlands as "dune-marsh **ecotone**." Dr. Adams gives a particularized view of the frequency of flooding in the area in question:

"The dune-marsh **ecotone** is an irregular zone of change from vegetation characterizing high marsh to that typical of dune or sand knoll vegetation. Flooding by salt water occurs only during storms."

Environmental Assessment of the Bald Head Development, Administrative Record, Vol. III, at p. A–11. Conservation Council of North Carolina v. Costanzo, 398 F.Supp. 653, 661–2 (E.D.N.Car.1975).

ECS (electroconvulsive shock) See *shock therapy*, under *therapy*.

E.C.T. (electroconvulsive therapy) See *therapy, electroconvulsive*.

ectopia (ek-to′pe-ah) [Gr. *ektopos* displaced + *-ia*] displacement or malposition, especially if congenital.

He further noticed that Joe Dial was developing an **ectopia** of the left lower eyelid, which is a drawing down of the eyelid. The result of this **ectopia** was an exposure of the eyeball. Subsequently, this happened to the upper eyelid exposing the upper eyeball. Wry v. Dial, 503 P.2d 979, 984 (Ct.App.Ariz. 1972).

ectopic beat See *beat, ectopic*.

eczema (ek′zĕ-mah) [Gr. *ekzein* to boil out] 1. a superficial inflammatory process involving primarily the epidermis, characterized early by redness, itching, minute papules and vesicles, weeping, oozing, and crusting, and later by scaling, lichenification, and often pigmentation. It is not a disease entity or an acceptable diagnosis. 2. atopic dermatitis.

To explain further the doctor's testimony, we borrow from the opinion of the referee.

"Dr. Weiss characterized the eruption, also described as hand **eczema**, in its various stages as symptoms of the allergic contact dermatitis. Although SAIF attempted to establish ... that the hand **eczema** ... and other manifestations of the dermatitis, and the decree thereof, were secondary disease processes also constituting a compensable condition, Dr. Weiss' testimony does not support that position. Dr. Weiss ... testifies, that those manifestations are symptoms. There is no other medical evidence." Matter of Compensation of Baer, 652 P.2d 873–4 (Ct.App.Or.1982).

His history, based upon his history to me and also the review of the previous records, would indicate that he did have an **eczematous** type of dermatitis involving primarily his exposed parts.... Quintana v. Weinberger, 385 F.Supp. 1102 (D.D. Col.1974).

He testified that **eczema** is a response by the skin to a variety of stimulations; that the causes are various, such as poison ivy; and that in some instances crude petroleum oils are primary irritants. The treatments for **eczema** are various, depending upon the cause and the symptoms. In acute **eczema** oils should not be used because in some cases they are an irritant, and they should be used in no case because they tend to dam up the accretions of the skin and provide a good medium on which bacteria can flourish....

... Based upon his knowledge, training and experience in the field of dermatology crude petroleum oil applied either externally or internally is not an appropriate or effective treatment for all types of **eczema**. Colusa Remedy Co. v. U.S., 176 F.2d 554, 558 (8th Cir. 1949).

eczematous (ek-zem′ah-tus) affected with or of the nature of eczema.

edema (ĕ-de′mah) [Gr. *oidēma* swelling] the presence of abnormally large amounts of fluid in the intercellular tissue spaces of the body; usually applied to demonstrable accumulation of excessive fluid in the subcutaneous tissues. Edema may be localized, due to venous or lymphatic obstruction or to increased vascular permeability, or it may be systemic due to heart failure or renal disease. Collections of edema fluid are designated according to the site, e.g., ascites (peritoneal cavity), hydrothorax (pleural cavity), and hydropericardium (pericardial sac). Massive generalized edema is called *anasarca*.

She accurately defined **edema** as "swelling or excessive tissue liquid in the tissue." Bevevino v. Saydjari, 574 F.2d 676, 678 (2d Cir. 1978).

Further, Dr. Harvey testified:

"Q. I will ask you whether you agree with this:

" 'Edema'—and by the way, that is swelling of the soft tissue?

"A. That is correct." Harvey v. Kellin, 566 P.2d 297, 301 (Ariz.1977).

"Edema" means the condition of an excess of water in the body which occurs when the body does not eliminate a sufficient quantity through the kidneys, thereby resulting in a back pressure through the veins pushing water and fluid through the capillaries out into the tissues causing such conditions as congestive heart failure, chronic lung disease, chronic cirrhosis and kidney failure. U.S. v. Ciba Geigy Corp., 508 F.Supp. 1118, 1122 (D.N.J.1976).

Other Authorities: Klofta v. Mathews, 418 F.Supp. 1139, 1143 (E.D.Wis.1976).

edema, angioneurotic recurring attacks of transient edema suddenly appearing in areas of the skin or mucous membranes and occasionally of the viscera, often associated with dermatographism, urticaria, erythema, and purpura. In the hereditary form, transmitted as an autosomal dominant trait, it tends to involve more visceral lesions than the sporadic form, especially of the respiratory and gastrointestinal tracts; two types of the familial form have been identified: one involves failure of synthesis of the inhibitor of complement component C1, the other involves the synthesis of an abnormal protein. Called also *acute circumscribed e., Milton's e., Quincke's e., wandering e., angioedema,* and *giant urticaria.*

Both medical and lay evidence described claimant as suffering from edema (swelling). A lay witness described the swelling as occurring at irregular intervals and as causing claimant's face, hands and arms to swell, with hard knots in her arms, back and chest....

... An examining physician referred to claimant's nervousness and discussed, in a manner implying that they are related, hypertension and swelling of the arms, face, hands, forearms and feet. A pathologist, who made a consultative examination, referred to "hypertensive vascular disease." A report from still another doctor, who treated claimant for several years, refers repeatedly to "angioneurotic edema." McGee v. Weinberger, 518 F.2d 330–1 (5th Cir. 1975).

edema, brain an excessive accumulation of fluid in the brain substance (*wet brain*); it may be due to various causes, including trauma, tumor, and increased permeability of the capillaries occurring as a result of anoxia or exposure to toxic substances.

Dr. Leander also said that Leeper suffered from a chemical reaction of alcohol and the cortical cells or gray matter of the brain. The reaction produced a condition known as "wet brain", which is an absorption of fluid from the blood vessels into the brain causing blackout or amnesia. A person in this condition is unable to realize and appreciate the nature and consequences of his acts....

... Dr. Alderete noted that an electroencephalogram and psychological testing revealed no evidence of structural brain damage. This, he said, negated the possibility of "wet brain" which is normally accompanied by brain damage. He felt that it would be extremely unlikely for Leeper to have had an amnesic episode lasting three days. U.S. v. Leeper, 413 F.2d 123, 125–6 (8th Cir. 1969).

edema, laryngeal See *epinephrine* (Wright case).

edema, pretibial

Pre-tibial edema is a swelling and softening of the tissue between the knee and the ankle. Magruder v. Richardson, 332 F.Supp. 1363, 1367 (E.D.Mo.1971).

edema, pulmonary abnormal, diffuse, extravascular accumulation of fluid in the pulmonary tissues and air spaces due to changes in hydrostatic forces in the capillaries or to increased capillary permeability; it is characterized clinically by intense dyspnea and, in the intra-alveolar form, by voluminous expectoration of frothy pink serous fluid and, if severe, by cyanosis.

He testified that Bruney had developed **edema of the lungs**. He also stated that there was infiltration for pneumonia present in the lungs. He stated that the **edema** was a result of a combination of things, including an enlarged heart and lung infiltrate. Bruney v. City of Lake Charles, 386 So.2d 950, 952 (Ct.App.La.1980).

"Mr. Ianelli died of heart and lung damage that resulted from exposure to a number of toxic environmental conditions and toxic gases that he was exposed to over a six or seven hour period in fighting the paper fire." He explained that the smoke indicated the presence of carbon dioxide and an insufficient amount of oxygen. He said that paper fires produced cyanide gas. This exposure to heat, carbon monoxide, cyanide gas and lack of oxygen, according to the witness, was responsible for the fatal **pulmonary edema**, in that the irritation produced by inhalation of the smoke "caused fluid to pour out into the spaces of the lungs." Matter of Ianelli, 384 A.2d 1104, (Super.Ct.N.J.1978).

Ms. Seacrist relies almost entirely on materials contained in Hurwitz & Koulack, Pneumoconiosis: Attorney's Textbook of Medicine, Vol. 8A, Ch. 25, ¶ 205.35(3). In response to the first inquiry, she states that "[pulmonary edema] is a lung disease which can be caused by interference with pulmonary blood circulation created by fibrosis and hyalinization induced by an irritating stimulus such as coal dust particles. Moreover, 2035(d)(ii) of the Coal Miner's Manual describes **pulmonary edema** as a 'cardiopulmonary disease.' "...

The government disagrees:

Pulmonary edema is an accumulation of fluid in the lungs, with resulting shortness of breath and congestion. It occurs most often as a complication of left ventricular failure due to heart disease. Left heart failure upsets the balance of pressures in the lungs, causing the accumulation of fluids. **Pulmonary edema** is not a chronic dust disease or other disease of the lung within the meaning of the Act....

... **Pulmonary edema** is neither an independent cause of death nor a "disease" but rather the natural physiological result of left heart failure. Seacrist v. Weinberger, 538 F.2d 1054, 1056 (4th Cir. 1976).

edema of lungs See *edema, pulmonary.*

edematous (ĕ-dem'ah-tus) pertaining to or affected by edema.

> The patient remained in traction for 11 days. Defendant saw him every day. The boy's legs were never lowered to a horizontal position. The bandages on his legs were never removed. On July 9, defendant loosened the bandages so that he could examine portions of the patient's legs....
>
> ... Defendant testified that the blood circulation to the legs was good at that time....
>
> ... The nurse's notes for the 7 A.M. to 3 P.M. shift indicate: "Dr. Vitacco here L [left] foot **edematous**" (subject to a swelling caused by an abnormal accumulation of fluid). Garfield Park Community Hospital v. Vitacco, 327 N.E.2d 408, 410 (App.Ct.Ill.1975).

edetate (ed'ĕ-tāt) any salt or ester of edetic acid (ethylenediaminetetraacetic acid, EDTA). Formerly called *edathamil.*

edetate disodium [USP] chemical name: N,N'-1,2-ethanediylbis[N-(carboxymethyl)glycine disodium salt. A metal complexing agent, $C_{10}H_{14}N_2Na_2O_8 \cdot 2H_2O$, used as a chelating pharmaceutic aid. It is also used in poisoning with lead and other heavy metals and, because of its affinity for calcium, in the treatment of hypercalcemia. Called also *edathamil disodium.* See also, *therapy, chelation.*

> The common chelating agent, Na_2 **EDTA**, was originally discovered by I. G. Farben in the 1930's and is widely used as a food preservative. **EDTA** intravenous treatment is often recommended for lead poisoning and other diseases requiring removal of heavy metals from the body. Chelation treatments were widely used during World War II in treating sailors who had contracted poisoning from leaded paint. Since World War II more than 1500 scientific articles and studies have been published concerning practically every application of the chelating process in the body. Many of those articles are contained in the record. Rogers v. State Bd. of Med. Examiners, 371 So.2d 1037, 1039 (Dist.Ct.App.Fla.1979).

edrophonium chloride (ed"ro-fo'ne-um) [USP] chemical name: N-ethyl-3-hydroxy-N,N-dimethylbenzenaminium chloride. A cholinergic, $C_{10}H_{16}ClNO$, occurring as a white, crystalline powder; used as an antidote for curare principles, as a diagnostic aid in myasthenia gravis, and in the treatment of myasthenic crises, administered intramuscularly and intravenously.

> ... the child remained in the operating room under assisted respiration until approximately 11:40 A.M., at which time she was given ¼ cc of Tensilon, intravenously, to restore spontaneous breathing....
>
> ... He stated that the better practice recognized everywhere is never give **Tensilon** to cure or reverse a Phase II Block. He conceded **Tensilon** might be given cautiously, slowly, and in small dosage to test for the presence of a Phase II or desensitizing Block. He explained that **Tensilon** breaks down the cholinesterase which inhibits Anectine thereby prolonging the effects of Anectine. In Dr. Small's opinion, Dr. Wyly mistakenly gave the patient **Tensilon** to reverse or cure what Dr. Wyly considered a Phase II Block. In so doing, the **Tensilon** tem-

porarily relieved the child's respiratory distress, as shown by the chart which indicates that the heartbeat improved and spontaneous respiration resumed following administration of the **Tensilon**. This, according to Dr. Small, caused Dr. Wyly to mistakenly assume the Phase II Block was permanently reversed. Instead, when the effect of the **Tensilon** wore off after 15 or 20 minutes, the blockage resumed....

> ... he warns that Anectine and **Tensilon** should never be given during the same operation, and that **Tensilon** should never be employed to overcome the effects of Anectine. He acknowledged a wide divergence of equally reputable medical authority concerning whether **Tensilon** should ever be used at all. Chapman v. Argonaut-Southwest Insurance Co., 290 So. 2d 779, 781, 783 (Ct.App.La.1974).

EDTA See *edetate.*

EEG See *electroencephalogram.*

EFA (essential fatty acids) See *acid, fatty, essential.*

effect (ĕ-fekt') the result produced by an action.

effect, Doppler the relationship of the apparent frequency of waves, as of sound, light, and radio waves, to the relative motion of the source of the waves and the observer, the frequency increasing as the two approach each other and decreasing as they move apart.

> ... we quoted from People v. Abdallah (1967), 82 Ill.App.2d 312, at page 315, 226 N.E.2d 408, at page 410:
>
> > "The 'radar' device presently in common use by law enforcement agencies for the determination of speeds of moving vehicles, ... operates on the **Doppler principle**, that is, the emission of a continuous electromagnetic wave which enables the speed of a target object to be determined by measuring the difference in frequency between the wave emitted from the radar device and the wave reflected from the object. Kopper, The Scientifc Reliability of Radar Speedmeters, 33 N.C.L.Rev. 343. It is presently so well settled that the **Doppler principle** is an accurate means of determining the speed of a moving object that a court may take judicial notice thereof; and expert testimony is unnecessary to establish the usefulness of the method. (Citations.)" People v. Stankovich, 255 N.E.2d 461, 463 (App.Ct.Ill.1970).

effect, placebo the nonspecific psychologic or psychophysiologic effect produced by a placebo.

> People who are given medication for an ailment frequently feel better because they think they should, even though the product has no therapeutic value. This is known as the **placebo effect**. In order to eliminate the bias of the placebo effect in a clinical study, it is common practice to "blind" the participants, i.e., dispense to the control group a placebo which simulates in taste, smell, and appearance the product being tested. Similarly, to neutralize any subconscious bias of the examiner, it is important to blind him, i.e., prevent him from knowing which subjects received the medication and which did not. A study in which both the subjects and the examiner are blinded is referred to as "double-blind." Warner-Lambert Co. v. F.T.C., 562 F.2d 749, 754 (D.C.Cir.1977).

effusion (ĕ-fu'zhun) [L. *effusio* a pouring out] 1. the escape of fluid into a part or tissue, as an exudation or a transudation. 2. an effused material, which may be classified according to protein content as an exudate or transudate.

On examination the left knee revealed no **effusion** (escape of fluid into a part or tissue). Pruchniewski v. Weinberger, 415 F.Supp. 112, 114 (D.Md.1976).

effusion, pericardial

... a "**pericardial**" (the sac around the heart) **effusion** was made and 300 cc's of yellow cloudy fluid was obtained.... Prudential Insurance Co. of America v. Beaty, 456 S.W.2d 164, 169 (Ct.Civ.App.Tex.1970).

effusion, pleural the presence of liquid in the pleural space.

Pleural effusion is the presence of fluid in the pleural cavities of the lungs. Poore v. Mathews, 406 F.Supp. 47, 49 (E.D.Tenn. 1975).

There was no **pleural effusion** (fluid in the chest cavity). Magruder v. Richardson, 332 F.Supp. 1363, 1367 (E.D.Mo.1971).

"eggshell skull" rule

So read, the finding would be inconsistent with the "thin skull" or "**eggshell skull**" or "you take your victim as you find him" rule of the common law. The substantive law of Wisconsin is conceded to govern this case, see 28 U.S.C. § 1346(b); and, by an odd coincidence, what has come to be the leading case announcing the eggshell skull rule is a Wisconsin case, Vosburg v. Putney, 80 Wis. 523, 50 N.W. 403 (1891), though it is not the earliest eggshell skull case even in Wisconsin, see Stewart v. City of Ripon, 38 Wis. 584, 590–91 (1875). Stoleson v. United States, 708 F.2d 1217, 1221 (7th Cir. 1983).

ego (e′go) [L. *ego* I] that portion of the psyche which possesses consciousness, maintains its identity, and recognizes and tests reality; the conscious sense of the self.

He stated that psychiatrically the **ego** is that function which permits an individual to perceive reality and react appropriately to the realistic situation. If an individual is overburdened by stress and is unable to defend himself against this stress he retreats to a lower level and loses contact with reality which may result in an assaultive or physical violence. When his hemeostasis balance is regained the individual may return to a relatively normal pattern of action.... People v. Harrington, 317 N.E.2d 161, 164 (App.Ct.Ill.1974).

ego rupture

... **ego rupture** may be very temporary with prompt restoration of normal function. The doctor stated that **ego rupture** is an extremely common occurrence. He concluded that defendant had been put through a succession of stresses and the night of March 3d was the final stress which caused the defendant to totally break from reality for a brief period. People v. Harrington, 317 N.E.2d 161, 164 (App.Ct.Ill.1974).

EI See *ethylene imine*.

EIP See *environmental impact statement*.

ejaculation (e-jak″u-la′shun) [L. *ejaculatio*] a sudden act of expulsion, as of the semen.

ejaculation, retrograde

A "dry climax" or, as it is known medically, **retrograde ejaculation**, is a common side-effect of a properly performed TUR. Dessi v. U.S., 489 F.Supp. 722, 730 (E.D.Va.1980).

elase

Because of the necrotic tissue, he ordered **elase** (a form of debridement).... Stogsdill v. Manor Convalescent Home, Inc., 343 N.E.2d 589, 594 (App.Ct.Ill.1976).

elbow (el′bo) [L. *cubitus*] the bend of the arm; the joint that connects the arm and forearm; called also *cubitus* [NA].

The **elbow** is commonly understood as the arm joint. There are actually three separate joints which comprise the **elbow** joint: the humeroulnar (the humerus is the bone of the upper arm), the humeroradial, and the proximal radioulnar. Blakiston's New Gould Medical Dictionary (2d ed, 1956), Tables of Joints and Ligaments, Elbow, p. 1378; 3 Schmidt, Attorney's Dictionary of Medicine, Elbow Joint, p. E–23. Dobbs v. Villa Capri Restaurant, 329 N.W.2d 503, 505–6 (Ct.App.Mich.1982).

As a result, she sustained a fracture to her left **elbow** with displacement of the joint surfaces....

... The **elbow** fracture was reduced by surgery requiring insertion of a one inch screw, leaving her with a permanent loss of extension between 35 and 40 degrees. Stewart v. West Bradford Corp., 453 N.Y.S.2d 255–6 (3d Dep't 1982).

elbow, tennis a painful condition localized to the outer aspect of the elbow, due to inflammation or irritation of the extensor tendon attachment to the lateral humeral condyle; called also *external humeral epicondylitis*, and *radiohumeral bursitis* or *epicondylitis*.

... he had diagnosed as a **tennis elbow**. She related a history of bursitis "years ago" and said her present symptoms recurred 8 months prior to her consulting our Clinic, and that they had grown worse steadily since. Hughes v. Richardson, 342 F.Supp. 320, 323 (W.D.Mo.1971).

elective (e-lek′tiv) subject to the choice or decision of the patient or physician; applied to procedures that are advantageous to the patient but not urgent.

In Riedinger v. Colburn, 361 F.Supp. 1073, 1075–76 (D.Idaho 1973), the court defined "**elective** surgery" as one that was "not necessary as a matter of life and death, but rather is a matter of choice to the patient depending on his or her desire to try to eliminate problems of discomfort." Of course, the surgery involved in this case was so optional that it would not qualify even as "**elective** surgery" as defined by the Riedinger court. Cowman v. Hornaday, 329 N.W.2d 422, 424–5 (Iowa 1983).

The term "**elective** surgery" would appear to cover nontherapeutic abortions. McKee v. Likins, 261 N.W.2d 566, 576 (Minn.1977).

First, that the surgery Mrs. Riedinger consented to can be termed major "**elective**" surgery. It is major in the sense that it is not without the same risks inherent in any operation involving an attack on body tissues under a general anesthetic. It is "**elective**" in the sense that it is not necessary as a matter of life and death, but rather is a matter of choice to the patient depending upon his or her desire to try to eliminate problems of discomfort. Riedinger v. Colburn, 361 F.Supp. 1073, 1075–6 (D.Idaho 1973).

electric shock See *therapy, electroconvulsive.*

electrical muscle stimulator See *stimulator, electronic.*

electrocardiogram (e-lek″tro-kar′de-o-gram″) [*electro* + Gr. *kardia* heart + *gramma* mark] a graphic tracing of the variations in electrical potential caused by the excitation of the heart muscle and detected at the body surface. The normal electrocardiogram shows deflections resulting from atrial and ventricular activity. The first deflection, P, is due to excitation of the atria. The QRS deflections are due to excitation (depolarization) of the ventricles. The T wave is due to recovery of the ventricles (repolarization). The U wave is a potential undulation of unknown origin immediately following the T wave, seen in normal electrocardiograms and accentuated in hypokalemia. Abbreviated ECG or EKG. See also *lead* [2].

An **electrocardiogram** was done (some times called an EKG, some times an ECG), and it appeared normal to Dr. Crawley (dep. 29). A single EKG, however, may not be a reliable indication that an infarction is not about to happen....

... "[S]ometimes the evidence of a myocardial infarction takes a couple of days to manifest itself on a [sic] **electrocardiogram**" (dep. 13).... Schales v. U.S., 488 F.Supp. 33, 35–6 (E.D.Ark.1979).

An **electrocardiogram** taken at that time showed the old healed infarct with stable first degree AV block and unequivocal posterior coronary insufficiency. Kelley-Rickman, Inc. v. Hartford Life Ins., 557 F.2d 639, 641 (8th Cir. 1977).

An **electrocardiogram** (EKG) is a tracing showing the changes in electrical potential produced by heart contractions and is an important tool in diagnosing disruption of normal heart function. Hamil v. Bashline, 364 A.2d 1366, 1371 (Super.Ct.Pa. 1976), vacated 392 A.2d 1280.

Other Authorities: Brown v. U.S., 419 F.2d 337, 338 (8th Cir. 1969); U.S. v. Article Consisting of 2 Devices, etc., 255 F.Supp. 374, 381 (W.D.Ark.1966).

electrocardiograph (e-lek″tro-kar′de-o-graf″) an instrument for performing electrocardiography, i.e., for making electrocardiograms.

electrocautery (e-lek″tro-kaw′ter-e) an apparatus for cauterizing tissue, consisting of a platinum wire in a holder which is heated to a red or white heat when the instrument is activated by an electric current.

Upon removal of a mouth gag that had been employed to facilitate access to Lisa's throat, she was discovered to have two blisters on her face. The blebs ruptured. Upon healing, noticeable scars remained. The evidence showed that an **electrocauterizer** was used by Dr. Cherry during the operation. Stevens v. Union Memorial Hospital, 424 A.2d 1118–19 (Ct. Spec.App.Md.1981).

electroconvulsive therapy See *therapy, electroconvulsive.*

electrodesiccation (e-lek″tro-des″ĭ-ka′shun) dehydration of tissue by the use of a high frequency electric current. See also *fulguration.*

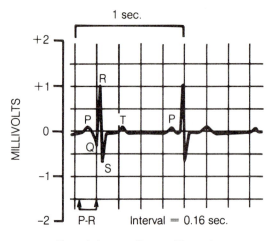

Normal electrocardiogram (Guyton).

Plaintiffs alleged that defendant negligently removed a malignant melanoma from the left chest wall of the decedent by **electrodesiccation** on October 8, 1973. Williams v. Grant, 417 N.E.2d 586–7 (Ct.App.Ohio 1979).

electroencephalogram (e-lek″tro-en-sef′ah-lo-gram″) a recording of the potentials on the skull generated by currents emanating spontaneously from nerve cells in the brain. The dominant frequency of these potentials is about 8 to 10 cycles persecond and the amplitude about 10 to 100 microvolts. Variations in wave characteristics

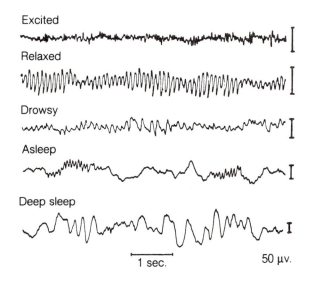

Electroencephalogram

Recordings made while the subject was excited, relaxed, and in various stages of sleep. During excitement the brain waves are rapid and of small amplitude, whereas in sleep they are much slower and of greater amplitude. The regular waves characteristic of the relaxed state are called alpha waves. (From Jasper, in Epilepsy and Cerebral Localization, by Penfield and Erickson.)

correlate well with neurological conditions and so have been useful as diagnostic criteria. Abbreviated EEG.

Doctor Leoni also testified that an **electroencephalogram** taken on April 27, 1979, revealed that the electrical discharge to the brain was slower than normal. He said that this slowing of the brain can make one slow mentally. Vallot v. Camco, Inc., 396 So.2d 980, 985 (Ct.App.La.1981).

From the time of the accident until the time of trial in the spring of 1978, plaintiff suffered from intermittent numbness and weakness on the left side of his body. An **electroencephalogram** (EEG), a test which records brain wave activity over the cortex of the brain, was administered to the plaintiff in November of 1975 and again in May of 1978. Both tests showed a slowing of brain wave activity over that portion of the brain which controls the left side of the body. Doering v. Janssen, 394 N.E.2d 721, 722–3 (App.Ct.Ill.1979).

In an effort to ascertain the cause of the coma, Dr. Morse conducted a brain scan, an angiogram, an **electroencephalogram** (EEG), a lumbar tap and several other tests. The first three are related to the brain and are conducted, according to the testimony, with the object of finding an injury or insult to the brain, such as a subdural hematoma or the like, or for ascertaining any abnormality in the brain activity patterns. The latter is particularly true of the EEG where electrodes are placed on the skull. The measurement is made of cortical neurons. The neuron is basically a conducting cell of nervous energy. The recordings are made on awake and sleep cycles. The awake recorded data, referred to in the testimony as alpha rhythm or activity, indicates a frequency of pattern which can be compared against normal frequencies or patterns to determine whether any abnormality exists. The EEG establishes the existence or nonexistence of normal patterns. It does not precisely locate the insult or lesion causing, in this case, the unconsciousness. Matter of Quinlan, 348 A.2d 801, 808 (Super. Ct.N.J.1975)

Other Authorities: Intrater v. Thomas, 369 N.E.2d 1339, 1342 (Ill.App.1977); Smith v. Jugosalvenska Linijska Plovidea, 278 F.2d 176, 178 (4th. Cir. 1960).

electroencephalograph (e-lek″tro-en-sef′ah-lo-graf″) an instrument for performing electroencephalography.

An **electroencephalograph** test, however, was not normal but showed a multiple of small spikes on the right occipital lobe of the brain. The doctor stated that these were not particularly indicative ''at times'' of anything but they would best satisfy the picture of epilepsy. Skaug v. Johnson, 330 N.E.2d 265, 267 (App.Ct.Ill.1975).

electroencephalography (e-lek″tro-en-sef″ah-log′rah-fe) the recording of the electric currents developed in the brain, by means of electrodes applied to the scalp, to the surface of the brain (*intracranial e.*), or placed within the substance of the brain (*depth e.*). See also *electroencephalogram.*

electrolyte (e-lek′tro-līt) [*electro-* + Gr. *lytos* that may be dissolved] a substance that dissociates into ions when fused or in solution, and thus becomes capable of conducting electricity; an ionic solute.

Briefly, **electrolytes** are electrically charged substances, such as sodium and potassium, which are found in the blood. A particular balance or concentration of these substances in the blood stream is necessary for sustaining life. An imbalance produces detrimental results ranging from disorientation and weakness to coma and death. An imbalance may result from increased ingestion of fluids or rapid loss thereof, as by continued vomiting or diarrhea. Sears v. Cooper, 574 S.W.2d 612, 614 (Ct.Civ.App.Tex.1978).

electromyogram (e-lek″tro-mi′o-gram) the record obtained by electromyography.

After Slater complained of paralysis, Kehoe ordered an **electromyogram** for January 27 to test the nerve function of the right arm and shoulder. An **electromyogram** is of limited value in determining whether there is nerve injury if performed within 18 to 21 days following the trauma, but is of diagnostic value in eliminating preexisting neurological disease which might give abnormal electromyographic readings. Slater v. Kehoe, 113 Cal.Rptr. 790, 793 (Ct.App.Cal.1974).

electomyograph See *electromyography.*

electromyographic See *electromyography.*

electromyography (e-lek″tro-mi-og′rah-fe) [*electro* + *myography*] the recording and study of the intrinsic electrical properties of skeletal muscle (1) by means of surface or needle electrodes to determine merely whether the muscle is contracting or not (useful in kinesiology) or (2) by insertion of a needle electrode into the muscle and observing by cathode-ray oscilloscope and loud-speaker the action potentials spontaneously present in a muscle (abnormal) or induced by voluntary contractions, as a means of detecting the nature and location of motor unit lesions; or (3) recording the electrical activity evoked in a muscle by electrical stimulation of its nerve (called also *electroneuromyography*), a procedure useful for study of several aspects of neuromuscular function, neuromuscular conduction, extent of nerve lesion, reflex responses, etc. Abbreviated EMG.

When Dr. Miller first examined Abernathy, more than a year before giving him the **electromyograph test**, the only observable symptom of a continuing back problem was that Abernathy's left buttock was thinner than the right (how much thinner the record does not reveal). Miller attributed the asymmetry to the accident's having injured the nerve running into the buttock from the spine. The **EMG** provided objective corroboration of his diagnosis—originally based just on visual observation—and of his testimony that Abernathy was 35–50 percent disabled as a result of the accident. Abernathy v. Superior Hardwoods, Inc., 704 F.2d 963, 969 (7th Cir. 1983).

On April 8, 1977, an **electromyographic** (EMG) study was conducted which revealed the presence of fibrillations and positive sharp waves, a sign of denervation in the peripheral nervous system. McDonald v. U.S., 555 F.Supp. 935, 942 (M.D. Pa.1983).

Nerve conduction studies and **electromyogram** of the muscles in the left leg showed no evidence of abnormalities. Field v. Winn Dixie Louisiana, Inc., 427 So.2d 616–17 (Ct.App.La. 1983).

Other Authorities: Sanden v. Mayo Clinic, 495 F.2d 221, 224 (8th Civ. 1974).

embolus, pulmonary

Mrs. Belmon was admitted to Cabrini on August 11, 1980, with a diagnosis of a possible **pulmonary embolus** (a blood clot lodged in the lung). Belmon v. St. Frances Cabrini Hospital, 427 So.2d 541–2 (Ct.App.La.1983).

Plaintiff is the widow of Perry M. Kuntz, who died as the result of a **pulmonary embolus** (a blood clot in the lung) he sustained as a consequence of heart surgery. Kuntz v. Kern Cty. Emp. Retirement Ass'n, 134 Cal.Rptr. 501–2 (Ct.App.Cal.1976).

embouchure

These changes in jaw movement and changes in physical formation have resulted in a concomitant change in the plaintiff's "**embouchure**" [bouche, mouth] which in turn adversely affects Petersen's ability to play the trumpet or any other wind instrument. This handicap in playing wind instruments is due to the loss of muscle control and sensitivity in the lips, realignment or change in jaw formation, and facial muscular control in the mouth, all of which Petersen has sustained as a result of the injuries incurred in this accident. Petersen v. Head Construction Co., 367 F.Supp. 1072, 1077 (D.D.C.1973).

embryo (em'bre-o) [Gr. *embryon*] in animals, those derivatives of the fertilized ovum that eventually become the offspring, during their period of most rapid development, i.e., after the long axis appears until all major structures are represented. In man, the developing organism is an embryo from about two weeks after fertilization to the end of seventh or eighth week.

It is by now commonly accepted that at conception the egg and sperm unite to jointly provide the genetic material requisite for human life. Thus, various courts have gradually come to recognize that the **embryo**, from the moment of conception, is a separate organism that can be compensated for negligently inflicted prenatal harm. (See, e.g., Sinkler v. Kneale (1960), 401 Pa. 267, 273, 164 A.2d 93, 96; Smith v. Brennan (1960), 31 N.J. 353, 366, 164 A.2d 497, 504.... Renslow v. Mennonite Hospital, 367 N.E.2d 1250, 1254 (Ill.1977).

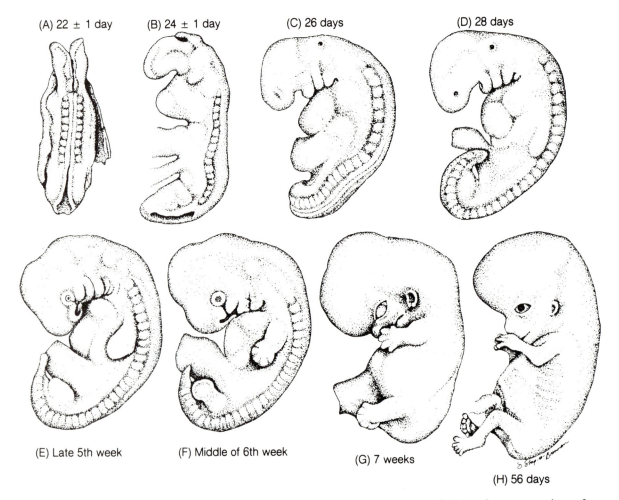

(A) 22 ± 1 day   (B) 24 ± 1 day   (C) 26 days   (D) 28 days

(E) Late 5th week   (F) Middle of 6th week   (G) 7 weeks   (H) 56 days

Human embryo at various stages of development, as indicated. The relative size has been distorted to better show correspondence of parts. (Adapted as follows: *A* and *D*, from photography by Nislimura; *B*, from a drawing by Key; *C, E, F, G*, from Carnegie Collection.)

The pregnant woman cannot be isolated in her privacy. She carries an **embryo** and, later, a fetus, if one accepts the medical definitions of the developing young in the human uterus. See Dorland's Illustrated Medical Dictionary 478–479, 547 (24th ed. 1965). Roe v. Wade, 410 U.S. 113, 159, 93 S.Ct. 705, 35 L.Ed.2d 147 (1973).

Other Authorities: YWCA of Princeton, N.J. v. Kugler, 342 F.Supp. 1048, 1083 (D.N.J.1972).

emergency (e-mer'jen-se) [L. *emergere* to raise up] an unlooked for or sudden occasion; an accident; an urgent or pressing need.

An **emergency** is statutorily defined as a situation wherein, in competent medical judgment, the proposed surgical or medical treatment procedures are reasonably necessary, and a person authorized by statute to consent is not readily available, and any delay in treatment could reasonably be expected to jeopardize the life or health of the person affected or could reasonably result in disfigurement or impair faculties. La.R.S. 40:1299.54. Karl J. Pizzalotto, M.D., Ltd. v. Wilson, 437 So. 2d 859, 862 (La.1983).

Emergency has been defined as an unforeseen combination of circumstances which calls for immediate action and is synonymous with crisis, pinch, strait, necessity, Lutzken v. City of Rochester, 7 A.D.2d 498, 184 N.Y.S.2d 483, and as an unforeseen occurrence or combination of circumstances which calls for immediate action leaving no time for deliberation, Helvich v. George A. Rutherford Co., 96 Ohio App. 367, 114 N.E.2d 514.

While Dr. Lipton may have been operating under stress, no **emergency** situation is depicted by the available testimony. There was time for deliberation and the application of available skills....

... Dr. Lipton abdicated his role as surgeon in that operating room and permitted the judgment and skills of a layman to prevail. Mr. MacKay's involvement in the surgical procedure extended far beyond instruction as to the use or manner of implant of the device he sold. People v. Smithtown General Hospital, 402 N.Y.S.2d 318, 321 (Sup.Ct.Suffolk Cty. 1978).

emergency procedure See *procedure, quickstep.*

EMG See *electromyogram.*

EMI See *scintiscan.*

EMI scan See *scanner, EMI*; and *scanning, radioisotope.*

eminentia (em"ĭ-nen'she-ah), pl. *eminen'tiae* [L.] [NA] an eminence: a general term for a prominence or projection, especially one on the surface of a bone.

eminentia intercondylaris [NA]; eminentia intercondyloidea; eminentia intermedia intercondylar eminence: an eminence on the proximal extremity of the tibia, surmounted on either side by a prominent tubercle, on to the sides of which the articular facets are prolonged; called also *intermediate eminence* and *tuberculum intercondyloideum.*

Dr. Heinen's diagnosis revealed that Fontenot had a fractured tibial tubercle (posterior). Fontenot v. American Fidelity Fire Ins. Co., 386 So.2d 165, 169 (Ct.App.La.1980).

emission (e-mish'un) [L. *emissio*, a sending out] a discharge; specifically an involuntary discharge of semen.

emission, fugitive

Most relevant to this case was the stance the EPA took with regard to **fugitive emissions**—i.e., matter having a negative impact on air quality which does not originate from a stack or vent, including, but not limited to, dust from ore storage piles, road dust and dust from nonindustrial urban sources. National Steel Corp., Great Lakes Steel v. Gorsuch, 700 F.2d 314, 318 (6th Cir. 1983).

emotion (e-mo'tion) [L. *emovere* to disturb] a state of mental excitement characterized by alteration of feeling tone and by physiological behavioral changes. See also *shock* (Pathfinder case).

emotional (e-mo'shun-al) pertaining to the emotions. See also *emotion.*

emotional distress

The danger of illusory claims for mental distress is no greater than in cases of physical injury, especially when the injury is slight.[3] The opportunity for fraud is as likely in such a case as one absent any physical injury. "The problem is one of adequate proof, and it is not necessary to deny a remedy in all cases because some claims may be false." Prosser, Law of Torts (4 Ed.1971) 327–328, Section 54.... [[3] Courts have allowed recovery for **emotional distress** accompanied by the slightest injury. "When there is evidence of any injury, no matter how slight, the mental anguish suffered by plaintiff becomes an important element in estimating the damages sustained." Clark Restaurant Co. v. Rau (1931), 41 Ohio App. 23, 26, 179 N.E. 196 [31 O.O. 576]. In Wolfe v. Great A & P Tea Co. (1944), 143 Ohio St. 643, 56 N.E.2d 230 [28 O.O. 520], the plaintiff was allowed to recover for mental suffering, after eating food contaminated with worms, if any physical injury was proven. See, also, Ward Baking Co. v. Trizzino (1928), 27 Ohio App. 475, 161 N.E. 557.]

Having carefully examined the arguments in support of the contemporaneous physical injury rule, it is clear that continued adherence to the rule makes little sense. Legal scholars who have considered the rule denying recovery in the absence of contemporaneous physical injury or impact are unanimous in condemning it as unjust and contrary to experience. The justifications for the doctrine are no longer valid and the reasons for abrogating it are strong. Consequently, the earlier cases upholding the doctrine are overruled. Miller, [85 N.E. 499 (Ohio 1908)] and Davis v. Cleveland Ry. Co. (1939), 135 Ohio St. 401, 21 N.E.2d 169 [14 O.O. 307]. [Two bibliographical footnotes omitted.] Schultz v. Barberton Glass Co., 447 N.E.2d 109, 111–113 (Ohio 1983).

emphysema (em"fĭ-se'mah, em"fĭ-ze'mah) [Gr. "an inflation"] a pathological accumulation of air in tissues or organs; applied especially to such a condition of the lungs. See also *glomectomy*; and *emphysema, pulmonary.*

Dr. Schimke testified that respondent's chest x-rays indicated the development of emphysema for at least ten to fifteen years prior to examination and that there was no new disease traceable to the incident on December 18. Ridenour v. Equity Supply Co., 665 P.2d 783, 785 (Mont.1983).

An autopsy revealed no evidence of coronary artery disease or a heart attack, but microscopic examination of employee's lungs showed that he had had severe **emphysema** with honeycombing of upper lobes of the lungs and also had had massive pulmonary fibrosis with siderotic nodules. Dunn v. Vic Mfg.Co., 327 N.W.2d 572–3 (Minn.1982).

At trial, Dr. Phillips described the accepted medical treatment for **emphysema** as follows: (1) encourage the patient to stop smoking and to move to a dry, pollution-free climate; (2) use medication to lessen the bronchical spasm; (3) use machines to aid the patient in breathing; and (4) employ oxygen therapy....

Dr. Erin Longfield, Chief of Staff of the Veterans Administration Hospital located in Houston and a specialist in chest diseases, testified there was only one accepted medical treatment for **emphysema**; namely, the use of drugs and machines to assist the patient in breathing. Dr. Longfield asserted carotid surgery would not benefit anyone suffering from **emphysema** and that the performance of such surgery would be negligence. To his knowledge, such surgery was not used in any veterans' hospital. Hood v. Phillips, 554 S.W.2d 160, 162 (Tex.1977).

Other Authorities: Griffin v. Phillips, 542 S.W.2d 432, 435 (Ct. Civ.App.Tex.1976); International Harvester Co. v. Industrial Com'n, 305 N.E.2d 529, 531 (Ill.1973); Linville v. Steel Fixture Mfg. Co., 469 P.2d 312, 315 (Kan.1970); Insurance Co. of North America v. Stroburg, 456 S.W.2d 402, 405 (Ct.Civ. App.Tex.1970); Reilly v. Industrial Com'n, 398 P.2d 920, 921 (Ct.App.Ariz.1965); Harris v. Ribicoff, 198 F.Supp. 861, 864 (W.D.N.Car.1961).

emphysema, interstitial presence of air in the peribronchial and interstitial tissues of the lungs; called also *Hamman's disease.*

emphysema, panacinar; emphysema, panlobular generalized obstructive emphysema affecting all lung segments, with atrophy and dilatation of the alveoli and destruction of the vascular bed.

emphysema, pulmonary a condition of the lung characterized by increase beyond normal in the size of air spaces distal to the terminal bronchioles, either from dilatation of the alveoli (*panacinar e.*), or from destruction (*interstitial e.*) of their walls. See also *emphysema, interstitial*; and *emphysema, panlobular* (vesicular).

The expert testimony also established that while not all of the causes of **pulmonary emphysema** are known, it is known that the disease can be caused by ingestion of perilla mint (the most common cause of **pulmonary emphysema** in Louisiana) and by changing cattle from an overgrazed pasture to a lush pasture....

... Both of these veterinarians testified that labored breathing and gas bubbles trapped under the skin of the back of the cow are classic signs of **pulmonary emphysema**. Both symptoms were exhibited by some of plaintiff's cattle. Further, the two doctors necropsied one of the cows and found that the lungs were distended with air trapped inside, another classic sign of **pulmonary emphysema**. Gaar v. State Through Dep't of Highways, 389 So.2d 426–8 (Ct.App.La.1980).

emphysema, vesicular See *emphysema, panlobular.*

emphysematous (em″fi-sem′ah-tus) of the nature of or affected with emphysema.

We note that the plaintiff does not contend that cement dust directly causes carcinoma. However, both Dr. Whittaker and one of the defendant's experts stated that **emphysematous** lungs are more likely to become cancerous. Totherow v. Penn Dixie Industries, Inc., 589 S.W.2d 375–6 (Tenn.1979).

emphysematous bleb See *bleb*; and *emphysema.*

empyema (em″pi-e′mah) [Gr. *empyema*] accumulation of pus in a cavity of the body; when used without a descriptive qualifier, it refers to thoracic empyema. See also *empyema, thoracic.*

The appellant developed a chronic **empyema**, a collection of pus in a localized area, in the chest cavity which required extensive hospitalization and resulted in serious physical impairment. Laws v. Harter, 534 S.W.2d 449–50 (Ct.App.Ky.1975).

... two medical experts who testified that the cause of death, to the best of their medical knowledge, was a blow to the decedent's head, which resulted in a sub-dural hematoma which became secondarily infected, culminating in death-causing sub-dural **empyema**. SKF Industries, Inc. v. Cody, 276 A.2d 356, 359 (Commonwealth Ct.Pa.1971).

Empyema is an infection of the pleura, the membrane covering the lung, characterized by pus in the pleural cavity often leading to collapse of the lung. Alden v. Providence Hospital, 382 F.2d 163, 165 (D.C.Cir.1967).

empyema, thoracic suppurative inflammation of the pleural space; called also *pyothorax.*

enamel (en-am′el) the white, compact, and very hard substance that covers and protects the dentin of the crown of a tooth; called also *enamelum* [NA] and *substantia adamantina dentis.*

Enamel is the hardest body tissue. It covers the dentin on the crown of each tooth. Sullivan v. Russell, 338 N.W.2d 181, 184 (Mich.1983).

enantiomorphism (en-an″te-o-mor′fizm) [Gr. *enantios* opposite + *morphē* form] a special type of optical isomerism in which a nonsuperimposable, mirror-image relationship exists at all times between the respective molecules of the compounds. Enantiomorphic isomers always rotate the plane of polarized light to the same degree but in opposite directions; otherwise most of their chemical and physical properties are identical, the principal exceptions being biological reactions catalyzed by enzymes. The molecules are always asymmetric, very often as the result of possession of one or more asymmetric carbon atoms. Thus lactic acid, $CH_3CHOHCOOH$, possessing one such carbon atom, exists in a *dextro* and a *levo* form. The molecules of some enantiomorphic compounds (e.g., certain biphenyl or spirane compounds) are asymmetric as a whole, but do not possess any asymmetric carbon atoms. Cf. *diastereoisomerism.*

encapsulated (en-kap′su-lāt-ed) [Gr. *en* in + L. *capsula* a little box] enclosed within a capsule. See also *encapsulation.*

... inflamed reactive tissue at the "Bo-plant" site was discovered, with the "Bo-plant" not fused but walled off or **encapsulated**; and the "Bo-plant" was removed. The hospital's pathologist determined that the reactive type tissue was a result of a rejection of a foreign body, and that it was the incompatible cow protein which was the cause of the reaction. E. R. Squibb & Sons, Inc. v. Jordan, 254 So.2d 17–18 (Dist.Ct.App. Fla.1971).

encapsulation (en-kap"su-la'shun) any act of inclosing in a capsule.

encephalitis (en"sef-ah-li'tis), pl. *encephalit'ides* [*encephalo-* + *-itis*] inflammation of the brain.

. . . she was hospitalized at St. Vincent's Hospital, Indianapolis, Indiana with a neurological and muscular disorder which was diagnosed as **encephalitis** and which left her with a permanent disability. [Footnote omitted.] Sheffield v. Eli Lilly and Co., 192 Cal.Rptr. 870, 874 (Ct.App.Cal.1983).

It is plaintiff's position that the illness from which Mr. Warner ultimately died was the neurological disorder of postvaccinal **encephalitis** or encephalopathy caused by the swine inoculation. On the other hand, defendant contends not only that the swine flu vaccine did not cause **encephalitis** or encephalopathy but that neither postvaccinal **encephalitis** nor encephalopathy was the cause of Mr. Warner's death. . . .

. . . He emphatically asserted that Mr. Warner's illness was not **encephalitis**, which he stated is an acute viral disease. Warner v. U.S., 522 F.Supp. 87–8, 90 (M.D.Fla.1981).

In this action against the United States, F. H. Harries and his wife seek damages for loss sustained when Harries contracted **encephalitis** following a border smallpox vaccination administered by employees of the United States.[1] [[1] **Encephalitis** is a clinical term descriptive of an inflammation of the brain.] Harries v. U.S., 350 F.2d 231–2 (9th Cir. 1965).

encephalitis, acute disseminated See *encephalitis, postinfection.*

encephalitis, hemorrhagic herpes encephalitis in which there is inflammation of the brain with hemorrhagic foci and perivascular exudate; called also *Strümpell-Leichtenstern type of encephalitis.*

I find that Mrs. Stich has failed to establish by a preponderance of the credible evidence that the condition she is suffering from is GBS, or that it is causally related to the swine flu inoculation which she received. I find instead that the most probable diagnosis of Mrs. Stich's condition is **herpes simplex encephalitis** ("HSE") of a viral etiology unrelated to the swine flu inoculation she received. See Caputo v. United States, 157 F.Supp. 568, 571 (D.N.J.1957); Szczytko v. Public Service Coordinated Transport, 21 N.J.Super. 258, 264, 91 A.2d 116 (App.Div.1952). . . .

. . . A physical examination by Dr. Tsairis on October 14, 1981, found her spastic in all four extremities. She still exhibited bilateral Babinski reflexes, and could not follow objects or fingers with her eyes. She had a mild left ptosis (drooping of the eyelid) and would attempt to put into her mouth any object that would come into her visual field. As is clear from this summary, Mrs. Stich's residual intellectual impairment is substantial. . . .

It has been known for some time that **HSE**, being primarily a focal encephalitis, may be detected through the use of Computer Axial Tomography ("CAT") and technetium radionucleid-type brain scans and electroencephalographs ("EEGs") which may reveal the location of focal lesions in the brain. The pres-

ence of such focal lesions would support the diagnosis of **HSE** and contraindicate the diagnosis of postvaccinal encephalitis. The Collaborative Study Group has found that the EEG, brain scan and CAT scan are the three best noninvasion (non-biopsy) tools or studies to correctly predict an **HSE** diagnosis. Clinical findings alone, such as fever, CSF pleocytosis, consciousness and convulsions, have been found insufficient in and of themselves to predict or confirm such a diagnosis, although they may create the initial suspicion. . . .

Encephalitis is an inflammation of the brain. Viral encephalitis is the most common form of encephalitis and is usually characterized by localized lesions in the brain. **HSE**, in turn, is the most frequently found viral encephalitis in humans, and is caused by the herpes simplex virus. This virus is usually benign, but for unknown reasons it may attack the temporal lobe or the inferior part of the frontal lobe, thereafter sometimes extending back into the occipital, parietal and frontal areas.

In **HSE** cases the virus typically causes localized involvement first, with affected brain cells becoming swollen and edematous. The disease, as detected by such edema, normally begins in the gray matter, but may spread through the white matter (neural tissue which typically underlies the cortical gray matter, or is gathered into central tracts and peripheral nerves) as the infection progresses. The acute phase of **HSE**, with the virus infecting the cortex and subcortical white matter, leads eventually to severe necrosis. The host eventually may bring the virus under control, but not before irreversible brain damage is done. Where **HSE** is untreated, the infection may become bilateral, meaning that the opposite side of the brain may become involved, and the virus may continue its destructive process.[16]

HSE, as a predominantly focal disease, usually produces neurological signs on the opposite side of the body from the sector of the brain which is involved; such signs include central nervous system weakness, focal seizures, one-sided pathological responses, and hemiparesis (implying frontal area involvement) or hemianopsia (implying occipital area involvement). Onset of **HSE** is typically accompanied by fever and headache, focal neurological symptoms, behavioral disturbances, and altered consciousness. **HSE** is the most common non-epidemic cause of fatal rapid-onset disorder of the central nervous system; it is a devastating condition which is fatal for approximately 75% of all patients. Those who survive suffer a severe neurologic deficit due to destruction of part of the brain. The typical residual disabilities include hemiparesis and disorders of cognition, thought and memory. . . .

Finally, the course of Mrs. Stich's condition, from onset until today, is typical for **HSE**. The onset of the plaintiff's disease was typical, manifested by high fever, abnormal behavior, focal seizures, eyes deviated to the left, elevated protein, white cells in CSF, and rapid progress toward coma.

After onset, the course remained typical of **HSE**, presenting severe motor difficulties of the upper motor neuron type (i.e., originating in the central nervous system). These upper motor neuron motor difficulties included the left hemiparesis noted at Columbia, the left upper motor neuron facial paralysis, the left arm and left leg spasticity, the severe disorder of all four extremities, predominantly the left side. This course was indicative of supra-temporal destruction of brain with residuals caused by **HSE**. The signs of central nervous system involvement included exaggerated reflexes, the Babinski reflex, spasticity, ankle clonus, and abnormal EEG. (Gluck at 2674.)

Mrs. Stich's mental status deteriorated as coma eventually resolved into a persistent vegetative state. Today, marked memory disorder and numerous problems in the cognitive spheres continue to persist, all of which are hallmarks of **HSE**. The present condition shows obvious sequelae of severe encephalitis, including serious dysfunction of cognition, memory, behavioral changes, and impaired higher cortical functions; there continues to be marked upper motor neuron type (i.e., central nervous system) difficulty in all four extremities, predominantly the left, and especially in the legs. The continued spasticity today is another example of a typical residual of **Herpes Simplex Encephalitis**, and it is noted that medications for spasticity have continued since the early course of this disease. [16] Upon biopsy of autopsy of the brain in an **HSE** case, the presence of the virus will be found bilaterally but in larger quantities where the disease began.] Stich v. U.S., 565 F.Supp. 1096, 1098–1100, 1112–13, 1118–19 (D.N.J.1983).

encephalitis, herpes; encephalitis, herpes simplex; encephalitis, herpetic a disease caused by herpesvirus, resembling equine encephalomyelitis. See also *encephalitis, hemorrhagic.*

encephalitis, postinfection an acute disease of the central nervous system seen in persons who are convalescing from infectious diseases, usually one of viral origin; called also *acute disseminated e., acute disseminated encephalomyelitis, acute demyelinating disease,* and *acute perivascular myelinoclasis.*

ADEM is a diffuse disease of the white matter of the brain, often having the same clinical presentation as post-vaccinal encephalitis. ADEM is a disorder or a group of disorders which is mediated on an immune or allergic basis....

... The CAT scans in this case are not what one would expect in ADEM: the middle to higher cuts of the earlier CAT scans, which should be the site of ADEM, are normal and uninvolved. This lack of pathology in the higher cuts is evidence against ADEM. A donut-type lesion, which appeared in the February 17, 1977 CAT scan, affects the cortex of the brain (that is, the gray matter covering the brain), which is more consistent with HSE than ADEM. ADEM is not a cortical disease....

... ADEM is a very rare disease which has become even more rare. It is virtually unreported in the medical literature of CAT scans. Stich v. U.S., 565 F.Supp. 1096, 1121–2 (D.N.J. 1983).

encephalitis, viral

On the other hand, **viral encephalitis** is characterized by a gradual onset of symptoms, long illness with a slow recovery that often results in residual brain damage. Lethargy, rapid heartbeat, and the elevation of the white blood count in the spinal fluid are also important symptoms of **viral encephalitis**. Skogen v. Dow Chemical Co., 375 F.2d 692, 698 (8th Cir. 1967).

encephalomalacia (en-sef"ah-lo-mah-la'she-ah) [*encephalo-* + Gr. *malakia* softness] softening of the brain.

Her death certificate, dated June 26, 1950, showed: "Disease or condition directly leading to death—Gliora with En-

cephalomalacia'' (meaning brain tumor or a growth in the tissues of the brain)....

... Contestant's additional medical testimony tended to show that if a tumor or growth in the brain tissues makes pressure upon it, the pressure begins to interfere with and to alter the speech and to affect the mind, causing one to become forgetful, "and so forth." ...

... Acute cerebral **encephalomalacia** (a diseased condition of brain tissues, a sudden softening of the brain substance itself). Glover v. Bruce, 265 S.W.2d 346, 351 (Mo.1954).

encephalomyelitis (en-sef"ah-lo-mi"ĕ-li'tis) inflammation involving both the brain and the spinal cord.

encephalomyelitis, acute disseminated See *encephalitis, postinfection.*

encephalomyeloradiculopathy (en-sef"ah-lo-mi"ĕ-lo-rah-dik"u-lop'ah-the) disease involving the brain, spinal cord, and spinal nerve roots.

Dr. Medinets has been practicing neurology and neurosurgery since 1950. He felt that Mrs. Stich suffered from **encephalomyeloradiculopathy**. He testified that she had both peripheral nervous system and CNS involvement. Boiled down, it was Dr. Medinets' conclusion that Mrs. Stich's peripheral neuropathy could be classified as a GBS and her CNS pathology as a meningo-encephalitis. While I have considerable regard for Dr. Medinets' qualifications, I find that his opinion as to diagnosis and causation is unpersuasive. Stich v. U.S., 565 F.Supp. 1096, 1109 (D.N.J.1983).

encephalopathy (en-sef"ah-lop'ah-the) [*encephalo-* + Gr. *pathos* illness] any degenerative disease of the brain.

Defendant Sherman vaccinated Mark, at that time healthy in body and mind, with either Quadrigen, manufactured by Parke-Davis, or Compligen, manufactured by Dow, on January 18, 1961. On January 23, 1961 Mark was admitted to Nassau County's Meadowbrook Hospital with a very high fever later measured at 108° and subsequently diagnosed as postvaccinal **encephalopathy** ("PVE"), which is known to cause brain damage, convulsive seizures, blindness, deafness, paralysis, mental retardation, and possibly death. Ezagui v. Dow Chemical Corp., 598 F.2d 727, 730 (2d Cir. 1979).

Further hospitalization for 13 days after March 11, 1976 was based upon diagnosis of post traumatic **encephalopathy**, right frontal skull defect.... Sears, Roebuck & Co. v. Tatum, 586 P.2d 734, 736 (Okl.1978).

Both doctors agreed that he was peculiarly susceptible to traumatic injury to his brain, having suffered a degree of **encephalopathy** on various prior occasions when stress, trauma or infection "aggravated the preexisting disposition towards this type of result." Buccery v. General Motors Corp., 132 Cal.Rptr. 605, 608 (Ct.App.Cal.1976).

Other Authorities: Sears v. Cooper, 574 S.W.2d 612, 614 (Ct.Civ.App.Tex.1978); Glover v. Bruce, 265 S.W.2d 346, 348 (Mo.1954).

encephalopathy, anoxic

... severe **anoxic encephalopathy**, meaning a lack of oxygen in the brain. So that, superimposed on Peter's other catastrophic illnesses, residuals and disabilities, he has sustained irreversible diffuse damage to both hemispheres of the brain at the cortical and subcortical levels. Application of Lydia E. Hall Hospital, 455 N.Y.S.2d 706, 708 (Sup.Ct.Nassau Cty.1982).

encephalopathy, hepatic a condition usually occurring secondarily to advanced disease of the liver but also seen in the course of any severe disease or in patients with portacaval shunts. It is marked by disturbances of consciousness which may progress to deep coma (hepatic coma), psychiatric changes of varying degree, flapping tremor, and fetor hepaticus. Called also *portal-systemic encephalopathy*.

Her condition worsened, resulting in some brain damage due to **hepatic encephalopathy**. Her treating physician, Dr. McCleery, diagnosed Mrs. Coffran as suffering from hepatitis caused by the June exposure to halothane. Coffran v. Hitchcock Clinic, Inc., 683 F.2d 5, 7 (1st Cir. 1982).

The physicians in attendance concluded that the unfortunate youngster who, in the month before admission, had twice "mainlined" heroin, was in the terminal stage of **hepatic coma** and that, absent some radical procedure to stimulate liver regeneration, accumulation of toxins would shortly end his life. Jones v. City of New York, 395 N.Y.S.2d 10–11 (1st Dep't 1977).

encephalopathy, hypoxic

During the tubal ligation procedure the patient suffered an episode of cardiac arrest with resulting massive brain damage, seizures and convulsions.[4] She has died since this appeal was brought. [4 The patient's condition was referred to as **hypoxic encephalopathy** (inadequate blood supply and inadequate oxygen to the nerve cells of the brain and spinal cord.)] Thompson v. Presbyterian Hosp., Inc., 652 P.2d 260, 262 (Okl.1982).

The principal cause of death was **hypoxic encephalopathy**, lack of oxygen to the brain. Marek v. U.S., 639 F.2d 1164, 1166 (5th Cir. 1981).

encephalopathy, lead brain disorder caused by lead poisoning; called also *saturnine e.* See also *poisoning, lead* (Lead Industries Ass'n case).

The more severe neurological effects of high level lead exposure are the clinical syndrome of **lead encephalopathy**. Early symptoms include dullness, restlessness, irritability, headaches, muscular tremor, hallucinations, and loss of memory. These symptoms rapidly progress (sometimes within 48 hours) to delirium, mania, convulsions, paralysis, coma, and death. Id. at 11–15, JA 1237. Lead Industries Ass'n v. Environmental Protection, 647 F.2d 1130, 1140 (D.C.Cir.1980).

encephalopathy, posttraumatic See *syndrome, postconcussional*.

encysted (en-sist'ed) [Gr. *en* in + *kystis* sac, bladder] enclosed in a sac, bladder, or cyst.

During the ensuing year the plaintiff suffered headaches which grew progressively more excruciatingly painful and were accompanied by dizziness and nausea. In early 1964 an Austrian neurologist, Dr. Strasser, X-rayed the plaintiff's skull and on March 7, 1964 he advised the plaintiff that pantopaque globules **encysted** on brain tissues were the primary cause of his illness. Toal v. U.S., 438 F.2d 222, 224 (2d Cir. 1971).

end stage kidney disease See *disease, end stage kidney*.

endarterectomy (end"ar-ter-ek'to-me) excision of the thickened, atheromatous tunica intima of an artery.

An **endarterectomy** is a surgical procedure where the plaque from the inside of the carotid arteries is removed, thereby increasing the arteries' blood flow capacity....

The technique employed in performing an **endarterectomy** is fairly standard. An incision is made between muscles in the neck. The carotid sheath is opened and the carotid artery is separated from the vagus nerve and the judgular vein. The carotid artery is clamped to prevent blood flow or, in the alternative, a temporary carotid shunt is used. An incision is then made in the artery, the plaque is cleaned out and finally the artery is closed. The clamps or shunt are removed and the incision in the neck is also closed. Lemke v. U.S., 557 F.Supp. 1205, 1207–8 (D.N.Dak.1983).

The October 1968 operation is described as a bilateral aortoiliac **endarterectomy**, the operation performed by Dr. Nosti. He removed obstructive plaque from the left and right common iliac arteries (which branch off from the aorta in a Y shape)....

... Dr. Nosti did not further elaborate on that statement to explain that sexual impairment was a risk known to be associated with an aortoiliac **endarterectomy**, or that the damage was irreparable. Hulver v. U.S., 562 F.2d 1132, 1135 (8th Cir. 1977).

endemic (en-dem'ik) [Gr. *endēmos* dwelling in a place] a disease of low morbidity that is constantly present in a human community, but clinically recognizable in only a few.

"Q. What do you mean by endemic area?
"A. That it is found in great part only in this area and not in other areas...." Crawford v. Industrial Com'n, 534 P.2d 1077, 1080 (Ct.App.Ariz.1975).

endocarditis (en"do-kar-di'tis) exudative and proliferative inflammatory alterations of the endocardium, characterized by the presence of vegetations on the surface of the endocardium or in the endocardium itself, and most commonly involving a heart valve, but sometimes affecting the inner lining of the cardiac chambers or the endocardium elsewhere. It may occur as a primary disorder, or as a complication of or in association with another disease.

endocarditis, bacterial infectious endocarditis (q.v.), acute or subacute, caused by various bacteria, including streptococci, staphylococci, enterococci, gonococci, gram-negative bacilli, etc.

"On September 14, 1972, the plaintiff was treated by the defendant dentist for an abscessed tooth. It is alleged that the defendant dentist was negligent in his treatment. In December of 1972 the plaintiff developed a heart problem which resulted in his hospitalization from December of 1972 through February 1973. His condition was diagnosed as **bacterial endocarditis**. In February of 1973 an aortic valve transplant was performed. On or about February 20, 1973 the plaintiff learned that the condition had resulted from the negligence of the defendant dentist in failing to properly treat the abscessed tooth in September of 1972...." Shadle v. Pearce, 430 A.2d 683–4 (Super.Ct.Pa.1981).

endocardium (en″do-kar′de-um) [*endo-* + Gr. *kardia* heart] [NA] the endothelial lining membrane of the cavities of the heart and the connective tissue bed on which it lies.

endocervicitis (en″do-ser″vĭ-si′tis) [*endo-* + L. *cervix* neck] inflammation of the mucous membrane of the cervix uteri; called also *endotrachelitis.*

... **endocervicitis**, chronic (inflammation of the cervix) within the body of the uterus. Glover v. Bruce, 265 S.W.2d 346, 351 (Mo.1954).

endodontics (en″do-don′tiks) [*end-* + Gr. *odous* tooth + *-ics*] that branch of dentistry which is concerned with the etiology, prevention, diagnosis, and treatment of diseases and injuries that affect the tooth pulp, root, and periapical tissue. Called also *endodontology.*

Dr. Joseph Caldwell was qualified as an expert witness in **endodontics** primarily dealing with root canals. Wiley v. Karam, 421 So.2d 294, 297 (Ct.App.La.1982).

While at dental school he took a course in **endodontics**, the study of the contents of the pulp of the tooth. However, Dr. Davis is not a certified specialist in **endodontics**....

''... There is a classification of a specialty in **endodontics**, and there are endodontists in Wichita. Limit their practice to **endodontics**. To become board qualified you take a two-year training program or a number of post graduate programs satisfying the requirements of the American Board of Endodontists. Also submitting a number of satisfactorily completed cases, I have not attempted to become board qualified for **endodontics**, I have taken post-graduate courses in dentistry....'' Simpson v. Davis, 549 P.2d 950, 952, 955 (Kan.1976).

He explained that he could remove the tooth or treat it through **endodontic** procedures, i.e., removal of the infected pulp tissue within the tooth. She chose the latter alternative. Dufrene v. Faget, 260 So.2d 76, 78 (Ct.App.La.1972).

endometrial See *endometrium.*

endometrial polyp See under *polyp*; and *endometrium.*

endometrioma (en″do-me″tre-o′mah) a solitary, non-neoplastic mass containing endometrial tissue.

... an **endometrioma** (an ovarian cyst internally caused by severe endometriosis), in either case complicated by pelvic inflammatory disease. Karl J. Pizzalotto, M.D., Ltd. v. Wilson, 437 So.2d 859, 861 (La.1983).

endometriosis (en″do-me″tre-o′sis) [*endometrium* + *-osis*] a condition in which tissue more or less perfectly resembling the uterine mucous membrane (the endometrium) and containing typical endometrial granular and stromal elements occurs aberrantly in various locations in the pelvic cavity; called also *adenomyosis externa* and *endometriosis externa.* See also *adenomyosis.*

Dr. Stewart also diagnosed the pain as attributable to a pelvic inflammation and **endometriosis**, a disease whereby the endometrium, the lining of the uterus, backs up into the uterus, fallopian tubes and ovaries rather than being emptied from the uterus during the menstrual period. Once it backs up, the endometrium passes through the surface of the reproductive organs causing cysts and adhesions that form in reaction to blood

irritating the surface of the organs. The adhesions cause the reproductive and other pelvic organs to become attached to one another and increasingly distorted until, if not treated, sterility results. Karl J. Pizzalotto, M.D., Ltd. v. Wilson, 437 So.2d 859, 861 (La.1983).

... the uterus had markedly enlarged in size possibly resulting from a fibroid condition or **endometriosis** (internal menstruation). Again, a total hysterectomy was recommended. LaCaze v. Collier, 434 So.2d 1039, 1041 (La.1983).

Even plaintiffs' expert conceded that the **endometriosis** which required the hysterectomy was only discoverable surgically and not upon the basis of a mere pelvic examination. Gayle v. Neyman, 457 N.Y.S.2d 499, 502 (1st Dep't 1983).

Other Authorities: Pugsley v. Privette, 263 S.E.2d 69, 71 (Va. 1980); Hammock v. Allstate Ins. Co., 124 Ga.App. 854, 855–6, 186 S.E.2d 353 (1971); Bly v. Rhoads, 222 S.E.2d 783, 785 (Va.1976); Carmichael v. Reitz, 95 Cal.Rptr. 381, 384 (Ct.App. Cal.1971).

endometritis (en″do-mĕ-tri′tis) [*endometrium* + *-itis*] inflammation of the endometrium.

Since she had the I.U.D., he suspected **endometritis**, which is inflammation or infection of the lining of the uterus and caused menstrual-type pain. Baker v. Beebe, 367 So.2d 102, 105 (Ct. App.La.1979).

endometrium (en-do-me′tre-um), pl. *endome′tria* [*endo-* + Gr. *metra* uterus] the inner mucous membrane of the uterus, the thickness and structure of which vary with the phase of the menstrual cycle. It is functionally divisible into three layers: the stratum basale, stratum spongiosum, and stratum compactum; the latter two layers together form the *stratum functionale.* Accepted by NA as an alternative term for *tunica mucosa uteri.*

On July 31, 1971, she was admitted to St. Mary's Hospital, Milwaukee, Wisconsin, for treatment of cancer of the **endometrium** (mucous membrane lining the uterus) and a fractured right hip. On October 15, 1971.... Klofta v. Mathews, 418 F.Supp. 1139, 1140 (E.D.Wis.1976).

In humans, chronic estrogenic stimulation of the uterus, whether due to excessive ovarian production or abnormalities of the reproductive cycle, results in increased cancer of the **endometrium**....

... Such cancer has also been observed to develop in women during or following estrogen therapy. Women in these two categories show a higher incidence of cancer of the **endometrium** than women who are not subject to such additional endogenous or exogenous estrogens. Bell v. Goddard, 366 F.2d 177, 180 (7th Cir. 1966).

endoneural (en″do-nu′ral) pertaining to or situated within a nerve.

An **endoneural** injection is an injection into a nerve root or into a nerve. Funke v. Fieldman, 512 P.2d 539, 544 (Kan.1973).

endoscopic (en″do-skop′ik) performed by means of an endoscope; pertaining to endoscopy.

endoscopy (en-dos′ko-pe) visual inspection of any cavity of the body by means of an endoscope.

... there was substantial evidence that plaintiff has been, and will continue to be limited in the future in his professional activities, and otherwise, particularly with regard to his ability to perform **endoscopic** surgery by virtue of the injury to his eye. Thomas v. American Cystoscope Makers Inc., 414 F.Supp. 255, 258 (E.D.Pa.1976).

He alleged that the presence of the foreign body went undiscovered until its removal by **endoscopy** on October 14, 1975. Keating v. Zemel, 421 A.2d 1181–2 (Super.Ct.Pa.1980).

endothelium (en″do-the′le-um), pl. *endothe′lia* [*endo-* + Gr. *thēlē* nipple] [NA] the layer of epithelial cells that lines the cavities of the heart and of the blood and lymph vessels, and the serous cavities of the body, originating from the mesoderm.

endothelium, corneal the portion of the endothelium of the anterior chamber of the eye that covers the posterior surface of the cornea.

The first operative procedure was a curettement of the **endothelium** by Dr. Kleinhandler with Dr. Paton in attendance, which had for its purpose the scraping of an underlying layer of diseased tissue. The second operation, the corneal transplant, was performed by Dr. Kleinhandler with Dr. Doctor supervising. The third operation was performed by Dr. Paton for a secondary glaucoma. The ultimate result of the surgical procedures is a bulging opaque corneal transplant with the iris completely adherent to the posterior surface of the cornea and perception limited to light and shadows. McDermott v. Manhattan Eye Ear & Throat Hospital, 228 N.Y.S.2d 143, 147 (1st Dep't 1962).

endotoxin (en″do-tok′sin) a heat-stable toxin present in the bacterial cell but not in cell-free filtrates of cultures of intact bacteria. They are found primarily in gram-negative organisms, in which they are identical with the somatic antigen. They occur in the cell wall as a lipopolysaccharide complex extractable in trichloracetic acid and glycols. The endotoxins are pyrogenic and increase capillary permeability, the activity being substantially the same regardless of the species of bacteria from which they are derived. Called also *bacterial pyrogen*. See also *lipopolysaccharide* (Ezagui case).

endotracheal (en″do-tra′ke-al) [*endo-* + *trachea*] 1. within or through the trachea. 2. performed by passage through the lumen of the trachea. See also *tracheostomy*.

endotracheal tube See *tube, endotracheal*.

endrin (en′drin) chemical name: 1,2,3,4,4,10,10-hexachloro-6,7-epoxy-1,4,4a,5,6,7,8,8a-octahydro-1,4,5,8 - endo-endo-dimethono-naphthalene; a highly toxic insecticide of the chlorinated hydrocarbon group.

Endrin is a chlorinated hydrocarbon first introduced about 1950.[2] It has been used as a pesticide for several decades, and is currently used for pest control on crops including cotton and sugar cane....

Evidence concerning the dangers of **endrin** to public health and the environment has been produced over the years since **endrin** was first introduced. In 1965, results from a study using rats suggested that it was carcinogenic. *See* 41 Fed.Reg. 31316 (1976). EPA has found that **endrin** has caused fifty-two

reported fish and wildlife kills, largely the result of leakage or runoff during agricultural use. Id. at 31317. However, a massive fish kill in the lower Mississippi in 1963 was traced to discharges from Velsicol's Memphis plant. 42 Fed.Reg. 2591. **Endrin** is suspected in particular of threatening the brown pelican, an endangered species sensitive to **endrin**. 42 Fed. Reg. 2591; 41 Fed.Reg. 31317. [Footnotes omitted.][2] Encyclopedia Britannica (Micropedia) 215 (1974) (definition of aldrin, a related substance).] Hercules, Inc. v. Environmental Protection Agcy., 598 F.2d 91, 98 (D.C.Cir.1978).

Enduron (en′du-ron) trademark for a preparation of methyclothiazide. See also *methyclothiazide*.

enema (en′e-mah), pl. *enemas* or *enem′ata* [Gr.] a clyster or injection; a liquid injected or to be injected into the rectum. See also *appendicitis* (Koch case).

energy (en′er-je) [Gr. *energeia*] the capacity to operate or work; power to produce motion, to overcome resistance, and to effect physical changes.

"And then there is another fundamental component, and this is **energy**. Although **energy** may be defined in many ways, I suspect that perhaps one of the simplest definitions is one in which it is defined simply as that component of the universe which makes matter move. Without **energy** in this universe of ours all of the things which we see, feel, and touch would be absolutely stationary; there would be no motion...." Chiropractice Ass'n of New York, Inc. v. Hilleboe, 227 N.Y.S.2d 309, 345 (Sup.Ct.Albany Cty.1961).

enophthalmos (en-of-thal′mos) [Gr. *en* in + *ophthalmos* eye] a backward displacement of the eyeball into the orbit.

... she had an **enophthalmos** (a sinking of the left eye).... Yarrow v. U.S., 309 F.Supp. 922, 927 (S.D.N.Y.1970).

Enovid (en-o′vid) trademark for preparations of mestranol and norethynodrel. See also *mestranol; norethynodrel; and contraceptive, oral*.

Norman Elliot Brewer testified that his wife, Sandra, began taking **Enovid** for birth control purposes about one month following the birth of their son in 1963....

... In the early part of 1965 Sandra experienced and complained of blackouts or memory lapses, dizziness, headaches and tingling in the fingers....

... Dr. Prewitt testified that he suspected that **Enovid**, the contraceptive pills Sandra had been taking, were responsible for the thrombosis....

... Dr. Prewitt testified that it was his opinion that **Enovid** causally contributed to Sandra's death. The fact that she had been taking the drug for several years did not rule out the contraceptive as the cause of the condition resulting in her death....

... Dr. Winter noted that prior to 1960 it was known for at least 20 years that the synthetic hormones used in the manufacture of **Enovid** produced metabolic changes in humans. He noted that these hormones had been found to affect certain factors involved in the blood clotting process. Mahr v. G. D. Searle & Co., 390 N.E.2d 1214, 1220, 1222–3 (App.Ct.Ill. 1979).

The subject birth control drug **Enovid** is an endocrine preparation which substitutes for the natural hormones, estrogen and
progesterone. Like the natural hormones, **Enovid** secretes matter directly into the bloodstream. The function of the pituitary
gland in the brain is thereby suppressed to the extent of preventing the release of an egg by the ovary. **Enovid** is a "prescription drug" as provided by statute and by the regulations
of the United States Food and Drug Administration. It was
placed on the market for control of menstrual disturbances in
1957, and later, in 1960, it was additionally approved for use
as an oral contraceptive. It continues to be so approved today. Lawson v. G. D. Searle & Company, 331 N.E.2d 75, 86
(App.Ct.Ill.1975).

Dr. Reitz decided to prescribe **Enovid**,[15] which he considered
the drug of choice, for plaintiff's problems since pregnancy,
which he considered to be the optimal treatment, had not
been achieved. He did not feel that surgery was called for at
the time in view of the seriousness of surgical procedure. He
examined plaintiff for pregnancy because **Enovid** taken during
pregnancy can cause masculinization of a female infant. He
prescribed the pill for the purposes of: treating the endometriosis (including premenstrual tension syndrome); treating the
heavy ("characterized by the passage of clotted blood") and
painful menstrual flow (dysmenorrhea); and assisting in achieving pregnancy....

Dr. Reitz testified that he advised plaintiff of the risks and
hazards of breakthrough bleeding, nausea, and vomiting in
taking **Enovid**, and instructed her that if she had problems with
the medicine to contact him. Plaintiff testified that Dr. Reitz
discussed endometriosis with her; that it caused blood cysts;
that he informed her that in some instances **Enovid** might be
helpful in treating endometriosis and that a purpose for prescribing **Enovid** was to treat the endometriosis.... [15 Dr.
Reitz testified that **Enovid** is "a combination of two agents;
one is progesterone and one is estrogen."]

... Exhibit "A", as well as Code 364 dated March 16,
1964, attached to Exhibit "A", listed under contraindications:
"3. Previous Thrombophlebitis or Pulmonary Embolism. **Enovid**
is contraindicated in these patients unless the reason for its use
in the judgment of the physician is overwhelming." Carmichael
v. Reitz, 95 Cal.Rptr. 381, 388, 401 (Ct.App.Cal.1971).

enteric-coated (en-ter"ik-kōt'ed) a term designating a special coating applied to tablets or capsules which prevents
release and absorption of their contents until they reach
the intestines.

An **enteric coating** is applied to a medicament for the purpose
of transporting the medicament unaltered through the acidic
environment of the stomach and into the small intestine....
... A typical claim is Claim (1) as follows:
"An article of manufacture for the introduction of trypsin into
the blood stream for systemic treatment of inflammation
which comprises an orally administrable dosage unit in which
the effective therapeutic ingredient consists of 10 to 50 mgs,
of trypsin, said dosage unit being enterically coated the **enteric coating** being of sufficient thickness so as to resist dissolution and disintegration of the dosage unit in passing
through the gastrointestinal tract until it reaches the ileum in
which it disintegrates permitting liberation of the trypsin and
absorption of the trypsin into the blood stream." Armour

Pharmaceutical Co. v. Richardson-Merrell, Inc., 396 F.2d
70–1 (3d Cir. 1968).

enteritis (en"ter-i'tis) [enter- + -itis] inflammation of the
intestine, applied chiefly to inflammation of the small
intestine. See also *enterocolitis*.

Enteritis refers to inflammation of the small intestine. Anderson
v. Moore, 275 N.W.2d 842, 846 (Neb.1979).

enterococcus (en"ter-o-kok'us), pl. *enterococ'ci* [entero- +
coccus] any streptococcus of the human intestine; the
enterococcus group includes *Streptococcus faecalis, S.
durans, S. liquefaciens,* and *S. zymogenes.*

After the orchiectomy, Stanley's left testicle was sent to the
hospital's laboratory for examination. The pathological report
showed that there was a hematoma with an abscess as a result
of an infection of **enterococcus** and E. coli bacteria. In addition, there was an area of hemorrhage found in the left testicle. [In this case, it traveled outside the intestine, where it is
usually found. Ed.] Stanley v. Fisher, 417 N.E.2d 932–3 (Ct.
App.Ind.1981).

The laboratory reported on September 11 that with respect to
the knee fluid there was "gram-positive cocci—identification
pending," and on September 12 or 13 a further report was
issued reading "Culture-Rare Hemolytic Enterococci." Dr.
Tadros testified that, particularly because the cocci was
"rare," it was normal for the laboratory to take extra time to
identify the type. Dr. Tadros defined "**enterococcus**" as being
a normal inhabitant in the bowel but a cause of infection if
present in other areas such as in a knee wound....

After plaintiff was released he asked Dr. Borders what
caused the infection, and Borders said: "Well, it's either three
things: Either a glove or a tool that wasn't well sterilized or a
defective mask and one of the persons that was operating
breathed into it." Contreras v. St. Lukes Hospital, 144 Cal.
Rptr. 647, 651–2 (Ct.App.Cal.1978).

enterocolitis (en"ter-o-ko-li'tis) [entero- + colitis] inflammation involving both the small intestine and the colon.
See also *enteritis*.

enterocolitis, pseudomembranous an acute inflammation
of the bowel mucosa with the formation of pseudomembranous plaques overlying an area of superficial ulceration, and the passage of the pseudomembranous material
in the feces; it may result from shock and ischemia or be
associated with antibiotic therapy. Called also *necrotizing
e.* and *pseudomembranous colitis* or *enteritis*.

We note the following colloquy between counsel for Upjohn
and Dr. Walker:
Q.   And with regard to—Doctor, I am going to ask you this:
You said that you didn't know about **pseudomembranous colitis** at the time, but even if you had known about it, knowing
that the Cleocin was the best drug on the market to give Mr.
Mauldin, you would have given it to him, anyway, wouldn't
you?
A.   I probably would have at the time because there was
really no adequate substitute to use....
... Dr. McHardy was of the opinion that the Upjohn warning did not notify the practicing physician of the danger of
pseudomembranous colitis as a possible adverse reaction to
the use of Cleocin or Lincocin nor advise of any method of

treatment for complications arising from the use of the drugs. Mauldin v. Upjohn Co., 697 F.2d 644, 646–7 (5th Cir. 1983).

He further stated that the only side effects of or reaction to terramycin of which he was aware by reason of his own experience, "and that would include possibly any case that has ever been in Research Hospital," was "**pseudo-mucinous enterocolitis**" which is a reaction that occurs in the bowel resulting from the antibiotic killing off normal bacteria as well as the infection producing bacteria. Fisher v. Wilkinson, 382 S.W.2d 627, 629 (Mo.1964).

enterostomy (en"ter-os'to-me) [entero- + Gr. stomoun to provide with an opening, or mouth] the formation of a permanent opening into the intestine through the abdominal wall, usually by surgical means; also, the opening so created.

enterotoxin (en"ter-o-tok'sin) an exotoxin that is protein in nature and relatively heat stable, produced by staphylococci, primarily by coagulase-positive *Staphylococcus pyogenes* var. *aureus*. Enterotoxin, which on ingestion produces violent vomiting and diarrhea, is the primary factor in staphylococcal food poisoning.

Both parties have stipulated that the **enterotoxin** produced by coagulase positive Staphylococcus aureus is a poisonous and deleterious substance injurious to the health of the consuming human....

Dr. Zehren testified, as an expert witness, that cheese containing either **enterotoxin** or coagulase positive Staphylococcus aureus capable of producing **enterotoxin** is unsafe and unfit for its intended use. Safeway Stores, Inc. v. L.D. Schreiber Cheese Co., 326 F.Supp. 504, 507 (W.D.Mo.1971).

enterovirus (en"ter-o-vi'rus) one of a subgroup of the picornaviruses infecting the gastrointestinal tract and discharged in the excreta, including poliovirus, the coxsackieviruses, and the echoviruses. See also *poliovirus*.

envelope (en've-lōp) an encompassing structure or membrane. In virology, a coat surrounding the capsid and usually furnished at least partially by the host cell. In bacteriology, the cell wall and the plasma membrane considered together.

He had a tear of the **envelope** which surrounds the brain in the right base of the skull so that spinal fluid leaked out of the right ear. Hampton v. State Highway Com'n, 498 P.2d 236, 251 (Kan.1972).

environment (en-vi'ron-ment) [Fr. environner to surround, to encircle] the sum total of all the conditions and elements which make up the surroundings and influence the development of an individual.

environmental impact statement

Plaintiffs sought in their complaint (1) to require the defendants to prepare and file an **environmental impact statement** pursuant to the requirements of Section 102(2)(C) of the National Environmental Policy Act of 1969 (NEPA)....

... Plaintiffs contended that the construction of the marina itself will adversely affect the aesthetic and environmental well-being of the area and is the key for plans for further destruction of the environment of Bald Head Island. Conserva-

tion Council of North Carolina v. Costanzo, 398 F.Supp. 653, 656 (E.D.N.Car.1975).

enzyme (en'zīm) [Gr. *en* in + *zymē* leaven] a protein produced in a cell and capable of greatly accelerating by its catalytic action the chemical reaction of a substance (the substrate) for which it is often specific. Enzymes perform this function without being destroyed or altered. They are divided into six main groups: oxidoreductases, transferases, hydrolases, lyases, isomerases, and ligases.

More importantly, the warm and fluent meat contains **enzymes** (live tissues) that metabolize (consume) residual internal oxygen. Bird Provision Co. v. Owens Country Sausage, Inc., 568 F.2d 369, 372 (5th Cir. 1978).

Because **enzymes** (i.e., naturally produced organic catalysts) were known to trigger other types of sugar conversion, research workers had, for some years prior to Marshall's work, been on the look-out for an **enzyme** which would convert dextrose into levulose. CPC International, Inc. v. Standard Brands Inc., 385 F.Supp. 1057–8 (D.Del.1974).

Modern science has not been able to chemically define **enzymes**.[1] They are usually described by what they do, not by what they are.... [[1] Definitions of "**Enzyme**", "Enzyme Preparation having Starch-Glucogenase Activity" and "Transglucosidase" were stipulated as follows: "**Enzyme:** Specific, cell-independent catalysts of biological origin, which are proteinaceous and can be destroyed by heating." "Enzyme Preparation having Starch-Glucogenase Activity: Any **enzyme**-containing substance which gives a positive value when subjected to the procedure and calculations described in U.S. 2, 531,999, column 3, lines 14 to 51."]

The **enzymes** mentioned in this case are derived from fungi (molds). They excrete through their cell walls **enzymes** of various digestive abilities or activities. A large number of **enzymes** of "activities" are produced by a culturing of a single kind of mold such as Aspergillus oryzae or Aspergillus niger. Among these activities is an amylase, which hydrolyses starch to dextrose. Baxter Laboratories, Inc. v. Corn Products Co., 394 F.2d 892–3 (7th Cir. 1968).

enzyme, proteolytic one that catalyzes the hydrolysis of proteins and various split products of protein, the final product being small peptides and amino acids.

"The '93 patent teaches the use of enteric coated **proteolytic enzymes**, notably trypsin and chymotrypsin, as orally administered anti-inflammatory agents....

"... These enzymes are derived from pancreatin which is a substance derived from the freshly ground pancreas of hogs and cattle...." Armour Pharmaceutical Co. v. Richardson-Merrell, Inc., 396 F.2d 70–1 (3d Cir. 1968).

eosin (e'o-sin) [Gr. *ēōs* dawn] a rose-colored stain or dye: typically the sodium salt of tetrabromfluorescein, $C_{20}H_6Br_4Na_2O_5$, C.I. 45380. Commercially, several other red coal tar dyes are called eosin. All the eosins are bromine derivatives of fluorescin. Eosin is an important plasma stain, used especially with hematoxylin, methylene blue, and methyl green.

eosinophil (e"o-sin'o-fil) [eosin + Gr. *philein* to love] a structure, cell, or histologic element readily stained by eosin, especially a granular leukocyte with a nucleus that usually has two lobes connected by a slender thread of chromatin, and cytoplasm containing coarse, round granules that are uniform in size; called also *acidocyte, eosinocyte, eosinophilic leukocyte*, and *Rindfleisch's cell*.

In any case, the court's primary reliance was clearly on the Clinic's failure to perform an **eosinophil** test in June. This is a test which determines the percentage of **eosinophils**—a type of white cell—in the blood. Plaintiffs argued that if it had been performed, it would have warned of Mrs. Coffran's sensitivity to halothane, and thus would have led to more tests and the choice of a different anesthetic in June. Coffran v. Hitchcock Clinic, Inc., 683 F.2d 5, 9 (1st Cir. 1982).

eosinophilia (e"o-sin"o-fil'e-ah) [*eosin* + Gr. *philein* to love] 1. the formation and accumulation of an abnormally large number of eosinophils in the blood. 2. the condition of being readily stained with eosin.

Plaintiffs' expert anesthesiologist, Dr. Barnett Greene, testified that 50 percent of those who are sensitized to halothane exhibit "**eosinophilia**," or an abnormally high eosinophil count. He also testified that a high eosinophil count Mrs. Coffran had in July 1970 was evidence that she was among the 50 percent who do show **eosinophilia** as a marker of halothane sensitization. Defendant's expert, Dr. Nicholas Greene, disputed this evidence, however. Coffran v. Hitchcock Clinic, Inc., 683 F.2d 5, 11 (1st Cir. 1982).

"... the extreme degree of edema and **eosinophilia** [rose colored stain] suggest an allergic response." Rainer v. Buena Community Memorial Hospital, 95 Cal.Rptr. 901, 905 (Ct. App.Cal.1971).

epicondylitis (ep"ĭ-kon"dĭ-li'tis) inflammation of the epicondyle or of the tissues adjoining the epicondyle of the humerus. See also *condyle; condylus*; and *epicondylus*.

However, Dr. Gritzka, in a letter to claimant's attorney, related claimant's condition to his employment at Dave's:

"In my opinion, there is no question that [claimant's] underlying condition of bilateral humeral **epicondylitis** was made worse due to the work activities at Dave's Bunker Hill Shell Station. The forearm motions, required working as a mechanic, are especially stressful to the epicondylar area, and typically exacerbate underlying **epicondylitis** or tennis elbow...." SAIF v. Gupton, 663 P.2d 1300–1 (Ct.App.Or. 1983).

Examination and X-rays revealed a mild scoliosis of her upper spine and an inflammation of the lateral **epicondyle** of her left elbow, commonly called tennis elbow. Negrete v. Western Elec. Co., Inc., 326 N.W.2d 681–2 (Neb.1982).

... left lateral elbow **epicondylitis**. Gotschall v. Weinberger, 391 F.Supp. 73–4 (D.Neb.1975).

epicondylus (ep"ĭ-kon'dĭ-lus), pl. *epicon'dyli* [L.] [NA] epicondyle: a general term for an eminence upon a bone, above its condyle.

epidemic (ep"ĭ-dem'ik) [Gr. *epidēmios* prevalent] 1. attacking many people in any region at the same time; widely diffused and rapidly spreading. 2. a disease of high morbidity which is only occasionally present in a human community.

Wyeth produced eight expert medical and epidemiological witnesses, each of whom testified that in his opinion a polio **epidemic** existed in Hidalgo County, Texas in May 1970. To arrive at this conclusion, Wyeth's experts employed an "epidemiological definition" of **epidemic**, according to which two cases within a given city, county, or metropolitan area in a four week period may constitute a polio **epidemic**.[47] Dr. Ramiro R. Casso, the Hidalgo County general practitioner who testified as Reyes's medical expert, referred to a medical dictionary to define "**epidemic**" as "[disease] attacking many people in any region at the same time"[48]....

... But for our purpose here I am going to tell you that under the law that the term **epidemic** is a relative term, and the question of how many cases constitute an **epidemic** is a question of fact depending upon the prevailing circumstances. This term **epidemic** in its common and ordinary meaning applies to any disease which is widely spread or generally prevailing at a given place and time. That is what an **epidemic** is. You will be guided by that definition. [[47] This definition, which appeared as part of the 1969 Recommendations of the United States Public Health Service's Advisory Committee on Immunization Practice, is as follows: "An '**epidemic**' of poliomyelitis is defined as two or more cases caused by the same polio virus type and occurring within a four-week period in a circumscribed population such as that of a city, County or metropolitican area."[48] This definition was the first, of three, appearing in Dorlan's [sic] Illustrated Medical Dictionary, Twenty-Fourth Edition, which Dr. Casso testified was "the most generally accepted dictionary by medical people."] Reyes v. Wyeth Laboratories, 498 F.2d 1264, 1290 (5th Cir. 1974).

epidemiology (ep"ĭ-de"me-ol'o-je) [*epidemic* + *-logy*] 1. the study of the relationships of the various factors determining the frequency and distribution of diseases in a human community. 2. the field of medicine concerned with the determination of the specific causes of localized outbreaks of infection, such as hepatitis, of toxic disorders, such as lead poisoning, or any other disease of recognized etiology.

Dr. Goldfield defines **epidemiology** as "the study of the distribution and determination of human affections." Dr. Langmuir defines **epidemiology** as

that branch of scientific study and analysis of the important chronology factors of the occurrence of disease in populations... It's distinct from clinical medicine in that clinical medicine deals with disease in the single person and epidemiology deals with a disease in a community, a number of cases in measured populations. Varga v. U.S., 566 F.Supp. 987, 990 (N.D.Ohio 1983).

Epidemiology is the study of the patterns and causes of disease in human populations. Epidemiologists investigate factors or events that are associated with disease in an effort to determine which of the factors or events are causing the disease.

Epidemiologists are the professionals who are trained to study the cause and effect relationship. They are trained to work with groups of people and populations, analyze reports of disease in relation to the populations, determine incidence rates in the groups, and interpret the differences in various incidence rates. Epidemiologists are qualified to evaluate the level of association, and explanations for the association other than causality. Padgett v. U.S., 553 F.Supp. 794, 799–800 (W.D.Tex.1982).

"**Epidemiology**", the field of expertise of a number of Wyeth's experts, was defined in the defendant's trial brief as a "specialized field of medicine dealing with public health", which is "based on the observation of the occurrence of disease and thereafter, by statistical methods trying to arrive at a conclusion as to the possible source of the disease". Reyes v. Wyeth Laboratories, 498 F.2d 1264, 1271 (5th Cir. 1974).

epididymectomy (ep″ĭ-did″ĭ-mek′to-me) [*epididymis* + Gr. *ektomē* excision] surgical removal of the epididymis. See also *epididymitis*; and *epididymis*.

... contracted epididymytis of the left testicle while incarcerated in a prisoner of war camp. In 1959 he had a recurrence or flareup of the epididymitis resulting in an **epididymectomy** requiring the surgical removal of his left testicle. Miller v. U.S., 431 F.Supp. 988–9 (S.D.Miss.1976).

epididymis (ep″ĭ-did′ĭ-mis), pl. *epididym'ides* [*epi-* + Gr. *didymos* testis] [NA] the elongated cordlike structure along the posterior border of the testis, whose elongated coiled duct provides for storage, transit, and maturation of spermatozoa and is continuous with the ductus deferens. It consists of a head (caput epididymis), body (corpus epididymis), and tail (cauda epididymis). Called also *parorchis*.

epididymitis (ep″ĭ-did″ĭ-mi′tis) inflammation of the epididymis. See also *torsion*.

Dr. Daniels' examination of Parent revealed swelling and tenderness around the left groin area. He diagnosed Parent's ailment as **epididymitis**, an inflammation of the cord and testicle. Parent v. Great Northern Paper Co., 424 A.2d 1099, 1100 (Sup.Jud.Ct.Me.1981).

Dr. Smith states that as torsion most commonly occurs in young men between the ages of twelve and sixteen, while Cradle was twenty-three in 1968, the treating physician treated the condition as an infection (**epididymitis**) [sic] which also occasionally occurs. However, as Dr. Smith found during surgery, plaintiff lost his left testicle due to torsion, which Dr. Smith states probably occurred during this period in 1968. Cradle v. Superintendent, Correctional Field Unit No. 7, 374 F.Supp. 435, 437 (W.D.Va.1973).

epidural (ep″ĭ-du′ral) situated upon or outside the dura mater. See also *dura mater*.

epidural block See *block, epidural*.

epidural space See *cavum, epidurale*.

epiduravenogram See *phlebogram*.

epigastric See *epigastrium*.

epigastrium (ep″ĭ-gas′tre-um) [Gr. *epigastrion*] the upper middle region of the abdomen, located within the sternal angle; called also *regio epigastrica* [NA].

She gave a history of respiratory distress and tenderness in the abdomen in the left upper quadrant and **mid-epigastric** region. Sellers v. Breaux, 422 So.2d 1231, 1234 (Ct.App.La.1982).

On October 30, 1974, plaintiff was admitted to Hutchinson Hospital complaining of acute **epigastric** pain (pain in the up-

per abdomen). Manigan v. Califano, 453 F.Supp. 1080, 1083 (D.Kan.1978).

Plaintiff was admitted to the New York Veterans Administration Hospital on April 4, 1966 for intractable **epigastric** pain, seemingly indicative of a peptic ulcer. Denton v. Weinberger, 412 F.Supp. 450, 452 (S.D.N.Y.1976).

epiglottis (ep″ĭ-glot′is) [*epi-* + Gr. *glōttis* glottis] [NA] the lid-like cartilaginous structure overhanging the entrance to the larynx and serving to prevent food from entering the larynx and trachea while swallowing.

Dr. Johnson testified that the **epiglottis** works by reflex action entirely; that aspiration of vomitus is not a natural thing. It is not usual and it is undesigned. It is "... not foreseeable by the victim." In other words, the accidental means which resulted in death was the unanticipated failure of the epiglottis to close the air passage and prevent material other than air going into the tubes and the lungs. 379 F.2d 871. Cobb v. Aetna Life Ins. Co., 274 N.W.2d 911, 914 (Minn.1979).

The opinion stated in the deposition of Dr. Stivers, the medical examiner who performed the autopsy, was that Olin Lee died when his **epiglottis**, the small flap which normally prevents food from entering the air passage, failed as Lee regurgitated, allowing gastric acids and partially digested food particles to enter the lungs. The lung tissue was extremely swollen from stomach fluids, and severely burned by the acid. This condition prevented the deceased from inhaling sufficient amounts of oxygen, and resulted in his death by asphyxiation. Lee v. Fidelity & Cas. Co. of New York, 567 F.2d 1340–1 (5th Cir. 1978).

epilation (ep″ĭ-la′shun) [L. *e* out + *pilus* hair] the removal of hair by the roots.

He also noted that "severe enough radiation to produce lens changes would cause **epilation**, falling out of the lashes...." (In their case in chief, plaintiffs had put in testimony that these opacities were early radiation cataracts. McVey v. Phillips Petroleum Co., 288 F.2d 53, 55 (5th Cir. 1961).

epilepsy (ep′ĭ-lep″se) [Gr. *epilēpsia* seizure] paroxysmal transient disturbances of brain function that may be manifested as episodic impairment or loss of consciousness, abnormal motor phenomena, psychic or sensory disturbances, or perturbation of the autonomic nervous system. Symptoms are due to paroxysmal disturbance of the electrical activity of the brain. On the basis of origin, epilepsy is idiopathic (cryptogenic, essential, genetic) or symptomatic (acquired, organic). On the basis of clinical and electroencephalographic phenomenon, four subdivisions are recognized: (1) *grand mal e.* (major e., haut mal e.)—subgroups: generalized, focal (localized), jacksonian (rolandic), (2) *petit mal e.*, (3) *psychomotor e.* (temporal lobe e., psychic, psychic equivalent, or variant)—subgroups: psychomotor proper (tonic with adversive or torsion movements or masticatory phenomena), automatic (with amnesia), and sensory (hallucinations, or dream states or déjà vu), (4) *autonomic e.* (diencephalic), with flushing, pallor, tachycardia, hypertension, perspiration, or other visceral symptoms. Called also *epilepsia*.

Dr. Stowe's affidavit indicates that, although the plaintiff's **epileptic** condition was "another aspect of the known, pre-existent head injury," the condition was "undiagnosable" until its post-judgment manifestation and "[n]o amount of care could have revealed this pre-existing condition until its manifestation...." Vanalstyne v. Whalen, 445 N.E.2d 1073, 1077 (App.Ct.Mass.1983).

The doctor testified substantially as follows: that the son is now 47 years of age and has suffered from all forms of **epilepsy** since he was a boy; that these forms of **epilepsy** are termed "the petit mal", "the grand mal" and "the psychomotor seizure". Will of Arneson, 374 N.Y.S.2d 973, 976 (Surr.Ct. Westch.Cty.1975).

... the court determined that Smith had been subject to convulsive seizures since age six; that these seizures have continued with some degree of regularity; that he had no convulsive seizures for about two years prior to the accident; that he suffered a seizure while in the hospital about twelve days after the accident; and that his raging and maniacal condition prior to the seizure while he was in the hospital indicates that Smith not only suffers from occasionals attacks of **epilepsy**, but also from some personality disorder which affects his activity. The court, relying primarily upon the testimony of Dr. Frederick G. Woodson, an expert witness described as "specialty board certified" in neurology and psychiatry, concluded that while the injury to the head did not aggravate the **epilepsy** grand mal condition there was some aggravation of the personality disorder which accompanied the epileptic condition. [Footnote omitted.] Smith v. Jugosalvenska Linijska Plovidea, 278 F.2d 176–78 (4th Cir. 1960).

epilepsy, grand mal epilepsy, frequently preceded by an aura, in which a sudden loss of consciousness is immediately followed by generalized convulsions; called also *grand mal, major e.,* and *haut mal e.* Cf. *petit mal e.* See also *epilepsy, jacksonian.*

He further stated that the **grand mal** is manifested by convulsive seizure. Will of Arneson, 374 N.Y.S.2d 973, 976 (Surr.Ct. Westch.Cty.1975).

He said that he believed the initial seizure preceded the fall, and based this conclusion on the reports of a witness that respondent "cried out" before he fell, because "this is a classical finding in a **grand mal** seizure." The doctor added, however, that "it's important to know ... what [the witness] means by 'crying out' ". H. P. Foley Electric Co. v. Industrial Com'n, 501 P.2d 960–1 (Ct.App.Ariz.1972).

Dr. Frank, a prison doctor who had treated petitioner over several months, testified that the kind of **epilepsy** from which petitioner suffered—"Gran Mal" [sic]—was not usually characterized by long "twilight periods," but generally only by attacks of momentary length. In Re Downs, 478 P.2d 44, 46 (Cal.1970).

Other Authorities: Moore v. Guthrie Hospital, Inc., 403 F.2d 366, 370 (4th Cir. 1968).

epilepsy, jacksonian epilepsy characterized by unilateral clonic movements that start in one group of muscles and spread systematically to adjacent groups, reflecting the march of the epileptic activity through the motor cortex. The seizures are due to a discharging focus in the contralateral motor cortex; called also *Bravais-jacksonian e.* and *rolandic e.*

From the description of the movements supplied by the husband to the emergency room nurse, Dr. Goodall diagnosed Sandra's condition as being a **Jacksonian** type seizure. Mahr v. G. D. Searle & Co., 390 N.E.2d 1214, 1221 (App.Ct.Ill. 1979).

Finally, the plaintiff's fungal infection and resulting brain damage has left him with partial paralysis of the left upper and lower extremities, as well as **Jacksonian** and grand mal epilepsy. McLean v. U.S., 446 F.Supp. 9, 13 (E.D.La.1977).

epilepsy, myoclonus slowly progressive hereditary epilepsy beginning in childhood and characterized by attacks of intermittent or continuous clonus of muscle groups, resulting in difficulties in voluntary movement; there is mental deterioration, sometimes progressing to complete dementia, and the presence of Lafora bodies in various cells, including those of the nervous system, retina, heart, muscle, and liver. It is transmitted as an autosomal recessive trait. Called also *Lafora's disease, progressive familial myoclonic e., Unverricht's disease* or *syndrome,* and *myoclonia epileptica.*

Petitioner suffers from a rare or unique disease characterized as "**myoclonic epilepsy**." He has frequent seizures and little control over his body. Strong light, loud noises, high temperatures, and similar nervous stress can cause a severe seizure during which petitioner, if unassisted, could choke to death. Since he lacks sufficient muscle control to summon help during a seizure, his physician has prescribed that he have a personal attendant to assist him during his waking hours, about 15 hours a day. Roberts v. Brian, 489 P.2d 1378–9 (Cal.1971).

epilepsy, petit mal epilepsy in which there is sudden momentary loss of consciousness with only minor myoclonic jerks, seen especially in children, and accompanied by 3-c.p.s. spike and wave discharges on the electroencephalogram; called also *petit mal* and *absence seizure.* Cf. *grand mal e.*

Petit Mal Epilepsy involves a neurological disorder characterized by recurrent and unpredictable seizures. While symptoms vary in severity, the SSI regulations require that attacks recur frequently and that they be accompanied by alteration of awareness or loss of consciousness and antisocial behavior. Winfield v. Mathews, 571 F.2d 164, 169 (3d Cir. 1978).

He described the **petit mal** as the smallest attack, one that may simply be a momentary lapse of consciousness which may last only a matter of seconds. Will of Arneson, 374 N.Y.S.2d 973, 976 (Surr.Ct.Westch.Cty.1975).

epilepsy, post-traumatic recurring convulsions due to head injury.

The underlying facts are that Renn, while employed for S.L.C. Leasing, struck his head on an air conditioning unit. In the resulting fall, he struck his head again on an automobile bumper....

Renn's treating physician from January of 1974 through the time of the hearings was G. Scott Tyler, M.D., a neurologist. He testified that, on the basis of the patient's history and an extensive battery of tests, Renn was suffering from **posttraumatic epilepsy** as a result of the June, 1973 industrial accident....

... Dr. Eisenbeiss concurred with Dr. Tyler that if Renn had been unconscious following the blow, that fact would support Dr. Tyler's diagnosis of **posttraumatic epilepsy.** S.L.C. Leasing v. Industrial Com'n, 543 P.2d 795–6 (Ct.App.Ariz.1975).

epilepsy, psychomotor epileptic seizures associated with disease of the temporal lobe and characterized by variable degrees of impairment of consciousness, the patient performing a series of coordinated acts which are out of place, bizarre, and serve no useful purpose and for which he is amnesic.

Sometime following both consummation of the settlement and enrollment of the judgment, Irene developed **epileptic** symptoms that were diagnosed by a neurologist at Georgetown University Hospital as indicating a post-traumatic **psychomotor seizure** disorder resulting from a brain injury she sustained in the 1975 accident. Bernstein v. Kapneck, 430 A.2d 602, 604 (Ct.App.Md.1981).

These seizures, referred to as "**psychomotor epilepsy,**" are generally "short-term episodes," which are characterized by fumbling of the hands, and forgetfulness or inattention. Silverstein v. Sisters of Charity, 614 P.2d 891, 896 (Ct.App.Colo. 1979).

... resulted in a "permanent minimal brain dysfunction syndrome [brain damage] with associated multiple **psychomotor seizures** [permanent epilepsy]"....

... He indicated not only that the minimal brain damage would prevent Brian from reaching his proper level in life, but that "it is complicated by the fact that he is taking medications for epilepsy which further depress an already difficult learning situation." Healy v. White, 378 A.2d 540, 543–4 (Conn. 1977).

Other Authorities: Ex parte Hagans, 558 S.W.2d 457, 460 (Ct.Crim.App.Tex.1977). Will of Arneson, 374 N.Y.S.2d 973, 976 (Surr.Ct.Westch.Cty.1975); People v. Williams, 99 Cal. Rptr. 103, 117–20 (Ct.App.1972); In re Downs, 478 P.2d 44, 46 (Cal.1970).

epileptic (ep"ĭ-lep'tik) [Gr. *epilēptikos*] a person affected with epilepsy.

epileptic, deteriorated

The doctor testified further that the son had unsuccessfully undergone preventive surgery to remedy his condition and that he is medically termed a "**deteriorated epileptic**", i.e. "a person who starts out with epilepsy and whose normal intellectual function worsens over the years", that the son is no longer able to function as an independent normal individual within society and requires large amounts of medication (twice the normal amount) to prevent him from having frequent seizures; that the process of deterioration "was fully developing" in January and February 1974; that he had lucid periods between seizures which in the case of some epileptics means "during their lucid interval [they may] be completely undeteriorated and quite capable of full normal mental activity"— however, the son was "not such a person".

The doctor further pointed out that epilepsy affects a person not only when he is having a seizure, but when he is not having one as well and thus the deterioration does not vanish during the lucid period; further that the son does not have good power of concentration and that he is both a "distractable and a distracting person". Will of Arneson, 374 N.Y.S.2d 973, 976–7 (Surr.Ct.Westch.Cty.1975).

epileptiform (ep"ĭ-lep'tĭ-form) [Gr. *epilēptikos* + [L.] *forma* shape] 1. resembling epilepsy or its manifestations. 2. occurring in severe or sudden paroxysms.

... he had an arrest of speech. This was due to **epileptiform** discharges from the speech area of the left temporal lobe hemisphere, as evidenced on EEG. Resolution of the problem followed institution of Dilantin therapy. There was no motor deficit. Vanalstyne v. Whalen, 445 N.E.2d 1073, 1076 (App. Ct.Mass.1983).

epimer (ep'ĭ-mer) either of two diastereomers that differ in the configuration around one asymmetric carbon atom.

If two compounds are identical at all but a single position at which one compound has a configuration opposite that of the other, the two compounds are known as "**epimers**" of one another. Pfizer, Inc. v. International Rectifier Corp., 538 F.2d 180, 187 (8th Cir. 1976).

epinephrine (ep"ĭ-nef'rin) chemical name: 4-[1-hydroxy-2-(methylamino)ethyl]-1,2-benzenediol. A hormone, $C_9H_{13}NO_3$, secreted by the adrenal medulla in response to splanchnic stimulation, and stored in the chromaffin granules; it is released also in response to hypoglycemia. It is a potent stimulator of the sympathetic nervous system (adrenergic receptors), and a powerful vasopressor, increasing blood pressure, stimulating the heart muscle, accelerating the heart rate, and increasing cardiac output. It also increases such metabolic activities as glycogenolysis and glucose release. The official preparation [USP], produced synthetically as the levorotatory form (*l*-form), occurs as white to nearly white, microcrystalline powder or granules, and is used chiefly as a topical vasoconstrictor, cardiac stimulant, and bronchodilator; administered intranasally, orally, and parenterally, or by inhalation. Called also *adrenaline* (Great Britain).

He entered the shed and was overcome by a high concentration of grain dust produced by an unloading operation which was taking place below. He could hardly see but he made his way to the man-lift and descended to the main floor. As he proceeded down, he experienced extreme breathing difficulties. The claimant was immediately taken to a physician. The teating physician prescribed **epinephrine** to relieve bronchial spasm, and diagnosed Ridenour's condition as acute asthmatic bronchitis. Ridenour v. Equity Supply Co., 665 P.2d 783–4 (Mont.1983).

Based on his conclusion that Mr. Wright was salvageable when he arrived at the hospital, because of the facts that he was sitting up and still able to breathe, Dr. Adriani strongly felt that the immediate line of treatment to deal with Mr. Wright's problem, an acute allergic reaction to penicillin, was to give him an injection of the drug **Epinephrine.** According to him, **Epinephrine** acts quickly on swelling and within one or two minutes Mr. Wright's swelling could have gone down. It is considered the drug of first choice in treating an emergency allergic reaction....

Dr. Clay made two significant points. First, he was of the opinion that the longer the time which elapses following an anaphylactoid reaction, the less chance there is for drug response, and after twenty minutes, there would probably be no response to any drug. According to him, in full blown laryngeal edema, which would occur in twenty minutes, **Epinephrine** no longer has an effect on the swelling. The reason he gives for this opinion is that **Epinephrine** can only stop further release of allergens which cause the edemous condition; it cannot reverse the swelling that already exists. On the other hand, if it is administered at an early stage in the swelling process, it is possible that it would stop the release of tissue allergens and additional swelling. . . .

Three other doctors called by defendant—Drs. Van Meter, Moore and McSwain—supported Dr. Clay's position that **Epinephrine** either would not have helped or was contraindicated. Dr. Keith Van Meter, Director of the Emergency Department at the Jo Ellen Smith Memorial Hospital in New Orleans, agreed that normally **Epinephrine** is the drug of first choice with laryngeal edema. However, he felt that its use was extremely dangerous on an anoxic patient. In addition, he was of the opinion that there is a point at which edema becomes "fixed" and at which **Epinephrine**, or like drugs, will not have the desired effect. Wright v. U.S., 507 F.Supp. 147, 152–4 (E.D.La.1980).

Xylocaine is an anesthetic. **Epinephrine** is a vasoconstricting drug, i.e., one which compresses the diameter of the blood vessels. It is administered in combination with Xylocaine to contain the latter in the injected area so as to extend the duration of the anesthetic effect. A consequence of administering **Epinephrine** is to increase the patient's blood pressure. It is for this reason that the use of **Epinephrine** is contraindicated in cases where the patient suffers from hypertension (high blood pressure). In a hypertensive patient the bursting point of the blood vessels is reached very quickly upon elevation of the blood pressure. Only a minute amount of **Epinephrine** is required to raise the pressure. . . .

. . . Medical testimony showed that the **Epinephrine**-bearing compound injected by defendant aggravated Mrs. Sanzari's already hypertensive condition, causing the cerebral hemorrhage and ensuing death. . . .

. . . and that in cases where vasopressor drugs (**Epinephrine**) are contraindicated (dangerous) Xylocaine can be used alone. From this evidence the jury could reasonably conclude that defendant knew or should have known that it was dangerous to administer **Epinephrine** to a hypertensive patient. Sanzari v. Rosenfeld, 167 A.2d 625, 627, 633 (N.J.1961).

Other Authorities: Daniels v. Hadley Memorial Hospital, 566 F.2d 749, 753 (D.C.Cir.1977).

epichlorohydrin See *epoxy* (Pereira case).

epiphyseal See *epiphysis*.

epiphysis (ĕ-pif'ĭ-sis), pl. *epiph'yses* [Gr. "an ongrowth; excrescence"] [NA] 1. the end of a long bone, usually wider than the shaft, and either entirely cartilaginous or separated from the shaft by a cartilaginous disk. 2. part of a bone formed from a secondary center of ossification, commonly found at the ends of long bones, on the margins of flat bones, and at tubercles and processes; during the period of growth, epiphyses are separated from the main portion of the bone by cartilage. Called also *apophysis ossium*.

He stated at his deposition that a mere "superficial infection," "abrasion," or "breakage in the skin" would be insufficient to cause osteomyelitis. He reasoned that, "[t]he bacteria to get into an osteomyelitis occur between the . . . growing points of the bone at the **epiphysis**. Sprague v. Director, Office of Workers' Comp., etc., 688 F.2d 862, 867 (1st Cir. 1982).

X–RAYS: Multiple views of the vertebral zone reveals no disalignment. Vertebral bodies are generally uniform in height, width and density. However, superior margins of the first lumbar segment and the adjacent inferior margin of the 12th dorsal segment are irregular in outlines suggesting residual change of prior **epiphyseal** variation. Chabert v. City of Westwego Police Pension, 423 So.2d 1190, 1193 (Ct.App.La. 1982).

epiphysitis (ĕ-pif"ĭ-si'tis) inflammation of an epiphysis or of the cartilage that separates it from the main bone. See also *epiphysis*.

The physician described **epiphysitis** as a "growth disturbance in the bodies of the vertebrae, the cause of which we do not know, which makes an irregularity of the vertebrae at the tip and at the bottom." . . .

. . . The X rays definitely established the **epiphysitis** condition but would not show the ligamentous damage, at least not until calcification set in. Colgan v. Raymond, 146 N.W.2d 530, 532 (Minn.1966).

episiotomy (ĕ-piz"e-ot'o-me) [*episio-* + Gr. *tomē* a cutting] surgical incision into the perineum and vagina for obstetrical purposes. See also *vulva*.

He then called in Dr. J. G. Matthews, an obstetrician, who immediately performed an **episiotomy** (surgical enlargement of the lower part of the birth canal). Dr. Matthews was then able to deliver the baby's legs, hips, torso and arms. Roark v. Allen, 633 S.W.2d 804, 807 (Tex.1982).

No anesthesia was administered, no **episiotomy** was done, and plaintiffs allege that no member of defendant doctors' group was present when Betty Friel delivered the child. Friel v. Vineland Obstetrical, etc., 400 A.2d 147, 149 (Super.Ct.N.J. 1979).

Dr. Rook testified that he delivered Mrs. Hiatt's first child; that it was a normal obstetrical delivery without complications; that in that delivery he used an **episiotomy**, which is an incision in the lower part of the vagina, either lateral or posterior. He said the purpose of the incision is to admit delivery of the baby's head and body a little easier. Dr. Rook further testified that ordinarily an **episiotomy** is done with a sedative. He also testified that an **episiotomy** is done by a trained physician or surgeon who knows where to cut. Hiatt v. Groce, 523 P.2d 320, 327 (Kan.1974).

episode (ep'ĭ-sōd) a noteworthy happening or series of happenings occurring in the course of continuous events, as an episode of illness; a separate but not unrelated incident.

episode, acute reactive psychotic

He stated that an **acute reactive psychotic episode** is characterized by loss of the control of an individual, reality is not tested in its usual way, one's judgment is impaired, and one does not react or behave in the usual controlled manner. The episode could vary from a short time to a prolonged period of time, and people are prone to episodes such as defendant exhibited who have altered ego structures and lots of other personality deficits. The defendant manifested an early history of ego weakness and problems, but there was no evidence of a history of psychotic depression, activities, or episodes prior to March 3d that the doctor knew of from the defendant. The doctor explained defendant's episode was caused by a crescendo of many life threatening events. People v. Harrington, 317 N.E.2d 161, 164 (App.Ct.Ill.1974).

epistropheus (ep″ĭ-stro′fe-us) [Gr. "the pivot"] the second cervical vertebra (axis [NA]). See also *vertebrae, cervical.*

epithelium (ep″ĭ-the′le-um), pl. *epithe′lia* [*epi-* + Gr. *thēlē* nipple] [NA] the covering of internal and external surfaces of the body, including the lining of vessels and other small cavities. It consists of cells joined by small amounts of cementing substances. Epithelium is classified into types on the basis of the number of layers deep and the shape of the superficial cells.

Dr. Michaile also found a condition of tenderness of the **epithelium,** the first layer of the cornea.... Rohm & Haas v. Workmen's Comp. App. Bd., 414 A.2d 163–4 (Com.Ct.Pa. 1980).

The **epithelium** is a tissue which acts as a protective covering for the cornea. To maintain its normal structure, function, and metabolism, the **epithelial** tissue requires a constant supply of oxygen. Normally, the cornea receives oxygen directly from the air through diffusion by the tear layer. But since a "hard" contact lens is not permeable, it must be designed to permit adequate tear flow underneath it in order to supply the **epithelial** cells it covers with oxygen. If it does not do so, these cells will be altered or die. People ex rel. Watson v. House of Vision, 322 N.E.2d 15, 17 (Ill.1975).

épluchage (a″ploo-shahzh′) [Fr. "cleaning," "picking"] removal of the contused and contaminated tissues of a wound. Cf. *débridement.*

epoxy (ĕ-pok′se) 1. containing one atom of oxygen bound to two different carbon atoms. 2. a resin composed of epoxy polymers and characterized by adhesiveness, flexibility, and resistance to chemical actions.

Dow manufactures and distributes DER 599 and DER 331, the latter of which is purchased by General and resold under the name of GenEpoxy 190. Both of these products are liquid **epoxies,** used by Midcor in the manufacture of airplane galley doors, and were delivered to Midcor in 55-pound metal drums. DER 599 is a reaction product of epichlorohydrin and brominated phenol and Gen 190 (DER 331) is a reaction product of epichlorohydrin and bisphenol. Both epichlorohydrin and phenol can be toxic, irrespective of the route of exposure—skin contact or inhalation of vapors—and epichlorohydrin has cumulative potential. Pereira v. Dow Chemical Co., 129 Cal.App.3d 865, 871, 181 Cal.Rptr. 364, 367 (Ct.App.Cal.1982).

Equanil (ek′wah-nil) trademark for preparations of meprobamate. See also *meprobamate.*

Simple squamous

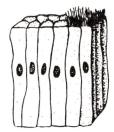
Simple cuboidal · Simple columnar

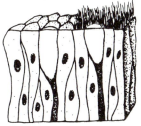
Pseudostratified columnar · Stratified columnar

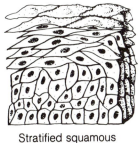
Stratified squamous · Transitional

Epithelium of different types (after Colard Keen, in Bloom and Fawcett).

equilibrium (e″kwĭ-lib′re-um) [L. *aequus* equal + *libra* balance] a state of balance or equipoise; a condition in which opposing forces exactly counteract each other.

He described the sensation as a "stoned, completely numb feeling inside my head" (N.T. 3–14)....

... From Amsterdam to Philadelphia, the stoned, deep numbness feeling continued (N.T. 3–18), and that evening, on the way home, he experienced **equilibrium** loss—a "floating feeling"—which he testified continues to this day (N.T. 3–18–19)....

... He also testified that because of the absence of prior **equilibrium** problems, "one can attribute his present clinical picture to what transpired when his symptoms first began" on May 20, 1972 (N.T. 5–37); that the inner ear dysfunction "took place as a result of rapid decompression" (N.T. 5–58); a decompression was "indicate[d] strongly" by the presence of his symptoms and those of others as well (N.T. 5–58); that "permanent and complete disability" from pressure changes is known and reported, and in this case "it has" been "produced by rapid decompression'' (N.T. 5–124).... DeMarines v. KLM Royal Dutch Airlines, 433 F.Supp. 1047, 1050, 1054 (E.D. Pa.1977).

equivalent (e-kwiv′ah-lent) [L. *aequivalens*, from *aequus* equal + *valere* to be worth] 1. having the same value; neutralizing or counterbalancing each other. 2. chemical equivalent.

equivalent, chemical that weight in grams of a substance which will produce or react with one mole of hydrogen ion or one mole of electrones; called also *gram e.*

Drug products are said to be **chemically equivalent** when they contain the same amount of the same active ingredient in the same dosage form. American Medical Ass'n v. Mathews, 429 F.Supp. 1179, 1206 (N.D.Ill.1977).

equivalent, therapeutic

They are said to be **therapeutic equivalents** when they produce the same therapeutic effect with no difference in toxicity or side-effects.... Hearings Before the Subcommittee on Monopoly of the Select Committee on Small Business of the U.S. Senate, 94th Cong., 1st Sess., pt. 26, p. 11656 (1975). American Medical Ass'n v. Mathews, 429 F.Supp. 1179, 1186 (N.D.Ill.1977).

Erb-Duchenne paralysis (erb′du-shen′) [Willhelm Heinrick *Erb;* Guillaume Benjamen Amand *Duchenne*, French neurologist, 1806–1875]. See under *paralysis.*

erection (ĕ-rek′shun) [L. *erectio*] the condition of being made rigid and elevated; as erectile tissue when filled with blood.

His inability to obtain an **erection**—the urologist said he would never have a "complete" one—is owing to a disruption of the retropubic veins and the veins coming from the penis, "almost totally negat[ing] the penile venous flow," accompanied with a disruption from the crushing injury to the integrity of the nerve.... Gretchen v. U.S., 618 F.2d 177, 180 (2d Cir. 1980).

Erect: Standing up or out from a body; characterized by firm or rigid straightness; not leaning or bent (Plaintiff's Exhibit 22A, p. 770; definitions 1(b) and (d). Shaw v. E. B. & A. C. Whiting Co., 157 U.S.P.Q. 405, 410 (D.Vt.1967).

ergotamine (er-got′ah-min) an alkaloid derived from ergot, consisting of lysergic acid, ammonia, proline, phenylalanine, and pyruvic acid combined in amide linkages; used in the treatment of migraine.

Ergotamine is a vasoconstrictant; excessive intake can cause vascular insufficiency and gangrene of the extremities. **Ergotamine** can also cause gastrointestinal problems. The literature accompanying the drug—introduced into evidence—indicates that Cafergot is contraindicated for patients suffering from certain vascular problems, including hypersensitivity to any of its components and peripheral vascular disease. Hemingway v. Ochsner Clinic, 722 F.2d 1220–1 (5th Cir. 1984).

erosion (e-ro′zhun) [L. *erosio*, from *erodere* to eat out] an eating or gnawing away; a kind of ulceration. In dentistry, the wasting away or loss of substance of a tooth by a chemical process that does not involve known bacterial action. In dermatology, a gradual breakdown or very

shallow ulceration of the skin which involves only the epidermis and heals without scarring.

erosion, corneal

Dr. Hechter's report concluded:

"Miss Jakubielski gives a definate [sic] history of recurrent **corneal erosion** of the right eye. The physical examination of the cornea in the right eye appears to support this diagnosis. This is a condition which usually comes after a foreign body enters the cornea and the area involved does not seem to heal properly, that is, there can be a slough of the tissue in the area of the wound subsequent to a period of time where one would assume there was complete healing. The situation may be chronic and/or may heal itself spontaneously at any time. The present regimen of Lacrilube ointment may be all that she requires. If the foreign body sensation does not relieve itself in the next few weeks I would strongly recommend a therapeutic bandage, soft contact lens...." Thrall Car Mfg. Co. v. Industrial Com'n, 427 N.E.2d 141, 143 (Ill. 1981).

eruption (e-rup′shun) [L. *eruptio* a breaking out] visible efflorescence lesions of the skin due to disease, and marked by redness, prominence, or both; a rash. See also *exanthem.*

eruption, drug an eruption or a solitary skin lesion caused by a drug taken internally; called also *drug rash* and *dermatitis medicamentosa.*

In Dr. Rotman's final summary the same diagnosis of **dermatitis medicamentosa** is contained. Under diagnosis, that condition is referred to as "probably secondary to Doriden," whereas under impression it is stated as "possibly due to Doriden." Finley v. U.S., 314 F.Supp. 905, 908 (N.D.Ohio 1970).

erysipelas (er″ĭ-sip′ĕ-las) [Gr. *erythros* red + *pella* skin] a contagious disease of skin and subcutaneous tissue due to infection with *Streptococcus pyogenes* and marked by redness and swelling of affected areas, with constitutional symptoms; sometimes accompanied by vesicular and bullous lesions. See also *lysergide* (Ward case).

... she has an infection in her hand, a streptococcal infection. Ordinarily the infection travels with rapidity up the arms and becomes a systemic infection. This is called **erysipelas**. It can be fatal but it rarely becomes localized unless it gets caught in a tonsil. But it rarely becomes localized. It tends to spread very rapidly. In the case of a massive streptococcal infection in the hand, usually it simply diffuses itself out and disappears up the arm, lymph nodes and so forth. Ward v. Kovacs, 390 N.Y.S.2d 931, 935 (2d Dep't 1977).

erythema (er″ĭ-the′mah) [Gr. *erythēma* flush upon the skin] a name applied to redness of the skin produced by congestion of the capillaries, which may result from a variety of causes, the etiology or a specific type of lesion often being indicated by a modifying term. See also *radiodermatitis* (McCarthy case).

"... had been in recently good health until one week prior to admission when he had the onset of left thigh pain. The pain gradually progressed and increased in intensity. He noted some **erythemia** [sic] of the medial aspect of his left thigh. Several days prior to admission this **erythemia** [sic] descended and he felt that his left leg was swollen. Because of the increasing severity of the pain and persistence of the symptoms, he sought medical attention today." Claim of Bromley, 330 N.W.2d 498–9 (N.Dak.1983).

Some ten days after her admission to the hospital she developed a rash and an itching sensation over much of her body which was described by Dr. Jay Barnhart as "severe generalized **erythematous** rash, especially on the back where she has many self-inflicted excoriations which are bleeding. This rash looks like a contact dermatitis and may be due to the neosporin ointment." Stevens v. Barnhart, 412 A.2d 1292–3 (Ct. Spec.App.Md.1980).

There is present in the X-ray a type of ray that produces **erythema** on the skin. This can be modified by filters on the X-ray machine or by variation in the kilovoltage, but when **erythema** appears on a patient it is not appropriate to reduce the kilovoltage. When **erythema** appears the filters are not filtering all of the soft rays. No change in filters was made during the course of the plaintiff's treatment. Dr. Branca further testified that it is good medical practice to apply radiation therapy to an area of the body to the extent that blisters and ulceration develop in that area of the skin; but it is not good medical practice to apply radiation to the skin to the extent that ulcers develop to a diameter of four inches and a depth of half an inch. McCarthy v. Boston City Hospital, 266 N.E.2d 292, 294 (Mass.1971).

erythema induratum a chronic necrotizing vasculitis, usually occurring on the calves of young women, which was thought to be a form of tuberculosis of the skin complicated by vasculitis, but now the role of tuberculosis is in dispute; called also *Bazin's disease, tuberculosis cutis indurativa*, and *tuberculosis indurativa*.

In November 1961 plaintiff was hospitalized, reciting on her admission a 15 year history of ankle swelling, pain and reddish bumps on the skin of her lower legs. This was diagnosed as **erythema induratum** and treated with antituberculosis drugs. Andreola v. Weinberger, 409 F.Supp. 55–6 (D.Mass.1976).

erythema multiforme a symptom complex characterized by vivid erythematous, urticarial, bullous, more or less purpuric lesions which appear suddenly in a symmetrical distribution, usually on the face, neck, forearms, legs, and dorsal surfaces of the hands and feet. The lesions may appear as separate rings (*e. annulare*), as vesicles or bullae (*e. bullosum*), as concentric rings (*e. iris*), in round patches with elevated edges (*e. marginatum*), or in variously figured arrangements (*e. figuratum*). The disease has also been classified according to severity as a mild form (*Hebra's disease*) and the severe form (*Stevens-Johnson syndrome*), with constitutional symptoms, involvement of the oronasal and anogenital mucosa and the eyes, and visceral involvement. Individual attacks are usually self-limited, but recurrences are the rule. The severe form may be fatal.

The pigmentation of the rash with blister formation had increased; there was a diffuse ulceration and purulence of oral mucosa, fever and other symptoms. Claimant was then diagnosed at the correctional facility as suffering from a form of **Erythema Multiforme**, and was immediately transferred to the Glens Falls Hospital where he was diagnosed as suffering from Stevens-Johnson Syndrome, a relatively uncommon and severe type of **Erythema Multiforme**. Littlejohn v. State, 451 N.Y.S.2d 225–6 (3d Dep't 1982).

erythema multiforme bullosa See *syndrome, Stevens-Johnson*.

erythemia See *erythema*.

erythematous (er″ĭ-them′ah-tus) characterized by erythema.

erythroblastemia (ĕ-rith″ro-blas-te′me-ah) the presence in the peripheral blood of abnormally large numbers of nucleated red cells; erythroblastosis.

erythroblastosis (ĕ-rith″ro-blas-to′sis) the presence of erythroblasts in the circulating blood; erythroblastemia.

erythroblastosis fetalis; erythroblastosis neonatorum hemolytic anemia of the fetus or newborn infant, caused by the transplacental transmission of maternally formed antibody, usually secondary to an incompatibility between the blood group of the mother and that of her offspring, characterized by accelerated destruction of erythrocytes and consequent jaundice and by increased red cell regeneration (nucleated red cells in the blood) and hepatosplenomegaly. In infants with severe jaundice, kernicterus may result. The most severe form is *hydrops fetalis*. Called also *hemolytic disease of newborn*.

Erythroblastosis fetalis is a disease of the fetus and the newborn resulting from blood group incompatibility between a mother and child. If an Rh-negative mother conceives an Rh-positive fetus and some of the fetus's blood crosses the placental barrier into the mother's blood-stream, the mother's system forms antibodies. Generally the fetus is unaffected. But if the mother subsequently conceives another Rh-positive fetus, the mother's antibodies may cross the placental barrier into this fetus and destroy its red blood cells, producing bilirubin. Schnebly v. Baker, 217 N.W.2d 708, 711–12 (Iowa 1974).

The dispute herein involves the respective trade-marks given by the parties to a drug used principally in the treatment of Rh **hemolytic disease of the newborn**, a malady which may result in children being stillborn, or if born alive, may bring about illness, deformity or death (Norman J–14 para. 2; Freda T. p. 606–24 to p. 607–4).

The disease occurs as follows: When an Rh negative female, impregnated by an Rh positive male, gives birth to an Rh positive first child, the child may trigger the mother's "immune response": that is to say, the Rh positive blood cells from the child will pass through the placenta in large amounts into the mother's blood stream, usually at the time of labor and delivery, and thereby trigger in the mother's blood stream the creation of an Rh antibody, sensitizing the mother's blood to any future contact with Rh positive blood. The first child will escape Rh hemolytic disease, but in the case of a future Rh positive child, the antibodies which have been developed in the mother's blood will pass over into that child's blood during pregnancy and attach themselves to that child's red cells, causing the Rh **hemolytic disease** and its serious consequences (Freda T. p. 606–7–23; Pollack J–34 p. 15.9–3 to p. 15.10–14). Ortho Pharmaceutical Corp. v. American Cyanamid Co., 361 F.Supp. 1032–4 (D.N.J.1973).

Erythroblastosis fetalis is a malady suffered by babies of parents with incompatible Rh blood factors. In such unions there is usually no difficulty with the first or second pregnancies. However, prior pregnancies tend to "sensitize" the mother, that is, the Rh positive cells which the fetus has inherited from the father filter through the placenta to enter the bloodstream of the mother. As a protective mechanism the mother develops a protein substance, or antibody, which destroys the foreign substance in her blood. These antibodies, however, themselves sometimes filter through the placenta to the fetus and destroy red blood cells. The liver then produces large quantities of bile to eliminate the dead red cells from the bloodstream of the baby. The result is **erythroblastosis fetalis**....

The presence of **erythroblastosis fetalis** in a newborn child is disclosed by a combination of clinical symptoms and laboratory tests. The clinical symptoms are anemia, jaundice, enlargement of the spleen or liver and difficulty with respiration. Perhaps the most significant of these is the development of jaundice within the first few days of life....

... no follow-up hemoglobin test was ordered, in spite of the fact that the second blood count, made on November 6th, showed a significant drop in the hemoglobin, admittedly diagnostic evidence of the presence of **erythroblastosis fetalis**. Price v. Neyland, 320 F.2d 674, 676 (D.C.Cir.1963).

erythrocyte (ĕ-rith′ro-sit) [*erythro-* + Gr. *Kytos* hollow vessel] one of the elements found in peripheral blood; called also *red blood cell* or *corpuscle*. Normally, in the human, the mature form is a non-nucleated, yellowish, biconcave disk, adapted, by virtue of its configuration and its hemoglobin content, to transport oxygen. For immature forms in the erythrocytic series. See also *normoblast*.

A major function of the hematological system is the production of red blood cells (**erythrocytes**) which carry oxygen to the cells of the body by chemically binding oxygen to the protein hemoglobin, one of the components of **erythrocytes**. Lead Industries Ass'n v. Environmental Protection, 647 F.2d 1130, 1139 (D.C.Cir.1980).

erythrocytosis (ĕ-rith″ro-si-to′sis) increase in the total red cell mass secondary to any of a number of nonhematopoietic systemic disorders in response to a known stimulus (*secondary polycythemia* [q.v.]), in contrast to erythremic or primary polycythemia (polycythemia vera).

The internist replied: "**Erythrocytosis**." (Erythrocytosis is another name for polycythemia.) Young v. Park, 417 A.2d 889, 894 (R.I.1980).

erythrocytosis, stress See *polycythemia*.

erythroderma (ĕ-rith″ro-der′mah) [*erythro-* + Gr. *derma* skin] abnormal redness of the skin, usually applied to a condition of abnormal redness over widespread areas of the body, a phase of exfoliative dermatitis.

erythroderma, maculopapular a reddish eruption composed of macules and papules.

erythrodermatitis See *dermatitis, exfoliative*.

The hearing officer found—and we do not perceive any serious objection to that finding—that exfoliative **erythrodermatitis** is not an occupational disease within the definitions and

requirements found in A.R.S. §§ 23–901(9)(c) and 23–901.01, supra. According to the medical testimony, it is an idiopathic disease (no known cause). In any event, Slayton had the skin condition for some 20-plus years prior to his employment with KRUX....

"... My skin was very sensitive to changes of temperature, and living in the Bay area, anybody knows that there is considerable change of temperature, even though there isn't a wide variance of, well, degree reading of the thermometer. So if it is the least bit cold, my hands turn very blue; the least bit of sunshine, they get very red....

"... Then we moved to Ventura, California, and I noticed that I was unable to perspire, that I was losing my hair faster, and little pus marks were evident around the hair follicles of my legs. In other words, in each pore there would be a little particle of pus, and then pretty soon the hair was all gone from my legs.

"We moved back to Arizona in 1967. I lost all of my hair. My sweat glands were destroyed...." Slayton v. Industrial Com'n, 550 P.2d 246, 247–9 (Ct.App.Ariz.1976).

escalator, mucociliary

Along the way, nearly all fibers are removed, either through expectoration, by means of the physiological filters in the nose and throat, through being carried back up and out by the **mucociliary escalator**, or sometimes by being taken away by an alveolar macrophage through the lymphatic system or the **mucociliary escalator**. Eagle-Picher Industries v. Liberty Mut. Ins. Co., 523 F.Supp. 110, 115 (D.Mass.1981).

Escherichia (esh″er-i′ke-a) a genus of microorganisms of the tribe Escherichieae, family Enterobacteriaceae, order Eubacteriales, made up of gram-negative, motile or non-motile short rods, widely distributed in nature, and occasionally pathogenic for man.

Escherichia coli a species of organisms constituting the greater part of the intestinal flora of man and other animals. Characteristically positive to indol and methyl red tests, and negative to the Voges-Proskauer and citrate tests. Divided into physiological types on the basis of sucrose and salicin fermentation by some workers. Separable into serotypes on the basis of distribution of heat-stable O antigens, envelope antigens of varying heat stability, and flagellar antigens that are heat labile. Usually nonpathogenic, but pathogenic strains, often hemolytic, and predominantly certain serotypes are common. Pathogenic strains are the cause of scours in calves and the hemorrhagic septicemia Winckel's disease in newborn children, are one of the most frequently encountered causes of urinary tract infection and of epidemic diarrheal disease, especially in children, and are found infrequently in localized suppurative processes. They often become the predominant bacteria in the flora of the mouth and throat during antibiotic therapy. See illustration accompanying *bacterium*. Called also *colibacillus* or *colon bacillus*, and *Escherich's bacillus*.

A culture taken from the surgical wound site showed the presence of **Escherichia Coli Bacteria (E. Coli Bacteria)**, a common infection. Harwell v. Pittman, 428 So.2d 1049, 1051 (Ct.App. La.1983).

Plaintiff's affidavits are based on the belief that the experiment here in question will be conducted utilizing a common strain of **escherichia coli (E coli)** as the host-vector....

The research is now restricted by these guidelines to implanting any new genes into enfeebled strains of **E coli,** a human gut bacteria that has been modified even further to make it safe as the new DNA's laboratory host. In the planned experiment a derivative of **E coli K–12,** which has been specifically designed to "self destruct", will be employed. **E coli K–12** is unable to colonize within the human intestinal tract and causes no known human or animal disease.... This **EK2** host-vector system will not survive passage through the intestinal tract of animals and will "die" because of its dependency on chemicals not found in nature. Mack v. Califano, 447 F.Supp. 668–9 (D.D.C.1978).

The survival capability of fecal **coliform bacteria** in a permanent resident population, as found in ocean bottom sediments, is significantly greater than in the water....

The EPA tested for total **coliform bacteria,** which are found in the feces of warm-blooded animals, and for **fecal coliform,** which is that portion of the total coliform found only in the gut and feces of warm-blooded animals. The coliform count is used to determine the presence of pathogens. Referring to G–54 (bacteriological results of sludge taken from defendants' plants), the testimony revealed that the samples showed very high levels of fecal bacteria and a high level of disease-producing micro-organisms, especially since salmonella bacteria was isolated, it was concluded that these levels were much higher than usually found in recreational beach areas. U.S. v. City of Asbury Park, 340 F.Supp. 555, 565–6 (D.N.J.1972).

esophagitis (ĕ-sof″ah-ji′tis) [*esophagus* + *-itis*] inflammation of the esophagus.

esophagitis, peptic inflammation of the esophagus caused by a reflux of acid and pepsin from the stomach; usually associated with hiatus hernia, duodenal ulcer, indwelling tubes, or prolonged vomiting.

Mrs. Hoard was hospitalized for two days in September 1979, with **reflux esophagitis,** an inflammation of the esophagus. Her doctor testified that this condition was brought on by the emotional stress she was under at the time, the fact that she had increased smoking from one pack to three packs of cigarettes a day following the accident, and because she was not eating properly during this time. Hoard v. Shawnee Mission Medical Ctr., 662 P.2d 1214, 1218 (Kan.1983).

Following discharge the plaintiff continued to experience the symptoms of post concussion syndrome, including vomiting, nausea and ataxia. The plaintiff was hospitalized on July 10, 1978 for a stomach disorder known as **reflux esophagitis.** Although Mrs. Prats had a previous history of this problem, Dr. Mary testified that this condition was caused by the accident. Prats v. Moffett, 391 So.2d 1299, 1301 (Ct.App.La.1980).

... it was felt that the cause of plaintiff's pain was mild **reflux esophagitis** (inflammation of the esophagus caused by reflux of acid and pepsin from the stomach), and reflux induced esophageal spasm. Manigan v. Califano, 453 F.Supp. 1080, 1085 (D.Kan.1978).

Other Authorities: Bellard v. Woodward Wight & Co., Ltd., 362 So.2d 819, 822 (Ct.App.La.1978).

esophagitis, reflux See *esophagitis, peptic.*

esophagocardiomyotomy (ĕ-sof″ah-go-kar″de-o-mi-ot′o-me) incision through the muscular coats of the esophagus and cardiac part of the stomach, the incision extending equal distances above and below the esophagogastric junction; done in achalasia of the esophagus. Called also *cardiomyotomy.*

esophagojejunogastrostomosis (ĕ-sof″ah-go-je″ju-no-gas″tros-to-mo′sus) the operation of mobilizing a loop of jejunum and implanting its proximal end in the esophagus and its distal end in the stomach: done in cases of esophageal stricture.

... no definite ulcer was found, but a bilateral truncal vagotomy and antrectomy with **gastrojejunostomy** was performed. Matthews v. Matthews, 415 F.Supp. 201–2 (E.D.Va.1976).

esophagojejunogastrostomy See *esophagojejunogastrostomosis.*

esophagoscopy (ĕ-sof″ah-gos′ko-pe) endoscopic examination of the esophagus.

The defendant requested Dr. Pittman's advice on the use of **esophagoscopy** (inspection of the esophagus through a lighted tube through which bleeding sites can be visualized) and the use of a Senstaken-Blakemore tube. Dr. Pittman recommended against **esophagoscopy** until the incision was enlarged. His advice was accepted by the defendant. Fitzgerald v. Manning, 679 F.2d 341, 344 (4th Cir. 1982).

Dr. Rex performed an **esophagoscopy** on appellant to relieve the blockage. During the surgical procedure, Dr. Rex removed several small portions of meat, eventually reducing the size of the portion to allow its passage into appellant's stomach. Brannan v. Lankenau Hospital, 417 A.2d 196, 198 (Pa.1980).

In view of these urgent complaints of Mr. Chester and his wife disclosing symptoms consistent with cancer of the esophagus, the doctors in the Hospital were negligent, and through them the Government, in not ordering an **esophagoscopy,** upper gastro-intestinal x-rays, an esophagram, biopsy and a barium swallowing test to rule out a diagnosis of cancer of the esophagus. Chester v. U.S., 403 F.Supp. 458–9 (W.D.Pa.1975).

esophagus (ĕ-sof′ah-gus) [Gr. *oisophagos,* from *oisein* to carry + food] [NA] the musculomembranous passage extending from the pharynx to the stomach. Called also *gullet.* See also *carcinoma* (Chester case).

Dr. Rex left the hospital without informing Dr. West that the forceps broke during the operation and possibly perforated the **esophagus**....

... Appellant proceeded against Dr. Rex on the multiple theories of negligence, alleging that Dr. Rex (1) negligently punctured appellant's **esophagus** during surgery when the forceps he used broke, (2) failed to diagnose and treat appellant's punctured **esophagus** in a timely manner, (3) did not obtain appellant's "informed consent" to this surgical procedure, and (4) failed to inform Dr. West of the forcep problem. Brannan v. Lankenau Hospital, 417 A.2d 196, 198–9 (Pa.1980).

I find that in the light of Mr. Chester's history, his familial history of cancer, his symptoms and urgent complaints, that it was foreseeable as early as August and especially in November, 1972, that he might have been afflicted with cancer of the esophagus or stomach, and the failure of the Hospital doctors during that period to administer a barium swallowing test and other esophageal tests was negligence which fell short of the recognized and accepted medical practice in this community. If there was a possibility that Mr. Chester had carcinoma of the esophagus, the Hospital doctors had no right to gamble with his life on the theory that he was suffering only from hypertension. Chester v. U.S., 403 F.Supp. 458, 460 (W.D.Pa. 1975).

... plaintiff had a perforation of the esophagus and a partially collapsed lung. Presumably these injuries were sustained when attempts were made to remove the M-A tube. Stumper v. Kimel, 260 A.2d 526–7 (Super.Ct.N.J.1970).

esophoria (es"o-fo're-ah) [*eso-* + Gr. *phorein* to bear] a form of heterophoria in which there is a deviation of the visual axis of an eye toward that of the other eye after the visual fusional stimuli have been eliminated; called also *esodeviation.*

... who found that she had esophoria, i.e., her eyes were focusing in too much at close range. She had one degree of esophoria for distance vision of twenty feet, which is considered acceptable, and three degrees for vision as close as sixteen inches, which is abnormal. Dr. Perrin noted that with regard to vision at twenty feet the Civil Aeronautics Administration would permit an individual to fly a plane with two degrees of esophoria (where the eyes turn in) or exophoria (where the eyes turn out) since a person's eyes would pull that much. He concluded that plaintiff had no impairment of distance vision....

... He said he could not definitely say that the esophoria was caused by the accident, but that plaintiff told him she had never had it before and that she had a blow on her head which had been known to cause muscle imbalance, and, therefore, it was a medical probability that the esophoria resulted from the accident. Perry v. Bertsch, 441 F.2d 939–41 (8th Cir. 1971).

esotropia (es"o-tro'pe-ah) [*eso-* + Gr. *trepein* to turn] strabismus in which there is manifest deviation of the visual axis of an eye toward that of the other eye, resulting in diplopia. Called also *cross-eye* and *convergent* or *internal strabismus.*

In October and November of 1973, Timothy's mother noticed Timothy's eyes crossing....

... Dr. Shank made an extended examination and diagnosed Timothy's eye condition as an accommodative esotropia correctable by eyeglasses....

... Esotropia, meaning pointing inward....

... Esotropia in a child of four, Timothy's age in 1973, is a serious matter. Dr. Black states that esotropia in a four year old child is very rare. Most cases of congenital esotropia caused by muscle imbalance develop before age two. This condition is correctable by an operation on the muscles of the eye. Accommodative esotropia, such as diagnosed by Dr. Shank in December, 1973, develops in most cases at age two to two and a half, although it occasionally develops as late as age four or five. This condition is correctable by eyeglasses and the esotropia usually corrects itself after eyeglasses are worn. Steele v. U.S., 463 F.Supp. 321–2, 324–6 (D.Alas. 1978).

Diagnosis: Concomitant esotropia of 20 [prism diopters]. U.S. ex rel. Kempf v. Commanding Officer, etc., 339 F.Supp. 320, 323 (S.D.Iowa 1972).

essential fatty acid See *acid, fatty, essential.*

E.S.T. (electroshock therapy) See *electroconvulsive therapy,* under *therapy.*

ester (es'ter) any compound formed from an alcohol and an acid by the removal of water; the esters are named as if they were salts of the acid. Called also *compound ether.*

An ester is a combination of an "alcohol type" compound with an "acid." In this instance a catechol ester of 2-chloroethyl phosphonic acid (catechol being the name of the particular alcohol used) was provided to Amchem. GAF Corp. v. Amchem Products, Inc., 399 F.Supp. 647, 650 (E.D.Pa.1975).

ester—a product which results when an organic acid is mixed with an alcohol. More importantly to the problems at hand, esters fall into one of two classes, normal or reverse, according to the manner of their chemical bonding. Eli Lilly & Co. v. Generix Drug Sales, Inc., 460 F.2d 1096, 1100 (5th Cir. 1972).

estoppel theory on discovery of injury See *injury, discovery of, estoppel theory.*

estradiol (es"trah-di'ol, es-tra'de-ol) chemical name: estra-1,3,5(10)-triene-3,17β-diol. The most potent naturally occurring ovarian and placental estrogen in human subjects, $C_{18}H_{24}O_2$, the chief functions of which are to prepare the uterus for implantation of the fertilized ovum and to induce and maintain the female secondary sex characteristics; it has also been isolated from hog ovaries and the urine of pregnant mares and has been produced semisynthetically. Estradiol exists in two isomeric forms: the most active isomer is *estradiol-17β* (formerly called β-estradiol), much less active *estradiol-17α* (formerly called α-estradiol). The official preparation [NF], occurring as white or creamy white, small crystals or crystalline powder, is administered by intramuscular injection or implanted subcutaneously in pellets. Called also (rarely) *dihydroxyestrin, dihydrofolliculin,* and *dihydrotheelin.* See also *estrogen* for functions and uses.

estriol (es'tre-ol) chemical name: estra-1,3,5(10)-triene-3,16α,-17β-triol. A reduction product of estradiol and estrone, $C_{18}H_{24}O_3$, having relatively weak estrogenic activity and detectable in high concentrations in the urine, especially human pregnancy urine. The official preparation [USP], rarely used clinically, occurring as a white, microcrystalline powder, is administered orally. Called also *trihydroxyestrin.* See also *estrogen* for uses.

estrogen (es'tro-jen) a generic term for estrus-producing steroid compounds; the female sex hormones. In humans, estrogen is formed in the ovary, the adrenal cortex, the testis, and the fetoplacental unit, and it has various functions in both sexes. It is responsible for the development of the female secondary sex characteristics, and during the menstrual cycle it acts on the female genitalia to produce an environment suitable for the fertilization, implantation, and nutrition of the early embryo. Estrogen is used in oral contraceptives and as a palliative in cancer of the breast after menopause, and of the prostate; other uses include the relief of the discomforts of menopause, inhibition of lactation, and treatment of osteoporosis, threatened abortion, ovarian disease, and severe menorrhagia. See also *estradiol; estrone; estriol; dienestrol* (Schering Corp. case); *endometrium* (Bell case); and *insufficiency, cerebral vascular.*

They pointed out that the loss of **estrogen** from her ovaries would cause the appellee to undergo physical changes, although the use of Premarin would minimize such changes. Thimatariga v. Chambers, 416 A.2d 1326, 1329 (Ct.Spec.App. Md.1980).

Humans, both male and female, under **estrogen** therapy have been observed to develop cancer of the breast. Human breast cancers in the female are sustained and grow upon the **estrogens** normally secreted by the ovaries and adrenals; the adrenals normally secrete from 15–50 micrograms per day. Removal of those organs results in observable clinical improvement of female breast cancer. Bell v. Goddard, 366 F.2d 177, 180 (7th Cir. 1966).

DES is a synthetic organic compound which, when administered to man or animals, has all the biological effects of the naturally-occurring female sex hormones known as **estrogens.** Except for quantitative differences, the effects of DES or other estrogenic substances, on either humans or animals are identical, however administered.

DES and other **estrogens**, when administered to test animals in controlled experiments, have been shown to cause cancers of the breast, endometrium, uterine cervix, pituitary, testes, ovaries, adrenals, and kidneys, and leukemia, in mice, rats, rabbits, hamsters and dogs; often more than one of these cancers appear in a particular species or strain. In addition, fibroid tumors have been produced in guinea pigs. Bell v. Goddard, 366 F.2d 177, 180 (7th Cir. 1966).

Other Authorities: Mahr v. G. D. Searle & Co., 390 N.E.2d 1214, 1227 (App.Ct.Ill.1979); Carmichael v. Reitz, 95 Cal. Rptr. 381, 387 (Ct.App.1971).

estrogens, conjugated [USP], a mixture of the sodium salts of the sulfate esters of estrogenic substances, principally estrone and equilin, that are of the type excreted by pregnant mares, occurring as a buff-colored, amorphous powder; the actions and uses are those of estrogens (q.v.), administered orally.

They did say that the use of **Premarin** increased the risk of breast cancer, gall bladder diseases and caused thickening of the blood. Thimatariga v. Chambers, 416 A.2d 1326, 1329 (Ct.Spec.App.Md.1980).

Testimony of Dr. Gerald Fenichel, p. 309:

Q. Doctor, is it your opinion and within that, that Premarin is accepted therapy for cerebral vascular insufficiency?

A. No, it is not.

Q. Is there anyone in this community of neurologists or neurosurgeons that you have knowledge of that uses Premarin in the treatment of cerebral vascular insufficiencies?

A. I can only speak for the neurologists in the city. There are nine. At our last society meeting, of which seven were present, all said they had never used Premarin for the treatment of cerebral vascular insufficiency. . . .

BY THE COURT:. . . . Are you saying, doctor, that it's ineffective, is that what you are saying?

A. It has never been demonstrated to be effective as a treatment for cerebral vascular insufficiency.

Testimony of Dr. Ray W. Hester, p. 78:

Q. Do you of your knowledge know of anyone in this community that's a neurosurgeon or a neurologist that prescribes **Premarin** in the treatment of cerebral vascular insufficiency other than Dr. McClure?

A. Well, Dr. McClure did, and of my own personal knowledge, I don't know of any of the other neurosurgeons who do, No, sir.

Page 91:

Q. Now, based on that, and based on your knowledge and based on reasonable medical certainty, etc. should that drug [Premarin] have been used on Boyce Chumbler for anything other than prostatic carcinoma?

A. Again, that's a difficult question to answer. First of all, we have just quoted two articles that one is for and the other is against. Now there are other articles in the literature where the drug has been used and has been tried and they also have conflicting evidence. . . . Chumbler v. McClure, 505 F.2d 489, 493 (6th Cir. 1974).

estrone (es'trōn) chemical name: 3-hydroxyestra-1,3,5(10)-triene-17-one. An oxidation product of estradiol, $C_{18}H_{22}O_2$, the first of the estrogens isolated in pure form, found in human pregnancy urine, male human urine, human plasma, mare pregnancy urine, stallion urine, human ovarian follicular fluid and placenta, and palm kernel oil; also produced synthetically. Less potent than estradiol but more so than estriol, it is secreted by the ovary but circulating estrone is for the most part derived from peripheral metabolism of estradiol and especially androstenedione. The official preparation [NF], occurring as small, white crystals or as a white to creamy white, crystalline powder, is administered by intramuscular injection. Called also *folliculin, ketohydroxyestrone, ketohydroxyestrin,* and *thelykinin.* See also *estrogen* for uses.

ethane (eth'ān) a hydrocarbon of the methane series, C_2H_6, forming a constituent of natural gas, which occurs as a colorless, odorless, flammable gas.

Ethane, the next lowest hydrocarbon molecule, consists of two carbon atoms joined with six hydrogen atoms. Ethane is formulated as $CH_3 - CH_3$. . . . Ziegler v. Phillips Petroleum Co., 483 F.2d 858, 862 (5th Cir. 1973).

ether (e'ther) [L. *aether*, Gr. *aithēr* "the upper and purer air"] 1. [USP] chemical name: diethyl ether. A colorless, transparent, mobile, very volatile liquid, $C_2H_5 \cdot O \cdot C_2H_5$, with a characteristic odor, and highly inflammable: used by inhalation as a general anesthetic. Called also *ethyl ether* and *ethyl oxide.*

The reason an incubator's heater-surface temperature is important is that **ether**, when heated above about 300°F., may decompose into formaldehyde, a poisonous gas. In consequence, a dangerous situation exists whenever **ether** is present in an incubator of the isolation type, in which the baby's breathing air is recirculated. This may occur when an isolation incubator is employed for post-surgical care of a baby that has had **ether** anesthetc. A baby may, under those circumstances, exhale **ether** during the postoperative period; and the **ether**, on being recirculated through the incubator heater, may decompose and form formaldehyde. (Mendenhall-Jenicek paper, J.A.M.A., June 11, 1960, DX A, Tab 38). Air-Shields, Inc. v. Air Reduction Co., 331 F.Supp. 673, 683 (N.D.Ill.1971).

ethical drug See *drug, ethical.*

ethics (eth′iks) [Gr. *ēthos* the manner and habits of man or of animals] the rules or principles which govern right conduct.

ethics, medical the values and guidelines that should govern decisions in medicine.

The doctor admitted that he had spoken in the living room of his home with that attorney on the eve of the trial and had allowed him to examine a medical file compiled during Downey's earlier consultation in Dr. Brady's office. With that much established, plaintiff's counsel then undertook to show by further cross-examination of Dr. Brady that such pretrial disclosure of plaintiff's medical records without Downey's permission and out of his presence violated the Hippocratic Oath and the Principles of **Medical Ethics** of the American Medical Association.[3] [[3] There is no dispute that under the Act of June 7, 1907, P.L. 462, § 1, 28 P.S. § 328, Dr. Brady could have been and was subject to judicial compulsion in revealing the same information about Downey's condition at trial....] Downey v. Weston, 301 A.2d 635, 638 (Pa.1973).

ethmoid bone See *os ethmoidale.*

ethyl (eth′il) [*ether* + Gr. *hylē* matter] the univalent alcohol radical, $CH_3 \cdot CH_2$. Symbol Et.

ethyl mercaptan a thioalcohol, C_2H_5SH, which has a revolting odor and contributes to the odor of feces.

Because propane is odorless an odorizing agent is added to make its presence perceptible to the human nose. The propane delivered to the Smiths was odorized with **ethyl mercaptan**, which has a foul smell described by all witnesses as being like that of rotten eggs or a dead mouse. Jones v. Hittle Service, Inc., 549 P.2d 1383, 1388 (Kan.1976).

ethylene (eth′ĭ-lēn) a colorless gas, $CH_2=CH_2$, somewhat lighter than air, and having a slightly sweet taste and odor; used for inducing general anesthesia. Called also *aethylenum, ethene,* and *olefiant gas.*

The compound here involved is called an **ethylene**, or derivative of **ethylene**, because of the central nucleus of the two carbon atoms (C=C).... E. I. DuPont de Nemours and Co. v. Ladd, 328 F.2d 547, 555 (D.C.Cir.1964).

Ethylene: An unsaturated hydrocarbon compound having at least one double bond between two carbon atoms (C = C). Ritter v. Rohm & Haas Co., 271 F.Supp. 313, 154 U.S.P.Q. 518, 554 (S.D.N.Y.1967).

Other Authorities: Ziegler v. Phillips Petroleum Co., 483 F.2d 858, 862–3 (5th Cir. 1973).

ethylene imine

The case for the carcinogenicity of EI, however, is weaker. The Walpole study with rats was carried out almost 20 years ago and that of Innes is unclear as to whether the tumors produced

in mice were malignant and specifically cautions against extrapolating from his data as to the carcinogenic effect in rodents to that in man....

... Based on this summary of the evidence, we conclude that the most that can be said is that DCB and EI pose a "potential" cancer hazard to man. Dry Color Mfrs.Ass'n, Inc. v. Dep't of Labor, 486 F.2d 98, 103–4 (3d Cir. 1973).

There is agreement between the parties that **ethylene imine** is highly corrosive and capable of causing severe burns. Dr. Lorenc said it would cause necrosis, or death of tissue, on contact. Lorenc v. Chemirad Corp., 179 A.2d 401 (N.J.1962).

ethylene oxide a bactericidal agent, occurring as a colorless gas with a pleasant ethereal odor; used as a disinfectant, especially for disposable equipment.

... **ethylene oxide** (EtO), a synthetic organic chemical. Used, *inter alia,* as a sterilizing agent, fumigant, pesticide, and industrial chemical additive, EtO is critically employed as a sterilant in the health care and medical products industries. The exposure of workers who work near sterilizing equipment in the health care industry is the principal focus of this case....

The current OSHA standard for EtO has been in effect for well over a decade; it allows a permissible exposure limit in the workplace of 50 parts per million (ppm) averaged over an eight hour workday ("time-weighted average" or TWA). 29 C.F.R. § 1910.1000. That level, information now available reveals, poses a serious risk of causing chromosomal abnormalities and cancer in exposed animals and humans....

... The chemical is both mutagenic and carcinogenic in animals and humans. One uncontradicted study finds significant chromosomal aberrations in workers chemically exposed to 36 ppm, App. 996–1003; another study shows similar results for concentrations described, more generally, as within the current 50 ppm standard. App. 1488–99. In addition, dose responsive relationships between exposure to EtO and fertility in rats have been observed. 47 Fed.Reg. 3568 (Jan. 26, 1982); App. 172. Public Citizen Health Research Group v. Auchter, 702 F.2d 1150–2, 1154 (D.C.Cir.1983).

ethylenediaminetetraacetate See *edetate.*

etiology (e″te-ol′o-je) [Gr. *aitia* cause + *-logy*] the study or theory of the factors that cause disease and the method of their introduction to the host; the cause(s) or origin of a disease. Cf. *pathogenesis.*

A. "Etiology" means a known cause for a given condition. 'Etiology' refers to a cause of an abnormality.

Q. Because of what?

A. Of any given abnormality or disease process.... The **etiology** of the changes described, which we already referred to yesterday of changes in the aortic wall, the cause for this is not known to the medical profession. It is open to speculation. We have our thoughts but we have no proof. This is why he says there is no etiologic basis known. Woodall Industries, Inc. v. Massachusetts Mutual Life Insurance Co., 483 F.2d 986, 999 (6th Cir. 1973).

EtO See *ethylene oxide.*

eugenics (u-jen′iks) [*eu-* + Gr. *gennan* to generate] the study and control of procreation as a means of improving the hereditary characteristics of a race; called also *orthogenics*. Cf. *dysgenics*. See also *abortion, eugenic*.

The originator of the term "**eugenics**" defined it as "the study of agencies under social control that may improve or impair ... future generations either physically or mentally." Ferster, Eliminating the Unfit—Is Sterilization the Answer?, 27 Ohio St. L.J. 591 (1966).

> [T]he **eugenics** movement ... had a two-fold aim: (1) positive **eugenics**—encouragement of the propagation of the biologically fit and (2) negative **eugenics**—discouragement of the reproduction of inferior stock.... The proponents ... decided that mental illness, mental retardation, epilepsy, criminality, pauperism and various other defects were hereditary. Considerable agitation for corrective action was based upon the premise that these various conditions were hereditary. Since attempts at cure were considered futile for hereditary defects, measures which would prevent reproduction by "the unfit" appeared to be the only way to eliminate these conditions. [Id. at 592]. In re Grady, 426 A.2d 467, 472 (N.J.1981).

eugenics, negative that concerned with prevention of reproduction (procreation) by individuals possessing inferior or undesirable traits.

eugenics, positive that concerned with promotion of optimal mating of individuals possessing superior or desirable traits.

euphoria (u-fo're-ah) [Gr. "the power of bearing easily"] bodily comfort; well-being; absence of pain or distress. In psychiatry, an abnormal or exaggerated sense of well-being, particularly common in the manic state.

Euphoria is defined as "a feeling of well-being or elation, especially one that is groundless, disproportionate to its cause, or inappropriate to one's life situation." Webster's Third New International Dictionary (unabridged 1964)....

... Witnesses described **euphoria** as a state of artificial happiness or elation of mood; or, an abnormal state of well-being, quite different in quality and intensity from a healthy state of well-being. Carter-Wallace, Inc. v. Gardner, 417 F.2d 1086, 1094 (4th Cir. 1969).

eustachian tubes See *tuba auditiva (Eustachii)*.

euthanasia (u"thah-na'zhe-ah) [*eu-* + Gr. *thanatos* death] mercy killing; the deliberate ending of life of a person suffering from an incurable and painful disease. See also *dysthanasia*.

These extraordinary means of preserving a person's "existence" in an irreversible vegetative coma have little to do with the continuation or the ending of "life", and removal of such systems under highly restricted circumstances cannot reasonably be construed as violative of the constitutional prohibition against **euthanasia**. In re P.V.W., 424 So.2d 1015, 1022 (La. 1982).

There are, however, abundant manifestations of both the breadth and depth of interest and concern on the part of the medical profession, theologians, ethicists, moralists, sociologists and criminologists, as well as of the public at large [1]....

... The question before us is whether, and under what circumstances, a surrogate decision can be made on behalf of the patient when he is incompetent to make it himself, where he has been diagnosed as incurably ill, and where the decision relates to the withholding or withdrawal of extraordinary life support medical procedures. The question poses the problem of judicial involvement in passive **euthanasia** (sometimes called "dysthanasia")—the deliberate withholding or withdrawal of available clinical means for the prolongation of the life of a patient for whom there is little or no hope of recovery or survival [2]....

There is reliable information that for many years physicians and members of patients' families, often in consultation with religious counselors, have in actuality been making decisions to withhold or to withdraw life support procedures from incurably ill patients incapable of making the critical decisions for themselves.[3] [[1] (See, e.g., Kutner, Euthanasia: Due Process For Death with Dignity; The Living Will, 54 Ind.L.J. 201; Ufford, Brain Death/Termination of Heroic Efforts to Save Life—Who Decides, 19 Washburn L.J. 225; Note, Informed Consent and the Dying Patient, 83 Yale L.J. 1632; Survey, Euthanasia: Criminal, Tort, Constitutional and Legislative Considerations, 48 Notre Dame Lawyer 1202; Fletcher, Ethics and Euthanasia, 73 Am.J.Nursing 670; Williamson, Prolongation of Life or Prolonging the Act of Dying?, 202 JAMA 162; 3 Houts, Courtroom Medicine, § 1.06, p. 1–53; Pope Pius XII, Prolongation of Life, 4 Am.Q. Papel Doctrine 393; Burt, Taking Care of Strangers: The Rule of Law in Doctor-Patient Relations.) [2] Because "**euthanasia**:" can have two meanings, to avoid any possible misunderstanding I explicitly disclaim any intention, expressly or by implication, to invite consideration of "active" **euthanasia**—the deliberate use of a life shortening agent for the termination of life. [3] (Levisohn, Voluntary Mercy Deaths, 8 J. For Med. 57, 68 [Levisohn conducted a survey of the Chicago Medical Convention which revealed that 61% of the physicians present believed that **euthanasia** was being practiced by members of the profession]; Euthanasia Questions Stir New Debate, Med. World News, Sept. 14, 1973, p. 75 [87% of respondents to a poll of the Association of American Physicians reported they approved of passive **euthanasia**]; see also, e.g., Harrison's Principles of Internal Medicine [9th ed.], pp. 6–7; Survey, Euthanasia: Criminal, Tort, Constitutional and Legislative Considerations, 48 Notre Dame Lawyer 1202, 1213; Wilkes, When Do We Have The Right To Die?, Life, Jan. 14, 1972, p. 48; Medical Ethics: The Right To Survival Hearings Before The Subcommittee On Health Of The Committee On Labor & Public Welfare, 93 Cong., 2d Sess. 9 [1979].)] Matter of Storar, 438 N.Y.S.2d 266, 276–8 (N.Y.1981).

"**Euthanasia**", literally "good death", generally connotes the willful putting to death of an individual. Some observers have sought to differentiate between "active" **euthanasia** (i.e., causing someone to die) and "passive" **euthanasia** (merely allowing someone to die) (see, e.g., Rachels, Active and Passive Euthanasia, 292 N.E.J.Med. 78; Note, The "Living Will": The Right to Death with Dignity? 26 Case W.Res.L.Rev. 485, 487; Note, Informed Consent and the Dying Patient, 83 Yale L.J. 1632, 1649–1650; Louisell, Euthanasia and Biathanasia, On Dying and Killing, 22 Cath.U.L.Rev. 723, 724). (For further discussion of the euthanasia controversy, see Beneficent Euthanasia [M. Kohl ed., 1975]; Euthanasia and the Right to Death:

The Case for Voluntary Euthanasia [A. Downing ed., 1970].) Eichner v. Dillon, 426 N.Y.S.2d 517, 533 (2d Dep't 1980).

euthyroid (u-thi'roid) having a normally functioning thyroid gland.

Dr. Carl E. Ervin testified that "**euthyroid**" is a medical term to describe a state in which the patient's thyroid is brought as close as possible to a normal situation. Dunham v. Wright, 423 F.2d 940, 943 (3d Cir. 1970).

eutrophication (u"tro-fi-ka'shun) the accidental or deliberate promotion of excessive growth (multiplication) of an organism to the disadvantage of other organisms in the same ecosystem by oversupplying it with nutrients.

The announced purpose of the total phosphate detergent ban is the retardation and reduction of the **eutrophication** of Dade County waters. **Eutrophication** is "the process of nutrient enrichment of water accompanied by a depletion of oxygen." Environment Reporter, Vol. 2, No. 16, Monograph 9.... Soap and Detergent Ass'n v. Clark, 330 F.Supp. 1218, 1220 (S.D.Fla.1971).

eutrophication, cultural

Cultural eutrophication is the acceleration of the eutrophication of a body of water by reason of discharge into it of man-derived nutrients, particularly phosphorus and nitrogen. A body of water normally has a life span of thousands of years in natural conditions, progressing from its pristine state through stagnant waters, to a swamp and finally to dry land. But the death of the waterway through **cultural eutrophication** can take place in a fraction of the time required for natural eutrophication. The immediate result of **cultural eutrophication** is increased production of algae and aquatic plants. Soap and Detergent Ass'n v. Clark, 330 F.Supp. 1218, 1220 (S.D.Fla. 1971).

evacuator (e-vak'u-a-tor) an instrument for removing fluid or small particles from a body cavity or container; formerly applied to one for compelling evacuation of the bowels or bladder.

During the use of the **Ellick Evacuator**, many things can be absorbed into the circulatory system, including air. While the human body can handle small amounts of air in the venous circulation with no real difficulty, a large volume of air, such as 50, 75 or 100 cc's, can result in an air embolism. Although Dr. Streeter had never encountered a clinically detectable air embolism in the 100 TURs he had personally performed, an air embolism is a recognized and reported risk of the TUR surgical procedure. Chiero v. Chicago Osteopathic Hospital, 392 N.E.2d 203, 206 (App.Ct.Ill.1979).

eventration (e"ven-tra'shun) [L. *eventratio* disembowelment, from *e* out + *venter* belly] protrusion of the bowels from the abdomen.

However, the possibility of **eventration** through the weakness of the abdominal wall remains, and for this reason we have advised the patient to consult a surgeon on his arrival in the U.S.A. Report of Dr. A. de J. Manzanilla, Chief Medical Officer, Cardon Hospital. Graham v. Alcoa S.S.Co., 201 F.2d 423–4 (3d Cir. 1953).

evert (e-vert') [L. *e* out + *vertere* to turn] to turn inside out; to turn outward.

evidence, clinical

Clinical verification and **clinical evidence** are not limited to objective evidence. **Clinical evidence** means the recognition, assessment, and evaluation by a physician of a subjective complaint, such as pain, or of objective evidence, such as physical manifestations. In other words, **clinical evidence** is evidence applying to either objective or subjective symptoms. Homm v. Gardner, 267 F.Supp. 926 (D.C.Mo.) [Dissent.] Jenkins v. Gardner, 430 F.2d 243, 264 (6th Cir. 1970).

evisceration (e-vis"er-a'shun) [L. *evisceratio; e* out + *viscus* the inside of the body] extrusion of the viscera, or internal organs; disembowelment. When used in connection with the eye, it denotes removal of the contents of the eyeball, with the sclera being left intact.

The only testimony with respect to a specific cause for Mrs. Trichel's wound **evisceration** was given by Dr. Texada, who opined that it resulted from a hematoma....

... However, he also stated that, while the incidence of such events is less than one in one thousand, a wound dehiscence can happen to anybody. Thus, it is evident that, although this is an unusual occurrence, it can and does occur without negligence. Trichel v. Caire, 427 So.2d 1227, 1231 (Ct.App.La.1983).

examination (eg-zam"ĭ-na'tion) [L. *examinare*] inspection or investigation, especially as a means of diagnosing disease, qualified according to the methods employed, as physical examination, roentgen examination, cystoscopic examination, etc.

Section 314 of The Pennsylvania Workmen's Compensation Act requires an injured employe to submit himself for physical **examination**, and provides that refusal or neglect to do so, without reasonable cause or excuse, shall deprive him of the right to compensation. Under this section, an order requiring further physical examination is a matter for the sound discretion of the compensation authorities, and nothing less than a manifest abuse of that discretion will justify the interference of the court: Roach v. Oswald Lever Co., 274 Pa. 139, 117 A. 785. Cf. Gabersek v. Hillman C. & C. Co., 107 Pa.Super. 1, 162 A. 503; Rennard v. Rouseville Cooperage Co., 141 Pa. Super. 286, 15 A.2d 48. [Footnote omitted.] Bostic v. Dreher, 213 A.2d 118, 120 (Super.Ct.Pa.1965).

examination, physical

A comprehensive and specific set of guidelines which may be helpful to courts in exercising discretion in these matters is found in Richardson v. Johnson, 60 Tenn.App. 129, 444 S.W.2d 708 (Ct.App.1969). While some of the guidelines are procedural and not applicable to the issue at bar, the opinion does collate the factors which are operative in disposing of motions to compel a party to submit to various types of **physical examinations**. The guidelines are here summarized, drawn from the opinion cited, 444 S.W.2d at 710:

1. The power to order a **physical examination** must be exercised with great restraint and with careful attention to the rights of the plaintiff.

2. The application must be supported by affidavit setting forth pertinent facts and reasons to justify the examination.

3. The **physical examination** should not be ordered where it appears that the information to be elicited would be merely cumulative.

4. Compelling considerations of justice on behalf of the defendant-applicant must be established.

5. The burden is upon the defendant-applicant to affirmatively establish that the requested **physical examination** can be conducted without considerable pain and danger to the plaintiff.

6. Adequate and appropriate precautions should be imposed so that privacy of the person is insured. Duprey v. Wager, 451 A.2d 416, 420 (Super.Ct.N.J.1982).

exanthem (eg-zan'them) [Gr. *exanthēma*] 1. any eruptive disease or eruptive fever. 2. the eruption which characterizes an eruptive fever. Called also *rash*. See also *eruption*.

excipient (ek-sip'e-ent) [L. *excipiens*, from *ex* out + *capere* to take] any more or less inert substance added to a prescription in order to confer a suitable consistency or form to the drug; a vehicle.

A drug product normally includes an active ingredient and various inactive ingredients, known collectively as **excipients**. **Excipients** may include binders mixed with the active ingredient to form a tablet, coatings, colorings, flavors, etc. Premo Pharmaceutical Laboratories, Inc. v. U.S., 475 F.Supp. 52, 54 (S.D. N.Y.1979).

excision (ek-sizh'un) [L. *excisio*, from *ex* out + *caedere* to cut] removal, as of an organ, by cutting.

excision (nail)

It would appear from the testimony of each that there are several methods of treatment of ingrown toenails. The issue was not so much the method, but whether what was done by appellant was in fact radical surgery for which the charges were made. One method of performing a radical excision involves cutting through a layer of skin, removing the matrix (nail root) and then closing the wound with sutures and bandaging. There would be some degree of bleeding and ordinarily there would be scarring. Matter of Silberman, 404 A.2d 1164, 1166–7 (Super.Ct.N.J.1979).

excision (nail), phenol method

Another method [of radical excision] consists of the use of a powerful caustic acid (**phenol**) to destroy the matrix and nail bed, and the cleansing of the area or the washing of the area with isopropyl alcohol following the use of **phenol**. According to Dr. Nieuwenhuis, no scar is generally left when he uses the **phenol** alcohol technique, because it is not a skin-cutting procedure. Matter of Silberman, 404 A.2d 1164, 1167 (Super.Ct. N.J.1979).

excision (nail), phenol-bur method

The method espoused by appellant and by Dr. Roven, and which appellant testified that he performed, was the phenol-bur process. This type was described as inducting anesthesia into the toe with adrenaline or epinephrine to control bleeding. A nail splitter is used to remove the offending section, which can be as small as $1/16$ of an inch. The entire section is removed, right down to the root. A hemostat or similar instrument is used to remove the offending nail section and a surgical bur (similar to that used by dentists) is used to destroy the matrix. Phenol is used as a supplement to make sure the growth center is destroyed. Matter of Silberman, 404 A.2d 1164, 1167 (Super.Ct.N.J.1979).

exercise (ek'ser-sīz) the performance of physical exertion for improvement of health or the correction of physical deformity.

exercise, isometric active exercise performed against stable resistance, without change in the length of the muscle.

The exact language of the text "warning readers of the extreme dangers of isometric exercises" is as follows.

"**Isometric exercises** have gone out of favor for another reason: They can be dangerous. Applying maximum force during **isometric exercises** usually closes the glottis, the narrowest part of the windpipe, between the vocal cords. A closed glottis prevents exhalation. Thus as the muscles (including those of the chest) contract vigorously, the pressure in the lungs rises sharply. This pressure travels through the thin walls of the lungs to the veins in the chest region. The pressure compresses the veins and reduces blood flow into the heart and to the brain; the reduction in blood flow may cause dizziness, spots before the eyes or even fainting.

Perhaps more serious, the contraction of muscles in **isometric exercises** greatly increases their resistance to blood flow. This causes a sharp rise in blood pressure and a consequent increase in the work load of the heart. For this reason, people with heart or blood-vessel disease should not perform **isometric exercises**. Even those without this ailment conceivably could harm themselves with isometrics. Fatal brain hemorrhages have been induced not by exercise but by strain similar to that caused by isometric exertion—in some instances trying too hard to move too heavy a box has burst blood vessels in the brain. Better and safer for everyone are rhythmic isotonic exercises, which promote steady blood flow and result in little increase in blood pressure.

The plaintiff also alleges that portions of this passage are incorrect. Amended Complaint ¶29 ("Defendant makes certain wrongful, deliberate and erroneous statements including inter alia ... stating that the muscle contraction involved therein 'closes the glottis' of the throat and 'prevents exhalation,' [and] stating that such exercises result in compression of blood vessels thereby 'reduc[ing] blood flow to the heart and brain' and 'may cause dizziness, spots before the eyes, fainting' and 'fatal brain hemorrhages.' "). Charles Atlas, Ltd. v. Time-Life Books, Inc., 570 F.Supp. 150, 153 (S.D.N.Y.1983).

exhaustion (eg-zawst'yun) [*ex-* + L. *haurire* to drain] 1. privation of energy with consequent inability to respond to stimuli; lassitude. 2. withdrawal. 3. condition of emptiness caused by withdrawal. 4. emptying by a process of withdrawal.

The appellant's theory being that death of the insured was the result of physical **exhaustion** brought on by his strenuous exertion at the cattle pens, our attention is directed toward the meaning of the term "physical **exhaustion**."

We have noted that this term has no known medical meaning, nor can a definition of the term be found in reported decisions. The dictionary definition of "physical" is as follows:

physical ... 4a: of or relating to the body ([physical] strength)—often opposed to *mental* b: concerned or occupied with the body and its needs. ... Merriam-Webster New International Dictionary 1706 (3rd ed. 1965)

"Exhaustion" has been given the following medical definition:

Exhaustion.... 1. Privation of energy with consequent inability to respond to stimuli. 2. Withdrawal. 3. Condition of emptiness caused by withdrawal.... Dorland's Illustrated Medical Dictionary 523 (24th ed. 1965). Watkins v. Underwriters at Lloyd's, London, 473 P.2d 464, 469 (Ct.App.Ariz. 1970).

exhaustion, heat an effect of excessive exposure to heat occurring commonly among workers in furnace rooms, foundries, etc., although it may occur from exposure to the sun's heat. It is marked by subnormal temperature, with dizziness, headache, nausea, and sometimes delirium and/or collapse. Distinguished from heat stroke, in which the body temperature may be dangerously elevated. Called also *heat prostration*. Cf. *sunstroke*.

exhibitionism (ek″sĭ-bish′ŭ-nizm″) an abnormal tendency to display one's body or parts for the purpose, conscious or unconscious, of attracting sexual interest; it is most commonly seen in males and when severe leads to exposure of the genitals, sometimes accompanied by sexual gratification.

... the diagnosis made at the hospital in October 1962 when Millard was first committed: the appellant was not and is not psychotic, but suffers from a personality disorder categorized as a "passive-aggressive personality, passive-dependent type, **exhibitionism**." None of the remaining expert witnesses criticized this diagnosis. All of the witnesses testified that the appellant is unable to enter into a mature relationship with women. The sexual misconduct which precipitated the 1962 commitment, **exhibitionism**, is the product of this difficulty. The psychiatrists testified that, when he was experiencing difficulties with his marriage, Millard would react by exhibiting himself in public, and sometimes masturbating. On occasion the triggering event for his misconduct would be some other disturbing occurrence, such as the loss of his job. Millard v. Harris, 406 F.2d 964, 974 (D.C.Cir.1968).

exogenous (eks-oj′ĕ-nus) [*exo-* + Gr. *gennan* to produce] growing by additions to the outside; developed or originating outside the organism, as exogenous disease.

The major **exogenous** (introduced into the body) cause of hypoglycemia is insulin. People v. Archerd, 477 P.2d 421, 424 (Cal.1970).

exogenous (obesity)

Dr. Obenour made no examination of her to ascertain whether her obesity was **exogenous** but merely gave that as "his impression." "**Exogenous**" means that there is no physical malfunction of the body which causes obesity. Recognized causes of involuntary obesity include psychological factors. See opinion of Judge Edwards in Mefford v. Gardner, 383 F.2d 748, 765 (C.A. 6), dissenting from the majority opinion only as to

cause of disability. [Dissent.] Jenkins v. Gardner, 430 F.2d 243, 268 (6th Cir. 1970).

exophoria (ek-so-fo′re-ah) [*exo-* + Gr. *phorein* to bear] a form of heterophoria in which there is deviation of the visual axis of one eye away from that of the other eye in the absence of visual fusional stimuli. Called also *exodeviation*.

Dr. Perrin noted that with regard to vision at twenty feet the Civil Aeronautics Administration would permit an individual to fly a plane with two degrees of esophoria (where the eyes turn in) or **exophoria** where the eyes turn out) since a person's eyes would pull that much....

... found that instead of having esophoria as before, where her eyes turned in, she then had **exophoria**, where the eyes tend to turn out. She had two prism diopters for distance and eight for near (ten inches from the nose). She had symptoms of blurring, some discomfort when reading, her eyes would tire, and close work troubled her. Perry v. Bertsch, 441 F.2d 939–40, 942 (8th Cir. 1971).

exophthalmos (ek″sof-thal′mos) [*ex-* + Gr. *ophthalmos* eye] abnormal protrusion of the eyeball.

exophthalmos, endocrine exophthalmos associated with disorder of an endocrine gland, commonly thyrotoxicosis.

Before and at the time the cataract surgery was performed the husband had a condition medically known as **endocrine exophthalmos** (protrusion of the eyeballs), which was symptomatic of his inactive thyroid. Edema of the eyelids (puffiness) was a manifestation of the **endocrine exophthalmos** which had beset the husband. Miller v. Scholl, 594 S.W.2d 324, 326 (Mo.Ct. App.1980).

exostosis (ek″sos-to′sis) [*ex-* + Gr. *osteon* bone] a benign bony growth projecting outward from the surface of a bone, characteristically capped by cartilage.

Dr. Hull, whose testimony was based upon five visits by claimant and extensive x-ray examination, testified that claimant had an "extra bone deposited at the site of the [sternum] fracture and had persistent inflammatory process going on, which I felt was probably related to the injury, probably triggered by the injury" and an "unusual condition called sternocostoclavicular hyperostosis...."

"... The condition in his sternum is unusual. It is not a condition that occurs following an accident then disappears completely. Not necessarily does that. The nature of this disorder is that it is an inflammatory continuing process that has ups and downs much the same way that other types of arthritis have ups and downs. It—it takes time for the appearance on x-ray. Deposition of new bone and I would not be surprised that a diagnosis of this condition was not made at that time and in addition to that, it's a very unusual condition and it's more apt to be in the area of rheumatology than it would be in orthopedics." Andrews v. Pine Hill Wood Co., 426 So.2d 196, 200–1 (Ct.App.La.1983).

Radical excision of nail, partial or complete, including destruction of nail matrix, with or without removal of subungual **exostosis** (permanent surgical removal of chronic ingrown or deformed nail). Matter of Silberman, 404 A.2d 1164, 1166 (Super.Ct.N.J.1979).

X rays taken just prior to trial of the right knee showed complete healing and one can see marked bony **exostosis** or projection in the knee joint which as it rotates back and forth on the thigh bone will tear up what articular surface is left. Carter v. Consolidated Cabs, Inc., 490 S.W.2d 39, 45 (Mo.1973).

Other Authorities: Ballard v. Commanding General, Fort Leonard Wood, Mo., 355 F.Supp. 143, 148 (W.D.Mo.1973); Southall v. Gabel, 293 N.E.2d 891, 892 (Franklin Cty.Munic. Ct.Ohio 1972).

exotropia (ek″so-tro′pe-ah) [*exo-* + Gr. *tropos* a turning + *-ia*] strabismus in which there is permanent deviation of the visual axis of one eye away from that of the other, resulting in diplopia; called also *divergent* or *external strabismus*, and *walleye*.

... he is entitled to an award for "structural" changes in the eye, especially the disfiguring effects of a turning out of the eyeball (**exotropia**). Englishman v. Faber Cement Block Co., 349 A.2d 75–6 (Super.Ct.N.J.1975).

explode (eks-plōd′) [L. *explodere*, from *ex* out + *plaudere* to clap the hands] to undergo sudden and violent decomposition or combustion.

"Q. What is the difference between a substance that is flammable and a substance that is **explosive**?

"A. An **explosion** is simply an accelerated flame. In other words, it is an uncontrolled flammable occasion. In other words, when you look at, the example, an automobile engine or some other example, once the detonation has started, you can't control it. One is rapid and one is slow and controlled. In other words, a flame, we think of, as being a slower, much less flame velocity than an explosion. An **explosion** has a high flame velocity. It's the difference in flame velocity, in other words.

"Q. Well, you take the substances such as methane or gasoline—certain mixtures with oxygen, they are **explosive**, aren't they?

"A. Yes, sir.

"Q. What is the difference that makes—what is it that makes it **explosive**?

"A. It's the uncontrolled carburation that makes them sometimes lethal, whereas sometimes when the carburation of the adjustment of these things are used, they are very useful...." Eddleman v. Scalco, 484 S.W.2d 122, 125 (Ct.Civ. App.Tex.1972).

exploration (eks″plo-ra′shun) [L. *exploratio*, from *ex* out + *plorare* to cry out] investigation or examination for diagnostic purposes.

The two counts were essentially the same, alleging negligent **exploration** of Plaintiff's arm for the presence of embedded glass and a failure to use antibiotics and a drain upon the completion of surgery. Washington v. Walton, 423 So.2d 176, 179 (Ala.1982).

explosion (eks-plo′zhun) [L. *explosio*] the act of exploding. See also *explode* (Eddleman case).

Although the ordinance itself does not define "explosion", it is elsewhere technically defined as a chemical reaction which results in the instantaneous release of gases and heat. See, e.g., 49 C.F.R. § 173.50 (DOT Regulations).[2] [[2] The Federal Department of Transportation Regulations, 49 C.F.R. § 173.50 provides: "An **explosive**. (a) For the purpose of Part 170.189 of this Chapter, an explosive is defined as any chemical compound, mixture, or device, the primary or common purpose of which is to function by **explosion**, i.e., with substantially instantaneous release of gas and heat, unless such compound, mixture or device is otherwise specifically classified in Parts 170–189 of this Chapter."] Snap-N-Pops, Inc. v. Browning, 432 F.Supp. 360, 363 (E.D.Va.1977).

The common understanding of the term "explosion" includes the notion of a bursting caused by an internal force or pressure. See Webster's New International Dictionary, **explosion**, **explode**, burst. One definition emphasizes an internal force as the causative element in an **explosion**:

The term 'explosion' has been defined as a bursting with violence and loud noise, caused by internal pressure .... 22 Am.Jur. 126, Explosions and Explosives § 2.

[2–4] In American Alliance Ins. Co. v. Keleket X-Ray Corp., 6th Cir., 248 F.2d 920, the following definition was approved:

It [explosion] may be defined as a sudden accidental, violent bursting, breaking, or expansion caused by an internal force or pressure which may be and usually is accompanied by some noise.

Although the cases admit that "explosion" is a term insusceptible of fixed definition, they make it clear that in order for an occurrence to constitute an **explosion** there must be a sudden breaking forth of a confined substance as a result of an internal force. The evidence is insufficient to support a finding of **explosion**. American Casualty Co. of Reading, Pa. v. Myrick, 304 F.2d 179, 182–3 (5th Cir. 1962).

exposure (eks-po′zhur) the condition of being subjected to something, as to infectious agents, extremes of weather or radiation, which may have a harmful effect.

exposure, extraterrestrial

(b) "Extraterrestrially exposed" means the state or condition of any person, property, animal or other form of life or matter whatever, who or which has:

(1) Touched directly or come within the atmospheric envelope of any other celestial body; or

(2) Touched directly or been in close proximity to (or been exposed indirectly to) any person, property, animal or other form of life or matter who or which has been **extraterrestrially exposed** by virtue of paragraph (b)(1) of this section.

For example, if person or thing "A" touches the surface of the Moon, and on "A's" return to the Earth, "B" touches "A" and, subsequently, "C" touches "B," all of these—"A" through "C" inclusive—would be **extraterrestrially exposed** ("A" and "B" directly; "C" indirectly). 14 C.F.R. Sect. 1211.102(b).

exsanguinate (eks-sang′gwĭ-nāt) [*ex-* + L. *sanguis* blood] 1. to deprive of blood. 2. bloodless; anemic.

Where plaintiff's own qualified experts cannot say that it is more likely than not that decedent **exsanguinated** as a result of the alleged negligent postpartum care by her doctors and nurses.... Maslonka v. Hermann, 414 A.2d 1350, 1354 (Super.Ct.N.J.1980).

exsanguination (eks-sang″wĭ-na′shun) extensive loss of blood due to internal or external hemorrhage.

... the patient was undergoing an uneventful recuperation when suddenly, on July 2, she began to hemorrhage from the vagina. Fearing a fatal **exsanguination**, the hospital authorities immediately rushed her to the operating room—not sparing the time to put her into a transfer stretcher....

... Determining that it was critical to find the cause of the bleeding, the surgeons again entered the abdominal cavity, and "after a number of hours of searching" they finally tied off the bleeding blood vessel which had caused the hemorrhage. Denneny v. Siegel, 407 F.2d 433, 435 (3d Cir. 1969).

extension (ek-sten′shun) [L. *extensio*] a movement which brings the members of a limb into or toward a straight condition.

... **extension** of the left wrist was a little over half of normal. Zipp v. Gasen's Drug Stores, Inc., 449 S.W.2d 612, 622 (Mo. 1970).

extension, nail extension exerted on the distal fragment of a fractured bone by means of a nail or pin (Steinmann pin) driven into the fragment. See also *rod, Hansen-Street intramedullary.*

extensor (eks-ten′sor) [L.] [NA] a general term for any muscle that extends a joint.

The **extensor tendon** controlling her right thumb was severed and three to five ribs were fractured. Koehler v. Burlington Northern, Inc., 573 S.W.2d 938, 946 (Mo.Ct.App.1978).

exteriorize (eks-te′re-or-īz) to transpose an internal organ to the exterior of the body.

An appendectomy and ileostomy were performed. Attempted repair of the ileum was not considered suitable at that time. Instead, the bowel was divided at the affected area and the two segments were **exteriorized**. The peritoneal cavity was thoroughly irrigated and drains were inserted for the pelvic abscess. Plaintiff's recovery was somewhat slow because of the infection and a fistula which developed following surgery. She was released from the hospital on October 5, 1974, at which time she went home and was cared for by her mother. An ileostomy bag was attached to the **exteriorized** bowel. Anderson v. Moore, 275 N.W.2d 842, 846 (Neb.1979).

external (eks-ter′nal) [L. *externus* outside] situated or occurring on the outside; many anatomical structures formerly called external are now more correctly termed lateral.

I have been asked if I have an opinion on whether byssinosis is also an inflammation of the **external** contact surface. I think it truly has to be considered, as we have for many years in the study of lung disease, that the entire respiratory surface of the lung is an **external** contact surface. That is what all our air pollution legislation is based on. There is solid experimental and epidemiologic evidence that though we have something in the neighborhood of one-half to two square meters of body surface which is skin, we have in the neighborhood of 180 square meters or roughly the size of a tennis court of body surface, which is lung, and both are in the same intimate contact with the air which we walk around in and beathe. (sic) But one is 100 times as extensive as the other, so that plus the fact the lung is sort of one thin cell thick and the skin is many cells thick.

So, in terms of being responsive to environmental materials, whether they are natural or manmade, the lung is an **external** contact surface which is responsive to this material, whatever it be, that we get in this mixture which we breathe and call air....

... The key word is "**external**", and we construe its commonly accepted and ordinary usage to mean something capable of being perceived outwardly, something situated or relating to the outside or outer part of the object under consideration. See Webster's 3d New Int'l Dict. (unabridged). Our construction is supported by the fact that effective 1 July 1963, G.S. 97–53(13) was amended to include "internal organs" of the body, a term which clearly includes the lungs. Taylor v. Cone Mills Corp., 289 S.E.2d 60, 65–6 (Ct.App.N. Car.1982).

The better reasoned authorities from other jurisdictions conclude that death results from **external** means if the result obtained from ingestion and from internal means if it results from regurgitation: food in the process of being swallowed distinguished from regurgitated matter that had been in the digestive tract....

Finally, in McCallum v. Mutual Life Insurance Co. of New York, 175 F.Supp. 3 (D.C.Va.1959), the district court, holding an insured's death as a result of aspiration of gastric contents into the trachea was not from an **external** means, reasoned:

The ultimate question is the distinction, if any, between choking on food as it is being ingested, and choking on food reduced to matter as it is regurgitated from the stomach....

... The substance, as contained within the stomach, was inside the body and on its way outside during the vomiting process. This, in no sense, constitutes an "**external** means."

For a discussion of this question see 98 A.L.R.2d 318. Jones v. Liberty Nat. Life Ins. Co., 357 So.2d 976, 978 (Ala.1978).

The concept of "**external**," in the context of death or injury, is that the causative means acts from without the body. The term "force" relates to the cause of the injury or death. Thus the connotation of "**external** force" is an outside force applied to the body, or to which the body is exposed, resulting in injury, whether **external** or internal, or death. In this regard, one normally envisages a solid, physical object coming into contact with the body, such as a falling beam striking a fireman at the scene of a fire. Cf. Still v. Bd. of Trustees, Pub. Emp. Ret. Syst., 144 N.J.Super. 103, 364 A.2d 793 (App.Div.1976), certif. den. 73 N.J. 46, 372 A.2d 311 (1977). But we are unable to discern any sound reason for excluding smoke, fumes and gases from the classification of **external** forces, particularly since it has been held that where one dies from the inhalation of gas, the death, in such circumstances, results from an **external** agency, and is violent, in the sense that it was not in the ordinary course of nature. Caffaro v. Metropolitan Life Ins. Co., 14 N.J.Misc. 167, 183 A. 200, 201 (Sup.Ct.1936), aff'd 117 N.J.L. 146, 187 A. 143 (E. & A.1936). See also, Standard Acc. Ins. Co. v. Van Altena, 67 F.2d 836, 839 (7 Cir. 1933). Matter of Iannelli, 384 A.2d 1104, 1109 (Super.Ct.N.J.1978).

Other Authorities: Metropolitan Life Ins. Co. v. Main, 383 F.2d 952, 959–60 (5th Cir. 1967).

external force See *external.*

extra- (eks'trah) [L.] a prefix meaning outside of, beyond, or in addition.

extract (eks'trakt) [L. *extractum*] a concentrated preparation of a vegetable or animal drug obtained by removing the active constituents therefrom with a suitable menstruum, evaporating all or nearly all the solvent, and adjusting the residual mass or powder to a prescribed standard. Extracts are prepared in three forms: semiliquid or of syrupy consistency, pilular or solid, and as dry powder.

extract, belladonna [USP], a preparation, available in pilular and powdered form, containing in each 100 grams, 1.15–1.35 gm. of the alkaloids of belladonna leaf; used as an anticholinergic for the same purposes as atropine and hyoscyamine.

extraction (eks-trak'shun) [L. *ex* out + *trahere* to draw] the process or act of pulling or drawing out.

Defendant testified that he anaesthetized her locally and opened up the gum to expose the tooth. He found the tooth imbedded in the bone. He was unable to loosen the tooth from the bone by use of an elevator so he laid about a third of the buccal bone away down to the bifurcation of the crown. After doing this, he was able to loosen the tooth with the elevator and wiggle it out with a small-tipped forcep. Negaard v. Estate of Feda, 446 P.2d 436, 438 (Mont.1968).

extraction, breech extraction of the infant from the uterus in breech presentation, i.e., when the buttocks of the fetus is presented in labor.

extraction, tooth the removal of a tooth.

Defendant testified as to the procedure used to remove the tooth. First he tried to use forceps, but the crown fractured; so he made an incision in the gum to remove the tooth fragments. The roots of the tooth were bifurcated with one root curving to the rear. He stated that there was nothing unusual in this **extraction**, that he performed it in a careful manner, and that this was an "everyday procedure." The notes on his clinical record indicated that he warned plaintiff of a possible numb lip. Grubb v. Jurgens, 373 N.E.2d 1082–4 (App.Ct.Ill.1978).

Dr. Henry testified that he stood behind Cousins on the right side, with the patient's head positioned by means of a head rest. He held the **extracting** instrument in his right hand and his left hand "**extracts**" the cheek, allowing access to the operative area. Tooth removal was accomplished by gripping the tooth with the **extracting** instrument, rotating it from side to side, and then, when loosened, **extracting** it sideways toward the cheek. He points out that the upward pulling procedure described by Cousins is not used because of danger of damage to the upper teeth. Not much force was necessary and he describes the entire event as a normal procedure without any particular difficulty arising in the course thereof. Cousins v. Henry, 332 So.2d 506, 508 (Ct.App.La.1976).

The oral surgeon, Dr. Mead, a conceded expert, then testified for appellant as to the accepted methods of wisdom **tooth extraction**. He said that dentists will, as appellee did herein, first x-ray a patient's jaw in order to make a prior determination of the force level which should not be exceeded. Then, dentists generally break the tooth and remove its pieces, or, as

was done here, cut around the tooth and raise it with an "elevator."...

... He also testified that wisdom **tooth extractions** do not, if the accepted procedures are being observed, normally result in jaw bone fractures....

... Appellant testified that she kept a dental appointment with appellee for the purpose of having the wisdom tooth pulled. At the end of an unusually prolonged and apparently difficult extraction, in the course of which appellee assertedly exhibited signs of growing impatience and frustration, appellant sensed a snapping sound in her jaw.[1] [[1] Appellant's testimony was that, as the extraction effort proceeded, appellee remarked that it was giving him the most difficulty he had had "in forty years." She also said that, as time wore on into the second hour, appellee was "getting impatient," "more and more upset," "excited, heated," "red in the face," and "breathing heavily." When the tooth finally came out, she "felt as though my ear had been wrenched out;" and appellee characterized the tooth as "really a monster." Appellant then "heard a crack, and I looked up and I realized [appellee] was bending over me, and I said 'Doctor, what was that?' and he said, 'I don't know.' "] Raza v. Sullivan, 432 F.2d 617–18 (D.C.Cir. 1970).

Other Authorities: Henderson v. Milobsky, 595 F.2d 654, 659, 660 (D.C.Cir.1978); Cassano v. Hagstrom, 159 N.E.2d 348, 350 (N.Y.1959); Carr v. Dickey, 329 P.2d 539, 540 (Dist. Ct.App.Cal.1958); Simone v. Sabo, 231 P.2d 19, 20–21 (Cal. 1951).

extraction, vacuum See *aspiration, vacuum.*

extradural (eks"trah-du'ral) situated or occurring outside the dura mater. See also *dura mater.*

On August 24, 1979, Dr. L. M. Heinz performed a lumbar myelogram on Daney and determined that he had an "**extradural** defect L4–5 on the left anterolaterally" and that these findings were "compatible with herniated nucleus pulposus." Daney v. Argonaut Ins. Co., 421 So.2d 331, 333 (Ct.App.La.1982).

extrahepatic (eks"trah-hĕ-pat'ik) situated or occurring outside the liver.

... they erroneously diagnosed the plaintiff as having an **extra-hepatic** obstruction, a gallstone, and subjected her to two operations that were unnecessary. Brown v. City of N.Y., 405 N.Y.S.2d 253–4 (1st Dep't 1978).

extramedullary (eks"trah-med'u-la"re) situated or occurring outside any medulla, especially the medulla oblongata. See also *medulla oblongata.*

... **extramedullary** in nature, that is outside the substance of the spinal cord. Tyminski v. U.S., 481 F.2d 257, 260 (3d Cir. 1973).

extraordinary See *life support (system)* (Eichner case).

extrapyramidal (eks"trah-pi-ram'ĭ-dal) outside of the pyramidal tracts. See also *syndrome, extrapyramidal*; and *system, extrapyramidal.*

Among the **extrapyramidal** side effects [of Prolixin], the two most common are akinesia and akathesia. Rennie v. Klein, 462 F.Supp. 1131, 1138 (D.N.J.1978).

vitreous humor fills the space back of the lens, and is a clear, jelly-like substance containing mucin. It is surrounded by the *hyaloid membrane*. The *lens*, or *crystalline humor*, is a double convex transparent body between the vitreous and aqueous humors, and is held in place by an elastic *capsule* and *suspensory* ligament. The arteries of the eye are the short ciliary, the long ciliary, the anterior ciliary, and the central artery of the retina. The nerves are the optic and the long and short ciliary nerves. See illustration. See also *accommodation.*

The pellets entered the **eye** through the conjunctivia; passed through the cornea, the lens at its margin, the vitreous, and the retina; and came to rest on the ora. The penetration of the gunshot into the **eye** caused hemorrhaging in the anterior chamber and the vitreous as well as a leakage of the vitreous. Gleason v. Hall, 555 F.2d 514, 516 (5th Cir. 1977).

eye, abducting See *abduct*; and *eye.*

eye, panophthalmitis See *panophthalmitis.*

eyeglass (i'glas) a lens for aiding the sight.

The definition found in the current regulation provides: " 'Eyeglasses' means lenses, including frames, and other aids to vision prescribed by a physician skilled in diseases of the eye or an optometrist.'' 42 C.F.R. § 440.120(d) (1978). Simpson v. Wilson, 480 F.Supp. 97, 102 (D.Vt.1979).

The class members are poor persons who, though not suffering from eye disease, need **eyeglasses** to correct refractive error. Under the Pennsylvania Department of Public Welfare's regulations, **eyeglasses** are provided only for treatment of eye disease or pathology.[1] [[1] The pertinent portion of the DPW-PA manual reads as follows: "9743 GLASSES, Glasses are not provided for ordinary refractive errors; glasses are authorized only in cases which are primarily pathologic and in which glasses would be expected to have therapeutic or sight-saving value in adjunct to medical care such as in the following general conditions: a. Glaucoma; b. Uveitis; c. Aphakia, when acuity in the aphakic eye or eyes can be increased to a beneficial degree; d. Congenital cataract; e. Dislocated lens, when indicated; f. Convergent Squint; g. Divergent strabismus; h. Residual, or quiescent disease of the eyes; i. Amblyopia exanopsia under treatment; j. Diplopia aided by prisms; k. One eye enucleated, or one eye which cannot be corrected to $^{20}/_{400}$ ($^3/_{60}$) or better. 'Safety' lens (plastic, case hardened or three millimeter safety glass) and glass safety frames as approved by the American Standards Association are authorized in all cases. Maximum fees for glasses are listed in Section XII, Appendix I of Section 9411."] White v. Beal, 555 F.2d 1146, 1148 (3d Cir. 1977).

eyepiece (i'pēs) the lens or system of lenses in a microscope (or telescope) that is nearest to the eye of the user and that serves to further magnify the image produced by the objective.

ACMI manufactured and sold two basic types of **eyepieces**: a standard **eyepiece** and what was termed a photographic **eyepiece**, which permitted a camera or other attachments to be used with the instrument for purposes other than direct viewing. Dr. Thomas, however, at the time of his injury, was using a resectoscope equipped with a photographic **eyepiece** with his naked eye. . . .

According to the testimony ACMI first marketed the "photographic" **eyepiece** in 1963. Its original composition was of aluminum, and, as already noted, it was intended to be used only with various special viewing attachments. In 1969, however, the company admittedly became aware that surgeons might be using this uninsulated device for direct viewing, when it began to receive instruments back for normal repairs and servicing with photographic **eyepieces** attached. Apparently in response, ACMI introduced a new photographic **eyepiece** that same year which was made of non-conductive nylon material. The evidence is quite clear, however, that no warnings or other instructions were sent out at that time nor had any previously been issued to advise physicians of the appropriate limited use to be made of the photographic **eyepiece**. It was this later model **eyepiece** that Dr. Thomas was using when he was injured, and yet, it is not disputed, that even it was not fully insulated. The metallic end of the telescope shaft remained exposed, though slightly recessed in its center when the **eyepiece** was affixed to the resectoscope. Thomas v. American Cystoscope Makers, Inc., 414 F.Supp. 255, 259, 266 (E.D.Pa.1976).

F

fabere Patrick test See *test, Patrick's.*

facet joint See *joint, facet.*

facial nerve See *nervus, facialis.*

facies (fa'she-ēz), pl. *fa'cies* [L.] the expression or appearance of the face.

facies, Parkinson's; facies, parkinsonian a stolid masklike expression of the face, with infrequent blinking, pathognomonic of parkinsonism; see also *parkinsonian syndrome*, under *syndrome*, and see *paralysis agitans.*

factitial (fak-tish'al) produced by artificial means; unintentionally produced.

Dr. Bains testified:
"A. I thought the wound was **factitial**, self-imposed. I confronted Mr. Rowe with this and he denied it. I stated so in my records and I still have that opinion. . . .
"Q. Did you say the original graft at one point was completely healed?
"A. There were two areas of about two millimeters in diameter which mysteriously would not heal, but to all intents and purposes he had a healed wound for six weeks, from the time of the grafting until this mysterious disease appeared in the center of the graft. . . .
. . . I realize I am sticking my neck out but on the other hand I have treated patients many times for **factitial** wounds and I suppose being sensitized to the problem makes it easy to ar-

rive at a conclusion." Rowe v. Industrial Com'n, 510 P.2d 388, 391–2 (Ct.App.Ariz.1973).

factor (fak'tor) [L. "maker"] an agent or element that contributes to the production of a result, such as a chemical compound that is essential to a reaction (e.g., a coagulation factor; a quantity or symbol employed in a specific formula or, in the study of heredity, a particular gene; a property of immunoglobulins by which they can be identified by a given set of reagents.

factor, Castle's intrinsic factor, the mucoprotein in gastric juice necessary for the absorption of cyanocobalamin.

factor, intrinsic a glycoprotein secreted by the parietal cells of the gastric glands, necessary for the absorption of vitamin B_{12} (cyanocobalamin, extrinsic factor). Lack of intrinsic factor, with consequent deficiency of vitamin B_{12}, results in pernicious anemia.

Factor V proaccelerin: a heat- and storage-labile material, present in plasma but not in serum, functioning in both the intrinsic and extrinsic pathways of blood coagulation. Deficiency of this factor, an autosomal recessive trait, leads to a rare hemorrhagic tendency, known as Owen's disease or parahemophilia, which varies greatly in severity. Called also *accelerator globulin* (*AcG*) and *labile factor*.

Factor VIII antihemophilic factor (AHF): a relatively storage-labile factor participating only in the intrinsic pathway of blood coagulation. Deficiency of this factor, when transmitted as a sex-linked recessive trait, causes classical hemophilia (hemophilia A). More than one molecular form of this factor has been discovered. Called also *antihemophilic globulin* (*AHG*) and *antihemophilic factor A*.

Factor IX plasma thromboplastin component (PTC): a relatively storage-stable substance involved only in the intrinsic pathway of blood coagulation. Deficiency of this factor results in a hemorrhagic syndrome called hemophilia B or Christmas disease, which is similar to classical hemophilia (hemophilia A). More than one molecular form has been discovered. Called also *autoprothrombin II, Christmas factor*, and *antihemophilic factor B*. See also *Konyne*.

Dr. Larsen's letter, in part, reads as follows:
"It is obvious that this patient has a **Factor IX** deficiency **(Christmas disease)**. This hemophilia B, as it is sometimes called, usually is a mild disease and with his 20% activity this gives the reason for his very minimal problems during his life. There is no therapy indicated for this with the exception of the fact that if surgery were contemplated then therapy with fresh frozen plasma or the new **Factor IX Konyne** could be used." Fogo v. Cutter Laboratories, Inc., 137 Cal.Rptr. 417, 420 (Ct.App.Cal.1977).

Factor XII Hageman factor: a stable factor activated by contact with glass or other foreign surfaces, which initiates the intrinsic process of blood coagulation *in vitro*. Deficiency of this factor results in prolonged *in vitro*

blood clotting but overt clinical bleeding is rare. Called also *glass, contact*, or *activation factor*.

PTT reagents for use in performing the PTT test are of two kinds—non-activated reagents and activated reagents. Non-activated PTT reagents include a platelet substitute, and activated PTT reagents include both a platelet substitute and an activator of **Hageman factor**, one of the factors of blood. PTT tests performed with non-activated reagents are usually performed in glass test tubes, and the **Hageman factor** in the plasma is activated by the glass wall of the test tube. In PTT tests performed with activated reagents, the **Hageman factor** is activated by the activator in the reagent. Non-activated PTT times for PTT tests performed on normal plasma in glass test tubes generally fall in the range of about forty (40) to eighty (80) seconds, and activated PTT times for normal plasma using activated reagents fall in a much narrower and lower range. Ortho Pharmaceutical Corp. v. Amer. Hospital Supply Corp., 186 U.S.P.Q. 501, 504 (S.D.Ind.1975).

factor, Rh; factor, Rhesus antigens (agglutinogens) present on the membrane of red blood cells. See also *blood group*.

factors, coagulation substances in the blood that are essential to the clotting process and hence, to the maintenance of normal hemostasis. They are designated by Roman numerals, to which the notation "a" is added to indicate the activated state. Platelet factors, designated by Arabic numerals, also play a role in coagulation. *platelet factor 1*, adsorbed Factor V from the plasma. *platelet factor 2*, an accelerator of the thrombin-fibrinogen reaction, attached to platelets. *platelet factor 3*, a substance, probably a lipoprotein, extracted from platelets, which contributes to the interaction of plasma coagulation proteins in the generation of intrinsic prothrombin converting principle. *platelet factor 4*, an intracellular protein component of blood platelets, capable of neutralizing the antithrombic activity of heparin in the fibrinogen-fibrin reaction and the inhibitory effect of heparin in the thromboplastin generation test.

factors, platelet factors important in hemostasis which are contained in or attached to the platelets. See *platelet factors 1, 2, 3,* and *4*, under *coagulation f's*. See also *platelet cofactors*, under *cofactor*.

fallopian aqueduct (arch), artery, ligament, tube (fallo'pe-an) [Gabriele *Falloppio* (L. *Fallopius*), 1523–1562; an important Italian anatomist, pupil of Vesalius, and later professor at Padua] see *canalis facialis, arteria uterina, ligamentum inguinale*, and *tuba uterina*.

family practice See *medicine, family*.

fascia (fash'e-ah), pl. *fas'ciae* [L. "band"] [NA] a sheet or band of fibrous tissue such as lies deep to the skin or forms an investment for muscles and various organs of the body.

The ulcer was worse ... it was possibly a little deeper. The infection was down to the **fascia**. Stogsdill v. Manor Convalescent Home, Inc., 343 N.E.2d 589, 594 (App.Ct.Ill.1976).

It [the bowel] was between the skin and the **fascia** which is the fat layer. Richardson v. Holmes, 525 S.W.2d 293, 296 (Ct.Civ. App.Tex.1975).

He did admit to finding a localized muscle tenderness in the area of the right scapula, which he believed was caused by an inflammation of the **fascia** (a thin layer of tissue connecting muscles), and stated: "In this case I thought it was caused by a muscle stretch." Motorola, Inc. v. Industrial Com'n, 265 N.E.2d 99, 101 (Ill.1970).

fascia of Gerota; Gerota's fascia a fibrous capsule enclosing the kidney and extending for a variable distance down the ureter. See also under *capsule*.

fascia lata femoris [NA], the external investing fascia of the thigh.

He decided that the best suture material for part of this operation would be **fascia lata**, which he obtained from the patient's left thigh, and he said he informed the patient of his plan to do this but did not tell him all the possible complications which might result from the two surgical procedures because it was not accepted medical practice to do so in the Houston area in 1960. Goodnight v. Phillips, 458 S.W.2d 196, 198–9 (Ct.Civ. App.Tex.1970).

fasciitis (fas"e-i'tis) inflammation of fascia.

The apparent plantar **fasciitis** present in the left foot, as previously noted on two separate occasions by Dr. Lytton-Smith, still exists. It is the consultants' opinion that although this is not directly related to either of the three previous foot injuries, it may well be interfering somewhat with his work and again recommendation is made for Kylocaine and Steroid suspension injection into the plantar fascia origin from the os calcis. One or two injections will more than likely suffice to make this foot asymptomatic. Apolinar v. Industrial Commission, 507 P.2d 698, 700 (Ct.App.Ariz.1973).

fasciotomy (fash"e-ot'o-me) [*fascia* + Gr. *temnein* to cut] surgical incision or transection of fascia. See also *fascia*.

The following morning Richard had a high fever and severe swelling of the leg. Fever, swelling and marked discoloration of the toes and foot persisted and a **fasciotomy** to combat the inflammation was done on November 16. On November 17 the youth was transferred to a Memphis hospital and amputation was narrowly averted. Treatment required several hospital stays and the final result was a severe and permanent injury, the injured leg being one and a half inches shorter, the right ankle being fused. Hively v. Edwards, 646 S.W.2d 688, 689 (Ark.1983).

At that point, she began receiving blood transfusions and was taken to an operating room where a **fasciotomy** was performed upon her upper leg and left abdominal region. She died while upon the operating table....

... Absent that [amputation of a lower limb], the best treatment [for gas gangrene] is a **fasciotomy**, or a cutting into the tissue of the muscles so as to bring oxygen to the area immediately and thus kill the bacilli. Harris v. State Through Huey P. Long Mem. Hosp., 378 So.2d 383, 387 (La.1979).

Thereafter, the cast was spread apart by Dr. Robberson, and later that day a **fasciotomy**—the cutting of the tissue around

the muscle—was performed on both the front and back of the leg from the knee to the ankle to increase circulation. Flamm v. Ball, 476 S.W.2d 710, 712 (Ct.Civ.App.Tex.1972).

Other Authorities: DeWitt v. Brown, 669 F.2d 516, 519 (8th Cir. 1982); White v. Mitchell, 568 S.W.2d 216, 218 (Ark. 1978); Buck v. U.S., 433 F.Supp. 896, 903 (M.D.Fla.1977).

fast (fast) abstention from food.

Carlton was introduced to the concept of extended **fasting** by a friend at work and decided to pursue this alternative form of treatment prior to submitting to the surgical removal of his colon. Joan Carlton described the decedent's decision to pursue **fasting** at trial:

We had been introduced to the natural health hygiene way of thinking and possibility of undertaking a **fast** to allow the body to rest, cure itself....

... after reading Dr. Shelton's book—Fasting Can Save Your Life—he contacted the Shelton Health School and consulted with Dr. Vetrano. Dr. Vetrano recommended an extended **fast** for the treatment of Carlton's condition, urged him to quit taking the medication prescribed for Carlton by his doctors, and enrolled Carlton in the Shelton Health School's **fasting** program....

... twenty-nine days later and sixty pounds lighter, William Carlton expired shortly after being admitted to Baptist Memorial Hospital in San Antonio, Texas....

... The evidence presented to the jury demonstrated that Dr. Vetrano literally allowed Carlton to starve to death. For twenty-nine days, the decedent was given nothing more than distilled water, usually only two cups of water a day. No vitamins or food supplements were administered and virtually no record of the decedent's progress was kept by Dr. Vetrano. The decedent's vital signs were not monitored and recorded on a daily basis and blood or urine samples were never tested. Indeed, the record reflects that Dr. Vetrano would not even see the decedent for as long as four days at a time. Carlton was unable to leave his bed for almost four days before Dr. Vetrano ultimately had him transported to Baptist Memorial Hospital and, upon arrival, the doctors noted that he could not sit up and became completely exhausted by simply moving his hands. Record, vol. 1 at 175, 197, 252, 253, 261....

... The deteriorated state of Carlton's condition when Dr. Vetrano finally sought competent medical assistance was described by the Bexar County Medical Examiner at trial:

When he came in he was in a very serious condition, a critical condition. His blood tests revealed that the constituents of his blood were such that he was sort of, I guess you would say, balanced on a knife edge.... If he had died five minutes after admission I would not have been surprised in the least. Carlton v. Shelton, 722 F.2d 203–5 (5th Cir. 1984).

fatty acid, essential See *acid, fatty, essential*.

Federal Licensing Examination See *test, FLEX*.

feeding (fed'ing) the taking or giving of food.

feeding, intravenous

The procedure for the **intravenous feeding** included the insertion of a flexible catheter tubing, commonly referred to as an intravenous pressure catheter, into the plaintiff's arm....

... The x-rays showed a radiopaque catheter fragment approximately 12 to 15 centimeters in length (4½ to 5½ inches) in the right atrium of plaintiff's heart. An attempt to remove the catheter was unsuccessful. The radiopaque catheter fragment lodged in plaintiff's heart is the type used for intravenous fluids; ... Smothers v. Butler, 398 N.E.2d 12, 14 (App.Ct.Ill. 1979).

fellatio (fĕ-la'she-o) [L. *fellare* to suck] oral stimulation or manipulation of the penis.

female (fe'māl) [L. *femella* young woman] 1. an individual organism of the sex that bears young or that produces ova or eggs. 2. feminine.

It is Dr. Federman's opinion that the Barr body test reliably and inexpensively ($15.00) determines the presence of a second x chromosome in the "normal **female**". He says:

The cells of a normal **female** contain 22 pairs of chromosomes which are identical to those of a normal male. In addition, there is a pair of sex chromosomes. In the **female**, there are two like structures, two x-chromosomes. In the male, the sex chromosomes are unlike—a larger x and a smaller y. Richards v. U.S. Tennis Ass'n, 400 N.Y.S.2d 267, 269 (Sup. Ct.N.Y.Cty.1977).

femoral artery See *arteria femoralis*.

femoral nerve See *nervus femoralis*.

femoral shaft See *corpus femoris*; and *femur*.

femoral vein See *vena femoralis*.

femoral vein, common See *vena femoralis*.

femur (fe'mur), pl. *fem'ora* [L.] [NA] the bone that extends from the pelvis to the knee, being the longest and largest bone in the body; its head articulates with the acetabulum of the hip bone, and distally the femur, along with the patella and tibia, forms the knee joint. See illustration accompanying *skeleton*. Called also *thigh bone* and *femoral bone*. See also *rod, Hanson-Street intramedullary* (Pfeiffer case).

In addition to generalized bodily contusions and abrasions he received a comminuted (segmented) fracture of the midshaft of his right **femur**. Coleman v. Jackson, 422 So.2d 179, 184 (Ct. App.La.1982).

Plaintiff suffered a broken left **femur** (large upper leg bone) when a forklift he was riding overturned. Surgery was required. Hester v. Ridings, 388 So.2d 1218, 1219 (Ct.Civ.App.Ala. 1980).

His experience was limited to non-complicated fractures in which the healing period for a bone such as the **femur** is from two to three months, during which period it is very essential to avoid motion. The bone must be kept quiet to obtain proper healing and X-rays are usually taken to check the healing prior to the allowance of weight bearing. Largess v. Tatem, 291 A.2d 398, 401 (Vt.1972).

Other Authorities: Graeff v. Baptist Temple of Springfield, 576 S.W.2d 291, 296 (Mo.1978); Safeway Stores, Inc. v. Industrial Com'n, 558 P.2d 971–2 (Ct.App.Ariz.1976); Bradshaw v. State of New York, 24 A.D.2d 930, 264 N.Y.S.2d 725 (3d

Dep't N.Y.1965); King v. Celebrezze, 223 F.Supp. 457, 461–2 (W.D.Ark.1963).

femur, neck of See *collum femoris*.

fenthion See *phosphate*.

The FDA granted Diamond approval on February 12, 1969, to market Talodex, a new drug to be administered by injection to dogs suffering from mange, heartworm, hookworm, ringworm, ticks and fleas. The principal ingredient of Talodex is **fenthion**, an organic phosphate. Organic phosphates are commonly used as insecticides and pesticides. Diamond Laboratories, Inc. v. Richardson, 452 F.2d 803, 805 (8th Cir. 1972).

fertilization (fer'tĭ-lĭ-za'shun) the act of rendering gametes fertile or capable of further development; fecundation. Fertilization begins with contact between spermatozoon and ovum, leading to their fusion, which stimulates the completion of ovum maturation with release of the second polar body. Male and female pronuclei then form and perhaps merge; synapsis follows, which restores the diploid number of chromosomes and results in biparental inheritance and the determination of sex. The process of fertilization leads to the formation of a zygote and ends with the initiation of its cleavage.

fertilization, in vitro

Lifchez describes **in vitro fertilization** as a six-step procedure. These steps are: (1) surgical removal of mature ovum or ova from the female ovary; (2) examination of the fluid removed from the ovary to confirm the presence of a mature ovum or ova; (3) placement of the mature ovum in a nourishing medium; (4) introduction of a specimen of the husband's semen into the medium in a manner that encourages fertilization; (5) incubation of the fertilized ovum ("conceptus") for several days in an environment that duplicates the female body (during this time period, the conceptus is observed to determine if it is dividing normally); and (6) reimplantation of the conceptus in the woman's uterus after several days. Lifchez also states that a conceptus will not be reimplanted if severe problems in cell division are determined after fertilization because the conceptus will not survive and would likely abort spontaneously. Smith v. Hartigan, 556 F.Supp. 157, 159 (N.D.Ill.1983).

fetal (fe'tal) of or pertaining to a fetus; pertaining to *in utero* development after the embryonic period. See also *embryo*; and *zygote*.

fetal death See *death, fetal*.

fetal distress See *syndrome, respiratory distress, of newborn*.

fetus (fe'tus) [L.] the unborn offspring of any viviparous animal; specifically, the unborn offspring in the postembryonic period, after major structures have been outlined, in man from seven or eight weeks after fertilization until birth. See also *death, wrongful* (fetus) (Justus case); *life, intrauterine* (Abele case); and *viability*.

A "**fetus**" is a developing human being in posse which means "that which is not, but may be." "A child before birth is in posse; after birth, in esse." Black's Law Dictionary, p. 894 (Rev. 4th Ed. 1968). ...

Courts which create a new right of action travel the medical route. They say a **viable fetus** is a person because it has been put into existence separate from its mother by medical science. To me, "medical existence is not legal existence." Neither can the medical profession create a right of action at law. A seed planted in the earth that grows to the surface and dies cannot become a mighty oak. [Dissent.] Salazar v. St. Vincent Hospital, 619 P.2d 826, 832, 834 (Ct.App.New Mex.1980).

The Legislature thereupon chose to extend the statute to the case of the unborn child, but did so by creating a new category of murder victims: rather than redefine the term "human being" to include a **fetus**, the Legislature declared that murder is now the unlawful and malicious killing of "a human being, or a **fetus**" (Stats.1970, ch. 1311, § 1, p. 2440).[13] . . . [[13] The disjunctive form must be deemed deliberate, because earlier versions of the bill had proposed to redefine human being to "include" a fetus. (Assem. Bill No. 816, 1970 reg. sess.) The version actually adopted confirms our reading of the original statute in Keeler. We note also that in the Therapeutic Abortion Act the Legislature uses the term "fetus" to refer to the product of human conception regardless of the duration of the pregnancy. (Health & Saf.Code, § 25956, subd. (a).)]

In conclusion, we agree with one of the latest reported expressions of judicial opinion on this issue, in which a unanimous Missouri Supreme Court held that "a wrongful death action may not be maintained for the death of an unborn child. It is our view that a **fetus** is not a 'person' within the meaning of our wrongful death statute until there has been a live birth." Justus v. Atchison, 565 P.2d 122, 132–3 (Cal.1977).

The pregnant woman cannot be isolated in her privacy. She carries an embryo and, later, a **fetus**, if one accepts the medical definitions of the developing young in the human uterus. See Dorland's Illustrated Medical Dictionary 478–479, 547 (24th ed. 1965). Roe v. Wade, 410 U.S. 113, 159, 93 S.Ct. 705 (1973).

Other Authorities: Abele v. Markle, 351 F.Supp. 224, 229 (D.Conn.1972); Justus v. Atchison, 565 P.2d 122, 124 (Cal. 1977).

fever (feʹver) [L. *febris*] any disease characterized by fever.

fever, rheumatic a febrile disease occurring as a delayed sequela of infections with group A hemolytic streptococci and characterized by multiple focal inflammatory lesions of the connective tissue structures, especially of the heart, blood vessels, and joints (polyarthritis), and by the presence of Aschoff bodies in the myocardium and skin. Typically, the onset is signalled by the sudden occurrence of fever and joint pain, followed by manifestations of heart and pericardial disease, abdominal pain, skin changes, and chorea. Atypical manifestations, particularly in adults, are not uncommon. Called also *acute articular rheumatism, acute rheumatic fever* or *arthritis*, and *polyarthritis rheumatica acuta.*

The other condition is my theory that he had **rheumatic disease** when the rest of the kids in the family had it and that is the reason he has a persistent fibrillation because **rheumatic disease** affects the heart muscle and the conduction system and

the blow on the chest doesn't. Costanzo v. Workmen's Comp. App.Bd., 410 A.2d 967, 969 (Commonwealth Ct.Pa.1980).

fever, Rocky Mountain spotted infection with *Rickettsia rickettsii*, transmitted by various ticks, including *Dermacentor andersoni, D. variabilis, Amblyomma americanum*, and the rabbit tick *Haemaphysalis leporispalustris*. First reported in Rocky Mountain states, the disease has since been reported in the eastern U.S. and most other states, as well as in Canada, Mexico, Colombia, and Brazil. The infection follows tick bite by a few days and begins with fever, muscle pain, and weakness, with headache followed in two to four days by a macular petechial eruption that begins on the hands and feet and spreads centripetally to the trunk and face. The sensorium is clouded. The localization of rickettsiae in the intima of arterioles is responsible for microangiopathic thrombohemolytic anemia, nephritis, and meningoencephalitis. Called also *Choix f., pinta f.*, and *tickborne typhus*. It is also known by various names according to geographic area.

She alleged that the physicians, both pediatricians practicing in the City of Richmond-Henrico County metropolitan area, negligently failed to diagnose and treat **Rocky Mountain spotted fever** which caused her child's death. . . .

On May 20, 1974, plaintiff's decedent awoke suffering from neck pain and from discomfort behind one ear. Noticing that a "gland" behind the boy's ear appeared swollen, the mother took her son to the Henrico County office of the defendants, who were associated in the practice of pediatrics. . . .

. . . The child was examined by defendant Jaffe who concluded that David had a virus. The only treatment recommended was use of a non-prescription medication, Tylenol. The mother testified that subsequent to the diagnosis but before leaving the physicians' office, she remembered that David had previously told her that his head was "sore." She stated that she then called this complaint to Jaffe's attention who, upon examination, pointed out to her a "tick bite" on the side of the head. She testified that thereafter the diagnosis was not changed and she took David home. Noll v. Rahal, 250 S.E.2d 741, 742 (Va.1979).

fever, shipping a disease of cattle caused by *Pasteurella haemolytica* in association with a virus; infection occurs when the resistance of the animal is lowered by stress.

The witness was of the opinion that the fibrinous pleuritis with blood in the pleural cavity [of the cow] was not symptomatic of arsenic poisoning but symptomatic of **shipping fever**, or virus diseases with organism pasturella; . . . . Marian v. Lena Pellet Co., 256 N.E.2d 93, 96 (App.Ct.Ill.1970).

fiber (fiʹber) an elongated, threadlike structure; see also *fibra* [NA].

fibers, asbestos fibers formed in degenerating hyaline cartilage by ossification of the collagen fibers.

" 'Asbestos fibers' means asbestos fibers longer than 5 micrometers." 29 C.F.R. § 1910.1001(a)(2). R. T. Vanderbilt Co. v. Occ. Saf. & H. Rev. Com'n, 708 F.2d 570, 572 (11th Cir. 1983).

fibers, collagenous the soft, flexible, white fibers which are the most characteristic constituent of all types of connective tissue, consisting of the protein collagen, and composed of bundles of fibrils that are in turn made up of smaller units (microfibrils) which show a characteristic crossbanding with a major periodicity of 65 nm. See also *fibrous long-spacing collagen* and *segment long-spacing collagen*, under *collagen*, and see also *tropocollagen*.

fiberglas See *tracheobronchitis*.

By 1970, the ACGIH threshold limit committee had determined that "there was no evidence to indicate that **fiberglas** was a problem;" it therefore classified airborne **fiberglas** particles as "nuisance" dust—one with "a long history of little adverse effect on lungs" and that did not produce "significant organic disease or toxic effect when exposures are kept under reasonable control." Upon reaching this conclusion, the AC-GIH raised the TLV for **fiberglas** as a nuisance dust to 15 milligrams per cubic meter of air. Murphy v. Owens-Corning Fiberglas Corp., 447 F.Supp. 557, 563 (D.Kan.1977).

fiberoptics (fi"ber-op'tiks) the transmission of an image along flexible bundles of coated parallel glass or plastic fibers that propagate light by internal reflections.

fiberscope (fi'ber-skōp) a flexible endoscope whose lumen is coated with glass or plastic fibers having special optical properties; see *fiberoptics*. See also *operation* (Cooper case).

The device used for the gastroscopic examination of appellant was a **fiberscope**, a fiberglass instrument, about ¼" in diameter containing some 150,000 glass fibers. The **fiberscope** could be lowered into the stomach of a patient to photograph that area for purposes of diagnosis and treatment. The device had been in use for approximately five years at the time of appellant's examination; during that time, there had been no reported punctures, and appellee Cohen had utilized the device in 250 examinations without mishap. The **fiberscope** was considered an improvement over its forerunner, the semi-rigid scope, in terms of comfort for the patient, visibility of the area under examination, and safety. The incidence of perforation with the semi-rigid scope was approximately 1 in 2500, or .0004%. Cooper v. Roberts, 286 A.2d 647–8 (Super.Ct.Pa. 1971).

fibrillate

The medical testimony here indicates that the blow to the chest aggravated this preexisting condition and caused the claimant's heart to **fibrillate**—to beat in a very rapid and irregular manner. Costanzo v. Workmen's Comp. App. Bd., 410 A.2d 967–8 (Commonwealth Ct.Pa.1980).

fibrillation (fi-bri-la'shun) a small, local involuntary contraction of muscle, invisible under the skin, resulting from spontaneous activation of single muscle cells or muscle fibers.

The **fibrillation**, in the presence of a preexisting deformed aortic valve in claimant's heart, presented a dangerous health situation requiring corrective surgery. On September 9, 1975, Dr. George J. D'Angelo performed open heart surgery and replaced the defective valve....

Q. To paraphrase, Doctor Lowe said **fibrillation** is when the electrical hook up of the heart goes wrong as far as the sinus rhythm but that once **fibrillation** stops there is no permanent damage caused by the **fibrillation**. Do you agree with that? A. Oh yes. Costanzo v. Workmen's Comp. App. Bd., 410 A.2d 967–9 (Commonwealth Ct.Pa.1980).

fibrillation, atrial atrial arrhythmia characterized by rapid randomized contractions of the atrial myocardium, causing a totally irregular, often rapid ventricular rate.

Shortly after those tests and surgery, decedent developed an **atrial fibrillation**, a potentially lethal irregularity in the heartbeat. Quinidine quelled the problem at that time. A few months later he suffered the infarction which was the immediate cause of his death. Sears, Roebuck & Co. v. Workmen's Comp. App. Bd., 409 A.2d 486–7 (Commonwealth Ct.Pa. 1979).

The **atrial fibrillation** and treatment of it by blood thinner was a contributing cause. [of death]. Tschohl v. Nationwide Mut. Ins. Co., 418 F.Supp. 1124, 1127 (D.Minn.1976).

Other Authorities: Kirnan v. Dakota Midland Hosp., 331 N.W.2d 72, 73 (S.Dak.1983); Phillips v. Celebrezze, 330 F.2d 687, 690 (6th Cir. 1964).

fibrillation, auricular See *fibrillation, atrial*.

fibrillation, paroxysmal atrial

Plaintiff's own physician, Dr. Doyle, gave the following answer to a question as to whether there was anything wrong with the top part of the doctor's heart, "By **paroxysmal atrial fibrillation** is meant a functional disorder which may occur in the absence of anatomically demonstrable disease."...

... As to the absence of heart disease, what the doctors did not clearly say was that **paroxysmal atrial fibrillation** has a definite systemic cause whether discovered or not (it does not fall from the sky); but they did testify that usually **paroxysmal atrial fibrillation** is caused by heart disease and any other cause is exceptional, and a first year medical student knows that the most common causes are coronary artery disease, rheumatic mitral valvular disease and hyperthyroidism. Vander Veer v. Continental Casualty Co., 346 N.Y.S.2d 655, 660–661 (3d Dep't 1973).

fibrillation, ventricular arrhythmia characterized by fibrillary contractions of the ventricular muscle due to rapid repetitive excitation of myocardial fibers without coordinated contraction of the ventricle, an expression of randomized circus movement or of an ectopic focus with a very rapid cycle. See also *arrhythmia*.

Dr. Theodore A. Keith testified that in his opinion, Bingham died a sudden cardiac death, most likely that of **ventricular fibrillation**—rapid, irregular heart rhythm precipitated by a bout of severe myocardial ischemia or an acute myocardial infarction. Bingham v. Smith's Transfer Corp., 286 S.E.2d 570, 572 (Ct.App.N.Car.1982).

While on the scene, Captain Hill collapsed as a result of a heart attack and was taken by ambulance to Rahway Hospital. Upon arrival he was in **ventricular fibrillation**, with his skin mottled and without measurable blood pressure. Dr. Melvin W. Lipowitz, a qualified internist, examined him and concluded that "the heart, for all intents and purposes, has stopped beating effectively," causing the cessation of a blood flow to the vital organs. Matter of Hill, 390 A.2d 131, 133 (Super.Ct.N.J. 1978).

In Hastings v. City of Fort Lauderdale Fire Department, 178 So.2d 106 (Fla.1965), the deceased employee of the Fire Department of the City of Fort Lauderdale sustained a **ventricular fibrillation** or arrhythmia. The deputy awarded benefits based upon evidence showing a causal relationship between the heart attack and unusual physical effort exerted and mental stress and strain experienced by decedent immediately prior to his attack. We held that the deputy's order was supported by competent substantial evidence. Richard E. Mosca & Co., Inc. v. Mosca, 362 So.2d 1340, 1344 (Fla.1978).

Other Authorities: U.S. v. Narciso, 446 F.Supp. 252, 287 (E.D. Mich.1977); Republic Nat. Life Ins. Co. v. Bullard, 399 S.W.2d 376, 379 (Ct.Civ.App.Tex.1966); Britt v. Travelers Ins. Co., 556 F.2d 336, 341 (5th Cir. 1977); Community Life & Health Ins. Co. v. McCall, 497 S.W.2d 358, 361 (Ct.App.Tex.1973); Wilkins v. American Export Isbrandtsen Lines, Inc., 446 F.2d 480, 482 (2d Cir. 1971).

fibrin (fiʹbrin) the insoluble protein formed from fibrinogen by the proteolytic action of thrombin during normal clotting of blood. Fibrin forms the essential portion of the blood clot.

On that day plaintiff, with his consent, was taken to the operating room, incision was made under a general anesthetic, cloudy yellow fluid and **fibrin** clots were removed, the wound was irrigated, an input tube and an output suction tube were placed, and a new cast was applied. Contreras v. St. Luke's Hosp., 144 Cal.Rptr. 647, 651 (Ct.App.Cal.1978).

"I don't know what actually initiates this first clot formation. Now, once a clot starts to form then the state is set for additional **fibrins**, which is the material to be deposited, and for additional red cells and white cells and platelets to become enmeshed in this clot. . . . That may close off the lumen." This is what happened. Flannery v. Industrial Com'n, 412 P.2d 297, 299 (Ct.App.Ariz.1966).

fibroadipose (fiʺbro-adʹĭ-pōs) both fibrous and fatty.

Dr. Abarbanel performed a "sliver biopsy" which was given to Dr. Seifert for study. Dr. Seifert reported that the mass was "**fibroadipose** tissue, post chronic inflammatory," and not malignant. Jines v. Abarbanel, 143 Cal.Rptr. 818, 821 (Ct.App. Cal.1978).

fibrocystic disease of breast See *disease, Schimmelbusch's.*

fibromatosis (fiʺbro-mah-toʹsis) the formation of a fibrous, tumor-like nodule arising from the deep fascia with a tendency to local recurrence, as in desmoid tumor.

In the same area, though, the surgery, also revealed **fibromatosis**, which the patient was known to have had long before the accident and which is characterized by bony and soft tissue tumors. Figliomeni v. Board of Ed. of City School Dist., 341 N.E.2d 557, 559 (N.Y.1975).

fibromyoma uterus See *leiomyoma, uteri.*

fibromyositis (fiʺbro-miʺo-siʹtis) [*fibro-* + Gr. *mys* muscle + *-itis*] inflammation of fibromuscular tissue.

In his deposition the claimant's physician stated that claimant was suffering from generalized muscular **fibromyositis**, an inflammatory condition of the muscles and soft tissues; . . . . Teledyne Standard, etc. v. Workmen's Comp., 415 A.2d 113, 114 (Commonwealth Ct.Pa.1980).

Dr. Cooper, who treated Walker beginning in October 1971, had repeatedly expressed the view that Walker suffered from sprain and strain of muscles and ligaments in his back and from **fibromyositis** involving the right rhomboid muscle. [Dissent.] Walker v. Rothschild Intern. Stevedoring Co., 526 F.2d 1137, 1141 (9th Cir. 1975).

fibro-nodose See *nodose.*

. . . that it was his opinion that Williams was "affected by" or "susceptible to" silicosis since the X-ray films indicated "**fibro-nodose** infiltration of the lungs." Williams v. Clinchfield Coal Co., 192 S.E.2d 751 (Va.1972).

fibroplasia (fiʺbro-plaʹse-ah) the formation of fibrous tissue, as occurs normally in the healing of wounds and abnormally in some tissues.

fibroplasia, retrolental a bilateral retinopathy occurring in premature infants treated with excessively high concentrations of oxygen, characterized by vascular dilatation, proliferation, and tortuosity, edema, and retinal detachment, with ultimate conversion of the retina into a fibrous mass that can be seen as a dense retrolental membrane; usually, growth of the eye is arrested and may result in microophthalmia, and blindness may occur. Called also *retinopathy of prematurity, RLF,* and *Terry's syndrome.* See also *oxygen* (Burton case).

Plaintiff, blind since infancy from a disease known as **retrolental fibroplasis (RLF)**, caused by his exposure to a prolonged liberal application of oxygen, has recovered a substantial judgment for medical malpractice against New York Hospital, where he was treated as a premature infant, and two of its physicians, all of whom appeal. . . .

. . . **RLF** is a progressive disease consisting of five stages. Initially, the blood vessels to the retina constrict. In the second stage the vessels enlarge, causing hemorrhaging into the retina. Further bleeding into the inside of the eye develops in the third stage, and in the fourth a localized tear in the retina ("retinal detachment") occurs. Finally, the retina detaches and a fibroid mass develops over the crystalline lens of the eye. The disease is irreversible in the fourth and fifth stages. Burton v. Brooklyn Doctors Hosp., 452 N.Y.S.2d 875, 877 (1st Dep't 1982).

. . . while in the incubator from April 27 to May 6, Rusty was administered oxygen of 32% to 40% on a continuous basis; resulting in his developing **retrolental fibroplasia (RLF)** which rendered him totally and permanently blind. . . .

. . . There is evidence that **RLF** is usually caused by giving a premature infant oxygen; that excessive oxygen is a significant factor in causing **RLF**; that oxygen such as received by Rusty would be calculated to produce **RLF**; that Rusty's blindness was caused by exposure to oxygen; that Rusty's blindness was caused by the oxygen administered during the first days of his life. Air Shields, Inc. v. Spears, 590 S.W.2d 574, 576, 578 (Ct. Civ.App.Tex.1979).

The theory behind this oxygen treatment was that maintenance of premature babies in an oxygen environment would sustain life and prevent brain damage. Shortly after the birth of the twins, a Cooperative Study of **Retrolental Fibroplasia** and the Use of Oxygen conducted for the National Institute for Neurological Diseases and Blindness indisputably established that the course of treatment was tragically mistaken. The study showed that, while the use of oxygen might mitigate brain damage, it did not reduce the mortality rate at all, and did cause **retrolental fibroplasia (RLF)**, resulting in blindness in many infants. This was the result here. Toth v. Community Hospital at Glen Cove, 239 N.E.2d 368, 370 (N.Y.1968).

Other Authorities: Beary v. City of Rye, 406 N.Y.S.2d 9, 11 (N.Y.1978).

fibrosarcoma (fi″bro-sar-ko′mah) a sarcoma derived from fibroblasts that produce collagen.

X-rays revealed that a soft tissue mass had invaded the bone at the point of fracture. An excisional biopsy was performed, revealing a **fibrosarcoma** (cancer of the bone) of low-grade malignancy. Gradel v. Inouye, 421 A.2d 674, 676 (Pa.1980).

The frozen section report differed in its analysis of the type of tumor from reports of prior excisions which had described the tumor as showing elements of **fibrosarcoma**. Clemens v. Regents of University of California, 87 Cal.Rptr. 108, 113 (Ct. App.Cal.1970).

fibrosis (fi-bro′sis) the formation of fibrous tissue; fibroid or fibrous degeneration.

He expressed the opinions that employee's death was directly related to his hypoxemia, that this condition was directly related to the condition of employee's lungs, and that his **fibrosis** had been a significant factor in the development of the hypoxemia. Dr. Drage also held the opinion that employee's **fibrosis** had been caused by work exposure to iron oxides and probably to silica. Dunn v. Vic Mfg. Co., 327 N.W.2d 572, 574 (Minn.1982).

Continuous breathing of asbestos-laden air will cause an eventual concentration of the particles in the lung tissue. Once in the lung, the particles cannot be coughed out and remain there permanently. The noxious effect of these rock particles causes the body to set up an inflammation until eventually **fibrosis** occurs. Through **fibrosis** the body lays down scar tissue in the lung surrounding the asbestos fibers. Porter v. American Optical Corp., 641 F.2d 1128, 1133 (5th Cir. 1981).

At that time he had essentially no hip or knee motion and had an almost board-like hardness of the muscle tissue extending from his lower rib cage down to his ankles. According to testimony of Dr. Kissam and other doctors, that condition was due to the continuous use of injectable talwin, which transforms normal muscle tissue into a **fibrotic** condition like scar tissue. Dr. Kissam diagnosed Poole's condition as muscle **fibrosis** or brawny edema. Southern Bell Tel. & Tel. Co. v. Poole, 388 So. 2d 330, 332 (Dist.Ct.App.Fla.1980).

Other Authorities: Moore v. Industrial Comn, 492 P.2d 1222–3 (Ct.App.Ariz.1972); Glover v. Bruce, 265 S.W.2d 346, 351 (Mo.1954).

fibrosis, cystic See *fibrosis, cystic of the pancreas.*

fibrosis, cystic of the pancreas a generalized, hereditary disorder of infants, children, and young adults, in which there is widespread dysfunction of the exocrine glands; characterized by signs of chronic pulmonary disease (due to excess mucus production in the respiratory tract), pancreatic deficiency, abnormally high levels of electrolytes in the sweat, and occasionally by biliary cirrhosis. Pathologically, the pancreas shows obstruction of the pancreatic ducts by amorphous eosinophilic concretions, with consequent deficiency of pancreatic enzymes, resulting in steatorrhea and azotorrhea. The degree of involvement of organs and glandular systems may vary greatly, with consequent variations in the clinical picture. It is transmitted as an autosomal recessive trait. Called also *fibrocystic disease of the pancreas* and *mucoviscidosis.*

Cystic fibrosis is an inherited disease present at birth, although indications of it may not appear immediately. The disease cannot be cured. The only treatment for it is supportive. Its symptoms include lung insufficiency, instability of the pancreatic glands and thick mucous secretions which tend to block various organs of the body....

... Dr. Marano, defendant's other medical expert, testified that **cystic fibrosis** while congenital, and, therefore, present at birth, may not manifest symptoms "until years after birth or may not be recognized until later." However, he said that in Matthew's case the diagnosis of meconium ileus confirmed on the third day of his life, was pathognomonic of **cystic fibrosis** and amounted to a diagnosis of that disease at that time....

... The record indicates that while **cystic fibrosis** is a generalized disease, the symptomotology is variable. Inter alia, it may appear as an intestinal condition, and upper respiratory condition or a liver condition. The problem is to recognize the particular condition as a certain manifestation of **cystic fibrosis**. Dr. Sank and Dr. Marano both testified that Matthew's meconium ileus was a symptom or characteristic sign of **cystic fibrosis**. Dr. Schiffman, on the other hand, disagreed and said that there are cases of children with meconium ileus who are not cystics, i.e., that meconium ileus may or may not be indicative of **cystic fibrosis**. Kissil v. Beneficial National Life Ins. Co., 319 A.2d 67, 69–70 (N.J.1974).

fibrosis, diffuse interstitial pulmonary See *fibrosis, idiopathic pulmonary.*

fibrosis, idiopathic pulmonary chronic inflammation and progressive fibrosis of the pulmonary alveolar walls, with steadily progressive dyspnea, resulting finally in death from oxygen lack or right heart failure. Called also *diffuse interstitial pulmonary f.* The acute, rapidly fatal form is often called *Hamman-Rick syndrome.*

His condition was diagnosed as **pulmonary fibrosis**. After taking Mr. Ferebee's history and performing a number of tests,[9] the treating physicians identified paraquat poisoning as the cause of the **pulmonary fibrosis**. All other known causes of **pulmonary fibrosis** were ruled out,[10] and, as Drs. Yusuf and Crystal testified at trial, the diagnosis of paraquat poisoning was made, to a reasonable degree of medical certainty, long before Mr. Ferebee's death. [9 These included pulmonary function tests, a liver biopsy, gallium scans, and x-rays. [10 As defendant pointed out over and over again at trial, a substantial number of cases of **pulmonary fibrosis** are "idiopathic," i.e., their cause is unknown. At trial, defendant and its experts characterized **idiopathic pulmonary fibrosis (IPF)** as a distinct disease, with an identifiable pattern of symptoms. Plaintiffs and their experts, on the other hand, characterized **IPF** as a group of **pulmonary fibrosis** types with different, as-yet-unknown, causes. They claimed to have identified paraquat poisoning as the cause of one type of **pulmonary fibrosis** that would have been characterized as **IPF** if the history of paraquat exposure had not been known.] Ferebee v. Chevron Chemical Co., 552 F.Supp. 1293, 1295–6 (D.D.C.1982).

... he was disabled from further employment due to chronic obstructive lung disease or **pulmonary fibrosis**....

... He asserted that his pulmonary disability resulted from negligence, in that the defendant had.... (3) failed to remove minute fibrous glass particles and dust from the general plant area;.... Murphy v. Owens-Corning Fiberglas Corp., 447 F.Supp. 557, 561 (D.Kan.1977).
Other Authorities: Duquesne Light Co. v. W.C.A.B. (Shaffer), 465 A.2d 1340 (Cmwlth.Ct.Pa.1983). Consolidation Coal Co. v. Workmen's Compensation, 391 A.2d 14, 17, 18 (Cmwlth. Ct.Pa.1978). Harrison v. Flota Mercante Grancolombiana, S.A., 577 F.2d 968, 976 (5th Cir. 1978). Hunter v. Penn Galvanizing Co., 319 A.2d 214–15 (Cmwlth.Ct.P.1974); Magruder v. Richardson, 332 F.Supp. 1363, 1368, 1371 (E.D.Mo.1971).

fibrosis, interstitial See *fibrosis, idiopathic pulmonary.*

fibrosis, pulmonary See *fibrosis, idiopathic pulmonary.*

fibrosis, retroperitoneal deposition of fibrous tissue in the retroperitoneal space, producing vague abdominal discomfort, and often causing blockage of the ureters, with resultant hydronephrosis and impaired renal function, which may result in renal failure.

Dr. Harter testified that an exploratory operation on the stomach was necessitated because of a suspected **retroperitoneal fibrosis** and during the course of this exploratory operation the sponge was removed. No **retroperitoneal fibrosis** was discovered. Laws v. Harter, 534 S.W.2d 449, 450 (Ky.1975).

fibrothorax (fi"bro-tho'raks) a condition characterized by adhesion of the two layers of pleura, the lung being covered by a thick layer of nonexpansible fibrous tissue; often a consequence of traumatic hemothorax or of effusion.

A biopsy of the fibrous tissue revealed the presence of asbestos particles. Surgical procedures were undertaken in an attempt to clear the lung and chest cavity of the fibrous tissue and to re-expand the lower left lung. Subsequently complications developed, including air leaks and emphysema, and after several days in this condition Clarence Nelson suffered a cardiac arrest and died on April 5, 1975. The final diagnosis was left **fibrothorax** due to asbestosis with pleural effusion. The deceased expired due to complications of the surgery necessitated by that condition. Nelson v. Industrial Commission, 585 P.2d 887, 888 (Ct.App.Ariz.1978).

fibrotic tissue See *tissue, fibrous.*

fibrous scar tissue See *tissue, cicatricial.*

fibula (fib'u-lah) [L. "buckle"] [NA] the outer and smaller of the two bones of the leg, which articulates proximally with the tibia and distally is joined to the tibia in a syndesmosis. See illustration accompanying *skeleton.*

The lower leg consists of two bones: the **fibula**, which is the outer, smaller bone, and the tibia, which is the inner, larger bone. Both bones were fractured as a result of the fall. Jones v. Recreation and Park Commission, 395 So.2d 846–7 (Ct. App.La.1981).
Other Authorities: White v. Mitchell, 568 S.W.2d 216–17 (Ark.1978).

filling (fil'ing) the restoration of the crown with appropriate material after removal of the carious tissue from a tooth.

Although there are a number of restorative procedures, the procedure discussed here is that which is commonly called a **filling. Fillings** are ordinarily placed in teeth in order to restore the integrity of the tooth following the removal of dental decay....
The type of **filling** material used in restorations may vary according to the extent of the cavity and the location of the tooth. The Ohio Medical Assistance Program provides reimbursement for amalgam or composite restorations without prior authorization at the rate of $5.00 for one surface, $8.00 for two surfaces, and $10.00 for three surfaces. Silicate, acrylic or plastic restorations (normally used in anterior teeth) are reimbursed without prior authorization at the rate of $8.00 for each **filling**, regardless of which surface is treated. U.S. v. Talbott, 460 F.Supp. 253, 258–9 (S.D.Ohio 1978).

filter (fil'ter) [L. *filtrum*] in radiology, a solid screen usually of varying thickness of metal (aluminum, copper, tin, lead, etc.) which when placed in the pathway of the radiation beam prevents transmission of beta particles and photons of longer wavelengths.

The tube of the x-ray machine would be lowered so that the x-ray **filter** which had been attached to the tube would rest on plaintiff's body....
The defendants explained that in order to insure no overlap, it was essential that the **filter** be centered exactly in the middle of the field of exposure every time the treatment was given ....
Two different **filters** were used in the course of the treatment. One was round, 15 centimeters in diameter. The other was square, 15 centimeters on a side. Naturally, the square **filter** covered a larger area than its circular counterpart. Fifteen centimeters measures just a speck shy of six inches.
Doctor Hunt was somewhat imprecise as he described defendants' technique of centering the **filter**. He said that when treating the upper right mediastinal area, the **filter** was centered "about five to eight centimeters" to the right of the midline of the body. This specialist stated that when it was time to radiate the hilar of the left lung, the **filter** was centered a "little below" the left nipple and from six to seven centimeters to the left of the midline. Finally, when the filter was positioned for treatment to the left upper lung, it was placed "approximate-

ly'' five to six centimeters below the center of the clavicle. Wilkinson v. Vesey, 295 A.2d 676, 684 (R.I.1972).

filth

As previously stated, the green beans in issue are adulterated, under (a)(3), if they consist in whole or part of any **filthy** substance. The courts which have had occasion to interpret the word ''filthy'', as used in that section, have been unanimous in applying a common, everyday definition, rather than attempting to define it in a scientific or technical sense. See, e.g. United States v. Cassaro, Inc., 443 F.2d 153 (1st Cir. 1971); United States v. 44 Cases, Etc., 101 F.Supp. 658 (E.D.Ill.1951); United States v. Swift & Co., 53 F.Supp. 1018 (M.D.Ga.1943). Under such a definition, there can be no question, and the defendants do not assert otherwise, that Geotrichum mold fragments constitute **filth**. See United States v. Swift & Co., supra. U.S. v. General Foods Corp., 446 F.Supp. 740, 743 (N.D.N.Y.1978).

fimbria (fim'bre-ah) [L. *fimbriae* (pl.) a fringe] a fringe, border, or edge; [NA] a general term for such a structure. See also *fimbria, ovarian*; and *fimbriae of uterine tube.*

. . . the left tube was identified by its **fimbriated** extremity and the **fimbria** crushed with a hemostat followed by two ties of O Tycron suture. The tube was then inspected for hemostasis and found to be satisfactory. . . . McNeal v. U.S., 689 F.2d 1200, 1201 (4th Cir. 1982).

fimbria, ovarian; fimbria ovarica [NA], the longest of the processes that make up the fimbriae tubae uterinae, extending along the free border of the mesosalpinx; called also *fimbriated extremity.*

fimbriae of uterine tube the numerous divergent fringelike processes on the distal part of the infundibulum of the uterine tube.

finding (find'ing) an observation; a condition discovered.

''Medical **findings**'' are defined as ''symptoms,'' ''signs,'' or ''laboratory findings,'' each of which is defined. 20 C.F.R. § 404.1528. Gallagher on Behalf of Gallagher v. Schweiker, 697 F.2d 82–3 (2d Cir. 1983).

finger (fing'ger) any of the five digits of the hand. See also *metacarpus.*

Recent cases involving Section 306(c)(24) have upheld awards for specific loss of the use of a hand where amputation was limited to one or more **fingers**; [4] in each, the impairment to the hand was not confined to the loss of the **fingers**. See Gindy Manufacturing Co. v. Workmen's Compensation Appeal Board, 32 Pa. Commonwealth Ct. 128, 378 A.2d 492 (1977) (inclement weather caused pain in partially-amputated **fingers** and in hand generally); Reading Tube Corp. v. Workmen's Compensation Appeal Board, 12 Pa. Commonwealth Ct. 45, 315 A.2d 678 (1974) (nerve condition developed in hand and feeling was lost in middle **finger**); and Wall v. Workmen's Compensation Appeal Board, 12 Pa. Commonwealth Ct. 12, 315 A.2d 656 (1974) (remainder of hand suffered loss of bone structure and anatomical disarrangement). [4 Section 306(c) contains specific benefit provisions for loss of a thumb, index finger, middle finger, fourth finger, little finger, and portions

thereof. See 77 P.S. § 513(9)–(16).] Lykouras v. W.C.A.B. (Lyk-Math Inc.), 463 A.2d 1203, 1205 (Commonwealth Ct.Pa. 1983).

Immediately after the surgery Luna's left hand was numb and he could not bend his **fingers**. Within two days after the surgical procedures the long, ring and little **fingers** on this hand began to retract and are presently permanently curled inward, or clawed. Luna v. Nering, 426 F.2d 95, 97 (5th Cir. 1970).

finger, index the second digit of the hand, the thumb being considered the first; the forefinger.

She still complains of some deformity and lack of suppleness in her left **index finger**, but no loss of function there has been shown, although there is a potential need for corrective surgery in the future. Doyle v. U.S., 441 F.Supp. 701, 707 (D.S. Car.1977).

finger, lock one that is fixed in a flexed position, owing to the presence of a small fibrous growth in the sheath of the flexor tendon.

finger, trigger a finger liable to be affected with a momentary spasmodic arrest of flexion or extension, followed by a snapping into place; it is due to stenosing tendovaginitis, or a nodule in the flexor tendon (see *lock f.*).

Dr. Shucker notes that plaintiff complains of weakness and numbness in both hands and has **trigger fingers**; . . . . Longo v. Weinberger, 369 F.Supp. 250, 254 (E.D.Pa.1974).

fire ant See *Solenopsis.*

fissura (fis-su'rah), pl. *fissu'rae* [L.] [NA] fissure: a general term for a cleft or groove, especially a deep fold in the cerebral cortex that involves its entire thickness.

fissure (fish'ūr) [L. *fissura*] any cleft or groove, normal or otherwise; especially a deep fold in the cerebral cortex which involves the entire thickness of the brain wall. See *fissura.* Cf. *sulcus.*

fistula (fis'tu-lah), pl. *fistulas* or *fis'tulae* [L. "pipe"] an abnormal passage or communication, usually between two internal organs, or leading from an internal organ to the surface of the body; frequently designated according to the organs or parts with which it communicates, as anovaginal, bronchocutaneous, hepatopleural, pulmonoperitoneal, rectovaginal, urethrovaginal, and the like (see illustrations). Such passages are frequently created experimentally for the purpose of obtaining body secretions for physiologic study.

A **fistula** or hole had developed in the wall of her urethra at the site of the diverticulectomy. Dr. Scarzella operated on Ms. Saxon again in June 1976, in an effort to close the **fistula**, but the attempt was largely unsuccessful. A third operation, performed by another doctor in November 1977, resulted in some improvement, but the **fistula** remains. As a result, Ms. Saxon suffers from an uncontrolled discharge of urine, and the **fistula** has affected her sexual relationship with her husband. Scarzella v. Saxon, 436 A.2d 358, 359 (Ct.App.D.C.1981).

Later when urine began seeping from the wound plaintiff returned to the hospital. X rays and another cystoscopy revealed a **fistula** or small opening in the right ureter in the same area where the partial blockage had originally been encountered. This **fistula** had developed from pressure on the ureter from ligatures, sutures and adhesions in the area resulting from the hysterectomy. . . .

"I think, based upon my judgment and my findings, that the **fistula** in this ureter was caused by ligatures placed in the proximity of this ureter which, in turn, along with swelling and edema and reaction, caused pressure on this ureter to interfere with the blood supply to a small portion of this ureter which, under most circumstances would heal by—would heal satisfactorily but in this patient did not heal and close off as we had expected." Cronin v. Hagan, 221 N.W.2d 748, 750, 752 (Iowa 1974).

As used here a **fistula** is a medical term for an abnormal passage or tunnel which starts in the colon and comes out the skin or body surface. Treatment or repair of a **fistula** is made by inserting a small wire through the tunnel until it comes within the colon. The wire serves as a guide to the surgeon who attempts to repair the **fistula** by excising the infected tissue and converting the tunnel or passage into a trough. The trough is then expected to heal and close in from the bottom or interior. Ross v. Sher, 483 S.W.2d 297, 298 (Ct.Civ.App.Tex.1972).

fistula, rectovaginal one between the rectum and vagina.

. . . while plaintiff was in the hospital recovering from an operation performed by defendant, a nurse, in administering an enema, forced a hard rectal tube from plaintiff's rectum into her vagina. This created a **recto-vaginal fistula**, a small hole in the wall between the vagina and the rectum. The next day defendant, in attempting surgical repair, stitched the fistula with stainless steel sutures not absorbable by the body. Brown v. Colm, 522 P.2d 688, 689 (Cal.1974).

Other Authorities: Rainer v. Buena Community Memorial Hospital, 95 Cal.Rptr. 901, 906 (Ct.App.Cal.1971).

fistula, urinary an abnormal passage communicating with the urinary tract.

Shortly after discharge she developed bleeding and a **urinary fistula**, an abnormal tract from the urinary system that discharged urine to the abdominal incision. Therefore she returned to the hospital for reinsertion of the catheter that had been in place after the surgery but had been removed before discharge. Buckelew v. Grossbard, 435 A.2d 1150, 1153 (N.J.1981).

fistula, vesical an abnormal passage communicating with the urinary bladder.

fistula, vesicovaginal one from the bladder to the vagina. See also *fistula, vesical.*

Dr. Collier became concerned that she might have developed a **vesico-vaginal fistula**,[2] and made an appointment for her to see a urologist. . . .

. . . It was stipulated at trial that a **vesico-vaginal fistula** will not heal itself through the natural processes of the body. Absent corrective surgery, the condition is permanent. [[2] A fistula is an abnormal opening between two organs of the body, in

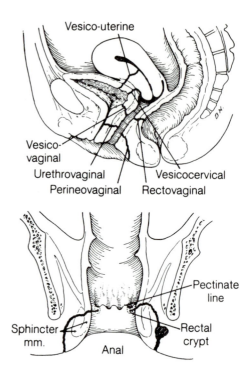

Various types of fistulae, designated according to site or to the organs with which they communicate.

this case between the bladder and the vagina. Medical evidence presented indicated that the usual cause of a **vesicovaginal fistula** forming is a stitch that may be inadvertently taken into the bladder during the closing of the vaginal cuff. In time, the stitch would pull through the bladder wall. Other possible causes are nicking the bladder with the knife or damaging the blood supply to a portion of the bladder wall with a blunt instrument or clamp. **Vesico-vaginal fistulae** typically measure only a few millimeters in size, and, once formed, retain their initial size until corrected.] LaCaze v. Collier, 434 So.2d 1039, 1041, 1048 (La.1983).

Dr. Warren diagnosed plaintiff's condition as a **vesicovaginal fistula**. Dr. Warren tried various means in attempting to control the bladder leakage and saw plaintiff every two weeks until April when examinations were continued on a monthly basis. Dr. Warren testified that in the beginning there was an opening between the bladder and the vagina which he denominated a fistula; that it was approximately one and one-half centimeters in diameter and that it had reduced in size to approximately one-half centimeter by September. Dr. Warren testified that because of the reduction in size he had hopes of a spontaneous closing of the fistula; however, that did not come about. Surgery was performed by Dr. Warren on September 15, 1969, which corrected the condition. . . .

. . . They agreed that a **vesicovaginal fistula** in connection with an hysterectomy could be caused by (1) cutting the bladder; (2) clamping the bladder and vagina together; (3) stitching or suturing the bladder and vagina together; (4) a cancer of the vagina or of the bladder and a complication of radium, cobalt, and x-rays; and (5) an abscess which can rupture both ways—into the vagina on the one side and into the bladder on the other. Tatro v. Lueken, 512 P.2d 529, 532–3 (Kan.1973).

After the operation was completed plaintiff suffered a severe spasm whenever she voided, and about ten days later there was a leakage of urine from the vagina. Dr. Weber examined her and found a **vesicovaginal fistula**, which is an opening through the wall of the bladder and the vagina . . . .

It is known that such fistulas result from devascularization and necrosis (cutting off of the blood supply and death of tissue) in the place where the fistula is formed; a number of factors can contribute to the devascularization and necrosis, and ordinarily it cannot be determined which of them were operative in a specific case. Among these factors are bruising of the bladder during the necessary separation of the uterus from the bladder, sutures or ligatures in the wall of the bladder to control bleeding caused in the separation, infection present in the cervix of the uterus and the vagina vault adjacent to the bladder, and the tissue reaction of the individual to surgery and suture materials. Siverson v. Weber, 372 P.2d 97–8 (Cal.1962).

fixation (fik-sa'shun) [L. *fixatio*] the condition of being held in a fixed position.

She had **fixation** of both elbows, in flexion and across the chest, with the fingers flexed, pronated and deformed in terms of their relationship to each other.

Her left leg could be extended when I saw her, but not completely, and it now seems to be more extensible than it was in 1963. The right leg was **fixed** in extension at that time and is still fixed in extension, with a spastic paralysis where the leg cannot be bent at the knee. Talcott v. Holl, 224 So.2d 420, 423 (Dist.Ct.App.Fla.1969).

fixation, external pin a method for stabilizing fractures by means of pins drilled into the bony parts through the overlying skin and connected by metal bars.

She underwent her seventh operation on April 10, 1979, a six-hour procedure, for the **external fixation** of the fracture and placement of a Hoffman apparatus on plaintiff's leg. Three holes were drilled for a length of six to eight inches through the bone at various levels and two pins were inserted near the ankle below the fracture and three pins were inserted above the fracture. Long devices were applied on the outside of the leg to which clamps, screws, nuts, bolts and washers were utilized. It was hoped that in time this would compress the bones together. Warmsley v. City of New York, 454 N.Y.S.2d 144, 145 (2d Dep't 1982).

fixation, intraosseous the open reduction and stabilization of fractured bony parts by direct fixation to one another with surgical wires, screws, pins, and/or plates.

. . . a hip fixation device used by orthopedic surgeons to set fractures of the femur in the neck region between the head and shaft of the femur, and fractures in the intertrochanteric region of the femur.

The device comprises a metal plate having a rectangular thick head portion and a leg portion which is attached to the shaft of the femur. These portions have a continuous concave cylindrical surface which conforms to and abuts the lateral cortex of the femur for a substantial longitudinal extent.

The head portion has a substantially central bore which accommodates an elongated fixation nail. The bore extends through the plate at an angle of about 135 degrees to the plate. This angle corresponds to the angular relation between the axes of the femur neck and shaft. The head portion also contains a plurality of holes extending along axes parallel to and spaced substantially symmetrically radially of the bore axis. In one embodiment there are eight holes arranged in a substantially square pattern around the bore. These holes are adapted to receive fixation pins slidably extending therethrough and guided to extend through the neck of the femur and terminate in the proximal cortex of the femur head. The plate, nail and pins coact to provide a massive fixation of the fracture, thereby immobilizing it against shearing and torsion forces while maintaining contact of bone fragments and accommodating bone absorption or healing at the fracture site. Deyerle v. Wright Mfg. Co., 496 F.2d 45, 49 (6th Cir. 1974).

flagellum (flah-jel'um), pl. *flagel'la* [L. "whip"] a long, mobile, whiplike projection from the free surface of a cell, serving as a locomotor organelle; it is composed of nine pairs of microtubules arrayed around a central pair. Arising from basal bodies, flagella are common to all mastigophoran protozoa and occur in such specialized cells as spermatozoa. Bacterial flagella are thinner and simpler, being composed of tightly wound chains of strands that contain flagellin. Bacteria having a single flagellum are *monotrichous*, those with two or more at one end are *lophotrichous*, those with one flagellum at each end are *amphitrichous*, and those with flagella around the entire surface are *peritrichous*. Cf. *cilium*.

flail (flāl) exhibiting abnormal or paradoxical mobility, as flail joint, flail chest, or flail valve.

Plaintiff's right arm had to be amputated on November 16, 1972. Dr. Hocker stated that Mr. Aretz "has a **flail** elbow with the substance of the elbow joint being absent,. . . ." Aretz v. U.S., 456 F.Supp. 397, 404 (S.D.Ga.1978).

flammable See *explode.*

flap (flap) a mass of tissue for grafting, usually including skin, only partially removed from one part of the body so that it retains its own blood supply during its transfer to a new location; used to repair defects in an adjacent or distant part of the body.

flap, bladder

Plaintiff testified that after the examination Dr. Weber pointed to a chart on his desk and said, "I must have put a suture through the flap of the bladder there which caused the fistula." There was evidence that "**bladder flap**" is an informal term used to refer to the "vesico uterine reflection of the parietal peritoneum." . . . .

. . . Dr. Weber denied making the statement ascribed to him by Mrs. Siverson and explained that a suture through the "**flap of the bladder**" is "normal procedure," that "it is done in every case, and in doing so you can't cause a fistula." Siverson v. Weber, 372 P.2d 97–8 (Cal.1962).

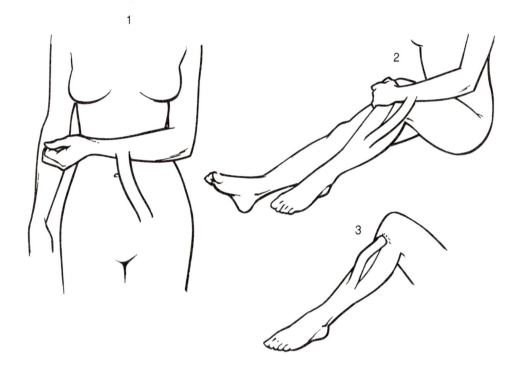

Tubed pedicle flap raised from the abdomen and (1) sutured to the arm to preserve blood supply, (2) transferred from abdomen to leg, and (3) from arm to leg.

flap, pedicle a flap consisting of the full thickness of the skin and the subcutaneous tissue, attached by a pedicle.

On 25 June 1971 the petitioner first saw Eugene Migray, M.D., a plastic surgeon. Dr. Migray performed a **Pedicle flap** on 26 July 1971. In the process the forearm is bound to the abdominal wall for about four weeks. Rowe v. Industrial Com'n, 510 P.2d 388, 392 (Ct.App.Ariz.1973).

flashback

Q.   Doctor, I am going to ask you about a term now, and you will have to explain the term. What are **flashbacks**?

A.   **Flashbacks** are events that occur that are characterized with LSD, but they can occur with some other drugs. An individual can be sitting here just as we are now and, with no warning, no apparent precipitating cause, there will be a behavioral change, and he will experience the same thing that he experienced, or similar to what he experienced at the time that he took this drug. The greatest danger of the **flashback** that I have been personally aware of was when an airline pilot, particularly a co-pilot, had taken LSD some twenty months previously and had a **flashback** during a landing, I think, of a jet aircraft. This basically is a broad description of what the **flashback** is. But the **flashback** can be precipitated by other causes.

Q.   What, for instance, Doctor?

A.   Stimulants can precipitate the **flashback**. If an individual has taken LSD, say, a year or two years ago, or even longer—

again this is unknown as to the precise time—and then took a diet pill, or amphetamine, it has been shown that amphetamines will produce the **flashback**. Brinkley v. U.S., 498 F.2d 505, 511–12 (8th Cir. 1974).

flat (flat) lying in one plane; having an even surface.

flatfoot (flat'foot) a condition in which one or more of the arches of the foot have flattened out; called also *pes pla-novalgus, pes planus,* and *pes valgus.* See illustration, next page.

Further examination reveals severe bilateral **flat foot** deformity with flattening of the longitudinal arches to a severe degree probably grade III. Ballard v. Commanding General, Fort Leonard Wood, Mo., 355 F.Supp. 143, 148 (W.D.Mo.1973).

flavonoid (fla'vo-noid) a generic term for a group of aromatic oxygen heterocyclic compounds derived from 2-phenylbenzopyran or its 2,3-dehydro derivative. They are widely distributed in higher plants, one subgroup, the anthocyanins, accounting for the majority of yellow, red, and blue pigmentation. Another subgroup, varying somewhat in structure, has physiologic properties formerly referred to as "vitamin P" activity, now called *bioflavonoids,* e.g., citrin, rutin, etc. The flavonoids are grouped in order of increasing oxidation state: catechins; leucoanthocyanidins and flavanones, flavanols, flavones, and anthocyanidins; and flavonols.

Print soles (*A*) of normal foot and (*B*) of one with flatfoot (Albert).

FLEX test See *test, FLEX.*

flexion (flek′shun) [L. *flexio*] the act of bending or condition of being bent.

Although he is able to flex his knee, there is still 35% to 40% loss of **flexion**—"approximately 40 percent range of normal motion." This condition is considered by the physician as permanent.

Dr. Powell stated his opinion that "I don't think that he will ever regain any significant improvement in knee **flexion**." Means v. Sears, Roebuck & Co., 550 S.W.2d 780, 783 (Mo. 1977).

flexion, dorsa

He also noted "no **dorsa flexion**," or inability to flex or raise foot up. Hale v. Venuto, 187 Cal.Rptr. 357, 359 (Ct.App.Cal. 1982).

flexor (flek′sor) [L.] any muscle that flexes a joint; see *Table of Musculi.*

flexor spasm See *spasm;* and *flexor.*

fluid (floo′id) [L. *fluidus*] 1. a liquid or a gas. 2. composed of elements or particles which freely change their relative positions without their separating. See also *liquid, liquor,* and *solution.*

fluid, cerebral See *fluid, cerebrospinal (C.S.F.).*

fluid, cerebrospinal (C.S.F.) the fluid contained within the four ventricles of the brain, the subarachnoid space, and the central canal of the spinal cord; it is formed by the choroid plexus and brain parenchyma, is circulated through the ventricles into the subarachnoid space, and is absorbed into the venous system. Called also *liquor cerebrospinalis* [NA].

... she received follow-up medical care for leakage of **cerebral fluid** and for her other injuries. Doyle v. U.S., 441 F.Supp. 701, 706 (D.S.Car.1977).

fluorescein (floo″o-res′e-in) chemical name: resorcinolphthalein. The simplest of the fluorane dyes and the parent compound of eosin; used intravenously in tests to

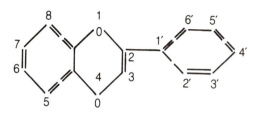

Flavonoid.

assess by its fluorescence the adequacy of the circulation, and combined with radioactive iodine in localization of brain tumors, etc. Called also *dihydroxyfluorane.* See also *fluorescein, soluble.*

To determine whether or not the lens is touching the cornea, **fluorescein** dye is introduced into the eye with a strip of paper moistened with an eye irrigating solution and impregnated with **fluorescein** at one end. The **fluorescein** mixes with tears in the eye and is activated when viewed under an ultraviolet or black light. In this manner, the tears can be viewed under the lens to determine if the lens is touching the cornea or floating over it as it should....

... The resulting **fluorescein** pattern in this test affects the determination of the base or fitting curve of the lenses ultimately selected or ordered. State ex rel. Londerholm v. Doolin, 497 P.2d 138, 142 (Kan.1972).

fluorescein, sodium; fluorescein, soluble chemical name: resorcinolphthalein sodium. An odorless, water-soluble, orange-red powder, $C_{20}H_{10}Na_2O_5$, used in dilute solution to reveal corneal lesions and as a test of circulation in the extremities and retina. Called also *uranin.*

He went to the emergency room of the Mt. Sinai Hospital at 11 p.m. where personnel irrigated his right eye and conducted a **fluorscein** examination for foreign bodies. Johnson v. Connecticut Transit Management, 463 A.2d 625, 627 (Super.Ct. Conn.1983).

To determine proper tear flow, the fitter places a clear, nontoxic chemical, **fluorescein**, in the wearer's eye. He then examines the part of the eye covered by the contact lens with a magnifier equipped with an ultraviolet light which causes the **fluorescein** to glow green. By observing the depth of the **fluorescein** color the fitter determines whether there is proper tear flow behind the lens and what its rate of circulation is. He also determines whether any part of the trial lens is too tight or too loose on the cornea. There is no machine or chart to aid the fitter in reading these **fluorescein** patterns, which may be misinterpreted for a number of reasons. This is a skill which is acquired through training and experience. People ex rel. Watson v. House of Vision, 322 N.E.2d 15, 17 (Ill. 1975).

fluoridation (floo″or-ĭ-da′shun) treatment with fluorides; specifically, the addition of fluoride to the public water supply as part of the public health program to prevent or reduce the incidence of dental caries.

The studies which were begun in the 1930's to determine the effect of fluoride on teeth have continued to date and have established beyond any serious question that persons who use waters containing 1.0 to 1.5 ppm of fluoride, either naturally or artificially, from infancy to the age of 10 or 12 years have significantly fewer dental caries in their permanent teeth and without dental fluorosis to an unacceptable degree.

This widespread acceptance of **fluoridation** as an effective means to prevent dental caries has led to the controlled **fluoridation** of the water supplies in over 4,800 communities in the United States and these communities include most of the large cities in the nation. There are presently about 100 million people in this country consuming water having a fluoride content between .7 ppm and 1.5 ppm. In Minnesota over 90% of the more than 650 communities having a municipal water supply have fluoridated the same.... A substantial majority of the citizens of this state presently drink fluoridated water and most of this majority have been doing so for more than 15 years.

Fluoridation of public water supplies has been advocated or recommended by more than forty national professional and scientific organizations including the American Medical Association, American Dental Association, American Institute of Nutrition, American Association for the Advancement of Science, American Association of Dental Schools, American Cancer Society and many others of like standing and repute. **Fluoridation** now has and for many years has had the enthusiastic endorsement and support of the U.S. Public Health Service. Minn.State Bd. of Health v. City of Brainerd, 241 N.W.2d 624, 629 (Minn.1976).

fluoride (floo'o-rīd) a binary compound of fluorine (q.v.). See also *fluorosis.*

The cosmetically undesirable mottling of the tooth enamel that results from excessive **fluoride** occurs in a severity proportional to the concentration of **fluoride** in the drinking water. Environmental Defense Fund, Inc. v. Costle, 578 F.2d 337, 347 (D.C. Cir.1978).

... it is important to understand the factual background of fluoridation. For this purpose we quote at length from the trial court's memorandum in MOFF v. City of Brainerd and Minnesota State Board of Health:

Fluoride, the substance in question, is the ion of the element fluorine. It is never found in nature in an isolated form but always in association with other elements, most commonly with calcium. **Fluoride** is found in all minerals, rocks and soil; it is present in all foods and water consumed by human beings. The addition of **fluoride** to drinking water, at least in the amounts here contemplated, affects neither the color nor the taste of the water. **Fluoride**, in common with many other substances such as oxygen, ordinary table salt, vitamin A and vitamin B is toxic when ingested in relatively large amounts. The natural drinking waters of this country vary in **fluoride** content from a barely discernible trace up to about 15 milligrams per liter or, as it is otherwise expressed, up to about 15 parts per million (ppm). Minn. State Bd. of Health v. City of Brainerd, 241 N.W.2d 624, 628 (Minn.1976).

fluorine (floo'ŏ-rēn) [from *fluor spar,* from which it is derived] a nonmetallic, gaseous element, belonging to the halogen group; symbol, F; atomic number, 9; atomic weight, 18.998. Fluorine, in the form of fluoride, is incorporated into the structure of bone and teeth and provides protection against dental caries; an excess of fluorine may result in fluorosis.

fluoroscope (floo'ŏ-ro-skōp) [*fluorescence* + Gr. *skopein* to examine] a device used for examining deep structures by means of roentgen rays; it consists of a screen (*fluorescent screen*) covered with crystals of calcium tungstate on which are projected the shadows of x-rays passing through the body placed between the screen and the source of irradiation.

The fluoroscopic equipment used consisted of a tube underneath the table on which the patient would lie. X-rays would pass through the table and the body of the patient onto a fluoroscent screen augmented by a television system which improved the clarity of the image. Because the screen must be positioned above and rather close to the portion of the body being visualized there is insufficient space to allow for manipulation of the biopsy needle and the screen can be used only intermittently. The **fluoroscope** is not energized any longer than necessary in order to minimize radiation to the patient and the hands of the surgeon. Logan v. Greenwich Hosp. Ass'n., 465 A.2d 294, 297 (Conn.1983).

Dr. Rich's findings were made only with the use of a **fluoroscope**,.... Statzer v. Weinberger, 383 F.Supp. 1258, 1262 (E.D.Ky.1974).

fluoroscopy (floo"or-os'ko-pe) examination by means of the fluoroscope.

The examining physician reported that **fluoroscopy** revealed "fine nodulation throughout both lung fields indicating an early stage of silicosis." Ansel v. Weinberger, 529 F.2d 304, 305 (6th Cir. 1976).

fluorosis (floo"o-ro'sis) a condition due to exposure to excessive amounts of fluorine or its compounds. Fluoride intoxication may occur as a result of such factors as accidental ingestion of fluoride-containing insecticides and rodenticides, chronic inhalation of industrial dusts or gases containing fluorides, or prolonged ingestion of water containing large amounts of fluorides; it is characterized by skeletal changes, consisting of combined osteosclerosis and osteomalacia (osteofluorosis) and by mottled enamel of the teeth when exposure occurs during enamel formation (see *dental f.*). A similar condition is seen in cattle, sheep, and other livestock, and is due to the same factors that cause intoxication in humans and also to ingestion of animal feed containing toxic levels of fluorides and grazing on pastures contaminated with fluorides in industrial dusts or gases. Called also *chronic endemic f.* and *chronic fluoride,* or *fluorine, poisoning.*

The MCL for fluoride specified by the interim regulations is based on the principle that drinking water may usefully contain sufficient fluoride to provide optimal protection against dental caries, but that the amount by which such levels are exceeded should be limited, so as to avoid undue side-effects—primarily mottling of the teeth (**fluorosis**), a condition with only esthetic significance....

There is serious question as to whether mottling can be regarded as an "adverse effect on health" within the meaning of the Act. See, e.g., HEW letter of June 4, 1973, to EPA at 2. "We believe that in the context of discussing limits to avoid concentrations of substances that may be hazardous to health, dental **fluorosis** should not be termed harmful. The more severe dental **fluorosis** caused by highly excessive concentrations is described in the literature as unesthetic, cosmetically objectionable, or disfiguring, but is not described as hazardous to health.'' Environmental Defense Fund, Inc. v. Costle, 578 F.2d 337, 341, 347 (D.C.Cir.1978).

fluorosis, dental a form of enamel hypoplasia, largely of the permanent teeth, resulting from ingestion of excessive amounts of fluoride in the natural water supply used for drinking and for food preparation during the period of enamel calcification; it is manifested by a mottled discoloration of the tooth enamel, the affected teeth having a dull, chalky white appearance on eruption and later, in areas with higher fluoride concentration, may show a brown stain. Called also *mottled enamel.*

fluorouracil (floo″o-ur′ah-sil) [USP] chemical name: 5-fluoro-2,4(1*H*,3*H*)-pyrimidinedione. A pyrimidine analogue that acts as an antimetabolite to uracil, $C_4H_3FN_2O_2$, occurring as a white to practically white, crystalline powder; used as an antineoplastic in the palliative management of carcinoma of the gastrointestinal tract, breast, and pancreas, administered intravenously. Also used topically in the treatment of actinic keratoses.

In addition the government expert has testified—and the court accepts his testimony as true—that at this time there is only one ''acceptable'' treating agent for pancreatic cancer— Flourouracil. The fact that this drug is highly toxic is borne out by the manufacturer's brochure accompanying it:

Flourouracil is a highly toxic drug with a narrow margin of safety. Therefore, patients should be carefully supervised since therapeutic response is unlikely to occur without some evidence of toxicity. Patients should be informed of expected toxic effects, particularly oral manifestations. White blood counts with differential are recommended before each dose. Severe hematological toxicity, gastrointestinal hemorrhage and even death may result from the use of Flourouracil despite meticulous selection of patients and careful adjustment of dosage. Although severe toxicity is more likely in poor risk patients, fatalities may be encountered occasionally even in patients in relatively good condition. Rizzo v. U.S., 432 F.Supp. 356, 359–60 (E.D.N.Y.1977).

Fluothane (floo′o-thān) trademark for a preparation of halothane. See also *halothane.*

fluphenazine (floo-fen′ah-zēn) chemical name: 4-[3-[2-(trifluoromethyl)-10*H*-phenothiazin-10-yl]-propyl]-1-piperazineethanol. The 2-trifluromethyl derivative of perphenazine, $C_{22}H_{26}F_3N_3OS$, the most potent of the phenothiazine tranquilizers.

fluphenazine hydrochloride [USP], the dihydrochloride salt of fluphenazine, $C_{22}H_{26}F_3N_3OS \cdot HCl$, occurring as a white or nearly white, crystalline powder; used as a tranquilizer in the treatment of manifestations of psychotic disorders, and as an antiemetic, administered orally and intramuscularly. See also *psychotropic.*

The doctor's drug of choice was Prolixin because of its benefits, and since it is administered by injection only once every two weeks, it avoids a need for the patient to be disturbed more often. Matter of B, 383 A.2d 760, 761 (Super.Ct.N.J. 1977).

He was subdued by deputy sheriffs using mace and a dosage of **prolixin** was injected in him by the jail doctor while movant was restrained by deputy sheriffs....

... She testified that **prolixin** ''slows the thinking, but it is not to impair the thinking.'' Cavallaro v. State, 465 S.W.2d 635–7 (Mo.1971).

flux (fluks) [L. *fluxus*] a borax-containing substance that maintains the cleanliness of metals to be united and facilitates the easy flow and attachment of solder. See also *neuritis, retrobulbar* (Skinner case).

Using a torch, sunglasses, a ''solder'' and ''Blue Label'' **flux**,[1] claimant welded copper surfaces of some kind....

... Dr. Lewin was extensively examined and cross-examined; the substance of his testimony was that it was unlikely that the fluoride vapors produced by welding with Blue Label Sil Flux had been the cause of claimant's disease. [[1] The noun ''flux'' is used here to denote a substance applied to surfaces to be joined by soldering, brazing or welding to clean and free them from oxide and promote their union.] Skinner v. Dawson Metal Products, 575 S.W.2d 935, 938, 942 (Mo.Ct.App. 1978).

foci (fo′si) [L.] plural of *focus.*

focus (fo′kus), pl. *fo′ci* [L. ''fire-place''] the chief center of a morbid process.

However, two or three days later, Dr. Hunt received the results of the paraffin test. These results showed conclusively that the tissue removed from Mrs. Steele contained ''**foci**''[5] of carcinoma in situ. [[5] Foci translates into layman's terms as localized areas. (Tr. p. 388)] Steele v. St. Paul Fire & Marine Ins. Co., 371 So.2d 843, 846 (Ct.App.La.1979).

folic acid See *acid, folic.*

follicle (fol′lĭ-k′l) 1. a sac or pouchlike depression or cavity; see also *folliculus.* 2. a former name for a lymph nodule.

folliculitis (fŏ-lik″u-li′tis) inflammation of a follicle or follicles; used ordinarily in reference to hair follicles, but sometimes in relation to follicles of other kinds. See also *follicle.*

His examination revealed **folliculitis**, an inflammation of the follicles, on Green's chest, back, shoulders, neck, face, and scalp. Dr. Wise pointed out that such a disorder is quite responsive to treatment and usually does not disrupt an individual's ability to work except in presence of excessive heat or irritating chemical exposure. Green v. Schweiker, 694 F.2d 108, 111 (5th Cir. 1982).

folliculus (fo-lik′u-lus), pl. *follic′uli* [L., dim. of *follis* a leather bag] [NA] a follicle; [NA] a general term for a very small excretory or secretory sac or gland.

fontanelle (fon″tah-nel′) [Fr., dim. of *fontaine* spring, filter] a soft spot, such as one of the membrane-covered spaces (*fonticuli cranii* [NA]) remaining in the incompletely ossified skull of a fetus or infant. See also *fonticulus.*

The infant's **fontanelle**, or soft spot, was markedly bulging and tense, and the doctor also noticed a small scar and some abrasions. State v. Goblirsch, 246 N.W.2d 12–13 (Minn. 1976).

fonticulus (fon-tik'u-lus), pl. *fontic'uli* [L., dim. of *fons* fountain] [NA] fontanelle; a soft spot; one of the membrane-covered spaces remaining in the incompletely ossified skull of the fetus or infant.

food (fōōd) anything which, when taken into the body, serves to nourish or build up the tissues or to supply body heat; aliment; nutriment.

Congress defined ''**food**'' in Section 321(f) as ''articles used as **food**.'' This definition is not too helpful, but it does emphasize that ''**food**'' is to be defined in terms of its function as **food**, rather than in terms of its source, biochemical composition or ingestibility. Plaintiffs' argument that starch blockers are **food** because they are derived from **food**—kidney beans—is not convincing; if Congress intended **food** to mean articles derived from **food** it would have so specified. Indeed some articles that are derived from **food** are indisputably not **food**, such as caffeine and penicillin. In addition, all articles that are classed biochemically as proteins cannot be **food** either, because for example insulin, botulism toxin, human hair and influenza virus are proteins that are clearly not **food**. . . .

. . . The term ''**food**'' as defined in [21 U.S.C.] Section 321(f) means (1) articles used for **food** or drink for man or other animals, (2) chewing gum, and (3) articles used for components of any such article. Nutrilab, Inc. v. Schweiker, 713 F.2d 335, 336–7 (7th Cir. 1983).

On April 22, 1976, the President signed Public Law 94–278, extensively amending the Food, Drug and Cosmetic Act. Section 501(a) added to the Act § 411.

(c)(1) For purposes of this section, the term **food** to which this section applies means a **food** for humans which is a **food** for special dietary use—

(A) which is or contains any natural or synthetic vitamin or mineral, and

(b) which—

(i) is intended for ingestion in tablet, capsule, or liquid form, or

(ii) if not intended for ingestion in such a form, does not simulate and is not represented as conventional **food** and is not represented for use as a sole item of a meal or of the diet. National Nutritional Foods Ass'n v. Kennedy, 572 F.2d 377, 381 (2d Cir. 1978).

food additive See *additive, food.*

foot (foot) [L. *pes*] the distal portion of the primate leg, upon which an individual stands and walks. It consists, in man, of the tarsus, metatarsus, and phalanges and the tissues encompassing them. See also *pes* and *talipes.*

The present guideline for distinguishing between leg and **foot** amputations was adopted in 1953, 1953 P.A. 198, § 10:

An amputation between the knee and **foot** 7 or more inches below the tibial table (plateau) shall be considered a **foot**, above that point a leg. (Except for stylistic changes, the present version is the same as the 1953 amendment. See now M.C.L. § 418.361, subds. [2][i] and [2][k]; M.S.A. § 17.237[361], subds. [2][i] and [2][k].) Dobbs v. Villa Capri Restaurant, 329 N.W.2d 503, 505 (Ct.App.Mich.1982).

. . . he slipped and caught his **foot** in the turning parts of a Wheelabarator, a machine used to abrade and clean steel. Flesh and skin were torn from the top of his **foot** leaving bone and tendons exposed. Additionally, nerves and extensor tendons to some of his toes were severed. Lattin v. Hica Corp., 395 So.2d 690, 692 (La.1981).

foot, dangle; foot, drop a condition in which the foot hangs in a plantar-flexed position, due to lesion of the peroneal nerve.

On July 27, 1976, respondent doctor performed a hip replacement operation on appellant. After surgery, appellant's leg was placed in a traction device. When appellant complained of pain, attending nurses advised appellant that the device was not to be altered; that the postoperative pain was not unusual.

On or about August 11, 1976, according to appellant's complaint, appellant ''first discovered that she lacked any feeling or sensation in the toes of her left foot, [and] left leg between the ankle and the knee. [She also] noticed that the toes of her left foot appeared curled downward and [she] was unable to exercise any motor control in the region of her lower left leg and foot. [Upon inquiry she] was told that it was not unusual or permanent and that physical therapy would result in an improvement thereof.'' If caused by nerve damage, such a condition is known as ''**dropped foot**.'' Massey v. Litton, 669 P.2d 248–9 (Nev.1983).

A procedure was performed to remove the aneurysm, but following the operation the then 60-year-old plaintiff suffered ''**foot drop**'', a partial paralysis of the right foot. Spitzer v. Ciprut, 437 N.Y.S.2d 27–28 (2d Dep't 1981).

It was subsequently discovered that during the operation, the peroneal nerve had been transected or cut resulting in peroneal palsy, a condition which results in ''**drop foot**'', an abnormal gait, muscular atrophy, and limitation of function. Welsh v. State of N.Y., 51 A.D.2d 602, 377 N.Y.S.2d 790 (3d Dep't 1976).

Other Authorities: McKeague v. Talbert, 658 P.2d 898, 907 (Intermed.Ct.App.Hawaii 1983); Storey v. Lambert's Limbs & Braces, Inc., 426 So.2d 676, 677 (Ct.App.La.1982). Aretz v. U.S., 456 F.Supp. 397, 403 (S.D.Ga.1978); Allen v. Weinberger, 552 F.2d 781, 785 (7th Cir. 1977); DuBose v. Matson Navigation Co., 403 F.2d 875, 877 (9th Cir. 1968); Honeywell v. Rogers, 251 F.Supp. 841, 844 (W.D.Pa.1966).

foot, march painful swelling of the forefoot, often associated with fracture of one of the metatarsal bones, following excessive foot strain.

footdrop (foot'drop) dropping of the foot from paralysis of the anterior muscles of the leg.

foramen (fo-ra'men), pl. *foram'ina* [L.] a natural opening or passage; [NA] a general term for such a passage, especially one into or through a bone.

He also found a 50–60% narrowing of the neural **foramina**, the space between the vertebra through which the nerve fibers pass, in the C4, C5, C6 levels of the Appellant's neck. His conclusion, reported on March 2, 1978, was that cervical spondylosis was indicated and that the condition had not changed significantly since the performance of previous tests. Broadbent v. Harris, 698 F.2d 407, 409 (10th Cir. 1983).

foramen, epiploic; foramen epiploicum [NA], an opening connecting the two sacs of the peritoneum, situated below and behind the porta hepatis.

We know the common bile duct—under normal conditions the common bile duct, the porta vein and the hepatic artery, that's the artery to the liver, run in this band called the porta hepatis. This opening here is a true opening and empties into a cavity here, it's called the foramen of Winslow or the **epiploic foramen**. Now, as I testified before, when you palpate a common duct, you are palpating for a hard object because the common duct is a soft object. Bronwell v. Williams, 597 S.W.2d 542, 552 (Ct.Civ.App.Tex.1980).

foramen, intervertebral; foramen intervertebrale [NA], the passage formed by the inferior and superior notches on the pedicles of adjacent vertebrae; it transmits a spinal nerve and vessels.

He suffered some straightening of the forward curvature of the spine and narrowing of the **intervertebral foramin** on the left side between 3 cervical discs and on the right side between 5 cervical discs as a result of the accident. Landry v. Aetna Ins. Co., 422 So.2d 1287, 1290 (Ct.App.La.1982), remanded 429 So.2d 150.

Dr. Brodsky testified that the fifth lumbar root at that point was "bound down" in scar tissue and adhesions to the disc and to the lateral wall of the bony canal. He stated that the nerve was compressed in the **intervertebral foramen** which is the canal the nerve travels through to get out of the spine into the soft tissue; that he "freed that up." French v. Brodsky, 521 S.W.2d 670, 683 (Ct.Civ.App.Tex.1975).

foramen mandibulae; foramen mandibulare the opening on the medial surface of the ramus of the mandible, leading into the mandibular canal.

The nerves governing sensation in the lower jaw, teeth and chin enter the jaw through the **mandibular foramen**, an opening at the rear of the lower jaw. LaRocque v. LaMarche, 292 A.2d 259–60 (Vt.1972).

foramen, mental; foramen mentale [NA], an opening on the lateral part of the body of the mandible, opposite the second biscuspid tooth, for passage of the mental nerve and vessels.

Fairly well forward on the jaw a branch of the inferior alveolar nerve exits through a jaw opening called the **mental foramen**. LaRocque v. LaMarche, 292 A.2d 259–60 (Vt.1972).

foramen of Winslow See *foramen epiploicum.*

foraminotomy (for"am-ĭ-not'o-me) [*foramina* + Gr. *tomē* a cutting] the operation of removing the roof of intervertebral foramina, done for the relief of nerve root compression.

He performed a **foraminotomy**, or unroofing of the nerve root as it comes out of the bony canal. Field v. Winn Dixie Louisiana, Inc., 427 So.2d 616–17 (Ct.App.La.1983).

Conservative treatment proved to be a failure. Dr. Starr consequently performed an interlaminar dissection of the C–6, C–7 level, left, with decompressive **forminotomy** [sic] over a hard spur. After the operation plaintiff felt improved sensation and immediately showed increased strength in his left arm. Pain, spasm and soreness in the neck muscles remained. Four months after surgery the patient was still complaining of pain, particularly of soreness in his neck and upper back and still had a certain amount of spasm in the neck muscles. However, he had no further signs of impaired nerve supply to the upper left extremity. Webb v. Insurance Co. of North America, 396 So.2d 508, 513 (Ct.App.La.1981).

. . . opening up the foramen where the nerve goes out to relieve any bony impression on the nerve and this is also the lateral portion of the spine, and then removing the disc. A. P. Green Refractories Co. v. Workmen's Comp. App. Bd., 301 A.2d 914–15 (Commonwealth Ct.Pa.1973).

force, external See *external* (Iannelli case).

forceps (fōr'seps) [L.] an instrument with two blades and a handle for compressing or grasping tissues in surgical operations, and for handling sterile dressings and other surgical supplies. See illustration, next page.

forceps, Piper a special obstetrical forceps for an aftercoming head.

The Court also finds that the attending physicians were negligent in failing to use **Piper forceps** during a difficult vaginal delivery of the child's head. The child was in a breech position which, according to all of the medical testimony, significantly increases the chances of complications and serious injury during delivery. . . .

. . . However, all who were present testified that "**Piper forceps**", a basic and well-recognized tool for use in just such an emergency situation, were not used. Williams v. Lallie Kemp Charity Hosp., 428 So.2d 1000, 1005–6 (Ct.App.La.1983).

However, the child's head became lodged in the mother's pelvis. In order to aid delivery, Dr. Matthews employed **Piper forceps** to grasp the child's head. As he was pulling on them, the forceps slipped off the child's head. Dr. Matthews reapplied the forceps and successfully delivered the child, a boy, who was named Robert Ryan Roark.

The infant Roark had an indentation on either side of its head. Roark v. Allen, 633 S.W.2d 804, 807 (Tex.1982).

forceps, Simpson's a form of obstetrical forceps. See also *forceps, Tucker-McLean* (Wale case).

forceps, Tucker-McLean a long obstetrical forceps with a solid blade.

After waiting for further spontaneous movement and birth of the child, the doctor concluded that these events would not occur. He thereupon decided to use forceps for the delivery. The instrument used is what is known in the medical profession as long **Tucker-McLane forceps** [sic]. (The two types of forceps look like long-handled tongs. The **Tucker-McLane forceps** [sic] has thin, solid blades and a narrower shaft than does the Simpson forceps, with its solid, somewhat thicker and wider blades and slightly larger shaft.). . . .

. . . He considered the **Tucker-McLane type forceps** [sic] as practically obsolete for mid forceps delivery, especially where there is a molded head involved. [The Supreme Court (Florida) noted that in such a situation they are "no longer recognized as proper".] Another type forceps (Simpson) was considered by him to be less likely to slip and cause injury. Wale v. Barnes, 261 So.2d 201, 202–4 (Dist.Ct.App.Fla.1972), quashed 278 So.2d 601, 605 (Fla.1972).

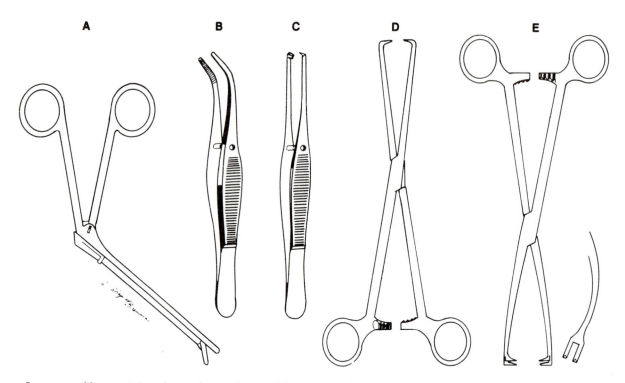

Some types of forceps: *A*, Struycken ear forceps; *B*, serrated forceps; *C*, Iris forceps, fine mouse tooth; *D*, Schroeder tenaculum forceps; *E*, Schroeder vulsellum forceps (with side view of blade).

Dr. Barnes then measured her and based upon his judgment, he manually turned the child (without forceps) in an attempt to ease delivery. However, this procedure did not cause childbirth and Dr. Barnes decided to use forceps. He chose **Tucker-McLane forceps** [sic] even though the baby's head was "considerably molded" (elongated) and applied the forceps to the baby's face several times during the delivery....

... Upon the issue of negligence, Dr. Kahn's testimony suffices: that the **Tucker-McLane** [sic] were the wrong **forceps** to use in these circumstances. He further stated that **Tucker-Mc-Lane forceps** [sic] are no longer recognized as proper in deliveries involving a molded or elongated head. Wale v. Barnes, 278 So.2d 601, 603, 605 (Fla.1973).

forearm (fōr'arm) the part of the upper limb of the body between the elbow and the wrist; called also *antebrachium* [NA]. See also *radius*.

Neither the language of the Act nor the cases decided under it preclude "loss of use" benefits for injuries involving amputation. Section 306(c)(24) provides: "Amputation between the wrist and elbow shall be considered as the loss of a **forearm** ...;" yet in the same paragraph it states that "[p]ermanent loss of the use of a(n) ... arm ... shall be considered as the loss of such ... arm...." In Pater v. Superior Steel Co., 263 Pa. 244, 106 A. 202 (1919), a claimant's arm was badly crushed, requiring its amputation an inch below the elbow. Notwithstanding that the Act then provided that amputation between the wrist and elbow was to be considered as the loss of a hand, our Supreme Court upheld a referee's finding that,

due to the closeness of the amputation to the elbow and the restricted motion of the joint from infection and interference with its muscles, the claimant had permanently lost the use of the entire arm. Lykouras v. W.C.A.B. (Lyk-Math Inc.), 463 A.2d 1203, 1205 (Commonwealth Ct.Pa.1983).

... he fell from a bench while at work, fracturing his right **forearm** (comminuted distal radius fracture). Patin v. Continental Cas. Co., 424 So.2d 1161, 1163 (Ct.App.La.1982).

... with anterior dislocation of the **forearm** on the elbow....

... multiple comminuted fracture fragments were excised and the triceps tendon was reattached to the distal ulna. Dardar v. State of La., 322 F.Supp. 1115, 1119 (E.D.La.1971).

foreign body See *object, foreign; rongeur;* and *care, standard of.*

foreign substance See *object, foreign.*

formaldehyde (fōr-mal'dĕ-hīd) a powerful disinfectant gas, HCHO, formerly used as a disinfectant for rooms, clothing, etc. A 37 per cent solution of formaldehyde gas in water (formalin) is widely used as a fixing fluid for pathologic specimens or as a preservative, and dilutions have also been used as a surgical and general antiseptic and as an astringent. See also *ether* (Air Shields, Inc. case).

Formaldehyde is a colorless gas composed of carbon, hydrogen, and oxygen. It is present in every cell in the human body and in the atmosphere. Formaldehyde has been in widespread commercial use for almost a century. Seven billion pounds per year are produced in the United States. According to the industry, **formaldehyde** is a component of products aggregating 8% of this country's Gross National Product. Approximately half of the **formaldehyde** produced in the United States is used in preparing bonding resins. These resins are used in producing plywood, particleboard, fiberboard and permanent press products, in addition to UFFI. Such products as shampoo, toothpaste, cosmetics, and paper towels also contain **formaldehyde**. . . .

. . . The industry next contends that the numerous studies of humans exposed to **formaldehyde** in the workplace discredit the Commission's finding that **formaldehyde** is carcinogenic at low levels. Eleven epidemiologic studies involving a total of 10,000 workers were introduced into the record. None of the studies' authors found a statistically significant increase in the number of cancers among workers exposed to **formaldehyde** compared to the general population. The largest studies were conducted by Dr. Marsh, who found no nasal cancer and no dose-response relationship between **formaldehyde** exposure and other respiratory cancers among 2,490 **formaldehyde** workers; Drs. Walrath and Fraumeni of the National Cancer Institute, who found no nasal cancer mortality and no unusual respiratory cancer mortality in their study of 1,106 morticians; and Dr. Wong of Tabershaw Occupational Medical Associates, who found no nasal cancer mortality or excess respiratory cancer mortality among 2,026 formaldehyde workers. Dr. Wong concluded that "at this point there is no epidemiologic evidence that **formaldehyde** is a human carcinogen." [Footnote omitted.] Gulf South Insul. Co. v. U.S. Consumer Prod. Safety Com'n, 701 F.2d 1137, 1140, 1145 (5th Cir. 1983).

General background. The trial judge made the following findings. **Formaldehyde** is a colorless, gaseous compound of carbon, hydrogen, and oxygen. It is present, with other aldehydes, in the atmosphere, where it is continuously introduced through natural processes of photochemical generation in plants. Automobiles also inject **formaldehyde** into the atmosphere as a by-product of the incomplete burning of hydrocarbon fuels. It is produced by emissions from industrial and power plants, by smoking, by the use of gas stoves, and even by the heating of cooking oils. . . .

. . . On November 1, 1979, the commissioner, acting under the authority of G.L. c. 94B, §§ 1, 2 & 8, issued regulations effective November 14, 1979, which declared **formaldehyde** and UFFI to be toxic and hazardous substances, banned the sale of UFFI, and required its repurchase in certain circumstances. 105 Code Mass.Regs. 650.000–650.990 (1979). . . .

. . . The judge found that "[f]ormaldehyde, . . . at some level of concentration, becomes an irritant. . . . [F]urther . . . as this abrasive level of exposure is increased, the exposure level becomes toxic." We accept this finding. Since **formaldehyde** meets the definition of hazardous substance, we conclude that **formaldehyde** is properly regulated under G.L. c. 94B. Borden, Inc. v. Commissioner of Public Health, 448 N.E.2d 367 (Sup.Jud.Ct.Mass.1983).

Under no rational view of this overwhelming evidence could the air in the defendant's plant be deemed "harmful."

The plaintiff's only evidence to the contrary consisted of testimony by Dr. William E. Evans, M.D., to the effect that (1) inhalation of **formaldehyde** vapors causes irritation to the mucous membranes of the lungs and reduces the ability of pulmonary cilia to rid the lungs of foreign materials. . . . Murphy v. Owens-Corning Fiberglas Corp., 447 F.Supp. 557, 563 (D.Kan.1977).

Other Authorities: Hallinan v. Prindle, 220 Cal. 46, 50, 55, 29 P.2d 202 (1934).

formaldehydogenic (for-mal"dĕ-hīd"o-jen'ik) [*formaldehyde* + *-genic*] producing formaldehyde; pertaining to the production of formaldehyde by certain compounds when subjected to chemical reactions (i.e., steroids with α-ketol grouping in the C–17 position which on treatment with periodic acid liberate formaldehyde).

formalin See *formaldehyde.*

formula (fōr'mu-lah), pl. *formulas* or *formulae* [L., dim. of *forma* form] a specific statement, using numerals and other symbols, of the composition of, or of the directions for preparing, a compound, such as a medicine, or of a procedure to follow for obtaining a desired value or result; a simplified statement, using numerals and symbols, of a single concept. See also formula, *chemical.*

formula, chemical a combination of symbols used to express the chemical constitution of a substance; in practice, different types of formulas, of varying complexity, are employed. See also formula, empirical; formula, molecular; formula, spatial; formula structural.

formula, empirical a chemical formula which expresses the proportions of the elements present in a substance. For substances composed of discrete molecules, it expresses the relative numbers of atoms present in a molecule of the substance in the smallest whole numbers. For example, the *empirical formula* for ethane is written CH_3, whereas its actual *molecular formula* is C_2H_6.

formula, molecular a chemical formula giving the number of atoms of each element present in a molecule of a substance, without indicating how they are linked.

formula, spatial a chemical formula giving the numbers of atoms of each element present in a molecule of a substance, which atom is linked to which, the types of linkages involved, and the relative positions of the atoms in space.

formula, straight

"Straight formulation" means a dosage form product containing only one therapeutically active product. Hydrochlorothiazide in straight formulation is a tablet or other dosage form that contains hydrochlorothiazide as the only therapeutically active ingredient. U.S. v. Ciba Geigy Corp., 508 F.Supp. 1118 (D.N.J.1976).

formula, structural a chemical formula telling how many atoms of each element are present in a molecule of a substance, which atom is linked to which, and the type of linkages involved; for convenience, abbreviated structural formulas are sometimes used. Called also *constitutional f., graphic f.,* and *rational f.*

formulary (fōr'mu-lār"e) a collection of recipes, formulas, and prescriptions. See also *National Formulary.*

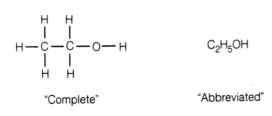

"Complete"   "Abbreviated"

Structural formulas for ethyl alcohol.

Georgia has historically administered its prescription drug program on the basis of a drug "**formulary**", or in other words, a restricted list of drugs for which Medicaid will reimburse provider pharmacists. Thus, any drug not specifically included on the list will not be reimbursed unless prior approval is granted by the defendants. The drug **formulary** currently being utilized in this state consists of approximately 10,000 drugs, and although reimbursement is restricted to those drugs specifically included on the list, the breadth of that list is tantamount to an open **formulary** with certain narrowly carved out exceptions.[2] [2 The current categorical exceptions to the present **formulary** include certain appetite suppressants, most intravenous treatment except for insulin, and certain dietary supplements.] Dodson v. Parham, 427 F.Supp. 97, 100–1 (N.D.Ga.1977).

formulary, (controlled medical assistance drug list [CMADL]

On the other hand, **CMADL**, the drug **formulary** sought to be implemented, contains approximately 5,000 automatically reimbursable pharmaceutical drugs, although at the same time it has broadened the items reimbursable to include certain "medicine-chest" and "over-the-counter" items, such as laxatives, aspirin, and milk of magnesia. Dodson v. Parham, 427 F.Supp. 97, 101 (N.D.Ga.1977).

formulary (Moore-Mikael)

At the end of December, 1975, two doctors of pharmacy and professors at the School, Doctors Moore and Mikael, after intensive studies of similar **formularies**, drug package inserts, relevant medical literature, and other reference materials, submitted a report and proposed drug **formulary** [hereinafter the "Moore-Mikael list"] containing approximately 4,000 drugs listed generically. Cost savings as a result of the new list were projected at approximately $6,000,000.00 annually to the State. Dodson v. Parham, 427 F.Supp. 97, 101 (N.D.Ga. 1977).

fossa (fos'ah), pl. *fos'sae* [L.] a trench or channel; [NA] a general term for a hollow or depressed area.

fossa cranii posterior [NA], posterior cranial fossa: the posterior subdivision of the floor of the cranial cavity, lodging the cerebellum, pons, and medulla oblongata; it is formed by portions of the sphenoid, temporal, parietal, and occipital bones.

fossa, orbital

... traumatic contusion to the left **orbital fossa** (blow to the eye socket);.... Schmiedeck v. Gerard, 166 N.W.2d 136, 141 (Wis.1969).

founder (fown'der) the crippled condition of a horse afflicted with laminitis.

fracture (frak'chur) [L. *fractura*, from *frangere* to break] a break or rupture in a bone. See also *angulation; apposition; elbow; rod, Hansen-Street intramedullary* (Pfeiffer case); *therapy, electroconvulsive* (Collins case); and *wrist*.

There has been no showing whatsoever that Doctor Cayer's decision to treat LaDonna Paul's **fractured** arm through manipulation and casting constituted such negligence that it excluded every other reasonable hypothesis or represented the most plausible explanation for the problems that later developed....

... In this regard, the trial judge correctly determined:
According to Dr. Strange's deposition, closed reduction with casting is one of the accepted methods for managing a broken bone such as was involved in LaDonna Paul's case. Paul v. St. Paul Fire & Marine Ins. Co., 430 So.2d 285, 287–8 (Ct. App.La.1983).

In an effort to clean out the cement so that he could reinsert a new prosthesis, Dr. Lipton **fractured** the femur. The result was described by Mr. MacKay as a "mess". The tension in the operating room mounted. At this point, Dr. Lipton was "making overtures about doing a girdle stone procedure". He was dissuaded from that course by Mr. MacKay [the general sales manager of the company which sold the Charnley-type prosthesis used for that purpose] who stated that he could fix the "thing" and put it back. With the consent of Dr. Lipton, he sat down on a stool and removed the cement which had cured in the shaft. He did that with tiny curettes in a careful procedure which took him about three and a half hours picking it out piece by piece.
   Q.   How did you fix the **fracture**?
   A.   As I said, I reapproximated all the fragments and I took what are called parabands which are little flat pieces of metal about eight inches long and I ran them around the femur in two places and then I had Dave Lipton mix up a batch of cement for me. We put cement down the shaft and I held the shaft together with lowman (phoenetically) bone clamps because when you put the cement in you create a compressive force from inside. I put the prosthesis down in it, let it cure and put wire around it and the **fracture** was reduced. People v. Smithtown General Hospital, 402 N.Y.S.2d 318, 321 (Sup.Ct.Crim.Term, Suffolk Cty.1978).

fracture, bimalleolar See *malleolus.*

fracture, closed a fracture which does not produce an open wound in the skin; called also *simple f.*

Dr. Prisinzano erroneously interpreted the x-rays as showing merely a **simple fracture** of plaintiff's heel bone with no involvement of the subtalar joint. Prisinzano thereupon applied a cast from midcalf to toes; a few days later, he attached a steel support outside the cast to facilitate walking. Keen v. Prisinzano, 100 Cal.Rptr. 82, 84 (Ct.App.Cal.1972).

fracture, Colles' fracture of the lower end of the radius in which the lower fragment is displaced posteriorly (see illustration). If the lower fragment is displaced anteriorly, it is a *reverse Colles' fracture* (Smith's fracture).

Larsen fell from a stack stool at his home in Anoka on Saturday, April 22, 1972, and sustained a severely comminuted Col-

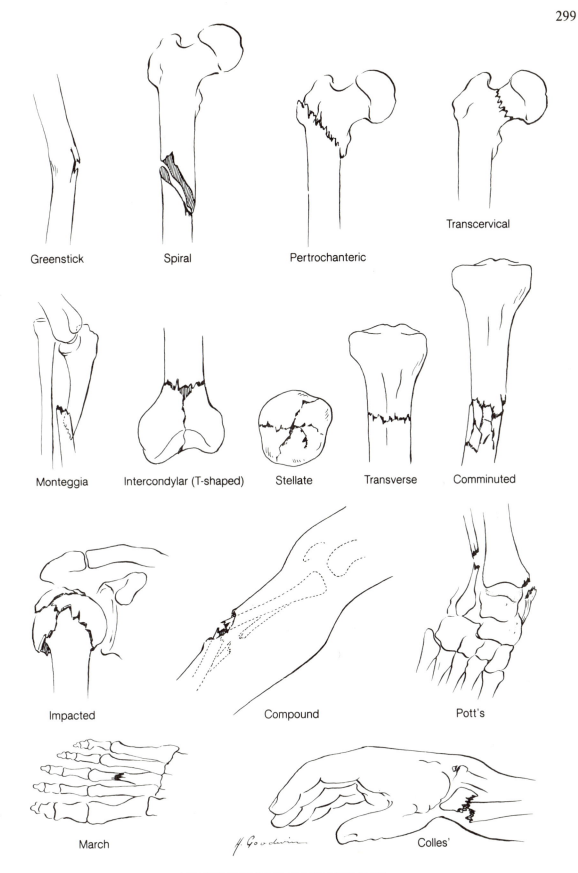

Greenstick

Spiral

Pertrochanteric

Transcervical

Monteggia

Intercondylar (T-shaped)

Stellate

Transverse

Comminuted

Impacted

Compound

Pott's

March

H. Goodwin

Colles'

VARIOUS TYPES OF FRACTURES

les fracture of the right wrist (a fracture in which the bone was splintered)....

... He explained that this type of fracture is usually treated by a special technique called pins and plaster, in which pins are placed for traction purposes through the hand and through the elbow, then incorporated into a plaster cast. Larsen v. Yelle, 246 N.W.2d 841, 843 (Minn.1976).

The wrist bones were broken into multiple fragments with displacement of the fragments. This type of injury is referred to as a "**Colles fracture**." No reduction of the fractures was attempted other than that incidental to the application of circular plaster casts to each wrist. Lieder v. Maus, 203 N.W.2d 393–4 (Minn.1973).

This examination indicated a "**Colles fracture**" of the left wrist consisting of a "fracture of the distal radial metaphysis with marked posterior and lateral displacement of the distal fragment which is rotated posteriorly and over-rides the proximal fragment for about 1 cm". Donaldson v. Maffucci, 156 A.2d 835–7 (Pa.1959).

fracture, comminuted one in which the bone is splintered or crushed (see illustration). See also *reduction, open* (Zipp case).

An orthopedic surgeon testified at the trial that she had sustained a **comminuted fracture** of the pelvic bone—that is, broken into large number of pieces—which would result in a permanent disability of from 30 to 50% of her lower extremity.... Cleere v. Humphreys, 280 So.2d 23–4 (Dist.Ct. App.Fla.1973).

fracture, comminuted open

... had sustained a **communited [sic] open fracture** (opening in the skin where the bone apparently came through the skin) of the femur and a closed fracture of the tibia. Dr. Brooks set the fractures by surgically placing pins in the bone which left a six inch scar on the thigh and caused the child to be nonambulatory for at least ten days. Cupit v. Grant, 425 So.2d 847, 852 (Ct.App.La.1982).

A **compound comminuted fracture** is one in which the bone has been splintered or crushed, and some portion of the fractured bone has penetrated the skin surface and created an open wound. Dorland's Illustrated Medical Dictionary 616–17 (25th Ed. 1974). Pollard v. Goldsmith, 572 P.2d 1201–2 (Ct. App.Ariz.1977).

fracture, compound See *fracture, open.*

fracture, compression one produced by compression; e.g., vertebral fracture.

Mrs. Leavitt fell while attempting to get in or out of her bed without assistance. She complained immediately of back pain and an x-ray revealed a slight **compression fracture** of "L–1," the first lumbar vertebra. Leavitt v. St. Tammany Parish Hosp., 396 So.2d 406–7 (Ct.App.La.1981).

Dr. Sherman's examination uncovered a chronic **compression fracture** in the area of the 12th vertebra which was confirmed by x-rays made after the March 8, 1976 incident. In response to the inquiry as to which of the two injuries caused the **compression fracture**, the Doctor responded:

Well, she had two injuries. And I honestly can't tell you which of these injuries caused the **compression fracture**, which is an

objective finding. But when she described this snapping in her back at the time of the second injury on March 8, 1976, I certainly would have to feel this may have been the precipitating cause, but honestly can't say. Halaski v. Hilton Hotel, 409 A.2d 367, 369 (Pa.1979).

He took x-rays on December 9 which showed a fracture on the anterior-superior portion of the twelfth vertebra. Apparently there had been a **compression fracture** of the same vertebra at the time Kitsch was hit by the tree limb, but it had not previously been noticed on the x-rays taken at the time....

... Dr. Fritsch compared the x-rays of Kitsch's back taken after the injury caused by the falling limb with those taken after the automobile accident. The difference which he found was that, in the latter x-rays, a piece of bone which was merely impacted in the earlier pictures had been knocked completely off the vertebra. Kitsch v. Goode, 362 N.E.2d 446, 448–9 (App.Ct.Ill.1977).

Other Authorities: Hammond v. Estate of Rimmer, 643 S.W.2d 222, 224 (Ct.App.Tex.1982).

fracture, condylar fracture of the humerus in which a small fragment including the condyle is separated from the inner or outer aspect of the bone.

Dr. Claringdon testified, in answer to a hypothetical question, that there are three ways of treating a **condylar fracture** that has become stuck: unilateral, or one side condylectomy; bilateral, or both sides; or unilateral with attempt to reconstruct the joint; that the third method is of more recent origin; and that a unilateral ends up with "maybe a cross bite". A bilateral "will most probably end up with an open bite due to vertical shortening of the bones." Campbell v. Oliva, 424 F.2d 1244, 1249 (6th Cir. 1970).

fracture, depressed a fracture of the skull in which a fragment is depressed.

The films confirmed that Thomas sustained, as a result of being struck by a puck, a four milimeter **depressed skull fracture** supralateral to the left orbit on the frontoparietal bone. Benjamin v. State, 453 N.Y.S.2d 329, 332 (Ct.Cl.1982).

fracture, double fracture of a bone in two places; called also *segmental f.*

With respect to the pelvic fractures, there was a **segmental fracture** of the inferior public ramus on the left and a fracture on the superior border. Carter v. Consolidated Cabs, Inc., 490 S.W.2d 39, 44 (Mo.1973).

fracture, fatigue a fracture attributed to the strain of prolonged walking or exercise. See also fracture, march.

In April of 1968 a further operation was performed on his back to correct **fatigue fractures** of his lumbar fusion. Southern Bell Tel. & Tel.Co. v. Poole, 388 So.2d 330–1 (Dist.Ct.App.Fla. 1980).

fracture, impacted fracture in which one fragment is firmly driven into the other.

The X-rays indicated, inter alia, an **impacted fracture** of the left femoral neck. Bryant v. Rankin, 332 F.Supp. 319, 321 (S.D. Iowa 1971), judgment affirmed 468 F.2d 510 (8th Cir. 1972).

fracture, intracapsular one within the capsule of a joint.

*The plaintiff tripped over the step and fractured the right femur at the neck of the femur just below the ball and socket joint. The doctor referred to the injury as an **intracapsular fracture**. St. Gregory's Church v. O'Connor, 477 P.2d 540, 542 (Ct. App.Ariz.1970).*

fracture, Le Fort's bilateral horizontal fracture of the maxilla. Le Fort fractures are classified as follows: *Le Fort I f.*, a horizontal segmented fracture of the alveolar process of the maxilla, in which the teeth are usually contained in the detached portion of the bone; called also *Guérin's f.* and *horizontal maxillary f. Le Fort II f.*, unilateral or bilateral fracture of the maxilla, in which the body of the maxilla is separated from the facial skeleton and the separated portion is pyramidal in shape; the fracture may extend through the body of the maxilla down the midline of the hard palate, through the floor of the orbit, and into the nasal cavity. Called also *pyramidal f.*

Le Fort *nasal maxillary fracture of zygoma. Yarrow v. U.S., 309 F.Supp. 922–3 (S.D.N.Y. 1970).*

fracture, LeFort III a fracture in which the entire maxilla and one or more facial bones are completely separated from the craniofacial skeleton; such fractures are almost always accompanied by multiple fractures of the facial bones. Called also *craniofacial disjunction* and *transverse facial f.*

LeFort III fracture *of the maxilla with comminution and craniofacial dysjunction. Titus v. Smith, 330 F.Supp. 1192–3 (E.D.Pa. 1971).*

fracture, linear a fracture extending lengthwise of the bone.

*A nondepressed **linear skull fracture** is ordinarily detectable only by X-ray examination. Landeros v. Flood, 551 P.2d 389, 391 (Cal.1976).*

fracture, linear skull See *fracture, linear.*

fracture, march fracture of a bone of the lower extremity, developing after repeated stresses, as seen in soldiers; called also *fatigue f.* Cf. *march foot.*

fracture, open one in which there is an external wound leading to the break of the bone; called also *compound f.*

*The scaffolding gave way and the pipe fell on his left knee, causing a **compound fracture** of both bones of the lower left leg. Reese v. Gas Engineering and Construction Co., 548 P.2d 746, 749 (Kan.1976).*

fracture, Pott's fracture of the lower part of the fibula, with serious injury of the lower tibial articulation, usually a chipping off of a portion of the medial malleolus, or rupture of the medial ligament; called also *Dupuytren's f.*

fracture, segmental See *fracture, double.*

fracture, spiral one in which the bone has been twisted apart; called also *torsion f.*

*Dr. Ruskin ordered x-rays of the body and discovered a **spiral** or twisting **fracture** of the left upper arm. People v. Frost, 362 N.E.2d 417–8 (App.Ct.Ill.1977).*

fracture, splintered a comminuted fracture in which the bone is splintered into thin, sharp fragments.

*Surgical inspection by means of a craniotomy, performed by drilling burr holes through the skull, were reported to have disclosed a **splintered**, depressed **fracture** of the frontal bone. Figliomeni v. Board of of Ed. of City School Dist., 341 N.E.2d 557, 559 (N.Y.1975).*

fracture, subcapital fracture of a bone just below its head; especially an intracapsular fracture of the neck of the femur at the junction of the head and neck.

*... he made a diagnosis of a "completely displaced, **subcapital fracture** of the right hip." Ray v. Industrial Com'n, 284 N.E.2d 272–3 (Ill.1972).*

fracture, transverse a fracture at right angles to the axis of the bone.

*She had sustained a complete **transverse fracture** of the C–2 cervical vertebra presenting an immediate and acute danger of total paralysis or death. Rue v. State, Dept. of Highways, 376 So.2d 525–6 (Ct.App.La.1979).*

*The admission x-rays revealed a **transverse fracture** of the right ankle and marked soft tissue swelling was noted. Flamm v. Ball, 476 S.W.2d 710–11 (Ct.Civ.App.Tex.1972).*

*The accident on the M. V. LUBECK resulted in a compound **transverse fracture** of plaintiff's left thumb, the proximal phalanx (bone of the finger), with almost complete amputation. Sanchez v. Lubeck Linie A.G., 318 F.Supp. 821, 823 (S.D.N.Y. 1970).*

fracture, trimalleolar fracture of the medial and lateral malleoli and the posterior tip of the tibia.

*Kathryn Malpass, a fifty-five-year-old woman, slipped and fell on the premises of the Park Shores Apartments sustaining a fracture of all three ankle bones.[1] The immediate effects of her injury were that she was hospitalized for ten days, immobilized in a full leg cast for six weeks, and rendered unable to care for her totally disabled husband, Alvin. The long range and permanent effects were a ten per cent disability of the ankle, continued pain, muscle atrophy, swelling, and a limp. [[1] In medical terminology, a **trimalleolar fracture**.] Malpass v. Highlands Ins. Co., 387 So.2d 1042 (D.C.App.Fla.1980).*

frame (frām) a structure, usually rigid, designed for giving support to or for immobilizing a part.

frame, Stryker one consisting of canvas stretched on anterior and posterior frames, on which the patient can be rotated around his longitudinal axis.

*He underwent eight skin graft operations, many of which required that he be put upon a **Stryker frame** which suspended him upside down for days. Arnold v. Eastern Air Lines, Inc., 681 F.2d 186, 203 (4th Cir. 1982).*

*He is on a **Stryker Frame**, a device which prevents bed sores. Webb v. Aggrey, 447 F.Supp. 17, 18 (N.D.Ohio 1977).*

Franconi's syndrome See *syndrome, Franconi's.*

frank breech See *presentation, breech, frank.*

frenulum (fren'u-lum), pl. *fren'ula* [L., dim. of *frenum*] a small bridle; [NA] a general term for a small fold of integument or mucous membrane that checks, curbs, or limits the movements of an organ or part. See also *frenum.*

As Dr. Banowsky was removing enamel below the gum line, the burr became entangled in fibrous material which was either a **frenum** attachment or a mental nerve. . . .

Q. And the drill became entangled in this **frenum** attachment?

A. In the ligamentous strands of the endings of this **frenum** attachment.

Q. What caused that?

A. In my judgment, it was because this attachment extended up higher than one would normally look for." Williford v. Banowsky, 563 S.W.2d 702, 705 (Ct.Civ.App.Tex. 1978).

frenum (fre′num), pl. *fre′na* [L. "bridle"] a restraining structure or part. See also *frenulum.*

frequency (fre′kwen-se) 1. the number of occurrences of a periodic process in a unit of time. 2. the number of vibrations made by a particle or ray in one second; in electricity, the rate of oscillation or alternation in an alternating current; the number of complete cycles produced by an alternating current generator per second.

Frequency and intensity are important speech characteristics involved in voice analysis. **Frequency** determines the pitch of the sound. It is delineated by the time interval between successive vocal cord vibrations and the speed at which air molecules are vibrated thereby. U.S. v. Williams, 583 F.2d 1194, 1196 (2d Cir. 1978).

friable (fri′ah-b′l) [L. *friabilis*] easily pulverized or crumbled.

Mrs. Cameron complained of intermittent bleeding and the tissue was **friable**—i.e., it bled easily. The gum tissue surrounding the extraction site, as opposed to the extraction site itself, appeared normal. O'Brien v. Stover, 443 F.2d 1013–14 (8th Cir. 1971).

frigidity (fri-jid′ĭ-te) coldness; especially sexual unresponsiveness, usually applied to this state in the female. Analogous to impotence in the male.

Doctor Burnett then referred to an article which appeared in the January, 1968 issue of the OB-GYNE NEWS, written by a Doctor Maurice Martin, a recognized authority in the field and a consultant in psychiatry at the Mayo Clinic, Rochester, Minnesota, entitled "Frigidity is Difficult to Treat". The article sets forth three types of problems which comprise psychological relations for **frigidity** or impotency. The first one is fear, either conscious fear of being hurt or fear of pregnancy. This results in the holding back of emotions. It could be unconscious fear of being hurt when involved in the sexual act. The second problem involves displaced love, either conscious love for another person, resulting in the loss of interest in the spouse, or the type of unconscious displaced love in an unresolved Oedipal situation as in the son-mother or daughter-father complex. The third problem involves a hostility, either conscious anger directed toward the spouse or unconscious hostility towards members of the opposite sex. T v. M, 242 A.2d 670, 672 (Super.Ct.N.J.1968).

frontal lobe See *lobus frontalis.*

frontoparietal (frun″to-pah-ri′e-tal) pertaining to the frontal and parietal bones.

Dr. Leonard Bruno performed a right **frontopariatal** craniotomy with evacuation of a subdural hematoma and clipping of the right posterior communicating aneurysm. Polischeck v. U.S., 535 F.Supp. 1261, 1265 (E.D.Pa.1982).

frontoparietal bone See *os frontale*; and *os parietale.*

fructose (fruk′tōs) [L. *fructus* fruit] chemical name: D-fructose. A ketohexose, $C_6H_{12}O_6$, occurring in honey and many sweet fruits and a component of many di- and polysaccharides; it is obtainable by inversion of aqueous solutions of sucrose and subsequent separation of fructose from glucose. The official preparation [USP], occurring as colorless crystals or as a white, crystalline powder, is administered intravenously as a fluid and nutrient replenisher. Called also *fructopyranose, fruit sugar*, and *levulose.*

The patent-in-suit relates to a process for the enzymatic conversion of dextrose (also known as glucose or corn sugar) into levulose (also known as **fructose** or fruit sugar)—a "sweeter" sugar. CPC International, Inc. v. Standard Brands, Inc., 385 F.Supp. 1057–58 (D.Del.1974).

fugue (fūg) [L. *fuga* a flight] a dissociative reaction in which amnesia is accompanied by physical flight from customary surroundings.

He described the defendant's condition that morning as hysterical amnesia ("**fugue**"): he was confused, slow to make associations, and had blocked out part of the event. He was suffering from a "progressive depressive reaction" which brought on the amnesic state. In this **fugue** condition he would perform normally certain mechanical acts and make intelligent decisions on some matters, but would depart otherwise from his normal patterns and do things he could not later recall. Com. v. Goulet, 372 N.E.2d 1288, 1292 (Sup.Jud.Ct.Mass. 1978).

fulguration (ful″gu-ra′shun) [L. *fulgur* lightning] destruction of living tissue by electric sparks generated by a high frequency current. This may be direct or indirect. *Direct:* An insulated fulguration electrode with a metal point is connected to the uniterminal of the high frequency apparatus and a spark of electricity is allowed to impinge on the area to be treated. *Indirect:* In this procedure the patient is connected directly by a metal handle to the uniterminal and the operator utilizes an active electrode to complete an arc from the patient.

Those allegations are in substance as follows: Plaintiff employed defendant, a licensed physician and surgeon, for a compensation not to exceed $150—to operate upon him for the purpose of removing a growth by **fulguration**—a procedure which would not involve entry through the abdominal wall by incision. . . .

. . . Instead, in breach of the contract, defendant attempted in an unworkmanlike, unprofessional and unskilled manner to perform the operation by **fulguration** but as a result of his unskillfulness and his unworkmanlike procedure he twice punctured one of plaintiff's organs and thus necessitated a major operation including the opening of the abdominal wall by incision. Robins v. Finestone, 127 N.E.2d 330–31 (N.Y.1955).

fulminate (ful'mĭ-nāt) to occur suddenly with great intensity.

fumigation (fu″mĭ-ga'shun) [L. *fumus* smoke, steam, vapor] exposure of an area or object to disinfecting fumes.

If the infestation has not entered inside the bags, the **fumigation** can effectively save the flour so as to remain suitable for human consumption. If the infestation has entered the bags but is localized, **fumigation** can effectively save the surrounding stacks of flour not yet so infested. U.S. v. Central Gulf Steamship Corp., 321 F.Supp. 945, 951–2 (E.D.La.1970).

function (funk'shun) [L. *functio* a performance] the special, normal, or proper action of any part or organ.

function, impairment of

Q. You have heard the term **impairment of function**?
A. I have heard the term **impairment of function**.
Q. Are you familiar with its meaning?
A. Well, from a legal point of view?
Q. No, from a medical point of view.
A. Yes, I think so.
Q. Would there be any **impairment of function** in the Claimant because of this allergy to flour?
A. I think it is possible that there could be.
Q. Do you have an opinion as to whether or not there is?
A. Whether or not there was? I have to believe there was. If a man is not well, he doesn't function well. And if he is sneezing and coughing and so on, I don't want to eat his bread either. So I think this bears on function in some ways. Sutton v. Industrial Com'n, 509 P.2d 234, 235 (Ct.App.Ariz. 1973).

function, visual

By **visual function** I mean the ability of the patient really to not only see directly straight ahead but to see on the sides, to work under all different types of condition whether they be glare, smoke, pollution, in other words any of our normal activities or the normal activities which the patient finds in his occupation.
Q. Could this patient see better in general using the injured left eye in connection with his good right eye than by using the right eye alone?
A. In my opinion he could see better using the right eye alone.
Q. Are you saying that the left eye detracted from his vision?
A. No I didn't say it detracted from his vision. I said it disturbed his vision. Rohm & Haas Co. v. Workmen's Comp. App. Bd., 414 A.2d 163–5 (Commwth.Ct.Pa.1980).

functional (funk'shun-al) of or pertaining to a function; affecting the functions, but not the structure; said of disturbances of function with no detectable organic cause. In chemistry, denoting the group within a molecule that participates in a chemical reaction, e.g., the—OH group of an alcohol, or the—NH_2 group of an amine.

"I feel it was **functional**" (**functional** means the disturbance of an organ's function). . . . Vander Veer v. Continental Casualty Co., 346 N.Y.S.2d 655, 661 (3d Dep't 1973).

functional disorder See *disorder, functional.*

fundi (fun'di) [L.] plural of *fundus.*

fundoscopic See *fundus.*

fundus (fun'dus), pl. *fun'di* [L.] the bottom or base of anything; [NA] a general term for the bottom or base of an organ, or the part of a hollow organ farthest from its mouth.

Each time he checked the boy for increased intracranial pressure by determining with an ophthalmoscope that the veins in the back of the eye (**fundus**) were pulsating normally and by feeling the soft spot where the hole had been made in his skull in connection with the brain surgery to determine if it was pulsating normally. Gendusa v. St. Paul Fire & Marine Ins. Co., 435 So.2d 479, 481 (Ct.App.La.1983).

A **fundoscopic** examination is, in other words, an ophthalmoscopic examination. [DISSENT.] Jenkins v. Gardner, 430 F.2d 243, 285 (6th Cir. 1970).

fundus of eye See *fundus oculi.*

fundus oculi fundus of the eye: the back portion of the interior of the eyeball, as seen by means of the ophthalmoscope.

It was also reported that his **fundi**—the part of his eye opposite the pupil—could not be visualized and that he had pain with dull light, occasional double vision, blurring coupled with inflammation, and that his eyes moved abnormally and involuntarily from side to side. McBrayer v. Secretary of Health and Human Serv., 712 F.2d 795, 798 (2d Cir. 1983).

An examination with an ophthalmoscope of the **fundus of the eye** (the retina, the back of the eye where the optic nerve enters the eyeball) revealed no evidence of any foreign bodies or of any eye disease. He was of the opinion her complaints were functionally induced. Maryland Casualty Co. v. Davis, 464 S.W.2d 433, 437 (Ct.Civ.App.Tex.1971).

funeral director See *mortician.*

fungate (fung'gāt) to produce fungus-like growths; to grow rapidly, like a fungus.

It is the consensus of all doctors to avoid hitting the mole at all times. If it is in a spot where it will receive irritation, as under a belt or a bra line most doctors will urge its removal rather than take a chance on the irritation causing the melanoma to begin **fungating** or growing. Cox v. Ulysses Cooperative Oil and Supply Co., 544 P.2d 363, 366 (Kan.1975).

fungicide (fun'jĭ-sīd) an agent that destroys fungi. See also *diquat.*

A **fungicide** is an economic poison. Q.V. See 7 U.S.C.A. § 135(a), (d). Throughout this opinion the terms "economic poison" and "pesticide" will be used interchangeably. First Nat. Bk. in Albuquerque v. U.S., 552 F.2d 370, 372 (10th Cir. 1977).

fungus (fung'gus), pl. *fun'gi* [L.] a general term used to denote a group of eukaryotic protists, including mushrooms, yeasts, rusts, molds, smuts, etc., which are characterized by the absence of chlorophyll and by the presence of a rigid cell wall composed of chitin, mannans, and sometimes cellulose. They are usually of simple morphological form or show some reversible cellular specialization, such as the formation of pseudoparenchymatous tissue in the fruiting body of a mushroom. The dimorphic fungi grow, according to environmental conditions, as molds or yeasts.

F.U.O. fever of undetermined origin.

However, the high temperature remained. Because of the "fuo" (fever of undetermined origin), Dr. Woodard sent Mrs. Cade to the Radiology Department at Mid-City Hospital on August 5, 1969, for a chest x-ray. Cade v. Mid-City Hospital Corp., 119 Cal.Rptr. 571–2 (Ct.App.Cal.1975).

Furacin (fu′rah-sin) trademark for preparations of nitrofurazone. See also *nitrofurazone*.

Furadantin (fur″ah-dan′tin) trademark for preparations of nitrofurantoin. See also *nitrofurantoin*.

furfurol (fur′fu-rol) [L. *furfur* bran] an aromatic compound, from the distillation of bran, sawdust, etc. It causes convulsions in animals.

The Quaker Oats plant produces "furfurol," which is an amber colored liquid used primarily in the production of plastics, adhesives, abrasives, motor oils, and other varied products. Hodgson v. Sugar Cane Growers Coop. of Florida, 346 F.Supp. 132, 135 (S.D.Fla.1972), judgment affirmed in part, reversed in part, sub nom. Brennan v. Sugar Cane Growers Coop. of Florida, 486 F.2d 1006 (5th Cir. 1973).

furosemide (fu-ro′sĕ-mīd) [USP] chemical name: 5-(aminosulfonyl)-4-chloro-2-[2-furanylmethyl)amino]benzoic acid. A sulfonamide, $C_{12}H_{11}ClN_2O_5S$, occurring as a white to slightly yellow, crystalline powder; used as a diuretic in the treatment of disorders in which edema is a symptom and in hypertension, administered orally, intramuscularly, and intravenously. Called also *frusemide* and *fursemide*.

Plaintiff's **furosemide** purports to be a "me-too" of Hoechst's Lasix, approved for years as a diuretic and recently approved as an anti-hypertensive. Pharmadyne markets the drug for both indications. Pharmadyne Laboratories, Inc. v. Kennedy, 466 F.Supp. 100, 106 (D.N.J.1979).

fusiform (fu′zĭ-form) [L. *fusus* spindle + *forma* form] spindle shaped.

... the fingers of the right hand are **fusiform** and are fixed in extension. Pl.Ex. 3, (Vol. I). Aretz v. U.S., 456 F.Supp. 397, 404 (S.D.Ga.1978).

X-rays of both hands showed **fusiform** type swelling about the proximal interphalangeal joints of the fingers consistent with arthritic changes. This also involved some of the metacarpal bones of the left hand and also the greater multangular bone of the left hand. Byrd v. Richardson, 362 F.Supp. 957, 961 (D.S.Car.1973).

fusion (fu′zhun) [L. *fusio*] 1. the merging or coherence of adjacent parts or bodies. 2. the operative formation of an ankylosis or arthrodesis (*f. of joint*).

A decompressive laminectomy attempts to relieve the pressure on the nerves and the **fusion** attempts to properly realign and secure the vertebrae to prevent further destruction. Zimmer-

man v. New York City Health & Hospitals, 458 N.Y.S.2d 552, 554 (1st Dep't 1983).

In estimating the results of a **fusion** operation, which involves an excision of the ruptured disc, possibly with a **fusion** of the spine, both in the neck and in the lumbar area in this case, Dr. Parisien testified that the results for pain relief are not one hundred percent, but may reach only fifty to seventy percent and, in some cases, people are made worse by this type of surgery. Michaud v. Steckino, 390 A.2d 524, 529 (Sup.Jud.Ct. Me.1978).

This surgeon suggested a brace to slow the ankle's deterioration and to relieve pain, and also indicated that plaintiff will probably need a major operation—an ankle **fusion**—to reduce the pain. Such an operation permanently removes all flexion from the ankle. Kelty v. Wiseman Construction Co., Inc., 349 N.E.2d 108, 110 (App.Ct.Ill.1976).

Other Authorities: West v. Richmond, F. + P.R. Co., 528 F.2d 290, 292 (4th Cir. 1975).

fusion, cervical

Due to continued pain, and after physical therapy proved unsuccessful, Simonson underwent surgery on January 13, 1976. Dr. W. S. Pollard performed a **cervical fusion** at C 4–5 and C 5–6. Although he experienced relief from pain immediately following surgery, Simonson testified his back and neck have become progressively stiffer and more painful since the operation. Simonson v. Schweiker, 699 F.2d 426–7 (8th Cir. 1983).

On May 21, 1980, Naquin was admitted into Lakeside Hospital for a total myelogram which revealed a large defect at the cervical 5–6 level. On May 22, 1980, Dr. Jackson performed surgery to correct the ruptured disc by performing an anterior **cervical fusion** at the 5–6 level. Naquin v. Texaco, Inc., 423 So.2d 31, 34 (Ct.App.La.1982).

The operation planned is known as an anterior **cervical fusion** and procedurally includes the removal of a bone plug from the vertebrae at the C 5–6 interspace by means of a surgical tool and replacing it with a donor plug contemporaneously removed from the patient's hip....

Procedurally, Dr. Kauffman made an incision in plaintiff's neck and the neck muscles were held back by tractors. The cervical spine at the location where the plug was to be inserted is 2.5 cm. thick. The hole where the plug was to be placed is drilled only to a depth of 1.0 cm., as in the donor plug. Dr. Kauffman testified that he measured the plug cutter to 1.0 cm. and tightened the hexagonal screw allowing for a 1.5 cm. margin between the cut and the spinal cord. The entire drilling procedure for a 1.0 cm. plug is normally completed in a few seconds and in the instant operation Dr. Kauffman noticed that the drill was cutting quite quickly which he attributed to the sharpness of the new drill. Dr. Kauffman stated in his postoperative report and likewise testified that in spite of his tightening the screw, securing the guard, the guard slipped allowing the drill to penetrate farther than he had expected. When he removed the drill he found that it had taken a full depth of vertebrae tissue and penetrated to the postinor cortex. Anticipating spinal shock Dr. Kauffman and his assistants inspected the spinal cord and posterior longitudinal ligament for bleeding. Upon finding no bleeding, Dr. Beller directed them to insert the donor plug and complete the operation. Grubb v. Albert Einstein Medical Center, 387 A.2d 480, 483–4 (Super.Ct.Pa.1978).

Other Authorities: Hughes v. Richardson, 342 F.Supp. 320, 329–30 (W.D.Mo.1971).

fusion, spinal See *spondylosyndesis.*

fusion, vertebral See *ankylosis.*

However, he did discuss the possibility of **vertebral fusion** with the plaintiff as a possible alternative to eliminating some of her pains. This discussion was a very general one—the Doctor describing in general and simplified terms the procedure involved, i.e., that he would perform the same operation as was performed in Seattle, except that a small chunk of bone would be removed from her hip bone (iliac crest) which would be shaped to be inserted between the 5th and 6th cervical vertebrae to bring about fusion and, hopefully, more neck stability. Riedinger v. Colburn, 361 F.Supp. 1073, 1075 (D.Idaho 1973).

fusion, wrist See *ankylosis.*

The medical evidence was that if the plaintiff continued to work as he then was he would have to have a **wrist fusion** in one to five years, after which he would be unable to work as a brakeman. A **wrist fusion** is an operation which "obliterate[s]" the joint at the wrist. The pain ceases after that, but the wrist will not bend. West v. Richmond, F. & P.R. Co., 528 F.2d 290, 292 (4th Cir. 1975).

G

γ the third letter of the Greek alphabet; see *gamma.* Symbol for *microgram* and *immunoglobulin.*

Gaenslen's sign (test) (genz'lenz) [Frederick Julius *Gaenslen*, Milwaukee surgeon, 1877–1937] See under *sign.*

gag reflex See *reflex, pharyngeal.*

gain (gān) an increase in amount or value; a benefit or advantage; the increase achieved by amplification of a signal.

gain, epinosic a secondary psychic or social advantage derived from a symptom or illness, as opposed to paranosic gain. Called also *secondary g.* See also *ambivalence* (Loughran case).

"Q. Doctor, you have also used the term '**secondary gain** elements'; would you describe that term to the court?
A. Yes. A symptom has sort of—the primary purpose of the symptom is sort of a compromise between the person's conflict. **Secondary gain** refers to what else that symptom can accomplish for the individual. For example, perhaps a physical illness, which has hysterical qualities to it, might result in a pension for the individual; or a soldier who breaks down in combat, the secondary gain—his original breakdown would be because of all kinds of pressure, the second would be that he would avoid returning to combat. This would be sort of a bonus. In hysterical symptoms, secondary symptoms is a way—not a way, but is a procedure where the person can avoid distressful situations." In re Loughran, 276 F.Supp. 393, 410 (Centr.D.Cal.1967).

gain, secondary See *gain, epinosic.*

gait (gāt) the manner or style of walking. See also *reaction, conversion* (Anunti case).

gait, gluteal the gait characteristic of paralysis of the gluteus medius muscle, marked by a listing of the trunk toward the affected side at each step; called also *Trendelenburg g.*

Strandberg was subsequently examined by two orthopedic specialists who testified, that because of the manner in which his hip had healed, Strandberg had developed a Trendelenburg's gait, described as a "listing gait over the hip," his left leg had shortened measurably, and he walked with a limp. Strandberg v. Reber Co., 587 P.2d 18, 19 (Mont. 1978).

gait, spastic a walk in which the legs are held together and move in a stiff manner, the toes seeming to drag and catch.

Dr. Fresh also found Terry Dale to have an aspastic walk. Such a condition describes an impairment of the free flowing movement of the arm and leg. With such an impairment, Dr. Fresh states Terry Dale is incapable of walking at a quick pace, climbing, bending, squatting and might later incur back problems in the form of scoliosis (curvature of the spine). Cupit v. Grant, 425 So.2d 847, 852 (Ct.App.La.1982).

gait, Trendelenburg See *gait, gluteal.*

galea (ga'le-ah) [L.] a helmet; [NA] a general term for a helmet-like structure.

galea aponeurotica [NA], the aponeurotic structure of the scalp, connecting the frontal and occipital bellies of the occipitofrontalis muscle.

The skull fracture was accompanied by extensive subgaleal hemorrhage (bleeding between the outer skull surface and the overlying skin), which extended from ear to ear over the top of the skull as well as forward beneath the skull,.... State v. Durand, 465 A.2d 762–3 (R.I.1983).

gallbladder (gawl'blad-der) the pear-shaped reservoir for the bile on the posteroinferior surface of the liver, between the right and the quadrate lobe; from its neck, the cystic duct projects to join the common bile duct. Called also *cholecyst* and *vesica fellea* [NA]. See also *ductus, choledochus* (Bronwell case).

The **gall bladder** rests on the liver. During the course of the removal of the **gall bladder**, plaintiff's liver was lacerated, apparently by a retractor used in the surgery. There is no allegation that defendant was at fault in lacerating the liver, an apparently not infrequent occurrence in gall bladder surgery. White v. McCool, 395 So.2d 774–5 (La.1981).

For better understanding of the contentions of the respective parties, we are told that the **gall bladder** is located on the underside of the liver and that it discharges concentrated bile through the cystic duct into the common bile duct which in turn discharges into the upper end of the small intestine. Bile (not concentrated) is also discharged directly from the liver through the hepatic duct into the common bile duct. Thus severance of the common bile duct permitted bile to be freely discharged from the liver into the upper abdominal area. Yerzy v. Levine, 260 A.2d 533–4 (Super.Ct.N.J.1970).

gallbladder [disease]

Medication and diet adjustment are used to relieve the patient's symptoms. The only medical cure for **gallbladder disease** is surgical removal, and such surgical removal is the generally recommended treatment for patients with **gallbladder disease**. Harwell v. Pittman, 428 So.2d 1049, 1053 (Ct.App. La.1983).

gallbladder echogram See *echography.*

gallbladder test See *test, gallbladder.*

gallstone (gawl′stōn) a concretion, usually of cholesterol, formed in the gallbladder or bile duct. See also *cholelithiasis.*

During the course of the surgery, it was determined that a stone was lodged in the distal part of the common bile duct. The stone was removed during the surgery....

Plaintiff contends that Bruney's activities during the fire of February 4th caused a **gallstone** to be dislodged from the gall bladder and to become impacted in the common bile duct....

Dr. Robert E. Brierty testified that the only documented cause of dislodging of a stone, of which he was aware, is the presence of food in the gastrointestinal tract, causing the gall bladder to propel bile and the stone out of the gall bladder into the common bile duct. Bruney v. City of Lake Charles, 386 So.2d 950, 952–3 (Ct.App.La.1980).

Diagnosis of **gallstones** is made by establishing a patient's history, performing a clinical examination, taking x-rays, and making a work-up verification. Kathleen Cardamone had a history which was consistent with his diagnosis of **gallstones.**

The diagnosis of **gallstones** was not positive until x-rays were taken on April 1, 1974. **Gallstones** are concretions formed by a layering of stagnant bile. Although he has no idea how long they take to develop, **gallstones** the size of those removed from plaintiff would take longer than one month to form. Cardamone v. Allstate Ins. Co., 364 N.E.2d 460, 462 (App. Ct.Ill.1977).

galvanism (gal′vah-nizm) [Luigi *Galvani*] the therapeutic use of direct current.

He put her on a course of treatment twice a week consisting of ''chiropractice adjustments'' and therapy consisting of ''pulse **galvanism**'' which he defined as electrical current for pain. Carter v. Woolco Dept. Store, 379 So.2d 759–60 (Ct.App.La. 1979).

galvanometer (gal″vah-nom′e-ter) [*galvanism* + Gr. *metron* measure] an instrument for measuring current by electromagnetic action. See also *polygraph* (Romero case).

The polygraph machine is an electromechanical instrument which measures and records these physiological fluctuations that are detected with the aid of three basic components: ... (3) the **galvanometer** which measures the galvanic skin reflex or electrodermal response—skin resistance to electrical current (perspiration on the palmar surfaces of the hands will increase the flow of electrical current). U.S. v. Alexander, 526 F.2d 161, 163 (8th Cir. 1975).

gamete (gam′ēt) [Gr. *gametē* wife, *gametēs* husband] a reproductive element; one of two cells produced by a gametocyte, male (spermatozoon) and female (ovum), whose union is necessary, in sexual reproduction, to initiate the development of a new individual. The conjugation of male and female gametes produces a zygote.

gamma (gam′ah) 1. the third letter in the Greek alphabet, γ; used as part of a chemical name to distinguish the third in a series of compounds or to designate the position of the third carbon atom of an aliphatic chain or the position opposite the alpha position on the naphthalene ring. 2. microgram. 3. a unit of intensity of magnetic field, γ = 0.00001 gauss. 4. a numerical expression of the degree of development of a photographic negative.

gamma benzene hexachloride See *lindane.*

gamma globulin See *globulin;* and *immunoglobulin.*

ganglion (gang′gle-on), pl. *ganglia* or *ganglions* [Gr. "knot"] 1. a knot, or knotlike mass. 2. a benign cystic tumor occurring on an aponeurosis or tendon, as in the wrist or dorsum of the foot; it consists of a thin fibrous capsule enclosing a clear mucinous fluid. See also *cyst.*

In September 1970 petitioner had right-hand surgery for a double **ganglion** cyst. Camp v. Lockheed Electronics, Inc., 429 A.2d 615, 618 (Super.Ct.N.J.1981).

... appellant herein, suffered a contusion and sprain of the right wrist area. Subsequent to the wrist injury, a **ganglion** formed which required surgery on three occasions including

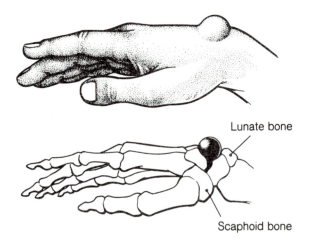

Lunate bone

Scaphoid bone

Ganglion of wrist arising from a tendon.

October 1967, July 1968, and May 1970. State ex. rel. Wallace v. Industrial Com'n, 386 N.E.2d 1109–10 (Ohio 1979).

The injured wrist failed to respond to the treatments prescribed by Dr. Florio, and several weeks later a **ganglion** (a cyst or tumor filled with liquid) developed in the injured area. . . .

The plaintiffs did not call Dr. Sharpless as a witness, but the defendant did. He expressed the opinion that a single act of trauma cannot cause a **ganglion**, ...

. . . He persisted in this position, although he admitted on cross-examination that certain well-recognized medical authorities do not agree with his view that a single act of trauma can never cause a **ganglion**. Abrams v. Philadelphia Suburban Transportation Co., 264 A.2d 702–4 (Pa.1970).

Other Authorities: Sellars v. Sec. Dept. of Health, Ed. & Welf., 331 F.Supp. 1103, 1105 (E.D.Mo.1971), reversed 458 F.2d 984 (8th Cir. 1972).

ganglion, cervicothoracic; ganglion cervicothoracicum [NA], a ganglion on the sympathetic trunk at the level of the 7th cervical and 1st thoracic vertebra, anterior to the 8th cervical and 1st thoracic nerves; it has two components, the inferior cervical and first thoracic ganglia, which are usually fused, partially or completely. Its postganglionic fibers are distributed to the head and neck, heart, and upper limb. Called also *stellate g.* and *g. stellatum* [NA alternative].

Contrary to Nennhaus's findings, Spiegler found plaintiff's artery constricted but not blocked. He recommended plaintiff have a stellate ganglion block. The **stellate ganglion** is a nerve junction located in one's neck which controls the nerve fibers which go down into arteries of the arm and cause arteries to constrict. Blockage of the **stellate ganglion** causes the arteries to open up. This procedure could be performed by a physiatrist, an anesthesiologist or a neurosurgeon. Spiegler explained to plaintiff that the risks were slight with little or no potential for serious injury, and that if she did not have it done she might have persistent spasms, increased pain, and impaired circulation to the hand which might become permanent. Plaintiff rejected the recommendation. Crawford v. Anagnostopoulos, 387 N.E.2d 1064, 1067 (App.Ct.Ill.1979).

ganglion, Gasser's; ganglion, gasserian See *ganglion trigeminale.*

ganglion, popliteal See *popliteal*; and *posterior.*

DuBose's affliction was diagnosed as **popliteal ganglion**, a cystic tumor connected to the tendon sheath on the back of his knee joint. DuBose v. Matson Navigation Co., 403 F.2d 875, 877 (9th Cir. 1968).

ganglion, sensory ganglia of the peripheral nervous system which transmit sensory impulses; also, the collective masses of nerve cell bodies in the brain subserving sensory functions.

ganglion, stellate See *ganglion cervicothoracicum.*

ganglion, trigeminal; ganglion of trigeminal nerve; ganglion trigeminale [NA], a ganglion on the sensory root of the fifth cranial nerve, situated in a cleft within the dura mater (trigeminal cave) on the anterior surface of the petrous portion of the temporal bone, and giving off the

ophthalmic and maxillary and part of the mandibular nerve; it contains the cells of origin of most of the sensory fibers of the trigeminal nerve. Called also *semilunar g.*, and *g. semilunare* [*Gasseri*]. See also *nervus, trigeminus.*

An injection of hyperbaric alcohol or phenol into the fifth cranial nerve root, the **Gasserian ganglion**, causes destruction of the nerve fibers by caustic action of the injected solution. Hales v. Pittman, 576 P.2d 493, 496 (Ariz.1978).

On August 31, 1967, plaintiff was operated on by Dr. Robert J. Goodall, who performed a retro-gasserian resection of the sensory root of the right trigeminal nerve. Derryberry v. Hollier, 334 F.Supp. 677–8 (W.D.La.1971).

ganglionectomy (gang"gle-o-nek'to-me) [*ganglio-* + Gr. *ektome* excision] excision of a ganglion.

He also found scar tissue on a nerve near the site of the injury and he cut the nerve itself, a "sensory **ganglionectomy**," to lessen it as a source of leg pain. Davis v. Becker & Associates, Inc., 608 F.2d 621, 623 (5th Cir. 1979).

ganglionectomy, sensory See *ganglionectomy.*

gangrene (gang'grien) [L. *gangraena*; Gr. *gangraina* an eating sore, which ends in mortification] death of tissue, usually in considerable mass and generally associated with loss of vascular (nutritive) supply and followed by bacterial invasion and putrefaction. Cf. *necrosis* and *necrobiosis.* See also *Clostridium* (Garza case).

A medical examination by Dr. Filippone indicates that Quackenbush has **gangrene** in both legs. On his left leg the skin is black from the knee down, is partially mummified and the foot is dangling, about to fall off. On the left leg, there is an open sore, which is draining fluid and in which the tibia (shinbone) and tendons are exposed. His right leg is in a similar condition except that the black skin and mummified condition extend from midcalf down. Matter of Quackenbush, 383 A.2d 785, 787 (Morris Ct.Ct.Prob.Div.1978).

gangrene, diabetic moist gangrene occurring in a person with diabetes; called also *glycemic g.*

Dr. Mason described **diabetic gangrene** as a "wet gangrene" which occurs as the result of an infection as opposed to a "dry gangrene" which results from poor circulation. II Rec. 242. Brown v. Arlen Management Corp., 663 F.2d 575, 577 (5th Cir. 1981).

When the infection persisted plaintiff was readmitted to the hospital on December 26 at which time, because **diabetic gangrene** had set in, her entire toe was amputated. When the condition continued to spread she underwent three more operations, the last, an amputation, extending to her mid thigh. With the final amputation the infection was contained and healing took place. Eventually, an artificial leg was fitted. . . .

. . . Dr. Slobodien testified that "diabetics have problems with regard to healing, particularly with infection." As to the reasons for this he stated, "Basically, one of them is that the blood vessels are older than the individual is, and the second is that because of the fluctuating sugar levels in the body, infection itself tends to recede more slowly than it would in individuals without diabetes." He added that, "[D]iabetes affects blood vessels in the body, primarily arteries of the middle size. Because these vessels are involved, the blood flow through

Dr. Adams took a history of the child which indicated that the child had been vomiting repeatedly with the vomitus becoming greenish. Dr. Adams performed an examination of the child and concluded that the child had **gastroenteritis**, an irritation of the stomach and intestines. Kern v. St. Luke's Hospital Ass'n of Saginaw, 273 N.W.2d 75, 77 (Mich.1978).

... plaintiff was experiencing vomiting and diarrhea....

... At that time she was in acute distress, in a mild degree of shock and was dehydrated. He diagnosed her condition as suffering from severe **gastro-enteritis**. Ohligschlager v. Proctor Community Hospital, 303 N.E.2d 392, 394 (Ill.1973).

Dr. Couch treated Main on December 24, 1962, for **gastroenteritis**, usually called 24 to 48 hour flu by laymen. He gave him a liter of glucose intravenously and an anti-diarrhea preparation. Metropolitan Life Ins. Co. v. Main, 383 F.2d 952, 955 (5th Cir. 1967).

Other Authorities: Manigan v. Califano, 453 F.Supp. 1080, 1083 (D.Kan.1978); Swihel v. Richardson, 346 F.Supp. 930, 933 (D.Neb.1972); Sinkey v. Surgical Associates, 186 N.W.2d 658, 660 (Iowa.1971); Jenkins v. Gardner, 430 F.2d 243, 256 (6th Cir. 1970).

gastroenterology (gas"tro-en"ter-ol'o-je) [*gastro-* + Gr. *enteron* intestine + *-logy*] the study of the stomach and intestines and their diseases.

Gastroenterology is a sub-specialty which includes the study of liver illnesses. Coffran v. Hitchcock Clinic, Inc., 683 F.2d 5, 8 (1st Cir. 1982).

Other Authorities: Rainer v. Buena Community Memorial Hospital, 95 Cal.Rptr. 901, 904 (Ct.App.Cal.1971).

Gastrografin (gas"tro-graf'in) trademark for a preparation of meglumine diatrizoate. See also *meglumine diatrizoate*.

gastrointestinal (gas"tro-in-tes'tĭ-nal) [*gastro-* + *intestinal*] pertaining to or communicating with the stomach and intestine, as a gastrointestinal fistula.

gastrointestinal hemorrhage See *gastritis, hemorrhagic*.

gastrointestinal tract See under *tract*.

gastrojejunostomy (gas"tro-jĕ-ju-nos'to-me) [*gastro-* + *jejunostomy*] surgical creation of an anastomosis between the stomach and jejunum; also, the anastomosis so established. See also *esophagojejunogastrostomosis*.

However, fearing that even with this the valve would cease to function, he performed a **gastrojejunostomy**, which, in other terms, supplied an alternate route in case the pylorus became blocked. Drains were installed so as to allow drainage in the area of the spleen, along the liver, under the diaphragm on both sides, and in the area of the stomach. These drains were for control of infection or leakage through the closures made. Insurance Co. of North America v. Stroburg, 456 S.W.2d 402, 409 (Ct.Civ.App.Tex.1970), reversed 464 S.W.2d 827 (Tex. 1971).

gastroscopy See *fiberscope* and *operation* (both Cooper case).

gastrostomy (gas-tros'to-me) [*gastro-* + Gr. *stomoun* to provide with an opening, or mouth] surgical creation of an artificial opening into the stomach; also, the opening so established.

It was determined that a large thoracic aortic aneurysm was displacing his esophagus. Surgery (a **gastrostomy**) was performed to relieve the esophagus obstruction caused by the thoracic aortic aneurysm. Griffin v. Time, DC, Inc., 661 P.2d 579–80 (Ct.App.Ore.1983).

As the defendant recalled it, Dr. Wellons had "no specific" suggestions "except that we should esophagoscope the patient before carrying out any exploration if the patient bled again ... [and] that we make a tube **gastrostomy** [that is an opening in the stomach through which we put a tube leading to the outside] to check more easily on any recurrent bleeding and to allow any nasogastric tube to be removed after a day or two.' Fitzgerald v. Manning, 679 F.2d 341, 344 (4th Cir. 1982).

A feeding **gastrostomy** was also performed, which was "difficult because of the adhesions and scarring from his previous operation." Overstreet v. U.S., 528 F.Supp. 838, 840 (M.D. Ala.1981).

gastrostomy, Beck's creation of a gastric fistula by the formation of a tube from the greater curvature of the stomach to the surface of the abdominal wall.

She is unable to feed herself because she cannot properly swallow, and is therefore fed with specially prescribed nutrients every two or three hours through a surgically implanted **gastrostomy tube**. This tube requires attention on a daily basis and periodical surgical intervention. Pisel v. Stamford Hospital, 430 A.2d 1, 16 (Conn.1980).

gastrotomy (gas-trot'o-me) [*gastro-* + Gr. *temnein* to cut] incision into the stomach.

It was too late to surgically resect the cancerous lesion, and a **gastrotomy tube** was inserted into his stomach to provide sustenance. Chester v. U.S. 403 F.Supp. 458, 460 (W.D.Pa. 1975).

GBS (Guillain-Barre syndrome) See *polyneuritis, acute febrile*.

gender (jen'der) sex; the category to which an individual is assigned on the basis of sex.

gender [change]

Dr. Brown determined that it was medically necessary and reasonable to perform surgery, which would involve the removal of the male sex organs and construction of female genitalia....

Dr. Leibman asserted that G.B. "must have this [**gender change**] surgery to alleviate her emotional problems, prevent them from exacerbation, and to rehabilitate her to the point where she can function as a normal person and participate fully in society."...

Dr. Tennant concluded a discussion of this type of surgery as follows: "Denial of this valid medical treatment can lead to a further deterioration in the psychological health of the transsexual resulting in self-mutilating acts and in some cases suicide." G.B. v. Lackner, 145 Cal.Rptr. 555–6 (Ct.App.Cal. 1978).

gene (jēn) [Gr. *gennan* to produce] the biologic unit of heredity, self-reproducing and located at a definite position (locus) on a particular chromosome. The concept of gene is still evolving. From the standpoint of function, genes are conceived of as structural, operator, and regulator genes. From another standpoint, they are conceived of as cistrons, mutons, and recons. As classically construed, the gene is approximately synonymous with cistron. See also *mutation* (Chiropractic Ass'n of New York, Inc. case).

The hereditary units or **genes** are arrayed in a linear series along these chromosomes, many hundreds, or even thousands of **genes** making up any one chromosome, and so it also follows that for every **gene** inherited from the mother of an individual there is a corresponding **gene** inherited from the father of the individual. Chiropractic Ass'n of New York, Inc. v. Hilleboe, 227 N.Y.S.2d 309, 363 (Sup.Ct.Albany Cty.1961).

gene, recessive a gene that produces an effect in the organism only when it is transmitted by both parents, i.e., only when the individual is homozygous. See also *syndactyly* (Two Rivers Co. case).

generic (jĕ-ner'ik) [L. *genus, generis* kind] nonproprietary; denoting a drug name not protected by a trademark, usually descriptive of its chemical structure; sometimes called *public name*.

By my latest count, 31 states have enacted **generic** substitution laws. See, e.g., N.J.Stat.Ann. 24:6E–1 et seq. (West Supp. 1978); Pa.Stat.Ann. tit. 35, §§ 960.1–960.7 (Purdon Supp. 1978); Del.Code Ann. tit. 24, § 2589 (1976). Although these laws vary, they all provide a mechanism whereby the less expensive generic equivalent of a name brand drug may be substituted when the name brand is prescribed. It was established at oral argument that no post-1962 pioneer or ''me-too'' drug has to date been marketed without premarketing clearance by the FDA. Tr. at 39–41....

Dr. Crout says that 34 states have enacted such laws. I will accept his word for it. The count of 31 such laws I mention in the opinion was made a year ago in connection with another case....

Chlorothiazide with reserpine is a ''me-too'' of Merck's Diupres, an anti-hypertensive. Pharmadyne Laboratories, Inc. v. Kennedy, 466 F.Supp. 100, 106, 110 (D.N.J.1979).

genesis (jen'ĕ-sis) [Gr. *genesis* production, generation] the coming into being of anything; the process of originating. Often used as a word termination to denote the production, formation, or development of the object or state indicated by the word stem to which it is affixed, as biogenesis, gametogenesis, and pathogenesis.

genitalia (jen″ĭ-ta'le-ah) [L., pl.] the reproductive organs (organa genitalia [NA]).

''Private Parts'' means the penis, scrotum, mons veneris, vulva or vaginal area. Brown v. Brannon, 399 F.Supp. 133, 139 (M.D.N.Car.1975).

genotype (jen'o-tip) [*geno-* + Gr. *typos* type] the entire genetic constitution of an individual; also, the alleles present at one or more specific loci.

gentamicin (jen″tah-mi'sin) an antibiotic complex isolated from the actinomycetes *Micromonospora purpurea* and *M. echinospora*, consisting of components designated A, B, C, etc. The form in medicinal use is a mixture of three fractions of the C component (C_1, C_{1a}, C_2); it is bactericidal for a wide range of pathogens, being highly effective against many gram-negative bacteria, especially *Pseudomonas* species, as well as some gram-positive species, especially *Staphylococcus aureus*. See also *aminoglycoside*.

gentamicin sulfate [USP], the sulfate salt of the antibiotic substances isolated from *Micromonospora purpurea*. It is used as an antibacterial in the treatment of infections caused by susceptible organisms involving almost all body organs and systems, especially in gram-negative bacillary infections of the urinary tract, in burns contaminated by *Pseudomomas*, sepsis, and toxemias. It is administered intramuscularly, intravenously, or applied topically to the skin, and is also applied topically to the conjunctiva in eye infections due to responsive bacteria. See also *ototoxicity* (O'Brien case).

An operation was performed on August 7, 1977 for the removal of the plate and screws and the wound was irrigated with Garamycin. After plaintiff's discharge from St. Mary's Hospital, she continued as an outpatient for approximately seven months. Antibiotics, including **Gentamicin**, were prescribed. She remained in the plaster cast. However, there was no progress as the fracture was still not united notwithstanding the immobilization, and it was still infected. Warmsley v. City of New York, 454 N.Y.S.2d 144–5 (2d Dep't 1982).

The evidence adduced at trial shows that the recommended dosage of **Garamycin** for a person of appellant's weight, as set forth by the Schering Corporation's product insert, is 60 milligrams three times daily. However, for a patient determined to be in a life threatening condition, the manufacturer recommends a dosage for a person of appellant's weight of approximately 77 milligrams three times daily. The product insert indicates further that use of **Garamycin** in excess of recommended dosages might cause certain side effects, including impairment of the auditory function. The evidence is undisputed that appellant was not informed of this potential adverse consequence of using **Garamycin**. O'Brien v. Angley, 407 N.E.2d 490, 492 (Ohio 1980).

The jury further found that Schering represented to Dr. Edwards that **Garamycin** would cause only temporary partial hearing loss; that such representation was false; that Dr. Edwards relied on the representation; and that Dr. Edward's reliance was a producing cause of Walter K. Giesecke's total and permanent hearing loss. Schering Corp. v. Giesecke, 589 S.W.2d 516, 518 (Ct.Civ.App.Tex.1979).

gentian (jen'shun) the dried rhizome and roots of *Gentiana lutea* L. (Gentianaceae); it has been used as a bitter tonic. It contains gentiin, gentiamarin, gentisin, gentisic acid, gentiopicrin, gentianose, and pectin. Also known as *yellow* or *pale gentian*.

gentian violet [USP], chemical name: *N*-[4-[bis[4-(dimethylamino)phenyl]-methylene]-2,5-cyclohexadiene-1-ylidene]-[*N*-methylmethanaminium chloride. Hexamethylpararosaniline chloride, usually admixed with penta- and tetramethylpararosaniline chlorides, occurring as a dark green powder or greenish glistening pieces having a metallic luster. It is a dye with antibacterial, antifungal, and anthelmintic properties, applied topically in the treatment of infections of the skin and mucous membranes associated with gram-positive bacteria and molds, and administered orally in pinworm and liver fluke infections. It has been given orally, intravenously, and by transduodenal intubation in strongyloidosis. See also *anthelmintic*.

... products containing **gentian violet** (methylrosaniline chloride)....

... The record is thus devoid of evidence probative of general expert recognition of the safety of **gentian violet** as a food additive and the trial court's finding that **gentian violet** has been shown to be generally recognized by experts as safe under the conditions of its intended use must be set aside as clearly erroneous. U.S. v. Naremco, Inc., 553 F.2d 1138, 1140, 1143 (8th Cir. 1977).

geotrichosis (je"o-tri-ko'sis) infection by *Geotrichum candidum*, which may attack the bronchi, lungs, mouth, or intestinal tract; its manifestations resemble those of candidiasis.

Geotrichum (je-ot'ri-kum) a genus of yeastlike imperfect fungi of the family Cryptococcaceae, order Moniliales. *G. candidum*, found in the feces and in dairy products, is the etiologic agent of geotrichosis.

Microscopic examinations of those samples revealed the presence in all five of **Geotrichum** mold, commonly known as machinery mold....

... The chemist then looked for the very characteristic features of **Geotrichum**, including a feathery texture, crossed walls, and series of at least three branches growing off the main trunk at 45° angles, with tapered growing ends....

Geotrichum, commonly referred to within the food processing industry as machinery mold, also known as dairy mold, oospora and oidium, is one whose spores are generally isolated from soil, sewage, and surfaces of fruits and vegetables growing in the field. **Geotrichum** is not harmful to humans when consumed in food. In fact, it is intentionally introduced into several types of cheese (Limburger, Camemberti, and Brie) as a curing agent, and as such both live and dead **Geotrichum** is present in those cheeses as part of the finished products. **Geotrichum** would be killed when subjected to a blanch of 5–6 minutes at 212° F., such as that utilized by the defendants at Fulton, but the dead mycelium would remain unless otherwise removed....

When **Geotrichum** begins to grow, it generally takes 4–8 hours to become visible. As it grows, the mold generally appears gray or white in color, although in a food packaging plant its surface would generally take on the color of the juices flowing from whatever food was being processed at the time. The mold accumulation generally has a slimy texture. U.S. v. General Foods Corp., 446 F.Supp. 740, 743, 749–51 (N.D. N.Y.1978).

Geritol

The Commission's Order requires that not only must the **Geritol** advertisements be expressly limited to those persons whose symptoms [3] are due to an existing deficiency of one or more of the vitamins contained in the preparation, or due to an existing deficiency of iron, but also the **Geritol** advertisements must affirmatively disclose the negative fact that a great majority of persons who experience these symptoms do not experience them because they have a vitamin or iron deficiency; that

for the great majority of people experiencing these symptoms, **Geritol** will be of no benefit. [Footnote omitted.] [[3] The use of the word "symptoms" will include the symptoms of tiredness, loss of strength, run-down feeling, nervousness or irritability.] J. B. Williams Co. v. F.T.C., 381 F.2d 884, 886 (6th Cir. 1967).

gestation (jes-ta'shun) [L. *gestatio*, from *gestare* to bear] the period of development of the young in viviparous animals, from the time of fertilization of the ovum until birth. See also *pregnancy*.

Schatkin, Disputed Paternity Proceedings (Third Edition) in Chapter XV under the discussion of The Duration of Pregnancy on pages 519 and 520 states as follows:

The duration of pregnancy, or period of **gestation**, is the interval in days between the time of impregnation and the beginning of labor. The normal period of **gestation**, according to the consensus of medical testimony, is approximately 9 calendar months—10 lunar months—or 280 days, calculated from cessation of the last menstruation. In the United States, the courts will judicially notice that a period of 9 calendar months is the usual period of **gestation**.

In the Fourth Edition of Schatkin, Disputed Paternity Proceedings the discussion of the topic of Duration of Pregnancy is contained in Chapter XXII from pages 567 through 585. Most of the discussion contained in those pages by that authority consists of quotations from the dissenting opinion of Mr. Justice Woodside in Commonwealth of Pennsylvania v. Watts (1955), 179 Pa.Super. 398, 116 A.2d 844.

On page 570 in the first paragraph there is stated the following:

"The average duration of human pregnancy, counting from the first day of the last menstrual period is about 280 days or 10 lunar months."

On page 585 the author on his own comes to a conclusion as follows:

"In computing the period of **gestation**, and in predicting the expected date of confinement, where there is extended cohabitation (such as a married woman) or a long sexual association (which may be present in a paternity case) the date of the last menses may be useful and necessary in predicting the expected date of confinement. However, where the petitioner alleges a single act of sexual intercourse, she rests her case on that sole occurrence and we may disregard the date of her last menses, for she herself has designated the date of impregnation, and from that date we predict the expected date of confinement." [**Gestation** is defined, according to said authority, [Dorland's Illus. Med. Dict. 24th Ed.] as the period of development of the young in viviparous animals from the time of fertilization of the ovum. Leonard v. Couse, 372 N.Y.S.2d 527, 529–31 (Fam.Ct.Otsego Cty.1975).

gesture, suicidal

"**Suicidal gesture** is more designed to demonstrate to everyone around that the person is in great conflict, is in great distress. The **suicidal gesture** is not designed to commit suicide. It usually will involve something quite dramatic. And as a rule the person escapes most injuries. Occasionally there will be a minor injury. It is quite rare for the person who makes **suicidal gestures** to commit suicide. It does occur sometimes by miscalculation; where you had expected to be rescued at the last minute and the rescuer didn't show up on time. That, of course, can lead to a disaster. But as a rule **suicidal gestures** are not particularly serious. . . .

"A. She described one event, which occurred, I believe, about a year ago, and I don't know the—she didn't tell me about the circumstances, she did mention that she had cut one wrist twice. I asked her if this was deep enough to have cut the tendons. She stated no.

"The other event she mentioned, and her attorney mentioned it to me also, occurred I believe Thursday night when it was alleged that she jumped out of a moving car in front of, I believe, the Beverly Wilshire Hotel, and ran down the middle of Wilshire Boulevard.

"I asked her about injuries, and she stated that she hadn't even received a minor injury from this occurrence.

"Q. With reference to these two incidents, it is your professional judgment that these were two **suicidal gestures** as opposed to suicidal tendencies, is that your testimony, Doctor?

"A. Yes, sir." In re Loughran, 276 F.Supp. 393, 411 (C.D. Cal.1967).

ghost surgery See *surgery, ghost.*

gibbous (gib′us) [L. *gibbosus*] convex; humped; protuberant; humpbacked.

gibbous, dorsal

Dr. Schreiber stated that, upon examining claimant, he detected a **dorsal gibbous** (outward bowing) at the T–12/L–1 level, severe spasm of the lower back muscles, and limited back motion and flexion. Inland Steel Coal Co. v. Industrial Com'n, 405 N.E.2d 781–2 (Ill.1980).

gingivae (jin-ji′ve, jin′ji-ve) [L., plural of *gingiva*] [NA] the gums: the mucous membrane, with the supporting fibrous tissue, which overlies the crowns of unerupted teeth and encircles the necks of those that have erupted.

gingival (jin′ji-val, jin-ji′val) pertaining to the gingivae.

gingivectomy (jin″ji-vek′to-me) [*gingiva* + Gr. *ektomē* excision] surgical excision of all loose infected and diseased gingival tissue to eradicate periodontal infection and reduce the depth of the gingival sulcus.

A **gingivectomy** is the surgical removal of gum tissue surrounding the cervical portion of the tooth. Such treatment is ill-advised for pregnant women. U.S. v. Talbott, 460 F.Supp. 253, 261 (S.D.Ohio 1978).

gingivitis (jin″ji-vi′tis) [*gingiva* + -*itis*] inflammation involving the gingival tissue only.

ginseng (jin′seng) [Chinese *jin-tsan* life of man] any herb of the genus *Panax*, especially *P. schinseng* (Chinese ginseng) and *P. quinquefolius* (American ginseng), whose roots are used by the Chinese as a tonic, stimulant, and aphrodisiac.

A woodland herb [ginseng] reputed to have medicinal qualities and used primarily in the Orient. Appalachian Power Co. v. LaForce, 201 S.E.2d 768–9 (Va.1974).

girdle stone procedure See *operation, girdle stone.*

glabella (glah-bel′ah) [L. *glaber* smooth] 1. the smooth area on the frontal bone between the superciliary arches.

2. the most prominent point in the midsagittal plane between the eyebrows; used as an anthropometric landmark.

. . . a severe hurt to the face, described by her doctor as an "extensive deep irregular laceration of the forehead which extended from the **glabella** area down across the nose." Bernstein v. Kapneck, 430 A.2d 602–3 (Ct.App.Md.1981).

gland (gland) [L. *glans* acorn] an aggregation of cells, specialized to secrete or excrete materials not related to their ordinary metabolic needs; called also *glandula* [NA]. See also *cortisone* (Dupuy case). See illustration.

The hypothalamus, pituitary and adrenal **glands** are suppressed by cortisone, necessitating slow withdrawal of the drug. Dupuy v. Tilley, 380 So.2d 634, 635 (Ct.App.La.1979).

gland, adrenal a flattened body situated in the retroperitoneal tissues at the cranial pole of either kidney. In man, the adrenal gland is the result of fusion of two organs, recognizable as cortex and medulla. The adrenal cortex, under control of the pituitary hormone corticotropin, elaborates steroid hormones—glucocorticoids, 17-ketosteroids, mineralocorticoids, estrogens, androgens, and progestins. The adrenal medulla elaborates the catecholamines epinephrine and norepinephrine. Called also *glandula suprarenalis* [NA] and *suprarenal g.*

An autopsy performed by Dr. William S. Randall, Pathologist, resulted in his attributing the cause of death to adrenal insufficiency, based on a finding that the **adrenal glands** were ⅕th normal size, and were therefore hypofunctioning. Dr. Randall explained that the abnormally small glands were incapable of producing sufficient adrenal fluids to sustain life under surgical stress. Chapman v. Argonaut-Southwest Ins. Co., 290 So.2d 779, 781 (Ct.App.La.1974).

gland, mesenteric See *nodi lymphatici mesenterici.*

gland, parathyroid small bodies in the region of the thyroid gland, developed from the entoderm of the branchial clefts, occurring in a variable number of pairs, commonly two (*glandula parathyroidea inferior* and *glandula parathyroidea superior* [NA]) (see inset on accompanying Plate). The parenchyma consists of masses and cords of epithelial cells, which have been divided into two main types: chief cells and oxyphil cells, but intermediate forms exist. The parathyroid glands secrete parathyroid hormone and are concerned chiefly with the metabolism of calcium and phosphorus. Called also *epithelial* or *parathyroid bodies.*

The **parathyroid glands**, located adjacent to the thyroid, regulate the amount of calcium in the blood stream. . . .

. . . Because of their small size and their location, these glands are difficult to identify during surgery. According to the pathology report, made after the operation, the mass removed by Dr. Kiledjian contained no parathyroid tissue. Nevertheless, it is undisputed that after the surgery all such glands had either been removed or had ceased to function.[2] [[2] Although an individual normally has four **parathyroid glands**, a person needs only one such gland to regulate the calcium flow into the bloodstream.] O'Neill v. Kiledjian, 511 F.2d 511–12 (6th Cir. 1975).

314

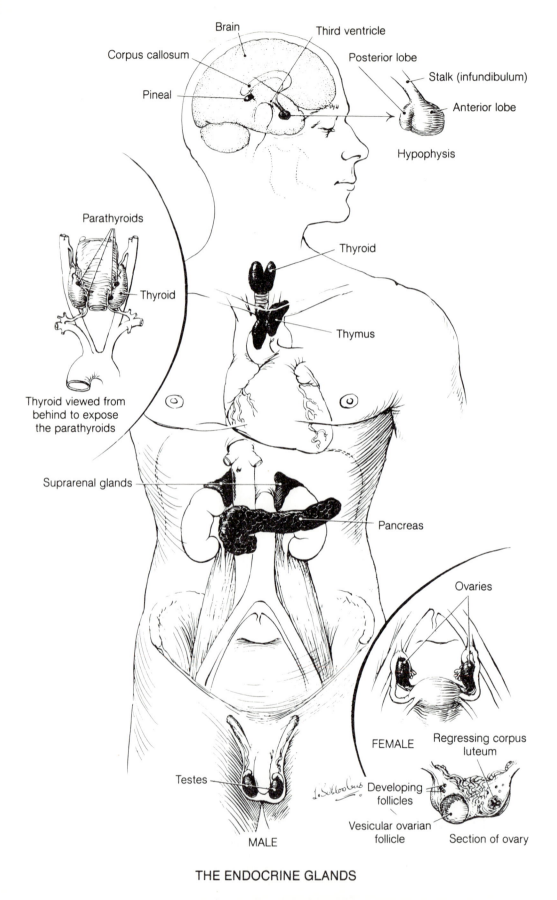

Brain

Corpus callosum

Third ventricle

Pineal

Posterior lobe

Stalk (infundibulum)

Anterior lobe

Hypophysis

Parathyroids

Thyroid

Thyroid viewed from
behind to expose
the parathyroids

Thyroid

Thymus

Suprarenal glands

Pancreas

Ovaries

Regressing corpus
luteum

FEMALE

Developing
follicles

Vesicular ovarian
follicle

Section of ovary

Testes

MALE

THE ENDOCRINE GLANDS

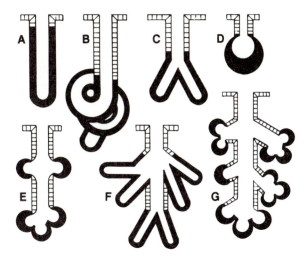

Schematic diagram of various forms of glands: *A*, simple tubular; *B*, simple coiled tubular; *C*, simple branched tubular; *D*, simple alveolar; *E*, simple branched alveolar; *F*, compound tubular; *G*, compound alveolar.

gland, parotid the largest of the three chief, paired salivary glands; see *glandula parotis* [NA].

gland, sudoriferous; gland sudoriparous See *glandulae sudoriferae*.

gland, sweat See *glandulae sudoriferae*.

gland, thyroid one of the endocrine glands, normally situated in the lower part of the front of the neck and consisting of two lobes, one on either side of the trachea and joined in front by a narrow isthmus. It secretes, stores, and liberates as necessary the thyroid hormones (thyroxine and triiodothyronine), which require iodine for their elaboration and which are concerned in regulating the metabolic rate. It also secretes thyrocalcitonin. Called also *glandula thyroidea* [NA] and *thyroid body*.

Another physician advised her—again in October, 1968—that she had a marked lack of thyroid function, which could account for anemia. He prescribed thyroid tablets and said that she would have to take them daily for the rest of her life. Another physician said in November, 1968, that Mrs. Coleman had an underactive **thyroid gland** and was unable to work. Coleman v. Weinberger, 538 F.2d 1045–6 (4th Cir. 1976).

Five years later, in 1971, she again was afflicted with a hyperactive **thyroid** condition. On this occasion, she sought care from the clinic at St. Joseph Hospital in Memphis. A second operation was performed, and the thyroid remaining on the right side was removed. Within a year of this operation and soon after she had given birth to a child, plaintiff was again hospitalized at St. Joseph Hospital because of a **thyroid** problem. On September 20, 1972, the defendant, then the chief surgical resident at the hospital, operated to remove the portion of the **thyroid** remaining on the left side of the neck. O'Neill v. Kiledjian, 511 F.2d 511–12 (6th Cir. 1975).

gland, vestibular greater See *glandula vestibularis major*.

glandula (glan'du-lah), pl. *glan'dulae* [L.] [NA] a gland: an aggregation of cells, specialized to secrete or excrete materials not related to their ordinary metabolic needs.

glandulae parathyroideae [NA], small bodies in the region of the thyroid gland occurring in a variable number of pairs, commonly two, named *glandula parathyroidea superior* and *glandula parathyroidea inferior*, according to their position; see *parathyroid glands*, under *gland*.

glandula parotis [NA], parotid gland: the largest of the three chief, paired glands which, together with numerous small glands in the mouth, constitute the salivary glands; it is located below the zygomatic arch, below and in front of the external acoustic meatus.

Dr. Oakey explained to Mr. DeFulvio that the biopsy would involve an incision about 1″ long and the removal of the suspected tumor on his **parotid** (salivary) gland. DeFulvio v. Holst, 414 A.2d 1087, 1089 (Super.Ct.Pa.1979).

He diagnosed the lump as a ''mixed'' or benign tumor in appellant's **parotid gland**.[1] [[1] The parotid is one of the major saliva-secreting glands.] LeMons v. Regents of the Univ. of Cal., 582 P.2d 946–7 (Cal.1978).

glan'dulae sudorif'erae [NA], sudoriferous or sweat glands: the glands that secrete sweat, situated in the corium or subcutaneous tissue, and opening by a duct on the surface of the body. They are of two types: The ordinary or *eccrine sweat glands* are unbranched, coiled, tubular glands that are distributed over almost all of the body surface, and promote cooling by evaporation of their secretion. The *apocrine sweat glands* are large, branched, specialized glands that empty into the upper portion of a hair follicle instead of directly onto the skin surface, and are found only on certain areas of the body, such as around the anus and in the axilla. Called also *sudoriparous glands*. See also *sweat*.

Located beneath the surface of the skin are glands known as **sweat glands**, each having an opening or duct at the surface of the skin, referred to as the mouth of the sweat gland....

    Sweat glands function most of the time in at least some small degree in all human beings, but much of the time the secretion produced is so small in amount that it dries off too quickly for a person to see of feel any of the secretion. Carter Products v. F.T.C., 186 F.2d 821, 823–4 (7th Cir. 1951).

glandula suprarena'lis [NA], a flattened body situated in the retroperitoneal tissues at the superior pole of either kidney; see *adrenal gland*, under *gland*.

glandula thyroidea [NA], thyroid gland: one of the endocrine glands, normally situated in the front of the lower part of the neck and consisting of two lobes, one on either side of the trachea and joined in front by a narrow isthmus. It secretes, stores, and liberates as necessary the thyroid hormones (thyroxine and triiodothyronine), which require iodine for their elaboration and are concerned in regulating the rate of metabolism. It also secretes thyrocalcitonin. Called also *thyroid body*. See also *thyroid*.

glandula vestibularis major [NA], either of two small reddish yellow bodies in the vestibular bulbs, one on each side of the vaginal orifice; they are homologues of the bulbourethral glands in the male. Called also *Bartholin's gland* and *greater vestibular gland.*

In October 1975 Kranda consulted Dr. Keim Houser, an obstetrician-gynecologist employed by Norborg-Houser Medical Corporation, concerning problems she was having with vaginal warts. At this time, Dr. Houser also noted a **Bartholin** cyst deep within the tissue on the left side of her vagina. From Kranda's medical history, Dr. Houser knew that a similar cyst had been surgically removed from the same area in 1972 and that Kranda suffered from Crohn's disease. Kranda v. Houser-Norborg Medical Corp., 419 N.E.2d 1024, 1031 (Ct.App. Ind.1981).

glasses (glas'ez) spectacles; a pair of lenses arranged in a frame holding them in the proper position before the eyes, as an aid to vision. See also *prism;* and *spectacles.*

glasses, contact See *lens, contact.*

glaucoma (glaw-ko'mah) [Gr. *glaukōma* opacity of the crystalline lens (from the dull gray gleam of the affected eye)] a group of eye diseases characterized by an increase in intraocular pressure which causes pathological changes in the optic disk and typical defects in the field of vision. See also *tonometer, Schiotz'* (Gates case).

Dr. Wilson tested Ms. Harris' intraocular pressure, found it to be extremely high, and diagnosed an acute glaucoma attack. (Glaucoma is an increase in fluid pressure in the eye which may result in damage to the optic nerve.)...

... Flashing lights and a feeling of pressure centered in the eye are common symptoms of **glaucoma**. In addition, steroids may induce **glaucoma** in a small number of susceptible persons. Two physicians testified that, because of this possibility, the intraocular pressure of any patient on steroids should be tested regularly. [Footnote omitted.] Harris v. Robert C. Groth, M.D., Inc., 663 P.2d 113–14 (Wash.1983).

Dr. Hargiss then examined Mrs. Gates' optic nerves with a direct ophthalmoscope to determine whether the discs, or surfaces, of the nerves showed the exacerbated "cupping" which is characteristic of **glaucoma**. There was evidence at trial that observation of the nerve discs in Mrs. Gates' case was particularly difficult with the direct ophthalmoscope when the pupils were not dilated. Nonetheless Dr. Hargiss did not dilate Mrs. Gates' pupils. He could see no evidence of abnormality and made no further tests for **glaucoma**. In response to Mrs. Gates' inquiry about the pressure test, he said he had checked for **glaucoma** but found everything all right. He diagnosed her problem as difficulties with the contact lenses she wore and treated her accordingly....

The significant facts in this case are that Dr. Hargiss neither told Mrs. Gates he had found high pressure in both eyes which put her in a borderline **glaucoma** area, nor that her risk of **glaucoma** was increased considerably by this high pressure and her myopia. Furthermore, Dr. Hargiss had available to him two additional diagnostic tests for **glaucoma** which are simple, inexpensive, and risk free. The first was to use the standard drops for dilating the pupils to obtain a better view of the optic nerve discs. The second was to have Mrs. Gates take a visual field examination to determine whether she had suffered any loss in her field of vision. Dr. Hargiss did not tell Mrs. Gates of the existence of these simple procedures, and he did not administer the tests. Gates v. Jensen, 595 P.2d 919, 921 (Wash. 1979).

... he discovered that she was having an early case of **glaucoma** in her left eye and he prescribed pilocarpine drops in both eyes because **glaucoma** is a disease that usually affects both eyes. The doctor testified in cross-examination as follows: "Q. You thought, Doctor, on November 17, 1952 you saw evidence of **glaucoma**? A. I saw cupping of the left optic nerve, that is the eye that I first operated for cataract and that was the first chance that I had to see that optic nerve for quite sometime and it had not been cupped before. I interpreted that as early evidence of **glaucoma**. I made a sketch of that. He also testified as follows: "A. Yes, I have a note here which I failed to notice yesterday, written in the same ink and on the same sheet and dated July 7, 1952 that the pressure of the right eye was one plus, pressure of left eye was normal as determining measurement with my fingers. Q. What does the one plus on the right eye indicate to you? A. It indicates to me that there is probably **glaucoma** present.''...

... A reading of the evidence also reveals that **glaucoma** is a disease of the eye which requires continuous observation and treatment in order to keep it in control and that it is a disease of the eye which is never completely cured. Thorpe v. Schoenbrun, 195 A.2d 870, 872–3 (Super.Ct.Pa.1963).

Other Authorities: Winkjer v. Herr, 277 N.W.2d 579, 584 (N.Dak.1979). Excelsior Leather Washer Co. v. Industrial Com'n, 297 N.E.2d 158–60 (Ill.1973).

glaucoma, closed-angle See *glaucoma, narrow-angle.*

glaucoma, narrow-angle a form of primary glaucoma in an eye characterized by a shallow anterior chamber and a narrow angle, in which filtration is compromised as a result of the iris blocking the angle; called also *angle-closure g., closed-angle g.,* and *acute congestive g.*

Their evidence tended to prove that Ms. Harris' glaucoma attack was of a type known as **closed-angle glaucoma** which comes on in a matter of hours and would therefore not have been detected by intraocular pressure tests. Harris v. Robert C. Groth, M.D., Inc., 663 P.2d 113, 115 (Wash.1983).

glenoid (gle'noid) [Gr. *glēnē* socket + *eidos* form] resembling a pit or socket. See also *cavitas glenoidalis.*

glioblastoma (gli"o-blas-to'mah) [*glio-* + Gr. *blastos* germ + *-oma*] a general term for malignant forms of astrocytoma. See also *glioblastoma multiforme;* and *astrocytoma.*

The angiogram revealed a large malignant brain tumor (**glioblastoma**). His condition deteriorated until his death on May 14, 1973....

... Though there is no negligence upon which to base an award of damages, the court finds that Riddlesperger was suffering from a terminal condition which was finally diagnosed as a malignant **glioblastoma** located in the posteroparietal area of the brain. Due to the rapid onset of symptoms and its size and the malignancy of the tumor, he could not have lived more than six to 12 months, and would never have been able to return to a productive livelihood. Riddlesperger v. U.S., 406 F.Supp. 617, 619, 623 (N.D.Ala.1976).

glioblastoma multiforme an astrocytoma of Grade III or IV; it is a rapidly growing tumor, usually confined to the cerebral hemispheres and composed of a mixture of spongioblasts, astroblasts, and astrocytes. Called also *spongioblastoma multiforme* and *anaplastic astrocytoma*.

glioma (gli-o'mah) [*glio-* + *-oma*] a tumor composed of tissue which represents neuroglia in any one of its stages of development. The term is sometimes extended to include all the primary intrinsic neoplasms of the brain and spinal cord, including astrocytomas, ependymomas, neurocytomas, etc. See also *neuroglia*.

... the defendant did render neurosurgical treatment to the plaintiff, diagnosing and operating on what he considered a brain stem **glioma**. Gattis v. Chavez, 413 F.Supp. 33, 35 (D.S. Car.1976).

gliosis (gli-o'sis) an excess of astroglia in damaged areas of the central nervous system.

Dr. Winston, admitted on cross-examination that the destruction of brain tissue, such as occurred here, would leave "some adjacent reparative **gliosis**," which he also stated some experts would term a scar. Tr. at 238. Beins v. U.S., 695 F.2d 591, 608 (D.C.Cir.1982).

Other Authorities: Roth v. Law, 579 S.W.2d 949, 954 (Ct.Civ. App.Tex.1979).

glissando

The **glissando** is part of the electroshock equipment and is used to cause slow application of electricity to the patient's body in order to prevent a sudden jolt of the body. This device was part of the equipment at Eugenia when the therapy was administered to Miss Collins. Collins v. Hand, 246 A.2d 398, 402 (Pa.1968).

globulin (glob'u-lin) [L. *globulus* globule] a class of proteins characterized by being insoluble in water, but soluble in saline solutions (euglobulins), or water soluble proteins (pseudoglobulins) whose other physical properties closely resemble true globulins. See *globulin, serum*.

globulin, gamma a group of plasma globulins which, in neutral or alkaline solutions, have the slowest electrophoretic mobility and which have sites of antibody activity. See also *immunoglobulin*.

Doctor explained that because the needle may have been used on another person suffering from a liver disease, Patient may have been exposed to a risk of infectious hepatitis.

Patient then was required to undergo a series of massive **gamma globulin** injections. These injections, continuing from June through November, 1970, were described as extremely painful. It was necessary also to suspend methotrexate therapy for her psoriasis during the course of the **gamma globulin** injections because continuance of that therapy would confuse the required tests incident to the anti-hepatitis procedures. Suburban Hospital Ass'n, Inc.v. Hadary, 322 A.2d 258, 260 (Ct.Spec.App.Md.1974).

globulin, immune; globulin, immune human serum [USP], a sterile solution containing many antibodies normally present in adult human blood; it contains 15 to 18 gm. of protein per 100 ml., not less than 90 per cent of which is gamma globulin. Each lot is derived from an original plasma or serum pool representing venous or placental blood from at least 1000 individuals; used for passive immunization of susceptible contacts against infectious hepatitis, poliomyelitis, rubella, rubeola, and varicella, and in the treatment of gamma globulin deficiency, administered intramuscularly. Called also *gamma g.* and *immune serum g. (human)*.

The general procedure for the use of Rh **immune globulin** in hospitals is as follows: (i) if the patient is an Rh negative mother, umbilical cord blood is taken at the time of birth and sent to the blood bank or laboratory to determine if the child is Rh positive or Rh negative; (ii) the mother's physician is advised of the findings and if the child is Rh positive, the physician will order that Rh **immune globulin** be administered to the mother, normally by writing the order on the patient's chart; (iii) a nurse then will transcribe the physician's order from the patient's chart to a requisition form by means of which Rh **immune globulin** is ordered from the blood bank; (iv) at the blood bank the mother's blood is cross-matched against the Rh **immune globulin** to insure against incompatibility; (v) the blood bank personnel process the requisition and send out the Rh **immune globulin** for administration to the patient, usually by a nurse who may or may not be the nurse who received the order to administer the product from the physician (Queenan T. p. 158–21 to T. p. 169–11; Freda T. p. 627–23 to T. p. 632–3; Dyer J–41 p. 27–19 to p. 32–24; Goodkin J–38 p. 40–8 to p. 45–7). Ortho Pharmaceutical Corp. v. American Cyanamid Co., 361 F.Supp. 1032, 1039 (D.N.J.1973).

globulin, serum a group of proteins precipitated from plasma (or serum) by half saturation with ammonium sulfate; further fractionation of globulins into subgroups may be carried out by solubility, chromatography, electrophoresis, and ultracentrifugation. The principal groups include the α-, β-, and γ-globulins, which differ with respect to their association with lipids or carbohydrates and their content of physiologically significant features. The fractions include immunoglobulins (anti-bodies) in the β and γ fractions, lipoproteins in the α and β fractions, gluco- or mucoproteins, and metal-binding and metal-transporting proteins. Also present in globulin fractions are prothrombin, macroglobulin, plasminogen, euglobulin, fibrinogen, cryoglobulin, and antihemophilic globulin.

globulin, tetanus immune human [USP], a sterile solution of gamma globulins derived from the blood plasma of adult human donors who have been immunized with tetanus toxoid, containing 10 to 18 gm. of protein per 100 ml., of which not less than 90 per cent is gamma globulin; used in the prophylaxis and treatment of tetanus, administered intramuscularly. Called also *tetanus immune g. (human)*.

In his deposition, Dr. Goldsmith admitted that he accepted as authority the guidelines prepared by the Committee on Trauma of the American College of Surgeons, entitled "Prophylaxis Against Tetanus and Wound Management." One of the procedures required by the guidelines is that **human-immune globulin** be given to patients with wounds which indicate an overwhelming possibility that tetanus will develop. Pollard v. Goldsmith 572 P.2d 1201, 1203 (Ct.App.Ariz.1977).

Appellant sells the plasma to pharmaceutical firms which use it to produce the **immune globulin** for treating or preventing tetanus. Mirsa, Inc. v. State Medical Board, 329 N.E.2d 106, 108 (Ohio 1975).

glomectomy (glo-mek′to-me) excision of a glomus, especially of the glomus caroticum.

Thereafter, defendant performed **glomectomy** surgery on plaintiff. The procedure involved removing the carotid body and related nerves from plaintiff's neck. Plaintiff contends the surgery was unnecessary and an improper treatment for emphysema. Griffin v. Phillips, 542 S.W.2d 432, 435 (Ct.Civ.App. Tex.1976).

glomerulonephritis (glo-mer″u-lo-ně-fri′tis) [*glomerulus* + *nephritis*] a variety of nephritis characterized by inflammation of the capillary loops in the glomeruli of the kidney. It occurs in acute, subacute, and chronic forms and may be secondary to hemolytic streptococcal infection. Evidence also supports possible immune or autoimmune mechanisms.

Glomerulonephritis is a disease in which the vessels within the kidney have been damaged or hardened through the exertion of pressure....

... He was hospitalized for 140 days and became totally disabled as a result of the disease. Ranieli v. Mutual Life Ins. Co. of America, 413 A.2d 396–7 (Super.Ct.Pa.1979).

glomerulonephritis, subacute persistence of acute glomerulonephritis, with or without periods of remission, which may develop into the lobular or malignant forms.

Dr. McLaughlin noted the following in that portion of the autopsy report entitled ''Clinical-Pathological Correlation:''
Death in this case was caused by recent myocardial infarct of the anterior wall of the left ventricle interventricular septum. This was secondary to recent thrombosis of the anterior descending branch of the left coronary artery. It was further complicated by **subacute glomerulonephritis** type of renal failure terminally. (Tr. 94). Poore v. Mathews, 406 F.Supp. 47, 50 (E.D.Tenn.1975).

glomus (glo′mus), pl. *glom′era* [L. ''a ball''] [NA] a small, histologically recognizable body, composed primarily of fine arterioles connecting directly with veins, and possessing a rich nerve supply.

glucagon (gloo′kah-gon) 1. a polypeptide hormone secreted by the alpha cells of the islets of Langerhans in response to hypoglycemia or to stimulation by the growth hormone of the anterior pituitary; it stimulates glycogenolysis in the liver by inducing activation of liver phosphorylase. Called also *hyperglycemic-glycogenolytic factor (HGF)*. 2. [USP] the polypeptide occurring in the pancreas of those domestic mammals used for food by man, $C_{153}H_{225}N_{43}O_{49}S$, which has the property of increasing the blood glucose concentration, occurring as a fine, white or faintly colored crystalline powder; used in the form of the hydrochloride salt as an antihypoglycemic, administered parenterally.

A new hormone called **glucagon**—developed late in 1960—largely eliminates the need for intravenous injection of glucose in such emergencies. Injected under the skin, it has the remark-

able ability to raise the blood sugar to normal levels promptly and consistently. Facts about Diabetes. [Am. Diabetes Ass'n, Inc. 1966, N.Y.]

Within ten minutes after receiving one ampule of glucagon the patient is usually sufficiently awake to eat. Recovery after an insulin reaction is usually prompt and complete. Often a person feels well again within fifteen to thirty minutes. ADA Forecast, published by American Diabetes Association, Inc. 1967. U.S. v. Dunavan, 464 F.2d 1166, 1178 (6th Cir. 1972).

gluteal (gloo′te-al) [Gr. *gloutos* buttock] pertaining to the buttocks.

... she had permanent residual limping, characterized as a ''**gluteal** lurch;'' a permanent weakness in the left thigh and **gluteal** muscles.... Lycon v. Walker, 279 F.2d 478, 485 (8th Cir. 1960).

glutethimide (gloo-teth′ĭ-mīd) [USP] chemical name: 3-ethyl-3-phenyl-2,6-piperidinedione. A nonbarbiturate structurally related to phenobarbital, $C_{13}H_{15}NO_2$, occurring as a white, crystalline powder; used as a sedative and hypnotic, administered orally.

Pursuant to this authority and its general rule-making authority (Code Ann. § 79A–208 (Ga.L.1967, pp. 296, 304); Code Ann. § 79A–909 (Ga.L.1967, pp. 296, 354)), the Georgia State Board of Pharmacy duly promulgated Rule No. 480–9–.01(2)(3)(iii), which classifies the substance **glutethimide** (**Doriden**) as a ''depressant or stimulant'' drug within the purview of § 79A–903(b), par. 4, supra. State v. Pettus, 212 S.E.2d 9, 11 (Ct.App.Ga.1974).

Entries by both Dr. Rotman and Dr. Glen on Mr. Finley's clinical records and medical records during the term of his hospitalization also express the opinion that the patient was suffering from a dermatitis medicamentosa possibly related to a drug reaction from the taking of **Doriden**. The records also reflected an anemic condition on blood serum testing, as to which the resident physician in hematology stated that ''this anemia could possibly be related to **Doriden** intake, although I am unaware of this side effect.''...

... The question is: Did the extensive dermatitis, which is presumably due to **Doriden** relate in any way to hair loss and to vitiligo? I believe the relationship, if one exists, would be indirect. That is, the patient would have an exfoliative dermatitis because of an allergic reaction to **Doriden**. The dermatitis, in turn, could have predisposed him to develop vitiligo and hair loss at the particular time he did. Ordinarily, a patient predisposed to vitiligo requires little in the way of trauma to the skin to have loss of pigment. If the patient was a potential candidate for vitiligo the generalized dermatitis would certainly be sufficient trauma for development of total vitiligo.
I do not believe that **Doriden** has a direct effect on the pigment cells. In fact, no one has ever reported that any drug can produce vitiligo. One has been sought for but not yet found....

... Based on all the foregoing, it is the Court's conclusion that, while there is no known drug which can cause a total loss of pigmentation, the plaintiff's taking of **Doriden**, although not in and of itself the direct cause of the plaintiff's leukoderma, produced in Mr. Finley a drug reaction, the drug reaction manifested itself in the form of severe exfoliative dermatitis, and the severe exfoliative dermatitis was such a trauma to the plaintiff's system that it triggered a latent predisposition to total depigmentation. Therefore, the taking of the **Doriden** by the plaintiff was the proximate cause, as that term is understood in the law, of his depigmentation....

... While there is evidence that **Doriden** is known to produce skin rash, there is no proof as to the incidence of such side-effect in relation to the use of the drug. Finley v. U.S., 314 F.Supp. 905, 909–10, 915 (N.D.Ohio 1970).

goiter (goi'ter) an enlargement of the thyroid gland, causing a swelling in the front part of the neck.

goiter, toxic See *disease, Graves'*.

gonad (go'nad, gon'ad) [L. *gonas*, from Gr. *gonē* seed] a gamete-producing gland; an ovary or testis.

Q. Doctor, the **gonads** are the reproductive cells, are they not? A. They contain the reproductive cells; that's correct.

Q. The **gonads** of the male are the testes and the spermatozoa? A. The **gonads** of the male are the testes and contain spermatozoa, among other cells.

Q. And the **gonads** of the female are what? A. Are the ovaries and they contain ova in various stages of development.

Q. In those **gonads** of the male and the female are contained the hereditary material from which the human beings in existence came, and from which the generations yet unborn are to come? A. That's correct. Chiropractic Ass'n of New York, Inc. v. Hilleboe, 227 N.Y.S.2d 309, 347 (Sup.Ct.Albany Cty.1961).

gonorrhea (gon"o-re'ah) [*gono*- + Gr. *rhein* to flow] infection due to *Neisseria gonorrhoeae* transmitted venereally in most cases, but also by contact with infected exudates in neonatal children at birth, or by infants in households with infected inhabitants. It is marked in males by urethritis with pain and purulent discharge, but is commonly asymptomatic in females, although it may extend to produce suppurative salpingitis, oophoritis, tubo-ovarian abscess, and peritonitis. Bacteremia occurs in both sexes, resulting in cutaneous lesions, arthritis, and rarely meningitis or endocarditis.

From the findings of fact, it appears that petitioner is guilty of no more than a series of erroneous diagnoses of **gonorrhea** which resulted from the use of a direct smear or gram stain test rather than a culture test; that the culture procedure is the most accurate and currently acceptable method of testing for the presence of **gonorrhea** in the female patient. Gentry v. Dep't of Pro. & Oc. Reg., St. Bd. of M.E., 293 So.2d 95, 97 (Dist.Ct. App.Fla.1974).

Gonyaulax (gon"e-aw'laks) a genus of protozoa of the order Dinoflagellata, class Phytomastigophora, found in salt, fresh, or brackish waters, and having yellow to brown chromatophores.

Gonyaulax catanella a poisonous flagellate protozoon which may cause *gonyaulax poisoning* and which helps to form the destructive red tide in the ocean. See also *gonyaulax poison*, under *poison*.

good health See *health, good*.

Goodpasture's syndrome See *syndrome, Goodpasture's*.

graft (graft) 1. any tissue or organ for implantation or transplantation. 2. to implant or transplant such tissues. See also *flap; site, donor;* and *transplantation*.

... she underwent a skin **graft** operation because a significant percentage of the burned area "continued to manifest itself as third degree." Holloway v. Hauver, 322 A.2d 890, 892 (Ct.Spec.App.Md.1974).

graft, bone a piece of bone taken from an animal or from some bone of the patient and used to take the place of a removed bone or bony defect. See also *autogenous; antigen* (Squibb case); *heterogenous;* and *homogenous*.

At that time Dr. Reidland decided that the union of the fracture was progressing slowly and that Guerra would have to be later hospitalized for a fusion. Guerra was hospitalized for the fourth time on April 12, 1969. At that time a **bone graft** was performed using bone taken from his hip and grafted into the fracture site of his leg. South Texas Natural Gas Gathering Co. v. Guerra, 469 S.W.2d 899, 915 (Ct.Civ.App.Tex.1971).

The relevant evidence adduced at trial was that, at the time of Mrs. Jordan's first operation, there were three different types of bones which Dr. Davis could have used for the grafting procedure: (1) [autogenous bone—bone coming from the patient's own body;] (2) [homogenous bone—human bone taken from another human being;] and (3) [heterogenous bone—bone from a species other than a human being (in this case, "Bo-plant").] It was established by experience, medical journals, and various other testimony and reports, that the order of effectiveness in grafting procedures such as this was autogenous, homogenous and then heterogenous bone, although at least one of appellant's witnesses testified that the use of "Bo-plant" proved to be as effective as homogenous bone. E.R. Squibb & Sons, Inc. v. Jordan, 254 So.2d 17, 19 (Dist.Ct.App. Fla.1971).

X-rays ... showed that the broken bones were not going to unite and Zipp was readmitted to Barnes Hospital on July 27 for **bone graft**. On July 28, an operation was performed, under general anesthetic, and bone from the iliac crest was packed around the fracture sites. Zipp v. Gasen's Drug Stores, Inc., 449 S.W.2d 612, 621 (Mo.1970).

graft, bypass See *bypass, femoropopliteal* (Walstad case).

graft, fillet flap See *amputation, closed* (Trovatten case).

graft, patch a graft of living tissue or prosthetic material used to close a vascular incision in order to enlarge the lumen of the vessel.

Dr. Lillehei found a small obstruction of the artery at the site of the incision made by Dr. Murray for the catheterization, which Dr. Lillehei rectified by taking a little piece of vein and patching the artery so as to widen it at that point (a **patch graft** angioplasty). During this operation it became apparent that Donna's collateral blood vessels were in poor condition as they did not satisfactorily serve as detours for blood flow to her lower leg. Walstad v. Univ. of Minnesota Hospitals, 442 F.2d 634, 637 (8th Cir. 1971).

graft, pinch a piece of skin about ¼ in. in diameter, obtained by elevating the skin with a needle and slicing it off with a knife; the thickness of the graft may vary, but it is always free of fat.

Although there were some unpleasant problems in relation to the graft, the graft appeared to be substantially successful with a supplemental **pinch graft** which was performed on 15 September 1971. Rowe v. Industrial Com'n, 510 P.2d 388, 392 (Ct.App.Ariz.1973).

graft, skin a piece of skin transplanted to replace a lost portion of the body skin surface; it may be a full-thickness, thick-split, or split-skin graft.

... a **skin graft** five inches long and one and one-half inches wide was taken from two places on plaintiff's right thigh and grafted onto the site of the wound in an attempt to close the hole. This procedure proved unsuccessful and resulted in further infection. Warmsley v. City of New York, 454 N.Y.S.2d 144–5 (2d Dep't 1982).

Joe Dial was taken to surgery under general anesthesia and an intermediate **skin graft** was made. An intermediate thickness **skin graft** is an area of skin which is $^{15}/_{1000}$ of an inch thick. It was taken from the patient and applied to the burned raw areas of his left upper and lower eyelids, his left cheek, his forehead and his nose. The grafts took quite well with no significant loss of the grafts. Wry v. Dial, 503 P.2d 979, 983 (Ct. App.Ariz.1972).

... all of the tissue and part of the bone of the right side of plaintiff's face had to be removed. To cover the exposed area, a massive **skin graft** was moved from the abdomen. The procedure entailed a series of stages over about a month's time, and caused the plaintiff extreme discomfort. Gorsalitz v. Olin Mathieson Chemical Corp., 429 F.2d 1033, 1044 (5th Cir. 1970).

graft, split-skin a skin graft consisting of only a portion of the skin thickness. See also *graft, skin*; and *graft, split-thickness*.

Michael pulled his father from the chair and extinguished the flames. However, plaintiff suffered second- and third-degree burns over 30 percent of his body. Ten surgical procedures were required to debride the burned area and apply **split-thickness skin grafts**. Christy v. Saliterman, 179 N.W.2d 288, 293 (Minn.1970).

graft, split-thickness a graft, varying in thickness, containing only mucosal elements and no subcutaneous tissues.

Between May 18 and July 10 the plaintiff underwent eight separate operations for the removal of dead bone and other tissue and procedures for the placement of **split-thickness skin grafts** over the open wounds. The skin for the grafts had a tissue paper diameter, and was taken from the plaintiff's upper thigh and abdomen....

During the plaintiff's stay at St. Bernard's, Dr. Kurth, a specialist in skin grafting, performed several operations, covering the raw areas with **split-thickness skin grafts**. The aim was to prevent the loss of body fluids, and to promote healing. The effect of removing skin from plaintiff's abdomen, hips and thighs for the graft was to leave these areas raw and painful....

... In his opinion, **split-thickness grafts**, which are only $^{10}/_{1000}$ to $^{16}/_{1000}$ of an inch and contain no subterraneous fat, would not support a prosthesis. At most, in his opinion, the plaintiff could hope for only limited mobility. Raines v. New York Central Railroad Co., 283 N.E.2d 230, 236–7 (Ill.1972).

Gram's method, stain, solution (gramz) [Hans Christian Joachim *Gram*, Danish physician, 1853–1938] See *Table of Stains and Staining Methods*, under *stain*, and see *gram-negative* and *gram-positive*.

gram-negative (gram-neg'ah-tiv) losing the stain or decolorized by alcohol in Gram's method of staining, a primary characteristic of bacteria having a cell wall surface more complex in chemical composition than do the gram-positive bacteria.

gram-positive (gram-poz'ĭ-tiv) retaining the stain or resisting decolorization by alcohol in Gram's method of staining, a primary characteristic of bacteria whose cell wall is composed of peptidoglycan and teichoic acid. See also *Gram's method* under *Table of Stains and Staining Methods*.

granulation tissue See *tissue, granulation*.

granuloma (gran"u-lo'mah) a tumor-like mass or nodule of granulation tissue, with actively growing fibroblasts and capillary buds, consisting of a collection of modified macrophages resembling epithelial cells (*epithelioid cells*), surrounded by a rim of mononuclear cells, chiefly lymphocytes and sometimes a center of giant multinucleate cells, either of the Langhans' or foreign body type; it is due to a chronic inflammatory process associated with infectious disease, such as tuberculosis (see *tubercle*), syphilis, sarcoidosis, leprosy, lymphogranuloma, etc., or with invasion by a foreign body.

Following the vasectomy plaintiff developed pain in the scrotal area. He returned to defendant who diagnosed a sperm **granuloma** on both sides. Medication failed to dissipate the sperm **granuloma** on the left side and it was surgically removed on February 21, 1977. Cowman v. Hornaday, 329 N.W.2d 422–4 (Iowa 1983).

The x-rays revealed that there is evidence of healed calcified **granulomotous** disease with minimal parenchymal scarring and slight overexpansion of the lungs consistent with chronic obstructive pulmonary disease. Swink v. Cone Mills, Inc., 300 S.E.2d 848, 850 (Ct.App.N.Car.1983).

Some time after the surgery, [a stapedectomy] Ramirez began to experience vertigo and a continued loss of hearing. To eliminate the condition, Ramirez underwent surgery a second time, in October 1973. The stapes prosthesis was removed. After the second operation, it was confirmed that Ramirez suffered a sensory hearing loss caused by a **granuloma**, a reaction to the stapes prosthesis that occurs in a small percentage of cases. Ramirez v. U.S., 567 F.2d 854–5 (9th Cir. 1977).

granuloma, thorium

In May of 1971 plaintiff was admitted to a hospital in New Mexico due to a progressive and recurrent abdominal pain. On May 15, 1971, plaintiff was diagnosed by the treating physicians to have a **thorium granuloma** with chylous peritonitis, a condition which plaintiff alleges was proximately caused by the injection of Thorotrast. Thrift v. Tenneco Chemicals, Inc., Heyden Div., 381 F.Supp. 543–4 (N.D.Tex.1974).

granulomatous (gran"u-lom'ah-tus) composed of granulomas.

Graves' disease See *disease, Graves'*.

gray (gra) a proposed unit of absorbed radiation dose equal to 100 rads. Abbreviated Gy.

grinding (grīnd'ing) rubbing together with force; wearing away or polishing by rubbing. See also *bruxism*.

grinding, selective the modification of the occlusal forms of teeth by grinding according to a plan.

He said, "These teeth look so much better rounded." And, with that he filed off the side of my lateral tooth....

... But, apparently, he was displeased. And, he came back, and he proceeded to round off this tooth that was down on a point. And, he tried to round it off to make it look right, I guess. And then, he went on to the other teeth so they would all kind of shape up....

... Upon examining tooth No. 10, he saw that "the contact points, the corners of the tooth were fractured off", i.e., the enamel around the dentin was fractured and the tooth shortened. Although he could not say whether that condition was caused by dental **grinding** or natural wear, it would be very unusual for that one tooth to wear down as he found it, i.e., the opposing lower tooth would exhibit similar wear, but it did not. Indeed, plaintiff's other teeth exhibited only normal wear. A dentist would not grind that much off unless treating a malocclusion, i.e., an improper bite, and then would inform the patient of the need for a return visit. Sullivan v. Russell, 338 N.W.2d 181, 183–4 (Mich.1983).

grip (grip) a grasping or seizing.

Because of residual weakness, Dr. Nawas commented, plaintiff is unable to execute a full **gripping** motion, has lost "some of the fine motions in his fingers," cannot make a fist, is unable to bring the tips of his fingers back towards his wrist, and "does not have the normal strength in the muscles to function normally, and to be able to carry heavy things like a regular person," the carrying ability of his hand being limited to "10 to 15 pounds." Harrelson v. Louisiana Pacific Corp., 434 So. 2d 479, 484–5 (Ct.App.La.1983).

groggy

Where a word has been used with intent that it convey a recognized meaning, then the meaning intended by the user must be accepted; and some other unintended meaning may not be inferred and imposed upon the user merely because it is also a recognized definition. There is no evidence to indicate that the patient's **grogginess** was other than described by the nurse, and other unintended meanings of the word "**groggy**" cannot supply the lack of evidence....

... Plaintiff insists that "**groggy**," means in a semi-comatose condition. The nurse who made the entry testified that she used "**groggy**" in its meaning of "unsteady" on the feet, and that this referred to difficulty in walking and standing because of intense back pain. No judicial definition of the word "**groggy**" has been found....

In Spivey v. St. Thomas Hospital, 31 Tenn.App. 12, 211 S.W.2d 450 (1947), cited by plaintiff, the patient was in delirium on admission and was not properly restrained. The case is not in point. "**Groggy**" does not mean "in delirium." Perkins v. Park View Hospital, Inc., 456 S.W.2d 276, 283–4 (Ct.App. Tenn.1970).

groin (groin) [L. *inguen*] the junctional region between the abdomen and thigh; called also *inguen* [NA].

The witness was then asked to define the word "groin" as to precise location and he replied: "I placed it [the milliroentgen chamber] between the legs as far up as it was possible to place it." Chiropractic Ass'n of New York, Inc. v. Hilleboe, 227 N.Y.S.2d 309, 338 (Sup.Ct.Albany Cty.1961).

guanethidine (gwan-eth'ĭ-dēn) chemical name: [2-(hexahydro-1(2*H*)-azocinyl)ethyl]guanidine; an adrenergic blocking agent, $C_{10}H_{22}N_4$, which has prolonged and marked hypotensive effects.

Guanethedine [sic] is a very potent antihypertensive drug which lowers blood pressure in even the most severe cases where the patient has not responded adequately to other medication. U.S. v. Ciba Geigy Corp., 508 F.Supp. 1118, 1154 (D.N.J.1976).

guanidine (gwan'ĭ-din) a poisonous base, the amidine of amino carbamic acid, $NH:C(NH_2)_2$.

guarded, long term

His prognosis was "short term—favorable, long term—guarded." By "long term—guarded" he meant that his long term prognosis was unpredictable. Exxon Corp. v. Brecheen, 519 S.W.2d 170, 178 (Ct.Civ.App.Tex.1975), reversed 526 S.W.2d 519.

guide (gīd) a device by which another object is led in its proper course, such as a grooved sound, or a filiform bougie over which a tunneled sound is passed, as in stricture of the urethra.

guide wire

The **guide wire** used in the procedure on plaintiff was known to the radiologists as a "large one." Depending on where it was measured, its outside diameter was from .0526 to .0527 of an inch. The tolerance of Kifa wires was from 52 to 54½. Converted to inches, this meant a diameter of from 52 thousandths to 54.5 thousandths. Thus the wire used on Mrs. Frerker fell within this tolerance. Picker X-Ray Corp. v. Frerker, 405 F.2d 916, 918 (8th Cir. 1969).

Guillain-Barre syndrome See *polyneuritis, acute febrile*.

gusset

The surgical wound was reopened and Dr. Spense created a **gusset** to allow the spinal cord greater room in which to pulsate. Canterbury v. Spence, 464 F.2d 772, 777 (D.C.Cir. 1972).

gutta-percha (gut"ah-per'chah) [USP] the coagulated, dried, purified latex of trees of the genera *Palaguium* and *Payena*, most commonly *Palaguium gutta;* used as a dental restoration agent and in orthopedics for fracture splints.

The second method [of obturation] is referred to as **gutta percha**. This method also consists of the placement of an inert substance into the pulp chamber and root canal. U.S. v. Talbott, 460 F.Supp. 253, 257 (S.D.Ohio 1978).

Gy See *gray*.

Gymnodinium (jim"no-din'e-um) a genus of protozoa of the order Dinoflagellata, class Phytomastigophora, most species of which have many colored (yellow, brown, green, or blue) chromatophores. They inhabit salt, fresh, or brackish waters and, when present in great numbers, cause the discoloration known as red tide, which may result in the death of many fish and invertebrates.

Expert testimony elicited by the County unveiled the ominous possibility of an outbreak of the Red Tide in Biscayne Bay simi-

lar to the one presently affecting the Tampa Bay region. The Red Tide is caused by a marine dinoflagellate, **gymnodium brevis**, [sic] which requires a high degree of phosphates to flourish. Once the Red Tide organism blooms, it secretes a toxin which kills fish and poses other serious health hazards. Soap and Detergent Ass'n v. Clark, 330 F.Supp. 1218, 1220–1 (S.D. Fla.1971).

H

habit (hab'it) [L. *habitus*, from *habere* to hold] predisposition or bodily temperament; see under *type*.

habituation (hah-bit″u-a′shun) a condition resulting from the repeated consumption of a drug, with a desire to continue its use, but with little or no tendency to increase the dose; there may be psychic, but no physical dependence on the drug, and detrimental effects, if any, are primarily on the individual.

habitus (hab′ĭ-tus) [L. "habit"] physique; see also under *habit* and *type*.

Hageman factor See *factor, coagulation, XII.*

hair See *ammonia thioglycolate* (Hussey case).

hallucination (hah-lu″sĭ-na′shun) [L. *hallucinatio;* Gr. *alyein* to wander in the mind] a sense perception without a source in the external world; a perception of an external stimulus object in the absence of such an object. See also *pentazocine.*

hallucinogen (hah-lu′sĭ-no-jen″) [*hallucin*ation + Gr. *gennan* to produce] an agent which induces hallucinations. See also *lysergide* (Brinkley case).

The main characteristic which unites the **hallucinogens** is the alteration of the perception of the user. (See V. Uelmen and G. Haddox, Drug Abuse and the Law 77–80 (1974); Note, "Hallucinogens," 68 Colum.L.Rev. 521 (1968)). Although the specific effects of a substance such as psilocyn vary according to the user and according to the circumstances under which the psilocyn is taken (Panton and Fischer, "Hallucinogenic Drug-Induced Behavior Under Sensory Attenuation," 28 Archives of Gen. Psychiatry 434 (1973)), some generalizations can be made. As Dr. Siegel testified, individuals often initially feel a sense of euphoria, which gives way to a distortion of perception. Siegel stated that blurred vision occurs, accompanied by a more vivid perception of colors. Sounds may be "seen" and colors may be "heard;" this effect is known as synesthesia. While sources disagree concerning the frequency of **hallucinations**, in which the individual sees objects which are not there, it is apparent that they do occur. More common appear to be alterations of the individual's perception of space and time relationships. This, according to Dr. Siegel, would seriously affect a person's ability to judge distances. People v. Dunlap, 442 N.E.2d 1379, 1387 (App.Ct.Ill.1982).

Section 404.01(3), F.S., originally enacted as Section 2, Chapter 67–136, reads as follows:

(3) The words "**hallucinogenic** drug" mean "cannabis" as defined in subsection (12), "lysergic acid" and "lysergic acid

amide", "LSD" (lysergic acid diethylamide), "DMT" (dimethyltryptamine), "peyote", "mescaline", "psilocyn", "psilocybin", including their salts and derivatives, or any compounds, mixtures and every substance neither chemically nor physically distinguishable from them, and any and all derivatives of same and any other drug to which the drug abuse laws of the United States apply, and rivea corymbosa (ololiuqui) when used as a **hallucinogen**.

We believe that it would be improper to arbitrarily permit a substantive inclusion by reference into the reach of a Florida statute of a particular item embraced in a subsequently enacted or adopted federal law or federal administrative rule, whether it involved a specific drug, article in trade, a new federal regulation, or provision of law or other conceivable thing or subject merely by virtue of the adoption of the biennial revision of prior general laws which includes the pertinent original Florida law. State v. Camil, 279 So.2d 832–4 (Fla.1973).

The drugs psilocybin, peyote, mescaline and what is commonly called LSD are examples of the **hallucinogens**. People v. Mc-Cabe, 275 N.E.2d 407, 411 (Ill.1971).

hallux (hal′uks), pl. *hal′luces* [L.] [NA] the great toe, or first digit of the foot.

hallux rigidus painful flexion deformity of the great toe in which there is limitation of motion at the metatarsophalangeal joint.

For nearly two years prior to her December 27, 1979 application for disability insurance benefits, she complained of pain and swelling in her left foot. She was admitted April 11, 1979 to The Parkway Hospital where she was diagnosed as suffering from **hallux rigidus** of the left foot and underwent surgery for the removal of a benign bone growth on her big toe. Varela v. Secretary of Health and Human Services, 711 F.2d 482–3 (2d Cir. 1983).

hallux valgus angulation of the great toe away from the midline of the body, or toward the other toes; the great toe may ride under or over the other toes.

The orthopedic effect asserted for the modification in the specifications is that, by providing "an anatomically correct positioning of the toes when the sandal is put on," the modification "prevent[s] the formation of crooked toes, and alleviate[s] or counteract[s] conditions such as **hallux valgus**." Scholl, Inc. v. S. S. Kresge Co., 580 F.2d 244, 247 (7th Cir. 1978).

halogen (hal′o-jen, ha′lo-jen) [*halo-* + Gr. *gennan* to produce] an element of a closely related chemical family, all

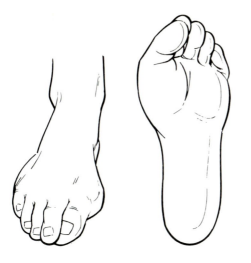

Hallux valgus.

of which form similar (saltlike) compounds in combination with sodium and most other metals. The halogens are bromine, chlorine, fluorine, iodine, and astatine.

All halogenated anesthetics contain **halogens** which are a group of elements consisting primarily of fluorine and bromine. Carlsen v. Javurek, 526 F.2d 202, 204 (8th Cir. 1975).

haloperidol (hah″lo-per′ĭ-dol) [USP] chemical name: 4-[4-(4-chlorophenyl)-4-hydroxy-1-piperidinyl]-1-butanone. A tranquilizer, $C_{21}H_{23}ClFNO_2$, which also has antiemetic, hypotensive, and hypothermic actions, occurring as a white to faintly yellowish, amorphous or microcrystalline powder; used especially in the management of psychoses and for the control of the vocal utterances and tics of Gilles de la Tourette's syndrome, administered orally and intramuscularly.

When B. earlier received **Haldol**, he said he slept up to 20 hours a day. The medical literature describes excessive drowsiness as a relatively common side effect of **Haldol** and other psychotropic drugs. Matter of B, 383 A.2d 760, 761 (Super. Ct.N.J.1977).

halothane (hal′o-thān) [USP] chemical name: 2-bromo-2-chloro-1,1,1-trifluoroethane. A general anesthetic, $C_2HBrClF_3$, occurring as a colorless, mobile, nonflammable, heavy liquid; administered by inhalation.

She was operated on the next day, at which time she received **halothane**, an anesthetic which defendant's expert testified is used in one-third of all operations, and is considered in most instances particularly safe and effective. This was the second time in her life that **halothane** had been administered to her, the first being in 1964. The April hernia repair was not completely satisfactory, and Mrs. Coffran was re-admitted on June 4, 1970 for further surgery. During the operation on June 5, she again received **halothane**. After returning home, she became jaundiced about June 15 . . . .

Although it was known in 1970 that a tiny number of patients who received **halothane** later contracted hepatitis, there was

some question among experts within the medical profession whether the hepatitis was actually caused by the **halothane**. Those who believed that **halothane** caused hepatitis—and the evidence suggests that the believers outnumbered the disbelievers—posited a ''sensitization'' theory, as follows. A patient who is susceptible to **halothane** hepatitis is sensitized to **halothane** by exposure; there is no hepatitis at this time. After a subsequent exposure to **halothane**, however, the sensitized patient does contract hepatitis. This sensitization process is to be distinguished from direct toxic disease reactions, whereby liver damage is caused by the first exposure to a drug, and by a very different mechanism. Those doctors who did not accept the validity of the **halothane** sensitization thesis believed that **halothane** had been mistakenly incriminated in cases of viral hepatitis which became clinically evident after operations using **halothane**. Regardless of whether the **halothane** actually caused the hepatitis, or was merely innocently associated with it, the incidence of hepatitis following use of **halothane** was very rare: one study of fatal hepatic occurrences reported only nine otherwise unexplained fatal hepatic occurrences out of 250,000 administrations of **halothane**. Coffran v. Hitchcock Clinic, Inc., 683 F.2d 5, 7 (1st Cir. 1982).

Fluothane is the trade name for the anesthetic; **halothane** is its generic name. It is a widely used and nearly ideal anesthetic agent. . . .

Dr. Knutson had never had a patient suffer liver failure as a result of administration of **Fluothane** in some 20,000 operations, including successive uses of the anesthetic within 30 and 60 days. It was his opinion that **Fluothane** could be used successively in a 30-day period. He also was aware of the results of the National Halothane Study, which found **Fluothane** to be a comparatively safe anesthetic. . . .

. . . Dr. Wier, an anesthesiologist, would have testified that ''the warning was inadequate [in] that it did not advise anesthesiologists that if **Halothane** was to be administered on successive occasions within a thirty to ninety day period of time that [they] should . . . perform certain liver tests in order to rule out whether or not there has been a hypersensitivity reaction to **Halothane** on the first administration.'' Cornfeldt v. Tongen, 262 N.W.2d 684, 690, 698 (Minn.1977).

hammering See *toe, hammer.*

hammertoe See *toe, hammer.*

hand (hand) [L. *manus*] the part of the upper limb distal to the forearm: the carpus, metacarpus, and fingers together; called also *manus* [NA]. See also *finger* (Lykouras case).

M.C.L. § 418.361(2); M.S.A. § 17.237(361)(2), provides in pertinent part:

''(h) **Hand**, 215 weeks.

''(i) **Arm**, 269 weeks.

''An amputation between the elbow and wrist that is 6 or more inches below the elbow shall be considered a **hand**, and an amputation above that, point shall be considered an arm. . . .

. . . Because there are two bones ''below the elbow'' and because the top of the radius is below the top of the ulna, we hold that the length of the radius is the measurement called for in M.C.L. § 418.361, subds. (2)(h) and (2)(i); M.S.A.

§ 17.237(361), subds. (2)(h) and (2)(i). Dobbs v. Villa Capri Restaurant, 329 N.W.2d 503–6 (Ct.App.Mich.1982).

During his hospitalization at Oschner he was also operated on by an orthopedist who did a tendon transfer from the brachial radialis to the extensor carpi to help improve the use of his **hand** which was virtually useless because of extreme weakness of his fingers. Warner v. City of Bay St. Louis, 408 F.Supp. 375, 379–80 (S.D.Miss.1975).

hand, trench contracture or other incapacity of the hand from frostbite in the trenches; called also *main de tranchées.*

. . . a condition in his hands which his physician referred to as **trenchhand** or cold-exposure arteritis, a condition of insufficient blood supply to an extremity. His fingers had become chronically sore, cold and at times extremely painful. Sears, Roebuck & Co. v. Workmen's Comp. Appeal Bd., 409 A.2d 486–7 (Commonwealth Ct.Pa.1979).

Hand Board

After several weeks, when no improvement was shown, Kalar was referred to the "**Hand Board**" of the Industrial Commission of Arizona. This board consists of physicians who specialize in the treatment of the hand, wrist, and arm, and who advise the Commission as to treatment and determine for the Commission the percent of disability from an injury. Carroll v. Kalar, 545 P.2d 411–13 (Ariz.1976).

handicap (han'dǐ-kap) any physical or mental defect or characteristic, congenital or acquired, preventing or restricting a person from participating in normal life or limiting his capacity to work.

K.S.A.1974 Supp. 44–566(b) provided in part:
"A '**handicapped** employee' means one afflicted with or subject to any physical or mental impairment, or both, whether congenital or due to an injury or disease of such character the impairment constitutes a **handicap** in obtaining employment or would constitute a **handicap** in obtaining reemployment if the employee should become unemployed and his **handicap** is due to any of the following diseases or conditions
"16. Any physical deformity or abnormality;
"17. Any other physical impairment, disorder or disease, physical or mental, which is established as constituting a **handicap** in obtaining or in retaining employment." Hinton v. S. S. Kresge Co., 592 P.2d 471, 473–4 (Ct.App.Kan.1978).

(c) "Physically **handicapped** child" means a person under twenty-one years of age who, by reason of a physical defect or infirmity, whether congenital or acquired by accident, injury or disease, is or may be expected to be totally or partially incapacitated for education or for remunerative occupation, as provided in the education law, or is physically **handicapped**, as provided in section two thousand five hundred eighty-one of the public health law. [Family Ct. Act. § 232(c).]. . .

. . . Until 1967, Education Law § 4401 defined physically **handicapped** children in words identical to those in § 232(c) of the Family Court Act, supra. In 1967, Education Law § 4401 was amended (L.1967, c. 786, § 3) to eliminate the distinction between physical and other **handicaps** and to make explicit that the definition encompassed children **handicapped** for "emotional reasons". The purpose was to provide "a simple definition which [was] intended to cover all **handicaps**, whether physical, mental or emotional".[3] At the same time, the qualifying word "physically" was deleted before the word "**handicapped**" in § 4403 of the Education Law which relates to Family Court proceedings. L.1967, c. 786, § 3. [[3] Memorandum of Senator J. Speno, 1967 N.Y.State Legis.Annual 130.] In Matter of Jessup, 379 N.Y.S.2d 626, 630 (Fam.Ct. N.Y.Cty.1975).

References are to K.S.A.
44–566(4) defines a "**handicapped** employee" as a person afflicted with or subject to any physical or mental impairment, or both, whether congenital or due to an injury or disease of such character that the impairment constitutes a **handicap** in obtaining employment or would constitute a **handicap** in obtaining re-employment if the employee should become unemployed, and his **handicap** is due to any of sixteen enumerated diseases or conditions—among them being "physical deformity". Hardwick v. General Motors Corp., 476 P.2d 244–5 (Kan.1970).

handicapped See *disabled, permanently and totally.*

handicapped child

"The Family Court (also) has jurisdiction over physically handicapped children" (Family Court Act § 232(a)), and over "proceedings concerning physically handicapped and mentally defective or retarded children" (Family Court Act § 115, subd. (b))

"(c) 'Physically handicapped child' means a person under twenty-one years of age who, by reason of physical defect or infirmity, whether congenital or acquired by accident, injury or disease, is or may be expected to be totally or partially incapacitated for education or for remunerative occupation, as provided in the education law, or is physically handicapped, as provided in section two thousand five hundred eighty-one of the public health law" (Family Court Act § 232, subd. (c)).

"As defined in the Education Law "A '**handicapped child**' is one who, because of mental, physical or emotional reasons, cannot be educated in regular classes but can benefit by special services and programs to include, but not limited to, transportation, the payment of tuition to boards of cooperative educational services and public school districts, home teaching, special classes, special teachers, and resource rooms." (Education Law § 4401, subd. 1).

"Physically handicapped children" are defined in the Public Health Law as follows: "As used in this article: 1. 'Physically handicapped children' means any person under twenty-one years of age who are handicapped by reason of a defect or disability, whether congenital or acquired by accident, injury, or disease, or who are suffering from long-term disease, including but without limiting the generality of the foregoing, cystic fibrosis, muscular dystrophy, nephrosis, rheumatic fever and rheumatic heart disease, blood dyscrasies, cancer, brain injured, and chronic asthma, or from any disease or condition likely to result in a handicap in the absence of treatment, provided, however, no child shall be deprived of a service under the provisions of this chapter solely because of the degree of mental retardation." (Public Health Law § 2581). In Re Sampson, 317 N.Y.S.2d 641, 647–8 (Fam.Ct.Ulster Cty.1970).

handicapped individual

(7)(A) Except as otherwise provided in subparagraph (B), the term "handicapped individual" means any individual who (i) has a physical or mental disability which for such individual constitutes or results in a substantial handicap to employment and (ii) can reasonably be expected to benefit in terms of employability from vocational rehabilitation services provided pursuant to subchapters I and III of this chapter.

(B) Subject to the second sentence of this subparagraph, the term "handicapped individual" means, for purposes of subchapters IV and V of this chapter, any person who (i) has a physical or mental impairment which substantially limits one or more of such person's major life activities, (ii) has a record of such an impairment, or (iii) is regarded as having such an impairment. For purposes of sections 793 and 794 of this title as such sections relate to employment, such term does not include any individual who is an alcoholic or drug abuser whose current use of alcohol or drugs prevents such individual from performing the duties of the job in question or whose employment, by reason of such current alcohol or drug abuse, would constitute a direct threat to property or the safety of others. 29 U.S. C.A. § 706(7).

hang-up

The patient states she had (**hang up**) in the knees and the left elbow. By **hang up** the patient means the knee will not move and she does not have use of the knees or elbow. Dean v. Califano, 439 F.Supp. 730, 733 (W.D.Ark.1977).

Hansen's disease See *leprosy.*

Hansen-Street intramedullary rod See under *rod.*

hardening of the arteries See *arteriosclerosis.*

harm

Harm with reference to a living, active structure (as the body is) means essentially that the structure no longer functions as it should. **Harm** also embraces the impairment of use or control of physical structures directly caused by the accident. Bailey v. American General Insurance Company [279 S.W.2d 315 (Tex. 1955)]. Hartford Acc. & Indem. Co. v. Thurmond, 527 S.W.2d 180, 188 (Ct.Civ.App.Tex.1975).

harm, injury distinguished from See *injury* (Hall case).

Hashimoto's disease, struma, thyroiditis (hash″ĭ-mo′tōz) [Hakaru *Hashimoto*, Japanese surgeon, 1881–1934] struma lymphomatosa.

hashish (hash-ēsh′) [Arabic "herb"] a preparation of the unadulterated resin scraped from the flowering tops of cultivated female hemp plants, *Cannabis sativa* L. (Cannabaceae), which is smoked or chewed for its intoxicating effects. It is far more potent than marihuana. See *cannabis.* Also referred to as *charas* or *churus.*

The hash oil extraction procedure is contrasted to the procedure for obtaining **hashish** from the cannabis plant. **Hashish** is a resin which is oozed out of the flowery part of the plant, collected, and pressed into bricks. **Hashish** generally contains a higher concentration of THC than that found in the cannabis plant as a whole. The crime lab classifies **hashish** as marijuana rather than Schedule I THC because **hashish** retains plant fi-

bers, i.e., the "gross morphological features" of the cannabis plant. Aycock v. The State, 246 S.E.2d 489 (App.Ct.Ga.1978).

The State produced Gary Ray Howell, the chief forensic chemist of the Regional Crime Laboratory. Mr. Howell stated **hashish** is defined as an extraction of the active ingredients of marihuana. He stated "so the absence of plant material plus the presence of the extractable tetrahydrocannabinol and other cannabinoids would be **hashish**." At another point Mr. Howell stated he distinguished between marihuana and **hashish** mostly by physical appearance. He stated "if it is not a green leafy material and shows to be an extraction under the microscope, it is **hashish**." Mr. Howell further stated **hashish** would be the result if the plant material were destroyed and then pressed into a fine block which would result in a pressed block of material high in concentration of tetrahydrocannabinol "THC". Mr. Howell also referred to **hashish** as a refined form of marihuana. . . .

The other chemist produced by the State, Edward Covey, stated **hashish** is a form of marihuana. . . .

. . . Since **hashish** is included in the definition of marihuana, there is no separate crime for the possession of **hashish**, and the conviction on Count 2 for possession of **hashish** is reversed. State v. Randall, 540 S.W.2d 156, 158–9 (Mo.Ct. App., Kansas City Dist.1976).

Hauser procedure, modified

The defendant performed a "**Modified Hauser**" surgical procedure which has the effect of realigning the entire mechanism controlling the kneecap in order to correct the attendant knee dislocation. During the operation a pneumatic tourniquet was applied to plaintiff's leg for the purpose of facilitating the operation procedure by cutting off the blood supply to the leg to create a dry (bloodless) surgical field. Following surgery plaintiff's leg was wrapped with a padded dressing consisting of expandable bandage extending from the toes to the groin. . . .

. . . Dr. Johnson did not believe that the surgical incision made in performing the **Modified Hauser procedure** could have caused the problem because the incision is made "anteriorly and far away from where the nerves are." Hale v. Venuto, 187 Cal.Rptr. 357, 359–60 (Ct.App.Cal.1982).

hazard

Hazard is a function of toxicity and exposure and is the probability that injury will result from the use of a substance in a given formulation, quantity, or manner. If taken in sufficient quantities, even water will cause death. Florida Peach Grow. Ass'n v. U.S. Dept. of Lab., 489 F.2d 120, 131 (5th Cir. 1974).

hazardous substance See *substance, hazardous.*

Hb symbol for *hemoglobin.*

HCT hematocrit.; hydrochlorothiazide.

headache See *clavus hystericus.*

Heaf test [England] See *test, tuberculin Sterneedle.*

health (helth) a state of optimal physical, mental, and social well-being, and not merely the absence of disease and infirmity.

health, good

"In connection with the above Special Issue you are instructed that **GOOD HEALTH** does not mean perfect health, but means state of health free from any disease or bodily infirmity of substantial nature which affects general soundness and healthfulness of system seriously or materially increases risk to be assumed by the insurance company."

The defendant did not object to this definition. State Reserve Life Ins. Co. v. Ives, 535 S.W.2d 400, 403 (Ct.Civ.App.Tex. 1976).

You are instructed that by the term "**Good Health**" as used here, is meant "A state of health free from any disease or bodily infirmity of a substantial nature which affects the general soundness and healthfulness of the system seriously, or materially increased the risk to be assumed by the insured." Prudential Insurance Co. of America v. Beaty, 456 S.W.2d 164–5 (Ct.Civ.App.Tex.1970).

Admittedly, the term "**good health**" as used in life policies such as that issued to Mr. Britton is a relative one, but in my opinion, it is a matter of common knowledge that any person suffering from angina to the extent that it is necessary to take a powerful drug in order to dilate the blood vessels cannot be said to be in "**good health**". Great American Reserve Ins. Co. v. Britton, 406 S.W.2d 901, 908 (Tex.1966).

hearing aid See *aid, hearing.*

hearing loss (hēr-ing los') partial or complete loss of hearing. See also *audiogram; chloroquine; deafness; neomycin;* and *nervus tympanicus.*

While in the hospital she was examined and treated by Dr. I. Novak for bilateral **hearing loss**, which was revealed by an audiogram indicating mixed conductive and sensory neuro **hearing loss** on the right with pure tone of 58 decibels and sensory neuro **hearing loss** on the left with pure tone of 27 decibels. Adams v. Schweiker, 557 F.Supp. 1373, 1376–7 (S.D.Tex.1983).

It also sets forth the formula to be followed in measuring the **hearing loss.** U.C.A., 1953, § 35–2–60 reenacts the identical formula verbatim, which reads as follows:

In measuring **hearing loss,** a medical panel of medical and paramedical professionals appointed by the commission shall measure the loss in each ear at the three frequencies 500, 1000 and 2000 cycles per second which shall be added together and divided by three to determine the average decibel loss. To allow for presbycusis, there shall be deducted from the average decibel loss one-half a decibel for each year of the employee's age over forty at the time of the last exposure to harmful industrial noise. To determine the percentage of **hearing loss** in each ear, (after deduction of the loss in decibels for presbycusis) the average decibel loss for each decibel of loss exceeding fifteen decibels shall be multiplied by 1½% up to the maximum of 100% which is reached at 82 decibels. Wayman v. Western Coal Carrier Corp., 665 P.2d 1294–5 (Utah 1983).

Prior to a hearing on Fishel's claim, the parties stipulated, inter alia, that the nature and extent of the injury was a noise induced, occupationally-related **hearing loss**, and that a portion of the total **hearing loss** arose out of and in the course of Fishel's employment at Newport News. Newport News Ship-

building & Dry Dock Co. v. Fishel, 694 F.2d 327–8 (4th Cir. 1982).

Other Authorities: Capaldi v. Weinberger, 391 F.Supp. 502, 504–5 (E.D.Pa.1975); Portis v. U.S., 483 F.2d 670–1 (4th Cir. 1973); Petition of United States, 303 F.Supp. 1282, 1328 (E.D.N.Car.1969); Rubley v. Louisville & Nashville Ry. Co., 208 F.Supp. 798, 800 (E.D.Tenn.1962).

hearing loss, conductive hearing loss due to a defect of the sound conducting apparatus, i.e., of the external auditory canal or middle ear. Called also *transmission h.l.*

Air conduction deafness, first means the inability to hear sounds transmitted through the air to the ear drum, and then through the small bones of the middle ear to the oval window. Sound vibrations may also be conducted through the bone of the skull, but low-volume conversation cannot practically be sensed through such transmission. Hearing aids often are useful for persons who have good bone conductive hearing, because they boost the sound volume sufficiently to cause vibrations of the inner ear fluid through bone transmission of the sound vibrations. Sensineural deafness, damage to the nerve, is not remedial. (N.T. 91–92). Warshaw v. Trans World Airlines, Inc., 442 F.Supp. 400, 402–3 (E.D.Pa.1977).

hearing loss, perceptive See *deafness, sensorineural.*

hearing loss, sensorineural hearing loss due to a defect in the inner ear or the acoustic nerve. See also under *deafness.*

hearing loss, transmission See *hearing loss, conductive.*

heart (hart) [L. *cor;* Gr. *kardia*] the viscus of cardiac muscle that maintains the circulation of the blood. Called also *cor* [NA]. It is divided into four cavities—two atria and two ventricles. The left atrium receives oxygenated blood from the lungs. From there the blood passes to the left ventricle, which forces it via the aorta through the arteries to supply the tissues of the body. The right atrium receives the blood after it has passed through the tissues and given up much of its oxygen. The blood then passes to the right ventricle, and then to the lungs, to be oxygenated. The major valves are four in number: the *left atrioventricular* (*bicuspid,* or *mitral*), between the left atrium and ventricle; the *right atrioventricular* (*tricuspid*), between the right atrium and ventricle; the *aortic,* at the orifice of the aorta; and the *pulmonary,* at the orifice of the pulmonary trunk. The heart tissue itself is nourished by the blood in the coronary arteries. See illustration.

The **heart** is simply a mechanical pump, like any other mechanical pump, which requires energy in the form of blood and oxygen in order to do its job. It normally, at rest, the **heart** is working at about 30% of its capacity. As physical or occasionally emotional activity increases, the **heart** simply responds by increasing the cardiac output in order to meet the demand that the body and its tissues are demanding. The **heart** will do this, in a manner of speaking, with total disrespect for its own welfare. If there is significant atherosclerosis of the coronary arteries and the **heart** continues to try to meet the demands that are placed on it, then eventually in many cases, the cardiac muscle becomes ischemic [deprived of adequate blood supply] and this can lead to death of the muscle cells or

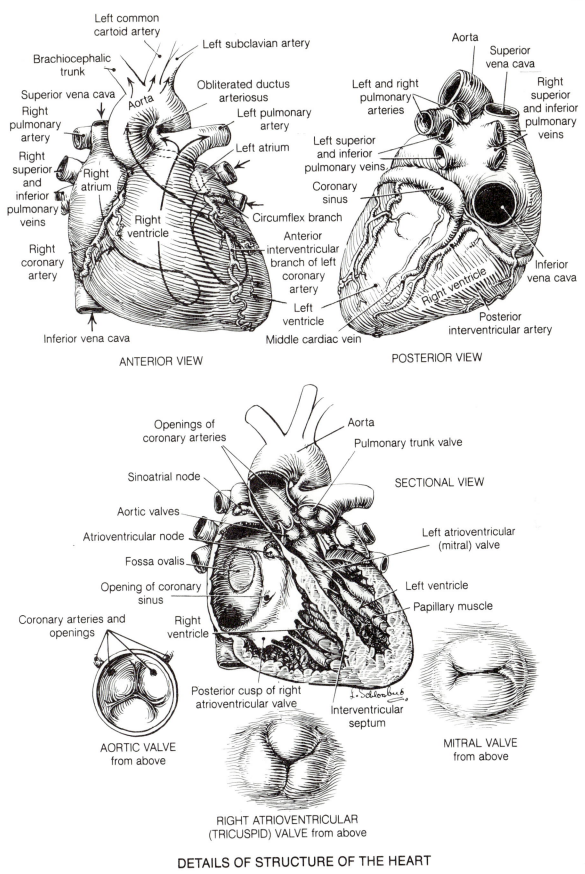

ANTERIOR VIEW

Left common cartoid artery
Left subclavian artery
Brachiocephalic trunk
Obliterated ductus arteriosus
Superior vena cava
Aorta
Right pulmonary artery
Left pulmonary artery
Left atrium
Right superior and inferior pulmonary veins
Right atrium
Right ventricle
Circumflex branch
Anterior interventricular branch of left coronary artery
Right coronary artery
Left ventricle
Inferior vena cava
Middle cardiac vein

POSTERIOR VIEW

Aorta
Superior vena cava
Left and right pulmonary arteries
Right superior and inferior pulmonary veins
Left superior and inferior pulmonary veins
Coronary sinus
Inferior vena cava
Right ventricle
Posterior interventricular artery

SECTIONAL VIEW

Openings of coronary arteries
Aorta
Pulmonary trunk valve
Sinoatrial node
Aortic valves
Left atrioventricular (mitral) valve
Atrioventricular node
Fossa ovalis
Opening of coronary sinus
Left ventricle
Papillary muscle
Right ventricle
Coronary arteries and openings
Posterior cusp of right atrioventricular valve
Interventricular septum

AORTIC VALVE from above

RIGHT ATRIOVENTRICULAR (TRICUSPID) VALVE from above

MITRAL VALVE from above

DETAILS OF STRUCTURE OF THE HEART

a heart attack. Kempner's and Dodson Ins. Co. v. Hall, 646 S.W.2d 31, 33 (Ct.App.Ark.1983).

Dr. Becker further testified that "the **heart** is an active pumping organ which goes basically through two phases of action, one is the active contraction of the heart muscle which results in a pumping out of a blood volume which has collected inside the heart chamber. This part of the active contraction we call 'systole.'

"Then, after the contraction, the heart muscle basically relaxes and is filled with a blood volume which it has to pump out again. This is called 'diastole.'...'' Woodall Industries, Inc. v. Massachusetts Mutual Life Insurance Co., 483 F.2d 986, 993 (6th Cir. 1973).

The autopsy disclosed that Brown's **heart** was tremendously enlarged, "about some of the largest we have seen." Its weight was 725 grams as compared to about 300 grams for a normal man of Brown's size and age. Brown v. U.S., 419 F.2d 337, 340 (8th Cir. 1969).

heart, artificial a pumping mechanism that duplicates the output, rate, and blood pressure of the natural heart. It may replace the function of the entire heart or a portion of it, and may be an intracorporeal, extracorporeal, or paracorporeal heart.

Medical history was made in 1969 when Dr. Denton A. Cooley, a thoracic surgeon, implanted the first totally mechanical heart in 47-year-old Haskell Karp. This threshold orthotopic cardiac prosthesis also spawned this medical malpractice suit by Mr. Karp's wife, individually and as executrix of Mr. Karp's estate, and his children, for the patient's wrongful death....

In the event cardiac function cannot be restored by excision of destroyed heart muscle and plastic reconstruction of the ventricle and death seems imminent, I authorize Dr. Cooley and his staff to remove my diseased heart and insert a mechanical cardiac substitute. I understand that this mechanical device will not be permanent and ultimately will require replacement by a heart transplant. I realize that this device has been tested in the laboratory but has not been used to sustain a human being and that no assurance of success can be made.

"I said, 'what's mechanical device?'

"And he said, 'well you know, Mrs. Karp, when we operate on a heart we have to take the heart out of the body. So what we do is use what's commonly known as a heart lung machine and we attach the pipes from the machine to the different arteries that they sever to take the heart out. And this here keeps the flow of blood going through the body and the oxygen so that there will not be any damage to the body.'

"So he says the reason that he put that into the consent was because the one that they had in the operating room, I believe he said, worked for a matter of maybe two hours or something and this here one was a new model and it was proven in the laboratory, but he [sic] hasn't been used on a human being yet. But that this here should sustain him if he should die on the table. He says it would sustain him for at least thirty minutes in order to get the donor heart into my husband's body."

Mrs. Karp also testified that Dr. Cooley did not state that the device was any different from the heart-lung device ordinarily used for open heart surgery, stating that it was a "newer model" that had not been used before. She said Dr. Cooley told her there was a donor heart available in a nearby hospital, and that the mechanical device would be used for only 30 minutes while the donor was being prepared.

... Dr. Cooley described his discussion of this device:

I told him that it was a heart pump similar to the one that we used in open-heart surgery; that it was a reciprocating-type pump with the membrane, in which the pumping element never became in contact with the bloodstream; that it was designed in such a manner that it would not damage the bloodstream or it would cause minimal damage to the bloodstream; that it would be placed in his body to take over the function of the dead heart and to propel blood throughout his body during this interim until we could have a heart transplant.

... I told him that we had been successful in keeping an animal alive for more than forty hours with the device, but that this was a calf. It was a 300-pound animal in which the demands on the pump were far greater than would be in the human body, and that I was reasonably confident that this device would sustain his life until we could get a heart transplant. But no guarantees were made at all." [Footnote omitted.] Karp v. Cooley, 493 F.2d 408 (5th Cir. 1974).

heart attack See *heart failure.*

heart block (hart'blok) impairment of conduction in heart excitation; often applied specifically to atrioventricular heart block (q.v.).

heart block, atrioventricular a form in which the block occurs in the atrioventricular junctional tissue (atrioventricular node, bundle of His, or its branches); it is called *first degree h.b.* when conduction time is prolonged but all atrial beats are followed by ventricular beats; *second degree (partial) h.b.* when some, but not all, atrial beats are conducted; and *third degree (complete) h.b.* when no impulses whatsoever are conducted by the junctional tissues, owing to pathologic factors. The condition may be permanent or paroxysmal and if syncopal attacks occur, it is known as *Adams-Stokes disease.*

heart block, bundle-branch a form in which one ventricle is excited before the other because of absence of conduction in one of the branches of the bundle of His.

Dr. Petrie testified, however, that he had noticed no heart murmur during his physical examinations of the defendant. He did not testify as to what disease or disability a heart murmur might indicate. He testified that the **bundle branch block** was "a normal variance in a small percentage of people" and that, as a cardiologist, he did not feel the need to investigate it further because the defendant did not show any symptoms. City of Rochester v. Smith, 403 A.2d 421, 423 (N.H.1979).

heart disease [classification] See *classification, functional.*

heart disease, congenital

Q. Now, I am curious as to exactly how many conditions the man had that pre-existed? A. **Congenital heart disease.** Q. When you speak of that—let's define that, you are speaking of closing of an aortic valve, aren't you? A. That is right. He was born that way with a small opening in his aortic valve and it makes extra work for the pump and it leaks back. Costanzo v.

Workmen's Comp. App. Bd., 410 A.2d 967, 969 (Commonwealth Ct.Pa.1980).

heart failure (hart'fāl-yer) a clinical syndrome characterized by distinctive symptoms and signs resulting from disturbances in cardiac output or from increased venous pressure. Most often applied to myocardial failure with increased pressures distending the ventricle (high end-diastolic pressure [EDP]) and a cardiac output inadequate for the body's needs; often subclassified as right- or left-sided heart failure depending on whether the systemic or pulmonary veins are predominantly distended. See also *cardiac arrest*, under *arrest; edema, pulmonary; infarction, myocardial*; and *stress*.

The cause of death was a **heart attack** as the result of ventricular fibrillation. The decedent's heart disease was so advanced that the physicians seem to agree that his death could have been caused if he were asleep. Also, it appears that mental and emotional stress, as a result of the accident, would have caused his death by virtue of his heart disease. The coroner and pathologist, both of whom are physicians, were of the latter opinion. Dr. Olash, appointed pursuant to KRS 342.121, was of the former opinion, that the work-related situation was in no way related to his death. . . .

The accident suffered by Loy on the morning of October 19, 1972, while operating the truck of Smith's Transfer Corporation clearly arose out of and in the course of his employment by Smith's Transfer Corporation. He suffered a slight injury to his nose as a result of that accident. Giving the board's findings of fact their reasonable and obvious meaning, we conclude that the board found as a fact that the ventricular fibrillation which caused the fatal **heart attack** was a result of the mental and emotional stress which Loy suffered as a result of the accident which arose out of and in the course of his employment. . . .

. . . In a long line of cases, this state's highest court has held that apportionment was required when a **heart attack** was not wholly, but only partially, work connected. See Grimes v. Goodlett and Adams, Ky., 345 S.W.2d 47 (1961); Hudson v. Owens, Ky., 439 S.W.2d 565 (1969) (dictum); . . . Yocom v. Loy, 573 S.W.2d 645, 648, 650 (Ky.1978).

However, in Baird v. T.E.I.A., 495 S.W.2d 207, 211 (Tex. 1973), this court recently reaffirmed that a **heart attack** caused by strain or over-exertion is an accidental injury to the physical structure of the body within the meaning of the Workmen's Compensation Act. . . .

. . . On cross-examination, Dr. DeLeon stated that "[g]enerally speaking most people die either from physical activity or work—tennis, working out or doing other enjoyable things. . . . So, that if the man had been working, this could have produced his enlarged myocardium which could have led to sudden arrhythmia and sudden death." We believe that this is some evidence that the **heart attack** was caused by Henderson's strenuous work on the day of his death. . . .

. . . A **heart attack** precipitated or brought on by the activity of the job is an injury sustained in the course of employment. A claimant must prove activity and then prove that the activity was a cause of this particular attack or injury. The proof cannot stop at possibility—nor need it reach certainty; it is enough to prove the probability. The claimant need only produce evidence and obtain findings that it is more likely than not

that the workman's activity at his work overstrained his heart and precipitated his death. Henderson v. Travelers Ins. Co., 544 S.W.2d 649, 650–1, 653–4 (Tex.1976).

Once the heart begins to fail as a pump, activity increases its failure. A person who is in **heart failure** should not perform physically strenuous work because this will aggravate the damage to the heart by placing a greater load on it. Smith v. Workmen's Comp. App. Bd., Co. of Los Angeles, 455 P.2d 822, 824 (Cal.1969).

Other Authorities: Richard E. Mosca & Co., Inc. v. Mosca, 362 So.2d 1340, 1342, 1344 (Fla.1978); Hartford Acc. & Indem. Co. v. Thurmond, 527 S.W.2d 180, 188 (Ct.Civ.App. Tex.1975).

heart failure, congestive a clinical syndrome due to heart disease and characterized by breathlessness and abnormal sodium and water retention, resulting in edema. The congestion may occur in the lungs or in the peripheral circulation, or in both, depending on whether the heart failure is right-sided, left-sided, or general.

Dr. Anderson saw plaintiff the following day and, after a more thorough examination, changed his diagnosis to **congestive heart failure** (CHF). Plaintiff remained hospitalized for several days for treatment. His symptoms of shortness of breath subsided. . . .

Dr. Anderson went further than the cardiologists. He was of the opinion that the exertion of plaintiff's climb aggravated the plaintiff's heart condition and such aggravation contributed to his disability. . . .

. . . It is undisputed that plaintiff incurred at least a sudden intensification of symptoms of his heart condition which intensification was caused by the physical exertion needed to climb the ladder. This sudden intensification of symptoms is an injury that is measureable in damages. Bonsack v. Keystone Shipping Co., 425 So.2d 869–70 (Ct.App.La.1982).

He further stated that when the heart was unable to pump blood from the pulmonary circulation, "fluids backed up." This, he said, was **congestive heart failure**. Matter of Iannelli, 384 A.2d 1104, 1107 (Super.Ct.N.J.1978).

The proof disclosed that the government's physician, relying primarily on Pastor's description of his own subjective symptoms (mostly pain), diagnosed his condition as "mild" **congestive heart failure** (which is not a heart attack but insufficient pumping of blood) and prescribed 7 to 10 days rest. U.S. v. Pastor, 557 F.2d 930, 935 (2d Cir.1977).

heart implant See *heart, artificial*.

heart, mechanical See *heart, artifical*.

heart murmur See *murmur, cardiac*.

heart transplant See *heart, artificial*.

heart trouble

To resolve this issue, the phrase "**heart trouble**" must be defined. . . .

. . . An attorney general's opinion interpreting this phrase as used in the County Employees Retirement Law of 1937 (Gov. Code, §§ 31450–31898) [4] concluded that "**heart trouble**" referred to "any injury or disease to that portion of the body which, from an anatomical standpoint, is the heart" (55 Ops. Cal.Atty.Gen. 24, 26). It also noted that "there is nothing in the Government Code section or the Labor Code sections that restricts the term 'heart trouble' to arteriosclerosis or its sequelae.'' (Id., at 25.) [⁴ Labor Code section 3212 was also enacted in 1937 with an amendment in 1939 to include ''heart trouble'' within the definition of ''injury'' under the statute.]

As to those specific afflictions which have been found to be ''heart trouble,'' the more restrictive interpretations have arisen from appeals board decisions which have not been reviewed by appellate courts. Injuries excluded from the meaning of ''heart trouble'' have included an aneurysm of the arch of the aorta (Fitzgerald v. City of Napa, 8 Cal.Comp.Cas. 90) and a cerebral hemorrhage causing a stroke in an arteriosclerotic hypertensive individual (Agrella v. Industrial Acc. Com., 9 Cal.Comp.Cas. 240; Smith v. Workmen's Comp. App. Bd., 34 Cal.Comp.Cas. 198.)

On the other hand, in cases which have for the most part received appellate review, the presumption of these Labor Code sections containing the phrase ''heart trouble'' has been extended to individuals with acute and chronic arteriosclerotic occlusive disease in the iliac arteries (Stephens v. Workmen's Comp. App. Bd., 20 Cal.App.3d 461, 97 Cal.Rptr. 713), atherosclerosis of the coronary artery (Id.), valvular lesions and scarring due to rheumatic fever (State Employees' Retirement System v. Workmen's Comp. App. Bd., 267 Cal.App.2d 611, 73 Cal.Rptr. 172), arteriosclerotic heart disease or coronary artery disease (Gillette v. Workmen's Comp. App. Bd., 20 Cal. App.3d 312, 97 Cal.Rptr. 542; Bussa v. Workmen's Comp. App. Bd., 259 Cal.App.2d 261, 66 Cal.Rptr. 204; Turner v. Workmen's Comp. App. Bd., 258 Cal.App.2d 442, 65 Cal. Rptr. 825),. and heart attack diagnosed as heart insufficiency (Ferris v. Industrial Acc. Com., 237 Cal.App.2d 427, 46 Cal. Rptr. 913). [O]ther more generalized afflictions of the heart and even those characterized as ''cardiovascular complaints'' have also been found to fall within the meaning of ''heart trouble.'' (See Lamb v. Workmen's Comp. App. Bd., 11 Cal.3d 274, 113 Cal.Rptr. 162, 520 P.2d 978 (claimant initially suffered from hypertension, but died of arrhythmia or ventricular fibrillation); Horn v. Industrial Acc. Com., 128 Cal.App.2d 837, 276 P.2d 673 (claimant suffered from coronary artery insufficiency); see also, Thobe v. Workmen's Comp. App. Bd., 35 Cal.Comp.Cas. 114 (essential hypertension was described as a ''cardiovascular disability''); Morgan v. Industrial Acc. Com., 23 Cal.Comp.Cas. 132 (claimant had hypertensive heart disease).)

Furthermore, ''heart trouble'' has also been found to arise through interaction of the heart with other bodily disorders. . . .

Given these cases and the mandate that section 3212 is to be liberally construed and that statutory language is to be given its commonly understood meaning, the phrase ''heart trouble'' assumes a rather expansive meaning. Muznik v. Worker's Comp. App. Bd. of Cty. of Los Angeles, 124 Cal.Rptr. 407, 413–415 (Ct.App.Cal.1975).

heat rash See *miliaria rubra.*

heating device See *machine, Aquamatic K-Thermia.*

heating pad See *pad, heating.*

heatstroke See *stroke, heat.*

Heberden's nodes See *nodes, Heberden's.*

heel (hēl) the hindmost part of the foot; called also *calx* [NA]. See also *calcaneus.*

heel bone See *calcaneus.*

Heller procedure See *operation, Heller's.*

helix (he'liks) [Gr. "snail," "coil"] a coiled structure, such as the coil of wire in an electromagnet.

helix, double; helix, Watson-Crick a double helix, each chain of which contains information completely specifying the other chain, representing a structural formulation of the mechanism by which the genetic information in DNA reproduces itself; see *illustration.*

hemangioma (hĕ-man"je-o'mah) [*hem- + angioma*] a benign tumor made up of new-formed blood vessels. See also *angioma* and *lymphangioma.*

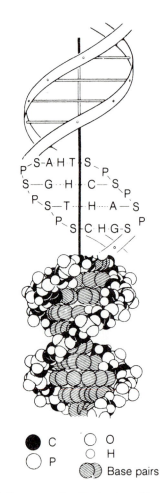

C O
P H
Base pairs

The DNA helix, representing the structure of deoxyribonucleic acid. *Upper:* as a spiral staircase. *Middle:* as an arrangement of organic molecules (A = adenine, C = cytosine, G = guanine, P = phosphate, S = sugar, T = thymine) and hydrogen bonds. *Lower:* as an arrangement of atoms of carbon, hydrogen, oxygen, and phosphorus, and base pairs as shown. (From Swanson: The Cell, Prentice-Hall, Inc., 1960.)

A **hemangioma** is a benign skin lesion, containing many capillary blood vessels. Generally, a **hemangioma** will blanch upon pressure. A melanoma should not blanch because of the pigment. Williams v. Grant, 417 N.E.2d 586–7 (Ct.App.Ohio 1979).

Hemangioma of the liver (gross) (a hemorrhagic condition in the liver, a blood clot in the liver itself). Glover v. Bruce, 265 S.W.2d 346, 351 (Mo.1954).

hemarthrosis (hem″ar-thro′sis) [*hem-* + Gr. *arthron* joint] extravasation of blood into a joint or its synovial cavity.

The patient appears to have suffered a dislocation of the patella recently, with a traumatic **hemarthrosis**, and this is still resolving....

... He may in fact have an osteochondritis lesion of his patella, but he most definitely does have a subluxing left patella. U.S. v. Poczik, 362 F.Supp. 101, 105 (W.D.N.Y.1973).

Other Authorities: Voegeli v. Lewis, 568 F.2d 89, 91 (8th Cir. 1977).

hematocrit (he-mat′o-krit) [*hemato-* + Gr. *krinein* to separate] the volume percentage of erythrocytes in whole blood. Originally applied to the apparatus or procedure used in its determination, but now also used to designate the result of the determination. Abbreviated HCT.

... a **hematocrit** (a blood test measuring the ratio of the volume of blood cells to the volume of whole blood). Mirsa v. State Medical Board, 329 N.E.2d 106–7 (Ohio 1975).

Dial was instrumental in developing two separate instruments which the laboratory is now using. One measures the capillary **hematocrit** (a concentration of red cells in the capillaries).... Wry v. Dial, 503 P.2d 979, 981 (Ct.App.Ariz.1972).

hematogenous (hem″ah-toj′ĕ-nus) produced by or derived from the blood; disseminated by the circulation or through the blood stream.

The ALJ also relied generally on the testimony of Drs. Dominici and Evans, stating that "[i]t is significant to note that two of the three treating physicians testified that within reasonable medical probability the staph was carried **hematogenously** from the right great toe to the left fibula." Sprague v. Director, Office of Workers' Comp., etc., 688 F.2d 862, 867 (1st Cir. 1982).

hematology (hem″ah-tol′o-je) [*hemato-* + *-logy*] that branch of medical science which treats of the morphology of the blood and blood-forming tissues. Cited in Carmichael v. Reitz, 95 Cal.Rptr. 318, 390 (Ct.App.1971).

hematoma (hem″ah-to′mah), pl. *hemato′mas* [*hemato-* + *-oma*] a localized collection of blood, usually clotted, in an organ, space, or tissue, due to a break in the wall of a blood vessel. See also *nodule*.

While returning from her second trip to the freezer, at approximately 5 p.m., claimant felt a numbness in her right leg. The numbness progressed up her leg, and she was subsequently hospitalized. It was later found that claimant had suffered an intracerebral **hematoma**, the cause of which was an arteriovenous malformation. Doyle v. Industrial Com'n, 449 N.E.2d 1352–3 (Ill.1983).

Around 7:30 a.m. Mrs. Belmon began to experience pain in the right arm both below and above the elbow, as well as discoloration and swelling....

... Nurse Bardwell stated that she saw no **hematoma** (which would have been evidenced by discoloration) at 11:50 or any other time....

... Arriving ten minutes later at ICU, he discovered a large **hematoma**. He wrapped the arm and elevated it and immediately reduced the Heparin therapy by one-half....

It was Dr. Knoepp's opinion that Mrs. Belmon's **hematoma** was a secondary hemorrhagic complication due to the combination of heparin, venepuncture and blood pressure cuff trauma. Further explaining, he said that the blood pressure cuff could have ruptured smaller blood vessels, or she could have had a venous or an arterial **hematoma** from the needle stick and this was aggravated by the blood pressure cuff. Belmon v. St. Frances Cabrini Hospital, 427 So.2d 541–3 (Ct.App.La. 1983).

At 12:45 p.m. the pressure from the expanding **hematoma** caused a portion of the brain to herniate by protruding into a sinus cavity. An hour later Dr. Joseph Cauthen, a neurosurgeon, bored emergency and temporary burr holes to relieve the pressure. Subsequently, complete surgical procedures were employed to remove the **hematoma**. Schackow v. Medical-Legal Consulting, etc., 416 A.2d 1303, 1305 (Ct.Spec. App.Md.1980).

Other Authorities: Abernathy v. Superior Hardwoods, Inc., 704 F.2d 963, 973 (7th Cir. 1983); Trichel v. Caire, 427 So.2d 1227, 1231 (Ct.App.La.1983); Cowman v. Hornaday, 329 N.W.2d 422, 424 (Iowa 1983); Hirn v. Edgewater Hospital, 408 N.E.2d 970, 973 (App.Ct.Ill.1980); U.S. v. Choice, 392 F.Supp. 460, 462 (E.D.Pa.1975); Ins. Co. of North America v. Chinowith, 393 F.2d 916, 918 (5th Cir. 1968).

hematoma, epidural accumulation of blood in the epidural space, due to damage to the middle meningeal artery and producing compression of the dura mater and thus compression of the brain. Unless evacuated, it may result in herniation through the tentorium, and death.

It appears that the noted head trauma resulted in an acute **epidural hematoma**. The patient was taken to the neurosurgical operating room where the treating physicians performed an evacuation of the acute **epidural hematoma**. Schaffer v. Califano, 433 F.Supp. 1218, 1220 (D.Md.1977).

The District Court, however, found that the paraplegia was caused by post-operative bleeding within the operative site which collected in the potential space outside the dura, forming an **epidual** [sic] **hematoma** and causing pressure on the spinal cord. The pressure of the hematoma created a block of the spinal cord. An **epidural hematoma** in these circumstances, the District Court found, requires immediate treatment consisting of a second operation for the purpose of removing the accumulated blood and stopping the source of the bleeding. The failure to re-operate and stop the post-operative bleeding was found to be the proximate cause of the paraplegia. The defendant's negligence consisted in failing to recognize the symptoms of paralysis as caused by the hematoma and in failing to re-operate and stop the post-operative bleeding. Tyminski v. U.S., 481 F.2d 257, 260 (3d Cir. 1973).

hematoma, retroperitoneal

A **retroperitoneal hematoma**, which had formed as a result of the bleeding, was also removed. Reichman v. Wallach, 452 A.2d 501, 504 (Super.Ct.Pa.1982).

hematoma, subdural accumulation of blood in the subdural space. In the severe *acute* form, both blood and cerebrospinal fluid enter the space as a result of laceration of the brain and a tear in the arachnoid, adding subdural compression to the direct injury to the brain. In the *chronic* form, only blood effuses into the subdural space as a result of rupture of the bridging veins, usually due to closed head injury. The effusion is a gradual process resulting, weeks after the injury, in headache, progressive stupor, and hemiparesis, followed by dilating pupil, a sign of herniation of the tentorium.

Dr. Swenson then performed a subdural tap which revealed blood. Since the doctor testified that a **subdural hematoma** caused by infection does not usually have blood in it, the presence of blood suggested trauma. State v. Goblirsch, 246 N.W.2d 12, 13 (Minn.1976).

Pt was putting on his trousers and fell against the wall in his room, bumping back of head....

... He was diagnosed as having a **subdural hematoma**. Surgery was immediately performed to relieve the pressure on plaintiff's brain caused by the large blood clot or hematoma. Plaintiff suffered residual brain damage....

... However, plaintiffs introduced substantial expert testimony that **subdural hematoma** is a progressive condition in which pressure due to intracranial bleeding builds up in the skull to the point where unconsciousness results. The testimony of Dr. I. Joshua Speigel, a neurosurgeon, was that a **subdural hematoma** could be treated by simple burr hole procedure, instead of extensive surgery such as that undergone by Stahlin, if the condition was detected early enough. Stahlin v. Hilton Hotels Corp., 484 F.2d 580, 582–3 (7th Cir. 1973).

One of plaintiffs' medical experts was of the opinion that the cause, within reasonable medical probability, of the chronic **subdural hematomas** was the traumatic or injurious forceps delivery of this child in which the head was injured....

... The parties conceded that **subdural hematomas** may be caused without negligence by a difficult trip down the birth canal. Wale v. Barnes, 261 So.2d 201, 203–4 (Dist.Ct.App. Fla.1972).

Other Authorities: Brissette v. Schweiker, 566 F.Supp. 626, 629 (E.D.Mo.1983); Beins v. U.S., 695 F.2d 591, 595 (D.C.Cir. 1982); Wages v. Snell, 360 So.2d 807–8 (D.C.App.Fla.1978); U.S. v. Grady, 481 F.2d 1106–7 (D.C.Cir.1973); Wale v. Barnes, 278 So.2d 601, 603 (Fla.1973).

hematopoietic (hem″ah-to-poi-et′ik) [*hemato-* + Gr. *poiein* to make] pertaining to or effecting the formation of blood cells.

The Criteria Document concluded that, among the major organ systems, the **hematopoietic** (blood-forming) and neurological systems are the areas of prime concern. CD 1–12, JA 1116. Its discussion of the effects of lead on these two organ systems is central to our review of the lead standards. Lead Industries Ass'n v. Environmental Protection, 647 F.2d 1130, 1136 (D.C. Cir.1980).

hematuria (hem″ah-tu′re-ah) [*hemat-* + Gr. *ouron* urine + *-ia*] blood in the urine.

Plaintiff's injuries consisted of a ''contusion of the right kidney with microscopic **hematuria**.'' (**Hematuria** indicates the presence of blood in the urine.) Todd v. Dabkowski, 372 A.2d 350 (Super.Ct.N.J.1977).

heme (hēm) the nonprotein, insoluble, iron protoporphyrin constituent of hemoglobin, various other respiratory pigments and of many cells, both animal and vegetable. It is $C_{34}H_{33}O_4N_4FeOH$, an iron compound of protoporphyrin, with the iron in the ferrous, or Fe (II), state, and so constitutes the pigment portion or protein-free part of the hemoglobin molecule. It is responsible for the characteristic coloring and oxygen-carrying properties of hemoglobin. Formerly known as *hematin*.

Heme, one of the components of hemoglobin, is formed through a series of biochemical steps (**heme** synthesis), the final step in which is incorporation of iron into the protein protoporphyrin IX....

... This process takes place in the mitochondria of the cell, and one of the ways in which lead affects **heme** synthesis is by interfering with this final step. The result is that protoporphyrin IX, without iron, is incorporated in the hemoglobin molecule in the erythrocytes. This phenomenon is detected as an elevation of protoporphyrin in the erythrocyte, i.e., EP elevation. CD 11-7–11-14, JA 1229–1236. [See under ''Poisoning, Lead,'' this case.] Lead Industries Ass'n v. Environmental Protection Agency, 647 F.2d 1130, 1139 (D.C.Cir.1980).

hemianopia (hem″e-ah-no′pe-ah) [*hemi-* + *an-* neg. + Gr. *ōpē* vision + *-ia*] defective vision or blindness in half of the visual field.

hemianopia, homonymous hemianopia affecting the right halves or the left halves of the visual fields of the two eyes.

The left **homonymous hemianopsia**, a central nervous system disorder, has continued to the present time. The left hand and arm disorders are upper motor neuron type, as is the continued inability of cerebral functioning such as inability to recognize objects and words. Stich v. U.S., 565 F.Supp. 1096, 1119 (D.N.J.1983).

In [Title 20, Section 404.1538 Appendix] Section 2.01, the ''Category of Impairments, Special Sense Organs,'' is set forth. In Section 2.05, one of these impairments is ''Complete **homonymous hemianopsia**,'' or half sight, or vision, of uncrossed images of an object seen double; where the image seen by the right eye is on the right side and that by the left, on the left side; and when one image is above the other, the result is vertical diplopia, as above defined. [Dissent.] Jenkins v. Gardner, 430 F.2d 243, 296 (6th Cir. 1970).

hemianopsia See *hemianopia*.

hemicolectomy (hem″e-ko-lek′to-me) [*hemi-* + *colectomy*] excision of approximately half of the colon.

The doctor performed a right **hemi-colectomy** with ileotransverse colostomy, a surgical procedure by which a mass in the intestines is removed and the intestines sewed back together. Babin v. St. Paul Fire and Marine Ins. Co., 385 So.2d 849, 852 (Ct.App.La.1980).

hemigastrectomy (hem″e-gas-trek′to-me) excision of one half of the stomach.

... suffering from a duodenal ulcer which, it was thought, may have been bleeding. The doctors performed a **hemigastrectomy** and a vagotomy.... Kelly v. U.S., 554 F.Supp. 1001–2 (E.D.N.Y.1983).

hemilaminectomy (hem″e-lam″ĭ-nek′to-me) surgical removal of a vertebral lamina on one side only.

Following the epiduravenogram, Dr. Applebaum performed a **hemilaminectomy** in the lumbar area at the L–4–5 and L–5, S–1 interspaces on the left side. Looking into the L–4–5 interspace on the left, Dr. Applebaum found the L–5 nerve root to be bound with mild scar tissue coming off at a rather acute angle from the dura sac. Field v. Winn Dixie Louisiana, Inc., 427 So.2d 616–17 (Ct.App.La.1983).

On September 7, 1969, plaintiff was again admitted to the Addison Gilbert Hospital, this time for a **hemi-laminectomy** (removal of layers of bone attached to the vertebrae by ligaments) and the removal of the ruptured disc. Sousa v. M/V Caribia, 360 F.Supp. 971, 974 (D.Mass.1973).

Dr. Polakoff described the operation as follows:

The operation performed is known as a **hemilaminectomy**. That is taking off a small portion of the bone over the area where the nerve and disc are located, foraminotomy which is opening up the foramen where the nerve goes out to relieve any bony impression on the nerve and this is also in the lateral portion of the spine, and then removing the disc. A. P. Green Refractories Co. v. Workmen's Comp. App. Bd., 301 A.2d 914–15 (Commonwealth Ct.Pa.1973).

Other Authorities: Poltorak v. Sandy, 345 A.2d 201, 209 (Super.Ct.Pa.1975).

hemiparesis (hem″e-par′e-sis) [*hemi-* + *paresis*] muscular weakness or partial paralysis affecting one side of the body.

Dr. Tobias, a neurosurgeon who had examined plaintiff shortly after the surgery, testified that plaintiff had suffered **hemiparesis** (muscular weakness affecting one side) and that he did not know if the condition was permanent. He did not consider a global oxygen loss to be a logical explanation of plaintiff's condition. He felt that the most likely cause would be a spasm of the blood vessel to the brain. Vuletich v. Bolgla, 407 N.E.2d 566, 568 (App.Ct.Ill.1980).

As to plaintiff's injuries, the evidence showed he suffered amnesia, a contusion which left him with **hemiparesis** (weakness and stiffness or partial paralysis similar to a condition after a stroke) and some brain damage as a result of the accident....

... At that time, her diagnosis of the plaintiff was that of left **hemiparesis** post-traumatic. In layman's terms, this is very similar to the picture of a stroke victim. In her opinion, the plaintiff would not be able to work as a carpenter, nor would he be able to engage in any occupational activity that would require coordination of both left and right side of the body. Hyatt v. Sierra Boat Co., 145 Cal.Rptr. 47, 51, 58–59 (Ct.App.Cal. 1978).

A lumbar puncture was performed which showed the spinal fluid to be clear and of normal pressure, though the protein count was 132 milligrams per cent, which was abnormal. Based upon this information, the attending physician formulated a working diagnosis of right **hemiparesis**, hereinafter referred to as "incomplete stroke," and prescribed treatment of anticoagulants (heparin, coumadin, and, to increase blood supply, rheomacrodex). Riddlesperger v. U.S., 406 F.Supp. 617, 619 (N.D.Ala.1976).

Other Authorities: Belshaw v. Feinstein, 65 Cal.Rptr. 788, 792 (Ct.App.Cal.1968).

hemiparesthesia (hem″e-par″es-the′ze-ah) [*hemi-* + *paresthesia*] perverted sensation on one side of the body.

Dr. Leuschke's final diagnosis was "left **hemiparesthesia**" of undetermined etiology. Daniels v. U.S., 704 F.2d 587, 590 (11th Cir. 1983).

hemipelvectomy (hem″e-pel″vek′to-me) amputation of a lower limb through the sacroiliac joint.

As treatment, he underwent a **hemipelvectomy** (amputation of one leg and half the pelvis). In her complaint, plaintiff alleges that, despite this surgery, a subsequent spread of the malignancy caused Mr. Hawkins' death on January 27, 1976. Hawkins v. Regional Med. Laboratories, P.C., 329 N.W.2d 729–30 (Mich.1982).

Claimant had a wart-like lesion on the bottom of his foot which had never caused him any trouble until he stepped on a sharp piece of steel which penetrated his shoe sole and pierced the wart. The wart raised up a quarter of an inch above surrounding tissue and when excised, examination revealed a malignant melanoma. The upshot was a **hemipelvectomy**—amputation of the entire leg and half of the pelvis. Cox v. Ulysses Cooperative Oil and Supply Co., 544 P.2d 363, 370 (Kan.1975).

hemiplegia (hem″e-ple′je-ah) [*hemi-* + Gr. *plēgē* stroke] paralysis of one side of the body.

It is our opinion that the patient has a mild leftsided **hemiplegia** of upper motor neuron type, due to a head injury and skull defect. There is a reactive depression of mild degree. Associated with the depression, there is a mild degree of inadequacy of personality, with an associated tendency toward passive-dependent behavior patterns (augmented by a mildly paranoid resentment over being impaired by his injury). DePaepe v. Richardson, 464 F.2d 92, 97 (5th Cir. 1972).

Respondent had suffered an injury at birth that had resulted in a partial paralysis of her right side and limbs (**hemiplegia**) which in turn resulted in a somewhat atrophied condition in her right side. Domagalski v. Victoria's Restaurant, 306 N.Y.S.2d 273–4 (3d Dep't 1970).

hemisacralization (hem″e-sa″kral-i-za′shun) fusion of the fifth lumbar vertebra to the first segment of the sacrum on only one side.

This patient represents a regressing sprain of the cervical, thoracic and lumbosacral spine, in a spine characterized by congenital changes consisting of **hemisacralization** of lumbar 5 on the right side.... Gotschall v. Weinberger, 391 F.Supp. 73–4 (D.Neb.1975).

Hemodialysis (he″mo-di-al′ĭ-sis) the removal of certain elements from the blood by virtue of the difference in the rates of their diffusion through a semipermeable membrane, e.g., by means of a hemodialyzer.

The ward was suffering from "end-stage kidney disease," which required him to undergo **hemodialysis** treatment (filtering of the blood) three days a week, five hours a day. Matter of Spring, 405 N.E.2d 115, 118 (Sup.Jud.Ct.Mass.1980).

The guardian relies heavily on the decision of the Kentucky Court in Strunk v. Strunk, 445 S.W.2d 145 (Ky.1969). In that case, the proposed donee of the kidney was suffering from endstage renal disease, as is Stephen in the case before us, and, again, like Stephen, he was being kept alive by **hemodialysis**, which consists of filtering the blood of the afflicted person through an external artificial kidney. Little v. Little, 576 S.W.2d 493, 496 (Ct.Civ.App.Tex.1979).

hemodialyzer (he"mo-di'ah-liz"er) an apparatus by which hemodialysis may be performed, blood being separated by a semipermeable membrane from a solution of such composition as to secure diffusion of certain elements out of the blood. Popularly called *artificial kidney*.

hemodynamics (he"mo-di-nam'iks) [*hemo-* + Gr. *dynamis* power] the study of the movements of the blood and of the forces concerned therein.

It is my opinion that the man developed, as the result of the thrombus found in the coronary artery, an acute condition which interfered with the proper functioning of his heart. This, in turn, brought about an abrupt change of the body's **hemodynamics**—or we might call it a circulatory failure—with the result that he died due to lack of sufficient oxygen to the vital tissues of his body, the lack of oxygen being due to the embarrassment of the heart function. Follmer Trucking v. Stump, 286 A.2d 1, 4 (Commonwealth Ct.Pa.1972), reversed and remanded 292 A.2d 294.

hemoglobin (he"mo-glo'bin) the oxygen-carrying pigment of the erythrocytes, formed by the developing erythrocyte in bone marrow. It is a conjugated protein containing four heme groups and globin, and having the property of reversible oxygenation. A molecule of hemoglobin contains four globin polypeptide chains. They are designated α, β, γ, δ, in the adult; and each is composed of several hundred amino acids. Different types of hemoglobin are determined by the specific combination of these chains, the number of chains of the different types in the molecule being indicated by subscript numerals. For example, *hemoglobin F* (*fetal h.*), which is the predominant type in the newborn, may be written as $\alpha_2{}^A\gamma_2{}^F$. *Hemoglobin A* (*adult h.*), which is normally predominant in the adult is designated $\alpha_2{}^A\beta_2{}^A$ or $\alpha_2\beta_2$. Another hemoglobin, *hemoglobin A$_2$* (designated $\alpha_2{}^A\delta_2{}^A$ or $\alpha_2{}^A\delta_2$), is usually present in limited minor concentrations. Many hemoglobins with differing electrophoretic mobilities and characteristics have been reported, for example, S, C, D, E, G, H, I, J, K, L, M, N, Q, Norfolk, Barts, and many others. (See also *hemoglobinopathy*.) Because refined biochemical techniques may lead to the discovery of additional hemoglobins, certain standards for nomenclature have been devised. The hemoglobin electrophoretic mobility is designated by a capital letter; if two or more hemoglobins have the same mobility, the geographic area of discovery is indicated as a subscript, for example, hemoglobin M$_S$, or M$_{Saskatoon}$, and hemoglobin M$_M$, or M$_{Milwaukee}$. To restrict the increasing use of capital letters new hemoglo-

bins are named simply for the laboratory, hospital, or town where they were discovered, for example, hemoglobin $_{Norfolk}$. When known, the number of each amino acid substituting in each polypeptide(s) in the molecule should be indicated by the appropriate superscript numeral. Symbol *Hb*. See also *anemia, iron deficiency* (J. B. Williams Co. case).

Hemoglobin is the protein which transports life-sustaining oxygen from the respiratory system to all cells in the body. CD 11–8, JA 1230. It consists of a combination of heme and globin, and lead interferes with **hemoglobin** synthesis by inhibiting synthesis of the globin moiety and affecting several steps in synthesis of the heme molecule. See CD 11–13—11–14, JA 1235–1236. Lead Industries Ass'n v. Environmental Protection Agency, 647 F.2d 1130, 1138 (D.C.Cir.1980).

Approximately 70% of all the iron in the normal adult is in the circulating blood as a component of **hemoglobin**, the red material in the red blood cells. In the creation of **hemoglobin**, iron is an essential major constituent. **Hemoglobin** carries oxygen which is essential for the functioning of cells throughout the body. J. B. Williams Co. v. F.T.C., 381 F.2d 884, 887 (6th Cir. 1967).

hemoglobin H a rapidly migrating, abnormal hemoglobin composed of four beta chains, having a high oxygen affinity, found in a form of α-thalassemia in various ethnic groups, manifested by chronic hemolytic anemia associated with splenomegaly clinically and hypochromia, anisocytosis, and poikilocytosis of the red blood cells, with inclusion bodies detectable by supravital staining.

hemolysis (he-mol'ĭ-sis) [*hemo-* + Gr. *lysis* dissolution] the liberation of hemoglobin. Hemolysis consists of the separation of the hemoglobin from the red cells and its appearance in the plasma. It may be caused by hemolysins, by chemicals, by freezing or heating, or by distilled water.

Hemolysis due to the presence of beta hemolytic streptococci is evidenced by breakdown in the blood red appearance of the culture medium. Fink v. SmithKline Corp., 186 U.S.P.Q. 262, 268 (N.D.Cal.1975).

Taking one large sample, then separating it into smaller samples, is unsatisfactory because of the (i) quickness of harmful coagulation, and (ii) ease of causing **hemolysis** of the blood. "Hemolysis" is destruction of blood cells, and can be caused by applying physical force such as that in sudden contact with hard surfaces. Becton, Dickinson & Co. v. Sherwood Medical Ind. Inc., 516 F.2d 514–15 (5th Cir. 1975).

The donor is also warned that a "**hemolytic transfusion reaction**" may result if he would happen to receive another donor's blood cells during the process. The possibility that one could go into shock and die as a result of this reaction is explained. . . . Mirsa v. State Medical Board, 329 N.E.2d 106–7 (Ohio 1975).

Other Authorities: Young v. Park, 417 A.2d 889, 894 (R.I.1980).

hemolytic (he"mo-lit'ik) pertaining to, characterized by, or producing hemolysis.

hemolytic disease [of newborn] See *erythroblastosis fetalis*.

hemolytic enterococci See *Streptococcus pyogenes*.

hemophilia (he"mo-fil'e-ah) [*hemo* + Gr. *philein* to love + *ia*] a hereditary hemorrhagic diathesis due to deficiency of coagulation Factor VIII, and characterized by spontaneous or traumatic subcutaneous and intramuscular hemorrhages; bleeding from the mouth, gums, lips, and tongue; hematuria; and hemarthroses. It affects males, being transmitted as an X-linked recessive trait. Called also *h. A, classical h.,* and *Factor VIII deficiency*. See also *factor, coagulation (factor IX)*.

Petitioner was born with **hemophilia**, a condition of the circulatory system characterized by delayed clotting of the blood and difficulty in controlling hemorrhage. As a result of hemorrhages during his growth years, Petitioner lost nearly all of the motion in his knees and ankles. Cook v. Com., Bur. of Vocational Rehabilitation, 405 A.2d 1000–1 (Commonwealth Ct. Pa.1979).

James Fogo had suffered throughout his life from a mild form of **hemophilia** as the result of which he experienced more bleeding episodes from lacerations and trauma than would normal persons. Although the condition was not life-threatening he had a history of bleeding following tooth extractions, when the sockets would ooze some blood for periods as long as two weeks. Fogo v. Cutter Laboratories, 137 Cal.Rptr. 417, 419 (Ct.App.Cal.1977).

If, however, the damage is done in the ovum there is a slightly higher probability that the defects will be manifested in the immediate offspring of the irradiated ovum, because there are sex-linked genes that male offspring inherit from their mother and not from their father that can show up in the next generation. **Hemophilia**, or failure of the blood to clot properly, is an example of such a defect. Chiropractic Ass'n of New York v. Hilleboe, 227 N.Y.S.2d 309, 367 (Sup.Ct. Albany Cty.1961).

hemophilia B Factor IX deficiency. See *coagulation factors*, under *factor*.

Hemophilus (he-mof'ĭ-lus) a genus of hemophilic bacteria of the family Brucellaceae, order Eubacteriales, made up of small gram-negative rods and characterized by a nutritional requirement for the constituents of fresh blood, including hemoglobin and certain allied compounds, called X factor, and for V factor. Spelled also *Haemophilus*.

Hemophilus influenzae a species once thought to be the cause of epidemic influenza in man; it produces a serious form of meningitis, especially in infants.

... in the absence of acute inflammation doctors proceed to operate even if they know HI is present in a patient's throat because it is impossible to clear a throat of bacteria.[1] Also HI is extremely prevalent and found in 10 to 20 percent of healthy persons and is not considered as ordinarily pathogenic, i.e., disease producing. When it becomes pathogenic it attacks children more frequently than adults. [[1] Common knowledge affords an assumption that the mouth and throat are subject to constant bacterial invasion. There is thus an inference that a culture negative for HI taken two or three days before a tonsillectomy would afford no indication that HI or any other bacteria would not be present at the time of the operation.]

Among children, it can cause meningitis (an inflammation of the lining of the brain), middle ear infections and croup. Among adults it can induce bronchitis where there is chronic respiratory infection, conjunctivitis (pink eye) and in rare cases, pneumonia....

... Dr. Keller stated that he knew that HI could attack the meninges (lining of the brain) but that he knew little else about HI. A subsequent motion to strike the opinion on the basis of lack of sufficient knowledge was granted. Folk v. Kilk, 126 Cal. Rptr. 172, 177, 181 (Ct.App.Cal.1976).

hemoptysis (he-mop'tĭ-sis) [*hemo-* + Gr. *ptyein* to spit] the expectoration of blood or of blood-stained sputum.

There is no mention in the doctor's notes of that date of any complaint of wheezing or **hemoptysis** (spitting up of saliva mixed with blood). Joynt v. Barnes, 388 N.E.2d 1298, 1302 (App. Ct.Ill.1979).

In October of 1966 Dr. Williams found the plaintiff had experienced **hemoptysis** (expectoration of blood or blood tinged sputum) and as a result of this finding he sent the plaintiff to Charity Hospital for a diagnostic workup. Claborn v. Cohen, 303 F.Supp. 167, 168 (E.D.La.1969).

... the coughing of blood (**hemoptysis**) and the suspicious cells for malignancy on the bronchial washings were the result of the dust inhalation due to petitioner's employment. Bedel v. Industrial Com'n, 428 P.2d 134–5 (Ct.App.Ariz.1967).

Other Authorities: Black v. Richardson, 356 F.Supp. 861, 866 (D.S.Car.1973).

hemorrhage (hem'or-ij) [*hemo-* + Gr. *rhēgnynai* to burst forth] the escape of blood from the vessels; bleeding. Small hemorrhages are classified according to size as petechiae (very small), purpura (up to 1 cm.), and ecchymoses (larger). The massive accumulation of blood within a tissue is called a hematoma.

hemorrhage, cerebral a hemorrhage into the cerebrum. See also *stroke syndrome*, under *syndrome*.

hemorrhage, expulsive hemorrhage of the eye, breaking through both the choroid and the retina and extruding the ocular contents before it; usually occurring during the course of intraocular surgical procedure.

The earlier gaping of the "wound", the extrusion of the vitreous, and the "grey tissue" observed suggested an **expulsive** (the rapidity with which it occurs) **choroidal hemorrhage**. In turn, they also suggested excessive intraocular pressure. According to the evidence **expulsive choroidal hemorrhages** are rare and their incidence of occurrence during cataract surgery is less than one percent. Miller v. Scholl, 594 S.W.2d 324, 327 (Mo.Ct.App.1980).

hemorrhage, interstitial

Pulmonary congestion and edema with **interstitial hemorrhage** (congestion of the lungs with the blood escaping out of the vessels into the tissues, an abnormal amount of fluid in the lungs). Glover v. Bruce, 265 S.W.2d 346, 351 (Mo.1954).

hemorrhage, intracerebral hemorrhage within the cerebrum. See also *hemorrhage, cerebral*.

On November 19, 1974, appellant suffered a spontaneous **intracerebral hemorrhage**. The major symptom of appellant's hemorrhage was loss of his entire right field of vision in both eyes. Beins v. U.S., 695 F.2d 591, 595 (D.C.Cir.1982).

hemorrhage, intracranial bleeding within the cranium, which may be extradural, subdural, subarachnoid, or cerebral. See also *stroke syndrome*, under *syndrome*.

An emergency operation was performed on his brain to relieve a diagnosed blood clot. The operation was unsuccessful and he expired on May 7. The cause of death was certified by Dr. Lawrence T. Sanders who attended him as "Intra-cranial hemorrhage in left temporal lobe due to or as a consequence of anticoagulation with Warfarin." Tschohl v. Nationwide Mut. Ins. Co., 418 F.Supp. 1124, 1126 (D.Minn.1976).

hemorrhage, pial See *pia mater*.

. . . secondary to **pial hemorrhage** of mild degree occurring at time of accident January 1959, wherein tailgate of his car was allegedly whiplashed by DSR bus. . . .

Dr. Lewis' meticulous diagnosis (supported by Dr. Bolton's report) also found brain damage caused by "a little **pial hemorrhage** occurring in the medulla dorsally" and resulting in a postconcussive neurosis, which he related to plaintiff's complaints of excessive emotionalism in human contacts, excessive tendency toward weeping, and excessive argumentativeness. Phillips v. Celebrezze, 330 F.2d 687, 689–90 (6th Cir.1964).

hemorrhage, retinal

He explained that the longer a person has diabetes the greater the possibility of **retinal hemorrhage** because the weakened blood vessels might break if blood pressure increases and this is compounded by an emotional trauma or fall. He described the condition of claimant's right eye as entirely due to diabetes. Excelsior Leather Washer Co. v. Industrial Com'n, 297 N.E.2d 158, 160–1 (Ill.1973).

hemorrhage, retrobulbar

Dr. Lazenby . . . treated the hemorrhage by placing ice packs around the eye. He later performed a second successful operation, but Mr. Beisel can only see light from this eye.

Retrobulbar hemorrhages generally heal without treatment and cause no damage. However, occasionally the elevated pressure inside the eye produces a loss of vision, and there was general agreement that this occurred in Mr. Beisel's case. Lazenby v. Beisel, 425 So.2d 84–5 (D.Ct.App.Fla.1982).

hemorrhage; subarachnoid intracranial hemorrhage into the subarachnoid space. See also *cavum, subarachnoideale; puncture, lumbar* (Polischeck case).

An arteriogram was performed which showed a large subdural hematoma and a right posterior communicating artery aneurysm, demonstrating that plaintiff's decedent had suffered a **subarachnoid hemorrhage**. . . .

. . . The symptoms of **subarachnoid hemorrhage** are the sudden onset of a severe headache, nausea and vomiting, perhaps a decreased level or loss of consciousness, and perhaps weakness, followed in time by elevated temperature, malaise, photophobia, and nuchal rigidity (stiffness of the neck). Deposition of Dr. Neal Kassell, at 26. These symptoms of **subarachnoid hemorrhage** are commonly taught in medical school to all medical students. Id. Thus, as both plaintiff's and defendant's experts agreed, any physician, regardless of specialty, possessing and employing the skill and knowledge usually pos-

sessed by physicians in Philadelphia in 1978, would have known and recognized that the presence of the above-named symptoms in a patient would suggest the possibility of a **subarachnoid hemorrhage**. Id.; Testimony of Dr. Hubert Mickel. Polischeck v. U.S., 535 F.Supp. 1261, 1265 (E.D.Pa.1982).

At Charity Hospital it was determined that Cunningham had sustained a **sub-arachnoid hemorrhage** caused by an aneurysm of the anterior communicating (cerebral) artery. Cunningham v. Am. Mut. Ins. Co., 390 So.2d 1372–3 (Ct.App.La. 1980).

The cause of Zorn's death was a massive **subarachnoid hemorrhage** resulting from the rupture of a blood vessel in the brain just below the area known as the Circle of Willis. Zorn v. Aetna Life Insurance Co., 260 F.Supp. 730–1 (E.D.Tex.1965).

hemorrhage, vitreous See *vitreous*.

In Timothy's case, however, Dr. Bleything would distinguish between an active **vitreous hemorrhage** and an inactive **vitreous hemorrhage**. He classifies an inactive **vitreous hemorrhage** as a scar and suggests referral to a medical doctor is indicated only in the event that an active **vitreous hemorrhage** were detected. It is implicit by this reasoning that to Dr. Bleything a scar is not an indication of existing disease. Scar tissue, according to Dr. Bleything's opinion, when old or inactive, is typically black. This is consistent with Dr. Shank's testimony that the **vitreous hemorrhage** detected in his December examination was old because it appeared black or dark.

Actually a black or dark color in a **vitreous hemorrhage** has nothing at all to do with its age, but rather is a result of its magnitude or extent. The black or dark color indicates a lack of reflected light from the retina behind the hemorrhage. Blood in a **vitreous hemorrhage** is not black; it is only the shadow that appears black. Indeed, as Dr. Black states in his deposition, an old **vitreous hemorrhage** would appear as white strands in the vitreous and settle to the lower part of the vitreous. And Dr. Kinn testified that he had personally observed hemorrhages in the vitreous more than a year old which were red in color. He explained that a hemorrhage would appear to be black because it was sufficiently thick with blood to absorb all the light reflecting off the retina during an examination, not because of an innate darkness of color. Steele v. U.S., 463 F.Supp. 321, 324–5 (D.Alaska 1978).

hemorrhoid (hem'o-roid) [Gr. *haimorrhois*] a varicose dilatation of a vein of the superior or inferior hemorrhoidal plexus, resulting from a persistent increase in venous pressure.

Hemorrhoids are dilated veins superficially close to the surface, located at the lower part of the rectum, very close to the exit point, and are very common. Woodall Industries, Inc. v. Massachusetts Mutual Life Insurance Co., 483 F.2d 986, 993 (6th Cir. 1973).

The Commission used the medical approach in defining the term "hemorrhoid." Its conclusions in this regard are based upon the testimony of nine physicians who specialize in diseases of the rectal area including hemorrhoids. Their testimony showed that hemorrhoids or "piles" are dilated or varicose veins located in the lower portions of the rectal area. These are divided into two types, namely, internal and external.

The medical proof further showed that symptoms of hemorrhoids often disappear within periods of time ranging from sev-

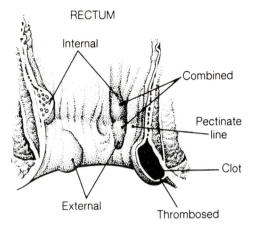

RECTUM

Internal

Combined

Pectinate line

Clot

External

Thrombosed

Hemorrhoids.

eral days to several weeks, but the underlying cause, namely, the dilated vein will persist unless corrected and will cause recurring periods of such symptoms. Surgical removal is the only means by which hemorrhoids can be cured....

... [W]e conclude that there is substantial evidence that hemorrhoids can be permanently cured only through the surgical removal of the affected varicose vein; that petitioner's products will not shrink the hemorrhoidal vein itself, nor eliminate the need for surgery where it is indicated, nor eliminate all itching and all pain due to hemorrhoids in every case. However, in our opinion, there is no substantial evidence that will support the Commission's findings that the Pazo products will not afford temporary relief from the pain and itching connected with hemorrhoids in many cases, nor that these products will not help to reduce swelling associated with hemorrhoids and caused by edema, infection, or inflammation, except to the extent that such swelling is in the varicose vein itself. Grove Laboratories v. Federal Trade Commission, 418 F.2d 489, 494–6 (5th Cir. 1969).

Much of the controversy centers around the definition of "hemorrhoids." The Commission defined the term as follows: " 'Hemorrhoids' are masses of dilated weak-walled veins located underneath the mucous membrane of the lower portions of the rectum and under the skin of the anal canal and the perianal area." In other words, they are varicose veins located in the rectal area. Depending upon their location, these varicose veins may be classified as internal or external. Internal hemorrhoids are in the top part of the anal canal and are covered by mucosa; external hemorrhoids are in the lower portion of the anal canal and are covered by skin....

... But, hemorrhoids as just defined are not in themselves medically significant. It is only when the varicose veins become symptomatic, involving the skin or mucosa around them, that they become troublesome.

Hemorrhoids become symptomatic at various times because of one or more complicating factors, such as constipation, diarrhea, straining, trauma, infections, or conditions or activities which increase pressure on the hemorrhoidal veins. There is some inference that an individual's mental attitude may cause

hemorrhoidal veins to become symptomatic. Symptoms may include bleeding, pain, protrusion, swelling, discharge, itching, and a sense of discomfort or fullness at the anus. These symptoms also may be caused or accompanied by inflammation, edema, ulceration, or infection in tissue adjacent to the varicose veins. The severity and duration of the symptoms may range from mild and short-lived to very severe and long-lasting. Treatment is not an absolute prerequisite for the remission of hemorrhoidal symptoms. The symptoms may disappear or be alleviated by the body's own healing processes. After such remission they may never reappear or they may cause further trouble periodically. However, remission ordinarily will be more rapid and long-lasting if treatment is utilized.... The only realistic definition of "hemorrhoid," as used in petitioner's advertisements, is to regard it as including not only the varicose vein itself but also the tissue contiguous to the vein. This is what the term means to the average person, and it is the average person with whom we are here concerned. In this manner, symptoms and attendant difficulties associated with hemorrhoids are recognized in the definition. The question then is whether the petitioner's representations are false in regard to its product's effect on hemorrhoids and the attendant symptoms commonly associated with hemorrhoids. American Home Products Corp. v. F.T.C., 402 F.2d 232, 235–6 (6th Cir. 1968).

hemorrhoid, external a varicose dilatation of a vein of the inferior hemorrhoidal plexus, situated distal to the pectinate line and covered with modified anal skin.

... **external hemorrhoids** occur in the lower portions of the anal canal below the pectinate line....

... The most common symptoms of **external hemorrhoids** are pain and swelling which is frequently caused by blood clot (thrombosis) inflammation, swelling, or ulceration. Itching is not a common symptom of either type of hemorrhoids, but is believed to be caused by some other disease. Grove Laboratories v. Federal Trade Commission, 418 F.2d 489, 494 (5th Cir. 1969).

hemorrhoid, internal a varicose dilatation of a vein of the superior hemorrhoidal plexus, originating above the pectinate line, and covered by mucous membrane.

Internal hemorrhoids occur in the top part of the anal canal....

... The most common symptoms of **internal hemorrhoids** are bleeding and "prolapse." Grove Laboratories v. Federal Trade Commission, 418 F.2d 489, 494 (5th Cir. 1969).

hemorrhoidectomy (hem"o-roid-ek'to-me) excision of hemorrhoids.

In her complaint she alleged that defendants had subjected her to extensive anal surgery, which she had not authorized, including a negligently performed radical **hemorrhoidectomy**, as a result of which her anal sphincter was irreparably injured, causing her permanent incontinence of the feces, as well as other disabilities. Sanden v. Mayo Clinic, 495 F.2d 221, 223 (8th Cir. 1974).

hemosiderin (he"mo-sid'er-in) [*hemo-* + Gr. *sidēros* iron] an insoluble form of storage iron in which the micelles of ferric hydroxide are so arranged as to be visible microscopically both with and without the use of specific staining methods.

A minimal amount of **hemosiderin** which is a blood breakdown product pigment is present. York v. Daniels, 259 S.W.2d 109, 116 (Springfield Ct.App.Mo.1953).

hemostasis (he"mo-sta′sis, he-mos′tah-sis) [*hemo-* + Gr. *stasis* halt] the arrest of bleeding, either by the physiological properties of vasoconstriction and coagulation or by surgical means.

After the procedure is performed, pressure should be applied to the blood vessel for five minutes and then an additional five more minutes if bleeding persists. In most instances, **hemostasis** is achieved after the first five to ten minutes. Because of the close proximity of the femoral artery and vein, Dr. Blazek would not consider it a deviation from the standard of care for a cardiologist performing a renal arteriography to hit the vein two or three times. If the vein is punctured slight pressure on it causes **hemostasis**. [Footnote omitted.] Hirn v. Edgewater Hospital, 408 N.E.2d 970, 974 (App.Ct.Ill.1980).

The brochure stated that Epinephrine is administered with Xylocaine to prolong the anesthetic effect of the latter drug; that to achieve greater constriction of the blood vessels (**haemostasis**) the concentration of Epinephrine should be increased;... Sanzari v. Rosenfeld, 167 A.2d 625, 633 (N.J. 1961).

hemostat (he′mo-stat) a small surgical clamp for constricting a blood vessel.

Many of the x-rays clearly revealed the presence of two scissor shaped foreign objects in Mr. Easter's left side. These objects proved to be **hemostats**, or clamps used to control bleeding during an operation, five and three-quarters inches in length and resting in a vertical position, pointed ends directed downward, against Mr. Easter's intestines....

... The plaintiff's decedent carried two five and three-quarters inch scissor shaped objects in his abdominal cavity from the date of the operation until his death, over ten months later. The jury found that the presence of these **hemostats** caused him suffering and discomfort for most of the last year of his life. When finally made aware of them, and that their presence had been deliberately concealed from him, the decedent became emotionally distraught, and remained upset over the situation for the rest of his life. Easter v. Hancock, 346 A.2d 323, 325, 328 (Super.Ct.Pa.1975).

The products consist of (a) a disposable instrument in the form of either a **hemostat** (clamp) or a long slender tube which is used to locate bleeders and apply a nylon ligature loop and a nylon lock in the shape of a minute button, (b) the nylon ligature loop, and (c) the nylon lock. AMP Inc. v. Gardner, 275 F.Supp. 410–11 (S.D.N.Y.1967).

hemothorax (he"mo-tho′raks) [*hemo-* + Gr. *thōrax* chest] a collection of blood in the pleural cavity.

The lungs are encased in an envelope-like sac, called the pleural cavity, which is a vacuum. It is necessary to maintain this vacuum to sustain the mechanics of respiration. Anything which breaks the "seal" will cause the lung to collapse. If it is blood, the condition is called **hemothorax**; ... Earlin v. Cravetz, 399 A.2d 783, 785 (Super.Ct.Pa.1979).

... probable tear of the great vessels around the heart, and **hemothorax**; that is blood in the chest. In re Bagge's (Dependents') Case, 338 N.E.2d 348, 351 (Sup.Jud.Ct.Mass.1975).

heparin (hep′ah-rin) an acidic mucopolysaccharide composed of D-glucuronic acid and D-glucosamine, present in many tissues, especially the liver and lungs, and having potent anticoagulant properties. It is believed to act by inhibiting conversion of prothrombin to thrombin, and thus fibrinogen to fibrin. Heparin also has lipotrophic properties, promoting transfer of fat from blood to the fat depots by activation of lipoprotein lipase. See also *time, prothrombin* (Raitt case).

Her treating physician, Dr. James D. Knoepp, prescribed **Heparin** therapy, the recognized treatment for a suspected pulmonary embolism. **Heparin** is a potent anti-coagulant drug. Dr. Knoepp ordered the immediate administration of a 7500 unit bolus of **Heparin** in the emergency room. He then placed Mrs. Belmon in the hospital's intensive care unit (ICU), and ordered that she receive the anti-coagulant by continuous I.V. (intravenous) drip at the rate of 2000 units per hour to achieve maximum Heparinization....

The medical testimony was unanimous that hemorrhage is a substantial risk in **Heparin** therapy. The most common is bleeding into the skin or soft tissues at needle puncture sites. Belmon v. St. Frances Cabrini Hospital, 427 So.2d 541–3 (Ct.App.La. 1983).

... the decision is most difficult as to when if ever, to go to the use of **Heparin** after surgery because of the risks of using the drug as distinct from the benefits to be achieved if, indeed, the patient is clotting and going to throw an embolism and suffer that kind of complication. Raitt v. Johns Hopkins Hospital, 322 A.2d 548, 563 (Ct.Spec.App.Md.1974), reversed and remanded 336 A.2d 90 (Ct.App.Md.1975).

Other Authorities: Mahr v. G. D. Searle & Co., 390 N.E.2d 1214, 1222 (App.Ct.Ill.1979).

heparinize (hep′er-ĭ-nīz″) to treat with heparin in order to increase the clotting time of the blood.

The trial court found that Cabrini breached its duty toward Mrs. Belmon because neither the nurse nor the med tech approached their duties with a proper understanding of the hemorrhage-prone vulnerability of a **Heparinized** patient. As a consequence, the med tech drew blood in ignorance of the fact that plaintiff was **Heparinized** and without observing the extra precautions required in such cases.

... Medical scientists disagree as to the parameters, expressed in PTT value, of adequate **Heparinization**. One school of thought—and some of the doctors who testified in this case belonged to that school—believe that **Heparinization** is achieved when clotting time is increased to two and a half times the base, which in Mrs. Belmon's case would have been about 70 seconds. At higher levels the risk of hemorrhage outweighs the benefits of increased clotting time. Nurse Kevil was taught according to this school and based her evaluation of an ICU nurse's duties on its precepts.

Another school, of which Dr. Knoepp was a proponent, thinks the risk of hemorrhage does not increase apace with clotting time, and that **Heparinization** in life threatening situations is not achieved until the maximum reading on the PTT machine is attained, 180 seconds. This was the extent to which

Mrs. Belmon was **Heparinized**. Belmon v. St. Frances Cabrini Hospital, 427 So.2d 541, 544–5 (Ct.App.La.1983).

She stated in her opinion there was no evidence here the child suffered from **overheparinization**. In addition, she noted, had the infant been **overheparinized**, she would have metabolized the substance in three or four hours, assuming a normal liver function as was this child's, and there would not have been this type of bleeding without some trauma. Vecchione v. Carlin, 168 Cal.Rptr. 571, 574 (Ct.App.Cal.1980).

hepatic (hĕ-pat'ik) [L. *hepaticus;* Gr. *hēpatikos*] pertaining to the liver.

hepatic duct See *ductus, choledochus.*

hepatitis (hep"ah-ti'tis), pl. *hepatit'ides [hepat-* + *-itis*] inflammation of the liver. See also *halothane* (Coffran case); *isoniazid* (Moodie case); and *tattooing.*

At the hospital, Mr. Santoni was diagnosed as suffering from **hepatitis**. There is no treatment for the disease, only care to prevent complications. Despite the absence of any complications, Mr. Santoni's condition deteriorated rapidly and he died on July 3, 1972. Expert testimony placed the cause of death as a toxic reaction to isoniazid, causing **hepatitis**. 48 Md.App. at 503–04, 428 A.2d 94. Moodie v. Santoni, 441 A.2d 323–4 (Ct.App.Md.1982).

A second report, also dated June 28, 1976, discussed the possible causes of Everett's **hepatitis**. Dr. Lewis listed the three usual causes: exposure to another person so inflicted (infectious hepatitis); internal contact with contaminated blood (serum hepatitis), a common source for those who use syringes, as do morticians (Everett was a mortician), and ingestion of contaminated food (infectious hepatitis). Johnsee v. Stop & Shop Cos., Inc., 416 A.2d 956, 958 (Super.Ct.N.J.1980).

He testified that **hepatitis** is an inflammatory disease of the liver. Symptoms are fever, weakness, usually abdominal pain, often nausea, vomiting with dehydration as a result, malaise. Treatment is bed rest, intravenous feeding including glucose and water. It is a liver disease. It can be mild or severe and fulminating. Jaundice or yellowing is a development of the disease. It is first visible in the white of the eyeball. Torrez v. Raag, 357 N.E.2d 632, 634 (App.Ct.Ill.1976).

Other Authorities: State v. Weiner, 41 N.J. 21, 23 (1963).

hepatitis A See *hepatitis, viral, type A.*

hepatitis B See *hepatitis, viral, type B.*

hepatitis, infectious See *hepatitis, viral, type A.*

hepatitis, serum See *hepatitis, viral, type B.*

hepatitis, viral a third form, caused by non-A, non-B hepatitis virus, closely resembles viral hepatitis type B. See *viral h. type A* and *viral h. type B.*

There was expert testimony at trial that the incubation period for **hepatitis** can be 30–60 days for Type A (infectious hepatitis) and 4–6 months for Type B (serum hepatitis). It was the belief of appellant's doctor that she had contracted Type A. . . .

There was conflicting expert testimony introduced at trial regarding the mode by which the **hepatitis** virus, Type A, is transmitted. Appellant's treating physician and an expert medical witness called by appellant at trial both testified that Type A may be transmitted by blood transfusions, although the primary means of transmission is oral, through contaminated food or water. The expert medical witness called by the defendant, a physician affiliated with the hospital, testified that the Type A virus is believed to be transmitted orally, while Type B is linked to injections with contaminated needles and transfusions of impure blood. Fisher v. Sibley Memorial Hospital, 403 A.2d 1130–1 (D.C.Cir.1979).

hepatitis, viral, type A an acute viral illness of worldwide distribution, occurring most commonly in children and young adults. It is usually transmitted by oral ingestion of infected material, but may also be transmitted parenterally (see *viral H. type B*). Although the viral agent (hepatitis virus A) has not been isolated or detected by immunological tests, transmission studies and electron microscopy indicate that patients with viral hepatitis type A excrete the infective agent in their stools for a period of weeks in the prodromal and early icteric period of illness. The incubation is short (about 15 to 50 or 60 days). The prodromal (*preicteric*) stage usually begins abruptly with fever, malaise, and nonspecific gastrointestinal symptoms (anorexia, nausea, upper abdominal discomfort, and vomiting); the *icteric stage* usually reaches a peak within two weeks and is characterized by jaundice, variable pruritus, dark urine, pale stool, and liver enlargement with tenderness; the *posticteric period* refers to the period of convalescense, when malaise, tiredness, and minor abnormalities of hepatic function may persist. During the acute phase, characteristic pathological findings include necrosis of liver cells and portal and parenchymal infiltration, chiefly by mononuclear cells. Called also *h. A, epidemic h.* or *jaundice, infectious h., MS–1 h.,* and *short-incubation h.*

Nothing was done which would help differentiate ordinary **infectious hepatitis**, from the usual unknown sources (another person carrying the virus) from food contamination source. We do know now, however, that he was Australian antigen positive. The odds now begin to shift in the direction of contamination of his blood, possibly as a result of his professional work as I previously explained. In ordinary **infectious hepatitis** only 20% of patients become Australian antigen positive. Johnesee v. Stop & Shop Cos., Inc., 416 A.2d 956, 958 (Super.Ct.N.J.1980).

Plaintiff-respondent's decedent, a young man of seventeen, was admitted to Metropolitan Hospital where, after tests, his ailment was diagnosed as **acute viral hepatitis**. His condition did not improve and he became comatose and, in less than a week after admission, moribund. Jones v. City of New York, 395 N.Y.S.2d 10, 11 (1st Dep't 1977).

The Official Package Circular for Blood Services' blood provides the following warning:

HOMOLOGOUS SERUM JAUNDICE (**VIRAL HEPATITIS**): The transmission of **viral hepatitis** is an inherent and unavoidable risk which is present each time a unit of whole blood is given. There is no known laboratory tests which will detect the presence of the virus in the donor blood. The incubation period is usually 15 to 180 days and the disease is sometimes severe and protracted and may be fatal. Heirs of Fruge v. Blood Services, 365 F.Supp. 1344, 1348 (W.D.La.1973), affirmed in part, reversed in part 506 F.2d 841 (5th Cir. 1975).

Other Authorities: State v. Weiner, 41 N.J. 21, 23, 194 A.2d 467 (1963).

hepatitis, viral, type B an acute illness caused by hepatitis B virus, formerly considered to be transmitted only by parenteral exposure (contaminated needles and administration of blood or blood products), but now known also to be transmitted by oral ingestion of contaminated material. The incubation period is long—50 to 160 or as many as 180 days. Prodromal symptoms and signs may be insidious in onset and include urticarial skin lesions and arthritis, and the acute illness tends to be more prolonged than in viral hepatitis type A; otherwise, the clinical and pathological symptoms are similar (see *viral h. type A*). Anicteric, icteric, fulminant, cholestatic, recurrent, chronic and persistent forms have been characterized. Serum antigens detected include hepatitis B surface and core antigens and e antigen, as have complete virions or Dane particles and DNA polymerase. Called also *h. B, inoculation h., long-incubation h., MS–2H., serum h., transfusion h.*, and *homologous serum h.* or *jaundice*. See also *Carrier* (N.Y. State Ass'n case).

Serium [sic] **hepatitis** contracted from contaminated blood, some 80% become positive. The odds, obviously shift, in the direction of so-called **serium** [sic] **hepatitis** (now known as **hepatitis-B**). Johnesee v. Stop & Shop Cos., Inc., 416 A.2d 956, 958 (Super.Ct.N.J.1980).

Hepatitis B is a virus which may ultimately have a debilitating effect on the liver. When introduced into a susceptible person, the virus undergoes a long period of incubation, generally two to three months. The acute stage, which is a rather rare phenomenon, is sometimes accompanied by jaundice and inflammation of the liver and in some cases may be very serious and even lead to death. There is no known cure for **hepatitis B**, although optimism was expressed as to the development of an effective vaccine within the next four years. In other cases, however, particularly among children, the acute phase of **hepatitis B** may be very mild and be mistaken for a passing flu and fever. . . .

The epidemiology of **hepatitis B** was discussed at length during the hearing. Unlike hepatitis A, which is highly contagious, **hepatitis B** is of limited communicability. It is generally communicated solely by the parenteral, or blood-to-blood route, by means of transfusions of infected blood, or by use of a contaminated needle. Long believed to be found only in the blood, or in body fluids where blood is present, recent studies indicate that **hepatitis B** antigen may also be present, on occasion, in saliva. Dr. Bakal testified with respect to one study he had read where the disease was experimentally transmitted by placing infected saliva into the mouth of a recipient. However, according to a Center for Disease Control study issued in May 1976,

[a]lthough [**hepatitis B** antigen] has been detected in many human biological fluids during acute infection, transmission of disease by saliva or other body fluids containing antigen has not yet been convincingly demonstrated. United States Public Health Service, Center for Disease Control, Morbidity and Mortality Weekly Report, Vol. 25, No. 17, May 7,

1976, at 4. New York State Ass'n, etc. v. Carey, 466 F.Supp. 479, 482–3 (E.D.N.Y.1978).

The other form of viral hepatitis is "**serum**" hepatitis, and this is transmitted directly into the blood stream by the injection of contaminated material. The State's case depended upon the thesis that the decedents died of **serum hepatitis**, transmitted into their veins by the injections and infusions which we have already mentioned and which we will shortly describe. . . .

. . . One such difference is that the rate of fatality is distinctly higher in the case of **serum hepatitis**. Another is that the incubation period with respect to infectious hepatitis is two to six weeks, while the period in the case of **serum hepatitis** is six weeks to six months, or, according to some testimony, as much as one year. State v. Weiner, 41 N.J. 21, 23–4, 194 A.2d 467 (N.J.1963).

hepatolienography (hep"ah-to-li"ĕ-nog'rah-fe) [*hepato-* + L. *lien* spleen + Gr. *graphein* to record] roentgenography of the liver and spleen after intravenous injection of an opaque medium.

. . . and for **hepatolienography** (visualization of the liver and spleen). Application of Papesch, 315 F.2d 381, 389 (U.S.Ct. Cust. & Pat.App.1963).

hepatomegaly (hep"ah-to-meg'ah-le) enlargement of the liver.

. . . also congestive **hepatomegaly** (swelling of the liver). Magruder v. Richardson, 332 F.Supp. 1363, 1368 (E.D.Mo.1971).

heptabarbital (hep"tah-bar'bĭ-tal) chemical name: 5-(1-cyclohepten-1-yl)-5-ethyl-2,4-6(1H,3H,5H)-pyrimidine-trione. A short-acting barbiturate, $C_{13}H_{18}N_2O_3$, occurring as a white, crystalline powder, used as a sedative and hypnotic, administered orally.

Main had used **Medomin** and Elixir of Butibel to relax him and aid him in going to sleep on retiring for the night, and he had used Equanil from time to time, when needed to relieve tension, acting under the direction of his then physician, who had given him prescriptions therefor. **Medomin** and Butibel are barbiturates. . . .

. . . Dr. Crouch, after some discussion with Main, gave him a prescription for the **Medomin** and for Butibel, because he was of the opinion Main needed them to relax him and aid him in going to sleep at bedtime. . . .

. . . He further testified that in his opinion it was the synergistic action of the **Medomin** and the alcohol present in the blood stream and spinal fluid at the same time that depressed the center of the brain controlling breathing, blood circulation, and blood pressure and caused a respiratory arrest and Main's death. Metropolitan Life Ins. Co. v. Main, 383 F.2d 952–4, 957 (5th Cir. 1967).

herbicide (her'bĭ-sĭd) [L. *herba* herb + *caedere* to kill] an agent that is destructive to weeds or causes an alteration in their normal growth. See also particular kinds of herbicides, e.g., *paraquat*.

herbicide, phenoxy

The **phenoxy herbicides** are a group of selective herbicides widely used in crop production and in the management of forests, rangelands, aquatic habitats, and industrial and urban sites. These herbicides, which are related to naturally-occur-

...urn problem is a **hiatus hernia**. She notices ...mach, some pressure in her chest when she ...like a heart attack....

...astrointestinal X-rays revealed a large **hiatus** ...akes for easy regurgitation of food on stoop- ...g, increasing intra-abdominal pressure.... ...inberger, 361 F.Supp. 247, 249, 251 (E.D.Mo. ...d and remanded 490 F.2d 1187 (8th Cir. 1974).

...mination, defendant's counsel was permitted to ...n, over objection, if during surgery he had discov- ...cted an esophageal **hiatal hernia**. He answered ...not. Wagner v. Reading Co., 428 F.2d 289–90 (3d ...

incisional hernia occurring through an old abdom- ...ncision. See also *herniorrhaphy*.

...mes was of this opinion:

...ughing would tend to increase the chances of developing ...*separation*, a deep separation with subsequent or later ...evelopment of an **incisional hernias** [sic] but from the stud- ...s that have appeared in the literature, most separations ...purely depend on the nutritional status of the patient and ...upon the cement substance of the body, the ability of the ...body to form collagen to make that incision stick together. ...Dr. James also described appellant as being moderately ...bese at the time of the hysterectomy and said that it was his ...xperience a moderately obese woman would have a greater ...hance of developing an **incisional hernia** than a person of ...ormal weight and height. Pendleton v. Cilley, 574 P.2d 1303, ...306 (Ariz.1978).

...nia, inguinal hernia into the inguinal canal. An *indirect* ...guinal hernia (*external* or *oblique* hernia) leaves the ...domen through the deep inguinal ring, and passes ...wn obliquely through the inguinal canal, lateral to the ...rior epigastric artery. A *direct* inguinal hernia (*inter-* ... hernia) emerges between the inferior epigastric artery ...the edge of the rectus muscle. See also *anulus in-* ...alis profundus; anulus inguinalis superficialis; and ...lis inguinalis.

...s the workmen's compensation referee found, "the dece- ...was helping to unload bags of lime from a chute; he ...d himself to catch a bag which weighed approximately ...und extended his arms to stop [the] bag from falling to ...our and felt a pull in his right inguinal region." On ...ry 1968, the decedent was operated on for the ...ght **inguinal hernia**, and on March 13, 1968, ...e hospital, he died. Czankner v. Sky Top Lodge, ...911–12 (Commonwealth Ct.Pa.1973).

...rainerd observed an enlarged inguinal ring and ...defendant suffered from a right **inguinal hernia** ...sence of "true protruding". Several other pri- ...observed enlarged inguinal rings without pro- ...mpanied by "striking" or "gurggling." The re- ...dle, another Brainerd physician indicates a ...ernia on the right side", but later inquiry re- ...was only an opinion and the doctor did not ...ernia and there was no protrusion....

...ct results from the fact that several qualified ...drew different conclusions from substantially

similar symptoms. U.S. v. Hansen, 327 F.Supp. 1090, 1093 (D.Minn.1971).

It is my impression that this man has a minimal right **inguinal hernia** which can be probably well controlled by the use of an appliance. He did not have the appliance with him when he was examined by me. It is my opinion that this man had proba- bly some weakness of the anatomical structures in the right inguinal area and that the repeated trauma undoubtedly con- tributed to the production of what is now the right **inguinal hernia**. Hurlburt v. Fidelity Window Cleaning Co., 160 A.2d 251, 255 (Super.Ct.Pa.1960).

hernia, real traumatic

§ 23–1043. Hernias classified for compensation pur- poses....

1. **Real traumatic hernia** is an injury to the abdominal wall of sufficient severity to puncture or tear asunder the wall, and permit the exposure or protrusion of the abdominal viscera or some part thereof. Such injury will be compensated as a temporary total disability and as a partial permanent disabil- ity, depending upon the lessening of the injured individual's earning capacity. Figueroa v. Industrial Com'n, 529 P.2d 1188, 1191 (Ct.App.Ariz.1974), vacated 543 P.2d 785 (Ariz.1975).

hernia, ventral hernia through the abdominal wall.

Dr. Samuel Borssuck, the operating physician, noted that the claimant had developed a **ventral hernia**, and he was of the opinion that his patient "should do no lifting." Purdham v. Cel- ebrezze, 349 F.2d 828–9 (4th Cir. 1965).

He is suffering, and has suffered for some time in the past, from a traumatic **ventral hernia** which is the direct result of the gun shot, the operation in Venezuela, and the operation in Balti- more and which requires correction by surgery....

... defendant, being aware of that medical background, should have known, when Dr. Parker found a bulging in plain- tiff's abdomen, that that bulge indicated that he had a hernia and that surgery should then have been advised and offered .... Graham v. Alcoa S.S. Co., 201 F.2d 423–4 (3d Cir. 1953).

Other Authorities: Pendleton v. Cilley, 574 P.2d 1303–4 (Ariz. 1978).

herniated disk See *herniation of intervertebral disk*.

herniated nucleus pulposus See *herniation of nucleus pulposus*.

herniation (her"ne-a'shun) the abnormal protrusion of an organ or other body structure through a defect or natural opening in a covering membrane, muscle, or bone. See also *hematoma* (Schakow case).

Due to the **herniation** of his brain, caused by delay in proper medical treatment, Mr. Dixon was rendered cortically blind and a quadriplegic. Schackow v. Medical-Legal Consulting, etc., 416 A.2d 1303, 1305 (Ct.Spec.App.Md.1980).

He testified further that a radiating pain down one's leg, a tingling sensation in the foot and a footdrop condition are all signs of great pressure on a nerve root and are symptoms which indicate that the adjustment preceding them could have aggravated a herniated disc or caused a **herniation**. Cham- ness v. Odum, 399 N.E.2d 238, 245 (App.Ct.Ill.1979).

ring plant growth regulators, kill plants by causing malfunctions in growth processes. They are useful primarily because of their selectivity: broad-leaved plants are generally susceptible, while most grasses, coniferous trees, and certain legumes are relatively resistant.

The phenoxy acids form a family of compounds having similar chemical and biological properties but differing in details that affect their activity on individual plants, their cost, and other characteristics. The ones presently in use as herbicides in the United States include 2,4-dichlorophenoxyacetic acid (2,4–D), 2,4,5-trichlorophenoxyacetic acid (2,4,5–T), 2–(2,4,5-trichlorophenoxy) propionic acid (2,4,5–TP or silvex), 2,4–DP or dichloroprop, mecoprop, 2,4–DB, 2,4–DEP, erbon, MCPA, and MCPB. Of the **phenoxy herbicides**, 2,4–D, 2,4,5–T, and silvex are used the most extensively. Citizens Against Toxic Sprays, Inc. v. Bergland, 428 F.Supp. 908, 913–14 (D.Ore. 1977).

hereditary (he-red'ĭ-ter-e) [L. *hereditarius*] genetically transmitted from parent to offspring.

hermaphrodite (her-maf'ro-dīt) [Gr. *hermaphroditos*] an individual exhibiting hermaphroditism (q.v.).

hermaphroditism (her-maf'ro-di-tizm″) [Gr. *hermaphroditos* a person partaking of the attributes of both sexes] originally, a state characterized by the presence of both male and female sex organs. In humans, *true hermaphroditism* is caused by anomalous differentiation of the gonads, with the presence of both ovarian and testicular tissue and of ambiguous morphologic criteria of sex. If only testicular tissue is present, but there are some female morphological criteria of sex, it is known as *male pseudohermaphroditism*. If only ovarian tissue is present, but there are some male morphological criteria of sex, it is known as *female pseudohermaphroditism*. See also *intersex; pseudohermaphroditism*; and *transsexual* (Hartin case).

hermaphroditism, true coexistence, in the same individual, of both ovarian and testicular tissue, with somatic characters typical of both sexes; called also *true intersex*.

. . . **true hermaphroditism**, which is a rare condition in humans characterized by the co-existence of both ovarian and testicular tissue. Hartin v. Director of Bureau of Records, etc., 347 N.Y.S.2d 515, 517 (Sup.Ct.N.Y.Cty.1973).

hernia (her'ne-ah) [L.] the protrusion of a loop or knuckle of an organ or tissue through an abnormal opening. See also *traumatic* (Figueroa case). See illustration.

However, on this occasion his physician attempted repair of the **hernia** by use of Marlex fiber screen which was sewn into the fascia because of the lack of sufficient tissue to close the herniation. Dr. Kittrell, the treating physician, testified that Mr. Taylor would never again be able to do any heavy work. Northern Assurance Co. of America v. Taylor, 540 S.W.2d 832–3 (Ct.Civ.App.Tex.1976).

By statute, in Arizona **hernias** parallel the medical grouping, being classified for compensation purposes in two categories. A.R.S. § 23–1043 provides:

. . . the following rules for rating hernias shall govern:

1. Re
of sufficie
wall. . . . [C
2. All oth
considered dise
sidered to be as
ed from birth, to h
[Category 2]
. . . The vital distinc
cause of the herniation,
abnormal weakness of th
from birth, or which formed
debilitating disease, or both.
It is to be concluded, therefo
the two categories is primarily a
by whether a contributing cause
normal weakness of the muscular
abdomen as set forth in the statute.
ness exists, it is a category 2 **hernia**
category 1 **hernia**. Figueroa v. Indust.
P.2d 785, 787–8 (Ariz.1975).

Chapter 2 Army Regulations 40–501 simply
nia other than small asymptomatic umbilical or
cause for rejection from service in the Armed F
elsewhere defined as, "[t]he protrusion of a lo
an organ or tissue through an abdominal ope
Medical Dictionary, (24th ed.); accord Black's
(4th ed. 1968). "Ordinarily a **hernia**, or ruptu
nonymous term, involves the extrusion of one
abdominal viscera through an abnormal openin
largement of a normal opening in the abdomi
Jur. Proof of Facts, Hernia, at 700, U.S.
F.Supp. 1090–1, 1095 (D.Minn.1971).

hernia, frank
Q. Were these hernias that you found?
A. This is a rather difficult question to
be considered a **frank hernia**, but a defi
abdominal floors, the inguinal area.
Q. When you say a **frank hernia**, d
not hernias by definition; that they had
cess of becoming a hernia?
A. In other words, when I say **f**
separated the muscular wall to the
contents and viscera were protru
wall. Matthews v. Industrial Com
App.Ariz.1971).

hernia, hiatal; hernia, hiatus
through the esophageal hia
ally a sliding or paraesop

In December, 1974 the d
hernia (which he stated is
pressure and can be car
. . . This physician, H
all of the medical rec
not cause a **hiatal h**
by direct blow to t
the dashboard an
room, and he w
stomach pain
Wight & Co.,

Claimant's heart
cramps in her st
eats, and it feel
. . . Upper G
hernia, which
ing or
Landess W
1973), r

On cro
ask Dr.
ered o
that he
Cir. 1

hernia
inal
Dr.
C

her
in
ab
do
inf
na
and
guin
can

. . .
dent
brac
80 p
the
Febru
repair
while
Inc., 3
Dr. Me
conclu
despite
vate ph
trusion
port of C
"small
vealed
definitel
medical

ring plant growth regulators, kill plants by causing malfunctions in growth processes. They are useful primarily because of their selectivity: broad-leaved plants are generally susceptible, while most grasses, coniferous trees, and certain legumes are relatively resistant.

The phenoxy acids form a family of compounds having similar chemical and biological properties but differing in details that affect their activity on individual plants, their cost, and other characteristics. The ones presently in use as herbicides in the United States include 2,4-dichlorophenoxyacetic acid (2,4–D), 2,4,5-trichlorophenoxyacetic acid (2,4,5–T), 2–(2,4,5-trichlorophenoxy) propionic acid (2,4,5–TP or silvex), 2,4–DP or dichloroprop, mecoprop, 2,4–DB, 2,4–DEP, erbon, MCPA, and MCPB. Of the **phenoxy herbicides**, 2,4–D, 2,4,5–T, and silvex are used the most extensively. Citizens Against Toxic Sprays, Inc. v. Bergland, 428 F.Supp. 908, 913–14 (D.Ore. 1977).

hereditary (he-red′ĭ-ter-e) [L. *hereditarius*] genetically transmitted from parent to offspring.

hermaphrodite (her-maf′ro-dīt) [Gr. *hermaphroditos*] an individual exhibiting hermaphroditism (q.v.).

hermaphroditism (her-maf′ro-di-tizm″) [Gr. *hermaphroditos* a person partaking of the attributes of both sexes] originally, a state characterized by the presence of both male and female sex organs. In humans, *true hermaphroditism* is caused by anomalous differentiation of the gonads, with the presence of both ovarian and testicular tissue and of ambiguous morphologic criteria of sex. If only testicular tissue is present, but there are some female morphological criteria of sex, it is known as *male pseudohermaphroditism*. If only ovarian tissue is present, but there are some male morphological criteria of sex, it is known as *female pseudohermaphroditism*. See also *intersex; pseudohermaphroditism;* and *transsexual* (Hartin case).

hermaphroditism, true coexistence, in the same individual, of both ovarian and testicular tissue, with somatic characters typical of both sexes; called also *true intersex.*

… true hermaphroditism, which is a rare condition in humans characterized by the co-existence of both ovarian and testicular tissue. Hartin v. Director of Bureau of Records, etc., 347 N.Y.S.2d 515, 517 (Sup.Ct.N.Y.Cty.1973).

hernia (her′ne-ah) [L.] the protrusion of a loop or knuckle of an organ or tissue through an abnormal opening. See also *traumatic* (Figueroa case). See illustration.

However, on this occasion his physician attempted repair of the hernia by use of Marlex fiber screen which was sewn into the fascia because of the lack of sufficient tissue to close the herniation. Dr. Kittrell, the treating physician, testified that Mr. Taylor would never again be able to do any heavy work. Northern Assurance Co. of America v. Taylor, 540 S.W.2d 832–3 (Ct.Civ.App.Tex.1976).

By statute, in Arizona hernias parallel the medical grouping, being classified for compensation purposes in two categories. A.R.S. § 23–1043 provides:

… the following rules for rating hernias shall govern:

1.   Real traumatic hernia is an injury to the abdominal wall of sufficient severity to puncture or tear asunder the wall…. [Category 1]

2.   All other hernias … whatsoever the cause … are considered diseases … but … the causes thereof are considered to be as shown by medical facts to have either existed from birth, to have been years in formation, or both…. [Category 2]

… The vital distinction in category 2 hernias is that as a cause of the herniation, concurring with the strain, there is the abnormal weakness of the muscular structure, either existing from birth, or which formed through muscular wasting, old age, debilitating disease, or both.

It is to be concluded, therefore, that the difference between the two categories is primarily a medical one to be determined by whether a contributing cause of the herniation was the abnormal weakness of the muscular structure of the walls of the abdomen as set forth in the statute. If such a muscular weakness exists, it is a category 2 hernia. But, otherwise, it is a category 1 hernia. Figueroa v. Industrial Commission, 543 P.2d 785, 787–8 (Ariz.1975).

Chapter 2 Army Regulations 40–501 simply states that, "hernia other than small asymptomatic umbilical or hiatal," shall be cause for rejection from service in the Armed Forces. Hernia is elsewhere defined as, "[t]he protrusion of a loop or knuckle of an organ or tissue through an abdominal opening," Dorlands Medical Dictionary, (24th ed.); accord Black's Law Dictionary (4th ed. 1968). "Ordinarily a hernia, or rupture, which is a synonymous term, involves the extrusion of one or more of the abdominal viscera through an abnormal opening or the enlargement of a normal opening in the abdominal wall." 5 Am. Jur. Proof of Facts, Hernia, at 700. U.S. v. Hansen, 327 F.Supp. 1090–1, 1095 (D.Minn.1971).

hernia, frank

Q.   Were these hernias that you found?

A.   This is a rather difficult question to answer. It would not be considered a frank hernia, but a definite weakness in the abdominal floors, the inguinal area.

Q.   When you say a frank hernia, do you mean they were not hernias by definition; that they had not completed the process of becoming a hernia?

A.   In other words, when I say frank hernia, it has not yet separated the muscular wall to the point where the abdomen contents and viscera were protruding through the abdominal wall. Matthews v. Industrial Commission, 490 P.2d 29, 31 (Ct. App.Ariz.1971).

hernia, hiatal; hernia, hiatus protrusion of any structure through the esophageal hiatus of the diaphragm, but usually a sliding or paraesophageal hernia.

In December, 1974 the doctor surgically repaired the hiatal hernia (which he stated is caused by increased interabdominal pressure and can be caused by trauma)….

… This physician, having examined plaintiff and reviewed all of the medical records, opined that a whiplash injury does not cause a hiatal hernia, which is traumatically caused only by direct blow to the abdomen (plaintiff was thrown beneath the dashboard and complained of chest pain in the emergency room, and he was a thin, young man who had never suffered stomach pain prior to the accident). Bellard v. Woodward Wight & Co., Ltd., 362 So.2d 819, 822 (Ct.App.La.1978).

Claimant's heartburn problem is a **hiatus hernia**. She notices cramps in her stomach, some pressure in her chest when she eats, and it feels like a heart attack. . . .

. . . Upper Gastrointestinal X-rays revealed a large **hiatus hernia**, which makes for easy regurgitation of food on stooping or bending, increasing intra-abdominal pressure. . . . Landess v. Weinberger, 361 F.Supp. 247, 249, 251 (E.D.Mo. 1973), reversed and remanded 490 F.2d 1187 (8th Cir. 1974).

On cross-examination, defendant's counsel was permitted to ask Dr. Rowan, over objection, if during surgery he had discovered or detected an esophageal **hiatal hernia**. He answered that he had not. Wagner v. Reading Co., 428 F.2d 289–90 (3d Cir. 1970).

hernia, incisional hernia occurring through an old abdominal incision. See also *herniorrhaphy*.

Dr. James was of this opinion:

Coughing would tend to increase the chances of developing a separation, a deep separation with subsequent or later development of an **incisional hernias** [sic] but from the studies that have appeared in the literature, most separations purely depend on the nutritional status of the patient and upon the cement substance of the body, the ability of the body to form collagen to make that incision stick together.

Dr. James also described appellant as being moderately obese at the time of the hysterectomy and said that it was his experience a moderately obese woman would have a greater chance of developing an **incisional hernia** than a person of normal weight and height. Pendleton v. Cilley, 574 P.2d 1303, 1306 (Ariz. 1978).

hernia, inguinal hernia into the inguinal canal. An *indirect* inguinal hernia (*external* or *oblique* hernia) leaves the abdomen through the deep inguinal ring, and passes down obliquely through the inguinal canal, lateral to the inferior epigastric artery. A *direct* inguinal hernia (*internal* hernia) emerges between the inferior epigastric artery and the edge of the rectus muscle. See also *anulus inguinalis profundus; anulus inguinalis superficialis;* and *canalis inguinalis.*

. . . as the workmen's compensation referee found, "the decedent was helping to unload bags of lime from a chute; he braced himself to catch a bag which weighed approximately 80 pounds, extended his arms to stop [the] bag from falling to the ground, and felt a pull in his right inguinal region." On February 27, 1968, the decedent was operated on for the repair of a right **inguinal hernia**, and on March 13, 1968, while still in the hospital, he died. Czankner v. Sky Top Lodge, Inc., 308 A.2d 911–12 (Commonwealth Ct.Pa.1973).

Dr. Meller of Brainerd observed an enlarged inguinal ring and concluded that defendant suffered from a right **inguinal hernia** despite the absence of "true protruding". Several other private physicians observed enlarged inguinal rings without protrusion but accompanied by "striking" or "gurggling." The report of Dr. Cardle, another Brainerd physician indicates a "small indirect hernia on the right side", but later inquiry revealed that this was only an opinion and the doctor did not definitely find a hernia and there was no protrusion. . . .

. . . The conflict results from the fact that several qualified medical experts drew different conclusions from substantially similar symptoms. U.S. v. Hansen, 327 F.Supp. 1090, 1093 (D.Minn.1971).

It is my impression that this man has a minimal right **inguinal hernia** which can be probably well controlled by the use of an appliance. He did not have the appliance with him when he was examined by me. It is my opinion that this man had probably some weakness of the anatomical structures in the right inguinal area and that the repeated trauma undoubtedly contributed to the production of what is now the right **inguinal hernia**. Hurlburt v. Fidelity Window Cleaning Co., 160 A.2d 251, 255 (Super.Ct.Pa.1960).

hernia, real traumatic

§ 23–1043. Hernias classified for compensation purposes. . . .

1. **Real traumatic hernia** is an injury to the abdominal wall of sufficient severity to puncture or tear asunder the wall, and permit the exposure or protrusion of the abdominal viscera or some part thereof. Such injury will be compensated as a temporary total disability and as a partial permanent disability, depending upon the lessening of the injured individual's earning capacity. Figueroa v. Industrial Com'n, 529 P.2d 1188, 1191 (Ct.App.Ariz.1974), vacated 543 P.2d 785 (Ariz.1975).

hernia, ventral hernia through the abdominal wall.

Dr. Samuel Borssuck, the operating physician, noted that the claimant had developed a **ventral hernia**, and he was of the opinion that his patient "should do no lifting." Purdham v. Celebrezze, 349 F.2d 828–9 (4th Cir. 1965).

He is suffering, and has suffered for some time in the past, from a traumatic **ventral hernia** which is the direct result of the gun shot, the operation in Venezuela, and the operation in Baltimore and which requires correction by surgery. . . .

. . . defendant, being aware of that medical background, should have known, when Dr. Parker found a bulging in plaintiff's abdomen, that that bulge indicated that he had a hernia and that surgery should then have been advised and offered . . . . Graham v. Alcoa S.S. Co., 201 F.2d 423–4 (3d Cir. 1953).

Other Authorities: Pendleton v. Cilley, 574 P.2d 1303–4 (Ariz. 1978).

herniated disk See *herniation of intervertebral disk.*

herniated nucleus pulposus See *herniation of nucleus pulposus.*

herniation (her"ne-a'shun) the abnormal protrusion of an organ or other body structure through a defect or natural opening in a covering membrane, muscle, or bone. See also *hematoma* (Schakow case).

Due to the **herniation** of his brain, caused by delay in proper medical treatment, Mr. Dixon was rendered cortically blind and a quadriplegic. Schackow v. Medical-Legal Consulting, etc., 416 A.2d 1303, 1305 (Ct.Spec.App.Md.1980).

He testified further that a radiating pain down one's leg, a tingling sensation in the foot and a footdrop condition are all signs of great pressure on a nerve root and are symptoms which indicate that the adjustment preceding them could have aggravated a herniated disc or caused a **herniation**. Chamness v. Odum, 399 N.E.2d 238, 245 (App.Ct.Ill.1979).

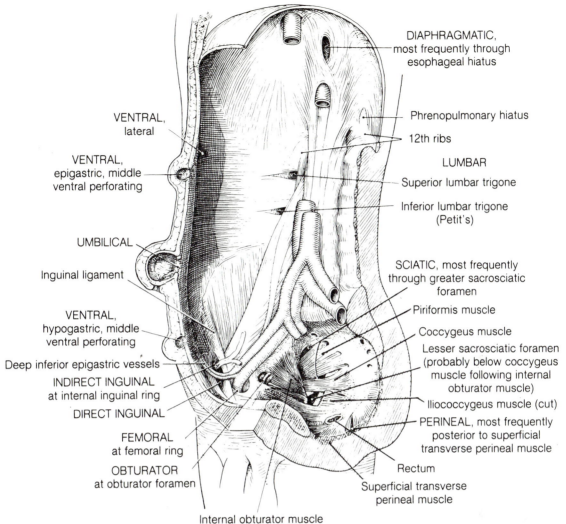

DIAPHRAGMATIC, most frequently through esophageal hiatus

Phrenopulmonary hiatus

12th ribs

LUMBAR

Superior lumbar trigone

Inferior lumbar trigone (Petit's)

VENTRAL, lateral

VENTRAL, epigastric, middle ventral perforating

UMBILICAL

Inguinal ligament

SCIATIC, most frequently through greater sacrosciatic foramen

Piriformis muscle

Coccygeus muscle

Lesser sacrosciatic foramen (probably below coccygeus muscle following internal obturator muscle)

VENTRAL, hypogastric, middle ventral perforating

Deep inferior epigastric vessels

INDIRECT INGUINAL at internal inguinal ring

DIRECT INGUINAL

FEMORAL at femoral ring

OBTURATOR at obturator foramen

Iliococcygeus muscle (cut)

PERINEAL, most frequently posterior to superficial transverse perineal muscle

Rectum

Superficial transverse perineal muscle

Internal obturator muscle

TYPES OF INTESTINAL HERNIA: ABDOMINAL AND PELVIC OPENINGS

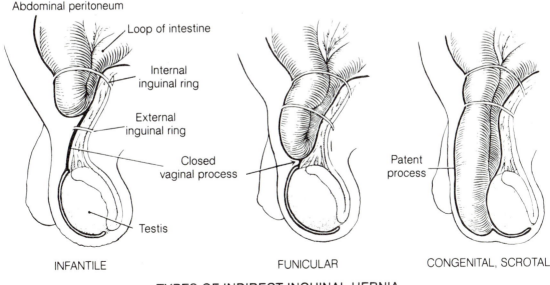

Abdominal peritoneum

Loop of intestine

Internal inguinal ring

External inguinal ring

Closed vaginal process

Testis

Patent process

INFANTILE

FUNICULAR

CONGENITAL, SCROTAL

TYPES OF INDIRECT INGUINAL HERNIA

herniation of intervertebral disk protrusion of the nucleus pulposus or annulus fibrosus of the disk, which may impinge on nerve roots.

Dr. Richard H. Eppright, who consulted with Dr. Brodsky with respect to Mr. French's third operation, testified that a "herniated" disc is one in which a hole has developed in the posterior longitudinal ligament. He testified that a disc might protrude without rupturing but that a **herniated disc** is one which has protruded and then ruptured. He stated that after a protruding disc has ruptured, it is no longer protruded because like a burst balloon, there is a hole through which the disc material leaves its normal space....

Dr. Brodsky described a **herniated disc** as follows:

A disc is a gristle-like substance which is like the cushion between two vertebrae. There is one between each of the two vertebrae, up and down the spine. It's held in space by ligaments all around it. And when a disc herniates, it means that first it changes its interior consistency, becoming more fluid and more what we call sequestrated. It bulges. The ligament has to stretch or tear, and then a bulge takes place. That bulge can be, well, of different kinds. It can be a diffused bulge or it can be a localized knot, or the ligament may tear and a piece of ruptured disc may come out, like cooked crab meat may through the hole, either part way out the hole and all the way out the hole, and when that happens we call it ruptured.

If it bulges or has a blister on it or a protrusion, we call it herniated. French v. Brodsky, 521 S.W.2d 670, 680 (Ct.Civ. App.Tex.1975).

Dr. Klinghoffer, an orthopedic surgeon testified that the necessity for the **herniated disc** operation and the spinal fusions, which resulted in the disability, was the result of the over-exertion of the claimant in lifting the tar roll when his back "popped". Barber v. Fleming-Raugh, Inc., 222 A.2d 423, 426 (Super.Ct.Pa.1966).

Dr. Otto further testified that he made a diagnosis of **herniated disc**. This diagnosis was not based on the myelogram and X-rays performed and taken at the Perryville Hospital, which he said did not show positive evidence of a **herniated disc** but, on the usual tests given, straight leg raising together with the man's reaction to those tests and the localization of pain, a combination of objective and subjective symptoms....

... during that interval there was absent the classic symptoms of a **herniated disc**, extreme pain in the back which radiated into the hip and legs. Welker v. MFA Central Co-operative, 380 S.W.2d 481, 485–7 (St. Louis Ct. of App.1964).

herniation of nucleus pulposus rupture or prolapse of the nucleus pulposus into the spinal canal.

This time the myelogram showed a "**Herniated nucleus pulposus**, L4, L5 interspace on the right." Taweel v. Starn's Shoprite Supermarket, 276 A.2d 861, 864 (N.J.1971).

herniorrhaphy (her″ne-or′ah-fe) [*hernia* + Gr. *rhaphē* suture] surgical repair of a hernia.

Dr. Singer discovered a ventral hernia and referred appellant to Dr. David James, a specialist in general surgery. Dr. James found a long midline suprapubic incisional hernia and performed a successful Martex graft operation, called a **herniorrhaphy**, to correct the problem. Pendleton v. Cilley, 574 P.2d 1303–04 (Ariz.1978).

Petitioner first suffered a left inguinal hernia on January 6, 1971 while in the course of his employment. Thereafter a successful **herniorrhaphy** was performed and petitioner returned to work. Figueroa v. Industrial Commission, 543 P.2d 785–6 (Ariz.1975).

heroin See *diacetylmorphine*.

herpes (her′pēz) [L.; Gr. *herpēs*] any inflammatory skin disease characterized by the formation of small vesicles in clusters. The term was once used to denote any creeping vesicular skin disorder, including many fungal disorders, e.g., herpes circinatus (see tinea circinata) and herpes tonsurans maculosus (see pityriasis rosea), but is now usually restricted to such diseases caused by herpesviruses. When used alone, the term may refer to *herpes simplex* (dermatology) or to *herpes zoster*.

herpes simplex encephalitis See *encephalitis, hemorrhagic*.

herpes zoster an acute, unilateral self-limited inflammatory disease of the cerebral ganglia and ganglia of the posterior nerve roots and peripheral nerves in a segmented distribution, caused by the virus of chickenpox. It is characterized by groups of small vesicles on inflammatory bases occurring in the cutaneous areas supplied by the affected segments and associated with neuralgic pain. Called also *acute posterior ganglionitis, shingles, zoster,* and *zona*.

Dr. George Farber, a dermatologist testified for the plaintiff. He diagnosed Mrs. Villetto's blister as a **herpes zoster** viral infection, that is, "shingles." The condition usually appears on the upper trunk and when it does not it is often misdiagnosed. If treatment is begun within 24–36 hours there will be less scarring, swelling and pain. The treatment would be applications of a drying agent such as a topical steroid salve if it would not interfere with the bond healing. If the cast could not be removed a window could be made in it and the shingles treated with silver nitrate or ultraviolet light. Villetto v. Weilbaecher, 377 So.2d 132, 134 (Ct.App.La.1979).

The affidavits state that **herpes zoster** is hard to diagnose, runs a variable course, and causes pain—a symptom difficult to measure objectively. Cooper Laboratories, Inc. v. Commissioner, Fed. F.D.A., 501 F.2d 772, 778 (D.C.Cir.1974).

There is uncontradicted medical evidence from more than one source to the effect that **herpes zoster** and chickenpox are infectious diseases communicable by direct contact and that they occur from exposure to the same virus or a virus so similar that they can be crossinfected. Wilhelm v. Workmen's Compensation Appeals Bd., 62 Cal.Rptr. 829–30 (Ct.App.Cal. 1967).

heterogenous (het″er-oj′ĕ-nus) derived from a different source or species. See also *xenograft*.

It is because of the disadvantages and undesirable results which flow from the use of both autogenous and homogenous bone as grafting material that efforts were made over a period of many years to develop a process whereby readily available animal bone could be made acceptable for this purpose.

In response to the foregoing need, Squibb inaugurated in the 1950's a program of studies and experiments with bovine bone in an effort to develop a process which would make it a useable implant material in orthopedic bone grafting procedures. Bone of this type is characterized by the medical profession as **heterogenous** bone to distinguish it from the other two types of bone taken from human beings. E. R. Squibb & Sons, Inc. v. Stickney, 274 So.2d 898, 900–1 (Dist.Ct.App.Fla. 1973).

Other Authorities: E. R. Squibb & Sons, Inc. v. Jordan, 254 So. 2d 17, 19 (Dist.Ct.App.Fla.1971).

heterosexuality (het″er-o-seks″u-al′ĭ-te) sexual desire directed toward persons of the opposite sex, as distinguished from homosexuality.

heterotropia (het″er-o-tro′pe-ah) [*hetero-* + Gr. *tropē* a turn, turning + *-ia*] failure of the visual axes to remain parallel when fusion is a possibility. See also *strabismus.*

heterotropia, comitant; heterotropia; concomitant deviation of a visual axis in which the angular relation between the two visual axes remains fairly constant, whatever the position of the fixing eye.

A distinction exists between incomitant heterotropia and **comitant heterotropia**. Incomitant heterotropia is a condition in which the amount of deviation in the squinting eye varies according to the direction in which the eyes are turned. The deviation of **comitant heterotropia** is fairly constant in whatever direction the eyes are turned and one with that affliction has less ability to fuse than one with incomitant heterotropia. The prognosis for obtaining binocular vision by strabismus surgery for one with **comitant heterotropia** is not as good as one with incomitant heterotropia, and while persistent post-operative diplopia is rare in either case, there is a measure of possibility of its occurrence in **comitant heterotropia** that may require a disclosure to a patient who seeks surgery for cosmetic purposes.

It is not a standard medical practice among ophthalmologists to inform patients with incomitant heterotropia of the less than one percent possibility that strabismus surgery could cause long term or permanent double vision. Walker v. North Dakota Eye Clinic, Ltd., 415 F.Supp. 891, 893 (D.N.Dak.1976).

heterotropia, incomitant See *heterotropia, noncomitant; heterotropia, comitant.*

heterotropia, noncomitant deviation in which the angular relation between the visual axes is not maintained.

hexachlorophene (hek″sah-klo′ro-fēn) [USP] chemical name: 2,2′-methylenebis-(3,4,6-trichlorophenol). An antibacterial, $C_{13}H_6Cl_6O_2$, occurring as a white to light tan, crystalline powder, effective against gram-positive organisms; used as a topical anti-infective and detergent, mainly in soaps and dermatological preparations, and in veterinary medicine to combat flukes in ruminants.

... the Examiner continued his rejection of the claims, primarily on the grounds that **hexachlorophene** was a well known bactericide, and that there was no invention in applying **hexachlorophene** to plant diseases....

... In his final rejection, the Examiner again clearly stated that **hexachlorophene** is a well known germicidal and bactericidal agent for use on skin, kitchen utensils and textiles as well as plants.... Nationwide Chemical Corp. v. Wright, 458 F.Supp. 828, 832–3 (M.D.Fla.1976).

hexylresorcinol (hek″sil-rĕ-zor′sĭ-nol) [USP] chemical name: 4-hexyl-1,3-benzenediol. An anthelmintic, $C_{12}H_{18}O_2$, occurring as white, or yellowish white, needle-shaped crystals; used in the treatment of roundworm and trematode infections, administered orally.

The principal ingredient of Jayne's RW Vermifuge tablets is **hexylresorcinol. Hexylresorcinol** is made by adding to the six-carbon ring in resorcinol a six-carbon straight change....

... None of the witnesses, expert or lay, knew of any human death from **hexylresorcinol**. It has long been known that the drug causes superficial erosion of the mucous membrane of the mouth when it comes in contact with the tissues of the mouth, and it may act as a gastric irritant. Relatively little of it is absorbed, however, and in case of overdosage, it acts as its own emetic and is also carried off by the kidneys. The purpose of covering the drug with a heavy outer surface is so that the contents will not be released until the pill reaches the intestinal tract. Holbrook v. Rose, 458 S.W.2d 155–7 (Ct.App.Ky. 1970).

Hgb hemoglobin.

hiatus (hi-a′tus) [L.] [NA] general term for a gap, cleft, or opening.

The **hiatus** is the opening in the diaphram through which the esophagus normally passes into the stomach. Stringer v. Zacheis, 434 N.E.2d 50, 52 (App.Ct.Ill.1982).

hidradenitis (hi″drad-ĕ-ni′tis) [Gr. *hidrōs* sweat + *adēn* gland + *-itis*] inflammation of a sweat gland, usually of the apocrine type.

They are also in agreement that he must avoid dishwashing. Dr. Lorio's diagnosis also includes **hydrosis**, a malfunction of the sweat glands.... Varady V. D & D Catering Serv., Inc., 450 F.Supp. 182–3 (E.D.La.1978).

hilar (hi′lar) pertaining to a hilus.

hilar lymph See *hilus nodi lymphatici.*

hilar structure See *hilus pulmonis.*

hilus (hi′lus), pl. *hi′li* [L. "a small thing"] [NA] a general term for a depression or pit at that part of an organ where the vessels and nerves enter. Called also *hilum.*

hilus nodi lymphatici [NA], hilus of lymph node: the indentation on a lymph node where the arteries enter and the veins and efferent lymphatic vessels leave; called also *h. lymphoglandulae.*

... that there was a prolonged expiratory phase of respiration and on "asculation" (sic) there was scattered ronchi throughout, and that the chest X-ray revealed discrete nodular densities scattered throughout both lung fields with rather pronounced **hilar lymph** adenopathy. Young v. Marsillett, 473 S.W.2d 128–9 (Ct.App.Ky.1971).

hilus pulmonis [NA], hilus of the lung: the depression on the mediastinal surface of the lung where the bronchus and the blood vessels and nerves enter.

The films have two significant abnormalities. The first abnormality is the appearance of a mask lesion rather nodular in outline located peripherally in the right upper lobe and well seen also on the lateral projection. Its peripheral nature is beautifully demonstrated by clear lung between the **hilar structures**, the central bronchi in other words, and the lesion itself. Utter v. Asten-Hill Mfg. Co., 309 A.2d 583, 587 (Pa.1973).

hip (hip) 1. the area of the body lateral to and including the hip joint; called also *coxa* [NA] 2. loosely, the hip joint. See also *arthroplasty; arthroplasty, hip; intertrochanteric;* and *joint, hip.*

One procedure involved the complete removal of a **hip**, its reconstruction, and its replacement. This required the removal of fragmented bones, their rearrangement to proper alignment, screwing them together, and the recreation of the hip socket. Westfall was in a cast from his chest to his toes for a period of two months. A less complete leg cast was needed for an additional period. Painful physical therapy then ensued. When he is older, Westfall will require a **hip** replacement and may also require a replacement of a knee joint. Westfall by Terwilliger v. Kottke, 328 N.W.2d 481, 484 (Wis.1983).

Marla sustained fractures to her left **hip**, her right lower leg and her right foot. Immediately after the accident, surgery was performed involving an open reduction of the **hip** fracture, and she was placed in a two-leg body cast that extended from her ribs to her toes. Metal pins were placed in her **hip** which were removed in a subsequent operation....

... Dr. Pete Rhymes, an orthopedic surgeon who treated Marla, testified he believes she is likely to develop arthritis in her **hip** and at least once during her life an artificial **hip** will have to be inserted....

... Although a healthy and active child before the accident, Marla must now be a mere spectator as she observes her friends running, dancing, skating and participating in sports. These aspects of her injury are grave in themselves, but the most egregious aspect is that she must anticipate at least one, and probably several, serious operations whereby the natural bone of her **hip** will be replaced by plastic and steel. Dr. Rhymes testified once the artificial **hip** is inserted, it would have to be replaced every ten to fifteen years. (For this reason he wanted to delay the initial surgery for as long as possible.) Therefore, depending upon the date of the first operation, Marla could face as many as seven such operations during her lifetime. Herndon v. Neal, 424 So.2d 1180, 1182 (Ct.App.La. 1982).

hip arthroplasty See *arthroplasty, hip.*

hip fixation device See *fixation, intraosseous.*

hip replacement See *replacement, total hip.*

hip socket See *acetabulum.*

histiocyte (his'te-o-sīt") [*histio-* + Gr. *kytos* hollow vessel] macrophage.

histiocytic See *histiocytosis.*

histiocytoma (his"te-o-si-to'mah) [*histiocyte* + *-oma*] a tumor containing histiocytes (macrophages). See also *macrophage.*

Very shortly after his transfer to Ann Arbor, Mr. Hawkins' condition was diagnosed as a malignant fibrous **histiocytoma** (cancerous tumor). Hawkins v. Regional Med. Laboratories, P.C., 329 N.W.2d 729–30 (Mich.1982).

histiocytoma, fibrous See *dermatofibroma.*

histiocytosis (his"te-o-si-to'sis) a condition marked by the abnormal appearance of histiocytes (macrophages) in the blood. See also *macrophage.*

Dr. Orr's written report states that the three pathologists felt that a "benign lesion" was represented "although it has manifestation [sic] of a most unusual **histiocytic** proliferating pattern."...

On November 17, Dr. Milner performed a second biopsy, taking more tissue from the mass. Dr. Orr again examined the tissue, prepared slides, and submitted a written report stating that "the overall pattern is that of severe inflammatory response within a lymphoid tissue with rather active **histiocytosis** reaction demonstrated." Jeanes v. Milner, 428 F.2d 598, 600 (8th Cir. 1970).

histology (his-tol'o-je) [*histo-* + *-logy*] that department of anatomy which deals with the minute structure, composition, and function of the tissues; called also *microscopical anatomy.*

histology, pathologic the histology of diseased tissues; histopathology.

By contrast, the other pathologists consulted during the suspension proceeding generally believe that cancer can be reliably diagnosed by observation of tissue cells under a microscope (**histopathological** evidence) without evidence, or very much evidence, of invasion or metastasis. Environmental Defense Fund, Inc. v. E.P.A., 548 F.2d 998, 1007 (D.C.Cir.1976).

histopathological See *histology, pathologic.*

histopathology See *histology, pathologic.*

histoplasmosis (his"to-plaz-mo'sis) infection resulting from inhalation or, infrequently, the ingestion of spores of *Histoplasma capsulatum.* Worldwide in distribution, it is particularly common in midwestern United States. The infection is asymptomatic in most cases, but in 1–5 per cent, it causes acute pneumonia, or disseminated reticuloendothelial hyperplasia with hepatosplenomegaly and anemia, or an influenza-like illness with joint effusion and erythema nodosum. Reactivated infection involves the lungs, meninges, heart, peritoneum, and adrenals in that order of frequency. It can be diagnosed by culture, or by demonstration of a rise in complement-fixing antibody titers in serum.

The question presented is whether the Industrial Commission abused its discretion by deciding that **histoplasmosis** as contracted by Forrest L. Ellars is a compensable occupational disease under the Workmen's Compensation Act....

Although the disease doesn't appear to have a litigious history, its contraction has been the subject of actions against employers who (1) had ordered an employee to clean out an attic where quite a few decomposed "animals" thought to be birds were present, without furnishing a mask (Mowry v. Schmoll [C.A.8, 1971], 441 F.2d 1271), and (2) had allowed "large amounts of pigeon excretion" to remain in the structure in which an employee worked. Myers v. Plattsburgh (N.Y. 1961), 13 A.D.2d 866, 214 N.Y.S.2d 773. [Footnote omitted.] State ex. rel. Ohio Bell Telephone Co. v. Krise, 327 N.E. 2d 756, 758 (Ohio 1975).

In March 1967, plaintiff was hospitalized with what was diagnosed as acute disseminated **histoplasmosis**, a systemic disease caused by a fungus....

... Another witness, Dr. Cross, specializing in internal medicine, testified that the disease is "contracted by inhaling dust from an area in which **histoplasmosis** spores have been deposited in large numbers." He said that "[t]his is classically associated with bird droppings, either chickens, bats, pigeons, something of this nature." Close environment usually is compatible with contracting the disease. Mowry v. Schmoll, 441 F.2d 1271–2 (8th Cir. 1971).

hives See *urticaria.*

HLA test See *test, HLA paternity blood.*

HLW (high level radioactive waste) See under *waste.*

Hodgkin's disease See *disease, Hodgkin's.*

Hoffmann's reflex See *sign, Hoffmann's.*

holosystolic (hol″o-sis-tol′ik) [*holo-* + *systole*] pertaining to the entire systole.

holosystolic murmur See *murmur, pansystolic.*

Homans' sign (ho′manz) [John *Homans,* American physician, 1877–1954] see under *sign.*

homeopathy (ho″me-op′ah-the) [*homeo-* + Gr. *pathos* disease] a system of therapeutics founded by Samuel Hahnemann (1755–1843), in which diseases are treated by drugs which are capable of producing in healthy persons symptoms like those of the disease to be treated, the drug being administered in minute doses. Cf. *allopathy.*

homeostasis (ho″me-o-sta′sis) [*homeo-* + Gr. *stasis* standing] a tendency to stability in the normal body states (internal environment) of the organism. It is achieved by a system of control mechanisms activated by negative feedback; e.g., a high level of carbon dioxide in extracellular fluid triggers increased pulmonary ventilation, which in turn causes a decrease in carbon dioxide concentration. See also *ego* (People v. Harrington).

homogenize (ho-moj′ĕ-nīz) to render homogeneous, or of uniform quality or consistency throughout.

Except for buttermilk and chocolate milk, all the milk was then "**homogenized**," by fracturing the butterfat cells into smaller portions so that they would not rise to the top of the bottle. Glowacki v. Borden, Inc., 420 F.Supp. 348, 351 (N.D.Ill. 1976).

homogenous (ho-moj′ĕ-nus) having a similarity of structure because of descent from a common ancestor.

Another type of bone grafting material used in orthopedic bone grafting procedures is known medically as **homogenous** bone. This type of bone is taken from another human being and procured either from a live donor or from a bone bank in which the bones of deceased humans are stored. The utilization of **homogenous** bone in orthopedic procedures is highly impracticable because of the lack of donors, the scarcity of bone banks over the country, and the difficulties experienced in storing and preserving the bone until needed. E. R. Squibb & Sons, Inc. v. Stickney, 274 So.2d 898, 900 (Dist.Ct.App.Fla. 1973).

... **homogenous** bone—human bone taken from another human being.... E. R. Squibb & Sons, Inc. v. Jordan, 254 So. 2d 17, 19 (Dist.Ct.App.Fla.1971).

homograft See *allograft.*

homolog See *homologue.*

homologous (ho-mol′o-gus) [Gr. *homologos* agreeing, correspondent] corresponding in structure, position, origin, etc., as (*a*) the feathers of a bird and the scales of a fish, (*b*) antigen and its specific antibody, (*c*) allelic chromosomes. Cf. *analogous.* See also *homologue.*

homologue (hom′o-log) in chemistry, one of a series of compounds, each of which is formed from the one before it by the addition of a constant element or a constant group of elements, as in the homologous series CH_4, C_2H_6, C_3H_8, etc.; called also *homologen.*

... **homologue**—one of a series of similar molecules which vary by a regular difference in atomic structure, especially the members of a series which vary by only one carbon and two hydrogen atoms. Eli Lilly & Co., Inc. v. Generix Drug Sales, Inc., 460 F.2d 1096, 1100 (5th Cir. 1972).

A **homolog** is a member of a series of compounds in which each member differs from the next member by a constant number of atoms. Monsanto Company v. Rohm & Haas Company, 456 F.2d 592, 596 (3d Cir. 1972).

"A **homologous** series is a family of chemically related compounds, the composition of which varies from member to member by CH_2 (one atom of carbon and two atoms of hydrogen).... Chemists knowing the properties of one member of a series would in general know what to expect in adjacent members." Application of Henze, 37 C.C.P.A. (Pat.) 1009, 1014, 181 F.2d 196, 200–201 (1950). Brenner v. Manson, 383 U.S. 519, 522, 86 S.Ct. 1033, 16 L.Ed.2d 69 (1966).

Other Authorities: GAF Corp. v. Amchem Products, Inc., 399 F.Supp. 647, 651 (E.D.Pa.1975), reversed and remanded 570 F.2d 457 (3d Cir. 1978).

homopolymer

... the word "**homopolymer**" defines a polymer made from one single monomer, such as polyvinylidene fluoride alone. International Tel. & Tel. Corp. v. Raychem Corp., 538 F.2d 453, 459 (1st Cir. 1976).

homosexual (ho″mo-seks′u-al) an individual who is sexually attracted toward a person of the same sex, as opposed to heterosexual.

When it comes to sex, the problem is complex. Those "who fail to reach sexual maturity (hetero-sexuality), and who remain at a narcissistic or **homosexual** stage" are the products "of heredity, of glandular dysfunction, [or] of environmental circumstances." Henderson, Psychopathic Constitution and Criminal Behaviour, in Mental Abnormality and Crime 105, 114 (Radzinowicz & Turner ed.1949).

The **homosexual** is one, who by some freak, is the product of an arrested development:

All people have originally bisexual tendencies which are more or less developed and which in the course of time normally deviate either in the direction of male or female. This may indicate that a trace of homosexuality, no matter how weak it may be, exists in every human being. It is present in the adolescent stage, where there is a considerable amount of undifferentiated sexuality. Abrahamsen, Crime and the Human Mind 117 (1944). [Dissent.] Boutilier v. Immigration Service, 387 U.S. 118, 127, 87 S.Ct. 1563, 18 L.Ed.2d 661 (1967).

homosexuality (ho″mo-seks″u-al′ĭ-te) [*homo-* + *sexuality*] sexual attraction toward those of the same sex. Cf. *heterosexuality*.

Sigmund Freud wrote in 1935:

"**Homosexuality** is assuredly no advantage, but it is nothing to be ashamed of, no vice, no degradation, it cannot be classified as an illness; we consider it to be a variation of the sexual function produced by a certain arrest of sexual development. Many highly respectable individuals of ancient and modern times have been homosexuals, several of the greatest men among them (Plato, Michelangelo, Leonardo da Vinci, etc.). It is a great injustice to persecute **homosexuality** as a crime, and cruelty too. If you do not believe me, read the books of Havelock Ellis." Ruitenbeek, The Problem of Homosexuality in Modern Society 1 (1963). [Dissent.] Boutilier v. Immigration Service, 387 U.S. 118, 130, 87 S.Ct. 1563, 18 L.Ed.2d 661 (1967).

homozygous (ho″mo-zi′gus) possessing a pair of identical alleles at a given locus or loci.

The testimony of various doctors established that a child of an Rh positive **homozygous** father and a sensitized Rh negative mother would be Rh positive and, in all probability, would suffer from erythroblastosis fetalis at birth. Price v. Neyland, 320 F.2d 674, 676 (D.C.Cir.1963).

hook (hook) a curved instrument, usually with a sharp point, designed for holding, elevating, or exerting traction on a tissue.

hook, Kodt

The petitioner could not tolerate work and Dr. Petersen therefore performed a surgical fusion of the sacroiliac joint at L–4–5 and of the previously treated joint at L–5 and S–1....

In attempting to explain objectively the continuing complaints of the petitioner, Dr. Petersen stated that there were **Kodt hooks** remaining in the petitioner's back which had been used to hold the fusion together. However, the doctor asserted that it was highly unlikely that they were the cause of the petitioner's symptoms.... Martin Young Enterprises, Inc. v. Industrial Com'n, 281 N.E.2d 305–7 (Ill.1972).

hormone (hor′mōn) [Gr. *hormaein* to set in motion, spur on] a chemical substance, produced in the body by an organ or cells of an organ which has a specific regulatory effect on the activity of a certain organ; originally applied to substances secreted by various endocrine glands and transported in the blood stream to the target organ on which their effect was produced, the term was later applied to various substances not produced by special glands but having similar action. See also *endocrine system*, under *system*.

Though liver fractions of some practical utility had been developed, the medical and scientific worlds remained quite ignorant of the nature of the anti-pernicious anemia principle. There were those who thought it to be a **hormone**. This

seemed logical since it was found in the liver of cattle, and, by definition, a **hormone** is, while a vitamin is not, produced in the body of the animal. Merck & Co. v. Olin Mathieson Chemical Corp., 253 F.2d 156, 158 (4th Cir. 1958).

Horner's syndrome See *syndrome, Horner's.*

hospital (hos′pit-'l) [L. *hospitalium; hospes* host, guest] an institution for the treatment of the sick. "An institution suitably located, constructed, organized, managed and personneled, to supply, scientifically, economically, efficiently and unhindered, all or any recognized part of the complex requirements for the prevention, diagnosis, and treatment of physical, mental, and the medical aspect of social ills; with functioning facilities for training new workers in the many special professional, technical and economic fields essential to the discharge of its proper functions; and with adequate contacts with physicians, other hospitals, medical schools and all accredited health agencies engaged in the better health program."—Council on Medical Education.

Since the dispositive issue on appeal is whether plaintiff-Tranquilaire is a "**hospital**" within the terms of the policy, we deem it appropriate to set out such provisions, in pertinent part, as follows:

"**Hospital**" means a legally constituted institution which is licensed as a **hospital** (if **hospital** licensing is required where it is situated), which is open at all times and is operated primarily for the care and treatment of sick and injured persons as in-patients, which has a staff of one or more licensed physicians available at all times, which continuously provides 24-hour nursing service by graduate registered nurses, which provides organized facilities for diagnosis and major surgery and which is not primarily a clinic, nursing, rest or convalescent home, or similar establishment.

Initially, defendant contends plaintiff is not a **hospital** since it does not treat the "sick and injured" but instead treats those with psychiatric disorders. We do not agree with this contention. Mobile Psychiatric Service Inc. v. Employers Life Ins. Co., 362 So.2d 244, 246 (Ct.Civ.App.Ala.1978).

Present-day **hospitals**, as their manner of operation plainly demonstrates, do far more than furnish facilities for treatment. They regularly employ on a salary basis a large staff of physicians, nurses, internes, as well as administrative and manual workers, and they charge patients for medical care.... The Standards for Hospital Accreditation, the state licensing regulations and the defendant's bylaws demonstrate that the medical profession and other responsible authorities regard it as both desirable and feasible that a **hospital** assume certain responsibilities for the care of the patient. [Darling v. Charleston Community Memorial Hospital, 33 Ill.2d 326, 211 N.E.2d 253, 257, 14 A.L.R.3d 860 (1965), cert. den. 383 U.S. 946, 86 S.Ct. 1204, 16 L.Ed.2d 209 (1966).] Stumper v. Kimel, 260 A.2d 526, 528 (Super.Ct.N.J.1970).

A **hospital**, as its name implies, is a hostel with special services, but it is nonetheless essentially a custodial institution, albeit a very high form of custody. Obviously this does not mean that it is sufficient for a **hospital** to admit a patient to its premises and then close its eyes to whatever befalls him....

... It is not the function of a private **hospital** to diagnose or treat patients except as the agent of the patient's private physician and under his explicit order. This is because it is the physician, not the **hospital**, who is the healer. Diagnosis and treatment are the functions of the physicians, not the private proprietary **hospital**. It "serves the function only of a specialized facility, not a direct service healing institution," Fiorentino v. Wenger, 19 N.Y.2d 407, 280 N.Y.S.2d 373, 227 N.E.2d 296, 299 (1967). Of course there can be exceptions to this rule.... [Concurring and Dissenting Opinion.] Alden v. Providence Hospital, 382 F.2d 163, 166–7 (D.C.Cir.1967).

hospital record See *record, hospital.*

hospital (rules and regulations) See *surgery (rules and regulations).*

The excised rules were offered as well as testimony concerning their contents. The court denied the admission.

The rules are:

Duties of the Chief of the Department of Anesthesiology will be: ... (e) General supervision of the procurement and maintenance of equipment and the procurement of supplies. General supervision is further defined:

8. All equipment, supplies, drugs, etc. will be purchased, provided and maintained up-to-date and in good condition by the hospital. A suitable person will be employed by the hospital to be in charge of the maintenance of all equipment and the requisition of all anesthesia supplies. While employed by the hospital administration, this individual will serve under the direction of the Chief of the Department of Anesthesiology.

The Chief of Anesthesiology testified that although he noted a slight variance in the thermal capacity as recorded on the machine on a prior occasion, he notified no one nor did he believe he was responsible for the maintenance.

The individual responsible for the maintenance as described in section 8 above was never identified; on the contrary, everyone disclaimed responsibility....

The admission of the two rules was objected to on the ground that they would be misleading when taken out of context of the entire regulation. The trial court refused to admit the rules on this basis. Weeks v. Latter-Day Saints Hospital, 418 F.2d 1035, 1039 (10th Cir. 1969).

HSE See *encephalitis, hemorrhagic.*

human-immune globulin See *globulin, tetanus immune human.*

humerus (hu′mer-us), pl. *hu′meri* [L.] [NA] the bone that extends from the shoulder to the elbow articulating proximally with the scapula and distally with the radius and ulna; see illustration accompanying *skeleton.*

The medical findings revealed a fracture of a previous bone graft of the **humerus** from the elbow to the shoulder. The **humerus** was completely and permanently detached from his left shoulder resulting in the hanging arm held together by soft tissue. Misfud v. Allstate Ins. Co., 456 N.Y.S.2d 316 (Civ.Ct.City of N.Y. Kings Cty.1982).

Dr. Bretz, a radiologist employed by Medical Radiologists, a professional group regularly performing professional services at Good Samaritan under a promise of service, read the X-rays, and contrary to the diagnosis of the treating physician, found that there was indeed a fracture of the distal portion of the **humerus** in the area of the elbow with an eight millimeter

displacement. Phillips v. Good Samaritan Hospital, 416 N.E.2d 646–7 (Ct.App.Ohio 1979).

The capsule affected here encloses the head of the **humerus** (the long bone of the upper arm) and part of the shoulder blade. Slater v. Kehoe, 113 Cal.Rptr. 790, 793 (Ct.App.Cal. 1974).

Other Authorities: Redepenning v. Dore, 201 N.W.2d 580, 586 (Wis.1972); Downs v. American Employment Ins. Co., 423 F.2d 1160, 1164 (5th Cir. 1970).

humidifier (hu-mid′ĭ-fi″er) an apparatus for controlling humidity by adding to the content of moisture in the air of a room.

humoral response See *response, humoral.*

hyaline (hi′ah-lin) [Gr. *hyalos* glass] glassy and transparent or nearly so. See also under *membrane.*

hydradenitis See *hidradenitis.*

hydramnios (hi-dram′ne-os) [*hydr-* + *amnion*] excess of amniotic fluid.

... an X-ray which he had ordered taken disclosed a condition called **polyhydramnios** (excessive amniotic fluid). Lhotka v. Larson, 238 N.W.2d 870, 872 (Minn.1976).

hydrocarbon (hi″dro-kar′bon) an organic compound that contains carbon and hydrogen only. The hydrocarbons are divided into *alicyclic, aliphatic,* and *aromatic* hydrocarbons, according to the arrangement of the atoms and the chemical properties of the compounds.

The most basic organic chemicals, formed solely from the elements carbon and hydrogen, are referred to as **hydrocarbons**. Ziegler v. Phillips Petroleum Co., 483 F.2d 858, 862 (5th Cir. 1973).

hydrocephalus (hi-dro-sef′ah-lus) [*hydro-* + Gr. *kephale* head] a condition marked by dilatation of the cerebral ventricles, most often occurring secondarily to obstruction of the cerebrospinal fluid pathways (see *ventricular block,* under *block*), and accompanied by an accumulation of cerebrospinal fluid within the skull; the fluid is usually under increased pressure, but occasionally may be normal or nearly so. It is typically characterized by enlargement of the head, prominence of the forehead, brain atrophy, mental deterioration, and convulsions, and may be congenital or acquired, and be of sudden onset (*acute h.*) or be slowly progressive (*chronic* or *primary h.*).

Dr. Wilson diagnosed the plaintiff as not having multiple sclerosis, but that he in fact had a massive brain tumor which had grown to such a size that it created a **hydrocephalus** or stopped the normal draining of brain fluids, thus causing an acute pressure problem which required the immediate placement of a shunt to drain off the brain fluids. Swanson v. U.S. By and Through Veterans Admin., 557 F.Supp. 1041, 1044 (D.Idaho 1983).

This showed a buildup of fluid in the ventricles (**hydrocephalus**) and a narrowing (stenosis) of the connecting aqueduct. Gendusa v. St.Paul Fire & Marine Ins. Co., 435 So.2d 479, 481 (Ct.App.La.1983).

Dr. Livingston's report also stated that the hydrocephalic condition is a blockage of the communication of fluid between the brain and spinal canal, and was a result of damage to the brain substance. Normally, the fluid constantly circulates with absorption which maintains a specific tension in the whole system. If circulation of the fluid is blocked, as the tests revealed in Triplett's case, **hydrocephalus** occurs. Mid Central Tool Co. v. Industrial Com'n, 382 N.E.2d 222, 225 (Ill.1978).

hydrocephalus, obstructive hydrocephalus due to ventricular block (q.v.); called also *noncommunicating h.* See also *block, ventricular.*

At the follow-up appointment, on Wednesday, December 28, decedent reported blurring of vision and difficulty in opening one eye, in addition to the headache and nausea. After being examined, she was hospitalized, because the examining internist suspected increased intra-cranial pressure. After a CAT scan and electroencephalogram were performed, UOHSC doctors suspected that a brain tumor was obstructing the flow of cerebrospinal fluid between ventricles of decedent's brain, causing enlargement of one ventricle and increased intra-cranial pressure. Blood tests showed her white blood cell count to be elevated. An arteriogram was performed on Friday, December 30. It confirmed that decedent was suffering from **obstructive hydrocephalus.** Mendez v. State of Oregon, 669 P.2d 364–5 (Ct.App.Or.1983).

hydrochloride (hi″dro-klo′rīd) an addition salt of hydrochloric acid, for instance with quinine. The hydrochloric acid adds on in such a way that the valence of the basic nitrogen is changed from three to five. In a sense the alkaloid hydrochlorides may be looked on as derivatives of ammonium chloride:

hydrochlorothiazide (hi″dro-klo″ro-thi′ah-zīd) [USP] chemical name: 6-chloro-3,4-dihydro-2*H*-1,2,4-benzothiadiazine-7-sulfonamide-1,1-dioxide. An orally effective diuretic and antihypertensive, $C_7H_8ClN_3 \cdot O_4S_2$, occurring as a white or nearly white, crystalline powder.

"Hydrochlorothiazide" (hereinafter referred to as HCT) is the generic name for one benzothiadiazine derivative covered by United States Letters Patent 3,163,645, which issued to CIBA on December 29, 1964 and which will expire on December 29, 1981....

A commonly employed drug treatment for hypertension is the use of HCT plus reserpine, an antihypertensive and calming agent. The ratio of the HCT to the reserpine that produces the maximum therapeutic effect varies from patient to patient. The various combination products of this type, however, are marketed in the form of a fixed ratio of the two therapeutically active ingredients....

HCT has also been sold in dosage form in combination with other drugs by the companies and under the trade names listed below: [Oreticyl (Abbott); Caplaril, Miluretic (Carter); Apresoline-Esidrex, Esidrex-K, Esimil, Ser-Ap-Es, Serpasil-Esidrex, Singoserp-Esideix (CIBA); Butiserpazide, Butizide (McNeil); Aldoril, Cyclex, Hydropres (Merck); Aldactizide (Searle); Dyazide (Smith, Kline & French); Perithiazide (Warner).] U.S. v. Ciba Geigy Corp., 508 F.Supp. 1118, 1122–3 (D.N.J.1976). **Other Authorities:** Gudlis v. Califano, 452 F.Supp. 401, 403 (N.D.Ill.1978).

Hydrochloride.

hydrocholeresis (hi″dro-ko″lĕ-re′sis) [*hydro-* + Gr. *cholē* bile + *hairesis* a taking] choleresis characterized by increase in water output, or induction of the excretion of bile relatively low in specific gravity, viscosity, and total solid content.

hydrocholeretic (hi″dro-ko″lĕ-ret′ik) pertaining to, characterized by, or producing hydrocholeresis. See also *acid, dehydrocholic.*

On the other hand, Ames' brief stresses that Decholin is different from bile salts and its affidavit of Dr. G. Gordon McHardy, formerly of the faculty of the Tulane University School of Medicine and the only one of claimant's experts who attempted to describe the specific function of Decholin, refers to the drug as a "hydrocholeretic," an agent which only "increases the watery component of the bile." U.S. v. Article of Drug Labeled Decholin, 264 F.Supp. 473, 477 (E.D.Mich. 1967).

hydrocollator See *pack, hydrocollator steam.*

hydrocortisone (hi″dro-kor′tĭ-sōn) chemical name: 11β,-17α,21-trihydroxypregn-4-ene-3,20-dione. The major glucocorticoid, $C_{21}H_{30}O_5$, elaborated by the human adrenal cortex (or *cortisol*, as it is usually referred to by biochemists), or the same substance produced synthetically; it has life-maintaining properties and also has appreciable mineralocorticoid activity. The official preparation [USP] and its salts are used in the treatment of inflammations, allergies, pruritus, collagen diseases (rheumatoid arthritis, lupus erythematosus, etc.), some neoplasms, acute or chronic adrenocortical deficiency, severe status asthmaticus, and shock.

hydrocortisone sodium succinate [USP], a water-soluble ester of hydrocortisone, $C_{25}H_{33}NaO_8$, occurring as a white or nearly white crystalline powder, having actions and uses similar to those of the base; administered intravenously or intramuscularly, especially for acute adrenocortical insufficiency.

Solu-Cortef is a form of corticosteroid. Daniels v. Hadley Memorial Hospital, 566 F.2d 749, 755 (D.C.Cir.1977).

hydrogen (hi′dro-jen) [*hydro-* + Gr. *gennan* to produce] the lightest element, an odorless, tasteless, colorless gas that is inflammable and explosive when mixed with air. It is found in water and in almost all organic compounds. Its ion is the active constituent of all acids in the water system. Its symbol is H; atomic number, 1; atomic weight, 1.00797; specific gravity, 0.069. Hydrogen exists in three isotopes: ordinary, or light, hydrogen is the mass 1 isotope, also called *protium;* heavy hydrogen is the mass 2 isotope, also called *deuterium;* mass 3 isotope is *tritium.*

hydrogen cyanide an extremely poisonous colorless liquid or gas, HCN, used as a rodenticide and insecticide, its toxic effect being due to its inhibition of the oxidation of cytochrome, resulting in suppression of cellular respiration; it can cause tachypnea, dyspnea, paralysis, and respiratory arrest. Called also *hydrocyanic acid.*

When **hydrogen cyanide** is present in the human body at a rate greater than the body's ability to detoxify the **hydrogen cyanide**, cyanide poisoning, manifested by labored breathing, vomiting, ataxia, convulsions and death occurs. . . .

. . . The lethal dose of **hydrogen cyanide** in human beings ranges between 50 and 280 mg for an 80 kg person. U.S. v. General Research Laboratories, 397 F.Supp. 197–9 (C.D.Cal. 1975).

hydrogen, heavy See *hydrogen.*

hydrogen sulfide an offensive and poisonous gas, H$_2$S, used as a chemical reagent; called also *hydrosulfuric* or *sulfhydric acid.*

Finally it is clear that Vy Lactos's chemist knew that the proteinaceous fish solubles were subject to natural decomposition, that the decomposition process would produce **hydrogen sulfide gas**, and that **hydrogen sulfide gas** in sufficient concentration poses a serious hazard of death or physical injury. Brennan v. Occupational Safety & Health Review Commission, 494 F.2d 460, 464 (8th Cir. 1974).

hydrogenate (hi'dro-jen-āt") to cause to combine with hydrogen; to reduce with hydrogen.

Hydrogenation has two effects in an oil. 1) Hydrogen is absorbed at the hydrogen-deficiency points of the poly- and mono-unsaturates, converting linoleic into oleic, and oleic into saturated fatty acid. 2) Disturbances are created in the carbon-atom chains such that existing hydrogen-deficiency points change in character or shift position along the chains without absorbing hydrogen, thereby creating man-made substances called "isomers" that differ in melting point and other characteristics from the natural components of the oil. Corn Products Co. v. Standard Brands, Inc., 359 F.2d 739, 741 (7th Cir. 1966).

hydrolysate (hi-drol'ĭ-zāt) a compound produced by hydrolysis.

hydrolysis (hi-drol'ĭ-sis), pl. *hydrol'yses* [*hydro-* + Gr. *lysis* dissolution] the splitting of a compound into fragments by the addition of water, the hydroxyl group being incorporated in one fragment, and the hydrogen atom in the other.

In the process of **hydrolysis**, starch usually is suspended in a relatively large amount of water. This starch suspension is frequently referred to as "substrate." Since the starch chains molecule is relatively stable, the process of **hydrolysis** does not readily occur. A catalyst is required to initiate and assist the reaction. An acid or an enzyme may be added to the substrate. The reaction then proceeds through the initial thinning of the starch to the final formation of the dextrose molecules. The resulting "hydrolyzate" is a liquid solution which contains small amounts of reversion products and the residual acid or enzyme. Baxter Laboratories, Inc. v. Corn Products Co., 394 F.2d 892–3 (7th Cir. 1968).

hydrolyzate See *hydrolysate;* and *hydrolysis* (Baxter Laboratories, Inc. case).

hydrolyze (hi'dro-līz) to subject to hydrolysis.

Hydrolyze: To react with water. In the Ritter process, hydrolysis normally performs two separate functions. First, it adds a molecule of water to each molecule of intermediate ("quench"); second, it removes the bisulfate ion from the intermediate ("neutralize"). Ritter v. Rohm & Haas Co., 154 U.S.P.Q 518, 554 (S.D.N.Y.1967).

hydromorphone (hi"dro-mor'fōn) chemical name: 4,5α-epoxy-3-hydroxy-17-methyl-methylmorphinan-6-one. A morphine alkaloid, C$_{17}$H$_{19}$NO$_3$, occurring as a fine, white or practically white, crystalline powder, having narcotic analgesic effects similar to but greater and of shorter duration than those of morphine; administered as the sulfate salt by subcutaneous injection.

hydromorphone hydrochloride [USP], the hydrochloride salt of hydromorphone, C$_{17}$H$_{19}$NO$_3$ · HCl, having the same actions as the base; administered orally and subcutaneously. Called also *dihydromorphinone hydrochloride.*

Appellant Stewart, was charged in the District Court for the District of New Mexico in a two-count indictment with unlawful sale of **dilaudid**, a narcotic drug, in violation of 26 U.S.C. § 4705(a). . . . U.S. v. Stewart, 443 F.2d 1129–30 (10th Cir. 1971).

hydronephrosis (hi"dro-nĕ-fro'sis) [*hydro-* + Gr. *nephros* kidney] distention of the pelvis and calices of the kidney with urine, as a result of obstruction of the ureter, with accompanying atrophy of the parenchyma of the organ.

Postoperative intravenous pyelogram on November 7, 1968 showed persistent **hydronephrosis** (distention of kidney with atrophy of tissue) of the kidney and dilation of the ureter. Hurst v. Mathews, 426 F.Supp. 245–6 (E.D.Va.1976).

(**hydronephrosis**, according to prior medical testimony, in this case was a mild hydronephrosis on the left side of the kidney, which meant a slight swelling in the left kidney and ureter.) Ausley v. Johnston, 450 S.W.2d 351, 353 (Ct.App.Tex.1970). Other Authorities: Capaldi v. Weinberger, 391 F.Supp. 502, 505 (E.D.Pa.1975).

hydrosalpinx (hi"dro-sal'pinks) [*hydro-* + Gr. *salpinx* trumpet] a collection of watery fluid in a uterine tube, occurring as the end-stage of pyosalpinx.

Dr. Lund determined that decedent had a chronic pelvic inflammatory disease and a resultant **hydrosalpinx** (puss mass in fallopian tube covered with water) requiring removal of the uterus. Cline v. Lund, 107 Cal.Rptr. 629, 632 (Ct.App.Cal.1973).

hydrosis See *hidradenitis.*

hydrothorax (hi"dro-tho'raks) [*hydro-* + Gr. *thorax* chest] a collection of watery fluid in the pleural cavity; pleural effusion with transudate.

The lungs are enclosed in an envelope-like sac, called the pleural cavity, which is a vacuum. It is necessary to maintain this vacuum to sustain the mechanics of respiration. Anything which breaks the "seal" will cause the lung to collapse . . . if it is water, its [sic] called **hydrothorax**. Earlin v. Cravetz, 399 A.2d 783, 785 (Super.Ct.Pa.1979).

The cause of death recited in the official death certificate was "pulmonary **hydrothorax** due to extensive metastasis from melanocarcinoma". In lay language this meant that a watery collection on the lungs was the immediate cause of death, but this condition was caused by one of the many forms of cancer. Insurance Company of North America v. Chinowith, 393 F.2d 916–17 (5th Cir. 1968).

hydrotroping See *hydrotropism.*

hydrotropism (hi-drot'ro-pizm) [*hydro-* + Gr. *tropē* a turn, turning] a growth response of a nonmotile organism elicited by the presence of water or moisture.

Appellant defines **hydrotroping** agents as:

Compounds such as potassium toluene sulfonate, which cosolubilize inorganic builder salts and organic detergents in concentrated aqueous compositions to permit the formulation of homogeneous detergent compositions. Application of Smith, 398 F.2d 849–50 (U.S.Ct.Cust. & Pat.App.1968).

hydroxyprogesterone capraote (hi-drok"se-pro-jes'ter-ōn) [USP] chemical name: 17α-[(1-oxohexyl)oxy]pregna-4-ene-3,20-dione. A synthetic progestin, $C_{27}H_{40}O_4$, occurring as a white or creamy white, crystalline powder; used in the treatment of functional uterine bleeding, abnormalities of the menstrual cycle, threatened abortion, and uterine cancer, administered intramuscularly. Called also *h. hexanoate.*

This suit involves a mother to whom, during the course of her pregnancy, **Delalutin**, a drug manufactured and marketed by the defendants Squibb, was administered by the defendant doctor. The baby was born without limbs and with other deformities, all alleged to have been produced by the drug. [Dissent.] Vaccaro v. Squibb Corp., 418 N.E.2d 386 (N.Y.1980).

hydroxyzine (hi-drok'sĭ-zēn) chemical name: 2-[2-[4-[(4-chlorophenyl)phenylmethyl]-1-piperazinyl]ethoxy]ethanol. A synthetic drug, $C_{21}H_{27}ClN_2O_2$, with central nervous system depressant, antispasmodic, antihistaminic, and antifibrillatory actions.

More specifically, the plaintiff alleges that medical doctors at the above facility negligently administered a drug known as **Vistaril**, a tranquilizer used in the treatment of those suffering from nervous disorders, which undisputably produced antihistaminic effects. Miller v. U.S., 431 F.Supp. 988–9 (S.D.Miss. 1976).

Vistaril is a commonly used drug, and is administered to patients in combination with morphine on a daily basis at Candler Hospital. Its purpose is to increase the activity of the narcotic or pain relieving drug, thereby decreasing the amount of morphine required; additionally it has a mild sedative effect. The manufacturer's vials containing **vistaril**, which are sold to hospitals, have instructions thereon as to the effect that the medicine is to be injected intramuscularly, not subcutaneously. Su v. Perkins, 211 S.E.2d 421, 424 (Ct.App.Ga.1974).

hygienist (hi-je'nist, hi'je-en"ist) a specialist in hygiene.

hygienist, dental an auxiliary member of the dental profession who has been trained in the art of removing calcareous deposits and stains from the surfaces of the teeth and in providing additional services and information on the prevention of oral disease; such persons are employed in private dental offices or are active in school or public health programs.

The board has defined the procedures which a **dental hygienist** may perform by further defining the function in the regulations as follows:

Dental hygienist—One who is legally licensed as such by the Board to remove tartar, deposits, accretions, and stains from the exposed surfaces of the teeth and directly beneath the free margin of the gums and to make application of medicaments as defined and approved by the Board to the exposed surfaces of the teeth for the prevention of dental caries, in the office of a dentist, in any public or private institutions . . . or in state health care under the general supervision of a licensed and registered dentist. Oppenheim v. Com., Dep't of State, etc., 459 A.2d 1308, 1314 (Commonwealth Ct.Pa. 1983).

hygroma, cystic See *lymphangioma, cystic.*

hymen (hi'men) [Gr. *hymēn* membrane] [NA] the membranous fold which partially or wholly occludes the external orifice of the vagina.

When a female plaintiff alleges a cause of action arising from injury to her reproductive organs, the possibility that a physical examination [hysterosalpingography] will necessitate rupture of her **hymen** weighs heavily against ordering such an examination. A court will not order a procedure as part of a physical examination of a woman claiming to be a maiden "which would destroy the seal of appellee's virginity and would cause pain and a flow of blood." Kokomo M. & W. Traction Co. v. Walsh, 58 Ind.App. 182, 194, 108 N.E. 19, 23 (App.Div. 1915). In the language of another court, a plaintiff must not be required to "have appellee's person exposed, suffering humiliation and the loss of the evidence of her virginity," by submitting to an examination which would rupture the **hymen** and inflict pain associated with the vaginal exploration. Louisville Ry. Co. v. Hartlege, 25 Ky.L.Rep. 152, 153, 74 S.W. 742, 743 (Ct.App.1903). Duprey v. Wager, 451 A.2d 416, 420 (Super. Ct.N.J.1982).

". . . The hymen itself had been, or maidenhead had been included in the tear or in the laceration." Hester v. State, 310 So.2d 455–6 (Dist.Ct.App.Fla.1975).

hymenotomy (hi"men-ot'o-me) [Gr. *hymēn* membrane + *temnein* to cut] surgical incision of the hymen.

"This 27 year old female was admitted to the hospital on 10/31/71 for **hymenotomy**, complaining of redness and itching around the vulva and has been treated recently for vulvitis with some effect and was found to have almost completely intact hymen.". . .

. . . So we proceeded with the rest of the operation, which took only—not more than a minute. Because you just made two cuts in it and then dilate the opening of the vagina with your fingers. That's the end of the procedure. Holloway v. Hauver, 322 A.2d 890, 892, 895 (Ct.Spec.App.Md.1974).

hyoscine See *scopolamine.*

hypalgesia (hi"pal-je'ze-ah) [Gr. *hypo* under + *algēsis* pain] diminished sensitiveness to pain.

She continues to have the residual **hypalgesia** [diminished sensitiveness to pain] C6 and C8 distribution in both upper extremities. Ascough v. Workmen's Comp. Appeals Board, 98 Cal.Rptr. 357, 360 (Ct.App.Cal.1971).

hyperaldosteronism See *aldosteronism.*

hyperalgesia (hi"per-al-je'ze-ah) [*hyper-* + Gr. *algēsis* pain] excessive sensitiveness or sensibility to pain.

At that time, there was diffused pain in her left foot, accompanied by swelling, stiffness and **hyperalgesia** (extreme sensitivity to pain). Zick v. Industrial Com'n, 444 N.E.2d 164, 166 (Ill. 1982).

hyperbaric (hi"per-băr'ik) [*hyper-* + Gr. *baros* weight] characterized by greater than normal pressure or weight; applied to gases under greater than atmospheric pressure, as hyperbaric oxygen, or to a solution of greater specific gravity than another taken as a standard of reference.

In the early evening of December 29, Mrs. Germann's jaws became more painful and her speech became impaired....

... She was removed to Mt. Sinai Hospital in New York City for treatment in a **hyperbaric** chamber. Unfortunately, this treatment was unsuccessful and Mrs. Germann died two days later....

The cause of death was given as tetanus. Germann v. Matriss, 260 A.2d 825, 828 (N.J.1970).

hyperbilirubinemia (hi"per-bil"ĭ-roo"bĭ-ne'me-ah) excessive concentrations of bilirubin in the blood, which may lead to jaundice; the hyperbilirubinemias are classified as conjugated or unconjugated, according to the predominant form of bilirubin in the blood. See also *bilirubin;* and *syndrome, Crigler-Najjar.*

Plaintiff's six-count complaint for negligence and willful and wanton misconduct alleges that in October of 1965, when her mother was 13 years of age, the defendants, on two occasions, negligently transfused her mother with 500 cubic centimeters of Rh-positive blood. The mother's Rh-negative blood was incompatible with, and was sensitized by, the Rh-positive blood....

The resulting sensitization of the mother's blood allegedly caused prenatal damage to plaintiff's hemolitic processes, which put her life in jeopardy and necessitated her induced premature birth. Plaintiff was born on March 25, 1974, jaundiced and suffering from **hyperbilirubinemia**. She required an immediate, complete exchange transfusion of her blood and another such transfusion shortly thereafter. It is further alleged that, as a result of the defendants' acts, plaintiff suffers from permanent damage to various organs, her brain, and her nervous system. Renslow v. Mennonite Hospital, 367 N.E.2d 1250–1 (Ill.1977).

hypercapnia (hi"per-kap'ne-ah) [*hyper-* + Gr. *kapnos* smoke] excess of carbon dioxide in the blood.

The purpose of the preparations made by Mr. Tommie, according to the medical testimony, was to heighten sexual pleasure during masturbation by reducing the supply of blood, and therefore the supply of oxygen, to the brain by gradually tightening the rope around his neck. The reduced oxygen to the brain produces a state of **hypercapnia**, or an increase of carbon dioxide in the blood, and a state of hypoxia, or a decrease in oxygen in the blood, which is supposed to increase the intensity of orgasm....

... There is also evidence that a state of **hypercapnia** simply alters the amount of oxygen in the brain, thus heightening or intensifying certain body sensations, and that it may be accomplished by various drugs as well as by other means. Connecticut General Life Ins. Co. v. Tommie, 619 S.W.2d 199, 201–3 (Ct.Civ.App.Tex.1981).

hypercholesterolemia (hi"per-ko-les"ter-ol-e'me-ah) [*hyper-* + *cholesterol* + Gr. *haima* blood + *-ia*] excess of cholesterol in the blood.

I therefore feel that 75 percent of this lady's permanent disability was not related to her work, but related to her high cholesterol, a metabolic and genetic predisposition to coronary artery disease.... Franklin v. Workers' Comp. Appeals Bd., 145 Cal.Rptr. 22, 27 (Ct.App.Cal.1978).

On August 4, 1962, the Council on Foods and Nutrition of the American Medical Association, published in the American Medical Association Journal, a comprehensive report titled "The Regulation of Dietary Fat." The article advised physicians that the preferred treatment for **hypercholesteremia** (abnormally high cholesterol content in the blood plasma, a condition claimed to be associated with high incidence of heart attack and strokes) is a diet in which "the ratio of poly-unsaturated fatty acids to saturated fatty acids ranges from 1.1:1 to 1.5:1 (an L/S ratio of 1.1 to 1.5)". The article also recommended specific diets for use in such cases in which "Special" margarine is a mandatory substitute for ordinary margarine and butter. Corn Products Co. v. Standard Brands, Inc., 359 F.2d 739, 741 (7th Cir. 1966).

hyperemesis (hi"per-em'ĕ-sis) [*hyper-* + Gr. *emesis* vomiting] excessive vomiting.

hyperemesis gravidarum pernicious vomiting during pregnancy.

At all times material to this litigation, Eastern's medical benefits plan has provided major medical benefits for the following complications of pregnancy: **Hyperemsis** [sic] **Gravidarum** (pernicious vomiting); ... Burwell v. Eastern Air Lines, Inc., 458 F.Supp. 474, 480 (E.D.Va.1978).

hyperextension (hi"per-ek-sten'shun) extreme or excessive extension of a limb or part.

Another doctor, describing Riley's condition shortly after he entered the hospital, noted: "[M]ost of his work is overhead type and involves quite a bit of **hyperextension** of the neck. That means that most of his work he will have to do with his neck bending upwards." [Dissent.] U.S. Industries/Federal Sheet Metal, Inc. v. Director, OWCP, 455 U.S. 608, 619, 102 S.Ct. 1312, 71 L.Ed.2d 495 (1982).

The doctor's opinion was that the break was about two or three weeks old and had probably been caused by **hyperextension** of the arm, or bending it the way it shouldn't bend. People v. Atkins, 125 Cal.Rptr. 855, 858 (Ct.App.Cal.1975).

hyperflexia

... the **hyperflexia**, or the increased reflexes,... Pratt v. Stein, 444 A.2d 674, 682 (Super.Ct.Pa.1982).

hyperglycemia (hi"per-gli-se'me-ah) [*hyper-* + Gr. *glykys* sweet + *haima* blood + *-ia*] abnormally increased content of sugar in the blood.

This condition [diabetes mellitus] produces **hyperglycemia** (abnormal increase in the glucose level in the blood) and may result in acidosis and coma. Application of Lydia E. Hall Hospital, 455 N.Y.S.2d 706–7 (Sup.Ct.Nassau Cty.1982).

The evidence clearly establishes that the immediate cause of Maltempo's death was strangulation on his own vomit. There is a conflict in the evidence as to whether the vomiting was caused by **hyperglycemia** (high blood sugar) or.... Maltempo v. Cuthbert, 504 F.2d 325, 328 (5th Cir. 1974).

hyperimmunization (hi″per-im″u-ni-za′shun) the practice of establishing a heightened state of actively acquired immunity by the administration of repeated (booster) doses of antigen, or of passively acquired immunity by the injection of hyperimmune gamma globulin.

At this time, the receptionist informs the donor of the possibility of "**hyperimmunization**," an allergic reaction to the presence of antigens which are later injected into the donor's system. He is told that he may go into shock if **hyperimmunization** occurs. Mirsa, Inc. v. State Medical Board, 329 N.E.2d 106–7 (Ohio 1975).

hyperinsulinism (hi″per-in′su-lin-izm″) excessive secretion of insulin by the pancreas, resulting in hypoglycemia.

... **hyperinsulinism** (a concentration of glucose in the blood at below normal levels), but the examining physician was unable to obtain sufficient details to verify this condition....

... Although the term "hypoglycemia" does not appear on the Surgeon General's list of disqualifying medical conditions and physical defects, the condition to which hypoglycemia relates is inextricably bound to "**hyperinsulinism**." Allan, "Hyperinsulinism, Hypoglycemia, Hypoglycosis," in The Cyclopedia of Medicine, Surgery, Specialities vol. VI, at 906 (1971 rev. ed.); McNalty (ed.), Butterworth's Medical Dictionary 703–04 (24th ed. 1965); Derick, "Spontaneous Hyperinsulinism and Allied States: Hypoglycemic Syndrome," in Christian (ed.), The Oxford Medicine 178(27) (1949). U.S. v. D'Arcey, 471 F.2d 880–1 (9th Cir. 1972).

hyperkalemia (hi″per-kah-le′me-ah) abnormally high potassium concentration in the blood, most often due to defective renal excretion. It is characterized clinically by electrocardiographic abnormalities (elevated T waves and depressed P waves, and eventually by atrial asystole). In severe cases, weakness and flaccid paralysis may occur. Called also *hyperpotassemia*.

The major risk associated with the drug therapy was **hyperkalemia** (high serum potassium), and Dr. Varon testified that he ran a serum-potassium test on Andrea's third visit in September, 1975. At that time, she was not hyperkalemic. Mendoza v. Varon, 563 S.W.2d 646, 653 (Ct.Civ.App.Tex. 1978).

hyperkinesia (hi″per-ki-ne′ze-ah) [*hyper-* + Gr. *kinēsis* motion + *-ia*] abnormally increased motor function or activity; hyperactivity. See also *hyperkinetic syndrome*, under *syndrome*.

Hospital personnel found that J.L. was mentally ill and diagnosed his illness as "Hyperkinetic Reaction of Childhood 308.00."...

This nomenclature is derived from the Diagnostic and Statistical Manual of Mental Disorders published by the American Psychiatric Association. J.L. v. Parham, 412 F.Supp. 112, 117 (M.D.Ga.1976).

hyperkinetic See *hyperkinesia*.

hyperlipemia (hi″per-li-pe′me-ah) [*hyper-* + Gr. *lipos* fat + *haima* blood + *-ia*] elevated concentration of triglycerides in the plasma. See also *hyperlipoproteinemia*.

Dr. Olash also found **hyperlipodemia** [sic] which is an elevation of fats in the blood being cholesterols and triglycerides. Pierce v. Kentucky Galvanizing Co., Inc., 606 S.W.2d 165, 167 (Ct.App.Ky.1980).

... type IV **hyperlipidemia** [sic] (an increase in the amount of fats in the blood stream, causing hardening of the arteries). Matter of Iannelli, 384 A.2d 1104, 1108 (Super.Ct.N.J.1978).

hyperlipoproteinemia (hi″per-lip″o-pro″te-in-e′me-ah) an excess of lipoproteins in the blood, due to a disorder of lipoprotein metabolism, and occurring as an acquired or familial condition.

hyperostosis (hi″per-os-to′sis) [*hyper-* + Gr. *osteon* bone + *-osis*] hypertrophy of bone; exostosis. See also *exostosis*.

hyperphoria (hi″per-fo′re-ah) [*hyper-* + Gr. *phorein* to bear] a form of heterophoria in which there is permanent upward deviation of the visual axis of an eye after the visual fusional stimulus has been eliminated. See also *strabismus*.

It was further his opinion that Plaintiff, as her eyes moved right, unconsciously compensated by pulling the images together to the point of suppressing the vision in her left eye, thereby eliminating the double vision. When fatigued or ill, she would have more difficulty maintaining fusion and this resulted in symptoms commonly called eye strain, and caused headaches with severe pressure behind the eyes, all of which were symptoms of **hyperphoria**. Walker v. North Dakota Eye Clinic, Ltd., 415 F.Supp. 891–2 (D.N.Dak.1976).

hyperplasia (hi″per-pla′ze-ah) [*hyper-* + Gr. *plasis* formation] the abnormal multiplication or increase in the number of normal cells in normal arrangement in a tissue. See also *hypertrophy*.

... high blood pressure would be likely in a man with nodular **hyperplasia** of the adrenal cortices, as I described in my protocol. Henderson v. Travelers Ins. Co., 544 S.W.2d 649, 652 (Tex.1976).

A further condition, called **hyperplasia** of the islets of the pancreas might have the same symptoms as the islet cell tumor but is obvious to the pathologist on examination of the pancreas cell. People v. Archerd, 477 P.2d 421, 424 (Cal.1970).

hyperplasia, giant follicular a disorder of the lymph nodes, generally confined to the cervical lymph nodes, which may simulate follicular lymphoma, but cytologically the follicles contain both macrophages and lymphoblasts.

In July 1969, a Mayo Clinic pathologist amended Jewson's 1942 diagnosis of lymphosarcoma to follicular and reticular **hyperplasia**. Jewson v. Mayo Clinic, 691 F.2d 405, 407 (8th Cir. 1982).

hyperpyrexia (hi″per-pi-rek′se-ah) [*hyper-* + Gr. *pyressein* to be feverish] a highly elevated body temperature. See also *pneumothorax* (Vogan case).

... decedent's rectal temperature of 107.8° "strongly suggests" that death was caused by malignant **hyperpyrexia** or hyperthermia (a chemical reaction to anesthesia causing an extreme rise in body temperature), instead of a tension pneumothorax as originally diagnosed....

... The majority opinion indicates that the observations formed by Dr. Van Kirk were the basis for Dr. Zeiler's newly cast and changed opinion. The addendum, however, also reveals that he considered other sources, all of them hearsay. It recites that Dr. Zeiler's views were based in part on a symposium in 1968 on the subject of "Hyperpyrexia During Anesthesia" of the International Anesthesia Research Society. His views were also based upon a "review of the literature including the important article of Britt and Kalow, 'Hyperrigidity and Hyperthermia Associated with Anaesthesia', in the Annals, New York Academy of Sciences, 1968." None of these additional sources were tested under cross-examination. Vogan v. Byers, 447 F.2d 543, 545–6 (3d Cir. 1971).

hyperpyrexia, malignant See *hyperthermia*.

hyperreflexia (hi″per-re-flek′se-ah) [*hyper-* + *reflex* + *-ia*] exaggeration of reflexes.

It follows as a corollary to this required absence or depression of DTRs [in GBS (acute febrile polyneuritis)] that the related pathological reflexes or signs, such as the Babinski and Hoffman, would be similarly absent. The presence of either these pathological reflexes or of increased DTRs (**hyperreflexia**) would be an indication of central nervous system disease. Stich v. U.S., 565 F.Supp. 1096, 1101 (D.N.J.1983).

Involvement of the central nervous system is often associated with an increase of reflex, or **hyperreflexia**. Smith v. U.S., 557 F.Supp. 42, 47 (W.D.Ark.1982).

hypersensitivity (hi″per-sen′sĭ-tiv″ĭ-te) a state of altered reactivity in which the body reacts with an exaggerated response to a foreign agent. Hypersensitivity reactions are pathologic processes induced by immune responses and may be classified as immediate or delayed, or as: *type I*, the immediate hypersensitivity reactions (e.g., anaphylaxis); *type II*, in which injury is produced by antibody against tissue antigens (e.g., nephrotoxic nephritis); *type III*, in which injury is produced by antigen-antibody complex, especially by soluble complexes formed by slight antigen excess (e.g., Arthus reaction and serum sickness); and *type IV*, the delayed hypersensitivity reactions (e.g., contact dermatitis).

It is not unusual for drug **hypersensitivity** to develop in persons who have been receiving long courses of treatment. Fever is a common symptom, as well as ... hepatitis, and others. "Tuberculosis," Current Therapy, p. 91 (1963). See also, Physician's Desk Reference, 1963, 1964, pp. 702–03; Goodman & Gilman, The Pharmacological Basis of Therapeutics, 1322–1327 (1965); "Tuberculosis," Current Therapy, pp. 111–114 (1965). Brick v. Barnes-Hines Pharmaceutical Co., Inc., 428 F.Supp. 496–7 (D.D.C.1977).

hypertension (hi″per-ten′shun) [*hyper-* + *tension*] persistently high arterial blood pressure. Various criteria for its threshold have been suggested, ranging from 140 mm. Hg systolic and 90 mm. Hg diastolic to as high as 200 mm. Hg systolic and 110 mm. Hg diastolic. Hypertension may have no known cause (*essential* or *idopathic h.*) or be associated with other primary diseases (*secondary h.*). See also *pressure, blood*; and *aneurism* (Cunningham case).

Hypertension increases the possibility of leakage and stressful situations are frequent causes of bleeding. Cunningham v. Am. Mut. Ins. Co., 390 So.2d 1372, 1375 (Ct.App.La.1980).

There were medical findings which established that appellant suffered from **hypertension** (high blood pressure), mild diabetes, obesity, and was a light smoker—all basic risk factors associated with heart attacks....

... **Hypertension** is associated with the build-up of arterial plaque. Pierce v. Kentucky Galvanizing Co., Inc., 606 S.W.2d 165, 167 (Ct.App.Ky.1980).

"**Hypertension**" means an elevation of the blood pressure within the arterial system of the body which is in excess of the generally accepted level of 140 cystolic or pumping pressure and 90 diastolic or resting pressure. There are different degrees of **hypertension** generally referred to as mild, moderate, moderate to severe, and severe, depending upon the extent of the elevation of the blood pressure. It is generally believed in the medical profession that, as has ben [sic] demonstrated by short-term and long-term studies, such elevation of the blood pressure is directly contributory to the early onset of strokes, heart attacks, kidney failure, etc....

Hypertension is also treated by the use of combinations of HCT and other drugs, such as deserpidine, syrosingopine, butabarbital, meprobamate, methyldopa, guanethedine sulfate, and hydralazine-hydrochloride. As in the case of reserpine, for any given patient there exists an optimum ratio of the benzothiadiazine to the other therapeutically active product or products....

From a medical point of view, the preferred initial medication for **hypertension** is today a diuretic. U.S. v. Ciba Geigy Corp., 508 F.Supp. 1118, ____, ____, ____ (D.N.J.1976).

Other Authorities: U.S. v. DePalma, 466 F.Supp. 920, 925 (S.D.N.Y.1979); McClaflin v. Califano, 448 F.Supp. 69, 74 (D.Kan.1978); Muznik v. Workers' Comp. App. Bd. of Cty. of Los Angeles, 124 Cal.Rptr. 407, 410–11 (Ct.App.Cal.1975); James H. Boyle & Son, Inc. v. Prudential Ins. Co., 268 N.E.2d 651–2 (Sup.Jud.Ct.Mass.1971); Sanzari v. Rosenfeld, 167 A.2d 625, 627 (N.J.1961); Glover v. Bruce, 265 S.W.2d 346, 351 (Mo.1954).

hypertension, benign intracranial See *pseudotumor cerebri*.

hypertension, borderline a condition in which the arterial blood pressure is sometimes within the normotensive range and sometimes within the hypertensive range; called also *labile h.*

The jury found that Dr. Varon was not negligent in prescribing treatment for **labile hypertension** (intermittent high blood-pressure). Mendoza v. Varon, 563 S.W.2d 646, 650–1 (Ct.Civ.App.Tex.1978).

hypertension, labile See *hypertension, borderline*.

hypertensity See *hypertension*.

hyperthermia (hi"per-ther'me-ah) [*hyper-* + Gr. *thermē* heat + *-ia*] abnormally high body temperature, especially that induced for therapeutic purposes. See also *hyperpyrexia* (Vogan case).

Plaintiff claims that her husband suffered a fatal reaction to anesthesia diagnosed as malignant **hyperthermia**. King v. Retz, 454 N.Y.S.2d 594 (Sup.Ct.Onondaga Ct.1982).

Dr. Zeiler speculated in the Addendum that decedent's rib was broken by heart massage during the operation and that, in light of recent advances in medical knowledge, decedent's rectal temperature of 107.8° "strongly suggests" that death was caused by malignant hyperpyrexia or **hyperthermia** (a chemical reaction to anesthesia causing an extreme rise in body temperature), instead of a tension pneumothorax as originally diagnosed. The Addendum further stated that the condition noted has a familial tendency and for this reason should be explained to the family....

    ... His views were also based upon a "review of the literature including the important article of Britt and Kalow, 'Hyperrigidity and Hyperthermia Associated with Anaesthesia', in the Annals New York Academy of Sciences, 1968." None of these additional sources were tested under cross-examination. Vogan v. Byers, 447 F.2d 543, 545–6 (3d Cir. 1971).

hyperthyroidism (hi"per-thi'roi-dizm) excessive functional activity of the thyroid gland, characterized by increased basal metabolism, goiter, and disturbances in the autonomic nervous system and in creatine metabolism. This term is sometimes used to refer to *Graves' disease.*

During this physical examination, the doctor noted two unusual things: "One was the rate and intensity with which the deep tendon reflexes appear; and the other ... that when stretching the hands there was a small tremor present in the fingertips." These factors combined with a slightly larger than normal thyroid suggested possible **hyperthyroidism.** Carmichael v. Reitz, 95 Cal.Rptr. 381, 387 (Ct.App.Cal.1971).

hypertriglyceridemia (hi"per-tri-glis"er-i-de'me-ah) an excess of triglycerides in the blood; an inherited form occurs in familial hyperlipoproteinemia, types IIb and IV.

    ... hypertriglyceridemia (fats in the blood). Manigan v. Califano, 453 F.Supp. 1080, 1084 (D.Kan.1978).

hypertrophic See *hypertrophy.*

hypertrophy (hi-per'tro-fe) [*hyper-* + Gr. *trophē* nutrition] the enlargement or overgrowth of an organ or part due to an increase in size of its constituent cells. Cf. *hyperplasia.* See also *ray, roentgen* (Greenberg case).

They [the experts] also agreed that Mr. Van Hook had **hypertrophy,** which is a condition associated with sudden death in a small but identifiable group of individuals. Van Hook v. Aetna Life Ins. Co., 550 F.Supp. 888, 892 (E.D.Mich.1982).

He had **hypertrophic,** or growing boney arthritis in 1973–74, and it could be a condition that any 54-year-old man would be likely to have. Lovely v. Cooper Indus. Products, Inc., 429 N.E.2d 274–5 (Ct.App.Ind.1981).

The examination, performed by Dr. Pickens on April 6, 1972, revealed a trabeculated bladder which suggested that small obstructing tissue in the middle lobe of the prostate gland was causing the strain in urination. On the basis of the patient's complaints, medical history and lab reports, Dr. Pickens diagnosed the condition as benign prostatic **hypertrophy.** Dessi v. U.S., 489 F.Supp. 722, 724 (E.D.Va.1980).

Other Authorities: Eller and Co. v. Golden, 620 F.2d 71, 73 (5th Cir. 1980); City of Philadelphia v. Collins, 320 A.2d 421, 423 (Commonwealth Ct.Pa.1974); Swihel v. Richardson, 346 F.Supp. 930, 933 (D.Neb.1972).

hypertrophy, benign prostatic

BPH, according to the evidence before the Postal Service, is a condition of enlargement of the prostate gland in older men that tends to compress the urethra; its symptoms include difficulty in voiding, frequency of urination, urgency to urinate, nocturia, and dribbling after urination. Kurzon v. U.S. Postal Service, 539 F.2d 788–9 (1st Cir. 1976).

hypertrophy, coronary

    ... **coronary hypertrophy** (an enlarged heart).... Britt v. Travelers Ins. Co., 556 F.2d 336, 339 (5th Cir. 1977).

hypertrophy, prostatic

In January, 1975, he was hospitalized, with a diagnosis of **prostatic hypertrophy** (enlarged prostate). McClaffin v. Califano, 448 F.Supp. 69, 71 (D.Kan.1978).

hypertrophy, ventricular hypertrophy of the myocardium of a ventricle.

hypertropia (hi"per-tro'pe-ah) [*hyper-* + Gr. *trepein* to turn] strabismus in which there is permanent upward deviation of the visual axis of an eye. See also *strabismus.*

The more the eye moved to the right, the more the left eye would move up, until the pupil would disappear under the eyelid, a condition known as **hypertropia,** a type of strabismus squint. This condition is also medically described as incomitant heterotropia, and it was the doctor's opinion it was a condition that had existed with the Plaintiff for a long time. Walker v. North Dakota Eye Clinic, Ltd., 415 F.Supp. 891–2 (D.N.Dak. 1976).

hyperventilation (hi"per-ven"ti-la'shun) 1. a state in which there is an increased amount of air entering the pulmonary alveoli (increased alveolar ventilation), resulting in reduction of carbon dioxide tension and eventually leading to alkalosis. 2. abnormally prolonged, rapid, and deep breathing, frequently used as a test procedure in epilepsy and tetany.

Dorland's Illustrated Medical Dictionary, 24th Edition, defines **hyperventilation** as rapid and deep breathing. Expert witness testimony also reflected that "**hyperventilation**" implies depth. Considering all the testimony and the totality of the circumstances, we reject as clearly erroneous the trial court's conclusion that the degree of **hyperventilation** indicating salicylate poisoning was not present when Dr. Finley made the examination. Dr. Finley's explanation of the manifested "overbreathing" of Joann Rewis is entitled to little weight when juxtaposed with the uncontradicted documentary notation of "**hyperventilating**".... Rewis v. U.S. 445 F.2d 1303, 1305 (5th Cir. 1971).

hypesthesia See *hypoesthesia.*

hypnosis (hip-no'sis) an artificially induced passive state in which there is increased amenability and responsiveness to suggestions and commands, provided that these do not conflict seriously with the subject's own conscious or unconscious wishes.

Dr. Spiegel testified that **hypnotism** is a state of great attentive/receptive concentration. He stated that different individuals have different and fixed abilities to go into this trance state. Mr. Neely, in his opinion, is a person of low hypnotizability, does not have a rich fantasy life, but instead exercises his critical faculties before reaching conclusions, and it follows that he is not unduly subject to suggestion while in the hypnotic state. U.S. v. Narciso, 446 F.Supp. 252, 280 (E.D. Mich.1977).

Dr. Baker claimed that he verified defendant's truthfulness by placing him under **hypnosis** and stated that people under **hypnosis** always tell the truth.[4] The jury was not bound to believe Dr. Baker's unsupported conclusion as to the reliability of **hypnosis**. Vol. 9 of the Encyclopaedia Britannica (1974) at pg. 139 on the subject of **hypnosis** states:

> **Hypnosis** has not been found reliable in obtaining truth from a reluctant witness. Even if it were possible to induce **hypnosis** against one's will, it is well documented that the hypnotized individual still can willfully lie.[5] [[4] There is a question about the admissibility of the results of **hypnosis** when used not as a diagnostic test but in order to determine the subject's veracity. See Annot. 41 A.L.R.3d pp. 1369 et seq.[5] This article was co-authored by Dr. Martin T. Orme, M.D., Professor of Psychiatry & Director of Unit for Experimental Psychiatry, University of Pennsylvania and A. Gordon Hamner, Professor of Psychology, MacQuarie University, North Ryde, Australia.] State v. Allen, 557 P.2d 176, 182 (Ct.App.Ariz.1976).

hypnotic (hip-not'ik) [Gr. *hypnōtikos*] a drug that acts to induce sleep. See also *tranquilizer* (In re Cameron case).

Dr. Burbridge, distinguished the reasons that a tranquilizer like Thorazine produces sleep from the reasons that a **hypnotic** drug would produce sleep. Tranquilizers and **hypnotic** drugs operate upon different levels of the brain. A **hypnotic** drug will induce sleep because it operates upon the area of the brain that controls thought process and consciousness. An individual under the influence of a **hypnotic** drug is rendered unconscious. In re Cameron, 439 P.2d 633, 641 (Cal.1968).

hypnotism See *hypnosis*.

hypo- [Gr. *hypo* under] a prefix signifying beneath, under, or deficient. In chemistry, it denotes that the principal element in the compound is combined in its lowest state of valence.

hypoallergenic See *allergen; allergenic;* and *hypo-*.

In general, the regulation being challenged here, Regulation 700.100 of the Food and Drug Administration, limits the use on cosmetic labels of the term "hypoallergenic" and of phrases such as "allergy tested" and "dermatologist tested" which convey "the same meaning" as that term. More specifically, it demands that cosmetic manufacturers who use such terms: (1) accompany the word or phrase with the explanation "less likely to cause adverse reactions than some competing products" and (2) conduct certain scientific studies to demonstrate that the product for which the claim is made is in fact less likely to cause a reaction than a significant number of competitive

products. 21 C.F.R. § 701.100, 40 Fed.Reg. 24450–51 (June 6, 1975)....

... However, [plaintiffs] they suggested to the Commissioner that the term be defined as "very unlikely to cause adverse reactions," arguing that such a definition would better facilitate economic, efficient and accurate testing by providing an objective standard chosen by the Commissioner against which a manufacturer could measure a particular cosmetic's risk of producing an adverse reaction....

... The Commissioner thereafter considered the alternative objective tests that various commenters proposed as substitutes for the proposed rule test. He determined that no objective test had been suggested which would come sufficiently close to assuring that only those cosmetics which were "less likely to produce adverse reactions than a significant number of their competitors" would be permitted to use the term "hypoallergenic" on their labels. 40 Fed.Reg. 24444 (June 6, 1975). It is this Court's opinion, based on the foregoing, that the Commissioner's decision to retain the comparative test in the regulation was a rational and reasonable one. Almay, Inc. v. Weinberger, 417 F.Supp. 758, 760–2 (D.D.C.1976).

hypocalcemia (hi"po-kal-se'me-ah) [*hypo-* + *calcium* + Gr. *haima* blood + *-ia*] reduction of the blood calcium below normal; manifestations include hyperactive deep tendon reflexes, Chvostek's sign, muscle and abdominal cramps, and carpopedal spasm.

Shortly thereafter, Mrs. O'Neill went into **hypocalcemic** shock, an infrequent complication of thyroid surgery. O'Neill v. Kiledjian, 511 F.2d 511–12 (6th Cir. 1975).

hypocapnia (hi"po-kap'ne-ah) [*hypo-* + Gr. *kapnos* smoke + *-ia*] deficiency of carbon dioxide in the blood, resulting from hyperventilation and eventually leading to alkalosis.

Hypocapnia is a deficiency of carbon dioxide in the blood. Dorland's Medical Dictionary. Plaintiff's deficiency is not severe enough to be totally disabling. See 20 C.F.R. § 410.424 & Appendix to Subpart D. Jeffries v. Mathews, 431 F.Supp. 1030, 1032 (E.D.Tenn.1977), vacated and remanded without published opinion 575 F.2d 1337 (6th Cir. 1978).

hypochlorhydria (hi"po-klor-hi'dre-ah) [*hypo-* + Gr. *chlōros* green + *hydōr* water + *-ia*] deficiency of hydrochloric acid in the gastric juice. Cf. *achlorhydria*.

... **hypochlorhydria** (insufficient production of hydrochloric acid in digestive system).... Palik v. Mathews, 422 F.Supp. 547, 549 (D.Neb.1976).

hypochondria See *hypochondriasis*.

hypochondriacal (hi"po-kon-dri'ah-kal) affected with hypochondriasis.

hypochondriasis (hi"po-kon-dri'ah-sis) [so called because the hypochondrium, and especially the spleen, was supposed to be the seat of this disorder] morbid anxiety about one's health, often associated with numerous and varying symptoms which cannot be attributed to organic disease; called also *hypochondria*.

The administrative law judge viewed the psychiatrists as having concluded that the plaintiff's complaints were "largely **hypochondriacal**;" it was his conclusion that the "medical evidence does not demonstrate a condition either mental or physical which is so severe it would constitute 'disability' under the Act and Regulations.'' Transcript, p. 34. Meek v. Califano, 488 F.Supp. 26, 29–30 (D.Neb.1979).

Other Authorities: Leslie v. Richardson, 320 F.Supp. 580–1 (E.D.Tenn.1970).

hypochromia (hi"po-kro'me-ah) [*hypo-* + Gr. *chrōma* color + *-ia*] abnormal decrease in the hemoglobin content of the erythrocytes.

Severe iron deficiency can be diagnosed when an examination of the blood shows that the red blood cells are pale (**hypochromic**) and the red cells are abnormally small (microcytic) from a lack of sufficient hemoglobin to color and fill them. J. B. Williams Co. v. F.T.C., 381 F.2d 884, 887 (6th Cir. 1967).

hypochromic (hi"po-kro'mik) pertaining to or marked by hypochromia.

hypodermoclysis (hi"po-der-mok'lĭ-sis) [*hypo-* + Gr. *derma* skin + *klyzein* to wash out] introduction into the subcutaneous tissues of fluids, especially physiologic sodium chloride solution, to replace inadequate intake or loss of water and salt during illness or operation.

Dr. Root stated that one of the immediate first treatments should be external cooling, followed by prevention of imbalance of electrolyte fluid and acid bases, accomplished either by intravenous injection of solutions or by **hypodermoclysis** (injection subcutaneously). Cortez v. Macias, 167 Cal.Rptr. 905, 908 (Ct.App.Cal.1980).

hypoesthesia (hi"po-es-the'ze-ah) [*hypo-* + Gr. *aisthēsis* sensation + *-ia*] abnormally decreased sensitivity to stimulation.

Hypoesthesia, an abnormally decreased sensitivity of the skin, was detected over the distribution of nerves on the C5 and C6 level. Broadbent v. Harris, 698 F.2d 407, 409 (10th Cir. 1983).

Among other things, he found **hypesthesia** [sic] (impairment or lessening of tactile sensibility) in the thigh, leg, foot and toe areas of petitioner's legs. Ascough v. Workmen's Comp. Appeals Board, 98 Cal.Rptr. 357, 362 (Ct.App.Cal.1971).

Current physical examination reveals sensory changes of **hypoesthesia** involving the L5 neural segment on the right. Cline v. Secretary of Health, Education and Welfare, 444 F.2d 289–90 (6th Cir. 1971).

Other Authorities: Miracle v. Celebrezze, 351 F.2d 361, 366 (6th Cir. 1965).

hypogastric artery See *arteria iliaca interna.*

hypoglossal nerve See *nervus hypoglossus.*

hypoglycemia (hi"po-gli-se'me-ah) [*hypo-* + Gr. *glykys* sweet + *haima* blood + *-ia*] an abnormally diminished content of glucose in the blood, which may lead to tremulousness, cold sweat, piloerection, hypothermia, and headache, accompanied by confusion, hallucinations, bizarre behavior, and ultimately, convulsions and coma.

Petitioner suffers from a disease known as **hypoglycemia**, a condition caused by abnormally low blood sugar in the body. It can cause permanent damage to the nervous system and brain, and often results in various psychological disorders and diabetes, as well as chronic exhaustion of the adrenal gland

and pancreas. Leona Von Kalb v. Com., 37 TCM 1511, 1512 [CCH Dec. 35,406(M)] (1978).

After an introductory technical paragraph, Dr. Fee concluded: Reactive **Hypoglycemia** is rarely disqualifying for entry into military service, and there is no standard glucose value used to diagnose the problem. The diagnosis is made by close correlation between glucose values and the man's symptoms as reflected in the individual's history and as observed by a physician during the actual conduct of the test. U.S. v. D'Arcey, 471 F.2d 880, 885 (9th Cir. 1972).

It was the opinion of fifteen experts at the trial, including attending physicians, autopsy surgeons and experts in the fields of diabetes and **hypoglycemia**, pathology, insulin and research and its relation to pathology and insulin shock therapy, that all six of the victims died from **hypoglycemia** caused by an injection or injections of insulin, none had any prior history of **hypoglycemia**, none had ever evidenced or complained of any of its symptoms.

Hypoglycemia is a state in which the blood sugar is lowered below normal levels. Some forms have never been reported as fatal. Among the forms that may result in death there are two classifications. The first are those causes which are obvious and readily recognizable either by the physician or autopsy surgeon. These include liver disease which cause obvious changes; non-pancreatic tumors which are never reported less than the size of a grapefruit and cannot possibly be overlooked by an autopsy surgeon; more rare types of cancer of the adrenal glands, stomach, cecum and lungs, which are also of obvious size. As a general rule each is accompanied by prolonged period of progressive symptoms; a person is not normally healthy one day and dead of **hypoglycemia** the next. The major remaining cause of severe **hypoglycemia** that may be more obscure in manifesting its origin relates to the pancreas, and is always accompanied by a long period of progressive symptoms of **hypoglycemia** before severe symptoms result. History of these symptoms, and of weight gain over a period of time (the afflicted person learns that increased caloric intake can alleviate the symptoms) are important. People v. Archerd, 477 P.2d 421, 424 (Cal.1970).

Other Authorities: Brown v. Crews, 363 So.2d 1121–2 (Dist. Ct.App.Fla.1978); Ressegiue v. Secretary of H.E.W. of United States, 425 F.Supp. 160, 163 (E.D.N.Y.1977); Goodwin v. Richardson, 357 F.Supp. 540, 547 (E.D.Mo.1973), U.S. v. Dunavan, 464 F.2d 1166, 1178 (6th Cir. 1972).

hypoglycemia, endogenous

Endogenous hypoglycemia may be caused by failure of the adrenal or pituitary glands, but this is always accompanied by symptoms such as a prolonged history of weakness, weight loss, loss of appetite, changes in texture and color of the skin, headaches, with episodes of low blood pressure, prolonged periods of no food and anatomical changes that will not be missed by an autopsy surgeon. People v. Archerd, 477 P.2d 421, 424 (Cal.1970).

hypoglycemic (hi"po-gli-se'mik) an agent that acts to lower the level of glucose in the blood.

. . . a diagnosis of diabetes was rendered. Shortly before discharge from the hospital, Dr. Crews treated Mrs. Brown with a drug known as Dymelor, described as an oral **hypoglycemic** designed to reduce the amount of sugar in the blood. Brown v. Crews, 363 So.2d 1121–2 (Dist.Ct.App.Fla.1978).

hypogonadal See *hypogonadism*; and *gonad*.

hypogonadism (hi"po-go'nad-izm) a condition resulting from or characterized by abnormally decreased functional activity of the gonads, with retardation of growth and sexual development.

The District Court made the following findings with regard to the meaning of these terms.

"**Hypogonadal** impotence is impotence caused by insufficient functioning of the testes to secrete testosterone, that is, impotence caused by androgen deficiency...." U.S. v. 1,048,000 Capsules, More or Less, "Afrodex", 494 F.2d 1158, 1163 (5th Cir. 1974).

hypokinemia (hi"po-ki-ne'me-ah) [*hypo-* + Gr. *kinein* to move + *haima* blood + *-ia*] subnormal cardiac output.

hypokinesia (hi"po-ki-ne'ze-ah) [*hypo-* + Gr. *kinēsis* motion + *-ia*] abnormally decreased mobility; abnormally decreased motor function or activity, having multiple causes.

In April of that year, a coronary arteriogram was performed, and it was discovered that the left ventricle of decedent's heart was **hypokinetic**. Kuntz v. Kern Cty. Emp. Retirement Ass'n, 134 Cal.Rptr. 501, 503 (Ct.App.Cal.1976).

hypokinetic (hi"po-ki-net'ik) pertaining to or characterized by hypokinesia.

hypomagnesemia (hi"po-mag"nĕ-se'me-ah) an abnormally low magnesium content of the blood plasma, manifested chiefly by neuromuscular hyperirritability. It may result from malabsorption, dehydration, alcoholism, or renal disease.

... **hypomagnesemia** (abnormally low amount of magnesium in the blood).... Chester v. Oklahoma Natural Gas Co., 619 P.2d 1266, 1268 (Ct.App.Okla.1980).

hypomania (hi"po-ma'ne-ah) [*hypo-* + Gr. *mania* madness] mania of a moderate type.

"Although I stated it was a mild state of **hypomania**, it is severe enough to interfere with her functioning as a teacher." Newman v. Bd. of Ed. of City Sch. Dist. of N.Y., 443 F.Supp. 994, 1000 (E.D.N.Y., 1977), reversed and remanded 594 F.2d 299 (2d Cir. 1979).

hypometabolism (hi"po-mĕ-tab'o-lizm) [*hypo-* + *metabolism*] abnormally decreased utilization of any substance by the body in metabolism; low metabolic rate.

It goes on to state, however, that the primary problem, as of April, 1967, was that of "borderline **hypometabolism**", metabolic processes insufficient to provide the energy she required. Magruder v. Richardson, 332 F.Supp. 1363, 1368 (E.D.Mo. 1971).

hyponatremia (hi"po-nah-tre'me-ah) deficiency of sodium in the blood; salt depletion.

Plaintiff was diagnosed as having acute pyelonephritis, acute tubular necrosis, **hyponatremia** (sodium depletion), and frequent premature ventricular beats. Smith v. U.S., 557 F.Supp. 42, 46 (W.D.Ark.1982).

hypoparathyroidism (hi"po-par"ah-thi'roid-izm) the condition produced by greatly reduced function of the parathyroids or by the removal of those bodies. The lack of parathyroid hormone leads to a fall in plasma calcium level—which may result in increased neuromuscular excitability and, ultimately, tetany—followed by a rise in plasma phosphate level, resulting in a decrease in bone resorption and consequent density of bone. There may also be dermatologic, ophthalmologic (cataracts), psychiatric, and dental symptoms.

An abnormally low amount of calcium in the blood, or hypocalcemia, is caused by **hypoparathyroidism** resulting from damage to or removal of all of an individual's parathyroid glands. O'Neill v. Kiledjian, 511 F.2d 511–12 (6th Cir. 1975).

hypopharynx (hi"po-far'inks) that division of the pharynx which lies below the upper edge of the epiglottis and opens into the larynx and esophagus.

hypoplasia (hi"po-pla'ze-ah) [*hypo-* + Gr. *plasis* formation + *-ia*] incomplete development or underdevelopment of an organ or tissue; it is less severe in degree than aplasia.

hypoplasia, enamel incomplete or defective development of the enamel of the teeth; it occurs in a hereditary form, as in amelogenesis imperfecta, usually affecting both the deciduous and permanent teeth and generally involving only the enamel, or in an environmental form due to various factors, e.g., vitamin deficiency, exanthematous diseases, congenital syphilis, fluorosis, and local injury or trauma. See also *tetracycline* (Dalke case).

Enamel hypoplasia has also been reported. Tetracycline drugs, therefore, should not be used in this age group unless other drugs are not likely to be effective or are contraindicated....
  A condition in which enamel flakes away from the dentin of the tooth. Dalke v. Upjohn Co., 555 F.2d 245, 247–8 (9th Cir. 1977).

hypoplastic (hi"po-plas'tik) marked by hypoplasia.

A **hypoplastic** defect is a pit or fissure which provides a sanctuary for bacteria and debris. Such defects occur when something (such as illness) interferes with the normal formation of the tooth. Since **hypoplastic** defects develop in the formation process of the teeth, these defects are normally found in a rainbow pattern reflecting the pattern in which the teeth are formed. That is, the mid-coronal portion of the incisors and the tips of the cuspids would be involved. If **hypoplastic** defects are discovered before dental decay has occurred, these defects may be removed through a procedure known as a prophylactic odontonomy. In this procedure the tooth surface is reformed to remove the pit or fissure, but no filling is inserted. U.S. v. Talbott, 460 F.Supp. 253, 258 (S.D.Ohio 1978).

hyporeflexia (hi"po-re-flek'se-ah) weakening of the reflexes.

Involvement of the peripheral nervous system is associated with a decrease of reflexes (**hyporeflexia**) or total reflexia. Involvement of the central nervous system is often associated with an increase of reflex, or hyperreflexia. Smith v. U.S., 557 F.Supp. 42, 47 (W.D.Ark.1982).

hyposomnia See *insomnia*.

hypotension (hi"po-ten'shun) abnormally low blood pressure; seen in shock but not necessarily indicative of it. See also *pressure, blood*.

hypotension, orthostatic a fall in blood pressure associated with dizziness, syncope, and blurred vision occurring upon standing or when standing motionless in a fixed position; it can be acquired or idiopathic, transient or chronic, and occur alone or secondary to a disorder of the central nervous system, such as the Shy-Drager syndrome (see under *syndrome*). Called also *postural o.* and *postural syncope*.

The patient also reported a new symptom, **postural hypotension** (dizzy feelings following a sudden change in position), said by the doctor not to be unusual in people over fifty-five. Cebula v. Benoit, 652 S.W.2d 304–6 (Mo.Ct.App.1983).

hypotension, postural See *hypotension, orthostatic*.

hypothenar (hi-poth'ĕ-nar) [*hypo-* + Gr. *thenar* palm] 1. [NA] the fleshy eminence on the palm along the ulnar margin.

On his left forearm there was atrophy of the **hypothenar** (palm) muscles. He was able to make a fist with poor strength. Long v. Richardson, 334 F.Supp. 305, 309 (W.D.Va.1971).

hypothermia (hi"po-ther'me-ah) [*hypo-* + Gr. *thermē* heat + *-ia*] a low body temperature, as that due to exposure in cold weather or a state of low temperature of the body induced as a means of decreasing metabolism of tissues and thereby the need for oxygen, as used in various surgical procedures, especially on the heart, or in an excised organ being preserved for transplantation. See also *machine, hypothermia*.

The process of destruction of brain cells may be delayed by **hypothermia** (body temperature below 90° F) or central nervous system depressants, such as barbiturates. Ad Hoc Committee of Harvard Medical School to Examine the Definition of Brain Death, A Definition of Irreversible Coma, 205 J.A.M.A. 337 (1968). Matter of Dinnerstein, 380 N.E.2d 134–6 (App. Ct.Mass.1978).

Edith Fogal was injured as the result of the use of a **hypothermia** blanket to cool her body temperature during surgery. After exposure to the cold, Mrs. Fogal's feet, thighs and buttocks became necrotic necessitating excision of parts of her legs and buttocks and amputation of parts of both feet. She died February 21, 1971 before the trial of this action from causes unrelated to these injuries....

... Because this surgery involves stopping the blood supply to portions of the body for extended periods of time, recognized surgical practice suggested the use of **hypothermia** to cool and slow the body's metabolism during the operation. Dr. Geary ordered this procedure. It was administered by the anesthesiologist, defendant Dr. Templeton, by use of an Aquamatic K-Thermia machine which was manufactured by defendant Gorman-Rupp Industries, Inc. and sold to The Genesee Hospital by defendant American Hospital Supply Co., Inc.....

The **hypothermia** was accomplished by use of a blanket placed under the patient's body on the operating table. The blanket was cooled or warmed by circulating alcohol through tubes in it at pre-set temperatures. The points at which the body rested on the blanket were covered to prevent contact injuries and there is no claim here that Mrs. Fogal's injuries resulted from contact with the blanket. The temperature of the coolant is regulated by control units, either automatic or manual, monitored by the anesthesiologist. By pre-setting the "cold" dial to a desired temperature, in this case 48 degrees F., the blanket will cool to that level. Similarly, there is a "high" dial for warming liquid to that level. The temperature at which it is desired to maintain the body during surgery is established by a third dial adjustment, in this case set at 89.6 degrees F. (later raised to 93.2 degrees F.). When set on automatic the machine is designed to cool until the desired body temperature (89.6 degrees F.) is reached and then the automatic adjustment takes over and recirculates the warm liquid in the tubes in place of the cold to warm the blanket so that it maintains the patient at the prescribed body temperature. The hot and cold liquids alternate to keep the temperature of the body constant as recorded by an esophogeal probe or thermometer. Fogal v. Genesee Hospital, 344 N.Y.S.2d 552, 556–7 (4th Dep't 1973).

They also knew that the telethermometer, which was attached to the **hypothermia machine** (an apparatus to lower body temperature) was not always accurate....

Hypothermia as used and understood by Hakim and Hospital's employees is a mechanical cooling process consisting of a blanket placed on the patient. The blanket contained tubing through which cooling material circulated. The blanket was connected to a machine which caused the circulation of the cooling material. The machine may be set to operate automatically at the desired constant temperature and if working properly it maintains that temperature or a temperature within a permissible variable one-half degree. A telethermometer is a part of this equipment and through a tube records the temperature rectally. If in proper working condition, it records the actual body temperature. Rose v. Hakim, 335 F.Supp. 1221, 1226 (D.D.C.1971), remanded with directions in part and otherwise affirmed, 501 F.2d 806 (D.C.Cir. 1972).

hypotonia (hi"po-to'ne-ah) [*hypo-* + Gr. *tonos* tone + *-ia*] a condition of diminished tone of the skeletal muscles; diminished resistance of muscles to passive stretching.

Examination of the central nervous system showed an active infant with normal neurological findings except for mild **hypotonia** (reduced muscular tone). Re Wintersgill and Minister of Social Services, 131 D.L.R. 184, 186 (Unified Fam.Ct., Sask. 1981).

hypovolemia (hi"po-vo-le'me-ah) [*hypo-* + *volume* + Gr. *haima* blood + *-ia*] abnormally decreased volume of circulating fluid [plasma] in the body.

He noted that before administering Dopamine, it should be determined whether the patient is suffering from **hypovolemia**, i.e., a decrease in the amount of circulating fluid in the bloodstream. Erickson v. U.S., 504 F.Supp. 646, 649 (D.S.Dak. 1980).

hypoxia (hi-pok'se-ah) reduction of oxygen supply to tissue below physiological levels despite adequate perfusion of the tissue by blood. Cf. *anoxia*. See also *abruptio* *placentae* (Friel case); *complication, permanent* (Eichelberger case); and *respirator, Bird* (Rose case).

Dr. G testified that the patient's **hypoxia** [lack of oxygen] resulted from insufficient breathing while she was under a spinal anesthesia and narcotized with Demerol. The insufficient uptake of oxygen was viewed as having been occasioned by a failure to monitor the patient while under the anesthesia. Thompson v. Presbyterian Hosp., Inc., 652 P.2d 260, 265 (Okla.1982).

The etiology of **hypoxia**, developing as a result of fresh water near drowning, is such that each moment that the victim suffers a deprivation of oxygen contributes significantly to the **hypoxia** and ultimate brain damage or death. Nazaroff v. Super.Ct. in and for Cty. of Santa Cruz, 145 Cal.Rptr. 657, 659 (Ct.App. Cal.1978).

Through the course of this delivery [by caesarian section], Brian allegedly suffered through a period of **hypoxia** and/or anoxia which caused serious injuries, including brain damage, to him. Bergstreser v. Mitchell, 448 F.Supp. 10, 12 (E.D.Mo. 1977).

Other Authorities: Eichelberger v. Barnes Hosp., 655 S.W.2d 699, 705–7 (Mo.Ct.App.1983); Dunn v. Vic Mfg. Co., 327 N.W.2d 572, 575 (Minn.1982); Vuletich v. Bolgla, 407 N.E.2d 566, 568 (App.Ct.Ill.1980); Bergstreser v. Mitchell, 577 F.2d 22, 24 (8th Cir. 1978); Burrow v. Widder, 368 N.E.2d 443, 447, 450 (App.Ct.Ill.1977); Rose v. Hakim, 335 F.Supp. 1221, 1227 (D.C.Cir.1971).

hypoxic (hi-pok'sik) pertaining to or characterized by hypoxia.

Moreover, he noticed that his complexion was ashen gray, indicating that Mr. Wright was becoming **hypoxic**. Wright v. U.S., 507 F.Supp. 147, 150 (E.D.La.1981).

Dr. Kelly stated that "I had no way of determining how long he had been **hypoxic**, which means has a lessened concentration of oxygen, to produce enough oxygen going to the brain prior to his sudden arrest. There was no way of determining that. It could have been a matter of a minute, it could have been as long as five or six minutes." Eichner v. Dillon, 426 N.Y.S.2d 517, 527 (2d Dep't 1980).

hypoxic encephalopathy See *encephalopathy, hypoxic.*

hysterectomy (his″tĕ-rek′to-me) [*hystero-* + Gr. *ektomē* excision] the operation of excising the uterus, performed either through the abdominal wall (*abdominal h.*) or through the vagina (*vaginal h.*). See also *abortion* (Am. College case); and *fistula, vesicovaginal.*

Although she had undergone a total **hysterectomy**, i.e., complete removal of the uterus, Mrs. Trichel continued to have light monthly bleeding....

... The evidence with regard to the failure of Dr. Donald to completely remove the cervix in the emergency **hysterectomy** showed that it is difficult, at best, to detect whether the entire uterus, fundus (body) and cervix (neck), has been successfully removed in a postpartal **hysterectomy**....

... It was testified that a postpartal **hysterectomy** is not a common operation, and is more difficult than an elective **hysterectomy** because of the abnormal size of the female organs, especially after a vaginal delivery. Trichel v. Caire, 427 So.2d 1227, 1229, 1231 (Ct.App.La.1983).

In fact, both doctors specifically stated that a vesico-vaginal fistula is a recognized hazard of all **hysterectomies** and may occur without any negligence, even when the surgery is performed under ideal conditions, by the most skillful surgeon....

... In performing a **hysterectomy**, it is necessary to separate the uterus from the bladder. This can usually be accomplished by the use of a blunt instrument, often the fingers. In respondent's case, the bladder and uterus were joined by multiple adhesions and petitioner determined that sharp dissection was necessary. It was during this procedure that respondent's bladder was inadvertently entered. Sims v. Helms, 345 So.2d 721–3 (Fla.1977).

A **hysterectomy**, as disclosed by the medical testimony, involves surgical removal of the uterus and repair of any weaknesses in the bladder or the entrance of the urethra into it....

Expert medical testimony showed that in performing a **hysterectomy** it is necessary to place sutures or ligatures within approximately one and one half centimeters of the ureters. This operation was no exception and ligatures were necessarily placed in close proximity to plaintiff's right ureter; there were no ligatures placed through or around the ureter, however....

"Q. And ligatures, those ligatures that you saw, were the result of the **hysterectomy**? A. These ligatures were the result of tying off the blood vessels necessary to control bleeding at the time of the **hysterectomy**." Cronin v. Hagan, 221 N.W.2d 748, 749, 752 (Iowa 1974).

Other Authorities: Hammock v. Allstate Ins. Co., 186 S.E.2d 353–4 (Ct.App.Ga.1971); Siverson v. Weber, 372 P.2d 97–8 (Cal.1962).

hysterectomy, abdominal excision of the uterus through an incision in the abdominal wall.

Dr. James' testimony on deposition was that a vertical midline incision is one of the accepted and recognized techniques for performing an **abdominal hysterectomy** and that going through an existing scar is traditional and within the accepted standard of care in Phoenix, Arizona. Pendleton v. Cilley, 574 P.2d 1303, 1305 (Ariz.1978).

The standards of good medical practice in the performance of an **abdominal hysterectomy** were clearly established and cutting, clamping or stitching the bladder in an uncomplicated operation were clearly identified as deviations from good medical practice. Tatro v. Lueken, 512 P.2d 529, 533 (Kan.1973).

hysterectomy, subtotal hysterectomy in which the cervix is left in place.

Q. Is a hysterectomy, **supracervical hysterectomy**, removal of the tubes and ovaries, a type of surgery which in ordinary course, is likely to lead and have as one of its results, now, in the ordinary course, mind you, in the ordinary course, likely to lead to and have as one of its results, in the absence of any negligence, the formation of fecal vaginal fistulas?

A. This is a rare and unusual complication of hysterectomies. Spidle v. Steward, 402 N.E.2d 216, 219 (Ill.1980).

hysterectomy, total hysterectomy in which the uterus and cervix are completely excised; called also *panhysterectomy.*

Dr. Lund did a **total abdominal hysterectomy** (removal of uterus and cervix).... Cline v. Lund, 107 Cal.Rptr. 629, 632 (Ct. App.Cal.1973).

hysteria (his-tēr′e-ah) [Gr. *hystera* uterus + *-ia*] a psychoneurosis, the symptoms of which are based on conversion and which is characterized by lack of control over acts and emotions, by morbid self-consciousness, by anxiety, by exaggeration of the effect of sensory impressions, and by simulation of various disorders. Symptoms may take the form of hyperesthesia; pain and tenderness in the region of the ovaries, spine, and head; anesthesia and other sensory disturbances; choking sensation; dimness of vision; paralysis; tonic spasms; convulsions; retention of urine; vasomotor disturbances; fever, hallucinations, and catalepsy.

Q.   What do you mean by "**hysterical** symptoms"?

A.   **Hysterical** symptoms are psychological symptoms that result from a conflict within the individual. They can take many forms, from all kinds of pains to trouble with seeing; it could affect practically any part of the body....

... She was at that time in a state of high excitement, being practically **hysterical**, in tears, panicky, and utterly distraught, being somewhat incoherent, obviously as the result of anxiety, making all kinds of threats in regard to her self-destruction; therefore I advised, in order to have her calm down and to give us a chance to observe her, that she be immediately hospitalized, which was a suggestion that I communicated to you and communicated to the brother-in-law, aside from the patient herself. And after some hesitation she accepted that, and we forthwith hospitalized her at the closed psychiatric ward of St. Francis Hospital in Lynwood, California, where she has been since yesterday afternoon. In re Loughran, 276 F.Supp. 393, 409, 418 (C.D.Cal.1967).

Other findings are characteristic of **hysteria** by virtue of the changing nature of the deformity (such as the appearance and disappearance of dorsal lordosis) & [sic] the absence of set pattern (such as the bizarre hysterical gait, staggering in the direction of objects upon which to lean; etc....

... This case is one for preference regarding a legal hearing, since hysterics who remain untreated for from 3–5 years usually develop hysterical paralysis, followed by dis-use atrophy and then fixed joint contractures, creating an actual physical and non-reversible disability which remains after the **hysteria** subsides. Weinstein v. Levy, 18 A.D.2d 398, 400–1, 239 N.Y.S.2d 752 (2d Dep't 1963).

hysteria, conversion See *conversion* (Bourne case); and *neurosis, hysterical.*

hysteric (his-ter′ik) pertaining to or characterized by hysteria.

Dr. DeMinico wrote in a consultation report that his initial impression of the government's witness was:

Conversion Reaction with dissociative traits. [The patient] has all the classical symptoms of a Hysterical Personality in all aspects of her past life history, her interpersonal relationships, her marital histories, and her personal psychological maladjustments. [She] admitted, to a certain degree, the manipulation of one fasting blood sugar test and passed that off casually with some sort of vague rationalization. Howev-

er, she denied any conscious knowledge of having taken insulin to modify the results of the glucose tolerance test. To explain this she wove an intricate fabrication in a bland, detached way that is typical of "la belle indifference" of a classical Freudian **hysteric**. U.S. v. Lindstrom, 698 F.2d 1154, 1164 (11th Cir. 1983).

hysterical (his-ter′ĭ-kal) characterized by hysteria.

In denying Dolly's claim, the Bureau found that she was not credible because she has a **hysterical** personality with hypochondriacal neurosis....

... Dr. Ramos stated his opinion, through his deposition, that Dolly has a **hysterical** personality which he defined as someone who "overdramatizes events or feelings." Roberts v. North Dakota Workmen's Comp. Bur., 326 N.W.2d 702, 706 (N.Dak.1982).

hysterosalpingogram

I feel a **hysterosalpingogram** would invade the privacy of my person and impede my chances of eventually marrying because of the absence of a hymen which is considered a prerequisite by many of my countrymen before marriage....

... On the motion before this court it appears that whatever value the findings of a **hysterosalpingogram** would produce, that value would be exacted by the loss of the physical attribute of plaintiff's virginity. Additionally, the invasive procedure contemplated would not only inflict such permanent physical residuals, but those residuals would have far-reaching cultural dimensions in the ability of the plaintiff to contract marriage. These considerations are of far greater weight and substance than assertions of feminine modesty and embarrassment. Duprey v. Wager, 451 A.2d 416–17, 420 (Super.Ct.N.J.1982).

... she then returned for a **hysterosalpingogram**, a painful x-ray procedure, to verify the success of the second sterilization. Ochs v. Borrelli, 445 A.2d 883, 886 (Conn.1982).

hysterosalpingography (his″ter-o-sal″ping-gog′rah-fe) [*hystero-* + Gr. *salpinx* tube + *graphein* to record] roentgenography of the uterus and uterine tubes after the injection of opaque material. Called also *uterosalpingography, uterotubography, hysterotubography, metrosalpingography, metrotubography.*

Hysterosalpingography involves the injection of radiopaque substances into the uterus and fallopian tubes for diagnostic purposes. Usually a cannula or catheter is inserted into the uterine cervical canal after visualization of the cervix through an appropriate speculum. A water-soluble opaque material is introduced into the uterine cavity. The procedure is carried out in a dark room and intermittent X-ray screening will show the shape of the uterus, filling of the tubes and peritoneal spill if it occurs. Browne, J. C. McClure, Postgraduate Obstetrics and Gynaecology (4 ed.1973), at 362.

Both parties have offered the reports of their respective experts describing the procedure, its purposes and the complications that may attend such a procedure. To perform this procedure a speculum is placed in the vagina and the cervix must be exposed. Plaintiff's expert maintains the procedure can "be painful normally and with the absence of tubes will be of even greater pain." The risk of infection is present, according to the medical expertise of both plaintiff's and defendant's physicians. Further complications that may result, according to defendant's expert, are hemorrhage and venous or lymphatic intravasation. Finally, plaintiff's expert states that no useful information can be obtained from that X-ray; it is only 70% accurate at the optimum and to subject plaintiff, who is a virgin, to this procedure would be unnecessarily cruel and painful, causing unusual physical and psychological trauma. Duprey v. Wager, 451 A.2d 416, 418 (Super.Ct.N.J.1982).

Other Authorities: Carmichael v. Reitz, 95 Cal.Rptr. 381, 388 (Ct.App.Cal.1971).

hysterotomy (his"ter-ot'o-me) [*hystero-* + Gr. *temnein* to cut] incision of the uterus. See also *abortion* (Am. College case).

Another method of performing abortions which may be used after the first trimester is **hysterotomy**, a surgical entry into the uterus, similar to a cesarean section, in which the fetus is removed. Legalized Abortion, [National Academy of Sciences, 1975] at 138. All parties agree that this method poses a substantially greater risk of complications and death to the wo-

man than saline abortions. Because of this increased danger, **hysterotomy** is not an adequate substitute for saline amniocentesis. Wynn v. Scott, 449 F.Supp. 1302, 1324 (N.D.Ill. 1978).

hysterotomy, vaginal incision of the uterus through the vagina.

The petitioner admitted to the Erie County Medical Examiner that he had performed a **vaginal hysterotomy**, which consists of an incision in the cervix and manual extraction of the fetus. There was testimony at the trial from doctors that **vaginal hysterotomy** was not a commonly used method of abortion, especially at the stage of pregnancy that the victim had reached, was somewhat dangerous and more properly considered major medical procedure of the type normally performed only in a hospital. Ketchum v. Ward, 422 F.Supp. 934, 937, 939 (W.D.N.Y.1976).

Hytrol-D See *dripolene*.

I

iatrogenic (i-at"ro-jen'ik) [*iatro-* + Gr. *gennan* to produce] resulting from the activity of physicians. Originally applied to disorders induced in the patient by autosuggestion based on the physician's examination, manner, or discussion, the term is now applied to any adverse condition in a patient occurring as the result of treatment by a physician or surgeon.

Dr. Fischer further stated that, in the absence of a fracture, the surgery was unnecessary and "may be **iatrogenic**." He defined "**iatrogenic**" as a condition caused by overtreatment. Zick v. Industrial Com'n, 444 N.E.2d 164, 166 (Ill.1982).

The doctor who treated appellee when she was first admitted to the hospital (after receiving appellant's injections) noted on his report that the patient was suffering from a pneumothorax and his conclusion was that it was "**iatrogenic**" (i.e. caused by a doctor). Earlin v. Cravetz, 399 A.2d 783, 786 (Super.Ct.Pa. 1979).

Slater suffered from regressive depression and **iatrogenic** (medically induced) complications secondary to the treatment of bursitis. Slater v. Kehoe, 113 Cal.Rptr. 790, 794 (Ct.App. 1974).

Other Authorities: Dupuy v. Tilley, 380 So.2d 634–5 (Ct.App. La.1979).

IBA See *isobutyl acrylate*.

I/C See *catheterization, intermittent*.

ictus (ik'tus), pl. *ic'tus* [L. "stroke"] a seizure, stroke, blow, or sudden attack. See also *seizure*.

idea (i-de'ah) [Gr. "form"] a mental impression or conception.

idea of reference; idea, referential the assumption by a patient that the words and actions of others refer to himself or the projection of the causes of his own imagi-

nary difficulties upon someone else; called also *delusion of reference*.

At the trial of the cases sub judice, Dr. David Vernon Hicks defined "**ideas of reference**" as being an illogical tendency to relate external events to one's self. See Transcript of Testimony of Dr. David Vernon Hicks at 66. Johnson v. U.S., 409 F.Supp. 1283, 1286 (M.D.Fla.1976), reversed and remanded 576 F.2d 606 (5th Cir. 1978).

ideation (i"de-a'shun) the distinct mental presentation of objects.

ideation, paranoid See *paranoia*.

identification (i-den"ti-fi-ka'shun) a mental mechanism of the unconscious by which the ego attaches or transfers to itself qualities or properties belonging to other persons or objects.

identification, voice

Voice analysis thus rests on the non-likelihood that two individuals would have identical vocal cavities and identical dynamic patterns of articulator manipulation, and on the inability of an individual to change or disguise the particular voice characteristics created by his unique combination of cavities and articulator manipulative patterns. U.S. v. Williams, 583 F.2d 1194, 1197 (2d Cir. 1978).

idiocy (id'e-o-se) severe mental retardation; a former category of mental retardation, which comprised individuals having an IQ of less than 25. See also *mental retardation*, under *retardation*. Cf. *imbecility* and *moronity*.

idiocy, amaurotic familial former name for cerebral sphingolipidosis. See also under *sphingolipidosis*.

idiogram (id'e-o-gram") [*idio-* + -*gram*] a diagrammatic representation of a chromosome complement, based on measurement of the chromosomes of a number of cells. Cf. *karyotype*.

iodipamide (i″o-dip′ah-mīd) [USP] chemical name: 3,3′-[(1,6-dioxo-1,6-hexanediyl)diimino]bis[2,4,6-triiodobenzoic acid]; a radiopaque medium, $C_{20}H_{14}I_6N_2O_6$, used as the meglumine and sodium salts.

iodipamide meglumine; iodipamide methylglucamine [USP], the meglumine salt of iodipamide, $(C_7H_{17}NO_5)_2 \cdot C_{20}H_{14}I_4N_2O_6$; used as a radiopaque medium in cholangiography and cholecystography, administered intravenously.

idiopathic (id″e-o-path′ik) of the nature of an idiopathy; self-originated; of unknown causation.

As defendant pointed out over and over again at trial, a substantial number of cases of pulmonary fibrosis are "idiopathic," i.e., their cause is unknown. Ferebee v. Chevron Chemical Co., 552 F.Supp. 1293, 1296 (D.D.C.1982).

The general rule is that injuries caused by **idiopathic** falls do not arise out of employment unless the employment in some way contributes to the risk personal to the claimant or aggravates the injury. Foxworth v. Florida Industrial Commission, 86 So.2d 147, 151 (Fla.1955); Federal Electric Corp. v. Best, 274 So.2d 886 (Fla.1973); Southern Convalescent Home v. Wilson, 285 So.2d 404 (Fla.1973); Honeywell v. Scully, 289 So. 2d 393 (Fla.1974). See also 1 Larson, Workmen's Compensation Law, § 12.10, 3–252 (1978). Legakis v. Sultan & Sons, 383 So.2d 938–9 (Dist.Ct.App.Fla.1980).

idiosyncrasy (id″e-o-sin′krah-se) [idio- + Gr. synkrasis mixture] an abnormal susceptibility to some drug, protein, or other agent which is peculiar to the individual.

Dr. Boyle was of the opinion that Mrs. Boyd died as the result of an **idiosyncratic** reaction to the shot of Demerol. He explained that an **idiosyncratic** reaction refers to a "sensitivity peculiar to that individual." Fraijo v. Hartland Hospital, 160 Cal.Rptr. 246, 251 (Ct.App.Cal.1979).

idiosyncratic (id″e-o-sin-krat′ik) pertaining to or characterized by idiosyncrasy.

idiot (id′e-ot) [Gr. idiōtēs one in private station, ignoramus] a person without intellect and understanding; a former name for a mentally retarded person of the lowest order, i.e., having an IQ of less than 25. See also *mental retardation*, under *retardation*. Cf. *imbecile* and *moron*.

Ig immunoglobulin of any of the five classes: IgA, IgD, IgE, IgG, or IgM. See also *immunoglobulin*.

ileal (il′e-al) pertaining to the ileum.

ileitis (il″e-i′tis) inflammation of the ileum.

ileitis, regional; ileitis, terminal Crohn's disease affecting the ileum.

In the 1950s Mrs. Eichelberger developed a condition known as Chron's Disease which inflames the small and large intestines and affects the body's ability to absorb nutrition. Between 1958 and the date of trial, plaintiff experienced periodic flare-ups of Chron's Disease which forced her to be hospitalized twelve times....

On July 3, 1977, plaintiff's condition of Chron's Disease rapidly deteriorated and she was taken to the emergency room at Barnes Hospital. Doctor Bernard Hirschel, a resident in the emergency room treated Mrs. Eichelberger, who weighed 75 pounds at the time of her admission. Doctor Hirschel testified that due to her dehydrated state, plaintiff needed fluids and calories but because of the Chron's Disease, it was impossible to give her these fluids orally. Doctor Hirschel testified that he first attempted to insert an intravenous line into her arm but he was unsuccessful in locating the vein. Eichelberger v. Barnes Hosp., 655 S.W.2d 699, 702 (Mo.Ct.App.1983).

The thrust of the complaint filed by Richard R. DeNardo is that while he was being treated by Dr. Carneval at Doctors Osteopathic Hospital, he was suffering from **regional ileitis** with abscess formation involving the terminal cecum and the ileum with the fistulous tract extending into the right ileopsoas space, which in turn created a right ileopsoas abscess. Denardo v. Carneval, 444 A.2d 135–6 (Super.Ct.Pa.1982).

Doctor Dunn testified that what he thought she had was **regional ileitis** because the complications that she developed and the findings at the surgery were consistent with complications of **regional ileitis**, those being an abscess formation and a fistula formation. "There are other things that can cause those complications, but those two are definitely associated with **regional ileitis**." During later questioning, Doctor Dunn stated that in his opinion earlier medical or surgical treatment would have avoided the ileostomy. Anderson v. Moore, 275 N.W.2d 842, 848 (Neb.1979).

ileostomy (il″e-os′to-me) [ileo- + Gr. stoma mouth] surgical creation of an opening into the ileum, usually by establishing an ileal stoma on the abdominal wall.

It was then necessary to form an urethroileo conduit, and an **ileostomy** was performed. This is a method of urinary diversion effected by opening a hole in the stomach, a stoma, to which a bag-type "artificial bladder" is attached. Rodriguez v. McDonnell Douglas Corp., 151 Cal.Rptr. 399, 414 (Ct.App.Cal. 1978).

... a loop or venting **ileostomy** was performed to divert the fecal matter from the rectum because it was being driven into the vagina from the rectum through a rectovaginal fistula (the suture line) which needed time to heal. [Footnote omitted.] Rainer v. Buena Community Memorial Hospital, 95 Cal.Rptr. 901, 903, 906 (Ct.App.Cal.1971).

Other Authorities: Paris v. Schweiker, 674 F.2d 707–8 (8th Cir. 1982).

ileum (il′e-um) [L.] [NA] the distal portion of the small intestine, extending from the jejunum to the cecum; called also *intestinum ileum*.

... he underwent an **ileal** loop operation consisting of the urethra being **anastomosed** to a loop of intestine and the urinary bladder bypassed. Warner v. City of Bay St. Louis, 408 F.Supp. 375, 380 (S.D.Miss.1975).

Since the vivisection work had indicated that the optimal point of absorption was the **ileum**—the lower third of the small intestine—Martin's application directed that the trypsin be coated to resist disintegration until it reached the **ileum**. Armour Pharmaceutical Co. v. Richardson-Merrell, Inc., 396 F.2d 70, 72–3 (3d Cir. 1968).

Other Authorities: Harrigan v. U.S., 408 F.Supp. 177, 179 (E.D.Pa.1976). Rainer v. Buena Community Memorial Hosp., 95 Cal.Rptr. 901, 903 (Ct.App.Cal.1971).

ileus (il'e-us) [L.; Gr. *eileos*, from *eilein* to roll up] obstruction of the intestines.

After surgery Mrs. Seeley developed complications evidenced by abdominal distention, fever, and an "**ileus**" (a cessation of muscular activity of the colon, resulting in an inability to pass fecal matter). Seeley v. Eaton, 506 S.W.2d 719, 721 (Ct.Civ. App.Tex.1974).

Plaintiff's stomach was not functioning properly at that time. It was in a state of **ileus**, which apparently is a condition of temporary, partial paralysis. This condition generally lasts "from a day and a half to two or three days and sometimes up to five days after an operation." . . .

. . . The witness expressed the opinion, however, that the **ileus** was in existence when plaintiff was given the liquid diet on August 16. He wanted plaintiff's stomach to remain empty until the **ileus** was resolved. If food or fluid or air is allowed into the stomach while the patient has the **ileus**, a whole series of complications can develop. Patients with **ileus** are prone to swallow air, and "they get the small intestine full of air, the stomach and small intestine which is unable to pass except in small increments and gradually causes a distention of the abdomen." This causes the patient a great deal of distress. It can cause obstructions, tension on the suture lines, a variety of complications. "The main reason I personally use a Levin tube is to prevent this **ileus** from becoming so pronounced that it will cause complications on its own." Lenger v. Physician's General Hosp., Inc., 455 S.W.2d 703, 707 (Tex.1970).

ileus, adynamic ileus resulting from inhibition of bowel motility, which may be produced by numerous causes, most frequently by peritonitis.

He thought the Jasper doctors recognized and adequately treated the **paralytic ileus**. The limits of this disorder would probably be put "at anywhere from one day to ten days, . . . [b]ut on the fifth or sixth day of an unresponding **paralytic ileus**, an astute physician starts looking for hidden factors. And on the sixth and seventh day he does everything within his power to find other factors. . . . [Y]ou should be very, very alarmed when the sixth and seventh day come around. [I]n my opinion, it is perfectly acceptable for the 'occasional abdominal surgeon' to handle his own **paralytic ileus** up through the third and fourth day. Beyond that the condition is not common enough in the ordinary occasional abdominal surgeon's practice for him to be conversant with it unless he has special skills." Richardson v. Holmes, 525 S.W.2d 293, 297 (Ct.Civ. App.Tex.1975).

As a result of their consultations, it was their impression that the boy had some bleeding into the peritoneal cavity which was causing **paralytic ileus**—a failure of the contractibility of the intestines—with a resulting reduction of the ability of the intestines to pass along gas and solid matter, and subsiding gastroenteritis. Rogers v. U.S., 334 F.2d 931, 933 (6th Cir. 1964).

ileus, meconium ileus in the newborn due to blocking of the bowel with thick meconium; a manifestation of fibrocystic disease (mucoviscidosis). See also *fibrosis, cystic fibrosis of the pancreas.*

In the instant case, Matthew was born on June 1, 1969 with a mucous blockage of his intestinal tract which required immedi-

ate surgery. His condition was diagnosed as **meconium ileus**. The condition results from enzyme, mucous gland and pancreatic malfunctions. All of the experts agreed that some degree of correlation exists between **meconium ileus** and cystic fibrosis. There was testimony that 10% of all cystic children are born with **meconium ileus**. Conversely, most, if not all, **meconium ileus** children develop cystic fibrosis. Defendant's medical expert, Dr. Marano, said that **meconium ileus** is conclusively pathognomonic (indicative or characteristic) of cystic fibrosis. However, plaintiff's expert, Dr. Schiffman, testified that not all infants born with a condition of **meconium ileus** become cystic. Kissil v. Beneficial National Life Ins. Co., 319 A.2d 67, 69 (N.J.1974).

ileus, paralytic; ileus paralyticus See *ileus adynamic.*

ileus, reflex

. . . he wrote a report to Dr. Meyer on the x-rays of Joy Sinkey in which it was stated his "impression" was "localized **reflex ileus** [stoppage of the bowel] secondary to appendicitis". His impression was formed on a statistical basis as appendicitis headed the list of possibilities. Sinkey v. Surgical Associates, 186 N.W.2d 658, 660 (Iowa 1971).

iliac (il'e-ak) [L. *iliacus*] pertaining to the ilium.

iliac artery See *arteria, iliaca interna; externa.*

iliac dissection and perfusion See *prophylaxis, chemotherapeutical* (Sherrill case).

iliotibial (il"e-o-tib'e-al) pertaining to or extending between the ilium and tibia.

Dr. Drez's associate, Dr. Gunderson, noted that Coleman's pain was occurring in Coleman's **iliotibial** band (knee area). Dr. Drez stated that such tenderness was consistent with the injury, subsequent casting, and return to function. Coleman v. Jackson, 422 So.2d 179, 185 (Ct.App.La.1982).

ilium (il'e-um), pl. *il'ia* [L.] the expansive superior portion of the hip bone (os coxae); it is a separate bone in early life. See illustration accompanying *skeleton*. Called also *os ilium* [NA]. See also *graft, bone* (Zipp case).

When we got to the cancellous bone of the **ilium**, the bone looked abnormal. [In this case the bone was apparently both "cancellous" or spongy and "cancerous"—Ed.] Insurance Company of North America v. Chinowith, 393 F.2d 916, 919 (5th Cir. 1968).

illness (il'ness) a condition marked by pronounced deviation from the normal healthy state; sickness.

This court declared that "**Illness**, in insurance law, is 'a disease or ailment of such a character as to affect the general soundness and healthfulness of the system seriously, and not a mere temporary indisposition which does not tend to undermine or weaken the constitution of the insured,' ". . . [24 S.E.2d 815] Mutual Life Ins. Co. of New York v. Bishop, 209 S.E.2d 223, 227 (Ct.App.Ga.1974).

illness, radiation See *sickness, radiation.*

illusion (ĭ-lu'zhun) [L. *illusio*] a false or misinterpreted sensory impression; a false interpretation of a real sensory image. Cf. *delusion.*

imbecile (im'bĕ-sil) a former name for a mentally retarded person of the second lowest order, i.e., having an IQ of 25 to 49. See also *mental retardation*, under *retardation*. Cf. *idiot* and *moron*.

imbecility (im"bĕ-sil'ĭ-te) [L. *imbecillitas*] mental retardation; a former category of mental retardation comprising individuals having an IQ of 25 to 49. See also *mental retardation*, under *retardation*. Cf. *idiocy* and *moronity*.

... the following comprehensive test set forth at 403 Mich. 63, 85 [268 N.W.2d 28]:

" 'We conclude that a worker's mental illness is "insanity" if he suffers severe social dysfunction and that a worker's intellectual impairment is "imbecility" if he suffers severe cognitive dysfunction....' " Modreski v. Gen. Motors Corp., Fisher Body, 337 N.W.2d 231, 234 (Mich.1983).

imbedded See *impaction, dental.*

IMD See *institution for mental diseases.*

imino- (ĭ-me'no) a prefix used to denote the presence of the bivalent group > NH attached to nonacid radicals.

Imino: An organic compound characterized by a nitrogen atom doubly bonded to a carbon atom (N = C). Ritter v. Rohm & Haas Co., 154 U.S.P.Q. 518, 554–5 (S.D.N.Y.1967).

imipramine hydrochloride (ĭ-mip'rah-mēn) [USP] chemical name: 10,11-dihydro-N,N-dimethyl-5H-dibenz[bf] azepine-5-propanamine monohydrochloride. A tricyclic antidepressant, $C_{19}H_{24}N_2 \cdot HCl$, occurring as a white to off-white, crystalline powder; used especially in the treatment of endogenous depression and in childhood enuresis, administered orally.

The pathology report indicated that Stupy died from an overdose of desipramine or **imipramine**, both pharmacologically related drugs which are used as antidepressants. Stuppy v. U.S., 560 F.2d 373, 375 (8th Cir. 1977).

Tofranil is an anti-depressant drug. Collins v. Hand, 246 A.2d 398, 402 (Pa.1968).

immobilize (im-mo'bil-īz) [L. *in* not + *mobilis* movable] to render incapable of being moved, as by a cast or splint.

At trial, the defense presented evidence that the pin fractured out of the bone while Wisdom was working on his truck without an arm **immobilizer** on his right arm, contrary to Dr. Swan's instructions. Swan v. Wisdom, 386 So.2d 574–5 (Dist.Ct.App. Fla.1980).

immobilizer See *immobilize.*

immunoglobulin (im"u-no-glob'u-lin) a protein of animal origin endowed with known antibody activity, synthesized by lymphocytes and plasma cells. Immunoglobulins function as specific antibodies and are responsible for the humoral aspects of immunity. They are found in the serum and in other body fluids and tissues, including the urine, spinal fluid, lymph nodes, spleen, etc. Molecularly, each immunoglobulin is made up of two light chains and two heavy chains, this basic four-chain unit being repeated in the higher molecular weight forms, as in the pentameric IgM molecule. There are five antigenically different kinds of heavy chains, which form the basis of the five classes of immunoglobulins (IgA, IgD, IgE, IgG, IgM; see Table). In addition there are two types of light chains, designated κ and λ, which are common to all five classes, although an individual immunoglobulin molecule has either κ or λ chains, not both. Symbol Ig or γ.

immunoglobulin G

A spinal fluid analysis indicated a slightly elevated total protein level and an abnormally high ratio of total protein to IgG (**immunoglobulin G**) of 22%, the normal being approximately 10%. McDonald v. U.S., 555 F.Supp. 935, 941 (M.D.Pa. 1983).

immunology (im"u-nol'o-je) that branch of biomedical science concerned with the response of the organism to antigenic challenge, the recognition of self from not self, and all the biological (*in vivo*), serological (*in vitro*), and physical chemical aspects of immune phenomena.

Dr. Krakauer explained that the science of **immunology** is the study of the body's ability or any organism's ability, for that matter, to maintain an internal environment free of foreign material. That is, the ability to recognize what is foreign and eliminate it and the ability to recognize what is self and leave it alone. Varga v. U.S., 566 F.Supp. 987, 1010–11 (N.D.Ohio 1983).

impaction (im-pak'shun) [L. *impactio*] the condition of being firmly lodged or wedged. In obstetrics, the indentation of any fetal parts of one twin onto the surface of its co-twin, so that the simultaneous partial engagement of both twins is permitted.

impaction, dental the condition in which a tooth is embedded in the alveolus so that its eruption is prevented, or is locked in position by bone, restoration, or surfaces of adjacent teeth, preventing either its normal occlusion or its routine removal.

... plaintiff returned to defendant's office where she was shown the x-rays, told that she had an **imbedded wisdom tooth** but was not showing any irritation from her plates, and was advised by defendant that he could not see any reason for extracting the tooth. Negaard v. Estate of Feda, 446 P.2d 436 (Mont.1968).

impairment

Section 223(d)(3) [of the Social Security Act (42 U.S.C. § 423[d][3])] define "physical or mental **impairment**" for all disability claimants as "an **impairment** that results from anatomical, physiological, or psychological abnormalities which are demonstrable by medically acceptable clinical and laboratory diagnostic techniques." Gallagher on Behalf of Gallagher v. Schweiker, 697 F.2d 82–3 (2d Cir. 1983).

20 C.F.R. § 404.1502(a) (1968). Appendix 1 of the regulations, the "Listing of Impairments", was introduced in 1968 to describe in detailed diagnostic terms, quantified where possible, those **impairments** "which are of a level of severity deemed sufficient to preclude an individual from engaging in any gainful activity". § 404.1506 (1968). A claimant suffering from a "listed **impairment**", if actually unemployed, was entitled to disability benefits without any need to consider the ef-

MOLECULAR STRUCTURE OF IMMUNOGLOBULINS
THE FIVE CLASSES

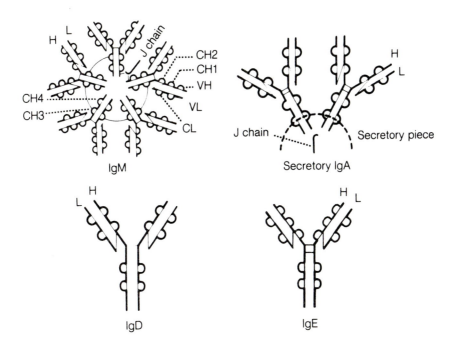

STRUCTURE OF IMMUNOGLOBULIN G & A SUBCLASSES

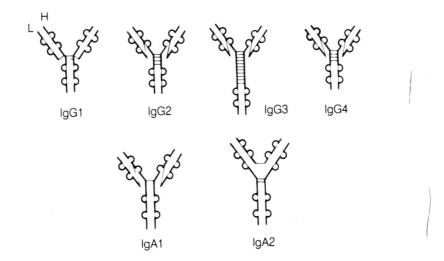

Schematic representation of the basic four polypeptide chain, monomeric unit structure of immunoglobulin molecules. Heavy (H) chains determine *class*. Those in IgG are gamma, in IgM are mu, in IgA are alpha, in IgD are delta, and in IgE are epsilon. The two *types* of light (L) chains (kappa and lambda) are shared in common by all five immunoglobulin classes, although only one *type* is present in any individual molecule. Both heavy and light chains have looped structures referred to as domains or regions. Heavy chains possess one variable (VH) (wherein the antigen-binding site resides) and three constant (CH1, CH2, CH3) regions, with the exception of IgM and IgE which contain one variable (VH) and four constant regions (CH1, CH2, CH3, CH4). Light chains contain one variable (VL) and one constant (CL) region each. The heavy and light chains are fastened together by disulfide bonds as well as noncovalent forces. The disulfide bonds differ in number at the *hinge* (inter H chain) region according to immunoglobulin subclass. Antigen-binding sites are located in the variable (amino-terminus) regions of each immunoglobulin monomer. IgM and dimeric or multimeric IgA molecules have J chains which are associated with the ability of these molecules to form polymers. Secretory IgA contains a secretory piece made by epithelial cells and believed to protect the molecule from enzymatic cleavage in the hinge region. Serum IgA2 has no heavy to light chain disulfide bonds, whereas IgA1 has a classic structure.

HUMAN IMMUNOGLOBULIN CLASSES: SOME PHYSICAL AND BIOLOGIC PROPERTIES

CLASS	MEAN SERUM CONCEN- TRATION (mg/100 ml)	MOLECULAR WEIGHT	$S_{20,w}$	MEAN SURVIVAL T/2 (days)	BIOLOGIC FUNCTION	HEAVY CHAIN DESIG- NATION	NO. OF SUB- CLASSES
γG or IgG	1240	150,000	7	23	1. Fix complement 2. Cross placenta 3. Heterocytotropic antibody	γ	4
γA or IgA	280	170,000	7, 10, 14	6	1. Secretory antibody	α	Θ
γM or IgM	120	890,000	19	5	1. Fix complement 2. Efficient agglutination	μ	1
γD or IgD	3	150,000	7	2.8	1. Lymphocyte surface receptor	δ	2
γE or IgE	.03	196,000	8	1.5	1. Reaginic antibody 2. Homocytotropic antibody	ε	

From Bellanti: Immunology.

fect of his age, education, or work experience on his ability to do other work. . . .

In 1978, the Secretary issued new regulations, 43 F.R. 55349,[3] which were modified in 1980, 45 F.R. 55566. [[3] The preamble to these regulations, 43 F.R. 55349–51, contains a valuable discussion of the history.] Chico v. Schweiker, 710 F.2d 947, 949–50 (2d Cir. 1983).

Dr. Mallin rated this physical **impairment** under the A.M.A. guidelines as "not more" than 5%.[1] . . . [[1] A.C.R.R. R4–13–113(D) requires a physician to rate any functional impairment according to the American Medical Association "Guides to the Evaluation of Permanent Impairment." The ratings in the guides are specifically related to loss of motion at a joint, or amputation.]

Since petitioner was employed as a weight lifter, he contends that a 75% loss of strength at maximum output was a 75% "loss of use" of his arm under A.R.S. § 23–1044(B)(21). Respondents contend that any **impairment** rating for loss of strength should not be based exclusively on petitioner's occupation as a weight lifter under A.R.S. § 23–1044(B)(21). In any event, respondents contend that the 75% rating is unacceptable, both because it is not founded on the A.M.A. guides and because it fails to recognize the many "uses" of the arm at less than maximum output. . . .

. . . It is apparent from the record of this case that petitioner has suffered a permanent **impairment** as that term is defined in Arizona law. See Smith v. Industrial Commission, 113 Ariz. 304, 305 n. 1, 552 P.2d 1198, 1199 (1976). We further hold that loss of strength may constitute a loss of "use" under A.R.S. § 23–1044(B)(21) for which compensation must be paid. The difficulty we perceive is in rating the loss-of-strength **impairment** for purposes of determining permanent partial scheduled disability. Dutra v. Industrial Com'n of Arizona, 659 P.2d 45–6 (Ct.App.Ariz.1982), vacated 659 P.2d 18 (Ariz. 1983).

Other Authorities: Sullivan v. Weinberger, 493 F.2d 855, 860 (5th Cir. 1974); Jenkins v. Gardner, 430 F.2d 243, 266 (6th Cir. 1970).

impairment of function See *function, impairment of.*

impairment, mild

Mild: suspected impairment of slight importance which does not affect ability to function; . . . Camp v. Schweiker, 643 F.2d 1325, 1330 (8th Cir. 1981).

impairment, moderate

Moderate: an impairment which affects but does not preclude ability to function; . . . Camp v. Schweiker, 643 F.2d 1325, 1330 (8th Cir. 1981).

impairment, moderately severe

Moderately Severe: an impairment which seriously affects ability to function; . . . Camp v. Schweiker, 643 F.2d 1325, 1330 (8th Cir. 1981).

impairment, severe

Severe: extreme impairment of ability to function. Camp v. Schweiker, 643 F.2d 1325, 1330 (8th Cir. 1981).

implant (im'plant) material (e.g., tissue, inert material, or radioactive material) inserted or grafted into the body.

Dr. Rothenberg performed a mammary augmentation operation on Mrs. Henderson, inserting artificial breast **implants** manufactured by Heyer-Schulte Corporation. The **implants** consisted of silicone envelopes filled with a soft silicone gel. After inserting each **implant**, Dr. Rothenberg intentionally slit the envelope to allow the gel to escape into the retro-mammary pockets. Henderson v. Heyer-Schulte Corp., etc., 600 S.W.2d 844, 846 (Ct.Civ.App.Tex.1980).

implant, subperiosteal a metal appliance made to conform to the shape of a bone and placed on its surface beneath the periosteum, with lugs protruding through the mucosa to support an overlying denture.

... he told plaintiff about the **subperiosteal implant** that he said he had been using successfully since 1948. The plaintiff said that defendant had told her there was a permanence about this type of implant. The defendant, however, testified that he had warned her of the risk involved....

The implant was installed in two stages. The first, described by defendant as preparatory, consisted in incising the gum tissue and folding it back so as to expose the bone, of which an impression was made. The gum tissue was then sutured and the impression forwarded to the laboratory where the prosthetic implant was made so as to conform to the impression. Once the prosthetic implant was made, the gum tissue was again opened, the prosthetic was fitted onto the bone, and the gum tissue resutured over the implant.[1] [[1] A detailed description of the prosthetic implant is unnecessary. Suffice it to note that it is a one-piece prosthetic device made of vitalium, generally horseshoe in shape, with four posts which, after implantation, protrude vertically through the gum tissue. A roofless denture or row of teeth is then attached to these posts.] Kelly v. Gershkoff, 312 A.2d 211–13 (R.I.1973).

implant, hair

The procedure, as performed by the defendant, involved a number of steps—marking the part of the scalp where the **implant** was to be inserted; injecting the scalp with an anesthetic; implanting synthetic hair fibres by attaching three or four fibres to a needle and injecting the needle into the scalp; removing the needle leaves the fibres in the scalp. This whole process is then repeated a number of times....

Natural hair transplantation, the most widely used permanent hair restoration technique, is a generally accepted medical procedure as practiced by dermatologists, plastic surgeons, general surgeons, and others.

If this implant procedure is used, recognized medical studies have shown that the list of complications is long and painful—marked facial edema, bleeding, foreign body reaction, infection, spontaneous loss of fibers, pain, numbness, itchiness, natural hair loss, severe scarring and more. There have been cases of resulting endocarditis (inflammation of the lining of the heart and its valves) and osteomyelitis (inflammatory disease of the bone). Concern is great that the future holds progressive post-inflammatory sclerosing (hardening of tissue) and carcinoma of the scalp.[10] [[10] Lepaw M: Commentary—The Synthetic Fiber Implant Scam. The International Journal of Dermatology 18:468, July–August, 1979.]

Efforts by dermatologists to repair the damage usually begin with trying to control the infections which do not always respond to antibiotics and removing any remaining fibers. Removal is almost impossible when the knot technique was utilized. In many cases, the entire scalp has been removed in a Juri flap operation whereby scalp flaps, raised form hair bearing areas, are rotated and sutured onto non-hair bearing areas covering the scarring.[11] The full extent of physical and psychological damage cannot be determined at this time but it may be considered life-threatening in many cases. [[11] Supra, note 3, p. 2688.] People v. Rubin, 424 N.Y.S.2d 592–5 (Crim. Ct.Queens Cty.1979).

implantodontia See *implantodontics.*

implantodontics (im″plan-to-don′tiks) that branch of dentistry that deals with implanting alloplastic materials into or onto the jaw bones to support overlying dental appliances.

... a specialist in the field of prothodontia and **implantodontia**—i.e., "implant dentistry". Strake v. R. J. Reynolds Tobacco Co., 539 S.W.2d 715, 719–20 (Mo.Ct.App.1976).

impotence (im′po-tens) [L. *in* not + *potentia* power] lack of power, chiefly of copulative power in the male due to failure to initiate an erection or to maintain an erection until ejaculation. It may be *atonic*, due to paralysis of the motor nerves (nervi erigentes) without evidence of lesion of the central nervous system; *paretic*, due to lesion in the central nervous system, particularly in the spinal cord; *psychic*, dependent on mental complex; *symptomatic*, due to some other disorder, such as injury to nerves in the perineal region, by virtue of which the sensory portion of the erection reflex arc is interrupted.

All of the experts in this case testified that **impotence** occurs in a small percentage of patients following a TUR. These doctors could only speculate as to what aspect of a TUR causes impotence, although they seemed to agree that the condition is usually psychogenic, rather than organic. The evidence suggests that the patient's prior sexual ability and mental preparedness for surgery are crucial factors in cases of post-TUR **impotence**. Two urologists, Drs. Decker and Poutasse, testified that, if a patient enjoys a regular sex life before the operation, in most instances, he will be potent thereafter. However, if a man is experiencing problems with his sexual ability, a TUR may be enough to render him totally **impotent**. Therefore, both doctors attempt to determine prior to the operation the level or frequency of sex the patient enjoys and then advise him accordingly of the risks involved....

Diagnosis of a subjective condition such as psychogenic **impotence** depends to a great degree upon the history and symptoms related to the physician by the patient. See Kaufman v. Kaufman, 164 F.2d 519, 520 (D.C.Cir.1947). The patient's credibility is thus an important consideration in the physician's evaluation of the complaint. Dessi v. U.S., 489 F.Supp. 722, 729–30 (E.D.Va.1980).

Testimony by numerous government witnesses, notably Dr. Schoolar, indicated that the vast majority of cases of **impotence** were psychogenic in origin and that in such cases androgen replacement therapy through administration of methyltestosterone was not a beneficial treatment since there was no androgen deficiency to begin with. U.S. v. 1,048,000 Capsules, More or Less, "Afrodex", 494 F.2d 1158, 1162–3 (5th Cir. 1974).

This action to annul a marriage on the ground of **impotence** is a case of novel impression in New Jersey and, perhaps, in this country, in that the wife, while still a virgin, with an intact hymen, suffered a miscarriage during the marriage. The husband seeks the annulment, charging his wife with being physically and incurably **impotent**....

It was his opinion "that this woman is **impotent**." He defined **impotency** as the lack of ability to perform the sexual act—he stressed the word "perform"—which could be absolute or relative; in women, "it is the lack of ability to allow penetration for the performance of the sexual act."...

... **Impotency** is the inability to have sexual intercourse; **impotence** is not sterility. Donati v. Church, 13 N.J.Super. 454, 80 A.2d 633 (App.Div.1951); Kirschbaum v. Kirschbaum, 92 N.J.Eq. 7, 111 A. 697 (Ch.1920)....

... By statute in New Jersey, **impotence** is a ground for nullity of marriage. N.J.S. 2A:34–1, N.J.S.A. provides for a number of grounds for nullity. Sub-paragraph c. dealing with **impotency**, provides as follows:

The parties, or either of them, were at the time of marriage physically and incurably **impotent**, provided the party making the application shall have been ignorant of such **impotency** or incapability at the time of the marriage, and has not subsequently ratified the marriage...

Impotence was at the time of the common law a canonical disability and was treated in the ecclesiastical courts where, according to Canon 1068 of the Code of Canon Law, "inability to perform the marital act was a diriment impediment, and thus invalidated the marriage." 52 Iowa Law Review 768 (1967). T v. M, 242 A.2d 670–4 (Super.Ct.N.J.1968).

impotence, hypogonadal

The District Court made the following findings with regard to the meaning of these terms.

"**Hypogonadal impotence** is impotence caused by insufficient functioning of the testes to secrete testosterone, that is, impotence caused by androgen deficiency." U.S. v. 1,048,000 Capsules, More or Less, "Afrodex", 494 F.2d 1158, 1163 (5th Cir. 1974).

impressio (im-pres′se-o), pl. *impressio′nes* [L.] an impression, indentation, or concavity; [NA] a general term for an indentation produced in the surface of one organ by pressure exerted by another.

impression (im-presh′un) [L. *impressio*] 1. a slight indentation or depression; see *impressio*. 2. a negative copy or counterpart of some object made by bringing into contact with the object, with varying degrees of pressure, some plastic material which later becomes solidified, as a dental impression. 3. an effect produced upon the mind, body, or senses by some external stimulus, or agent.

Dr. Boggs argues that "**impressions**" is a term of art to the dental profession which refers only to the functional **impression** made in a reddish brown wax substance from which dentures are fabricated. He says that the **impressions** described by the witnesses did not fall within the statutory meaning because such **impressions** were used only to determine the size, shape and design of a patient's mouth before making a functional **impression**. We are unconvinced by this argument. The statute does not define or qualify "**impressions**." In Webster's New International Dictionary (2d ed. 1948) an **impression** is defined as "[a]n imprint of the surfaces of the teeth and adjacent portions of the jaw." Regardless of what substance was used in making imprints of the patients' mouths, and for whatever purpose they were used by the dentist, they were "**impressions**" within the meaning of the statute. Boggs v. Virginia State Board of Dental Examiners, 196 S.E.2d 81, 83 (Va. 1973).

On cross-examination he testified: "The difference between an '**impression**' and a diagnosis is that an **impression** means something that I think it could be by looking at the shadows on films. A diagnosis, to me, means that this is it; all things fit together; this is the final answer." Sinkey v. Surgical Associates, 186 N.W.2d 658, 660 (Iowa 1971).

On that day the doctor took an **impression** of the upper teeth and the roof of her mouth in order to have an acrylic denture ready for insertion in her mouth upon completion of the extractions. Germann v. Matriss, 260 A.2d 825, 827 (N.J.1970).

incapacity See *disability*.

incapacity, partial

The Texas Pattern Jury Charges defines "**partial incapacity**" in Section 22.02 as follows:

Partial incapacity is any degree of incapacity less than total incapacity, and means that a person's earning capacity is reduced because he can perform only part of the usual task of a workman or can only do lower paying work than he could do before his injury, but can get and keep employment suitable to his condition. 2 State Bar of Texas, Texas Pattern Jury Charges (1970). [Emphasis added.]

Consequently, under the quoted definition, a party may secure a finding of **partial incapacity** when there is or has been both a degree of incapacity less than total and a reduction in earning capacity. Select Ins. Co. v. Boucher, 561 S.W.2d 474, 478–9 (Tex.1978).

incapacity, total

The term "**total incapacity**" implies a disability to perform the usual tasks of a workman and not merely the usual tasks of any particular one trade or occupation. Texas Employers' Ins. Ass'n v. Mallard, 143 Tex. 77, 182 S.W.2d 1000, 1001 (1944); Texas Employers Ins. Ass'n v. Hawkins, 369 S.W.2d 305, 307 (Tex.1963). A person's disability is total within the meaning of the Compensation Act if he can no longer secure and hold employment for physical labor such as he was required to do prior to his injury. It does not mean that he must be wholly unable to do any work at all. Traders & General Ins. Co. v. Collins, 179 S.W.2d 525, 529 (Tex.Civ.App.—Galveston, 1944, writ ref'd w.o.m.); Aetna Life Ins. Co. v. Bulgier, 19 S.W.2d 821, 824 (Tex.Civ.App.—Dallas, 1929, writ ref'd). Gulf Ins. Co. v. Gibbs, 534 S.W.2d 720, 723–4 (Ct.Civ.App. Tex.1976).

inception See *contract*.

incision (in-sizh′un) [L. *incidere* (in + *caedere*), to cut open, to cut a cut, or a wound produced by cutting with a sharp instrument.

incision, ab externo

An **ab externo incision** was then made at the 12:00 o'clock position where the sclera (the "white of the eye") and the cornea (a "transparent structure" covering the iris) meet. By way of explanation, an **ab externo incision** refers to an incision which is made by a series of small "scrapes" on the surface with a sharp instrument thereby effecting a slow entry and gradually, as opposed to suddenly, exposing the inner eye to atmospheric pressure. The **ab externo incision** was then lengthened to the horizontal on each side by the use of surgi-

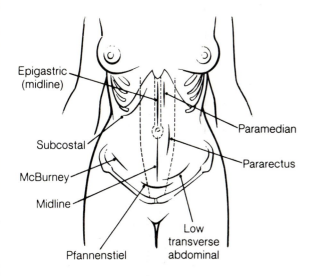

Epigastric
(midline)

Paramedian

Subcostal

Pararectus

McBurney

Midline

Low
transverse
abdominal

Pfannenstiel

Various abdominal incisions.

cal scissors. After the **ab externo incision** had been lengthened
the "wound" gaped, meaning, that the lips of the "wound"
began to separate. Miller v. Scholl, 594 S.W.2d 324, 327
(Mo.Ct.App.1980).

incision, lateral rectus

Consequently, the physician decided to make a **right rectus incision** instead of the usual type of appendectomy incision. The purpose of this incision, as explained by Abramson, was that in case he found something other than an
appendix problem, he could extend the incision readily to
handle any other problems he might encounter. Babin v. St.
Paul Fire and Marine Ins. Co., 385 So.2d 849, 853 (Ct.
App.La.1980).

incision, McBurney's an abdominal incision parallel to
the fibers of the external oblique muscle, about one-
third the distance along a line from the anterior superior iliac spine to the umbilicus, half the incision being above and the remainder below this point. The
skin and subcutaneous fat are incised down to the
external oblique, the fibers of which are split; the
underlying internal oblique and transversus
abdominalis are then split and separated.

Under general anesthesia, surgery began at 11 a.m. with a
McBurney incision. A large amount of pus exudate, less than a
quart, was drained from the abdomen; and the appendix,
which was ruptured, was removed. Hawkins v. Ozborn, 383
F.Supp. 1389, 1392 (N.D.Miss.1974).

incision, paramedian

Definite rebound tenderness present now, guarding deep tenderness. Surgery will have to be done. The whole situation is
peculiar and I will do a R **paramedian incision.** Babin v. St. Paul
Fire and Marine Ins. Co., 385 So.2d 849, 853 (Ct.App.La.
1980).

incisor (in-si′zer) [L. *incidere* to cut into] any of the four
anterior teeth in either jaw; a tooth that is mesial to the
canines. See also *tooth, incisor.*

Fractured upper central **incisor** with a questionable prognosis.... This tooth had been capped prior to the accident....
The **incisor** was fractured horizontally in the accident and the
portion which remained in plaintiff's mouth was loose. Later it
appeared that the root was fractured lengthwise with the result that the tooth had to be extracted and a fixed bridge constructed.... Yarrow v. U.S., 309 F.Supp. 922, 926 (S.D.N.Y.
1970).

incisura (in-si-su′rah), pl. *incisu′rae* [L.] a cut, notch, or
incision; [NA] a general term for an indention or depression, chiefly on the edge of a bone or other structure.
Called also *incisure* and *notch.*

incompetence (in-kom′pe-tens) [L. *in* not + *competens*
sufficient] physical or mental inadequacy or insufficiency.
See also *retardation, mental* (Ruby case).

incompetence, professional

The standards employed by the State Medical Board were
those found in AS 08.64.330(b) and 12 AAC 40.970 (amended
1980, 1981) defined "**professional incompetence**" as follows:
As used in AS 08.64 and these regulations, "**professional
incompetence**" means lacking sufficient knowledge or skills
or both, in that field of practice in which the physician concerned engages, to a degree likely to endanger the health
of his patients.

... Based on the cumulative evidence presented, Hearing Officer Snow concluded that Dr. Storrs demonstrated a pattern
of inadequacy which "greatly increased the exposure of his
patients to risks of injury, pain and death." "The patterns of
inadequacy and failure suggested by these cases include the
inability to foresee and recognize common complications, the
inability to recognize a need for a consultation regarding a
developing complication, and the inability to identify and apply the most direct and appropriate diagnostic and corrective
measures once a complication has developed." Storrs v. State
Medical Bd., 664 P.2d 547, 549, 555–6 (Alaska 1983).

incompetency See *incompetence.*

incompetent (in-kom′pe-tent) 1. an individual who is unable to perform the required functions of everyday living.
2. a person determined by the court to be unable to
manage his own affairs. See also *life-prolonging* (Sup't of
Belchertown case).

Appellants argue that this finding is inadequate to bring
Thomas within the terms of Probate Code section 1460, au-
thorizing the appointment of a guardian for an **incompetent**
person, and that instead the trial court should have made a
finding in accordance with the definition of "**incompetent**" in
section 1460 as to whether or not Thomas was a person "who
by reason of old age, disease, weakness of mind, or other
cause, is unable, unassisted, properly to manage and take
care of himself or his property, and by reason thereof is likely
to be deceived or imposed upon by artful or designing persons." Guardianship of Estate of Brown, 546 P.2d 298, 303
(Cal.1976).

We determine that he is mentally **incompetent**, the apparent cause being Chronic Brain Syndrome due to cerebrovascular insufficiency and diabetes. Commitment not recommended.

"3. ... his propensities are that he is oriented to time, person, and place, restless, mood swings, subject to periods of agitation. Takes Mellaril for agitation. Borderline abnormal EEG.

"4. ... he does require mechanical restraint to prevent him from self-injury or violence to others....

... This finding is not sufficient to sustain the order adjudicating appellant **incompetent**. In re Moyer, 263 So.2d 286–7 (Dist.Ct.App.Fla.1972).

incontinence (in-kon'ti-nens) [L. *incontinentia*] inability to control excretory functions, as defecation (fecal i.) or urination (urinary i.).

Dr. Sher performed a fistulectomy on the plaintiff on September 8, 1964. Plaintiff contends that the operation brought on **incontinence**, an inability to control bowel movement. Ross v. Sher, 483 S.W.2d 297–8 (Ct.Civ.App.Tex.1972).

Q. All right now. You have used the word "**incontinent**," and just so I have this explained, does she have any control over her bladder or going to the bathroom? A. No, she has none. Q. And the same way with bowel movements? A. Yes, sir. Q. She has no control? A. No control. Talcott v. Holl, 224 So.2d 420, 424 (Dist.Ct.App.Fla.1969).

incontinence, stress involuntary discharge of urine due to anatomic displacement which exerts an opening pull on the bladder orifice, as in straining or coughing.

As a result of the latter injury [tear of the bladder neck (urethra)] she developed "**Stress Incontinence**", a condition which causes a loss of urine when a person coughs or sneezes. Brunner v. Slupe, 290 N.E.2d 327–8 (App.Ct.Ill.1972).

incubation (in"ku-ba'shun) [L. *incubatio*] the induction of development, as (*a*) the development of an infectious disease from the entrance of the pathogen to the appearance of clinical symptoms (see also under *period* and cf. *decubation*); (*b*) the development of disease-producing microorganisms in an intermediate or in the ultimate host; or (*c*) the development of microorganisms or other cells in appropriate media.

The opinions of the various doctors and dentists as to the **incubation** period of the tetanus bacillus following introduction of the spore into the tooth sockets ranged from two days to several weeks. Dr. Hook fixed the average time as seven to fourteen days. Dr. Graubard said it would be four to ten days. They all agreed, however, that the nearer the brain the portal of entry of the spore, the shorter the **incubation** time. Thus so far as the **incubation** period is concerned a tetanus spore could have been in Mrs. Germann's mouth before the extractions or could have gotten into an extraction cavity either during the removal or thereafter until December 27. Germann v. Matriss, 260 A.2d 825, 832 (N.J.1970).

incubation period See *incubation; period, incubation.*

incubator (in'ku-ba-ter) an apparatus for maintaining a premature infant in an environment of proper temperature and humidity.

The **incubator** and supplemental oxygen permit many premature infants to live who would otherwise die, but too much oxygen causes RLF and blindness in the infant. Formerly less than 40% oxygen was believed safe, but in 1967 or 1968 Air Shields learned there was no safe level and that duration of exposure to oxygen as well as concentration was a factor in causing RLF....

... The **incubator** provides an environment for a premature infant. It controls the temperature, the humidity, and permits oxygen to be either at room air concentrations (about 20%) or increased. The **incubator** has an oxygen limiter, which prevents the concentration of oxygen from exceeding 40% unless a red flag device on the **incubator** is raised. Air Shields, Inc. v. Spears, 590 S.W.2d 574, 578 (Ct.Civ.App.Tex.1979).

The **isolation incubator**, universally used today in caring for premature babies, has been aptly called a "Room within a Room", providing "Individual Air-Conditioning for Each Patient" (DX D, p. 3). The baby compartment of such an incubator is supplied, by associated air-conditioning machinery, with a continuous flow of recirculated air, accurately controlled as to temperature, humidity, and oxygen content. Enough fresh air to replace the carbon dioxide generated by the baby's breathing is brought in through a filter, and the air pressure in the baby's chamber is maintained slightly above atmospheric, so that air leaks out of the baby chamber and into the adjoining nursery, rather than vice versa. Thus is the baby effectively protected against infection from his environment.... Air-Shields, Inc. v. Air Reduction Co., 331 F.Supp. 673, 675 (N.D. Ill.1971).

incubator, non-isolation

The original infant incubators—dating back at least to 1893 ... were the type now known as "**non-isolation incubators**". They consisted essentially of an enclosed crib provided with a means for heating, and in some cases humidifying, the air supplied to it. Such a device afforded a baby an enclosed living space in which the temperature and humidity were controlled, but it did not isolate the infant from the nursery environment, for there was a continuous flow of air from the nursery into the incubator and out again into the nursery. (**Non-isolation incubators** had no forced air draft; they depended for ventilation on the natural convection that resulted from heating the incoming air.) While **non-isolation incubators** are still used in hospitals for non-critical purposes such as post-operative care of full-term babies, they are not normally used in the care and treatment of premature infants, having been supplanted in that field of use by the so-called "isolation incubator".... Air-Shields, Inc. v. Air Reduction Co., 331 F.Supp. 673, 675 (N.D. Ill.1971).

incubator, servo control

In the fall of 1958, a noted pediatrician named Dr. William Silverman, renowned for several important contributions to the science of treating premature infants ... released to the press ... information concerning so-called "**servo control**" infant incubators which he had developed with the help of technical advisers at Columbia University.... Those incubators had the feature that the baby occupants themselves, by means of a sensor taped to their abdomens, "acted as their own thermostats". That is, the heat source was controlled by electric signals from the abdominal unit, being turned on whenever the baby's temperature dropped below the desired value and being turned off the instant the baby's temperature rose above that value.... Air-Shields, Inc. v. Air Reduction Co., 331 F.Supp. 673, 677 (N.D.Ill.1971).

incus (ing'kus) [L. "anvil"] [NA] the middle of the three ossicles of the ear, which, with the stapes and malleus, serves to conduct vibrations from the tympanic membrane to the inner ear. See illustration accompanying *ear*. Called also *anvil*.

Anunti was then referred to an otolaryngologist, who initially diagnosed his hearing and balance problems as resulting from a disruption of the **incus** and stapes. That diagnosis was confirmed by surgery performed on his left ear in 1971. Anunti v. Payette, 268 N.W.2d 52, 54 (Minn.1978).

indentation (in"den-ta'shun) [L. *indentatio; dens* tooth] a condition of being notched; a notch, pit, or depression.

Dr. Matthews testified he was at first concerned that his use of the forceps might have fractured the child's skull. This fear was allayed when Dr. Roig, a pediatrician, examined the child and found no neurological damage. Drs. Roig, Matthews and Allen, together, concluded that these were soft-tissue **indentations** which would resolve themselves within a short time and Dr. Allen so advised the Roarks. The **indentations** did not, however, resolve themselves and, when the child was about five weeks old, Dr. Roig X-rayed Robert and determined that he suffered from bilateral fractures of the skull. Dr. Roig referred the Roarks to Dr. Morris Sanders, a neurosurgeon, who, on March 18, operated on Robert and successfully elevated the fractures. Robert fully recovered with no neurological impairment. Roark v. Allen, 633 S.W.2d 804, 807 (Tex.1982).

Inderal (in'der-al) trademark for a preparation of propranolol hydrochloride. See also *propanolol hydrochloride*.

index (in'deks), pl. *indexes* or *in'dices* [L.]

Cumulated I. Medicus, an annual publication of the National Library of Medicine, comprising the twelve monthly issues of the Index Medicus.

Index Medicus a monthly publication of the National Library of Medicine in which the world's leading biomedical literature is indexed by author and subject. See also *Cumulated I. Medicus.*

The MEDLARS system is used in various ways by the library. Some of the stored information is printed in various medical bibliographies, e.g., **Index Medicus,** which are distributed worldwide.... SDC Development Corp. v. Mathews, 542 F.2d 1116–7 (9th Cir. 1976).

index, Merck

Defendant ("Merck"), a New Jersey corporation, is a diversified chemical and pharmaceutical company. As a service to customers and others, it publishes and sells **The Merck Index** (hereinafter "Index"), advertising it as "an encyclopedia of chemicals and drugs [which] contains ... information of value to chemists, biochemists, pharmacists, botanists, physicists, chemical engineers, and others interested in the life sciences." The Index offers information about some 10,000 chemicals, drugs and biologicals with respect to their "general, medical, or veterinary uses as well as

toxicity." Demuth Development Corp. v. Merck & Co., Inc., 432 F.Supp. 990–1 (E.D.N.Y.1977).

On the other hand the **Merck Index** (a compilation of various chemical compounds commonly used by industry which shows toxicity) indicates that Butanone "may be irritating to the eyes." Tucson Industries, Inc. v. Schwartz, 487 P.2d 12, 16 (Ct.App.Ariz.1971).

Indocin (in'do-sin) trademark for a preparation of indomethacin. See also *indomethacin*.

indomethacin (in"do-meth'ah-sin) [USP] chemical name: 1-(4-chlorobenzoyll)-5-methoxy-2-methyl-1H-indole-3-acetic acid. A nonsteroidal anti-inflammatory agent, $C_{19}H_{16}ClNO_4$, which also has antipyretic and analgesic properties, occurring as a pale yellow to yellow-tan powder; used in the treatment of rheumatoid arthritis, rheumatoid spondylitis, osteoarthritis of the hip, and acute gouty arthritis in selected patients, administered orally.

Q. In your opinion, is **Indocin** an analgesic?
A. I will have to qualify that because if it is considered anti-inflammatory, it has to take care of pain, heat and swelling, so if it is anti-inflammatory, it has to alleviate all of those conditions. Conway v. State Horse Racing Com'n, 276 A.2d 840–2 (Commonwealth Ct.Pa.1971).

It is noted that the medical testimony in the record indicates that the drug **Indocin** is seldom used by persons with stomach ulcers due to the possibility of the drug causing internal bleeding. Mr. Stott was known to have had trouble with stomach ulcers. Stott v. Houston Lighting and Power Co., 453 S.W.2d 364–5 (Ct.Civ.App.Tex.1970).

infant (in'fant) [L. *infans; in* neg. + *fans* speaking] a young child; considered to designate the human young from birth or from the termination of the newborn period (the first four weeks of life) to the time of assumption of erect posture (12 to 14 months); it is regarded by some to extend to the end of the first 24 months.

infant, premature one usually born after the twenty-seventh week and before full term, and arbitrarily defined as an infant weighing 1000 to 2499 grams (2.2 to 5.5 lbs.) at birth, having poor to good chance of survival, depending on the weight. In countries where adults are smaller than in the United States, the upper limit is 2250 grams (5 lbs.). Other criteria such as crown-heel length (less than 47 cm.) and occipitofrontal diameter (less than 11.5 cm.) have also been used.

A premature delivery is the termination of a pregnancy after the twentieth week but prior to full term. Burwell v. Eastern Air Lines, Inc., 458 F.Supp. 474, 486 (E.D.Va.1978), affirmed in part, reversed in part 633 F.2d 361 (4th Cir. 1980).

infarct (in'farkt) [L. *infarctus*] an area of coagulation necrosis in a tissue due to local ischemia resulting from obstruction of circulation to the area, most commonly by a thrombus or embolus. See also *infarction*.

He said that he treats about 20 acute myocardial **infarcts** per year, and that upset stomach and nausea frequently are symptoms of posterior or posterior lateral **infarcts**. The doctor presumed that the decedent had coronary artery disease. Interlake, Inc. v. Industrial Com'n, 447 N.E.2d 339, 342 (Ill.1983).

infarction (in-fark'shun) [L. *infarcire* to stuff in] 1. the formation of an infarct. 2. an infarct.

Emergency measures were taken including intracardiac administration of adrenaline, external cardiac massage and electric shock therapy. The patient's heart rhythm was restored and his vital signs stabilized. His condition was diagnosed as an acute massive anterior wall **infarction**. . . .

Dr. Lipowitz testified that the death-dealing attack of September 7 was related to the myocardial **infarction** *of January 6, 1975. It was his opinion that decedent, who suffered an acute myocardial* **infarction** *together with ventricular fibrillation and heart failure, was thereby subject to a "greater risk of death in the near term after successful resuscitation from same," and that as a consequence the event of January 6 was a material factor contributing to his death on September 7. Matter of Hill, 390 A.2d 131, 133 (Super.Ct.N.J.1978).*

A. The immediate cause of death was due to an **infarction** *of the small bowel. Q. Can you be a little more general as to the nature of that type of condition for us, Doctor? A. All right. Mrs. Holcombe had a blockage of the blood supply to the small bowel which was incompatible with life. . . .*

. . . Q. And the infarction was as I understand your testimony due to generalized arteriosclerosis, is that right, sir? A. The **infarction** *was due to a blockage, or is a blockage of the arteries. Allstate Insurance Co. v. Holcombe, 207 S.E.2d 537–9 (Ct.App.Ga.1974).*

infarction, myocardial gross necrosis of the myocardium, as a result of interruption of the blood supply to the area, as in coronary thrombosis. See also *injury* (Creek case).

Dr. Clark's medical summary stated that petitioner's atherosclerosis was accelerated by his diabetes, smoking, and high levels of cholesterol, and explained that physical activity causes an increased demand on the heart muscle which in turn requires an increased blood supply to these muscles. Dr. Clark further explained that where severe coronary artery disease is present, this blood supply cannot be delivered, and thus physical activity may "precipitate" **myocardial infarction**. *Dr. Patton opined that moderate to heavy lifting could precipitate a* **myocardial infarction** *in a person with moderately severe vascular disease. . . .*

. . . Petitioner notes that Dr. Heller's report states that the **myocardial infarction** *was the cause of his subsequent cardiac problems:*

Once the extensive heart muscle damage had occurred, the patient's subsequent cardiac problems were inevitable. Given the extensive degree of heart muscle damage from the **myocardial infarction**, *an excessive intake of salt and fluid would have been expected to produce overt heart failure. This was, in fact, what happened in the March 1975 episode, and this episode cannot in any way be considered work related. Riley v. Industrial Com'n, 447 N.E.2d 799, 801 (Ill.1983).*

It is my professional opinion that there can definitely be causal connection between effort, emotion, stress, exertion and other job-related activities to the precipitation of a **myocardial infarction** *if the primary cause is present, that is, coronary atherosclerosis. . . .*

. . . **Myocardial infarction** *has been generally defined as an actual injury to the heart resulting in the death of cells. When*

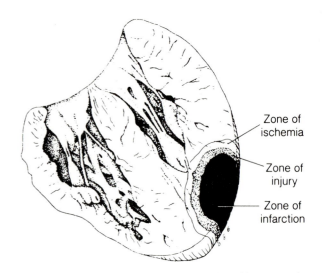

Myocardial infarction shown in cross-section of heart (ventricles only).

enough cells have died an enzyme change in blood samples occurs. Where **myocardial infarction** *is shown to have been aggravated or precipitated by the employment, awards of benefits have been sustained. Reynolds Metals Co. v. Cain, 243 Ark. 483, 420 S.W.2d 872 (1967); Hoerner Waldorf Corp. et al. v. Alford, 255 Ark. 431, 500 S.W.2d 758 (1973). Kempner's and Dodson Ins. Co. v. Hall, 646 S.W.2d 31–33 (Ct.App.Ark.1983).*

Dr. Pruitt testified that death of heart cells is a **myocardial infarction** *and is different from angina pectoris. Dr. Pruitt stated that it is conceivable that Mr. Black could have drastically increased his exercise and caused a* **myocardial infarction**, *but that it is interesting that Mr. Black did not have a* **myocardial infarction** *despite the documented exercise. Black v. Riverside Furniture Co., 642 S.W.2d 338, 340 (Ct.App.Ark.1982).*

Other Authorities: *Harris v. Rainsoft of Allen Ct., Inc., 416 N.E.2d 1320–2 (Ct.App.Ind.1981); Pierce v. Kentucky Galvanizing Co., Inc., 606 S.W.2d 165, 167 (Ct.App.Ky.1980); Fain v. St. Paul Ins. Co., 602 S.W.2d 577, 579, 581 (Ct.App.Tex. 1980); Savage v. Christian Hospital, 543 F.2d 44, 47 (8th Cir. 1976); Hamil v. Bashline, 364 A.2d 1366, 1371 (Super.Ct.Pa. 1976); Com'l Standard Fire & Marine Co. v. Thornton, 540 S.W.2d 521–2 (Ct.Civ.App.Tex.1976); Hartford Acc. & Indem. Co. v. Thurmond, 527 S.W.2d 180, 184 (Ct.Civ.App. Tex.1975); Barbato v. Alsan Masonry & Concrete, Inc., 318 A.2d 1, 3 (N.J.1974); Goldklang v. Metropolitan Life Ins. Co., 326 A.2d 690, 697 (Super.Ct.N.J.1974); Todd Shipyards Corp. v. Donovan, 300 F.2d 741, 743 (5th Cir. 1962).*

infarction pulmonary localized necrosis of lung tissue caused by obstruction of the arterial blood supply, most often due to pulmonary embolism. Clinical manifestations range from the nonexistent to pleuritic chest pain, dyspnea, hemoptysis, and tachycardia.

Pulmonary infarction is defined as "infiltration of an airless area of lung with blood cells, resulting from obstruction of the pulmonary artery by an embolus [a blood clot which obstructs circulation] or thrombus [a clot in a blood vessel of the heart which remains at its point of formation]." Dorland, 478, 738, 1580. [24th Ed. 1965] Poore v. Mathews, 406 F.Supp. 47, 49 (E.D.Tenn.1975).

infection (in-fek'shun) invasion and multiplication of microorganisms in body tissues, which may be clinically inapparent or result in local cellular injury due to competitive metabolism, toxins, intracellular replication, or antigen-antibody response. The immunological response may be transient or prolonged, and consists of a cellular response (delayed hypersensitivity) or the production of specific (immunoglobulin) antibody to the components of the infecting organism or its toxins. See also *leukemia* (Sevigny's case).

Dr. Pittman considered it a wound **infection** and superficial skin **infection**, since there was no purulent drainage from the separate incisional drain which had been removed the day before. Harwell v. Pittman, 428 So.2d 1049, 1051 (Ct.App.La.1983).

Upon admission he was perceived to have an open wound on the inside of his right hand which appeared to the admitting nurse to be oozing. His temperature was above normal and a blood analysis showed an abnormal white blood corpuscle count of 10,100 as well as other signs of **infection**. . . .

On the next day, December 30, 1979, plaintiff's **infection** appears to have attracted the attention of a nurse who noted that the patient "has open deep wound in the 2nd and 3rd joint of finger on right hand. Wound is draining thick yellowish foul smelling drainages." Kernall v. U.S., 558 F.Supp. 280, 282 (E.D.N.Y.1982).

In non-medical vernacular the word "**infection**" carries a pejorative connotation which is not entirely deserved. For example, many common vaccinations are "**infections**" which elicit the body's defense mechanisms and lead to the creation of an immunity to a later, more virulent **infection**. Plummer v. U.S., 420 F.Supp. 978, 984 (M.D.Pa.1976).

Other Authorities: Williams v. Bennett, 610 S.W.2d 144–5 (Tex.1980); Contreras v. St. Luke's Hosp., 144 Cal.Rptr. 647, 653 (Ct.App.Cal.1978); Casey v. Penn, 360 N.E.2d 93, 95 (App.Ct.Ill.1977); Kelly v. Gershkoff, 312 A.2d 211, 214 (R.I. 1973).

infection, fungal See *brain* (McLean case).

Plaintiff sustained burns over sixty to sixty-five percent of his body. Furthermore, as a direct result of his injuries, the plaintiff developed a **fungal infection** of the brain. This infection necessitated at least three surgical procedures during which portions of the plaintiff's skull and brain were excised. McLean v. U.S., 446 F.Supp. 9, 12 (E.D.La.1977).

infection, toxic purulent septic

He diagnosed the infection as a "**toxic purulent septic infection**"[3] which was so far advanced as to present a surgical problem. [3 He defined this as "an overwhelming infection that has secondary effects on the general systemic body, on the body itself, rather than just a local affair."] Lewin v. Metropolitan Life Ins. Co., 394 F.Supp. 608–10 (3d Cir. 1968).

infection, upper respiratory

Dr. Weiss' medical records for the plaintiff's March 4 and 7, 1977, visits contain Dr. Weiss' impression that the plaintiff's condition was an **upper-respiratory infection** (URI).

On March 8, 1977, the plaintiff visited a general practitioner in Seguin, Texas, Joseph B. Gastring, M.D., and gave a history of "fever on and off for eight days, from 100 to 101 in the p.m., malaise, medication and fever." Dr. Gastring also noted that a swine influenza vaccination had been administered to the plaintiff on November 14, 1976. His impression was "viral and/or nonpyogenic sinusitis." Padgett v. U.S., 553 F.Supp. 794–5 (W.D.Tex.1982).

infestation (in-fes-ta'shun) parasitic attack or subsistence on the skin and its appendages, as by insects, mites, or ticks; sometimes used to denote parasitic invasion of the tissues or organs, as by helminths. Cf. *infection*.

At that time Woody discovered substantial evidence of live **infestation**. Large numbers of larvae and adult insects were found. Woody reported that there were as many as fifty or sixty insects per bag in his examination of about one-fourth of the total shipment. U.S. v. Central Gulf Steamship Corp., 340 F.Supp. 473, 482 (E.D.La.1972), vacated and remanded 517 F.2d 687 (5th Cir. 1975).

infiltration (in"fil-tra'shun) [L. *in* into + *filtration*] the diffusion or accumulation in a tissue or cells of substances not normal to it or in amounts in excess of the normal. Also, the material so accumulated. Cf. *degeneration*. See also *extravasation* (Ohligschlager case).

infirmity (in-fir'mĭ-te) [L. *infirmitas*] a disease or condition producing weakness. See also *disease* (Watkins case).

However, in reviewing the cases in other jurisdictions, it was found that there are several cases in which it was specifically decided that an aneurysm is a bodily **infirmity**. See cases collected in Annotation, 75 A.L.R.2d 1238. No case has been found in which a contrary result was reached.

In Black's Law Dictionary an "**infirmity**" is defined as an ailment or disease of a substantial character, which apparently in some material degree impairs the physical condition and health of the insured and increases the chance of his death or sickness. An abnormal weakness in the wall of a blood vessel plainly falls within such definition. Thus, the Court finds and concludes that the pre-existing aneurysm in the blood vessel in Zorn's brain constituted a "bodily **infirmity**" within the meaning of the exclusionary clause of the insurance policy, . . . Zorn v. Aetna Life Insurance Co., 260 F.Supp. 730, 733 (E.D. Tex.1965).

inflammation (in"flah-ma'shun) [L. *inflammatio; inflammare* to set on fire] a localized protective response elicited by injury or destruction of tissues, which serves to destroy, dilute, or wall off (sequester) both the injurious agent and the injured tissue. It is characterized in the acute form by the classical signs of pain (dolor), heat (calor), redness (rubor), swelling (tumor), and loss of function (functio laesa). Histologically, it involves a complex series of events, including dilatation of arterioles, capillaries, and venules, with increased permeability and blood flow; exudation of fluids, including plasma proteins; and leukocytic migration into the inflammatory focus.

inflammation, granulomatous an inflammation, usually chronic, characterized by the formation of granulomas. See also *granuloma*.

Since a **granulomatous inflammation** is a cellular reaction to a foreign object, treatment would be taken to block the reaction. Steroids are a recognized form of treatment for **granulomatous inflammation**. Steele v. U.S., 463 F.Supp. 321, 329 (D.Alaska 1978).

inflammatory bowel disease See *disease, inflammatory bowel.*

influenza (in″flu-en′zah) [Ital. "influenza"] an acute viral infection involving the respiratory tract, occurring in isolated cases, in epidemics, or in pandemics striking many continents simultaneously or in sequence. It is marked by inflammation of the nasal mucosa, the pharynx, and conjunctiva, and by headache and severe, often generalized myalgia. Fever, chills, and prostration are common. Involvement of the myocardium and of the central nervous system occur infrequently. A necrotizing bronchitis and interstitial pneumonia are prominent features of severe influenza and account for the susceptibility of patients to secondary bacterial pneumonia due to *Streptococcus pneumoniae, Haemophilus influenzae,* and *Staphylococcus aureus.* The incubation period is one to three days and the disease ordinarily lasts for three to ten days. Influenza is caused by a number of serologically distinct strains of virus, designated A (with many subgroups), B, and C. See also *influenza virus,* under *virus.*

influenza A the most common variety of influenza caused by the type A strain of influenza virus; epidemics of this form occur at two- to three-year intervals. The causative strain is subject to wide variations in antigenic type, called antigenic shift, and outbreaks of influenza A caused by such antigenic types have been called *Asian i., Spanish i., Russian i.,* and so on. See also *influenza virus,* under *virus.*

influenza, swine a highly contagious disease of hogs caused by simultaneous infection with *Hemophilus influenzae* and a virus. See also *polyneuritis, acute febrile.*

informed consent See *consent, informed.*

infrared (in-frah-red′) denoting thermal radiation of wavelength greater than that of the red end of the visible spectrum, between the red waves and the radio waves, having wavelengths between 0.75 and 1000μm. Infrared rays emanating from tissues are the basis of thermography.

Infrared Therapy, [Pertaining to or designating those rays which lie just beyond the red end of the visible spectrum, such as are emitted by a hot nonincandescent body. They are invisible and nonactinic and are detected by their thermal effect. Their wave lengths are longer than those of visible light and shorter than those of radio waves.] U.S. v. Article Consisting of 2 Devices, etc., 255 F.Supp. 374, 381 (W.D.Ark.1966).

infusion (in-fu′zhun) the therapeutic introduction of a fluid other than blood, as saline solution, into a vein. NOTE—An *infusion* flows in by gravity, an *injection* is forced in by a syringe, an *instillation* is dropped in, an *insufflation* is blown in, and an *infection* slips in unnoticed.

The **infusion** procedure was the same in both cases. To the bottle containing the solution there was attached a plastic tube of some six feet in length, called a Ven-O-Pak. At the other end of the tube was an adapter designed for attachment to the needle after the syringe was detached from it. The adapter came covered with a removable tip to keep it sterile. Before the **infusion** was begun, the sterile tip was removed and the solution permitted to run through the tube to clear it of air. If this was done by a nurse employed by defendant, the adapter was recapped with the sterile tip, to be removed by defendant when he connected the adapter to the needle. The bottle was hung in a position well above the patient so that the solution could flow by gravity into the vein. State v. Weiner, 194 A.2d 467 (N.J.1963).

inguen (ing′gwen), pl. *in'guina* [L.] [NA] the groin; the junctural region between the abdomen and thigh.

inguinal (ing′gwĭ-nal) [L. *inguinalis*] pertaining to the inguen, or groin.
Q. On this examination of April 23rd, 1969, in which you found the weakness in the quadrants, were these weaknesses in the femoral walls?
A. Yes, sir, this is in the general area I referred to as the **inguinal** areas. Matthews v. Industrial Commission, 490 P.2d 29, 31 (Ct.App.Ariz.1971).

inguinal canal See *canalis inguinalis.*

inguinal hernia See *hernia, inguinal.*

inguinal ligament See *ligamentus inguinale.*

inguinal ring, external See *anulus, inguinalis superficialis.*

INH trademark (from *iso nicotine hydrazine*) for preparations of isoniazid. See also *isoniazid.*

injection (in-jek′shun) [L. *injectio*] the act of forcing a liquid into a part, as into the subcutaneous tissues, the vascular tree, or an organ. Cf. *infusion.*

Dr. Burgess gave support to plaintiff's theory by testifying that the **injection** of cortisone and xylocaine into the shoulder does not usually cause the sort of pain which plaintiff described and that an **injection** from the back of the shoulder might get close to the affected nerves if the needle penetrated to that depth. He also testified that the nerve cord lay approximately one and one half to two inches from the surface and that if the **injection** had been directed into the proper place, it would not have hit the nerves that suffered damage. In addition, defendant testified that she used a needle two and one half to three inches long in order to perform the **injections.** Bardessono v. Michels, 478 P.2d 480, 483 (Cal.1970).

injection, bolus See *bolus.*

A **bolus injection** is a rapid injection of a dose of a drug into a patient's bloodstream through the intravenous lines. **Bolus injections** are also known as "i.v. push" injections. This form of injection produces rapid effects on the patient. U.S. v. Narciso, 446 F.Supp. 252, 307 (E.D.Mich.1977).

injection, intramuscular an injection into the substance of a muscle. See also *neomycin* (Portis case).

The evidence is uncontradicted that **intramuscular injections** of chymar and penicillin were proper medication for Moore and that it was an acceptable practice to allow a nurse to administer the injections in the absence of the doctor. Moore v. Guthrie Hospital, Inc., 403 F.2d 366, 368 (4th Cir. 1968).

The defendant's expert medical testimony was that the proper area for **intramuscular injections** was the upper outer quadrant of the buttock. If we were to superimpose the face of a clock upon the face of the left buttock this would be the area between the hands at nine o'clock and twelve o'clock. The upper outer quadrant guide was used for two reasons: to stay away from the sciatic nerve as much as possible and to place the medication into the large muscle at the outer periphery of this quadrant so that it would be absorbed more readily. However, the medical witnesses admit that in using the standard of the upper outer quadrant there should be no injection into the medial portion of this quadrant. It was shown by anatomical charts that the lower corner, or the apex of the lines which form the angle of the quadrant, was the area where the sciatic nerve would be found. The medical witnesses admitted that an injection given in this area could damage the sciatic nerve and that no injection should be given in this medial area according to standard medical practice. Honeywell v. Rogers, 251 F.Supp. 841, 844–5 (W.D.Pa.1966).

injection, intravenous an injection made into a vein.

He then placed Mrs. Belmon in the hospital's intensive care unit (ICU), and ordered that she receive the anti-coagulant by continuous I.V. (**intravenous**) drip at the rate of 2000 units per hour to achieve maximum Heparinization. Belmon v. St. Frances Cabrini Hospital, 427 So.2d 541–2 (Ct.App.La.1983).

Without contradiction, expert witnesses testified that an injection of chymar into the bloodstream is improper. On the record before us, proof of an **intravenous injection** would establish negligence, especially in the light of Dr. Guthrie's specific instructions for intramuscular injection. Moore v. Guthrie Hospital, Inc., 403 F.2d 366, 368 (4th Cir. 1968).

injection, retrobulbar

Frederick Beisel suffered from cataracts in both eyes. He consulted Dr. William Lazenby, an ophthalmologist, who decided to place a lens implant in the right eye. During the surgery, Dr. Lazenby gave Mr. Beisel a **retrobulbar injection** behind the eye. Within thirty seconds of the injection, the doctor noticed that the eyelids were beginning to bulge, a sign of retrobulbar hemorrhage. Lazenby v. Beisel, 425 So.2d 84–5 (D.Ct.App. Fla.1982).

injection, "Z-track"

... the evidence shows that he directed that this **injection** be given with a "Z-track" technique. This technique was fully explained by several of the witnesses in this case consisting of drawing the skin to one side when making the injection so that the skin would slide back over the site of the injection into the subcutaneous tissue and seal the injected material off from direct access to the puncture which the needle made in the skin. This was advisable in the administration of Imferon because if the injected material would leak out of the site into the area of the skin puncture it would permanently stain the skin. This tends further to explain the evidence of some of the medical witnesses that they found such a stain on the buttock of the minor patient which extended down toward or over the sciatic nerve area of the buttock. Honeywell v. Rogers, 251 F.Supp. 841, 847 (W.D.Pa.1966).

injury (in'ju-re) [L. *injuria; in* not + *jus* right] harm or hurt; a wound or maim. Usually applied to damage inflicted to the body by an external force. See also *accident; heart failure.*

No question is raised as to the inclusion of a myocardial infarction within the definition of **injury** found in § 27–12–102(a)(xii), W.S.1977, and we take it to be settled as the law in Wyoming that cardiac conditions can be **injuries** within that definition....

... This court summarized the requirements imposed upon a claimant by this statute in coronary condition cases as follows in State ex rel. Worker's Compensation Division v. McCarley, Wyo., 590 P.2d 1333, 1335–1336 (1979):

(1) The claimant must establish a period of employment stress unusual or abnormal for employees in claimant's occupations;

(2) Claimant must show that he or she engaged in some exertion during the period of unusual or abnormal employment stress;

(3) Claimant must establish by competent medical evidence a direct causal connection between such exertion and the myocardial infarction; and

(4) Claimant must show that the acute symptoms of the cardiac difficulty were clearly manifested within four hours after the alleged causative exertion. Creek v. Town of Hulett, 657 P.2d 353, 355 (Wyo.1983).

The approach taken in the panel opinion here is different from the approaches of other courts in two significant respects. First, it defines the "**injury**" that triggers insurance coverage not merely as exposure to asbestos fibers or manifestation of the symptoms of asbestosis, mesothelioma or lung cancer, but also—at least in the case of asbestosis—as the process by which the victim's body resists, adapts, and tries to accommodate itself to a foreign matter—a process, which we understand from the medical testimony elicited at trial, is a major, if not primary, factor in the development of asbestosis. In short, the "**injury**" is taking place every year that the asbestos fiber remains in situs until tissue damage in the lungs is significant enough to be detected by X-rays or to produce symptomatic effects of asbestosis, mesothelioma or lung cancer....

... I agree with this more comprehensive definition of "**injury**," encompassing the period from initial exposure to manifestation, because it comports with what we know and do not know about the etiology and progress of the diseases. This process-oriented definition not only provides a flexible formula for adjudicating the legal issues associated with asbestos-related diseases, but also sets a useful precedent for other product-exposure **injuries**, as of yet unknown in origin. Further, the more comprehensive definition will give much needed certainty to the insurance industry, currently rent asunder by advocates of exposure and manifestation, whose fluctuating positions often depend upon their economic interests in a particular case, and by differing judicial rulings which seem to depend at least partially upon the equities of each case. [Concurring Opinion.] Keene Corp. v. Ins. Co. of North America, 667 F.2d 1034, 1058 (D.C.Cir.1981).

Under the rationale of Osborne v. Johnson, Ky., 432 S.W.2d 800 (1968), he does not have any occupational disability unless he has sustained (1) an **injury** of appreciable proportions (2) which will probably impair his future earning capacity through a reduction of his work life or a limitation of his work opportunities.

It was established that claimant's **injury** is permanent, but not all permanent **injuries** may be classified as **injuries** of "appreciable proportions". In Harry Gordon Scrap Materials, Inc. v. Davis, Ky., 478 S.W.2d 731 (1972), it was held that "appreciable proportions" means substantial or of significant consequence, and an **injury** which resulted in a fractured wrist and in which the attending physician expressed the opinion that Davis had a permanent impairment of the right extremity but could nevertheless perform all types of manual labor was held not to be of appreciable proportions.

The **injury** here is a change in the texture of the tissue lining the mucous membranes and nasal passages. It causes head congestion and discomfort but has not disabled claimant from working. Chemetron Corp. v. McKinley, 574 S.W.2d 332, 334 (Ct.App.Ky.1978).

The Restatement (Second) of Torts § 7, Comment (1965), carefully distinguishes between "harm" and "injury". "Harm" is defined as "the existence of loss or detriment in fact of any kind to a person resulting from any cause." Thus, harm in a malpractice context consists of the loss of health or other physical state which might be expected to follow medical treatment. "Injury," on the other hand, is defined as "the invasion of any legally protected interest of another." **Injury** in a malpractice context connotes the actual wrong done to a patient, the act of malpractice itself. Hall v. Musgrave, 517 F.2d 1163, 1168 (6th Cir. 1975).

Other Authorities: Kondzielski v. W.C.A.B. (Northwestern Electric), 463 A.2d 1221-2 (Commonwealth Ct.Pa.1983); Stanton v. Ben Rubin Ajax Cleaners-Dyers, 460 A.2d 1219, 1221 (Commonwealth Ct.Pa.1983); Massey v. Litton, 669 P.2d 248, 251-2 (Nev.1983); Ridenour v. Equity Supply Co., 665 P.2d 783, 787 (Mont.1983); Newport News Shipbuilding & Dry Dock Co. v. Fishel, 694 F.2d 327, 329-30 (4th Cir. 1982); Hale v. Venuto, 187 Cal.Rptr. 357, ___ (Ct.App.Cal.1982); Daney v. Argonaut Ins. Co., 421 So.2d 331, 336 (Ct.App.La. 1982); Roberts v. North Dakota Workmen's Comp. Bur., 326 N.W.2d 702, 705 (N.Dak.1982); Scott v. Houston Independent School Dist., 641 S.W.2d 255-7 (Ct.App.Tex.1982); Hensley v. Washington Metro. Area Transit Auth., 655 F.2d 264, 268 (D.C.Cir.1981); Eagle-Picher Industries v. Liberty Mut. Ins. Co., 523 F.Supp. 110, 115 (D.Mass.1981); Lovely v. Cooper Indus. Products, Inc., 429 N.E.2d 274, 276-7 (Ct. App.Ind.1981); Bowes v. Inter-Community Action, Inc., 411 A.2d 1279-80 (Commonwealth Ct.Pa.1980); Halaski v. Hilton Hotel, 409 A.2d 367, 370 (Pa.1979); Transportation Ins. Co. v. Maksyn, 580 S.W.2d 334, 336 (Tex.1979); Liberty Mut. Ins. Co. v. Graves, 573 S.W.2d 249, 255 (Ct.Civ.App.Tex.1978); Cooper Stevedoring Co. v. Washington, 556 F.2d 268, 274 (5th Cir. 1977); Tschohl v. Nationwide Mut. Ins. Co., 418 F.Supp. 1124, 1128 (D.Minn.1976); Reese v. Gas Engineering and Constr. Co., 548 P.2d 746, 749 (Kan.1976); Northern Assur. Co. of America v. Taylor, 540 S.W.2d 832, 834 (Ct.Civ. App.Tex.1976); Barlow v. Thornhill, 537 S.W.2d 412, 418 (Mo.1976); Haycraft v. Corhart Refractories Co., 544 S.W.2d 222, 224-5 (Ky.1976); Hunyadi v. San Enterprises, Inc., 48 Ohio App.2d 251, 253, 356 N.E.2d 747, ___ (Ct.App.Ohio 1975); Hartford Acc. & Indem. Co. v. Thurmond, 527 S.W.2d 180, 187-8 (Ct.Civ.App.Tex.1975); Bewley v. American Home Assur. Co., 450 F.2d 1079-80 (10th Cir. 1971); Robi-

nette v. Kayo Oil Co., 171 S.E.2d 172, 174 (Sup.Ct.App.Va. 1969); Aetna Cas. & Sur. Co. v. Moore, 361 S.W.2d 183, 186 (Tex.1962).

injury, accidental

The key to the application of the term "**accidental injury**," is whether the occurrence was an unusual or unexpected happening in the course of employment. Thus, if a stenographer was suddenly subjected to another employee's striking him or her in the elbow with great force, the resulting injury would at a minimum be unusual, unexpected, and surprising. It would, in any event, not be a commonplace happening. Consequently, the stenographer would properly be said to have incurred an **accidental injury** within the meaning of the Workmen's Compensation Law.

On the other hand, a professional football player is engaged in an occupation in which physical contact with others is not only expected, commonplace, and usual, but is a requirement. Injury to the player is a frequent event. Indeed, risk of injury is an integral part of the game and possibly accounts for the reason players receive the salaries they are paid....

... Whenever a person engages in an occupation requiring violent physical contact with others similarly inclined, he must expect that injury may arise therefrom. The injury is neither unusual nor extraordinary. Therefore, we hold that an injury sustained by a professional football player as the result of legitimate and usual physical contact with other players, whether under actual or simulated game conditions, cannot be said to be an "**accidental injury**" within the meaning of the Maryland Workmen's Compensation Law. See Palmer v. Kansas City Chiefs Football Club, 621 S.W.2d 350 (Mo.App.1981)....

We do not herein decide whether injury caused to the player as the direct result of extraordinary violence is compensable. That decision must await another day. Rowe v. Baltimore Colts, 454 A.2d 872, 878 (Ct.Spec.App.Md.1983).

injury, accidental bodily

Q. Well, in formulating such an opinion as to whether or not his death was caused by, "**Accidental bodily injury**", what meaning or definition did you attach to the phrase, "**Accidental bodily injury**"?

A. Well, I attached to it what we recognize in pathology and in medicine as circumstances which in themselves may produce either organic or functional abnormalities of the body capable of producing an individual's death either directly or by influencing other already existing conditions.

Q. Well, then, the meaning of the definition of the phrase as you have just given me, what bodily injury did Mr. Boring sustain which caused his death on July 17, 1967?

A. Well, I think that Mr. Boring sustained, as a result of the episode in which he was involved, a stress situation which caused his body to react under the influence of pressors [sic] arising out of the experience which resulted in his attempt to develop an increased coronary artery volume flow from his heart, which was already diseased, and that, as a result of that, he developed a functional situation which we recognize as acute coronary insufficiency complicated by cardiac arrest.

Q. Well, Doctor, you do recognize that nowhere in this material which you have handed me is there any references to or any finding of, any bruises, abrasions, contusions, cuts, fractures, or any physical injury, don't you?

A.   No, I think it is equivocated a little bit in the pathology report, but nothing definite is identified as being evident in the form of external bodily trauma. Boring v. Hayes, 496 P.2d 1385, 1388 (Kan.1972).

injury, bodily

While the definition of **bodily injury** includes sickness or disease in the policies before me, the definition also specifically includes injury to the body within its terms. Because of the extensive medical testimony that tissue injury is sustained long before a worker can be termed diseased, the plain meaning of the term "bodily injury" requires coverage at the time of the insult of asbestos that follows upon exposure. Ins. Co. of No. Am. v. Forty-Eight Insulations, Inc., 451 F.Supp. 1230, 1242 (E.D.Mich.1978).

In our view, therefore, the ordinary, natural meaning of "bodily injury" as used in article 17 connotes palpable, conspicuous physical injury,[11] and excludes mental injury with no observable "bodily", as distinguished from "behavioral", manifestations.... [[11] "In its broadest legal meaning **bodily (corporelle) injury** is an injury which can be seen, which one can touch". Henry P. de Vries' translation: H. and L. Mazeaud and A. Tunc, Traité Théorique et Pratique de la Responsabilitè Civile Délictuelle et Contractuelle, 377 (5th ed., 1957).]

... But in this case there is absolutely no dispute over the proper translation of the liability provisions of the Convention, i.e., that the French phrase "mort, de blessure, ou de toutes autres lésion corporelle" in article 17 means "death or wounding ... or any other **bodily injury**" in English. Although they would attach different connotations to these terms, the parties agree that "lésion corporelle" means "bodily injury". Both sides urge one and the same translation of the Convention's liability provisions—that contained in the United States Statutes at Large (49 U.S.Stat. 3018). Where a translation which fairly comprehends the meaning and scope of the foreign terms is agreed upon, the court's inquiry should proceed toward determining the ordinary meaning of those terms and arriving at a reasonable interpretation which will effectuate the treaty's purposes....

... For example, if plaintiff Herman's skin rash was caused or aggravated by the fright she experienced on board the aircraft, then she should be compensated for the rash and for the damages flowing from the rash. It follows that, if proved at trial, she should be compensated for her mental anguish, suffered as a result of the rash, since this anguish would have flowed from the "bodily injury".

Thus, as we read article 17, the compensable injuries must be "bodily" but there may be an intermediate causal link which is "mental" between the cause—the "accident"—and the effect—the "bodily injury". And once that predicate of liability—the "bodily injury"—is established, then the damages sustained as a result of the "bodily injury" are compensable including mental suffering....

... We hold, therefore, that defendant is liable for plaintiff's palpable, objective **bodily injuries**, including those caused by the psychic trauma of the hijacking, and for the damages flowing from those **bodily injuries**, but not for the trauma as such or for the nonbodily or behavioral manifestations of that trauma. Rosman v. Trans World Airlines, Inc., 314 N.E.2d 848, 850–1, 855–7 (N.Y.1974).

injury, deceleration

an injury sustained by sudden deceleration in the movement of the body, as in a motor vehicle accident; the brain is especially liable to such trauma.

Two neurosurgeons, Dr. George Bryar and Dr. Sherman Kaplitz, found that Reeves suffered a severe bruising of the brain, a basal skull fracture, and multiple fractures of his face and jaw bone. Dr. Bryar and Dr. Marshall Matz, a neurosurgeon testifying for defendants, testified that the "sudden stopping" of the head may cause severe brain damage even without a direct blow to the head or penetration of the skull. The sudden stopping of the skull causes the brain, which is still in motion, to strike against the skull's inner surfaces. This is called a **deceleration injury**. Walker v. Maxwell City, Inc., 453 N.E.2d 917, 920 (App.Ct.Ill.1983).

injury, discovery of

This question of the reasonableness of an individual's conduct in attaining the appropriate level of knowledge, which must be had before the statute of limitation will start to run in a personal injury case, has been a source of much litigation since the "discovery rule" was enunciated in Ayers v. Morgan, 397 Pa. 282, 154 A.2d 788 (1959). Recently, this Court in Stein v. The Washington Hospital, 302 Pa.Super. 124, 448 A.2d 558 (1982), filed July 16, 1982, addressed this question and stated:

The test by which the time at which a discovery is made is determined by the following standard which we recently discussed in Anthony v. Koppers Co., Inc., 284 Pa.Super. 81, 96–97, 425 A.2d 428, 436 (1981), reversed on other grounds 496 Pa. 119, 436 A.2d 181 (1981).

There has been some dispute or confusion, as to the exact level of knowledge a plaintiff must have before the statute of limitations will start to run. Judge Harry TAKIFF of the Court of Common Pleas of Philadelphia has recently set forth an excellent statement of the rule, as follows:

Ayers' progeny have struggled primarily with the question of reasonableness of plaintiff's conduct in attaining the appropriate level of cognitive knowledge which ultimately prompts a timely lawsuit. With the question of "reasonableness" as a constant qualification running through the decisional law, the principle emerges that three independent phases of knowledge must be known or knowable to plaintiff before the limitation period commences: (1) knowledge of the injury; (2) knowledge of the operative cause of the injury; and (3) knowledge of the causative relationship between the injury and the operative conduct. (P. ___, 448 A.2d 558) Petri v. Smith, 453 A.2d 342, 346 (Super.Ct.Pa.1982).

injury, discovery of, estoppel theory

The "estoppel theory" exception is premised on the concept that when an injured party is lulled into a sense of false security or misled by the party discovered to be culpable, which results in a delay in bringing suit beyond the statutory period, then the culpable party will be estopped from advocating a statute of limitations' bar. Walters v. Ditzler, 424 Pa. 445, 227 A.2d 833 (1967). It is axiomatic that before such exception can be applied, it must be demonstrated that the concealing screen was erected by appellant's adversaries. Nesbitt v. Erie Coach Company, 416 Pa. 89, 204 A.2d 473 (1964). Petri v. Smith, 453 A.2d 342, 346 (Super.Ct.Pa.1982).

injury, occupational

(a) ''**Injury**'' means a personal injury caused by an accident arising out of and in the course of any employment covered by the workmen's compensation law....

(c) ''Injury'' and ''personal injury'' shall be construed to include only an injury caused by an accident, which results in violence to the physical structure of the body. The terms shall in no case be construed to include an occupational disease and only such nonoccupational diseases as result directly from an injury. I.C. § 72–102(14). Yeend v. United Parcel Service, Inc., 659 P.2d 87, 89 (Idaho 1982).

''Injury'' is defined in § 65–01–02(8), N.D.C.C.:

''8. ''Injury'' shall mean an injury by accident arising out of and in the course of employment including an injury caused by the willful act of a third person directed against an employee because of his employment, but such term shall not include an injury caused by the employee's willful intention to injure himself or to injure another, nor any injury received because of the use of narcotics or intoxicants while in the course of the employment. If an injury is due to heart attack or stroke, such heart attack or stroke must be causally related to the worker's employment, with reasonable medical certainty, and must have been precipitated by unusual stress. Such term, in addition to an injury by accident, shall include:

''a. Any disease which can be fairly traceable to the employment. Ordinary diseases of life to which the general public outside of the employment is exposed shall not be compensable except where the disease follows as an incident to, and in its inception is caused by a hazard to which an employee is subjected in the course of his employment. The disease must be incidental to the character of the business and not independent of the relation of employer and employee. The disease includes impairment and effects from radiation fairly traceable to the employment. It need not have been foreseen or expected, but after it is contracted, it must appear to have had its origin in a risk connected with the employment and to have flowed from that source as a rational consequence.

''b. An injury to artificial members.'' Satrom v. N.Dak. Workmen's Compensation Bureau, 328 N.W.2d 824, 827 (N.Dak.1982).

injury, personal

''**Personal injury**'' is defined in M.C.L. § 750.520a(f); M.S.A. § 28.788(1)(f) as follows:

'' '**Personal injury**' means bodily injury, disfigurement, mental anguish, chronic pain, pregnancy, disease, or loss or impairment of a sexual or reproductive organ.''...

As a result of the attack [rape], she incurred pain in her spine and had trouble sitting for two weeks after the incident. She also suffered scratches on her chin and some internal pain which lasted for three to four days after the incident. There was also evidence that complainant received a small bruise on her lower back.

To satisfy the bodily injury component, the injuries suffered need not be permanent or substantial. People v. Kraai, 92 Mich.App. 398, 285 N.W.2d 309 (1979), lv. den. 407 Mich. 954 (1980). People v. Jenkins, 328 N.W.2d 403–5 (Ct.App. Mich.1982).

In Pinkston v. Rice Motor Co., 180 Kan. 295, 303 P.2d 197 (1956), a proceeding under the workmen's compensation act, it was held that the term ''**personal injury**'' as used in the act is to be construed as meaning any lesion or change in the physical structure of the body, causing damage or harm thereto and it is not essential that the disorder be of such character as to present external or visible signs of its existence. We see no reason for the application of any different rule here. Boring v. Haynes, 496 P.2d 1385, 1394 (Kan.1972).

injury, preexisting

The acceleration, aggravation or ''lighting up'' of a **preexisting** nondisabling condition is an injury in the employment causing it. (Fred Gledhill Chevrolet Co. v. Industrial Acc. Com., 62 A.C. 45, 47, 41 Cal.Rptr. 170, 396 P.2d 586.) The employer takes the employee as he finds him; thus compensation may be granted even though the employee's physical condition subjects him to industrial disability to which a healthy person would be relatively immune. Peter Kiewit Sons v. Industrial Accident Com'n, 44 Cal.Rptr. 813, 817 (Dist.Ct.App.Cal.1965).

injury, prenatal

Missouri has expanded the right of action for **prenatal personal injuries** to allow a surviving infant to bring an action for injuries received after conception. Steggall v. Morris, 258 S.W.2d 577 (Mo.1953). However, a wrongful death action may not be maintained for the death of an unborn or stillborn child. Hardin v. Sanders, 538 S.W.2d 336 (Mo.1976). The decisions in Steggall and Hardin are clear indications that the right of a child to bring an action for damages incurred prior to birth is contingent upon being born alive....

In looking to the decisions of the other states, there are several decisions which hold that a child has a cause of action for injuries resulting from negligent acts committed prior to conception. Jorgensen v. Meade Johnson Laboratories, Inc., 483 F.2d 237 (10th Cir. 1973); Renslow v. Mennonite Hospital, 348 Ill.2d 367, 10 Ill.Dec. 484, 367 N.E.2d 1250 (1977); Park v. Chessin, 88 Misc.2d 222, 387 N.Y.S.2d 204 (Sup.Ct. Queens County 1976). Bergstreser v. Mitchell, 448 F.Supp. 10, 14 (E.D.Mo.1977).

... see also Sinkler v. Kneale, 401 Pa. 267, 164 A.2d 93, 96 (treating the cause of a Mongoloid condition as a factual one requiring medical proof); Womack v. Buchhorn, 384 Mich. 718, 187 N.W.2d 218, 219, 222 (referring to advances in medical knowledge in the context of a suit for **prenatal injuries**); Smith v. Brennan, 31 N.J. 353, 157 A.2d 497, 503; Bennett v. Hymers, 101 N.H. 483, 147 A.2d 108, 110. And such treatment of the problem would accord with the predominant view that an action may be maintained for **prenatal injuries** negligently inflicted if the injured child is born alive. See Sinkler v. Kneale, supra, 164 A.2d at 94–96, and cases there collected; Womack v. Buchhorn, supra, 187 N.W.2d at 220–222, and cases there collected; Annotation, Liability For Prenatal Injuries, 40 A.L.R.3d 1222, 1228. Jorgensen v. Meade Johnson Laboratories, Inc., 483 F.2d 237, 240 (10th Cir. 1973).

injury, serious bodily

Section 18–1–901, C.R.S.1973, the definition section, differentiates between ''Bodily injury'' and ''**Serious bodily injury**.'' It states:

(c) "Bodily injury" means physical pain, illness, or any impairment of physical or mental condition. . . .

(p) "Serious bodily injury" means bodily injury which involves a substantial risk of death, serious permanent disfigurement, or protracted loss or impairment of the function of any part or organ of the body. People v. Martinez, 540 P.2d 1091, 1094 (Colo.1975).

injury, soft tissue

Bodily injury confined solely to the soft tissue for the purpose of this section means, injury in the form of sprains, strains, contusions, lacerations, bruises, hematomas, cuts, abrasions, scrapes, scratches, and tears confined to the muscles, tendons, ligaments, cartilages, nerves, fibers, veins, arteries and skin of the human body.

Plaintiff argues that injury to the kidney is an injury to an organ and not to soft tissue. Medical testimony at the trial suggested that, in a medical sense, an injury to an organ could not be referred to as a "soft tissue injury." . . .

The term "soft tissue injury" is peculiar to the New Jersey statute and is not found in comparable legislation in other states. Schermer, Automobile Liability Insurance (rev.ed.1975) § 8.01 et seq., at 8–1 through 8–27. . . .

Giving this statute a liberal construction so as to effect its purpose, N.J.S.A. 39:6A–16, we conclude that the obvious purpose of the statute and in particular the tort exemption provisions thereof can best be effected by holding that injuries to organs, such as the kidneys, are injuries "confined solely to the soft tissue" of the body. Todd v. Dabkowski, 372 A.2d 350–1 (Super.Ct.N.J.1977).

injury, straddle type

A straddle type injury was described as a situation when one's foot slips from the pedal of a bicycle and trauma occurs, crushing the urethra between the arch of the symphysis and the bar of the bicycle. Langton v. Brown, 591 S.W.2d 84, 87 (Mo.Ct. App.1979).

injury, whiplash a nonspecific term applied to injury to the spine and spinal cord at the junction of the fourth and fifth cervical vertebrae, occurring as the result of rapid acceleration or deceleration of the body. Because of their greater mobility, the four upper vertebrae act as the lash, and the lower three act as the handle of the whip.

Dr. Anderson testified by deposition that his diagnosis was whiplash—multiple soft tissue injuries of the back, shoulders and neck. Considering the absence of complaints of this type before the accident, Dr. Anderson concluded that the injury was the result of the accident. He provided plaintiff with ultrasonic treatment, muscle relaxants, anti-inflammatory agents and pain tablets. . . .

Plaintiff testified that her condition is getting worse. Her back pain is more constant, and becoming worse in her lower back. Her left arm had developed shooting pains if she lifted it too far, but in September, 1977, it got worse and she couldn't use it for three weeks. Just before trial she found she was losing her grip, dropping things, and could not type accurately. . . .

Dr. Badgley testified by deposition that when plaintiff visited him in November, 1975, she complained of cervical, dorsal and lumbar spine pain radiating into the shoulders and sometimes arms, aggravated by lifting of arms over the head; inter-

mittent sharp shooting leg pain; and headaches. He diagnosed residual cervical, dorsal, lumbar spine sprain. . . .

. . . Sometimes when she sits, her legs get numb or go to sleep. She wears a neck collar at home, and is currently taking valium and muscle relaxants. Pohl v. Gilbert, 280 N.W.2d 831–3 (Ct.App.Mich.1979).

Plaintiff Slowik stated that the impact pushed her forward, toward the steering wheel, and then back into the seat. She testified that she did not come into contact with any part of the interior. . . .

. . . Dr. Rentschler testified that Mrs. Slowik was suffering from a flexion extension type injury of the cervical spine, or, in layman's language, a "whiplash." The doctor found muscle spasm in the neck and shoulder area. He prescribed the continued use of the cervical collar, ultrasonic treatments, a home traction unit and additional pain medication. Slowik v. Schrack, 395 N.E.2d 753–5 (App.Ct.Ill.1979).

. . . she had been involved in an elevated railway train accident in which she was thrown forward and hit her face, shoulder, and arm on the seat in front of her. . . .

. . . She experienced extreme pain on turning her head or flexing or extending the head on the neck. This indicated to Dr. Wittelle that there was damage to the nerves coming out between the cervical vertebrae and that she had what is commonly called a severe whiplash injury plus contusions of the shoulder, right arm, neck, and face. McSwain v. Chicago Transit Authority, 362 N.E.2d 1264, 1267 (App.Ct.Ill.1977).

Other Authorities: Michaud v. Steckino, 390 A.2d 524, 528 (Sup.Jud.Ct.Me.1978). Raisovich v. Giddings, 201 S.E.2d 606–7 (Va.1974); Phillips v. Celebrezze, 330 F.2d 687, 689–90 (6th Cir. 1964).

insane (in-sān') [L. in not + sanus sound] mentally deranged. See also insanity.

The Doctor also said that Currens was not "insane" in the sense that that legal, non-medical, term is employed, that the term "sociopathic personality" is not a term precisely indicating a mental illness but that it does have "mental implications". He stated also that: "It is a very fine line, as I pointed out before, between the psychopathic type of personality and a true mental psychotic personality.", and that "We do not use the word 'sane' or 'insane' in medicine." U.S. v. Currens, 290 F.2d 751, 756 (3d Cir. 1961).

insanitary (in-san'ĭ-ter-e) not in a good sanitary condition; not conducive to good health; unclean.

. . . the manner of processing can surely give rise to the survival, with attendant toxic effects on humans, of spores which would not have survived under stricter "sanitary" conditions. In that sense, treating "insanitary conditions" in relation to the hazard, the interpretation of the District Court which described the word "sanitary" as merely "inelegant" is a fair reading, emphasizing that the food does not have to be actually contaminated during processing and packing but simply that "it may have been rendered injurious to health," § 342(a)(4), by inadequate sanitary conditions of prevention. U.S. v. Nova Scotia Food Products Corp., 568 F.2d 240, 247 (2d Cir. 1977).

insanity (in-san'ĭ-te) [L. insanitas, from in not + sanus sound] mental derangement or disorder. The term is a

social and legal rather than a medical one, and indicates a condition which renders the affected person unfit to enjoy liberty of action because of the unreliability of his behavior with concomitant danger to himself and others. See also *chromosome Y* (People v. Tanner case); *rule, M'Naghten.*

Defendants contend that even if they were required to show a change in circumstances, such a change was shown because the legal definition of incurable **insanity**, for workers' compensation claims purposes, changed between the time the 1973 award was entered and the date that the Board entered its decision in this case. At the time that the 1973 award was entered, decisions concerning claims of incurable **insanity** were governed by the definition stated in Sprute v. Herlihy Mid-Continent Co., 32 Mich.App. 574, 189 N.W.2d 89 (1971). In 1978, the Supreme Court overruled Sprute and announced a new more restrictive standard. Redfern v. Sparks-Withington Co., 403 Mich. 63, 268 N.W.2d 28 (1978). Selk v. Detroit Plastic Products, 328 N.W.2d 15, 22 (Ct.App.Mich. 1982).

Section 6–2 of the Criminal Code (Ill.Rev.Stat.1971, ch. 38, par. 6–2(a)) provides:

Insanity. (a) A person is not criminally responsible for conduct if at the time of such conduct, as a result of mental disease or mental defect, he lacks substantial capacity either to appreciate the criminality of his conduct or to conform his conduct to the requirements of law. People v. Harrington, 317 N.E.2d 161, 165 (App.Ct.Ill.1974).

insanity (ALI test)

We shall explain why we have concluded that we should discard the M'Naghten language, and update the California test of mental incapacity as a criminal defense by adopting the test proposed by the American Law Institute [3] and followed by the federal judiciary and the courts of 15 states. [[3] "A person is not responsible for criminal conduct if at the time of such conduct as a result of mental disease or defect he lacks substantial capacity either to appreciate the criminality [wrongfulness] of his conduct or to conform his conduct to the requirements of law." (Model Pen.Code, Proposed Official Draft (1962) § 4.01, subpart (1).)] People v. Drew, 583 P.2d 1318–19 (Cal.1978).

insanity (M'Naghten test)

For over a century California has followed the **M'Naghten** test [2] to define the defenses of insanity and idiocy. The deficiencies of that test have long been apparent, and judicial attempts to reinterpret or evade the limitations of M'Naghten have proven inadequate. [Footnote omitted.] [[2] "[T]o establish a defence on the ground of insanity, it must be clearly proved that, at the time of the committing the act, the party accused was labouring under such a defect of reason, from disease of the mind, as not to know the nature and quality of the act he was doing; or, if he did know it, that he did not know he was doing what was wrong." (M'Naghten's Case (1843) 10 Clark & Fin. 200, 210 [8 Eng.Rep. 718, 722].)] People v. Drew, 583 P.2d 1318–19 (Cal.1978).

insemination (in-sem″ĭ-na′shun) [L. *inseminatus* sown, from *in* into + *semen* seed] the deposit of seminal fluid within the vagina or cervix.

insemination, artificial introduction of semen into the vagina or cervix by artificial means.

The process of **artificial insemination** allows one sire to artificially inseminate thousands of cattle in its lifetime while a bull in natural service can sire no more than 125–150 offspring in the same span of time. These techniques allow a breeder access to many different bulls without incurring the cost of maintaining a large number of bulls. Two Rivers Co. v. Curtiss Breeding Service, 624 F.2d 1242, 1244 (5th Cir. 1980).

insemination, donor; insemination, heterologous artificial insemination in which the semen used is that of a man other than the woman's husband; called also A.I.D. Cited in In re Adoption of Anonymous, 345 N.Y.S.2d 430–1 (Sur.Ct.Kings Cty.1973).

insemination, homologous artificial insemination in which the husband's semen is used; called also A.I.H.

As a preliminary, there are two types of **artificial insemination. Homologous insemination** is the process by which the wife is artificially impregnated with the semen of her husband. This procedure is referred to as AIH (Artificial Insemination Husband) and creates no legal problems since the child is considered the natural child of the husband and wife....

(See Note "A Legislative Approach to Artificial Insemination", 53 Cornell L.Rev. 497 [1968].) New York City has a health ordinance and regulations confining AID treatment to the medical profession and regulating procedures and required records. (N.Y.C. Health Code § 112; for code and regulations see Boardman's N.Y. Family Law § 217.) Neither the code nor the regulations declare the legal rights of the parties....

... Biskind "Legitimacy of a Child Born by Artificial Insemination", 5 J. Family L. 39, 47 [1965]; Smith "Artificial Insemination—No Longer a Quagmire", 3 Family L.Q. 1 [1969]. In Re Adoption of Anonymous, 345 N.Y.S.2d 430–2 (Surrog.Ct., Kings Cty.1973).

insert (in′sert) something that is implanted. See also *instructions, manufacturers.*

insert, manufacturer's

As the name suggests, a **package insert** is the legally required document which the manufacturer includes in the drug package....

... As noted, **package inserts** are included within the drug package when it is shipped to the pharmacy. The pharmacist, however, often removes and discards the insert in the process of affixing his own gummed label to the actual container. There is no system for insuring, or even making it likely, that the physician sees the insert. (See Dixon, Drug Product Liability, § 6.10[4].) Consequently, "[m]any prescribing physicians would not come into contact with **package inserts** or warning labels attached to the drug when the pharmacist filed the prescription". (Stevens v. Parke Davis & Co., 9 Cal.3d 51, 107 Cal.Rptr. 45, 54, 507 P.2d 653, 662.) Baker v. St. Agnes Hospital, 421 N.Y.S.2d 81, 83, 86 (2d Dep't 1979).

insomnia (in-som′ne-ah) [L. *in* not + *somnus* sleep + *-ia*] inability to sleep; abnormal wakefulness.

Insomnia is a "subjective" illness. It cannot be detected by medical methods or examination, but no one questions that it causes great distress. **Insomnia** is medically described as "inability to sleep, abnormal wakefulness." Dorland's Medical Dictionary, 25th Edition. In Cecil-Loeb's Textbooks of Medicine, Beeson McDermott, page 96, it is stated:

Too little sleep is known as **insomnia** or hyposomnia. **Insomnia** . . . most frequently results from something other than structural diseases of the nervous system. . . . **Insomnia** has three patterns: difficulty in falling asleep after retiring; intermittent waking through the period of attempted sleep; and early awakening. Direct observation on patients suffering from **insomnia** almost always reveals they are less wakeful than they think and there is little evidence that chronic **insomnia** takes any physical toll. Nevertheless, even brief difficulty in falling asleep, or staying asleep, causes great subjective distress, leads to a large consumption of sedatives in the United States. . . .

The government undercover agents and government counsel seemed to pretend to be ignorant of the fact that **insomnia** is a common affliction that causes great subjective distress leading to a large consumption of sedatives in the United States, according to medical authorities, and that the only remedy to alleviate this distressing affliction, known personally by practically everybody, is sedatives, as stated in books written by the medical profession. [Dissent.] U.S. v. Carroll, 518 F.2d 187, 190, 197 (6th Cir. 1975).

institution for mental diseases

"[Medicaid program]," 42 U.S.C. § 1302 (Supp. V 1981), and pursuant to this authority the Secretary has promulgated regulations that define the term "**institution for mental diseases**." The regulations define "institution" as "an establishment that furnishes (in single or multiple facilities) food, shelter, and some treatment or services to four or more persons." 42 C.F.R. § 435.1009 (1982).

An IMD is specifically defined as:

an institution that is primarily engaged in providing diagnosis, treatment or care of persons with mental diseases, including medical attention, nursing care and related services. Whether an institution is an **institution for mental diseases** is determined by its overall character as that of a facility established and maintained primarily for the care and treatment of individuals with mental diseases, whether or not it is licensed as such. Id. . . .

HHS has further interpreted this definition of an IMD in a series of internal documents in the Field Staff Information and Instruction Series (FSIIS). These FSIIS documents were issued by the Medical Services Administration of the Social and Rehabilitation Service, the predecessor agency of the Health Care Financing Administration (HCFA), as guidelines for its regional officials. The most important one, for purposes of this case, is FSIIS FY–76–44, which directed the use of the World Health Organization's International Classification of Diseases (ICD) for determining what constitutes a "mental disease." Granville House v. Dep't of Health & Human Serv., 715 F.2d 1292, 1295 (8th Cir. 1983).

instructions, manufacturer's

The term "**manufacturers' instructions**" will be used to denote generally all the information and exhibits introduced at trial by both sides which purported to establish the guidelines under which physicians would conduct themselves in the prescription and administration of the drugs in question. Chief among the exhibits introduced were the manufacturers' "inserts"—the printed use instructions which are "inserted" as part of the packaging of any given drug—and the 1969 Physicians' Desk Reference to Pharmaceutical Specialties and Biologicals, a standard medical reference work which summarized between its covers much of the information contained in the manufacturers' inserts. Lhotka v. Larson, 238 N.W.2d 870, 874 (Minn. 1976).

instrument (in'stroo-ment) [L. *instrumentum; instruere* to furnish] any tool, appliance, or apparatus.

instrument pack

The Hospital supplied the instruments in the form of an **instrument pack**. This pack is a set of instruments of a type and number prescribed by the Hospital sufficient to perform the operation scheduled by the surgeon. The packs are assembled by employees of the Hospital. The rules of the Hospital do not require that the number of instruments be verified by their operating room staff by either a preoperation or preclosing instrument count. However, the Hospital does require its operating room staff to make a post operation count at the time the instruments are cleaned, to keep count of the number of scalpel blades used and to report any deficiency. No such report was made here either to the hospital administration or the operating surgeon. If a scalpel blade becomes dull during an operation it is the duty of the operating room staff on request of the surgeon to obtain a new blade, replace the dull one on the handle and dispose of the used blade. No one recalls whether such a replacement was made here. City of Somerset v. Hart, 549 S.W.2d 814, 816 (Ky.1977).

insufficiency (in"sŭ-fish'en-se) [L. *insufficientia*, from *in* not + *sufficiens* sufficient] the condition of being insufficient or inadequate to the performance of the allotted duty.

insufficiency, cerebral vascular

Q. Doctor, do you know whether or not, basing your knowledge upon the factors that you know about in the practice of medicine in Davidson County, Tennessee, is Premarin used for the treatment of **cerebral vascular insufficiency**?

A. Yes, sir.

Q. How is it used and why is it used for that purpose?

A. . . . Now the important thing is to enlarge the diameter of these blood vessels so that more blood can get through and at the same time use some kind of drug that will decrease the physiological age of these blood vessels. Chumbler v. McClure, 505 F.2d 489, 495 (6th Cir. 1974).

insufficiency, coronary decrease in flow of blood through the coronary blood vessels.

. . . an episode of **coronary insufficiency** (meaning that the coronary arteries were not supplying the heart with an adequate supply of blood). Stoleson v. U.S., 708 F.2d 1217, 1219 (7th Cir. 1983).

This was an explanation of what happens when insufficient blood flows through the arteries to the heart (**coronary insufficiency**). Wilkins v. American Export Isbrandtsen Lines, Inc., 446 F.2d 480, 482 (2d Cir. 1971).

It was the doctor's opinion that Bullard had not had an outright coronary thrombosis, but rather a **coronary insufficiency**. This deprives the heart muscle of blood over a period of time and this causes changes to be shown in the electrocardiogram. Republic National Life Ins. Co. v. Bullard, 399 S.W.2d 376, 378 (Ct.Civ.App.Tex.1966).

insulase See *chlorpropamide.*

insulin (in'su-lin) [L. *insula* island (of the pancreas) + *-in*] a double-chain protein hormone formed from proinsulin in the beta cells of the pancreatic islets of Langerhans. The major fuel-regulating hormone in humans, it is secreted into the blood in response to a rise in concentration of glucose in the blood and also to a rise in amino acid concentration. Insulin promotes the storage of glucose in the liver, skeletal muscle, and adipose tissue, promotes the uptake of amino acids by skeletal muscle, increases protein synthesis, accelerates lipid synthesis, and inhibits lipolysis and gluconeogenesis. A sterile solution of this hypoglycemic principle of the pancreas (regular insulin), prepared in accordance with USP standards, containing 40, 80, 100, and 500 USP insulin units per milliliter, and suitable for intravenous and intramuscular injection, is used in the treatment of diabetes mellitus.

"In 1921 a young Canadian surgeon, recently back from service in World War I, and a young Canadian graduate student performed one of the most notable experiments in medical history. Into dogs dying of diabetes—brought on by removal of the pancreas—the researchers injected an extract obtained from the pancreas of a normal dog. The dogs didn't die.

"The surgeon and the graduate student—Frederick Grant Banting and Charles H. Best—tested the safety of the new extract by injecting it into themselves. Then on Jan. 11, 1922, it was given for the first time to a diabetic patient.

"In those days, an adult with diabetes had a life expectancy of only five or ten years. But many of the patients treated with the new extract in 1922 are still living, and today the life expectancy of the adult diabetic approaches the average for the general population....

"What Banting and Best discovered was, of course, the life-giving hormone, insulin." Facts about Diabetes, published by the American Diabetes Association, Inc., 1966, New York. U.S. v. Dunavan, 464 F.2d 1166, 1177–8 (6th Cir. 1972).

insulin reaction See *hypoglycemia.*

insulin shock See *hypoglycemia; shock, insulin.*

intelligence (in-tel'ĭ-jens) [L. *intelligere* to understand] the ability to comprehend or understand. See also under *quotient.*

Brother Fox had lapsed into a coma with attendant lack of comprehension of surroundings and "[i]n general ... a loss of all the functions that we think [of] as **intelligence**." Eichner v. Dillon, 426 N.Y.S.2d 517, 527 (2d Dep't 1980).

intelligence quotient See under *quotient.*

intensity (in-ten'sĭ-te) [L. *intensus* intense; *in* on + *tendere* to stretch] the condition or quality of being intense; a high degree of tension, activity, or energy.

Intensity is loudness, and is a function of the number of air molecules vibrating at a given frequency. U.S. v. Williams, 583 F.2d 1194, 1196 (2d Cir. 1978).

interarticular (in"ter-ar-tik'u-lar) [*inter-* + L. *articulus* joint] situated between articular surfaces.

interdental splint See *splint, interdental.*

interferon (in"ter-fēr'on) a class of small soluble proteins produced and released by cells invaded by virus, which induce in noninfected cells the formation of an antiviral protein that inhibits viral multiplication; although not virus-specific, interferons are more effective in animal cells of the same species that produced them. Type I, or classical, interferon is produced by leukocytes, as well as nonlymphoid cells, in response to virus infection. Interferon production may also be induced by certain bacteria, rickettsiae, etc., and by specifically sensitized lymphocytes following interaction with specific antigen or antigen-antibody complex. The latter form, known as *Type II* or *immune interferon,* is capable of affecting antibody production and cell-mediated immunity.

On November 4, 1976 plaintiff was placed on a 30-day treatment program with the experimental drug, **interferon**. He responded with a partial decrease in lymph node size. Plaintiff reacted to **interferon** treatment with high fever, appetite and hair loss, nausea and general weakness. Marek v. Professional Health Services, Inc., 432 A.2d 538, 540 (Super.Ct.N.J.1981).

intermediate (in"ter-me'de-it) [*inter-* + L. *medius* middle] a substance formed in a chemical process that is essential to the formation of the end product of the process. Cited in Ritter v. Rohm & Haas Co., 271 F.Supp. 313 (S.D. N.Y.1967).

intern (in'tern) [Fr. *interne*] a graduate of a medical or dental school serving and residing in a hospital preparatory to being licensed to practice medicine or dentistry. Cf. *resident.*

These **interns** (who are not licensed physicians, but are allowed to practice only under direct supervision) were never given any course of training at all in emergency room procedures except for practical experience. Other departments of the hospital had actual formal training programs, but the emergency room department had none (T. 635–645). [Dissent.] Washington v. City of Columbus, 222 S.E.2d 583, 593 (Ct. App.Ga.1975).

internal (in-ter'nal) [L. *internus*] situated or occurring within or on the inside; many anatomical structures formerly called internal are now correctly termed medial. See also *external* (Jones case).

internal mammary visualization See *visualization, internal mammary.*

internal medicine See *medicine, internal.*

interphalangeal (in"ter-fah-lan'je-al) [*inter-* + *phalangeal*] situated between two contiguous phalanges.

The accident happened when a large metal fire door closed on plaintiff's left index finger, amputating it at the distal **interphalangeal** joint. Moazzami v. Bd. of Sup'rs of La. State Univ., 424 So.2d 1112 (Ct.App.La.1982).

The diagnosis for the December 10 readmission shows "recurrent dislocation of proximal **interphalangal** joint left little finger." In this operation fixation was attempted with two metal appliances. Thompson v. U.S., 368 F.Supp. 466, 469 (W.D.La. 1973).

He is unable to eat with his left hand and cannot tie his shoe laces because of the permanently partially flexed position of the **interphalangeal** joint. He suffers and will suffer numbness of the thumb, adhesions of the extensor and flexor apparatus which causes the **interphalangeal** joint to be in fixed partial flexion. He has lost 50 percent of the use of his left thumb which represents about 25 percent of the left hand. Sanchez v. Lubeck Linie A.G., 318 F.Supp. 821, 823 (S.D.N.Y.1970).

intersex (in'ter-seks) an individual who shows intermingling, in varying degrees, of the characters of each sex, including physical form, reproductive organs, and sexual behavior. See also *hermaphrodite; pseudohermaphroditism.*

intersexuality (in"ter-seks"u-al'ĭ-te) the intermingling, in varying degrees, of the characters of each sex, including physical form, reproductive organs, and sexual behavior, in one individual, as a result of some flaw in embryonic development. See also *intersex; hermaphroditism; pseudohermaphroditism.*

interstitial fibrosis See *fibrosis, idiopathic pulmonary.*

intertrochanteric (in"ter-tro"kan-ter'ik) [*inter- + trochanter*] situated in or pertaining to the space between the greater and the lesser trochanter. See also *trochanter major; trochanter minor.*

X-rays were taken, and the injury was diagnosed as a comminuted **intertrochanteric** fracture of the left hip....

... Dr. Chard is an acknowledged specialist in orthopedic surgery with unquestioned qualifications in the field and extensive experience in **intertrochanteric** hip fractures. Dr. Chard recommended open reduction and internal fixation of the fracture fragments by an internal fixation device known as the "Jewett nail". Largess v. Tatem, 291 A.2d 398, 409–10 (Vt.1972).

intestine (in-tes'tin) [L. *intesti'nus* inward, internal; Gr. *enteron*] the portion of the alimentary canal extending from the pyloric opening of the stomach to the anus; called also *bowel* and *gut.* See also *bowel; intestinum.*

When the abdomen was opened there was seen the burn in the **bowel** which was caused in the performance of that procedure. Some seven centimeters of it were removed and the **bowel** re-anastomosed, put back end-to-end again,... Raitt v. Johns Hopkins Hospital, 322 A.2d 548, 562 (Ct.Spec.App. Md.1974), reversed and remanded 336 A.2d 90 (Ct.App. 1975).

intestinum (in"tes-ti'num), pl. *intesti'na* [L., from *intestinus* inward, internal] intestine: the portion of the alimentary canal extending from the pyloric opening of the stomach to the anus: it is a membranous tube, comprising the intestinum tenue and the intestinum crassum, whose function is to complete the processes of digestion, to provide the body (through absorption) with water, electrolytes, and nutrients, and to move along and store fecal wastes until they are expelled.

intima (in'tĭ-mah) [L.] [NA] a general term denoting an innermost structure. See also *tunica intima vasorum.*

The lining is called the **intima**.... I don't know that I can say exactly what starts this thin collection to form on the surface of the **intima**. Flannery v. Industrial Com'n, 412 P.2d 297, 299 (Ct.App.Ariz.1966).

intoxication (in-tok"sĭ-ka'shun) [L. *in* intensive + Gr. *toxikon* poison] 1. poisoning; the state of being poisoned. 2. the condition produced by excessive use of an alcohol, especially ethanol. See also *test, Bogen's.*

In Clowney v. State, Fla., 1958, 102 So.2d 619, the Supreme Court of Florida held that, "a person is intoxicated when he is under the influence of intoxicants to such an extent as to deprive him of full possession of his normal faculties. **Intoxication** is generally associated with imbibing vinous, malt or spirituous liquors. But with the advent of the pervasive illegal traffic in drugs which our society is experiencing, the definition of **intoxication** has been extended generally to their use also." Trivette v. State, Fla., 244 So.2d 173. An excellent annotation is found in 17 A.L.R.3rd 815. Leu v. City of Mountain Brook, 386 So.2d 483, 486 (Ct.Crim.App.Ala.1980).

Upon the trial of any civil or criminal action or proceeding arising out of acts alleged to have been committed by any person while driving a vehicle while under the influence of intoxicating liquor, the amount of alcohol in the person's blood at the time of the chemical test or tests authorized by this chapter as shown by chemical analysis of the person's blood, urine, breath shall be admissible as evidence and give rise to the following presumptions:...

3. If there was at that time 0.10 percent or more by weight of alcohol in the person's blood, it shall be presumed that the person was under the influence of intoxicating liquor.

4. Percent by weight of alcohol in the blood shall be based upon milligram of alcohol per one hundred cubic centimeters of blood.

Ala.Code tit. 36, § 155(a) (Supp.1974). Watkins v. U.S., 589 F.2d 214, 218 (5th Cir. 1979).

The distinction between "in an intoxicated condition" and "under the influence of alcohol" is not mere semantics in this case: it is a distinction which section 493 [V.I.Code, Title 20] itself makes. For the evidentiary purpose of determining **intoxication**, section 493(b) c & d provide:

(c) evidence that there was, at the time, ten hundredths of one per centum, or more, by weight of alcohol in his blood, may be admitted as prima facie evidence that the defendant's ability to operate a motor vehicle was impaired by the consumption of alcohol; (d) evidence that there was, at the time, fifteen-hundredths of one per centum, or more, by weight of alcohol in his blood, may be admitted as prima facie evidence that the defendant was in an intoxicated condition. Government of Virgin Islands v. Brown, 571 F.2d 773, 776 (3d Cir. 1978).

Other Authorities: Hyatt v. Sierra Boat Co., 145 Cal.Rptr. 47, 52 (Ct.App.Cal.1978); Arnold v. Reynolds, 211 S.E.2d 46–7 (Va.1975). Pfeffer v. Dep't of Public Safety, 221 S.E.2d 658–9 (Ct.App.Ga.1975). People v. Van Tuyl, 359 N.Y.S.2d 958, 961, 963 (Sup.Ct.App.Term 1974); Kissinger v. Frankhouser, 308 F.2d 348, 353 (4th Cir. 1962).

intoximeter

For all of the reasons stated above it is the ultimate conclusion of this Court that processes used by and incorporated in the Intoximeter 3000 are generally accepted in the scientific community and in the fields in which they belong, and that the Intoximeter 3000 reliably and accurately detects and measures the quantity of ethyl alcohol in the blood of a driver to the exclusion of any other substance. People v. Jones, 461 N.Y.S.2d 962, 969 (Albany Ct.Ct.1983).

Isaacs followed them to headquarters, and was present when Officer Holtage, who was certified by the State Board of Health as qualified to operate the photo-electric intoximeter machine, attempted to administer the test to appellant. Appellant made three attempts to blow into the machine but was unable to exhale a sufficient amount of air to obtain a meter reading. . . .

Officer Gene Holtage gave appellant the Miranda rights and warnings and explained the requirements of taking the PEI test. He set up the machine and appellant made three unsuccessful attempts to blow into the tube which inflates the bag. Leu v. City of Mountain Brook, 386 So.2d 483, 485 (Ct.Crim. App.Ala.1980).

intracapsular (in"trah-kap'su-lar) within a capsule.

The other surgical procedure for removing cataracts is called intracapsular surgery. It involves a 180 degree incision into the eye. The entire cataract is removed intact in the membrane surrounding it. Lambert v. Park, 597 F.2d 236, 239 (10th Cir. 1979).

intracardiac (in"trah-kar'de-ak) within the heart. Cited in Daniels v. Hadley Memorial Hospital, 566 F.2d 749, 752 (D.C.Cir.1977).

intracordical blood clot See *clot, intracordical blood.*

intrahepatic (in"trah-hĕ-pat'ik) within the liver.

. . . she was instead suffering from an intra-hepatic obstruction, hepatitis induced by a drug named Thorazine. Brown v. City of N.Y., 405 N.Y.S.2d 253–4 (1st Dep't 1978).

intramedullary (in"trah-med'u-lăr"e) within the marrow cavity of a bone. See also *rod, Hansen-Street intramedullary.*

An intermedullary rod was inserted in the left leg. Following reduction of the fractures, full leg casts were applied to both legs. Borowski v. Von Solbrig, 328 N.E.2d 301, 304 (Ill.1975).

intramuscular (in"trah-mus'ku-lar) [*intra-* + L. *musculus* muscle] within the substance of a muscle. Cited in Daniels v. Hadley Memorial Hospital, 566 F.2d 749, 752 (D.C.Cir.1977).

intraoral (in"trah-o'ral) within the mouth.

". . . I performed an intra-oral X-ray series," revealing severe recurrent caries in six designated teeth, a post perforation/root fracture in one tooth "rendering a hopeless prognosis for that tooth and probable root perforation in [another] tooth," . . . Jobson v. Dooley, 296 S.E.2d 388, 390 (Ct.App.Ga. 1982).

intrauterine device See *device, intrauterine (IUD).*

intrauterine growth retarded baby See *baby, intrauterine growth retarded.*

intravenous (in"trah-ve'nus) within a vein or veins. Cited in Daniels v. Hadley Memorial Hospital, 566 F.2d 749, 752 (D.C.Cir.1977).

introcele

. . . an introcele, a protrusion of the bowel from the peritoneal cavity into the vagina. Kerbeck v. Suchy, 270 N.E.2d 291–2 (App.Ct.Ill.1971).

introitus (in-tro'ĭ-tus), pl. *intro'itus* [L., from *intro* within + *ire* to go] [NA] a general term for the entrance to a cavity or space.

In the area where she had the laceration, the lacerations are categorized by degrees. And this child had a second degree laceration of the vagina and perineum, meaning that it extended through the vaginal mucose, through the introitus, which is the opening in the vagina, and down to but not through the anal sphincter. Hester v. State, 310 So.2d 455–6 (Dist.Ct. App.Fla.1975).

introitus, marital

. . . he came to the conclusion that Barbara has, what he would call, a marital introitus which he said, would mean, there had been sexual intercourse." People v. McGillen, 220 N.W.2d 689, 693 (Mich.1974).

introtus vaginae See *ostium vaginae.*

intubation (in"tu-ba'shun) [L. *in* into + *tuba* tube] the insertion of a tube into a body canal or hollow organ, as into the trachea or stomach.

Intubation is a process by which a tube is inserted into a patient's trachea (windpipe) in order that the patient's airway remains open. Battles v. Aderhold, 430 So.2d 307, 309 (Ct.App. La.1983).

Intubation is the insertion of a breathing tube through a patient's mouth into the lungs which renders speech impossible. U.S. v. Narciso, 446 F.Supp. 252, 287 (E.D.Mich.1977).

Intubation is the insertion of a tube into the patient's nose or mouth for the dual purpose of administering anesthesia and/or assisting in respiration during surgery, should the latter become necessary. Chapman v. Argonaut-Southwest Insurance Co., 290 So.2d 779, 786 (Ct.App.La.1974).

Other Authorities: Ascher v. Gutierrez, 533 F.2d 1235–6 (D.C.Cir.1976).

intubation, endotracheal insertion of a tube into the trachea for administration of anesthesia, maintenance of an airway, aspiration of secretions, ventilation of the lungs, or prevention of entrance of foreign material into the tracheobronchial tree.

intubation, nasal insertion of a tube into the respiratory or gastrointestinal tract through the nose.

While Dr. Faber had been working on the incision, a Major Least, a nurse-anesthetist who had responded to the Core 0, had performed a nasal intubation, that is, passing an endotracheal tube through the nose. Marek v. U.S., 639 F.2d 1164, 1166 (5th Cir. 1981).

intussusception (in"tus-sus-sep'shun) [L. *intus* within + *suscipere* to receive] a receiving within; specifically: (1) the prolapse of one part of the intestine into the lumen of an immediately adjoining part (Treves, 1899). There are four varieties: *colic*, involving segments of the large intestine; *enteric*, involving only the small intestine; *ileocecal*, in which the ileocecal valve prolapses into the cecum, drawing the ileum along with it; and *ileocolic*, in which the ileum prolapses through the ileocecal valve into the colon. (2) In physiology, the reception into an organism of matter, such as food, and its transformation into new protoplasm.

A mass seemed to be present in the child's abdomen, and a possible bowel blockage by **intussusception**[1] was diagnosed.... [[1] A blockage caused by a telescoping of the bowel or intestine.]

On Sunday morning, Kyle's condition became worse, and at noon Dr. Rice operated. He found a bowel blockage by **intussusception** with about six inches of intestine gangrenous, which he removed and then rejoined the bowel. Kyle's post-operative recovery appeared to be normal, and his parents went home, but were called back when the child's temperature became extremely high due to the gangrene. As a result, Kyle suffered permanent and irreversible brain damage and is now totally disabled. Kern v. St. Luke's Hospital Ass'n of Saginaw, 273 N.W.2d 75, 77–8 (Mich.1978).

invasion (in-va'zhun) [L. *invasio; in* into + *vadere* to go] the infiltration and active destruction of surrounding tissue, a characteristic of malignant tumors.

The objective evidence Velsicol charges is lacking is evidence that the tumors induced during the feeding studies had properties of **invasion** (spreading of a tumor into adjacent tissues). Environmental Defense Fund, Inc. v. E.P.A., 548 F.2d 998, 1007 (D.C.Cir.1976).

invasive (in-va'siv) 1. having the quality of invasiveness. 2. involving puncture or incision of the skin or insertion of an instrument or foreign material into the body; said of diagnostic techniques.

The Pathology Department of the University of Minnesota Hospitals thereupon performed a biopsy which revealed an "in situ" carcinoma of the cervix about one millimeter in size. The hospital's gynecology department, however, diagnosed the carcinoma as "early **invasive.**" Ray v. Wagner, 176 N.W.2d 101–2 (Minn.1970).

invasiveness (in-va'siv-nes) 1. the ability of a microorganism to enter the body and to spread more or less widely throughout the tissues; the organism may or may not cause an infection or a disease. 2. the ability to infiltrate and actively destroy surrounding tissue; said of malignant tumors.

in vitro (in ve'tro) [L.] within a glass; observable in a test tube; in an artificial environment. See also *in vivo*.

I told him this device had not been used in human beings; that it had been used in the laboratory; that we had been able to sustain the circulation in calves and that it had not been used in human beings. It had been used on the bench in what we call **in vitro** experiments, **in vitro** as opposed to in vivo. In vivo means using it in live or experimental animals. **In vitro** means using it in

Schema for an intussusception: *A*, intussuscipiens; *B*, entering layer; *C*, intussusceptum (Stevens).

some type of testing device where you test the hydraulic factors concerned with the pump. I told him it had been tested in the laboratory, it had not been used in a human being, but I was confident that it would support his circulation.... Karp v. Cooley, 493 F.2d 408, 414 (5th Cir. 1974).

Other Authorities: Pfizer, Inc. v. International Rectifier Corp., 538 F.2d 180, 190 (8th Cir. 1976).

in vitro fertilization See *fertilization, in vitro.*

in vivo (in ve'vo) [L.] within the living body. See also *in vitro.*

Pfizer responds that doxycycline is vastly superior to the McCormick compound in antibacterial activity against most organisms both **in vitro** (in test tubes) and **in vivo** (in experiments on animals). Pfizer, Inc. v. International Rectifier Corp., 538 F.2d 180, 190 (8th Cir. 1976).

In vivo means using it in live or experimental animals. Karp v. Cooley, 493 F.2d 408, 414 (5th Cir. 1974).

ion (i'on) [Gr. *ion* going] an atom or radical having a charge of positive (cation) or negative (anion) electricity owing to the loss (positive) or gain (negative) of one or more electrons. Substances that form ions are called electrolytes. See also *ionic theory*, under *theory.*

involuntary (in-vol'un-ter"e) [L. *involuntarius; in* against + *voluntas* will] performed independently of the will; contravolitional. See also *voluntary* (U.S. ex rel. Townsend case).

An act is "**involuntary**", then, where the actor's body is moved by overmastering physical force (vis absoluta) or where the actor's movements are a reflex or convulsion, or are performed during unconsciousness, sleep, or hypnosis....

... Thus, for example, if a prisoner has an epileptic fit during which he falls over the prison wall, ...

The second way in which the term "voluntary" is used refers to exercise of the free will, rather than mere exercise of the will. In this context, an act is said to be "**involuntary**" where the will of an actor is subject to such coercive pressure (vis compulsiva) that it is overborne, and the actor—"against his own will"—chooses to violate the law rather than obey it. Thus, for example, if a prisoner is forced at gunpoint to walk out of prison "against his own will", then he has not acted "voluntarily". U.S. v. Bailey, 585 F.2d 1087, 1118 (D.C.Cir. 1978).

ion, carbonium

Carbonium Ion: An organic ion carrying a positive charge at a carbon location owing to an electron deficiency, i.e., the presence of an extra proton. Ritter v. Rohm & Haas Co., 271 F.Supp. 313 (S.D.N.Y.1967).

iophendylate (i"o-fen'dĭ-lāt) [USP] chemical name: iodo-ι-methylbenzene decanoic acid. A radiopaque medium, $C_{19}H_{29}IO_2$, occurring as a colorless to pale yellow, viscous liquid; used in myelography, administered intrathecally or by special injection. See also *paraplegia* (Swan case).

The myelogram was done with a contrast medium known as **Pantopaque**....

... Shortly thereafter, she visited Dr. Butler and asked him if she had a claim against anyone. He replied no, that "there is always some [**Pantopaque**] left after a myelogram and there are thousands of people walking around with it in their bodies with no complaints".... Fidler v. Eastman Kodak Co., 714 F.2d 192, 194–5 (1st Cir. 1983).

... known retention of **pantopaque**, an iodized radiopaque contrast medium used in myelograms, in the plaintiff's lumbar sac: ... Tyminski v. U.S., 481 F.2d 257, 264 (3d Cir. 1973).

This diagnostic procedure involved the introduction of an iodized radiopaque contrast medium, called **pantopaque**, into plaintiff's spine by means of a lumbar puncture. As the dye circulated through the spinal fluid, X-rays scanned the spinal column. When the filming was completed, the table upon which the patient lay was tilted to permit the **pantopaque** to collect in the lumbar sac, from which, in the course of customary practice, the dye was then aspirated through a needle. In plaintiff's case, however, the **pantopaque** was not removed from the plaintiff's spine. Dr. Elliott attempted to withdraw the **pantopaque** but failed, and no further efforts were made to extract it....

... he asked Dr. Elliott whether the retained **pantopaque** might prove harmful. Dr. Elliott assured the plaintiff that **pantopaque** retention would not injure him, that "we normally leave it [the **pantopaque**] in; it's standard procedure in ... a lot of hospitals," that the dye would in time be absorbed and that the plaintiff "had nothing to worry about."...

... Dr. Strasser, X-rayed the plaintiff's skull and on March 7, 1964 he advised the plaintiff that **pantopaque** globules encysted on brain tissues were the primary cause of his illness. Toal v. U.S., 438 F.2d 222–4 (2d Cir. 1971).

IPPB intermittent positive pressure breathing. See also under *breathing*.

I.Q. (intelligence quotient) See under *quotient*.

iridectomy (ir"ĭ-dek'to-me) [*irid-* + Gr. *ektomē* excision] surgical excision of part of the iris; called also *corectomy*.

... and performed further surgery on the left eye for removal of a cataract on October 12, 1966 (described as "a full **iridectomy** to complete the peripheral **iridectomy** that had been previously done ..."). The record of the cataract surgery describes certain steps taken "to continue the extraction of the lens." State Compensation Ins. Fund v. Workmen's Comp. App. Bd., 88 Cal.Rptr. 469, 471 (Ct.App.Cal.1970).

iridectomy, peripheral surgical excision of a peripheral portion of the iris.

A peripheral iridectomy was then performed, i.e., a small incision was made in the iris of the eye. This was done to prevent a form of secondary glaucoma. Sometimes it also effects a reduction of intraocular pressure. Miller v. Scholl, 594 S.W.2d 324, 327 (Mo.Ct.App.1980).

On August 7, 1962, surgery, **peripheral iridectomy** with scleral cautery was performed on the right eye. Her left eye was beyond redemption, and was enucleated in 1975 elsewhere. Wolfe v. Califano, 468 F.Supp. 1018, 1021 (W.D.Pa.1979).

iridocyclitis (ir"ĭ-do-si-kli'tis) [*irido-* + Gr. *kyklos* circle + *-itis*] inflammation of the iris and of the ciliary body; anterior uveitis.

Dr. Winter's initial diagnosis was that Mrs. Grill had **iridocyclitis**, which is an allergic condition, in this case causing an inflammation of the iris and ciliary body. Her loss of color vision in the left eye indicated to him a possible involvement of the optic nerve, because color vision fibers are very sensitive to inflammatory changes of that nerve. Grill v. U.S., 552 F.Supp. 505–6 (E.D.N.Y.1982).

iris (i'ris), pl. *ir'ides* [Gr. "rainbow," "halo"] 1. [NA] the circular pigmented membrane behind the cornea, perforated by the pupil; the most anterior portion of the vascular tunic of the eye, it is made up of a flat bar of circular muscular fibers surrounding the pupil, a thin layer of smooth muscle fibers by which the pupil is dilated, thus regulating the amount of light entering the eye, and posteriorly two layers of pigmented epithelial cells. 2. the rhizome of *Iris versicolor*, formerly used as a purgative, emetic, and diuretic.

iritis (i-ri'tis) [*iris* + *-itis*] inflammation of the iris, usually marked by pain, congestion in the ciliary region, photophobia, contraction of the pupil, and discoloration of the iris. See also *atropine* (Harris case).

As treatment for Ms. Harris' **iritis**, Dr. Groth prescribed topical corticosteroids (eyedrops) and systemic corticosteroids (pills). He also prescribed a drug called atropine in topical form. Ms. Harris claims that she faithfully took these medications at least through March 1977, though Dr. Groth claims she could not have continually taken the systemic corticosteroids during this period because she did not have enough prescribed. Harris v. Robert C. Groth, M.D., Inc., 663 P.2d 113–14 (Wash.1983).

He further said that both eyes suffered from **iritis**, a condition he characterized as an inflammation of the iris of the eye. Ex-

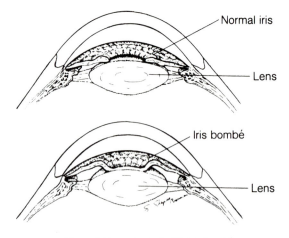

Normal iris contrasted with iris bombé.

celsior Leather Washer Co. v. Industrial Com'n, 297 N.E.2d 158, 160 (Ill.1973).

iron (i'ern) [A.S. *iren;* L. *ferrum*] a metallic element found in certain minerals, in nearly all soils, and in mineral waters: atomic number 26; atomic weight, 55.847; specific gravity, 7.85–7.88; symbol, Fe. Iron is an essential constituent of hemoglobin, cytochrome, and other components of respiratory enzyme systems. Its chief functions are in the transport of oxygen to tissues (hemoglobin) and in cellular oxidation mechanisms. Depletion of iron stores may result in iron-deficiency anemia (see under *anemia*). Iron is used to build up the blood in anemia. The compounds of iron are astringent and styptic.

An understanding of the function of **iron** in the human body and how it is lost is essential to an understanding of the issues in this case and the medical testimony relating to these issues.

The human body does not synthesize **iron**. Consequently, all **iron** in the human must come from outside sources, normally from food. The adult body will have an average of 2.6 grams of **iron** for a small woman, and six grams of **iron** for a large adult male. The daily amount of **iron** in the average American adult diet has been estimated at from 7 mg. to 15 mg. **Iron** is generally conserved and reutilized.

Approximately 70% of all the **iron** in the normal adult is in the circulating blood as a component of hemoglobin, the red material in the red blood cells. In the creation of hemoglobin, **iron** is an essential major constituent. Hemoglobin carries oxygen which is essential for the functioning of cells throughout the body.

A minute amount of **iron** (one mg. or less) is lost each day in the feces, sweat, and urine. Blood loss, either present or past, accounts for the major loss of **iron** in the body. In the male, this is usually due to severe nose bleeds, bleeding from the gums, peptic ulcer, cancer of the stomach, cancer of the bowels and hemorrhoids. In the woman, the major cause of **iron** loss occurs from bleeding during the menstrual period, and **iron** given to the fetus during pregnancy. Inadequacy of **iron** in the diet and malabsorption of **iron** account for only a small amount of **iron** loss. J. B. Williams Co. v. F.T.C., 381 F.2d 884, 887 (6th Cir. 1967).

irradiation (i-ra"de-a'shun) [L. *in* into + *radiare* to emit rays] treatment by photons, electrons, neutrons, or other ionizing radiations.

Dr. Allen concluded that "there was no significant exposure to radiation.... They had none of the symptoms that I could refer to radiation syndrome...." Dr. Allen was followed by an eye specialist, Dr. Goar. He testified that, because of their shape, he did not believe the "opacities" observed in the eyes of McVey and Northway were caused by **irradiation**. McVey v. Phillips Petroleum Co., 288 F.2d 53, 55 (5th Cir. 1961).

irrigation (ir"ĭ-ga'shun) [L. *irrigatio; in* into + *rigare* to carry water] 1. washing by a stream of water or other fluid. See also *lavage.* 2. a liquid used for irrigation.

irrigation, Ringer's [USP], a sterile solution containing, in each 100 ml., 820–900 mg. of sodium chloride, 25–35 mg. of potassium chloride, and 30–36 mg. of calcium chloride in water for injection; used as a topical physiological salt solution. Called also *Ringer's mixture* and *Ringer's solution.*

A 1000 c.c. lactated **ringer solution** was administered. This is a mixture of water and sodium and is used to expand the blood volume to prohibit shock. U.S. v. Choice, 392 F.Supp. 460–1 (E.D.Pa.1975).

irritability (ir"ĭ-tah-bil'ĭ-te) [L. *irritabilitas,* from *irritare* to tease] the quality of being irritable, or of responding to stimuli.

irritability, ventricular

Dr. Kritzer defined **ventricular irritability** as "skipped beats" which might occur with or without heart disease. Muznik v. Workers' Comp.App.Bd. of Cty. of Los Angeles, 124 Cal.Rptr. 407, 411 (Ct.App.Cal.1975).

irritant (ir'ĭ-tant) [L. *irritans*] an agent that produces irritation.

(8) "**Irritant**" means any substance not corrosive within the meaning of section 2(i) of the act [Consumer Product Safety Act 15 U.S.C. 2051–81] (restated in paragraph (b)(7) of this section) which on immediate, prolonged, or repeated contact with normal living tissue will induce a local inflammatory reaction. 16 C.F.R. § 1500.3(b)(8).

irritation (ir"ĭ-ta'shun) [L. *irritatio*] a state of overexcitation and undue sensitivity.

ischemia (is-ke'me-ah) [Gr. *ischein* to suppress + *haima* blood + *-ia*] deficiency of blood in a part, due to functional constriction or actual obstruction of a blood vessel.

Suddenly plaintiff became faint and pale, began to stutter badly, and asked for help. He could not stand or walk unassisted. McNabb tried to support him to the shop, but plaintiff's legs were giving out and he wanted to go in the wrong direction....

... The emergency room nurse called Dr. Looney, telling him only that a patient was there who had had a fainting spell, but that the patient was then all right. The doctor told the nurse to release him to go home. Minutes later, the nurse called Dr. Looney again, telling him that the patient was unable to move his arm and leg and was exhibiting facial weakness and slurred speech. The nurse felt these symptoms indicated a classic ischemic attack....

According to the medical testimony an **ischemia** occurs when there is insufficient oxygen to the brain. A transient attack will leave no damage because the oxygen supply has not been cut off long enough to cause damage. A person suffering a transient ischemic attack will be no worse off afterwards. Dr. Looney likened transient **ischemia** to angina pectoris. He said both were symptoms, transient **ischemia** manifesting itself in a temporary oxygen deficiency to the brain, caused by arteriosclerosis in the vessels leading to the brain and angina manifesting itself in temporary oxygen deficiency to the heart muscle, caused by arteriosclerosis in the vessels leading to the heart. Transient **ischemia** does not cause damage to the brain cells, and angina pectoris does not cause damage to heart muscle; hence, according to the medical testimony, the patient is no worse off after the attack than before. Daily v. Bechtel Power Corp., 420 So.2d 1337, 1339–40 (Ct.App.La.1982).

Following her discharge, an infection developed at the site of the incision in each toe resulting in further hospitalization. A debridement procedure followed, occasioning loss of tissue and some bone from both toes. Plaintiff characterizes this as an "amputation"—defendants look askance at such word with all its connotations and prefer to speak in terms of "partial loss." Antibiotics were first tried, but when it became apparent that they would not control the infection the doctor made the decision to debride the area. The medical term for plaintiff's condition following the surgery is **ischemia**. Brown v. St. John's Hospital, 367 N.E.2d 155–6 (App.Ct. of Ill.1977).

The occluded coronary artery mentioned above was not able to accommodate the full flow of blood which the heart was attempting to force through it, and a blood clot developed. This blood clot then moved about one centimeter from its point of origin and completely blocked off the left anterior descent coronary artery. This caused "**ischemia**", or general deprivation of blood supply throughout the heart, which in turn resulted in marked irritability of the heart muscle. This caused the heart to be erratic in its rhythm. The onset of this abnormal rhythm was accompanied by a feeling of dizziness; within a few minutes the abnormal rhythm caused the heart to stop beating and death resulted. Watkins v. Underwriters at Lloyd's London, 481 P.2d 849, 852 (Ariz.1971).

Other Authorities: Ward v. Kovacs, 390 N.Y.S.2d 931, 934 (2d Dep't 1977); Com'l Standard Fire & Marine Co. v. Thornton, 540 S.W.2d 521–2 (Ct.Civ.App.Tex.1976); Hartford Acc. & Indem. Co. v. Thurmond, 527 S.W.2d 180, 186 (Ct.Civ.App. Tex.1975).

ischemia, myocardial deficiency of blood supply to the heart muscle, due to obstruction or constriction of the coronary arteries.

Plaintiffs' evidence tended to show that decedent had been hospitalized in 1975 for an acute myocardial infarction (a heart attack), and that he was diagnosed as suffering from **myocardial ischemia**, or transient decreased blood flow to the heart muscle. Bingham v. Smith's Transfer Corp., 286 S.E.2d 570–1 (Ct.App.N.Car.1982).

In 1974 a stress test revealed that he suffered from **ischemic heart disease**, a shortage of blood to the heart caused by a buildup of atherosclerotic plaque within the coronary arteries. Doyle v. Industrial Com'n, 427 N.E.2d 1223–4 (Ill.1981).

On April 1, 1965, in a regular visit to the Clinic an electrocardiogram was taken by Dr. Levitt which pictured an atypical T-wave pattern, indicating an insufficient supply of blood to the heart (**myocardial ischium**) due to narrowing of the coronary arteries caused by arteriosclerosis. Brown v. U.S., 419 F.2d 337–8 (8th Cir. 1969).

Other Authorities: Todd Shipyards Corp. v. Donovan, 300 F.2d 741, 744 (5th Cir. 1962).

ischemia, subendocardial See *subendocardial; endocardium.*

... he may have some degree of muscle damage that's not measured, that can't be measured, so-called "**subendocardial ischemia**." This, of course, he could have death to a small amount of muscle and not be reflected either in electrocardiograms and/or serum enzyme studies, which is the means that we have of detecting any serious muscle damage. Hartford Acc. & Indem. Co. v. Thurmond, 527 S.W.2d 180, 187 (Ct.Civ. App.Tex.1975).

ischemic (is-kem'ik) pertaining to, or affected with, ischemia.

ischemic bowel disease See *disease, ischemic bowel.*

ischemic contracture syndrome See *contracture, Volkmann's.*

ischemic heart disease See *ischemia, myocardial.*

isobutyl acrylate

Isobutyl acrylate is an industrial chemical used in the manufacture of plastics, latex paints, synthetic rubber, lacquer, and varnish. It is a highly reactive substance, readily reacting with amines, fats, and proteins, and will react with itself unless accompanied by an inhibitor during shipment. It is strong smelling and is known to cause burning and itching of the eyes, nose, and throat, but because it is not easily soluble in body fluids it does not readily penetrate the skin layers or other tissues. R.Vol. III, 486....

... While in the hold, the plaintiff inhaled **IBA** fumes and the liquid splashed upon his clothing. The plaintiff experienced burning and stinging of the eyes and skin, as well as a sore throat and a headache....

... During the ensuing five or six weeks, the plaintiff remained on the job but experienced a worsening condition of shortness of breath, itching and burning of the skin, and headaches. He then became seriously ill and is now totally disabled....

... In particular, Dr. Mailman testified concerning the thin and fragile nature of lung tissue and the effect upon the respiratory system which may result when **IBA** reacts with the proteins, fats, and amines found in the cells which comprise the lung. Basically, the testimony reveals that inhalation of **IBA** may destroy the structural integrity of the cell membrane, causing the cell to die. He concluded that such reaction will produce scar or fibrous tissue and the resulting symptoms exhibited by the plaintiff....

... Comstock testified that **IBA** may pass through skin tissue and pass to the lungs, a target area for toxic substances....

... The testimony of Dr. Mailman that **IBA** is more toxic than butyl acrylate, referred to above as capable of causing "serious systemic injury, even death," was uncontradicted. Supp.R. Vol. II, 508–509. Harrison v. Flota Mercante Grancolombiana, S.A., 577 F.2d 968, 972, 974–5, 978 (5th Cir. 1978).

isocyanate See *asthma, isocyanate; isocyanide.*

... claimant breathed fumes at his place of employment containing **isocyanates**, a substance in paint hardening compounds used in acrylic enamel paint. As a result, claimant experienced respiratory problems and on January 4, 1977, claimant experienced a serious episode of bronchospasm which resulted in his total incapacity to work. Therefore, the judge found that claimant sustained injury by accident on January 4, 1977; that the inhalation of the **isocyanates** aggravated claimant's pulmonary disease; and that the fume inhalation at work was a substantive contributing cause of claimant's total disability. Thornton Chevrolet, Inc. v. Morgan, 252 S.E.2d 178 (App.Ct.Ga.1979).

isocyanide (i"so-si'ah-nīd) one of a class of organic cyanides characterized by their disagreeable odor and formed by heating silver cyanide with alkyl iodides; called also *carbylamine.*

isoerythrolysis, neonatal

The evidence shows instances where package inserts for Anaplaz were amended to include a warning of a possibility of **neonatal isoerythrolysis (NI)** in calves through the use of Anaplaz, and a notice that it could be used only on order of a licensed veterinarian. Haste v. American Home Products Corp., 577 F.2d 1122–3 (10th Cir. 1978).

Necropsies were performed by Dr. Stuart Nelson, DVM, Dr. Loren D. Kintner, and Dr. Charles Counts, DVM, each of them finding the animals in an extremely yellow and jaundice condition. The calves were diagnosed as having **neonatal isoerytholysis ("NI")**, a form of hemolytic anemia.

Neonatal isoerytholysis can result under the following set of circumstances: A red blood cell antigen must be introduced into the dam or brood cow and that cow's system must produce antibodies to such antigen. If a cow is then bred to a bull having a blood characteristic similar to such antigen and if the cow has made antibodies to combat such antigen, and if at the time of birth the calf has inherited the bull's blood characteristics, then, when the calf sucks the cow's colostrum, the colostrum or first milk will convey the hostile antibodies to the calf. These antibodies will attack the calf's red blood cells and produce **neonatal isoerytholysis**, which is the lysing of the red blood cells. Waller v. Fort Dodge Laboratories, 356 F.Supp. 413–14 (E.D.Mo.1972).

isolation perfusion process See *perfusion.*

isolette See *incubator.*

From the moment of their birth they were dangerously ill. Their pediatrician, fearful for their lives, immediately ordered that they be placed in an **isolette**, a type of incubator, and that oxygen be administered to them. His written orders were to the effect that the infants should receive oxygen at the rate of 6 liters per minute for the first 12 hours and thereafter at the rate of 4 liters per minute.[1] [[1] Six liters per minute meant that the atmosphere in the isolette consisted approximately of 50–60% oxygen. At 4 liters per minute, the oxygen concentration would be about 30–40%.] Toth v. Community Hospital at Glen Cove, 239 N.E.2d 368, 370 (N.Y.1968).

isomer (i'so-mer) [*iso-* + Gr. *meros* part] any compound exhibiting, or capable of exhibiting, isomerism. An isomer may be structural or stereochemical. See also *isomerism.*

The first D.E.A. expert to testify defined an "**isomer**" of a substance as "anything that has the same empirical formula." The record demonstrates that cocaine compound may exist in as many as eight molecular arrangements but each one is isomeric to the others. There can be no doubt that the substance involved in the present case is derived from coca leaves and falls within the statutory definition. See United States v. Fince, 670 F.2d 1356 (4th Cir. 1982); United States v. Ortiz, 610 F.2d 280 (5th Cir. 1980); United States v. Orzechowski, 547 F.2d 978 (7th Cir. 1976). U.S. v. Kolenda, 697 F.2d 149–50 (6th Cir. 1983).

On cross-examination, Medina stated that cocaine, like most organic compounds, has many "**isomers**." **Isomers** are two or more compounds which have the same molecular formula but different molecular structures. The variations in structure may give rise to different chemical characteristics. U.S. v. Hall, 552 F.2d 273–4 (9th Cir. 1977).

Isomers are related compounds that have the same molecular formula but different three dimensional structures. GAF Corp. v. Amchem Products, Inc., 399 F.Supp. 647, 651 (E.D.Pa. 1975), reversed and remanded 570 F.2d 457 (3d Cir. 1978).

Other Authorities: Monsanto Co. v. Rohm & Haas Co., 456 F.2d 592, 596 (3d Cir. 1972).

isomerase (i-som'er-ās) a major class of enzymes comprising those that catalyze the process of isomerization, such as the interconversion of aldoses and ketoses, or the shift of a double bond, e.g., 3-ketosteroid-Δ^4,Δ^5-isomerase.

isomerase, xylose an enzyme that catalyzes the aldose-ketose interconversion of D-xylose to D-xylulose.

One enzyme which had received special attention was "**xylose isomerase**"—that is, the enzyme known to be capable of converting the sugar called "xylose" into its sweeter relative "xylulose." CPC International, Inc. v. Standard Brands Inc., 385 F.Supp. 1057–8 (D.Del.1974).

isomerism (i-som'ĕ-rizm) [*iso-* + Gr. *meros* part] the possession by two or more distinct compounds of the same molecular formula, each molecule possessing an identical number of atoms of each element, but in different arrangement. Isomerism is divided into two broad classifications: *structural isomerism* and *stereochemical isomerism,* or *stereoisomerism.*

isomerism, structural the possession by two or more compounds of the same molecular formula but of different structural formulas, the linkages of the atoms being different, in contrast to stereoisomerism, in which the structural arrangements of the atoms are the same.

isometric exercise See *exercise, isometric.*

isoniazid (i"so-ni'ah-zid) [USP] chemical name: 4-pyridinecarboxylic acid hydrazide. An antibacterial, $C_6H_7N_3O$, occurring as colorless or white crystals or white, crystalline powder; used as a tuberculostatic, administered orally and intramuscularly.

The program involved Mr. Santoni's taking the drug **isoniazid** (INH) daily in pill form. This drug has been used widely in the treatment and prevention of tuberculosis....

... Soon after he began taking the pills, he started to experience fatigue and decreased appetite. Then he noted fullness, abdominal discomfort, and increased flatulence. Then he could not tolerate fatty foods, his stools became lighter, his urine became darker, and he began to feel very tired....

... Despite excellent hospital treatment and no complications, Mr. Santoni died on July 3, 1972, of hepatitis, caused by a toxic reaction to **isoniazid**. Santoni v. Moodie, 452 A.2d 1223, 1225 (Ct.Spec.App.Md.1982).

For purposes of preventative therapy he was placed on the drug known as **Isoniazid** (INH), which had been widely used for a number of years for the prevention and treatment of tuberculosis. However, there came a time when the United States Public Health Service had some doubts relative to the safety of the drug. It believed that **INH** might be a cause of hepatitis. Moodie v. Santoni, 441 A.2d 323–4 (Ct.App.Md.1982).

Isoniazid is a well-known prescription drug used worldwide for many years in the treatment of tuberculosis. Its relative safety and effectiveness had, of course, been documented under the Federal Food, Drug, and Cosmetic Act, see 21 U.S.C. § 355, by another company which sponsored the drug....

Decedent was administered **isoniazid** over a period of 18 months by a V.A. hospital. As a result she developed liver ailments, hepatitis and cirrhosis, which eventually caused her death....

... The uncontested fact is that the danger of liver damage and hepatitis was generally known and identified, and that decedent fell victim to this previously established side effect of the drug.

It is also clear that the warning given by Xttrium was adequate. Where prescription drugs are involved the manufacturer's duty to warn is limited to advising physicians of any potential danger. Brick v. Barnes-Hines Pharmaceutical Co., Inc., 428 F.Supp. 496–7 (D.C.Cir.1977).

Other Authorities: Plummer v. U.S., 420 F.Supp. 978, 980–1 (M.D.Pa.1976); Prudential Ins. Co. of America v. Beaty, 456 S.W.2d 164, 169 (Ct.Civ.App.Tex.1970).

isoproterenol (i″so-pro″tĕ-re′nol) chemical name: 4-[1-hydroxy-2-[(1-methylethyl)amino]ethyl]-1,2-benzenediol. A synthetic adrenergic, $C_{11}H_{17}NO_3$, derived from norepinephrine, having powerful bronchodilator and cardiac stimulant actions.

Dr. Katz, Chairman of the Mt. Sinai Department of Anesthesia, who was on duty as a circulator to respond to emergencies, immediately recognized the bronchospasm and promptly administered an ampule of **isuprel**, a drug which relaxes the involuntary muscles of the body including those that constrict the breathing passages. He injected **isuprel** twice the strength of a normal dose. Shortly afterwards, Siegel's bronchospasm was broken and his respiration and pulse returned. Siegel v. Mt. Sinai Hospital of Cleveland, 403 N.E.2d 202, 206 (Ct.App. Ohio 1978).

Isuprel (i′su-prel) trademark for a preparation of isoproterenol. See also *isoproternol.*

isopto-carpine See *atropine* (Harris case).

itching (ich′ing) an unpleasant cutaneous sensation that provokes the desire to scratch or rub the skin. A symptom in various skin diseases, it may also occur idiopathically. Called also *pruritus.*

The uncontradicted testimony of plaintiff and the lay witnesses is exactly that of Dr. Delgado, who testified that the constant **itching** which Whitaker experiences is characteristic of keloid scars.... Whitaker v. Church's Fried Chicken, Inc., 387 So.2d 1093, 1096 (La.1980).

IUD intrauterine contraceptive device.

IUGR See *baby, intrauterine growth retarded.*

IVP See *pyelography, intravenous.*

J

Jacksonian seizure See *epilepsy, jacksonian.*

jar (jar) a wide-mouthed, glass or earthenware container.

jar, Coplin

The **Coplin** jar, which has been used in the field of microbiology for many years prior to the filing of the application for the '859 patent, is used for staining of specimens, such as sputum or tissue sections, which are on microscope slides. Inside the jar, which may be of square configuration, are opposing slots in which the slides are seated so as to prevent the faces of the slides bearing the specimens from touching each other. Fink v. Smithkline Corp., 186 U.S.P.Q. 262, 268 (N.D.Cal.1975).

jaundice (jawn′dis) [Fr. *jaunisse,* from *jaune* yellow] a syndrome characterized by hyperbilirubinemia and deposition of bile pigment in the skin, mucous membranes and sclera with resulting yellow appearance of the patient; called also *icterus.*

Mrs. Cornfeldt's recovery appeared to be going well, but after a few days **jaundice** was evident in her eyes and skin. By July 31, after a series of tests performed the day before, it was clear that her liver was seriously malfunctioning, and Dr. Alfonzo A. Belsito, a gastroenterologist specializing in liver disorders, was called in. On August 1, Mrs. Cornfeldt was transferred to University of Minnesota Hospitals, where desperate measures, including a liver transplant, were unsuccessfully taken. Mrs. Cornfeldt died from hepatitis on September 20, 1973. Cornfeldt v. Tongen, 262 N.W.2d 684, 691 (Minn. 1977).

The most obvious physical finding he observed was that Rivas was deeply **jaundiced**. Rivas also had a distended gall bladder. **Jaundiced** means a yellowish tint to the skin and mucous membranes due to the retention of a high level of a substance called bilirubin....

... **Jaundice** can be caused by the absorption of blood into the system and can also be precipitated by a head injury or shock. It was his opinion that the accident of May 25, 1969 was a producing cause, or a contributing cause of Rivas' death. He concurred with Dr. Caballero's opinion that a stone in the cystic duct will not cause **jaundice**. Rivas v. United States Fire Insurance Co., 470 S.W.2d 249, 253 (Ct.Civ.App.Tex. 1971).

jaundice, obstructive that which is due to an impediment to the flow of the bile from the liver cells to the duodenum.

Dr. Warden felt that Rivas was suffering from an **obstructive jaundice**. He explained that the liver produces bile which is then concentrated by the gall bladder and subsequently flows into the duodenum to serve its function in the digestion of food. If the bile duct is pinched off between its point of origin in the liver and where it empties into the gall bladder the bile cannot get out of the liver and it then flows back into the blood, causing jaundice. Rivas v. United States Fire Insurance Co., 470 S.W.2d 249–50 (Ct.Civ.App.Tex.1971).

jaundice, pathologic See *kernicterus*.

Pathologic jaundice deposits bile pigments in the brain stem, causing brain damage known as kernicterus. Michele Neyland has kernicterus....

... When the child was six months old she had a seizure in Dr. Price's office, in his presence. Yet the mother was still not advised that her child was suffering from brain damage which would make her a hopeless cripple and limit her life span to five to ten years....

... The recognized treatment for **pathologic jaundice** in this area was in 1953, and is now, an exchange transfusion in which the blood of the baby is replaced with healthy blood. While the incidence of mortality in such operations was, in 1953, ten per cent, the alternative is paralyzing brain damage and early death, and the recognized medical practice at that time, as now, was to undertake the exchange transfusion. Price v. Neyland, 320 F.2d 674, 676–7 (D.C.Cir.1963).

jaundice, physiologic mild icterus neonatorum lasting the first few days after birth.

There are, however, two types of jaundice, physiologic and pathologic. **Physiologic jaundice** is benign and common in normal babies. Price v. Neyland, 320 F.2d 674, 676 (D.C.Cir. 1963).

jaw (jaw) either of the two bony structures (mandible and maxilla) in the head of vertebrates, bearing the teeth (in dentate species) and enabling carnivores to seize their prey and others to bite and chew food. See also *condylectomy* (Campbell case); *mandibula; maxilla*.

As a proximate result of the accident in question, plaintiff Petersen suffered three fractures to his **jaw**, i.e., fracture of the mandible symphysis, fracture of the right condyle mandible and fracture of the left condyle mandible. In addition, he suffered a laceration of the left auditory canal and a small chin laceration.

After appropriate treatment, Petersen has regained the normal use of his **jaw** for the purposes of eating, speaking and appearance. **Jaw** movement or mobility, however, has not been completely restored. Forward protrusion of the lower **jaw** has been impaired. Lateral movement of the **jaw** is not equal as a result of a restriction on movement to the right side. Petersen v. Head Construction Co., 367 F.Supp. 1072, 1077 (D.D.C.1973).

Part of the lower right **jaw** has been removed and the upper **jaw** bone is exposed. All of his teeth on the lower right **jaw** have been removed. He can't go out to dinner because "I'm messy, trying to get it stuffed in the hole. I can't drink anything unless it's through a straw. I don't have any teeth on this side. I only chew on this side. It takes me three times as long to eat as what it does a normal person." The lack of soft tissue and gum tissue causes poor nutrition and pieces of bone from the upper right **jaw** will continue to slough out. Gorsalitz v. Olin Mathieson Chemical Corp., 429 F.2d 1033, 1044 (5th Cir. 1970).

jaw [fracture]

Appellant testified that she kept a dental appointment with appellee for the purpose of having the wisdom tooth pulled. At the end of an unusually prolonged and apparently difficult extraction, in the course of which appellee assertedly exhibited signs of growing impatience and frustration, appellant sensed a snapping sound in her **jaw**.[1] [[1] Appellant's testimony was that, as the extraction effort proceeded, appellee remarked that it was giving him the most difficulty he had had "in forty years." She also said that, as time wore on into the second hour, appellee was "getting impatient," "more and more upset," "excited, heated," "red in the face," and "breathing heavily." When the tooth finally came out, she "felt as though my ear had been wrenched out;" and appellee characterized the tooth as "really a monster." Appellant then "heard a crack, and I looked up and I realized [appellee] was bending over me, and I said 'Doctor, what was that?' and he said, 'I don't know.' "] Raza v. Sullivan, 432 F.2d 617–18 (D.C.Cir. 1970).

jawbone, lower See *mandibula*.

jejuno See *jejunum*.

jejunostomy (jě"joo-nos'to-me) [*jejuno-* + Gr. *stomoun* to provide with an opening, or mouth] the surgical creation of a permanent opening between the jejunum and the surface of the abdominal wall; also, the opening so established.

jejunostomy, feeding

Later, a second surgical procedure was performed, called a "feeding jejunostomy," by which a tube was placed into the small bowel below where the leakage was occurring so that he could be fed. Insurance Co. of North America v. Stroburg, 456 S.W.2d 402, 409 (Ct.Civ.App.Tex.1970), reversed and remanded 464 S.W.2d 827 (Tex.1971).

jejunum (jě-joo'num) [L. "empty"] [NA] that portion of the small intestine which extends from the duodenum to the ileum; called also *intestinum jejunum*.

... this person underwent an operation for a **jejuno-ileal bypass** in order to help her reduce her weight which at the time was over two hundred pounds. The operation procedure was a success and the patient has responded favorably to weight reduction type diet. Dean v. Califano, 439 F.Supp. 730, 732 (W.D.Ark.1977).

jerk (jerk) a sudden reflex or involuntary movement.

jerk, triceps surae a twitchlike contraction of the triceps surae muscle, elicited by sharply tapping the muscle or the Achilles tendon; called also *ankle jerk*.

The **Achilles reflex** on the right was normal, but was absent on the left, which indicated severe nerve root involvement of the left lower extremity. Consolidated Freightways, Inc. v. Industrial Com'n, 356 N.E.2d 51, 53 (Ill.1976).

Jewitt brace See *brace, Jewitt*.

Jewett nail (joo'et) [Eugene Lyon *Jewett*, American surgeon, born 1900] see under *nail, Jewett*.

jock itch See *tinea cruris*.

Jockex See *antifungal* (Pennwalt case).

joint (joint) [L. *junctio* a joining, connection] an articulation: the place of union or junction between two or more bones of the skeleton, especially a junction that admits of more or less motion of one or more bones. See also *articulatio; junctura.*

joint, facet the articulations of the vertebral column.

I think Mr. Jones's injury caused injury to these lower **facet joints** as well as probably some disruption in the cartlidaginous [sic] junction at his spondylolysis. His injury therefore, not only brought about new facet injury, but aggravated the preexisting condition of his spondylolysis. Jones v. North Dakota Workmen's Comp. Bureau, N.D., 334 N.W.2d 188, 190 (N.Dak. 1983).

joint, hip the joint formed at the head of the femur and the acetabulum of the hip bone; called also *articulatio coxae* [NA] and *articulation of the hip.* Loosely called *hip.*

In the case of the **hip joint**, the most common type of externally-caused trauma or injury resulting in reduced blood supply to the bones of the hip joint is a protracted stretch through the capsula of the **hip joint**, otherwise described as a strain through the groin or **hip joint**....

... X-rays constitute the only means other than radio isotopes by which a physician can determine with certainty whether a vascular condition exists in a **hip joint**. (N.T. 246.)

Rosario v. American Export—Isbrandtsen Lines, Inc., 395 F.Supp. 1192, 1202 (E.D.Pa.1974), reversed and remanded 531 F.2d 1227 (3d Cir. 1978).

joint, temporomandibular See *mandibula.*

A blunt injury even to the chin may be transmitted to the brain because the mandible is connected to the skull by means of the **temporomandibular joint**, which is one of the sidewalls of the brain cavity. Walker v. Maxwell City, Inc., 453 N.E.2d 917, 920 (App.Ct.Ill.1983).

On December 6, 1969, she returned there, complaining of pain over both **temporomandibular joints**. (These connect the lower jaw to the temporal bone [skull] and are similar to a ball and socket.) Rosario v. New York City Health & Hospitals, 450 N.Y.S.2d 805–6 (1st Dep't 1982).

junction (junk'shun) the place of meeting or of coming together, as of two different organs or types of tissue. See also *joint; junctura.*

junctura (junk-tu'rah), pl. *junctu'rae* [L. "a joining"] a general term used in anatomical nomenclature to designate the site of union between different structures. See also *articulatio; joint.*

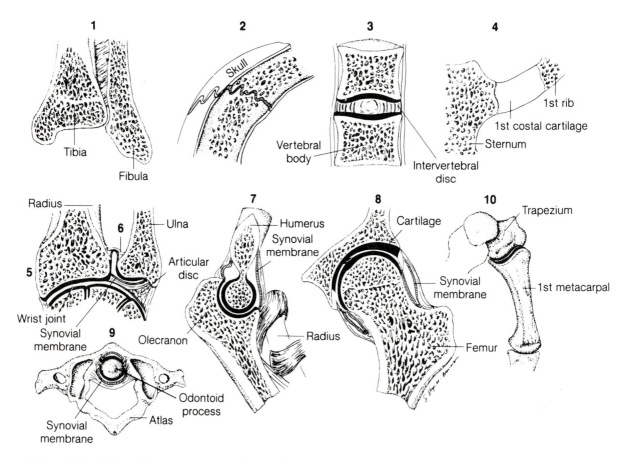

Various kinds of joints: *Fibrous*—1. syndesmosis (tibiofibular). 2. suture (skull). *Cartilaginous*—3. symphysis (vertebral bodies). 4. synchondrosis (1st rib and sternum). *Synovial*—5. condyloid (wrist). 6. gliding (radioulnar). 7. Hinge or ginglymus (elbow). 8. Ball and socket (hip). 9. Pivot (atlanto-axial). 10. Saddle (carpometacarpal of thumb).

junctura, cervicothoracic

The technicians tried to obtain a picture of plaintiff's **cervicothoracic junction**, the point at which the cervical and thoracic portions of the spine join, by a cervical lateral film and six or seven "swimmer's views." The technicians changed their technique on approach from film to film in order to get a clear picture.

"Q. Were you concerned then in any way about a possible fracture in the C–7/T–1 area?

"A. Well, not per se. The clinical symptoms didn't point to that. The clinical symptoms that he had would have pointed to a lesion, as I said, somewhere from about D–10 centrally towards the skull and could have been anywhere from there on up. We did not see, as everyone I'm sure has heard endlessly, the entirety of his cervical-thoracic spine on x-ray to our satisfaction in that first set of several days of x-rays. But there was no more reason to suspect a lesion there than there might have been in other areas, no more clinical reason, excuse me."

Nevertheless, plaintiff had a fracture at the cervical thoracic junction resulting from the fall and when he was dangled the fracture compressed the spinal cord, paralyzing plaintiff from the shoulders down. Simpson v. Sisters of Charity of Providence, etc., 588 P.2d 4, 7–8 (Or. 1978).

Juri-flap procedure See *procedure, Juri-flap.*

K

K

The designation "K" derives from the "keratometer," an instrument used to measure the curvature of the central or optical zone of the cornea. Accordingly, a lens is said to be "on K", "flatter than K" or "steeper than K" depending on whether the radius of curvature of the lens corresponds to, is greater than, or is less than the central corneal curve of the eye in question. Butterfield v. Oculus Contact Lens Co., 332 F.Supp. 750, 754 (N.D.Ill.1971).

kanamycin (kan"ah-mi'sin) chemical name; *O*-3-amino-3-deoxy-α-D-glucopyranosyl-(1 → 6)-*O*-[6-amino-6-deoxy-α-D-glucopyranosyl-(1 → 4)]-2-deoxy-D-streptamine. A water-soluble antibiotic derived from *Streptomyces kanamyceticus,* first isolated in Japan in 1957; it is effective against some gram-positive, many gram-negative, and some acid-fast bacteria.

Both **Kanamycin** and **Garamycin** belong to a class of drugs known as Aminoglycosides and are effective in combating gram-negative infections. Both are broad spectrum bacterial agents, and both are eliminated through the kidneys. **Garamycin** and **Kanamycin** are potentially ototoxic (affecting hearing and/or balance) and nephrotoxic (affecting the kidneys). Schering Corp. v. Giesecke, 589 S.W.2d 516, 518 (Ct. Civ.App.Tex.1979).

kanamycin, sulfate [USP], the sulfate salt of kanamycin, $C_{18}H_{36}N_4O_{11} \cdot H_2SO_4$, occurring as a white, crystalline powder; used especially in the treatment of infections due to gram-negative bacteria, such as *Klebsiella, Aerobacter,* some *Proteus* species, *Serratia,* an *Escherichia coli,* and has been used in the treatment of pulmonary tuberculosis, administered orally, intramuscularly, and intravenously.

Kantrex is the trade name for **kanamycin sulfate** and is one of about seven antibiotics which may be used to treat the type of bacteria discovered in plaintiff's infection....

The 1970 Physicians' Desk Reference (PDR) states in part regarding the dosage of **Kantrex**: "In well-hydrated adult patients with normal kidney function receiving a total dose of 15 grams or less, the risk of ototoxic reactions is minimal." Bristol-Myers Co. v. Gonzales, 561 S.W.2d 801, 803 (Tex.1978).

Dr. Gonzalez testified that if he had known that use of **Kantrex** was totally wrong when other less dangerous antibiotics were available, he would have used a different drug.

Dr. Gonzalez further testified that he decided to use **Kantrex** based upon the following statement contained in the 1970 PDR.

Kantrex Injection . . . in concentrations of 0.25 per cent . . . has been used satisfactorily as an irrigating solution in abscess cavities, plueral space, peritoneal and ventricular cavities.

This statement was bolstered by the testimony of all the physician witnesses who stated that irrigation encompassed several methods including the type administered by Dr. Gonzalez to the plaintiff. Dr. Gonzalez said that although he knew of the ototoxic propensities of **Kantrex** when injected intramuscularly, he did not know of such propensities when **Kantrex** was used as an irrigant. Bristol-Myers Co. v. Gonzales, 548 S.W.2d 416, 424 (Ct.Civ.App.Tex.1976).

Other Authorities: Marsh v. Arnold, 446 S.W.2d 949–50, 952 (Ct.Civ.App.Tex.1969).

Kantrex (kan'treks) trademark for preparations of kanamycin. See also *kanamycin.*

karyotype (kar'e-o-tip) [*karyo-* + *type*] the chromosomal constitution of the nucleus of a cell; by extension, the photomicrograph of chromosomes arranged according to the Denver classification. Cf. *idiogram,* and see illustration accompanying *chromosome.*

In October and November, 1977, Dr. Bass ordered blood **karyotypes** of both Mrs. Phillips and Randy; these tests, performed by Dr. Jorgenson and Mr. Rogers at MUSC, revealed that the child suffered from the translocational variety of Down's syndrome and that Mrs. Phillips was a carrier of this chromosomal translocation. Transcript at 75; Pl. Ex. 2. Dr. Bass' explanation of these tests was the first indication given to Mrs. Phillips that Down's syndrome could be an inheritable defect and that she could transmit the defect to her offspring. [Footnote omitted.] Phillips v. U.S., 566 F.Supp. 1, 4 (D.S.Car. 1981).

. . . the Barr body test does not determine the presence or absence of any chromosome. Individuals with chromosomal defects may not therefore be definitely classified by the Barr test alone. The **Karyotype** test, involving blood sampling and culture, will, though it is more expensive ($150.00–$300.00) and takes at least one week for the test results. Richard v. U.S. Tennis Ass'n, 400 N.Y.S.2d 267, 270 (Sup.Ct.N.Y.Cty.1977).

keloid (ke'loid) [Gr. *kēlē* tumor + *eidos* form] a sharply elevated, irregularly-shaped, progressively enlarging scar due to the formation of excessive amounts of collagen in the corium during connective tissue repair. See also *scar, hypertropic* (Maguire case).

Dr. Marsh excised a **keloid scar** formation at the location of the previous injury, probed the area and removed a piece of glass situated beneath the skin. He next sutured the wound and instructed Ms. Washington to return in several days to have the stitching removed. When she returned, there was no sign that the area was infected. Washington v. Walton, 423 So.2d 176, 178 (Ala.1982).

The scar underneath the chin is actually a **keloid** and is red in color. There are two **keloid** formations on the chest. There was an attempt to remove one by excision, but the result was a scar worse than the one removed. Young v. Caribbean Associates, Inc., 358 F.Supp. 1220, 1223 (D.V.I.1973).

At the time of the second hospitalization plaintiff had a large **keloid scar** on the left thigh which Dr. Immermann excised on either side and made an incision to take it out. Maguire v. Waukegan Park District, 282 N.E.2d 6, 8 (App.Ct.Ill.1972).

Other Authorities: Wry v. Dial, 503 P.2d 979, 984 (Ct.App. Ariz.1972).

Kenalog (ken'ah-log) trademark for preparations of triamcinolone acetonide. See also *triamcinolone acetonide.*

keratitis (ker"ah-ti'tis) [*kerato-* + *-itis*] inflammation of the cornea.

... a long history of past ocular difficulties consisting of what was referred to as "a granular like **kerotitis**" in both eyes, together with a past history of trachoma. American National Ins. Co. v. Carbajal, 530 S.W.2d 642–4 (Ct.Civ.App.Tex. 1975).

keratitis, chemical

The next day Mrs. Schwartz was examined by an ophthalmologist who diagnosed the condition of her eyes as **chemical keratitis**, an inflammation of the cornea of the eye caused by chemical exposure. The medical evidence was sufficient to allow a jury to determine that the resulting glaucoma, surgery, and cataracts suffered by Mrs. Schwartz were the result of her exposure to fumes in the Frontier Carpet Office. Tucson Industries, Inc. v. Schwartz, 487 P.2d 12, 15 (Ct.App.Ariz.1971), affirmed in part, reversed in part 501 P.2d 936 (Ariz.1972).

keratoconjunctivitis (ker"ah-to-kon-junk"tĭ-vi'tis) inflammation of the cornea and conjunctiva.

keratoconjunctivitis sicca a condition marked by hyperemia of the conjunctiva, lacrimal deficiency, thickening of the corneal epithelium, itching and burning of the eye, and often reduced visual acuity.

He was of the further opinion that the menopause is not a cause of keratoconjunctivitis, that trauma is a contributing factor to keratoconjunctivitis, and that while **keratoconjunctivitis sicca** (lack of tears) may be caused by rheumatoid arthritis,

Mrs. Davis had bacterial keratoconjunctivitis. Maryland Casualty Co. v. Davis, 464 S.W.2d 433, 436 (Ct.Civ.App.Tex. 1971).

keratoconus (ker"ah-to-ko'nus) [*kerato-* + Gr. *kōnos* cone] a noninflammatory, usually bilateral protrusion of the cornea, the apex being displaced downward and nasally. It occurs most commonly in females at about puberty. The cause is unknown, but hereditary factors may play a role. Called also *conical cornea.*

... an observed condition as bilateral **keratoconus**—raised corneas in both eyes—and suggested as a possible cause plaintiff's prior treatment with steroids. Kupchella v. Finch, 314 F.Supp. 256, 259 (W.D.Pa.1970).

keratometer (ker"ah-tom'ĕ-ter) [*kerato-* + Gr. *metron* measure] an instrument for measuring the curves of the cornea.

The first step in this procedure is the measuring of the approximate spherical curvature of the wearer's cornea. This is done by using an optical analytical device known as a **keratometer**. Because the **keratometer** is incapable of measuring an irregular cornea, this process is only the starting point for a fitting. Three **keratometer** readings are taken and averaged together, after which the fitter uses a chart to translate the result into a specific lens shape. People ex rel. Watson v. House of Vision, 322 N.E.2d 15, 17 (Ill.1974).

Next, an instrument called a **keratometer** is used to make measurements of the curvature of the cornea of the eye. Two readings are taken for each eye to try to arrive at the same figure. This measures the front center area of the cornea and is accomplished by light reflection to focus on a series of targets inside the **keratometer**. This information is written on a work sheet and constitutes a starting place for selection of a trial diagnostic lens. This reading helps to determine the curvature of the diagnostic lens....

The court [North Carolina] also held that the use of the **keratometer** was merely technical or mechanical and stated:

A **keratometer** (or ophthalmometer) is a mechanical instrument or device used for measuring the curvature of the cornea of the human eye. As we interpret the evidence, its use

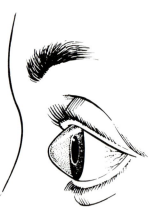

Keratoconus.

has no relation whatever to the methods used by medical doctors, oculists or optometrists in the measuring of the powers of vision.... (p. 630, 129 S.E.2d p. 304.) State ex rel. Londerholm v. Doolin, 497 P.2d 138, 142, 149 (Kan.1972).

The designation "K" derives from the "keratometer," an instrument used to measure the curvature of the central or optical zone of the cornea. Accordingly, a lens is said to be "on K", "flatter than K" or "steeper than K" depending on whether the radius of curvature of the lens corresponds to, is greater than, or is less than the central corneal curve of the eye in question. Butterfield v. Oculus Contact Lens Co., 332 F.Supp. 750, 754 (N.D.Ill.1971).

keratopathy (ker″ah-top′ah-the) a noninflammatory disease of the cornea.

On direct examination this treating eye specialist testified that at the time of the first treatment his diagnosis was a "massive keratopathy of the left eye." His testimony as to causation, in light of reasonable medical probability, was that the injury was causally related to the presence of the wrinkle cream in the eye, based upon the history related to him by Mrs. Sheppard....

... the plaintiff's treating physician could not ascribe the traumatic injury to the cream apart from Mrs. Sheppard's medical history. Next, there were significant time lapses involved from the application to the pain, and from the pain to the treatment at the hospital. Lastly, the expert testimony was undisputed that there was no adulteration or foreign substance present in the wrinkle cream and there was no evidence adduced as to the pH of the cream, which would indicate its acidity or alkalinity. Sheppard v. Revlon, Inc., 267 So.2d 662–3 (Dist.Ct.App.Fla.1972).

keratoplast See *keratoplasty.*

keratoplasty (ker′ah-to-plas″te) [kerato- + Gr. *plassein* to form] plastic surgery of the cornea; corneal grafting.

Dr. Burden on March 19, 1968 performed a lamellar keratoplast (cornea transplant) on plaintiff's right eye. This improved his vision with a contact lens to ²⁰⁄₆₀. In January 1970, Dr. Burden performed another lamellar keratoplast on plaintiff, this time on plaintiff's left eye, resulting in his post operative vision of ²⁰⁄₆₀ minus 1. After each of these operations there was nothing to indicate that the operations were not a success.... American National Ins.Co. v. Carbajal, 530 S.W.2d 642, 644 (Ct.Civ.App.Tex.1975).

keratoplasty, refractive that in which a section of cornea is removed from the patient or a donor, shaped to the desired curvature, and inserted either between (keratophakia) layers of or on (keratomileusis) the patient's cornea to change its curvature and correct optical errors.

Throughout this time, as Dr. Bores was aware, all forms of "refractive keratoplasty," including radial keratotomy, were considered by the National Advisory Eye Council to be "experimental," and clinical procedures involving human patients were discouraged until the results of animal experiments employing the technique were available. (Bores Affidavit ¶6). [Footnotes omitted.] Vest v. Waring, 565 F.Supp. 674, 677 (N.D.Ga.1983).

keratosis (ker″ah-to′sis), pl. *kerato′ses* [kerato- + -osis] any horny growth, such as a wart or callosity, usually either an actinic keratosis or a seborrheic keratosis.

keratosis punctata a form of hyperkeratosis in which the lesions are localized in multiple points on the palms and soles; it is transmitted as an autosomal dominant.

After gradual development of painful eruptions on his hands and feet, he ceased working in August of 1972 with what was diagnosed by three dermatologists as Keratosis Punctata, a disease attended by horny growths in which the lesions are localized in multiple points (Dorland's Medical Dictionary [23d ed.], p. 711), the etiology of which disease is unknown. Lopez v. Hercules Corrugated Box Box Corp., 377 N.Y.S.2d 745–6 (3d Dep't 1975).

keratosis, seborrheic; keratosis seborrheica a benign, noninvasive tumor of epidermal origin, characterized by hyperplasia of the keratinocytes, ordinarily developing in middle life in the form of numerous yellow or brown, sharply marginated, oval, raised lesions; called also *seborrheic wart, verruca senilis, basal cell acanthoma,* and *basal cell papilloma.*

During the summer of 1971, Phelps noticed some small growths on his penis under the foreskin and went to the Clinic on August 5, 1971, where he was seen by Dr. Hedenstrom....
... Dr. Anderson removed some small warts from Phelps' eyelid and took a biopsy of one of the penile lesions, sending it to the Charles T. Miller Hospital for examination by the pathology department. Soon thereafter a pathology report was sent to Dr. Anderson, diagnosing the lesion as a nonmalignant seborrheic keratosis. Phelps v. Blomberg Roseville Clinic, 253 N.W.2d 390, 391 (Minn.1977).

keratotomy (ker″ah-tot′o-me) [Gr. *keras* cornea + *temnein* to cut] surgical incision of the cornea.

keratotomy, radial an operation in which a series of incisions is made in the cornea from its outer edge toward its center in spoke-like fashion; done to flatten the cornea and thus to correct myopia.

This lawsuit, filed on February 19, 1982, involves a surgical procedure known as radial keratotomy that is performed on the cornea of the eye in an attempt to correct nearsightedness....
As the principal advisory body to the National Eye Institute, the federal government's chief source of support for vision research, the National Advisory Eye Council would like to express grave concern about potential widespread adoption of an operation intended to correct nearsightedness, a common condition that can be easily and safely corrected by the use of eyeglasses or contact lenses. The operation, called radial keratotomy, has received widespread publicity during the last year. It involves cutting the conea with a series of deep incisions that extend from the sclera toward, but not into, the center of the cornea. The incisions are intended to be deep enough to weaken the tissue so that internal eye pressure causes the edge of the cornea to bulge slightly, thereby flattening the central portion of the cornea which improves focusing. The incisions result in permanent corneal scars. Vest v. Waring, 565 F.Supp. 674, 676, 678 (N.D.Ga.1983).

kernicterus (ker-nik'ter-us) [Ger. "nuclear jaundice"] a condition with severe neural symptoms, associated with high levels of bilirubin in the blood. It is characterized by deep yellow staining of the basal nuclei, globus pallidus, putamen, and caudate nucleus, as well as the cerebellar and bulbar nuclei, and gray substance of the cerebrum, and is accompanied by widespread destructive changes. It is commonly a sequela of icterus gravis neonatorum. Called also *bilirubin encephalopathy.*

Accumulated bilirubin in a newborn child causes cell death, and when that cell death occurs in the central nervous system including the brain, the damage is irreversible. Brain damage caused by bilirubin is called **kernicterus**. See Price v. Neyland, 115 U.S.App.D.C. 355, 320 F.2d 674 . . . .

. . . On the basis of the evidence, the trial court described the child thus:

Kelly Schnebly exhibits all of the classical findings of severe kernicterus; namely, profound mental retardation; profound failure of growth and development; profound involvement of the central nervous system, manifested by quadraplegia. . . .

A profound athetosis [a nervous disorder marked by continual slow movements]. . . .

. . . bilirubin staining and damage; apparent deafness, whether by input without recognition or by true nerve damage; bilateral nerve involvement of both eyes; sixth nerve palsy, bilaterally, preventing voluntary turning to either side; characteristic contractures of the extremities and body; responsiveness limited almost entirely to tactile stimuli; lack of but limited light perception and inability to follow objects visually; and an inability to recognize difference in strangers, possibly recognizing his mother and father only in a primitive way. Schnebly v. Baker, 217 N.W.2d 708, 712, 716 (Iowa 1974).

Pathologic jaundice deposits bile pigments in the brain stem, causing brain damage known as **kernicterus**. Michele Neyland has **kernicterus**. . . .

. . . the record is replete with medical testimony describing the manner in which **kernicterus** develops from erythroblastosis fetalis. It is also replete with medical diagnoses that Michele has **kernicterus**. Price v. Neyland, 320 F.2d 674, 676 (D.C.Cir. 1963).

Kernig test See *test, Kernig.*

kerotitis See *keratitis.*

ketoacidosis (ke″to-ah″sĭ-do'sis) acidosis accompanied by the accumulation of ketone bodies (ketosis) in the body tissues and fluids, as in diabetic acidosis. See also *Ketone*; and *Ketosis.*

The physician's testimony and the hospital records indicate that Neal suffered a cerebrovascular accident and diabetic **ketoacidosis** precipitated by the severe heat exhaustion. Ex parte Neal, 423 So.2d 850, 852 (Ala.1982).

Her abdomen was tender in the right lower quadrant, though Dr. Winter found no rebound tenderness. The turgor of her skin demonstrated that she was dry and dehydrated. She was lethargic. Her sugar was strong and positive, and there was acetone in the urine. Dr. Winter recorded her history and ordered blood tests. The tests showed high hemoglobin and hematocrit readings, and an elevated white blood cell count. On the basis

of the history, physical examination and his interpretation of the blood tests, Dr. Winter formed a clinical diagnosis of **ketoacidosis** (a state of metabolic imbalance). . . .

Dr. Winter, co-defendant internist, testified that a patient in metabolic acidosis is both a surgical and an anesthetic risk. Dr. Widder, co-defendant anesthesiologist, testified that the previous physical status of the patient, the fact that she had been in a state of **ketoacidosis**, contributed to the weakening of the heart, and this sudden change in her condition caused the cardiac arrest. Burrow v. Widder, 368 N.E.2d 443, 445 (App.Ct. Ill.1977).

ketone (ke'tōn) any of a large class of organic compounds containing the carbonyl group, $C=O$, whose carbon atom is joined to two other carbon atoms, that is, with the carbonyl group occurring within the carbon chain. See also under *body.*

They were using a PVC pipe cleaner marketed under the brand name of Plum-O, PVC-ABS Cleaner. According to the label on the can, the cleaner contained methyl-ethyl-**ketone**. While using this cleaner, the Claimant felt a burning sensation in his throat and eyes. . . .

. . . Not only did the exposure to Plum-O cause the Claimant's nose to bleed, but it also caused his diabetic condition to become uncontrollable. . . .

. . . Considering the nature of the methyl-ethyl-**ketone** and its toxic effect on one with a pre-existing diabetic condition, we hold that the record contains competent, substantial evidence to support a finding of causal relationship between claimant's exposure at work and the claimant's nose bleeds and general physical deterioration. City of Bonifay v. Faulk, 390 So.2d 791–2 (Dist.Ct.App.Fla.1980).

ketosis (ke-to'sis) a condition characterized by an abnormally elevated concentration of ketone bodies in the body tissues and fluids; it is a complication of diabetes mellitus and starvation.

ketosis a condition in which the body uses fat for energy and produces acetone in the body. **Ketosis** is detected by the presence of more than a trace of acetone in the patient's urine and is treated by administering a large dose of insulin, 100 units or more, to the patient within 24 hours after the condition is discovered. Severe **ketosis** can render a person unable to perform such normal functions as walking or driving an automobile. U.S. v. McGuire, 381 F.2d 306, 317 (2d Cir. 1967).

kidney (kid'ne) [L. *ren;* Gr. *nephros*] either of the two organs in the lumbar region that filter the blood, excreting the end-products of body metabolism in the form of urine, and regulating the concentrations of hydrogen, sodium, potassium, phosphate, and other ions in the extracellular fluid. Called also *ren* [NA]. Each kidney is about four inches long, two inches wide, and one inch thick, and weighs from four to six ounces. The kidney is of characteristic shape, and presents a notch on the inner, concave, border, known as the *hilus*, which communicates with the cavity or sinus of the kidney and through which the vessels, nerves, and ureter pass. The kidney consists of a *cortex* and a *medulla*. The medullary substance forms pyramids, whose bases are in the cortex and whose apices, which are called *papillae*, project into the calices of the kidney. The renal pyramids number from

399

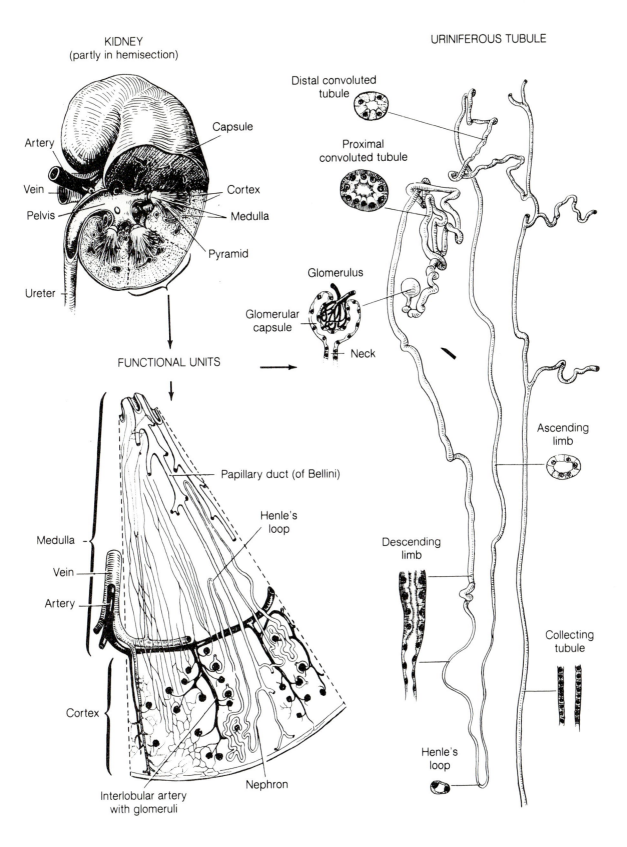

KIDNEY
(partly in hemisection)

URINIFEROUS TUBULE

Artery

Vein

Pelvis

Ureter

Capsule

Cortex

Medulla

Pyramid

Distal convoluted
tubule

Proximal
convoluted tubule

Glomerulus

Glomerular
capsule

Neck

FUNCTIONAL UNITS

Papillary duct (of Bellini)

Henle's
loop

Medulla

Vein

Artery

Cortex

Interlobular artery
with glomeruli

Nephron

Ascending
limb

Descending
limb

Collecting
tubule

Henle's
loop

DETAILS OF STRUCTURE OF THE KIDNEY

10 to 15. The parenchyma of each kidney is composed of about one million *renal tubules* (nephrons, the functional unit of the kidney), held together by a little connective tissue. Each tubule begins blindly in a renal corpuscle, consisting of a glomerulus and its capsule, situated within the cortex. After a neck or constriction below the capsule, it becomes the proximal convoluted tubule, Henle's loop, distal convoluted tubule, arched collecting tubule, and then the straight collecting tubule, which opens at the apex of a renal papilla. The straight collecting tubules converge as they descend, forming groups in the center, known as *medullary rays*. See illustration. See also *cystoscope*; disease, polycystic of kidneys; and terms formed from the root "nephro" or "nephr".

Plaintiff argues that injury to the kidney is an injury to an organ and not to soft tissue. Medical testimony at the trial suggested that, in a medical sense, an injury to an organ would not be referred to as a "soft tissue injury." Plaintiff's doctor testified that a **kidney** is a special vital organ consisting of arteries, veins, special tubes or tubulars (which in turn consist, in part, of muscle), special tissue, some nerves and a capsule or lining. Todd v. Dabkowski, 372 A.2d 350–1 (Super.Ct.N.J.1977).

Examination at the Arecibo District Hospital, where the claimant receives treatment, shows that he has a good functioning left **kidney**. The blood urea nitrogen on January 14, 1963 was 15 mg. %, and the urea in the blood on March 12, 1963 was 10.2 cc. This would indicate **kidney** performance in the range of normal. Torres v. Celebrezze, 349 F.2d 342, 344 (1st Cir. 1965).

kidney, polycystic See *disease, polycystic of kidneys.*

kidney disease, end stage See *disease, end stage, kidney.*

kidney stone See *calculus, renal.*

Kifa guide wire See *guide;* and *wire, Kifa guide.*

kingdom (king'dum) [Anglosaxon *cyningdom*] classically, one of the three categories into which natural objects are usually classified: the *animal kingdom*, including all animals; the *plant kingdom*, including all plants; and the *mineral kingdom*, including all objects and substance without life. A fourth kingdom, the *Protista*, includes all single-celled organisms.

I understand, of course, that in the language of taxonomy, categories of "**kingdoms**" are based upon more gross distinctions, than those involved in categories of classes, subclasses, orders, families, genuses, and species, and I understand that the distinctions among **kingdoms**, specifically, are far more gross than the distinctions among species. But the decisive point, it seems to me, is that those whose very function is to weigh the significance of distinctions between plants within a genus—the plant taxonomists—consider the distinctions among Cannabis sativa L. and Cannabis indica Lam. sufficient to categorize them as different species. It does not seem to me decisive whether those engaged in botanical taxonomy had addressed and investigated this question deliberately and consciously, and had arrived at some scholarly consensus, prior to 1938 or prior to 1970, when Congress acted, or whether this came later. U.S. v. Lewallen, 385 F.Supp. 1140, 1142–3 (W.D.Wis.1974).

knee (ne) the site of articulation between the thigh (femur) and leg; called also *genu* [NA]. See also *chondromalacia; ligamenta collaterale fibulare; osteotomy* (Monahan case); *synovectomy* (Monahan case).

Dr. Mitchell Sheinkop, the government's expert, testified that the treatment Weise received, which consisted of bed rest with initial immobilization of the **knee** followed within twelve days by gradual weight bearing, was among the medically accepted treatments for a **knee** fracture. Weise v. U.S., 724 F.2d 587–8 (7th Cir. 1984).

It was on this date that the plaintiff underwent her first **knee** operation. Dr. Kilroy testified this surgical procedure involved the removal of the cushion from the kneecap and prevented Mrs. Perry from engaging in any excessive kneeling. Dodd v. Nicolon Corp., 422 So.2d 398, 401 (La.1982).

He noted that there was still tenderness over the intrapatella ligament and that she had reached maximum improvement even though she was still somewhat symptomatic. He felt that she could continue to have pain and discomfort over that area for a considerable time in the future and that the exacerbation of pain was quite common with this type of injury. . . .

. . . She was unable to kneel for any length of time because the pressure caused pain and discomfort, and additionally motions such as stepping down from a curb or up from a curb caused a snapping sensation over the lateral aspect of the **knee**. The doctor attributed this snapping sensation to the ligament slipping over the edge of the **knee** joint, resulting from scar tissue in the ligament as a result of her injury. He noted that even though she had recently bumped her **knee** and some discoloration was present at the time of this examination, that the injuries reported above were due entirely to the original blow she received at the hands of Mrs. Meyers. The doctor noted that it was not unusual for such symptoms to persist over a long period of time but that it was consistent with the injuries she received and the symptoms would persist from time to time in the future. Fernandez v. Meyers, 396 So.2d 425–6 (Ct.App. La.1981).

Other Authorities: Hale v. Venuto, 187 Cal.Rptr. 357, 359 (Ct. App.Cal.1982); Pruchniewski v. Weinberger, 415 F.Supp. 112, 114 (D.Md.1976).

knee joint See *articulatio genus.*

kneecap See *patella.*

knowledge

In assessing the awareness required to trigger the statute of limitations, it is essential to distinguish between "**knowledge**" and "belief." For one to have **knowledge** of fact "x," three requisites must exist: (1) "x" must be true, (2) the person must believe "x" to be true, and (3) the belief must be reasonably based. A. Flew, A Dictionary of Philosophy (1979); A. Quinton, "Knowledge and Belief," Encyclopedia of Philosophy (1967). "Belief," which is a component of **knowledge**, requires only requisites (1) and (2)—"x" must be true and the person must believe it to be true. As a consequence, conclusions based on dreams, intuitions, suspicion, conjecture, ESP, speculation, or faulty reasoning, even if true, are merely "belief." Absent a reasonable basis, these conclusions do not rise to the level of "**knowledge**." Harrison v. U.S., 708 F.2d 1023, 1027–8 (5th Cir. 1983).

knuckle (nuk″l) the dorsal aspect of any phalangeal joint, especially of the metacarpophalangeal joints of the flexed fingers.

knuckle-bender

Plaintiff was given a "knuckle-bender," an outrigger device designed to improve movement in his fingers.

On November 14, 1979, plaintiff returned to Dr. Morgan complaining of a poor grip and weakness in his left hand. Plaintiff had not been wearing his knuckle-bender. Parnell v. Reed & Sims, Inc., 428 So.2d 899, 902 (Ct.App.La.1983).

Koebner's syndrome See *phenomenon, Koebner's.*

Konyne See *factor, coagulation [factor IX].*

At the trial Dr. Milton Mozen, a PhD in biochemistry employed by Cutter Laboratories as director of chemical and biological research, testified that Konyne is a Factor IX concentrate developed by Cutter through use of a fractionation process wherein this particular coagulation factor is removed from plasma extracted from the pooled blood obtained from thousands of donors. . . .

The hepatitis virus is undetectable. Dr. Mozen testified that while some plasma products can be made in processes which allow for the destruction of the hepatitis virus, those processes cannot be conducted in the production of Konyne because it would lose its coagulation activity. Fogo v. Cutter Laboratories, Inc., 137 Cal.Rptr. 417, 420 (Ct.App.Cal.1977).

K-wire See *wire, Kirschner.*

Kwell (kwel) trademark for preparations of lindane. See also *lindane.*

kyphoscoliosis (ki″fo-sko″le-o′sis) [*kyphosis* + *scoliosis*] backward and lateral curvature of the spinal column, as in vertebral osteochondrosis (Scheuermann's disease).

The plaintiff at the time of his application for the policy suffered from kyphoscoliosis (curvature of the spine) caused by a childhood disease. After his fall his back condition was diagnosed as "acute lumbarsacral strain and kyphoscoliosis." Biathrow v. Continental Cas. Co., 356 N.E.2d 451 (Mass. 1976).

Curvature of the upper spine (kyphoscoliosis) was also diagnosed. Reading v. Mathews, 542 F.2d 993, 995 (7th Cir. 1976).

kyphosis (ki-fo′sis) [Gr. *kyphōsis* humpback] abnormally increased convexity in the curvature of the thoracic spine as viewed from the side; hunchback. Cf. *lordosis* and *scoliosis.*

Plaintiff suffers from kyphosis (increase in chest diameter) because of overinflation from the lung disease and because of spine curvature with aging. . . .

. . . There is evidence, mirrored in Finding of Fact No. 9, that plaintiff's byssinosis has aggravated his kyphosis. Dr. Sieker explained that changes in plaintiff's air flows were due to an overinflated chest, caused by "obstructive lung disease" and kyphosis. "Kyphosis," he stated, "is often seen in conjunction with chronic obstructive lung disease." Garner v. J.P. Stevens and Co., Inc., 289 S.E.2d 68–70 (Ct.App.N.Car.1982).

He testified that the automobile collision of December 7, 1971, had thrown the back alignment out, resulting in what is known as a kyphosis (backward curvature of the spine). Kitsch v. Goode, 362 N.E.2d 446, 449 (App.Ct.Ill.1977).

Other Authorities: McCalip v. Richardson, 333 F.Supp. 1207, 1210 (D.Neb.1971), reversed and remanded 460 F.2d 1124 (8th Cir. 1972).

kyphosis dorsalis juvenilis; kyphosis, juvenile; kyphosis, Scheuermann's See *Osteochondrosis.*

Examination of her chest revealed that she had partial scoliosis and kyphosis of the dorsal spine. Tr. 143. Movement of the dorsal spine was painful and restrictive but there was no motor or sensory loss. Adams v. Schweiker, 557 F.Supp. 1373, 1376 (S.D.Tex.1983).

He stated that plaintiff had a dorsal kyphosis, or curvature of the spine, relative to a juvenile epiphysitis. Caterpillar Tractor Co. v. Industrial Com'n, 440 N.E.2d 861, 864 (Ill.1982).

Ingram was examined by Dr. William L. Patterson, an orthopedic surgeon, who found that he was a fairly thin individual with an increased dorsal kyphosis and noted that on standing he elevated his left pelvis ¼ to ⅜ inch with a slight compensatory left scoliosis and no disturbance of his gait. . . . Ingram v. Richardson, 471 F.2d 1268, 1273 (6th Cir. 1972).

L

labia See *vulva.*

labile (la′bil) [L. *labilis* unstable, from *labi* to glide] gliding; moving from point to point over the surface; unstable; fluctuating. See also *lability.*

lability (lah-bil′ĭ-te) the quality of being labile. In psychiatry, emotional instability; a tendency to show alternating states of gaiety and somberness.

In addition, examinations conducted at government expense show the plaintiff as a labile personality, whose complaints may be of non-organic or psychosomatic origin related to chronic anxiety. Plouse v. Richardson, 334 F.Supp. 1086, 1088 (W.D.Pa.1971).

Most of his present difficulty is "nervousness" when he is with people. He is unable to talk, his friends have noted some emotional lability such as crying at intervals of time. Phillips v. Celebrezze, 330 F.2d 687, 689 (6th Cir. 1964).

labor (la′bor) [L. "work"] the function of the female organism by which the product of conception is expelled from the uterus through the vagina to the outside world. Labor may be divided into three stages: The first (the stage of dilatation) begins with the onset of regular uterine contractions and ends when the os is completely dilated and flush with the vagina, thus completing the birth canal. The second stage (stage of expulsion) extends from the end of the first stage until the expulsion of the infant is completed. The third stage (placental stage) extends from the expulsion of the child until the placenta and membranes are expelled and contraction of the uterus is completed. Called also *accouchement, childbirth, confinement, delivery, parturition,* and *travail.* See also *labor pains,* under *pain.*

As noted in defendant's brief, the three stages of **labor** are:
First Stage: From meaningful contractions until complete dilation of the cervix. (10 Centimeters)
Second Stage: From complete dilation of the cervix until delivery of the child.
Third Stage: From delivery of the child to delivery of the placenta (afterbirth). Grindstaff v. Tygett, 655 S.W.2d 70, 72 (Mo.Ct.App.1983).

Various factors to be considered in determining the imminence of childbirth are: dilation; the progress of dilation; station of the child; the frequency and intensity of the contractions. Hiatt v. Groce, 523 P.2d 320, 326 (Kan.1974).

laboratory (lab'o-rah-to"re) [L. *laboratorium*] a place equipped for performing experimental work or investigative procedures, for the preparation of drugs, chemicals, etc.

laboratory, clinical a laboratory for examination of materials derived from the human body for the purpose of providing information on diagnosis, prevention, or treatment of disease.

The subject of this lawsuit in our original jurisdiction is the following proposed regulations of the Department of Health, published at Vol. 5, Number 35, Page 2129 of the Pennsylvania Bulletin:
§ 5.1. Definitions.
For the purpose of these regulations, the following definitions shall apply.
(a) "Clinical Laboratory":
(1) Any place, establishment or institution organized and operated primarily for the performance of all or any bacteriological, biochemical, hematological, microscopical, serological or parasitological or other tests by the practical application of one or more of the fundamental sciences to material originating from the human body, by the use of specialized apparatus, equipment and methods, for the purpose of obtaining scientific data which may be used as an aid to ascertain the state of health. This definition includes, but is not limited to, all independent hospital, industrial, state, county and municipal laboratories and to all clinical laboratories operated in private offices and clinics of practitioners of the healing arts.
(2) Provided, however, that the term "Clinical Laboratory" shall not apply to the office or clinic of a licensed practitioner of the healing arts who performs only the following procedures as part of his or her examinations of the patient to obtain results which are essential for the immediate diagnosis and therapy of the patient:
(i) Chemical examinations of urine by 'Dipstik' and/or tablet methods.
(ii) Microscopic examination of urine sediment.
(iii) Pregnancy tests.
(iv) Red and white blood cell counts.

(v) Sedimentation rate of blood.
(vi) Gram stain.
(vii) Primary culturing for transmittal to a licensed laboratory including preincubation, if required.
(viii) Qualitative chemical examination of stool specimens.
(ix) Test for pinworms.
(x) Test for Trichomonas vaginalis. Masland v. Bachman, 361 A.2d 473, 475 (Commonwealth Ct.Pa.1976).

labyrinth (lab'ĭ-rinth) [Gr. *labyrinthos*] a system of intercommunicating cavities or canals, especially that constituting the internal ear (auris internus [NA]).

Dr. Suckle, a neurologist, stated that he believed she had a concussion of the **labyrinth** (the balance mechanism in the middle ear), which was caused by the accident and that this accounts for her continued dizziness. Suckle's opinion was made with knowledge of the fact that earlier in Julia's life she suffered from Meniere's disease. There was evidence that Julia was struck behind the left ear, which is consistent with an aggravation if not the sole cause of her dizziness after the accident. Redepenning v. Dore, 201 N.W.2d 580, 586 (Wis.1972).

labyrinthitis (lab"ĭ-rin-thi'tis) inflammation of the labyrinth; otitis interna.

One diagnosed a condition preexisting her accident, **labyrinthitis,** which manifests itself, among other things, by dizziness. Another, a neurologist, also testified she suffered from **labyrinthitis,** and with such a condition, a sudden turn of the head could produce vertigo, causing her to lose her balance and fall. Legakis v. Sultan & Sons, 383 So.2d 938-9 (Dist.Ct. App.Fla.1980).

labyrinthosis

Dr. Bernard Ronis, an otolaryngologist (ear, nose and throat), testified that in his opinion the plaintiff was suffering from **labyrinthosis,** which is a dysfunction of the inner ear (N.T. 5-33). Various causes for plaintiff's equilibrium loss, such as a stroke (N.T. 2-74), a neurological disorder (N.T. 5-108-109, 111) and pre-existing medical conditions (N.T. 5-29, 5-31, 5-126) were ruled out by him and plaintiff's treating doctor, Dr. Miraldo....
... He has a disorder termed **labyrinthosis,** which is a dysfunction or abnormal action of the inner structure of its connections. DeMarines v. KLM Royal Dutch Airlines, 433 F.Supp. 1047, 1053 (E.D.Pa.1977), reversed and remanded 580 F.2d 1193 (3d Cir. 1978).

laceration (las"er-a'shun) [L. *laceratio*] a torn, ragged, mangled wound.

Matthew sustained a four and one-half inch **laceration** on the left side of his scalp down to his skull, a one and one-half inch avulsion on his left cheek, a two and one-half inch **laceration** extending from the left upper eyelid over to the nose area, a two inch **laceration** on the right front of his scalp, a two and one-half inch **laceration** on his right cheek and a three inch **laceration** on his left forehead. In addition, a portion of his ear was torn away. Blanchard v. City of Bridgeport, 463 A.2d 553, 556 (Conn.1983).

The **laceration** to Sasha's thigh required nine inside and twenty outside stitches to close the wound. The scar is "v" shaped about 1" × 1½" in length. Gibbons v. Orleans Parish School Bd., 391 So.2d 976, 978 (Ct.App.La.1980).

... the most obvious injury was his left lower limb where there was a large **laceration** of approximately one half the circumference of his lower thigh with a bone protruding from the wound. Graeff v. Baptist Temple of Springfield, 576 S.W.2d 291, 296 (Mo.1978).

Other Authorities: Albert v. Alter, 381 A.2d 459, 468 (Super. Ct.Pa.1977); Hester v. State, 310 So.2d 455–6 (Dist.Ct.App. Fla.1975). Hiatt v. Groce, 523 P.2d 320, 323 (Kan.1974).

Laetrile (la'ĕ-tril) trademark for *l*-mandelonitrile-β-glucuronic acid, derived by hydrolysis of amygdalin and oxidation of the resulting *l*-mandelonitrile-β-glucoside; it is alleged to have antineoplastic properties. The term is sometimes used interchangeably with *amygdalin*. See also *amygdalin*.

lamina (lam'ĭ-nah), pl. *lam'inae* [L.] a thin flat plate, or layer; [NA] a general term for such a structure, or a layer of a composite structure. The term is often used alone to mean the lamina arcus vertebrae.

The appellants' expert witness, a veterinarian, characterized laminitis as an inflammation of the **laminae** which are the membranes located between the sensitive and insensitive structure of the hoof of a horse. The affliction is caused by overexertion on hard footing and often is secondary to conditions such as digestive disturbances and bio-chemical changes resulting from overeating or overdrinking. Campbell v. C.I.R., 504 F.2d 1158, 1163 (6th Cir. 1974).

laminagram (lam'ĭ-nah-gram) a roentgenogram of a selected layer of the body made by body-section roentgenography.

A **laminogram** is an x-ray taken by special technique which brings out the details at a particular depth of the structure while blurring the details of other depths or planes. A series of such x-rays taken at differing depths provide a fairly detailed picture of a given structure. However, it is estimated that between 5 to 10% of tracheal tumors, benign and malignant, will go undetected by **laminograms**. Joynt v. Barnes, 388 N.E.2d 1298, 1304 (App.Ct.Ill.1979).

laminectomy (lam'ĭ-nek'to-me) [L. *lamina* layer + Gr. *ektomē* excision] excision of the posterior arch of a vertebra. See also *chymopapain; diskectomy* (Hankel case).

The operation performed was a thoracic **laminectomy** at T–9, 10, 11, and 12 of the spinal column. Tyminski was not informed of the risks involved in the operation.

The details of the operation were found by the District Court to include the removal of the spinous processes and laminae of the spinal column with incisions made in both the dura and arachnoid. The arachnoid was adherent to the AVA and was cleared of several of the adhesions. The bones removed during the operation, the spinous processes and laminae, were not replaced; thus, there existed a potential "dead" space where these bones had been. In addition, clearing the arachnoid involved some manipulation of the spinal cord which could cause edema of the spinal cord. Within days of the operation Tyminski began progressively to lose control of the bodily functions in his lower extremities. Tyminski v. U.S., 481 F.2d 257, 260 (3d Cir. 1973).

Dr. Spence told appellant that he would have to undergo a **laminectomy**—the excision of the posterior arch of the verte-

bra—to correct what he suspected was a ruptured disc. Canterbury v. Spence, 464 F.2d 772, 777 (D.C.Cir.1972).

Midline incision is made in upper border of the spine of L4 downward in the midline to the upper sacrum. Dissection is carried down and in the subperiosteal space exposing the interspaces at L4–5 and L5 S1. At each interspace, partial **laminectomy** is carried out on the left and of the bone adjacent to the interspace followed by resection of the intervening ligament in order that the interspace could be thoroughly explored both by inspection as well as by palpation. In each instance, there was no protrusion of the disc identified. Further resection downward over the sacrum is carried out in order that we do not overlook the fragment of disc that may have extruded extra-durally in this space but none is found. Richardson v. Perales, 402 U.S. 389, 391 (1971).

Other Authorities: District of Columbia v. Barriteau, 399 A.2d 563, 565 (D.C.Ct.App.1979); Dill v. Skuka, 279 F.2d 145, 150 (3d Cir. 1960).

laminectomy, cervical

Plaintiff saw Dr. Gerald Litel, a neurosurgeon, before and after the operation. Dr. Litel testified that even with a good recovery from the operation nothing over fifty pounds should be lifted by a person who has had a **cervical laminectomy**. Dr. Litel further stated that plaintiff could not assume any awkward positioning of the body. Webb v. Insurance Co. of North America, 396 So.2d 508, 513 (Ct.App.La.1981).

Plaintiff's pain continued and another doctor found a pinching of the nerve between the sixth and seventh neck bone. In order to correct this, a **cervical laminectomy** was performed. This operation is a dangerous one and can result in paralysis or death. The operation seemed to be a success and plaintiff was able to work again. However, the pain returned to plaintiff's left shoulder and arm and a second **cervical laminectomy** was performed. Decker v. Norfolk & Western R. Co., 265 N.W.2d 785, 792 (Ct.App.Mich.1978).

The myelogram disclosed some type of obstruction in the spinal canal in the area of the neck.

As a result of his findings, Dr. Culberson performed a **cervical laminectomy**. This operation required the doctor to cut approximately three to four inches into Mrs. Fritsche's neck and to expose her spine. He then removed the bone to expose the cord of nerves which runs through the spine and which carries the impulses to the various parts of the body. Fritsche v. Westinghouse Electric Corp., 261 A.2d 657, 659 (N.J.1970).

laminectomy, decompressive

The surgery performed was a **decompressive spinal laminectomy** and fusion. A **decompressive laminectomy** attempts to relieve the pressure on the nerves and the fusion attempts to properly realign and secure the vertebrae to prevent further destruction. Zimmerman v. New York City Health & Hospitals, 458 N.Y.S.2d 552, 554 (1st Dep't 1983).

Dr. Llewellyn again repaired the disc and performed a **decompressive laminectomy** (removal of bone from the spine). Davis v. Becker & Associates, Inc., 608 F.2d 621, 623 (5th Cir. 1979).

laminitis (lam"ĭ-ni'tis) inflammation of a lamina, and especially of the laminae of a horse's foot. See also *founder*.

empirically to be 2100:1—i.e., for every part of alcohol found in deep lung air, there are 2100 parts of alcohol in the blood stream. This ratio was adopted by the National Highway Safety Council's Committee on Tests for Intoxication in 1952 and has been questioned and reaffirmed since then. In 1972, for example, an Ad Hoc Committee on Blood-Breath Alcohol Relationship sponsored by Indiana University endorsed the continued use of the 2100:1 ratio. (See: 4 Gray, Attorneys' Textbook Medicine, Section 133.73(1)). People v. Jones, 461 N.Y.S.2d 962–3 (Albany Cy.Ct.1983).

law of independent assortment the members of gene pairs segregate independently during meiosis.

law, Mendel's; law, mendelian in the inheritance of certain traits or characters, the offspring are not intermediate in character between the parents but inherit from one or the other parent in this respect. For example, if a pea plant with the factor tallness (TT) is mated with one with the factor shortness (SS) then some of the offspring will inherit TT, some TS, and some SS in the ratio: TT, 2TS, SS. The TT's are homozygous (pure) tall, the SS's are homozygous short, and the TS's are heterozygous. Which parent the TS ones resemble will depend on whether T or S is dominant. The TT's mated with TT's breed pure as do the SS's with SS's. The TS's mated with TS's again produce TT's, TS's and SS's in the same ratio as above. TS's mated with TT's or SS's give the same combinations but in a different ratio. Today, Mendel's law is usually expressed as the *law of independent assortment* (q.v.) and the *law of segregation* (q.v.).

The agglutinogens and agglutinins present in an individual's blood are hereditary characteristics and therefore capable of being used for identification purposes. To understand adequately how identification can be possible, it is necessary to explain, briefly, the genetic laws originally formulated by Gregor Mendel (**Mendelian Laws**). A person's biological makeup (color of hair, physical characteristics, blood types, etc.) becomes fixed at the time of impregnation of the mother's ovum by the father's sperm. The inheritance of these biological substances is governed by genes, which occur in rod-like groups or lumps called chromosomes. When reproduction takes place the two groups of chromosomes separate, each joining with some other chromosome to later form a new cell. This pairing of chromosomes takes place according to the biological character of each chromosome or gene. For example, the maternal chromosome that contains the color of eyes pairs off with the corresponding paternal chromosome controlling eye color, and the maternal blood type chromosome pairs off with the corresponding paternal blood type combination. Thus, if the blood groupings of both mother and father are known, the blood grouping of the child may be predicted. Conversely, if the blood groupings of one parent and the child are known, the blood grouping of the other parent can also be determined.

Both the existence of various blood types and **Mendel's Law of Hereditary Characteristics** are universely accepted in scientific fields. 1 Wigmore on Evidence Section 165a (3d ed. 1940). Anonymous v. Anonymous, 460 P.2d 32, 34 (Ct.App. Ariz.1969).

law of segregation in each generation the ratio of (*a*) pure dominants, (*b*) dominants giving descendants in the proportion of three dominants to one recessive, and (*c*) pure recessives is 1:2:1. This ratio follows from the fact that the two alleles of a gene cannot be a part of a single gamete, but must segregate to different gametes. See also *meiosis*.

layer (la'er) a sheetlike mass of tissue of nearly uniform thickness, several of which may be superimposed, one above another, as in the epidermis; called also *lamina* and *stratum*.

LD lethal dose; (perception of) light difference.

LD$_{50}$ median lethal dose; a dose that is lethal for 50 per cent of the test subjects.

L.D. 50 means lethal dose for 50%. It represents that amount of material necessary to kill half of a given number of test animals in accordance with their weight. The amount necessary of the particular product tested is indicated in the test symbolization by a numeral or numerals following the test symbol, as L.D. 50–10 indicates 10 milligrams per kilogram of body weight. This represents that one-half of the test animals fed 10 milligrams of a particular product would die. Therefore, the lower the number the greater the toxicity. Skogen v. Dow Chemical Co., 375 F.2d 692, 697 (8th Cir. 1967).

lead (led) [L. *plumbum*] a soft, grayish blue metal with poisonous salts; symbol, Pb; atomic number, 82; atomic weight, 207.19. See also *anemia; heme; hemoglobin; mitochondria* (Lead Industries Ass'n case); *poisoning, lead*.

After reviewing the available evidence, EPA reached the following general conclusions. First, ''lead exposure is a major health problem'' that results from the cumulative impact of ''a combination of sources, including food, water, air, leaded paint and dust.''. . .

When EPA first issued lead-content regulations in 1973, there was no firm evidence that gasoline lead was harmful, only a ''significant risk'' that it was. Ethyl Corp., 541 F.2d at 12. Today, in contrast, there is compelling evidence that gasoline lead is a major cause of lead poisoning in young children. . . .

See Memorandum by Dr. Joel Schwartz, Office of Policy and Resource Management, Energy Policy Division, EPA, on Health Effects of Gasoline Lead Emissions 9–10 (May 11, 1982), J.A. at 274, 286–91; I. Billick, Prediction of Pediatric Blood Levels from Gasoline Consumption (unpublished HUD report, Apr. 21, 1982).

See ICF, Inc., The Relationship Between Gasoline Lead Emissions and Blood Poisoning in Americans 11–12 (unpublished EPA report, Oct. 1982), J.A. at 1255, 1269–70 (food lead); D. Hsia, Blood Lead of Chicago Children and Its Sources, 1967–1980, at 9 (unpublished EPA report, July 1982) (concluding that gasoline is responsible for 55% of blood lead levels in Chicago children, lead paint for only 25%). Also, adults consume little lead paint, and infants less than a year old consume little canned food (an important source of food lead), yet both adults and small infants show drops in mean blood lead levels similar to other age groups. ICF, Inc., supra, at 12–13, J.A. at 1270–71; Memorandum by Dr. Joel Schwartz, supra note 48, at 8–9, J.A. at 285–86. Small Ref. Lead Phase-Down Task

Force v. U.S.E.P.A., 705 F.2d 506, 523–4, 527–9 (D.C.Cir. 1983).

lead (lēd) any of the conductors connected to the electrocardiograph. Also any of the records made by the electrocardiograph, varying with the part of the body from which the current is led off. It is customary to use three peripheral leads; lead I, right arm and left arm; lead II, right arm and left leg; lead III, left arm and left leg; and at least six leads from the precordial region. Called also *derivation*.

lead encephalopathy See *encephalopathy, lead.*

lead paint poisoning See *poisoning, lead.*

lead poisoning See *poisoning, lead.*

leavator muscle See *musculus levator palpebrae superioris.*

leg (leg) the lower limb, especially the part from knee to foot; called also *crus* [NA]. See also *foot* (Dobbs case).

As Murphy trimmed limbs off a fallen tree, the chain-saw blade caught in a bush and was thrown into the calf area of his inside lower left **leg**, cutting a gash approximately sixteen (16) inches long and one and one-half (1½) inches deep. King v. Murphy, 424 So.2d 547 (Miss.1982).

The blood supply was diminished to her right **leg** and, subsequently, the **leg** was amputated....

... There was considerable controversy in the testimony as to the symptoms exhibited by the **leg** and when diagnosis of the diminished blood supply was possible. At issue in the postoperative care of Mrs. Hoeke was whether the **leg** was properly monitored and procedures taken to determine the status of the blood supply. Hoeke v. Mercy Hospital of Pittsburgh, 445 A.2d 140, 142–3 (Super Ct.Pa.1982).

The lower **leg** consists of two bones: the fibula, which is the outer, smaller bone, and the tibia, which is the inner, larger bone. Both bones were fractured as a result of the fall. Jones v. Recreation and Park Commission, 395 So.2d 846–7 (Ct. of App.La.1981).

Other Authorities: Baloney v. Carter, 387 So.2d 54, 61 (Ct. App.La.1980); Safeway Stores, Inc. v. Industrial Com'n, 558 P.2d 971–2 (Ct.App.Ariz.1976); Roeder v. Industrial Com'n, 556 P.2d 1148, 1150 (Ct.App.Ariz.1976).

Legg-Calvé-Perthes disease (leg'-kal-va'-per'tez) [Arthur T. *Legg;* Jacques *Calvé,* French orthopedist, 1875–1954; Georg Clemens *Perthes,* German surgeon, 1869–1927] osteochondritis of the capitular epiphysis of the femur. See also *osteochondrosis.*

leiomyoma (li"o-mi-o'mah) [*leio-* + Gr. *mys* muscle + *-oma*] a benign tumor derived from smooth muscle, most commonly of the uterus; called also *fibroid.*

When none of these actions reduced substantially the flow of blood, the defendant made a provisional diagnosis of "probable acute bleeding, duodenal or gastric ulcer, some tumor, such as **Leiomyoma**, possible, alcoholic gastritis, doubtful," and concluded that there was "no alternative to operating [in order] to go in and see what was causing [the bleeding]." Fitzgerald v. Manning, 679 F.2d 341, 343 (4th Cir. 1982).

leiomyoma uteri a leiomyoma of the uterus, usually occurring in the third and fourth decades, characterized by the development, most commonly within the myometrium, of multiple, sharply circumscribed, uncapsulated, gray-white tumors, which are firm, usually round, and show a whorled pattern on cut section; called also *fibromyoma uteri, myoma previum,* and, colloquially, *fibroids.* Cited in Landess v. Weinberger, 361 F.Supp. 247, 250 (E.D.Mo.1973), reversed and remanded 490 F.2d 1187 (8th Cir. 1974).

lens (lenz) [L. "lentil"] 1. a piece of glass or other transparent substance so shaped as to converge or scatter the rays of light, especially the glass used in appropriate frames or other instruments to increase the visual acuity of the human eye. See also *glasses; prism; spectacles.* 2. [NA] the transparent biconvex body of the eye situated between the posterior chamber and the vitreous body, constituting part of the refracting mechanism of the eye. See also *eye.* Called also *l. crystallina* or *crystalline l.*

"Lenses" as used in the statute is a generic term, the dictionary definitions of which are and in 1921 were broad enough to include contact lenses....

... On the contrary we are of the opinion that in using the general, all-inclusive term "**lenses**" it was intended to grant authority to optometrists to prescribe and fit contact lenses. The trial court concluded that "Contact lenses are **lenses** within the meaning of Section 336.010, R.S.Mo.1959" and we reach that same conclusion of law. State ex inf. Danforth v. Dale Curteman, Inc., 480 S.W.2d 848, 851 (Mo.1972).

lens, adaptation of

The phrase "**adaptation of lenses**" does not refer to the fitting of spectacle frames containing prescription lenses to the face and head of the wearer. In such cases all of the lens curvatures have been previously formulated by an optometrist or ophthalmologist specifically to aid the vision of the person involved, and the optician's job is to position the lenses correctly in front of the wearer's eyes. He does not make any determinations regarding the curvatures of the lenses.

The fitting of contact lenses, on the other hand, requires the optician to determine some of the curvatures of the lenses themselves in order to properly fit them to the wearer's eye. Thus, his efforts are directed at making the lenses suitable for the eye, rather than making the frames suitable for the face. In

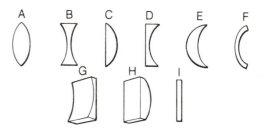

Lenses: *A-F.* Spherical lenses: *A.* biconvex; *B.* biconcave; *C.* planoconvex; *D.* planoconcave; *E.* concavoconvex; *F.* convexoconcave; *G, H.* cylindrical lenses, concave and convex; *I.* ordinary flat lens.

doing this the optician uses procedures that require him to come into actual contact with the customer's eyeball. . . .

In our opinion the construction given to the word "adaptation" by the Attorney General was correct. Courts of other jurisdictions have given the same construction to similar statutes. See State ex rel. Danforth v. Dale Curteman, Inc. (Mo. 1972), 480 S.W.2d 848; State ex rel. Reed v. Kuzirian (1961), 228 Or. 619, 365 P.2d 1046, 88 A.L.R.2d 1284; Pennsylvania Optometric Association, Inc. v. DiGiovanni (C.P.Phila.County 1968), 45 Pa.D. & C.2d 245; Fields v. District of Columbia (D.C.Ct.App.1967), 232 A.2d 300; Florida Association of Dispensing Opticians v. Florida State Board of Optometry (Fla. 1970), 238 So.2d 839; contra, State ex rel. Londerholm v. Doolin (1972), 209 Kan. 244, 497 P.2d 138; High v. Ridgeway's Opticians (1963), 258 N.C. 626, 129 S.E.2d 301; State Board of Optometry v. Chester (1964), 251 Miss. 250, 169 So.2d 468. People ex rel. Watson v. House of Vision, 322 N.E.2d 15, 19–20 (Ill.1975).

lens, contact a curved shell of glass or plastic applied directly over the globe or cornea to correct See also *lens* (Danforth case); *lens, adaptation of*; *lens, scleral*; *optometry*.

On the evening of April 3, while practicing inserting and removing the **lenses**, she was unable to remove the left **lens**, and the eye became bloodshot and puffy. Assuming that Appellant's office was closed, Mrs. Weiss did not attempt to contact him, but went instead to the emergency room at Einstein Hospital where an opthalmologist removed the lens. Chaby v. State Bd. of Optometrical Examiners, 386 A.2d 1071–2 (Commonwlth Ct.Pa.1978).

The Trial Court found the following facts as being undisputed. . . .

"In fitting the wearer, Defendant makes use of the prescription written by the ophthalmologist which shows the refractive error or correction for spectacles. He uses certain instruments including a corneal microscope, keratometer and keratascope. He also inserts a fluoresciein dye under the eyelid. Defendant also takes the patient's medical history although it presumably has been already taken by the ophthalmologist.

"In order to obtain the data necessary for the Defendant to order the **contact lenses** from the laboratory certain measurements and computations are made by Defendant.

"Defendant also instructs the wearer in the procedures for handling, inserting and removing the **contact lenses**. . . ." State ex rel. State, etc. v. Kuhwald, 389 A.2d 1277–8 (Del. 1978).

We think that if "lenses" in [G.L. c. 112] § 66 include **contact lenses** then "lenses" in [G.L. c. 112] § 73C equally include **contact lenses**. We further think that "the human face" in § 73C includes the human eye, just as we think it includes the human nose and human ears. We recognize that the statutes are not entirely free from ambiguity in these respects, but we think that if the Legislature wishes to treat **contact lenses** as something other than lenses or to distinguish the eyes from the face it must say so more clearly. Attorney General v. Kenco Optics, Inc., 340 N.E.2d 868, 871 (Sup.Jud.Ct.Mass.1976).

Other Authorities: People ex rel. Watson v. House of Vision, 322 N.E.2d 15, 17–18 (Ill.1974); State ex rel. Londerholm v. Doolin, 497 P.2d 138, 141 (Kan.1972); State ex. inf. Danforth v. Dale Curteman, Inc., 480 S.W.2d 848, 852 (Mo.1972); But-

terfield v. Oculus Contact Lens Co., 332 F.Supp. 750, 753 (N.D.Ill.1971).

lens, lacrimal

The layer of tears under the lens is called the tear lens or **lacrimal lens**. State ex rel. Londerholm v. Doolin, 497 P.2d 138, 142 (Kan.1972).

lens, scleral

The **scleral lens**, which rests on the white part (sclera) of the eyeball and covers the cornea without touching it, is fitted in a slightly different manner from the corneal lens.

A **scleral lens** is fitted by first taking an impression mold of the wearer's eyeball. After the necessary refractive qualities are ground into this lens, it is fitted to the wearer's eyeball and any corrections necessary to secure a proper fit are made. Although the corneal lens is fitted without the taking of impression molds, its fitting procedure resembles the latter stages of a **scleral lens** fitting. People ex rel. Watson v. House of Vision, 322 N.E.2d 15, 18–19 (Ill.1975).

leprosarium (lep"ro-sa're-um) [L.] a hospital or colony for the treatment and isolation of leprosy patients.

The state has statutorily conferred upon leprosy patients an entitlement to treatment at some state leprosarium.[5] [[5] Haw. Rev.Stat. § 326–1 provides: Establishment of hospitals, etc.; treatment and care of persons affected with leprosy. The department of health, subject to the approval of the governor, shall establish hospitals, settlements and places as it deems necessary for the care and treatment of persons affected with leprosy. At every such hospital, settlement, and place there shall be exercised every reasonable effort to effect a cure of such persons, and all such persons shall be cared for as well as circumstances will permit, and given such liberties as may be deemed compatible with public safety and in the light of advances in medical science and in accordance with accepted practices elsewhere.] Brede v. Director for Dept. of Health, etc., 616 F.2d 407, 411 (9th Cir. 1980).

leprosy (lep'ro-se) [Gr. *lepros* scaly, scabby, rough] a chronic communicable disease, caused by a specific microorganism, *Mycobacterium leprae*, which produces various granulomatous lesions in the skin, the mucous membranes, and the peripheral nervous system. Two principal or polar types are recognized: lepromatous and tuberculoid. A combination of these types is called *borderline* or *dimorphous leprosy*. Called also *lepra, elephantiasis graecorum*, and *Hansen's disease*.

Leprosy, which is also known as **Hansen's disease**, is a mildly infectious degenerative disease caused by the micro-organism Mycobacterium leprae. The disease produces lesions in the skin, the mucous membranes, and the peripheral nervous system. In its more advanced stages, it affects internal organs and renders its sufferers vulnerable to other diseases such as diabetes and cancer. See Dorland's Illustrated Medical Dictionary 849 (25th ed. 1974). **Leprosy** is endemic to subtropical climates such as that of Hawaii. In 1952, there were more cases of **leprosy** in Hawaii than there were in the remainder of the United States. See S.Rep. No. 1335, 82d Cong. 2d Sess. reprinted in [1952] U.S.Code Cong. & Admin.News, pp. 1630, 1631. [Hereinafter Senate Report]. Brede v. Director for Dept. of Health, etc., 616 F.2d 407, 409 (9th Cir. 1980).

leptospirosis (lep"to-spi-ro'sis) infection by *Leptospira*. The infections are transmitted to man from dogs, swine, and rodents or by contact with contaminated water, as in swamps, canals, or ponds. All pathogenic leptospiral species (or serotypes) are probably capable of causing any of the clinical syndromes, including lymphocytic meningitis, hepatitis, and nephritis, separately or in combinations. Epidemics of meningitis, of febrile disease, or of hepatitis have been named for the regions in which they occurred or for the leptospiral species, implying a specific relationship between a species and a single clinical syndrome.

Claimant attempted to prove before the referee that the Decedent's death was not caused primarily by bronchopneumonia, but by the disease of **leptospirosis** contacted in the course of his employment. **Leptospirosis** organisms or spirochetes are carried by animals, including rats, and are found in water contaminated by the infected animals. When **leptospirosis** organisms enter a human's system, e.g., through a break in the skin, death may eventually result, usually from damage to kidneys, liver and, in rare instances, to the lungs. . . .

. . . The pathologist Dr. Brody testified unequivocally that **leptospirosis** was a cause of death and that **leptospirosis** was the primary disease leading to bronchopneumonia as the medical cause of death. He asserted that his autopsy report confirmed this diagnosis in its statement that the organisms of **leptospirosis** were recognized when the cerebrospinal fluid drawn from Decedent's body was examined microscopically. . . .

Dr. Satz pointed out that when **leptospirosis** results in death, it usually occurs through damaging of the kidneys and the liver, and in rare instances the lungs. Though Decedent suffered extensive tissue damage of these organs, "no convincing spirochetes" were found in them according to Dr. Brody's autopsy report.

Dr. Satz further testified that the **leptospirosis** spirochete is one of many types of spirochetes similar in structure, so that a diagnosis should only be made after culturing tissues in a laboratory, in addition to observing them under a microscope. According to Dr. Satz, many other diseases produce symptoms similar to **leptospirosis**. Despite Dr. Satz' testimony which was unfavorable to Claimant, Dr. Satz could not state conclusively that Decedent did not have **leptospirosis**. [Footnote omitted.] Novak v. Workmen's Compensation Appeal Bd., 430 A.2d 703, 705–6 (Commonwealth Ct.Pa.1981).

lesion (le'zhun) [L. *laesio; laedere* to hurt] any pathological or traumatic discontinuity of tissue or loss of function of a part. See also *trauma* (Cox case).

The films have two significant abnormalities. The first abnormality is the appearance of a mask **lesion** rather nodular in outline located peripherally in the right upper lobe and well seen also on the lateral projection. Its peripheral nature is beautifully demonstrated by clear lung between the hilar structures, the central bronchi in other words, and the **lesion** itself. This is similarly demonstrated on the lateral projection where again the main bronchi area seemed to be several inches away from this peripheral neoplasm **lesion**. Utter v. Asten-Hill Mfg. Co., 309 A.2d 583, 587 (Pa.1973).

Dr. Orr's written report states that the three pathologists felt that a "**benign lesion**" was represented "although it has mani-

festation [sic] of a most unusual histiocytic proliferating pattern." Jeanes v. Milner, 428 F.2d 598, 600 (8th Cir. 1970).

lesion, Bowen's See *disease, Bowen's.*

lesion, cerebral

His impression was that Stephen had sustained a left **cerebral lesion**, traumatic, likely a contusion, meaning a bruise of the left side of his brain resulting in a speech defect and in a weakness of the right side of his body. . . .

. . . He had some confusion knowing the right side from the left side, and he had some evidence of perseveration. There was some incoordination in the upper extremities, some spasticity in the muscles in the right leg and ankle, and weakness in the right hip and leg. There was some evidence of abnormal reflexes on both sides in the upper extremities, and sensation was decreased on the right side. He diagnosed Stephen as having cerebral trauma with a contusion of the left frontal lobe of the brain and decreased memory and language disturbance. Kinsey v. Kolber, 431 N.E.2d 1316, 1322–3 (App.Ct. Ill.1982).

lesion, discharging

An electroencephalogram revealed the presence of a "**discharging lesion**" in the left temporal lobe area of plaintiff's brain. Dr. Blonsky explained that such a lesion merely meant a region in the brain which irregularly "discharged electrically" its impulses. It did not indicate a space-occupying lesion, such as a tumor. . . .

. . . [The doctor explained that a discharging lesion merely indicated a portion of the brain which was irregularly "discharging electrically."] Intrater v. Thomas, 369 N.E.2d 1339, 1342, 1344 (App.Ct.Ill.1977).

lethal dose See *dose, lethal.*

leukemia (loo-ke'me-ah) [Gr. *leukos* white + *haima* blood + *-ia*] a progressive, malignant disease of the blood-forming organs, characterized by distorted proliferation and development of leukocytes and their precursors in the blood and bone marrow. Leukemia is classified clinically on the basis of (1) the duration and character of the disease—*acute* or *chronic;* (2) the type of cell involved—*myeloid (myelogenous), lymphoid (lymphogenous),* or *monocytic;* (3) increase or nonincrease in the number of abnormal cells in the blood—*leukemic* or *aleukemic (subleukemic).* See also *benzene* (Industrial Union case).

"Q. **Leukemia** is cancer of the blood-forming cells of the bone, is it not? A. Yes. It is a disease, neoplastic in nature, which affects the blood-forming tissues.

"The referee: Which we call cancer.

"The witness: Yes.

"Q. Cancer of the— A. Blood-forming tissues. . . .

. . . The effect of radiation on biological tissues is one which not only affects the genetic elements of the reproductive organs, but also the other cells of the body, including the cells which are involved in the process of forming blood. Now, scientific evidences are perhaps not as extensive in this area as in the genetic field, yet, I think the evidence is rather conclusive on one or two points. Number 1: That radiation of the blood-forming tissues can produce **leukemia**. Chiropractic Ass'n of New York, Inc. v. Hilleboe, 227 N.Y.S.2d 309, 356 (Sup.Ct. Albany Cty.1961).

The expert for the dependents testified that he had seen five hundred cases of **leukemia** and that in six of them an ''infection was a possible producing cause'' (emphasis supplied). He also stated that the opinions of medical authorities are about equally divided whether there is a causal connection between infection and **leukemia** (''50–50 all along the line''). He apparently recognized that there was less evidence that bacterial infection might be a contributing cause of **leukemia** than that viruses might be such a cause.[3] The expert relied considerably on medical writings, set forth in the record, to support his views. These writings, however, indicate that the matter is still an unresolved medical problem. In the expert's own experience in about one per cent of the cases observed by him, there was a possibility, but no more than that, that bacterial infection was a contributing cause. [[3] The ''cause of **leukemia** as one agent causing one disease is unknown. However, many conditions being described seem to be outstanding in the history of patients who have come to develop **leukemia**; among them are chemicals, drugs, traumatic infection, both bacteria and due to viruses.... As to infection, especially virus, there is a tremendous body of evidence that transmission of virus may in fact be responsible.... [A]t least in animal **leukemia** you have very good evidence for the viral theory.''] In Re Sevigny's Case, 151 N.E.2d 258, 262 (Sup.Jud.Ct.Mass. 1958).

leukemia, acute See *leukemia, promyelocytic.*

This witness testified that **acute leukemia** is a form of malignant cancer with wild growth which affects the bone marrow and results in an increase in the white blood cells and a reduction of normal red blood cells so that a patient develops anemia. He expressed his opinion that the employee was suffering from monoblastic leukemia which is known for a very rapid course so that a patient survives for a shorter time after attack than with other types of leukemia. In Re Sevigny's Case, 151 N.E.2d 258, 260 (Sup.Jud.Ct.Mass.1958).

leukemia, lymphatic; leukemia, lymphoblastic; leukemia, lymphocytic; leukemia, lymphogenous; leukemia, lymphoid leukemia associated with hyperplasia and overactivity of the lymphoid tissue, in which the leukocytes are lymphocytes or lymphoblasts. See also *chemotherapy; lymphoblast; lymphocyte; series; lymphocytic.*

Acute **lymphocytic leukemia** is a disease of the blood characterized by the appearance in the lymph tissue of excessive numbers of white cells and abnormal cells. The disease is attended by such symptoms as enlargement of the lymph glands, internal bleeding, anemia, and a high susceptibility to infection. Left untreated, the disease is fatal. Custody of a Minor, 379 N.E.2d 1053, 1056–7 (Sup.Jud.Ct.Mass.1978).

leukemia, monoblastic See *leukemia, monocytic; monoblast.*

... the employee, who had always been active about the house, had become listless and complained of being tired. His gums were bleeding and his palate was large and swollen....

... The next day she saw that his face was swollen and he had a cough and a temperature....

... and was readmitted to the hospital on the same day where a diagnosis of **monoblastic leukemia** was made. In Re Sevigny's Case, 151 N.E.2d 258–9 (Sup.Jud.Ct.Mass.1958).

leukemia, monocytic leukemia in which the predominating leukocytes are identified as monocytes. The disease is generally divided into two main categories: the Naegeli type, in which many of the cells resemble myeloblasts, or cells of the myeloid series; and the Schilling type, in which the cells more truly resemble monocytes or histiocytes.

leukemia, myeloblastic leukemia in which myeloblasts predominate.

leukemia, promyelocytic a subvariety of acute granulocytic leukemia in which the predominant cells are promyelocytes, rather than myeloblasts, often associated with abnormal bleeding secondary to thrombocytopenia, hypofibrinogenemia, and decreased levels of Factor V.

leukemogen (loo-ke′mo-jen) any substance that causes or produces leukemia.

During the 1970's several additional studies reported a statistically significant increased risk of leukemia among workers occupationally exposed to high levels of benzene and concluded benzene was a **leukemogen**. American Pet. Institute v. Occupational Safety, 581 F.2d 493, 498 (5th Cir. 1978).

leukemogenic (loo-ke″mo-jen′ik) causing leukemia.

''The evidence in the record conclusively establishes that benzene is a human carcinogen. The determination of benzene's **leukemogenicity** is derived from the evaluation of all the evidence in totality and is not based on any one particular study. OSHA recognizes, as indicated above that individual reports vary considerably in quality, and that some investigations have significant methodological deficiencies. While recognizing the strengths and weaknesses in individual studies, OSHA nevertheless concludes that the benzene record as a whole clearly establishes a causal relationship between benzene and leukemia.'' [43 Fed.Reg. 5931 (1978).] Industrial Union v. American Petroleum, 448 U.S. 607, 100 S.Ct. 2844, 2849, 2860, 65 L.Ed.2d 1010 (1980).

leukemogenicity See *leukemogenic.*

leukocyte (loo′ko-sīt) [*leuko-* + Gr. *kytos* cell] white blood cell or corpuscle. The varieties of leukocytes may be classified into two main groups: *granular l's* and *nongranular l's.*

leukocytes, granular (granulocytes) leukocytes with abundant granules in the cytoplasm, which are divided into three groups: (1) *Neutrophils,* cells with fine neutrophilic granules in the cytoplasm and an irregular lobed nucleus; see *neutrophil.* (2) *Eosinophils,* cells with coarse eosinophilic granules in the cytoplasm and a bilobed nucleus; see *eosinophil.* (3) *Basophils,* cells with coarse basophilic granules in the cytoplasm and a bent nucleus that is partially constricted into two lobes; see *basophil* (def. 2). See also *granulocytic series,* under *series.*

leukocytes, nongranular leukocytes without specific granules in their cytoplasm, including the lymphocytes and monocytes. Called also *agranular l's* and *lymphoid l's.*

leukocyte, polymorphonuclear any of the fully developed, segmented cells of the granulocytic series, especially a neutrophil, whose nuclei contain three or more lobes joined by filamentous connections. See also *neutrophil.*

Another type of white cells in the CSF are **polymorphonuclear leukocytes**, which are also a sign of the body fighting acute infection, especially bacterial infections. Because HSE is a viral infection, these cells are not normally found in such cases. Stich v. U.S., 565 F.Supp. 1096, 1119 (D.N.J.1983).

leukocytosis (loo″ko-si-to′sis) a transient increase in the number of leukocytes in the blood, resulting from various causes, as hemorrhage, fever, infection, inflammation, etc.

Doctor Baldini was then asked to define the term "**leukocytosis.**" "**Leukocytosis**," he said, is an abnormal increase "of the white cell count in the peripheral blood." When asked, "And what causes that, doctor, as a rule?" the reply was the same as it was when the question was asked in direct examination that "one hundred twenty causes are responsible." Young v. Park, 417 A.2d 889, 894 (R.I.1980).

A decision was made to operate on plaintiff's left knee, but the surgery was cancelled because of the presence of **leukocytosis** (increase in the number of white blood cells). (Tr. 127). Pruchniewski v. Weinberger, 415 F.Supp. 112–13 (D.Md. 1976).

leukoderma (loo″ko-der′mah) [*leuko-* + Gr. *derma* skin] an acquired type of localized loss of melanin pigmentation of the skin, differing from vitiligo only in that the cause may be more or less apparent.

The term "**leukoderma**," as defined by Dr. Kenney, means a depigmentation for which the cause is known. He stated that, in his opinion, the cause of Mr. Finley's problem was known. He testified that the taking of Doriden caused the initial drug reaction, the drug reaction caused the exfoliative dermatitis, and the exfoliative dermatitis caused the depigmentation. Finley v. U.S., 314 F.Supp. 905, 909 (N.D.Ohio 1970).

leukokoria (loo″ko-ko′re-ah) [*leuko-* + Gr. *korē* pupil + *-ia*] a condition characterized by appearance of a whitish reflex or mass in the pupillary area back of the lens.

When Dr. Wolf examined Timothy on June 17th he found Timothy's visual acuity in the right eye limited to hand motion although capable of perceiving light. Essentially Timothy's right eye was blind. The doctor diagnosed **Leucocoria**, right eye, with right esotropia. In his medical opinion the inflammatory cause was a vitreous hemorrhage with possible involvement of toxocara canis or retinoblastoma. Steele v. U.S., 463 F.Supp. 321, 323 (D.Alas.1978).

leukopenia (loo″ko-pe′ne-ah) [*leukocyte* + Gr. *penia* poverty] reduction in the number of leukocytes in the blood, the count being 5000 per cu. mm. or less. See also *benzene* (American Petroleum Inst. case).

[Attributed to benzene]: A decline in the white blood cell count (**leukopenia**) reduces the capacity of the body to defend against disease and is characterized by recurrent infections. American Pet. Institute v. Occupational Safety, 581 F.2d 493, 498 (5th Cir. 1978).

levarterenol (lev″ar-tĕ-re′nol) the levorotatory isomer of norepinephrine (q.v.), a much more potent pressor agent than the natural dextrorotatory isomer.

levarterenol bitartrate See *norepinephrine bitartrate.*

Dr. Edmonds, who directed the autopsy, testified—in answer to questions by the judge—that in his view thorazine and electroshock standing alone would not have caused death, but that death was caused when this treatment was followed by administration of another drug, **levophed**, a combination that resulted in infarction of deceased's bowels. Dr. Schulman contested that the **levophed**, which he himself had prescribed, contributed to death. Thus, there was a conflict in the testimony as to the cause of death. Kosberg v. Washington Hospital Center, Inc., 394 F.2d 947, 949 (D.C.Cir.1968).

levonorgestrel

The crucial active ingredient in Ovranette, and the substance alleged to have caused Ms. Howell's stroke, is the synthetic progestogen **levonorgestrel**. Bewers v. American Home Products Corp., 459 N.Y.S.2d 666, 669 (Sup.Ct.N.Y.Cty.1982).

Levophed See *levarterenol bitartrate; norepinephrine bitartrate.*

levopropoxyphene napsylate (le″vo-pro-pok′sĕ-fēn nap′sĭ-lāt) [USP] chemical name: $[R-(R^*,S^*)]$-α-[2-(dimethylamino)-1-methylethyl]-α-phenylbenzenethanol propanoate (ester) compound with 2-naphthalenesulphonic acid (1:1) monohydrate. The napsylate salt of the levo isomer of propoxyphen, $C_{22}H_{29}NO_2 \cdot C_{10}H_8O_3S \cdot H_2O$, occurring as a white powder; used as an antitussive, administered orally.

levulose See *fructose.*

lincomycin (lin″ko-mi′sin) chemical name: (2S-*trans*)-methyl-6,8-dideoxy-6-[[(1-methyl-4-propyl-2-pyrrolidinyl) carbonyl] amino]-1-thio-D-*erythro*-α-D-*galacto*-octopyranoside. An antibiotic, $C_{18}H_{34}N_2O_6S$, primarily a gram-positive specific antibacterial, produced by a variant of *Streptomyces lincolnesis*. See also *enterocolitis.*

Librium (lib′re-um) trademark for preparations of chlordiazepoxide hydrochloride. See also *chlordiazepoxide hydrochloride.*

lidocaine (li′do-kān) [USP] chemical name: 2-(diethylamino)-*N*-(2,6-dimethylphenyl)acetamide. A drug, $C_{14}H_{22}N_2O$, having anesthetic, sedative, analgesic, anticonvulsant, and cardiac depressant activities, occurring as a white or slightly yellow, crystalline powder; used as a local anesthetic, applied topically to the skin and mucous membranes.

. . . she was mistakenly administered a massive overdose of **lidocaine** by a hospital nurse. Mrs. Sharrow suffered a cardiac arrest, but was resuscitated by the supervising doctors, Gary Archer and Richard Anschuetz.

Following this incident, Archer expressed some doubt as to whether the arrest was drug-induced, and told the nurses they were not to mention the drug overdose either to the patient or in the chart. Sharrow v. Archer, 658 P.2d 1331–2 (Alas.1983).

. . . it confirmed the findings of the other two previous examinations that certainly he had objective evidence of pain; was not malingering; and definitely had bonified [sic] objective evidence of injury of the spine. Mr. Chabert was treated with injection therapy of injecting these trigger areas with a 1% **Hydrocortisone Acetate** solution in ½% **Xylocaine Hydorchloride** with satisfactory results. Whereas he could hardly move prior to getting on the table, examination following the treatment revealed an absence of pain following treatment. Chabert v. City of Westwego Police Pension, 423 So.2d 1190, 1194 (Ct. of App.La.1982).

The defendant subsequently injected the plaintiff with **xylocaine**, a local anesthetic containing epinephrine, which is a vasoconstrictor. He then performed the oral surgery....

... The Physicians Desk Reference contains warnings about the use of **xylocaine** containing epinephrine with patients suffering from hypertension, high blood pressure, or cardiovascular disease....

... Dr. Tuby concluded in his affidavit:

That it is his opinion that Claude LeBeuf was probably suffering from hypertension accompanied by high blood pressure at the time he was operated on by Dr. Atkins, and that the injections of **Xylocaine** with epinephrine probably caused the ensuing damage to Claude LeBeuf's central nervous system and it is more likely than not that this resulted in a subarachnoid hemorrhage. LeBeuf v. Atkins, 594 P.2d 923–5 (Ct.App.Wash.1979), reversed and remanded with directions 604 P.2d 1282 (Wash.1980).

Other Authorities: Wallace v. State, 215 S.E.2d 703–4, 706 (Ct.App.Ga.1975); Sanzari v. Rosenfeld, 167 A.2d 625, 627 (N.J.1961).

life (līf) [L. *vita;* Gr. *bios* or *zōe*] the aggregate of vital phenomena; a certain peculiar stimulated condition of organized matter; that obscure principle whereby organized beings are peculiarly endowed with certain powers and functions not associated with inorganic matter. Generally, living things share, in varying degrees, the following characteristics: organization, irritability, movement, growth, reproduction, and adaptation.

life, intrauterine; life, uterine the period of life spent in the uterus; i.e., embryonic and fetal life.

The Legislature was undoubtedly aware that biologists, fetologists, and medical science commonly accept conception as the beginning of human life and the formation of an individual endowed with its own unique genetic pattern (Tr. 205); that the heart functions and circulates blood through the human fetus at three to five weeks (Tr. 286) and that blood groupings may be ascertained at eight weeks (Tr. 206); that while nutrients are fed to the baby from the mother through the placenta and the waste similarly excreted, the placenta is really part of the baby. (Tr. 284); and that the latter's heart pumps its own blood through the umbilical vessels and lives as a separate entity suspended in amniotic fluid. (Tr. 210)....

They had available to them medical information that, as early as seven weeks, brain waves are detectable in the unborn child and that it is known to react to drugs (Tr. 212); that physical reflexes such as contraction of the limbs, movements of the mouth, the eyelids, and general contraction of the body have been elicited from the maturing infant as early as six weeks; and that unborn babies weighing as little as 395 grams (13 ounces) have been known to survive outside the mother (Tr. 295–296). They were also aware that medical research in the field of fetal medicine is a comparatively new branch of

medicine (Tr. 252) and that the transplantation of life to artificial placentas is presently being studied. Abele v. Markle, 351 F.Supp. 224, 235–6 (D.Conn.1972).

life-prolonging

The nature of the choice has become more difficult because physicians have begun to realize that in many cases the effect of using extraordinary measures to **prolong life** is to "only prolong suffering, isolate the family from their loved one at a time when they may be close at hand or result in economic ruin for the family." Lewis, Machine Medicine and Its Relation to the Fatally Ill, 206 J.A.M.A. 387 (1968).

Recognition of these factors led the Supreme Court of New Jersey to observe "that physicians distinguish between curing the ill and comforting and easing the dying; that they refuse to treat the curable as if they were dying or ought to die, and that they have sometimes refused to treat the hopeless and dying as if they were curable." In re Quinlan, 70 N.J. 10, 47, 355 A.2d 647, 667 (1976)....

... The interest of the State in **prolonging a life** must be reconciled with the interest of an individual to reject the traumatic cost of that prolongation. There is a substantial distinction in the State's insistence that human life be saved where the affliction is curable, as opposed to the State interest where, as here, the issue is not whether but when, for how long, and at what cost to the individual that life may be briefly extended....

... For reasons discussed at some length in subsection A, supra, we recognize a general right in all persons to refuse medical treatment in appropriate circumstances. The recognition of that right must extend to the case of an incompetent, as well as a competent, patient because the value of human dignity extends to both. Superintendent of Belchertown v. Saikewicz, 370 N.E.2d 417, 423, 425–7 (Sup.Jud.Ct.Mass.1977).

life support [system] See *euthanasia.*

In Louisiana, the Legislature has not yet established a procedure for parents, tutors or curators of an incompetent person to withdraw **life support systems** when the person has entered a permanent and irreversible comatose condition. However, the Legislature in Act 339 of 1982 has at least indirectly recognized the incompetent person's right to have such systems terminated....

... See Collester, Death, Dying and the Law: A Prosecutorial View of the Quinlan Case, 30 Rutgers L.Rev. 304, 310–311 (1977). In re P.V.W., 424 So.2d 1015, 1019, 1021 (La.1982).

In describing **life-support systems**, extraordinary is apparently not a medical term and the distinction between "ordinary" and "extraordinary" measures remains hazy. One commonly quoted description is as follows: "Ordinary means are all medicines, treatments, and operations which offer a reasonable hope of benefit and which can be obtained and used without excessive pain, or other inconvenience. Extraordinary means are all medicines, treatments and operations which cannot be obtained or used without excessive expense, pain, or other inconvenience, or if used, would not offer a reasonable hope of benefit" (Kelly, The Duty to Preserve Life, 12 Theol. Studies 550, quoted in, Byrne, Agathanasia and the Care of the Dying, 112 Can.Med.A.J. 1396; see, also, Hirsch & Donovan, The Right to Die: Medico-Legal Implications of In Re Quinlan, 30 Rutgers L.Rev. 267, 290, n. 132, 291, n. 138). In the context of this proceeding, the use of a respirator for an individual who does not spontaneously respirate is accepted as an "extraordinary" means of **life support**. Eichner v. Dillon, 426 N.Y.S.2d 517, 527 (2d Dep't 1980).

life-sustaining

Life sustaining procedures are medical procedures which utilize mechanical or other artificial means to sustain, restore, or supplant a vital function, which serve only or primarily to prolong the moment of death, and where, in the judgment of the attending and consulting physicians, as reflected in the patient's medical records, death is imminent if such procedures are not utilized. John F. Kennedy Memorial Hosp. v. Bludworth, 432 So.2d 611, 619 (Dist.Ct.App.Fla.1983), quashed 452 So.2d 921 (Fla.1984).

life-sustaining device See *device, life-sustaining.*

life, wrongful

In Curlender v. Bio-Science Laboratories (1980) 106 Cal.App. 3d 811, 165 Cal.Rptr. 477, the appellate court held that a child had a cause of action for damages for pain and suffering to be endured in its life span, and the appellate court created a cause of action that has become known in the legal literature as "**wrongful life.**" The Supreme Court in Turpin v. Sortini (1982) 31 Cal.3d 220, 237, 182 Cal.Rptr. 337, 643 P.2d 954, recently dealt with the issue and held that recovery should be denied for a child's pain and suffering, where the allegation is that if the parents knew of the hereditary condition, they would not have conceived the baby. The Supreme Court in Turpin held recovery should be denied for the child's pain and suffering and other general damages, because it is impossible to determine whether plaintiff has in fact suffered an injury in being born rather than in not being born and it is impossible to assess general damages in any fair, nonspeculative manner. However, the Turpin court held that, even though general damages may not be recovered in such a case, damages for extraordinary expenses for specialized teaching and training and special equipment that plaintiff will need because of her defect are recoverable. Call v. Kezirian, 185 Cal.Rptr. 103, 105–6 (Ct.App.1982).

In recent times, a few jurisdictions appear to have allowed such a cause of action, but only under very limited circumstances. See generally Morrison, Torts Involving the Unborn—A Limited Cosmology, 31 Baylor L.Rev. 131 (1979). At oral argument, counsel for the Nelsons conceded that Texas has yet to recognize affirmatively a cause of action for **wrongful life**. He contended, however, that the decision in Jacobs v. Theimer, 519 S.W.2d 846 (Tex. 1975), provides, at least impliedly, support for Mark's claim for **wrongful life**. We do not agree.

Mark's pleadings, liberally construed, seek two general types of damages: (1) those for having been born at all and (2) those for the expenses related to his defect or deformity. With respect to damages for having been born at all, Jacobs is of no assistance. It denied the parents any recovery for such damages. The rationale relied on by the Court for denying recovery of these damages to the parents applies with equal force to deny recovery to a minor child, i.e., the impossibility of measuring the value of existence with physical defects against the value of non-existence, and the notion that life, no matter how defective or unsatisfactory, is preferable to non-

existence. Nelson v. Krusen, 635 S.W.2d 582, 585 (Ct.App. Tex.1982).

A "**wrongful life**" claim is one "brought on behalf of a severely defective infant, against a physician, . . . contend[ing] that the physician negligently failed to inform the child's parents of the possibility of their bearing a severely defective child, thereby preventing a parental choice to avoid the child's birth." Cohen, Park v. Chessin: The Continuing Judicial Development of the Theory of "Wrongful Life," 4 Am.J.L. & Med. 211, 211 (1979).

The child does not allege that the physician's negligence caused the child's deformity. Rather, the claim is that the physician's negligence—his failure to adequately inform the parents of the risk—has caused the birth of the deformed child. The child argues that but for the inadequate advice, it would not have been born to experience the pain and suffering attributable to the deformity.

Comment, "Wrongful Life": The Right Not to be Born, 54 Tulane L.Rev. 480, 485 (1980) (emphasis in original). E.g., Gleitman v. Cosgrove, 49 N.J. 22, 227 A.2d 689 (1967). The corresponding action by the parents for damages they may suffer in such a situation is denominated one for "wrongful birth." E.g., Berman v. Allen, 80 N.J. 421, 404 A.2d 8 (1979); Trotzig, The Defective Child and the Actions for Wrongful Life and Wrongful Birth, 14 Fam.L.Q. 15 (1980). For a complete discussion of the terminological distinctions, see 54 Tulane L.Rev. 480, 483–85 (1980) (including definitions of "wrongful pregnancy" and "dissatisfied life"). . . .

. . . The issues have also been thoroughly and cogently analyzed by various commentators. E.g., Capron, Tort Liability and Genetic Counseling, 79 Columbia L.Rev. 619 (1979); Capron, Informed Decision Making in Genetic Counseling: A dissent to the "Wrongful Life" Debate, 48 Ind.L.J. 581 (1973); Cohen, supra, note 1; Kelly, Wrongful Life, Wrongful Birth & Justice in Tort Law, 1979 Wash.U.L.Q. 919 (1979); Tedeschi, On Tort Liability for "Wrongful Life," 1 Israel L.Rev. 513 (1966), reprinted in 7 J.Fam.L. 465 (1967); Trotzig, supra note 1; 2 Am.J.Trial Advocacy 107 (1978); 27 Buffalo L.Rev. 537 (1978); 8 Hofstra L.Rev. 257 (1979); 55 Minn.L.Rev. 58 (1970); 10 Seton Hall L.Rev. 952 (1980); 54 Tulane L.Rev. 480 (1980); 55 Wash.L.Rev. 701 (1980). Phillips v. U.S., 508 F.Supp. 537–9 (D.S.C.1980).

Other Authorities: Curlender v. Bio-Science Laboratories, 165 Cal.Rptr. 477, 481, 489–90 (Ct.App.1980); Becker v. Schwartz, 413 N.Y.S.2d 895, 898, 386 N.E.2d 807, 810, 812 (N.Y.1978); Johnson v. Yeshiva Univ., 364 N.E.2d 1340–1 (N.Y.1977); Sherlock v. Stillwater Clinic, 260 N.W.2d 169, 172 (Minn.1977); Park v. Chessin, 400 N.Y.S.2d 110, 114–15 (2d. Dep't 1977); Bowman v. Davis, 356 N.E.2d 496, 499 (Ohio 1976).

ligament (lig'ah-ment) a band of fibrous tissue that connects bones or cartilages, serving to support and strengthen joints; see *ligamentum.*

A **ligament** is a structure that holds bones together, and those structures can be stretched or sometimes torn, and they are productive of pain when this happens. Colgan v. Raymond, 146 N.W.2d 530, 532 (Minn.1966).

ligament, collateral; fibular See *ligamentum collaterale fibulare.*

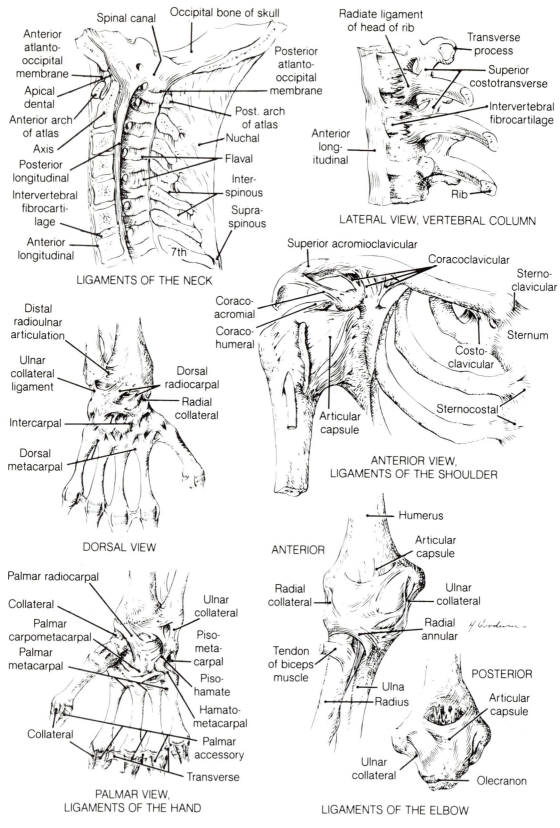

LIGAMENTS OF THE NECK

Anterior atlanto-occipital membrane
Apical dental
Anterior arch of atlas
Axis
Posterior longitudinal
Intervertebral fibrocartilage
Anterior longitudinal
Spinal canal
Occipital bone of skull
Posterior atlanto-occipital membrane
Post. arch of atlas
Nuchal
Flaval
Inter-spinous
Supra-spinous
7th

LATERAL VIEW, VERTEBRAL COLUMN

Radiate ligament of head of rib
Transverse process
Superior costotransverse
Intervertebral fibrocartilage
Anterior long-itudinal
Rib

DORSAL VIEW

Distal radioulnar articulation
Ulnar collateral ligament
Intercarpal
Dorsal metacarpal
Dorsal radiocarpal
Radial collateral

ANTERIOR VIEW, LIGAMENTS OF THE SHOULDER

Superior acromioclavicular
Coracoclavicular
Coraco-acromial
Coraco-humeral
Articular capsule
Sterno-clavicular
Sternum
Costo-clavicular
Sternocostal

PALMAR VIEW, LIGAMENTS OF THE HAND

Palmar radiocarpal
Collateral
Palmar carpometacarpal
Palmar metacarpal
Collateral
Ulnar collateral
Piso-meta-carpal
Piso-hamate
Hamato-metacarpal
Palmar accessory
Transverse

LIGAMENTS OF THE ELBOW

ANTERIOR
Humerus
Articular capsule
Radial collateral
Ulnar collateral
Radial annular
Tendon of biceps muscle
Ulna
Radius
POSTERIOR
Articular capsule
Ulnar collateral
Olecranon

H. Goodwin

ARTICULAR LIGAMENTS

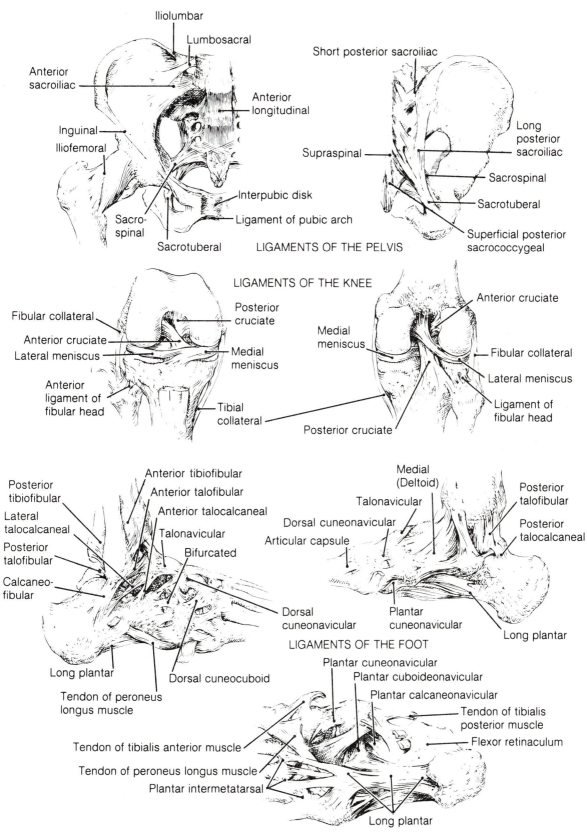

Iliolumbar

Lumbosacral

Anterior sacroiliac

Anterior longitudinal

Inguinal

Iliofemoral

Interpubic disk

Ligament of pubic arch

Sacro-spinal

Sacrotuberal

Short posterior sacroiliac

Long posterior sacroiliac

Supraspinal

Sacrospinal

Sacrotuberal

Superficial posterior sacrococcygeal

LIGAMENTS OF THE PELVIS

LIGAMENTS OF THE KNEE

Fibular collateral

Posterior cruciate

Anterior cruciate

Lateral meniscus

Medial meniscus

Anterior ligament of fibular head

Tibial collateral

Anterior cruciate

Medial meniscus

Fibular collateral

Lateral meniscus

Ligament of fibular head

Posterior cruciate

Posterior tibiofibular

Anterior tibiofibular

Anterior talofibular

Anterior talocalcaneal

Lateral talocalcaneal

Talonavicular

Posterior talofibular

Bifurcated

Calcaneo-fibular

Long plantar

Dorsal cuneocuboid

Tendon of peroneus longus muscle

Dorsal cuneonavicular

Medial (Deltoid)

Talonavicular

Dorsal cuneonavicular

Articular capsule

Posterior talofibular

Posterior talocalcaneal

Plantar cuneonavicular

Long plantar

LIGAMENTS OF THE FOOT

Plantar cuneonavicular

Plantar cuboideonavicular

Plantar calcaneonavicular

Tendon of tibialis posterior muscle

Flexor retinaculum

Tendon of tibialis anterior muscle

Tendon of peroneus longus muscle

Plantar intermetatarsal

Long plantar

ARTICULAR LIGAMENTS

ligament, inguinal See *ligamentum inguinale.*

ligament, patellar See *ligamentum patellae.*

ligament, supraspinal; ligament supra spinous See *ligamentum supraspinale.*

ligament, medial collateral See *ligamentum, collaterale fibulare.*

ligamentum (lig″ah-men′tum), pl. *ligamen′ta* [L. "a bandage," from *ligare* to bind] [NA] a ligament: a band of tissue that connects bones or supports viscera. Some ligaments are distinct fibrous structures; some are folds of fascia or of indurated peritoneum; still others are relics of fetal organs. For names of specific structures, see *Table of Ligamenta.*

TABLE OF LIGAMENTA

ligamentum collaterale fibulare [NA], collateral fibular ligament: a strong, round fibrous cord on the lateral side of the knee joint, entirely independent of the capsule of the knee joint; it is attached superiorly to the posterior part of the lateral epicondyle of the femur and inferiorly to the lateral side of the head of the fibula just in front of the styloid process.

The hospital records contain an "operative record" signed by Dr. Borders as of that date stating among other things that the **medial collateral ligament** "had detached itself from the undersurface of the superficial portion proximally..."

"[T]here was some significant tearing on anterior, medial, and posterior portions of this portion of the ligament; and it was completely separated from its proximal attachment," that these tears were all repaired, and that a "long-leg cast" going from his foot to his thigh was applied. Contreras v. St. Luke's Hosp., 144 Cal.Rptr. 647, 650 (Ct.App.Cal.1978).

ligamentum hepatogastricum [NA], hepatogastric ligament: a peritoneal fold, part of the lesser omentum, that passes from the under surface of the liver to the lesser curvature of the stomach.

ligamentum inguinale [NA], inguinal ligament: a fibrous band running from the anterior superior spine of the ilium to the spine of the pubis.

... claimant had suffered bruises of the sacral region and also "a permanent stretching of the right **inguinal ligament**, and enlargement of the external inguinal opening". Hurlburt v. Fidelity Window Cleaning Co., 160 A.2d 251, 254 (Super.Ct. Pa.1960).

ligamentum patellae [NA], patellar ligament: the continuation of the central portion of the tendon of the quadriceps femoris muscle distal to the patella; it extends from the patella to the tuberosity of the tibia.

Dr. Powell removed all the fragments of the fractured patella and sutured the quadriceps muscle tendon to the **patellar ligament**. Means v. Sears, Roebuck & Co., 550 S.W.2d 780, 783 (Mo.1977).

ligamentum popliteum arcuatum [NA], arcuate popliteal ligament: a band of variable and ill-defined fibers at the posterolateral part of the knee joint; it is attached inferiorly to the apex of the head of the fibula, arches superiorly and medially over the popliteal tendon, and merges with the articular capsule. Called also *popliteal arch* and *arcuate ligament of knee.*

ligamentum popliteum obliquum [NA], oblique popliteal ligament: a broad band of fibers that arises from the medial condyle of the tibia, merges more or less with the tendon of the semimembranosus, and passes obliquely across the back of the knee joint to the lateral epicondyle of the femur. It contains large openings for the passage of vessels and nerves.

ligamentum supraspinale [NA], supraspinal ligament: a single long, vertical fibrous band passing over and attached to the tips of the spinous processes of the vertebrae from the seventh cervical to the sacrum; it is continuous above with the ligamentum nuchae.

His preliminary diagnosis was that plaintiff had a residual injury to the area of the **supraspinal ligament** at the level of the L4 interspace. Wheat v. Ford, Bacon and Davis Const.Corp., 424 So.2d 293, 295 (Ct.App.La.1982).

---

ligamentous injury See *sprain.*

ligate (li′gāt) to tie or bind with a ligature. See also *ligation; ligature.*

During the operation itself [hysterectomy], excessive and profuse bleeding occurred in the operative area and, in the middle of the operation, Dr. Kairys sent for Dr. Cushing, a cardiovascular surgeon. Drs. Kairys and Cushing attempted to **ligate** the arteries involved to stop the massive bleeding and a right hypogastric artery ligation was performed. Hoeke v. Mercy Hospital of Pittsburgh, 445 A.2d 140, 142 (Super Ct.Pa.1982).

ligation (li-ga′shun) [L. *ligatio*] the application of a ligature. See also *ligature.* Cited in Carmichael v. Reitz, 95 Cal.Rptr. 381, 390 (Ct.App.Cal.1971).

ligation, tubal sterilization of the female by constricting the uterine tubes by means of ligatures; the tubes may, in addition, be severed or crushed.

At the same time, Hartke had herself resterilized by a **tubal ligation**, which involves actually cutting the Fallopian tubes. The record suggests that this method of sterilization involves about the same risk of subsequent pregnancy as cauterization. Hartke v. McKelway, 707 F.2d 1544, 1547 (D.C.Cir.1983).

In July 1973, the plaintiff Carol Ochs arranged for the individual defendant, a licensed physician and surgeon, to perform a sterilization procedure known as a laparoscopic **tubal ligation**. Ochs v. Borrelli, 445 A.2d 883, 883–4 (Conn.1982).

There was uncontradicted expert testimony that pregnancies occur in some instances in spite of the non-negligent performance of such an operation. The physician who delivered the plaintiff's third child and performed a second **tubal ligation**, but by a different procedure, testified that there is a rate of "failure" for all **tubal ligation** procedures which varies in the range of "one per two-hundred and fifty cases, one per five hundred, one per one thousand." Clevenger v. Haling, 394 N.E.2d 1119, 1122 (Sup.Jud.Ct.Mass.1979).

Other Authorities: Thompson v. Presbyterian Hosp., Inc., 652 P.2d 260, 262 (Okl.1982); Sard v. Hardy, 379 A.2d 1014, 1017–18 (Ct.App.Md.1977); Walker v. Pierce, 560 F.2d 609, 611 (4th. Cir. 1977); Raitt v. Johns Hopkins Hosp., 322 A.2d 548, 560–1 (Ct.Spec.App.Md.1974).

ligation, tubal (Pomeroy) See *operation, Pomeroy's.*

ligation, vein

The "vein ligation" was a surgical operation involving the tying of the patient's veins; evidently, Thompson suffered from varicose veins, and the ligation was necessary to relieve this condition. Thompson v. Occidental Life Insurance Co. of Cal., 513 P.2d 353, 359 (Cal.1973).

ligature (lig'ah-chūr) [L. *ligatura*] any substance, such as catgut, cotton, silk, or wire, used to tie a vessel or strangulate a part. See also *hysterectomy* (Cronin case).

During the surgical procedures involving the removal of the uterus and the ovary, it was necessary to control normal bleeding and Dr. Ricks utilized **ligatures** (a form of tied suture) as well as standard sutures (threading with a needle) for this purpose....

... The evidence showed that during the operation, Dr. Ricks apparently tied a **ligature** (loop) inadvertently around the left ureter. Either because of the normal tension of the **ligature** or because of its subsequent displacement, the **ligature** formed an obstruction of the left ureter and blocked the flow from the left kidney to the bladder. Williams v. Ricks, 263 S.E.2d 457–8 (Ct.App.Ga.1979).

This operation revealed **ligatures** or sutures and adhesions very close to the blocked area of the ureter. However, there were no **ligatures** or stitches going through or around the ureter. The **ligatures** and adhesions in the area of the partial blockage of the ureter were a result of the hysterectomy and were putting pressure on the ureter. Dr. Howard was easily able to "free up" the ureter at this time. Cronin v. Hagan, 221 N.W.2d 748, 749 (Iowa 1974).

The baron ligation method [of treating hemorrhoids] consists of placing a rubber **ligature** around the hemorrhoidal vein, thereby cutting off blood circulation into the vein. American Home Products Corp. v. F.T.C., 402 F.2d 232, 236 (6th Cir. 1968).

Other Authorities: AMP Inc. v. Gardner, 275 F.Supp. 410–11 (S.D.N.Y.1967).

limb (lim) 1. one of the paired appendages of the body used in locomotion or grasping. In man, an arm or a leg with all its component parts; called also *membrum* [NA] and, formerly, *extremitas*. In embryology, the limbs are divided into four main parts: the *zonoskeleton*, comprising the scapula and clavicle (as a unit) and the hip bone; the *stylopodium*, comprising the humerus and femur; the *zygopodium*, comprising the radius and ulna and the tibia

and fibula; and the *autopodium*, comprising the hand and the foot.

limb, artificial See *prosthesis.*

limb, phantom the sensation, after amputation of a limb, that the absent part is still present; there may also be paresthesias, transient aches, and intermittent or continuous pain perceived as originating in the absent limb.

However, he suffered from the **phantom pain syndrome** in which "the brain still thinks that the nerve conduction fibers are still there." (Tr. p. 197). Dr. Hocker testified that "I'm not sure we're ever going to get rid of this type of pain." (Tr. p. 204). Aretz v. U.S., 456 F.Supp. 397, 404 (S.D.Ga.1978).

Raines also suffered what Doctors Meany and McNabola called **phantom pains**—that is, even though the legs were severed, he complained of pain in his feet and toes. **Phantom pains** are not uncommon in these kinds of amputations, Dr. Meany testified, and result from the cutting of the femoral and sciatic nerves, which have their origin in the spinal cord. Raines v. New York Cent. Railroad Co., 283 N.E.2d 230, 236 (Ill. 1972).

limp

Westfall walks with a permanent **limp**. One leg is one and one-half inches shorter than the other. He has constant pain and will develop arthritis as the result of the injury. Westfall by Terwilliger v. Kottke, 328 N.W.2d 481, 485 (Wis.1983).

Lincocin (lin-ko'sin) trademark for a preparation of lincomycin hydrochloride. See also *lincomycin hydrochloride.*

Mauldin severely injured his hand in March 1974 while working on a lake barge. He was treated by Dr. Herman E. Walker, Jr., who prescribed Lincocin as a guard against infection. Mauldin v. Upjohn Co., 697 F.2d 644–5 (5th Cir. 1983).

She told the doctor and his nurse that she had had a reaction to penicillin and streptomycin the previous year; that her internist had advised her not to take any antibiotics and displayed to the doctor a medical alert bracelet that she wore reading "Penicillin—Streptomycin allergy" which had been prescribed by her internist. Dr. Wurster advised that he would use **Lincocin** and that she would have no ill effects therefrom....

... Her testimony was that on the 8th of August, she felt a little under par and was tense. On the 10th or 11th of August, she was experiencing a breaking-out on her face and severe itching. At that time she called her internist Dr. Lundgren. She was treated with ACTH and given creams for the swelling and breaking-out on her hands, face, neck and ears. Her condition temporarily improved but soon got worse again. She had swelling, breaking out, itching and blistering on her hands and arms, face, neck and ears, and over large portions of the rest of her body. The condition was such that the skin between her fingers broke....

... At the time of the trial she had itching, rash and swelling, and was not able to pursue her normal activities....

... Among other things, the insert stated "Patients with otitis media [plaintiff's condition] ... have been treated with good clinical results in the majority of cases." It was also stated "**Lincocin** has been administered to over 460 persons with known allergies (including persons reported to be allergic to penicillin). No serious hypersensitivity reactions have been reported in these patients and many patients have received repeated courses of **Lincocin** without developing evidence of hypersensitivity." Further, the insert advised "Cross resistance has not been demonstrated with penicillin, . . . streptomycin. . . ."

Under the heading "Adverse Reactions", the following appeared:

"The most frequently observed side effect has been loose stools or diarrhea. As expected, this was observed almost exclusively in patients on oral therapy. Other adverse reactions reported in a small per cent of patients have been nausea, vomiting, abdominal cramps or pain, skin rash, rectal irritation, vaginitis, urticaris, and itching.

"Angioneurotic edema, serum sickness, anaphylaxis or other serious hypersensitivity reactions have not been reported. "Intramuscularly, **Lincocin** has demonstrated excellent local tolerance and reports of pain following injection have been infrequent. . . .

. . . For all the evidence shows Mrs. Johnston may be the first person to have such a severe reaction or a reaction in any way different from those described. Johnston v. Upjohn Co., 442 S.W.2d 93–4 (Mo.Ct.App.1969).

She told Dr. Denicourt that she had hoped he might be able to save the implant. Doctor Denicourt agreed to try but gave her little encouragement. Accordingly, he prescribed massive doses of an antibiotic, specifically **lincocin**, with temporary positive results. However, the infection recurred, and on December 8, 1967, Dr. Denicourt was convinced that the implant would have to come out. Kelly v. Gershkoff, 312 A.2d 211, 213 (R.I.1973).

lincomycin hydrochloride [USP], the monohydrated monohydrochloride salt of lincomycin, $C_{18}H_{34}N_2O_6S \cdot HCl \cdot H_2O$, occurring as a white or practically white, crystalline powder; used as an antibacterial, mainly in the treatment of infections due to susceptible strains of streptococci, pneumococci, and staphylococci, administered intramuscularly and intravenously.

lindane (lin'dān) [USP] chemical name: $1\alpha,2\alpha,3\beta,4\alpha,$ $5\alpha,6\beta$-hexachlorocyclohexane. The gamma isomer of benzene hexachloride, $C_6H_6Cl_6$, occurring as a white, crystalline powder; an insecticide more potent than chlorophenothane (DDT), it is used as a pediculicide and scabicide, applied topically to the skin. Called also *gamma benzene hexachloride.*

"Kwell" is a parasiticide used in the treatment of scabies and lice and is a poison. Hardt v. Board of Naturopathic Examiners, 606 P.2d 1169–70 (Ct.App.Or.1980).

Petitioner manufactures three smoke insecticides containing a chemical known as "**lindane**."[5] Because **lindane** is an economic poison, the products have been registered with the Department of Agriculture since 1955.[6] [[5] **Lindane** is the accepted common name for the gamma isomer of benzene hexachloride and is known chemically as 1,2,3,4,5,6-hexachlorocyclohexane. [6] The products and their labels differ in various respects which are not material to the issues here. "Smo-Cloud" contains 10.2% **lindane**; "Bug-Tab" contains 20% **lindane**; and "Moth Cloud" contains 10.5% **lindane**.]

Among [the Hearing Examiner's] specific findings were the following:

"11. **Lindane** is absorbed in the body; is not readily stored; and is excreted comparatively rapidly.

"15. The labeled uses of subject products do not expose people or vertebrates to toxicologically significant amounts of **lindane**; and do not create toxicologically significant residues in food tightly covered." A.54. Continental Chemiste Corp. v. Ruckelshaus, 461 F.2d 331–2, 334 (7th Cir. 1972).

line (līn) [L. *lin'ea*] a stripe, streak, mark, or narrow ridge; often an imaginary line connecting different anatomical landmarks. Called also *linea* [NA].

line, Bryant's 1. the vertical side of the iliofemoral triangle. 2. a test line for detecting shortening of the femur.

linear (lin'e-ar) [L. *linearis*] pertaining to or resembling a line.

Linear (adjective): Describes a polymer wherein the molecules are chemically bonded together end to end to form a chain without any appreciable branching. Shaw v. E. B. & A. C. Whiting Co., 157 U.S.P.Q. 405, 410 (D.Vt.1967).

lingual nerve See *nervus lingualis.*

Lipiodol (lip-i'o-dol) trademark for iodized oil used as a contrast medium. See also *oil, iodized.*

lipoma (lĭ-po'mah) [*lipo-* + *-oma*] a benign tumor usually composed of mature fat cells. At times the tumor may be composed partly or entirely of fetal fat cells (hibernoma).

A **lipoma** is a benign deposit of fatty tissue. Steinbach v. Barfield, 428 So.2d 915, 918 (Ct.App.La.1983).

Dr. Diaz opined that it was either a lipoma (fatty accumulation above the kneecap or a hypertropy . . . Eller and Co. v. Golden, 620 F.2d 71, 73 (5th Cir. 1980).

In March of 1975, Dr. Spencer surgically removed a tumor-like mass from the hip of Mr. Hawkins. A specimen of this mass was examined by Dr. Collins, a member of Regional Medical Laboratories, who diagnosed it as a benign **lipoma** (noncancerous). After the surgery the wound did not heal as expected, and there was an accumulation of fluid and drainage. A specimen of the fluid was examined by Dr. Walters who found no elements of malignancy present. Hawkins v. Regional Medical Laboratories, 314 N.W.2d 450–1 (Ct.App.Mich.1979).

lipopolysaccharide (lip"o-pol"e-sak'ah-rīd) a molecule or compound in which lipids and polysaccharides are linked, as in cell membranes. See also *endotoxin.*

One of these endotoxins, the **lipopolysaccharide**, was known to cause a fever which could lead to convulsions and brain damage, as occurred in this case. Ezagui v. Dow Chemical Corp., 598 F.2d 727, 731 (2d Cir. 1979).

lipping (lip'ing) the development of a bony overgrowth in osteoarthritis.

X-rays of plaintiff's thoracic and lumbar spine revealed the old compression fracture and **lipping** (formation of a lip-like structure) at the L1 level. Brissette v. Schweiker, 566 F.Supp. 626, 631 (E.D.Mo.1983), remanded 730 F.2d 548 (8th Cir. 1984).

. . . a moderate narrowing of the space between the fifth and six cervical vertebrae, and some anterior "**lipping**" of the same two vertebrae. He explained that "**lipping**" is frequently normal even in the absence of disease, that it could result from a slipped disc or from degeneration caused by the thrusting of "abnormal strain and stresses on the ligaments in this spot," and testified it could be assumed in this case that the "lipping" was caused by degeneration, inasmuch as there had been a narrowing of the disc space. On cross-examination, he conceded that trauma could aggravate a pre-existing condition and that the stretching of joint tissue beyond normal was trauma, but stated there was no way of knowing whether the "lipping" and narrowing were pre-existing conditions and that he did not see that any "real trauma" had been sustained by the claimant. Motorola, Inc. v. Industrial Com'n, 265 N.E.2d 99–100 (Ill.1970).

Spinal X-rays showed moderate osteoarthritic **lipping** of the upper dorsal vertebrae although the cervical and lumbosacral spine appeared normal. Abshire v. Gardner, 271 F.Supp. 927, 931 (S.D.W.Va.1967).

liquid (lik'wid) [L. *liquidus; liquere* to flow] 1. a substance that flows readily in its natural state. 2. flowing readily; neither solid nor gaseous. See also *fluid, liquor, mixture; solution.*

liquor (lik'er, li'kwor), pl. *liquors, liquo'res* [L.] 1. a liquid, especially an aqueous solution containing a medicinal substance. 2. a general term used in anatomical nomenclature for certain fluids of the body. See also *fluid; liquid; solution.*

liquor, intoxicating

"The term 'intoxicating beverage' and the term '**intoxicating liquor**' shall include only those liquors, wines and beers containing more than three and two-tenths per cent of alcohol by weight." [Laws of Florida § 561.01.] Castlewood International Corp. v. Wynne, 305 So.2d 773, 775 (Fla.1974).

Listerine

. . . [the Commission found that the ability of **Listerine** to kill germs by millions on contact is of no medical significance in the treatment of colds or sore throats. Expert testimony showed that bacteria in the oral cavity, the "germs" which **Listerine** purports to kill, do not cause colds and play no role in cold symptoms. Colds are caused by viruses. Further, "while **Listerine** kills millions of bacteria in the mouth, it also leaves millions. It is impossible to sterilize any area of the mouth, let alone the entire mouth."] Warner-Lambert Co. v. F.T.C., 562 F.2d 749, 754 (D.C.Cir.1977).

lithium (lith'e-um) [Gr. *lithos* stone] a white metal; atomic number, 3; atomic weight, 6.939; symbol, Li; its oxide, lithia, Li_2O, is alkaline; its salts are solvents of uric acid to a certain extent in the test tube: based on this, it was formerly erroneously thought to be indicated in gout and rheumatic conditions. Lithium salts (lithium carbonate) are used in treating the manic phase of manic-depressive disorders.

lithium carbonate [USP], chemical name: carbonic acid dilithium salt. A white, granular powder, Li_2CO_3, used in the treatment of acute manic states and in the prophylaxis of recurrent affective disorders manifested by depression or mania only, or those in which both mania and depression occur occasionally, administered orally.

Dr. Martinez further testified that his treatment of Mrs. Lindsay is a delicate task because the drug **lithium carbonate** which he prescribed for her manic-depressive condition causes a person to retain fluids and that fluid retention increases the potential for convulsions in a person with a predisposition towards them. Lindsay v. Appleby, 414 N.E.2d 885, 888 (App.Ct.Ill.1980).

Lithium carbonate is now established as the most effective treatment available for mania, an affective disorder marked by extreme elation, hyperactivity, grandiosity, and accelerated thinking and speaking. It also prevents the recurrence of both the manic and depressive episodes which alternately afflict patients with bipolar manic-depression. Winick, supra at 787; Pepper, Tr. VIII, 40; Testimony of Dr. Richard F. Limoges, Tr. XII, 27–29, 4/20/78. However, in a bipolar case, an antidepressant such as tofranil, amitripyene or imipramine must be added to prevent depression. Rennie v. Klein, 462 F.Supp. 1131, 1138 (D.N.J.1978).

lithotomy position See *position, lithotomy.*

livedo (lī-ve'do) [L.] a discolored spot or patch on the skin, commonly due to passive congestion; commonly used alone to refer to *l. reticularis.*

livedo reticularis a peripheral vascular condition characterized by a reddish blue netlike mottling of the skin of the extremities; called also *asphyxia reticularis, l. annularis* and *l. racemosa.*

liver (liv'er) [L. *jecur;* Gr. *hēpar*] a large gland of a dark-red color situated in the upper part of the abdomen on the right side. Called also *hepar* [NA]. Its domed upper surface fits closely against and is adherent to the inferior surface of the right diaphragmatic dome, and it has a double blood supply from the hepatic artery and the portal vein. It comprises thousands of minute lobules (lobuli hepatitis), the functional units of the liver (see also *liver acinus,* under *acinus,* and *portal lobule,* under *lobule*). Its manifold functions include the storage and filtration of blood, the secretion of bile, the excretion of bilirubin and other substances formed elsewhere in the body, and numerous metabolic functions, including the conversion of sugars into glycogen, which it stores. It is essential to life.

As to him, plaintiff argues that the abnormal test results indicated **liver** disease, and since surgery in the presence of **liver** disease may be of considerable risk to the patient's life and health, those results reflected a significant risk that Dr. Tongen should have disclosed to Mrs. Cornfeldt. Cornfeldt v. Tongen, 262 N.W.2d 684, 702 (Minn.1977), modified on appeal after remand 295 N.W.2d 638 (Minn.1980).

"Well, it is my opinion that the patient became jaundiced at the time of or following the fall because of a load or stress placed on the **liver** by the damage of the tissues of the body as a result of the fall, and subsequently, because of the **liver's** function in healing the entire body and regulation of the clotting of the blood, this strain caused the liver to decompensate and he became jaundiced." . . .

. . . He also testified that the reason cirrhosis is terminable is because the **liver** is no longer able to metabolize toxic materials out of the bloodstream. He testified "the **liver**, like you say, does not metabolize any more, and you have toxics, and not only the heart but everything else deteriorates."...

...He stated that a liver does have the power to regenerate but an unhealthy one does this very slowly. He said that the liver can get to the state where it is not capable of repairing any more, and in this case that Rivas lapsed into a coma from which he did not recover. Rivas v. United States Fire Insurance Co., 470 S.W.2d 249, 250–1, 253–4 (Ct.Civ.App.Tex. 1971).

lixivium (liks-iv'e-um) [L.] any alkaline filtrate obtained by leaching ashes or other similar powdered substance; lye.

lobe (lōb) [L. *lobus;* Gr. *lobos*] a more or less well-defined portion of any organ, especially of the brain, lungs, and glands. Lobes are demarcated by fissures, sulci, connective tissue, and by their shape.

lobe, frontal the anterior portion of the pallium. See also *lobus frontalis.*

lobe, occipital the posterior portion of the cerebral hemisphere. See also *lobus occipitalis.*

He removed a blood clot that was about two and a half inches inside the occipital lobe (located in the left rear of the brain). Beins v. U.S., 695 F.2d 591, 595 (D.C.Cir.1982).

lobectomy (lo-bek'to-me) [Gr. *lobos* lobe + *ektomē* excision] excision of a lobe, as of the thyroid, liver, brain, or lung. See also *lobotomy.*

... she underwent a right thoracotomy and middle lower lobectomy to remove the destroyed lung tissue. Black v. Richardson, 356 F.Supp. 861, 866 (D.S.C.1973).

lobotomy (lo-bot'o-me) incision into a lobe; in psychosurgery, surgical incision of all the fibers of a lobe of the brain.

Dr. Burbridge described the effect of administering a 300 mg. initial dose of Thorazine to a subject with a .18 percent alcohol blood level as a "drug-induced lobotomy within reasonable medical probabilities." Dr. Jackson, one of the prosecution's doctors, described a lobotomy as a procedure during which the anxiety or worry nerves are severed, so that messages conveying anxiety or worry are prevented from reaching the brain. In re Cameron, 439 P.2d 633, 640–1 (Cal. 1968).

lobotomy, frontal; lobotomy, prefrontal an operation in which, through holes drilled in the skull, the white matter of the frontal lobe is incised with a leukotome passed through a cannula; called also *leukotomy.*

Plaintiff alleges that, as a proximate result of these negligent actions and omissions, he suffered a brain abscess for which he had to undergo surgery for an en bloc removal of the entire anterior portion of the right frontal lobe of his brain (prefrontal lobotomy). Barton v. Owen, 139 Cal.Rptr. 494, 496 (Ct.App. Cal.1977).

lobule (lob'ūl) a small lobe. See also *lobulus.*

lobule, portal a polygonal mass of liver tissue, larger than a liver acinus, containing portions of three adjacent hepatic lobules, and having a portal vein at its center and a central vein peripherally at each corner.

lobulus (lob'u-lus), pl. *lob'uli* [L., dim of *lobus*] a lobule, or small lobe; [NA] a general term for a small lobe or one of the primary divisions of a lobe.

lobus (lo'bus), pl. *lo'bi* [L.] a lobe; a more or less well defined portion of any organ; [NA] a general term for such subdivisions, especially of the brain, lungs, and various glands, demarcated by fissures, sulci, or connective tissue septa.

lobus frontalis [NA], frontal lobe: the anterior portion of the cerebral hemisphere, extending from the frontal pole to the sulcus centralis.

He testified that plaintiff's injury was to her frontal lobe area. The frontal lobe affects a person's reliability, emotional stability, ability to reason, and ability to maintain self control. According to Doctor Leoni, an injury to the frontal lobe region can produce permanent residual damage....

Since the accident, however, plaintiff has been a very nervous person who will not stay alone. She is a slow talker and is very forgetful. She can no longer care for her plants. She needs someone to help her with her housework, and she can no longer sew because she cannot concentrate....

... According to the medical evidence, all of plaintiff's personality changes are attributable to her frontal lobe injury. Vallot v. Camco, Inc., 396 So.2d 980, 985–6 (Ct.App.La. 1981).

lobus occipitalis [NA], occipital lobe: the posterior portion of the cerebral hemisphere, extending from the posterior pole to the parieto-occipital fissure on the medial surface, but continuous with the parietal lobe on the lateral surface.

lockjaw See *trismus.*

Lomotil (lo'mo-til) trademark for preparations of diphenoxylate hydrochloride and atropine. See also *atropine; colitis, ulcerative* (Wilson case); *diphenoxylate hydrochloride.*

longevity (lon-jev'ĭ-te) [L. *longus* long + *aevum* age] the condition or quality of being long lived.

lordosis (lor-do'sis) [Gr. *lōrdosis*] the anterior concavity in the curvature of the lumber and cervical spine as viewed from the side. The term is used to refer to abnormally increased curvature (hollow back, saddle back, swayback) and to the normal curvature (normal lordosis). Cf. *kyphosis* and *scoliosis.*

In a 1979 report to the Florida Retirement Commission, included in the transcript, Dr. Prevatt stated that Mr. Bloodsworth had marked limitation of the motion of the spine with loss of the normal lordosis and that he had centralized osteoarthritis and disc disease of the lumbar spine and pain on any prolonged standing, sitting, bending or lifting. Bloodsworth v. Heckler, 703 F.2d 1233, 1241 (11th Cir. 1983), affirmed 799 F.2d 131 (4th Cir. 1986).

The medical testimony was that plaintiff had preexisting conditions of mild lordosis (sway back) and mild scoliosis (curvature of the spine), which were aggravated by the low back strain. The treatment prescribed by both specialists, Dr. Lowery of Alexandria and Dr. Starr of Beaumont, was conservative— pain medication, muscle relaxers and exercise to strengthen the muscles of the lower back. Culp v. Belden Corp., 432 So. 2d 847, 849 (La.1983).

The x-rays showed loss of cervical **lordosis**, an objective finding which usually indicates that the patient is moving his, or her head in response to pain. . . .

. . . The lack of normal cervical **lordosis** is an objective finding and is indicative of trauma sufficient to cause precipitation of multiple sclerosis. McSwain v. Chicago Trans. Authority, 362 N.E.2d 1264, 1266, 1274 (App.Ct.Ill.1977).

Other Authorities: Adams v. Schweiker, 557 F.Supp. 1373, 1377 (S.D.Tex.1983); Consolidated Freightways, Inc. v. Indus. Com., 356 N.E.2d 51, 53 (Ill.1976); Fritsche v. Westinghouse Electric Corp., 261 A.2d 657–8 (N.J.1970); Bluebonnet Express, Inc. v. Foreman, 431 S.W.2d 45, 47 (Ct.Civ.App.Tex. 1968).

lordotic (lor-dot'ik) pertaining to or characterized by lordosis.

Lotrimin (lo-trim'in) trademark for preparation of clotrimazole. See also *clotrimazole*.

LSD lysergic acid diethylamide. See also *lysergide*.

The testimony of the experts indicated that there was a range of **longevity** among patients with liver metastasis. According to Dr. Cunningham, this range could, for some patients, extend at least as far as six years. Where a particular patient fell within this range of **longevity** could not, according to Dr. Cunningham, be predicted, absent clinical signs of imminent death. Continental Ill.Nat.B. & T. Co. of Chicago v. U.S., 504 F.2d 586, 592 (7th Cir. 1974).

lude See *methaqualone*.

Ludwig's angina (lood'vigz) [Wilhelm Friedrich von *Ludwig*, German surgeon, 1790–1865] See *angina*.

lumbar (lum'ber) pertaining to the loins, the part of the back between the thorax and the pelvis.

lumbar neural arch See *arcus vertebrae*.

lumbar spine See *vertebra, lumbar; vertebra, thoracic*.

lumbarization (lum"ber-i-za'shun) a condition in which the first segment of the sacrum is not fused with the second, so that there is one additional articulated vertebra and the sacrum consists of only four segments.

Records from St. Joseph's Hospital, Albuquerque, New Mexico, indicate that the plaintiff was hospitalized on September 16, 1974, upon the advice of Ronald W. Racca, M.D., suffering from **lumbarization** of the first sacral vertebrae. The purpose of the hospitalization was to determine if he had any type of retrodisc or radicuoopathy. All of the test results were negative. On September 21, 1974, the plaintiff was released from the hospital wearing a lumbosacral corset. Gonzales v. Califano, 452 F.Supp. 411, 413 (D.N.M.1978).

lumbosacral (lum"bo-sa'kral) pertaining to the loins and sacrum.

X-ray examination of the **lumbosacral** spine showed no evidence of fracture or dislocation, and the alignment of the vertebra was satisfactory. Dr. Wilson diagnosed Chisholm's problem as a musculo-ligamentous strain to the **lumbosacral**

region. Chisholm v. L. S. Womack, Inc., 424 So.2d 1138, 1141 (Ct.App.La.1982).

Other Authorities: McClaflin v. Califano, 448 F.Supp. 69, 73 (D.Kan.1978).

lumen (loo'men), pl. *lu'mina* [L. "light"] the cavity or channel within a tube or tubular organ.

The suction **lumen** [of a Miller-Abbott tube] communicates with the interior gastric system through holes at the end of the tube. It is through this **lumen** that the gastric contents may be extracted. Stumper v. Kimel, 260 A.2d 526–7 (Super.Ct.N.J. 1970).

The artery itself varies in its caliber throughout its course, and as a result of its hardening this occlusion took place at one of the narrower portions, and gradually filled up until the **lumen** or passageway was blocked. It builds up over a period of time. I would say that what I saw here probably took several hours to build up. . . .

The **lumen** is the passageway itself. Flannery v. Industrial Com'n, 412 P.2d 297–9 (Ct.App.Ariz.1966).

lumen, tubal

After Mrs. Bowman was discharged from the hospital, appellant received a laboratory analysis of portions of the removed tissue. It stated that the **tubal lumen**, the distinctively lined channel in the fallopian tube through which the egg passes, had not been "seen" in either sample. Bowman v. Davis, 356 N.E.2d 496–7 (Ohio 1976).

lunate (loo'nāt) [L. *luna* moon] moon-shaped, or crescentic. See also *os lunatum*.

lung (lung) [L. *pulmo;* Gr. *pneumōn* or *pleumōn*] the organ of respiration; called also *pulmo* [NA]. Either of the pair of organs that effect the aeration of the blood. The lungs occupy the lateral cavities of the chest, separated from each other by the heart and mediastinal structures. The right lung is composed of superior, middle, and inferior lobes, and the left, of superior and inferior lobes. Each lobe is subdivided into two to five bronchopulmonary segments which are separated by connective tissue septa. Pulmonary disorders may be confined to, or localized in, one or more of these segments. Each lung consists of an external serous coat (the visceral layer of the pleura), subserous areolar tissue, and lung parenchyma. The latter is made up of lobules, which are bound together by connective tissue. A primary lobule consists of a terminal bronchiole, respiratory bronchioles, and alveolar ducts, which communicate with many alveoli, each alveolus being surrounded by a network of capillary blood vessels. It is between the alveoli and capillaries that gas exchange takes place. See illustrations. See also *external* (Taylor case); *pleura*; terms formed from the root "*pneumo*".

The right **lung** consists of three lobes, and since it is undisputed that only two segments of the upper lobe of the right **lung** were removed, and not the entire right **lung**, the employer contends that no compensation should have been awarded under the quoted provision of the statute. . . .

There is no legislative history to assist us in determining the intention of the legislature, and we know of no precedents that are of very significant assistance. An easy solution would be to

422

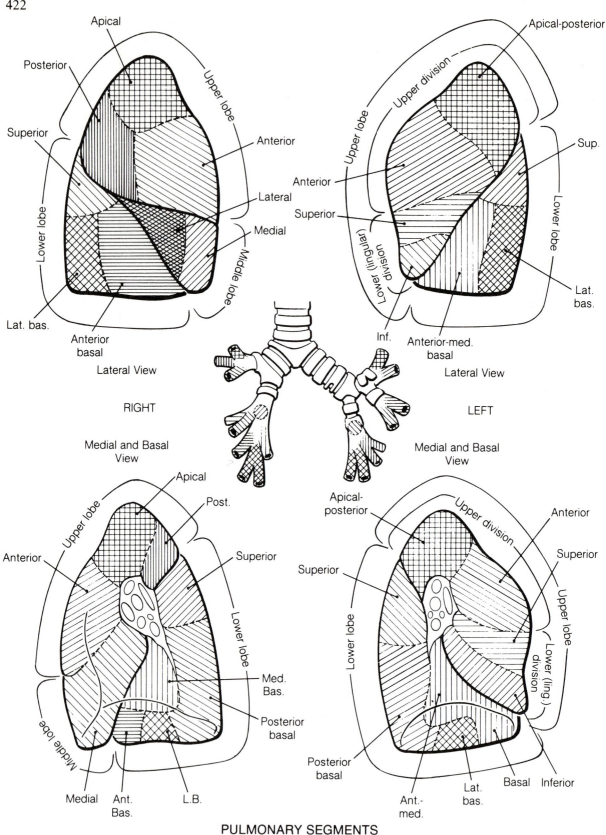

Apical

Posterior

Apical-posterior

Superior

Anterior

Upper lobe

Upper division

Lateral

Medial

Sup.

Superior

Anterior

Lower lobe

Lower lobe

Superior

Lat. bas.

Lat. bas.

Anterior
basal

Inf.

Anterior-med.
basal

Lower (lingular)
division

Lateral View

Lateral View

RIGHT

LEFT

Medial and Basal
View

Medial and Basal
View

Apical

Post.

Apical-
posterior

Anterior

Upper lobe

Superior

Upper division

Superior

Anterior

Upper lobe

Superior

Lower lobe

Lower lobe

Med.
Bas.

Posterior
basal

Lower (ling.)
division

Middle lobe

Medial

Ant.
Bas.

L.B.

Posterior
basal

Ant.-
med.

Lat.
bas.

Basal

Inferior

PULMONARY SEGMENTS

Tracheobronchial branching correlated with subdivision of the lungs. Each bronchus is marked the same as the segment it branches out to supply, and should be designated by the same name. The terminology used is that suggested by Jackson and Huber (Diseases of the Chest, volume 9, 1943).

say, as the employer would have us say, that "a lung" does not mean "a part of a lung." But such a literal construction would mean that no compensation would be awarded so long as part of the lung remained, even though what remained performed no useful function whatever. It is unlikely that the legislature intended that result. On the other hand, we agree with the employer that the legislature did not intend that the "slightest loss of lung tissue either through biopsy or perhaps the puncturing of the lung by a rib fracture" would qualify as removal of a lung. Boyer-Rosene Moving Service v. Industrial Com'n, 268 N.E.2d 415–17 (Ill.1971).

lung cancer See *carcinoma, bronchogenic.*

lung collapse See *pneumothorax.*

lupus (loo'pus) [L. "wolf" or "pike"] a name originally given to a destructive type of skin condition, implying "a local degeneration, strumous in its origin, essentially chronic in its character, and 'attended with more or less hypertrophy, with absorption, and with ulceration'. As one or other of these characters is most marked, ... a special name [is applied]," e.g., lupus erythematosus, lupus tuberculosus. Although the term is frequently used alone to designate lupus vulgaris and sometimes lupus erythematosus, without a modifier it has no specific meaning.

lupus erythematosus an inflammatory dermatitis; see *l. erythematosus, discoid,* and *l. erythematosus, systemic.*

An autopsy revealed that Mr. Cartwright died of severe pneumonia, and that he did have systemic lupus erythematosus. Lupus erythematosus is a progressive and degenerating disease of the body's connective tissue affecting every system and organ. Its symptoms include fever, pleurisy, arthritis resembling rheumatoid arthritis, skin lesions on the upper body and extremities, leukemia, and inflammation of the heart lining. Cartwright v. Maccabees Mut.Life Ins.Co., 247 N.W.2d 298, 301–2 (Mich.1976).

lupus erythematosus, discoid; lupus erythematosus discoides a chronic, superficial inflammation of the skin, marked by red macules up to 3 or 4 cm. in width, and covered with scanty adherent scales, which extend into patulous follicles, which fall off, leaving scars. The lesions typically form a butterfly pattern over the bridge of the nose and cheeks, but other areas may be involved. Clinical variants include *l. erythematosus hypertrophicus, l. erythematosus profundus,* and *l. tumidus.*

lupus erythematosus, systemic a generalized connective tissue disorder, affecting mainly middle-aged women, ranging from mild to fulminating, and characterized by skin eruptions similar to those seen in discoid lupus erythematosus, arthralgia, arthritis, leukopenia, anemia, visceral lesions (including renal involvement, pericarditis, and pleurisy), neurologic manifestations, lymphadenopathy, fever, and other constitutional symptoms. Typically, there are many abnormal immunologic phenomena, including hypergammaglobulinemia and hypocomplementemia, deposition of antigen-antibody complexes, and the presence of antinuclear antibodies and LE cells.

lye (li) an alkaline percolate from wood ashes; lixivium. Household lye is a crude mixture of sodium hydroxide with some sodium carbonate. See *sodium hydroxide.*

The chemical constitutent sodium hydroxide is more commonly known as lye. Liquid-plumr was designed as an all-purpose drain cleaner for use in both the kitchen and bathroom. It is clear, however, that liquid-plumr is more effective on kitchen drain problems because of its chemical design. The product is essentially an organic decomposer that dissolves grease through a process of saponification. The sodium contained in the solution attacks the grease, rapidly turning it into molten soap. Considerable internal heat is created by the chemical reaction which further speeds the process....

Mr. Levy's opinion would appear to be contrary to that of Dr. Lucian L. Leape whose article "Accidental Ingestion of Liquid Lye Drain Cleaners," Medical Trial Technique Quarterly, 1973 Annual at 30–35, was introduced into evidence at trial. Therein Dr. Leape states "An alkali, like lye, is much more likely to cause esophageal injury than acid, presumably because of its greater tissue penetrating characteristics," at 30–31, Drayton v. Jiffee Chemical Corp., 395 F.Supp. 1081, 1085, 1087 (N.D.Ohio 1975).

lymph (limf) [L. *lympha* water] a transparent, slightly yellow liquid of alkaline reaction, found in the lymphatic vessels and derived from the tissue fluids. It is occasionally of a light-rose color from the presence of red blood corpuscles, and is often opalescent from particles of fat. Under the microscope, lymph is seen to consist of a liquid portion and of cells, most of which are lymphocytes. Lymph is collected from all parts of the body and returned to the blood via the lymphatic system. Called also *lympha* [NA]. See illustration.

lymph gland See *node, lymph.*

lymph hilar See *hilus nodi lymphatici.*

lymph node See *node, lymph.*

lymphadenectomy (lim-fad"ĕ-nek'to-me) [*lymphaden* + Gr. *ektomē* excision] surgical excision of one or more lymph nodes.

In order adequately to expose the bifurcation of the trachea as well as the subcarinal nodes the arch of the aorta was retracted laterally to the left. The carina was thus adequately exposed and a subcarinal lymphadenectomy performed. Campbell v. U.S., 325 F.Supp. 207–8 (M.D.Fla.1971).

lymphadenitis (lim-fad"ĕ-ni'tis) [*lymph-* + Gr. *adēn* gland + *-itis*] inflammation of lymph nodes.

Upon his advice and recommendation, Mrs. Sindler underwent surgery at Montefiore Hospital on July 6, 1971 and the growth, an enlarged lymph node, was removed from the left side of the base of her neck. (N.T. 26, 27). The condition was diagnosed as chronic, nonspecific lymphadenitis. (N.T. 99). Mrs. Sindler was released from the hospital the same day but had to return to Dr. Goldman's office on July 8 to have a drain removed from the surgical wound. (N.T. 28). She complained of pain in her left arm during this visit but was advised that the pain would go away. Sindler v. Goldman, 454 A.2d 1054–5 (Super.Ct.Pa.1982).

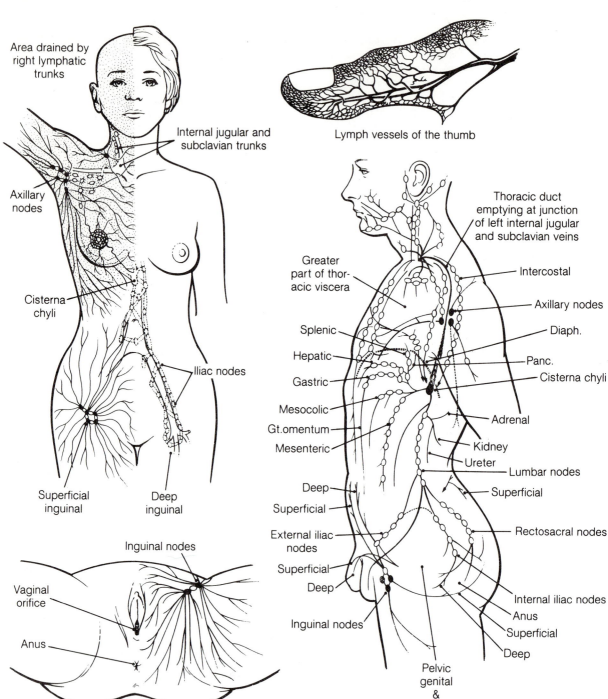

Area drained by right lymphatic trunks

Internal jugular and subclavian trunks

Axillary nodes

Cisterna chyli

Iliac nodes

Superficial inguinal

Deep inguinal

Lymph vessels of the thumb

Thoracic duct emptying at junction of left internal jugular and subclavian veins

Greater part of thoracic viscera

Intercostal

Axillary nodes

Splenic

Diaph.

Hepatic

Panc.

Gastric

Cisterna chyli

Mesocolic

Gt.omentum

Adrenal

Mesenteric

Kidney

Ureter

Deep

Lumbar nodes

Superficial

Superficial

External iliac nodes

Rectosacral nodes

Superficial

Deep

Internal iliac nodes

Inguinal nodes

Anus

Superficial

Deep

Pelvic genital & urinary organs

Inguinal nodes

Vaginal orifice

Anus

DIAGRAMMATIC REPRESENTATION OF LYMPHATIC DRAINAGE
OF VARIOUS PARTS OF THE BODY

lymphadenitis, mesenteric a condition clinically resembling acute appendicitis, in which there is inflammation of the mesenteric lymph nodes receiving lymph from the intestine. A septal form, which is frequently fatal, and a milder form, which is self-limited, are caused by *Yersinia (Pasteurella) pseudotuberculosis.* Called also *mesenteric adenitis.*

lymphangioma (lim-fan"je-o'mah) a tumor composed of new-formed lymph spaces and channels; called also *angioma lymphaticum.*

lymphangioma, cystic; lymphangioma cysticum a cystic growth occurring almost exclusively in the neck or groin and more commonly in children than in adults, and thought to originate from some anomaly in development of the primitive lymphatic spaces. The symptoms are largely the result of compression of adjoining structures by the mass.

In April, 1978, a subtotal excision of a **cystic hygroma** was performed on the plaintiff's neck at the defendant hospital. Over a course of several years the plaintiff had required several surgical procedures for this disorder. Although the disease had in the past been life threatening, the April, 1978, procedure was done purely for cosmetic reasons. Harnish v. Children's Hosp. Med. Center, 439 N.E.2d 240, 244 (Sup.Jud.Ct. Mass.1982).

lymphasis See *lymph; lymphedema.*

lymphatic drainage See under *drainage.*

lymphatic system See *system, lymphatic.*

lymphedema (lim"fe-de'mah) [*lymph-* + *edema*] chronic unilateral or bilateral edema of the extremities due to accumulation of interstitial fluid as a result of stasis of lymph, which is secondary to obstruction of lymph vessels or disorders of the lymph nodes.

The doctors noted mild to moderate edema of the right arm due to lymphasis. In his report, Dr. Tapp reported plaintiff as stating that if she had to live with the fluid in her arm she would rather be dead.

... he found plaintiff had "moderate to advanced residual **lymphedema** of entire (right) upper extremity associated to weakness & about 20% limitation of motion." Sellers v. Sec. Dept. of Health, Ed. & Welf., 331 F.Supp. 1103, 1105–6 (E.D. Mo.1971), reversed and remanded 458 F.2d 984.

Nodules can be felt on the skull surface and there is widespread lymphatic metastasis manifested by moderate **lymphedema** of the right lower extremity. Sowell v. Richardson, 319 F.Supp. 689, 692 (D.S.C.1970).

lymphoblast (lim'fo-blast) [*lympho-* + Gr. *blastos* germ] the immature, nucleolated precursor of the mature lymphocyte.

lymphocyte (lim'fo-sit) [*lympho-* + *-cyte*] a mononuclear leukocyte 7μ to 20μ in diameter, with a deeply staining nucleus containing dense chromatin, and a pale-blue-staining cytoplasm. It is chiefly a product of lymphoid tissue and participates in humoral and cell-mediated immunity. See also *lymphocytic series,* under *series.*

Vaccines confer protection against diseases by introducing antigens into the body which stimulate the production of immunizing antibodies. This process occurs when **lymphocytes,** cells contained in the lymph glands, absorb the antigens and produce an antitoxin against the particular disease. Ezagui v. Dow Chemical Corp., 598 F.2d 727, 731 (2d Cir. 1979).

lymphoma (lim-fo'mah) a general term applied to any neoplastic disorder of the lymphoid tissue, including Hodgkin's disease. Benign lymphoma is rare; the term *lymphoma* often is used alone to denote malignant lymphoma. Recent classifications of malignant lymphomas are based on the predominant cell type and its degree of differentiation; the various categories may be subdivided into nodular and diffuse types depending on the predominant pattern of cell arrangement. See also *lymphosarcoma.*

Dr. Lea strongly suspected that the decedent had **lymphoma,** a terminal malignant cancer related to the lymph glands. Lewis v. U.S., 75–2 Tax Cases Par. 13,087 at 88,830, 88,832 (N.D. Ga.1975).

A chest x-ray taken on July 28 and a fluroscope examination conducted on July 30 were interpreted by the two radiologists. A report dated July 30 and signed by Dr. Hunt, but embodying both defendants' conclusions, states that Winifred had "probably a **lymphoma** of the mediastinum or possibly a substernal thyroid." [Footnote omitted] Wilkinson v. Vesey, 295 A.2d 676, 681 (R.I.1972).

lymphoma, malignant, poorly differentiated lymphocytic a form in which the predominant cell is morphologically similar to the lymphoblast and contains a fine nuclear chromatin structure with one or more nucleoli; called also *lymphoblastoma, lymphoblastic l.,* and *lymphoblastic lymphosarcoma.*

On January 21, A.F.I.P. diagnosed the tissue as **malignant lymphoma, poorly differentiated lymphocytic** type. Jeanes v. Milner, 428 F.2d 598, 600 (8th Cir. 1970).

lymphoma, malignant, well-differentiated lymphocytic a form in which the predominant cell is the mature lymphocyte; called also *lymphocytoma, lymphocytic l.,* and *lymphocytic lymphosarcoma.*

Dr. Gee diagnosed plaintiff's disease process as a Stage 4 diffuse, **well-differentiated lymphocytic lymphoma.** Stage 4 is the ultimate of four stages in the classification of lymphoma. It is the most extensive, involving the spread of the disease beyond localized lymph nodes to the liver, kidneys, bone marrow, brain and other organs.

    Q. And what is "lymphocytic lymphoma, Stage 1"?

    A. A lymphoma is a tumor of the lymph gland in which the main cells are a certain type of blood cell. In this case lymphocytes—and these are blood vessels which, of course, are normally found in the blood in a relatively small percent; but when they become tumorous, they grow excessively; and in this case they were growing in this man's or this patient's lymph node, the one on the right.

    Now, the staging in this condition is extremely important medically because there are four stages. Stage 1 means that there's only one lymph gland involved; and the reason it is important is because if the patient is treated at Stage 1, the chance of successful therapy and almost sometimes complete cure or certainly a prolonged period of life is very, very good; whereas if it is not diagnosed until he gets Stage 4, it completely changes the outlook; and that's why we as doctors put such emphasis on stages of these patients.

Q. Can you tell us with any more precision than you just have as to the difference between Stage 1 and Stage 4 in terms of life expectancy?

A. Yes. If this type of condition is diagnosed while it's still Stage 1, that's a single lymph node involvement and treated promptly and appropriately, the life expectancy of these patients then improves so that 50 to 70 percent of such patients have a good chance of living for 5 years or more; and that "more" can be almost indefinite. The word "more" there is indefinite.

I mean, some people go on. I know. I have one patient that's going 30 years, but that would be unusual.

In other words, it's far, far greater than the five—the five years is not a cutoff. It's just a starting point.

Q. What about Stage 4?

A. Stage 4 is the reverse. In Stage 4 almost all of these patients are gone by the end of 3 or 4 years. Anyone who goes beyond that would be a fortunate survivor. Marek v. Professional Health Services, Inc., 432 A.2d 538, 540–1 (Super. Ct.N.J.1981).

lymphosarcoma (lim″fo-sar-ko′mah) a general term applied to malignant neoplastic disorders of lymphoid tissue, but not including Hodgkin's disease. See also *lymphocyte; lymphoma; radiation* (Cullum case).

Lymphosarcoma is a malignant disease of the lymph system. It is more commonly known today as "histiocytic non-Hodgkins lymphoma." Brief of Mayo Clinic at 3 n.1. Jewson v. Mayo Clinic, 691 F.2d 405, 406 (8th Cir. 1982).

On January 6, 1966, the Pathology Department at Barnes examined the slides sent to it and made a diagnosis of malignant lymphoma—**lymphosarcoma**. . . .

. . . the plaintiff's expert witness, Dr. Bauer, testified that his diagnosis of **lymphosarcoma** was based upon his finding that the tissue examined had "effacement of architecture by sheets of large lymphocytes . . . many of which show mitotic figures," that the "many histiocytes present [gave] a 'starry sky' pattern," and that these conditions were rarely observed in benign tissue. Dr. Bauer testified on cross-examination that interpretation of slides is a matter of judgment on which competent pathologists differ and that the judgment is ordinarily a difficult one to make. . . .

The plaintiff's expert witnesses testified that early diagnosis and treatment of **lymphosarcoma** is of the greatest importance. One of the experts, Dr. Komet, testified that if the cancer is treated in Stage One, when it is still localized, there is a 35% rate of survival; that in Stage Two, when it spreads to adjacent areas, the rate of survival decreases to 24%; and in Stage Three, when it becomes systemic, the rate of survival is reduced to 0–5%. Dr. Komet further testified that when he first saw Tommy in January, 1966, the **lymphosarcoma** was in Stage Two and that if the cancer was present at all on September 16, it was in Stage One. Thus, the cancer passed from Stage One to Stage Two between these two dates, and every day's delay was prejudicial to Tommy's recovery. Dr. Milner himself testified that early diagnosis means earlier treatment and possibly longer survival. Jeanes v. Milner, 428 F.2d 598, 600–1 (8th Cir. 1970).

Dr. Wandling, a defense witness, testified that if a lymph node in a given area of the body swells because of **lymphosarcoma** and the cause is known, "the patient will do better on radiation" if it's localized, with no other evidence of spread. He testified that treatment of **lymphosarcoma** alleviates for awhile needless suffering by the patient, and makes survival more comfortable; that delay in treatment of the disease does "not in every case" allow the progress of the **lymphosarcoma**, for the disease is one "that can remain dormant for a long period of time." Cullum v. Seifer, 81 Cal.Rptr. 381, 385 (Ct.App.Cal. 1969).

lyse (līz) to cause or produce disintegration of a compound, substance, or cell.

These antibodies will attack the calf's red blood cells and produce neonatal isoerytholysis, which is the **lysing** of the red blood cells. Waller v. Fort Dodge Laboratories, 356 F.Supp. 413, 415 (E.D.Mo.1972).

Lysenkoism

. . . "Lysenkoism."[5] [[5] Soviet geneticist T. D. Lysenko, controversial dictator of "communistic" biology during the Stalin period, stultified the science of genetics in the U.S.S.R. for at least a generation. He imposed the "state sanctioned alternative," the curious idea that environmentally acquired characteristics of an organism could be transmitted to the offspring through inheritance. Thus, the Stalinist concept of ideological conformity politically implanted in genetics paralyzed this important branch of Soviet science.] People v. Privitera, 153 Cal. Rptr. 431, 448 (Cal.1979).

lysergide (li′ser-jīd) chemical name: *N,N*-diethyllysergamide. A hallucinogenic compound, $C_{20}H_{25}N_3O$, derived from lysergic acid; it has been used experimentally in the study and treatment of mental disorders. The substance has also been found to be antagonistic to serotonin in its action on smooth muscle. The side effects include bizarre behavior and, reportedly, psychosis and chromosomal damage. Called also *LSD* and *lysergic acid diethylamide*. See also *flashback*.

". . . Something else must interfere with the blood supply to the hand to allow this infection to be uncontrolled and to produce death of the tissues and it is my opinion that some other factor was involved and **LSD** seems to be the most reasonable conclusion of this. It has to be something else. I have never seen nor are there any reports of digital gangrene such as I have seem in this young lady in just a streptococcal infection. Could be the first one in the history of medicine. I don't think so." Ward v. Kovacs, 390 N.Y.S.2d 931, 935 (2d Dep't 1977).

In light of the changing state of medical knowledge regarding hallucinogens, we think that the district court may have underestimated the unique and potentially dangerous impact that prolonged use of **LSD** appears to have on the psychological state and behavioral patterns of some users. See Lunter, "The Effect of Drug-Induced Intoxication on the Issue of Criminal Responsibility," 8 Crim.L.Bull. 731 (1972); Comment, "LSD—Its Effect on Criminal Responsibility," 17 DePaul L.Rev. 365 (1968). Testimony presented by the defense at trial drew attention to the existence of such effects.[3] [[3] At the trial, Dr. Edwin Barron, a physician in family practice, testified for the defense in a general way as to the possible effects that **LSD** might have on an individual.

Q. Can **LSD** be dangerous?

A. Yes, it certainly can.

Q. What are some of the effects?

A. The effects of **LSD**, while there can be very wild moods, swings, there can also be fits of depression. There can be a manic behavior manifested. There can also be behavior exhibited so far as to result in suicide. And there have been medical articles published that have indicted **LSD** in suicide cases.

Q. Are there other catastrophic reactions? And what are they?

A. **LSD** has been described as having catastrophic results. I will just refer to you from a pharmacologic text I have here: "The catastrophic reactions to **LSD** cause a severe disruption of psychological defense mechanism and they do cause repressions and denial in an individual precariously defended against confrontation of conflict material." . . .

Q. Can a user of **LSD** be on a long trip without taking **LSD**?

A. Yes, he certainly can. In the text referred to by Dr. Goff, the estimate there is 25 to 50 trips; that after 25 to 50 trips on **LSD**, or taking **LSD**, that a person can be maintained or sustained in a permanent trip; that he finds that it's no longer necessary at all to take **LSD**. He doesn't have to have the **LSD**. And this is the type of thing that is feared especially

in experimentation with the drug.] Brinkley v. U.S., 498 F.2d 505, 511 (8th Cir. 1974).

Also placed under the Drug Abuse Control Act are the hallucinogens or the "psychedelics." **LSD** is the best known and one of the highly potent forms of these drugs. Less potent hallucinogens include psilocybin, peyote, and mescaline and hashish (another derivative of the plant from which marijuana comes). As with marijuana usage, a true physical addiction does not occur with **LSD**, in that withdrawal effects do not follow abstinence. Frequent use of **LSD** will lead rapidly, however, to the development of a high tolerance. Psychological dependence develops as it does with exposure to almost any substance which alters the state of consciousness. During **LSD**-intoxication severe panic and paranoid reactions are encountered. Attempts at suicide as well as uncontrolled aggression are among the dangers to the intoxicant. Hallucinations are common, accompanied by feelings of grandiosity and omnipotence. Recurrences of the **LSD** experience weeks or months after the last drug intake are well known. Various emotional disorders have been observed following exposure to **LSD**. A chronic anxiety state is the most common. Prolonged psychotic reactions also have been identified with **LSD**. Too, there is also growing evidence that **LSD** can cause chromosomal damage. People v. McCabe, 275 N.E.2d 407, 411 (Ill. 1971).

Other Authorities: U.S. v. Kuch, 288 F.Supp. 439, 442 (D.D.C. 1968).

M

M-A tube See *tube, Miller-Abbott.*

macerate (mas′er-āt) to soften by wetting or soaking. See also *maceration.*

maceration (mas″er-a′shun) [L. *maceratio*] the softening of a solid by soaking. In histology, the softening of a tissue by soaking, especially in acids, until the connective tissue fibers are so dissolved that the tissue components can be teased apart. In obstetrics, the degenerative changes with discoloration and softening of tissues, and eventual disintegration, of a fetus retained in the uterus after its death.

Between 8:55 p.m. and 9:40 p.m., the plaintiff spontaneously delivered a **macerated** still-born fetus and placenta. Mercurdo v. County of Milwaukee, 264 N.W.2d 258–9 (Wis. 1978).

The primary advantage of this tape over prior tapes is its substantial elimination of the hydrated, whitened and wrinkled condition of the skin known as **maceration**. Minnesota Mining & Mfg. Co. v. Johnson & Johnson, 179 U.S.P.Q. 216–17 (N.D. Ill. 1973).

Q. How does dampness contribute to this problem?

A. Moisture and in prolonged contact with the skin actually draws fluid out and macerates the skin.

Q. Does what?

A. **Macerates.** All of you are familiar with when we immerse our body in water, a swimming pool or anything, how the skin shrivels and puckers. This is caused by the fluid in the

skin being drawn out by the water. The medical word is **maceration**. It causes the tissues of the skin to undergo changes which requires good circulation in order to heal. A diabetic doesn't have this good circulation. The **maceration** caused by the water continues, gets worse, blisters, and makes a greater demand on the circulation because of infection being present, and the circulation is not able to supply this demand, and, consequently, gangrene sets in. Isgett v. Seaboard Coast Line RR Co., 332 F.Supp. 1127, 1135 (D.S.Car. 1971).

machine (mah-shēn′) [L. *machina*] a contrivance or apparatus for the production, conversion, or transmission of some form of energy or force.

machine, Aquamatic K-Thermia

Dr. Hruska used an **Aquamatic K-Thermia machine** to control the infant's temperature during the operation.

The machine contains a reservoir of fluid which may be heated or cooled to provide circulating fluid for a rubber mattress which is placed under the patient. Corrugated indentations contained in the mattress evidence the channels or tubes through which the thermally controlled fluid circulates. A pillow slip was used to cover the mattress upon which appellee was placed. The temperature of the circulating fluid is set manually by control knobs which indicate maximum and minimum temperature extremes. Dr. Hruska set the extremes at 40°F minimum and 102°F or 103°F maximum. Weeks v. Latter-Day Saints Hospital, 418 F.2d 1035, 1037 (10th Cir. 1969).

machine, Bovie

The surgical function is accomplished by means of high frequency electrical energy supplied by the **Bovie machine** to the resectoscope cutting loop. Thomas v. American Cystoscope Makers, Inc., 414 F.Supp. 255, 259 (E.D.Pa.1976).

He had used the **Bovie machine** "very extensively". He described it as an electronic device "that works on an electromagnetic wave principle that produces waves that are manufactured by the machine to produce coagulation of tissues." It can be used to cauterize and "as with a scalpel to cut and cauterize simultaneously." The witness gave a "qualified yes" to the question "In your use of the **Bovie machine**, have you ever noticed that when you approach tissue with the scalpel and that the power is on that there will be an electric arc between the scalpel and the tissue?"...

Dr. Aubrey Haines, a plastic and reconstructive surgeon, testified that he was familiar with the Bovie electro-surgical unit. He explained how it is used:

Well the machine is usually on a stand in close proximity to the operating table. There is a power cord that runs from some point in the machine to a plug in the wall. When the machine is turned on there are usually two wires leading out of the machine, one which goes to an active electrode and one which goes to a ground plate. The ground plate is usually placed under the patient at some convenient point where a wide surface area is in contact, and the machine is then operated by a foot pedal so that when the foot pedal is turned on current will flow from the active electrode to whatever part of the patient's body or to an instrument on this part of the patient's body to pass current through this area for the coagulation of tissues. Holloway v. Hauver, 322 A.2d 890, 893–4 (Ct.Spec.App.Md.1974).

Dr. Darner, one of the Appellees, testified to the operation of the **Bovie machine** in "lay" terms. He stated that "when you deliver the current into a patient's body if you deliver it over a wide surface, and the entire surface is in contact with the electrode, there will be no burning...." When Dr. Darner was asked how he was familiar with the theory of an electrosurgical machine, he stated that it was developed by one of his former medical chiefs and that he, Dr. Darner, had written a treatise on the subject. Monk v. Doctors Hospital, 403 F.2d 580, 582–3 (D.C.Cir.1968).

machine, heart-lung a combination blood pump (artificial heart) and blood oxygenator (artificial lung) used in open-heart surgery.

During the connection of the **heart-lung machine**, the lines to and from the machine were reversed, resulting in oxygen-depleted blood being sent to Mrs. Green's brain. She suffered extensive, irreversible brain damage and has been a patient at the Veterans Administration Hospital at Wood, Wisconsin, under extensive nursing care, almost continuously since the operation. Green v. U.S., 530 F.Supp. 633, 636 (E.D.Wis.1982).

machine, hypothermia

They also knew that the telethermometer, which was attached to the **hypothermia machine** (an apparatus to lower body temperature) was not always accurate. Rose v. Hakim, 335 F.Supp. 1221, 1225 (D.D.C.1971).

Macrodantin (mak″ro-dan′tin) trademark for a preparation of nitrofurantoin. See also *nitrofurantoin*.

macrophage (mak′ro-fāj) [*macro-* + Gr. *phagein* to eat] any of the large, mononuclear highly phagocytic cells with a small, oval, sometimes indented nucleus and inconspicuous nucleoli, occurring in the walls of blood vessels (adventitial cells) and in loose connective tissue (histiocytes, phagocytic reticular cells). Derived from monocytes, they are components of the reticuloendothelial system and are usually immobile (fixed macrophages, resting wandering cells), but when stimulated by inflammation become actively mobile (free macrophages, wandering histiocytes). Macrophages also interact with B- and T-lymphocytes to facilitate antibody production.

Dr. Krakauer thus described **macrophages:**

A **macrophage** is a cell or—it is called a pheochromocytic cell, which can engulf, ingest and eliminate material from the body.

So, for example, as an example, some foreign material which has been identified and coated by an antibody may then be engulfed by a **macrophage** which then will carry it through the blood elsewhere and get rid of it.

Dr. Krakauer was asked by counsel, "Are these what are known as clean-up cells or garbage collectors?" He responded, "Yes. They are garbage collectors." Varga v. U.S., 566 F.Supp. 987, 1011 (N.D.Ohio 1983).

macrophage, alveolar See *phagocyte, alveolar.*

macula (mak′u-lah), pl. *mac′ulae* [L.] 1. a stain, spot, or thickening; [NA] a general term for an area distinguishable by color or otherwise from its surroundings. Often used alone to refer to the macula retinae. 2. a moderately dense scar of the cornea that can be seen without special optical aids, appreciated as a gray spot intermediate between a nebula and a leukoma.

On this visit Dr. Becker found that appellee was developing macular degeneration in each eye....
... [Dr. Willcockson examined appellee and found that she had inability to see beyond 20 per cent with either eye, with or without glasses, and that she had specific toxic destruction in the **macula** of the retina of both eyes.] Sterling Drug, Inc. v. Yarrow, 408 F.2d 978, 983–4 (8th Cir. 1969).

macula retinae [NA], an irregular yellowish depression on the retina, about 3 degrees wide, lateral to and slightly below the optic disk; it is the site of absorption of short wavelengths of light, and it is thought that its variation in size, shape, and coloring may be related to variant types of color vision. Called also *m. lutea retinae.*

But esotropia may also indicate some type of retinal or vitreous pathology in the visual axis. This will often involve a disease in the **macula**, the central part of the retina. This condition reduces visual acuity in the eye and as a result the eye turns inward. Steele v. U.S., 463 F.Supp. 321, 325 (D.Alaska 1978).

macular (mak′u-lar) pertaining to or characterized by the presence of macules; pertaining to the macula retinae.

magma (mag′mah) [Gr. *massein* to knead] a thin, pastelike substance composed of organic material.

Magma is a paste-like mix of raw sugar and sugar syrup. The moisture content of **magma** is approximately 7% to 8%. Sucrest Corp. v. M/V Jennifer, 455 F.Supp. 371, 375 (D.Me. 1978).

Majzlin Spring See *device, intrauterine (IUD).*

malacosis senilis See *osteomalacia, senile.*

malalignment (mal"ah-lin'ment) displacement out of line, especially displacement of the teeth from their normal relation to the line of the dental arch. See also *fracture.*

Since Dr. Gamburg undertook to correct the **malalignment** of the broken bone in LaDonna Paul's arm only two days after Dr. Cayer's treatment, the limits recognized as reasonable by Dr. Strange for such follow up treatment had not been exceeded. Paul v. St. Paul Fire & Marine Ins. Co., 430 So.2d 285, 288 (Ct.App.La.1983).

Malassezia See *Pity rosporon.*

malatal

Malatal is a sugar which sucks water out of the eye and makes it soft. Lazenby v. Beisel, 425 So.2d 84–5 (D.Ct.App.Fla. 1982).

male (māl) an organism of the sex that begets young or that produces spermatozoa. See also *chromosome Y; sex.*

The Committee concluded, after careful consideration of the many aspects of change of sex on the birth certificate of a transsexual, that:
   1. male-to-female transsexuals are still chromosomally **males** while ostensibly females;
   2. it is questionable whether laws and records such as the birth certificate should be changed and thereby used as a means to help psychologically ill persons in their social adaptation. The Committee is therefore opposed to a change of sex on birth certificates in transsexualism. Hartin v. Director of Bureau of Records, etc., 347 N.Y.S.2d 515, 517 (Sup. Ct.N.Y.Cty.1973).

male climacteric See *climacteric.*

malformation (mal"for-ma'shun) [L. *malus* evil + *formatio* a forming] defective or abnormal formation; deformity; an anatomical aberration, especially one acquired during development.

malformation, arteriovenous

Dr. Cascino, a neurosurgeon, stated that an **arteriovenous malformation** is a malformed blood vessel, which is usually congenital in nature. Dr. Cascino explained that when a strain is placed on such a blood vessel, it may rupture, allowing blood to escape and causing a hematoma. Such a blood vessel was located in the area of claimant's brain and did in fact rupture and cause her condition of ill-being. Doyle v. Industrial Com'n, 449 N.E.2d 1352, 1354 (Ill.1983).

malingerer (mah-ling'ger-er) [Fr. *malingre* sickly] an individual who is guilty of malingering.

With respect to Dr. Moore's testimony, the record reflects that he was being cross-examined by the attorney for Mr. Pierce concerning malingering generally and the meaning of the word "malingerer" and in the course of the questioning the following appears:

"Q. You find **malingerers** usually where there is a motive such as material gain or money damage? A. Yes, that is why he is malingering because he has a motive. Q. So that you would expect to find **malingerers** then more commonly among your patients who have litigation pending than in patients that have no motive? A. No, I would say the need for a neurosis is more severe there because they are honest people and that they have to have symptoms in order to get what they call justice. . . ."
  . . . As to the testimony of Dr. Moore, there was no timely objection made. The court did not abuse its discretion in refusing to grant a mistrial. Barlow v. Thornhill, 537 S.W.2d 412, 422 (Mo.1976).

malingering (mah-ling'ger-ing) the willful, deliberate, and fraudulent feigning or exaggeration of the symptoms of illness or injury, done for the purpose of a consciously desired end. See also *neurosis, traumatic.*

malleoli (mal-le'o-li) [L.] plural of *malleolus.*

There are patch avulsion and brush burns of approximately 4 × 6 cm. areas of skin over the medial and lateral **malleoli**. Landry v. Offshore Logistics, Inc., 544 F.2d 757, 759 (5th Cir. 1977).

malleolus (mal-le'o-lus), pl. *malle'oli* [L., dim. of *malleus* hammer] a rounded process, such as the protuberance on either side of the ankle joint; [NA], a general term for such a process.

It was there diagnosed that plaintiff had suffered a **bimalleolar** fracture dislocation of the right ankle. Alexander v. Mt. Carmel Medical Center, 383 N.E.2d 564–5. (Ohio 1978).

X-rays revealed that the **malleolus** shaft of her left ankle was fractured. She was hospitalized for 12 days. . . .
  Malleolus is the rounded lateral projection on each bone of the leg at the ankle. Albert v. Alter, 381 A.2d 459, 467–8 (Super.Ct.Pa.1977).

The shattered bones of her left ankle were put back into place. All three **malleola** having been snapped off in the accident, two were sewn into place, and one had to be kept in place with a bone screw. Williams v. Steuart Motor Co., 494 F.2d 1074, 1085 (D.C.Cir.1974).
  Other Authorities: Clark v. Gibbons, 426 P.2d 525, 528 (Cal. 1967).

Malleolus medialis [NA], medial malleolus: the rounded protuberance on the medial surface of the ankle joint, produced by the m. medialis tibiae.

There was tremendous comminution of this fracture, described by the treating doctor as "a bag of bones." Numerous fragments were broken off from the **medial malleolus** and large amounts of bone were missing from the cancellous portion. Bohme v. Southern Pacific Co., 87 Cal.Rptr. 286, 288 (Ct.App. Cal.1970).

malocclusion (mal"o-kloo'zhun) such malposition and contact of the maxillary and mandibular teeth as to interfere with the highest efficiency during the excursive movements of the jaw that are essential for mastication; originally classified by Angle into four major groups, depending on the anteroposterior jaw relationship as indicated by interdigitation of the first molar teeth, but

Class IV is not used (see table). See also *bite, underhung; occlusion.*

Its author, Dr. Samuel Herder, suggests making a model of the patient's teeth, employing artificial stone for the teeth. Below the "stone" teeth is one-eighth inch of wax, and the gums and base are of plaster of Paris. The "stone" teeth are moved to normal occlusion by heating the wax. The author found the final model useful in diagnosis and prognosis of **malocclusion** cases. T.P. Laboratories, Inc. v. Huge, 371 F.2d 231, 234 (7th Cir. 1966).

ANGLE'S CLASSIFICATION OF MALOCCLUSION

Class I (Neutroclusion). Normal anteroposterior relationship of the jaws, as indicated by correct interdigitation of maxillary and mandibular molars, but with crowding and rotation of teeth elsewhere, i.e., a dental dysplasia or an arch length deficiency.

Class II (Distoclusion). The lower dental arch is posterior to the upper in one or both lateral segments; the lower first molar is distal to the upper first molar.

Division 1. Bilaterally distal with narrow maxillary arch and protruding upper incisors.

Subdivision, unilaterally distal with other characteristics the same.

Division 2. Bilaterally distal with normal or square-shaped maxillary arch, retruded maxillary central incisors, labially malposed maxillary lateral incisors, and an excessive overbite.

Subdivision. Unilaterally distal with other characteristics the same.

Class III (Mesioclusion). The lower arch is anterior to the upper in one or both lateral segments; lower first molar is mesial to upper first molar.

Division. Mandibular incisors are usually in anterior crossbite.

Subdivision. Unilaterally mesial, with other characteristics the same.

Class IV. The occlusal relations of the dental arches present the peculiar condition of being in distal occlusion upon one lateral half, and in mesial occlusion upon the other half of the mouth.

malpractice (mal-prak'tis) [L. *mal* bad + *practice*] improper or injurious practice; unskillful and faulty medical or surgical treatment.

malpractice, medical See *care, standard of.*

A plaintiff's burden of proof in a **medical malpractice** suit is set forth in LSA-RS 9:2794 which reads as follows:

A. In a **malpractice** action based on the negligence of a physician licensed under R.S. 37:1261 et seq., or a dentist licensed under R.S. 37:751 et seq., the plaintiff shall have the burden of proving:

(1) The degree of knowledge or skill possessed or the degree of care ordinarily exercised by physicians or dentists licensed to practice in the state of Louisiana and actively practicing in a similar community or locale and under similar circumstances; and where the defendant practices in a particular specialty and where the alleged acts of medical negligence raise issues peculiar to the particular medical specialty involved, then the plaintiff has the burden of proving the degree of care ordinarily practiced by physicians or dentists within the involved medical specialty.

(2) That the defendant either lacked this degree of knowledge or skill or failed to use reasonable care and diligence, along with his best judgment in the application of that skill, and

(3) That as a proximate result of this lack of knowledge or skill or the failure to exercise this degree of care the plaintiff suffered injuries that would not otherwise have been incurred. Battles v. Aderhold, 430 So.2d 307, 310–11 (Ct. App.La.1983).

There appears to be no definition of "**medical malpractice**" contained within the CPLR. However subdivision 2 of section 681 of the Insurance Law contains the following:

" '**Medical malpractice** insurance' means insurance against legal liability of the insured, and against loss, damage, or expense incident to a claim of such liability arising out of death or injury of any person due to medical or hospital malpractice by any licensed physician or hospital." . . .

Subdivision 1 of section 148–a of the Judiciary Law mandates the establishment of a **medical malpractice** panel to facilitate the disposition of **medical malpractice** cases. McGinness v. Rosen, 415 N.Y.S.2d 744, 745 (Supr.Ct.Queens Cty. 1979).

"**Malpractice**", also sometimes called "malapraxis" means bad or unskillful practice, resulting in injury to patient, and comprises all acts and omissions of physician or surgeon as such to a patient as such, which may make physician or surgeon either civilly or criminally liable. Bakewell v. Kahle, 125 Mont. 89, 232 P.2d 127, 129.

It has also been said that

A "**malpractice**" action presents a claim of a hybrid nature, in that in one aspect it is based upon negligence and in another upon breach of contract, and the term "**malpractice**" may be applied to a single act or to a course of treatment. Giambozi v. Peters, 127 Conn. 380, 16 A.2d 833, 835.

The Texas Supreme Court in considering **malpractice** cases has followed traditional principles enunciated in Bowles v. Bourdon, 148 Tex. 1, 219 S.W.2d 779 (1949):

It is definitely settled with us that a patient has no cause of action against his doctor for **malpractice**, either in diagnosis or recognized treatment, unless he proves by a doctor of the same school of practice as the defendant: (1) that the diagnosis or treatment complained of was such as to constitute negligence and (2) that it was a proximate cause of the patient's injuries. . . .

Therefore, Texas courts in **medical malpractice** cases have required negligence and proximate cause proven by medical testimony and have held the doctrine of res ipsa loquitur inapplicable except where the alleged malpractice and injuries are plainly within the common knowledge of laymen. Such cases include negligence in the use of mechanical instruments, operating on the wrong part of the body, or leaving surgical equipment inside the body. Irick v. Andrew, 545 S.W.2d 557 (Tex. Civ.App.—Houston (14th Dist.) 1976, writ ref. n.r.e.); Hunter v. Robison, 488 S.W.2d 555 (Tex.Civ.App.—Dallas 1972, writ ref. n.r.e.); Harle v. Krchnak [422 S.W.2d 810 (Tex.Civ.App.— Houston (1st Dist.) 1967, writ ref. n.r.e.)], . . . Williford v. Banowsky, 563 S.W.2d 702–6 (Ct.Civ.App.Tex.1978).

Other Authorities: Donohue v. Martin, 413 N.Y.S.2d 99–101 (Sup.Ct.Rensselaer Cty.1979).

malpractice panel See *panel, malpractice.*

mal rouge a syndrome occurring after inhalation or ingestion of calcium cyanamide followed by drinking an alcoholic beverage, marked by intense flushing, rapid pulse and pounding heart, panting respiration, and perception of the taste and smell of acetaldehyde in the exhaled breath, which may be followed by nausea, vomiting, and a precipitous fall in blood pressure; the extent and severity of the symptoms depend on the amount of calcium cyanamide and alcohol in the system. The reactions are due to the inhibition by calcium cyanamide of one or more of the enzymes required for oxidation of acetaldehyde formed from alcohol, resulting in the accumulation of acetaldehyde and the altered vascular reaction to it. A similar syndrome, also due to accumulation of acetaldehyde, occurs on ingestion of disulfiram followed by drinking an alcoholic beverage, but in addition there is impaired taste, unpleasant breath and perspiration, and lessened sexual potency.

mammary visualization See *visualization internal mammary.*

mammectomy (mah-mek'to-me) [*mamma* + Gr. *ektome* excision] excision of the breast; mastectomy.

mammogram (mam'o-gram) a roentgenogram of the breast.

A **mammogram** is a diagnostic X-ray examination of the breasts employed to determine the presence of cancerous tissue. Davis v. Caldwell, 445 N.Y.S.2d 63, 65 (N.Y.1981).

mandible (man'di-b'l) the bone of the lower jaw. See also *mandibula.*

mandibula (man-dib'u-lah), pl. *mandib'ulae* [L.] [NA] the mandible: the horseshoe-shaped bone forming the lower jaw; the largest and strongest bone of the face, presenting a body and a pair of rami, which articulate with the skull at the temporomandibular joints.

The jaw bone is called the **mandible**; the ball at the upper extremity of the **mandible**, which fits into the socket in the skull is called the condyle. Rosario v. New York City Health & Hospitals, 450 N.Y.S.2d 805–6 (1st Dep't 1982).

At some time during the extraction, plaintiff's **mandible** was broken. As a result plaintiff was hospitalized and ultimately underwent two operations to repair the fracture....

... The findings of fact which are basic to this appeal can be summarized as follows: (1) that plaintiff's fractured **mandible** was not a consequence that would ordinarily have occurred if due care had been exercised by defendant in extracting plaintiff's tooth, (2) that defendant failed to inform plaintiff prior to the extraction that her **mandible** was extremely porous, atrophic and brittle or that there was insufficient buccal plate left that was thick enough to withstand the pressure that was needed to extract the tooth....

Expert dental testimony at the trial did establish that ordinarily speaking, a fracture of the **mandible** is not to be anticipated in pulling a wisdom tooth if proper procedure and reasonable care is exercised, but that each case presents its own situation. In plaintiff's case, a fracture was a definite possibility. Other expert opinion evidence established that although fractured **mandibles** do occur from the extraction of teeth, they are not common. Negaard v. Estate of Feda, 446 P.2d 436, 438–9 (Mont.1968).

mandibular (man-dib'u-lar) pertaining to the lower jaw bone, or mandible.

mandibular nerve See *nervus mandibularis.*

maneuver (mah-noo'ver) any dextrous proceeding; applied especially to procedures employed by the obstetrician in manual delivery of an infant. See also entries under *method; technique,* etc.

mangled

Dr. Nawas stated that Mr. Harrelson's hand "was really badly injured, and it falls in the category of what we call '**mangled** hand,' where he had severe injury to the soft tissue, to the tendons, and to the bone, and to the skin.... [F]ortunately, his hand was saved; and we did not need to amputate it." Harrelson v. Louisiana Pacific Corp., 434 So.2d 479, 484 (Ct. App.La.1983).

manic-depressive (ma'nik-de-pres'iv) alternating between attacks of mania and depression. See also under *psychosis.*

manifest See *latent* (Director case).

Plaintiffs initially contend that Kathleen Cardamone's sickness first **manifested** itself after the 30 day exclusionary period. They assert that the phrase "first **manifests** itself" is ambiguous. Citing Black's Law Dictionary which defines "**manifest**" as "[E]vident to the mind ... and ... synonymous with clear ... unmistakable [and] indubitable...." (Black's Law Dictionary, 1115 (4th ed. 1951).), they argue that her illness did not **manifest** itself until revealed by x-ray on April 1, 1974....

... Admittedly, Dr. Giardina only had an "impression" at this time that she had gallstones. However, this "impression" proved later to be correct. Moreover, the exclusionary clause does not require that the diagnosis occur within 30 days of the issuance of the policy, but in rather that the sickness **manifest** itself within this time. In the instant case it clearly did. See, Dowdall v. Commercial Travelers Mutual Accident Association of America (1962), 344 Mass. 71, 181 N.E.2d 594. Cardamone v. Allstate Ins. Co., 364 N.E.2d 460, 462–3 (App. Ct.Ill.1977).

The word "**manifest**" is defined in Continental Casualty Company v. Robertson, 5 Cir., 245 F.2d 604, 607, where recovery on a polio policy was upheld, although said polio was clearly contracted and in existence prior to the issuance of the policy, but the disease was not "**manifest**" to the insured until after issuance of the policy.... It inserted a word possessing a more exacting connotation, one contemplating the advancement of the disease beyond the point of origin and to the state where its presence was plain, distinct or beyond question or doubt. Hammock v. Allstate Insurance Co., 186 S.E.2d 353, 355–6 (Ct.App.Ga.1971).

manifestation

Having found in favor of **manifestation**, a workable definition of the term "**manifestation**" remains to be delineated. The parties have proferred several possibilities. These include the date on which an asbestosis victim "knows or has reason to know" he has the disease, the date on which a victim's symptoms become "capable of medical diagnosis," the date of actual diagnosis, or the date of death....

... I conclude that with respect to all claims under the insurance policies at issue in this case, coverage shall be provided when the asbestos-related disease becomes manifest, as measured by the date of actual diagnosis or, with respect to those cases in which no diagnosis was made prior to death, the date of death. Eagle-Picher Industries v. Liberty Mut. Ins. Co., 523 F.Supp. 110, 118 (D.Mass.1981).

manipulation (mah-nip″u-la′shun) [L. *manipulare* to handle] skillful or dextrous treatment by the hand. In physical therapy, the forceful passive movement of a joint beyond its active limit of motion.

On the date of the accident, plaintiff saw Dr. Barry M. Rills, an orthopedic surgeon, who performed a closed **manipulation** of plaintiff's right forearm and applied a long arm cast. Patin v. Continental Cas. Co., 424 So.2d 1161, 1163 (Ct.App.La. 1982).

Peeples also testified that Dr. Sargent described the **manipulation** "as a simple process in which I would be put under anesthetic and he would manipulate my arm in order to get rid of the muscular adhesions." Dr. Sargent stated that while Peeples was under anesthesia he intended "to move the shoulder through the various ranges where he was limited." Peeples v. Sargent, 253 N.W.2d 459, 462 (Wis.1977).

... rather, plaintiff pointed to the back of his neck and said "Crack my neck." This was described as a simple **manipulation** and part of osteopathic treatment, which the defendant had been performing for a number of years. Nimmer v. Purtell, 230 N.W.2d 258, 261 (Wis.1975).

Other Authorities: Slater v. Kehoe, 113 Cal.Rptr. 790, 793, 798 (Ct.App.Cal.1974); Dardar v. State of La., 322 F.Supp. 1115, 1119 (E.D.La.1971).

manipulation, lumbar roll

On cross-examination, Dr. Halterman testified that if the thrust in a **lumbar roll manipulation** is done with sufficient force it could cause a herniation or an aggravation of a herniated disc. Chamness v. Odum, 399 N.E.2d 238, 245 (App.Ct.Ill. 1979).

man-rem See *rem.*

A **man-rem** is [t]he summation of the environmental dose of radioactive effluents to the population. It is used to relate the radiation dose delivered to the general public resulting from reactor operations. This measure is the product of the dose delivered per unit time to an individual at a particular location multiplied by the number of individuals that spend their time at that location. Brief for intervenor at x. York Com. for a Safe Envir. v. U.S. Nuclear Reg., 527 F.2d 812, 815 (D.C.Cir.1975).

manufacturer's inserts or instructions See *instructions, manufacturer's.*

Marfan's puncture (epigastric puncture, method) sign, syndrome (mar-fahnz′) [Bernard-Jean Antonin *Marfan,* French pediatrician, 1858–1942]. See under *puncture; sign; syndrome.*

margarine (mar′jar-in) [Gr. *margaron* pearl] a food product containing 80 per cent of fat, manufactured primarily from refined cottonseed and soybean oils—sources of vitamin E and essential fatty acids—and fortified to supply a minimum of 15,000 U.S.P. units of vitamin A per pound; called also *oleomargarine.*

Margarine, to be readily saleable, must closely approximate the physical characteristics of butter as to (a) firmness at refrig-

erator temperatures (50°F.) which permits manufacture and wrapping in the form of quarter-pound prints (sometimes called "printability"); (b) retention of form at room temperature (70°F.) (sometimes called "stand-up" or "nonslumping"); (c) resistance to oil-staining of cartons in warm weather (80°F.), and (d) quick melting just below human body temperature (92°F.) which enables the emulsion to break up on the tongue and thus release flavors,—otherwise the product would have a greasy taste such as a kitchen shortening if spread on the tongue. Corn Products Co. v. Standard Brands, Inc., 359 F.2d 739–40 (7th Cir. 1966).

Marie-Tooth disease (mah-re′-tooth′) [Pierre *Marie;* Howard Henry *Tooth,* English physician, 1856–1926] progressive neuropathic (peroneal) muscular atrophy.

marihuana (mar″ĭ-hwan′ah) [Portuguese] a crude preparation of the leaves and flowering tops of (male or female plants) *Cannabis sativa* L. (Cannabaceae), usually employed in cigarets and inhaled as smoke for its euphoric properties. See also *cannabis; hashish* (State v. Randall case); *tetrahydrocannabinol.*

Marijuana's primary short-term physical effects are inducement of a mild pleasant euphoria, enhancement of perception and a slight slowing of temporal perceptions. These may be something the law should require people to forego, but they do not present a danger to society comparable to the encouragement of violence by barbiturates and amphetamines or the total misperception of reality and hallucinations LSD can cause....

The classification of **marijuana** with opiates is irrational and denies Ms. Bourassa the equal protection of law promised by Florida's constitution. This does not mean **marijuana's** use or possession may not be regulated or even prohibited and punished. It only means that the danger to the public presented by **marijuana** and its use is so different and less severe than that presented by opiates that it may not constitutionally be treated as if it presented the same dangers. [Footnote omitted.] Bourassa v. State, 366 So.2d 12, 16, 19 (Fla.1978).

In 1970 Congress enacted the Controlled Substances Act, a comprehensive statute designed to rationalize federal control of dangerous drugs....

... In drafting the CSA Congress placed **marihuana** in Schedule I,[7] the classification that provides for the most severe controls and penalties. [[7] **See** § 202(c), 21 U.S.C. § 812(c); 21 C.F.R. § 1308.11. For purposes of the CSA **marihuana** is defined as follows: The term "**marihuana**" means all parts of the plant Cannabis sativa L., whether growing or not; the seeds thereof; the resin extracted from any part of such plant; and every compound, manufacture, salt, derivative, mixture, or preparation of such plant, its seeds or resin. Such term does not include the mature stalks of such plant, fiber produced from such stalks, oil or cake made from the seeds of such plant, any other compound, manufacture, salt, derivative, mixture, or preparation of such mature stalks (except the resin extracted therefrom), fiber, oil, or cake, or the sterilized seed of such plant which is incapable of germination.] Nat. Organization for Reform, etc. v. Drug Enforcement, 559 F.2d 735, 737 (D.C. Cir.1977).

" 'Marihuana' means all parts of the plant Cannabis sativa L., whether growing or not, the seeds thereof, the resin extracted from any part of the plant and every compound, manufacture, salt, derivative, mixture or preparation of the plant, its seeds or resin. It does not include the mature stalks of the plant, fiber produced from the stalks, oil or cake made from the seeds of the plant, any other compound, manufacture, salt, derivative, mixture or preparation of the mature stalks, except the resin extracted therefrom, fiber, oil, or cake or the sterilized seed of the plant which is incapable of germination." (K.S.A. 65–4101[o].) . . .

. . . We conclude the definition of **marihuana** contained in K.S.A. 65–4101(o) of the Kansas Uniform Controlled Substances Act, enacted in 1972, was intended to include those parts of **marihuana** which contain the chemical tetrahydrocannabinol, to exclude those parts which do not, and to outlaw all plants popularly known as **marihuana** to the extent they possess the chemical regardless of the possible existence of more than one species of **marihuana**. State v. Luginbill, 574 P.2d 140–1, 143 (Kan.1977).

Other Authorities: State v. Vail, 274 N.W.2d 127, 130 (Minn. 1979). Aycock v. State, 246 S.E.2d 489, 493 (Ga.App.1978). State v. Woods, 522 P.2d 967, 969 (Kan.1974). U.S. v. Maiden, 355 F.Supp. 743, 745 (D.Conn.1973). In re Jones, 110 Cal.Rptr. 765, 768–9 (Ct.App.Cal.1973). People v. McCabe, 275 N.E.2d 407, 410–11 (Ill.1971).

Marijuana See *marihuana.*

Marjolin's ulcer See *ulcer.*

marrow (mar'o) the soft organic material that fills the cavities of the bones; called also *medulla.* See also *medulla ossium.*

masochism (mas'o-kizm) [Leopold von Sacher-*Masoch*, an Austrian novelist, 1836–1895] a form of sexual perversion in which cruel or humiliating treatment gives sexual gratification to the recipient.

mass (mas) [L. *massa*] a lump or body made up of cohering particles. See also *massa.*

Furthermore, Dr. Brougham's testimony supports a finding that the tumor itself was not the sole cause of the condition that led to the surgery and resulting disability. Instead, his testimony suggests that Corbett's painful condition was caused by a "**mass**" consisting of tumor cells and old blood clots intruding into the confined area around the vertebrae. As the **mass** expanded, it impinged on the nerves radiating from the spinal column, causing the pain and thus requiring surgery. Corbett v. Riley-Stoker, Corp., 425 A.2d 1335–6 (Sup.Jud.Ct.Me.1981).

massa (mas'ah), pl. *mas'sae* [L.] a unified lump or mass of material; [NA] a general term for an accumulation of cells or cohesive tissue. Called also *mass.*

massage (mah-sahzh') [Fr.; Gr. *massein* to knead] the systematic therapeutical friction, stroking, and kneading of the body.

On July 8, 1974, defendant, City of East Moline, a non-home rule unit, enacted an ordinance, effective immediately, extensively regulating "Massage Establishments and Massage Services" performed in such establishments . . . .

On September 16, 1974, the city enacted an amendment, effective immediately, to modify its act entitled "Massage Establishments and Massage Services" . . . .

. . . "**Massage**" is defined in the ordinance as "[a]ny method of pressure on or friction against, or stroking, kneading, rubbing, tapping, pounding, vibrating, or stimulating of the external soft parts of the body with the hands or with aid of

any mechanical electrical apparatus or appliances with or without such supplementary aids as rubbing alcohol, liniments, antiseptics, oils, powder, creams, lotions, ointments, or other similar preparations commonly used in this practice." Clevenger v. City of East Moline, 357 N.E.2d 719, 722 (App.Ct.Ill. 1976).

Section 1. A new section, designated Section 13–31, is added at the end of Section 13 of the Durham City Code as follows:

Section 13–31. Massage of Private Parts for Hire Prohibited.

It shall be unlawful for any person to **massage** or to offer to **massage** the private parts of another for hire. "**Massage**" means the manipulation of body muscle or tissue by rubbing, stroking, kneading or tapping, by hand or mechanical device. Brown v. Brannon, 399 F.Supp. 133, 139 (M.D.N.Car.1975).

massage, cardiac rhythmic compression of the heart by pressure applied manually over the sternum (closed cardiac massage) or directly to the heart through an opening in the chest wall (open cardiac massage); done to reinstate and maintain circulation.

The third action was to restore the patient's blood circulation so that both the oxygen and the adrenalin could be transported through the patient's blood stream. This required external **cardiac massage**, which makes the heart muscle expand and contract, thereby causing the blood to circulate. Daniels v. Hadley Memorial Hospital, 566 F.2d 749, 752–3 (D.C.Cir. 1977).

mastectomy (mas-tek'to-me) [*mast-* + Gr. *ektomē* excision] excision of the breast; mammectomy.

On June 17, 1976 plaintiff Joan Davis underwent a bilateral subcutaneous **mastectomy**, resulting in the removal of substantial portions of both breasts, accompanied by breast reconstruction with silicone implants. [Footnote omitted.] Davis v. Caldwell, 445 N.Y.S.2d 63–4 (N.Y.1981).

. . . "scirrhous carcinoma, **mastectomy**", that is, surgical removal of a breast due to a hard malignant tumor. Sellars v. Secretary of Dep't of Health, Ed. & Welf., 331 F.Supp. 1103–4 (E.D.Mo.1971), reversed and remanded 458 F.2d 984 (8th Cir. 1972).

When malignancy was discovered, a radical **mastectomy** was performed. Lopez v. Swyer, 279 A.2d 116, 119 (Super.Ct.N.J. 1971).

Other Authorities: Dietze v. King, 184 F.Supp. 944, 948 (E.D. Va.1960).

Master "2-step" exercise test See under *tests.*

mastoidal (mas-toi'dal) pertaining to the mastoid process of the temporal bone.

mastoidal process See *processus mastoideus ossis temporalis.*

mastoidectomy (mas"toi-dek'to-me) [*mastoid* + Gr. *ektomē* excision] excision of the mastoid cells or the mastoid process of the temporal bone.

Another more detailed report of three medical associates [Emil P. Liebman, Bernard J. Ronis and Max Lee Ronis, Transcript p. 168, Ex. 31], who are ear, nose and throat specialists, discloses that she had undergone a **mastoidectomy** in 1945, that after another operation was performed around 1964 in an attempt to improve her hearing the ear began to drain, and that sometime later a radical **mastoidectomy** was done, but the ear continued to drain. Capaldi v. Weinberger, 391 F.Supp. 502, 504 (E.D.Pa.1975).

When plaintiff visited the defendant again on November 5, he was advised that it was necessary to perform an operation on the mustoid and clear out all the diseased tissue and relieve the pressure. The hearing in that ear had already been destroyed and the plaintiff was advised that failure to operate could result in meningitis, brain absess or death.

The surgery, known as a left radical **mastoidectomy**, was performed on November 18, 1968. The defendant found granulations, pus and debris which obscured the cranial nerve but which he considered necessary to remove. Because the debris and pus were so thick it could not be removed by air suction. Therefore, defendant proceeded to remove the debris by scraping. Livengood v. Howard, 295 N.E.2d 736, 738 (App.Ct.Ill.1973).

mastoidectomy, tympano See *tympanum.*

Another ear doctor [Felice J. Santore, Transcript p. 170, Ex. 33] wrote that in 1964 a **tympano-mastoidectomy** was performed upon her for otitis media and conductive deafness, and that she complained of vertigo. Capaldi v. Weinberger, 391 F.Supp. 502, 504 (E.D.Pa.1975).

mastopathy (mas-top'ah-the) [*masto-* + Gr. *pathos* disease] disease of the mammary gland. Cited in Davis v. Caldwell, 445 N.Y.S.2d 63, 65 (N.Y.1981).

material (mah-te're-al) substance or elements from which a concept may be formulated, or an object constructed.

material, radioactive

"The legislative history of the Act reflects that the term '**radioactive materials**' as included within the definition of 'pollutant' in section 502 of the Act covers only **radioactive materials** which are not encompassed in the definition of source, byproduct, or special nuclear materials as defined by the Atomic Energy Act of 1954, as amended, and regulated pursuant to the latter Act. Examples of **radioactive materials** not covered by the Atomic Energy Act and, therefore, included within the term 'pollutant' are radium and accelerator produced isotopes." 40 CFR § 125.1(y) (1975) (citations omitted). Train v. Colorado Pub. Int. Research Group, 426 U.S. 1, 8, 96 S.Ct. 1938, 1941 (1976).

material, radioactive (airborne)

"**Airborne radioactive material**" means any radioactive material dispersed in the air in the form of dusts, fumes, mists, vapors, or gases; . . . 10 C.F.R. § 20.3(a)(2) (1982).

material, radioactive (byproduct)

"**Byproduct material**" means any radioactive material (except special nuclear material) yielded in or made radioactive by exposure to the radiation incident to the process of producing or utilizing special nuclear material; . . . 10 C.F.R. § 20.3(a)(3) (1982).

42 U.S.C. § 2014(e) defines "**byproduct material**" as "any radioactive material (except special nuclear material) yielded in or made radioactive by exposure to the radiation incident to the process of producing or utilizing special nuclear material." Colorado Public Interest Research Group, Inc. v. Train, 373 F.Supp. 991, 993 (D.Col.1974), reversed and remanded 507 F.2d 743 (10th Cir. 1974).

material, radioactive (source)

"**Source material**" means: (i) Uranium or thorium, or any combination thereof, in any physical or chemical form; or (ii) ores which contain by weight one-twentieth of one percent (0.05%) or more of (a) uranium, (b) thorium or (c) any combination thereof. **Source material** does not include special nuclear material. 10 C.F.R. § 20.3(a)(15) (1982).

42 U.S.C. § 2014(z) defines "**source material**" as "(1) uranium, thorium, or any other material which is determined by the Commission pursuant to the provisions of section [61] to be **source material**; or (2) ores containing one or more of the foregoing materials, in such concentration as the Commission may by regulation determine from time to time." Colorado Public Interest Research Group, Inc. v. Train, 373 F.Supp. 991, 993 (D.Col.1974), reversed and remanded 507 F.2d 743 (10th Cir. 1974).

material, special nuclear

"**Special nuclear material**" means: (i) Plutonium, uranium 233, uranium enriched in the isotope 233 or in the isotope 235, and any other material which the Commission, pursuant to the provisions of section 51 of the act, determines to be **special nuclear material**, but does not include source material; or (ii) any material artificially enriched by any of the foregoing but does not include source material; . . . 10 C.F.R. § 20.3(a)(16) (1982).

42 U.S.C. § 2014(aa) defines "**special nuclear material**" as "(1) plutonium, uranium enriched in the isotope 233 or in the isotope 235, and any other material which the Commission, pursuant to the provisions of section [51], determines to be **special nuclear material**, but does not include source material; or (2) any material artificially enriched by any of the foregoing, but does not include source material." Colorado Public Interest Research Group, Inc. v. Train, 373 F.Supp. 991, 993 (D.Col.1974), reversed and remanded 507 F.2d 743 (10th Cir. 1974).

matrix (ma'triks), pl. *ma'trices* [L.] the intercellular substance of a tissue, as bone matrix, or the tissue from which a structure develops, as hair or nail matrix.

matrix unguis [NA], the nail matrix: the tissue upon which the deep aspect of the nail rests; called also *nail bed.* The term is also used to denote the proximal portion of the nail bed from which growth chiefly proceeds.

The **matrix** consists of the cells which comprise the nail root and allow it to regrow. Destruction of the **matrix** usually prevents or in some cases merely impedes growth of the nail. Matter of Silberman, 404 A.2d 1164, 1166 (Super.Ct.N.J.1979).

maxilla (mak-sil'ah), pl. *maxil'las, maxil'lae* [L.] [NA] the irregularly shaped bone that with its fellow forms the upper jaw; it assists in the formation of the orbit, the nasal cavity, and the palate, and lodges the upper teeth.

[T]here was an additional . . . fracture at the **maxilla**-zygomatic suture line where the two bones come together . . . that required fixation. . . . We drilled a hole where we could pad the fixation to stabilize it. Cooperider v. Dearth, 420 So.2d 220, 221 (Ct.App.La.1982).

The medical examination revealed that the **maxillary bone** (the area of bone beneath the eyes and into which the teeth are inserted) was completely dissociated from the rest of the skull, i.e., it was free-floating or attached only by muscle and facial attachments. McCoy v. McNutt, 227 N.W.2d 219, 220 (Ct. App.Mich.1975).

. . . a diagnosis that plaintiff had a bilateral fracture of the **maxilla** or upper jaw running through the sinuses on each side. Yarrow v. U.S., 309 F.Supp. 922, 924 (S.D.N.Y.1970).

maxilla-zygomatic suture line See *maxilla; os zygomaticum.*

maxillary (mak'si̇̆-ler"e) [L. *maxillaris*] pertaining to the maxilla.

maxillofacial (mak-sil"o-fa'shal) pertaining to the maxilla and the face.

The record contains no definition of the term "**maxillofacial surgery**." The parties stipulated that "**maxillofacial** is a recognized specialty" in the practice of dentistry. Associates for Oral Surg., Ltd. v. Assoc. for Surg., 350 N.E.2d 109, 112 (App.Ct.Ill.1976).

MCL maximum contamination level.

McMurray sign See *sign, McMurray.*

MDM mechanically deboned meat See also *meat.*

measles (me'zelz) a highly contagious viral infection involving primarily the respiratory tract and reticuloendothelial tissues. Called also *rubeola.* A prodrome of three to five days duration begins about eight days after inhalation of the virus in droplets derived from a person in the prodromal or early eruptive phase of the infection. Coryza, cervical lymphadenitis, Koplik's spots, palpebral conjunctivitis, photophobia, myalgia, malaise, and a harassing cough with steadily mounting fever precede the skin eruption. The skin becomes covered with red papules that appear behind the ears and on the face before spreading rapidly down the trunk then onto the arms and legs. The papules are discrete but gradually become more confluent. The lesions flatten, turn brown, and slowly desquamate on about the sixth day, when the temperature has returned to normal. It may be complicated by bacterial pneumonia, otitis media, and by a demyelinating encephalitis. Fatalities are due to the severity of measles itself, or to the bacterial or immunological complications.

measles, German See *rubella.*

meat

The Secretary argues that MDM containing bone particles or products containing MDM cannot be adulterated because the bone is actually "**meat**" under the Department's 1938 definition of **meat**, found at 9 C.F.R. § 301.2(tt). That section provides:

> **Meat.** The part of the muscle of any cattle, sheep, swine, or goats, which is skeletal or which is found in the tongue, in the diaphragm, in the heart, or in the esophagus, with or without the accompanying and overlying fat, and the portions of bone, skin, sinew, nerve, and blood vessels which normally accompany the muscle tissue and which are not separated from it in the process of dressing. Community Nutrition Institute v. Butz, 420 F.Supp. 751, 755 (D.D.C.1976).

Meat is defined as "the properly dressed, clean, sound flesh derived from cattle, swine or sheep. . . ." M.S.A. § 12.964(1) (h), M.C.L.A. § 289.581(h). . . . Armour & Co. v. Ball, 468 F.2d 76, 86 (6th Cir. 1972).

meatus (mea'tus), pl. *meat'tus* [L., "a way, path, course"] an opening or passage; [NA] a general term for an opening or passageway in the body.

meatus, urethra See *meatus, urinary.*

meatus urinarius; meatus, urinary the external urethral orifice: the opening of the urethra on the body surface through which urine is discharged. See also *ostium urethrae externum femininae; ostium urethrae externum masculinae.*

The child had an abrasion and some oozing blood at the ure-**thra meatus**.[2] [[2] The opening of the urethra on the penis.] In re Sharpe, 374 A.2d 1323–4 (Super.Ct.Pa.1977).

mebutamate (mĕ-bu'tah-māt) chemical name: 2-methyl-2-(1-methylpropyl)-1,3-propanediol dicarbamate. A mildly tranquilizing, antihypertensive agent, $C_{10}H_{20}N_2O_4$, occurring as a white, crystalline powder; used alone or in conjunction with diuretics and other hypotensive drugs, administered orally.

Subsequently, Carter discovered another drug called **mebutamate**, a sedative with antihypertensive effects, which Carter eventually patented and marketed under the trade name Capla. U.S. v. Ciba Geigy Corp., 508 F.Supp. 1118, 1139 (D.N.J.1976).

mechanical heart See *heart, artificial.*

mechanotherapy (mek"ah-no-ther'ah-pe) [*mechano-* + Gr. *therapeia* treatment] the use of mechanical apparatus in the treatment of disease or its results, especially as an aid in performing therapeutic exercises.

According to Rule MB–1–05(G), **mechanotherapy** is understood to be "the use of manual, physical, or mechanical measures for the treatment of disease." . . .

Applying the various statutory provisos to the facts in this case, we conclude that the exemption from the optometry licensing provisions of R.C. Chapter 4725, which is set forth in R.C. 4725.14(A), is applicable only to persons holding the degree of doctor of medicine or doctor of osteopathy. This exemption does not include persons licensed to practice only a limited branch of medicine or surgery pursuant to R.C. 4731.15 through R.C. 4731.21. Specifically, this exemption does not include licensed **mechanotherapists**, and the latter may not practice optometry under favor of the exemption. State v. DeMido, 308 N.E.2d 749, 751–2 (Ohio 1974).

ers, 413 A.2d 882, 885 (Del.1980); People v. Rubin, 424 N.Y.S.2d 592–3, 598 (Crim.Ct.Queens Cty.N.Y.1979); McGinness v. Rosen, 415 N.Y.S.2d 744–5 (Supr.Ct.Queens Cty. N.Y.1979); Norville v. Miss. State Medical Ass'n, 364 So.2d 1084, 1086 (Miss.1978); Bilbrey v. Industrial Comm., 556 P.2d 27–8 (Ct.App.Ariz.1976); People v. Amber, 76 Misc.2d 267–8, 349 N.Y.S.2d 604 (Sup.Ct.Queens Cty.N.Y.1973); U.S. v. Article Consisting of 2 Devices, etc., 255 F.Supp. 374, 378 (W.D.Ark.1966); Chiropractic Ass'n of New York, Inc. v. Hilleboe, 227 N.Y.S.2d 309, 336 (Sup.Ct.Albany Cty.N.Y.1961).

medicine, family See under *practice*.

medicine, internal that branch of medicine dealing especially with the diagnosis and medical treatment of diseases and disorders of the internal structures of the human body.

Dr. Ray, a specialist in colon and rectal surgery, was the treating physician at Ochsner's Foundation Hospital after the cancer was discovered. He also testified that the diagnosis of cancer in the colon is not limited to the practice of **internal medicine**. Since Dr. Ray performed both surgeries on Mrs. Steinbach for her cancer, it is apparent that the treatment of cancer is not limited to **internal medicine**. Steinbach v. Barfield, 428 So.2d 915, 920 (Ct.App.La.1983).

medicine, school of

A **school of medicine** relates to the system of diagnosis and treatment. While the law recognizes that there are different **schools of medicine**, it does not favor, or give exclusive recognition to, any particular school or system of medicine, as against the others. When a patient selects a practitioner of a recognized school of treatment he adopts the kind of treatment common to that school, or, as otherwise stated, he is presumed to elect that the treatment shall be according to the system or school of medicine to which such practitioner belongs. Whitehurst v. Boehm, 255 S.E.2d 761, 766 (Ct.App.N.Car.1979).

medicine and surgery

The Statutory Construction Act, however, provides that "medicine and surgery" unless otherwise provided by law, is "[t]he art and science having for their object the cure of diseases of and the preservation of the health of man, including all practice ... or without drugs." [1 Pa.Con.Stat. § 1991.] American College of Obstetricians, etc. v. Thornburg, 552 F.Supp. 791, 810 (E.D.Pa.1982).

medium (me'de-um), pl. *mediums* or *me'dia* [L. "middle"] 1. a substance which transmits impulses. 2. a substance used in the culture of bacteria. See also *culture medium*, under C.

medium, culture a substance used to support the growth of microorganisms or other cells. See also *culture medium*, under C.

MEDLARS (med'larz) [*MED*ical *L*iterature *A*nalysis and *R*etrieval *S*ystem] a computerized bibliographic system of the National Library of Medicine, from which the Index Medicus is produced.

One of the services provided by the library pursuant to its statutory mandate is the Medical Literature Analysis and Retrieval System (**MEDLARS**), a computerized system for storing, indexing, and retrieving medical bibliographical data. The core of the system consists of the **MEDLARS** tapes, on which are

stored citations and abstracts of two million articles from approximately 3000 medical and scientific journals published throughout the world. The National Library [of Medicine] continually updates these tapes. SDC Development Corp. v. Mathews, 542 F.2d 1116–17 (9th Cir. 1976).

MEDLINE (med'līn) [from *MEDLARS* on-*line*] a computerized bibliographic retrieval system, an on-line segment of MEDLARS.

The MEDLARS system is used in various ways by the library. Some of the stored information is printed in various medical bibliographies, e.g., Index Medicus, which are distributed worldwide. Direct access to the MEDLARS data bank is available on a subscription basis through **MEDLINE**, the National Library's on-line terminal reference retrieval system. SDC Development Corp. v. Mathews, 542 F.2d 1116–17 (9th Cir. 1976).

Medomin See *heptabarbital*.

medulla (mě-dul'ah), pl. *medul'lae* [L.] the inmost part; [NA] a general term for the inmost portion of an organ or structure. Called also *marrow*.

medulla oblongata [NA], the truncated cone of nerve tissue continuous above with the pons and below with the spinal cord; it lies anterior to the cerebellum, and the upper part of its posterior surface forms the floor of the lower part of the fourth ventricle; it contains ascending and descending tracts, and important collections of nerve cells that deal with vital functions, such as respiration, circulation, and special senses. It is derived (developed) from the myelencephalon of the embryo. See also *brain stem*, under *B*.

medulla ossium bone marrow: the soft material filling the cavities of the bones, made up of a meshwork of connective tissue containing branching fibers, the meshes being filled with marrow cells, which consist variously of fat cells, large nucleated cells or myelocytes, and giant cells called megakaryocytes. See *medulla ossium flava*.

medulla ossium flava [NA], yellow bone marrow: ordinary bone marrow of the kind in which the fat cells predominate.

medulla ossium rubra [NA], red bone marrow: marrow of developing bone, of the ribs, vertebrae, and many of the smaller bones; it is the site of production of erythrocytes and granular leukocytes.

medullary (med'u-lār"e) [L. *medullaris*] pertaining to the marrow or to any medulla; resembling marrow.

Kimmick was employed by United Industrial on October 27, 1972, when he sustained a left femoral fracture, falling approximately 87 feet in a work-related accident. An **intermedullary** rod was surgically implanted in his leg....
... On December 5, 1973, he underwent surgery for the removal of the rod. United Indus. Maint. v. W.C.A.B., 405 A.2d 1360–1 (Commonwealth Ct.Pa.1979).

megacolon (meg"ah-ko'lon) abnormally large or dilated colon; the condition may be congenital or acquired, acute or chronic.

meglumine (meg'lu-mēn) [USP] chemical name: 1-deoxy-1-(methylamino)-*D*-glucitol. A crystalline base, $C_7H_{17}NO_5$, occurring as white to faintly yellowish white, crystals or powder; used in the preparation of certain radiopaque media. Called also *methylglucamine*. See also under *diatrizoate; iodipamide*.

meglumine diatrizoate a salt of 3,5-diacetamido-2,4,6-triiodobenzoic acid, $C_{18}H_{26}I_3N_3O_9$, occurring as a clear, colorless to pale yellow, slightly viscous liquid; used as a diagnostic radiopaque medium for intravascular use in angiocardiography and excretory urography.

... a **gastrografin** swallow test on August 22 revealed a gastric leak on the lower curvature of Carol's stomach.... Mercer v. Thornton, 646 S.W.2d 375, 378 (Mo.Ct.App.1983).

meiosis (mi-o'sis) [Gr. *meiōsis* diminution] a special method of cell division, occurring in maturation of the sex cells, by means of which each daughter nucleus receives half the number of chromosomes characteristic of the somatic cells of the species. See illustration. Cf. *mitosis*.

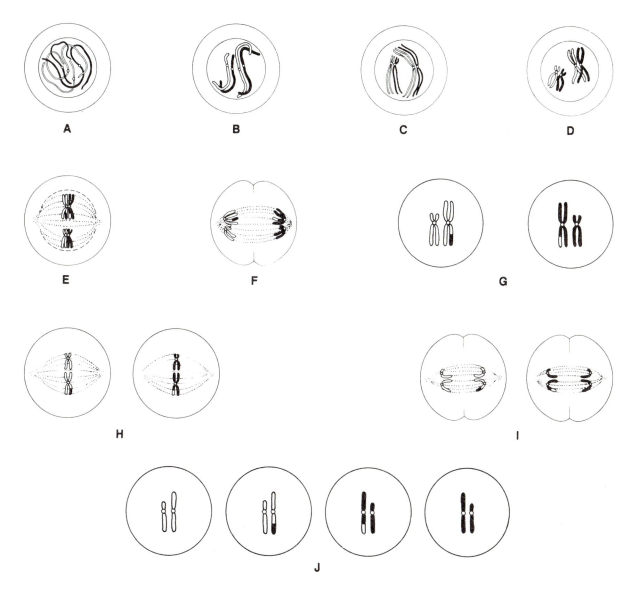

Meiosis (only two of the 23 human chromosome pairs are shown, the chromosomes from one parent in black, from the other parent in outline). FIRST MEIOTIC DIVISION: *A, leptotene*—first appearance of chromosomes as thin threads; *B, zygotene*—pairing (synapsis) of chromosomes; *C, pachytene*—chromosomal thickening and shortening, the individual chromatids becoming visible; *D, diplotene*—longitudinal separation of chromatids, the centromere remaining intact and a chiasma being formed (NOTE: prophase includes *A* to *D* plus diakinesis [not shown]); *E, metaphase*—movement of chromosomes into the equatorial plane; *F, anaphase*—separation of pairs, one member going to each pole; *G, telophase*—cell division, each of the two daughter cells being haploid. SECOND MEIOTIC DIVISION: *prophase* (not shown)—chromosomes become visible; *H, metaphase*—movement of chromosomes into equatorial plane; *I, anaphase*—division of centromeres, the chromatids going to opposite poles; *J, telophase*—cell division, each daughter cell being diploid. (Thompson and Thompson.)

melancholia (mel"an-ko'le-ah) [*melano-* + Gr. *cholē* bile + *-ia*] a depressed and unhappy emotional state with abnormal inhibition of mental and bodily activity.

melancholia, involutional a major affected disorder occurring during involution, and marked by agitation, worry, anxiety, somatic preoccupation, severe insomnia, and sometimes paranoid reactions; formerly thought to be associated with the climacteric. Called also *involutional psychosis.*

This report shows admission of claimant in April 1972 with a diagnosis of "involutional melancholia" with a prognosis of "fair." . . .

. . . In oral testimony claimant described her "bad nerves" and headaches so severe that two to three days was required to recover from each episode. McGee v. Weinberger, 518 F.2d 330–1 (5th Cir. 1975).

melanocarcinoma See *melanoma, malignant.*

. . . "pulmonary hydrothorax due to extensive metastasis from **melanocarcinoma**". In lay language this meant that a watery collection on the lungs was the immediate cause of death, but this condition was caused by one of the many forms of cancer. Insurance Company of North America v. Chinowith, 393 F.2d 916, 917 (5th Cir. 1968).

melanoma (mel"ah-no'mah) [*melano-* + *-oma*] a tumor made up of melanin-pigmented cells. When used alone, the term refers to malignant melanoma. See also *hemangioma* (Williams case); *trauma* (Cox case).

Appellant Linda Sherrill, having had a malignant **melanoma** on her right foot excised, requested her Tulsa, Oklahoma, surgeon to obtain an opinion regarding post-operative treatment from the M. D. Anderson Hospital and Tumor Institute of the University of Texas at Houston. Appellee, Dr. Charles McBride of the hospital's department of surgery, responded to the Tulsa surgeon's inquiry in a letter stating that the preferred treatment at M. D. Anderson was an iliac dissection and perfusion. Sherrill v. McBride, 603 S.W.2d 365–6 (Ct.Civ.App.Tex. 1980).

Chinowith had had a rather extensive **melanoma** removed from his body in 1959 but periodic x-rays had been negative up to a not definitely fixed time prior to his death. It appears that in 1953 he had injured his back in a fall from a tree. Insurance Company of North America v. Chinowith, 393 F.2d 916–17 (5th Cir. 1968).

melanoma, malignant a malignant tumor, usually developing from a nevus and consisting of black masses of cells with a marked tendency to metastasis. Called also *melanocarcinoma, melanoepithelioma, melanosarcoma, melanoscirrhus,* etc.

Pathological examination of the excised mass of lymph nodes resulted in a diagnosis of metastic **malignant melanoma** (cancer which has spread). In the search for the primary site of the cancer, the slide of the 1971 mole specimen sent to the state laboratory was recovered and reexamined. This resulted in the disclosure that an erroneous diagnosis had been made by the state pathologist in his biopsy of the mole and that the correct diagnosis at that time should have been melanoma. Hunter v. Office of Health Services, etc., 385 So.2d 928, 931 (Ct.App. La.1980).

The lesion previously referred to was "a mole" approximately one centimeter by two centimeters. A **malignant melanoma** is a skin cancer first noticeable as a pigmented spot on the skin and is darker than a normal spot on the skin . . . .

. . . Defendant claimed that he removed a hemangioma by electric cautery and that this was a normal and accepted practice. Plaintiffs claimed that the lesion was a **malignant melanoma** and should have been removed by a wide incision and sent to a pathologist for examination and that timely and appropriate treatment should have followed. Williams v. Grant, 417 N.E.2d 586–7 (Ct.App.Ohio 1979).

We think it is to be concluded from Dr. Williams' testimony that decedent's preexisting mole, whether cancerous or not, was injured and aggravated in the course of his employment; and that the injury and aggravation, as shown by the sequence of symptoms and the doctor's testimony, caused or hastened the spread of the **malignant melanoma**, ultimately resulting in death . . . .

" 'It has been recognized that trauma does play a part in the development of malignant lesions, and this is particularly true of malignant melanomas. Almost all cases of melanoma will give a history of some form of injury or chronic irritation to a preexisting lesion. The direct effect is difficult to prove except by inference.' " [Charleston Shipyards v. Lawson, 227 F.2d 110, 112.] Cox v. Ulysses Cooperative Oil and Supply Co., 544 P.2d 363, 371 (Kan.1975).

Other Authorities: Silverman v. Lathrop, 403 A.2d 18–19 (Super.Ct.N.J.1979).

melanosarcoma See *melanoma, malignant.*

Mellaril (mel'ah-ril) trademark for preparations of thioridazine hydrochloride. See also *thioridazine hydrochloride.*

membrana (mem-brah'nah), pl. *membra'nae* [L.] a membrane, or thin skin; [NA] a general term for a thin layer of tissue covering a surface, lining a cavity, or dividing a space or organ.

membrana synovialis capsulae articularis [NA], synovial membrane of articular capsule: the inner of the two layers of the articular capsule of a synovial joint, composed of loose connective tissue and having a free smooth surface that lines the joint cavity. It secretes the synovial fluid. Called also *stratum synoviale capsulae articularis.*

. . . "[t]here was one small rent in the **synovium** just above the cartilage,". . . Contreras v. St. Luke's Hosp., 144 Cal.Rptr. 647, 650 (Ct.App.Cal.1978).

membrane (mem'brān) a thin layer of tissue which covers a surface, lines a cavity, or divides a space or organ. See also *membrana.*

membrane, hyaline a layer of eosinophilic hyaline material lining the alveoli, alveolar ducts, and bronchioles, found at autopsy in infants who have died of respiratory distress syndrome of the newborn. Called also *asphyxial membrane* and *vernix membrane.* See also *respiratory distress syndrome,* under *syndrome.*

. . . **hyaline membrane** is believed to be a disease of premature babies and this child was believed to be fully mature. Hogan v. Almand, 205 S.E.2d 440, 442 (Ct.App.Ga.1974).

membrane, synovial, of articular capsule See *membrana synovialis capsulae articularis.*

Mendel's law See *law, Mendel's.*

mendelian (men-de'le-an) named for Gregor Johann *Mendel;* see under *character,* and see *Mendel's law,* under *law.*

Meniere's disease (syndrome) (men"e-ārz') [Prosper Meniere, French physician, 1799–1862. The spelling *Meniere* appears on his birth certificate, *Menière* and *Ménière* on his works. Ménière was the choice of his son]. See under *disease; labyrinth.*

meninges (mĕ-nin'jēz) [Gr. pl. of *mēninx* membrane] [NA] the three membranes that envelop the brain and spinal cord: the dura mater, pia mater, and arachnoid.

At 8:00 a.m. Dr. West for the first time diagnosed appellant's condition as a perforated esophagus. By way of treatment, he then ordered the administration of antibiotics.

Appellant received the first dosage of antibiotics at 12:30 p.m., more than four hours after Dr. West's order. By that time infection had set in. As a result of the infection, appellant suffered a **meningeal** stroke, was forced to undergo several additional surgical procedures and lost the full use of his right arm and left leg. Brannan v. Lankenau Hospital, 417 A.2d 196, 198 (Pa.1980).

. . . Dr. Keller stated that he knew that HI [Hemophilus influenzae] could attack the **meninges** (lining of the brain) but that he knew little else about HI. Folk v. Kilk, 126 Cal.Rptr. 172, 181 (Ct.App.Cal.1975).

Other Authorities: York v. Daniels, 259 S.W.2d 109, 111 (Springfield Ct.App.Mo.1953).

meningioma (mĕ-nin"je-o'mah) [*meninges* + *-oma* tumor] a hard, slow-growing, usually vascular tumor which occurs mainly along the meningeal vessels and superior longitudinal sinus, invading the dura and skull and leading to erosion and thinning of the skull.

George Szimonisz committed suicide on September 16, 1976. An autopsy was performed which revealed a **parasagittal meningioma**, a benign tumor of the covering of the brain, which was about the size of an egg. The tumor had not been diagnosed by the Veteran's Administration physicians despite the fact that such tumors grow slowly and George Szimonisz had been hospitalized and treated in the Veteran's Administration Hospital on numerous occasions over a period of four years. Such a tumor is readily detectable by means of either Computerized Axial Tomography (CAT scan) or the more widely available isotope brain scan. . . .

. . . The plaintiff's evidence established that Szimonisz was suffering from the effects of a relatively large, non-cancerous brain tumor at the time of his suicide. Such tumors of the brain covering are called **meningiomas**, they expand slowly and produce inexorable pressure on and displacement of the soft tissues of the brain. The testimony established that such **meningiomas** can be successfully removed through surgery. The risks of the procedure are not much greater than the usual hazards present in all surgery, and the vast majority of the patients recover without major complications or significant residual disability. The testimony also established that such tumors are highly vascular and are, therefore, readily apparent on an isotope brain scan or CAT scan.

The clinically-observable symptoms of such a tumor include, in addition to possible mental disturbances, a certain spasticity or uncertainty of gait attended by occasional loss of balance; a nystagmus or trembling of the eyeballs; headaches, lethargy and difficulties in spatial orientation. Szimonisz v. U.S., 537 F.Supp. 147–9 (D.Or.1982).

meningitis (men"in-ji'tis), pl. *meningit'ides* [Gr. *mēninx* membrane + *-itis*] inflammation of the meninges. When it affects the dura mater, the disease is termed *pachymeningitis;* when the arachnoid and pia mater are involved, it is called *leptomeningitis,* or meningitis proper.

A spinal tap was performed which revealed a very severe case of meningitis.[2] (T-p. 55). . . . [[2] This was later diagnosed as H-Flu meningitis. It was explained that this bacterial organism was in no way connected with the viral disorder commonly known as "flu." (T-pp. 137–138)]

. . . He had some mild improvement, but the H-Flu **meningitis** has left him with brain damage and a crippled body. (T-pp. 55–58). . . .

Matthew McNeill is profoundly retarded, although he was "normal" prior to the illness which befell him. His spine has become curved, and he exercises no effective control over his body. McNeill v. U.S., 519 F.Supp. 283, 286 (D.S.Car.1981).

Throughout the early hours of Tuesday, December 1, she checked plaintiff several times to see whether he could touch his chin to his chest without difficulty. At about 5:30 a.m. Speed could not carry out the chin-to-chest test without experiencing stiffness and pain, which is a recognized symptom of **meningitis**. Speed v. State, 240 N.W.2d 901, 903 (Iowa 1976).

Among children, [HI] it can cause **meningitis** (an inflammation of the lining of the brain), middle ear infections and croup. Folk v. Kilk, 126 Cal.Rptr. 172, 177 (Ct.App.Cal.1975).

meningitis, pneumococcal bacterial

He was transferred that morning to the Wichita General Hospital where he was diagnosed to have **pneumococcal bacterial meningitis**. . . .

. . . This form of meningitis in conjunction with head trauma develops with extraordinary rapidity and invariably causes serious injury and is often fatal.

The effects of the meningitis on plaintiff were severe. He suffers from muscle atrophy and partial permanent paralysis of both his legs and left arm. He cannot walk unaided. Sebree v. U.S., 567 F.2d 292, 295 (5th Cir. 1978).

meningitis, spinal inflammation of the meninges of the spinal cord.

Eleanore had neither physical handicaps nor mental impairment until 1930 when she was attacked by **spinal meningitis**. She was in a coma for a considerable time, during which she could not recognize people or make sounds. After three or four months she was barely conscious and had no memory of the attack. After some sixteen months, she was able to walk but with some permanent impairment or paralysis of her right arm and leg. Her condition improved gradually, but her recollection was poor and she spoke as a child. . . .

Dr. Foster stated that one of the unhappy sequelae of an acute attack of meningitis is damage to the brain. The records of St. Joseph Hospital also showed Eleanore's right side paralysis and probable Jacksonian seizures indicative of continuing illness. Mayo records showed the beginning of headaches in her right frontal region, also indicative of progressive illness. Such records also showed loss of sensation and paralysis and weakness of the right side, indicative of damage to the left side of the brain.

The Missouri Baptist records showed diagnosis by pneumoencephalogram of distal or enlarged ventricle on the left side of the brain, indicative of brain damage and shrinkage. She underwent brain surgery at Missouri Baptist and a biopsy showed progressive brain damage and disease. Dilantin and Mezantoin were prescribed for control of convulsive seizures and she continued the prescriptions through the years. In Dr. Foster's opinion, all this evidence indicated brain damage resulting in personality and character structure changes, all as a result of her **spinal meningitis**. Simmons v. Inman, 471 S.W.2d 203–4 (Mo.1971).

meniscectomy (men″ĭ-sek′to-me) excision of an intra-articular meniscus, as in the knee joint.

Claimant sustained the knee injury in December, 1978, when a metal door fell against his right knee, causing a tear of the medial meniscus. He underwent an arthroscopic **meniscectomy** in May, 1979, performed by Dr. Manley, who noted that the synovial fluid in the knee joint was cloudy. Matter of Compensation of Aquillon, 653 P.2d 264–5 (Ct.App.Or.1982).

… Dr. Schneider performed a lateral **meniscectomy** and a chondrectomy of the kneecap. Plaintiff contends he is disabled as a result of his knee injury. Istre v. Hudson Engineering Corp., 386 So.2d 366–7 (Ct.App.La.1980).

… surgical procedures known as arthrotomy and **meniscectomy** were performed on the infant claimant at the New York State Rehabilitation and Research Hospital at West Haverstraw for the removal of damaged cartilage from her right knee joint. Welsh v. State of N.Y., 377 N.Y.S.2d 790, 791 (3d Dep't N.Y.1976).

meniscus (mĕ-nis′kus), pl. *menis′ci* [L.; Gr. *mēniskos*, crescent] [NA] a general term for a crescent-shaped structure of the body. Often used alone to designate one of the crescent-shaped disks of fibrocartilage attached to the superior articular surface of the tibia.

meniscus, medial, of knee joint; meniscus medialis articulationis genus [NA] a crescent-shaped disk of fibrocartilage attached to the medial margin of the superior articular surface of the tibia; called also *m. medialis articulationis genu.*

Surgery performed on McGuire's left knee revealed a torn **medial meniscus** (cartilage) which was removed. McGuire v. National Super Markets, Inc., 425 So.2d 1315–16 (Ct.App.La. 1983).

The injury was sufficiently serious to require corrective surgery to remove the **medial meniscus**—fibrocartilage of the knee joint—from that knee. Potomac Elec. Power Co. v. Director, etc., 606 F.2d 1324–5 (D.C.Cir.1979).

… he underwent an arthrotomy (surgical incision of a joint) for excision of the left **medial meniscus** (internal semilunar cartilage of the knee joint). He was discharged on August 4, 1970, with diagnoses of degenerative osteoarthritis of the left

knee, and tear of the left **medial meniscus**. Pruchniewski v. Weinberger, 415 F.Supp. 112–13 (D.Md.1976).

Other Authorities: Moore v. Industrial Com'n, 492 P.2d 1222–4 (Ct.App.Ariz.1972); U.S. v. Ehret, 431 F.2d 1146, 1148 (9th Cir. 1970).

menometrorrhagia (men″o-met″ro-ra′je-ah) excessive uterine bleeding occurring both during the menses and at irregular intervals.

… an operation commonly known as a "D & C" was performed to stop the excessive uterine bleeding (**menometrorrhagia**).… Hammock v. Allstate Insurance Co., 186 S.E.2d 353, 354 (App.Ct.Ga.1971).

menorrhagia (men″o-ra′je-ah) [*meno-* + Gr. *rhēgnynai* to burst forth] excessive uterine bleeding occurring at the regular intervals of menstruation, the period of flow being of greater than usual duration.

She was not seen by the gynecologist until October 18, 1974, when he diagnosed the condition as **menorrhagia** (excessive menstruation) and prescribed birth control pills to control her menstruation. Todaro v. Ward, 431 F.Supp. 1129, 1142 (S.D. N.Y.1977).

menses (men′sēz) [L., pl. of *mensis* month] the monthly flow of blood from the genital tract of women. See also *menstruation.*

menstruation (men″stroo-a′shun) the cyclic, physiologic discharge through the vagina of blood and muscosal tissues from the nonpregnant uterus; it is under hormonal control and normally recurs, usually at approximately four-week intervals, in the absence of pregnancy during the reproductive period (puberty through menopause) of the female of the human and a few species of primates. It is the culmination of the menstrual cycle; see illustration accompanying *cycle.*

mental (men′tal) [L. *mens* mind] pertaining to the mind; psychic.

mental defect See *mental disease.*

mental disease See *disorder, mental.*

The definition of **mental disease** or defect is any "congenital or traumatic mental condition" with certain enumerated exceptions. It is not limited to psychosis. See State v. Montague, 510 S.W.2d 776 (Mo.App.1974).… State v. Pike, 516 S.W. 2d 505, 507 (Mo.Ct.App.1974).

The concern that medical terminology not control legal outcomes culminated in McDonald v. United States, 114 U.S. App.D.C. 120, 312 F.2d 847, 851 (en banc, 1962), where this court recognized that the term, **mental disease** or defect, has various meanings, depending upon how and why it is used, and by whom. **Mental disease** means one thing to a physician bent on treatment, but something different, if somewhat overlapping, to a court of law. We provided a legal definition of **mental disease** or defect, and held that it included "any abnormal condition of the mind which substantially affects mental or emotional processes and substantially impairs behavior controls." (312 F.2d at 851). "Thus the jury would consider testimony concerning the development, adaptation and functioning of these processes and controls." Id.…

Our ruling today includes our decision that in the ALI rule as adopted by this court the term "**mental disease** or defect" includes the definition of that term provided in our 1962 en banc McDonald opinion, as follows:

[A] **mental disease** or defect includes any abnormal condition of the mind which substantially affects mental or emotional processes and substantially impairs behavior controls. McDonald v. United States, 114 U.S.App.D.C. at 124, 312 F.2d at 851. U.S. v. Brawner, 471 F.2d 969, 978, 983 (D.C. Cir.1972).

mental illness See *disorder, mental; mental disease.*

meperidine hydrochloride (mĕ-per′ĭ-dēn) [USP] chemical name: 1-methyl-4-phenyl-4-piperidinecarboxylic acid ethyl ester. A synthetic narcotic analgesic, $C_{15}H_{21}NO_2 \cdot$ HCl, occurring as a fine, white, crystalline powder, used as a preanesthetic medication, postoperative sedative, obstetric analgesic, and when a relatively short duration of analgesia is desired; administered orally in tablets or intramuscularly or subcutaneously. Abuse of this drug may lead to dependence. Called also *isonipecaine* and *pethidine hydrochloride.*

Demerol is an anesthetic given to a patient before administration of a spinal block....

The record is barren of proof to the effect that the surgeon could reasonably anticipate the synergistic effect of **Demerol** in combination with the saddle block would repress the patient's breathing. All expert medical testimony indicated that, under the circumstances adduced, the use of **Demerol** in connection with a saddle block was not below acceptable medical standards....

Dr. G explained that the surgeon's choice of **Demerol**, a narcotic which depresses breathing, started "the chain of events," that it was an "essential factor," a "contributing factor," which bore "a direct causal connection" to patient Dorothy Thompson's brain damage from lack of oxygen. [Dissent.] Thompson v. Presbyterian Hosp., Inc., 652 P.2d 260, 262, 264, 270 (Okl.1982).

Demerol, it developed at trial, is a narcotic, frequently used to combat pain; it is **meperidine hydrochloride**, manufactured by Winthrop Laboratories. The Phenergan is given with **Demerol** to facilitate the latter's effectiveness. The literature provided with **Demerol** by the manufacturer included, in 1972, a warning that "**Meperidine** should be used with extreme caution in patients having an acute asthmatic attack, ... [i]n such patients, even usual therapeutic dosages of narcotics may decrease respiratory drive while simultaneously increasing airway resistance to the point of apnea." Fraijo v. Hartland Hospital, 160 Cal.Rptr. 246, 249 (Ct.App.Cal.1979).

Defendant's unprofessional conduct consisted of writing 11 prescriptions for the controlled substance **Demerol** [3] in the name of individuals who then gave the drug to defendant for his own use. Defendant testified that he used the drug due to chronic mastoiditis, which caused him severe pain in his right ear. [3 A trademark for **meperdine**, a synthetic narcotic drug used as an analgesis, sedative and antispasmodic.] State Bd. of Dentistry v. Blumer, 261 N.W.2d 186–7 (Ct.App.Mich. 1977).

Other Authorities: Petri v. Smith, 453 A.2d 342–3 (Super.Ct. Pa.1982); Eli Lilly and Co., Inc. v. Generix Drug Sales, Inc., 324 F.Supp. 715, 717 (S.D.Fla.1971).

mephenesin (mĕ-fen′ĕ-sin) chemical name: 3-(2-methylphenoxy)-1,2-propanediol. A skeletal muscle relaxant, $C_{10}H_{14}O_3$, occurring as a white crystalline powder; administered orally.

... a chemical compound, which he had discovered in 1947, known as **mephenesin** and used both as a tranquilizer and for the treatment of muscle spasms. Carter-Wallace, Inc. v. Riverton Laboratories, Inc., 433 F.2d 1034–5 (2d Cir. 1970).

mepivacaine hydrochloride (mĕ-piv′ah-kān) [USP] chemical name: *N*-(2,6-dimethylphenyl)-1-methyl-2-piperidinecarboxamide monohydrochloride. An analogue of lidocaine, $C_{15}H_{22}N_2O \cdot$ HCl, occurring as a white, crystalline solid; used to produce local anesthesia by infiltration injection, peripheral nerve block, and epidural block.

Appellant began cleaning the wound and injected the drug **Carbocaine**, a local anesthetic, which enabled him to clean it without causing pain. King v. Murphy, 424 So.2d 547–8 (Miss. 1982).

meprobamate (mĕ-pro′bah-māt, mep″ro-bam′āt) [USP] chemical name: 2-methyl-2-propyl-1,3-propanediol. A carbamate derivative, $C_9H_{18}N_2O_4$, occurring as a white powder, having tranquilizing, muscle relaxant, and anticonvulsant actions. It is used as an oral sedative for the relief of anxiety and tension, as an adjunct in the treatment of conditions in which anxiety and tension are manifested, and to promote sleep in anxious tense patients; it is also used in musculoskeletal disorders and as an anticonvulsant in petit mal epilepsy. An intramuscular injection is used as adjunctive therapy in tetanus. See also *carisoprodol* (Perkins case).

Claim 4 of the patent is upon a therapeutic agent called **meprobamate**, a drug used in the treatment of disorders of the central nervous system, and among other purposes, as a tranquilizer. It is known popularly by such trade names as **Miltown** and **Equanil**. Carter-Wallace, Inc. v. Wolins Pharmacal Corp., 326 F.Supp. 1299 (E.D.N.Y.1971).

The patent covers three organic compounds in the class of 2, 2-disubstituted-1,3-propanediol dicarbamates, one of which is the compound "2-methyl-2-n-propyl-1,3-propanediol dicarbamate," generically known as **meprobamate** and marketed under certain trade names, of which "**Miltown**" and "**Equanil**" are the most common....

... Drs. Berger and Ludwig filed an application for a patent on the compounds, asserting that the compounds possessed "marked anticonvulsant properties ... possessing an action of considerable duration and intensity."...

... The results showed it had utility as an anticonvulsant and afforded resistance to electroshock seizures. Carter-Wallace, Inc. v. Riverton Laboratories, Inc., 433 F.2d 1034, 1035, 1040 (2d Cir. 1970).

Meprobamate is one of a group of drugs known as minor tranquilizers which are used for the symptomatic relief of anxiety and tension associated with psychoneurotic disorders. It was first used in clinical trials in 1952, and it has been widely distributed commercially since 1955 in tablets or capsules of 200 and 400 milligram doses. Carter-Wallace has produced enough of the drug to make approximately 14 billion tablets. It may be dispensed only by prescription, and an estimated 500 million prescriptions have been written. The maximum recommended adult dosage is 2,400 milligrams daily. **Meprobamate** is a safe, effective drug when it is taken in accordance with the manufacturer's recommendation under a physician's direction. Carter-Wallace, Inc. v. Gardner, 417 F.2d 1086, 1089 (4th Cir. 1969).

Other Authorities: U.S. v. Ciba Geigy Corp., 508 F.Supp. 1118, 1139 (D.N.J.1976); Metropolitan Life Ins. Co. v. Main, 383 F.2d 952–3 (5th Cir. 1967).

meralgia (me-ral′je-ah) [*mero-* (2) + *-algia*] pain in the thigh.

meralgia paresthetica a disease marked by paresthesia, pain, and numbness in the outer surface of the thigh, in the region supplied by the lateral femoral cutaneous nerve, due to entrapment of the nerve at the inguinal ligament. Called also *Bernhardt's disturbance of sensation.*

According to Dr. Redler, plaintiff exhibited symptoms of **meralgia paraesthetica**, which is an irritation of a nerve running from the pelvic area to the thigh and can be traumatic in origin. Muller v. Lykes Bros. Steamship Co., 337 F.Supp. 700, 707 (E.D.La.1972).

Other Authorities: Ascough v. Workmen's Comp.App.Bd., 98 Cal.Rptr. 357, 361 (Ct.App.Cal.1971).

Merck index See *index, Merck.*

mercuric (mer-ku′ric) pertaining to mercury as a bivalent element.

mercurous (mer′ku-rus) pertaining to mercury as a monovalent element.

mercury (mer′ku-re) [L. *mercurius,* or *hydrargyrum*] a metallic element, liquid at ordinary temperatures; quicksilver. Its symbol is Hg; atomic number, 80; atomic weight, 200.59; specific gravity, 13.546. It is insoluble in ordinary solvents, being only partially soluble in boiling hydrochloric acid. It may be dissolved, however, in nitric acid. Mercury forms two sets of compounds—*mercurous,* in which a single atom of mercury combines with a monovalent radical, and *mercuric,* in which a single atom of mercury combines with a bivalent radical. Mercury and its salts have been employed therapeutically as purgatives; as alteratives in chronic inflammations; as antisyphilitics, intestinal antiseptics, disinfectants, and astringents. They are absorbed by the skin and mucous membranes, causing chronic mercury poisoning (see under *poisoning*). Because of toxicity, the use of mercurials is diminishing. The mercuric salts are more soluble and irritant than the mercurous. See also *mercuric; mercurous; poisoning, mercury.*

Mercury is often combined with organic chemical compounds to form what are known as "organic mercurials." These serve a wide variety of purposes. In agriculture, it was discovered that organic mercurials were effective as fungicides and that methylmercury was one of the most effective. First Nat. Bk. in Albuquerque v. U.S., 552 F.2d 370, 373 (10th Cir. 1977).

mercury poisoning See *poisoning, mercury.*

Merthiolate (mer-thi′o-lāt) trademark for preparations of thimerosal. See also *thimerosal.*

mescaline (mes′kah-lin) a poisonous alkaloid, 3,4,5-trimethoxy-phenylethylamine, $(CH_3 \cdot O)_3C_6H_2 \cdot CH_2 \cdot CH_2 \cdot NH_2$, in the form of a colorless alkaline oil from the flowering heads (mescal buttons) of *Lophophora williamsii* (Lemaire) Coult. (Cactaceae). It produces an intoxication with delusions of color and music.

mesencephalotomy (mes″en-sef″ah-lot′o-me) [*mesencephalon* + Gr. *tomē* a cutting] surgical production of lesions in the midbrain, especially in the pain-conducting pathways for the relief of intractable pain.

mesenchyma (mĕ-seng′kĭ-mah) [*meso-* + Gr. *enchyma* infusion] the meshwork of embryonic connective tissue in the mesoderm from which are formed the connective tissues of the body, and also the blood vessels and lymphatic vessels.

mesenteric adenitis See *adenitis, mesenteric* (Incollingo case).

mesentery (mes′en-ter″e) a membranous fold attaching various organs to the body wall. Commonly used with specific reference to the peritoneal fold attaching the small intestine to the dorsal body wall. Called also *mesenterium* [NA]. See also *mesocolon.*

The body appeared to be extensively bruised and Dr. Ruskin discovered that approximately one-third of the child's blood supply had drained into the abdominal cavity. In Dr. Ruskin's opinion, the deceased bled to death after suffering tears in the two **mesentery** membranes which enclose numerous vessels supplying blood to the vital organs. People v. Frost, 362 N.E.2d 417–19 (App.Ct.Ill.1977).

A loop of small bowel showed a near complete transection in the body's midline and the small bowel **mesentery**, which is the tissue that supplies the bowel proper with blood and lymph vessels showed a laceration. State v. Mendell, 523 P.2d 79, 81 (Ariz.1974).

It is his opinion that a hole or opening had first appeared in the **mesentery** or mesocolon, which is the tissue joining the colon to the abdominal wall. This hole or opening, which should not have been there, was underneath the colon at the point where the ends were sutured during the first operation. Lenger v. Physician's General Hosp., Inc., 455 S.W.2d 703, 706 (Tex. 1970).

mesentery gland See *adenitis, mesenteric.*

mesocolon (mes″o-ko′lon) [*meso-* + Gr. *kolon* colon] [NA] the process of the peritoneum by which the colon is attached to the posterior abdominal wall. It is divided into ascending, transverse, descending, and sigmoid or pelvic portions, according to the segment of the colon to which it gives attachment.

mesophilic (mes″o-fil′ik) [*meso-* + Gr. *philein* to love] fond of moderate temperature; said of bacteria which develop best at temperatures between 20° and 45° C. Cf. *psychrophilic* and *thermophilic.*

mesothelial (mes"o-the'le-al) pertaining to the mesothelium.

meso- [Gr. *mesos* middle] a prefix signifying "middle," either situated in the middle or intermediate.

mesothelioma (mes"o-the"le-o'mah) a malignant tumor derived from mesothelial tissue (peritoneum, pleura, pericardium); it appears as broad sheets of cells, with some regions containing spindle-shaped, sarcoma-like cells and other regions showing adenomatous patterns. Pleural mesotheliomas have been linked to exposure to asbestos. See also *asbestosis; cancer, lung* (Pierce case); *injury* (Keene Corp. case).

The medical evidence consisted of the opinions of two physicians who reported that a peculiar feature of **mesothelioma** is a lengthy period between exposure to asbestos and the presence of a tumor. Both of the physicians agreed that it was extremely unlikely that any exposure to asbestos after 1963 (within 15 years of the tumor's appearance) contributed to the development of the tumor. Indus. Indem. Co. v. Workers' Comp. App. Bd., 193 Cal.Rptr. 471, 475 (Ct.App.Cal.1983).

According to plaintiff's theory, this exposure resulted in Mr. Murphree contracting **mesothelioma**, a cancer of the lining of the chest. This disease ultimately caused his death. All of the expert witnesses who testified at trial agreed that Mr. Murphree's disease resulted from his occupational exposure to asbestos-containing products. Murphree v. Raybestos-Manhattan, Inc., 696 F.2d 459–60 (6th Cir. 1982).

Mesothelioma is a malignant tumor of the lining of the lungs or the lining of the peritoneum, which surrounds the organs of the gastrointestinal tract. It is well-established that prolonged inhalation of asbestos fibers causes **mesothelioma**. The disease can develop many years after inhalation ceases, and can manifest itself several months after it begins to develop. Keene Corp. v. Ins. Co. of North America, 667 F.2d 1034, 1038 (D.C.Cir.1981).

Other Authorities: Wilson v. Johns-Manville Sales Corp., 684 F.2d 111, 113 (D.C.Cir.1982); Nelson v. Industrial Com'n of Arizona, 656 P.2d 1230, 1233 (Ariz.1982); Neubauer v. Owens-Corning Fiberglas Corp., 686 F.2d 570–1 (7th Cir. 1982); Ins. Co. of N.A. v. Forty-Eight Insulations, Inc., 657 F.2d 814–15 (6th Cir. 1981); 451 F.Supp. 1230, 1237 (E.D. Mich.1978); Arndt v. Workers' Comp. App. Bd., 128 Cal.Rptr. 250–2 (Ct.App.Cal.1976); U.S. v. Reserve Mining Co., 380 F.Supp. 11, 40 (D.Minn.1974); Borel v. Fibreboard Paper Products Corp., 493 F.2d 1076, 1082–3 (5th. Cir. 1973); Linnell, Choate & Webber v. Heyde, 330 F.Supp. 170–1 (D.Me. 1971).

mesothelium (mes"o-the'le-um) [*meso-* + *epithelium*] [NA] the layer of flat cells, derived from the mesoderm, which lines the coelom or body cavity of the embryo. In the adult, it forms the simple squamous epithelium which covers all true serous membranes (peritoneum, pericardium, pleura).

mestranol (mes'trah-nōl) [USP] chemical name: 3-methyoxy-19-nor-17α-pregna-1,3,5(10)-triene-20-yne-17α-01. The 3-methyl ether of ethinyl estradiol, $C_{21}H_{26}O_2$, occurring as a white to creamy white, crystalline powder; used as the estrogen component of several progestin-estrogen oral contraceptives.

metabolic (met"ah-bol'ik) pertaining to or of the nature of metabolism.

Doctor Fazekas has contributed 204 articles to the medical literature, most of them dealing with metabolic disturbances. He defined **metabolic** as alterations in the "biological or biochemical activity of various cells under various conditions" and related it to the translation of ingested food into the make-up of the body. U.S. v. 60 28–Capsule Bottles, More or Less, etc., 211 F.Supp. 207, 209 (D.N.J.1962).

metabolism (mĕ-tab'o-lizm) [Gr. *metaballein* to turn about, change, alter] the sum of all the physical and chemical processes by which living organized substance is produced and maintained (anabolism), and also the transformation by which energy is made available for the uses of the organism (catabolism).

metabolism, basal the minimal energy expended for the maintenance of respiration, circulation, peristalsis, muscle tonus, body temperature, glandular activity, and the other vegetative functions of the body. The rate of basal metabolism (basal metabolic rate) is measured by means of a calorimeter, in a subject at absolute rest, 14 to 18 hours after eating, and is expressed in calories per hour per square meter of body surface.

Basal Metabolism, [The changes going on continually in living cells, by which energy is provided for vital processes and activities in the body, and new material is produced to repair the waste.] U.S. v. Article Consisting of 2 Devices, etc., 255 F.Supp. 374, 381 (W.D.Ark.1966).

metacarpal (met"ah-kar'pal) 1. pertaining to the metacarpus. 2. a bone of the metacarpus.

metacarpal bone See *bone, metacarpal.*

metacarpophalangeal (met"ah-kar"po-fah-lan'je-al) pertaining to the metacarpus and phalanges. See also *metacarpus*; and *phalanges.*

There was tenderness in the right wrist and about the **metacarpophalangeal** joints, but no deformity. Camarata v. Benedetto, 420 So.2d 1146, 1148 (Ct.App.La.1982).

. . . he was admitted to the Faulkner Hospital and was treated for a staphylococcus aureus infection of the second **metacarpophalangeal** joint of his right hand. In Re Sevigny's Case, 151 N.E.2d 258–9 (Sup.Jud.Ct.Mass.1958).

"He states that at irregular intervals, particularly when his hand is tired and warm, he experiences a sudden sharp pain extending from the **metacarpophalangeal** joints of the middle and ring fingers to the elbow. When this occurs he frequently drops any object he may be holding. He states that for perhaps one hour he experiences 'cramps' in the hand. Cold weather does not affect his condition, but in warm weather it is worse...." Liberty Mut. Ins. Co. v. Industrial Accident Commission, 199 P.2d 302, 304 (Cal.1948).

metacarpus (met"ah-kar'pus) [*meta-* + Gr. *karpos* wrist] [NA] the part of the hand between the wrist and the fingers, its skeleton being five cylindric bones (metacarpals) extending from the carpus to the phalanges.

... where Dr. Rifat Nawas, his treating physician, diagnosed plaintiff's injury as fractures of four of the five **metacarpals**— the long bones in the hand which extend from the wrist to the knuckle—in the right hand. Harrelson v. Louisiana Pacific Corp., 434 So.2d 479, 482 (Ct.App.La.1983).

In essence, a debridement was performed which involved the amputation of the little and ring fingers through the distal **metacarpals**, amputation of the index finger at the proximal metacarpal level, and amputation of the mid finger at the level of the PIP joint. The thumb was not amputated.... Grable v. Sec. of Health, Ed. & Welfare, 442 F.Supp. 465, 468 (W.D. N.Y.1977).

As a result of the injury, plaintiff's left thumb had to be amputated except for one-quarter inch of **metacarpal** bone. This restricts plaintiff's ability to pinch or grip with his left hand. Swoffer v. Marmac Industries, Inc., 204 N.W.2d 344–5 (Ct. App.Mich.1972).

Other Authorities: In re Sharpe, 374 A.2d 1323–4 (Super.Ct. Pa.1977).

metal (met''l) [L. *metallum;* Gr. *metallon*] any element marked by luster, malleability, ductility, and conductivity of electricity and heat and which will ionize positively in solution.

metal, heavy

The so-called **heavy metals** are lead, cadmium, zinc, mercury and iron and, while aluminum is not a heavy metal, aluminum may be considered as such for the purposes hereinafter mentioned as it tends to some extent to be chelated by the processes concerned. U.S. v. Evers, 453 F.Supp. 1141, 1143 (M.D.Ala.1978).

metaplasia (met''ah-pla'ze-ah) [*meta-* + Gr. *plassein* to form] the change in the type of adult cells in a tissue to a form which is not normal for that tissue.

Referring to one of the slides, the doctor said it showed a "highly malignant undifferentiated neoplasm," and that the outermost covering of the affected area of the body, known as the epithelium, showed marked changes from normal tissue, the changes being known as **metaplasia**. ZeBarth v. Swedish Hospital Medical Center, 499 P.2d 1, 4 (Wash.1972).

metaplasia, myeloid the occurrence of myeloid tissue in extramedullary sites; specifically, a syndrome characterized by splenomegaly, anemia, the presence of nucleated erythrocytes and immature granulocytes in the circulating blood, and extramedullary hematopoiesis in the liver and spleen. The primary form is also known as *agnogenic myeloid metaplasia, myelosclerosis,* and *myelofibrosis.* The secondary or symptomatic form may be associated with various diseases, including carcinomatosis, tuberculosis, leukemia, and polycythemia vera.

metaraminol (met''ah-ram'ĭ-nol) [USP] chemical name: α-(1-aminoethyl)-3-hydroxybenzenemethanol[R-(R^*,R^*)]-2,3-dihydroxybutanedioate (1:1) (salt). An adrenergic with potent vasopressor activity; $C_9H_{13}NO_2 \cdot C_4H_6O_6$, used especially for the prevention and treatment of acute hypotensive states occurring with spinal anesthesia and for adjunctive therapy of hypotension due to hemorrhage, reactions to medications, surgical complication, and shock associated with brain damage due to trauma or tumor, administered intramuscularly and intravenously.

In order to prevent Murphy from going into shock, appellant prescribed the minimum recommended dosage of the drug **Aramine**, a vasoconstrictor, which reduces the blood supply in the extremities and concentrates it in the vital organs. This procedure stabilized Murphy's blood pressure. King v. Murphy, 424 So.2d 547–8 (Miss.1982).

metastasis (mĕ-tas'tah-sis) [*meta-* + Gr. *stasis* stand] Pl. *metastases.* A growth of pathogenic microorganisms or of abnormal cells distant from the site primarily involved by the morbid process.

"Metastasis" is the spreading of malignant cells through the bloodstream to the other organs of the body, particularly the lungs. Gradel v. Inouye, 421 A.2d 674, 676 (Pa.1980).

A pathologist diagnosed the biopsy sample as cancerous, whereupon Dr. Kelley performed a radical mastectomy. The pathologist reported the size of the cancerous lesion to be 4 by 3 by 2.2 centimeters, and further indicated the presence of carcinomic **metastasis** into nine of twenty-one lymph nodes in the plaintiff's lower armpit. The size of the malignant tumor removed was disputed by the medical experts. Dettmann v. Flanary, 273 N.W.2d 348, 350 (Wis.1979).

... **metastasis** (spreading of malignant cells into nonadjacent tissues)—characteristics two of their witnesses considered essential definitional elements of "cancer." Environmental Defense Fund, Inc. v. E.P.A., 548 F.2d 998, 1007 (D.C.Cir.1977). Other Authorities: Grassetti v. Weinberger, 408 F.Supp. 142, 144 (N.D.Cal.1976); Lopez v. Swyer, 279 A.2d 116, 119 (Super.Ct.N.J.1971); Sowell v. Richardson, 319 F.Supp. 689, 692 (D.S.C.1970).

metastasis, liver See *longevity.*

When asked to give his opinion as to the percentage of persons with **liver metastasis** who live one year or 18 months, Dr. Cunningham stated that approximately 10 to 15 percent survive one year and probably about 5 to 10 percent survive 18 months. Continental Ill.Nat.B. & T. Co. of Chicago v. U.S., 504 F.2d 586, 592 (7th Cir. 1974).

metastasize (me-tas'tah-sīz) to form new foci of disease in a distant party by metastasis.

... the condition had **metastasized** or broken loose from the parent tumor. Sawyer v. Sigler, 320 F.Supp. 690, 694 (D.Neb. 1970).

metatarsalgia (met''ah-tar-sal'je-ah) [*meta-* + Gr. *tarsos* tarsus + *-algia*] pain and tenderness in the metatarsal region.

metatarsophalangeal (met''ah-tar''so-fah-lan'je-al) pertaining to the metatarsus and the phalanges of the toes. See also *metatarsus*; and *phalanges of toes* under *ossa digitorum pedis.*

On September 5, 1979, the entire **metatarsophalangeal** joint in her left foot was replaced with an artificial joint. Varela v. Secretary of Health and Human Services, 711 F.2d 482–3 (2d Cir. 1983).

metatarsus (met''ah-tar'sus) [*meta-* + Gr. *tarsos* tarsus] [NA] the part of the foot between the tarsus and the toes, its skeleton being the five long bones (the metatarsals) extending from the tarsus to the phalanges.

This operation [the Sympathectomy, Q.V.] was successful but six months later petitioner was forced to submit to yet another operation to remove a piece of bone over the ball of the great toe. Petitioner's medical witness testified that there is still a hazard of more surgery because "this is just a mess of bones"—"the **metatarsal** has been completely crushed"—"the joint is completely lost"—"the overall black appearance of the bone"—"indicates decalcification or demineralization"—"the nourishment to the foot is so bad that the skin shows the unhealthy condition of the foot." Grunenthal v. Long Island R. Co., 393 U.S. 156, 162, 89 S.Ct. 331, 335 (1968).

metatarsus adductus a congenital deformity of the foot in which the fore part of the foot deviates toward the midline.

Catherine was born with two orthopedic problems, forefoot **metatarsus adductus** and flatfoot. Although the forefoot adductus was corrected by casts and exercise, the flatfoot condition and a mild knock-knee continue. Ochs v. Borrelli, 445 A.2d 883–4 (Conn.1982).

methadone hydrochloride (meth'ah-don) [USP] chemical name: 6-(dimethylamino)-4,4-diphenyl-3-hepanone hydrochloride. A synthetic narcotic, $C_{21}H_{27}NO \cdot HCl$, occurring as colorless crystals or white, crystalline powder, possessing pharmacologic actions similar to those of morphine and heroin and almost equal addiction liability; used as an analgesic and as a narcotic abstinence syndrome suppressant in the treatment of heroin addiction, administered orally, intramuscularly, and subcutaneously. See also *narcotic blockade* under *blockade*.

Methadone is a synthetic narcotic and a central nervous system depressant. If injected into the bloodstream with a needle, it can produce basically the same effects as heroin.

Methadone has been used, under medical controls, as a pain killer. Also, **methadone** is used in "detoxification units" of hospitals to take addicts off of heroin. This is done by switching a heroin addict to **methadone** and gradually reducing the doses of **methadone** to zero over a period of about three weeks. The patient thus detoxified is drug free. Moreover, it is hoped that the program of gradually reduced doses of **methadone** leaves him without the withdrawal symptoms, or the "physical dependence" on a narcotic. Beazer v. New York City Transit Authority, 399 F.Supp. 1032, 1038 (S.D.N.Y.1975).

Methadone proved to be as active an analgesic as morphine, but also proved to be equally high in addiction liability. Eli Lilly and Co., Inc. v. Generix Drug Sales, Inc., 324 F.Supp. 715, 717–18 (S.D.Fla.1971).

A five day course of medication was prescribed for Miranda involving the twice daily administration of diminishing doses of **Methadone**, "a dependence-inducing, morphine-like narcotic analgesic" used in the treatment of drug addiction (see Note: Methadone Maintenance for Heroin Addicts, 78 Yale L.J. 1175, 1185 n. 36 [1969]). Miranda v. U.S., 325 F.Supp. 217, 220 (S.D.N.Y.1970), reversed and remanded 437 F.2d 1255 (2d Cir. 1971).

methamphetamine (meth"am-fet'ah-mēn) chemical name: (*S*)-*N*,α-dimethylbenzeneethanamine. A sympathomimet-

ic amine of the amphetamine group, $C_{10}H_{15}N$. Abuse of this drug may lead to dependence. See also *amphetamine*, def. 1.

Special mention should be made of one particular amphetamine, **methamphetamine**, commonly called "speed." Its effects are generally the same as other amphetamines, only markedly intensified. There is evidence that large doses result in permanent brain damage. The drug's lethal qualities are well documented. The potential for violence, paranoia and physical depletion are substantially more severe. People v. McCabe, 275 N.E.2d 407, 411 (Ill.1971).

methamphetamine hydrochloride white crystals or white, crystalline powder, $C_{10}H_{15}N \cdot HCl$, used chiefly for its central stimulant effects in the treatment of mental depression, psychopathic states, narcolepsy, and exogenous obesity, and for its calming effects in hyperkinetic children. It also has pressor effects and is used in various hypotension states, especially in regional and spinal anesthesia and after ganglionic blockade.

. . . and an unlawful sale of **desoxyn**, a stimulant drug known as "speed," in violation of 21 U.S.C. § 331(q)(2). U.S. v. Stewart, 443 F.2d 1129–30 (10th Cir. 1971).

methane (meth'ān) a colorless, odorless, inflammable gas, CH_4, produced by decomposition of organic matter, which may explode when mixed with air or oxygen; it is the first member of a homologous series of saturated hydrocarbons, including butane, ethane, hexane, pentane, and propane. Called also *marsh gas*.

Methane, the smallest hydrocarbon molecule, consists of one carbon atom joined with four atoms of hydrogen. The chemist's formula for methane is CH_4. . . . Ziegler v. Phillips Petroleum Co., 483 F.2d 858, 862 (5th Cir. 1973).

methanol (meth'ah-nol) [USP] a clear, colorless, flammable liquid, CH_3OH, with characteristic odor, miscible with alcohol, ether, and water; used as a solvent. See also *alcohol, isopropyl* (Intoximeters, Inc. case).

methaqualone (mĕ-thah'kwah-lōn) [USP] chemical name: 2-methyl-3-(2-methylphenyl)-4(3*H*)-quinazolinone. A hypnotic and sedative, $C_{16}H_{14}N_2O$, occurring as a white, crystalline powder; administered orally.

Platt and Rivera appeal their convictions for aiding and abetting in possessing, with intent to distribute, approximately 100,000 **Methaqualone** tablets (commonly known as quaaludes) (Count 1). U.S. v. Rivera, 775 F.2d 1559–60 (11th Cir. 1985).

Methaqualone tablets—called quaaludes or ludes—are powerful depressants. They work on the central nervous system just like alcohol. It is frightening to realize that one **methaqualone** pill is the equivalent of 8 ounces of 100 proof whiskey, and frequently our young people are taking two of these pills at a time. Hearings before the Sen.Comm. on Labor and Human Resources on Health Promotion and Disease Prevention Amend. on S. 771, 98th Cong., 1st Sess. 1, 302 (1983).

Methergine (meth'er-jin) trademark for preparations of methylergonovine maleate. See also *methylergonovine maleate*.

methocarbamol (meth″o-kar′bah-mol) [USP] chemical name: 3-(2-methoxyphenoxy)-1,2-propanediol 1-carbamate. A skeletal muscle relaxant, $C_{11}H_{15}NO_5$, occurring as a white powder; administered orally, intramuscularly, and intravenously.

Robaxin is a muscle-relaxant and is administered to prevent spasm of the muscles. Collins v. Hand, 246 A.2d 398, 403 (Pa. 1968).

method (meth′ud) [Gr. *methodos*] the manner of performing any act or operation; a procedure or technique. See also under *maneuver; stains; tests;* and *treatment.*

method, acid hematin (*for hemoglobin*): dilute the blood in tenth normal HCl and compare the color with a standard heme solution or glass standards.

method, Crede's 1. method of expressing the placenta by forcing the uterus down into the pelvis and at the same time squeezing the uterus from all sides so that its contents are expelled. 2. a similar method for expressing urine from the bladder, especially in paralytic bladder. 3. the placing of a drop of 2 per cent solution of silver nitrate in each eye of a newborn child for the prevention of ophthalmia neonatorum.

Crede—This procedure is placing pressure on the bladder by pressing on the belly with one's hands. Plaintiff was unable to do it, and it would be dangerous for another person to do it. Harrigan v. U.S., 408 F.Supp. 177, 181 (E.D.Pa.1976).

methods for hemoglobin See *method, acid hematin; method, Sahli's; tests.*

method, Kroener

. . . the path in the right tube was interrupted by the "Kroener" method in which the distal fimbriated end of the tube is excised and the tube sutured with a non-absorbable suture. McNeal v. U.S., 689 F.2d 1200–1 (4th Cir. 1982).

method, Pavlov's study of the changes in the salivary reflex produced by psychic influence. See also *conditioned response*, under *response*; and *conditioning.*

Pavlovian conditioning is based on the theory that when environmental stimuli or the kinetic stimuli produced by the incipient movements of the punished act are made contiguous with punishment, they take on some of the aversive properties of the punishment itself. The next time the organism begins the act, particularly in the same environment, it produces stimuli which through classical conditioning have become aversive. It is these aversive stimuli which then prevent the act from occurring. Singer, Psychological Studies of Punishment, 58 Calif.L. Rev. 405, 423 (1970). Knecht v. Gillman, 488 F.2d 1136–7 (8th Cir. 1973).

method, Sahli's (*for estimation of hemoglobin*): convert the hemoglobin into acid hematin by adding HCl and compare the color with a standard color scale.

method, Sargenti See *therapy, root canal (Sargenti method).*

method, scientific See *science*

method, silver point See *therapy, root canal (silver point method).*

methotrexate (meth″o-trek′sāt) [USP] chemical name: *N*-[4-[[(2,4-diamino-6-pteridinyl)methyl]methylamino] benzoyl]-ʟ-glutami acid. A folic acid antagonist, $C_{20}H_{22}N_8O_5$, occurring as an orange-brown, crystalline powder; used as an antineoplastic agent in the treatment of acute and subacute lymphocytic and meningeal leukemia, gestational choriocarcinoma, chorioadenoma destruens, hydatidiform mole, and advanced stages of lymphosarcoma, and as an antipsoriatic agent, administered orally and intramuscularly. It has also been used as an immunosuppressive agent in immunologically mediated disorders. See also *antineoplastic.*

The methotrexate therapy was effective in controlling the psoriasis to the point that her dermatologist said represented 75 to 80% improvement. . . .

Methotrexate therapy for psoriasis was described as posing a potential hazard to a patient's liver. Accordingly, to rule out liver damage from the therapy, her dermatologist on May 12, 1970 referred Patient to Dr. Sidney J. Malawer, one of the appellants, for a liver biopsy. Suburban Hospital Ass'n v. Hadary, 322 A.2d 258–9 (Ct.Spec.App.Md.1974).

methoxyflurane (mĕ-thok″se-floo′răn) [USP] chemical name: 2,2-dichloro-1,1-difluoro-1-methoxyethane. A general anesthetic with analgestic action, $C_3H_4Cl_2F_2O$, occurring as a clear, colorless, mobile liquid; administered by inhalation.

The surgery was performed under Penthrane (Methoxyflurane), a general halogenated anesthetic.

Dr. Trinidad testified he was aware that there were two schools of thought in the medical profession concerning the propriety of administering a halogenated anesthetic such as Penthrane to patients with a prior history of hepatitis.

The defendants presented an anesthesiologist, Dr. Michael Weingarten, director of the Department of Anesthesia at St. Francis Hospital in Milwaukee, Wisconsin, as an expert witness and introduced a report into evidence entitled the "National Halothane Study" to support the proposition that notwithstanding Mrs. Carlsen's prior history of hepatitis 16 years earlier, Penthrane was the proper anesthetic for the operation.[4] [[4] Dr. Weingarten gave his opinion that under the circumstances, Penthrane was the best anesthetic which could have been used.]

The package insert accompanying Penthrane contained the following relevant warnings:

PRECAUTIONS: Cirrhosis, a history of viral hepatitis or other abnormalities involving liver dysfunction may be the basis for selecting an anesthetic other than a halogenated agent. . . .

ADVERSE REACTIONS: Hepatic dysfunction and fatal hepatic necrosis following Penthrane (Methoxyflurane) anesthesia have been reported. . . . (Emphasis added). Carlsen v. Javurek, 526 F.2d 202, 204, 206 (8th Cir. 1975).

methyclothiazide (meth″ĭ-klo-thi′ah-zīd) [USP] chemical name: 6-chloro-3-(chloromethyl)-3,4-dihydro-2-methyl-2*H*-1,2,4-benzothiadiazine-7-sulfonamide 1,1-dioxide. An orally effective diuretic and antihypertensive drug, $C_9H_{11}Cl_2N_3O_4S_2$, occurring as a white or practically white, crystalline powder; used in the treatment of hypertension and in edema associated with congestive heart failure, hepatic cirrhosis, chronic renal disease, pregnancy, premenstrual syndrome, obesity, and corticosteroid and estrogen therapy.

Mrs. Cooper complained to Dr. Sears of not feeling well and of having a slight puffiness, or edema, in her face and hands. Dr. Sears prescribed **Enduron**, a moderate diuretic manufactured by Abbott Laboratories, for treatment of the edema. [Footnote omitted.] Sears v. Cooper, 574 S.W.2d 612–13 (Ct.Civ.App.Tex.1978).

methyl (meth'il) [Gr. *methy* wine + *hylē* wood] the chemical group or radical CH_3—, sometimes abbreviated Me.

methyl alcohol See *methanol*.

methyl ethyl-ketone See *ketone* (City of Bonifay case).

methylene (meth"ĭ-lēn) the bivalent hydrocarbon radical, CH_2.

methylene chloride; methylene dichloride a volatile anesthetic liquid, CH_2Cl_2, resembling chloroform, formerly used as an anesthetic in minor operations.

Central distributed **methylene chloride** to Midcor. This is a chemical solvent manufactured by Dow for use as a paint, metal, and carbon remover. The vapor from that liquid chemical compound is harmful and Dow's material safety data sheet for 599 suggests using **methylene chloride** to clean up a 599 spill. **Methylene chloride** was also one of the chemicals to whose vapors Mr. Pereira was exposed during his employment. Dr. Donald Whorton's declaration allows that a nephrotic syndrome may be causally related to chronic solvent exposure. Pereira v. Dow Chemical Co., 181 Cal.Rptr. 364, 367 (Ct.App. Cal.1982).

methylergonovine maleate (meth"il-er"go-no'vēn) [USP] chemical name: 9,10-didehydro-*N*-[1-(hydroxymethyl)propyl]-6-methylergoline-8β(*S*)-carboxamide (*Z*)-2-butenedioate (1:1) (salt). An oxytocic, $C_{20}H_{25}N_3O_2 \cdot C_4H_4O_4$, occurring as a white to pinkish tan, microcrystalline powder; used especially to prevent or combat postpartum hemorrhage and atony, administered orally, intramuscularly, and intravenously.

Following delivery, **Methergine**, a medication which has the occasional side-effect of increasing blood pressure in conjunction with the desired effect of contracting the uterus and decreasing uterine bleeding, had been given. Dr. Weiss interpreted the hospital chart as showing that decedent's blood pressure increased from $^{130}/_{90}$ shortly after admission to $^{180}/_{100}$ by 6:45 a.m. Maslonka v. Hermann, 414 A.2d 1350, 1352 (Super.Ct.N.J.1980).

methylmercuri See *cyanoguanidine*.

methylmercury dicyandiamide See *cyanoguanidine*.

methylphenidate hydrochloride (meth"il-fen'ĭ-dāt) [USP] chemical name: (R^*,R^*) -(±)-α-phenyl-2-piperidineacetic acid methyl ester hydrochloride. A central stimulant, $C_{14}H_{19}NO_2 \cdot HCl$, occurring as a white, fine, crystalline powder; used in the treatment of hyperkinetic children, various types of depression, and narcolepsy, administered orally.

... defendant Williams failed to prepare and maintain complete and accurate records with respect to the receipt and distribution of Ritalin 20 mg. tablets, a Schedule II preparation containing **methylphenidate**. U.S. v. Williams, 416 F.Supp. 611–12 (D.D.C.1976).

methyltestosterone (meth"il-tes-tos'ter-ōn) [USP] chemical name: 17β-hydroxy-17α-methylandrost-4-en-3-one. A synthetic androgen derived from cholesterol, $C_{20}H_{30}O_2$, occurring as white or creamy white crystals or crystalline powder, having actions similar to those of testosterone (q.v.); used as replacement therapy for androgen deficiency in males, in the palliation of certain inoperable mammary cancers, and to prevent postpartum breast pain and engorgement in the non-nursing mother, administered orally or sublingually.

A major portion of the expert testimony heard in this suit centered around the safety and efficacy of the component **methyltestosterone**. Expert testimony was also taken concerning yohimbine and extract of nux vomica, as well as the combination of these ingredients in the amounts contained in the drug Afrodex....

In addition to the evidence concerning liver damage there was specific testimony that a dosage of **methyltestosterone** even smaller than that contained in Afrodex could activate latent cancer of the prostate....

This testimony was corroborated by the testimony of Dr. Joseph Schoolar, a professor of pharmacology and psychiatry, who testified that liver disease was a generally recognized side effect of **methyltestosterone**....

Dr. Russell Scott, Jr., a professor of urology and an expert on cancer of the prostate, testified as follows:

Q. Dr. Scott, what amount of **methyltestosterone**, in your opinion, would be required possibly to activate carcinoma of the prostate?...

The point, is that any testosterone, I think, would be dangerous in a man with latent cancer of the prostate, when we know the treatment is to remove all hormones, certainly not to give him any, but to remove what he has. U.S. v. 1,048,000 Capsules, More or Less, "Afrodex", 494 F.2d 1158, 1161–2 (5th Cir. 1974).

Methyltestosterone is a synthetic form of the male hormone testosterone, which is a part of the group of male hormones called androgens....

He enumerated certain side effects of **methyltestosterone**, including the retention of sodium and water which may cause edema, acceleration of latent cancer of the prostate, and liver damage resulting in jaundice. He found **methyltestosterone** to be contraindicated in persons having congestive heart failure for which edema could be fatal, known or suspected cancer of the prostate or any preexisting liver disease. U.S. v. 1,048,000 Capsules More or Less, 347 F.Supp. 768, 772–3 (S.D.Tex.1972).

methyltryptamine

... unlawfully and knowingly possessing **dimethyltryptamine**, a "depressant or stimulant drug" within the meaning of Title 21, U.S.C. § 321(v)(3) and 21 C.F.R. 166.3.... U.S. v. Moore, 452 F.2d 569–71 (6th Cir. 1971).

"me-too" drug See *generic*.

MicaTin (mi'kah-tin) trademark for preparations of miconazole nitrate. See also *miconazole nitrate*.

Michaelis constant See *constant, Michaelis.*

miconazole nitrate (mĭ-kon′ah-zōl) chemical name: 1-[2-(2,4-dichlorophenyl)-2-[(2,4-dichlorophenyl)methoxy] ethyl]-1*H*-imidazole mononitrate. A synthetic antifungal agent, $C_{18}H_{14}Cl_4N_2O \cdot HNO_3$, used topically in the treatment of tinea pedis, tinea cruris, and tinea corpora due to *Trichophyton rubrum, T. mentagrophytes*, and *Epidermophyton floccosum;* of cutaneous candidiasis, and of tinea versicolor; and intravaginally in the treatment of vulvovaginal candidiasis.

Until the FDA's approval of an expanded spectrum for **Micatin**, Lotrimin had a broader approved spectrum than any other topical product for treatment of such a wide range of fungal infections. Delbay Pharmaceuticals v. Department of Commerce, 409 F.Supp. 637, 641 (D.D.C.1976).

microangioma

Dr. Winston mentioned a possible left frontal **microangioma** (a small tumor composed chiefly of blood vessels) and a suspect right parietal (upper posterior wall) **microangioma**. Beins v. U.S., 695 F.2d 591, 595 (D.C.Cir.1982).

microbiology (mi″kro-bi-ol′o-je) [*micro-* + Gr. *bios* life + *-logy*] the science which deals with the study of microorganisms, including bacteria, fungi, viruses, and pathogenic protozoa.

That spoilage is hastened by the natural action of bacterial agents in the air is an elementary principle of **microbiology** obvious to anyone who has relaxed too long before wrapping and refrigerating leftovers from the evening meal. Bird Provision Co. v. Owens Country Sausage, Inc., 568 F.2d 369, 378 (5th Cir. 1978).

microcirculation (mi″kro-sir″ku-la′shun) the flow of blood in the entire system of finer vessels (100 microns or less in diameter) of the body (the microvasculature).

Because of Joe Dial's expertise in the field of electrical engineering, he was working with Dr. Johnson to develop special instrumentation in the field of **microcirculation**.[2] [2 The study of the travel of red blood cells through the capillaries, and some of the factors which control the circulation of blood throughout the tissues of the body.] Wry v. Dial, 503 P.2d 979, 981 (Ct.App.Ariz.1972).

microcurie (mi″kro-ku′re) a unit of radioactivity, being one one-millionth (10^{-6}) curie, or the quantity of radioactive material in which the number of nuclear disintegrations is 3.7×10^4 per second. Abbreviated μC. See also *radioactivity.*

(j)(1) "Microcurie" means that amount of radioactive material which disintegrates at the rate of 37 thousand atoms per second. 10 C.F.R. § 30.4(j)(1).

He then translated the 8,000 count per minute reading into one-third of a **microcurie**, which is about three times the amount of radiation given off by a wrist watch with a radium dial. McVey v. Phillips Petroleum Co., 288 F.2d 53, 55 (5th Cir. 1961).

microcyte (mi′kro-sīt) [*micro-* + *-cyte*] an abnormally small erythrocyte, i.e., one 5 microns or less in diameter.

Severe iron deficiency can be diagnosed when an examination of the blood shows that the ... red cells are abnormally small (**microcytic**) from a lack of sufficient hemoglobin to color and fill them. J. B. Williams Co. v. F.T.C., 381 F.2d 884, 887 (6th Cir. 1967).

microgram (mi′kro-gram) a unit of mass (weight) of the metric system, being one-millionth of a gram (10^{-6} gm.), or one one-thousandth of a milligram (10^{-3} mg.). Abbreviated μg. or mcg. Symbol γ.

One thousand **micrograms** (μg) equal one milligram. Citizens Against Toxic Sprays, Inc. v. Bergland, 428 F.Supp. 908, 928 (D.Or.1977).

microorganism (mi″kro-or′gan-izm) [*micro-* + *organism*] a minute living organism, usually microscopic. Those of medical interest are bacteria, rickettsiae, viruses, molds, yeasts, and protozoa.

They [writings on microbiology cited in the opinion] indicate that the many kinds of **microorganisms** are classified by various characteristics and by the relative ease or difficulty with which they may be killed, as well as by the number of available materials or methods that can be used. Evidently, the "vegetative bacteria" are the easiest to kill, and the "bacterial spores" are the most difficult, with "lipid viruses", "non-lipid viruses," "fungi" and the "tubercle bacillus" falling between. Poncy v. Johnson & Johnson, 460 F.Supp. 795, 800 (D.N.J.1978).

Yet, so far as the category of harmful micro-organisms is concerned, there is only a single provision, 21 U.S.C. § 344, which directly deals with "**micro-organisms**." That provision is limited to emergency permit controls dealing with any class of food which the Secretary finds, after investigation, "may, by reason of contamination with **micro-organisms** during the manufacture, processing or packing thereof in any locality, be injurious to health, and that such injurious nature cannot be adequately determined after such articles have entered interstate commerce, [in which event] he then, and in such case only, shall promulgate regulations providing for the issuance... of permits...." U.S. v. Nova Scotia Food Products Corp., 568 F.2d 240, 247 (2d Cir. 1977).

microsecond (mi′kro-sek″und) one-millionth of a second; abbreviated μsec.

... an industry producing EDP systems which perform an almost limitless variety of electronic data processing operations at the seemingly incredible speed of a millionth of a second (**microsecond**).... Honeywell Inc. v. Sperry Rand Corp., 1974 Trade Cases Par. 74,874 at 95,882 (D.Minn.1973).

microtrauma (mi″kro-traw′mah) a slight trauma or lesion; a microscopic lesion.

Compensable disability may be caused by the cumulative contribution of daily work strains, as well as by a single traumatic incident. (Firemen's Fund Indem. Co. v. Industrial Acc. Com., 39 Cal.2d 831, 834, 250 P.2d 148; Beveridge v. Industrial Acc. Com., 175 Cal.App.2d 592, 594–595, 346 P.2d 545; Argonaut Ins. Co. v. Industrial Acc. Com., 231 A.C.A. 136, 141–142, 41 Cal.Rptr. 628; 2 Hanna, The Law of Employee Injuries and Workmen's Compensation 133–134.) "**Microtraumata**" is a convenient medical term, describing the piecemeal physical strains whose cumulative effect is disability. (See Argonaut v. Industrial Acc. Com., supra, 231 A.C.A. at pp. 141, 142, 41 Cal.Rptr. 628.) The phenomenon is characteristic of compensation cases involving disabling back conditions among persons engaged in heavy manual labor. Peter Kiewit Sons v. Industrial Accident Com'n, 44 Cal.Rptr. 813, 816 (Dist. Ct.App.Cal.1965).

microwave (mi'kro-wāv) a wave typical of electromagnetic radiation between far infrared and radio waves, generally regarded as extending from 300,000 to 100 megacycles (wavelength of 1 mm. to 30 cm.).

microwave radiation sickness See *sickness, radiation.*

microwave sickness See *sickness, microwave.*

midwifery (mid'wi-fer-e) the practice of assisting in childbirth. See also *nurse-midwife*; and *obstetrics.*

An applicant for a license to practice **midwifery** must possess qualifications, under Section 485.031(4)(b), Florida Statutes (1977), including the requirement that the applicant
(b) Have attended under the supervision of a duly licensed and registered physician not less than 15 cases of labor and have had the care of at least 15 mothers and newborn infants during lying-in period of at least 10 days each.... State, Dep't of Health, etc. v. McTigue, 387 So.2d 454–5 (Dist.Ct.App.Fla.1980).

[Business and Professions Code] Section 2137 permits those with a valid certificate to practice surgery and other modes of medical treatment, while section 2140 authorizes those with a valid certificate to practice **midwifery**, defined as attendance upon normal childbirth without use of drugs or instruments. Bowland v. Mun. Ct. for Santa Cruz Cty., etc., 556 P.2d 1081, 1084 (Cal.1976).

mil (mil) contraction of *milliliter.*

miliaria (mil"e-a're-ah) [L. *milium* millet] a syndrome of cutaneous changes associated with sweat retention and extravasation of sweat occurring at different levels in the skin; when used alone, it refers to *miliaria rubra.*

miliaria rubra a condition resulting from obstruction to the ducts of the sweat glands, probably caused in part by prolonged maceration of the skin surface; the sweat escapes into the epidermis, producing pruritic erythematous papulovesicles. The severity of the symptoms fluctuates with the heat load of the individual. Called also *prickly heat.*

... claimant developed a skin irritation which was diagnosed as **miliaria rubra**, secondarily infected by pyoderma, a disorder which is often called heat rash....

In fact, any member of the general public staying in a motor vehicle for long periods of time during hot weather, under the same conditions as that of the claimant, may contract **miliaria rubra**. A dermatologist testified that this type of rash is a disorder caused by failure of the sweat mechanism induced by heat and that claimant was apt to develop this rash whenever he became excessively hot. Brooks v. State Dep't of Transportation, 255 So.2d 260–2 (Fla.1971).

milium (mil'e-um), pl. *mil'ia* [L. "millet seed"] a tiny, spheroidal, white epithelial cyst lying superficially within the skin, usually of the face, containing lamellated kera-

tin and often associated with vellus hair follicles; milia commonly occur in large numbers and are found especially over the eyelids, cheeks, and forehead. Popularly called *whitehead.*

Mrs. Rosenblum went to Dr. Bloom's office for treatment of four or five skin blemishes on her face called "**whiteheads**", and also to have Dr. Bloom examine a freckled spot on her chin. Rosenblum v. Bloom, 492 S.W.2d 321–2 (Ct.Civ.App. Tex.1973).

milk (milk) [L. *lac*] the fluid secretion of the mammary gland forming the natural food of young mammals.

"Milk" means raw milk produced by cows prior to pasteurization.... U.S. v. Associated Milk Producers, Inc., 1975 Trade Cases Par. 60,327 at 66,342 (W.D.Mo.1975).

The United States Public Health Service Milk Ordinance and Code (1953) contains the following definitions:
Milk.—Milk is hereby defined to be the lacteal secretion, practically free from colostrum, obtained by the complete milking of 1 or more healthy cows, which contains not less than 8¼ percent **milk** solids-not-fat and not less than 3¼ percent milkfat. Odle v. Shamrock Dairy of Phoenix, Inc., 441 P.2d 550, 552 (Ct.App.Ariz.1968).

Milk is about 87% water, 4% butterfat and 9% "**milk** solids not fat," which include casein, albumin and globulin, lactose, and inorganic chemical elements, including calcium, sodium, phosphorus and postassium. M & R Dietetic Laboratories, Inc. v. Dean Milk Co., 203 F.Supp. 130, 132 (N.D.Ill.1961).

milk, fluid

"Fluid milk" means pasteurized milk sold for human consumption in fluid form.... U.S. v. Associated Milk Producers, Inc., 1975 Trade Cases Par. 60,327 at 66,341 (W.D.Mo.1975).

milk, reconstituted

Reconstituted or Recombined Milk.—Reconstituted or **recombined milk** is a product which results from the recombining of milk constituents with water, and which complies with the standards for milkfat and solids-not-fat of milk as defined herein. Odle v. Shamrock Dairy of Phoenix, Inc., 441 P.2d 550, 552 (Ct.App.Ariz.1968).

milk, skimmed milk from which the cream has been removed.

Skim Milk.—Skim milk is milk from which a sufficient portion of milkfat has been removed to reduce its milkfat content to less than 3¼ percent. Odle v. Shamrock Dairy of Phoenix, Inc., 441 P.2d 550, 552 (Ct.App.Ariz.1968).

Miller-Abbott tube See *tube, Miller-Abbott.*

millicurie (mil"ĭ-ku're) a unit of radioactivity, being one one-thousandth (10^{-3}) curie, or the quantity of radioactive material in which the number of nuclear disintegrations is 3.7×10^7 per second; abbreviated mc. See also *radioactivity.*

(i)(2) "Millicurie" means that amount of radioactive material which disintegrates at the rate of 37 million atoms per second. 10 C.F.R. § 30.4(i)(2).

milliliter (mil'ĭ-le"ter) [*milli-* + *liter*] a unit of volume in the metric system, being one one-thousandth (10^{-3}) liter, or the equivalent of 0.033815 of a fluid ounce; abbreviated ml.

> ... and that the term "5 Mil." represents .5 **milliliters**, a dosage recommended for an adult, which should not be given to a child. Caron v. U.S., 410 F.Supp. 378, 385 (D.R.I.1975).

Miltown (mil'town) trademark for a preparation of meprobamate. See also *meprobamate*.

Mirex

> After extensive analysis of and experimentation with over 400 chemicals, the chlorinated hydrocarbon **Mirex** was selected by the Department of Agriculture cs the safest, effective, currently available chemical for control of the imported fire ant....
>
> When administered in large doses, **Mirex** is directly toxic to shrimp, crabs and other marine organisms. **Mirex** bait is toxic to other species of ants, especially oil-feeding ants. **Mirex** in heavy doses induces tumors in animals in laboratory tests and is a potential danger as a carcinogen for man. Environmental Defense Fund v. Hardin, 325 F.Supp. 1401, 1405 (D.D.C. 1971).

miscarriage (mis-kar'ij) loss of the products of conception from the uterus before the fetus is viable; spontaneous abortion.

> A **miscarriage** is defined as the termination of a pregnancy before the twentieth week. Burwell v. Eastern Air Lines, Inc., 458 F.Supp. 474, 486 (E.D.Va.1978), affirmed in part, reversed in part 633 F.2d 361 (4th Cir. 1980).

misdiagnosis See *diagnosis*; and *discovery*.

mitochondria (mi"to-kon'dre-ah, mit"o-kon'dre-ah), pl. of *mitochondrion* [*mito-* + Gr. *chondrion* granule] small spherical to rod-shaped components (organelles) found in the cytoplasm of cells, enclosed in a double membrane, with an internal membrane space between the two units, the inner one infolded into the interior of the organelle as a series of projections (cristae). They are the principal sites of the generation of energy (in the form of ion gradients and adenosine triphosphate [ATP] synthesis) resulting from the oxidation of foodstuffs, and they contain the enzymes of the Krebs and fatty acid cycles and the respiratory pathway. Mitochondria also contain RNA and DNA, by means of which they can independently replicate and code for the synthesis of some of their proteins. Called also *chondriosomes*.

> ... an impairment in the functioning of the **mitochondria**, the subcellular units which play a crucial role in the production of energy in the body, and in cellular respiration. CD 1–6, 11–11, 11–14, 13–5, JA 1110, 1233, 1236, 1335. Lead Industries Ass'n v. Environmental Protection Agency, 647 F.2d 1130, 1139 (D.C.Cir.1980).

mitosis (mi-to'sis), pl. *mito'ses* [*mito-* + *-osis*] a method of indirect division of a cell, consisting of a complex of various processes, by means of which the two daughter nuclei normally receive identical complements of the number of chromosomes characteristic of the somatic cells of the species. Mitosis, the process by which the body grows and replaces cells, is divided into four phases. 1. *Prophase:* Formation of paired chromosomes; disap-

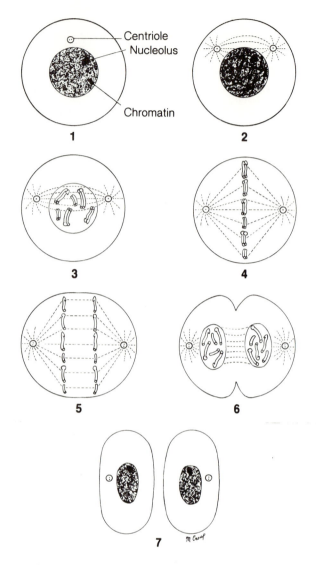

Mitosis shown as occurring in a cell of a hypothetical animal with a diploid chromosome number of six (haploid number three); one pair of chromosomes is short, one pair is long and hooked, and one pair is long and knobbed. *1*. Resting stage. *2*, Early prophase: centriole divided and chromosomes appearing. *3*, Later prophase: centrioles at poles, chromosomes shortened and visibly doubled. *4*. Metaphase: chromosomes arranged on equator of spindle. *5*, Anaphase: chromosomes migrating toward poles. *6*, Telophase: nuclear membranes formed, chromosomes elongating; cytoplasmic divisions beginning. *7*, Daughter cells: resting phase. (Villee.)

pearance of nuclear membrane; appearance of the achromatic spindle; formation of polar bodies. 2. *Metaphase:* Arrangement of chromosomes in the equatorial plane of the central spindle to form the monaster. Chromosomes separate into exactly similar halves. 3. *Anaphase:* The two groups of daughter chromosomes separate and move along the fibers of the central spindle, each toward one of the asters, forming the diaster. 4. *Telophase:* The daughter chromosomes resolve themselves into a reticulum and the daughter nuclei are formed; the cytoplasm divides, forming two complete daughter cells. NOTE: The term *mitosis* is used interchangeably with cell division, but strictly speaking it refers to nuclear division, whereas *cytokinesis* refers to division of the cytoplasm. In some cells, as in many fungi and the fertilized eggs of many insects, nuclear division occurs within the cell unaccompanied by division of the cytoplasm and formation of daughter cells. Cf. *meiosis*.

mitral insufficiency See *regurgitation, mitral*.

mitral valve See *valva atrioventricularis sinistra*.

mitro-commissurotomy See *commissurotomy*.

mixture (miks'tūr) [L. *mixtura, mistura*] a combination of different drugs or ingredients, as a fluid resulting from mixing a fluid with other fluids, or with solids, or a suspension of a solid in a liquid.

M'Naghten (McNaughten) rule (mik-naw'ten) [from *M'Naghten*, a person who in 1843 was acquitted by a British court of murder on the ground of insanity]. See under *rule*.

MMPI See *Minnesota Multi-phasic Personality Inventory* under *test*.

mobility (mo-bil'ĭ-te) [L. *mobilitas*] capability of movement, of being moved, or of flowing freely.

The plaintiff testified that the pain was constant, mostly in her hips and knees but also in her hands and elbows. In the morning she is very stiff and it may take several hours before she can get any **mobility**, although on what she describes as bad days she cannot acquire **mobility** at all. She testified that she is unable to do most ordinary activities including housework and playing bridge with her friends. Flippen v. Mathews, 423 F.Supp. 135–6 (E.D.Va.1976).

modality (mo-dal'ĭ-te) a method of application of, or the employment of, any therapeutic agent; limited usually to physical agents.

"Appropriate **modalities**" are any forms of treatment medically appropriate for a particular patient with a particular condition. Alternative forms of treatment have been "exhausted" when they have been tried and found insufficient. The legislative intent is to make the more radical procedures the treatments of "last resort" and to require medically appropriate alternative therapies be attempted first. Aden v. Younger, 129 Cal.Rptr. 535, 544–5 (Ct.App.Cal.1976).

molasses (mo-las'ez) [L. *mellaceus* like honey] a thick, sweet syrup, the residue left after crystallization of sugar; treacle.

... "molasses" means any grade, type or form of product commonly so defined, including but not limited to, **molasses**, black strap **molasses**, and all industrial grades of sugar obtained from sugar beet or sugar cane....

Molasses is an entirely different product, with its own quality, quantity and distribution variations, and it is addressed to a different market. As one example, while cane and beet refined sugars chemically are identical, cane **molasses** and beet **molasses** are so substantially different that, among other things,

the latter is never sold for human consumption. Sugar Industry, 1977–1 Trade Cases, Par. 61,373 at 71,319; 71,323–4 (N.D. Cal.1976).

mold (mōld) any of a large group of parasitic and saprophytic fungi that cause mold or moldiness and that exist as multicellular filamentous colonies; also, the deposit or growth produced by such fungi. The dimorphic fungi exist, according to environmental conditions, as molds or unicellular (yeast) forms. The common molds are *Mucor, Penicillium, Rhizopus*, and *Aspergillus*. See illustration.

"**Mold** and bacterial slime develop on the surface of cooked sausages and similar products held for long periods under good refrigeration or for shorter periods at higher temperatures. The appearance of **mold** and other surface growth serves to alert consumers to the condition of the product...." Chip Steak Co. v. Hardin, 332 F.Supp. 1084, 1090 (N.D.Cal.1971).

moldicide

Sorbates are most effective **moldicides** and bactericides for products with high acidity, i.e., a pH of 5 or below. These chemicals are not effective in products such as cooked sausages since their pH ranges from 5.9 to 6.2. Chip Steak Co. v. Hardin, 332 F.Supp. 1084, 1090 (N.D.Cal.1971).

mole (mōl) [L. *moles* a shapeless mass] 1. a fleshy mass or tumor formed in the uterus by the degeneration or abortive development of an ovum. 2. a nevocytic nevus; the term is also used to designate a pigmented fleshy growth, and is applied loosely to any blemish of the skin.

... plaintiff consulted defendant Torre, a dermatologist, and requested that he examine a dark **mole** on her left ankle. Torre excised the **mole** and submitted a specimen to defendant Central Health Laboratories, Inc. (Laboratories), for a pathology report. About one week later, Torre informed plaintiff that the laboratory report was negative and "therefore nothing further had to be done".

Plaintiff saw Torre at least eight more times between May 10, 1974 and September 13, 1976. During that period, plaintiff sought medical attention for various other ailments, but also complained about continued pain and a grayish color in her ankle. Torre re-examined the ankle several times and referred to the earlier biopsy report at least once. On each occasion, and even at plaintiff's last visit, Torre reassured her that there was no cause for concern....

Later developments proved the earlier diagnosis to be wrong. [Footnotes omitted.] McDermott v. Torre, 452 N.Y.S.2d 351, 353 (N.Y.1982).

In October 1971, Mr. Cox scratched the **mole** on a nail while at work. Claimant testified that prior to this incident the **mole** was "real dark brown", about the size of a large pea, and that the decedent had had no previous problem with it because it was flat. After the **mole** was scratched there was a change in its appearance "It was raised up and had gotten bigger around."...

Early in January 1972 Mr. Cox went to see Dr. Evan R. Williams about the **mole**. Dr. Williams found a "4 cm by 4 cm lesion" which appeared to be a malignant melanoma. On January 19, 1972, Dr. Williams surgically removed the growth and submitted it to a pathologist, who reported "malignant mela-

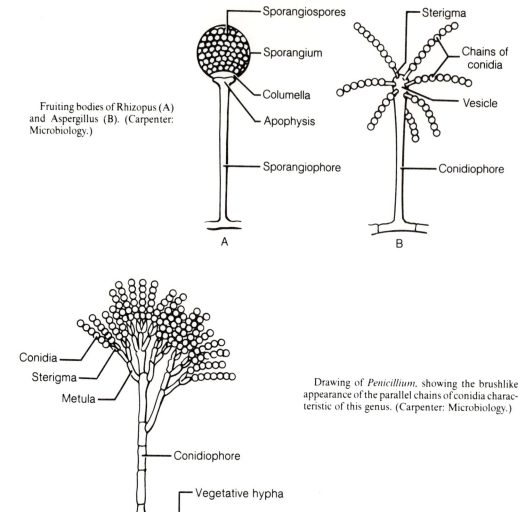

Fruiting bodies of Rhizopus (A) and Aspergillus (B). (Carpenter: Microbiology.)

A labels: Sporangiospores, Sporangium, Columella, Apophysis, Sporangiophore

B labels: Sterigma, Chains of conidia, Vesicle, Conidiophore

Conidia
Sterigma
Metula
Conidiophore
Vegetative hypha

Drawing of *Penicillium*, showing the brushlike appearance of the parallel chains of conidia characteristic of this genus. (Carpenter: Microbiology.)

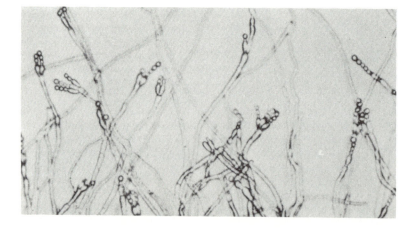

Photomicrograph of a *Penicillium*, showing twisted, branching hyphae and a few chains of conidia. (Courtesy of The Abbott Laboratories, North Chicago, Ill.)

CHARACTERISTIC STRUCTURES OF COMMON MOLDS

noma, adequately excised." Cox v. Ulysses Cooperative Oil and Supply Co., 544 P.2d 363, 365 (Kan.1975).

mole, hydatid; mole hydatidiform an abnormal pregnancy resulting from a pathologic ovum, with proliferation of the epithelial covering of the chorionic villi and dissolution and cystic cavitation of the avascular stroma of the villi. It results in a mass of cysts resembling a bunch of grapes. Called also *cystic* or *vesicular m.*

He diagnosed a **hyatidiform mole** and indicated that another D&C operation would be necessary to clear the uterus of this abnormal tissue growth. During the course of the subsequent surgery, Dr. Hobson found fetal tissue in appellant's uterus. Schenck v. Government of Guam, 609 F.2d 387, 389 (9th Cir. 1979).

mole, malignant (metastasizing) See *chorioadenoma destruens.*

mongolism (mon'go-lizm) [*Mongol*, a member of one of the chief ethnological divisions of Asiatic peoples] Down's syndrome; so called because of facial characteristics typical of this condition. See also *syndrome, Down's.*

Dr. Thomas Bumbalo conducted a "double blind" study on a group of children having **mongolism**, the results of which were published in the American Medical Association Journal. Ubiotica Corp. v. Food and Drug Administration, 427 F.2d 376, 379 (6th Cir. 1970).

mongoloid (mon'go-loid) [see *mongolism*] an individual with Down's syndrome. See also *chromosome* (with accompanying illustration); and *syndrome, Down's.*

Monilia (mo-nil'e-ah) [L. *monile* necklace] a former name for a genus of fungi now called *Candida.*

monitor (mon'ĭ-tor) [L. "one who reminds," from *monere* to remind, admonish] an apparatus used to observe or record such physiological signs as respiration, pulse, and blood pressure in an anesthetized patient or one undergoing surgical or other procedures. See also *syndrome, respiratory distress, of newborn.*

monitor, fetal

Beat to beat variability is a factor derived from the readings of the **fetal monitor**, which measures the fetus' heart rate and the mother's contractions over a period of time. The **fetal monitor's** measurements are displayed as a pair of continuous tracings on a strip chart, with the fetal heart rate drawn on top of the chart and the mother's contractions on the bottom. In a normal childbirth, the two "beat" measurements will vary— that is, the fetus' heart rate will be unaffected by the mother's contractions. If, however, the heart rate begins to fluctuate in direct correlation with the contractions, then fetal distress should be suspected. For example, the umbilical cord may be in such a position that the contractions compress it, causing an interruption of the fetus' oxygen supply and a corresponding alteration of the fetus' heart rate; the alteration of the heart rate would appear on the fetal monitor at a time corresponding to the contraction, thus indicating a loss of the normal beat to beat variability. Haught v. Maceluch, 681 F.2d 291, 294 (5th Cir. 1982).

monoblast (mon'o-blast) [*mono-* + Gr. *blastos* germ] the earliest precursor in the monocytic series, which matures to develop into the promonocyte; monoblasts have a fine chromatin structure and nucleoli are usually visible. They are not normally seen in the bone marrow or peripheral blood, but may be seen in monocytic anemia.

monomania (mon"o-ma'ne-ah) [*mono-* + Gr. *mania* madness] psychosis on a single subject or class of subjects.

At age 90 when the testatrix died and 89 when she executed the will, she was unable to see or walk well, was feeble and becoming senile in that she would forget things and lose track of conversations. She was angry with her husband because he had threatened to leave her when she was accusing him of stealing her things. He claims she even glued the lamps, vases and nicnacs to the tables, although he did not see her do this.

"**Monomania** means a mental disease, not merely the unreasonable conduct of a sane person. **Monomania** is partial insanity; ... The **monomaniac** is subject to hallucinations and insane delusions as to one or a few subjects and yet is perfectly rational as to others; ... **Monomania** is a diseased condition of the mind and is distinguished from ill will, bad judgment, animosity, prejudice, erroneous conclusions from facts, illogical views, and other conditions of mind which can be co-existent with sanity ...." I Redfearn, Wills and Administration in Georgia § 42 (3d Ed. 1965)....

Construing this evidence most favorably to the caveator, Irvin, we find no evidence of insanity and thus no **monomania** as a matter of law. Cobb v. Thompson, 236 Ga. 261, 223 S.E.2d 658 (1976); Thornton v. Hulme, 218 Ga. 480, 128 S.E.2d 744 (1962). Irvin v. Askew, 246 S.E.2d 682–3 (Ga.1978).

"**Monomania** is insanity only upon a particular subject and with a single delusion of the mind, but it may so limit the testamentary capacity as to prevent the testator from bringing into mental review matters essential to the validity of a will...." Yarbrough v. Yarbrough, 202 Ga. 391(5), 43 S.E.2d 329. See also Moreland v. Word, 209 Ga. 463(3), 74 S.E.2d 82. Powell v. Thigpen, 199 S.E.2d 251–2 (Ga.1973).

monomer (mon'o-mer) a simple molecule of a compound of relatively low molecular weight; a substance consisting of simple unrepeated structural units, but capable of reaction to form a dimer, trimer, polymer, etc. See also *polymer.*

monounsaturate

Mono-unsaturates are fatty acid radicals that have a hydrogen-deficiency at one place. The only **mono-unsaturate** occurring in nature is oleic acid. Corn Products Co. v. Standard Brands, Inc., 359 F.2d 739, 740 (7th Cir. 1966).

monovalent (mon"o-va'lent) denoting an antibody capable of combining with only one antigenic specificity, or an antigen capable of combining with only one antibody specificity.

Lucy McDonald received the swine flu vaccination on November 14, 1976 at the Pittston Area High School. Because of her diabetic condition, she was administered the bivalent, rather than the **monovalent**, vaccine.[6] [6 The bivalent vaccine was administered principally to those inoculees over 65 and those with certain chronic illnesses to protect against both swine influenza and A/Victoria influenza.] McDonald v. U.S., 555 F.Supp. 935, 938 (M.D.Pa.1983).

Wilson, a 1912 publication, states regarding dead bacterial vaccines:

"... In veterinary medicine bacterial vaccines are used chiefly for the treatment of suppurative conditions. The vaccine may be **monovalent**—that is, contain but one strain of bacteria; or polyvalent, containing two or more strains...." Application of Davis, 305 F.2d 501, 503 (U.S. Ct.Cust. & Pat.App.1962).

monster (mon'ster) [L. *monstrum*] a fetus or infant with such pronounced developmental anomalies as to be grotesque and usually nonviable. Called also *teras*.

monstrum (mon'strum), pl. *mon'stra* [L.] a monster.

moron (mo'ron) [Gr. *mōros* stupid] in a former classification, a mentally retarded person with an IQ of 50 to 69. Cf. *idiot* and *imbecile*. See also *mental retardation* under retardation.

moronity (mo-ron'ĭ-te) the condition of being a moron.

morphine (mor'fēn) [L. *morphina, morphinum*] chemical name: 7,8-didehydro-4,5-epoxy-17-methylmorphinan-3,6-diol. The principal and most active narcotic alkaloid of opium (q.v.), $C_{17}H_{19}NO_3$, occurring as a white, crystalline powder or as white, acicular crystals, and having powerful analgesic action and some central stimulant action. In the United States, it is usually used in the form of the sulfate salt, while in Germany and Great Britain, the hydrochloride salt is usually preferred. Abuse of morphine and its salts leads to dependence. See also *spectrofluorometer*; and *spectrophotometer*.

If the blood and/or urine test demonstrated the presence of **morphine** and alcohol, they would significantly bolster defendant's theory that Schindehette died from a respiratory failure induced by a combination of alcohol and heroin, rather than from the blow to his head.[2] [2 **Morphine** is the end-product resulting from the body's injection of heroin.] People v. Drake, 236 N.W.2d 537, 542 (Ct.App.Mich.1975).

morphine sulfate [USP], the pentahydrate sulfate salt of morphine, $(C_{17}H_{19}NO_3)_2.H_2SO_4.5H_2O$, occurring as white, feathery, silky crystals, cubical masses or crystals, or white, crystalline powder, and having the same actions as the base; used as a narcotic analgesic, administered parenterally. It is the form usually preferred in the United States.

Miranda was immediately given a ¼ grain dose of **morphine sulfate**, a narcotic with analgesic and sedative qualities. United States Dispensatory and Physician's Pharmacology [hereafter U.S. Dispensatory] 737–741 (26th ed. 1967). Miranda v. U.S., 325 F.Supp. 217, 219 (S.D.N.Y.1970).

mortician (mor-tish'an) [L. *mors* death] an undertaker; a person trained to care for the dead.

Michigan Compiled Laws Annotated Section 338.866 provides that no person may receive a license to be an embalmer or to practice mortuary science unless that person has, inter alia, "served as a resident trainee for one year under the personal supervision and instruction of a licensed embalmer, or

the holder of a license for the practice of mortuary science in this state...." Sharp v. Brown and Co. Funeral Home, Inc., 14 EPD par. 7748 at 5675 (E.D.Mich.1977).

"The examination may include both practical demonstrations and written and oral tests and shall embrace the subjects of sanitary science, health regulations in relation to the handling of dead human bodies, measures used by **funeral directors** for the prevention of the spread of diseases, and such other subjects relating to the care and handling of dead human bodies as the Department by rule may prescribe." (Ill.Rev.Stat.1955, chap. 111½, par. 73.6.) Specifically, the plaintiff argues that it would be futile to take the examination for a **funeral director's** certificate because the board is authorized to include questions covering the field of embalming, and is not limited to questions concerning the qualifications of **funeral directors**. Plaintiff has not taken the examination, and we cannot assume improper questioning by the board. Gholson v. Engle, 138 N.E.2d 508, 512 (Ill.1956).

Morton's neuroma See *metatarsalgia*; and *neuroma*.

mortuary science See *mortician*.

mottling (mot'ling) a condition of spotting with patches of color. See also *fluorosis*.

moulage (moo-lahzh') [Fr. "molding"] the making of molds or models in wax or plaster, as of a structure or a lesion; also such a mold or model.

Since the scars on Dial's nose and the corners of his eyes still presented a problem, Dr. Aronoff made a model of Dial's face, a **moulage**. From this **moulage** the doctor fashioned a mask made of orthoplast, a malleable material. This mask was worn to keep pressure on the scars, with experience showing that such pressure on keloidal scar tissue does tend to have some beneficial effect. The mask looks like a white Halloween mask with eyes cut out. Wry v. Dial, 503 P.2d 979, 985 (Ct. App.Ariz.1972).

moxa (mok'sah) [Japanese] a tuft of soft, combustible substance to be burned upon the skin, popularly used in the Orient as a cautery.

moxibustion (mok"sĭ-bus'chun) cauterization by the burning of moxa upon the skin. See also *moxa*.

Acupuncture is often, but need not be, conducted in concert with a process known as "**moxabustion**," [sic] the heating of the acupuncture points, either through or in the absence of the needles, with a slow burning herb (artemesia vulgaris) commonly called "moxa." Electricity may also be passed through the needles by attaching them to a low-voltage battery, a process called electroacupuncture. Andrews v. Ballard, 498 F.Supp. 1038, 1043 (S.D.Tex.1980).

mucocilary escalator See *escalator, mucociliary*.

multangular bone See *os carpal (carpi); os centrale; os trapezium*; and *os trapezoideum*.

multicatheter

... a **multicatheter**—a tube placed in the blood stream to measure blood pressure and gas flow in the blood stream. McAdory v. Scientific Research Instruments, Inc., 355 F.Supp. 468–9 (D.Md.1973).

multiple sclerosis See *sclerosis, multiple.*

mumps (mumps) a contagious paramyxovirus disease occurring mainly in children and conferring a resultant persisting immunity. It is acquired by aspiration, the heaviest inoculation of virus being in the salivary glands, the parotids more so than submandibular or sublingual. The incubation period is 18 to 22 days. Infection is symptomatic in approximately 75 per cent of cases. In these, parotitis occurs in 70 per cent, and meningitis in 10–15 per cent (with asymptomatic pleocytosis in half of these). Epididymo-orchitis develops in 20 per cent of postpubertal males, but subsequent sterility is rare. Other manifestations are less common and consist of pancreatitis, arthritis, myocarditis, oophoritis, thyroiditis, and mastitis. Fever and painful inflammation of the involved part are most pronounced during the first two days and subside slowly over the next four or five. More than one area may be involved simultaneously; occasionally the involvement is sequential, the entire disease lasting for two or three weeks. Meningoencephalitis with attendant lasting neurological injury is rare. Called also *epidemic parotitis.*

mumps titer See *titer, mumps.*

murmur (mur'mur) [L.] an auscultatory sound, benign or pathologic, particularly a periodic sound of short duration of cardiac or vascular origin.

A TABLE OF ENDOCARDIAL MURMURS

TIME OF OCCURRENCE	SITE OF GREATEST INTENSITY	DIRECTION OF TRANSMISSION	SEAT OF LESION	NATURE OF LESION
Systolic	At cardiac apex	Along left fifth and sixth ribs—in left axilla—in the back, at inferior angle of left scapula	Mitral orifice	Incompetency—Regurgitation
Systolic	At junction of right second costal cartilage with sternum	To junction of right clavicle with sternum—in course of right carotid	Aortic orifice	Narrowing—Obstruction
Systolic	At ensiform cartilage	Feebly transmitted.	Tricuspid orifice	Incompetency—Regurgitation
Systolic	At left second intercostal space, close to sternum	Feebly transmitted	Pulmonary orifice	Narrowing—Obstruction
Diastolic	At junction of right second costal cartilage with sternum	To midsternum—in course of sternum	Aortic orifice	Incompetency—Regurgitation
Diastolic	At left second intercostal space, close to sternum	In course of sternum	Pulmonary orifice	Incompetency—Regurgitation
(Diastolic) presystolic	Over body of heart	To apex of heart	Mitral orifice	Narrowing—Obstruction
(Diastolic) presystolic	At ensiform cartilage	Feebly transmitted	Tricuspid orifice	Narrowing—Obstruction

murmur, cardiac a sound of finite length generated by blood flow through the heart.

Dr. Becker informed Vye that "he had a significant **heart murmur** which I considered secondary to a defective aortic valve." Woodall Industries, Inc. v. Massachusetts Mutual Life Insurance Co., 483 F.2d 986–7 (6th Cir. 1973).

Cardiac murmurs are graded one through six as to audibility. Grade one is audible only on careful examination, grade six without artificial means of ausculation. The tremors of grade four are frequently palpated as well as heard. Magruder v. Richardson, 332 F.Supp. 1363, 1367 (E.D.Mo.1971).

murmur, diastolic one occurring during diastole, i.e., after the second sound of the heart. Heard at the apex, it is a sign of mitral obstruction; at the base of the heart, it is due to aortic regurgitation; more rarely to pulmonary regurgitation. See also *heart* (Woodall Industries, Inc. case).

A **diastolic murmur** is medically significant as showing a defect of the valves of the heart....

"The diastole, as I explained already, the inactive part of the heart muscle, the heart muscle is filled passively, is filled after the second sound, which terminates the action, contraction part.

"Anything after the second sound occurring until the first sound comes in again would be diastole...." Woodall Industries, Inc. v. Massachusetts Mutual Life Insurance Co., 483 F.2d 986, 991, 994 (6th Cir. 1973).

murmur, diastolic apical See *murmur, apical diastolic.*

murmur, holosystolic See *murmur, pansystolic.*

murmur, pansystolic a cardiac murmur that extends through systole; called also *holosystolic m.*

There was a Grade II/VI systolic ejection murmur and a **holosystolic murmur** at the apex radiating into the axilla. Richardson v. Richardson, 333 F.Supp. 890, 893 (W.D.Va.1971).

murmur, systolic one during systole; usually due to mitral or tricuspid regurgitation, or to aortic or pulmonary obstruction.

The examinations of Donna Walstad revealed very weak leg pulses and many abnormalities, the most serious being a **systolic murmur**, characteristic of a mitral valve insufficiency due to rheumatic fever. Walstad v. Univ. of Minnesota Hospitals, 442 F.2d 634, 636 (8th Cir. 1971).

murmurs, apical diastolic murmurs at the apex of the heart indicative of mitral stenosis and consisting essentially of low-frequency vibrations, which account for their rumble quality.

muscle (mus'el) an organ which by contraction produces the movements of an animal organism. Called also *musculus* [NA]. Muscles are of two varieties: *striated*, or *striped*, including all the muscles in which contraction is voluntary and the heart muscle; *unstriated, nonstriated, smooth,* or *organic,* including all the involuntary muscles except the heart, such as the muscular layer of the intestines, bladder, blood vessels, etc. Striated muscles are covered with a thin layer of connective tissue (*epimysium*) from which septa (*perimysium*) pass, dividing the muscle into bundles of fibers, or *fasciculi.* Each fasciculus contains a number of parallel fibers separated by connective tissue septa (*endomysium*). Each fiber consists of sarcoplasm which is cross-striated or composed of alternate light and dark portions (whence the name *striated muscle*); each contains embedded in it the *myofibrils* and each is surrounded by *sarcolemma*. Smooth muscles are composed of elongated, spindle-shaped, nucleated cells arranged parallel to one another and to the long axis of the muscle, and these cells are often grouped into bundles of varying size. The muscles, bundles, and cells are enclosed in an indifferent connective tissue material much as is found in striated muscles.

muscle, abductor of great toe See *musculus abductor hallucis.*

muscle, abductor of little finger See *musculus abductor digiti minimi manus.*

muscle, abductor of little toe See *musculus abductor digiti minimi pedis.*

muscle, abductor of thumb, long See *musculus abductor pollicis longus.*

muscle, abductor of thumb, short See *musculus abductor pollicis brevis.*

muscle, adductor, great See *musculus adductor magnus.*

muscle, adductor, long See *musculus adductor longus.*

muscle, adductor, short See *musculus adductor brevis.*

muscle, adductor, smallest See *musculus adductor minimus.*

muscle, adductor of great toe See *musculus adductor hallucis.*

muscle, adductor of thumb See *musculus adductor pollicis.*

muscle, biceps of arm See *musculus biceps brachii.*

muscle, cremaster See *musculus cremaster.*

muscle, flexor of fingers, deep See *musculus flexor digitorum profundus.*

muscle, flexor of fingers, superficial See *musculus flexor digitorum superficialis.*

muscle, flexor of great toe, long See *musculus flexor hallucis longus.*

muscle, flexor of great toe, short See *musculus flexor hallucis brevis.*

muscle, flexor of little finger, short See *musculus flexor digiti minimi brevis manus.*

muscle, flexor of little toe, short See *musculus flexor digiti minimi brevis pedis.*

muscle, flexor of thumb, long See *musculus flexor pollicis longus.*

muscle, flexor of thumb, short See *musculus flexor pollicis brevis.*

muscle, flexor of toes, long See *musculus flexor digitorum longus.*

muscle, flexor of toes, short See *musculus flexor digitorum brevis.*

muscle, gastrocnemius See *musculus gastrocnemius.*

muscles, interosseous of hand, dorsal See *musculi interossei dorsales manus.*

muscle, levator of upper eyelid See *musculus levator palpebrae superioris.*

muscle, oblique of abdomen, external See *musculus obliquus externus abdominis.*

muscles, paralumbar See *musculi interspinales lumborum.*

muscle, piriform See *musculus piriformis.*

muscle, psoas, greater See *musculus psoas major.*

muscle, quadriceps of thigh See *musculus quadriceps femoris.*

muscle, sartorius See *musculus sartorius.*

muscle, scalene, anterior See *musculus scalenus anterior.*

muscle, trapezius See *musculus trapezius.*

musculoskeletal (mus"ku-lo-skel'ĕ-tal) pertaining to or comprising the skeleton and the muscles, as musculoskeletal system.

It is believed that the foregoing findings are substantially in accord with the majority view expressed in ''Cause of Musculoskeletal Condition'' set forth in 2 A.L.R.3d, pp. 294–353 . . . .

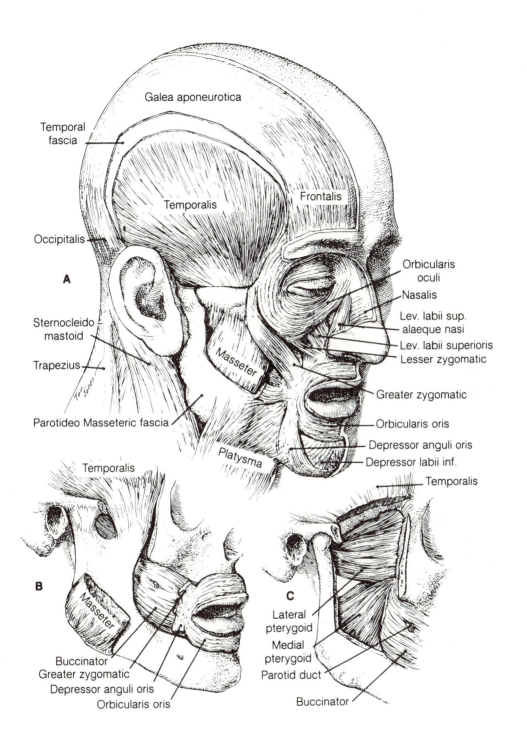

MUSCLES OF THE HEAD AND FACE

A, muscles of face and scalp, showing insertion of platysma; B, buccinator and orbicularis oris; C, pterygoid muscles. (Jones and Shepard.)

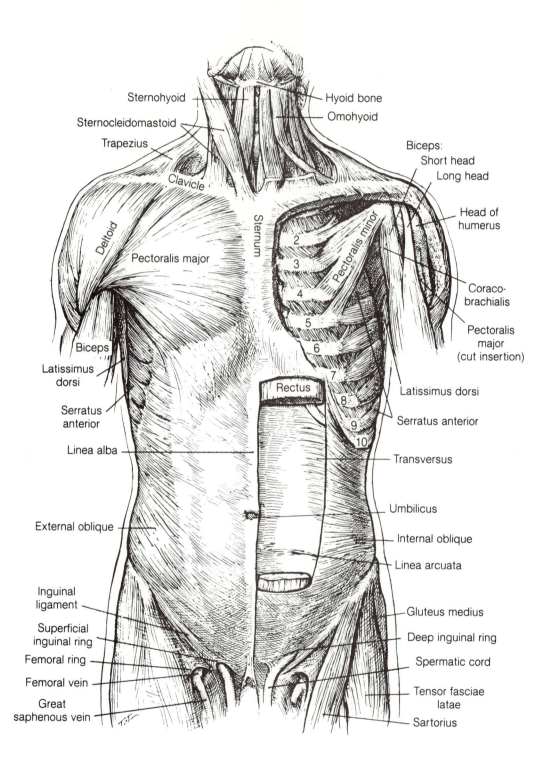

Sternohyoid

Sternocleidomastoid

Trapezius

Clavicle

Deltoid

Pectoralis major

Sternum

Biceps

Latissimus dorsi

Serratus anterior

Linea alba

External oblique

Inguinal ligament

Superficial inguinal ring

Femoral ring

Femoral vein

Great saphenous vein

Hyoid bone

Omohyoid

Biceps:
Short head
Long head

Head of humerus

Pectoralis minor

Coraco-brachialis

Pectoralis major (cut insertion)

Latissimus dorsi

Serratus anterior

Rectus

Transversus

Umbilicus

Internal oblique

Linea arcuata

Gluteus medius

Deep inguinal ring

Spermatic cord

Tensor fasciae latae

Sartorius

2 3 4 5 6 7 8 9 10

MUSCLES OF TRUNK, ANTERIOR VIEW

The left sternocleidomastoid, pectoralis major, external oblique, and a portion of the deltoid have been removed to show underlying muscles. A portion of the rectus abdominis has been cut away to expose the posterior part of its sheath. (Jones and Shepard.)

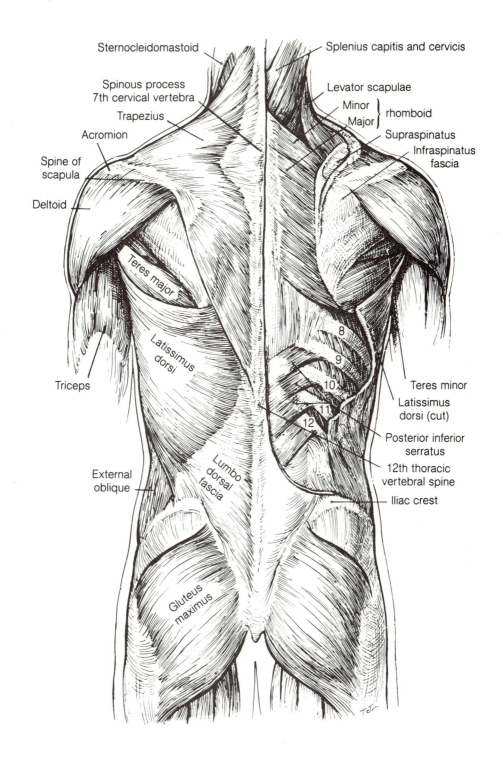

MUSCLES OF THE TRUNK, POSTERIOR VIEW

The latissimus dorsi and trapezius on the right side have been cut away to expose the underlying muscles. (Jones and Shepard.)

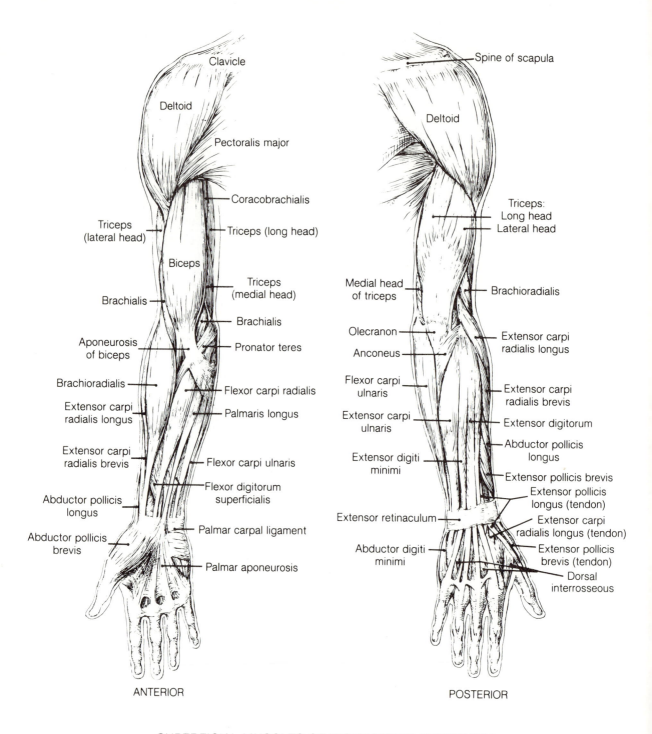

SUPERFICIAL MUSCLES OF RIGHT UPPER EXTREMITY
(Jones and Shepard)

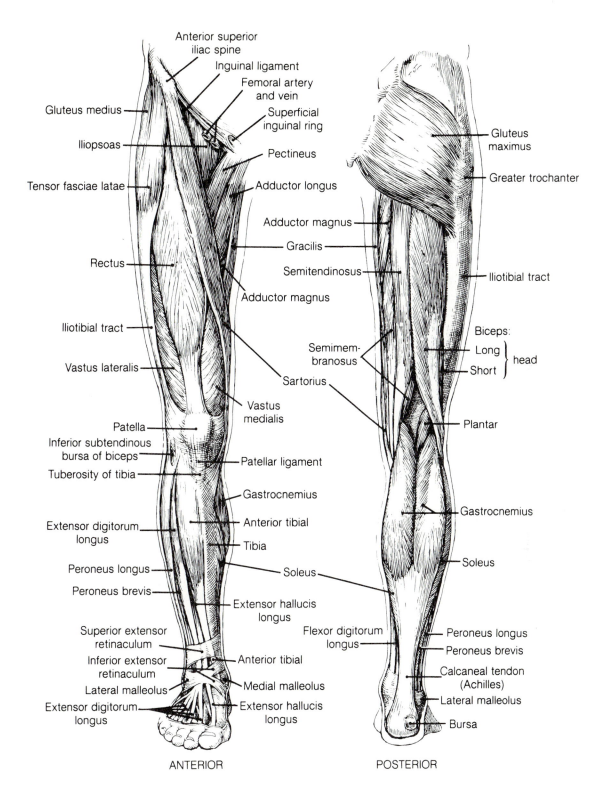

Anterior superior
iliac spine

Inguinal ligament

Femoral artery
and vein

Superficial
inguinal ring

Gluteus medius

Iliopsoas

Pectineus

Tensor fasciae latae

Adductor longus

Adductor magnus

Gracilis

Rectus

Semitendinosus

Adductor magnus

Iliotibial tract

Vastus lateralis

Semimem-
branosus

Sartorius

Vastus
medialis

Patella

Inferior subtendinous
bursa of biceps

Tuberosity of tibia

Patellar ligament

Gastrocnemius

Anterior tibial

Extensor digitorum
longus

Tibia

Peroneus longus

Soleus

Peroneus brevis

Extensor hallucis
longus

Superior extensor
retinaculum

Inferior extensor
retinaculum

Anterior tibial

Lateral malleolus

Medial malleolus

Extensor digitorum
longus

Extensor hallucis
longus

Gluteus
maximus

Greater trochanter

Iliotibial tract

Biceps:

Long
head
Short

Plantar

Gastrocnemius

Soleus

Flexor digitorum
longus

Peroneus longus

Peroneus brevis

Calcaneal tendon
(Achilles)

Lateral malleolus

Bursa

ANTERIOR

POSTERIOR

SUPERFICIAL MUSCLES OF RIGHT LOWER EXTREMITY
(Jones and Shepard)

There is minimal support for the five-year estimate in that the musculature was wasting away at the rate of 3% per annum. Petition of U.S., 303 F.Supp. 1282, 1320 (E.D.N.Car.1969).

musculus (mus'ku-lus), pl. *mus'culi* [L., dim. of *mus* mouse, because of a fancied resemblance to a mouse of a muscle moving under the skin] [NA] an organ which by its contraction and relaxation produces movements of certain organs or of the entire animal organism. See also *muscle*. For names and description of specific muscles see *Table of Musculi.*

TABLE OF MUSCULI

musculus abductor digiti minimi manus [NA], abductor muscle of little finger: *origin*, pisiform bone, flexor carpi ulnaris tendon; *insertion*, medial surface of base of proximal phalanx of little finger; *innervation*, ulnar; *action*, abducts little finger.

musculus abductor digiti minimi pedis [NA], abductor muscle of little toe: *origin*, medial and lateral tubercles of calcaneus, plantar fascia; *insertion*, lateral surface of base of proximal phalanx of little toe; *innervation*, superficial branch of lateral plantar; *action*, abducts little toe.

musculus abductor hallucis [NA], abductor muscle of great toe: *origin*, medial tubercle of calcaneus, plantar fascia; *insertion*, medial surface of base of proximal phalanx of great toe; *innervation*, medial plantar; *action*, abducts, flexes great toe.

musculus abductor pollicis brevis [NA], short abductor muscle of thumb: *origin*, scaphoid, ridge of trapezium, transverse carpal ligament; *insertion*, lateral surface of base of proximal phalanx of thumb; *innervation*, median; *action*, abducts thumb.

musculus abductor pollicis longus [NA], long abductor muscle of thumb: *origin*, posterior surfaces of radius and ulna; *insertion*, radial side of base of first metacarpal bone; *innervation*, posterior interosseous; *action*, abducts, extends thumb.

musculus adductor brevis [NA], short adductor muscle: *origin*, outer surface of inferior ramus of pubis; *insertion*, upper part of linea aspera of femur; *innervation*, obturator; *action*, adducts, rotates, flexes thigh.

musculus adductor hallucis [NA], adductor muscle of great toe (2 heads): *origin*, Caput Obliquum—bases of second, third, and fourth metatarsals, and sheath of peroneus longus, Caput Transversum—capsules of metatarsophalangeal joints of three lateral toes; *insertion*, lateral side of base of proximal phalanx of great toe; *innervation*, lateral plantar; *action*, adducts great toe.

musculus adductor longus [NA], long adductor muscle: *origin*, crest and symphysis of pubis; *insertion*, linea aspera of femur; *innervation*, obturator; *action*, adducts, rotates, flexes thigh.

Dr. Springer examined the **adductor muscles** of plaintiff's left leg, which ran along the inside of the thigh, from knee to the pelvic bone, about two inches from the hip socket. (N.T. 156, 157, 160)....

... the upper ends of the **adductor muscles** lie at the periphery of the hip joint, control motion through the hip joint, and are thus intimately associated with the hip joint. Accordingly, when the hip joint goes awry for any number of reasons, the adductor muscles will become tender. Persistence of tenderness in the upper adductor muscles thus constitutes extremely high cause for suspicion of a possible hip derangement. (N.T. 245–247, 250, 262.) Rosario v. Amer. Export-Isbrandtsen Lines, Inc., 395 F.Supp. 1192, 1201, 1211 (E.D.Pa.1974), reversed and remanded 531 F.2d 1227 (3d Cir. 1978).

musculus adductor magnus [NA], great adductor muscle (2 parts): *origin*, Deep Part—inferior ramus of pubis, ramus of ischium, Superficial Part—ischial tuberosity; *insertion*, Deep Part—linea aspera of femur, Superficial Part—adductor tubercle of femur; *innervation*, Deep Part—obturator, Superficial Part—sciatic; *action*, Deep Part—adducts thigh, Superficial Part—extends thigh.

"... He was having a lot of spasm in the muscles on the inner aspect of the leg and hip called the **adductor muscles.**" Arrendale v. U.S., 469 F.Supp. 883, 890 (N.D.Tex.1979).

musculus adductor minimus smallest adductor muscle: a name given the anterior portion of the adductor magnus muscle; *insertion*, ischium, body and ramus of pubis; *innervation*, obturator and sciatic; *action*, adducts thigh.

musculus adductor pollicis [NA], adductor muscle of thumb (2 heads: *origin*, Caput Obliquum—sheath of flexor carpi radialis, anterior carpal ligament, capitate bone, and bases of second and third metacarpals, Caput Transversum—lower two-thirds of anterior surface of third metacarpal; *insertion*, medial surface of base of proximal phalanx of thumb; *innervation*, ulnar; *action*, adducts, opposes thumb.

musculus biceps brachii [NA], biceps muscle of arm (2 heads): *origin*, Caput Longum—upper border of glenoid cavity, Caput Breve—apex of coracoid process; *insertion*, radial tuberosity and fascia of forearm; *innervation*, musculocutaneous; *action*, flexes forearm, supinates hand.

"Q. Does the **biceps tendon** have anything to do with the shoulder?
"A. Well, it attaches to the glenoid process of this joint.
"Q. The shoulder joint?
"A. The shoulder joint...." Hartford Accident and Indemnity Co. v. Helms, 467 S.W.2d 656, 658 (Ct.Civ.App.Tex. 1971).

musculus cremaster [NA], cremaster muscle: *origin*, inferior margin of internal oblique muscle of abdomen; *insertion*, pubic tubercle; *innervation*, genital branch of genitofemoral; *action*, elevates testis.

musculus flexor accessorius [NA] alternative for *musculus quadratus plantae.*

musculus flexor carpi radialis [NA], radial flexor muscle of wrist: *origin*, medial epicondyle of humerus; *insertion*, base of second metacarpal; *innervation*, median; *action*, flexes and abducts wrist joint.

The surgeon discovered the **flexor carpi-radialis**, a tendon in the forearm, had been severed completely. The median nerve was partially severed. The defendant surgeon attended, reattached the tendon, sutured the median nerve, and treated the injury. Webb v. Lungstrum, 575 P.2d 22–24 (Kan.1978).

musculus flexor carpi ulnaris [NA], ulnar flexor muscle of wrist (2 heads): *origin*, Caput Humerale—medial epicondyle of humerus, Caput Ulnare—olecranon, ulna, intermuscular septum; *insertion*, pisiform, hook of hamate, proximal end of fifth metacarpal; *innervation*, ulnar; *action*, flexes and adducts wrist joint.

musculus flexor digiti minimi brevis manus [NA], short flexor muscle of little finger: *origin*, hook of hamate bone, transverse carpal ligament; *insertion*, medial side of proximal phalanx of little finger; *innervation*, ulnar; *action*, flexes little finger.

musculus flexor digiti minimi brevis pedis [NA], short flexor muscle of little toe: *origin*, base of fifth metatarsal, plantar fascia; *insertion*, lateral surface of base of proximal phalanx of little toe; *innervation*, lateral plantar; *action*, flexes little toe.

musculus flexor digitorum brevis [NA], short flexor muscle of toes: *origin*, medial tuberosity of calcaneus, plantar fascia; *insertion*, middle phalanges of four lateral toes; *innervation*, medial plantar; *action*, flexes toes.

musculus flexor digitorum longus [NA], long flexor muscle of toes: *origin*, posterior surface of shaft of tibia; *insertion*, distal phalanges of four lateral toes; *innervation*, posterior tibial; *action*, flexes toes and extends foot.

musculus flexor digitorum profundus [NA], deep flexor muscle of fingers: *origin*, shaft of ulna, coronoid process; *insertion*, distal phalanges of fingers; *innervation*, ulnar and anterior interosseous; *action*, flexes distal phalanges.

Dr. Herbert B. Niestat, in his diagnosis of July 19, 1971, writes:
"This 22-year old University of South Carolina student states that about three months ago he sustained a laceration just proximal to the volar DIP crease of his left long finger with a hunting knife. He was seen and the laceration was sutured by Dr. Skinner; however, after this he developed some difficulty with flexion at the discal joint... I believe this was an injury of the **flexor digitorem profundes**. Repair will probably entail flexor tendon graft in this case. Skipper v. U.S. Fidelity & Guaranty Co., 448 F.Supp. 74–5 (D.S.Car.1978).

musculus flexor digitorum superficialis [NA], superficial flexor muscle of fingers (2 heads): *origin*, Caput Humeroulnare—medial epicondyle of humerus, coronoid process of ulna, Caput Radiale—oblique line of radius, anterior border; *insertion*, middle phalanges of fingers; *innervation*, median; *action*, flexes middle phalanges.

musculus flexor hallucis brevis [NA], short flexor muscle of great toe: *origin*, under surface of cuboid, lateral cuneiform; *insertion*, base of proximal phalanx of great toe; *innervation*, lateral and medial plantar; *action*, flexes great toe.

musculus flexor hallucis longus [NA], long flexor muscle of great toe: *origin*, posterior surface of fibula; *insertion*, base of distal phalanx of great toe; *innervation*, posterior tibial; *action*, flexes great toe.

musculus flexor pollicis brevis [NA], short flexor muscle of thumb: *origin*, transverse carpal ligament, ridge of trapezium; *insertion*, base of proximal phalanx of thumb; *innervation*, median, ulnar; *action*, flexes and adducts thumb.

musculus flexor pollicis longus [NA], long flexor muscle of thumb: *origin*, anterior surface of radius and coronoid process of ulna; *insertion*, base of distal phalanx of thumb; *innervation*, anterior interosseous; *action*, flexes thumb.

musculus gastrocnemius [NA], gastrocnemius muscle (2 heads): *origin*, Caput Mediale—popliteal surface of femur, upper part of medial condyle, and capsule of knee, Caput Laterale—lateral condyle and capsule of knee; *insertion*, aponeurosis unites with tendon of soleus to form calcaneal tendon (Achilles tendon); *innervation*, tibial; *action*, plantar flexes ankle joint, flexes knee joint.

Plaintiff had a weakness in his left **gastrocnemius** (a muscle in the calf), "with a tendency to a calcaneus foot." Tr. 185. Brissette v. Schweiker, 566 F.Supp. 626, 631 (E.D.Mo.1983), remanded 730 F.2d 548 (8th Cir. 1984).

His fall produced a rupture of the **gastrocnemius muscle**, the principal muscle of the lower leg. Bickel v. City of Chicago, 323 N.E.2d 832, 839–40 (App.Ct.Ill.1975).

musculi interossei dorsales manus [NA], dorsal interosseous muscles of hand (4): *origin*, by two heads from adjacent sides of metacarpal bones; *insertion*, extensor tendons of second, third, and fourth fingers; *innervation*, ulnar; *action*, abduct, flex proximal phalanges.

In this report, Dr. Danforth recognized the difficulty in qualifying Mr. Broadbent's complaints, but found a motor weakness in the grip and a slight atrophy of the **interosseous muscle** between the thumb and forefinger. Broadbent v. Harris, 698 F.2d 407, 409 (10th Cir. 1983).

musculi interspinales lumborum [NA], interspinal muscles of loins: paired bands of muscle fibers extending between spinous processes of contiguous lumbar vertebrae, innervated by spinal nerves, and acting to extend the vertebral column.

She was tender, however, over the right paralumbar muscles, a large bundle of muscles which extend on both sides of the lumbar spine to hold the trunk in a normal position to keep the body erect, and she had tension or spasm there. Perry v. Bertsch, 441 F.2d 939, 941 (8th Cir. 1971).

musculus levator palpe brae superioris [NA], levator muscle of upper eyelid: *origin*, upper border of optic foramen; *insertion*, tarsal plate of upper eyelid; *innervation*, oculomotor; *action*, raises upper lid.

... fracture of the right orbital area and **leavator muscle** which controls the upper eyelid of the right eye....
At that particular time it was noted that the lid, the upper lid on the right side dropped as compared to the lid on the left side,.... Masters v. Alexander, 225 A.2d 905, 911 (Pa.1967).

musculus obliquus externus abdominis [NA], external oblique muscle of abdomen; *origin*, lower eight ribs at costal cartilages; *insertion*, crest of ilium, linea alba through rectus sheath; *innervation*, lower intercostal; *action*, flexes and rotates vertebral column, compresses abdominal viscera.

The "Report of Operation" describes the incident as follows: "In closing the initial **oblique muscle**, closing loosely to the internal oblique, a tiny bit of the sweged needle was lost in it and rather than losing time for this particular incident, the operation was continued...." Horn v. Citizens Hosp., 425 So. 2d 1065–6 (Ala.1982).

musculus piriformis [NA], piriform muscle: *origin*, ilium, second to fourth sacral vertebrae; *insertion*, upper border of greater trochanter; *innervation*, first and second sacral; *action*, rotates thigh laterally.

Dr. Willner's notes on his first examination of Mrs. Rothman were to the effect that:

> The patient presents the cardinal findings of a peripheral neuritis secondary to a saddle block, to the right sciatic nerve; to the **peraformis** [sic] **muscle**, without any motor, sensory or reflex changes, have advised 1,000 m.g. B–12 three times a week, plus Darvon comp. one BID plus conservative measures. Rothman v. Silber, 216 A.2d 18, 20 (Super.Ct.N.J. 1966).

musculus psoas major [NA], greater psoas muscle: *origin*, lumbar vertebrae and fascia; *insertion*, lesser trochanter of femur; *innervation*, second and third lumbar; *action*, flexes trunk, flexes and rotates thigh medially.

Well the **psoas major muscle** rotates the lower limb outward and since his rotator, his external rotator, the effect of the psoas is gone. He will have difficulty in rolling his thigh outward. Moreover, when the **psoas major** goes into action, contraction, by reflex action, I am certain there must be some disturbance as it pulls on the lesser trochantal portion of bone to which it is still attached in a position where it has no business to be. King v. Celebrezze, 223 F.Supp. 457, 462 (W.D.Ark. 1963).

musculus quadratus plantae [NA], quadrate muscle of sole: *origin*, calcaneus and plantar fascia; *insertion*, tendons of flexor digitorum longus; *innervation*, lateral plantar; *action*, aids in flexing toes. Called also *m. flexor accessorius* [NA alternative] or *accessory flexor muscle*.

musculus quadriceps femoris [NA], quadriceps muscle of thigh: a name applied collectively to the rectus femoris, vastus intermedius, vastus lateralis, and vastus medialis, inserting by a common tendon that surrounds the patella and ends on the tuberosity of the tibia, and acting to extend the leg upon the thigh. See individual components. See also *musculus rectus femoris, musculus vastus intermedius, musculus vastus lateralis and musculus vastus medialis*.

Placing his full weight on his left leg, however, continued to cause pain. His left **quadriceps** remained weakened and slightly atrophied. Delamater v. Schweiker, 721 F.2d 50, 52 (2d Cir. 1983).

"... He felt that he was 'unable to do all of these things because of pain in his left hip.' On physical examination the doctor noted that the claimant walked with a single crutch. He walked all right without the crutch and without a limp. He had a full range of motion in his left hip. There was a 1 inch atrophy of the left quadriceps...." Whitson v. Finch, 437 F.2d 728, 730 (6th Cir. 1971).

Plaintiff's **quadriceps** (thigh muscles) and hamstrings were weaker in the left than the right leg. He had diminished sensation in his left leg. Brissette v. Schweiker, 566 F.Supp. 626, 631 (E.D.Mo.1983), remanded 730 F.2d 548 (8th Cir. 1984).

The other doctor who testified for appellees, Dr. Botkin, testified that his examination revealed atrophy in the left **quadriceps femoris** (anterior thigh) muscle and an inability to maintain full active knee extension. Stringe v. S & S Maintenance Co., 303 A.2d 874–5 (Commonwealth Ct.Pa.1973).

musculus rectus femoris [NA], *origin*, anterior inferior iliac spine, rim of acetabulum; *insertion*, patella, tubercle of tibia; *innervation*, femoral; *action*, extends leg, flexes thigh.

musculus sartorius [NA], sartorius muscle: *origin*, anterior superior iliac spine; *insertion*, medial side of proximal end of tibia; *innervation*, femoral; *action*, flexes thigh and leg.

musculus scalenus anterior [NA], anterior scalene muscle: *origin*, transverse processes of third to sixth cervical vertebrae; *insertion*, tubercle of first rib; *innervation*, second to seventh cervical; *action*, raises first rib. Called also *m. scalenus anticus*.

Doctor Terrien testified that his conclusion was that Mrs. West "had a cervical neck sprain with irritation of the scalene muscle...."

> Transcript of Trial at 63. Doctor Terrien described the **scalene muscle** as follows: "A **scalene muscle** is not a very dramatic muscle in the human, but in the horse, that is how he flicks the flies off his neck." West v. Jutras, 456 F.2d 1222, 1224 (2d Cir. 1972).

musculus scalenus medius [NA], middle scalene muscle: *origin*, transverse processes of second to sixth cervical vertebrae; *insertion*, first rib; *innervation*, second to seventh cervical; *action*, raises first rib.

musculus scalenus minimus [NA], smallest scalene muscle: a band occasionally found between the m. scalenus anterior and the m. scalenus medius.

musculus scalenus posterior [NA], posterior scalene muscle: *origin*, tubercles of fourth to sixth cervical vertebrae; *insertion*, second rib; *innervation*, second to seventh cervical; *action*, raises first and second ribs.

musculus sphincter ani externus [NA], external sphincter muscle of anus: *origin*, tip of coccyx and surrounding fascia; *insertion*, tendinous center of perineum; *innervation*, inferior rectal and fourth sacral; *action*, closes anus.

Dr. Willibald Nagler, head of the Department of Physical Medicine and Rehabilitation, New York Hospital and Cornell University testified that he found the nerves which supply the **anal sphincter muscles** to be damaged. Sanden v. Mayo Clinic, 495 F.2d 221, 225 (8th Cir. 1974).

It was plaintiff's contention in the trial court that the incontinence was occasioned by Dr. Sher's negligently severing the **sphincter** and levator **muscles** in the process of the operation. These are muscles by which bowel movement is controlled. Ross v. Sher, 483 S.W.2d 297, 298 (Ct.Civ. App.Tex.1972).

musculus sphincter ani internus [NA], internal sphincter muscle of anus: a thickening of the circular lamina of the tunica muscularis at the caudal end of the rectum.

Dr. Essam Awad, a professor at the University of Minnesota Medical School, specializing in neuromuscular diseases, testified that he had discovered "definite evidence of denervation in the **inner sphincter**." Sanden v. Mayo Clinic, 495 F.2d 221, 225 (8th Cir. 1974).

musculus spinalis [NA], the medial division of the erector spinae, including the *m. spinalis capitis, m. spinalis cervicis,* and *m. spinalis thoracis.*

musculus sternocleidomastoideus [NA], sternocleidomastoid muscle (2 heads): *origin,* sternum and clavicle; *insertion,* mastoid process and superior nuchal line of occipital bone; *innervation,* accessory nerve and cervical plexus; *action,* flexes vertebral column, rotates head.

He discerned stiffness in the cervical area with practically no range of motion. He found further tenderness and muscle spasm over the neck muscles and the muscles between the neck and shoulder. Examination revealed pain radiating down the entire back, although there was no tenderness over the lumbosacral junction. Muscle relaxants and a pain killer were prescribed. Dr. Bertucci's diagnosis was a strain of both **sternocleidomastoid** and paravertebral **muscles.** Duchmann v. Allstate Ins. Co., 389 So.2d 896, 898 (Ct.App.La.1980).

musculus supraspinatus [NA], supraspinous muscle: *origin,* supraspinous fossa of scapula; *insertion,* greater tubercle of humerus; *innervation,* suprascapular; *action,* abducts humerus.

The muscles involved are in the shoulder. There was testimony of some atrophy of the **supraspinatus muscle,** which lies along the upper part of the shoulder blade. Safeway Stores, Inc. v. Industrial Com'n, 558 P.2d 971, 973 (Ct.App.Ariz.1976).

musculus trapezius [NA], trapezius muscle: *origin,* occipital bone, ligamentum nuchae, spinous processes of seventh cervical and all thoracic vertebrae; *insertion,* clavicle, acromion, spine of scapula; *innervation,* accesso-

ry nerve and cervical plexus; *action,* rotates scapula to raise shoulder in abduction of arm, draws scapula backward.

Dissatisfied, Mrs. Sindler consulted other medical experts and it was thereby determined that there was a loss of function in the superior portion of the left **trapezius muscle.** It was also concluded that the left **trapezius muscle,** which is controlled by the spinal accessory nerve, had hollowed out or atrophied. Sindler v. Goldman, 454 A.2d 1054–5 (Super.Ct.Pa.1982).

However, six weeks after the accident, on November 14, 1975, he saw her again and she complained of "pain of the left **trapezius muscle,** which is the left side of the neck...."

A week later she was seen again by him and he reported she had "mild tenderness of the **trapezius muscle,** which is the base of the left neck," but he thought it so minimal that he discharged her from further treatment. Pisciotta v. Allstate Ins. Co., 385 So.2d 1176, 1180 (La.1979).

He found also a strain of the uppermost portion of the **trapezius muscles** between the neck and shoulder. Duchmann v. Allstate Ins. Co., 389 So.2d 896, 898 (Ct.App.La.1980).

Other Authorities: Sindler v. Goldman, 389 A.2d 1192–3 (Super.Ct.Pa.1978).

musculus vastus intermedius [NA], *origin,* anterior and lateral surfaces of femur; *insertion,* patella, common tendon of quadriceps femoris; *innervation,* femoral; *action,* extends leg.

musculus vastus lateralis [NA], *origin,* capsule of hip joint, lateral aspect of femur; *insertion,* patella, common tendon of quadriceps femoris; *innervation,* femoral; *action,* extends leg.

musculus vastus medialis [NA], *origin,* medial aspect of femur; *insertion,* patella, common tendon of quadriceps femoris; *innervation,* femoral; *action,* extends leg.

The doctor stated that plaintiff would not be able to walk again. He summarized his reasons as marked arthritis in both knees, laxity of the ligaments of the knees, complete nonunion of the left hip, fracture of the right hip with a prosthetic replacement, marked muscle wasting of his legs, the **vastus medialis** is completely gone, and legs are completely atrophied through inability to use them. Carter v. Consolidated Cabs, Inc., 490 S.W.2d 39, 45 (Mo.1973).

---

mushroom (mush'room) the fruiting body of any of a variety of basidiomycetous, fleshy fungi of the order Agaricales, especially one that is edible; poisonous species are popularly called *toadstools.* Called also *basidiocarp.* See also *agaric.*

The hallucinogenic properties of certain **mushrooms** have long been a matter of common knowledge in several native American cultures. In Mexico, these **mushrooms,** in addition to being ingested in aid of religious ritual, also took on a symbolic character. (P. Furst, Hallucinogens and Culture 75–88 (1976)). Contemporary interest in these varities of **mushrooms** may be traced to anthropological studies of surviving "**mushroom** cults" in Mexico, which studies were begun in the 1950s, as well as to the first extraction of pure psilocybin from the **mush-**

rooms themselves in 1958. (F. Brown, Hallucinogenic Drugs 81–83 (1972); B. Wells, Psychedelic Drugs 52–53 (1973)). People v. Dunlap, 442 N.E.2d 1379, 1387–8 (App.Ct.Ill. 1982).

mutagenesis (mu"tah-jen'ĕ-sis) [*mutation* + *genesis*] the induction of genetic mutation. Cited in Dow Chemical Co. v. Ruckelshaus, 477 F.2d 1317, 1320 (8th Cir. 1973).

mutagenicity (mu"tah-jĕ-nis'ĭ-te) the property of being able to induce genetic mutation. Cited in Citizens Against Toxic Sprays, Inc. v. Bergland, 428 F.Supp. 908, 916 (D.Or.1977).

mutarotation (mu"tah-ro-ta'shun) a special type of tautomerism involving either (*a*) the transformation of one optical isomer into another, or (*b*) the transformation of one structural isomer into another (both possessing asymmetric centers and optical activity). With each type the rotatory power of a freshly prepared solution of the compound will change, under a variety of conditions, until an equilibrium value is set up which (unlike in racemization) will not be zero.

mutation (mu-ta'shun) [L. *mutatio*, from *mutare* to change] in genetics, a permanent transmissible change in the genetic material, usually in a single gene; the change may be in the form of a loss (deletion), gain (translocation), or exchange (transduction) of genetic material. Also, an individual exhibiting such a change. Called also (in classical genetics) a *sport*.

"Q. Doctor, if in the mating process when a reproductive cell, including its gene and chromosome, has been damaged by radiation, if in the mating process that joins with an ova or sperm, depending on the sex, will that visible genetic damage necessarily show in the first generation?

"A. No, it may not.

"Q. Will you explain what you mean by that? A. Well, if the **mutation** is one which results in what is termed in genetics a dominant type of **mutation**, even though the ovum or sperm, as the case may be, unites with a normal corresponding cell, the **mutation** will show in the first generation.

"On the other hand if it is a recessive type of **mutation**, that is one which takes another one of the same type from the opposite party then this, of course, may not show up until there are enough of these **mutations** in the population to produce the chance of mating of an ovum and a sperm with this type of **mutation** present; so there is great variability here.

"Q. That's right. But the visible genetic damage to offspring is possible to occur as long as the individual carrying that inherited damaged chromosome continues to be available for reproductive purposes? A. That's right. I think you can say that as long as this abnormal chromosome or gene is present, even though it may be a recessive type, as long as it is being reproduced generation after generation, an abnormal individual possibly may result if a mating with a similar abnormal gene exists or takes place.

"Q. Doctor, what happens then, if in the master plan a male sperm cell that has been damaged by **mutation** from X-ray exposure unites with a female ovum in the reproduction process? A. Theoretically all mutations, an overwhelming majority of them, produce damage. This damage may be evident in the immediate offspring or only in subsequent generations, even to the fortieth, or later, generation. The types of damage which may arise can affect virtually any part or system of the body. These might include: Mental or nervous defects and disorders, such as epilepsy, for example; neuromuscular disorders; defects of vision or hearing, such as deafness; defects in the growth of the skeletal system, such as dwarfness; defects of a hematological kind, such as inability of the blood to clot properly; or endocrine disorders, such as diabetes, or modifications; congenital deformities and defects of the heart, of the digestive tract, or of the urinary and genital organs. Everything can be covered. This is because the genes control the pattern of normal develop-

ment—the master plan, as you called it, of development is in the gene. When a gene is mutated it is unable to perform its normal function either entirely or partly. Chiropractic Ass'n of New York, Inc. v. Hilleboe, 227 N.Y.S.2d 309, 349–50, 353, 366–7 (Sup.Ct.Albany Cty.1961).

mutism (mu'tizm) [L. *mutus* unable to speak, inarticulate] inability or refusal to speak.

mutism, akinetic a state in which the individual makes no spontaneous movement or sound.

Deborah did not regain consciousness. She remains in a permanent semi-comatose condition, variously described as a state of "akinetic mutism" or a "persistive vegetative" state. Burrow v. Widder, 368 N.E.2d 443, 447 (App.Ct. of Ill.1977).

muton (mu'ton) [*mutation* + Gr. *on* neuter ending] in molecular genetics, the smallest element of DNA whose alteration can give rise to a mutant form of organism, possibly as small as one nucleotide base. Cf. *cistron* and *recon*.

myasthenia (mi"as-the'ne-ah) [*my-* + Gr. *astheneia* weakness] muscular debility; any constitutional anomaly of muscle.

myasthenia gravis; myasthenia gravis pseudoparalytica a disorder of neuromuscular function thought to be due to the presence of antibodies to acetycholine receptors at the neuromuscular junction; clinically there is fatigue and exhaustion of the muscular system with a tendency to fluctuate in severity and without sensory disturbance or atrophy. The disorder may be restricted to a muscle group or become generalized with severe weakness and, in some cases, ventilatory insufficiency. It may affect any muscle of the body, but especially those of the eye, face, lips, tongue, throat, and neck. See also *test, Tensilon*.

When Triplett came out of surgery, he testified he suffered a paralysis on the left side, which affected his arm and leg. He was suffering from headaches, and his nerves were bothering him. Also, while he was in the hospital, he began to notice that he was having difficulty in chewing. His jaws would become tired, and he could not chew a number of certain meats. The muscles in his neck and eyelids would grow tired and, as a result, his eyelids drooped. These were the symptoms of **myasthenia gravis**. . . .

For **myasthenia gravis**, he was given drugs called Mestinon and Mestinon Timespan. After leaving the hospital, and while continuing to see Dr. Schultz, he noticed that the weakness in his arms and legs was becoming worse. In addition, he was unable to use the muscles of his jaws to chew and was only capable of eating soft foods. Dr. Schultz increased the dosages of Mestinon and Mestinon Timespan. During this same period of time, Triplett continued to suffer from dizziness and headaches. . . .

The hospital report introduced into the record also shows that following the injury Triplett had a **myasthenia gravis** condition, a destruction, to a certain extent, of the ability of the nerves to transmit impulses. Mid Central Tool Co. v. Industrial Com'n, 382 N.E.2d 222, 224–5 (Ill.1978).

mycelial (mi-se'le-al) pertaining to a mycelium.

mycelium (mi-se'le-um), pl. *myce'lia [myc- +* Gr. *hēlos* nail] the mass of threadlike processes (hyphae) constituting the fungal thallus. See also *thallus.*

A **mycelial** fragment of Geotrichum is generally defined as three or more thread-like strands joined at one end of a branched filament. U.S. v. General Foods Corp., 446 F.Supp. 740, 749 (N.D.N.Y.1978).

mycobacteriosis (mi"ko-bak-te"re-o'sis) any tuberculosis-like disease caused by mycobacteria other than *Mycobacterium tuberculosis;* these include Group I–IV mycobacteria. Called also *atypical tuberculosis.*

In September 1966 he was hospitalized for a form of pulmonary tuberculosis called atypical **mycobacteriosis**, an infection of the lungs caused by an organism known as the Battey bacillus Type III. The germ, generally believed to be endemic to the soil in rural areas of the southeastern United States, is capable of lying dormant in the lungs for extended periods. Respiratory infection can occur when the lung's biological defenses attenuate, activating these organisms....

The suspected causation was grounded on Fulks' exposure to airborne concentrations of silica particles caused by sandblasting operations. Fulks v. Avondale Shipyards, Inc., 637 F.2d 1008, 1010 (5th Cir. 1981).

mycobacterium (mi"ko-bak-te're-um), pl. *mycobacte'ria,* an organism of the genus *Mycobacterium,* a slender, acid-fast microorganism resembling the bacillus which causes tuberculosis. Cited in U.S. v. City of Asbury Park, 340 F.Supp. 555, 566 (D.N.J.1972).

mycotoxicosis (mi"ko-tok"sĭ-ko'sis) poisoning caused by a fungal or bacterial toxin.

... without the use of pesticides and stored in air conditioned warehouses at a certain humidity point and at a certain temperature. According to the presentation, this special method of growing tobacco prevented the development of molds on the tobacco leaves, which, when broken down, produced a **mycotoxy**. This **mycotoxy** was described as being actually more harmful in human consumption than the tars and nicotines everyone blamed for causing cancer. Securities & Exch. Com'n v. Continental Tobacco Co. of S.C., 463 F.2d 137, 144 (5th Cir. 1972).

mycotoxy See *mold;* and *mycotoxicosis.*

myelin (mi'ĕ-lin) [Gr. *myelos* marrow] the substance of the cell membrane of Schwann's cells that coils to form the myelin sheath (see under *sheath*); it has a high proportion of lipid to protein and serves as an electrical insulator. Called also *white substance of Schwann.*

In GBS patients, lymphocytes attack the **myelin**, the fatty substance that surrounds or "insulates" the peripheral nerves. Padgett v. U.S. 553 F.Supp. 794–5 (W.D.Tex.1982).

Myelin is the coating on the cells of the nervous system which insulates, nourishes and conducts impulses along the axons of the nervous system. McSwain v. Chicago Transit Authority, 362 N.E.2d 1264–5 (App.Ct.Ill.1977).

myelin sheath See *sheath, myelin.*

myelitis, transverse See *myelopathy, transverse.*

myelofibrosis (mi"ĕ-lo-fi-bro'sis) replacement of the bone marrow by fibrous tissue, occurring in association with a myeloproliferative disorder or secondary to another, unrelated condition; called also *myelosclerosis.* See also *myeloid metaplasia,* under *metaplasia.*

Subsequent medical examination resulted in medical opinion that petitioner was suffering from **myelofibrosis**, which petitioner contends was caused by his employment related exposure to volatile hydrocarbons. Priedigkeit v. Industrial Com'n, 514 P.2d 1045–6 (Ct.App.Ariz.1973).

myelogram (mi'ĕ-lo-gram) 1. a roentgenogram of the spinal cord. 2. a graphic representation of the differential count of cells found in a stained preparation of bone marrow.

A **myelogram** is an X-ray visualization or photograph of the spinal cord after the injection of a contrast medium into the spine. As the contrast medium flows, first toward the patient's head and then back again, it forms a column which can be scanned by X-ray. Deviations, obstructions or deformities in the column suggest to a physician the locus of a patient's difficulties, thus aiding in diagnosis and treatment. Fidler v. Eastman Kodak Co., 714 F.2d 192, 194 (1st Cir. 1983).

Dr. Applebaum recommended that the plaintiff undergo a cervical **myelogram** to rule out the possibility of a herniated disc. The **myelogram**, which involves inserting a needle in the patient's lumbar area, was performed at Touro Infirmary on March 26, 1979. Field v. Winn Dixie Louisiana, Inc., 427 So. 2d 616, 619 (Ct.App.La.1983).

The **myelogram** was performed April 19th. Complications resulted from this test. A blood patch had to be done a few days later to stop the leakage of spinal fluid which had occurred following the myelogram. The **myelogram** demonstrated a herniated disc. Dr. Moore recommended an anterior cervical fusion. Plaintiff sought another opinion. Webb v. Insurance Co. of North America, 396 So.2d 508, 513 (Ct.App.La.1981).

Other Authorities: Roberts v. Industrial Com'n, 445 N.E.2d 316–17 (Ill.1983); Martin v. H. B. Zachry Co., 424 So.2d 1002, 1004 (La.1982); Green v. Larkin, 245 N.W.2d 454–5 (Minn.1976); Canterbury v. Spence, 464 F.2d 772, 776–7 (D.C.Cir.1972); Toal v. U.S., 438 F.2d 222–3 (2d Cir. 1971); Fritsche v. Westinghouse Electric Corp., 261 A.2d 657, 659 (N.J.1970); Bostic v. Dreher, 213 A.2d 118–19 (Super.Ct.Pa. 1965).

myelogram, cervical air See *puncture, cisternal.*

myelogram, refusal of See *treatment, refusal of* (Bostic case).

myelography (mi"ĕ-log'rah-fe) [*myelo- +* Gr. *graphein* to write] roentgenography of the spinal cord after injection of a contrast medium into the subarachnoid space.

The manufacturer's statement of directions was introduced as an exhibit....

"Clinical reports indicate that the incidence and the severity of the side effects following Pantopaque myelography with aspiration of the medium are but slightly greater than with ordinary lumbar puncture. In 10–30 percent of such cases there may be transient symptomatic reactions consisting of slight temperature elevation and increase of symptoms referable to a back condition. When the medium is not removed, similar transient side effects occur with a slight elevation of temperature in a greater percent of patients. To reduce the reactions to a minimum, Pantopaque should be removed by aspiration after **myelography**.

"Occasional severe arachnoiditis occurs producing headache, fever, meningismus, pains in the back and extremeties and elevations in the white blood count and the protein content of the cerebrospinal fluid. The incidence and severity of arachnoiditis are generally increased when active subarachnoid bleeding has been induced by the lumbar puncture.

"Rare instances of the development of lipoid granulomas, obstruction of the ventricular system and venous intravasation producing pulmonary emboli have been reported." Wasem v. Laskowski, 274 N.W.2d 219, 222 (N.Dak.1979).

myeloma (mi"ĕ-lo'mah) [*myelo-* + *-oma*] a tumor composed of cells of the type normally found in the bone marrow. See also *multiple myeloma.*

The undisputed evidence disclosed that Parks suffered a compensable industrial accident, a compression fracture of the L-3 vertebra, and that in combination with the **myeloma** (a condition of plasma cell leukemia) Parks was permanently totally disabled.[2] [2 This latent disease apparently results in a weakening or softening of the bones.] Sheller-Globe Corp., Hardy Division v. Parks, 393 N.E.2d 264, 267 (Ct.App.Ind.1979).

myeloma, multiple a malignant neoplasm of plasma cells usually arising in the bone marrow and manifested by skeletal destruction, pathologic fractures, and bone pain, and by the presence of anomalous circulating immunoglobulins (paraproteins), Bence Jones proteinuria, and anemia; it is the most common from of monoclonal gammopathy. Called also *plasma cell m.* See also *plasmacytoma.*

The parties stipulated that on February 19, 1974, Parks suffered a compression fracture of the L-3 vertebra in an accident arising out of and in the scope of his employment with Sheller-Globe. The Board found as fact that the injury was the catalyst in activating a pre-existing dormant condition of **multiple myeloma**, a form of plasma cell leukemia. Parks v. Sheller-Globe Corp., Hardy Division, 380 N.E.2d 110–11 (Ct.App. Ind.1978).

Carlton Baker sustained a fracture of his right arm in the course of his employment. While in the hospital for treatment of this injury it was discovered that he had **multiple myeloma**, a form of bone cancer, which antedated the accidental injury. Subsequent Injury Fund v. Baker, 392 A.2d 94–5 (Ct.Spec.App.Md. 1978).

Multiple myeloma is a malignant, fatal disease originating in the bone marrow, and is excruciatingly painful. The cause is not known. It always spreads until it is either removed surgically by amputation or destroyed by X-ray. The choices of treatment of the plaintiff's condition were amputation, intensive radiation, or chemical therapy. None of these is ever entirely curative. The purpose of intensive radiation is to kill the cancerous lesion in an effort to save the patient's life and at the same time to relieve the pain. McCarthy v. Boston City Hospital, 266 N.E.2d 292–3 (Mass.1971).

Other Authorities: James v. U.S., 483 F.Supp. 581, 584 (N.D. Cal.1980).

myelomeningocele (mi"ĕ-lo-mĕ-ning'go-sēl) [*myelo-* + *meningocele*] hernial protrusion of the cord and its meninges through a defect in the vertebral canal. See also *spina bifida.*

Amber Tatro is a five year old female suffering from **myelomenengocele**, commonly known as spinal bifida. As a result of this birth defect, Amber suffers from orthopedic and speech impediments and a neurogenic bladder. Tatro v. State of Tex., 516 F.Supp. 968, 970–1 (N.D.Tex.1981).

myelopathy (mi"ĕ-lop'ah-the) [*myelo-* + Gr. *pathos* disease] a general term denoting functional disturbances and/or pathological changes in the spinal cord; the term is often used to designate nonspecific lesions, in contrast to inflammatory lesions (myelitis).

". . . The final pertinent diagnosis was incomplete **transverse myelopathy** due to arterio venus angimatous malformation of the spinal cord." Tyminski v. U.S., 481 F.2d 257, 262 (3d Cir. 1973).

Other Authorities: Broadbent v. Harris, 698 F.2d 407, 410 (10th Cir. 1983).

myelopathy, transverse myelopathy which extends across the spinal cord.

The Defendant's position is that the Plaintiff's illness is not GBS, but **Transverse Myelitis** (TM), a disease of the spinal cord, which the Defendant contends has no causal relationship to the swine flu vaccine.

TRANSVERSE MYELITIS

Transverse myelitis is an internal, inflammatory process which results in the production of a spinal cord lesion. Its evolution is generally acute, but may be subacute, and the presenting symptoms often consist either of diffuse tingling sensations in the lower extremities, a burning sensation in the girdle surrounding the affected spinal cord segment, or severe back pain. Plum and Olson, Myelitis and Myelopathy, Ch. 36 in Clinical Neuropathy at 26 (Baker & Baker ed. 1973). The lesion transects the spinal cord horizontally but is generally limited vertically to one or a few spinal segments. All sensation is lost below the level of the lesion and deep tendon reflexes are nearly always intact but hyperactive. Wilson, Neurology at 226 (2d ed. 1955). It is more commonly associated with a sharp sensory level and pain and also with spasticity in the affected extremities and autonomic components, i.e., the bowel, bladder and sphincter. It is generally of unknown etiology but is believed to represent an abnormal autoimmune response to an antigen such as a viral infection or vaccine. Plum and Olson, supra at 24, 26. . . .

He described **TM** as a transection of the cord, etiology unknown but thought to have an immunological basis. He stated that initially with TM there may be some spinal cord shock and that spasticity is a hallmark of **TM**. Symptoms of **TM** often vary with how much of the cord is involved or destroyed. He says that, in contrast, GBS patients have peripheral nerve system involvement and that GBS patients are unlikely to have long term bowel and bladder involvement, but it is possible. In **TM**, he noted that the lower motor neuron can be destroyed and the peripheral nerves all the way out to the muscles therefore, may die. This is a significant observation in the doctor's opinion, since it makes it difficult and perhaps, he says, almost impossible to decide whether the peripheral nerve damage or the injury to the spinal cord came first in a case such as the

Plaintiff's. McDonald v. U.S., 555 F.Supp. 935, 938, 943, 951 (M.D.Pa.1983).

myeloradiculoneuropathy

Dr. Poser stated that specifically the Plaintiff's neurological disorder can be considered a **myeloradiculoneuropathy**, a term, he pointed out, which is generally accepted as being synonymous with GBS. McDonald v. U.S., 555 F.Supp. 935, 950 (M.D.Pa.1983).

myeloradiculopathy (mi"ĕ-lo-rah-dik"u-lop'ah-the) disease of the spinal cord and spinal nerve roots.

Mylanta

The second medication prescribed by Dr. Wald was called **Mylanta** liquid, which was a liquid antacid for treatment of an upper gastrointestinal tract upset or stomach distress of which Richardson was complaining. Watkins v. U.S., 589 F.2d 214, 224 (5th Cir. 1979).

Myleran (mil'er-an) trademark for a preparation of busulfan. See also *busulfan.*

myo-, my- [Gr. *mys* muscle] a combining form denoting relationship to muscle.

"Myo" means muscle and "carditis" refers to the inflammation of that muscle. State Reserve Life Ins. Co. v. Ives, 535 S.W.2d 400, 403 (Ct.Civ.App.Tex.1976).

myocardial See *myocardium.*

myocardiopathy (mi"o-kar"de-op'ah-the) any noninflammatory disease of the muscular walls (myocardium) of the heart. See also *hypertrophy, ventricular.*

myocardiopathy, alcoholic a form attributed to ingestion of large amounts of alcohol over an extended period of time, characterized chiefly by enlargement of the heart and myocardial degenerative changes, particularly evident on electron microscopy.

During this sojourn in the hospital the doctors noted that Smith's heart disease could possibly be attributed to **alcoholic myocardiopathy**. The term "**myocardiopathy**" is defined as a disease of the muscle of the heart....

He unfortunately has some form of **myocardiopathy**, which is enlarging his heart, causing left ventricular hypertrophy, progressive heart failure, and which has a rather poor future prognosis. From the history ... the diagnosis of **alcoholic myocardiopathy** is a good one. This, however, is a rather difficult diagnosis to make; it is purely dependent upon the history of alcoholism. The only other conceivable diagnosis is the form of ventricular hypertrophy that is secondary to some form of idiopathic myocarditis; the etiology of this is unknown....

At the April 8 hearing Dr. Kritzer, called as a witness by the employer's insurance carrier, testified as follows: Smith's death was due to congestive heart failure secondary to **myocardiopathy**. Where there is myocardial damage the heart breaks down in its function as a pump; the blood backs up into the venous system and heart failure results. Treatment for such a condition includes medication and bed rest. The cause of acute **myocardiopathy** is usually unknown but there is a form of the disease which is connected with a history of alcoholism....

On cross-examination, Dr. Kritzer stated that, although the only direct evidence regarding Smith's alcoholic intake indicat-

ed that he consumed only half a pint of liquor a week, this amount was "like poison" to a man suffering from **alcoholic myocardiopathy**. Smith v. Workmen's Comp.App.Bd., Co. of Los Angeles, 455 P.2d 822–4 (Cal.1969).

myocarditis (mi"o-kar-di'tis) [*myo-* + Gr. *kardia* heart + -*itis*] inflammation of the myocardium; inflammation of the muscular walls of the heart.

An autopsy was performed by Dr. A. M. Hand, pathologist at Schumpert Medical Center, which disclosed that decedent had a cardiac condition known as **myocarditis** (an inflammation of the heart muscle) which was subacute and diffuse. Brown v. Allen Sanitarium, Inc., 364 So.2d 661, 663 (Ct.App. La.1978).

myocarditis, acute postviral

However, Dr. Wood, after test procedures, diagnosed Mr. Thornton's condition as **acute post viral myocarditis** at the time Mr. Thornton was discharged from the clinic. This last medical term means a virus infection of the heart muscles, a disease of the heart. It is not caused by physical exertion; but it may weaken heart muscles to the extent that exertion may overtax the heart and cause injury. Diagnosis of **post viral myocarditis** was influenced by Mr. Thornton's medical history of having had an acute upper viral respiratory infection six or seven weeks before the time of examination and failure of usual tests to clearly show myocardial infarction. Com'l Standard Fire & Marine Co. v. Thornton, 540 S.W.2d 521, 523 (Ct.Civ. App.Tex.1976).

myocarditis, chronic chronic myocardial inflammatory disease; often used loosely to indicate any myocardial deficiency.

He ran an EKG and reached the conclusion that the nerves in his heart which caused the blood to go through a certain artery were being interfered with, and the patient had had a mild heart attack. The precise diagnosis was **chronic myocarditis**. He explained that this means an "inflammation of the muscle" of the heart. "Myo" means muscle and "carditis" refers to the inflammation of that muscle. State Reserve Life Ins. Co. v. Ives, 535 S.W.2d 400, 403 (Ct.Civ.App.Tex.1976).

myocardium (mi"o-kar'de-um) [*myo-* + Gr. *kardia* heart] [NA] the middle and thickest layer of the heart wall, composed of cardiac muscle.

Cut surfaces of **myocardium** or heart muscle showed the muscle to be red-brown, soft and well developed. There was no evidence of infarction. Watkins v. Underwriters at Lloyd's, London, 473 P.2d 464, 467 (Ct.App.Ariz.1970), affirmed 107 Ariz. 56, 481 P.2d 849 (Ariz.1971).

myoclonic (mi"o-klon'ik) relating to or marked by myoclonus.

myoclonus (mi-ok'lo-nus) [*myo-* + Gr. *klonos* turmoil] shock-like contractions of a portion of a muscle, an entire muscle, or a group of muscles, restricted to one area of the body or appearing synchronously or asynchronously in several areas.

... he was again hospitalized with confusion and involuntary movements in all four extremities simulating **myoclonic** jerks. Warner v. U.S., 522 F.Supp. 87, 88 (M.D.Fla.1981).

myofascial See *myofascitis.*

myofascitis (mi"o-fah-si'tis) [*myo-* + *fascitis*] inflammation of a muscle and its fascia, particularly of the fascial insertion of muscle to bone.

There was trial testimony that the morning after the accident plaintiff consulted Dr. Thomas Johnson, a physician, who diagnosed a **myofascial** injury to the neck and back and a traumatic umbilical hernia. Murray v. Walter, 269 N.W.2d 47–8 (Minn. 1978).

She concluded that Walker was suffering from a **myofascial** sprain or strain, an injury to the soft tissue of the back. [Dissent.] Walker v. Rothschild Intern. Stevedoring Co., 526 F.2d 1137, 1141 (9th Cir. 1975).

Traumatic **myofascitis** of the dorsolumbar spine musculature. Cline v. Secretary of Health, Education and Welfare, 444 F.2d 289, 291 (6th Cir. 1971).

myofascitis, lumbosacral

It is undisputed that **lumbosacral myofascitis** and herniated lumbar disc are separate and distinct conditions. Appellee's expert medical witness defined **lumbosacral myofascitis** as a low back sprain. One of appellant's expert medical witnesses defined it as a backache. Appellant's other expert medical witness stated that **myofascitis** is an inflammation of a muscle and its lining, the fascia. Amie v. General Motors Corp., 429 N.E.2d 1079, 1083 (Ct.App.Ohio 1980).

myomectomy (mi"o-mek'to-me) [*myoma* + Gr. *ektomē* excision] surgical removal of a myoma (leiomyoma).

Finding abnormal swelling, defendant referred Lorna to a gynecologist (Dr. Tanz), who determined through radiological testing that Lorna had two fibroid tumors in her uterus. Tanz treated Lorna through January 1975, reporting to defendant that he favored a conservative approach because growth of these benign tumors had "plateaued", because they were not causing any significant problems, and because **myomectomy** (surgical removal of the fibroids) would be risky due to their location. Gayle v. Neyman, 457 N.Y.S.2d 499–500 (1st Dep't 1983).

myometrium (mi-o-me'tre-um) [*myo-* + Gr. *mētra* uterus] the smooth muscle coat of the uterus which forms the main mass of the organ. NA alternative term for tunica muscularis uteri.

myonecrosis (mi"o-ně-kro'sis) necrosis or death of individual muscle fibers. See also *gangrene, gas* (Harris case).

The government's expert witness concluded that the doctors who performed the operation erred in concluding both preoperatively and post-operatively that the proper diagnosis of plaintiff's condition was gas gangrene or anaerobic **myonecrosis**. In order to sustain this opinion, the government's expert read the detailed operation report as finding no necrotic muscle tissue. However, a fair reading of the report makes clear that necrotic muscle tissue—a clear indicia of gas gangrene or of another **myonecrotic** infection—was found and removed....

What the cultures suggest is that the "**myonecrosis**" (muscle death) and gas formation observed during the surgery in plaintiff's forearm may not have been produced by the anaerobic clostridial bacteria associated with gas gangrene (the full name for which is clostridial **myonecrosis**) but rather by other bacteria.... Kernall v. U.S., 558 F.Supp. 280, 283 (E.D.N.Y. 1982).

myonecrosis, clostridial See *gangrene, gas.*

myopathy (mi-op'ah-the) [*myo-* + Gr. *pathos* suffering] any disease of a muscle. Cited in Bolton v. Sec. of Health & Human Services, 504 F.Supp. 288, 290 (E.D.N.Y. 1980).

myosarcoma (mi"o-sar-ko'mah) a malignant tumor derived from myogenic cells.

myositis (mi"o-si'tis) [Gr. *myos* of muscle + *-itis*] inflammation of a voluntary muscle.

The second injury is termed **myositis ossificans**. This condition occurs when there has been an acute injury to a portion of the body, in this case appellee's right shoulder and arm, and the impact is such that significant bleeding occurs in the area of the tear. This bleeding lead to calcification instead of the production of fibrous tissue, and, as a result, bone tissue built within the muscle tissue. This in turn resulted in pain, limitation of motion and the loss of muscle strength. This injury is not correctable by surgery and will remain indefinitely. Klug v. Keller Industries, Inc., 328 N.W.2d 847, 848 (S.D.1982).

On this visit she complained of pain in her left arm and right leg. Dr. Barnes began treating the plaintiff for acute **myositis**, which treatment consisted of therapy, medications and heat. Urbina v. Alois J. Binder Bakery, Inc., 423 So.2d 765–6 (Ct. App.La.1982).

Some three months after leaving the hospital, appellee's doctor amended his diagnosis to include chronic **myositis** (inflammation of a muscle) of the right thigh. Peavy v. Flowers, 390 N.E.2d 832–3 (Ohio 1979).

In spite of the lack of positive findings, Dr. Schull felt that claimant "probably had a disturbance involving connecting tissue and/or muscle and ascribed the diagnosis of **Myositis** to him." Miles v. Secretary of Health, Education & Welfare, 322 F.Supp. 1132, 1135 (W.D.Tenn.1971).

Other Authorities: Dodson v. Parham, 427 F.Supp. 97, 106 (N.D.Ga.1977).

myositis, anterior thoracic

... **anterior thoracic myositis** (sore superficial chest muscle).... Chester v. Oklahoma Natural Gas Co., 619 P.2d 1266, 1268 (Ct.App.Okl.1980).

myositis ossificans myositis which is characterized by bony deposits or by ossification of muscles.

Dr. Massie diagnosed the appellant as suffering from "**myositis ossificans**, left hip with a functional hip flexion contracture." He reported that the physical examination showed the left hip as being fixed in a 10° external rotation and no internal rotation, and that X rays showed marked tilting of the sacrum, and the hips and pelvis showed a left hip irregularity of the joint space....

... or whether appellant was suffering from **myositis ossificans**, a condition of inflammation and bony deposits, or ossification of muscle, it was his function to weigh the conflicting medical evidence and to distinguish the actual medical facts from the unproven medical conclusions. Colwell v. Gardner, 386 F.2d 56, 64, 73 (6th Cir. 1967).

myositis ossificans traumatica myositis ossificans due to injury.

... he found no conclusive evidence of an ulnar nerve problem, but did find the claimant was suffering from **traumatic myositis**. Funke v. State Acc. Ins. Fund, 619 P.2d 668–9 (Ct.App. Or.1980).

myringoplasty (mĭ-ring′go-plas″te) [*myringo-* + Gr. *plasein* to form] surgical restoration of a perforated tympanic membrane by grafting. See also *tympanoplasty*.

myringotomy (mir″in-got′o-me) [*myringo-* + Gr. *tomē* a cutting] surgical incision of the membrana tympani; tympanotomy.

As Hakim completed the tonsillectomy and adenoidectomy he positioned the infant plaintiff's head to perform a **myringotomy**, the surgical procedure to correct the ear involvement. Rose v. Hakim, 335 F.Supp. 1221, 1224 (D.D.C.1971), remanded with directions in part and otherwise affirmed 501 F.2d 806 (D.C.Cir. 1974).

Mysoline (mi′so-lēn) trademark for preparations of primidone. See also *primidone*.

myxoma (mik-so′mah), pl. *myxomas* or *myxo′mata* [*myxo-* + *-oma*] a tumor composed of primitive connective tissue cells and stroma resembling mesenchyme.

myxomatous (mik-so′mah-tus) of the nature of a myxoma.

myxosarcoma (mik″so-sar-ko′mah) a sarcoma containing myxomatous tissue. See also *mesenchyma*; and *myxoma*.

Fifteen minutes after the tumor was submitted to him, the pathologist reported that, based upon the frozen section, the tumor appeared to be a **myxosarcoma**, a "low grade malignant mesenchymal tumor" and that it might have been "cleared," i.e., removed, by the surgery. The frozen section report was, however, not conclusive as to the nature of the tumor and could not be completely accurate in its estimate that all tumor cells had been excised since tentacles or lesions may have remained which were not disclosed by the section. Clemens v. Regents of University of California, 87 Cal.Rptr. 108, 112–113 (Ct.App.1970).

N

nail (nāl) 1. [L. *unguis;* Gr. *onyx*] the horny cutaneous plate on the dorsal surface of the distal end of a finger or toe. See also *unguis*. 2. a rod of metal, bone, or other material used for fixation of the ends or the fragments of fractured bones.

Dr. Deyerle testified concerning the meaning of the term "**fixation nail**" in the patent claim:

It meant a rod of varying stiffness, of varying shape, some triflanged, some with rolled-on threads, some with cut-in threads, the varying sizes, and a **nail** or pin, the words are practically interchangeable, to me, and to the orthopedic profession, and people I had contact with and people I was teaching with, and to my opinion as an orthopedist as a whole, this is their interpretation. It is almost interchangeable with the word "pin" and it encompassed many things, even the Lorenzo screw, the others that have been mentioned, it had no specific limiting factors by usage. One doctor who used nothing, let's say, but Moore pins, where he said he was going to pin a hip, to him he meant he was going to use "Moore pins", that was the natural thing to do.

Another that used Smith-Petersen **nail**, he may use Smith-Petersen **nail**, the word "pin" or "**nail**" don't have too much limited factors in terms of the orthopedist's thought about it.

In my own thought, I think a little bit more of a **nail** as something that is pounded, would, like you [171] hammer a tack or a **nail**. This is just my feeling. This is the way I feel about it. I think a pin may be pounded, but more often is twisted in, drilled in, sometimes even pins are tapped in, even very small ones. So there are not many limiting factors, and it does cover a tremendous area. [Dissent.] Deyerle v. Wright Mfg. Co., 496 F.2d 45, 56 (6th Cir. 1974).

nail, Jewett a nail for internal fixation of a trochanteric fracture; the nail is fastened to a plate for fixing the head and neck of the bone to the shaft.

... alleged negligent treatment of a hip fracture sustained by her, and against Zimmer Company for alleged defects in a so-called "**Jewett nail**". This is a hip fixation device manufactured by Zimmer Company and was used in the fixation of the fracture in question....

The fixation device, the "**Jewett nail**", was not designed to permit full early weight bearing nor was it so recommended; it was in fact packaged with a printed admonition to the effect that "no implant can be expected to withstand the unsupported stresses of full weight bearing" (Finding 7)....

This admonition (contained in plaintiff's Exhibit # 22) was also accompanied by a printed instruction as follows:

"4. POST OPERATIVE CARE IS IMPORTANT. The patient should be instructed in the limitations of his metallic implant and should be cautioned regarding weight bearing and body stresses on the appliance prior to secure bone healing." Largess v. Tatem, 291 A.2d 398–400 (Vt.1972).

nail Küntscher a tubular metal nail for the intramedullary fixation of fractures.

In the judgment of the surgeons, the treatment indicated for the fracture was an operation known as intramedullary nailing by use of a **Kuntscher Cloverleaf Intramedullary Nail**.[1] This involves the insertion of a long metal rod or nail into the medullary canal (containing the marrow) of the femur (or thigh bone), in order to stabilize the broken fragments. The advantage sought by this method is an early union and weight-bearing without the necessity of a plaster cast.... [[1] The nail is named for Dr. Kuntscher, a German who originally devised the nailing operation during World War II. The nail is tubular but the hollow is not circular; it has indentations running the length of the nail, which give it the appearance, viewed from either end, of a cloverleaf; hence its name.]

... These **Kuntscher nails** usually have imprinted upon them two figures signifying their dimensions, e.g., 9 × 40, 10 × 42, but the imprint or label does not explain the meaning of these figures. It is agreed by the parties that the larger figure is understood to represent the length of the nail in centimeters. According to the plaintiff's expert witnesses, the interpretation placed upon the smaller figure by orthopedists is that the nail will fit into a hole having a width or diameter corresponding in millimeters to the figure on the nail. This follows from the necessity that the nail shall fit tightly into the canal previously prepared by a reamer of corresponding diameter. Orthopedic Equipment Co. v. Eutsler, 276 F.2d 455, 457–8 (4th Cir. 1960).

nail, Smith—Petersen a flanged nail for fixing the head of the femur in fracture of the femoral neck.

Although the only specific operative embodiments described in the patent relate to a **Smith-Peterson nail** as the central fixation device, the specification refers to the central nail as a "fixation nail" or a nail of the "Smith-Peterson type or the like." A **Smith-Peterson nail** is a triflanged nail and is considerably larger than a fixation pin. Deyerle v. Wright Mfg. Co., 496 F.2d 45 (6th Cir. 1974).

He performed an open reduction of the fracture and inserted a **Smith-Petersen nail.** Ray v. Industrial Com'n, 284 N.E.2d 272–3 (Ill.1972).

... he inserted a **Smith-Peterson nail** and applied a Wilkie boot. It is conceded that he performed this operation without the availability of a portable X-ray machine (the hospital having none) which the medical testimony indicated was "an absolute necessity" during this type of operation. On December 11 an X ray revealed that the fragments were still rotating and that the **nail** had been driven through the head of the femur and acetabulum into the pelvic cavity. Bradshaw v. State of New York, 264 N.Y.S.2d 725, 726 (3d Dep't N.Y.1965).

Nalline (nal′lēn) trademark for a preparation of nalorphine. See also *nalorphine.*

nalorphine (nal′or-fēn, nal-or′fēn) chemical name: 17-allyl-7,8-didehydro-4,5α-epoxymorphinan-3,6-α-diol. A drug structurally related to morphine, $C_{19}H_{21}NO_3$, which acts as an antagonist to morphine and related narcotics. Called also *allorphine* and *antorphine.*

Ten minutes after birth, 0.2 milligrams of **Nalline** were administered to the child.[5] ...

The instructions on **Nalline** specifically stated that it could be used in newborn infants for the treatment of asphyxia resulting from maternal narcotization. [[5] **Nalline** is a synthetic narcotic typically used in the treatment of severe narcotic-induced respiratory depression.] Lhotka v. Larson, 238 N.W.2d 870, 873–4 (Minn.1976).

nanosecond (na″no-sek′ond) one-billionth (10^{-9}) of a second; abbreviated ns. or nsec.

... or even a billionth of a second (**nanosecond**) and of persisting in the work for hours on end, and thus completing tasks beyond the capacity of human bodies and minds. Honeywell, Inc. v. Sperry Rand Corp., 1974 Trade Cases Par. 74,874 at 95,882 (D.Minn.1973).

naphtha See *petroleum benzin* under *benzin.*

narcissism (nar′sĭ-sizm) [from *Narcissus*, a character in Greek mythology who fell in love with his own image reflected in water] self-love, which may or may not include genital excitation. In psychoanalysis, *primary n.* is the original energy embodied in the infantile ego; *secondary n.* denotes libidinous attachments withdrawn from others and directed back onto the self, as in schizophrenia.

(A **narcissistic** personality was defined by the psychiatrist as one who needs an emotional crutch.) Pace v. Pace, 372 So.2d 775–6 (Ct.App.La.1979).

narcissistic See *narcissism.*

narcotic (nar-kot′ik) [Gr. *narkōtikos* benumbing, deadening] an agent that produces insensibility or stupor.

... The characteristics of **narcotic** drugs are that they (1) botanically, are related to the opium poppy; (2) pharmacologically, are psychoactive depressants; (3) physiologically, are addicting, that is, they produce tolerance and withdrawal. Tolerance means that with continued use the body will require a larger amount of the drug to produce the same effect. When the drug is withdrawn from the user a 'withdrawal syndrome' will occur with a variety of unpleasant symptoms.... [People v. McCarty, 86 Ill.2d 247, 56 Ill.Dec. 67, 427 N.E.2d 147 (Ill. 1981).] People v. Key, 328 N.W.2d 609, 612 (Mich.Ct.App. 1982).

The term **narcotic** is derived from the word narcosis, or in the original Greek, narkotikon, which means numbness or sleep. Any drug which produces sleep or drowsiness, has traditionally been defined as a narcotic. Drugs stemming from the opiate family, especially opium, morphine, heroin, and a variety of synthetic drugs which act as a depressant upon the central nervous system are narcotic drugs. U.S. v. Castro, 401 F.Supp. 120 (N.D.Ill.1975).

The term "**narcotic** drug" as used in the statute just read, means "Opium or any compound or derivative or preparation of opium."

Heroin is a derivative of morphine, and morphine and morphine hydrochloride are both products of opium. Heroin is therefore a **narcotic** drug as defined by law. Verdugo v. U.S., 402 F.2d 599, 607 (9th Cir. 1968).

Other Authorities: Leu v. City of Mountain Brook, 386 So.2d 483, 486 (Ct.Crim.App.Ala.1980); State v. Zornes, 475 P.2d 109, 111, 114, 123 (Wash.1970).

nasopharynx (na″zo-far′inks) [*naso- + pharynx*] the part of the pharynx which lies above the level of the soft palate (pars nasalis pharyngis [NA]).

... he saw Mary Ann for a condition he diagnosed as "acute catarrhal **rhinopharyngo tonsillitis.**" Incollingo v. Ewing, 282 A.2d 206, 211 (Pa.1971).

National Formulary a book of standards for certain pharmaceuticals and preparations that are not included in the USP. It is revised every five years, and recognized as a book of official standards by the Pure Food and Drugs Act of 1906. Abbreviated NF.

National Swine Flu Immunization Program of 1976 See *polyneuritis, acute febrile.*

The Swine Flu Act no longer appears in title 42, See Health Services and Centers Amendments of 1978, Pub.L. No. 95–626, 92 Stat. 3551.

The **National Swine Flu Immunization Program of 1976** was an attempt by the federal government to inoculate the entire adult population of the United States against the perceived threat of a swine flu epidemic. From its commencement on October 1, 1976 until its suspension on December 16, 1976, over forty-five million Americans were vaccinated, resulting in the largest immunization program ever in this country's history. See Administration of the National Influenza Immunization Program of 1976, Final Report to Congress by Department of Health, Education and Welfare (1978). The historical genesis of this mass inoculation effort and the legislative response thereto has been exhaustively discussed on numerous occasions by other courts and commentators and need not be repeated here. See Hunt v. United States, 636 F.2d 580, 589–593 (D.C.Cir.1980); Unthank v. United States, 533 F.Supp. 703, 716–21 (D.Colo.1982); Bean v. United States, 533 F.Supp. 567, 571–72 (D.Colo.1980); Baynes, Liability for Vaccine Related Injuries: Public Health Considerations and Some Reflections on the Swine Flu Experience, 21 St.Louis L.J. 44, 62–69 (1977). McDonald v. U.S., 555 F.Supp. 935, 937–8 (M.D.Pa.1983).

naturopathy (na"tūr-op'ah-the) a drugless system of therapy, making use of physical forces such as air, light, water, heat, massage, etc. See also *physician* (Rastetter case).

Under ORS 685.030(2), a **naturopathic** physician may not "administer or write prescriptions for or dispense drugs." Hardt v. Board of Naturopathic Examiners, 606 P.2d 1169–70 (Ct.App.Or.1980).

Naturopathic theory and practice are not based upon the body of basic knowledge related to health, disease, and health care which has been widely accepted by the scientific community. Moreover, irrespective of its theory, the scope and quality of **naturopathic** education do not prepare the practitioner to make an adequate diagnosis and provide appropriate treatment. HEW, Independent Practitioners Under Medicare: A Report to the Congress, (1968). Rastetter v. Weinberger, 379 F.Supp. 170, 174 (D.Ariz.1974).

Nevertheless the provision defining **naturopathy** contemplates a practice which certainly is "non-surgical", if not "non-medical". A.R.S. § 32–1501, subsec. 2 states:

"**Naturopathy**" includes all forms of physiotherapy and means a system of treating the abnormalities of the human mind and body by the use of drugless and nonsurgical methods, including the use of physical, electrical, hygienic and sanitary measures incident thereto.

And other decisions by our Supreme Court have made it clear that naturopaths, like chiropractors, are wholly prohibited by statute from prescribing or administering any type of internal or external drug, or performing any surgical operation. See Kuts-Cheraux v. Wilson, 71 Ariz. 461, 229 P.2d 713, supplemented on rehearing, 72 Ariz. 37, 230 P.2d 512 (1951); Nethken v. State, 56 Ariz. 15, 104 P.2d 159 (1940). Chalupa v. Industrial Com'n, 498 P.2d 228, 232 (Ct.App.Ariz.1972).

Other Authorities: Griffith v. Dep't of Motor Vehicles, 598 P.2d 1377, 1380–1 (Ct.App.Wash.1979).

navicular bone See *os scaphoideum.*

nebulizer (neb'u-līz"er) an atomizer; a device for throwing a spray.

After he informed Dr. Tramer of his (Siegel's) asthmatic condition, which was noted in the hospital record, Dr. Tramer authorized him to take his **nebulizer** [1] with him when he reported to the hospital. [[1] A **nebulizer** is a spray with a rubber bulb attached. Medication is put into the receptacle and when squeezed, the fluid that is put into this apparatus is sprayed either into the throat or nose.] Siegel v. Mt. Sinai Hospital of Cleveland, 403 N.E.2d 202, 204 (Ct.App.Ohio 1978).

The Croupette [a humidity and oxygen tent] included a "**nebulizer**"—i.e., vaporizing unit—by means of which air was drawn out of the oxygen tent, humidified by a fine spray from an atomizer, and recirculated through the tent. Air-Shields, Inc. v. Air Reduction Co., 331 F.Supp. 673, 676 (N.D.Ill.1971).

necessity (ně-ses'ĭ-te) something necessary or indispensable.

necessity, medical See *neocolporrhaphy.*

The State of Iowa does not appear to challenge the use of "**medically necessary**" as the standard for determining when it must provide coverage, but rather argues that sex reassignment surgery simply is considered not "**medically necessary**," but more in the nature of cosmetic surgery. This standard of **medical necessity** is not explicit in the statute, but has become judicially accepted as implicit to the legislative scheme and is apparently endorsed by the Supreme Court. Beal v. Doe, 432 U.S. 438, 444–45 & n. 9, 97 S.Ct. 2366, 2370–71, 53 L.Ed. 2d 464 (1977). Pinneke v. Preisser, 623 F.2d 546, 548 (8th Cir. 1980).

neck (nek) a constricted portion, such as the part connecting the head and trunk of the body (collum [NA]), or the constricted part of an organ, as of the uterus (cervix uteri), or other structure (e.g., collum dentis).

. . . plaintiff had previously suffered a broken **neck**. Further, Dr. Mattson informed Simpson that he had had the broken **neck** for a long time. Thereafter, a Dr. Gail referred plaintiff to a Dr. Sanders for treatment of the improperly healed **neck**. In addition to the above problems, Dr. Sanders discovered plaintiff had also suffered an odontoid fracture in the **neck**. The neck has seven bones. Dr. Mattson informed plaintiff of problems at the C–5 level; additionally, Dr. Sanders found problems at the C–1 and C–2 level. Obviously, although separate bones of the vertebrate are involved, they are closely allied and in the same immediate area. Simpson v. Dep't of Health & Human Resources, 423 So.2d 71–2 (Ct.App.La.1982).

neck of femur See *collum femoris.*

necrobiosis (nek"ro-bi-o'sis) [*necro-* + Gr. *biōsis* life] swelling, basophilia, and distortion of collagen bundles in the dermis, sometimes with obliteration of normal structure, but short of actual necrosis, characteristic especially of granuloma annulare and necrobiosis lipoidica diabeticorum. Cf. *gangrene* and *necrosis.*

necrophilia (nek"ro-fil'e-ah) morbid attraction to corpses; sexual intercourse with a dead body.

The pathologist testified that the mutilation and dismemberment of the bodies were done after death and that his findings were consistent with the psychiatric condition known as **necrophilia**, that is, the perverse sexual attraction to dead bodies. The pathologist further described the numerous stab wounds and slashing-type wounds, which he inferred from his findings were all inflicted after death. In each case there was evidence of sexual abuse. Commonwealth v. Costa, 274 N.E.2d 802, 806 (Mass.1971).

necropsy (nek'rop-se) [Gr. *nekros* dead + *opsis* view] examination of a body after death. See also *autopsy*.

Several cows died and Dr. Pray performed **necropsies** on them, removing organs and tissue samples for analysis. Gaar v. State Through Dep't of Highways, 389 So.2d 426–7 (Ct.App. La.1980).

necrosis (ně-kro'sis), pl. *necro'ses* [Gr. *nekrōsis* deadness] the sum of the morphological changes indicative of cell death and caused by the progressive degradative action of enzymes; it may affect groups of cells or part of a structure or an organ.

. . . a **necrosis** had developed over the bone and steel plate, and this left a large hole in the leg through which there was drainage of pus and a bad odor. These conditions required a surgical procedure to debride the wound and remove bone and the necrotic tissue. Warmsley v. City of New York, 454 N.Y.S.2d 144–5 (2d Dep't 1982).

The hemorrhaging was due to the **necrosis** of tissue (death of tissue prior to death of the patient) in various reproductive organs. Commonwealth v. Mace, 341 A.2d 505, 507 (Super.Ct. Pa.1975).

This patient had a wound infection which resulted in **necrosis**, which means that it was the—the infection was of a severe enough nature to have destroyed muscle tissue and skin. And it is incumbent upon the doctor in charge of the patient to recognize the infection early enough to start antibiotic therapy and also to establish drainage. Majetich v. Westin, 80 Cal.Rptr. 787–8 (Ct.App.1969).

Other Authorities: Ohligschlager v. Proctor Community Hospital, 303 N.E.2d 392, 395 (Ill.1973). Gorsalitz v. Olin Mathieson Chemical Corp., 429 F.2d 1033–4 (5th Cir. 1970); Lewin v. Metropolitan Life Ins. Co., 394 F.2d 608–9 (3d Cir. 1968); Appleman v. U.S., 338 F.2d 729–30 (7th Cir. 1964).

necrosis, aseptic increasing sclerosis and cystic changes in the head of the femur which sometimes follow traumatic dislocation of the hip. A similar condition sometimes develops in the head of the humerus after shoulder dislocation. See also *necrosis, avascular*.

That surgeon took x-rays and informed appellant that they revealed "aseptic necrosis" in the right femoral head. Plaintiff underwent a bone graft on his right femur. Budzichowski v. Bell Tel. Co., 445 A.2d 811–12 (Super.Ct.Pa.1982).

Aseptic necrosis of the femoral heads is a condition wherein the upper part of the thigh bones die, because of loss of blood supplied to those parts . . . .

This condition in which the bones in my hip are dissolving can be reasonably corrected with a plastic hip. . . . Niblack v. U.S., 438 F.Supp. 383–4, 386 (D.Col.1977).

. . . the record contains sufficient evidence from which the referee and Board could conclude that Muniz suffered an **aseptic necrosis** of the carpal lunate in the right wrist, which is the death of bone in the wrist, frequently occurring about six months (or later) after a "crush-type" injury. United States Steel Corp. v. Workmen's Comp. App. Bd., 308 A.2d 200–1 (Commonwealth Ct.Pa.1973).

Other Authorities: Carroll v. Kalar, 545 P.2d 411, 413 (Ariz. 1976); Ray v. Industrial Com'n, 284 N.E.2d 272, 274 (Ill. 1972).

necrosis, avascular that due to deficient blood supply.

Avascular necrosis is a condition of bone deterioration or bone death resulting from the disruption of the blood supply to certain areas of the skeletal system . . . .

. . . Dr. Robinson had described the possible complications of the bone displacement injury, how such an injury could affect the femur's blood supply, and could cause **avascular necrosis**. Johns Hopkins Hospital v. Lehninger, 429 A.2d 538, 541 (Ct.Spec.App.Md.1981).

Aseptic or **avascular necrosis** is the medical term used to designate a condition in which bone tissue has died because the blood supply to that tissue has been cut off. (N.T. 181).

The most common cause for such a reduction in blood supply to bone tissue is trauma or injury which will occlude to some degree the vessels which supply blood to the bone tissue. (N.T. 248). . . .

Had x-rays been taken of plaintiff's left hip on June 7, 1970, such x-rays would have revealed the **avascular necrosis** in plaintiff's left femoral head. (Deposition of Dr. Klinghoffer, pp. 45, 48).

Had x-rays been taken of plaintiff's left hip on August 28, 1970, such x-rays would have revealed the existence of the aseptic or **avascular necrosis** in that hip. (N.T. 257, 354).

When such necrosis or death occurs in bone tissue, the tissue becomes very soft. (N.T. 182). Rosario v. American Export, Isbrandtsen Lines, Inc., 395 F.Supp. 1192, 1202 (E.D.Pa.1974).

He had performed around 175 hip fracture operations. He had encountered two main types of complications in this type of surgery: non-union failure of the fracture to heal in the neck of the femur and **avascular necrosis** [3] of the head of the femur. [[3] Doctor Rankin defined this term as being synonymous with "aseptic necrosis," (non-infectious) loss of blood supply to an area of bone causing death of bone. [But see Dorland's] Dr. Schnell testified "avascular necrosis" could result from infection or trauma or both.] Bryant v. Rankin, 332 F.Supp. 319, 323 (S.D.Iowa 1971), affirmed 468 F.2d 510 (8th Cir. 1972).

necrosis, coagulation necrosis of a portion of some organ or tissue, with the formation of fibrous infarcts, in which a relatively small part seems to have been deprived of the afflux of blood by the plugging of its vessels with coagula.

He entered the room, felt the boy's feet and legs, which he found "cold", removed him from traction and told the nurse to notify the doctor. Some four hours later, Dr. Stamler checked the boy and found the left leg had color, warmth and minimal motion. On the right leg he found sensation still absent from the foot and no motion. While the patient's fractured left leg responded to treatment, the right leg had developed a circulatory deficiency known as **ischemic necrosis** (death from reduced blood circulation) and subsequently required amputation. Garfield Park Community Hospital v. Vitacco, 327 N.E.2d 408, 410 (App.Ct.Ill.1975).

The infiltration of the penicillin into the plaintiff's forearm caused **ischemic necrosis** (dead tissue from lack of blood supply) and the blackened tissue later sloughed off. Mercurdo v. County of Milwaukee, 264 N.W.2d 258, 259 (Wis.1978).

necrosis, gangrenous cell death caused by a combination of ischemia and superimposed bacterial infection, combining the features of coagulation and colliquative necrosis.

Cepon testified that the arm had an open wound that extended from the wrist to the elbow which was several inches wide. The tissue was eaten away (**necrosis**, a form of **gangrene**), and the bone was partly exposed. The wound contained drainage fluid filled with blood, the arm was swollen and the fingers were slightly bluish in color and cold to the touch. Casey v. Penn, 360 N.E.2d 93, 97, affirmed 45 Ill.App.3d 1068, 6 Ill.Dec. 453, 362 N.E.2d 1373 (App.Ct.Ill.1977).

necrosis, ischemic See *necrosis, coagulation.*

necrosis, phloem

Phloem necrosis first appeared in Champaign County, Illinois, in the early 1950's. It is a virus which enters the cells of the phloem of a tree, the woody connective tissue of the tree just beneath the bark. The virus is carried by an insect called a leaf hopper which after feeding on an infected tree, sucking up the sap, moves on to a healthy tree into which it injects the virus while feeding thereon....

There is testimony in the record from which the jury could have concluded that the bite of but one leaf hopper carrying the virus is sufficient to infect an elm tree; that the infected tree inevitably dies from the disease, usually in about a month; that there was nothing which a property owner could do to save the elm tree once it was infected. Appleman v. U.S., 338 F.2d 729, 731 (7th Cir. 1964).

necrosis, pressure necrosis due to insufficient local blood supply as in decubitus ulcers.

... it was not unusual for a foot to become cool following a leg fracture or for it to be mottled in color. A cast which is too tight can cause **pressure necrosis.** Flamm v. Ball, 476 S.W.2d 710, 713 (Ct.Civ.App.Tex.1972).

"... that even though there was a small amount of blood stain in the cast, there still could have been a large collection of blood beneath the skin, subcutaneously, that could have caused **pressure necrosis** of the tissues involved." Majetich v. Westin, 80 Cal.Rptr. 787, 789 (Ct.App.Cal.1969).

necrotic (nĕ-krot'ik) pertaining to or characterized by necrosis.

Dr. Woldow found a massive infection, with the foot and leg swollen and inflamed to mid-calf and pus exuding from the undersurface of the foot from a large wound with **necrotic** tissue [2] underneath it. [[2] Dr. Woldow defined **necrotic** tissue to be "... almost dead tissue. It is whitish, pusy looking, not fresh and red as you would see if you had cut yourself. This is a sort of a dirty greenish-white tissue ... destroyed ... by in-

fection."] Lewin v. Metropolitan Life Insurance Co., 394 F.2d 608–9 (3d Cir. 1968).

needle (ne'd'l) [L. *acus*] a sharp instrument for suturing or puncturing. See also *syringe* (Earlin case); and *ventriculogram* (Harrison case).

Shortly after he began stitching, Dr. Benoit realized that the **needle** point had broken, leaving him with only half a **needle.** Concerned that the point may have fallen into the chest cavity, he lifted an edge of the sternum and examined the cavity both visually and by feel. He called for a magnet to be brought into the operating room to search for the **needle** fragment on the floor. The search was unproductive. Cebula v. Benoit, 652 S.W.2d 304–5 (Mo.Ct.App.1983).

We are of the opinion that the above factors, particularly appellant's inability to remember with certainty what size **needle** he used or to produce any documentation as to what was used, made the issue of causation, i.e. did the **needle** penetrate appellee's pleural cavity, one to be decided by medical opinion testimony. Earlin v. Cravetz, 399 A.2d 783, 786 (Super.Ct.Pa.1979).

needle, acupuncture See *piqûre.*

needle, Menghini a needle that does not require rotation to cut loose the tissue specimen in a biopsy of the liver.

The biopsy required insertion of a **menghini needle** into the liver. A syringe attached to the needle withdrew liver tissue into the bulb of the needle for laboratory analysis. That analysis showed the liver to be entirely normal. Suburban Hospital Ass'n v. Hadary, 322 A.2d 258, 260 (Ct.Spec.App.Md.1974).

needle, swaged one permanently attached to the suture material. See also *object, foreign* (Bowlin Horn case).

negative (neg'ah-tiv) [L. *negativus*] indicating a lack or absence, as chromatin negative or Wassermann negative.

Dr. Applebaum recommended plaintiff undergo a cervical myelogram to rule out the possibility of a herniated disc; the result of which was normal (that is **negative**). Field v. Winn Dixie Louisiana, Inc., 427 So.2d 616–17 (Ct.App.La.1983).

negligence See *care, standard of.*

neo- (ne'o) [Gr. *neos* new] a combining form meaning new or strange.

neocolporrhaphy See *colporrhaphy; necessity, medical;* and *neo-.*

We have prescribed this treatment, sex reassignment surgery, for [J.D.] in the knowledge that surgery is the only medically recognized therapy for this disorder, gender dysphoria syndrome....

On May 6, 1976, Dr. Laub filed a treatment authorization request with Medi-Cal for a surgical procedure described as: **neocolporrhaphy** with split thickness skin graft or surgical removal of the male genitalia and construction of female genitalia....

As stated in G.B. v. Lackner: We do not believe, by the wildest stretch of the imagination, that such surgery can reasonably and logically be characterized as cosmetic. J.D. v. Lackner, 145 Cal.Rptr. 570–2 (Ct.App.1978).

neomycin (ne'o-mi"sin) a broad-spectrum antibacterial antibiotic produced by the growth of *Streptomyces fradiae,*

effective against a wide range of gram-negative organisms, including *Escherichia coli, Aerobacter aerogenes,
Proteus vulgaris, Salmonella* and *Shigella species,
Pseudomonas aeruginosa*, and *Mycobacterium tuberculosis*, and most gram-positive bacteria.

Following the surgery, Dr. Gonzalez started continuous irrigation (washing) of the wound with alternating solutions of Kantrex and Upjohn's **neomycin**. It is not known how much of these
solutions was absorbed into plaintiff's body, but it is uncontradicted that plaintiff's deafness was produced by excessive administration, by tablets, injections, and irrigation, of these two
drugs. Bristol-Myers Co. v. Gonzales, 561 S.W.2d 801, 803
(Tex.1978).

It is undisputed that **neomycin** was properly used for preoperative care, since it sterilizes the intestine but is not absorbed in
significant amounts in the blood stream. . . .

Two of the reference books did not list the recommended
dosage for intraperitoneal instillation. The third contained the
following statement:

For intraperitoneal instillation a 0.5 to 1 percent solution of
neomycin in sterile water or normal saline is used. For adults,
no more than 100 ml. of solution or 1 Gm. of antibiotic
should be instilled per day for 1 to 3 days. The 3-day limit on
duration of dosage must not be exceeded.

Dr. Thian testified that he was aware of the recommended
dosage, but defended the dosage he prescribed on two bases. First, he asserted that the reference books were merely
guidelines intended to assist physicians in exercising medical
judgment in given circumstances. Second, he contended that
he used an "irrigation dosage" which did not really exceed
the recommended maximum, since a major portion of the drug,
used as a lavage in this area (which is not an open space, but is
filled with intestines) runs out through the drain and is not absorbed. DaRoca v. St. Bernard General Hospital, 347 So.2d
933–5 (Ct.App.La.1977).

In preparation for this operation, a staff physician prescribed
one gram of **Neomycin** to be given to Leslie every six hours.
The drug was to be administered orally, but tragically, an unidentified government nurse administered seven doses of it hy-
podermically. This negligent muscular injection of **Neomycin**
immediately caused acute kidney poisoning nearly resulting in
Leslie's death. The renal toxicity was soon corrected and Leslie was discharged from the hospital in November 1963—apparently none the worse for her near-mortal experience.

A possible side effect of intramuscularly administered **Neomycin** is damage to the auditory (eighth cranial) nerve. Hearing
impairment may result from destruction of small hair cells in the
inner ear. Portis v. U.S., 483 F.2d 670–1 (4th Cir. 1973).
Other Authorities: Pratt v. Stein, 444 A.2d 674, 680, 683–4
(Super.Ct.Pa.1982); Kubrick v. U.S., 581 F.2d 1092–4 (3d Cir.
1978); U.S. v. Kubrick, 444 U.S. 111, 114, 100 S.Ct. 352,
355, 62 L.Ed.2d 259 (1979).

neomycin sulfate [USP], the sulfate salt of neomycin, occurring as a white to slightly yellow powder or cryodessi-
cated solid; used in the treatment of urinary tract, eye,
skin, ear, and enteric infections due to susceptible bacteria and for preoperative disinfection, administered orally,
intramuscularly, and topically. See also *azotemia* (Richards case).

The 1971 PDR indicated that the drug could be used topically,
and stated that "[n]eomycin sulfate . . . may be used effectively as wet dressings, packs, or irrigations in secondarily infected wounds. . . ."

It is undisputed that **neomycin sulfate** can cause deafness.
Upjohn has publicly acknowledged this fact in the information
about the drug which it published in the PDR, in 1971, '72, and
'73. The PDR's warn that significant amounts of the drug may
be absorbed when used repeatedly for irrigation and that high
blood levels increase the risk of ototoxicity. Richards v. Upjohn
Co., 625 P.2d 1192, 1194–5 (Ct.App.N.M.1980).

neonatology (ne"o-na-tol'o-je) the art and science of diagnosis and treatment of disorders of the newborn infant.

The extent of specialization of modern medicine is shown
here: one witness was a pediatric pathologist and another
was an expert in **neonatology** which is the care and study of
diseases in new born infants. Hogan v. City-County Hospital
of LaGrange, 227 S.E.2d 796, 798 (Ct.App.Ga.1976).

neopallium (ne"o-pal'le-um) [*neo-* + L. *pallium* cloak]
that portion of the pallium (cerebral cortex) showing
stratification and organization characteristic of the most
highly evolved type of cerebral tissue. It consists of six
layers: layer I, the molecular or plexiform layer; layer II,
the external granular layer; layer III, the pyramidal layer; layer IV, the internal granular layer; layer V, the
ganglionic layer; layer VI, the multiform or polymorphic
layer. Called also *homotypical cortex, isocortex, ne-
ocortex*, and *nonolfactory cortex*. Cf. *archipallium*.

neoplasia (ne"o-pla'ze-ah) the formation of a neoplasm,
i.e., the progressive multiplication of cells under conditions that would not elicit, or would cause cessation of,
multiplication of normal cells.

neoplasm (ne'o-plazm) [*neo-* + Gr. *plasma* formation] any
new and abnormal growth; specifically a new growth of
tissue in which the growth is uncontrolled and progressive (see neoplasia). Malignant neoplasms are distinguished from benign in that the former show a greater
degree of anaplasia and have the properties of invasion
and metastasis. Called also *tumor*. See also *lesion* (Utter
case).

In May of 1977 Dr. David Strayhorn examined Lashley. He found
that plaintiff had a mild speech impediment, was slightly weak in
the right hand, and was noticeably unsteady when standing on
one foot. Dr. Strayhorn stated: "His symptoms at the present time
in addition to his speech trouble consist of generalized weakness
and some difficulty with his memory." Dr. Strayhorn opined that
plaintiff could have a **neoplasm** or mass occupying lesion in his
brain. Lashley v. Secretary of Health and Human Services, 708
F.2d 1048, 1050 (6th Cir. 1983).

The pleural fluid was withdrawn through the process known as
thoracentesis, and a number of large cells were discovered
which appeared to be **neoplastic**. Petition of U.S., 303
F.Supp. 1282, 1310 (E.D.N.Car.1969).

neoplasm, intracranial

The doctor testified that: "An **intracranial neoplasm** means a
tumor, either benign or malignant, within the cranial cavity."
Whitfield v. Roth, 519 P.2d 588, 591 (Cal.1974).

neoplastic See *neoplasm*.

neosporin

The application of **neosporin** to the abrased area of her arm was stopped. Thereafter the progress notes indicate that she was treated for the rash and that the rash condition seemed to have improved....

... He agreed that if the rash started where the **neosporin** was applied and that the rash condition improved when it was not applied, it was not unreasonable to suspect that the rash was caused by the **neosporin**. Stevens v. Barnhart, 412 A.2d 1292–3 (Ct.Spec.App.Md.1980).

Neo-Synephrine (ne"o-sĭ-nef'rin) trademark for preparations of phenylephrine hydrochloride. See also *phenylephrine hydrochloride.*

The plaintiffs argued that another cause of injury to the patient was the administration of **neosynephrine** in order to raise her blood pressure. Since the consequence of administering **neosynephrine** is to constrict the blood vessels, the plaintiffs contended that its injection caused the dye in effect to be squeezed into the patient's spinal cord. They presented evidence that a qualified anesthesiologist would have known that the administration of **neosynephrine** in such circumstances was improper. Medvecz v. Choi, 569 F.2d 1221, 1223 (3d Cir. 1977).

neovascularization See *vascularization.*

... and evidence of **neovascularization**, meaning the formation of new blood vessels on the cornea at the stroma. Rohm & Haas v. Workmen's Comp. App. Bd., 414 A.2d 163–4 (Commwlth.Ct.Pa.1980).

nephrectomy (nĕ-frek'to-me) [*nephr-* + Gr. *ektomē* excision] excision of a kidney.

The reports from the hospital in March show that the claimant made a good recovery from the right **nephrectomy** [removal of the right kidney].... Torres v. Celebrezze, 349 F.2d 342, 344 (1st Cir. 1965).

nephritis (nĕ-fri'tis), pl. *nephrit'ides* [Gr. *nephros* kidney + *-itis*] inflammation of the kidney; a focal or diffuse proliferative or destructive process which may involve the glomerulus, tubule, or interstitial renal tissue. See also *glomerulonephritis.* Cf. *nephrosis.* Cited in Capaldi v. Weinberger, 391 F.Supp. 502, 505 (E.D.Pa.1975).

nephrology (nĕ-frol'o-je) [*nephro-* + *-logy*] scientific study of the kidney, its anatomy, physiology, and pathology. See also *kidney.*

Dr. Norma Lee Wenger, an internist specializing in **nephrology**, has treated Peter Cinque since 1979. She testified that his kidneys were destroyed, do not function and cannot remove toxic waste. He requires maintenance hemo dialysis three times a week, for a total of twelve hours, in order to survive. Without dialysis Peter Cinque will be dead within one week or sooner. Application of Lydia E. Hall Hospital, 455 N.Y.S.2d 706, 708 (Sup.Ct.Nassau Cty.1982).

nephrosclerosis (nef"ro-skle-ro'sis) [*nephro-* + Gr. *sklēr-ōsis* hardening] sclerosis or hardening of the kidney; the condition of the kidney due to renovascular disease.

nephrosclerosis, arteriolar nephrosclerosis involving chiefly the arterioles; it is frequently associated with hypertension, and characterized by insidious onset, cylindruria, edema, hypertrophy of the heart, degeneration of the renal tubules, and fibrotic thickening of the glomeruli (glomerulonephritis), resulting in renal insufficiency, congestive heart failure, and cerebral hemorrhage. Called also *intercapillary n.* and *glomerulosclerosis.* Cited in Britt v. Travelers Ins. Co., 556 F.2d 336, 339 (5th Cir. 1977).

nephrosis (nĕ-fro'sis), pl. *nephro'ses* [*nephr-* + *-osis*] any disease of the kidney, especially any disease of the kidneys characterized by purely degenerative lesions of the renal tubules—as opposed to nephritis—and marked by edema (noninflammatory), albuminuria, and decreased serum albumin (the nephrotic syndrome).

nephrostomy (nĕ-fros'to-me) [*nephro-* + Gr. *stomoun* to provide with an opening, or mouth] the creation of a permanent fistula leading directly into the pelvis of the kidney.

To enable the fistula to heal, Dr. Berger performed a **nephrostomy**, diverting the flow of urine through a tube inserted through the patient's side into the kidney a tube which remained until the first of December 1974. Pugsley v. Privette, 263 S.E.2d 69, 72 (Va.1980).

nephrotoxic (nef"ro-tok'sik) toxic or destructive to kidney cells. See also *kanamycin* (Schering Corp. case).

Upjohn had published warnings in the Physician's Desk Reference (PDR) and in the package inserts of the neomycin sulfate it sold that the drug was ... **nephrotoxic** (toxic to the kidneys).... Richards v. Upjohn Co., 625 P.2d 1192, 1194 (Ct. App.N.M.1980).

neptunium (nep-tu'ne-um) [from planet Neptune] a radioactive element of atomic number 93 and atomic weight 237, occurring in certain earths and obtained by splitting the uranium atom with neutrons. It is unstable and changes into plutonium. Symbol Np.

nerve (nerv) [L. *nervus;* Gr. *neuron*] a cordlike structure, visible to the naked eye, comprising a collection of nerve fibers which convey impulses between a part of the central nervous system and some other region of the body. Called also *nervus* [NA]. A nerve consists of a connective tissue sheath (epineurium) enclosing bundles (funiculi or fasciculi) of nerve fibers, each bundle being surrounded by its own sheath of connective tissue (perineurium), the inner surface of which is formed by a membrane of flattened mesothelial cells. Very small nerves may consist of only one funiculus derived from the parent nerve. Within each such bundle, the individual nerve fibers, which are microscopic in size, are surrounded by interstitial connective tissue (endoneurium). An individual nerve fiber (an axon with its covering sheath) consists of formed elements in a matrix of protoplasm (axoplasm), the entire structure being enclosed in a thin membrane (axolemma). Each nerve fiber is enclosed by a cellular sheath (neurilemma), from which it may or may not be separated by a lipid layer (myelin sheath) derived from neurilemmal cells. See generally *nervi, Table of* (page 487).

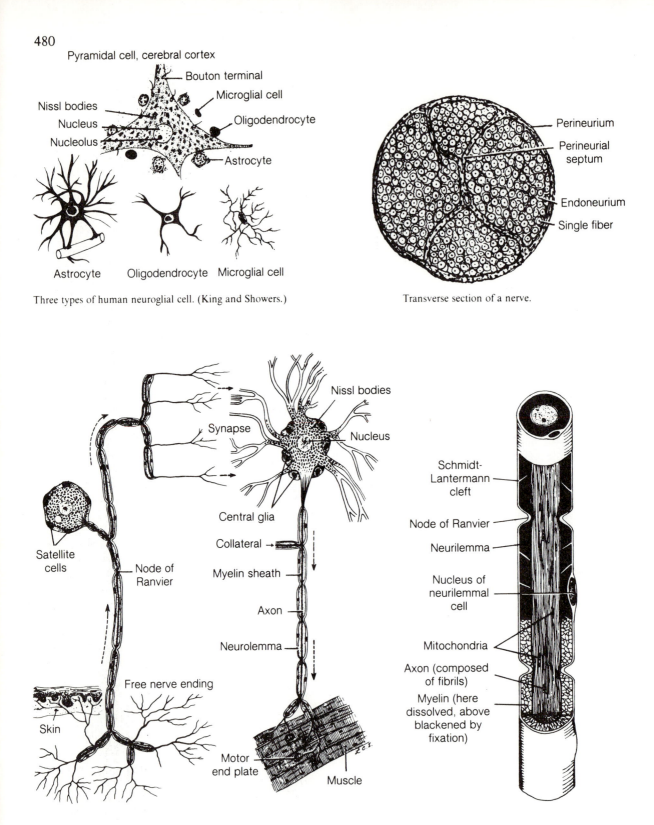

Pyramidal cell, cerebral cortex

Bouton terminal

Microglial cell

Nissl bodies

Oligodendrocyte

Nucleus

Nucleolus

Astrocyte

Astrocyte   Oligodendrocyte   Microglial cell

Three types of human neuroglial cell. (King and Showers.)

Perineurium

Perineurial septum

Endoneurium

Single fiber

Transverse section of a nerve.

Nissl bodies

Synapse

Nucleus

Central glia

Collateral →

Myelin sheath

Axon

Neurolemma

Satellite cells

Node of Ranvier

Free nerve ending

Skin

Motor end plate

Muscle

SENSORY NEURON   MOTOR NEURON

Diagrammatic representation of two types of neurons. (King and Showers.)

Schmidt-Lantermann cleft

Node of Ranvier

Neurilemma

Nucleus of neurilemmal cell

Mitochondria

Axon (composed of fibrils)

Myelin (here dissolved, above blackened by fixation)

Longitudinal section of a nerve fiber (Leeson and Leeson).

DETAILS OF STRUCTURE OF COMPONENTS OF NERVE TISSUE

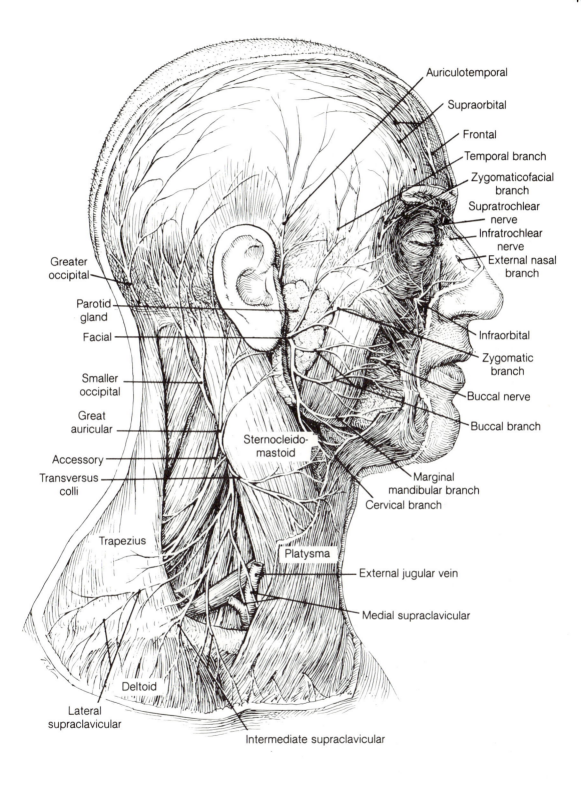

SUPERFICIAL NERVES AND MUSCLES OF HEAD AND NECK

Portions of the parotid gland and platysma muscle are shown cut away. (Jones and Shepard.)

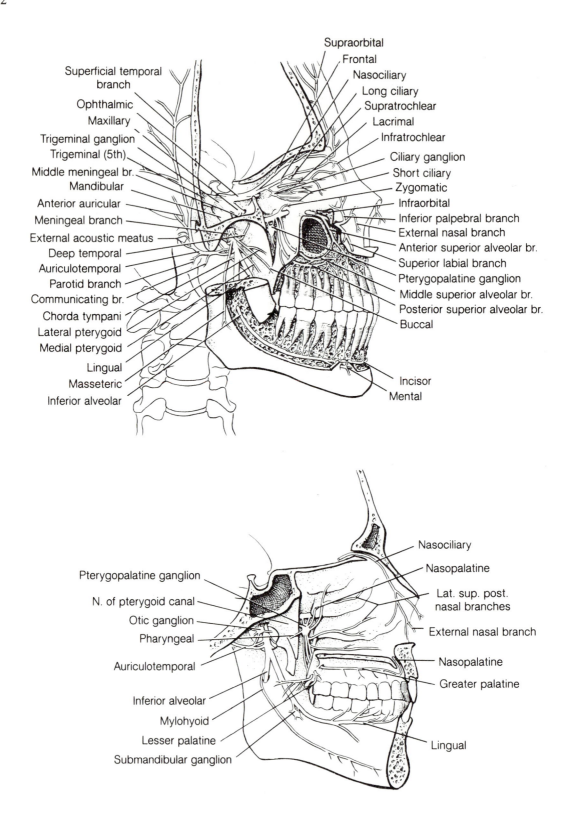

Superficial temporal branch
Ophthalmic
Maxillary
Trigeminal ganglion
Trigeminal (5th)
Middle meningeal br.
Mandibular
Anterior auricular
Meningeal branch
External acoustic meatus
Deep temporal
Auriculotemporal
Parotid branch
Communicating br.
Chorda tympani
Lateral pterygoid
Medial pterygoid
Lingual
Masseteric
Inferior alveolar

Supraorbital
Frontal
Nasociliary
Long ciliary
Supratrochlear
Lacrimal
Infratrochlear
Ciliary ganglion
Short ciliary
Zygomatic
Infraorbital
Inferior palpebral branch
External nasal branch
Anterior superior alveolar br.
Superior labial branch
Pterygopalatine ganglion
Middle superior alveolar br.
Posterior superior alveolar br.
Buccal

Incisor
Mental

Pterygopalatine ganglion
N. of pterygoid canal
Otic ganglion
Pharyngeal
Auriculotemporal
Inferior alveolar
Mylohyoid
Lesser palatine
Submandibular ganglion

Nasociliary
Nasopalatine
Lat. sup. post. nasal branches
External nasal branch
Nasopalatine
Greater palatine
Lingual

DEEP NERVES SHOWN IN RELATION TO BONES OF FACE

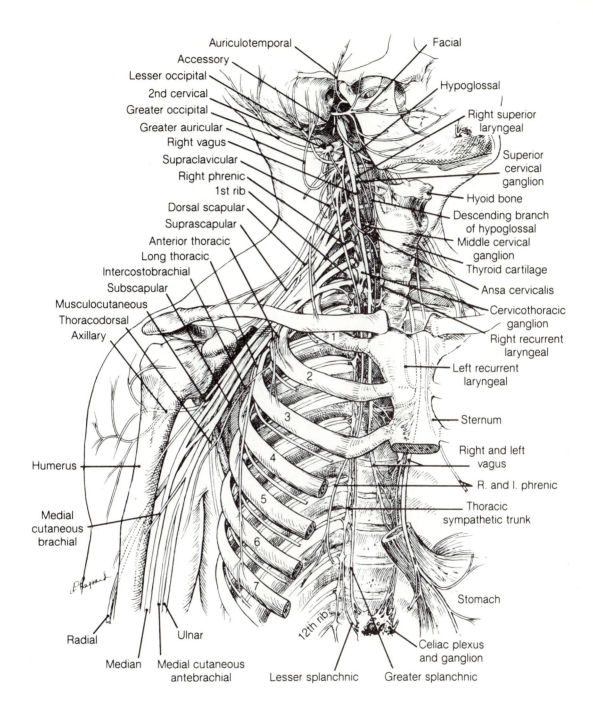

DEEP NERVES OF NECK, AXILLA, AND UPPER THORAX

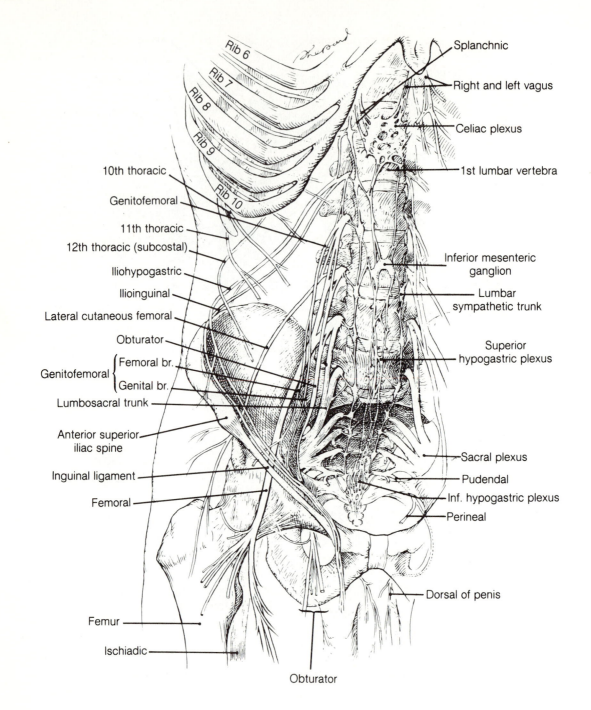

Splanchnic

Right and left vagus

Celiac plexus

1st lumbar vertebra

Rib 6
Rib 7
Rib 8
Rib 9
Rib 10

10th thoracic

Genitofemoral

11th thoracic

12th thoracic (subcostal)

Iliohypogastric

Ilioinguinal

Lateral cutaneous femoral

Obturator

Genitofemoral { Femoral br.
                Genital br.

Lumbosacral trunk

Anterior superior iliac spine

Inguinal ligament

Femoral

Inferior mesenteric ganglion

Lumbar sympathetic trunk

Superior hypogastric plexus

Sacral plexus

Pudendal

Inf. hypogastric plexus

Perineal

Dorsal of penis

Femur

Ischiadic

Obturator

DEEP NERVES OF LOWER TRUNK

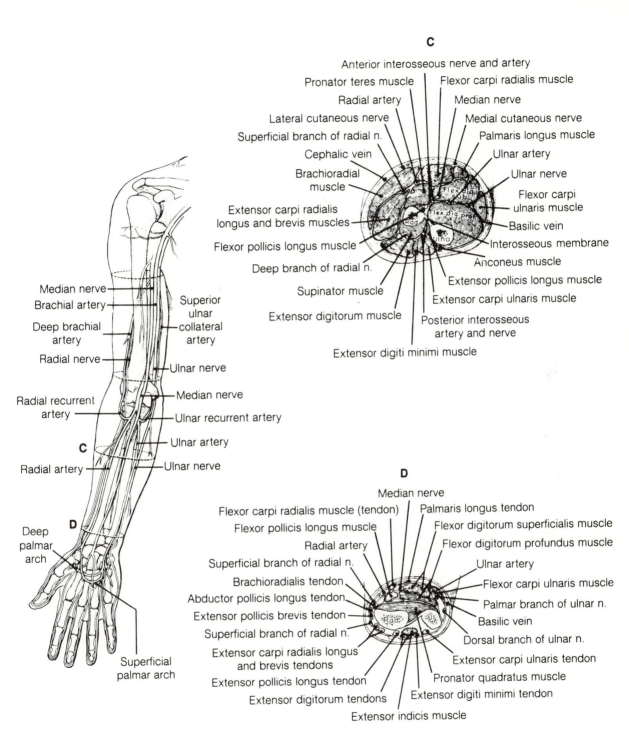

C

Anterior interosseous nerve and artery
Pronator teres muscle
Radial artery
Lateral cutaneous nerve
Superficial branch of radial n.
Cephalic vein
Brachioradial muscle
Extensor carpi radialis longus and brevis muscles
Flexor pollicis longus muscle
Deep branch of radial n.
Supinator muscle
Extensor digitorum muscle

Flexor carpi radialis muscle
Median nerve
Medial cutaneous nerve
Palmaris longus muscle
Ulnar artery
Ulnar nerve
Flexor carpi ulnaris muscle
Basilic vein
Interosseous membrane
Anconeus muscle
Extensor pollicis longus muscle
Extensor carpi ulnaris muscle
Posterior interosseous artery and nerve
Extensor digiti minimi muscle

Median nerve
Brachial artery
Deep brachial artery
Radial nerve
Radial recurrent artery

Superior ulnar collateral artery
Ulnar nerve
Median nerve
Ulnar recurrent artery
Ulnar artery
Ulnar nerve

C

Radial artery

Deep palmar arch

D

Superficial palmar arch

D

Median nerve
Flexor carpi radialis muscle (tendon)
Flexor pollicis longus muscle
Radial artery
Superficial branch of radial n.
Brachioradialis tendon
Abductor pollicis longus tendon
Extensor pollicis brevis tendon
Superficial branch of radial n.
Extensor carpi radialis longus and brevis tendons
Extensor pollicis longus tendon
Extensor digitorum tendons
Extensor indicis muscle

Palmaris longus tendon
Flexor digitorum superficialis muscle
Flexor digitorum profundus muscle
Ulnar artery
Flexor carpi ulnaris muscle
Palmar branch of ulnar n.
Basilic vein
Dorsal branch of ulnar n.
Extensor carpi ulnaris tendon
Pronator quadratus muscle
Extensor digiti minimi tendon

NERVES OF RIGHT UPPER EXTREMITY

Front view shows principal nerves and arteries in relation to the bones, *C* and *D* are cross sections made at levels indicated on drawing at left. (Jones and Shepard.)

486

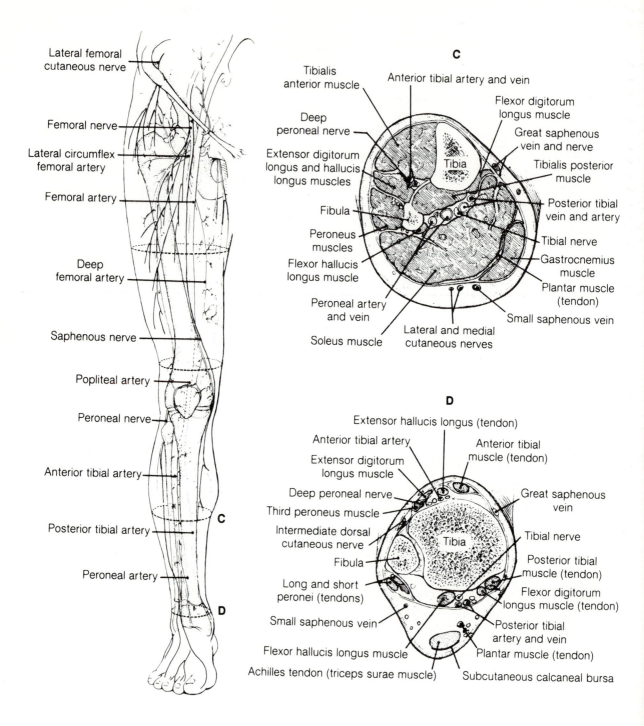

NERVES OF RIGHT LOWER EXTREMITY

Front view shows principal nerves and arteries in relation to the bones, *C* and *D* are cross sections made at levels indicated on drawing at left. (Jones and Shepard.)

nerve, abducent See *nervus abducens*

nerve, accessory; nerve, accessory, spinal See *nervus accessorius.*

nerve, alveolar, inferior See *nervus alveolaris inferior.*

nerve, auditory See *nervus vestibulocochlearis.*

nerves, ciliary, long See *nervi ciliares longi.*

nerves, cranial the twelve pairs of nerves connected with the brain. See also *nervi craniales* [NA].

nerve, cranial, eighth See *nervus vestibulocochlearis.*

nerve, cutaneous See *nervus cutaneus.*

nerve, cutaneous of thigh, posterior See *nervus cutaneus femoris posterior.*

nerve, facial See *nervus facialis.*

nerve, femoral See *nervus femoralis.*

nerve, frontal See *nervus frontalis.*

nerve, hypoglossal See *nervus hypoglossus.*

nerve, ischiadic See *nervus ischiadicus.*

nerve, laryngeal See *thyroidectomy* (Jones case).

nerve, laryngeal, recurrent See *nervus laryngeus recurrens*; and *adenoma* (Schroeder case).

nerve, laryngeal, superior See *nervus laryngeus superior.*

nerve, lingual See *nervus lingualis.*

nerve, mandibular See *nervus mandibularis.*

nerve, median See *nervus medianus.*

nerve, mental See *nervus mentalis.*

nerve, ophthalmic See *nervus ophthalmicus.*

nerve, optic See *nervus opticus.*

nerve, peroneal, common See *nervus peroneus communis.*

nerve, peroneal, deep See *nervus peroneus profundus.*

nerve, phrenic See *nervus phrenicus.*

nerve, plantar, medial See *nervus plantaris medialis.*

nerves, sacral the five pairs of nerves arising from the sacral segments of the spinal cord. See also *nervi sacrales.*

nerve, sixth See *nervus abducens.*

nerves, spinal the thirty-one pairs of nerves arising from the spinal cord. See also *nervi spinales.*

nerve, supraorbital See *nervus supraorbitalis.*

nerve, supratrochlear See *nervus supratrochlearis.*

nerve, tympanic See *nervus tympanicus.*

nerve, ulnar See *nervus ulnaris.*

nerve, vagus See *nervus vagus.*

nerve, vestibulocochlear See *nervus vestibulocochlearis.*

nerve block See *anesthesia, regional.*

nerve conduction study

> The **nerve conduction studies**, which measure the function of the peripheral nerve, disclosed a mild slowing, indicating an abnormality.... Cook v. Marshall Bros. Lincoln-Mercury, Inc., 427 So.2d 655, 657 (Ct.App.La.1983).

nerve root See *roots, nerve*; and *radix.*

nerve root compression See *decompression, nerve.*

nerve root, spinal See *radices spinales nervi accessorii* under *radix.*

nervous system See under *system.*

nervous system, central See *system, central nervous.*

nervous system, peripheral See *system, peripheral nervous.*

nervus (ner'vus), pl. *ner'vi* [L.] [NA] a nerve: a cordlike structure, visible to the naked eye, comprising a collection of nerve fibers which convey impulses between a part of the central nervous system and some other region of the body. See also *nerve.* For names and description of specific nerves, see *Table of Nervi.*

TABLE OF NERVI

nervus abducens [NA], abducens nerve (6th cranial): *origin*, a nucleus in the pons, beneath the floor of the fourth ventricle, emerging from the brain stem anteriorly between the pons and medulla oblongata; *distribution*, lateral rectus muscle of eye; *modality*, motor.

> ... "sixth nerve paresis," i.e., a weakness of the sixth nerve, causing her eyes to turn in. Perry v. Bertsch, 441 F.2d 939, 941 (8th Cir. 1971).

nervus accessorius [NA], accessory nerve (11th cranial); *origin*, by cranial roots from the side of the medulla oblongata, and by spinal roots from the side of the spinal cord (from the upper three or more cervical segments); the roots unite and the nerve thus formed divides into an internal branch (cranial portion) and an external branch (spinal portion); *distribution*, the internal branch to the vagus and thereby to the palate, pharynx, larynx, and thoracic viscera; the external branch to the sternocleidomastoid and trapezius muscles; *modality*, parasympathetic and motor.

> Ms. Peterson has raised a fact question on whether the risk of injury to the **accessory nerve** could influence a reasonable person in making the decision to undergo surgery. Dr. Durcan testified that nerves "must be treated with the utmost gentleness." Dr. Durcan also testified the **accessory nerve** "could be either cut or traumatized ... by the manipulations necessary to free the lymph glands ... if they were adherent to the structure." When asked whether there is a risk to the **accessory nerve** during a lymph node biopsy, Dr. Durcan testified: "Yes.

There is a definite risk.'' Peterson v. Shields, 652 S.W.2d 929, 931 (Tex.1983).

It was also concluded that the left trapezius muscle, which is controlled by the spinal **accessory nerve**, had hollowed out or atrophied. (N.T. 105, 175). The **spinal accessory nerve** is located in that area upon which Dr. Goldman operated. Sindler v. Goldman, 454 A.2d 1054–5 (Super.Ct.Pa.1982).

nervus alveolaris inferior [NA], inferior alveolar nerve: *origin*, mandibular nerve; *branches*, mylohyoid, inferior dental, mental, and inferior gingival nerves; *distribution*—see individual branches, in this table; *modality*, motor and general sensory.

Dr. Gordon Burch, an expert in neurology, testified that he made two examinations of plaintiff in February 1976 and April or May 1977, and on the basis of his examination, he concluded that plaintiff was suffering from a sensory change consistent with abnormal function in the **inferior alveolar nerve** on the left side, in that, the nerve was conducting electrical impulses abnormally. Furthermore, Dr. Burch felt that in his opinion, it was highly unlikely that plaintiff's condition would change. Dr. Burch also testified, over objection, that it was his belief that the **inferior alveolar nerve** had been injured at the time of the local anesthetic undertaken on the left side. . . .

. . . Dr. Angellilo stated that the incision by defendant on the left side of plaintiff's mouth could not have damaged the **inferior alveolar nerve** since, in his opinion, nerve damage produces an immediate altered sensation. Cozart v. Chapin, 251 S.E.2d 682, 684–5 (Ct.App.N.C.1979).

See also Tr. 60, 69 (appellee's testimony). Dr. Stevens explained that the mandibular branch of the trigeminal nerve was involved in the loss of sensation, and that the **alveolar nerve** is a branch of the mandibular. Tr. 74. . . .

A lower right wisdom tooth is very close to the **alveolar nerve**, which through two filaments supplies sensation to the chin and lips; it is closer in some individuals than in others. Appellee stated from the witness stand that appellant's lower right wisdom tooth ''strattled'' the **alveolar nerve**, ''almost touching'' it. No wonder it was that, as appellee conceded, any application of pressure demanded caution with respect to both amount and direction to avoid damage to the nerve, which in turn could cause loss of sensation in that region of the face. [Footnotes omitted.] Henderson v. Milobsky, 595 F.2d 654, 656, 662 (D.C.Cir.1978).

The nerve involved is called the **inferior alveolar** and is a branch of the trigeminal nerve, sometimes called the dental nerve. On each side of the jaw the **inferior alveolar** follows the mandibular canal forward innervating the lower teeth up to the midline of the chin. . . .

The dispute about treatment relates to the two foramen or jaw openings for the passage of the **inferior alveolar**. In making injections of anesthesia it is important not to injure the nerve by striking it with the hypodermic needle. The testimony indicated that injection at the rear or mandibular foramen is preferred because of more effective sensory blocking and a lessened chance of injury to nerve tissue. LaRocque v. LaMarche, 292 A.2d 259–60 (Vt.1972).

nervi ciliares longi [NA], long ciliary nerves: *origin*, nasociliary nerve, from ophthalmic nerve; *distribution*, dilator pupillae, uvea, cornea; *modality*, sympathetic and general sensory.

. . . widely dilated pupil right, secondary to irritation of the sympathetic nerves traveling the long **ciliary nerves** from ophthalmic division of trigeminal right, and by corneal analgesia right by reason of injury to these same long **ciliary sensory nerves**. Phillips v. Celebrezze, 330 F.2d 687, 689 (6th Cir. 1964).

nervi craniales [NA], cranial nerves: the twelve pairs of nerves that are connected with the brain, including the nervi olfactorii (I), and the opticus (II), oculomotorius (III) trochlearis (IV), trigeminus (V), abducens (VI), facialis (VII), vestibulocochlearis (VIII), glossopharyngeus (IX), vagus (X), accessorius (XI), and hypoglossus (XII). Called also *nervi cerebrales*.

As one doctor testified: ''There are risks of injury to the nerves, particularly the **cranial nerves** or nerves in the head that control certain of the facial muscles and the eyes. Harrington v. Cohen, 374 N.E.2d 344–5 (App.Ct.Mass.1978).

nervus cutaneus [NA], cutaneous nerve: a peripheral nerve that supplies a region of the skin, many of them not being specifically named.

Dr. Williams found injury to the **cutaneous nerves** which supply the area of the thigh which causes pain in the knee when the leg is used. Pike v. Roe, 516 P.2d 972–3 (Kan.1973).

nervus cutaneus femoris posterior [NA], posterior cutaneous nerve of thigh: *origin*, sacral plexus—S1–S3; *branches*, inferior clunial nerves and perineal rami; *distribution*, skin of buttock, external genitalia, and back of thigh and calf; *modality*, general sensory.

Nurse Rodriguez knew, as the result of her recent training, that an injection into or near the **sciatic nerve** located in the lower back would cause immediate and irreparable damage to the nerve. She knew that care must be taken to inject the needle perpendicularly to the point of entry. Frantz v. San Luis Medical Clinic, 146 Cal.Rptr. 146, 149 (Ct.App.Cal.1978).

nervi digitales palmares proprii nervi mediani [NA], proper palmar digital nerves of median nerve: *origin*, common palmar digital nerves; *distribution*, first two lumbrical muscles, skin and joints of both sides and palmar aspect of thumb, index, and middle fingers radial side of ring finger, and back of distal aspect of these digits; *modality*, general sensory and motor.

This surgery disclosed that a branch of the brachial plexus nerve network known as the **lateral cord of the median nerve** had been severed and that scar tissue had formed and was pressing against the rest of the major nerve bundle. This scar tissue appeared to be the cause of the clawing. The severed nerve serves only the thumb. Its severance would cause loss of feeling and movement to that digit alone. Luna v. Nering, 426 F.2d 95, 97 (5th Cir. 1970).

nervus facialis [NA], facial nerve (7th cranial), consisting of two roots: a large motor root, which supplies the muscles of facial expression, and a smaller root, the nervus intermedius (q.v.). *Origin*, inferior border of pons, between olive and inferior cerebellar peduncle; *branches* (of motor root), stapedius and posterior auricular nerves, parotid plexus, digastric, temporal, zygomatic, buccal, lingual, marginal mandibular, and cervical rami, and a communicating ramus with the tympanic plexus; *distribution*—see individual branches, in this table and under *ramus; modality*, motor, parasympathetic, general sensory, special sensory.

On November 16th, an operating team headed by Dr. Ward performed the parotidectomy. In cutting the tissue toward the parotid gland, Dr. Ward unintentionally severed appellant's **facial nerve** before identifying it. After discovering the severed nerve, Dr. Ward removed the cyst (which proved to be benign), sutured the nerve ends back together, and completed the operation.

Following the operation, the left side of appellant's face was completely paralyzed. LeMons v. Regents of the Univ. of Cal., 582 P.2d 946–7 (Cal.1978).

During the course of the surgery [a mastoidectomy] the nerve [**nervus facialis** (7th cranial nerve)] became frayed or partially severed. Realizing the frayed nerve should be repaired, he called in Dr. Alcocer, another ear specialist, to help him. Dr. Alcocer, in repairing the injured nerve, used a surgical microscope which afforded magnification up to ten times that of the binocular loop used by defendant. Following the surgery the left side of plaintiff's face drooped and was paralyzed. Livengood v. Howard, 295 N.E.2d 736, 738 (App.Ct.Ill.1973).

nervus femoralis [NA], femoral nerve: *origin*, lumbar plexus—L2–L4; descending behind the inguinal ligament to the femoral triangle; *branches*, saphenous nerve, muscular and anterior cutaneous rami; *distribution*, the skin of the thigh and leg, the muscles of the front of the thigh, and the hip and knee joints—see individual branches, in this table and under *ramus; modality*, general sensory and motor.

Dr. Neil Allen, a neurologist who treated the plaintiff in consultation after the procedure, testified that the plaintiff's nerve injury was caused either by pressure from the hematoma or by a direct puncture of the **femoral nerve** during the renal arteriography. Hirn v. Edgewater Hospital, 408 N.E.2d 970, 973 (App.Ct.Ill.1980).

nervus frontalis [NA], frontal nerve: *origin*, ophthalmic division of trigeminal nerve; enters the orbit through the superior orbital fissure; *branches*, supraorbital and supratrochlear nerves; *distribution*, chiefly to the forehead and scalp—see individual branches, in this table; *modality*, general sensory.

... numbness of the forehead,[15] and headaches caused by the skull fracture. [[15] It was explained by plaintiff's physician that the nerves which supply the forehead go up and over the forehead on each side, that the cut across the plaintiff's forehead severed both of these nerves, resulting in the numbness of which plaintiff complained.] Williams v. Steuart Motor Co., 494 F.2d 1074, 1086 (D.C.Cir.1974).

nervus hypoglossus [NA], hypoglossal nerve (12th cranial): *origin*, several rootlets in the anterolateral sulcus between the olive and the pyramid of the medulla oblongata; it passes through the hypoglossal canal to the tongue; *branches*, lingual rami; *distribution*, styloglossus, hypoglossus, and genioglossus muscles and intrinsic muscles of the tongue; *modality*, motor.

The plaintiff underwent an operation to remove a tumor in her neck. During the procedure, her **hypoglossal nerve** was severed, allegedly resulting in a permanent and almost total loss of tongue function....

... The procedure resulted in severance of the **hypoglossal nerve** with resulting severe dysfunctions in speech, mastication, saliva management, and swallowing. Harnish v. Children's Hosp. Med. Center, 439 N.E.2d 240–1, 244 (Sup.Jud.Ct. Mass.1982).

nervus ischiadicus [NA], sciatic nerve, the largest nerve of the body: *origin*, sacral plexus—L4–S3; it leaves the pelvis through the greater sciatic foramen; *branches*, divides into the tibial and common peroneal nerves, usually in lower third of thigh; *distribution*—see individual branches, in this table; *modality*, general sensory and motor.

... She also has a **sciatic nerve** pain in her hip which was severe in July of 1970. At that time she got 'down in her back' and was almost paralyzed. The doctor took x-rays and told her that she had a disintegrated disc and a huge calcium deposit which was pinching the nerve.... Landess v. Weinberger, 361 F.Supp. 247, 249 (E.D.Mo.1973), reversed and remanded 490 F.2d 1187 (8th Cir. 1974).

The **sciatic nerve** bundle, which at this point contains several subsidiary nerves, is located in the approximate center of the buttock although somewhat upward and outward from the center of the cheek of the buttock. These two areas are not concentric as was shown by an anatomical illustration at the trial. The location of the upper outer quadrant is not capable of exact definition. The exact location of the **sciatic nerve** in this area varies in individuals. Testimony that it was accepted and recognized by all doctors and nurses that no injection of any kind should be made in the **sciatic nerve** area and that such injection if done would be in violation of recognized standard medical, nursing and hospital procedures, was elicited from the defendant, Dr. Rogers; from Mrs. Cook, the chief nurse of the pediatric section of defendant hospital, and from Dr. Wiley, the director of defendant hospital's department of physical medicine, in addition to testimony of plaintiffs' witnesses. (Honeywell v. Rogers, 251 F.Supp. 841, 844 (W.D.Pa.1966).

Throughout this treatment it was apparent that Mr. Hart was having a revert pain down his left **sciatic nerve** (this nerve goes down into the hip and back of the left leg), which was caused by "involvement of the nerve roots" in Mr. Hart's lower back. Hart v. Van Zandt, 399 S.W.2d 791, 793 (Tex.1965).

nervus laryngeus recurrens [NA], recurrent laryngeal nerve: *origin*, vagus nerve (chiefly the cranial part of the accessory nerve); *branches*, inferior laryngeal nerve, tracheal, esophageal, and inferior cardiac rami; *distribution*—see individual branches, in this table and under *ramus; modality*, parasympathetic, visceral afferent, and motor.

A physical examination revealed that he suffered left vocal cord paralysis characteristic of loss of innervation by the **recurrent laryngeal nerve**. Lemke v. U.S., 557 F.Supp. 1205, 1208 (D.N.D.1983).

Dr. Tiesenga indicated that to either side of the thyroid gland there is a nerve, the **recurrent laryngeal nerve**, and that he identified the recurrent nerve on the right side but made no attempt to locate the **recurrent nerve** on the left side....

Dr. Tiesenga admitted that the first thing a surgeon should do in performing thyroid surgery is to identify and isolate the **recurrent nerve**. He explained, however, that he knew the nerves would not be in their normal location due to the prior surgery and that in removing tissue from the left side he made a wide cut so as to avoid the area where the nerve might possibly be. Dr. Tiesenga explained that this is the most difficult type of thyroid surgery that can be performed, that the nerve is very delicate and could have been injured in an attempt to locate it, and that it was more prudent not to attempt to locate the nerve on the left side. Dr. Tiesenga did not view the patient's vocal chords before or after the operation.

Dr. Tiesenga also indicated that he agreed with the textbook procedure of first exposing and identifying the **recurrent laryngeal nerve** in those cases where the patient had no previous thyroid surgery. Walski v. Tiesenga, 368 N.E.2d 573–4 (App. Ct.Ill.1977).

The **recurrent laryngeal nerves** control the motion of adduction, that is, the movement of the vocal chords away from each other. The **recurrent laryngeal nerve** which controls the movement of the right vocal chord now fails to function. Roberts v. Wood, 206 F.Supp. 579, 582 (S.D.Ala.1962).

nervus laryngeus superior [NA], superior laryngeal nerve: *origin*, inferior ganglion of vagus nerve; *branches*, external, internal, and communicating rami; *distribution*, inferior constrictor of the pharynx, cricothyroid muscle, and mucous membrane of back of tongue and larynx—see individual branches, under *ramus; modality*, motor, general sensory, visceral afferent, and parasympathetic.

The **superior laryngeal nerves** control the motion of adduction, that is, the movement of the vocal cords towards each other. Roberts v. Wood, 206 F.Supp. 579, 582 (S.D.Ala.1962).

nervus lingualis [NA], lingual nerve: *origin*, mandibular nerve, descending to the tongue, first medial to the mandible and then under cover of the mucous membrane of the mouth; *branches*, sublingual nerve, lingual ramus, ramus to the isthmus of the fauces, and rami communicating with the hypoglossal nerve and chorda tympani; *distribution*—see individual branches, in this table and under *ramus; modality*, general sensory.

Plaintiff's complaint alleged, inter alia, that defendant cut, severed, or damaged the left **lingual nerve** in the course of removal of a wisdom tooth.... Grubb v. Jurgens, 373 N.E.2d 1082, 1084 (App.Ct.Ill.1978).

nervus mandibularis [NA], mandibular nerve, one of three terminal divisions of the trigeminal nerve, passing through the foramen ovale to the infratemporal fossa. *Origin*, trigeminal ganglion; *branches*, meningeal ramus, masseteric, deep temporal, lateral and medial pterygoid, buccal, auriculotemporal, lingual, and inferior alveolar nerves; *distribution*, extensive distribution to muscles of mastication, skin of face, mucous membrane of mouth, and teeth—see individual branches, in this table and under *ramus; modality*, general sensory and motor.

It appears that, in the removal of the tooth, the **mandibular nerve** was bruised or severed. As a result, at the time of the trial, Simone had a numbness of a portion of the lower lip and jaw which may be permanent.

Simone presented the testimony of an expert tending to prove that it is customary for a general practitioner to refer the extraction of impacted lower bicuspids to an exodontist or oral surgeon. Such a tooth, the testimony shows, is invariably in close proximity of a branch of the **mandibular nerve**, and the extraction constitutes "considerable danger to the mental nerve"....

... Traumatization of the **mandibular nerve**, he said, occurs in approximately 25 per cent of extractions such as that performed by Dr. Sabo. However, he did not know in what percentage of cases the nerve was severed. His opinion, based upon an examination of Simone, was that the nerve had been traumatized, but not severed. Simone v. Sabo, 231 P.2d 19, 21–2 (Cal.1951).

nervus maxillaris [NA], maxillary nerve, one of the three terminal divisions of the trigeminal nerve, passing through the foramen rotundum, and entering the pterygopalatine fossa. *Origin*, trigeminal ganglion; *branches*, meningeal ramus, zygomatic nerve, posterior superior alveolar rami, infraorbital nerve, pterygopalatine nerves, and, indirectly, the branches of pterygopalatine ganglion; *distribution*, extensive distribution to skin of face and scalp, mucous membrane of maxillary sinus and nasal cavity, and teeth—see individual branches, in this table and under *ramus; modality*, general sensory.

nervus medianus [NA], median nerve: *origin*, lateral and medial cords of brachial plexus—C6–T1; *branches*, anterior interosseous nerve of forearm, common palmar digital nerves, and muscular and palmar rami, and a communicating branch with the ulnar nerve; *distribution*, ultimately, skin on front of lateral part of hand, most of flexor muscles of front of forearm, most of short muscles of thumb, and elbow joint and many joints of hand—see individual branches, in this table and under *ramus; modality*, general sensory.

This surgery disclosed that a branch of the brachial plexus nerve network known as the lateral cord of the **median nerve** had been severed and that scar tissue had formed and was pressing against the rest of the major nerve bundle. This scar tissue appeared to be the cause of the clawing. The severed nerve serves only the thumb. Its severance would cause loss of feeling and movement to that digit alone. Luna v. Nering, 426 F.2d 95, 97 (5th Cir. 1970).

nervus mentalis [NA], mental nerve: *origin*, inferior alveolar nerve; *branches*, mental and inferior labial rami; *distribution*, skin of chin, and lower lip; *modality*, general sensory.

This nerve supplies feeling to the chin and soft tissue of the forward area of the jaw. It is known as the **mental nerve** or **mental branch**. The plaintiff's **mental nerve** was cut in the area of the mental foramen to relieve pain in that location....

... Injections at the mental foramen apparently carry a higher risk of such injury [to the nerve]. LaRocque v. LaMarche, 292 A.2d 259–60 (Vt.1972).

nervus ophthalmicus [NA], ophthalmic nerve, one of the three terminal divisions of the trigeminal nerve. *Origin*, trigeminal ganglion; *branches*, tentorial rami, frontal, lacrimal, and nasociliary nerves; *distribution*, eyeball and conjunctiva, lacrimal gland and sac, nasal mucosa and frontal sinus, external nose, upper eyelid, forehead, and scalp—see individual branches, in this table and under *ramus; modality*, general sensory.

nervus opticus [NA], optic nerve (2nd cranial): the nerve of sight, consisting chiefly of axons and central processes of cells of the ganglionic layer of the retina, which leave the orbit through the optic canal, join the optic chiasm (the medial ones crossing over to opposite side), and continue as the optic tract.

Dr. Delavasio also stated that Mr. Naylor's injuries have caused a functional blindness in his right eye, in which the **optic nerves** have simply ceased to operate. Naylor v. La. Dep't of Public Highways, 423 So.2d 674, 685 (Ct.App.La.1982).

Doctor Dahrling explained that plaintiff's visual field was less than five degrees in the left eye, which gave rise to concern about the possibility of neurologic problems in the **optic nerve**. However, he said that any injury to the **optic nerve** would be indicated by a whitening of the nerve within two (2) to six (6) months and that no evidence of nerve damage had yet appeared. Davidson & Graham Const. Co. v. McKee, 562 S.W.2d 426–7 (Tenn.1978).

nervus peroneus communis [NA], common peroneal nerve: *origin*, sciatic nerve in lower part of thigh; *branches and distribution*, supplies short head of biceps femoris muscle (while still incorporated in sciatic nerve), gives off lateral sural cutaneous nerve and peroneal communicating branch as it descends in popliteal fossa, supplies knee and superior tibiofibular joints and tibialis anterior muscle, and divides into superficial and deep peroneal nerves; *modality*, general sensory and motor. Called also *n. fibularis communis* [NA alternative] or *common fibular nerve*. See also *arthrotomy*; and *foot, drop* (both Welsh case).

nervus peroneus profundus [NA], deep peroneal nerve: *origin*, a terminal branch of common peroneal nerve; *branches and distribution*, winds around the neck of the fibula and descends on the interosseous membrane to the front of the ankle; muscular branches are given off to the tibialis anterior, extensor hallucis longus, extensor digitorum longus, and peroneus tertius muscles, and a twig to the ankle joint; a lateral terminal division supplies the extensor digitorum brevis muscle and tarsal joints; the medial terminal division, or digital branch, divides into dorsal digital nerves for the skin and joints of the adjacent sides of the big and second toes; *modality*, general sensory and motor. Called also *n. fibularis profundus* [NA alternative] or *deep fibular nerve*.

Electromyogram tests performed on plaintiff subsequent to surgery indicated involvement of both the **peroneal** and tibial **nerves** which control the upward and downward motion of the foot. Hale v. Venuto, 187 Cal.Rptr. 357, 360 (Ct.App.Cal. 1982).

nervus phrenicus [NA], phrenic nerve: *origin*, cervical plexus—C4–C5; *branches*, pericardiac and phrenicoabdominal rami; *distribution*, pleura, pericardium, diaphragm, peritoneum, and sympathetic plexuses; *modality*, general sensory and motor.

Her shortness of breath was attributed to pressure on the **phrenic nerve**, which controls the diaphragm. Badke v. Barnett, 316 N.Y.S.2d 177–8 (2d Dep't 1970).

nervus plantaris medialis [NA], medial plantar nerve: *origin*, the larger of the terminal branches of tibial nerve; *branches*, common plantar digital nerves and muscular rami; *distribution*, abductor hallucis, flexor digitorum brevis, flexor hallucis brevis, and first lumbrical muscles, and cutaneous and articular twigs to the medial side of the sole, and to the first to fourth toes—see individual branches, in this table and under *ramus; modality*, general sensory and motor.

In his opinion, claimant now suffers from an entrapment of the **medial plantar nerve** in the great toe, which precipitates considerable pain and resulting disability. Zick v. Industrial Com'n, 444 N.E.2d 164, 166 (Ill.1982).

nervi sacrales [NA], sacral nerves: the five pairs of nerves that arise from the sacral segments of the spinal cord; the ventral branches of the first four pairs participate in the formation of the sacral plexus.

An electromyogram was administered on May 8, 1979 and it revealed a nerve lesion of the fifth lumbar and the first **sacral nerve** root. Coleman v. Douglas Public Service, Inc., 423 So. 2d 1205, 1207 (Ct.App.La.1982).

... numbness over the right side of the perinium (this is the crotch area), scrotum and penis. In other words, Mr. Hart had a lack of natural feeling in and around the above described areas....
    The sensory feeling in the area wherein Mr. Hart is numb is supplied by **sacral nerves**. Hart v. Van Zandt, 399 S.W.2d 791, 794 (Tex.1965).

nervi spinales [NA], spinal nerves: the thirty-one pairs of nerves that arise from the spinal cord and pass out between the vertebrae, including the eight pairs of cervical, twelve of thoracic, five of lumbar, five of sacral, and one pair of coccygeal nerves.

It was also concluded that the left trepazius muscle, which is controlled by the **spinal accessory nerve** had hollowed out or atrophied (N.T. 105, 175). The **spinal accessory nerve** is located in that area upon which Dr. Goldman operated. Sindler v. Goldman, 454 A.2d 1054–5 (Super.Ct.Pa.1982).

Dr. Sheptak, one of plaintiff's experts, testified that the **spinal accessory nerve**, which is the eleventh cranial nerve, activates the trapezius muscle. Record at 172. See L. Wolfstone, J. Leibman, R. Bingham, & C. Parnell, 2 Courtroom Medicine § 7.20 (1975). Sindler v. Goldman, 389 A.2d 1192–3 (Super. Ct.Pa.1978).

nervus supraorbitalis [NA], supraorbital nerve: *origin*, continuation of frontal nerve, from ophthalmic nerve; *branches*, lateral and medial rami; *distribution*, leaves orbit through supraorbital notch or foramen, and supplies the skin of upper eyelid, forehead, anterior scalp (to vertex), mucosa of frontal sinus; *modality*, general sensory.

... a resection of the **supra-orbital** and supra-trachlear [sic] nerves in May 1972, but the pain persisted to the point that plaintiff discontinued work in November 1974. Cornett v. Califano, 590 F.2d 91–2 (4th Cir. 1978).

nervus supratrochlearis [NA], supratrochlear nerve: *origin*, frontal nerve, from ophthalmic nerve; *distribution*, leaves orbit at medial end of supraorbital margin and supplies the forehead and upper eyelid; *modality*, general sensory.

... a resection of the supra-orbital and **supra-trachlear** [sic] nerves in May 1972, but the pain persisted to the point that plaintiff discontinued work in November 1974. Cornett v. Califano, 590 F.2d 91–2 (4th Cir. 1978).

nervus trigeminus [NA], trigeminal nerve (5th cranial), which emerges from the lateral surface of the pons as a motor and a sensory root, together with some intermediate fibers. The sensory root expands into the trigeminal ganglion, which contains the cells of origin of most of the sensory fibers, and from which the three divisions of the nerve arise. See also *nervus mandibularis, nervus maxillaris,* and *nervus ophthalmicus.* The trigeminal nerve is sensory in supplying the face, teeth, mouth, and nasal cavity, and motor in supplying the muscles of mastication.

nervus tympanicus [NA], tympanic nerve: *origin,* inferior ganglion of glossopharyngeal nerve; *branches,* helps form tympanic plexus; *distribution,* mucous membrane of tympanic cavity, mastoid air cells, auditory tube, and, via lesser petrosal nerve and otic ganglion, the parotid gland; *modality,* general sensory and parasympathetic.

The tinnitus can only be medically corrected by surgery of the **tympanic nerve,** which surgery would result in complete loss of hearing in the right ear. Feaga has sustained some loss of hearing acuity but no functional loss of hearing. Doyle v. U.S., 441 F.Supp. 701, 706–7 (D.S.Car.1977).

nervus ulnaris [NA], ulnar nerve: *origin,* medial and lateral cords of brachial plexus—C7–T1; *branches,* muscular, dorsal, palmar, superficial, and deep rami; *distribution,* ultimately to skin on front and back of medial part of hand, some flexor muscles on front of forearm, many short muscles of hand, elbow joint, many joints of hand—see individual branches, under *ramus; modality,* general sensory and motor.

While pitching for the San Francisco Giants in 1974, claimant underwent surgery to his left elbow, which relocated the **ulnar nerve.** Sielicki v. New York Yankees, 388 So.2d 25 (Dist.Ct. App.Fla.1980).

Claimant's problem is "**ulnar nerve** subluxation with **ulnar nerve** neuropathy." That is, the **ulnar nerve** moves in and out of a groove in claimant's left elbow, which movement results in irritation to the nerve (neuropathy) with resultant tingling and numbness in certain portions of his left hand....

... He acknowledged that, particularly in view of the unusual kind of **ulnar nerve** which claimant possessed, it was possible that an accident of the kind claimant experienced might cause the nerve to become subluxated at the elbow. Funke v. State Acc. Ins. Fund, 619 P.2d 668–9 (Ct.App.Or.1980).

Damage-causing stretching or compression of the [**ulnar**] **nerve** can most easily occur while one is anesthetized (or sedated) and the body's muscles are relaxed and protective reactions to pain are eliminated (or reduced). The unsedated person whose arm is pulled pulls back, preventing stretching; one whose arm is compressed (to the point that fingers tingle)

moves his arm, relieving the compression. Holloway v. Southern Baptist Hospital, 367 So.2d 871, 874 (Ct.App.La.1978).

Other Authorities: Jones v. W.C.A.B. (First Pa. Bank), 463 A.2d 1266–7 (Comwlth.Ct.Pa.1983); Hampton v. Cristina, 362 So.2d 1180, 1182 (Ct.App.La.1978).

nervus vagus [NA], vagus nerve (10th cranial): *origin,* by numerous rootlets from lateral side of medulla oblongata in the groove between the olive and the inferior cerebellar peduncle; *branches,* superior and recurrent laryngeal nerves, meningeal, auricular, pharyngeal, cardiac, bronchial, gastric, hepatic, celiac, and renal rami, pharyngeal, pulmonary, and esophageal plexuses, and anterior and posterior trunks; *distribution,* descending through the jugular foramen, it presents a superior and an inferior ganglion, and continues through the neck and thorax into the abdomen. It supplies sensory fibers to the ear, tongue, pharynx, and larynx, motor fibers to the pharynx, larynx, and esophagus, and parasympathetic and visceral afferent fibers to thoracic and abdominal viscera—see individual branches, in this table and under *ramus; modality,* parasympathetic, visceral afferent, motor, general sensory.

Neither the **vagus** nor the recurrent laryngeal nerves were visible during surgery. However, the **vagus nerve** is visible in only 30 to 40 percent of the procedures and the recurrent laryngeal nerve is rarely seen. When the nerves are not visible during the endarterectomy the surgeon will not probe for, locate or expose them, since such manipulation may cause nerve injury. Lemke v. U.S., 557 F.Supp. 1205, 1211 (D.N.Dak.1983).

... cut the **vagus nerve** (which causes the stomach to produce acid), and removed 40% of plaintiff's stomach. Bellard v. Woodward Wight & Co., Ltd., 362 So.2d 819, 822 (Ct.App. La.1978).

... respondent operated with the assistance of Dr. Moore and purported to repair the hernia. In the course of the operation, respondent severed both branches of the **vagus nerve,** which controls the secretion of acids in the stomach. Nichols v. Smith, 507 S.W.2d 518–19 (Tex.1974).

Other Authorities: Nichols v. Smith, 489 S.W.2d 719, 724 (Ct. Civ.App.Tex.1973).

nervus vestibulocochlearis [NA], vestibulocochlear nerve (8th cranial), which emerges from the brain between the pons and the medulla oblongata, at the cerebellopontine angle and behind the facial nerve. It consists of two sets of fibers, the pars vestibularis nervi octavi from the utricle, saccule, and semicircular ducts, and the pars cochlearis nervi octavi from the cochlea, and is connected with the brain by corresponding roots, the radix superior and the radix inferior nervi vestibulocochlearis. Called also *n. acusticus, n. octavus* [NA alternative], and *acoustic nerve.*

A possible side effect of intramuscularly administered Neomycin is damage to the **auditory (eighth cranial) nerve.** Hearing impairment may result from destruction of small hair cells in the inner ear. Portis v. U.S., 483 F.2d 670–1 (4th Cir. 1973).

neural arch See *arcus vertebrae.*

neuralgia (nu-ral'je-ah) [*neur- + -algia*] paroxysmal pain which extends along the course of one or more nerves. Many varieties of neuralgia are distinguished according to the part affected or to the cause, as brachial, facial, occipital, supraorbital, etc., or anemic, diabetic, gouty, malarial, syphilitic, etc.

He noted **neuralgia** concerned itself with the fifth trigeminal nerve, which could have been caused by trauma or independent process. McSwain v. Chicago Trans. Authority, 362 N.E.2d 1264, 1269 (App.Ct.Ill.1977).

neuralgia, trigeminal excruciating episodic pain in the area supplied by the trigeminal nerve, often precipitated by stimulation of well-defined trigger points. Called also *Fothergill's n., trifocal n.,* and *tic douloureux.*

Trigeminal **neuralgia** is defined as excrutiating episodic pain in the area supplied by the trigeminal nerve, (i.e., the fifth cranial nerve). It is often precipitated by stimulation to well defined trigger points. Dorland's Illustrated Medical Dictionary 1038 (25th ed. 1974). At times talking, eating, or brushing the teeth can serve as a trigger. 1 Textbook of Medicine 612 (ed. P. Beeson & W. McDermott, 14th ed. 1975). Lurch v. U.S., 719 F.2d 333, 335 (10th Cir. 1983).

At the time of the supplementary hearing, plaintiff suffered from a facial condition known as a **tic douloureux**. This condition caused excruciating pain in the left side of his face, according to plaintiff's own testimony. He stated that the pain from this condition was constant but could be kept at a lower level through the use of medication. DeBolt v. Califano, 445 F.Supp. 893, 897 (S.D.Ill.1978).

Abraham R. Derryberry, Jr. brought this action against the defendant, Dr. Bernard C. Hollier, Jr., seeking to recover damages for injuries suffered as a result of the allegedly negligent performance of an operation for correction of the condition known as tic douloureux....

... The operative report states that the operation consisted of an avulsion of the infra-orbital portion of the second division of the right fifth cranial nerve and avulsion of the mental portion of the third division of the right cranial nerve. Derryberry v. Hollier, 334 F.Supp. 677–8 (W.D.La.1971).

Other Authorities: Hales v. Pittman, 576 P.2d 493, 495–6 (Ariz.1978).

neurasthenia See *neurasthenic neurosis* under *neurosis.*

During the fall of 1977 she had several stressful encounters with H.I.S.D. supervisors. She spent the Christmas holidays home in bed because she felt "wiped out." On the first day of school following the holidays, Scott forgot her lesson plans....

... Arriving at her classroom a few minutes late, she found her principal waiting for her. Scott was reprimanded in front of the class for being tardy. She became so upset she was unable to continue working and left for home. Her family found her in bed unable to even rise and dress herself.

She was taken to an emergency room and, several days later, was hospitalized under the care of a psychiatrist. Her condition was diagnosed as **neurasthenia**, a general term encompassing a class of nervous disorders including "anxiety neurosis." It is characterized by a group of symptoms formally

ascribed to debility or exhaustion of the nerve centers. Scott v. Houston Independent School Dist., 641 S.W.2d 255–6 (Ct. App.Tex.1982).

Neurasthenia, as used in the labeling of Afrodex, is an archaic, obsolete term used to describe a general condition of weakness or nervous fatigue. Testimony reflects that **neurasthenia** refers to symptoms rather than to specific diseases or malfunctions. The condition of **neurasthenia** is viewed as psychogenic in origin.[2] ...

... The Court also notes with interest an admission by the claimant:

As to the term **neurasthenia**, the witnesses agree that it is a vague term, susceptible of many meanings. They also agree that it is an old term, not in current use as a diagnostic term, although it has only recently been redefined as a term in psychiatry. U.S. v. 1,048,000 Capsules, More or Less, 347 F.Supp. 768, 772–3 (S.D.Tex.1972). [[2] Dr. Schoolar testified that, although the use of the term **neurasthenia** as defined here is obsolete, the term has a valid use in the speciality of psychiatry.]

Dr. Armstrong opined that plaintiff had several neurotic processes, of which the primary one was "**Neurasthenic neurosis** manifested by exhaustion, frequent fatigue and retreat from usual physical activity." Richardson v. Richardson, 333 F.Supp. 890, 894 (W.D.Va.1971).

neurasthenic (nu"ras-then'ik) pertaining to or affected with neurasthenic neurosis.

neurasthenic neurosis See *neurasthenia.*

neurectomy (nu-rek'to-me) [*neur- +* Gr. *ektomē* excision] the excision of a part of a nerve.

A **neurectomy** was performed on April 7, 1980 resulting in a residual loss of sensation on the backside of the hand. Tests performed after surgery showed that plaintiff's gross grip and pinch strength had decreased and she was continuing to have pain and swelling. The doctor felt plaintiff's pain and swelling would diminish in six to eight months eventually reaching a partial permanent impairment of 12%. The doctor was of the opinion that disuse of the hand tends to intensify the pain and recommended increased utilization of the hand. He explained that pain resulting from this type of injury was always out of proportion to the injury, but he did not feel that the pain was excruciating or severe enough to be incapacitating. [Footnote omitted.] Harrington v. Starline, Inc., 425 So.2d 307, 309 (Ct. App.La.1982).

In an effort to relieve her pain the plaintiff has submitted to two surgical procedures: a nerve block **neurectomy**.... Cornett v. Califano, 590 F.2d 91–2 (4th Cir. 1978).

Here, in addition to the leg and hip involvement Mrs. Rodenski is suffering from back pains caused by the degenerated lumbo sacral intervertebral disc, she underwent an obturator **neurectomy** which did not succeed in relieving the pain, and there is no evidence which refutes her testimony of constant pain and resultant inability to work. Ray v. Industrial Com'n, 284 N.E.2d 272, 275 (Ill.1972).

neuritis (nu-ri'tis) [*neur- + -itis*] inflammation of a nerve, a condition attended by pain and tenderness over the nerves, anesthesia and paresthesias, paralysis, wasting, and disappearance of the reflexes. In practice, the term is also used to denote noninflammatory lesions of the peripheral nervous system. See also *neuropathy.*

The plaintiff's hand as a result of the accident was severely contused on the backside of the wrist and on the thumbside of the hand. There was pain and tenderness on the backside of the hand and wrist. The plaintiff was diagnosed as having radial nerve **neuritis** with causalgic associated pain syndrome. Harrington v. Starline, Inc., 425 So.2d 307, 309 (Ct.App.La. 1982).

Undisputed testimony from four doctors, each of whom is a specialist, is that claimant has suffered a disabling physical injury, ulnar **neuritis**. Claimant now has weakness in his left hand, loss of motion in his arm, pain, and occasional numbness in the arm. Those doctors who expressed opinions on claimant's prognosis concurred that claimant will never professionally pitch again; that he is now unemployable as a professional pitcher. The medical testimony related the ulnar nerve **neuritis** to the strain of pitching. Sielicki v. New York Yankees, 388 So. 2d 25–6 (Dist.Ct.App.Fla.1980).

We may here note the distinction between ulnar **neuritis** and ulnar neuropathy with causalgia. The **neuritis** is a transitory, inflammatory condition which occurs with some frequency as a result of even moderately prolonged compression of the nerve. The neuropathy is a permanent degenerative condition, far more seldom seen. Much testimony (including some by Dr. Schramel) spoke of a **neuritis**, and assigned innocent causes, such as lying in bed with one's arms folded over the abdomen. We find the clear preponderance of the evidence is that these innocent possibilities would not explain plaintiff wife's condition of neuropathy with causalgia. Holloway v. Southern Baptist Hospital, 367 So.2d 871, 874 (Ct.App.La.1978).

neuritis, optic inflammation of the optic nerve; it may affect the part of the nerve within the eyeball (*neuropapillitis*) or the portion behind the eyeball (*retrobulbar neuritis*).

It is undisputed that both plaintiffs developed severe eye problems within a month after receiving a swine flu shot. Plaintiffs claim the condition was **optic neuritis**, an inflammation of the optic nerve, which runs back from the retina of the eye into the brain. **Optic neuritis** has many known causes and associations, including certain drugs and chemicals such as lead and carbon tetrachloride, viral problems, an autoimmune process, and toxins. It is also associated with multiple sclerosis. Plaintiffs claim here that the swine flu vaccine caused a hypersensitive autoimmune reaction which resulted in demyelinization of the optic nerve. Plaintiffs argue that the onset of eye problems soon after the administration of the vaccine, coupled with the symptoms exhibited and the medical opinions in evidence, satisfy their burden of proving causation. . . .

Defendant contends that the only probative evidence here is temporal, that the incidence of **optic neuritis** in vaccine recipients was no greater than its incidence in the general population, that there are many other possible causes of **optic neuritis**, and that the causes in these cases were vascular problems for Mr. Healy and a slow growing tumor on the optic nerve of Mrs. Grill. Grill v. U.S., 552 F.Supp. 505–6 (E.D.N.Y.1982).

Optic neuritis is a very common early symptom of multiple sclerosis. (Defendant's exhibits 32 and 35; Plaintiffs' exhibit 4.) Hitchcock v. U.S., 479 F.Supp. 65, 67 (D.D.C.1979).

neuritis, paralytic brachial See *amyotrophy, neuralgic.*

neuritis, peripheral inflammation of the nerve endings or of terminal nerves.

His only persistent health problems in the years prior to his death were a disorder of the nerves in the skin of his feet (**peripheral neuritis**).[3] . . . [[3] By 1973 this was being treated through the use of a small electric stimulator and acupuncture treatments.] Cobb v. Aetna Life Ins. Co., 274 N.W.2d 911–12 (Minn.1979).

The work the claimant was doing required him to lower metal products into a large tank containing trichloroethylene in order to remove the grease from the said metals.

He first consulted a doctor on January 30, 1959 complaining of pain and a numbing sensation in both arms and legs and occasional substernal chest pain. The doctor, after examination, made a diagnosis of **peripheral neuritis** and sent him to an internist who agreed with the diagnosis and recommended hospitalization. Hassell v. Oxford Filing Supply Co., Inc., 16 A.D.2d 534, 535, 230 N.Y.S.2d 866, 67 (3d Dept. 1962).

Peripheral neuritis is defined as "inflammation of the nerve endings or terminal nerves," Dorland's Medical Dictionary 1039 (25th ed. 1974), which can lead to loss of reflex and some loss of weight, but certainly could not be considered a threat to life itself. Blair v. Inter-Ocean Ins. Co., 589 F.2d 730–1 (D.C.Cir.1978).

neuritis, retrobulbar inflammation in that portion of the optic nerve which is posterior to the eyeball.

His examination consisted entirely of a physical examination of the eyes, plus x-rays of orbit and optic canals. His diagnosis was a **retrobulbar neuritis** in the right eye, which he explained was an inflammation of the optic nerve behind the eye, a condition that usually affects only one eye. Among its possible causes are medication, virus infection, multiple sclerosis and other neurological abnormalities.

Dr. Howard approximated that 20 to 25% of the cases of **retrobulbar optic neuritis** have no known cause. In his report he mentioned that the swine flu vaccination was a possible cause of Mr. Healy's optic neuritis; however, he explained that he was stating that not to a reasonable degree of medical certainty, but only as a probability in the absence of any other indicated cause. Grill v. U.S., 552 F.Supp. 505, 510 (E.D.N.Y. 1982).

. . . there is evidence that at least one of the chemicals to which he was exposed is a cause of or a precipitating factor in the onset of **retrobulbar neuritis**, a condition associated with the onset of Leber's Optic Atrophy. Parsons Corp. of Cal. v. Director, Office of Wkrs., 619 F.2d 38, 42 (9th Cir. 1980).

The doctor's diagnosis was **retrobulbar neuritis** of the right eye. The usual treatment for that ailment is oral steroids, which were prescribed.

Dr. Prater described this disease in this language:

Retrobulbar neuritis infers an inflammatory process of some nature that occurs along the optic nerve, that is not visible by looking at the head of the optic nerve on examination so it is made by inference. Since there is a central scotoma in [sic] visual loss the inflammation, therefore, is somewhere behind the eye along the optic nerve before it reaches the brain. [R. 145].

Asked to give the causes of claimant's disease, Dr. Prater responded:

Retrobulbar neuritis is poorly understood and to give you exact causes would be difficult. I think infection or inflammation of any type, particularly in an adjacent structure, which would be a sinus, could be a cause ... I think that it also can be caused by toxic agents, particularly the type that may be taken by mouth. I think there are also several neurological diseases which can cause this retrobulbar neuritis and the most outstanding would be multiple sclerosis....

... Dr. Ridgeway gave it as his opinion that the claimant welded with an irritating material [flux, q.v.] and consequently suffered an acute sinusitis with resultant retrobulbar neuritis and loss of vision in the right eye. Skinner v. Dawson Metal Products, 575 S.W.2d 935, 939, 942 (Mo.Ct.App.1978).

Other Authorities: McConnell v. Richardson, 321 F.Supp. 1397, 1399 (W.D.Pa.1971).

neuritis, traumatic that which follows and is caused by an injury.

neurodermatitis (nu"ro-der"mah-ti'tis) [*neuro-* + Gr. *derma* skin + *-itis*] a general term for a dermatosis presumed to be caused by itching due to emotional causes; it is also used to refer to n. circumscripta (*lichen simplex chronicus*) and sometimes n. disseminata (*atopic dermatitis*).

The Commission necessarily overlooked the fact that Dr. Jeruss' diagnosis of neurodermatitis is not the same condition, i.e., contact dermatitis, treated by Dr. Cirlin. The evidence demonstrates that the diagnosis made by Dr. Cirlin and Dr. Jeruss pertain to entirely different diseases. Inasmuch as Dr. Jeruss said that neurodermatitis was not related to cement poisoning, the neurodermatitis must have resulted from some other unconnected disease. Phelps v. Gunite Construction and Rentals, Inc., 279 So.2d 829, 831 (Fla.1973).

"In my opinion, she has a localized neurodermatitis (lichen simplex chronicus) which is neither caused by nor has it been aggravated by the conditions of her employment. It is further my opinion that she does not have a compensable disease." Norman v. Morrison Food Services, 245 So.2d 234, 238 (Fla.1971).

neurofibromatosis (nu"ro-fi"bro-mah-to'sis) a familial condition characterized by developmental changes in the nervous system, muscles, bones and skin and marked superficially by the formation of multiple pedunculated soft tumors (neurofibromas) distributed over the entire body associated with areas of pigmentation. Called also *multiple neuroma, neuromatosis,* and *von Recklinghausen's disease.*

The infant suffers from neurofibromatosis, a crippling disease of the nervous system. The parents did not want a child and took measures to prevent conception and birth because of their deep-rooted fear that such a child would be born with this hereditary disease. The child's father and the child's two sisters also suffer from neurofibromatosis. Mason v. Western Pennsylvania Hosp., 428 A.2d 1366–7 (Super.Ct.Pa.1981), complaint reinstated in part 499 Pa. 484, 453 A.2d 974 (Pa. 1982).

Plaintiff has suffered since childhood from **Von Recklinghausen's disease,** a disorder which causes tumors to grow

on the nerves, spinal cord and brain. When a tumor enlarges rapidly, it is often removed because of the danger of malignancy. Plaintiff has undergone surgical procedures for removal of tumors from various parts of her body since childhood. Lowery v. Newton, 278 S.E.2d 566, 569 (Ct.App.N.C.1981).

The boy, Kevin Sampson, who is now fifteen years of age, having been born on January 25, 1955, suffers from extensive neurofibromatosis or Von Recklinghausen's disease which has caused a massive deformity of the right side of his face and neck. The outward manifestation of the disease is a large fold or flap of an overgrowth of facial tissue which causes the whole cheek, the corner of his mouth and right ear to drop down giving him an appearance which can only be described as grotesque and repulsive. Fortunately, however, the disease has not yet progressed to a point where his vision has been affected or his hearing impaired....

... However, the massive deformity of the entire right side of his face and neck is patently so gross and so disfiguring that it must inevitably exert a most negative effect upon his personality development, his opportunity for education and later employment and upon every phase of his relationship with his peers and others. In Re Sampson, 317 N.Y.S.2d 641, 643–4 (Fam.Ct.Ulster Cty.1970).

neuroglia (nu-rog'le-ah) [*neuro-* + Gr. *glia* glue] the supporting structure of nervous tissue (Virchow, 1854). It consists of a fine web of tissue made up of modified ectodermal elements, in which are enclosed peculiar branched cells known as *neuroglial cells* or *glial cells*. The neuroglial cells are of three types: astrocytes and oligodendrocytes (collectively macroglia, which are of ectodermal origin), and microglia, said to be of mesodermal origin. Astrocytes and oligodendrocytes appear to play a role in myelin formation, transport of material to neurons, and maintenance of the ionic environment of neurons. Called also *bind web* and *glia.*

neurologist (nu-rol'o-jist) an expert in neurology or in the treatment of disorders of the nervous system.

There are two specialties in neurology, the neurologist and neurosurgeon who does the surgery. The neurologist is responsible for the care, treatment, and diagnosis of multiple sclerosis. McSwain v. Chicago Trans. Authority, 362 N.E.2d 1264, 1276 (App.Ct.Ill.1977).

neurology (nu-rol'o-je) [*neuro-* + *-logy*] that branch of medical science which deals with the nervous system, both normal and in disease.

The care and treatment and diagnosis, with regard to the disease of multiple sclerosis come primarily within the field of neurology. There are two specialties in neurology, the neurologist and neurosurgeon who does the surgery. McSwain v. Chicago Transit Authority, 362 N.E.2d 1264, 1276 (App.Ct. Ill.1977).

neurolysis (nu-rol'ĭ-sis) [*neuro-* + Gr. *lysis* dissolution] the operative breaking up of perineural adhesions.

While recovering from that surgery, she fell; during the course of that fall she applied pressure to the right hand. This event prolonged her recovery but she did return to work. Thereafter, in October of 1979, and as a result of the fall, a neurolysis of the median nerve of the right wrist was performed. Negrete v. Western Elec. Co., Inc., 326 N.W.2d 681–2 (Neb.1982).

neuroma (nu-ro'mah) [*neuro-* + *-oma*] a tumor or new growth largely made up of nerve cells and nerve fibers; a tumor growing from a nerve.

The plaintiff did undergo physical therapy for several weeks, but it was interrupted when she developed a **neuroma** of her left knee. This **neuroma** was surgically removed on January 22, 1980. Dodd v. Nicolon Corp., 422 So.2d 398, 400 (La.1982).

On June 28, 1977, Circello received severe electrocution burns of the right arm which resulted in the arm being amputated 4 inches below the elbow. These injuries rendered him totally and permanently disabled and there is no claim for loss of wages in these proceedings. On January 23, 1979, Circello consulted Dr. Harry H. Philibert, a family physician emphasizing relief from pain, for treatment of nerve tumors and multiple **neuromas** in his right arm stump. During the period of January 23, 1979, through October 10, 1979, Circello had approximately 20 visits with Dr. Philibert for this condition. The primary treatment administered was the injection of the problem areas of the stump with steroids to relieve pain. Circello v. Government Employees Ins. Co., 425 So.2d 239, 244 (Ct.App.La. 1982).

Defendant diagnosed plaintiff's problem as a Morton's **neuroma** (scar tissue on a nerve) and indicated that the **neuroma** tissue could be removed by minor surgery in defendant's office. Whitehurst v. Boehm, 255 S.E.2d 761, 763 (Ct.App.N.C. 1979).

Other Authorities: Lattin v. Hica Corp., 395 So.2d 690, 692 (La.1981). Webb v. Lungstrum, 575 P.2d 22, 24 (Kan.1978). Knott v. Califano, 559 F.2d 279–80 (5th Cir. 1977). Abrams v. Philadelphia Suburban Transp. Co., 264 A.2d 702, 704 (Pa. 1970).

neuroma, acoustic a progressively enlarging, benign tumor within the auditory canal arising from the eighth cranial (acoustic) nerve; the symptoms, which vary with the size and location of the tumor, may include hearing loss, headache, disturbances of balance and gait, facial numbness or pain, and tinnitus. It may be unilateral or bilateral. Called also *acoustic neurilemoma* or *neurinoma*, and *schwannoma*.

On April 5, 1972, plaintiff became aware that he was suffering from an **acoustic neuroma** (a slow-growing benign brain tumor), which resulted in severe injuries to him. Gattis v. Chavez, 413 F.Supp. 33, 35 (D.S.C.1976).

neuronitis (nu"ro-ni'tis) a term applied by Foster Kennedy to a disorder of unknown origin involving the more proximal part of the peripheral nervous system, characterized by breakdown of nerve fibers, sometimes in association with inflammatory-cell reaction. Currently seldom used, it was in the past one of numerous synonyms used for *acute febrile polyneuritis*. See also *polyneuritis, acute febrile.*

Approximately 20 days after receiving the flu shot, she started suffering the symptoms of the disease [Guillain-Barre Syndrome, a form of infectious **neuronitis**]. Her first symptoms were partial paralysis of her hands and feet and the disease progressed by the paralysis extending upward in both her arms and legs....

This was the first case tried under the National Swine Flu Immunization Program of 1976, 42 U.S.C. § 247b(j)(1). Overton v. U.S., 619 F.2d 1299, 1302 (8th Cir. 1980).

neuropathic See *neuropathy.*

neuropathy (nu-rop'ah-the) a general term denoting functional disturbances and/or pathological changes in the peripheral nervous system. The etiology may be known (e.g., *arsenical n., diabetic n., ischemic n., traumatic n.*), or unknown. *Encephalopathy* and *myelopathy* are corresponding terms relating to involvement of the brain and spinal cord, respectively. The term is also used to designate noninflammatory lesions in the peripheral nervous system, in contrast to inflammatory lesions (neuritis). See also *nervus ulnaris* (Funke case).

The Government, after this suit was filed, had a board certified neurologist, Dr. Gordon J. Kirschberg, examine the appellant. Dr. Kirschberg's diagnosis was that appellant had suffered a localized brachial **neuropathy** due to the swine flu vaccination. Daniels v. U.S., 704 F.2d 587, 590 (11th Cir. 1983).

Plaintiff wife had healthy arms when she entered an operating room for heart surgery. By the time she returned to her room after a week's stay in recovery room and surgical intensive care unit, she was experiencing left arm pain which heralded a left ulnar **neuropathy** with causalgia. Despite major surgical efforts at ulnar nerve relocation and autonomic nerve system excisions (including removal of her uppermost rib), she remains afflicted today with the **neuropathy** and causalgia which have caused atrophy and disability of the left arm. Holloway v. Southern Baptist Hospital, 367 So.2d 871–2 (Ct.App.La. 1978).

Examination and testing in August, 1973, resulted in a diagnosis by Dr. Snyder of peripheral **neuropathy**, "either secondary to infectious polyneuritis or some type of toxic **neuropathy**," "probable toxic **neuropathy**." A second visit to Dr. Snyder in August, 1973, showed little change in Estes' condition and the doctor recommended he avoid any job which required him to have any exposure to chemicals, "since his findings suggested the possibility of a causal relationship with his general **neuropathy**." Estes v. Noranda Aluminum, Inc., 574 S.W.2d 34–5 (Mo.Ct.App.1978).

Other Authorities: Shepard v. Midland Foods, Inc., 666 P.2d 758, 763 (Mont.1983). Funke v. State Acc. Ins. Fund, 619 P.2d 668–9 (Ct.App.Or.1980), Sears, Roebuck & Co. v. Tatum, 586 P.2d 734, 736 (Okl.1978).

neuropathy, optic

Optic neuropathy refers to a disorder of optic nerve function which may be secondary to a mass, an inflammation or an occlusion of a blood vessel. In Dr. Tenner's opinion Mrs. Grill does not have an optic neuritis because she did not show an inflammatory lesion of the optic nerve....

Dr. Wolintz' conclusion was that Mr. Healy suffered from right **optic neuropathy** of a "segmental" type. His segmental visual field loss indicated to him that a vascular cause would be the primary consideration. He reasoned that since the branches of the ophthalmologic artery are disposed in a segmental fashion, one can assume that if the visual field involvement is segmental, then one of the branches of the ophthalmic artery, called the posterior ciliary arteries, has been involved. A blockage of one of the approximately 20 branches of the ophthalmic artery causes a loss of only a segment of a person's field of vision. Grill v. U.S., 552 F.Supp. 505, 509, 511 (E.D.N.Y.1982).

neuropathy, peripheral

... they all developed **peripheral neuropathy**. This is damage to the nerves controlling the muscles of the extremities. The symptoms of this damage were generally numbness, coldness and marked tremors in both hands and legs, and an eventual loss of grip in the hands and difficulty in walking, both continuing for sometime. Ruiz v. Minnesota Mining & Mfg. Co., 93 Cal.Rptr. 270, 273 (Ct.App.Cal.1971).

neurosis (nu-ro'sis), pl. *neuro'ses* [*neur- + -osis*] an emotional disorder due to unresolved conflicts, anxiety being its chief characteristic. The anxiety may be expressed directly or indirectly, as by conversion, displacement, etc. In contrast to the psychoses, the neuroses do not involve gross distortions of external reality or disorganization of personality. Called also *psychoneurosis.*

Dr. Rosecrans diagnosed the plaintiff's injury as "anxiety neurotic" which he testified was causally related to the accident....

... In Fruehauf Corp. v. Prater, Ala.Civ.App., 360 So.2d 999, cert. den., Ala., 360 So.2d 1003 (1978), we held that if it is established by legal evidence that an employee has suffered a physical injury or trauma in the line and scope of his employment and he develops a **neurosis** as a proximate result of such injury or trauma which neurosis causes or contributes to an occupational or physical disability, such disability is compensable. Abex Corp. v. Coleman, 386 So.2d 1160–2 (Ct.Civ.App. Ala.1980).

The pertinent regulation promulgated by the Secretary, 20 C.F.R. § 404.1504(a)(2) (1979), provides that "[m]edical considerations which justify a finding that an individual is under a disability are those that bring an individual's impairment(s) under the listing in Appendix 1 of this subpart...." Among the impairments included in this listing are various mental disorders, including "Neurotic disorders" [2].... [[2] 20 C.F.R. § 12.00(B)(3)(b) of Appendix 1 to Subpart P, at 376 (1979), reads as follows: "Neurotic disorders (e.g., anxiety, depressive, hysterical, obsessive-compulsive, and phobic neuroses). In these conditions there are no gross falsifications of reality such as observed in the psychoses in the form of hallucinations or delusions. Neuroses are characterized by reactions to deep-seated conflicts and are classified by the defense mechanisms the individual employs to stave off the threat of emotional decompensation (e.g., anxiety, depression, conversion, obsessive-compulsive, or phobic mechanisms). Anxiety or depression occurring in connection with overwhelming external situations (i.e., situational reactions) are self-limited and the symptoms usually recede when the situational stress diminishes."] Crespo v. Harris, 484 F.Supp. 1167, 1171 (S.D.N.Y. 1980).

neurosis, accident a neurosis with hysterical symptoms caused by accident or injury. See also *asthenia, neurocirculatory* (Chester case).

neurosis, anxiety neurosis characterized by morbid and unjustified dread, sometimes extending to panic and frequently associated with somatic symptoms; it occurs without apparent external cause. Called also *anxiety reaction.*

The question we address in this case is whether an employee, who is totally disabled by **anxiety neurosis** which manifests itself as a phobia that his continued exposure to radioactive materials will cause death, can recover for that disability under the Act. We hold that he can....

When petitioner returned to work following his eye surgery, he began to suffer from headaches, excessive fatigue, dizziness, nausea, and feelings of extreme anxiousness and nervousness. He continued to be exposed to and come in contact with radioactive materials. Petitioner's illness increased to a point that he was totally unable to work. Martinez v. University of California, 601 P.2d 425–6 (N.M.1979).

The discovery that he had this physical condition, [a tendency to faint] coupled with the dismissal from employment and its resulting financial problems, led to a loss of self-esteem and the development of an **anxiety neurosis**, which petitioner claims is compensable as a result of the industrial injury. To support this contention petitioner constructs a causal chain: if not for the accident, however minor, he would not have fainted; had he not fainted, his underlying condition of vasovagal bradycardia would not have been discovered; had the underlying condition not been discovered, he would not have been dismissed from employment and so not suffered financial problems; without the anxiety and loss of self-esteem evoked by his physical, employment, and financial problems petitioner would not have developed his disabling **anxiety neurosis**.

To support this causal chain petitioner relies on testimony by a neurologist, Dr. Masland, who felt that the industrial episode was "contributory" to the anxiety, and a psychiatrist, Dr. Schorsch, who testified that the industrial episode was "a precipitant or stimulus to his loss of self-esteem and his following anxiety." Ramonett v. Industrial Com'n, 558 P.2d 923–4, 926 (Ct.App.Ariz.1976).

Thereafter the doubts built up, and upon returning that evening for the wake, claimant, in a state of extreme distress, examined the corpse more closely and verified that it was not that of her mother. At this point, claimant became "very, very hysterical", and had to be helped from the funeral chapel.

The hospital was called, and the mistake confirmed. Claimant's mother was alive and well in another wing of the hospital.

After this incident, claimant did not work in her employment for more than 11 days. She complained of "[r]ecurrent nightmares, terrifying dreams of death, seeing the coffin ... difficulty in concentrating, irritability, inability to function at work properly, general tenseness and anxiety." Her psychiatrist testified that "She appeared to be somewhat depressed, tremulous. She seemed to be under a considerable amount of pressure. She cried easily when relating events that occurred. I though that she spoke rather rapidly and obviously perspiring." Both her psychiatrist and that of the State agreed that, as a result of the incident, claimant suffered "excessive anxiety", that is, **anxiety neurosis**. Johnson v. State, 334 N.E.2d 590–1 (N.Y.1975).

Other Authorities: Englishman v. Faber Cement Block Co., 349 A.2d 75–6 (Super.Ct.N.J.1975).

neurosis, cardiac See asthenia, neurocirculatory.

neurosis, conversion See *reaction, conversion.*

neurosis, hypochondriacal a neurosis characterized by persistent preoccupation with the body and fear of presumed diseases of various organs.

On this reading, when he referred to Mrs. Stoleson's "**hypochondriacal neurosis**" he meant her symptoms, not the underlying psychological condition on which a traumatic event might act to produce symptoms of ill health. This usage would not be surprising. Hypochondria is usually defined in terms of its symptoms rather than its underlying psychological structure, which anyway is not well understood....
    ... "Hypochondriasis, or hypochondria, is an exaggerated concern for one's health that is not based on any physical illness, although the patient feels ill." The Harvard Guide to Modern Psychiatry 35 (Nicholi ed. 1978). "[I]t is a chronic disorder characterized by a persistent preoccupation with the functions of one's body and intractable fears that one is suffering from physical illness." Id. at 195. "Little is known about the cause, nature, or effective treatment of hypochondria." See id. at 195–96. Stoleson v. U.S., 708 F.2d 1217, 1220, 1222 (7th Cir. 1983).

neurosis, hysterical a neurosis characterized by sudden involuntary psychogenic loss or disorder of function in response to emotional stress, occurring in two types: a *conversion type*, which is manifested by disorders of the special senses or the voluntary nervous system and produces such symptoms as blindness, deafness, anesthesia, paresthesia, paralysis, and impaired muscular coordination, and a *dissociative type*, which is manifested by alterations in the state of consciousness or in identity and produces such symptoms as amnesia, somnambulism, fugue, and multiple personality.

neurosis, neurasthenic a neurosis characterized by chronic weakness, easy fatigability, and sometimes exhaustion; believed by some to be one of the psychophysiologic, or psychosomatic, disorders. Called also *neurasthenia, psychophysiologic asthenic reaction,* and *psychophysiologic nervous system reaction.*

neurosis, postconcussive

"2. **Postconcussive neurosis,** anxiety hysteria with depression, grade intermediate, as manifested by increased emotional and nervous tension, tiredness and fatigability, great circumstantiality, emotional instability as evidenced in resort to weeping, combativeness and argumentativeness without provocation, development of modified claustrophobia as manifested in continuing sensation that he is walking under a heavy beam and that he is not going to make it...." Phillips v. Celebrezze, 330 F.2d 687, 689–90 (6th Cir. 1964).

neurosis, posttraumatic

In May 1973 a consulting psychiatrist diagnosed appellant's condition as **post-traumatic neurosis** manifested by depression, headaches, weakness, easy fatigueability, impotence, poor sleep, and increased dependency on his wife. Lewis v. Weinberger, 515 F.2d 584, 586 (5th Cir. 1975).

neurosis, traumatic one which results from an injury. See also *conversion.*

"[T]he term **traumatic neurosis** implies that a person unconsciously feels the pain or unconsciously believes that they have injury; as distinguished from the term malingering, where the patient consciously attempts to deceive the examiner." Bourne v. Washburn, 441 F.2d 1022, 1025 (D.C.Cir.1971).

neurostimulator

In addition she was referred to a physiotherapist, and a transcutaneous **neurostimulator** was prescribed for her. This was a cumbersome device which Mrs. Thomasee attached to her arm at night. It sent out electric shocks that eased the pain to allow plaintiff to sleep. Thomasee v. Liberty Mut. Ins. Co., 385 So. 2d 1219, 1223 (Ct.App.La.1980).

neurosurgery (nu″ro-sur′jer-e) surgery of the nervous system.

Neurosurgery is that portion of general medicine which deals with the diagnosis and treatment, more particularly the surgical treatment of conditions that involve the nervous system, that is the brain, the spinal cord, and the nerves that emanate from these structures. McSwain v. Chicago Transit Authority, 362 N.E.2d 1264, 1275 (App.Ct.Ill.1977).

neurotic (nu-rot′ik) a nervous person in whom emotions predominate over reason.

A Sheldon Gelburd, Ph.D., a clinical psychologist associated with Psychiatric Services, reported:
    In summary, this man appears to be a chronic **neurotic**, characterized by feelings of helplessness, having lapsed into dependency, somatizing conflicts, and general regressing. He appears to be a poor to guarded rehabilitation prospect and this examiner would be surprised if he could adjust to a job, however simple. Ingram v. Richardson, 471 F.2d 1268, 1273 (6th Cir. 1972).

neurotoxicity (nu″ro-tok-sis′ĭ-te) the quality of exerting a destructive or poisonous effect upon nerve tissue.

At oral argument, Dr. Choi's counsel stressed that the literature on the **neurotoxicity** of the dye [radiopaque] is in medical journals that an anesthesiologist would not likely read. However, in his deposition, Dr. Choi said that he was aware that the dye could have neurotoxic effects. See Appendix at 332a–333a. Medvecz v. Choi, 569 F.2d 1221, 1223 (3d Cir. 1977).

neurovirulence (nu″ro-vir′u-lens) the competence of an infectious agent to produce pathologic effects on the nervous system.

The regulation governing the evaluation of monkey **neurovirulence** testing at all times pertinent to this action was 42 CFR 73.114(b)(1)(iii) promulgated March 25, 1961, which reads as follows:
    Determination of **neurovirulence.**
    At the conclusion of the observation period comparative histopathological examinations shall be made of the lumbar cord, cervical cord, lower medulla, upper medulla and mesencephalon of each monkey in the groups injected with virus under test and those injected with the NIH Reference Attenuated poliovirus, except that for animals dying during the test period, these examinations shall be made immediately after death. The animals shall be examined to ascertain

whether the distribution and histological nature of the lesions are characteristic of poliovirus infection. Griffin v. U.S., 351 F.Supp. 10, 15 (E.D.Pa.1972).

neutral (nu'tral) [L. *neutralis; neuter,* neither] in chemistry, neither acid nor basic.

neutralize (nu'tral-īz) to render neutral. See also *neutral.*

Neutralize: To remove an acid ion from a compound, producing a stable, uncharged product. In Ritter, the removal of the bisulfate ion, by either an excess of water or other neutralizing agents (sodium acetate). Ritter v. Rohm & Haas Co., 271 F.Supp. 313 (S.D.N.Y.1967).

neutrophil (nu'tro-fil) [L. *neuter* neither + Gr. *philein* to love] a granular leukocyte having a nucleus with three to five lobes connected by slender threads of chromatin, and cytoplasm containing fine inconspicuous granules; neutrophils have the properties of chemotaxis, adherence to immune complexes, and phagocytosis; called also *polymorphonuclear, polynuclear,* or *neutrophilic leukocytes.* Their counterparts in nonhuman mammals are heterophils.

nevus (ne'vus), pl. *ne'vi* [L. *naevus*] a circumscribed stable malformation of the skin and occasionally of the oral mucosa, which is not due to external causes and therefore presumed to be of hereditary origin. The excess (or deficiency) of tissue may involve epidermal, connective tissue, adnexal, nervous, or vascular elements.

nevus, pigmented; nevus pigmentosus a nevus containing melanin; the term is usually restricted to nevocytic nevi, or moles, but may be applied to other pigmented nevi, e.g., nevus spilus and Becker's nevus.

In 1971 Gail Hunter, who was then 29 years old, had a mole removed by Dr. Jacob Segura, a general practitioner in Mansfield. Dr. Segura sent the specimen to the state laboratory in New Orleans for a biopsy. He received a response some seven days later which diagnosed the specimen as "pigmented nevus, compound type," indicating it was benign or not cancerous. Hunter v. Office of Health Services, etc., 385 So.2d 928, 931 (Ct.App.La.1980).

NF See *National Formulary.*

NI See *isoerytholysis, neonatal.*

nikethamide (nĭ-keth'ah-mīd) chemical name: *N,N*-diethyl-3-pyridinecarboxamide. A central and respiratory stimulant, $C_{10}H_{14}N_2O$, occurring as a colorless to pale yellow, somewhat viscous liquid; used to counteract respiratory and central nervous system depression and circulatory failure, administered intramuscularly and intravenously.

She then administered **Coramine**, a heart stimulant by hypodermic needle, in the arm. . . . People v. Penny, 285 P.2d 926, 928 (Cal.1955).

Nissen repair See *repair, Nissen.*

nitrile (ni'tril) an organic compound containing trivalent nitrogen attached to one carbon atom, · C∷N.

Nitrile: An organic compound characterized by a triple bond between a carbon atom and a nitrogen atom (CN); a cyanide. Ritter v. Rohm & Haas Co., 271 F.Supp. 313 (S.D.N.Y.1967).

nitrofurantoin (ni"tro-fu-ran'to-in) [USP] chemical name: 1-[[(5-nitro-2-furanyl)methyl]amino]-2,4-imidazolidinedione. A synthetic antibacterial, $C_8H_6N_4O_5$, occurring as lemon-yellow crystals or fine powder, effective against many gram-negative and gram-positive organisms, including *Escherichia coli, Staphylococcus pyogenes, Streptococcus pyogenes, Aerobacter aerogenes,* and *Paracolobactrum* species; used in the treatment of urinary tract infections due to susceptible bacteria, administered orally.

Hospital records show that a urinary tract infection was observed some eight days prior to her November 30, 1977, discharge, and that an antibiotic, **Furodantin**, was prescribed by Dr. Payne of TOC. The laboratory test results placed in evidence show that the particular disease organisms present in Mrs. Wade's urine were resistant to this antibiotic. Wade v. Thomasville Orthopedic Clinic, 306 S.E.2d 366, 367 (Ct.App. Ga.1983).

Dr. Bush also indicated that in 1970 the plaintiff had taken the drug **macrodantin** and that medical literature reveals more than 100 cases of pulmonary fibrosis resulting from an adverse reaction to the drug. Harrison v. Flota Mercante Grancolombiana, S.A., 577 F.2d 968, 975 (5th Cir. 1978).

nitrofurazone (ni"tro-fu'rah-zōn) [USP] chemical name: 2-[(5-nitro-2-furanyl)methylene]hydrazinecarboxamide. An antibacterial $C_6H_5N_3O_4$, occurring as as a lemon yellow, crystalline powder, effective against a wide variety of gram-negative and gram-positive organisms. It is used topically as a local anti-infective in many skin lesions, including wounds, burns, skin infections, and ulcers; to aid healing and prevent infection of skin grafts; and in the treatment of otitis media and externa, urethritis, and eye infections. It has also been used orally in the treatment of African trypanosomiasis.

The blaze was immediately extinguished, and after the operation, **Furacin** dressings were applied to the burns, which consisted of two areas of burns, one on each buttock and each measuring about 5 inches square. The patient's hospitalization was for one week, and she was discharged 10/29/71 receiving daily dressings of **Furacin** to the burns. Holloway v. Hauver, 322 A.2d 890, 892 (Ct.Spec.App.Md.1974).

nitroglycerin (ni-tro-glis'er-in) chemical name: glyceryl trinitrate. A colorless to yellow liquid, $C_3H_5N_3O_9$, formed by the action of nitric and sulfuric acids on glycerine. It explodes on concussion, but is rendered safe when compounded in tablets with mannitol. The official preparation [USP] is used in medicine chiefly in the prophylaxis and treatment of angina pectoris, administered sublingually. See also *vasodilatation.*

He was convinced by her experience and that of several of her coworkers, who had similar symptoms, that excessive exposure to **nitroglycerin** had caused their coronary arteries to expand—much as **nitroglycerin** tablets given for the treatment of coronary artery disease do—and that the sudden withdrawal of **nitroglycerin** on the weekends had caused the arteries to contract violently. See Lange, et al., Nonatheromatous Ischemic Heart Disease Following Withdrawal from Chronic Industrial Nitroglycerin Exposure, 46 Circulation 666 (1972). Stoleson v. U.S., 708 F.2d 1217, 1219–20 (7th Cir. 1983).

During his hospitalization, one of the medications given to plaintiff was **nitroglycerin**, a vasodilatant which dilates the blood vessels to the heart and allows a greater flow of blood. Bishop v. Capitol Life Insurance Co., 545 P.2d 1125, 1127 (Kan.1976).

Nitro-glycerine is a common remedy for coronary insufficiency. U.S. v. Stegmaier, 397 F.Supp. 611, 615 (E.D.Pa.1975).

nitrous (ni′trus) pertaining to nitrogen in its lowest valency.

nitrous oxide a colorless gas, N_2O, having a sweetish taste and a pleasant odor and used as a general anesthetic or analgesic; called also *nitrogen monoxide, factitious air,* and *laughing gas.*

This is an action by Dr. Ronald Strauss (plaintiff), a licensed podiatrist, to enjoin the State Board of Podiatry Examiners of Delaware (Board) from enforcing a resolution which bans the use by podiatrists of **nitrous oxide** (commonly called "laughing gas"). . . .

By a resolution adopted on November 17, 1975, the Board announced that it had determined nitrous oxide to be a general anesthetic and, as such, may not be administered by a podiatrist. In other words, the Board concluded that the use of **nitrous oxide** by a Delaware podiatrist is prohibited by § 501. The Board then gave notice to all Delaware podiatrists that continued use of **nitrous oxide** would result in suspension of license. Strauss v. Silverman, 399 A.2d 192–3 (Del.1979).

On cross-examination Cheryl Carr testified:

It's normal practice after a person has had **nitrous oxide** that you take off the **nitrous oxide** and continue to use oxygen for a period of five minutes, to get rid of all the nitrous out of their system. I didn't do that on that occasion. I suppose one might feel, after taking the gas, a drunkenness effect. Another assistant and I have tried it after hours. We have gotten a drunken effect out of it. One would become incoherent at times depending on the amount that you took. If a person takes enough **nitrous oxide**, they can pass completely out. Simpson v. Davis, 549 P.2d 950, 954 (Kan.1976).

"no code" order

They have joined with the doctor and the hospital in bringing the instant action for declaratory relief, asking for a determination that the doctor may enter a **"no-code"** order [3] on the patient's medical record. [3 The terminology derives from the development in recent years, in acute care hospitals, of specialized "teams" of doctors and nurses trained in the administration of cardiopulmonary resuscitative measures. If a patient goes into cardiac or respiratory arrest, the nurse in attendance causes a notice to be broadcast on the hospital's intercommunications system giving a code word and the room number. The members of the code team converge on the room immediately from other parts of the hospital. In the hospital in question, if the code is broadcast at night, all doctors then in the hospital for whatever reason are expected to respond to the code. A **"no-code"** order entered in a patient's medical record instructs the nursing staff, as part of the attending physi-

cian's ongoing instructions to the nursing staff for the care of the patient, not to summon the code team in the event of cardiac or respiratory arrest. A **no-code order** is sometimes called ONTR (order not to resuscitate) (Rabkin, Gillerman, & Rice, Orders Not to Resuscitate, 295 New Eng. J. Med. 364 [1976]) or DNR (do not resuscitate) (In re Quinlan, 70 N.J. 10, 29, 355 A.2d 647, cert. denied sub nom. Garger v. New Jersey, 429 U.S. 922, 97 S.Ct. 319, 50 L.Ed.2d 289 [1976]).] Matter of Dinnerstein, 380 N.E.2d 134, 136 (App.Ct.Mass. 1978).

nocturnal penile tumescent study See *test, nocturnal penile tumescent.*

node (nōd) [L. *nodus* knot] a small mass of tissue in the form of a swelling, knot, or protuberance, either normal or pathological. See also *nodule*; and *nodus.*

He also noted, for the first time, that Tommy had a tender jugulodigastric **node** in the left parapharyngeal area. Jeanes v. Milner, 428 F.2d 598, 600 (8th Cir. 1970).

nodes, Bouchard's cartilaginous and bony enlargements of the proximal interphalangeal joints of the fingers in degenerative joint disease. Such nodules in the terminal interphalangeal joints are called *Heberden's nodes.*

nodes, Heberden's small hard nodules, formed usually at the distal interphalangeal articulations of the fingers, produced by calcific spurs of the articular cartilage and associated with interphalangeal osteoarthritis. Heredity is an important etiologic factor. Called also *Heberden's sign.* Cf. *Bouchard's n's.*

Upon examination of the hands, there was no **Heberden's nodes** present. There are indeed no deformities about the fingers. There are no contractures of any of the finger joints. There is no swelling. Byrd v. Richardson, 362 F.Supp. 957, 962 (D.S.C.1973).

node, lymph any of the accumulations of lymphoid tissue organized as definite lymphoid organs, varying from 1 to 25 mm. in diameter, situated along the course of lymphatic vessels (see illustration accompanying *lymph*), and consisting of an outer cortical and an inner medullary part. The lymph nodes are the main source of lymphocytes of the peripheral blood and, as part of the reticuloendothelial system, serve as a defense mechanism by removing noxious agents, such as bacteria and toxins, and probably play a role in antibody production. Called also *nodus lymphaticus* [NA].

Upon his advice and recommendation, Mrs. Sindler underwent surgery at Montefiore Hospital on July 6, 1971 and the growth, an enlarged **lymph node**, was removed from the left side of the base of her neck. (N.T. 26, 27). The condition was diagnosed as chronic, nonspecific lymphadenitis. Sindler v. Goldman, 454 A.2d 1054–5 (Super.Ct.Pa.1982).

In April 1974, as a result of metastasis to a **lymph node** in the left groin, Dr. Duthoy performed an exploratory operation removing 100 additional **lymph nodes** in Phelps' abdomen. Phelps v. Blomberg Roseville Clinic, 253 N.W.2d 390, 392 (Minn.1977).

Metastasis was suspected during surgery, as a result of which "all lymph glands that they could find in the axilla . . . everyone in sight" were also removed.... Lopez v. Swyer, 279 A.2d 116, 119 (Super.Ct.N.J.1971).

nodose (no'dōs) [L. *nodosus*] having nodes or projections.

nodule (nod'ūl) [L. *nodulus* little knot] a small boss or node which is solid and can be detected by touch. See also *nodulus*.

Stated another way, Plaintiff contends that the injury, which occasioned her claim for malpractice against Dr. Walton, first occurred in November of 1979 with the appearance of the **nodule** at the site of her original wound. Washington v. Walton, 423 So.2d 176, 181 (Ala.1982).

And other than for a small **nodule** in the thigh, he seemed to have made a complete recovery. The **nodule** was a little knot which is under the skin, which is palpable, and which we felt was a hematoma or a collection of probably old blood and fluid from his initial injury. The **nodule** was in the subcutaneous tissue, it was not a part of the bone and was freely movable. Insurance Company of North America v. Chinowith, 393 F.2d 916, 918–19 (5th Cir. 1968).

nodules, siderotic focal fibrotic lesions characterized by the presence of crystals of iron on the degenerated elastic tissue fibers, seen in the spleen in Banti's disease.

The witness said the **siderotic nodes**, resulting from iron oxide deposits in the lungs, could be identified on microscopic examination. Silica particles could not be thus identified, but the presence of refractile bodies under polarized light also suggested to him that employee had been exposed to silica. Dr. John Coe agreed that silicosis could not be ruled out. Dunn v. Vic Mfg. Co., 327 N.W.2d 572, 574 (Minn.1982).

nodulus (nod'u-lus), pl. *nod'uli* [L., dim. of *nodus*] a nodule or small knot; used in anatomical nomenclature as a general term to designate a comparatively minute collection of tissue.

nodus (no'dus), pl. no'di [L.] a node or knot; used in anatomical nomenclature as a general term to designate a small mass of tissue.

nodus lymphaticus jugulodigastricus [NA], one of the deep cervical lymph nodes lying on the internal jugular vein at the level of the greater cornu of the hyoid bone.

He also noted, for the first time, that Tommy had a tender **jugulodigastric node** in the left parapharyngeal area. Jeanes v. Milner, 428 F.2d 598, 600 (8th Cir. 1970).

nodi lymphatici mesenterici mesenteric lymph nodes: nodes that lie at the root of the mesentery, receiving lymph from the parts of the small intestine, cecum, appendix, and large intestine; called also *lymphoglandulae mesentericae*. See also *adenitis, mesenteric* (Incollingo case).

nomenclature (no'men-kla"tūr, no-men'kla"tūr) [L. *nomen* name + *calare* to call] a classified system of names, as of anatomical structures, organisms, etc. See also *Nomina Anatomica*.

nomenclature, Geneva system of

Preliminarily, it should be noted that the so-called "Geneva" **system of nomenclature**, from which the name tetracya-

noethylene is derived, is a standard system of identification for various chemical compounds. E. I. DuPont de Nemours and Co. v. Ladd, 328 F.2d 547, 554–5 (D.C.Cir.1964).

Nomina Anatomica (no'mĭ-nah an-ah-tom'ĭ-kah) [L. "anatomical names"] the official body of anatomical nomenclature, applied specifically to that revised by the International Anatomical Nomenclature Committee appointed by the Fifth International Congress of Anatomists held at Oxford in 1950, and approved by the Sixth, Seventh, and Eighth International Congresses of Anatomists held in Paris, 1955, New York, 1960, and Wiesbaden, 1965. Abbreviated NA.

nonosseous tissue See *tissue, nonosseous*; and *tissue, osseous*.

nonresectable

The question still remains, however, whether this Court should, under the circumstances of this case, order this boy to undergo a risky surgical procedure, which the surgeons concede will not cure him of the disease. Dr. Hoffmeister, one of the plastic surgeons who testified in this case concedes, "we would certainly leave a tumor behind. This is a **non-resectable** lesion." Dr. Maccomber, the other surgeon also was frank in admitting the limitations upon the surgeon's skill when he said: "well, you can remove—you can't get it all, this is for sure." Although the results of the surgery would be to change his physical appearance, Dr. Maccomber conceded that "he can't be returned to a normal face, impossible." In Re Sampson, 317 N.Y.S.2d 641, 654 (Fam.Ct.Ulster Cty.1970).

nonunion (non-ūn'yun) failure of the ends of a fractured bone to unite.

This stay was for the eighth operation and involved one of the newest methods of bone-healing techniques for "**non-union**" whereby electrodes were inserted into plaintiff's right leg. It was believed that the electrical stimulation of the bones would bring them back to life and allow healing. Warmsley v. City of New York, 454 N.Y.S.2d 144–5 (2d Dep't 1982).

One of the reasons for **non-union** of fractures may be improper reduction. Another possible cause could be premature weight-bearing. Downer v. Veilleux, 322 A.2d 82, 86 (Sup.Jud. Ct.Me.1974).

The employer's doctor, who had treated Lee after the accident, testified that, although the bone chip had not united, the injury had healed routinely and the **nonunited** fracture would not cause any difficulty. Upon Lee's complaints of pain, however, the doctor suggested minor surgery. Shortly before trial, plaintiff was examined by an orthopedic surgeon, who also found the fracture not to have united, but who did not recommend further surgery because of the possible discomfort from scar tissue which would be created by removal of the bone fragments. Lee v. Kisen, 475 F.2d 1251, 1253 (5th Cir. 1973).

nonunited See *nonunion*.

norepinephrine (nor"ep-ĭ-nef'rin) one of the naturally occurring catecholamines; a neurohormone released by the postganglionic adrenergic nerves, which is the principal neurotransmitter of adrenergic neurons, having predominately α-adrenergic but some β-adrenergic activity. It is also secreted by the adrenal medulla in response to splanchnic stimulation and is stored in the chromaffin granules, being released predominately in response to hypotension. Norepinephrine is a powerful vasopressor and is used in the form of the bitartrate salt. Called also *arterenol* and *noradrenalin*.

norepinephrine bitartrate [USP], the bitartrate salt of norepinephrine, $C_6H_{11}NO_3 \cdot C_4H_6O_6 \cdot H_2O$, occurring as a white or faintly gray, crystalline powder, having the vasoconstrictor actions of the parent compound; used to restore the blood pressure in certain cases of acute hypotension, and as an adjunct in the treatment of cardiac arrest and profound hypotension, administered by intravenous infusion. Called also *levarterenol bitartrate*.

"Levophed," the trade name for **norepanefrin** [sic] a substance chemically similar to the secretions of the adrenal glands, is an exceedingly potent drug used for major shock. The drug functions by radically constricting the arteries and veins and may produce undesirable side effects. Necrosis (death of tissue) in the immediate vicinity is a well recognized complication of the use of the drug. The drug and other substances were administered intravenously through appellant's right arm. Sanchez v. Rodriguez, 38 Cal.Rptr. 110, 112 (Dist.Ct.App.Cal.1964).

norethynodrel (nor"ĕ-thi'no-drel) [USP] chemical name: 17-hydroxy-19-nor-17α-pregn-5(10)-en-20-yn-3-one. A progestin, $C_{20}H_{26}O_2$, occurring as a white or nearly white, crystalline powder; used in combination with an estrogen component as an oral contraceptive, to control endometriosis, for the treatment of hypermenorrhea, to produce cyclic withdrawal bleeding, and to produce amenorrhea for medical or sociological reasons.

norgestrel (nor-jes'trel) [USP] chemical name: $(+)13\beta$-ethyl-17-hydroxy-18,19-dinor-17α-pregn-4-en-20-yn-3-one. A potent progestin, $C_{21}H_{28}O_2$, occurring as a white or nearly white, crystalline powder; used in combination with an estrogen component as an oral contraceptive.

A crucial active ingredient in Ovran, and the ingredient alleged to have caused the injuries complained of in Action Nos. 1 and 2, is **norgestrel**. Bewers v. American Home Products Corp., 459 N.Y.S.2d 666, 669 (Sup.Ct.N.Y.Cty.1982), reversed 99 A.D.2d 949, 472 N.Y.S.2d 637 (1st Dep't 1984).

normoblast (nor'mo-blast) [*normo-* + Gr. *blastos* germ] a nucleated precursor cell in the erythrocyte series; four developmental stages are recognized: the pronormoblast and the basophilic, polychromatic, and orthochromatic normoblasts.

nose (nōz) [L. *nasus;* Gr. rhis] the specialized structure of the face that serves as an organ of the sense of smell and as part of the respiratory apparatus. The receptor cells for the sense of smell (olfactory cells) lie in the olfactory membrane, in the superior portion of each nostril. In its respiratory function, the nose serves to warm the inspired air as it passes along the surfaces of the septum and turbinate bones and to moisten and filter the air. Called also *nasus* [NA].

Following surgery the plaintiff "couldn't breath through the left side of my **nose** and I was having nosebleeds and a lot of pain." She developed a sinus infection which caused headaches and a discharge down her throat containing pus. When

the swelling went down the plaintiff's **nose** "was way off to the right side of my face."

Dr. Sleeper assured the plaintiff that these were natural postoperative discomforts which would go away in time. When she pressed Dr. Sleeper about the miserable state of her **nose**, inside and out, he said that whatever was wrong with the **nose** had been caused by the anesthesiologist. A bump also appeared on the plaintiff's **nose** which had not been there before the oral surgery. In the eyes of the plaintiff's mother, "[H]er face had changed, her **nose** had changed shape ... it changed the length of her **nose** in such a way that it just wasn't her **nose**.". . .

... Dr. Wysocki also gave it as his opinion, assuming the plaintiff's **nose** to be straight and regular before oral surgery, that intubation through a nasal passage with the No. 7 endotracheal tube was a most likely cause of her broken **nose** and deviated septum....

... His postoperative notes describe his observation of "an obvious nasal fracture" and that "the site of the old fracture and subsequent deviation of the **nose** could be palpated." McCarthy v. Hauck, 447 N.E.2d 22, 24 (App.Ct.Mass.1983).

Prior to the accident, Eric had not suffered from nosebleeds or swelling of the **nose** and face, and there was no evidence of any trauma or other cause for such bleeding and swelling having occurred or developed after the accident. Hence, it was reasonable to conclude that his continued nosebleeds and swelling of the **nose** and face and the congestion of the mucosa of the **nose** were all attributable to the injuries he received when he fell from the device. Hart v. Western Investment and Development Co., 417 F.2d 1296, 1299 (10th Cir. 1969).

nosebleed See *bleeding*; and *nose*.

notch (noch) an indentation or depression, especially one on the edge of a bone or other organ. See also *incisura*.

notch, thyrohyoid

Dr. Faber made the incision in the neck at the **thyrohyoid notch**, between the hyoid bond and thyroid cartilage. Marek v. U.S., 639 F.2d 1164–5 (5th Cir. 1981).

NPT See *test, nocturnal penile tumescent*.

nuchal (nu'kal) pertaining to the nucha, or back of the neck.

The absence of **nuchal** rigidity [stiffness of the neck] in a patient who exhibits all other symptoms of a subarachnoid hemorrhage does not foreclose the possibility that such a hemorrhage has occurred. Polischeck v. U.S., 535 F.Supp. 1261, 1265 (E.D.Pa.1982).

nuclear material See under *material*.

numbness (num'nes) a lack or diminution of sensation in a part.

The **numbness** continued and covered "most of the front of the cheek on the left side; that part of the front of the cheek from the eye down to about the corner of the mouth, and of the nose on that side, and that of the lip on that side." Dr. Davenport further stated that, to a reasonable degree of medical certainty, the **numbness** was permanent. Krause v. Milwaukee Mutual Ins. Co., 172 N.W.2d 181, 191 (Wis.1969).

Numorphan (nu-mor'fan) trademark for preparations of oxymorphone hydrochloride. See also *oxymorphone hydrochloride*.

nurse (ners) a person who is especially prepared in the scientific basis of nursing and who meets certain prescribed standards of education and clinical competence. See also *care, standard of* (nurse).

Frequently, if not most often, the hospital **nurse** or other employee who is temporarily lent to the physician or surgeon, in every realistic sense continues to carry on her hospital duties. Her work is of mutual interest to both of two employers, the physician or surgeon and the hospital, and is performed to effect their common purpose. The doctrine of respondeat superior is therefore equally applicable to both employers. Dickerson v. American Sugar Refining Co., supra. Martin v. Perth Amboy General Hospital, 104 N.J.Super. 335, 250 A.2d 40 (1969). Tonsic v. Wagner, 458 Pa. 246, 329 A.2d 497 (1974). City of Somerset v. Hart, 549 S.W.2d 814, 817 (Ky.1977).

nurse, registered a graduate nurse who has been legally authorized (registered) to practice after examination by a state board of nurse examiners or similar regulatory authority, and who is legally entitled to use the designation R.N.

R.N. applicants are persons who have graduated from nursing school but have not received the results from their State Board examinations. They are given a permit to practice as a **registered nurse** and are allowed to perform the duties of a **registered nurse** while awaiting their State Board results. Battles v. Aderhold, 430 So.2d 307, 309 (Ct.App.La.1983).

nurse-anesthetist

A **nurse-anesthetist** is a nurse specializing in the giving and administering of an anesthesia (R. 169). An anesthesiologist is a medical doctor specializing in this area (R. 170). Marek v. U.S., 639 F.2d 1164, 1167 (5th Cir. 1981).

nurse-midwife (ners-mid'wīf) an individual educated in the two disciplines of nursing and midwifery, who possesses evidence of certification according to the requirements of the American College of Nurse-Midwives. Abbreviated C.N.M. (Certified Nurse-Midwife).

nursing (ners'ing) the provision, at various levels of preparation, of services that are essential to or helpful in the promotion, maintenance, and restoration of health and well-being or in the prevention of illness, as of infants, of the sick and injured, or of others for any reason unable to provide such services for themselves. Sometimes designated according to the age of the patients being cared for (e.g., pediatric or geriatric nursing), or their particular health problems (e.g., gynecologic, medical, obstetrical, orthopedic, psychiatric, surgical, urological nursing, or the like), or the setting in which the services are provided (e.g., office, school, or occupational health nursing). See also *nurse*.

S.D. Compiled Laws Ann. 36–9–3.[7] [7 The text of that section reads: The "practice of professional **nursing**" means the performance for compensation of any act in the observation, care, evaluation, and counsel of the ill, injured or infirm, or in the maintenance of health or prevention of illness of others or in the supervision and teaching of other personnel, or the administration of medications and treatments as prescribed by a licensed physician or licensed dentist; requiring substantial specialized judgment and skill and based on knowledge and application of principles of biological, physical and social science. The professional nurse may perform in addition to the foregoing, such special acts, with appropriate training, delegated by a physician licensed under the Medical Practice Act of South Dakota or by the medical staff of an employing medical facility licensed by the state of South Dakota. The foregoing shall not be deemed to include the practice of medicine, dentistry, or pharmacy.] Carlsen v. Javurek, 526 F.2d 202, 208 (8th Cir. 1975).

The practice of **nursing** is more precisely defined today. (Tex. Rev.Civ.Stat.Ann., art. 4518, sec. 5, (Vernon Supp. 1980–1981)). The statutory definition includes:

... The administration of ... treatments as prescribed by a licensed physician....

Thus, nurses can lawfully perform medical functions delegated to them by physicians. When nurses do perform delegated medical tasks, they do so with the knowledge that administering these delegated treatments is part of the practice of **nursing** and recognized as such in the state statutes defining **nursing** practice. When performing CIC as ordered by a physician for a particular patient, the nurse is practicing **nursing** as it is contemplated in the statutes. Tatro v. State of Tex., 516 F.Supp. 968, 989 (N.D.Tex.1981).

nursing facility, skilled

A **skilled nursing facility** is an institution which is "primarily engaged in providing inpatients skilled nursing care and related services for patients who require medical or nursing care." 42 U.S.C. Sec. 1395x(j). Klofta v. Mathews, 418 F.Supp. 1139, 1142 (E.D.Wis.1976).

nursing manual See *protocol, nursing*.

nursing protocol See *protocol, nursing*.

nut (nut) [L. *nux*; Gr. *karyon*] a seed element, as of various trees, usually enclosed in a coating of variable hardness.

nux See *nut*.

nux vomica the dried ripe seed of *Strychnos nux-vomica* L. (Loganiaceae), containing several alkaloids, principally strychnine and brucine. It has been used as a bitter tonic and central nervous system stimulant, and in veterinary medicine it is used as a bitter tonic and in the treatment of inappetence, atony of the rumen, and chronic indigestion.

Extract of **nux vomica** is an alkaloid preparation of strychnine which relaxes inhibitions and allows nervous stimulation. U.S. v. 1,048,000 Capsules More or Less, 347 F.Supp. 768, 772 (S.D.Tex.1972).

Nyloxin

Nyloxin is attenuated cobra venom which apparently lessens pain by deadening the nerve endings. These shots caused swelling so great in his arm that the needle could not penetrate the welts there. Shots were then given in his legs. The nurse was unable to get the medicine to flow through the needle into his left leg. Gonzales said that when the needle was inserted into his leg, it felt like acid. Immediately after the leg injections,

Gonzales became quite ill and suffered some sort of paralysis for about two weeks that prevented his leaving his bed. He experienced low back pains, numbness in the lower extremities, and developed a bilateral limp. Western Casualty and Surety Co. v. Gonzales, 518 S.W.2d 524–5 (Tex.1975).

nystagmus (nis-tag'mus) [Gr. *nystagmos* drowsiness, from *nystazein* to nod] an involuntary rapid movement of the eyeball, which may be horizontal, vertical, rotatory, or mixed, i.e., of two varieties.

Anunti was taken from the scene by ambulance to a hospital and was hospitalized initially for 2½ days, complaining of dizziness and headaches, back pains, and pain in his left arm and right leg. Following his discharge from the hospital he continued to complain of the same problems and developed, in addition, difficulty in maintaining his balance. Two weeks after the accident, Anunti was hospitalized again, this time by a neurosurgeon who diagnosed the cause of his problems as a **nystagmus** which could be related either to the labyrinthine system within the petrous bone of the skull or to problems within the brain stem. Anunti v. Payette, 268 N.W.2d 52, 54 (Minn.1978).

The toxicologist who conducted the analysis testified that 0.12 percent blood alcoholic content produces "**nystagmus**," a condition which causes "a distracting effect on the vision"; the eyes "have a tendency to wander back and forth until [focus] is voluntarily directed." Arnold v. Reynolds, 211 S.E.2d 46–7 (Va.1975).

Dr. Robitaille experienced some dizziness (positional vertigo) and oscillations of the eyeball (**nystagmus**) which were attributed by Dr. E. J. Sacks, a Navy otorhinolaryngologist, to the acoustic trauma Dr. Robitaille suffered in 1961. Guardian Life Ins. Co. of America v. Robitaille, 495 F.2d 890, 893 (2d Cir. 1974).

Other Authorities: Cornett v. Califano, 590 F.2d 91–2 (4th Cir. 1978); McSwain v. Chicago Transit Authority, 362 N.E.2d 1264, 1270, 1275 (App.Ct.Ill.1977); Denby v. Davis, 188 S.E. 2d 226, 228 (Va.1972); Ascough v. Workmen's Comp. Appeals Bd., 98 Cal.Rptr. 357, 362 (Ct.App.Cal.1971).

nystagmus, disconjugate See *sclerosis, multiple.*

Disconjugate nystagmus is definitely a sign of a small injury within the very sensitive brain stem posterior to the head mechanisms that control eye movements, and it is evidence of a small myelin injury there, and it is extremely suggestive of multiple sclerosis in this age group, suggesting a lesion. McSwain v. Chicago Transit Authority, 362 N.E.2d 1264, 1272 (App.Ct. Ill.1977).

nystagmus, vertical an up-and-down movement of the eyes.

She also had **vertical nystagmus**, that is the same kind of jerky irregular movements, but this is in a vertical plane. This was present on a lateral vision in either direction, was disconjugate, not the same in both eyes. It was greater in the abducting eye, the eye looking away from the body, than the adducting eye, the eye looking forward. McSwain v. Chicago Trans. Authority, 362 N.E.2d 1264, 1272 (App. Ct.Ill.1977).

O

oat cell cancer See *carcinoma, oat cell*; and *cells, oat.*

obesity (o-bēs'ĭ-te) [L. *obesitas*] an increase in body weight beyond the limitation of skeletal and physical requirement, as the result of an excessive accumulation of fat in the body.

Obesity itself presents as a spectrum ranging from mildly inconvenient and/or unattractive "overweight" to massive and often lifethreatening excess poundage. Its treatment likewise involves measures ranging from relatively modest dietary restriction to intestinal surgery. Above all, **obesity** almost invariably involves a complex interplay between physiology and behavior, so that the physician must perforce combine purely physiologic and medical measures with the skills of the psychologist and educator. Largely for this reason there is no "standard" treatment that will serve to manage most obese patients or even a large fraction of them. In each case, treatment must be geared to the specific problems, habits, personality, and life-style of the patient. U.S. v. Zwick, 413 F.Supp. 113, 115 (N.D.Ohio 1976).

Dr. Crowell testified (as did the other experts) that weight is lost only by restricting caloric intake or increasing physical activities so as to burn more calories than one's particular intake happens to be (15–17); that SCMC had a medically recognized use as a laxative (52) but not for treatment for **obesity**; that the ingestion of that product "in the dosages indicated on this label" would have no effect on appetite. Institute for Weight Control, Inc. v. Klassen, 348 F.Supp. 1304, 1310 (D.N.J.1972).

We find, too, that plaintiff's life expectancy is quite limited and very substantially less than average, because of his almost lifelong gross **obesity**, which has been a prime factor in causing or contributing to his many serious medical and mental problems. He has long and persistently failed to cooperate with his own physician's medical advice, which included a low calorie diet. Both of his parents died at ages substantially lower than average. The concurrence of gross **obesity** and diabetes is not conducive to longevity. Zanos v. Marine Transport Lines, Inc., 315 F.Supp. 321, 323 (E.D.Pa.1970).

object, foreign See *broach, root-canal* (Bean case); *feeding, intravenous* (Smothers case); and *hemostat* (Easter case).

On 20 November 1979, he performed surgery on plaintiff to remove a "**foreign substance**" disclosed by x-ray. He found a mass of tissue near and involving plaintiff's spleen, near the site where a hiatal hernia operation would take place. The tissue removed by Dr. Newman included the remains of a surgical sponge. Tice v. Hall, 303 S.E.2d 832, 834 (Ct.App.N.C. 1983).

Melinda Bowlin Horn, appellant, was at the time of her appendectomy on April 21, 1971, an unmarried 13-year-old. Her physician, Dr. E. H. Roberts, allowed a piece of a sweged needle that broke off during the operation to remain embedded in the thick wall of the girl's abdomen. Bowlin Horn v. Citizens Hosp., 425 So.2d 1065–6 (Ala.1982).

For about three months the pain remitted and then it exacerbated. Hart again sought the aid of a family physician.

This physician treated Hart with analgesics and prostate massage. His symptomatology of pain and bloody urination continued to worsen. In August of 1971 he was referred to another surgeon who examined him and took x-rays. The x-rays revealed a bladder stone from which a scalpel blade protruded.

Shortly thereafter Hart's urinary system became completely obstructed with blood clots. The second surgeon admitted Hart to a second hospital. A second major operation was performed and the clots, stone and blade were removed. It was established that the pain, bleeding and clots were caused by the stone and blade irritating the wall of the bladder. . . .

It is beyond cavil in this case that the accurate accounting for scalpel blades is "of mutual interest to both" the surgeon and the hospital, that such an accounting "effects their common purpose", i.e., the cure of the patient, and that the surgeon issued no orders to the operating room staff in regard to the accounting for scalpel blades which conflicted with those of the Hospital. Consequently, the operating room staff acted as servants of both the surgeon and the hospital as a matter of law.

The facts of this case which we have so tediously related mandate the application of the doctrine of "res ipsa loquitur". Jewish Hospital Association of Louisville v. Lewis, Ky., 442 S.W.2d 299 (1969). Once the doctrine is applied the jury had a right to infer, as it did, that the operating room staff failed in its duty to accurately account for scalpel blades and that such failure was a substantial factor in causing the scalpel blade to be left in Hart's bladder with attendant and protracted bad results. This negligence is of course, as chargeable to the hospital as it is to the surgeon. City of Somerset v. Hart, 549 S.W.2d 814–815, 817 (Ky.1977).

Other Authorities: Reis v. Cox, 660 P.2d 46, 49 (Idaho 1982); Keating v. Zemel, 421 A.2d 1181–2 (Super.Ct.Pa.1980); Brannan v. Lankenau Hospital, 417 A.2d 196, 198 (Pa.1980); Laws v. Harter, 534 S.W.2d 449–50 (Ct.App.Ky.1975); Bryan v. Luverne Community Hosp., 217 N.W.2d 745–6 (Minn.1974); Rothman v. Silber, 216 A.2d 18, 22 (Super.Ct.N.J.1966); Dietze v. King, 184 F.Supp. 944, 948–9 (E.D.Va.1960).

objective (ob-jek'tiv) [L. *objectivus*] perceptible to the external senses. See also *subjective*.

On cross-examination, the doctor defined the difference between subjective and **objective** findings and testified that muscle spasm was an **objective** finding usually present in a case of serious injury to the neck or back. Whyatt v. Kukura, 321 P.2d 860–1 (Dist.Ct.App.Cal.1958).

obstetrics (ob-stet'riks) [L. *obstetricia*] that branch of surgery which deals with the management of pregnancy, labor, and the puerperium.

In **Houck**, the Supreme Court, 32 Wash.2d at page 691, 203 P.2d at page 699, defines "Obstetrics" as "The branch of medicine that cares for women during pregnancy, labor, and the puerperium." . . .

. . . it is clear that the practice of assisting pregnant women to give birth to their children sought to be undertaken by plaintiff through "natural childbirth" is the practice of **obstetrics** which drugless healers are prohibited from performing . . . .

We believe that petitioner Griffith reads the language of the injunction too literally. The definition of **obstetrics** must be construed to include only the care for a woman during pregnancy, labor and the puerperium that deals with the same. Likewise, the subject order logically proscribes those practices of medicine, surgery and midwifery involving **obstetrics**. But if a drugless healer's practice includes procedures of care independent of the practices of medicine and surgery or midwifery, which constitute **obstetrics**, those parts of his practice would not be affected by such an order any more than would be the practice of dentistry to a licensed dentist. We can immediately conceive of at least two examples where the drugless healer could continue to render legitimate naturopathic services to a pregnant woman (a) in the case of a patient who has been receiving regular care and attention from a naturopathic physician and becomes pregnant; or (b) that of a female who has sought the particular type of expertise and care of a drugless healer because she is pregnant and particularly concerned with her nutritional balance and personal biochemistry. Griffith v. Dep't of Motor Vehicles, 598 P.2d 1377, 1380, 1382–4 (Ct.App.Wash.1979).

obstetrics (standard of care) See *care, standard of (obstetrics)*.

obturation (ob"tu-ra'shun) the act of closing or occluding; a form of intestinal obstruction. See also *Silver point method* and *Sargenti method*, both under *therapy, root canal*.

The final step in the root canal procedure is the **obturation** or filling of the void space in the tooth. The purpose of **obturation** is to provide a seal between the periapical tissue at the apex of the root and the oral cavity. **Obturation** is generally accomplished by one of three methods. U.S. v. Talbott, 460 F.Supp. 253, 257 (S.D.Ohio 1978).

obturator (ob'tu-ra"tor) [L.] a disk or plate, natural or artificial, which closes an opening, such as a prosthetic appliance used to close a congenital or acquired opening in the palate.

Plaintiff must wear an eye patch, and an **obdurator** [sic] is attached to his remaining teeth to assist in speaking and eating. Schwartz v. U.S., 230 F.Supp. 536, 539 (E.D.Pa.1964).

occipital (ok-sip'ĭ-tal) [L. *occipitalis*] pertaining to the occiput; located near the occipital bone, as the occipital lobe.

With posterior cervical pain she also has **occipital** [pertaining to the back part of head] headaches. Ascough v. Workmen's Comp. Appeals Board, 98 Cal.Rptr. 357, 361 (Ct.App.Cal. 1971).

occipito- See *occiput*.

occipito-parietal See *os occipitale*; and *os parietale*.

occiput (ok'sĭ-put) [L.] [NA] the back part of the head; called also *o. cra'nii* and *o. of cranium*.

While working for Brown & Root, John Fillwock was struck in the head, in the area of his **occiput**, by an angle iron which fell from scaffolding set up inside a water tank he was painting. Fillwock v. Brown & Root, Inc., 422 So.2d 458–9 (Ct.App.La. 1982).

occlusion (ŏ-kloo′zhun) [L. *occlusio*] 1. the act of closure or state of being closed; an obstruction or a closing off. 2. the relation of the maxillary and mandibular teeth when in functional contact during activity of the mandible.

Although an **occlusion** such a was diagnosed in McCall can be caused from a sudden emotion, there must be existing arteriosclerosis or a heart attack will not occur, and an **occlusion** or a clot, such as was found in McCall, would not be brought on by suddenly getting out of a pickup truck into cold water without the existence of a pre-existing arteriosclerosis disease. Community Life & Health Ins. Co. v. McCall, 497 S.W.2d 358, 363 (Ct.App.Tex.1973).

Mrs. Bohlen engaged the services of another dentist for follow-up dental work in the nature of realigning and grinding her teeth to correct the separation of the maxilla (jaw) from the cranium, a condition which had so changed her "**bite**" that her upper and lower teeth did not meet. Bohlen v. Weinberger, 483 F.2d 918, 920 (3d Cir. 1973).

"Q. Doctor, isn't it your opinion that the **occlusion** of the popliteal artery and the major occlusive disease of Mr. Lewin seriously affected his ability to withstand any infection that he had in his right leg in June and July of 1960?

"A. I am not sure that the **occlusion** of the popliteal artery was particularly important in this situation. I think that if he had **occlusions** of arteries further down, particularly in the foot, they would have had more likely a significant influence on the blood flow to those tissues which were involved in the injuries and subsequent infection and would have made it more difficult to heal.

"It is entirely possible for a patient to have a totally occluded popliteal artery and normal blood flow to the skin of the foot." Lewin v. Metropolitan Life Insurance Co., 394 F.2d 608, 612–13 (3d Cir. 1968).

Other Authorities: Matter of Iannelli, 384 A.2d 1104, 1108 (Super.Ct.N.J.1978); Henderson v. Travelers Ins. Co., 544 S.W.2d 649, 652 (Tex.1976); Brock v. Gunter, 292 So.2d 328, 330 (Ct.App.La.1974).

occlusion, coronary complete obstruction of an artery of the heart, usually from progressive atherosclerosis (sometimes complicated by thrombosis), rarely from embolism, arteritis, or dissecting aneurysm.

The doctor conceded that appellant may have had a coronary condition for many years, but in his opinion "the precipitating event of the **coronary occlusion**, the closure of the blood vessel, was the work she was doing that day"—and he never deviated from that opinion. Kirnan v. Dakota Midland Hosp., 331 N.W.2d 72, 75 (S.Dak.1983).

An investigation of thousands of attacks of **coronary occlusion** has led a majority of the physicians in the field of cardiology to reach the conclusion that **coronary occlusion** is the end result of the arteriosclerotic process and is unrelated to external events. Heart Disease and Industry, by Meyer Texon, M.D., 1954, page 283 et seq. Williams v. Fuqua, 101 S.E.2d 562, 566 (Sup.Ct.App.Va.1958).

occlusion, traumatic occlusion in which the contact relation of the masticatory surfaces of the teeth is directly the result of trauma.

Dr. Berman examined plaintiff and observed that the bridge was in "**traumatic occlusion**," i.e., that the bridge hit her lower teeth before her natural uppers hit her natural lowers . . . .

During the trial, Dr. Berman testified to the following effect: **traumatic occlusion** is one of the major causes of abscess; root canal treatment is an urgent procedure since the untreated abscess destroys the adjoining bone as it gets larger. . . . Evans v. Ohanesian, 112 Cal.Rptr. 236, 238 (Ct.App.Cal.1974).

occult (ŏ-kult′) [L. *occultus*] obscure; concealed from observation; difficult to be understood.

Sherry Bergstreser suffered an **occult** rupture of the uterus. Plaintiffs allege that this rupture was caused by the negligent performance by defendants of the Caesarean section on February 22, 1972. As a result of this rupture, Sherry Bergstreser was forced to undergo a premature emergency Caesarean section to accomplish the delivery of Brian. Bergstreser v. Mitchell, 448 F.Supp. 10, 12 (E.D.Mo.1977).

Expert testimony is necessary "where the truth is **occult** and can be found only by resorting to the sciences." (State Comp. Ins. Fund v. Industrial Acc. Com., 195 Cal. 174, 184, 231 P. 996, 1000.) Peter Kiewit Sons v. Industrial Accident Com'n, 44 Cal.Rptr. 813, 818 (Dist.Ct.App.Cal.1965).

occupational disease See *disease, occupational.*

occurrence

The medical evidence establishes that each tiny deposit of scar-like tissue causes injury to a lung. Each such insult causing injury is an "**occurrence**" for the purpose of determining which coverage applies. Ins. Co. of No. Am. v. Forty-Eight Insulations, 451 F.Supp. 1230, 1239 (E.D.Mich.1978).

oculocephalic reflex See *reflex, oculocephalogyric.*

oculovestibular reflex See *reflex, oculovestibular.*

odd lot doctrine See *disability, total.*

"Under the **odd lot doctrine**, a claimant is considered totally disabled if his injury makes him an odd lot in the labor market, that is, one capable of obtaining employment periodically but one whose services are so limited in quality, dependability or quantity that a reasonably stable market for his services does not exist. An odd lot claimant need not be absolutely helpless to qualify for total disability. If the claimant can prove that his physical condition, mental capacity, education, training, age or other factors combine to place him at a substantial disadvantage in the competitive labor market, he has made out a prima facie case for classification in the odd lot category. . . ." [Louisiana Supreme Court in Lattin v. Hica Corporation, 395 So.2d 690 (La.1981).] Gilcrease v. J. A. Jones Const. Co., 425 So.2d 274, 276 (Ct.App.La.1982).

The **odd lot doctrine** is also applicable to substantial pain cases because a worker who, due to his injury, can function only with substantial pain or with the help of fellow workers may not be considered a particularly desirable employee. Thus, if a claimant's pain appreciably limits the types of work available to him and greatly diminishes his ability to compete in the labor market, he can be treated as an odd lot worker and be awarded total disability, unless there is proof that jobs are realistically available to him. On the other hand, if a worker cannot perform the same work that he did before his injury because it causes him substantial pain, but he has the mental capacity to perform other jobs which are available, he should be considered partially disabled. Dusang v. Henry C. Beck Builders, Inc., [389 So.2d 367 (La.1980).] Lattin v. Hica Corp., 395 So.2d 690, 693–4 (La.1981).

The so-called odd lot theory was stated in Oster [v. Wetzel Printing, Inc., 390 So.2d 1318 (La.1980)]: "Simply stated, this doctrine is that a claimant may be considered totally disabled if, after his injury, he is considered an 'odd lot' in the competitive labor market, i.e., that he may be capable of holding various jobs from time to time, but that the kind of work he may perform is so limited in quality, dependability or quantity that a reasonably stable market for that work does not exist....

"... the essence of the **'odd lot' doctrine** ... is the probable dependability with which claimant can sell his services in a competitive labor market, undistorted by such factors as business booms, sympathy of a particular employer or friends, temporary good luck or the superhuman efforts of the claimant to rise above his crippling handicaps...." Fancher v. Overhead Doors, Inc., 425 So.2d 965–6 (Ct.App.La.1983).

odontoid (o-don'toid) [*odonto-* + Gr. *eidos* form] toothlike; resembling a tooth.

Dr. Sanders discovered plaintiff had also suffered a **odontoid** fracture in the neck. Simpson v. Dep't of Health & Human Resources, 423 So.2d 71–2 (Ct.App.La.1982).

oil (oil) [L. *oleum*] an unctuous, combustible substance which is liquid, or easily liquefiable, on warming, and is soluble in ether but insoluble in water. Such substances, depending on their origin, are classified as animal, mineral, or vegetable oils. Depending on their behavior on heating, they are classified as volatile or fixed.

oil, crude See *petroleum.*

oil, iodized an iodine addition product of vegetable oil; used as radiopaque medium in roentgenography of the uterus and uterine tubes.

X-rays taken at the Veterans Administration clinic in 1945 without the insertion of any contrast material showed the presence in the left antrum of an opaque substance which was assumed to be **lipiodol**, a non-radioactive **iodized oil** which was commonly used in X-ray studies. Schwartz v. U.S., 230 F.Supp. 536–8 (E.D.Pa.1964).

olecranon (o-lek'rah-non) [Gr. *ōlekranon*] [NA] the proximal bony projection of the ulna at the elbow, its anterior surface forming part of the trochlear notch.

In May 1973 claimant was again examined by a physician at the request of the C.T.A. This physician's diagnosis indicated a "healed fracture of the left **olecranon** with considerable restriction of motion" and "considerable osteoarthritis of the right knee." The physician observed that improvement would occur if the screw was removed from the elbow and the "overlying bursa resected." After discussing the matter with counsel for the C.T.A. this physician later concluded that there was no reason "why this man [claimant] should not have been able to carry on his work for a substantial period of time prior to my examination." Chicago Transit Authority v. Industrial Commission, 329 N.E.2d 198, 201 (Ill.1975).

Other Authorities: Firestone Tire & Rubber Co. v. Industrial Com'n, 390 N.E.2d 907, 909 (Ill.1979), Cinch Mfg. Corp. v. Industrial Com'n, 74 N.E.2d 872–3 (Ill.1947).

olefin (o'le-fin) [*oleo-* + L. *facere* to make] an unsaturated hydrocarbon; alkene.

Ethylene, propylene, and butadiene, related gases generally obtained from the petroleum industry, are the monomers involved in this suit. These monomers have at least one double bond between two carbon atoms in their small chains, called an olefinic bond, and are known as **olefins**. Ziegler v. Phillips Petroleum Co., 483 F.2d 858, 862 (5th Cir. 1973).

Olefin: An unsaturated hydrocarbon containing at least one double bond $(C=C)$. Ritter v. Rohm & Haas Co., 271 F.Supp. 313 (S.D.N.Y.1967).

olefin, alpha

An **alpha-olefin** is a chemically active hydrocarbon containing one carbon-to-carbon double bond connecting the first carbon atom in the chain to the adjacent carbon atom. Hercules Inc. v. Exxon Corp., 434 F.Supp. 136, 141 (D.Del.1977).

The double bond $(=)$ connecting the adjacent carbon atoms [in ethylene for example] is referred to by chemists synonomously as an olefinic bond or an unsaturated bond. Where this bond occurs between the first and second carbon atoms of the hydrocarbon chain, the hydrocarbon is called an **alpha olefin**. Ziegler v. Phillips Petroleum Co., 483 F.2d 858, 863 (5th Cir. 1973).

omentum (o-men'tum), pl. *omen'ta* [L. "fat skin"] a fold of peritoneum extending from the stomach to adjacent organs in the abdominal cavity. See also *omentum majus;* and *omentum minus.*

It was the opinion of the surgeon who operated on Kurtis that the rupture in the small intestine and split in the **omentum** (the apron of tissue over the transverse colon), which he attempted to repair, was caused by a sharp blow which squeezed those organs against Kurtis' spine. People v. Atkins, 125 Cal.Rptr. 855, 859 (Ct.App.Cal.1975).

... resection of a portion of the **omentum** of the right colon.... Zanos v. Marine Transport Lines, Inc., 315 F.Supp. 321–2 (E.D.Pa.1970).

The fecal material which had escaped into the body cavity had contaminated the **omentum**, or fat apron which covers the abdominal area, so it was removed so as to remove as much contamination as possible from the area. Insurance Co. of North America v. Stroburg, 456 S.W.2d 402, 409 (Ct.Civ. App.Tex.1970), reversed and remanded 464 S.W.2d 827 (Tex.1971).

omentum, greater See *omentum majus.*

omentum, lesser See *ligamentum hepatogastricum;* and *omentum minus.*

omentum majus [NA], greater omentum: a prominent peritoneal fold suspended from the greater curvature of the stomach and passing inferiorly a variable distance in front of the intestines; it is attached to the anterior surface of the transverse colon.

omentum minus [NA], lesser omentum: a peritoneal fold joining the lesser curvature of the stomach and the first part of the duodenum to the porta hepatis.

oncogenic (ong"ko-jen'ik) giving rise to tumors or causing tumor formation; said especially of tumor- inducing viruses. Cf. *tumorigenic.*

oncogenicity (ong"ko-jĕ-nis'ĭ-te) the quality or property of being able to cause tumor formation.

oncology (ong-kol'o-je) [*onco-* + *-logy*] the sum of knowledge concerning tumors; the study of tumors.

oncologist See *oncology.*

... oncologist, i.e., a specialist in the field of tumors.... Sherrill v. McBride, 603 S.W.2d 365–6 (Ct.Civ.App.Tex. 1980).

ONTR (order not to resuscitate) See *"no code" order.*

oophorectomize (o"of-o-rek'to-mīz) to deprive of the ovaries by surgical removal.

oophorectomy (o"of-o-rek'to-me) [*oophor-* + Gr. *ektomē* excision] the removal of an ovary or ovaries; called also *ovariectomy.*

... a partial left oophorectomy (removal of a part of the left ovary).... Gayle v. Neyman, 457 N.Y.S.2d 499–500 (1st Dep't 1983).

After the mastectomy the patient was referred to Dr. John Hurley, a cancer specialist. He recommended an oophorectomy, a surgical procedure removing Mrs. Dettmann's ovaries in order to minimize the hormone stimulation upon the estrogen receptive cancer cells. Dettmann v. Flanary, 273 N.W.2d 348, 350 (Wis.1979).

Dr. Money, who Dr. Richards has consulted professionally, states that

For all intents and purposes, Dr. Richards functions as a woman; that is her internal sex organs resemble those of a female who has been hysterectomized and ovariectomized (i.e. panhysterectomized). Also, her external organs and appearance, as well as her psychological, social and endocrinological makeup are that of a woman. Richards v. U.S. Tennis Ass'n, 400 N.Y.S.2d 267, 271 (Sup.Ct.N.Y.Cty.1977).

operation (op"er-a'shun) [L. *operatio*] any act performed with instruments or by the hands of a surgeon; a surgical procedure. See also *surgery.*

"By definition a surgical operation is a procedure carried out on a living body for effecting a cure by altering an existing abnormal state or condition, as distinguished from medical. A biopsy is defined as the removal of tissue, cells, or fluids from the living body for examination or study for diagnostic purposes." Massachusetts Mutual Life Insurance Company v. Allen, 416 P.2d 935, 941 (Okl.1965). Farmers & Bankers Life Ins. Co. v. Allingham, 457 F.2d 21, 24 (10th Cir. 1972).

The law of Louisiana is that an injured person must submit to reasonable treatment, including an operation if it is shown that the operation will alleviate the disability. Donovan v. New Orleans Railway & Light Co., 132 La. 239, 61 So. 216 (1913);[1] Welch v. Ratts, 235 So.2d 422 (La.App.1970). "An injured person may not refuse to accept treatment which the best medical advisers believe to be necessary and then claim compensation for the additional disability which, in such case, has resulted not so much from the original injury as from the refusal to submit...." [[1] The medical profession has made great strides since 1913, when the Donovan court remarked, with reference to a hernia operation, "surgical operations are not looked upon with the horror that they inspired in former years. It requires only ordinary resignation."] Stark v. Shell Oil Co., 450 F.2d 994, 997–8 (5th Cir. 1971).

There was some dispute as to whether the gastroscopic examination qualified as a surgical operation. Appellant was anesthetized and transported to a special area for the examination, occurrences which seem to closely relate the examination to the normal surgical procedure. However, if there is any distinction between the two types of procedures, such a distinction is immaterial for purposes of this issue. The same duty of disclosure obtains whether or not the treatment can be technically termed operative. Cooper v. Roberts, 286 A.2d 647, 649 (Super.Ct.Pa.1971).

operation, Billroth's 1. partial resection of the stomach with anastomosis of the severed end of the duodenum to the partially closed end of the resected stomach (Billroth I), or with anastomosis of the resected stomach to the jejunum through the transverse mesocolon (Billroth II).

After Dr. Whitehurst's visitation with the appellant, he recommended that the appellant undergo a Billroth II procedure and a vagotomy. These two procedures consist of the removal of the lower portion of the stomach and a reconnection of the small intestine to a different area of the stomach. The vagus nerve extending to the lower stomach would also be removed to further reduce the secretion of acid into the stomach....

... Testimony by Dr. Avery established that the Billroth II procedure always involved some risk of injury to the pancreas, even when the surgery is performed competently and by the best of surgeons. Johnson v. Whitehurst, 652 S.W.2d 441, 444, 447 (Ct.App.Tex.1983).

operation, Blalock-Taussig the anastomosis of the subclavian artery to the pulmonary artery in order to shunt some of the systemic circulation into the pulmonary circulation; performed in cases of congenital pulmonary stenosis.

... it was decided that Mahmood should be transferred to defendant's surgery branch for a Blalock-Taussig shunt operation. This operative procedure is recognized medically as a palliative operation, intended to strengthen the patient so that further surgery can correct the congenital defect. Johnson v. National Institutes of Health, 408 F.Supp. 730–1 (D.Md. 1976).

operation, Caldwell-Luc the operation of opening into the maxillary sinus by way of an incision into the supradental fossa opposite the premolar teeth.

The affidavits of the treating physicians establish that appellant sustained in an accident a fractured nose with severe nose bleed. A surgical procedure described as a "right Caldwell-Luc procedure with ligation of the internal maxillary artery" was performed the day after the accident. It is not patently clear how the physicians failed to exercise ordinary care in the treatment of Mr. Dobbs or how his blindness in one eye could have resulted from such negligence, if any. Dobbs v. Cobb E.N.T. Associates, P.C., 299 S.E.2d 141, 143 (Ct.App.Ga. 1983).

operation, duration of

This case, Vasquez [371 S.W.2d 119], is also authority for denying the contention of appellant that the second operation recommended for appellee was but a continuation of the first operation. The court approved the definition of the **duration of an operation** as beginning "[W]hen the opening is made into the body and ends(ing) when this opening has been closed." Texas Employers' Insurance Ass'n v. Shirey, 391 S.W.2d 75, 78 (Ct.Civ.App.Tex.1965).

operation, Elliot's a method of trephining the sclerocornea for the relief of increased tension in glaucoma.

operation, girdle stone

. . . an operation known as a **Girdle Stone Procedure** was performed in which the ball part of the hip joint was removed and the hip allowed to ride out of the socket. As a result of this procedure the leg was shortened and somewhat weakened. Bryant v. Rankin, 332 F.Supp. 319, 321 (S.D.Iowa 1971), affirmed 468 F.2d 510 (8th Cir. 1972).

operation, Heller's cardiomyotomy for relief of obstruction of the esophagogastric junction.

The appellant was admitted to St. Joseph's Infirmary where thoracic surgery known as a **Heller Procedure** was performed on February 29, 1968, by the appellee Dr. John S. Harter. Laws v. Harter, 534 S.W.2d 449–50 (Ct.App.Ky.1975).

operation, Hibbs' an operation for Pott's disease by fracturing the spinous processes of the vertebrae and pressing the tip of each downward to rest in the denuded area caused by the fracture of its elbow below.

operation, Holth's excision of the sclera by punch operation.

operation, Lagrange's See *sclerectoiridectomy*.

operation, Pomeroy's a method of sterilization in the female, in which the fallopian tube is picked up about two inches from the uterine cornua, a chronic catgut ligature tied around the loop without crushing it, and the tied loop is then resected.

Plaintiffs alleged in their First Amended Original Petition that their last child, Kirk Patrick, was born to them as the result of negligence on the part of Doctor Robert E. Shirley, Jr. in performing an unsuccessful **Pomeroy bilateral tubal ligation**. La-Point v. Shirley, 409 F.Supp. 118–19 (W.D.Tex.1976).

operation, scleral buckle See *retina*; and *sclera*.

About a week later, he felt a sharp pain in his left eye and lost all vision in it. Thereafter, it was confirmed that plaintiff's retina had detached as a result of the original injury, and a **scleral buckle operation** was performed by Dr. Taylor Smith at the Massachusetts Eye and Ear Infirmary on October 29, 1969, to reattach the retina. The operation was successful and the retina was put back into fairly good position. Central vision was not and cannot be restored. Plaintiff's vision out of his left eye is limited to counting fingers at two feet. He has lost true depth perception. Although he does have side vision, he sees double

images at night. The vision in his left eye is $^{20}/_{2300}$ or 2400 at best and he is legally blind in that eye. Hagenbuch v. Snap-on Tools Corp., 339 F.Supp. 676, 684 (D.N.H.1972).

operation, spinal-jack

The surgeon recommended a drastic or radical procedure, known as a **spinal-jack operation**, rather than the customary protracted treatment involving spinal fusion (also a major operation) and the use of a body cast. . . .

The surgeon himself had devised the **spinal-jack operation** and had performed it previously some 35 times. One of these had resulted in paralysis and, eventually, a death which was arguably related to the operation. Some four other operations had been followed by serious complications. The surgeon's procedure had been constantly improved, however, based on his experience with the earlier operations. Concededly, the surgeon was the only one in this country using his technique and at the very best it was not commonly used elsewhere in the world.

The operation performed on decedent lasted $5\frac{1}{2}$ hours. Two inches were excised from each of seven ribs, and a similar number of bony processes were removed from the spine. The principal artery, the aorta, was detached from the spine so that it would hang freely, and evidently the same was done to the vena cava, the principal vein. Other organs were temporarily pushed aside. Holes were then drilled into vertebrae to receive two screws. The upper screw was $2\frac{1}{2}$ inches long, and the lower somewhat longer. A metal bar of about four inches in length with a turnbuckle was then attached to the screws. First by manual pressure and then by wrench applied to the turnbuckle the spine was straightened. Throughout the operation X rays were taken to verify placement and alignment of the devices. The drastic or radical nature of the operation (and it has been described variously as that) is evident even from this brief statement. Further description would emphasize the gruesome character of the operation, especially, of course, to laymen. The claimed advantage of the operation is that, if successful, it is more certain of achieving the desired result and the patient is ready for normal activity after a brief period of convalescence compared with the year or longer period involved in the spinal fusion and body cast procedure, the usual treatment for this condition.

The operation was performed September 11, 1958. While still in the hospital, the boy developed untoward symptoms and on September 29, 1958 he died of a massive hemorrhage with external effusion of blood. Fiorentino v. Wenger, 227 N.E.2d 296, 298 (N.Y.1967).

operation, Thal

In the **Thal Procedure** an opening was made in the chest wall through the scar tissue formed by the incision for the Heller Procedure. The **Thal Procedure** was considerably more complicated because once entry was gained to the chest cavity an additional incision was made through the diaphragm so that the surgeon had access to both the chest cavity and the abdominal cavity. Laws v. Harter, 534 S.W.2d 449–50 (Ct.App. Ky.1975).

operation, "tummy tuck"

The "**tummy tuck**" **operation** is a procedure wherein a large patch of skin is removed from the area below the patient's navel; the skin above the navel is detached from the underlying tissue; the muscles are tightened; the skin from above the navel is stretched and pulled down to cover the portion of the abdomen that is exposed; the flaps of skin are sewn together; and a new navel is cut into the skin to which the umbilicus is attached. After the operation, a surgical dressing in the form of a cast is applied to keep the skin flat against the underlying tissue and to prevent pressure on the stitches. Stone v. Foster, 164 Cal. Rptr. 901, 904 (Ct.App.Cal.1980).

operation, Vineberg's an operation to establish a collateral blood supply to the heart, in which an internal mammary artery is implanted in the myocardium, the artery being pulled into a myocardial tunnel after blunt dissection between the muscle bundles.

The result of the first coronary arteriogram and aortic arch procedures showed that Morgenroth had a complete occlusion of his right coronary artery and a 50 percent narrowing of the main branch of the left coronary artery. . . .

. . . Thereafter, on March 6, 1967, Dr. Kerth performed a **Double Vineberg operation** on Morgenroth.[2] In this procedure, the internal mammary arteries on each side of the chest are cut open and introduced into the heart muscle, with the hope that the blood coming through the arteries will sprout into a new channel that will then connect with those that have inadequate blood supply. [[2] As to the **Vineberg operation**, Morgenroth was advised of the risks involved, including the risk of death that occurred in 4–5 percent of the cases.] Morgenroth v. Pacific Medical Center, Inc., 126 Cal.Rptr. 681, 684 (Ct.App.Cal.1976).

operations register See *register of operations*.

ophthalmia (of-thal'me-ah) [Gr., from *ophthalmos* eye] severe inflammation of the eye or of the conjunctiva or deeper structures of the eye.

ophthalmia, sympathetic granulomatous inflammation of the uveal tract of the uninjured eye (the sympathizing eye) following some weeks after a wound involving the uveal tract of the other eye (the exciting eye). The end result is bilateral granulomatous inflammation of the entire uveal tract. Called also *sympathetic uveitis*.

A third possible complication resulting from the eye injury is **sympathetic ophthalmia**, Dr. Breffeilh identified the condition as an inflammatory reaction resulting from a wound to one eye that affects the functioning of the good eye. Such a sympathetic reaction in the uninjured eye can lead to blindness. Dr. McPherson testified that such a reaction is "very rare", "it's one out of many thousands and thousands and thousands of cases". Dr. Breffeilh rejected those statistics but agreed that the likelihood that **sympathetic ophthalmia** will develop is "remote". Gleason v. Hall, 555 F.2d 514, 517 (5th Cir. 1977).

"The Plaintiff's basic charges of negligence were that (a) Dr. Reichel had allowed iris matter to remain incarcerated in the right eye following the operation, thus leading to the infection and **sympathetic ophthalmia**, and (b) Dr. Reichle failed properly to diagnose the condition of the Plaintiff's right eye in July, 1965, and having missed the diagnosis, failed to enucleate the right eye soon enough to prevent the irreversible spread of the disease to the left eye." App. Brief P. 3. McPhee v. Reichel, 461 F.2d 947, 949 (3d Cir. 1972).

ophthalmic (of-thal'mik) [Gr. *ophthalmikos*] pertaining to the eye.

ophthalmic dispenser See *dispenser, ophthalmic*.

ophthalmologist (of"thal-mol'o-jist) a physician who specializes in the diagnosis and medical and surgical treatment of diseases and defects of the eye and related structures.

Plaintiff **ophthalmologists**, practicing in the Seattle area, specialize in all aspects of treating eye disease and conditions. They diagnose, perform surgery, administer drugs, medicines and chemicals, prescribe and fit glasses and other devices, and, in short, do and perform all medical services necessary to the complete medical care of human vision. Ketcham v. King County Medical Service Corp., 502 P.2d 1197–9 (Wash. 1972).

ophthalmology (of"thal-mol'o-je) [*ophthalmo-* + *-logy*] that branch of medicine dealing with the eye, its anatomy, physiology, pathology, etc.

ophthalmoscope (of-thal'mo-skōp) [*ophthalmo-* + Gr. *skopein* to examine] an instrument containing a perforated mirror and lenses used to examine the interior of the eye.

ophthalmoscopy (of-thal-mos'ko-pe) the examination of the interior of the eye with the ophthalmoscope.

In the handbook, "Office Management of Ocular Diseases," by Dr. William F. Hughes, published in 1953, Professor and Head, Department of Ophthalmology, University of Illinois College of Medicine, Ophthalmologist in Chief, Illinois Eye and Ear Infirmary, and Attending Ophthalmologist, Presbyterian Hospital, Chicago, he states:

Ophthalmoscopic examination of the ocular fundus is important not only for the diagnosis and treatment of ocular diseases, but also for the recognition of certain systemic diseases, such as hypertension and diabetes. [Dissent.] Jenkins v. Gardner, 430 F.2d 243, 285 (6th Cir. 1970).

opiate (o'pe-at) a remedy containing or derived from opium; also any drug that induces sleep. See also *opium*.

In terms of effects, narcotics such as the **opiates** are generally addictive, running rapidly to tolerances, and causing severe physical withdrawal symptoms upon termination. U.S. v. Castro, 401 F.Supp. 120, 123 (N.D.Ill.1975).

opisthotonos (o"pis-thot'o-nos) [*opistho-* + Gr. *tonos* tension] a form of spasm in which the head and the heels are bent backward and the body bowed forward.

The child was readmitted to the Mason City hospital about noon that day. He was somewhat rigid at times which indicated **opisthotonos**, a sign of brain damage. Schnebly v. Baker, 217 N.W.2d 708, 714 (Iowa 1974).

opium (o'pe-um) [L.; Gr. *opion*] [USP] an air-dried milky exudate obtained by incising the unripe capsules of *Papaver somniferum* L. (Papaveraceae) or its variety, *album*, yielding not less than 9.5 per cent of anhydrous morphine. Called also *crude o.* and *gum o.* Various principles and derivates of opium, including some 20 alkaloids, notably morphine, codeine, paperavine, and thebaine, are used for their narcotic and analgesic effects.

Opisthotonus.

Because it is highly addictive, the production of opium is restricted, and the cultivation of the plants from which it is obtained is prohibited by most nations under an international agreement.

One researcher has summarized this addiction as follows: "Of all the drugs of abuse the **opiates** present the most complex set of problems. It is hard to motivate the **opiate** user to abstain because the drug produces a state of total drive satisfaction in the user: nothing needs to be done because all things are as they should be. At the same time, the physiological and psychological dependence force the opiate dependent person to extreme measures to obtain the drug." (Arthur D. Little, Inc., Drug Abuse and Law Enforcement, Submitted to the President's Commission on Law Enforcement and Administration of Justice, 1967, p. S–1.) . . .

The United States Supreme Court recognized in 1925 that **opiate** addiction was a disease subject to proper medical treatment. (Linder v. United States, 268 U.S. 5, 18, 45 S.Ct. 446, 69 L.Ed. 819.) Thirty-six years later, in Robinson v. California, 370 U.S. 660, 667, 82 S.Ct. 1417, 8 L.Ed.2d 758, the court again asserted that **opiate** addiction was an illness and struck down a California statute prescribing criminal sanctions for the status of narcotics addition. . . .

. . . The court's holding in Robinson has subsequently been interpreted as precluding criminal punishment of an individual because of a particular status, i.e., addiction, but allowing the imposition of criminal sanctions for the acts or use, possession or sale of contraband even though necessary to support an addictive habit, as well as sanctions for disorderly public conduct by the addict while under the influence of the addicting substance. In Re Foss, 519 P.2d 1073, 1079 (Cal.1974).

optic (op'tik) [Gr. *optikos* of or for sight] of or pertaining to the eye. See also *neuritis, optic*; and *neuropathy*.

optic atrophy See *atrophy, optic*.

optic disk See *discus nervi optici*.

optic nerve See *nervus opticus*.

optician (op-tish'an) an expert in opticianry. See also *optometrist*; and *optometry*.

In contrast [to an optometrist], a registered dispensing **optician** is licensed by the Division of Allied Health Professions of the Board of Medical Quality Assurance. Dispensing **opticians** fill prescriptions for glasses or contact lenses from optometrists and ophthalmologists (physicians or surgeons who specialize in eye care and treatment). Dispensing **opticians** do not examine eyes and dispense ophthalmic goods only on prescription. Cal. Ass'n of Disp. Opticians v. Pearle Vision, 191 Cal. Rptr. 762, 766 (Ct.App.Cal.1983).

For many years optical dispensers were known as "**opticians**" and usually confined their activities to the grinding of lenses and the fitting of spectacles to the human eye upon prescription of a physician. In the latter part of the nineteenth century some of these dispensing **opticians** took upon themselves the additional responsibility and function of refracting human eyes to determine the amount of power correction needed by the patient. Until that time it had been assumed that the refraction of human eyes was exclusively a medical responsibility. Thus, **opticians** in the latter part of the nineteenth century were divided into "dispensing **opticians**" and "refracting **opticians**." State ex rel. Londerholm v. Doolin, 497 P.2d 138, 141 (Kan. 1972).

"A dispensing **optician** . . . is a person who prepares and dispenses lenses . . . to the intended wearer thereof on written prescriptions from a duly registered physician or optometrist, and, in accordance with such prescriptions, interprets, measures, adapts, fits and adjusts such lenses . . . to the human face for the aid or correction of visual or ocular anomalies of the human eyes." [G.L. c. 112] § 73C. We think that if "lenses" in § 66 include contact lenses then "lenses" in § 73C equally include contact lenses. We further think that "the human face" in § 73C includes the human eye, just as we think it includes the human nose and human ears. We recognize that the statutes are not entirely free from ambiguity in these respects, but we think that if the Legislature wishes to treat contact lenses as something other than lenses or to distinguish the eyes from the face it must say so more clearly. Accord, Florida Ass'n of Dispensing Opticians v. Florida State Bd. of Optometry, 238 So.2d 839, 842 (Fla.1970); State ex rel. Londerholm v. Doolin & Shaw, 209 Kan. 244, 262, 497 P.2d 138 (1972); State Bd. of Optometry v. Chester, 251 Miss. 250, 259–260, 169 So.2d 468 (1964); High v. Ridgeway's Opticians, 258 N.C. 626, 629, 129 S.E.2d 301 (1963). But cf. Fields v. District of Columbia, 131 U.S.App.D.C. 346, 404 F.2d 1323 (1968) (opticians not licensed); Burt v. People, 161 Colo. 193, 195–196, 421 P.2d 480 (1966) (no violation of injunction under explicit statute); People ex rel. Watson v. House of Vision, 59 Ill.2d 508, 513, 322 N.E.2d 15 (1974), cert. denied, 422 U.S. 1008, 95 S.Ct. 2631, 45 L.Ed.2d 671 (1975) (**opticians** not licensed); Commonwealth ex rel. Kentucky Bd. of Optometric Examiners v. Economy Optical Co., 522 S.W.2d 444, 445 (Ky.1975) (explicit statute); Attorney Gen. ex rel. Bd. of Examiners in Optometry v. Peterson, 4 Mich.App. 612, 615–616, 145 N.W.2d 386 (1966), aff'd, 381 Mich. 445, 164 N.W.2d 43 (1969) (explicit statute); State ex rel. Danforth v. Dale Curteman, Inc., 480 S.W.2d 848, 856 (Mo.1972) (**opticians** not licensed); New Jersey State Bd. of Optometrists v. Reiss, 83 N.J.Super. 47, 54, 198 A.2d 816 (App.Div.1964) (explicit statute); State ex rel. Reed v. Kuzirian, 228 Or. 619, 621, 365 P.2d 1046 (1961) (**opticians** not licensed); Pennsylvania Optometric Ass'n v. DiGiovanni, 45 Pa.

D. & C.2d 245, 268 (C.P. of Phila. County 1968) (**opticians** not licensed); South Carolina Bd. of Examiners in Optometry v. Cohen, 256 S.C. 13, 19, 180 S.E.2d 650 (1971) (explicit statute). Attorney General v. Kenco Optics, Inc., 340 N.E.2d 868, 871 (Sup.Jud.Ct.Mass.1976).

optician, dispensing

For many years optical dispensers were known as "opticians" and usually confined their activities to the grinding of lenses and the fitting of spectacles to the human eye upon prescription of a physician....

Meanwhile, the "**dispensing opticians**" continued their historic functions of grinding lenses and fitting spectacles to the eyes of patients referred to them by both medical doctors and "refracting opticians." As the field of human eye care became more and more complex and thus more specialized, the **dispensing opticians** secured licensing legislation in several states in the early to middle part of the twentieth century. Kansas does not have a licensing statute regulating the practice of **dispensing opticians**. State ex rel. Londerholm v. Doolin, 497 P.2d 138, 141 (Kan.1972).

optician, refracting

In the latter part of the nineteenth century some of these dispensing opticians took upon themselves the additional responsibility and function of refracting human eyes to determine the amount of power correction needed by the patient. Until that time it had been assumed that the refraction of human eyes was exclusively a medical responsibility. Thus, opticians in the latter part of the nineteenth century were divided into "dispensing opticians" and "**refracting opticians**." State ex rel. Londerholm v. Doolin, 497 P.2d 138, 141 (Kan.1972).

opticianry (op-tish′an-re) the science, craft, and art of optics as applied to the translation, filling, and adapting of ophthalmic prescriptions, products, and accessories.

optometrist (op-tom′ĕ-trist) a person trained and licensed to examine and test the eyes and to treat visual defects by prescribing and adapting corrective lenses and other optical aids, and by establishing programs of visual training. See also *lens*; and *lens, contact*.

As the "refracting opticians" extended their sphere of influence they successfuly obtained legislation in various states recognizing their right to examine eyes for the purpose of determining refractive error. Around the turn of the century the "refracting opticians" took upon themselves the name of "**optometrists**" and in 1904 formed the American Optical Association. This in turn became the American Optometric Association in 1918. State ex rel. Londerholm v. Doolin, 497 P.2d 138, 141 (Kan.1972).

"The term '**optometrist**' means a person who practices optometry in accordance with the provisions of this act." [63 P.S. § 231] Chaby v. State Bd. of Optometrical Examiners, 386 A.2d 1071, 1073–4 (Commonwlth.Ct.Pa.1978).

An **optometrist**, say the opthalmologists, is not authorized to use drugs for dilation of the eye, and no matter how highly trained an **optometrist** may be, he will be unable to detect many diseases of the eye without dilating the pupil with eyedrops....

... He said that RCW 18.53.100(14) contemplates that licensing of **optometrists** means the capability "to demonstrate in manner satisfactory to the director, their practical ability to correctly measure eyes, fit glasses, adjust frames and neutralize lenses correctly." Ketcham v. King County Medical Service Corp., 502 P.2d 1197, 1201–2 (Wash.1972).

optometry (op-tom′ĕ-tre) measurement of the powers of vision and the adaptation of prisms or lenses for the aid thereof, utilizing any means other than drugs. See also *optometrist*.

Optometrists in California are licensed and regulated by the Board. **Optometry** is regarded as a learned profession. To become licensed as an optometrist an individual must have at least three years of undergraduate education in a scientific field and four years of optometry school culminating in a doctor of **optometry** degree. Upon admission to practice, optometrists are allowed to correct refractive errors and to detect eye disease. Most optometrists also dispense ophthalmic products consisting of eye glasses and contact lenses. Cal. Ass'n of Disp. Opticians v. Pearle Vision, 191 Cal.Rptr. 762, 765–6 (Ct.App.1983).

Other Authorities: Simpson v. Wilson, 480 F.Supp. 97, 101–2 (D.Vt.1979); State ex rel. State, Etc. v. Kuhwald, 389 A.2d 1277, 1278 (Del.1978); Chaby v. State Bd. of Optometrical Examiners, 386 A.2d 1071, 1073–4 (Commonwlth Ct.Pa. 1978); Steele v. U.S., 463 F.Supp. 321, 330 (D.Alas.1978); Attorney General v. Kenco Optics, Inc., 340 N.E.2d 868, 870–1 (Sup.Jud.Ct.Mass.1976); Commonwealth, Etc. v. Economy Optical Co., 522 S.W.2d 444, 445–6 (Ky.1975); People ex rel. Watson v. House of Vision, 322 N.E.2d 15, 16–19 (Ill. 1974); State ex Inf. Danforth v. Dale Curteman, Inc., 480 S.W.2d 848, 851 (Mo.1972); State ex rel. Londerholm v. Doolin, 497 P.2d 138, 149 (Kan.1972).

ora (o′rah), pl. *o′rae* [L.] an edge or margin.

The pellets entered the eve through the conjunctivia: passed through the cornea, the lens at its margin, the vitreous, and the retina; and came to rest on the **ora**. Gleason v. Hall, 555 F.2d 514, 516 (5th Cir. 1977).

oral surgery See *surgery, oral*.

orbiculare See *processus lenticularis incudis*.

orchiectomy (or″ke-ek′to-me) [*orchio-* + Gr. *ektomē* excision] excision of one or both testes.

The day after his admission to the hospital Stanley's scrotal sac ruptured. This rupture was enlarged by Lee so that the old blood contained within Stanley's scrotal sac could drain. However, the swelling had not diminished significantly by March 5. Fisher then informed Stanley that Lee would lance his scrotum to drain all of the blood which was within it. However, on the same afternoon Lee informed Stanley that an **orchiectomy** would have to be performed, and this operation took place on March 9th. Stanley v. Fisher, 417 N.E.2d 932–3 (Ct. App.Ind.1981).

... an **orchiectomy**, an excision of the left testis and complete excision of the cord, was performed at the prison hospital of the Texas Department of Corrections. Sawyer v. Sigler, 320 F.Supp. 690, 694 (D.Neb.1970).

orchiopexy (or″ke-o-pek′se) [*orchio-* + Gr. *Pēxis* fixation] surgical fixation in the scrotum of an undescended testis.

During the examination, decedent informed Dr. Stish that the physician who examined decedent for Foster after his injury had recommended that decedent undergo a bilateral **orchiopexy** to correct a congenital defect of undescended testis. Foster Wheeler Energy Corp. v. Ustonofski, 417 A.2d 1334–5 (Commonwealth Ct.Pa.1980).

order not to resuscitate See *"no code" order.*

organoleptic (or"gah-no-lep′tik) [*organo- + *Gr. *lambanein* to seize] 1. making an impression on an organ of special sense. 2. capable of receiving a sense impression.

To some extent, all of us have God-given **organoleptic** expertise. We exercise the powers of sight, smell, taste and feel to reject unpalatable food. As used in food and drug matters, the **organoleptic** test is a mere refinement in that people can be trained to detect why the food is offensive. . . .

. . . but in the final result, the **organoleptic** examination is not far removed from that daily performed by the housewife. If the food smells bad, she rejects it. And yet, it is generally approved by the most exacting of scientists as proper. More importantly, in civil cases, it has been recognized by the courts for at least 50 years. United States v. 443 Cans of Frogen Egg Product, 193 F. 589 (3rd Cir. 1912); Knapp v. Callaway, 52 F.2d 476 (S.D.N.Y.1931); United States v. 284 Barrels of Dried Eggs, 52 F.Supp. 661 (W.D.Tenn.1943); United States v. 1851 Cartons, etc., 55 F.Supp. 343 (D.Colo.1944); United States v. 310 Cans, More or Less, etc., 170 F.Supp. 16 (N.D. Ill.1959); United States v. Ocean Perch Fillets, 196 F.Supp. 255 (D.Maine 1961) [Footnote omitted.]. . . . U.S. v. 1,200 Cans, Pasteurized Whole Eggs, 339 F.Supp. 131, 137–8 (N.D. Ga.1972).

organophosphate (or"gan-o-fos′fāt) phosphate esterified to organic compounds such as glucose or sorbitol. See also *organophosphorus.*

The Growers argue that there is a substantial and significant difference in the toxicity per se of an organophosphorous pesticide and that of any of its residues that may remain on sprayed foliage, because the **organophosphates** start to decompose rapidly immediately upon application. They, therefore, challenge the Secretary's citation of sources cataloging the symptoms of severe **organophosphate** poisoning, because they describe the afflictions of persons having primary contact with pure or active **organophosphates**. . . .

. . . From time to time a group of workers will experience nausea, excessive salivation and perspiration, blurred vision, abdominal cramps, vomiting, and diarrhea, in approximately that sequence. There is substantial evidence that farmworkers occupationally exposed to **organophosphate** residues on foliage may experience headache, fatigue, and vertigo. . . .

. . . A severe case of **organophosphate** poisoning may result in tremors, paroxysmal tachycardia (abrupt attacks of excessively rapid heart action), respiratory difficulty, convulsions, pinpoint pupils, pulmonary edema (effusion of serous fluid into the lungs), collapse, and coma. The toxicity of the **organophosphates** results from inhibition of the enzyme cholinesterase, which plays an important role in the appropriate cessation of nerve impulse transmission. In this they are similar to agents of chemical warfare ("nerve gas"). Absorption can occur through the eyes, the unbroken skin, and the respiratory

and intestinal tracts. Florida Peach Grow. Ass'n v. U.S. Dept. of Lab., 489 F.2d 120, 131–2 (5th Cir. 1974).

organophosphorus (or"gah-no-fos′fō-rus) a compound containing phosphorus bound to an organic molecule; many organophosphorus compounds are powerful acetylcholinesterase inhibitors and are used as insecticides.

organum (or′gah-num), pl. *or′gana* [L.] [NA] an organ: a somewhat independent part of the body that is arranged according to a characteristic structural plan, and performs a special function or functions; it is composed of various tissues, one of which is primary in function Called also *organon.*

organa genitalia feminina [NA], female genital organs: the various organs in the female that are concerned with reproduction, including the ovary, uterine tube, uterus, vagina, labia, and clitoris. Called also *organa genitalia muliebria.* See illustration accompanying *system.*

As Dr. DiVincenti testified, during the operation he was able to see and examine plaintiff's **reproductive organs**, including both ovaries, her fallopian tubes and her uterus. Baker v. Beebe, 367 So.2d 102, 104 (Ct.App.La.1979).

oropharyngeal See *oropharynx.*

oropharynx (o"ro-far′inks) [*oro-*(1) + *pharynx*] that division of the pharynx which lies between the soft palate and the upper edge of the epiglottis (pars oralis pharyngis [NA]).

She inserted an **oropharyngeal** airway and maintained anesthesia with cyclopropane and oxygen. Burrow v. Widder, 368 N.E.2d 443, 446 (App.Ct. of Ill.1977).

orthocephalic (or"tho-sĕ-fal′ik) [Gr. *orthos* straight + *kephalē* head] having a head with a vertical index of 70.1 to 75.

Dr. Marlowe examined plaintiff again in December, 1975, and found him to have dyspnea on exertion and to be "four pillow **orthocephalic.**" (Tr. p. 192.) Plaintiff testified that he had to sleep propped upright on pillows in order to avoid the "smothering" feeling. McDaniel v. Califano, 446 F.Supp. 1080, 1082 (W.D.N.C.1978).

orthodontia See *orthodontics*; and *positioner.*

orthodontics (or"tho-don′tiks) [*ortho- + Gr. *odous* tooth] that branch of dentistry which deals with the development, prevention, and correction of irregularities of the teeth and malocclusion, and with associated facial abnormalities.

The patents in issue relate to that branch of dentistry known as **orthodontia** which is concerned with the straightening of irregular teeth. T.P. Laboratories, Inc. v. Huge, 261 F.Supp. 349, 350 (E.D.Wis.1965).

Ortho-Novum

Ortho is a New Jersey corporation which manufactures an oral contraceptive called **Ortho-Novum**. This drug is used principally for birth control purposes and is obtainable only by prescription. . . .

... Although the numbness and tingling sensations were not then as severe as before, she had developed some brown facial blotches. Because of the blotches, Dr. Harris advised plaintiff to stop using **Ortho-Novum** and recommended instead the use of a diaphragm. Lindsay v. Ortho Pharmaceutical Corp., 637 F.2d 87, 89–90 (2d Cir. 1980).

Ortho manufactures pharmaceutical products, including **Ortho-Novum**. This product is a combination of a progestational compound, norethindrone, and an estrogenic compound, mestranol, which was tested and shown to be effective and reliable for the prevention of conception....

The 1964 Physicians' Desk Reference (PDR) listed the following precautionary note with regard to the prescription of **ORTHO-NOVUM**: "Physicians should be alert to the possible occurrence of thrombophlebitis or phlebothrombosis in patients to whom **ORTHO-NOVUM** is prescribed, even though a causal relationship has not been proved or disproved. This possibility should be given particular attention if **ORTHO-NOVUM** is considered for administration to patients with thrombo-embolic disease or a history of thrombophlebitis." Leibowitz v. Ortho Pharmaceutical Corp., 307 A.2d 449, 451–2 (Super.Ct.Pa.1973).

orthopedic (or"tho-pe'dik) [ortho- + Gr. pais child] pertaining to the correction of deformities of the musculoskeletal system; pertaining to orthopedics.

... the injured child had sustained a permanent injury to his leg which would result in his left leg being shorter than his right leg for the remainder of his natural life and that he would be required to wear an **orthopedic** shoe or a shoe with a lift built under the shoe in order to compensate for the difference in leg lengths. Campbell v. Government Employees Ins. Co., 306 So. 2d 525, 528 (Fla.1974).

orthopedics (or"tho-pe'diks) [ortho- + Gr. pais child] that branch of surgery which is specially concerned with the preservation and restoration of the function of the skeletal system, its articulations and associated structures.

The field of **orthopedics** relates to the field of prosthetics in that the orthopedic surgeon amputates and the prosthetist replaces the amputated part or organ. Daw Industries, Inc. v. U.S., 561 F.Supp. 433, 435 (U.S.Ct.Int.Trade 1983), reversed 714 F.2d 1140 (Fed.Cir.1983).

Other Authorities: Sandford v. Howard, 288 S.E.2d 739–40 (Ct.App.Ga.1982); Employers Mut. L. Ins. Co. of Wis. v. Industrial Com'n, 500 P.2d 308, 311 (Ct.App.Ariz.1972), opinion vacated, commission award reinstated 109 Ariz. 383, 509 P.2d 1030 (Ariz.1973).

orthopnea (or"thop-ne'ah) [ortho- + Gr. pnoia breath] difficult breathing except in an upright position. Cf. *platypnea*.

He disputed Dr. Goodman's analysis of **orthopnea**—difficulty in breathing while lying down. Barbato v. Alsan Masonry & Concrete, Inc., 318 A.2d 1, 3 (N.J.1974).

Other Authorities: Dir., Office of Workers' Comp. Programs v. Rowe, 710 F.2d 251, 254 (6th Cir. 1983).

os (os), gen. *os'sis*, pl. *os'sa* [L.] bone; [NA] a general term which is qualified by the appropriate adjective to designate a specific type of bony structure or a specific segment of the skeleton.

os calcis NA alternative of *calcaneus*.

os carpal See *ossa carpi*.

ossa carpi [NA], carpal bones: the eight bones of the wrist (carpus), including the o. capitatum, o. hamatum, o. lunatum, o. pisiforme, o. scaphoideum, o. trapezium, o. trapezoideum, and o. triquetrum.

Dr. Gleason described the injuries "... exquisite swelling and tenderness ... crushed fracture of the multangular (**carpal**) bone of the wrist." Anderson v. Safeco Ins. Co., 396 So.2d 322, 324 (Ct.App.La.1981).

os centrale [NA], central bone: an accessory bone sometimes found on the back of the carpus.

os cuneiforme mediale [NA], medial cuneiform bone: the medial and largest of the three wedge-shaped tarsal bones located medial to the cuboid and between the navicular and the first three metatarsal bones; called also *o. cuneiforme primum*.

In late 1974 he had an arthrodesis of the first **coneiform** bone with the first metatarsal. The claimant was walking with a mildly elevated right shoe with an ankle brace without motion being present and as of December 15, 1975, he was still in a surgical boot. The diagnosis as of December 15, 1975 was status postoperative ankle fusion with triple arthrodesis of the right foot....

... painful partial stiffening navicular **cuneiform** joint right foot. Minney v. Secretary of Health, Ed. & Welfare, 439 F.Supp. 706, 707 (W.D.Ark.1977).

os cuneiforme primum See *os cuneiforme mediale*.

ossa digitorum pedis [NA], the 14 bones that compose the skeleton of the toes; called also *phalanges digitorum pedis* or *phalanges of toes*.

os ethmoidale [NA], ethmoid bone: the cubical bone located between the orbits and consisting of the lamina cribrosa, the lamina perpendicularis, and the paired lateral masses.

os frontale [NA], frontal bone: a single bone that closes the front part of the cranial cavity and forms the skeleton of the forehead; it is developed from two halves, the line of separation sometimes persisting in adult life.

os, internal

... in order to effect an abortion by instrumentation the internal os (mouth of womb) would have to be entered.... Russo v. Commonwealth, 148 S.E.2d 820, 824 (Va.1966).

os lunatum [NA], lunate bone: the bone in the proximal row of carpal bones lying between the scaphoid and triquetral bones.

... the record contains sufficient evidence from which the referee and Board could conclude that Muniz suffered an aseptic necrosis of the **carpal lunate** in the right wrist, which is the death of bone in the wrist, frequently occurring about six months (or later) after a "crush-type" injury. United States Steel Corp. v. Workmen's Comp.App.Bd., 308 A.2d 200–1 (Commonwealth Ct.Pa.1973).

ossa metacarpalia I–V [NA], metacarpal bones: the five cylindric bones of the hand, articulating proximally with bones of the carpus and distally with the proximal phalanges of the fingers; numbered from that articulating with the proximal phalanx of the thumb to the most lateral one, articulating with the proximal phalanx of the little finger. *Os metacarpale III*, the middle metacarpal bone, is characterized by the presence of the styloid process at its base.

... dislocation of the index **metacarpal** ... [surgically] reduced by [inserting] a pin [and] K-wire...." Anderson v. Safeco Ins. Co., 396 So.2d 322, 324 (Ct.App.La.1981).

os occipitale [NA], occipital bone: a single trapezoid-shaped bone situated at the posterior and inferior part of the cranium, articulating with the two parietal and two temporal bones, the sphenoid bone, and the atlas; it contains a large opening, the foramen magnum.

... contusions to scalp—**occipito** parietal area.... Krezinski v. Hay, 253 N.W.2d 522–3 (Wis.1977).

os parietale [NA], parietal bone: either of the two quadrilateral bones forming part of the superior and lateral surfaces of the skull, and joining each other in the midline at the sagittal suture.

os scaphoideum [NA], scaphoid bone: the most lateral bone of the proximal row of carpal bones; called also *o. naviculare manus*.

X-ray films taken at that time demonstrated, inter alia, a fracture of the **navicular (or scaphoid) bone** in Mrs. Lipsius's right wrist. It was Dr. Fielding's opinion that symptoms referable to such an injury are similar to those of carpal tunnel syndrome and that sequelae of the former were sufficient to constitute the competent producing cause of the injuries complained of. Lipsius v. White, 458 N.Y.S.2d 928, 931 (2d Dep't 1983).

Dr. MacCollum treated the wrist as a possible fracture of the **navicular bone**....

... Part of the **navicular bone** was removed and a piece of bone taken from Kalar's hip was fused with the lunate and radius bones. The fusion was unsuccessful and two further operations were required. Carroll v. Kalar, 545 P.2d 411–13 (Ariz. 1976).

... the x-ray report was made revealing that the **navicular bone** in the plaintiff's right wrist had been fractured....

In August, when the cast was removed from his wrist, the plaintiff was informed that the two segments of the **navicular bone** had failed to knit. U.S. ex rel. Fear v. Rundle, 506 F.2d 331–3 (3d Cir. 1974).

ossa sesamoidea sesamoid bones: a type of short bone occurring mainly in the hands and feet, and found embedded in tendons and joint capsules.

os temporale [NA], temporal bone: one of the two irregular bones forming part of the lateral surfaces and base of the skull, and containing the organs of hearing.

He was taken to a hospital where X rays revealed that he had sustained two skull fractures. One fracture was through the "squamous portion of the **temporal bone** extending to the base of the skull." C.S.T. Erection Company v. Industrial Com'n, 335 N.E.2d 419–20 (Ill.1975).

os trapezium [NA], trapezium bone: the most lateral bone of the distal row of carpal bones; called also *o. multangulum majus*.

os trapezoideum [NA], trapezoid bone: the bone in the distal row of carpal bones lying between the trapezium and capitate bones; called also *o. multangulum minus*.

os zygomaticum [NA], zygomatic bone: the quadrangular bone of the cheek, articulating with the frontal bone, the maxilla, the zygomatic process of the temporal bone, and the great wing of the sphenoid bone.

"The depressed **cheek bone** was corrected through incision inside the hairline...." Cooperider v. Dearth, 420 So.2d 220–1 (Ct.App.La.1982).

ossa (os'ah) [L.] plural of *os*, bone. See also *os*.

ossicle (os'sĭ-k'l) [L. *ossiculum*] a small bone.

ossiculum (ŏ-sik'u-lum), pl. *ossic'ula* [L.] [NA] a general term for a small bone, or ossicle.

ossicula auditus [NA], auditory ossicles: the malleus, incus, and stapes, the small bones of the middle ear, which transmit the vibrations from the tympanic membrane to the oval window.

ossolopsia

... he suffers from double vision and **ossolopsia** (jiggly eyes).... Swanson v. U.S. By and Through Veterans Admin., 557 F.Supp. 1041, 1044 (D.Idaho 1983).

osteo- (os'te-o) [Gr. *osteon* bone] a combining form denoting relationship to a bone or to the bones.

osteoarthritic See *osteoarthritis*.

osteoarthritis (os"te-o-ar-thri'tis) [*osteo-* + Gr. *arthron* joint + *-itis*] noninflammatory degenerative joint disease occurring chiefly in older persons, characterized by degeneration of the articular cartilage, hypertrophy of bone at the margins, and changes in the synovial membrane. It is accompanied by pain and stiffness, particularly after prolonged activity. Called also *degenerative arthritis, hypertrophic arthritis,* and *degenerative joint disease.* See also *osteomalacia.*

On the basis of x-rays taken at that examination, Dr. Butler determined that Ibbitson had suffered from an **osteoarthritic** condition of the upper and mid-dorsal spine prior to the work incident. It was Dr. Butler's diagnosis that the work incident caused an acute ligamentous strain of Ibbitson's upper and mid-dorsal spine and also aggravated the preexisting **osteoarthritic** condition in that area. Ibbitson v. Sheridan Corp., 463 A.2d 735–6 (Maine 1983).

Dr. McCurley's professional opinion was that Mrs. Urbina had an **osteoarthritic** condition on July 14, 1976, at the time of her fall, and that the fall converted the asymptomatic osteoarthritis condition into a symptomatic one....

Dr. Stokes was of the opinion that if Mrs. Urbina had a preexisting **osteoarthritic** condition which had been aggravated by a fall in July of 1976, and if she was still symptomatic from that condition, then she would have had a restricted range of motion and would not have been able to touch her toes or execute the various maneuvers he put her through on March 2,

1977. Urbina v. Alois J. Binder Bakery, Inc., 423 So.2d 765, 767–8 (Ct.App.La.1982).

"All of us know as we get older we shrink, and the shrinkage is due to the fact the cushions between our vertebrae begin to deteriorate, and we begin to form bone spurs which is described as osteophytes, and this leads to **osteoarthritis** of the spine. This is present in 75 per cent of the people over the age of 55...." West v. Jutras, 456 F.2d 1222, 1224 (2d Cir. 1972).

Other Authorities: Bloodsworth v. Heckler, 703 F.2d 1233, 1236 (11th Cir. 1983); Shepard v. Midland Foods, Inc., 666 P.2d 758–60 (Mont.1983); Simpson v. Schweiker, 691 F.2d 966, 970 (11th Cir. 1982); Starlings v. Ski Roundtop Corp., 493 F.Supp. 507, 510 (M.D.Pa.1980); Peavy v. Flowers, 390 N.E.2d 832–3 (Ohio 1979); Arceneaux v. Domingue, 370 So. 2d 1262–3 (Ct.App.La.1979); Flippen v. Mathews, 423 F.Supp. 135, 137 (E.D.Va.1976); Micucci v. Industrial Com'n, 494 P.2d 1324, 1326–7 (Ariz.1972); Floyd v. Finch, 441 F.2d 73, 91 (6th Cir. 1971); Colwell v. Gardner, 386 F.2d 56, 61 (6th Cir. 1967); Lumbermen's Mutual Casualty Co. v. Einbinder, 343 F.2d 338, 344 (D.C.Cir.1965); Celebrezze v. Bolas, 316 F.2d 498, 504 (8th Cir. 1963); Whyatt v. Kukura, 321 P.2d 860–1 (Dist.Ct.App.Cal.1958).

osteochondritis (os″te-o-kon-dri′tis) [*osteo-* + Gr. *chondros* cartilage + *-itis*] inflammation of both bone and cartilage.

osteochondritis deformans juvenilis osteochondrosis of the capitular epiphysis of the femur. See also *osteochondrosis.*

osteochondritis dissecans osteochondritis resulting in the splitting of pieces of cartilage into the joint, particularly the knee joint or shoulder joint.

One letter read as follows:

This is to inform you that Charles Poczik was treated by me in October of 1965 with complaints of intermittent locking of his elbow and cramping of his arm.

Xrays demonstrated an **osteochondritis dissecans** of the elbow joint with a loose body. He was admitted to St. Joseph's Intercommunity Hospital and an arthrotomy of the elbow joint was performed with removal of the loose pieces of bone. His postoperative course was uneventful. When he was last examined on August 9, 1966 there was mild restriction of elbow extension. I have not seen him since that time, but would presume that he would have a mild permanent partial disability involving his elbow.

A second states:

[Poczik] was operated upon elsewhere in June of 1966 for an **osteochondritis dissecans** of the right elbow in which four loose bodies were excised. He has complained of pain in the arm, chiefly centered at the elbow aggravated by pushing, pulling, etc.

On examination he presents a healed scar over the lateral aspect of the elbow. The head of the radius is abnormally prominent. Extension lacks 5°. He has full flexion, full pronation and supination. There is tenderness over the lateral aspect of the elbow.

Xrays show the head of the radius to be enlarged. There are no loose bodies. In my opinion the condition described above is permanent in nature. U.S. v. Poczik, 362 F.Supp. 101, 103–4 (W.D.N.Y.1973).

osteochondrosis (os″te-o-kon-dro′sis) a disease of the growth or ossification centers in children which begins as a degeneration or necrosis followed by regeneration or recalcification. Called also eiphyseal ischemic necrosis (q.v.). It may affect (1) the Calcaneus (os calcis), a condition sometimes called *apophysitis;* (2) the Capitular Epiphysis (head) of the Femur, a condition known as *Legg-Calvé-Perthes disease, Perthes disease, Waldenström's disease, coxa plana,* and *pseudocoxalgia;* (3) the Ilium; (4) the Lunate (Semilunar) Bone, known as *Kienböck's disease;* (5) Head of the Second Metatarsal Bone, known as *Freiberg's infraction;* (6) the Navicular (Tarsal Scaphoid), known as *Köhler's tarsal scaphoiditis;* (7) the Tuberosity of the Tibia, called *Osgood-Schlatter disease, Schlatter's disease;* (8) the Vertebrae, called *Scheuermann's disease* or *kyphosis, juvenile kyphosis, vertebral epiphysitis,* and *kyphosis dorsalis juvenilis*; (9) *the capitellum of the humerus,* called *Panner's disease.* See also *revascularization* (Arrendale case).

More x-rays were taken and after they were returned Dr. Hood diagnosed Terrance's ailment as hip damage resulting from **Legg-Perthes Disease,**[1] which the doctor described to the plaintiff as a deterioration of the femur head (hip ball) resulting from inadequate blood supply.... [[1] According to Dorland's Illustrated Medical Dictionary, the ailment is known variously as **Legg's Disease** or the **Legg-Calvé-Perthes disease,** the pathological name of which is **Osteochondritis demormans juvenilis.** It was named for Arthur T. Legg, a Boston surgeon; Jacques Calvé, a French orthopedist; and Georg Clemens Perthes, a German surgeon.]

Dr. Yount describes **Legg-Perthes disease** as one of unknown etiology whose pathology is known to be a vascular demise with resulting necrosis to the femur head or, in layman's terms, death and disintegration of the hip ball resulting from cessation of the blood flow to the hip ball area. The disease was previously considered infectious but this has more recently been ruled out. Dr. Yount testified that to pinpoint **Legg-Perthes Disease** a doctor should look for pain in the hip, a limp resulting from this pain, and a restriction of movement. Dr. Yount further testified that in some cases knee pain such as that suffered by Terrance is the first symptom of the disease, and that a diligent doctor who failed to find a basis for knee pain in x-rays should consider the possibility of the disease, which Dr. Yount has always done....

Legg-Perthes Disease is a four step process involving initially the necrosis stage in which the blood flow ceases, next a degenerative stage involving disintegration of the femur head from lack of blood, then a regenerative stage, hopefully, where the blood flow is reinstated and the femur head resumes growth, and, finally, in a few cases, a restoration stage in which the femur head achieves its proper place in the hip socket. The medical testimony in this case reveals clearly that treatment for the disease is not available in the degenerative stage beyond containment of the head in the socket, and that regeneration cannot be externally initiated.

... He describes the basic treatment as containment of the head in the hip socket, the feasibility of which depends upon the extent of the femur head involvement. Where containment is feasible by use of a brace, Dr. Yount supports the type of tendon removal surgery as was conducted by Dr. Hood. Arrendale v. U.S., 469 F.Supp. 883, 885–8 (N.D.Tex.1979).

osteodegenerative See *osteo-*; and *degeneration*.

osteogenic (os"te-o-jen'ik) [*osteo-* + Gr. *gennan* to produce] derived from or composed of any tissue which is concerned in the growth or repair of bone.

osteoid (os'te-oid) [*osteo-* + Gr. *eidos* form] 1. resembling bone. 2. the organic matrix of bone; young bone which has not undergone calcification.

osteomalacia (os"te-o-mah-la'she-ah) [*osteo-* + Gr. *malakia* softness] a condition marked by softening of the bones (due to impaired mineralization, with excess accumulation of osteoid), with pain, tenderness, muscular weakness, anorexia, and loss of weight, resulting from deficiency of vitamin D and calcium. Cited in W.P. Fuller and Co. v. Industrial Accident Com'n, 27 Cal.Rptr. 401, 404 (Dist.Ct.App.Cal.1962).

osteomalacia senile softening of bones in old age due to vitamin D deficiency.

... all the doctors had decided that Mock was suffering from a degenerative disease of the right femur caused by lack of circulation in the bone, which antedated the injury of December 17, 1957. It was diagnosed as malacosis senilis, a localized osteoarthritis, a disease which becomes progressively worse although in some cases it can be arrested by an operation. Lumbermen's Mutual Casualty Co. v. Einbinder, 343 F.2d 338, 340 (D.C.Cir.1965).

osteomyelitis (os"te-o-mi"ĕ-li'tis) [*osteo-* + Gr. *myelos* marrow] inflammation of bone caused by a pyogenic organism. It may remain localized or may spread through the bone to involve the marrow, cortex, cancellous tissue, and periosteum.

Furthermore, x-rays taken of Sprague's entire left leg on August 14, 1975 did not reveal the onset of **osteomyelitis**, a bacterial bone infection which caused Sprague's disability in this case....

... **Osteomyelitis** may occur in two ways: (1) through direct "innoculation" of a bone with bacteria that has entered the skin through an open wound located near the bone; and (2) through transmission of bacteria through the blood stream from one part of the body to a bone in another part of the body. The claimant contends that Sprague's **osteomyelitis** was caused by entry of staph bacteria through wounds on his left leg received at BIW in July 1975. BIW, however, contends that staph entered Sprague's body through the non-work-related ulcer on his right toe and traveled through his blood stream to his left leg. Sprague v. Director, Office of Workers' Comp., etc., 688 F.2d 862, 864–5 (1st Cir. 1982).

Dr. Greenberg and a treating radiologist, orthopedist, and neurosurgeon agreed that appellant suffered from spinal **osteomyelitis** (degeneration of the bone)....

... infections which occur in the bladder and in the vagina and in the uterus and in the rectum may be associated with **osteomyelitis**; particularly with the spine, and that is why, say, in pyelonephritis or acute kidney infections **osteomyelitis** of the spine is more common than any other kind of **osteomyelitis** because this drainage of material which may be infected in it and the bacteria tends to go back into this portion of the body. Rimmele v. Northridge Hosp. Foundation, 120 Cal.Rptr. 39, 41, 47 (Ct.App.Cal.1975).

Dr. Stover did not want to do a tissue biopsy because if the condition were **osteomyelitis**, an infection of the bone and surrounding soft tissue, he feared that making an incision necessary for the tissue biopsy would aggravate the infection and possibly cause it to spread. The doctors then arrived at a diagnosis of chronic **osteomyelitis**, and Dr. Stover prescribed an antibiotic to treat it....

The second defense offered is that there were two schools of thought with relationship to the treatment of **osteomyelitis**. One is that surgery is indicated and the infected bone and surrounding tissue should be taken out as soon as possible. The other advocates a more conservative approach initially, because the surgical procedure involves a risk of spreading the infection into other sensitive areas, which could have serious, possibly even fatal, consequences. Therefore, treatment by antibiotics is initially preferred and if this is unsuccessful, then surgery is performed. O'Brien v. Stover, 443 F.2d 1013, 1015–17 (8th Cir. 1971).

Other Authorities: Union Packing Co. of Omaha v. Klauschie, 314 N.W.2d 25, 27 (Neb.1982); Kubrick v. U.S., 581 F.2d 1092–3 (3d Cir. 1978); Raines v. New York Railroad Co., 283 N.E.2d 230, 237 (Ill.1972); Jones v. Stess, 268 A.2d 292–4 (Super.Ct.N.J.1970); Orthopedic Equipment Co. v. Eutsler, 276 F.2d 455, 458 (4th Cir. 1960).

osteopath (os'te-o-path) a practitioner of osteopathy.

I find that **osteopaths** are trained in a manner which qualifies them, upon proper licensing, to cure disease and perform such acts as are necessary to preserve and protect health.

... Further, I note that the definition of "medicine and surgery" contained in the Statutory Construction Act is virtually identical to the definition of "osteopathic medicine and surgery" contained in the Osteopathic Medical Practice Act. See Pa.Stat.Ann. tit. 63, § 271.2....

Thus, based on the present record, it appears that **osteopaths** were intended by the legislature to be included within the definition of "physician." American College of Obstetricians, etc. v. Thornburg, 552 F.Supp. 791, 810 (E.D.Pa. 1982).

osteopathic See *osteopathy*.

osteopathy (os"te-op'ah-the) [*osteo-* + Gr. *pathos* disease] a system of therapy founded by Andrew Taylor Still (1828–1917) and based on the theory that the body is capable of making its own remedies against disease and other toxic conditions when it is in normal structural relationship and has favorable environmental conditions and adequate nutrition. It utilizes generally accepted physical, medicinal, and surgical methods of diagnosis and therapy, while placing chief emphasis on the importance of normal body mechanics and manipulative methods of detecting and correcting faulty structure.

The **osteopathic** approach to treatment arose in the United States in the late 19th Century. That approach centered on the belief that the proper functioning of the various parts of the musculoskeletal system is crucial to maintaining health and preventing or curing disease. Historical **osteopathic** practice used only techniques of bio-mechanics to manipulate the neuromusculoskeletal system in order to return the various bodily systems to their naturally harmonious state. Prescription drugs and surgery were not accepted treatment modalities.

Osteopathy no longer defers the use of drugs and other medications and measures in the treatment of disease, but **osteopathic** medical schools require their students to take courses in **osteopathic** theory and manipulation. There are presently 14 **osteopathic** medical schools in the United States, and each such school provides medical education which is at least minimally equivalent in both substance and quality to that which is provided in the American nonosteopathic medical schools. In New Jersey, **osteopathic** medical schools are required by the Board to provide the same minimum curriculum as is required of all other approved medical schools.

It is the expressed legislative policy of the State as well as the policy of the Board to recognize graduates of **osteopathic** medical schools as fully competent in every respect to practice medicine and surgery. There are over 21,000 licensed M.D.'s in New Jersey (including graduates of foreign medical schools) and there are approximately 1,600 licensed D.O.'s. Eatough v. Bd. of Medical Examiners, 465 A.2d 934, 936 (Super.Ct. N.J.1983).

§ 459.002(3), Fla.Stat.:

"Practice of **osteopathic** medicine" means the diagnosis, treatment, operation or prescription for any human disease, pain, injury, deformity or other physical or mental condition, which practice is based in part upon educational standards and requirements which emphasize the importance of the musculoskeletal structure and manipulative therapy in the maintenance and restoration of health.

Osteopathic physicians are licensed under Ch. 459. Gulf Coast Hosp. v. Dep't of Health, etc., 424 So.2d 86, 89 (Dist. Ct.App.Fla.1982).

osteopetrosis (os"te-o-pe-tro'sis) [*osteo-* + Gr. *petra* stone + *-osis*] a rare hereditary disease characterized by abnormally dense bone, probably due to faulty bone resorption. The disorder occurs in two forms: a severe autosomal recessive form occurring in infancy or childhood, and a benign autosomal dominant form occurring in adolescence or adulthood. In the recessive form, the proliferation of bone obliterates the marrow cavity, causing anemia, and the nerve foramina of the skull, causing compression of cranial nerves, which may result in deafness and blindness. Fractures are common in both forms. Called also *Albers Schönberg disease, ivory bones,* and *marble bones.*

Examination by the treating orthopedist, Dr. Elliot J. Friedel, revealed that although the fracture to the right foot was well healed, there had been bone wash-out, known as **osteopetrosis**, resulting from a lack of use of the right leg. Giant Food, Inc. v. Coffey, 451 A.2d 151, 153 (Ct.Spec.App.Md.1982).

osteophyte (os'te-o-fit") [*osteo-* + Gr. *phyton* plant] a bony excrescence or osseous outgrowth. See also *osteoarthritis* (West case).

Dr. Sorensen's review of the X-rays indicated what he termed to be a severe degeneration at the C4, C5, and C6 vertebra with some posterior **osteophytes** (abnormal bone-type growth) encroaching on the intervertebral foramen. Broadbent v. Harris, 698 F.2d 407, 410 (10th Cir. 1983).

. . . In oblique projection, **osteophytic** spurring is noted in the superior margins of the first lumbar segment. Chabert v. City of

Westwego Police Pension, 423 So.2d 1190, 1193 (Ct. of App.La.1982).

Dr. Upshaw found a small bony overgrowth, an **osteophyte**, which was causing pressure on a nerve root and also some disk pressure. He did a curet and removed the disk from one of the disk spaces and the **osteophyte**. An **osteophyte**, such as observed in Mr. Chinowith's back, is somewhat a part of the normal aging process. In younger people they often develop at sites of trauma or as a result of abnormal stress or strain. The **osteophyte** [spur, in common language] would grow at the site of an injury and in a man of his age, probably. Insurance Company of North America v. Chinowith, 393 F.2d 916, 919 (5th Cir. 1968).

osteophytic See *osteophyte.*

osteophytosis (os"te-o-fi-to'sis) a condition characterized by the formation of osteophytes.

Two views of thoracic spine reveal just minimal degenerative **osteophytosis** in lower thoracic spine at the level of thorocolumbar junction. . . .

. . . In addition, there is paravertebral calcification on the right side at the level of L–2–L–3.

"Above this area there is degenerative **osteophytosis** with complete bridging of intervertebral disc space. A similar thing is identified at the level of L–5–S–1 disc interspace. The findings are compatible with an old TB. Foster v. Mathews, 423 F.Supp. 117, 120 (W.D.N.C.1976).

osteoporosis (os"te-o-po-ro'sis) [*osteo-* + Gr. *poros* passage + *-osis*] abnormal rarefaction of bone, seen most commonly in the elderly. Depending on the extent of demineralization of bone, it may be accompanied by pain, particularly of the lower back; deformities, such as loss of stature; and pathological fractures. It may be idiopathic or secondary to other diseases, such as thyrotoxicosis. See also *cortisone* (Dupuy case).

Dr. Rhymes testified the accident had caused an **osteoporosis** condition of the left foot which would become aggravated as the years go by. Herndon v. Neal, 424 So.2d 1180, 1183 (Ct. App.La.1982).

Dr. Klinghoffer X-rayed both feet, which revealed some demineralization in both feet and evidence of "**osteoporosis**" in both ankles. These findings, according to Dr. Klinghoffer, suggested a diffuse metastatic disease that was destroying the bone in both feet. Dr. Klinghoffer then testified that it was this condition that was disabling the Claimant, and that this condition was not related to the previous work injury. Jones v. Workmen's Comp. Appeal Bd., 412 A.2d 686–7 (Commonwealth Ct.Pa.1980).

In 1973, he developed back pain and was diagnosed to have **osteoporosis**, a loss of calcium in the bones. Cataracts and **osteoporosis** of the types that plaintiff exhibited are both characteristic side effects of steroid treatment. Hill v. Squibb & Sons, E.R., 592 P.2d 1383, 1386 (Mont.1979).

Other Authorities: Harrelson v. Louisiana Pacific Corp., 434 So.2d 479, 485 (Ct.App.La.1983); Warner v. Schweiker, 551 F.Supp. 789, 791 (E.D.Mo.1982) reversed 722 F.2d 428 (8th Cir. 1983); Jackson v. City of Alexandria, 424 So.2d 1265–6 (Ct.App.La.1982); Marcus v. Califano, 615 F.2d 23, 26 (2d Cir. 1979); Pruchniewski v. Weinberger, 415 F.Supp. 112, 114

(D.Md.1976); Coulter v. Weinberger, 527 F.2d 224, 226 (3d Cir. 1975); Draper v. Liberty Mutual Ins. Co., 484 S.W.2d 135, 137–8 (Ct.Civ.App.Tex.1972); Collins v. Hand, 246 A.2d 398, 401 (Pa.1968); Celebrezze v. Bolas, 316 F.2d 498, 503–4 (8th Cir. 1963); Leavell v. Alton Ochsner Medical Foundation, 201 F.Supp. 805–6 (E.D.La.1962).

osteoporosis, post-traumatic loss of bone substance following an injury in which there is damage to a nerve, sometimes due to an increased blood supply caused by the neurogenic insult, or to disuse secondary to pain.

Although, according to Dr. Florence's testimony, tremendous swelling should have been anticipated, some of the swelling of Larsen's wrist area might have been associated with **Sudeck's atrophy**. Dr. Yelle testified that **Sudeck's atrophy** is a rarely encountered complication which, when it occurs, usually occurs in fractures of the wrist and ankle and is characterized by the very small blood vessels in the extremity going into spasm, causing poor circulation and consequent swelling from blood still being pumped to the area. The treatment for **Sudeck's atrophy** is to encourage mobilization of the affected area. Larsen v. Yelle, 246 N.W.2d 841, 843 (Minn.1976).

osteoporotic (os″te-o-po-rot′ik) pertaining to or characterized by osteoporosis. See also *osteoporosis*.

Once the bone is **osteoporotic** there is so little can be done . . . in Mr. Bolas, it is occurring at the pelvis and at the vertebra of the back; that the arthritis was not related to the osteoporosis; that Bolas was suffering the pain of both; that in April 1954 "we felt that he was in a situation that he was permanently disabled as far as carrying on any sustained activity" . . . . Celebrezze v. Bolas, 316 F.2d 498, 503 (8th Cir. 1963).

osteosarcoma See *osteogenic sarcoma* under *sarcoma*.

osteosynthesis (os″te-o-sin′thĕ-sis) [*osteo-* + Gr. *synthesis* a putting together] surgical fastening of the ends of a fractured bone by sutures, rings, plates, or other mechanical means.

On June 30, 1980, plaintiff underwent a six-hour **osteosynthesis** operation with "AO" compression plating of the right tibia-fibula. Thus, an eight- to nine-inch-long steel plate was screwed into the fracture site with nine screws. In conjunction with the insertion of the steel plate, another operative procedure was performed on the plaintiff's hip to obtain bone grafts for emplacement at the fracture site. This entailed making another incision in her hip to expose the bone and slices of bone in various dimensions were removed and inserted in the area of the fracture for support. The grafting meant another operation and left a permanent scar at her hip where the bone grafts were taken. Warmsley v. City of New York, 454 N.Y.S.2d 144, 146 (2d Dep't 1982).

osteotomy (os″te-ot′o-me) [*osteo-* + Gr. *temnein* to cut] the surgical cutting of a bone.

In an effort to improve plaintiff's condition and to relieve pain, defendant performed a supracondylar femoral wedge **osteotomy** on each knee, after which both knees were placed in casts for five to six weeks. When the casts were removed, it was found that the bones in plaintiff's knees had fused (ankylosed), thus making it impossible for plaintiff to bend his knees

at all. Monahan v. Weichert, 461 N.Y.S.2d 633–4 (4th Dep't 1983).

Defendant performed a supracondylar femoral wedge **osteotomy** on plaintiff's left leg on July 27, 1972 and on the right leg on August 3, 1972. These operations were designed to correct the knee flexion contractures by removing a piece of bone from the femur just above the knee and artificially joining the femur with a plate and screws to form a compensating angle to permit knee flexation. Following surgery plaintiff's legs were placed in plaster casts. When the casts were removed five weeks later plaintiff's legs were stiff and he never regained mobility in either knee despite recommended physiotherapy. Monahan v. Weichert, 442 N.Y.S.2d 295–7 (4th Dep't 1981).

The plaintiff brought a malpractice action against the defendant, a licensed podiatrist (Ill.Rev.Stat.1973, ch. 91, par. 73 *et seq.*), for an allegedly negligent **osteotomy** (surgical cutting of a bone) performed on his left foot in 1974. Dolan v. Galluzzo, 396 N.E.2d 13–14 (Ill.1979).

Other Authorities: Benjamin v. State, 453 N.Y.S.2d 329, 332 (Ct.Cl.1982).

osteotomy, vertical

Dr. Phillips performed a "**vertical osteotomy**". Essentially, the operation consists of cutting the bone of the jaw on each side and repositioning the lower jaw to align it as ideally as possible with the upper jaw. The operation was performed under general anesthesia and in this instance required approximately six hours for completion. Carter v. Phillips, 365 So.2d 48 (Ct. App.La.1978).

ostium (os′te-um), pl. *os′tia* [L.] a door, or opening; used in anatomical nomenclature as a general term to designate an opening into a tubular organ, or between two distinct cavities within the body. Called also *orificium*, *orifice*, and *opening*.

ostium urethrae externum femininae [NA], external orifice of female urethra: the opening of the urethra into the vestibule; it is surrounded by a sphincter of striated muscle derived from the bulbocavernosus muscle. Called also *orificium urethrae externum muliebris*.

ostium urethrae externum masculinae [NA], external orifice of male urethra: the slitlike opening of the urethra on the tip of the glans penis; called also *orificium urethrae externum virilis*.

ostium vaginae [NA], the external orifice of the vagina, situated just posterior to the external urethral orifice; called also *orificium vaginae*. See also *pudendum, feminium*; and *vulva*.

He then cited from Delee Greenhill, Principles and Practice of Obstetrics, 9th ed., page 9, where, referring to copulation, this authority stated: "Copulation is not absolutely necessary if the semen is injected into the vagina or even on the introitus **vulva** which is the external opening to the vagina, conception may take place." T v. M, 242 A.2d 670, 673 (Super Ct.N.J. 1968).

ostomate (os′to-māt) one who has undergone enterostomy or ureterostomy. See also *enterostomy*; and *ureterostomy*.

Policing was facilitated by the fact that foreign **ostomates**, for reasons not altogether clear, tend to use a much higher rate of closed, as distinguished from drainable, pouches than do their American counterparts. Bruce Drug, Inc. v. Hollister, Inc., 688 F.2d 853, 858 (1st Cir. 1982).

ostomy (os'to-me) a general term referring to any operation in which an artificial opening is formed between two hollow organs or between one or more such viscera and the abdominal wall for discharge of intestinal contents or of urine.

Defendant Hollister Incorporated is the nation's leading manufacturer and supplier of **ostomy** appliances and related products for ostomates, viz., pouches, etc., used for the collection of body wastes which drain through a surgically created opening in the abdomen of individuals whose intestinal or urinary tracts have been fully or partly removed by surgery. Bruce Drug, Inc. v. Hollister, Inc., 688 F.2d 853–4 (1st Cir. 1982).

otitis (o-ti'tis) [*ot-* + *-itis*] inflammation of the ear, which may be marked by pain, fever, abnormalities of hearing, hearing loss, tinnitus, and vertigo.

otitis interna inflammation of the internal ear; labyrinthitis.

otitis media inflammation of the middle ear; tympanitis.

Another ear doctor [Felice J. Santore, Transcript p. 170, Ex. 33] wrote that in 1964 a tympano-mastoidectomy was performed upon her for **otitis media** and conductive deafness, and that she complained of vertigo. Capaldi v. Weinberger, 391 F.Supp. 502, 504 (E.D.Pa.1975).

On the occasion now being considered, Mrs. Johnston had a hurting in her ear and consulted Dr. Wurster who diagnosed her condition as **otitis media** (an infection of the middle ear) and indicated that she needed antibiotic treatment. Johnston v. Upjohn Co., 442 S.W.2d 93–4 (Kansas City, Mo.Ct.App. 1969).

Other Authorities: Reading v. Mathews, 542 F.2d 993, 995 (7th Cir. 1976).

otolaryngology (o"to-lar"in-gol'o-je) that branch of medicine concerned with medical and surgical treatment of the head and neck, including the ears, nose, and throat.

otolaryngologist See *otolaryngology.*

Dr. Bernard Ronis, an **otolaryngologist** (ear, nose and throat), testified that in his opinion the plaintiff was suffering from labyrinthosis, which is a dysfunction of the inner ear (N.T. 5–33). DeMarines v. KLM Royal Dutch Airlines, 433 F.Supp. 1047, 1053 (E.D.Pa.1977), reversed and remanded 580 F.2d 1193 (3d Cir. 1978).

otologist (o-tol'o-jist) a physician who specializes in otology. See also *ear* (specialist).

otology (o-tol'o-je) [*oto-* + *-logy*] that branch of medicine which deals with the medical treatment and surgery of the ear, and its anatomy, physiology, and pathology.

otosclerosis (o"to-skle-ro'sis) [*oto-* + Gr. *sklērōsis* hardening] a pathological condition of the bony labyrinth of the ear, in which there is formation of spongy bone (otospongiosis), especially in front of and posterior to the footplate of the stapes; it may cause bony ankylosis of the

stapes, resulting in conductive hearing loss. Cochlear otosclerosis may also develop, resulting in sensorineural hearing loss.

Mr. LePellev was suffering from a disease known as **otosclerosis** causing severe hearing loss. LePelley v. Grefenson, 614 P.2d 962, 964 (Idaho 1980).

One cause of deafness is a condition known as **otosclerosis**; that condition is one in which there is calcification of the bones of the middle ear. Calcification is the deposit of additional bone; its effect is to cement the middle ear bones and to anchor the stapes footplate in the oval window. thereby impeding passage of the sound vibrations and causing air conduction deafness. Warshaw v. Trans World Airlines, Inc., 442 F.Supp. 400, 402 (E.D.Pa.1977).

. . . she suffered from severe hearing loss. It was caused by **otosclerosis**, a hereditary progressive affliction which affects the middle ear. Her hearing loss was about 80 percent in her left ear and 50 percent in her right ear. In Re Estate of Lamb, 97 Cal.Rptr. 46–7 (Ct.App.Cal.1971).

ototoxic (o"to-tok'sik) having a deleterious effect upon the eighth nerve, or upon the organs of hearing and balance. See also *Kanamycin* (Schering Corp. case).

Upjohn had published warnings in the Physicians' Desk Reference (PDR) and in the package inserts of the neomycin sulfate it sold that the drug was **ototoxic** (toxic to the nerve controlling hearing) and nephrotoxic (toxic to the kidneys), and could cause deafness. Richards v. Upjohn Co., 625 P.2d 1192, 1194 (Ct.App. New Mex.1980).

Plaintiff did not contend that Bristol-Myers' drug, Kantrex, was adulterated or was itself defective, but rather that the drug was "**ototoxic**" (having the potential to cause deafness) and that the warnings given by Bristol-Myers for its use were inadequate and improper. Bristol-Myers Co. v. Gonzales, 561 S.W.2d 801, 803 (Tex.1978).

Both Bristol's Kantrex and Upjohn's neomycin were known to be "**ototoxic**" (having potential to cause deafness). The mechanical way in which each drug affects hearing (damage to the eighth cranial nerve) is the same. It is not disputed that some portion of the Kantrex and neomycin used in the irrigation was absorbed in the blood and that the cumulative effect of all those **ototoxic** drugs in the blood, the unknown amount of absorbed Kantrex and neomycin plus the injected Kantrex, resulted in Ramon's deafness. Bristol-Myers Co. v. Gonzales, 548 S.W.2d 416, 422 (Ct.Civ.App.Tex.1976), reversed and remanded 561 S.W.2d 801 (Tex.1978).

ototoxicity (o"to-toks-is'ĭ-te) the quality of being poisonous to or of exerting a deleterious effect upon the eighth nerve or upon the organs of hearing and balance.

On October 20, 1972, appellant experienced dizziness and partial hearing loss. On November 9, 1972, she consulted an otolaryngolist who diagnosed her problem as gentamicin **ototoxicity**; a loss of hearing due to a toxic reaction to Garamycin. O'Brien v. Angley, 407 N.E.2d 490, 492 (Ohio 1980).

Petitioner is the manufacturer of a drug product marketed under the name of Garamycin. Plaintiffs' complaint alleged that as a result of the use of such drug, plaintiff husband developed ototoxicity. Schering Corp. v. Thornton, 280 So.2d 493 (Dis. Ct.App.Fla.1973).

outbreak

The term ''outbreak'' is a flexible one. While one ''outbreak'' reported in the record affected 94 workers, a number of whom required hospitalization for a day or two, another consisted of 10 workers who consulted physicians complaining of nausea, vomiting, and diarrhea. Florida Peach Grow. Ass'n v. United States Dep't of Labor, 489 F.2d 120, 131 (5th Cir. 1974).

ovariectomize See *oophorectomize.*

ovariectomy See *oophorectomy.*

overdose (o'ver-dōs'') an excessive dose.

By December 1977, Mrs. Sharrow had been informed of her overdose [of Lidocaine] by Dr. Mayer and had specifically stated to Dr. Rhyneer that she had been given an **overdose**. Once she knew that the **overdose** was the cause of her cardiac arrest, Mrs. Sharrow should have realized that the only way to reconcile the conflicting accounts of her treatment and its relationship to the cardiac arrest was that Dr. Archer and the hospital had concealed the true facts . . . .

. . . I was convinced that there was no ''proof'' that I had received an **overdose**. In addition, my treating physician during the period of the alleged **overdose**, Dr. Archer, had continuously led me to believe my ''heart attack'' had been the result of a pre-existing condition and never disclosed the true facts of the **overdose** and cover-up. . . .

I don't recall that she told me exactly how much Lidocaine that she received, but my understanding was that she thought she had received an excessive amount of it. Sharrow v. Archer, 658 P.2d 1331, 1334–6 (Alas.1983).

overheparinize See *heparinize.*

overlay (o'ver-la) an increment; a later addition superimposed upon an already existing mass, state, or condition.

overlay, emotional See *overlay, psychogenic.*

overlay, functional

At argument counsel for the insurer described ''**functional overlay**'' as an ''over-reaction or over-response to pain'' and as a ''psychological or psychiatric condition which develops subsequent to compensable injury in some occasions and in some cases exists prior to a compensable injury. It manifests itself by perhaps phantom pain, perhaps an over-response to pain.'' . . .

. . . Applying these definitions to this case **functional overlay** may be explained as the psychological component of the injury claimant sustained to his back and it manifests itself in the pain and discomfort he continues to experience after the structural causes of his injury are no longer apparent. Claimant alleges that it is the **functional overlay** which causes his disability. Such a disability has been compensated in Oregon. See Eilliott v. Precision Castparts Corp., 30 Or.App. 399, 401, 567 P.2d 566, rev. den. 280 Or. 171 (1977), and Guerra v. Transport Indemnity, 30 Or.App. 415, 417, 567 P.2d 573, rev. den. 279 Or. 301 (1977). [Footnotes omitted.] Barrett v. Coast Range Plywood, 661 P.2d 926, 928 (Or.1983).

overlay, psychogenic the emotionally determined increment to an existing symptom or disability which has been of an organic or of a physically traumatic origin.

''. . . a considerable degree of **emotional overlay**,'' reflecting a reaction to the organic injury more than would be expected from a person with normal stability, i.e., in terms of how much a person is bothered and worried by pain. Bourne v. Washburn, 441 F.2d 1022, 1025 (D.C.Cir.1971).

Ovran See *norgestrel.*

The women sue for serious personal injuries claimed to have resulted from ingestion of prescribed oral contraceptives. . . .

In Action No. 1 plaintiff Gwendoline Bewers claims that on the advice of her physician and without knowledge of the high risk of dangerous side effects she bought and used **Ovran** for approximately three years in accordance with the instructions included with the drug and that on April 17, 1977 she suffered a severe and disabling thromboembolic accident resulting, inter alia, in impairment of left-side bodily function, partial paralysis and impairment of speech. She claims that she can neither move nor speak normally and that she is incapable of gainful employment. Bewers v. American Home Products Corp., 459 N.Y.S.2d 666, 668 (Sup.Ct.N.Y.Cty.1982), reversed 99 A.D.2d 949, 472 N.Y.S.2d 637 (1st Dep't 1984).

Ovranette See *levonorgestrel.*

Ovrette (ov-ret') trademark for a preparation of norgestrel. See also *norgestrel.*

oxygen (ok'sĭ-jen) [Gr. *oxys* sour + *gennan* to produce] a gaseous element existing free in the air and in combination in most nonelementary solids, liquids, and gases; atomic number, 8; atomic weight, 15.999; symbol, O. Oxygen exists in three isotopes, with atomic weights of 16, 17 and 18 (heavy oxygen). Oxygen constitutes 20 per cent by weight of the atmospheric air; it is the essential agent in the respiration of plants and animals and, although noninflammable, is necessary to support combustion. It forms the characteristic constituent of ternary acids. It is administered by inhalation in some pulmonary and cardiac disorders. See also *fibroplasia, retrolental* (Air Shields, Inc. case).

Since 1954 prolonged exposure to **oxygen** has been uniformly recognized as the leading cause of RLF. Burton v. Brooklyn Doctors Hosp., 452 N.Y.S.2d 875, 879 (1st Dep't 1982).

Dr. Watson's testimony was that lack of **oxygen** causes dizziness and lightheadedness, and eventually causes a person to pass out. Smith v. Clayton and Lambert Mfg. Co., 488 F.2d 1345, 1347 (10th Cir. 1973).

oxygenate (ok'sĭ-jĕ-nāt) to add oxygen to.

Dr. Johnston, the anesthesiologist, agreed that ''if [the patient] does not get oxygen to his brain, he is going to die very quickly.'' She also stated that for a patient in Mr. Miller's condition the very first thing in importance was to ''**oxygenate** the patient'':

''Q. When you said **oxygenation**, what do you mean?

''A. **Oxygenate** the patient, give oxygen to the patient.

''Q. How?

''A. Whichever is the easiest and the fastest way to do it, intubate the patient, **oxygenation** by intermittent positive pressure breathing manually with mask or intubate the patient with endotracheal tube."...

"Q. When you say **oxygenation** as the No. 1 step you are talking about intermediate pressure through an ambu bag and pressure breathing?

"A. Yes, whichever is the fastest, the ambu bag and mask if it is the fastest and followed by intubation if you can intubate; there are cases when you cannot intubate, then the mask may be satisfactory." Daniels v. Hadley Memorial Hospital, 566 F.2d 749, 758 (D.C.Cir.1977).

oxymorphone hydrochloride (ok"se-mor′fōn) [USP] chemical name: 4,5α-epoxy-3,14-dihydroxy-17-methyl-morphinan-6-one hydrochloride. A semisynthetic compound, $C_{12}H_{19}NO_4 \cdot HCl$, occurring as a white or slightly off-white, odorless powder; used as a narcotic analgesic.

A rather painstaking search of the citation given in the Federal Register has failed to reveal the word "Numorphan". We assume the reason we are unable to find the above-mentioned drug is that the Federal Register lists narcotic drugs by the actual chemical ingredients contained within the substance, and not by trade names. See 33 Fed.Reg. 14831 (Oct. 3, 1968). The fact that the narcotic compound in Numorphan is **Oxymorphone**, and the latter substance is listed in the Federal Register of 1968, supra, is a matter that was not mentioned at the preliminary hearing, nor was it mentioned at any time in this record. State v. Osborn, 494 P.2d 773, 775 (Ct.App.Ariz. 1972).

oxyphenbutazone (ok"se-fen-bu′tah-zōn) [USP] chemical name: 4-butyl-1-(4-hydroxyphenyl)-2-phenyl-3,5-pyrazolidinedione monohydrate. A derivative of phenylbutazone, $C_{19}H_{20}N_2O_3 \cdot H_2O$, having similar anti-inflammatory, analgesic, and antipyretic actions; administered orally in the treatment of arthritis, gout, and similar conditions.

A diagnosis of Carpal Tunnel Syndrome was made and she was treated with **Tanderil** and **Deltasone** which are anti-inflammatory agents used in the treatment of this disorder.... Segar v. Garan, Inc., 388 So.2d 164–5 (Miss.1980).

oxytetracycline (ok"se-tet″rah-si′klēn) [USP] chemical name: 4-(dimethyl-amino)-1,4,4α,5α,6,11,12a-octahydro-3,5,6,10,12a-hexahydroxy-6-methyl-1,11 dioxa-2-naphthacenecarboxamide. A broad-spectrum antibiotic of the tetracycline group, produced by *Streptomyces rimosus*, $C_{22}H_{24}N_2O_9 \cdot 2H_2O$, occurring as a yellow crystalline powder, and used chiefly as an antibacterial, administered intramuscularly. See also *enterocolitis, pseudomembranous*.

The "package insert" or "package brochure" supplied in 1958 by Chas. Pfizer & Company with **terramycin** and available to members of the medical profession, contained a paragraph headed "Precautions," and therein it was stated that "Glossitis and dermatitis as reactions of an allergic nature may

occur but are rare. If adverse reactions occur or individual idiosyncracy or allergy occur, discontinue medication." Fisher v. Wilkinson, 382 S.W.2d 627, 629 (Mo.1964).

oxytetracycline calcium [USP], the calcium salt of oxytetracycline, $C_{44}H_{46}Ca_4O_{18}$, occurring as a yellow to light brown, crystalline powder; used as a antibacterial, administered orally.

oxytocic (ok-se-to′sik) an agent that hastens evacuation of the uterus by stimulating contractions of the myometrium.

Dr. Zearfoss administered an **oxytocic** drug called **Tocosamine** which is used to stimulate the uterus to contract more powerfully, thus forcing the baby's head down through the pelvic canal. Rutherford v. Zearfoss, 272 S.E.2d 225–6 (Va.1980).

oxytocin (ok″se-to′sin) an octapeptide, one of two hormones formed by the neuronal cells of the hypothalamic nuclei and stored in the posterior lobe of the pituitary, the other being vasopressin. It has uterine-contracting and milk-ejection actions.

Pursuant to her physician's order for the inducement of uterine contractions, she was infused intravenously with the prescription drug, **Pitocin**. The product information disseminated to the medical profession by the defendant did not contraindicate the use of **Pitocin** for this purpose. On or about the same date, the child, delivered by the vaginal route, was born with brain damage, permanent blindness and quadriplegia. The complaint alleges that the use of **Pitocin** was the proximate cause of the child's injuries, and....

... that defendant's failure to warn physicians and patients of the danger in using **Pitocin** while a fetus is in high station rendered the drug "not reasonably safe." Woodill v. Parke Davis & Co., 402 N.E.2d 194–5 (Ill.1980).

He testified that the appellee had violated accepted medical standards by failing to administer immediately prior to the abortion or during the procedure a drug known as **pitocin** which would have caused the uterus to contract and become more firm. Hitch v. Hall, 399 A.2d 953, 955 (Ct.Spec.App.Md. 1979).

The Robbins alleged that the intense and frequent uterine contractions which occurred after Dr. Footer administered the drug "**pitocin**" to stimulate Mrs. Robbins' labor process sharply limited their child's supply of oxygen, jeopardizing his life and rendering him highly susceptible to injury from the subsequent forceps delivery. Robbins v. Footer, 553 F.2d 123, 125 (D.C.Cir.1977).

Other Authorities: Haught v. Maceluch, 681 F.2d 291, 294 (5th Cir. 1982); Maslonka v. Hermann, 414 A.2d 1350, 1353 (Super.Ct.N.J.1980); Friel v. Vineland Obstetrical, etc., 400 A.2d 147, 149 (Super.Ct.N.J.1979); Mercurdo v. County of Milwaukee, 264 N.W.2d 258–9 (Wis.1978); Long v. Johnson, 381 N.E.2d 93, 96 (Ct.App.Ind.1978).

P

P.A. See *physician assistant.*

pacemaker (pās′māk-er) an object or substance that influences the rate at which a certain phenomenon occurs; often used alone to indicate the natural cardiac pacemaker or an artificial cardiac pacemaker. In biochemistry, a substance whose rate of reaction sets the pace for a series of interrelated reactions.

When the [diathermy] machine was turned on, decedent suffered cardiac arrest due to interference with his **pacemaker** by the machine. Mr. Armstrong never regained consciousness and subsequently died. There was an x-ray in Dr. Williams' file showing that Armstrong was fitted with a **pacemaker**. It was also obvious upon direct physical examination. Armstrong v. Stearns-Roger Elec. Contractors, 657 P.2d 131–2 (Ct.App. N.M.1982).

A **pacemaker**, in the form of an electrical conducting wire, may be fed through a large blood vessel directly to the heart's surface to stimulate contractions and to regulate beat. Matter of Dinnerstein, 380 N.E.2d 134–5 (App.Ct.Mass.1978).

pacemaker, artificial See *pacemaker, cardiac, artificial.*

pacemaker, asynchronous an implanted cardiac pacemaker in which the induced ventricular rhythm is independent of the atrium; it is usually set at a fixed rate of ventricular stimulation.

An **asychronous pacemaker** artificially stimulates the heart independent of the heart's natural pulse beat. An **asynchronous pacer** is set at a predetermined pulse rate and it stimulates the ventricle at this preset rate regardless of the natural atrial pulse rate. The runaway inhibited pacemaker disclosed in the Greatbatch patent is an **asynchronous pacemaker**. Medtronic, Inc. v. Cardiac Pacemakers, Inc., 555 F.Supp. 1214, 1218, (D.Minn.1983).

pacemaker, cardiac the group of cells rhythmically initiating the heart beat, characterized physiologically by a slow loss of membrane potential during diastole. Usually the pacemaker site is the sinoatrial node.

pacemaker, cardiac, artificial a device designed to stimulate, by electrical impulses, contraction of the heart muscle at a certain rate; used particularly in heart block or in absence of normal function of the sinoatrial node; it may be connected from the outside or implanted within the body. Popularly called *pacemaker.*

pacemaker, demand an implanted cardiac pacemaker in which the generator stimulus is inhibited for a set interval (refractory period) by a signal derived from depolarization (normal or ectopic), thus minimizing the risk of pacemaker-induced ventricular fibrillation.

A **demand pacemaker** is programmed to artificially stimulate the heart only when the heart "demands" assistance. A **demand pacer** senses the natural pulse beat of the heart and will lie dormant while the heart naturally beats above a predetermined rate. When the natural pulse falls below the predetermined rate, the **demand pacer** is activated to artificially stimulate the heart asynchronously at a present rate. Medtronic,

Inc. v. Cardiac Pacemakers, Inc., 555 F.Supp. 1214, 1218 (D.Minn.1983).

pacemaker, synchronous an implanted cardiac pacemaker that synchronizes the electromechanical events in the atrium with those of the ventricle; the pacemaker stimulates the ventricle when triggered by the P wave from the atrium.

There are three general types of pacemakers: synchronous, asynchronous and demand. A **synchronous pacemaker** stimulates the heart in synchrony with the physiological pulse beat of the heart. A **synchronous pacer** senses the natural pulse of the atrium of the heart and correspondingly provides a delayed but amplified pulse to the ventricle of the heart. Medtronic, Inc. v. Cardiac pacemakers, Inc., 555 F.Supp. 1214, 1218 (D.Minn.1983).

pacing (pās′ing) setting of the pace, or regulation of the rate of.

pacing, cardiac regulation of the rate of contraction of the heart muscle by an artificial cardiac pacemaker.

This litigation involves one aspect of **artificial cardiac pacing**, a medical technique that allows a person's heartbeat to be steadied, stimulated, or re-established. This artificial pacing of the heartbeat has been achieved by means of a pulse generator which transmits regular electrical impulses to the heart. The pulse generator is connected to the heart by, and relays the electrical impulses to the heart through, electrical leads. The leads are attached to the heart either on the outside of the organ, that is, through the epicardium to the myocardium, by means of a surgical procedure, or the inside of the organ by means of a transvenous procedure, in which case the lead is termed transvenous or endocardial. Goldberg v. Medtronic, Inc., 686 F.2d 1219–21 (7th Cir. 1982).

pack (pak) treatment by wrapping a patient in blankets or sheets or a limb in towels, wet or dry and either hot or cold; also the blankets, sheets, or towels used for this purpose.

pack, Hydrocollator steam

Essentially this patient's symptoms at this time are only mild and mostly referable to the right posterior neck. Should the patient be bothered by it **Hydrocollator steam packs** could be tried together with medicines such as Tylenol, etc. Bolton v. MFA Mut. Ins. Co., 386 So.2d 144–5 (Ct.App.La.1980).

package insert See *insert, manufacturer's.*

pad (pad) a cushion-like mass of soft material.

pad, heating

"It is an extremely safe means of applying heat. In fact, the safest that I know of." When asked why he ordered the **aqua pad** rather than moist towels, his reply was: "It is the most superior appurtenance or instrument or applicable form of heat that I know of. It is used standard in my treatment as well as other orthopedic surgeons." . . .

Dr. Gozansky corroborated the testimony of Dr. Sciarretta in regard to the propriety of using an **aqua pad** under the particular circumstances. When he first saw the patient on Sunday, November 7, he was aware that the pad had been ordered for application to the left hip. Knowing the patient's condition of diabetes and his incapacity, he still felt that the order and the treatment were proper. He said that **aqua pads** are preferable to other forms of heat because they are known not to burn a patient. The pad's highest range of temperature (105 degrees) is a proper temperature. Hale v. Holy Cross Hospital, Inc., 513 F.2d 315, 317 (5th Cir. 1975).

pain (pān) [L. *poena, dolor;* Gr. *algos, odynē*] a more or less localized sensation of discomfort, distress, or agony, resulting from the stimulation of specialized nerve endings. It serves as a protective mechanism insofar as it induces the sufferer to remove or withdraw from the source. See also *dystrophy, reflex sympathetic* (Culp case); *mobility; stress; subjective*; and *symptom.*

Pain can be disabling "even when its existence is unsupported by objective medical evidence if linked to a medically determinable impairment." Scharlow v. Schweiker, 655 F.2d 645, 648 (5th Cir. 1981). Simpson v. Schweiker, 691 F.2d 966, 970 (11th Cir. 1982).

The evidence that Whitaker works in constant **pain** greatly preponderates. A finding of substantial **pain** requires that plaintiff be held disabled. Phillips v. Dresser Engineering Co., 351 So.2d 304 (La.App. 3 Cir.1977), writ denied 353 So.2d 1048 (La.1978); Rachal v. Highlands Insurance Co., 355 So.2d 1355 (La.App. 3 Cir.1978), writ denied La., 358 So.2d 645; Wright v. Liberty Mutual Insurance Co., 357 So.2d 1213 (La.App. 3 Cir.1978), writ denied La., 360 So.2d 1180; Ashworth v. Elton Pickering, Inc., 361 So.2d 940 (La.App. 3 Cir.1978), writ denied La., 362 So.2d 1119; Bonnette v. Travelers Insurance Co., 367 So.2d 1261 (La.App. 3 Cir.1979); Simmons v. State Department of Transportation, 368 So.2d 770 (La.App. 2 Cir.1979); Jones v. Arnold, 371 So.2d 1258 (La.App. 3 Cir. 1979); Guidry v. Ford, Bacon & Davis Construction Corp., 376 So.2d 352 (La.App. 3 Cir. 1979). See the article by Professor H. Alston Johnson, III at 39 La.Law Review 883, which points out that the "working in **pain** jurisprudence", 39 La.L.Rev. 886, continues to be viable under the definition of total disability in the 1975 amendments to the compensation act. Whitaker v. Church's Fried Chicken, Inc., 387 So.2d 1093, 1096 (La.1980).

"... Then they, the studies talk about emotional stress, but **pain** is emotionally stressful. I don't think we can get away from the fact that the perception of **pain** is emotional stress, just like the apprehension of anxiety, the feeling of anxiety, or the feeling of worry, or the feeling of depression, or the feeling, of frustration, or the feeling of working under a tight time schedule. All of these things are emotional stress, and although the types of emotional stress that we can perceive are several, the ways in which the body mechanism can react to emotional stresses are limited." Lewis v. Workers' Comp. Appeals Bd., 128 Cal.Rptr. 752, 755 (Ct.App.Cal.1976).

Other Authorities: Simonson v. Schweiker, 699 F.2d 426, 429 (8th Cir. 1983); Marcus v. Califano, 615 F.2d 23, 27 (2d Cir. 1979); U.S. v. Pastor, 557 F.2d 930, 942 (2d Cir. 1977); Mc-Swain v. Chicago Transit Auth., 362 N.E.2d 1264, 1267 (App. Ct.Ill.1977); Generella v. Weinberger, 388 F.Supp. 1086, 1089–90 (E.D.Pa.1974); Ascough v. Workmen's Comp. App. Bd., 98 Cal.Rptr. 357, 360 (Ct.App.Cal.1971); Bourne v. Washburn, 441 F.2d 1022, 1025 (D.C.Cir.1971).

pain and suffering

Pain and suffering is a generic name for several types of damages falling under that head, including mental and physical pain and suffering, past, present and future. The measure of damage in such cases is the enlightened conscience of impartial jurors. The award for future **pain and suffering** does not have to be reduced to present cash value. St. Paul Fire & Marine Insurance Company v. Dillingham, 112 Ga.App. 422, 424, 145 S.E.2d 624. . . .

The term "**pain and suffering**" covers disfigurement and deformity. Ableman v. Ormond, 53 Ga.App. 753, 187 S.E. 393; Fulton Bakery Incorporated v. Williams, 37 Ga.App. 780, 141 S.E. 922; Langran v. Hodges, 60 Ga.App. 567, 4 S.E.2d 489. Aretz v. U.S., 456 F.Supp. 397, 401, 402 (S.D.Ga.1978).

pain, chest (cardiac origin)

Chest pain of **cardiac origin** is considered to be pain which is precipitated by effort and promptly relieved by sublingual nitroglycerin or rapid-acting nitrates or rest. The character of the pain is classically described as crushing, squeezing, burning, or oppressive pain located in the chest. Excluded is sharp, sticking, or rhythmic pain. Pain occurring on exercise should be described specifically as to usual inciting factors (kind and degree), character, location, radiation, duration, and response to nitroglycerin or rest. [20 C.F.R., Ch. III, App. I, Part A, § 4.00E.] Jackson v. Schweiker, 696 F.2d 630, 632 (8th Cir. 1983).

pain, labor the rhythmic pains of increasing severity and frequency, caused by contractions of the uterus during childbirth.

pain, neuroma

The referee found that the claimant suffered from **neuroma pain** caused by the original injury and that the pain rendered him disabled. The referee further characterized the **neuroma pain** as an extreme sensitivity in the central nervous system of the claimant which causes an extreme response to contact or anticipated contact, and prevents the claimant from doing his former work or any activities involving his left hand. . . .

. . . Dr. Novak testified, as follows, regarding Durr's condition after the second amputation:

"Q. Is there a name for this type of difficulty that he had?

"A. The name is **neuroma pain**, because it is the easiest name to understand. And the explanation to (sic) the pain is that the nerve heals with a neuroma. It is a small tumor of the nerve where the little fibers of the nerve grow out and form a little button. In some people, these buttons are completely insensitive. In other people, they can be awfully painful. . . . When we see this pain, the patient is very disabled, because of this pain, and it is rare. . . . I see in my practice 500 to 700 amputees a year and about one percent of my patients have this kind of **neuroma pain**." Truck Lubricating v. Workmen's Compensation, 421 A.2d 1251–3 (Commonwealth Ct. Pa.1980).

pain, phantom limb pain felt as though arising in an absent (amputated) limb. See also *limb, phantom.*

Ultimately, a twelfth surgical procedure was performed in which Musial's right leg was amputated below the knee— more than three years after the original injury. Since the amputation, Musial has suffered "**phantom pain**" of his lower right leg and suffers continuing back pain resultant from the awkward manner in which he is required to walk with his prosthesis. Musial v. A & A Boats, Inc., 696 F.2d 1149, 1152 (5th Cir. 1983).

However, following the removal of her leg, the plaintiff continued to suffer "**phantom pain**", which Dr. Friedman testified was a frequent reaction of the body to an amputation. Warmsley v. City of New York, 454 N.Y.S.2d 144, 146 (2d Dep't 1982).

pain, precordial

... the petitioner complained of "a typical pain, what we call **precordial pain**, pain along the—over the—left chest with pain down his left arm." Yeomans v. Jersey City, 143 A.2d 174, 179 (N.J.1958).

pain, radiating

Dr. DeNaples, the surgeon who operated on appellee, testified that **radiating pain**. i.e., pain which extends from the back down into the legs, involves nerve root irritation which is often caused by a ruptured or damaged disc. Liberty Mut. Ins. Co. v. Graves, 573 S.W.2d 249, 255 (Ct.Civ.App.Tex.1978).

palindromic (pal"in-dro'mik) returning; recurrent.

The report concluded that plaintiff was suffering from **palindromic** (recurrent) rheumatism aggravated by possible psychological problems and general tenseness and anxiety. Hamm v. Richardson, 324 F.Supp. 328, 330 (N.D.Miss.1971).

pallidotomy (pal"ĭ-dot'o-me) [*pallidum* + Gr. *tomē* a cutting] a stereotaxic surgical technique for producing lesions in the globus pallidus for treatment of extrapyramidal disorders.

palpation (pal-pa'shun) [L. *palpatio*] the act of feeling with the hand; the application of the fingers with light pressure to the surface of the body for the purpose of determining the consistence of the parts beneath in physical diagnosis.

Chisholm complained of some pain on forward flexion and deep **palpation** of the lumbosacral spine area. Chisholm v. L. S. Womack, Inc., 424 So.2d 1138, 1141 (Ct.App.La.1982).

It is the standard and accepted practice in trauma cases for the examining physician to **palpate** the area of suspected injury or fracture to determine the response to pain that might point to the location of an injury. The medical records do not record any such **palpation** although both doctors now testify that they did **palpate** the thoracic area. Brazil v. U.S., 484 F.Supp. 986, 988 (N.D.Ala.1979).

palsy See *paralysis.*

palsy, cerebral a persisting qualitative motor disorder appearing before the age of three years, due to a non-progressive damage to the brain.

Cherie was expelled from the uterus into the abdomen, and her oxygen supply was compromised, resulting in severe and permanent brain damage. More specifically, she has a condition known as **cerebral palsy**.

Although Cherie is mentally alert, and she has no physical impairment, due to the anoxic condition (lack of oxygen) in which she was born, Cherie has a severe neurological impairment. Long v. Johnson, 381 N.E.2d 93, 97 (Ct.App.Ind.1978).

palsy, peroneal

As a result of this [knee] surgery, plaintiff suffers from combined **peroneal and tibial palsy** of her left foot, a condition evidenced by numbness in her big toe and three adjoining toes, the numbness extending about half way up her foot on both the top and the bottom. Hale v. Venuto, 187 Cal.Rptr. 357, 359 (Ct.App.Cal.1982).

palsy, sixth nerve See *nervus abducens.*

Plaintiff was admitted to the Hospital with **sixth nerve palsy**, a condition that resulted from intracranial pressure, which caused his loss of vision. If radical and immediate treatment to alleviate this pressure were not taken, permanent loss of vision, loss of consciousness, and sudden death could have occurred. Niblack v. U.S., 438 F.Supp. 383, 387 (D.Col.1977).

palsy, suprascapular nerve

Upon awakening in the recovery room following surgery, appellee experienced severe pain in her neck, left shoulder, and left arm. This pain was diagnosed as resulting from a **suprascapular nerve palsy** allegedly caused by the malpositioning of the patient. Jones v. Harrisburg Polyclinic Hosp., 410 A.2d 303, 305 (Super.Ct.Pa.1979), reversed 496 Pa. 465, 437 A.2d 1134 (Pa.1981).

palsy, tardy median See *syndrome, carpal tunnel.*

palsy, tardy ulnar nerve

Tardy ulnar nerve palsy—As a likely result of either the accident or the lengthy bed rest required of him, Worthington developed **tardy ulnar nerve palsy** of the left hand, which initially caused severe loss of grip and loss of sensation in the left hand. Ultimately, Worthington's left elbow was operated on to relieve pressure on the nerve. Worthington v. Bynum, 281 S.E.2d 166, 170 (Ct.App.N.Car.1981), reversed and cause remanded 305 N.C. 478, 290 S.E.2d 599 (N.Car.1982).

pancreas (pan'kre-as), pl. *pan'creáta* [Gr. *pan* all + *kreas* flesh] a large, elongated, racemose gland situated transversely behind the stomach, between the spleen and the duodenum. Its right extremity, the *head*, is the larger, and directed downward; the left extremity, or *tail*, is transverse, and terminates close to the spleen. The external secretion or juice of the pancreas, which passes into the duodenum through the pancreatic duct, contains a variety of digestive enzymes. An internal secretion, insulin, produced in the beta cells, is concerned with the regulation of carbohydrate metabolism. Glucagon, a glycogenolytic-hyperglycemic factor, is produced in the alpha cells. Both the alpha and beta cells, along with the delta cells, form aggregates known as islets of Langerhans, scattered throughout the pancreas.

Plaintiff claims that he was given three different explanations for the performance of the second operation: A Dr. Oxman said it was to "scrape the **pancreas**," on which the first operation had revealed scar tissue. A Dr. Weiss said that "Dr. Oxman punctured the **pancreas** in the first operation." A Dr. Smith said that "the stitches hadn't been pulled tight enough on the first operation." Kelly v. U.S., 554 F.Supp. 1001–2 (E.D.N.Y.1983).

Scientific evidence tended, then, to show a probability that if there were asbestos in the **pancreas**, any co-existent pancreatic carcinoma would be asbestos-related, and that, therefore, that death from pancreatic carcinoma in such circumstances would probably be industrially-related. Baptist v. W.C.A.B. of State of Cal., 187 Cal.Rptr. 270–1 (Ct.App.Cal. 1982).

The tail of the **pancreas**, which lies way in the back of the abdominal cavity, showed a near complete crushing transection in the midline. State v. Mendell, 523 P.2d 79, 81 (Ariz. 1974).

pancreatic pseudocyst See *pseudocyst, pancreatic.*

pancreatin (pan′kre-ah-tin) [USP] a substance obtained from the pancreas of the hog or the ox, which contains enzymes, chiefly amylase, protease, and lipase, and having the same action as do the enzymes of the pancreatic juice; used as a digestive aid in conditions of pancreatic insufficiency, and also to peptonize milk and other foods.

These enzymes are derived from **pancreatin** which is a substance derived from the freshly ground pancreas of hogs and cattle. Prior to the disclosures of the '93 patent **pancreatin** had long been used as a digestive aid, designed to supplement the natural secretions of the human pancreas and facilitate digestion of the complicated protein molecule. In this use as a digestive supplement, **pancreatin** had been enterically coated and orally administered to persons whose own production of proteolytic enzymes was insufficient. Armour Pharmaceutical Co. v. Richardson-Merrell, Inc., 396 F.2d 70–1 (3d Cir. 1968).

pancreatitis (pan″kre-ah-ti′tis) acute or chronic inflammation of the pancreas, which may be asymptomatic or symptomatic, and which is due to autodigestion of a pancreatic tissue by its own enzymes. It is caused most often by alcoholism or biliary tract disease; less commonly it may be associated with hyperlipemia, hyperparathyroidism, abdominal trauma (accidental or operative injury), vasculitis, or uremia.

Other secondary causes of death included focal acute **pancreatitis**, associated along with pancreatic and duodenal abscesses following gall bladder surgery. Bruney v. City of Lake Charles, 386 So.2d 950–1 (Ct.App.La.1980).

This major surgery disclosed that Mrs. Campbell was afflicted with acute **pancreatitis**, an inflammation of the pancreas. Bellaire General Hospital, Inc. v. Campbell, 510 S.W.2d 94–5 (Ct.Civ.App.Tex.1974).

pancreatitis, acute See *pancreatitis, acute hemorrhagic.*

pancreatitis, acute hemorrhagic a condition due to autolysis of pancreatic tissue caused by the escape of enzymes into its substance, resulting in hemorrhage into the parenchyma and surrounding tissues. Blood staining of the lateral abdominal wall (Grey Turner's sign) or periumbilical area (Cullen's sign) may result.

The doctor testified that the decedent's death resulted from the disease of ''acute **pancreatitis**'' which in turn caused ''acute renal failure and shock.'' The witness explained that **acute pancreatitis** is ''the digestion of the tissues of the pancreas ... by its own enzymes.'' Edwards v. Jackson, 171 S.E. 2d 854–5 (Va.1970).

pancuronium bromide (pan″ku-ro′ne-um) chemical name: 1,1′-[(2β,3α,5α,16β,17β)-3,17-bis(acetyloxy)androstane-2,16-diyl]-bis[1-methyl]piperidinium dibromide. A nondepolarizing skeletal muscle relaxant, $C_{35}H_{60}Br_2N_2O_4$, with curariform action; used as an adjunct to anesthesia, and may be used to facilitate mechanical ventilation, administered intravenously.

The Grand Jury charged, and the government sought to prove, that the defendants, registered nurses employed in the Intensive Care Unit of the Veterans Administration Hospital in Ann Arbor, Michigan, conspired together and did in fact poison and murder various patients in that institution by injecting a powerful muscle relaxant drug, known as **pavulon**, into the victims' intravenous (i.v.) apparatus....

... She described the clinical symptoms of persons who have been given each of the two broad types of muscle relaxants, succinylcholine and turbocurare, a sub-type of which is **pavulon**. U.S. v. Narciso, 446 F.Supp. 252, 306 (E.D.Mich. 1977).

pancytopenia (pan″si-to-pe′ne-ah) [*pan-* + *-cyte* + Gr. *penia* poverty] deficiency of all cell elements of the blood; aplastic anemia.

During that period he was exposed on the job to xylene, toluene and trichlorethylene....

... he worked for still a third employer where he handled cleaning materials containing, according to his testimony, carbon tetrachloride....

... Dr. Bunting's initial or tentative diagnosis was ''**pancytopenia** with hypoplastic marrow, etiology unknown. Exposure to volatile hydrocarbon suspected....'' Priedigkeit v. Industrial Com'n, 542 P.2d 1140–1 (Ct.App.Ariz.1975).

panel (pan′el) a list of names, a number of individuals participating in a specific discussion or activity, especially a list of names of the medical men who are willing to care for insured persons for a stipulated yearly fee under the system of medical insurance carried on by insurance groups under the supervision of the government in Great Britain, or the list of the insured persons assigned as clients to a physician under the British National Health Insurance Act.

panel, malpractice

The medical **malpractice panel** procedure was instituted in 1974 to expedite the disposition of malpractice cases and reduce litigation costs. Bryant v. University of Rochester, 72 A.D. 2d 965, 422 N.Y.S.2d 262; Musso v. Westfield Memorial Hospital, 64 A.D.2d 851, 407 N.Y.S.2d 605. It was anticipated that many nonmeritorious cases would be eliminated by unanimous findings of no liability that would eventually result in similar jury verdicts, and that trial calendars would be reduced by pre-trial settlements subsequent to a panel recommendation. Recent study suggests that these hopes have not been realized and that the malpractice ''problem'' has been exacerbated by the panel process. Rosa v. Mohan Kulkarni Unibell Anesthesia, P.C., 113 Misc.2d 39, 448 N.Y.S.2d 400.

A **malpractice panel** serves in a quasi-judicial capacity. De-Camp v. Good Samaritan Hospital, supra. Although a jury is not bound by the panel's unanimous recommendation (Bernstein v. Bodean, supra.), the panel's recommendation and a panelist's testimony provide the jury with expert testimony or evidence to influence and assist the jury in reaching its verdict. Luce v. St. Peter's Hospital, supra. Indeed, it appears that the Legislature intended the panel recommendation to impact upon the jury. Bernstein v. Bodean, supra 53 N.Y.S.2d at p. 527, 443 N.Y.S.2d 49, 426 N.E.2d 741; Rosa v. Mohan Kulkarni Unibell Anesthesia, P.C., supra. Under the circumstances, the panelists must be viewed no differently than judges in terms of their qualifications to resolve the issues of law and fact. King v. Retz, 454 N.Y.S.2d 594, 596, 598–9 (Sup.Ct.Onondaga Ct. 1982).

panogen See *cyanoguanidine.*

panograph

The third type of X-ray is **panograph**. This X-ray depicts all of the teeth in both jaws in panoramic fashion. It is used to reflect the general oral hygiene of the patient. U.S. v. Talbott, 460 F.Supp. 253, 256 (S.D.Ohio 1978).

panophthalmitis (pan″of-thal-mi′tis) [*pan-* + Gr. *ophthalmos* eye + *-itis*] inflammation of all the structures or tissues of the eye.

The ear, nose, and throat specialist testified that in his expert opinion on 25 September, appellant's condition "was a severe condition. It was so severe, that it spread not only to the front sinuses, while waiting for a bed in the hospital, he developed what we call **pan-ophthalmitis** eye. His eye was pushed forward, as it was a secondary condition." Graham v. Roberts, 441 F.2d 995, 998 (D.C.Cir.1970).

pansinusitis (pan″si-nu-si′tis) [*pan-* + *sinus* + *-itis*] inflammation involving all of the paranasal sinuses on one side.

The appellant Graham, a patient of the appellee Roberts, did not allege that the dentist was negligent in extracting an upper molar, but rather that the dentist was negligent in continuing to treat a worsening condition of **pansinusitis** over a period of four months, instead of referring appellant's condition to a properly qualified medical specialist for treatment when appellant's condition became apparent to the appellee. The appellee's testimony showed that the removal of an upper molar created a communication channel between the mouth and the maxillary sinus. Following the extraction in May 1963, appellant developed a sinus infection which drained through the opening created by the extraction into his mouth. This sinus infection became progressively worse and by September it required surgery, 22 days' hospitalization, and six months' follow-up treatment before appellant was fully recovered....

... The appellee himself testified that he as a dentist would not try to cure an infected sinus, but would rather close off the connection between the mouth and the sinus and refer the patient to a specialist for proper treatment....

... At that time, according to appellee, appellant had "a fistula draining at the extraction site," an "infection of the socket and an infection of the sinus." Appellee "Treat[ed] the infection at the site of the socket," but did not attempt to treat the sinus infection. Graham v. Roberts, 441 F.2d 995–7 (D.C. Cir.1970).

Pantopaque (pan-to-pāk′) trademark for a preparation of iophendylate. See also *iophendylate.*

Pap smear See *test, pap.*

Pap test See *test, Papanicolaou's.*

papilla (pah-pil′ah), pl. *papil′lae* [L.] a small nipple-shaped projection or elevation; [NA] a general term for such a structure.

papilledema (pap″il-ĕ-de′mah) choked disk; edema of the optic disk (papilla), most commonly due to increased intracranial pressure, malignant hypertension, or thrombosis of the central retinal vein. See also *pressure, intracranial* (Gendusa case).

Dr. Giorlando diagnosed his condition as bilateral **papilledema** or swelling of the optic nerve and referred plaintiff to Dr. Robert Cangelosi, an ophthalmologist....

... Dr. Pailet testified unequivocally that **papilledema** of a short term does not cause decreased visual acuity to the extent of 20/40 and 20/50 as measured by Dr. Cangelosi on October 29th. He went on to say that once the decrease was present it would continue to decrease even with adequate relief of intracranial pressure and that an "irreversible condition due to a decrease in visual acuity at the time of the initial examination by Dr. Cangelosi" had already begun leading to optic atrophy....

... He explained that when he examined the boy in April there was no **papilledema** and no sign of intracranial pressure. There was optic atrophy, or deadness of the optic nerve. He went on to explain that while **papilledema** may not show up where there is optic atrophy because the nerve fibers are dead and less likely to swell you could see "signs of wrinkling of the retina or hemorrhages" with increased pressure but there were none. We have concluded that Dr. Cangelosi's overall testimony supports the conclusion that more probably than not the final condition was caused by the initial **papilledema** with only a possibility remaining that some undetected increase in pressure between January and April contributed significantly to the final condition. Gendusa v. St. Paul Fire & Marine Ins. Co., 435 So.2d 479, 481, 484 (Ct.App.La.1983).

... its [pseudotumor cerebri] accompanying symptoms of **papilledema** (swelling of the retina at the optic disc), headaches, dizziness and brief memory lapses....

On October 9, 1973, plaintiff was examined at Meyer's eye clinic for complaints of headaches, blurring of vision and spots before his eyes. Neurological examination revealed bilateral **papilledema** and it was recommended that plaintiff be admitted for re-evaluation as soon as possible. Marbury v. Matthews, 433 F.Supp. 1081, 1083 (W.D.N.Y.1977).

papilloma (pap″ĭ-lo′mah) [*papilla* + *-oma*] a branching or lobulated benign tumor derived from epithelium.

... a California appeals court held that a chiropodist could not testify in an action against a hospital and its radiologist for burns suffered through the use of radiation therapy for **papillomae** (warts on the skin or the mouth). Bennett v. Los Angeles Tumor Institute [227 P.2d 473 (1971)]. Ragan v. Steen, 331 A.2d 724, 736 (Super.Ct.Pa.1974).

papilloma, intraductal

The examination revealed a lump in the upper right quadrant of the plaintiff's right breast. Dr. Gryniewicz attributed the condition to Mrs. Dettmann's pregnancy, explaining the lump to be a benign milk duct cyst referred to as **intraductal papilloma**, a condition which would dissolve in due course. According to Dr.

Gryniewicz the size of the cyst was one centimeter by one centimeter. Dettmann v. Flanary, 273 N.W.2d 348–9 (Wis. 1979).

para- [Gr. *para* beyond] a prefix meaning beside, beyond, accessory to, apart from, against, etc. In chemistry, the prefix indicates the substitution in a derivative of the benzene ring of two atoms linked to opposite carbon atoms in the ring. The abbreviation is *p-*.

para-aminosalicylic acid See *acid, aminosalicylic.*

paraffin section See *section, paraffin.*

paragrammatism (par″ah-gram′ah-tizm) impairment of speech, with confusion in the use and order of words and grammatical forms.

paraldehyde (par-al′dĕ-hīd) [USP] chemical name: 2,4,6-trimethyl-1,3,5-trioxane. A polymerization product of acetaldehyde, $C_6H_{12}O$, occurring as a colorless, transparent liquid and having rapid-acting sedative and hypnotic properties; used to control insomnia, excitement, agitation, delirium, and convulsions, administered rectally and intramuscularly and by intravenous infusion.

That evening plaintiff visited with his family until about 10 p.m., at which time his wife gave him a dosage of **paraldehyde**. Since **paraldehyde** is a quick-acting, sleep-inducing hypnotic, plaintiff retired immediately.

The jury could find that, in addition to being affected by the electroshock treatment, plaintiff may have been unhinged by the effect of **paraldehyde**, which is a fast-acting drug described as a colorless liquid with a strong taste, aromatic odor, and a burning disagreeable taste. This drug, which is taken orally, usually insures sleep within 10 or 15 minutes. About a half hour is required for it to reach maximal concentrations in the brain after oral administration. Chronic **paraldehyde** intoxication results in tolerance and dependence. The drug is used in the treatment of alcoholism, and in spite of its taste and odor the patient may prefer it to alcohol. A tolerance to it is acquired, and addiction is not infrequent. Christy v. Saliterman, 179 N.W.2d 288, 293–5 (Minn.1970).

paralysis (pah-ral′ĭ-sis), pl. *paral′yses* [para- + Gr. *lyein* to loosen] loss or impairment of motor function in a part due to lesion of the neural or muscular mechanism; also, by analogy, impairment of sensory function (sensory paralysis). In addition to the types named below, paralysis is further distinguished as *traumatic, syphilitic, toxic,* etc., according to its cause; or as *obturator, ulnar,* etc., according to the nerve, part, or muscle specially affected. For other varieties see also *hemiplegia; paraplegia; paresis;* and *polyneuritis, acute febrile.*

On July 5, 1973, plaintiff had surgery performed on his left eye to correct a muscle disorder which allowed his eye to wander and turn out. After surgery, he was paralyzed on his right side and at the time of trial, he had a spastic right-sided **paralysis** of 50 percent in the right shoulder, a loss of fine finger movement in his right hand, an inability to heel gait on the right side, a right circumductive walk, and a right-sided numbness. Vuletich v. Bolgla, 407 N.E.2d 566, 568 (App.Ct.Ill.1980).

"So that the essence of her neurological disability is that this patient has extensive involvement of the central nervous system, with **paralysis** of both upper extremities in spastic flexion, **paralysis** of the right lower extremity in extension, some involvement of the left lower extremity, which is persistent, and disturbances in thinking and mentation and mood from excessive crying which is reported as well as repetitious speech, and some disorientation in time and her recent retention...." Talcott v. Holl, 224 So.2d 420, 423 (Dist.Ct.App.Fla.1969).

paralysis agitans a form of parkinsonism of unknown etiology usually occurring in late life, although a juvenile form has been described. It is a slowly progressive disease characterized by masklike facies, a characteristic tremor of resting muscles, a slowing of voluntary movements, a festinating gait, peculiar posture, and weakness of the muscles. There may be excessive sweating and feelings of heat. Pathologically, there is degeneration within the nuclear masses of the extrapyramidal system and a characteristic loss of melanin-containing cells from the substantia nigra and a corresponding reduction in dopamine levels in the corpus striatum. Called also *Parkinson's disease* and *shaking palsy.*

Plaintiff did not respond to the treatment and on September 8 Dr. Romito referred him to another neurologist, Dr. Stanley Skillicorn, who positively diagnosed **Parkinson's disease**. This is a progressive, degenerative disorder of the central nervous system, that is, a portion of the brain, characterized by disturbances of ability to move one or both sides, by disturbances in gait, and by tremor. It is essentially an involvement of the extraparamental tract or basal ganglia section of the brain, which may result in involuntary movements of various kinds. The great majority of persons afflicted with the disease follow a fairly predictable pattern, in fact, in due time they will progress to a condition of considerable and eventual total disability. There is no true cure for the disease. Belshaw v. Feinstein, 65 Cal.Rptr. 788, 790 (Ct.App.Cal.1968).

paralysis, brachial paralysis of an arm from lesion of the brachial plexus. See also *Erb-Duchenne paralysis*; and *Klumpke-Dejerine paralysis.*

paralysis, Erb-Duchenne the upper-arm type of brachial paralysis; paralysis of the upper roots of brachial plexus due to destruction of the fifth and sixth cervical roots and characterized by absence of involvement of the small hand muscles.

The expert further testified that this use of traction was the competent producing cause of the injury to the infant's left brachial plexus, which injury resulted in a condition known as **Erb's paralysis** or **Erb's palsy** in the infant's left arm. Mulligan v. Shuter, 419 N.Y.S.2d 13–14 (2d Dep't 1979).

Dr. Sargent concluded Peeples was suffering from a complete **brachial plexus palsy**. Complete **brachial plexus palsy** results in loss of all sensation and all motor ability of the arm. Peeples couldn't move his hand and had no sensation in his arm. Peeples was taken to the x-ray room and then to the operating room where Dr. Sargent reduced the dislocation and put the shoulder back in the socket. Peeples v. Sargent, 253 N.W.2d 459, 464 (Wis.1977).

paralysis, flaccid paralysis with loss of tone of the muscles of the paralyzed part and absence of tendon reflexes. Cf. *spastic p.*

After Dr. Dostal arrived and upon examination found Sendejar to be suffering from **flaccid paralysis** from the waist down due to a spinal cord injury, Dr. Dostal then directed that the patient be transferred to Memorial Hospital in Corpus Christi, Texas, where he would be treated by Dr. Rufino Gonzales....

... He testified that in his opinion the paralysis commenced on Sunday and was caused by injuries to the soft tissues and the swelling and bleeding in the spinal cord. He testified that the paralysis came on gradually and that the function of the spinal cord was lost in increments....

Dr. Craig Norstrom and Dr. Joseph G. Klotz, both neurosurgeons, testified that they saw Sendejar after he arrived at Memorial Hospital in Corpus Christi. They testified that as a result of x-ray studies, they were of the opinion that Sendejar's spinal cord was severely crushed and severed at the time of the automobile accident and that such injuries caused immediate paralysis at that time. Sendejar v. Alice Physicians & Surgeons Hosp., Inc., 555 S.W.2d 879, 884 (Ct.Civ. App.Tex.1977).

paralysis, hysterical apparent loss of power of movement in a part seen in hysteria, in the absence of a neurological cause.

Comfort did not believe that Slater suffered from **hysterical paralysis** because he showed a loss of electromyographic potential, which does not occur where there is **hysterical paralysis**. Slater v. Kehoe, 113 Cal.Rptr. 790, 794 (Ct.App.Cal. 1974).

paralysis, Klumpke's; paralysis, Klumpke-Dejerine the lower-arm type of brachial paralysis; atrophic paralysis of the muscles of the arm and hand, from lesion of the eighth cervical and first dorsal nerves. It often occurs in infants delivered by breech extraction.

paralysis, spastic paralysis marked by spasticity of the muscles of the paralyzed part and increased tendon reflexes, due to upper motor neuron lesions. Cf. *flaccid p.*

paralysis, Werdnig-Hoffmann a hereditary, progressive, infantile form of muscular atrophy, transmitted as an autosomal recessive trait, usually occurring in siblings rather than in successive generations, and resulting from degeneration of the anterior horn cells of the spinal cord. It is marked by early onset (usually at about six months of age, but sometimes in fetal life), hypotonia and wasting of the muscles, complete flaccid paralysis, and death, usually in early life. Called also *familial spinal muscular atrophy, Hoffmann-Werdnig syndrome,* and *progressive spinal muscular atrophy of infants.* Cf. *Kugelberg-Welander disease.*

... his son suffered from a genetically transmitted disease known as **Werdnig-Hoffman** disease from which a previous son had died a year earlier at the age of five months. [Footnote omitted.] Williams v. Travelers Insurance Co., 123 Cal. Rptr. 83–4 (Ct.App.Cal.1975).

paralytic (par″ah-lit′ik) [Gr. *paralytikos*] 1. affected with or pertaining to paralysis. 2. a person affected with paralysis.

paralytic brachial neuritis See *amyotrophy, neuralgic.*

paralumbar See *lumbar;* and *para-.*

paralumbar muscles See *muscucli interspinales lumborum.*

paralyze (par′ah-līz) to put into a state of paralysis.

paramedic See *paramedical.*

paramedical (par″ah-med′ĭ-kal) having some connection with or relation to the science or practice of medicine; adjunctive to the practice of medicine in the maintenance or restoration of health and normal functioning. Paramedical workers include physical, occupational, and speech therapists, medical social workers, pharmacists, technicians, and so on. See also *physician assistant.*

While the definition places special emphasis upon the **paramedic's** training in all aspects in cardiopulmonary resuscitation, the act does not limit a **paramedic's** authority to act in situations involving other than cardiopulmonary resuscitation. The act implicitly recognizes that the **paramedics** may encounter a variety of emergencies. The statute's grant of immunity includes all those acts which can fall within the term "emergency lifesaving service."....

Laws of 1971, 1st Ex.Sess., ch. 305, § 2, provided in part:
" '[P]hysician's trained mobile intensive care **paramedic'** means a person who:
(1) has successfully completed an advanced first aid course equivalent to the advanced industrial first aid course prescribed by the Division of Safety, Department of Labor and Industries; and
(2) is trained by a licensed physician:
(a) to carry out all phases of cardio-pulmonary resuscitation;
(b) to administer drugs under written or oral authorization of a licensed physician; and
(c) to administer intravenous solutions under written or oral authorization of a licensed physician; and
(3) has been examined and certified as a physician's trained mobile intensive care paramedic by a county health officer or by the University of Washington's School of Medicine or by their designated representatives." Malone v. City of Seattle, 600 P.2d 647, 650 (Ct.App.Wash.1979).

parametrium (par″ah-me′tre-um) [*para-* + Gr. *mētra* uterus] [NA] the extension of the subserous coat of the supracervical portion of the uterus laterally between the layers of the broad ligament.

paranoia (par″ah-noi′ah) [*para-* + Gr. *nous* mind + *-ia*] a chronic, slowly progressive mental disorder (personality disorder) characterized by the development of ambitions or suspicions into systematized delusions of persecution and grandeur which are built up in a logical form. The condition does not appear to interfere with the rest of the personality and thinking. Cf. *paranoid schizophrenia.*

Q. Doctor, what is **paranoid** ideation?

A. Being overly suspicious, accusatory, being overly concerned with sexual matters of another individual. Mass. Mut. Life Ins. Co. v. Tate, 391 N.Y.S.2d 667, 672 (2d Dep't 1977), reversed 42 N.Y. 1046, 399 N.Y.S.2d 211, 369 N.E.2d 767 (N.Y.1977).

"Now, the word **paranoid** means having a systematized delusion of persecution. The word itself, paranoid, by itself, does not mean necessarily that a person is insane, because there are people who think they are being picked on and persecuted all the time, and are not necessarily insane...." State v. Spivey, 319 A.2d 461, 465 (N.J.1974).

Dr. Bailey's report to the agency on August 30, 1966, concluded with the following diagnosis:

Paranoid personality, manifested by hostility, feelings of persecution and long history of strained interpersonal relationships.

I do not feel that this patient has a separate psychiatric illness at this time. It appears that his personality is conducive to anger, frustrations, etc. Richardson v. Perales, 402 U.S. 389, 394, 91 S.Ct. 1420, 28 L.Ed.2d 842 (1971).

Other Authorities: In Interest of Rambousek, 331 N.W.2d 548, 651 (N.D.1983).

paranoid (par'ah-noid) resembling paranoia. See also *paranoia*.

A **paranoid** person may interpret a reality skewed by suspicions, antipathies or fantasies. U.S. v. Lindstrom, 698 F.2d 1154, 1160 (11th Cir. 1983).

... psychological tests revealed a personality
with a latent **paranoid** thinking disorder ... from the record this is a man who has difficulty in getting along with people ... we have evidence of a pattern of responses consistent with a **paranoid** schizophrenic condition....

"After a complete review of the available documents and the information of all sorts already available in our clinical record, it is my opinion that an appropriate diagnostic label for this man would be a **paranoid** personality. He shows the sensitivity, the suspiciousness, the stubbornness and the tendency to utilize the mechanism of projection, characteristic of such a personality type. I do not believe however, that his psychological state is disabling at this time nor does it seem likely to become so in the foreseeable future. He is accordingly fit for duty at sea psychiatrically." Hendry v. U.S., 418 F.2d 774, 778 (2d Cir. 1969).

paranoid schizophrenia See under *schizophrenia*.

paraparesis (par"ah-par'ĕ-sis) [*para-* + Gr. *paresis* paralysis] a partial paralysis of the lower extremities.

... **paraparesis** (partial paralysis affecting the lower limbs) ensued and he was not expected to survive. Pratt v. Stein, 444 A.2d 674, 680 (Super.Ct.Pa.1982).

His medical diagnosis is that of **paraparesis**, or partial paralysis of the lower extremities, and not paraplegia, or total paralysis. Brazil v. U.S., 484 F.Supp. 986, 989 (N.D.Ala.1979).

In some cases, sudden **paraparesis** or paraplegia was stated to occur as a result of spontaneous thrombosis or bleeding within the spinal cord and that minor effort such as lifting or abdominal strain or compression may unleash such a spinal vascular accident. Tyminski v. U.S., 481 F.2d 257, 262 (3d Cir. 1973).

parapharyngeal See *pharynx*.

paraphasia (par"ah-fa'ze-ah) [*para-* + *aphasia*] partial aphasia in which the patient employs wrong words, or uses words in wrong and senseless combinations (*choreic p.*).

paraphernalia, drug

La.R.S. 40:1031. Definitions
A. As used in this Part, unless the context clearly otherwise indicates, the term "**drug paraphernalia**" shall mean and include, but not be limited to:
(1) All equipment, products, and materials of any kind which are used, intended for use, or designed for use in planting, propagating, cultivating, growing, harvesting, manufacturing, compounding, converting, producing, processing, preparing, testing, analyzing, packaging, re-packaging, storing, containing, concealing, injecting, ingesting, inhaling, or otherwise introducing into the human body a controlled substance in violation of the Uniform Controlled Dangerous Substances Law, as scheduled in R.S. 40:964.
La.R.S. 40:1031(A)(2)–(12) provides:
(2) Kits used, intended for use, or designed for use in planting, propagating, cultivating, growing, or harvesting of any species of plant which is a controlled substance or from which a controlled substance can be derived.
(3) Kits used, intended for use, or designed for use in manufacturing, compounding, converting, producing, processing, or preparing controlled substances.
(4) Isomerization devices used, intended for use, or designed for use in increasing the potency of any species of plant which is a controlled substance.
(5) Testing equipment used, intended for use, or designed for use in identifying, or in analyzing the strength, effectiveness, or purity of controlled substances.
(6) Diluents and adulterants, such as quinine, hydrochloride, mannitol, mannite, dextrose, and lactose, used, intended for use, or designed for use in cutting controlled substances.
(7) Separation gins and sifters used, intended for use, or designed for use in removing twigs and seeds from, or in otherwise cleaning or refining marijuana.
(8) Blenders, bowls, containers, spoons, and mixing devices used, intended for use, or designed for use in compounding controlled substances.
(9) Capsules, balloons, envelopes, and other containers used, intended for use, or designed for use in packaging small quantities of controlled substances.
(10) Containers and other objects used, intended for use, or designed for use in storing or concealing controlled substances.
(11) Hypodermic syringes, needles, and other objects used, intended for use, or designed for use in parenterally injecting controlled substances into the human body.
(12) Objects used, intended for use, or designed for use in ingesting, inhaling, or otherwise introducing marijuana, cocaine, hashish, or hashish oil into the human body, such as:
(a) Metal, wooden, acrylic, glass, stone, plastic, or ceramic pipes with or without screens, permanent screens, hashish heads, or punctured metal bowls.
(b) Water pipes.
(c) Carburetion tubes and devices.
(d) Smoking and carburetion masks.
(e) Roach clips, meaning objects used to hold burning material, such as a marijuana cigarette, that has become too small or too short to be held in the hand.
(f) Miniature cocaine spoons, and cocaine vials.
(g) Chamber pipes.

(h) Carburetor pipes.

(i) Electric pipes.

(j) Air-driven pipes.

(k) Chillums.

(l) Bongs.

(m) Ice pipes or chillers. Tobacco Accessories, Etc. v. Treen, 681 F.2d 378, 380–1 (5th Cir. 1982).

paraphilia (par″ah-fil′e-ah) [*para-* + Gr. *philein* to love + *-ia*] aberrant sexual activity; sexual deviation; expression of the sexual instinct in practices which are socially prohibited or unacceptable, or biologically undesirable. See also *cunnilingus; fellatio*; and *sodomy*.

A **deviate sexual act** is defined by Section 130.002(2) of the Penal Law as:

"Deviate sexual intercourse" means sexual conduct between persons not married to each other consisting of contact between the penis and the anus, the mouth and penis, or the mouth and the vulva. . . .

It cannot be said that acts of deviate sexual intercourse are, in and of themselves, intrinsically harmful or unnatural, causing in the participants any deviation from fundamental human nature.[15] [[15] . . . Studies indicate that most unmarried persons engage in the sexual conduct characterized as deviate sexual intercourse. Of unmarried heterosexual persons between the ages of 18 and 24 years old, 72% of those studied performed fellatio, 69% performed cunnilingus. One-sixth of all persons under 25 years of age who have ever had coitus have engaged in anal intercourse. M. Hunt, Sexual Behavior in the 1970's, pp. 166–7 (1974). Studies also reveal that 20 to 25% of all males over the age of 15 have engaged in oral or anal sex with another male and 10–20% of all females over 19 years of age have engaged in oral sex with another female. Hunt, supra at 312; Kinsey, Sex and the Human Male (1948); Kinsey, Sex and the Human Female (1953).] In re Dora P., 400 N.Y.S.2d 455, 458, 462–3 (Family Ct.N.Y.Cty.1977), reversed and remanded 68 A.D.2d 719, 418 N.Y.S.2d 597 (1st Dep't 1979).

paraplegia (par″ah-ple′je-ah) [*para-* + Gr. *plēgē* stroke + *-ia*] paralysis of the legs and lower part of the body.

He stated that Mrs. Swan's **paraplegia** was due to trauma which occurred principally at the time of surgery. As described by this witness, the irritation to the nerve roots caused by non-removal of the pantopaque caused them to be inflamed or injured. Said injury was compounded when the nerve roots were traumatized upon surgical removal of the posterior arch, thus producing immediate paralysis. Swan v. Lamb, 584 P.2d 814, 816 (Utah 1978).

Dr. Long returned to Shreveport on Sunday, February 3, which was six days into plaintiff's postoperative period. Samuels then had developed total **paraplegia** with sensory level at L–1. . . .

Plaintiff contends that the infection has rendered him a lifelong paraplegic. [Footnote omitted.] Samuels v. Doctors Hospital, Inc., 414 F.Supp. 1124, 1126 (W.D.La.1976).

The permanent result was complete **paraplegia**, with total loss of all sensation and motor control below the severance of the spinal cord. This includes loss of control of bowel movements and the passage of urine and the inability to perform sexual acts. . . .

With the **paraplegia** goes the prospect of almost certain recurring medical problems, notably infections of the kidney-ureter-bladder system, stone formation in that system, ulcers on the hip bone pressure points, and depression. Hampton v. State Highway Com'n, 498 P.2d 236, 251 (Kan.1972).

paraplegia, flaccid paraplegia with loss of muscle tone of the paralyzed part and absence of tendon reflexes. Cf. *spastic p*. See also under *paralysis*.

Within days of the operation Tyminski began progressively to lose control of the bodily functions in his lower extremities. . . . Tyminski's neurological condition deteriorated into **flaccid paraplegia**. Within a month of the operation the complete paraplegia in the lower extremities of Tyminski's body became spastic.

Tyminski was persistently informed by the defendant's physicians that the paraplegia was due to the natural progression of the congenital AVA. The District Court, however, found that the paraplegia was caused by post-operative bleeding within the operative site which collected in the potential space outside the dura, forming an epidual hematoma and causing pressure on the spinal cord. Tyminski v. U.S., 481 F.2d 257, 260 (3d Cir. 1973).

paraplegia, Pott's that which is due to vertebral caries or spinal tuberculosis; called also *Pott's paralysis*.

paraplegia, spastic paraplegia marked by spasticity of the muscles of the paralyzed part and increased tendon reflexes, due to damage to the corticospinal tract. Cf. *flaccid p*.

paraplegic (par″ah-plej′ik) pertaining to or of the nature of paraplegia; by extension, sometimes used to designate an individual affected with paraplegia.

According to Dr. Carter, the primary problems of the **paraplegic** are as follows:

"The major problems that would face any **paraplegic** would be two very significant ones. One, of course, is urinary tract infection, which may ascend from the bladder to the kidneys and compromise the kidneys' function, and/or result in kidney stones, which may result in the same type of thing. The second major problem is that of involving the skin, which because of the anesthesia and alteration of its own circulation is more sensitive to thermal injury from either severe hot sun or external heat of any type, hot water, et cetera, as well as an increased sensitivity to pressure, that the individual cannot feel, to pressure ulceration as we mentioned before. The third area, not quite as common as the first two, depending on the level of the spinal injury, would be that of a lowered resistance where the patient may get a respiratory infection, which then has to be treated with a little more vigor and a little more intelligence than in the normal individual, because of some impairment of ability to cough and clear secretions out of the lung." Cobb v. Insured Lloyds, 387 So.2d 13, 16 (Ct.App.La.1980).

parapsoriasis (par″ah-so-ri′ah-sis) a name applied by Brocq to a group of maculopapular scaly erythrodermas of slow development. They are marked by persistent red, scaling patches or papules devoid of subjective symptoms and resistant to treatment. There are three principal forms, the guttate, lichenoid, and patchy. See also *erythrodermatitis*.

"[In 1969 I'd] lost all my hair, sweat glands were destroyed, skin was very flaky, continuously coming off....

... he biopsied me, consulted with every member of his staff, and they came up with a diagnosis of retiform **parapsoriasis**, and he told me at that time, he said that this very well could lead in later life to lymphoma, Hodgkins disease, leukemia and things of this nature. Slayton v. Industrial Com'n, 550 P.2d 246, 249 (Ct.App.Ariz.1976).

parapsoriasis, retiform See *retiform*.

"Then we moved to Ventura, California, and I noticed that I was unable to perspire, that I was losing my hair faster, and little pus marks were evident around the hair follicles of my legs. In other words, in each pore there would be a little particle of pus, and then pretty soon the hair was all gone from my legs....

... and they came up with a diagnosis of retiform **parapsoriasis**, and he told me at that time, he said that this very well could lead in later life to lymphoma, Hodgkins disease, leukemia and things of this nature...." Slayton v. Industrial Com'n, 550 P.2d 246, 249 (Ct.App.Ariz.1976).

parapsychology (par"ah-si-kol'o-je) [*para-* + *psychology*] a branch of psychology dealing with those psychical effects and experiences which appear to fall outside the scope of physical law, e.g., telepathy and clairvoyance.

The American Society for Psychical Research was formally organized in 1906, principally through the efforts of William James, thought generally to be the most eminent of American psychologists....

One of the stated purposes of the Society is psychical research in all of its aspects, of which "survival research" is one of its recognized subdivisions. As Dr. Murphy explained, "Psychical research is the study of psychological processes for which we have no physical explanation as physics now exist." Dr. Murphy further explained that most of the phenomena associated with the field of psychical research are some type of telepathy or clairvoyance or related processes....

As to "survival research" itself, the American Society for Psychical Research studies and disseminates information as to "crisis apparitions" (whereby a person receives a "vision" of another person undergoing a crisis experience, often death, at another place), "deathbed visions" (whereby a dying person appears to undergo a transformation allowing him to see into another world), "physical changes in the surroundings" (whereby the death of a person is signaled by the disturbance of a physical object some distance away), and "out-of-the-body experiences" (whereby a person in a sleeping or comatose state appears to himself to wander forth from his body and take up a station some distance away, purportedly sometimes to be seen there by others)....

Dr. Joseph Gaither Pratt, whose testimony on behalf of the Psychical Research Foundation was referred to in the majority opinion, indicated that the general field of **parapsychology** includes:

crisis apparitions, deathbed visions, out-of-the-body experiences, clairvoyance, audiopsychometry, psychokinesis, poltergeist phenomena, ESP, and working with sensitives. In Re Estate of Kidd, 479 P.2d 697, 702, 712 (Ariz.1971).

paraquat (par'a-kwat) a poisonous dipyridilium compound whose dichloride and dimethylsulfate salts are used as contact herbicides. Contact with concentrated solutions causes irritation of the skin, cracking and shedding of the nails, and delayed healing of cuts and wounds. After ingestion of large doses, renal and hepatic failure may develop, followed by pulmonary insufficiency. See also *fibrosis, idiopathic pulmonary*.

... the treating physicians identified **paraquat** poisoning as the cause of the pulmonary fibrosis....

Paraquat is excreted from the body very soon after it is taken in. The doctors therefore had to rely on the history of **paraquat** exposure rather than any detection of **paraquat** in Mr. Ferebee's body. Ferebee v. Chevron Chemical Co., 552 F.Supp. 1293, 1296, 1299–1300 (D.D.C.1982).

parasagittal See *sutura, sagittalis*.

parasagittal meningioma See *meningioma*.

paraspinous muscle spasm See *spasm, paraspinous*.

parathion (par"ah-thi'on) chemical name: diethyl-*p*-nitrophenyl thiophosphate. An agricultural insecticide, $C_{10}H_{14}NO_5PS$, highly toxic to humans and animals.

He said that from reading the labels on the drums he had learned that **Parathion** DDT was "poison, that's one thing, for sure, I can remember. It does say they are poison." And during his spraying operations over the years he had had employees who became ill from the chemical and he had taken them to doctors and hospitals for treatment. The supervisor, Caldwell, said that the chemical had a distinct odor and he knew that it was dangerous and "believed it would" kill human beings....

The conspicuous label in black and red type on yellow paper, together with skull and crossbones, had this warning in capital letters: "WARNING. POISONOUS IF SWALLOWED, INHALED OR ABSORBED THROUGH SKIN."....

... the death certificate reciting that death was caused by "chemical poisoning toxic corn spray."

... Dr. Sarno saw Ronnie wheeled into the hospital and he said, "When I first saw him, he was cyanotic or blue, couldn't breathe. He had a thick jelly-like mucus coming from his nose and from his mouth. His eyes were watering. He smelled as though his bowels had been moving and he had a diarrhea. He was unconscious, could not talk. His muscles were very rigid and when you touched him he just went into convulsions and spasms and his muscles seemed to be twitching all over. Dr. Sarno's diagnosis was that "this boy had died of a chemical poisoning when I heard the history of the type of work he had been doing, and it was obviously a case of **parathion** poisoning, insecticide poisoning." On cross-examination the doctor said that Ronnie "had some of the symptoms" of sunstroke but he repeated the symptoms and again said "there is no doubt in my mind that this boy died of **parathion** poisoning."...

... As to how **parathion** enters the body, Dr. Sarno said, "It can enter in several ways. It can enter by contact with the skin, direct exposure of the skin or mucous membranes to the insecticide. It can enter by breathing it in. It can enter by swallowing it or getting it in your eye." Tripp v. Choate, 415 S.W.2d 808–12 (Mo.1967).

paravertebral (par"ah-ver'tĕ-bral) beside the vertebral column.

... a slight spasm of the **paravertebral** muscles on the left (located in the back of the neck, slightly to the side of the spine). This finding of spasm "was based on an objective finding, something that I saw and felt." Bourne v. Washburn, 441 F.2d 1022, 1024 (D.C.Cir.1971).

paravertebral muscle spasm See *spasm*; and *paravertebral*.

parenchyma (pah-reng'kĭ-mah) [Gr. "anything poured in beside"] the essential elements of an organ; used in anatomical nomenclature as a general term to designate the functional elements of an organ, as distinguished from its framework, or stroma.

The latter, acting greatly in reliance on a pathologist's conclusion that the pulmonary autopsy slides failed to show asbestosis,[1] found "Baptist's demise unrelated to ... his occupation ...." [[1] However, we note that the pathologist, Dr. Chung, limited his conclusion by the caveat "if this slide is representative of the pulmonary **parenchyma** as a whole."] Baptist v. W.C.A.B. of State of Cal., 187 Cal.Rptr. 270–1 (Ct.App.Cal. 1982).

parenteral (pah-ren'ter-al) [*para-* + Gr. *enteron* intestine] not through the alimentary canal but rather by injection through some other route, as subcutaneous, intramuscular, intraorbital, intracapsular, intraspinal, intrasternal, intravenous, etc.

Fetal immaturity constituted a contraindication only if the drug was administered **parenterally** (by injection). Lhotka v. Larson, 238 N.W.2d 870, 874 (Minn.1976).

He tried injecting these compounds at the site of the inflammation (**parenteral** administration) and found them to be efficacious in reducing inflammation. Armour Pharmaceutical Co. v. Richardson-Merrell, Inc., 396 F.2d 70–1 (3d Cir. 1968).

paresis (pah-re'sis, par'ĕ-sis) [Gr. "relaxation"] slight or incomplete paralysis; often used alone to mean general paresis (dementia paralytica).

Marcella suffered **paresis** (slight paralysis or muscle weakness) and loss of voice volume after the surgery. She now has difficulty walking unassisted and can only whisper rather than talk. Ritz v. Florida Patient's Compensation Fund, 436 So.2d 987–8 (Dist.Ct.App.Fla.1983).

... weaknesses on the right side of the body known as **paresis**, caused by injury to the brain. There had been a fracture of L2 of the spine. Kinsey v. Kolber, 431 N.E.2d 1316, 1323 (App.Ct.Ill.1982).

paresis, sixth nerve

... "sixth nerve **paresis**," i.e., a weakness of the sixth nerve, causing her eyes to turn in. He said he could not definitely say that the esophoria was caused by the accident, but that plaintiff told him she had never had it before and that she had a blow on her head which had been known to cause muscle imbalance, and, therefore, it was a medical probability that the esophoria resulted from the accident. Perry v. Bertsch, 441 F.2d 939, 941 (8th Cir. 1971).

paresthesia (par"es-the'ze-ah) [*para-* + Gr. *aisthēsis* perception] morbid or perverted sensation; an abnormal sensation, as burning, prickling, formication, etc.

The admitting report indicated that Plaintiff could not hold a cup of tea and she experienced weakness in the hands and has had **paresthesiae** over the arms and hands....

... Dr. Price further noted that Plaintiff suffered from an altered sensation in the hands and that the problem was not that she did not have feeling but that she had a tingly feeling which is **paresthesia**, not anesthesia. Adams v. Schweiker, 557 F.Supp. 1373, 1376–7 (S.D.Tex.1983).

Plaintiffs instituted this action against defendant, Dr. Marvin E. Chapin, D.D.S., alleging that he was negligent in removing an impacted wisdom tooth of the plaintiff, Sara Cozart, and his alleged negligent dental treatment proximately caused **paresthesia** or an altered sensation in her lower lip. Cozart v. Chapin, 251 S.E.2d 682, 683 (Ct.App.N.C.1979).

Several months after his discharge, Dr. Robitaille developed a burning sensation (**paresthesias**) in both legs. His condition worsened and, when he developed a weakness of the right leg, he was "no longer able to carry on." Guardian Life Ins. Co. of America v. Robitaille, 495 F.2d 890, 892 (2d Cir. 1974).

Other Authorities: Gates v. U.S., 707 F.2d 1141, 1143 (10th Cir. 1983); Jimison v. North Dakota Workmen's Comp. Bur., 331 N.W.2d 822–4 (N.D.1983); Hale v. Venuto, 187 Cal. Rptr. 357, 359 (Ct.App.Cal.1982); Henderson v. Milobsky, 595 F.2d 654, 656 (D.C.Cir.1978); McSwain v. Chicago Trans. Auth., 362 N.E.2d 1264–5, 1269 (App.Ct.Ill.1977); Lugo v. Joy, 205 S.E.2d 658–9 (Va.1974); Ascough v. Workmen's Comp. App. Bd., 98 Cal.Rptr. 357, 361 (Ct.App.Cal. 1971); Long v. Richardson, 334 F.Supp. 305, 308 (W.D.Va. 1971).

parietal (pah-ri'ĕ-tal) [L. *parietalis*] 1. of or pertaining to the walls of a cavity. 2. pertaining to or located near the parietal bone, as the parietal lobe. See also *bone, parietal*.

parkinsonism (par'kin-sun-izm") a group of neurological disorders characterized by hypokinesia, tremor, and muscular rigidity. See also *parkinsonian syndrome*, under *syndrome*; and *paralysis agitans* (Parkinson's disease).

Parkinson's disease, facies (sign) (par'kin-sunz) [James *Parkinson*, English physician, 1755–1824] See also *paralysis agitans; facies, Parkinsons*; and *parkinsonism*.

Parnon

The statements in the MGH records at issue in this case include diagnoses of the plaintiff's eye condition as "toxic" in origin and conclusions that the toxic agent causing the blindness was **Parnon**, or "insecticide" (probably a mislabel for fungicide). In their context at trial, the judge could find that these opinions did not satisfy the criteria of reliability. [Footnote omitted.] Diaz v. Eli Lilly & Co., 440 N.E.2d 518, 520 (App.Ct.Mass. 1982).

parotid gland See *glandula, parotis*.

parotidectomy (pah-rot"ĭ-dek'to-me) [*parotid* + Gr. *ektomē* excision] excision of the parotid gland.

Mr. DeFulvio testified that appellant did not explain to him that the operation she planned to perform (a **parotidectomy**) differed from a biopsy. He testified further that she did not inform him of the risks involved, the six-inch scar which would result, and the concavity in his neck which would exist after the operation. . . .

The operation left Mr. DeFulvio with a six-inch scar, concavity in his neck, pain, and a feeling of numbness which persisted at the time of trial. DeFulvio v. Holst, 414 A.2d 1087, 1089 (Super.Ct.Pa.1979).

Dr. Ward advised appellant that the parotid tumor was more serious than the nasal cyst and should be removed. Appellant was reluctant to have the parotid surgery (i.e., a **parotidectomy**), since she had been aware of the lump for at least 10 years and it had never bothered her. Nevertheless, Dr. Ward considered the lump potentially malignant and capable of spreading quickly, thereby endangering the nearby facial nerve. LeMons v. Regents of the Univ. of Cal., 582 P.2d 946–7 (Cal.1978).

paroxysmal auricular tachycardia See *tachycardia, paroxysmal.*

pars (parz), pl. *par'tes* [L.] a division or part; [NA], a general term for a particular portion of a larger area, organ, or structure.

pars interarticularis See *articular; interarticular;* and *pars.*

Dr. Schultz stated that X rays showed that petitioner had a condition called **pars interarticularis** defect. The **pars interarticularis** is a structure in the lower back which is part of the vertebra. Dr. Schultz explained that this structure acts as a hook on either side which prevents one vertebra from sliding forward on another. D'Alfonzo v. Industrial Com'n, 440 N.E.2d 883–4 (Ill.1982).

pars nasalis pharyngis [NA], nasopharynx: the part of the pharynx that lies above the level of the soft palate.

pars oralis pharyngis [NA], the division of the pharynx lying between the soft palate and the upper edge of the epiglottis; called also *oropharynx.*

pars petrosa ossis temporalis [NA], petrous portion of temporal bone: a pyramid of dense bone located at the base of the cranium; one of the three parts of the temporal bone, it houses the organ of hearing.

pars pylorica ventriculi [NA], the caudal one-third of the stomach, consisting of the pyloric antrum and canal, and distinguished by the presence of the pyloric glands and by the absence of parietal cells.

The stomach operation for the removal of a **pre-pyloric** ulcer occurred in April of 1970. The medical evidence did not show that she had excessive weight loss, malnutrition, or serious stomach disorder before March 31, 1959. Capaldi v. Weinberger, 391 F.Supp. 502, 504 (E.D.Pa.1975).

pars squamosa ossis temporalis [NA], squamous part of temporal bone: the flat, scalelike, anterior and superior portion of the temporal bone; called also *squama temporalis.*

One fracture was through the "**squamous** portion of the **temporal bone** extending to the base of the skull." C.S.T. Erection Company v. Industrial Com'n, 335 N.E.2d 419–20 (Ill.1975).

pars superior duodeni [NA], the part of the duodenum adjacent to the pylorus, forming the superior flexure; called also *duodenal cap.*

He was placed on a peptic ulcer regimen and a complete "work-up" was done, including gastric analysis and a GI series, which revealed a huge ulcer crater with a deformity of the **duodenal cap.** Denton v. Weinberger, 412 F.Supp. 450, 452 (S.D.N.Y.1976).

Upper G.I. series showed a lot of pylorospasm with a contracted **duodenal bulb.** Matthews v. Matthews, 415 F.Supp. 201–2 (E.D.Va.1976).

particulate (par-tik'u-lāt) composed of separate particles.

The standards relevant to the case before us are those governing total suspended **particulates** in the air.[1] The limitations on **particulate** matter were set at levels deemed necessary to protect the public health and welfare. [[1] The EPA defines **particulate** matter as follows: "**Particulate** matter consists of a broad range of chemically and physically diverse substances that exist as discrete particles in the air." (Resp. Br. at p. 3.)] National Steel Corp., Great Lakes Steel v. Gorsuch, 700 F.2d 314, 316 (6th Cir. 1983).

. . . while "**particulate** matter" is defined as "any finely divided liquid or solid material, other than uncombined water, as measured by Method 5." 40 C.F.R. § 60.41(c). In the instance of both acid mist and **particulate** matter alternative methods of measurement other than the opacity test are promulgated. See 40 C.F.R. §§ 60.42(a), 60.83(a), which set quantitative limits based upon emissions actually detected by appropriately objective test methods. Essex Chemical Corp. v. Ruckelshaus, 486 F.2d 427, 432 (D.C.Cir.1973).

PAS See *acid, aminosalicylic.*

passage (pas'ij) a channel.

passage, false an unnatural channel or meatus in a body structure, created by trauma or by disease.

Respondents testified that although the physicians at the Mayo Clinic observed a **false passage**, reference thereto did not clarify whether the **false passage** was caused by disease or improper instrumentation. They testified that a **false passage** could be produced by an infected bladder, improper instrumentation, self-instrumentation or straddle type injuries. [Footnote omitted.] Langton v. Brown, 591 S.W.2d 84, 86–7 (Mo.Ct.App.1979).

pasteurization (pas″ter-i-za'shun) [Louis *Pasteur*] the process of heating milk or other liquids, e.g., urine, to a moderate temperature for a definite time, often to 60°C. for thirty minutes. This exposure kills most species of pathogenic bacteria and considerably delays other bacterial development.

The next step was "**pasteurization**," which involved killing the enzymes in the milk. Glowacki v. Borden, Inc., 420 F.Supp. 348, 351 (N.D.Ill.1976).

past-pointing

". . . and she presented neurological signs of **past-pointing**," i.e., she was unable to touch her nose when instructed to do so. Fritsche v. Westinghouse Electric Corp., 261 A.2d 657, 659 (N.J.1970).

PAT See *tachycardia, paroxysmal.*

patch graft See *graft, patch.*

patching

The general objective findings that relate to multiple sclerosis are evidence of **patching** involved in the nervous system, which means that more than one area of the nervous system dysfunctions. McSwain v. Chicago Transit Authority, 362 N.E.2d 1264, 1274 (App.Ct.Ill.1977).

patella (pah-tel'ah) [L., dim. of *patera* a shallow dish] [NA], a triangular sesamoid bone, about 5 cm. in diameter, situated at the front of the knee in the tendon of insertion of the quadriceps extensor femoris muscle. Called also *knee cap.*

Dr. Berkebile testified that plaintiff sustained a nondisplaced fracture of the right **patella** which has resulted in a 5% permanent-partial disability of the right lower extremity. Stoltz v. Stonecypher, 336 N.W.2d 654, 656 (S.D.1983).

patella alta

Dr. Euliano, who recommended an operation after he examined x-rays showing evidence of **patella alta**, i.e., a raised kneecap....

... Dr. Euliano said in his opinion Claimant's **patella alta** condition was something that was present for a long time and that that condition could not have been caused by a fall such as that sustained by the Claimant. The doctor testified further that only an extreme forceable blow to the knee which would jam it up against the thighbone would aggravate Claimant's pre-existing condition. Girovsky v. Workmens Comp. Appeal Bd. (Corry Foam Products, Inc.), 453 A.2d 723, 70 Pa.Cmwlth. 536 (1982).

patellar ligament See *ligamenta patellae.*

patellectomy (pat"ĕ-lek'to-me) [*patella* + Gr. *ektomē* excision] excision or removal of the patella.

"In about 1967, she again injured the knee and sustained a fractured patella. She was off work for 2 weeks at that time, and improved.

"In Feb. 1972 the knee was again injured and she was treated conservatively by Dr. M. E. Robinson. On 4–10–73, Dr. Ronald Vinyard did a **patellectomy** and joint policing....

"She stated that since her last surgery she falls frequently due to the right knee 'giving way'...." Howard v. State Acc. Ins. Fund, 584 P.2d 325–6 (Ct.App.Or.1978).

After an examination which showed a comminuted fracture of the left patella, Mr. Means was taken to surgery and a total **patellectomy** was performed. Means v. Sears, Roebuck & Co., 550 S.W.2d 780, 783 (Mo.1977).

patellofemoral (pah-tel"o-fem'o-ral) pertaining to the patella and the femur.

patellofemoral arthritis See *arthritis, patellofemoral.*

patent ductus arteriosus See *ductus arteriosus, patent.*

paternity test See *test, HLA paternity blood.*

pathogen (path'o-jen) [*patho-* + Gr. *gennan* to produce] any disease-producing microorganism.

Although the tests were capable of recovering only a very small percentage of the viruses which can occur in human feces, it was established that if one **pathogen** (disease-producing organism) is found, there is a high scientific probability that many others are also present. U.S. v. City of Asbury Park, 340 F.Supp. 555, 564–5 (D.N.J.1972).

pathogenesis (path"o-jen'ĕ-sis) [*patho-* + *genesis*] the development of morbid conditions or of disease; more specifically the cellular events and reactions and other pathologic mechanisms occurring in the development of disease.

pathogenic (path-o-jen'ik) giving origin to disease or to morbid symptoms.

All viruses are **pathogenic**; that is, they can cause disease or infection. U.S. v. City of Asbury Park, 340 F.Supp. 555, 565 (D.N.J.1972).

pathognomonic (path"og-no-mon'ik) [*patho-* + Gr. *gnōmonikos* fit to give judgment] specifically distinctive or characteristic of a disease or pathologic condition; a sign or symptom on which a diagnosis can be made.

Defendant's medical expert, Dr. Marano, said that meconium ileus is conclusively **pathognomonic** (indicative or characteristic) of cystic fibrosis. However, plaintiff's expert, Dr. Schiffman, testified that not all infants born with a condition of meconium ileus become cystic. Kissil v. Beneficial Nat. Life Ins. Co., 319 A.2d 67, 69 (N.J.1974).

Dr. Hardy explained he could have no final diagnosis unless he had something **pathognomonic**, which he has defined as "clear cut" or "that it has got to be this, nothing else" or "I have a laboratory report confirming this tentative diagnosis". O. M. Franklin Serum Co. v. C. A. Hoover & Son, 437 S.W.2d 613, 616 (Ct.Civ.App.Tex.1969), reversed 444 S.W.2d 596 (Tex.1969).

pathologist (pah-thol'o-jist) an expert in pathology.

A **pathologist** is defined by Dr. Maynard as follows:
"A. A **pathologist** is fundamentally the scientist with an M.D. degree who specializes in the causation of disease...." Meeks v. Industrial Com'n, 436 P.2d 928, 932 (Ct.App.Ariz.1968).

A. **Pathologist** is one learned in that branch of medicine, which treats of the essential nature of disease, especially of the structural and functional changes caused by disease. York v. Daniels, 259 S.W.2d 109, 111 (Springfield Ct.App.Mo. 1953).

pathology (pah-thol'o-je) [*patho-* + *-logy*] that branch of medicine which treats of the essential nature of disease, especially of the structural and functional changes in tissues and organs of the body which cause or are caused by disease.

Pathology has to do with the laboratory side of the practice of medicine, and involves mainly diagnostic procedures. Pathologists examine tissue for evidence of disease, including tissues removed in surgical operations, biopsies, and autopsies. Metropolitan Life Ins. Co. v. Main, 383 F.2d 952, 955 (5th Cir. 1967).

pathology, anatomic

"In **anatomic pathology**, it is the part pertaining to the diagnosis of surgical specimens removed by the surgeon and examination of tissues at autopsy...." Meeks v. Industrial Com'n, 436 P.2d 928, 932 (Ct.App.Ariz.1968).

pathology, clinical pathology applied to the solution of clinical problems, especially the use of laboratory methods in clinical diagnosis.

"In **clinical pathology**, it is the study of the body fluids removed from the individual and sent to the laboratory, and supervision of medical technologists in bacteriology, serology, hematology, and chemistry, as well as lesser phases of medical technology." Meeks v. Industrial Com'n, 436 P.2d 928, 932 (Ct.App.Ariz.1968).

patient (pa'shent) [L. *patiens*] a person who is ill or who is undergoing treatment for disease.

patient (mental)

The words "**patient**" and "**institution**" are defined in N.J.S.A. 30:4–23:

"**Patient**" includes any person or persons alleged to be mentally ill, tuberculous, or mentally retarded whose admission to any institution for the care and treatment of such class of persons in this State has been applied for. In Re Grady, 426 A.2d 467, 476 (N.J.1981).

Patrick's test (sign) (pat'riks) [Hugh Talbot *Patrick*, neurologist in Chicago, 1860–1938] See under *tests*.

Pavlov's method (pahv'lovz) [Ivan Petrovich *Pavlov*, Russian physiologist, 1849–1936; winner of the Nobel prize for medicine in 1904] See under *method*.

Pavlovian conditioning See *method, Pavlov's*.

Pavulon (pav'u-lon) trademark for a preparation of pancuronium bromide. See also *pancuronium bromide*.

PCP See *phencyclidine hydrochloride*.

PDR See *Physician's Desk Reference*.

pectus (pek'tus) [L.] the breast: the chest or thorax.

pectus excavatum [L. "hollowed breast"] undue depression of the sternum; called also *funnel breast* or *chest*.

On July 17, 1975, Eric Ewen was scheduled for a relatively simple cosmetic surgery to correct a **pectus excavatum** (or sunken chest). Eric was eleven years old at the time and, except for the sunken chest condition, was in good health. Ewen v. Baton Rouge General Hospital, 378 So.2d 172, 174 (Ct. App.La.1979).

pedicle (ped'ĭ-k'l) a footlike, stemlike, or narrow basal part or structure, as the stalk by which a nonsessile tumor is attached to normal tissue, or the narrow strip of flap tissue through which it receives its blood supply.

This report also indicated that the polyp rested upon a **pedicle** (i.e., a stalk) and resembled a mushroom in form. Spotts v. Reidell, 497 A.2d 630, 632 (Super.Ct.Pa.1985).

pedodontics (pe-do-don'tiks) [*pedo*-(1) + Gr. *odous* tooth] the branch of dentistry concerned with the diagnosis and treatment of conditions of the teeth and mouth in children.

Appellants contend that the untimely demise occurred as a result of the combined negligence of Dr. Michal, DDS, a **Pedodontist** (general dentistry for children), who performed the surgery, and Dr. Wyly, Anesthesiologist, who administered anesthesia for the operation. Chapman v. Argonaut-Southwest Ins. Co., 290 So.2d 779, 780 (Ct.App.La.1974).

pedodontist See *pedodontics*.

pelvic inflammatory disease See *disease, pelvic inflammatory*.

pelvis (pel'vis), pl. *pel'ves* [L.; Gr. *pyelos* an oblong trough] [NA] the lower (caudal) portion of the trunk of the body, bounded anteriorly and laterally by the two hip bones and posteriorly by the sacrum and coccyx. The pelvis is divided by a plane passing through the terminal lines into the *false pelvis* (*p. major* [NA]) above and the *true pelvis* (*p. minor* [NA]) below. The upper boundary of the cavity of the pelvis is known as the *inlet, brim,* or *superior strait of the pelvis*. The true pelvis is limited below by the *inferior strait*, or *outlet*, bounded by the coccyx, the symphysis pubis, and the ischium of either side. The outlet of the pelvis is closed by the coccygeus and levator ani muscles and the perineal fascia, which form the *floor of the pelvis*. The inlet and outlet of the pelvis each have three important diameters—an anteroposterior (conjugate), an oblique, and a transverse, the relations of which determine types variously classified by different authors (see entries under *diameter*). The term pelvis is applied also to any basin-like structure, such as the renal pelvis (pelvis renalis [NA]).

There is a healed fracture of the **pelvis** which appears to have involved both the rami of both sides of the **pelvis** with a considerable deformity of the pelvic ring....

"A. There is a sign of an old fracture through the inferior ramus of the pubic bone. The entire **pelvis** left side has been broken and shoved up so that the left side of the **pelvis** is a half to three-quarters of an inch higher than the right...." King v. Celebrezze, 223 F.Supp. 457, 461–3 (W.D.Ark. 1963).

pelvis, android a pelvis characterized by a wedge-shaped inlet and narrowness of the anterior segment; used as a general designation of a female pelvis showing characters typical of the pelvis in the male.

pelvis, anthropoid a female pelvis characterized by a long anteroposterior diameter of the inlet, which equals or exceeds the transverse diameter.

pelvis, gynecoid a pelvis having a rounded oval shape with a well rounded anterior and posterior segment; it represents the normal female pelvis.

pelvis, platypellic; pelvis platypelloid a pelvis characterized by flattening of the pelvic inlet, with a short anteroposterior and a wide transverse diameter.

pemphigus (pem'fĭ-gus) [Gr. *pemphix* blister] a name applied to a distinctive group of diseases characterized by

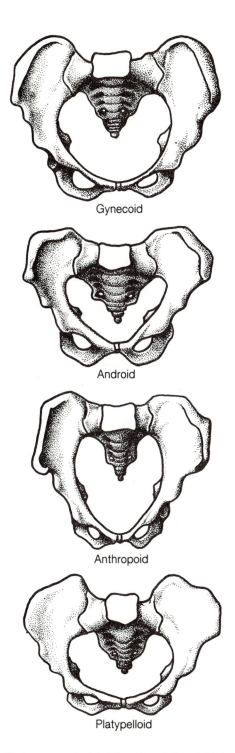

Gynecoid

Android

Anthropoid

Platypelloid

Various types of pelvic inlets (Greenhill and Friedman).

successive crops of bullae, the specific type usually being indicated by a modifying term. Frequently used alone to designate pemphigus vulgaris. See also *bulla*.

On the remand considerable additional medical testimony was taken, as to this rare disease, about which much is vague and unknown, but there is sufficient evidence upon which the board could find that the decedent died of **pemphigus** acutus, or butchers **pemphigus**. De Tura v. Eastern Meat Markets, Inc., 221 N.Y.S.2d 188 (3d Dep't 1961).

pemphigus vulgaris a rare relapsing disease manifested by suprabasal, intraepidermal bullae of the skin and mucous membranes; invariably fatal if untreated, but remission has been obtained by use of corticosteroid hormones and immunosuppressive drugs.

penectomy

Phelps saw Dr. Duthoy and learned that he would have to undergo a partial **penectomy**. On March 29, 1974, Dr. Duthoy removed 2 inches of the distal end of Phelps' penis, and the inguinal lymph glands in his groin. Phelps v. Blomberg Roseville Clinic, 253 N.W.2d 390, 392 (Minn.1977).

penicillamine (pen"ĭ-sil-ah-mēn) [USP] chemical name: 3-mercapto-D-valine. A degradation product of penicillin, $C_{15}H_{11}NO_2S$, occurring as a white or almost white, crystalline powder, which chelates certain heavy metals; used orally to reduce the blood copper level in the treatment of hepatolenticular degeneration and to promote excretion of cystine by forming a more soluble penicillamine-cystine disulfide. It has been used in the treatment of rheumatoid arthritis.

Penicillamine is a drug currently used to treat Wilson's Disease, cystinuria, and rheumatoid arthritis. At the time it was prescribed for Mrs. Reinhardt, **penicillamine** was approved by the Food and Drug Administration for only Wilson's Disease and cystinuria, and not for rheumatoid arthritis. **Penicillamine** is a toxic drug with a potential for causing a variety of adverse reactions, including bone marrow suppression (i.e., destruction of certain blood cell making capacities causing, among other things, aplastic anemia). Reinhardt v. Colton, 337 N.W.2d 88, 90 (Minn.1983).

penicillin (pen"ĭ-sil'in) any of a large group of natural or semisynthetic antibacterial antibiotics derived directly or indirectly from strains of fungi of the genus *Penicillium* and other soil-inhabiting fungi grown on special culture media, which exert a bacteriocidal as well as a bacteriostatic effect on susceptible bacteria by interfering with the final stages of the synthesis of peptidoglycan, a substance in the bacterial cell wall. The penicillins, despite their relatively low toxicity for the host, are active against many bacteria, especially gram-positive pathogens (streptococci, staphylococci, pneumococci); clostridia; some gram-negative forms (gonococci, meningococci); some spirochetes (*Treponema pallidum* and *T. pertenue*); and some fungi. Certain strains of some target species, e.g., staphylococci, secrete the enzyme penicillinase, which inactivates penicillin and confers resistance to the antibiotic.

Both of these witnesses agreed that **penicillin** in a concentrated form would be caustic and could damage the tissues surrounding the I.V. site if the penicillin got out of the vein.

When the I.V. was given to the plaintiff, she immediately complained of pain and when the later I.V. "push" was administered she suffered more intense pain and her arm began to swell. She developed a blister which became black and her hospital bracelet had to be removed. This blistering was caused by the infiltration of the I.V. fluids in the tissue around the I.V. site. Mercurdo v. County of Milwaukee, 264 N.W.2d 258–9 (Wis.1978).

Defendant ordered that plaintiff be given hot, wet pack compresses and continued on **penicillin. Penicillin** normally has no effect on a gram-negative bacteria. Casey v. Penn, 360 N.E.2d 93, 97; affirmed 45 Ill.App.3d 1068, 6 Ill.Dec. 453, 362 N.E.2d 1373 (App.Ct.Ill.1977).

Thereupon, defendant injected intravenously a treatment of Bicillin (a pharmaceutical trade name for a preparation of **penicillin**). That afternoon plaintiff experienced some itching and discomfort. Sunday his condition became worse, with swelling about the face. Monday he was hospitalized in serious condition. He went through a critical stage and finally recovered, but suffered loss of the sight of one eye and serious impairment of vision of the other. Johnston v. Brother, 12 Cal.Rptr. 23–4 (Dist.Ct.App.Cal.1961).

penicillin, phenoxymethyl See *penicillin V.*

penicillin V [USP], a semisynthetic oral penicillin prepared from cultures of the mold *Penicillium* in the presence of 2-phenoxyethanol with an autolysate of yeast as the source of nitrogen. It is a broad-spectrum antibiotic having pharmacologic and toxic properties similar to those of other penicillins, and is less potent than penicillin G. Called also *phenoxymethyl p.*

For treatment of the strep throat infection, he prescribed a medication called **Pen Vee Kee** of 250 milligram tablets, which is **Penicillin**, to be taken by mouth at the rate of one tablet 4 times a day for 10 days. This was a treatment for a bacterial infection and the dosage was for a period of 10 days. [Dissent.] Watkins v. U.S., 589 F.2d 214, 223 (5th Cir. 1979).

Penicillium (pen″ĭ-sil′e-um) [L. *penicillum* brush, roll] a genus of Fungi Imperfecti (family Moniliaceae, order Moniliales) that develop fruiting organs resembling a broom, or the bones of the hand and fingers. When identified, the perfect (sexual) stage is classified with the ascomycetous fungi in the family Eurotiaceae, order Eurotiales. See also *penicillin.*

Penrose drain (pen′rōz) [Charles Bingham *Penrose*, Philadelphia gynecologist, 1862–1925] See *drain, cigarette.*

pentazocine (pen-taz′o-sēn) [USP] chemical name: 1,2,3,4,5,6-hexahydro-*cis*-6,11-dimethyl -3-(3-methyl-2-butenyl)-2,6-methano-3-benzazocin-8-ol. A synthetic analgesic, $C_{27}H_{27}NO$, occurring as a white or very pale tan-colored powder; used in the form of the hydrochloride and lactate salts.

DeLuryea developed severe ulcerations on her left thigh with necrotic tissue caused by injections of **Talwin** over a period of time. Later she developed tissue necrosis of her other thigh and her hips, shoulders, and upper arms. Sterling stipulated

that DeLuryea's tissue problems were caused by her use of **Talwin.** . . .

DeLuryea produced testimony from Dr. McCarthy DeMere that the warnings given prior to May 1974 regarding tissue damage at injection sites were inadequate to warn the medical profession of the danger involved. He stated that the manufacturer knew in 1967, prior to marketing, that **Talwin** would cause tissue damage after prolonged use. An adequate warning could have been given at that time. . . .

Talwin was held to be an unavoidably unsafe product in Crocker v. Winthrop Laboratories, 514 S.W.2d 429, 432–33 (Tex.1974). DeLuryea v. Winthrop Laboratories, etc., 697 F.2d 222, 224, 229 (8th Cir. 1983).

At this time, Dr. Edward Kissam, who had treated Poole since 1966 and had performed all of his back operations, found that Poole was probably habituated or addicted to **talwin**, which he had been taking by injection daily for at least the past year. . . .

After he began the use of **talwin**, Poole noticed a gradual stiffening of his lower extremities. . . .

. . . Dr. Toyama continued to give Poole prescriptions for injectable **talwin.** Poole's stiffness grew worse until he was admitted to the hospital under Dr. Kissam's care in June 1977. At that time he had essentially no hip or knee motion and had an almost board-like hardness of the muscle tissue extending from his lower rib cage down to his ankles. According to testimony of Dr. Kissam and other doctors, that condition was due to the continuous use of injectable **talwin**, which transforms normal muscle tissue into a fibrotic condition like scar tissue. Southern Bell Tel. & Tel. Co. v. Poole, 388 So.2d 330–2 (Dist.Ct.App. Fla.1980).

Crocker told Dr. Palafox that he liked the relief he received from **talwin**, and Dr. Palafox responded that this was fortunate because **talwin** had no addicting side effect.

Crocker did develop an addiction to **talwin**, however, and was able to obtain prescriptions from several doctors as well as to cross the Mexican border to Juarez and acquire the same drug without a prescription under the name of "sosigon." . . .

Subsequent experience has proved that **talwin** is an extremely useful drug for the relief of pain but that it cannot be regarded as non-addictive. Crocker v. Winthrop Lab. Div. of Sterling Drug, Inc., 514 S.W.2d 429–30 (Tex.1974).

Other Authorities: Contreras v. St. Luke's Hosp., 144 Cal.Rptr. 647, 651 (Ct.App.Cal.1978).

Penthothal See *thiopental sodium.*

Penthrane See *methoxyflurane.*

pentothal See *thiopental sodium.*

Pen Vee Kee See *penicillin V.*

pentosuria (pen″to-su′re-ah) [*pentose* + Gr. *ouron* urine + *-ia*] a benign error of metabolism due to a defect in the activity of the enzyme L-xylulose dehydrogenase, which results in high levels of L-xylulose in the urine. It is transmitted as an autosomal recessive trait. Called also *L-xylulosuria.*

peraformis muscle See *musculus, piriformis.*

Percogesic

He also stated that it was not medically acceptable to substitute a tranquilizer for a pain killer (**Percogesic**).... Com. v. DeLaCruz, 443 N.E.2d 427, 430 (App.Ct.Mass.1982).

perforation (per"fo-ra'shun) [L. *perforare* to pierce through] a hole made through a part or substance.

She declared that appellees were negligent in **perforating** the bowel, in not recognizing during the operation that the intestine had been **perforated**, and in failing promptly to repair the **perforation**. Raitt v. Johns Hopkins Hospital, 322 A.2d 548, 555 (Ct.Spec.App.Md.1974), reversed and remanded 274 Md. 489, 336 A.2d 90 (Ct.App.1975).

perfusion (per-fu'zhun) the act of pouring over or through, especially the passage of a fluid through the vessels of a specific organ.

perfusion, iliac and dissection See *prophylaxis, chemotherapeutical* (Sherrill case).

perfusion, isolation

He informed appellant that there was another newer technique [as opposed to a forequarter amputation], the **isolation perfusion**. Gaal explained the **isolation perfusion** process in detail. He stated that the method involved the lowering of body temperature of the patient, the isolation of the blood supply to the portion of the body to be treated, the injection of toxic chemicals into the isolated portion, and the properties of the chemicals in destroying cells in general and tumor tissue in particular. Gaal told appellant that the **isolation perfusion** carried inherent risks including the possible risk of an inflammation in the artery which might result in the loss of the arm or some portion of it. Clemens v. Regents of University of California, 87 Cal. Rptr. 108, 111 (Ct.App.Cal.1970).

periapical (per"e-ap'ĭ-kal) [*peri-* + L. *apex* tip] relating to tissues encompassing the apex of a tooth, including periodontal membrane and alveolar bone.

In connection with certain dental work Sundstrand requires **periapical** X-rays (full mouth) to be taken as a pre-condition of payment under the plan. Pfluger v. Sundstrand Corp., 405 N.E.2d 12, 14 (App.Ct.Ill.1980).

periapical (radiograph)

The second type of X-ray is called a **periapical radiograph**. This type of X-ray depicts the entire tooth (crown and root) and usually includes several teeth in a single jaw. **Periapical radiographs** are generally used to diagnose periodontal disease and detect periapical lesions which normally indicate diseased or necrotic pulp tissue....

... the **periapical radiograph** is the most useful in diagnosing the conditions which render root canal therapy as proper treatment. Periapical lesions appear on these radiographs as a radioluscent or non-opaque area around the apex of the root. These lesions signify bone loss or potential bone loss surrounding the root and are indicative of an unsatisfactory pulp condition. U.S. v. Talbott, 460 F.Supp. 253, 256 (S.D. Ohio 1978).

periapical disease See *disease, periapical*.

pericardectomy See *pericardiectomy*.

pericardial sac See *pericardium*.

pericardiectomy (per"ĭ-kar"de-ek'to-me) [*pericardium* + Gr. *ektomē* excision] excision of the pericardium.

... an anterior "**pericardectomy**" or removal of the heart sac.... Prudential Insurance Co. of America v. Beaty, 456 S.W.2d 164, 169 (Ct.Civ.App.Tex.1970).

pericarditis (per"ĭ-kar-di'tis) [*pericardium* + *-itis*] inflammation of the pericardium.

Pericarditis is an inflammation of the fibroserous sac that surrounds the heart. Dorland's Illustrated Medical Dictionary, 469, 1125 (24th ed. 1965). [hereinafter cited as Dorland]. Poore v. Mathews, 406 F.Supp. 47, 49 (E.D.Tenn.1975).

pericardium (per"ĭ-kar'de-um) [L.; *peri-* + Gr. *kardia* heart] [NA] the fibroserous sac that surrounds the heart and the roots of the great vessels, comprising an external layer of fibrous tissue (*pericardium fibrosum* [NA]) and an inner serous layer (*pericardium serosum* [NA]). The base of the pericardium is attached to the central tendon of the diaphragm.

Dr. Butts further was of the opinion that the fluid entered the **pericardial sac** through a hole in the right atrium which was caused by a catheter. Warren v. Canal Industries, Inc., 300 S.E.2d 557, 559 (Ct.App.N.C.1983).

perinatal (per"ĭ-na'tal) [*peri-* + L. *natus* born] pertaining to or occurring in the period shortly before and after birth; variously defined as beginning with completion of the twentieth to twenty-eighth week of gestation and ending 7 to 28 days after birth.

Perinatal refers to the time when a baby is in the uterus and immediately after it is born. Dr. Hayashi was stating that, of the IUGR babies which weigh less than 2500 grams and have a gestation period of more than 37 weeks, there is a 95% mortality rate. Freed v. Priore, 372 A.2d 895, 898 (Super.Ct. Pa.1977).

perineal (per"ĭ-ne'al) pertaining to the perineum.

perineum (per"i-ne'um) [Gr. *perineos* the space between the anus and scrotum] 1. [NA] the pelvic floor and the associated structures occupying the pelvic outlet; it is bounded anteriorly by the pubic symphysis, laterally by the ischial tuberosities, and posteriorly by the coccyx. 2. the region between the thighs, bounded in the male by the scrotum and anus and in the female by the vulva and anus.

... his condition of cancer was discovered too late to arrest the carcinoma in question which required surgery in the nature of an abdominal **perineal** resection resulting in a colostomy.... Bennett v. Raag, 431 N.E.2d 48–9 (App.Ct.Ill.1982).

The most Dr. Rook would admit in his testimony was that he "put a few sutures" in the laceration of the **perineum**. Hiatt v. Groce, 523 P.2d 320, 323 (Kan.1974).

This is where a wall of the vagina is repaired and "the muscles of the **perineum**, that is, the bundle of muscles between the vagina and the rectum, are strengthened and shortened as need be". Harris v. Campbell, 409 P.2d 67, 69 (Ct.App.Ariz. 1965).

period (pe're-od) [*peri-* + Gr. *hodos* way] an interval or division of time; the time for the regular recurrence of a phenomenon.

period, incubation the interval of time required for development; the period of time between the moment of entrance of the infecting organism into the body and the first symptoms of the consequent disease, or between the moment of entrance into a vector and the time at which the vector is capable of transmitting the disease. Called also *incubative stage.*

By incubation period is meant the period of time dating from the time the virus entered the mouth, to the time of the onset of the first illness. From the first sign of illness to the time paralysis develops, may involve a further period as long as 25 days. Wardrop v. City of Manhattan Beach, 326 P.2d 15, 20 (Dist. Ct.App.Cal.1958).

periodontal (per"e-o-don'tal) [*peri-* + Gr. *odous* tooth] situated or occurring around a tooth; pertaining to the periodontium.

periodontal disease See *periodontitis; periodontosis; periodontium*; and *gingivitis.*

periodontics (per"e-o-don'tiks) [*peri-* + Gr. *odous* tooth] that branch of dentistry dealing with the study and treatment of diseases of the periodontium.

periodontist (per"e-o-don'tist) a dentist who specializes in periodontics.

According to Dr. Jackson, a periodontist is a dentist who specializes in treating diseases of the teeth and disorders of the bite and jaw. Sullivan v. Russell, 338 N.W.2d 181, 184 (Mich. 1983).

periodontitis (per"e-o-don-ti'tis) [*peri-* + Gr. *odous* tooth + *-itis*] inflammatory reaction of the tissues surrounding a tooth (periodontium), usually resulting from the extension of gingival inflammation (gingivitis) into the periodontium.

Dr. Karam's examination revealed approximately twelve missing molars, acute infection of the gums, and moderate periodontal disease (loss of bone structure holding the teeth). Wiley v. Karam, 421 So.2d 294–5 (Ct.App.La.1982).

When Armstrong first examined the plaintiff within two weeks of her last visit to defendant, Armstrong determined that she had "advanced periodontal disease". Armstrong testified that this disease, of which the dental profession had become "rather acutely aware" during "the past ten years", affects the tooth and the gum around the tooth, resulting in destruction of the bone. He stated that the disease, which develops slowly and gets progressively worse if untreated, is caused by inflammation which in turn is caused by bacteria.

The first oral examination by Armstrong revealed bone loss around most of the teeth, dental decay, red gum margins and looseness of teeth. A probing examination, conducted with a hand instrument calibrated in millimeters and placed between the tooth and the gum, revealed "pocket depths" far in excess of a "normal" depth of two millimeters. The plaintiff's medical testimony indicated that the gum tissue is usually attached very tightly within "a couple of millimeters of where the edge of the gum line is" and when periodontal disease develops, "this at-

tachment migrates or comes away from the tooth" and a "pocket" or "space" results. Farley v. Goode, 252 S.E.2d 594, 596–7 (Va.1979).

Dr. Gunter confirmed the presence of severe periodontal disease and existing loss of a portion of the bony support for both upper and lower teeth. He suggested he perform treatment consisting of scraping and curretaging under the gum area to arrest the disease. Plaintiff's four upper front teeth were found to be extremely loose. Brock v. Gunter, 292 So.2d 328–9 (Ct.App.La.1974).

periodontium (per"e-o-don'she-um), pl. *periodon'tia* [*peri-* + Gr. *odous* tooth] the tissues investing and supporting the teeth, including the cementum, periodontal ligament, alveolar bone, and gingiva. Anatomically [NA], the term is restricted to the connective tissue interposed between the teeth and their bony sockets, i.e., the periodontal ligament; called also *periosteum alveolare.*

periodontosis (per"e-o-don-to'sis) a degenerative, noninflammatory condition of the periodontium, originating in one or more of the periodontal structures and characterized by destruction of the tissues. See also *periodontitis; periodontium*; and *gingivitis.*

"Q. [Mr. Kelly]: And, the reason for the extraction of the remaining eleven upper jaw teeth was their looseness? Is that correct?
"A. Correct.
"Q. And wasn't the basic cause of the looseness a preexisting periodontal disease?
"A. Yes, she had periodontal disease. Certainly a certain amount of this had to be preexisting prior to the accident. Periodontal disease isn't something that occurs in a matter of months.
"Q. There may be possibly some involvement with the traumatic blow, but the basic reason was the preexisting periodontal decay over a long period of time?
"A. I would say yes to that." McCoy v. McNutt, 227 N.W.2d 219, 222–3 (Ct.App.Mich.1975).

periorbital (per"e-or'bĭ-tal) situated around the orbit, or eye socket.

Plaintiff's left eye has receded 4 millimeters and dropped 2½ millimeters within the orbit as a result of the atrophy of the periorbital fat surrounding the eye (249–255, 259–260, 264). Yarrow v. U.S., 309 F.Supp. 922, 925 (S.D.N.Y.1970).

periosteal See *periosteum.*

periosteum (per"e-os'te-um) [*peri-* + Gr. *osteon* bone] [NA] a specialized connective tissue covering all bones of the body, and possessing bone-forming potentialities; in adults, it consists of two layers that are not sharply defined, the external layer being a network of dense connective tissue containing blood vessels, and the deep layer composed of more loosely arranged collagenous bundles with spindle-shaped connective tissue cells and a network of thin elastic fibers.

... petitioner had a "periosteal tear at the joint area between the distal sacral segment at the first coccygeal segment." Camp v. Lockheed Electronics, Inc., 429 A.2d 615, 617 (Super.Ct.N.J.1981).

periosteum, lingual

Plaintiff's whole theory of action was that defendant had negligently severed the two nerves in question by improperly allowing his drill to penetrate the **lingual periosteum** which lies between the extracted tooth and these two nerves....

... These two nerves are separated from the tooth which was extracted by the periosteum (described as a fibrous layer, fairly strong, about as thick as two pieces of paper) and the mandibular bone. Cassano v. Hagstrom, 159 N.E.2d 348, 350 (N.Y.1959).

periostitis (per″e-os-ti′tis) inflammation of the periosteum. The condition is generally chronic, and is marked by tenderness and swelling of the bone and an aching pain. Acute periostitis is due to infection, is characterized by diffuse suppuration, severe pain, and constitutional symptoms, and usually results in necrosis. See also *periosteum.*

... **periostitis** (splints) both right and left medial splint bones, front legs. Southall v. Gabel, 293 N.E.2d 891–2 (Franklin Cty. Munic.Ct.Ohio 1972).

peripheral vision See *vision, peripheral.*

periproctitis (per″ĭ-prok-ti′tis) [*peri-* + Gr. *prŏktos* anus + *-itis*] inflammation of the tissues surrounding the rectum and anus.

Dr. Charles H. Peete, Jr., as a result of his examination, found principally proctitis and **periproctitis**, a type of inflammation involving the large and small bowel, with swelling and tenderness. This was the result of infection in and around the lower bowel, with swelling, a lot of scar tissue and inflammation. Morgan v. Schlanger, 374 F.2d 235, 237–8 (4th Cir. 1967).

perirectal (per″ĭ-rek′tal) around the rectum. See also abscess, perirectal.

peristalsis (per″ĭ-stal′sis) [*peri-* + Gr. *stalsis* contraction] the wormlike movement by which the alimentary canal or other tubular organs provided with both longitudinal and circular muscle fibers propel their contents. It consists of a wave of contraction passing along the tube for variable distances.

At plaintiff's initial dilatation sessions, the string method was attempted by Dr. DeMeules. Because of the lack of **peristalsis** in the plaintiff's transposed esophagus, the string was never able to anchor itself so as to allow the procedure to be performed. Battick v. Stoneman, 421 F.Supp. 213, 218 (D.Vt. 1976).

Now, that injury to the bowel, and in this case the injury to this lady's bowel, was at a point—the bowel moves, there is a **peristalsis**, the bowels move—mine may be moving now a little more actively than yours because of what I am doing, although it shouldn't be—but this organ moves within the body cavity, a good healthy bowel will do that. Raitt v. Johns Hopkins Hospital, 322 A.2d 548, 561 (Ct.Spec.App.Md.1974), reversed and remanded 274 Md. 489, 336 A.2d 90 (Ct.App.1975).

peritoneal cavity See *cavum, peritonaei.*

peritoneoscope (per″ĭ-to′ne-o-skōp″) an instrument for performing peritoneoscopy.

peritoneoscopy (per″ĭ-to″ne-os′ko-pe) [*peritoneum* + Gr. *skopein* to examine] examination of the peritoneal cavity by an instrument inserted through the abdominal wall.

peritoneum (per″i-to-ne′um) [L.; Gr. *peritonaion,* from *per* around + *teinein* to stretch] [NA] the serous membrane lining the abdominopelvic walls (*parietal p.*) and investing the viscera (*visceral p.*). A strong, colorless membrane with a smooth surface, it forms a closed sac in the male and is continuous with the mucous membrane of the uterine tubes in the female.

The most inner layer is called the **peritoneum**. It is a lining of the abdominal cavity. That is the first thing that is closed. Tice v. Hall, 303 S.E.2d 832, 834 (Ct.App.N.Car.1983).

Proceeding "very slowly" he just kept on incising and found "a substantial amount of scar tissue under the skin." Finally he "got down to what I thought was the peritonea (sic: **peritoneum**, the serous membrane lining the interior of the abdominal cavity and surrounding the organs contained therein). And I made a very small incision into what I thought was a peritonea and after making a small incision it did not look like peritonea to me. And we stopped at this point and I put a probe into the point where I thought the peritonea was, but this was the incision and it turned out to be the urinary bladder." Buckelew v. Grossbard, 435 A.2d 1150, 1154 (N.J.1981).

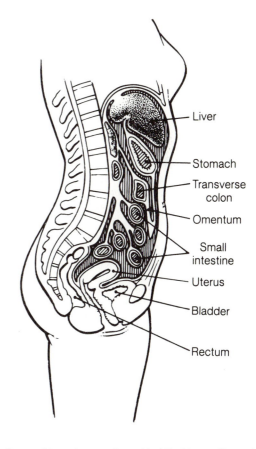

Course of the peritoneum (heavy black line) in a median sagittal section of a female.

Q. What is the danger of releasing a patient that has a surgical incision all the way open to the **peritoneum**?

A. If the primary wound itself is open infection can develop; however, there are occasions in which patients are released from the hospital with a drain through a stab wound that goes through all of the layers that causes no problem; but the tearing of an abdominal wound, the primary danger would be one of infection. Cleveland v. Edwards, 494 S.W.2d 578, 580 (Ct.Civ.App.Tex.1973).

peritoneum, parietal; peritoneum parietale [NA], the peritoneum that lines the abdominal and pelvic walls and the undersurface of the diaphragm. Cited in Siverson v. Weber, 372 P.2d 97–8 (Cal.1962).

peritoneum, visceral; peritoneum viscerale [NA], a continuation of the parietal peritoneum reflected at various places over the viscera, forming a complete covering for the stomach, spleen, liver, ascending portion of the duodenum, jejunum, ileum, transverse colon, sigmoid flexure, upper end of rectum, uterus, and ovaries; it also partially covers the descending and transverse portions of the duodenum, the cecum, ascending and descending colon, the middle part of the rectum, the posterior wall of the bladder, and the upper portion of the vagina. The peritoneum serves to hold the viscera in position by its folds, some of which form the *mesenteries*, connecting portions of the intestine with the posterior abdominal wall; other folds, the *omenta*, are attached to the stomach; and still others form the *ligaments* of the liver, spleen, stomach, kidneys, bladder, and uterus. The potential space between the visceral and the parietal peritoneum is the peritoneal cavity, which consists of the *pelvic peritoneal cavity* below and the *general peritoneal cavity* above. The general peritoneal cavity communicates by the epiploic foramen with the cavity of the greater omentum, which is also known as the *lesser peritoneal cavity*.

peritonitis (per″ĭ-to-ni′tis) inflammation of the peritoneum; a condition marked by exudations in the peritoneum of serum, fibrin, cells, and pus. It is attended by abdominal pain and tenderness, constipation, vomiting, and moderate fever.

Dr. Reams removed one of the tubes twenty-four hours after surgery. On June 14, 1973, Dr. Reams left town for three days without leaving written orders for the patient's care, though he had arranged for Dr. Wendell Lyon to fill in for any emergencies. The remaining tube was not cleaned nor properly monitored after Dr. Reams' departure and finally became clogged causing stump blow-out. Stutler's precarious condition was not known until June 15, 1973, when a nurse noticed his stomach was distended. Emergency surgery was performed seven hours later, but Stutler died on the operating table of peritonitis from gastronomy tube leakage....

... In any event, the warning signs should have been detected earlier, as Dr. McElhinney found evidence of **peritonitis** twenty-four to thirty-six hours before the emergency surgery of June 15, 1973. Reams v. Stutler, 642 S.W.2d 586–8 (Ky. 1982).

Briefly summarized, appellant alleged in her petition that on January 29, 1970, and continuing through March 31, 1970, appellee negligently examined, diagnosed and treated Ralph,

and that appellee allowed Ralph's appendix to burst resulting in **peritonitis** and the spreading of the deadly carcinoma cells through Ralph's abdominal cavity, either expediting or causing Ralph's death. Parsons v. Wood, 584 P.2d 1332–3 (Okla. 1978).

The operation performed by Dr. Boles on January 4 revealed that the child then had severe generalized **peritonitis**, which had caused a strangulation, or kink, in the intestine. Rogers v. U.S., 334 F.2d 931, 933 (6th Cir. 1964).

Other Authorities: Babin v. St. Paul Fire and Marine Ins. Co., 385 So.2d 849, 855 (Ct.App.La.1980). Raitt v. Johns Hopkins Hospital, 322 A.2d 548, 562 (Ct.Spec.App.Md.1974), reversed and remanded 274 Md. 489, 336 A.2d 90 (Ct.App. 1975).

permanent wave See *ammonia thioglycolate* (Hussey case).

peroneal See *nervus peroneus communis; nervus peroneus profundus.*

peroneal nerve, common See *nervus, peroneus communis.*

peroneal neuromuscular atrophy See *atrophy, progressive neuropathy (peroneal) muscular.*

personality (per″sŭ-nal′ĭ-te) that which constitutes, distinguishes, and characterizes a person as an entity over a period of time; the total reaction of a person to his environment.

personality, antisocial a personality disorder marked by a basic lack of socialization, behavior resulting in repeated conflict with society, and an incapacity to be loyal to individuals, groups, or social codes; it is associated with low tolerance to frustration, impulsiveness, selfishness, inability to feel guilty and to learn from experience and punishment, callousness, and a tendency to blame others for inappropriate behavior or to offer rationalizations for it, and by irresponsibility. Those who exhibit this type of personality have been called psychopaths and sociopaths. Called also *psychopathic p.* and *sociopathic p.*

Mr. Justice Douglas, with whom Mr. Justice Fortas concurs, dissenting.

The term "psychopathic personality" is a treacherous one like "communist" or in an earlier day "Bolshevik." A label of this kind when freely used may mean only an unpopular person. It is much too vague by constitutional standards for the imposition of penalties or punishment.

Cleckley defines "psychopathic personality" as one who has the following characteristics:

(1) Superficial charm and good "intelligence." (2) Absence of delusions and other signs of irrational "thinking." (3) Absence of "nervousness" or psychoneurotic manifestations. (4) Unreliability. (5) Untruthfulness and insincerity. (6) Lack of remorse or shame. (7) Inadequately motivated antisocial behavior. (8) Poor judgment and failure to learn by experience. (9) Pathologic egocentricity and incapacity for love. (10) General poverty in major affective reactions. (11) Specific loss of insight. (12) Unresponsiveness in general interpersonal relations. (13) Fantastic and uninviting behavior with drink and sometimes without. (14) Suicide rarely carried out. (15) Sex life imperson-

al, trivial and poorly integrated. (16) Failure to follow any life plan. Cleckley, The Mask of Sanity 238–255 (1941). . . .

. . . I have already quoted from clinical experts to show what a wide range the term "**psychopathic personality**" has. Another expert [4] classifies such a person under three headings:

Acting: (1) inability to withstand tedium, (2) lack of a sense of responsibility, (3) a tendency to "blow up" under pressure, (4) maladjustment to law and order, and (5) recidivism.

Feeling: they tend to (1) be emotionally deficient, narcissistic, callous, inconsiderate, and unremorseful, generally projecting blame on others, (2) have hair-trigger emotions, exaggerated display of emotion, and be irritable and impulsive, (3) be amoral (socially and sexually) and (4) worry, but do nothing about it.

Thinking: they display (1) defective judgment, living for the present rather than for the future, and (2) inability to profit from experience, i.e., they are able to realize the consequences intelligently, but not to evaluate them.

. . . the term **psychopathic personality** has been used to designate every conceivable type of abnormal character." Curran & Mallinson, Psychopathic Personality, 90 J. Mental Sci. 266, 278. See also Guttmacher, Diagnosis and Etiology of Psychopathic Personalities as Perceived in Our Time, in Current Problems in Psychiatric Diagnosis 139, 154 (Hoch & Zubin ed. 1953); Tappan, Sexual Offences and the Treatment of Sexual Offenders in the United States, in Sexual Offences 500, 507 (Radzinowicz ed. 1957). It is much too treacherously vague a term to allow the high penalty of deportation to turn on it. [[4] Caldwell, Constitutional Psychopathic State (Psychopathic Personality) Studies of Soldiers in the U.S. Army, 3 J. Crim. Psychopathology 171–172 (1941).] Boutilier v. Immigration and Naturalization Service, 387 U.S. 118, 124–7, 131, 87 S.Ct. 1563, 1570, 18 L.Ed.2d 661 (1967).

personality, passive-aggressive a personality characterized by aggression exhibited in passive ways, as by pouting, stubbornness, procrastination, and passive obstructionism.

My diagnosis of Miss Francine Newman's mental status is **Passive-aggressive Personality**, aggressive type, severe, precipitated by death of her mother and manifested by many instances of impulsive behavior, difficulties with pupils, co-workers, and superiors, excessive irritability, lack of judgment, and no insight. In my opinion, Miss Newman is not fit to perform the duties of a teacher. Newman v. Bd. of Ed. of City Sch. Dist. of N.Y., 443 F.Supp. 994, 1002 (E.D.N.Y.1977).

perspiration (per″spĭ-ra″shun) [L. *perspira're* to breathe through] sweat.

In a more restricted sense, and as the term generally is used, "perspiration" refers to the secretion of the sweat glands after it passes through the skin and appears on the surface thereof, plus accumulated dirt or debris which has collected on the skin from various sources, and when both are left on the surface of the skin, the combination generates an odor characterized as the odor of sweat. **Perspiration** is either sensible (which can be seen or felt) or insensible (which can neither be seen nor felt). Carter Products v. F.T.C., 186 F.2d 821, 823 (7th Cir. 1951).

pertussis See *whooping cough.*

pertussis vaccine See *vaccine, pertussis.*

pes (pes), pl. *pe'des*, gen. *pe'dis* [L.] [NA] the foot: the terminal organ of the leg, or lower limb. Used also as a general term to designate a footlike part.

petechia (pe-te'ke-ah), pl. *pete'chiae* [L.] a pinpoint, nonraised, perfectly round, purplish red spot caused by intradermal or submucous hemorrhage. See also *ecchymosis.*

At about 5:00 p.m. Dr. German examined plaintiff and observed soft palate **petechiae** (small red spots on the soft palate) and redness of the lids of both eyes. Speed v. State, 240 N.W.2d 901, 903 (Iowa 1976).

Petri dish See *Dish, Petri.*

petroleum (pĕ-tro'le-um) [L. *petra* stone + *oleum* oil] a thick natural oil obtained from beneath the earth. It consists of a mixture of various hydrocarbons of the paraffin and olefin series. It has been used as an expectorant, diaphoretic, and vermifuge; also in skin diseases, etc.

In his opinion **crude oil** applied to the skin would act as an emollient; it would soften the skin, and act as an irritant to a slight extent. It would tend to block the hair folicles of the sebaceous glands and probably produce an infection of the plugged glands. In his opinion there is no pharmacological basis for the use of **crude oil** as beneficial action. Colusa Remedy Co. v. U.S., 176 F.2d 554, 558 (8th Cir. 1949).

petrous bone See *pars petrosa ossis temporalis.*

peyote (pa-o'te) a stimulant drug from mescal buttons, the flowering heads of *L. williamsii*, used by North American Indians in ceremonies and feasts to produce a state of intoxification marked by feelings of ecstasy. The active euphoric principle is the major alkaloid, mescaline. Called also *peyotl.*

"**Peyote's** principal constituent is mescaline. When taken internally by chewing the buttons or drinking a derivative tea, peyote produces several types of hallucinations, depending primarily upon the user. In most subjects it causes extraordinary vision marked by bright and kaleidoscopic colors, geometric patterns, or scenes involving humans or animals. . . ." [People v. Woody, 61 Cal.2d 716, 40 Cal.Rptr. 69, 394 P.2d 813 (1964).] U.S. v. Kuch, 288 F.Supp. 439, 448–9 (D.D.C.1968).

PFB See *pseudofolliculitis.*

pH the symbol relating the hydrogen ion (H^+) concentration or activity of a solution to that of a given standard solution. Numerically the pH is approximately equal to the negative logarithm of H^+ concentration expressed in molarity. pH 7 is neutral; above it alkalinity increases and below it acidity increases.

pH is a logarithmic expression of the concentration of hydrogen ions. At a **pH** of 7, the hydrogen and hydroxyl ion concentrations are essentially equal and the water is neutral. A **pH** value below 7 indicates acidity, a higher value indicates alkalinity. Tanners' Council of America, Inc. v. Train, 540 F.2d 1188, 1190–1 (4th Cir. 1976).

pH is a measure of hydrogen ion concentration. A solution having a **pH** of 7 is neutral. As the **pH** of a solution decreases, the hydrogen ion concentration increases, and the solution becomes correspondingly more acidic. Conversely, as the **pH**

increases the solution becomes less acidic and more alkaline. Rawlings v. National Molasses Co., 328 F.Supp. 913, 917 (C.D.Cal.1971).

Term used in expressing relative acidity and alkalinity. M & R Dietetic Laboratories, Inc. v. Dean Milk Co., 203 F.Supp. 130, 132 (N.D.Ill.1961).

phacoemulsification (fak″o-e-mul″sĭ-fĭ-ka′shun) a method of cataract extraction in which the lens is fragmented by ultrasonic vibrations and simultaneously irrigated and aspirated.

Before engaging in this all important task, a brief explanation of the procedure known as **phacoemulsification** is in order. A "rather elaborate" piece of equipment is required to extract a cataractous lens by the procedure known as **phacoemulsification**. Basically, the equipment was described as a probe "containing an irrigating and aspirating cannula . . . [with] a tip that goes 'buzz' . . . [which] fragments the lens." The fragmented lens is then "aspirated" by the "rather elaborate" piece of equipment. A less generous incision is required to insert the "probe" or "tip" of the **phacoemulsification** equipment than is required to insert the probe used in a "standard cryophake delivery." The less generous incision employed in the **phacoemulsification** procedure, and the filling of the less generous incision "with the aspirator-irrigator tip, perhaps . . . could maintain the innerocular pressure better. . . ." According to the record, on April 17, 1973, the date of the operation in question, the **phacoemulsification** procedure was in its infancy and there was no **phacoemulsification** equipment in Kansas City, Missouri, at that time. Miller v. Scholl, 594 S.W.2d 324, 329–30 (Mo.Ct.App.1980).

The operation in this case, **phacoemulsification**,[8] involved surgical removal of a cataract. [8 **Phacoemulsification** is a surgical procedure first used about ten years before the surgery in this case. It entails a three millimeter incision in the eye, into which a small needle is inserted. The needle then vibrates at 45,000 vibrations per second. When it touches the cataract, the vibrations emulsify the cataract and the particles are removed from the eye by a suction technique.] Lambert v. Park, 597 F.2d 236, 239 (10th Cir. 1979).

Dr. McPherson confirmed that there is an increased danger that a cataract will develop as a result of the penetration of the eye by the pellets and the resulting scar tissue. She also testified that there was at the time of her last examination no evidence of cataract development. With a new surgical procedure known as **phacoemulcification**, Dr. McPherson estimated the likelihood that a cataract could be successfully removed from the lens of Kevin's eye was from ninety to ninety-five percent. Dr. Breffeilh testified that he did not agree with those figures but did not indicate how high he would estimate the rate of success. Gleason v. Hall, 555 F.2d 514, 517 (5th Cir. 1977).

phagocyte (fag′o-sīt) [phago- + -cyte] any cell that ingests microorganisms or other cells and foreign particles. In many cases but not always the ingested material is digested within the phagocyte. Fixed phagocytes (fixed macrophages) are potentially phagocytic, and free phagocytes (free macrophages, polymorphonuclear leukocytes) are intensely phagocytic.

He rejected Fulks' claim that exposure to sandblasting was the originating cause of his atypical mycobacterial disease. However, there was medical evidence that the inhalation of silica crystals can destroy **phagocytes**, cells capable of defending against infection caused by the Battey bacillus. Fulks v. Avondale Shipyards, Inc., 637 F.2d 1008, 1011 (5th Cir. 1981).

phagocyte, alveolar rounded granular phagocytic cells within the alveoli of the lungs, which ingest inhaled material; called also *alveolar macrophages* and *dust cells*.

Before even sub-clinical injury can occur, the asbestos fiber must pass a number of dichotomously branching tubes in the nose and throat which get progressively narrower, must reach the lung and become depositioned there, and must be enveloped by a scavenger cell, an **alveolar macrophage** which may then begin to produce destructive enzymes in a futile attempt to destroy the indestructible asbestos fiber. Because the fiber is not biodegradable, the macrophage continues to secrete enzymes which eventually destroy surrounding tissue and produce scarring. Eagle-Picher Industries, Inc. v. Liberty Mut. Ins. Co., 523 F.Supp. 110, 115 (D.Mass.1981).

phalanges (fah-lan′jēz) plural of *phalanx*.

phalanx (fa′lanks), pl. *phalan'ges* [Gr. "a line or array of soldiers"] [NA] a general term for any bone of a finger or toe.

phalanx media digitorum manus [NA], middle phalanx of fingers: any one of the four bones of the fingers (excluding the thumb) situated between the proximal and distal phalanges; called also *p. secunda digitorum manus*.

phalanx, middle See *phalanx media digitorum manus*.

phalanx proximalis digitorum manus [NA], proximal phalanx of fingers: any one of the five bones of the fingers that articulate with the metacarpal bones and, except in the thumb, with the phalanx media; called also *p. prima digitorum manus*.

He developed a non-union which required a bone graft operation for the fracture of the **proximal phalanx**, but the bone graft incompletely canalized. Sanchez v. Lubeck Linie A.G., 318 F.Supp. 821, 823 (S.D.N.Y.1970).

phalanx proximalis digitorum pedis [NA], proximal phalanx of toes: any one of the five bones of the toes that articulate with the metatarsal bones and, except in the great toe, with the phalanx media; called also *p. prima digitorum pedis*.

phantom pain syndrome See *limb, phantom*.

pharmacist (fahr′mah-sist) one who is licensed to prepare and sell or dispence drugs and compounds, and to make up prescriptions; an apothecary, druggist, or (British) chemist.

pharmacologist (fahr″mah-kol′o-jist) one who makes a study of the actions of drugs.

. . . a trained **pharmacologist**, i.e., one who deals in the study of drugs per se and their chemical effect on patients. Dodson v. Parham, 427 F.Supp. 97, 107 (N.D.Ga.1977).

pharmacology (fahr"mah-kol'o-je) [*pharmaco-* + *-logy*] the science that deals with the origin, nature, chemistry, effects, and uses of drugs; it includes pharmacognosy, pharmocokinetics, pharmacodynamics, pharmacotherapeutics, and toxicology.

Dr. Irwin G. Gross, Ph. D., M.D., head of the Department of Pharmacology at the University of Iowa, testified that **pharmacology** is the study of drugs as to their chemistry, source, physical properties, preparation and physiological effects on living tissue, whether they be used in therapeutic amounts or otherwise, their absorption, their fats, their excretion and therapeutic indications for their use. Colusa Remedy Co. v. U.S., 176 F.2d 554, 558 (8th Cir. 1949).

Other Authorities: Harrison v. Flota Mercante Grancolombiana, S.A., 577 F.2d 968, 975 (5th Cir. 1978).

pharmacy (fahr'mah-se) [Gr. *pharmakon* medicine] 1. the branch of the health sciences dealing with the preparation, dispensing, and proper utilization of drugs. 2. a place where drugs are compounded or dispensed.

Chapter 30, Article 5 of our Code is titled "Pharmacists, Assistant Pharmacists and Drugstores." Its Section 18 prohibits retail sale of poisonous, deleterious, or habit-forming drugs by any person other than a registered pharmacist. Its Section 3, among other things, prohibits any person not a registered pharmacist to conduct a **pharmacy** for the purpose of "retailing, compounding or dispensing medicines, poisons or narcotic drugs...." Section 1 has definitions, among which is subsection (5): "The term '**pharmacy**' or 'drugstore' or 'apothecary' shall be held to mean and include every store or shop or other place (a) where drugs are dispensed, or sold at retail, or displayed for sale at retail; or (b) where physicians' prescriptions are compounded...."

Code, 30–5–21 excludes from the prohibitions of the article "... any legally qualified practitioner of medicine, ... in the compounding of his own prescriptions, or to prevent him from supplying to his patients such medicines as he may deem proper if such supply is not made as a sale." [Our emphasis] Ye Olde Apothecary v. McClellan, 253 S.E.2d 545–6 (Sup.Ct. App.W.Va.1979).

pharyngitis (far"in-ji'tis) [*pharyngo-* + *-itis*] inflammation of the pharynx.

... he appeared at defendant's office in the morning with inflamed throat and eyes. Defendant diagnosed plaintiff's malady as acute **pharyngitis** and acute conjunctivitis. Believing the cause to be some form of pathogenic streptococci, defendant asked plaintiff if he was allergic to penicillin. Plaintiff answered that he didn't know if he had ever had any penicillin, and may also have stated that his children did have such allergy. Johnston v. Brother, 12 Cal.Rptr. 23–4 (Dist.Ct.App.Cal.1961).

Pharyngitis is an inflammation of the pharynx—that part of the alimentary canal between the base of the tongue and the esophagus—usually accompanied by pain in the throat and fever. Rotan v. Greenbaum, 273 F.2d 830–1 (D.C.Cir.1959).

pharynx (far'inks) [Gr. "the throat"] [NA] the musculomembranous passage between the mouth and posterior nares and the larynx and esophagus. The part above the level of the soft palate is the *nasopharynx*, which communicates with the auditory tube. The lower portion consists of two sections—the *oropharynx*, which lies between the soft palate and the upper edge of the epiglottis, and the *hypopharynx*, which lies below the upper edge of the epiglottis and opens into the larynx and esophagus.

Phemerol (fe'mer-ol) trademark for preparations of benzethonium.

phenacetin (fĕ-nas'ĕ-tin) [USP] chemical name: *N*-(4-ethoxyphenyl)acetamide. An analgesic and antipyretic, $C_{10}H_{13}NO_2$, occurring as white, glistening crystals or fine, white, crystalline powder; administered orally. Called also *acetophenetidin* and *acetphenetidin*.

See Michael v. Warner/Chilcott, 91 N.M. 651, 579 P.2d 183 (Ct.App.1978), involving the warning on the label of a nonprescription sinus decongestant containing **phenacetin**, a medically known producer of kidney disease if taken in large amounts for a prolonged period. The court there reversed a summary judgment in favor of defendant, holding that that risk was required to be unequivocally and unambiguously communicated to the buyer and that the duty to warn as to use of the product could not be discharged simply by a label instruction that the remedy not be taken for longer than 10 days without consulting a physician. Torsiello v. Whitehall Laboratories, 398 A.2d 132, 139 (Super.Ct.N.J.1979).

Phenaphen

Phenaphen #3, he stated, while also a drug with little addictive tendency, is a depressant. He also testified that any of these drugs including [Valium and Darvon N], when given to a person who is otherwise depressed, could make that depression worse. He also stated that a man's judgment could be impaired so much that he could not distinguish right from wrong, "in the sense that a person's sense of values would be quite, quite distorted, and he might well feel impelled to do something that otherwise he would not be impelled to do." Texas Employers' Ins. Ass'n v. Saunders, 516 S.W.2d 242–3 (Ct.Civ.App.Tex.1974), reversed and remanded 526 S.W.2d 515 (Tex.1975).

phencyclidine See *phencyclidine hydrochloride*.

phencyclidine hydrochloride (fen-si'klĭ-dēn) chemical name: 1-(1-phenylcyclohexyl)piperidine hydrochloride; a potent analgesic and anesthetic, $C_{17}H_{25}N \cdot HCl$, used in veterinary medicine. Abuse of this drug may lead to serious psychological disturbances. Abbreviated PCP.

The appellant was found guilty of having unlawfully possessed and sold a controlled substance, **phencycladine** [sic] (which is used by veterinarians for tranquilizing horses). Foley v. State, 565 S.W.2d 128 (Ark.1978).

Phencyclidine hydrochloride was found to be a depressant or stimulant drug by the State Board of Pharmacy. See Rule 480–9.01(3). Rules of the Georgia State Board of Pharmacy. Sundberg v. State, 216 S.E.2d 332–3 (Ga.1975).

... a hallucinogenic drug, to-wit: **Phenycylidine Hydrochloride**, a/k/a "PCP."...

PCP is not specifically listed in F.S. Section 404.01, F.S.A., but is brought under the statute, if at all, by the language of F.S. Section 404.01(3), F.S.A.: "and any other drug to which the drug abuse laws of the United States apply." This language was added by the Legislature to Section 404.01(3) in

July, 1967. At that time **PCP** was not a prohibited drug under the United States law.

PCP was added to the drug abuse laws of the United States by Congress on October 27, 1970. State v. Camil, 279 So.2d 832–3 (Fla.1973).

Phenergan (fen'er-gan) trademark for preparations of promethazine hydrochloride. See also *promethazine hydrochloride.*

phenmetrazine hydrochloride (fen-met'rah-zēn) [USP] chemical name: 3-methyl-2-phenyl morpholine hydrochloride. A central nervous system stimulant, $C_{11}H_{15}NO \cdot HCl$, occurring as a white to off-white crystalline powder, used as an anorexic. Abuse of this drug may lead to habituation. See also *amphetamine.*

Dr. Eichenwald testified that the prescribed combination of drugs violated community standards of practice, and particularly noted that the use of **preludin**, an amphetamine, in a patient with hypertension, such as Andrea, was dangerous. This was because the amphetamine increases blood pressure. Mendoza v. Varon, 563 S.W.2d 646, 652 (Ct.Civ.App.Tex. 1978).

. . . defendant Williams failed to prepare and maintain complete and accurate records with respect to the receipt and distribution of Preludin 75 mg. Endurets, a Schedule II preparation containing **phenmetrazine** and its salts. U.S. v. Williams, 416 F.Supp. 611–12 (D.D.C.1976).

phenobarbital (fe″no-bar′bĭ-tal) [USP] chemical name: 5-ethyl-5-phenyl-2,4,6(1*H*,3*H*,5*H*)pyrimidinetrione. A long-acting barbiturate, $C_{12}H_{12}N_2O_3$, occurring as white, glistening, small crystals, or white, crystalline powder; used as a sedative, hypnotic, and anticonvulsant, administered orally. Called also *phenobarbitone* and *phenylethylbarbituric acid.*

He prescribed the drug **Phenobarbital**, an anti-seizure medication, and told John's mother to give John one capsule in the morning and two at bedtime. . . .

. . . He had used the drug before on many occasions and never had a patient who suffered an allergic reaction. He stated that it was not standard medical procedure for a pediatrician to warn that Stevens-Johnson syndrome or other severe allergic reactions could occur as a result of the use of the drug. He said it was "very unlikely that the drug treatment would result in Stevens-Johnson syndrome."

The plaintiffs offered the medical testimony of Dr. Martha D. Yow, Professor and Department Chairman at Baylor College of Medicine. Dr. Yow testified that **Phenobarbital** was "a very commonly prescribed drug. It is one of the safest drugs that we use for sedation of children, . . . that rarely patients have side effects, such as somnolence, lethargy, and occasionally rashes." Menefee v. Guehring, 665 S.W.2d 811, 814–15 (Ct. App.Tex.1983).

Her only problem was that she was depressed. She was taking her medication and had no other complaints. The major side effect of **phenobarbital** is drowsiness. A person's mood may be affected and they either may be depressed or hyper-excitable. It could be expected to last three to four weeks at the most. Camarata v. Benedetto, 420 So.2d 1146, 1150 (Ct. App.La.1982).

The doctor administered an injection of ⅛ grain of **phenobarbital** and ¹⁄₂₃₀ grain of hyoscine. **Phenobarbital** has a tranquilizing effect, and the subject may experience a sense of euphoria or elation. U.S. ex rel. Townsend v. Twomey, 452 F.2d 350, 367 (7th Cir. 1971).

phenol (fe'nol) [USP] an extremely poisonous, colorless to light pink, crystalline compound, $C_6H_5 \cdot OH$, obtained by the distillation of coal tar, and converted, by the addition of 10 per cent water, into a clear liquid with a peculiar odor and a burning taste. Used as an antimicrobial agent. Called also *carbolic acid, hydroxybenzene, oxybenzene, phenic acid, phenylic acid,* and *phenylic alcohol.* See also *excision (nail), phenol method*; and *poisoning; phenol.*

There was no specification by Dr. Graubard as to the strength or the temperature of the **carbolic acid** required to accomplish effective sterilization, or as to the necessity or duration of immersion required. Furthermore he did not say anything about the effect of **carbolic acid** or alcohol on an acrylic denture or on the mouth or gums of the patient. . . .

. . . Furthermore, **carbolic acid** and acrylic dentures are not compatible and such acid would destroy the shape, form and contour of the denture. . . .

. . . **Carbolic acid** would destroy it, and he had never used that acid himself nor ever heard of any dentist using it on such a denture. . . .

. . . At his office that evening he inserted in the **carbolic acid** an acrylic denture of the same kind as that given to Mrs. Germann. Within a few minutes the denture was completely destroyed even though it was thereafter immersed in alcohol. (Both the bottle of acid and the ruined denture were marked in evidence.) The doctor said the acid and the acrylic material are not at all compatible, and that even if he had just washed the denture in **carbolic acid** it would eat into the pores of the denture and remain there. . . .

For an illustration of the damage of **carbolic acid** to the skin and tissues, See Picheloup v. Gibbons, 9 La.App. 380, 120 So. 504 (1928), where a dentist carelessly spilled the acid on a patient's hands and thigh. Germann v. Matriss, 260 A.2d 825, 829–32 (N.J.1970).

phenol-bur See *phenol; bur*; and *excision (nail), phenol-bur method.*

phenomenon (fĕ-nom'ĕ-non), pl. *phenom'ena* [Gr. *phainomenon* thing seen] any sign or objective symptom; any observable occurrence or fact.

phenomenon, doll's head an abnormal extraocular muscle manifestation of many ophthalmologic syndromes and conditions: the eyes depress as the head is bent backward.

See *reflex, doll's eye*; and *reflex, oculocephalogyric.*

As part of this test . . . the head is also moved front and back, the neck is flexed in the back movement, causing the eyelids to open. This phenomenon is called "**doll's—eyelid response.**" Matter of Quinlan, 348 A.2d 801, 807 (Super.Ct.N.J.1975).

phenomenon, Koebner's the appearance of isomorphic lesions at the site of an injury in psoriasis, verruca plana, lichen nitidus, or lichen planus; called also *isomorphic effect.*

... another illustration of the **Koebner phenomenon** which Dr. Mitchell provided at another point in his deposition: that "it's well established that the mild, repeated trauma to the knees and elbows of patients accounts for the characteristic distribution of psoriasis, and this is a form of **Koebner's phenomenon.**"....

... His physician, Dr. Mitchell, corroborated the testimony that he had pustular lesions on his hands and feet, App. at 30. These lesions constituted a dermal injury giving rise to a diagnosis of **Koebner's syndrome**, one form of which occurs when "mild, repeated trauma" penetrates the dermal level of the skin causing a flare-up in the psoriatic patient's condition. See App. at 34–5....

The dissent makes much of the fact that by the time the company's doctor examined him nine months later, he had lesions all over his body. It is entirely consistent with the pattern of psoriasis that the emotional stress caused by the appearance of some lesions in one area precipitates lesions in other areas as well. Thus a person may simultaneously have some lesions that are a result of **Koebner's syndrome**, i.e., caused or aggravated by physical trauma, and others that are not. See generally 6 P. Cantor, Traumatic Medicine and Surgery for the Attorney 640–41 (1962). Hensley v. Washington Metro. Area Transit Auth., 655 F.2d 264, 269, 272 (D.C.Cir.1981).

phenomenon, Raynaud's intermittent bilateral attacks of ischemia of the fingers or toes and sometimes of the ears or nose, marked by severe pallor, and often accompanied by paresthesia and pain; it is brought on characteristically by cold or emotional stimuli and relieved by heat, and is due to an underlying disease or anatomical abnormality. When the condition is idiopathic or primary it is termed *Raynaud's disease*. See also *disease, Raynaud's*; and *scleroderma*. (Stark case).

Raynaud's phenomenon is a vascular disorder marked by recurrent spasm of the capillaries, especially those of the fingers and toes. Concomitant symptoms include pallor, cyanosis and redness in succession, numbness and pain. The symptoms are usually most pronounced during cold weather. In severe cases, the disease may lead to local gangrene. Stark v. Weinberger, 497 F.2d 1092, 1096 (7th Cir. 1974).

... the patient has had a suggestion of **Raynaud's phenomenon** for a long time on plunging her hands into cold water. The patient states that the pain waxed and waned for a while and then became a kind of chronic dull ache down the right arm, especially on pronation or supination of the arm. The patient could not raise her arm above her head. Hughes v. Richardson, 342 F.Supp. 320, 324 (W.D.Mo.1971).

phenothiazine (fe″no-thi′ah-zēn) a greenish, tasteless compound, $C_{12}H_9NS$, prepared by fusing diphenylamine with sulfur; used as a veterinary anthelmintic. Called also *dibenzothiazine, thiodiphenylamine*.

Rath discloses in Example 15 of his patent the compound **1,9-diazaphenothiazine**, which is the diaza analogue of plaintiff's 1-monoaza compound. Rath is the only one of the four references relied upon by the defendant which provides some indication of therapeutic utility for the disclosed compounds, which are said "to be distinguished by relatively low toxicity and valuable physiological effects based on their capacity of stabilizing the vegetative and central nervous system, accom-

panied by essentially reduced side effects". Deutsche Gold- und Silber-Scheideanstalt v. Comm. of Patents, 251 F.Supp. 624, 627 (D.D.C.1966).

phenotype (fe′no-tīp) [Gr. *phainein* to show + *typos* type] the entire physical, biochemical, and physiological make-up of an individual as determined both genetically and environmentally, as opposed to genotype. Also, any one or any group of such traits.

Apparently, until August 1976, there had been no sex determination test in the 95-year history of the USTA National Championships, other than a simple **phenotype test** (observation of primary and secondary sexual characteristics)....

"... I rejected reliance solely on the Barr body test and instead chose to rely on the **Phenotype test** which concerns itself with the observation of primary and secondary sexual characteristics...." Richards v. U.S. Tennis Ass'n, 400 N.Y.S. 2d 267–9 (Sup.Ct.N.Y.Cty.1977).

phenotype test See *phenotype*.

phenyl (fen′il, fe′nil) the univalent radical, C_6H_5. Symbol Ph.

phenylbutazone (fen″il-bu′tah-zōn) [USP] chemical name: 4-butyl-1,2-diphenyl-3,5-pyrazolidinedione. A congener of aminopyrine and antipyrine, $C_{19}H_{20}N_2O_2$, occurring as a white to off-white, crystalline powder, having analgesic, antipyretic, anti-inflammatory, and mild uricosuric properties; used especially in the treatment of gout, rheumatoid arthritis, ankylosing spondylitis, and other rheumatoid conditions, administered orally. Called also *diphebuzol*.

Plaintiff brings this suit to recover damages for injuries allegedly sustained while he was a cadet at the United States Air Force Academy in Colorado. He says that he was a member of the varsity football team at the Academy in 1969 and 1970, and that in those years the team physicians prescribed **Butazolodin**, an anti-inflammatory drug, so that he could play with a hurt knee. He graduated in June 1971 and became a commissioned officer in the Air Force.

He claims that the drug caused damage to his bone marrow and that he developed chronic mononucleosis, chronic anemia, dangerous alteration of heartbeat, and other ills. These started to manifest themselves after his graduation but it was not until after he had been retired for disability in 1975 that his personal physician discovered that the drug was the cause of the disability. He alleges that as a result of the negligence of the Air Force doctors he has been reduced from a two hundred and twenty pound tackle to a chronically ill one hundred and forty pound weakling. Fischer v. U.S., 451 F.Supp. 918–19 (E.D.N.Y.1978).

Through expert testimony of two physicians it was established that **butazolidin** alka is an "anti-inflammatory agent" sometimes used for treatment of arthritis. However, its use is limited because scientific tests have proved that approximately 40 per cent of the persons using said drug have severe orientation problems. The adverse side effects that the drug has been found to cause include a "confusional state," lethargy, vertigo, unsteadiness afoot, blurred vision and possibly even slurred speech. The drug has a "half life" interval of 36 to 72 hours which means that one-half of its dosage remains in the central nervous system so that potential adverse effects might not occur until the fourth or fifth day of continual medication. An average dosage of two tablets per day could cause the side effects mentioned above. People v. Van Tuyl, 359 N.Y.S.2d 958, 960 (Sup.Ct.App.Term 1974).

Out of a quantity of 200 ml of urine, 6.2 mg of the drug **Butazolidin IV**, or **Phenylbutazone**, was recovered. This drug is commonly used in the treatment of ailing race horses to combat arthritic disorders, to relieve pain, and to reduce inflammation and fever....

... also gave the horse an intravenous injection of **Butazolidin IV**, a drug also known as **Phenylbutazone**, and known commonly in the trade as "**Bute**," in the amount of ten cubic centimeters or two grams, a dosage which the doctor described as a small one. Dr. King characterized **Butazolidin** as an anti-inflammatory drug which also acts as a pain reliever so that the horse can be trained, preferably by walking the horse on the two days following the tapping. Commonwealth v. Webb, 274 A.2d 261, 263, 269 (Commonwealth Ct.Pa. 1971).

Other Authorities: Baldino v. Castagna, 454 A.2d 1012, 1014–15 (Super.Ct.Pa.1982).

phenylephrine hydrochloride (fen″il-ef′rin) [USP] chemical name: (S)-3-hydroxy-α-[(methylamino)methyl] benzenemethanol hydrochloride. An adrenergic with strong alpha-receptor stimulant activity, $C_9H_{13}NO_2 \cdot$ HCl, occurring as white or nearly white crystals; used as vasoconstrictor to decongest nasal and laryngeal mucous membranes, to produce mydriasis without cycloplegia, to maintain blood pressure during spinal and inhalation anesthesia, to treat vascular failure in drug-induced shock, shocklike states, and hypotension, to prolong spinal anesthesia, and to treat supraventricular tachycardia. It is applied topically or administered by intramuscular or intravenous injection or infusion.

phenylketonuria (fen″il-ke″to-nu′re-ah) an inborn error of metabolism attributable to a deficiency of or a defect in phenylalanine hydroxylase, the enzyme that catalyzes the conversion of phenylalanine to tyrosine. The lack permits the accumulation of phenylalanine and its metabolic products in the body fluids. It results in mental retardation (phenylpyruvic oligophrenia), neurologic manifestations (including hyperkinesia, epilepsy, and microcephaly), light pigmentation, eczema, and a mousy odor, unless treated by administration of a diet low in phenylalanine. The disorder is transmitted as an autosomal recessive trait. Abbreviated PKU. Two variants of classic **phenylketonuria** have been recognized: a mild variant, in which the patient tolerates higher levels of phenylalanine in the diet, and a transient variant, in which tolerance increases during infancy and early childhood.

Plaintiff alleges that the defendant negligently failed to discover that Brian had a condition at birth known as **phenylketonuria** ("PKU"), which is an inborn or inherited error of metabolism which may result in mental retardation, and that defendant negligently failed to discover and treat Brian's condition. Flippin v. Jarrell, 261 S.E.2d 257–8 (Ct.App.N.C. 1980).

phenylthiocarbamide See *phenylthiourea.*

phenylthiourea (fen″il-thi″o-u-re′ah) a compound, $C_6H_5NHCSNH_2$, used in genetic research in dry crystal form or in 5 per cent solution. The ability to taste it is inherited as a dominant trait, the compound being intensely bitter to approximately 70 per cent of the population, and nearly tasteless to the rest. Called also *phenylthiocarbamide* or *PTC*.

phenytoin (fen′ĭ-to-in) [USP] chemical name: 5,5-diphenyl-2,4-imidazolidinedione. An anticonvulsant and cardiac depressant, $C_{15}H_{12}N_2O_2$, occurring as a white powder; used in the treatment of all forms of epilepsy except petit mal and as an antiarrhythmic, administered orally. Called also *diphenylhydantoin.*

To prevent seizures which might result from the injuries she received in the accident he also prescribed **dilantin**; this medication could not be given to her immediately after the accident because she was then pregnant and **dilantin** has been linked to birth defects....

Plaintiff testified that her use of **dilantin** produced unpleasant side effects, including an upset stomach if taken at times other than after eating; irritation to the gums and tongue; loss of energy and drowsiness; headaches when she doesn't wear sunglasses outside; she developed a mustache and it has adverse sexual effects upon her. In addition to these drug-related side effects she testified that she continued to have severe headaches once a week which last for approximately eight hours. Lindsay v. Appleby, 414 N.E.2d 885, 888 (App.Ct.Ill. 1980).

He has treated some 2,000 epilepsy patients with **phenytoin**. Since the rate of absorption of different brands of **phenytoin** varies, he has found it best if a patient becomes stabilized on one brand, not to change to another. Because there are various undesirable side effects from use of the drug, Dr. Booker's practice and recommendation is that only the minimum amount of **phenytoin** that will suffice to prevent epileptic seizures in the particular patient should be administered. Among these side effects are overgrowth of gums, stimulation of the growth of body hair, interference with the functioning of Vitamins D and K, and formation of folic acid. U.S. v. Articles of Drug Labeled Colchicine, 442 F.Supp. 1236, 1240 (S.D.N.Y.1978).

phlebitis (flĕ-bi′tis) [*phleb-* + *-itis*] inflammation of a vein. The condition is marked by infiltration of the coats of the vein and the formation of a thrombus. The disease is attended by edema, stiffness, and pain in the affected part, and in the septic variety by pyemic symptoms. See also *phlebogram* (Smith case). Cited in Thompson v. Occidental Life Ins. Co. of Cal., 513 P.2d 353, 360 (Cal. 1973); Carmichael v. Reitz, 95 Cal.Rptr. 381, 388 (Ct. App.Cal.1971).

phlebitis, reactive

The pain in Ms. Smith's arm persisted and soon a dark streak appeared. A week after the IVP, she visited Dr. Lynberg, who diagnosed **reactive phlebitis**. **Reactive phlebitis** is an inflammation of the vein in reaction to some irritant. Renographin-60, the contrast agent used in the IVP, is an irritant. Smith v. Shannon, 666 P.2d 351, 353 (Wash.1983).

phlebogram (fleb′o-gram) [*phlebo-* + Gr. *gramma* a writing] 1. roentgenogram of a vein filled with contrast medi-

Jugular
venous pulse

Phlebogram: *a*, a positive wave due to contraction of the right atrium; *c*, a venous wave due to contraction of the right ventricle, with downward movement of the tricuspid valve; *x*, a small negative wave due to atrial relaxation; *v*, the early diastolic wave, a positive wave occurring during ventricular contraction and reflecting the filling of the right atrium (also [not shown] the exaggerated positive wave related to reflux of blood through an incompetent atrioventricular valve); *y*, a negative wave due to emptying of the right atrium; *h*, an occasional, late filling wave.

um. 2. a tracing of the venous pulse made with a phlebograph or sphygmograph. See also *test, Graham's.*

The doctor did not perform a preoperative **venogram** (vein test) on plaintiff. There were inherent risks involved in such a test. Also, the three clinical signs which would indicate the need for a venogram were not present. Ziegert v. South Chicago Community Hospital, 425 N.E.2d 450, 455 (App.Ct.Ill. 1981).

At trial, Dr. Luckett testified that phlebitis is a known complication to a **venogram** and appellant's expert witnesses agreed. Smith v. Luckett, 271 S.E.2d 891, 893 (Ct.App.Ga.1980).

... he noticed a vein in his left buttock getting more enlarged and painful. He consulted a private physician, Dr. James Boland, who recommended that he have a **venogram** performed. He did so in August 1970. After examining the **venogram**, Dr. Boland concluded that the femoral vein, which had been severed during the vein stripping operation, had become blocked, probably within a few days or weeks after the anastomosis. Dr. Boland and another doctor who was consulted, Dr. Joseph Schanno, both agreed that this blockage could not be corrected by surgery and that the only possible treatment was the continued use of supportive stockings. Bridgford v. U.S., 550 F.2d 978, 980 (4th Cir. 1977).

Other Authorities: Field v. Winn Dixie Louisiana, Inc., 427 So. 2d 616–17 (Ct.App.La.1983); Carmichael v. Reitz, 95 Cal. Rptr. 381, 390 (Ct.App.Cal.1971).

phlebotomy (flĕ-bot'o-me) [*phlebo-* + Gr. *tomē* a cutting] incision of a vein, as for the letting of blood; venesection.

Doctor Fischer first saw Young in October 1962 and prescribed a course of therapy which called for periodic **phlebotomies**. A **phlebotomy**, Dr. Fischer explained, "is simply withdrawing blood," and he reminded the jurors that a **phlebotomy** is performed any time an individual donates blood. The withdrawal lowers the number of blood cells. Young v. Park, 417 A.2d 889, 891 (R.I.1980).

phloem (flo'em) [Gr. *phloios* bark] a form of vascular tissue in plants which conducts synthesized nutrients, such as glucose, both up and down the stem or root, characterized by the presence of sieve tubes. See also *xylem.*

"Phloem" is a complex tissue in the vascular system of higher plants consisting mainly of sieve tubes and companion cells

and usually also of fibre and parenchyma cells. It is part of the conductive tissue conveying the materials nourishing the plant. Appleman v. U.S., 338 F.2d 729–30 (7th Cir. 1964).

phobia (fo'be-ah) [Gr. *phobos* fear (*phobein* to be affrighted by) + *-ia*] any persistent abnormal dread or fear. Used as a word termination designating abnormal or morbid fear of or aversion to the subject indicated by the stem to which it is affixed.

He testified, and her own testimony corroborated, that she developed a **phobia** about sex after the searches which not only caused her to break off her first sexual relationship, but later manifested itself as a severe sexual dysfunction. Blackburn v. Snow, 771 F.2d 556, 572 (1st Cir. 1985).

In other words, the appellant's initial problems with diarrhea, led to a fear of flying, which in turn now, when faced with flying causes aggravation of the condition. In short, the appellant's diarrhea now is due to fear of flying.

OPM's finding that the appellant's problems are situational rather than an inherent disease are supported by the facts of this case and there is no precedent for awarding disability retirement based on an individual's **phobias**....

... The attempt by OPM and MSPB to disparage petitioner's medical condition as a mere "**phobia**" not only ignores the physical manifestation of petitioner's disease but also overlooks the fact that phobic reactions are clinically defined as mental illnesses, see American Psychiatric Association, Diagnostic and Statistical Manual of Mental Disorders 225–34 (3d ed. 1980); equally compelling, OPM has never before suggested that **phobias**, as a class, are excluded from the statute's coverage of disabling mental diseases, see, e.g. Your Retirement System, supra, § F–21, at 17. Turner v. Office of Personnel Management, 707 F.2d 1499, 1501–02 (D.C.Cir. 1983)....

In stressful situations Ms. Doe employed a "numbers game" as a blocking technique to avoid dealing with the problem. This numbers game essentially involved adding random numbers in her head. Also, she had experienced a plane crash on her way to interview for the job in Mississippi, and for a time had an irrational **phobia** about planes. In addition, for a time she "day-dreamed" that a monster was chasing her through a cemetery. Doe v. Region 13 Mental Hlth-Mental Retard Com'n, 704 F.2d 1402, 1404 (5th Cir. 1983).

pholic acid See *acid, folic.*

phonetics (fo-net'iks) the science of vocal sounds; phonology.

... he defined **phonetics** as a study of the way in which people talk; both the study of the sounds insofar as they combine to make different words and as they combine to distinguish different speakers. People v. King, 72 Cal.Rptr. 478, 489 (Ct. App.Cal.1968).

phonology (fo-nol'o-je) [*phono-* + *-logy*] the science which treats of vocal sounds; phonetics.

phosphatase (fos'fah-tās") [*phosphate* + *-ase*] an enzyme that hydrolyzes monophosphoric esters, with liberation of inorganic phosphate, found in practically all tissues, body fluids, and cells, including erythrocytes and leukocytes.

phosphatase, acid a phosphatase active in an acid medium; such enzymes are found in mammalian erythrocytes and yeast (optimal activity at pH 6), prostatic tissue, epithelium, spleen, kidney, blood plasma, liver, and pancreas, and in rice bran (optimal activity at pH 5) and Taka-diastase (optimal activity at pH 3–4).

He explained that **acid phosphatase** is a chemical which is found in large quantities in the seminal fluid released by the male at the time of sexual climax, but it is not found in the vagina in amounts detectable with the tests used unless semen is deposited there....

... With **acid phosphatase** there is a steady decrease in the quantitative measurement after intercourse depending upon variable factors, but the decrease continues whether the body into which it is deposited is alive or dead. It is detectable for as long as 12 to 24 hours after deposit. A significantly large amount would be designated as "four plus" on a test scale which descends to "one plus," "a trace," and "absent." People v. Bynum, 483 P.2d 1193–5 (Cal.1971).

phosphatase, alkaline a phosphatase active in an alkaline medium; such enzymes are found in blood plasma or serum, bone, kidney, mammary gland, spleen, lung, leukocytes, adrenal cortex, and seminiferous tubules (optimal activity at about pH 9.3).

On the SMA–12 graph (a battery of 12 tests of the blood), the **alkaline phosphatase** reading was 145, compared with a normal range of 30 to 85....

... These tests are not in themselves specifically diagnostic, since they indicate increased levels of enzymes in the blood that may be caused by several organs.[1] [[1] An elevated **alkaline phosphatase** level indicates the possibility of either liver or bone disease. A rise in the level of SGOT may be indicative of liver, heart, or muscle damage.] Cornfeldt v. Tongen, 262 N.W.2d 684, 690 (Minn.1977).

phosphate (fos′fāt) [L. *phosphas*] any salt or ester of phosphoric acid. Phosphates are distributed throughout the body. Inorganic phosphates occur chiefly in the skeleton in association with calcium, where they play a role in the mineralization of bone, and in body fluids, where they play a role in the regulation of acid-base balance. Organic phosphates are incorporated in such macromolecules as sugar phosphates, phospholipids, phosphoproteins, and nucleic acids. See also *cholinesterase*.

The FDA granted Diamond approval on February 12, 1969, to market Talodex, a new drug to be administered by injection to dogs suffering from mange, heartworm, hookworm, ringworm, ticks and fleas. The principal ingredient of Talodex is fenthion, an organic **phosphate**. Organic **phosphates** are commonly used as insecticides and pesticides. Fenthion and other organic **phosphates** cause inhibition of cholinesterase, an enzyme the presence of which is vital to the transmission of nerve impulses. Excessive exposure to organic **phosphates** results in organic **phosphate** poisoning, which may cause death. Diamond Laboratories, Inc. v. Richardson, 452 F.2d 803, 805 (8th Cir. 1972).

The more prevalent view in the scientific community is that phosphorus is the most likely nutrient for controlling eutrophication because of its comparative abundance in the waters and the more ready means for reducing its input into the waters. Based upon scientific testimony, **phosphates** are the limiting nutrient in the waters of Biscayne Bay to a wide variety of different species of algae, and may well be a limiting nutrient in the inland waters of Dade County. Therefore, reducing the level of phosphorus in the waters will produce a direct effect on the amount of algae and retard the eutrophication of the waterways. Soap and Detergent Ass'n v. Clark, 330 F.Supp. 1218, 1220 (S.D.Fla.1971).

phosphocreatine (fos″fo-kre′ah-tin) a creatine—phosphoric acid compound, $(OH)_2PO \cdot NH \cdot C(:NH) \cdot N(CH_3) \cdot CH_2 \cdot COOH$, occurring in muscle metabolism, being broken down into creatine and inorganic phosphorus. It is an important storage form of high-energy phosphate, the energy source in muscle contraction. The phosphate group is transferred to ADP on muscle contraction to yield creatine and ATP. Called also *creatine phosphate*.

phosphorus (fos′fō-rus) [Gr. *phōs* light + *phorein* to carry] a nonmetallic, allotropic element: poisonous and highly inflammable; symbol, P; atomic number, 15; atomic weight, 30.974. It occurs in three forms—*white* (yellow), *red*, and *black*. It is obtainable from bones, urine, and especially minerals, such as apatite. Ordinary white phosphorus is the kind once used in medicine, and is very inflammable and exceedingly poisonous. Phosphorus is an essential element in the diet; it is a major component of the mineral phase of bone and is abundant in all tissues, being involved in some form in almost all metabolic processes. Free phosphorus causes a fatty degeneration of the liver and other viscera, and the inhalation of its vapor often leads to necrosis of the lower jaw. Therapeutically, it was once used in rickets, osteomalacia, nervous and cerebral diseases, scrofula, and tuberculosis, as a genital stimulant in sexual exhaustion, and as a tonic in conditions of exhaustion. See also *detergent; Gymnodinium*; and *phosphate* (Soap and Detergent Ass'n case).

photocoagulation (fo″to-ko-ag″u-la′shun) condensation of protein material by the controlled use of an intense beam of light (e.g., xenon arc light or argon laser); used especially in treatment of retinal detachment and destruction of abnormal retinal vessels, or of intraocular tumor masses.

Six weeks later, and more than six months after the accident, Merritt was sent to an Indianapolis hospital for treatment of his left eye. The surgeons at the hospital did not perform a vitrectomy on the left eye. Instead, they performed an argon laser **photocoagulation** on Merritt's right eye, even though his vision in his right eye was 20/25 and he had never complained about his right eye. Following his trip to the hospital, Merritt's vision in his right eye deteriorated, and he became functionally blind in both eyes. Merritt v. Faulkner, 697 F.2d 761–2 (7th Cir. 1983).

photon (fo′ton) a particle (quantum) of radiant energy.

"Q. Now, it is the protons, or the radiation, which actually go right through the body tissue of the patient and land onto that film in back of the patient or on the side of the patient, that produce the picture on the film, is that so? A. The word is 'photon.'...

"Q. In other words, Doctor, X-rays are ionizing radiation or energy in motion resulting from the collision of high energy electrons which strike a tungsten tube inside the vacuum of the X-ray tube thereby producing myriads of these electromagnetic waves or protons—A. **Photons**,

"Q. —that are commonly spoken of as X-rays, is that true? A. Again the word is '**photons.**'

"Many of them stay inside. . . .?

"When an X-ray beam is projected through a structure, and if that structure is a human being . . . most of the X-ray **photons** are absorbed or scattered. . . ?

"In the case of an anterior-posterior film involving the abdomen, those **photons** which pass through the abdomen, about 99 per cent. are absorbed or scattered, and only about 1 per cent. emerge on the other side for photographic purposes. . . ." Chiropractic Ass'n of New York, Inc. v. Hilleboe, 227 N.Y.S.2d 309, 347 (Sup.Ct.Albany Cy.1961).

photophobia (fo"to-fo'be-ah) [*photo-* + Gr. *phobein* to be affrighted by] abnormal visual intolerance of light.

Dr. Kassell. Garman performed an abbreviated neurologic examination which revealed **photophobia** but no nuchal rigidity. . . .

. . . Dr. SanFelipe had to examine decedent with an opthalmoscope twice because decedent was winking and blinking at the light. Testimony of Harold Polischeck. The doctor admits this indicated **photophobia** and that she didn't mark this symptom on the chart. Polischeck v. U.S., 535 F.Supp. 1261, 1263–4 (E.D.Pa.1982).

photosensivity (fo"to-sen"si-tiv'ĭ-te) abnormal reactivity of the skin to sunlight.

Well from the patient's history and from my observations of him, I felt that using both eyes with the glare phenomenon being so permanent in the left eye, the patient was actually getting poor[er] vision than if he used just the right eye alone and shielded off the left eye. In other words when the left eye had this excessive **photo-sensivity** it sympathetically involved the right eye which caused the patient really to have poor[er] vision than if he used the right eye alone, or poor[er] visual function, let me put it that way didn't change his visual acuity in that eye but visual function. Rohm & Haas v. Workmen's Comp. App. Bd., 414 A.2d 163–4 (Commwlth.Ct.Pa.1980).

phrenic nerve See *nervus phrenicus.*

phthisis (ti'sis) [Gr. *phthisis,* from *phthiein* to decay] tuberculosis especially of the lungs.

This case involves only pulmonary tuberculosis. **Phthisis,** the proper name for pulmonary tuberculosis, has already been held to be a dust disease. Felcoskie v. Lakey Foundry Corp., 382 Mich. 438, 446, 170 N.W.2d 129, 132 (1969). Cotton v. Campbell, Wyant & Cannon Foundry, 225 N.W.2d 187, 190 (Ct.App.Mich.1974).

physical examination See *examination, physical.*

physical therapy See *therapy, physical.*

physician (fĭ-zish'un) an authorized practitioner of medicine, as one graduated from a college of medicine or osteopathy and licensed by the appropriate board. See also *doctor.*

. . . plaintiff argues that a medical corporation is neither a licensed **physician** nor a licensed hospital.

We disagree. A **physician** is a person who practices medicine (i.e., diagnoses and treats human ailments) (People ex rel. Gage v. Siman (1917), 278 Ill. 256, 257–58, 115 N.E. 817), and section 2 of the Medical Corporation Act authorizes the formation of corporations "for the study, diagnosis and treatment of human ailments and injuries. . . ." (Ill.Rev.Stat. 1979, ch. 32, par. 632; compare, People by Kerner v. United Medical Service, Inc. (1936), 362 Ill. 442, 454, 456, 200 N.E. 157 (decided before the Medical Corporation Act was enacted; holding that Illinois law prohibited corporations from practicing medicine.) Moreover, a corporation formed to practice medicine must be licensed by the State. (Ill.Rev.Stat. 1979, ch. 32, pars. 635–42.) Therefore, a corporation formed under the Medical Corporation Act can lawfully practice medicine, just like any individual who is a licensed **physician.** . . .

. . . We are convinced that the legislature did not intend this discrepancy, and we hold that the word "**physician,**" as used in section 21.1 of the Limitations Act, includes corporations formed to practice medicine under the Medical Corporations Act. Real v. Kim, 445 N.E.2d 783, 790 (App.Ct.Ill.1983).

The word "**physician**", as used in the statute, has a plain and ordinary meaning usually denoting a practitioner of medicine, a person duly authorized or licensed to treat diseases (Black's Law Dictionary, Third Edition); a person skilled in the art of healing; specifically, a doctor of medicine (Webster's Seventh New Collegiate Dictionary). State, Dep't of Health, Etc. v. McTigue, 387 So.2d 454, 455 (Dist.Ct.App.Fla.1980).

physician assistant one who has been trained in an accredited program and certified by an appropriate board to perform certain of a physician's duties, including history taking, physical examination, diagnostic tests, treatment, certain minor surgical procedures, etc., all under the responsible supervision of a licensed physician. Abbreviated P.A. See also *Medex.*

A **physician's assistant** is a paramedically trained member of armed forces personnel. To become a **physician's assistant,** a person receives one year of classroom instruction at **physician's assistant** school, studying a variety of basic medical topics, followed by one year of clinical rotation in a hospital or hospitals alongside full-time medical students. Polischeck v. U.S., 535 F.Supp. 1261–3 (E.D.Pa.1982).

Physician's Desk Reference (PDR)

In particular, he did not inform her of 10 other risks which are mentioned in the Physicians' Desk Reference (**PDR**). The **PDR** is a book published by drug manufacturers which describes the uses, effects, and dangers of various drugs. Smith v. Shannon, 666 P.2d 351, 354 (Wash.1983).

As an additional measure, Lilly, for a time, published information on Dicumarol in the **Physician's Desk Reference (PDR),** the compendium often relied upon by physicians to obtain knowledge of the proper uses and hazards of drugs. Baker v. St. Agnes Hospital, 421 N.Y.S.2d 81, 83 (2d Dep't 1979).

PDR is prepared from information provided by pharmaceutical companies, and includes all potential risks, no matter how slight. Depos. of Dr. Ryan at 28–29. Niblack v. U.S., 438 F.Supp. 383, 388 (D.Colo.1977).

physiology (fiz"e-ol'o-je) [*physio-* + *-logy*] the science which treats of the functions of the living organism and its parts, and of the physical and chemical factors and processes involved.

Physiology is the study of how the body functions and the various biochemical and physical events which cause the body to function under normal conditions. Harrison v. Flota Mercante Grancolombiana, S.A. 577 F.2d 968, 974 (5th Cir. 1978).

pial (pi'al) pertaining to the pia mater.

pial hemorrhage See *hemorrhage, pial.*

pia mater (pi'ah ma'ter) [L. "tender mother"] the innermost of the three membranes (meninges) covering the brain and spinal cord, investing them closely and extending into the depths of the fissures and sulci; it consists of reticular, elastic, and collagenous fibers. Cited in York v. Daniels, 259 S.W.2d 109, 11 (Springfield Ct.App.Mo.1953).

pica (pi'kah) [L.] a craving for unnatural articles of food; a depraved appetite, as seen in hysteria, pregnancy, and in malnourished children.

Pica, the habitual ingestion of nonfood substances, is a particularly important source of lead exposure for children who live in urban areas. Lead Industries Ass'n v. Environmental Protection, 647 F.2d 1130, 1136 (D.C.Cir.1980).

PID See *disease, pelvic inflammatory.*

pilocarpine (pi"lo-kar'pin) chemical name: (3*S-cis*)-3-ethyldihydro-4-[(1-methyl-1*H*-imidazol-5-yl)methyl]-2(3*H*)-furanone. An alkaloid, $C_{11}H_{16}N_2O_2$, obtained from the leaves of *Pilocarpus jaborandi* or *P. microphyllus*, which has cholinergic activity. See also *pilocarpine hydrochloride*; and *pilocarpine nitrate.*

pilocarpine hydrochloride [USP], the monohydrochloride salt of pilocarpine, $C_{11}H_{16}N_2O_2 \cdot HCl$, occurring as colorless, translucent crystals; used mainly as an ophthalmic cholinergic to produce miosis and to decrease intraocular pressure in the treatment of glaucoma, applied topically to the conjunctiva.

They also stated in their depositions that **pilocarpine** is probably the most common first-prescribed drug for treating glaucoma and phospholine iodide is one of a number of drugs which are often tried second. Winkjer v. Herr, 277 N.W.2d 579, 584 (N.Dak.1979).

pilocarpine nitrate [USP], the nitrate salt of pilocarpine, $C_{11}H_{16}N_2 \cdot HNO_3$, occurring as shining, white crystals, having the same actions and uses as the hydrochloride salt.

pimple (pim'p'l) a papule or pustule, usually of the face, neck, or upper trunk, most often due to acne vulgaris.

The evidence disclosed that **pimples** are a low inflammatory lesion of the skin, caused by a specific germ, and that they range in size from scarcely visible bumps to the proportion of boils, and usually are surrounded by an area of redness. There also was testimony that the primary treatment of **pimples** is a thorough washing of the face or affected parts with soap and water, although ultraviolet rays and vaccines are occasionally used. Folds v. Federal Trade Commission, 187 F.2d 658–9 (7th Cir. 1951).

pin (pin) a long slender metal rod for the fixation of the ends of fractured bones; in dentistry, a peg or dowel by means of which an artificial crown is fixed to the root of a tooth or by which supplemental retention is provided to any dental restoration. See also *nail.*

On November 18, 1976, plaintiff underwent an open reduction operation during which a **Webb bolt** was inserted across the fracture site and a bone graft was performed to fill in the defect in the tibia. Warner v. Schweiker, 551 F.Supp. 789, 791 (E.D.Mo.1982), reversed 722 F.2d 428 (8th Cir. 1983).

Avery Wisdom was a twenty-nine-year-old man when he dislocated his right clavicle while playing football. He was treated by Dr. Swan, who repositioned Wisdom's arm and stabilized it with a **pin**. The **pin** migrated and punctured the right lung. This caused blood and air to accumulate in the cavity between the lung and chest wall. Further surgery was required to drain the cavity. Swan v. Wisdom, 386 So.2d 574–5 (Dist. Ct.App.Fla.1980).

pin, Harrington

A laminectomy was performed on that date, and **Harrington pins** were installed to maintain the alignment and to stabilize the spinal column. Brazil v. U.S., 484 F.Supp. 986, 989 (N.D. Ala.1979).

pin, Steinmann's a metal rod for the internal fixation of fractures. See also *nail extension*, under *extension.*

The normal gliding movement was completely destroyed in both knees. Both legs were initially placed in traction and a **Steinman** [sic] **pin** was placed through the left leg below the knee. He developed osteomyelitis from the **Steinman** [sic] **pin** and the infected and dead bone was scraped from the wound. Carter v. Consolidated Cabs, Inc., 490 S.W.2d 39, 44 (Mo.1973).

pineal See *body, pineal.*

pins and plaster technique See *technique, pins and plaster.*

piperazine (pi-per'ah-zēn) [USP] a compound, $C_4H_{10}N_2$, prepared by the action of alcoholic ammonia on ethylene chloride, or by other methods, occurring as white to slightly off-white lumps or flakes. Its salts are used orally as anthelmintics. Called also *diethyl diamine, dispermine,* and *p. hexahydrate.*

". . . 'Piperazine' is used in the treatment of human pinworms and roundworm. . . ."

. . . He testified that he prescribed **piperazine** as a local anesthetic for the removal of an infestation of roundworms from the intestine. Hardt v. Board of Naturopathic Examiners, 606 P.2d 1169–71 (Ct.App.Or.1980).

piqûre (pe-koor') [Fr.] puncture, especially Bernard's (diabetic) puncture.

The **piqure** is made by the use of acupuncture needles. Those currently in general use are required to be very fine, hairlike, flexible, unbreakable and stainless. The lengths vary according to the usage; the long needle (three inches or more) is used for deep **piqure** in the region of the buttocks; the medium needle (two to three inches) is used for the deep points of the limbs and trunk; and the short needle (one to two inches) or the very short needle (less than one inch) is used on superficial points.

The **piqure**, once placed, must remain there for a determined time at a determined depth.

The **piqures** are inserted and manipulated in accordance with the "great law of Pu-Hsieh and the rule of Shou Fa", which constitute the keystone of acupuncture, its procedure being to supply energy where it is lacking or to calm or retire an excess of energy where such excess is present. Ideally, it restores the equilibrium of the Yin and Yang and as a consequence the person's state of health is restored. People v. Amber, 349 N.Y.S.2d 604, 610 (Sup.Ct.Queens Cty.N.Y.1973).

piston action

The mechanical problem relates to the rubbing and **piston action**, causing abrasion of the skin of the residual limb. The **piston action** is the result of up and down movement of the artificial limb. According to the witness the residual limb has a tendency to change in size and volume. As a result mechanical injuries may occur since the residual limb becomes tighter or looser in the socket of the artifical limb. Daw Industries, Inc. v. U.S., 561 F.Supp. 433, 436 (U.S.Ct.Int.Trade 1983), reversed 714 F.2d 1140 (Fed.Cir.1983).

pityriasis (pit"ĭ-ri'ah-sis) [Gr. *pityron* bran + *-iasis*] a name originally applied to a group of skin diseases characterized by the formation of fine, branny scales, but now used only with a modifier.

pityriasis rosea a dermatosis characterized by scaling pink oval macules arranged with the long axes parallel to the lines of cleavage of the skin.

Pityrosporon (pit"ĭ-ros'po-ron) a genus of imperfect fungi of the family Cryptococcaceae, which are yeastlike and produce no mycelium; called also *Malassezia*.

PKU See *phenylketonuria*.

placebo (plah-se'bo) [L. "I will please"] an inactive substance or preparation given to satisfy the patient's symbolic need for drug therapy, and used in controlled studies to determine the efficacy of medicinal substances. Also, a procedure with no intrinsic therapeutic value, performed for such purposes. See also *effect, placebo*.

People who are given medication for an ailment frequently feel better because they think they should, even though the product has no therapeutic value. This is known as the **placebo effect**. Warner-Lambert Co. v. F.T.C., 562 F.2d 749, 754 (D.C.Cir.1977).
Other Authorities: U.S. v. 60 28-Capsule Bottles, More or Less, etc., 211 F.Supp. 207, 209 (D.N.J.1962).

placenta (plah-sen'tah), pl. *placentas* or *placen'tae* [L. "a flat cake"] an organ characteristic of true mammals during pregnancy, joining mother and offspring, providing endocrine secretion and selective exchange of soluble, but not particulate, blood-borne substances through an apposition of uterine and trophoblastic vascularized parts. According to species, the area of vascular apposition may be diffuse, cotyledonary, zonary, or discoid; the nature of apposition may be labyrinthine or villous; the intimacy of apposition may vary according to what layers are lost of those originally interposed between maternal and fetal blood (maternal endothelium, uterine connective tissue, uterine epithelium, chorion, extraembryonic mesoderm,

and endothelium of villous capillary). The chorion may be joined by and receive blood vessels from either the yolk sac or the allantois, and the uterine lining may be largely shed with the chorion at birth (deciduate) or may separate from the chorion and remain (nondeciduate). The human placenta is discoid, villous, hemochorial, chorioallantoic, and deciduate. After birth, it weighs about 600 gm. and is about 16 cm. in diameter and 2 cm. thick, discounting a principal functional part, the maternal blood in the intervillous space (which leaks out at birth) into which the chorionic villi dip. The villi are grouped into adjoining cotyledons making about 20 velvety bumps on the side of the placenta facing outward to the uterus; the inner side of the placenta facing the fetus is smooth, being covered with amnion, a thin avascular layer that continues past the edges of the placenta to line the entire hollow sphere of chorion except where it is reflected to cover the umbilical cord, which joins fetus and placenta. The cord usually joins the placenta near the center but may insert at the edge, on the nonplacental chorion, or on an accessory placenta.

In the next case, a 1975 case involving a woman in childbirth who had a retained **placenta**, Dr. Storrs did not take steps to remove those portions of the **placenta** which had not been expelled or removed after the birth. Inordinate delay in removing a retained **placenta**, according to one physician practicing obstetrics and gynecology, involves a risk of infection and bleeding. Storrs v. State Medical Bd., 664 P.2d 547, 556 (Alas.1983).

placenta abruptio See *abruptio placentae*.

plane (plān) [L. *planus*] a superficial incision in the wall of a cavity or between tissue layers, especially in plastic

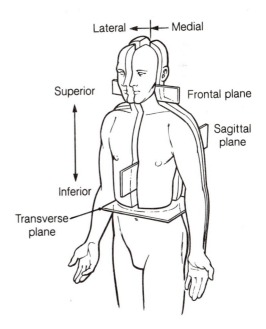

Planes of the body (Davenport). Anterior view, in the anatomical position, with standard planes of reference shown by cleavages.

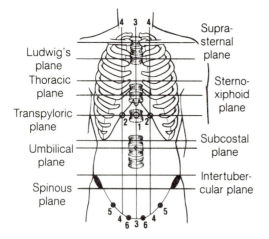

Ludwig's plane
Thoracic plane
Transpyloric plane
Umbilical plane
Spinous plane

Supra-sternal plane
Sterno-xiphoid plane
Subcostal plane
Intertuber-cular plane

Planes of the trunk (Rawling).

surgery, made so that the precise point of entry into the cavity or between the layers can be determined.

planes, Addison's a series of planes used as landmarks in the topography of the thorax and abdomen.

planing (pla'ning) the plastic surgery procedure of abrading disfigured skin to promote reepithelialization with minimal scarring. It may be done by means of sandpaper, emery paper, low- or high-speed wire brushes, etc. (surgical planing; dermabrasion), or by application of caustic substances such as phenol or trichloracetic acid (chemical planing; chemabrasion).

plantar (plan'tar) pertaining to the sole of the foot.

The cushioning effect, according to Dr. Lehneis, is analogous to the cushioning of the **plantar** surface of the foot (sole). Daw Industries, Inc. v. U.S., 561 F.Supp. 433, 436 (U.S.Ct.Int.Trade 1983), reversed 714 F.2d 1140 (Fed.Cir.1983).

On November 24, 1981, plaintiff consulted Dr. David with a second degree burn on the **plantar** surface (bottom) of his foot and toes. This burn was not present at any of the times of Dr. David's prior examinations. Dr. David testified that the only history plaintiff gave on November 24 "was that he had the foot exposed to the sun and that possibly he got burned in the sun". Jackson v. City of Alexandria, 424 So.2d 1265–6 (Ct. App.La.1982).

plantar fascia See *aponeurosis, plantar.*

plantar nerve, medial See *nervus plantaris medialis.*

plantar wart See *verruca plantaris.*

plaque (plak) [Fr.] any patch or flat area. See also *pleura* (Industrial Indemnity Co. case).

plaques, Hollenhorst atheromatous emboli containing cholesterol crystals in the retinal arterioles, a warning sign of impending serious cardiovascular disease such as stroke, myocardial infarction, aortic aneurysm, or occlusion of the retinal arterioles.

At the operation, it was found that the incision into the artery made for the insertion of the catheter for the procedures of coronary arteriogram and aortic arch studies had been made

through a very large **atheromatous plaque.** Such a plaque is composed of a fatty substance that grows over with fibrous tissue and very often develops some calcium or lime salt in it. . . .

. . . If, in fact, these fatty plaques are present in other parts of the circulation, then one of the well recognized risks of doing a catheter procedure in the patient is the risk of knocking off one of the plaques. If a plaque is knocked off, it will be swept into the circulation and will eventually lodge in a place where the artery becomes too small for it; if this should be in the brain, then there is a probability of a stroke. Morgenroth v. Pacific Medical Center, Inc., 126 Cal.Rptr. 681, 684 (Ct.App. Cal.1976).

plasm (plazm) plasma; formative substance.

plasm, germ (*obs.*), Weismann's term for the reproductive and hereditary substance of individuals which is passed on from the germ cell in which an individual originates in direct continuity to the germ cells of succeeding generations. By it new individuals are produced and hereditary characters are transmitted. Cf. *somatoplasm.*

plasma (plaz'mah) [Gr. "anything formed or molded"] the fluid portion of the blood in which the particulate components are suspended. *Plasma* is to be distinguished from *serum,* which is the cell-free portion of the blood from which the fibrinogen has been separated in the process of clotting. See also *blood plasma.*

Diagnostic testing of the clotting of blood in laboratories for disorders such as hemophilia is routinely performed on **plasma** which is anti-coagulated with either sodium citrate or sodium oxalate to inactivate the calcium which is present in blood. For this purpose, a patient's blood is drawn, anti-coagulated, and then centrifuged to remove red and white cells and most of its platelets and thus separate the solid portions of the blood from the liquid part. The resulting liquid is called "**plasma**". **Plasma,** being relatively clear, assists the technician in detecting the point of beginning of the formation of the clot so that the clotting time can be accurately determined. Such anti-coagulated **plasma** is routinely tested by recalcifying the **plasma** and measuring the time to form a clot. Commonly used recalcification clotting tests designed to detect the different bleeding disorders include the prothrombin time test, the Hicks-Pitney test, thromboplastin generation test and the PTT test. The Speck patent in suit directly relates to a reagent for use in the PTT test. Ortho Pharmaceutical Corp. v. Amer. Hospital Supply Corp., 186 U.S.P.Q. 501, 504 (S.D.Ind.1975).

plasmacytoma (plaz"mah-si-to'mah) [*plasmacyte* + *-oma*] any focal neoplasm of plasma cells, including those of multiple myeloma. Isolated plasma cell tumors may occur outside the bone marrow (extramedullary plasmacytomas), affecting such tissues as the nasal, oral, and pharyngeal mucosa and visceral organs. Called also *peripheral plasma cell myeloma* and *plasma cell tumor.*

plasmacytosis (plaz"mah-si-to'sis) the presence of excess plasma cells in the blood.

plasmapheresis (plaz"mah-fĕ-re'sis) [*plasma* + Gr. *aphairesis* removal] the removal of plasma from withdrawn blood, with retransfusion of the formed elements into the donor; generally, type-specific fresh frozen plasma or albumin is used to replace the withdrawn plasma. The procedure may be done for purposes of collecting plasma components or for therapeutic purposes.

Plasmapheresis is a process in which whole blood is removed from a donor and immediately centrifuged to separate the red blood cells from the plasma or watery part of the blood. The red blood cells are then transfused back into the donor's body. As a donor can safely give whole blood only about eight times per year but can give blood plasma as often as twice a week, the use of **plasmapheresis** dramatically increased the volume of antibodies that could be taken from appellant during any given period of time. This process is generally repeated twice at a session and requires about an hour and a half to recover a pint of plasma; due to the small size of appellant's veins, however, it usually took her two and a half hours. . . .

. . . The process of **plasmapheresis** also involved pain and discomfort. On occasion the technician would have difficulty situating the needle properly in the veins in appellant's arms, allowing blood to seep into the tissues around the vein creating a minor hematoma or even hitting a nerve. These difficulties could produce lingering soreness and stiffness of the arms. In addition, Garber inevitably suffered a certain amount of scarring of the veins in her arms and ran the remote risk of contracting hepatitis or having an air bubble introduced into her bloodstream. An expert testified at trial, however, that there should be no untoward effects if the process is done properly. U.S. v. Garber, 589 F.2d 843, 845 (5th Cir. 1979), reversed and remanded 607 F.2d 92 (5th Cir. 1979).

Appellant is engaged in the business of collecting blood plasma from donors by a process known as "**plasmapheresis.**" This technique, involving more complicated procedures than the taking of whole blood, may be described in the following manner. . . .

The donor is taken to the donor room where a paramedical technician performs the veni-puncture and collects the requisite amount of blood in a bag. The bag is then placed in a centrifuge which separates the plasma from the blood cells, and the plasma is extracted into a pooling bag. After that step is completed, the remaining blood cells are mixed with a saline solution, and the mixture is allowed to run through a filtering tube back into the donor's vein at a set rate. This procedure of taking whole blood, and returning the blood cells to the donor, is then repeated to obtain the agreed upon amount of plasma. Mirsa, Inc. v. State Medical Board, 329 N.E.2d 106–7 (Ohio 1975).

Thus, in Mirsa v. State Medical Board (1975), 42 Ohio St.2d 399, 329 N.E.2d 106, this court held that the practice of "plasmapheresis," by which a blood-donor center removes and specially processes blood plasma from a donor, constituted the practice of medicine within the meaning of R.C. 4731.34. State v. Rich, 339 N.E.2d 630, 632 (Ohio 1975).

plasmid (plaz′mid) [*plasm* + *-id*] any extrachromosomal self-replicating element of a cell. In bacteria, plasmids are circular DNA molecules that reproduce themselves and are thus conserved, apart from the chromosome, through successive cell divisions; they include the F factor and R factor. Plasmids that may also become integrated into the chromosome are sometimes called *episomes*.

Plasmids are hereditary units physically separate from the chromosomes of the cell. In prior research, Chakrabarty and an associate discovered that **plasmids** control the oil degradation abilities of certain bacteria. Diamond v. Chakrabarty, 447 U.S. 303, 100 S.Ct. 2204, 2205, 65 L.Ed.2d 144 (1980).

plate (plāt) [Gr. *platē*] a flat structure or layer, such as a thin layer of bone. See also *lamina*; and *layer*, etc.

plate, bone a metal bar with perforations for the insertion of screws, used to immobilize fractured segments.

A heavy metal **plate**, some eight to ten inches in length was attached to the broken bone [a left femur] by eight metal screws around the fracture site. The plaintiff suffered severe pain in and around the area where the **plate** was installed. He was referred to several doctors in an attempt to determine the cause of and to arrest the severe pain. The **plate** was removed after eight months; the plaintiff stayed on crutches for about ten months; and the visits to these doctors continued for some fourteen months. Hester v. Ridings, 388 So.2d 1218–19 (Ct. Civ.App.Ala.1980).

plateau (plah-to′) an elevated and level area.

plateau, tibial either of the bony surfaces of the tibia, internal and external, closest to the condyles of the femur.

The cause of employee's disability was a severely comminuted depression fracture of the lateral **tibial plateau** of his right leg (the area which is the leg portion of his knee joint). Williamson v. Besco's Services, 270 N.W.2d 297–8 (Minn.1978).

platelet (plāt′let) a disk-shaped structure, 2 to 4μ in diameter, found in the blood of all mammals and chiefly known for its role in blood coagulation; platelets, which are formed in the megakaryocyte and released from its cytoplasm in clusters, lack a nucleus and DNA but contain active enzymes and mitochondria. See also *coagulation factor* under *factor*; and *thrombocytic series*, under *series*. Called also *blood platelet* and *thrombocyte*.

Platelets may be simply referred to as the glue that holds the white and red blood cells together and prevents bleeding. Vallot v. Central Gulf Lines, Inc., 641 F.2d 347, 349 (5th Cir. 1981).

platypnea (plah-tip′ne-ah) [*platy-* + Gr. *pnoia* breath] dyspnea induced by assumption of the upright position and relieved by assumption of a recumbent position; the opposite of orthopnea.

pleocytosis (ple″o-si-to′sis) presence of a greater than normal number of cells in the cerebrospinal fluid.

It should be further noted that the presence of white cells in this case, particularly lymphocytes, when accompanied by increased CSF protein, is a condition of **pleocytosis** which is a characteristic of HSE and practically unknown in GBS cases. Stich v. U.S., 565 F.Supp. 1096, 1118 (D.N.J.1983).

pleura (ploor′ah), pl. *pleur′ae* [Gr. "rib," "side"] [NA] the serous membrane investing the lungs and lining the thoracic cavity, completely enclosing a potential space known as the pleural cavity. There are two pleurae, right and left, entirely distinct from each other. The pleura is moistened with a serous secretion which facilitates the movements of the lungs in the chest. See also *empyema*.

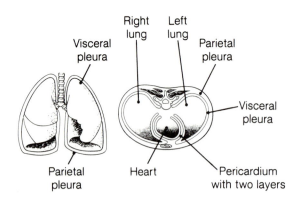

Pleura; for purposes of illustration, the pleural cavity is shown as an actual space. (Williams.)

Dr. W. G. Hughson reported the same history of applicant's exposure to asbestos on February 11, 1982, and found that the applicant has **pleural plaque**, one of the signs of asbestosis, in his left lung due to his exposure to asbestos at National [Steel & Shipbuilding]. Indus. Indem. Co. v. Workers' Comp. App. Bd., 193 Cal.Rptr. 471, 473 (Ct.App.Cal.1983).

He gave her an injection for bursitis in her back. He used a needle that was an inch to an inch and one-half long. He estimated thickness of the muscle wall at the point of injection to be an inch and one-half. Inside the muscle wall at that point is the **pleura**, the outer lining of the lung. Dr. Whittle, another doctor who treated Mrs. Baker, testified that, as Mrs. Baker was very thin, her chest wall would be three-quarters of an inch to an inch thick. Baker v. Chastain, 389 So.2d 932–3 (Ala. 1980).

In the normal person the pleural cavity is at a low pressure so the lung which is highly elastic, having a higher pressure within, due to the connection with atmosphere through the bronchial tubes, is expanded to fill the pleural cavity. Thus, the parietal **pleura** and the visceral **pleura** are in contact and there is in effect no pleural cavity since the lung entirely fills the space. During breathing when the rib cage is expanded and the diaphragm lowered, the parietal **pleura** moves outwardly to enlarge the pleural cavity and thus to reduce the pressure therein. The lung then expands against its elasticity to fill the cavity. Similarly, when the rib cage is compressed and the diaphragm raised the natural elasticity of the lung permits it to decrease in size and force air therefrom. Deknatel, Inc. v. Bentley Sales, Inc., 173 U.S.P.Q. 129, 130 (C.D.Cal.1971).

pleural (ploor'al) pertaining to the pleura.

Q. Right. And they found you had some type of an abnormality in the lower two-thirds on the right side of your chest, what the radiologist calls apparent **pleural** thickening. Is that what you're talking about?...

A. **Pleural** density in the lower two-thirds of the right side of the chest. Areas of apparent **pleural** thickening are demonstrated. Lundy v. Union Carbide Corp., 695 F.2d 394–5, 397 (9th Cir. 1982).

pleural cavity See *pleura*; and *cavum, pleurae*.

pleurisy (ploor'ĭ-se) [Gr. *pleuritis*] inflammation of the pleura, with exudation into its cavity and upon its surface. It may occur as either an acute or a chronic process. In acute pleurisy the pleura becomes reddened, then covered with an exudate of lymph, fibrin, and cellular elements (the *dry* stage); the disease may progress to the second stage, in which a copious exudation of serum occurs (stage of *liquid effusion*). The inflamed surfaces of the pleura tend to become united by adhesions, which are usually permanent. The symptoms are a stitch in the side, a chill, followed by fever and a dry cough. As effusion occurs there is an onset of dyspnea and a diminution of pain. The patient lies on the affected side.

Dr. Starnes determined that she was ill with **pleurisy**, which he described as an inflammation or infection of the pleura, the membraneous sacs which surround the lungs. He said that if a person could not withstand the pain resulting from **pleurisy**, they could not breathe as deeply as at other times. The visual pleura are part of the respiratory system. It was Dr. Starnes' impression that the Demerol caused respiratory depression. Fuller v. Starnes, 597 S.W.2d 88, 91–2 (Ark.1980).

pleurisy, fibrinous pleurisy characterized by deposition of large amounts of fibrin in the pleural space.

The cow showed a **fibrinous pleuritis** on necropsy with blood in the pleural cavity. The liver showed 4 P.P.M. of lead and the bowel content was negative. Marian v. Lena Pellet Co., 256 N.E.2d 93, 96 (App.Ct.Ill.1970.)

pleuritis See *pleurisy*.

plexus (plek'sus), pl. *plexus* or *plexuses* [L. "braid"] a network or tangle; [NA] a general term for a network of lymphatic vessels, nerves, or veins.

plexus, brachial; plexus brachialis [NA], a plexus originating from the ventral branches of the last four cervical spinal nerves and most of the ventral branch of the first thoracic spinal nerves. Situated partly in the neck and partly in the axilla, it is composed successively of ventral branches and trunks (supraclavicular part) which are related to the subclavian artery and which give off the dorsal scapular, long thoracic, subclavius, and suprascapular nerves. The infraclavicular part consists of divisions which lie approximately behind the clavicle and cords and branches in the axilla in relation to the axillary artery. Its branches are medial and lateral pectoral, medial brachial cutaneous, medial antebrachial cutaneous, median, ulnar radial, subscapular, thoracodorsal, and axillary nerves. See also *nervus medianus* (Luna case).

Dr. Jarrott was convinced that the January accident caused the cervical disc rupture based on Dr. Gomila's initial findings of **brachial plexus** tenderness and radiation of pain into the right arm. Villavaso v. State Farm Mut. Auto Ins. Co., 424 So.2d 536, 540 (Ct.App.La.1982).

The doctor thought there were two possible causes for her symptoms: either she had "stretched some portions of her **brachial plexus**, that is, the nerves that come down from the spine in the region of the neck to go down the arm," or that she had been struck by an object in that area. Pisciotta v. Allstate Ins. Co., 385 So.2d 1176, 1181 (La.1979).

The appellant doctors testified that their surgical procedure was to follow the path the shrapnel had taken as it entered and lodged in Luna's shoulder. This did not require them to expose any portion of the major nerve network in the shoulder, known by the technical name, **brachial plexus.** No nerve was observed in the surgical field at any time during the operation. Severance of a nerve by the missile or by surgery would have caused immediate detectable evidence of such damage . . .

. . . This surgery disclosed that a branch of the **brachial plexus** nerve network known as the lateral cord of the median nerve had been severed and that scar tissue had formed and was pressing against the rest of the major nerve bundle. This scar tissue appeared to be the cause of the clawing. The severed nerve serves only the thumb. Its severance would cause loss of feeling and movement to that digit alone. Luna v. Nering, 426 F.2d 95, 97 (5th Cir. 1970).

Other Authorities: Lowery v. Newton, 278 S.E.2d 566, 569 (Ct.App.N.C.1981); Harrington v. Cohen, 374 N.E.2d 344–5 (App.Ct.Mass.1978); Slater v. Kehoe, 113 Cal.Rptr. 790, 793–5 (Ct.App.Cal.1974); Bardessono v. Michels, 478 P.2d 480, 483 (Cal.1970).

plexus, prevertebral autonomic nerve plexuses situated in the thorax, abdomen, and pelvis, anterior to the vertebral column; they consist of visceral afferent fibers, preganglionic parasympathetic fibers, preganglionic and postganglionic sympathetic fibers, and ganglia containing sympathetic ganglion cells, and they give rise to postganglionic fibers. The major plexuses are cardiac, pulmonary, esophageal, celiac, mesenteric, and hypogastric. All are closely related to the aorta; those in the abdomen and pelvis supply adjacent viscera by subdivisions which accompany the branches of the aorta and which are named usually after these branches, but sometimes according to the organ supplied.

. . . one thing, he had considerable enlargement of his **prevertebral plexus;** in other words, the veins about the dural sac anterior to the dural sac and posterior to the disc. Perry v. Industrial Com'n, 539 P.2d 178, 181 (Ct.App.Ariz.1975), decision vacated and award of Industrial Commission reinstated 542 P.2d 1096 (Ariz.1975).

plication (pli-ka'shun) the taking of tucks in any structure to shorten it, or in the walls of a hollow viscus; a folding.

Plication: Dr. Dahlquist explained it as a "suturing off instead of tying the vessel off completely. . . . It leaves a sieve-like quality." Carmichael v. Reitz, 95 Cal.Rptr. 381, 390 (Ct.App. Cal.1971).

plutonium (ploo-to'ne-um) [named for the planet *Pluto*] a heavy, metallic, radioactive element of atomic number 94, atomic weight 242, obtained by the addition of neutrons to uranium, thereby changing it into neptunium and then into plutonium. Symbol Pu. See also *radioactivity.*

pneumoconiosis (nu"mo-ko"ne-o'sis) [*pneumo-* + Gr. *konis* dust] a condition characterized by permanent deposition of substantial amounts of particulate matter in the lungs, usually of occupational or environmental origin, and by the tissue reaction to its presence. It may range from relatively harmless forms of anthracosis or siderosis to the destructive fibrosis of silicosis. See also *aluminosis; anthracosis; asbestosis; fibrosis, idiopathic pulmonary; siderosis; silicosis;* and *test, ventilation.*

Plaintiff's treating physician and expert, Dr. Morton Brown, is a specialist in internal medicine and pulmonary diseases. He diagnosed plaintiff as having **pneumoconiosis**, a medical classification encompassing lung diseases caused by dusts of various types. . . . Howard v. Johns-Manville Sales Corp., 420 So.2d 1190, 1192 (Ct.App.La.1982).

It is well-established medically that **pneumoconiosis** is a progressive disease which frequently defies diagnosis. (See, 1972 U.S.Code Congressional and Administrative News, pp. 2313–2320.) There is no single effective method that can be used in diagnosing its presence. Thus, it was recognized by Congress that negative chest X-rays are not always definitive proof of absence of the disease. 30 U.S.C. § 921(c)(4). Because of the progressive nature of the disease and the difficulty in making accurate diagnosis, many miners who were in fact disabled as a result of black lung disease were denied compensation. In recognition of this difficulty the circuit opinions heretofore cited have ameliorated the harsh position that total disability must be unqualifiedly shown to have existed as of June 30, 1973, by adopting the position that medical evidence obtained after that date can be used in determining eligibility dating back to June 30, 1973. Medical evidence obtained after the cut-off date is to be considered relevant in ascertaining when disability commenced. Paluso v. Mathews, 573 F.2d 4, 10 (10th Cir. 1978).

He held the opinion that the claimant was not suffering from **pneumoconiosis** because as both doctors agreed, the claimant's condition of pulmonary fibrosis improved from time to time, which does not occur with **pneumoconiosis**. Hunter v. Penn Galvanizing Co., 319 A.2d 214–15 (Commonwealth Ct. Pa.1974).

Other Authorities: Colt Industries v. Borovich, 403 A.2d 1372, 1374 (P. Commonwealth Ct.1979); Gibson v. Consolidation Coal Co., 588 S.W.2d 290, 292–3 (Tenn.1979); Hash v. Califano, 451 F.Supp. 383, 386 (S.D.Ill.1978). Ansel v. Weinberger, 529 F.2d 304, 306–7 (6th Cir. 1976); Massey v. Celebrezze, 345 F.2d 146, 150 (6th Cir. 1965).

pneumoconiosis, bauxite rapidly progressive pneumoconiosis leading to extreme pulmonary emphysema, frequently accompanied by pneumothorax, caused by inhalation of bauxite fumes containing fine particles of alumina and silica. Called also *bauxite workers' disease* and *Shaver's disease.*

There is considerable, albeit contradicted, evidence that claimant suffers from "**Shaver's Disease**," that **Shaver's Disease** is caused by the inhalation of aluminum oxide dust, and that claimant was exposed to a significant amount of aluminum oxide dust at the employer's plant. Spartan Abrasive Co., Inc. v. Workmen's Comp., 405 A.2d 594–5 (Commonwealth Ct.Pa. 1979).

pneumoconiosis of coal workers a form caused by deposition of large amounts of coal dust in the lungs, and typically characterized by centrilobular emphysema; called also *coalminer's* or *miner's lung, black phthisis,* and *miner's phthisis.* Cf. *anthracosis.*

Pneumoconiosis is a slow progressive disease which ravages the health of coal miners. The incidence of this devastating disease is markedly higher in miners who have worked more than fifteen years. See Hill v. Califano, 592 F.2d 341 (6th Cir. 1979).

... The Federal Coal Mine Health and Safety Act of 1969 ("Act"), as amended, 30 U.S.C § 901 et seq., was passed to "compensate miners, and the widows and children of miners, whose lives and health have been sacrificed in the production of that critical energy source—coal." S.Rep. No. 92–743, 92d Cong., 2d Sess. (1972), U.S.Code Cong. & Admin. News, p. 2305 quoted in Morris v. Mathews, 557 F.2d 563, 566, 570 (6th Cir. 1977) and Miniard v. Califano, 618 F.2d 405, 410 (6th Cir. 1980). . . .

... Section 921(c)(3) provides the claimant with an irrebuttable presumption of disability due to **pneumoconiosis** if the x-ray or autopsy yields one or more large opacities greater than one centimeter in diameter. The Act, however, is also sensitive to the difficulty of diagnosing **pneumoconiosis** using an x-ray or any other single medical test. . . .

First, an x-ray is merely a static portrait of an on-going dynamic process. An x-ray is a photograph of a claimant's lung field on a specific date. **Pneumoconiosis**, however, is a slow, progressive disease. Consequently, a negative diagnosis in one year is not probative of the existence of **pneumoconiosis** on subsequent dates. See Singleton v. Califano, 591 F.2d 383, 385 (6th Cir. 1979). On any given date **pneumoconiosis** may not be detectable or may not have destroyed enough of the claimants lungs to be diagnosed as category I. The disease, nevertheless, may progress and later destroy sufficient lung tissue to be characterized as category I. Therefore, the negative diagnosis in 1971 and the subsequent positive readings in 1974 are not "conflicting". The Secretary never had an occasion to resolve "conflicting" x-ray evidence in Lawson. The different diagnoses are a poignant illustration of the progressive nature of **pneumoconiosis**. Haywood v. Secretary of Health & Human Services, 699 F.2d 277, 281, 284 (6th Cir. 1983).

Coal workers' pneumoconiosis—black lung disease—affects a high percentage of American coal miners with severe, and frequently crippling, chronic respiratory impairment. The disease is caused by long-term inhalation of coal dust.[2] **Coal workers' pneumoconiosis** (hereafter **pneumoconiosis**) is generally diagnosed on the basis of X-ray opacities indicating nodular lesions on the lungs of a patient with a long history of coal dust exposure. . . . [[2] Coal workers' pneumoconiosis is a distinct clinical entity, and is not the only type of pneumoconiosis. The remarks of the Surgeon General, reproduced in H.R. Rep. No. 91–563, supra, at 15, indicate that the pathological condition of pneumoconiosis may also be caused by inhalation of other dusty materials, such as cotton fibers or silica.]

According to the Surgeon General, **pneumoconiosis** is customarily classified as "simple" or "complicated." Simple **pneumoconiosis**, ordinarily identified by X-ray opacities of a limited extent, is generally regarded by physicians as seldom productive of significant respiratory impairment. Complicated **pneumoconiosis**, generally far more serious, involves progressive massive fibrosis as a complex reaction to dust and other factors (which may include tuberculosis or other infection), and usually produces significant pulmonary impairment and marked respiratory disability. This disability limits the victim's physical capabilities, may induce death by cardiac failure, and may contribute to other causes of death. [Footnotes omitted.] Usery v. Turner Elkhorn Mining Co., 428 U.S. 1, 6–7, 96 S.Ct. 2882, 49 L.Ed.2d 752 (1976).

... and that he was at the time totally disabled due to **pneumoconiosis**[2]; or that his death was attributable to **pneumoconiosis**. 20 C.F.R. § 410.210. [[2] A chronic dust disease of the lung arising out of employment in a coal mine. 30 U.S.C. § 902(b).] Statzer v. Weinberger, 383 F.Supp. 1258, 1261 (E.D.Ky.1974).

Other Authorities: Collins v. Mathews, 547 F.2d 795–6 (4th Cir. 1976).

pneumoencephalogram (nu"mo-en-sef'ah-lo-gram)   the roentgenogram obtained by pneumoencephalography. See also *ventriculogram* (Harrison case).

At 5:30 p.m. on Friday, December 30, the decedent's father gave his consent for the next diagnostic procedure, a **pneumoencephalogram**. Because the procedure requires surgical standby and the availability of an anesthetist, an operating room and an x-ray technician, it is not normally performed on weekends or holidays, except in cases of emergency. Mendez v. State of Oregon, 669 P.2d 364–5 (Ct.App.Or.1983).

After that operation, there was eventual regression and a **pneumoencephalogram** was done, which showed a shift of ventricles from the left to the right side of the head so that there was pressure on the left part of the brain. Figliomeni v. Board of Ed. of City School District, 341 N.E.2d 557, 564 (N.Y.1975).

The beneficiary contended that as the **pneumoencephalogram** was a diagnostic test leading up to treatment and not tending to cure or relieve the physical condition the death caused thereby was not the result of medical or surgical treatment. McKay v. Bankers Life Co., 187 N.W.2d 736, 738 (Iowa 1971).

pneumoencephalography (nu"mo-en-sef"ah-log'rah-fe) radiographic visualization of the fluid-containing structures of the brain after cerebrospinal fluid is intermittently withdrawn by lumbar puncture and replaced by air, oxygen, or helium.

pneumograph (nu'mo-graf) [*pneumo-* + Gr. *graphein* to write] an instrument for registering the respiratory movements. See also *polygraph* (Romero case).

The polygraph machine is an electromechanical instrument which measures and records these physiological fluctuations that are detected with the aid of three basic components: (1) the **pneumograph** which monitors the respiration rate of the examinee. . . . U.S. v. Alexander, 526 F.2d 161, 163 (8th Cir. 1975).

pneumonectomy (nu"mo-nek'to-me) [*pneumono-* + Gr. *ektomē* excision] the excision of lung tissue, especially of an entire lung.

In August, 1974, a **pneumonectomy** was performed. Snyder's left lung and part of his chest wall were removed. However, the chest pains continued even after several other procedures were performed to try to alleviate this pain. Snyder v. U.S., 717 F.2d 1193–4 (8th Cir. 1983).

pneumonia (nu-mo'ne-ah) [Gr. *pneumōnia*] inflammation of the lungs with consolidation. See also *Pseudomonas*.

Pathologically, Dr. Custodio stated, surgery and **pneumonia** are separate entities, but, clinically speaking, they can be related in that surgery predisposes the patient to **pneumonia**. Dr. Custodio could not with any degree of certainty pinpoint when the decedent contracted **pneumonia** other than to state that she had had it a few days before her death. People v. Love, 373 N.E.2d 1312, 1315 (Ill.1978).

pneumonia, aspiration pneumonia due to the entrance of foreign matter, such as food particles, into the respiratory passages (bronchi).

Basically, **aspiration pneumonitis** occurs in individuals who have become too weak to gag. As a result, these individuals inhale their own saliva and vomit and are inflicted with bronchial disorders resulting from the inhaled substances. Carlton v. Shelton, 722 F.2d 203–4 (5th Cir. 1984).

pneumonitis (nu"mo-ni'tis) [Gr. *pneumōn* lung + *-itis*] inflammation of the lungs.

Q. When Dr. Freedman had you in Moses Cone Hospital the last time in 1965 did he say anything to you about the work at Cone Mills causing your breathing problems?
A. He said, "That cotton dust will kill you." . . .
The final diagnoses when [decedent] was discharged . . . were . . . allergic **pneumonitis** due to exposure to cotton fibers and hypertensive vascular disease. McCall v. Cone Mills Corp., 300 S.E.2d 245, 247 (Ct.App.N.C.1983).

pneumonitis, aspiration See *pneumonia, aspiration*.

pneumothorax (nu"mo-tho'raks) [*pneumo-* + Gr. *thōrax* thorax] an accumulation of air or gas in the pleural space, which may occur spontaneously or as a result of trauma or a pathological process, or be introduced deliberately. See also *block, brachial; artificial pneumothorax; diagnostic pneumothorax*; and *syringe* (Earlin case).

While using the small anesthetic needle to locate the vein, Doctor Hirschel punctured the pleural space around plaintiff's right lung. Mrs. Eichelberger immediately complained of shortness of breath at which point an x-ray confirmed that she had indeed suffered a **pneumothorax**, or puncture of the pleural space around the lung. A surgical intern who was present in the emergency room inserted a chest tube to reinflate the lung. Eichelberger v. Barnes Hosp., 655 S.W.2d 699, 703 (Mo.Ct. App.1983).

Dr. Wideman recommended a form of anesthesia known as a brachial block, to which Napier consented. During the operation, on the morning of January 6, 1970, the anesthetist's needle punctured the patient's right lung, causing a partial deflation known as a **pneumothorax**. . . .
. . . The complaint, as abstracted, alleged that Dr. Northrum negligently punctured Napier's lung in administering the brachial block, that Dr. Northrum and Dr. Wideman failed to warn Napier of recognized complications in this type of anesthesia, and that all three defendants failed to provide proper post-operative care, with the result that Napier suffered unnecessary pain and mental anguish for about 9½ hours while his lung was collapsing. Napier v. Northrum, 572 S.W.2d 153, 155 (Ark.1978).

At trial, plaintiffs sought to prove that one of decedent's ribs had been broken in the accident and had punctured his left lung; that the pressurized anesthetic used in the operation had leaked through this puncture into the chest cavity, causing a tension **pneumothorax** which led to cardiac arrest, anoxia, and finally death. . . . Vogan v. Byers, 447 F.2d 543–4 (3d Cir. 1971).

Other Authorities: Smith v. U.S., 557 F.Supp. 42, 46 (W.D.Ark. 1982); Simons v. Georgiade, 286 S.E.2d 596–9 (Ct.App.N.C. 1982); Baker v. Chastain, 389 So.2d 932–3 (Ala.1980); Earlin v. Cravetz, 399 A.2d 783, 785 (Super.Ct.Pa.1979); Barker v. Cole, 396 N.E.2d 964, 969 (Ct.App.Ind.1979); Jones v. City of New York, 395 N.Y.S.2d 10–11 (1st Dep't 1977). In re Bagge's (Dependents') Case, 338 N.E.2d 348, 351 (Sup.Jud. Ct.Mass.1975); Bray v. Yellow Freight System, Inc., 483 F.2d 500, 506 (10th Cir. 1973).

pneumothorax, artificial pneumothorax induced intentionally by artificial means, employed for the purpose of allowing the lung to collapse in the treatment of pulmonary tuberculosis. Called also *induced p.* and *therapeutic p.* Cf. *collapse therapy*, under *therapy*.

pneumothorax, diagnostic temporary artificial pneumothorax employed for the purpose of clearly demonstrating the parietal or visceral pleura on chest films in order to detect and localize tumors of the pleura.

pneumothorax, spontaneous pneumothorax without known cause.

Also, testimony by appellant's own expert (Dr. Makous) tended to eliminate all the known causes of "**spontaneous pneumothorax**" (lung collapse without any visible trauma to the body). Earlin v. Cravetz, 399 A.2d 783, 786 (Super.Ct.Pa. 1979).

He suggested the possibility of a pulmonary embolism, a myocardial infarction, or a **spontaneous pneumothorax** (collapse of a lung) as the cause of death. Fraijo v. Hartland Hospital, 160 Cal.Rptr. 246, 250 (Ct.App.1979).

pneumothorax, tension closed pneumothorax in which the tissues surrounding the opening into the pleural cavity act as valves, allowing air to enter but not to escape. The resultant positive pressure in the cavity displaces the mediastinum to the opposite side, with consequent embarrassment of respiration. Called also *pressure p.*

At trial, plaintiffs sought to prove that one of decedent's ribs had been broken in the accident and had punctured his left lung; that the pressurized anesthetic used in the operation had leaked through this puncture into the chest cavity, causing a **tension pneumothorax** which led to cardiac arrest, anoxia, and finally death. . . . Vogan v. Byers, 447 F.2d 543–4 (3d Cir. 1971).

podiatry (po-di'ah-tre) [Gr. *pous* foot + *iatreia* healing] the specialized field that deals with the study and care of the foot, including its anatomy, pathology, medical and surgical treatment, etc. Formerly called *chiropody*. See also *nitrous oxide* (Strauss case).

Podiatry is statutorily defined as "the diagnosis, medical, surgical, mechanical, manipulative and electrical treatment limited to the ailments of the human foot and leg. No podiatrist shall do any amputation or use any anesthetic other than local.'' Code Ann. § 84–601. From the statute we can discern that, insofar as the human foot and leg are concerned, a podiatrist is capable of rendering the same treatment an orthopedist may give, short of amputation. Sandford v. Howard, 288 S.E.2d 739, 740 (Ct.App.Ga.1982).

The Delaware Code defines the practice of **podiatry** as follows:

''. . . the diagnosis and the medical, surgical, mechanical, manipulative and electrical treatment of all ailments of the human foot and leg, excepting amputation of the foot or leg or the administration of an anesthetic other than local.'' 24 Del.C. § 501(a). Strauss v. Silverman, 399 A.2d 192, 193 (Del.1979).

Section 7001 of the Education Law defines the practice of **podiatry** as follows:

''The practice of the profession of podiatry is defined as diagnosing, treating, operating and prescribing for any disease, injury, deformity or other condition of the foot or operating on the bones, muscles or tendons of the feet for the correction of minor deficiencies and deformities of a mechanical and functional nature. The practice of **podiatry** includes treating simple and uncomplicated fractures of the bones of the foot; administering only local anesthetics for therapeutic purposes as well as for anesthesia; treating under general anesthesia administered by authorized persons; using nonnarcotic post-operative sedatives; but not treating any other part of the human body nor treating fractures of the malleoli or cutting operations upon the malleoli. A podiatrist licensed to practice **podiatry**, only after certification by the education department of the state of New York, in accordance with qualifications established by the commissioner, shall have the right to administer or prescribe narcotics.'' McGinness v. Rosen, 415 N.Y.S.2d 744, 745 (Supr.Ct. Queens Cty.1979).

Other Authorities: Whitehurst v. Boehm, 255 S.E.2d 761, 765 (Ct.App.N.Car.1979); Alexander v. Mt. Carmel Medical Center, 383 N.E.2d 564, 567 (Ohio 1978); Godfrey v. Massachusetts Medical Service, 270 N.E.2d 804, 808–9 (Sup.Jud. Ct.Mass.1971).

podophyllin See *resin, podophyllun.*

poikilothermy (poi″kĭ-lo-ther′me) [*poikilo-* + Gr. *thermĕ* heat] the exhibition of body temperature which varies with the environmental temperature.

Dr. Levy testified further that the stump skin is different from other skin because it is ''poikilthermic'' (it picks up the environmental temperature). Daw Industries, Inc. v. U.S., 561 F.Supp. 433, 436 (U.S.Ct.Int.Trade 1983), reversed 714 F.2d 1140 (Fed.Cir.1983).

point (point) [L. *punctum*] a small area or spot; the sharp end of an object.

point, Addison's the midpoint of the epigastric region.

He conducted **Adson [sic] maneuvers**, which consist of raising the arms, turning the head from one side to the other, putting the shoulder in different positions, and simultaneously feeling the pulse to test the blood supply to the arm. . . .

. . . The records from Research Hospital indicated that plaintiff had a negative **Adson [sic] sign** on March 18, 1973, which

defendant conceded was not consistent with severe thoracic outlet syndrome. Cress v. Mayer, 626 S.W.2d 430, 432–3 (Mo.Ct.App.1981).

poison (poi′zn) [L. *potio* draft; *toxicum;* Gr. *toxikon*] any substance which, when ingested, inhaled or absorbed, or when applied to, injected into, or developed within the body, in relatively small amounts, by its chemical action may cause damage to structure or disturbance of function. See also *poisoning;* and *toxin.*

The court further approved use of the following dictionary definitions of ''**poison:**'' (1) any substance which, when introduced into the animal organization, is capable of producing morbid, noxious, or deadly effect upon it; and (2) any substance which, introduced in small quantities in the animal economy, seriously disturbs or destroys the vital functions. It was further noted that there are ''many different modes in which **poisons** operate,'' and that included under the heading of ''**poisons**'' are ''obviously . . . a vast number of bodies belonging to the mineral, vegetable, and animal kingdoms, some solid, others fluid, and others gaseous, and deleterious vapors and miasmata imperceptible to the senses.'' 36 Kan. at 20–21, 12 P. at 328–29. A similar approach to the definition of ''**poisoning**'' in a workmen's compensation context was expressly condoned by the Kansas Supreme Court in Weimer v. Sauder Tank Company, 184 Kan. 422, 337 P.2d 672 (1959). Accordingly, the jury in this case should have been informed of the substance of the relevant occupational disease statutes and instructed to determine whether any part of the plaintiff's disability was attributable to ''**poisoning**'' for which K.S.A. § 44–5a01 provided the exclusive remedy. Murphy v. Owens-Corning Fiberglas Corp., 447 F.Supp. 557, 571 (D.Kan.1977).

poison, economic

The Act defines an ''**economic poison**'' as follows, 7 U.S.C.A. § 135(a):

(1) any substance or mixture of substances intended for preventing, destroying, repelling, or mitigating any insects, rodents, nematodes, fungi, weeds, and other forms of plant or animal life or viruses, except viruses on or in living man or other animals, which the Secretary shall declare to be a pest, and (2) any substance or mixture of substances intended for use as a plant regulator, defoliant, or dessicant. First Nat. Bk. in Albuquerque v. U.S., 552 F.2d 370, 372 (10th Cir. 1977).

poison, gonyaulax the neurotoxic principle produced by members of the genus *Gonyaulax* and related dinoflagellates; ingestion of shellfish that feed on these organisms causes a severe neurologic reaction which may end in paralysis and death. Called also *clam p., mussel p., paralytic shellfish p., mytilotoxin,* and *saxitoxin.*

poisoning (poi′zuh-ning) the morbid condition produced by a poison. See also *intoxication.*

When toxicologists speak of **poisoning** they are not referring to the layman's concept of the victim turning blue, twitching convulsively, etc. Rather a person is ''**poisoned**'' if any of his body functions has been impaired through introduction of a foreign substance into his system. This definition says nothing about the degree of impairment. Thus episodes of ''acute organophosphate **poisoning**'' cover a considerable gamut, from cases in which symptoms are no more distressing than those of a common cold to those in which a patient is veritably snatched from the jaws of death by heroic therapeutic measures and to death despite such measures. Florida Peach Growers, Ass'n v. United States Dep't of Labor, 489 F.2d 120, 132 (5th Cir. 1974).

poisoning, arsenic poisoning due to systemic exposure to inorganic pentavalent arsenic. *Acute arsenic poisoning*, which may result in shock and death, is marked by erythematous skin eruptions, vomiting, diarrhea, abdominal pain, muscular cramps, and swelling of the eyelids, feet, and hands. *Chronic arsenic poisoning*, due to the ingestion of small amounts over a long period of time, is marked by pigmentation of the skin accompanied by scaling, hyperkeratosis of the palms and soles, transverse white lines on the fingernails (Mees' lines), headache, peripheral neuropathy, and confusion. Called also *arsenicalism* and *arsenism*.

Initial symptoms of **arsenic poisoning** include listlessness, scouring, lack of appetite and weight loss....

... Dr. Every testified that **arsenic poisoning** will usually result in death within two weeks; if the poisoned cow survives that period of time, it will usually recover. Gaar v. State Through Dep't of Highways, 389 So.2d 426–7 (Ct.App.La. 1980).

poisoning, food, clostridial food poisoning caused by *Clostridium botulinum*. See also *allantiasis*; and *botulism*. 2. food poisoning caused by *Clostridium perfringens;* meat, particularly poultry, is usually the vehicle of infection.

poisoning, lead poisoning due to the absorption or ingestion of lead or one of its salts. The symptoms include loss of appetite, weight loss, colic, constipation, insomnia, headache, dizziness, irritability, moderate hypertension, albuminuria, anemia, a blue line at the edge of the gums (lead line), encephalopathy (especially in children), and peripheral neuropathy leading to paralysis. Called also *plumbism*.

EPA concluded that these studies of low-level health effects, while not fully conclusive, were "suggestive of a potentially lower maximum safe level of blood lead [than 30 ug/dl]." 47 Fed.Reg. at 38,077/1. Even a moderate cut in the "safe" blood lead level from 30 ug/dl to 25 ug/dl would almost double the number of children with excessive blood lead levels, and a major cut to, say, 10 ug/dl would put half of the children in the U.S. at risk of lead poisoning.[59] ... [[59] See Memorandum by Dr. James Pirkle, supra note 53, at 2, J.A. at 306 (in NHANES II study, 2.1% of children tested during 1978–1980 had blood lead levels of 30 ug/dl or higher; 3.7% had blood lead levels of 25 ug/dl or higher). Ten ug/dl was the mean blood lead level for all persons in 1980, according to NHANES II data. See Figure 1 supra. Mean blood lead levels for small children were somewhat higher. Annest, Mahaffey, Cox & Roberts, Blood Lead Levels for Persons 6 Months-74 Years of Age: United States, 1976–80, in National Center for Health Statistics, Advance Data from Vital and Health Statistics 4–5 (No. 79, May 12, 1982).]

In sum, the demonstrated connection between gasoline lead and blood lead, the demonstrated health effects of blood lead levels of 30 ug/dl or above, and the significant risk of adverse health effects from blood lead levels as low as 10–15 ug/dl, would justify EPA in banning lead from gasoline entirely. Necessarily, then, there are health benefits from any intermediate reduction. Small Ref. Lead Phase-Down Task Force v. U.S.E.P.A., 705 F.2d 506, 529–31 (D.C.Cir.1983).

[The acronym NHANES II stands for Second National Health and Nutrition Examination Survey of the Center for Disease Control-Ed.]

The relative abundance of lead in the earth's crust makes it unique among the toxic heavy metals. EPA's "Air Quality Criteria For Lead" (hereinafter cited as CD) 1–1, Joint Appendix (JA) 1105....

... Lead is a poison which has no known beneficial function in the body, id. 1–12, JA 1116, but when present in the body in sufficient concentrations lead attacks the blood, kidneys, and central nervous and other systems and can cause anemia, kidney damage, severe brain damage, and death. Id. 1–6–1–9, JA 1110–1113.[2]... [[2] See generally EPA's "Air Quality Criteria For Lead" (hereinafter cited as CD), Chapter 11, Joint Appendix 1223–1276.]

... Among the most deleterious effects of **lead poisoning** are those associated with severe central nervous system damage at high exposure levels. The Criteria Document noted that neurological and behavioral deficits have long been known to be among the more serious effects of lead exposure, but it pointed out that there is disagreement about whether these effects are reversible, and about what exposure levels are necessary to produce specific deleterious effects. CD 11–14, JA 1236....

Lead also affects the renal, reproductive, endocrine, hepatic, cardiovascular, immunologic, and gastrointestinal systems. CD Chapter 11, JA 1223–1276. Lead Industries Ass'n v. Environmental Protection, 647 F.2d 1130, 1135–6, 1139–40 (D.C.Cir.1980).

There was medical testimony for the city as follows: that **lead poisoning** is a serious health hazard, and it is "epidemic" in St. Louis; that it is particularly dangerous to children who crawl about, explore, and eat paint chips, or chew on painted windowsills or rails; that the principal danger is from ingesting the material, and this occurs in the older housing units; that very serious and permanent results are frequent in children, including retardation and other brain damage; that even one per cent of lead in paint is not safe.... City of St. Louis v. Brune, 520 S.W.2d 12, 14 (Mo.1975).

Other Authorities: City-Wide Coalition, etc. v. Philadelphia Hous. Auth., 356 F.Supp. 123, 125–6 (E.D.Pa.1973). Marian v. Lena Pellet Co., 256 N.E.2d 93, 96 (App.Ct.Ill.1970); Steiner v. Mitchell, 350 U.S. 247, 249–50, 76 S.Ct. 330, 100 L.Ed. 267 (1956).

poisoning, mercury acute or chronic disease caused by mercury and its salts. The *acute* form, due to ingestion, is marked by severe abdominalgia, metallic taste in the mouth, vomiting, bloody diarrhea with watery stools, oliguria or anuria (usually at onset), and corrosion and ulceration of the entire digestive tract. The *chronic* form, due to absorption by the skin and mucous membranes, inhalation of vapors, or ingestion of mercury salts, is marked by stomatitis, metallic taste in the mouth, a blue line along the border of the gum, sore hypertrophied gums that bleed easily, loosening of the teeth, erethism, excessive secretion of saliva, tremors, and incoordination. Called also *mercurialism* and *hydrargyrism*.

Alkyl mercury is a highly toxic substance. Once ingested, it moves rapidly through the body and is absorbed, rather than passed off, by the body. As the hog ate the treated grain every day, the mercury level in its body increased and remained there at the time when the hog was slaughtered. When the Hucklebys began eating the meat from the hog, the level of alkyl mercury in their bodies gradually increased also. However, because **alkyl mercury** poisoning normally affects only the young, the adult Hucklebys, Ernest and Lois, escaped injury. . . .

Alkyl mercury poisoning does irreversible damage to the central nervous system. It affects sight, speech, locomotion and the ability to grasp objects or otherwise use one's hands properly. First Nat. Bk. in Albuquerque v. U.S., 552 F.2d 370–1 (10th Cir. 1977).

"In view of the insidious nature of **alkyl mercury poisoning** and the irreversible injury to the central nervous system, we firmly believe that this class of compounds should be discontinued for seed treatment. . . .

. . . He averred that alkyl mercury can produce permanent damage to the central nervous system, and that there are no known effective antidotes for chronic poisoning by that substance. . . .

. . . He stated that alkyl mercury compounds have a propensity to accumulate in the central nervous tissues, particularly in the brain. Nor-Am Agricultural Products, Inc. v. Hardin, 435 F.2d 1151, 1153–4 (7th Cir. 1970).

poisoning, organophosphate

A severe case of **organophosphate poisoning** may result in tremors, paroxysmal tachycardia (abrupt attacks of excessively rapid heart action), respiratory difficulty, convulsions, pinpoint pupils, pulmonary edema (effusion of serous fluid into the lungs), collapse, and coma.

The toxicity of the organophosphates results from inhibition of the enzyme cholinesterase, which plays an important role in the appropriate cessation of nerve impulse transmission. In this they are similar to agents of chemical warfare ("nerve gas"). Absorption can occur through the eyes, the unbroken skin, and the respiratory and intestinal tracts. Florida Peach Growers, Ass'n v. United States Dep't of Labor, 489 F.2d 120, 131 (5th Cir. 1974).

Organo-phosphate poisoning is characterized by a rapid onset of symptoms, short duration of illness, and either complete recovery or death. The victim also has pinpoint pupils, slow heartbeat, insomnia, nervousness, tearing, muscle twitching, diarrhea, excessive salivation, and lung congestion. Skogen v. Dow Chemical Co., 375 F.2d 692, 698 (8th Cir. 1967).

poisoning, phenol poisoning due to ingestion or absorption through the skin of phenol; the symptoms include colic, weakness, collapse, and local irritation and corrosion. Called also *carbolism.*

The finding, after an autopsy had been had, was that the immediate cause of death was **phenol (carbolic acid) poisoning** and edema of the glottis due to "application of phenol-containing mixture to the face and neck." Other findings were that 5.1 milligrams of phenol per 100 grams were found in the liver and 2.9 milligrams of phenol per 100 grams were found in the

blood of the victim. It was the opinion of Dr. Newbarr, prosecution witness and Chief Autopsy Surgeon for the Los Angeles coroner's office, that these findings were the result of the application of a solution containing more than 10% phenol to the face and neck of the victim. It was the opinion of Mr. Abernathy, the toxicologist, that the reddish-brown discoloration of the victim's face was a third degree burn caused by phenol, and that the normal finding of phenol in a normal human being would be practically zero. People v. Penny, 285 P.2d 926, 928 (Cal.1955).

poisoning, toluene

On the other hand, in support of their theory that their illness was caused by their constant exposure at work to EC 2125, plaintiffs introduced evidence . . . that **toluene**, as a dissolvant of fat, damaged the nerves in plaintiffs' extremities by dissolving the myelin sheaths surrounding them; that plaintiffs experienced at least two of the many symptoms of **toluene poisoning** found by Dr. Sokol in his research on the effects of **toluene poisoning** on human beings, namely, numbness and marked tremors of the extremities. . . .

One of plaintiffs' witnesses in their case in chief was the previously mentioned Dr. Jacob Sokol, an internist in private practice, who had been chief physician at the Central Juvenile Hall in Los Angeles for close to five years. There he examined over a thousand youngsters for the immediate physical and psychological effects of glue sniffing, i.e., **toluene poisoning**. Prior to Dr. Sokol's research from January 1962 to 1966 very little was known of the effects upon human beings of **toluene poisoning**. Among the 18 symptoms of **toluene poisoning** which Dr. Sokol found in one child or another were tremors and numbness of the extremities. Ruiz v. Minnesota Mining & Mfg. Co., 93 Cal. Rptr. 270, 273 (Ct.App.Cal.1971).

poisonous (poi'son-us) pertaining to, due to, or of the nature of a poison; toxic; venomous.

The Supreme Court, in an opinion rendered in 1914, quoted one of the Congressional sponsors of the original Food and Drugs Act of 1906, a predecessor of the Act involved here, as follows:

As to the use of the term "**poisonous**," let me state that everything which contains poison is not poison. It depends on the quantity and the combination. A very large majority of the things consumed by the human family contain, under analysis, some kind of poison, but it depends upon the combination, the chemical relation which it bears to the body in which it exists as to whether or not it is dangerous to take into the human system. United States v. Lexington Mill Co., 232 U.S. 399, 412, 34 S.Ct. 337, 341, 58 L.Ed. 658 (1914). Millet, Pit & Seed Co., Inc. v. U.S., 436 F.Supp. 84, 88 (E.D. Tenn.1977), vacated and remanded 627 F.2d 1093 (6th Cir. 1980).

polio See *poliomyelitis.*

poliomyelitis (po″le-o-mi″ĕ-li′tis) [*polio-* + Gr. *myelos* marrow + *-itis*] an acute viral disease, occurring sporadically and in epidemics, and characterized clinically by fever, sore throat, headache, and vomiting, often with stiffness of the neck and back. In the *minor illness* these may be the only symptoms. The *major illness*, which may or may not be preceded by the minor illness, is characterized by involvement of the central nervous system, stiff neck, pleocytosis in the spinal fluid, and perhaps paralysis. There may be subsequent atrophy of groups of muscles, ending in contraction and permanent deformity. The major illness is called *acute anterior p., infantile paralysis*, and *Heine-Medin disease*. The disease is now largely controlled by vaccines. See also *epidemic* (Reyes case); and *poliovirus*.

Polio is, of course, an anterior horn cell disease. The Lovelace EMG finding of a disease process at the anterior horn cell level is consistent with the findings one would expect in the EMG of a muscle affected many years before with clinical or subclinical old polio. Accordingly, the electromyographic findings which have been interpreted as indicative of anterior horn cell disease may indeed arise from the polio involvement that plaintiffs' experts chose to ignore. Stich v. U.S., 565 F.Supp. 1096, 1112 (D.N.J.1983).

The average incubation period for poliomyelitis is one to two weeks but symptoms may develop between three and thirty-five days after exposure. Sheffield v. Eli Lilly and Co., 192 Cal. Rptr. 870, 874 (Ct.App.Cal.1983).

APPENDIX B: POLIOMYELITIS

It was not until about 1950 that scientists and physicians really began to understand how poliomyelitis attacks its victims. They learned that polio is caused by an enterovirus which grows in the intestinal tract, but that the virus is introduced into the body orally, through the mouth. After entering the body, the virus reproduces rapidly in the alimentary tract, and when it reaches the lower intestinal tract its growth causes what could be termed an "infection". This does not mean that the individual "infected" has contracted polio; upwards of 80 percent of the population is naturally immune to polio virus, and only about one of every hundred persons who experience the intestinal viral infection will later manifest clinical symptoms of polio. When disease does result, medical scientists believe, the virus moves, perhaps through the bloodstream, from the intestinal tract or alimentary tract to the spinal column, where it attacks the anterior horn cells, the "grey matter" within the spinal column. Destruction of sufficient "grey matter" will result in "motor neuron disease", that is, muscular paralysis. Reyes v. Wyeth Laboratories, 498 F.2d 1264, 1295–6 (5th Cir. 1974).

Other Authorities: Stahlheber v. American Cyanamid Co., 451 S.W.2d 48, 50 (Mo.1970).

poliomyelitis, bulbar a serious form of poliomyelitis in which the medulla oblongata is affected, and in which there may be dysfunction of the swallowing mechanism, and respiratory and circulatory distress.

Her case was diagnosed as that of bulbar poliomyelitis. She remained at this hospital for approximately five weeks. She was placed in an iron lung. She was then taken to Rancho Los Amigos and was there for approximately one and one-half years. After staying there for approximately one year, she was able to go home on weekend passes.

At the time of trial in March, 1957, almost three years from the time of her infection, her whole body from the neck to her knees and legs, was enclosed in a cast. Each leg was in a separate cast. The child could not bend at the waist. She has had three surgical operations and there are three contemplated surgical procedures. With reference to her future the testimony was that the possibility of return of muscle function is

slight after two and one-half years. "The main thing is to give the child a stable trunk". Wardrop v. City of Manhattan Beach, 326 P.2d 15, 21 (Dist.Ct.App.Cal.1958).

poliomyelitis, spinal paralytic the classic form of acute anterior poliomyelitis, in which the appearance of flaccid paralysis, usually of one or more limbs, makes the diagnosis quite definite.

poliomyelitis virus See *poliovirus*.

poliovirus (po"le-o-vi'rus) the etiologic agent of poliomyelitis, separable, on the basis of specificity of neutralizing antibody, into three serotypes, designated types 1, 2, and 3. Over the years, type 1 has been responsible for about 85 per cent of all paralytic poliomyelitis and for most epidemics, and type 3 for about 10 per cent of paralytic poliomyelitis and for occasional epidemics. Type 2 has been responsible for about 5 per cent of paralytic poliomyelitis. Epidemics caused by poliovirus are now largely controlled by vaccines. See also *attenuation* (Reyes case); and *period, incubation* (Wardrop case).

The first breakthrough resulted from the research of Dr. Jonas Salk, who perfected a "killed virus" vaccine to be administered by innoculation. To produce this vaccine, polio virus is grown in a tissue culture and clinically "killed", that is, rendered incapable of causing disease. In killing the virus, however, no chemical alteration occurs and when it is introduced into the body in the vaccine, the virus acts as an antigen to prompt the production of antibodies....

For a further discussion of the development of polio vaccine, and the elaborate testing procedures, see, e.g. Davis v. Wyeth Laboratories, Inc., 9 Cir. 1969, 399 F.2d 121; Griffin v. United States, E.D.Pa.1972, 351 F.Supp. 10; Stahlheber v. American Cyanamid Co., Mo.Sup.Ct.1970, 451 S.W.2d 48. Reyes v. Wyeth Laboratories, 498 F.2d 1264, 1296, 1298 (5th Cir. 1974).

Around 1950, however, a number of discoveries paved the way toward the development of an effective vaccine, among them the fact that polio virus was an enterovirus, which grew first in the intestinal tract and spread afterward to the Central Nervous System through the blood, and the further fact that there were not a huge number of types of polio virus, as in the case of the common cold for instance, but rather only three types which were immunogenically homogeneous. Griffin v. U.S., 351 F.Supp. 10, 23 (E.D.Pa.1972).

The germ connected with poliomyelitis is called the virus of poliomyelitis. It affects human beings only. The virus grows only in the human body. It grows all along the digestive tract, from the mouth all the way to the bowel. The two major areas where it proliferates in large amounts are in the tonsils and in the walls of the small bowel. The virus usually enters through the mouth and proliferates in the mouth and tonsils and persists there in fairly large quantities for a few days. The virus is usually found in the mouth and tonsils for only two or three days and then the virus goes rapidly down to the stomach and to the bowel and proliferates in the small bowel and it will persist or exist there for several days, in most individuals for a week or 10 days but sometimes longer, and even occasionally for several weeks and months....

The experiments of some scientists have shown that the virus exists for weeks, at least, in cesspools, can be found in sewage, and will persist in storage sewage water. Dr. Rosenthal testified that the virus can live for as long as seven months. Wardrop v. City of Manhattan Beach, 326 P.2d 15, 20 (Dist. Ct.App.Cal.1958).

pollicization (pol"is-i-za'shun) [L. *pollex* thumb] the replacement or rehabilitation of a thumb, especially surgical construction of a thumb from a portion of the index finger.

To correct this [loss of a thumb] a hand specialist recommended an operation known as **pollicization**. This surgical procedure involves removing the index or middle finger on the injured hand and fusing it onto the thumb metacarpal to act as a thumb. It is an established medical practice among orthopedic surgeons. Swoffer v. Marmac Industries, Inc., 204 N.W.2d 344–5 (Ct.App.Mich.1972).

pollutant

The legislative history of the FWPCA speaks with force to the question whether source, byproduct, and special nuclear materials are "pollutants" subject to the Act's permit program. The House Committee Report was quite explicit on the subject:

The term "pollutant" as defined in the bill includes "radioactive materials." These materials are those not encompassed in the definition of source, byproduct, or special nuclear materials as defined by the Atomic Energy Act of 1954, as amended, and regulated pursuant to that Act. "Radioactive Materials" encompassed by this bill are those beyond the jurisdiction of the Atomic Energy Commission. Examples of radioactive material not covered by the Atomic Energy Act, and, therefore, included within the term "pollutant," are radium and accelerator produced isotopes. H.R. Rep. No. 92–911, p. 131 (1972), 1 Leg.Hist. 818....[10] [[10] Citations to "Leg. Hist." refer to a two-volume Committee print for the Senate Committee on Public Works, A Legislative History of the Water Pollution Control Act Amendments of 1972, 93d Cong., 1st Sess. (1973).] Train v. Colorado Pub. Int. Research Group, 426 U.S. 1, 11, 96 S.Ct. 1938, 48 L.Ed.2d 434 (1976).

The Federal Water Pollution Control Act [33 U.S.C. § 1362(6)] defines **pollutants**, and, included in a list of specified **pollutants** are "radioactive materials." The Environmental Protection Agency has in effect defined the "radioactive materials" included under its control in 38 Fed.Reg. 13530, published May 22, 1973:

... the term radioactive materials as included within the definition of **pollutant** in section 502 of the Act covers only radioactive materials which are not encompassed in the definition of source, byproduct or special nuclear materials as defined by the Atomic Energy Act of 1954. Colorado Public Interest Research Group, Inc. v. Train, 373 F.Supp. 991, 993 (D.Col.1974).

pollution (pŏ-lu'shun) [L. *pollutio*] the act of defiling or making impure.

polycystic (pol"e-sis'tik) [*poly-* + Gr. *kystis* cyst] containing or made up of many cysts. See also *disease, polycystic, of kidneys.*

polycythemia (pol"e-si-the'me-ah) [*poly-* + Gr. *kytos* cell + *haima* blood + *-ia*] an increase in the total red cell

mass of the blood. See also *absolute polycythemia*; and *relative polycythemia.*

Young, a toolmaker by trade, attributed his malaise to the odor of paint which permeated his work area in a Cranston machine shop. Doctor Grzebien made a series of clinical tests, which included an analysis of Young's hemoglobin.

In speaking to the jury in layman's terms, Dr. Grzebien defined **polycythemia** as an overproduction of red cells. Thanks to Dr. Grzebien and a number of physicians who followed him as witnesses at the trial, the jury soon became aware that **polycythemia** is a disease that causes an abnormal elevation in the number of red blood cells, thereby increasing the blood's viscosity and correspondingly multiplying the risk of blood clots. There are two types of **polycythemia**: primary and secondary. The cause of **primary polycythemia** is unknown, whereas **secondary polycythemia** can be attributed to such factors as heart disease, emphysema, or a prolonged residence at high altitudes....

... Young at that time had a tumor on his upper right gum. Laboratory tests performed at St. Joseph's Hospital confirmed the presence of **polycythemia**. Young v. Park, 417 A.2d 889, 891 (R.I.1980).

... **polycythemia** (an abnormal increase in red blood cells)....

... Dr. Chretien testified that he prescribed withdrawal of Boyle's blood as treatment for **polycythemia**, from which Boyle was aware that he was suffering. James H. Boyle & Son, Inc. v. Prudential Ins. Co., 268 N.E.2d 651–2 (Sup.Jud.Ct. Mass.1971).

polycythemia, absolute an increase in red cell mass caused by a sustained overactivity of the erythroid component of the bone marrow, which may occur as a compensatory physiologic response to tissue hypoxia (see *secondary p.*), or as the principal manifestation of polycythemia vera. Cf. *relative p.*

polycythemia, myelopathic; polycythemia, primary See *polycythemia vera.*

polycythemia, relative a decrease in plasma volume without change in red blood cell mass so that the erythrocytes become more concentrated (elevated hematocrit); it may occur as an acute transient condition due to marked loss of body fluid or lowered fluid intake or a combination of both, or it may be a chronic condition associated with a low normal plasma volume and a high normal red cell mass or with other factors. Cf. *absolute p.* See also *polycythemia, stress.*

polycythemia, secondary any absolute increase in the total red cell mass other than polycythemia vera, occurring as a physiologic response to tissue hypoxia. It may be compensatory and *appropriate*, adjusting for general tissue hypoxia, such as that occurring in association with pulmonary disease, alveolar hypoventilation, cardiovascular disease, and prolonged exposure to high altitude or occurring as a result of defective hemoglobin or drugs. Or it may be *inappropriate*, reflecting excessive erythropoietin production due to renal or extrarenal disorders. Called also *erythrocytosis.*

polycythemia, stress chronic relative polycythemia (q.v.) usually affecting white, middle-aged, mildly obese males who are active, anxiety-prone, and hypertensive, occurring without the characteristic symptoms associated with polycythemia vera, i.e., without leukocytosis, splenomegaly, and thrombocytosis. Called also *benign p., Gaisböck's disease* or *syndrome*, and *stress erythrocytosis.* See also *erythrocytosis, stress.*

While it was absolutely clear that Chuy did not have this serious disease, there was some question in the minds of the Eagles consultant Dr. Harrell whether he may have suffered from **stress polycythemia** which is a form of related polycythemia observed in active, anxiety-prone individuals, in whom there is a moderate increase in the red cell mass. See N. T. Perry 30–31; N.T. 5th & 6th Day 341. Chuy v. Philadelphia Eagles Football Club, 431 F.Supp. 254, 257 (E.D.Pa.1977).

polycythemia vera a myeloproliferative disorder of unknown etiology, characterized by abnormal proliferation of all hematopoietic bone marrow elements and an absolute increase in red cell mass and total blood volume, associated frequently with splenomegaly, leukocytosis, and thrombocythemia. Hematopoiesis is also reactive in extramedullary sites (liver and spleen). In time, myelofibrosis occurs. Called also *erythremia, erythrocythemia, p. ruba, splenomegalic p., myelopathic p., erythrocytosis megalosplenica, Osler's disease, Vaquez's disease,* and *Vasquez-Osler disease.* Cf. *secondary p.*

The terms "polycythemia vera" and "polycythemia primary" are synonymous. Young v. Park, 417 A.2d 889, 891 (R.I.1980).

What resulted was a story in the Bulletin and, via the wire services in newspapers all over America, reporting that Dr. Nixon had stated that Chuy was suffering from a rare blood disease known as **polycythemia vera** which would prevent him from playing professional football again.[2] Chuy read the article and became panic stricken. [2 According to the trial testimony **polycythemia vera** is a disease characterized by a striking increase in red cell mass and total blood volume. Although the disease is ultimately terminal life may be prolonged for many years with treatment.] Chuy v. Philadelphia Eagles Football Club, 431 F.Supp. 254, 257 (E.D.Pa.1977).

Polycythemia vera is defined in the record as "A disease marked by a persistent increase of the red blood corpuscles due to excessive formation of erythroblasts by the bone marrow. It is accompanied by increased thickness of the blood, and enlargement of the spleen. The disease extends over many years and gradually causes death by complications." Gozan v. Mutual Life Ins. Co. of New York, 358 N.E.2d 499, 500 (N.Y.1976).

polydrug

"Polydrug" is a new word that has sprung up to describe a troublesome new problem: two or more drugs used simultaneously. The two drugs most frequently used are alcohol and marihuana. One national survey reported that more than 80 percent of young people in treatment were involved in multiple drug use. Hearings before the Sen.Comm. on Labor and Human Resources on Health Promotion and Disease Prevention Amend. on S. 771, 98th Cong., 1st Sess. 1, 302 (1983).

polygraph (pol'ĕ-graf) [*poly-* + Gr. *graphein* to write] an instrument for simultaneously recording various physiological responses as represented by mechanical or electrical impulses, such as respiratory movements, pulse wave, blood pressure, and the psychogalvanic reflex. Such phenomena reflect emotional reactions which are of use in detecting deception. Popularly known as *lie detector.* See also *spectrography.*

Polygraph test results are no more than a set of lines and squiggles on the **polygraph** read-out which record the physiological reactions of the subject when answering questions put to him by the examiner. Unlike a vocabulary test or mathematics examination, the results of which a lay person might be able to evaluate independently, the **polygraph** read-out is meaningless to the general public. Only through a polygrapher's interpretation can the results be in any real way available to a jury. State v. Finn, 417 A.2d 554–5 (Super.Ct.N.J.1980).

The **polygraph** technique is based on the premise that an individual's conscious attempt to deceive engenders various involuntary physiological changes due to an acute reaction in the sympathetic parts of the autonomic nervous system. The **polygraph** machine is an electromechanical instrument which measures and records these physiological fluctuations that are detected with the aid of three basic components: (1) the pneumograph which monitors the respiration rate of the examinee; (2) the cardiosphygmograph which gauges blood pressure and pulse rate; and (3) the galvanometer which measures the galvanic skin reflex or electrodermal response—skin resistance to electrical current (perspiration on the palmar surfaces of the hands will increase the flow of electrical current). Some of the more recent **polygraph** machines have incorporated a device that detects unobservable muscular activity believed to accompany intentional attempts to control the other responses that are recorded by the **polygraph**....

... All of the physiological responses detected by these components are transmitted by a recording pen onto a constantly moving piece of graph paper, a polygram....

... It is clear, therefore that the **polygraph** does not detect lies, but merely records physiological phenomena which are assumed to be related to conscious deception....

In applying the scientific acceptability standard to polygraph tests, all United States courts of appeals addressing the issue have excluded the results of unstipulated **polygraph** tests. These courts reason that the **polygraph** does not command scientific acceptability and that it is not generally believed to be sufficiently reliable in ascertaining truth and deception to justify its utilization in the trial process. Consequently, they have held that the results of an unstipulated **polygraph** examination are either per se inadmissible or that the trial court did not abuse its discretion in refusing admission of the test results. Most of these cases manifest rather laconic discussions of why **polygraph** results should be inadmissible and their stated authority for exclusion is generally Frye v. United States, [293 F. 1013 (Ct.App.D.C.1923)] and its progeny. Frye held that the Marston "systolic blood pressure deception" test lacked scientific acceptability and thus its results were inadmissible. However, the **polygraph** used in Frye measured only variations in the examinee's blood pressure and was a relatively unsophisticated precursor to the modern **polygraph** machine which measures many other physiological responses. The key issue on this appeal is whether the modern **polygraph** machine and technique have attained sufficient scientific acceptance among experts in polygraphy, psychiatry, physiology, psychophysiology, neurophysiology ... to justify the admission of the results of an unstipulated polygraph examination in evidence....

Further complicating the problem of reliability that can be affected by extraneous stimuli not connected with guilt is the apparent fact that the **polygraph** will not operate reliably on a class of persons who for one reason or another is emotionally unresponsive. According to Highleyman:

An examiner cannot detect deception if the subject is unresponsive in character or nature, or if the subject has no fear of detection because of a fatalistic attitude, rationalization of his behavior, "circumscribed amnesia," or a condition of shock or exhaustion. In addition, the **polygraph** cannot be used successfully on pathological liars, children, the mentally dull, or other subjects who are unable to distinguish between truth and falsehood. (Footnotes omitted.)

Highleyman, The Deceptive Certainty of the "Lie Detector", 10 Hastings L.J. 47, 58–59 (1958)....

After careful review of the numerous materials presently available discussing polygraphy, we conclude that the results of unstipulated **polygraph** examinations should not be admissible in evidence at a criminal trial. While the polygraphic science and its instruments have advanced significantly since the Frye case, we are still unable to conclude that there is sufficient scientific acceptability and reliability to warrant the admission of the results of such tests in evidence. [Footnotes omitted.] U.S. v. Alexander, 526 F.2d 161, 163–4, 166 (8th Cir. 1975).

No reported Texas decision has described the machine and it is perhaps well to do so here.

The **polygraph** machine ordinarily consists of a cardiograph which registers pulse rate, a sphygmograph which measures blood pressure, a pneumograph which measures respiration, and usually a galvanometer which measure electrodermal responses. The theory for using the **polygraph** to detect lies is that the act of lying causes conscious conflict in the mind of the examinee, which produces an emotion of fear or anxiety, manifested by fluctuations in pulse rate, blood pressure, breathing, and perspiration. Pulakis v. State, 476 P.2d 474, 477–478 (Alaska Sup.1970). Romero v. State, 493 S.W.2d 206, 209 (Ct.Crim.App.Tex.1973).

Other Authorities: U.S. v. Urquidez, 356 F.Supp. 1363, 1365, 1367 (C.D.Cal.1973).

polygraphist

The function of polygraph practitioners, or **polygraphists**, is to study and interpret the markings on the polygram and make a determination as to whether the recorded physiological reactions evince the psychological and emotional pressures which normally accompany intentional attempts to deceive. U.S. v. Alexander, 526 F.2d 161, 163 (8th Cir. 1975).

polyhydramnios See *hydramnios*.

polymer (pol'ĭ-mer) [*poly-* + Gr. *meros* part] a compound, usually of high molecular weight, formed by the linear combination of simpler repeating molecules, or monomers. In immunology, immunoglobulins that form aggregates of more than one four-chain monomeric unit structure. For example, IgM and IgA both contain J chains

which are associated with polymerization of the molecules.

A **polymer** is a chemical compound, or mixture of chemical compounds, which consists essentially of repeated structural units. The individual units are called "monomers". Polyethylene, for example, is a chain of successive ethylene, CH_2, units. Polyvinylidene fluoride is a chain of vinylidene fluoride, CF_2-CH_2, units. International Tel. & Tel. Corp. v. Raychem Corp., 538 F.2d 453, 454 (1st Cir. 1976).

Synthetic **polymers** are produced by causing hydrocarbon molecules, called monomers, which are generally in liquid or gaseous form, to link together in long chains. These long chains are called **polymers**. Ziegler v. Phillips Petroleum Co., 483 F.2d 858, 862 (5th Cir. 1973).

Synthetic **polymers** are formed by causing small molecules, referred to as monomers and which are generally in the form of gases or liquids, to link together in long chains forming the polymers. Ziegler v. Phillips Petroleum Co., 171 U.S.P.Q. 44, 45 (N.D.Tex.1971).

Other Authorities: Shaw v. E.B. & A.C. Whiting Co., 157 U.S. P.Q. 405, 410 (D.Vt.1967).

polymer, linear

The patent defines **linear polymers** as "combination whose molecules are long chains built up from repeating units." ... It discloses a high degree of orientation along the fiber axis.... Shaw v. E.B. & A.C. Whiting Co., 417 F.2d 1097, 1100 (2d Cir. 1969).

polymerization (pol"ĭ-mer"ĭ-za'shun) the act or process of forming a compound (polymer), usually of high molecular weight, by the combination of simpler molecules.

The linking of the monomers is termed a **polymerization** reaction, and the **polymerization** catalyst is what causes the monomers to link together to form polymers. Ziegler v. Phillips Petroleum Co., 483 F.2d 858, 862 (5th Cir. 1973).

polymorphonuclear (pol"e-mor"fo-nu'kle-ar) [*poly-* + Gr. *morphē* form + *nucleus*] having a nucleus deeply lobed or so divided that it appears to be multiple.

Plaintiff underwent a splenectomy. Pathology of the spleen revealed that it was hyperplastic, with a diffuse infiltration of **polymorphonuclear** cells (cells having nuclei of varied forms), which suggested that the spleen was in an aseptic condition (a condition in which living organisms are absent). Brissette v. Schweiker, 566 F.Supp. 626, 629 (E.D.Mo.1983), remanded 730 F.2d 548 (8th Cir.1984).

polymyalgia (pol"e-mi-al'je-ah) myalgia affecting several muscles.

polymyalgia rheumatica a syndrome in the elderly characterized by proximal joint and muscle pain, high erythrocyte sedimentation rate, and a self-limiting course; it is frequently associated with temporal arteritis.

He further stated that the claimant may have had **polymyalgia rheumatica** but that this diagnosis could not be made with certainty because the peripheral neuropathy clouded the clinical picture. Miles v. Secretary of Health, Education & Welfare, 322 F.Supp. 1132, 1137 (W.D.Tenn.1971).

polymyeloencephaloradiculoneuropathy See *polyneuritis, acute febrile.*

polymyositis (pol"e-mi"o-si'tis) [*poly-* + Gr. *mys* muscle + *-itis*] inflammation of several or many muscles at once, along with degenerative and regenerative changes marked by muscle weakness out of proportion to the loss of muscle bulk. When developing in adults, it is often associated with cancer. When accompanied by skin lesions, it is known as *dermatomyositis.*

The plaintiff related a three (3) months history of substantial muscle pain involving much of his body....
... Clinically it was felt that the claimant had **polymyositis** with an effort made to determine if there was an underlying malignancy. No malignancy was found, however. Miles v. Secretary of Health, Education & Welfare, 322 F.Supp. 1132, 1135 (W.D.Tenn.1971).

polyneuritis (pol"e-nu-ri'tis) [*poly-* + Gr. *neuron* nerve + *-itis*] inflammation of many nerves at once; multiple, or disseminated, neuritis.

A neurological examination at that time indicated normal motor strength in her upper extremities but marked weakness of the hips, knees, and ankles. Reflexes were absent at the ankles and diminished at the knees. The initial diagnosis was an ascending **polyneuritis**, an inflammation of a large number of the spinal nerves.... Gates v. U.S., 707 F.2d 1141, 1143 (10th Cir. 1983).

polyneuritis, acute febrile; polyneuritis, acute idiopathic; polyneuritis, acute infective; polyneuritis, acute postinfectious rapidly progressive ascending motor neuron paralysis of unknown etiology, frequently following an enteric or respiratory infection. An autoimmune mechanism following viral infection has been postulated. It begins with paresthesias of the feet, followed by flaccid paralysis and weakness of the legs, ascending to the arms, trunk, and face, and is attended by slight fever, bulbar palsy, absent or lessened tendon reflexes, and an increase in the protein of the cerebrospinal fluid without corresponding increase in cells. Called also *Barré-Guillain syndrome, Guillain-Barré polyneuritis* or *syndrome, acute ascending spinal paralysis, acute postinfectious polyneuropathy, neuronitis,* and *postinfectious p.*

Guillain-Barre Syndrome is a neurological disorder of unknown cause....
... Beginning approximately on December 1, 1976 plaintiff experienced a general fatigability and loss of energy. On March 1, 1977, plaintiff developed a flu-like illness characterized by diarrhea, fever of 103 degrees, abdominal cramps, runny nose, and chills. The day before being hospitalized, plaintiff experienced blurry vision, numbness of his mouth, and weakness in his legs. On the morning of March 7, 1977, plaintiff's symptoms worsened—his vision was blurred and he developed a lisp in his speech....
Upon admission to the hospital, plaintiff was diagnosed as suffering from **GBS**. Plaintiff remained hospitalized for almost three months. During that time he was severely paralyzed and underwent surgery to assist his breathing. His respiratory muscles, cranial nerves, and limbs had been paralyzed....
... Dr. Ringel then testified that smoldering **GBS** is without evidentiary support in the neurological literature....

Because the cause of **GBS** is unknown, both parties placed considerable emphasis on epidemiologic evidence. The principal epidemiologic study is reported in Schonberger, et al., Guillain-Barre Syndrome Following Vaccination in the National Influenza Program, United States, 1976–1977, 110 Am.J. Epidemiology 105 (1979) ("CDC study")....
... The authors of the CDC study concluded that there is no relation between swine flu vaccine and the onset of **GBS** more than ten weeks after vaccination. Lima v. U.S., 708 F.2d 502, 503–6 (10th Cir. 1983).

The symptoms manifested by plaintiff during his illness are strongly supportive of a diagnosis of **GBS**. His symptoms included progressive motor weakness of more than one limb and areflexia (loss of tendon jerks). In addition, his disease was marked by the following clinical features: rapid onset of motor weakness; relative symmetry in his extremit'es; sensory symptoms; recovery or cessation of progression of symptoms within four weeks; autonomic dysfunction in the form of tachycardia; and absence of fever. O'Gara v. U.S., 560 F.Supp. 786, 788 (E.D.Pa.1983).

Mrs. Grill received her swine flu vaccine on October 15, 1976 when she was 50 years of age. She had experienced no prior eye trouble, except she did use glasses for reading. Immediately after the shot, she suffered the normal post-vaccinal sensations of burning and swelling of the left arm, followed by flu-like symptoms of a mild temperature, chills and aching lungs. She testified that she also felt a slight pain during this period, in her left eyeball. Suddenly, on November 6, 1976, she could not see out of her left eye....
Dr. Winter suspected the swine flu vaccine as a cause, because he had read in the literature that optic neuritis is a condition which sometimes follows vaccinations. His treatment of Mrs. Grill was as if she had an inflammatory condition; he gave her cortisone, varying the amount to determine the smallest amount that would keep her comfortable and keep her vision level tolerable. He found that if he reduced the dosage, her pain increased and the quality of her vision deteriorated. Grill v. U.S., 552 F.Supp. 505–6 (E.D.N.Y.1982).
Other Authorities: Gates v. U.S., 707 F.2d 1141–2, 1144 (10th Cir. 1983); Fraysier v. U.S., 566 F.Supp. 1085, 1087–9 (S.D.Fla.1983); Stich v. U.S., 565 F.Supp. 1096, 1100–2 (D.N.J.1983); McDonald v. U.S., 555 F.Supp. 935, 938, 942–5, 949 (M.D.Pa.1983); Smith v. U.S., 557 F.Supp. 42, 46, 49 (W.D.Ark.1982); Padgett v. U.S., 553 F.Supp. 794–6, 798 (W.D.Tex.1982); Warner v. U.S., 522 F.Supp. 87–8 (M.D.Fla. 1981). In re Swine Flu Immunization Products Liability Litigation, 446 F.Supp. 244–6 (Jud.Panel on Multidist.Litig.1978).

polyneuropathy (pol"e-nu-rop'ah-the) [*poly-* + Gr. *neuron* nerve + *pathos* disease] a disease which involves several nerves.

He also explained that a **polyneuropoly** [sic] meant multiple damages to her nerves, which could have resulted from numerous factors. Intrater v. Thomas, 369 N.E.2d 1339, 1344 (App. Ct. of Ill.1977).

polyolefin

Polyolefin is a generic term for polymers made from certain types of organic compounds—hydrocarbon chemicals. Polyethylene is a **polyolefin**. International Tel. & Tel. Corp. v. Raychem Corp., 538 F.2d 453–4 (1st Cir. 1976).

polyoma (pol"e-o'mah) a tumor caused by an oncogenic virus of broad host range, originally isolated from parotid gland tumors of mice inoculated with Gross leukemia virus.

Plaintiff asserts that defendants are planning to conduct experiments with **polyoma**, a virus known to cause cancer in mice. He states that the nature of the organisms to be created by the research is such that even a miniscule quantity, if released, in the environment would represent a threat to life and health. Mack v. Califano, 447 F.Supp. 668–9 (D.D.C.1978).

polyp (pol'ip) [Gr. *polypous* a morbid excrescence] a morbid excrescence, or protruding growth, from mucous membrane; classically applied to a growth on the mucous membrane of the nose, the term is now applied to such protrusions from any mucous membrane.

The development of a mass lesion (i.e., the **polyp**) was indicative of the possible development of cancer. This possibility made an operation mandatory, since in his opinion the whole colon was diseased calling for its total excision. He also testified that no medication would provide protection against such a mass in the colon. Rainer v. Buena Community Memorial Hospital, 95 Cal.Rptr. 901, 905 (Ct.App.Cal.1971).

... other than a small **polyp** (benign tumor) at the opening of her cervix, there were no organic findings to account for her complaints. Maryland Casualty Co. v. Davis, 464 S.W.2d, 433, 439 (Ct.Civ.App.Tex.1971).

polyps, endometrial small, sessile, benign projecting masses on the endometrium, composed of an edematous stroma containing cystically dilated glands.

At the time of the hysterectomy it was discovered that there was an **endometrial polyp** in the uterine cavity. When ulcerated, a **polyp** could cause bleeding, but Dr. Gentry testified there was "no evidence" that it had ulcerated. Ketcham v. Thomas, 283 S.W.2d 642, 649 (Mo.1955).

polyp, rectal

Mr. Vye also had "a very small **polyp**," which is a wart-like growth of the lining of the rectum—eight millimeters in circumference, of benign appearance, and which Dr. Becker linked with the rectal bleeding. The treatment for such bleeding is sitz baths, suppositories, and a local ointment, all designed to act against inflammation, and to avoid recurrences of bleeding, which Dr. Becker prescribed. Woodall Industries, Inc. v. Massachusetts Mutual Life Insurance Co., 483 F.2d 986, 991 (6th Cir. 1973).

polypectomy (pol"ĭ-pek'to-me) [*polyp* + Gr. *ektomē* excision] surgical removal of a polyp. See also *colonoscopy* (Ogden case); and *colotomy*.

Appellant's suit alleged that Dr. Reidell fell below the medical standard of care when he elected to perform a resection of the colon instead of a snare wire **polypectomy**.[2] [2 In this procedure, the snare wire is passed through the colonoscope, looped around the polyp, and then tightened to remove portions of the polyp.] Spotts v. Reidell, 497 A.2d 630, 632–3 (Super.Ct.Pa.1985).

polypharmacy (pol"e-fahr'mah-se) [*poly-* + Gr. *pharmakon* drug] the administration of many drugs together.

The practice of **polypharmacy**, the concurrent use of multiple drugs, was not warranted by industry standards given Timothy's status and the types of drugs involved. Cf. Ronnie v. Klein, 653 F.2d 836, 844–48 (3rd Cir. 1981) (the least intrusive means of treatment must be used, striking an acceptable balance between need for use of a psychotropic drug and the detriment to the patient to whom it is administered). The use of **polypharmacy** impeded the detection process of Timothy's growing problem and increased the likelihood Timothy's adverse reactions to the drugs would be more severe and permanent. Clites v. State, 322 N.W.2d 917, 920 (Ct.App.Iowa 1982).

polytypic

Despite these publications from which it has been clear that the genus Cannabis is **polytypic** (that is, that the genus includes more than one species), until about 1973, and specifically in 1938 and 1970, the genus Cannabis had been generally considered monotypic. U.S. v. Lewallen, 385 F.Supp. 1140, 1142 (W.D.Wis.1974).

polyunsaturated (pol"e-un-sach'ĕ-ra-ted) denoting a fatty acid, e.g., linoleic acid, having more than one double bond in its hydrocarbon chain.

Poly-unsaturates are fatty acid radicals, which, at two or more places, along the carbon-atom chain, have a deficiency in hydrogen and are capable of adding it there. The most abundant **polyunsaturate** is natural linoleic acid having two hydrogen-deficiency points, which comprises nearly 50% or more of corn, cottonseed and soybean oils. Animal fats and coconut oil, in contrast, contain only a very small percentage of linoleic acid. Corn Products Co. v. Standard Brands, Inc., 359 F.2d 739–40 (7th Cir. 1966).

polyvalent (pol"e-va'lent; po-liv'ah-lent) having more than one valency. See also *monovalent* (Davis case).

polyvinylchloride (pol"e-vi"nil-klōr'īd) a substance formed by the polymerization of vinyl chloride; a tasteless, odorless, clear hard resin, which changes color on exposure to ultraviolet light or heat.

Second, there are the manufacturers of **polyvinyl chloride** (PVC). Virtually all vinyl chloride is polymerized into thermoplastic PVC resin which serves as the basis for a wide variety of useful plastic products....

Innumerable firms throughout the country, employing thousands of workers, compound **PVC** with plasticizers, heat stabilizers, lubricants, light stabilizers, flame retardants, or impact modifiers to produce an astounding variety of wares, such as pipes and conduits for building and construction, flooring, wire and cable, furniture, phonograph records, and packaging. In fabrication, residual VCM that has been entrapped in the **PVC** resin escapes during the heating process, and in this way workers in the fabricating industry are also exposed to vinyl chloride. Society of Plastics Industries, Inc. v. Occupational S. & H.A., 509 F.2d 1301, 1304–5 (2d Cir. 1975).

polyvinylpyrrolidone See *povidone*.

Pomeroy technique See *technique, Pomeroy*.

pons (ponz), pl. *pon'tes*, gen. *pon'tis* [L. "bridge"] [NA] that part of the central nervous system lying between the medulla oblongata and the mesencephalon, ventral to the cerebellum, and consisting of a pars dorsalis and a pars ventralis; called also *bridge of Varolius*, *p. cerebelli*, *p. varolii*, and *commissura cerebelli*. See illustration accompanying *brain*. See also *brain stem*.

... the decerebrate rigidity showed an injury to the **pons**, the middle portion of the brain stem, located just above the medulla....

One of the plaintiff's experts, Dr. Leestma, a board-certified neuropathologist, testified that he was certain that the needle penetrated the medulla and possibly also the **pons**. He testified that a lesion of the **pons** could occur even if the needle penetrated the medulla but not the **pons**, because the medullary injury could be "transferred" upward into the **pons** by bleeding, edema, progressive necrosis or destruction of tissue. McClain v. U.S., 490 F.Supp. 485–6 (E.D.Wis.1980).

pontic (pon'tik) [L. *pons, pontis* bridge] the portion of a bridge which substitutes for an absent tooth, both esthetically and functionally; it usually, but not necessarily, occupies the space formerly filled by a natural tooth.

Prior to the preparation of the permanent bridge and the application of **pontics** on teeth to be crowned, Dr. Gunter consulted plaintiff about the desired shade of color for the teeth. Brock v. Gunter, 292 So.2d 328–9 (Ct.App.La. 1974).

Pontocaine (pon'to-kān) trademark for preparations of tetracaine. See also *tetracaine*.

popliteal (pop-lit'e-al; pop″lĭ-te'al) [L. *poples* ham] pertaining to the posterior surface of the knee. See also *ligamentum popliteum arcuatum*; and *ligamentum popliteum obliquum*.

popliteal artery See *arteria poplitea*.

porosis (po-ro'sis) 1. [Gr. *pōrōsis* callosity] the formation of the callus in the repair of a fractured bone. 2. [Gr. *pōros* pore] cavity formation.

porotic (po-rot'ik) pertaining to or characterized by porosis favoring the growth of connective tissue. See also *porosis*.

She complained of pain in the ankle, which was swollen, and she had difficulty in walking. Dr. Mueller took x-rays "which showed that most of the bones in ankle area and the foot were **porotic**...." The word "**porotic**" means a loss of mineral in the bone. "This can be the after effects of trauma" but usually demineralization is not associated with trauma. Demineralization can be painful. When the doctor saw Stella, she was using a crutch and "I am sure she needed it because her ankle looked to me like it would be painful." Blackburn v. Katz Drug Co., 520 S.W.2d 668, 674 (Mo.Ct.App.1975).

port, AP See *beam*.

position (po-zish'un) [L. *positio*] 1. a bodily posture or attitude assumed by the patient to achieve comfort in certain conditions, or the particular disposition of the body and extremities to facilitate the performance of certain diagnostic or therapeutic procedures. 2. in obstetrics, the situation of the fetus in the pelvis, determined and described by the relation of a given arbitrary point (point of direction or reference point) in the presenting part to a given arbitrary point in the coronal plane of the maternal pelvis. For the various possible positions see the table (from Greenhill and Friedman's Obstetrics). Cf. *presentation*.

POSITIONS OF THE FETUS IN VARIOUS PRESENTATIONS
CEPHALIC PRESENTATION

1. Vertex—occiput, the point of direction

Left occipito-anterior	L.O.A.
Left occipitotransverse	L.O.T.
Right occipitoposterior	R.O.P.
Right occipitotransverse	R.O.T.
Right occipito-anterior	R.O.A.
Left occipitoposterior	L.O.P.

2. Face—chin, the point of direction

Right mentoposterior	R.M.P.
Left mento-anterior	L.M.A.
Right mentotransverse	R.M.T.
Right mento-anterior	R.M.A.
Left mentotransverse	L.M.T.
Left mentoposterior	L.M.P.

3. Brow—the point of direction

Right frontoposterior	R.F.P.
Left fronto-anterior	L.F.A.
Right frontotransverse	R.F.T.
Right fronto-anterior	R.F.A.
Left frontotransverse	L.F.T.
Left frontoposterior	L.F.P.

BREECH OR PELVIC PRESENTATION

1. Complete Breech—sacrum, the point of direction (feet crossed and thighs flexed on abdomen)

Left sacro-anterior	L.S.A.
Left sacrotransverse	L.S.T.
Right sacroposterior	R.S.P.
Right sacro-anterior	R.S.A.
Right sacrotransverse	R.S.T.
Left sacroposterior	L.S.P.

2. Incomplete breech—sacrum, the point of direction. Same designations as above, adding the qualifications footling, knee, etc.

TRANSVERSE LIE OR SHOULDER PRESENTATION

Shoulder—scapula, the point of direction

Left scapulo-anterior	L.Sc.A.	Back anterior positions
Right scapulo-anterior	R.Sc.A.	
Right scapulo-posterior	R.Sc.P.	Back posterior positions
Left scapulo-posterior	L.Sc.P.	

position, breech See *delivery, breech; extraction, breech*; and *presentation, breech*.

position, dorsal the posture of a person lying on his back; called also *supine p.*

570

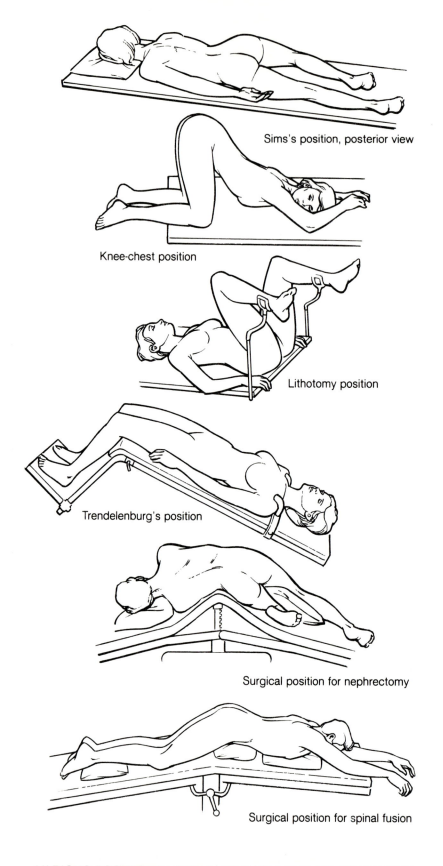

Sims's position, posterior view

Knee-chest position

Lithotomy position

Trendelenburg's position

Surgical position for nephrectomy

Surgical position for spinal fusion

VARIOUS POSITIONS USED IN EXAMINATION OR TREATMENT

Subsequent to the laparoscopy, the patient's legs were removed from the stirrups and the table returned to a **supine position** parallel to the floor. Jones v. Harrisburg Polyclinic Hosp., 437 A.2d 1134, 1136 (Pa.1981).

position, lithotomy the patient in dorsal decubitus with hips and knees flexed and the thighs abducted and externally rotated; called also *dorsosacral p.*

The D&C was performed with the patient in a flat (modified **lithotomy) position** with the operating table parallel to the floor and the patient's legs in stirrups. Jones v. Harrisburg Polyclinic Hosp., 437 A.2d 1134, 1136 (Pa.1981).

position, occipitotransverse a position of the fetus in cephalic presentation in labor, with its occiput directed toward the right (R.O.T.) or left (L.O.T.) iliac fossa of the maternal pelvis.

The baby's head was in the left "**occiput traverse position**." This means the baby was turned on its side with the back of the head towards the mother's left side. Defendant attempted a manual rotation of the child's head but was unsuccessful. Grindstaff v. Tygett, 655 S.W.2d 70, 72 (Mo.Ct.App.1983).

position, occiput transverse See *position, occipitotransverse.*

position, Trendelenburg's one in which the patient is supine on the table or bed, the head of which is tilted downward 30 to 40 degrees, and the table or bed angulated beneath the knees. See illustration.

Appellee's position on the operating table changed during the course of the operative procedures performed on her. During the D. & C., she was placed in a modified dorsal lithotomy or supine position which entailed her laying on her back in a flat position with her feet in stirrups. To facilitate the laparoscopy, appellee was placed in the **Trendelenberg position**. In this position, the patient's abdomen and legs are raised, and her head and shoulders are lowered. Appellee's position was again altered for the laparotomy procedure. For that procedure, the **Trendelenberg position** again was employed, but the degree of slant of the table was more severe than that used for the laparoscopy procedure. Jones v. Harrisburg Polyclinic Hosp., 410 A.2d 303–4 (Super.Ct.Pa.1979), reversed 437 A.2d 1134 (Pa.1981).

positioner (po-zish'un-er) a resilient elastoplastic removable appliance fitted over the occlusal surfaces of the teeth to obtain limited tooth movement and stabilization, usually at the end of orthodontic treatment.

The subject matter of the patents in suit is an orthodontic appliance comprising a body of resilient and deformable material, which as described in the introduction to the **Positioner** Patent "... is adapted to surround the teeth of a wearer for directing the teeth and the arch forms towards the assumption of preselected ideal positions ...." and to the method of making said appliance.

The **Positioner**, as made by the plaintiff in accordance with the teaching of the patents is a rubber appliance which fits within the mouth of a patient. It contains impressions of the upper and lower teeth of the patient. All of these impressions do not correspond with the natural position of the teeth in the patient's mouth for some are located in different positions which are selected by the orthodontist as the ultimate position the teeth are intended to assume.

The **Positioner** is intended for use and is so used by the profession—primarily after basic treatment with the conventional type wires and bands. Thus, after major tooth movements have been accomplished, the positioner provides for the final artistic positioning and retention of the teeth. The **positioner** is not inserted in the mouth of a patient as a permanent appliance, as is the case during basic treatment, but is worn only part-time during the day and at night during sleep. The rubber allows it to stretch over the teeth and while it is being worn, its resiliency influences each tooth toward the pre-selected position. T.P. Laboratories, Inc. v. Huge, 261 F.Supp. 349, 351 (E.D.Wis. 1965).

positioner, tooth See *positioner.*

postconcussional syndrome See under *syndrome.*

posterior (pos-tēr'e-or) [L. "behind"; neut. *posterius*] situated in back of, or in the back part of, or affecting the back part of a structure; [NA] a term used in reference to the back or dorsal surface of the body. In lower animals, it refers to the caudal end of the body.

post partum (pōst par'tum) [L.] after childbirth, or after delivery.

Nurse Bennett concluded that the nurse-defendants' depositions and the nurses' notes evinced poor **postpartum** care because (1) the notes were poorly kept, (2) the notes were possibly made after the pronouncement of death, (3) the notes suggested poor communication among the nursing staff about the patient's care and condition, (4) the patient's vital signs were poorly monitored, and (5) "a nursing diagnosis ... could have led [nurse] T. Bastinelli to conclude hemorrhage was possible." Maslonka v. Hermann, 414 A.2d 1350, 1353 (Super. Ct.N.J.1980).

... the **post-partum** period following pregnancy after the giving of birth).... Leibowitz v. Ortho Pharmaceutical Corp., 307 A.2d 449, 462 (Super.Ct.Pa.1973).

post-traumatic stress disorder See *disorder, posttraumatic stress.*

potassium (po-tas'e-um) [L.] a metallic element of the alkali group, many of whose salts are used in medicine. It is a soft, silver-white metal, melting at 58° F.; atomic number, 19; atomic weight, 39.102; specific gravity, 0.87; symbol, K (L. *kalium*). Potassium is the chief cation of muscle and most other cells (intracellular fluid). See also *sodium-potassium pump,* under *pump.*

potassium iodide [USP], KI, occurring as crystals that are colorless and transparent or somewhat opaque and white, or as a white, granular powder; used as an expectorant, as a source of iodine in thyrotoxic crisis and in the preparation of thyrotoxic patients for thyroidectomy, and as an antifungal in the treatment of lymphocutaneous sporotrichosis; administered orally.

Chemical analysis of the autopsy specimens revealed the presence of **potassium iodide** in various concentrations throughout the body. A medical expert stated that **potassium iodide** was a corrosive substance when it is in a concentrated state and gave the opinion that the chemical had been injected into the victim's system in such a strong concentration as to cause cardiac arrest and general collapse of the circulatory system, and to coagulate the protein molecules in the body tissue, thus creating massive hemorrhaging. In the doctor's opinion, the specific cause of Mrs. Maley's death from shock was the introduction of a strong concentration of **potassium iodide** into her system....

... One expert testified that, in his opinion, the concentration of the chemical when it was first injected was between seven and eight percent. In that concentration, **potassium iodide** is a corrosive substance which could cause cardiac arrest, collapse of the circulatory system, and coagulation of protein molecules in the body tissue causing hemorrhaging into the coagulated areas. Commonwealth v. Mace, 341 A.2d 505, 507 (Super.Ct.Pa.1975).

potassium sorbate [NF] chemical name: 2,4-hexadienoic acid potassium salt. A mold and yeast inhibitor, $C_6H_7O_2$, occurring as white crystals or as a powder; used as a preservative in pharmaceutical preparations. See also *acid, sorbic.*

potential (po-ten'shal) [L. *potentia* power] electric tension or pressure, as measured by the capacity of producing electric effects in bodies of a different state of electrization. When bodies of different potentials are brought into communication, a current is set up between them; if they are of the same potential, no current passes between them.

potential, spike the initial very large change in potential of an excitable cell membrane during excitation.

Pott's aneurysm, disease, etc. (pots [Sir Percivall *Pott,* English surgeon, 1714–1788]. See under *abscess; curvature; fracture*; and *paraplegia; varix, aneurysmal*; and *tuberculosis of spine.*

povidone (po'vĭ-dōn) [USP] chemical name: 1-ethenyl-2-pyrrolidinone homopolymer. A synthetic polymer occurring as a white to creamy white, odorless powder, principally consisting of linear 1-vinyl-2-pyrrolidone groups, produced as a series of products having mean molecular weights ranging from about 10,000 to about 700,000; used as a dispersing and suspending agent, and has been used as a tablet binder, coating agent, and viscosity-increasing agent in pharmaceutical preparations. Formerly called *polyvinylpyrrolidone (PVP).* See also *povidone-iodine.*

povidone-iodine (po'vĭ-dōn i'o-dīn) [USP], a complex produced by reacting iodine with the polymer povidone, which slowly releases iodine; it occurs as a yellowish brown, amorphous powder and is used as a topical anti-infective. Abbreviated PVP-I.

P.P.D. (purified protein derivative [of tuberculin]) See under *tuberculin.*

P.P.D. (purified protein derivative) test See *test, tuberculin Sterneedle.*

practice (prak'tis) [Gr. *praktikē*] the utilization of one's knowledge in a particular profession, the practice of medicine being the exercise of one's knowledge in the practical recognition and treatment of disease.

practice, family the medical specialty concerned with the planning and provision of the comprehensive primary health care of all members of a family, regardless of age or sex, on a continuing basis.

Dr. Mitchell, a specialist in **family practice**, testified that the **family practice** specialty is broad and encompasses pediatrics, internal medicine, surgery, psychiatry, obstetrics and gynecology. It provides care like that of an internist. He further testified that the diagnosis of abdominal and gastrointestinal conditions, such as cancer of the colon, is included in this specialty. Steinbach v. Barfield, 428 So.2d 915, 920 (Ct.App.La. 1983).

practitioner (prak-tish'un-er) one who has complied with the requirements of and who is engaged in the practice of medicine.

The term '**practitioner**' means a physician or other person licensed, registered, or otherwise permitted by the United States or the jurisdiction in which he practices, to distribute, dispense, or administer a controlled substance in the course of professional practice....

Though the court read to the jury the statutory definition of "**practitioner**" as a physician or other person licensed to dispense or administer controlled substances, it did not advise them that physicians are exempt from the provisions of the drug abuse statute when they dispense or prescribe controlled substances in good faith to patients in the regular course of professional practice. U.S. v. Carroll, 518 F.2d 187–9 (6th Cir. 1975).

precancerous (pre-kan'ser-us) pertaining to a pathologic process that tends to become malignant.

Dr. Alan L. Jacobs, one of the treating physicians, asserted that the chronic ulceration indicates potential malignancy. He characterized the condition as probably **premalignant**, and said that when burns constantly reopen and ulcerate "there is a strong danger of malignancy." Lorenc v. Chemirad Corp., 37 N.J. 56, 74, 179 A.2d 401 (1962).

preclampsia

Preeclampsia is the development of hypertension due to pregnancy. Sard v. Hardy, 379 A.2d 1014, 1018 (Ct.App.Md. 1977).

preconception

If a child after birth has no right of action for injuries arising out of **preconception** negligent conduct, there is a wrong inflicted for which there is no remedy. The Court finds no logical reason to deny recovery to a person simply because he had not yet been conceived when the wrongful action took place. Bergstreser v. Mitchell, 448 F.Supp. 10, 14 (E.D.Mo.1977).

Prednefrin See *prednisolone acetate.*

prednisolone (pred-nis'o-lōn) [USP] chemical name: 11β17α-21-trihydroxypregna-1,4-diene-3,20-dione. A synthetic glucocorticoid derived from cortisol, $C_{21}H_{28}O_5$, occurring as a white to practically white, crystalline powder; administered orally in the treatment of various conditions responsive to the anti-inflammatory action of glucocorticoids, including rheumatoid arthritis and other collagen diseases, allergic conditions, neoplastic and gastrointestinal disease, and blood dyscrasias.

Over the last five months of his treatment by Dr. Marks, up to his final visit on January 18, 1971, plaintiff was treated with a total of 1450 mg. of **sterane**, an oral steroid, and 440 mg. of

Kenalog-40 by injection. Hill v. Squibb & Sons, E.R., 592 P.2d 1383, 1385 (Mont.1979).

prednisolone acetate [USP], the 21-acetate ester of prednisolone, $C_{23}H_{30}O_4$, occurring as a white to practically white, crystalline powder, having actions and uses similar to those of the base; administered by intra-articular or intramuscular injection.

Prednefrin 0.12% has been on the market since 1957. It is an admittedly pure drug, the principal ingredient of which is a steroid, **Prednisolone Acetate**. It is a prescription drug which is prohibited by law from being dispensed except on the written prescription of a licensed physician. Increased intraocular pressure is and was a known side effect in susceptible persons, and it is undisputed that extended or prolonged use should be allowed only when there is direct supervision by a medical doctor....

... The average treatment with the drug is two to four weeks, and that adverse or side reactions are negligible. The drug is not to be used for a period in excess of six weeks and for the majority of the people for less than four weeks. The manufacturer's testing results were good. The doctor knew that the drug could cause increased intraocular pressure if administered for prolonged periods of time to susceptible persons, and that the drug could not damage anybody's eyes in three weeks unless it was improperly used. Over a million bottles of the drug had been dispensed by 1965 without any report of cataracts. However, the drug can cause a rise in intraocular pressure and cataracts if it is misused. If topical steroid is put in the eyes for a prolonged period of time, about 30% to 33% of the users will receive intraocular pressure. Ortiz v. Allergan Pharmaceuticals, 489 S.W.2d 135, 138 (Ct. Civ.App.Tex.1972).

prednisone (pred'nĭ-sōn) [USP] chemical name: 17α,21-dihydroxypregna-1,4-diene-3,11,20-trione. A synthetic glucocorticoid derived from cortisone, $C_{21}H_{26}O_5$, but having reduced mineralocorticoid activity; it occurs as a white to practically white, crystalline powder and is used orally in the treatment of various conditions responsive to the anti-inflammatory action of glucocorticoids. Called also *deltacortisone*. See also *prednisolone*; and *stria* (Robbins case).

Dr. Wexler told Robbins that the stria were directly caused by the **Prednisone** and that, because of his young age, the drug should not have been given to him. Robbins v. U.S., 624 F.2d 971–2 (10th Cir. 1980).

Dr. Webb stated that **Prednisone** could cause mental disturbances such as euphoria, depression and psychotic effects. Dr. Webb admitted, however, that Dresser had not suffered from severe depression bordering on psychosis and that Dresser had been able to appreciate the consequences of this conduct while under the effects of **Prednisone**. U.S. v. Dresser, 542 F.2d 737, 741 (8th Cir. 1976).

This man received and had to have a very long period of time, **Prednisone**, which is a sort of Cortisone for the treatment of his severe emphysema. This has an effect on bones of causing a weakening, softening of their structure, so that they are more vulnerable to injury, and very probably that was a contributing factor. Drake v. State Dep't of Soc. Welf.-Larned State Hosp., 499 P.2d 532, 537 (Kan.1972).

Other Authorities: Segar v. Garan, Inc., 388 So.2d 164–5 (Miss.1980).

preexisting See *aggravation; "eggshell skull" rule*; and *latent*.

For many years it has been the rule in Montana that the employer takes his employee as he finds him, and as we said in Gaffney v. Ind. Acc. Board (1955), 129 Mont. 394, 401, 287 P.2d 256, 259, "[t]he fact that an employee was suffering from a preexisting disease or disability does not preclude compensation if the disease or disability was aggravated or accelerated by an industrial injury which arose out of and in the course of the employment." Consequently, the question here is whether or not Mr. Ridenour's COPD was aggravated or accelerated by the inhalation incident on December 18, 1978. Ridenour v. Equity Supply Co., 665 P.2d 783, 787–8 (Mont. 1983).

preexisting

Although the ligamentous strain had resolved itself sometime before October 1, 1979, Dr. Butler stated his opinion that Ibbitson's current incapacity was caused, at least in part, by the aggravation of his **preexisting** condition. Our prior cases make it clear that "an employee is entitled to disability compensation for any period of disability that is shown to result from the combined effects of work-related activity and a **preexisting** condition of the employee." Bryant v. Masters Machine Co., 444 A.2d 329, 335 (Me.1982); see also Canning v. State Department of Transportation, 347 A.2d 605, 609 (Me.1975); Soucy, 267 A.2d at 922. Even though the **preexisting** condition is not completely asymptomatic before the work-related incident, the employee is entitled to benefits "at least for the period during which the impact and the condition combine to produce some disability." Bryant, 444 A.2d at 335; see also Canning, 347 A.2d at 609; Soucy, 267 A.2d at 921....

In view of Dr. Butler's testimony that the work accident not only caused a ligamentous strain but aggravated or "lit up" a **preexisting** condition, the Commissioner's findings did not completely answer the question whether the work incident had ceased to be a factor contributing to Ibbitson's continuing incapacity. Merely finding that the ligamentous strain had resolved itself did not conclusively establish that the work injury had ceased to have an effect on Ibbitson's condition. Ibbitson v. Sheridan Corp., 463 A.2d 735, 738 (Maine 1983).

Dr. Kilroy admitted: "she had more spasm and she was hurting more" when she was admitted to the hospital in December than she had in September. (TR.108.) In Dr. Kilroy's opinion, Peggy Napoli had had a relapse when he admitted her to the hospital. He did not attribute the relapse to trauma, but admitted that the accident could have aggravated her condition.

Dr. John Tassin, a general practitioner, testified that there was a definite correlation between the accident and Peggy Napoli's subsequent hospitalization and surgery.

Dr. David Klein, a neurological surgeon, said that trauma can aggravate a **pre-existing** condition, particularly a degenerative situation involving the spine. It was difficult in Ms. Napoli's case to "be certain, absolutely certain that the accident was an aggravating factor" but that was a reasonable suspicion. (TR.137.)

Dr. Robert Hanchey, a neurosurgeon, saw Peggy Napoli in the hospital on December 6, 1977. She was in severe pain with muscle spasms in the cervical and shoulder region. According to Dr. Hanchey, a disc problem can be aggravated by movement or injury; the accident could have aggravated Ms. Napoli's condition. Napoli v. State Farm Mut. Auto Ins. Co., 395 So.2d 720–1 (La.1981).

Other Authorities: Kondzielski v. W.C.A.B. (Northwestern Elec.), 463 A.2d 1221–2 (Commonwealth Ct.Pa.1983); International Harvester Co. v. Industrial Com'n, 305 N.E.2d 529, 533–4 (Ill.1973).

preexisting injury See *injury, preexisting.*

pregnancy (preg′nan-se) [L. *praegnans* with child] the condition of having a developing embryo or fetus in the body, after union of an ovum and spermatozoon. In women duration of pregnancy is about 266 days. Pregnancy is marked by cessation of the menses; nausea on arising in the morning (morning sickness); enlargement of the breasts and pigmentation of the nipples; progressive enlargement of the abdomen. The absolute signs of pregnancy are fetal movements, sounds of the fetal heart, and demonstration of the fetus by x-ray or ultrasound.

Pregnancy generates physiological changes in a woman's body and produces certain side effects which, Eastern maintains, impair her functioning as a flight attendant. Two dramatic changes are an increase in blood volume and an increase in cardiac output. The blood volume of an expectant mother can increase by as much as 40–45% . Simultaneously, the percentage of red cells per unit of blood decreases. The resulting decrease in hemoglobin concentration is termed physiological anemia and is a normal condition in pregnant women; it means that greater amounts of oxygen exist in the blood, but in a less concentrated form. Cardiac output also increases during **pregnancy**. The combination of these factors means that more blood and oxygen are available for the body's organs at any given time than are available to a non-pregnant person.

A pregnant woman also experiences an expansion in her abdominal area, a loosening of the pelvic joints, and increased girth. The rate at which the fetus and uterus grow is basically exponential, increasing most rapidly during the later stages of **pregnancy**. Prior to the twentieth week of **pregnancy**, these changes have little or no effect on a woman. The rate of growth after the twentieth week varies from woman to woman. The combination of abdominal expansion and increased girth decreases a woman's agility. Consequently, many women become more accident-prone during the later stages of **pregnancy**. By the end of the twenty-eighth week, these physiological changes significantly affect the agility and mobility of virtually all women.

Many pregnant women complain of fatigue, loss of strength, fainting and morning sickness during various stages of their **pregnancy**. The degree to which a pregnant woman becomes fatigued during **pregnancy** is largely dependent upon her general state of health and the level of activity to which she is normally accustomed. An active woman who continues her employment during her **pregnancy** is less likely than an inactive, non-working woman to become fatigued during early stages of **pregnancy**.

Fainting occurs most frequently when a person, pregnant, or non-pregnant, stands suddenly after being in a fixed position, and least frequently when a person is on her feet moving around. Fainting in pregnant women is most common in the

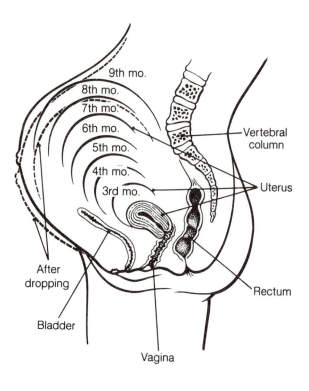

Pregnancy—Uterine levels.

very early weeks and after the twenty-eighth week of **pregnancy**.

Morning sickness or nausea affects at least 50% of all pregnant women. This condition is rarely disabling and can be ameliorated through diet regulation. Dr. Hellegars has observed that engaging in some activity such as work will take a pregnant woman's mind off of her nausea and thus lessen its effects. Burwell v. Eastern Air Lines, Inc., 458 F.Supp. 474, 485–6 (E.D.Va.1978), reversed in part, affirmed in part, and remanded 633 F.2d 361 (4th Cir. 1980).

Other Authorities: Leonard v. Couse, 372 N.Y.S.2d 527, 530 (Fam.Ct.Otsego Cty.1975).

pregnancy, ectopic development of the fertilized ovum outside of the uterine cavity; called also *extrauterine p.* Cited in Clark v. U.S., 402 F.2d 950–1 (4th Cir. 1968).

pregnancy, splash

When asked how a pregnancy could occur in a woman whose hymen was intact he testified that this was possible and that it was not unknown in medical science. To use his own expression, it was a "**splash pregnancy**". T v. M, 242 A.2d 670, 672 (Super.Ct.N.J.1968).

pregnancy, wrongful See *birth, wrongful.*

In contradistinction to a "wrongful birth" claim, an action for "**wrongful pregnancy**" or "wrongful conception" is generally brought by the parents of a healthy, but unwanted, child against a pharmacist or pharmaceutical manufacturer for negligently filling a contraceptive prescription, or against a physician for negligently performing a sterilization procedure or an

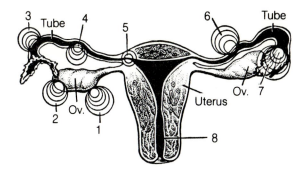

Diagram showing locations of ectopic (extrauterine) pregnancy: (1) primary abdominal; (2) ovarian; (3) ampullar; (4) tubal—rupture into broad ligament; (5) interstitial; (6) tubal—rupture into peritoneal cavity; (7) tubo-ovarian; (8) cervical (Greenhill).

abortion. E.g., Coleman v. Garrison, 349 A.2d 8 (Del.1975); Troppi v. Scarf, 31 Mich.App. 240, 187 N.W.2d 511 (1971); Robertson, Civil Liability Arising from "Wrongful Birth" Following an Unsuccessful Sterilization Operation, 4 Am.J.L. & Med. 131 (1978); Comment, Pregnancy After Sterilization: Causes of Action for Parent and Child, 12 J.Fam.L. 635 (1972). Thus, " 'wrongful pregnancy' actions typically involve a healthy, but unwanted, child. 'Wrongful birth' actions, on the other hand, usually involve planned children who are born deformed." 54 Tulane L.Rev. 480, 485 (1980). There can, however, be some overlap between these categories; for example, a few "wrongful pregnancy" cases involve unplanned children who, coincidentally, were born with congenital defects. E.g., La-Point v. Shirley, 409 F.Supp. 118 (W.D.Tex.1976); Bowman v. Davis, 48 Ohio St.2d 41, 356 N.E.2d 496 (1976); Speck v. Finegold, 268 Pa.Super. 342, 408 A.2d 496 (Pa.Super.1976). It should also be noted that judicial adherence to this terminology has not been uniform, with many courts utilizing the term "wrongful birth" to describe "wrongful pregnancy" claims. E.g., Custodio v. Bauer, 251 Cal.App.2d 303, 59 Cal.Rptr. 463 (1967); Annot., 83 A.L.R.3d 15 (1978). Nonetheless, the recent decisions have been more precise in their language, e.g., Sherlock v. Stillwater Clinic, 260 N.W.2d 169 (Minn. 1977); Becker v. Schwartz, 46 N.Y.2d 401, 386 N.E.2d 807, 413 N.Y.S.2d 895 (1978), and this court feels that these distinctions are essential to the development of a functional analytic framework. Perhaps the most compelling justification for this terminology is provided by those jurisdictions that recognize "wrongful birth" claims, but not "wrongful pregnancy" claims. Compare Jacobs v. Theimer, 519 S.W.2d 846 (Tex. 1975) and Dumer v. St. Michael's Hosp., 69 Wis.2d 766, 233 N.W.2d 372 (1975) with Terrell v. Garcia, 496 S.W.2d 124 (Tex.Civ.App.1973), cert. denied, 415 U.S. 927, 94 S.Ct. 1434, 39 L.Ed.2d 484 (1974) and Rieck v. Medical Protective Co., 64 Wis.2d 514, 219 N.W.2d 242 (1974). Phillips v. U.S., 508 F.Supp. 544, 545 (D.S.Car.1981).

Preludin See *phenmetrazine hydrochloride.*

premalignant See *precancerous.*

Premarin (prem'ah-rin) trademark for preparations of conjugated estrogens. See also *estrogens, conjugated.*

premature delivery See *infant, premature.*

premonitory (pre-mon'ĭ-to-re) [L. *praemonitorius*] serving as a warning.

prenatal (pre-na'tal) [*pre-* + L. *natalis* natal] existing or occurring before birth, with reference to the fetus. Cf. *antepartal.*

The recognition of a cause of action for **prenatal** injuries has been recent in Missouri, as elsewhere. See generally W. Prosser. The Law of Torts 335–38 (4th ed. 1971). In Missouri, the right of a child to bring an action for injuries incurred prior to birth is currently contingent upon the child's having been born alive. See Hardin v. Sanders, 538 S.W.2d 336, 337 (Mo. 1976); Steggall v. Morris, 363 Mo. 1224, 258 S.W.2d 577 (1953). A wrongful death action may not be maintained in Missouri for the death of an unborn child or for a stillborn child. Hardin v. Sanders, supra at 338. Bergstreser v. Mitchell, 577 F.2d 22, 25 (8th Cir. 1978).

prenatal injury See *injury, prenatal.*

preoperative (pre-op'er-a"tiv) preceding an operation.

Pre-operative orders are instructions to the nursing staff with respect to the patient's preparation for surgery. The orders include a prescription for **pre-operative** medication. Thompson v. Presbyterian Hosp., Inc., 652 P.2d 260, 262 (Okl.1982).

preparation (prep"ah-ra'shun) [L. *praeparatio*] the act or process of making ready.

preparation, crown

Dr. Banowsky testified that to prepare a tooth for a crown it was necessary for the enamel to be removed. This is accomplished by grinding the tooth down with a high-speed-rotary instrument. In order to prevent tooth decay at the point where the crown and tooth meet, it is necessary to remove the enamel below the gum line from two to three millimeters. To go below the gum line, a long tapered "burr", which would cause less bleeding than the larger instrument used in removing the enamel for the rest of the tooth, was used. Williford v. Banowsky, 563 S.W.2d 702, 704 (Ct.Civ.App.Tex.1978).

Preparation H See *hemorrhoid* (American Home Products Corp. case).

preponderance (pre-pon'der-ans) [*pre-* + L. *pondere* to weigh] the condition of having greater weight, force, or influence.

preponderance, ventricular disproportionate hypertrophy between the ventricles of the heart; diagnosed by the electrocardiograph.

Left **ventricular preponderance** on x-ray, means that this was a little more prominent than usual and would go along with the possibility of the aneurysm.... Fain v. St. Paul Ins. Co., 602 S.W.2d 577, 580 (Ct.App.Tex.1980).

prepyloric (pre"pi-lor'ik) in front of or just proximal to the pylorus or the pyloric part of the stomach. See also *pars pylorica ventriculi.*

presbycusis (pres"bĕ-ku'sis) [*presby-* + Gr. *akousis* hearing] a progressive, bilaterally symmetrical perceptive hearing loss occurring with age. See also *hearing loss.*

The issue presented by this writ of review is whether **presbycusis**, a loss of hearing generally associated with the aging process, is compensable by the Second Injury Fund. We conclude that it is not. . . .

. . . the medical panel acknowledged that it had not applied the statutory correction for **presbycusis**,[2] and after having done so, found that the hearing impairment represented not twelve percent but zero percent of the whole body. [[2] As provided by the provisions of U.C.A., 1953, § 35–2–60.] Wayman v. Western Coal Carrier Corp., 665 P.2d 1294–5 (Utah 1983).

Other Authorities: Matter of Compensation of Hughes, 658 P.2d 548, 551 (Ct.App.Or.1983).

presbyopia (pres″be-o′pe-ah) [*presby-* + Gr. *ōps* eye + *-ia*] hyperopia and impairment of vision due to advancing years or to old age; it is dependent on diminution of the power of accommodation from loss of elasticity of the crystalline lens, causing the near point of distinct vision to be removed farther from the eye.

. . . **presbyopia** (loss of ability to focus the eye on objects near at hand). . . . Cornett v. Califano, 590 F.2d 91–2 (4th Cir. 1978).

" . . . The claimant has an aphacic eye condition, whereby the lens has been removed, and this does not allow the claimant to use lenses under the exception to the Director's Rules 51–8–9 for **presbyopia** (normal old sight), which has a medical definition as: 'The condition of vision in the aged due to diminished power of accommodation from impaired elasticity of the crystalline lens. . . .' In one case there is no lens, and in the other case there is a lens that does not function normally. . . ." Piper v. Kansas Turnpike Authority, 436 P.2d 396, 398 (Kan.1968).

prescription (pre-skrip′shun) [L. *praescriptio*] a written direction for the preparation and administration of a remedy. A prescription consists of the heading or *superscription*—that is, the symbol ℞ or the word Recipe, meaning "take"; the *inscription*, which contains the names and quantities of the ingredients; the *subscription*, or directions for compounding; and the *signature*, usually introduced by the sign S. for *sig′na*, "mark," which gives the directions for the patient which are to be marked on the receptacle. See also *drug, over-the-counter*.

In the Revised Statutes governing pharmacies, the following requirement regarding the labeling of **prescriptions** is found at Chapter 37, Section 1195:

B. All receptacles containing compounded or filled **prescriptions** shall bear a label showing the prescription number, the name of the person actually and personally filling, compounding or dispensing the **prescription**, the directions for its use internally or externally, as specified by the prescriber, the date of its compounding or filling, and the name of the store or the proprietor thereof. Cazes v. Raisinger, 430 So.2d 104, 107 (Ct. of App.La.1983).

"**Prescribed** drugs" are any simple or compounded substance or mixture of substances prescribed as such or in other acceptable dosage forms for the cure, mitigation or prevention of disease, or for health maintenance, by a physician or other licensed practitioner of the healing arts within the scope of his professional practice. . . . 45 C.F.R. § 249.10(b)(12)(i). Dodson v. Parham, 427 F.Supp. 97, 104 (N.D.Ga.1977).

presentation (pre″zen-ta′shun) [L. *praesentatio*] in obstetrics: (*a*) the relationship of the long axis of the fetus to that of the mother (called also *lie*); (*b*) the presenting part, i.e., that portion of the fetus which is touched by the examining finger through the cervix, or during labor, is bounded by the girdle of resistance. See also *extraction*; and *position*.

The **presentation** of the child was not normal, and Dr. Smith observed that a prolapse of the child's arm had occurred. He thereupon spent a period of time, of disputed duration, attempting to perform a "version and extraction," that is, attempting manually to turn the child in such a way as to permit a normal delivery. Hernandez v. Smith, 552 F.2d 142–4 (5th Cir. 1977).

presentation, breech presentation of the buttocks or feet of the fetus in labor. See also *longitudinal presentation*.

presentation, breech, complete presentation of the buttocks of the fetus in labor, with the feet alongside of the buttocks, the fetus being in the same attitude as in vertex presentation, but with polarity reversed.

presentation, breech, double See *presentation, breech, complete*.

presentation, breech, frank presentation of the buttocks of the fetus in labor, with the legs extended against the trunk and the feet lying against the face.

These X-rays revealed that the child was in the **frank breech position**—i.e., the child was in a scissorlike position with its legs pointing up toward its head. The child's buttocks were at the top of the birth canal. Dr. Allen determined from the X-rays that the child could be delivered vaginally and that a Caesarean section would be unnecessary. Roark v. Allen, 633 S.W.2d 804, 807 (Tex.1982).

Other Authorities: Petri v. Smith, 453 A.2d 342–3 (Super.Ct. Pa.1982).

presentation, breech, incomplete presentation of the fetus in labor, with one or both feet or one or both knees of the fetus prolapsed into the maternal vagina.

presentation, breech, single See *presentation, breech, frank*.

presentation, longitudinal the situation of the fetus in labor in which the long axis of the fetal body lies parallel to that of the mother. Normally, the head presents first, but sometimes the breech is the first to appear.

pressure (presh′ur) [L. *pressura*] stress or strain, whether by compression, pull, thrust, or shear.

pressure, blood the pressure of the blood on the walls of the arteries, dependent on the energy of the heart action, the elasticity of the walls of the arteries, and the volume and viscosity of the blood. The maximum pressure occurs near the end of the stroke output of the left ventricle of the heart and is termed *maximum* or *systolic* pressure. The minimum pressure occurs late in ventricular diastole and is termed *minimum* or *diastolic* pressure. *Mean blood pressure* is the average of the blood pressure levels. *Basic blood pressure* is the pressure during quiet rest or basal

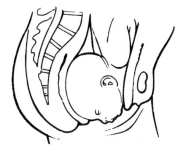

Face presentation

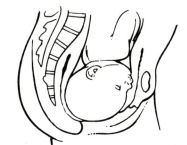

Brow presentation

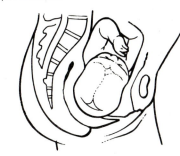

Parietal presentation

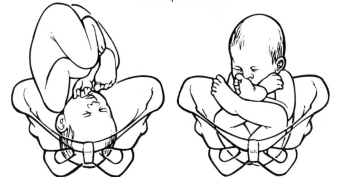

Vertex presentation

Breech presentation

Shoulder presentation

VARIOUS PRESENTATIONS

conditions. See also *hypertension; hypotension*; and *sympathectomy*.

Normal **blood pressure** is generally considered to be in the vicinity of 120 over 80. Medvecz v. Choi, 569 F.2d 1221, 1223 (3d Cir. 1977).

Upon examination, his **blood pressure** was 180/100. Medication was prescribed. Eight days later the pressure had been reduced to 130/90 and the medication was cut in half. On April 3, pressure stood at 160 or 170/90 and medication was continued. Life Insurance Co. of Virginia v. Shifflet, 359 F.2d 501, 503 (5th Cir. 1966).

pressure, intracranial the pressure in the space between the skull and the brain, i.e., the pressure of the subarachnoidal fluid.

At this point on May 6th Dr. Coulon hospitalized plaintiff for the purpose of installing a shunt.

While this installation was being made and the catheter was inserted into the right lateral ventricle the fluid from the brain "shot out approximately one foot" from the catheter dramatically demonstrating the presence of increased **intracranial pressure**. Gendusa v. St. Paul Fire & Marine Ins. Co., 435 So. 2d 479, 482 (Ct.App.La.1983).

She claims inability to work beginning November 27, 1974 due to **intracranial pressure**, which is either due to or complicated by dizziness, a constant severe headache.... Cornett v. Califano, 590 F.2d 91–2 (4th Cir. 1978).

pressure, intraocular the pressure of the fluids of the eye against the tunics. It is produced by continual renewal of the fluids within the interior of the eye, and is altered in certain pathological conditions (e.g., glaucoma). It may be roughly estimated by palpation of the eye or measured, directly or indirectly, with specially devised instruments, the tonometers.

The depositions and affidavits disclosed that some persons can have elevated **intraocular pressure** with no resulting disc damage. These persons are termed as having ocular hypertension for which generally no treatment is prescribed as there is no resulting injury. Although there may in some cases be characteristics commonly associated with glaucoma that are not found in ocular hypertension, the only sure method of distinguishing if a person with elevated **intraocular pressure** has glaucoma or ocular hypertension is through a test of time to determine if there is subsequent ocular disc damage. Winkjer v. Herr, 277 N.W.2d 579, 584 (N.D.1979).

Other Authorities: Harris v. Robert C. Groth, M.D., Inc., 663 P.2d 113, 114 (Wash.1983).

pressurized container See *aerosol*.

prickly heat See *miliaria rubra*.

primary site See *site, primary*.

primidone (prim′ĭ-dōn) [USP] chemical name: 5-ethyldihydro-5-phenyl-4,6(1*H*,5*H*)-pyrimidinedione. An anticonvulsant, $C_{12}H_{14}N_2O_2$, occurring as a white, crystalline powder; used in the treatment of grand mal, focal, and psychomotor epileptic seizures, administered orally. Called also *desoxyphenobarbital*.

... the Physician's Desk Reference (PDR), a guide to prescription medications commonly used by the medical profession, published for the first time the following warning in relation to Mysoline: "Recent reports strongly suggest an association between the use of anticonvulsant drugs by women with epilepsy and an elevated incidence of birth defects in children born to these women. Reference has been made to **primidone** [Mysoline] in several cases in which it was used in combination with other anticonvulsants; but its teratogenicity has not been conclusively demonstrated." Dillashaw v. Ayerst Laboratories, Inc., 190 Cal.Rptr. 68, 70 (Ct. of App.1983).

prism (prizm) [Gr. *prisma*] a solid with a triangular or polygonal cross section. A triangular prism splits up a ray of light into its constituent colors, and turns or deflects light rays toward its base. Prisms are used to correct deviations of the eyes, since they alter the apparent situation of objects. See also *spectacles, prismatic*.

When the diplopia persisted, Dr. Prochaska prescribed **prism** lenses that he referred to in his discussions with Plaintiff as training glasses, and which, when worn, restored binocular vision in all fields of gaze except up. The plan was to gradually reduce the **prism** in the glasses as the eye muscles achieved the ability to fuse without the aid of corrective glasses. Walker v. North Dakota Eye Clinic, Ltd., 415 F.Supp. 891–3 (D.N. Dak.1976).

private parts See *genitalia*.

probability

The fact that the experts testified as to "odds" and percentages was acceptable. "Odds" as used in this context is defined as "the ratio of probability that one thing is so rather than another or that one thing will happen rather than another." (Emphasis added.) Webster's Third New International Dictionary. The expert testimony in this case concerning odds or percentages was all clearly in terms of the probable permanence of Brian's conditions. Such testimony is therefore distinguishable from the expert opinion in the case on which the defendants rely, where a physician testified that there was a "fifty-fifty chance" that the plaintiff's low back condition attributable to the accident would be permanent. Davis v. P. Gambardella & Son Cheese Corporation, 147 Conn. 365, 373, 161 A.2d 583. In such a situation the ratio of **probability** is exactly even, and the witness (unlike the witnesses in the present case) is testifying as to possibilities and not **probabilities**. "For medical opinion testimony to have any probative value, it must at least advise the jury that the inference drawn by the doctor is more probably correct than incorrect. If the **probabilities** are in balance, the matter is left to speculation. Speculation filtered through a jury is still speculation." (Emphasis added.) Crawford v. Seufert, 236 Or. 369, 388 P.2d 456, 459; see annot., 2 A.L.R.3d 354, 360. The jurors were correctly instructed by the trial court that the "law requires proof within the realm of reasonable **probabilities** ... and ... possibility cannot form the basis for proving a fact." Healy v. White, 378 A.2d 540, 544 (Conn.1977).

Pro-Banthine (pro-ban-thīn′) trademark for preparations of propantheline bromide. See also *propantheline bromide*.

procaine (pro′kān) chemical name: 4-aminobenzoic acid 2-(diethylamino)ethyl ester; a local anesthetic, $C_{13}H_{20}N_2O_2$.

At the hearing one Frances Oldhan Kelsey, who holds the degree of doctor of philosophy in Pharmacology, gave expert testimony showing that **Procaine-PVP** is not recognized among experts as safe and effective for any use other than as a local anesthetic. It is clear that no application with respect to **Procaine-PVP** has been approved or exemption claimed under any Federal Act. We gather from an amicus curiae brief filed by loyal patients of Dr. DeMarco and from other references in the proceedings that Dr. DeMarco has used the drug as a specific for a number of ailments, including cardiovascular ailments, scleroderma, circulatory troubles, heart disease, bronchial asthma, phlebitis, and general debility. DeMarco v. Com. Dep't of Health, 397 A.2d 61, 63 (Cmwlth.Ct.Pa.1979).

procaine-PVP See *procaine*.

procedure (pro-se′jur) [L. *procedere*, from *pro* forward + *cedere* move] a series of steps by which a desired result is accomplished.

procedure, Claggett's

The remainder of the left lung was found to be "pretty much destroyed by infection" and was removed. Later, the customary **Claggett's procedure** (a process of sterilizing against infection the space created by the removal of the lung), used whenever a lung is removed, was performed. Fitzgerald v. Manning, 679 F.2d 341, 346 (4th Cir. 1982).

procedure, Juri-flap

Because the strips had failed under optimal circumstances, Dr. Peters recommended a **Juri-flap procedure** which involved rotating a flap of hair-bearing scalp on the head with one end still attached to the head. The rotated flaps in the **Juri-flap procedure** carry their own blood supply with them when rotated; the strips of hair-bearing scalp do not depend upon the surrounding scalp for blood supply as was the case with the unsuccessful procedure. Dixon v. Peters, 306 S.E.2d 477, 479 (Ct.App.N.C.1983).

procedure, quickstep

The "Quickstep Procedure" is an emergency procedure adopted by the medical staff of Rapides General Hospital. It is designed to notify certain personnel that an emergency has occurred and to secure the presence of these personnel, together with certain emergency equipment, at the scene of the emergency.

The written policy of the hospital requires that a **Quickstep** shall be instituted when the patient sustains an actual cardiac arrest, respiratory arrest or displays dilated or contracted pupils. The **Quickstep procedure** may also be instituted if in the judgment of the nurse, the procedure needs to be called. Battles v. Aderhold, 430 So.2d 307, 313 (Ct.App.La.1983).

process (pros′es; pro′ses) [L. *processus*] a series of operations, events, or steps leading to the achievement of a specific result; used also as a verb to designate subjection to such a series designed to produce desired changes in the original material, or achieve other result. See also *processus*.

Plaintiff contends that Claim 41 is really a "**process**" claim, according to the following special definition of the term in 35 U.S.C. § 100(b):

The term "**process**" means process, art or method, and includes a new use of a known **process**, machine, manufacture, composition of matter, or material. Clinical Products Ltd. v. Brenner, 255 F.Supp. 131-2 (D.D.C.1966).

process, mastoid See *processus mastoideus ossis temporalis*.

process, transverse, of vertebrae, accessory See *processus accessorius vertebrarum lumbalium*.

process, xiphoid the pointed process of cartilage, supported by a core of bone, connected with the lower end of the body of the sternum; called also *processus xiphoideus* and *xiphisternum*.

processus (pro-ses′us), pl. *processus* [L.] a process: a prominence or projection; [NA] a general term for such a mass projecting from a larger structure.

processus accessorius vertebrarum lumbalium [NA], accessory process of lumbar vertebrae: a small nodule that projects backward from the posterior surface of the transverse process of a lumbar vertebra. It is situated lateral to and below the mamillary process and varies in size.

The transverse processes and body are, however, all part of one solid, bony structure with, so far as this record indicates, no separation whatsoever. Nor does the medical testimony indicate what, if any, distinction exists between the effect of a fracture of the transverse process and a fracture occurring elsewhere in the vertebra. In this connection it is noteworthy that the treating physician in his report states "There was a fracture of the spinal processes *of the body* of the vertebrae" (emphasis ours), and that the employer's medical witness agreed that a "**process**" meant anything that protrudes "from the remainder of the body." C.R. Winn Drilling Co. v. Industrial Com'n, 203 N.E.2d 904, 906 (Ill.1965).

processus coracoideus scapulae [NA], coracoid process of scapula: a strong curved process that arises from the upper part of the neck of the scapula and overhangs the shoulder joint.

... and a complete disruption of the "coracoclavicular ligament". In laymen's terms, the residual condition could be described as a chronic or permanent shoulder separation. Eggleston v. Industrial Com'n, 539 P.2d 918 (Ct.App.Ariz.1975).

processus lenticularis incudis [NA], lenticular process of incus: a small process on the medial side of the tip of the long limb of the incus, which articulates with the head of the stapes.

processus mastoideus ossis temporalis [NA], mastoid process of temporal bone: a conical process projecting forward and downward from the external surface of the petrous part of the temporal bone just posterior to the external acoustic meatus.

The hospital records, which bear his name as resident, indicate that plaintiff was involved in an accident, had trauma or injury to the right front side of the neck from the **mastoidal process** (behind the ear) to the clavicle (below the shoulder). McSwain

v. Chicago Trans. Authority, 362 N.E.2d 1264, 1266 (App.Ct. III.1977).

processus xiphoideus [NA], xiphoid process: the pointed process of cartilage, supported by a core of bone, connected with the lower end of the body of the sternum.

... an incision from the breast bone (**xiphoid**) to a point below the navel (pubic bone). Koehler v. Burlington Northern, Inc., 573 S.W.2d 938, 946 (Mo.Ct.App.1978).

prochlorperazine (pro"klŏr-per'ah-zēn) [USP] chemical name: 2-chloro-10-[3-(4-methyl-1-piperazinyl) propyl]-10H-phenothiazine. A phenothiazine derivative, $C_{20}H_{24}ClN_3S$, occurring as a clear, pale yellow, viscous liquid; used chiefly as an antiemetic, administered rectally. Called also *prochlorpemazine*.

prochlorperazine maleate [USP], the maleate salt of prochlorperazine, occurring as a white or pale yellow, crystalline powder; used as an antiemetic and tranquilizer, administered orally.

After the emetic had served its purpose, Miss Webb was given an injection of **Compazine**, an anti-emetic, for the purpose of controlling the nausea which had been induced by the Ipecac. Webb v. U.S., 446 F.2d 760–1 (5th Cir. 1971).

procidentia (pro"si-den'she-ah) [L.] a prolapse, or falling down, especially prolapse of the uterus to such a degree that the cervix protrudes from the vaginal outlet. See also *prolapse*.

proctitis (prok-ti'tis) [*proct-* + *-itis*] inflammation of the rectum.

Dr. Charles H. Peete, Jr., as a result of his examination, found principally **proctitis** and periproctitis, a type of inflammation involving the large and small bowel, with swelling and tenderness. This was the result of infection in and around the lower bowel, with swelling, a lot of scar tissue and inflammation. Morgan v. Schlanger, 374 F.2d 235, 237–238 (4th Cir. 1967).

proctosigmoidectomy (prok"to-sig"moi-dek'to-me) [*procto-* + *sigmoid* + Gr. *ektomē* excision] excision of the anus, rectum, and sigmoid flexure.

proctosigmoidectomy, Babcock-Bacon

Purcell performed a "cancer operation" called a "**Babcock-Bacon proctosigmoidectomy**." This procedure was first described by and is named after Drs. Babcock and Bacon and is also called a "**pull-through**" operation.

In doing the "**pull-through**" Purcell first opened the abdomen and removed a piece of the bowel. The uppermost portion of what was removed was three inches above the point of the lesion. Purcell then took the end of the remaining bowel (called the proximal end) and "pulled it through" the peritoneal reflection into the rectum, where he attached it at the anus. All of the bowel and rectum below the proximal end of the resection were thus discarded....

The surgeons were relatively unanimous in the opinion that a "**pull-through**" was an operation designed only for disease located below the peritoneal reflection and that where, as in Zimbelman's case, the problem is located above the peritoneal reflection, even if low-down, there is no indication for doing

a "**pull-through**." [Footnote omitted.] Purcell v. Zimbelman, 500 P.2d 335, 339–40 (Ct.App.Ariz.1972).

prodromal (pro-dro'mal) premonitory; indicating the onset of a disease or morbid state.

And that four days later she began to manifest, that is four days after being informed of the contents of this letter in the newspaper—four days after that, she began to develop her **prodromal** symptoms of acute myocardial infarction.

THE REFEREE: Excuse me. Define for the Referee "**prodromal**." I never heard of the term....

... In a great majority of the patients with a myocardial infarction, there is the stage, the **prodromal** stage—prodrom means the symptomatology that just proceeds [sic] the actual event....

Q. What were they in this case, Doctor?

A. Her pains. Her pains were the clinical manifestation of the **prodromal** stage of her myocardial infarction....

"... To be more specific, I would say that the **prodromal** state of her myocardial infarction was connected causally to the emotional disturbance evoked by the information in that letter." Bowes v. Inter-Community Action, Inc., 411 A.2d 1279, 1281 (Cmwlth.Ct.Pa.1980).

product (prod'ukt) something produced.

product, drug

A drug product is a particular drug made by a particular manufacturer. Thus Diabinese and Insulase are different **drug products**, even though their active ingredients are the same. Premo Pharmaceutical Laboratories, Inc. v. U.S., 475 F.Supp. 52–54 (S.D.N.Y.1979), reversed and remanded with directions to dismiss 629 F.2d 795 (2d Cir. 1980).

progestational (pro"jes-ta'shun-al) denoting a class of pharmaceutical preparations that have effects similar to those of progesterone; used in such disorders as dysfunctional uterine bleeding and recurrent abortion. See also under *agent*.

progesterone (pro-jes'tĕ-ron) chemical name: pregn-4-ene-3,20-dione. The principal progestational hormone of the body, $C_{21}H_{30}O_2$, liberated by the corpus luteum, adrenal cortex, and placenta, whose function it is to prepare the uterus for the reception and development of the fertilized ovum by transformation of the endometrium from the proliferative to the secretory stage. Also [USP], the same principle isolated from pregnant sows or prepared synthetically, occurring as a white or creamy white, crystalline powder, and containing, calculated on the dry basis, between 98 and 102 per cent of progesterone; used, usually in the form of synthetic derivatives, as a progestin in the treatment of functional uterine bleeding, abnormalities of the menstrual cycle, and threatened abortion, administered orally and intramuscularly. Called also *luteohormone* and *progestational hormone*. Cited in Carmichael v. Reitz, 95 Cal.Rptr. 381, 388 (Ct.App.Cal.1971).

progestin (pro-jes'tin) the name originally given (Corner and Allen, 1930) to the crude hormone of the corpora lutea. It has since been isolated in pure form and is now known as *progesterone*. The name progestin is used for certain synthetic or natural progestational agents. See *progestational agents*, under *agent*.

progestogen (pro-jes'to-jen) a term applied to any substance possessing progestational activity.

prognathism (prog'nah-thizm) the condition of being prognathous; marked protrusion of the jaw.

Miss Carter was referred by her regular dentist, a Dr. Bailey, to Dr. Phillips because of a pronounced underbite: her lower jaw protruded and she had difficulty in chewing, which caused food digestion problems. Apparently, there were also cosmetic considerations in the desire to correct the protruding jaw or what is described in medical terms as a "mandibular **prognathism**." Carter v. Phillips, 365 So.2d 48 (Ct.App.La.1978).

prognathous (prog'nah-thus, prog-na'thus) [*pro-* + Gr. *gnathos* jaw] having projecting jaws, having a gnathic index above 103, the teeth being in mesioclusion.

prognosis (prog-no'sis) [Gr. *prognōsis* foreknowledge] a forecast as to the probable outcome of an attack of disease; the prospect as to recovery from a disease as indicated by the nature and symptoms of the case.

prognosis, dim

Dim **prognosis** is interpreted to mean no successful operation can take place that will return the patient to a cognitive sapient life. The operation in this case is projected to be successful. Dim **prognosis** is not interpreted to mean a successful operation with possible lifetime confinement to a wheelchair or, alternatively, dependence upon artificial legs and prosthetic devices in remaining years that will be spent at a nursing home. If the latter interpretation was considered, then certainly, in Quackenbush's eyes, there is a dim **prognosis**. Matter of Quackenbush, 383 A.2d 785, 789 (Morris Ct.Ct.Prob.Div. 1978).

progrometer

. . . complained of numbness in his hands. Dr. Howard advised him to try light work, but that he was not capable of doing heavy strenuous activities. Dr. Howard described Shatoska's condition as indicating **progrometer** warnings (possible future problems). Shatoska v. Intern. Grain Transfer, Inc., 430 So.2d 1255, 1258 (Ct.App.La.1983).

prolapse (pro-laps') [L. *prolapsus; pro* before + *labi* to fall] the falling down, or sinking, of a part or viscus; procidentia. See also *presentation* (Hernandez case).

The baby's death certificate listed the cause of death as the **prolapsed** umbilical cord with amnionitis as a possible contributing condition. Lindsey v. The Clinic for Women, 253 S.E.2d 304, 306 (Ct.App.N.C.1979).

And he acknowledged the possibility that muscular movement of the uncovered eye, application of compresses, or the suturing of the laceration near the eye in the emergency room could have exerted sufficient pressure to cause the **prolapse**. . . .

Furthermore, the jury could have inferred from the testimony of all three ophthalmologists and in particular from that of Dr. Gaynin that the cause of the **prolapsed** retina was the pressure from compresses, muscle movements or suturing the wound near the eye, coupled with the failure promptly to treat the eye surgically. Bevevino v. Saydjari, 574 F.2d 676, 682–3 (2d Cir. 1978).

prolapse of uterus downward displacement of the uterus so that the cervix is within the vaginal orifice (*first-degree p.*), the cervix is outside the orifice (*second-degree p.*), or the entire uterus is outside the orifice (*third-degree p.*).

Dr. Loyacano, who testified as an expert in the field of obstetrics and gynecology as well as plaintiff's gynecologist, stated that during the course of the operation he observed that:

. . . the uterus was deeply recessed in the cul-de-sac and a little bit larger than usual and a little softer or mushier. The uterus a little bit on the abnormal size and being recessed means that it was deeply placed down, way down in the pelvic tunnel. And this was giving the patient the feeling of **prolapse**, that is, that feeling as if her bottom was going to fall out. Baker v. Beebe, 367 So.2d 102, 105 (Ct.App.La. 1979).

Prolixin (pro-lik'sin) trademark for preparations of fluphenazine hydrochloride. See also *fluphenazine hydrochloride*; and *psychotic* (Guillory case).

prolongevity

. . . considerable controversy has developed from the ability of modern medical science, by various sophisticated devices, to keep life in existence or "vital functions [continuing] long after a patient's awareness has departed." William D. Poe, "Do We Need Restraint in Medicine?" The Christian Century, September 19, 1973, at 914.

Although we are unaware of any generic term for the particular subject, such as euthanasia in an allied area of discussion, "**prolongevity**" might well be used. Continental Ill. Nat. B. & T. Co. of Chicago v. U.S., 504 F.2d 586, 592 (7th Cir. 1974).

promazine hydrochloride (pro'mah-zēn) [USP] chemical name: *N,N*-dimethyl-10*H*-phenothiazine-10-propanamine mono-hydrochloride. A phenothiazine derivative, $C_{17}H_{20}N_2S \cdot HCl$, occurring as a white to slightly yellow, crystalline powder; used as an antipsychotic agent, as an antiemetic, and as an analegesic- and anesthetic-potentiating agent, administered orally, intramuscularly, and intravenously.

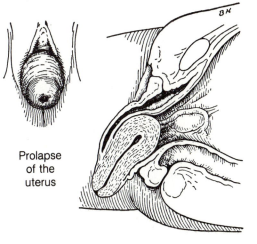

Prolapse
of the
uterus

The testimony shows that the purpose of the intravenous feeding was to correct plaintiff's dehydrated condition and the **Sparine** was added to the intravenous solution to stop the vomiting. . . .

. . . The manufacturer's instructions that came with the **Sparine** cautioned: "**Sparine** (Promazine Hydrochloride, Wyeth) when used intravenously should be used in a concentration no greater than 25 m.g. per c.c. The injection should be given slowly. Suitable dilution of the more concentrated solution, 50 m.g. per c.c., with an equivalent volume of physiological saline is advised if used intravenously. . . . care should be exercised during intravenous administration not to allow perivascular extravasation since under such circumstances chemical irritation may be severe. The intravenous administration . . . in a concentration of 50 m.g. per c.c. has resulted in localized thrombophlebitis . . . in an extremely small number of cases. . . . That injection be made only into vessels previously undamaged by multiple injections or trauma." . . .

. . . He stated that if **Sparine** was injected directly into the tubing during an intravenous feeding it could cause a reaction and might cause a thrombosis or breakdown of the blood vessel wall, and fluid in the vein would leak into surrounding tissue. He explained that this breakdown would not happen immediately, that it took time for the substance to corrode the inside wall of the blood vessel, and that the length of time depended on the concentration and different solutions used, the blood vessel, and the individual anatomy of the person involved. Ohligschlager v. Proctor Community Hospital, 303 N.E.2d 392, 395 (Ill.1973).

promethazine hydrochloride (pro-meth'ah-zēn) [USP] chemical name: N,N,α-trimethyl-10H-phenothiazine-10-ethanamine. A phenothiazine derivative, $C_{17}H_{20}N_2S \cdot HCl$, occurring as a white to faint yellow, crystalline powder, having marked antihistaminic activity as well as sedative and antiemetic actions; used to provide bedtime, surgical, and obstetrical sedation, to potentiate the action of central depressants, and to manage nausea and vomiting associated with surgery, pregnancy, and motion sickness, administered orally, intramuscularly, and intravenously.

One instruction was to inject plaintiff with 50 milligrams of **Phenergan**, commonly used as a mild tranquilizer to relieve anxiety and dispel nausea. **Phenergan** also contains a caustic agent known as Phenol. Frantz v. San Luis Medical Clinic, 146 Cal.Rptr. 146, 149 (Ct.App.Cal.1978).

Phenergan is an obstetrical sedative. Lhotka v. Larson, 238 N.W.2d 870, 872 (Minn.1976).

pronation (pro-na'shun) [L. *pronatio*] the act of assuming the prone position, or the state of being prone. Applied to the hand, the act of turning the palm backward (posteriorly) or downward, performed by medial rotation of the forearm. Applied to the foot, a combination of eversion and abduction movements taking place in the tarsal and metatarsal joints and resulting in lowering of the medial margin of the foot, hence of the longitudinal arch. Cf. *supination*.

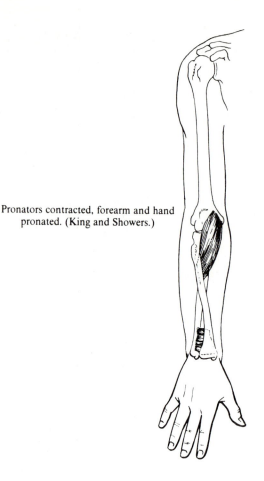

Pronators contracted, forearm and hand pronated. (King and Showers.)

Pronation

. . . **pronation** [of the left hand] to one sixth of normal flexion. . . . Zipp v. Gasen's Drug Stores, Inc., 449 S.W.2d 612, 622 (Mo.1970).

. . . with the fingers flexed, **pronated** and deformed in terms of their relationship to each other. Talcott v. Holl, 224 So.2d 420, 423 (Dist.Ct.App.Fla.1969).

propane (pro'pān) a hydrocarbon of the methane series, $CH_3 \cdot CH_2 \cdot CH_3$, which is a constituent of natural gas and crude petroleum, and occurs as a colorless flammable gas with a characteristic odor.

Propane gas in its natural state is odorless, colorless, volatile, inflammable, and when mixed with air it is explosive. It is also heavier than air, so it has a tendency to collect in low places like the Smiths' storm cellar. Jones v. Hittle Service, Inc., 549 P.2d 1383, 1388 (Kan.1976).

Three carbon atoms may join together with eight hydrogen atoms to form the hydrocarbon propane. **Propane** is formulated as $CH_3-CH_2-CH_3$. . . . Ziegler v. Phillips Petroleum Co., 483 F.2d 858, 862 (5th Cir. 1973).

propantheline bromide (pro-pan'thĕ-lēn) [USP] chemical name: N-methyl-N-(1-methylethyl)-N-[2-[(9H-xanthen-9-ylcarbonyl)oxy]ethyl]-2-propanaminium bromide. An anticholinergic, $C_{23}H_{30}BrNO_3$, occurring as white or nearly white crystals, which inhibits gastrointestinal hypermotility and hyperacidity; used especially as adjunctive therapy in the treatment of peptic ulcer, administered orally, intravenously, and intramuscularly.

Probanthine serves the purpose of reducing pancreatic secretions. Dr. Dyer testified that it is also possible to surgically remove part or all of the pancreas, but that he considered removal as a radical procedure. Bellaire General Hospital, Inc. v. Campbell, 510 S.W.2d 94–5 (Ct.Civ.App.Tex.1974).

propellant

(e) ''Propellent'' means a liquefied or compressed gas in a container, where a purpose of the liquefied or compressed gas is to expel material from the container. The material to be expelled may be the propellant itself and/or a material different from the propellent. 16 C.F.R. Sect. 1401.3(e) (1982).

prophylaxis (pro"fi-lak'sis) [Gr. *prophylassein* to keep guard before] the prevention of disease; preventive treatment.

prophylaxis, chemotherapeutical See *chemoprophylaxis.*

An iliac dissection and perfusion is a chemotherapeutical prophylaxis. The patient's limb is isolated from the rest of the body; circulation is provided by use of a heart-lung apparatus; catheters are inserted into the major artery and vein going into the extremity, an incision having been made in the groin; a tourniquet is placed over the catheters to prevent the drug which will be introduced through the catheters from entering the rest of the body; and the leg is completely wrapped in order to raise its temperature significantly during the operation. At the conclusion of the treatment the drug is completely washed out of the leg, circulation is restored to the rest of the body and the leg is undraped. Sherrill v. McBride, 603 S.W.2d 365–6 (Ct.Civ.App.Tex.1980).

prophylaxis, dental the use of appropriate procedures and/or techniques to prevent dental and oral disease and malformations.

Mrs. Prescott testified that (1) as a licensed dental hygienist, she could recognize the performance of a prophylaxis procedure and that she (2) witnessed the dentists instruct their unlicensed assistants to perform prophylaxis, (3) saw the assistants use an ultrasonic cleaner, scale mouths with scaling instruments, and take a polishing cup and polish teeth....

... Mrs. Prescott testified as follows:
A. Okay. I noticed that two of their dental assistants were going into the waiting room, taking patients back to another room, proceeding to take X rays....
They then proceeded to take the ultrasonic cleaner, the Cavitron in this case, go through the entire mouth, after which they would take scaling instruments, go through the entire mouth and complete with a polishing.
Q. Now, on approximately 60 occasions when you testified you observed these three people doing prophys, how did you know that they were doing prophys as opposed to doing some other procedure?
A. Okay. Well, they would begin by using the ultrasonic cleaner. And, to my knowledge, that is not used for much more than removing calculus and stain and plaque. I have never heard of it being used to polish amalgams. Then they would take their scaling instruments and proceed to scale

around the entire mouth. And then lastly they would take the polishing cup and polish the teeth. Oppenheim v. Com., Dep't of State, etc., 459 A.2d 1308, 1312 (Commonwealth Ct.Pa.1983).

prophys See *prophylaxis, dental.*

propoxyphene (pro-pok'se-fēn) chemical name: (*S*)-α-[2-(dimethylamino)-1-methylethyl]-α-phenylbenzeneethanol propanoate. An analgesic, $C_{22}H_{29}NO_2$, structurally related to methadone. Called also *dextropropoxyphene.* See also *levopropoxyphene napsylate.*

propoxyphene hydrochloride [USP], the hydrochloride salt of propoxyphene, $C_{22}H_{29}NO_2 \cdot HCl$, occurring as a white, crystalline powder; used as an analgesic to provide relief in mild to moderate pain, administered orally.

He testified that Darvon N is a drug that is chemically related to some of the pain relieving opiates, but is not addictive. He also testified that it has little effect on thinking and emotion. Texas Employers' Ins. Ass'n v. Saunders, 516 S.W.2d 242–3 (Ct.Civ.App.Tex.1974), reversed and remanded 526 S.W.2d 515 (Tex.1975).

The Pohland analgesic propoxyphene hydrochloride satisfied a long-felt need for a synthetic analgesic having the pain-relieving properties of morphine but without addiction liability. That search began in the late 1920's and was accelerated in later years by two events. The first of those events was the scarcity of morphine during the second World War....

Lilly submitted Pohland's propoxyphene for testing at the University of Michigan and later at Lexington. The compound proved to be the first synthetic analgesic of the morphine class (i.e., centrally acting) having negligible hazard of addiction. Lilly introduced Darvon commercially in 1957, and since then Darvon has remained unique as the only such analgesic commercially available.

That Pohland's compound, propoxyphene hydrochloride, satisfied a long-felt need for such a product is shown by the dramatic commercial success it has achieved. After it was commercially introduced in 1957, sales increased substantially each year to a current annual rate of sales being in the order of $65,000,000. Since the introduction of the product on the market, total wholesale sales have aggregated in excess of $450,000,000. Eli Lilly and Co., Inc., v. Generix Drug Sales, Inc., 324 F.Supp. 715, 717–18 (S.D.Fla.1971).

propranolol (pro-pran'o-lōl) chemical name: 1-[(1-methylethyl)amino]-3-(1-naphthalenyloxy)-2-propanol. A beta-adrenergic blocking agent, $C_{16}H_{21}NO_2$, which decreases cardiac rate and output, reduces blood pressure, and is effective in the prophylaxis of migraine.

propranolol hydrochloride, [USP], the hydrochloride salt of propranolol, $C_{16}H_{21}NO_2 \cdot HCl$, occurring as a white to off-white, crystalline powder. It is used as an antiarrhythmic, and also as an antihypertensive, in the management of hypertrophic aortic stenosis, and in conjunction with an alpha-adrenergic blocking agent in the symptomatic treatment of inoperable pheochromocytoma. It is also effective in the prophylaxis of migraine. Administered orally or intravenously.

Inderal is used primarily to slow the heart rate and correct heart irregularities such as atrial fibrillation. It may be described as a "pace-maker" type of medication. Lea v. Family Physicians, P.A., 517 F.2d 797–8 (5th Cir. 1975).

proptosis (prop-to'sis) [Gr. *proptōsis* a fall forward] a forward displacement or bulging, especially of the eye; see *exophthalmos*.

There was no swelling of the eyeball itself, no **proptosis (bulging)** of the eyeball, no impairment of eye movement or double vision. Weiby v. Wente, 264 N.W.2d 624, 626 (Minn.1978).

By this time one of plaintiff's eyes was beginning to bulge out of its socket, a condition called **proptosis**.

Plaintiff was then taken to the Neurology Department, where he was given the anticoagulant Heparin and massive doses of the antibiotic Ampicillin. The **proptosis** increased, extending to both eyes. Speed v. State, 240 N.W.2d 901, 903 (Iowa 1976).

propylene (prop'ĭ-lēn) chemical name: propene. A gaseous hydrocarbon, $CH_3 \cdot CH:CH_2$, of the olefin series, which has anesthetic properties. See also *ethylene*.

prostaglandin (pros"tah-glan'din) a group of naturally occurring, chemically related, long-chain hydroxy fatty acids that stimulate contractility of the uterine and other smooth muscle and have the ability to lower blood pressure, regulate acid secretion of the stomach, regulate body temperature and platelet aggregation, and to control inflammation and vascular permeability; they also affect the action of certain hormones. First found in semen, prostaglandins have since been found in menstrual fluid and various tissues of many species, and have been synthesized chemically. There are six types, A, B, C, D, E, and F, the degree of saturation of the side chain of each being designated by subscripts 1, 2, and 3. The types of prostaglandin are abbreviated PGE_2, PGF_2, and so on. Prostaglandin E_2 is also known as *dinoprostone;* $PGF_{2\alpha}$ as *dinoprost*. See also *abortion* (Am. College case).

The third method of performing abortions after the first trimester is chemical induction of labor by injection of a **prostaglandins** solution into the amniotic sac. This process is similar to that used in saline abortions, but the risk to the woman is not as great. The fetus is expelled from the uterus sooner after the injection than is the case in saline abortions. Complications from **prostaglandins** include vomiting and diarrhea, but there appears to be no risk to the central nervous system if the **prostaglandins** enter the bloodstream....

According to the description, use of **prostaglandins** is contraindicated in women who have acute pelvic inflammatory disease and in women who are hypersensitive to the drug. The description also indicates that **prostaglandins** should be used with caution in patients with a history of asthma, glaucoma, hypertension, cardiovascular disease, or past history of epilepsy. The instructions as to dosage and administration recommend that the physician inject a small amount of the drug slowly before proceeding to determine possible sensitivity to **prostaglandins**. Finally, the description states that in a group of 229 patients, 14% failed to abort completely. When a **prostaglandins** abortion is incomplete, other measures should be taken to assure complete abortion, and the method contemplated is saline amniocentesis. [Footnote omitted.] Wynn v. Scott, 449 F.Supp. 1302, 1325–6 (N.D.Ill.1978).

prostaglandin $F_{2\alpha}$ tromethamine See *dinoprost tro methamine*.

prostate (pros'tāt) [Gr. *prostates* one who stands before, from *pro* before + *histanai* to stand] a gland in the male which surrounds the neck of the bladder and the urethra. Called also *prostata* [NA]. It consists of a median lobe and two lateral lobes, and is made up partly of glandular matter, the ducts from which empty into the prostatic portion of the urethra, and partly of muscular fibers which encircle the urethra. The prostate contributes to the seminal fluid a secretion containing acid phosphatase, citric acid, and proteolytic enzymes which account for the liquefaction of the coagulated semen.

Dr. Miller, the urologist who testified for the Government, offered a simple explanation: "The **prostate** [when enlarged] produces symptoms ... because it constricts the urethra, so anything else that will constrict the urethra will give the same sort of symptoms." Kurzon v. U.S. Postal Service, 539 F.2d 788, 791 (1st Cir. 1976).

prostatectomy (pros"tah-tek'to-me) [*prostate + ektomē* excision] surgical removal of the prostate or of a part of it.

prostatectomy, retropubic prevesical removal of the prostate through a suprapubic incision but without entering the urinary bladder.

"Q. All right. Doctor, tell me what you tell a patient upon whom you are going to perform a **retropubic prostatectomy**.

"A. I tell him that he will have an incision in his abdomen, that the enlargement of his prostate will be removed without entering his bladder, that he will wear a catheter through his urethra for a period of five to seven days, and that he will have a small rubber drain in his incision....

"... He will have bottles of water irrigating his bladder for the first 24 to 48 hours, but he will be out of bed the day of operation in most instances...." Jeffries v. McCague, 363 A.2d 1167, 1169–70 (Super.Ct.Pa.1976).

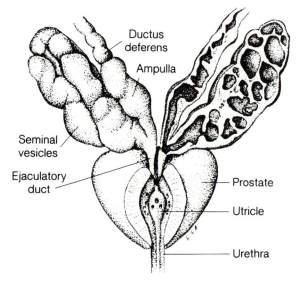

Prostate and seminal vesicles.

prostatectomy, suprapubic transvesical removal of the prostate through an incision above the pubis and through the urinary bladder.

"I explain to him that the **superpubic** [sic] **prostatectomy** is, as far as he is concerned, indistinguishable from the retropubic prostatectomy, except that he will have more pain if the **superpubic** [sic] **prostatectomy** is done, and it will always be done in case he needs vesical drainage in addition to his prostatectomy...." Jeffries v. McCague, 363 A.2d 1167, 1170 (Super.Ct.Pa.1976).

prostatectomy, transurethral See *resection, transurethral.*

prostatitis (pros"tah-ti'tis) inflammation of the prostate.

Guardian claimed that Dr. Robitaille should have disclosed further information concerning his **prostatitis**, specifically, a complete urinary retention. Guardian Life Ins.Co. of America v. Robitaille, 495 F.2d 890, 893 (2d Cir. 1974).

The examination revealed "a very boggy prostate", and a smear showed "many pus cells". The diagnosis was "**prostatitis** chronic", and hospitalization was not recommended. McMullen v. Celebrezze, 335 F.2d 811, 815 (9th Cir. 1964).

Prostex

Prostex is a combination of three amino acids, glycine, alanine and glutamic acid, and is sold as a remedy for the symptoms of benign prostatic hypertrophy (BPH). Kurzon v. U.S. Postal Service, 539 F.2d 788–9 (1st Cir. 1976).

prosthesis (pros-the'sis), pl. *prosthe'ses* [Gr. "a putting to"] an artificial substitute for a missing body part, such as an arm or leg, eye or tooth, used for functional or cosmetic reasons, or both. See also *Fracture* (People v. Smithtown General Hosp. case); *replacement, total hip*; and *stump* (Raines case).

The injury to Boyd's arm in 1972 necessitated the insertion of an elbow **prosthesis**. Dr. McCarthy, appellee's treating physician in 1973, reported that he considered the treatment successful and that appellee would regain functional use of her right arm. Dr. Moreau, to whom appellee was referred by Dr. McCarthy for additional tests in October 1973, felt that the movement was within the normal range and that she had good strength in the arm. Boyd v. Heckler, 704 F.2d 1207, 1210 (11th Cir. 1983).

The aura of apparent success remained until May, 1974, when the plaintiff found himself unable to bear any weight on the replaced joint without pain. A subsequent examination showed "a fracture and resulting separation between the rounded head and the narrowed neck of the metal femoral component of the **prosthetic device**." The condition was corrected by an operation on May 28, 1974. Expert testimony was presented at the trial relative to the defendant's negligence in the manufacture and testing of the device. Hoffman v. Howmedica, Inc., 364 N.E.2d 1215–16 (Sup.Jud.Ct.Mass.1977).

[He was walking with the aid of a cane in the right hand, protecting full weight-bearing through a patellar tendon bearing **prosthesis** having a thigh suspension cuff and SACH foot. The **prosthesis** was at least ¼" over-length. It tended to in-toe and there was excessive wear along the medial border of the sole and heel. A soft liner showed signs of excessive pressure points and had become dry and had a large buckled area in

the posterior wall.] Alexander v. Weinberger, 536 F.2d 779, 782 (8th Cir. 1976).

Other Authorities: Daw Industries, Inc. v. U.S., 561 F.Supp. 433, 435–40 (U.S.Ct.Int. Trade 1983), reversed 714 F.2d 1140 (Fed.Cir. 1983)); Raines v. New York Cent. Railroad Co., 283 N.E.2d 230, 238 (Ill.1972).

prosthesis, Austin-Moore

The operation in which the **Austin-Moore prosthesis** was inserted involved two steps.

First, surgeons removed a portion of the normal anatomical structure of plaintiff's left femoral neck and the entirety of the normal anatomical structure of plaintiff's left femoral head. (N.T. 198)

Second, surgeons then inserted into plaintiff's left femur an **Austin-Moore prosthesis**, consisting of a metal ball on a rod. Such metal ball is designed to replace the natural femoral head and to rotate in the hip socket. (N.T. 199)

The **Austin-Moore prosthesis** was necessitated in plaintiff's case by the extent of the deformity and destruction of plaintiff's left femoral head. (N.T. 259, 260) Rosario v. Amer. Export-Isbrandtsen Lines, Inc., 395 F.Supp. 1192, 1204 (E.D.Pa. 1974), reversed and remanded 531 F.2d 1227 (3d Cir. 1976).

prosthesis, orthotopic cardiac See *heart, artificial.*

prosthesis, Starr-Edwards a caged-ball cardiac valve prosthesis consisting of a retaining cage made of silicone-coated nonferrous metal containing a Silastic ball for occluding the orifice and preventing the reflux of blood. See also *valva aortae.*

Loomis had undergone heart surgery in which his aortic valve was replaced with an artificial valve known as a **Starr-Edwards Model 2320 prosthesis**, and it was this "medical circumstance" which the Federal Air Surgeon found "to be incompatible with flying safety." Loomis v. McLucas, 553 F.2d 634–5 (10th Cir. 1977).

prosthetic (pros-thet'ik) serving as a substitute; pertaining to the use or application of prostheses.

prosthetic articles

The standard dictionary meaning of "prosthetic" comprises, as one would expect of an adjective, more than prostheses themselves: it refers to (in this case) articles that relate to or pertain to prostheses. While obviously we would not want to stretch that relationship too far, it includes at least items intimately or exclusively used, and intended to be used, with prostheses.

It should be evident that such a definition encompasses these sheaths and socks. They are designed for use with prostheses; they are used specifically to overcome certain problems with prostheses; and they have, as far as the record shows, no other use.

. . .

In conclusion, we hold that the sheaths and socks are not prostheses but that they are other prosthetic articles. Further, even if they are describable as wearing apparel they are relatively more specifically described, and are therefore classifiable as, other prosthetic articles. The decision of the Court of International Trade is reversed. Daw Industries, Inc. v. U.S., 714 F.2d 1140, 1142, 1144 (Fed.Cir.1983).

prosthetic device See *prosthesis*; and *implant, subperiosteal.*

prosthetic implant See *implant, subperiosteal.*

prosthetics (pros-thet′iks) the field of knowledge relating to prostheses, their design, use, etc.

The field of **prosthetics**, according to Dr. Lehneis is "the replacement or substitution of parts of the human body". Daw Industries, Inc. v. U.S., 561 F.Supp. 433, 435 (U.S.Ct.Int.Trade 1983), reversed 714 F.2d 1140 (Fed..Cir.1983).

prosthodontics (pros″tho-don′tiks) [*prosthesis* + Gr. *odous* tooth] that branch of dentistry concerned with the construction of artificial appliances designed to restore and maintain oral function by replacing missing teeth and sometimes other oral structures or parts of the face.

The field of **prosthodontics**, which includes the constructing and applying of dentures, clearly affects the health and well-being of persons who have lost their natural teeth. The current delivery system ensures that a licensed dentist is involved to some extent in every step leading to the construction of a denture and places full responsibility with the dentist for every completed denture and its eventual effect upon the patient's health. Missouri Dental Bd. v. Alexander, 628 S.W.2d 646, 649 (Mo.1982).

Prostin F2 Alpha (pros′tin) trademark for preparations of dinoprost tromethamine. See also *dinoprost tromethamine.*

Protamide

In 1944 the FDA approved an NDA for **Protamide**, an injectible colloidal solution f denatured proteolytic enzyme, upon a finding that the drug was safe for human use, and **Protamide** was thereafter marketed for symptomatic treatment of herpes zoster (popularly known as shingles), ophthalmic herpes zoster, tabes dorsalis, and neuritis....

... **Protamide** was evaluated by three such panels, which reported their conclusions in 1969. The Panel on Neurological Drugs found **Protamide** "ineffective" for neuritis and herpes zoster; the Panel on Drugs Used in Dermatology III found the drug "ineffective" for herpes zoster; and the Panel on Drugs Used in Ophthalmology found the drug "possibly effective" for treatment of ophthalmic herpes zoster. Cooper Laboratories, Inc. v. Commissioner, Fed.F.D.A., 501 F.2d 772–5 (D.C. Cir.1974).

proteinuria (pro″te-in-u′re-ah) [*protein* + Gr. *ouron* urine + *-ia*] the presence of an excess of serum proteins in the urine; called also *albuminuria.*

Proteinuria is a kidney malfunction where large amounts of protein are expelled by the body through the urine. Director, Office of Workers' Comp. v. Newport News, 676 F.2d 110, 112 (4th Cir. 1982).

proteolysis (pro″te-ol′ĭ-sis) [*protein* + Gr. *lysis* dissolution] the splitting of proteins by hydrolysis of the peptide bonds with formation of smaller polypeptides; the process may be catalyzed by proteolytic enzymes, by acids, or by bases. See also *enzyme* (Armour case).

proteolytic (pro″te-o-lit′ik) 1. pertaining to, characterized by, or promoting proteolysis. 2. an enzyme that promotes proteolysis.

Proteus (pro′te-us) [Gr. *Prōteus* a many-formed deity] a genus of microorganisms of the tribe Proteeae, family Enterobacteriaceae, order Eubacteriales, made up of gram-negative, generally active, motile, rod-shaped bacteria of limited pathogenicity, usually found in fecal and other putrefying material.

Thus his testimony was that the **proteus** organism was introduced into the blood stream at the time of the manipulation, not that it was brought into the body at that time. He specifically testified that he was not saying that unsterile instruments introduced the **proteus** organisms into Mr. Quick's system. The evidence is unequivocal on this point....

... "Q. Doctor, I think you answered one of Mr. Rossner's questions and said that it was your opinion that probably the **proteus** that was found in the urine cultures and the blood cultures came from the same source. Is that correct? A. That's right.... Q. What was the source, in your opinion? A. Most likely, I would think, a local source in the lower urinary tract, bladder, prostate, urethra, something of that nature." Quick v. Thurston, 290 F.2d 360, 363, 365 (D.C.Cir.1961).

Proteus mirabilis a species which is usually saprophytic and occasionally found as a human pathogen.

Interestingly enough, he said that the second most common clinical situation involving **Proteus mirabilis** involves people who have ulcers on their feet as a result of diabetes and who have had a previous infection where it comes in as a secondary invader. Union Packing Co. of Omaha v. Klauschie, 314 N.W.2d 25, 28 (Neb.1982).

prothrombin time See *time, prothrombin.*

prothrombin time test See *test, prothrombin*; and test, Quick's.

protium (pro′te-um) the mass one isotope of hydrogen, symbol ^{1}H; ordinary, or light, hydrogen. See also *hydrogen*. Cf. *deuterium* and *tritium.*

protocol (pro′to-kol) the original notes made on a necropsy, an experiment, or on a case of disease.

A **protocol** is a plan for the investigation of a new drug which outlines how the drug is to be used, the number of patients, the conditions under which the drug is to be given, the doses, and other relevant data. Ubiotica Corp. v. Food & Drug Administration, 427 F.2d 376, 379 (6th Cir. 1970).

protocol, nursing

According to the doctor, a **nursing protocol** was "a manual for nurses, written by nurses." Washington Hospital Center v. Martin, 454 A.2d 306–7 (D.C.Ct.App.1982.)

To fill that gap the plaintiff sought to introduce the hospital's Nursing Procedure Manual. The court ruled that there had been no showing that any of the standards had been violated and that therefore the proffered manual was irrelevant.

In the transcript the bulky single-spaced manual comprises about 31 pages. Napier v. Northrum, 572 S.W.2d 153, 156 (Ark.1978).

protocol, stress test

During the course of the trial, plaintiffs attempted to bolster the testimony of their expert witness by introducing into evidence an article entitled "Maximal Exercise Testing." The article was written by Dr. Robert A. Bruce, who devised the Bruce-Protocol, which was used as the basis for the stress test taken by plaintiff William Tart. A **stress test protocol** is a set of directions that describes how a treadmill stress test should be conducted. It indicates, for example, the proper speed and incline of the treadmill at various stages of the test. Tart v. McGann, 697 F.2d 75, 77 (2d Cir. 1982).

prototropy (pro-tot′ro-pe) [*proton* + Gr. *tropē* a turning] the more usual type of tautomerism, which is the result of a mobile hydrogen ion. See also *anionotropy*.

pseudarthrosis (soo″dar-thro′sis) [*pseud-* + Gr. *arthrōsis* joint] a pathologic entity characterized by deossification of a weight-bearing long bone, followed by bending and pathologic fracture, with inability to form normal callus leading to existence of the "false joint" that gives the condition its name.

. . . he was again admitted to the hospital for recurrent herniation of the nucleus at L4 and L5 and continuing **pseudoarthrosis** [sic], or deterioration and instability of the lumbar fusion. Southern Bell Tel. & Tel. Co. v. Poole, 388 So.2d 330–1 (Dist. Ct.App.Fla.1980).

He testified that there was a possible **pseudoarthrosis** [sic], or nonfusion, causing the petitioner's pain, and that if this could be demonstrated by exploratory surgery, a refusion could be done and the Kodt hooks removed. However, he cautioned that the existence of a nonfusion was uncertain from the X rays, and that only exploratory surgery would determine it. Martin Young Enterprises, Inc. v. Industrial Com'n, 281 N.E.2d 305, 307 (Ill.1972).

There is no conflict in the medical testimony in this case to the effect that the claimant is disabled from doing any kind of physical work as a result of the failure of the spinal fusion, i.e., **pseudoarthrosis** [sic] of the lumbosacral spine, has disabled the claimant. There is conflict as to causation. . . .

. . . In his testimony, the causal relationship between the over-exertion and the injuries which the Claimant now has, is definitely established." The doctor stated unequivocally when asked for his opinion, as follows: "Having begun at the time, **pseudoarthrosis** [sic] is not the result of the incident, but the result of something that occurred as a result of the incident. The pain problem is the **pseudoarthrosis** [sic] which is the result of an unsuccessful attempted spinal fusion which was performed because of the incident in August of 1960." Barber v. Fleming-Raugh, Inc., 222 A.2d 423, 426–7 (Super.Ct.Pa. 1966).

Other Authorities: Spaulding v. Califano, 427 F.Supp. 982, 984 (W.D.Mo.1977).

pseudocyst (soo′do-sist) [*pseudo-* + *cyst*] an abnormal or dilated space resembling a cyst but not lined by epithelium as is a true cyst.

With the approval of Mrs. Lane, defendant Wersich performed exploratory kidney surgery which disclosed no tumor or malignancy. Some months later a **pseudocyst** was discovered at the operative site and a doctor, other than the defendants, removed the right kidney. Lane v. Wallace, 579 F.2d 1200, 1201–2 (10th Cir. 1978).

pseudocyst, pancreatic an encapsulated collection of pancreatic juice and celluar debris that has escaped from the pancreas, the wall being formed by inflammatory fibrosis of serosal surfaces of adjacent organs; pseudocysts most commonly occur in the lesser sac of the peritoneum.

. . . she underwent surgery for a **pancreatic pseudocyst**. Cannon v. Harris, 651 F.2d 513, 515 (7th Cir. 1981).

pseudofolliculitis (soo″do-fo-lik″u-li′tis) a chronic disorder occurring chiefly in the beard of Negroes, most often in the submandibular region of the neck, the characteristic lesions of which are erythematous papules, less commonly pustules, containing buried hairs whose tips can easily be freed up; in contrast to sycosis barbae (q.v.), which is most frequently seen in bearded men, this disorder affects exclusively those who shave.

pseudofolliculitis barbae See *sycosis vulgaris*.

pseudogout (soo′do-gowt) an apparently hereditary, arthritic condition marked by attacks of goutlike symptoms, usually affecting a single joint (particularly the knee) and associated with chondrocalcinosis. See also *chondrocalcinosis*.

Respondent relies on statements by Dr. Taylor and Dr. Griffin that Mr. Shepard's "main problem" was degenerative arthritis of the knees and **pseudogout** caused by chondrocalcinosis. Shepard v. Midland Foods, Inc., 666 P.2d 758, 762 (Mont. 1983).

pseudohermaphroditism (soo″do-her-maf′ro-dīt-izm″) a condition in which the gonads are of one sex but one or more contradictions exist in the morphologic criteria of sex. See also *intersexuality*; and *hermaphroditism*.

pseudologia (soo″do-lo′je-ah) [*pseudo-* + Gr. *logos* word + *-ia*] the writing of anonymous letters to people of prominence, to one's self, etc.

pseudologia fantastica a tendency to tell extravagant and fantastic falsehoods centered about one's self.

"Confabulation is to be differentiated from **pseudologia fantastica** (q.v.), which occurs mainly in the 'psychopathic' group and in other conditions in which acting-out is prominent. In **pseudologia fantastica**, the phantasy is believed only momentarily and will quickly be dropped if the patient is confronted with contradictory evidence. The confabulator, in contrast, will stick steadfastly to his story." Hinsie and Campbell, Psychiatric Dictionary (3d ed. 1960), Oxford University Press, p. 147. U.S. v. Currens, 290 F.2d 751, 754 (3d Cir. 1961).

Pseudomonas (soo″do-mo′nas) a genus of microorganisms of the family Pseudomonadaceae, suborder Pseudomonadineae, order Pseudomonadales, occurring usually as monotrichous, lophotrichous, or nonmotile straight rods. Some of the 149 described species are pathogenic for plants or for warm- and cold-blooded vertebrates.

The defendant also testified that **pseudomonas** is always present in plaintiff's skin and is an organism that is easily killed off by a healthy blood supply. . . .

. . . He asserts that failure to treat the **pseudomonas** after the first culture was negligence, but failure to treat it after several examinations constituted wilful and wanton conduct. We disagree. Wilson v. Clark, 417 N.E.2d 1322, 1324–5 (Ill. 1981).

In testifying about the "cause of the causes", Dr. Milam said that the cause of the pneumonia was a germ or bacteria called **pseudomonas**, which he said was a type of pneumonia that has shown up in other patients undergoing heart transplants as well as non-transplant and non-cardiovascular patients. Karp v. Cooley, 493 F.2d 408, 418 (5th Cir. 1974).

pseudopolyp (soo″do-pol′ip) a hypertrophied tab of mucous membrane resembling a polyp, but caused by ulceration surrounding and sometimes undermining a portion of intact mucosa; frequently observed in chronic inflammatory diseases, such as ulcerative colitis.

pseudotumor cerebri a condition caused by cerebral edema, marked by raised intracranial pressure with headache, nausea, vomiting, and papilledema without neurological signs except occasional sixth-nerve palsy. Called also benign *intracranial hypertension* and *meningeal hydrops*.

. . . **pseudotumor cerebri** (a false, specious tumor of the mass of the brain). . . . Cornett v. Califano, 590 F.2d 91–2 (4th Cir. 1978).

He was suffering from severe visual impairment, nausea, and headaches. Dr. Ronald Ignelzi, a neurosurgeon, correctly diagnosed Plaintiff's illness as **pseudotumor cerebri** a swelling of the brain that mimics brain tumors and jeopardizes vital functions. Dr. Ignelzi immediately commenced treatment of Plaintiff with Decadron. Plaintiff's condition improved rapidly under a course of treatment with Decadron, which was administered in decreasing dosages until its discontinuation on January 2, 1971. . . .

The "mainstay" treatment for lowering intracranial pressure due to **pseudotumor cerebri** is the administration of corticosteroids. Deposition of Donald W. Ryan, M.D., at 12, 26. It is to Dr. Ignelzi's credit that such treatment was initiated on the day of Plaintiff's admission to the Denver VA Hospital. Id. at 23. Plaintiff was admitted to the Hospital with sixth nerve palsy, a condition that resulted from intracranial pressure, which caused his loss of vision. If radical and immediate treatment to alleviate this pressure were not taken, permanent loss of vision, loss of consciousness, and sudden death could have occurred. Id. at 22–23. Niblack v. U.S., 438 F.Supp. 383, 385, 387 (D.Colo.1977).

Plaintiff's claim for disability insurance benefits is based primarily upon his diagnosed condition of **pseudotumor cerebri** (benign intracranial hypertension). . . .

. . . He testified that **pseudotumor cerebri** was a condition which involved swelling of the brain due to infiltration by lymphocytes. It was his opinion that such condition generally runs its course and is asymptomatic in six to eight months. Marbury v. Matthews, 433 F.Supp. 1081, 1083, 1085 (W.D.N.Y.1977).

psilocin (si′lo-sin) a hallucinogenic substance closely related to psilocybin. See also *mushroom* (People v. Dunlap case); and *psilocybin*.

The physiological effects of psilocyn were described at trial by Dr. Siegel, who, as noted above, has done research on **psilocyn** [sic] under laboratory conditions. He testified that the substance generally begins to affect the subject within 15 minutes to one-half hour after ingestion. It has been said that the first

half-hour following the ingestion of the companion substance psilocybin is "rather unpleasant and typified by dizziness, nausea and anxiety" and the next half-hour includes "further somatic affects such as sweating and ataxia." (B. Wells, Psychedelic Drugs 53 (1973)). It begins to excite electrical activity in the brain, it can alter breathing patterns somewhat, and it may change the subject's blood pressure. The pupils of the subject frequently become dilated, as may the blood vessels of the skin and neck, producing a flushed appearance. Dr. Siegel has recorded a skin temperature drop of up to 3° (F) in his subjects. These physiological symptoms usually disappear four hours after ingestion, by which time the presence of **psilocyn** in the blood and tissues of the body has dropped to an immeasurable quantity. Dr. Siegel remarked that a dosage of 3 to 4 milligrams of **psilocyn** [sic] could be toxic, while it would probably take 20 or 30 milligrams to constitute a lethal dose.

As a result of his investigations, Dr. Siegel concluded that **psilocyn** [sic] is not a dangerous drug. He stated that **psilocyn** [sic] was not physically addictive because one does not build up a tolerance to it, and because there are no withdrawal symptoms which occur when a **psilocyn** [sic] user ceases to take the substance. Dr. Siegel also contended that, because the **psilocyn** [sic] experience is not as intensely euphoric and short-lived as that produced by heroin or cocaine, it is not likely to produce psychological dependence. . . .

As Dr. Siegel testified, there are several possible adverse psychological reactions to **psilocyn** [sic]. First, an individual may feel a sense of panic with all of the sensory changes which the substance tends to induce. Second, a temporary psychosis may be produced in someone who is not psychologically well balanced. Dr. Siegel stated that he knew of no evidence to suggest that **psilocyn** [sic] led to any long-term mental effects, but it should be noted that Dr. Siegel's research was performed under laboratory conditions on subjects who were selected because they were psychologically stable. Other case studies have indicated that longer lasting psychological complications can be produced. (See Hyde, Glancy, Omerod, Hall and Taylor, "Abuse of Indigenous Psilocybin Mushrooms: A New Fashion and Some Psychiatric Complications," 132 Brit. J. of Psychiatry 602 (1978)). People v. Dunlap, 442 N.E.2d 1379, 1386 (App.Ct.Ill.1982).

psilocybin (si″lo-si′bin) chemical name: 3-[2-(dimethyl amino)-ethyl]indol-4-ol dehydrogen phosphate ester. A hallucinogenic crystalline compound, $C_{13}H_{18(20)}O_3N_2P_2$, possessing indole characteristics, isolated from the mushroom *Psilocybe mexicana* Heim. See also *psilocin*.

psoas See *Table of Musculi.*

psoas major muscle See *musculus psoas major.*

psoriasis (so-ri′ah-sis) [Gr. *psōriasis*] a chronic, hereditary, recurrent, papulosquamous dermatosis, the distinctive lesion of which is a vivid red macule, papule, or plaque covered almost to its edge by silvery lamellated scales. It usually involves the scalp and extensor surfaces of the limbs, especially the elbows, knees, and shins. See also *phenomenon, Koebner's.*

Dr. Mitchell found petitioner to be in severe pain and unable to use his hands and feet; his **psoriasis** was extensive with pustular lesions on the palms and the soles of his feet. App. at 30–3. . . .

... But when I would grip the wheel and be out there on the job for a while, then it would crack open and bleed from the work, from doing the job, from holding the steering wheel; it would actually crack open and my hand would bleed....

Dr. Thomas P. Nigra, M.D., to whom claimant was referred by Dr. Mitchell, said:

When I saw him, he had physically disabling **psoriasis** of his left hand. He is a Metro Bus driver, and there is little question that he uses his hands in his work.

Psoriasis is a capricious disease which waxes and wanes and comes and goes without cause. However, we definitely do know that trauma to an area of skin in a patient who has extensive **psoriasis** will result in a flare of **psoriasis** in the traumatic area. It is my opinion that using his hands in his work the way Mr. Hensley does as a bus driver could result in trauma and therefore flaring of his basic condition.... App. at 154.

... Medical texts on the disease recognize the fact that some kinds of trauma to the skin of a **psoriatic** patient may precipitate or aggravate the condition, see, e.g., 6 P. Cantor, Traumatic Medicine and Surgery for the Attorney 640–41 (1962) ("Chronic pressure caused by gripping tools may precipitate a **psoriatic** eruption of the palms.... The role of trauma in aggravating a pre-existing **psoriasis** has to be accepted.").... Hensley v. Washington Metro. Area Transit Auth., 655 F.2d 264, 266–7, 270, 274 (D.C.Cir.1981).

In 1972 Robbins, who was fifteen years old, developed **psoriasis**, a skin disease, and consulted Dr. R. Fleischmann, a physician at Loring Air Force Base where Robbins' father was stationed. In August 1972, Dr. Fleischmann prescribed the oral drug Prednisone for Robbins' condition. Robbins v. U.S., 624 F.2d 971–2 (10th Cir. 1980).

Norma T. Hadary had suffered from **psoriasis** from about 1964 or 1966. She said that the disease evidenced itself by spots over the trunk or torso, on the thighs and in her scalp, inside her ears, in the corner of the nose, on her elbows. She said her toenails thickened and became deformed and distorted. She said her skin was rough and scaly. Suburban Hospital Ass'n v. Hadary, 322 A.2d 258–9 (Ct.Spec.App.Md.1974).

psoriasis guttata; psoriasis, guttate psoriasis in which the lesions are small (about the size of drops of water) and distinct. This form may begin suddenly after sunburn or an acute infection, such as streptococcal sore throat, and has a better prognosis than other forms.

His psoriasis was what we call **guttate** type of **psoriasis**,[1] drop-like, all over the body. And he had extensive pustular lesions on the palms and soles. [[1] Guttate lesions are lesions having a drop-like appearance. 6 P. Cantor, Traumatic Medicine and Surgery for the Attorney 643 (1962).] Hensley v. Washington Metro. Area Transit Auth., 655 F.2d 264, 275 (D.C.Cir.1981).

psychiatry (si-ki'ah-tre) [*psyche* + Gr. *iatreia* healing] that branch of medicine which deals with the study, treatment, and prevention of mental illness.

Defendants urge that when a psychiatric condition is the basis of a lawsuit, "all aspects of a plaintiff's past life are in issue." Thus, in this case about the prescription of drugs, they claim to be entitled to inquire about the drinking habits of her parents, her childhood feelings, her reactions to the sight of her father nude, her anxieties, her fears, her sexual reactions, her fantasies, and all she revealed about her love affairs in her confes-

sions to her **psychiatrist**. The areas of inquiry would thus be virtually without limitation. The court cannot agree. Gordon v. Roche Lab., Div. of Hoffman-La Roche, 456 N.Y.S.2d 291, 293 (Sup.Ct.N.Y.Cty.1981).

psychical research See *parapsychology* and *psychology* (both Kidd case).

psychodelic See *hallucinogen*.

psychogenic (si"ko-jen'ik) of intrapsychic origin; having an emotional or psychologic origin (in reference to a symptom), as opposed to a physicogenic, or organic, basis.

The plaintiff's injury was also described by Dr. Herlihy as "**psychogenic** musculoskeletal reaction." This disorder occurs when a psychic disturbance within a person causes physical pain. The individual experiences anxiety which translates into physical-muscular tension. An example of this disorder would be a tension headache. As a result of this disorder the plaintiff has pain in his back from the accident despite the fact that he suffers from no apparent physical disability. The plaintiff is unable to sit or stand for long periods of time, has pain going down the back of his leg, and is unable to exercise. The plaintiff also has problems sleeping, has nightmares about the accident, and is unable to do physical labor.... Abex Corp. v. Coleman, 386 So.2d 1160–1 (Ct.Civ.App.Ala.1980).

Q. Doctor, when you say there were findings that you made outside of those that could be classified physical in origin, what do you mean?
A. Well, that they are **psychogenic**. They are not reflecting any physical disease of the nervous system and must be attributed to psychiatric or emotional factors. Poltorak v. Sandy, 345 A.2d 201, 206 (Super.Ct.Pa.1975).

The claimant appeared to be mildly depressed and unhappy with his environment. Although cautious, Dr. Harvie again attributed part of the symptoms to **psychogenic** factors, since the symptoms seemed out of proportion to the objective evidence. Richardson v. Richardson, 333 F.Supp. 890, 893 (W.D.Va. 1971).

psychologist (si-kol'o-jist) a qualified specialist in psychology.

psychology (si-kol'o-je) [*psycho-* + *-logy*] that branch of science which deals with the mind and mental processes, especially in relation to human and animal behavior.

Dr. Pratt testified that there are two principal areas in the field of **psychology**, the conventional, which is largely dedicated to attempting to understand behavior in human nature in terms of physical principles, and the parapsychological, which are those exceptional things which occur which come about by noting that there are exceptions that do not fit into the ordinary conventional physical considerations. In Re Estate of Kidd, 479 P.2d 697, 703 (Ariz.1971).

psychomotor seizure See *epilepsy, psychomotor.*

psychoneurosis (si"ko-nu-ro'sis), pl. *psychoneuroses* [*psycho-* + Gr. *neuron* nerve + *-osis*] an emotional disorder due to unresolved conflicts, anxiety being its chief characteristic. The anxiety may be expressed directly or indirectly, as by conversion, displacement, etc. In contrast to the psychoses, the psychoneuroses do not involve gross distortions of external reality or disorganization of personality. Called also *neurosis*.

This patient has a most severe and disabling **psychoneurosis** with depressive symptoms, anxiety features and will not except (sic) any psychiatric diagnosis or help. She will probably tend to continue to be admitted to the hospital because of various complaints. [Tr. 261]. Palik v. Mathews, 422 F.Supp. 547, 549 (D.Neb.1976).

Dr. George L. Gee, Jr. made another report dated February 11, 1969, in which he stated:

I still adhere to the original diagnosis given of a **psychoneurotic** reaction aggravated in the involutional period and lapsed into invalidism and dependency. His depression is more obvious than two years ago and there is great somatization present.... Ingram v. Richardson, 471 F.2d 1268, 1273 (6th Cir. 1972).

The psychologist found that the claimant was of at least average intelligence, but that he was "timid, anxious, obsessional and overdependent", generally diagnosed as "**Psychoneurotic** reaction in an immature, dependent personality." Richardson v. Richardson, 333 F.Supp. 890, 894 (W.D.Va.1971).

Other Authorities: Leslie v. Richardson, 320 F.Supp. 580–1 (E.D.Tenn.1970); McMullen v. Celebrezze, 335 F.2d 811, 815–16 (9th Cir. 1964).

psychoneurotic See *psychoneurosis*.

psychopath (si'ko-path) a person who has an antisocial (psychopathic) personality (q.v.). See also *antisocial personality*, under *personality*.

The word "**psychopath**" according to some means "a sick mind." Guttmacher & Weihofen, Psychiatry and the Law 86 (1952):

"In the light of present knowledge, most of the individuals called psychopathic personalities should probably be considered as suffering from neurotic character disorders. They are, for the most part, unhappy persons, harassed by tension and anxiety, who are struggling against unconscious conflicts which were created during the very early years of childhood. The nature and even the existence of these conflicts which drive them restlessly on are unknown to them. When the anxiety rises to a certain pitch, they seek relief through some anti-social act. The frequency with which this pattern recurs in the individual is dependent in part upon the intensity of the unconscious conflict, upon the tolerance for anxiety, and upon chance environmental situations which may heighten or decrease it. One of the chief diagnostic criteria of this type of neurotically determined delinquency is the repetitiveness of the pattern. The usual explanation, as for example, that the recidivistic check-writer has just 'got in the habit of writing bad checks' is meaningless." Id., at 88–89. [Dissent.] Boutilier v. Immigration and Naturalization Service, 387 U.S. 118, 126, 87 S.Ct. 1563, 1568, 18 L.Ed.2d 661 (1967).

It is readily apparent that this objection to the inclusion of **psychopaths** among those entitled to raise the defense of insanity assumes a particular definition of psychopathy; viz., that the term psychopathy comprehends a person who is a habitual criminal but whose mind is functioning normally. Perhaps some laymen and, indeed some psychiatrists, do define the term that broadly; and insofar as the term psychopathy does merely indicate a pattern of recurrent criminal behavior we would cer-

tainly agree that it does not describe a disorder which can be considered insanity for purposes of a defense to a criminal action. But, we are aware of the fact that psychopathy, or sociopathy, is a term which means different things to experts in the fields of psychiatry and psychology. Indeed, a confusing welter of literature has grown up about the term causing some authorities to give up its use in dismay, labelling it a "waste basket category." See, e.g., Partridge, C.E., Current Conceptions of Psychopathic Personality, 10 American Journal of Psychiatry, pp. 53–59 (1930).

We have examined much of this literature and have certainly found it no less dismaying than those authorities to which we have just referred. Our study has, however, revealed two very persuasive reasons why this court should not hold that evidence of **psychopathy** is insufficient, as a matter of law, to put sanity or mental illness in issue. First, it is clear that as the majority of experts use the term, a **psychopath** is very distinguishable from one who merely demonstrates recurrent criminal behavior. For example, Dr. Winfred Overholser, Superintendent of Saint Elizabeths Hospital in the District of Columbia, has stated that the Hospital takes the unequivocal position that sociopathy is a mental disease. Dr. Overholser in stating that this is the position of the Hospital uses the words "the Hospital" in the same sense that a judge uses the term "the court" in expressing the judgment of his tribunal. Moreover, the American Psychiatric Association in 1952 when it published its Diagnostic and Statistical Manual, Mental Disorders (Mental Hospital Service), altered its nomenclature, p. 38, removing sociopathic personality disturbance and psychopathic personality disturbance from a non-disease category and placing them in the category of "Mental Disorders". See also note 11, cited to the text, p. 16, in the concurring opinion of Judge Burger in Blocker v. United States, D.C.Cir.1961, 288 F.2d 853....

... Our second reason for not holding that **psychopaths** are "sane" as a matter of law is based on the vagaries of the term itself. In each individual case all the pertinent symptoms of the accused should be put before the court and jury and the accused's criminal responsibility should be developed from the totality of his symptoms. A court of law is not an appropriate forum for a debate as to the meaning of abstract psychiatric classifications. The criminal law is not concerned with such classifications but with the fundamental issue of criminal responsibility. Testimony and argument should relate primarily to the subject of the criminal responsibility of the accused and specialized terminology should be used only where it is helpful in determining whether a particular defendant should be held to the standards of the criminal law.

It is for such reasons that we feel sure that the Court of Appeals for the District of Columbia Circuit has applied the Durham formula to all types of mental illness including psychopathy or sociopathy. Whether a **psychopath** or a psychotic suffers from illness of such a nature that he should not be held to criminal responsibility is a jury question in the District of Columbia. Taylor v. United States, 1955, 95 U.S.App.D.C. 373, 222 F.2d 398, 404; Stewart v. United States, 1954, 94 U.S. App.D.C. 293, 214 F.2d 879, 881. Indeed in the case last cited a charge to the jury that a **psychopath** "is not insane within the meaning of the law" has been held by the Court of Appeals for the District of Columbia Circuit to be reversible error. U.S. v. Currens, 290 F.2d 751, 761–3 (3d Cir. 1961).

psychopath, sexual an individual whose sexual behavior is manifestly antisocial and criminal.

The record contains no allegations that appellant has ever committed a violent sexual offense, and the testifying psychiatrists agreed that because of "the lack of aggressiveness, inferiority, timidity and heterosexual immaturity of the [typical] exhibitionist," such individuals are markedly less likely to commit violent sexual crimes than other types of sexual offenders. . . .

In 1948 Congress enacted the Sexual Psychopath Act [1] under which in 1962 Maurice Millard was committed. The key definitional section of that statute defines a **sexual psychopath** as "a person, not insane, who by a course of repeated misconduct in sexual matters has evidenced such lack of power to control his sexual impulses as to be dangerous to other persons because he is likely to attack or otherwise inflict injury, loss, pain, or other evil on the objects of his desire." 22 D.C. Code § 3503(1). [[1] 62 Stat. 347 (1948), 22 D.C.Code §§ 3501–3511 (1967).] Millard v. Harris, 406 F.2d 964, 978–80 (D.C.Cir.1968).

psychopathy (si-kop'ah-the) [*psycho-* + Gr. *pathos* disease] a disorder of the psyche, whether or not associated with subnormal intelligence. See also *psychopath.*

psychosis (si-ko'sis), pl. *psycho'ses* [*psych-* + *-osis*] 1. a general term for any major mental disorder of organic and/or emotional origin characterized by derangement of the personality and loss of contact with reality, often with delusions, hallucinations, or illusions. Cf. *neurosis.* See also *episode, acute reactive psychotic* (People v. Harrington case).

He stated that this condition was a **psychosis** and defined it as follows:

Well, in a **psychosis**, people, . . . they are not realistic, and they react to things in a bizarre and illogical manner.

He stated that persons with such a **psychosis** are removed from reality and are disoriented in their thinking. . . .

. . . He testified that when he first saw Mr. Brecheen he considered him to be **psychotic** which means that he had lost the capacity for reality testing and did not have the capacity to determine whether what's going on either inside him or around him was real. He considered that at the time of his discharge the **psychotic** aspect of his illness had cleared. An individual may be **psychotic** at times, and at other times may not be. Exxon Corp. v. Brecheen, 519 S.W.2d 170, 178–9 (Ct.Civ. App.Tex.1975), reversed and remanded 526 S.W.2d 519 (Tex.1975).

That "mental illness" is by no means a static concept but rather one of degree of deviation from the "norm" is illustrated by the very ambiguity in the definition which embraces "a **psychosis** or other disease which substantially impairs mental health." [57] [[57] Even what may viscerally appear to be precise to the layman—the term "**psychosis**"—is deceptively broad: Psychotic Disorders. These disorders are characterized by a varying degree of personality disintegration and failure to test and evaluate correctly external reality in various spheres. In addition, individuals with such disorders fail in their ability to relate themselves effectively to other people or to their own work. American Psychiatric Association, Diagnostic and Statistical Manual—Mental Disorders 24 (13th ed. 1960).] In Re Ballay, 482 F.2d 648, 665 (D.C.Cir.1973).

"It is clear that we are dealing with a fairly serious disorder. There are grave disturbances in the patient's affective life as well as in foresight and the control and organization of behavior. Cleckley considers the condition serious enough to be classed as a **psychosis**. Although the patient outwardly presents a 'convincing mask of sanity' and a 'mimicry of human life,' he has lost contact with the deeper emotional accompaniments of experience and with its purposiveness. To this extent he may be said to have an incomplete contact with reality, and it is certainly very hard to approach him and influence him therapeutically."

Professor Robert W. White's, The Abnormal Personality (Ronald Press 1948) at p. 401. U.S. v. Currens, 290 F.2d 751, 762 (3d Cir. 1961).

psychosis, manic-depressive a major affective disorder characterized by severe mood swings and a tendency to remission and recurrence. It is seen in a *manic type,* consisting of manic episodes characterized by excessive elation, irritability, talkativeness, flight of ideas, and psychomotor overactivity; in a *depressed* or *unipolar type,* consisting of depressive episodes characterized by severely depressed mood and by mental and motor retardation that may progress to stupor; and in a *circular* or *bipolar type,* consisting of at least one depressive episode and a manic episode. Called also *manic-depressive illness* or *reaction.* See also *manic-depressive.*

Dr. Salvatore Martinez, a psychiatrist with training in neurology testified he had diagnosed her as suffering from a **manic-depressive** condition; a mental illness which, in his opinion, was unrelated to the collision. He testified that during the manic stage of this condition, the brain overproduces certain chemicals which stimulate it and can result in a convulsion, especially if a person has a propensity towards seizures. Lindsay v. Appleby, 414 N.E.2d 885, 887 (App.Ct.Ill.1980).

Furthermore, **manic depression** actually is a **psychosis**. See: Hinsie and Campbell, Psychiatric Dictionary, 3d ed. (1960). Moreover, Dr. van der Meer himself testified that electroshock would considerably shorten the hospitalization of a **manic-depressive** and, as previously noted, Dr. Hadden also testified that electroshock treatment is standard treatment for a "**manic-depressive** state, agitated." Collins v. Hand, 246 A.2d 398, 402 (Pa.1968).

psychosomatic (si"ko-so-mat'ik) [*psycho-* + Gr. *sōma* body] pertaining to the mind-body relationship; having bodily symptoms of psychic, emotional, or mental origin; called also *psychophysiologic.* See also under *disorder.*

Psychosomatic medicine deals with the treatment of physiological, psychological, and emotional functions of a patient. Leona Von Kalb v. Com., 37 TCM 1511, 1512 [CCH Dec. 35,406(M)] (1978).

One of the reasons Dr. Moore gave for his opinion was that plaintiff was a chronic **psychosomatic** complainer, so that it was difficult to tell whether her complaints were real or imaginary and that one could not rely upon her complaints. This was confirmed by the other doctors who had treated plaintiff. Dr. Wayman characterized her as a "chronic complainer" and noted that "The more complaints, the less obvious a condition is," Dr. Morgan, plaintiff's own witness, agreed that an accurate diagnosis would be rendered more difficult by many diverse complaints and indicated that the period of time the plaintiff had under his care had been a "rather trying experience" because of her difficult attitudes. He noted that "I can purely by memory recall that there were many complaints with no organic reason." Clark v. U.S., 402 F.2d 950, 954 (4th Cir. 1968).

psychosurgery (si"ko-ser'jer-e) brain surgery performed for the relief of mental and psychic symptoms.

Psychosurgery, as defined in [Welfare & Insts. Code] section 5325(g), as amended, includes those operations "referred to as lobotomy, psychiatric surgery, and behavioral surgery...."

The distinctive feature of such **psychosurgical procedures** is the destruction, removal, or disconnection of brain tissue in order to modify or control "thoughts, feelings, actions, or behavior" when the tissue is normal or when there is no evidence any abnormality has caused the behavioral disorder.[4] **Psychosurgery** is also distinguished from "shock" therapy by its experimental nature.[5] **Psychosurgery** is an irreversible alteration of the brain and its functions that presents serious risks to patients, some of which risks are unknown. The court in Kaimowitz, supra, at page 475 concluded that the dangers of such surgery are undisputed. Such a procedure often leads to "the blunting of emotions, the deadening of memory, the reduction of affect, and limits the ability to generate new ideas" (Kaimowitz, supra, at p. 478.) [[4] The lack of tissue abnormality, or causal relation between an abnormality and character or behavior disorder is the primary feature of the definition in section 5225(g)(1), (2) and (3). This characteristic is emphasized in the definitions adopted by the court in Kaimowitz v. Department of Mental Health for the State of Michigan, civil action No. 73–19434–AW (Cir.Ct. Wayne County, Mich., July 10, 1973) (reported in 2 Prison L.Rptr. 433, 473–474 August 1973). [[5] Kaimowitz, supra, at 475. This view of the nature of **psychosurgery** is concurred in by the American Psychiatric Association in their Position Statement of the American Psychiatric Association on Possible Revision of the Standard #9 of the April 13, 1972 Decree in Wyatt v. Stickney, filed in Wyatt v. Hardin, (Civ. Action No. 3195–N—M.D.Ala. Feb. 28, 1975.) December 20, 1974, p. 9. Petitioners and amici curiae in support of the petition do not seriously contend otherwise.] Aden v. Younger, 129 Cal.Rptr. 535, 540–1 (Ct.App.Cal.1976).

psychotic (si-kot'ik) 1. pertaining to, characterized by, or caused by psychosis. 2. a person exhibiting psychosis. See also *episode, acute reactive psychotic* (People v. Harrington case).

Guillory was given Thorazine, Stelazine, Cogentin, and Prolixin, drugs he had been given since the diagnosis of his condition in 1975.[1] [[1] All of these drugs are used to treat individuals with **psychotic** disorders. The record indicates that these drugs have a significant effect upon the nervous system and are strong sedatives. The medical community concludes that heavy sedation is the easiest way to deal with such emotionally disturbed individuals. In the instant case, the record indicates that Guillory was given very large dosages of these drugs.] Guillory on Behalf of Guillory v. U.S., 699 F.2d 781, 783 (5th Cir. 1983).

Mental illness may tend to produce bias in a witness' testimony. A **psychotic's** veracity may be impaired by lack of capacity to observe, correlate or recollect actual events. U.S. v. Lindstrom, 698 F.2d 1154, 1160 (11th Cir. 1983).

He testified that when he first saw Mr. Brecheen he considered him to be **psychotic** which means that he had lost the capacity for reality testing and did not have the capacity to determine whether what's going on either inside him or around him was real. He considered that at the time of his discharge the **psychotic** aspect of his illness had cleared. An individual may be psychotic at times, and at other times may not be. Exxon Corp. v. Brecheen, 519 S.W.2d 170, 178 (Ct.Civ.App.Tex. 1975), reversed and remanded 526 S.W.2d 519 (Tex.1975).

psychotropic (si"ko-trop'pik) [*psycho-* + Gr. *tropē* a turning] exerting an effect upon the mind; capable of modifying mental activity; usually applied to drugs that affect the mental state. See also *dyskinesia, tardive* (Rennie case).

Prolixin or Fluphenazine belongs to a group of chemicals variously described as antipsychotic or **psychotropic** drugs. It comes in long-acting (prolixin decanoate) and short-acting (prolixin hydrochloride) form. Prolixin Decanoate is the only **psychotropic** drug to come in a form that will last approximately two weeks. Bugaoan, Tr. IV, 124, 1/16/78; Zander, Prolixin Decanoate: A Review of the Research, in 2 Mental Disability L.Rep. 37 (1977)....

In the past twenty years, **psychotropic** drugs have played an increasingly important role in the treatment of mental illness, and are now widely used. **Psychotropic** drugs tend to shorten hospital stays and allow patients to function in the community. Many consider use of these drugs necessary in any treatment program, especially for schizophrenics. Winick, Psychotropic Medication and Competence to Stand Trial, 1977 Am.B. Found.Res.J. 769, 773–74; Zander, supra....

However, the court can appropriately make certain generalizations even at this stage of scientific knowledge. **Psychotropic** drugs are effective in reducing thought disorder in a majority of schizophrenics....

Unfortunately, all of the **psychotropic** drugs cause dysfunctions of the central nervous system called extrapyramidal symptoms, as well as other side effects. All these vary among individuals. Zander, supra at 39. On the average, among all patients, no one drug is much worse than the others at any given therapeutic dosage.

A number of short term autonomic side effects have commonly been reported. These include blurred vision, dry mouth and throat, constipation or diarrhea, palpitations, skin rashes, low blood pressure, faintness and fatigue. [Footnote omitted.] Rennie v. Klein, 462 F.Supp. 1131, 1136–8 (D.N.J.1978).

Psychotropics is the name given to a group of drugs utilized by professionals to reduce a patient's psychotic symptoms and allow the hospitalized patient's return to and maintenance in the community....

Prolixin and Haldol are two of a group of major tranquilizers affecting the central nervous system which are used in the treatment of schizophrenia. In a significant percentage of patients, **psychotropic** drugs are known to produce effects similar to the symptoms of Parkinson's disease, such as loss of muscular control, involuntary grimaces and twitching, among other symptomatology. While such symptoms are temporary in most cases and are controlled by anti-Parkinsonian drugs, the effects are sometimes permanent and known as tardive dyskinesia, a neurologic disorder. Matter of B, 383 A.2d 760–2 (Super.Ct.N.J.1977).

psychrophilic (si″kro-fil′ik) [*psychro-* + Gr. *philein* to love] fond of cold; said of bacteria that grow in the cold, often growing best between 15° and 20°C. See also *mesophilic*; and *thermophilic*.

Fresh pork sausage can be held at high temperatures for a period of 3 to 4 hours before appreciable bacterial growth begins. Therefore, the Bird Provision process is able to control bacterial spoilage by controlling the initial level of **psychophilic** bacteria (those which grow at temperatures below 50°) and by packaging the sausage within 3½ hours. Bird Provision Co. v. Owens Country Sausage, Inc., 568 F.2d 369, 372 (5th Cir. 1978).

PTC plasma thromboplastin component (blood coagulation Factor IX); phenylthiocarbamide.

ptosis (to′sis) [Gr. *ptōsis* fall] prolapse of an organ or part.

... **ptosis** of the stomach and transverse colon ["ptosis" means the slipping or sagging of an organ]. See generally Dorland's Illustrated Medical Dictionary, 24th Edition. Swihel v. Richardson, 346 F.Supp. 930, 933 (D.Neb.1972).

... **ptosis** of the right eyelid.... Masters v. Alexander, 225 A.2d 905, 911 (Pa.1967).

PTT See *partial thromboplastin time* under *tests.*

pudendum (pu-den′dum), pl. *puden′da* [L., from *pudere* to be ashamed.] the external genitalia of humans, especially of the female. See also *pudendum femininum.*

pudendum femininum [NA], female pudendum: that portion of the female genitalia comprising the mons pubis, labia majora, labia minora, vestibule of the vagina, bulb of the vestibule, greater and lesser vestibular glands, and vaginal orifice. Commonly used to denote the entire external female genitalia (partes genitales femininae externae). Called also *p. muliebre* and *vulva.*

puerperium (pu″er-pe′re-um) [L.] the period or state of confinement after labor.

"pull-through" operation See *proctosigmoidectomy, Babcock-Bacon.*

pulmonary fibrosis See *fibrosis, idiopathic pulmonary.*

pulp (pulp) [L. *pulpa* flesh] any soft, juicy animal or vegetable tissue, such as that contained within the spleen or the pulp chamber of a tooth. See also *pulp, dental.*

pulp, dental the richly vascularized and innervated connective tissue contained in the pulp cavity of a tooth, constituting the formative, nutritive, and sensory organ of the dentin; called also *pulpa dentis* [NA].

pulp, necrotic dental pulp which has been deprived of its blood and nerve supply and is no longer composed of living tissue, as evidenced by its insensitivity to stimulation by electricity, heat, cold, or trauma.

... he diagnosed plaintiff's dental problems as pulpitis of both teeth (the upper left central incisor and the upper right lateral incisor) progressing to necrosis or death of the **pulp** within three or four weeks following placement of the bridge.... Evans v. Ohanesian, 112 Cal.Rptr. 236, 239 (Ct. App.Cal.1974).

pulp, red; pulp, splenic the dark, reddish brown substance which fills up the interspaces of the sinuses of the spleen; called also *pulpa lienis.*

pulp, white sheaths of lymphatic tissue surrounding the arteries of the spleen.

pulpitis (pul-pi′tis), pl. *pulpit′ides* inflammation of the dental pulp.

He testified that Mrs. Dufrene entered his office on December 23, 1966, complaining of a severe toothache which he diagnosed as acute **pulpitis** of the lower left second bicuspid tooth. Dufrene v. Faget, 260 So.2d 76, 78 (Ct.App.La.1972).

pulposus, herniated nucleus

Bloodsworth had surgery in 1962 and 1964 for lumbar disc disease and a **herniated nucleus pulposus** (ruptured disc). Bloodsworth v. Heckler, 703 F.2d 1233, 1236 (11th Cir. 1983).

A report from appellant's second treating physician, Dr. Herbstein, diagnosed her condition as a **herniated nucleus pulposis** (a ruptured disc). Marcus v. Califano, 615 F.2d 23, 26 (2d Cir. 1979).

pulpotomy (pul-pot′o-me) [*pulp* + Gr. *tomē* a cutting] surgical excision of the coronal portion of a vital pulp.

Root canal therapy is a distinct endodontic treatment from a **pulpotomy**. A **pulpotomy** consists of debridement, chemical disinfection and obturation of the coronal or crown portion of the pulp chamber without extension into the root canals. This procedure is most commonly used on deciduous teeth rather than adult teeth. Although it may be used as an interim or final treatment on an adult tooth, the potential risk of re-infection to exposed pulp renders **pulpotomies** on adult teeth generally unacceptable. Adult teeth in need of endodontic treatment are therefore usually given root canal therapy or a pulp capping procedure in which the pulp is not exposed or is exposed only minutely.

Compared to a root canal procedure, a **pulpotomy** is a relatively swift and easy procedure, since the root canals need not be negotiated. U.S. v. Talbott, 460 F.Supp. 253, 257–8 (S.D. Ohio 1978).

pulse (puls) [L. *pulsus* stroke] the rhythmic expansion of an artery which may be felt with the finger. The *pulse rate* or number of pulsations of an artery per minute normally varies from 50 to 100. See also *beat.*

According to Dr. Lewis' testimony, he inspected the leg at 7:05 p.m., following a telephone report by Nurse Preston that the leg appeared mottled and cold and Voegeli could not move his toes. Lewis did not take a **pulse** at that time. He testified that he returned to the room alone a few minutes later, however, and checked for a **pulse**. Finding one, he noted this on the chart....
... Nonetheless, Dr. Gross testified that no rule of medicine required Dr. Lewis to take a **pulse**, and "if he used his clinical judgment in assessing the circulation of that leg, and felt it was adequate at the time, then I don't think there's any law or rule that holds him to take a **pulse**." ....
There seems to be no disagreement that immediate attention is required once a circulatory problem has been identified. The successful taking of a distal **pulse** provides an indication that

circulation is present; failure to find a **pulse**, while not conclusive, puts the treating person on notice of a possible impairment. [Footnote omitted.] Voegeli v. Lewis, 568 F.2d 89, 92–93 (8th Cir. 1977).

pump (pump) 1. an apparatus for drawing or forcing fluids or gases. 2. to draw or force fluids or gases.

pump, sodium; pump, sodium-potassium the mechanism of active transport, involving membrane-bound ATPase, by which sodium (Na+) is extruded from a cell and potassium (K+) is brought in, so as to maintain the low concentration of Na+ and the high concentration of K+ within the cell with respect to the surrounding medium, the high concentration of K+ being necessary for vital processes such as protein biosynthesis, certain enzymes activities, and maintenance of the membrane potential of excitable cells. Called also Na+-K+ p.

puncta See *punctum, lacrimale.*

punctum (punk'tum), pl. *punc'ta* [L.] an extremely small spot, or point; used in anatomical nomenclature as a general term to designate an extremely small area, or point of projection.

punctum lacrimale [NA], lacrimal point: the opening on the lacrimal papilla of an eyelid, near the medial angle of the eye, into which tears from the lacrimal lake drain to enter the lacrimal canaliculi.

Eric was 16 months old and suffered from a congenital eye defect, the absence of the **lacrimal puncta**, i.e., tear duct, from his left eye. Winfield v. Mathews, 571 F.2d 164–5 (3d Cir. 1978).

puncture (punk'tūr) [L. *punctura*] 1. the act of piercing or penetrating with a pointed object or instrument. 2. a wound so made.

puncture, Bernard's in experimental medicine, puncture on a definite point of the floor of the fourth ventricle causing glycosuria; called also *diabetic p.*

puncture, cisternal puncture of the cisterna cerebellomedullaris through the occipitoatlantoid ligament for the purpose of withdrawing cerebrospinal fluid.

The **cisternal puncture**, cervical air myelogram is performed in two stages. In stage one, a needle, between three and a half to four and a half inches in length, is inserted from the back of the neck into the cisterna magna subarachnoid space. After the needle is inserted in the cisterna magna, cerebral spinal fluid is withdrawn and air or oxygen is injected incrementally. In stage two, after the needle is withdrawn and the air is caused to move through the spinal canal to the patient's lumbar spine by elevating the lower half of the body and lowering the upper half, X-rays are then taken of the lumbar spine. The air serves as a "contrast medium," enabling the radiologist to detect the presence and location of any tumors or other disorders. The diagnostic tools of the procedure include the lumbar X-rays and laboratory analysis of the cerebral spinal fluid.

One of the known risks associated with the **cisternal puncture** procedure is that the needle may pass through the cister-

na magna and penetrate the brain stem, which lies just a few millimeters beyond the cisterna magna. This can occur if the patient moves suddenly while the needle is in place in the cisterna magna, if the needle initially is inserted too far, or if the doctor performing the procedure moves the needle after it is correctly placed in the cisterna magna. If the needle passes through the cisterna magna and becomes lodged in the brain stem, it will not be possible to withdraw cerebral spinal fluid, and certain critical respiratory and cardiac functions controlled by the brain stem may be interrupted. McClain v. U.S., 490 F.Supp. 485–6 (E.D.Wis.1980).

puncture, epigastric pericardiocentesis in which the trocar is passed just below the xiphoid cartilage in the middle line, directed obliquely from below upward, passing 2 cm. along the posterior surface of the sternum. It is then directed somewhat obliquely backward, passing into the gap in the sternal insertion of the diaphragm, entering the pericardium at its base. Called also *Marfan's method* and *Marfan's epigastric p.*

puncture, lumbar the tapping of the subarachnoid space in the lumbar region, usually between the third and fourth lumbar vertebrae.

A diagnosis of subarachnoid hemorrhage can be confirmed by performing a **lumbar puncture**, a medical procedure in which a long needle is inserted between two vertebrae into the fluid-filled cavity around the spinal cord and a sample of the fluid is allowed to drip off. After a subarachnoid hemorrhage, the fluid, which is normally colorless, will be bloody or pink or slightly discolored. Laboratory analysis of the specimen can demonstrate whether a result uncertain to the naked eye is positive or negative. Deposition of Dr. Neal Kassell, at 29–30. Polischeck v. U.S., 535 F.Supp. 1261, 1266 (E.D.Pa.1982).

A **spinal tap** revealed bloody spinal fluid which indicated hemorrhaging somewhere between the brain and the point of the tap. State v. Goblirsch, 246 N.W.2d 12–13 (Minn.1976).

"I made the initial **spinal tap** at the L2–3 interspace. [This is the interspace between the second lumbar vertebra and the third lumbar vertebra.] This is the highest possible interspace at which the procedure can be safely done because in the average person, the spinal cord comes down to the L1–2 interspace. If the initial tap is done higher than the L2–3 interspace there is a danger of traumatizing the spinal cord which would cause nerve or spinal cord damage that would result in weakness in one of the legs. Funke v. Fieldman, 512 P.2d 539, 543 (Kan.1973).

puncture, Marfan's epigastric See *puncture, epigastric.*

purified protein derivative test See *test, tuberculin Sterneedle.*

Puritan Pot See *humidifier; tracheostomy* (Walstad case).

purpura (pur'pu-rah) [L. "purple"] a group of disorders characterized by purplish or brownish red discoloration, easily visible through the epidermis, caused by hemorrhage into the tissues. Small punctate hemorrhages are called *petechiae;* large hemorrhages are called *ecchymoses* (bruises; black and blue marks).

purpura, Schönlein-Henoch a form of nonthrombo-cytopenic purpura probably due to a vasculitis of unknown cause, most commonly observed in children and associated with a variety of clinical symptoms including urticaria and erythema, arthropathy and arthritis, gastrointestinal symptoms, and renal involvement. Called also *allergic p.*, *anaphylactoid p.*, and *Schönlein-Henoch disease.*

Dr. Perucca diagnosed the child's ailment as **allergic purpura**, a predominantly childhood condition manifested by discoloration of the skin, swelling of the lips or head and welts on the skin. People v. Frost, 362 N.E.2d 417–18 (App.Ct.Ill.1977).

purpura, thrombocytopenic, thrombotic a disease of undefined cause, characterized by thrombocytopenia, hemolytic anemia, bizarre neurological manifestations, azotemia, fever, and thromboses in terminal arterioles and capillaries; called also *microangiopathic hemolytic anemia* and *Moschcowitz's disease.*

... **thrombotic thrombocytopenic purpura** is an extremely different disease from stroke. **TTP's** attributes include a simultaneous hyper-and hypo-coagulability of the blood. Zeck v. U.S., 559 F.Supp. 1345, 1350 (D.S.Dak.1983).

PVC See *polyvinylchloride.*

PVE See *encephalopathy.*

pyarthrosis (pi"ar-thro'sis) [Gr. *pyon* pus + *arthron* joint + *-osis*] suppuration within a joint cavity; acute suppurative arthritis.

On that day plaintiff, with his consent, was taken to the operating room, incision was made under a general anesthetic, cloudy yellow fluid and fibrin clots were removed, the wound was irrigated, an input tube and an output suction tube were placed, and a new cast was applied. At this time no "gross pus" was found but the area was described as "infected," "infectious," and indicating "**pyarthrosis**." Contreras v. St. Luke's Hospital, 144 Cal.Rptr. 647, 651 (Ct.App.1978).

pyelitis (pi"ĕ-li'tis) [*pyel-* + *-itis*] inflammation of the pelvis of the kidney. It is attended by pain and tenderness in the loins, irritability of the bladder, remittent fever, bloody or purulent urine, diarrhea, vomiting, and a peculiar pain on flexion of the thigh. See also *pyelonephritis.* Cited in Swihel v. Richardson, 346 F.Supp. 930, 933 (D.Neb.1972).

pyelogram (pi'ĕ-lo-gram") [*pyelo-* + Gr. *gramma* mark] a roentgenogram of the kidney and ureter, especially showing the pelvis of the kidney. See also *pyelography, intravenous.*

Dr. Shannon was to administer an intravenous **pyelogram** (IVP) to Ms. Smith and take X-rays of her kidneys and ureters, the ducts that carry urine away from the kidneys to the bladder. Smith v. Shannon, 666 P.2d 351, 353 (Wash.1983).

... plaintiff was admitted to MCV complaining of right flank pain. An intravenous **pyelogram** showed a small urethral stone, and corrective surgery was performed on October 10, 1968. Hurst v. Mathews, 426 F.Supp. 245–6 (E.D.Va.1976).

While in the hospital Dr. Carl Ambler, a hospital radiologist, began the first of a number of procedures necessary for an intravenous **pyelogram**. Ausley v. Johnston, 450 S.W.2d 351, 353 (Ct.App.Tex.1970).

Other Authorities: Clark v. U.S., 402 F.2d 950–1 (4th Cir. 1968).

pyelography (pi"ĕ-log'rah-fe) [*pyelo-* + Gr. *graphein* to draw] roentgenography of the renal pelvis and ureter after the structures have been filled with a contrast solution.

pyelography, intravenous pyelography in which an intravenous injection is made of a contrast medium which passes quickly into the urine.

An IVP (Intravenous Pyleogram [sic]) which is a test of the functioning of the kidneys was normal. Harrigan v. U.S., 408 F.Supp. 177, 180 (E.D.Pa.1976).

pyelolithotomy (pi"ĕ-lo-lĭ-thot'o-me) [*pyelo-* + Gr. *lithos* stone + *tomē* a cutting] the operation of excising a renal calculus from the pelvis of the kidney.

After admission to St. Joseph's Hospital in 1977 and upon examination and consultation an operation for kidney stones (right **pyelolithotomy**) was recommended. Perna v. Pirozzi, 442 A.2d 1016 (Super.Ct.N.J.1982), reversed and remanded 457 A.2d 431 (N.J.1983).

pyelonephritis (pi"ĕ-lo-nĕ-fri'tis) [*pyelo-* + Gr. *nephros* kidney + *-itis*] inflammation of the kidney and its pelvis, beginning in the interstitium and rapidly extending to involve the tubules, glomeruli, and blood vessels; due to bacterial infection.

On December 5, 1976, plaintiff was hospitalized at the Spring dale Memorial Hospital, and was diagnosed as having an urinary tract infection (UTI), causative agent e. coli, with migraine headaches. The final diagnosis was acute **pyelonephritis** (inflammation of the kidney). Smith v. U.S., 557 F.Supp. 42, 44 (W.D.Ark.1982).

Robert was advised that she suffered from an acute kidney infection with a diagnosis of **pyelonephritis** acute right etiological mechanism E. Coli and streptococcus faecalis. Sanders v. U.S., etc., 551 F.2d 458–9 (D.C.Cir.1977).

... an examination revealed the presence of **pyelonephritis** (inflammation of both the pelvis and the substance of the kidney). Capaldi v. Weinberger, 391 F.Supp. 502, 505 (E.D.Pa. 1975).

Other Authorities: Torres v. Celebrezze, 349 F.2d 342–3 (1st Cir. 1965). Quick v. Thurston, 290 F.2d 360, 363 (D.C.Cir. 1961).

pyelonephritis of pregnancy a renal infection during pregnancy characterized by dilatation of the renal pelvis and the ureters; some degree of ureteric obstruction may be caused by the gravid uterus.

... an examination revealed the presence of **pyelonephritis** (inflammation of both the pelvis and the substance of the kidney).... Capaldi v. Weinberger, 391 F.Supp. 502, 505 (E.D. Pa.1975).

pyloroplasty (pi-lo'ro-plas"te) [*pyloro-* + Gr. *plassein* to form] a plastic operation to relieve pyloric obstruction or to accelerate gastric emptying.

When a complete vagotomy is performed, the digestive processes are materially affected and it is necessary to enlarge the valve at the end of the stomach to provide more adequate drainage. This latter procedure, called a **pyloroplasty**, was not performed on Mrs. Nichols. She has suffered from disorders of her digestive system ever since the operation and eventually had corrective surgery which did not fully alleviate her problems. It is necessary that she take drugs to supplement her digestive processes, and she constantly suffers from diarrhea, constipation, and nausea. Nichols v. Smith, 507 S.W.2d 518–19 (Tex.1974).

pylorospasm (pi-lo′ro-spazm) [*pyloro-* + Gr. *spasmos* spasm] spasm of the pylorus or of the pyloric portion of the stomach.

Upper G.I. series showed a lot of **pylorospasm** with a contracted duodenal bulb. Matthews v. Matthews, 415 F.Supp. 201–2 (E.D.Va.1976).

pylorus (pi-lo′rus) [Gr. *pyloros,* from *pylē* gate + *ouros* guard] [NA] the distal aperture of the stomach surrounded by a strong band of circular muscle, and through which the stomach contents are emptied into the duodenum. It is variously used to mean pyloric part of the stomach, pyloric antrum, pyloric canal, pyloric opening, and pyloric sphincter.

The doctor diagnosed a hiatal hernia, esophagitis, and a deformed **pylorus** secondary to peptic ulcer disease. Bellard v. Woodward Wight & Co., Ltd., 362 So.2d 819, 822 (Ct.App. La.1978).

Since the stomach perforation was in the area of the **pylorus**, or junction between the stomach and the small bowel, Dr. Moskovitz peformed a pyloroplasty closure of the perforation so that the valve would continue to function. Insurance Co. of North America v. Stroburg, 456 S.W.2d 402, 409 (Ct.Civ. App.Tex.1970).

pyoderma (pi″o-der′mah) [*pyo-* + Gr. *derma* skin] any purulent skin disease.

... claimant developed a skin irritation which was diagnosed as miliaria rubra, secondarily infected by **pyoderma**, a disorder which is often called heat rash. Brooks v. State Dep't of Transportation, 255 So.2d 260–1 (Fla.1971).

pyogenic (pi″o-jen′ik) producing pus; pyopoietic.

pyosalpinx (pi″o-sal′pinks) [*pyo-* + Gr. *salpinx* tube] a collection of pus in an oviduct.

pyridoxine (pēr″ĭ-dok′sēn) chemical name: 5-hydroxy-6-methyl-3,4-pyridinedimethanol. One of the forms of vitamin B_6; see *Table of Vitamins,* under *vitamin.*

pyridoxine hydrochloride [USP], the hydrochloride salt of pyridoxine, $C_8H_{11}NO_3 \cdot HCl$, occurring as colorless or white crystals or white crystalline powder; used in the prophylaxis and treatment of vitamin B_6 deficiency. It has also been used in neuromuscular and neurological diseases, in dermatoses, and in the management of nausea and vomiting of pregnancy and irradiation sickness.

pyuria (pi-u′re-ah) [Gr. *pyon* pus + *ouron* urine + *-ia*] the presence of pus in the urine.

pyuria, hemorrhagic

... she had **hemorrhagic pyuria**, or blood in the urine accompanied by pain in the lower abdomen. A regimen of whirlpool baths was prescribed and commenced on March 11. Wade v. Thomasville Orthopedic Clinic, 306 S.E.2d 366–7 (Ct.App. Ga.1983).

Q

q.i.d. abbreviation for L. *qua'ter in di'e,* four times a day.

Finally the use of t.i.d. (3 times per day) and **q.i.d.** (4 times per day) dosage schedules for 14% of the patients receiving psychotropic medications was questioned. Rone v. Fireman, 473 F.Supp. 92, 108 (E.D.Ohio 1979).

Quaalude (kwa′lood) trademark for a preparation of methaqualone. See also *methaqualone.*

quadrantanopia (kwod″rant-ah-no′pe-ah) [L. *quadrans* a fourth part + Gr. *an-* neg. + *ōpē* vision + *-ia*] defective vision or blindness in one fourth of the visual field, bounded by a vertical and a horizontal radius. Called also *tetartanopia.*

Diffuse slowing on the left side by virtue of his EEG obtained at Scott & White. I felt—my impression was that he may have a low pressure hydrocephalus rather than the hydrocephalus ex vacuo. **Quadrantanopia** could possibly be explained by the occipital lobe contusion at the time of the automobile accident. Fitzwater v. Lambert and Barr, Inc., 539 F.Supp. 282, 288 (W.D.Ark.1982).

quadriceps (kwod′rĭ-seps) [*quadri-* + L. *caput* head] four headed; possessing four heads. See *Table of Musculi.*

Quadrigen

Parke-Davis developed **Quadrigen** during the 1950's as a quadruple antigen product, combining diphtheria toxoids, tetanus toxoids, Salk polio vaccine, and pertussis (whooping cough) vaccine....

In 1953 Dr. Jonas Salk developed a polio vaccine. Following commercial development of the Salk Vaccine, Parke-Davis decided to add the new polio vaccine to its "Triogen" product in order to develop a four-way antigen product, whereby one shot would protect against polio as well as diphtheria, tetanus, and pertussis. This new product Parke-Davis marketed under the trade name **Quadrigen**, beginning in July, 1959. Ezagui v. Dow Chemical Corp., 598 F.2d 727, 731 (2d Cir. 1979).

This diversity products liability action, instituted pursuant to the provisions of 28 U.S.C.A. § 1332, involves a multiple antigen product marketed by Parke-Davis and Company under its trade name "**Quadrigen.**" This product was intended for use in simultaneous immunization against four major diseases of children: diphtheria, tetanus, pertussis (whooping cough) and poliomyelitis....

Shane was born in Grand Forks, North Dakota, on May 24, 1959 and was inoculated with **Quadrigen** by a technician under the direction of Dr. John H. Graham, the family physician, on August 26 and October 1, 1959. Following the second inoculation, plaintiff suffered a convulsion and thereafter suffered other convulsions. There is no dispute that he sustained serious and permanent brain damage, disabling him both mentally and physically to the extent that for his lifetime he will require constant attention and perhaps institutional care. Parke-Davis & Co v. Stromsodt, 411 F.2d 1390–2 (8th Cir. 1969).

quadriparesis

Plaintiff's Exhibit Number 8, being MDL Document Number 103, is Chapter 56 from the textbook, Peripheral Neuropathy, edited by Doctor Peter Dyck. This particular chapter is authored by Doctor Barry G. W. Arnason and is entitled "Inflammatory Polyradiculoneuropathies". In this article, he points out on page 1135 that the illness may begin with a mild distal weakness and progress at a slow tempo to **quadriparesis**. Grubbs v. U.S., 581 F.Supp. 536, 538 (N.D.Ind.1984).

Alternatively, plaintiff contends that she experienced chronic inflammatory polyradiculoneuropathy shortly after she was vaccinated. Plaintiff's experts relied on the following passage from Dr. Arnason's description of "chronic inflammatory polyradiculoneuropathy (hypertrophic neuropathy)": The illness may begin as a mild distal weakness and progress at a slow tempo to **quadriparesis**. Migliorini v. U.S., 521 F.Supp. 1210, 1215 (M.D.Fla.1981).

quadriparetic

Karla has impairment of bulbar function which prevents her from talking and chewing, and barely permits her to swallow; in addition she has frequent trouble with aspiration; she experiences major and minor seizures which carry a risk of further brain damage; Karla is a **quadriparetic**—nearly paralyzed in all four extremities; she is susceptible to infection because of her lack of bladder and bowel control; her mental function is probably at the level of six to fourteen months; she can see and hear in only a limited way; she is tremendously frustrated since she functions "at a one year level of insight, feeling and emotion." Karla's condition is permanent. Foskey v. U.S., 490 F.Supp. 1047, 1060 (D.R.I.1979).

quadriplegia (kwod″rĭ-ple′je-ah) paralysis of all four limbs; tetraplegia.

quadriplegic See *quadriplegia*.

Mrs. Miller had an accident while using the vehicle, sustaining serious injuries which resulted in a **quadriplegic** condition. She will, in all probability, be confined to a bed or wheelchair the rest of her life, totally dependent on others for all aspects of her care, even for breathing, for which she requires the use of a respirator. Miller v. Honda Motor Co., Ltd., 779 F.2d 769–70 (1st Cir. 1985).

According to Lisa Salmine's amended complaint, she fell more than thirty inches from Dennis and Julie Knagins' carport, suffered a broken neck, and ever since has been a **quadriplegic** paralyzed from the neck down. Salmine v. Knagin, 645 P.2d 148 (Alas.1982).

quarantine (kwor′an-tēn) [Ital. *quarantina*] 1. a period (usually of forty days' duration) of detention of ships or persons coming from infected or suspected ports. 2. the place where persons are detained for inspection. 3. to detain or isolate on account of suspected contagion. 4. restrictions placed on the entrance to and exit from the

place or premises where a case of communicable disease exists.

As part of her duties, the Commissioner has the power to control, by licensing or other means, the treatment in institutions such as hospitals and prisons of persons suffering from communicable diseases, including the disinfection and **quarantine** of persons. See Minn.Stat. 144.12 subd. 1(7). DeGidio v. Perpich, 612 F.Supp. 1383, 1390 (D.Minn.1985).

The USDA administers a strictly-regulated program controlling the importation of birds into the United States. The primary purpose of this program is to protect American poultry from a highly contagious disease known as Viscerotropic Velogenic Newcastle's Disease ("VVND").

As part of this program, all importers of birds are required to maintain **quarantine** facilities. When a shipment of birds arrives in the United States, it is met by USDA officials and transported to a sanitized quarantine facility for a thirty day observation period. [Footnote omitted.] U.S. v. Slocum, 708 F.2d 587, 591 (11th Cir. 1983).

Unquestionably, the inherent police power of a state allows a state to establish **quarantines** to control disease in animals. See, e.g., Smith v. St. Louis and Southwestern Ry. Co., 181 U.S. 248, 255–58, 21 S.Ct. 603, 605–606, 45 L.Ed. 847 (1901). States can even destroy diseased cattle if essential for public safety. E.g., Lawton v. Steele, 152 U.S. 133, 136, 14 S.Ct. 499, 500, 38 L.Ed. 385 (1894). The means used by the state, however, cannot go beyond the necessities of the case or unreasonably burden constitutional rights. Reid v. Colorado, 187 U.S. 137, 151, 23 S.Ct. 92, 97, 47 L.Ed. 108 (1902). Johansson v. Board of Animal Health, 601 F.Supp. 1018, 1021 (D.Minn.1985).

Other Authorities: Ideal Waste Systems, Inc. v. Provo City Corp., 605 F.Supp. 100, 105 (D.Utah 1985); Arizona Attorney General, slip opinion, May 25, 1977; Battic v. Stoneman, 421 F.Supp. 213, 231 (D.Vt.1976).

Queckenstedt's sign (phenomenon, test) (kwek′en-stets″) [Hans Heinrich Georg *Queckenstedt*, German physician, 1876–1918] See under *sign*.

Quervain's disease (kār′vanz) [Fritz de *Quervain*, Swiss surgeon, 1868–1940] See *de Quervain's disease* under *disease*.

quick (kwik) pregnant and able to feel the fetal movements.

. . . "**Quick** Child"—For the purposes of this section "**quick** child" shall mean an unborn child whose heart is beating, who is experiencing electronically-measurable brain waves, who is discernibly moving, and who is so far developed and matured as to be capable of surviving the trauma of birth with the aid of usual medical care and facilities available in this state. Rodos v. Michaelsonm, 396 F.Supp. 768, 770–1 (D.R.I.1975), reversed and dismissed 527 F.Supp. 582 (1st Cir. 1975).

We received into evidence the view of a gynecologist that a fetus normally becomes **quick** at about four and a half months after conception. Dorland's Illustrated Medical Dictionary (24th ed. 1965) defines "**quick**" as "Pregnant and able to feel the fetal movements." "Quickening" is defined as "The first recognizable movements of the fetus in utero, appearing usually from the sixteenth to the eighteenth week of pregnancy." Babbitz v. McCann, 310 F.Supp. 293, 299 (E.D.Wis.1970).

quickening (kwik′en-ing) the first recognizable movements of the fetus, appearing usually from the sixteenth to the eighteenth week of pregnancy. See also *quick.*

quinacrine hydrochloride (kwin′ah-krin) [USP] chemical name: N^4-(6-chloro-2-methoxy-9-acridinyl)-N^1,N^1-diethyl-1,4-pentanediamine dihydrochloride dihydrate. An antimalarial, antiprotozoal, and anthelmintic, $C_{23}H_{30}ClN_3 \cdot 2HCl \cdot 2H_2O$, occurring as a bright yellow, crystalline powder; used especially for suppressive therapy of malaria and in the treatment of giardiasis and tapeworm infestations, administered orally. Called also *chinacrin hydrochloride* and *mepacrine hydrochloride.*

The excerpt reads in full: "QUINACRINE HYDROCHLORIDE (MEPACRINE, CHINACRIN, ATABRINE, ATEBRIN). This synthetic drug has been used as an antimalarial since 1931. In a very large majority of the many thousands of individuals who have been given this drug there have been no alarming untoward effects. In persons taking the drug a yellow coloration of the skin develops in many, and the urine becomes deep yellow when acidified, although renal function is unimpaired. In some instances, in addition to coloration of the skin and mucous membranes, there are nausea, vomiting, cramps, diarrhea, vertigo, and pains in the muscles and joints. Enormous doses may prove fatal. The concurrent administration of quinacrine and primaquine, an 8-aminoquinoline antimalarial, is likely to produce methemoglobinemia and hemolysis and is contraindicated (Goodman and Gilman). This drug does not produce retinopathy." The particular ambiguity relied upon is that the words "this drug" in the last sentence could refer either to quinacrine [7] alone (quinacrine is another name for Atabrine) or to quinacrine and primaquine. When the excerpt is interpreted according to principles of standard grammatical usage, however, no such ambiguity appears. [[7] According to one of the plaintiff's experts, quinacrine and mepacrine are synonyms for atabrine.] Cross v. Huttenlocher, 440 A.2d 952, 957 (Conn. 1981).

quinidine (kwin′ĭ-din) chemical name: 6-methoxycinchonan-9-ol. The dextrorotatory isomer of quinine, $C_{20}H_{24}N_2O_2$, obtained from various species of *Cinchona* and their hybrids, and from *Remijia pedunculata*, or prepared from quinine. It has cardiac depressant activity, and is as potent an antimalarial as quinine but is rarely used for the latter effect except in those having an idiosyncrasy to quinine.

Defendant Alexander examined him initially and diagnosed atrial fibrillation with marked hypertension. Dr. Alexander admitted plaintiff's father to the hospital and placed him on the drug **Quinidine** in an effort to control his abnormal heart rhythm. Haney v. Alexander, 323 S.E.2d 430–1 (Ct.App.N. Car.1984).

The problem of atrial fibrillation was first treated with digitalis preparation of **quinidine** which resulted in atrial fibrillation flutter. Thereafter, Moser's heart was returned to a normal sinus rhythm by Lee Schocket, M.D., a cardiologist, who prescribed and performed electrocardioversion on July 29. Allstate Ins. Co. v. Industrial Com'n, 616 P.2d 100–01 (Ct.App.Ariz.1980).

Mr. Burns was told that he had a heart valve hardening. He took empirin and codeine for chest pain and had been told to take **quinidine** if he ever felt that his heart was going rapidly. **Quinidine** is a depressant for the heart which calms irregular

beatings and is used for certain types of fibrillation. Burns v. Prudential Ins. Co. of America, 20 Cal.Rptr. 535, 537 (Ct. of App.Cal.1962).

Other Authorities: Vander Veer v. Continental Casualty Co., 356 N.Y.S.2d 13–14 (N.Y.1974).

quinidine gluconate [USP], the gluconate salt of quinidine, occurring as an odorless, white powder with a very bitter taste; administered intramuscularly or intravenously for the treatment of cardiac arrhythmias.

quinidine polygalacturonate a salt of quinidine, $(C_{20}H_{24}N_2O_2 \cdot C_6H_{10}O_7 \cdot H_2O)_x$, having actions and uses the same as the other salts of quinidine; administered orally.

quinidine sulfate [USP], the sulfate salt of quinidine, occurring as fine, needle-like crystals or as a fine, white powder, which is odorless, has a bitter taste, and darkens on exposure to light; administered orally for the treatment of cardiac arrhythmias.

quinine (kwin′in, kwin-ēn′, kwi′nīn) [L. *quinina*] an alkaloid of cinchona, $C_{20}H_{24}N_2O_2 \cdot 3H_2O$, occurring as a white microcrystalline powder, which suppresses the asexual erythrocytic forms of all malarial parasites and has a slight effect on the gametocytes of *Plasmodium vivax* and *P. malariae* but none on those of *P. falciparum.* Once widely used to prevent and control malaria, it has been largely replaced by less toxic and more effective synthetic antimalarials, and is now used chiefly (usually in the form of one of its soluble salts) in the treatment of falciparum malaria resistant to other antimalarials. Quinine also has analgesic antipyretic, mild oxytocic, cardiac depressant, and sclerosing properties, and it decreases the excitability of the motor endplate.

In his "Brief in Support of Confirmation of the Wholesaler-Retailer Class", the plaintiff states that: "All of the relevant products are derived from the bark of the cinchona tree, most of which comes from plantations located in Indonesia and in the Republic of the Congo. Quinine is extracted from the bark of the cinchona tree and combined with acids to form a variety of salts used for medicinal purposes, including the treatment and prevention of malaria. Most of the world's supply of quinidine is synthesized by isomerization of quinine. Its principal use is to restore and maintain a normal heartbeat in people suffering from irregular heartbeat or cardiac arrhythmia." Sol S. Turnoff Drug Dist., Inc. v. N. V. Nederlandsche, 51 F.R.D. 227–8 (E.D.Pa.1970).

quinine and urea hydrochloride a double salt of quinine and urea hydrochloride, $C_{20}H_{24}N_2O_2 \cdot HCl \cdot CH_4N_2O_2 \cdot HCl \cdot 5H_2O$, occurring as colorless translucent prisms, white granules, or white powder. It has been used to produce sclerosing, thrombosis, and obliteration of internal hemorrhoids and varicose veins, and as a local anesthetic.

quotient (kwo′shent) a number obtained as the result of division.

quotient, intelligence the measure of intelligence obtained by dividing the patient's mental age, as ascertained by the Binet-Simon scale, by his chronological age and multiplying the result by 100. Abbreviated I.Q.

The first usable I.Q. tests were developed in France in 1905 by Alfred Binet, who sought to distinguish between "backward" and "normal" children in Paris. He had no illusions that his test could measure innate traits. He sought to develop diagnostic tools to help those who needed to improve their intellectual skills. Binet insisted that "it was necessary to react against and protest the brutal pessimism of those who regarded the test as measuring some fixed and unchanging quantity." Kamin 849. This admonition, however, was not heeded when Binet's test was transplanted in American soil.

The early leaders of the I.Q. testing movement in the United States were quick to assume that the Binet tests measured an innate capacity fixed in the genes. Typical and of particular interest for the California story were the views of Professor Lewis Terman of Stanford, the well-known developer of the Stanford-Binet I.Q. test in 1916.

Detailed information on the history of the I.Q. test and of special education in California can be obtained from the following two works: L. Kamin, The Science and Politics of IQ (1974); J. Simmons, A Historical Perspective of Special Education in California, Vol. 1 (unpublished doctoral dissertation, 1973). Both Professor Kamin and Dr. Simmons testified at the trial.

L. Terman, The Measurement of Intelligence 6–7 (1916)....

I.Q. tests, like other ability tests, essentially measure achievement in the skills covered by the examinations....

Originally an I.Q. of 100 was supposed to mean that the child had a "mental age" 100 percent equivalent to the child's chronological age. Thus a child of five who had a mental age of an average four-year-old would be considered to possess an I.Q. score of 80—four-fifths of 100. I.Q. scores are no longer designed to represent mental ages....

The I.Q. tests must be recognized as artificial tools to rank individuals according to certain skills, not to diagnose a medi-

cal condition. The ranking is done in a manner useful for statistical analysis. [Footnote omitted.] Larry P. v. Riles, 495 F.Supp. 926, 935, 952–53 (N.D.Cal.1979), affirmed in part, reversed in part 793 F.2d 969 (9th Cir. 1986).

Dr. Paul F. Bramwell, Ph.D., a licensed clinical psychologist, testified that he interviewed appellant on October 19, 1980, and administered the Wechsler Adult Intelligence Scale (WAIS). Dr. Bramwell had previously evaluated appellant in 1976. Appellant's full-scale I.Q. on both occasions was 76.

Dr. Bramwell explained that the WAIS is designed to measure the whole range of intelligence through use of different subtests. From the scores on the subtests, an aggregate score, commonly known as **intelligence quotient**, or I.Q., is computed. Wechsler defined intelligence as "the aggregate or global capacity of an individual to act purposefully, to think rationally, and to deal effectively with his environment."

Dr. Bramwell said that test scores are not precise: there is statistically a standard error of measurement in any test, as well as variance in the test subject's attention and emotional state on the day of the test, and a subjective element in scoring on the Wechsler and Stanford-Binet. Dr. Bramwell said that he prefers to speak in terms of a range of intelligence rather than a specific score; appellant's range was between 70 and 80. Money v. Krall, 180 Cal.Rptr. 376, 386–7 (Ct.App. Cal.1982).

A psychological evaluation was conducted by LaVern Ells, school psychologist, on May 3, 1968. Mr. Ells reported, in part, as follows: "The Stanford-Binet Intelligence Scale was administered and the following results were obtained: M.A. 13–8; I.Q. 86 which would place her in the dull normal range of intellectual functioning." McCalip v. Richardson, 333 F.Supp. 1207, 1209 (D.Neb.1971), reversed and remanded 460 F.2d 1124 (8th Cir. 1972).

R

℞ symbol for L. *rec'ipe*, take. See also *prescription*.

rabies (ra′bēz, ra′be-ēz) [L. *rabere* to rage] an acute infectious disease of the central nervous system usually fatal in mammal species ranging from bats to cattle. It is caused by an RNA virus (rhabdoviridae). Human infection results from the bite of a rabid animal, such as a bat, wolf, dog, cat, mongoose, or other mammal. The incubation period in man is from one to three months, being shorter following bites near the brain than after those farther away. The earliest symptoms are numbness and tingling around the site of infection; soon afterwards generalized hyperexcitability occurs, followed by fever, by paralysis of the muscles of deglutition and glottal spasm at first provoked by the drinking of fluids or by the sight of fluids, and by maniacal behavior. Convulsions, tetany, and respiratory paralysis are the inevitable terminal event. The diagnosis can be confirmed during life by viral isolation (from saliva, cerebrospinal fluid, urine) or by demonstration of neutralizing antibody, and after death by the appearance of cytoplasmic inclusion bodies (Negri bodies) in degenerated neurons. Called also *hydrophobia* and *lyssa*. See also under *vaccine*.

racemate (ra′se-māt) an equimolecular mixture of two enantiomorphic isomers, being optically inactive in solution because of the presence of the same number of dextro- and levo-rotatory molecules. In the solid state it may have the properties of a loosely bound molecular compound. Called also *racemic form, racemic mixture,* or *racemic modification.*

> ... **racemate**—a name coined by Pasteur for a compound consisting of equal parts of a dextro and a levo isomer, also referred to as a racemic mixture. Eli Lilly & Co. v. Generix Drug Sales, Inc., 460 F.2d 1096, 1100 (5th Cir. 1972).

racemization (ra″sĕ-mi-za′shun) the transformation of one half of the molecules of an optically active compound into molecules which possess exactly the opposite (mirror-image) configuration, with complete loss of rotatory power because of the statistical balance between equal numbers of dextro- and levorotatory molecules. Cf. *mutarotation.*

rad [acronym for *radiation absorbed dose*] a unit of measurement of the absorbed dose of ionizing radiation; it corresponds to an energy transfer of 100 ergs per gram of any absorbing material (including tissues). The biological effect of 1 rad varies with the kind of radiation the tissue is exposed to. Cf. *gray*.

The **rad**, as used in this part, is a measure of the dose of any ionizing radiation to body tissues in terms of the energy absorbed per unit mass of the tissue. One **rad** is the dose corresponding to the absorption of 100 ergs per gram of tissue. (One millirad (mrad)＝0.001 **rad**.) 10 C.F.R. § 20.4(b) (1982).

radar See *effect, Doppler*.

radiation (ra-de-a'shun) [L. *radiatio*] electromagnetic waves, such as those of light, or particulate rays, such as alpha, beta, and gamma rays, given off from some source. See also *carcinoma, basal cell* (Vasily case); *erythema* (McCarthy case); *rays, roentgen*; and *sickness, radiation*.

... **radiation** of the pelvic area to destroy as much of the tumor as possible....

Subsequent to the completion of the **radiation** therapy, Albert began urinating normally rather than through the ileal loop. He informed Dr. Frankel of this about January 17, 1977, who advised Albert this was a complication from the **radiation**. In February 1977, Albert was hospitalized at Winona Hospital. He had stopped urinating and became extremely ill. Surgery then was performed on February 12, 1977, and a tube was put directly into the kidney. Two months later, further surgery was performed, the original intention of which was to refix the ileal loop. However, the ileal loop and ureters had been destroyed by the **radiation** and the ileal loop was not functioning. The removal of the bladder, prostate, and seminal vesicles was then performed. The Nahmiases were informed by Dr. Frankel in April or May of 1977 that the ileal loop was damaged, the ureters were eaten up, and that such was the result of **radiation** damage. Nahmias v. Trustees of Indiana University, 444 N.E.2d 1204–05 (Ct.App.Ind.1983).

Port said that at the times in question it was well known "that **radiation** might or could cause cancerous growths in the human body" and that "such knowledge was readily available to the radiological and medical community." He stated that this information should have been known to the defendant. Port also said that at the times in question the technology was available to shield tissue adjacent to areas being treated and that proceeding without such shielding was "an unsafe and hazardous practice." With regard to the hazards inherent in X-**radiation** therapy, plaintiffs' expert concluded that "based upon a reasonable degree of radiological and physical certainty" defendant should have known that the use of **radiation** included the hazard of tumor development in tissues adjacent to the tonsils, including the thyroid gland. Finally, Port concluded that at the times in question there were techniques available, including animal studies, which would have enabled defendant to ascertain the longterm effects of irradiation and thereby determine the benefit and risk associated with **radiation** of the tonsils. He said that the failure to do so created a practice which was "unnecessarily hazardous." Greenberg v. Michael Reese Hospital, 415 N.E.2d 390, 392 (Ill.1980).

... that the cobalt treatment of the neck nodes caused typical regression and stopped, at least temporarily, the progression in the case treated; that the **radiation** "destroy[s] [the cancer cells'] growth processes, their reproductive processes, therefore, allowing the body to take over and have a better defense against the ... cancerous process"; and that this form of cancer is more sensitive to **radiation** than some other forms,

and [treatment] helps the patient. Cullum v. Seifer, 81 Cal.Rptr. 381, 385–6 (Ct.App.Cal.1969).

Other Authorities: 10 C.F.R. § 20.3(a)(12) (1982); Ahern v. Veterans Administration, 537 F.2d 1098–1101 (10th Cir. 1976); Ragan v. Steen, 331 A.2d 724, 727–8, 732 (Super.Ct. Pa.1974); ZeBarth v. Swedish Hosp. Med. Center, 499 P.2d 1, 5 (Wash.1972); Lopez v. Swyer, 279 A.2d 116, 119 (Super.Ct. N.J.1971); Crowther v. Seaborg, 312 F.Supp. 1205, 1228–9 (D.Colo.1970). Chiropractic Ass'n of New York, Inc. v. Hilleboe, 227 N.Y.S.2d 309, 336 (Sup.Ct.Albany Cty.1961).

radiation, dosage

In a recognized textbook entitled "Radiotherapy of Benign Disease" published in 1965, Dr. Stephen B. Dewing observes at 221: "If a single dose is to be used, either 1,000 or 1,200r will suffice for most lesions not over a centimeter in diameter. Some prefer to use larger doses, going up to 1,800r for a single dose.... Others vary the dose in inverse proportion to the size of the lesion, as in the schedule of Pipkin et al. which varies from 1,000r for a wart of 12 mm. diameter, to 2,720 for a 2 or 3 mm. wart...." Ragan v. Steen, 331 A.2d 724, 732 (Super.Ct.Pa.1974).

radiation, illness See *sickness, radiation*.

radiation, ionizing high-energy radiation (x-rays and gamma rays) which interacts to produce ion pairs in matter.

... the studies and experiments in the structure of the atom pointed toward physiological chemistry (and physics) leading prominent scientists to the conclusion that **ionizing radiation** causes changes in the male and female genital organs capable of producing deleterious effects upon future generations. The details of these interesting and important concepts and experiments are for scientists rather than judges and lawyers. It is sufficient for present purposes that the record discloses the existence of a substantial quantity of reliable scientific opinion that future generations may sustain absence of portions of the brain, absence of a finger or ear or other bodily members, defects in the neuro-muscular system, the circulatory system, the genito-urinary system, the gastro-intestinal system, the skin, or other deformities due to the effect of **ionizing radiation**....

... Their testimony amply supports the explicit findings of the Referee and the Appellate Division that the effect of X-ray exposure to the reproductive life is deleterious, additive and cumulative. The bad effects, according to this testimony, vary according to the total of **ionizing radiation** to which the individual is subjected. Chiropractic Ass'n of New York, Inc. v. Hilleboe, 187 N.E.2d 756–7 (N.Y.1962).

radiation, microwave See *microwave*.

One of the crucial questions presented, and one which resulted in conflicting views, was the amount of **microwave radiation** to which decedent was exposed; whether it exceeded permissible standards and whether those standards themselves are within acceptable levels. Yannon v. New York Telephone Co., 450 N.Y.S.2d 893–4 (3d Dep't 1982).

radiation, sickness See *sickness, radiation*.

radical (rad'ĭ-kal) [L. *radicalis*] a group of atoms which enters into and goes out of chemical combination without change, and which forms one of the fundamental constituents of a molecule.

Radical (R): A group of atoms replaceable by a single atom, or remaining unchanged during a series of reactions and hence conveniently regarded as playing the part of a single atom; in Ritter, often a hydrocarbon chain. Ritter v. Rohm & Haas Co., 271 F.Supp. 313 (S.D.N.Y.1967).

radiculitis (rah-dik"u-li'tis) [L. *radicula* radicle + *-itis*] inflammation of the root of a spinal nerve, especially of that portion of the root which lies between the spinal cord and the intervertebral canal.

His diagnosis was acute lumbosacral sprain with evidence of **radiculitis** involving the left S1 nerve. Jackson v. Maloney Trucking & Storage, Inc., 424 So.2d 1037–9 (Ct.App.La. 1982).

In a letter to plaintiff's counsel dated January 23, 1976, Dr. Hart indicated that plaintiff demonstrated some evidence of **radiculitis** (inflammation of the root of a spinal nerve), which was probably associated with a systemic arthritis disorder. McClaflin v. Califano, 448 F.Supp. 69, 71 (D.Kan.1978).

... traumatic **radiculitis** (involvement of the nerves coming out between the cervical vertebrae and joining up with the nerves over the shoulder on her right side). Pain was severe and constant and was only partially controlled by medication. Plaintiff complained of weakness on her right side. ...

... Movement of her right arm was restricted and painful. **Radiculitis** has been known, in many cases where the original injury was severe, to be a permanent condition. McSwain v. Chicago Transit Authority, 362 N.E.2d 1264, 1267 (App.Ct. Ill.1977).

Other Authorities: Napoli v. State Farm Mut. Auto Ins. Co., 395 So.2d 720–1 (La.1981); Carter v. Woolco Dept. Store, 379 So.2d 759–60 (Ct.App.La.1979).

radiculitis, cervical

She also had **cervical radiculitis**—an inflammation of the spinal nerve roots—and exhibited signs of severe depression because of her prolonged illness. Fritsche v. Westinghouse Electric Corp., 261 A.2d 657, 660 (N.J.1970).

radiculopathy (rah-dik"u-lop'ah-the) disease of the nerve roots.

Dr. Shara found a positive straight leg raising reaction on the left which indicated "an L5 **radiculopathy**", but that this diagnosis was tentative because Daney otherwise had normal reflexes. Daney v. Argonaut Ins. Co., 421 So.2d 331, 333 (Ct. App.La.1982).

Plaintiff's allegedly disabling condition consists of low back pain with **radiculopathy** that transmits itself to his legs, neck and head, and which subjects plaintiff to feelings of exhaustion. Masone v. Califano, 482 F.Supp. 525–7 (S.D.N.Y.1979).
Other Authorities: Broadbent v. Harris, 698 F.2d 407, 410 (10th Cir. 1983).

radiculopathy, lumbar

He defined "lumbar **radiculopathy**" as a sciatic nerve root irritation secondary to his back injury. Hartford Accident & Indemnity Co. v. Contreras, 498 S.W.2d 419, 421 (Ct.Civ.App. Tex.1973).

radio frequency coagulation See under *coagulation*.

radioactive (ra"de-o-ak'tiv) having the property of radioactivity. See also *pollutant* (Colorado Public Interest Re-

search Group case); *radioactive (byproduct) material; radioactive (source) material*; and *radioactive (special nuclear) material* all under *material*; and *radioactivity*.

radioactive material See under *material*.

radioactive substance See *material, radioactive; substance, radioactive*; and *thorium dioxide*.

radioactive waste See *waste, radioactive*.

radioactivity (ra"de-o-ak-tiv'ĭ-te) the quality of emitting or the emission of corpuscular or electromagnetic radiations consequent to nuclear disintegration, a natural property of all chemical elements of atomic number above 83, and possible of induction in all other known elements.

Radioactivity is commonly, and for purposes of the regulations in this part shall be, measured in terms of disintegrations per unit time or in curies. One curie $= 3.7 \times 10^{10}$ disintegrations per second (dps) $= 2.2 \times 10^{12}$ disintegrations per minute (dpm). Commonly used submultiples of the curie are the millicurie and the microcurie:
   (1) One millicurie $(mCi)^1 = 0.001$ curie $(Ci)^1 = 3.7 \times 10^7$ dps.
   (2) One microcurie $(\mu Ci)^1 = 0.000001$ curie $= 3.7 \times 10^4$ dps.
[25 FR 10914, Nov. 17, 1960, as amended at 38 FR 29314, Oct. 24, 1973; 39 FR 23990, June 28, 1974; 40 FR 50705, Oct. 31, 1975]. 10 C.F.R. § 20.5 (1982).

"This suit is based on an alleged incident occurring March 13, 1957 when two **radioactive** pellets upon opening the reactor can became pulverized and contaminated the air as **radioactive** dust. ..." McVey v. Phillips Petroleum Co., 288 F.2d 53, 56 (5th Cir. 1961).

radiocarpal (ra"de-o-kar'pal) pertaining to the radius and carpus.

... a bone chip was removed from the lateral **radiocarpal** joint of the left leg. Southall v. Gabel, 293 N.E.2d 891–2 (Franklin Cty.Munic.Ct.Ohio 1972).

radiodermatitis (ra"de-o-der-mah-ti'tis) a cutaneous inflammatory reaction occurring as a result of exposure to biologically effective levels of ionizing radiation.

Novy consulted with a dermatologist who diagnosed the condition as **radiodermatitis**, an injury resulting from exposure to x-rays. The exposure to such radiation occurred in the course of Novy's practice. Dr. Novy had used a fluoroscope to x-ray fractures while he set them, and in so doing he had repeatedly exposed his hands to the x-rays. Upon discovering the source of his affliction the doctor ceased all work with x-rays. However, the effects of the exposure to radiation were irreversible and the problems with his hands worsened. The doctor testified that in late 1967 his hands began to stiffen, forcing him to give up the surgical and obstetrical procedures in his practice. Continental Cas. Co. v. Novy, 437 N.E.2d 1338, 1340–1 (Ct. App.Ind.1982).

After about two weeks of the third series of treatments, the plaintiff noticed that the skin of his left hip (in the area where he had received X-ray radiation treatment) had started to get hard and red, that it was sore, and that small blisters had started to develop. About one week after the last X-ray radiation treatment, the plaintiff visited the skin clinic of the hospital because the blisters began to break. He was instructed to use a Dakin solution. The outpatient department records of the skin clinic contained a note dated April 26, 1963, as follows: "Diagnosis is acute **radio dermatitis**, early."....

There is present in the X-ray a type of ray that produces erythema on the skin. This can be modified by filters on the X-ray machine or by variation in the kilovoltage, but when erythema appears on a patient it is not appropriate to reduce the kilovoltage. When erythema appears the filters are not filtering all of the soft rays. No change in filters was made during the course of the plaintiff's treatment. Dr. Branca further testified that it is good medical practice to apply radiation therapy to an area of the body to the extent that blisters and ulceration develop in that area of the skin; but it is not good medical practice to apply radiation to the skin to the extent that ulcers develop to a diameter of four inches and a depth of half an inch. McCarthy v. Boston City Hospital, 266 N.E.2d 292, 294 (Sup.Jud.Ct.Mass.1971).

radiograph (ra′de-o-graf″) a film produced by radiography. See also *bite-wing; panograph*; and *periapical*.

Radiographs and examination revealed: (1) chip fracture off antero-lateral aspect of distal left radius.... Southall v. Gabel, 293 N.E.2d 891–2 (Franklin Cty.Munic.Ct.Ohio 1972).

radiographer

(n) "**Radiographer**" means any individual who performs or who, in attendance at the site where the sealed source or sources are being used, personally supervises radiographic operations and who is responsible to the licensee for assuring compliance with the requirements of the [Nuclear Regulatory] Commission's regulations and the conditions of the license.... 10 C.F.R. 30.4(n).

radiography (ra″de-og′rah-fe) [*radio-* + Gr. *graphein* to write] the making of film records (radiographs) of internal structures of the body by passage of x-rays or gamma rays through the body to act on specially sensitized film. See also *roentgenography*.

radiologist (ra″de-ol′o-jist) a specialist in the use of radiant energy (x-rays, etc.) in the diagnosis and treatment of disease.

There is no **radiologist** in the x-ray room while the x-ray technicians are performing their duties and normally the **radiologist** does not see or consult with the patient....

... It is the **radiologist** who reads the film and who decides whether it is sufficient to enable a diagnosis of the area about which there is concern. While a technician is supposed to be skilled in the taking of x-rays, he is not an expert in deciding whether they are sufficient for the purpose of a specific diagnosis. Simpson v. Sisters of Charity of Providence, etc., 588 P.2d 4, 11 (Or.1978).

radiolucency (ra″de-o-lu′sen-se) the property of being radiolucent.

The tests showed a suspicious **radiolucency** or lesion on her right renal pelvis. Lane v. Wallace, 579 F.2d 1200–01 (10th Cir. 1978).

radiolucent (ra-de-o-lu′sent) [*radio-* + L. *lucere* to shine] permitting the passage of radiant energy, such as x-rays, yet offering some resistance to it, the representative areas appearing dark on the exposed film.

The **radiolucent** area shown in the X ray on tooth number 19 gave all the indications of decay. It was either decay, or a

wasting away of the tooth. The condition had just about reached the nerve of the tooth. There was a discoloration in or close to the nerve. A **radiolucent** area in an X ray indicates that there is a lesion in the tooth, a wasting away of the tooth, indicating a loss of tooth structure. It can indicate decay or a change in density of the tooth. After reexamining the X ray he came to the conclusion that plaintiff's pain was coming from tooth No. 19. He based this conclusion upon the fact that the **radiolucent** area was on the back surface of the tooth, below the gum line in the root of the tooth. When decay reaches the nerve of a tooth, extraction is one remedy. Plaintiff had stated that taking hot or cold substances into her mouth caused pain. Carr v. Dickey, 329 P.2d 539, 541 (Dist.Ct.App.Cal.1958).

radionuclide (ra″de-o-nu′klīd) a radioactive nuclide; one that disintegrates with the emission of corpuscular or electromagnetic radiations.

The monitoring of the flared gas provides a measure of the quantity af [sic] the **radionuclides** released in the gas. However, in order to determine the actual exposure of individuals, it is essential to establish concentrations of **radionuclides** in the environment of the exposed individuals. Crowther v. Seaborg, 312 F.Supp. 1205, 1224 (D.Colo.1970).

radiopaque (ra″de-o-pāk′) [*radio-* + L. *opacus* dark, obscure] not permitting the passage of radiant energy, such as x-rays, the representative areas appearing light or white on the exposed film.

Renographin-60, the contrast agent used in the IVP, is an irritant. Smith v. Shannon, 666 P.2d 351, 353 (Wash.1983).

Part of that procedure is to inject the patient with a dye which causes clear images of the kidneys to appear on the x-ray films. The dye is injected intravenously.

Admitted into evidence was an exhibit containing the manufacturer's recommendations for the use of the dye. In pertinent part these provide: "Severe, life-threatening reactions suggest hypersensitivity to the **radiopaque** agent, which has prompted the use of several pretesting methods, none of which can be relied upon to predict severe reactions. Many authorities question the value of any. A history of bronchial asthma or allergy, a family history of allergy, or a previous reaction to a contrast agent warrant special attention. McMillen v. Carlinville Area Hosp., 450 N.E.2d 5, 7–8 (App.Ct.Ill.1983).

Both parties conceded that the **radiopaque** dye used in the operation has neurotoxic properties, and that the patient's paralysis resulted from the movement of the dye from her blood vessels, where it had been injected, into her spinal cord. Yet, the parties differed as to the precise medical cause of the transfer of dye into the spinal cord. Medvecz v. Choi, 569 F.2d 1221, 1223 (3d Cir. 1977).

radiotherapy (ra″de-o-ther′ah-pe) [*radio-* + Gr. *therapeia* cure] the treatment of disease by ionizing radiation. See also *beam*.

radiowave sickness See *sickness, microwave*.

radius (ra′de-us), pl. *ra′dii* [L. "spoke" (of a wheel)] [NA] the bone on the outer or thumb side of the forearm, articulating proximally with the humerus and ulna and distally with the ulna and carpus; see illustration accompanying *skeleton*. See also *wrist*.

He was there taken to a hospital, where examination by a physician disclosed that he had suffered a severe comminuted fracture of the distal right **radius** which extended into the joint. West v. Richmond, F. & P.R. Co., 528 F.2d 290–1 (4th Cir. 1975).

X-rays were taken and it was determined that Mrs. Lieder had comminuted fractures of the distal **radius** bilaterally of both wrists. Lieder v. Maus, 203 N.W.2d 393–4 (Minn.1973).

radix (ra'diks), pl. *rad'ices* [L.] the lowermost part, or a structure by which something is firmly attached; [NA] a general term for the lowermost part, or a part by which a structure is anchored, as the portion of a hair, nail, or tooth that is buried in the tissues, or the part of a nerve adjacent to the center to which it is connected. Called also *root*. See also *compression, spinal* (Stark case).

radix dentis [NA], root of tooth: the portion of a tooth which is covered by cementum, proximal to the neck of the tooth and ordinarily embedded in the dental alveolus; called also *anatomical root*.

... this doctor who testified on the trial found a **root** tip in Mrs. Gorsalitz's gum and advised having same removed at once as it could cause trouble. Gorsalitz v. Harris, 410 S.W.2d 956–7 (Ct.Civ.App.Tex.1966).

radices spinales nervi accessorii [NA], the spinal roots of the accessory nerve. Originating from the gray matter of the spinal cord and emerging from the side of the cord as far down as a level between the third and seventh cervical nerves, they form a trunk that ascends in the vertebral canal, passes through the foramen magnum, and unites with the cranial portion in the jugular foramen. The constituent fibers then form the external branch, which supplies the sternocleidomastoid and trapezius muscles.

There was also a compression fracture of a vertebra. The diagnosis was post-traumatic nerve root damage to certain spinal nerves resulting in impairment of bowel and bladder sensation and function. The doctor testified: "the most probable thing is they will be permanent" and "there won't be any cure." Hammond v. Estate of Rimmer, 643 S.W.2d 222, 224 (Ct.App.Tex.1982).

radon (ra'don) a heavy, colorless, gaseous, radioactive element, symbol Rn, atomic weight 222, atomic number 86, obtained by the breaking up of radium, and used in radiotherapy. Called also *radium emanation* (*RE*).[219] Rn is a radioactive isotope of the actinium radioactive series.[220] Rn is a radioactive isotope of the thorium radioactive series.

Radon is a colorless, odorless, tasteless gas and is a by-product of decaying uranium that can cause lung cancer, according to DER [Pennsylvania Dep't of Environmental Resources]. 17 BNA Env.Rptr. 119 (May 30, 1986).

Barnes told the conference that 5,000 to 20,000 lung cancer deaths each year are attributable to **radon**, but that definitive epidemiological studies on the cancer-causing air pollutant are four to five years away.... Panelist Robert Yuhnke, an attorney with Environmental Defense Fund, claimed that EPA's guideline for danger from **radon** exposure is "much too high." EPA's upper threshold for safe exposure to **radon** is 4 picocuries per liter. Yuhnke said this would result in a "one-in-65" chance of getting lung cancer. 17 BNA Env.Rptr. 971–2 (Oct. 24, 1986).

Radon is a naturally occurring radioactive gas created by the decay of uranium and radium deposits in soil. National concern over the threat posed by **radon** increased rapidly in 1985 with the discovery of unusually high levels of the gas in homes located on the Reading Prong, a geological formation extending across highly populated areas of New Jersey, New York and Pennsylvania. 17 BNA Env.Rptr. 596–7 (Aug. 22, 1986).

rale (rahl) [Fr. *râle* rattle] an abnormal respiratory sound heard in auscultation, and indicating some pathologic condition. Rales are distinguished as *dry* or *moist*, according to the absence or presence of fluid in the air passages, and are classified according to their site of origin as *bronchial, cavernous, laryngeal, pleural, tracheal*, and *vesicular, (crepitant)*. Cited in Magruder v. Richardson, 332 F.Supp. 1363, 1367 (E.D.Mo.1971).

rale, moist a rale produced by the presence of liquid in the bronchial tubes. Cited in Harris v. Ribicoff, 198 F.Supp. 861, 864 (W.D.N.C.1961).

rale, sibilant a hissing sound resembling that produced by suddenly separating two oiled surfaces. It is produced by the presence of a viscid secretion in the bronchial tubes or by thickening of the walls of the tubes; heard in asthma and bronchitis.

This time Dr. Hyde's diagnosis concluded that she was a well developed, and undernourished female appearing chronically ill, suffering from **sibilant rales** (a whistling sound). Harris v. Ribicoff, 198 F.Supp. 861, 864 (W.D.N.Car.1961).

rami (ra'mi) [L.] plural of *ramus*.

ramus (ra'mus), pl. *ra'mi* [L.] a branch; [NA] a general term for a smaller structure given off by a larger one, or into which the larger structure, such as a blood vessel or nerve, divides.

ramus inferior ossis pubis [NA]; **ramus, inferior, of pubis** the short flattened bar of bone that projects from the body of the pubic bone in a posteroinferolateral direction to meet the ramus of the ischium.

As a result of the occurrence, plaintiff suffered fractures of the right **inferior** and **superior pubic rami** and right hip joint. Johnson v. Chicago Transit Authority, 329 N.E.2d 395, 396 (App. Ct.Ill.1975).

ramus, inferior pubic See *ramus, inferior ossis pubis*.

ramus of mandible; ramus mandibulae [NA], a quadrilateral process projecting superiorly from the posterior part of either side of the mandible. See also *mandibula*.

Fracture of the left **ramus of the mandible**. Titus v. Smith, 330 F.Supp. 1192–3 (E.D.Pa.1971).

ramus, pelvic

Mr. Choice was later x-rayed and it was found that there was a fracture of the left inferior **pelvic rami**, which is the bridge of bone in front of the penis. U.S. v. Choice, 392 F.Supp. 460, 462 (E.D.Pa.1975).

ramus superior ossis pubis [NA]; **ramus, superior, of pubis** the bar of bone projecting from the body of the pubic bone in a posterosuperolateral direction to the iliopubic eminence, and forming part of the acetabulum.

ramus, superior pubic See *ramus superior ossis pubis*.

rash (rash) a temporary eruption on the skin, as in urticaria; a drug eruption or viral exanthem.

rash, heat See *miliaria rubra*.

rattlesnake bite See *bite, rattlesnake (Buck case)*.

ravocaine

> Rather, plaintiff suffered a reaction to the anesthetic, **ravocaine**, one of the drugs of the novocaine family commonly used as an oral anesthetic. Surabian v. Lorenz, 40 Cal.Rptr. 410–11 (Dist.Ct.App.Cal.1964).

ray (ra) [L. *radius* spoke] a line emanating from a center, as (*a*) a more or less distinct portion of radiant energy (light or heat), proceeding in a specific direction (used in the plural as a general term for any form of radiant energy, whether vibratory or particulate), or (*b*) one of the individual elements at the distal end of the limb of an early embryo, foretelling development of the metacarpal or metatarsal bones and the phalanges of the digits.

rays, roentgen electromagnetic vibrations of short wavelengths (from 5 A.U. down) or corresponding quanta (wave mechanics) that are produced when electrons moving at high velocity impinge on various substances, especially the heavy metals. They are commonly generated by passing a current of high voltage (from 10,000 volts up) through a Coolidge tube (see under *tube*). They are able to penetrate most substances to some extent, some much more readily than others, and to affect a photographic plate. These qualities make it possible to use them in taking roentgenograms of various parts of the body, thus revealing the presence and position of fractures or foreign bodies or of radiopaque substances that have been purposely introduced. They can also cause certain substances to fluoresce and this makes fluoroscopy possible, by which the size, shape and movements of various organs such as the heart, stomach and intestines can be observed. By reason of the high energy of their quanta, they strongly ionize tissue through which they pass by means of the photoelectrons, both primary and secondary, which they liberate. Because of this effect they are used in treating various pathological conditions. Called also *x-rays*. See also *chromosome; leukemia; mutation* (Chiropractic Ass'n of New York, Inc. case); *erythema* (McCarthy case); *filter* (Wilkinson case); and *suppuration* (Lopez case).

Dr. Cohen stated that "based on a reasonable degree of medical and radiological certainty, the administration of **X-ray** therapy for hypertrophic lymphoid tissue in the pharynx was standard and customary and ordinarily used by hospitals and physicians" at the times in question. Greenberg v. Michael Reese Hospital, 415 N.E.2d 390, 392 (Ill. 1980).

Thus, what we have said with regard to electricity applies equally to x-radiation. Just as electricity has been held to be personal property despite its intangible nature ... and a product within the meaning of 402A [Restatement (Second) of Torts (1965)] ....

X-radiation presented no danger as it contained no inherent defect. Rather, the dangerous condition was brought about by the medical decision to use certain amounts of **X-radiation** in treatment of plaintiffs' disease....

We, therefore, find that the appellate court erred in finding **X-radiation** to be a product subject to the doctrine of strict liability in tort. For the reasons stated, the judgment of the appellate court is reversed and the judgment of the circuit court is affirmed. Dubin v. Michael Reese Hospital, 415 N.E.2d 350, 352 (Ill.1981).

After plaintiff thought the surgery was completed, she said, " 'Did you get the tooth' and he said, 'No,' he had read the **x-ray** backwards and that there was no tooth there.' " Defendant then anesthetized the right side of plaintiff's mouth and removed the impacted wisdom tooth....

Dr. Cockerham testified that he could not state with any degree of certainty whether he told plaintiff the location of the one remaining wisdom tooth. In his normal practice, he would have placed the **x-rays** in the view box, oriented the impacted wisdom tooth on the right side, and explained that the **x-rays** were placed in the view box so that the left side of the patient's **x-ray** would be sitting on the right side of the view box. It was the duty of a dentist to orient an **x-ray** properly with a patient's mouth if a dentist was going to use it. Dr. Cockerham forwarded an **x-ray**, plaintiff's Exhibit #2, to defendant. Dr. Cockerham also testified that excluding one additional filling since 15 April 1975, there were three teeth on one side of plaintiff's mouth, which would be a way to orient the **x-ray**. Cozart v. Chapin, 251 S.E.2d 682–4 (Ct.App.N.C.1979).

Other Authorities: Simpson v. Sisters of Charity of Providence, etc., 588 P.2d 4, 7–8 (Or.1978); Ragan v. Steen, 331 A.2d 724, 732 (Super.Ct.Pa.1974); Wilkinson v. Vesey, 295 A.2d 676, 681 (R.I.1972); Lopez v. Swyer, 279 A.2d 116, 119 (Super.Ct.N.J.1971); Leavell v. Alton Ochsner Medical Foundation, 201 F.Supp. 805, 808 (E.D.La. 1962); Chiropractic Ass'n of New York, Inc. v. Hilleboe, 227 N.Y.S.2d 309, 336–7, 345–9 (Sup.Ct. Albany Cty. 1961).

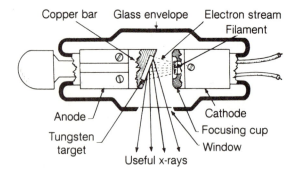

Standard stationary anode x-ray tube; diagram in longitudinal section. (Meschan.)

ray, roentgen reader

This same X-ray was reread by Dr. G. Joseph Rosenstein, who is a Board certified radiologist, and who, according to the government's brief, is known to be a certified "B" reader of coal miner's X-rays.[1] [[1] A certification as a "B" reader is the highest possible rating a physician may attain and is awarded only after he has successfully passed a specially designed proficiency examination given by or on behalf of the Appalachian Laboratory for Occupational Respiratory Diseases.] Hash v. Califano, 451 F.Supp. 383, 386 (S.D.Ill.1978).

rays, x the name given by Röntgen to roentgen rays.

Raynaud's phenomenon See *phenomenon, Raynaud's*; and *disease, Raynaud's*.

reaction (re-ak'shun) [*re-* + L. *agere* to act] in psychology, the mental and/or emotional state that develops in any particular situation.

reaction, acute situational a transient disorder, occurring in an individual without underlying mental disorder, in response to overwhelming environmental stress.

The psychiatrists diagnosed Richardson's disorder as "an acute and chronic situational reaction manifested by hysteria, anxiety, and depression." Watkins v. U.S., 589 F.2d 214–15 (5th Cir. 1979).

reaction, anaphylactic See *anaphylaxis*; and *shock, anaphylactic*.

reaction, byssinotic

Stevens' diagnosis was mild chronic obstructive pulmonary disease with a history of byssinotic reaction. Dr. Stevens gave plaintiff a note suggesting that he return to work immediately but avoid undue dust. Donnell v. Cone Mills Corp., 299 S.E.2d 436–7 (Ct.App.N.C.1983).

reaction, cell-mediated See *response, immune*.

reaction, conversion the conversion type of hysterical neurosis. See also *neurosis, hysterical*.

He also testified that he had developed an irritable and quarrelsome disposition and a limp, described at trial as a bizarre gait, which requires his body to be at an angle when he walks....

... Medical experts also testified that his bizarre gait was the result of a conversion reaction caused by the collision and the events following it. Anunti v. Payette, 268 N.W.2d 52, 54–5 (Minn.1978).

Mayo's diagnosis was post-traumatic syndrome and tinea cruris, pedis, and manus. No objective evidence of any neurologic impairment was found nor was there objective evidence of spinal cord disease or cervical or lumbar radiculopathy. A psychiatrist at Mayo believed Mr. Barlow was demonstrating a conversion reaction....

... He found nothing organically abnormal with the patient from a neurological standpoint. Dr. Moore's diagnosis was a post-traumatic psychoneurosis with conversion reaction, marked traumatic fixation with total invalid reaction, all of which the doctor explained to the jury. Barlow v. Thornhill, 537 S.W.2d 412, 415–16 (Mo.1976).

At that time he felt that Mr. Brecheen's condition was the same that had been bothering him for the past two years, that is, his schizophrenic reaction and conversion reaction. It converted his emotional tensions into physical symptoms of "headaches and vomiting, etc." Exxon Corp. v. Brecheen, 519 S.W.2d 170, 179 (Ct.Civ.App.Tex.1975), reversed and remanded 526 S.W.2d 579 (Tex.1975).

Other Authorities: Sullivan v. Weinberger, 493 F.2d 855, 858–9 (5th Cir. 1974).

reaction, depressive any neurotic depressive reaction in which insight is impaired to a lesser degree than in psychotic depression. See also *depression* (def. 3).

Dr. Herlihy's diagnosis was that the plaintiff was suffering from a "depressive illness" or "depressive reaction" which was precipitated by the accident. Abex Corp. v. Coleman, 386 So. 2d 1160–1 (Ct.Civ.App.Ala.1980).

reaction, gross stress an acute emotional reaction incident to severe environmental stress, e.g., in military operations or civilian disasters; called also *stress r.*

After several consultations with various doctors, he was hospitalized for psychiatric evaluation which revealed he was suffering from "gross stress reaction manifested by psychotic decompensation." Select Ins. Co. v. Boucher, 561 S.W.2d 474, 476 (Tex.1978).

reaction, insulin See *hypoglycemia*.

reaction, Moro's an eruption of pale or red papules on a cutaneous area after application of an ointment of 5 ml. of old tuberculin and 5 gm. of anhydrous lanolin; other percutaneous tests, e.g., the Vollmer patch test, have replaced Moro's test.

reaction, ophthalmic local reaction of the conjunctiva following instillation into the eye of toxins of typhoid fever and tuberculosis. The reaction is much more severe in persons affected with these diseases than in the healthy or those affected with some other disease. Called also *Calmette's ophthalmoreaction*. See also *Calmette's tuberculin*, under *tuberculin*.

reaction, Pirquet's appearance of a papule with a red areola 24–48 hours after introduction of two small drops of old tuberculin by slight scarification; a positive test indicates previous infection but does not distinguish clinical disease. Called also *dermotuberculin r.*, *Pirquet's test*, *scarification test*, and *von Pirquet's cutireaction* or *test*.

reaction, schizophrenic See *schizophrenia, reactive*.

He defined the term "a schizophrenic reaction" as being a split mind in that one could be realistic and appropriate in some aspects of his life, but in other aspects such a person could be "very unrealistic and unappropriate and unlogical and sick." Exxon Corp. v. Brecheen, 519 S.W.2d 170, 178 (Ct.Civ.App.Tex.1975), reversed and remanded 526 S.W.2d 579 (Tex.1975).

reagent (re-a'jent) [*re-* + L. *agere* to act] a substance employed to produce a chemical reaction so as to detect, measure, produce, etc., other substances.

reagent, Stokes' (*for oxyhemoglobin*), a solution containing 2 per cent of ferrous sulfate and 3 per cent of tartaric or citric acid; for use, add ammonium hydroxide to a small portion until the precipitate redissolves, thus forming ammonium ferrotartrate.

reamer (re′mer) an instrument used in dentistry for enlarging root canals.

He testified that the breaking of a root canal **reamer** in the canal is not necessarily negligence (breach of duty). He testified that the root canal **reamer** can be broken off intentionally as part of treatment, can break because it is defective, or can break from too much pressure. He further testified that the breaking of the root canal **reamer** does not necessarily preclude a successful final result. Wiley v. Karam, 421 So.2d 294, 297 (Ct.App.La.1982).

This suit was brought by plaintiffs, alleging that Dr. Harold Faget was guilty of dental malpractice which resulted in Mrs. Dufrene's swallowing a small needlelike instrument known as a root canal **reamer.** Surgery was subsequently necessary to remove this instrument, which measured approximately 1¼ inches in length, from the plaintiff's duodenum. Dufrene v. Faget, 260 So.2d 76–7 (Ct.App.La.1972).

reanastomosis See *anastomosis.*

reassignment, sex

Plaintiff's surgeon, Dr. Roberto Granato, who performed the **sex reassignment** operation on plaintiff, asserts that the male genitalia of Dr. Richards were removed and that as the result of the surgery the external genital appearance of Dr. Richards is that of female. Further:

> With respect to Dr. Richard's internal sex, due to the operation I performed, one would say that Dr. Richards' internal sexual structure is anatomically similar to a biological woman who underwent a total hysterectomy and ovariectomy. Richards v. U.S.Tennis Ass'n, 400 N.Y.S.2d 267, 271 (Sup.Ct. N.Y.Cty.1977).

recanalization

There was testimony from which the jury could infer that prior to the operation Dr. McKelway failed to disclose to Hartke that there was a risk of **recanalization**—where a Fallopian tube spontaneously reopens—of one to three out of one thousand. Hartke and her boyfriend, with whom she had lived for four years and whom she later married, also testified that the boyfriend offered to undergo a vasectomy if there was any risk of subsequent pregnancy, but that McKelway told them that the procedure was "a 100 percent sure operation," and that Hartke would not have to worry about becoming pregnant again. Record Excerpts (R.E.) at 33; accord id. at 34. Hartke v. McKelway, 707 F.2d 1544, 1547 (D.C.Cir.1983).

recessive (re-ses′iv) tending to recede; not exerting a ruling or controlling influence; in genetics, incapable of expression unless the responsible allele is carried by both members of a pair of homologous chromosomes. A recessive allele or trait.

... **recessive** defects which require that before the trait is clearly manifested it must be inherited both from the father and from the mother....

The **recessive** ones will not be manifested perhaps for many generations. Chiropractic Ass'n of New York, Inc. v. Hilleboe, 227 N.Y.S.2d 309, 367 (Sup.Ct.Albany Cty.1961).

recombinant (re-kom′bĭ-nant) 1. the new cell or individual that results from genetic recombination. 2. pertaining or relating to such cells or individuals. See also under *DNA.*

Significantly, the NIH guidelines "prohibit certain kinds of **recombinant** DNA experiments which include virtually all the known hazards—for example, those involving known infectious agents." Mack v. Califano, 447 F.Supp. 668–9 (D.D.C.1978).

recombination (re″kom-bĭ-na′shun) the reunion, in the same or a different arrangement, of formerly united elements which have become separated. In genetics, the formation of new combinations of genes as a result of crossing over between homologous chromosomes.

recon (re′kon) [*rec* combination + Gr. *on* neuter ending] the smallest unit of genetic material capable of recombination, presumably a series of three nucleotide bases (a triplet). Cf. *cistron* and *muton.*

record (rek′ord) a permanent or long-lasting account of something (as on film, in writing, etc.); in dentistry, a registration.

record, hospital See *chart, anesthesiological;* and *register of operations.*

In 1975 the code provisions governing the organization and administration of a hospital were set forth in 10 N.Y.C.R.R. Part 720 as established pursuant to the provisions of Public Health Law 2803.

In Section 720.13, subd. (g), there is the requirement that a **register of operations** be maintained in a bound book in the operating suite which should include the following information for each surgical procedure performed:

> "4.   Name of surgeon, anesthetists, assistants and nurses;
> "5.   Surgical procedures performed and anesthetic agents used; and
> "6.   Complications of surgery."

There is a further requirement [10 N.Y.C.R.R.] (720.20) that the hospital maintain a medical record department under supervision of a medical record administrator or other qualified person and that a complete medical record be maintained including surgical reports which "shall be completed promptly, authenticated and signed by a physician" (subd. j).

The testimony of the Chief of Surgery of the Smithtown General Hospital and a representative of the Suffolk County Department of Health Services includes statements that the surgeon's report should list the name of his assistants as well as a statement of the complications that may have occurred. People v. Smithtown General Hospital, 402 N.Y.S.2d 318, 321, 323 (Sup.Ct.Crim.Term, Suffolk Cty.1978).

Here we have statements written by a business manager of a hospital relating to an incident occurring in the hospital. One statement was made at least four hours after the incident; the other four days after the incident. That he knew the incident could result in a lawsuit is certain from the fact that he notified the University's attorney and its insurance carrier. Thus the statements have none of the usual safeguards of a res gestae statement and clearly were inadmissible under the res gestae theory advanced by counsel. . . .

We believe that incident reports, a requirement in many hospitals, are proper. This opinion, therefore, is not a condemnation of such reports or of the interest of the business manager in recording what happens in the hospital. We feel, however, that the statute under which **hospital records**, including incident reports, are sometimes received in evidence as business records, was never intended to include ex parte statements gathered under the circumstances and for the purposes and persons for whom Exhibits 8A and 12 were prepared. . . .

. . . When their primary utility is litigation and not hospital administration or technique, and when they are made by one not a participant as a supplement to an incident report previously prepared by a participant and make reference to insurance, or an insurance company, or contain other irrelevant or incompetent matter, they are not business records of the kind intended to be received in evidence under the business records acts. [Footnote omitted.] Picker X-Ray Corp. v. Frerker, 405 F.2d 916, 922–4 (8th Cir. 1969).

recovery room See *room, recovery.*

rectocele (rek′to-sēl) [*recto-* + Gr. *kēlē* hernia] hernial protrusion of part of the rectum into the vagina; called also *proctocele.*

The patient's knee struck her abdomen causing her to involuntarily void urine. The unanimous medical opinion is that she suffered a **rectocele** and cystocele (i.e., hernias in which the rectum and bladder protrude into the vaginal space). The doctors agree that these herniated structures prevent her from heavy lifting. LaMountain v. Alice Hyde Hospital Ass'n, 406 N.Y.S.2d 914–15 (3d Dep't 1978).

. . . and a slight **rectocele** (hernia of the rectum), known as anatomical defects. Hammock v. Allstate Insurance Co., 186 S.E.2d 353–4 (Ct.App.Ga.1971).

Other Authorities: Buckelew v. Grossbard, 435 A.2d 1150, 1153 (N.J.1981); Kerbeck v. Suchy, 270 N.E.2d 291–2 (App. Ct.Ill.1971).

rectosigmoid (rek″to-sig′moid) the lower portion of the sigmoid and upper portion of the rectum. See also *rectum*; and *sigmoidoscope* (both Purcell case).

A barium enema x-ray report showed a complete obstruction in the area of the **rectosigmoid** junction. Purcell v. Zimbelman, 500 P.2d 335, 339 (Ct.App.Ariz.1972).

rectum (rek′tum) [L. "straight"] [NA] the distal portion of the large intestine, beginning anterior to the third sacral vertebra as a continuation of the sigmoid and ending at the anal canal; called also *intestinum rectum.*

A barium enema x-ray report showed a complete obstruction in the area of the rectosigmoid junction.[3] [3 The **rectum** is the last part of the colon. The sigmoid is the part of the colon preceding the **rectum**. Both parts are continuous and represent arbitrary divisions of the large bowel, mainly for convenience of reference.] Purcell v. Zimbelman, 500 P.2d 335, 339 (Ct. App.Ariz.1972).

recurrence (re-kur′ens) [L. *re-* again + *currere* to run] the return of symptoms after a remission.

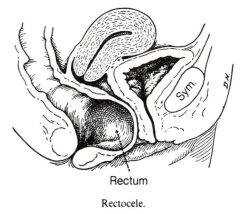

Rectum

Rectocele.

Dr. Fahey himself indicated that the claimant had "signs and symptoms which were slightly suggestive of **recurrence** of discogenic disease." We think it unlikely that Dr. Fahey only inadvertently used the word "**recurrence**" when he really intended to refer to the "existence" of discogenic disease. Purdham v. Celebrezze, 349 F.2d 828, 830 (4th Cir. 1965).

recurrence (distinguished from aggravation) See *aggravation.*

red See *redbird.*

red tide See *Dinoflagellata; Gonyaulax;* and *Gymnodinium.*

redbird See *black mollie* (Lapp case).

"Reds" or "**Redbirds**" are shown by the evidence to be "downers" or depressants. . . .

. . . and that the "reds" or red capsules contained a barbituric acid derivative, same being a barbiturate. Lapp v. State, 519 S.W.2d 443, 445–6 (Ct.Crim.App.Tex.1975).

reduce (re-dūs′) [*re-* + L. *ducere* to lead] to restore to the normal place or relation of parts, as to *reduce* a fracture. See also *reduction.*

Dr. Shaughnessy chose to continue the conservative treatment he had begun, rather than to try to **reduce** the hip (replace the head of the femur back into the hip socket). Reeg v. Shaughnessy, 570 F.2d 309, 312 (10th Cir. 1978).

reduction (re-duk′shun) [L. *reductio*] the correction of a fracture, luxation, or hernia.

reduction, closed the manipulative reduction of a fracture without incision.

Dr. Robert Miller, Weise's expert witness, testified that the preferable course of treatment for Weise's fracture would have been open reduction (surgery), although non-operative **closed reduction** was an acceptable alternative treatment.[1] [1 **Closed reduction** is a procedure that involves manipulation of the bone. Anesthesia must be used during the procedure.] Weise v. U.S., 724 F.2d 587–8 (7th Cir. 1984).

A **closed reduction** and manipulation was performed with reference to the multiple fractures of the right tibia. . . . Warmsley v. City of New York, 454 N.Y.S.2d 144–5 (2d Dep't 1982).

Fugle attempted **closed reduction** of the dislocated shoulder....

... Katzowitz admitted attempting a **reduction** by placing his foot on the plaintiff's chest while he pulled on his arm. Katzowitz attempted the **reduction** some 16 hours after the dislocation occurred. Plaintiff was given no anesthetic. There is some indication that plaintiff was experiencing muscle spasms at that time. Grewe v. Mount Clemens General Hospital, 253 N.W.2d 805–6 (Ct.App.Mich.1977).

Other Authorities: White v. Mitchell, 568 S.W.2d 216–17 (Ark.1978); Donaldson v. Maffucci, 156 A.2d 835, 837 (Pa. 1959).

reduction, open reduction of a fracture after incision into the fracture site.

On March 11, 1977, an **open reduction** and internal fixation was performed. Clamps were used to hold the fractured pieces of bone together and then a six-inch-long steel plate was screwed into the site with eight screws in an attempt to restore the bones to their original position. Warmsley v. City of New York, 454 N.Y.S.2d 144–5 (2d Dep't 1982).

Only after the passing of several months were Paula's parents first to learn through consultation of another physician that their child had been suffering from a broken arm. A medical procedure known as an "**open reduction**" involving calcium removal and the physical realignment of the fractured area was then required. Phillips v. Good Samaritan Hospital, 416 N.E.2d 646, 648 (Ct.App. Ohio 1979).

He received an open comminuted fracture of the radius and ulna of the left forearm....

... A considerable area of necrotic muscle tissue was removed. Incisions were made over the lower end of the radius and ulna, the ends of the bones exposed, and drill holes made in the ends of the bones and a rush rod inserted. The fracture of each bone was **reduced** and the rush rod passed across the fracture into the bone above the fracture on each bone. Swelling prevented the wound being brought together and the wound was left open. Zipp v. Gasen's Drug Stores, Inc., 449 S.W.2d 612, 621 (Mo.1970).

Other Authorities: Johns Hopkins Hospital v. Lehninger, 429 A.2d 538, 540 (Ct.Spec.App.Md.1981); Castellanos v. Industrial Com'n, 488 P.2d 675–6 (Ct.App.Ariz.1971); Dobson v. Myers, 247 F.Supp. 427, 430 (M.D.Pa.1965); Donaldson v. Maffucci, 156 A.2d 835, 837 (Pa.1959).

reflection, periotoneal

The trouble in Zimbelman's case was located above the **peritoneal reflection.**[2] [[2] The bottom of the abdomen.] Purcell v. Zimbelman, 500 P.2d 335, 339 (Ct.App.Ariz.1972).

reflex (re′fleks) [L. *reflexus*] a reflected action or movement; the sum total of any particular involuntary activity. See also *arc, reflex*; and *action, reflex.*

reflex, Achilles tendon See *jerk, triceps surae.*

reflex, Babinski's (1896), dorsiflexion of the big toe on stimulating the sole of the foot; it occurs in lesions of the pyramidal tract, and indicates organic, as distinguished from hysteric, hemiplegia. Called also *Babinski's sign* or *toe sign.*

In explaining that the Plaintiff has a positive **Babinski response** in one of her legs, he said this would not rule out GBS because while she has significant loss of the nerve and muscle fibers of the leg, there would be enough fibers remaining to allow an involuntary movement such as a **Babinski response.** [Footnote omitted.] McDonald v. U.S., 555 F.Supp. 935, 945 (M.D.Pa. 1983).

... the findings of pathologic reflex or reflexes at one time or another in one or both legs, called a **Babinski response**, or a withdrawal response, or a Chaddock response.... Pratt v. Stein, 444 A.2d 674, 682 (Super.Ct.Pa.1982).

The leg—or the foot rather, was inverted as it is today, with the foot turned inwards in a spastic condition, and she had what was described then and still has now, from simple observation, tonic **Babinski toe sign.** A **Babinski sign** is named after the man who described this. It is elicited by stroking the sole of the foot. The normal response to stroking the sole of the foot is a downward movement or a grasping movement of the toes.

"When certain brain and spinal cord pathways are involved, this response is replaced by an upward extension of the big toe and a fanning or partial flexion of the little toes. She has this position even without stimulation of the sole of the foot, in which case it is called a tonic or a constant **Babinski sign** rather than one elicited by stimulation...." Talcott v. Holl, 224 So.2d 420, 423 (Dist.Ct. App.Fla.1969).

reflex, cremasteric stimulation of the skin on the front and inner side of the thigh retracts the testis on the same side. The presence of this reflex indicates integrity of the first lumbar nerve segment of the spinal cord or its root; absence indicates damage of the first lumber nerve segment or its root or lesion of the corticospinal tract. Cf. *Geigel's r.* See also *musculus cremaster.*

The **cremasteric reflexes** are absent. Bartlett v. Secretary of Dept. of Health, Ed. & Welf., 330 F.Supp. 1273, 1278 (E.D. Ky.1971).

reflex, deep one elicited by a sharp tap on the appropriate tendon or muscle to induce brief stretch of the muscle, followed by contraction. Called also *tendon r.*

reflex, Geigel's a reflex in the female corresponding to the cremasteric reflex in the male; i.e., on stroking of the inner anterior aspect of the upper thigh there is a contraction of the muscular fibers at the upper edge of Poupart's ligament.

reflex, Hoffmann's See under *sign.*

reflex, Moro's; reflex, Moro embrace flexion of an infant's thighs and knees, fanning and then clenching of the fingers, with the arms first thrown outward then brought together in an embrace attitude, produced by a sudden stimulus, such as striking the table on either side of the child. It is seen normally in infants up to 3 to 4 months of age. Called also *embrace r.* and *startle r.*

Blood tests for bilirubin are not invariably accurate; hence the physician also regularly observes the child for signs of heightened bilirubin levels. These signs include jaundice, lessened suck reflex and **Moro's reaction** instinctive embracing grasp when jarred.... Schnebly v. Baker, 217 N.W.2d 708, 712 (Iowa 1974).

reflex, oculocephalogyric the reflex by which the movements of the eye, the head, and the body are directed in the interest of visual attention.

The **oculocephalic reflex** test consists of turning the head from side to side with the eyes open. In a positive response, when the head is rotated to the right, the eyes deviate to the left. Matter of Quinlan, 348 A.2d 801, 807 (Super.Ct.N.J.1975).

reflex, oculovestibular

The **oculovestibular reflex** ascertained by a caloric stimulation test consists of the slow introduction of ice water into the ear canal. The eyes drift or move toward the irrigated ear. It is a lateral eye movement test. Matter of Quinlan, 348 A.2d 801, 807 (Super.Ct.N.J.1975).

reflex, pharyngeal contraction of the constrictor muscle of the pharynx elicited by touching the back of the pharynx; called also *gag r.*

reflex, tendon involuntary contraction of a muscle after brief stretching caused by percussion of its tendon; tendon reflexes include the biceps reflex, triceps reflex, quadriceps reflex, etc. Called also *deep r., tendon jerk* or *reaction.*

reflex, triceps surae plantar flexion of the foot elicited by a tap on the Achilles tendon preferably while the patient kneels on a bed or chair, the feet hanging free over the edge; ankle jerk.

He had an absence of the **Achilles tendon reflex** on both sides and that its absence means that there is some lack of impulses getting to that, either because of pressure on the nerve at some level or to degenerative changes that have been there for a long period of time. Hitchcock v. Weddle, 304 F.2d 735, 737 (10th Cir. 1962).

reflux (re'fluks) [*re-* + L. *fluxus* flow] a backward or return flow.

The doctor determined the problem was caused by bile **reflux** into the stomach and performed a surgical revision of the bile flow. Bellard v. Woodward Wight & Co., Ltd., 362 So.2d 819, 822 (Ct.App.La.1978).

Reflux is the condition where urine backs up in the bladder and flows back up the ureters. **Reflux** is likely to lead to infection in the ureters and kidneys. Harrigan v. U.S., 408 F.Supp. 177, 180 (E.D.Pa.1976).

refraction (re-frak'shun) 1. the act or process of refracting; specifically the determination of the refractive errors of the eye and their correction by glasses. 2. the deviation of light in passing obliquely from one medium to another of different density. The deviation occurs at the surface of junction of the two mediums, which is known as the refracting surface. The ray before refraction is called the *incident ray;* after refraction it is the *refracted ray.* The point of junction of the incident and the refracted ray is known as the *point of incidence.* The angle between the incident ray and a line perpendicular to the refracting surface at the point of incidence is known as the *angle of incidence;* that between the refracted ray and this perpendicular is called the *angle of refraction.* The sine of the angle of incidence divided by the sine of the angle of refraction gives the *relative index of refraction.*

The affidavits of two ophthalmologists and one optometrist reveal that **refractive error** is not a disease of the eye, but rather a physical state of the structural components of the eye that in some cases can cause greater visual impairment than a disease. **Refractive error** does not generally lead to blindness, but can be so substantial that it renders an individual legally blind. [Footnote omitted.] Simpson v. Wilson, 480 F.Supp. 97, 99–100 (D.Vt.1979).

The affidavits explain that a **refractive error** is a physical state of the eye components causing visual impairment. The severity of the **refractive error** depends on the size and shape of the eye with respect to the optical system. An eye that is too long will produce nearsightedness (myopia), and one that is too short causes farsightedness (hyperopia). Eyeglasses will correct **refractive errors** when there is significant visual impairment but may not be necessary when the **refractive error** is minor in degree. White v. Beal, 555 F.2d 1146, 1150 (3d Cir. 1977).

We first consider whether the defendants prescribe lenses to correct **refractive errors. Refraction** is the deviation of light passing obliquely from one medium to another of different density. As this relates to the human eye it is the process by which light rays come to focus on the retina. A "**refraction**," optometrically speaking, is taken to determine if such a focusing does take place and, if it does not, the "**refraction**" reveals the degree of error. State ex rel. Londerholm v. Doolin, 497 P.2d 138, 151 (Kan.1972).

refraction, ocular the refraction of light produced by the mediums of the normal eye and resulting in the focusing of images upon the retina.

refractive error See *refraction;* and *refraction, ocular.*

refusal of treatment See *treatment, refusal of* (Bostic case).

regio (re'je-o), pl. *regio'nes* [L. "a space enclosed by lines"] a region: a plane area with more or less definite boundaries; [NA] a general term for certain areas on the surface of the body within certain defined boundaries.

region (re'jun) a plane area with more or less definite boundaries. See also *regio.*

register of operations

In 1975 the code provisions governing the organization and administration of a hospital were set forth in 10 N.Y.C.R.R. Part 720 as established pursuant to the provisions of Public Health Law 2803.

In Section 720.13, subd. (g), there is the requirement that a **register of operations** be maintained in a bound book in the operating suite which should include the following information for each surgical procedure performed:

"4. Name of surgeon, anesthetists, assistants and nurses;
"5. Surgical procedures performed and anesthetic agents used; and
"6. Complications of surgery." People v. Smithtown General Hospital, 402 N.Y.S.2d 318, 323 (Sup.Ct.Suffolk Cty.1978).

registered nurse See *nurse, registered.*

regurgitation (re-gur"ji-ta'shun) [*re-* + L. *gurgitare* to flood] a backward flowing, as the casting up of undigested food, or the backward flowing of blood into the heart, or between the chambers of the heart when a valve is incompetent.

regurgitation, mitral backflow of blood from the left ventricle into the left atrium, owing to inadequate functioning (insufficiency) of the mitral valve.

Two days later on October 6, Donna Walstad was discharged with a heart diagnosis of severe **mitral regurgitation** and was informed that heart surgery would ultimately have to be performed. Walstad v. University of Minnesota Hospitals, 442 F.2d 634, 637 (8th Cir. 1971).

... he concluded that there was a possibility of some **mitral insufficiency** (inefficient valve operation, not caused by disease). Magruder v. Richardson, 332 F.Supp. 1363, 1368 (E.D. Mo.1971).

rehabilitation (re"hah-bil"ĭ-ta'shun) the restoration of an ill or injured patient to self-sufficiency or to gainful employment at his highest attainable skill in the shortest possible time.

Our reading of the statute leads us to conclude that non-medical treatment is available as an alternative to medicine and that, under the circumstances, vocational **rehabilitation** does not constitute non-medical treatment designed to treat, cure, relieve or restore physical health of the appellant. It is a step taken to educate a person thereby increasing his job marketability rather than a treatment taken to cure an injury or disease. Interpreting the statute as a whole, with reference being made to related statutes, we find that the legislative intent in extending the employer's duty beyond medical and pharmaceutical expenses, so as to include "non-medical treatment", was to provide the injured worker with therapeutic expenses such as chiropractic services rather than vocational **rehabilitation**. LSA–C.C. Arts. 16–18. Koslow v. E. R. Desormeaux, Inc., 428 So.2d 1275, 1277 (La.Ct. of App.1983).

relaxant (re-lak'sant) [L. *relaxare* to loosen] an agent that lessens tension.

relaxant, muscle an agent that specifically aids in reducing muscle tension, as those acting at the polysynaptic neurons of motor nerves (e.g., meprobamate) or at the myoneural junction (curare and related compounds).

Dr. Marcelle Willock, an anesthesiologist, testified at length concerning the nature and action of **muscle relaxants**. She described the clinical symptoms of persons who have been given each of the two broad types of **muscle relaxants**, succinylcholine and turbocurare, a sub-type of which is pavulon. She then testified that to produce a certain cluster of symptoms (which, it would come to pass, resembled those suffered by the patients named in the indictment), it would be necessary to have injected the **muscle relaxant**, probably pavulon, into the intravenous tubing in a rapid, "bolus" fashion. U.S. v. Narciso, 446 F.Supp. 252, 307 (E.D.Mich.1977).

release, carpal tunnel See *tunnel, carpal;* and *decompression.*

release, slow

The specification of the application in suit relates to the adsorption of drugs on ion-exchange resins to provide **slow and even release** of the drug in the gastro-intestinal tract over an extended period of time. Clinical Products Ltd. v. Brenner, 255 F.Supp. 131, 134–5 (D.D.C.1966).

rem (rem) [*roentgen-equivalent–man*] the quantity of any ionizing radiation which has the same biological effectiveness as 1 rad of x-rays; 1 rem = 1 rad × **RBE** (relative biological effectiveness).

The **rem**, as used in this part, is a measure of the dose of any ionizing radiation to body tissues in terms of its estimated biological effect relative to a dose of one roentgen (r) of X-rays. (One millirem (mrem)=0.001 **rem**.) The relation of the **rem** to other dose units depends upon the biological effect under consideration and upon the conditions of irradiation. For the purpose of the regulations in this part, any of the following is considered to be equivalent to a dose of one **rem**:

(1) A dose of 1 r due to X– or gamma radiation;

(2) A dose of 1 rad due to X–, gamma, or beta radiation;

(3) A dose of 0.1 rad due to neutrons or high energy protons;

(4) A dose of 0.05 rad due to particles heavier than protons and with sufficient energy to reach the lens of the eye; If it is more convenient to measure the neutron flux, or equivalent, than to determine the neutron dose in rads, as provided in paragraph (c)(3) of this section, one **rem** of neutron radiation may, for purposes of the regulations in this part, be assumed to be equivalent to 14 million neutrons per square centimeter incident upon the body; or, if there exists sufficient information to estimate with reasonable accuracy the approximate distribution in energy of the neutrons, the incident number of neutrons per square centimeter equivalent to one **rem** may be estimated from the following table:

NEUTRON FLUX DOSE EQUIVALENTS

Neutron energy (Mev)	Number of neutrons per square centimeter equivalent to a dose of 1 rem (neutrons/cm^2)	Average flux to delivery 100 millirem in 40 hours (neutrons/cm^2 sec.)
Thermal	970 · 10^6	670
0.0001	720 · 10^6	500
0.005	820 · 10^6	570
0.02	400 · 10^6	280
0.1	120 · 10^6	80
0.5	43 · 10^6	30
1.0	26 · 10^6	18
2.5	29 · 10^6	20
5.0	26 · 10^6	18
7.5	24 · 10^6	17
10	24 · 10^6	17
10 to 30	14 · 10^6	10

10 C.F.R. § 20.4(c) (1982).

"The **rem** . . . is a measure of the dose of any ionizing radiation to body tissue in terms of its estimated biological effect relative to a dose of one roentgen (r) of X-rays. (One millirem (mrem)=0.001 **rem**)." 10 C.F.R. § 20.4(c) (1975). York Com. for a Safe Envir. v. U.S. Nuclear Reg., 527 F.2d 812, 814 (D.C. Cir.1975).

The "dose" to a human being from exposure to radiation is measured in **rems**. A **rem** is the absorbed dosage of radiation (measured in rads) multiplied by the appropriate quality factor. The absorbed dosage depends upon the energy level and concentration of the radionuclide producing the radiation. The quality factor is a number which expresses the radiobiological effect of the radiation, its ability to damage living cells. Crowther v. Seaborg, 312 F.Supp. 1205, 1227 (D.Colo.1970).

remission (re-mish'un) [L. *remissio*] a diminution or abatement of the symptoms of a disease; also the period during which such diminution occurs.

Moreover, while most patients survive chemotherapy, **remission** of the leukemia is achieved in only thirty to fifty per cent of the cases. **Remission** is meant here as a temporary return to normal as measured by clinical and laboratory means. If **remission** does occur, it typically lasts for between two and thirteen months although longer periods of **remission** are possible. Superintendent of Belchertown v. Saikewicz, 370 N.E.2d 417, 420 (Sup.Jud.Ct.Mass.1977).

Finally, Dr. Taylor agreed with Dr. Cunningham that spontaneous **remission** was a medical fact and could occur in any cancer patient prior to the emergence of clinical signs of imminent death. Continental Ill. Nat. B. & T. Co. of Chicago v. U.S., 504 F.2d 586, 592 (7th Cir. 1974).

Renographin-60 See *radiopaque.*

repair (re-pār') the physical or mechanical restoration of damaged or diseased tissues by the growth of healthy new cells or by surgical apposition.

repair, Nissen

The depositions and affidavits in this case reveal that Dr. Zacheis performed a **Nissen repair** of a hiatal or diaphragmatic hernia on plaintiff on January 22, 1976....

... The sphincter at the end of the esophagus was not closing because of the dilatation at the lower end of the esophagus. This caused a reflux from the stomach into the esophagus causing pressure and gas pains. The **Nissen repair** attempted to solve this problem through sewing the upper part of the stomach around the esophagus so the esophagus stops the contents of the stomach from coming back up. In making this repair, a bougie, which is a dilator, is pushed down like a tube through the esophagus, so the repair will not be made too tight and the surgeon will have something to stabilize the esophagus enabling him to wrap the stomach around it. Stringer v. Zacheis, 434 N.E.2d 50, 52 (App.Ct.Ill.1982).

replacement, total hip

A **total hip replacement** involves the surgical insertion of a plastic socket into the socket of the hip, and a metal shaft, with a ball on the end, into the femur. The new ball and socket approximate the natural bony structures they replace....

... Ordinarily, following a **total hip replacement** a patient will stay in a horizontal position in his hospital bed for several days, because (1) sitting could cause the hip to dislocate, and (2) patients suffer from dizziness as a result of the loss of blood during surgery. The preferred medical practice is to begin physical therapy as soon as the patient is able to tolerate it. One important aspect of the physical therapy is to have the patient walk between and with the support of parallel bars, under the supervision of a physical therapist employed by the hospital. The patient is moved from lying down to standing by

the use of a tilt table, a mechanized table with controls on the side operated by the physical therapist. Forsyth v. Sisters of Charity of Providence, 593 P.2d 1270–1 (Ct.App.Or.1979).

"Q. Can you tell us exactly what encompasses a hip replacement, from a medical standpoint?

"A. Well, a **total hip replacement**, such as Mr. Roeder had involving replacing both sides of the hip joint, replacing the sockets with a plastic socket, composed of high-density polyethylene, and the ball or the upper end of the femur is replaced with a stainless steel prosthesis. Both of these devices are then attached to the respective sides of the hip joint with methacrylates, which is a type of foam cement.

"Q. I wonder if we could concentrate for a second on the socket site, Doctor. Is there something done to round out the socket area, or what is done?

"A. Yes, the acetabulum is deepened and expanded to about two inches in diameter to accept the plastic socket that's put in place there." Roeder v. Industrial Com'n, 556 P.2d 1148–9 (Ct.App.Ariz.1976).

replacement, total hip, Charnley-Mueller

On October 9, 1974, the appellant underwent a **Charnley-Mueller total hip replacement** in which his hip was reduced and replaced by a prosthesis. Scheideler v. Elias, 309 N.W.2d 67, 69 (Neb.1981).

report, adverse reaction See *adverse reaction report.*

reproduction (re"pro-duk'shun) [L. *re-* again + *productio* production] the production of offspring by organized bodies.

"Q. And that is what happens at conception, the instant of conception. A. That's correct.

"Q. Then, almost instantaneously, that single cell begins its divisive process to go on to form over the course of approximately the next nine months the human being that is to be born? A. Yes. Every time a cell divides this is preceded by the **reproduction** of replication, as geneticists call the process, of the chromosomes; and then one duplicate of each chromosome goes to each daughter cell, so that when the original fertilized egg has forty-six chromosomes each daughter cell will have forty-six chromosomes, identical with those that were in the original fertilized egg cell; and if a fractured chromosome or a mutated gene is present in one of the chromosomes of the fertilized egg cell either coming from the ovum or coming from the sperm, it will be replicated and transferred to all of the cells of the body of the offspring, including the prospective reproductive cells which would be used in the next generation." Chiropractic Ass'n of New York, Inc. v. Hilleboe, 227 N.Y.S.2d 309, 364–5 (Sup. Ct.Albany Cty.1961).

reproductive organs See *organa genitalia feminina* under *organum.*

res ipsa loquitur

The doctrine of **res ipsa loquitur** permits an inference of defendant's negligence "where (a) the occurrence itself ordinarily bespeaks negligence; (b) the instrumentality was within the defendant's exclusive control; and (c) there is no indication in the circumstances that the injury was the result of the plaintiff's own voluntary act or neglect." Bornstein v. Metropolitan Bottling Co., 26 N.J. 263, 269, 139 A.2d 404 (1958)....

... Courts of this state have long recognized that depending upon the probabilities, the **res ipsa loquitur** doctrine can apply in a medical malpractice context. Sanzari v. Rosenfeld, 34 N.J. 128, 140, 167 A.2d 625 (1961) ("Where, for example, a surgical sponge is left inside a patient after an operation, it is reasonable to say the probability is that someone has been negligent." Ibid.); Magner v. Beth Israel Hosp., 120 N.J. Super. 529, 533, 295 A.2d 363 (App.Div.1972); Terhune v. Margaret Hague Maternity Hosp., 63 N.J.Super. 106, 164 A.2d 75 (App.Div.1960); Becker v. Eisenstodt, 60 N.J.Super. 240, 158 A.2d 706 (App.Div.1960); Toy v. Rickert, 53 N.J. Super. 27, 146 A.2d 510 (App.Div.1958); Steinke v. Bell, 32 N.J.Super. 67, 107 A.2d 825 (App.Div.1954); Gould v. Winokur, 98 N.J.Super. 544, 237 A.2d 916 (Law Div.1968), aff'd, 104 N.J.Super. 329, 250 A.2d 38 (App.Div.1969). Each of the above malpractice cases implicated the proposition that as a matter of common knowledge within the ken of lay jurors, the accident in question would not have occurred had the defendant adhered to the appropriate standard of his profession. When that principle is applicable, plaintiff need not produce expert testimony to demonstrate defendant's deviation from the standard. We continue to endorse that proposition, which remains undiminished in this jurisdiction. However, the instant case is not suited to its application, for we cannot say that on the facts before us, as a matter of common understanding, the injury to plaintiff's bladder raises an inference of negligence. Buckelew v. Grossbard, 435 A.2d 1150, 1157–8 (N.J.1981).

resection (re-sek'shun) [L. *resectio*] excision of a portion of an organ or other structure.

resection, anterior See *colostomy* (Purcell case).

Purcell testified that he could not have performed an **anterior resection** [7] on Zimbelman because the lesion was low down in a cylindrical pelvis, he had an inadequate cuff and had no room to work. [7 The procedure ordinarily used by surgeons in treating a ruptured diverticulum. In performing the operation the fecal stream is diverted by a temporary colostomy, the diseased section of the bowel is cut out, the bowel is then resected and the temporary colostomy is closed.] Purcell v. Zimbelman, 500 P.2d 335, 340 (Ct.App.Ariz.1972).

resection, colon

A **colon resection** was performed at that time to remove a cancerous growth located in the middle transverse section of the colon. Lenger v. Physician's General Hospital, Inc., 455 S.W. 2d 703, 705 (Tex.1970).

resection, transurethral resection of the prostate by means of an instrument passed through the urethra. See also *evacuator* (Chiero case).

To correct this obstructing tissue, Dr. Pickens recommended a **transurethral resection** of the prostate (**TUR**). . . .

If plaintiff had made these inquiries, we believe he also would have discovered that impotency is a known slight risk in the **TUR** procedure. Dessi v. U.S., 489 F.Supp. 722, 724, 726 (E.D.Va.1980).

Dr. Streeter explained that a **TUR** surgical procedure involves the removal of the fibromuscular portion of the prostate gland by the use of electorcautery. Chips and pieces of the prostate gland are carried into the bladder by an irrigating solution. The chips and pieces and the irrigating solution are then re-

moved from the bladder by an Ellick Evacuator. Chiero v. Chicago Osteopathic Hospital, 392 N.E.2d 203, 206 (App.Ct.Ill. 1979).

On May 26, 1971, the plaintiff, Doctor Samuel Dwane Thomas, then a urology resident at Episcopal Hospital, was performing a transurethral prostatectomy using a surgical instrument known as a resectoscope. . . .

According to the testimony, the source of plaintiff's claimed loss of earnings was his inability to perform **transurethral resections**, called **TUR's** for short, which are one of the mainstays of a urologist's practice. Thomas v. American Cystoscope Makers Inc., 414 F.Supp. 255, 258, 269 (E.D.Pa.1976). **Other Authorities:** Miller v. U.S., 431 F.Supp. 988, 990 (S.D. Miss.1976); Jeffries v. McCague, 363 A.2d 1167, 1170 (Super.Ct.Pa.1976).

resection, wedge removal of a triangular wedge of tissue, as from the ovary in an operation designed to stimulate ovarian function in patients with Stein-Leventhal syndrome.

Dr. Beazley had generally discussed various surgical procedures with Mr. Karp including the possibility of a heart transplant, but Mr. Karp desired to have the **wedge resection** or excision of diseased heart muscle attempted as the initial procedure. . . .

The mechanical heart implant was actually the second stage of a three stage procedure. On April 4, 1969, Dr. Cooley first attempted a **ventriculoplasty**, or as sometimes termed a **wedge excision**, or **wedge resection**. That proved unsuccessful, and it was then that the mechanical heart was implanted in Mr. Karp, where it sustained Mr. Karp for approximately sixty-four hours. Karp v. Cooley, 493 F.2d 408, 411, 415 (5th Cir. 1974).

resectoscope (re-sek'to-skōp) an instrument with a wide-angle telescope and an electrically activated wire loop for transurethral removal or biopsy of lesions of the bladder, prostate, or urethra. See also *cystoscope; eyepiece* (both Thomas case); and *machine, Bovie*.

The crux of the action, of course, is the product itself [a **resectoscope**]. The device in question here is an instrument commonly used in urological surgery. It is part of a complex and highly sophisticated electro-surgical unit and is comprised of several component parts. Chief among them, and relevant for our consideration, is an optical telescope (a cystoscope) which permits so called closed surgery by insertion of the instrument directly into the patient's body. The surgeon is able to see and to operate internally by viewing through a monocular eyepiece affixed to the end of the telescope shaft.

When incorporated with other component parts, including a **resectoscope** working element, cutting loop, and sheath, and connected to a light source and electrical power supply known as a Bovie machine, the instrument is complete. In its integrated configuration, the **resectoscope** is hand-held and measures approximately 15 inches in length. The surgical function is accomplished by means of high frequency electrical energy supplied by the Bovie machine to the **resectoscope** cutting loop. Thomas v. American Cystoscope Makers Inc., 414 F.Supp. 255, 258–9 (E.D.Pa.1976).

reserpine (res'er-pēn, rĕ-ser'pin) [USP] chemical name: 3,4,5-trimethoxybenzoyl methyl reserpate. An alkaloid,

$C_{33}H_{40}N_2O_9$, isolated from the root of *Rauwolfia serpentina* and other species of *Rauwolfia*, and occurring as a white or pale buff to slightly yellowish crystalline powder; used as an antihypertensive, and also as a sedative, administered orally and intramuscularly. See also *hydrochlorothiazide*.

A commonly employed drug treatment for hypertension is the use of HCT plus **reserpine**, an antihypertensive and calming agent. The ratio of the HCT to the **reserpine** that produces the maximum therapeutic effect varies from patient to patient. U.S. v. Ciba Geigy Corp., 1976–1 Trade Cases, Par. 60,908 at 68,933; 68,936 (D.N.J.1976).

resident (rez′ĭ-dent) a graduate and licensed physician receiving training in a specialty in a hospital.

residual functional capacity See *capacity, residual functional*.

resin (rez′in) [L. *resina*] a solid or semisolid, amorphous, organic substance, of vegetable origin or produced synthetically. True resins are insoluble in water, but are readily dissolved in alcohol, ether, and volatile oils.

resins, acrylic a class of thermoplastic resins, ethylene derivatives containing a vinyl group, produced by polymerization of acrylic or methacrylic acid or their derivatives; used in the fabrication of medical prostheses and dental restorations and appliances.

An **acrylic** material in dough form was placed in the mold, boiled in water, put into a steam bath and cooked for four hours. On removal from the bath it was polished and cleansed by scouring and scrubbing with an antiseptic soap the elements of which were compatible with the composition of acrylic dentures. Germann v. Matriss, 260 A.2d 825, 827 (N.J.1970).

resin, podophyllum [USP], a powdered mixture of resins removed from podophyllum by percolation with alcohol and subsequent precipitation upon addition of acidified water; used as a topical caustic in the treatment of certain papillomas as a 25 per cent dispersion in compound benzoin tincture, or as a solution is alcohol. Formerly used as a cathartic. Called also *podophyllin*.

Dr. Anderson sent a letter to Dr. Hedenstrom who had referred Phelps, stating that the several lesions on the penis were warts and "one lesion was biopsied to make sure it was a wart and later these were treated with **podophyllin** [sic]."...

Dr. Anderson proceeded to treat the lesions with a 20-percent solution of **podophyllin** [sic] during six subsequent visits by Phelps, from August 18, 1971, to November 10, 1971. Phelps v. Blomberg Roseville Clinic, 253 N.W.2d 390, 391 (Minn. 1977).

resorcin See *resorcinol*.

resorcinol (rĕ-zor′sĭ-nol) [USP] chemical name: 1,3-benzenediol. A bactericidal, fungicidal, keratolytic, exfoliative, and antipruritic agent, $C_6H_6O_2$, occurring as white, or nearly white, needle-shaped crystals or powder; used especially as a topical keratolytic in the treatment of acne and other dermatoses, such as seborrheic dermatitis. Called also *resorcin*.

... **resorcin**, in the concentration of 1% to 2% used in the Kleerex formula, is antiseptic, antipruritic, and analgesic (pain relieving).... Folds v. Federal Trade Commission, 187 F.2d 658–9 (7th Cir. 1951).

resorption (re-sorp′shun) [L. *resorbere* to swallow again] the loss of substance through physiologic or pathologic means, such as loss of dentin and cementum of a tooth, or of the alveolar process of the mandible or maxilla.

resorption, apical

... **apical resorption** (loss of substance of the apex of two teeth).... Jobson v. Dooley, 296 S.E.2d 388, 390 (Ct.App. Ga.1982).

respiration (res″pĭ-ra′shun) [L. *respiratio*] the exchange of oxygen and carbon dioxide between the atmosphere and the cells of the body. The process includes ventilation (inspiration and expiration), the diffusion of oxygen from pulmonary alveoli to the blood and of carbon dioxide from the blood to the alveoli, and the transport of oxygen to and carbon dioxide from the body cells.

"Respiratory arrest" meant that Henderson was not breathing on his own. He was revived by cardio-pulmonary resuscitation. Henderson v. Life and Cas. Ins. Co., 574 S.W.2d 634–5 (Ct. Civ.App.Tex.1978).

respirator (res′pĭ-ra″tor) an apparatus to qualify the air that is breathed through it, or a device for giving artificial respiration or to assist in pulmonary ventilation.

He seeks, with full approval of his adult family, to have the **respirator** removed from his trachea, which act, according to his physician, based upon medical probability, would result in "a reasonable life expectancy of less than one hour". Satz v. Perlmutter, 362 So.2d 160–1 (Dist.Ct.App.Fla.1978).

Upon entry to the St. Clare's I.C.U. she was placed on a MA–1 **respirator**, which provides air to her lungs on a controlled volume basis. It also has a "sigh volume," which is a periodic increase in the volume of air to purge the lungs of any accumulation of fluids or excretions. The machine takes over completely the breathing function when the patient does not breathe spontaneously.[1] [[1] See Bellegie, "Medical Technology As It Exists Today," 27 Baylor L.Rev. 31, 32, describing the functioning of a **respirator**, wherein the author states, "This apparatus can maintain a person's respiratory functions indefinitely, and does so on many occasions where it is a matter of life and death."] Matter of Quinlan, 348 A.2d 801, 807 (Super.Ct.N.J.1975).

When asked about the use of **respirators**, Borel replied that they were not furnished during his early work years. Although **respirators** were later made available on some jobs, insulation workers usually were not required to wear them and had to make a special request if they wanted one. Borel stated that he and other insulation workers found that the **respirators** furnished them were uncomfortable, could not be worn in hot weather, and—"you can't breathe with the **respirator**." Borel further noted that no **respirator** in use during his lifetime could prevent the inhalation of asbestos dust. As an alternative precaution, therefore, he would sometimes wear a wet handkerchief over his nostrils or apply mentholatum, but these methods were also unsatisfactory and did not exclude all the dust. Borel

v. Fibreboard Paper Products Corp., 493 F.2d 1076, 1082 (5th Cir. 1973).

Other Authorities: Eichner v. Dillon, 426 N.Y.S.2d 517, 527 (2d Dep't 1980); Society of Plastics Industries, Inc. v. Occupational S. & H.A., 509 F.2d 1301, 1306 (2d Cir. 1975).

respirator, Bird

There was no resuscitator available in the intensive care unit and a nurse gave mouth to tube resuscitation for a period of 10 to 15 minutes until a **Bird respirator** was brought from the Hospital's inhalation therapy unit and connected to infant plaintiff....

... At 6:50 A.M. of that day the nurse assigned to infant plaintiff noted that he was not getting proper air exchange, that is he was being deprived of the necessary amount of oxygen. She called the inhalation therapy unit. A member of that unit arrived at 7 A.M. and discovered an obvious kink in one of the tubes of the **Bird respirator** and corrected it....

... Commencing with the first grand mal convulsion infant plaintiff was unable to do his own breathing. The hospital chart maintained by the nursing staff records no breathing—respiration—by infant plaintiff between 1:45 A.M., the time of the first grand mal convulsion, and 2:10 A.M. on February 22. Nor was any respiration recorded for 7:15 A.M., the approximate time of the kinking of the tube in the **respirator**. The **Bird respirator** had to perform or assist his breathing for some considerable period of time. It was not until April 18, 1968, and thereafter that the **respirator** was no longer used at any time to breathe for him or to assist him in breathing. Rose v. Hakim, 335 F.Supp. 1221, 1226–7 (D.D.C.1971).

respiratory (re-spi'rah-to"re) [*re-* + L. *spirare* to breathe] pertaining to respiration.

response (re-spons') [L. *respondere* to answer, reply] an action or movement due to the application of a stimulus.

response, anamnestie in immunology, the rapid reappearance of antibody in the blood following the administration of an antigen to which the subject had previously developed a primary immune response; called also *memory r.*, *recall r.*, *booster r.*, *second set r.*, and *secondary immune r.*

According to Dr. Randall Krakauer: An **anamnestic response** is a response that is exacerbated in degree and usually occurs in a shorter period of time as a result of an organism's prior experience with that antigen. That is, the first experience with an antigen primes an organism for a more—for a quicker and more intense response later. Varga v. U.S., 566 F.Supp. 987, 1009 (N.D.Ohio 1983).

response, conditioned one that does not occur naturally in the animal but that may be developed by regular association of some physiological function with an unrelated outside event, such as ringing of a bell or flashing of a light. Soon the physiological function starts whenever the outside event occurs (Pavlov, 1911). Called also *conditioned reflex.*

response, humoral

A **humoral response**, he said,

is one that is mediated by antibodies which are proteins, which have the ability to themselves recognize antigens, ei-

ther self or foreign, and damage them or initiate damage in their own rate....

Asked whether either a cell-mediated response, or a **humoral response**, or both, may cause Guillain-Barre Syndrome, Dr. Krakauer responded:

My opinion would be that perhaps the humoral immunity is playing a larger role than cellular, but that is—I would not care to state that as a conclusion.

Further asked, "Is that because at this point, Doctor, as a clinical immunologist, you just don't possibly know?" He answered, "That is correct." Thus, Dr. Krakauer is unsure about Dr. Poser's theory that "humoral factors" cause the "breakdown of myelin." Varga v. U.S., 566 F.Supp. 987, 1011 (N.D. Ohio 1983).

response, immune specifically altered reactivity of the animal body following exposure to antigen, manifested as antibody production, cell-mediated immunity, or immunological tolerance; called also *immune reaction.*

A cell-mediated reaction is an **immune reaction** in which cells at a particular site may proliferate, release pheochromocytic cells of inflammation, collect macrophages at the site, and literally gobble up the tissue and get rid of it. Varga v. U.S., 566 F.Supp. 987, 1011 (N.D.Ohio 1983).

restoration (res"to-ra'shun) the partial or complete reconstruction of a body part, or the device used as its replacement. In dentistry, the act of restoring a tooth to its original condition by the filling of a cavity and replacement of lost parts, or the material used in such a procedure.

For purposes of this discussion, Appellant asks us to visualize a tooth as a three-dimensional box, having four side surfaces and one top surface. When a dentist restores (fills) a tooth, the size and location of the decay will determine the number of surfaces affected by the **restoration**. Moses v. Com., State Dental Council & Examining Bd., 400 A.2d 664, 667 (Commonwealth Ct.Pa.1979).

restraint (re-strānt') the forcible confinement of a violently psychotic or irrational person. See also *care, standard of* (Wash. Hosp. Center case).

restraint, chemical the quieting of a violently psychotic or irrational person by means of narcotics.

resuscitation (re-sus"ĭ-ta'shun) [L. *resuscitare* to revive] the restoration to life or consciousness of one apparently dead; it includes such measures as artificial respiration and cardiac massage.

In this situation her attending physician has recommended that, when (and if) cardiac or respiratory arrest occurs, **resuscitation** efforts should not be undertaken. Such efforts typically involve the use of cardiac massage or chest compression and delivery of oxygen under compression through an endotracheal tube into the lungs. An electrocardiogram is connected to guide the efforts of the **resuscitation** team and to monitor the patient's progress. Various plastic tubes are usually inserted intravenously to supply medications or stimulants directly to the heart. Such medications may also be supplied by direct injection into the heart by means of a long needle. Matter of Dinnerstein, 380 N.E.2d 134–5 (App.Ct.Mass.1978).

Place one hand under the patient's chin and the other on top of his head. Lift up on the chin and push down on the top of the head to tilt the head backwards.

While holding the jaw forward pinch the nostrils closed with the other hand to prevent leakage of air through the nose.

Blowing into the lungs causes the chest to expand. When the chest has expanded adequately remove your mouth from the patient's so that he can exhale.

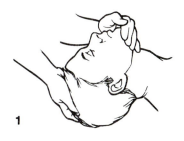

1

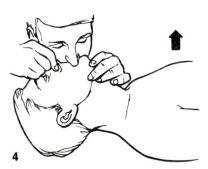

3

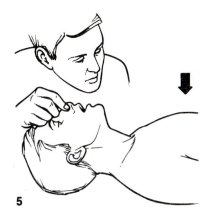

5

Put the thumb of the hand under the jaw into the patient's mouth; grasp the jaw and pull it forward.

Take a deep breath; place your mouth tightly over the patient's and blow forcefully into his lungs.

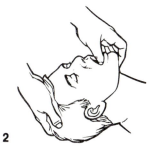

2

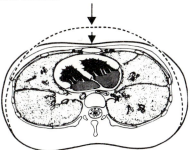

4

Repeat this sequence of maneuvers every 3 to 4 seconds until other means of ventilation are available.

If you cannot open his mouth blow through his nose. In infants cover both mouth and nose with your mouth. Blow gently into a child's mouth, and in infants use only small puffs from your cheeks.

The patient is placed in a supine position on a rigid support so that there is no give under the patient as pressure is applied. The individual applying the pressure stands or kneels at right angles to the patient. He places the heel of one hand with the heel of the other on top of it on the sternum, just cephalad to the xiphoid process.

Firm pressure is applied vertically downward about 60 times a minute. At the end of each pressure stroke the hands are relaxed to permit full expansion of the chest. The position of the operator should be such that he can use his body weight while applying the pressure. Sufficient pressure should be exerted to move the sternum 3 or 4 cm. toward the vertebral column.

Children up to 10 years of age require the force of only one hand.

Only moderate pressure by the finger tips on the middle third of the sternum should be used on infants.

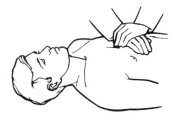

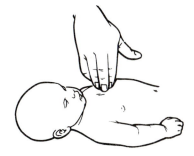

*Kouwenhoven, W. B., Jude, J. R., and Knickerbocker, G. G.: Closed Chest Cardiac Massage. J.A.M.A. *173:*1064, 1960.

TECHNIQUE OF RESUSCITATION BY CLOSED CHEST CARDIAC MASSAGE

(Kouwenhoven, Jude, and Knickerbocker, J.A.M.A. 173:1064, 1960.)

About one minute and ten seconds after external cardiac massage began, it was interrupted so that Dr. Prabhaker could inject adrenalin by the intracardiac route. Oxygenated blood was observed in the syringe prior to injection. A cardiac monitor was brought into the operating room and connected. About two minutes and ten seconds elapsed from the time the crisis was announced before a normal oscillographic tracing appeared. At that time Dr. Widder confirmed a recordable and low normal pulse and returning blood pressure. Sometime after **resuscitation**, surgery was completed. Burrow v. Widder, 368 N.E.2d 443, 447 (App.Ct. of Ill.1977).

resuscitation, cardiopulmonary (CPR) the reestablishing of heart and lung action as indicated for cardiac arrest or apparent sudden death resulting from electric shock, drowning, respiratory arrest, and other causes. The two major components of CPR are artificial ventilation and closed chest cardiac massage; see illustration accompanying *respiration.*

There is at least some question whether the use of **cardiopulmonary resuscitation** would be regarded as sound medical practice in the case of cardiac or respiratory arrest which occurs as the anticipated or expected end of a terminal illness. See National Conference on Standards for Cardiopulmonary Resuscitation and Emergency Cardiac Care, Standards for Cardiopulmonary Resuscitation (CPR) and Emergency Cardiac Care (ECC), 227 J.A.M.A. 837, 864 (1974): "The purpose of **cardiopulmonary resuscitation** is the prevention of sudden, unexpected death. **Cardiopulmonary resuscitation** is not indicated in certain situations, such as in cases of terminal irreversible illness where death is not unexpected or where prolonged cardiac arrest dictates the futility of resuscitation efforts. Resuscitation in these circumstances may represent a positive violation of an individual's right to die with dignity. When **CPR** is considered to be contraindicated for hospital patients, it is appropriate to indicate this in the patient's progress notes. It also is appropriate to indicate this on the physician's order sheet for the benefit of nurses and other personnel who may be called upon to initiate or participate in **cardiopulmonary resuscitation**." Matter of Dinnerstein, 380 N.E.2d 134, 139 (App.Ct.Mass.1978).

resuscitator (re-sus′ĭ-ta″tor) an apparatus for initiating respiration in cases of asphyxia.

[It is my] opinion the anesthetist gave too much ether to the child... More than indicated by the circumstances ... [and] that was the cause of the darkening of the blood... [W]hen that kind of danger takes place ... the anesthetist usually immediately stops the flow of ether and artificial respiration is immediately instituted... This time I turned the suction over to my mother and [began giving artificial] respiration ... with my hands, but the best way is by a mechanical **resuscitator**, which applies carbon dioxide and oxygen into the lungs ... the very best procedure is to apply the ... **resuscitator** ... at once....

The doctors stated also that the mechanical **resuscitator** was "standard equipment for hospital surgery rooms" which "we expect ... to be present in any kind of an operation," and it "should be immediately available, ... it is not always present right in the room, but should be there or close by." A doctor would normally "expect to find it in the room, although it is not always there." The hospital stipulated that "it is standard practice in the hospitals in San Francisco to have a **resuscitator**

available for use in the operating rooms." Cavero v. Franklin General Benev. Soc., 223 P.2d 471, 473–4 (Cal.1950).

retardation (re″tar-da′shun) [L. *retardare* to slow down, impede] delay; hindrance; delayed development.

retardation, mental subnormal general intellectual development, originating during the developmental period, and associated with impairment of either learning and social adjustment or maturation, or both. The disorder is classified according to intelligence quotient as follows: *borderline*, 68–83; *mild*, 52–67; *moderate*, 36–51; *severe*, 20–35; and *profound*, less than 20. Formerly called *feeblemindedness* and *mental deficiency.*

Mental retardation is listed as a mental disorder in the International Classification of Diseases (ICD), but Title XIX specifically allows reimbursement to residents in facilities for the mentally retarded. See 42 U.S.C. § 1396d(d) (1976). Granville House v. Dep't of Health & Human Serv., 715 F.2d 1292, 1295 (8th Cir. 1983).

The American Association on Mental Deficiency definition of **mental retardation** has the widest acceptance:

... **Mental retardation** refers to sub-average general intellectual functioning which originated during the developmental period and is associated with impairment in adaptive behavior.[4]

Mental retardation is commonly classified from profound to mild, according to IQ scores. The most profoundly retarded attain IQ scores under 20. They require virtually constant care and have major physical and sensory impairment. Those with scores of 20–35 are severely retarded. They manifest retarded speech, language and motor development. Persons in the moderate range (IQ scores 36–51) are usually slow or retarded in general development and require supervision in a sheltered environment. The mildly (IQ scores 52–67) and borderline (IQ scores 68–83) retarded frequently can work at suitable jobs and achieve a considerable degree of independence. Generally, those with IQ scores 50–75 have been classified as educable and those with 30–50 IQ as trainable.

These categories are general; the number levels are arbitrary. It cannot be said too often: an IQ score is merely a guide. [4 Baumeister, Mental Retardation 1 (1967).] Matter of Grady, 405 A.2d 851, 855 (Super.Ct.N.J.1979), vacated and remanded 426 A.2d 467 (N.J.1981).

There is a difference between **mental retardation** which refers to significantly subaverage general intellectual functioning existing concurrently with defects in adaptive behavior manifested during the developmental period, cf. North Carolina Ass'n for Retarded Children v. North Carolina, 420 F.Supp. 451, 453 (M.D.N.C.1976), and mental incompetency, which is the mental inability to comprehend the consequences of one's actions. See Conn.Gen.Stat. § 19–569g. Ruby v. Massey, 452 F.Supp. 361, 363 (D.Conn.1978).

Other Authorities: J.L. v. Parham, 412 F.Supp. 112, 117 (M.D. Ga.1976); In re Ballay, 482 F.2d 648, 660 (D.C.Cir.1973).

retarded See *retardation, mental.*

reticulocyte (rĕ-tik′u-lo-sīt″) a young red blood cell showing a basophilic reticulum under vital staining.

reticulocytosis (rĕ-tik″u-lo-si-to′sis) an increase in the number of reticulocytes in the peripheral blood.

Reticulocytosis, the production of reticulocytes, young red blood cells, was usually observable shortly after administration of the active liver fractions, but not necessarily at the same rate as the subsequently observable erythropoiesis, the production of red corpuscles. Merck & Co. v. Olin Mathieson Chemical Corp., 253 F.2d 156, 158 (4th Cir. 1958).

reticulum (rĕ-tik′u-lum), pl. *retic′ula* [L., dim. of *rete* net] a network, especially a protoplasmic network in cells, as the flattened double membrane sheets of the endoplasmic reticulum.

retiform (re′tĭ-form, ret′ĭ-form) [L. *rete* net + *forma* form] resembling a network.

retina (ret′ĭ-nah) [L.] [NA] the innermost of the three tunics of the eyeball, surrounding the vitreous body and continuous posteriorly with the optic nerve. It is divided into the *pars optica*, which rests upon the choroid, the *pars ciliaris*, which rests upon the ciliary body, and the *pars iridica*, which rests upon the posterior surface of the iris. Grossly, the retina is composed of an outer, pigmented layer (stratum pigmenti) and an inner, transparent layer, the optic part of which is the cerebral stratum (stratum cerebrale). The latter consists of nine layers, named from within outward, as follows (see illustration): (1) the membrana limitans interna; (2) the nerve fiber layer; (3) the layer of ganglion cells; (4) the inner molecular, or plexiform, layer; (5) the inner nuclear layer; (6) the outer molecular, or plexiform, layer; (7) the outer nuclear layer; (8) the membrana limitans externa; (9) the layer of rods and cones (called also *Jacob's membrane* and *bacillary layer*). The pigmentary layer overlying the optic portion is continued forward over the inner surface of the ciliary body, constituting the *pars ciliaris retinae*. The various layers are connected transversely by fibers of connective tissue (*fibers of Müller*). The layer of rods and cones forms the percipient element of the retina (i.e., the element that responds to visual stimuli by a photochemical reaction), and is connected with the nerve fiber layer by nerve fibers which join to form the optic nerve. In the center of the posterior part of the retina is the *macula lutea*, the most sensitive portion of the retina; and in the center of the macula lutea is a depression, the *fovea centralis*, from which the rods are absent. About 0.25 cm. inside the fovea is the point of entrance of the optic nerve and its central artery (*central artery of the retina*). At this point the retina is incomplete and forms the *blind spot*. See also *detachment of retina*.

At trial, Dr. Smith explained to the jury the observations which he gleaned from the drawings. He explained that the pictures showed extensive scarrings, extensive gliosis (dried blood caked on the **retina**), cyst formation impigmentation (suggesting trauma) and blood vessels growing into the gliosis (suggesting that the damage had been present for some time). In addition, he stated that the **retina** appeared fixed and folded (also suggesting that the damage had occurred quite some time in the past). We think Dr. Smith's opinion was based upon fact rather than opinion. Roth v. Law, 579 S.W.2d 949, 954 (Ct.Civ.App.Tex.1979).

Doctor Dahrling testified that when he examined plaintiff on January 14, 1976, his **retinas** looked good, and he explained

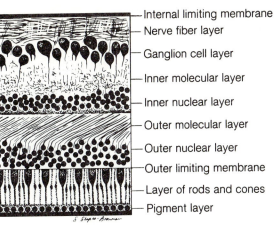

— Internal limiting membrane
— Nerve fiber layer
— Ganglion cell layer
— Inner molecular layer
— Inner nuclear layer
— Outer molecular layer
— Outer nuclear layer
— Outer limiting membrane
— Layer of rods and cones
— Pigment layer

Schematic representation of the layers of the adult human retina.

to plaintiff that, ''we really didn't see anything wrong, that we felt that perhaps he was suffering some of this distortion from traction on the **retina** by the vitreous and told him that we'd like to check him again in three months.''...

... The witness said that he advised plaintiff of **retinal** symptoms on April 6, 1976, and had a notation on his record to that effect. Davidson & Graham Const. Co. v. McKee, 562 S.W. 2d 426–8 (Tenn.1978).

He diagnosed arteriosclerosis of the **retinal** vessels in both eyes, and optic atrophy in the left eye. In response to a questionnaire sent him by ALJ Stillerman, Dr. Domanskis stated that plaintiff's condition was ''deteriorating'' and that lifting, stretching, pushing, pulling, stooping, or prolonged reading would ''probably not'' aggravate the condition, presumably meaning that it would not hasten the ongoing deterioration. Gudlis v. Califano, 452 F.Supp. 401, 404 (N.D.Ill.1978).

retinal (ret′ĭ-nal) pertaining to the retina. See also *hemorrhage, retinal* (Excelsior case).

retinal detachment See *detachment of retina*.

Dr. Smith testified that the making of **retinal drawings** follows a standardized procedure such that any ophthalmologist could interpret the drawing even if he or she could not see the retina. In general, such drawings are hand sketched reproductions of what the doctor views when looking into the patient's dilated eye. Further, according to Dr. Smith, the drawings are usually very accurate because they are made in preparation for surgery so that the surgeon will know where to work on the eye. In addition, they are prepared for future reference by the treating doctor and for reference by other doctors who might need to become involved with the patient. Dr. Smith did state, however, that some ophthalmologists would be better skilled than others in making **retinal drawings** but that essentially ophthalmologists, as a group, would give the same rendition of a certain ocular condition. Roth v. Law, 579 S.W.2d 949, 953 (Ct.Civ.App.Tex.1979).

retinitis (ret″ĭ-ni′tis) inflammation of the retina; used in the older ophthalmological literature to denote impairment of sight, perversion of vision, edema, and exudation into the retina, and occasionally by hemorrhages into the retina.

retinitis, granulomatous

The laboratory report revealed total retinal detachment of the eye with giant reaction and massive disorganization of the retina. The pathological examination ruled out a retinoblastoma but concluded the cause of the disease to be **granulomatous retinitis**,[2] etiology unknown. [2 Retinitis is an inflammation which chiefly involves the retina. "Granulomatous" is a type of inflammation. Thus, the pathology conclusion was that of a general retinal inflammation of unknown origin.] Steele v. U.S., 463 F.Supp. 321, 323 (D.Alas.1978).

retinitis pigmentosa

a group of diseases, frequently hereditary, marked by progressive loss of retinal response (as elicited by the electroretinogram), retinal atrophy, attenuation of the retinal vessels, and clumping of the pigment, with contraction of the field of vision. It may be transmitted as a dominant, recessive, or X-linked trait and is sometimes associated with other genetic defects.

Generally, **retinitis pigmentosa** is an hereditary disease of the retina which is marked by a slowly progressive withering of the nerve cells, a deterioration of blood vessels and a wasting of the optic disk. It is marked by a constriction (reduction in size) of the field of vision. Helms v. Monsanto Co., 558 F.Supp. 928, 930 (N.D.Ala.1982), reversed and remanded 728 F.2d 1416 (11th Cir. 1984).

retinitis, serous

simple inflammation of the superficial layers of the retina.

Mrs. Hitchcock was examined by an opthalmologist for a complaint of blurred vision in her right eye. Examination at that time revealed central **serous retinitis**. The blur later cleared slightly but vision was not as bright in the right eye as in the left eye. (Defendant's exhibit 32.) Hitchcock v. U.S., 479 F.Supp. 65, 67 (D.D.C.1979).

retinoblastoma

(ret"ĭ-no-blas-to′mah) a tumor arising from retinal germ cells.

On examination the medical team observed a retinal detachment involving a grayish yellow tumor. The doctors diagnosed the cause of the tumor as possibly **retinoblastoma** or toxocara canis. Eye condition at that point in time made it impossible to differentiate between either disease. Because of the danger of **retinoblastoma**, a particularly fast-spreading and life-threatening malignancy, the doctors recommended to Timothy's parents that his right eye be removed....

Retinoblastoma is an extremely dangerous malignancy sometimes found in the eyes of young children. When diagnosed, **retinoblastoma** requires removal of the diseased eye to prevent the malignancy from escaping outside the eye, possibly through the optic nerve into the brain. Steele v. U.S., 463 F.Supp. 321, 323, 327 (D.Alas.1978).

retinopathy

(ret"ĭ-nop′ah-the) [*retina* + Gr. *pathos* disease] any noninflammatory disease of the retina. See also *retina.*

By reason of the **retinopathy** (degenerative disease of the retina) he became, within the last few years, totally blind. Application of Lydia E. Hall Hospital, 455 N.Y.S.2d 706–7 (Sup.Ct. Nassau Cty.1982).

Chloroquine **retinopathy** is a damaged condition of the retina which can result from the long continuous use of chloroquine drugs. Hoffman v. Sterling Drug, Inc., 485 F.2d 132, 135 (3d Cir. 1973).

retinopathy, alterior sclerotic

His eye examination, which included an inspection of the deeper eye structures, indicated that she had **alterior sclerotic retinopathy** in both eyes and this diagnosis was more pronounced in the left eye. This condition was described as a thinning of the artery walls and an engorging of the veins resulting in a diminution of vision. Excelsior Leather Washer Co. v. Industrial Com'n, 297 N.E.2d 158, 161 (Ill.1973).

retinopathy, diabetic

retinopathy associated with diabetes mellitus, which may be of the background type, progressively characterized by microaneurysms, intraretinal punctate hemorrhages, yellow, waxy exudates, cotton-wool patches, and macular edema, or of the proliferative type, characterized by neovascularization of the retina and optic disk, which may project into the vitreous, proliferation of fibrous tissue, vitreous hemorrhage, and retinal detachment. Called also *diabetic retinitis.* See also *detachment, tractional* (George case).

Claimant has been a diabetic for roughly 25 years and at the time of his injury suffered from **diabetic retinonathy**, a serious deteriorative condition of the eyes and a manifestation of a diabetic condition. According to the findings of the referee, Claimant's left eye was in an advanced proliferative stage of this condition, which would eventually result in tractional detachment of the retina. George v. Workmen's Comp.App.Bd, 437 A.2d 521–2 (Pa.Commonwealth Ct.1981).

Dr. Seiverson stated that in his opinion a pre-existing condition of **diabetic retinopathy** might have been aggravated by the accident thereby precipitating a hemorrhage in the left eye. He explained that the longer a person has diabetes the greater the possibility of retinal hemorrhage because the weakened blood vessels might break if blood pressure increases and this is compounded by an emotional trauma or fall. He described the condition of claimant's right eye as entirely due to diabetes....

... He described claimant's condition of **diabetic retinopathy** as progressive and stated that any person so afflicted might sustain a hemorrhage at any time but that such occurrence might also be caused by an aggravating incident. Excelsior Leather Washer Co. v. Industrial Com'n, 297 N.E.2d 158, 160–1 (Ill.1973).

retractor

(re-trak′tor) an instrument for maintaining operative exposure by separating the edges of a wound and holding back underlying organs and tissues; many shapes, sizes, and styles are available.

The average incision is five to six inches in length. It goes all the way down through the four layers of the abdominal wall. At that particular stage of the operation you put in surgical **retractors**, and those surgical **retractors** are lined with sponges so that they will not damage the patient's tender skin and muscles. The **retractors** are made of stainless steel.... Tice v. Hall, 303 S.E.2d 832, 836 (Ct.App.N.C.1983).

retrobulbar (ret″ro-bul′bar) [*retro-* + L. *bulbus* bulb] behind the eyeball. See also *hemorrhage, retrobulbar;* and *injection*.

. . . has a **retro bulbar** hemorrhage; lower bulbar conjunctiva is pushed out across eyelid [illegible] by the deep subconjunctival hemorrhage. Pupil is small, cornea is clear. Prognosis guarded. Diagnosis: **retro bulbar** hemorrhage. Recommendations: sterile vaseline to cover the inverted conjunctiva. Bevevino v. Saydjari, 574 F.2d 676, 679 (2d Cir. 1978).

retrobulbar neuritis See *neuritis, retrobulbar*.

retrocecal (ret″ro-se′kal) behind the cecum.

. . . that when he looked into Emanuel's opened abdomen he saw that the appendix was **retrocecal** and that it had perforated along the end of the stalk. . . . Emanuel v. Bacon, 615 S.W.2d 847, 850 (Ct.Civ.App.Tex.1981).

retroflexed (ret′ro-flekst) [*retro-* + L. *flexus* bent] bent backward; in a state of retroflexion.

Dr. Elswick testified also that the uterus of Miss Gaskins was **retroflexed** and "this means that it was bent on itself and had fallen back. In the normal position the womb is up, and it had fallen back at the time of my examination." Russo v. Commonwealth, 148 S.E.2d 820, 823 (Va.1966).

retroflexion (ret″ro-flek′shun) [L. *retroflexio*] the bending of an organ so that its top is turned backward; specifically, the bending backward of the body of the uterus toward the cervix, resulting in a sharp angle at the point of bending.

retrogasserian See *ganglion, trigeminal*.

retrolental fibroplasus See *fibroplasus, retrolental*.

retrolisthesis

In November, since his back was getting worse rather than better, the claimant was examined by orthopedic specialist, Dr. Banks. The examination revealed that he has a **retrolisthesis** of the L5 vertebra on the S1 vertebra. Dr. Banks described this as a relative backward displacement of the body of the L5 on the S1. The symptoms of this condition are localized back pain, pain on hyperextension, i.e., lifting one's arms up above one's head, and occasionally sciatic pain due to irritation of the first sacral nerve root. Mr. Gilcrease's symptoms were found to be consistent with this diagnosis. Dr. Banks testified that any lifting or twisting motion would produce pain. Gilcrease v. J. A. Jones Const. Co., 425 So.2d 274–5 (Ct. App.La.1982).

retroperitoneal hematoma See *hematoma, retroperitoneal*.

retroversion (ret″ro-ver′zhun) [L. *retroversio; retro* back + *versio* turning] the tipping of an entire organ backward.

retroversion of uterus the turning backward of the entire uterus in relation to the pelvic axis.

He noted at the time that she had a **retroverted (tipped) uterus**, could be characterized as obese, and had given birth to five children by the time she was 23 years old. Lawson v. G. D. Searle & Company, 331 N.E.2d 75, 88 (App.Ct.Ill.1975), reversed 356 N.E.2d 779 (Ill.1976).

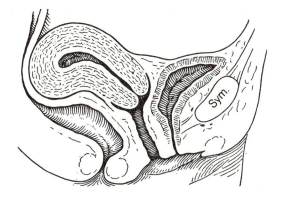

Retroflexion of uterus.

retroverted (ret″ro-vert′ed) in a condition of retroversion. See also *retroversion of uterus* (Lawson case).

revascularization (re-vas′ku-lar-i-za′shun) the restoration of an adequate blood supply to a part by means of a blood vessel graft, as in aortocoronary bypass. See also *vascularization*.

Dr. Harmon has had previous experience with Legg-Perthes Disease in his career among some of his patients. He states that the onset of the disease results in a progression of the necrosis, or dying of the bone. He describes the cure for the disease as **revascularization**—restoration of the blood flow to the femur head. Arrendale v. U.S., 469 F.Supp. 883, 887 (N.D.Tex.1979).

Rh 1. chemical symbol for *rhodium*. 2. symbol for *rhesus factor* (see under *factor*).

Rh (Rhesus) factor See *blood group, Rh*; and *factor, Rhesus*.

rheumatic disease See *fever, rheumatic*.

rheumatism (roo′mah-tizm) [L. *rheumatismus;* Gr. *rheumatismos*] any of a variety of disorders marked by inflammation, degeneration, or metabolic derangement of the connective tissue structures of the body, especially the joints and related structures, including muscles, bursae, tendons and fibrous tissue. It is attended by pain, stiffness, or limitation of motion of these parts. Rheumatism confined to the joints is classified as arthritis.

rheumatoid (roo′mah-toid) [Gr. *rheuma* flux + *eidos* form] resembling rheumatism. See also *arthritis*.

rheumatologist (roo″mah-tol′o-jist) a specialist in rheumatic conditions.

Dr. Hull, a qualified **rheumatologist** specializing in inflammations of the musculo-skeletal system, corroborated the testimony of the other doctors as to the symptomatic and medically verifiable nature of Mr. Andrews' injury. Andrews v. Pine Hill Wood Co., 426 So.2d 196, 200 (Ct.App.La.1982.)

rhinitis (ri-ni′tis) [*rhin-* + *-itis*] inflammation of the mucous membrane of the nose.

Appellee, Frank McKinley, who suffered from various allergies, developed a condition known as chronic **rhinitis** from inhaling toxic chemical substances during his work as a janitor....

The chronic **rhinitis** resulted from a change in the tissue lining his mucous membranes and nasal passages. It is a permanent condition and the evidence, though meager, sufficiently establishes the probability of a causal relationship between the condition and the condition of his work.

As a result of the chronic **rhinitis**, McKinley is subjected to nasal congestion and drainage, will likely be more susceptible to upper respiratory infections and should avoid breathing toxic chemical fumes. Chemetron Corp. v. McKinley, 574 S.W.2d 332–3 (Ct.App.Ky.1978).

rhinitis, allergic; rhinitis, anaphy lactic a general term used to denote any allergic reaction of the nasal mucosa; it may occur perennially (*nonseasonal allergic rhinitis*) or seasonally (*hay fever*).

Dr. Salzmann diagnosed claimant's condition as **allergic rhinitis** (hayfever) and asthma. United Airlines, Inc. v. Industrial Com'n, 405 N.E.2d 789, 791 (Ill.1980).

rhinitis, atrophic a chronic form marked by wasting of the mucous membrane and the glands.

... and finally and most important, extensive infestation with **atrophic rhinitis**.

Dr. Kadel described **rhinitis** as an inflammation of the nasal cavity of a hog which results in the decrease in the size of the cone shaped nasal ethmoid turbinate bones on either side of the hog's nose. These structures filter, cool or heat the air as it comes from the outside to the lungs. As a result of the **rhinitis**, air gets to the lungs without either filtration, heating or cooling. The disease, Dr. Kadel testified, was not a killer in its own right, but has a debilitating effect on the ability of the animal to purify the air it breathes and to make natural adjustments to its temperature. Clinical signs of **atrophic rhinitis** are sneezing, coughing, rougher hair coat and a poor rate of weight gain. According to the testimony, hogs so infected frequently develop secondary pneumonia, cough a lot, contract fever, and may eventually die of pneumonia. Arlie Larimer & Sons, Inc. v. Kleen-Leen, Inc., 523 F.2d 865, 867 (6th Cir. 1975).

rhinitis, atrophic, of swine a disease of very young swine that may result in marked displacement or atrophy of the turbinate bones in severe cases, due to severe persistent inflammation of the nasal mucosa; the primary inflammatory reaction may be caused by a variety of agents, including a virus. See also *rhinitis, inclusion-body.*

From the record we learn that **atrophic rhinitis** is a transmissible wasting of the delicate turbinate of the nasal cavity. The actual tissue changes are primarily a stunting and a resorption of this delicate, scroll-like bone and a failure of the development to a limited extent of the denser bones that make up the nasal cavity.

Another witness tells us that **atrophic rhinitis** is a disease of the hog; the nose is infected with organisms and as a result of that infection, there may be damage to the internal bones called turbinates, and the lining of those bones to a varying degree will erode away or be reabsorbed and thereby cause problems in filtering out the air as it passes through the nose into the lungs. **Rhinitis** is normally associated with a decrease in rate of gain in the efficiency with which market hogs being

fed for slaughter will convert feed into gain. They are usually more susceptible to secondary respiratory infections. It is caused only by a disease organism known as bordetella. There is a difference of opinion among experts here as to whether there is a distinction between **infectious atrophic rhinitis** and **atrophic rhinitis**. Winter v. Honeggers' & Co., Inc., 215 N.W.2d 316, 318 (Iowa 1974).

rhinitis, inclusion-body atrophic rhinitis of swine due to a viral infection, frequently marked by atrophy of the turbinate bones and distortion of the snout, sneezing, stunting of growth, and, histologically, by the presence of inclusion bodies in scrapings of the nasal mucous membranes.

rhinopharyngo See *nasopharynx.*

rhinoplasty (ri'no-plas"te) [*rhino-* + Gr. *plassein* to form] a plastic surgical operation on the nose, either reconstructive, restorative, or cosmetic.

In addition, ''the Board of Trustees has permitted surgeons who specialize in the field of plastic or cosmetic surgery to perform certain types of procedures, including but not limited to **rhinoplasty**, [known colloquially as plastic nose surgery] [and] skin graphs [sic].'' Hathaway v. Worcester City Hospital, 475 F.2d 701, 704 (1st Cir. 1973).

Rhizobium (ri-zo'be-um) a genus of microorganisms of the family Rhizobiaceae, order Eubacteriales, made up of gram-negative, rod-shaped, symbiotic nitrogen-fixing bacteria, producing nodules on the roots of leguminous plants and fixing free nitrogen in this symbiosis. It includes six species, *R. japo'nicum, R. leguminosa'rum, R. lupi'ni, R. melilo'ti, R. phase'oli,* and *R. trifo'lii.*

[O]nce nature's secret of the non-inhibitive quality of certain strains of the species of **Rhizobium** was discovered, the state of the art made the production of a mixed inoculant a simple step. Even though it may have been the product of skill, it certainly was not the product of invention....

... That is to say, there is no invention here unless the discovery that certain strains of the several species of these bacteria are non-inhibitive and may thus be safely mixed is invention. Armour Pharmaceutical Co. v. Richardson-Merrell, Inc., 396 F.2d 70, 74 (3d Cir. 1968).

rhizotomy (ri-zot'o-me) [*rhizo-* + Gr. *tome* a cutting] interruption of the roots of spinal nerves within the spinal canal.

At this time they reopened the fusion to expose the nerve and found that the nerve roots were being squeezed by the bone. A **rhizotomy** was performed in which the nerve root or sensory part of the nerve is clipped to relieve pain....

... According to Dr. Correa, when a **rhizotomy** is performed the patient is exchanging pain for numbness in the area. Dr. Correa stated that Linda Brown had no feeling in certain areas of her leg. He stated further that patients learn to accommodate this numbness but the **rhizotomy** is permanent. Brown v. Fidelity & Cas. Co. of New York, 385 So.2d 572, 574 (Ct.App.La.1980).

In December of 1967, he had a **rhizotomy** in an attempt to relieve him of his groin and flank pain. This operation was described by Dr. Alfred Uihlein of the Mayo Clinic as follows:

On December 5, 1967, under x-ray control, the sensory component of the 1st lumbar nerve root on the right side was divided between silver clips. (Tr–173).

At the hearing in December of 1968, the plaintiff contended that the operation did not stop the pain; that "I still got the pains right now yet what I went up there for to get rid of, and before my operation I could walk. I had no trouble at all except when the pains would hit me. I could walk, hop up and down off that truck, walk up and down off steps and everything else, but after the operation I can't." (Tr–56–57). Bartlett v. Secretary of Dep't of Health, Ed. & Welf., 330 F.Supp. 1273, 1275 (E.D.Ky.1971).

rhizotomy, posterior division of the posterior or sensory spinal nerve roots; done for relief of intractable pain.

The procedure is called a **posterior fozza rhizotomy**. III R. 18. Lurch v. U.S., 719 F.2d 333, 335 (10th Cir. 1983).

rhizotomy, subtemporal See *decompression, subtemporal.*

The **subtemporal rhizotomy** [for relief from trigeminal neuralgia] involves a direct surgical entrance at the base of the skull exposing the fifth cranial nerve. The second and third division nerves are then selectively severed. Hales v. Pittman, 576 P.2d 493, 496 (Ariz.1978).

rhytidoplasty (rit′ĭ-do-plas″te) plastic surgery for the elimination of wrinkles from the skin.

Dr. Gerow recommended that Mrs. Rosenblum get a "face lift" operation (the technical name of which is "rhytidoplasty"). Rosenblum v. Bloom, 492 S.W.2d 321, 323 (Ct. Civ.App.Tex.1973).

rifampicin (rif′am-pĭ-sin) the international nonproprietary name for rifampin.

rifampin (rif′am-pin) [USP] chemical name: 3-[[(4-methyl-1-piperazinyl)imino]methyl]rifamycin. A semisynthetic derivative of rifamycin SV, $C_{43}H_{58}N_4O_{12}$, occurring as a red-brown, crystalline powder, having the antibacterial actions of the rifamycin (q.v.) group of antibiotics; administered orally. Called also *rifampicin.*

Some biomedical theorists suggest, Dr. Grassetti among them, that **Rifampicin** actually favors the formation of metastases (or secondary cancer tumors) due to its immunosuppressant properties. Grassetti v. Weinberger, 408 F.Supp. 142, 144 (N.D.Cal.1976).

rigidity (rĭ-jid′ĭ-te) [L. *rigiditas; rigidus* stiff] stiffness or inflexibility, chiefly that which is abnormal or morbid; rigor.

rigidity, decerebrate the posture produced in an experimental animal by decerebration (q.v.), marked by rigid extension of the legs. It occurs in man as a result of lesions of the upper part of the brain stem and is manifested as follows: the patient lies in rigid extension with his arms internally rotated at the shoulder, extended at the elbow, and pronated, his fingers flexed at the interphalangeal joints and extended at the metacarpophalangeal joints, and his legs extended at the hips and knees, with the ankles and toes flexed.

rigor (rig′or, ri′gor) [L.] rigidity.

rigor mortis the stiffening of a dead body, accompanying the depletion of adenosine triphosphate in the muscle fibers.

ring (ring) [L. *annulus, circulus, orbiculus*] any annular or circular organ or area.

rings, annular round or oval opacities surrounding a translucent area in the roentgenogram, indicative of cavitation of the lung in tuberculosis; called also *pleural rings.*

On redirect examination, Dr. Holland stated that the literature available to chiropractors contains references to cases in which chiropractic manipulation has caused a ruptured disc. He also indicated that it is fairly common knowledge among chiropractors that the **annular ring** in a thirty-eight year old man who has had a prior disc injury is fragile and that chiropractic manipulation could cause the extrusion of a disc's internal material. Chamness v. Odum, 399 N.E.2d 238, 244 (App. Ct.III.1979).

ring, Bandl's pathologic retraction ring. See also *ring, retraction.*

ring, constriction a contracted area of the uterus, allegedly possible at any level, occurring where the resistance of the uterine contents is slight, as over a depression in the contour of the fetal body, or below the presenting part. Cf. *retraction r.*

ring, retraction a ringlike thickening and indentation occurring in normal labor at the junction of the isthmus and corpus uteri, delineating the upper contracting portion and the lower dilating portion (*physiologic retraction r.*), or a persistent retraction ring in abnormal or prolonged labor that obstructs expulsion of the fetus (*pathologic retraction r.*). Cf. *constriction r.*

At 9:46 to 9:50 there was a sudden change in the contour of Wanda's abdomen, and, according to Wanda's testimony, she experienced a terrible pain in the pit of her stomach. Her abdomen then resembled the shape of an hourglass, a condition diagnosed by Johnson (and later by other experts) as a **Bandl's ring**, which is a strong contraction of the uterus which is not released. Expert testimony established that a **Bandl's ring** is the precursor of a uterine rupture. Expert testimony further established that when abnormal contractions begin to develop they may be reversed very quickly by stopping or slowing down the flow of Pitocin. Long v. Johnson, 381 N.E.2d 93, 97 (Ct.App.Ind.1978).

Ringer's solution See *irrigation, Ringer's.*

risus (ri′sus) [L.] laughter.

risus sardonicus a grinning expression produced by spasm of the facial muscles; so called from a plant of Sardinia, probably one of the genus *Ranunculus*, or crowfoot, which was believed to produce it.

Dr. Winsor explained that Nash's laughing attempt to hoist himself back on the yacht was not actually what it seemed to be to those observing the incident; his facial expression was probably contorted into a grimace known as "risus sardonicus," evidence of a convulsive state. Dr. Winsor maintained, in addition, that it was possible for a person in the throes of a fatal thrombosis to swim some distance before final collapse. Nash v. Prudential Insurance Co. of America, 114 Cal.Rptr. 299, 301–2 (Ct.App.Cal.1974).

Ritalin (rit'ah-lin) trademark for preparations of methylphenidate hydrochloride. See also *methylphenidate hydrochloride*.

RLF See *fibroplasia, retrolental*.

Robaxin (ro-bak'sin) trademark for preparations of methocarbamol. See also *methocarbamol*.

Rocky Mountain spotted fever See under *fever*.

rod (rod) a straight, slim mass of substance; specifically, one of the rodlike bodies of the retina. See also *retinal rods*.

rod, Hansen-Street intramedullary

He could have treated the plaintiff's fracture by either of two methods. One was "the conservation method of traction," and the other was by the insertion of the **Hansen-Street intramedullary rod**. He used the latter method. The rods come in varying lengths and thicknesses. They may be cut with a hacksaw, but he did not cut the one he used. The rod he used was diamond shaped, about eighteen inches long and less than one-half inch thick. He made an incision at the fracture site and then drove the rod into the marrow of the femur upward until it went through the saddle of the greater trochanter. An incision was made in the skin at the upper end to permit the rod to protrude. After the lower end of the rod was driven up to the point of the fracture, it was then driven downward into the marrow of the part of the femur below the fracture. Good medical practice requires that it be driven down to the extent "that you don't have the end of the rod sticking up more than an inch and a half" above the saddle of the greater trochanter. It is not accepted medical practice to have the rod stick up two to three inches. Pfeiffer v. Salas, 271 N.E.2d 750, 752 (Mass.1971).

rods, retinal highly specialized cylindrical segments of the visual cells containing rhodopsin; together with the retinal cones they form the light-sensitive elements of the retina; called also *rod cells*.

roentgen (rent'gen) [for Wilhelm Conrad *Röntgen*, German physicist, 1845–1923, who discovered roentgen rays in 1895; winner of the Nobel prize in physics for 1901] the international unit of x- or γ-radiation. It is the quantity of x- or γ-radiation such that the associated corpuscular emission per 0.001293 gm. of air produces in air ions carrying 1 electrostatic unit of electrical charge of either sign. Abbreviated R.

roentgenogram (rent-gen'o-gram") a film produced by roentgenography.

A total body scanner takes x-ray scans of the whole body, including the brain. Cobb Cty., etc. v. Prince, 249 S.E.2d 581, 583 (Ga.1978).

roentgenograph See *roentgenogram*.

roentgenography (rent"gen-og'rah-fe) [*roentgen* + Gr. *graphein* to write] the making of a record (roentgenogram) of internal structures of the body by passage of x-rays through the body to act on specially sensitized film. See also *radiography*.

roentgenography, body section a special technique to show in detail images of structures lying in a predetermined plane of tissue, while blurring or eliminating detail in images of structures in other planes. Called also *analytical roentgenography* and *sectional roentgenography*. Various mechanisms and methods for such roentgenography have been given various names, such as *laminagraphy, laminography, planigraphy, radiotomy, stratigraphy,* and *vertigraphy*. See also *tomography*.

The **CAT Scan** revealed an area of atrophy where the blood clot had been removed....

... Dr. Stevens explained that the **CAT Scan** revealed an absence of circulation of blood in an area of atrophy, and that "the consensus would hold that there is an accompanying scar." Tr. at 401, 403. Beins v. U.S., 695 F.2d 591, 596, 608 (D.C.Cir.1982).

roentgenology (rent"gĕ-nol'o-je) [*roentgen rays* + *-logy*] the branch of radiology which deals with the diagnostic and therapeutic use of roentgen rays.

roentgenoscope (rent-gen'o-skōp) a fluoroscope; an apparatus for examining the body by means of the fluorescent screen excited by the roentgen rays.

Romberg's disease (trophoneurosis), sign, spasm, station (rom'bergz) [Moritz Heinrich *Romberg*, physician in Berlin, 1795–1873] See *facial hemiatrophy*, under *hemiatrophy*; and see under *sign; spasm;* and *station*.

rombergism (rom'berg-izm) the tendency of a patient to fall when he closes his eyes while standing still with his feet close together (Romberg's sign), due to loss of joint position sensation, as in tabes dorsalis.

rongeur (raw-zhur') [Fr. "gnawing, biting"] an instrument for cutting tissue, particularly bone.

... plaintiff was operated on by defendant Dr. Somberg at St. James Hospital (hospital) for the removal of an intravertebral disc at the L4–5 level. During the course of the surgery the cup of one of the jaws of the metal pituitary **rongeurs** (forceps) being used to remove disc material broke off and remained within the surgical cavity....

The instrument in question was an angulated pituitary **rongeur** manufactured by defendant Lawton Instrument Company (Lawton) who sold it to defendant Reinhold-Schumann, Inc. (Reinhold). Reinhold, in turn, sold the instrument to the hospital on or about August 25, 1963. It appears that the pituitary **rongeur** was used only in laminectomies, perhaps five times a year....

John Carroll, an expert witness for Lawton, testified that he examined the instrument in question, performed laboratory tests upon it and found no evidence of faulty workmanship. He was of the opinion that the failure was a result of the instrument being over-strained. He said that the pattern of fracture of the **rongeur** indicated that the strain was caused by a twisting motion (which Dr. Graubard testified should be avoided in the use of this instrument). Carroll said that the strain could have occurred during the course of one operation or many operations. He also indicated that if the instrument had previously suffered the strain, it could thereafter break even through normal use. He could not pinpoint the time when the instrument was strained. Anderson v. Somberg, 338 A.2d 35–7 (Super.Ct. N.J.1973).

ronnel (ron'el) chemical name: phosphorothioic acid, *O,O*-dimethyl *O*-(2,4,5-trichlorophenyl) ester; a cholinesterase inhibitor, $C_8H_8Cl_3O_3PS$, used as an insecticide, effective against flies, roaches, screw worms, and cattle grub.

The scientific evidence dealt with the properties of **Ronnel**, which the defendants admit is, at least, a mild cholinesterase inhibitor, belonging to that class of compounds known as organo-phosphates, while the plaintiffs contend that a chemical phenomenon known as $P = O$ Bond causes the chemical to become highly toxic....

Tests required by the Federal Food and Drug Administration indicate that **Ronnel** is five times less toxic than any substance which the Food and Drug Administration would classify as highly toxic under the Hazardous Substance Labeling Act. And **Ronnel** was found to be one thousand times more toxic to flies than to humans. L.D. 50 tests show that **Ronnel** is low in toxicity as compared with other economic poisons, while it is high in toxicity for pests. Skogen v. Dow Chemical Co., 375 F.2d 692, 696–7 (8th Cir. 1967).

room (rōōm) a place in a building enclosed and set apart for occupancy or for performance of certain procedures.

room, recovery a hospital unit adjoining operating or delivery rooms, with special equipment and personnel for the care of postoperative or postpartum patients until they may safely be returned to general nursing care in their own rooms or wards.

The lower court observed, and we agree: "The record fairly indicates that the general functions of the **recovery room** are three-fold: (1) to monitor the patient's vital signs; (2) to administer medical care in achieving post-operative recuperation; and (3) to advise the attending physician on any significant problems with respect to the patient's condition of which the physician should be made aware. Reichman v. Wallach, 452 A.2d 501, 507 (Super.Ct.Pa.1982).

root (root) the lowermost part, or a structure by which something is firmly attached. For official names of various anatomical structures, see under *radix*.

Dr. Hand testified that the practice in the New Bern community is that when an extraction is done and the dentist knows that there is a broken **root** tip, an x-ray is taken to determine if it's feasible to leave it. That if an x-ray was not taken at the time the broken **root** tip was left in and the patient returned complaining of pain, it would be in accordance with good and accepted practice and procedure to take an x-ray at that time. Dailey v. N.C.State Bd. of Dental Examiners, 299 S.E.2d 473, 477 (Ct.App.N.C.1983).

root canal therapy See *canal, root (of tooth); debridement (Talbott case); disinfection (root canal); obturation; pulpotomy*; and *therapy, root canal*.

roots, nerve the series of paired bundles of nerve fibers which emerge at each side of the spinal cord, termed dorsal or posterior (see *radix dorsalis*), or ventral or anterior (see *radix ventralis*) according to their position. There are 31 pairs (8 cervical, 12 thoracic, 5 lumbar, 5 sacral, and 1 coccygeal), each corresponding dorsal and ventral root joining to form a spinal nerve. Called also *spinal r's*. Certain cranial nerves, e.g., the trigeminal, also have nerve roots.

In a letter to Dr. Brent before the discogram, Dr. Jackson apprised him that his interpretation of the myelogram revealed a "large dilated **nerve root**" at the L–5 level, on the right side, which could have been caused by a disc bulge compressing the **nerve root**. This bulge would have been the cause of the plaintiff's pain. Martin v. H. B. Zachry Co., 424 So.2d 1002, 1004–5 (La.1982).

Rorschach test See *test, Rorschach*.

rotator cuff See *cuff, rotator*.

rubella (roo-bel'ah) German measles: a mild viral infection characterized by a pink discrete and confluent macular exanthem. After an incubation period of 14 to 21 days, lymph node enlargement (postauricular, posterior cervical, and elsewhere) often precedes the appearance of a pink, macular eruption, occurring first on the face before spreading rapidly to involve the trunk and finally the extremities. No rash occurs in up to 40 per cent of those with the infection. Rhinorrhea, sore throat, bulbar and occasionally palpebral conjunctivitis precede or accompany the exanthem, which lasts little more than 3 to 4 days before fading. Arthralgia is common, and monoarticular arthritis occurs in 20 per cent of patients, more so in adults than children. Transplacental infection of the fetus in the first trimester produces developmental abnormalities of the heart, eyes, brain, bone, and ears in up to 40 per cent of cases without interrupting the pregnancy. See also under *syndrome*. In certain non-English-speaking countries, the disease is called *rubeola*. See also *syndrome, rubella*.

Mrs. Robak, who was then approximately one month pregnant, had developed a rash and a fever. She was examined by Dr. Joshua Roth, who performed a pregnancy test and a blood test for **rubella** (german measles)....

... Neither Dr. Roth nor anyone else at the hospital, however, ever informed Mrs. Robak that she had contracted **rubella**. She was also never advised of the serious consequences that the **rubella** virus could have upon her unborn fetus. [Footnote omitted.] Robak v. U.S., 658 F.2d 471, 473 (7th Cir. 1981).

ruga (roo'gah), pl. *ru'gae* [L.] a ridge, wrinkle, or fold, as of mucous membrane.

rugae of stomach large folds of the mucous membrane of the stomach, occurring especially in the corpus, which are seen when the stomach is empty or undistended.

rule (rōōl) [L. *regula*] a statement of conditions commonly observed in a given situation, or a statement of a prescribed course of action to obtain a result.

rule, M'Naghten "to establish a defense on the ground of insanity, it must be clearly proved that at the time of committing the act the party accused was laboring under such a defect of reason from disease of the mind as not to know the nature and quality of the act he was doing, or, if he did know it, that he did not know he was doing what was wrong."

The **M'Naghten rule** is no longer the standard for deciding criminal responsibility in Texas—see V.T.C.A., Penal Code, § 8.01....

In the instant case, although both the issues of insanity at the time of the commission of the offense and insanity at the time of trial (present insanity) (incompetency) were submitted to the jury, only the **M'Naghten standard** was given to the jury to determine both issues. This was an improper standard with regard to the competency issue. Ex Parte Hagans, 558 S.W.2d 457, 462 (Ct.Crim.App.Tex.1977).

"run the bowel"

He **ran the bowel** (a process whereby the entire twenty-four to twenty-eight feet of bowel are passed between the surgeon's fingers to inspect for tears or interference with the blood supply) and found no other damage. Hitch v. Hall, 399 A.2d 953, 955 (Ct.Spec.App.Md.1979).

rupture (rup′chur) forcible tearing or disruption of tissue. See also *hernia*.

Sherry Bergstreser suffered an occult **rupture** of the uterus. Plaintiffs allege that this **rupture** was caused by the negligent performance by defendants of the Caesarean section on February 22, 1972. As a result of this **rupture**, Sherry Bergstreser was forced to undergo a premature emergency Caesarean section to accomplish the delivery of Brian. Bergstreser v. Mitchell, 448 F.Supp. 10, 12 (E.D.Mo.1977).

Dr. Eppright further testified that the terms "herniated" or "ruptured" might be used interchangeably, the latter being a lay term for a herniated intervertebral disc. Dr. Eppright testified that he had not heard the term "offending disc" used in medicine. French v. Brodsky, 521 S.W.2d 670, 680 (Ct.Civ. App.Tex.1975).

ruthenium (roo-the′ne-um) a rare, very hard metallic element; symbol, Ru; atomic weight, 101.07; atomic number, 44.

... the statement in Claim 1 of the patent that the noble metal **Ruthenium** is a "preferred" and "entirely operative" catalyst for producing doxycycline by hydrogenolysis. Pfizer, Inc. v. International Rectifier Corp., 538 F.2d 180, 192 (8th Cir. 1976).

S

sac (sak) [L. *saccus;* Gr. *sakkos*] a pouch; a baglike organ or structure.

sac, amniotic See *amnion*.

sac, pericardial See *pericardium*.

sacral (sa′kral) [L. *sacralis*] pertaining to or situated near the sacrum.

sacral nerves See *nervi sacrales*.

sacralization (sa″kral-i-za′shun) anomalous fusion of the fifth lumbar vertebra to the first segment of the sacrum, so that the sacrum consists of six segments.

The medical report, as well as the deposition of Dr. Racca indicates that the plaintiff has a congenital defect in the low back, a **sacralization** of the fifth lumbar vertebrae, which was aggravated by the March accident. Gonzales v. Califano, 452 F.Supp. 411, 413 (D.New Mex.1978).

sacroiliac (sa″kro-il′e-ak) pertaining to the sacrum and ilium; denoting the joint or articulation between the sacrum and ilium and the ligaments associated therewith. See also *symphysis pubis* (Campbell case).

sacrum (sa′krum) [L. "sacred"] the triangular bone just below the lumbar vertebrae, formed usually by five fused vertebrae (sacral vertebrae) that are wedged dorsally between the two hip bones; called also *os sacrum* [NA]. See illustration accompanying *skeleton*.

... the transverse process on the right side was incorporated into the **sacrum** (tailbone), so that Plaintiff has only four lumbar vertebrae on the right side, but five lumbar vertebrae on the left side. Robinson v. Charter Oak Fire Ins. Co., 551 S.W.2d 794, 797 (Ct.Civ.App.Tex.1977).

sadism (sad′izm) [Marquis de *Sade*, 1740–1814] sexual perversion in which satisfaction is derived from humiliating or hurting another.

sadomasochistic (sad″o-mas″o-kis′tik) characterized by both sadism and masochism. See also *sadism*; and *masochism*.

"Sexual conduct" is defined in § 39–1–18(14)–(16)....
(16) "**Sado-Masochistic** Abuse" means flagellation or torture by or upon a person who is nude or clad in undergarments or in a sexually revealing or bizarre costume, or the condition of such person being fettered, bound or otherwise physically restrained, in an apparent act of sexual stimulation or gratification. People v. Austin, 257 N.W.2d 120, 122 (Ct. App.Mich.1977).

... [18 Pa.C.S. § 5903(c)] (5) "**Sadomasochistic** abuse" means flagellation or torture by or upon a person clad in undergarments, a mask or bizarre costume, or the condition of being fettered, bound or otherwise physically restrained on the part of one so clothed.... Commonwealth v. MacDonald, 347 A.2d 290, 296 (Pa.1975).

Saint Vitus' dance See *chorea, Sydenham's*.

salivary gland See *glanula parotis*.

Salmonella (sal″mo-nel′ah) [Daniel Elmer *Salmon*, American pathologist, 1850–1914] a genus of microorganisms of tribe Salmonelleae, family Enterobacteriaceae, order Eubacteriales, made up of rod-shaped, gram-negative, usually but not invariably motile bacteria set apart from other enteric bacilli by failure to ferment lactose. It includes the typhoid-paratyphoid bacilli and bacteria usually pathogenic for lower animals which are often transmitted to man. The genus is separated into species or serotypes on the basis of O and H antigens, the latter occurring in two phases and identified by antigenic formulae taking the general form: O antigen: phase 1 ⇄ phase 2 in which the O antigens are designated by Roman numerals, the phase 1 antigens by lower case letters, and the phase 2 antigens by Arabic numerals. More than 1000 different serotypes have been described.

The evidence further revealed that fecal pollution is one of the worst types of water pollutants in terms of containing disease-producing bacteria; that is, salmonella, shigella, brucella, mycobacterium, and vibrio. **Salmonella** [19] produces gastroenteritis.... [[19] **Salmonella**, however, dies very quickly in salt water. In a few days, 90% will die, and only 10% will persist up to 30 days.] U.S. v. City of Asbury Park, 340 F.Supp. 555, 566 (D.N.J.1972).

... the government **Salmonella** expert completed the cultures and isolated the bacteria as **Salmonella Worthington**.

Salmonella itself is a well-recognized pathogen. There are some 1400 types, all felt by medical scientists to be deleterious. As such, **Salmonella** constitutes a serious threat to public health, particularly to the old, the young, and the sickly....

... However, one of the greatest benefits of the pasteurization process is that it normally destroys all **Salmonella** getting into the product, but improper processing or recontamination is possible. U.S. v. 1,200 Cans, Pasteurized Whole Eggs, 339 F.Supp. 131, 136 (N.D.Ga.1972).

DR. SCHAEFFER: **Salmonella** are bacteria which produce diseases, such as typhoid fever, food poisoning, blood poisoning, and dysentery. Infection in an individual can spread to others causing an epidemic. The failure of the mail order laboratories or any other laboratory to identify these organisms may have very serious consequences and this is very shocking, indeed. United Medical Labs v. Columbia Broadcasting System, Inc., 404 F.2d 706, 715 (9th Cir. 1968).

Salmonella Worthington

Salmonella Worthington is particularly found in fowl and can be cultured from a carcass or from the feces of an infected chicken. An infected chicken generally contaminates an egg with this **Salmonella**.... U.S. v. 1,200 Cans, Pasteurized Whole Eggs, 339 F.Supp. 131, 136 (N.D.Ga.1972).

salpingectomy (sal"pin-jek'to-me) [*salpingo-* + Gr. *ektomē* excision] surgical removal of the uterine tube.

During her prenatal care, Mrs. Bowman was advised by the doctors to undergo a bilateral partial **salpingectomy**, or tubal ligation, immediately after childbirth in order to avoid the hazards of a future pregnancy. Bowman v. Davis, 356 N.E.2d 496, 497 (Ohio 1976).

It is therefore ordered that Carolyn Sue Tucker submit to a **salpingectomy**, or such other operation as will insure sterilization, to be performed by a licensed physician in an approved hospital. Wade v. Bethesda Hospital, 356 F.Supp. 380, 383 (S.D.Ohio 1973).

salpingitis (sal"pin-ji'tis) [*salpingo-* + *-itis* inflammation] inflammation of the uterine tube.

Her pelvis was still tender but there were no masses. There was some fullness on the right side indicating **salpingitis** or inflammation of the uterine tube. Anderson v. Moore, 275 N.W.2d 842, 845 (Neb. 1979).

salpingo-oophorectomy (sal-ping"go-o"of-o-rek'to-me) surgical removal of a uterine tube and ovary.

Dr. Lund did a total abdominal hysterectomy (removal of uterus and cervix) and left **salpingo-oophorectomy** (removal of left fallopian tube and left ovary). Cline v. Lund, 107 Cal.Rptr. 629, 632 (Ct.App.1973).

saluresis (sal"u-re'sis) [L. *sal* salt + Gr. *ourēsis* a making water] the excretion of sodium and chloride ions in the urine.

saluretic (sal"u-ret'ik) an agent that promotes saluresis. See also *saluresis*.

"Saluretic" means a pharmaceutical product which causes increased excretion of salt in the urine. U.S. v. Ciba Geigy Corp., 508 F.Supp. 1118, 1122 (D.N.J.1976).

sanitary (san'ĭ-ta"re) [L. *sanitarius*] promoting or pertaining to health. See also *insanitary*.

saphenous See *vena, saphena* (*accessoria* and *magna*).

saphenous vein, greater See *vena saphena magna*.

sarcoid (sar'koid) [*sarco-* + Gr. *eidos* form] 1. tuberculoid; characterized by noncaseating epithelioid cell tubercles. 2. pertaining to or resembling sarcoidosis.

sarcoid of Boeck See *sarcoidosis*.

sarcoidosis (sar"koi-do'sis) a chronic, progressive, generalized granulomatous reticulosis of unknown etiology, involving almost any organ or tissue, including the skin, lungs, lymph nodes, liver, spleen, eyes, and small bones of the hands and feet. It is characterized histologically by the presence in all affected organs or tissues of noncaseating epithelioid cell tubercles. Laboratory findings may include hypercalcemia and hypergammaglobinemia; there is usually diminished or absent reactivity to tuberculin, and, in most active cases, a positive Kveim reaction. The acute form has an abrupt onset and a high spontaneous remission rate, whereas the chronic form, insidious in onset, is progressive. Formerly called *Besnier-Boeck disease, Boeck's disease, benign lymphogranulomatosis*, and *sarcoid of Boeck*. See also *reticuloendothelial system* under *system*.

"He had apparently a proven diagnosis of gout. He had been diagnosed as having **Boeck's sarcoid** a number of years previously, and it is my opinion that he probably had an old degenerative joint disease." Micucci v. Industrial Com'n, 494 P.2d 1324, 1326 (Ariz.1972).

sarcoma (sar-ko'mah), pl. *sarcomas* or *sarco'mata* [*sarco-* + *-oma*] a tumor made up of a substance like the embryonic connective tissue; tissue composed of closely packed cells embedded in a fibrillar or homogeneous substance. Sarcomas are often highly malignant. See also *chondrosarcoma; fibrosarcoma; lymphosarcoma; melanosarcoma; myxosarcoma;* and *osteosarcoma*.

This operation was cancelled, however, when further examination revealed a large mass, which was later determined to be a **sarcoma**, or malignant tumor, in the patient's pelvic area. Easter v. Hancock, 346 A.2d 323, 325 (Super.Ct.Pa.1975).

... **sarcoma** is a tumor deriving from cells of an internal layer of the skin (epithelium). ZeBarth v. Swedish Hospital Medical Center, 499 P.2d 1, 3–4 (Wash.1972).

sarcoma, Hodgkin's Hodgkin's disease of the lymphocytic depletion type. See also *disease, Hodgkin's*.

He concluded, as did other specialists, that, at the time plaintiff entered the defendant clinic, he was suffering from the "subgroup of malignant lymphoma" identified more particularly as "**Hodgkin's sarcoma**" or, as it is otherwise described, "reticulum cell sarcoma." [Referring to one of the slides, the doctor said it showed a "highly malignant undifferentiated neoplasm," and that the outermost covering of the affected area of the body, known as the epithelium, showed marked changes from normal tissue, the changes being known as metaplasia.] ZeBarth v. Swedish Hospital Medical Center, 499 P.2d 1, 4 (Wash.1972).

Sarcoma, osteogenic a malignant primary tumor of bone composed of a malignant connective tissue stroma with evidence of malignant osteoid, bone, and/or cartilage formation. Depending on which component is dominant, three major subtypes are recognized: osteoblastic, fibroblastic, and chondroblastic. Called also *osteosarcoma, osteoid s.* and *osteolytic s.*

sarcoma, reticulum cell malignant lymphoma of the undifferentiated or histiocytic type, depending on the degree of differentiation of the malignant cells.

Dr. Lea definitely diagnosed the decedent as having "**reticulum cell sarcoma**," a terminal cancer of the lymph glands. Lewis v. U.S., 75–2 Tax Cases Par. 13,087 at 88,830, 88,833 (N.D.Ga.1975).

Sargenti method See *therapy, root canal (Sargenti method)*.

saturated (sach'ĕ-rāt"ed) denoting a fatty acid having only single bonds in its carbon chain.

Saturates are fatty acid radicals which have no hydrogen deficiency point and cannot add hydrogen. They comprise about 10 to 15% of corn and soybean oils and about 23 to 25% of cottonseed oil. They comprise nearly 50% of the animal fats and almost 90% of coconut oil. Corn Products Co. v. Standard Brands, Inc., 359 F.2d 739–40 (7th Cir. 1966).

sausage

The Michigan Comminuted Meat Law governs the sale of "meat that has been subjected to a process whereby it has been reduced to minute meat particles." **Sausage**, by definition, is a comminuted meat....

... **Sausage**, by definition, is a meat food product for which federal regulations provide marking, labeling, and ingredient requirements. The only meat food product involved in this case is **sausage**.... Armour & Co. v. Ball, 468 F.2d 76, 79 (6th Cir. 1972).

scale (skāl) [L. *scala*, usually pl., *scalae*, a series of steps] a scheme or device by which some property may be evaluated or measured, such as a linear surface bearing marks at regular intervals, representing certain predetermined units.

scale, microringelmann

On April 21, 1971, an air pollution inspector for the city of Cincinnati observed a non-black plume of smoke spewing from the vent stack of the defendant. The smoke plume was observed for eleven minutes. The opacity of the plume was compared by the inspector to the opacity gradients of a **microringelmann scale**, which is a visual indicator device measuring smoke density by a shade matching technique. The inspector determined that the density of the smoke plume from the vent stack ranged above the number three level on the ringelmann standard smoke chart. City of Cincinnati v. M & M Metals, Inc., 288 N.E.2d 836, 838 (Ct.App.Ohio 1972).

scalene muscle See *musculus scalenus anterior; musculus scalenus medius; musculus scalenus minimus;* and *musculus scalenus posterior*.

scalenectomy (ska"lĕ-nek'to-me) [*scalenus* + Gr. *ektomē* excision] the operation of resecting a scalenus muscle.

The surgeon also performed a **scalelonectomy**, [sic] and prescribed traction for claimant's back. Sears, Roebuck & Co. v. Tatum, 586 P.2d 734, 736 (Okl.1978).

scalenlonectomy See *scalenectomy*.

scalenus (ska-le'nus) [L.; Gr. *skalēnos*] uneven; a name given to various muscles of the neck. See *Table of Musculi*.

scalenus syndrome See *syndrome, scalenus*.

scalpel (skal'pel) [L. *scalpellum*] a small surgical knife with a straight handle and, usually, a blade with a convex edge. See also *foreign object*.

scan (skan) shortened form of *scintiscan*, q.v.; variously designated, according to the organ under examination, as *brain scan, kidney scan, thyroid scan*, etc.

scanner (skan'er) something that scans; a scintiscanner. See also *roentgenograph; roentgenography; tomograph;* and *tomography*.

scanner, brain See *tomograph, brain*.

scanner, EMI an instrument for reconstructing tomographic images for display on a cathode ray tube. See also *computerized axial tomography*, under *tomography*.

At this point Mrs. Gendusa decided to bring plaintiff to another neurosurgeon, Dr. Richard Coulon, who examined the boy on April 29th and May 2nd when an **EMI scan** was made. This is a procedure whereby X-rays are taken of slices of the skull enabling the viewer to see the condition of each part of the brain. Gendusa v. St. Paul Fire & Marine Ins. Co., 435 So.2d 479, 481 (Ct.App.La.1983).

scanner, total body See *roentgenography, body section*.

A **total body scanner** takes x-ray scans of the whole body, including the brain. Cobb Cty., etc. v. Prince, 249 S.E.2d 581, 583 (Ga.1978).

scanning (skan'ning) the act of examining visually, as a small area or different isolated areas, in detail.

scanning, radioisotope the production of a two-dimensional picture (scintiscan, or scan), representing the gamma rays emitted by a radioactive isotope concentrated in a specific tissue of the body, such as the brain or thyroid gland.

William Real suffered from an unidentified neurological ailment and, as part of a medical evaluation, he was referred to Northwestern Memorial Hospital in April of 1976 for what the complaint calls "an **EMI scan** with and without infusion.". . .

According to the complaint, this diagnosis was incorrect because proper interpretation of the results of the **EMI test** would have "disclosed the presence of an abnormality." In the alternative, the complaint alleges that the defendants failed to properly conduct the test, or failed to report that the test results were so equivocal that they were "of no diagnostic value." Real v. Kim, 445 N.E.2d 783, 785 (App.Ct.Ill.1983).

scapula (skap'u-lah), pl. *scap'ulae* [L.] [NA] the flat, triangular bone in the back of the shoulder; the shoulder blade. See illustration.

. . . complaints of pain and stiffness in the neck and right **scapula** area. He had abrasions and contusion of both legs, of the "seat belt" type. Sinclair v. Lumbermen's Mut. Cas. Co., 388 So.2d 417–18 (Ct.App.La.1980).

Examination revealed that plaintiff had suffered a separation of his clavicle (collarbone) at its joint with his **scapula** (shoulder blade). Vest v. City National Bank and Trust Co., 470 S.W.2d 518–19 (Mo.1971).

"Q. Does the **scapula** have any function separate and apart from the operation of the arm?
"A. Not really. Heredia v. Industrial Com'n, 460 P.2d 43–4 (Ct.App.Ariz.1969).
Other Authorities: Hartford Acc. & Indem. Co. v. Helms, 467 S.W.2d 656–7 (Ct.Civ.App.Tex.1971).

scar (skahr) [Gr. *eschara* the scab or eschar on a wound caused by burning] a mark remaining after the healing of a wound or other morbid process; a cicatrix. By extension applied to other visible manifestations of an earlier event. See also *disfigurement; gliosis;* and *keloid.*

The photographs in the record reveal severe **scarring** over most of his body below the waist. Several of these **scars** show that portions of the flesh have been gouged out. Westfall by Terwilliger v. Kottke, 328 N.W.2d 481, 484–5 (Wis.1983).

The trial record establishes that claimant suffered, as a result of his work-related injury, an L-shaped **scar** approximately two inches long above his left eyebrow as well as a second **scar** running from the top of his forehead back into his receding hairline. This facial **scarring** was accompanied by the severance of a nerve and many months of numbness and loss of normal sensation. Andrews v. Pine Hill Wood Co., 426 So.2d 196, 202 (Ct.App.La.1983).

Plaintiff's expert proposed four possibilities of the cause of the injury. The first, and in his opinion most probable, was cast burn. Contact with the skin by a cast can cause a burn, and plaintiff's **scars** appeared to be burn **scars**. The second possibility was any minor injury, such as abrasion, with infection. The third possibility was any kind of chemical burn. The final possibility postulated by the witness was burning from beneath the skin by liquid silicone. Plaintiff had her breasts injected with

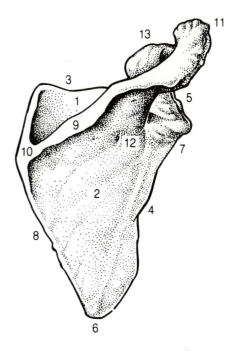

Right scapula, dorsal view: 1, supraspinous fossa. 2, infraspinous fossa. 3, superior margin. 4, lateral margin. 5, glenoid cavity. 6, inferior angle. 7, neck of scapula. 8, medial margin. 9, spine. 10, triangular commencement of spine, upon which the tendon of the trapezius muscle moves. 11, acromion. 12, arterial foramen. 13, coracoid process.

liquid silicone years earlier and liquid silicone tends to migrate. If some of the silicone from plaintiff's breast injections had migrated to her abdomen, when defendant disturbed the flesh under the skin, the silicone could have come in contact with the skin and thus caused the condition. Stone v. Foster, 164 Cal. Rptr. 901, 905 (Ct.App.Cal.1980).
Other Authorities: Evans Bros. Co. v. Labor & Industry R. Com'n, 335 N.W.2d 886–8 (Ct.App.Wis.1983). Blanchard v. City of Bridgeport, 463 A.2d 553, 556 (Conn.1983). Camarata v. Benedetto, 420 So.2d 1146, 1149 (Ct.App.La.1982); Hukill v. U.S. Fidelity & Guaranty Co., 386 So.2d 172–4 (Ct.App. La.1980); Villetto v. Weilbaecher, 377 So.2d 132, 135 (Ct. App.La.1979); Graeff v. Baptist Temple of Springfield, 576 S.W.2d 291, 297 (Mo.1978); Sharpe v. Grindstaff, 329 F.Supp. 405, 411 (M.D.N.C.1970).

scar, cortical

Dr. Stevens also stated that a **cortical scar**, such as he believed existed here, is a potential source of epilepsy. Tr. at 408. Beins v. U.S., 695 F.2d 591, 608 (D.C.Cir.1982).

scar, hypertrophic one formed by exuberant cicatrization, giving it the appearance of a keloid but without the latter's tendency to progressive extension, and recurrence after excision. See also *hypertrophy.*

On June 17, the boy was again admitted to the hospital for several injections of steroids into the **hypertrophic scarred** areas. **Hypertrophic scarred** areas are scars that are thickened and raised from the healthy, normal skin. Young v. Caribbean Associates, Inc., 358 F.Supp. 1220, 1223 (D.V.I.1973).

... development of his thick hypertrophic or keloid scars....
Dr. Delgado gave detailed testimony about the burn scars, which he regarded as unstable, subject to irritation, infection, and ulceration, followed by additional scarring in a vicious cycle. Whitaker v. Church's Fried Chicken, Inc., 387 So.2d 1093, 1095 (La.1980).

He found that she had an extensive linear scar running down the thigh and the side of the leg in excess of 4 inches in length and approximately 1/3rd inch in width. There was another scar above this area which was perhaps less than an inch in length. Both scars were raised, irregular, and very red. The Doctor characterized the larger **scar** as **hypertrophic** bordering on keloidal. He defined **hypertrophic** as a scar which is an excessive response to injury and almost within normal range contrasted with a keloid which continues to grow and tends to invade under the skin. He found evidence of blood vessels penetrating the scars, indicating that the scars were still active and continuing to grow. Since operating on an active scar would tend to stimulate it, the Doctor felt that it could not be attempted until the scar was more mature, which might take an indeterminate period depending on the child's maturation. X-ray treatments would possibly have to be used in the removal. The removal would be in 3 stages, each involving surgery under general anesthesia and a minimum of 2 days hospitalization. After each stage the child would be immobilized for 10 days to 2 weeks, and kept from physical exercise for approximately 1 month. Removal of the scar could only be partial, and some permanent scarring would remain. Maguire v. Waukegan Park District, 282 N.E.2d 6, 8 (App.Ct.Ill.1972).

scar, keloid See *keloid*.

scar, pleural

By December 1975, after seeing several doctors, all that Lundy knew with any degree of certainty was that his chest X rays revealed some **pleural scarring** that the doctors attributed to tuberculosis or pneumonia, among other causes. Lundy himself raised the possibility that the **scarring** could have resulted from his exposure to asbestos, but Dr. Vitums apparently did not think this probable. Lundy v. Union Carbide Corp., 695 F.2d 394, 397 (9th Cir. 1982).

scar tissue See *tissue, cicatrical*.

scar tissue, fibrous See *tissue, cicatrical*.

Scarpa's triangle See *trigonum, femorale*.

scarring See *scar*.

scheduled

As used in this opinion, the term "**scheduled**" refers to those permanent disabilities for which compensation is provided under the provisions of A.R.S. § 23–1044B. Roeder v. Industrial Com'n, 556 P.2d 1148–9 (Ct.App.Ariz.1976).

scheduled permanent disability See under *disability*.

Schistosoma (shis", skis"to-so'mah) [*schisto-* + Gr. *sōma* body] a genus of trematode parasites or flukes; the blood flukes; sometimes called also *Bilharzia*.

schistosomiasis (shis", skis"to-so-mi'ah-sis) the state of being infected with flukes of the genus *Schistosoma*; sometimes called *bilharziasis*.

It was discovered that claimant had a spinal tumor, which was removed, and his condition was pathologically diagnosed as **schistosomiasis**, a parasitic infestation of the spinal cord which caused inflammation of the spinal tissue leading to paraplegia....
... One of claimant's experts, Dr. Rosner, who saw claimant in May, 1967 submitted reports stating that the **schistosomiasis** of the spinal cord was aggravated by the back injury and also referred to the lifting incident as the precipitant cause of the injury. In his testimony at the hearing, Dr. Rosner explained his opinion as to aggravation. He noted that upon lifting heavy objects there is an increase in spinal pressure which in the normal individual is tolerable. He concluded that the diseased spinal cord of the claimant was probably not able to resist this pressure and this led to the subsequent events. Garcia v. Gallo Original Iron Works, Inc., 312 N.Y.S.2d 467, 468 (3d Dept. 1970).

schizoid (skiz'oid, skit'soid) resembling schizophrenia: a term applied by Bleuler to the shut-in, unsocial, introspective type of personality (see under *personality*) and by Kretschmer to the physical type resembling that of persons with dementia praecox, i.e., the asthenic dysplasic type. Cf. *syntonic*.

Schizoid: "Resembling the division, separation or split of the personality that is characteristic of schizophrenia." Hinsie & Campbell, Psychiatric Dictionary, 3d ed., 1960, Oxford Univ. Press at p. 658. U.S. v. Currens, 290 F.2d 751, (3d Cir. 1961).

schizophrenia (skiz"o-fre'ne-ah, skit"so-fre'ne-ah) [*schizo-* + Gr. *phrēn* mind + *-ia*] any of a group of severe emotional disorders, usually of psychotic proportions, characterized by misinterpretation and retreat from reality, delusions, hallucinations, ambivalence, inappropriate affect, and withdrawn, bizarre, or regressive behavior. Popularly and erroneously called *split personality*. In the U.S., formerly called *dementia praecox*, a term still used in Europe for process schizophrenia. See also *schizophrenia, reactive* (Exxon Corp. case).

In 1975, David Guillory, Sr., a member of the armed forces, was diagnosed as suffering from acute **schizophrenia**, a permanent and incurable condition....
... He was suffering from active auditory hallucinations, posturing, thought disorders, chaos, and delusions of persecution. Guillory on Behalf of Guillory v. U.S., 699 F.2d 781, 783 (5th Cir. 1983).

She was admitted in a psychotic state with an admitting diagnosis of **schizophrenia**. At the hospital she complained that the light bulb burning in her head had broken and that she had broken glass in her ear that hurt. She did not recognize her parents, was withdrawn, almost catatonic, agitated, confused and had poor motor coordination. Pisel v. Stamford Hospital, 430 A.2d 1, 5 (Conn.1980).

Dr. Sconzo went on to say:
I think this case illustrates what may be a stumbling block in the understanding of non-psychiatric agencies; namely, that **schizophrenia** is not a simple disease entity which falls neatly into one sub-category or another. Most individuals who have

longstanding or recurrent disorders show various phases of the schizophrenic process at different times, such as catatonic stupor, paranoid ideation, thinking disorders, associational and emotional disturbances, general inability to cope with simple but realistic every day demands etc. Chernicoff v. Richardson, 400 F.Supp. 448, 453 (W.D.N.Y.1975).

Other Authorities: Exxon Corp. v. Brecheen, 519 S.W.2d 170, 178 (Ct.Civ.App.Tex.1975), reversed and remanded 526 S.W.2d 579 (Tex.1975); U.S. v. Shackelford, 494 F.2d 67, 72 (9th Cir. 1974); McCalip v. Richardson, 333 F.Supp. 1207, 1211 (D.Neb.1971), reversed 460 F.2d 1124 (8th Cir. 1972).

schizophrenia, childhood schizophrenia having the onset before puberty, characterized by autism, withdrawal, and atypical behavior.

Matter of David H., 72 Misc.2d 59, 337 N.Y.S.2d 969 (**schizophrenia of childhood**, evidenced by a short attention span, inability to conform to classroom routines, hyperactivity and distractibility, auditory hallucinations, fears and phobias and a thinking disorder). In Matter of Jessup, 379 N.Y.S.2d 626, 632 (Fam.Ct.N.Y.Cty.1975).

schizophrenia, latent a susceptibility to the development of schizophrenia, without a previous history of a psychotic schizophrenic episode.

The examiner concluded that the patient exhibited signs of **latent schizophrenia** which he defined as a category for patients having clear symptoms of schizophrenia but no history of psychotic schizophrenic episode. The report relates that due to family background, plaintiff has a long standing emotional difficulty which culminated in a brief stay at Spring Grove Hospital Center. However, following that hospitalization the report relates that Mr. Schaffer developed a workable obsessional way of handling the inner-emotional turmoil which enabled him to function socially in an adequate fashion. Dr. Silver characterized that earlier adjustment as excellent in spite of a poor prognosis. However, Mr. Schaffer's adjustment following his unfortunate disfiguring accident has not been the best. Schaffer v. Califano, 433 F.Supp. 1218, 1225 (D.Md. 1977).

schizophrenia, paranoid a psychotic state characterized by delusions of grandeur or persecution, often accompanied by hallucinations; called also *dementia paranoides* and *heboid paranoia*.

He explained that **paranoid schizophrenia** is a severe mental illness characterized by disorganization of thinking, paranoid ideas, hallucinations and delusions....

... Dr. Guild stated that during appellant's hospitalization, appellant had actually threatened to kill him and that in the event appellant was released from the hospital, he would be dangerous to himself and others. Further, he stated that he feared appellant, currently taking medication for his mental condition, would not take the medication after leaving the hospital. In such event, the likelihood of his becoming psychotic would increase greatly and perhaps produce another violent incident. Bethany v. Stubbs, 393 So.2d 1351–3 (Miss.1981).

B.'s condition has been diagnosed as **paranoid schizophrenia**. He apparently hears voices, which he believes to be God's and which he obeys. On one occasion those voices directed

him to assault another inmate. Matter of B, 383 A.2d 760, 762 (Super.Ct.N.J.1977).

... the defendant was diagnosed as suffering from "**dementia praecox, paranoid type**," which is a mental disease characterized by disassociation of ideas, emotions and motor activities....

... He also stated that the defendant had auditory hallucinations when he was admitted to Kings County Hospital in New York. In addition, defendant had exhibited impulsive behavior in the past....

Dr. Haines also testified that **dementia praecox** was the same as schizophrenia but that this didn't necessarily classify one as legally sane or insane. He said that a person with a psychopathic personality would be more liable to act due to an irresistible passion. People v. Childs, 281 N.E.2d 631, 633–4 (Ill.1972).

Other Authorities: U.S. v. Shackelford, 494 F.2d 67, 72 (9th Cir. 1974); State v. Spivey, 319 A.2d 461, 465 (N.J.1974); Hendry v. U.S., 418 F.2d 774, 785 (2d Cir. 1969).

schizophrenia, process severe, progressive schizophrenia seldom resulting in remission or recovery, believed by many to be caused by organic brain changes although definitive evidence is lacking; cf. *reactive s.*

schizophrenia, reactive schizophrenia attributed chiefly to environmental conditions, with the expectation of a benign prognosis; cf. *process s.*

He defined the term "a **schizophrenic reaction**" as being a split mind in that one could be realistic and appropriate in some aspects of his life, but in other aspects such a person could be "very unrealistic and unappropriate and unlogical and sick." He stated that this condition was a psychosis and defined it as follows:

Well, in a psychosis, people, ... they are not realistic, and they react to things in a bizarre and illogical manner.

He stated that persons with such a psychosis are removed from reality and are disoriented in their thinking. Exxon Corp. v. Brecheen, 519 S.W.2d 170, 178 (Ct.Civ.App.Tex.1975).

schizophrenia, residual a condition manifested by individuals with symptoms of schizophrenia who, after a psychotic schizophrenic episode, are no longer psychotic.

When he discharged Mr. Brecheen from the hospital he gave a discharge diagnosis of **schizophrenia residual type**, which means simply that there continued to be evidence of perhaps defective functioning of his personality. He showed evidence of personality disorders without manifest symptoms that were incapacitating. Exxon Corp. v. Brecheen, 519 S.W.2d 170, 178 (Ct.Civ.App.Tex.1975), reversed and remanded 526 S.W.2d 579 (Tex.1975).

schizophrenia, undifferentiated

"THE WITNESS: Yes **Schizophrenia** comes in a number of varieties, and many so-called ambulatory schizophrenics get along very well in life and never see a psychiatrist and never had an acute psychotic break. Their reasons are very simple, and they have a very peculiar logic, and they have a way of blaming it on other things. For instance, if his marriage is maladjusted, it isn't wrong that he is doing it. It has to be somebody else doing it, which he related in the first interview. It has a lack of clarity, lack of objectivity, lack of realism. It's called

undifferentiated schizophrenia. Martinez v. Industrial Com'n, 498 P.2d 153, 155–6 (Ct.App.Ariz.1972).

schizophrenic (skiz"o-fren'ik) a person affected with schizophrenia. See also *schizophrenia*.

A **schizophrenic** may have difficulty distinguishing fact from fantasy and may have his memory distorted by delusions, hallucinations and paranoid thinking. A paranoid **schizophrenic**, though he may appear normal and his judgment on matters outside his delusional system may remain intact, may harbor delusions of grandeur or persecution that grossly distort his reactions to events. U.S. v. Lindstrom, 698 F.2d 1154, 1160 (11th Cir. 1983).

school of medicine See *medicine, school of*.

sciatic nerve See *nervus ischiadicus*.

sciatic nerve-small See *nervus cutaneus femoris posterior*.

sciatica (si-at'ĭ-kah) [L.] a syndrome characterized by pain radiating from the back into the buttock and into the lower extremity along its posterior or lateral aspect, and most commonly caused by prolapse of the intervertebral disk; the term is also used to refer to pain anywhere along the course of the sciatic nerve.

At the time of the trial Abernathy still had some **sciatica** (a pain running up and down the leg, typically caused by pressure on a nerve), though he was not taking any pain killers. Dr. Miller testified that he might recommend, although he had not yet done so, an operation on Abernathy's back to fuse the damaged vertebrae in order to alleviate the **sciatica**. Abernathy v. Superior Hardwoods, Inc., 704 F.2d 963, 973 (7th Cir. 1983).

Dr. Licciardi saw Mrs. Urbina on September 7, 1976 at which time she complained of low back pain. X-rays showed some physical evidence of nerve root irritation on the right side, which the doctor called **sciatica**. Urbina v. Alois J. Binder Bakery, Inc., 423 So.2d 765, 767 (Ct.App.La.1982).

Chisholm complained of pain on the straight leg raising test at 60 degrees. Dr. Flynn felt that the shooting pains in the leg possibly could be caused by irritation of the nerve root (**sciatica**). An electromyelogram and a lumbar myelogram were performed and the results were normal, indicating no nerve root irritation. Chisholm v. L. S. Womack, Inc., 424 So.2d 1138, 1141 (Ct.App.La.1982).

Other Authorities: Lovely v. Cooper Indus. Products, Inc., 429 N.E.2d 274–5 (Ct.App.Ind.1981); Barats v. Weinberger, 383 F.Supp. 276, 280 (E.D.Pa.1974).

science (si'ens) [L. *scientia* knowledge] the systematic observation of natural phenomena for the purpose of discovering laws governing those phenomena.

For example, Dr. Arthur J. Backrach, head of the Department of Psychology at Arizona State University, defined his understanding of the **scientific** approach or method as follows:

"A. Well, briefly, I would say that **scientific method** is a self-correcting method in the sense that it starts off with collection of data and facts.

"It is then tested by setting up hypotheses and experiments in research to test our theoretical positions or hypothetical prospects based on these facts, and then to correct the hypotheses by confirming or refuting them, adding to the store of knowledge which then is in need of further testing.

"I think one of the things that characterizes the **scientific method** is that it is always self-correcting and always seeking for further information.

"It is fundamentally an experimental method in terms of conducting controlled studies based on amassing facts, and the testing of hypotheses show that there is not such thing as a final answer in the **scientific method**. It assumes that you are always studying, and that as you get more and more information this opens up more and more areas of reresearch so that it is very much of, if I may say so, an ethical kind of approach in the sense that it is based on respect for truth, integrity, and that data are important and not individuals in the sense that no person, no matter how venerable himself, can long stand if he does not have the facts or his theoretical propositions don't hold.

"I think this is the **science** of self-correction, which is the best phrase for this, and continual search for truth." In Re Estate of Kidd, 479 P.2d 697, 706–7 (Ariz.1971).

scientific method See *science*.

scintiscan (sin'tĭ-skan) a two-dimensional representation (map) of the gamma rays emitted by a radioisotope, revealing its varying concentration in a specific tissue of the body, such as the brain, kidney, or thyroid gland.

It was further admitted by the defendant that if the **scan** had been done by the Veterans Administration in 1976, such a **scan** would have disclosed a brain stem lesion or the tumor that was later found in 1980. Swanson v. U.S. By and Through Veterans Admin., 557 F.Supp. 1041, 1043 (D.Idaho 1983).

Dr. Winter interpreted a **CAT (computed axial tomography) scan** of Mrs. Grill's optic nerve and felt strongly that the enlargement on the optic nerve was not a tumor, primarily because he felt that a tumor could not respond so dramatically to cortisone, which is a drug that reduces inflammatory reactions. A second **CAT scan** showed, in his opinion, no enlargement of the elongated tortuous optic nerve. Grill v. U.S., 552 F.Supp. 505, 507 (E.D.N.Y.1982).

scintiscanner (sin"tĭ-skan'er) the system of equipment used in the making of a scintiscan.

sclera (skle'rah), pl. *sclerae* [L.; Gr. *skleros* hard] [NA] the tough white outer coat of the eyeball, covering approximately the posterior five-sixths of its surface, and continuous anteriorly with the cornea and posteriorly with the external sheath of the optic nerve.

Doctor Arnold testified that McKee sustained a laceration of the **sclera**, that it was punctured, and some fluid leaked out. Surgery was performed at the hospital to repair the laceration and excise the iris prolapse. Davidson & Graham Const. Co. v. McKee, 562 S.W.2d 426–7 (Tenn.1978).

Apparently physicians later discovered that this type tubing [a hollow polyethylene ring] creates a problem of erosion through the **sclera** (the white portion of the eye which is a membrane). In procedures thereafter a softer type plastic was used. Holton v. Pfingst, 534 S.W.2d 786–7 (Ct.App.Ky.1975).

sclerectoiridectomy (skle-rek"to-ir"ĭ-dek'to-me) the operation of excision of a portion of the sclera and of the iris for glaucoma; called also *Lagrange's operation*.

sclerectomy (skle-rek'to-me) [*sclero-* + Gr. *ektomē* excision] excision of the sclera by scissors (Lagrange's operation), by punch (Holth's operation), or by trephining (Elliot's operation).

The records of Dr. Richards, introduced in evidence and uncontradicted, reflect that he treated Hill for glaucoma of both eyes, performed surgery for glaucoma on both eyes on November 7, 1960 (described as irido-corneal **sclerectomies**).... State Compensation Ins. Fund v. Workmen's Comp. App. Bd., 88 Cal.Rptr. 469, 471 (Ct.App.Cal.1970).

scleroderma (skle"ro-der'mah) [*sclero-* + Gr. *derma* skin] chronic hardening and shrinking of the connective tissues of any part of the body, including the skin, heart, esophagus, kidney, and lung. The skin may be thickened, hard, and rigid, and pigmented patches may occur. It may be generalized (*systemic* or *diffuse s.*) limited to the distal parts of the extremities and face (*acrosclerosis*) or to the digits (*sclerodactyly*), or localized to oval or linear areas a few centimeters across (*morphea*).

First, Ms. Stark suffered from a precisely diagnosable impairment (**scleroderma**) with well known developmental stages,[8] so that the doctor was able to accurately estimate the seriousness of claimant's condition at a given time in the past. [[8] **Scleroderma** has been defined as a chronic mesenchymal disease of undetermined origin, characterized by connective tissue proliferation in the dermis and in many internal organs. The onset is insidious, with stiffness of the hands, sweating of the hands and feet, and Raynaud's phenomenon. The skin eventually becomes hard, thick and glossy, and the fingers and toes become fixed. Gradually the entire integument becomes involved, and ulcerations, pigmentation, and calcification may occur. Dysphagia, disturbed gastrointestinal motility, respiratory embarrassment, pneumonia and heart failure and renal involvement are due to connective tissue proliferation of the viscera. The condition is usually slowly progressive over many years, and death is usually due to renal or cardiac failure or to sepsis. Treatment is symptomatic and supportive. The Handbook of Medical Treatment 386 (12th ed. 1970), quoted in Stark v. Weinberger, (497 F.2d 1092 [7th Cir. 1974]) at 1094.] Lieberman v. Califano, 592 F.2d 986, 991 (7th Cir. 1979).

Plaintiff has been afflicted with **scleroderma**, a progressive, incurable disease, since the late 1930's....

... They establish that the onset of **scleroderma** is insidious and its progression slow; while its cutaneous manifestations may, on occasion, regress, the disease nevertheless follows its fatal course. Raynaud's phenomenon, pain, ulcerations and increasing tightness of the skin are all associated with the disease in its initial, as well as subsequent, stages....

... There is no cure for **scleroderma**. One medical authority, who was cited by the administrative law judge, concluded:

Patients with slowly progressive systemic sclerosis can lead productive and useful lives. The most important goal in therapy is to preserve function in and prevent injury to the hands. Vocational and/or climatic change may be indicated. Hand care must be stressed, including instructions for active and passive exercises to prevent flexion contracture. Early signs of local infection in fingertips must be treated immediately before they progress to large ulcerations.

C. Loeb, Textbook of Medicine 813 (13th ed. 1971). Under this medical evidence it is clear that, for a person who works only with his hands, **scleroderma** should be considered disabling before the disease reaches its most advanced and crippling stages. [Footnotes omitted.] Stark v. Weinberger, 497 F.2d 1092, 1094, 1097–8 (7th Cir. 1974).

sclerosing (skle-rōs'ing) causing or undergoing sclerosis.

... a **sclerosing** drug known as Sotradecol was injected into the capsule of the tissue around her right condyle, and both condyles, respectively. This was done to cause scarring of the tissue under the belief that this scarring would tighten the capsules and prevent the condyle from slipping out. Rosario v. New York City Health & Hospitals, 450 N.Y.S.2d 805–6 (1st Dep't 1982).

sclerosis (skle-ro'sis) [Gr. *sklērōsis* hardness] an induration, or hardening; especially hardening of a part from inflammation and in diseases of the interstitial substance. The term is used chiefly for such a hardening of the nervous system due to hyperplasia of the connective tissue or to designate hardening of the blood vessels.

Also, the X-ray showed a **sclerosis** along the mid-portion of the right sacroiliac joints. Robinson v. Charter Oak Fire Ins. Co., 551 S.W.2d 794, 797 (Ct.Civ.App.Tex.1977).

Considerable narrowing of the lumbosacral disc space was seen with subchondral **sclerosis** and spurring along the articular aspects of L5 and S1 bodies. Barats v. Weinberger, 383 F.Supp. 276, 281 (E.D.Pa.1974).

sclerosis, amyotrophic lateral a disease marked by progressive degeneration of the neurons that give rise to the corticospinal tract and of the motor cells of the brain stem and spinal cord, and resulting in a deficit of upper and lower motor neurons; it usually ends fatally within two to three years. Called also *Charcot's syndrome* and *Dejerine type.*

Seventy-three year old Abe Perlmutter lies mortally sick in a hospital, suffering from **amyotrophic lateral sclerosis** (Lou Gehrig's disease) diagnosed in January 1977. There is no cure and normal life expectancy, from time of diagnosis, is but two years. In Mr. Perlmutter, the affliction has progressed to the point of virtual incapability of movement, inability to breathe without a mechanical respirator and his very speech is an extreme effort. Even with the respirator, the prognosis is death within a short time. Notwithstanding, he remains in command of his mental faculties and legally competent. Satz v. Perlmutter, 362 So.2d 160–1 (Dist.Ct.App.Fla.1978).

... **amyotrophic lateral sclerosis** (a terminal degenerative disease of unknown etiology affecting the central nervous system).... Mattson v. Prospect Foundry, Inc., 219 N.W.2d 435 (Minn.1974).

Subsequently appellant's condition was diagnosed as **amyotrophic lateral sclerosis** (sometimes herein "ALS"), a relatively rare neurological disorder characterized by progressive deterioration and death of nerve cells located in the spinal column. As the nerve cells die, muscular stimulation is impeded and ultimately blocked altogether; atrophy and paralysis ensue. At the time of trial, appellant was almost totally paralyzed and had a life expectancy of four years....

... In all, the record contains hundreds of pages of testimony by these six expert witnesses, virtually all of which is devoted to the question of causation and all of which conclusively demonstrates but one fact: the best minds of medical science are nowise in agreement as to the etiology of **amyotrophic lateral sclerosis**. . . .

... All of the defense medical witnesses had stated that based on the information now available to medical science, it was unlikely that trauma—physical injury to living tissue—could cause the onset of **amyotrophic lateral sclerosis**, a disease involving the selective degeneration and death of only the lower motor neurons of the anterior horn cells located in the spinal cord. Plaintiff offered to prove in rebuttal through Dr. Wycis that such selective destruction of the anterior horn cells can be caused by trauma. Downey v. Weston, 301 A.2d 635, 638, 640–1 (Pa.1973).

sclerosis, multiple a disease in which there are patches of demyelination throughout the white matter of the central nervous system, sometimes extending into the gray matter. Typically, the symptoms of lesions of the white matter are weakness, incoordination, paresthesias, speech disturbances, and visual complaints. The course of the disease is usually prolonged, with remissions and relapses over a period of many years. The etiology is unknown. Called also *disseminated s.* and *insular s.*

Multiple sclerosis is a classic disease of the myelin. Myelin is the coating on the cells of the nervous system which insulates, nourishes and conducts impulses along the axons of the nervous system. The cause of **multiple sclerosis** is unknown but experts hypothesize that it is caused by a virus which is present in the body of a susceptible person prior to age fifteen and which is activated, precipitated or exacerbated upon some triggering event such as trauma (especially injury to the neck), fever, excessive fatigue, infections, emotional distress or other factor.

Multiple sclerosis is characterized initially by inflammation or swelling of the myelin around the nerve endings resulting, in the later stages of the disease, in scarring of the myelin, which is destroyed and broken down, creating "multiple" lesions in the nervous system. "Multiple" also applies to the fact that patients have multiple attacks of the disease. At one point the disease may affect the patient's gait (inflammation stage). They can recover slowly (remission) and be able to walk with less difficulty (scarring stage). The next episode may involve inflammation of another area of the central nervous system which may, for example, affect the vision, producing diplopia, then improved vision, and then almost normal, but weakened, vision which will eventually deteriorate as the lesions become more numerous or more severe and the myelin is destroyed creating more scarring. Ultimately the damage can be irreversible and permanent.

The following are some of the classical symptoms of **multiple sclerosis**: ocular disturbances; nystagmus (involuntary oscillation of the eyeballs); diplopia (double vision); diminished eyesight; difficulty with speech; difficulty with performing with the extremities; weakness with seizures of spasticity; weakness in arms or hands such as inability to grip; ataxia (difficulty in walking characterized by stumbling, wobbling, falling); increased or abnormal reflexes; hyperflexia indicated by Babinski or other abnormal signs; intention tremor; clonus (extreme weakness in the legs); atrophy; paresthesia (numbness or other abnormal spontaneous sensation such as burning or pricking); loss of abdominal reflexes; urinary incontinence; bladder difficulties; rectal functions interfered with.

Multiple sclerosis is extremely difficult to diagnose partly because an involvement of any of these areas may last from weeks to months, then the patient enters a period of remission during which the symptomology abates, and after which the same symptoms or other symptoms recur and may be exacerbated. **Multiple sclerosis** is a debilitating disease in which, typically, the possibility of further disability in the future is very high. Patients who have attacks tend to have more attacks. There is presently no known cure for multiple sclerosis. . . .

Trauma can precipitate the symptoms of **multiple sclerosis**. The care and treatment and diagnosis, with regard to the disease of **multiple sclerosis** come primarily within the field of neurology. . . .

One of the most vexing problems of **multiple sclerosis** has to do with diagnosis. It is a disease that strikes in insidious ways. It takes a very trained observer making a very careful study to really be able to make a diagnosis of **multiple sclerosis** when it does not manifest itself in the classic form, when it is not in its most advanced stages.

In **multiple sclerosis** you usually find some motor nerve involvement. This refers to movement. Weakness is both an objective and subjective motor finding. Weakness such as not being able to hold a fork or to hold anything in her hand, weakness of the limb or right arm would be a motor finding such as the one he was talking about. And, if that sort of finding occurred within days or weeks of an injury to the neck that would meet one of the requirements that he was talking about of trauma and precipitation of **multiple sclerosis**. That sort of complaint in conjunction with a doctor's diagnosis of radiculitis could go to substantiate motor nerve root involvement.

One of the other requirements was difficulty with speech. He stated that plaintiff exhibited "an area of suspicion with regard to speech."

One of the real problems with **multiple sclerosis** is the fact that you have inflammation of the central nervous system where you have periods of exacerbation and remission. If they are in a period of remission, the symptomology might not be present or may be lessened.

The accepted treatment for **multiple sclerosis** includes muscle relaxants, high vitamin intake, tranquilization, drugs that open up blood vessels and ACTH steroid treatment.

From a subjective point of view a patient who had suffered a neck injury and then complains of weakness in a limb shortly thereafter would fall classically within the framework of the diagnosis or the beginning signs of **multiple sclerosis**. McSwain v. Chicago Transit Authority, 362 N.E.2d 1264–5, 1274, 1276–7 (App.Ct.Ill.1977).

Mrs. Hitchcock's symptoms closely resemble **multiple sclerosis**. Several doctors have diagnosed her disease as **multiple sclerosis**. **Multiple sclerosis** is a demyelinating disease for which there is no known cause or cure. (Testimony of Drs. Herskovits and Schulein.) [Footnote omitted.] Hitchcock v. U.S., 479 F.Supp. 65, 68 (D.D.C.1979).

... a diagnosis of **multiple sclerosis**, a tragic degenerative disease of the nervous system. . . .

Finally, in early 1969, Dr. Robitaille experienced a "vague sensory disturbance" in his right leg and a numbness in his hands, which he mentioned to Dr. T. A. Grossi during his annual naval physical in April. The numbness was described as a "pins and needles" sensation which Dr. Grossi attributed to Dr. Robitaille's habit of leaning his elbows on his desk as he worked....

... in April 1969 he described his physical findings to Dr. Leland Patterson, a neurologist. During their casual conversation, Dr. Robitaille asked whether his symptoms could be associated with any neurological disease or **multiple sclerosis**. Dr. Patterson conducted an unofficial neurological examination (not reported in Navy records) which proved negative, as had Dr. Grossi's several days earlier. Accordingly, Dr. Patterson found, and informed Dr. Robitaille in emphatic terms, that he did not have any neurological disorder....

In December, 1969, Dr. Kramer, supporting Dr. Robitaille's application for a medical discharge from the Navy, reported his conversation with him in the spring of that year and stated: "It seems clear to me that there can be no question now that the symptoms he related did present evidence of **multiple sclerosis** at that time. This combination of symptoms—dysfunction on a chance basis alone could not occur in a young man in the absence of neurological disease." Guardian Life Ins. Co. of America v. Robitaille, 495 F.2d 890, 892–3, 904 (2d Cir. 1974).

Other Authorities: McConnell v. Richardson, 321 F.Supp. 1397, 1399–1400 (W.D.Pa.1971).

sclerosis tuberosa; sclerosis, tuberous a congenital familial disease characterized pathologically by tumors on the surfaces of the lateral ventricles and sclerotic patches on the surface of the brain and marked clinically by progressive mental deterioration and epileptic convulsions. There may be adenoma sebaceum, congenital tumor of the eye (phakoma), and tumors of the viscera, especially the kidney and heart muscle. Called also *Bourneville's disease* and *epiloia*.

Within a few weeks the Juges noticed the child was having "seizures" which involved a tensing of the body for a few seconds....

... After careful examination and testing she diagnosed the child as having **tuberous sclerosis**. This is an inherited condition which involves over-growth of tissue, particularly within the central nervous system. The child was found to be profoundly retarded and his condition was described as a permanent one....

... She testified the condition was not related to trauma but was an inherited birth defect. She stated unequivocally that in her opinion there was no relation whatsoever between the accident and the child's condition....

Although the disease is classified as an "inherited" disease, 80% of the persons contracting it get it from a "new mutation," i.e., there is no evidence of it elsewhere in the family. Juge v. Cunningham, 422 So.2d 1253, 1255–6 (Ct.App.La. 1982).

scoliosis (sko"le-o'sis) [Gr. *skoliōsis* curvation] an appreciable lateral deviation in the normally straight vertical line of the spine. Cf. *kyphosis* and *lordosis*. See also *operation, spinal-jack*.

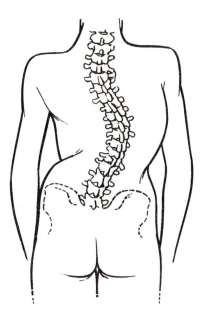

Scoliosis.

A set of dorsal spine x-rays revealed **scoliosis** concave on the left side with hypoertrophic changes of arthritis. Adams v. Schweiker, 557 F.Supp. 1373, 1376 (S.D.Tex.1983).

The minor plaintiff suffered from a severe spinal deformity, or **scoliosis**, which became more pronounced as she grew older. When she was thirteen years old, a group of doctors, including the defendant, recommended that she undergo a complicated and risky orthopedic procedure, the first stage of which involved setting her spine in rigid traction aimed at straightening it mechanically to whatever extent reasonably possible. The second stage involved an operation which would effect a fusion of portions of her spine, so that extreme deformity would not recur. She would then remain in another type of rigid traction until the process of fusion was complete, perhaps as long as six months. Harrington v. Cohen, 374 N.E.2d 344–5 (App.Ct.Mass.1978).

He was found to have **scoliosis** (curvature) of the lumbar spine. The curvature was described as being "several inches" in nature. Neurological signs included positive straight leg raising tests. There was narrowing of intervertebral discs in the lumbar area and evidence of inflammation and of muscle spasm. He was fitted with a lumbo-sacral brace, and discharged improved. Foster v. Mathews, 423 F.Supp. 117–18 (W.D.N.Car. 1976).

Other Authorities: Long v. Martin Timber Co., Inc., 395 So.2d 931–2 (Ct.App.La.1981). Albert v. Alter, 381 A.2d 459, 469 (Super.Ct.Pa.1977). Sousa v. M/V Caribia, 360 F.Supp. 971, 974 (D.Mass.1973). Maguire v. Waukegan Park District, 282 N.E.2d 6, 8 (App.Ct.Ill.1972). McCalip v. Richardson, 333 F.Supp. 1207, 1210 (D.Neb.1971).

scoliosis, myopathic See *scoliosis, paralytic*.

scoliosis, paralytic lateral curvature of the spinal column due to muscle paralysis; called also *myopathic s.*

In addition, Ricky now suffers from **paralytic scoliosis** (94% curvature of the spine). Green Appeal, 307 A.2d 279, 280 (Pa. 1973).

scoliosis, static that which is due to difference in the length of the legs.

Various neurological tests were positive, and Dr. Wentworth concluded the claimant suffered from a **static**, or paralytic or myopathic **scoliosis** of the lumbo sacral area. Miles v. Secretary of Health, Education & Welfare, 322 F.Supp. 1132, 1137 (W.D.Tenn.1971).

scopolamine (sko-pol'ah-mēn) chemical name: α-(hydroxymethyl) benzeneacetic acid 9-methyl-3-oxa-9-azatricyclo[3.3.1.0^{2,4}]non-7-yl ester. An anticholinergic alkaloid, $C_{17}H_{21}NO_4$, derived from several solanaceous plants, including *Atropa belladonna* L., *Hyoscyamus niger* L., *Datura* species, and *Scopolia* species. It has effects on the autonomic nervous system similar to those of atropine. Called also *hyoscine.*

Hyoscine, also known as "truth serum," had at one time been used as a method of narco-interrogation, but by 1954, had been considered outdated as a technique. **Hyoscine** has a tendency to cause the subject to hallucinate and become disoriented from his environment. The administration of these drugs to Townsend was in violation of the rules of the Chicago Police Department.

. . . Dr. Freedman stated that **hyoscine** (or **scopalomine**) [sic] causes amnesia and hallucination. It tends to give its subject a "heightened motivation to cooperate." The actual effect of the drug, he said, must be measured with the "subject's previous background, the stresses, tensions, hopes and fears operating at a given time, the physiological mechanism of action of the drug given, the milieu of contacts at the time, the stimuli to which the subject is exposed at the time." The district court summarized Dr. Freedman's testimony:

He testified that **scopalomine** [sic] [or **hyoscine**] either alone or in combination with phenobarbital was not the proper medication for a narcotic addict and that the administration of **scopalomine** [sic] was the improper medication for Townsend under all the circumstances. . . .

Dr. Freedman said that in the hundreds of hours he spent examining prisoners under drugs, he was virtually never able to treat the statements given by them as evidence of objective reality but rather as evidence of subjective personality characteristics. U.S. ex rel. Townsend v. Twomey, 452 F.2d 350, 367–8 (7th Cir. 1972).

score (skōr) a rating, usually expressed numerically, based on achievement or the degree to which certain qualities are present.

score, Apgar a numerical expression of the condition of a newborn infant, usually determined at 60 seconds after birth, being the sum of points gained on assessment of the heart rate, respiratory effort, muscle tone, reflex irritability, and color. Cf. *recovery s.*

Following delivery Matthew was in a very depressed state. On an "APGAR" scoring system that awards points to various vital signs of a baby at one minute after birth, with ten as the highest rating and zero, or death, the lowest, Matthew registered a score of one. He had marked molding of the head and, while still in the hospital, had a number of seizures. Rutherford v. Zearfoss, 272 S.E.2d 225–6 (Va.1980).

Tina could not breathe on her own at birth. She was given an **Apgar rating** of "one." [4 Within a minute or so of birth she was connected to a resuscitator which administered positive-pressure oxygen. [⁴ The **Apgar rating** indicated the child's condition. A perfect score is 10; a stillborn child would score 0. At birth, Tina's heart rate was slow, her color "blue," her muscle tone "flaccid," her respiratory effort "absent."] Lhotka v. Larson, 238 N.W.2d 870, 873 (Minn.1976).

score, recovery a number expressing the condition of an infant at various intervals, which should be stipulated, greater than 1 minute after birth, based on the same features assessed by the Apgar score at 60 seconds after birth.

scotoma (sko-to'mah), pl. *scoto'mata* [Gr. *skotōma*] an area of depressed vision within the visual field, surrounded by an area of less depressed or of normal vision.

In October 1968, Dr. Robitaille noticed a blurring of vision in his right eye which Dr. Dunbar Hoskins, a Navy ophthalmologist, examined and believed to be caused by congenital nuclear cataracts. Dr. Robitaille disclosed this finding to Guardian's medical examiner, Dr. Greer, but the condition was subsequently recognized at Massachusetts General as a **scotoma** or isolated area of depressed vision.⁵ According to uncontradicted testimony at trial, a **scotoma** does not necessarily impair vision and, indeed, Dr. Robitaille's vision remained 20/20. [⁵ There was considerable disagreement at trial concerning the likely origin of the **scotoma**. Guardian's witnesses testified that **scotoma** is evidence of optic neuritis, although they could not state that this was true in Dr. Robitaille's case. Dr. Robitaille testified, on the contrary, that **scotoma** is not necessarily of neurological origin and that, in fact, there had never been a definitive connection made between his **scotoma** and any neurological disorder.] Guardian Life Ins. Co. of America v. Robitaille, 495 F.2d 890, 893 (2d Cir. 1974).

scotoma, central an area of depressed vision corresponding with the point of fixation and interfering with or entirely abolishing central vision.

Dr. Prater found a "large **central scotoma**" in the right eye, which indicated a loss of vision, primarily in her right eye. Skinner v. Dawson Metal Products, 575 S.W.2d 935, 939 (Mo.Ct. App.1978).

Dr. Willcockson charted a large central total blind spot (**central scotoma**) in each of appellee's eyes, which left her with only peripheral vision. Glasses, in his opinion, cannot improve this permanent partial blindness. Sterling Drug, Inc. v. Yarrow, 408 F.2d 978, 984 (8th Cir. 1969).

scotoma, paracentral an area of depressed vision situated near the point of fixation.

Numerous other reports of the toxic effects of chloroquine appeared in the United States. Dr. Mayer reported field defects, retinal damage, and **paracentral scotoma** from the use of chloroquine. Sterling Drug, Inc. v. Yarrow, 408 F.2d 978, 986 (8th Cir. 1969).

scours (skowrz) diarrhea or dysentery, especially in new-born animals. See also *white scours*.

Autopsies performed upon a number of the swine under the direction of Wade Kadel, a veterinarian and director of the Kentucky Diagnostic Laboratory, revealed the existence of a variety of diseases and conditions adversely affecting the health of the herd including **scours** (diarrhea probably caused by E Coli).... Arlie Larimer & Sons, Inc. v. Kleen-Leen, Inc., 523 F.2d 865, 867 (6th Cir. 1975).

scours, white an acute infectious disease of calves, lambs, and foals during the first few days after birth, caused by enteropathogenic strains of *Escherichia coli* and marked by fever, dehydration, depression, and diarrhea, with fetid feces that are light in color but may be blood-stained late in the disease.

scrotum (skro'tum) [L. "bag"] [NA] the pouch which contains the testes and their accessory organs. It is composed of skin, the dartos, the spermatic, cremasteric, and infundibuliform fasciae, and the tunica vaginalis.

That night he developed **scrotal** hematoma, resulting in a four-day hospitalization during which the **scrotum** was reopened, drained and packed with gauze that remained for ten days to two weeks. In about seven weeks when the drainage stopped and the wound healed, atrophy of the left testicle was evident. Cowman v. Hornaday, 329 N.W.2d 422, 424 (Iowa 1983).

The next day Stanley saw Fisher at his office, and by this time Stanley's **scrotum** was swollen to the size of a cantaloupe or three to four times the normal size. Fisher told him to continue the use of ice. On the 25th, Fisher contacted Stanley to come in for an examination, which he did. Fisher informed Stanley that he had a hematoma on the left side, and he was to use heat on his **scrotum**. Stanley v. Fisher, 417 N.E.2d 932–3 (Ct. App.Ind.1981).

Seba-Nil

Mrs. Wilson first cleansed off Mrs. Rosenblum's face with **Seba-Nil** a rapid-drying cleansing fluid with an alcohol base, using a cotton ball. Rosenblum v. Bloom, 492 S.W.2d 321–2 (Ct.Civ.App.Tex.1973).

secobarbital (se"ko-bar'bĭ-tal) [USP] chemical name: 5-(1-methylbutyl)-5-(2-propenyl)-2,4,6($1H,3H,5H$)pyrimidinetrione. A short-acting barbiturate, $C_{12}H_{18}N_2O_3$, occurring as a white, amorphous or crystalline powder; used as a hypnotic and sedative, administered orally. Called also *quinalbarbitone*.

Seconal is a brand of sodium **secobarbital**, a barbiturate. It is used as a sedative to ease apprehension....

... More specifically, plaintiffs charge that the use of **Seconal** was absolutely contraindicated in cases of premature labor. Lhotka v. Larson, 238 N.W.2d 870, 872–3 (Minn.1976).

There was expert testimony that **Seconal** is a barbituric acid which is controlled under Schedule III....

It may be observed that this case is concerned with the dispensing of a remedy for insomnia. All the requests by the government undercover men were for remedies for sleeplessness, or loss of sleep, for which **Seconal** capsules, a sedative, are frequently prescribed as a common remedy. U.S. v. Carroll, 518 F.2d 187–8, 190 (6th Cir. 1975).

Seconal See *secobarbital*.

secondary (sek'un-der"e) [L. *secundarius; secundus* second] second or inferior in order of time, place, or importance; derived from or consequent to a primary event or thing.

secondary gain See *gain, epinosic*.

secondary to

Turning to the second question, she answers: "Clearly 'secondary' used here is in the sense of an independent cause of death...."

The government disagrees....

"**Secondary to**" as used in the autopsy report, and in medical parlance generally means "resultant from" or "consequent to." The term was used to indicate that the edema resulted from the left heart failure, in turn caused by arteriosclerosis. It was not used in the sense of "independent though less significant." This is clear from the report itself and from the death certificate, both of which require contributing or noncomitant conditions to be listed. None were found.... Seacrist v. Weinberger, 538 F.2d 1054, 1056 (4th Cir. 1976).

Furthermore, the doctor's statement that in his opinion Owens' costo chondritis was "**secondary to** his occupation" very well could be interpreted as an express opinion of causation, because the word "**secondary**" has in some contexts, and especially in medical usage, a meaning of causation or derivation. See Webster's Third New International Dictionary, Merriam-Webster. Hutchinson v. Owens, 458 S.W.2d 442–3 (Ct.App. Ky.1970).

section (sek'shun) [L. *sectio*] a cut surface.

section, paraffin a section cut by a microtome from tissue which has been embedded in paraffin.

An analysis by the pathology department of the hospital of a **paraffin section** had revealed that the suspicious cells removed during the earlier operation were "atypical." A slide of the tissue then had been sent to a professor of pathology at the University of Minnesota who determined that cancer was present. Cornfeldt v. Tongen, 262 N.W.2d 684, 690 (Minn. 1977).

sedapap

Following the surgery, he prescribed penicillin and **Sedapap**, an alcohol/barbiturate combination. An overdose of this medication could cause drunkenness and/or drowsiness, he testified. Harris v. State, 230 S.E.2d 1, 4 (Ga.1976).

sedentary (sed'en-ter"e) [L. *sedentarius*] 1. sitting habitually; of inactive habits. 2. pertaining to a sitting posture. See also *semisedentary*.

"**Sedentary** work" is defined by 20 C.F.R. § 404.1567 as follows:

(a) Sedentary work. **Sedentary** work involves lifting no more than 10 pounds at a time and occasionally lifting or carrying articles like docket files, ledgers, and small tools. Although a **sedentary** job is defined as one which involves sitting, a certain amount of walking and standing is often necessary in carrying out job duties. Jobs are **sedentary** if walking and standing are required occasionally and other **sedentary** criteria are met.

The obvious requirement that the claimant have the capacity to sit for long periods of time is recognized by 20 C.F.R. § 1567(b) which defines "light work" in pertinent part as follows:

(b) Light work. . . . If someone can do light work, we determine that he or she can also do **sedentary** work, unless there are additional limiting factors such as loss of fine dexterity or inability to sit for long periods of time. Carroll v. Secretary of Health & Human Services, 705 F.2d 638, 641 (2d Cir. 1983).

Other Authorities: Bolton v. Sec. of Health & Human Services, 504 F.Supp. 288, 292 (E.D.N.Y.1980).

seizure (se'zhur) 1. the sudden attack or recurrence of a disease. 2. an attack of epilepsy. See also *ictus;* and *epilepsy.*

The technologist was also in the corridor and noticed that the plaintiff was having a **seizure.** In his words, "her whole neck and head . . . went rigid and went straight back into the chair." McMillen v. Carlinville Area Hosp., 450 N.E.2d 5, 8 (App.Ct.Ill.1983).

One week prior to his admission, plaintiff's head had jerked uncontrollably towards the right. Plaintiff then lost consciousness and fell out of his chair. An observer stated that plaintiff had a generalized **seizure** for about one minute, followed by a period of confusion and disorientation in which plaintiff's eyes stared blankly straight ahead and then closed for several hours. Brissette v. Schweiker, 566 F.Supp. 626, 629 (E.D.Mo. 1983), remanded 730 F.2d 548 (8th Cir. 1984).

seizure, convulsive

He testified that trauma such as a concussion can cause scarring of the brain tissue, which in turn can trigger **convulsive seizures** and that a scarring of brain tissue creates a propensity for **convulsive seizures**. . . .

Dr. Martinez described a **convulsive seizure** as a symptom or an effect of an underlying brain disorder such as a birth defect, tumor or of brain tissue scars from illness or injury. Such a seizure can also be brought on by loud noises or over consumption of alcohol as well as the overproduction of certain chemicals in the brain of a person suffering from a manic-depressive condition. Lindsay v. Appleby, 414 N.E.2d 885, 887–8 (App.Ct.Ill.1980).

seizure, extrapyramidal See *tract, pyramidal;* and *extra.*

Dr. Philibert testified that he found severe spasms of the lumbar spine which he identified as **extrapyramidal seizures** and had Circello admitted to the Metairie Hospital. Circello v. Government Employees Ins. Co., 425 So.2d 239, 244 (Ct.App.La. 1982).

seizure, Jacksonian type See *epilepsy, Jacksonian.*

Seldinger technique See *technique, Seldinger.*

self-instrumentation

[Self-instrumentation:] Internal masturbation, often by the use of a broomstraw or spark plug wire. Langton v. Brown, 591 S.W.2d 84, 87 (Mo.Ct.App.1979).

semen (se'men), gen. *sem'inis* [L. "seed"] the thick, whitish secretion of the reproductive organs in the male; composed of spermatozoa in their nutrient plasma, secretions from the prostate, seminal vesicles, and various other glands, epithelial cells, and minor constituents.

Semen is not recognizable as **semen** in the vagina five minutes after emission because it then looks like any clear liquid. It can be detected on clothes a matter of months later. People v. Bynum, 483 P.2d 1193, 1195 (Cal.1971).

seminal vesicle See *vesicula seminalis.*

seminoma (se"mĭ-no'mah) [*semen* + *-oma*] a radiosensitive, malignant neoplasm of the testis, thought to be derived from primordial germ cells of the sexually undifferentiated embryonic gonad, and occurring as a gray to yellow-white nodule or mass; three histologic variants are recognized: *classical* (typical), the most common type; *anaplastic;* and *spermatocytic.* The classical tumor is composed of fairly well-differentiated sheets or cords of uniform polygonal or round cells (seminoma cells), each cell having abundant clear cytoplasm, distinct cell membranes, a centrally placed round nucleus; and one or more nucleoli. In the female, a grossly and histologically identical neoplasm, known as *dysgerminoma,* occurs. See also *carcinoma, embryonal* (Sawyer case).

semisedentary

He used the term "**semisedentary**" to describe a person's work in a sitting position for a total accumulated time of four hours (not continuously or at one sitting) out of eight. Ascough v. Workmen's Comp. App. Bd., 98 Cal.Rptr. 357, 363 (Ct.App. Cal.1971).

semi-stuporous See *stupor.*

Dr. Fred Pitts, a neurosurgeon, testified he first saw the plaintiff in Madison the day after the accident and found the plaintiff's condition to be "**semi-stuporous**", i.e., "With stimulation he could be aroused, . . . give verbal responses to questions . . . he knew where he was. But when left undisturbed he would generally lapse off to sleep." Krause v. Milwaukee Mutual Ins. Co., 172 N.W.2d 181, 191 (Wis.1969).

senescence (se-nes'ens) [L. *senescere* to grow old] the process or condition of growing old, especially the condition resulting from the transitions and accumulations of the deleterious aging processes. Cf. *aging.*

sensation (sen-sa'shun) [L. *sensatio*] an impression conveyed by an afferent nerve to the sensorium.

Q. As we go over to December 8, 1972, is the finding at that time, Dr. Tabor, of the notation as set forth in the progress note at 8:30 a.m., 'patient has good circulation; can move toes but says there is no **sensation** in toes.' Is that of any significance?

A. Yes. It would be of some significance.

Q. Why would that be?

A. The lack of **sensation** would indicate that something was wrong as far as the extremity is concerned. It could be a number of features but at least it's a factor that indicates that something is different than it should be at that stage of the game. The loss of **sensation** would imply that either there was something wrong with the circulation or that there was something wrong with the nerve supply to that extremity. It would be a warning signal at this point." White v. Mitchell, 568 S.W.2d 216, 222 (Ark.1978).

... a brain injury which resulted in a loss of **sensation**, the claimant testified, in the left side, including his face, shoulder, arm and hand....

... He does not feel that the left arm is part of his body. Dr. George Roulhac, a neurosurgeon who attended the claimant, testified to his sensory loss on his left side and particularly in his arm. The claimant did not suffer from muscle weakness, he said, but he did suffer a loss of sense of position in his left hand. That is, he was unable to identify the position of his hand unless he was looking at it. Bradford Supply Co. v. Industrial Com'n, 277 N.E.2d 854, 856-7 (Ill.1971).

sensation (loss) See *anesthesia* (Carter case).

sensitivity (sen"sĭ-tiv'ĭ-te) the state or quality of being sensitive; often used to denote a state of abnormal responsiveness to stimulation, or of responding quickly and acutely.

If the culture test is "positive," i.e., if the test shows that abnormal bacteria or pathogens are present, then a **sensitivity test** is performed. This test consists of dropping on the culture tiny discs containing various antibiotics to determine the specific antibiotic to which the bacteria or pathogens are sensitive. The resulting information is then relayed to the physician who, in turn, can prescribe the correct antibiotic for treating the patient from whom the specimen came. U.S. v. Halper, 590 F.2d 422, 425 (2d Cir. 1978).

sensitivity test See *sensitivity*.

sensitization (sen"sĭ-ti-za'shun) the initial exposure of an individual to a specific antigen, resulting in an immune response; subsequent exposure then induces a much stronger (secondary or anamnestic) immune response. Said especially of such exposure resulting in a hypersensitivity reaction.

sensitization, Rh the process or state of becoming sensitized to the Rh factor (i.e., Rh antigen(s), especially D antigen) as when an Rh-negative woman is pregnant with an Rh-positive fetus. See also *blood group Rh*.

It has long been known that **sensitization** occurs in 90% of Rh-negative women who have received multiple transfusions of Rh-positive blood (W. Nelson, Textbook of Pediatrics 1034 (8th ed. 1964)), and that about 85% of white Americans and a higher percentage of American Negroes and Chinese are Rh-positive (N. Eastman, Williams Obstetrics 1074, 1076, 1078 (12th ed. 1961)). It has been likewise long known that the Rh-positive fetus of an Rh-negative woman previously **sensitized** is "at high risk." (S. Robbins, Pathologic Basis of Disease 557 (1974).) Thus, it has been pointed out that "it must be an absolute rule that Rh-positive blood is never transfused to an Rh-negative female who is below the age of menopause." (P. Mollison, Blood Transfusion in Clinical Medicine 418 (1961).) For these reasons, routine Rh typing has been established practice since at least 1961. (N. Eastman, Williams Obstetrics 1080 (12th ed. 1961).) Renslow v. Mennonite Hospital, 367 N.E.2d 1250, 1253 (Ill.1977).

As a result of extensive research begun in 1959, Ortho developed a product which prevents Rh hemolytic disease of the newborn by preventing **Rh "sensitization"** (passive immunization with Rh antibody) of the mother (Pollack J–34 p. 15.15–17 to p. 15.19–12; Freda T. p. 608–5 to 609–5). After clinical

tests established that the product was safe and effective, it was licensed by the Bureau of Biologics in April 1968 (Freda T. p. 609–4–5; Norman J–14 para. 3; Johnson T. p. 415–13–15). The development of this new drug was described "as one of the major breakthroughs in obstetrics and gynecology of the decade." (Queenan T. p. 151–5–6). Ortho Pharmaceutical Corp. v. American Cyanamid Co., 361 F.Supp. 1032, 1034 (D.N.J.1973).

sensitizer (sen'sĭ-tīz-er) obsolete term for antibody.

sensitizer, strong

(9) "**Strong sensitizer**" means a substance which will cause on normal living tissue through an allergic or photodynamic process a hypersensitivity which becomes evident on reapplication of the same substance and which is designated as such by the Commission [Consumer Product Safety]. Before designating any substance as a **strong sensitizer**, the Commission, upon consideration of the frequency of occurrence and severity of the reaction, shall find that the substance has a significant potential for causing hypersensitivity. 16 C.F.R. Sec. 1500.3(b)(9).

sensorineural hearing loss See *deafness, sensorineural*.

sensorium (sen-so're-um) [L. *sentire* to experience, to feel the force of] the seat of sensation, located in the brain (*s. commu'ne*); the term is often used to designate the condition of a subject relative to his consciousness or mental clarity.

Senstaken-Blakemore tube See *tube, Senstaken-Blakemore*.

sepsis (sep'sis) [Gr. *sēpsis* decay] the presence in the blood or other tissues of pathogenic microorganisms or their toxins; the condition associated with such presence. See also *septicemia*.

Dr. Berger, the attending urologist, found Mrs. Privette in a comatose state and said her condition was "ultracritical," due primarily to **sepsis**, which is an overwhelming systemic bloodstream infection. Pugsley v. Privette, 263 S.E.2d 69, 72 (Va. 1980).

[A] Febrile condition with positive urine cultures are symptoms of a condition called **sepsis**. Harrigan v. U.S., 408 F.Supp. 177, 180 (E.D.Pa.1976).

septicemia (sep"tĭ-se'me-ah) [*septic* + Gr. *haima* blood + *-ia*] systemic disease associated with the presence and persistence of pathogenic microorganisms or their toxins in the blood. Called also *blood poisoning*.

The plaintiff was seriously ill with **septicemia** (a system-wide infection) when he was admitted to the VA hospital in January of 1977. Fraysier v. U.S., 566 F.Supp. 1085, 1089 (S.D.Fla. 1983).

In September 1972, she underwent a kidney transplant operation. Some time after the operation, the insured contracted peritonitis which developed into **septicemia**, a generalized infectious condition throughout the body. The death certificate listed the cause of death as "overwhelming sepsis"....

... Sepsis is synonymous with **septicemia**. Body v. United Ins. Co. of America, 391 N.E.2d 19–21 (App.Ct.Ill.1979).

County General Hospital. On admission her temperature was 105 degrees and her condition was listed as critical. The plaintiff was apparently suffering from **septicemia**, a blood stream infection, caused by the incompletely aborted fetus. Mercurdo v. County of Milwaukee, 264 N.W.2d 258–9 (Wis.1978).

Other Authorities: Matter of Quackenbush, 383 A.2d 785, 787 (Morris Cty.Ct.Prob.Div.1978); Speed v. State, 240 N.W.2d 901, 903 (Iowa 1976); Quick v. Thurston, 290 F.2d 360, 364 (D.C.Cir.1961), reversed and remanded 464 S.W.2d 827 (Tex.1971).

septicemia, gram-negative See *gram-negative*; and *gram-positive*.

Soon after, Mr. Stroburg began to hallucinate, and had high fevers and a loss of blood pressure. One of two explanations for this was the development of **gram negative septicemia**, an infection of the blood due to gram negative bacteria from the colon. A later blood culture showed that there were gram negative bacteria in the blood stream. Insurance Co. of North America v. Stroburg, 456 S.W.2d 402, 409 (Ct.Civ.App.Tex. 1970).

septum (sep′tum), pl. *sep′ta* [L.] a dividing wall or partition; [NA] a general term for such a structure. The term is often used alone to refer to the septal area (see under *area*) or to the septum pellucidum.

septum, deviated See *septum, sinuum frontalium*; and *sinus frontalis osseus*.

He diagnosed a **septum deviated** markedly to the left side and recommended a submucous resection, an operation he performed in March, 1975. This improved the patient's nasal breathing, but the infection and drainage problem persisted. Dr. Klotz performed a second operation to improve the draining of the afflicted sinus cavity....

There was evidence from an expert witness called by the plaintiff, Dr. Wysocki, that a **deviated septum** is usually traumatic in origin and that a nose fracture and a **deviated septum** are "concomitant injuries." McCarthy v. Hauck, 447 N.E.2d 22, 24 (App.Ct.Mass.1983).

Doctor Alldredge found swelling and bruising of the face, a prominent hump on top of plaintiff's nose, and a **deviated septum** causing airway problems. X-rays revealed a nasal fracture which caused the septal deviation. Doctor Alldredge testified that a surgical reconstruction would be required to straighten plaintiff's nose and correct the septal deviation. Thibodeaux v. Hulin Marble & Granite Works, 386 So.2d 136, 139 (Ct.App. La.1980).

septum, pellucid; septum pellucidum [NA], a triangular double membrane separating the anterior horns of the lateral ventricles of the brain; situated in the median plane, it is bounded by the corpus callosum and the body and columns of the fornix.

septum sinuum frontalium [NA], septum of frontal sinuses: a thin lamina of bone, in the lower front part of the frontal bone, that lies more or less in the median plane and separates the frontal sinuses.

sequela (se-kwe′lah), pl. *seque′lae* [L.] any lesion or affection following or caused by an attack of disease.

He also testified that the plaintiff would have "**sequela**," including adhesions in the abdomen and permanent scarring in the left chest cavity, and that these residual effects of the acci-

dent would cause "distress." Wagner v. Reading Co., 428 F.2d 289, 291 (3d Cir. 1970).

sequential multiple analysis test See *test, SMA–12.*

sequestra (se-kwes′trah) [L.] plural of *sequestrum.*

sequestrectomy (se″kwes-trek′to-me) [*sequestrum* + Gr. *ektomē* excision] the surgical removal of a sequestrum.

Much of the bone in the right humerus was destroyed by magnesium burns. Two **sequestrectomies** (surgical removal of dead bone) were performed. The right arm could not be saved. Aretz v. U.S., 456 F.Supp. 397, 402 (S.D.Ga.1978).

sequestrum (se-kwes′trum), pl. *seques′tra* [L.] a piece of dead bone that has become separated during the process of necrosis from the sound bone. See also *osteomyelitis.*

Dr. Turner, an orthopedic surgeon with experience in the treatment of amputees, testified that he had examined him approximately one week before the trial, and he had taken certain X rays, which were introduced into evidence. The pictures showed that approximately four inches of right thigh bone and 3½ to 4 inches of left thigh bone remained. They also showed a **sequestra**, indicating an osteomyelitis....

... **Sequestra** appearing in an X ray of stumps, he admitted in response to a question, was one of the "classical findings" of osteomyelitis. Raines v. New York Railroad Co., 283 N.E. 2d 230, 237–8 (Ill.1972).

... four months after the accident, for a **sequestra** of a bone spike or fragment at the fracture site. South Texas Natural Gas Gathering Co. v. Guerra, 469 S.W.2d 899, 915 (Ct.Civ.App. Tex.1971).

series (sēr′ēz) [L. "row"] a group or succession of objects or substances arranged in regular order or forming a kind of chain. In electricity, an arrangement of the parts of a circuit by connecting them successively to form a single path for the current. Parts thus arranged are in series.

series, granulocyte; series, granulocytic the succession of developing cells that ultimately culminates in the mature granulocyte or granular leukocyte (*basophil, eosinophil,* or *neutrophil*); it begins with the myeloblast, which matures to form sequentially the promyelocyte, myelocyte, metamyelocyte, and mature segmented (polymor-

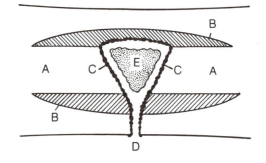

Illustrating the formation of a sequestrum: *A, A,* sound bone; *B, B,* new bone; *C, C,* granulations lining involucrum; *D,* cloaca; *E,* sequestrum (DaCosta).

phonuclear) cell. Called also *myeloid, myelocytic,* or *leukocytic s.* See also *granular leukocytes,* under *leukocyte.*

series, lymphocyte; series, lymphocytic the succession of developing cells that ultimately culminates in the lymphocyte; it begins with the lymphoblast which matures to form sequentially the lymphoblast, prolymphocyte, and mature lymphocyte.

series, thrombocyte; series, thrombocytic the succession of developing cells that ultimately culminates in the blood platelets (thrombocytes); it begins with the megakaryoblast, which matures to form sequentially the promegakaryocyte, megakaryocyte, and the mature cell.

Seromycin (ser′o-mi″sin) trademark for preparations of cycloserine. See also *cycloserine.*

serosal layer of the bowel See *tunica serosa intestini tenuis.*

serotonin (ser″o-to′nin) chemical name: 3-(2-aminoethyl)-5-indolol. A vasoconstrictor, $C_{10}H_{12}N_2O$, found in various animals from coelenterates to vertebrates, in bacteria, and in many plants. In humans, it is released by the blood platelets and is found in high concentrations in many body tissues, including the intestinal mucosa, pineal body, and central nervous system. Produced enzymatically from tryptophan by hydroxylation and decarboxylation, serotonin has many physiologic properties; e.g., it inhibits gastric secretion, stimulates smooth muscle, serves as a central neurotransmitter, and is a precursor of melatonin. Called also *enteramine, thrombocytin, thrombotonin, 5-hydroxytryptamine,* and *5-HT.* See also *carcinoid.*

As to those causes he had suggested, Dr. Buckingham stated that in his 32 years of practice he had become aware of only a half dozen cases of death caused by the production of **serotonin.** Interlake, Inc. v. Industrial Com'n, 447 N.E.2d 339, 343 (Ill.1983).

serum (se′rum), pl. *serums* or *se′ra* [L. "whey"] 1. the clear portion of any animal liquid separated from its more solid elements; especially the clear liquid (*blood s.*) which separates in the clotting of blood from the clot and the corpuscles. 2. blood serum from animals that have been inoculated with bacteria or their toxins. Such serum, when introduced into the body, produces passive immunization by virtue of the antibodies which it contains.

The administrative regulations in effect at the time of the 1944 revision defined a **serum** as "the product obtained from the blood of an animal by removing the clot or clot components and the blood cells." ...

"Serum" is "1) the clear portion of any animal liquid separated from its more solid elements; especially the clear liquid which separates in the clotting of blood from the clot and the corpuscles. 2) Blood **serum** from animals that have been inoculated with bacteria or their toxins." [6] **Serum's** principal, if not sole, therapeutic function is as a passive immunological agent; that is, therapeutic **serum** contains antitoxic or antibacterial antibodies which neutralize or counteract toxins or bacteria. [6 Dorland, American Illustrated Medical Dictionary 1311 (21st ed. 1948).] Blank v. U.S., 400 F.2d 302–4 (5th Cir. 1968).

serum, antivenomous a serum used as a remedy for snake bite, prepared from the blood of animals which have been immunized against the venom of serpents; called also *Calmette's s.* See also *antivenin.*

serum, blood See *blood serum.*

serum, truth a misnomer for the drugs sometimes employed to facilitate interviews; especially applied to sodium amobarbital and sodium thiopental when used in criminal interrogation. The agent used is not a serum and its use does not guarantee truthfulness. See also *scopolamine.*

The Supreme Court in Townsend v. Sain, supra, 372 U.S. at 307–308, 83 S.Ct. at 754 (1963), an earlier appeal in this case, stated that:

These standards are applicable whether a confession is the product of physical intimidation or psychological pressure and, of course, are equally applicable to a drug-induced statement. It is difficult to imagine a situation in which a confession would be less the product of a free intellect, less voluntary, than when brought about by a drug having the effect of a "**truth serum.**" U.S. ex rel. Townsend v. Twomey, 452 F.2d 350, 367 (7th Cir. 1971).

sesamoid (ses′ah-moid) [L. *sesamoides;* Gr. *sēsamon* sesame + *eidos* form] 1. denoting a small nodular bone embedded in a tendon or joint capsule. 2. a sesamoid bone. See under *bone.*

sesamoid, bilateral

On cross-examination, Dr. Smith stated that, in his opinion, claimant suffered from a separated or fractured tibia or sesamoid bone in her left foot, a condition resulting from trauma. He did not recall if there was any callus formation in the area of the injury. Nor did he recall if there was a congenital **bipartite lateral sesamoid** beneath the bone of the first metatarsal. Dr. Smith described a **bilateral sesamoid** as a congenital condition in which the sesamoid bone develops in two pieces instead of one. He did not believe she had this condition because it is not painful....

... Dr. Fischer concurred with the roentgenologist's report. He stated that claimant suffered from a congenital **bipartite lateral sesamoid** bone beneath the distal first metatarsal of the left foot. This condition is characterized by the smooth margins and concentric trabecular lines of the two bone pieces. He stated that, if the bone were fractured, the bone margins would be rough and the trabecular line would be broken. Further, between September and November of 1979, there was no callus formation or other indicia of healing characteristic of a fracture....

Dr. William Meszaros, a physician specializing in radiology, was also deposed by respondent. He did not examine claimant but did review her X rays. He concurred with Dr. Fischer's analysis that claimant suffered from a **bipartite lateral sesamoid** bone beneath the distal first metatarsal of the left foot. He stated that this was a relatively rare congenital anomaly which was not caused by any trauma. In his opinion, there was no evidence of any fracture. Zick v. Industrial Com'n, 444 N.E.2d 164, 166–7 (Ill.1982).

sesamoid, bipartite lateral See *sesamoid, bilateral.*

severance

The policy defines the loss as follows: "Loss" as used with reference to hand ... means **severance** at or above the wrist....

Admittedly, the loss of the hand must occur at or above the wrist. But **severance** does not mean amputation. A hand may be severed but need not be amputated. Amputation is irreparably cutting off of a limb while to sever may limit its use, but not necessarily cause amputation. The **severance** of the humerus satisfies the meaning of "loss". Misfud v. Allstate Ins. Co., 456 N.Y.S.2d 316–17 (Civ.Ct.City of N.Y. Kings Cty.1982).

sewage (su'ij) the matters found in sewers; it consists of the excreta of man and animals, and other waste material from homes and other structures inhabited by man.

sewage, domestic sewage from dwellings, business buildings, factories, or institutions.

sewage, raw See *sewage, domestic.*

Raw sewage, by definition, is the water supply of a community after it has been fouled by various uses. From the standpoint of source, it is a combination of the liquid or water-carried wastes from residences and business and industry, together with ground water, surface water and storm water. It also is composed of suspended solids and dissolved solids, including human fecal material. U.S. v. City of Asbury Park, 340 F.Supp. 555, 560 (D.N.J.1972).

sex (seks) [L. *sexus*] the fundamental distinction, found in most species of animals and plants, based on the type of gametes produced by the individual or the category into which the individual fits on the basis of that criterion; ova, or macrogametes, are produced by the female, and spermatozoa, or microgametes, are produced by the male, the union of these distinctive germ cells being the natural prerequisite for the production of a new individual in sexual reproduction.

It is Dr. Federman's view that sexual identity is a complex pattern of which some features are immutable (the nuclear and chromosomal); some can be effaced but not converted to their opposite (the gonadal and ductal structures); some are alterable by surgery or drugs (the external genitalia and hormonal balance); and some are largely subjective (the psychological and social **sex**). Under no circumstances can transsexual surgery produce the internal ductal organs or the gonadal identity of the opposite **sex**. Richards v. U.S. Tennis Ass'n, 400 N.Y.S.2d 267, 269–70 (Sup.Ct.N.Y.Cty.1977).

sex change See *reassignment, sex.*

sex chromatin test See *chromatin-positive.*

sex reassignment See *reassignment, sex.*

SGOT (serum glutamic-oxaloacetic transaminase) See *glutamic-oxaloacetic transaminase,* under *transaminase.*

Shaver's disease See *pneumoconiosis, bauxite.*

sheath (shēth) [L. *vagina;* Gr. *thēkē*] a tubular structure enclosing or surrounding some organ or part.

sheath, myelin the sheath surrounding the axon of some (the myelinated) nerve cells, consisting of concentric layers of myelin, formed in the peripheral nervous system by the plasma membrane of Schwann cells, and in the central nervous system by oligodendrocytes. It is interrupted at intervals along the length of the axon by gaps known as nodes of Ranvier. Myelin is an electrical insulator that serves to speed the conduction of nerve impulses.

The predominate theory regarding the dynamics of GBS is that for some unknown reason the antibodies that occur normally within the human immune system act in a confused way by attacking the covering of the nerves. This results in a breakdown of the **myelin sheath** (the covering of the nerve) and inhibits the ability of signals to move along the nerves. Lima v. U.S., 708 F.2d 502, 504 (10th Cir. 1983).

sheath, thermometer

... a "thermometer sheath". This is a device made up of several layers of flexible, translucent plastic sheet material, fabricated to fuse the sheets with an impressed form, shaped with a die, in a width and length such that a typical fever thermometer can be inserted. The tip end, where the mercury thermometer bulb would rest, is closed. The other end, through which the thermometer is inserted, has a flared shape, somewhat like the bell of a trumpet, to make insertion easier (i.e., the "throat")....

The concept of the plastic **thermometer sheath** is to cover the glass thermometer with a new, unused sheath each time the thermometer is used. In principle, the plastic covering would provide a barrier between the thermometer and the patient such that it would not matter that the thermometer is not sterilized. Poncy v. Johnson & Johnson, 460 F.Supp. 795–7 (D.N.J.1978).

Shigella (shǐ-gel'ah) [Kiyoshi *Shiga*] a genus of microorganisms of tribe Salmonelleae, family Enterobacteriaceae, order Eubacteriales, made up of nonmotile, rod-shaped, gram-negative bacteria. These microorganisms, which cause dysentery and for that reason are called dysentery bacilli, are separated into the non-mannitol-fermenting and the mannitol-fermenting type; the former make up Group A, and the latter are subdivided into Groups B, C, and D, each group making up a species. See also *Shigella boydii; Shigella dysenteriae; Shigella flexneri;* and *Shigella sonnei.* Cited in U.S. v. City of Asbury Park, 340 F.Supp. 555, 566 (D.N.J.1972).

Shigella boydii the species name given to Group C dysentery bacilli, the cause of an acute diarrheal disease in man, especially in tropical regions; culturally identical with *S. flexneri* but serologically unrelated, the species includes 15 independent numbered serotypes.

Shigella dysenteriae the species name given to Group A dysentery bacilli, and separated into numbered serotypes. TYPE 1, the classic Shiga bacillus, which is set apart from other dysentery bacilli by the production of a potent exotoxin, is more common in tropical regions and causes severe dysentery. TYPE 2, the Schmitz bacillus, is a non-mannitol-fermenting organism serologically related to *Escherichia coli* type 0112. Of limited pathogenicity, but occasionally the cause of epidemic diarrheal disease in man, the organism has been found in the chimpanzee but not in other lower animals. The other numbered types include the Large-Sachs group of parashiga bacilli. Formerly called *Bacillus dysenteriae* and *Bacterium dysenteriae*. See also *Shigella parashigae*.

Shigella flexneri a species name given to Group B dysentery bacilli, one of the commonest causes of acute diarrheal disease in man, occurring as eight related serotypes, designated by numbers 1 to 6 and letters X and Y. Called also *S. paradysenteriae* and *Flexner's bacillus*.

Shigella parashigae a name formerly given to a group of non-mannitol-fermenting dysentery bacilli serologically differentiable from the Shiga bacillus (now *S. dysenteriae* type 1); also known as the Large-Sachs group of parashiga bacilli, they are now known as *S. dysenteriae*, types 3 to 7, inclusive.

Shigella sonnei a species name given to Group D dysentery bacilli, one of the commonest causes of bacillary dysentery in temperate climates; slow (5–14 days) lactose fermenters, the organisms are serologically homogeneous, but two antigens, designated I and II, occur in varying proportions. Called also *Sonne-Duval bacillus* and formerly *Bacterium sonnei*.

shingles See *herpes zoster*.

shock (shok) 1. a sudden disturbance of mental equilibrium. 2. a condition of acute peripheral circulatory failure due to derangement of circulatory control or loss of circulating fluid. It is marked by hypotension, coldness of the skin, usually tachycardia, and often anxiety. See also under *therapy*.

The claimant experienced a sudden severe emotional **shock**, which would be the reaction of a person of normal sensibilities who, attempting to aid an injured coworker, reached in and drew a severed hand from the press....

... We must conclude that an employee who, like the claimant here, suffers a sudden, severe emotional shock traceable to a definite time, place and cause which causes psychological injury or harm has suffered an accident within the meaning of the Act, though no physical trauma or injury was sustained....

... As to the category of mental stimulus causing nervous injury, with no "physical" involvement, although the cases are now sharply divided, the strength of the trend toward coverage suggests that the time is perhaps not too far off when compensation law generally will cease to set an artificial and medically unjustifiable gulf between the "physical" and the "nervous." The test of existence of injury can then be greatly simplified. The single question will be whether there was a harmful change in the human organism—not just its bones and muscles, but its brain and nerves as well. (Larson, Mental & Nervous Injury in Workmen's Compensation, 23 Vand.L.Rev. 1243, 1260 (1970).) ...

... we must decide the underlying question of whether an employee who suffers a sudden, severe emotional **shock**, traceable to a definite time and place and to a readily perceivable cause, which produces psychological disability, can recover under the Workmen's Compensation Act (III.Rev.Stat. 1973, ch. 48, par. 138.1 et seq.), though the employee suffered no physical injury. Pathfinder Co. v. Industrial Com'n, 343 N.E.2d 913, 916–919 (III.1976).

Upon her admission to the hospital, the victim's condition was diagnosed as that of **shock**, a broad medical term which does not comprehend specific causes. See Dorland's Illustrated Medical Dictionary 1374 (24th ed. 1965). Commonwealth v. Mace, 341 A.2d 505, 507 (Super.Ct.Pa.1975).

The defendant doctor testified that when he examined the plaintiff in the emergency room he also found but did not record in the hospital records that the plaintiff was shaking, cold, clammy and staring into space; that he had extreme pallor and was unconscious at times and did not answer questions; that the pupils of his eyes were dilated. He further testified that on the basis of these findings he diagnosed but did not record that the plaintiff was in a severe state of **shock** and had sustained a brain concussion with possible brain damage and that there was a possibility of a basal skull fracture....

... Besides the other symptoms of **shock** previously observed, the plaintiff's blood pressure had dropped to $^{80}/_{60}$. Borowski v. Von Solbrig, 328 N.E.2d 301, 304 (III.1975).
Other Authorities: Commonwealth v. Wright, 328 A.2d 514, 517 (Pa.1974).

shock, anaphylactic a violent attack of symptoms produced by a second injection of serum or protein and due to anaphylaxis. See also *anaphylaxis*.

His opinion was that she died from "anaphylactic shock," a sudden, violent reaction with complete collapse and death in a matter of two or three minutes. It was his opinion that the swollen area in the right hip was "a probable area of injection of some substance."...

... When asked how **anaphylactic shock** "shows itself in a body" he said "Nearly nothing." State v. Baker, 453 S.W.2d 918, 920 (Mo.1970).

On the contrary, the uncontradicted expert medical evidence is to the effect that **anaphylactic shock** can, and often does, strike suddenly without previous symptom or warning. Perkins v. Park View Hospital, Inc., 456 S.W.2d 276, 284 (Ct.App.Tenn. 1970).

An autopsy card was admitted in evidence without objection during the testimony of the Deputy Coroner. The card reported the result of an autopsy on the daughter held June 7, 1956, the day after her death. **Anaphylactic shock**—hypersusceptibility—due to penicillin reaction was reported on the card to have been found. The Deputy Coroner also testified without objection as follows: "The history says she received it [the penicillin injection] for mumps." Rotan v. Greenbaum, 273 F.2d 830–1 (D.C.Cir.1959).

shock, cardiogenic shock resulting from diminution of cardiac output in heart disease, as in myocardial infarction.

When they came back, he was on the floor unconscious. The family rushed him to the nearest hospital, 23 miles away in Salem, Arkansas. He died a few minutes after reaching the hospital. Michael Neal Moody, M.D., who saw Mr. Schales at the hospital, stated that he was "in **cardiogenic shock**" (dep. 3) on arrival. In Dr. Moody's opinion, which the Court accepts, Mr. Schales died of an acute myocardial infarction (dep. 8). Schales v. U.S., 488 F.Supp. 33, 36 (E.D.Ark.1979).

shock, electric the effects produced by the passage of an electric current through any part of the body. When the current is intense, it may cause (*a*) reversible loss of consciousness or death, owing to effects on the nervous system or heart, (*b*) coagulation of tissue and resultant necrosis due to heat, and (*c*) violent tetanic muscular contractions which may lead to injury. See also *electroconvulsive therapy*, under *therapy*.

The central factual allegation postulated by plaintiff was that his eye was burned when an electrical current passed from the instrument's eyepiece by a phenomenon commonly called "arcing", since admittedly there was at least some distance between his eye and the eyepiece at the critical moment of the incident. . . .

Defendant argues from his own assessment of the evidence that all of the engineering experts agreed that, absent some abnormal or extraordinary occurrence in the functioning of the surgical unit which might cause "arcing" to occur, the plaintiff would not have sustained an **electrical shock** without virtually direct contact with the uninsulated eyepiece. Thomas v. American Cystoscope Makers, Inc., 414 F.Supp. 255, 260 (E.D.Pa. 1976).

shock, hematogenic shock due to diminished blood volume; hypovolemic shock.

There were multiple blisters filled with bloody fluid located on the medial aspect of her upper left thigh. His first impression was **hypervolemic shock** due to loss of blood and he felt bleeding from the fractured pelvis had increased the size of the thigh. Harris v. State, Through Huey P. Long Hospital, 371 So.2d 1221, 1224 (Ct.App.La.1979).

shock, hypovolemic See shock, *hematogenic*.

shock, insulin a condition of circulatory insufficiency resulting from overdosage with insulin which causes too sudden reduction of blood sugar. It is marked by tremor, sweating, vertigo, diplopia, convulsions, and collapse. See also *hypoglycemia*; and *insulin coma therapy*, under *therapy*.

The evidence clearly establishes that the immediate cause of Maltempo's death was strangulation on his own vomit. There is a conflict in the evidence as to whether the vomiting was caused by hyperglycemia (high blood sugar) or **insulin shock** (low blood sugar). . . .

Cuthbert's theory is that an improperly administered shot of insulin entered a vein and caused **insulin shock**, the inference being that that shot was an independent, efficient cause of death. However, although the man who gave the shot was wholly inexperienced, there is no direct evidence that he hit a vein; that possibility is speculation at best. Maltempo v. Cuthbert, 504 F.2d 325, 328 (5th Cir. 1974).

He had the opportunity to give injections of insulin, under supervision; was trained to observe danger signals while the patient was under **insulin shock** and to give necessary therapeutic measures to protect the patient; and was allowed to give injections of glucose to bring patients out of shock. . . .

Dr. Grace Fern Thomas, a psychiatrist and an expert in **insulin shock** therapy, and director of the **insulin shock** department at the time defendant was at Camarillo, testified as to the procedures on the ward. A precise dosage of insulin was measured for each person at a particular time. At a specific level that patient would go into shock in approximately two hours

after the injection. Patients do not progress at the same level. Careful watch must be kept of the pulse, color, blood pressure, general condition, and neurological signs, such as pupillary changes and body motions. When a patient is going into progressive stages of coma he sweats very profusely and breathes very heavily. Saliva is secreted in large amounts, mucous flows freely and mixes with the saliva, and the patient must be carefully watched, turned, or assisted so that he does not aspirate the fluid into his lungs. Otherwise bronchopneumonia may develop, leading to death. The gag reflex and the cornea reflex are lost. Convulsions may occur, and medication is given to prevent this. The extremities may stiffen. People v. Archerd, 477 P.2d 421, 424–5 (Cal.1970).

shock lung syndrome See *syndrome, shock lung.*

shock treatment See *cingulumotomy* (Kapp case); *defibrillation; therapy, electroconvulsive;* and *therapy; shock.*

shoulder (shōl'der) the junction of the arm and trunk; also that part of the trunk which is bounded at the back by the scapula. See also *arm* (Safeway Stores, Inc. case).

The **shoulder** is a distinct anatomical entity in medical, legal, and lay understanding. It makes little sense to disregard this distinct entity for purposes of workmen's compensation awards. . . .

Other jurisdictions which have considered the question here presented have determined that:

. . . the **shoulder** is not part of the arm and where the injury is to the **shoulder** it is not proper to base the award on the proportionate loss to the use of the arm. M. R. Thomason & Assoc. v. Jones, 48 Ala.App. 67, 261 So.2d 899, 902 (1972). . . .

All the cases therein discussed recognize that the **shoulder** is a distinct anatomical entity, not part of the arm. . . .

. . . In fact, the **shoulder**, which also is not a part of the arm, separates the collarbone and the arm. Safeway Stores, Inc. v. Industrial Com'n, 558 P.2d 971, 974 (Ct.App.Ariz.1976).

shoulder, frozen See *capsulitis, adhesive.*

shoulder-blade (shōl'der-blād) the scapula.

shrimp

". . . Like other crustaceans, they wear their skeletons outside their bodies in order to shield their savory pink and white flesh against predators, including man. They also carry their intestines, commonly called veins, in bags (or sand bags) that run the length of their bodies. For **shrimp** to be edible it is necessary to remove their shells. In addition, if the vein is removed, **shrimp** become more pleasing to the fastidious as well as more palatable." [1] [[1] The Laitram Corporation v. Deepsouth Packing Co., Inc., 301 F.Supp. 1037, 1040, 406 U.S. 518, 519, 92 S.Ct. 1700, 1702 (1969).] Deepsouth Packing Co., Inc. v. Laitram Corp., 173 (1972).

shunt (shunt) 1. a passage or anastomosis between two natural channels, especially between blood vessels. Such structures may be formed physiologically (e.g., to bypass a thrombosis), or they may be structural anomalies. See also *cardiovascular shunt.* 2. a surgically created anastomosis; also, the operation of forming a shunt. See also *anastomosis.*

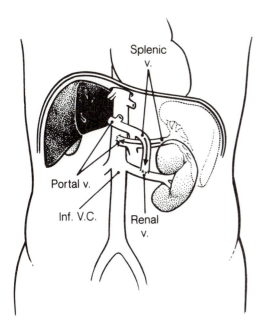

Portal shunts, showing two types of portal to systemic venous shunt. (Blakemore and Vorhees, Jr.)

He later had an episode wherein he had an infection of the **shunt**, which was treated. The plaintiff will be required to continue with the **shunt**, which presently drains brain fluids into his abdomen, for the remainder of his lifetime. Swanson v. U.S. By and Through Veterans Admin., 557 F.Supp. 1041, 1044 (D.Idaho 1983).

Although there was some suggestion by plaintiff that Dr. Pisarello should have installed a **shunt**, a permanent apparatus which relieves intracranial pressure in the event it should reoccur, plaintiff specifically renounced any claim of negligence with respect to Dr. Pisarello's operative procedures including his decision not to install the **shunt**. Gendusa v. St.Paul Fire & Marine Ins. Co., 435 So.2d 479, 481 (Ct.App.La.1983).

In October and November of 1975 the New York V.A. physician performed "**shunt**" operations to relieve the increased intercranial pressure caused as a result of the lesion. Dundon v. U.S., 559 F.Supp. 469, 471 (E.D.N.Y.1983).

shunt, cardiovascular an abnormality of blood flow between the sides of the heart or between the systemic and pulmonary circulation. See also *left-to-right shunt*; and *right-to-left shunt*.

shunt, left-to-right diversion of blood from the left side of the heart to the right side or from the systemic to the pulmonary circulation through an anomalous opening such as a septal defect or patent ductus arteriosus.

shunt, right-to-left diversion of blood from the right side of the heart to the left side or from the pulmonary to the systemic circulation through an anomalous opening such

as a septal defect or patent ductus arteriosus; called also *reversed s.*

shunt, ventriculo-atrial See *ventriculoatriostomy*.

sick sinus syndrome See *syndrome, sick sinus*.

sickle cell disease See *disease, sickle cell*.

sickness (sik´nes) any condition or episode marked by pronounced deviation from the normal healthy state; illness.

Although technically synonymous, these words [**sickness**, illness, disease] have assumed clear and divergent meanings when employed in disability insurance clauses delaying coverage until a stipulated date. **Sickness** has been deemed to have its inception when the disease first becomes manifest or active, or when there is a distinct symptom or condition from which one learned in medicine can with reasonable accuracy diagnose the disease. E.g., Keller v. Orion Insurance Company, 422 F.2d 1152 (8th Cir. 1970); Mutual Hospital Ins., Inc. v. Klapper, 153 Ind.App. 555, 288 N.E.2d 279 (1972); Dirgo v. Associated Hospitals Service, Inc., 210 N.W.2d 647 (Iowa 1973); Southards v. Central Plains Insurance Co., 201 Kan. 499, 441 P.2d 808 (1968); State National Life Insurance Co. v. Stamper, 228 Ark. 1128, 312 S.W.2d 441 (1958); Malone v. Continental Life and Accident Co., 89 Idaho 77, 403 P.2d 225 (1965); Horace Mann Mutual Insurance Co. v. Burrow, 213 Tenn. 262, 373 S.W.2d 469 (1963); 43 Am.Jur.2d Insurance § 1205 (1969); 45 C.J.S. Insurance § 893 (1946). See generally 53 A.L.R.2d 686 (1957). Ranieli v. Mutual Life Ins. Co. of America, 413 A.2d 396, 400–1 (Super.Ct.Pa.1979).

Sickness has been defined to embrace the term "**sickness** and injury." **Sickness** is any affection of the body which deprives the body temporarily of the power to fulfill its usual functions. See Globe Life Insurance Co. of Alabama v. Howard, 41 Ala. App. 621, 147 So.2d 853 (1962). Furthermore, it has been generally stated that a hospital is a place for the care of the sick, whether in mind or body. See Bennett v. Bennett, 27 Ill. App.2d 24, 169 N.E.2d 172 (1960).

In this instance, the term "sick and injured" within the policy provision would include a psychiatric disorder in that, to this court, such disorder is clearly a **sickness**. Mobile Psychiatric Service v. Employers Life Ins., 362 So.2d 244, 246 (Ct.Civ. App.Ala.1978).

Moreover, whatever the definition of "**sickness**" may have been in earlier epochs, it now encompasses "[a] condition or an episode marked by pronounced deviation from the normal healthy state", Borland's [sic Dorland's] Illustrated Medical Dictionary, 24th ed., or "a disordered, weakened, or unsound condition", Webster's New International Dictionary, 3d ed. Removal of tonsils or an appendix highly susceptible to infection or, as the stipulation describing the appellee's services notes, "excisions of benign tumors which could cause subsequent neurological problems", would seem not only required by sound medical practice but consistent with a more expansive reading of "**sickness**". Hathaway v. Worcester City Hospital, 475 F.2d 701, 704–5 (1st Cir. 1973).

sickness, decompression a disorder characterized by joint pains, respiratory manifestations, skin lesions, and neurologic signs, occurring in aviators flying at high altitudes and following rapid reduction of air pressure in persons who have been breathing compressed air in caissons and diving apparatus.

sickness, microwave

Claimant's leading expert, Dr. Milton Zaret, provided the board with ample evidence of the existence of a disease identified as "**microwave or radiowave sickness**". Dr. Zaret's own studies, including those performed for the United States Government, and excerpts of reports from the Warsaw Conference of 1973 which documented the diagnosis of such a disease in other countries, substantiate this conclusion. Yannon v. New York Telephone Co., 450 N.Y.S.2d 893–4 (3d Dep't 1982).

sickness, radiation a condition sometimes produced by exposure to sources of ionizing radiation; it is characterized by malaise, nausea, emesis, diarrhea, leukopenia, etc.

The Administrative Law Judge awarded claimant benefits and the board affirmed, finding that decedent's death resulted from an occupational **radiation disease**, one within the meaning of section 3 (subd. 2, par. 30) of the Workers' Compensation Law, and that said disease and his ultimate death were directly related to his exposure to microwave radiation while employed by the New York Telephone Company. Yannon v. New York Telephone Co., 450 N.Y.S.2d 893–4 (3d Dep't 1982).

A third case, State Compensation Fund v. Yazzie, Ariz.App., 541 P.2d 415 (1975), was heard at the same time as these two cases and it presented this same question. We held in Yazzie that "lung cancer caused by an excessive amount of exposure to ionizing radiation is embraced within the term of '**radiation illness**,'" as it is defined in A.R.S. § 23–1102(12). State Compensation Fund v. Joe, 543 P.2d 790, 792–3 (Ct.App.Ariz. 1975).

siderosis (sid″er-o′sis) pneumoconiosis due to the inhalation of iron particles.

Based on chest X-rays obtained in June 1979, he thought employee had had silicosis or **siderosis** which was "simple" (nodules not more than dime size) and said that **siderosis** is a fairly benign condition and that silicosis, if present, was not work related because employee presumably was not exposed to silica in his work. Dunn v. Vic Mfg. Co., 327 N.W.2d 572, 575 (Minn. 1982).

siderotic (sid″er-ot′ik) pertaining to or characterized by siderosis.

siderotic node See *nodules, siderotic.*

sigmoid (sig′moid) [L. *sigmoides;* Gr. *sigmoeidēs*] the sigmoid colon.

sigmoidoscope (sig-moi′do-skōp) [*sigmoid* + Gr. *skopein* to examine] an endoscope with appropriate illumination for examining the sigmoid flexure.

. . . and, now with reference to his complaint, the rectal examination, which included both a finger examination and examination by a **sigmoidoscope**. This is a term which we use when we use a tubular instrument which is inserted into the lower rectum for a certain length. It allows us to directly inspect the inside lining of the rectum, lower part of the colon, large bowel, and discloses to us any visible abnormality which, for in-

stance, could have led to bleeding. Woodall Industries, Inc. v. Massachusetts Mutual Life Insurance Co., 483 F.2d 986, 993 (6th Cir. 1973).

Zimbelman was also given a sigmoidoscopic examination by Purcell which consists of the insertion of a tube-like instrument called a **sigmoidoscope** through the anus, up the rectum and into the colon. According to the testimony of Purcell the **sigmoidoscope** passed 17 cm. from the outlet of the anus, which meant that it passed through the entire rectum, through the peritoneal reflection and into the rectosigmoid junction. This meant that the diseased portion of the bowel was located at least 17 cm. above the outlet of the anus. Purcell v. Zimbelman, 500 P.2d 335, 339 (Ct.App.Ariz.1972).

sigmoidoscopy (sig″moi-dos′ko-pe) inspection of the sigmoid flexure through a sigmoidoscope.

Dr. Fainer performed a **sigmoidoscopy**, which is an examination of the colon between the descending colon and rectum by means of a speculum. Rainer v. Buena Community Memorial Hospital, 95 Cal.Rptr. 901, 904 (Ct.App.Cal.1971).

sign (sīn) [L. *signum*] an indication of the existence of something; any objective evidence of a disease, i.e., such evidence as is perceptible to the examining physician, as opposed to the subjective sensations (symptoms) of the patient.

signs, Babinski's 1. loss or lessening of the Achilles tendon reflex in sciatica: this distinguishes it from hysteric sciatica. 2. Babinski's reflex. 3. in hemiplegia, the contraction of the platysma muscle in the healthy side is more vigorous than on the affected side, as seen in opening the mouth, whistling, blowing, etc. 4. the patient lies supine on the floor, with arms crossed upon his chest, and then makes an effort to rise to the sitting posture. On the paralyzed side, the thigh is flexed upon the pelvis and the heel is lifted from the ground, while on the healthy side the limb does not move. This phenomenon is repeated when the patient resumes the lying posture. It is seen in organic hemiplegia, but not in hysterical hemiplegia. 5. when the paralyzed forearm is placed in supination, it turns over to pronation: seen in organic paralysis. Called also *pronation sign.*

As testified by Drs. Johnson, C. Sisco, Poser, Tyler and Lucy, the presence of a **Babinski sign** is a clear indication of a central nervous involvement. Smith v. U.S., 557 F.Supp. 42, 48 (W.D.Ark.1982).

Furthermore, claimant was tested for the **Babinski sign** with positive results, which, assertedly, reveals progression of the spinal cord injury. Inland Steel Coal Co. v. Industrial Com'n, 405 N.E.2d 781–2 (Ill.1980).

At a relatively deep level of coma the Babinski test (scratching the sole of the foot in a certain manner) will cause a reflex known as the **Babinski response** (toes fan out). The patient must be brought out of the coma within 10–15 minutes thereafter. People v. Archerd, 477 P.2d 421, 425 (Cal.1970).

Other Authorities: Hammond v. Estate of Rimmer, 643 S.W.2d 222, 224 (Ct.App.Tex.1982).

sign, Gaenslen's with the patient on his back on the operating table, the knee and hip of one leg are held in flexed position by the patient, while the other leg, hanging over the edge of the table, is pressed down by the examiner to produce hyperextension of the hip: pain occurs on the affected side in lumbosacral disease.

The **Gaenslen test**, which is another test for lumbosacral disease, was also positive bilaterally. Consolidated Freightways v. Industrial Com'n, 356 N.E.2d 51–2 (Ill.1976).

sign, Hoffmann's a sudden nipping of the nail of the index, middle, or ring finger produces flexion of the terminal phalanx of the thumb and of the second and third phalanx of some other finger; called also *digital reflex, Hoffmann's reflex,* and *Trömmer's s.*

Her reflexes were active and were not symmetrical. They were greater on the right than the left, and she had an abnormal **Hoffmann reflex** on the right. The asymmetry of the reflexes is always abnormal, and this suggests a second lesion within the brain because the lesion that controls the eyes could not cause the reflex abnormality. McSwain v. Chicago Transit Authority, 362 N.E.2d 1264, 1272 (App.Ct.Ill.1977).

sign, Homans' discomfort behind the knee on forced dorsiflexion of the foot; a sign of thrombosis in the veins of the calf.

Dr. Magsaysay also noted a positive **Homan's sign**. This is a pain or discomfort behind the knee generally associated with a thrombosis or blood clot in the leg. The doctor diagnosed her condition as a possible pulmonary embolism or obstruction of a pulmonary vein. He ordered heparin, an anticoagulant drug. A pulmonary scan was also ordered. Ziegert v. South Chicago Community Hospital, 425 N.E.2d 450, 453 (App.Ct. Ill.1981).

He testified that there was a **Homan's sign**, definitely showing thrombophlebitis and recurrent pulmonary emboli. Carmichael v. Reitz, 95 Cal.Rptr. 381, 396 (Ct.App.Cal.1971).

sign, Lasègue's in sciatica, flexion of the hip is painful when the knee is extended, but painless when the knee is flexed. This distinguishes the disorder from disease of the hip joint.

The **Lasègue and straight leg-raising tests**, both standard objective tests, as well as the Patrick test, were all severely positive, demonstrating sacroiliac joint damage. Flexion, extension, abduction, and internal rotation were all "markedly restricted" on the right and "moderately restricted" on the left. Gretchen v. U.S., 618 F.2d 177, 180 (2d Cir. 1980).

Laseque's [sic] signs: To do with movement of limb. McClaflin v. Califano, 448 F.Supp. 69, 74 (D.Kan.1978).

sign, McMurray occurrence of a cartilage click during manipulation of the knee; indicative of meniscal injury.

MacMurray's [sic] sign (occurrence of a cartilage click during manipulation of the knee) was negative bilaterally, and all ligaments were described as stable. Pruchniewski v. Weinberger, 415 F.Supp. 112, 114 (D.Md.1976).

sign, Marfan's a red triangle at the tip of a coated tongue indicates typhoid fever; a rarely observed phenomenon.

sign, Queckenstedt's when the veins in the neck are compressed on one or both sides, there is a rapid rise in the pressure of the cerebrospinal fluid of healthy persons, and this rise quickly disappears when pressure is taken

off the neck. But when there is a block in the vertebral canal the pressure of the cerebrospinal fluid is little or not at all affected by this maneuver.

In the post-operative recovery room Dr. Kauffman administered a lumbar spinal tap which showed no bleeding within the spinal column. A **Queckenstedt test** also showed that the fluid pressure within the spinal column was normal. From the foregoing test results Dr. Kauffman concluded that the plaintiff suffered from spinal shock. Grubb v. Albert Einstein Medical Center, 387 A.2d 480, 484 (Super.Ct.Pa.1978).

There remain genuine issues of material fact in the case including whether the defendant, consistent with the standards of reasonable medical care in the community, promptly administered and properly read the results of a **Queckenstedt test** given the plaintiff to determine the presence of blockage of cerebral spinal fluid.... Cooper v. Fenton Brace & Limb Co., 350 So.2d 1106, 1108 (Dist.Ct.App.Fla.1977).

sign, Romberg's swaying of the body or falling when standing with the feet close together and the eyes closed; observed in tabes dorsalis. See also *rombergism.*

It was Dr. Livingston's opinion that Triplett suffered brain damage secondary to the head injury sustained in the fall. He further stated that as a result of the injury, Triplett had suffered a disturbance of the labyrinth, which impaired the balancing mechanisms extending from the ear to the brain. This condition resulted in ataxia and the positive **Romberg**, or falling to the right. Mid Central Tool Co. v. Industrial Com'n, 382 N.E.2d 222, 225 (Ill.1978).

He had the patient place her feet together in an erect posture and close her eyes. This is called the **Romberg sign** and she performed it accurately, showing good stability and coordination. Her gait was normal. She had normal movement of her neck and lower back. McSwain v. Chicago Trans. Authority, 362 N.E.2d 1264, 1275 (App.Ct.Ill.1977).

Silastic (sĭ-las'tĭk) trademark for polymeric silicone substances having the properties of rubber; it is biologically inert and used in surgical prostheses.

Dr. Cheris, called by the defendants, testified that he removed the disc, the capsule and part of the condyle and inserted a **silastic** block to fill the space between the condylar stump and the fossa of the temporal bone. The implant was kept in place by wires which went through the lower portion of the temporal bone. Rosario v. New York City Health & Hospitals, 450 N.Y.S.2d 805, 806 (1st Dep't 1982).

silica (sil'ĭ-kah) [L. *silex* flint] silicon dioxide, SiO_2, or silicic anhydride. It may occur in various allotropic forms, some of which are used in dental materials. See also *siderotic.*

Silica, which is another name for silicon dioxide, is the chief constituent of sand. Totherow v. Penn Dixie Industries, Inc., 589 S.W.2d 375, 376 (Tenn.1979).

silicon (sil'ĭ-kon) [L. *silex* flint] a nonmetallic light element whose dioxide is silica; symbol, Si; atomic number, 14; atomic weight, 28.086. See also *scar* (Stone case).

silicon dioxide See *silica.*

siliconoma

She later developed numerous small lumps or nodules under the skin of her chest and abdomen; these were later diagnosed as **siliconomas**, caused by accumulations of migrating silicone gel. The testimony is in dispute as to whether the **siliconomas** arose after other doctors had operated on her. Although she has undergone over twenty surgical operations to remove the **siliconomas**, they continue to appear. In addition, Mrs. Henderson has suffered several deformities in the shape and placement of her breasts. She has consulted many other physicians and has undergone subsequent augmentation procedures, some of which were sought to further increase the size of her breasts. Henderson v. Heyer-Schulte Corp., etc., 600 S.W.2d 844, 846 (Ct.Civ.App.Tex.1980).

silicosis (sil"ĭ-ko'sis) [L. *silex* flint] pneumoconiosis due to the inhalation of the dust of stone, sand, or flint containing silicon dioxide, with formation of generalized nodular fibrotic changes in both lungs. Called also *grinders' disease.*

His report, dated August 4, 1972, states that Haywood suffers from silicosis [3] Stage ⅔q and could not extinguish a match held six inches from his mouth. [[3] Silicosis is a disease encompassed within the definition of pneumoconiosis. See 20 C.F.R. § 410.401(b)(1).] Haywood v. Secretary of Health & Human Services, 699 F.2d 277, 279–80 (6th Cir. 1983).

Q. **Silicosis** or the general classification of pneumoconiosis, silicosis would be considered a chronic obstructive pulmonary disease.
A. Right....
Q. I understand your testimony to be that the possibility of his survival is decreased because he has this **silicosis** condition.
A. Right. The possibility of his surviving the heart attack when he had it there was decreased because of that silicosis, in that the prime thing is the amount of oxygen supplied to the heart muscle that gingered, and if they have the chronic obstructive pulmonary disease, the oxygen concentration getting into that heart muscle is decreased much more than just the heart attack. So, it really aggravates the infarction and heart attack markedly....

... The medical testimony is that **silicosis** was not the cause of death; rather the testimony describes silicosis as a condition which can operate to impair the ability to recover from a myocardial infarction. McCloskey v. W.C.A.B., 460 A.2d 237, 242 (Pa.1983).

The evidence establishes that **silicosis** and coal worker's pneumoconiosis are diseases of the lungs resulting from exposure to dust. Both are classified medically in the broad category of pneumoconiosis. The medical evidence, including the testimony of Dr. Schmidt, Williams' own expert, establishes that it is impossible to distinguish between the two diseases by X-ray examination. Both diseases manifest themselves on the X-ray film as nodules or shadows. It is only after a study of the history of exposure, whether to silica dust, coal dust or both, that the physician can make a calculated medical guess as to whether the disease is **silicosis** or coal worker's pneumoconiosis. Williams v. Clinchfield Coal Co., 192 S.E.2d 751, 753 (Va. 1972).

Other Authorities: Fulks v. Avondale Shipyards, Inc., 637 F.2d 1008, 1013 (5th Cir. 1981); Gibson v. Consolidation Coal Co., 588 S.W.2d 290, 294 (Tenn.1979); Froust v. Coating Specialists, Inc., 364 F.Supp. 1154–5 (E.D.La.1973); Graber v. Peter Lametti Construction Co., 197 N.W.2d 443, 445–6 (Minn.1972); Johnson v. American Gen. Ins. Co., 464 S.W.2d 83, 86 (Tex.1971); Young v. Marsillett, 473 S.W.2d 128–9 (Ct.App.Ky.1971); Massey v. Celebrezze, 345 F.2d 146, 150 (6th Cir. 1965).

silver fork deformity See *deformity, silver fork.*

silver point method See *therapy, root canal (silver point method).*

sinus (si'nus), pl. *si'nus* or *sinuses* [L. "a hollow"] a cavity, or channel; [NA] a general term for such spaces as the dilated channels for venous blood in the cranium, or the air cavities in the cranial bones.

In answer to hypothetical questions, Dr. Roberts himself testified that he, as a dentist practicing in the District of Columbia, would not attempt to treat a **sinus** infection, but would close off the passage from the **sinus** to the mouth, and then refer the patient to a specialist for treatment. Viz., the following colloquy:
Q. How would you go about treating [the extraction site] in a hope of curing the infected **sinus**?
A. I would not try to cure an infected **sinus**.
Q. You just said you would.
A. I would try at the site of the extraction.
Q. How would you treat the infected **sinus**? Do not tell me about the extraction. Tell me about the **sinus**.
A. I would approach it, lance it, and flush it out and put a flap up.
Q. In what way would this relieve the infection in the **sinus**?
A. It would not relieve the infection of the **sinus** but it would close up the infection of the mouth.
Q. How about the infection already there?
A. He could be referred.
Q. But then in order to treat the infected **sinus**, you refer him to a specialist, is that right, sir, is that right?
A. Right. Graham v. Roberts, 441 F.2d 995, 997–8 (D.C. Cir.1970).

... to have the upper right first molar tooth pulled. The doctor extracted this tooth and in doing so, left a root tip in the gum. In removing this tooth, Dr. Harris broke the floor of the **sinus** chamber which is not uncommon in removing this tooth according to Dr. Curl, the dental surgeon who testified in the case....
... The hole in the floor of the **sinus** which Dr. Curl was called upon to close was a result of the pulling of the tooth by Dr. Harris. The root of the tooth had extended into the **sinus** chamber and when the tooth was removed, the floor of the **sinus** chamber was left with a hole in the same. This is not uncommon according to Dr. Curl. Gorsalitz v. Harris, 410 S.W.2d 956–7, 959 (Ct.Civ.App.Tex.1966).

sinus caroticus [NA]; **sinus, carotid** the dilated portion of the internal carotid artery, situated above the division of the common carotid artery into its two main branches, or sometimes on the terminal portion of the common carotid artery, containing in its wall pressoreceptors that are stimulated by changes in blood pressure. Called also *bulbus caroticus.*

sinus cavernosus [NA]; sinus, cavernous an irregularly shaped venous space in the dura mater at either side of the body of the sphenoid bone, extending from the medial end of the superior orbital fissure in front to the apex of the petrous temporal bone behind. It receives the superior ophthalmic vein, the superficial middle cerebral vein, and the sphenoparietal sinus, and communicates with the opposite cavernous sinus and with the transverse sinus and internal jugular vein by way of the petrosal sinuses. Commonly comprising one or more main venous channels, it contains the internal carotid artery and abducent nerve.

An infection, probably originating in the ethmoid sinuses, traveled back into plaintiff's cranium and caused blood clotting—thrombosis—in the veins passing through an area in the center of the head called the **cavernous sinus**. These veins include those going to the eyes. Blockage of these veins resulted in the stoppage of the arterial flow of blood to the eyes, which in turn caused the retinae in the eyes to die. Speed v. State, 240 N.W.2d 901, 904 (Iowa 1976).

sinus, coccygeal a sinus or fistula situated just over or close to the tip of the coccyx, being the remains of the end of the neurenteric canal. See also *pilonidal sinus.*

sinus, ethmoidal; sinus ethmoidalis [NA], one of the paranasal sinuses, located in the ethmoid bone, consisting of the cellulae ethmoidales collectively, and communicating with the ethmoidal infundibulum and bulla and with the superior and highest meatuses of the nasal cavity. See also *os ethmoidale.*

On Tuesday afternoon, surgeons at the Hospital operated on plaintiff and removed his **ethmoid sinuses**. During the next days plaintiff received intensive medical care. The physicians and surgeons saved his life but not his sight; he emerged permanently blind. Speed v. State, 240 N.W.2d 901, 903–4 (Iowa 1976).

sinus frontalis osseus [NA], bony frontal sinus: an irregular air cavity situated in the frontal bone on either side, deep to the superciliary arch; separated from its fellow of the opposite side by a bony septum, and communicating with the middle meatus of the bony nasal cavity on the same side.

sinus maxillaris [NA]; sinus maxillaris [Highmori] maxillary sinus: one of the paired paranasal sinuses, located in the body of the maxilla on either side and communicating with the middle meatus of the nasal cavity on the same side. Called also *antrum of Highmore.* See also *sinus maxillaris osseus.*

The repair of the **maxillary antrum**—that's the sinus that was fractured in its wall—it had to be approached through the inside of the mouth.... Cooperider v. Dearth, 420 So.2d 220, 221 (Ct.App.La.1982).

The blow that he received was severe enough to render him unconscious, cause a cerebral concussion, a fracture of the anterior wall of the left **maxillary sinus**—a sinus bone—in the left cheek through which the roots of teeth go, and the loosening of two teeth so that they had to be removed. Powell v. Hellenic Lines, Ltd., 347 F.Supp. 855, 857 (E.D.La.1972).

The appellee's testimony showed that the removal of an upper molar created a communication channel between the mouth and the **maxillary sinus**. Following the extraction in May 1963, appellant developed a sinus infection which drained through the opening created by the extraction into his mouth. This sinus infection became progressively worse and by September it required surgery, 22 days' hospitalization, and six months' follow-up treatment before appellant was fully recovered....

... The appellee himself ... as a dentist would not try to cure an infected sinus, but would rather close off the connection between the mouth and the sinus and refer the patient to a specialist for proper treatment. Graham v. Roberts, 441 F.2d 995, 996 (D.C.Cir.1970).
Other Authorities: Schwartz v. U.S., 230 F.Supp. 536–7 (E.D. Pa.1964); Hazelwood v. Adams, 95 S.E.2d 917–18 (N.C. 1957).

sinus maxillaris osseus [NA], bony maxillary sinus: an air cavity of variable size and shape located in the body of each maxilla, communicating with the middle meatus of the bony nasal cavity on the same side.

sinus, maxillary See *sinus maxillaris.*

sinus, pilonidal a suppurating sinus containing a tuft of hair, occurring chiefly in the coccygeal region, but also in other regions of the body. See also *coccygeal sinus.*

site (sīt) a place, position, or locus.

site, donor

The doctor obtained skin for the skin grafts from the boy's left and right thighs. These areas are approximately six inches long and two and-a-half inches wide. These are called "donor sites" which will eventually become less noticeable, but, as indicated, they may always appear as "patches". Young v. Caribbean Associates, Inc., 358 F.Supp. 1220, 1223 (D.V.I.1973).

site, primary

... the **primary site** of action of the benzodiazepines. Primary site of action is defined to mean to [sic (the)] location in the brain where a drug at the lowest dose will produce an effect. Hoffman-La Roche, Inc. v. Kleindienst, 478 F.2d 1, 8 (3d Cir. 1973).

situational reaction, acute See *reaction, acute situational.*

skeleton (skel'ĕ-ton) [Gr. "a dried body, mummy"] the hard framework of the animal body, especially the bony framework of the body of higher vertebrate animals; the bones of the body collectively. See illustration.

skin (skin) the outer integument or covering of the body, consisting of the corium, or dermis, and the epidermis, and resting upon the subcutaneous tissues; called also *cutis [NA].*

He found the **skin** puckered over the scarring and somewhat atrophic, which meant that it was thinner than normal **skin**. Being thinner, it would be more susceptible to further chemical burns or to blows or to scrubbing with a brush in preparation for an operation. It is "possible," he said, that scrubbing would cause the thin **skin** to break down but he did not think it was probable; the **skin** could take "almost as much punish-

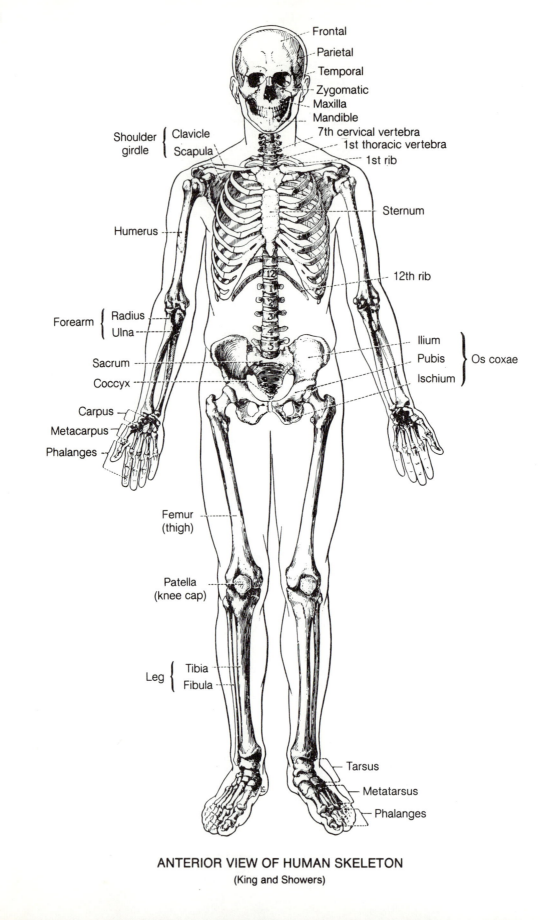

ANTERIOR VIEW OF HUMAN SKELETON
(King and Showers)

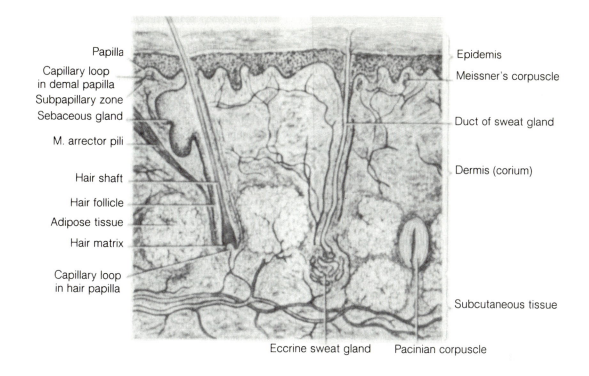

Papilla
Capillary loop
in demal papilla
Subpapillary zone
Sebaceous gland
M. arrector pili

Hair shaft
Hair follicle
Adipose tissue
Hair matrix

Capillary loop
in hair papilla

Epidemis
Meissner's corpuscle

Duct of sweat gland

Dermis (corium)

Subcutaneous tissue

Eccrine sweat gland   Pacinian corpuscle

The skin and its appendages (Domonkos).

ment'' as normal tissue. Lorenc v. Chemirad Corp., 37 N.J. 56, 79–80, 179 A.2d 401 (1962).

skin atrophy See *atrophy*.

skin, piebald a term sometimes applied to the lesions of partial albinism.

skin test (for tubercule bacilli) See *test, tuberculin Sterneedle*.

skull (skul) the bony framework of the head, composed of the cranial bones and the bones of the face. It includes the ethmoid, frontal, hyoid, lacrimal, nasal, occipital, palatine, parietal, sphenoid, temporal, and zygomatic bones, and the inferior nasal conchae, mandible, maxillae, and vomer. Called also *cranium*. See also *fracture, depressed* (Benjamin case).

A diagnosis of basilar fracture of the **skull** was made and she was transported in a comatose condition to, and hospitalized at, the Medical University of South Carolina Hospital, in Charleston, South Carolina, for treatment of a concussion, laceration of the right mastoid area, right basilar **skull** fracture, draining blood from her right ear, and a fracture of the left index finger. Doyle v. U.S., 441 F.Supp. 701, 706 (D.S.Car. 1977).

skull fracture, basilar See *basilaris cranii*.

slough (sluf) necrotic tissue in the process of separating from viable portions of the body.

The defendant examined the plaintiff on that occasion and found that she would benefit cosmetically from plastic surgery. On January 11, 1974, plaintiff underwent surgery. Postoperative complications arose, however. On examination on January 21, 1974, defendant noticed **sloughing** of skin on both of plaintiff's cheeks. This was the result of blood clotting under the cheeks and resultant tissue breakdown. As a consequence of the **sloughing**, plaintiff suffered permanent facial scarring. Granger v. Wisner, 656 P.2d 1238–9 (Ariz.1982).

sloughing (sluf'ing) the formation or separation of a slough.

sludge (sluj) a suspension of solid or semisolid particles in a fluid which itself may or may not be a truly viscous fluid. See also *virus*; and *Escherichia coli* (both U.S. v. City of Asbury Park case).

The **sludge**, which is composed of water, organic matter and inorganic matter, in varying percentages, is retained in holding tanks during the year and is pumped into the ocean during the three-month period between December 15th and March 15th.

Sludge, generally, is composed of human excretion, household waste from food preparation, laundry waste, commercial waste, dirt, etc. Items such as corn kernels, tomato seeds and prophylactics, sanitary napkins, pieces of orange peel, sand, shaving brushes, toothbrushes, plastic diaper liners, plastic toys and filter-tip cigarettes are some of the items frequently found in primary **sludge**. Further, **sludge** is not homogeneous; that is, unless it is mixed, the lighter materials will rise to the surface, with the heavier particles falling to the bottom.

Experts for all parties defined and characterized **sludge** in a number of ways: a thin suspension of solids; a slurry of solids in a water vehicle—"slurry" being defined as a mixture of insoluble material in water (gasoline was offered as an example of a pure liquid or fluid); **sludge** is a plastic solid because it has rigidity and shearing force; **sludge** is a fluid because it will flow where a shearing force is applied—"shearing force" being defined as a force applied tangentially; **sludge** is definitely a liquid if its solids content is less than 15%; **sludge** is a liquid because it flows; **sludge** is a liquor—that is, it contains two states, a solid state and a liquid state. U.S. v. City of Asbury Park, 340 F.Supp. 555, 557, 559 (D.N.J.1972).

SMA (sequential multiple analysis) See under *test*.

smear (smēr) a specimen for microscopic study prepared by spreading the material across the glass slide.

smear, cytological See *cytology, exfoliative*.

This time Dr. Stover took a **cytological smear** of the affected area for pathological evaluation. Here a distinction between a **cytological smear** and a tissue biopsy is necessary. Both are tests done to discover a tissue cancer. A **cytological smear** consists of scraping cells from the surface of the affected area for microscopic examination....

... A **cytological smear** is not a very good diagnostic device. It is a good screening device—i.e., a good method of discovering unsuspected cancers in the general population, as is commonly done with cervical cancers in women. But where there are other symptoms leading one to suspect a cancer is present, it is not a good method of getting a definitive diagnosis because of the danger of getting a "false negative"—i.e., as compared to a tissue biopsy, a **cytological smear** has a much greater chance of failing to indicate a cancer which is actually present. Therefore, in order to get a definite diagnosis, a tissue biopsy should be done. O'Brien v. Stover, 443 F.2d 1013, 1015 (8th Cir. 1971).

smear test See *Papanicolaou's stain* under *Table of Stains*.

Smith-Petersen nail See *nail, Smith-Petersen*.

snake bite See *bite, rattlesnake* (Buck case).

snare (snār) a wire loop or noose for removing polyps and tumors by encircling them at the base and closing the loop. See also *tonsillectomy* (Civitarese case).

sociopath (so'se-o-path") a person with an antisocial (sociopathic) personality (q.v.). See also *personality, antisocial*.

In my opinion, Mr. Schoppel [sic] can be diagnosed as a **Sociopathic Personality** with marked emotional instability, impulsivity, lack of control and judgment, and paranoid trends. U.S. v. Schappel, 445 F.2d 716, 721 (D.C.Cir.1971).

She has a defect in terms of her formation of her personality. She has what is called a **sociopathic personality**. This is getting

off into a rather technical area. She is not what you might call the average, normal, healthy, contented human being, at best. She would deviate from the normal. Not that she would necessarily have symptoms, but that her life has not been a well organized, fruitful venture for her. It has been crises and, rather, disappointment.

"Q. Doctor, with reference to the term '**sociopathic personality**,' using more basic language, is that associated with what we call an anti-social personality?

"A. In general, yes...." In re Loughran, 276 F.Supp. 393, 416 (C.D.Cal.1967).

sociopathic (so"se-o-path'ik) pertaining to a person with an antisocial personality (q.v.); antisocial.

... subject "to a **sociopathic** personality disturbance, [an] antisocial reaction in an individual who tends to become schizophrenic under stressful circumstances, as manifested by a history of antisocial behavior, superficiality of affect and judgment, affability and psychological test evidence suggestive of schizophrenia."...

... He stated, nonetheless, that the schizoid personality and the **sociopathic** personality are closely related. U.S. v. Currens, 290 F.2d 751, 755–6 (3d Cir. 1961).

sociopathic personality See *sociopath*; and *personality, antisocial*.

socket (sok'et) a hollow or depression, into which a corresponding part fits.

socket, dry a condition sometimes occurring after tooth extraction, resulting in exposure of bone with localized osteomyelitis of an alveolar crypt, and symptoms of severe pain; called also *alveolar osteitis, alveolitis sicca dolorosa*, and *localized alveolar osteitis*.

If a **dry socket** developed in the area of the root tip the standard of practice is to leave the root tip in until after the **dry socket** is treated and cleared and then the dentist can make a determination about the removal of the root tip. Dailey v. N.C. State Bd. of Dental Examiners, 299 S.E.2d 473, 477 (Ct.App. N.C.1983).

sodium (so'de-um), gen. *so'dii* [L. *na'trium*, gen. *na'trii*] a soft, silver white, alkaline metallic element; symbol, Na; atomic number, 11; atomic weight, 22.990; specific gravity, 0.971. With a valence of 1, it has a strong affinity for oxygen and other nonmetallic elements. Sodium provides the chief cation of the extracellular body fluids. See also *sodium pump*, under *pump*. The salts of sodium are the most widely used salts in medicine. (Note: For sodium salts not listed below, see the name of the active ingredient.)

Sodium intake is of concern to individuals on sodium-restrictive diets—primarily those suffering from hypertension or congestive heart failure. Environmental Defense Fund, Inc. v. Costle, 578 F.2d 337, 341 (D.C.Cir.1978).

sodium amytal See *amobarbital*.

sodium arsenite

Sodium arsenite is highly soluble, more than nine times as toxic as arsenic trioxide and has a record of having caused human fatalities. **Sodium arsenite** would be classified as highly toxic to man (as measured by lethal effect in rats when the poison is administered orally) under standards contained in USDA Regulations (7 C.F.R. 362.8). Sodium arsenite has an LD50 toxicity of 42 mg./kg. in rats. Pax Company of Utah v. U.S., 324 F.Supp. 1335, 1341 (D.Utah 1970), reversed and remanded 454 F.2d 93 (10th Cir. 1972).

sodium barbital See *secobarbital.*

sodium carboxymethylcellulose

The Judicial Officer's opinion then follows:
   The only evidence before me as to the extent to which the stomach would be filled by a Skini-Mini tablet is that in the testimony of Dr. Cordaro who estimates the size of the mass produced by the amount of the **sodium carboxymethylcellulose** contained in a Skini-Mini to be approximately that of a walnut. Since the stomach capacity is approximately one quart the degree of filling indicated would not be substantial. [Postal Service Decision at p. 8.] Institute for Weight Control, Inc. v. Klassen, 348 F.Supp. 1304, 1311–12 (D.N.J.1972).

sodium casinate See *casein-sodium.*

sodium chloride common salt or table salt: a mineral, NaCl, soluble in water and occurring as colorless, cubic crystals or white, crystalline powder, found widely distributed over the earth, in sea water, etc., which is a necessary constituent of the body and consequently of the diet. It makes up over 90 per cent of the inorganic constituents of the blood serum and is the principal salt involved in maintaining osmotic tension of blood and tissues. It is used in medicine [USP] for many purposes, as in the preparation of isotonic and physiologic saline solutions; as a fluid and electrolyte replenisher, an isotonic vehicle for drugs, an antihypercalcemic, and an antidote to silver nitrate poisoning, administered by intravenous infusion; as a topical anti-inflammatory; to irrigate wounds and body cavities; as an enema to flush the colon and promote evacuation; as a mucolytic, administered by inhalation; and as a topical osmotic agent in ophthalmology. Also used widely as a food preservative and seasoning.

sodium hydroxide [NF], a caustic alkali, NaOH, occurring as white, or nearly white, fused masses, in small pellets, flakes, sticks, and other forms; used as an alkalizing agent in pharmaceutical preparations. Called also *caustic soda* and *s. hydrate.* See also *tissue, cicatricial* (Drayton case).

According to Professor Beroes, the chemical composition of liquid-plumr is such as to enable it to dissolve human tissue in a fraction of a second. The **sodium hydroxide** contained therein was extremely dangerous since, in solution, the sodium ions were freed to attack the tissue thereby forming yet another chemical compound, essentially that of soap....
   ... In his opinion, a severe **sodium hydroxide** burn has no antidote. The damage incurred is so rapid and so difficult to neutralize that it renders the victim virtually helpless. Contact with the skin results in an immediate chemical reaction which

itself generates considerable heat further speeding the saponification of the skin....
   ... His testimony was marked by frequent references to the highly caustic nature of **sodium hydroxide** which in solutions of 2% or more is corrosive to human tissue. Drayton v. Jiffee Chemical Corp., 395 F.Supp. 1081, 1089 (N.D.Ohio 1975).

sodium hypochlorite the sodium salt of hypochlorous acid, NaClO, having germicidal and disinfectant properties.

Sodium hypochloride [sic] emits chlorine gas, is highly unstable, and breaks down while in solution into hydrochloric and hydrochlorous acid. Although defendants knew that the chemicals were highly dangerous, the service men were not warned of this fact except that they were told to be careful not to get any of the chemicals in their eyes. McEvoy v. American Pool Corp., 195 P.2d 783, 785 (Cal.1948).

sodium nitrite [USP], a compound, $NaNO_2$, occurring as a white to slightly yellow, granular powder or as white or nearly white, opaque fused masses or sticks, used as an antidote for cyanide poisoning. It is also used in the relief of the pain of angina pectoris, Raynaud's disease, asthma, and such conditions as lead colic and spastic colitis.

The food additive of **sodium nitrite** may be safely used in conjunction with salt (NaCl) to aid in inhibiting the outgrowth and toxin formation from *Clostridium botulinum* type E in the commercial processing of smoked chub....
   ... [each fish shall be heated to] at least 160° F. for a minimum of 30 minutes [provided that it has not less than 3.5% of salt and a prescribed **sodium nitrite** content]. Note that whitefish at this temperature would require not less than 5% salt content under the regulation, 21 C.F.R. Part 122 (1977). U.S. v. Nova Scotia Food Products Corp., 568 F.2d 240, 244 (2d Cir. 1977).

The Statement further noted that "although **sodium nitrite** was not specifically authorized as an additive to prevent the development of Clostridium Botulinum, it did not seem appropriate to the [Agriculture] Department to ban its use when presently available evidence indicated its possible usefulness in preventing botulism and there was a lack of evidence demonstrating that ... [it] would be dangerous to human health." Schuck v. Butz, 500 F.2d 810–11 (D.C.Cir.1974).

sodium pentothal See *laryngospasm* (Ascher case); and *thiopental, sodium.*

sodium sorbate See *acid, sorbic.*

sodium warfarin See *warfarin, sodium.*

sodomy (sod'o-me) [after the city of *Sodom*] a form of paraphilia, variously defined by law to include sexual contact between humans and animals of other species, and mouth-genital or anal contact between humans; in medical usage, it is restricted to human-animal sexual contact and anal intercourse.

Deviate sexual intercourse, also a Class B misdemeanor, is made a crime under Section 130.38 of the Penal Law:
   Consensual **Sodomy**: A person is guilty of consensual **sodomy** when he engages in deviate sexual intercourse with another person....
   ... See Richards, Unnatural Acts and the Constitutional Right to Privacy: A Moral Theory, 45 Fordham L.Rev. 1281

(1977); Wolfenden, Report of the Commission on Homosexual Offenses and Prostitution, British Home Office Par. 287 p. 96 (1957)....

Seventeen states have repealed their consensual **sodomy** laws: Arkansas, California, Colorado, Connecticut, Delaware, Hawaii, Illinois, Indiana, Maine, New Hampshire, New Mexico, North Dakota, Ohio, Oregon, South Dakota, Washington. Comment, The Constitutionality of Sodomy Statutes, 45 Fordham L.Rev. 553, 592 (1976). In re Dora P., 400 N.Y.S.2d 455, 458, 463 (Family Ct.N.Y.Cty.1977), reversed and remanded 418 N.Y.S.2d 597 (1st Dep't 1979).

soft tissue See *tissue, soft.*

soft tissue injury See *injury, soft tissue.*

sole See *plantar.*

solenoid (so′lĕ-noid) [Gr. *sōleno-eides* pipe-shaped, grooved] a coil of wire spaced equally between turns, which acts like a magnet when an electric current is passed through it.

A **solenoid** is a device which uses electrical energy to create a magnetic field in a coil so that a movable core is drawn into the coil when a current flows. Republic Industries, Inc. v. Schlage Lock Co., 592 F.2d 963, 966 n. 7 (7th Cir. 1979).

Solenopsis (so″lĕ-nop′sis) a genus of stinging ants, including the fire ants that attack man and inflict painful burning stings and may cause severe local and systemic reactions; *S. geminata* is indigenous to the United States; *S. saevissima richteri* is a viciously aggressive South American species that has been imported into the United States and gained a strong foothold.

The imported fire ant (**Solenopsis saevissima**) was accidentally introduced into the Southern United States from South America sometime around 1918. It presently infests approximately 126 million acres in over 400 counties in the nine southeastern states of Alabama, Arkansas, Florida, Georgia, Louisiana, Mississippi, North Carolina, South Carolina, and Texas....

The imported fire ant is a pest that adversely affects human health. Its sting is painful and the resulting pustule and lesion presents the risk of secondary infection. In a small number of sensitized persons the ant sting can cause allergic or anaphylactic reactions which may cause death. The United States Department of Health, Education, and Welfare has concluded that on the whole the fire ant "presents a low health hazard to humans in the United States." Environmental Defense Fund v. Hardin, 325 F.Supp. 1401, 1404 (D.D.C.1971).

Solu-Cortef (sol″u-kor′tef) trademark for a preparation of hydrocortisone sodium succinate. See also *hydrocortisone sodium succinate.*

solute (so′lūt) a substance dissolved in a solvent; a solution consists of a solute and a solvent.

solution (so-lu′shun) [L. *solutio*] a homogeneous mixture of one or more substances (solutes) dispersed molecularly in a sufficient quantity of dissolving medium (solvent). The solute may be gas, liquid, or solid; the solvent is usually liquid, but may be solid, as in a solid solution of copper in silver (sterling silver). In pharmacology, a liquid preparation containing one or several soluble chemical substances usually dissolved in water and not, for various reasons, falling into another category.

solution, Dakin's; solution, Dakin's, modified See *solution, sodium hypochlorite, diluted.*

solution, Ringer's See under *irrigation.*

solution, sodium hypochlorite, diluted a colorless to light yellow liquid with a faint odor of chlorine, compounded of sodium hypochlorite solution, sodium bicarbonate, and water, each 100 ml. containing 450–500 mg. of sodium hypochlorite; used as a topical anti-infective. It is also used for wound irrigation, and has been used to irrigate the urinary bladder. Called also *Dakin's antiseptic, Dakin's fluid, Dakin's s., Dakin's modified s.,* and *surgical s. of chlorinated soda.* See also *Carrel's treatment,* under *treatment.*

... the infection was so severe, Dr. Meany testified, that it was necessary to apply **Dakin's solution**, a medicated solution containing chlorine. **Dakin's solution**, which disinfects and promotes healing tissue, is an irritant and causes pain when put on a raw, sensitive area. Raines v. New York Cent. Railroad Co., 283 N.E.2d 230, 236 (Ill.1972).

soma (so′mah) [Gr. *sōma* body] the body tissue as distinguished from the germ cells.

somatic (so-mat′ik) [Gr. *sōmatikos*] pertaining to or characteristic of the soma or body. See also *somatoplasm.*

"The referee: What do you mean by '**somatic**'?

"The witness: '**Somatic**' is to distinguish cells and tissues and organs from reproductive. It refers to all parts of the body which are not the reproductive organs and the reproductive cells...." Chiropractic Ass'n of New York, Inc. v. Hilleboe, 227 N.Y.S.2d 309, 366 (Sup.Ct. Albany Cty.1961).

somatization (so″mah-ti-za′shun) in psychiatry, the conversion of mental experiences or states into bodily symptoms.

Dr. Pearson stated that plaintiff had strong unconscious motivations to prolong his convalescence, and characterized plaintiff as undergoing a massive **somatization** reaction (physical expression of psychological conflicts) partially masking depression. Manigan v. Califano, 453 F.Supp. 1080, 1084 (D.Kan.1978).

somatoplasm (so-mat′o-plazm) [*somato-* + Gr. *plasma* anything formed or molded] the protoplasm of the body cells as distinguished from that of the germ cells. Cf. *germ plasm.*

sorbate See *acid, sorbic.*

sorbic acid See *acid, sorbic.*

sosigon See *pentazocine.*

Sotradecol See *sclerosing* (Rosario case).

sound (sownd) [L. *sonus*] 1. the effect produced on the organ of hearing and its central connections by the vibrations of the air or other medium. 2. mechanical radiant energy, the motion of particles of the material medium through which it travels (air, water, or solids) being along the line of transmission (longitudinal); such energy, of frequency between 8 and 20,000 cycles per second, provides the stimulus for the subjective sensation of hearing.

Sound consists essentially of pressure waves of varying frequencies and amplitudes. The pressure waves associated with speech are initiated when air is exhaled past the vocal cords. The resulting vibration of the vocal cords produces the pressure waves. U.S. v. Williams, 583 F.2d 1194, 1196 (2d Cir. 1978).

Simply stated, **sound** can be defined as energy in the form of waves or pulses caused by vibrations. In the speech process the initial wave-producing process originates in the vocal cords. If a **sound** wave strikes another medium, the energy from the **sound** wave causes the new medium to vibrate. The **sound** waves in the ear cause the eardrum to vibrate. The vibrating motion of the eardrum is then converted into impulses which are transferred to the brain and are "perceived as sounds we hear." [3] [[3] Moenssens, Moses and Inbau, "Spectrographic Voice Identification," Scientific Evidence in Criminal Case, The Foundation Press, Inc., 1973, Chapter 12, pp. 508–509.] People v. Rogers, 385 N.Y.S.2d 228, 232 (Sup.Ct. Kings Cty.1976).

sound, bowel

Dr. Collins also testified that he did not use a stethoscope to check for **bowel sounds**—high-pitched crescendo sounds that indicate intestinal blockage—because his pelvic examination did not give him a hint that there was any distended bowel suggesting a partial or impending obstruction at that time and because what plaintiff told him did not indicate that there was any trouble....

... If the **bowel sounds**, instead of being a normal, intermittent, low, rumbling type [is] a real high-pitched crescendo type, that indicates to us that there may be some blockage; and then we have to go further with maybe stronger enemas and possibly get an x-ray to see if there is what we call a paralytic ileus present, or, indeed, intestinal obstruction. Smithers v. Collins, 278 S.E.2d 286, 290 (Ct.App.N.C.1981).

sound, P–2 See *sound, pulmonic*.

sound, pulmonic

Although he found a rather prominent **pulmonary sound (P–2)**, an indication that something might be wrong with her pulmonary circulatory system, he concluded that plaintiff was "medically asymptomatic and in a reasonable state of clinical equilibrium while taking her daily anticoagulant and tranquilizer therapy." Carmichael v. Reitz, 95 Cal.Rptr. 381, 395 (Ct.App. 1971).

sound the uterus

He testified that the appellee had violated accepted medical standards by failing to measure the depth of Mrs. Hitch's uterus by not **"sounding" the uterus** (a procedure employed to measure the depth of the uterus).... Hitch v. Hall, 399 A.2d 953, 955 (Ct.Spec.App.Md.1979).

Sparine (spar'ēn) trademark for preparations of promazine hydrochloride. See also *promazine hydrochloride*.

sparteine (spar'te-in) [L. *spartium* broom] chemical name: dodecahydro-7,14-methano-2*H*,6*H*-dipyrido[1,2-*a*:1',2'-*e*][1,5]diazocine. An alkaloid $C_{15}H_{26}N_2$, obtained from the legumes *Cystisus scoparius* (L.) Link. (broom), *Lupinus luteus* L. (yellow lupin bean), *L. niger* Hort. (black lupin bean), and *Anagyris foetida* L. (Mediterranean stinkbush). It is poisonous, and acts like digitalis.

sparteine sulfate the pentahydrate sulfate salt of sparteine, $C_{15}H_{26}N_2 \cdot H_2SO_4 \cdot 5H_2$, used as an oxytocic for the induction of labor and stimulation of hypotonic or subnormal uterine contractions. Formerly used as a substitute for digitalis.

Appellant contends that **spartocin** speeds up uterine contractions which is undesirable in a breech delivery; appellee contends that **spartocin** does not speed up uterine contractions, but makes them more efficient. Freed v. Priore, 372 A.2d 895, 897 (Super.Ct.Pa.1977).

Spartocin See *sparteine sulfate*.

spasm (spazm) [L. *spasmus;* Gr. *spasmos*] a sudden, violent, involuntary contraction of a muscle or a group of muscles, attended by pain and interference with function, producing involuntary movement and distortion.

He noted a "painful and palpable **spasm** in the left paraspinal and scapular region;" and the range of mobility of the cervical spine was −3 of the basis of 0 to grade 4. Simonson v. Schweiker, 699 F.2d 426, 428 (8th Cir. 1983).

Daney advised Dr. Thomas that the pain continued in his lower back area with radiation into his left leg which cramped his calf muscles. Dr. Thomas' examination revealed "a man who is obviously in moderate distress from lower back pain with definite paralumbar muscle **spasm** on both forward and lateral bending and restricted secondary to muscle **spasm** and pain." Dr. Thomas determined that Daney was "suffering from a lumbar disc disease." Daney v. Argonaut Ins. Co., 421 So.2d 331, 334 (Ct.App.La.1982).

The consequent pressure on the affected nerves produced severe muscular contraction, known as a "**spasm**". Mrs. Badke was found to have tenderness and swelling of the posterior neck muscles, indicative of **spasms**. Badke v. Barnett, 316 N.Y.S.2d 177–8 (2d Dep't 1970).

spasm, ascending spinal

Furthermore, he testified that plaintiff's neck pains are a result of an **ascending spinal spasm**. Selk v. Detroit Plastic Products, 328 N.W.2d 15, 23 (Ct.App.Mich.1982).

spasm, bronchial spasmodic contraction of the muscular coat of the bronchial tubes, such as occurs in asthma. See also *bronchospasm*.

spasm, cadaveric rigor mortis causing movements of the limbs.

In a discussion of rigor mortis the authors of Scientific Evidence, at page 201, state: "A phenomenon known as **cadaveric spasm** adds another note of uncertainty to the variable onset of rigor mortis. It is characterized by instantaneous rigidity of the whole body or an appendage such as the hand gripping a weapon or a clump of the assailant's hair or clothing." People v. Garrett, 339 N.E.2d 753, 763 (Ill.1975).

spasm, flexor See *flexor*; and *spasm*.

He testified that a **flexor spasm** signifies "profound spinal cord disease" and this alone, in his opinion, is enough to make this a non-GBS case. McDonald v. U.S., 555 F.Supp. 935, 953 (M.D.Pa.1983).

They explained that the movement in his legs after being admitted to the hospital was due to **flexor spasms** which was a natural phenomenon following paraplegia. Sendejar v. Alice

Physicians & Surgeons Hosp., Inc., 555 S.W.2d 879, 884 (Ct. Civ.App.Tex.1977).

spasm, paraspinous

Dr. Plauche found no neurovascular deficit in either leg, but did note a moderate degree of **paraspinous muscle spasm** in the lumbosacral area bilaterally. Chisholm v. L. S. Womack, Inc., 424 So.2d 1138, 1141 (Ct.App.La.1982).

spasm, paravertebral muscle

Erickson complained of back pain with pain radiating into the left buttock and left calf. Dr. Idelkope's examination found a significant degree of **paravertebral muscle spasm** in the lumbar region of the back, stigmata of a stroke suffered 13 years ago, some right-sided weakness, and some cranial nerve abnormalities. Erickson by Erickson v. Gopher Masonry, Inc., 329 N.W.2d 40, 41 (Minn.1983).

spasm, Romberg's masticatory spasm of the muscles supplied by the fifth nerve.

spasm, trapezium muscle

Plaintiff was suffering from **trapezius muscle spasm**, which he described as a vicious cycle whereby the muscle contracts to limit motion in response to pain, which, self-defeating, causes more pain and more spasm and pain . . . .

Persons with this injury become depressed, weepy, cranky, unpredictable, and have temper tantrums. These personality changes are caused by muscle spasm compressing the vertebral artery as it goes into the skull, constricting blood flow. Pohl v. Gilbert, 280 N.W.2d 831, 833–4 (Ct.App.Mich.1979).

spasticity (spas-tis′ĭ-te) a state of hypertonicity, or increase over the normal tone of a muscle, with heightened deep tendon reflexes.

Upon questioning by the Court, Dr. Shane stated that not all nerve innervation is destroyed by GBS and, thus, you can have some partial function of the nerves that can elicit **spasticity**, i.e., a flexor spasm or withdrawal response, in an otherwise flaccid paralysis. McDonald v. U.S., 555 F.Supp. 935, 949 (M.D.Pa.1983).

Dr. Chester Fresh, a neurosurgeon, treated Terry Dale twenty months after the accident on a referral from Dr. Banks. Dr. Fresh found the child to have sufficient **spasticity** (sustained contracture of the muscles) from the elbow to the hand to significantly limit the use and function of his right hand. Cupit v. Grant, 425 So.2d 847, 852 (Ct.App.La.1982).

Movement both active and passive of the head and neck produced severe pain. He stated that movement against resistance aggravated the pain; muscle **spasticity** was 4 plus (the top degree of severity or intensity of pain). Movement of her right arm was restricted and painful. McSwain v. Chicago Trans. Authority, 362 N.E.2d 1264, 1267 (App.Ct.Ill.1977).

special nuclear material See under *material*.

specialist (spesh′al-ist) a physician whose practice is limited to a particular branch of medicine or surgery, especially one who, by virtue of advanced training, is certified by a specialty board as being qualified to so limit his practice. See also *care, standard of (specialist)*.

"[The] Court finds that Drs. Yamaguchi and Sherrod, being licensed physicians and having limited their practice to obstetrics and gynecology, and further having held themselves out as so limiting their practice, are '**specialists**' within the meaning of LSA-R.S. 40:1299.39(A)(4), and are therefore not entitled to the benefits of the 'locality rule.' White v. Edison, 361 So.2d 1292 (La.App. 1st Cir. 1978), writ den. 363 So.2d 915 (La. 1978). . . .'' Williams v. Lallie Kemp Charity Hosp., 428 So.2d 1000, 1005 (Ct.App.La.1983).

Physicians are deemed to be **specialists** in a variety of ways. The most common classification is on the basis of education and certification. A **specialist** generally is defined as a doctor who has served a residency, taken and successfully passed examinations for certification and one who limits his practice to a particular medical area. Lawyers Medical Encyclopedia, Vol. I, 13–18 §§ 1.8–1.10 (1966). A physician is also considered, in law, bound to the standard of a **specialist** if he holds himself out as such. . . .

. . . See also: 21 A.L.R.3d 953 (1968), ''Physicians & Surgeons: Standard or Skill and Care Required of a Specialist.'' Reeg v. Shaughnessy, 570 F.2d 309, 315 (10th Cir. 1978).

specialty see *specialist*.

specific adjustment See *adjustment*.

specific pathogen free See *SPF*.

spectacles (spek′tah-k′lz) [L. *spectacula; spectare* to see] a pair of lenses in a frame to assist vision. See also *glasses*; and *lens*.

spectacles, prismatic spectacles with prismatic lenses for correcting muscular defects.

spectrofluorometer (spek″tro-floo″or-om′ĕ-ter) an optical instrument for analysis of fluorescence spectra.

Gleason then traveled to the Texas Medical Center in Houston, where there was a morphone analyzer operating on a **spectroflorometer** [sic]. The machine, unlike the emit spectrophotor, was capable of determining whether urine contained morphine or codeine. Roberts v. State, 537 S.W.2d 461–2 (Ct.Crim.App.Tex.1976).

spectrogram See *phonetics*.

A **spectrogram** has been often called a ''voiceprint.'' We avoid the term as potentially leading to an unwarranted association with fingerprint evidence . . . .

In producing **spectrograms**, a tape is placed in the spectrograph. The spectrograph electronically scans the tape and generates electronic signals representative of the components of the sound. The signals are fed to a variable filter, which adjusts the position of a stylus. The stylus burns thin parallel lines on current-sensitive paper wrapped around a rotating drum. The stylus traces a horizontal line, representing a single frequency, the darkness of the linetrace varying as it progresses. At the end of each line, the stylus returns to trace out another line, representing a slightly higher frequency, and so on, producing a bar **spectrogram**.

The **spectrograms** of the same words and phrases are then compared visually, to determine whether they were made by the same speaker. The bar **spectrogram** indicates time along the horizontal axis, frequency along the vertical axis, and intensity by varying shades of darkness in the pattern. The unique speech characteristics of the individual whose voice is being analyzed produce unique **spectrogram** patterns of vocal energy at the various frequency levels. Though it is not necessary that two **spectrograms** be identical, there must be exhibited a sufficient number of similar **spectrogram** patterns, called "matches," to warrant a conclusion that they were produced by the same person. U.S. v. Williams, 583 F.2d 1194, 1197 (2d Cir. 1978).

The **spectrogram** (the "display" of a spectrograph machine) displays three main parameters of speech—time (horizontal axis), frequency (vertical axis), and intensity (degree of shading in the time/frequency regions). . . .

The **spectrogram** examiner listens to recordings of known and unknown voices and visually analyzes the **spectrograms** of each voice. If he finds sufficient points of similarity, he will indicate that the two exemplars, the known and the unknown, were made by the same person. People v. Rogers, 385 N.Y.S.2d 228, 232–3 (Sup.Ct.Kings Cty.1976).

This pictorial representation of a sound is called the **spectrogram**. The so-called "voiceprint" is the **spectrogram** (the photograph, a map or a diagram) of the signals produced by the spectrograph. To obtain a **spectrogram** the operator requires a magnetic tape recorder and a sound spectrograph. . . .

. . . Dr. Gerstman does not think it is scientifically possible to differentiate voices on **spectrograms** by unique vocal patterns. . . .

. . . He believes that it is extremely unlikely that it is possible to identify speakers by use of **spectrograms**. He testified that Kersta's tests are not affirmatively valid and reliable; that no one has acquired the knowledge to be able to identify and separate personal qualities as distinguished from qualities of the word being spoken. . . .

. . . Dr. Ladefoged was of the opinion that the high frequency percentage figure given by Kersta was meaningless since there was no indication of how Kersta arrived at the figure or how he verified the figure. He testified that the Acoustical Society passed a resolution opposing the admissibility of "voiceprints" in evidence on the basis of claims which have not yet been adequately evaluated scientifically. He stated that the claim that a speaker can be identified by a comparison of sound **spectrograms** is not generally accepted by competent authorities in the field. . . .

. . . Kersta's admission that his process is entirely subjective and founded on his opinion alone without general acceptance within the scientific community compels us to rule "voiceprint" identification process has not reached a sufficient level of scientific certainty to be accepted as identification evidence in cases where the life or liberty of a defendant may be at stake. People v. King, 72 Cal.Rptr. 478, 485, 489–90, 493 (Ct.App.Cal.1968).

spectrograph (spek'tro-graf) an instrument for photographing spectra on a sensitive photographic plate. See also *spectrum*.

The **spectrograph** is an electromagnetic instrument which analyzes sound and disperses it into an array of its time, frequency and intensity components. The array is graphically displayed in a spectrogram.

The **spectrograph** operator is supplied with two magnetic tapes—one with a known, the other with an unknown, voice. He listens for similar words and phrases on both tapes. The preferred cue words are: THE, TO, AND, ME, ON, IS, YOU, I, A, and IT. Spectrograms are then made of the portions of the tapes on which the selected words and phrases occur. [Footnote omitted.] U.S. v. Williams, 583 F.2d 1194, 1197 (2d Cir. 1978).

Before the evidence of **spectrograph** [4] analysis can be admitted, the prosecutor must lay a proper foundation of proof of the accuracy of the scientific and mechanical instruments used in the test. [[4] The **spectrograph** has been thus described: The sound **spectrograph** consists of 4 basic parts: (1) a magnetic recording device, (2) a variable electronic filter, (3) a paper-carrying drum that is coupled to the magnetic recording device, and (4) an electric stylus that marks the paper as the drum rotates. The magnetic recording device is used to record a short sample of speech. The duration of the speech sample corresponds to the time required for one revolution of the drum. Then the speech sample is played repeatedly in order to analyze its spectral contents. For each revolution of the drum, the variable electronic filter passes only a certain band of frequencies, and the energy in the frequency band activates the electric stylus so that a straight line of varying darkness is produced across the paper. The degree of darkness represents the varying amplitude of the speech signal at the specified time within the given frequency band. As the drum revolves, the variable electronic filter moves to higher and higher frequencies, and the electric stylus moves parallel to the axis of the drum. Thus, a pattern of closely-spaced lines is generated on the paper. This pattern, which is the spectrogram, has the dimensions of frequency, time, and amplitude. United States Department of Justice, Voice Identification Research—A Summary of the Report to the Law Enforcement Assistance Administration, Grant No. NI–70–004, February 1971, at 9.] People v. Tobey, 231 N.W.2d 403, 408 (Ct.App.Mich.1975).

A "**spectrograph**" is an apparatus or instrument for the photographing of or mapping a spectrum. The sound **spectrograph** shows how the speech spectrogram varies from instant to instant.

Other **spectrographs** are used in analyzing other types of spectrums in addition to sound **spectrographs**. Examples are spectrums in the field of chemistry and light.

A sound **spectrograph** is an instrument which can translate acoustical sounds made by voices, engines or machinery. The **spectrograph** translates by electronic process the sounds into a pictorial representation of the sounds. People v. King, 72 Cal.Rptr. 478, 485 (Ct.App.Cal.1968).

Other Authorities: People v. Rogers, 385 N.Y.S.2d 228, 232 (Sup.Ct.Kings Cty.1976).

spectrography

Spectrography is qualitatively different from polygraph evidence. In **spectrography**, the examiner merely compares spectrograms reflecting the purely physical characteristics of a voice. In polygraph analysis, the examiner must go on, to extrapolate a judgment of something not directly measured by the machine, i.e., the credibility of the person examined. Commonwealth v. Lykus, 367 Mass. 191, 327 N.E.2d 671 (1975). The skill of the polygraph examiner, the kinds of questions asked, natural variations in blood pressure among individuals, and in how accustomed they are to lying, are unpredictable variables that make the polygraph technique far more speculative than is **spectrographic** analysis. U.S. v. Williams, 583 F.2d 1194, 1197 (2d Cir. 1978).

spectrometer (spek-trom'ĕ-ter) 1. an instrument for measuring the index of refraction by measuring the external angle of a prism of the substance. 2. a spectroscope for measuring the wavelengths of rays of a spectrum.

spectrometer, mass an analytical instrument which identifies a substance by sorting a stream of electrified particles (ions) according to their mass; the sorting is most commonly done as follows: when the stream of charged particles enters a magnetic field, it is deflected into a semicircular path, ultimately striking a photographic plate or photomultiplier tube sensor. Called also *mass spectrograph*.

The principal product is a **mass spectrometer**, known commercially as "medspec," which is used in hospitals to monitor body fluids during operations. It is an expensive and complicated device which analyzes the compositions of these fluids by a computation of the different atomic weights, and it ranges in price from $15,800 to $30,000. McAdory v. Scientific Research Instruments, Inc., 355 F.Supp. 468–9 (D.Md.1973).

spectrophotometer (spek"tro-fo-tom'ĕ-ter) [*spectrum* + *photometer*] an apparatus for estimating the quantity of coloring matter in solution by the quantity of light absorbed (as indicated by the spectrum) in passing through the solution.

Gleason testified that he had performed **spectrophotometer** analysis upon appellant's urine, using an emit **spectrophotometer** machine. He was properly qualified as an expert in the theory and use of this machine. He interpreted the results of the test he performed upon appellant's urine as showing the urine contained "morphine or an opiate derivative." He agreed, however, that solely upon the basis of this test it was "impossible" to determine whether the urine contained morphine or codeine. Roberts v. State, 537 S.W.2d 461–2 (Ct. Crim.App.Tex.1976).

spectrum (spek'trum), pl. *spec'tra* [L. "apparition"] a charted band of wavelengths of electromagnetic vibrations obtained by refraction and diffraction. By extension, a measurable range of activity, such as the range of bacteria affected by an antibiotic (antibacterial s.) or the complete range of manifestations of a disease. See also *spectrum, invisible*; and *spectrum, visible*.

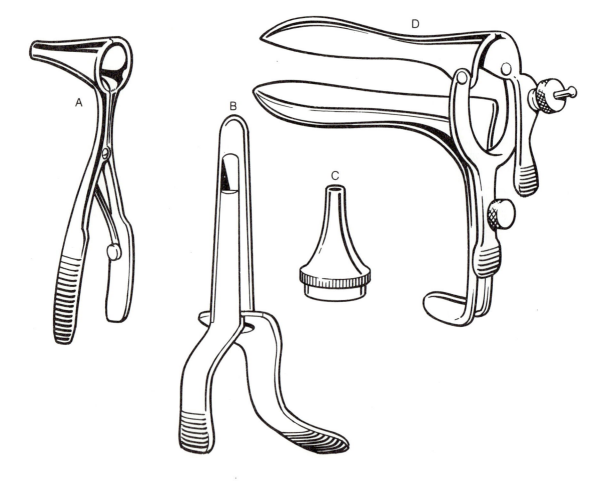

Specula: *A*. Vienna nasal speculum; *B*. Brinckerhoff rectal speculum; *C*. speculum for otoscope; *D*. Graves vaginal speculum.

A "**spectrum**" is a series of images. In this case the **spectrum** involves a series of radiant energies arranged in order of wave lengths. The speech **spectrum** is concerned with the frequency and intensity of each overtone of the speech wave. People v. King, 72 Cal.Rptr. 478, 484 (Ct.App.Cal.1968).

spectrum, invisible that made up of vibrations of wavelengths less than 3900 A.U. (ultraviolet, grenz rays, x-rays, and gamma rays) and between 7700 and 120,000 A.U. (infrared).

spectrum, visible that portion of the range of wavelengths of electromagnetic vibrations (from 7700 to 3900 A.U.) which is capable of stimulating specialized sense organs and is perceptible as light.

speculum (spek'u-lum), pl. *spec'ula* [L. "mirror"] an instrument for exposing the interior of a passage or cavity of the body.

A **speculum** is an appliance for opening a passage of the body to view. Rainer v. Buena Community Memorial Hospital, 95 Cal.Rptr. 901, 904 (Ct.App.1971).

... that he used a **speculum** to examine the uterus, which he thought was retroflexed, and he assumed "that we were going to deal with possibly a spontaneous abortion if nothing was done." Russo v. Commonwealth, 148 S.E.2d 820, 824 (Va.1966).

speech (spēch) the utterance of vocal sounds conveying ideas. See also *spectrogram*.

All **speech** is composed of several frequencies produced simultaneously; a fundamental frequency and several overtones having frequencies which are even multiples of the fundamental.

An individual's **speech** is created by a complex physiological and mechanical operation. The waves generated by the vocal cords are modified by vocal cavities (throat, nose, and cavities formed in the mouth by positioning the tongue), and by articulators (lips, teeth, tongue, palate and jaw muscles). The vocal cavities act as resonators which cause sound energy to be reinforced in specific sound spectrum areas, dependent upon the size, shape and interrelationship of the cavities. The articulators cooperate in a controlled dynamic interplay in the production of intelligible **speech**. The manner in which each of us manipulates his articulators when speaking has been developed by a process of imitation and trial and error. U.S. v. Williams, 583 F.2d 1194, 1196 (2d Cir. 1978).

According to Kersta, **speech** is produced by a complex physiological and mechanical operation within the body which, once developed basically never changes after puberty and cannot be disguised or concealed by mimicry, illness, passage of years or objects within the speaker's mouth. It is Kersta's contention that the unique pattern of **speech** once developed for an individual is substantially unchanged by age.

He testified that **speech** begins with the exhalation of air past vocal cords. The vocal cords are set in vibration and make a buzzing sound. The energy created by the vibration of the vocal cords is modified by two vocal tract functions. First, the vocal cavities affect the concentration of energy in certain parts of the pharyngeal or throat cavities. The size of these cavities is dependent upon the location of the tongue and the nasal cavities which exist in the nose and sinuses. People v. King, 72 Cal.Rptr. 478, 486 (Ct.App.Cal.1968).

speed See *methamphetamine*.

spermaceti (sper"mah-set'e) [Gr. *sperma* seed + *kētos* whale] a waxy substance obtained from the head of the sperm whale, *Physeter macrocephalus*, occurring as white, somewhat translucent, slightly unctuous masses, having a crystalline fracture and a pearly luster; used in the preparation of ointment bases, such as cold cream and rose water ointment. See also *Lotrimin*.

Lotrimin cream contains **spermaceti**, a waxy substance derived from the sperm whale....

The **spermaceti** utilized by the plaintiff in the manufacture of Lotrimin cream was purchased from the Werner G. Smith Company throughout the period 1974–1975. Delbay Pharmaceuticals v. Department of Commerce, 409 F.Supp. 637, 640 (D.D.C.1976).

spermatozoa (sper"mah-to-zo'ah) [Gr.] plural of *spermatozoon*.

spermatozoon (sper"mah-to-zo'on), pl. *spermatozo'a* [*spermato-* + Gr. *zōon* animal] a mature male germ cell, the specific output of the testes. It is the generative element of the semen which serves to fertilize the ovum. It consists of a head (or nucleus), a neck, a middle piece, and a tail with an end piece. Spermatozoa, formed in the seminiferous tubules, are derived from spermatogonia, which first develop into spermatocytes, which, in turn, undergo meiosis to produce spermatids; the spermatids then differentiate into spermatozoa.

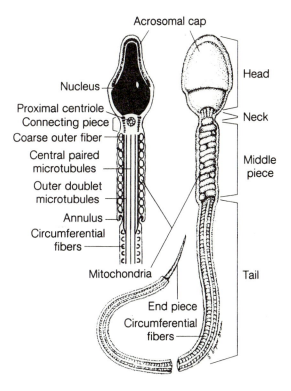

Human spermatozoon: side view (in cross-section) and flat view.

spermatozoon

Spermatozoa are recognizable much longer than the time mentioned for the physical appearance of semen. The detectable presence of **spermatozoa** diminishes but not in the same way as acid phosphatase. People v. Bynum, 483 P.2d 1193, 1195 (Cal.1971).

SPF specific-pathogen free, a term applied to animals reared for use in laboratory experiments, and known to be free of specific pathogenic miscroorganisms.

The Kleen-Leen program for delivering **SPF** stock is described in its sales brochure:

In the primary **SPF** process, pigs are taken from the sow by hysterectomy and raised in Kleen-Leen's laboratory environment for several weeks. Thus, the sow-to-pig disease link is broken, making new hog health standards possible. Pigs leave the laboratory free of virus pneumonia, atrophic rhinitis and vibrionic dysentery since the sow-to-pig disease link is broken.

"Freedom from these specific disease organisms, as well as freedom of parasites, lice and mange, passes from generation to generation, so long as hogs are not exposed to these diseases and parasites. Arlie Larimer & Sons, Inc. v. Kleen-Leen, Inc., 523 F.2d 865, 867 (6th Cir. 1975).

Plaintiff had started in a disease control program on breeding stock known as **SPF** in 1965 by purchasing some gilts and a boar from accredited herds. The initials stand for "**Specific Pathogen Free.**" It is a group that has been founded to administer a program for the control of the two chronic respiratory diseases of swine, atrophic rhinitis and the chronic mycoplasmal pneumonia formerly called virus pneumonia....

The swine must be tested for Brucellosis and a veterinarian must make a quarterly report in regard to health and disease. He makes visual inspection to determine the problems, if any, the farmer is having with his herd, what type of precautions he takes on his farm and what visitor control he might have. This report is sent to the national office in Conrad, Iowa.

It is further required that after the herd is started and sows farrow and the litter is brought along, 10 head of butcher hogs must be taken to slaughter for visual inspection before any can be sold. If they pass visually, they are then accredited. Winter v. Honeggers' & Co., Inc., 215 N.W.2d 316, 318 (Iowa 1974).

sphincter (sfingk'ter) [L.; Gr. *sphinktēr* that which binds tight] a ringlike band of muscle fibers that constricts a passage or closes a natural orifice; called also *musculus sphincter* [NA].

sphincter, O'Beirne's circular muscle fibers in the wall of the large intestine at the junction of the sigmoid colon and rectum.

According to expert testimony adduced at trial, the result of this repeated vomiting and nausea was an inflammation and scarring of the **sphincter** valve between Andrea's stomach and esophagus. This inflammation and scarring allegedly limited the effectiveness of the valve so that it could no longer keep the contents of the stomach from entering the esophagus. The entry of stomach contents produced further scarring, which, in turn, led to further regurgitation. Mendoza v. Varon, 563 S.W.2d 646–8 (Ct.Civ.App.Tex.1978).

sphincter muscle See *musculus sphincter ani externus.*

sphincter valve See *sphincter, O'Beirne's.*

sphincterotomy (sfingk"ter-ot'o-me) [*sphincter* + Gr. *tomēa* cutting] division of a sphincter.

In August, 1978, Dr. Ignatov performed a **sphincterotomy** at Evanston Hospital to remove the sphincter from the urinary canal. After the surgery David had no control over urination and needed a constant bag attachment. Kinsey v. Kolber, 431 N.E.2d 1316, 1319 (App.Ct.Ill.1982).

A **sphincterotomy** is the division of a sphincter. A sphincter is a ring-like band of muscle fiber that constricts a passage or closes a natural orifice.* [* Dorland's Illustrated Medical Dictionary (25th ed. 1974).] Langton v. Brown, 591 S.W.2d 84, 86 (Mo.Ct.App.1979).

sphingolipidosis (sfing"go-lip"ĭ-do'sis), pl. *sphingolipidoses.* A general designation applied to diseases characterized by abnormal storage of sphingolipids, such as Gaucher's disease, Niemann-Pick disease, generalized gangliosidosis, and Tay-Sachs disease.

sphingolipidosis, cerebral a group of hereditary disorders transmitted as an autosomal recessive trait and due to an inborn defect of lipid metabolism in which spingolipids accumulate in the brain. They are characterized by cerebromacular degeneration, progressive dementia, progressive loss of vision resulting in blindness, paralysis, and death, and are classified according to age of onset. The *infantile form* usually occurs between 4 and 6 months of age, chiefly affecting children of Jewish ancestry, and marked by a cherry-red spot with a gray-white border on both retinas; called also *Sachs'* or *Tay-Sachs disease.* The *late infantile form* occurs between 3 and 4 years of age, shows no racial predilection, and progresses more slowly than the infantile form. The cherry-red spot seen in the infantile form is frequently absent, but there are pigmentary changes of the retina. Called also *Bielschowsky's* or *Bielschowsky-Jansky disease.* The *juvenile form* shows no racial predilection, occurs between 5 and 10 years of age, and is marked by "salt and pepper" pigmentation of the retina; called also *Batten-Mayou, Spielmeyer-Vogt,* and *Vogt-Spielmeyer disease.* The *late juvenile,* or *adult, form* occurs between the ages of 15 and 26, and shows no racial predilection or occular lesions; clinical findings are those of cerebellar or basal ganglia disorders. Called also *Kufs' disease.* See also *disease, Tay-Sachs.*

sphygmograph (sfig'mo-graf) [*sphygmo-* + Gr. *graphein* to write] an instrument for registering the movements, form, and force of the arterial pulse. Vierordt's sphygmograph (1835) and Marey's (1860) were the earliest. The latter, variously modified, is the kind principally used. See also *polygraph* (Romero case).

sphygmomanometer (sfig"mo-mah-nom'ĕ-ter) an instrument for measuring blood pressure in the arteries. There are many forms of the instrument, each named for the person who devised it, as *Riva-Rocci s., Faught's s., Erlanger's s., Janeway's s., Mosso's s., Rogers' s., Staunton's s., Tycos s.*

Keen's testimony relating to her use of a **sphygmomanometer** to periodically check Robert Keen's blood pressure over a period of 10 to 15 years clearly "opened the door" for further cross-examination relating to the manner and degree her deceased husband was being treated for blood pressure related problems. Keen v. Detroit Diesel Allison, 569 F.2d 547, 553 (10th Cir. 1978).

spica (spi′kah) [L. "ear of wheat"] a figure-of-8 bandage with turns that cross one another usually at the shoulder or hip. See also under *bandage*.

spike (spīk) a sharp upward deflection in a curve, such as the main deflection of the oscillographic tracing of the action potential wave, the following smaller wave being called the *after-potential*. See also under *potential*.

On October 9 and 10 he had a "spiking" fever that varied from 99 to 103 degrees. Though the **spikes** were not ascending, those symptoms could indicate sepsis—a serious, continuing, blood infection. His pulse and blood pressure also fluctuated markedly, and four units of whole blood were administered. Franz v. Bd. of Medical Quality Assur., 642 P.2d 792, 795 (Cal.1982).

The surgery was uneventful and appellant made good progress in recovery except for his inability to swallow the 5:00 p.m. capsule and a **spiking** of temperature around 2:00 p.m. A **spiking** is a brief but pronounced elevation of temperature and is considered a normal response to tissue trauma but it may be caused by infectious organisms entering the blood stream. Folk v. Kilk, 126 Cal.Rptr. 172, 176 (Ct.App.Cal.1975).

spiking See *spike*.

spina (spi′nah), pl. *spi′nae* [L.] a spine: a thornlike process or projection; [NA] a general term for such a process.

spina bifida a developmental anomaly characterized by defective closure of the bony encasement of the spinal cord, through which the cord and meninges may (s. bifida cystica) or may not (s. bifida occulta) protrude.

Prompt surgical treatment can save children with **spina bifida** (exposure of the spinal cord) from death but cannot save them from a life of partial paralysis, moderate to severe mental retardation, and complete dependence upon others for the simplest body functions. American Academy of Pediatrics v. Heckler, 561 F.Supp. 395–6 (D.D.C.1983).

Appellant's prior condition is known as "**spina bifida**," . . . .
. . . In Mr. Green's case, the condition apparently resulted in the exposure of sacral nerve roots, which were injured or damaged during surgery. Had respondent discovered this condition before surgery, he would have utilized different surgical techniques which apparently would have avoided the injury. Green v. Larkin, 245 N.W.2d 454–5 (Minn.1976).

spina bifida cystica spina bifida in which there is protrusion through the defect of a cystic swelling involving the meninges (meningocele), spinal cord (myelocele), or both (meningomyelocele).

spina bifida occulta spina bifida in which there is a defect of the bony spinal canal without protrusion of the cord or meninges.

X-rays showed a spina bifida occulta of the first sacral segment of the spine. Generella v. Weinberger, 388 F.Supp. 1086, 1087 (E.D.Pa.1974).

A **spina bifida occulta** of S1 segment was noted. Barats v. Weinberger, 383 F.Supp. 276, 281 (E.D.Pa.1974).

spinal (spi′nal) [L. *spinalis*] pertaining to a spine or to the vertebral column. See also under *animal*; and *cord, spinal*.

spinal accessory nerve See *nervi spinales*; and *nervus accessorius*.

spinal anesthetic See *anesthesia, spinal*; and *puncture, lumbar*.

spinal cord See *cord, spinal*; and *decompression of spinal cord* (Warner case).

spinal fusion See *spondylosyndesis*.

spinal-jack operation See *operation, spinal-jack*.

spinal nerve root See *radices spinales nervi accessorii* under *radix*.

spinal tap See *puncture, lumbar*.

spine (spīn) the spinal column (columna vertebralis [NA]). See also *back; disk*; and *vertebra*.

The surgery would involve the removal of all bone and swollen tissue around the joints from the last two or three levels of the **spine**. The object of the operation is to allow the spinal fluids to flow freely through the spinal column. In this patient, the area from "L3 to the sacrum" were affected. The surgery, which is four or five times more involved than the surgery for a ruptured disc, requires a three week stay in the hospital, at a cost of approximately $5,600. The surgery involves the risk of possible death, paralysis, and a non-success rate of ten to twenty percent. After the operation, the plaintiff would be required to undergo physical therapy. He would have to wear a corset for the rest of his life and would experience pain for the rest of his life. Coleman v. Douglas Public Service, Inc., 423 So.2d 1205, 1207 (Ct.App.La.1982).

Petitioner's counsel inquired, "what area of the body do you consider to be the **spine**?" He answered: "When you say the **spine**, of course, I was asked for examination of the back. I think that should have been examination of the **spine** because the back doesn't include the neck, but when you say **spine**, the **spine** includes everything from the occiput [back of the head] where the first cervical vertebra attaches to the skull down to the end of the coccyx." It does not include the head. Ascough v. Workmen's Comp. Appeals Board, 98 Cal.Rptr. 357, 362 (Ct.App.Cal.1971).

By way of explanation, the human **spine** consists of various segments of bone. In between the vertebral bones is cartilaginous material, commonly referred to as discs, which take part in the movement of the **spine** and perform the function of a shock absorber. Starting from the top of the **spine** downward, the first seven vertebrae are called cervical vertebrae; the next twelve, thoracic (or dorsal); the next five lumbar, followed by the sacrum, and then the coccyx—commonly called the tail bone. The medical profession has assigned numbers to these various vertebrae, and those of the lumbar region from top to bottom are numbered L1, L2, L3, L4 and L5. The segments of the sacrum are also numbered, and the first segment is S1, followed by S2 and S3. When reference is made, for instance, to the L4 L5 interspace, this means the space between the fourth and fifth lumbar segments. Likewise, the L5 S1 intervertebral space refers to the space between the fifth lumbar and the first sacral segments which is occupied by the L5 S1 disc. Hart v. Van Zandt, 399 S.W.2d 791, 793 (Tex.1965).

spine, bamboo the ankylosed spine produced by rheumatoid spondylitis; so called because of the roentgenographic appearance caused by lipping of the vertebral margins.

Drs. Shanker and Stuhr found an arthritic condition known medically as ankylosing spondylitis, or "**bamboo spine.**" That condition conceivably would have rendered the spinal column more liable to fracture. Brazil v. U.S., 484 F.Supp. 986, 988 (N.D.Ala.1979).

spine, cervical See *vertebrae, cervical.*

spine, lumbar See *vertebrae, lumbar.*

spine, thoracic See *vertebrae thoracic.*

spirit (spir'it) [L. *spiritus*] a solution of a volatile material in alcohol.

spirit, camphor [USP], a solution of camphor and alcohol, each 100 ml. of which contains 9–11 gm. of camphor; used topically as a local irritant. It was formerly used for the treatment of diarrhea, and in hysteria and nervous excitement.

. . . that **spirits of camphor** has an astringent action on the skin and is also antipruritic. Folds v. Federal Trade Commission, 187 F.2d 658–9 (7th Cir. 1951).

spirits of camphor See *spirit, camphor.*

spirogram (spi'ro-gram) [L. *spirare* to breathe + Gr. *gramma* a writing] a tracing or graph of respiratory movements.

"Respiratory wise, I feel that his **spirogram** would suggest that he could do less than moderate activity." Long v. Richardson, 334 F.Supp. 305, 309 (W.D.Va.1971).

spirometry (spi-rom'ĕ-tre) the measurement of the breathing capacity of the lungs.

Dr. Emory performed **spirometry** testing to evaluate the appellant's breathing capacity and checked her arterial blood gases. The **spirometry** test was within normal limits and there was a mild reduction of oxygen in the arterial blood gases due to obesity. Sellers v. Breaux, 422 So.2d 1231, 1234 (Ct.App.La. 1982).

spironolactone (spi-ro"no-lak'tŏn) [USP] chemical name: 7α-(acetylthio)-17-hydroxy-3-oxo-pregn-4-ene-21-carboxylic acid γ-lactone acetate. A spirolactone, $C_{24}H_{32}O_4S$, occurring as a light-cream-colored to light tan, crystalline powder; it is an aldosterone antagonist, which increases urinary excretion of sodium and chloride, reduces excretion of potassium and ammonium and decreases the titratable acidity of urine. It is used in treatment of edema and ascites of hepatic cirrhosis, edema of congestive heart failure, and nephrotic syndrome.

Spironolactone is an anti-aldosterone agent, covered by a patent issued to Searle. Searle markets it under the trade name **Aldactone. Aldactone** is a potassium-sparing diuretic useful in the treatment of edema and in the treatment of hypertension. . . .

Spironolactone (a patented compound marketed by Searle) and triamterene (patented by SKF) are both potassium sparing diuretics. When used alone or in conjunction with other diuretics, such as thiazides, they reduce the potassium loss associated with those other diuretics. U.S. v. Ciba Geigy Corp., 508 F.Supp. 1118, 1131–2, 1154 (D.N.J.1976).

spleen (splēn) [Gr. *splēn;* L. *splen*] a large glandlike but ductless organ situated in the upper part of the abdominal cavity on the left side and lateral to the cardiac end of the stomach. Called also *lien* [NA]. It is of a flattened oblong shape and about 125 mm. long, the largest structure in the lymphoid system; it has a purple color and a pliable consistency, and is distinguished by two types of tissue: red pulp and white pulp (see under *pulp*). It disintegrates the red blood cells and sets free the hemoglobin, which the liver converts into bilirubin; gives rise to new red blood cells during fetal life and in the newborn; serves as a reservoir of blood, produces lymphocytes and plasma cells, and has other important functions, the full scope of which is not entirely determined. See also *polymorphonuclear* (Brissette case).

Surgery revealed the source of the bleeding to be a lacerated **spleen** which was surgically removed. Dr. Richter observed the **spleen** upon its removal and described it as looking like "an apple that's been cracked open." Dr. Richter did not recall any other signs of internal trauma. He stated that the condition of the **spleen** was the result of a traumatic injury, but could not identify the character of the injury other than to describe it as being like a "military injury," i.e., a major abdominal injury caused by an external force and one which was many hours old at the time it was first observed. . . .

On cross-examination, Dr. Richter described the location of the **spleen** as being in the upper left quadrant of the abdominal cavity and noted that the **spleen** can be torn by broken ribs. People v. Love, 373 N.E.2d 1312, 1314–15 (Ill.1978).

Generally, the doctors agreed that the functions of the **spleen**, after removal, are carried out by other organs in the body; and a person can carry out normal physiological functions without significant difficulty in the absence of the **spleen**, but that there are certain situations where it would be to one's advantage if it were still present. The **spleen**, being a part of the lymphatic system, traps infection as it comes through the bloodstream and would be needed most in the event of abdominal infection. . . .

From the testimony given by the several doctors, we can only conclude that plaintiff may have a healthy life without a **spleen**, but if attacked by serious infections its absence may be the difference between life and death. Huffman v. Young, 478 S.W.2d 332–3 (Mo.1972).

splenectomy (sple-nek'to-me) [splen- + Gr. *ektomē* excision] excision or extirpation of the spleen.

He considered pneumonia to be a common result following a **splenectomy** . . . .

... Aside from the surgical removal of the spleen, Dr. Custodio did not notice any other signs of trauma. People v. Love, 373 N.E.2d 1312, 1315 (Ill. 1978).

splint (splint) a rigid or flexible appliance for the fixation of displaced or movable parts. See also *splinting*.

splint, Gunning's an interdental splint used in treating fractured mandible or maxilla.

The final device mentioned by the District Court in connection with prior art was the **Gunning interdental splint**.[2] To make the **Gunning splint**, impressions are taken of the patient's teeth, and a cast model is made. At the point of fracture, the model is cut and the parts of the model comprising groups of teeth are adjusted and set to make a proper occlusion, thus moving any dislodged teeth to their normal position. The teeth are not dissected from the model in groups. [2 Dr. Gunning, a New York dentist, used such a splint to treat the broken jaw of Secretary of War Seward, who was injured at the time of President Lincoln's assassination.] T.P. Laboratories, Inc. v. Huge, 371 F.2d 231, 234 (7th Cir. 1966).

splint, interdental a plastic or metallic appliance for application to the dentition of the labial and/or lingual aspects to provide lugs for applying mandibular and/or maxillofacial traction or fixation. See also *splint, Gunning's*.

splinting (splint'ing) 1. in dentistry, the application of a fixed restoration to join two or more teeth into a single rigid unit. 2. rigidity of muscles occurring as a means of avoiding pain caused by movement of the part.

Dr. Behrans, who had been treating Walker since 1972, testified that she had observed muscle spasms on both the right and the left sides of Walker's back and further that she had noticed **splinting** of his back muscles when he moved. [Dissent.] Walker v. Rothschild Intern. Stevedoring Co., 526 F.2d 1137, 1141 (9th Cir. 1975).

At the trial the plaintiff's dentist testified that prior to the accident the plaintiff suffered from some loosening of teeth but that the violence of the collision, of which he was a victim, had further loosened his teeth, that they were "mobile," that "you could shake them with your fingers," and that he "**splinted** the teeth together to try to allow the bone to regenerate and tighten the teeth." Freer v. Parker, 192 A.2d 348–9 (Pa. 1963).

spondylitis (spon"dĭ-li'tis) inflammation of the vertebrae.

He testified that Alma had a congenital spinal defect, known as **spondylitis**, in the fifth lumbar vertebra. This defect consists of an incomplete development of the vertebra. Alma v. Manufacturers Hanover Trust Co., 684 F.2d 622, 624 (9th Cir. 1982).

spondylitis ankylopoietica; spondylitis ankylosans; spondylitis, ankylosing See *spondylitis rheumatoid*.

spondylitis, Marie-Strümpell See *spondylitis, rheumatoid*.

spondylitis, rheumatoid the form of rheumatoid arthritis that affects the spine. It is a systemic illness of unknown etiology, affecting young males predominantly, and producing pain and stiffness as a result of inflammation of the sacroiliac, intervertebral, and costovertebral joints; paraspinal calcification, with ossification and ankylosis of the spinal joints, may cause complete rigidity of the spine

and thorax. Called also *Bekhterev's disease* and *Marie-Strümpell disease*. See also *spine, bamboo*.

His diagnosis was that plaintiff suffers from **ankylosing spondylitis**, a type of rheumatoid arthritis that stiffens the joints and shows a predilection toward the central portion of the body....

... Based on the tests performed at Marianjoy Clinic along with his own examination, Dr. Rentschler stated that the **ankylosing spondylitis** was one of the reasons for the disability from which plaintiff is suffering, although he was somewhat equivocal about using the term ankylosing, which is a further state of development. Caterpillar Tractor Co. v. Industrial Com'n, 440 N.E.2d 861, 864 (Ill. 1982).

Dr. Kalmarides found positive straight leg raising at 10 degrees on the right side and 20 degrees on the left side, and "definite blurring of the L4–L5 facet in the right oblique view with ... evidence of loss of the joint space in this area." He also found "blurring of the joint space at the facet between L3 and L4 in the left oblique view." Dr. Kalmarides' opinion was that Mr. Aubeuf was suffering from "**spondylitis of the Marie-Strumpell type**." Aubeuf v. Schweiker, 649 F.2d 107, 111 (2d Cir. 1981).

The plaintiff's position on a stretcher and his pre-existing condition of **rheumatoid spondilitis**, which caused his head to tilt down and to the left side, made it difficult to obtain clear pictures. Simpson v. Sisters of Charity of Providence, etc., 588 P.2d 4, 7 (Or. 1978).

spondyloepiphyseal dysplasia See *syndrome, Morquio's*.

spondylolisthesis (spon"dĭ-lo-lis'the-sis) [*spondyl-* + Gr. *olisthanein* to slip] forward displacement of one vertebra over another, usually of the fifth lumbar over the body of the sacrum, or of the fourth lumbar over the fifth, usually due to a developmental defect in the pars interarticularis.

The child was suffering from a condition called **spondylolisthesis**, which causes destruction of ligaments and produces pressure on nerve structures because of an improper alignment of the vertebrae of the spinal column. Zimmerman v. New York City Health & Hospitals, 458 N.Y.S.2d 552, 554 (1st Dep't 1983).

He also testified that the X-rays revealed a significant displacement of this vertebra [fifth lumbar] at this point, a condition known as **spondylolisthesis**. It was his opinion that the fall had aggravated the congenital spinal defect, causing low back pain radiating down the right leg and resulting in permanent partial disability. Alma v. Manufacturers Hanover Trust Co., 684 F.2d 622, 624 (9th Cir. 1982).

Spondylolisthesis is a defect in one or more vertebrae....

This condition [**spondylolisthesis**] has two associations which are important. One is that patients who have a curvature of the spine of the idiopathic type, which this patient has, have a higher percentage of **spondylolisthesis** in the low back than the routine population. Second, the presence of **spondylolisthesis** tends to occur in families. In other words, if we have a patient with **spondylolisthesis**, the chances of another member in the family having it are much higher than one would find in the ordinary family. For a long time this led us to believe that the defect is an inherited defect, but subsequent studies have shown this is not always true. So current thinking is that the

662

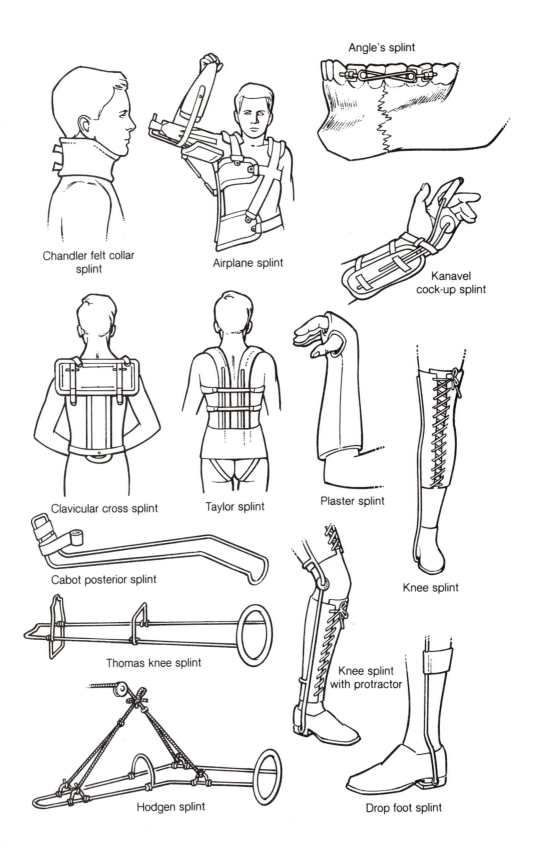

Angle's splint

Chandler felt collar
splint

Airplane splint

Kanavel
cock-up splint

Clavicular cross splint

Taylor splint

Plaster splint

Knee splint

Cabot posterior splint

Thomas knee splint

Knee splint
with protractor

Hodgen splint

Drop foot splint

VARIOUS TYPES OF SPLINT

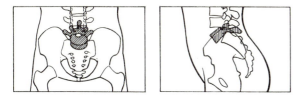

Spondylolisthesis of fifth lumbar vertebra over the sacrum (Meschan).

defect or tendency to develop a defect is inheritant. Albert v. Alter, 381 A.2d 459, 469 (Super.Ct.Pa.1977).

Other Authorities: D'Alfonzo v. Industrial Com'n, 440 N.E.2d 883–4 (Ill.1982); Furlong Const. Co. v. Industrial Com'n, 376 N.E.2d 1011–12 (Ill.1978); Strandberg v. Reber Co., 587 P.2d 18–19 (Mont.1978); Allen v. Weinberger, 552 F.2d 781, 785 (7th Cir. 1977); Spaulding v. Califano, 427 F.Supp. 982–4 (W.D.Mo.1977); Giles Industries v. Neal, 471 S.W.2d 5–6 (Ct.App.Ky.1971); Appalachian Regional Hospitals, Inc. v. Brown, 463 S.W.2d 323–4 (Ky.1971); W. P. Fuller and Co. v. Industrial Acc. Com'n, 27 Cal.Rptr. 401, 404 (D.Ct.App.Cal. 1962).

spondylolysis (spon″dĭ-lol′ĭ-sis) [*spondylo-* + Gr. *lysis* dissolution] dissolution of a vertebra; a condition marked by platyspondylia, aplasia of the vertebral arch, and separation of the pars interarticularis. See also *disease* (Giles Industries case).

Dr. Sonnier stated that in his examination of 1977 he had obtained x-rays on the plaintiff, which established a **spondylolysis** L–4, which put the plaintiff in a Class 4 category, unsuitable for heavy manual labor, which would not permit him to be hired by the Borden Company. The record indicates that **spondylolysis**, a defect of the bony architecture of the spine wherein fibral cartilage develops instead of true bone, is often asymptomatic and causes no problem. Trauma can aggravate the condition and make it symptomatic. In this regard, the trial judge noted that 10% of the population functioned well with such a congenital spinal defect. Alexander v. Leger, 423 So. 2d 731, 733 (Ct.App.La.1982).

He also introduced the testimony of Dr. Nettrour, his treating orthopedic surgeon, who testified by deposition that Claimant had a preexisting cervical **spondylolysis** (wear-and-tear changes) involving the lower cervical spine of which his employment as a butcher through vigorous use of his upper extremities was an aggravating condition. Lanzarotta v. Workmen's Compensation Appeal Bd., 400 A.2d 697, 699 (Commonwealth Ct.Pa.1979).

Dr. Casale diagnosed Yuhas' problem as "**spondylolysis** of the lumber spine". Dr. Casale defined this as follows:

Spondylolysis is a condition characterized by the failure of union, of portions of the posterior element of a vertebral segment. Such conditions are felt to be conductive to an underlying instability in the spine, thus effecting its function. Many of these cases remain asymptomatic until brought to light by some heavy exertion, accident or trauma....

... the referee had found that the moving of the piece of steel under the bundle, described hereinbefore, would have "required a good deal of exertion to release it". He also

found that "**spondylolysis** which is basically a displacement of the vertebrae due to degenerative joint disease" had been diagnosed as Yuhas' condition. Bethlehem Steel Corp. v. Yuhas, 303 A.2d 266–7 (Commonwealth Ct.Pa.1973).

Other Authorities: D'Alfonzo v. Industrial Com'n, 440 N.E.2d 883–4 (Ill.1982); McClaflin v. Califano, 448 F.Supp. 69, 71 (D.Kan.1978); Hinton v. S.S. Kresge Co., 592 P.2d 471, 474 (Ct.App.Kan.1978); Rund v. Cessna Aircraft Co., 518 P.2d 518, 522 (Kan.1974); Giles Industries v. Neal, 471 S.W.2d 5– 6 (Ct.App.Ky.1971).

spondylosis (spon″dĭ-lo′sis) ankylosis of a vertebral joint; also, a general term for degenerative changes due to osteoarthritis.

Doctor Borne stated that plaintiff had both a cervical and a lumbar **spondylosis**. He testified that **spondylosis** is a term which is employed to indicate degenerative changes in the spine. Basically, it refers to a normal aging process which occurs from wear and tear throughout an individual's life. He thought that the **spondylosis** was aggravated by trauma, and, based upon what plaintiff told him, the trauma he referred to was the accident of November 22, 1975. Arceneaux v. Domingue, 370 So.2d 1262–3 (Ct.App.La.1979).

... a diagnosis of **spondylosis** (a gradual degeneration of the spinal bone structure) was entered on Purdham's medical records. Purdham v. Celebrezze, 349 F.2d 828, 830 (4th Cir. 1965).

Other Authorities: Mattson v. Prospect Foundry, Inc., 219 N.W.2d 435 (Minn.1974).

spondylosis, cervical degenerative joint disease affecting the cervical vertebrae, intervertebral disks, and surrounding ligaments and connective tissue, sometimes with pain or paresthesia radiating down the arms as a result of pressure on the nerve roots.

He diagnosed the condition as **cervical spondylosis**, which is described as a "degenerative joint disease" affecting the vertebra in the neck area along with their surrounding ligaments and connecting tissue. See Dorland's Illustrated Medical Dictionary (25th Ed.). Dr. Heilbrun recommended conservative treatment utilizing a soft neck brace and analgesics. Broadbent v. Harris, 698 F.2d 407, 409 (10th Cir. 1983).

He still felt that Benny Harrison was suffering from **cervical spondylosis**, a degenerative disease. Harrison v. South Central Bell Tel. Co., 390 So.2d 219, 221 (Ct.App.La.1980).

... finding claimant to be totally and permanently disabled as a result of the accident which aggravated the preexistent latent condition of cervical degenerative disc disease or **cervical spondylosis**. Cooper Stevedoring of La., Inc. v. Washington, 556 F.2d 268, 270 (5th Cir. 1977).

spondylosis, discogenic

X-rays taken of his cervical spine showed that the disc space between his 5th and 6th cervical vertebrae had been compressed. This narrowing of space, termed **discogenic spondylosis**, caused loss of feeling in Gibbs' right arm. When such condition involves only one level of the spine, it is thought to be caused from a trauma or injury, rather than from degenerative age. Gulf Ins. Co. v. Gibbs, 534 S.W.2d 720, 723 (Ct. Civ.App.Tex.1976).

spondylosyndesis (spon"dĭ-lo-sin'de-sis) [*spondylo-* + Gr. *syndesis* a binding together] operative immobilization or ankylosis of the spine; spinal fusion. See also *operation, Hibbs.*

Of course his back may get worse, and not only is a **spinal fusion** a dangerous procedure, because there is a significant possibility of its causing paralysis, but it often is unsuccessful in relieving pain. Abernathy v. Superior Hardwoods, Inc., 704 F.2d 963, 973 (7th Cir. 1983).

By October 8, 1974, Ms. Gallo still had symptomatic spondylolisthesis and Dr. Donaldson decided to operate. On November 4, 1974, Dr. Donaldson performed a **spinal fusion** from the fourth lumbar vertebra across the fifth lumbar vertebra and onto the sacrum. This surgery required two incisions, because bone chips had to be taken from the pelvis to graft onto the vertebra....

... The **fusion** was successful and, as a result, she had permanent limited motion in the lower back. Albert v. Alter, 381 A.2d 459, 469 (Super.Ct.Pa.1977).

... a **fusion** operation of her spine from the level of the L–4 lumbar vertebra to the sacroiliac joints. The bone chips for the **fusion** were taken from her right ilium crest. Generella v. Weinberger, 388 F.Supp. 1086–7 (E.D.Pa.1974).

Other Authorities: Spaulding v. Califano, 427 F.Supp. 982–3 (W.D.Mo.1977); Halsey v. Richardson, 441 F.2d 1230–1 (6th Cir. 1971); E. R. Squibb & Sons, Inc. v. Jordan, 254 So.2d 17–18 (Dist.Ct.App.Fla.1971); Purdham v. Celebrezze, 349 F.2d 828, 830 (4th Cir. 1965).

sponge (spunj) [L., Gr. *spongia*] an absorbent pad of folded gauze or cotton.

It is not uncommon to miss a **sponge**. A **sponge** is not too difficult to lose within the cavities of the human body. They can be misplaced fairly easily. Being a gauze type material, they can and do assume the makeup that is in there and the mixture of the fluids and so on. They assume the coloration of those fluids. By virtue of that, they can become camouflaged and that is one of the reasons they can be missed in the procedure....

... you have to develop visibility. You put in **sponges** to pack off the liver to the left and to the stomach to the right and the intestines below and the diaphragm above. These **sponges** come from the operating room nurses. They are put in there by the entire team meaning the first assistant puts **sponges** in, the surgeon also puts **sponges** in and the first assistant and second assistant would also be putting **sponges** in. Everybody takes **sponges** out. The scrub nurse also handles **sponges** by handing them to the first assistant. Tice v. Hall, 303 S.E.2d 832, 835–6 (Ct.App.N.C.1983).

sponge count See *count, sponge.*

sponge, laparotomy See also *object, foreign.*

spontaneopneumothorax See *pneumothorax, spontaneous.*

spore (spōr) [L. *spora;* Gr. *sporos* seed] a refractile, oval body formed within bacteria, especially *Bacillus* and *Clostridium*, which is regarded as a resting stage during the life history of the cell, and is characterized by its

resistance to environmental changes. Called also *bacterial s.* See also *Clostridium tetani* (Germann case).

spotting See *bleeding, vaginal.*

... she began experiencing problems, such as bleeding between menstrual periods (**spotting**).... Hansen v. A. H. Robins Co., Inc., 715 F.2d 1265–6 (7th Cir. 1983).

Dr. Gentry, an expert witness called by plaintiff, stated that for a woman going through the change of life "excessive bleeding at menstrual times or the little **spotting** or bleeding at the ovulation time which she did is quite common ... but continuous bleeding, never," and that the symptoms of the plaintiff before the accident were typical of many women going through the change of life. Ketcham v. Thomas, 283 S.W.2d 642, 649 (Mo.1955).

sprain (sprān) a joint injury in which some of the fibers of a supporting ligament are ruptured but the continuity of the ligament remains intact.

He defined **sprain** as a tearing of supporting tissues around joints caused by movement of the joint beyond normal range. Pohl v. Gilbert, 280 N.W.2d 831, 833 (Ct.App.Mich.1979).

This patient represents a regressing **sprain** of the cervical, thoracic and lumbosacral spine....

... This type of spine, as characterized by the present x-rays, which show evidence of changes pre-existing this injury, is predisposed to strain, **sprain** or injury. Whereas the majority of **sprains** of this type tend to become quiescent in six to twelve weeks, as a general rule, with the presence of pre-existing changes in the spine and a congenital malposture, these symptoms will be markedly prolonged, in all likelihood. Gotschall v. Weinberger, 391 F.Supp. 73–4 (D.Neb.1975).

Ligamentous injury is another word for **sprain.**...

The attending physician defined the **ligamentous injury** in the lumbar area as a **sprain** similar to the reactions experienced from a sprained ankle, and his opinion, based upon X-ray evidence and symptoms of pain at the seat of the injury, was that the plaintiff sustained a 10-percent permanent impairment of the spine "as a whole." Colgan v. Raymond, 146 N.W.2d 530, 532 (Minn.1966).

Other Authorities: Hartford Acc. & Indem. Co. v. Contreras, 498 S.W.2d 419, 421 (Ct.Civ.App.Tex.1973).

sprain, lumbosacral

Dr. Edwards diagnosed claimant's injury as a **lumbosacral sprain** [a probable L4–5 disc on the right side, and possibly an L–5–S–1 disc on the right side]. Dr. Edwards found claimant to be in great pain which only moderated somewhat over the ensuing year....

"... Dr. Rambach also noted 'moderate paraspinal involuntary muscle spasm in the lower region of the spine and mid-lumbosacral area' (Page 5 of deposition, Line 5) and '... some weakness noted upon extension or straightening out or raising up of the great toe of the right foot' (Lines 17 and 18), etc., this on July 11, 1978...." Long v. Martin Timber Co. Inc., 395 So.2d 931–3 (Ct.App.La.1981).

sprue (sproo) a chronic form of malabsorption syndrome occurring in both tropical and nontropical forms; called also *catarrhal dysentery.*

Dr. Green testified that there is a disease called **sprue**, which is a defect in the lining membrane of the intestines that prevents food from being properly absorbed. Harrington v. State, 547 S.W.2d 616, 619 (Ct.Crim.App.Tex. 1977).

spur (sper) a projecting body, as from a bone. In dentistry, a piece of metal projecting from a plate, band, or other dental appliance. See also *osteophyte*.

Spurs also appeared on the left femur, and failure to remove them, he stated, would reduce the chances of clearing the infection and would cause pain if the plaintiff were to be fitted with a prosthetic appliance. Raines v. New York Cent. Railroad Co., 283 N.E.2d 230, 237 (Ill.1972).

spur, calcaneal a bone excrescence on the lower surface of the calcaneus which frequently causes pain on walking.

However, he noted a **calcaneal spur** on her left foot and described her ambulation as slow with short steps but without a limp. Lopez Diaz v. Secretary of Health, Ed. & Welfare, 585 F.2d 1137–8 (1st Cir. 1978).

spur, osteoarthropatic

At the expected place, the doctor found a ridge of bone three quarters of an inch long and a quarter of an inch wide which was pressing on and irritating the nerves. It was his opinion that this spur had compressed the spinal cord and damaged it. He removed the bone which he diagnosed as an **osteoarthropatic spur**. The operation left an eight inch scar on Mrs. Fritsche's neck. Fritsche v. Westinghouse Electric Corp., 261 A.2d 657, 659 (N.J.1970).

squamous portion of the temporal bone See *pars squamosa ossis temporalis*.

stable (sta′b'l) not moving, fixed, firm; resistant to change.

Stable (adjective): Durable; not subject to appreciable physical or chemical changes under normal environmental conditions, such as humidity and temperature, to which the material may be subjected. Shaw v. E.B. & A.C. Whiting Co., 157 U.S.P.Q. 405, 410 (D.Vt.1967).

By "**stable**" the doctor meant that the patient had improved to the extent that he was able to do some of his work without aggravation of pain to the severe degree he had at the onset of his condition. Welker v. MFA Central Co-operative, 380 S.W.2d 481, 485 (St.Louis Ct. of App. 1964).

staff (staf) the professional personnel of a hospital.

staff of Æsculapius a rod or staff with a snake entwined around it, which always appeared in the ancient representations of Æsculapius, the god of medicine. It is the symbol of medicine and is the official insignia of the American Medical Association.

staging (sta′jing) the determination of distinct phases or periods in the course of a disease, the life history of an organism, or any biological process.

He had supervised **staging** * of patients with lymphoma and testified that as a part of that procedure he had decided when and whether certain surgery should be performed. [* "**Staging**" refers to the investigative efforts of physicians to determine the extent of the disease, once the diagnosis is known. (R.T., Vol. II, pp. 169–170.)] Taylor v. Dirico, 606 P.2d 3, 9 (Ariz.1980).

stain (stān) any dye, reagent, or other material used in producing coloration, such as a substance used in coloring tissues or microorganisms for microscopical study. See *Table of Stains and Staining Methods* and names of specific compounds.

TABLE OF STAINS AND STAINING METHODS

stain, Gram's; Gram's method an empirical staining procedure devised by Gram in which microorganisms are stained with crystal violet, treated with 1:15 dilution of Lugol's iodine, decolorized with ethanol or ethanol-acetone, and counterstained with a contrasting dye, usually safranin. Those microorganisms that retain the crystal violet stain are said to be gram-positive, and those that lose the crystal violet stain by decolorization but stain with the counterstain are said to be gram-negative.

He further testified it is universal to do a **gram stain** with a culture sensitivity and that the clostridia bacteria which were detected by the test results of the 22nd of May could have shown on the 18th if the gram stain had been done. It was not too late to save the limb until the 18th. We are of the opinion that there is sufficient evidence to preclude an instructed verdict. Dr. Atchison's reply point is overruled.

Garza v. Keillor, 623 S.W.2d 669, 672 (Ct.Civ.App.Tex. 1981).

On September 10 it appeared from a laboratory report that a culture prepared with fluid taken from plaintiff's knee was "growing gram-positive bacteria," and Dr. Borders on the same day performed the second operation referred to above without waiting for the final laboratory analysis completed a day or two later. Contreras v. St. Luke's Hosp., 144 Cal.Rptr. 647, 654 (Ct.App.Cal.1978).

On Saturday, June 10th, defendant received the results from the culture and sensitivity tests which indicated that plaintiff had an aerobacter aerogenes bacteria that was **gram-negative**. Casey v. Penn, 360 N.E.2d 93, 97; supplemented 362 N.E.2d 1373 (App.Ct.Ill.1977).

Stain, Papanicolaou's a method of staining smears of various body secretions, from the respiratory, digestive or genitourinary tract, for the examination of exfoliated cells, to detect the presence of a malignant process.

Another test, known as the **smear test**, is used to determine in a general way the nature of the bacteria, i.e., gram-positive or gram-negative and spherical, rod-shaped or spiral. Defendant testified that it takes at least 48 hours to get the results from a culture and sensitivity test but that it takes less than 1 hour to get the results from a **smear test**, which would indicate the general class of drugs which would fight that type of bacteria. . . .

. . . A **smear test** was also done by the lab that day, the results of which indicated the plaintiff was infected with a gram-negative rod-shaped bacteria. Defendant testified that he did not see the report of the **smear test** results until two days later, on June 10th, although he was aware that it took less than one hour to make one. Casey v. Penn, 360 N.E.2d 93, 95, 97; supplemented 362 N.E.2d 1373 (App.Ct.Ill.1977).

---

staining, tooth See *tetracycline* (Dalke case).

standard of care See *care, standard of.*

stapedectomy (sta"pĕ-dek'to-me) [L. *stapes* stirrup + Gr. *ektomē* excision] excision of the stapes. See also *stapes.*

In July of 1973 Dr. Mark Grefenson performed a **stapedectomy** on appellant Lee LePelley, which is an operation involving the bones of the inner ear. . . .

. . . However, following the surgery, Mr. LePelley suffered even further hearing loss, dizziness and nausea. Following this unsuccessful surgery and several return visits to Dr. Grefenson which did not result in Mr. LePelley feeling any better, Mr. LePelley sought assistance from Dr. Goltry in Boise, who subsequently operated on Mr. LePelley and found a small bone fragment in his ear which was dropped during the **stapedectomy**. In his affidavit, Dr. Goltry stated that the dropping of a bone fragment in the ear is a risk of the **stapedectomy**. LePelley v. Grefenson, 614 P.2d 962, 964 (Idaho 1980).

A stapedectomy is surgery performed on persons who suffer air conduction hearing loss due to otosclerosis, but have not suffered severe bone conduction loss of hearing. The procedure is as follows: the middle ear is penetrated through an opening which has been made in the ear drum. The calcified stapes footplate and oval window are fractured, the pieces are removed, and a replacement is fashioned out of plastic, steel, fat, tissue, or other materials. Such an operation was performed on Mr. Warshaw's left ear in March, 1961; a piece of plastic tubing was used to replace the stapes, and a vein graft performed to close the oval window. The plastic tubing was fitted into the center of the vein graft; it transmits vibrations to the fluid in the inner ear. The vein graft, a flap of tissue taken from another vein in the body, closes off the opening to the inner ear and to the fluid chamber, while permitting vibrations to pass. The operation has a high probability of success when performed on patients who are amenable to such treatment; it was extremely successful in Mr. Warshaw's case. Warshaw v. Trans World Airlines, Inc., 442 F.Supp. 400, 403 (E.D. Pa.1977).

In July 1973, Ramirez underwent a surgical procedure called a **stapedectomy**, performed to alleviate a hearing problem. The procedure involves placement of a stapes prosthesis in the patient's ear. Ramirez v. U.S., 567 F.2d 854–5 (9th Cir. 1977).
Other Authorities: In re Estate of Lamb, 97 Cal.Rptr. 46–7 (Ct. App.Cal.1971).

stapes (sta'pēz) [L. "stirrup"] [NA] the innermost of the auditory ossicles, shaped somewhat like a stirrup; it articulates by its head with the incus, and its base is inserted into the fenestra vestibuli. Called also *stirrup*. See also *incus* (Anunti case); and *ossicula auditus* under *ossiculum.*

Some time after the surgery, Ramirez began to experience vertigo and a continued loss of hearing. To eliminate the condition, Ramirez underwent surgery a second time, in October 1973. The **stapes** prosthesis was removed. Ramirez v. U.S., 567 F.2d 854–5 (9th Cir. 1977).

staph See *Staphylococcus.*

Staphylococcus (staf"ĭ-lo-kok'us) [Gr. *staphyl* bunch of grapes + *kokkus* berry] a genus of microorganisms of the family Micrococcaceae, order Eubacteriales, that are the commonest cause of localized suppurative infections. Slightly less than 1μ in diameter and spherical in shape, they tend to form masses of cells.

Dr. Evans testified at his deposition that Sprague's diabetic condition was responsible for the ulcer on the right toe. A culture taken from this ulcer disclosed the presence of **staphylococcus aureus** [hereinafter "staph"], a type of bacteria. Sprague v. Director, Office of Workers' Comp., etc., 688 F.2d 862, 864 (1st Cir. 1982).

Dr. David found that plaintiff's burn was infected (**staphylococcus** infection) when he saw it on October 19, 1981, but he stated that such an infection was not a normal complication of a sprained ankle. Dr. David also stated with certainty that the wound appeared to be a burn with a secondary infection not a **staphylococcus** infection which looked like a burn. Jackson v. City of Alexandria, 424 So.2d 1265 (Ct.App.La.1982).

Dr. Bernard Siegel on redirect examination:
Q. What does the word 'staph' mean?
A. That is short for staphylococcus. . . .
Although no definition of "**staphylococcus**" was put in evidence, Dorland's Medical Dictionary describes it as a "spherical, gram-positive bacteria . . . Some species are pathogenic (giving origin to disease or morbid condition), and some are anaerobic (growing only in the absence of molecular oxygen), but most of the 20-odd species are non-pathogenic. The organisms are found in milk and other dairy products, or as free-living water forms. . . . Denneny v. Siegel, 407 F.2d 433, 436, 442 (3d Cir. 1969).

Staphylococcus aureus a species comprising the pigmented, coagulase-positive, mannitol-fermenting pathogenic form.

The experiment performed during the course of the Kehm trial and described by Chief Judge McManus, [Kehm v. Procter & Gamble Co., Civ. No. C 80–119 (N.D.Iowa June 29, 1982)] consisted of adding an enzyme, Betaglucosidase, to carboxymethyl-cellulose (CLD) chips taken from a Rely tampon with the intended result being the liquification of the chips into glucose. The experiment was intended to illustrate Dr. Tierno's theory that the staph infection associated with TSS is caused by the glucose acting as food for **staph aureus** bacteria. This results in increased production of **staph aureus** toxins which in turn combine with other factors to cause TSS. Wolf by Wolf v. Procter & Gamble Co., 555 F.Supp. 613, 626 (D.N.J.1982).

Dr. Coulter did not find any objective symptomatology other than a bacterial bronchitis which a sputum culture revealed to be caused by **staphylococcus aureus**. Sellers v. Breaux, 422 So.2d 1231, 1233 (Ct.App.La.1982).

"Staphylococci aureus" are microscopic plants, or bacteria, which are golden in pigment. Some of these organisms contain an enzyme termed "coagulase" which acts as a catalyst. **Staphylococci aureus** organisms that are "coagulase positive" may, under certain conditions, produce an "enterotoxin" which is poisonous to the human consumer. Safeway Stores, Inc. v. L. D. Schreiber Cheese Co., 326 F.Supp. 504, 507 (W.D.Mo.1971), reversed and remanded 457 F.2d 962 (8th Cir. 1972).

Other Authorities: Samuels v. Doctors Hospital, Inc., 414 F.Supp. 1124, 1126 (W.D.La.1976); Incollingo v. Ewing, 282 A.2d 206, 213 (Pa.1971); In re Sevigny's Case, 151 N.E.2d 258–9 (Sup.Jud.Ct.Mass.1958).

Staphylococcus epidermidis a species made up of non-pigmented, coagulase-negative, mannitol-negative nonpathogenic microorganisms commonly found on the skin.

He stated that both **staph epidermitis** [sic] and Proteus mirabilis are common in the environment and are no more likely to be found in a packing plant than in a home or hospital. However, **staph epidermitis** [sic] is part of the normal skin flora of human beings, and Proteus mirabilis is a part of the normal intestinal bacterial flora. He also offered that, with a couple of exceptions, it was almost unheard of for either bacteria to invade the skin in the absence of a preexisting wound or infection in that area. Union Packing Co. of Omaha v. Klauschie, 314 N.W.2d 25, 28 (Neb.1982).

. . . it was ultimately discovered that he had pneumonia and **staphylococcus epidermitis** [sic] which was resistant to the antibiotic (cloacillin) which the baby was receiving and he was switched to an "appropriate" antibiotic. . . .

. . . The **staph epidermitis** [sic] inhabits the skin of most people and it likely entered the baby through the skin. He said there was an unlikely possibility that it entered via the transfused blood. It could be via the intravenous, the umbilical arterial catheter or the endotracheal tube. Re Wintersgill and Minister of Social Services, 131 D.L.R. 184, 194 (Unified Fam.Ct., Sask.1981).

Starr-Edwards prosthesis See *prosthesis, Starr-Edwards.*

starvation (star-va′shun) long-continued deprival of food.

Assistant Medical Examiner Giles Green performed an autopsy on the body of the deceased. Dr. Green described the two year old child as follows:

This child was very small, a little girl, white girl. She was very thin, emaciated, ribs showing, little muscle development a

little muscle mass, at least in the arms or legs. She weighed, I think it was, twelve and three-quarters pounds, twenty-seven inches in height. . . .

Dr. Green's opinion was that the deceased had starved to death. She had been severely malnourished for a very substantial period of time. The child's death was the result of a very prolonged period of **starvation**. Harrington v. State, 547 S.W. 2d 616, 618 (Ct.Crim.App.Tex.1977).

stat. abbreviation for L. *sta′tim*, immediately.

In order to check for hemorrhage, at 10:50 p.m. Dr. Lund ordered an immediate ("stat") complete blood count. Although the lab technician normally goes home at 11 p.m., neither the hospital nor the doctor phoned the lab about the "stat" aspect of the blood count ordered. Cline v. Lund, 107 Cal.Rptr., 629, 633 (Ct.App.Cal.1973).

station (sta′shun) [L. *statio,* from *stare* to stand still] 1. the position assumed in standing; the manner of standing; in ataxic conditions it is sometimes pathognomonic. See *attitude.* 2. the location of the presenting part of the fetus in the birth canal, designated as -5 to -1 according to the number of centimeters the part is above an imaginary plane passing through the ischial spines, 0 when at the plane, and +1 to +5 according to the number of centimeters the part is below the plane. 3. a specified site to which the sick and wounded are brought.

station, Romberg the position assumed by the patient when the Romberg sign is being sought, i.e., standing upright with the feet close together.

stationary (sta′shun-er″e) [L. *stationarius*] not subject to variations or to changes of place.

"A [Dr. Peterson] Medically, when you say medically **stationary**, we assume it hasn't changed? And it hasn't changed any for months. So I guess we would have to consider it medically **stationary**." . . .

"The term '**stationary**' as used in the Arizona Workmen's compensation laws has not been statutorily defined, nor have we been able to find any indepth discussion of the term in Arizona case law. However, many Arizona appellate decisions have considered, in various contexts, whether an injured employee's condition has become '**stationary**' . . . . [Citations omitted] The thread running through all of these decisions is that the term '**stationary**' refers to that time when the physical condition of the employee resulting from the industrial injury has reached a relatively stable status so that nothing further in the way of medical treatment is indicated to improve that condition. We think that the meaning of the term '**stationary**' as used in workmen's compensation laws is well summarized by the Oregon Supreme Court in Dimitroff v. State Industrial Accident Commission, 209 Or. 316, 306 P.2d 398 (1957), as follows:

"We believe that the term '**stationary**', as applied to the condition of an injured workman, has become a 'term of art'. . . ."

"But we think it probable that in the administrative usage a workman's condition is considered "**stationary**" when he reaches the stage at which his restoration to a condition of self-support and maintenance as an able-bodied workman is found by the Commission on the basis of expert medical opinion to be as complete as it can be made by treatment." [Aragon v. Industrial Commission, 14 Ariz.App. 175, 481 P.2d 545

(1971).] Employers Mut.L.Ins.Co. of Wis. v. Industrial Com'n, 500 P.2d 308, 310–11 (Ct.App.Ariz.1972), opinion vacated and award of Commission reinstated 509 P.2d 1030 (Ariz. 1973).

status (sta'tus) [L.] state or condition.

status epilepticus a series of rapidly repeated epileptic convulsions without any periods of consciousness between them.

At that point, victim was apparently exhibiting some signs of a condition known as "**status epilepticus**," which is a condition of continuous seizures and which is fatal if intervening life saving measures are not taken. It seems, however, that defendant's manipulation and massaging of the victim afforded some relief and the seizure appeared to subside.

Several hours after the defendant left the residence the victim began suffering frequent and severe seizures which lasted over a period of about five hours from 6:00 p.m. to 11:00 p.m. After this series of seizures stopped the victim fell asleep. At about 5:00 a.m. the following morning, the victim died. People v. Cabral, 190 Cal.Rptr. 194–5 (Ct.App.Cal.1983).

Stelazine See *psychotic*; and *trifluoperazine hydrochloride*.

stellate (stel'āt) [L. *stellatus*] shaped like a star; arranged in a roset, or in rosets.

I believe that you stated that you found a rather large **stellate** wound in the kidney, star shaped wound in the kidney. Wolff v. Coast Engine Products, Inc., 432 P.2d 562, 567 (Wash.1967).

stenosis (stĕ-no'sis) [Gr. *stenōsis*] narrowing or stricture of a duct or canal.

In this worker's compensation case, a forty-two year old laborer with twenty-one consecutive years of apparent good health and essentially uninterrupted work record fainted at the conclusion of a strenuous work day. He was thereupon, for the first time, diagnosed as having had a long standing heart disease, aortic valvular **stenosis**.[1] . . . [[1] The disease is characterized by a constricted valve which restricts the amount of blood leaving the heart, and results in problems such as fainting, shortness of breath and/or chest pain.]

. . . The **stenosis**, or constriction, was brought on by the calcification of a defective valve over a period of years. Guillory v. U.S. Fidelity & Guar. Ins. Co., 420 So.2d 119–21 (La.1982).

The first of the seven operations, performed in January of 1974 by Dr. Woolam, was for a **stenosis** of the anastomosis, i.e., a stricture occurring after Dr. Bronwell's second operation at the place where the common duct had been cut. Bronwell v. Williams, 597 S.W.2d 542, 544 (Ct.Civ.App.Tex.1980).

The resultant condition, described by Dr. Booth as a **stenosis**, or scouring of the inner lining of the esophagus, a condition which restricts one's capacity to swallow, is likely to remain with Robert for an indeterminate period of time. Hawkins v. Ozborn, 383 F.Supp. 1389, 1392 (N.D.Miss.1974).

Other Authorities: Bergen v. Shah-Mirany, 404 N.E.2d 863–4 (App.Ct.Ill.1980).

stenosis, aortic a narrowing of the aortic orifice of the heart or of the aorta itself.

. . . an **aortic stenosis** situation, where work stress prompting an unsatisfied need for blood to the brain precipitated faint-ing. Daily v. Bechtel Power Corp., 420 So.2d 1337, 1342 (Ct.App.La.1982).

stenosis, mitral a narrowing of the left atrioventricular orifice (mitral orifice).

His condition was diagnosed as "**mitral stenosis** and insufficiency. Aortic insufficiency." An X-ray examination revealed findings "compatible with rheumatic mitral disease." Vecchiarello v. Board of Trustees, etc., 453 N.Y.S.2d 971–2 (Sup.Ct.N.Y.Cty.1982).

The initial operation was performed to relieve **mitral stenosis** caused by childhood rheumatic fever. The second operation was performed to replace a malfunctioning artificial mitral valve . . . . The abnormal valve removed demonstrated clot formations with fibrous tissue ingrowths which interfered with its function. Jamison v. Monarch Life Ins. Co., 652 P.2d 13, 15 (Ct.App.Wash.1982).

Mitral stenosis is a disease affecting the mitral valve in the heart. The valve gradually calcifies, deteriorates and closes, reducing pumping efficiency. Exhaustion, an enlarged liver, diastolic heart murmurs, varicose veins, and pretibial edema are all possible symptoms. . . .

. . . During the course of these visits he concluded that a **mitral stenosis** was present. He further testified that a narrow mitral valve opening cannot be seen and that his diagnosis of **mitral stenosis** was based on electrocardiograph interpretations provided by Dr. Gardner. Magruder v. Richardson, 332 F.Supp. 1363, 1367, 1370 (E.D.Mo.1971).

Other Authorities: Tschohl v. Nationwide Mut. Ins. Co., 418 F.Supp. 1124–5 (D.Minn.1976).

stenosis, spinal

Dr. Phillips posited that the plaintiff had **spinal stenosis**, which is a condition wherein the nerves of the back are encroached upon by an overgrowth of tissue from arthritis and an overgrowth of bone from the aging process. Dr. Phillips continued to treat the plaintiff with pain relievers and anti-inflamatory drugs and hospitalization was suggested. The plaintiff was required to wear a corset to prevent irritation of the affected area. Coleman v. Douglas Public Service, Inc., 423 So.2d 1205, 1207 (Ct.App.La.1982).

". . . In other words, to remove—I had to remove two laminae to get down into the canal. I found that this man had a much narrower canal than I had anticipated. The space that he had for his dural sac, I think, was probably about half of what I would normally see for a man of his build or for the normal lumbar vertebrae.

We have a name for this condition. It's called **spinal stenosis**, and it must be considered a congenital condition.

"Q.   All right.

"A.   In other words, he had adequate room for his nerve roots, but there wasn't any spare room. . . ." Perry v. Industrial Com'n, 539 P.2d 178, 181 (Ct.App.Ariz.1975), decision vacated and award of Industrial Commission reinstated 542 P.2d 1096 (Ariz.1975).

stent (stent) a mold for keeping a skin graft in place, made of Stent's mass or some acrylic or dental compound. By extension used to designate a device or mold of a suitable material, used to hold a skin graft in place or to provide support for tubular structures that are being anastomosed.

The tanning fluid fixes the valve in the inflated, closed position. After it is fixed, the valve is attached to a plastic ring, called a "**stent**", and is ready to be attached to a heart, which is done by suturing the **stent** to the heart wall. Hancock Laboratories v. American Hospital Supply, 199 U.S.P.Q. 279, 281 (N.D.III. 1978).

Sterane (ster'ān) trademark for preparations of prednisolone. See also *prednisolone*.

stereochemical (ste″re-o-kem'e-kal) pertaining to stereochemistry, or to the space relations of the atoms of a molecule.

The spacial arrangement of a molecule's substituents is known as its **stereochemical** configuration or orientation. Pfizer, Inc. v. International Rectifier Corp., 538 F.2d 180, 187 (8th Cir. 1976).

stereochemistry (ste″re-o-kem'is-tre) that chemical theory which supposes an arrangement of the atoms of certain molecules in three dimensional spaces; that branch of chemistry which treats of the space relations between atoms.

All three chemical compounds are molecules consisting of component groups of atoms, called substituents, in a configuration unique to each compound. Chemists are able to describe three dimensionally the molecular structure of each compound using the terminology of **stereochemistry**. The spacial arrangement of a molecule's substituents is known as its stereochemical configuration or orientation. Pfizer, Inc. v. International Rectifier Corp., 538 F.2d 180, 187 (8th Cir. 1976).

stereoencephalotomy (ster″e-o-en-sef″ah-lot'o-me) [*stereo-* + Gr. *enkephalos* brain + *tomē* a cutting] stereotaxic surgery. See also *mesencephalotomy; pallidotomy;* and *thalamotomy*.

As stated, a **stereotaxic operation** is a two-stage operative procedure utilizing special instruments, equipment and technique. During the course of the first stage, the inner square frame of a **stereotaxic frame** is affixed to the skull of the patient with three small inserts and skull screws. This enables the surgeon to remove the frame and later, during the second stage, accurately replace the frame in the same relative position on the patient's skull. The inner square frame of the **stereotaxic** instrument is calibrated upon three different planes. X-rays are taken of the patient's skull while the inner square frame is attached thereto. Through the use of the X-rays thus derived, the surgeon is able to locate his particular target with reference to all three dimensions and accurately chart the course that he will follow in reaching the selected area.

During the first stage, a trephine opening is made in the skull of the patient. A trephine is a circular cutting instrument used for penetrating the bone of the skull. In the instant case a d'Errico trephine with a 2-inch circumference was used. This instrument is applied to the patient's skull and then the circular blade is turned (with a tool similar to the carpenter's brace and bit), making an incision in the skull bone of the patient with the intent of cutting nearly through the skull bone leaving only a thin remaining shelf. During the course of the first stage, the button of bone thus made is not removed from the patient's skull but left in place until the performance of the second stage of the **stereotaxic procedure**. All of the first stage is performed while the patient is under a general anesthetic. After taking X-rays and incising a button of skull bone, the crevices in the skull are filled in with bone wax and gelfilm and the patient is released from the hospital to return home.

After a period of not less than six weeks convalescence the patient returns to the hospital for the performance of the second stage of the operation. The second stage of the two-step **stereotaxic operative procedure** is done under a local anesthetic. The inner square frame of the **stereotaxic** instrument is reaffixed to the skull of the patient using the prior small inserts to insure that the frame is accurately reaffixed in the same position that it was during the course of the first stage. The trephine instrument is then reapplied to the patient's skull and utilized to sever the fibrous tissue which has since grown in the crevice of bone and the remaining bone which was left after the incision of the first stage of the operation. The trephine is then tilted, breaking any slight remaining shelf of bone and the button of bone is lifted out. An electrode is then attached to the inner square frame of the **stereotaxic** instrument and set in a precise position in accordance with the prior calculations derived from the previously taken X-rays. This electrode is then introduced through the opening in the skull into the brain tissue of the patient to the target area the physician desires to inactivate. Through a testing procedure which entails the coordination of a considerable number of people: surgeon, anesthesiologist, electronic engineers, biophysicists, phychologists and assistant surgical personnel; the precise area is entered with the electrode and inactivated by causing a lesion due to heat. During this phase of the operation the patient is carefully and continuously monitored in order to see the degree of improvement and observe if anything untoward is happening. Belshaw v. Feinstein, 65 Cal.Rptr. 788, 790–1 (Ct.App.Cal.1968).

stereoisomer (ste″re-o-i'so-mer) a compound exhibiting, or capable of exhibiting, stereoisomerism.

stereoisomerism (ster″e-o-i-som'er-izm) [*stereo-* + *isomerism*] a type of isomerism in which two or more compounds possess the same molecular and structural formulas but different spatial or configurational formulas, the spatial relationships of the atoms being different, but not the linkages. Stereoisomerism is divided into two branches, *optical isomerism* (which includes enantiomorphism and diastereoisomerism), and *geometric isomerism*. See also *structural isomerism*, under *isomerism; mutarotation; racemization;* and *tautomerism*.

. . . **stereoisomerism**—a long known and predictable condition of certain chemical compounds in which two identical groups of atoms are linked in the same order, but differ in their arrangement in space. Simple analogies may be drawn to the left and right hand gloves from a single pair or to an object and its image in a mirror. The stereoisomers pertinent here are optical isomers, which means that one of the separate atomic groups, or isomers, will rotate a straight beam of light to the left and the other will rotate it to the right. The right rotating isomer is called the dextro or disomer, and its opposite is designated the levo or l-isomer. Eli Lilly & Co. v. Generix Drug Sales, Inc., 460 F.2d 1096, 1100 (5th Cir. 1972).

stereopsis See *vision, stereoscopic*.

When **stereopsis** is low, it means that the person's visual depth perception is low. [Dissent.] Jenkins v. Gardner, 430 F.2d 243, 253 (6th Cir. 1970).

stereoscopic (ste"re-o-skop'ik) having the effect of a stereoscope; giving to objects seen a solid or three-dimensional appearance.

stereotaxic (ste"re-o-tak'sik) 1. pertaining to or characterized by precise positioning in space; said especially of discrete areas of the brain that control specific functions. 2. pertaining to or exhibiting stereotaxis. See also *stereoencephalotomy*; and *surgery, stereotaxic*.

sterile (ster'il) [L. *sterilis*] aseptic; not producing microorganisms; free from living microorganisms. See also *Proteus* (Quick case).

An inanimate object, such as a thermometer, a sheath, a scalpel, a catheter, and the like, is said to be "sterile" when it is completely free of any kind of living microorganism. For this purpose, germicidal liquids or gases, as well as various forms of energy, such as heat, ultraviolet light and ultrasonic vibrations, may be used, the selection depending on a variety of applicable circumstances. Poncy v. Johnson & Johnson, 460 F.Supp. 795, 800 (D.N.J.1978).

The standards and regulations of the Maryland State Department of Health for the government of hospitals within the State included the following:

0405 **Sterile** Supply and equipment shall be stored in a suitable enclosed space, providing separation from unsterile supplies. Suburban Hospital Ass'n v. Hadary, 322 A.2d 258, 263 (Ct.Spec.App.Md.1974).

In fact the mouth is regarded as notoriously unsterile—ordinarily full of bacteria likely to produce infection at any time depending upon the condition and susceptibility of the person. For example see, Flanagan v. Smith, supra, 197 N.W. at 49; Mournet v. Sumner, supra, 139 So. at 731; Traverse v. Wing, supra, 152 N.E. at 355; Nevinger v. Haun, supra, 196 S.W. at 41. Germann v. Matriss, 260 A.2d 825, 831 (N.J.1970).

sterilize (ster'ĭ-liz) 1. to render sterile; to free from microorganisms. 2. to render incapable of reproduction.

In his opinion the proper procedure to **sterilize** an acrylic denture to be inserted in a patient's mouth immediately after the extraction of teeth would be first to cleanse it with carbolic acid and then to rinse it off in alcohol. That method would, in his opinion, eliminate any tetanus spores that might be on the denture. . . .

. . . At his office that evening he inserted in the carbolic acid an acrylic denture of the same kind as that given to Mrs. Germann. Within a few minutes the denture was completely destroyed even though it was thereafter immersed in alcohol. . . .

As has been indicated above, in light of all the evidence, we consider Dr. Graubard's testimony regarding the requirement for **sterilization** of the denture by means of carbolic acid and alcohol as quite insubstantial and ambiguous because he offered no real explanation as to how and under what conditions the **sterilization** should be done. Germann v. Matriss, 260 A.2d 825, 828, 831 (N.J.1970).

. . . the plaintiff, after giving birth to her second child, expressed a desire to have no more children and requested that she be **sterilized**. Two days later she underwent a bilateral tubal ligation performed by Doctors D. J. Hall and R. L. Hickok. After the surgery, Dr. Hickok filed an operation report and

submitted two excised portions of the fallopian tubes to the pathology department for examination. McNeal v. U.S., 689 F.2d 1200–01 (4th Cir. 1982).

Other Authorities: Ruby v. Massey, 452 F.Supp. 361, 366–7 (D.Conn.1978); Beary v. City of Rye, 406 N.Y.S.2d 9, 12 (N.Y. 1978); Walker v. Pierce, 560 F.2d 609, 611 (4th Cir. 1977); Bowman v. Davis, 356 N.E.2d 496, 498 (Ohio 1976); Walstad v. University of Minnesota Hospitals, 442 F.2d 634, 640 (8th Cir. 1971); State v. Weiner, 194 A.2d 467, 472–3 (N.J.1963).

sternocleidomastoid (ster"no-kli"do-mas'toid) pertaining to the sternum, clavicle, and mastoid process.

He had pains in the right groin and along the left **sternocleidomastoid**. Sinclair v. Lumbermen's Mut.Cas. Co., 388 So.2d 417–18 (Ct.App.La.1980).

sternocleidomastoid muscle See *musculus sternocleidomastoideus*.

sternocostoclabicular See *costoclavicular*.

sternum (ster'num) [L.; Gr. *sternon*] [NA] a longitudinal unpaired plate of bone forming the middle of the anterior wall of the thorax, and articulating above with the clavicles and along the sides with the cartilages of the first seven ribs. It consists of three portions, the manubrium, the body, and the xiphoid process.

Dr. Wadlington's final diagnosis was that plaintiff had received, in addition to head lacerations, contusions of the anterior chest cage and left ankle and a fracture of the **sternum** that was revealed by tomogram x-ray. Andrews v. Pine Hill Wood Co., 426 So.2d 196, 200 (Ct.App.La.1983).

steroid (ste'roid) a group name for lipids that contain a hydrogenated cyclopentophenanthrene-ring system. Some of the substances included in this group are progesterone, adrenocortical hormones, the gonadal hormones, cardiac aglycones, bile acids, sterols (such as cholesterol), toad poisons, saponins, and some of the carcinogenic hydrocarbons.

. . . an allegedly novel process for making certain known **steroids**.[1] [[1] The applicants described the products of their process as "2-methyl dihydrotestosterone derivatives and esters thereof as well as 2-methyl dihydrotestosterone derivatives having a C–17 lower alkyl group. The products of the process of the present invention have a useful high anabolic-androgenic ratio and are especially valuable for treatment of those ailments where anabolic or antiestrogenic effect together with a lesser androgenic effect is desired."] Brenner v. Manson, 383 U.S. 519, 520, 86 S.Ct. 1033, 1034, 16 L.Ed.2d 69 (1966).

A well recognized treatment of skin problems is the use of a class of drugs known as **steroids**, a kind of synthetic cortisone. Cortisone and all cortisone related drugs have significant and well-known side effects. Hill v. Squibb & Sons, E.R., 592 P.2d 1383, 1385 (Mont.1979).

Stevens-Johnson syndrome (ste'venz-jon'son) [Albert Mason *Stevens*, 1884–1945, and Frank Chambliss *Johnson*, 1894–1934, American pediatricians] See under *syndrome*.

stilbestrol See *diethylstilbestrol*.

Stilbetin See *diethylstilbestrol*.

stimulant (stim′u-lant) [L. *stimulans*] an agent or remedy that produces stimulation. See also *depressant* (Sundberg case and U.S. v. Schrenzel case).

[210 S.C.] § 321. Definitions; generally
For the purposes of this chapter— . . .
(v) The term "depressant or **stimulant** drug" means—
(1) any drug which contains any quantity of (A) barbituric acid or any of the sales of barbituric acid; or (B) any derivative of barbituric acid which has been designated by the Secretary under section 352(d) of this title as habit forming;
(2) any drug which contains any quantity of (A) amphetamine or any of its optical isomers; (B) any salt of amphetamine or any salt of an optical isomer of amphetamine; or (C) any substance which the Secretary, after investigation, has found to be, and by regulation designated as, habit forming because of its stimulant effect on the central nervous system; or
(3) lysergic acid diethylamide and any other drug which contains any quantity of a substance which the Secretary, after investigation, has found to have, and by regulation designates as having, a potential for abuse because of its depressant or **stimulant** effect on the central nervous system or its hallucinogenic effect; except that the Secretary shall not designate under this paragraph, or under clause (C) of subparagraph (2), any substance that is now included, or is hereafter included, within the classifications stated in section 4731, and marihuana as defined in section 4761 of Title 26. U.S. v. Robinson, 446 F.2d 562–3 (5th Cir. 1971).

stimulate (stim′u-lāt) to excite to functional activity.

stimulation (stim″u-la′shun) [L. *stimulatio*, from *stimulare* to goad] the act or process of stimulating; the condition of being stimulated.

The commercial exploitation of appellant's blood involved two separate steps: **stimulation** and plasmapheresis. **Stimulation** involved increasing the concentration of antibodies in her blood by injecting small amounts of selected human red blood cells into her blood; this procedure heightened her existing immunity to blood with a foreign Rh factor. . . .
The process of **stimulation** caused a number of unpleasant side effects, including dizziness, severe headaches and muscle aches, which lasted approximately two weeks after the injection of the foreign blood cells. U.S. v. Garber, 589 F.2d 843, 845 (5th Cir. 1979), reversed and remanded 607 F.2d 92 (5th Cir. 1979).

stimulator (stim″u-la′tor) any agent that excites functional activity.

. . . plaintiff wore a "transit nerve **stimulator**" consisting of two probes over the lower back that pulsate an electric current to ease pain. Caterpillar Tractor Co. v. Industrial Com'n, 440 N.E.2d 861, 863 (Ill.1982).

stimulator, electronic a device for applying electronic pulses or signals to activate muscles, to identify nerves, to treat muscular disorders, etc.

Electrical muscle stimulators are used to transmit a low voltage current through the skin, generally to trigger points in a muscle near the junction of nerves and muscle tissue thereby causing the muscle to contract. Dr. Wharton testified that he knew of no circumstances where a muscle stimulator would be used

with regard to the spine or spinal column. Norville v. Miss. State Medical Ass'n, 364 So.2d 1084–5 (Miss.1978).

stimulus (stim′u-lus), pl. *stim′uli* [L. "goad"] any agent, act, or influence that produces functional or trophic reaction in a receptor or in an irritable tissue.

stimulus, aversive one which, when applied following the occurrence of a response, decreases the strength of that response on later occurrences.

The summary of the evidence contained in the report of the magistrate showed that apomorphine had been administered at ISMF for some time prior to the hearing as "**aversive stimuli**" in the treatment of inmates with behavior problems. The drug was administered by intra-muscular injection by a nurse after an inmate had violated the behavior protocol established for him by the staff.
When it was determined to administer the drug, the inmate was taken to a room near the nurses' station which contained only a water closet and there given the injection. He was then exercised and within about fifteen minutes he began vomiting. The vomiting lasted from fifteen minutes to an hour. There is also a temporary cardiovascular effect which involves some change in blood pressure and "in the heart." This aversion type "therapy" is based on "Pavlovian conditioning." Knecht v. Gillman, 488 F.2d 1136–7 (8th Cir. 1973).

stimupulse

She has been fitted with a **stimupulse** which automatically administers electric shocks to reduce pain. Kosch v. Monroe, 433 N.E.2d 1062, 1070 (App.Ct.Ill.1982).

sting (sting) an injury caused by the venom of a plant or animal (biotoxin) introduced into the individual or with which he has come in contact, together with the mechanical trauma caused by the organ responsible for its introduction. See also *accident*.

Stokes-Adams See *disease, Adams-Stokes.*

stoma (sto′mah), pl. *sto′mas* or *sto′mata* [Gr. "mouth"] the opening established in the abdominal wall by colostomy, ileostomy, etc.; also the opening between two portions of the intestine in an anastomosis.

. . . passing the ileum out through an opening in the skin of the lower abdomen. The opening is called a **stoma** and an external collection device is cemented to the **stoma** to collect the urine passing out through the ileum. Harrigan v. U.S., 408 F.Supp. 177, 179 (E.D.Pa.1976).

stone (stōn) a mass of extremely hard and unyielding material, as a gallstone; a calculus.

stone, kidney See *calculus renal.*

strabismus (strah-biz′mus) [Gr. *strabismos* a squinting] deviation of the eye which the patient cannot overcome. The visual axes assume a position relative to each other different from that required by the physiological conditions. The various forms of strabismus are spoken of as tropias, their direction being indicated by the appropriate prefix, as *cyclo*tropia, *eso*tropia, *exo*tropia, *hyper*tropia, and *hypo*tropia. Called also *cast, heterotropia, manifest deviation*, and *squint*. See also *hypertropia.*

Kempf had **strabismus** according to Dr. Downing. U.S. ex rel. Kempf v. Commanding Officer, etc., 339 F.Supp. 320, 325 (S.D.Iowa 1972).

straight formulation See *formula, straight.*

strain (strān) an overstretching or overexertion of some part of the musculature. See also *stress.*

Counsel for Mrs. Draper never did go in to the curvature of the spine as the cause of her back pain, but he did get from Dr. Beachley the testimony that osteoperosis of the spine and an injury thereto in the low back, meaning muscle **strain** which refers to the pulling or tearing of muscle fiber, and should add in there muscle or ligament strain in this case. This causes pain in the fibers, the muscles and the other ligaments. Draper v. Liberty Mutual Insurance Co., 484 S.W.2d 135, 138 (Ct.Civ. App.Tex.1972).

strain, back

Appellee's medical expert explained that x-rays of Appellee's back

reveal a congenital abnormality which comprises a so-called unstable back, and ... this prior situation was made to become symptomatic as a result of a subtle low **back strain** that developed in the course of [Appellee's] recuperation from his foot injury and his limp.... [W]hile this man was recuperating from his foot problem, he was most certainly limping and that limp produced a certain **strain on his back**.... Mattox v. City of Philadelphia, 454 A.2d 46, 54 (Super.Ct. Pa.1982).

strain, cervical

... there is a diagnosis of a straining injury of the cervical muscles and of the ligamentous structure called **cervical strain**. Bluebonnet Express, Inc. v. Foreman, 431 S.W.2d 45, 48 (Ct. Civ.App.Tex.1968).

stramonium (strah-mo′ne-um) the dried leaf and flowering or fruiting tops of *Datura stramonium;* used like belladonna and in the treatment of asthma. Called also *thorn apple.* See also *atropine.*

strangle (strang′g′l) [L. *strangulare*] to choke, or to be choked by compression or other obstruction of the windpipe. See also *strangulation.*

I then grabbed her from behind with my right arm over her right shoulder, the forearm against her neck and my right hand above her left shoulder whereupon I grabbed my right hand with my left hand and pulled back. This is the way I had been trained to grab a person for a **strangle** hold in the Marine Corps. By pulling back with my left hand on my right hand I was able to apply pressure to her throat. I choked her for approximately ten seconds or until she was unconscious and then let her down to the floor. Knight v. State, 538 S.W.2d 101, 104 (Ct.Crim.App.Tex.1975).

strangulation (strang″gu-la′shun) [L. *strangulatio*] 1. choking or throttling arrest of respiration, due to occlusion of the air passage. 2. arrest of the circulation in a part, due to compression.

strength, loss (hip)

"Q. When we talk about **loss of strength**, are we talking about strength of what?

"A. Well, strength about the hip, abductor strength, extensor strength, flexor strength. Primarily the presence or absence of a limp. That most readily tells us about the strength of the hip." Roeder v. Industrial Com'n, 556 P.2d 1148, 1150 (Ct. App.Ariz.1976).

strep throat See *Streptococcus pyogenes.*

Streptococcus (strep″to-kok′us) [*strepto-* + Gr. *kokkos* berry] a genus of gram-positive, facultatively anaerobic cocci occurring in pairs or chains, assigned to the family Streptococcaceae. The genus is separable into the pyogenic group, the viridans group, the enterococcus group, and the lactic group. The first group includes the β-hemolytic human and animal pathogens, the second and third include α-hemolytic parasitic forms occurring as normal flora in the upper respiratory tract and the intestinal tract, respectively, and the fourth is made up of saprophytic forms associated with the souring of milk. See also *Streptococcus hemolyticus.*

streptococcus (strep-to-kok′us), pl. *streptococ′ci.* 1. a spherical bacterium occurring predominantly in chains of cells often surrounded by continuous capsular material as a consequence of failure of daughter cells to separate following cell division in one plane. 2. an organism of the genus *Streptococcus.*

streptococcus, hemolytic any streptococcus that is capable of hemolyzing red blood cells, or of producing a zone of hemolysis about the colonies on blood-agar. The great majority of streptococci found in pathologic processes belong to this type. The hemolytic streptococci have been classified as the *alpha* (α-hemolytic) or *viridans type,* which produces about the colony on blood-agar a zone of greenish discoloration considerably smaller than the clear zone produced by the beta type; and the *beta* (β-hemolytic) *type,* which produces a clear zone of hemolysis immediately surrounding the colony on blood-agar. On immunological grounds, the β-hemolytic streptococci may be divided into Group A (primarily pathogens of man), Group B (almost exclusively found in bovine mastitis), Group C (primarily pathogens of lower animals), Group D (found in cheese), Group E (found in milk), Group F, and so on. A further classification groups the hemolytic streptococci according to the presence of antigenic carbohydrates in the cell wall, and includes Groups A through O. See also *Lancefield classification,* under *classification.*

Streptococcus hemolyticus former name for *Streptococcus pyogenes.*

Streptococcus, microaerophilic gamma See *Streptococcus, micros.*

Streptococcus micros a microaerophilic or obligate anaerobe found in pulmonary gangrene and in puerperal infections.

... he discharged Mrs. Williams before the infection was identified by the laboratory report of January 1, 1975, as a "rare **microaerophilic gamma** streptococci." He erroneously reported in the discharge summary of Mrs. Williams' hospital record that the "culture was negative." Williams v. Bennett, 610 S.W.2d 144, 146 (Tex.1980).

Streptococcus pyogenes β-hemolytic, toxigenic pyogenic streptococci of group A, separable into numbered serotypes on the basis of the specificity and combination of the M and T antigens, and causing septic sore throat, scarlet fever, rheumatic fever, puerperal sepsis, acute glomerulonephritis, and other conditions in man.

sterilization (ster″ĭ-li-za'shun) 1. the complete elimination of microbial viability. 2. any procedure by which an individual is made incapable of reproduction, as by castration, vasectomy, or salpingectomy. See also *autoclave; cauterization, laparoscopic tubal; ligation, tubal; method, Kroener; salpingectomy;* and *technique, Pomeroy.*

From the time of the research done by Sir Joseph Lister, it has been a matter of general personal knowledge that **sterilization** of instruments is a sine qua non to surgery. This is not a case of alleged negligence in diagnosis or in the choice of a method of treatment. Here, the issue of negligence is not related to technical matters peculiarly within the knowledge of medical practitioners, but to circumstances where the exercise of the common knowledge and experience of reasonable men would be expected to make an assessment and evaluation of the conduct of professionals, without the necessity for the assistance of expert witnesses. Suburban Hospital Ass'n v. Hadary, 322 A.2d 258, 262–3 (Ct.Spec.App.Md.1974).

Sterilization may be said to destroy an important part of a person's social and biological identity—the ability to reproduce. It affects not only the health and welfare of the individual but the well-being of all society. Any legal discussion of **sterilization** must begin with an acknowledgment that the right to procreate is "fundamental to the very existence and survival of the race." Skinner v. Oklahoma, 316 U.S. 535, 541, 62 S.Ct. 1110, 1113, 86 L.Ed. 1655 (1942). This right is "a basic liberty" of which the individual is "forever deprived" through unwanted **sterilization**. Id....

A court must take particular care to protect the rights of the mentally impaired when considering the prospect of **sterilization**. Those rights have recently received increased attention from public authorities in this country. See, e.g., 42 U.S.C.A. § 6000 et seq.; N.J.S.A. 30:4–24 to –24.3 and 30:6D–1 et seq.; Joint Mental Health Subcommittee of the Senate and Assembly Institutions, Health and Welfare Committees, Final Report to the Legislature (1975); cf. Parham v. J.R., 442 U.S. 584, 99 S.Ct. 2493, 61 L.Ed.2d 101 (1979) (due process requirements of state commitment procedures). After a history of isolation and neglect, the mentally retarded members of our society are finally being accorded their basic civil rights. See generally F. de la Cruz & G. LaVeck (eds.), Human Sexuality and the Mentally Retarded 145–46 (1973); P. Friedman, The Rights of Mentally Retarded Persons (1976). In Re Grady, 426 A.2d 467, 472 (N.J.1981).

For treatment of the **strep throat** infection, he prescribed a medication called Pen Vee Kee of 250 milligram tablets, which is Penicillin, to be taken by mouth at the rate of one tablet 4 times a day for 10 days. This was a treatment for a bacterial infection and the dosage was for a period of 10 days. [Dissent.] Watkins v. U.S., 589 F.2d 214, 223 (5th Cir. 1979).

The laboratory reported on September 11 that with respect to the knee fluid there was "gram-positive cocci-identification pending," and on September 12 or 13 a further report was issued reading "Culture-Rare **Hemolytic Enterococci**." Dr. Tadros testified that, particularly because the cocci was "rare," it was normal for the laboratory to take extra time to identify the type. Contreras v. St. Luke's Hosp., 144 Cal.Rptr. 647, 651 (Ct.App.Cal.1978).

stress (stres) the sum of the biological reactions to any adverse stimulus, physical, mental, or emotional, internal or external, that tends to disturb the organism's homeostasis; should these compensating reactions be inadequate or inappropriate, they may lead to disorders. The term is also used to refer to the stimuli that elicit the reactions. See also *disorder, posttraumatic stress; pain* (Lewis case); and *reaction, gross stress.*

He subsequently visited a psychiatrist, H. Wayne Tobin, M.D., who diagnosed his condition as "Situational **Stress** reaction with anxiety, moderately severe, manifested by the symptoms described above in terms of feelings of anxiety, tension, difficulty with sleep, irritability and change in behavior at home, somatic equivalence such as headaches." Pomerleau v. United Parcel Service, 464 A.2d 206–7 (Me.1983).

This witness defined **stress** as the body's response to a perceived threat. He further stated that threats are idiosyncratically defined, apparently intending that they are peculiar to the individual. This witness went on to say that in his opinion the **stress** level that Darwin Creek suffered that night was definitely excessive and abnormal, although he conceded that in his work as a police department psychologist he had frequently encountered police officer **stress** based upon how members of the officer's family appeared in public. Creek¡ v. Town of Hulett, 657 P.2d 353–4 (Wyo.1983).

The physician further testified that the immediate precipitating cause of a myocardial infarction can be nothing, or that exertion, and conceivably a severe emotional upheaval, can cause enough spasm to cause a myocardial infarction and that it is conceivable that a heated argument with an employee could have been one of the things that contributed to the blockage. A cardiologist testified in response to a hypothetical question that, in his opinion, the emotional **stress** that was a result of a heated argument could be the precipitating factor bringing on a myocardial infarction. Cabe v. Union Carbide Corp., 644 S.W.2d 397–8 (Tenn.1983).

Other Authorities: Cook v. Marshall Bros. Lincoln-Mercury, Inc., 427 So.2d 655, 657 (Ct.App.La.1983); Vecchiarello v. Bd. of Trustees, etc., 453 N.Y.S.2d 971, 973 (Sup.Ct.N.Y.Cty. 1982); Ebarb v. Insurance Co. of North America, 424 So.2d 1266, 1268 (Ct.App.La.1982); Doyle v. Industrial Com'n, 427 N.E.2d 1223–4 (Ill.1981); City of Miami v. Rosenberg, 396 So.2d 163–5 (Fla.1981); Lewis v. Workers' Comp. Appeals Bd., 128 Cal.Rptr. 752, 754 (Ct.App.Cal.1976); Lamb v. Workmen's Compensation Appeals Bd., 520 P.2d 978, 980–1 (Cal.1974).

stress polycythemia See *polycythemia, stress.*

stress test See *tests, exercise.*

stress test protocol See *protocol, stress test.*

stria (stri'ah), pl. *stri'ae* [L. "a furrow, groove"] a streak, or line. See also *striae atrophicae.*

Robbins developed marks on the skin of his thighs, back and groin, which are called **stria**. In October of that year, Dr. Wexler, a dermatologist at the base, ordered Robbins to discontinue use of Prednisone. Robbins v. U.S., 624 F.2d 971–2 (10th Cir. 1980).

striae atrophicae linear, depressed, atrophic, pinkish or purplish, scarlike lesions that later become white (*striae albicantes, lineae albicantes*), occurring on the abdomen, breasts, buttocks, and thighs. They are due to weakening of the elastic tissues, and are associated with pregnancy (*striae gravidarum*), excessive obesity, rapid growth during puberty and adolescence, Cushing's syndrome, or topical or prolonged treatment with corticosteroids. Called also *striae distensae* and *lineae atrophicae.*

stricture (strik'chur) [L. *strictura*] decrease in the caliber of a canal, duct, or other passage, as a result of cicatricial contraction or the deposition of abnormal tissue.

He has **stricture** formation in his membranous urethra, about or near the prostate, affecting his ability to urinate and causing him on standing or in stress to lose varying amounts of urine. Gretchen v. U.S., 618 F.2d 177, 180 (2d Cir. 1980).

For some reason he began to retain urine in his bladder and a catheter was inserted for several days. Thereafter a **stricture**, or mass of scar tissue formed in his urethral canal, which restricted the passage of urine and caused difficulty in urinating. Richard v. Southwest Louisiana Hospital Ass'n, 383 So.2d 83, 85 (Ct.App.La 1980).

As to the **stricture** of the urethra, it is suggested that such obstructions tend to cause a continuing low-grade type of infection in the urinary tract. Whether or not this condition will continue to lend itself to treatment by dilation or cause future difficulty in passage of urine or emission of seminal fluid can not be resolved with certainty. Huffman v. Young, 478 S.W.2d 332–3 (Mo.1972).

Other Authorities: Manigan v. Califano, 453 F.Supp. 1080, 1083 (D.Kan.1978); Torres v. Celebrezze, 349 F.2d 342, 344 (1st Cir. 1965); Quick v. Thurston, 290 F.2d 360, 362–3 (D.C. Cir.1961).

stricture, urethral See *stricture.*

stridor (stri'dor) [L.] a harsh, high-pitched respiratory sound such as the inspiratory sound often heard in acute laryngeal obstruction. Cf. *laryngismus stridulus.*

Stridor is a term used to describe sounds that occur when a patient is having problems breathing. It generally refers to sounds that occur because of problems in the upper portion of the airway. Battles v. Aderhold, 430 So.2d 307, (Ct.App.La. 1983).

Although there is conflict in the evidence as to whether the administered oxygen completely controlled Mr. Wright's convulsive breathing (medically termed **stridor**), it appears that he was somewhat calm in the ambulance. Wright v. U.S., 507 F.Supp. 147, 149 (E.D.La.1980).

strip (strip) to excise lengths of large veins and incompetent tributaries by subcutaneous dissection and the use of a stripper.

The surgery, known as bilateral greater and lesser saphenous vein **stripping**, was performed on December 17, 1973. Ziegert

v. South Chicago Community Hospital, 425 N.E.2d 450, 453 (App.Ct.III.1981).

Bridgford, the dependent of a retired military officer, developed varicose veins in his left leg when he was 19 years old. Doctors at both Walter Reed Army Medical Center and Bethesda Naval Hospital [Bethesda] advised him to undergo a vein **stripping** operation to alleviate this condition. . . .

. . . The surgical procedure consisted of tying off and severing each varicose vein which was to be removed. Then a **stripping** rod was inserted and run through the vein, and it was pulled from the patient's leg. Bridgford v. U.S., 550 F.2d 978–80 (4th Cir. 1977).

stripping See *strip.*

stroke (strōk) a sudden and severe attack. See also *syndrome, stroke*; and *syndrome, Wallenberg's* (Nimmer case).

. . . he suffered a moderate cerebrovascular accident (CVA), i.e., **stroke**. He was hospitalized for a week, during which time he experienced difficulty with speaking and with motor coordination in his right hand. However by the time he was released, he could speak normally and his hand was much better. He has experienced no recurrence since and has no present disability of speech or hand.

Generally, a **stroke** results from a blockage in a blood vessel in the brain. In Meik's case, it was caused by an embolus that blocked the middle cerebral artery. The source of the embolus, which is defined as a mass of blood or other matter circulating in the blood stream, has never been determined. Meik v. National Trans. Safety Bd., 710 F.2d 584–5 (9th Cir. 1983).

Dr. Miller found that the **strokes** had adversely affected the right side of Lashley's body. In particular, his right leg was weak. It caused him to limp, and occasionally experience numbness. Periodically the leg collapsed beneath him. Lashley's right arm was similarly affected. It was clumsy and very unreliable. Lashley v. Secretary of Health and Human Services, 708 F.2d 1048, 1050 (6th Cir. 1983).

It was diagnosed that Sandra had suffered a cerebral vascular accident (**stroke**) resulting in the paralysis of the right side. Mahr v. G.D. Searle & Co., 390 N.E.2d 1214, 1220 (App.Ct. III.1979).

Other Authorities: Daily v. Bechtel Power Corp., 420 So.2d 1337, 1341 (Ct.App.La.1982); Sanzari v. Rosenfeld, 167 A.2d 625, 627 (N.J.1961).

stroke, heat a condition caused by exposure to excessive heat, natural or artificial, and marked by dry skin, vertigo, headache, thirst, nausea, and muscular cramps; body temperature may be dangerously elevated, contrasting with heat exhaustion in which the body temperature may be subnormal. Called also *heat apoplexy* and *thermoplegia.* Cf. *sunstroke.*

Upon arrival in the emergency room, Neal was in a coma with a body temperature of 108°F. He died shortly thereafter. The examining physician, Dr. Lightfoot, found the diagnosis to be compatible with **heat stroke**, which was indicated on the hospital records and his death certificate. Dr. Lightfoot testified that Neal, at age forty-five, obese and diabetic, was a high risk and that the weather conditions were inducive to **heat stroke**. Ex parte Neal, 423 So.2d 850–1 (Ala.1982).

stroke, sun See *sunstroke.*

stroma (stro'mah), pl. *stro'mata* [Gr. *strōma* anything laid out for lying or sitting upon] the supporting tissue or matrix of an organ, as distinguished from its functional element, or parenchyma.

stroma of cornae See *substantia propria corneae.*

stroma, Rollet's that part of a red blood cell which remains after the hemoglobin has been removed.

Upon hypothetical question, he testified that the red blood cell residual, or **stroma**, in the Anaplaz vaccine was the cause of NI in plaintiffs' herd. Further evidence indicated that neonatal isoerytholysis had not been diagnosed in cattle prior to the introduction of the vaccine, Anaplaz, manufactured by the Fort Dodge Laboratories. Waller v. Fort Dodge Laboratories, 356 F.Supp. 413, 415 (E.D.Mo.1972).

structure (struk'chur) [L. *struere* to build] the components and their manner of arrangement in constituting a whole.

structure of the body, physical

The term "**physical structure of the body**" was construed in Bailey v. American General Ins. Co., 154 Tex. 430, 279 S.W. 2d 315 (1955), to include coverage for an iron worker who suffered a severe neurosis after seeing his co-worker fall from a scaffold to his death. Bailey, however, became entangled in a cable and escaped death by falling onto the roof of a building. The event produced in Bailey such a disabling neurosis, an anxiety reaction, that he was incapable of pursuing his trade. Bailey recovered compensation on the basis of an accidental injury—not an occupational disease. The court permitted coverage as an accidental injury to the outer limits of the term "**physical structure of the body**." [2] [[2] The phrase "**physical structure of the body**", as it is used in the statute, must refer to the entire body, not simply to the skeletal structure or to the circulatory system or to the digestive system. It refers to the whole, to the complex of perfectly integrated and interdependent bones, tissues and organs which function together by means of electrical, chemical and mechanical processes in a living, breathing, functioning individual. To determine what is meant by "**physical structure of the body**", the structure should be considered that of a living person—not as a static, inanimate thing. 279 S.W.2d at 318.] Transportation Ins. Co. v. Maksyn, 580 S.W.2d 334, 336–7 (Tex.1979).

struma See *goiter.*

struma lymphomatosa a progressive disease of the thyroid gland, with extensive acidophilic degeneration of its epithelial elements and replacement by lymphoid and fibrous tissue; called also *Hashimoto's disease* or *thyroiditis.*

Her final diagnosis was possible **Hashimoto's disease**. Additional tests to determine her exact medical problem showed that there was no evidence that her thyroid was functioning and that thyroid replacement therapy should be continued. Coleman v. Weinberger, 538 F.2d 1045–7 (4th Cir. 1976).

strychnine (strik'nīn) an extremely poisonous alkaloid, $C_{21}H_{22}N_2O_2$, obtained chiefly from *Strychnos nux-vomica* and other species of *Strychnos*, which causes excitation of all portions of the central nervous system by blocking postsynaptic inhibition of neural impulses; it has been used as a central nervous system stimulant and was formerly used as a bitter tonic, circulatory stimulant, and with cathartic drugs. In veterinary medicine it is occasionally used as a tonic and stimulant. See also *strychninism.*

At 2:30 on the morning of December 9th, nurse Worrell, who had succeeded as the attending special nurse, administered the second bottle. One-half hour later the deceased was seized with a convulsion. She died one hour later at 4:00 o'clock. . . .

The toxicologist who performed the autopsy testified that he estimated from his three analyses of specified grams of brain, liver and of a composite sample of heart, brain, liver and blood that there were 3.7 grains of **strychnine** in the body of deceased. People v. Feldman, 85 N.E.2d 913, 916 (N.Y.1949).

strychninism (strik'nin-izm) a toxic condition due to the misuse of strychnine; chronic strychnine poisoning. Symptoms include increased acuity of hearing, vision, touch, taste, and smell, followed by tonic convulsions and vomiting; in severe cases, it may culminate in respiratory paralysis and death.

Stryker frame See *frame, Stryker.*

Stryker plug cutter

Dr. Kauffman used a number four **Stryker plug cutter** to remove the plug of bone from the vertebrae. This instrument is an electrically powered drill weighing between three and four pounds. The tool consists of four key parts; a serrated cutting edge; a sliding shield, a hexagonal fixation screw and a plunger used to remove the bone plug. The surgeon measures the depth to which he desires to drill and adjusts the shield accordingly, thereafter securing the shield (variously termed a guard, sleeve, guide or depth gauge at trial) by tightening the fixation screw with an allen-type wrench which is supplied by the manufacturer. Grubb v. Albert Einstein Medical Center, 387 A.2d 480, 483–4 (Super.Ct.Pa.1978).

study, aortic arch See *arch, aortic;* and *arcus aortae.*

The procedure of an **aortic arch study** entails the passing of a catheter to the orifice of each of the brain vessels in turn and similar pictures taken. Morgenroth v. Pacific Medical Center, Inc., 126 Cal.Rptr. 681, 684 (Ct.App.Cal.1976).

stump (stump) the distal end of the part of the limb left in amputation.

Before the plaintiff could be fitted with prostheses, it would be necessary to further revise both **stumps**, and bring soft tissue down over them by traction. In Dr. Turner's opinion the split-thickness grafts then on the **stumps** would not bear the weight of a prosthesis. When asked whether he knew of cases where an artificial limb was placed on an area where the bone protruded, he stated that although he had seen and heard of such attempts, he had never seen it done successfully.

Dr. Turner further testified that the usefulness of an artificial limb is proportional to the length of the **stump** on which it is placed, and one cannot readily move the appliance with **stumps** as short as those of the plaintiff. Given the extent of this amputation, a prosthesis on the right leg would be useless.

At best, the witness said, the plaintiff would always be obliged to use crutches to retain his balance, and he would always suffer some pain. He would periodically have to have the prosthesis changed. Raines v. New York Railroad Co., 283 N.E.2d 230, 237 (Ill.1972).

The surrounding terminal soft tissue was quite sensitive to any light to moderate pressure made through it, indicating inflammatory reaction. The **stump** surface elsewhere was in good shape though a slight pressure irritation was present from the socket over the internal condyle of the femur and there was some tendency to bursal formation laterally over the quadriceps tendon. The actual bone length of the **stump** was 8″, measured from the tibial plateau to the saw-cut level. Alexander v. Weinberger, 536 F.2d 779, 782 (8th Cir. 1976).

stump blowout See *gastrectomy* (Reams case).

stupor (stu′por) [L.] partial or nearly complete unconsciousness, manifested by responding only to vigorous stimulation. Also, in psychiatry, a disorder marked by reduced responsiveness.

styloid (sti′loid) [Gr. *stylos* pillar + *eidos* form] resembling a pillar; long and pointed; styliform. Cited in Donaldson v. Maffucci, 156 A.2d 835, 837 (Pa. 1959).

styloid, ulnar See *ulna*; and *ulnar*.

subarachnoid space See *cavum, subarachnoideale*.

subchondral (sub-kon′dral) beneath a cartilage.

Considerable narrowing of the lumbosacral disc space was seen with **subchondral** sclerosis and spurring along the articular aspects of L5 and S1 bodies. Barats v. Weinberger, 383 F.Supp. 276, 281 (E.D.Pa.1974).

subclavian (sub-kla′ve-an) situated under the clavicle, as the subclavian artery.

subclavian stick

Plaintiff Mary Eichelberger instituted this medical malpractice suit against Barnes Hospital alleging that defendant through its employee, Doctor Hirschel, negligently punctured the plaintiff's right lung while attempting to perform a medical procedure known as a **subclavian stick**....

According to the doctor, he then explained to Mrs. Eichelberger that the best alternative method of giving calories was through what is known as a **subclavian stick**, which requires insertion of a catheter under the collarbone and into the subclavian vein. This procedure involves using a small anesthetic needle to numb the area and locate the vein. Once the vein is located a much larger needle is then placed into the vein and a catheter is placed through the needle and is attached via a plastic line to the caloric solution....

There are two complications with performing a **subclavian stick**. One is bleeding and the other is a pneumothorax, or puncture of the pleural space around the lung. Eichelberger v. Barnes Hosp., 655 S.W.2d 699, 702–3 (Mo.Ct.App.1983).

subclavian vein See *vena, subclavia*.

subclinical (sub-klin′ĭ-kal) without clinical manifestations; said of the early stages, or a slight degree, of a disease.

According to the Criteria Document, "**subclinical**" effects "are disruptions in function, which may be demonstrated by special testing but not by the classic techniques of physical examination; using the term '**subclinical**' in no way implies that those effects are without consequences to human health." CD 13–4, JA 1334. [See under "Poisoning, Lead", this case.] Lead Industries Ass'n v. Environmental Protection Agency, 647 F.2d 1130, 1139 (D.C.Cir.1980).

subcutaneous (sub″ku-ta′ne-us) beneath the skin.

... in his opinion her condition was due to the improper administration of a medication into the **subcutaneous** tissue (just under the outer layer of skin) instead of intramuscular (into the muscle) as required by the medication. Su v. Perkins, 211 S.E.2d 421, 428 (Ct.App.Ga.1974).

Other Authorities: Daniels v. Hadley Memorial Hospital, 566 F.2d 749, 752 (D.C.Cir.1977).

subdural (sub-du′ral) situated between the dura mater and the arachnoid. See also *empyema* (SKF case).

... extensive **subdural** bleeding (bleeding in the area between the skull and the brain). State v. Durand, 465 A.2d 762–3 (R.I.1983).

subendocardial (sub″en-do-kar′de-al) beneath the endocardium. See also *endocardium; endothelium;* and *epithelium*.

His condition was diagnosed as a **sub-endocardial** infarction (a form of heart attack). Shatoska v. Intern. Grain Transfer, Inc., 430 So.2d 1255, 1258 (Ct.App.La.1983).

subgaleal See *galea aponeurotica*.

subjective (sub-jek′tiv) [L. *subjectivus*] pertaining to or perceived only by the affected individual; not perceptible to the senses of another person. See also *objective*.

It is clear that the conclusion of the administrative law judge was based on Mr. Poag's opinions and on his refusal to credit the testimony of plaintiff and his wife concerning plaintiff's **subjective** symptoms—his fainting spells, difficulty sleeping and constant chest pain....

Subjective evidence of pain or other symptoms may not be sufficient by itself to establish a disability; however, where such evidence is supported by objective indicators of disability it cannot be ignored. Thorne v. Weinberger, supra at 583; Nanny v. Matthews, 423 F.Supp. 548 (E.D.Va.1976); Kelly v. Matthews, 420 F.Supp. 359 (W.D.N.C.1976); Young v. Weinberger, 366 F.Supp. 81 (D.Md.1973). The record shows no objective medical evidence which would negate plaintiff's **subjective** claims. All the objective evidence clearly points to a chronic respiratory disease. McDaniel v. Califano, 446 F.Supp. 1080, 1084 (W.D.N.Car.1978).

subjective symptom See *symptom, subjective*.

subluxation (sub″luk-sa′shun) [*sub-* + L. *luxatio* dislocation] an incomplete or partial dislocation.

Dr. Taylor noted that the February 1980 x-rays indicated "multiple knee injuries [and] many, many **subluxations**" or small dislocations in both knees. Shepard v. Midland Foods, Inc., 666 P.2d 758, 761 (Mont.1983).

In the accident, Miss Modave suffered a sharp shock to the base of the neck, which apparently resulted in a partial dislocation or **subluxation** in the cervical region of the spine. The dislocation might have occurred in the accident, the experts testified, or the accident may merely have torn the supporting ligaments and permitted the dislocation to occur at a later time. In either case, the experts agreed that the condition was very serious and could lead to injury to the spinal cord, resulting in nerve damage or paralysis. Modave v. Long Island Jewish Medical Center, 501 F.2d 1065, 1069 (2d Cir. 1974).

On the basis of his examination and X-ray photographs which he took he diagnosed a chronical cervical thoracic **subluxation**, chronic sacroiliac and lumbar strain with radiculitis of the right leg. He defined the **subluxation** as a condition in the vertebra whereby it has lost its normal position in relationship to the one above and below, and radiculitis as a radiating type pain along the course of the nerve. He put her on a course of treatment twice a week consisting of ''chiropractic adjustments'' and therapy consisting of ''pulse galvanism'' which he defined as electrical current for pain. Carter v. Woolco Dept. Store, 379 So.2d 759–60 (Ct.App.La.1979).

Other Authorities: Funke v. State Acc. Ins. Fund, 619 P.2d 668–9 (Ct.App.Or.1980); Brazil v. U.S., 484 F.Supp. 986, 988 (N.D.Ala.1979); Badke v. Barnett, 316 N.Y.S.2d 177–8 (2d Dep't 1970); Chiropractic Ass'n of New York, Inc. v. Hilleboe, 227 N.Y.S.2d 309, 361 (Sup.Ct. Albany Cty.1961).

subluxation, vertebra

On February 25, in the course of performing regular housekeeping duties, Mrs. Arens fell down several basement stairs, apparently causing neck and lower back muscle strain and **vertebra subluxation** (misalignment). Arens v. Hanecy, 269 N.W.2d 924–5 (Minn.1978).

subperiosteal implant See *implant, subperiosteal.*

subscapular (sub-skap'u-lar) situated below or under the scapula. See also *scapula.*

Dr. Vogel, a neurosurgeon, examined the plaintiff and diagnosed that she had a **subcapular** herniated cervical disc. Monnier v. Boutte, 420 So.2d 725–6 (Ct.App.La.1982).

substance (sub'stans) [L. *substantia*] the material constituting an organ or body; called also *substantia* [NA]. See also *drug* (U.S. v. Schrenzel case).

substance, hazardous

The Commission's order and regulation are predicated on the Federal Hazardous Substances Act, 15 U.S.C. §§ 1261–1274. The act defines ''**hazardous substance[s]**'' to include certain toxic, corrosive, irritating, sensitizing, flammable, pressure generating, or radioactive materials which may cause substantial illness or injury as a proximate result of foreseeable use. 15 U.S.C. §§ 1261(f)(1)(A), (B) & (C). The Commission is authorized to adopt regulations declaring specific items to be **hazardous substances**. Id. § 1262(a).[3] [Footnote omitted.] [3 The Act specifically excludes certain fuels, pesticides, foods, drugs, cosmetics, and nuclear materials, which are subject to regulation under other statutes. 15 U.S.C. § 1261(f)(2), (3).] Pactra Industries v. Consumer Product Safety Com'n, 555 F.2d 677, 679 (9th Cir. 1977).

The FHSA [Federal Hazardous Substances Act], 15 U.S.C. § 1261, provides in part:

(f) The term ''**hazardous substance**'' means:

(1)(A) Any substance or mixture of substances which (i) is toxic, (ii) is corrosive, (iii) is an irritant, (iv) is a strong sensitizer,

(v) is flammable or combustible, or (vi) generates pressure through decomposition, heat, or other means, if such substances or mixture of substances may cause substantial personal injury or substantial illness during or as a proximate result of any customary or reasonably foreseeable handling or use, including reasonably foreseeable ingestion by children.
Certain pressurized products obviously fall within this definition. Chemical Specialities Mfrs. Ass'n, Inc. v. Lowery, 452 F.Supp. 431, 434 (2d Cir. 1971).

(4)(i) ''**Hazardous substance**'' means:

(A) Any substance or mixture of substances which is toxic, corrosive, an irritant, a strong sensitizer, flammable or combustible, or generates pressure through decomposition, heat, or other means, if such substance or mixture of substances may cause substantial personal injury or substantial illness during or as a proximate result of any customary or reasonably foreseeable handling or use, including reasonably foreseeable ingestion by children.

(B) Any substance which the Commission by regulation finds, pursuant to the provisions of section 3(a) of the act, meet the requirements of section 2(f)(1)(A) of the act (restated in (A) above).

(C) Any radioactive substance if, with respect to such substance as used in a particular class of article or as packaged, the Commission determines by regulation that the substance is sufficiently hazardous to require labeling in accordance with the act in order to protect the public health.

(D) Any toy or other article intended for use by children which the Commission by regulation determines, in accordance with section 3(e) of the act, presents an electrical, mechanical, or thermal hazard.

(ii) ''**Hazardous substance**'' shall not apply to pesticides subject to the Federal Insecticide, Fungicide, and Rodenticide Act, to foods, drugs, and cosmetics subject to the Federal Food, Drug, and Cosmetic Act, nor to substances intended for use as fuels when stored in containers and used in the heating, cooking, or refrigeration system of a house. ''**Hazardous substance**'' shall apply, however, to any article which is not itself a pesticide within the meaning of the Federal Insecticide, Fungicide, and Rodenticide Act but which is a **hazardous substance** which the meaning of section 2(f)(1) of the Federal Hazardous Substances Act (restated in paragraph (b)(4)(i) of this section) by reason of bearing or containing such a pesticide.

(iii) ''**Hazardous substance**'' shall not include any source material, special nuclear material, or byproduct material as defined in the Atomic Energy Act of 1954, as amended, and regulations issued pursuant thereto by the Atomic Energy Commission. 16 C.F.R.Sect. 1500.3(b)(4).

substance, proper, of cornea See *substantia propria corneae.*

substance, radioactive See *material, radioactive.*

''Radioactive substance'' means a substance which emits ionizing radiation. 16 C.F.R.Sect. 1500.3(b)(11).

substantia (sub-stan'she-ah), pl. *substan'tiae* [L.] material of which a tissue, organ, or body is composed; used as a general term in nomenclature. Called also *substance.*

substantia propria corneae [NA], proper substance of cornea: the fibrous, tough, and transparent main part of the cornea, between the anterior and the posterior limiting lamina; called also *stroma of cornea*.

On the first visit, Dr. Michaile did a complete opthalmological examination which disclosed severe damage to the cornea of Mr. Frederick's left eye in the **stromal layer**, consisting of a scar in the lower midportion of the cornea. The **stromal layer** is the third of the five layers of the cornea counting from the surface. Rohm & Haas v. Workmen's Comp.App.Bd., 414 A.2d 163–4 (Commonwealth Ct.Pa.1980).

substrate (sub'strāt) [L. *sub* under + *stratum* layer] a substance upon which an enzyme acts.

The affinity of an enzyme for any given "**substrate**"—i.e. material to be chemically converted—may be represented by a number called the "Michaelis constant".... CPC International, Inc. v. Standard Brands, Inc., 385 F.Supp. 1057, 1063 (D.Del.1974).

subtalar (sub-ta'lar) [*sub-* + L. *talus* ankle] beneath the talus, as the subtalar joint. See also *talus*.

An examination on December 11, 1979, revealed that Nettles was developing degenerative changes in the **subtalar** joint. By March 4, 1980, Dr. Dickson reported that Nettles had developed "a lot of **subtalor** [sic] arthritis" which is very painful and would probably require a triple arthrodesis. On April 15, 1980, the subtalar joint looked "very bad," and Nettles still required the use of a cane to walk. [Footnote omitted.] Nettles v. Schweiker, 714 F.2d 833, 835 (8th Cir. 1983).

... involvement of the **subtalar** joint (the joint separating the heel bone from the bone immediately above it). Keen v. Prisinzano, 100 Cal.Rptr. 82, 84 (Ct.App.Cal.1972).

subtemporal (sub-tem'por-al) beneath the temple or any temporal structure or part. See also under *decompression*.

subtemporal rhizotomy See *decompression, subtemporal; rhizotomy, subtemporal;* and *subtemporal*.

succinylcholine chloride (suk″sĭ-nil-ko'lēn) [USP] chemical name: 2,2'-[(1,4-dioxo-1,4-butanediyl)bis(oxy)]bis-[*N,N,N*-trimethylethanaminium]dichloride. A neuromuscular blocking agent, $C_{21}H_{22}H_2O_2$, occurring as a white, crystalline powder, which produces skeletal muscle relaxation by blocking transmission at the myoneural junction; used for its muscle relaxant action during shock therapy and such procedures as endotracheal intubation and endoscopy, and as an adjunct to surgical anesthesia, administered intravenously and intramuscularly.

... Succinylcholine di-Chloride, commonly called **Anectine**, which is used to relax or paralyze the skeletal muscles of the body to facilitate such an examination. Decedent was artificially respirated by Mrs. Meredith while under the influence of the **Anectine** as it also blocks the nerves controlling the diaphragm. Brown v. Allen Sanitarium, Inc., 364 So.2d 661–2 (Ct. App.La.1978).

... the patient was injected intravenously with a 1½ cc of **succinylcholine chloride**, a drug bearing the trade name "**Anectine**", a muscle relaxant employed to aid nasal intubation....

It is conceded **Anectine** is a synthetic drug which operates differently from, but produces effects similar to those induced by natural curare, namely, the capacity to relax a patient by

paralyzing the neuromuscular system. The drug produces almost instant relaxation and muscular paralysis lasting in most cases from three to five minutes. During this interval, the patient is unable to breathe spontaneously or unable to breathe sufficiently because of paralysis of muscles that operate the lungs and respiratory system. In this interval, respiration must be assisted. **Anectine** molecules are immediately attacked by an element in the blood plasma known as cholinesterase which breaks down **Anectine** into its components and destroys its efficacy. In the vast majority of cases, total dissipation of **Anectine** is achieved within 10 to 15 minutes, after which the patient breathes spontaneously. This initial result of **Anectine** is known in the medical profession as a Phase I Block. Although the advisability of giving **Anectine** is disputed, it is conceded that it is given by some anesthesiologists at the commencement of an operation to relax the patient so that intubation, either oral or nasal, may be accomplished with minimum trauma. Chapman v. Argonaut-Southwest Ins. Co., 290 So.2d 779, 781–2 (Ct.App. La.1974).

A defendant in the instant action, Dr. Milton Helpern, the Chief Medical Examiner of the City of New York, testified on the hearing in September 1966 that, in his opinion, the death of the plaintiff's wife was caused by an injection of **succinylcholine chloride**, a chemical muscle relaxant which induces apnea, or inability to breathe. Coppolino v. Helpern, 266 F.Supp. 930–1 (S.D.N.Y.1967).

succinylcholine di-chloride See *succinylcholine chloride*.

suction (suk'shun) [L. *sugere* to suck] aspiration of gas or fluid by mechanical means.

The naso-gastric **suction** is designed to remove stomach secretions and gases, so that the stomach will be more stationary. Bellaire General Hospital, Inc. v. Campbell, 510 S.W.2d 94–5 (Ct.Civ.App.Tex.1974).

Sudeck's atrophy See *atrophy, Sudeck's;* and *osteoporosis, posttraumatic*.

suffocation (suf″o-ka'shun) [L. *suffocatio*] asphyxiation; the stoppage of respiration, or the asphyxia that results from it.

At trial, plaintiffs' expert witnesses testified that the insured died of **suffocation** as a result of massive aspiration of his stomach contents. One of the experts, Dr. Tiffany, testified that this is extraordinary, unforeseen and unexpected, and not the result of disease. Cobb v. Aetna Life Ins. Co., 274 N.W.2d 911, 913 (Minn.1979).

sugar (shoog'ar) [L. *saccharum;* Gr. *sakcharon*] a sweet carbohydrate of various kinds, and of both animal and vegetable origin. It is an aldehyde or ketone derivative of polyhydric alcohols. The two principal groups of sugars are the disaccharides, having the formula $C_{12}H_{22}O_{11}$, and the monosaccharides, $C_6H_{12}O_6$; all are white, crystallizable solids, soluble in water and dilute alcohol. The disaccharides are sucrose or saccharose, *beet s., cane s., maple s., palm s., malt s.* (maltose), *milk s.* (lactose), and others. The monosaccharides include ordinary dextrose (δ-glucose) (*diabetic s., grape s., liver s., potato s., starch s.*), fructose (*fruit s.*), inositol (*heart s., muscle s.*). Besides these, a very considerable number of artificial and other sugars are known to chemistry.

sugar, beet sucrose derived from the root of the beet. Cited in Sugar Industry, 1977 Trade Cases, Par. 61,373 at 71,319; 71,323 (N.D.Cal.1976).

sugar, blood glucose, the form in which carbohydrate is carried in the blood, usually in a concentration of 70–100 mg. per 100 ml.

McMullen: Test four: **blood sugar**. The control laboratories reported that the specimen submitted was abnormally high in **blood sugar**—an indication of diabetes. Four of the mail order laboratories, reporting on the same specimen, said it was normal. Possible diabetes was undetected. The reports of 71 per cent of the mail order labs performing the test varied from the range of the control lab reports by from 20 to 104 per cent. Dr. Schaeffer.

Dr. Schaeffer: By medical standards, a variance of over 10 per cent in this test is unacceptable. Of course, the significance of not detecting diabetes is clear. But if it is detected the amount of insulin given a patient is determined by the amount of sugar in his blood. If the lab report is inaccurate on the low side he may not get a sufficient amount of insulin to help him. If the lab report is inaccurate on the high side, he may get too much insulin—and an overdose could put him into shock or kill him. United Medical Labs v. Columbia Broadcasting System, Inc., 404 F.2d 706, 715 (9th Cir. 1968).

sugar, cane sucrose obtained from sugar cane.

To produce **cane sugar**, sugar cane is ground into raw sugar at nearby grinding mills that operate seasonally. Thereafter, raw sugar is shipped to cane refineries normally located near seaports, which operate throughout the year by obtaining raw sugar from various worldwide cane growing areas having different harvest seasons. Thus, although pure refined beet and **cane sugar** are identical chemically, the difference in both technology and organization results in two separate products from the standpoint of industry economics. Sugar Industry, 1977–1 Trade Cases, Par. 61,373 at 71,319; 71,323 (N.D. Cal.1976).

sugar, refined

... "**refined sugar**" means any grade, type or form of saccharine product derived from the processing of sugar beets or in the refining of raw cane sugar, all of which contains sucrose, dextrose or levulose....

Refined sugar is produced regularly in at least the following grades and forms: (1) liquid sucrose sugar; (2) liquid invert sugar; (3) granulated sugar; (4) fine granulated sugar; (5) powdered sugar; (6) brown sugar; (7) bottlers sugar; (8) canners sugar; (9) bakers superfine sugar; (10) cubes; (11) industrial fine sugar; (12) coarse sugar; (13) individual packets; (14) bulk sugar; and (15) bagged sugar. Sugar Industry, 1977–1 Trade Cases, Par. 61,373 at 71,319; 71,323 (N.D.Cal.1976).

suicidal gesture See *gesture, suicidal.*

suicide (soo'ĭ-sīd) [L. *sui* of himself + *caedere* to kill] the taking of one's own life.

The evidence shows that he had attempted to take his own life and had threatened to do so in the following instances. He tried to commit **suicide** with a rifle while in the Air Force and a sergeant stopped him. Two years before the events in this case occurred, he threatened **suicide** and sought counsel from

a pastor and a psychiatrist. On another occasion he swallowed broken razor blades. While in a cell at Fort McClellan, he cut his wrist with a razor blade. At another time he had two pieces of razor blades in his mouth and later an x-ray picture showed another razor blade in his stomach which he said he ate the night before. He threatened to jump out of a window while in a psychiatric ward. Finally, he forced his wife and children to watch him for 45 minutes while he held a pistol to his head and threatened to shoot himself.... there was no evidence that he was taking Valium on these occasions Consequently, his attempts to commit **suicide** in the instant case, when there was no evidence that he was taking Valium at the time, was not unusual behavior for him. He apparently had suicidal mania. [Dissent.] Watkins v. U.S., 589 F.2d 214, 229–30 (5th Cir. 1979).

sulcus (sul'kus), pl. *sul'ci* [L.] a groove, trench, or furrow; [NA] a general-term for such a depression, especially one of those on the surface of the brain, separating the gyri. Cf. *fissure.*

The stump was well-contoured and had good soft-tissue coverage terminally, but there was a small, partially crusted area of erosion in a **sulcus** of the scar terminally between the tibial and fibular ends. Alexander v. Weinberger, 536 F.2d 779, 782 (8th Cir. 1976).

sulfameter (sul'fah-me"ter) chemical name: 4-amino-*N*-(5-methoxy-2-pyrimidinyl)benzenesulfonamide. A long-acting sulfonamide, $C_{11}H_{12}N_4O_3S$, occurring as a fine, white to yellowish-white, powder; used as an antibacterial, especially in the treatment of acute and chronic urinary tract infections, administered orally.

The plaintiff, Mrs. Roman, suffered from a recurring kidney infection and in June 1968, was given a prescription by her employer, Dr. Alberto Melgar, for **Sulla**, a drug produced by the defendant, A. H. Robins Co. She also received samples of the drug from a Robins Company representative at Dr. Melgar's request. On July 16, 1968 Mrs. Roman began having difficulties with her eyes....

... Here, although any mental disability that Mrs. Roman suffered must have been the result of the **Sulla**-induced Stevens-Johnson Syndrome, all the evidence indicates that this change in mental condition was a gradual thing—occurring over a period of time. Roman v. A. H. Robins Co., Inc., 518 F.2d 970–2 (5th Cir. 1975).

sulfapyridine (sul"fah-pir'ĭ-dēn) [USP] chemical name: N^1-2-pyridylsulfanilamide. An antibacterial compound, $C_{11}H_{11}N_3O_2S$, occurring as white or faintly yellowish white granules, crystals, or powder; used as an oral suppressant for dermatitis herpetiformis. It was formerly used in the treatment of pneumonia and streptococcal infections.

After some months of treatment, plaintiff was put on the drug **Sulfapyridine** but it caused some stomach upset. Late in 1968 plaintiff was put on the drug Avlosulfon prescribed either by Dr. Gordon or Dr. Rappaport. Plaintiff continued to be treated by Dr. Gordon through 1969 and 1970, seeing him once or twice a month....

... According to plaintiff's answer to a written interrogatory read into evidence, "[h]e [Dr. Rappaport] told me that the pills (Avlosulfon) I was taking were causing the wasting away of the muscles in my hand, legs and feet. He gave me a different pill to take (**Sulfapyridine**). In about six months I started to regain the use of part of my muscles. [¶] Dr. Harrah gave me a total disability about March 1973. In April 1974, I asked Dr. Harrah if I could try to go back to work. My muscles at that time were not back to normal, but I wanted to get back to work instead of lying around." Burgon v. Kaiser Foundation Hospitals, 155 Cal.Rptr. 763, 765 (Cal.App.1979).

Similarly in Berkowitz v. New York Life Insurance Company (256 App.Div. 324, 10 N.Y.S.2d 106), it was held that the death of the deceased was accidental where it was due to a hypersusceptibility to neosalvarsan with which the deceased had been injected as a treatment for syphilis. And in the same vein, in Escoe v. Metropolitan Life Insurance Company (178 Misc. 698, 699, 35 N.Y.S.2d 833) a recovery of double indemnity for accidental death was permitted where death resulted because of an allergy to a drug known as **sulfapyridine**, which had been injected to treat pneumonia. Bracey v. Metropolitan Life Insurance Company, 282 N.Y.S.2d 121, 124 (1967).

sulfate (sul'fāt) [L. *sulphas*] any salt of sulfuric acid.

Sulfates have a laxative effect on newcomers to a community whose water contains high **sulfate** levels. Environmental Defense Fund, Inc. v. Costle, 578 F.2d 337, 341 (D.C.Cir.1978).

sulfinpyrazone (sul"fin-pi'rah-zōn) [USP] chemical name: 1,2-diphenyl-4-[2-(phenylsulfinyl)ethyl]3,5-pyrazolidinedione. A sulfoxide analogue of phenybutazone, $C_{23}H_{20}N_2O_3S$, used as a uricosuric agent in treatment of gout.

An NDA [New Drug Application] had previously been approved for the use of **Anturane** in the treatment of chronic and intermittent gouty arthritis. Ciba-Geigy submitted the present NDA in support of its proposal to use the drug for the prevention of sudden death in survivors of heart attacks. Webb v. Dep't of Health and Human Services, 696 F.2d 101, 104 (D.C. Cir.1982).

sulfuric acid mist See *acid mist*.

Sulla (sul'ah) trademark for a preparation of sulfameter. See also *sulfameter*.

sulphate See *sulfate*.

sunstroke (sun'strōk) insolation, or thermic fever; a condition produced by exposure to the sun, and marked by convulsions, coma, and a high temperature of the skin. Cf. *heat exhaustion* and *heat stroke*.

The Industrial Commission awarded compensation on the basis that where peculiar conditions of employment subject an employee to the happening of a heatstroke to a greater extent than the public generally then such heatstroke is compensable. See also Connelly v. Hunt Furniture Co., 240 N.Y. 83, 147 N.E. 366 at page 368, 39 A.L.R. 867 (1925): "**Sunstroke**, strictly speaking, is a disease, but the suddenness of its approach and its catastrophic nature have caused it to be classified as an accident." Robinette v. Kayo Oil Co., 171 S.E.2d 172, 174 (Sup.Ct.App.Va.1969).

superficial (soo"per-fish'al) [L. *superficialis*] pertaining to or situated near the surface.

He testified that he prescribed piperazine as a local anesthetic for the removal of an infestation of roundworms from the intestine. The Board could properly find that petitioner's action was not taken in connection with minor surgery. Intestines are not within the common understanding of "**superficial** structures" of the body and the Board was entitled not to give credit to petitioner's testimony that he regarded the entire alimentary canal to be **superficial**. Hardt v. Board of Naturopathic Examiners, 606 P.2d 1169, 1171 (Ct.App.Or.1980).

superovulation (soo"per-ov"u-la'shun) extraordinary acceleration of ovulation.

Thus, the only potential issue raised for these plaintiffs under defendants' construction of the statute concerns the use of the technique of **superovulation** [13] to fertilize multiple embryos. [[13] **Superovulation** is a procedure designed to produce multiple ova. It involves the administration of hormones.] Smith v. Hartigan, 556 F.Supp. 157, 163 (N.D.Ill.1983).

supination (soo"pĭ-na'shun) [L. *supinatio*] the act of assuming the supine position, or the state of being supine. Applied to the hand, the act of turning the palm forward (anteriorly) or upward, performed by lateral rotation of the forearm. Applied to the foot, it generally implies

Supinators contracted; forearm, hand supinated. (King and Showers.)

Supination.

movements resulting in raising of the medial margin of the foot, hence of the longitudinal arch. Cf. *pronation*.

Supination of the left hand was limited by one half.... Zipp v. Gasen's Drug Stores, Inc., 449 S.W.2d 612, 622 (Mo. 1970).

supine (soo′pīn) [L. *supinus* lying on the back, face upward] lying with the face upward. See also *supination*.

supine position See *position, dorsal*.

suppuration (sup″u-ra′shun) [L. *sub* under + *puris* pus] the formation of pus; the act of becoming converted into and discharging pus.

The X-ray burn produced **suppuration** from the surgical incision. The pain was intense and constant. Not the least of the resultant injuries was that of radiation fibrosis of the lung. Spontaneous rib fractures occurred. A phrenic nerve block was employed as a palliative for the intense pain. She was hospitalized 15 times while under the care of Danon, Osder, and Stricker. In March 1967 Mrs. Lopez entered New York University Hospital for reconstructive surgery. She is still under medical supervision. Lopez v. Swyer, 279 A.2d 116, 119 (Super.Ct. N.J.1971).

suprascapular (soo″prah-skap′u-lar) situated on the upper part of the scapula. See also *scapula*.

Upon regaining consciousness, Mrs. Jones experienced intense pain in her neck, left shoulder and left arm. Mrs. Jones was diagnosed as having **suprascapular** nerve palsy which was allegedly caused by the malpositioning of her arm on the arm board and the changes in the angle of the operating table during the course of the surgery. Jones v. Harrisburg Polyclinic Hosp., 437 A.2d 1134, 1136 (Pa.1981).

supraspinal ligament See *ligamentum supraspinale*.

surgery (sur′jer-e) [L. *chirurgia*, from Gr. *cheir* hand + *ergon* work] that branch of medicine which treats diseases, injuries, and deformities by manual or operative methods. See also *trauma* (Exnicious case).

"Surgery" has been defined as "[t]herapy of a distinctly operative kind, such as cutting operations, the reduction and putting up of fractures and dislocations, and similar manual forms of treatment." Napier v. Greenzweig, 256 F. 196, 197 (2 Cir. 1919), and as "[t]he art or practice of healing by manual operation...." Black, Law Dictionary (4 ed.) p. 1612. Accord, Goss v. Goss, 102 Minn. 346, 351, 113 N.W. 690, 692 (1907) ("a surgeon is a physician who treats bodily injuries and ills by manual operations and the use of **surgical** instruments and appliances"). See, also, State v. Houck, 32 Wash.2d 681, 695, 203 P.2d 693, 701 (1949) (practice of obstetrics covered). See, generally, 40A Wd. & Phr. (Perm.ed.) p. 468. McKee v. Likins, 261 N.W.2d 566, 576 (Minn.1977).

... the meaning, in insurance law, of "medical or **surgical** attention," as used in the question in the application in controversy, is, "had the plaintiff, before signing of the application, received medical or **surgical** attention for an illness or an accident of such a character as to affect the general soundness and healthfulness of the system seriously? It does not mean a mere temporary indisposition which does not tend to undermine or weaken the constitution of the insured...." Mutual

Life Ins. Co. of New York v. Bishop, 209 S.E.2d 223, 227–8 (Ct.App.Ga.1974).

The term "**surgery**" as used in the Workmen's Compensation Act has been held to embrace "only cutting operations." Truck Insurance Exchange v. Seelbach, 161 Tex. 250, 339 S.W.2d 521. Texas Employers' Insurance Ass'n v. Shirey, 391 S.W.2d 75, 78 (Ct.Civ.App.Tex.1965).

surgery, anterior cervical

Plaintiff, Jannette Riedinger, suffered a "whiplash" neck injury in an automobile accident in May, 1967. In May of 1969, to correct problems sustained in that injury, plaintiff underwent corrective surgery known as "**anterior cervical excision**" at the Harborview Hospital, Seattle, Washington, performed by a Dr. White. The nature of that operation in a simplified fashion was to approach from the anterior and right side of plaintiff's neck, make a small incision slightly below the Adam's apple, spread various tissues to get at the site, then remove the intervertebral disc lying between the 5th and 6th cervical vertebrae. Those vertebrae were not fused, at that time. Riedinger v. Colburn, 361 F.Supp. 1073, 1075 (D.Idaho 1973).

surgery, cosmetic that department of plastic surgery which deals with procedures designed to improve the patient's appearance by plastic restoration, correction, removal of blemishes, etc.

The Department of Health has adopted a definition of **cosmetic surgery** which was approved by the California Medical Association. It defines **cosmetic surgery** as, "Surgery to alter the texture or configuration of the skin and its relationship with contiguous structures of any feature of the human body. [¶] This alteration would be considered by the average prudent observer to be within the range of normal and acceptable appearance for the patient's age and ethnic background and by competent medical opinion to be without risk to the patient's physical or mental health. [¶] It means only surgery which is sought by the patient for personal reasons and is not used to denote surgery which is needed to correct or improve physical features which may be functionally normal but which attracts undue attention or even ridicule by his peers, or which an average person would consider to be conspicuous, objectionable, abnormal or displeasing to others. [¶] Operations performed to correct congenital anomalies, to remove tumors, or restore parts which were removed in treatment of a tumor or repair a deformity or scar resulting from injury, infection, or other disease process is obviously not cosmetic even though the appearance may be improved by the procedure."

Surely, castration and penectomy cannot be considered surgical procedures to alter the texture and configuration of the skin and the skin's relationship with contiguous structures of the body. Male genitals have to be considered more than just skin, one would think....

It is clearly impossible to conclude that transsexual surgery is **cosmetic surgery**, even using the definition relied on by the Director. Drs. Leibman and Brown and Webster's dictionary define cosmetic as "beautifying, pertaining to or making for beauty," that which tends "to beautify or enhance the appearance of a person." G.B. v. Lackner, 145 Cal.Rptr. 555, 558–9 (Ct.App.Cal.1978).

surgery, elective See *elective*.

surgery, ghost

We now address the nature of the claim resulting from the performance of the operation by a physician other than the one named in the consent form, so called "**ghost surgery.**" If the claim is characterized as a failure to obtain informed consent, the operation may constitute an act of medical malpractice; if, however, it is viewed as a failure to obtain any consent, it is better classified as a battery....

The Judicial Council of the American Medical Association has declared:

To have another physician operate on one's patient without the patient's knowledge and consent is a deceit. The patient is entitled to choose his own physician and he should be permitted to acquiesce in or refuse to accept the substitution. The surgeon's obligation to the patient requires him to perform the surgical operation: (1) within the scope of authority granted by the consent to the operation; (2) in accordance with the terms of the contractual relationship; (3) with complete disclosure of all facts relevant to the need and the performance of the operation; and (4) to utilize his best skill in performing the operation. It should be noted that it is the operating surgeon to whom the patient grants consent to perform the operation. The patient is entitled to the services of the particular surgeon with whom he or she contracts. The surgeon, in accepting the patient is obligated to utilize his personal talents in the performance of the operation to the extent required by the agreement creating the physician-patient relationship. He cannot properly delegate to another the duties which he is required to perform personally.

Under the normal and customary arrangement with private patients, and with reference to the usual form of consent to operation, the surgeon is obligated to perform the operation, and may use the services of assisting residents or other assisting surgeons to the extent that the operation reasonably requires the employment of such assistance. If a resident or other physician is to perform the operation under the guidance of the surgeon, it is necessary to make a full disclosure of this fact to the patient, and this should be evidenced by an appropriate statement contained in the consent.

If the surgeon employed merely assists the resident or other physician in performing the operation, it is the resident or other physician who becomes the operating surgeon. If the patient is not informed as to the identity of the operating surgeon, the situation is "**ghost surgery.**"

Judicial Council of the American Medical Ass'n, Op. 8.12 (1982); **see also** "Questions and Answers," 209 J.A.M.A. 947 (1969) (describing the performance of surgery by a resident operating under the supervision of a surgeon, but without the consent of the patient, as a fraud and deceit); American College of Surgeons, "Statements on Principles," § I.A. (June 1981) (it is unethical to mislead a patient as to the identity of the doctor who performs the operation). Perna v. Pirozzi, 457 A.2d 431, 440 (N.J.1983).

surgery, minor surgery restricted to the management of minor problems and injuries.

ORS 685.010(3) provides:

" '**Minor surgery**' means the use of electrical or other methods for the surgical repair and care incident thereto of superficial lacerations and abrasions, benign superficial lesions, and the removal of foreign bodies located in the superficial struc-

tures; and the use of antiseptics and local anesthetics in connection therewith." Hardt v. Board of Naturopathic Examiners, 606 P.2d 1169, 1171 (Ct.App.Or.1980).

surgery, oral that branch of the healing arts which deals with the diagnosis and the surgical and adjunctive treatment of diseases, injuries, and defects of the mouth, the jaws, and associated structures.

"Oral surgery" is a term used to describe surgery which is associated with the teeth, jaws, and mouth structures (see Webster's Third New International Dictionary.... Associates for Oral Surg., Ltd. v. Assoc. for Surg., 350 N.E.2d 109, 113 (App.Ct.Ill.1976).

Dr. Smith defined **oral surgery** as

"... that part of dentistry that deals with the diagnosis, surgical and adjunctive treatment of injuries, disease, malformations of the human jaws and associated structures." Campbell v. Oliva, 424 F.2d 1244, 1248 (6th Cir. 1970).

surgery (rules and regulations)

In the present case the appellants were prevented from introducing into evidence the Arkansas Department of Health's "Rules and Regulations for Hospitals and Related Institutions in Arkansas," which specifically require that a complete history and physical work-up by a physician be in the chart of every patient prior to surgery. These standards are applicable statewide and would, therefore, be applicable as to the community in which appellee practiced at the time of the occurrence. [Dissent.] Hively v. Edwards, 646 S.W.2d 688, 693 (Ark.1983).

surgery, stereotactic; surgery stereotaxic a technique for the production of sharply circumscribed lesions in specific groups of cells in deep-seated brain structures after locating the discrete structure by means of three-dimensional coordinates; the lesions are made by such agents as heat, cold, x-ray or ultrasonic radiation, etc. Called also *stereoencephalotomy.*

Sus-Phrine (sus'frin) trademark for a preparation of epinephrine. See also *epinephrine.*

suture (su'chur) [L. *sutura* a seam] 1. material used in closing a surgical or traumatic wound with stitches. 2. a stitch or series of stitches made to secure apposition of the edges of a surgical or accidental wound; used also as a verb to indicate the application of such stitches.

... the doctor's alleged negligence in failing to properly **suture** Mrs. White's liver following a laceration which occurred in the course of the removal of her gall bladder. White v. McCool, 395 So.2d 774–5 (La.1981).

On two separate occasions, the plaintiff had to endure substantial pain during the removal of **sutures** from lacerations she had received. The first incident was shortly after the accident whereupon approximately one hundred twenty-five **sutures** had to be removed. Plaintiff testified that the pain was so severe that she perspired excessively during the procedure and had to hold on to two nurses until all the stitches were removed. The second time when stitches had to be removed was after the surgery performed by Dr. Henderson....

Dr. Henderson described the surgery he performed on the plaintiff as being very delicate in that the tissues were very thin and very near the eye. In addition to the one hundred twenty-

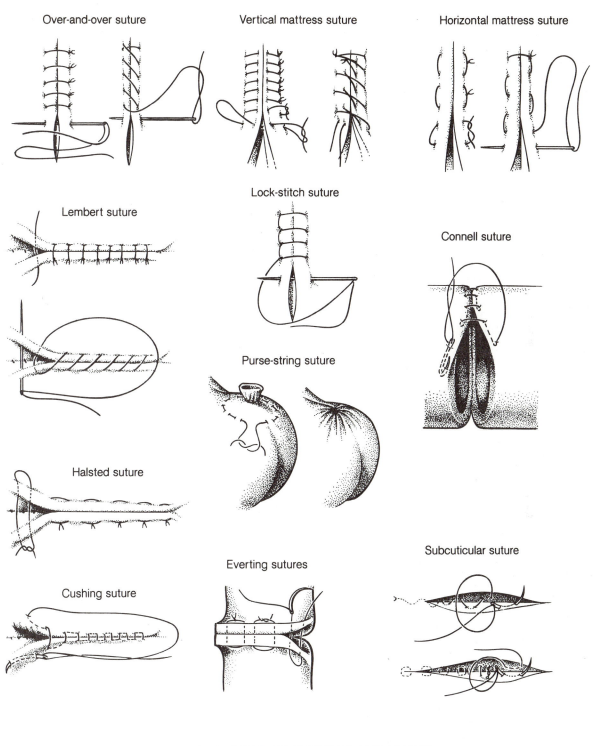

Over-and-over suture

Vertical mattress suture

Horizontal mattress suture

Lembert suture

Lock-stitch suture

Connell suture

Purse-string suture

Halsted suture

Cushing suture

Everting sutures

Subcuticular suture

VARIOUS TYPES OF SUTURES AND KNOTS
(Nealon)

five stitches originally taken in plaintiff's face, a myriad of other **sutures** were required. Hukill v. U.S. Fidelity and Guaranty Co., 386 So.2d 172, 174 (Ct.App.La.1980).

Dr. Lingenfelter did a very extensive repair job on the lacerations on his face. The cuts were irregular and ragged and required repairs by restoring the various anatomical portions to their normal position, which required three layers of **sutures**. Bray v. Yellow Freight System, Inc., 483 F.2d 500, 506 (10th Cir. 1973).

suture, catgut See *catgut.*

suture, interrupted a type of suture in which each stitch is made with a separate piece of material.

She argues he should have used **interrupted sutures** to close the peritoneal and fascial layers of her abdomen, put drains in the wound, and used large retention sutures around the incision to hold it together. Trichel v. Caire, 427 So.2d 1227, 1232 (Ct.App.La.1983).

suture, retention a reinforcing suture for abdominal wounds, utilizing exceptionally strong material like braided silk, stainless steel, or silkworm gut, and including a large amount of tissue in each stitch; intended to relieve pressure on the primary suture line and prevent postoperative disruption.

Dr. Texada is the only witness who testified he would have used these measures [both interrupted and **retention sutures**] because of the possibility of infection, her substantial loss of blood, and obesity. The other doctors testified they would not have expected poor healing, did not consider her overweight condition extreme enough to require **retention sutures** (which involve some discomfort).... Trichel v. Caire, 427 So.2d 1227, 1232 (Ct.App.La.1983).

suture, stainless steel

In 1968, Dr. Blodgett, a physician and surgeon practicing in the same geographic area as defendant, found in treating plaintiff that she had a recto-vaginal fistula. He proceeded to repair this condition surgically and in doing so discovered that the nonabsorbable **stainless steel sutures** employed by defendant in 1949 had become distorted into a figure-eight in the immediate area of the fistula. Brown v. Colm, 522 P.2d 688–9 (Cal.1974).

sweat (swet) the perspiration; the liquid secreted by the sweat glands (glandulae sudoriferae), having a salty taste and a pH that varies from 4.5 to 7.5. Sweat produced by the eccrine sweat glands is clear with a faint characteristic odor, and contains water, sodium chloride, and traces of albumin, urea, and other compounds; its composition varies with many factors, e.g., fluid intake, external temperature and humidity, and some hormonal activity. Sweat produced by the larger, deeper, apocrine sweat glands of the axillae contains, in addition, organic material which on bacterial decomposition produces an offensive odor.

Although often used interchangeably, the terms "**sweat**" and "perspiration" are not identical, and do not define or describe the same thing. Located beneath the surface of the skin are glands known as **sweat** glands, each having an opening or duct at the surface of the skin, referred to as the mouth of the

sweat gland. "Sweat" is the substance which is formed in the **sweat** glands before it appears on the surface of the skin. In a general sense, "perspiration" means any secretion which passes through the skin, which would include a secretion which passed through at a place where no **sweat** glands were located. Carter Products v. F.T.C., 186 F.2d 821, 823 (7th Cir. 1951).

sweat gland See *glandulae sudoriferae.*

sweat test See *test, sweat.*

swelling (swel'ing) a transient abnormal enlargement or increase in volume of a body part or area not caused by proliferation of cells.

In the case at bar the evidence was sufficient for the jury to conclude that a reasonably prudent man having and exercising the skill, care, knowledge, and attention ordinarily possessed and exercised by physicians in good standing would have recognized, first, that plaintiff's fracture was of such a nature [a Colles Fracture] that tremendous **swelling** would soon occur and, second, that if a circular plaster cast were applied, this **swelling** would require the loosening of the cast to such an extent that the bone fragments could not be held in a stable position, thereby resulting in deformity of the wrist. Larsen v. Yelle, 246 N.W.2d 841, 844 (Minn.1976).

swine flu See *polyneuritis, acute febrile.*

Swine Flu Act See *National Swine Flu Immunization Program of 1976.*

sycosis (si-ko'sis) [Gr. *sykōsis*, from *sykon* fig] a disease marked by inflammation of the hair follicles, especially of the beard.

sycosis barbae See *sycosis vulgaris.*

sycosis vulgaris an inflammatory, papulopustular staphylococcal infection of the bearded region in which the primary lesion is a follicular, pin-head sized pustule pierced by a hair, which, if neglected, may become chronic. Called also *barber's itch* and *s. barbae.* See also *pseudofolliculitis.*

... the plaintiff grew a beard on advice of his dermatologist in the treatment of a condition of **pseudofolliculitis barbae** ("**PFB**"), a condition that afflicts, almost exclusively, members of the black race.

PFB, colloquially known as "razor bumps" or "shaving bumps," is a condition far more common and much more severe among blacks than members of other races. It is caused by the ingrowing of hairs in the beard area of the face and neck. Regular shaving with a sharp blade is usually the precipitating stimulus, the hairs become sharpened points, and the natural curvature of the hair and the hair follicle—aggravated in blacks—facilitates ingrowth. Papules form where the hair is ingrown as the result of an inflammatory foreign body reaction. In severe reactions, papules may become pustules and subsequently abscesses. If the condition is not treated, a danger of permanent disfigurement of the face exists. Woods v. Safeway Stores, Inc., 420 F.Supp. 35, 37 (E.D.Va.1976).

sympathectomy (sim"pah-thek'to-me) [*sympathetic* + Gr. *ektomē* excision] the transection, resection, or other interruption of some portion of the sympathetic nervous pathways. Operations may be named according to the topographic location of the nerve, ganglion, or plexus operation on, as *cervical, dorsal, lumbar,* or *thoracolumbar s.,* or in reference to the diaphragm, as *subdiaphragmatic, supradiaphragmatic,* or *transdiaphragmatic s.*

When medication failed to dilate the blood vessels in the patient's foot, Dr. Ochsner performed a left lumbar **sympathectomy,** an operation in which nerves controlling the flow of blood to the leg are severed, allowing the blood to flow without restraint. In a few days the foot improved and Hemingway was discharged. Hemingway v. Ochsner Clinic, 722 F.2d 1220, 1222 (5th Cir. 1984).

Later, she underwent two surgical procedures. The first was for repair and removal of part of her fractured clavicle, and the second, a thoracic **sympathectomy,** to relieve pain by severing nerves to the upper extremity. Kosch v. Monroe, 433 N.E.2d 1062, 1070 (App.Ct.Ill.1982).

To relieve the acute discomfort caused by vasospasm, the treating specialist, Dr. Horwitz, recommended first an arteriogram and then a **sympathectomy,** a surgical procedure in which a sympathetic nerve regulating blood flow to the hand is severed in order to eliminate the contractions causing the spasms, so that circulation to the extremity could increase. Sears, Roebuck & Co. v. Workmen's Comp. Appeal Bd., 409 A.2d 486–7 (Commonwealth Ct.Pa.1979).

Other Authorities: Gerba v. Public Emp. Retirem. Sys. Trustees, 416 A.2d 314–15 (N.J.1980); Aretz v. U.S., 456 F.Supp. 397, 403 (S.D.Ga.1978); Grunenthal v. Long Island R. Co., 393 U.S. 156, 161–2, 89 S.Ct. 331, 334, 21 L.Ed.2d 309 (1968); New York Life Ins. Co. v. Eicher, 93 S.E.2d 269, 272 (Sup.Ct. App.Va.1956).

sympathectomy, chemical suppression of the activity of the sympathetic nervous system by appropriate drugs.

... was advised to undergo a "chemical sympathectomy" (injection of local anesthetic) to relieve the foregoing leg pain.
   Dr. Pellegrin also described the procedure for treatment by a **chemical sympathectomy.** He testified that the arteries are controlled by the sympathetic nervous system and that certain of the nerves are associated with the artery walls. He explained further that certain impulses cause the walls of a vessel to contract, thereby decreasing circulation. However, if such impulses are cut off the vessels are allowed to relax. The purpose of the **chemical sympathectomy** is to render ineffective those portions of the nervous system which cause the contractions. Thompson v. Occidental Life Insurance Co. of Cal., 513 P.2d 353, 360, 365–6 (Cal.1973).

sympathectomy, lumbar

After consultation with Dr. Story, Dr. Miller recommended that plaintiff undergo a **lumbarsympathectomy,** a surgical procedure involving the excision of a two- or three-inch section of the sympathetic nerve....
   During the operation Dr. Miller identified what appeared to him to be the sympathetic nerve chain. Upon instructions from Dr. Story, who also identified it as a nerve, Dr. Miller cut it. Immediately after the structure was cut it became apparent that Dr. Miller had cut the right ureter rather than the sympathetic nerve. Baker v. Story, 621 S.W.2d 639–40 (Ct.Civ.App. Tex.1981).

An operation known as a **lumbarsympathectomy** was performed. It involved removal of a section of the nerve in order that its fibers going to the injured limb are interrupted. Harrelson v. U.S., 420 F.Supp. 788, 791 (S.D.Ga.1976).

Upon arriving at Methodist Hospital, the boy underwent a **lumbar sympathectomy** and also a fasciotomy. The treatment was unsuccessful, and Curtis' right leg later had to be amputated just below the knee. Leong v. Wright, 478 S.W.2d 839, 842 (Ct.Civ.App.Tex.1972).

symphysis (sim'fĭ-sis), pl. *sym'physes* [Gr. "a growing together, natural junction"] a site or line of union; used in official anatomical nomenclature to designate a type of cartilaginous joint in which the apposed bony surfaces are firmly united by a plate of fibrocartilage; called also *fibrocartilaginous joint.*

symphysis, acetabular

Dr. Zurrow found that Willis Jones had an abnormal separation of the **acetabular symphysis** of the right ilium and ascending ramus of the right pubis which had healed. Dr. Jacobs indicated that the separation was not caused by the accident but was a normal condition and that by the time of the trial it had been filled with cartilage as part of the normal growth process. Jones v. U.S., 265 F.Supp. 858, 861 (S.D.N.Y.1967).

symphysis publica [NA]; **symphysis pubis** the joint formed by union of the bodies of the pubic bones in the median plane by a thick mass of fibrocartilage; called also *s. ossium pubis* and *pubic s.*

Carrier knew before trial that eight-year-old Larry Washington had suffered a pelvic injury manifested by separation of the **symphysis pubis** and separation of the sacroiliac joint, producing a difference in leg lengths of one and one-half inches which was a permanent deformity. Campbell v. Government Employees Ins.Co., 306 So.2d 525, 529 (Fla.1974).

They both likewise agreed that there was a separation of the **pubic symphysis.** Dr. Jacobs testified that this separation would produce local tenderness of a non-permanent nature and that there is no functional or disabling effect. Dr. Zurrow attempted to controvert this testimony only in the most general and unconvincing terms. Jones v. U.S., 265 F.Supp. 858, 861 (S.D.N.Y.1967).

The medical prognosis of plaintiff Dobson is as follows: he has weak spots on the scar seven and one-half inches long left of the midline below the **symphysis** to near the pubic bone which will develop into incisional hernias requiring surgery.... Dobson v. Myers, 247 F.Supp. 427, 430 (M.D.Pa.1965).

symptom (simp'tum) [L. *symptoma;* Gr. *symptōma* anything that has befallen one] any subjective evidence of disease or of a patient's condition, i.e., such evidence as perceived by the patient; a change in a patient's condition indicative of some bodily or mental state. See also *sign.*

The regulations take particular note of the manner in which **symptoms,** including pain will be evaluated:
   The effects of all symptoms, including severe and prolonged pain, must be evaluated on the basis of a medically determinable impairment which can be shown to be the cause of the symptom. We will never find that you are disabled based on your symptoms, including pain, unless medical signs or find-

ings show that there is a medical condition that could be reasonably expected to produce those symptoms.

20 C.F.R. § 404.1529. Gallagher on Behalf of Gallagher v. Schweiker, 697 F.2d 82–3 (2d Cir. 1983).

symptom, cardiac

Furthermore, Dr. Roberts testified without contradiction that the only one of Mrs. Stoleson's symptoms that is unequivocally a **cardiac symptom**—a pain in the left side of her chest that radiates down her left arm—she herself attributes not to heart disease but to some undefined, and apparently non-existent, lung ailment. Stoleson v. U.S., 708 F.2d 1217, 1223 (7th Cir. 1983).

symptom, subjective one that is perceptible to the patient only.

In Bittel v. Richardson, 3 Cir. 1971, 441 F.2d 1193, the court said:

> The Act and the regulations [20 C.F.R. § 404.1502(a)] promulgated by the Secretary pursuant to it require a **subjective** determination of the claimed disability. Symptoms which are real to the claimant, although unaccompanied by objective medical data, may support a claim for disability.... [Cases omitted.] [Id. at 1195.]
>
> ... Thus, Congress chose not to limit to laboratory techniques and evaluations the kind of evidence which may support a claim of disability, but instead adopted a broader standard encompassing all medical techniques. And as was stated in Ber v. Celebrezze, supra, 332 F.2d [293] at 299 [2 Cir. 1964]: "... even pain unaccompanied by objectively observable symptoms which is nevertheless real to the sufferer and so intense as to be disabling will support a claim for disability benefits." [Id. at 1195.] DePaepe v. Richardson, 464 F.2d 92, 99–100 (5th Cir. 1972).

symptoms, withdrawal symptoms which follow sudden abstinence from a drug to which a person has become addicted.

Another factor in determining a drug's potential for abuse is the existence of **withdrawal symptoms**. As to **withdrawal symptoms** associated with Librium and Valium, Finding 34 seems to us to be conclusive. That Finding states: "Dr. John G. Lofft, a psychiatrist and specialist in the treatment of alcoholism and allied addictions, testified that the abstinence syndrome associated with Librium and Valium withdrawal compares to that experienced after abrupt withdrawal from barbiturates (Tr. 550). It is characterized in its mildest form by insomnia and increased anxiety (Tr. 548–49). When the patient has been taking elevated doses for long periods of time the withdrawal syndrome is marked by restlessness, tremulousness, muscle pains, perspiration, hallucinations, and sometimes, although not frequently, convulsive seizures (Tr. 540, 543, 547). Hoffman-La Roche, Inc. v. Kleindienst, 478 F.2d 1, 10 (3d Cir. 1973).

synchondrosis (sin"kon-dro'sis), pl. *synchondro'ses* [Gr. *synchondrōsis* a growing into one cartilage] a type of cartilaginous joint that is usually temporary, the intervening hyaline cartilage ordinarily being converted into bone before adult life.

There is no spondylolisthesis and the sacro-iliac **synchondrosis** are patent. Chabert v. City of Westwego Police Pension, 423 So.2d 1190, 1193 (Ct. of App.La.1982).

syncope (sin'ko-pe) [Gr. *synkopē*] a temporary suspension of consciousness due to generalized cerebral ischemia; a faint or swoon.

... **syncopal** episodes (temporary loss of consciousness)....

... In a letter of November 19, 1974 Dr. Matthew N. Smith, a specialist in neurological surgery, stated that her syncopal episodes were suggestive of "minor seizures"....

... Since the spring of 1969 she has lost consciousness on many occasions both at home and at work. A number of lay witnesses, family, neighbors and former coemployees testified to having been present during one or more of these **syncopal** episodes. Following these episodes it is often necessary for claimant to stay in bed for several days before she can get up and resume her normal activities. Cornett v. Califano, 590 F.2d 91–2 (4th Cir. 1978).

Dr. Helm's diagnosis was **syncope**, or fainting, related to aortic valvular stenosis and caused by a deficiency in the amount of blood reaching the brain. Guillory v. U.S. Fidelity & Guar. Ins. Co., 420 So.2d 119, 121 (La.1982).

syndactylism See *syndactyly.*

syndactyly (sin-dak'tĭ-le) [Gr. *syn* with + *daktylos* finger] the most common congenital anomaly of the hand, marked by persistence of the webbing between adjacent digits, so they are more or less completely attached; generally considered an inherited condition, the anomaly may also occur in the foot.

Syndactylism is a genetic abnormality that can only appear when both the sire and the dam are carriers of the recessive gene. Therefore, Farro, as well as several of the heifers purchased by Two Rivers, were carriers. **Syndactylism** is exhibited by the fusion or nondivision of the functional digits of one or more feet of a cow. It is a hereditary genetic trait traced to the recessive gene. It is virtually impossible to detect the existence of a recessive genetic trait such as **syndactylism** until it is manifested by the union of two carriers.... Two Rivers Co. v. Curtiss Breeding Service, 624 F.2d 1242, 1244–5 (5th Cir. 1980).

syndrome (sin'drōm) [Gr. *syndromē* concurrence] a set of symptoms which occur together; the sum of signs of any morbid state; a symptom complex. In genetics, a combination of phenotypic manifestations. Cited in Bluebonnet Express, Inc. v. Foreman, 431 S.W.2d 45, 48 (Ct.Civ. App.Tex.1968).

Syndrome, acquired immune deficiency (AIDS)

The 1980's have seen the emergence of a new and deadly disease, **acquired immune deficiency syndrome** or, as it is more commonly referred to, **AIDS**. The disease is characterized by an improperly functioning immune system which results in a lack of the normal body defense mechanisms and leaves the victim vulnerable to a wide variety of opportunistic diseases. Johnson, AIDS, 52 Medico-Legal Journal 3 (1984). At present, there is no known cause or cure and the mortality rate is high.[3]

Medical researchers have identified a number of groups which have a high incidence of the disease and are labeled "high risk" groups. The overwhelming percentage of **AIDS** victims are homosexual or bisexual males with multiple sexual partners (72%) and intravenous drug users (17%).[4]

The public has reacted to the disease with hysteria. Reported accounts indicate that victims of **AIDS** have been faced with social censure, embarrassment and discrimination in nearly every phase of their lives, including jobs, education and housing.[5] It is with the above facts in mind that we analyze the respective interests in this case. [[3] The mortality rate may be as high as forty per cent (40%). Blodgett, Despite the public's hands-off attitude towards AIDS, those who discriminate against the disease's victims are finding no immunity from the law, 12 Student Law. 8 (Jan. 1984). [4] Other high risk groups are hemophiliacs (1%), heterosexual partners of AIDS victims (1%), and blood transfusion recipients (1%). Centers for Disease Control, United States Public Health Service, Morbidity and Mortality Weekly Report (June 22, 1984) at 1–2. [5] See, e.g., Flaherty, A Legal Emergency Brewing Over AIDS, Nat'l, L.J. July 9, 1984, at 1, col. 3; Pagano, Quarantine Considered for AIDS Victims, 4 Cal.Law. 17 (March 1984); Blodgett, supra, n. 3; Reaves, AIDS and the Law, 69 ABAJ 1014 (Aug. 1983).] South Florida Blood Service v. Rasmussen, 467 So.2d 798, 800 (Dist.Ct.App.Fla.1985).

Much of the information and statistical data on **AIDS** emanates from the United States Department of Health and Human Services, Public Health Service, Centers for Disease Control in Atlanta, Georgia [hereinafter "CDC"], which define **AIDS**, for purposes of epidemiologic surveillance, as "a reliably diagnosed disease that is at least moderately indicative of an underlying cellual immunodeficiency in a person who has had no known underlying cause of cellular immunodeficiency, nor any other cause of reduced resistance reported to be associated with that disease." [15]

Dr. John P. Hanrahan, an internal medicine specialist and epidemiologist at the CDC, testified that the cellular immunodeficiency referred to is a condition in which the body's immune system is compromised, impairing its ability to resist infections which, in the normal system, would be easily defeated.[16]

As a result of this dysfunction, the body becomes a defenseless host to an array of opportunistic infections or rare cancer disorders, notably, a previously exotic malignancy known as Kaposi's sarcoma [17] which, though formerly limited to males in Equatorial Africa and elderly men of eastern European descent,[18] has now appeared in 30% of all **AIDS** cases, and a variety of pneumonia—generally fatal for **AIDS** suffers—which has appeared in 50% of all AIDS cases.[19]

The immunodeficient condition produces symptoms which include enlarged lymph nodes ["swollen glands"], diarrhea, unexplained weight loss, and persistent skin markings associated with Kaposi's sarcoma.[20]

Its incubation period is uncertain and is variously said to range anywhere from 1 to 4 years.[21] [[15] Centers for Disease Control, MMWR, Vol. 32, No. 24, June 24, 1983. [16] H. Masur, An Outbreak of Community-Acquired Pneumocystis Carinii Pneumonia—Initial Manifestation of Cellular Immune Dysfunction, New England Journal of Medicine, Vol. 305, No. 24, December 10, 1981, p. 1431. [17] Acquired Immunodeficiency Syndrome Cause(s) Still Elusive, J.A.M.A. Vol. 248, No. 12, September 24, 1982, p. 1423. [18] Disease Control Bulletin, Vol. 2, No. 5, August 21, 1981; Sexually Trans-

mitted Disease Newsletter, Vol. 5, No. 6, June 1982; D. Durack, Opportunistic Infections and Kaposi's sarcoma in Homosexual Men, New England Journal of Medicine, Vol. 305, No. 24, p. 1465, December 10, 1981; Centers for Disease Control, MMWR, Vol. 30, No. 25, July 3, 1981, p. 305. [19] State of New York, Department of Health Memorandum, Series 83–27, March 30, 1983; H. Masur, An Outbreak of Community-Acquired Pneumocystis Carinii Pneumonia—Initial Manifestation of Cellular Immune Dysfunction, New England Journal of Medicine, Vol. 305, No. 24, December 10, 1981, p. 1431. [20] State of New York, Department of Health Memorandum, Series 83–27, March 30, 1983; City Health Information, Vol. 2, No. 11, March 16, 1983. [21] T. Andreani, et al., Acquired Immunodeficiency with Intestinal Cryptosporidiosis: Possible Transmission by Haitian Whole Blood, The Lancet, May 28, 1983, p. 1187; C. Harris, et al., Immunodeficiency in Female Sexual Partners of Men with the Acquired Immunodeficiency Syndrome, New England Journal of Medicine, Vol. 308, No. 20, May 19, 1983, p. 1181; Prevention of Acquired Immune Deficiency Syndrome, J.A.M.A., March 25, 1983, Vol. 249, No. 12, p. 1544.] LaRocca v. Dalsheim, 467 N.Y.S.2d 302, 305–6 (Sup.Ct.Duchess Cty.1983).

Unfortunately, we have learned this lesson the hard way through the situation we face with the current problem of **AIDS**, a disease that destroys the body's immune system, leaving the individual highly susceptible to life-threatening infections. This disease is rapidly becoming an uncontrolled epidemic in this country. Since **AIDS** was first identified in 1981, over 1,300 Americans have been afflicted with it. Of these victims, 489 have died. Fewer than 14 percent of **AIDS** victims have survived more than 3 years after being diagnosed, and no victim has recovered fully.

The incubation period for **AIDS** is anywhere from a few months to 2 years or more. According to the Centers for Disease Control—CDC—there will be more than 2,000 cases by the end of this year. Nearly 3 to 5 new cases are reported each day. Congressional Record, S. 6168 (May 5, 1983) [Daily ed.].

Other Authorities: Congressional Record H. 2286 (April 21, 1983); H. 2585–6 (May 3, 1983) [Daily Ed.].

syndrome, acute disk

Dr. Ferguson gave the following explanation of **acute disc syndrome:**

"It's not usually one episode that produces the disc. It's minute trauma until the fibers supporting the disc give way and then you have an acute episode and the disc starts pushing on the nerve root going down the leg. . . . It's mostly associated with degenerative discs and you see degenerative arthritis of the back produce a lot of symptoms down the back and it's like a bell-shape curve. . . .

"There was no evidence of acute trauma like a blow to the back. I think you were referring to that, there was no broken bone. There was no dislocation of the lower vertebrae joints, no acute trauma, acute injury, a sudden blow. And most discs don't fall in the category following "an acute trauma or acute blow." It's the constant wear and tear of the low back and if it weakens the back and if you don't have strong ligaments supporting the disc then the disc gives way and you can just go over and pick up a safety pin and have an acute disc. But when you really get the detailed history of that individual there's usually been a history of repetitive bending and lifting with the back to lead up to the fact when he bends over and picks up the pin he has acute disc. It's just by chance that happens. Just getting out [of] a chair you can see acute disc but when you go into the history of that individual he has a history of repetitive bending or extending the back." Satrom v. N.Dak. Workmen's Compensation Bureau, 328 N.W.2d 824, 829–30 (N.Dak. 1982).

syndrome, acute organic brain severe mental symptoms arising suddenly in a person previously psychologically normal, caused by head injury, infections, endogenous and exogenous intoxications, nutritional deficiency, etc. It is characterized by a host of symptoms, including delirium, confusional states, disorientation for time and place, distractibility, restlessness, and excitement. Such disorders are reversible.

syndrome, Albright's; syndrome, Albright-McCune-Sternberg fibrous dysplasia of bone, melanotic pigmentation of the skin, and sexual precocity in the female; called also *osteitis fibrosa disseminata*.

syndrome, amotivational

Another type of possible mental deterioration or subtle personality and behavioral changes associated with heavy long-termed cannabis use, is the **amotivational syndrome**. Its most extreme form depicts a loss of interest in virtually all activities other than cannabis use. "Recently the term has been used to describe the behavior of numbers of young Americans who are for a variety of reasons dropping out of school, refusing to prepare themselves for traditional adult roles and smoking marihuana.

"This type of social maladjustment is not comparable in magnitude to that described in other cultures. However, the individual may lose the desire to work, to compete, to face challenges. Old interests and concerns are lost and the individual's life becomes centered around his compulsive drug use. In addition, the individual may ignore personal hygiene, experience loss of sex drive and avoid social interaction." (Mirin et al., 1970; Smith, 1968). In Re Jones, 110 Cal.Rptr. 765, 769–70 (Ct.App.Cal.1973).

syndrome, anterior compartment See *syndrome, anterior tibial compartment*.

syndrome, anterior tibial compartment rapid swelling, increased tension, pain, and ischemic necrosis of the muscles of the anterior tibial compartment of the leg; the skin becomes glossy, erythematous, and edematous as the necrosis occurs. The cause is unknown, but usually there is a history of excessive exertion.

. . . claiming that Dr. Edwards was negligent in failing to diagnose an **anterior compartment syndrome** and by failing to take corrective measures promptly. Hively v. Edwards, 646 S.W.2d 688–9 (Ark.1983).

Dr. Tabor gave the following explanation of **anterior tibial compartment syndrome**:

"A. . . . An anterior compartment syndrome is a group of medical words we attach to a condition that occurs in the leg between the knee and ankle where the muscles run in and over the bones and around the bones we have a different compartment. We have a compartment in front of the leg

over the bone that runs down on the side and there are about three or four muscles in here that are contained with what we call a fascia compartment containment over this. This is a very light structure. It doesn't give. When anything happens in this space or this compartment, that increases pressure, we get what is called an anterior compartment syndrome. . . . It doesn't have much give to it and when increased pressure occurs in that compartment consequences occur which become dire if the pressure increases beyond a critical point." White v. Mitchell, 568 S.W.2d 216, 221–2 (Ark.1978).

syndrome, Axenfeld's a dominantly inherited syndrome consisting of posterior embryotoxon associated with adhesion of the base of the iris to Schwalbe's ring, defective development of the angular structures and trabecular region, and, frequently, glaucoma. Called also *Axenfeld's anomaly*.

. . . a diagnosis of congenital glaucoma and **Axenfeld's syndrome**. Her visual acuity when first seen was 20/70 in the right eye, and Hand Movements in the left. Wolfe v. Califano, 468 F.Supp. 1018, 1021 (W.D.Pa.1979).

syndrome, battered-child multiple traumatic lesions of the bones and soft tissues of young children, often accompanied by subdural hematomas; such lesions are usually willfully inflicted by an adult. Called also *abused child s.*

At trial, the medical examiner testified that the infant was a victim of homicide and that the underlying cause of death was **Child Abuse Syndrome**, which he described as death caused to a child by repeated episodes of abuse and repeated injury. He based this conclusion on the fact that most of the injuries occurred over a period of weeks or months. The bone fractures were relatively old and in varying stages of the healing process. The doctor estimated that the injury to the liver was more recent, probably only two weeks old. He stated, however, that the precipitating cause of death was the fracture of the skull, which would have caused almost immediate unconsciousness and death within thirty minutes, or forty-five minutes at the most. . . .

Generally, other jurisdictions have recognized **Child Abuse Syndrome** and have stated:

"This syndrome means that a child has received repeated and/or serious injuries by non-accidental means; characteristically, these injuries are inflicted by someone who is ostensibly caring for the child. There are several elements that are the criteria for the 'battered child syndrome.' They are (1) the child is usually under three years of age; (2) there is evidence of bone injury at different times; (3) there are subdural hematomas with or without skull fractures; (4) there is a seriously injured child who does not have a history given that fits the injuries; (5) there is evidence of soft tissue injury; (6) there is evidence of neglect. . . ." People v. Jackson, 18 Cal.App. 3d 504, 506, 95 Cal.Rptr. 919, 921 (1971). State v. Durand, 465 A.2d 762–3, 767 (R.I.1983).

He believed that the child exhibited the **battered-child syndrome** reflecting trauma which had been inflicted over a period of time by some other person. He found a depression on the back of Robin's skull which appeared to be a fracture. He testified that the severe injury to Robin's forehead and the bruises he saw on her abdomen and chest appeared to be caused by "deliberate beating over a period of one to two weeks." He also observed severe massive bruises on Robin's abdominal area and declared that it was impossible such injuries could result from grand mal seizures, as defendant had suggested....

Both Dr. Wiley and Dr. Mall characterized these bruises and injuries as typical of the "**battered-child syndrome**," a condition which occurs when a child has been physically abused over a period of time. Both verified that a number of photographs which were introduced in evidence accurately portrayed the bruises and discoloration on and about Robin's head and face. People v. Demond, 130 Cal.Rptr. 590, 593–4 (Ct.App.1976).

Dr. William Anderson, a pathologist who examined the infant after she died, testified that the brain injury, the external bruises, and the 13 fractures of her ribs which were then revealed were consistent with trauma, and that subdural hemorrhages and cerebral edema were the cause of death. Dr. Barranger testified that the size of the zones of recalcification on the infant's ribs indicated that the fractures were between 1 and 3 weeks old. Dr. Homer Venters, chief of the Department of Pediatrics at St. Paul-Ramsey Hospital in St. Paul, concurred with the opinion of the other doctors that the infant's injuries were not accidental in nature but instead indicative of the **battered child syndrome**....

... The phrase "**battered child syndrome**" is a widely recognized medical diagnosis which indicates that a child has been injured by other than accidental means. See, State v. Loss, supra; McCoid, The Battered Child and Other Assaults Upon the Family: Part One, 50 Minn.L.Rev. 1; Minn.St. 626.554, subd. 1. Although the phrase has an accusatory connotation, it is intended to indicate only that the child was not injured accidentally and does not constitute an opinion as to whether any particular person injured the child. See, People v. Jackson, 18 Cal.App.3d 504, 507, 95 Cal.Rptr. 919, 921 (1971); People v. Henson, 33 N.Y.2d 63, 74, 349 N.Y.S.2d 657, 665, 304 N.E.2d 358, 364 (1973). State v. Goblirsch, 246 N.W.2d 12–15 (Minn.1976).

Other Authorities: Landeros v. Flood, 551 P.2d 389, 393 (Cal. 1976).

syndrome, battering parent See *syndrome, battered child.*

[Dr. Wallace Kennedy, a clinical psychologist, took the stand to testify about the "**battering parent syndrome**."[2] ... [[2] This term is not Dr. Kennedy's, but clearly represents his concept. See Loebach v. State, 310 N.W.2d 58 (Minn.1981).]

... He testified that the characteristics of an adult who abuses a child in a life threatening fashion almost always are, first, that the parent herself is the product of a violent, abusive environment and usually commits violent acts with growing frequency; second, that the parent is under some kind of chronic environmental stress, caused by, for example, money or housing problems, and is frequently a single parent; third, that the parent has a history of poor social judgment, in that she tends to be impulsive or explosive under stress; fourth, that the child she abuses is the product of an unplanned, difficult, and unpleasant pregnancy and is prematurely born; fifth, that the abused child is a chronically difficult child, either sickly or frequently crying. Sanders v. State, 303 S.E.2d 13, 16 (Ga.1983).

syndrome, bilateral thoracic outlet compression See *syndrome, thoracic outlet.*

syndrome, carcinoid a symptom complex associated with carcinoid tumors (argentaffinoma) and characterized by attacks of severe cyanotic flushing of the skin lasting from minutes to days and by diarrheal watery stools, bronchoconstrictive attacks, sudden drops in blood pressure, edema, and ascites. Symptoms are caused by secretion by the tumor of serotonin, prostaglandins, and other biologically active substances. Called also *argentaffinoma s.*

syndrome, carpal tunnel a complex of symptoms resulting from compression of the median nerve in the carpal tunnel, with pain and burning or tingling paresthesias in the fingers and hand, sometimes extending to the elbow.

This is an action to recover damages for personal injuries based upon the alleged medical malpractice of the defendant physician, Dr. White, who in August, 1976 operated upon plaintiff Ruth Lipsius' right hand to relieve her of symptoms which he had diagnosed as evidencing **carpal tunnel syndrome**, a pathological process defined by Dr. White at trial as compression symptoms on the median nerve. As a result, Mrs. Lipsius claims that the use of her right hand is permanently impaired...

... It is never possible, the witness stated, for **carpal tunnel syndrome** to be present when there is a negative nerve conduction test. [Footnote omitted.] Lipsius v. White, 458 N.Y.S. 2d 928, 930–2 (2d Dep't 1983).

On September 9, 1979, plaintiff was hospitalized by Dr. Rills for a **carpal tunnel** release to relieve pressure on the nerve at the wrist near the fracture site that was causing pain and numbness in the hand. Patin v. Continental Cas. Co., 424 So.2d 1161, 1163 (Ct.App.La.1982).

"This patient was first seen in this clinic on April 2, 1976, complaining of swelling and numbness in her right hand. A diagnosis of **Carpal Tunnel Syndrome** was made and she was treated with Tanderil and Deltasone which are anti-inflammatory agents used in the treatment of this disorder.... The initial diagnosis of **Carpal Tunnel Syndrome** was continued, this being an inflammatory disorder in which the tendons in the wrist area which are bound down by ligaments in a band like fashion surrounding the wrists [become inflamed] due to excessive use especially that might be seen with factory type work where one movement, motion, or job is done continuously causing the reaction to begin. There is no notation in our office records as to the patient relating this to her work; however, it was noted that she was a seamstress and that she has not been able to do her work as well and was aware that her index finger was numb and not functioning well...." Segar v. Garan, Inc., 388 So.2d 164–5 (Miss.1980).

Other Authorities: Bastien v. Califano, 572 F.2d 908, 910 (2d Cir. 1978).

syndrome, cervical a condition caused by irritation or compression of the cervical nerve roots, marked by pain in the neck radiating into the shoulder, arm, or forearm, depending on which nerve root is affected.

He found that plaintiff had a fairly typical **cervical disc syndrome**, or a herniated disc in the neck, which was pinching a nerve going down his left arm. Dr. Starr was cognizant of plaintiff's previous cervical injury which occurred in 1975. He testified that the deterioration and the spur he found to be causing plaintiff's problem had obviously been there before the accident of May 22, 1979, that it may have dated back to his original injury, or even before that. Dr. Starr stated that the trauma of the accident of February 22, 1979, resulted in a jar to the existing deteriorated condition of the disc causing the nerve to swell. Under these circumstances, the swelling of the nerve persisted and would not respond to conservative treatment. As a result of the accident, plaintiff was suffering weakness in his wrist, weakness of his triceps muscles, diminished triceps reflex, and numbness to his index, middle and ring fingers. He also had pain, stiffness and muscle spasms in his neck. Webb v. Insurance Co. of North America, 396 So.2d 508, 513 (Ct.App.La.1981).

Although Mrs. Hampton related episodes of numbness, pulling and sensations of tightness in her right arm and fingers, which Dr. Llewellyn stated could be symptoms of nerve root irritation, he opined that the injury was a sprain rather than a ruptured disc. He treated her conservatively and in October, 1966 hospitalized her for cervical traction for 16 days, diagnosing "C6–C7 **cervical neurological syndrome** post-accident manifested by neck pain and right arm neuralgia". Hampton v. Cristina, 362 So.2d 1180–1 (Ct.App.La.1978).

syndrome, child abuse See *syndrome, battered-child.*

syndrome, chronic brain a syndrome resulting from or associated with relatively permanent and more or less irreversible diffuse organic impairment of cerebral tissue function; disturbances of memory, orientation, comprehension, and affect of greater or lesser degree are characteristically present. It may occur in dementia paralytica, cerebral arteriosclerosis, brain trauma, Huntington's chorea, Pick's disease, brain tumor, etc. Abbreviated CBS.

After March, 1978, his behavior at home became somewhat belligerent and destructive, and he became unable to care for himself. In October, 1978, he was diagnosed by a psychiatrist at the Bay State Medical Center in Springfield as having "**chronic organic brain syndrome**"; by January, 1979, his mental deterioration had progressed to the point where he had ceased to be able to recognize his wife and son....

... Although in appearance he does not differ from other patients in the nursing home, his mental confusion seems total, and his conversation is nonsense. He appears not to understand who or where he is. As mentioned before, he does not recognize his wife and son. He sometimes wanders about at night having, on occasion, to be physically restrained. His impulse to disruptive behavior is controlled through heavy sedation. Nevertheless, he has occasionally kicked nurses, resisted transportation for dialysis, and pulled the dialysis tubing from his body. Although the dialysis is accompanied by some pain, the evidence falls short, perhaps, of demonstrating that the ward resists dialysis particularly; it does warrant a finding that he has no understanding whatever of its purpose, and, due to his general disruptiveness, it is forced on him without his consent. His physical condition is generally good, but for the total loss of kidney function. His dementia is irreversible. In Matter of Spring, 399 N.E.2d 493, 495–6 (App.Ct.Mass.1979), reversed and remanded 405 N.E.2d 115 (Sup.Jud.Ct.Mass. 1980).

We determine that he is mentally incompetent, the apparent cause being **chronic brain syndrome** due to cerebrovascular insufficiency and diabetes. Commitment not recommended.

3. ... his propensities are that he is oriented to time, person and place, restless, mood swings, subject to periods of agitation. Takes Mellaril for agitation. Borderline abnormal EEG.

4. ... he does require mechanical restraint to prevent him from self-injury or violence to others.

This finding is not sufficient to sustain the order adjudicating appellant incompetent. In re Moyer, 263 So.2d 286–7 (Dist. Ct.App.Fla.1972).

syndrome, compartment

He also stated that in the course of leg surgery nerve damage can result from "**compartment syndrome**" or internal bleeding inside either the anterior (front) or posterior (back) leg compartments. However it was his opinion that plaintiff's injury could not be explained by the occurrence of a "**compartment syndrome**" because that would only explain the peroneal component and would not explain the posterior tibial component in the back of the leg. Hale v. Venuto, 187 Cal.Rptr. 357, 360 (Ct.App.Cal.1982).

syndrome, cri du chat a hereditary congenital syndrome characterized by hypertelorism, microcephaly, severe mental deficiency, and a plaintive catlike cry, due to deletion of the short arm of chromosome 5. Called also *cat's cry s.*

The plaintiff mother gave birth to the infant plaintiff, who, born a "**cri-du-chat**" child, was doomed by that condition to a life of helpless physical and mental retardation. Johnson v. Yeshiva Univ., 364 N.E.2d 1340 (N.Y.1977).

syndrome, Crigler-Najjar a congenital familial form of nonhemolytic jaundice, due to the absence of the hepatic enzyme glucuronide transferase, transmitted as an autosomal recessive trait. It is characterized by the presence in the blood of excessive amounts of unconjugated bilirubin and by kernicterus and severe disorders of the central nervous system. Called also *congenital hyperbilirubinemia* and *congenital nonhemolytic jaundice.*

syndrome, Cushing's 1. a condition, more commonly seen in females, due to hyperadrenocorticism resulting from neoplasms of the adrenal cortex or the anterior lobe of the pituitary, or to prolonged excessive intake of glucocorticoids for therapeutic purposes (*Cushing's s. medicamentosus* or *iatrogenic Cushing's s.*). The symptoms and signs may include rapidly developing adiposity of the face, neck, and trunk, kyphosis caused by osteoporosis of the spine, hypertension, diabetes mellitus, amenorrhea, hypertrichosis (in females), impotence (in males), dusky complexion with purple markings (striae), polycythemia, pain in the abdomen and back, and muscular wasting and weakness. When secondary to excessive pituitary secretion of adrenocorticotropin, it is known as Cushing's disease. Called also *Cushing's basophilism,* and *pituitary basophilism.* 2. in tumors of the cerebellopontine angle and acoustic tumors: subjective noises, impairment of hearing, ipsilateral cerebellar ataxia, and eventually ipsilateral impairment of the sixth and seventh nerve function together with elevated intracranial pressure.

Plaintiff, while under treatment by Dr. Tilley, developed **Cushing's Syndrome**, which is an indication of excessive cortisone in the body....

During the course of cross examination, appellant's attorney referred Dr. Tilley to a reference book, Dermatology, by Maschella, Pillsbury and Hurley. That portion of the text relevant to this matter reads as follows:

"A. Treatment is difficult and often ineffective. Intense antibiotic therapy is necessary, with frequent bacteriologic-antibiotic sensitivity studies to guide the selection and use of antibiotics as the disease progresses. Systemic corticosteroids are effective in controlling the process, but long-term therapy is necessary and their discontinuance often leads to a flare-up of the disease...." Dupuy v. Tilley, 380 So.2d 634, 635 (Ct.App.La.1979).

... possible **Cushings Syndrome** (a condition caused by any of several kinds of tumors). Marcus v. Califano, 615 F.2d 23, 26 (2d Cir. 1979).

syndrome, Down's a condition characterized by a small, anteroposteriorly flattened skull, short, flat-bridged nose, epicanthal fold, short phalanges, and widened space between the first and second digits of hands and feet, with moderate to severe mental retardation, and associated with a chromosomal abnormality, usually trisomy of chromosome 21 (Denver classification). Called also *mongolism* and *trisomy 21 s.*

Crown denied liability, claiming that because the child was afflicted by **Down's syndrome**, a congenital condition with devastatingly adverse and permanent mental and physical consequences, he was "disabled" and thus disqualified under the ... policy exclusion.... Crown Life Ins. Co. v. Garcia, 424 So.2d 893–4 (Dist.Ct.App.Fla.1982).

At birth she suffered from a chromosomal disorder known as **trisomy 21**. The nuclei of the cells in her body contain 47 rather than the usual 46 chromosomes. This disorder is not extremely rare. Various reports estimate its incidence as one in about 600 to 1,000 live births. The victim of **trisomy 21** manifests certain physical characteristics as well as mental and developmental disabilities. Together they are called **Down's syndrome**. In re Grady, 426 A.2d 467, 469 (N.J.1981).

Jorgensen v. Meade Johnson Laboratories, Inc. (10th Cir. 1973), 483 F.2d 237, is highly pertinent and persuasive of the question before us. There the mother sustained an alteration of her chromosome structure as a result of oral contraceptives prior to the conception of twin daughters. This alteration in the chromosome structure, according to the complaint, proximately caused a **Mongoloid** deformity in the fetus during the developmental period. Renslow v. Mennonite Hospital, 367 N.E.2d 1250, 1257 (Ill.1977).

Other Authorities: American Academy of Pediatrics v. Heckler, 561 F.Supp. 395–6 (D.D.C.1983); Call v. Kezirian, 185 Cal. Rptr. 103–4 (Ct.App.Cal.1982); Phillips v. U.S., 566 F.Supp. 1, 5, 8, 11 (D.S.C.1981); Matter of Grady, 405 A.2d 851, 853–5 (Super.Ct.N.J.1979); Little v. Little, 576 S.W.2d 493, 495 (Ct. Civ.App.Tex.1979); Becker v. Schwartz, 413 N.Y.S.2d 895–6 (N.Y.1978).

syndrome, dumping a complex reaction probably due to excessively rapid emptying of the gastric contents, manifested by nausea, weakness, sweating, palpitation, varying degrees of syncope, often a sensation of warmth, and sometimes diarrhea, occurring after ingestion of food by patients who have had partial gastrectomy and gastrojejunostomy. Called also *jejunal s.* and *postgastrectomy s.*

Defendant concedes that as a result of the surgical procedures performed at the VA hospital, plaintiff suffers from the "extremely unpleasant" gastrointestinal side effect known as "dumping syndrome."...

"... he now suffers from a '**dumping syndrome**' since surgery and eats six meals a day." Kelly v. U.S., 554 F.Supp. 1001, 1003 (E.D.N.Y.1983).

Dr. Baylor felt plaintiff was suffering from a **dumping syndrome** and possibly mild diabetes. Matthews v. Matthews, 415 F.Supp. 201, 204 (E.D.Va.1976).

Following such operation the plaintiff continued to have residuals and complications which have been described by Dr. Miguel E. Martinez, the plaintiff's treating physician, as a "dumping syndrome" (Tr. 77, 78, 79) and by Dr. José M. Berio, the Government's contracted physician, as a "post gastrectomy syndrome" (Tr. 81). The plaintiff's residuals include anemia, diarrhea and failure to gain weight (Tr. 77–80). LeBron v. Secretary of Health, Education & Welfare, 370 F.Supp. 403, 406 (D.Puerto Rico 1974).

syndrome, Ehlers-Danlos a congenital hereditary syndrome characterized by hyperextensibility of the joints and hyperelasticity and fragility of the skin with poor healing of wounds, leaving scars resembling parchment, by capillary fragility, and by subcutaneous mucinous or fatty nodules following trauma. It occurs in many types with wide variability of expression, the classic type being inherited as an autosomal dominant trait. Called also *Danlos's s., cutis elastica, cutis hyperelastica, elastic skin,* and *India rubber skin.*

A medical report dated June 26, 1975 from Dr. Victor A. McKusick, a Board certified internist, stated that Mrs. Flippen had signs of an underlying connective tissue disorder called **Ehlers-Danlos syndrome**. Flippen v. Mathews, 423 F.Supp. 135, 137 (E.D.Va.1976).

syndrome, extrapyramidal any of a group of clinical disorders characterized by abnormal involuntary movements, including parkinsonism, athetosis, and chorea.

Fortunately, he was observed during one of his spastic type of seizures and it was concluded by Dr. John Jackson, who happened to walk into the room at the time he was having an **extraparamidal seizure** due to medication which he had been given at a prior time...

... Mr. Chabert's injuries were being complicated by **extraparamidal seizures** which were causing such muscle spasms as to actually reinjure the contusion of his lumbosacral region each time he had a seizure. Chabert v. City of Westwego Police Pension, 423 So.2d 1190, 1195 (Ct.App.La.1982).

syndrome, Fanconi's 1. a rare hereditary disorder, transmitted in a recessive manner and having a poor prognosis, characterized by pancytopenia, hypoplasia of the bone marrow, and patchy brown discoloration of the skin due to the deposition of melanin, and associated with multiple congenital anomalies of the musculoskeletal and genitourinary systems. Called also *Fanconi's pancytopenia, pancytopenia-dysmelia s., congenital hypoplastic anemia, constitutional infantile panmyelopathy, Fanconi's anemia*, and *congenital pancytopenia*. 2. a general term for a group of diseases marked by dysfunction of the proximal renal tubules, with generalized hyperaminoaciduria, renal glycosuria, hyperphosphaturia, and bicarbonate and water loss; the most common cause is cystinosis (q.v.) but it is also associated with other genetic diseases and occurs in idiopathic and acquired forms. When unassociated with cystinosis, the disorder is also called *de Toni-Fanconi syndrome.*

The respondent has been diagnosed as having "**Fanconi's syndrome**, associated with Vitamin D resistant rickets", which results in severe osteoporosis. State Compensation Fund v. Banninster, 476 P.2d 875–7 (Ct.App.Ariz.1970).

syndrome, Gerstmann's a combination of finger agnosia, right-left disorientation, agraphia, acalculia, and often constrictional apraxia, due to a lesion in the angular gyrus of the dominant hemisphere.

". . . The current therapy program has been amazingly successful if one is aware of the fact that an individual with this type of stroke, a so-called '**Gerstmann's Syndrome**' rarely ever improves to the point Mr. King has already reached. . . ." U.S. v. King, 442 F.Supp. 1244–5 (S.D.N.Y. 1978).

syndrome, Gilles de la Tourette's a syndrome of facial and vocal tics with onset in childhood, progressing to generalized jerking movements in any part of the body, with echolalia and coprolalia; once thought to have an unfavorable prognosis but recently shown to be responsive to treatment with butyrophenones.

The neurologist diagnosed "Involuntary movement disorder—chorea & tics (could be **Gilles de la Tourette Syndrome**)." In further remarks, he added that it "could be basal ganglion disease or **Gilles de la Tourette Syndrome** or senile chorea." As to date of onset, he estimated "40 + years ago.". . .

". . . Tics are not normally disabling, and "**Gilles de la Tourette Syndrome**" is a form of tic "involving facial twitching, continuous gestures associated with echolalia, foul language, and obsessional ideas [which] is occasionally encountered in childhood. The disorder is progressive, and sometimes associated with marked personality changes." [Cecil and Loeb, Textbook of Med. 185 (13th Ed. 1971).] Lieberman v. Califano, 592 F.2d 986, 990 (7th Cir. 1979).

syndrome, Goodpasture's glomerulonephritis associated with hemoptysis, an uncommon, rapidly progressive, usually fatal condition affecting chiefly young men; it regularly begins with respiratory infection, variable pulmonary infiltrations, hemoptysis, and anemia, followed by a rapidly progressive renal disease in which hematuria, proteinuria, hypertension, and progressive azotemia are features. An antibody directed against the alveolar basement membrane of the lungs and the glomerular basement membrane of the kidneys has been implicated.

This court has recognized that caution should be used when evaluating medical testimony. In Boldt v. Jostens, Inc., 261 N.W.2d 92 (Minn.1977), the court evaluated testimony linking exposure to glue fumes with **Goodpasture's Syndrome**. Erickson by Erickson v. Gopher Masonry, Inc., 329 N.W.2d 40, 43 (Minn.1983).

He diagnosed her condition as **Goodpasture's Syndrome**, a rare disease which attacks the basement membrane of the kidneys and the alveolar lining cells of the lungs. It is irreversible, progressive, and generally fatal, although Dr. Dines felt in August 1974 that treatment thus far had resulted in "holding" employee's renal and pulmonary condition. Even when he saw her in May 1972, however, he found marked impairment of the lungs and by September of that year she needed oxygen at all times. The impaired condition of employee's lungs resulted in great strain on her heart, causing many episodes of heart failure from December 1973 until her death July 31, 1975. . . .

. . . Both physicians said that the etiology of **Goodpasture's Syndrome** is unknown. Dr. Dines said that it is an immunologic disease in which it is thought that the victim develops antibodies to some antigen (a substance to which he is hypersensitive) and that these antibodies react against the kidneys and lungs. He also said that the antigen to which a victim reacts "can probably be many different things and different for different people" and that it is not known whether the reaction results from one exposure to an antigen or from multiple exposures. Dr. Woellner said that it is not even known whether **Goodpasture's Syndrome** is produced by an antigen, and that he had no opinion as to the cause of employee's contracting the disease. Dr. Dines, however, expressed the opinion that employee's exposure to glue fumes "had a great deal to do with her illness, and certainly caused aggravation." Boldt v. Jostens, Inc., 261 N.W.2d 92–3 (Minn.1977).

Cf. Boldt v. Jostens, Inc., Minn., 261 N.W.2d 92, filed herewith, sustaining a finding of causal relation between employee's work environment and her contraction of **Goodpasture's Syndrome**, a disease also thought to be immunologic in character but admittedly of unknown etiology, against claims that the opinion on which the finding was based lacked foundation and was not based on reasonable medical certainty. Pommeranz v. State Dep't of Public Welfare, 261 N.W.2d 90–1 (Minn.1977).

syndrome, Guillain-Barré See *polyneuritis, acute febrile.*

syndrome, Horner's; syndrome, Horner-Bernard sinking in of the eyeball, ptosis of the upper eyelid, slight elevation of the lower lid, constriction of the pupil, narrowing of the palpebral fissure, anhidrosis and flushing of the affected side of the face; caused by paralysis of the cervical sympathetic nerves. Called also *Bernard's s., Bernard-Horner s.*, and *Horner's ptosis.*

I think with the skull fracture—I mean, she undoubtedly had some damage there, but with the **Horner's Syndrome**, and the subsequent development of this paralysis, rather rapidly, makes me believe, and with my experience this is the more common thing, is that she developed a clot in the region of her internal carotid artery in her neck. Poertner v. Swearingen, 695 F.2d 435–6 (10th Cir. 1982).

syndrome, hyperabduction thoracic outlet syndrome due to compression of the brachial plexus trunk roots and axillary vessels by the pectoralis minor muscle and the coracoid process when the arms are stretched above the head, as during sleep.

syndrome, hyperkinetic a childhood disorder that usually abates during adolescence, characterized by hyperactivity, fidgetiness, excitability, impulsiveness, distractibility, short attention span, low tolerance for frustration, and difficulties in learning and perceptual motor function. Some cases are believed to be associated with brain damage and psychoses, but the specific causes of most cases has not been determined. Called also *hyperactivity* and *hyperkinesia.*

syndrome, Klinefelter's condition characterized by infertility, variable degrees of masculinization, the presence of small testes with fibrosis and hyalinization of seminiferous tubules, variable impairment of function and clumping of Leydig cells, and by an increase in urinary gonadotropins; patients tend to be of eunuchoid habitus, and about half have gynecomastia. It is associated typically with an XXY chromosome complement, although variants include XXYY, XXXY, XXXXY, and several mosaic patterns (XY/XXY, XXY, XXXY, etc.).

Appellant argues that recently developed medical information indicates that an individual with the "XYY Syndrome" may, because of his chromosomal abnormality, be more aggressive and violent than an individual with a normal chromosomal makeup. Knight v. State, 538 S.W.2d 101, 106 (Ct.Crim.App. Tex.1975).

syndrome, Mallory-Weiss hematemesis or melena that follows typically upon many hours or days of severe vomiting and retching, traceable to one or several slitlike lacerations of the gastric mucosa, longitudinally placed at or slightly below the esophagogastric junction.

The plaintiff's affidavit saying she was not informed and was not aware of the location of the exploratory laparotomy and that no doctors or hospital staff members disclosed to her that her husband had died of a perforated esophagus after being treated for an ulcer, was not contradicted since there was no evidence to the contrary and at least the allegations as to her lack of knowledge must be taken as true for purposes of the motion to dismiss.

It is true that the death certificate disclosed the cause of plaintiff's husband's death as "Mallory Weiss Syndrome" but it is a rather cruel hoax to deny a widow and 4 minor children an opportunity to test their case on the merits because the widow failed to decipher this medical term. Fure v. Sherman Hospital, 380 N.E.2d 1376, 1385–6 (App.Ct.Ill.1978).

syndrome, Marfan's a congenital disorder of connective tissue characterized by abnormal length of the extremities, especially of fingers and toes, subluxation of the lens, cardiovascular abnormalities (commonly dilatation of the ascending aorta), and other deformities. It is inherited in an autosomal dominant manner with variable degrees of expression.

It would be my opinion, still, that the presence of an aortic valve prosthesis, with even the modern cloth covered metal poppet type, with its concomitant dangers of thrombo embolic complications, bacterial endocarditis, tissue over-growth

about the valve, for example, plus the fact that a pathology of the dilated aortic root showed a connective tissue disorder, indicating an inherent weakness of the aortic room, or a possible variant of Marfan's Syndrome, which would be incompatible with flying safety. Loomis v. McLucas, 553 F.2d 634, 636 (10th Cir. 1977).

Marfan's syndrome or Marfan's disease was described by Dr. Katterhagen as a "rare disease . . . of the connective tissue or cement substance of the body. It's a genetic-transmitted disease."

The doctor testified that David Wolff had this disease, and that while the disease was not aggravated by the collision or the injuries resulting therefrom, a person suffering from the disease "who is subjected to severe trauma, which David underwent, would in all probability suffer more than a young, healthy male the same age," and that it would take him longer to recover from his injuries. Wolff v. Coast Engine Products, Inc., 432 P.2d 562, 565 (Wash.1967).

syndrome, Meniere's See under *disease.*

syndrome, Morquio's a rare form of mucopolysaccharidosis which becomes evident when the affected infant starts to walk. The condition is marked by severe dwarfism, especially of the torso, short neck, prominent sternum, dorsolumbar kyphosis, genu valgum, flatfeet, and waddling gait. In contrast to Hurler's syndrome, the mental retardation is absent or slight, the facial deformities are less striking although marked by protruding mandible and short nose, the clouding of the cornea and deafness are mild, the muscles and ligaments are usually flaccid, and the cardiovascular changes are absent, except perhaps aortic valve disease. It is transmitted as an autosomal recessive trait. Called also *mucopolysaccharidosis IV, eccentro-osteochondrodysplasia, chondro-osteodystrophy, familial osteochondrodystrophy,* and *osteochondrodystrophia deformans.*

In the doctor's view she suffered from stunted bone growth (spondylo-epiphyseal dysplasia of congenital origin). . . .

The appellant has a long history of medical problems. She is only four feet seven inches tall due to a type of dwarfism. Reading v. Mathews, 542 F.2d 993, 995 (7th Cir. 1976).

syndrome, nephrotic a condition characterized by massive edema, heavy proteinura, hypoalbuminemia, and peculiar susceptibility to intercurrent infections; called also *Epstein's s.*

At this time, tests were conducted and Langley was diagnosed as suffering from nephrotic syndrome, which is a serious kidney disease. Director, Office of Workers' Comp. v. Newport News, 676 F.2d 110, 112 (4th Cir. 1982).

syndrome, organic brain any of the mental disorders caused by or associated with impairment of brain tissue function; they may be psychotic (e.g., senile dementia, alcoholic psychoses) or nonpsychotic, acute (reversible) or chronic (irreversible). Called also *organic psychosis.* See also *syndrome, acute*; and syndrome, *chronic organic brain.*

The hospital records where decedent was confined indicate that he suffered from an "organic brain syndrome" or a "degenerative central nervous system disease" or a "chronic brain syndrome'' of unknown etiology. There were, however, references in the record, by attending physicians, that decedent's symptomology could be related to microwave exposure. Yannon v. New York Telephone Co., 450 N.Y.S.2d 893–4 (3d Dep't 1982).

The doctor's conclusions are that Quackenbush is suffering from an **organic brain syndrome** with psychotic elements. He asserts that the **organic brain syndrome** is acute—i.e., subject to change—and could be induced by the septicemia. He bases his opinion on the patient's disorientation as to place—not aware of being in a hospital; his disorientation as to the people around him—not aware of talking to a nurse and doctor during the interview; his visual hallucinations—seeing but not hearing people in the room who are not there, are the inappropriateness of his responses to the discussions on the gravity of his condition and what might result. Matter of Quackenbush, 383 A.2d 785, 788 (Morris Ct.Ct.Prob.Div.1978).

Dr. Davidson believed Mr. Britt to be suffering from **organic brain syndrome**, a form of permanent brain damage that Dr. Davidson testified reveals itself in symptoms of anxiety, depression and lowered intelligence. Mr. Britt was given a wide range of achievement tests. His spelling, reading and mathematic comprehension had been reduced to that of a fourth grader. Some improvement occurred while at Whitfield but Mr. Britt remained depressed and anxious. Britt v. Travelers Ins. Co., 556 F.2d 336, 338 (5th Cir. 1977).

Other Authorities: Matter of Spring, 405 N.E.2d 115, 118 (Sup.Jud.Ct.Mass.1980).

syndrome, parkinsonian a form of parkinsonism due to idiopathic degeneration of the corpus striatum or substantia nigra, frequently occurring as a sequel of lethargic encephalitis, although cerebral arteriosclerosis, toxins, neurosyphilis, and trauma have also been implicated. It is characterized by muscular rigidity, immobile facies (Parkinson's facies), slow involuntary tremor (present at rest but tending to disappear during sleep and on volitional movement), abolition of associated automatic movements, festinating gait, stooped posture, and salivation. Called also *postencephalitic parkinsonism*. See also *paralysis agitans*.

syndrome, pickwickian the complex of obesity, somnolence, hypoventilation, and erythrocytosis.

The diagnosis made at that time indicated that Nye was suffering from diabetes, obesity, hypertension and **Pickwickian syndrome** (Def. Ex. R; Testimony of Dr. Marcus Bloomfield, hereinafter ''Bloomfield''). The latter syndrome is a complex of exogenous obesity (self-induced), somnolence, erythrocytosis and hyperventilation or a condition in which there is a reduced amount of air entering the pulmonary alveoli, resulting in elevation of the carbon dioxide tension (Dorland, Illustrated Medical Dictionary 717 [24th ed. 1965]). Nye v. A/S D/S Svendborg, 358 F.Supp. 145, 149 (S.D.N.Y.1973).

syndrome, post cerebral concussion See *syndrome, postconcussional*.

syndrome, postconcussional amnesia, headache, dizziness, tinnitus, irritability, fatigability, sweating, palpitations of the heart, insomnia, and difficulty in concentrating, occurring after concussion of the brain.

Dr. Richardson testified that plaintiff complained of cloudiness of thinking, blurred vision, nervousness, light headedness, unsteadiness, and a sensation of pressure behind her eyes all which were typical of **post-concussion syndrome**.... Villavaso v. State Farm Mut.Auto Ins. Co., 424 So.2d 536–7 (Ct. App.La.1982).

Mrs. Prats experienced vomiting, difficulty in walking, spots in front of her eyes and temper tantrums during the period of time between the emergency room visit the day after the accident and three weeks later when she was first hospitalized. This is reflected by the testimony of Dr. Manale and the plaintiff's daughter. Drs. Mary and Dysart indicated that the problems experienced by Mrs. Prats are characteristic of post traumatic encephalopathy, also known as **post concussion syndrome**. Mrs. Prats continued to exhibit these problems, as well as rambling speech and headaches, during the period of her first hospitalization from May 17 to 29, 1978. Prats v. Moffett, 391 So.2d 1299, 1301 (Ct.App.La.1980).

Plaintiff was sent to a neurosurgeon whose diagnosis was **post cerebral concussion syndrome**, which was the result of the injury to the head and the jarring of the brain, post traumatic cervical and epidural strain, and lypertrophic osteoarthritis of the spine. Decker v. Norfolk & Western R. Co., 265 N.W.2d 785, 792 (Ct.App.Mich.1978).

Other Authorities: Yarrow v. U.S., 309 F.Supp. 922, 928 (S.D. N.Y.1970).

syndrome, post gastrectomy See *syndrome, dumping*.

syndrome, respiratory distress, of newborn a condition of the newborn marked by dyspnea with cyanosis, heralded by such prodromal signs as dilatation of the alae nasi, expiratory grunt, and retraction of the suprasternal notch or costal margins, most frequently occurring in premature infants, children of diabetic mothers, and infants delivered by cesarean section, and sometimes with no apparent predisposing cause. The syndrome includes two patterns: (*a*) *hyaline membrane disease* or *syndrome*, in which affected infants frequently die of respiratory distress in the first few days of life and at autopsy have eosinophilic hyaline material lining the alveoli, alveolar ducts, and bronchioles, and (*b*) *idiopathic respiratory distress of newborn* in which the affected infants may live, but in those that die, only resorption atelectasis is seen and there is no formation of a hyaline membrane. Called also *congenital alveolar dysplasia* and *congenital aspiration pneumonia*.

''... All the doctors who testified admitted the importance of fetal heart monitoring since this is the test which monitors '**fetal distress**' which is an indication that the fetus is being deprived of oxygen and may become asphyxiated. The evidence showed that such monitoring could be done manually or with an electronic monitoring device....'' Williams v. Lallie Kemp Charity Hosp., 428 So.2d 1000, 1005 (Ct.App.La.1983).

syndrome, rubella a congenital syndrome due to intrauterine rubella infection (German measles), characterized most commonly by cataracts, cardiac anomalies (especially patent ductus arteriosus), deafness, microcephaly, and mental retardation. See also *rubella*.

Mrs. Robak gave birth to a daughter, Jennifer, on January 12, 1973. At the time of her birth, Jennifer had a rash all over her body. She was also suffering from a loss of hearing, bilateral cataracts, a slight heart defect and possible mental retardation—all common symptoms of a **rubella syndrome** child. Robak v. U.S., 658 F.2d 471, 473 (7th Cir. 1981).

On November 19, 1972, plaintiff-appellant Tanya Dumer was born with a "**rubella syndrome;**" she suffers permanent physical and mental retardation, cataracts, and heart malfunctions.

The plaintiffs allege that as a result of the negligent diagnosis by the defendants and their failure to advise Carol Dumer of the possible effects of rubella on the fetus and of the possibility of abortion, Tanya Dumer was not aborted, to her personal injury and to the financial injury to her parents. Dumer v. St. Michael's Hospital, 233 N.W.2d 372, 374 (Wis.1975).

syndrome, scalenus; syndrome scalenus anticus pain over the shoulder, often extending down the arm (cervicobrachial s.) or radiating up the back of the neck due to compression of the nerves and vessels between a cervical rib and the scalenus anticus muscle; called also *Naffziger's s.* and *cervical rib s.*

Additionally, tests conducted in December, 1973 by a Dr. Post, who performs electromyography and electroconduction studies, led that physician to the clinical impression that the etiology of Mrs. Lipsius' problem was **scalenus syndrome** and not carpal tunnel syndrome, the former condition being described by Dr. White as "thought to be a compression of the blood vessels that course underneath the . . . scalenus anticus muscle . . . a neck muscle that attaches to the clavicle". Dr. White explained that **scalenus syndrome** could produce symptoms similar to those presented by both thoracic outlet syndrome and carpal tunnel syndrome. Lipsius v. White, 458 N.Y.S.2d 928, 930 (2d Dep't 1983).

Dr. Kleinert states that the cause of appellant's pain and discomfort was a group of symptoms called "**scalenus anticus syndrome.**" This described condition is a developmental abnormality. It is inherent in the individual. It is observed among middle-aged women more frequently and among thin women in particular; it becomes symptomatic and painful when aging causes the neck muscles to lose their tone and elasticity and causes these muscles to sag and press against nerves and blood vessels which lead to the forearms. Keel v. Thomas Industries, 463 S.W.2d 919–20 (Ct.App.Ky.1971).

syndrome, shock lung

Dr. William McBride, an internal medicine expert, also attended Terry Dale on the day of the accident and stated that the child experienced "**shock lung syndrome.**" Such a condition describes damage to the small blood vessels in the lung (capillaries) due to lack of oxygen to the blood vessels. Fluid in the lungs often occurs as a result of this damage. Dr. McBride further testified that this type of injury can impair the oxygenation of the brain which, if long enough, can cause brain damage. Cupit v. Grant, 425 So.2d 847, 852 (Ct.App.La.1982).

syndrome, Shy-Drager a progressive disorder of unknown cause that results in severe disability or death, beginning with symptoms of autonomic insufficiency including impotence (in males), constipation, urinary urgency or retention, anhidrosis, and most importantly, orthostatic hy-potension, followed by signs of generalized neurologic dysfunction, such as parkinsonian-like disturbances, cerebellar incoordination, muscle wasting and fasciculations, and coarse tremors of the legs.

syndrome, sick sinus a complex cardiac arrhythmia manifested as severe sinus bradycardia alone, sinus bradycardia alternating with tachycardia, or sinus bradycardia with atrioventricular block.

He had a paroxysmal atrial flutter fibrillation, atrial premature beats, and post atrial extra systolic SA inhibition, indicating **sick sinus syndrome.** Dr. Phillips stated that any one of these disorders could result in sudden, unexpected death without any identifiable preceding cause. Ebarb v. Insurance Co. of North America, 424 So.2d 1266, 1268 (Ct.App.La.1982).

syndrome, Stein-Leventhal a clinical symptom complex characterized by oligomenorrhea or amenorrhea, anovulation (hence infertility), and regularly associated with bilateral polycystic ovaries; excretion of follicle-stimulating hormone and 17-ketosteroids is essentially normal. Called also *polycystic ovary disease* or *syndrome*.

syndrome, Stevens-Johnson the severe form of erythema multiforme in which, in addition to other symptoms, there is involvement of the oronasal and anogenital mucosa, the eyes, and viscera; constitutional symptoms include malaise, prostration, headache, fever, and arthralgia. It may be fatal. Called also *ectodermosis erosiva pluriorificialis, erythema multiforme exudativum*, and *Johnson-Stevens disease*. See also *erythema multiforme*.

According to Dr. Guehring's testimony, **Stevens-Johnson syndrome** is an allergic reaction that can be triggered by many kinds of drugs. Little blisters show up on the skin in places such as the corner of the lip and the eye, but high fever and ulcers inside the mouth, such as John developed, were not classic symptoms of the syndrome. He said that at the time he was treating John, there was an epidemic of herpes, i.e., cold sores, and when a bad case of herpes is developing, the children got ulcers in the mouth that looked exactly the same as the **Stevens-Johnson** blisters. Menefee v. Guehring, 665 S.W.2d 811, 813–14 (Ct.App.Tex.1983).

. . . he was diagnosed as suffering from **Stevens-Johnson Syndrome**, a relatively uncommon and severe type of Erythema Multiforme. . . .

. . . **Stevens-Johnson Syndrome** is not common and its origin is unclear. It is an acute inflammatory disease marked by a variety of eruptions appearing on different areas of the body. In many respects, it is similar to an allergic reaction, such as a reaction to penicillin. Claimant's expert admitted that in New York City he saw only about two or three such cases a year. Littlejohn v. State, 451 N.Y.S.2d 225–6 (3d Dep't 1982).

Based upon this initial examination, appellee gave appellant a two-week prescription of Butazolidin. Appellant subsequently developed **Stevens-Johnson syndrome**, which may have been caused by an allergic reaction to the Butazolidin. Haynes v. Hoffman, 296 S.E.2d 216–17 (Ct.App.Ga.1982).

Other Authorities: Roman v. A. H. Robins Co., Inc., 518 F.2d 970–1 (5th Cir. 1975); Johnston v. Brother, 12 Cal.Rptr. 23–4 (Dist.Ct.App.1961).

syndrome, stroke a condition with sudden onset caused by acute vascular lesions of the brain, such as hemorrhage, embolism, thrombosis, or rupturing aneurysm, which may be marked by hemiplegia or hemiparesis, vertigo, numbness, aphasia, and dysarthria; it is often followed by permanent neurologic damage. Called also *cerebrovascular accident* and *stroke*.

For example, the 1970 insert stated that "[t]he most serious known side effect is abnormal blood clotting which can be fatal" and the 1978 warning stated that "[a] clot can result in a **stroke** (if the clot is in the brain) a heart attack (if the clot is in a blood vessel of the heart). . . ."

Because an ischemic **cerebral vascular accident** involves an occlusion, a partial or complete closing off of the vessels that supply blood to the brain, the lay warnings, such as those above quoted, went to the heart of the medical issues in this case. Lindsay v. Ortho Pharmaceutical Corp., 637 F.2d 87, 93 (2d Cir. 1980).

On August 31, 1975, Mrs. Klink suffered a massive bilateral **stroke**. At the time of the stroke, she was taking Ovulen-21, a birth control pill prescribed by defendant Dr. Fields. She had been taking the pill for approximately 17 months. She presented expert testimony that the **stroke** was caused by the birth control pill. Klink v. G. D. Searle & Co., 614 P.2d 701, 703 (Ct.App.Wash.1980).

Shortly after the start of the coronary arteriography, and while the tip of the catheter was being repositioned in the orifice of the right coronary artery, Morgenroth had a serious **stroke**, becoming aphasic and hemiplegic. According to Dr. Kerth, the happening of the stroke was more probably a complication from the internal mammary visualization procedure study than it was a coincidence. According to Dr. Selzer, a **stroke** was an unusual but possible and recognized risk of a coronary arteriography. At the time of trial, Morgenroth's residual brain damage was such that he was unable to testify; he required care in a nursing home. Morgenroth v. Pacific Medical Center, Inc., 126 Cal.Rptr. 681, 686 (Ct.App.Cal.1976).

Other Authorities: Cook v. Marshall Bros. Lincoln-Mercury, Inc., 427 So.2d 655–6 (Ct.App.La.1983); U.S. v. King, 442 F.Supp. 1244–5 (S.D.N.Y.1978); Frazier v. State Central Savings Bank, 217 N.W.2d 238, 241 (Iowa 1974).

syndrome, superior vena cava suffusion and brawny edema of the face, neck, or upper arms due to increased venous pressure incident to compression of the superior vena cava, most commonly caused by metastatic mediastinal lymph node tumor in lung cancer.

Subsequent examinations revealed Joynt had developed **superior vena cava syndrome**, which meant that the cancer had become involved in the superior vena cava—the vein that drains the blood from the upper part of the body into the heart. Because the superior vena cava cannot be surgically removed or replaced, **superior vena cava syndrome** totally precluded a surgical remedy for Joynt's unfortunate malady. Joynt v. Barnes, 388 N.E.2d 1298, 1304 (App.Ct.Ill.1979).

syndrome, tarsal tunnel a complex of symptoms resulting from compression of the posterior tibial nerve or of the plantar nerves in the tarsal tunnel, with pain, numbness, and tingling paresthesia of the sole of the foot.

Fancher, whose profession was installing overhead commercial doors, sustained a comminuted fracture of the left ankle. . . .

Following surgery and the placement of four permanent screws in his ankle, Fancher developed **tarsal tunnel syndrome**, which is numbness caused by scar tissue adjacent to nerves. Fancher v. Overhead Doors, Inc., 425 So.2d 965–6 (Ct.App.La.1983).

syndrome, temporomandibular joint dysfunction of the temporomandibular joint marked by a clicking or grinding sensation in the joint and often by pain in or about the ears, muscle tiredness and slight soreness upon waking, and stiffness of the jaw or actual trismus; it results from mandibular overclosure, condylar displacement, or stress, with deforming arthritis an occasional factor.

The term **temporomandibular joint syndrome** is defined in Dorland's Medical Dictionary (25th edition, 1974) as a "dysfunction of the temporomandibular joint marked by a clicking or grinding sensation in the joint and often by pain in or about the ears, muscle tiredness and slight soreness upon waking, and stiffness of the jaw or actual trismus; it results from mandibular overclosure, condylar displacement, or stress, with deforming arthritis an occasional factor." (Id. at p. 1527.) "Temporomandibular," in turn, is defined as "pertaining to the temporal bone and the mandible." (Id. at p. 1546.) The temporal bone is "one of the two irregular bones forming part of the lateral surfaces and base of the skull, and containing the organs of hearing." (Id. at p. 219.) And the "mandible" is "the bone of the lower jaw." (Id. at p. 907.)

A leading text, Scopp, Oral Medicine (1973) describes some of the symptoms and causes of **temporomandibular joint disorders** more fully.

Organic disorders of the temporomandibular joint are similar to disorders of any other joints of the body. . . . Likewise, the type of pain in temporomandibular joint diseases is similar to afflictions of other joints. It consists of a steady dull ache of the joint with limited, painful movement . . . . Essentially, then, we are dealing with a pain-dysfunction syndrome similar to those found in other parts of the body. . . .

Temporomandibular joint disturbances are principally of traumatogenic, pathogenic, or psychogenic origin. (Id. at p. 154.)

Later in the chapter, the author defines traumatic causes to include externally generated fractures as from an automobile accident, dislocations, and traumatic occlusions. The pathogenic causes include traumatic arthritis—which itself can result "from a blow, . . . dental procedures, or even from overzealous endotracheal intubation"—osteoarthritis, rheumatoid arthritis, infectious arthritis, benign or malignant tumors, aplasia, hypoplasia, hyperplasia, rickets, Vitamin C deficiency, hyperpituitarism and hypothyroidism. Psychogenic causes include anxiety and hysteria. (Id. at pp. 157–66.)

The author likewise points out:

"Many temporomandibular joint disorders are not really true diseases of the joint itself but instead are muscular spasms. These contractures may be disguised as joint pain. Myofacial pain, usually unilateral, results from sustained contraction of the masseter, cervical, and temporal muscles. Accordingly, many temporomandibular joint disorders are pain-disfunction syndromes." (Id. at p. 155.) Ponder v. Blue Cross of Southern California, 193 Cal.Rptr. 632, 636 (Ct.App.Cal. 1983).

syndrome, thoracic outlet compression of the brachial plexus nerve trunks, characterized by pain in arms, paresthesia of fingers, vasomotor symptoms (pallor, acrocyanosis, secondary Raynaud's phenomenon, etc.), and weakness and wasting of small muscles of the hand; it may be caused by drooping shoulder girdle, a cervical rib or fibrous band, an abnormal first rib, continual hyperabduction of the arm, or (rarely) compression of the edge of scalenus anterior muscle. See also *syndrome, hyperabduction.*

... another doctor, Dr. Warren L. Gottsegen, a vascular and thoracic surgeon, examined the plaintiff. This doctor's diagnosis after examination was a **bilateral thoracic outlet compression syndrome.** After physical therapy failed to improve plaintiff's condition, the doctor recommended surgery. Monnier v. Boutte, 420 So.2d 725–6 (Ct.App.La.1982).

Her claim was based on a diagnosis of **thoracic outlet syndrome** and bilateral median and ulnar neuropathy. In laymen's terms, occlusion of the blood vessels leading from the chest to the arms and compression of major nerve roots were causing Mrs. Cassiday to experience pain in her chest and pain, numbness, tingling, and weakness in her arms and hands. Cassiday v. Schweiker, 663 F.2d 745–6 (7th Cir. 1981).

John Cress testified that the defendant examined him by raising his arm, turning his head from left to right and listening to a stethoscope, which lasted approximately 5–6 minutes. After taking plaintiff's medical history, the defendant told plaintiff he had **thoracic outlet syndrome.** Defendant doctor explained that plaintiff had an extra rib which was pressing on an artery and vein and that he might lose his arm if the rib were not removed....

Dr. Harold Kletschka, a thoracic surgeon, stated that he had treated hundreds of patients with **thoracic outlet syndrome** and had never performed surgery to treat the problem. He stated that at the least a period of observation is always necessary to determine if physiotherapy is required and that physiotherapy always has a presurgical role. It was his opinion from Cress' medical records that there was no indication for surgery....

... He testified that no case of **thoracic outlet syndrome** should be taken to surgery without first undergoing an exercise program or physical therapy and that 50–70 percent of patients with that problem respond to physical therapy. Cress v. Mayer, 626 S.W.2d 430, 432, 434 (Mo.Ct.App.1981).

Other Authorities: Lindsey v. H. A. Lott, Inc., 387 So.2d 1091–2 (La.1980).

syndrome, Tietze's [Alexander *Tietze*] idiopathic painful nonsuppurative swellings of one or more costal cartilages, especially of the second rib; the anterior chest pain may mimic that of coronary artery disease. Called also *costal chondritis* and *Tietze's disease.*

Dr. Crawley's diagnosis was **costochondritis**, a recognized condition involving pain in the chest that could be brought on by coughing. Schales v. U.S., 488 F.Supp. 33, 35 (E.D.Ark. 1979).

The Workmen's Compensation Board awarded Sampson Owens compensation for 25% permanent partial disability by reason of a condition of **costo chondritis** (a painful, noninfectious swelling of the joint between the sternal bone and adjoining ribs)....

... that **costo chondritis** can be caused by lifting and straining and usually is found where there has been "some evidence of trauma plus straining or lifting;"... Hutchinson v. Owens, 458 S.W.2d 442–3 (Ct.App.Ky.1970).

Other Authorities: Chester v. Oklahoma Natural Gas Co., 619 P.2d 1266, 1268 (Ct.App.Okl.1980).

syndrome, toxic shock a severe illness characterized by high fever of sudden onset, vomiting, diarrhea, and myalgia, followed by hypotension and, in severe cases, shock; a sunburn-like rash with peeling of the skin, especially of the palms and soles, occurs during the acute phase. The syndrome affects almost exclusively menstruating women using tampons, although a few women who do not use tampons and a few males have been affected. It is thought to be caused by infection with *Staphylococcus aureus.*

Toxic shock syndrome was first identified and named in a November 1978 article by Dr. James K. Todd of the University of Colorado. Dr. Todd listed as symptoms of **TSS** fever, vomiting, diarrhea, low blood pressure, rash, and subsequent skin peeling. Dr. Todd hypothesized that Staphylococcus aureus (Staph A), a bacterium, caused the symptoms. Dr. Todd had observed the disease only in children, but by early 1980, several state health departments had reported **TSS** in adult women. In May 1980, the federal Center for Disease Control (CDC) published a summary of reported cases which indicated a strong correlation between the disease and menstruation. Kehm v. Procter & Gamble Mfg.Co., 724 F.2d 613, 616–17 (8th Cir. 1983).

Plaintiffs allege that in March, 1980, Stacy Wolf contracted **Toxic Shock Syndrome** (hereinafter "TSS") as a result of using Rely tampons, a product manufactured and distributed by defendants....

The evidence sought to be introduced consists of complaints of rashes, allergic reactions, blackouts and weakness, vaginitis, infection, irritation, burning, disintegration of the tampon causing infection, severe cramping, abdominal pains, and ulcerations and lacerations caused by the tampon and the inserter. The symptoms of **TSS**, taken from the case definition formulated by the CDC (Center for Disease Control) consist of (1) fever; (2) rash; (3) desquamation of palms and soles; (4) hypotension; (5) involvement of three or more of the following organ systems: gastrointestinal, muscular, mucous membrane, renal, hepatic, hematologic, and central nervous system; and (6) negative results on the following tests, if obtained: blood, throat, or cerebrospinal fluid cultures, and serologic test for Rocky Mountain spotted fever, leptosirosis, or measles. I find no substantial similarity between the injuries alleged in the complaints sought to be introduced and the injury at issue in this case, namely **TSS**. Therefore, this evidence would not be admissible to establish product defect, negligence or causation. Wolf by Wolf v. Procter & Gamble Co., 555 F.Supp. 613, 616, 621 (D.N.J.1982).

syndrome, transverse carpal

Dr. Erskine, however, noted that appellant was suffering from a clinical condition called "**transverse carpal syndrome,**" i.e., a tightening of the ligament across the wrist which impairs the functioning of the nerve. He split the ligament and thereafter the wound healed and appellant recovered almost full use and sensation of her hand and fingers. Sanchez v. Rodriguez, 38 Cal.Rptr. 110, 113 (Ct.App.Cal.1964).

syndrome, Volkmann's See *contracture, Volkmann's.*

syndrome, Wallenberg's a syndrome due to occlusion of the posterior inferior cerebellar artery, marked by ipsilateral loss of temperature and pain sensations of the face and contralateral loss of these sensations of the extremities and trunk, ipsilateral ataxia, dysphagia, dysarthria, and nystagmus.

Following various tests, it was determined that the plaintiff had suffered a type of stroke known as a **Wallenberg syndrome**. Expert witnesses for both parties testified that the **Wallenberg syndrome** does not impair judgment or the ability to diagnose; people undergoing it are alert and oriented and it does not affect rationality. While the victim feels sick, he can tell that he is sick and knows what is going on around him. The testimony as to the cause of the stroke was in conflict; some was to the effect that the stroke was brought on by the manipulation of the neck, and other testimony was that the manipulation was not the cause but rather the stroke was the result of an arteriosclerotic plaquing of his posterior inferior cerebral artery. Nimmer v. Purtell, 230 N.W.2d 258, 263 (Wis.1975).

syndrome, Wolff-Parkinson-White the association of paroxysmal tachycardia (or atrial fibrillation) and preexcitation, in which the electrocardiogram displays a short P-R interval and a wide QRS complex which characteristically shows an early QRS vector (delta wave); called also *anomalous atrioventricular excitation.* Cited in Almonte v. Califano, 490 F.Supp. 127, 130 (S.D.N.Y.1980).

syndrome, XXY See *syndrome, Klinefelter's.*

syndrome, Zollinger-Ellison a triad comprising (1) intractable, sometimes fulminating, and in many ways atypical peptic ulcers; (2) extreme gastric hyperacidity; and (3) gastrin-secreting, non-beta islet cell tumors of the pancreas, which may be single or multiple, small or large, benign or malignant. The gastrinoma sometimes occurs in sites (e.g., the duodenum) other than the pancreas. See also *polyendocrine adenomatosis,* under *adenomatosis.*

The fact is, however, as we have learned from the probation report, that defendant, since age 11, has suffered from the **Zollinger-Ellison syndrome**, a very serious condition of the pancreas which results in an extreme acidic condition and ulcers of the stomach....

... The syndrome, as it applies to defendant, is associated with tumors of the pancreas and liver which are inoperable. Tiredness is apparently one of the results of the condition and rest is part of the treatment. Nevertheless, it is quite likely that the condition will worsen. People v. Young, 399 N.Y.S.2d 156, 157 (2d Dept. 1977).

synergism (sin'er-jizm) the joint action of agents so that their combined effect is greater than the algebraic sum of their individual effects.

Courts have long wrestled with the meaning of **synergism** and have formulated a number of definitions. The two most common have been that one of the elements functions differently in combination than it did previously, e.g., Burland v. Trippe

Manufacturing Co., 543 F.2d 588, 592, 191 USPQ 667, 670 (7th Cir. 1976), and that the combination results in an effect greater than the sum of the several parts taken separately. E.g., St. Regis Paper Co. v. Bemis Co., 549 F.2d 833, 838, 193 USPQ 8, 11 (7th Cir.), cert. denied, 434 U.S. 833, 195 USPQ 465 (1977).

At least in one basic sense, no result is actually greater than the sum of its parts. To the extent that some combination of elements appears **synergistic**, it is a function of our imperfect knowledge of the properties of the parts. If one could truly get more out of a combination than was put into it, it would amount to a creation of something out of nothing and would contravene the basic laws of nature as we understand them....

The term **synergism** derives from the Greek, syn, together, and ergos, work, to work together, cooperate. The Oxford English Dictionary (Clarendon Press 1919). See Rich, Laying the Ghost of the "Invention" Requirement, 1 Am.Pat.L.Q. 26, 43–44 (1972). Republic Industries, Inc. v. Schlage Lock Co., 592 F.2d 963, 970 n. 23 (7th Cir. 1979).

When alcohol and a barbiturate are ingested by a person sufficiently close in point of time that both are present in the blood and cerebrospinal fluid at the same time, a **synergism** occurs. A **synergism** is the cooperative action of two discrete, or individually distinct agencies or substances, which results in a total effect greater than the sum of their two effects when taken independently.[3] It is referred to as **synergistic** action. In Main's case the result was a greater depressant effect from the alcohol than would have occurred had the Medomin been absent, and a greater depressant effect from the Medomin than would have occurred had the alcohol been absent....

... Dr. Willey further testified that the **synergistic** effect of alcohol and drugs causes an injury of a chemical nature on that portion of the brain which controls respiration, and that such injury produces a respiratory arrest. [3 Webster's New International Dictionary, 2nd Edition.] Metropolitan Life Ins. Co. v. Main, 383 F.2d 952, 956, 958 (5th Cir. 1967).

synergistic (sin"er-jis'tik) acting together; enhancing the effect of another force or agent.

There is a **synergistic** effect associated with aging. As one function deteriorates, a person tends to rely more heavily on other functions. For example, a person may rely more heavily on vision to compensate for a hearing loss. Since the relied on function may also be deteriorating with age, the total effect of the aging process may be greater than the sum of its parts. U.S. Equal Employ. Oppor. v. City of Minneapolis, 537 F.Supp. 750, 755 (D.Minn.1982).

Given the evidence of **synergistic** effect of alcohol and Valium, the finding that Richardson did ingest the Valium, and his conduct in operating the automobile, we cannot hold clearly erroneous the judge's finding that Richardson's intoxication alone could not explain his actions. Watkins v. U.S., 589 F.2d 214, 219 (5th Cir. 1979).

The entire theory of the plaintiff's case at trial was that the *synergistic* reaction of "chemicals + heat + dust" produced the pulmonary disability for which relief was sought. The plaintiff disavowed the suggestion that any single component of this formula, or any combination of two such components, produced or could have produced the plaintiff's disability. Murphy

v. Owens-Corning Fiberglas Corp., 447 F.Supp. 557, 571 (D.Kan.1977).

Other Authorities: Metropolitan Life Ins. Co. v. Main, 383 F.2d 952, 957–8 (5th Cir. 1967).

synovectomy (sin″o-vek′to-me) [*synovia* + Gr. *ektomē* excision] excision of a synovial membrane, as of that lining the capsule of the knee joint, performed in treatment of rheumatoid arthritis of the knee, or of the synovial sheath of a tendon.

Synovectomy operations (removal of the lining of the knee joint, menisci and bony spurs from within the joint) were performed on both knees. Monahan v. Weichert, 442 N.Y.S.2d 295–6 (4th Dep't 1981).

It was alleged that they were negligent in recommending surgery for Kalar's wrist—a **synovectomy** and/or fusion of the wrist bones. Carroll v. Kalar, 545 P.2d 411–12 (Ariz.1976).

synovia (sĭ-no′ve-ah) [L.; Gr. *syn* with + *ōon* egg] [NA] a transparent alkaline viscid fluid, resembling the white of an egg, secreted by the synovial membrane, and contained in joint cavities, bursae, and tendon sheaths; called also *synovial fluid.* See also *synovitis* (Kern case).

During the next eight years, claimant experienced several episodes of pain and swelling and some instability in his knees. Doctors treated him by draining **synovial fluid** and injecting cortisone into the knee. Shepard v. Midland Foods, Inc., 666 P.2d 758, 760 (Mont.1983).

synovial See *synovia.*

synovial fluid See *synovia.*

synovitis (sin″o-vi′tis) inflammation of a synovial membrane. It is usually painful, particularly on motion, and is characterized by a fluctuating swelling, due to effusion within a synovial sac. Synovitis is qualified as *fibrinous, gonorrheal, hyperplastic, lipomatous, metritic, puerperal, rheumatic, scarlatinal, syphilitic, tuberculous, urethral,* etc.

At this time the doctor diagnosed possible transient **synovitis**, which is an inflammation of the inside of the hip joint and in 15% of the cases amounts to the beginning of Legg-Perthes Disease. Arrendale v. U.S., 469 F.Supp. 883, 889 (N.D.Tex. 1979).

Taking the medical testimony as a whole, we find that the consequences of chondromalacia patella resulting to petitioner are closely enough related and similar enough in effect as to be essentially no different from the symptoms of **synovitis** itself. Since we have determined earlier that the **synovitis** subsumes its irritating cause, we conclude that the hearing officer correctly limited relief to the Occupational Disease Disability Act....

... When the kneecap is irritated the lining of the knee joint (synovium) becomes irritated and produces a fluid (synovial fluid) which leads to swelling in the knee joint area. The latter condition is called **synovitis**....

... Petitioner was awarded permanent disability for the condition pursuant to A.R.S. § 23–1102(11), which provided that "**synovitis** ... of ... knee ... due to continual pressure or friction or to repeated trauma" is deemed an occupational disease for which an employee who is totally disabled is enti-

tled to compensation. Kern v. Industrial Commission, 588 P.2d 353–5 (Ct.App.Ariz.1978).

Synovitis is an inflammation of the synovial membrane which lines the various joint cavities in the wrist. Carroll v. Kalar, 545 P.2d 411–12 (Ariz.1976).

Other Authorities: Workmen's Compensation App. Bd. v. Gimbel Brothers, 338 A.2d 755, 758 (Commonwealth Ct.Pa. 1975).

synovitis, ankle

Her disability claim therefore rests on the condition of her feet and ankles, diagnosed as **ankle synovitis** and calcaneal spurs.[2] [[2] These conditions are a membrane inflammation, usually accompanied by pain and swelling of the joint, and growths on the heels.]

Claimant testified at the hearing that "my feet used to swell up very, very much and as I took a step, it would feel like I was being cut by glass underneath the foot. It was a piercing pain." She further stated that the pain forced her to walk on her toes, such action affecting her leg tendons and causing pain in her knee. Lopez Diaz v. Secretary of Health, Ed. & Welfare, 585 F.2d 1137–8 (1st Cir. 1978).

synovium (sĭ-no′ve-um) a synovial membrane. See also *membrana synovialis capsulae articularis.*

But Dr. Gilbert also explained that the **synovium** (membrane lining the knee joint), which was already weakened by the tuberculosis, was further traumatized by the injury. He testified:

... [Tuberculosis is] a disease process already in the synovium tissue, and then we get the trauma on top of it, and hemorrhage. We get a lot of blood or lot of white cells or debris in the joint space, and that aggravates the already existing tuberculus infection, and I think I can support strongly that the TB was already there.

It's not that we are aggravating the TB, but simply taking tissue already damaged with TB and put[ting] another process on top of it, which in this case happened to be trauma. The two, together, are aggravation.... Matter of Compensation of Aquillon, 653 P.2d 264, 266 (Ct.App.Or.1982).

It [the Hand Board, Q.V.] examined Kalar and reviewed X-rays that had been taken some five months earlier and concluded that Kalar had degenerative joint disease and suffered from synovitis. The board recommended surgery and, depending upon the findings from such surgery, the removal of the **synovium** and/or a fusion of the wrist. Carroll v. Kalar, 545 P.2d 411, 413 (Ariz.1976).

syntonic (sin-ton′ik) [*syn-* + Gr. *tonos* tension] a term applied by Bleuler to the stable integrated type of personality which responds normally to the environment, as contrasted with the schizoid type.

syringe (sĭ-rinj′, sir′inj) [L. *syrinxe;* Gr. *syrinx*] an instrument for injecting liquids into or withdrawing them from any vessel or cavity.

Dr. Herring, however, testified on redirect (R. 260a–265a) that in his opinion appellant had not used a 25 gauge **syringe** because the solution of hydrocortisone, xzlocaine and pontocaine would not flow through a 25 gauge needle, thus a **syringe** with a gauge on the order of "19", "20", or "21" would have had to be used, in which case those gauge needles could have easily penetrated the body far enough to have caused the "pneumothorax". Earlin v. Cravetz, 399 A.2d 783, 785 (Super.Ct.Pa.1979).

syringomyelia (sĭ-ring″go-mi-e′le-ah) [*syringo-* + Gr. *myelos* marrow + *-ia*] a condition marked by abnormal cavities filled with liquid in the substance of the spinal cord.

He has suffered since his late twenties from **syringomyelia**, a progressively disabling neurological disorder characterized by loss of sensation in the extremities, loss of balance and chronic back pain. . . .

. . . The symptoms of **syringomyelia** include loss of sensation to such a degree that plaintiff was, at the time of his hospitalization in late 1979, almost incapable of feeling pain in his extremities and was insensitive to changes in his body temperature. Kernall v. U.S., 558 F.Supp. 280–2 (E.D.N.Y.1982).

Plaintiff Richard Webb suffers from **Syringomyelia**, a disease of the central nervous system which leaves him totally dependent on others for his daily and personal care. Webb v. Aggrey, 447 F.Supp. 17–18 (N.D.Ohio 1977).

system (sis′tem) [Gr. *systēma* a complex or organized whole] a set or series of interconnected or interdependent parts or entities (objects, organs, or organisms) that function together in a common purpose or produce results impossible of achievement by one of them acting or operating alone.

system, automatic nervous the portion of the nervous system concerned with regulation of the activity of cardiac muscle, smooth muscle, and glands. See illustration accompanying *system*. See also *systema nervosum autonomicum*.

system, central nervous that portion of the nervous system consisting of the brain and spinal cord (systema nervosum centrale [NA]). Abbreviated CNS.

The **central nervous system** consists of the brain, brain stem, and the spinal cord. The peripheral nervous system begins where the nerves leave the spinal column and extends throughout the body. McDonald v. U.S., 555 F.Supp. 935, 945 (M.D. Pa.1983).

Other Authorities: Stich v. U.S., 565 F.Supp. 1096, 1100 (D.N.J.1983); Padgett v. U.S., 553 F.Supp. 794–5 (W.D.Tex. 1982).

system, circulatory the channels through which the nutrient fluids of the body circulate; often restricted to the vessels conveying blood.

The **circulatory system**, with its heart pump, circulates the blood carrying the oxygen to various parts of the body. The body organs require oxygen to live. Without oxygen there is necrosis. Daniels v. Hadley Memorial Hospital, 566 F.2d 749, 752 (D.C.Cir.1977).

system, conduction; system, conductive (of the heart) system comprising the sinoatrial node, the atrioventricular node, the atrioventricular bundle, and the Purkinje fibers.

system, cortical motor, of the brain

Dr. Fresh stated that these conditions [spasticity from elbow to hand and aspastic walk] were caused by direct trauma to the head and damage to the **cortical motor system of the brain**. Dr. Fresh finally stated that further recovery by Terry Dale would be minimal. Cupit v. Grant, 425 So.2d 847, 852 (Ct. App.La.1982).

system, endocrine the system of glands and other structures that elaborate internal secretions (hormones) which are released directly into the circulatory system and which influence metabolism and other body processes. Organs having endocrine function include the pituitary, thyroid, parathyroid, and adrenal glands, the pineal body, the gonads, the pancreas, and the paraganglia. The thymus is no longer considered to perform an endocrine function. See illustration accompanying *gland*.

system, extrapyramidal a functional, rather than anatomical, unit comprising the nuclei and fibers (excluding those of the pyramidal tract) involved in motor activities; they control and coordinate especially the postural, static, supporting, and locomotor mechanisms. It includes the corpus striatum, subthalamic nucleus, substantia nigra, and the red nucleus, along with their interconnections with the reticular formation, cerebellum, and cerebrum; some authorities include the cerebellum and the vestibular nuclei. Called also *extracorticospinal s.* or *tract* and *extrapyramidal tract*.

system, lymphatic the lymphatic vessels and the lymphoid tissue, considered collectively (systema lymphaticum [NA]).

The lymphatic circulation in the leg is affected so that as Pike uses the leg an obstruction occurs in the **lymphatic system** of the leg, causing the mass to become larger and harder which causes increased pain in its use. Pike v. Roe, 516 P.2d 972–3 (Kan.1973).

system, nervous the organ system which along with the endocrine system, correlates the adjustments and reactions of an organism to internal and environmental conditions. Called also *systema nervosum* [NA]. It comprises the central and peripheral nervous systems: the former is composed of the brain and spinal cord, and the latter includes all the other neural elements. See also *autonomic nervous system; parasympathetic nervous system*; and *sympathetic nervous system*.

Specifically, while her papers do speak of her "acute depression and psychological overlay", they also describe injuries to her "**nervous system**" (the "**nervous system**", as distinguished from "neurotic" or "psychotic" pathology, by any medical definition, is organic), along with repeated objective manifestations of "dizziness, vomiting and nausea". These allegations raised questions of fact as to whether she suffered independent personal injuries. [dissent.] Vaccaro v. Squibb Corp., 418 N.E.2d 386–7 (N.Y.1980).

system, parasympathetic nervous the craniosacral portion of the autonomic nervous system (pars parasympathica systematis nervosi autonomici [NA]). See illustration accompanying *system*.

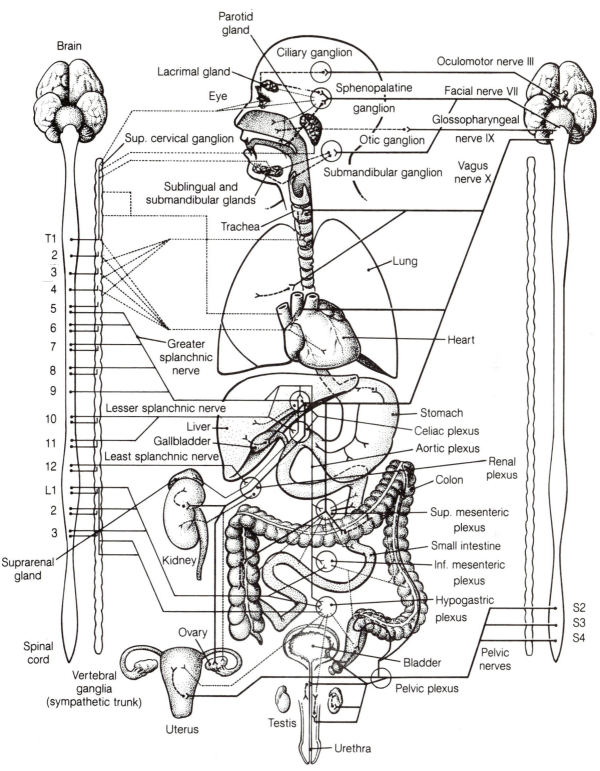

Brain

Parotid gland

Ciliary ganglion

Oculomotor nerve III

Lacrimal gland

Sphenopalatine ganglion

Facial nerve VII

Eye

Glossopharyngeal nerve IX

Sup. cervical ganglion

Otic ganglion

Submandibular ganglion

Vagus nerve X

Sublingual and submandibular glands

Trachea

Lung

T1
2
3
4
5
6
7
8
9
10
11
12
L1
2
3

Heart

Greater splanchnic nerve

Lesser splanchnic nerve

Liver

Stomach

Celiac plexus

Gallbladder

Aortic plexus

Least splanchnic nerve

Renal plexus

Colon

Sup. mesenteric plexus

Small intestine

Inf. mesenteric plexus

Kidney

Suprarenal gland

Hypogastric plexus

S2
S3
S4

Pelvic nerves

Spinal cord

Ovary

Bladder

Vertebral ganglia (sympathetic trunk)

Pelvic plexus

Uterus

Testis

Urethra

SYMPATHETIC
Thoracolumbar outflow

PARASYMPATHETIC
Craniosacral outflow

AUTONOMIC NERVOUS SYSTEM

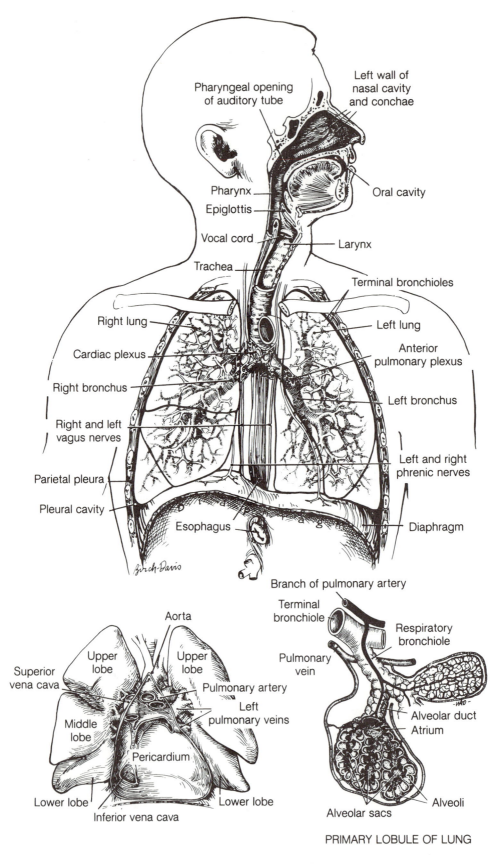

Pharyngeal opening
of auditory tube

Left wall of
nasal cavity
and conchae

Pharynx

Oral cavity

Epiglottis

Vocal cord

Larynx

Trachea

Terminal bronchioles

Right lung

Left lung

Cardiac plexus

Anterior
pulmonary plexus

Right bronchus

Left bronchus

Right and left
vagus nerves

Parietal pleura

Left and right
phrenic nerves

Pleural cavity

Esophagus

Diaphragm

Birch-Davis

Branch of pulmonary artery

Aorta

Terminal
bronchiole

Upper
lobe

Upper
lobe

Respiratory
bronchiole

Superior
vena cava

Pulmonary
vein

Pulmonary artery

Middle
lobe

Left
pulmonary veins

Alveolar duct

Atrium

Pericardium

Lower lobe

Lower lobe

Alveoli

Inferior vena cava

Alveolar sacs

PRIMARY LOBULE OF LUNG

ORGANS OF RESPIRATORY SYSTEM

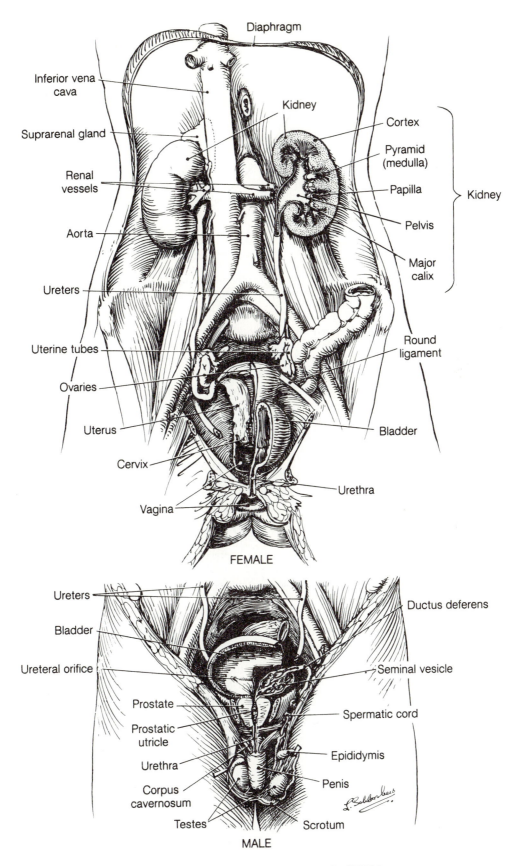

ORGANS OF THE UROGENITAL SYSTEM

system, peripheral nervous that portion of the nervous system consisting of the nerves and ganglia outside the brain and spinal cord (systema nervosum periphericum [NA]).

The **peripheral nervous system** begins where the nerves leave the spinal column, and extends throughout the body. Padgett v. U.S., 553 F.Supp. 794–5 (W.D.Tex.1982).

Other Authorities: Stich v. U.S., 565 F.Supp. 1096, 1100 (D.N.J.1983).

system, respiratory the tubular and cavernous organs and structures by means of which pulmonary ventilation and gas exchange between ambient air and the blood are brought about; called also *apparatus respiratorius* [NA]. See illustration accompanying system.

In describing the theory of plaintiff's case, we emphasize the difference between the circulatory system [Q.V.] and the **respiratory system**, because it was the District Court's confusion over their respective functions which lead it astray. The **respiratory system** supplies oxygen to the lungs where it is exchanged and infused into the blood....

... The real harm from the hospital's failure to assist respiration occurred because not enough oxygen was getting into the patient's blood stream. Thus the circulating blood was not carrying an adequate supply of oxygen to the patient's brain. Daniels v. Hadley Memorial Hospital, 566 F.2d 749, 752, 760 (D.C.Cir.1977).

system, reticuloendothelial a functional rather than anatomical system that serves as an important bodily defense mechanism, composed of highly phagocytic cells having both endothelial and reticular attributes and the ability to take up particles of colloidal dyes; these cells include macrophages lining the lymph sinuses and the blood sinuses of the liver (Kupffer's cells), spleen, and bone marrow, and the microglia, reticulum cells of lymphatic tissue, tissue macrophages, and circulating monocytes. Called also *macrophage s.*

system, sympathetic nervous 1. the thoracolumbar portion of the autonomic nervous system (pars sympathica systematis nervosi autonomici [NA]). See illustration accompanying system. See also *ureter* (Baker case).

system, urogenital the organs concerned in the production and excretion of urine, together with the organs of reproduction (apparatus urogenitalis or systema urogenitale [NA]). See illustration accompanying *system*.

system, vegetative nervous an old term for the autonomic nervous system (systema nervosum autonomicum [NA]).

He described her condition as a chronic or "persistent **vegetative state**". Dr. Fred Plum, a creator of the phrase, describes its significance by indicating the brain as working in two ways:

We have an internal vegetative regulation which controls body temperature, which controls breathing, which controls to a considerable degree blood pressure, which controls to some degree heart rate, which controls chewing, swallowing and which controls sleeping and waking. We have a more highly developed brain, which is uniquely human, which controls our relation to the outside world, our capacity to talk, to see, to feel, to sing, to think.... [See Dorland's definition set forth heretofore.] Brain death necessarily must mean the death of

both of these functions of the brain, vegetative and the sapient. Therefore, the presence of any function which is regulated or governed or controlled by the deeper parts of the brain which in layman's terms might be considered purely vegetative would mean that the brain is not biologically dead....

His description of Karen's posturing, reflexes, eyes, body movements and other conditions did not vary significantly from other experts. His diagnosis of the extent and area of the brain injury or lesion—in the cerebral hemisphere with brain stem involvement—essentially agrees with that of Dr. Morse. He described the upper brain area injury as a severe bilateral cerebral involvement with anoxia as the probable cause. He found a palmomental reflex, evidencing interruption in the brain stem fibre. He indicates the extensiveness of the reflex, a dimpling of the chin generated by stimulation of the palm, is greater than usually found because any stimulation along the entire arm generated it.

He described her condition as a persistent **vegetative state**. Matter of Quinlan, 348 A.2d 801, 810–12 (Super.Ct.N.J. 1975).

systema (sis-te'mah) [Gr. *systēma* a complex or organized whole] system: a series of interconnected or interdependent organs which together accomplish a specific function.

systema lymphaticum [NA], lymphatic system: the lymphatic vessels and the lymphoid tissue, considered collectively.

systema nervosum [NA], the nervous system: the chief organ system that correlates the adjustments and reactions of the organism to internal and environmental conditions, composed of the central and the peripheral nervous system; the former comprises the brain and spinal cord, and the latter includes all other neural elements.

systema nervosum autonomicum [NA], the autonomic nervous system: the portion of the nervous system concerned with regulation of activity of cardiac muscle, smooth muscle, and glands; usually restricted to the two visceral efferent peripheral components, the pars sympathica systematis nervosi autonomici (thoracolumbar part, or sympathetic nervous system) and the pars parasympathica systematis nervosi autonomici (craniosacral part, or parasympathetic nervous system). Called also *s. nervorum sympathicum.* See illustration accompanying *system*.

systema nervosum periphericum [NA], peripheral nervous system: that portion of the nervous system consisting of the nerves and ganglia outside the brain and spinal cord; called also *s. nervorum periphericum.*

systemic (sis-tem'ik) pertaining to or affecting the body as a whole.

That examination revealed cancer in the abdomen and small bowels. The malignancy had become **systemic**. Tommy died in June, 1967. Jeanes v. Milner, 428 F.2d 598, 601 (8th Cir. 1970).

systemic-cortico-steroid See *corticosteroid; steroid;* and *systemic.*

systole (sis'to-le) [Gr. *systolē* a drawing together, contraction] the contraction, or period of contraction, of the heart, especially that of the ventricles; sometimes divided into components, as pre-ejection and ejection periods, or isovolumic, ejection, and relaxation periods.

T

Table of Stains See *Stains, Table of.*

tachycardia (tak"e-kar'de-ah) [*tachy-* + Gr. *kardia* heart] excessive rapidity in the action of the heart; the term is usually applied to a heart rate above 100 per minute and may be qualified as atrial, junctional (nodal), or ventricular, and as paroxysmal.

He has a history of episodes of **tachycardia** for over one year, which we have documented as bouts of atrial fibrillation, and/or PAT, for which he takes Lanoxin prophylaxis one tablet daily and Quinidine 200 mg. three times a day with fairly decent control. He, however, had a bout of **tachycardia** requiring electrocardioversion while hospitalized two months ago for an infected right renal cyst. Wilson v. Schweiker, 553 F.Supp. 728, 732 (E.D.Wash.1982).

He had chest pain, shortness of breath, **tachycardia** (fast heartbeat—his pulse was 140), and had been vomiting (PX 1). Schales v. U.S., 488 F.Supp. 33, 35 (E.D.Ark.1979).

That report states that Dr. Brown believed the prime reason for the patient's cessation of work was the carbon tetrachloride accident:

As a result the W/E has "some liver damage" and episodes of **tachycardia** requiring hospitalization. . . .

. . . Dr. Voegele noted that the patient reported the attacks of **tachycardia** were associated with a "ball-like" substernal sensation which is also noted on exertion during the past nine months; the pain radiates to the left arm and becomes numb. Walker v. Ribicoff, 213 F.Supp. 32, 34–35 (N.D.Ohio 1962).

Other Authorities: Plouse v. Richardson, 334 F.Supp. 1086–7 (W.D.Pa.1971); Yeomans v. Jersey City, 143 A.2d 174, 179 (N.J.1958).

tachycardia, atrial a rapid cardiac rate, usually between 160 and 190 per minute, originating from an atrial locus.

tachycardia, paroxysmal a condition marked by attacks of rapid action of the heart having sudden onset and cessation; called also *Bouveret's disease* or *syndrome*. See also *tachycardia, atrial.*

The testing and observation at Jewish Memorial produced a final diagnosis that plaintiff was suffering from **paroxysmal supraventricular tachycardia** (excessively rapid heart action which comes and goes quite abruptly). . . . Almonte v. Califano, 490 F.Supp. 127, 130 (S.D.N.Y.1980).

Hayse further testified that throughout the suspension and investigation, he believed he was losing his job and was very upset because it was the sole source of support for his family. A few minutes after the hearing he was on his way to Airfreight in a van to confer with someone at the request of the President of the Local, when he felt a sharp pain, like a fist, in his chest. He felt cool and clammy and perspired heavily, his breath was short and he felt that he was going to pass out. . . .

During the next twelve days, Hayse said he had 10 to 15 recurrences, resulting in his going to the emergency room twice to see Dr. Simmons. He did not miss any work and his heart and E.K.G. were always normal when checked. On September 23, 1975, he was hospitalized for tests. Dr. Simmons, in his testimony, diagnosed Hayse's case as **paroxysmal auricular tachycardia** (P.A.T.) caused by the acute tension of the suspension incident. . . .

Dr. Simmons described the condition as a rapid, uncontrolled heart rate, which produces physical changes in the body, requiring medical treatment to prevent heart damage. Hayse v. Seaboard Fire & Marine Ins. Co., 562 S.W.2d 282–4 (Ct.Civ. App.Tex.1978).

McCall ". . . had bronchopneumonia and an acute **paroxysmal atrial tachycardia**, which means that he had a rapid heart action, paroxysmally, at a rate of 200 per minute." The normal rate, without exercising, is in the range of 70 to 90. Community Life & Health Ins. Co. v. McCall, 497 S.W.2d 358, 362 (Ct. App.Tex.1973).

tachycardia, ventricular an abnormally rapid ventricular rhythm with aberrant ventricular excitation (wide QRS complexes), usually in excess of 150 per minute, which is generated within the ventricle and is most commonly associated with atrioventricular dissociation. Minor irregularities of rate may also occur. Evidence implicates a reentrant pathway as the usual cause.

With regard to the safety of Quinaglute in the conversion of cardiac arrhythmias, the testimony at the trial indicated that it is definitely not safe for the conversion of the serious type of cardiac arrhythmia known as **ventricular tachycardia**, and such fact is admitted by the claimant in its brief (p. 67), to-wit:

"For **ventricular tachycardia**, which must be treated as promptly as possible and for which no oral medication is generally considered effective (testimony cited), all of the expert testimony given at the trial would indicate that neither Quinaglute nor quinidine sulfate should be employed (testimony cited). Consequently, if this court were to conclude that the new drug status of Quinaglute is to be determined under the current definition of a new drug in that Section 107(c)(4) of P.L. 87–781 is not applicable, claimant could not realistically dispute a finding of fact that, when offered for the conversion of **ventricular tachycardia**, Quinaglute is subject to new drug classification." U.S. v. Article of Drug, etc., 268 F.Supp. 245, 248 (E.D.Mo.1967).

tachypnea (tak"ip-ne'ah) [*tachy-* + Gr. *pnoia* breath] excessive rapidity of respiration; a respiratory neurosis marked by quick, shallow breathing.

He noticed **tachypnea**—rapid, difficult breathing—and an elevated pulse rate. He too suspected pulmonary embolism and considered the more-remote possibility of a ruptured stomach.

Franz v. Bd. of Medical Quality Assur., 181 Cal.Rptr. 732, 735 (Cal.1982).

taconite

Reserve produces merchantable iron ore in the form of pellets from **taconite**, a hard, gray rock in which are embedded fine particles of magnetite, a black magnetic oxide of iron. U.S. v. Reserve Mining Co., 380 F.Supp. 11, 30 (D.Minn.1974), remanded 498 F.2d 1073 (8th Cir. 1974).

talc, tremolytic See *tremolite (fiber)*.

talipes (tal'ĭ-pēz) [L. "clubfoot"] a congenital deformity of the foot, which is twisted out of shape or position; called also *clubfoot*.

Talodex See *fenthion*.

talus (ta'lus), pl. *ta'li* [L. "ankle"] 1. [NA] the highest of the tarsal bones and the one which articulates with the tibia and fibula to form the ankle joint; called also *ankle bone, astragalus, astragaloid bone*, and *os tarsi tibialis*. 2. the ankle (def. 1).

. . . the blow to Musial's heel crushed the calcenus (heel bone) and drove it up into the **talus** (the shaft of the ankle). Musial v. A & A Boats, Inc., 696 F.2d 1149, 1151 (5th Cir. 1983).

Plaintiff fell 10' to the frozen ground below, fracturing the weight-supporting **talus** bone of his ankle. Kelty v. Wiseman Construction Co., Inc., 349 N.E.2d 108–10 (App.Ct.Ill.1976).

These films do show a very slight tilt of the **talus** in the ankle mortise on a strain film. . . .

. . . It is my opinion that he has a chronic strain of the lateral collateral ligament and there is superimposed degenerative changes as manifested by the spur formation on the **talus** as reflected in the X-rays. Ballard v. Commanding General, Fort Leonard Wood, Mo., 355 F.Supp. 143, 148–9 (W.D.Mo. 1973).

Talwin (tal'win) trademark for preparations of pentazocine. See also *pentazocine*.

tampon (tam'pon) [Fr. "stopper, plug"] a pack; a pad or plug made of cotton, sponge, or other material; variously used in surgery to plug the nose, vagina, etc., for the control of hemorrhage or the absorption of secretions.

tampon, Rely

Rely tampons consist of two absorbent materials contained in a polyester bag, which is, in turn, enclosed in a plastic inserter. The two materials, carboxymethylcellulose (CMC) and polyester, are not used in other tampons. Kehm v. Procter & Gamble Mfg. Co., 724 F.2d 613, 616 (8th Cir. 1983).

. . . they allege that they thoroughly tested **Rely**, both prior to marketing it and continually during its lifetime; that at the time of Stacy Wolf's illness, the possible association between TSS and **Rely** or any other **tampon** was unknown; that they voluntarily withdrew **Rely** from the market at the first indication of a statistical correlation between it and TSS; and that they are presently funding, through unrestricted grants, TSS research. . . .

Plaintiffs contend that admissible evidence will show that defendants did not conduct basic microbiological tests prior to marketing **Rely**, which tests would have uncovered the dangers

inherent in its use, and that defendants failed to notify the FDA of a change in a component of **Rely** in order to avoid having the product retested for premarket approval, which retesting might have uncovered its defects. Wolf by Wolf v. Procter & Gamble Co., 555 F.Supp. 613, 618–19 (D.N.J.1982).

tamponade (tam"pon-ād') [Fr. *tamponner* to stop up] surgical use of the tampon; also pathologic compression of a part, as compression of the heart by pericardial fluid. See also *cardiac tamponade*.

tamponade, cardiac acute compression of the heart which is due to effusion of the fluid into the pericardium or to the collection of blood in the pericardium from rupture of the heart or penetrating trauma.

Dr. Butts was of the opinion that Joe's death was due to heart failure; that the heart failure was in the form of a **cardiac tamponade**; and that it was caused by the infusion of a large quantity of fluid into the pericardial sac. Warren v. Canal Industries, Inc., 300 S.E.2d 557, 559 (Ct.App.N.C.1983).

. . . and that it was the developing hemorrhage and dissection around that aorta which eventually resulted in rupture through the wall, and the development of the **cardiac tamponade** (aneurism of the heart). Woodall Industries, Inc. v. Massachusetts Mutual Life Insurance Co., 483 F.2d 986, 1004 (6th Cir. 1973).

Tandearil (tan-de'ah-ril) trademark for a preparation of oxyphenbutazone. See also *oxyphenbutazone*.

tangentiality

Tangentiality means that "a person is just going from one thought to the next with no logical connection between the two. . . ." Johnson v. U.S., 409 F.Supp. 1283, 1286 (M.D.Fla. 1976), reversed and remanded 576 F.2d 606 (5th Cir. 1978).

tank (tank) an artificial receptacle for liquids.

tank, septic a tank for the receipt of sewage, there to remain for a time in order that the solid matter may settle out and a certain amount of putrefaction occur from the action of the anaerobic bacteria present in the sewage; called also *anaerobic t.* and *hydrolytic t.*

A **septic tank** is basically a rectangular tank with a sloping bottom. As raw sewage enters the tank, those suspended solids with a specific gravity greater than water are pulled by gravity to the bottom of the tank. The suspended solids are both separated from raw sewage and permitted to decompose in the same tank. U.S. v. City of Asbury Park, 340 F.Supp. 555, 558 (D.N.J.1972).

tap (tap) to drain off fluid by paracentesis.

Medical testimony, previously referred to, showed that the quadrant **taps** are a procedure usually performed by a surgeon and are not intended or designed to strike or puncture organs. Washington v. City of Columbus, 222 S.E.2d 583, 589 (Ct.App.Ga.1975).

tap, spinal lumbar puncture.

tape (tāp) a long, narrow strip of fabric or other flexible material.

tape, adhesive [USP], a strip of fabric and/or film evenly coated on one side with a pressure-sensitive, adhesive mixture, the whole having high tensile strength, used for the application of dressings and sometimes to produce immobilization; formerly called *adhesive plaster.*

Claim 1 of Patent 3,121,021:

1. A nonwoven fibrous translucent microporous breathable surgical **adhesive tape** consisting essentially of: (A) a thin compacted tissue-like web of randomly interlaced staple textile fibers which are individually coated and are interbonded at their crossing points by a nontacky hydrophobic rubbery fibersizing polymer having a weight of about 30–70% of the total fabric weight, such as to provide water-repellant sized fibers and wet strength in a unified resilient reticular tissue-like fabric backing having a porous capillary structure capable of absorbing liquid perspiration and which is strong and tough enough for surgical tape functioning whether dry or wet; and (B) a thin smooth visibly-continuous hydrophobic transparent skin-adhering pressure-sensitive adhesive coating upon and interlocking with the fibers of one side of the backing to provide a unitary uniform but microporous fibro-adhesive web structure, the adhesive coating having a vast number per square inch of randomly-varying minute closely-spaced pores communicating with the inter-filar backing pores and sufficing to transmit perspiration in either liquid or vapor state when the tape is adhered to human skin such that the entire contacted skin area is maintained in a dry ventilated state under ordinary conditions; said adhesive coating essentially consisting of a water-insoluble hydrophobic aggressively-tacky highly-cohesive rubbery pressure-sensitive adhesive polymer, the adhesive having a composition that is relatively nonirritating to the human skin and being so firm and rubbery that the tape can be readily and comfortably removed from the skin after prolonged adhering contact. Minnesota Mining & Mfg. Co. v. Johnson & Johnson, 179 U.S.P.Q. 216–17 (N.D.Ill.1973).

tarsal tunnel syndrome See *syndrome, tarsal tunnel.*

tarsorrhaphy (tahr-sor'ah-fe) [*tarso*- + Gr. *rhaphē* suture] the operation of suturing together a portion of (*partial t.*) or the entire (*total t.*) upper and lower eyelids for the purpose of shortening or closing entirely the palpebral fissure. The terms *external t., median t.,* and *internal t.* are used to indicate the portion of the lids brought together in partial tarsorrhaphy. Called also *blepharorrhaphy.*

... If the situation becomes even worse, she may have to have a **tarsorraphy** [sic], that is, sewing margins of right lids together for a period of time to allow the epithelial area to heal, not be irritated by normal every day blinking reflexes." Thrall Car Mfg. Co. v. Industrial Com'n, 427 N.E.2d 141, 143 (Ill.1981).

tattooing (tah-too'ing) the insertion of permanent colors in the skin by introducing them through punctures.

Tattooing consists of puncturing the skin in the pattern desired and rubbing in coloring material so that the pattern is indelibly fixed. Encyclopedia Brittanica, Volume 16. Cf. Ormsby and Montgomery, Diseases of the Skin, Eighth Edition, 9 Proof of Facts 391. It is a matter of common knowledge that in making a tattoo, there are many entries by way of needle into the skin of a human body opening the way for infection and health impairment.

Relative to the relationship of regulation of the business of **tattooing** and the public health, the Supreme Court of New York, in upholding the constitutionality of Section 181.15 of the New York City Health Code making it unlawful for any person to tattoo a human being, with an exception being made for physician acting for medical purposes, declared:

"The record shows, to our minds conclusively, that the prohibition of lay **tattooing** was an advisable procedure for the security of life and health. It was established that hepatitis, a serious disease of the blood for which there is no known cure, is caused by a virus. This virus, which lives in the blood of infected persons, is transmitted to the healthy by injection into their blood or tissue of the blood or blood products of the infected. Such transmissions occur to persons who have been tattooed seven times more frequently than they occur in persons who have not been tattooed. Concededly, restricting the spread of hepatitis is a proper subject of Health Code regulations. And it would appear to be uncontradictable that **tattooing** is a source of the spread of this dread disease. It would therefore follow indisputably that the control of **tattooing** comes well within the field of securing the health of the community."
Grossman v. Baumgartner, 22 A.D.2d 100, 254 N.Y.S.2d 335, affirmed 17 N.Y.2d 345, 271 N.Y.S.2d 195, 218 N.E.2d 259 (1966).

It is our opinion and we hold that the method of **tattooing** is sufficient to bring it within the range of things directly affecting the public health and falls within the scope of the police power and that the subject regulation constitutes a reasonable restriction on the art of **tattooing** for the benefit of public health. Golden v. McCarty, 337 So.2d 388, 390–1 (Fla. 1976).

tautomerism (taw-tom'er-izm) [*tauto*- + Gr. *meros* part] a form of stereoisomerism in which the compounds are mutually interconvertible, under normal conditions, forming a mixture which is in dynamic equilibrium. See also *prototropy; anionotropy* and *mutarotation.*

taxon (tak'son), pl. *tax'a* [Ga. *taxis* a drawing up in rank and file + *on* neuter ending] a particular group (category) into which related organisms are classified; the main categories are (in ascending order): species, genus, family, order, class, phylum, and kingdom.

taxonomic (tak"so-nom'ik) pertaining to taxonomy.

taxonomy (tak-son'o-me) [L. *taxinomia;* Gr. *taxis* a drawing up in rank and file + *nomos* law] the orderly classification of organisms into appropriate categories (taxa) on the basis of relationships among them, with the application of suitable and correct names.

The **taxonomic** decision whether to dignify distinctions among plants within a genus by categorizing them as separate species involves an exercise of judgment, but it is an informed and disciplined judgment based upon well recognized factors, such as the geographical area in which the plant is found, its gross form (such as its height), its internal structure, its chemical characteristics, and so on. I understand, of course, that in the language of **taxonomy**, categories of "kingdoms" are based on more gross distinctions, than those involved in categories of classes, subclasses, orders, families, genuses, and species, and I understand that the distinctions among kingdoms, specifically, are far more gross than the distinctions among species.... U.S. v. Lewallen, 385 F.Supp. 1140, 1141–1142 (W.D.Wis.1974).

Tay-Sachs disease (ta saks') [Warren *Tay;* Bernard (Barney) *Sachs,* New York neurologist, 1858–1944] See *idiocy, amaurotic familial.*

TCA See *acid, trichloroacetic.*

TCDD See *dioxin;* and *Agent Orange.*

TDI See *toulene diisocyanate.*

technique (tek-nēk') [Fr.] the method of procedure and the details of any mechanical process or surgical operation. See also under *method; treatment; maneuver;* and *Table of Stains,* etc.

technique, pins and plaster

Dr. Florence testified that the purpose of the **pins and plaster technique** is to prevent residual deformity, and that if pins are not used the bone fragments in the comminuted area will settle back causing it to "clam up like an egg shell." In Dr. Florence's opinion, if the **pins and plaster technique** had been used in this case, deformity would have been minimized or eliminated. Larsen v. Yelle, 246 N.W.2d 841, 843 (Minn.1976).

technique, Pomeroy

By way of a de bene esse deposition Dr. Hickok testified that he closed the left fallopian tube through use of the "**Pomeroy**" **technique** whereby the mid-segment of the tube is doubly ligated and the segment distal to the ties is severed and removed.... McNeal v. U.S., 689 F.2d 1200–01 (4th Cir. 1982).

technique, Seldinger a technique for percutaneous puncture of arteries or veins, used in angiography. See also *arteriogram* (U.S. v. Choice case).

Tedral

At nights, he has difficulty sleeping and frequently must take Tedral [2] to minimize the smothering and wheezing sensations he experiences. [[2] **Tedral** is a prescription drug and a bronchial dilator which is used to treat asthmatics and others suffering from certain severe respiratory conditions.] Haywood v. Secretary of Health & Human Services, 699 F.2d 277, 279 (6th Cir. 1983).

teeth see *tooth.*

teeth, deciduous the teeth of the first dentition, which are shed and followed, in the dental arch, by the permanent teeth. The 20 deciduous teeth, 10 in each jaw, include 4 incisor, 2 canine, and 4 molar teeth. Called also *dentes decidui,* and *milk,* or *primary,* or *temporary teeth.*

teeth, incisor the four front teeth, two on each side of the midline in each jaw; the cutting teeth, each with one long root. Called also *dentes incisivi* [NA]. See also *incisor.*

teeth, molar [L. *molaris* to do with grinding], the most posterior teeth on either side in each jaw, totaling 8 in the deciduous dentition (2 on each side, upper and lower), and usually 12 in the permanent dentition (3 on each side, upper and lower). They are the grinding teeth, having large crowns with broad chewing surfaces. The upper molars characteristically have 4 major cusps and three roots. The lower first molars characteristically have 5 cusps, and the remaining lower molars 4 cusps. Normally

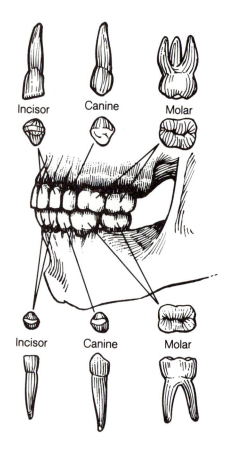

Typical deciduous teeth.

all lower molars have two roots. The third molars ("wisdom teeth") are often malformed, but when developed normally their crown and root form corresponds in general with neighboring molars in the same jaw. Called also *dentes molars* [NA].

... to have the upper right first **molar tooth** pulled. The doctor extracted this tooth and in doing so, left a root tip in the gum. In removing this tooth, Dr. Harris broke the floor of the sinus chamber which is not uncommon in removing this tooth according to Dr. Curl, the dental surgeon who testified in the case. Gorsalitz v. Harris, 410 S.W.2d 956–7, 959 (Ct.Civ.App.Tex. 1966).

According to the system used by defendant, the lower left wisdom tooth is designated number 17. That tooth had been extracted by defendant prior to the events here involved. The **molar** next to the wisdom tooth, the second lower left **molar**, and the back tooth after the wisdom tooth was removed, is designated as number 18. The next tooth in front of that or the first lower left **molar**, is designated as number 19. Carr v. Dickey, 329 P.2d 539, 540 (Dist.Ct.App.Cal.1958).

teeth, permanent the teeth of the second dentition; the 32 permanent teeth, 16 in each jaw. They include 4 incisor, 2 canine, 4 premolar, and 6 molar teeth in each jaw. Called also *dentes permanentes* [NA].

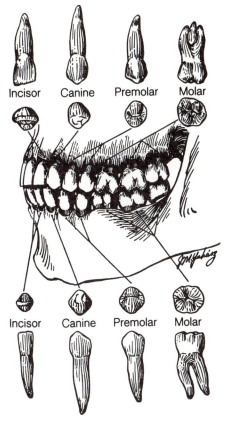

Incisor Canine Premolar Molar

Incisor Canine Premolar Molar

Typical permanent teeth.

Each **permanent tooth** in an adult's mouth is identified by both descriptive terminology and a numerical designation. Since this case involves some of plaintiff's upper teeth, it is necessary to explain the pertinent terminology and designations. The numerical designations begin on the far upper right (No. 1) and continue in numerical order to the far upper left (No. 16). Numbers 1 and 16 denote what are known as the third molars, commonly called the wisdom teeth. Numbers 8 and 9, i.e., the two upper middle front teeth, are known descriptively as the upper right central incisor and the upper left central incisor, respectively. The tooth immediately left of the latter is known as the upper left lateral incisor and is designated as No. 10. Continuing leftward, the next tooth is known as the upper left canine or cuspid and is designated as No. 11. The final tooth important for our purposes is designated as No. 12 and is known as the upper left first bicuspid or premolar. See, generally, 21 Encyclopaedia Britannica (1970), pp. 755–759. Sullivan v. Russell, 338 N.W.2d 181–2 (Mich.1983).

telepathy (tĕ-lep'ah-the) [*tele-*(2) + Gr. *pathos* feeling] extrasensory perception of the mental activity of another person. See also *clairvoyance*.

Q. What does **telepathy** mean?

A. **Telepathy** is the exchange of information from one person to another by means other than the sensory.

Q. Can you give an example?

A. In the collection of so-called spontaneous cases of **telepathy** you find, for example, the following: Mrs. Packet at work in her kitchen is suddenly overwhelmed by a vision of her brother being hurled to his death. She is sure that this means something that is not accidental. In time it turns out that her brother working on a tugboat in Chicago Harbor tripped over a rope and was thrown to his death approximately at the time.

These so-called spontaneous cases or crisis apparitions have been collected by the hundreds and are independent, of course, of certain natural studies. In re Estate of Kidd, 479 P.2d 697, 710 (Ariz.1971).

telescope, optical See *cystoscope* (Thomas case).

telethermometer (tel"ĕ-ther-mom'ĕ-ter) an apparatus for determining temperature on which the reading is made at a distance from the object or subject being studied.

A **telethermometer** is a part of this equipment [hypothermia machine] and through a tube records the temperature rectally. If in proper working condition, it records the actual body temperature. Rose v. Hakim, 335 F.Supp. 1221, 1226 (D.D.C. 1971).

Temik

Connie Riley and Carolyn Lord suddenly became ill while fertilizing potted plants which had been treated three and a half weeks previously with the highly toxic pesticide **Temik**. Claimants assert that they were exposed to the pesticide when their tennis shoes were soaked with water which had pooled on the black plastic placed under the potted plants.

The active ingredient in **Temik** is the organophosphate pesticide "aldecarb." Polk Nursery Co., Inc. v. Riley, 433 So.2d 1233–4 (Dist.Ct.App.Fla.1983).

temporomandibular See *mandibula*; and *bone, temporal* (os temporale).

temporal bone See *os temporale*.

temporomandibular joint See *joint, temporomandibular*.

temporomandibular joint syndrome See *syndrome, temporomandibular joint*.

tenaculum (te-nak'u-lum) a hooklike instrument for seizing and holding tissues.

"You did willfully fail to use medically proper sterilization techniques in the performance of abortions by . . . using unsterilized **tenaculums**, sounds and forceps. . . ." Sherman v. Com'n on Licensure to Practice, 407 A.2d 595, 598 (D.C.Ct. App.1979).

A I thought that there was possibly evidence of **tenaculum** marks in the anterior lip of the cervix. I couldn't be absolutely positive of this, because they heal very rapidly after the **tenac-**

Tenaculum (Da Costa).

ulum is withdrawn. A **tenaculum** is a sharp two-toothed or four-toothed instrument used to grasp tissues and hold them firm. Cooper v. State, 447 S.W.2d 179, 184 (Ct.Crim.App. Tex.1969).

tendinitis (ten″dĭ-ni′tis) inflammation of tendons and of tendon-muscle attachments. See also *capsulitis, adhesive.*

The record in this case contains substantial evidence [10] that plaintiff's **tendonitis** condition was most commonplace; that injections of cortisone and a local anesthetic were the normal, common treatment for this condition, and that untoward results were extremely rare. [[10] ... Plaintiff's present doctor was asked whether **tendonitis** is caused by physical exertion and he responded, "Usually, that is the usual cause of it."] Bardessono v. Michels, 478 P.2d 480, 488 (Cal.1970).

Other Authorities: Sielicki v. New York Yankees, 388 So.2d 25 (Dist.Ct.App.Fla.1980).

At 8:00 A.M., that morning, Tarport Conaway was examined by Dr. S. P. Dey, D.V.M., and was found to have **tendinitis** (swelling of the tendons) in both front legs. Sessa v. Riegle, 427 F.Supp. 760, 763 (E.D.Pa.1977).

One doctor felt that claimant's pain was primarily due to a biceps **tendonitis**, which is an inflammation in the major tendon that goes through the shoulder joint and is inserted within the joint itself. Safeway Stores, Inc. v. Industrial Com'n, 558 P.2d 971–2 (Ct.App.Ariz.1976).

tendo (ten′do), pl. *ten′dines* [L.] [NA] tendon: a fibrous cord of connective tissue in which the fibers of a muscle end and by which the muscle is attached to a bone or other structure.

tendo calcaneus [NA], calcaneal tendon: a powerful tendon at the back of the heel which attaches the triceps surae muscle to the tuberosity of the calcaneus; called also *tendo Achillis* or *Achilles tendon.*

On Sunday morning, November 19, 1972, he was playing tennis when he felt pain in his right ankle, after which he could not support his weight on his right foot....

... He diagnosed a ruptured **Achilles tendon** of the right ankle and recommended surgical repair of the tendon. Siegel v. Mt. Sinai Hospital of Cleveland, 403 N.E.2d 202, 204 (Ct. App.Ohio 1978).

tendon (ten′dun) [L. *tendo;* Gr. *tenōn*] a fibrous cord by which a muscle is attached. See also *tendo.*

tendon, quadriceps See *musculus quadriceps femoris.*

When the cast was taken off about six weeks later, he couldn't move his leg—"[t]he leg muscles were—I don't know what you call it, they were like jelly...."

By January, 1974, Mr. Means could not bend his left knee more than an inch, but did resume his regular duties in February. When Dr. Powell saw him in December, 1973, some four months after the operation, he "showed only about 10 degrees of active knee flexion and at this time it was apparent that the **quadriceps tendon** was bound down to the underlying femur and was sticking there which prohibited the tendon moving when he attempted to flex the knee, so he had only 10 degrees of active flexion." Means v. Sears, Roebuck & Co., 550 S.W.2d 780, 783 (Mo.1977).

tennis elbow See *epicondylitis.*

tenodesis (ten-od′ĕ-sis) [*teno-* + Gr. *desis* a binding together] tendon fixation; suturing of the end of a tendon to a bone.

... a **tenodesis** on the hypermobile biceps tendon of the right shoulder.... Claussell v. Secretary of Health, Education & Welf., 337 F.Supp. 717, 719 (S.D.N.Y.1972).

tenoplasty (ten′o-plas″te) [*teno-* + Gr. *plassein* to shape] plastic surgery of the tendons; operative repair of a defect in a tendon.

... a **tenoplasty** was performed on the fourth fingers of both claimant's hands. Longo v. Weinberger, 369 F.Supp. 250, 253 (E.D.Pa.1974).

tenosynovitis (ten″o-sin″o-vi′tis) inflammation of a tendon sheath. See also *disease, de Quervain's.*

Testing revealed that plaintiff's right hand had only half the grip strength of the left even though plaintiff was right handed. Dr. Cromwell felt that plaintiff had been cooperative. His diagnosis was a resultant or residual **tenosynovitis** involving the extensor tendons on the dorsum of the right wrist and hand and possibly involving the capsule or ligament which hold the carpal bones or the wrist together. The doctor explained that this condition is a reactive inflammation around the tendons caused by the scar tissue staying inflamed, sore and swollen. Harrington v. Starline, Inc., 425 So.2d 307, 309 (Ct.App.La. 1982).

Dr. Jones diagnosed Mrs. Thomasee's problem as **tenosynovitis** of the distal radio-ulna joint in her left wrist, or in lay terms, inflammation of the tendons about the joint at the end of the forearm of the left wrist. He had initially placed her in a long arm cast for three weeks....

... When she began seeing Dr. Jones he continued her in a splint and found her to have tenderness to palpation over the dorsum of the distal radio-ulna joint of the wrist, more simply described as an inflammation of the tendons and synovia about the joint. This inflammation was found to be located in the joints at the end of the forearm at the wrist. Dr. Jones had prescribed and continued to prescribe Clinorial, to decrease inflammation, and Elavil, a mood elevator. Thomasee v. Liberty Mut. Ins. Co., 385 So.2d 1219, 1222–3 (Ct.App.La.1980).

Appellant relies on National Stores, Inc. v. Hester, Ky., 393 S.W.2d 603 (1965). In that case, the claimant contracted the disease called **tenosynovitis** which is an attritional type of lesion caused by repeated movement of a tendon doing an unaccustomed type of motion....

... In the Morris case, [Turner, Day & Woolworth Handle Co. v. Morris, 267 Ky. 217, 101 S.W.2d 921.] **tenosynovitis** (a painful disease which inflames the sheath or membrane which surrounds a tendon) was regarded as a compensable result of a work-connected injury. Keel v. Thomas Industries, 463 S.W.2d 919–20 (Ct.App.Ky.1971).

Other Authorities: Knott v. Califano, 559 F.2d 279–80 (5th Cir. 1977); Longo v. Weinberger, 369 F.Supp. 250, 253–4 (E.D.Pa.1974); Hughes v. Richardson, 342 F.Supp. 320, 322 (W.D.Mo.1971); National Stores, Inc. v. Hester, 393 S.W.2d 603–4 (Ct.App.Ky.1965).

tenotomy (ten-ot′o-me) [*teno-* + Gr. *tomē* a cutting] the cutting of a tendon as for strabismus or clubfoot.

Dr. Prochaska concluded that to remedy her condition it would be necessary to perform a **tenotomy** to the left eye, a procedure known as strabismus surgery. This was intended to restore binocular vision in all fields of vision and relieve eye strain. Secondarily, it would remove psychological and social handicaps. The prognosis for fusion, after surgery, on gaze right without diplopia or suppression was excellent, and the doctor expected no complications. Walker v. North Dakota Eye Clinic, Ltd., 415 F.Supp. 891–2 (D.N.D.1976).

tenotomy, abductor

On July 29, 1975, Dr. Hood conducted a surgical procedure consisting of removal of some tendons in the groin area so that Terrance would be able to flex his left leg in the brace at a greater angle to aid in working the femur head back into its proper place in the hip socket. Dr. Hood described the procedure as a "**percutaneous abductor tenotomy** to relax the abductor tendons to obtain a better seating of the femoral head into the acetabulum." Arrendale v. U.S., 469 F.Supp. 883, 886 (N.D.Tex.1979).

Tensilon (ten'sĭ-lon) trademark for a solution of edrophonium chloride. See also *edrophonium chloride.*

Tensilon test See *test, Tensilon.*

TENS unit

Throughout the period of conservative treatment claimant continued to complain of severe pain.

In May of 1980 Dr. Massam prescribed a **TENS** unit, a stimulating device which can be worn by the patient. The **TENS** unit appeared to provide some relief to claimant but did not completely alleviate the pain. Sun 'N Lake Inn., Inc. v. Folsom, 426 So.2d 1265, (Dist Ct.App.Fla.1983).

tension (ten'shun) [L. *tensio;* Gr. *tonos*] the condition of being stretched or strained; the degree to which anything is stretched or strained.

Tension is not a disease or bodily or mental infirmity....

Dr. Crouch testified that **tension**, to a degree, is a normal condition in many persons; that it is desirable, in that one usually performs better under some **tension**, and that the **tension** under which Main at times worked was not a disease or a bodily or mental infirmity. Metropolitan Life Ins. Co. v. Main, 383 F.2d 952, 954, 958–9 (5th Cir. 1967).

teras (ter'as), pl. *ter'ata* [L.; Gr.] a monster.

teratism (ter'ah-tizm) [Gr. *teratisma*] an anomaly of formation or development; the condition of a monster. See also under *teras; monster; monstrum;* and names of specific monsters.

teratogen (ter'ah-to-jen) an agent or factor that causes the production of physical defects in the developing embryo.

More specifically, Merrell attacks the proof adduced to establish (1) that Bendectin is a **teratogen** (a potential cause of birth defects).... Mekdeci by and through Mekdeci v. Merrell Nat. Labs., 711 F.2d 1510, 1523 (11th Cir. 1983).

teratogenesis (ter'ah-to-jen'ĕ-sis) [*terato-* + Gr. *genesis* production] the production of physical defects in offspring in utero. Cited in Dow Chemical Co. v. Ruckelshaus, 477 F.2d 1317, 1320 (8th Cir. 1973).

teratogenic (ter"ah-to-jen'ik) tending to produce anomalies of formation, or teratism. See also *monster; teras;* and *teratism.*

Fortunately, the Thalidomide tranquilizers were not marketed in the United States, although they were in Europe. After their release it was found that they were **teratogenic**, that is they caused fetal skeletal deformities if taken during the first trimester of pregnancy. Pharmadyne Laboratories, Inc. v. Kennedy, 466 F.Supp. 100, 105 (D.N.J.1979).

... a study by the Bionetics Research Laboratories reported that 2,4,5–T caused **teratogenic** effects (birth defects) in mice and rats. Citizens Against Toxic Sprays, Inc. v. Bergland, 428 F.Supp. 908, 914 (D.Or.1977).

teratoma (ter"ah-to'mah), pl. *teratomas* or *terato'mata.* A true neoplasm made up of a number of different types of tissue, none of which is native to the area in which it occurs; most often found in the ovary or testis.

teratoma, immature See *teratoma, malignant.*

teratoma, malignant a solid, malignant ovarian tumor resembling a dermoid cyst but composed of immature embryonal and/or extraembryonal elements derived from all three germ layers. Called also *immature t.* and *solid t.*

Dr. Lindsay had seen that the **teratoma** contained both mature and immature tissue ("tissue that looks like the normal tissue of a fetus"). He knew that for many years there had been divergent opinions among pathologists as to whether immature tissue in a **teratoma** is potentially malignant. Jamison v. Lindsay, 166 Cal.Rptr. 443, 445 (Ct.App.Cal.1980).

term (term) [L. *terminus,* from Gr. *terma*] a definite period or specified time of duration, such as the culmination of pregnancy at the end of nine months. See also *gestation.*

A **term** baby would be one that was delivered either two weeks before or two weeks after the 280 days; one born after that period would be considered **post-term**; and one prior thereto as **pre-term**. Leonard v. Couse, 372 N.Y.S.2d 527, 531 (Fam.Ct.Otsego Cty.1975).

terminal (ter'mĭ-nal) [L. *terminalis*] forming or pertaining to an end; placed at the end.

Terminal condition means an incurable physical state caused by injury, disease, or illness which, regardless of the application of "life sustaining procedures," would produce death within a reasonable degree of medical probability, and where the application of life sustaining procedures serves only or primarily to postpone the moment of the patient's medico-legal death. John F. Kennedy Memorial Hosp. v. Bludworth, 432 So. 2d 611, 619 (Dist.Ct.App.Fla.1983).

For example, with regard to the impossibility of determining "who is **terminal**," the commissioner cited Dr. Peter H. Wiernik, Chief of the Clinical Oncology Branch of the National Cancer Institute's Baltimore Cancer Research Center, who stated "One major difficulty in making a particular chemical available for **terminal** patients only is that no one can prospectively define the term 'terminal' with any accuracy. A patient can be said to be **terminal** only after he dies. Many patients who are critically ill respond to modern day management of cancer." People v. Privitera, 591 P.2d 919, 925 (Cal.1979).

Terramycin (ter'ah-mi"sin) trademark for preparations of oxytetracycline. See also *oxytetracycline.*

test (test) [L. *testum* crucible] an examination or trial.

Well, analytical **tests** are divided into two broad categories, one a qualitative **test** which is used merely to indicate the presence [or] absence of something. The quanitative kind of **tests** are used to quantify or measure with some degree of precision how much of that substance is present. Reserve Mining Co. v. U.S., 498 F.2d 1073, 1080 (8th Cir. 1974).

A TABLE OF TESTS

(See also under *method; phenomenon; reaction; reagent; sign* and *symptom.*)

test, acid phosphatase

McMULLEN: Test three. The control labs agreed that the specimen submitted for the **Acid Phosphatase Test** was normal. But 25 per cent of the mail order labs said it was abnormal. Dr. Schaeffer.

DR. SCHAEFFER: An abnormal **Acid Phosphatase Test** could indicate that the patient had a bone tumor or a cancer of the prostate. If the test is inaccurate, unnecessary treatment or surgery could result. United Medical Labs v. Columbia Broadcasting System, Inc., 404 F.2d 706, 715 (9th Cir. 1968).

test, alkali denaturation: a moderately sensitive spectrophotometric method for determining the concentration of fetal (F) hemoglobin, which depends on the resistance of the hemoglobin molecule to denaturation of its globin moiety when exposed to alkali.

test, Almén's: 1. (*for albumin in urine*) one part of Almén's reagent is added to 6 parts of the urine; a cloudiness is produced when albumin is present. 2. (*for blood or blood pigment*) shake the suspected liquid with a mixture of equal parts of tincture of guaiacum and oil of turpentine; blood pigment, if present, will turn the mixture blue. 3. (*for dextrose*) heat the liquid with bismuth subnitrate dissolved in sodium hydroxide solution and sodium potassium tartrate; dextrose will cause the mixture to become dark brown or nearly black, and to deposit a black precipitate.

test, Ames (*for carcinogenicity*): a strain of *Salmonella typhimurium* that lacks the enzyme necessary for histidine synthesis is mixed with rat-liver extract and is plated thinly on an agar medium; a disk of filter paper containing the suspected carcinogen is then placed on the bacteria. If the substance causes DNA damage resulting in mutations, some of the bacteria will regain the ability to synthesize histidine and will proliferate to form colonies. The ability to cause mutations indicates that the substance is carcinogenic.

Senator DeConcini. Can you explain to me—I'm totally unfamiliar with this area—this **Ames test?**

Mr. Shirey. I am not familiar with it, really. It is a testing protocol used on chemical substances with an attempt to determine whether or not they are mutagenic. . . .

This is a test developed at the University of California. The purpose of the test is to determine whether the bacteria under test—whether they respond differently to different types of chemicals. From the type of response that this type of bacteria exhibits, and by testing chemicals that are known carcinogens or known not to be carcinogenic, they are able to determine

whether or not a new chemical is giving the same type of response as a known carcinogen.

If it does, then one of two assumptions are made. One, is that it is probably a human carcinogenic; or, second, that it certainly should be given further tests.

It is a brand new test. It is a pre-early indicator that is totally unrelated to feeding rats and mice—but it gives them an indication as to whether, perhaps, the type of studies that are carried out at national cancer institutes should be conducted. U.S. Cong. Sen. Hearings before the Judiciary Committee (Tris Hearing Panel) on S. 1503, 95th Cong. 1st Sess., 1977 at 53–54.

test, antigen (hepatitis) See *antigen, hepatitis B surface.*

test, audiological screening

Before he commenced employment at Newport News, Fishel underwent a pre-employment **audiological screening test** which revealed a binaural hearing loss of 25.3%.

As with his prior jobs, Fishel worked as a "burner" at Newport News which required the use of various types of torches to cut metal, usually in a noisy working environment. In May, 1979, after over seven years at that job, Fishel underwent a complete audiological exam which indicated that his binaural hearing loss had increased to 31.25%. Newport News Shipbuilding & Dry Dock Co. v. Fishel, 694 F.2d 327–8 (4th Cir. 1982).

test, Babinski's See under *sign.*

test, Bender gestalt; test, Bender visual-motor gestalt: a psychological test used for evaluating perceptual-motor coordination, for assessing personality dynamics, as a test of organic brain impairment, and for measuring neurological maturation. The subject is asked to make freehand copies of nine simple geometric designs presented separately on cards or sometimes to reproduce the design from memory.

As another example, the psychologist cited Mr. Schappel's response to the **Bender-Gestalt Test,** in which the patient is asked to copy certain geometric designs. Mr. Schappel chose to put several designs on a single piece of paper, in such a way that the designs were overlapping. Dr. Blum stated that this type of response has been correlated by past research with the personality traits of impulsiveness, and lack of emotional control. U.S. v. Schappel, 445 F.2d 716, 718 (D.C.Cir. 1971).

test, benzidine (*for blood*): to a saturated solution of benzidine in glacial acetic acid add an equal volume of 3 per cent hydrogen peroxide and 1 ml. of the unknown; a blue color indicates blood.

... plaintiff and several other inmates were subjected to a "benzidine test" to determine whether they had otherwise undetectable blood on their skin. The test involved the direct application of a chemical solution of benzidine, glacial acetic acid, and sodium perborate to the arms and upper portion of the inmates' bodies. If the solution had turned blue, it would have indicated the presence of blood on plaintiff's skin....

The evidence adduced at trial included the following: Dr. DiFanti purchased benzidine in bottles labelled "BENZIDINE WARNING! DUST HAZARDOUS RAPIDLY ABSORBED THROUGH SKIN MAY BE CARCINOGENIC AVOID BREATHING DUST OR VAPOR"....

... According to one of those experts, benzidine is considered a primary carcinogen, exposure to which, for as little as a minute, causes a permanent error to be imprinted in the DNA molecule and which, after a period of 14 to 30 years, may then result in bladder cancer. That expert also testified that because of plaintiff's exposure to benzidine, his risk of developing bladder cancer had increased from one in ten thousand to one in ten. [Footnote omitted.] Clark v. Taylor, 710 F.2d 4, 7, 10, 14 (1st Cir. 1983).

The deputy asked the witness: "And this test [the **benzidine test**] would show the presence of blood even though there was no blood visible to the naked eye?" Pinker replied: "So sensitive is it to blood that blood diluted 300 thousand times will still give the reaction. Amounts of blood that cannot be found with a microscope will give the reaction." The court then asked: "That is because of the presence of the hemoglobin?" Whereupon the witness gave an affirmative answer. People v. Schiers, 324 P.2d 981, 987 (Cal.Cr.App.1958).

test, blood alcohol

According to Dr. Brill, applicant was not suffering from any head injury but was in fact a chronic alcoholic, which explained the fact that he could tolerate such a high blood alcohol level without being rendered comatose.[2]...

... Dr. Brill diagnosed applicant as severely intoxicated and ordered a **blood alcohol test**. The result of that test was that the applicant had a blood alcohol level of .429. [2 The widely accepted data concerning the effects of alcohol are contained in a chart in "Lawyers Medical Cyclopedia of Personal Injuries & Allied Specialties", Rev., Vol. 3, section 24.6, page 470. That chart shows that a blood alcohol level of .35 produces coma.] Republic Indem. Co. of America v. W.C.A.B., 187 Cal.Rptr. 636, 638–9 (Ct.App.Cal.1982).

test, blood gas

Subsequently, the serial blood gas or arterial **blood gas examinations** were made. The tests indicate the degree of acidity (pH) in the blood, the level of oxygen (pO_2) in the blood and the level of carbon dioxide (pCO_2) in the blood. The latter is indicia of the extent carbon dioxide is discharged from the lungs. The pH reflects whether there is an excess of acid (acidosis) or an insufficiency of acid (alkalosis) in the blood. Matter of Quinlan, 348 A.2d 801, 807 (Super.Ct.N.J.1975).

test, Bogen's

A toxicologist took the stand for the plaintiff and explained to the jury the mechanics and meaning of the **Bogen method**. He

stated, "Well, obviously 2.5 is a marked degree of intoxication and there is no question that the person could not properly operate a motor vehicle"....

The **Bogen's method** of determination of the alcohol content of human blood is not a simple reading, such as a temperature taking, which a literate layman can make. Two stages are involved: the running of the test and then its evaluation. The testimony provides a somewhat complete description of the process. The necessary apparatus consists of two vertical test tubes, side by side, "with inlet tubes to the bottom of each and outlet tubes to each side". In the first tube are placed 4 ccs. of the blood specimen together with what is known as a Scott-Wilson reagent (to eliminate "acetone bodies in case of diabetics"). A defoaming element is also included. In the next or second tube—the receiving tube—are put 9 ccs. of Anstie's reagent, consisting of potassium dichromate and sulfuric acid. The tubes are then immersed in boiling water.

To the second tube is attached an aspirator, which is activated to reduce the pressure in the system. The alcohol in the blood in the first tube is volatilized by the heat of the water bath, and passes over into the second tube containing the Anstie's reagent. The "boiling and aspirating" in the distilling process must continue for a half hour. As the alcohol distills over, it condenses into a green chemical-chromic sulphate. By comparison of its hue with results of tests of known alcoholic content through the use of a colorimeter, the amount of alcohol in the specimen is assessed by the evaluator.* [* For a lucid, graphic and scholarly exposition of the entire process, see: Determination of Ethyl Alcohol in Blood, by Sidney Kaye, M.SC. and Harvey B. Haag, M.D., Journal of Forensic Medicine (October–December 1954) 373; and Emergency Toxicology (2d ed. 1961) by Sidney Kaye, M.SC. Ph.D., of Richmond, Va. [Dissent.]] Kissinger v. Frankhouser, 308 F.2d 348, 352–3 (4th Cir. 1962).

test, bone conduction: if a vibrating tuning-fork, when the handle is placed against the skull, is heard more distinctly than when held near the ear, it indicates loss in conduction through the middle ear.

The audiograms (i.e., the results of the examinations conducted) of each complaining witness were submitted into evidence and analyzed by at least one of the qualified experts. In virtually every instance, the review of the examination results established that appellant had failed to perform **bone conduction** and/or aided and unaided discrimination score testing. The record makes clear that these tests were essential to an adequate determination of possible medical pathology and the extent of hearing loss. Milligan v. Hearing Aid Dispensers Exam. Comm., 191 Cal.Rptr. 490, 493 (Ct.App.Cal.1983).

test, breath (alcohol)

10 NYCRR 59.4 lists four criteria for **breath-alcohol testing** devices. Interestingly the Intoximeter 3000 does, in fact, meet all of these criteria. The device does, in fact, collect and analyze a fixed volume of alveolar breath; it also is capable of analyzing and, in fact, does analyze reference samples of alcohol, and its analysis thereof has been shown to be within one-hundredth of one percent of the certified alcohol content of the reference solution. As to the final criteria (that the procedure's specificity be adequate and appropriate for the analysis of breath specimens for the determination of alcoholic concentration in traffic law enforcement), that is the very ques-

tion addressed in the hearings on this motion and in this opinion and which question the Court herein answers in the affirmative. People v. Jones, 461 N.Y.S.2d 962, 967 (Albany Cty.Ct. N.Y.1983).

test, breathalyzer

Hall testified that a **breathalyzer test** lacks probative value unless the machine has first been checked with a standardization test; that the sobriety of a person at the time of an earlier occurrence cannot be determined from the test; and that the test's validity is impaired if a subject smokes immediately before the test. People v. Godbout, 356 N.E.2d 865, 869 (App. Ct.Ill.1976).

The **breathalyzer** used in the test is an electrically powered apparatus designed to calculate the extent of alcohol in the suspect's circulatory system. The suspect blows into a tube and a sample of his breath is trapped inside the machine. The trapped sample is then permitted to bubble through a glass test ampoule containing three cubic centimeters of 0.025 percent potassium dichromate in a 50-percent-by-volume sulphuric acid solution which acts as a reagent to any alcohol suspended upon the suspect's breath. If alcohol is present in the sample, it produces a change in the color and the light transmissibility of the solution. Upon the passage of a light beam through the test ampoule, the relative light transmissibility of the solution is registered on a meter which calculates the percent of alcohol in the suspect's blood.

The machine is calibrated so as to provide a reading by establishing a correlation between the test ampoule and a reference ampoule which is identical in specification. It is essential to the accuracy of the test that a quantity of exactly three cubic centimeters of the solution be present in each. This is checked by a gauge in the machine and a test ampoule not meeting the requirement is discarded. People v. Hitch, 527 P.2d 361, 363 (Cal.1974).

test, carbon chloroform extract

The **carbon chloroform extract (CCE) test** procedure, which was the recommended standard for organic chemicals under the 1962 Public Health Service Drinking Water Standards, measures the total level of organic substances in drinking water, without identifying the individual component substances. While it may not detect all organics, it has the practical advantage of obviating the need to measure each substance individually, while providing a gross measure of the total organic content of water. See Drinking Water Standards: Report of the EPA Advisory Committee on the Revision and Application of the Drinking Water Standards (1973). Environmental Defense Fund, Inc. v. Costle, 578 F.2d 337, 345 (D.C. Cir.1978).

test, chemical (intoxication)

Counsel for the defendant makes two threshold arguments. First, that section 1193–a and 1194 of the Vehicle and Traffic Law permit only a "**chemical test**" of the breath, blood, urine, or saliva of a motor vehicle operator for the purpose of determining the alcoholic or drug content of his blood.

The defendant argues the Intoximeter 3000, based as it is on infrared and electrical analysis of a driver's breath, is not a "**chemical test**" and thus the results of such test are inadmissible.

The defendant's position is unrealistic and unfounded. There is no precedent in the State of New York on this issue, but a similar argument was made and rejected in courts of other states with regard to the Omicron Intoxilyzer (another breath-testing device utilizing infrared theory). In Ohio, a court held that even though the infrared test did not involve an actual chemical reaction, the definition of chemical analysis was broad enough to embrace the infrared process (City of Dayton v. Schenck, 63 Ohio Misc. 14, 409 N.E.2d 284). Similarly, in Delaware, the court held that the Intoxilyzer did perform a chemical analysis as required by State law regardless of the fact that the procedure was purely mechanical. The court concluded the term "**chemical test**" meant only an "analysis" of the substance being tested—that is, an examination of a substance to determine its component parts and proportions thereof, regardless of the method of testing (State of Delaware v. Moore, Del.Super., 307 A.2d 548). This Court likewise concludes that the term "**chemical test**" as used in Vehicle and Traffic Law 1193–a and 1194 was intended to mean an analysis of the chemistry of the substances therein referred to— breath, blood, urine or saliva—to determine the subject's blood-alcohol content, and was not intended to refer to the method of testing. Thus an analysis of breath as performed by the Intoximeter 3000, which utilizes established principles and laws of physics, is a **chemical test** within the meaning of that term in Vehicle and Traffic Law 1193–a and 1194. The position advanced by defendant seeks to restrict the meaning of "**chemical test**" to a process more appropriately called a chemical reaction. There is no authority in the law to require defendant's interpretation. People v. Jones, 461 N.Y.S.2d 962, 966 (Albany Cty.Ct.N.Y.1983).

test, coagulase: a test for coagulase activity in which bacteria are added to citrated or oxalated (human or rabbit) blood plasma; in the presence of coagulase, the plasma gels within three hours. Coagulase activity is also demonstrable by mixing bacteria with blood plasma on a slide; if positive, clumping occurs, with fibrin formation.

test, Coombs': a test for detection of antibodies to red cells by means of antiglobulin. In the *direct* Coombs test, used to detect cell-bound antibody, the red cells are washed free of serum and unbound antibody, and antiglobulin is added. Agglutination indicates the presence of antibody. This method is used to detect sensitized red cells in erythroblastosis fetalis and autoimmune hemolytic anemia. In the *indirect* Coombs' test, used to detect circulating antibody, a sample of the subject's serum is incubated with donor red cells (or bacteria), the cells are washed, and the antiglobulin is added. If antibody has adsorbed to the cells, they will be agglutinated. Called also *antiglobulin t.*

Dr. Price diagnosed Michele's jaundice as physiologic. His diagnosis was based primarily on laboratory tests which reported Michele's Rh factor and **Coombs test**, which would indicate the presence of antibodies in the red blood cells of the baby, as negative....

Before the baby was born, as shown on the mother's chart which was available to the pediatrician, Mrs. Neyland had a positive **Coombs test** showing her sensitivity to the Rh positive fetus she was carrying. Her condition became so acute that labor was prematurely induced. The child when born appeared healthy, but within 50 hours of life developed jaundice. Price v. Neyland, 320 F.2d 674, 676 (D.C.Cir.1963).

test, culture and sensitivity

There was also testimony by Dr. Barton that a **culture and sensitivity test** was the only method to reveal what was going on in the frontal sinus. . . .

It should be noted that there also was evidence that the **culture and sensitivity test** did not, in and of itself, assure a proper diagnosis of the exact nature of the infection. This is illustrated by the fact that the test performed on February 29, 1972, showed the infecting organism to be staphylococcus aureus coagulase positive bacteria, whereas the test performed on a specimen of the brain tissue after surgery revealed a streptococcus bacteria. Barton v. Owen, 139 Cal. Rptr. 494, 503 (Ct.App.Cal.1977).

test, Denver developmental

Dr. Schneier administered the **Denver Developmental Test** to James Sharpe. This is a standardized test used to assess the development of a child in social, verbal, fine motor and gross motor areas. In re Sharpe, 374 A.2d 1323–4 (Super.Ct.Pa. 1977).

test, diffusion

With the proliferation of the various types of antibiotics, doctors found a need for a screening test to help choose which antibiotic to use in treating a particular infection. A **diffusion test**, using antibiotic sensitivity discs like the one in question here, soon became a widely employed screening method.[3] In this test, a round paper disc, which has been impregnated with a specific antibiotic, is placed in contact with sample cultures, or isolates, of a patient's virus, grown in a special culture medium (agar) from a specimen of the patient's fluid (blood, spinal fluid, sputum, urine, etc.). In those places impregnated with an antibiotic to which the patient's infection is sensitive, no new isolate will grow, leaving a clear area (an "inhibition zone"); in those places impregnated with a drug to which the infection is resistant, the isolate will grow, leaving no clear area. The disc is used, in conjunction with a patient's specimen, in laboratory work exclusively, and never comes in contact with any part of the patient's body itself. [3 See generally Bauer, Kirby, Sherris, & Turck, Antibiotic Susceptibility Testing by a Standardized Single Disk Method, 45 American Journal of Clinical Pathology 493 (1966); Petersdorf & Sherris, Methods and Significance of In Vitro Testing of Bacterial Sensitivity to Drugs, 39 American Journal of Medicine 766 (1965); Gould, The Laboratory Control of Antibiotic Therapy, 3 Chemotherapia 477 (1961); Second Report of the Expert Committee on Antibiotics, Standardization of Methods for Conducting Microbic Sensitivity Tests, World Health Organization Technical Report Series No. 210, pp. 12–17 (1961).] U.S. v. Bacto-Unidisk, 394 U.S. 784, 787, 89 S.Ct. 1410, 1412, 22 L.Ed.2d 726 (1969).

test, Doppler blood velocity

Similarly, plaintiffs justified the use of the **doppler blood velocity test**, an ultrasonic probe placed over the patient's artery, on the ground that it could show aggravation of spinal nerves that controlled the circulatory system. Karaskiewicz v. Blue Cross and Blue Shield, 336 N.W.2d 757, 760 (Ct.App.Mich. 1983).

test, drug

The district court fully described the procedures in its opinion and it is unnecessary to repeat that description, except to state that the basic purposes of the **tests** are to determine the effective dose and the lethal dose of the chemical compound. Once these dosages are determined, **tests** on humans may begin. These are conducted in three stages with three different objectives: the first is to determine lack of toxicity, tolerance and safety; the second is to establish clinical effectiveness through repeated usage; and the third is to determine the addictive qualities of the drug. Carter-Wallace, Inc. v. Riverton Laboratories, Inc., 433 F.2d 1034, 1036 (2d Cir. 1970).

test, Ely heel-to-buttock See *test, Ely's.*

test, Ely's: with the patient prone, if flexion of the leg on the thigh causes the buttocks to arch away from the table and the leg to abduct at the hip joint, there is contracture of the lateral fascia of the thigh.

In the prone position, **Ely tests** are negative for lumbosacral pain. Chabert v. City of Westwego Police Pension, 423 So.2d 1190, 1193 (Ct.App.La.1982).

The **Ely heel-to-buttock test** for lumbosacral disease was positive bilaterally, which indicated an active disease or pathological changes occurring in that portion of the back. Consolidated Freightways v. Industrial Com'n, 356 N.E.2d 51–2 (Ill. 1976).

tests, exercise tests for detecting previously undetected coronary artery disease; they are graded tests of coronary fitness in which the subject performs exercise, as by walking a treadmill or pedaling a stationary bicycle, while under continuous electrocardiographic monitoring, usually by means by an oscilloscope, before, during, and after the exercise. Called also *stress t's.* See also *Master "2-step" exercise test.*

During the course of a **stress test** of the type at issue here, a patient walks or jogs at varying speeds and varying inclines on a treadmill while the physician monitors various lead systems attached to the patient's chest. Tart v. McGann, 697 F.2d 75, 76 (2d Cir. 1982).

test, FLEX

Both states use the Federal Licensing Examination (**FLEX Test**) to assess the qualifications of applicants. The **FLEX Test** covers the areas of basic science, clinical science, and clinical competence. Grades achieved on each of these sections are tabulated separately; they are not combined to obtain an average or total score. Grades from each section are weighted according to the importance placed on the area under consideration to demonstrate medical competency. Thus, basic science is given a weight of one; clinical science is given a weight of two; and clinical competence is given a weight of three. The score on each test is multiplied respectively by 1, 2 and 3, and the figure is then divided by 6 to arrive at a final weighted score.

Both New York and New Mexico require applicants to achieve a minimum score of 75 percent. The statutes, rules and regulations of both states do not provide any disparity. The only point of disparity is contained in the unwritten practice or custom of the Board. The Board has adopted a policy of not extending licensure by reciprocity under § 61–6–12, if the other state, which granted a medical license after requiring a **FLEX Test**, permitted the averaging of the highest grades attained on more than one examination to attain the 75 percent weighted average. New York's licensing authority does not impose this additional requirement upon the standard of 75 percent. Fiber v. New Mexico Bd. of Med. Examiners, 596 P.2d 510–12 (N.M.1979).

test, Gaenslen See *sign, Gaenslen's*.

test, gallbladder

In his opinion, the Cochran V.A. physicians failed to exercise proper medical judgment in not performing a series of tests or ultra sound on the gall bladder. Dr. Sapala testified that "99 percent" of all physicians would have automatically ordered **gall bladder tests** when ordering an upper G.I. Payne v. U.S., 711 F.2d 73, 76 (7th Cir. 1983).

test, Graham's: the intravenous or oral administration of tetraiodophthalein sodium prior to roentgenologic examination of the gallbladder.

Dr. Koehler, a radiologist, who was in charge of the section of abdominal roentgenology for the Institute, performed a **Graham dye test** or a venogram on Mrs. Frerker. In the course of the procedure a catheter is advanced by means of the guide wire into the location desired in the vessel. When the catheter is in position, the guide wire is then removed. In the procedure on plaintiff a part of the guide wire, described as the flexible tip, broke off and remained in plaintiff. This was discovered when the guide wire was withdrawn. Picker X-Ray Corp. v. Frerker, 405 F.2d 916, 918 (8th Cir. 1969).

test, Heller's: 1. (*for albumin in urine*) stratify cold nitric acid below the urine in a test tube; albumin will form a white coagulum between the urine and the acid. 2. (*for blood in the urine*) add potassium hydroxide solution and heat; the earthy phosphates are precipitated, and if blood is present, they are stained red by hematin. 3. (*for dextrose in urine*) add a solution of potassium hydroxide; sugar will cause a brownish or reddish precipitate.

test, hemoglobin See specific tests, including *alkali denaturation test; Almén's test* (2); *Heller's test* (2); *Katayama's test; Kobert's test; sand test* and *Stokes's test*. See also *hemoglobin, methods for,* under *method*.

. . . no follow-up **hemoglobin test** was ordered, in spite of the fact that the second blood count, made on November 6th, showed a significant drop in the hemoglobin, admittedly diagnostic evidence of the presence of erythroblastosis fetalis. Price v. Neyland, 320 F.2d 674, 676 (D.C.Cir.1963).

test, hemoglutination

She developed a reliable serologic test for the detection of toxocara which was announced in an article [5] published in the "American Journal of Tropical Medicine" in May, 1974. [[5] Hemoglutination Test for the Detection of Antibodies Specific for Ascaris and Toxocara Antigens in Patients with Suspected Visceral Larva Migrans.] Steele v. U.S., 463 F.Supp. 321, 327 (D.Alas.1978).

test, HLA paternity blood

That treatise, which appears in the Journal of Family Law,[2] explains in detail what the meaning of a percentage "probability of paternity" is . . . .

. . . It is the ratio of the probability that the known mother and the putative father would produce a child with the given genetic markers to the sum of such probabilities for the putative father and "a hypothetical man who is assumed to be random with respect serologic genotypes and unrelated to the putative father in question." [[2] Terasaki, "Resolution by HLA Testing of 1000 Paternity Cases Not Excluded by ABO Testing" (1978) 16 J.Fam.L. 543.] County of Ventura v. Marcus, 189 Cal.Rptr. 8, 11–12 (Ct.App.Cal.1983).

test, Katayama's (*for carbonyl-hemoglobin*): to 5 drops of blood add 10 ml. of water, 5 drops of orange-colored ammonium sulfide, and enough acetic acid to make the mixture acid. CO causes a rose-red color; normal blood, a dirty greenish gray.

test, Kernig

The supine attitude is assumed without difficulty. Straight leg raising permits elevation through an arc of seventy degrees. Hamstring muscle tightening is noted. There is no sciatic pain referral with these manipulations. **Kernig tests** are confirmatory. Chabert v. City of Westwego Police Pension, 423 So.2d 1190, 1193 (Ct.App.La.1982).

test, Kobert's (*for hemoglobin*): the suspected liquid is treated with zinc powder or a solution of zinc sulfate; the resulting precipitate is stained red by alkalis.

test, Lange's (*for acetone in urine*) 15 ml. of urine are mixed with 0.5 to 1 ml. of acetic acid, and a few drops of a freshly prepared concentrated solution of sodium nitroprusside added. The mixture is overlaid with ammonia. At the point of junction a characteristic violet ring is formed.

Dr. Klawans stated that the colloidal gold curve or **Lange gold curve** is a series of ten separate tests to give you information of the quality of the proteins in the spinal fluid extracted by lumbar puncture. Normally, the results should all be zeros or a few ones. Plaintiff's gold curve reads, as indicated in the hospital discharge summary: three, two, two, two, one, zero, zero, zero, zero, zero. This is what is known as a first zone elevation of the gold curve, and it is frequently found in patients with multiple sclerosis and is considered to be confirmatory evidence of the clinical diagnosis. McSwain v. Chicago Trans. Authority, 362 N.E.2d 1264, 1273 (App.Ct.Ill.1977).

test, Mantoux (*for tuberculosis*): give intracutaneous injection of 0.1 ml. of desired dilution of tuberculin and successive injections of gradually increasing concentration until a reaction occurs; called also *intracutaneous tuberculin t., Mantoux reaction*, and *Mendel's t.*

test, Marquis' (*for morphine*): evaporate the unknown to dryness on a white porcelain plate and touch with a mixture of 3 ml. of concentrated sulfuric acid and 2 drops of formalin. A purple-red color changing to violet and then to blue indicates morphine.

Agent Chesley testified that he had performed a "**Marquis reagent**" **field test** with the substance in the package and obtained a reaction indicating that it was a derivative of opium. Verdugo v. U.S., 402 F.2d 599, 607 (9th Cir. 1968).

test, Master "2-step" exercise (for coronary insufficiency): an electrocardiographic test, the tracings being recorded while the subject repeatedly ascends and descends two steps, each 9 inches high, immediately after cessation of the climbs, and then 2 and 6 minutes later. The amount of work (number of trips) is standardized for age, weight, and sex.

During those examinations he was given various tests to determine cardiovascular function. Although different interpretations were presented, the record indicates that the **Double Master's test** administered to Loomis in February 1973 produced a positive (i.e., abnormal) result. Loomis v. McLucas, 553 F.2d 634, 636 (10th Cir. 1977).

A **Masters test** (an electrocardiogram taken during and immediately after the stress of walking up and down a few steps) was taken and Morgenroth went 23 steps as compared with the 20 minimum requirement. Morgenroth v. Pacific Medical Center, Inc., 126 Cal.Rptr. 681, 683 (Ct.App.Cal.1976).

test, Minnesota Multi-Phasic Personality Inventory

Appellant introduced Dr. David Voit Myers, a clinical psychologist, who testified that appellant scored within normal range on the **Minnesota Multi-phasic Personality Inventory (MMPI)** [1] and that he could perform responsibly outside a hospital setting. [[1] The **MMPI** is a standard objective psychological battery containing 566 true-false items. Substantial clinical assessments are made by analysis of the item selections concerning emotional feelings, self-image, etc.] Bethany v. Stubbs, 393 So.2d 1351–2 (Miss.1981).

test, nocturnal penile tumescent

In November, 1978, plaintiff submitted to a **Nocturnal Penile Tumescent** study (NPT), a test which is designed to distinguish organic impotence from psychogenic impotence. The test is premised on the fact that all males have six to eight erections each night during the rapid eye movement (REM) cycle of sleep. Pressure transducers applied to the penis can thus indicate whether the subject is physically able to achieve an erection. The data from plaintiff's test shows that on two successive nights, he had more than one erection of significant duration. The experts agreed that these results effectively rule out any organic basis for plaintiff's complaint. Dessi v. U.S., 489 F.Supp. 722, 730 (E.D.Va.1980).

test, Pap; test, Papanicolaou: an exfoliative cytological staining procedure for the detection and diagnosis of various conditions, particularly malignant and premalignant conditions of the female genital tract (cancer of the vagina, cervix, and endometrium), in which cells which have been desquamated from the genital epithelium are obtained by smears, fixed and stained, and examined under the microscope for evidence of pathologic changes. Cytologic findings have commonly been expressed in terms of histologic lesions classified as Class I to Class V, but preferably each examination should have an individual histological description. The test is also used in evaluating endocrine function, and in the diagnosis of malignancies of other organs, as of the respiratory tract and lungs,

gastrointestinal tract, urinary tract, and breast. See also *Table of Stains*.

The record indicates that the **pap smear test** is an accurate detector of cervical cancer. Truman v. Thomas, 611 P.2d 902, 907 (Cal.1980).

It was brought out at trial that a **pap smear** is a method of diagnosing cancer in the cervix in its earliest stages. It is performed by obtaining cells from the cervix and testing them under a microscope. It was also shown that the particular pathologist employed in this case, Dr. Lehrue Stevens, used the most common method of classifying the results of the test. In this classification system, there are five classifications which are (Tr. pp. 355–359):

Class 1—This indicates a perfectly normal pap smear with no abnormalities.

Class 2—This indicates an inflammation or an infection in the cervix.

Class 3—This indicates the possibility of dysplasia (a precancerous change in the cells) or carcinoma in situ (cancer at its earliest stage).

Class 4—This indicates a stronger probability of cancerous cells.

Class 5—This indicates definite cancer in the cervix and possibly other areas of the female reproductive system. Steele v. St. Paul Fire & Marine Ins. Co., 371 So.2d 843, 846 (Ct.App.La.1979).

A colloquialism for Dr. George Papanicolaou. "**Papanicolaou's stain**: A method of straining smears of various body secretions, from the respiratory, digestive or genitourinary tract, for the examination of exfoliated cells, to detect the presence of a malignant process." Carmichael v. Reitz, 95 Cal.Rptr. 381, 387 (Ct.App.Cal.1971).

test, partial thromboplastin time: a one-stage clotting test used clinically to detect deficiencies of the components of the intrinsic thromboplastin system; in reality prolonged clotting time may reflect deficiency or absence of coagulation factors I, II, V, and VIII through XII, separately or in combination.

Most of the doctors and to some extent Nurse Kevil testified about the relationship between the **PTT** value and hemorrhage from Heparinization. The "**PTT** value" means the time in seconds it takes the blood to clot. Mrs. Belmon's normal **PTT** was 27.8 seconds. Belmon v. St. Frances Cabrini Hospital, 427 So.2d 541, 545 (Ct.App.La.1983).

The results of the **Partial Thromboplastin Time Test** (PTT, a measurement of clotting time), although above normal, ruled out a potential complication of excessive bleeding as the abnormality was "not significant." Ziegert v. South Chicago Community Hospital, 425 N.E.2d 450, 455 (App.Ct.Ill.1981).

The patent relates to a reagent for use in a **partial thromboplastin time test**, or PTT test. This is a test which is used to detect certain deficiencies in a person's blood which interfere with the ability of the blood to clot. The **PTT test** is performed on plasma, which is obtained by centrifuging blood to remove white and red blood cells and components of blood called platelets. An anti-coagulant is added to the blood as it is withdrawn from the patient to prevent clotting until the test is performed. The plasma is placed in a test tube, and a reagent which includes a material for providing clotting activity in place of the platelets, called a platelet substitute, is added to the plasma. Calcium chloride is then added to neutralize the anti-coagulant, and the time required for a clot to form is determined. This is the **PTT** time, and patients with certain coagulation disorders will have a longer **PTT** time than patients with normal blood....

... Dr. Brinkhous and associates developed the **PTT test**. That test is a test tube simulation of the intrinsic pathway of blood coagulation which tells the doctor whether the plasma contains dissolved components that will cause normal clotting. The test provides a fast, reliable method for detecting hemophiliacs or abnormal bleeders. A number of materials were evaluated by adding them to plasma in what was basically a recalcification clotting test. Some of the materials tested gave longer clotting times for hemophiliac blood than normal blood. Those materials which gave the longer times were recognized to function as a substitute for platelets and thus came to be known as platelet substitute of standard strength. Ortho Pharmaceutical Corp. v. Amer. Hosp. Supply Corp., 186 U.S. P.Q. 501, 503–4 (S.D.Ind.1975).

test, patch: a test for hypersensitiveness made by applying to the skin the substances in question by means of small pieces of linen or blotting paper impregnated with the substances; on removal of the patches the reactions of the skin are noted. The same method is used for applying tuberculin test for tuberculosis (*Vollmer's t.*).

He also gave claimant a **patch test** which indicated a 4-plus positive reaction to cement (a 4-plus reaction is the highest sensitivity)....

... The results of this test disclosed the presence of potassium dichromate and a 4-plus reaction to cement. This evidence coupled with his duties as a cement machine operator requiring his day by day contact with cement, which is uncommon to the members of the general public, constitutes the requisite evidence proving that claimant sustained a far greater exposure to cement during the course of his employment at Gunite in comparison to the hazards confronting the public generally. Phelps v. Gunite Construction and Rentals, Inc., 279 So.2d 829, 831–2 (Fla.1973).

test, Patrick's: with the patient supine, the thigh and knee are flexed and the external malleolus is placed over the patella of the opposite leg; the knee is depressed, and if pain is produced thereby arthritis of the hip is indicated. Patrick calls this test *fabere sign*, from the initial letters of movements that are necessary to elicit it, namely, flexion, abduction, external rotation, extension.

The Lasegue and straight leg-raising tests, as well as the **Patrick test**, were all severely positive, demonstrating sacroiliac joint damage. Flexion, extension, abduction and internal rotation were all "markedly restricted" on the right and "moderately restricted" on the left. Gretchen v. U.S., 618 F.2d 177, 180 (2d Cir. 1980).

There is a very positive **Fabre** [sic] **Patrick test** on the left. King v. Celebrezze, 223 F.Supp. 457, 460 (W.D.Ark.1963).

test, plythesmagraphic

The evidence at trial showed the **plythesmagraphic study** to be a pulse volume recording. By means of a light sensor attached to a patient's fingers or toes, the instrument recorded the volume of the patient's pulse. Plaintiffs justified the use of the test by chiropractors on the ground that irregular pulse patterns could indicate constricted blood vessels due to spinal nerve impingement. Karaskiewicz v. Blue Cross and Blue Shield, 336 N.W.2d 757, 760 (Ct.App.Mich.1983).

test, prothrombin: a test for prothrombin based on clotting time. See also *time, prothrombin*; and *Quick's test*.

These [tests] included refinements of the SGOT and alkaline phosphatase tests, additional enzyme tests, measurement of the bile in the urine, a test of the blood's capacity to clot (**prothrombin test**), and a differential blood count. Cornfeldt v. Tongen, 262 N.W.2d 684, 690 (Minn.1977).

McMULLEN: In the **Prothrombin Time Test**—which measures how quickly blood clots—the control labs found that the blood specimen submitted to them was in a normal range. The mail order labs, that reported on the same specimen, said the clotting time was between 50 to 53 per cent below normal.

DR. SCHAEFFER: A gross error in a Prothrombin Time Test, which measures the clotting time of blood, could cause very serious results. For example, doctors prescribe drugs to keep the clotting time of blood of their patients recovering from coronary heart attacks 15 to 20 per cent below normal. If the lab report shows that the clotting time is slow in the first place, an inadequate amount of drug may be given. That could cause another heart attack or possibly the death of the patient. United Medical Labs v. Columbia Broadcasting System, Inc., 404 F.2d 706, 715 (9th Cir. 1968).

Dr. Miles examined the patient, checked his **prothrombin time** [3] and decided to proceed with the aortogram. [[3] **Prothrombin time** is a test used to measure a substance that is in the blood which plays a major role in clotting.] Dill v. Scuka, 279 F.2d 145–6 (3d Cir. 1960).

test, pulmonary function

A **pulmonary function test** is designed to measure the degree to which breathing is obstructed. The subject is asked to inhale and exhale as hard as possible. A record is made of maximum breathing capacity (MBC or MVV) and forced expiratory volume (FEV_1). The values obtained are then correlated with the subject's height in order to determine the extent of dysfunction. Padavich v. Mathews, 561 F.2d 142, 146 (8th Cir. 1977).

test, Quick's: (*one-stage prothrombin time*) by adding an extrinsic thromboplastin such as dried rabbit brain and calcium to oxalated blood the integrity of the prothrombin complex, composed of factors II, V, VII, X, may be defined; used widely to control administration of coumarin-type anticoagulants.

test, Rinne: a hearing test made, with the opposite ear masked, with tuning forks of 256, 512, and 1024 Hz; by alternately placing the stem of the vibrating fork on the mastoid process of the temporal bone of the patient and holding it ½ inch from the external auditory meatus until it is no longer heard at one of these positions. When air conduction is greater than bone conduction, it indicates normal hearing or sensorineural hearing loss. When bone conduction is greater than air conduction, it indicates conductive hearing loss.

test, Rorschach: a projective test (q.v.) which is sensitive to disorders of thought and emotion. It consists of a series of 10 ink blot designs, some black and some in colors. The patient is directed to look at the cards and tell what he sees. He is then asked to indicate which aspect of the blot and which location suggest the percept he reports. See also *test, Bender gestalt.*

If anything, plaintiff's problems apparently have a psychological basis. A report by Dr. Edward W. Slockbower, a clinical psychologist, indicated that the results of the **Rorschach test** were those "of an hysterical man, conversion in type, and I feel that under stress he is capable of exaggerating any existing organic problems or developing somatic ones if the stress continues. However, what is most apparent is a very deep underlying depression and I feel, also, that many of his symptoms could be of a depressive equivalent. . . .

"I see this man's problems, at least as far as the tests reveal them, to be on neurotic, emotional basis with no evidence in any of the tests to suggest any involvement of the central nervous system." (Tr. 151–152). Gum v. Secretary of Dep't of Health, Educ. & Welf., 341 F.Supp. 611–12 (D.Md.1972).

Dr. Blum gave several examples of noteworthy test responses. On the **Rorschach Inkblot Test**, the patient is asked to interpret a standard set of abstract inkblots. Mr. Schappel repeatedly saw blood in the test cards, and in one card he saw a "little bloodied baby." Dr. Blum stated that this was part of a pattern of responses that indicated a basic pathological condition. U.S. v. Schappel, 445 F.2d 716, 718 (D.C.Cir.1971).

test, sand (*for bile and hemoglobin in urine*): a layer of white sand is spread on a plate and on this is poured some of the urine; if the urine contains pigments, a spot is left on the sand, which is brown with hemoglobin and greenish with bile pigment. Called also *Lipp's t.*

test, sequential multiple analysis See *test, SMA–12.*

test, serum bulirubin See *test, van den Bergh's.*

test, SMA–12

As explained by the government, an **SMA–12 test** is "a 12-component Sequential Multiple Analysis, done on auto-analytic equipment which in a matter of seconds performs 12 blood chemistry tests on a given specimen." U.S. v. Halper, 590 F.2d 422, 426 (2d Cir. 1978).

test, smear See *Papanicolaou's stain,* under *Table of Stains.*

test, Stokes's See under *reagent.*

tests, stress See *test, exercise.*

test, sweat

A **sweat test,** a reliable indicator of cystic fibrosis, measures the body's sodium chloride level. Cystic fibrosis children have a high level of sodium chloride. Kissil v. Beneficial Nat. Life Ins. Co., 64 N.J. 555, 559, 319 A.2d 67 (1974).

test, Tensilon (*for myasthenia gravis*): after administration of Tensilon (edrophonium chloride), the patient's eye signs (ptosis and extraocular muscle abnormalities) markedly decrease.

The test to determine the presence of myasthenia gravis is called a **tensolin** [sic] **test,** and in Triplett's case it was positive. Mid Central Tool Co. v. Industrial Com'n, 382 N.E.2d 222, 225 (Ill.1978).

test, tine; test, tine tuberculin (Rosenthal): four tines or prongs 2 mm. long, attached to a plastic handle and coated with dip-dried Old tuberculin (O.T.) are pressed into the skin of the volar surface of the forearm, where they deposit a dose of the tuberculin in the outer layer. The skin is checked 48 to 72 hours later for the presence of palpable induration; if the induration around one or more of the puncture wounds is 2 mm. or more in diameter, the test is considered positive.

Another medically acceptable, though less reliable, method which also measures skin reaction is the so-called **tine test.**

A positive PPD or **tine test** indicates nothing more than the presence of a tubercle bacillus, which may be dormant. Plummer v. U.S., 420 F.Supp. 978–9 (M.D.Pa.1976).

test, Trendelenburg's: the patient, standing erect, stripped, with back to the examiner, is told to lift one leg and then the other: when weight is supported by the affected limb, the pelvis on the sound side falls instead of rising; seen in disturbances of the gluteus medius mechanism, as in deformity of the femoral neck, dislocated hip joint, and weakness or paralysis of the gluteus medius muscle.

Trendelenburg tests are negative to instability at this time. In forward bending, the lordotic curvature gradually reverses. The patient is aware of tightness in the left ilio-lumbar zone with this effort. Chabert v. City of Westwego Police Pension, 423 So.2d 1190, 1193 (Ct. of App.La.1982).

test, tuberculin: a test for the existence of tuberculosis, consisting in the subcutaneous injection of 5 mg. of tuberculin. In healthy persons it produces no appreciable effect, but in tuberculous patients it produces a moderate fever, which lasts for several hours, and also a swelling and redness in tuberculous lesions of the patient. The test does not differentiate between infection in a resistant individual without the disease and a person with clinical features of the disease. See also *ophthalmic reaction; Pirquet's reaction; Moro's reaction* under *reaction;* and *Mantoux test.*

Mr. Santoni was required to undergo a physical examination, which included a **tuberculin skin test** and chest X-ray. Although the chest X-ray was clear, Mr. Santoni's **T.B. skin test** proved positive, indicating that he had been exposed to tubercle bacilli at some time in his life and was at a greater risk of developing the disease. Santoni v. Moodie, 452 A.2d 1223, 1225 (Ct.Spec.App.Md.1982).

A **tuberculin skin test** is a simple means of discovering if a tubercle bacillus has entered an individual's body . . . .

A positive **tuberculin skin test** indicates in a great majority of cases that the individual had exposure to tuberculosis in the past and that at some time at least one tubercle bacillus had entered his body. Plummer v. U.S., 420 F.Supp. 978–9 (M.D. Pa.1976).

test, tuberculin, Sterneedle: the needle points of the Sterneedle are dipped into 1 to 2 drops of tuberculin P.P.D. and then placed on the forearm, where the six needle points are caused to penetrate the skin (by means of a spring device in the handle), through the P.P.D. solution, to a depth of 1 mm., thus depositing tuberculin in the outer layer of the skin. Palpable, coalescing induration (edema) extending more than 5 mm. around the puncture wounds in three to seven days indicates a positive reaction. In England, it is known as the *Heaf test*.

The **PPD (Pure Protein Derivative) test**, which measures skin reaction to its injection, is a medically accepted method for ascertaining the presence of tubercle bacilli....

A positive **PPD** or tine test indicates nothing more than the presence of a tubercle bacillus, which may be dormant. Plummer v. U.S., 420 F.Supp. 978, 997–80 (M.D.Pa.1977).

test, tuberculin titer: a test for the hypersensitivity of the organism to tuberculin by a graduated cutaneous tuberculin test with varying concentrations of the tuberculin; called also *Ellerman-Erlandsen's t.*

test, urethral smear

The **urethral smear test**, done in this case for trichomonas, a nonvenereal disease of the urinary tract, is generally performed by obtaining fluid samples from the tip of the penis and subjecting them to various laboratory tests....

... According to the technician, he administered the test by inserting a cotton swab about a quarter-inch into the penis with appellant in a standing position....

... Dr. George Shargel, a board certified urologist and a member of the American College of Surgeons, who practiced in the state of Michigan. Dr. Shargel stated that although appearing simple, the **urethral smear test** involved a highly invasive procedure causing severe pain, particularly if there is disease or inflammation present. He testified that the insertion of a swab into the male organ produces a vasal vagal reflex in a patient which causes the blood to rush from the brain to the area being traumatized, thereby causing the patient to feel faint. For this reason, Dr. Shargel explained, the nationally accepted medical standard of care requires the test to be administered with the patient in a prone or sitting position. Moreover, Dr. Shargel testified that with respect to obtaining a good specimen, there was no qualitative difference between administering the test with the patient in a standing or prone position....

Appellees' final expert witness was Dr. William Dolan, a pathologist and director of the pathology laboratory at Arlington Hospital in Virginia. Dr. Dolan stated that he was not aware of any national standards for conducting the **urethral**

smear test, but that for the past thirty years he has always administered the test with the patient in a standing position. Morrison v. MacNamara, 407 A.2d 555, 558–9 (D.C.Cir. 1979).

test, van den Bergh's: a test for bilirubin in which diazotized serum or plasma is compared with a standard solution of diazotized bilirubin.

Dr. Price diagnosed Michele's jaundice as physiologic. His diagnosis was based primarily on laboratory tests which reported Michele's Rh factor and Coombs test, which would indicate the presence of antibodies in the red blood cells of the baby, as negative. As a matter of fact, these tests were wrong. No **Vandenbergh test**, which would probe the presence of bile in the brain, was given....

... The medical evidence also showed that where a child of an Rh positive homozygous father and an Rh negative mother developed jaundice in the first few days of life, a **Vandenburg test**[2] was strongly indicated. [[2] Also known as a serum bilirubin test.] Price v. Neyland, 320 F.2d 674, 676–7 (D.C.Cir. 1963).

test, ventilation: measurement of the quantity of air expired by a person during a period of exercise.

In a statement regarding the evaluation of **ventilatory function studies** Dr. Harold Passes, who appears to be the Administration's Chief Medical Officer, states that the results of **ventilatory function tests** are acceptable only where there are three tests with no more than a 2% variation in the results. (Tr. 92)....

... It appears that the **ventilatory function studies** are based on a claimant's blowing into a tube. Obviously it would be easy for a claimant simply not to blow as hard as he could and thereby achieve a lower value than he is entitled to. The medical analysis stating that Plaintiff's **ventilatory function studies** are unacceptable (Tr. 105) should be given the weight of expert testimony....

... [20 C.F.R. 410, 426(b)] provides a table of ventilatory study values for making a determination of totally disabling pneumoconiosis. Doctorman v. Weinberger, 417 F.Supp. 26, 29–30 (E.D.Okla.1976).

test, Vollmer's: trademark for a tuberculin patch test done with an adhesive strip on which are two test squares and one control square of filter paper, the test squares saturated with concentrated Old Tuberculin and the control square with uninoculated broth.

---

testicle See also *orchiectomy*; and *torsion* (Cradle case).

tetanus (tet′ah-nus) [Gr. *tetanos*, from *teinein* to stretch] 1. an infectious disease in which tonic muscle spasm and hyperreflexia result in trismus ("lockjaw"), generalized muscle spasm, arching of the back (opisthotonus), glottal spasm, seizures, and respiratory spasms and paralysis; it is caused by the neurotoxin of anaerobically vegetating *Clostridium tetani*, with onset one to two weeks after inoculation of spore forms into a traumatized area of the body. See also *Clostridium tetani; globulin, tetanus immune human*; and *incubation*.

Fortunately **tetanus** is a disease of rare occurrence, and it is extremely rare from oral infection. The testimony revealed that in recent years an over-all total of 250–300 cases a year from all portals of entry have been recorded in this country. No information was supplied as to whether any of these cases resulted from oral surgery. It was undisputed, however, that **tetanus** following tooth extraction is extremely rare. Germann v. Matriss, 260 A.2d 825, 829 (N.J.1970).

tetany (tet′ah-ne) a syndrome manifested by sharp flexion of the wrist and ankle joints (carpopedal spasm), muscle twitchings, cramps, and convulsions, sometimes with attacks of stridor. It is due to abnormal calcium metabolism and occurs in parathyroid hypofunction, vitamin D deficiency, alkalosis, and as a result of the ingestion of alkaline salts.

... before her death in the early morning hours of December 9th diagnosed her case as one of **tetany** accompanying pregnancy. That indicated a calcium deficiency. The five opinion witnesses called upon the trial all agreed that on December 7th, the deceased had ingested strychnine....

... The only troublesome symptom was that Mrs. Feldman complained of some tenderness in her feet. The doctor thought her condition was "strongly suggestive of hypocalcemic **tetany** of pregnancy" and finding the prognosis good he dictated a prescription consisting of "60 grains of calcium chloride in 150 c.c. of elixir lactate of pepsin" to be administered every four hours. People v. Feldman, 85 N.E.2d 913–15 (N.Y.1949).

tetracaine (tet′rah-kān) [USP] chemical name: 4-(butylamino)-benzoic acid 2-(dimethylamino)ethyl ester. A local anesthetic, $C_{15}H_{24}N_2O_2$, occurring as a white or light yellow, waxy solid; applied topically to the eyeball and conjunctivia.

There is nothing to indicate that the anesthetic (**Pontocaine**) was defective or was improper for the purpose used; that its use on plaintiff was contra-indicated, or that there was any want of skill in its administration. Rothman v. Silber, 216 A.2d 18, 25 (Super.Ct.N.J.1966).

tetrachlorodibenzoparadioxin See *Agent Orange*; and *dioxin*.

tetracyano-

... the **tetracyano** part of the name means that four cyano (CN) groups are attached to the ethylene nucleus. It seems, therefore, that the word tetracyanoethylene is little more than the structural formula of the compound converted into an utterable combination of letters. E. I. DuPont de Nemours and Co. v. Ladd, 328 F.2d 547, 555 (D.C.Cir.1964).

tetracyanoethylene

Tetracyanoethylene is described as an organic chemical compound having extraordinary properties. As indicated by the application, the substance reacts with certain other chemicals to produce strong permanent dyes for synthetic fibers, and its polymers and co-polymers are highly useful as insecticides, as well as motor coil and transformer wire insulation where high temperatures are encountered. E. I. DuPont de Nemours and Co. v. Ladd, 328 F.2d 547, 549 (D.C.Cir.1964).

tetracycline (tet″rah-si′klēn) any of a group of biosynthetic antibiotics isolated from certain species of *Streptomyces* or produced semisynthetically by catalytic hydrogenation of chlortetracycline or oxytetracycline. The tetracyclines, e.g., chlortetracycline (the first of the group to be discovered), oxytetracycline, tetracycline, demeclocycline, rolitetracycline, methacycline, doxycycline, and minocycline, are effective against a wide variety of organisms, including gram-positive and gram-negative bacteria, rickettsias, mycoplasmas, chlamydias, and certain viruses, protozoa, and actinomycetes.

She now suffers from permanent discoloration of her teeth alleged to be caused by her ingestion of **tetracycline**....

... As of 1965 the following warning appeared both in the package inserts of the drugs (under the heading "Precautions and Side Effects") and in the Physicians' Desk Reference ["PDR"]:

[Tetracyclines] may form a stable calcium complex in any bone forming tissue with no serious harmful effects reported thus far in humans. However, use of [any **tetracycline** drug] during tooth development (= last trimester of pregnancy, neonatal period and early childhood) may cause discoloration of the teeth (= yellow-gray-brownish). This effect occurs mostly during long-term use of the drug but it has also been observed in usual short treatment courses.

In 1971, for reasons that do not appear in the record, some package inserts were changed to read, under the heading "Warnings":

The use of drugs of the **tetracycline** class during tooth development (last half of pregnancy, infancy and childhood to the age of 8 years) may cause permanent discoloration of the teeth (yellow-gray-brown).

This adverse reaction is more common during long-term use of the drugs but has been observed following repeated short-term courses. Enamel hypoplasia has also been reported. **Tetracycline** drugs, therefore, should not be used in this age group unless other drugs are not likely to be effective or are contraindicated.

Thus from the period 1965 to 1971 there were these changes: the information was moved from the "side effects" heading to the "warning" heading, the word "permanent" was inserted in front of the word "discoloration", the danger of enamel hypoplasia was brought to the physician's attention, and a caveat as to limited use was added. Dalke v. Upjohn Co., 555 F.2d 245, 247 (9th Cir. 1977).

tetrahydrocannabinol (tet″rah-hi″dro-kah-nab′ĭ-nol) the active principle of cannabis, $C_{21}H_{30}O_2$, occurring in two isomeric forms: Δ^1-3,4-*trans* and Δ^6-3,4-*trans* tetrahydrocannabinol, both considered psychomimetically active. Abbreviated THC.

While there has been some recent evidence that not all Cannabis plants contain measurable amounts of **tetrahydrocannabinols (THC)**,[4] the active euphoric agent or intoxicant associated with marijuana, there is no scientific evidence that any of the species of the genus Cannabis lack THC. See, D. Bernheim, Defense of Narcotics Cases, § 4.04A at 4–36 (1975). THC is itself separately and specifically included as a Schedule I controlled substance. Minn.St. 152.02, subd. 2(3). Thus, if the definition of marijuana were held to exclude species other than Cannabis sativa L., those species would not be left in a statutory limbo but would still be proscribed, as "... material ... which contains ... **tetrahydrocannabinols**."[5] Minn.St. 152.02, subd. 2(3). [4 Small & Beckstead, Common Phenotypes in 350 Stocks of Cannabis, 17 Lloydia 144 (1973). 5 Several courts have concluded that the specific proscription of substances containing THC makes the botanic debate academic: U.S. v. Rothberg, 480 F.2d 534, 536 (2 Cir. 1973); certiorari denied, 414 U.S. 856, 94 S.Ct. 159, 38 L.Ed.2d 106 (1973); McKenzie v. State, 57 Ala.App. 69, 326 So.2d 135 (1976); See, also, Cassady v. Wheeler, 224 N.W.2d 649 (Iowa 1974).] State v. Vail, 274 N.W.2d 127, 131 (Minn.1979).

One of the most complete discussions of this issue is found in United States v. Walton, 168 U.S.App.D.C. 305, 514 F.2d

201 (1975). That court noted the defendant's expert testified that, applying the polytypic approach, four species existed other than sativa L. (indica, ruderalis, gigantea, and an Afghanistan species as yet unnamed) but conceded all five contain the toxic agent **tetrahydrocannabinol** which produces the hallucinogenic or euphoric effects which led to the congressional ban on marijuana. State v. Luginbill, 574 P.2d 140, 142 (Kan.1977).

He testified that each separate exhibit was subjected to the Duguenois-Lavine test for **tetrahydrocannabinal**, which is the active chemical ingredient in marijuana. This ingredient was present in each test and its presence confirmed his opinion that the contents of the bag and of the cigarette were marijuana, Cannabis sativa L. State v. Woods, 522 P.2d 967, 969 (Kan. 1974).

Other Authorities: Aycock v. State, 246 S.E.2d 489, 491–2 (App.Ct.Ga.1978); U.S. v. Lewallen, 385 F.Supp. 1140–1 (W.D.Wis.1974). In re Jones, 110 Cal.Rptr. 765, 768 (Ct.App. Cal.1973).

tetralogy (tĕ-tral′o-je) a combination of four elements or factors, such as four concurrent symptoms or defects.

tetralogy of Fallot a combination of congenital cardiac defects consisting of pulmonary stenosis, interventricular septal defect, dextroposition of the aorta so that it overrides the interventricular septum and receives venous as well as arterial blood, and right ventricular hypertrophy.

The infant's condition was diagnosed as **Tetralogy of Fallot**— the medical term for a congenital defect which develops between the left and right ventricle causing venous (blue) blood to flow into the aorta. This condition causes the heart to work harder and the body to receive less blood with adequate oxygen, resulting in a so-called "blue baby." Johnson v. National Institutes of Health, 408 F.Supp. 730 (D.Md.1976).

Thal procedure See *operation, Thal.*

thalamic See *thalamus.*

thalamotomy (thal″ah-mot′o-me) [*thalamus* + Gr. *tomē* a cutting] a stereotaxic surgical technique for the discrete destruction of specific groups of cells within the thalamus, as for the relief of pain or for relief of tremor and rigidity in Parkinson's disease.

thalamus (thal′ah-mus), pl. *thal′ami* [L.; Gr. *thalamos* inner chamber] [NA] a constituent of the thalamencephalon, being the middle and larger portion of the diencephalon, which forms part of the lateral wall of the third

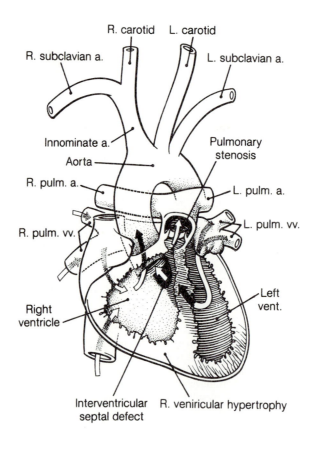

Tetralogy of Fallot. (Blalock and Taussig.)

ventricle and lies between the hypothalamus and the epithalamus. It comprises the medullary laminae and various nuclear groups, and is the main relay center for sensory impulses and cerebellar and basal ganglia projections to the cerebral cortex. Its nuclei include the anterior, central, intralaminar, lateral, medial, posterior, and reticular thalamic nuclei. The lateral and medial geniculate bodies (the metathalamus) are also considered by many to be part of the thalamus.

The x-rays clearly revealed that the needle had penetrated the **thalamus**. Further, immediately after receiving the x-rays Allen and Ashby discussed the damage that had been caused to the **thalamus**. Finally, the "work-up," which Ashby purported to be a complete summary of the tests, made no mention of the **thalamic** insult, despite the fact that notes taken by Allen at the time of the ventriculogram revealed the true nature of the damage: "x-rays demonstrated that tip of ventricular needle is penetrating floor of . . . **thalamus**." Harrison v. U.S., 708 F.2d 1023, 1026–7 (5th Cir. 1983).

thalassemia (thal"ah-se'me-ah) [Gr. *thalassa* sea (because it was observed originally in persons of Mediterranean stock) + *haima* blood + *-ia*] a heterogeneous group of hereditary hemolytic anemias which have in common a decreased rate of synthesis of one or more hemoglobin polypeptide chains and are classified according to the chain involved (α,β, δ); the two major categories are α- and β-thalassemia. It is manifested in homozygotes by profound anemia or death in utero, and in heterozygotes by relatively mild red cell anomalies. See also hemoglobin H.

During the second stay in Thailand, it was discovered that the daughter suffers from a rare form of anemia known as Alpha **Thalassemia** or Hemoglobin H disease. Mamanee v. Immigration & Naturalization Serv., 566 F.2d 1103, 1105 (9th Cir. 1977).

thalassemia, α-, that caused by decreased rate of synthesis of the alpha chains of hemoglobin. The *homozygous* form is incompatible with life, the stillborn infant displaying severe hydrops fetalis. The *heterozygous* form may be asymptomatic or marked by mild anemia.

thalassemia, β- that caused by diminished synthesis of beta chains of hemoglobin. The *homozygous* form (Cooley's anemia; Mediterranean anemia; erythroblastic anemia of childhood; thalassemia major) in which hemoglobin A is completely absent and which appears in the newborn period, is a severe form marked by a hemolytic, hypochromic microcytic anemia, pronounced hepatosplenomegaly, skeletal deformation, mongoloid facies, and cardiac enlargement. The *heterozygous* form (thalassemia minor), in which hemoglobin A synthesis usually is retarded, is asymptomatic, but there is sometimes moderate anemia and splenomegaly.

thalassemia, δ- that involving suppression of the delta chains of hemoglobin, but having no clinical significance.

thalassemia, δβ- a form of heterozygous thalassemia in which synthesis of both delta and beta chains of hemoglobin is decreased; clinically it resembles β-thalassemia.

thallus (thal'us) 1. a simple plant body not differentiated into root, stem, and leaf, which is characteristic of mycelial fungi and some algae. 2. the actively growing vegetative organism as distinguished from reproductive or resting portions, as in fungi.

THAM See *tromethamine.*

THC See *tetrahydrocannabinol.*

theory (the'o-re) [Gr. *theōria* speculation as opposed to practice] 1. the doctrine or the principles underlying an art as distinguished from the practice of that particular art. 2. a formulated hypothesis, or, loosely speaking, any hypothesis or opinion not based upon actual knowledge.

theory, ionic a theory that, on going into solution, the molecules of an electrolyte either completely or partially break up or dissociate into two or more portions, these portions being positively and negatively charged electrically, the positively charged portions being different chemically from those negatively charged. When an electric current is passed through the solution of an electrolyte the positively charged portions are attracted by the negative pole or electrode, and move toward it; the negatively charged portions are attracted by and migrate toward the positive electrode. From this property of moving toward one of the electrodes, these charged molecular fractions of electrolytes are called ions, from the Greek verb meaning "to move."

therapeutic See *curative.*

"Therapeutically active product" and "therapeutically active ingredient" each mean any chemical product possessing pharmacological or **therapeutic** utility in the treatment of humans or animals. U.S. v. Ciba Geigy Corp., 508 F.Supp. 1118, 1121 (D.N.J.1976).

The **therapeutic** property of a compound is its ability to heal or cure, in whole or significant part, a disorder in a human being or in any form of plant or animal life. Carter-Wallace, Inc. v. Riverton Laboratories, Inc., 433 F.2d 1034, 1040 (2d Cir. 1970).

therapist (ther'ah-pist) [Gr. *therapeutēs* one who attends to the sick] a person skilled in the treatment of disease; often combined with a term indicating the specific type of disorder treated (as *speech therapist*) or a particular type of treatment rendered (as *physical therapist*).

therapist, respiratory

Plaintiff is a trained **respiratory therapy** technician who would administer treatment directly to patients as prescribed by a physician at scheduled times or during unforeseen emergencies. Her duties would include the utilization of various machines to assist a patient's breathing, and the attachment and detachment of patients to and from the machines. Some of these patients have tracheal tubes inserted in the throat which must be connected to the machine. The machines are equipped with dials and the technician regulates the flow of air and oxygen and medicine content thereof. Silverstein v. Sisters of Charity, 614 P.2d 891, 896 (Ct.App.Colo.1979).

therapy (ther'ah-pe) [Gr. *therapeia* service done to the sick] the treatment of disease; therapeutics. See also under *treatment*.

therapy, chelation

Dr. Rogers, a practicing physician in Brevard County, was ordered by the Brevard County Medical Association to discontinue the use of **chelation therapy** [2] in the treatment of arteriosclerosis. [[2] The district court in its decision here under review explained in detail the nature of **chelation therapy**: The record reveals that **chelation therapy** consists of a series of intravenous injections of a chelating drug, usually disodium ethylenediamine tetraacetic acid (hereafter disodium EDTA, Na_2 EDTA, or EDTA). Each injection takes approximately three to four hours to administer, and a normal course of treatment usually involves twenty such injections. The treatments are specifically intended to treat arteriosclerosis (hardening of the arteries), therosclerosis (deposits on the inner lining of the arteries), and other generalized circulatory deficiencies caused by excess calcium in the circulatory vessels. . . . EDTA intravenous treatment is often recommended for lead poisoning and other diseases requiring removal of heavy metals from the body. **Chelation treatments** were widely used during World War II in treating sailors who had contracted poisoning from leaded paint. Since World War II more than 1500 scientific articles and studies have been published concerning practically every application of the chelating process in the body. Many of those articles are contained in the record. The precise chemical reaction whereby metals, or calcium, are removed from the body through chelation is not yet completely known nor understood. However, through the years, many doctors have observed that after EDTA infusion, the urine calcium level rises and remains at relatively high levels for some months after administration of the treatments. The theory, now generally agreed upon by chelation proponents, is that the chelating salt binds with ionic calcium in the blood, causing a temporary calcium deficiency in the blood. This is rapidly replaced by calcium in precipitate form ionizing in the bloodstream. This calcium, known as metastatic calcium, comes from the walls of the blood vessels and from calcium precipitate in every cell. Many experts believe that the metastatic calcium sludge in each cell causes the cells gradually to disfunction. This phenomenon, coupled with the better known effects of calcium deposits on the interior walls of the blood vessels, results in a gradual decline in blood flow and cell function. Thus, if the pernicious calcium buildup can be prevented or reversed, cells and vessels can continue to function well into old age, reducing the inevitable effects of hardening of the arteries and other vascular occlusive diseases. The record is replete with claimed instances of dramatic restoration of blood flow to the extremities resulting in arrest of gangrene, restored sensation, increased temperature and return of normal color to toes, fingers, hands and feet after chelation treatment. In one exceptionally dramatic case history, Reynolds Hall, a patient of petitioner, allegedly regained his sight during his seventh chelation treatment. **Chelation therapy** is, then, infusion of a chelating agent (generally Na_2 EDTA) into the bloodstream over several hours, a treatment which is repeated about 20 times, generally over a period of a month or more. 371 So.2d at 1038–39.] State Bd. of Medical Examiners v. Rogers, 387 So.2d 937–8 (Fla.1980).

therapy, electroconvulsive, (E.C.T.); therapy electroshock (E.S.T.) form of shock therapy that is most effective in the treatment of depression, in which unconsciousness and/or convulsions are induced by the passage of an electric current through the brain; in contemporary practice, the convulsions are minimized by the administration of a muscle relaxant prior to treatment. See also *therapy, shock*.

The decedent's headaches, vomiting and depression continued to plague him following his recovery from the suicide attempt. In the fall months of 1970 until his discharge from military service in December of 1970, the decedent received psychiatric care including **electroconvulsive therapy** in Veterans Administration hospitals in Pennsylvania and New York. Dundon v. U.S., 559 F.Supp. 469–70 (E.D.N.Y.1983).

In dealing with the problem of the cause of fractures during **electroshock therapy**, courts from other jurisdictions have consistently held that res ipsa loquitor is not applicable. This is attributed to the fact that fractures are a recognized risk of **electroshock therapy**. See: Johnston v. Rodis, 102 U.S.App. D.C. 209, 251 F.2d 917 (1958); Farber v. Olkon, 40 Cal.2d 503, 254 P.2d 520 (1953); Quinley v. Cocke, 183 Tenn. 428, 192 S.W.2d 992 (1946). . . .

Dr. Boerner described the normal procedure involved when **electroshock therapy** is given at Eugenia: "Q. You say you are stationed behind the head of the patient or top of the head? A. Yes, I am at the head of the bed, and there is an attendant on either side approximately at the chest of the patient. . . . Q. What do the aides do? What they are directed to do? A. One of the aides is directed to insert the rubber mouthpiece and hold the jaw firmly so that the mouthpiece cannot be pushed out and also to hold cotton on the arm, where I have injected the medication. The other aide has her hand on the shoulder and the other hand on the hand or head of the patient, depending." Mrs. Laura Buccino, a registered nurse in charge of the electroshock treatment room at Eugenia in 1959, testified: Q. When the patient, particularly Julia Collins, was on the bed, was she strapped down by any straps or anything like that? A. No. We never applied any straps. Collins v. Hand, 246 A.2d 398, 401, 404 (Pa.1968).

It is important to note that between June 29, and July 10, 1961, plaintiff received a series of **electroshock treatments**. In the administration of this treatment, two or more electrodes are placed on the side of the patient's head, and a measured electric current is passed through the brain. This treatment, which is calculated to relieve severe depression and agitation, induces lack of consciousness. The beneficial results derived are largely empirical in nature. Dr. Cranston testified:

> . . . I am afraid to say that it's by experience with the use of this form of therapy that we learn how valuable it is, and we do not quite understand and do not know the physiology, the anatomy, the chemistry that is involved.

Dr. Cranston testified that, although he has had patients who have worked through the course of an **electroshock treatment**, it ordinarily takes a week or two before the patient is ready to go back to work. This is because the patient suffers from fatigue as a result of the shock, and his memory is affected. Christy v. Saliterman, 179 N.W.2d 288, 294 (Minn.1970).

Other Authorities: Aden v. Younger, 129 Cal.Rptr. 535, 541, 544 (Ct.App.Cal.1976); Kosberg v. Washington Hospital Centers, Inc., 394 F.2d 947, 949 (D.C.Cir.1968).

therapy, collapse treatment of pulmonary tuberculosis by operative collapse of the diseased lung; called also *collapsotherapy.* Cf. *artificial pneumothorax,* under *pneumothorax.*

therapy, inhalation treatment aimed at restoring toward normal any pathophysiologic alterations of gas exchange in the cardiopulmonary system, as by the use of respirators, aerosol-producing devices, and the therapeutic use of oxygen, helium-oxygen, and carbon dioxide mixtures.

Appellants produced Dr. George A. Small, Anesthesiologist, Miami, Florida, whose sub-specialty is **inhalation therapy**, which is the treatment of pulmonary problems involving the chest and lungs, such as tuberculosis and emphysema. Chapman v. Argonaut-Southwest Ins. Co., 290 So.2d 779, 782 (Ct. App.La.1974).

therapy, insulin coma; therapy, insulin shock a form of shock therapy, now rarely used, primarily employed in the treatment of schizophrenia, in which hypoglycemic coma is induced by the injection of insulin; called also *hypoglycemic t.* See also *subcoma insulin therapy.*

therapy, metabolic

Metabolic therapy apparently refers to the prevention of disease by diet control. Millet, Pit & Seed Co., Inc. v. U.S., 436 F.Supp. 84, 90 (E.D.Tenn.1977), vacated and remanded 627 F.2d 1093 (6th Cir. 1980).

therapy, physical the treatment of disease by physical agents and methods to assist in rehabilitation and restoration of normal bodily function after illness or injury, including the use of massage and manipulation, therapeutic exercises, hydrotherapy, and various forms of energy (electrotherapy, actinotherapy, and ultrasound). Called also *physiotherapy.*

Section 6531 of the Education Law defines the practice of **physical therapy** as "treating by the use of actinotherapy; hydrotherapy, electric or medicated baths of all types, and colonic irrigations; mechanotherapy, including therapeutic exercises; thermotherapy and electrotherapy, exclusive of the X-ray. Such treatment shall be rendered pursuant to prescription or referral by physician and in accordance with physician's diagnosis." Vidra v. Shoman, 398 N.Y.S.2d 377, 378 (2d Dep't [N.Y.] 1977).

Yet, following the time this cause was filed, the definition of "physical therapy" was modified by statutory amendment, and it is the present law that must be applied in deciding this case. (Rios v. Jones, 63 Ill.2d 488, 348 N.E.2d 825 (1976)). The term no longer relates to the use of massage for "any condition" including even for gratification or enjoyment, but is restricted to "evaluation or treatment . . . for the purpose of preventing, correcting or alleviating a physical or mental disability." (Ill.Rev.Stat. (1975) c. 91, par. 22.1). Clevenger v. City of East Moline, 357 N.E.2d 719, 722 (App.Ct.Ill.1976).

therapy, root canal the treatment of diseases and injuries that affect the roots of the teeth and the pulp canals.

Root canal therapy is generally performed in an attempt to save a tooth in which an unsatisfactory condition of the dental pulp exists. The dental pulp consists of living tissue (mostly nerves and blood vessels) which is located in the central portion of the tooth surrounded by the dentin and enamel. The pulp extends from the pulp chamber in the center of the crown of the tooth (the visible portion of the tooth exposed to the oral cavity), along the root or roots of the tooth (the portion of the tooth which fixes its position in the jaw bone), to the apex or tip of the root where it emerges from the tooth. An unsatisfactory pulp condition may be caused by infection in the body which renders the pulp necrotic or dead, or by exposure resulting from serious decay or trauma.

An unsatisfactory pulp condition is diagnosed through clinical examination, patient symptoms, radiographs (X-rays), and professional judgment and experience. The clinical examination usually includes visual observation, palpation, percussion and perhaps thermal pulp testing. Important patient symptoms include pain and swelling. Radiographs or X-rays are important diagnostic tools when root canal therapy is considered. U.S. v. Talbott, 460 F.Supp. 253, 256 (S.D.Ohio 1978).

therapy, root canal (Sargenti method)

Over the course of several visits, Dr. Mahan performed a root canal on Ms. Thornton's tooth, using a procedure commonly known in the profession as the "Sargenti" method. . . .

. . . The procedure utilizes a motorized mechanism for packing the Sargenti "paste" into the repaired tooth, as opposed to the "guttapercha" and "silver point" methods, which apply their paste by hand.

Dr. Charles R. Yates, a Bessemer, Alabama, dentist and witness for the Defendant, testified that the State Board of Dentistry in Alabama had neither advocated nor prohibited the use of the "Sargenti" procedure. Dr. Yates submitted that, during the course of his practice, he had performed some two to three thousand root canals using the "Sargenti" method. Thornton v. Mahan, 423 So.2d 181–2 (Ala.1982).

The third method [of obturation] is the **Sargenti technique**. This method differs from silver point and gutta percha in that the filling substance, usually called Sargenti paste, contains an active ingredient. This active ingredient, paraformaldehyde, is a bacteriacidal agent. Sargenti paste, in its most common formulation, also contains zinc oxide as an inert filler and bismuth as radiopaque material. Each of these ingredients is in powder form which is mixed with a liquid, eugenol, to achieve a paste-like consistency. Following insertion into the tooth, this paste becomes semi-hard. As with the other methods, complete obturation is the goal. However, the void should not be overfilled with Sargenti paste since it is not desirable to force the paraformaldehyde beyond the apex of the tooth into the surrounding tissue. Thus, slight underfilling is preferred to overfilling. It is also thought that satisfactory results can be obtained with slight underfilling since the paste contains an active ingredient to fight infection. U.S. v. Talbott, 460 F.Supp. 253, (S.D.Ohio 1978).

therapy, root canal (silver point method)

One method [of obturation] is the so-called **silver point method**. In this method a silver wire is inserted into the root canal and cemented in place using an inert cement. U.S. v. Talbott, 460 F.Supp. 253, 257 (S.D.Ohio 1978).

therapy, shock the treatment of psychiatric illnesses, chiefly severe affective disorders, by convulsions induced by means of passing an electric current through the brain. Rarely convulsions are induced by the inhalation of Indoklon (flurothyl). Formerly comas were induced by the injection of insulin or the inhalation of carbon dioxide. Called also *shock treatment*. See also *cingulumotomy* (Kapp case); and *electroconvulsive therapy*.

Evidence was proffered to show that the patient received thirty **electric shock treatments** by order of Dr. Cassidy while she was under his care. Dr. Sovner wrote that the number of such treatments was "grossly excessive," and that the "psychiatric treatment" given the patient was "grossly improper medical care." Dr. Beuscher opined that the treatment of the patient by **electric shock** was based on an untenable diagnosis of manic depressive disease and that the treatment by **electric shock** before pursuing adequate trials of psychotherapy and chemotherapy was "irresponsible." Kapp v. Ballantine, 402 N.E.2d 463, 468 (Sup.Jud.Ct.Mass.1980).

The fact that an internist is not a specialist in psychiatry or neurology does not preclude him from testifying about the physical effects of **electroshock therapy** and the ability of a person in decedent's condition to withstand this treatment. See Baerman v. Reisinger, 124 U.S.App.D.C. 180, 363 F.2d 309 (1966). Such testimony, if believed by the jury, might have established both the standard of care and its violation. Kosberg v. Washington Hospital Center, Inc., 394 F.2d 947, 949 (D.C.Cir.1968).

therapy, subcoma insulin the induction of a state of drowsiness or somnolence short of coma by the administration of insulin; used to relieve anxiety, stimulate appetite, and produce a feeling of well-being. See also *insulin coma therapy*.

thermistor (ther-mis'tor) a thermometer whose impedance varies with the ambient temperature and so is able to measure extremely small changes in temperature.

The [Aquamatic K-Thermia] machine is also provided with a **thermistor** probe which is a temperature sensing device connected to the machine by an electric cord. This probe is inserted into the body of the patient and indicates, by means of a thermometer, the body temperature of the patient. Weeks v. Latter-Day Saints Hospital, 418 F.2d 1035, 1037 (10th Cir. 1969).

thermometer (ther-mom'ĕ-ter) [*thermo-* + Gr. *metron* measure] an instrument for determining temperatures. In principle, it makes use of some substance with a physical property that varies in magnitude with temperature, to determine a value of temperature on some defined scale. See also under *scale*.

thermometer, mercurial a liquid-in-glass thermometer in which mercury is the liquid used.

The standard **mercury-filled glass thermometer** is the major instrument in use for taking body temperature which, in turn, is one of the measurements needed by the medical staff (along with pulse, respiration rate, blood pressure and other measurements) to gauge the status and progress of a patient's condition of illness and recovery, as well as being a diagnostic

tool. Poncy v. Johnson & Johnson, 460 F.Supp. 795, 797 (D.N.J.1978).

thermometer sheath See *sheath, thermometer*.

thermophilic (ther"mo-fil'ik) [*thermo-* + Gr. *philein* to love] growing best at or having a fondness for high temperatures. Cf. *mesophilic* and *psychrophilic*.

thermoplastic (ther"mo-plas'tik) softening under heat and capable of being molded into shape with pressure, then hardening on cooling without undergoing chemical change. Cited in Shaw v. E.B. & A.C. Whiting Co., 157 U.S.P.Q. 405, 410 (D.Vt.1967).

thermosetting See *varnish* (Int. Tel. & Tel. case).

thiabendazole (thi"ah-ben'dah-zol) [USP] chemical name: 2-(4-thiazolyl)-1*H*-benzimidazole. A broad-spectrum anthelmintic, $C_{10}H_7N_3S$, occurring as a white to almost white powder; used in the treatment of pinworm, threadworm, whipworm, roundworm, and hookworm infections, and in cutaneous larva migrans, administered orally.

Her treatment for toxocara includes **thiabendazole** and steroids, generally used in combination. **Thiabendazole** is an anthelmintic medicine which kills the larva. Steele v. U.S., 463 F.Supp. 321, 329 (D.Alas.1978).

thiazide (thi'ah-zīd) any of a group of benzene disulfonamide derivatives, typified by chlorothiazide, that act as diuretics by inhibiting the reabsorption of sodium in the proximal renal tubule and stimulating chloride excretion, with resultant increase in excretion of water. Called also *benzothiadiazide, benzothiadiazine, thiadiazide*, and *thiadiazine*.

thigh (thi) the portion of the lower extremity situated between the hip above and the knee below; the femur.

Now, the portion between the knee and hip is referred to as the **thigh**, but, lay people generally don't make the distinction. So, that the leg means anything below the hips. (Tr. p. 162). Baloney v. Carter, 387 So.2d 54, 61 (Ct.App.La.1980).

thimerosal (thi-mer'o-sal) [USP] chemical name: ethyl(2-mercaptobenzoato-*S*)mercury sodium salt. An organomercurial antiseptic, $C_9H_9HgNaO_2S$, occurring as a light cream-colored, crystalline powder, which is actively antifungal and bacteriostatic for many nonsporulating bacteria; used as a topical anti-infective and as a preservative in pharmaceutical preparations. Called also *thiomersalate*.

Prior to the development of the Salk polio vaccine, the universal preservative was **merthiolate**. Although originally intended to maintain sterility, **merthiolate** was later shown to act as a stabilizer of the vaccine, decreasing toxity but maintaining potency. **Merthiolate**, however, adversely affected the polio vaccine. Ezagui v. Dow Chemical Corp., 598 F.2d 727, 738 (2d Cir. 1979).

He said that **Merthiolate** prep is an "alcohol preparation", and that it was inflammable....

He said that **Merthiolate** is commonly used with the electrocautery machine. He was asked: "Within the standard of medical practice in Washington County, what precautions should be taken when using an electro-cautery machine and a **Merthiolate** prep which contains alcohol?'' He replied: ''I think the standard for Hagerstown would be the same as the standard for anywhere, would be incidentally unrelated to the use of the Bovie or not. It would be either allowing the **Merthiolate** to dry or drying it with a sterile towel.'' He was asked the purpose in allowing it to dry. ''The purpose basically with the use of any alcohol prep in this fashion is so that there will not be any excessive irritation to the patient's skin because of the alcohol. . . . Secondarily, the chance that because it is a flammable liquid that there could be ignition of it.'' Holloway v. Hauver, 322 A.2d 890, 892–4 (Ct.Spec.App.Md.1974).

thiopental sodium (thi"o-pen′tal) [USP] chemical name: 5-ethyldihydro-5-(1-methylbutyl)-2-thioxo-4,6(1H,5H) pyrimidinedione monosodium salt. An ultra-short-acting barbiturate, $C_{11}H_{17}N_2NaO_2S$, occurring as a white to off-white, crystalline powder, or yellowish, hygroscopic powder; administered intravenously to produce general anesthesia of brief duration, for induction of anesthesia prior to administration of other anesthetics, to supplement regional anesthesia, as an anticonvulsive, and for narcoanalysis and narcosynthesis in psychiatric disorders.

Since the patient was still agitated, Dr. Gale then administered **thiopental** (**sodium pentothal**).

Dr. Viljoen (appellants' expert) considered everything appropriate prior to the administration of the **thiopental** (**sodium pentothal**). Dr. Viljoen testified that **thiopental** can cause constriction of the bronchia and can depress respiration. Dr. Mendelsohn testified ''it is thought to produce some bronchoconstriction.'' Dr. Gravenstein believes it is a drug that constricts rather than dilates bronchial tubes. Nevertheless, to Dr. Gale, **thiopental** does not routinely have a constricting effect. . . .

Dr. Mendelsohn, characterized by defense counsel as a ''witness worthy of belief as the one doctor whose testimony is given without bias or slant,'' testified that the injection of **thiopental** into the patient exacerbated the asthmatic attack which lead to bronchospasm. . . .

. . . In Dr. Viljoen's opinion, Dr. Gale was negligent in his treatment of the patient because **pentothal** ''was the straw that broke the camel's back'' and should not have been administered when the patient is suffering breathing difficulties. Dr. Gale, Dr. Gravenstein, Dr. Mendelsohn and Dr. Viljoen all agree that **pentothal** should not be used when the patient is undergoing respiratory embarrassment. Siegel v. Mt. Sinai Hospital of Cleveland, 403 N.E.2d 202, 210–11 (Ct.App. Ohio 1978).

''After considerable consultation with people familiar with lethal substances, the decision has been made to use **sodium thiopentol** in lethal doses. It will be administered by medical technicians knowledgeable in such procedure and a medical doctor will be present, but will not participate in any aspect of the execution other than to pronounce death.

''Very truly yours,

''/s/ W. J. Estelle, Jr.

SWORN TO AND SUBSCRIBED BEFORE ME by the said W. J. Estelle, Jr., this 7th day of September, 1977. . . .

''He explained that the drug **sodium thiopental** [5] was a paralytic agent, a rapidly acting barbiturate commonly used in pre-operative anesthesia. He stated a massive dosage of the drug would be calculated to kill any human if properly administered, and that records showed a lethal dosage of the drug ranges from two to five grams.[6] He explained that a solution of **sodium thiopental** in sterile water was commonly administered with syringe and needle and injected intravenously and that the only expected pain would be from the insertion of the needle.'' [[5] The witness stated another acceptable spelling of the drug's name was **sodium thiopentol**, and that its trade name was **sodium pentothal**.[6] He explained that tolerance of the drug varied from individual to individual and that a lethal dosage depended in part on the weight of the individual. . . . ''As described in the PHYSICIANS DESK REFERENCE, 534 (1977) adverse reactions to sodium thiopental (trade name Penthothal) include, 'respiratory depression, myocardial depression, cardiac arrhythmias . . . sneezing, coughing, bronchospasm, larongospasm and shivering.' The P.D.R. also states that, 'individual response to the drug is so varied that there can be no fixed dosage.' ''] Ex Parte Granviel, 561 S.W.2d 503, 508, 510 (Ct.Crim.App.Tex.1978).

Sodium pentothol is a hypnotic drug that is used with amnesics, as it enables the doctor to place the patient in a drug-induced hypnotic state and discover whether there is a memory despite the mental block. In Re Cameron, 439 P.2d 633, 642 (Cal. 1968).

thioridazine hydrochloride (thi"o-rid′ah-zēn) [USP] chemical name: 10-[2-(1-methyl-2-piperidyl)ethyl]-2-(methylthio)phenothiazine monohydrochloride. A tranquilizer, with sedative and behavioral effects, $C_{21}H_{26}N_2S_2 \cdot HCl$, occurring as a white to slightly yellow, granular powder; administered orally.

Thereafter, movant received one hundred milligrams of **mellaril** concentrate daily.

Movant testified at the hearing on his motion that he was under the influence of the medication at the time he pleaded guilty. ''I was in such a passive state and such an emotional cripple, that I don't believe I was capable of fully understanding what I was doing.''. . .

. . . She described **mellaril** as a tranquilizer, which likewise slowed the thinking process but did not impair it. She said that the dosage of **mellaril** movant received was ''very mild.'' Cavallaro v. State, 465 S.W.2d 635–7 (Mo.1971).

thixotropic (thik"so-trop′ik) pertaining to or characterized by thixotropy. See also *thixotropy.*

A **thixotropic** is a commodity the fluidity of which increases when a substantial force is applied against it. The greater the force, the more fluid the **thixotropic** becomes. A common example of a **thixotropic** is dripless paint. The force of gravity alone is insufficient to change the paint's gel-like, nonfluid consistency. When brushed, however, the paint flows because of the added force of the brush stroke. Sucrest Corp. v. M/V Jennifer, 455 F.Supp. 371, 379 (D.Me.1978).

thixotropy (thik-sot′ro-pe) [Gr. *thixis* a touch + *tropos* a turning] the property, exhibited by certain gels, of becoming fluid when shaken or stirred, and then becoming semisolid again.

Thomas collar See *collar, Thomas.*

thoracentesis (tho"rah-sen-te′sis) [*thoraco-* + Gr. *kentēsis* puncture] surgical puncture of the chest wall into the parietal cavity for aspiration of fluids; called also *pleurocentesis* and *thoracocentesis*.

The x-ray of the chest on admission showed a large soft tissue density obscuring the upper half of the left lung field, with some pleural fluid at the left base. The pleural fluid was withdrawn through the process known as **thoracentesis**, and a number of large cells were discovered which appeared to be neoplastic. [Footnote omitted.] Petition of U.S., 303 F.Supp. 1282, 1310 (E.D.N.C.1969).

On one occasion a **thoracentesis** was performed in which 600 cc's of cloudy yellow fluid was drawn from appellant's lung. Alden v. Providence Hospital, 382 F.2d 163, 165 (D.C.Cir. 1967).

thoracic (tho-ras'ik) [L. *thoracicus;* Gr. *thōrakikos*] pertaining to or affecting the chest.

thoracic outlet compression syndrome See *syndrome, thoracic outlet.*

thoracic spine See *vertebra, thoracic.*

thoracocentesis See *thoracentesis.*

thoracostomy (tho"rah-kos'to-me) [*thoraco-* + Gr. *stomoun* to provide with an opening, or mouth] surgical creation of an opening in the wall of the chest for the purpose of drainage; also, the opening so created.

thoracotomy (tho"rah-kot'o-me) [*thoraco-* + Gr. *tomē* a cutting] surgical incision of the wall of the chest. See also *thoracostomy.*

Dr. Benoit testified that he is a thoracic surgeon and has performed five to six thousand **thoracotomies** (open chest procedures). He operated on the plaintiff on January 4, 1979, to remove a partially solid, partially cystic benign tumor of the thymus gland. In doing so, he made a 10" midline chest incision, split the sternum (chest bone), and removed the tumor with little difficulty. Following the removal, he began to pull the sternum back into place by stitching the two halves together with wire sutures, using wire to which an extremely sharp needle was secured as an extension of the suture. Cebula v. Benoit, 652 S.W.2d 304–5 (Mo.Ct.App.1983).

The myocardial leads were implanted by means of a **thoracotomy**, a major surgical procedure involving the opening of the chest. The difficulty of this procedure, and its debilitating effects on the patient, made it unacceptable for the elderly or in emergency situations. Goldberg v. Medtronic, Inc., 686 F.2d 1219, 1221 (7th Cir. 1982).

Kimel performed a **thoracotomy** operation to repair the perforation and to remove the M-A tube. When the balloon was removed clear fluid came out of it which indicated that someone had improperly irrigated the M-A tube, preventing its removal in the normal manner and resulting in plaintiff's injuries. Stumper v. Kimel, 260 A.2d 526–7 (Super.Ct.N.J.1970). **Other Authorities:** Black v. Richardson, 356 F.Supp. 861, 866 (D.S.Car.1973); Campbell v. U.S., 325 F.Supp. 207–8 (M.D. Fla.1971); Bedel v. Industrial Com'n, 428 P.2d 134–5 (Ct.App. Ariz.1967).

Thorazine (thor'ah-zēn) trademark for preparations of chlorpromazine hydrochloride. See also *chlorpromazine hydrochloride;* and *psychotic.*

thorium (tho're-um) [*Thor*, a Norse deity] a rare, heavy gray metal, atomic number, 90; atomic weight, 232.038; symbol, Th. It is a radioactive metal with a half-life of the order of 10^{10} years, and the parent element of a radioactive disintegration series. Because of its radiopacity, various compounds of **thorium** have been used to facilitate visualization in roentgenography.

thorium dioxide ThO_2, used in roentgenography of the alimentary tract.

... a diagnostic procedure in which a radioactive substance called **Thorotrast** was used....

... The diagnostic procedure took place in February 1956; in March 1979 the **Thorotrast** was discovered to be still present in Mr. Allrid's body and was alleged to be the cause of Mr. Allrid's chronic sore throats, debilitated physical condition and, by amended complaint, his subsequent death. Allrid v. Emory University, 303 S.E.2d 486–7 (Ct.App.Ga.1983).

During the time in question in this case the defendant was engaged in the manufacture of the drug "**Thorium Oxide**" which was sold under the trade name "**Thorotrast**." This drug is a roentgen contrast medium containing radioactive **thorium dioxide** and is used for various medical investigations and tests. Thrift v. Tenneco Chemicals, Inc., Heyden Div., 381 F.Supp. 543–4 (N.D.Tex.1974).

For X-ray purposes a radioactive contrast dye, **umbrathor**,[1] was inserted into his sinus.... [[1] **Umbrathor** is a trade name for a non-stabilized colloidal solution of **thorium dioxide**. The stabilized solution of **thorium dioxide** is known as **thorotrast**. (See P.'s Exh. 38).]

... The **umbrathor** which was inserted in 1944 turned out to be an extremely dangerous drug. Grave warnings of the hazards of its use had appeared in major medical journals in the 1930's, and new research and case studies confirming its carcinogenic properties were documented and reported in the 1940's. Long before 1957, when the ravages of the disease had made necessary the radical surgery upon the plaintiff, the Government doctors therefore should have been aware of the dangers of the drug. Schwartz v. U.S., 230 F.Supp. 536–40 (E.D.Pa.1964).

Thorotrast See *thorium dioxide.*

threshold value See *value, liminal.*

thrombectomy (throm-bek'to-me) [Gr. *thrombos* clot + *ektomē* excision] removal of a thrombus from a blood vessel; properly indicative of such removal by excision.

"Right brachial artery **thrombectomy** and patch graft tomorrow."

On February 24, he performed the necessary surgery and removed a little clot from the brachial artery. This surgery restored the circulation and the radial pulse. Bergen v. Shah-Mirany, 404 N.E.2d 863, 865 (App.Ct.Ill.1980).

Dr. Nennhaus examined plaintiff and recommended that she have a brachial **thrombectomy**, a procedure to remove a clot from the artery. According to defendant, he advised Drs. Nennhaus and Strub not to perform the procedure. He thought that since plaintiff had a prolonged spasm of the brachial artery, a **thrombectomy** would only result in additional spasm and could be harmful. Crawford v. Anagnostopoulos, 387 N.E.2d 1064, 1067 (App.Ct.Ill.1979).

thromboangiitis (throm"bo-an"je-i'tis) [*thrombo-* + Gr. *angeion* vessel + *-itis*] inflammation of a blood vessel with thrombosis.

thromboangiitis obliterans an inflammatory and obliterative disease of the blood vessels of the extremities, primarily the lower extremities, occurring chiefly in young men and leading to ischemia of the tissues and gangrene; called also *Buerger's disease*.

The physician on Dr. Ochsner's staff who filled out the admission report noted "possible **Buerger's disease**," [5] a condition for which Cafergot is specifically contraindicated. [[5] **Buerger's disease** is a severe circulatory disease in which blood clots in the limbs cut off circulation.] Hemingway v. Ochsner Clinic, 722 F.2d 1220, 1222 (5th Cir. 1984).

thrombocytopenia (throm"bo-si"to-pe'ne-ah) [*thrombocyte* + Gr. *penia* poverty] decrease in the number of blood platelets.

Dr. Frawley diagnosed plaintiff as having idiopathic **thrombocytopenia** (a condition in which there are abnormally small numbers of platelets, of unknown origin), renal stones, and a convulsive disorder. Brissette v. Schweiker, 566 F.Supp. 626, 629 (E.D.Mo.1983), remanded 730 F.2d 548 (8th Cir. 1984).

The next day, Vallot discovered blood clots in his mouth, dark spots on all extremities of his body, and that he was urinating blood. Being taken off the vessel and examined by a Chittagong doctor, Vallot was diagnosed as having contracted **thrombocytopenia** purpura, a blood disease affecting the platelets.

The doctor who studied Vallot's record while hospitalized in the U.S. Public Health Service Hospital testified Vallot's illness developed over a period of time and was not a type which would have been caused by fear or the emotional upset of someone attacking him with a hatchet. Moreover, the doctor opined the type of **thrombocytopenia** Vallot had contracted could not be acquired by sniffing paint fumes, but instead was probably caused by a virus or a drug such as aspirin. Vallot v. Central Gulf Lines, Inc., 641 F.2d 347, 349 (5th Cir. 1981).

[Attributed to Benzene]: A decline in the platelet count (**thrombocytopenia**) results in an impaired clotting of the blood and is characterized by bleeding tendencies. American Pet. Institute v. Occupational Safety, 581 F.2d 493, 498 (5th Cir. 1978).

thromboembolism (throm"bo-em'bo-lizm) obstruction of a blood vessel with thrombotic material carried by the blood stream from the site of origin to plug another vessel.

Prior to the conference, a more detailed history of the plaintiff was obtained. What plaintiff had characterized as "flu" consisted of "generalized chest pain and symptoms of coryza" (common cold). There were also revealed episodes in 1961 and 1963 wherein plaintiff had experienced a sudden onset of pain in the right chest with low-grade fever, along with coughing of blood in 1963. Dr. Dahlquist testified that these symptoms were consistent with **thromboembolism**; that low-grade fever would generally cause a doctor to suspect **thromboembolism**. Carmichael v. Reitz, 95 Cal.Rptr. 381, 390 (Ct.App. Cal.1971).

thrombophlebitis (throm"bo-fle-bi'tis) [*thrombo-* + Gr. *phleps* vein + *-itis*] inflammation of a vein associated with thrombus formation. Cf. *phlebothrombosis*. See also *Enovid; sign, Homan's* (Carmichael case); and *warfin, sodium* (Carmichael case).

Dr. Marvin J. Towarnicky testified that **thrombophlebitis** is a condition in which blood clots form inside of a vein. Dr. Towarnicky also testified that physical injury is not the only cause of **thrombophlebitis**, and that it may result from a number of causes, including varicose veins, cancer, dehydration, complications with delivery, pelvic surgery, and injury or trauma to the vein. The doctor further testified that Bromley had varicose veins. [Footnote omitted.] Claim of Bromley, 330 N.W.2d 498, 501–2 (N.Dak.1983).

One of the risks of using **Renographin-60**, described by the PDR, is **thrombophlebitis**, a type of inflammation of the vein. Smith v. Shannon, 666 P.2d 351, 353 (Wash.1983).

After performing a veinogram on her legs, Dr. Juco, on May 22, 1976, told plaintiff she had **thrombophlebitis**, a condition of the vein marked by inflammation of the vein walls and the formation of clots and crusts of coagulated blood. Dr. Juco told plaintiff that the **thrombophlebitis** could have been caused by her use of the birth control pill, and he directed her to stop taking it. Witherell v. Weimer, 396 N.E.2d 268, 270 (App.Ct.Ill.1979), affirmed in part, reversed in part 421 N.E.2d 869 (Ill.1981).

Other Authorities: Buckelew v. Grossbard, 435 A.2d 1150, 1153 (N.J.1981); Ziegert v. South Chicago Community Hospital, 425 N.E.2d 450, 454 (App.Ct.Ill.1981); Lawson v. G. D. Searle & Co., 331 N.E.2d 75, 86 (App.Ct.Ill.1975), reversed 356 N.E.2d 779 (Ill.1976)); Leibowitz v. Ortho Pharmaceutical Corp., 307 A.2d 449, 459 (Super.Ct.Pa.1973); Cavanagh v. Ohio Farmers Ins. Co., 509 P.2d 1075, 1077 (Ct.App.Ariz. 1973); Carmichael v. Reitz, 95 Cal.Rptr. 381, 383–4 (Ct.App. Cal.1971).

thromboplastin (throm"bo-plas'tin) a substance having procoagulant properties or activity.

Blood clotting is an ancient art. By about 1860 the notion that it was motion that prevented blood from clotting was dispelled by experiments which proved that blood would not clot as long as it remained inside a vein or artery; contact with some foreign substance was established as the thing that caused blood to clot. Contact with air was early, but mistakenly, believed to cause clotting. Calcium was identified in 1875 to be necessary in the clotting of blood. By about 1900 it had been established that plasma, the watery, liquid part of blood, placed in a glass test tube would clot but if the glass tube was lined with paraffin the plasma would not clot. Thus, glass was early identified as a foreign substance that would promote clotting in blood clotting tests. In 1904 Morawitz taught that circulating blood contained calcium and proteins that under the influence of some factor produced a clot. He named the influencing factor "**Thromboplastin**". . . .

. . . By 1950 it was postulated that there were two types of **thromboplastin** resulting from two pathways of coagulation. The extrinsic pathway includes **thromboplastin** by its addition as tissue, i.e., skin, brain extract, etc. and this tissue **thromboplastin** causes clotting. The intrinsic pathway generates **thromboplastin** from components entirely within and dissolved in plasma. Ortho Pharmaceutical Corp., v. American Hospital Supply Corp., 186 U.S.P.Q. 501, 504 (S.D.Ind.1975).

thromboplastin, extrinsic the prothrombin activator formed as the result of interaction of coagulation Factors III, VII, and X which, with Factor IV, aids in the formation of thrombin; called *extrinsic* because not all of the components required for its production (e.g., Factor III, or tissue **thromboplastin**) are derived from intravascular sources.

By 1950 it was postulated that there were two types of **thromboplastin** resulting from two pathways of coagulation. The **extrinsic** pathway includes **thromboplastin** by its addition as tissue, i.e., skin, brain extract, etc. and this tissue **thromboplastin** causes clotting. The intrinsic pathway generates **thromboplastin** from components entirely within and dissolved in plasma. Ortho Pharmaceutical Corp. v. American Hospital Supply Corp., 186 U.S.P.Q. 501, 503–4 (S.D.Ind.1975).

thromboplastin, intrinsic the prothrombin activator formed as the result of interaction of coagulation Factors V, VIII, IX, X, XI, and XII and platelet factor 3 (PF–3) which, with Factor IV, aids in the conversion of prothrombin to thrombin: called *intrinsic* because the components required for its production are derived from intravascular sources. See *thromboplastin, extrinsic* (Ortho Pharmaceutical Corp. case).

thrombos, saddle See *embolism, saddle.*

thrombosis (throm-bo'sis) [Gr. *thrombōsis*] the formation, development, or presence of a thrombus.

All I can say is this: That one of the precipitating factors for an acute coronary **thrombosis** is a traumatic incident such as was described here or anything that would send the man's blood pressure up and precipitate the thing. Simon v. Lumbermens Mut. Cas. Co., 368 N.E.2d 344, 346–7 (App.Ct.Ill.1977).

... The Board concluded that ''the subsequent increase in the extent of paralysis was attributed to **thrombosis** in the affected spinal blood vessels... [T]he **thrombosis** is considered to be the proximate result of the demonstrated extreme deformity of the vessels rather than of any ordinary incident of surgery.'' Tyminski v. U.S., 481 F.2d 257, 262 (3d Cir. 1973).

thrombosis, brachial artery

At the site of the incision into the brachial artery made for the passage of the catheters, a clot formed, a condition called a **thrombosis of the brachial artery**. Morgenroth v. Pacific Medical Center, Inc., 126 Cal.Rptr. 681, 684 (Ct.App.Cal.1976).

thrombosis, cavernous sinus thrombosis affecting the cavernous sinus. See also *sinus, cavernous* (Speed case).

The doctors who treated plaintiff in the Neurology Department ultimately concluded that **cavernous sinus thrombosis** caused the blindness. Speed v. State, 240 N.W.2d 901, 904 (Iowa 1976).

thrombosis, cerebral thrombosis of a cerebral vessel, which may result in cerebral infarction.

Mr. Bewley developed a **cerebral thrombosis** or clot in the brain as a direct result of the fall he took on the night of January 12. Bewley v. American Home Assurance Co., 450 F.2d 1079–80 (10th Cir. 1971).

Dr. Nadler next provided a lengthy narrative explanation of the causality and symptomology of **cerebral thrombosis**. Dr. Nadler commented specifically in regard to the claimant's condition:

Now this man's artery process manifested itself in 1966 with the development of the end result of that process in that particular artery and that particular portion of his body resulting in a **cerebral thrombosis**. Now this can go on whether a man is lying in bed, is a white collar worker—as a matter of fact, it is presumed to be of higher incidence in the worrying types of occupations and white collar workers than in laborers. This is not a disease having to do with physical activity. (Tr. 160).

Dr. Nadler concluded his testimony by stating that only a very unusual physical effort might precipitate **cerebral thrombosis**.... Mid-Gulf Stevedores, Inc. v. Neuman, 333 F.Supp. 430, 434 (E.D.La.1971), reversed 462 F.2d 185 (5th Cir. 1972).

Cerebral thrombosis (a blood clot in the blood vessels in the brain tissues). Glover v. Bruce, 265 S.W.2d 346, 351 (Mo. 1954).

thrombosis, mesenteric formation of a clot in an artery or arteriole of the mesentery. See also *mesentery.*

It [the bowel] was between the skin and the fascia which is the fat layer. It was not inadvertently sewed into the fascia. There is no way to tell what caused it. It could be the result of an infection. His diagnosis of **mesenteric thrombosis** or gangrenous bowel was suspected before he opened the wound by the foul drainage. There was no way of knowing of the black bowel except opening the wound....

... A **mesenteric thrombosis** is a clotting of blood in the veins and arteries. It is very difficult in these cases to know when one should go back in. At the time he originally saw her, he did not suspect **mesenteric thrombosis**. ''The convincing factor as far as I was concerned was when I did this surgery and opened her wound.'' Her problems were caused by the clotting. Richardson v. Holmes, 525 S.W.2d 293, 296–7 (Ct. Civ.App.Tex.1975).

thrombus (throm'bus), pl. *throm'bi* [Gr. *thrombos* clot] an aggregation of blood factors, primarily platelets and fibrin with entrapment of cellular elements, frequently causing vascular obstruction at the point of its formation. Some authorities thus differentiate thrombus formation from simple coagulation or clot formation. Cf. *embolism.*

A **thrombus** is a plug or clot in a blood vessel or in one of the cavities of the heart, formed by coagulation of the blood, and remaining at the point of its formation. Leibowitz v. Ortho Pharmaceutical Corp., 307 A.2d 449, 459 (Super.Ct.Pa.1973).

... the terminal event occurred secondary to a plug or **thrombus** which formed in the left coronary artery, described as being severe, and that the artery itself was found to be affected by atherosclerosis, the degree described as being severe. Follmer Trucking v. Stump, 286 A.2d 1, 3 (Commonwealth Ct. Pa.1972), reversed and remanded 292 A.2d 294 (Pa.1972).

The coronary vessels showed marked atherosclerosis and a **thrombus** or blood clot was found to have completely occluded the left anterior descent coronary artery. The blood clot was located about one centimeter from its point of origin.

Watkins v. Underwriters at Lloyd's, London, 473 P.2d 464, 466–7 (Ct.App.Ariz.1970), vacated 481 P.2d 849 (Ariz.1971).

thumb (thum) [L. *pollex, pollux*] the first digit of the hand, being the most preaxial of the five fingers, having only two phalanges, and being apposable to the four other fingers of the hand. Called also *pollex* [NA]. See also *phalanx, proximalis digitorum manus* (Sanchez case).

thyroid (thi'roid) [Gr. *thyreoeidēs; thyreos* shield + *eidos* form] See *gland, thyroid.*

thyroidectomy (thi"roi-dek'to-me) [*thyroid* + Gr. *ektomē* excision] surgical removal of the thyroid.

The basic negligence alleged by plaintiff is that the defendant, in the course of performing a **thyroidectomy** upon the plaintiff, failed to use the appropriate standard of care during the operation and injured the recurrent laryngeal nerve. This resulted in the impairment of one of the vocal cords and left the plaintiff with permanent hoarseness.

The expert testimony indicates that damage to a laryngeal nerve is one of the risks, although infrequent, of a **thyroidectomy**. Plaintiff's expert testified that the defendant erred by starting the **thyroidectomy** and identifying the nerve superiorly rather than inferiorly. The defendant and his expert witness contradicted the claims of negligence. Jones v. Tranisi, 326 N.W.2d 190–2 (Neb.1982).

There is material evidence that a total **thyroidectomy** should be performed only when the gland is cancerous. O'Neill v. Kiledjian, 511 F.2d 511, 514 (6th Cir. 1975).

. . . a subtotal **thyroidectomy** was performed for the removal of a benign goiter. Black v. Richardson, 356 F.Supp. 861, 866 (D.S.C.1973).

Other Authorities: Battles v. Aderhold, 430 So.2d 307, 309 (Ct.App.La.1983); Dunham v. Wright, 423 F.2d 940, 942 (3d Cir. 1970); Roberts v. Wood, 206 F.Supp. 579, 581–2 (S.D. Ala.1962).

thyrotoxicosis (thi"ro-tok"sĭ-ko'sis) a morbid condition resulting from overactivity of the thyroid gland. See also *Graves' disease,* under *disease.*

tibia (tib'e-ah) [L. "a pipe, flute"] [NA] the shin bone: the inner and larger bone of the leg below the knee; it articulates with the femur and head of the fibula above and with the talus below. See illustration accompanying *skeleton.*

An x-ray taken in the emergency room revealed "a comminuted fracture of the proximal **tibia** with a major fragment representing the medial tibial plateau, where there is depression of at least a cm" (i.e., a break in the middle of plaintiff's shinbone in which the bone was broken into a number of pieces). Warner v. Schweiker, 551 F.Supp. 789, 791 (E.D.Mo. 1982), reversed 722 F.2d 428 (8th Cir. 1983).

The lower leg consists of two bones: the fibula, which is the outer, smaller bone, and the **tibia**, which is the inner, larger bone. Both bones were fractured as a result of the fall. . . .

. . . He stressed a broken **tibia** fracture was extremely painful and recovery varied a great deal from individual to individual. Jones v. Recreation and Park Commission, 395 So.2d 846–7, 849 (Ct. of App.La.1981).

. . . as a direct consequence of the fall, sustained a fracture of the **tibia**. [Footnote omitted.] White v. Mitchell, 568 S.W.2d 216–17 (Ark.1978).

tibial (tib'e-al) [L. *tibialis*] pertaining to the tibia.

tibial plateau See *plateau, tibial;* and *tibia.*

tic (tik) [Fr.] an involuntary, compulsive, repetitive, stereotyped movement, resembling a purposeful movement because it is coordinated and involves muscles in their normal synergistic relationships; tics usually involve the face and shoulders. See also *syndrome, Gilles de la Tourette's* (Lieberman case).

tic douloureux See *neuralgia, trigeminal.*

t.i.d.

Finally, the use of **t.i.d.** (3 times per day) and q.i.d. (4 times per day) dosage schedules for 14% of the patients receiving psychotropic medications was questioned. Rone v. Fireman, 473 F.Supp. 92, 108 (N.D.Ohio 1979).

time (tīm) [Gr. *chronos;* L. *tempus*] a measure of duration.

time, prothrombin the time required for clot formation after thromboplastin (brain extract) and calcium have been added to blood plasma.

So, when the order was given to do Heparin right away when the lady's **prothrombin time** that day—the **prothrombin time** is that time which is a measure of time during which blood will or will not clot and so you take **prothrombin time** to see what this lady's clotting time was immediately postoperative and when you found that her clotting time immediately postoperative was already in the anticoagulating condition the judgment was made not to go to Heparin, and that, we submit, is in good keeping with accepted standards, is good medical practice because of the dangers attendant to using Heparin had it at that time been employed. Raitt v. Johns Hopkins Hospital, 322 A.2d 548, 563 (Ct.Spec.App.Md.1974), reversed and remanded 336 A.2d 90 (Ct.App.Md.1975).

time weighted average

Time Weighted Average (TWA) represents a worker's cumulative exposure to a toxic substance during a 9-hour shift. Society of Plastics Indus. Inc. v. Occupational S. & H.A., 509 F.2d 1301, 1306 (2d Cir. 1975).

tincture (tink'tūr) [L. *tingere* to wet, to moisten] an alcoholic or hydroalcoholic solution prepared from animal or vegetable drugs or from chemical substances.

tincture, belladonna [USP], an alcoholic preparation of belladonna leaf, containing, in each 100 ml., 27–33 mg. of the alkaloids of belladonna leaf; used as an anticholinergic for the same purposes as atropine and hyoscyamine.

tine test See *test, tine.*

tinea (tin'e-ah) [L. "a grub, larva, worm"] a name applied to many different kinds of superficial fungal infection of the skin, the specific type (depending on characteristic appearance, etiologic agent, or site) usually being designated by a modifying term. Popularly called *ringworm.*

tinea circinata fungal infection of glabrous skin, characterized by presence of the annular lesions responsible for the appellation "ringworm."

tinea cruris a fungal infection common in males, starting in the crural or perineal folds, and extending onto the upper inner surfaces of the thighs; caused usually by *Epidermophyton floccosum* or species of *Trichophyton*.

Exh. C–2 consisted of (a) p. 1230 of the Physician's Desk Reference (1977), listing CRUEX and DESENEX as Pharmacraft products; (b) excerpts from the AMA "Current Medical Information and Terminology", for the entries "foot, athlete", "tinea pedis" and "**tinea cruris**" (no entry appeared for "jock itch"); Schmidt's Attorneys' Textbook of Medicine, p. J–3, showing no entry for "jock itch".

Exh. C–3 consisted of p. 654 of Stedman's Medical Dictionary (Williams & Wilkins, 1972) showing the use of "dhobie itch" and "jock itch" to refer to "**tinea cruris**".

Exh. C–4 consisted of excerpts from Dorland's Illustrated Medical Dictionary, 25th Ed. (W. B. Saunders, 1974), with p. 805 listing the same meanings as Exh. C–3, and pp. 1612–1613 listing the numerous fungal skin infections which include the term "tinea".

Exh. C–5 consisted of pp. 181–189 of "The Practitioner's Dermatology" (Dun-Donnelly, 1975), reviewing dermatoses due to fungi and including "tinea of the groin" at pp. 183–185.

Exh. C–6 consisted of Ch. 15 of Andrews' "Diseases of the Skin" 6th Ed. (W. B. Saunders, 1971), dealing with "diseases due to fungi", and discussing "**tinea cruris**" at pp. 331–332....

The term "jock itch" is also in the dictionary and is denoted as synonymous with the Latin term "tinea cruris," and the definition indicates that it is a fungus infection of the groin.

References to Latin dictionaries disclose that "tinea" means ringworm or the like and "cruris" is the genetive case of the noun "crus," meaning leg or shin. Thus, tinea cruris translates as ringworm of the groin for which the commonly recognized expression is "jock itch," doubtless due to association of the condition with an improperly fitted or inadequately washed jock strap. The medical texts show that it is a fungus condition. Pennwalt Corp. v. Becton, Dickinson & Co., 434 F.Supp. 758–60 (D.N.J.1977).

tinnitus (tĭ-ni'tus) [L. "a ringing"] a noise in the ears, as ringing, buzzing, roaring, clicking, etc. Such sounds may at times be heard by others than the patient. See also *nervus tympanicus*.

As a result of the accident, Feaga sustained permanent damage to the nerve in her right ear causing **tinnitus** (ringing). For many months, she suffered from, and was treated by neurologists and other physicians for, persistent dizziness, loss of equilibrium, pain in her right ear and face, headaches, and distress. She has recovered from these symptoms, except for the constant **tinnitus**, which condition is aggravated by fatigue or stress, and which is accompanied by occasional dizziness and loss of equilibrium. The **tinnitus** can only be medically corrected by surgery of the tympanic nerve, which surgery would result in complete loss of hearing in the right ear. Feaga has sustained some loss of hearing acuity but no functional loss of hearing. Doyle v. U.S., 441 F.Supp. 701, 706–7 (D.S.C.1977).

Appellant also complained of **tinnitus** or a ringing type sound in both ears which he had had for three years. Appellant had worked around loud machinery in a machine shop for about 20 years, and in such a work environment one very often develops a ringing in the ears, according to Dr. Draper. Similarly, the type of hearing loss which appellant had would be commonly called "boilermakers' deafness." Marsh v. Arnold, 446 S.W.2d 949, 951 (Ct.Civ.App.Tex.1969).

tissue (tish'u) [Fr. *tissu*] an aggregation of similarly specialized cells united in the performance of a particular function.

tissue, adipose fatty tissue; connective tissue made up of fat cells in a meshwork of areolar tissue.

tissue, adipose, brown a thermogenic type of adipose tissue containing a dark pigment, and arising during embryonic life in certain specific areas in many mammals, including man; it is prominent in the newborn of all species in which it occurs and remains a distinct and conspicuous tissue in the adults of certain species, especially those that hibernate. Called also *brown fat*. Cf. *white adipose t*.

tissue, adipose, white; tissue, adipose, yellow the adipose tissue comprising the bulk of the body fat. Cf. *brown adipose t*.

tissue, areolar connective tissue made up largely of interlacing fibers.

tissue, benign See *benign*.

tissue, cicatricial the dense fibrous tissue forming a scar or cicatrix and derived directly from granulation tissue; called also *scar t*.

To fully appreciate the catastrophic effect of the liquid-plumr it is essential to understand that much of Terri's face was not only repaired, but actually reconstructed. For example, her eyelids, composed mostly of **scar tissue**, are so taut that she must sleep with her eyes open. Her left ear has been reconstructed from cartilage extracted from her rib cage. Drayton v. Jiffee Chemical Corp., 395 F.Supp. 1081, 1095 (N.D.Ohio 1975).

The hematoma did not disappear following the injury. As a result the plaintiff was left with a permanent condition consisting of a doughy mass about the size of a fist in the upper leg area. The mass was described as a collection of fibrous **scar tissue** which is enmeshed in a series of lymphatic channels. Pike v. Roe, 516 P.2d 972–3 (Kan.1973).

tissue, fibrotic See *tissue, fibrous*.

tissue, fibrous the ordinary connective tissue of the body, made up largely of yellow or white fibers.

Upon surgically entering Mrs. Jines' abdominal cavity, the doctors encountered an unusual mass of tissue which contained "several entities" bound together by "dense adhesions." The large bowel was incorporated in this mass, as well as the left ovary and tube....

... Dr. Seifert reported that the mass was "**fibroadipose tissue**, post chronic inflammatory," and not malignant. Jines v. Abarbanel, 143 Cal.Rptr. 818, 820–1 (Ct.App.Cal.1978).

The **tissue** involved was quite **fibrotic**, which means scar tissue. Generally, the different tissues or muscles can be readily identified, but in Ross's case with the accumulated scar tissue involved, the tissues ran together and there was no recognizable line between them—all muscle layers and tissues being replaced by scars. Ross v. Sher, 483 S.W.2d 297, 300 (Ct.Civ. App.Tex.1972).

tissue, granulation the newly formed vascular tissue normally produced in the healing of wounds of soft tissue and ultimately forming the cicatrix; it consists of small, translucent, red, nodular masses or granulations that have a velvety appearance.

On February 3, 1980, plaintiff was discharged from the hospital on the basis of the absence of fever for the preceding four days and the fact that plaintiff's wound appeared to be doing well with **granulation tissue** present at the base of the abscess indicating healing process. Harwell v. Pittman, 428 So.2d 1049, 1051 (Ct.App.La.1983).

tissue, immature See *teratoma, malignant* (Jamison case).

tissue, nonosseous

... the injuries, resulting from the fall, to the **nonosseous tissues** of the nose and the facial area adjacent to the nose had not fully healed and such tissues had not returned to their normal condition. And Eric suffered from recurring nosebleeds and swelling of the **nonosseous tissues** of his nose and face just below his eyes from the time of the injuries on June 25, 1965, up to and during the time of the trial in January 1969. Hart v. Western Investment and Development Co., 417 F.2d 1296, 1299 (10th Cir. 1969).

tissue, osseous the specialized tissue forming the bones.

tissue, soft

Bodily injury confined solely to the **soft tissue** for the purpose of this section [N.J.S.A. 39:6A–8] means, injury in the form of sprains, strains, contusions, lacerations, bruises, hematomas, cuts, abrasions, scrapes, scratches, and tears confined to the muscles, tendons, ligaments, cartilages, nerves, fibers, veins, arteries and skin of the human body....

The term "**soft tissue** injury" is peculiar to the New Jersey statute and is not found in comparable legislation in other states. Schermer, Automobile Liability Insurance (rev.ed.1975) § 8.01 et seq., at 8–1 through 8–27.

In this case of first impression we are confronted with a specific statutory definition of "**soft tissue**" injury." One writer has observed that although the term "**soft tissue**" is used by physicians with some regularity, it is not specifically defined by medical science. Iavicoli, No Fault and Comparative Negligence in New Jersey, § 53 at 127 (1973). That writer inferentially includes organs as soft tissue in a discussion of the major injury limitation facet of this statute. "Injuries such as torn medial miniscus, subdural hematuria, collapsed lung, disfiguring facial scarring, ruptured bowel, etc., may arguably be confined solely to the **soft tissue**...." Id. at § 34....

Giving this statute a liberal construction so as to effect its purpose, N.J.S.A. 39:6A–16, we conclude that the obvious purpose of the statute and in particular the tort exemption provisions thereof can best be effected by holding that injuries to organs, such as the kidneys, are injuries "confined solely to the **soft tissue**" of the body. Todd v. Dabkowski, 372 A.2d 350–1 (Super.Ct.N.J.1977).

titer (ti'ter) [Fr. *titre* standard] the quantity of a substance required to produce a reaction with a given volume of another substance, or the amount of one substance required to correspond with a given amount of another substance.

Mumps titers are counteracting antibodies which develop in the blood of a person afflicted with mumps. Harries v. U.S., 350 F.2d 231, 233 (9th Cir. 1965).

titration (ti-tra'shun) [Fr. *titre* standard] determination of a given component in solution by addition of a liquid reagent of known strength until a given endpoint (e.g., change in color) is reached.

To calm the patient, Dr. Gale administered sedatives in small and repeated doses, a technique known as "**titration**." This permits an anesthesiologist to observe the effect of the particular drug on the patient. Siegel v. Mt. Sinai Hospital of Cleveland, 403 N.E.2d 202, 205 (Ct.App.Ohio 1978).

The medical evidence described the process of **titration**. This is a procedure used by clinicians to find the most effective drug or combination of drugs for use on a particular hypertensive patient. Basically it involves using a single drug in various dosages in order to obtain optimum control of the disease. If a single drug does not achieve good clinical results, drugs in free combination are tried until the clinical attainment is satisfactory. An experienced clinician need not go through all the basic steps of **titration**, but may be able to begin at a higher dosage or with a free or fixed combination. U.S. v. Ciba Geigy Corp., 508 F.Supp. 1118, 1154 (D.N.J.1976).

TLV See *value, liminal.*

T-max

T-max is the time after administration of the drug at which C-max [in determinings bioavailability. q.v.]. Premo Pharmaceutical Laboratories, Inc. v. U.S., 475 F.Supp. 52, 54 (S.D.N.Y. 1979), reversed and remanded with directions to dismiss 629 F.2d 795 (2d Cir. 1980).

tobacco (to-bak'o) [L. *tabacum*] the dried and prepared leaves of *Nicotiana tabacum* L. (Solenaceae), a solanaceous plant. Tobacco contains various alkaloids, the principal one being *nicotine*, and unites the qualities of a sedative narcotic with those of an emetic and diuretic. It is also a heart depressant and antispasmodic.

"Tobacco ranks with alcohol in widespread use among Americans; it is also the single major cause of heart and blood vessel disorders and cancer, which are the two most common causes of death in America. Nicotine, the primary active substance in **tobacco**, is a central nervous system stimulant similar to the amphetamines in its general effects. The harmful characteristics of nicotine are well-known. In addition to heart and blood vessel disorders and cancer of the lungs, mouth, larnyx and esophagus, **tobacco** smoking may also cause chronic bronchitis, emphysema and loss of vision (tobacco amplyopia). It is clear that tolerance develops to the use of nicotine and there is strong evidence that the phenomena accompanying discontinued use of **tobacco** constitute a withdrawal syndrome characteristic of true addiction." (supporting footnotes omitted) Soler, Of Cannabis and the Courts: A Critical Examination of Constitutional Challenges to Statutory Marijuana Prohibitions,

6 Conn.L.Rev. 601, 617–19 (1974). [Dissent.] State v. Mitchell, 563 S.W.2d 18, 32 (Mo.1978).

toe (to) any of the five digits of the foot.

Here, Appellee suffered the permanent loss of all the **toes** on his left foot. Appellee presented evidence of the continuous problems engendered by the amputation including difficulty in his maintaining stability, lifting objects, ascending a staircase, and walking long distances. Mattox v. City of Philadelphia, 454 A.2d 46, 54 (Super.Ct.Pa.1982).

In disposing of this issue, we are pleased to adopt, as our own, the trial court's cogent reasons which read as follows:

"Plaintiff's great **toe** of the right foot was mashed and most of it had to be amputated. He also had compound fractures of the second and third **toes**. He will have a permanent partial disability loss of use of the right foot directly attributable to the **toe** injuries variously estimated at from 15 percent to 17 percent.

Plaintiff contends, however, that the final effect of the accident is more serious than just the effect of the injury to three toes. He contends that an arthritic condition resulting from an old ankle injury in 1964 was aggravated by the gait and weight bearing changes brought on by the amputation of the great **toe** and the ununited fracture of the next two, and that these conditions together render him crippled and permanently disabled...." Johnson v. Alexander, 424 So.2d 1269, 1272 (Ct.App.La.1982).

toe, hammer a condition in which the proximal phalanx of a toe—most often that of the second toe—is extended and the second and distal phalanges are flexed, causing a clawlike appearance.

Plaintiff had weak toe flexors and extensor and a hammering deformity (condition in which there is permanent flexion at the midphalangeal joint of the toe) in his left big toe, with lesser **hammertoes** in the other toes. Brissette v. Schweiker, 566 F.Supp. 626, 631 (E.D.Mo.1983), remanded 730 F.2d 548 (8th Cir. 1984).

A **hammertoe** is basically a bent toe, occasioned by contraction of the inferior (bottom-foot) tendons of the foot and lengthening of the superior tendons, and the deformity of the bone itself as a result of this pulling. Matter of Silberman, 404 A.2d 1164, 1167 (Super.Ct.N.J.1979).

toenail (to'nāl) the nail on any of the digits of the foot. See also *nail* (def.1); and *unguis* [NA].

Tofranil (to-fra'nil) trademark for preparations of imipramine hydrochloride. See also *imipramine hydrochloride.*

tolerance (tol'er-ans) [L. *tolerantia*] the ability to endure without ill effect, unusually large doses of a drug, and to exhibit decreasing effect to continued use of the same dose of a drug.

"Tolerance" is described in Finding of Fact 19 as "... an adaptive process which contributes to abuse because, where it exists, a person tends continually to increase the amount of drug being taken. **Tolerance** has developed when, after repeated administration, a given dose of a drug produces a decreasing effect or conversely when increasingly larger doses must be administered to obtain the effects observed with the

original dose (Jaffe (1965), R–113, p. 285; Deneau, Tr. 1009)." 36 Fed.Reg., at 2557. We accept this definition. Hoffmann-La Roche, Inc. v. Kleindienst, 478 F.2d 1, 10 (3d Cir. 1973).

Repeated usage of these drugs [Heroin and Morphine] in a comparatively short time will result in the development of a **tolerance**, that is, a state which requires a gradually increasing dosage to permit the drug to attain the effect desired. People v. McCabe, 275 N.E.2d 407, 410 (Ill.1971).

toluene (tol'u-ēn) the hydrocarbon methylbenzene, $C_6H_5 \cdot CH_3$; a colorless liquid obtainable from tolu and other resins and from coal tar. It is an organic solvent used in rubber and plastic cements, paint removers, etc. Poisoning may result from ingesting the solvent or inhaling its concentrated vapors. Called also *toluol* and *methyl benzene.*

"**Toluene** is a vital or 'critical' material in wartime, because TNT, trinitrotoluene ... is undoubtedly the principal explosive in modern warfare. **Toluene** is used extensively as a solvent in the rubber, lacquer, and munition industries. It is poisonous when inhaled." A. Lowy & B. Harrow, An Introduction to Organic Chemistry, 242–43 (7th Ed. 1954)....

... Immediately after Earles and Woodford went into the tank, they breathed the poisonous fumes from the old cargo in that tank. Within twenty to thirty seconds after entering, they were overcome by the fumes, lost conciousness and fell on the floor of the tank with Earles' body lying in a puddle of the old chemical cargo. Plaintiff McNamer entered the tank to find out why the men were acting strangely, tried to rescue them and breathed the poisonous fumes. McNamer, however, was able to reach the ladder, climb out of the tank and flag down a passing boat before he, too, was overcome. Plaintiffs were treated for **toluene** exposure at a local hospital. Earles v. Union Barge Line Corp., 486 F.2d 1097, 1099–1100 (3d Cir. 1973).

toluene diisocyanate

She had been employed approximately four years when she began to develop headaches, breathing problems and nausea. An allergy specialist, Dr. John Argabrite, after extensive testing, recommended that she quit work as her condition had severely worsened and was becoming permanent. Dr. Argabrite concluded that the primary chemical causing Mrs. Hollman's condition was "**toluene diisocyanate**" (TDI). Hollman v. Liberty Mut. Ins. Co., 712 F.2d 1259–60 (8th Cir. 1983).

The complaint alleges that Olsen contracted asthma from exposure to a substance known as **TDI** [3] in the course of his employment by Western Electric Company. [3 **Toluene diisocyanate.**] Olsen v. Bell Telephone Laboratories, Inc., 445 N.E.2d 609–10 (Mass.1983).

toluene poisoning See *poisoning, toluene.*

tomogram (to'mo-gram) a roentgenogram of a selected layer of the body made by tomography.

Tomograms were also made of Brown's ankle which likewise indicated no new fracture. In Dr. Vesely's opinion, if Brown had suffered any injury, it had been a sprain or strain of the ankle, and he had suffered no resulting increase in permanent impairment to the ankle. Brown v. Pullman, Inc., 423 So.2d 250–1 (Ct.Civ.App.Ala.1982).

tomograph (to′mo-graf) an apparatus for moving an x-ray source in one direction as the film is moved in the opposite direction, thus showing in detail a predetermined plane of tissue while blurring or eliminating detail in other planes. See also *roentgenogram*.

Not only that, the radiologist recommended another x-ray study, diagnostic study which was not done and which could have determined whether or not probably the aseptic necrosis or a fracture actually did exist and those were **tomographs** or planographs, either one, of the wrist which could have determined bone density and whether or not there was a fracture. Carroll v. Kalar, 545 P.2d 411, 413 (Ariz.1976).

tomograph, brain

In October of 1975, the appellees began discussing among themselves the possibility of forming a group to purchase a computer assisted tomoscope (C.A.T.), hereinafter referred to as a brain scanner.[1] [1 A computer assisted **brain tomoscope** is a tool for the diagnosis of disorders of the brain. It uses a computer to analyze information produced by x-rays and prints out a picture of the brain. The machine makes an x-ray slice through the brain and feeds this information into the computer. The information is then processed by the computer and is printed out as a pattern of numbers corresponding to various types of brain tissue.] Cobb Cty., etc. v. Prince, 249 S.E.2d 581–2 (Ga.1978).

tomography (to-mog′rah-fe) [tomo- + Gr. *graphein* to write] the recording of internal body images at a predetermined plane by means of the tomograph; called also *body section roentgenography*.

tomography, computerized axial (CAT) that in which the emergent x-ray beam is measured by a scintillation counter, the electronic impulses are recorded on a magnetic disk, and then are processed by a mini-computer for reconstruction display of the body in cross-section on a cathode ray tube. Called also *computed t.* and *CAT scan*.

tomoscope See *tomograph*.

tone (tōn) [Gr. *tonos;* L. *tonus*] 1. the normal degree of vigor and tension; in muscle, the resistance to passive elongation or stretch. 2. a healthy state of a part; tonus.

tones, heart the sounds heard in the auscultation of the heart.

tone, heart (fetal) See *syndrome, respiratory distress, of newborn*.

The record indicates that **fetal heart tones** (an important test to monitor the condition of the fetus during labor) were taken only twice: at 4:30 a.m. and 7 a.m., both times by the medical student, Bajo. Although Lallie Kemp owned an electronic fetal heart monitor machine which would have provided for continuous monitoring of the fetal heart and which was available for use on Ms. Williams for at least some period of time prior to the time she was taken to the delivery room, the evidence is clear that the electronic fetal heart monitor machine was never used on her. Williams v. Lallie Kemp Charity Hosp., 428 So.2d 1000, 1003 (Ct.App.La.1983).

tonometer (to-nom′ĕ-ter) [tono- + Gr. *metron* measure] an instrument for measuring tension or pressure; usually used specifically in reference to an instrument by which intraocular pressure is measured.

tonometer, Schiotz' an instrument that registers intraocular pressure by direct application to the cornea, the reading on the scale being translated into millimeters of mercury by means of a conversion table.

Dr. Hargiss took eye pressure readings with a **Schiotz tonometer** and found the pressure in each eye registered 23.8 on the Goldman scale. This reading indicated Mrs. Gates was in the borderline area for glaucoma. Gates v. Jensen, 595 P.2d 919, 921 (Wash.1979).

tonometry (to-nom′ĕ-tre) the measurement of tension or pressure, especially the indirect estimation of the intraocular pressure from determination of the resistance of the eyeball to indentation by an applied force.

... a **tonometry** test (a test for glaucoma).... New York State Optometric Ass'n v. Whelan, 380 N.Y.S.2d 973, 975 (Sup.Ct.Albany Cty.1976).

Internal eye pressure, as an indication of glaucoma, he said, is measured by **tonometry** without the use of drugs. Ketcham v. King County Medical Service Corp., 502 P.2d 1197, 1202 (Wash.1972).

tonsil (ton′sil) a small rounded mass of tissue, especially of lymphoid tissue. The term is often used without qualification to designate the palatine tonsil. Called also *tonsilla*.

tonsillectomy (ton″sĭ-lek′to-me) [L. *tonsilla* tonsil + Gr. *ektomē* excision] surgical removal of a tonsil or tonsils. See also *Hemophilus influenzae* (Folk case).

The defendant removed the plaintiff's tonsils by ''dissection and snare,'' controlled the resultant bleeding by pressure of a ''Kelly'' instrument, and returned the patient to her room. Late that afternoon he received word that the plaintiff was bleeding from her right tonsil area. The next day, according to the hospital record, the patient was bleeding from both tonsil areas. The resident sutured the left tonsil area, applied silver nitrate to both areas and administered a two unit blood transfusion.

Dr. James Sacchetti, assistant superintendent of the Boston City Hospital, stated that the usual minimal standard preoperative tests for a **tonsillectomy** would include a urinalysis and a blood examination. The latter is primarily for blood typing and to determine if there is anemia. The urinalysis is to determine the possibility of kidney infection or kidney disease. Civitarese v. Gorney, 266 N.E.2d 668, 670 (Sup.Jud.Ct.Mass.1971).

tooth (tōōth), pl. *teeth*. One of a set of small hard structures in the jaws used for mastication of food (dens, *pl.* dentes [NA]), or a similar structure in various organisms other than man in the animal or plant kingdom. In man, there are two sets of teeth; the *deciduous teeth* and the *permanent teeth*. Each tooth has two main sections, a *crown* and a *root* or roots; the two divisions are further divided into crown, cervix (or neck), root, and apex. Clinical landmarks include the coronal portion, the cervical portion, the radicular portion and the apical portion. The tooth is solid except for a *pulp cavity* centered within it. The major portion of the tooth is made up of *dentin* or ivory. A layer of *enamel*, a very hard inorganic substance, covers the crown portion of the tooth, mostly in

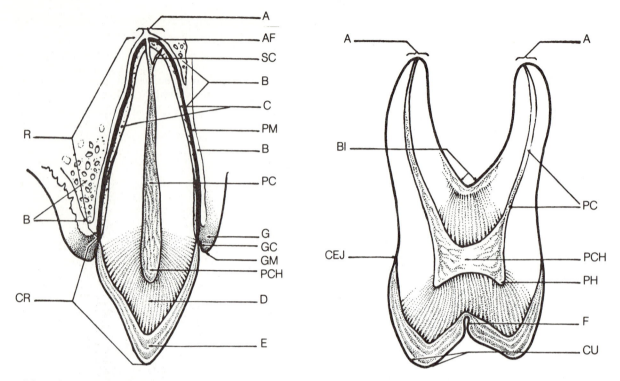

Schematic cross section of an anterior and a posterior tooth in upper jaw. **Left,** Anterior tooth: *A,* apex; *AF,* apical foramen; *SC,* supplementary canal; *C,* cementum; *PM,* periodontal membrane; *B,* bone; *PC,* pulp canal; *G,* gingiva; *GC,* gingival sulcus; *GM,* gingival margin; *PCH,* pulp chamber; *D,* dentin; *E,* enamel; *CR,* crown; *R,* root. **Right,** Posterior tooth; *A,* apices; *PC,* pulp canal; *PCH,* pulp chamber; *PH,* pulp horn; *F,* fissure; *CU,* cusp; *CEJ,* cemento-enamel junction; *BI,* bifurcation of roots. (Wheeler.)

evidence above the gum line, and a thin layer of *cementum* covers the root portion set in the jaw bones. Cementum (crusta petrosa) is true bone. The *pulp cavity* may be divided into two portions: the *pulp chamber,* mostly within the crown, and the *pulp canal* traversing the interior of the root, ending in a constricted opening at the root apex. There is at least one pulp canal in each root even when the tooth has multiple roots. The pulp cavity contains the *dental pulp,* a soft tissue containing connective tissue, blood vessels, and nerves. The *eruption* or "cutting" of the teeth follows generally an orderly schedule as follows: *Deciduous teeth*—first incisors, 6 to 8 months; second incisors, 7 to 9 months; first molars, 12 to 14 months; canines, 16 to 18 months; second molars, 20 to 24 months. *Permanent teeth*—first molars, 6 to 7 years; first incisors, 6 to 8 years; second incisors, 7 to 9 years; premolars, 10 to 12 years; canines, 9 to 12 years; second molars, 11 to 13 years; third molars, 17 to 21 years. See also *decay, dental; malocclusion; occlusion; restoration* (Moses case); *sinus* (Gorsalitz case); and *splinting* (Freer case).

The term "teeth", as used in Section 328.19 of Title 59 includes human **teeth** only and does not include prosthetic substitutes for natural **teeth.** Accordingly, we hold that the Trial Court erred in holding that the provisions of that Section include the cleaning of dentures within the definition of the prac-

tice of dentistry. Butler v. Bd. of Gov. of Registered Dentists, 619 P.2d 1262, 1266 (Okla.1980).

A loose **tooth** can always become looser. In fact, that is more or less the melancholy story of **teeth.**

A **tooth** first manifests the slightest variation from perpendicularity; then it leans a little more, but, like the Leaning Tower of Pisa, it is still firmly imbedded in the terra firma of the jaw bone. One day, however, the **tooth** bearer will note, as he masticates a tough steak or bites into a bit of gravel in his oyster sandwich, that the **tooth** under surveillance wobbles a little more, but it is still useful and still resolute for further masticatory assaults on foods of a stronger constituency than mush. A person may have a number of **teeth** in that state; they may even resemble a slightly pushed-over picket fence but they are still good **teeth,** still serviceable tusks. If, because of violence applied to the mandibles, the whole dental battery is jostled and the individual molars, bicuspids, grinders and incisors are shaken in their sockets, it is certainly proper to say that there has been a loosening of **teeth.** A further loosening, it is true, but still a loosening.

In whatever stage of looseness a man's dental pearls may be, he is entitled to keep them in that state, and if they are tortiously subjected to jostling, jarring and jouncing, the tortfeasor may not be excused from responsibility for the further chewing dilapidation of his victim on the basis that he had bad **teeth** anyway. Freer v. Parker, 192 A.2d 348, 350 (Pa.1963).

tooth (chart) See *mandibular*; and *maxillary*.

tooth, deciduous See *teeth, deciduous*.

tooth, incisor See *teeth, incisor*.

tooth, molar See *teeth, molar*.

tooth, permanent See *teeth, permanent*.

tooth, wisdom the third molar tooth, the tooth most distal from the medial line on either side in each jaw, so called because it is the last of the permanent dentition to erupt, usually at the age of 17 to 21 years. Called also *dens serotinus* [NA]. See also *extraction* (Raza case); *paresthesia* (Cozart case; and *teeth, molar*.

tooth positioner See *positioner*.

tooth staining See *tetracycline* (Dalke case).

torsion (tor'shun) [L. *torsio; torquere* to twist] the act of twisting; the condition of being twisted. In dentistry, the condition of a tooth when it is turned on its long axis. See also *epididymitis*.

According to Dr. Smith, at that time, Cradle's left testicle appeared small and wasted, and was probably non-functional due to "torsion." He defined **torsion** as a congenital condition that is usually manifest at or just after puberty, but which can occur at any age, in which a testicle rotates on its suspending cord resulting in blockage of the blood supply and death of the testicle—usually within twelve hours....

... According to Dr. Smith, once **torsion** occurs and a testicle dies, there is nothing that can be done save what was done in this case: surgery for cosmetic reasons, and fixation of the remaining testicle to prevent it from undergoing **torsion**. Cradle v. Superintendent, Correctional Field Unit #7, 374 F.Supp. 435, 437–8 (W.D.Va.1973).

tourniquet (toor'nĭ-ket) [Fr.] an instrument for the compression of a blood vessel by application around an extremity to control the circulation and prevent the flow of blood to or from the distal area. Tourniquets are of various kinds, named chiefly for their inventors.

As to the use of a **tourniquet** preparatory to knee surgery, Dr. Lambert testified that this was standard procedure and that although the surgeon rarely applies the **tourniquet** himself, the surgeon is responsible for the **tourniquet** because he "causes it to be put on and causes it to be removed." He also noted that from his experience **tourniquet** pressure ordinarily does not result in damage to the peroneal and tibial nerves unless "it is incorrectly applied or it is applied over a bony prominence or the **tourniquet** itself is defective." Hale v. Venuto, 187 Cal.Rptr. 357, 360 (Ct.App.Cal.1982).

toxaphene (toks'ah-fēn) a chlorinated hydrocarbon, $C_{10}H_{10}Cl_8$, used as an agricultural insecticide.

Toxaphene is also a chlorinated hydrocarbon pesticide. It has been used for several decades, and is currently used for pest control on cotton and livestock....

Evidence concerning the danger of **toxaphene** to public health and the environment, particularly to fish, has been produced in the years since the chemical was first introduced. Application of **toxaphene** to agricultural land surrounding several bird refuges resulted in massive bird kills in 1960–62. App. I 157. **Toxaphene** was identified as a cause of fish kills because

of the characteristic "broken back" syndrome it produces in fish. In 1969, strobane, a pesticide closely related to **toxaphene**, was identified as a carcinogen in mice. App. I 148. **Toxaphene** has been frequently found in clarified and treated municipal drinking water. App. I 152. Hercules, Inc. v. Environmental Protection Agcy., 598 F.2d 91, 98–99 (D.C.Cir.1978).

toxic (tok'sik) pertaining to, due to, or of the nature of a poison or toxin; manifesting the symptoms of severe infection.

(5) "Toxic" shall apply to any substance (other than a radioactive substance) which has the capacity to produce personal injury or illness to man through ingestion, inhalation, or absorption through any body surface. 16 C.F.R.Sect. 1500.3(b) (5).

toxic goiter See *disease, Graves'*.

toxic, highly

(6)(i) "Highly toxic" means any substance which falls within any of the following categories:

(A) Produces death within 14 days in half or more than half of a group of 10 or more laboratory white rats each weighing between 200 and 300 grams, at a single dose of 50 milligrams or less per kilogram of body weight, when orally administered; or

(B) Produces death within 14 days in half or more than half of a group of 10 or more laboratory white rats each weighing between 200 and 300 grams, when inhaled continuously for a period of 1 hour or less at an atmospheric concentration of 200 parts per million by volume of [or-sic] less of gas or vapor or 2 milligrams per liter by volume of less of mist or dust, provided such concentration is likely to be encountered by man when the substance is used in any reasonably foreseeable manner; or

(C) Produces death within 14 days in half or more than half of a group of 10 or more rabbits tested in a dosage of 200 milligrams or less per kilogram of body weight, when administered by continuous contact with the bare skin for 24 hours or less.

(ii) If the Commission finds that available data on human experience with any substance indicate results different from those obtained on animals in the dosages and concentrations specified in paragraph (b)(6)(i) of this section, the human data shall take precedence. 16 C.F.R.Sect. 1500.3(b)(6).

toxicity (tok-sis'ĭ-te) the quality of being poisonous, especially the degree of virulence of a toxic microbe or of a poison. See also *hazard*.

Toxicity is the inherent capacity of a substance to produce injury or death. Florida Peach Grow. Ass'n v. United States Dep't of Labor, 489 F.2d 120, 131 (5th Cir. 1974).

He said that after the plaintiff's admission to St. Bernard's on May 18, he had developed a toxic condition from the absorption of dead skin. This **toxicity** made him semicomatose. Between May 18 and May 21 his temperature was highly elevated, reaching 105 degrees at times. His stumps became infected.... Raines v. New York Railroad Co., 283 N.E.2d 230, 236 (Ill.1972).

Toxicity is a relative term. What would be highly toxic under one set of circumstances might be considered "low **toxicity**" under different circumstances and in a different part of the body where it would be quickly diluted by blood as in the case of aortography, here involved. Ball v. Mallinkrodt Chemical Works, 381 S.W.2d 563, 568 (Ct.App.Tenn.1964).

Other Authorities: U.S. v. Article of Drug Labeled Decholin, 264 F.Supp. 473, 476 (E.D.Mich.1967).

toxicology (tok"si-kol'o-je) the sum of what is known regarding poisons; the scientific study of poisons, their actions, their detection, and the treatment of the conditions produced by them. Cited in Harrison v. Flota Mercante Grancolombiana, S.A., 577 F.2d 968, 975 (5th Cir. 1978).

toxin (tok'sin) [L. *toxicum* poison, from Gr. *toxikos* of or for the bow] a poison; frequently used to refer specifically to a protein produced by some higher plants, certain animals, and pathogenic bacteria, which is highly toxic for other living organisms. Such substances are differentiated from the simple chemical poisons and the vegetable alkaloids by their high molecular weight and antigenicity.

Toxocara (tok"so-ka'rah) a genus of nematode worms of the superfamily Ascaridoidea.

Toxocara canis a nematode worm parasitic in the intestine of dogs; migrating larvae may cause lesions of the lung, liver, kidney, brain, and eye. In human infections, the larvae do not complete their cycle but cause visceral larva migrans. See also *retinoblastoma* (Steele case).

In Dr. Black's medical opinion the cause of the inflammation of Timothy's eye was probably **toxocara canis**. Dr. Black observed that although the larva was never found in the few sectionings of the eye, it is known that the larva may disintegrate or completely disappear in the eye.

Toxocara canis is a parasitic round worm frequently found in dogs. The eggs of the parasite may be ingested by children playing in dirt and the eggs hatch in the intestines of the child into a larva. The larva bores through the intestinal wall and enters the blood stream and is disseminated to different parts of the body. In every instance, with possible rare exception, the parasite is not able to complete its life cycle in a human host and the larva dies without developing into an adult worm. The most common locations where it has been found are in the liver or the lungs. Inflammation of the eye by toxocara is fairly rare. But when it does appear it tends to result in a massive inflammation which usually involves the retina and sometimes may intrude into other structures inside the eye. The presence of toxocara in the body often leads to visceral larva migrans syndrome. The child can have a fever and may have some type of lung disorder, his liver may be enlarged and tender and there may be some abnormalities in certain blood tests. However, an ocular toxocara inflammation frequently occurs without a visceral larva migrans syndrome occurring and some studies suggest that in only three or four percent of ocular toxocara inflammation is the syndrome present. With ocular toxocara, so long as the larva remains alive, there is usually not much effect on the eye. There may be a local inflammation in the retina or a small whitish elevated lesion in the retina at the site of the larva or where it penetrated the retina, but the stage at which the parasite usually becomes very damaging is when the larva dies and decomposes. This leads to an extensive lesion in the eye eventually resulting in a massive scar. If the larva is able to work itself into the vitreous cavity of the eye, it brings about an even more severe inflammatory process. Steele v. U.S., 463 F.Supp. 321, 327 (D.Alas.1978).

toxoid (tok'soid) [*toxo-* + Gr. *eidos* form] a modified bacterial exotoxin that has lost toxicity but retains the properties of combining with, or stimulating the formation of, antitoxin.

With some infectious diseases, such as diphtheria and tetanus, it has been possible to isolate the soluble toxin or poison excreted by these bacteria and to inactivate this toxin with formaldehyde, thereby converting the toxin into what is called a **toxoid**. This **toxoid** helps immunize the body against disease by stimulating the production of antibodies, but the **toxoid** will not cause disease because it has lost its poisonous qualities. Ezagui v. Dow Chemical Corp., 598 F.2d 727, 731 (2d Cir. 1979).

Other Authorities: Blank v. U.S., 400 F.2d 302, 304 (5th Cir. 1968).

toxoid, tetanus [USP], a sterile solution of formaldehyde-treated products of the growth of *Clostridium tetani*, used as an active immunizing agent.

After completion of this stage, the donor is asked if he will allow the injection of a **tetanus toxoid**. If he consents, he is given the toxoid in a stipulated schedule in order to proudce an antibody in his blood from which an immune globulin is produced for use in treating tetanus. The antibody is obtained if, as desired by appellant, the donor returns for subsequent donations. Mirsa v. State Medical Board, 329 N.E.2d 106–7 (Ohio 1975).

toxoplasmosis (tok"so-plaz-mo'sis) a protozoan disease of man caused by *Toxoplasma gondii. Congential toxoplasmosis* is characterized by lesions of the central nervous system, which may lead to blindness, brain defects, and death. The acquired form is of two types: *lymphadenopathic toxoplasmosis*, which closely resembles mononucleosis, and *disseminated toxoplasmosis*, in which lesions involve chiefly the lungs, liver, heart, skin, muscle, brain, and meninges and which is characterized by pneumonitis, hepatitis, myocarditis, and meningoencephalitis in varying degrees. Chorioretinitis invariably accompanies the congenital form, and may occur in the acquired form.

Louise Johnson, an inmate who had previously suffered from **toxoplasmosis** (parasitic infection) of the eye, complained of eye problems at the lobby clinic on January 27, 29, 30 and February 2, 3. Todaro v. Ward, 431 F.Supp. 1129, 1142 (S.D. N.Y.1977).

trachea (tra'ke-ah) [L.; Gr. *tracheia artēria*] [NA] the cartilaginous and membranous tube descending from the larynx and branching into the right and left main bronchi. It is kept patent by a series of about twenty transverse horseshoe-shaped cartilages.

Because of its location in the midst of the chest surrounded by bones, the heart, and major blood vessels, the **trachea** is a very difficult organ to examine. The evidence is that conventional x-rays are of little value in detecting a lesion in the **trachea**. A considerably more effective but by no means perfect diagnostic tool for the **trachea** is a specialized form of x-rays called laminograms. Joynt v. Barnes, 388 N.E.2d 1298, 1304 (App.Ct.Ill.1979).

An autopsy revealed that death resulted from total obstruction of the airway (**trachea**) from aspirated vomitus or food matter. The matter regurgitated was gastric contents. There was no evidence that death resulted from choking on or aspiration of food as it was being eaten or ingested. Jones v. Liberty Nat. Life Ins. Co., 357 So.2d 976–7 (Ala.1978).

Examination of the lungs involved opening widely the **trachea** (windpipe) from its beginning to where it divides into tubes leading into the lungs. These tubes which should normally be empty contained vomitus material, and several chunks of food, partially in digested state and some not partially digested. Similar material was found in the deep branches of these tubular structures. Jones v. Aetna Life Insurance Co., 439 S.W.2d 721, 723 (Ct.Civ.App.Tex.1969).

tracheitis (tra″ke-i′tis) inflammation of the trachea.

... the last time that Dr. Barnes had personally seen Joynt was in February 1973, when he had diagnosed him as having influenza syndrome with **tracheitis** (inflammation and infection of the trachea). Joynt v. Barnes, 388 N.E.2d 1298, 1302 (App. Ct.Ill.1979).

Because of her heart condition, it was necessary to insert a tube down Donna's throat in the course of administering the anesthetic. **Tracheitis** developed following the operation, so Dr. Stasiuk administered Ampicillin, a form of penicillin, to Donna for the purpose of treating the infection in her throat. Donna claims that when she complained of her sore throat to Dr. Stasiuk, he told her he was sorry, that he had used too big a tube. Dr. Stasiuk denies this conversation. Walstad v. University of Minnesota Hospitals, 442 F.2d 634, 637 (8th Cir. 1971).

tracheobronchitis (tra″ke-o-brong-ki′tis) inflammation of the trachea and bronchi.

Dolly again sought medical attention at the clinic from T. C. Corbett on May 18, 1978, complaining that, in spite of medication, her cough persisted, it was worse particularly in the evenings, and that she was producing small amounts of greenish phlegm from her throat when she coughed. Dr. Corbett admitted Dolly to the Mercy Hospital at Devils Lake on that date with a diagnosis of "persistent **tracheobronchitis** subsequent to fiberglass exposure.

Dolly's symptoms are consistent with those that can be caused by working with fiberglass materials according to the Good Practice Manual for Insulation Installers written in August, 1977, by the U.S. Department of Health, Education and Welfare. This manual, which was submitted for the record by Dolly's counsel, provides in relevant part:

"Fiberglass is one of the materials that can be highly irritating to your skin. It causes itching wherever it touches you. The tenderer the skin area, the more it will itch....

"The tiny fibers from fiberglass break off and stick into your skin. You can't see them, but you know they are there because they hurt or itch....

"Respiratory irritants are those which bother your nose, throat, and lungs. Some irritants make them itch and burn. Materials like dust and small fibers from glass or mineral wool can make your nose and throat sore. Also, dusts from other materials like vermiculite, perlite, and cellulose make you sneeze and cough." Roberts v. North Dakota Workmen's Comp. Bur., 326 N.W.2d 702, 704–5 (N.Dak.1982).

In any event, Dr. Laigon testified that he first saw the plaintiff "in late December 1963" and found him "ill with a febrile illness associated with a severe productive cough". On that basis and at that time, the doctor noted a preliminary "clinical impression" of "severe **tracheobronchitis**" for which treatment was initiated. (p. 22) Antibiotics, expectorants and bronchodilators were administered. Dabravalskie v. Gardner, 281 F.Supp. 919, 921 (E.D.Pa.1968).

tracheostomy (tra″ke-os′to-me) [*tracheo-* + Gr. *stomoun* to furnish with an opening or mouth] the surgical creation of an opening into the trachea through the neck, with the tracheal mucosa being brought into continuity with the skin; also, the opening so created. The term is also used to refer to creation of an opening in the anterior trachea for insertion of a tube to relieve upper airway obstruction and to facilitate ventilation. See also *endotracheal.*

Initially, an emergency **tracheostomy** was performed and a plastic tube and breathing mechanism remained in place for the major portion of her hospitalization. Warmsley v. City of New York, 454 N.Y.S.2d 144 (2d Dep't 1982).

Dr. Jones performed a classical **tracheostomy** in about ten minutes. According to him, it took this amount of time because it was an emergency as compared to the twenty to thirty minutes which would have been taken for an elective **tracheostomy**. Dr. Jones cut through the cartilaginous ring in the neck in a horizontal and transverse fashion in order to open the trachea. According to him, and the Court so finds, this was successful and there was a gush of air heard from Mr. Wright's lungs. A trach tube was then inserted which bypassed the edema in the vocal cords, and the patient was now breathing voluntarily. Wright v. U.S., 507 F.Supp. 147, 151 (E.D.La.1981).

On several occasions the Puritan Pot, which provided humidity for her throat condition in order to prevent her oral secretions from caking up, was without water. When Donna's sister, Mrs. Ione Kloster, visited her on the morning of April 14, she found Donna unattended and unable to talk, breathe or hold the oxygen mask. Mrs. Kloster fortunately was able to locate some nurses quickly, who in turn located the senior resident who immediately performed an emergency **tracheostomy**. Walstad v. Univ. of Minnesota Hospitals, 442 F.2d 634, 638 (8th Cir. 1971).

Other Authorities: Marek v. U.S., 639 F.2d 1164–5 (5th Cir. 1981).

tracheostomy tube See *tube, tracheostomy.*

tracheotomy (tra″ke-ot′o-me) [*tracheo-* + Gr. *tomē* a cutting] incision of the trachea.

A **tracheotomy** is a surgical procedure whereby the trachea is cut and a **tracheotomy** tube is inserted into the trachea so that the patient breathes directly through the **tracheotomy** tube. Battles v. Aderhold, 430 So.2d 307, 310 (Ct.App.La.1983).

In addition to both legs being fractured Mrs. Herndon suffered multiple fractures to her facial bones which were so severe she could not breathe on her own. A **tracheotomy** was performed and a breathing tube remained in place for several weeks, during which time she was fed intravenously. For several months after the accident her jaws were wired shut so the only way she could eat was to use a syringe and inject liquid foods into her mouth through her clenched teeth. Herndon v. Neal, 424 So.2d 1180, 1183 (Ct.App.La.1982).

None of the doctors ordered a **tracheotomy** either during the operation or during the post-operative period, a procedure which even defendants' expert, Dr. Cohen, testified "should always be considered in a case of Ludwig's Angina in order to prevent respiratory distress." Plaintiff's expert, Dr. Greene, also testified to the necessity of a **tracheotomy** to assure the protection of the patient's airway where there is a threat of respiratory obstruction. Spadaccini v. Dolan, 407 N.Y.S.2d 840, 842 (1st Dep't 1978).

trachoma (trah-ko'mah), pl. *trachomata* [Gr. *trachōma* roughness] a chronic infectious disease of the conjunctiva and cornea, producing photophobia, pain, and lacrimation, caused by an organism once thought to be a virus but now classified as a strain of the bacteria *Chlamydia trachomatis*. Clinically, it can be divided into four stages (MacCallan): (1) mild infection marked by tiny follicles on the eyelid conjunctiva and subepithelial infiltration; (2) enlargement of the follicles and inflammatory changes forming hard red papillae, usually with vascular invasion of the cornea marking the onset of pannus; (3) severe scarring and contraction resulting in symblepharon, entropion, trichiasis, and corneal scarring which may result in blindness; (4) complete arrest with permanent scarring, entropion, and symblepharon. Called also *Aret's t., Egyptian, granular,* or *trachomatous conjunctivitis, Egyptian ophthalmia,* and *granular lids.*

. . . plaintiff spent four or five months at the school for the blind. His condition was at that time diagnosed as **trachoma**. After taking certain tests at the school for the blind, showing that he had recovered sufficiently to be able to function adequately and go back to work, he was discharged. American National Ins. Co. v. Carbajal, 530 S.W.2d 642, 644 (Ct.Civ. App.Tex.1975).

tract (trakt) [L. *tractus*] a region, principally one of some length; specifically a collection or bundle of nerve fibers having the same origin, function, and termination (tractus [NA]), or a number of organs, arranged in series, subserving a common function.

tract, gastrointestinal the stomach and intestines in continuity.

Dr. Braswell, Mrs. Goss' local doctor, described the "**gastrointestinal tract**" as follows:

"The **gastro-intestinal tract** begins with the intake of food, which passes across the lips and into the oral cavity, the mouth, and is propelled down the pharynx by the tongue, the food then goes into the esophagus, and is propelled into the stomach, in which it is mixed with enzymes and acids of digestion. It is then emptied into the small bowel, where digestion is completed, and the contents of the food then empties into the colon, which is propelled into the rectum, and evacuated through the anus. This is the gastro-intestinal system, there are allied associated parts of the gastro-intestinal system, which would include the pancreas and the gall bladder and ducts, which are included in the gastro-intestinal system."...

. . . Dr. Haygood, the surgeon who removed Mrs. Goss' appendix, defined the "**gastro-intestinal tract**" in the following manner:

"Well, gastro means stomach. Intestinal means intestine, so the word 'gastro-intestinal' could strictly be limited to mean the stomach and the intestine, although when one speaks of the **gastro-intestinal tract** or GI tract, this generally refers to the entire alimentary canal, which starts with the mouth, the pharynx, the esophagus, the stomach, the entire small intestine, the entire large intestine, the rectum and ending at the anus. Embryologically, the appendix rises with the cecum, which is the right portion of the large intestine, and it communicates with and is a part of the **gastro-intestinal tract**." Mid-Western Life Ins. Co. of Texas v. Goss, 552 S.W.2d 430, 432 (Tex.1977).

tract, pyramidal a term applied to two groups of fibers (corticonuclear and corticospinal) arising chiefly in the sensorimotor regions of the cerebral cortex and descending in the internal capsule, cerebral peduncle, and pons to the medulla oblongata, the corticonuclear fibers synapsing with motor nuclei throughout the brain stem. Most of the corticospinal fibers cross in the decussation of the pyramids and descend in the spinal cord as the lateral pyramidal (lateral corticospinal) tract; most of the uncrossed fibers form the anterior pyramidal (anterior corticospinal) tract; both end by synapsing with internuncial and motor neurons. The pyramidal tract is a phylogenetically new tract, most prominent in man, which provides for direct cortical control and initiation of skilled movements, especially those related to speech and involving the hand and fingers. Called also *tractus pyramidalis* [NA], *corticospinal t.,* and *pyramidal system.*

tract, urinary the organs and ducts which participate in the secretion and elimination of the urine.

During this period of time he had a persistent **urinary tract** infection, and upon being readmitted on May 18 he was in urinary retention and was septic.

He is on continued urinary antibiotics and acidifying agents in an attempt to control his urinary infections, however, the possibility of eliminating the urinary infection is minimal. Warner v. City of Bay St. Louis, 408 F.Supp. 375, 380 (S.D.Miss. 1975).

traction (trak'shun) [L. *tractio*] the act of drawing or exerting a pulling force, as along the long axis of a structure.

One of the reasons why **traction** is not always effective is that the alternating muscle contractions would have some tendency to vary the traction on the fracture line. Downer v. Veilleux, 322 A.2d 82, 85–6 (Sup.Jud.Ct.Me.1974).

traction, Bryant's

Dr. Ramos had the boy admitted to the Hospital and put him into bilateral **Bryant's traction**. This apparatus caused both of his legs to be elevated to an acute degree so that the buttocks were raised off the bed. This was accomplished by weights appended to both legs. In accordance with defendant's instructions to Dr. Ramos, a weight of 10 pounds was used on each leg....

. . . Dr. David Petty, a qualified general surgeon, testified that there were dangers inherent in use of the **Bryant's traction**. In his opinion, this method was good for use with very small children but is practically useless in treatment of children over three years old. He felt that it should not be used on a child nine years of age but that if it is used for any reason, special daily care and precautions were required such as watching the circulation, bathing and cleaning of the skin. In his opinion, the use of the **Bryant's traction** in this particular case was not good medical practice.

Dr. Maurice S. Stamler, the orthopedic specialist who had come to the rescue of the patient, testified that he personally did not use **Bryant's traction** because he had seen complications from its use. However, it was his opinion that the use of this system was fairly common and he had seen other doctors use it. He suggested that the nurses should be advised to watch the patient but he testified that regardless of the method of traction used, the patient must "always" be watched. In his opinion, all methods of traction are similar but doctors have different opinions about the type of traction to be used. **Bryant's traction** was, in his opinion, an accepted medical procedure.

Dr. Donald S. Miller, a highly qualified and educated specialist in orthopedic and vascular surgery, testified that he was of the opinion that the limit in application of **Bryant's traction** depended upon the age and weight of the patient. He felt that the general age limit should be placed at about four years with the patient's weight in the area of 55 to 60 pounds but it could be used for older children up to seven who were very thin. Garfield Park Community Hospital v. Vitacco, 327 N.E.2d 408–411 (App.Ct.Ill.1975).

traction, elastic traction by an elastic force or by means of an elastic appliance.

Dr. Bedrick's treatment consisted of constructing and applying a headcap to reduce and fix the jaw fracture and hold it in place by means of **elastic traction** (289–290; Ex. 2, p. 11). Yarrow v. U.S., 309 F.Supp. 922, 924 (S.D.N.Y.1970).

traction, halopelvic traction applied to the spine by means of two metal hoops, one (the halo) applied to the skull and the other to the pelvis, connected by four extension rods which can be lengthened by turn screws.

She entered a hospital on February 18, 1970, and the defendant proceeded with the first stage, the application of a **halo-femoral traction** device. "Halo" refers to a band of metal wrapped around the skull, secured with four pins implanted in the skull, two over the eyes and two above and behind the ears. Other pins are driven into the patient's thigh bones, and metal traction rods then connect the head and thigh bone implants. The defendant implanted the pin over the minor plaintiff's left eye, and later relocated that pin. One or both of those pins were positioned in a negligent manner, lower than sound medical practice dictated. This caused severe pain and the pin site became infected, with the result that the halo had to be removed and the traction terminated before the second, or fusion, stage of the intended treatment was reached. Harrington v. Cohen, 374 N.E.2d 344–5 (App.Ct.Mass.1978).

traction, skeletal traction applied directly upon the long bones by means of pins, Kirschner's wire, etc.

As a result of Coleman's injury he was confined to the Lake Charles Memorial Hospital for about 48 days under the care of Dr. David Drez. Coleman remained confined in his hospital bed on his back in balanced **skeletal traction** for this length of time. A metal pin was surgically implanted in Coleman's leg just

below his knee. This pin was used to fascilitate the traction which was to re-align the fractured femur. Coleman v. Jackson, 422 So.2d 179, 184 (Ct.App.La.1982).

tractus (trak'tus), pl. *tractus* [L. "a track," "trail"] a tract: a region, principally one of some length; [NA] a general term, especially for a collection or bundle of nerve fibers having the same origin and termination, and serving the same function.

tractus pyramidalis See *tract, pyramidal.*

tranquilizer (tran"kwĭ-līz'er) [L. *tranquillus* quiet, calm + *-ize* verb ending meaning to make & *-er* agent] a large class of drugs used in the treatment of anxiety states, neuroses, and mental disorders. They are of two types; *major tranquilizers* (called also *antipsychotics* and *neuroleptics*) are used primarily for the treatment of psychoses and include the phenothiazines, thioxanthenes, and butyrophenones; *minor tranquilizers* (called also *anxiolytics*) are used primarily for the treatment of neuroses and anxiety states and include the benzodiazepines, certain barbiturates, and other drugs. See also *hypnotic* (In re Cameron case).

The use of major **tranquilizers** are appropriate under limited circumstances. One justification for their use is to curb severe aggression and self-abuse. The experts testified the drugs should not be used to control sexual behavior. The court noted the record was devoid of evidence of the severe aggression or self-abuse required to justify the extent to which major tranquilizers were administered. Clites v. State, 322 N.W.2d 917, 920 (Ct.App.Iowa 1982).

A **tranquilizer**, on the other hand, [as opposed to a hypnotic.def., 3, q.v.] does not operate upon the areas of the brain that control consciousness, but upon the areas of the brain that control the reactions of a conscious individual to his environment. **Tranquilizers** produce sleep by removing the anxiety or worry that is keeping the individual awake. He is then enabled to go to sleep. However, he can be roused from that sleep and will behave in a conscious manner, despite the fact that he is still under the influence of the drug. The drug is still having the effect of removing the normal anxiety or worry reactions the individual would have to his environment. With a hypnotic drug, on the other hand, the fact that the individual is conscious indicates that he is no longer under the influence of the drug. In re Cameron, 439 P.2d 633, 641 (Cal.1968).

transaminase (trans-am'ĭ-nās) an enzyme that catalyzes the reversible transfer of an amino group from an α-amino acid to an α-keto acid, usually α-ketoglutaric acid. Pyridoxal-5-phosphate and pyridoxamine phosphate act as coenzymes.

transaminase, glutamic-oxaloacetic, (GOT) an enzyme normally present in serum (SGOT) and in various body tissues, especially in the heart and liver; it is released into the serum as the result of tissue injury, hence the concentration in the serum may be increased in myocardial infarction or acute damage to hepatic cells.

... the SGOT reading (which measures the level of serum **glutamic-oxaloacetic transaminase**) was "off the chart," with a reading above 250, compared with a normal range of 10 to 50. Cornfeldt v. Tongen, 262 N.W.2d 684, 690 (Minn.1977).

transfer trauma See *trauma, transfer.*

transferase (trans'fer-ās) any of a class of enzymes that catalyze the transfer, from one molecule to another, of a chemical group that does not exist in the free state during the transfer.

Plaintiff's aspartate **aminotransferase** (SGOT) (an enzyme found in the blood) was 44 units, whereas normal is 0–33 units. Brissette v. Schweiker, 566 F.Supp. 626, 628 (E.D.Mo.1983), remanded 730 F.2d 548 (8th Cir. 1984).

transference (trans-fer'ens) in psychiatry, the shifting of an affect from one person to another or from one idea to another, especially the transfer by the patient to the analyst of emotional tones, either of affection or of hostility, based on unconscious identification. If the transfer is favorable it is *positive t.*, if unfavorable *negative t.*

According to expert testimony, **transference** is a common phenomenon in psychiatrist therapy in which the psychiatric patient transfers onto the psychiatrist emotions the patient has towards someone else. Mazza v. Huffaker, 300 S.E.2d 833, 840 (Ct.App.N.C.1983).

transference, counter See *countertransference.*

transfusion (trans-fu'zhun) [L. *transfusio*] the introduction of whole blood or blood component directly into the blood stream. Cf. *infusion.* See also *blood* (Foster case); and *hepatitis, viral* (Fisher case).

A. The blood **transfusion** was intended to correct the low hemoglobin thereby providing a better oxygen carrying capacity.

Q. What is the consequence to this child of this type of low hemoglobin contents in failure directed by that situation?

A. If a child is allowed in this particular situation where one has an infant who is requiring a large amount of oxygen to maintain a normal or near normal oxygen tension, the child is in a critical situation if his hemoglobin were to fall to low levels such that, so that in a marginal situation where the oxygen is already low, if the hemoglobin and red cell contents of the blood is low, then the child is going to suffer more from the effects of a low oxygen. And so it was thought to transfuse the infant. . . .

Q Why is the giving of blood a part of the treatment of this child?

A. In order for us to effectively treat a very sick infant of this nature, it is necessary to sample blood frequently. The sampling is for blood gasses as well as for other matters that other disorders of a chemical nature that very sick preterm infants are prone to. As an estimate, we have removed approximately one hundred and eighty-six cc's of blood from this infant from the time he was born until October the twenty-fourth. Now, this represents more than twice, approximately twice his circulating blood volume so that this would have to be replaced from time to time. Re Wintersgill and Minister of Social Services, 131 D.L.R. 184, 189–90 (Unified Fam.Ct., Sask. 1981).

Approximately forty-four states have enacted statutes precluding liability in blood procurement cases, many by characterizing blood **transfusions** as services. See Blood Transfusions, 24 Am.U.L.Rev. . . . . [367, 403–8 (1975)]. Fisher v. Sibley Memorial Hospital, 403 A.2d 1130, 1132 (D.C.App.1979).

The rationale for excluding blood transfers from the general products liability law is aptly set out in Heirs of Fruge v. Blood Services, 506 F.2d 841, 844–45 (5th Cir. 1975) (Louisiana law). "Six years ago, the Louisiana legislature—like many others—amended its laws to extinguish all causes of action except negligence against blood banks and hospitals supplying whole blood and its components. The reason for this unusual action was simple, and apparently cogent to the legislature: the obvious and overwhelming need for blood and blood products to be used in **transfusions** and in surgery was barely met by available supplies, and suppliers were threatened by crippling legal liability for a very small but—according to the majority of medical authorities—hard to avoid risk that their blood carried indetectable viral hepatitis.

Heirs of Fruge v. Blood Services, 365 F.Supp. 1344 (W.D.La. 1973) (footnote 3, affd., 506 F.2d 841 (5th Cir. 1975)), lists over 40 states with similar code provisions. McAllister v. American Nat. Red Cross, 240 S.E.2d 247, 249 (Ga.1977).

Other Authorities: Williamson v. Memorial Hosp. of Bay Cty., 307 So.2d 199, 201 (Dist.Ct.App.Fla.1975); Heirs of Fruge v. Blood Services, 365 F.Supp. 1344, 1350–1 (W.D.La.1973).

transglucosidase

"**Transglucosidase:** An enzyme which produces non-fermentable sugars, e.g., isomaltose and panose, from some starch hydrolysis products." Baxter Laboratories, Inc. v. Corn Products Co., 394 F.2d 892–3 (7th Cir. 1968).

transient

Defendant's argument is that the ischemic attacks, whether one or two, suffered by plaintiff on August 14, 1978 were **transient**, which by medical definition means that they passed without doing any damage, and that plaintiff was in exactly the same medical condition after the attacks as he was in before. Daily v. Bechtel Power Corp., 420 So.2d 1337, 1341 (Ct.App. La.1982).

Transient: A compound that may be momentarily formed during the course of a chemical reaction, but whose existence (if any) is so brief and structure so inherently unstable that there is no possible method, even theoretically, of proving the formation of the compound. The existence of such a compound can never be experimentally verified, unlike the existence of a genuine intermediate. Ritter v. Rohm & Haas Co., 154 U.S.P.Q. 518, 555 (S.D.N.Y.1967).

transit nerve stimulator See *stimulator.*

transplant (trans'plant) an organ or tissue taken from the body for grafting into another area of the same body or into another individual. See also *blood* (Foster case).

transplant, corneal See *endotheleum, corneal* (McDermott case).

Plaintiff sues for malpractice in an operation to **transplant the cornea** of plaintiff's left eye. . . .

. . . As to the second claim, the evidence is that the operation is one of extreme delicacy requiring minute sutures on a curved surface, during which period the **transplant** must be kept in exact position. Statistics in evidence show that the incidence of failure is as high as 35%. McDermott v. Manhattan Eye, Ear and Throat Hosp., 270 N.Y.S.2d 955, 956 (1st Dept. 1966).

The **transplant** in this case involved the excision of the central portion of plaintiff's cornea and its replacement with an identical piece cut from the cornea of a donor's eyeball.

Prior to 1952 no **corneal transplant** had ever been successfully performed on a patient with Fuch's dystrophy. Since then there have been a limited number of successful operations. Plaintiff's theory is that a **corneal transplant** is never indicated when the disease extends to the periphery of the cornea. Involvement of the periphery, argues the plaintiff, precludes a good result because the disease in the corneal periphery will invade the graft.

Plaintiff contends further that another prerequisite of a **corneal transplant** on a patient suffering from Fuch's dystrophy is that the patient's eyesight be not less than 20/200. Plaintiff's vision was considerably less than 20/200. McDermott v. Manhattan Eye Ear & Throat Hospital, 228 N.Y.S.2d 143, 146–7 (1st Dep't 1962).

transplant, hair See *procedure, Juri-flap.*

However, Dr. Peters, after a consultation with Dixon, recommended a surgical procedure whereby strips of scalp bearing hair would be surgically removed from the backside of Dixon's head and sutured into place on the front of his head to create a hairline. A later operation would be necessary to fill in, behind this newly created hairline, plugs of healthy hair.

An operation to **transplant** the strips was performed on 12 November 1976, but by 16 March 1977 no hair was growing on either of the two strips, although the transferred scalp was alive and well. Dixon v. Peters, 306 S.E.2d 477, 479 (Ct.App. N.C.1983).

transplant, heart See also *heart, artificial.*

transplantation (trans"plan-ta'shun) [*trans-* + L. *plantare* to plant] the grafting of tissues taken from the same body or from another. See also entries under *graft.* In dentistry, the insertion, into a prepared dental alveolus, of an autogenous or homologous tooth; it may be a developing tooth germ from the same mouth, or a frozen homologous transplant.

... and then went back to the hospital for a tissue **transplant** on her forearm. Skin was removed from the plaintiff's right thigh and grafted to the area on the left forearm. The grafted skin became black and a second **transplant** operation in the same area had to be performed....

The plaintiff's injury left a scar near her left wrist two to three inches wide and three to four inches long. The skin grafts from her right thigh caused three scars that were slightly larger than the one near her wrist. Mercurdo v. County of Milwaukee, 264 N.W.2d 258–60 (Wis.1978).

transposition (trans"po-zish'un) [*trans-* + L. *positio* placement] the operation of carrying a tissue flap from one situation to another without severing its connection entirely until it is united at its new location.

transposition, colon

On May 22, 1973, Dr. DeMeules performed a surgical procedure which is referred to as a right **colon transposition.** The operation replaced part of his severely damaged esophagus with a segment of the large intestine. Battick v. Stoneman, 421 F.Supp. 213, 217 (D.Vt.1976).

transsexual (trans-seks'u-al) 1. a person affected by transsexualism. 2. a person whose external anatomy has been changed to that of the opposite sex. See also *male* (Hartin case); *reassignment, sex; surgery, cosmetic* (G.B. case); and *transsexualism.*

Dr. Leibman asserted that G.B. "must have this [gender change] surgery to alleviate her emotional problems, prevent them from exacerbation, and to rehabilitate her to the point where she can function as a normal person and participate fully in society."

Dr. Richard Crews declared that, "As a general rule **transsexuals** have an improved psychological, social, and vocational adjustment after **transsexual** surgery. I believe this will prove to be the case for [G.B.]. Numerous attempts by way of therapy, pharmacology, behavioral and disciplinary approaches have generally been unavailing in treating the **transsexual.** Surgery is thus indicated for [G.B.] and I believe she would benefit significantly by it."...

... Adult male **transsexuals,** such as G.B., are not transvestites nor homosexuals but are males who have irreversibly accepted a gender identification as female. (See generally, Stoller, Sex and Gender (1968); Green & Money, Transsexualism and Sex Reassignment (1969) p. 268.) Medical experts agree that the etiology of transsexualism is unknown but that it occurs early in life and is a serious problem of gender role disorientation. (Benjamin, Should Surgery be Performed on Transsexuals, 25 Am.J. of Psychotherapy, pp. 75–75.)

Dr. Leibman, quoted above, describes **transsexuals** as a "... unique group of people who suffer from a profound disorder of sexual gender identity of an unknown cause.... This disorder is almost always associated with secondary emotional illnesses such as adjustment reactions, anxiety neuroses or depressive neuroses. [¶] Psychotherapy has been uniformly unsuccessful in alleviating the primary and secondary illnesses described above. The only treatment which has been found to be effective is hormonal feminization and eventual sex change surgery. In many cases the described illnesses are cured completely."

John Hoopes, M.D., of the Gender Identity Clinic at the Johns Hopkins Medical Institute points out: "Over the years, psychiatrists have tried repeatedly to treat these people without surgery, and the conclusion is inescapable that psychotherapy has not so far solved the problem. The patients have no motivation for psychotherapy and do not want to change back to their biological sex. The high incidence of suicide and self-mutilation among these people testifies to the magnitude of the problem. If the mind cannot be changed to fit the body, then perhaps we should consider changing the body to fit the mind." (Green & Money, Transsexualism and Sex Reassignment, supra, at p. 268.)

The severity of the problem of transsexualism becomes obvious when one contemplates the reality of the male **transsexual's** desperate desire to have normally functioning male genitals removed because the male sex organs are a source of immense psychological distress. **Transsexuals** consider themselves members of the opposite sex cursed with the wrong sexual apparatus. G.B. v. Lackner, 145 Cal.Rptr. 555–7 (Ct.App. Cal.1978).

What is a **transsexual**? A **transsexual** is an individual anatomically of one sex who firmly believes he belongs to the other sex. This belief is so strong that the **transsexual** is obsessed with the desire to have his body, appearance and social status altered to conform to that of his "rightful" gender. They are not homosexual. They consider themselves to be members of the opposite sex cursed with the wrong sexual apparatus. They desire the removal of this apparatus and further surgical assistance in order that they may enter into normal heterosexual relationships. On the contrary, a homosexual enjoys and uses his genitalia with members of his own anatomical sex. Medical Science has not found any organic cause or cure (other than sex reassignment surgery and hormone therapy) for transsexualism, nor has psychotherapy been successful in altering the **transsexual's** identification with the other sex or his desire for surgical change. (Cornell Law Review, vol. 56:963, Transsexualism, Sex Reassignment Surgery and the Law; also see Maryland Law Review, vol. XXXI, 1971, p. 236, Transsexuals in Limbo: The Search for a Legal Definition of Sex; and Connecticut Law Review, vol. 7:288, The Law and Transsexualism: A Faltering Response to a Conceptual Dilemma). Richards v. U.S. Tennis Ass'n, 400 N.Y.S.2d 267, 270–1 (Sup.Ct.N.Y.Cty.1977).

Medical affidavits accompanying the petition reveal that in April 1970, the petitioner underwent surgery removing the male sex organs and creating a functional female primary sex organ. This surgery was supplemented by breast implants in June 1970. The sum effect of these operations rendered the petitioner physiologically and psychologically a female, termed medically a **transsexual**.

The rationale for the rule is found in a report by the Committee on Public Health of the New York Academy of Medicine entitled "Change of Sex on Birth Certificates for Transsexuals" approved on October 4, 1965. The report embodies a study together with recommendations made at the request of the Board of Health of the City of New York with respect to modifications and amendments of birth certificates for **transsexuals**. The report reveals that the male-to-female **transsexual**, such as here, is anatomically and chromosomally a male who is deeply disturbed in his gender orientation and role. He has an overpowering desire to be a woman; to acquire her contour, to function sexually, and to be accepted socially and legally as a female. The male bodily configuration and genitalia are discordant factors which the **transsexual** strives to overcome through hormone treatment, and sometimes, by plastic surgery including the removal of the male genitalia and fashioning artificial female genitalia. Nonetheless, this abnormal individual, advises the report, is genetically a male as shown by chromosome and cell-chromatin studies, and the disorder manifests itself in various types of aberrations from minor to true hermaphroditism, which is a rare condition in humans characterized by the co-existence of both ovarian and testicular tissue....

... The minutes further reveal that the Board was of the opinion that surgery for the **transsexual** is an experimental form of psychotherapy by which mutilating surgery is conducted on a person with the intent of setting his mind at ease, and that nonetheless, does not change the body cells governing sexuality. Hartin v. Director of Bureau of Records, etc., 347 N.Y.S.2d 515–18 (Sup.Ct.N.Y.Cty.1973).

transsexualism (trans-seks'u-ah-lizm) a disturbance of gender identity in which the affected person has overwhelming desire to change anatomic sex stemming from the fixed conviction that he or she is a member of the opposite sex; such persons often seek hormonal and surgical treatment to bring their anatomy into conformity with their belief. Cf. *transvestism*. See also *neocolporrhaphy*; and *surgery, cosmetic* (G.B. case).

Pinneke began life as a male, but quickly became uncomfortable with the male gender identity. After extensive testing, doctors concluded that she had a transsexual personality, and required sex reassignment surgery....

... the District Court declared that the policy of denying Medicaid benefits for sex reassignment surgery where it is a medical necessity [q.v.] for treatment of **transsexualism** is contrary to the provisions of Title XIX of the Social Security Act, 42 U.S.C. § 1396 (1976), and therefore violates the supremacy clause of the United States Constitution....

From this record, it appears that radical sex conversion surgery is the only medical treatment available to relieve or solve the problems of a true transsexual. As noted by the Minnesota Supreme Court in Doe v. Minnesota Department of Public Welfare and Hennepin County Welfare Board, 257 N.W.2d 816, 819 (Minn.1977):

Given the fact that the roots of **transsexualism** are generally implanted early in life, the consensus of medical literature is that psychoanalysis is not a successful mode of treatment for the adult transsexual.... The only medical procedure known to be successful in treating the problem of **transsexualism** is the radical sex conversion surgical procedure requested by Doe in the present case:

It is the alternative that is sobering. In the light of present knowledge, there is no known approach to treatment of **transsexualism** other than the surgical route. Nothing else holds promise. Granted that the surgical route is difficult and clearly second-best to a method of preventing these tragic reversals of gender identity and role, yet it seems to be all that there is to offer at present. Hastings, Postsurgical Adjustment of Male Transsexual Patients, 1 Clinics in Plastic Surgery 335, 344. Pinneke v. Preisser, 623 F.2d 546–9 (8th Cir. 1980).

In 1975, the appellant, hereinafter referred to as G.B. consulted Dr. John Brown, a plastic surgeon, who diagnosed him as suffering from gender identity dysphoria or **transsexualism**....

... Dr. Hoopes, previously quoted, states at page 268: "You would probably never recognize a transsexual as such if you met him casually, or even if you knew him well. I cannot state too emphatically how completely these people assume the role of the opposite sex. The male transsexual looks, dresses, and acts exactly like a woman, and the same is true for his female counterpart. They are not simply transvestites, people who receive pleasure from just wearing the clothes of the opposite sex; nor are they homosexuals, as commonly defined." G.B. v. Lackner, 145 Cal.Rptr. 555–6, 558–9 (Ct.App. Cal.1978).

transurethral resection See *resection, transurethral*.

transverse carpal syndrome See *syndrome, transverse carpal*.

transverse process See *processus accessorius vertebrarum lumbalium*.

transvestism (trans-ves'tizm) [*trans-* + L. *vestitus* clothed] a sexual deviation characterized by overwhelming desire to assume the attire, and be accepted as a member, of the opposite sex; called also *cross dressing* and *eonism.* Cf. *transsexualism.*

The medical testimony was that Mr. Tommie had **transvestite** tendencies and that his sexual practices and fantasies were unusual, but that they were not such as would constitute a disease in either the medical or the ordinary sense of the word. Connecticut General Life Ins. Co. v. Tommie, 619 S.W.2d 199, 203 (Ct.Civ.App.Tex.1981).

transvestite (trans-ves'tīt) an individual exhibiting transvestism.

trapezius muscle See *musculus trapezius.*

trapezius spasm See *spasm;* and *musculus trapezius.*

trauma (traw'mah), pl. *traumas* or *trau'mata* [L.; Gr.] a wound or injury, whether physical or psychic.

In near drowning situations, the **trauma** consists of a continuing insult to the body, rather than a single event. In near drowning situations, when death is the result of hypoxia, the **trauma** continues until such time as adequate oxygenation has taken place to restore arterial blood gas and acid base levels. Nazaroff v. Super. Ct. in and for Cty. of Santa Cruz, 145 Cal. Rptr. 657, 659 (Ct.App.Cal.1978).

First, we cannot agree with the trial court that on receiving the 1960 diagnosis of traumatic arthritis, plaintiff had reason to believe even then that a **trauma** ("and **trauma** includes surgery") had coincided with a negligent act and some damage had resulted....

It is true that "**trauma**" has been defined as "an injury (as a wound)," to living tissue, with the example of surgery being given. Webster's Seventh New Collegiate Dictionary (1967), 942. The medical definition has been simply stated as "a wound or injury, whether physical or psychic," without a reference to surgery. Dorland's Illustrated Medical Dictionary, 25th ed. (1974), 1633. Exnicious v. U.S., 563 F.2d 418, 424 (10th Cir. 1977).

The evidence in question was the testimony of one of claimant's treating physicians who testified:

It has been recognized that **trauma** does play a part in the development of malignant lesions, and this is particularly true of malignant melanomas. Almost all cases of melanoma will give a history of some form of injury or chronic irritation to a preexisting lesion. The direct effect is difficult to prove except by inference. [Charleston Shipyards v. Lawson, 227 F.2d 110, 112 (4th Cir. 1955).] Cox v. Ulysses Cooperative Oil and Supply Co., 544 P.2d 363, 371 (Kan.1975).

Other Authorities: Matter of Iannelli, 384 A.2d 1104, 1108–10 (Super.Ct.N.J.1978); Hartford Acc. & Indem. Co. v. Contreras, 498 S.W.2d 419, 421–2 (Ct.Civ.App.Tex.1973); Sheppard v. Revlon, Inc., 267 So.2d 662–3 (Dist.Ct.App.Fla.1972).

trauma, psychic an emotional shock that makes a lasting impression on the mind, especially upon the subconscious mind.

In the absence of contemporaneous or consequential physical injury, courts have been reluctant to permit recovery for negligently caused **psychological trauma**, with ensuing emotional harm alone (see Restatement, Torts 2d, § 436A; Prosser, Torts [4th ed.], op. cit., pp. 328–330, and cases collected; 2 Harp-

er and James, Law of Torts, op. cit., pp. 1031–1032, and cases collected....

There have developed, however, two exceptions. The first is the minority rule permitting recovery for emotional harm resulting from negligent transmission by a telegraph company of a message announcing death....

The second exception permits recovery for emotional harm to a close relative resulting from negligent mishandling of a corpse (see Prosser, op. cit., pp. 329–330, and cases collected). Johnson v. State, 334 N.E.2d 590, 592 (N.Y.1975).

trauma, transfer

There has been considerable judicial and scientific recognition of the phenomenon known as "**transfer trauma**." See Bracco v. Lackner, 462 F.Supp. 436, 444–45 (N.D.Cal.1978); Klein v. Mathews, 430 F.Supp. 1005, 1009–10 (D.N.J.1977); Burchette v. Dumpson, 387 F.Supp. 812, 819 (E.D.N.Y.1974). **Transfer trauma** is characterized by physical and emotional deterioration as well as by increased rates of mortality. "The basic principle of the phenomenon is the recognition that the transfer of geriatric patients to any unfamiliar surroundings produces an increased rate of morbidity and mortality." Bracco v. Lackner, supra at 445. The degree to which this phenomenon is applicable to the leprosy patients presently resisting transfer from Hale Mohalu to Leahi Hospital is unclear on this record. Brede v. Director for Dept. of Health, etc., 616 F.2d 407, 412 (9th Cir. 1980).

traumatic (traw-mat'ik) [Gr. *traumatikos*] pertaining to, occurring as the result of, or causing trauma.

Accordingly, the Court stated that a "**traumatic** event" would ordinarily entail a **traumatic** injury suffered as a result of an external force or violence but might also "be found in some situations [having a "**traumatic** origin"] which do not literally fall within the external force or violence concept...." Gerba v. Public Emp. Retirem. Sys. Trustees, 416 A.2d 314, 319–20 (N.J.1980).

While the word "**traumatic**," itself, is often used in the sense of a blow only, by definition it also includes wounds such as sprains and dislocations....

... So, by the statute, a **traumatic** hernia is damage or harm of sufficient magnitude to tear the abdominal wall. Figueroa v. Industrial Commission, 543 P.2d 785, 788 (Ariz.1975).

A resort to the definition of terms in interpreting statutory enactments is often beneficial. State v. Harpham, 2 Ariz.App. 478, 410 P.2d 100 (1966). The Legislature's use of the word "**traumatic**" in subsection 1 [A.R.S. § 23–1043] is most significant. Black's Law Dictionary, 4th Edition Rev., defines "**traumatic**" as an adjective meaning "caused by or resulting from a wound or any external injury...." The term has received similar definition in workmen's compensation cases. In Smith v. Garside, 76 Nev. 377, 355 P.2d 849, 852 (1960), the Nevada Supreme Court said:

"**Traumatic**" (derived from the Greek trauma, a wound) is defined by Webster as "of, pertaining to, or resulting from a trauma; caused by a wound, injury or shock...." This is even further confined [sic] by the Funk & Wagnall definition relied on in Higgens v. Department of Labor & Industries, infra: "any injury to the body caused by violence." 355 P.2d at 852....

... The use of the word "traumatic" as defined above is not ambiguous. The inescapable conclusion is that the Legislature intended to differentiate those hernias resulting from a **traumatic** puncture or tear of the external abdominal wall from those which more typically result from a combination of a less severe injury or strain, and a congenital weakness of body tissue. Figueroa v. Industrial Com'n, 529 P.2d 1188, 1192–3 (Ct.App.Ariz.1975), vacated 543 P.2d 785 (Ariz.1975).

treacle (tre'k'l) [Gr. *thēriaka*] a syrupy substance or mixture; molasses.

treatment (trēt'ment) the management and care of a patient for the purpose of combating disease or disorder. See also under *maneuver; method; technique; tests* and *therapy.*

[In Lucito v. Louisiana Hospital Service, Inc., 392 So.2d 700 (La.App.3rd Cir. 1980), an action by an insured to recover medical benefits pursuant to a group hospitalization policy which did not define "**treatment**" or "diagnostic studies", this court resolved the ambiguity in favor of coverage and made the following observation:

In Baque v. Pan-American Life Insurance Company, 313 So. 2d 293 (La.App.3rd Cir. 1975), writ refused 318 So.2d 52 (La. 1975), this Court had occasion to define the word "**treatment**":

Although the Louisiana jurisprudence reveals no case defining "**treatment**", we find applicable the following definition of that term by the courts of sister states: "In common parlance and often in the law, '**treatment**' is the broad term covering all the steps taken to effect a cure of the injury or disease. It includes examination and diagnosis, as well as application of remedies", Hester v. Ford, 221 Ala. 592, 130 So. 203, 206 (1930). See also Stephens v. Williams, 226 Ala. 534, 147 So. 608 (1933); Kirschner v. Equitable Life Insurance Society, 157 Misc. 635, 284 N.Y.S. 506, 510 (1935); Permanent Edition, Words and Phrases, Volume 42A, Treatment, p. 45. We believe that the foregoing definition of the word "**treatment**" accords with logic and common sense.

Under this rather broad definition of the word "**treatment**" which this court has utilized, diagnostic tests may be properly regarded as part of the **treatment**.
392 So.2d 700, at 702. See also: Succession of Cormier, 80 So.2d 571 (La.App. 1st Cir. 1955) per Tate, J.]. Koslow v. E. R. Desormeaux, Inc., 428 So.2d 1275–1277 (La.Ct. of App. 1983).

... Schmit articulates three factors to be considered in determining when **treatment** ceases: (1) whether there is a relationship between physician and patient with regard to the illness; (2) whether the physician is attending and examining the patient; and (3) whether there is something more to be done. [Schmit v. Esser] 183 Minn. [354] at 358–59, 236 N.W. at 625. Jewson v. Mayo Clinic, 691 F.2d 405, 408 (8th Cir. 1982).

Significantly, however, for our purposes, this power of parents, managing conservators and guardians to consent to surgical intrusions upon the person of the minor or ward is limited to the power to consent to medical "**treatment**." See Tex. Fam.Code Ann. § 12.04(6) (Vernon Supp.1978–1979); Tex. Prob.Code Ann. § 229 (Vernon 1956); In re Guardianship of

Henson, 551 S.W.2d 136 (Tex.Civ.App.—Corpus Christi 1977, writ ref'd n.r.e.). Even ascribing to the word "**treatment**" its broadest definition, it is, nevertheless, limited to "the steps taken to effect a cure of an injury or disease ... including examination and diagnosis as well as application of remedies." Black's Law Dictionary 1673 (rev. 4th ed. 1968).

We cannot accept the guardian's argument that a donor nephrectomy constitutes medical **treatment** for the donor. Little v. Little, 576 S.W.2d 493, 495 (Ct.Civ.App.Tex.1979).
Other Authorities: Bickel v. City of Chicago, 323 N.E.2d 832, 835 (App.Ct.Ill.1975); Mutual Life Ins. Co. of New York v. Bishop, 209 S.E.2d 223, 228–9 (Ct.App.Ga.1974).

treatment, Carrel's; treatment, Carrel-Dakin treatment of wounds, based on thorough exposure of the wound, removal of all foreign material and divitalized tissue, meticulous cleansing, and repeated irrigation with a dilute sodium hypochlorite solution. The adjacent skin is protected with petrolatum gauze.

treatment, continuous

Initially, attention must be directed to whether the **continuous treatment** doctrine is applicable in the present case. Under that rule, the time in which to bring a malpractice action is stayed "when the course of treatment which includes the wrongful acts or omissions has run continuously and is related to the same original condition or complaint" (Borgia v. City of New York, 12 N.Y.2d 151, 155, 237 N.Y.S.2d 319, 187 N.E.2d 777). The concern, of course, is whether there has been **continuous treatment**, and not merely a continuing relation between physician and patient....

As a starting point, **continuous treatment** does not contemplate circumstances where a patient initiates return visits merely to have his or her condition checked (see id.). The Statute of Limitations may begin to run "once a hospital or physician considers the patient's treatment to be completed and does not request the patient to return for further examination" (1 Weinstein-Korn-Miller, NY Civ Prac, par. 214–a.03, p. 2–321; cf. Davis v. City of New York, 38 N.Y.2d 257, 379 N.Y.S.2d 721, 342 N.E.2d 516). This is not to say, however, that a complete discharge by a physician forever bars a finding of **continuing treatment**. Included within the scope of "**continuous treatment**" is a timely return visit instigated by the patient to complain about and seek treatment for a matter related to the initial treatment. Thus, there will be **continuing treatment** when a patient, instructed that he or she does not need further attention, soon returns to the doctor because of continued pain in that area for which medical attention was first sought. McDermott v. Torre, 452 N.Y.S.2d 351, 353–4 (N.Y.1982).

treatment, involuntary

A "person requiring treatment" is defined under Subsection 25–03.1–02(11), N.D.C.C.:
"11. 'Person requiring treatment' means either a person:
a. Who is severely mentally ill; or
b. Who is mentally ill, an alcoholic, or drug addict, and there is a reasonable expectation that if the person is not hospitalized there exists a serious risk of harm to himself, others or property. 'Serious risk of harm' means a substantial likelihood of:
"(1) Suicide as manifested by suicidal threats, attempts, or significant depression relevant to suicidal potential; or

"(2) Killing or inflicting serious bodily harm on another person, inflicting significant property damage, as manifested by acts or threats; or

"(3) Substantial deterioration in physical health, or substantial injury, disease, or death resulting from poor self-control or judgment in providing one's shelter, nutrition, or personal care."

For the court to order **involuntary treatment** of a respondent the petitioner must prove by clear and convincing evidence that the respondent is a person requiring treatment. Section 25–03.1–19, N.D.C.C. In Interest of Rambousek, 331 N.W.2d 548–9 (N.D.1983).

treatment, medcosonolator

... he was administered **medcosonolator treatments** (a combination of ultrasonic sound and electrical stimulation). Kelly v. International Union, etc., 386 So.2d 1060, 1062 (Ct.App.La. 1980).

treatment, non-medical See *rehabilitation*.

treatment, refusal of

In the case at bar, claimant's refusal to submit to a second myelogram was based upon his reaction to the first one, which assertedly resulted in the development of phlebitis. "Well, my legs swelled and the veins jumped out as big as my fingers. I hemorrhaged through the nose and mouth. I got chills and fever. A friend of mine had to rush me to the hospital. I couldn't walk". Claimant takes the position that a ruptured disc may be diagnosed and repaired without the performance of a myelogram, and that its indiscriminate use as a diagnostic technique can lead to serious and harmful side effects [3]. [[3] The following authorities are cited in claimant's brief before the lower court: "An Evaluation of Myelography in the Diagnosis of Intervertebral Disc Lesions of the Low Back" by Dr. J. Albert Key and Dr. Lee T. Ford, Journal of Bone and Joint Surgery, Volume 32A at page 306; "Court Room Medicine" by Marshall Houts at page 91; "Lesions of the Lumbar Intervertebral Disc" by Dr. R. Glen Spurling, at page 73. It is asserted that "the Mayo Clinic, in a recent study, rated the effectiveness of myelography at 72.7% and categorically condemned the indiscriminate use of myelography as a diagnostic technique."] Bostic v. Dreher, 213 A.2d 118, 121 (Super.Ct.Pa.1965).

treatment, surgical that in which surgical methods are those chiefly employed.

Benefits shall not be payable for any loss to which a contributing cause is

"(a) ...

"(b) disease, bodily or mental infirmity, or medical or **surgical treatment** thereof; or

"(c) ..."

The trial court recognized that "the great weight of authority is that '**surgical treatment**' includes a surgical procedure designed for diagnostic purposes" and cited many of the cases hereinafter considered. He believed however that a fact question was created because Dr. DeKraay made a medical distinction between diagnosis and treatment....

We do not believe that a doctor's technical distinction between "diagnosis" and "treatment" is sufficient to make a factual issue as to the meaning of the policy. The overwhelming weight of authority is that accidents resulting from diagnostic procedures are excluded from coverage by the language found in this policy as a matter of law.

The court said: " 'The meaning of the word "treatment" as used in the policy must be given a reasonable scope. It includes not merely the actual operation in a surgical case or the giving of a prescription in a nonsurgical case, but also the preliminary examination, including sometimes an exploratory operation or an exploratory examination. The treatment may, and generally does, include three stages: Preliminary, main, and final. Whatever is usually done to the patient or administered to him by a skilled physician or surgeon in any one of these stages is properly included under the term "treatment," even thought it may not be an indispensable prerequisite.' Order of United Commercial Travelers v. Shane, 8 Cir., 64 F.2d 55, 59. The opinion in this case quoted from, cites and relies upon International Travelers Association v. Yates, 29 S.W.2d 980, by the Texas Commission of Appeals and Flint v. Travelers Insurance Co., Tex.Civ.App., 43 S.W. 1079. We believe that the term 'medical and **surgical treatment**' has the legal significance and meaning, as is set out in the opinion quoted above. Within such legal meaning must be included not only what the physician or surgeon views as treatment, that is, things done in an effort to relieve or cure a physical disease or infirmity, but also all of the things performed by a doctor or a surgeon on the body of the patient in the diagnosis of or in preparation for cure...." McKay v. Bankers Life Co., 187 N.W.2d 736–8, 740 (Iowa 1971).

tremolite (fiber)

On January 19, 1977, after preliminary findings of NIOSH showed that workers exposed to **tremolytic talc** died from lung cancer and other respiratory diseases at significantly higher rates than normal populations, the Assistant Secretary cancelled FIM #74–92 [Osha Field Information Manual]. He expressly noted "that a **tremolite fiber** is an asbestos fiber under OSHA's asbestos standard."...

... The inspector took air and bulk samples to determine whether workers were exposed to asbestos. Laboratory analysis of the samples indicated the presence of anthophyllite and **tremolite fibers**, which are defined by OSHA as asbestos. See 29 C.F.R. § 1910.1001(a)(1). R. T. Vanderbilt Co. v. Occ. Saf. & H. Rev. Com'n, 708 F.2d 570, 573 (11th Cir. 1983).

trenchhand See *arteritis*; and *hand, trench*.

Trendelenberg position See *position, Trendelenberg's*.

Trendelenburg test See *test, Trendelenburg's*.

trephination See *trephine*.

trephine (trĕ-fīn′, trĕ-fēn′) [L. *trephina*] a crown saw for removing a circular disk of bone, chiefly from the skull.

On September 2, 1977, he underwent bilateral skull **trephination**, a surgical process in which small openings are made in the skull to contain undue accumulations of fluids between the surface of the brain and the undersurface of the skull. Naylor v. La. Dep't of Public Highways, 423 So.2d 674, 684–5 (Ct.App. La.1982).

Doctor Feinstein testified that he told Mrs. Belshaw that her husband had had a hemorrhage during surgery. He did not believe that he ever told her that it occurred during a **trephina-**

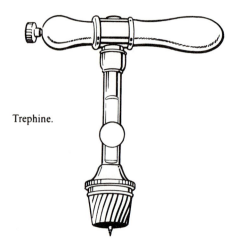

Trephine.

tion, nor did he ever tell the Belshaws that a surgical instrument had lacerated or cut plaintiff's brain....

... In using the **trephine** to cut out a bony segment of the skull there are four safeguards upon which the surgeon relies. There are: (1) the X-rays which indicate the thickness of the skull and which guide the surgeon in setting the guard on the **trephine**; (2) the guard on the **trephine**; (3) the fine probe which the surgeon may use to test the opening in the skull; and (4) the surgeon's own sense of touch which enables him to determine the difference between tissue and bone. Belshaw v. Feinstein, 65 Cal.Rptr. 788, 792, 796 (Ct.App.Cal.1968).

TRI See *trichloroethylene.*

triamcinolone (tri″am-sin′o-lōn) [USP] chemical name: 9-fluoro-11β,16 α,17,21-tetrahydroxypregna-1,4-diene-3,20-dione. A potent synthetic glucocorticoid, $C_{21}H_{27}FO_6$, occurring as a white or almost white, crystalline powder, having practically no mineralocorticoid activity; used in the treatment of various conditions responsive to the anti-inflammatory action of glucocorticoids, administered orally.

triamcinolone acetonide [USP], the acetonide ester of triamcinolone, $C_{24}H_{31}FO_6$, occurring as a white to cream-colored, crystalline powder; applied topically to the skin and oral mucosa or administered by intra-articular, intrabursal, intramuscular, and intradermal injection.

In 1965, Dr. Marks began using an injectible steroid called **Kenalog-40** which had recently been put on the market by defendant Squibb & Sons. From 1965 to 1970, Dr. Marks gave plaintiff injections of **Kenalog-40**, together with oral and topical steroids, at approximately two week intervals. Hill v. Squibb & Sons, E.R., 592 P.2d 1383, 1385 (Mont.1979).

triamcinolone hexacetonide [USP], the hexacetonide ester of triamcinolone, $C_{30}H_{41}FO_7$, occurring as a white to cream-colored powder; it is administered by intra-articular or by intralesional or sublesional injection for treatment of arthritis or of inflammatory skin lesions, respectively.

triangle (tri′ang-g'l) [L. *triangulum; tres* three + *angulus* angle] a three-cornered area, figure, or object. See also *trigone;* and *trigonum.*

Tribolium (tri-bo′le-um) a genus of small beetles that live in and are very destructive to flour and other cereal products. The two most common species, *T. confu'sum* and *T. casta'neum*, are reddish brown in color and 3.5 mm. in length.

Analysis of flour samples in Mobile by John Litton, an insect taxonomist with the Department of Agriculture, revealed that six species of insects were present: Lasioderma serricorne (cigarette beetle), Carpophilus diamiatus (corn sap beetle), Typhaea stercorea (hairy fungus beetle), Trogoderma glabrum (no common name given), **Triboleum** castaneum (red flour beetle), Oryaephilus surinamensis (saw toothed grain beetle).

The life cycle from egg to adult of these six insects is about thirty days but a life cycle of up to six weeks would not be unusual for most of them. The life span, i.e., the time from birth until death, of these six ranges from a month to several years. U.S. v. Central Gulf Steamship Corp., 340 F.Supp. 473, (E.D. La.1972), vacated and remanded 517 F.2d 687 (5th Cir. 1975).

Tribolium casteneum (Hbst.) is commonly called the red flour beetle....

... The red flour beetle and the saw-toothed grain beetle usually are found in cereal products. U.S. v. Central Gulf Steamship Corp., 321 F.Supp. 945, 951 (E.D.La.1970).

trichina (trĭ-ki′nah), pl. *trichi'nae*. an individual organism of the genus *Trichinella.*

trichinae (trĭ-ki′ne) plural of *trichina.*

Trichinella (trik″ĭ-nel′ah) [Gr. *trichinos* of hair] a genus of nematode parasites of the superfamily Trichuroidea.

Trichinella spiralis the etiologic agent of trichinosis, one of the smallest of the parasitic nematodes, being only about 1.5 mm. in length. It is found coiled in a cyst in the muscles of the bear, rat, pig, and man. When infected meat is eaten without proper cooking the cyst dissolves, the parasite matures, deposits its larvae in the deep mucosa, whence they enter the lymphatics, are carried to all parts of the body, and again encyst. An extract of *Trichinella* larvae is used in an intradermal skin test for trichinosis. Called also *pork worm.*

It has been scientifically established that thorough cooking to 137°F. will destroy all **trichinae**, and the trial court in the present case presumably took judicial notice of this fact. Huebner v. Hunter Packing Co., 375 N.E.2d 873, 875 (App.Ct.Ill.1978).

Trichinella spiralis encapsulated in muscle.

This case presents an issue of first impression in Arizona: whether the doctrine of strict liability should be applied against a defendant wholesale meat packer who sells fresh raw pork containing **trichina** larvae. A temperature of 137° is sufficient to kill **trichina** larvae. Scheller v. Wilson Certified Foods, Inc., 559 P.2d 1074–6 (Ct.App.Ariz.1976).

Under Evid.R. 9(2)(e) the court takes judicial notice of facts contained in two United States Department of Agriculture (U.S. D.A.) publications: "Facts About Trichinosis," Agriculture Research Bulletin ARS 91–72 (April 1969), and "Trichinosis," Leaflet No. 428, U.S.D.A. (revised September 1968). The disease is caused by parasitic worms called trichinae (**Trichinella spiralis**) and may infect humans eating raw or under-cooked pork in which the parasite is encysted. On ingestion of contaminated meat the parasites travel into the intestinal tract where they reproduce and move through the bloodstream to invade the voluntary muscles, growing and eventually becoming encysted therein. When the parasites reach the intestines they may cause upset stomach, vomiting, diarrhea and other symptoms of intestinal disorder. During the period of migration and encystment the host may have muscular pain, rising fever, headaches and prostration. When the larvae reach the muscles, swelling of the face and other parts of the body, sore eyes, hemorrhaging under the skin, sore throat, headache, fever and difficulty breathing commonly are experienced. After encystment these symptoms gradually may disappear although muscle stiffness can linger in severe cases. Most patients suffering from the disease recover with proper treatment....

... there is no completely effective method for detecting **trichinae** in raw pork. As a result the U.S.D.A. does not require inspection of unprocessed meat sold for human consumption. However, it is a known scientific fact that heating raw pork above a temperature of 137°F. will destroy the parasite and render the meat safe to eat. Thorough cooking is the only means of insuring that raw pork is completely free of **trichinae**. Hollinger v. Shoppers Paradise of New Jersey, Inc., 340 A.2d 687, 690–1 (Super.Ct.N.J.1975).

trichinosis (trik″ĭ-no′sis) a disease due to infection with trichinae. It is produced by eating undercooked meat containing *Trichinella spiralis*. It is attended in the early stages by diarrhea, nausea, colic, and fever, and later by stiffness, pain, swelling of the muscles, fever, eosinophilia, circumorbital edema, splinter hemorrhages, sweating, and insomnia. See also *Trichinella spiralis*.

Trichinosis is a disease caused in humans by eating the meat of an animal which contains trichinella spiralis larvae, or trichinae. When a human eats pork containing trichinae, the capsule in which they are encased is dissolved during the digestive process and the larvae pass into the small intestine. The trichinae then reach adulthood and reproduce, causing the disease to spread via the lymph glands through the body and to lodge in the muscles, including the heart. It is a severe and painful disease, although rarely fatal. 11 Proof of Facts 373 (Trichinosis) (1961). Huebner v. Hunter Packing Co., 375 N.E.2d 873, 875 (App.Ct.Ill.1978).

Trichinosis is a disease caused by eating raw or undercooked pork containing parasitic worms. "Facts About Trichinosis", 3, 4, Agricultural Research Service, U.S. Department of Agriculture (April 1969). Scheller v. Wilson Certified Foods, Inc., 559 P.2d 1074, 1076 (Ct.App.Ariz.1976).

Some of these chops were prepared by Mrs. Hollinger and consumed by her, her husband and their four children on October 10, 1971. Within sometime thereafter (the precise period is unclear) all the family members experienced some muscle pain, nausea and diarrhea; in the case of Mrs. Hollinger the symptoms were aggravated and included chest pains, heavy perspiration, skin rash and swelling of various parts of the body. This led to her hospitalization, where it was determined that she suffered from a parasitic infection diagnosed as **trichinosis**. Hollinger v. Shoppers Paradise of New Jersey, Inc., 340 A.2d 687, 690 (Super.Ct.N.J.1975).

trichloroacetic acid See *acid, trichloroacetic*

trichloroethylene (tri″klo-ro-eth′ĭ-lēn) chemical name: trichloroethene. A clear, colorless, or blue, mobile liquid, C_2HCl_3, used as an inhalation anesthetic for short operative procedures. It is widely used as an industrial solvent, and exposure to its vapor in high concentrations has caused some poisonings, some of which were fatal. Called also *ethinyl trichloride*.

There is undisputed evidence that **trichloroethylene**, a degreasing cleaning agent, was used by employees for many purposes in Employer's plant. Despite some discrepancy in terminology, the cleaning agent used in the plant had toxic properties.

... cleaning solvent occasioned when a full drum or bucket of the solvent spilled on the floor at Employer's plant. C.T.S. Corp. v. Schoulton, 383 N.E.2d 293–4 (Ind.1978).

Plaintiff, as administratrix, brought this diversity action against Hooker Chemical Corporation, a manufacturer of **trichloroethylene** (hereinafter called "TRI")....

Hooker had also prepared and submitted to Boeing a "Data Sheet for Toxicological and Safe Handling Information" which listed the following health hazards from inhalation of **TRI** vapor:

Victim may experience nausea and vomiting, drowsiness, acquire an attitude of irresponsibility and behave in a manner resembling any stage of alcoholic intoxication.

In addition to the warnings submitted by Hooker, Boeing had in its possession Chemical Safety Data Sheet SD–14 prepared by the Manufacturing Chemists Association (MCA) which discussed the safe handling and use of **TRI**. The fifteen page MCA data sheet listed several health hazards including the possibility of death from acute and subacute **TRI** poisoning....

The MCA data sheet provides in pertinent part:

10.1.   HEALTH HAZARDS

10.1.1.   **Trichloroethylene** may be harmful by inhalation, by contact with skin or mucous membranes or when taken by mouth However, if proper precautions are constantly observed, this compound may be handled with safety. Prolonged, excessive, or repeated exposures to the liquid, or to atmospheric concentrations of the vapor above those recommended below are hazardous....

10.1.4.1.   Acute Poisoning

When a worker inhales an excessive amount of **trichloroethylene** vapor within a short period of time, the symptoms are essentially those of production of anesthesia. There may be, at first, irritation of the eyes, nose and throat, then dizziness, nausea, vomiting and gradual suppression of consciousness. The picture which develops depends upon the concentration inhaled and the duration of inhalation. If the concentration is high and inhalation prolonged, there will eventually be complete suppression of pain sense and almost complete loss of muscular activity. After a period of very rapid breathing, the respiration and circulation may fall and death follow. High concentrations of **trichloroethylene** may prevent proper utilization of the oxygen of the blood by the tissues. When this condition is present, physical activity may lead to severe or even fatal circulatory failure....

10.1.4.2. **Subacute Poisoning**

Subacute **trichloroethylene** poisoning may result from prolonged or repeated work in an atmosphere containing high concentrations of **trichloroethylene** but under conditions in which the amount absorbed is not sufficient to cause loss of consciousness. Dougherty v. Hooker Chemical Corp., 540 F.2d 174–6, 180 (3d Cir. 1976).

The attending physician for the claimant, based upon his observation and treatment, together with reports from an internist and neurological consultant, gave his opinion that the claimant was suffering from peripheral neuritis, caused by **trichloroethylene** poisoning resulting from exposure to that solvent. Hassell v. Oxford Filing Supply Co., Inc., 230 N.Y.S.2d 866, 867 (3d Dept. 1962).

triethylene glycol

The source of the parties' controversy is the Index's treatment of **triethylene glycol**, a chemical indispensable to the operation of plaintiff's glycol vaporizer. It is **triethylene glycol** which, when vaporized in plaintiff's appliance, had been used as a germicidal agent to disinfect the air in hospitals, laboratories and other places where germ-free environments were required. Demuth Development Corp. v. Merck & Co., Inc., 432 F.Supp. 990–1 (E.D.N.Y.1977).

trifluoperazine hydrochloride (tri″floo-o-pār′ah-zēn) [USP] chemical name: 10-[3-(4-methyl-1-piperazinyl)propyl]-2-(trifluoromethyl)-10H-phenothiazine dihydrochloride. An antipsychotic agent, $C_{21}H_{24}F_3N_3S$ · 2HCl, occurring as a white to pale yellow, crystalline powder; administered orally and intramuscularly.

On September 1, he was placed on two milligrams of **stelazine** (an antipsychotic medication) three times a day; this dosage was increased until September 8, when the sergeant was receiving ten milligrams three times a day. Johnson v. U.S., 409 F.Supp. 1283, 1287 (M.D.Fla.1976), reversed and remanded 576 F.2d 606 (5th Cir. 1978).

trigger finger See *finger, trigger.*

trigeminal nerve See *nervus trigeminus.*

trigone (tri′gōn) a triangular area (trigonum [NA]). See also *triangle.*

trigonitis (trig″o-ni′tis) [*trigone* + *-itis*] inflammation or localized hyperemia of the trigone of the bladder. See also *trigonum vesicae.* Cited in Capaldi v. Weinberger, 391 F.Supp. 502, 505 (E.D.Pa.1975).

trigonum (tri-go′num), pl. *trigo′na* [L.; Gr. *trigōnon* triangle] a three-cornered area; [NA] a general term for a triangular area. Called also *triangle* and *trigone.*

trigonum femorale [NA], femoral trigone: a triangular area bounded superiorly by the inguinal ligament, laterally by the sartorius muscle, and medially by the adductor longus muscle; called also *Scarpa's triangle.* See also *ligamentum inguinale; musculus adductor longus;* and *musculus sartorius.*

The initial injury occurred in the area of his upper thigh close to the groin. It was described as a blood hematoma with the tearing of tissue and the lymphatic channels in an area known as **Scarpa's triangle.** Pike v. Roe, 516 P.2d 972–3 (Kan.1973).

trigonum vesicae [NA]; **trigonum vesicae** [Lieutaudi] trigone of bladder: a smooth triangular portion of the mucous membrane at the base of the bladder; it is bounded behind by the interureteric fold and ends in front in the uvula of the bladder.

trimalleolar See *malleolus.*

trimester (tri-mes′ter) a period of three months.

For the stage prior to approximately the end of the first **trimester**, the abortion decision and its effectuation must be left to the medical judgment of the pregnant woman's attending physician. Roe v. Wade, 410 U.S. 113, 164, 93 S.Ct. 705, 732, 35 L.Ed.2d 147 (1973).

triplegia (tri-ple′je-ah) [*tri-* + Gr. *plēgē* stroke] paralysis of three of the extremities.

Plaintiff Richard is **triplegic** as a result of this accident, paralyzed from the middle of the chest down. He has lost all bladder, bowel and sexual function. In addition, there are complications associated with the left side of his entire body, ranging from his left eye to a left arm which is practically useless. Rodriguez v. McDonnell Douglas Corp., 151 Cal.Rptr. 399, 413 (Ct.App.Cal.1978).

TRIS (tris[hydroxymethyl]aminomethane) See *tromethamine.*

trismus (triz′mus) [Gr. *trismos* grating, grinding] motor disturbance of the trigeminal nerve, especially spasm of the masticatory muscles, with difficulty in opening the mouth (lockjaw); a characteristic early symptom of tetanus.

He could not open her mouth because her jaws were locked in **trismus**, a muscle spasm, so he attempted to establish an airway by surgical means. Marek v. U.S., 639 F.2d 1164–5 (5th Cir. 1981).

Plaintiff Sacawa brought this malpractice action against defendant Polikoff, a licensed dentist, alleging that defendant was negligent in failing to take proper measures to prevent **trismus** (lockjaw) from developing after he had performed dental work on plaintiff. Sacawa v. Polikoff, 375 A.2d 279–80 (Super.Ct. N.J.1977).

tritium (trit′e-um, trish′e-um) [Gr. *tritos* third] the mass three isotope of hydrogen, ^3H, a radioactive gas obtained by bombardment of beryllium in the cyclotron with deuterium ions. It has a half-life of about 31 years and is used as an indicator or tracer in metabolic studies. Cf. *deuterium* and *protium.*

He testified that a dose of radiation from **tritium** is the same as a dose of radiation from X rays. He stated that the quality factor of **tritium** is to be revised downward from 1.7 to 1.0, meaning **tritium** has a lesser ability to damage living cells than was previously thought. In conventional terms, **tritium** does not concentrate in the human body....

... He stated that if 2,000 curies of **tritium** are released at the Rulison site over a one-year period (as the flaring plans contemplate), and this amount is deposited in the environment at a rate and in concentrations consonant with the normal precipitation pattern, the maximum dose any person will receive will be 0.0025 rem. Crowther v. Seaborg, 312 F.Supp. 1205, 1228 (D.Colo.1970).

trocar (tro'kar) [Fr. *trois quarts* three quarters] a sharp-pointed instrument equipped with a cannula, used to puncture the wall of a body cavity and withdraw fluid.

trochanter (tro-kan'ter) [L.; Gr. *trochantēr*] either of the two processes below the neck of the femur.

trochanter, greater See *trochanter major*.

trochanter, lesser See *trochanter minor*.

trochanter major [NA], greater trochanter: a broad, flat process at the upper end of the lateral surface of the femur, to which several muscles are attached.

The top end of the rod is anchored to the **greater trochanter** by use of an appropriate anchoring plate, and a cap is screwed on the top end of the rod. If you make the rod too long there will be irritation underneath the skin where the upper end of the rod sticks out of the saddle of the **greater trouchanter**. If it sticks out three inches you will get more irritation and will definitely get a bursitis which will become inflamed, redden, and eventually burst as in this case. Pfeiffer v. Salas, 271 N.E.2d 750, 752 (Mass.1971).

trochanter minor [NA], lesser trochanter: a short conical process projecting medially from the lower part of the posterior border of the base of the neck of the femur.

tromethamine (tro-meth'ah-mēn) [USP] chemical name: 2-amino-2-(hydromethyl)-1,3-propanediol. An amine base, $C_4H_{11}NO_3$, occurring as a white crystalline powder; used intravenously as an alkalizer for the correction of metabolic acidosis. Called also *THAM, TRIS* and *tris(hydroxymethyl)aminomethane*.

In February 1977, the National Cancer Institute published preliminary, unverified results of tests indicating that when **Tris** was fed daily in massive doses to cancer-prone rats and mice over extended periods of time, these rats and mice developed cancer. These testing procedures had not previously been applied to nonconsumable articles, such as children's sleepwear. Although there is no direct evidence linking **Tris** to cancer in humans based in large part on this very preliminary data, the Consumer Product Safety Commission issued regulations declaring **Tris** and all fabrics, yarns, and fibers treated with **Tris** and all apparel treated with **Tris** intended for use by children, to be "banned hazardous substances" under the Federal Hazardous Substance Act. U.S. Cong. Sen. Hearings before the Judiciary Comm. (Tris Hearing Panel) on S. 1503, 95th Cong. 1st Sess., 1977 at 5–6.

tropocollagen (tro"po-kol'ah-jen) [Gr. *tropē* a turning + *collagen*] the molecular unit of collagen fibrils, about 1.4 nm. wide and 280 nm. long. It is a helical structure consisting of three polypeptide chains, each chain composed of about a thousand amino acids coiled around each other to form a spiral; tropocollagen is rich in glycine, proline, and hydroxyproline and hydroxylysine, all types of collagen being formed by interaction of these units.

trypsin (trip'sin) [Gr. *tryein* to rub + pe*psin*] a proteolytic enzyme formed in the intestine by the action of enterokinase on trypsinogen, so named by Willy Kühne, in 1874. It is an endoproteinase, acting on peptide linkages containing the carboxyl group of either lysine or arginine. See also *enzyme*; and *ileum* (both Armour case).

TSS See *syndrome, toxic shock*.

tuba (too'bah), pl. *tu'bae* [L. "trumpet"] a tube: an elongated hollow cylindrical organ; [NA] a general term for such a structure.

tuba auditiva [NA]; **tuba auditiva [Eustachii]** auditory tube: a channel, about 36 mm. long, lined with mucous membrane, that establishes communication between the tympanic cavity and the nasopharynx and serves to adjust the pressure of air in the cavity to the external pressure. It comprises a pars ossea, located in the temporal bone, and a pars cartilaginea, ending in the nasopharynx. Called also *eustachian tube*.

One of the symptoms of the plaintiff's illness was an aggravation during this flight of the mucus lining of the **eustachian tubes**; these small passageways run from the throat to the middle ear, and ordinarily, either by swallowing or yawning, one is able to equalize the pressure between the middle and outer ear. Because of his illness, Mr. Warshaw's **eustachian tubes** were blocked both by mucus and by the swollen linings of the tubes; thus, the tubes did not permit the passage of air necessary to equalize the pressure. Warshaw v. Trans World Airlines, Inc., 442 F.Supp. 400, 402 (E.D.Pa.1977).

tuba uterina [NA]; **tuba uterina [Falloppii]** uterine tube: a long slender tube that extends from the upper lateral angle of the uterus to the region of the ovary of the same side; it is attached to the broad ligament by the mesosalpinx, and consists of an ampulla, an infundibulum, an isthmus, two ostia, and a pars uterina. Called also *fallopian tube*.

As he proceeded with the operation, according to the appellant, he observed that her left **Fallopian tube** had ruptured as a result of a tubal pregnancy and her left ovary had a large cyst. He removed both the left tube and the left ovary. Appellant further testified that in his opinion the condition of the right tube and the right ovary was such that the appellee would never be able to conceive a child and he decided it would be good surgical practice to remove them at that time. He thereupon removed the right tube, the right ovary and the uterus. Thimatariga v. Chambers, 416 A.2d 1326, 1329 (Ct.Spec. App.Md.1980).

At that time appellant purportedly removed portions of Mrs. Bowman's left and right **fallopian tubes**....

After Mrs. Bowman was discharged from the hospital, appellant received a laboratory analysis of portions of the removed tissue. It stated that the tubal lumen, the distinctively lined channel in the **fallopian tube** through which the egg passes, had not been "seen" in either sample....

At the trial, appellees introduced expert testimony (1) that tubal lumens are the major identifying characteristic of the **fallopian tube**; (2) that "it was unlikely," given Mrs. Bowman's early conception afterward, that the operation "was done in an acceptable" manner; (3) that it was "medically probable" that appellant had not cut Mrs. Bowman's **fallopian tubes** but had instead severed a neighboring "round ligament." Bowman v. Davis, 356 N.E.2d 496, 497 (Ohio 1976).

tubal (too'bal) pertaining to or occurring in a tube, as a tubal pregnancy.

tubal ligation See *ligation, tubal.*

tubal lumen. See *tuba uterina.*

tube (tūb) [L. *tubus*] an elongated hollow cylindrical organ or instrument.

tube, Coolidge a vacuum tube for the generation of roentgen rays in which the cathode consists of a spiral filament of incandescent tungsten, and the anode (the target) of massive tungsten.

tube, endotracheal an airway catheter inserted in the trachea in endotracheal intubation.

At bar, Dr. Eviatar testified that plaintiff's dentures could only have become lodged in his esophagus if his gag reflex was suppressed, his throat muscles were relaxed, and an outside force was applied. This particular combination of conditions occurred only during the time that Dr. Tang had placed an **endotracheal tube** in the patient's trachea to facilitate the administration of anesthesia before surgery. Cornacchia v. Mount Vernon Hosp., 461 N.Y.S.2d 348–9 (2d Dep't 1983).

When he gave his opinion that the **endotracheal tube** was the instrument of damage, Dr. Wysocki was asked to assume use of a tube which was shown to him at trial and which he was able to examine. The plaintiff had earlier introduced that tube as an exhibit, without objection. It was a clear plastic and semi-rigid tube marked "I.D. 7.0 nasal-oral tube/cuffed/true murphy tip and eye."

There was no dispute at trial that the plaintiff had been intubated with a No. 7 cuffed **endotracheal tube**. No testimony, however, had established that the clear plastic semi-rigid tube was representative of the seven millimeter (the dimension is that of the tube's interior diameter) tube used under the defendant's supervision when the plaintiff underwent oral surgery. Indeed, the only evidence in the case about the nature of the tube described something quite different and, for purposes of the case, significantly different. McCarthy v. Hauck, 447 N.E.2d 22, 26 (App.Ct.Mass.1983).

The oxygen was delivered to the baby's lungs by means of an **endotracheal tube**—a tube through the mouth into the trachea at a high concentration. A bag is connected to the tube and oxygen is pumped manually into it. Re Wintersgill and Minister of Social Services, 131 D.L.R. 184–6 (Unified Fam.Ct., Sask. 1981).

Other Authorities: Naylor v. La. Dept. of Public Highways, 423 So.2d 674, 684 (Ct.App.La.1982); Burrow v. Widder, 368 N.E.2d 443, 447 (App.Ct.Ill.1977).

tube, eustachian See *tuba auditiva [Eustachii].*

tube, Levin a gastroduodenal catheter of sufficiently small caliber to permit transnasal passage.

The next day his condition worsened, and the doctor ordered the insertion of a **Levin** [1] **tube** to relieve the distension.... [[1] This tube is passed through a patient's nostril down his throat and into his abdominal area in order to remove, by suction, excess gas from the area.]

The hospital's records indicate that on the night of May 9, 1973: "**Levin tube** attempted to be inserted, patient gagged and eviscerated." The doctor testified that Elizondo eviscerated because of strain, which he identified as: 1) the strain of distension; and 2) the strain from gagging....

Elizondo testified that he had always been sensitive about gagging when foreign objects were applied to his throat, and that he informed Nurse Aparicio of this when she entered his room to attempt insertion.... Elizondo v. Tavarez, 596 S.W.2d 667, 669, 672 (Ct.Civ.App.Tex.1980).

Koch was X-rayed once for obstruction of his intestinal tract. Two enemas were given for treatment purposes. Dr. Gertz also ordered a **Levine tube** inserted into Koch's stomach to further monitor his condition....

... Both Dr. Gertz and Dr. Santini testified that the decision to monitor stomach fluids with a **Levine tube** is a matter for the treating physician's judgment, and both discounted the importance of the change in stomach fluids shown in Koch's case. Koch v. Gorrilla, 552 F.2d 1170, 1172, 1176 (6th Cir. 1977).

The patient then began to have profuse bleeding from the stomach and esophagus. Bleeding from the esophagus was the result of ulcerations caused by a **Levine tube** which had been inserted, post operatively, to aid in keeping the abdomen decompressed. Hawkins v. Ozborn, 383 F.Supp. 1389, 1392 (N.D.Miss.1974).

Other Authorities: Lenger v. Physician's General Hosp., Inc., 455 S.W.2d 703, 705, 709 (Tex.1970).

tube, Levine See *tube, Levin.*

tube, Miller-Abbott a double-channel intestinal tube with an inflatable balloon at its distal end, for use in the treatment of obstruction of the small intestine; occasionally useful also as a diagnostic aid.

A **Miller-Abbott tube** is a device which is inserted through the patient's nostril and passes through the esophagus into the stomach and ultimately into the small intestine. The purpose of the device is to decompress the small intestine by extracting the gastric contents.

The device consists of a tubular rubber hose which surrounds two lumen. One lumen is used for suction; the other communicates with a balloon. The lumen do not communicate with each other. The tube has a forked metal tip; one fork is marked 'suction', the other 'balloon'. The markings are engraved in the metal. The tips communicate with their respective lumen. Stumper v. Kimel, 260 A.2d 526–7 (Super.Ct.N.J.1970).

tube, Sengstaken-Blakemore a device used for the tamponade of bleeding esophageal varices, consisting of three tubes: one leading to a balloon which is inflated in the stomach, to retain the instrument in place, and to compress the vessels around the cardia; another leading to a long narrow balloon by which pressure is exerted against the wall of the esophagus; and the third attached to a suction apparatus for aspirating contents of the stomach.

... the defendant, in an effort to stop the flow of blood, attempted without success to insert a **Senstaken** [sic]-**Blakemore tube** (a device containing two balloons which, when inflated, permits pressure to be applied to the walls of the esophagus or stomach, or both, in order to stop bleeding from small lacerations or bleeding sites on the walls of these parts of the bowel) in plaintiff's abdomen. When Dr. Pittman was in position to assist the defendant during the examination of the esophageal area, the defendant proceeded to enlarge the excision, and opened the lower stomach. Using an esophagoscope, both Dr. Manning and Dr. Pittman checked the esophageal area. They found no lesion or bleeding sites. The defendant then placed the **Senstaken** [sic] **tube** in the esophagus, inflated it properly and closed the esophagus. Fitzgerald v. Manning, 679 F.2d 341, 344 (4th Cir. 1982).

tube, stomach a tube for feeding or for irrigation of the stomach. See also *gastrectomy*; and *peritonitis*.

Dr. McElhinney testified that one of the two tubes, through which fluids could be sucked out of the stomach during the healing process, was prematurely removed. The remaining tube was not properly irrigated or monitored for drainage, which eventually resulted in occlusion. The blockage spawned increased pressure in the stomach causing the blown duodenal stump, the complications from which decedent died. Reams v. Stutler, 642 S.W.2d 586, 588 (Ky.1982).

tube, tracheostomy a curved tube to be inserted into the trachea through the opening made in tracheostomy.

Mr. Naylor is more susceptible to colds and upper respiratory infections because of his **tracheostomy tube**; however, Dr. Kirgis testified that he cannot close the throat incision, fearing that Mr. Naylor's inability to clear his throat without the tube would prove life-threatening. Naylor v. La. Dep't of Public Highways, 423 So.2d 674, 685 (Ct.App.La.1982).

tuber (too′ber), pl. *tubers* or *tu′bera* [L.] 1. a swelling, protuberance; [NA] a general term for such a structure. See also *tubercle; tuberculum; tuberositas* and *tuberosity*.

tubercle (too′ber-k′l) 1. any of the small, rounded, granulomatous lesions produced by infection with *Mycobacterium tuberculosis;* it is the characteristic lesion of tuberculosis, and consists of a translucent mass, gray in color, made up of a collection of modified macrophages resembling epithelial cells (*epithelioid cells*), surrounded by a rim of mononuclear cells, principally lymphocytes, and sometimes a center of giant multinucleate cells (*Langhans' giant cells*). Called also *gray t.* 2. a nodule, or small eminence, such as a rough, rounded eminence on a bone; called also *tuberculum* [N.A.]. See also *tuberculum*.

tubercle of tibia See *eminentia intercondylaris.*

tuberculin (too-ber′ku-lin) a sterile liquid containing the growth products of, or specific substances extracted from, the tubercle bacillus. The form first prepared (Old tuberculin) by boiling, filtering, and concentrating a bouillon culture of tubercle bacilli, was put forth as a cure for tuberculosis by Koch in 1890 (Koch's lymph paratoloid, paratoloidin). In various forms tuberculin is used in the diagnosis of tuberculosis infection, especially in children and cattle, and formerly also in the treatment of tuberculosis. The tuberculin test, as commonly applied, consists in the injection of tuberculin under or into the skin; the injection has no effect in nontuberculous subjects; but causes inflammation at the site of the injection in tuberculous subjects. See *tuberculin test*, under *tests*.

tuberculin, Calmette's purified tuberculin, prepared by precipitating Old tuberculin with alcohol, washing, dissolving in water, and filtering. When instilled in the conjunctiva of persons affected with tuberculosis or typhoid fever it produces a severe local reaction. Called also *tuberculin precipitation (T.P.).* See also *ophthalmic reaction*, under *reaction*.

tuberculin, purified protein derivative (P.P.D.) of [USP], a sterile, soluble partially purified product of growth of the tubercle bacillus prepared in a special liquid medium free from protein. It is used as a dermal reactivity indicator in the diagnosis of tuberculosis.

tuberculin skin test See *test, tuberculin.*

tuberculosis (too-ber″ku-lo′sis) any of the infectious diseases of man and animals caused by species of *Mycobacterium* and characterized by the formation of tubercles and caseous necrosis in the tissues. The common causative species are *M. tuberculosis, M. bovis,* and *M. avium,* but the disease is also caused by several atypical mycobacteria, including *M. kansasii* and others as yet unclassified. Atypical infections, which are clinically and morphologically indistinguishable from the typical disease, do not appear to be directly transmissible from man to man. Tuberculosis varies widely in its manifestations and has a tendency to great chronicity. Any organ may be affected, although in man the lung is the major seat of the disease and the usual portal through which the infection reaches other organs.

No doctor states that claimant's current condition stems solely from the **tuberculosis**. To the contrary, the undisputed medical evidence is that the two conditions are inextricably intertwined, in that the traumatic injury was superimposed on the tubercular infection, and the presence of the tubercular infection prolonged the effects of the traumatic injury to the synovium. Matter of Compensation of Aquillon, 653 P.2d 264, 266 (Ct.App.Or.1982).

1. **Tuberculosis** is an infectious disease caused by the invasion of tubercle bacilli.

2. Its symptomology ordinarily consists of anorea (loss of appetite), loss of weight, fatigue, night sweats, chills, coughing, hemoptysis (expectoration of blood) and abnormal temperature.

3 A tuberculin skin test is a simple means of discovering if a tubercle bacillus has entered an individual's body. (Undisputed)....

A positive tuberculin skin test indicates in a great majority of cases that the individual had exposure to **tuberculosis** in the past and that at some time at least one tubercle bacillus had entered his body....

Tuberculosis is proven by a chest X-ray plus bacteriological evidence by way of sputum culture or skin test....

Coughing, sneezing and singing commonly spread droplet nuclei containing the tubercle bacilli to an extent dependent upon the number of bacilli in the discharge, the size of the quarters and the ventilation conditions....

Although **tuberculosis** used to be treated by extended isolation, sometimes for years, it is now treated with safe, inexpensive drugs that can be taken orally....

Some individuals who have been infected have calcium nodules in their lungs which show up as "spots" in a chest X-ray. Plummer v. U.S., 420 F.Supp. 978–80 (M.D.Pa.1976).

Tuberculosis is a communicable disease and as such is not compensable under the Workmen's Compensation Act, either as an occupational disease or as a personal injury by accident. Linville v. Steel Fixture Mfg. Co., 469 P.2d 312, 316 (Kan.1970).

Other Authorities: Henning v. U.S., 311 F.Supp. 681 (E.D.Pa. 1970).

tuberculosis, acute miliary an acute form of tuberculosis in which minute tubercles are formed in a number of organs of the body, due to dissemination of the bacilli throughout the body by the blood stream.

... it was only after he had cut into various organ tissues that he discovered the minute lesions, and subsequently, a small number of bacteria (by microscope) which are evidence of an uncommon and lethal, if undetected, form of tuberculosis, namely, **miliary tuberculosis**.[3]... [3 "... by that time I completed the Rocitinsky and took a look at the kidneys and then started seeing millet seed type of nodules you expect to see with **miliary tuberculosis**, and I yelled for one of the men, whoever is doing the frozen, to stop, because with tuberculosis this is a good way to get exposure, during frozen section."]

The disease derives its name from the millet seed, because the lesions formed by the bacteria during the course of the disease are about the size of such a seed, approximately four or five millimeters in diameter, the size of a pinhead. This contrasts with the more common form of tuberculosis which is evidenced by large lesions in the lungs which may be seen by x-ray. Bacteria of the miliary type are airborne, enter the human bloodstream and attack various body organs, including the kidneys, the liver and the lungs. According to Dr. Fox, who testified for the defense at trial not only as an attending physician but as an expert on tuberculosis, the disease is more prevalent in children than adults and appears more often in groups which experience the conditions of poverty.

The disease is difficult to diagnose; it is now relatively rare, and is hard to detect because of the size of the lesions produced. Dr. Joseph Boyle, an expert on chest diseases who testified for the defense, stated that in 25% of the cases the lesions formed are so small that they would never be detected by x-ray; as the disease progresses, they may or may not be seen by this method. Cade v. Mid-City Hospital Corp., 119 Cal.Rptr. 571, 574 (Ct.App.Cal.1975).

tuberculosis of lungs infection of the lungs caused by *Mycobacterium tuberculosis*. Characteristically, the course of the untreated disease is as follows: tuberculous pneumonia, formation of tuberculous granulation tissue, caseous necrosis, calcification, and cavity formation. It may spread to other lung segments via the bronchi, or to other organs via the blood or lymph vessels. Symptoms may

include weight loss, lassitude and fatigue, night sweats, and wasting, with purulent sputum, hemoptysis, and chest pain. See also *phthisis*.

tuberculosis, miliary See *tuberculosis, acute miliary*.

tuberculosis, pericardial

... he was treated for "**pericardial tuberculosis**" (of the heart sac) with extensive effusion.... Prudential Insurance Co. of America v. Beaty, 456 S.W.2d 164, 169 (Ct.Civ.App.Tex. 1970).

tuberculosis, pulmonary See *tuberculosis of lungs*.

tuberculosis, spinal; tuberculosis of spine osteitis or caries of the vertebrae, usually occurring as a complication of tuberculosis of the lungs; it is marked by stiffness of the vertebral column, pain on motion, tenderness on pressure, prominence of certain of the vertebral spines, and occasionally abdominal pain, abscess formation, and paralysis. Called also *David's disease, dorsal phthisis, Pott's disease, spondylitis tuberculosa*, and *tuberculous spondylitis*.

Employee has suffered from tuberculosis since 1938. His condition, progressive degeneration of the hips and spine, is commonly called **Pott's disease** and required hip fusions in the early 1940's, and again in 1964 and 1968, and back fusion in 1950. He was hired by the employer in 1965 as part of a program to employ handicapped persons. Greene v. W & W Generator Rebuilders, 224 N.W.2d 157, 159 (Minn.1974).

tuberculum (too-ber′ku-lum), pl. *tuber′cula* [L., dim. of *tuber*] a tubercle, nodule, or small eminence; [NA] general term for such a structure. See also *tubercle; tuber; tuberositas*; and *tuberosity*.

tuberositas (too″bĕ-ros′ĭ-tas), pl. *tuberosita′tes* [L.] tuberosity: an elevation or protuberance; [NA] a general term for such a structure. See also *tuber; tubercle*; and *tuberculum*.

tuberosity (too″bĕ-ros′ĭ-te) an elevation or protuberance; called also *tuberositas*.

tubocurarine (too″bo-ku-rah′rin) an alkaloid isolated from the bark and stems of *Chondodendron tomentosum* R. & P. (Menispermaceae); it is the active principle of curare (q.v.).

"tummy tuck" operation See *operation, "tummy tuck"*.

tumor (too′mor) [L., from *tumere* to swell] a new growth of tissue in which the multiplication of cells is uncontrolled and progressive; called also *neoplasm*. See also *mass*.

On examination of Timothy July 9th, Dr. Wolf and Dr. Kinn observed a retinal detachment of the right eye with a subretinal **tumor**. "Tumor" in this context was defined as a mass rather than a malignancy. Steele v. U.S., 463 F.Supp. 321, 323 (D.Alas.1978).

The results of this initial examination disclosed that Ahern had a large **tumor** and was suffering from carcinoma of the rectum....

... The examining and consulting physicians were fearful that the **tumor** would obstruct the colon. The dimensions of the tumor were described by Dr. Lewis, Ahern's primary treating physician, as approximately eleven centimeters in length and seven centimeters above the anus. [R., Vol. X at 11]. Due to the unusual size of the tumor, it was concluded that the tumor was non-resectable. Preoperative radiation was thereupon employed in order to reduce the size of the tumor so that it could eventually be removed by surgery. Ahern v. Veterans Administration, 537 F.2d 1098–9 (10th Cir. 1976).

In June of 1958, a tumor about the size of a marble was excised from appellant's upper right arm by Dr. Kornblatt at Bay Cities Community Hospital. The tumor recurred higher on the arm. On August 4, 1961, when the tumor had grown to about 7 by 9 centimeters, it was again excised by Dr. Norcross at Gardena Hospital. Approximately three months later, the tumor reappeared, this time still further up the arm and extending into the armpit area. Dr. Norcross diagnosed the tumor as malignant. It was approximately the size of a baseball and appeared to be a fibrous tumor with strands or tentacles moving outward from the margin.

Dr. Norcross determined that his treatment of choice for the third recurrence of the tumor was a wide excision including the possibility of a forequarter amputation, the removal of the arm and the shoulder. Clemens v. Regents of University of California, 87 Cal.Rptr. 108, 111 (Ct.App.Cal.1970).

tumor, acoustic brain

The tests conducted at St. Paul Hospital indicated a possible answer to the mystery—Harrison had an acoustic brain tumor. In June 1968, Dr. Charles Simpson surgically removed a portion of the tumor. The location of the tumor prevented complete excision, and the possibility of regrowth remained.

The abatement of Harrison's pain was short-lived. The headaches, numbness, paralysis and burning sensation returned and were increasingly painful. Her life began to disintegrate. Constant pain forced closure of her small flower shop and interfered with her efforts to care for her invalid husband. Desperate to find an explanation for her suffering, Harrison became convinced that the tumor was growing anew. She returned to Simpson every other month for two years, insisting on x-rays of the tumor. No new growth was found. Though unable to identify the source of Harrison's pain, Simpson assured her that it was not the tumor. He refused to conduct further x-ray examinations, telling her "I'm going to burn your brain up." Harrison v. U.S., 708 F.2d 1023, 1025 (5th Cir. 1983).

tumor, benign one that lacks the properties of invasion and metastasis and that is usually surrounded by a fibrous capsule; its cells also show a lesser degree of anaplasia than those of malignant tumors.

tumor, bone

In May of 1978, Mr. Gramlich learned that he had a malignant bone tumor in the area of the injury and thereafter his left lower extremity was amputated. The cancerous condition eventually resulted in Mr. Gramlich's death on July 26, 1980. It is charged that defendants were negligent in failing to diagnose and treat the cancerous condition at an early stage. Gramlich v. Travelers Ins. Co., 640 S.W.2d 180, 182 (Mo.Ct.App. 1982).

tumor, brain

Testing by Dr. Pisarello confirmed the findings of the neurologists and he, like Dr. Cangelosi, diagnosed intracranial pressure caused by a brain tumor blocking the circulation of spinal fluid in the brain. Gendusa v. St. Paul Fire & Marine Ins. Co., 435 So.2d 479, 481 (Ct.App.La.1983).

tumor, epidermoid

This epidermoid tumor was described by the doctors as very difficult to remove in that in its process of growing it creeps into all crevices, and in the area of the cerebella pontine angle, critical nerves are involved so that it was impossible for the surgeon to completely remove the tumor without causing further debilitating damage to the plaintiff. Swanson v. U.S. By and Through Veterans Admin., 557 F.Supp. 1041, 1044 (D.Idaho 1983).

tumor, malignant one that has the properties of invasion and metastasis and that shows a greater degree of anaplasia than do benign tumors. See also *fibrosarcoma*.

Approximately three months later, the tumor reappeared, this time still further up the arm and extending into the armpit area. Dr. Norcross diagnosed the tumor as malignant. It was approximately the size of a baseball and appeared to be a fibrous tumor with strands or tentacles moving outward from the margin. Clemens v. Regents of University of California, 87 Cal. Rptr. 108, 111 (Ct.App.Cal.1970).

tumor, mullerian See *ductus paramesonephricus*.

tumor, retroperitoneal

Dr. Crouse examined appellant's abdomen and found an enlargement which seemed to be a tumor. X rays revealed a 9-centimeter retroperitoneal tumor adjacent to the right side of appellant's spinal column. Three pulmonary lesions were also found. Dr. Crouse concluded that the tumor was a recurrence of the appellant's ovarian teratoma, which probably had been malignant. At trial, Dr. Lindsay and a defense expert testified to the contrary: in their opinion the retroperitoneal tumor had not metastasized from the ovarian teratoma and the two growths were unrelated. Jamison v. Lindsay, 166 Cal.Rptr. 443, 445–6 (Ct.App.Cal.1980).

tumorigenic (too″mor-ĭ-jen′ik) giving rise to tumors; said especially of a cell or group of cells capable of producing a tumor. Cf. *oncogenic*.

tunic (too′nik) a covering or coat. See also *tunica*.

tunica (too′nĭ-kah), pl. tu′nicae [L.] a covering or coat; [NA] a general term for a membrane or other structure covering or lining a body part or organ. Called also *tunic*.

tunica intima vasorum [NA], the inner coat of the blood vessels, made up of endothelial cells surrounded by longitudinal elastic fibers and connective tissue.

"... He is there referring to the inner coating of the aorta, which is called 'intima'...." Woodall Industries, Inc. v. Massachusetts Mutual Life Insurance Co., 483 F.2d 986, 999 (6th Cir. 1973).

tunica muscularis uteri [NA], the smooth muscle coat of the uterus, which forms the mass of the organ; called also *myometrium* [NA alternative] and *mesometrium*.

tunica serosa intestini tenuis [NA], the serous coat of the small intestine.

In the meantime, Dr. Hall examined the bowel, and in addition to finding a tear in the uterus, found abrasions (bruises) in the **serosal (outer) layer of the bowel** in three places to the front of the perforation site. Hitch v. Hall, 399 A.2d 953, 955 (Ct. Spec.App.Md.1979).

tunnel (tun'el) a passageway of varying length, through a solid body, completely enclosed except for the open ends, permitting entrance and exit.

tunnel, carpal the osseofibrous passage for the median nerve and the flexor tendons, formed by the flexor retinaculum and the carpal bones. Called also *canalis carpi* [NA].

While in the hospital for an assortment of problems in June of 1979, she complained of tingling and numbness in her right hand. At one time she attributed numbness and tingling of her hands and heaviness in her shoulders to striking her head against the top of a car as the result of a 1975 automobile accident. Examination revealed she had a compression of the nerve at the wrist level. A **carpal tunnel** release of the right wrist was performed at that time. Negrete v. Western Elec. Co., Inc., 326 N.W.2d 681–2 (Neb.1982).

TUR See *resection, transurethral.*

TWA See *time weighted average.*

tyloxapol (ti-loks'ah-pōl) [USP] chemical name: 4-(1,1,3,3-tetramethylbutyl)phenol polymer with formaldehyde and oxirane. A nonionic liquid polymer of the alkyl aryl polyether alcohol type; used as a surfactant to aid liquefaction and removal of mucopurulent bronchopulmonary secretions, administered by inhalation through a nebulizer or with a stream of oxygen.

The FDA's notification included the following: "The Academy [the NAS-NRC] reports that ... [Alevaire is] ineffective in that there is no evidence that **tyloxapol** ... has any effect on secretions in the lung other than that of water in thinning secretions by simple dilution." Sterling Drug. Inc. v. Weinberger, 503 F.2d 675, 677 (2d Cir. 1974).

tympanic (tim-pan'ik) [L. *tympanicus*] bell-like; resonant.

Kurtis' abdomen was distended and **tympanic** (resonant or drum-like), which subsequent medical procedures disclosed to be the result of peritonitis due to abdominal injuries. People v. Atkins, 125 Cal.Rptr. 855, 859 (Ct.App.Cal.1975).

tympanic nerve See *nervus tympanicus.*

tympano-mastoidectomy See *mastoidectomy tympano.*

tympanoplasty (tim"pah-no-plas'te) [*tympanum* + Gr. *plassein* to form] surgical reconstruction of the hearing mechanism of the middle ear, with restoration of the drum membrane to protect the round window from sound pressure, and establishment of ossicular continuity between the tympanic membrane and the oval window. See also *myringoplasty.*

He was hospitalized for a modified radical mastoidectomy of the left ear and left **tympanoplasty** (surgical reconstruction of

the middle ear). Edwards v. Schweiker, 539 F.Supp. 650, 652 (E.D.Tex.1982).

The left eardrum of Mr. Aretz was ruptured in the explosion. In June, 1972 a mastoidectomy and **tympanoplasty** (surgical reconstruction of hearing mechanism of middle ear) was performed and a skin graft made to replace the eardrum. Aretz v. U.S., 456 F.Supp. 397, 403 (S.D.Ga.1978).

tympanosclerosis (tim"pah-no-sklĕ-ro'sis) a condition characterized by the presence of masses of hard, dense connective tissue around the auditory ossicles in the tympanic cavity.

Dr. Woodrow D. Schlosser, a noted surgeon specializing in the field of otolaryngology, performed an operation on the appellant's middle ear. The purpose of the surgery was to attempt a cure of **tympanosclerosis** which was causing loss of hearing to the appellant. Barshady v. Schlosser, 313 A.2d 296–7 (Super.Ct.Pa.1973).

tympanotomy (tim"pah-not'o-me) [*tympanum* + Gr. *tomē* a cutting] surgical puncture of the membrana tympani; myringotomy.

tympanum (tim'pah-num) [L.; Gr. *tympanon* drum] the cavity of the middle ear, located just medial to the tympanic membrane, and containing the auditory ossicles and connecting with the mastoid cells and auditory tube. Called also *auris media* [NA].

type (tīp) [L. *typus;* Gr. *typos* mark] the general or prevailing character of any particular case of disease, person, substance, etc. See also under *habit;* and *habitus.* Cf. *constitution* and *diathesis.*

typhus (ti'fus) [Gr. *typhos* stupor arising from fever] any of a group of related arthropod-borne infectious diseases caused by species of *Rickettsia* and marked by malaise, severe headache, sustained high fever, and a macular or maculopapular eruption which appears from the third to the seventh day. Called also *typhus fever.* In English-speaking countries, often used alone to refer to epidemic t., whereas in several European languages, it refers to typhoid fever.

While engaged in this work, plaintiff claims to have sustained "an accident when he was bit (sic) by an insect [flea], thereby causing him to contract a grave illness, Tyfus (**typhus**) fever."

On November 21, 1979, plaintiff was admitted to the St. Tammany Parish Hospital with initial symptoms of chills, high fever, and severe headache....

Q. Let me ask you, doctor, **typhus** fever you stated is a relatively rare condition. How is it contracted?

A. From a rat, flea bite.

When questioned about his diagnosis, Dr. Pittman stated:

A. ... The patient had certain symptoms. He had certain physical findings. He had a rash that was compatible of a rash that I had seen many times previously in reference to **typhus** fever and the laboratory findings were that you would find with **typhus** fever.

Q. Doctor, does **typhus** fever have a particular incubation period ...?

A. That could vary, I would say roughly seven to twenty days, somewhere in between seven and twenty days.

Oalmann v. Brock and Blevins Co., Inc., 428 So.2d 892–3, 896 (Ct.App.La.1983).

typhus, epidemic the classic form of typhus, caused by *Rickettsia prowazekii*, which is transmitted from man to man by the louse *Pediculus humanus*. After an incubation of 10 days to 2 weeks, the onset is usually abrupt, with severe headache, generalized aches and pains, and shaking chills. After a few days there is fever, lasting 10 to 14 days. A macular or maculopapular rash that becomes petechial appears about the fifth day, beginning on the back and covering the body except the face, palms, and soles; it fades with the fever. In the second week there may be delirium and stupor, progressing to coma and ending in death in 20 per cent of untreated cases.

U

UFFI See *urea-formaldehyde*.

ulcer (ul'ser) [L. *ulcus;* Gr. *helkōsis*] a local defect, or excavation, of the surface of an organ or tissue, which is produced by the sloughing of inflammatory necrotic tissue.

... that while even "blistering and ulceration is expected from x-ray treatments, it is not good medical practice to apply radiation to the skin to the extent that **ulcers** develop to a diameter of four inches and a depth of one half inch".... McCarthy v. Boston City Hospital, 266 N.E.2d 292, 295 (Mass.1971).

ulcer, decubital; ulcer, decubitus an ulceration caused by prolonged pressure in a patient allowed to lie too still in bed for a long period of time; called also *decubitus, bed sore*, and *pressure sore*.

Each time some adjustment was made, and Ms. Storey was told to continue wearing the brace. Eventually a **decubitous ulcer** developed on the outside edge of her right foot near the small toe as a result of the brace's continuous rubbing. Storey v. Lambert's Limbs & Braces, Inc., 426 So.2d 676, 678 (Ct. App.La.1982).

In addition, a major area of concern to a triplegic are ulcerated pressure sores, **decubitis**. Simple weightbearing produces these sores; while the triplegic cannot feel them, such sores may extend from the surface of the skin down to the bone, and osteomyelitis may develop, requiring amputation of the legs. The triplegic must shift position constantly and must avoid such small pressures as those resulting from wrinkled clothing. Dr. Billy De Shazo, a plastic surgeon, testified that he had operated on three extensive pressure sores developed by Richard, plugging the holes with skin taken from other parts of the body. Rodriguez v. McDonnell Douglas Corp., 151 Cal.Rptr. 399, 414 (Ct.App.Cal.1978).

Dr. Amanda C. Blount, an osteopathic physician, testified that leakage of urine from plaintiff's collection bag was contributing to maceration of tissue, and, therefore, aggravating plaintiff's **decubitus ulcers. Decubitus ulcers** are a breaking down of skin at pressure points over joints. Dr. Blount estimated that 25% of plaintiff's ulceration was caused by urine leakage. Harrigan v. U.S., 408 F.Supp. 177, 183 (E.D.Pa.1976).

Other Authorities: Stogsdill v. Manor Convalescent Home, Inc., 343 N.E.2d 589, 593–4, 598 (App.Ct.Ill.1976); Hale v. Holy Cross Hospital, Inc., 513 F.2d 315 (5th Cir. 1975); Matter of Quinlan, 348 A.2d 801, 808 (Super.Ct.N.J.1975).

ulcer, duodenal a peptic ulcer situated in the duodenum. See also *duodenum*.

In November 1973, according to a later report of Thomas F. Alderman, M.D., plaintiff's "severe and disabling back pain with radiation into the lower extremities" was compounded by the development of "a penetrating **duodenal ulcer** which (confirmed by X-ray), I believe was due in most part to the frequent ingestion of many analgesics, especially aspirin compounds." Spaulding v. Califano, 427 F.Supp. 982, 985 (W.D.Mo.1977).

ulcer, Hunner's a lesion occurring in chronic interstitial cystitis, involving all the layers of the bladder wall, and appearing as a small brownish red patch on the mucosa; it tends to heal superficially and is notoriously difficult to detect.

... appellee thought that his June 17th examination of appellant disclosed a condition called **interstitial cystitis (Hunner's Ulcer)**. Appellee thought that this condition accounted for the complaints that appellant was making, and his work with appellant thereafter was designed to cut down her pain and discomfort and relax her bladder. Ausley v. Johnston, 450 S.W.2d 351, 353 (Ct.App.Tex.1970).

ulcer, Marjolin's an ulcer seated upon an old cicatrix; it may degenerate into a squamous cell carcinoma with a propensity for metastasis.

The blood supply to the tissues is not good. Skin cancer sometimes occurs in burn scars. The type of cancer, **marjilons** [sic] **ulcer**, is usually more severe than the average type of skin cancer that individuals get on their forehead or face. The danger of this skin cancer is a very significant feature in Joe Dial's future. Dr. Aronoff has advised Dial to stay out of the sun and to protect his skin with oils and lubricants. Wry v. Dial, 503 P.2d 979, 985 (Ct.App.Ariz.1972).

ulcer, peptic an ulceration of the mucous membrane of the esophagus, stomach, or duodenum, caused by the action of the acid gastric juice. See also *pars superior duodeni* (Denton case).

ulcer, pressure See *ulcer, decubitus.*

ulcer, sluggish

> . . . the ulcer was a **sluggish ulcer**; one that does not get better or worse. She had, at that time, a fair circulation in the foot; the tibial artery was palpitating and the temperature of the toes was good. At all times when he treated her there was circulation in her foot and in his opinion it was adequate circulation to heal the ulcer. Stogsdill v. Manor Convalescent Home, Inc., 343 N.E.2d 589, 593 (App.Ct.III.1976).

ulcer, stress peptic ulcer, usually gastric, resulting from stress; possible predisposing factors include changes in the microcirculation of the gastric mucosa, increased permeability of the gastric mucosa barrier to H^+, and impaired cell proliferation.

> Following surgery [for removal of gallstones], Bruney developed serious complications, ultimately resulting in his death. The doctors who testified at trial were unanimous in the conclusion that the primary cause of death was massive gastrointestinal hemorrhage six weeks after surgery as a result of a **stress ulcer**. This type of ulcer develops from protracted serious sickness. Bruney v. City of Lake Charles, 386 So.2d 950–1 (Ct.App.La.1980).

ulna (ul'nah), pl. *ul'nae* [L. "the arm"] [NA] the inner and larger bone of the forearm, on the side opposite that of the thumb; it articulates with the humerus and with the head of the radius at its proximal end; with the radius and bones of the carpus at the distal end. See illustration accompanying skeleton.

> Plaintiff's injuries consisted primarily of an extensively comminuted fracture of the proximal portion of the ulna. . . .
>
> The fragmentation in the **ulna** was so great that it was impossible to reconstitute. Dardar v. State of La., 322 F.Supp. 1115, 1119 (E.D.La.1971).

ulnar (ul'nar) [L. *ulnaris*] pertaining to the ulna or to the ulnar (medial) aspect of the arm as compared to the radial (lateral) aspect. See also *ulna.*

ulnar nerve See *nervus ulnaris.*

ultrasonic (ul"trah-son'ik) [*ultra-* + L. *sonus* sound] pertaining to mechanical radiant energy having a frequency beyond the upper limit of perception by the human ear, that is, beyond about 20,000 Hz (cycles per second). See also *ultrasonics.* Cited in U.S. v. Article Consisting of 2 Devices, etc., 255 F.Supp. 374, 381 (W.D.Ark.1966), reversed and remanded 379 F.2d 29 (8th Cir. 1967).

ultrasonics (ul"trah-son'iks) that part of the science of acoustics dealing with the frequency range beyond the upper limit of perception by the human ear (beyond 20 kilocycles per second), but usually restricted to frequencies above 500 kilocycles per second. Ultrasonic radiation is injurious to tissues because of its thermal effects when absorbed by living matter, but in controlled doses it is used therapeutically to selectively break down pathologic tissues, as in treatment of arthritis and lesions of the nervous system, and also as a diagnostic aid by visually displaying echoes received from irradiated tissues, as in echocardiography and echoencephalography.

ultrasound (ul'trah-sownd) mechanical radiant energy (see *sound*), with a frequency greater than 20,000 cycles per second. See also *ultrasonics.*

> **Ultrasound**, according to Dr. Wharton, is energy in the form of a sound frequency. The **ultrasound** equipment can cause changes in the temperature of tissue and the purpose is to alter temperature selectively. As with microwave diathermy, it also produces some degree of increased circulation. According to Dr. Wharton, **ultrasound** penetrates more deeply than microwave diathermy. Among other dangers of the use of **ultrasound**, Dr. Wharton pointed out that if used in an area of an underlying tumor, the vibratory form of energy may spread malignancies through the bloodstream. A similar effect may occur if used over an area of infection. Norville v. Miss.State Medical Ass'n. 364 So.2d 1084–5 (Miss.1978).

> Sometime in 1949, Dr. Wild claimed, he ascertained by research that **ultrasound** echoes or waves could measure the thickness of a bowel wall. From this determination, he began using **ultrasound** techniques as a clinical aid to cancer detection. Wild v. Rarig, 234 N.W.2d 775, 782 (Minn.1975).

> Their testimony was to the effect that **ultrasound** is a deep heat modality and is used in making localized applications of heat in the tissues of the body; that **ultrasound** should be administered only after a careful medical examination and diagnosis to make certain that there are not present conditions for which the use of **ultrasound** is contraindicated, because the administration of **ultrasound** in the presence of such conditions could be harmful to the patient. Each of the physician witnesses enumerated a long list of such contraindications. Among the conditions mentioned were neurological defects, circulatory defects, tumors, bones, infections, nerves, pregnant uterus, rheumatic conditions, and eyes and face. They testified that many of these conditions, such as malignant tumors, infections, certain rheumatic conditions, pregnancy, and neurological and circulatory defects, could be reliably diagnosed only by a person with the training and experience of a medical doctor, and that the blind use of **ultrasound** without such an examination and diagnosis would be dangerous to the health of the patient. U.S. v. Article Consisting of 2 Devices, etc., 255 F.Supp. 374, 377 (W.D.Ark.1966), reversed and remanded 379 F.2d 29 (8th Cir. 1967).

ultraviolet (ul"trah-vi'o-let) beyond the violet end of the spectrum; said of electromagnetic rays or radiation between the violet rays and the roentgen rays, that is, with wavelengths between 4 and 400 nm. These rays have powerful actinic and chemical properties, inducing sunburn and tanning of the skin and producing ergocalciferol (vitamin D_2) by their action or ergosterol in the skin. Cited in U.S. v. Article Consisting of 2 Devices, etc., 255 F.Supp. 374, 381 (W.D.Ark.1966), reversed and remanded 379 F.2d 29 (8th Cir. 1967).

Umbrathor See *thorium dioxide.*

underbite See *bite, underhung;* and *prognathism.*

undermineralization

The x-ray revealed diffuse **undermineralization** of the skeleton. This lack of minerals in the skeleton results in increased susceptibility to bone trauma. In re Sharpe, 374 A.2d 1323–4 (Super.Ct.Pa.1977).

undertaker See *mortician.*

undifferentiation See *anaplasia* (James case).

unguis (ung'gwis), pl. *un'gues* [L.] 1. [NA] the horny cutaneous plate on the dorsal surface of the distal end of the terminal phalanx of a finger or toe, made up of flattened epithelial scales developed from the stratum lucidum of the skin. Called also *nail* (q.v.). 2. a collection of pus in the cornea; an onyx. 3. a nail-like part or structure.

union (ūn'yun) [L. *unio*] the process of healing; the renewal of continuity in a broken bone or between the edges of a wound. See also *healing;* and *nonunion.*

unobtrusive

On cross-examination when he was asked to explain what he meant by this description he testified: "The term **unobtrusive** means it is not grossly evident in my interpretation. When I saw her in the office it was not a particularly noticeable scar until I took the time of carefully watching the animation, and whatever variations there might be with animation". Rosenblum v. Bloom, 492 S.W.2d 321, 323–4 (Ct.Civ.App.Tex.1973).

unsaturated (un-sat'u-rāt″ed) not saturated; applied to (1) a chemical compound in which two or more atoms are united by double or triple bonds. These bonds have two or three pairs of shared electrons characterized by pi-electrons (π-electrons) with orbital overlap. Such compounds may still add atoms or groups to the unsaturated bonding atoms up to a limit of bonding power or saturation. Most commonly refers to carbon-carbon bonds, as in unsaturated fatty acids. (2) a solution in which more solute may still be dissolved under stated conditions.

Unsaturated: Any compound containing one or more double bonds, due to a deficiency of hydrogen. Ritter v. Rohm & Haas Co., 271 F.Supp. 313 (S.D.N.Y. 1967).

unscheduled

... "unscheduled" refers to those permanent disabilities for which compensation is provided under the provisions of A.R.S. § 23–1044C. Roeder v. Industrial Com'n, 556 P.2d 1148–9 (Ct.App.Ariz.1976).

unscheduled permanent disability See under *disability;* and *unscheduled.*

unsterile See *sterile.*

uranium (u-ra'ne-um) [L. *Uranus* a planet] a hard and heavy radioactive metallic element; symbol, U; atomic number, 92; atomic weight, 238.03; specific gravity, 18.68. Some of its compounds are medicinal. Naturally occurring uranium is composed of three isotopes of mass numbers 234, 235, and 238, respectively. Uranium 235 separated from U 238 undergoes fission with slow neutrons, giving up neutrons which can join the nucleus of U 238 to form neptunium, which in turn decays by beta particle emission to form plutonium. Cf. *neptunium* and *plutonium*. See also *radioactivity.*

urea (u-re'ah) the diamide of carbonic acid, $NH_2CO \cdot NH_2$, a white, crystallizable substance found in the urine, blood, and lymph. It is the chief nitrogenous constituent of the urine, and the chief nitrogenous end-product of the metabolism of proteins. It is formed in the liver from amino acids and from compounds of ammonia. See also *carbamide;* and *urea cycle*, under *cycle*. Cited in Rawlings v. National Molasses Co., 328 F.Supp. 913–14 (C.D.Cal. 1971).

urea-formaldehyde

The Commission found that UFFI presents an unreasonable risk of injury from irritation and cancer and that no feasible product standard exists that would adequately protect the public from these hazards. . . .

UFFI is a thermal insulation material used in residences and other buildings. It is manufactured at the job site by mixing a liquid resin containing formaldehyde, a foaming agent, and compressed gas. The resulting liquid foam, which resembles shaving cream, is pumped into the walls of the building being insulated. After a time the mixture solidifies. . . .

We are not unmindful that regulating in the face of scientific uncertainty within ever-tightening budgetary constraints presents the Commission with a difficult task. We nevertheless cannot abdicate our role in the regulatory process. Congress and our circuit's precedents require us to take a "harder look" to determine whether rules adopted under the Consumer Product Safety Act are supported by substantial evidence. That look discloses that the evidence is lacking here. The Commission's rule banning UFFI is VACATED. [Footnote omitted.] Gulf South Insul. Co. v. U.S. Consumer Prod. Safety Com'n, 701 F.2d 1137, 1139–40 (5th Cir. 1983).

urea nitrogen the nitrogen component of urea. The concentration of urea nitrogen in the blood (*blood urea nitrogen*, BUN) is measured in the determination of kidney function; elevated levels of blood urea nitrogen indicate a disorder of kidney function.

ureter (u-re'ter) [Gr. *ourētēr*] [NA] the fibromuscular tube which conveys the urine from the kidney to the bladder. It begins with the pelvis of the kidney, a funnel-like dilatation, and empties into the base of the bladder, being 16 to 18 inches long. It is divided into a pars abdominalis and a pars pelvina. See illustration accompanying *urogenital system*, under *system*. See also *cystoscopy* (Clark case).

On October 27, 1976, the urinary diversion was performed by Dr. Frankel, Albert's urologist. This was accomplished by means of an ileal loop, whereby the **ureters** were severed and connected to a loop of bowel which was then severed from the bowel, closed at one end, and drained through Albert's side. Nahmias v. Trustees of Indiana University, 444 N.E.2d 1204–5 (Ct.App.Ind.1983).

Dr. Shannon was to administer an intravenous pyelogram (IVP) to Ms. Smith ans take X-rays of her kidneys and **ureters**, the ducts that carry urine away from the kidneys to the bladder. Smith v. Shannon, 666 P.2d 351, 353 (Wash.1983).

Dr. Story testified that if a surgeon located the **ureter** and the structure he located looked like a **ureter** it would be a departure from standard medical practice for the surgeon, whose purpose was to cut a nerve ganglion, to cut the **ureter**.

While on the stand, Dr. Story testified as follows:

Q. All right. When you cut it, did it look like—when you cut it—examined it and cut the **ureter**, did it look like a **ureter** to you?

A. It must not have. It must have—when I cut it—or I didn't cut it, excuse me. Excuse me, when Dr. Miller cut it.

Q. When you looked at it and he cut it, it looked like a **ureter** to you then; didn't it?

A. It sure did....

There is testimony to the effect that, at the time it was cut, the **ureter** had rami-like filaments emanating from it and exhibited ganglial bulges, and that both the rami-like filaments and the ganglial bulges are characteristics of the sympathetic nerve chain. We cannot consider such testimony under the rule that only evidence favorable to the plaintiff may be considered. Baker v. Story, 621 S.W.2d 639, 642–3 (Ct.Civ.App. Tex.1981).

Other Authorities: Pugsley v. Privette, 263 S.E.2d 69, 71 (Va. 1980); Williams v. Ricks, 263 S.E.2d 457–8 (Ct.App.Ga.1979); Bly v. Rhoads, 222 S.E.2d 783, 785 (Va.1976); Cronin v. Hagan, 221 N.W.2d 748–9 (Iowa 1974); Clark v. U.S., 402 F.2d 950–2 (4th Cir. 1968).

ureteroileostomy (u-re″ter-o-il″e-os′to-me) anastomosis of the ureters to an isolated loop of the ileum, drained through a stoma on the abdominal wall.

... resident urologists performed a bilateral **ureteroileostomy**, which is a urinary diversion effected by cutting the ureters at the point they enter the bladder, connecting them to the ileum (a section of the small intestine), and passing the ileum out through an opening in the skin of the lower abdomen. The opening is called a stoma, and an external collection device is cemented to the stoma to collect the urine passing out through the ileum....

Dr. Abramson, professor at Albert Einstein College of Medicine in New York and an expert in both Physical Medicine and Rehabilitation and in Spinal Cord Injury cases, stated that indications for a bilateral **ureteroileostomy** are reflux and deterioration of the kidneys accompanied by infections. In Dr. Abramson's opinion, the operation was not indicated in plaintiff's case, because plaintiff had a normal urinary tract, showed good contraction of his bladder, secreted urine, and was able to void despite an obstruction. Dr. Abramson stated that the operation was a controversial procedure in 1967 and should only have been used at a later stage of decay in the plaintiff's urinary tract. Since the operation was irreversible, according to Dr. Abramson, less serious and more conservative forms of treatment should have been tried first. Harrigan v. U.S., 408 F.Supp. 177, 179–80 (E.D.Pa.1976).

ureterostomy (u″re-ter-os′to-me) [uretero- + Gr. stomoun to provide with an opening, or mouth] surgical formation of a permanent fistula through which a ureter may discharge its contents.

urethan (u′rĕ-than) [NF] chemical name: carbamic acid ethyl ester. An antineoplastic, $C_3H_7NO_2$, occurring as white crystals or white, granular powder; it has been used in the treatment of myeloid and lymphatic leukemia and

plasma cell myeloma, but has been replaced largely by superior drugs.

We note, moreover, that the proof shows that a researcher had in 1947 conducted an experiment in which pregnant mice were injected with **urethane**, an anesthetic administered to women during delivery, in order to determine if the offspring developed cancer from the drug.[9] Obviously, this researcher was concerned about a human transplacental carcinogen. [[9] (Larsen, Weed & Rhodes, Pulmonary Tumor Induction by Transplacental Exposure to Urethane, 8 J.Nat.Cancer Inst. 63 [1947].)] Bichler v. Eli Lilly and Co., 450 N.Y.S.2d 776, 778 (N.Y.1982).

urethane See *urethan.*

urethra (u-re′thrah) [Gr. *ourēthra*] the membranous canal conveying urine from the bladder to the exterior of the body. See illustration accompanying *urogenital system,* under *system.* See also *bladder, urinary* (Hall case).

The plastic repair of the ruptured **urethra** was commenced in May 1970, progressed in stages, and was finally completed in April 1971. Appellant effected a complete recovery. Hall v. Musgrave, 517 F.2d 1163–5 (6th Cir. 1975).

She also sustained fractures of the pelvis and a tear of the bladder neck (**urethra**). Brunner v. Slupe, 290 N.E.2d 327–8 (App.Ct.Ill.1972).

The treatment consisted of the insertion of certain instruments into the **urethra** to relieve the stricture and the administration of penicillin as a safeguard against infection. The urine drained during the treatment showed the presence of infection in the lower urinary tract, which was to be expected in view of the abnormal urinary retention. Quick v. Thurston, 290 F.2d 360–1 (D.C.Cir.1961).

urethral smear test See *test, urethral smear.*

urethritis (u″rĕ-thri′tis) inflammation of the urethra. Cited in Capaldi v. Weinberger, 391 F.Supp. 502, 505 (E.D. Pa.1975).

urethrocele (u-re′thro-sēl) [urethro- + Gr. kēlē tumor] 1. prolapse of the female urethra through the meatus urinarius. 2. a diverticulum of the urethral walls encroaching upon the vaginal canal.

During plaintiff's first visit Dr. Grossbard found that she had a **urethrocele** (a protrusion in the urethra).... Buckelew v. Grossbard, 435 A.2d 1150, 1153 (N.J.1981).

Other Authorities: Kerbeck v. Suchy, 270 N.E.2d 291–2 (App. Ct.Ill.1971).

urethroileo conduit See *ileostomy* (Rodriguez case).

urethroplasty (u-re′thro-plas″te) [urethro- + Gr. *plassein* to form] plastic surgery of the urethra; operative repair of a wound or defect in the urethra.

urethroplasty, Johannsen

The **Johannsen urethroplasty** was utilized to correct the strictures in plaintiff's urethral canal. On the first operation of September 21, 1976, an incision through the skin of the undersurface of the penis was made, carrying it down into the tip of the urethra, and split the urethra from the normal tissue from beyond the stricture to the normal tissue behind the stricture, and the skin margin was sewn down to the tube that had been split open. The incision is from the tip of the place where it joins into the scrotum. It is a longitudinal incision. The goal of the first operation was to sew skin onto the urethra that could subsequently be used on the second operation to rebuild the urethra. Concerning the second operation on January 17, 1977, Doctor Carlton stated: "We used the skin we had sewn to the urethra in the first operation to rebuild the tube and roll the skin up into a tube so he then had a new urethra from all the way from the tip of the penis back to the scrotum, and we put a catheter into the bladder to drain the urine." Richard v. Southwest Louisiana Hospital Ass'n, 383 So.2d 84–86 (Ct.App.La. 1980).

urethroplasty, patch

A "**patch urethroplasty**" is an operation to correct a urethral stricture. As explained by Doctor Melton, non-hair bearing skin is cut from the foreskin of the penis or the brachial plexus up in the neck, the skin is de-fatted, the mucosa strained, a "sound" is inserted, and then using sharp dissection the urethra is exposed. Then the scar tissue is cut out, and the non-hair bearing skin is sutured to replace the destroyed tissue. Richard v. Southwest Louisiana Hospital Ass'n, 383 So.2d 83, 85 (Ct.App.La.1980).

URI (upper respiratory infection) See *infection, upper respiratory.*

urinalysis (u″rĭ-nal′ĭ-sis) physical, chemical, or microscopic analysis or examination of urine.

However, a routine **urinalysis** indicated that there was an abnormal amount of protein in the urine as indicated by a +2 [albumin] test. Moreover, there were traces of acetone in the urine as well as traces of bilirubin. Moreover, there were traces of uroliduogen. This indicates there was an abnormal **urinalysis** and there was probably something wrong with Mr. Choice's liver which could have left him in pain. U.S. v. Choice, 392 F.Supp. 460, 462 (E.D.Pa.1975).

urinary tract See *tract, urinary.*

urine (u′rin) [L. *urina;* Gr. *ouron*] the fluid excreted by the kidneys, passed through the ureters, stored in the bladder, and discharged through the urethra. Urine, in health, has an amber color, a slight acid reaction, a peculiar odor, and a bitter, saline taste. The average quantity excreted under ordinary dietary conditions in twenty-four hours is about 1000 to 2000 ml. Specific gravity, about 1.024, varying from 1.005 to 1.030. One thousand parts of healthy urine contain about 960 parts of water and 40 parts of solutes, which consist chiefly of urea, 23 parts; sodium chloride, 11 parts; phosphoric acid, 2.3 parts; sulfuric acid, 1.3 parts; uric acid, 0.5 part; also hippuric acid, leukomaines, urobilin, and certain organic salts. The abnormal matters found in the urine in various conditions include ketone bodies, proteins, proteoses, bile, blood, cystine, glucose, hemoglobin, fat, pus, spermatozoa, epithelial cells, mucous casts, and crystals of sulfanilamide derivatives (crystalluria).

urogram (u′ro-gram) a roentgenogram of part of the urinary tract.

On December 7, 1977, an excretory **urogram** was performed and revealed the existence of an obstructive uropathy on the right side. It was believed that this was due to either a small non-opaque calculus or a recently passed calculus. Brissette v. Schweiker, 566 F.Supp. 626, 629 (E.D.Mo.1983), remanded 730 F.2d 548 (8th Cir. 1984).

On that day, August 1, an IVP was performed as well as a cystoscopy with an attempted right retrograde **urogram**. Clark v. U.S., 402 F.2d 950–1 (4th Cir. 1968).

urography (u-rog′rah-fe) roentgenography of a part of the urinary tract which has been rendered opaque by some opaque medium.

Urokon 70

As to Dr. Adams, the Court submitted to the jury the charge that, in performing the aortogram, he negligently selected **Urokon 70**, a toxic, unsafe and unsuitable substance, as the contrast agent for taking X-ray pictures of the renal arteries and that in obtaining Mrs. Ball's consent to the procedure he failed sufficiently to advise her of the danger of paralysis and other possible serious consequences. . . .

Almost immediately after the injection of **Urokon 70** by Dr. Adams, Mrs. Ball experienced the most excruciating pain in her chest and abdomen. This was shortly followed by a numbness and paralysis of both legs, one of which continues to be paralysed and almost, if not entirely, useless. The X-ray pictures taken during the test show that some of the solution escaped outside the aorta. It is the insistence of plaintiffs that it then migrated to the spinal cord causing damage which resulted in paralysis of Mrs. Ball's leg and some impairment of nerves controlling bowel and kidney action.

Conceding that Mrs. Ball suffered these injuries as the result of the use of **Urokon 70**, defendants insist that, in spite of the utmost skill and care on the part of the surgeon making the test, the escape of dye outside the aorta occurs in about five to ten per cent of the cases and that even where this occurs the extravasated dye is absorbed by the system without harmful effect except that it causes the patient severe pain for two or three hours. It is defendants' theory and insistence that the **Urokon 70** which caused the damage to Mrs. Ball's spinal cord passed through the needle into the aorta and thence into the arteries feeding the spinal cord and that this is a danger inherent in the test since it occurs in spite of all precautions which can be taken in about one per cent of all cases, no matter what contrast agent is used or how skillful the surgeon may be. . . .

Some of the foremost practicing and teaching surgeons testified that, knowing its toxic nature, they have used **Urokon 70** because it gives the best picture and, since the test is a severe and somewhat dangerous procedure used only in extreme cases when all else has failed, it is deemed unwise to have the patient undergo the test without a reasonable expectation that a satisfactory picture can be obtained.

The sales brochure stated in pertinent part as follows:

"Through extensive clinical uses **Urokon Sodium** has been found to be a comparatively safe preparation for the techniques described or referred to in the previous sections. Because of its low toxicity and high opacity to X-rays, it may prove to be useful in still other diagnostic procedures. However, this preparation is not recommended for use as a contrast medium in bronchography and venography at this time, since insufficient clinical data have been collected to assure the most suitable and safe method of administration in these techniques. Furthermore, while **Urokon Sodium** 30% is recommended for use in cerebral angiography, **Urokon** 50% and 70% must never be used in this procedure.''

Urokon 70 is exclusively a prescription product and used only by highly trained surgeons in this specialized field. Ball v. Mallinkrodt Chemical Works, 381 S.W.2d 563, 565–6, 568 (Ct.App.Tenn.1964).

urticaria (ur"tĭ-ka're-ah) [L. *urtica* stinging nettle + *-ia*] a vascular reaction of the skin marked by the transient appearance of smooth, slightly elevated patches (wheals) which are redder or paler than the surrounding skin and often attended by severe itching. The eruption rarely lasts longer than two days, but may exist in a chronic form. Certain foods (e.g., shellfish), drugs (e.g., penicillin), infection, or emotional stress may be the exciting cause. Called also *hives*.

The appellee, Lou Ethel Jarrell (hereinafter referred to as the employee) developed a breaking-out or rash, referred to in the medical testimony as **urticarial hives**, as a result of an allergic reaction to certain fabrics .... Princess Mfg. Co. v. Jarrell, 465 S.W.2d 45 (Ct.App.Ky.1971).

urticarial hives See *urticaria*.

uterus (u'ter-us), pl. *u'teri* [L.; Gr. *hystera*] the hollow muscular organ in female mammals in which the fertilized ovum normally becomes embedded and in which the developing embryo and fetus is nourished. In the nongravid human [NA], it is a pear-shaped structure, about 3 inches in length, consisting of a body, fundus, isthmus, and cervix. Its cavity opens into the vagina below, and into the uterine tube on either side above. It is supported by direct attachment to the vagina and by indirect attachment to various other nearby pelvic structures. See also "*sound the uterus*".

Well, under normal circumstances the mouth of the **womb** tends to be covered with a smooth homogeneous layer of tissue that will be dark bluish or reddish, but has its integrity intact. The tissues at the mouth of Miss _____ **womb** were a bright red color, and the architecture of the smoothness of the surface had been disrupted by some means. Cooper v. State, 447 S.W.2d 179, 184 (Ct.Crim.App.Tex.1969).

uterus, everted See *evert*.

The baby was delivered without incident and Dr. Donald left the hospital a short time later. Then, approximately an hour later, Mrs. Trichel began hemorrhaging severely due to an **everted uterus**, i.e., one which is turned inside out. Dr. Watson and Dr. Truly, an Ob-Gyn, both of whom happened to be at the hospital at the time, responded to the emergency and attempted unsuccessfully to revert the uterus by manually pushing it back to its original position. Trichel v. Caire, 427 So.2d 1227, 1229 (Ct.App.La.1983).

uvea (u've-ah) the vascular middle coat of the eye, comprising the iris, ciliary body, and choroid (tunica vasculosa bulbi [NA]).

uveitis (u"ve-i'tis) [*uvea* + *-itis*] inflammation of the uvea.

uveitis, anterior uveitis involving the structures of the iris and/or ciliary body; iridocyclitis.

V

vaccination, Swine flu See *polyneuritis, acute febrile*.

vaccine (vak'sēn) [L. *vaccinus*] a suspension of attenuated or killed microorganisms (bacteria, viruses, or rickettsiae), administered for the prevention, amelioration, or treatment of infectious diseases.

Vaccines confer protection against diseases by introducing antigens into the body which stimulate the production of immunizing antibodies. This process occurs when lymphocytes, cells contained in the lymph glands, absorb the antigens and produce an antitoxin against the particular disease. Ezagui v. Dow Chemical Corp., 598 F.2d 727, 731 (2d Cir. 1979).

vaccine, antirabies See *vaccine, rabies*.

vaccine, inactivated a vaccine containing nonreplicating microorganisms or viruses which are noninfectious but which retain their protective antigens. Viral vaccines are usually inactivated by agents such as formalin, phenol, or β-propiolactone; bacterial vaccines by heat, acetone, ultraviolet rays, formaldehyde, or phenol.

vaccine, killed See *poliovirus*.

A **killed virus vaccine** is made by growing virus in a tissue culture and killing it clinically to render it incapable of causing disease, but in such a way that the dead virus particles are not chemically altered, and will still, when introduced into the body, act as antigen and cause the body to produce an antibody which will, in the future, strangle any new live wild virus particles coming into the bloodstream, and therefore protect the central nervous system from infection and the inoculated person from disease. Salk developed a **killed virus vaccine** effective against each of the three polio types, and, after testing in the Frances Field trials, it was released for general use in 1955. Griffin v. U.S., 351 F.Supp. 10, 23–24 (E.D.Pa.1972).

vaccine, live a vaccine prepared from live microorganisms or viruses that have been attenuated but that retain their immunogenic properties.

vaccine, live virus hog cholera

The evidence shows that modified **live virus hog cholera vaccine** is manufactured by various American companies under license granted by the United States Department of Agriculture; and when used in conjunction with hog cholera serum concentrate, it is the best-known means of preventing hog cholera. The serum provides passive immunity for approximately 21 days and thus allows the modified **live virus vaccine**, injected at the same time, to produce a permanent immunity after 14 days. It is a known fact that the modified **live virus vaccine** is not 100% effective and may not provide immunity in from 5 to 15% of the hogs vaccinated. Inasmuch as the vaccine contains the **live cholera virus**, even though modified and attenuated, it can in certain circumstances cause a low-grade non-virulent type of hog cholera which, through shedding and passage of wastes, may possibly produce clinical hog cholera in other swine. Denman v. Armour Pharmaceutical Co., 322 F.Supp. 1370, 1372 (N.D.Miss.1970).

vaccine, pertussis [USP], a sterile bacterial fraction or suspension, in an isotonic sodium chloride solution or other suitable diluent, of killed pertussis bacilli (*Bordetella pertussis*) of a strain or strains selected for high antigenic efficiency; used as an active immunizing agent, administered subcutaneously.

Later reasearch, however, indicated that use of Phemerol caused certain endotoxins in the **pertussis vaccine** to leak out from the bacterial cell into the fluid which was injected.

... A jury could reasonably conclude from this evidence that the **pertussis vaccine** is capable of causing encephalopathy such as that experienced by Mark Ezagui, and that the combination in Quadrigen of the **pertussis vaccine** with other chemicals materially increased this risk. Ezagui v. Dow Chemical Corp., 598 F.2d 727, 731 (2d Cir. 1979).

Dr. Yazbak testified that in 1963 it was universally known that there was a definite risk in using **pertussis vaccine** in children who have family history of convulsive disorders and that "DPT", which has **pertussis vaccine** as part of the combination, should not be administered without first taking a detailed history and doing a complete physical. Caron v. U.S., 410 F.Supp. 378, 385 (D.R.I.1975).

vaccine, poliomyelitis; vaccine, polymyelitis, inactivated [USP], a sterile suspension of inactivated poliovirus of Types 1, 2, and 3, which are grown separately in primary cultures of monkey kidney tissue, and after inactivation are combined in suitable proportions; used as an active immunizing agent, administered intramuscularly and subcutaneously. Called also *Salk v.* See also *poliovirus vaccine live oral.*

The initial problem facing researchers attempting to develop a vaccine—cultivation of a growth of polio virus in tissue outside the body—was solved by Dr. Enders at Harvard University in 1949. The scientists also learned that polio virus was of three distinct types, and that to provide effective protection, a vaccine would have to immunize the vaccinee to all three types. . . .

... The first breakthrough resulted from the research of Dr. Jonas Salk, who perfected a "killed virus" vaccine to be administered by inoculation. To produce this vaccine, polio virus is grown in a tissue culture and clinically "killed", that is, rendered incapable of causing disease. In killing the virus, however, no chemical alteration occurs and when it is introduced into the body in the vaccine, the virus acts as an antigen to prompt the production of antibodies. Should a wild or virulent strain of polio virus enter the bloodstream, the antibodies generated as a reaction to the vaccine will destroy it and the vaccine will avoid polio. Reyes v. Wyeth Laboratories, 498 F.2d 1264, 1296 (5th Cir. 1974).

Salk vaccine had certain drawbacks which made it a reliable but rather slow tool in the war against polio. It was not the ideal vaccine for the ultimate in efficient immunization against polio, especially considering that polio struck hardest the low-

er socio-economic groups. First, **Salk vaccine** required hypodermic needle injection. Second, it required three separate injections. Third, it required booster shots every couple of years to remain effective. Fourth, it did not immunize the intestinal tract against infection by polio virus, so that persons immunized with **Salk vaccine** could still be links in the chain of infection of non-immunized persons. The **Salk vaccine** undoubtedly saved thousands upon thousands from the scourges of polio. However, many people felt that many thousands more could be saved if a more easily distributed cheaper vaccine could be developed, especially if that vaccine could provide intestinal immunity and also provide such permanent immunity that booster dosages were not necessary. Thus, in the late 1950's interest turned to the potentials of oral attenuated live-virus vaccine. Griffin v. U.S., 351 F.Supp. 10, 24 (E.D.Pa.1972).

vaccine, poliovirus, live oral [USP], a preparation of one or a combination of the three types of live, attenuated polioviruses, grown separately in primary cultures of monkey kidney tissue; used as an active immunizing agent against poliomyelitis, it is administered orally. Called also *Sabin oral v.*

Developed in the middle and late 1950's, the **Savin** [sic] **oral vaccine** introduced living but attenuated polio virus into the recipient's system. An attenuated polio virus is one which laboratory processes have rendered incapable of producing disease (to the extent of attenuation), but which retains sufficient strength to cause the production of antibodies to resist and destroy an attacking wild or virulent polio virus in the vaccinee's alimentary tract. Three types of "monovalent" vaccines were developed, one to deal with each type of polio virus, but through a "titering" or mixing process, a single "trivalent" oral vaccine can be produced which, upon ingestion, will provide protection against all three types of virus. Reyes v. Wyeth Laboratories, 498 F.2d 1264, 1296 (5th Cir. 1974).

vaccine, rabies [USP], a sterile preparation, in liquid or in dried form, of killed fixed virus of rabies, obtained from brain tissue of rabbits or from duck embryos, which have been infected with fixed rabies virus. It is used as an active immunizing agent in patients infected or contaminated with rabies virus, being administered subcutaneously daily for a minimum of 14 days. Called also *antirabies v.* and *hydrophobia v.* See also *disease, demyelinating* (Hitchcock case); and *Semple vaccine.*

In May and June, 1972, the Department routinely administered duck embryo-**derived antirabies vaccine** ("DEV") as pre-exposure prophylaxis for Foreign Service personnel assigned to Buenos Aires, Argentina, and to other particular stations. The DEV was routinely administered by a nurse, with no physician present. . . .

DEV is an **antirabies vaccine** introduced in 1955 and licensed for use in the United States in 1957. DEV was developed by Eli Lily and Company as an alternative to older nervous tissue vaccine ("NTV"). Serious post-vaccinal neurologic reactions to NTV, including paralysis and death, are not uncommon and make its use hazardous." (Plaintiff's exhibit 15, at 643.) For example, the rate of death for persons immunized with NTV has been estimated at 1 to 35,000. DEV is a suspension of 10% duck embryo tissue infected with a fixed virus and then inactivated. DEV is thought to contain little or none of the "paralytic factor" that causes paralysis and death after treatment with NTV. The identity of the "paralytic factor," however, is not known with certainty. DEV has been described as "markedly reducing" the hazard of post-vaccinal neurologic complications and as "relatively safe". Nevertheless, because DEV contains duck embryo protein, it is capable of causing neurologic reactions similar to NTV. Hitchcock v. U.S., 479 F.Supp. 65–6, 68 (D.D.C.1979).

vaccine, Sabin's oral See *vaccine, poliovirus, live oral.*

vaccine, Salk See *vaccine, poliomyelitis.*

vaccine, Semple an antirabies vaccine prepared from 4 per cent inoculated rabbit brain treated with 0.5 per cent phenol.

vaccine, swine flu See also *polyneuritis, acute febrile.*

Later that same day appellant began experiencing symptoms of nausea, weakness, aching muscles and chills. She was initially treated by her personal physician and subsequently, she was admitted to the hospital for a period of two days. The diagnosis at the hospital was "serum-type reaction" to the **swine flu vaccine.** Daniels v. U.S., 704 F.2d 587, 590 (11th Cir. 1983).

vaccine, triple a vaccine prepared from the cultures of three different species of organisms.

Originally, an oral live virus vaccine was administered separately for each of the three types of polio virus. Lederle was licensed by the Surgeon General of the United States for production of the separate or monovalent vaccine on March 27, 1962. On June 25, 1963, Lederle received a license for a **trivalent vaccine,** or one in which all three types of the attenuated live polio virus were used. The product was produced and sold by Lederle under the trade name "Trivalent Orimune." Stahlheber v. American Cyanamid Co., 451 S.W.2d 48, 51 (Mo.1970).

vaccine, trivalent See *vaccine, triple.*

vaccine, typhoid [USP], a sterile suspension, in buffered isotonic sodium chloride solution or other suitable diluent, of killed typhoid bacilli (*Salmonella typhosa*) of a strain selected for high antigenic efficiency, and containing approximately 1 billion typhoid bacilli in each milliliter; used as an active immunizing agent, administered subcutaneously. Called also *antityphoid v., typhobacterin, vaccinum antityphicum,* and *vaccinum typhosum.*

[A .5 milliliter dosage of **typhoid vaccine** is] almost sub-lethal for a child of four months. . . . Caron v. U.S., 410 F.Supp. 378, 386 (D.R.I.1976).

Vacutainer See *device, blood-letting.*

vagal (va'gal) pertaining to the vagus nerve. See also *nervus vagus.*

The automobile collision could have caused the respiratory arrest, in her opinion, by a **vagal** vagel response when the plaintiff hit the seat or something and quit breathing. Henderson v. Life and Cas. Ins. Co., 574 S.W.2d 634–5 (Ct.Civ.App.Tex. 1978).

vagina (vah-ji'nah), pl. *vagi'nae* [L.] [NA] the canal in the female, extending from the vulva to the cervix uteri, which receives the penis in copulation.

vaginal cuff See *cuff, vaginal.*

vaginismus (vaj"ĭ-niz'mus) [L.] painful spasm of the vagina due to local hyperesthesia; it is distinguished as *superficial* and *deep,* according as the seat is at the entrance of the vagina, or probably in the bulbocavernosus muscle, or in the levator ani muscle.

He is presently treating a patient who is seeking a church annulment for impotency due to **vaginismus.** It is interesting to note that this patient, who is impotent so far as her husband is concerned, was raped by a third party between the time the annulment proceeding was instituted and the time of the doctor's first examination of her, and she eventually gave birth to a child, the direct result of the rape.

Doctor Burnett concluded that in our case the wife's problem is obviously a psychogenic one, due to **vaginismus** producing impotency, "that if such a long trial by these partners with obvious positive direction, that this would support a conclusion that this case is incurable." . . .

. . . **Vaginismus,** physical or psychical, is a recognized cause of incurable impotency in New Jersey. D. v. C., 91 N.J.Super. 562, 221 A.2d 763 (Ch.1966); Godfrey v. Shatwell, 38 N.J. Super. 501, 119 A.2d 479 (Ch.1955); and, imperfect intercourse is not enough to rebut a finding of impotence. T v. M, 242 A.2d 670, 673 (Super.Ct.N.J.1968).

vaginismus, mental extreme aversion to coitus on the part of a woman, attended with contraction of the muscles when the act is attempted.

vaginismus, psychical See *vaginismus, mental.*

vaginismus, psychogenic See *vaginismus, mental.*

vagotomy (va-got'o-me) [*vagus* + Gr. *tomē* a cutting] interruption of the impulses carried by the vagus nerve or nerves; so called because it was first performed by surgical methods. See also *operation, Billroth's* (Johnson case); and *pyloroplasty.*

He testified that gall stones sometimes form as a consequence of a **vagotomy** and related the stone formation to his first surgery. Bellard v. Woodward Wight & Co., Ltd., 362 So.2d 819, 822 (Ct.App.La.1978).

The surgical severance of both branches of the vagus nerve is called a complete **vagotomy.** Nichols v. Smith, 507 S.W.2d 518–19 (Tex.1974).

vagus nerve See *nervus vagus.*

valgus (val'gus) [L.] bent outward, twisted; denoting a deformity in which the angulation of the part is away from the midline of the body, as in *talipes valgus.* The term valgus is an adjective and should be used only in connection with the noun it describes, as talipes valgus, genu valgum, coxa valga, etc. Cf. *varus.*

There was a mild **valgus** alignment of the foot. Osteomyelitis has been present in the past and it appeared to be relatively quiescent as of December 1975. There was found to be some compensatory shortening of the right lower extremity, secondary to the arthrodeses that have been carried out. The medical evidence further indicates that there is a loss of normal function and heel-toe gait pattern, right ankle and foot. Minney v. Secretary of Health, Ed. & Welfare, 439 F.Supp. 706–7 (W.D. Ark.1977).

Valium (val'e-um) trademark for a preparation of diazepam. See also *diazepam*.

valley fever See *coccidioidomycosis*.

value (val'u) a measure of worth or efficiency; a quantitative measurement of the activity, concentration, etc., of specific substances. See also *normal values*.

value, liminal that intensity of a stimulus which produces a just noticeable impression.

In determining whether the presence of such contaminants constituted a health hazard, the inspectors from Aetna referred to the so-called "threshold limit value" (TLV) published by a respected committee of the American Conference of Governmental Industrial Hygienists (ACGIH). The TLV established by the ACGIH committee for each particular contaminant was reviewed on a yearly basis and modified according to industrial experience and additional toxicological studies; TLV standards for humans were generally established at one tenth of the pollutant concentration level to which test animals could be exposed without suffering discernible harm. Because of this "safety factor" thus built into the TLV standards, each TLV represented conditions under which it was believed that nearly all workers could be "repeatedly exposed day after day without adverse effects." Murphy v. Owens-Corning Fiberglas Corp., 447 F.Supp. 557, 562–3 (D.Kan.1977).

A threshold value is that level of exposure below which no adverse health effects occur, while the dose-response relationship quantifies the association between disease-producing levels of exposure and the incidence of disease. Reserve Mining Co. v. U.S., 498 F.2d 1073, 1080 (8th Cir. 1974).

values, normal the range in concentration of specific substances found in normal healthy tissues, secretions, etc.

value, threshold See *value, liminal*.

valva (val'vah), pl. *val'vae* [sing. of L. *valvae* folding doors] [NA] a valve: a membranous fold in a canal or passage, which prevents the reflux of the contents passing through it.

valva aortae [NA], aortic valve: a valve composed of three semilunar cusps or segments (posterior, right, and left), guarding the aortic orifice in the left ventricle of the heart; it prevents backflow into the left ventricle. Called also *valvulae semilunares aortae* and *semilunar valve*.

van den Bergh's disease, test (van den bergz') [A. A. Hijmans (Hymans) *van den Bergh*, Dutch physician, 1869–1943]. See *enterogenous cyanosis*, under *cyanosis*; and see under *tests*.

Additionally Guillory may have had aortic insufficiency, a secondary **valve** problem, involving a valve distortion whereby blood leaving the heart through the valve flows back into the heart, with necessarily ill effect....

... On the day in question, the outflow **valve** from the left ventricular chamber of the heart had not opened wide enough to let sufficient blood pass through, and then had not completely closed, allowing some of the blood to rush back into the heart. Guillory v. U.S. Fidelity & Guar. Ins. Co., 420 So.2d 119–21 (La.1982).

Plaintiff's invention is a device for preparing heart valves for implantation into human coronary patients. In the human heart, blood is pumped out of the heart into the aortal artery, passing through the **aortic valve** which prevents it from flowing back into the heart. This valve consists of three flaps of tissue, or "cusps", located at the junction between the heart and the artery. When blood presses against the valve from the heart side, the cusps separate to permit it to flow through into the artery. However, when blood attempts to flow back through, the cusps close together, or "coapt", to prevent its passage. Hancock Laboratories v. American Hospital Supply, 199 U.S. P.Q. 279, 280 (N.D.Ill.1978).

It would be my opinion, still, that the presence of an **aortic valve** prosthesis, with even the modern cloth covered metal poppet type, with its concomitant dangers of thrombo embolic complications, bacterial endocarditis, tissue over-growth about the valve, for example, plus the fact that a pathology of the dilated aortic root showed a connective tissue disorder, indicating an inherent weakness of the aortic room, or a possible variant of Marfan's Syndrome, which would be incompatible with flying safety. Loomis v. McLucas, 553 F.2d 634, 636 (10th Cir. 1977).

valva atrioventricularis sinistra [NA], left atrioventricular valve: the valve between the left atrium and left ventricle of the heart; it usually has two cusps (anterior and posterior), but additional small cusps may be present. Called also *valvula bicuspidalis* [*mitralis*] and *bicuspid or mitral valve*.

In March, 1975, petitioner again entered a hospital and underwent open heart surgery for replacement of the **mitral valve** with a prosthetic device. His condition was diagnosed as "rheumatic heart disease." Vecchiarello v. Board of Trustees, etc., 453 N.Y.S.2d 971–2 (Sup.Ct.N.Y.Cty.1982).

valva ileocecalis [NA], ileocecal valve: a functional valve at junction of the ileum and cecum, consisting of circular muscle of the terminal ileum. The ileocecal opening has two folds, one above and one below, which project into the cecum. Called also *valvula coli*.

There are numerous scattered diverticula in the sigmoid colon. Remainder of the colon is probably within normal limits down to the region of the **ileocecal valve**. There is a large filling defect which probably represents lipomatous infiltration of the **ileocecal valve**. It has a little different appearance than the usual case of this condition and this may be because of the place of entrance of the **ileocecal valve** into the cecal region.... Steinbach v. Barfield, 428 So.2d 915, 918 (Ct.App. La.1983).

valve (valv) a membranous fold in a canal or passage, which prevents the reflux of the contents passing through it. See also *valva*; and *valvula*.

Dr. Phillips stated he knew Mr. Hood was an uneducated man and he described the carotid body as similar to a **valve** in an automobile tire because Mr. Hood would understand that explanation.[3] [3 The full response of Dr. Phillips to the question asked at trial regarding the "**valve**" explanation was as follows: Q. Now there is no **valve** effect with the carotid body that is removed, is there? A. This spasmodic element which causes a valve like effect, the mechanism of a **valve** like effect affects the entire bronchial tube tree. The operation is done in the neck and the sympathetic effect is to the lungs. There is no operation to the lungs at all. It is a sympathetic effect to the bronchial tubes. You see, the bronchial tubes have muscles in them, it is involuntary muscle, and when you go into a spasm or have a spasm in this vein those bronchial tubes close off. Now there is swelling or narrowing. Then the air gets in easier and when it closes by coughing or spasm, then the air has difficulty in getting out. It is merely.... There is no removal of the **valve**, it was just a method of attempting to explain to the patient air flow. For example, you have an air tire and you have a **valve** and you pump it up. The air goes in and none comes out. But if that **valve** is removed, why then you pump it up, the air immediately comes out. It was a method of explaining ... really there was no **valve** removed.] Hood v. Phillips, 554 S.W.2d 160, 162 (Tex.1977).

valve of aorta; valve, aortic See *valva aortae.*

valve, artificial a man-made cardiac valve.

valve, atrioventricular, left See *valva atrioventricularis sinistra.*

valve, Bjork-Shiley prosthetic

On May 16, 1975, Mrs. Jamison had congestive heart failure and underwent open heart surgery to correct a dysfunctional mitral valve caused by childhood rheumatic fever. Her natural valve was replaced with a **Bjork-Shiley prosthetic valve.** Jamison v. Monarch Life Ins. Co., 652 P.2d 13–14 (Ct.App.Wash. 1982).

valve, ileocecal; valve, ileocolic See *valva ileocecalis.*

valve, mitral See *valva atrioventricularis sinistra.*

valve, porcine artificial mitral

Dr. Henry Lang, M.D., her cardiologist, determined that the artificial heart valve was not functioning properly and Mrs. Jamison again underwent surgery to replace her failed valve with a **porcine artificial mitral valve.** Her recovery was normal. Jamison v. Monarch Life Ins. Co., 652 P.2d 13–14 (Ct.App. Wash.1982).

valve, sphincter See *sphincter, O'Beirne's.*

valvula (val'vu-lah), pl. *valvulae* [L., dim. of *valva*] a small valve; once used in official nomenclature as a general term to designate a valve, such as in the heart, but in NA restricted to designation of a cusp of the aortic valve or of the valve of the pulmonary trunk, or the valves of the anus, foramen ovale, navicular fossa, coronary sinus, inferior vena cava, or of the lymphatic vessels and veins.

varnish (var'nish) a solution of rosin, of resin, or of several resins in a suitable solvent or solvents, applied in a thin layer to form a hard, smooth surface; sometimes used in dentistry as a protective film for the dental pulp.

Varnish, a thermosetting material, does not soften and flow when heat is applied. Kynar is a thermoplastic material; it softens when heat is applied, and its oxygen permeability is thereby increased. International Tel. & Tel. Corp. v. Raychem Corp., 538 F.2d 453, 458 (1st Cir. 1976).

varus (va'rus) [L.] bent inward; denoting a deformity in which the angulation of the part is toward the midline of the body, as talipes varus. The term varus is an adjective

and should be used only in connection with the noun it describes, as talipes varus, genu varum, coxa vara, etc. Cf. *valgus.*

... "minimal **varus** deformity," or slight bowleggedness, was noted by a Dr. Hull in both of Mr. Shepard's knees. This condition is also consistent with degenerative arthritis....

... He noted that x-rays showed significant degenerative changes in Mr. Shepard's knees since 1972, and found "rather remarkable [**varus**] deformity." (bowleggedness) Dr. Griffin testified that such a deformity "means almost always that there's been significant bony change in one of the compartments of the knee.... Shepard v. Midland Foods, Inc., 666 P.2d 758, 760–1 (Mont.1983).

vas (vas), pl. *va'sa* [L.] a vessel: any canal for carrying a fluid; [NA] a general term for such channels, especially those carrying blood, lymph, or spermatozoa.

vas deferens See *ductus deferens.*

vascular (vas'ku-lar) pertaining to blood vessels or indicative of a copious blood supply.

Dr. Zarins currently practices **vascular** surgery at the University of Chicago. He also gives instruction at the medical school there on **vascular** disorders, such as diseases of the arteries and veins, clotting, and other circulatory problems. Weinstock v. Ott, 444 N.E.2d 1227, 1234 (Ct.App.Ind.1983).

Doctor Kairys' testimony reflects that he knew Mrs. Hoeke was suffering from **vascular** insufficiency, that he did not need vascular consultants to assist him in the diagnosis of this problem and that he recognized and appreciated the risk of the **vascular** insufficiency which was of course, the cause of the loss of Mrs. Hoeke's right leg. Hoeke v. Mercy Hospital of Pittsburgh, 445 A.2d 140, 145 (Super.Ct.Pa.1982).

Vascular, as above used [see **pia mater**], means full of vessels. York v. Daniels, 259 S.W.2d 109, 111 (Springfield Ct.App. Mo.1953).

vascularization (vas"ku-lar-i-za'shun) the process of becoming vascular, or the natural or surgically induced development of vessels in a tissue.

Ordinarily, the body will in time renew the blood supply to the bone tissue in which such necrosis has occurred. In the event the body fails so to revascularize the bone tissue, surgical procedures can accomplish the **revascularization**. (N.T. 263)

When **revascularization** occurs, whether by natural or surgical means, the bone tissue in which the necrosis has occurred will regain its hard character and will retain its normal anatomical structure. (N.T. 264).

Until such **revascularization** process has been completed, however, and while the bone tissue in which the necrosis has occurred is still soft, the bone may become deformed at the location of such soft tissue if external force is applied to such location. (N.T. 182, 187) Rosario v. Amer. Export-Isbrandtsen Lines, Inc., 395 F.Supp. 1192, 1202 (E.D.Pa.1974), reversed and remanded 531 F.2d 1227 (3d Cir. 1976).

vasculitis (vas"ku-li'tis) [L. *vasculum* vessel + *-itis*] inflammation of a vessel; angiitis.

Vasculitis is a general term for inflammation of the blood vessels, which can be caused by a reaction to drugs. Hemingway v. Ochsner Clinic, 722 F.2d 1220, 1222 (5th Cir. 1984).

vasectomy (vah-sek'to-me) [*vas* + Gr. *ektomē* excision] surgical removal of the ductus (vas) deferens, or of a portion of it; done in association with prostatectomy, or to induce infertility.

Plaintiff's petition alleged that on September 29, 1976, defendant performed a contraceptive bilateral **vasectomy** upon him. Further, "[t]hat previous to said surgery, the Defendant, neither personally nor through his agents, informed Plaintiff . . . of the risks involved in said surgical procedure, which were known or should have been known to the Defendant, such as the development of sperm granulomas, hematomas and testicular atrophy, and the probability of each such risk." . . .

The pleadings, depositions and interrogatory answers on file disclose that defendant asserts he told plaintiff at their first meeting about the complications of bleeding into the scrotum (scrotal hematoma), infection, sperm granuloma and several other "alleged possibil[ities]": rheumatoid arthritis, multiple sclerosis and Hodgkin's disease. Defendant was aware of the possibility of testicular atrophy, but did not inform plaintiff of that because the possibility is "extremely remote." Plaintiff denies he was informed of these possible complications. Cowman v. Hornaday, 329 N.W.2d 422–3 (Iowa 1983).

On February 20, 1976, Fisher performed the **vasectomy** in his office. The procedure lasted about one to one and one-half hours. Fisher used the bilateral incision method which entails making an incision of approximately one-fourth of an inch in length in both sides of the scrotum. Stanley v. Fisher, 417 N.E.2d 932, 933 (Ct.App.Ind.1981).

. . . in a small percentage of cases the operation will be unsuccessful even though the physician exercised the highest degree of care.

This is because the vas deferens, which is severed during a **vasectomy** operation, has a natural tendency to grow back together again, or recanalize. Because of the possibility of recanalization, most plaintiffs in malpractice actions do not attempt to prove that the **vasectomy** was negligently performed but instead allege negligent postoperative care. See Lombard, Vasectomy, 10 Suffolk U.L.Rev. 25; Note, 56 Geo.L.J. 976. Sherlock v. Stillwater Clinic, 260 N.W.2d 169, 171 (Minn. 1977).

Other Authorities: Maggard v. McKelvey, 627 S.W.2d 44, 46 (Ct.App.Ky.1981).

vasoconstriction (vas"o-kon-strik'shun) the diminution of the caliber of vessels, especially constriction of arterioles leading to decreased blood flow to a part.

vasoconstrictive (vas"o-kon-strik'tiv) pertaining to, characterized by, or producing vasoconstriction.

LSD, being an ergot derivative, is **vasoconstrictive**, could inhibit the flow of blood to the hand, and could have been a competent producing cause of the gangrene which developed. Ward v. Kovacs, 390 N.Y.S.2d 931, 934 (2d Dep't 1977).

vasoconstrictor (vas"o-kon-strik'tor) causing constriction of an agent (motor nerve or chemical compound) that causes constriction of the blood vessels.

Dr. Ochsner testified that a **vasoconstrictant** should not be given a patient being treated for acute arterial insufficiency. From the evidence introduced at trial, the jury could have concluded that a staff doctor gave Hemingway Cafergot, a **vasoconstrictant**, on July 9th, when he knew or should have known that the patient was being treated for acute arterial insufficiency. Hemingway v. Ochsner Clinic, 722 F.2d 1220, 1225 (5th Cir. 1984).

vasodilatation (vas"o-di-lah-ta'shun) a state of increased caliber of the blood vessels.

vasospasm (vas'o-spazm) spasm of the blood vessels, resulting in decrease in their caliber.

Spasmodic contractions of the small blood vessels in the fingers ("**vasospasm**") caused the extreme pain. Sears, Roebuck & Co. v. Workmen's Comp.Appeal Bd., 409 A.2d 486–7 (Commonwealth Ct.Pa.1979).

vastus medialis See *musculus vastus medialis.*

VCM See *vinyl chloride* (Society of Plastics Indus., Inc. case).

vegetative (vej'e-ta"tiv) functioning involuntarily or unconsciously, as the vegetative nervous system. See also *system, vegetative nervous.*

Since Brother Fox's EEG showed "minimal activity", he did not meet the criteria of "brain death" at the time of the hearing. A "**vegetative** state", on the other hand, "is a state where the individual is partially responsive . . . but . . . has no significant cognitive functions . . . [although he] does have some primitive cerebral reflexes." Brother Fox was in such a state at this time although Dr. Goldensohn was not certain whether this condition had stabilized. . . .

. . . that "[a]s a result of diffuse cerebral and subcortical anoxia brought on by cardiac arrest suffered on October 2, 1979, Brother Fox lost the ability to then respirate spontaneously and fell into a comatose, **vegetative** state in which he has since been maintained through use of a respirator. . . He is in a chronic **vegetative** and akinetic mute state as a result of which only certain lower **vegetative** functions operate. The higher functions of the brain, the so-called cognitive and sapient functions, have been lost and it is highly improbable that they will ever return. To the extent that any further improvements may occur, they will relate only to Brother Fox's **vegetative** functioning. . . It was the unanimous conclusion of the physicians who testified in this case, that, to a reasonable degree of medical certainty, there is no reasonable possibility that Brother Fox will ever return from the state he is now in to a condition in which the cognitive and sapient powers of the brain—the ability to feel, see, think, sense, communicate, feel emotions and the like—operate. The prognosis is that Brother Fox whether on or off the respirator, will die". . . . Eichner v. Dillon, 426 N.Y.S.2d 517, 529 (2d Dep't 1980).

vein (vān) [L. *vena*] a vessel through which blood passes from various organs or parts back to the heart. Called also *vena* [NA]. All veins except the pulmonary veins carry blood low in oxygen. Veins, like arteries, have three coats, an *inner, middle,* and *outer,* but the coats are not so thick, and they collapse when the vessel is cut. Many veins have *valves* formed of reduplications of their lining membrane, which prevent the backward flow of blood

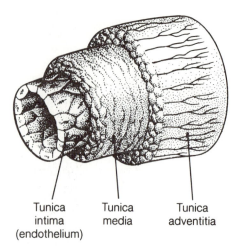

Tunica intima (endothelium)   Tunica media   Tunica adventitia

The three coats of a vein.

away from the heart. See illustrations accompanying the *Table of Venae*, under *vena*.

vein, central retinal See *vena centralis retinae.*

vein, saphenous (great) See *vena saphena magna.*

vein stripping See *strip.*

vein, varicose a dilated tortuous vein, usually in the subcutaneous tissues of the leg; incompetency of the venous valves is associated.

Dr. James Thompson testified for the defendant that Thompson suffered from two basic conditions: **varicose veins** (thrombophlebitis) and hardening of the arteries (arteriosclerosis). The doctor explained that **varicose veins** is a common ailment which results from thickening of the veins and has a tendency to make the legs swell. Such can have serious effects if a blood clot, which may form in the vein, breaks off and flows through the veins into the heart or lungs. Thompson v. Occidental Life Insurance Co. of Cal., 513 P.2d 353, 365 (Cal.1973).

vena (ve′nah), pl. *ve′nae* [L.] [NA] vein: a vessel that conveys blood to or toward the heart, or from the heart itself to the right atrium. See also *vein.* For names and description of specific veins, see *Table of Venae* and accompanying illustrations.

TABLE OF VENAE

vena cava inferior [NA], inferior vena cava: the venous trunk for the lower extremities and for the pelvic and abdominal viscera; it begins at the level of the fifth lumbar vertebra by union of the common iliac veins, passes upward on the right of the aorta, and empties into the right atrium of the heart. Cited in Carmichael v. Reitz, 95 Cal.Rptr. 381, 390 (Ct.App.Cal.1971).

... plaintiff was hospitalized after an episode of blurred and marred vision, which was diagnosed as thrombosis of the **central retinal vein**, left eye, resulting in $20/200$ vision, or functional blindness, in that eye. In her applications for relief, plaintiff complained of loss of vision and dizziness. Gudlis v. Califano, 452 F.Supp. 401–2 (N.D.Ill.1978).

vena centralis retinae [NA], central vein of retina: the vein that is formed by union of the retinal veins; it passes out of the eyeball in the optic nerve to empty into the superior ophthalmic vein.

vena femoralis [NA], femoral vein: a vein that lies in the proximal two-thirds of the thigh; it is a direct continuation of the popliteal vein, follows the course of the femoral artery, and at the inguinal ligament becomes the external iliac vein. NOTE: Vascular surgeons refer to the portion of the femoral vein proximal to the branching of the deep femoral vein as the *common femoral vein*, and to its continuation distal to the branching as the *superficial femoral vein.*

Dr. McClenathan discovered that a major leg vein, the **common femoral**, had been severed. Although this vein is normally much further below the surface of the leg than the superficial ones that are stripped, Dr. Raffaelly had apparently mistaken it for one which was to be removed. Bridgford v. U.S., 550 F.2d 978, 980 (4th Cir. 1977).

Petitioner complains that Dr. Bocian dissected and examined only a superficial vein from the right leg and did not dissect or examine the deep veins, i.e., the femoral and popliteal veins, which carry 90 per cent of the blood and through which emboli would be carried to the lungs. Foremost Dairies, Inc. v. Industrial Accident Com'n, 47 Cal.Rptr. 173, 183 (Ct.App.Cal. 1965).

vena poplitea [NA], popliteal vein: a vein following the popliteal artery, and formed by union of the venae comitantes of the anterior and posterior tibial arteries; at the adductor hiatus it becomes continuous with the femoral vein. See also *vena femoralis* (Foremost Dairies, Inc. case).

vena saphena accessoria [NA], accessory saphenous vein: a vein that, when present, drains the medial and posterior superficial parts of the thigh and opens into the great saphenous vein.

vena saphena magna [NA], great saphenous vein: the longest vein in the body, extending from the dorsum of the foot to just below the inguinal ligament, where it opens into the femoral vein.

"**Saphenous**" relates to the two chief superficial veins of the leg. Ziegert v. South Chicago Community Hospital, 425 N.E. 2d 450, 453 (App.Ct.Ill.1981).

To remedy the error, Dr. McClenathan immediately joined the remaining portion of the severed femoral vein to an intact portion of the **greater saphenous vein**. This surgical procedure, known as an anastomosis, restored the drainage of blood from Bridgford's leg. Drs. Ryskamp and Raffaelly then completed the vein stripping operation. Bridgford v. U.S., 550 F.2d 978, 980 (4th Cir. 1977).

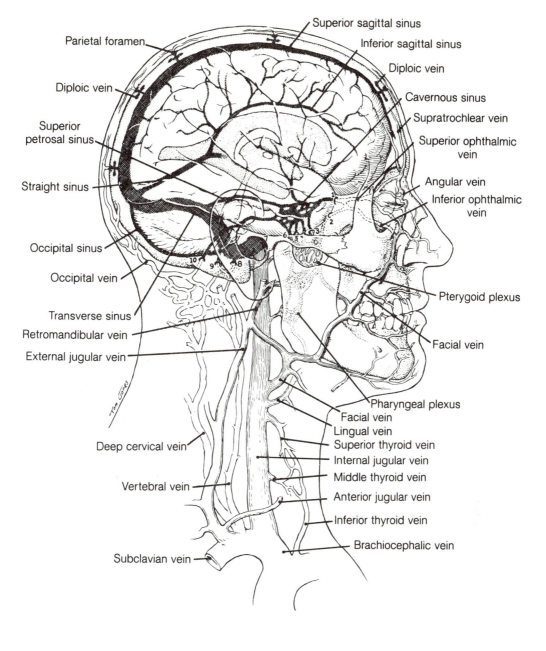

VEINS OF THE HEAD AND NECK
(Modified from Jones and Shepard.)

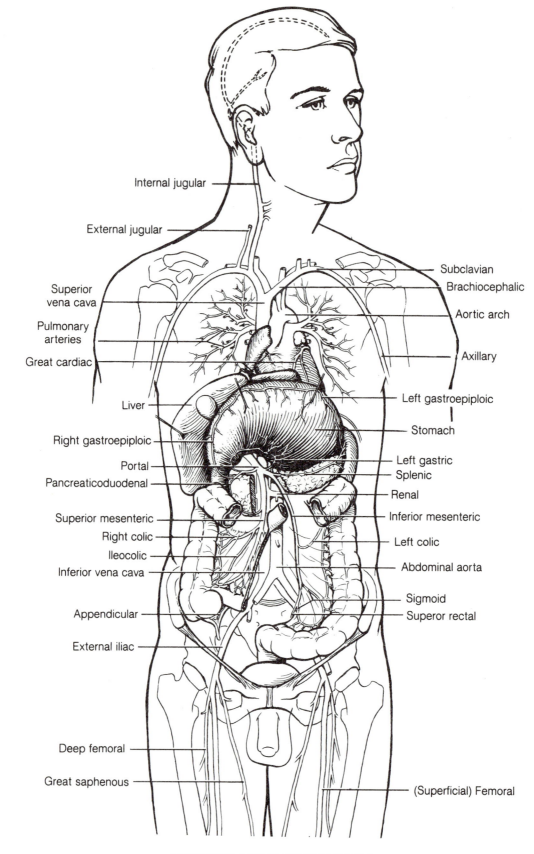

Internal jugular

External jugular

Superior vena cava

Pulmonary arteries

Great cardiac

Liver

Right gastroepiploic

Portal

Pancreaticoduodenal

Superior mesenteric

Right colic

Ileocolic

Inferior vena cava

Appendicular

External iliac

Deep femoral

Great saphenous

Subclavian

Brachiocephalic

Aortic arch

Axillary

Left gastroepiploic

Stomach

Left gastric

Splenic

Renal

Inferior mesenteric

Left colic

Abdominal aorta

Sigmoid

Superor rectal

(Superficial) Femoral

PRINCIPAL VEINS OF THE BODY

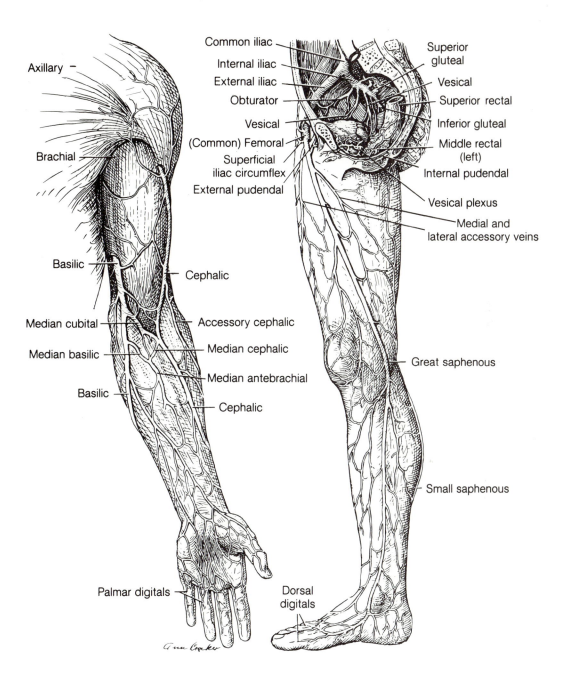

SUPERFICIAL VEINS OF THE EXTREMITIES

Because circulation in Donna's leg was still unsatisfactory on April 10, Dr. Lillehei reopened the area of the previous incisions and, using part of the **saphenous vein**, constructed a by-pass graft in the femoral artery around the site of the previous incisions. Walstad v. Univ. of Minnesota Hospitals, 442 F.2d 634, 637–8 (8th Cir. 1971).

vena subclavia [NA], subclavian vein: the vein that continues the axillary as the main venous stem of the upper member, follows the subclavian artery, and joins with the internal jugular vein to form the brachiocephalic vein.

First, Doctor Hirschel attempted to locate the **subclavian vein** on plaintiff's left side—the same side as her partially collapsed tuberculoid lung. However, the doctor could not find the vein so he attempted the same procedure on the right side. Eichelberger v. Barnes Hosp., 655 S.W.2d 699, 703 (Mo.Ct. App. 1983).

---

venogram See *phlebogram*.

venom (ven'um) [L. *venenum* poison] a poison; specifically, a toxic substance normally secreted by a serpent, insect, or other animal.

venom, cobra See *Nyloxin*.

ventilation (ven″tĭ-la'shun) [L. *ventilatio*] in respiratory physiology, the process of exchange of air between the lungs and the ambient air. *Pulmonary ventilation* (usually measured in liters per minute) refers to the total exchange, whereas *alveolar ventilation* refers to the effective ventilation of the alveoli, in which gas exchange with the blood takes place.

His report indicates that Haywood's maximum voluntary **ventilation** is less than the value set forth in interim regulations [4] for determining the existence of pneumoconiosis. Haywood's expiratory volume was slightly above the values set forth in the regulations. [[4] See 20 C.F.R. § 410.490(b)(ii).] Haywood v. Secretary of Health & Human Services, 699 F.2d 277, 280 (6th Cir. 1983).

As a result [of chest muscle paralysis induced by curare], the anesthesiologist had to "breathe" for him by squeezing a bag of oxygen into the lungs, a procedure called **ventilation**. People v. Stewart, 358 N.E.2d 487, 489–90 (N.Y.1976).

ventilatory function study See *test, ventilation*.

ventricle (ven'trĭ-k'l) a small cavity, such as one of the several cavities of the brain, or one of the lower chambers of the heart; called also *ventriculus*.

ventricle of heart one of a pair of cavities, with thick muscular walls, that make up the bulk of the heart. Called also *ventriculus cordis* [NA]. See also *ventriculus dexter cordis*; and *ventriculus sinister cordis*.

His electrocardiogram indicated that he had had a recent heart attack, with a possibility of some ballooning or dilation of the wall of the **left** ventricle, which is the main pumping chamber of the heart, due to the heart muscle damage he had sustained with his heart attack. Fain v. St. Paul Ins. Co., 602 S.W.2d 577, 580 (Ct.App.Tex.1980).

ventricular septal defect See *defect, ventricular septal*.

ventriculo-atrial shunt See *ventriculoatriostomy*.

ventriculoatriostomy (ven-trik″u-lo-a″tre-os'to-me) surgical creation of a passage, by means of subcutaneously placed catheters with a one-way valve, permitting drainage of cerebrospinal fluid from a cerebral ventricle to the right atrium by way of the jugular vein; performed for relief of hydrocephalus.

Decedent, who had reached the age of majority, see ORS 109.510, signed consent forms for the pneumoencephalogram on January 3, 1978, at 11:45 a.m., and for a pneumoencephalogram followed by a ventriculo-peritoneal shunt, **ventriculo-atrial shunt** or craniotomy at 5:00 p.m. that same day. Mendez v. State of Oregon, 669 P.2d 364–5 (Ct.App.Or.1983).

ventriculogram (ven-trik'u-lo-gram) a roentgenogram of the cerebral ventricles.

Doctors Benjamin Allen and Richard Ashby, Air Force medical officers, suspecting a brain tumor, decided to perform a **ventriculogram** and pneumoencephalogram. These very painful procedures involve the introduction of air into the brain and spinal cord, respectively, as a part of x-ray examination of the brain.

During the examination Harrison was placed in a special chair which could be positioned to permit the doctors to control the movement of the air bubble. Typically, the back of the chair is dropped, the patient is placed first in a supine position and is then rotated upside down. When the x-rays from the **ventriculogram** proved inconclusive, the doctors injected an air bubble into Harrison's spine. The needle used in the **ventriculogram** was left in Harrison's skull during the subsequent procedure.

During the course of the tests and while the chair was being moved, Harrison lost consciousness. Upon reviving, she noted a slight numbness in her arm, a condition the doctors described as a normal reaction to the tests. Other patients informed Harrison that they, too, had experienced transient numbness. As anticipated, Harrison's numbness soon disappeared....

... In less than a minute the decade-old mystery of Sibyl Harrison's enigmatic difficulties was solved: During the course of the tests at Wilford Hall the needle from the **ventriculogram** had plunged into the center of Sibyl Harrison's brain. Before beginning the spinal puncture Ashby and Allen had neglected to remove or secure the needle, or replace it with a safer, more flexible needle. While Harrison was being turned about, the needle was driven into her thalamus. Harrison v. U.S., 708 F.2d 1023–4, 1026 (5th Cir. 1983).

ventriculoplasty See *resection, wedge*.

ventriculus (ven-trik'u-lus), pl. *ventric'uli* [L., dim. of *venter* belly] [NA] a small cavity in an organ; called also *ventricle*.

ventriculus dexter cordis [NA], right ventricle of heart: the cavity of the heart that propels the blood through the pulmonary trunk and arteries into the lungs. See illustration accompanying heart.

ventriculus sinister cordis [NA], left ventricle of heart: the cavity of the heart that propels the blood out through the aorta into the systemic arteries. See illustration.

verbotonal program

The WPSD program, known as the "**verbotonal program**," appears to be centered around the development of the child's residual hearing ability. This method is relatively new to this country. WPSD is one of the very few verbotonal schools in the United States. Eberle v. Board of Public Ed. of Sch.Dist., 444 F.Supp. 41–2 (D.Pa.1977).

vermicide (ver′mĭ-sīd) [*vermis* + L. *caedere* to kill] an anthelmintic drug or medicine destructive to intestinal animal parasites.

With regard to the direct utility of plaintiff's claimed compounds as **vermicides** (anthelmintics), plaintiff introduced evidence which shows that the claimed 1-azaphenothiazine possesses more than one hundred times the anthelmintic effect on ascaris worms of unsubstituted 4-azaphenothiazine, the structural formula of which is suggested by Takahashi et al. Deutsche Gold-und Silber-Scheideanstalt v. Comm. of Patents, 251 F.Supp. 624, 627 (D.D.C.1966).

verruca (vĕ-roo′kah), pl. *verru′cae* [L.] one of the wartlike elevations developing on the endocardium in various types of endocarditis.

verruca plantaris plantar wart: a viral epidermal tumor on the sole.

. . . appellee consulted his family physician concerning a colony of **plantar warts** on his right foot. His doctor referred him to McKeesport Hospital to determine if x-ray treatment was advisable for removal of the warts. At the hospital he was seen by Dr. Steen, who was employed by the hospital as a radiologist. After two radiation treatments administered by Dr. Steen, appellee returned to his studies at Ohio University. A blister developed on the site which he had treated at the University Health Center and thereafter the area appeared to heal normally. However, in November 1970 the tissue in the area where the warts had been began to decompose and the appellee began to experience pain in his foot. He visited doctors in an attempt to remedy the increasing decomposition and finally in May 1971 surgery was performed. However, despite all efforts appellee remains with a permanent disability. . . .

Dr. Herring admitted that radiation therapy was an accepted course of treatment for **plantar warts** in 1968. Ragan v. Steen, 331 A.2d 724, 726–7, 732 (Super.Ct.Pa.1974).

version (ver-zhun) [L. *versio*] change of direction. In obstetrics, change of the polarity of the fetus with reference to the body of the mother, in order to convert an abnormal or relatively abnormal relation into a normal or relatively normal relation.

Dr. Smith observed that a prolapse of the child's arm had occurred. He thereupon spent a period of time, of disputed duration, attempting to perform a "**version** and extraction," that is, attempting manually to turn the child in such a way as to permit a normal delivery. Hernandez v. Smith, 552 F.2d 142–4 (5th Cir. 1977).

vertebra (ver′tĕ-brah), pl. *ver′tebrae* [L.] any of the thirty-three bones of the spinal column (columna vertebralis),

comprising the seven *cervical*, twelve *thoracic*, five *lumbar*, five *sacral*, and four *coccygeal* vertebrae.

vertebrae, cervical; vertebrae cervicales [NA], the upper seven vertebrae, constituting the skeleton of the neck.

He found plaintiff suffered from a disease of the **cervical vertebrae**, a condition which also involves the compression on nerve tissue causing pain in the arm and hand. Dr. Fox treated the condition by fusing three discs in the plaintiff's cervical spine. Lindsey v. H. A. Lott, Inc., 387 So.2d 1091–2 (La.1980).

Dr. Scheiner testified that in his opinion Mrs. Chavez suffered chronic musculo-ligamentous strain of the **cervical spine (neck)**. . . . Chavez v. Continental Ins. Co., 235 S.E.2d 335, 337 (Va.1977).

Q. And, actually, the surgery was in what's called the **cervical spine** or the neck area? A. The bottom part of the **cervical spine**, yes, which is just above the thoracic area, which is—it's not in this part of the neck; it's down a little bit. Perry v. Bertsch, 441 F.2d 939, 945 (8th Cir. 1971).
Other Authorities: York v. Daniels, 259 S.W.2d 109, 111 (Springfield Ct.App.Mo.1953).

vertebrae lumbales [NA]; **vertebrae, lumbar** the five vertebrae between the thoracic vertebrae and the sacrum.

The medical testimony established that a **lumbar vertebra** is a bony structure, various portions of which are medically termed "transverse process," "spinous process," "laminae", etc., the "body" seemingly referring to the main segment of which the others, specifically the transverse processes, are protruding portions, one on each side. C. R. Winn Drilling Co. v. Industrial Com'n, 203 N.E.2d 904, 906 (Ill.1965).

. . . **lumbar spine** (region of the pelvis). . . . Chavez v. Continental Ins.Co., 235 S.E.2d 335, 337 (Va.1977).

vertebrae; thoracic; vertebrae thoracales See *vertebrae thoracicae*.

When he saw David he had a fractured dislocation of T 12 on L 1, the junction between the **thoracic spine** and the lumbar spine, secondary to a motor vehicle accident which had occurred that day. He had a sensory level of T 12 with no sensibility below. He had no motor function or reflexes below the T 12 level. He testified that David was paralyzed and would not be able to move his legs. Kinsey v. Kolber, 431 N.E.2d 1316, 1319–20 (App.Ct.Ill.1982).

No **thoracic (dorsal) spine** X-ray was ordered. It was in the **thoracic spine** that the fracture had occurred. Brazil v. U.S., 484 F.Supp. 986, 988 (N.D.Ala.1979).

. . . **thoracic spine** (region of the shoulder blades). . . . Chavez v. Continental Ins. Co., 235 S.E.2d 335, 337 (Va.1977).

vertebrae thoracicae [NA], thoracic vertebrae: the vertebrae, usually twelve in number, situated between the cervical and the lumbar vertebrae, giving attachment to the ribs and forming part of the posterior wall of the thorax; called also *vertebrae thoracales*.

vertebrogenic (ver″tĕ-bro-jen′ik) arising in a vertebra or in the vertebral column.

Appellant argues that his disability meets the requirements found in section 1.05(C) [20 C.F.R.] of Appendix I:

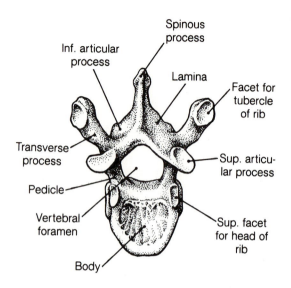

Inf. articular process

Spinous process

Lamina

Facet for tubercle of rib

Transverse process

Sup. articular process

Pedicle

Vertebral foramen

Sup. facet for head of rib

Body

Typical (sixth) thoracic vertebra viewed from above (King & Showers).

Other **vertebrogenic** disorders (e.g., herniated nucleus pulposus, spinal stenosis)... Bloodsworth v. Heckler, 703 F.2d 1233, 1243 (11th Cir. 1983).

vertigo (ver'tĭ-go, ver-ti'go) [L. *vertigo*] an illusion of movement; a sensation as if the external world were revolving around the patient (*objective vertigo*) or as if he himself were revolving in space (*subjective vertigo*). The term is sometimes erroneously used to mean any form of dizziness. Vertigo may result from diseases of the inner ear or may be due to disturbances of the vestibular centers or pathways in the central nervous system.

Between July and November of 1979, Naquin consulted Dr. Anna Plauche several times concerning dizziness that he had been experiencing since before the June accident, and the pain and numbness he had since the June accident. Dr. Plauche testified that she found a ''trigger area'' at the base of Naquin's skull which was consistent with his complaints of numbness in his right hand. Dr. Plauche also testified that her treatment was limited to the **vertigo** complaints, as she was under the impression that Dr. Marmande was treating Naquin for the back injury. Naquin v. Texaco, Inc., 433 So.2d 31, 33 (Ct.App. La.1982).

Regarding her **vertigo**, she stated that she was not astonished by the symptom itself because she had it ''all my life'' and that she would have dizzy spells every two weeks or once a month, that she would faint without warning, that the spells would last for several seconds, and that they would cause her to fall if she were standing at the time. She also stated that the reason for her three employment dismissals was because of her dizzy spells....

... She also added that since 1945 her right ear had been operated upon at least four more times in an effort to stop the drainage and remove the cause of the **vertigo** symptom....

... her main complaint was dizziness of two months duration, and that since she had a middle ear disease the symptom

of **vertigo** could not be considered unusual or highly significant....

... the evidence is ample to indicate that the condition in her right ear was severe during that period, and that middle ear disease such as she had commonly causes **vertigo**. Capaldi v. Weinberger, 391 F.Supp. 502, 504 (E.D.Pa.1975).

vertigo, positional See *vertigo, postural.*

vertigo, postural vertigo associated with a specific position of the head in space or changes in the position of the head in space; called also *positional v.* See also dizziness. Cited in Guardian Life Ins. Co. of America v. Robitaille, 495 F.2d 890, 893 (2d Cir. 1974).

vesicle (ves'ĭ-k'l) [L. *vesicula*, dim. of *vesica* bladder] a small bladder or sac containing liquid. See also *vesicula.*

vesicula (vĕ-sik'u-lah), pl. *vesic'ulae* [L., dim. of *vesica*] a vesicle: a small bladder or sac containing liquid; used as a general term in anatomical nomenclature.

vesicula seminalis [NA], seminal vesicle: either of the paired, sacculated pouches attached to the posterior part of the urinary bladder; the duct of each joins the ipsilateral ductus deferens to form the ejaculatory duct.

Dr. Arnold also obtained X-rays of the appellant's bladder, and these X-rays revealed an extremely rare condition, calcified **seminal vesicles**. Marsh v. Arnold, 446 S.W.2d 949, 951 (Ct.Civ.App.Tex.1969).

vesiculitis (vĕ-sik"u-li'tis) inflammation of a vesicle, especially of a seminal vesicle.

vesiculitis, seminal inflammation of a seminal vesicle.

He was merely asked, on cross-examination, whether **seminal vesiculitis** would produce pain in the area of the lower back and he replied in the affirmative. Petition of U.S., 303 F.Supp. 1282, 1327 (E.D.N.C.1969).

viability (vi"ah-bil'ĭi-te) ability to live after birth. See also *fetus.*

A. The Definition of Viability

Section 2(2) of the Act defines viability as ''that stage of fetal development when the life of the unborn child may be maintained outside the womb by natural or artificial life-supportive systems.'' Since several other provisions of the Act incorporate the words ''viable'' or ''viability,'' the constitutionality of this definition is critical. Plaintiffs contend that this definition is unconstitutionally vague and must be interpreted to mean the earliest age at which any fetus has ever survived, when read with the state policy that a fetus is a human being from the moment of conception. Plaintiffs also assert that the inconsistent definitions proposed by defendants prove that the definition is vague.

In *Danforth*, 428 U.S. 52, 96 S.Ct. 2831, 49 L.Ed.2d 788 (1976) the Court upheld a definition of viability very similar to the Illinois definition. The Missouri abortion statute in Danforth defined viability as ''that stage of fetal development when the life of the unborn child may be continued indefinitely outside the womb by natural or artificial life-support systems.'' The Court held that this definition was flexible and reflected the fact that **viability** was ''a matter of medical judgment, skill, and technical ability.'' Noting that this definition was consistent with the principles created in Wade, 410 U.S. 113, 93 S.Ct. 705, 35 L.Ed.2d 147 (1973) the Court specifically rejected the argument that unless the definition of **viability** is set at a specific gestational age, it is void for vagueness. Wynn v. Scott, 449 F.Supp. 1302, 1315 (N.D.Ill.1978).

They invoke the "weight of authority," pointing to the fact that 25 states now recognize a cause of action for the wrongful death of a fetus while at most 12 reject it. Next plaintiffs urge that when a developing fetus has reached the stage of "**viability**"—i.e., when it has become capable of living outside of its mother's body—its biological self-sufficiency should be reflected by according it legal independence as well. [Footnotes omitted that cite some 50 cases in these 37 states.] Justus v. Atchison, 565 P.2d 122, 125–6 (Cal.1977).

"**Viability** is usually placed at about seven months (28 weeks) but may occur earlier, even at 24 weeks." Roe v. Wade, 410 U.S., at 160. . . .

The definition of viability. Section 2(2) of the Act defines "**viability**" as "that stage of fetal development when the life of the unborn child may be continued indefinitely outside the womb by natural or artificial life-supportive systems." . . .

In Roe, we used the term "**viable**," properly we thought, to signify the point at which the fetus is "potentially able to live outside the mother's womb, albeit with artificial aid," and presumably capable of "meaningful life outside the mother's womb," 410 U.S., at 160, 163. We noted that this point "is usually placed" at about seven months or 28 weeks, but may occur earlier. Id., at 160.

We agree with the District Court and conclude that the definition of **viability** in the Act does not conflict with what was said and held in Roe. Planned Parenthood of Missouri v. Danforth, 428 U.S. 52, 61, 63, 96 S.Ct. 2831, 49 L.Ed.2d 788 (1976).

Other Authorities: Roe v. Wade, 410 U.S. 113, 163–4, 93 S.Ct. 705, 732, 35 L.Ed.2d 147 (1973).

viable (vi′ah-b′l) capable of living; especially said of a fetus that has reached such a stage of development that it can live outside of the uterus.

In 1978, Tennessee amended its act. Pub.Acts, ch. 742; § 1: "For purposes of this section, the word 'person' shall include a fetus which was viable at the time of injury. A fetus shall be considered **viable** if it had achieved a stage of development wherein it could reasonabley [sic] be expected to be capable of living outside the uterus." Salazar v. St. Vincent Hospital, 619 P.2d 826, 832 (Ct.App.New Mex.1980).

Vibrio (vib′re-o) a genus of microorganisms of the family Spirallaceae, suborder Pseudomonadineae, order Pseudomonadales, made up of short, slighly curved, actively motile gram-negative rods, occurring singly and occasionally found end-to-end. The 34 species described include the cholera and El Tor vibrios pathogenic for man, agents of specific disease in lower animals, and paracholera or cholera-like water vibrios (nonagglutinating, or NAG, vibrios). See also *vibrio.* Cited in U.S. v. City of Asbury Park, 340 F.Supp. 555, 566 (D.N.J.1972).

vibrio (vib′re-o), pl. *vib′rios* or *vibrio′nes.* An organism of the genus *Vibrio,* or other spiral motile organism.

Vietnamese syndrome See *disorder, posttraumatic stress.*

villi (vil′i) [L.] plural of *villus.*

villose (vil-lōs′) [L. *villosus*] shaggy with soft hairs; covered with villi.

villous See *villose.*

villus (vil′lus), pl. *vil′li* [L. "tuft of hair"] a small vascular process or protrusion, especially such a protrusion from the free surface of a membrane; [NA] a general term for such a structure.

The medical evidence adduced at the trial established that the abortion procedure used in this case should result in the fetus being broken up into pieces, which include **villi** (small projections that are part of the placenta) and these pieces pass through a suction tube into a container. Koehler v. Schwartz, 413 N.Y.S.2d 462, 465 (2d Dep't 1979).

vincristine sulfate (vin-kris′tēn) [USP] chemical name: 22-oxovincaleukoblastine sulfate (1:1) (salt). The sulfate salt of an alkaloid extracted from *Vinca rosea* L. (Apocynaceae), $C_{46}H_{56}N_4O_{10} \cdot H_2SO_4$, occurring as a white to slightly yellow, amorphous or crystalline powder; used as an antineoplastic, especially in the treatment of acute leukemia, administered intravenously.

Subsequently, plaintiff alleges that the decedent, while an outpatient at St. Luke's Medical Center, and being under the care of Dr. Wagner, was given an injection of a drug, **vincristine sulfate.** Plaintiff alleges that an employee of St. Luke's prepared the injection with the wrong dosage, injected it into the decedent, and as a result of the excessive dosage, the Hodgkins' disease advanced into a chronic progressive stage, forcing the decedent to undergo a long course of treatment and numerous hospitalizations until his death. Glover v. Wagner, 462 F.Supp. 308–9 (D.Neb.1978).

Vineberg's operation See *operation, Vineberg's.*

vinyl (vi′nil) the univalent group CH₂:CH—.

vinyl chloride a vinyl group to which an atom of chlorine is attached, $CH_2 \cdot CHCl$, the monomer which polymerizes to polyvinyl chloride. See also *polyvinylchloride.*

For some years, **vinyl chloride** commonly served as a propellant in aerosol cans manufactured to dispense paints, cosmetics, and other household products. . . .

. . . three of its employees who had been exposed to **vinyl chloride** at an industrial plant for approximately nineteen years had died from angiosarcoma of the liver, a rare form of cancer. Laboratory studies on animals who were administered varying dosages of **vinyl chloride** over extended periods further suggested that the chemical may be carcinogenic. As a result of this evidence, a number of federal agencies sought to protect industrial workers and the general public from exposure to **vinyl chloride.**[5] [5 On April 5, 1974, the Occupational Safety and Health Administration published an Emergency Temporary Standard setting an occupational exposure limit to **vinyl chloride.** 39 Fed.Reg. 12342 (1974). For later agency action, see 39 Fed.Reg. 16896 (1974) and 29 C.F.R. § 1910.1017 (1976). On April 22, 1974, the Food and Drug Administration published a notice of proposed rule-making concerning **vinyl chloride** used as an ingredient in drug and cosmetic aerosol products. 39 Fed.Reg. 14215 (1974). See 21 C.F.R.

§§ 310.506 & 700.14 (1976).] Pactra Industries v. Consumer Product Safety Com'n, 555 F.2d 677, 680 (9th Cir. 1977).

In brief, the Secretary has adopted a standard which requires that no worker is to be exposed to concentrations of **vinyl chloride** in excess of one part per million (ppm) averaged over any eight-hour period. 29 C.F.R. § 1910.93q(c)(1)....

A gas at ambient temperatures and pressure, **vinyl chloride** monomer (VCM) is primarily synthesized by the oxychlorination of ethylene in a handful of large outdoor production plants which resemble oil refineries....

It is now clear that the workers in all components of the **vinyl chloride** industry are subjected to a serious health risk from VCM. Although conclusive proof of the carcinogenic and, in turn, fatal character of VCM did not emerge until early in 1974 when the deaths of three workers in Goodrich's PVC plant at Louisville were reported, strong warning signals had appeared long before....

... The Assistant Secretary concluded that the evidence demonstrated VCM to be carcinogenic for man. See 39 Fed. Reg. 12342. Society of Plastics Indus., Inc. v. Occupational S. & H.A., 509 F.2d 1301, 1303 (2d Cir. 1975).

violet (vi'o-let) a violet-colored dye.

violet, gentian See under *gentian.*

virulence (vir'u-lens) [L. *virulen'tia,* from *virus* poison] the degree of pathogenicity of a microorganism as indicated by case fatality rates and/or its ability to invade the tissues of the host. It is measured experimentally by the median lethal dose (LD_{50}) or median effective dose (ED_{50}). By extension, the competence of any infectious agent to produce pathologic effects.

Although the viral population will decrease when stored, its **virulence** [13] can only be changed by passing the virus through another living host. **Virulence** is also affected by the phenomenon known as the "reversion factor"; that is, when polio vaccine is ingested for immunization purposes, some virus excreted in the recipient's feces will assume a more **virulent** form. In any event, the polio virus excreted cannot be less virulent than the virus found in vaccine. [[13] **Virulence** is a measure of a virus' disease or infection capability.] U.S. v. City of Asbury Park, 340 F.Supp. 555, 565 (D.N.J.1972).

virus (vi'rus) [L.] one of a group of minute infectious agents, with certain exceptions (e.g., poxviruses) not resolved in the light microscope, and characterized by a lack of independent metabolism and by the ability to replicate only within living host cells. Like living organisms, they are able to reproduce with genetic continuity and the possibility of mutation. They range from 200–300 nm. to 15 nm. in size and are morphologically heterogeneous, occurring as rod-shaped, spherical, or polyhedral, and tadpole-shaped forms; masses of the spherical or polyhedral forms may be made up of orderly arrays, to give a crystalline structure. The individual particle, or virion, consists of nucleic acid (the nucleoid), DNA or RNA (but not both) and a protein shell, or capsid, which contains and protects the nucleic acid and which may be multilayered. Viruses are customarily separated into three subgroups on the basis of host specificity, namely bacterial viruses, animal viruses, and plant viruses. They are also classified as to their origin (e.g., reoviruses),

mode of transmission (arboviruses, tickborne viruses), or the manifestations they produce (polioviruses, polyomaviruses, poxviruses). They are sometimes named for the geographical location in which they were first isolated (e.g., coxsackievirus).

The **viruses** found were of the type which multiply in or near the gastrointestinal tract of man, and are excreted by infected people in their feces. The **viruses** are thus found in raw sewage, and in sludge. **Viruses** will not multiply outside a living host, and will gradually die-off if stored in a sewage treatment plant holding tank....

... The **viruses** found in sludge are capable of producing a wide range of disease; for example, poliomyelitis, aseptic meningitis, herpangina, pleurodyne, myocarditis, rash diseases, diarrheal diseases, and respiratory diseases. Hepatitis is transmitted by **virus** found in human feces, and enters the ocean through sewage and sludge. The **virus** becomes concentrated in the flesh of shellfish, and thus may enter the human food chain. U.S. v. City of Asbury Park, 340 F.Supp. 555, 565 (D.N.J.1972).

Viruses are used in the preparation of viral vaccines. Blank v. U.S., 400 F.2d 302, 304 (5th Cir. 1968).

virus, attenuated one whose pathogenicity has been reduced by serial animal passage or by other means.

An **attenuated virus** is one which has, through laboratory procedures, been rendered incapable, to the degree at which it is attenuated, of producing disease. The virus employed in live polio vaccine is weakened so that it will not produce the disease in the person receiving it but it will cause the production of antibodies which will thereafter resist the attack by a wild or virulent virus. Stahlheber v. American Cyanamid Co., 451 S.W.2d 48, 51 (Mo.1970).

virus, influenza any of a group of myxoviruses that cause influenza, including at least three serotypes (A, B, and C) and several antigenic variations, classified on the basis of their surface antigens (hemagglutinin and neuraminidase) as H_1N_1, H_2N_2, etc. Serotype A viruses are subject to major antigenic changes (antigenic shifts) as well as minor gradual antigenic changes (antigenic drift) and cause the major pandemics. Serotype B viruses appear to undergo only minor antigenic changes (antigenic drift) and cause more localized epidemics. Serotype C viruses appear to be antigenically stable and cause only sporadic disease.

viscera See *viscus.*

viscus (vis'kus), pl. *vis'cera* [L.] any large interior organ in any one of the three great cavities of the body, especially in the abdomen; see illustration.

Diagnosis by appellee was that of a perforated **viscus** (abdominal organ) most probably perforated peptic ulcer or possibly as a consequence of recurrent aggravation of existing ulcerative colitis. Parsons v. Wood, 584 P.2d 1332, 1334 (Okla.1978).

vision (vizh'un) [L. *visio, videre* to see] 1. the act or faculty of seeing; sight. 2. visual acuity; symbol V. See also *pressure, intracranial* (Gendusa case).

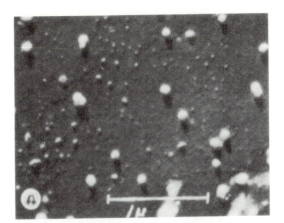

Influenza virus. (Williams and Wyckoff, S.A.B. LS-136.)

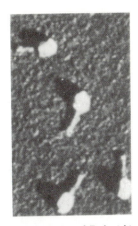

Bacteriophage (T$_2$) of *Escherichia coli.* (Williams and Frazer, Virology, vol. 2.)

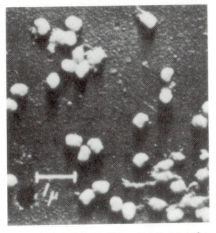

Vaccinia virus. (G. G. Sharp, S.A.B. LS-142.)

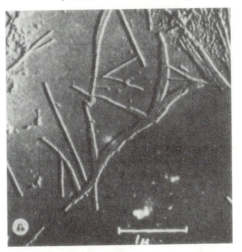

Tobacco mosaic virus. (Williams and Wyckoff, S.A.B. LS-135.)

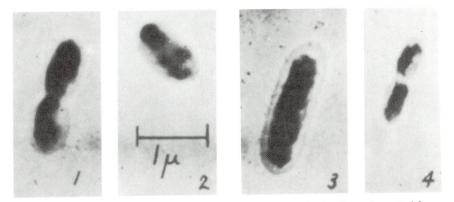

Rickettsiae: *1.* epidemic typhus fever; *2.* endemic typhus fever; *3.* Rocky Mountain spotted fever; *4.* American Q fever. (Plotz, Smadel, Anderson, and Chambers, S.A.B. LS-25.)

ELECTRON MICROGRAPHS OF VIRUSES AND RICKETTSIAE

778

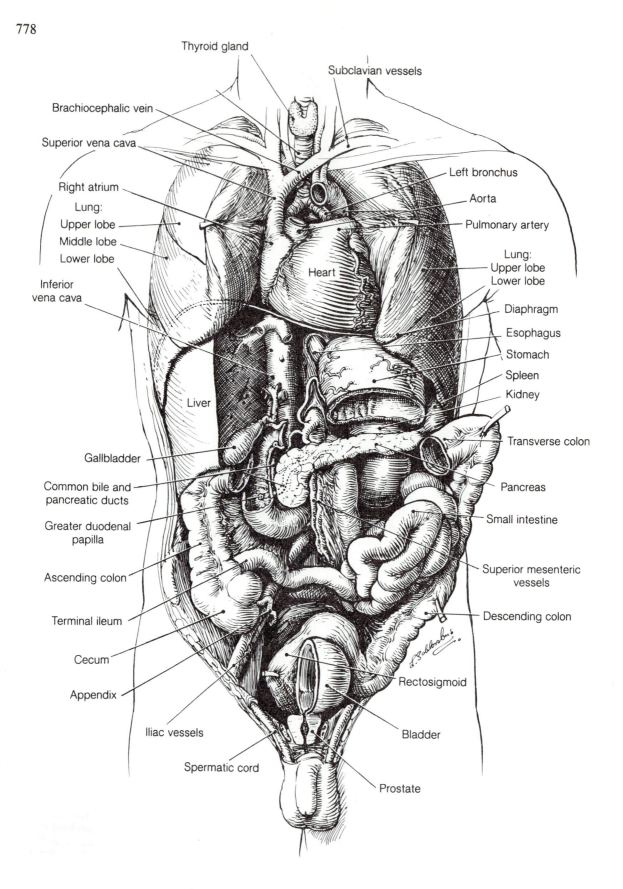

Thyroid gland

Subclavian vessels

Brachiocephalic vein

Superior vena cava

Right atrium

Lung:

Upper lobe

Middle lobe

Lower lobe

Inferior
vena cava

Left bronchus

Aorta

Pulmonary artery

Heart

Lung:
Upper lobe
Lower lobe

Diaphragm

Esophagus

Stomach

Spleen

Kidney

Liver

Transverse colon

Gallbladder

Common bile and
pancreatic ducts

Greater duodenal
papilla

Ascending colon

Terminal ileum

Cecum

Appendix

Iliac vessels

Spermatic cord

Pancreas

Small intestine

Superior mesenteric
vessels

Descending colon

Rectosigmoid

Bladder

Prostate

THORACIC AND ABDOMINAL VISCERA

vision, eccentric

Claimant had only **eccentric vision** in his left eye, which was described by Employer's medical witness as a loss of central vision, requiring Claimant to look to the side of an object in order to perceive it. [Footnote omitted.] George v. Workmen's Comp.App.Bd., 437 A.2d 521–2 (Pa.Commonwealth Ct.1981).

vision, peripheral that which is elicited by stimuli falling on areas of the retina distant from the macula. See also *epilepsy, post-traumatic* (S.L.C. Leasing case).

He concluded, based solely upon the visual tests, and without reference to other tests conducted by Dr. Tyler, that Renn was suffering a progressive loss of **peripheral vision**, and that such progressive loss was not characteristic of a traumatic etiology. S.L.C. Leasing v. Industrial Com'n, 543 P.2d 795–6 (Ct.App. Ariz.1975).

visual function See *function, visual.*

vision, stereoscopic perception of the relief of objects or of their depth; vision in which objects are perceived as having three dimensions, and not merely as two-dimensional pictures.

Vistaril (vis'tah-ril) trademark for preparations of hydroxyzine.

visual (vizh'u-al) [L. *visualis,* from *videre* to see] 1. pertaining to vision or sight. 2. a person in whom the visual centers are predominant in memory and learning.

visualization (vizh"u-al-i-za'shun) the act of viewing, or of achieving a complete visual impression of an object, as by roentgenography.

visualization, internal mammary

For the **internal mammary visualization**, a catheter is passed into an artery in the right groin and threaded to the arch of the aorta. The tip of the catheter is positioned into the orifice of each internal mammary artery, dye is injected, a fluoroscopic examination is made and X-ray pictures taken. The catheters used for the internal mammary procedure are then taken out. Morgenroth v. Pacific Medical Center, Inc., 126 Cal.Rptr. 681, 686 (Ct.App.Cal.1976).

vitamin (vi'tah-min) [L. *vita* life + *amine*] a general term for a number of unrelated organic substances that occur in many foods in small amounts and that are necessary in trace amounts for the normal metabolic functioning of the body. They may be water-soluble or fat-soluble. See *Table of Vitamins.* See also *dietary*; and *food* (both National Nutritional case).

This case [State v. Baker, 48 S.E.2d 61] cited by defendant states therefore that higher dosage **vitamins** used for therapeutic purposes are "drugs" but at the same time that not all **vitamin** preparations are classified as "drugs"....

Clearly all **vitamins** are not "drugs" but on a case by case basis and under the provisions of this contract the **vitamins** given by prescription of a physician absent a showing of fraud were covered. Palumberi v. Travelers Ins. Co., 404 N.Y.S.2d 939, 941 (Dist.Ct.Suffolk Cty.1976).

TABLE OF VITAMINS

Individual vitamins are listed here under their different designations (letters and subscript numbers or letters), with description or cross reference to the name of the specific compound.

vitamin A a fat-soluble vitamin occurring in nature in two forms: retinol and dehydroretinol. Deficiency in the diet causes (*a*) inadequate production and regeneration of the visual purple of the retina with resulting night blindness and (*b*) disturbances in epithelial tissue resulting in keratomalacia, xerophthalmia, and lessened resistance to infections through the epithelial surfaces. Vitamin A is present in the liver oils of the cod and other fish, in butter, egg yolk, cheese, and liver as well as in tomatoes and many other vegetable foods in most of which it exists in precursor form as carotene. Vitamin A is toxic when taken in excess; see *hypervitaminosis A.* The term vitamin A is used sometimes to mean retinol alone.

vitamin A₁, retinol.

vitamin A₂, dehydroretinol.

vitamin B, a member of the vitamin B complex.

vitamin B complex a group of water-soluble substances including thiamine, riboflavin, niacin (nicotinic acid), niacinamide (nicotinamide), the vitamin B₆ group (including pyridoxine, pyridoxal, pyridoxamine), biotin, pantothenic acid, folic acid, possibly para-a-minobenzoic acid, inositol, vitamin B₁₂, and possibly choline. Niacin and niancinamide are also known, together, as the pellagra-preventing factor, P.-P. factor, or antipellagra factor.

Vitamin B complex consists of a group of water-soluble substances, including: Thiamine (B₁), Riboflavin (B₂), Nicotinamide (B₃), Adenine (B₄), Pantothenic Acid (B₅), Pyridoxine Hydrochloride etc. (B₆ group), B₁₀, B₁₁, B₁₂, B₁₃, B₁₅, folic acid (Bc), para-aminobenzoic acid (possibly), inositol, and choline (possibly). Dorland's Medical Dictionary (25th ed. 1974). Nature's Bounty, Inc. v. Basic Organics, 432 F.Supp. 546, 549 (E.D.N.Y. 1977).

vitamin B₁, thiamine.

vitamin B₂, riboflavin.

vitamin B₆, water-soluble substances (including pyridoxine, pyridoxal, and pyridoxamine) found in most foods, especially meats, liver, vegetables, whole grain cereals, and egg yolk, and concerned in the metabolism of amino acids, in the degradation of tryptophan, and in the breakdown of glycogen to glucose-1-phosphate.

vitamin B₁₂, cyanocobalamin.

vitamin B₁₂ᵦ, hydroxocobalamine.

vitamin B₁₇

"Vitamin B–17" is not a recognized vitamin in human nutrition and has no known nutritional value. U.S. v. Articles of Food & Drug, 444 F.Supp. 266, 270 (E.D.Wis.1978).

vitamin Bᶜ, folic acid.

vitamin Bᶜ conjugate, folic acid.

vitamin C, ascorbic acid.

vitamin D, any one of several fat-soluble compounds, including cholecalciferol and ergocalciferol, which have antirachitic properties. Known collectively as *calciferol*, they may be produced artificially by the irradiation of ergosterol and a few related sterols. See *ergosterol*. Deficiency of vitamin D tends to cause rickets in children and osteomalacia and osteoporosis in adults. It is present in the liver oils of various fish, in butter and egg yolk, and is produced in the body on exposure to sunlight. Ingestion of excess amounts of vitamin D leads to hypercalcemia, weakness, loss of weight and other symptoms.

vitamin D₂, ergocalciferol.

vitamin D₃, cholecalciferol.

vitamin E, a fat-soluble vitamin necessary in the diet of many species for normal reproduction, normal development of muscles, normal resistance of erythrocytes to hemolysis, and various other biochemical functions. Chemically it is alpha-tocopherol, one of the three tocopherols (alpha, beta, and gamma) occurring in wheat germ oil, cereals, egg yolk, and beef liver. It is also prepared synthetically. Tocopherols act as antioxidants.

vitamin G, riboflavin.

vitamin H, biotin.

vitamin K, a group of fat-soluble vitamins (see *v. K₁, v. K₂, v. K₃*) which promote clotting of the blood by increasing the synthesis of prothrombin by the liver. They occur naturally in alfalfa, spinach, cabbage, putrefied fish meal, hog-liver fat, egg yolk, hempseed. Vitamin K and its synthetic analogues have an antihemorrhagic activity with a specific effect on prothrombin deficiency. They are used in obstructive jaundice, in hemorrhagic states associated with intestinal diseases and with disease of the liver, in the hypoprothrombinemia of the newborn, administered parenterally to the infant or to the mother during labor.

vitamin K₁, phytonadione.

vitamin K₂, menaquinone.

vitamin K₃, menadione.

vitamin M, folic acid.

vitamin L, a factor necessary for lactation in rats, L₁ is found in beef-liver extract, L₂ in yeast.

---

vitiligo (vit"ĭ-li'go) [L.] an idiopathic, probably autommune, condition characterized by destruction of melanocytes in small or large circumscribed areas of the skin, resulting in patches of depigmentation often having a hyperpigmented border, and often enlarging slowly. Cf. *piebald skin* and *leukoderma*.

The term "**vitiligo**," on the other hand, [as opposed to leukoderma] as defined by Dr. Kenney, means a depigmentation for which the cause is not known.

Dr. Lerner testified that, in his opinion, the cause of Mr. Finley's condition was not known. He stated that there are many possible causes for a total depigmentation and that it could not be said with any medical certainty that the taking of Doriden by Mr. Finley was the cause of his condition. He testified that many persons have a predisposition to **vitiligo**, and that a physical or emotional trauma can trigger the latent disorder. He stated that the history which he had of Mr. Finley reflected an emotional nature that would lend itself to the activation of a latent **vitiligo** condition. Finley v. U.S., 314 F.Supp. 905, 909–10 (N.D.Ohio 1970).

vitrectomy (vĭ-trek'to-me) [L. *vitreus* glassy + Gr. *ektomē* excision] surgical extraction via the pars plana of the contents of the vitreous chamber of the eye and their replacement by a physiological solution; done in diabetic retinopathy with vitreous hemorrhage.

Houck referred Merritt to a consulting surgeon for consideration of a **vitrectomy**, an operation which could remove fluid from Merritt's left eye. Merritt v. Faulkner, 697 F.2d 761–2 (7th Cir. 1983).

vitreitis

The only diagnosis of an organic condition made by Dr. Dahrling was **vitreitis**, a posterior vitreous detachment, and he found it difficult to account for the degree of loss of vision and the visual field loss on the basis of **vitreitis**. At one point in his testimony he described the degree of plaintiff's loss as "surprising if one tries to relate to the **vitreitis**." He indicated that **vitreitis** can usually be controlled by cortisone type preparations. Davidson & Graham Const. Co. v. McKee, 562 S.W.2d 426–7 (Tenn.1978).

vitreous (vit're-us) [L. *vitreus* glassy] glasslike or hyaline; often used alone to designate the vitreous body of the eye (corpus vitreum [NA]). See also *corpus vitreum*.

vitreous, primary persistent hyperplastic a congenital anomaly, usually unilateral, due to persistence of embryonic remnants of the fibromuscular tunic of the eye and part of the hyaloid vascular system. Clinically, there is a white pupil, elongated ciliary processes, and often microphthalmia; the lens, although clear initially, may become completely opaque.

The team of medical doctors who examined Timothy at Letterman Hospital in July considered four possibilities. The first was **persistent hyperplastic primary vitreous**, a congenital defect of the eye present at birth and generally noticed shortly after birth. With such a condition as **persistent hyperplastic primary** vitreous, the eye is usually a bit smaller. The front part of the eye is ordinarily not normal so there are distinguishing factors for that disease. The medical doctors at Letterman were able to rule out this possibility. Steele v. U.S., 463 F.Supp. 321, 326–7 (D.Alas.1978).

vitreum (vit're-um) the vitreous body of the eye (corpus vitreum [NA]).

vocal cord See *cord, vocal, true.*

voice identification See *identification, voice.*

voiceprint See *spectrograph.*

volar (vo'lar) pertaining to the palm or sole; indicating the flexor surface of the forearm, wrist, or hand.

The orthopedist simply notes that the patient "has open wound on the **volar** aspect (R) middle finger with flexor tendon exposed, abundant slough" for which he recommends hydrogen peroxide soaks. Kernall v. U.S., 558 F.Supp. 280, 283 (E.D.N.Y.1982).

Plaintiff was seen again on December 21 and then hospitalized on December 27 for a closed reduction and percutaneous pinning of the right forearm in an attempt to correct the **volar** tilting of the right arm. Patin v. Continental Cas. Co., 424 So. 2d 1161, 1163 (Ct.App.La.1982).

Volkmann's ischemic contracture syndrome See *contracture, Volkmann's.*

voluntary (vol'un-tār"e) [L. *voluntas* will] accomplished in accordance with the will. See also *involuntary.*

In one sense, the term "**voluntary**" has been used as meaning "volitionally". According to this usage, a "**voluntary**" act means only that an act is the product of the actor's will, regardless of whether that will is freely exercised. [Footnote omitted.]
. . . So, when the term "**voluntary**" is used as meaning "volitional", acts performed under duress are considered "**voluntary**" acts; even though they are not the products of the free will, they are nevertheless products of the will. U.S. v. Bailey, 585 F.2d 1087, 1118 (D.C.Cir.1978).

A confession is **voluntary** when it is the product of "a rational intellect and a free will." Blackburn v. Alabama, 361 U.S. 199, 208, 80 S.Ct. 274, 280, 4 L.Ed.2d 242 (1960). If the ". . . will [of the accused] was overborne by the interrogation and if he would have remained silent but for the improper influences on him." United States v. Hull, 441 F.2d 308, 309 (7th Cir. 1971), his confession must be held involuntary. Bram v. United States, 168 U.S. 532, 18 S.Ct. 183, 42 L.Ed. 568 (1897). . . .
. . . After reviewing the facts adduced in this and prior hearings, the district court stated:
This court is convinced that a dosage of ¹⁄₂₃₀th of a grain of hyoscine and ⅛th grain of phenobarbital at the time he was suffering from withdrawal symptoms in combination with co-existing factors would have left Townsend's mind in a disoriented condition and irresponsible and that under the co-existing factors his mind would have been overborne. . . . If there ever can be a confession obtained that is involuntary and coerced under the totality of the circumstances, this is such a case. U.S. ex rel. Townsend v. Twomey, 452 F.2d 350, 367–8 (7th Cir. 1971).

volutrol

The penicillin was administered by **volutrol**, an intravenous (I.V.) device. The **volutrol** is a small chamber attached to the I.V. apparatus and permits the drug to drip into a patient's body over a period of time along with the plain I.V. solution. Mercurdo v. County of Milwaukee, 264 N.W.2d 258–9 (Wis. 1978).

vomit (vom'it) [L. *vomitare*] to cast up from the stomach by the mouth.

vomit, bilious vomited matter stained with bile.

vomit, dark green See *vomit, bilious.*

She **vomited dark green** which Dr. Richardson said was bile from the gall bladder. Richardson v. Holmes, 525 S.W.2d 293, 295 (Ct.Civ.App.Tex.1975).

vomiting (vom'it-ing) the forcible expulsion of the contents of the stomach through the mouth.

vomiting, projectile vomiting in which the vomitus is ejected with force.

The **vomiting** at 10 P.M. that evening was "**projectile**"—or projected out. At 11:25 P.M. vomit was green, but her fever remained just over 99°. Richardson v. Holmes, 525 S.W.2d 293, 295 (Ct.Civ.App.Tex.1975).

She sustained bruises on her legs, arm and forehead and was bleeding from her ear. She was taken the same day to a doctor's office where she began **projectile vomiting** and was thereafter confined to bed for two days. Stimage v. Union Electric Co., 465 S.W.2d 23, 27 (St.Louis Ct.App.Mo.1971).

vomitus See *bile* (Jones case); and *vomit.*

Von Recklinghausen's disease See *neurofibromatosis.*

vortex (vor'teks), pl. *vor'tices* [L. "whirl"] a whorled arrangement, design, or pattern, as of muscle fibers, or of the ridges or hairs on the skin; [NA] a general term for a structure having a whorled arrangement, design, or pattern.

vortex of head

He stated that "the entire **vortex** which is the roof aspect of the head extending from the forehead to the absolute back of the head and then from each ear region, right and left, was component of the shotgun wound". People v. Garrett, 339 N.E.2d 753, 757 (Ill.1975).

voyeurism (voi'yer-izm) a form of paraphilia in which sexual gratification is derived from watching or looking at others, particularly the genitals, or from observing sexual objects or acts.

There was also some evidence in the hospital records that Millard admitted to assorted acts of **voyeurism** before his marriage. On the stand, however, he denied having been a peeping tom since then. Although there was testimony that **voyeurism** and exhibitionism are frequently associated, at least one psychiatrist, Dr. Dabney, testified that the two did not seem "tied up" in Millard's case. Millard v. Harris, 406 F.2d 964, 974 (D.C.Cir.1968).

vulva (vul'vah) [L.] the region of the external genital organs of the female, including the labia majora, labia minora, mons pubis, bulb of the vestibule, vestibule of the vagina, greater and lesser vestibular glands, and vaginal orifice. See also *pudendum feminimum* [NA].

"Under the established rule in this State, the penetration of the female sexual organ by the sexual organ of the male, which is necessary to constitute rape, need be only slight; it is not necessary that the vagina shall be entered or the hymen ruptured, but an entering of the anterior of the organ, known as the **vulva** or labia, is sufficient." Lee v. State, 197 Ga. 123(1), 28 S.E.2d 465. See Morris v. State, 54 Ga. 440; Addison v. State, 198 Ga. 249, 31 S.E.2d 393; Dean v. State, 204 Ga. 759, 51 S.E.2d 840; Bonner v. State, 206 Ga. 19(1), 55 S.E.2d 587; Payne v. State, 204 S.E.2d 128, 129 (Ga.1974).

Wallenberg's syndrome (vahl'en-bergz) [Adolf *Wallenberg*, German physician, 1862–1949] See under *syndrome*.

warfarin (war'fah-rin) [named for *Wisconsin Alumni Research Foundation*] chemical name: 4-hydroxy-3-oxo-1-phenylbutyl-2*H*-1-benzopyran-2-one. One of the synthetic coumarin anticoagulants, $C_{19}H_{16}O_4$. See also *hemorrhage, intracranial* (Tschohl case).

From 1967 to September 16, 1968, the deceased took **Warfarin** to thin his blood. His physician, Dr. Alois Scheidel, put him on **Warfarin** again on April 12, 1974 when deceased complained of dizziness. Its purpose was to reduce the likelihood of blood clotting. Tschohl v. Nationwide Mut. Ins. Co., 418 F.Supp. 1124–5 (D.Minn.1976).

warfarin, sodium [USP], the sodium salt of warfarin, $C_{19}H_{15}NaO_4$, occurring as a white, amorphous or crystalline powder, the anticoagulant action of which is of intermediate duration and cumulative; administered orally, intravenously, or intramuscularly. It is also used as a rodenticide.

The hospital's treatment included the use of **Coumadin**, an anticoagulating drug, to prevent the enlargement of the clot and to prevent the formation of more clots. Zeck v. U.S., 559 F.Supp. 1345, 1347 (D.S.Dak.1983).

Brief mention should be made of the medication known as **Coumadin** [sodium warfarin]. An artificial heart valve may induce bloodclotting, and to combat such, **Coumadin** is sometimes prescribed. **Coumadin** itself may lead to bleeding because of a thinning of the blood. Accordingly, **Coumadin** must be carefully prescribed. Loomis v. McLucas, 553 F.2d 634, 637 (10th Cir. 1977).

Although good clinical practice called for tapering off when taking a patient off of an anticoagulant Dr. Samuels in this instance suddenly stopped plaintiff's ingestion of **Coumadin**. He was aware of the hazard that thrombophlebitis could result from the "rebound" or "overshoot" reaction from suddenly stopping the taking of **Coumadin**. But he had advised plaintiff of this hazard as well as the hazard of having plaintiff take Enovid. In fact, this study on plaintiff was "a very hazardous life-threatening study." Carmichael v. Reitz, 95 Cal.Rptr. 381, 395 (Ct.App.Cal.1971).

warning See *contraindication*.

A "**warning**" usually relates to circumstances under which a drug may bring about a dangerous condition or side effect. A physician will consider the **warning** in weighing the risks and benefits of a drug for a particular patient. Baker v. St. Agnes Hospital, 421 N.Y.S.2d 81, 83 (2d Dep't 1979).

wart (wort) [L. *verruca*] an epidermal tumor caused by a papillomavirus; the term is also loosely applied to any of various benign, wartlike, epidermal proliferations of nonviral etiology, as a senile wart (seborrheic keratosis); called also *verruca*.

wart (cluster)

Dr. Steen testified that he administered two equal doses of 1000r's, totalling 2000r's, which he stated was the standard dosage for a **wart cluster** (a mosaic of many **warts** closely spaced). [Dissent.] Ragan v. Steen, 331 A.2d 724, 732 (Super. Ct.Pa.1974).

waste (wāst) useless and effete material, unfit for further use within the organism.

waste, industrial

Industrial **wastes** are defined as: "Any solid, liquid, or gaseous wastes, including cooling water, resulting from any industrial or manufacturing process or from the development, recovery or processing of natural resources." Chicago Allis Mfg. Corp. v. Metropolitan San. Dist., 288 N.E.2d 436, 438 (Ill. 1972).

waste, radioactive

"**Radioactive waste**" means HLW and any other radioactive materials other than HLW that are received for emplacement in a geologic repository. 10 C.F.R. § 60.2(o) (1982).

waste, radioactive-high level

(j) "**High-level radioactive waste**" or "**HLW**" means: (1) Irradiated reactor fuel, (2) liquid wastes resulting from the operation of the first cycle solvent extraction system, or equivalent, and the concentrated wastes from subsequent extraction cycles, or equivalent, in a facility for reprocessing irradiated reactor fuel, and (3) solids into which such liquid wastes have been converted. 10 C.F.R. § 60.2(j) (1982).

water (wah'ter) a tasteless, odorless, colorless liquid, $(H_2O)_n$, used as the standard of specific gravity and of specific heat. It freezes at 32°F. (0°C.) and boils at 212°F. (100°C.). It is present in all organic tissues and in many other substances, and is the most universal of the solvents.

water, potable water that is suitable for drinking purposes.

Drinking water normally contains no more than two or three solid parts per million. The United States Public Health Service allows up to 500 solid parts per million in soft **drinking water**, and in some sections of the Southwest **drinking water** can exceed 2,500 solid parts per million. U.S. v. City of Asbury Park, 340 F.Supp. 555, 560 (D.N.J.1972).

wave (wāv) a uniformly advancing disturbance in which the parts moved undergo a double oscillation; any wave-like pattern.

waves, alpha brain waves in the electroencephalogram which have a frequency of 8 to 13 per second; they are typical of the normal person awake and in a quiet resting state, and occur principally in the occipital region.

waves, beta brain waves in the electroencephalogram, which have a frequency of 18 to 30 per second; they are typical during periods of intense activity of the nervous system, and occur principally in the parietal and frontal regions.

waves, brain the fluctuations of electrical potential in the brain, as recorded by electroencephalography. See also *alpha, beta, delta,* and *theta waves.* Some observers distinguish three types of waves: (1) *trains,* which correspond to alpha waves; (2) *spindles,* short series with a frequency of 14 per second; and (3) *random waves,* irregular changes of potential with no fixed frequency which appear at the beginning of sleep.

The degree to which she is aware of her condition is in dispute. Her EEG's show primarily low level delta and theta activity—those **brainwaves** which are abnormal in an adult who is awake. However, a few alpha rhythms are present in some tests. Alpha rhythms are normal in an adult who is awake but who has closed eyes and is inattentive to surroundings. Green v. U.S., 530 F.Supp. 633, 645 (E.D.Wis.1982).

Dr. Walters also spoke of abnormality in the frontal leads (abnormal **brain waves**). People v. Williams, 99 Cal.Rptr. 103, 117 (Ct.App.Cal.1971).

waves, delta 1. waves in the electroencephalogram which have a frequency below 3½ per second; they are typical in deep sleep, in infancy, and in serious brain disorders. 2. an early QRS vector in the electrocardiogram characteristic of Wolff-Parkinson-White syndrome.

wave, T the second major deflection of the normal electrocardiogram, reflecting the potential variations occurring with repolarization of the ventricles. See also *electrocardiogram.*

It also appears from Dr. Cannon's deposition that an electrocardiogram was performed on Thurmond after the August 13, 1970, occurrence and such showed "non-specific **T-wave** changes". Dr. Cannon stated that the significance of that finding was that it was probably indicative of injury current which is caused by an injury of some kind. Hartford Acc. & Indem. Co. v. Thurmond, 527 S.W.2d 180, 186 (Ct.Civ.App.Tex.1975).

wave, theta brain waves in the electroencephalogram which have a frequency of 4 to 7 per second; they occur mainly in children but also in adults during periods of emotional stress.

Webb bolt See *pin.*

wedge

... "wedged" the cast (spread the cast open at the front of the left leg at the point of "circularization"), corrected the alignment and repaired the cast. DeWitt v. Brown, 669 F.2d 516, 518 (8th Cir. 1982).

wedging

Dr. Roger McBride, an osteopathic physician, took x-rays of the dorsal and lumbar spine which revealed "mild anterior **wedging** of the 4th and 5th lumbar" and a "mild anterior osteofied formation" on the lower vertebra. Simonson v. Schweiker, 699 F.2d 426, 428 (8th Cir. 1983).

Werdnig-Hoffman disease See *paralysis, Werdnig-Hoffman.*

wet brain See *edema, brain.*

wheal (hwēl, wēl) a smooth, slightly elevated area on the body surface, which is redder or paler than the surrounding skin; it is often attended with severe itching, and is usually evanescent, changing its size or shape, or disappearing, within a few hours. It is the typical lesion of urticaria, the dermal evidence of allergy, and in sensitive persons may be provoked by mechanical irritation of the skin.

At trial, defendant testified that a **wheal** could not be likened to a mosquito bite, but rather to a bite which had been scratched. He admitted that at his deposition he had defined a **wheal** as a raised, whitish area, rising above the surface of the skin like a large mosquito bite. Defendant also testified that he administered the test to plaintiff, and some minutes later he observed a minute elevation caused by the needle and an area of redness about the size of a dime. He considered the reaction to be negative, and had the remainder of the antitoxin administered to plaintiff. Anderson v. Martzke, 266 N.E.2d 137, 139 (App.Ct.Ill.1970).

whiplash See *injury, whiplash.*

whitehead See *milium.*

wine

§ 564.01 defines "**wine**" to mean all beverages made from fresh fruits, berries, or grapes, either by natural fermentation or by natural fermentation with brandy added.... Castlewood International Corp. v. Wynne, 305 So.2d 773, 776 (Fla.1974).

wine, fortified

Also, "**fortified wine**" is termed to mean all wines containing more than fourteen per cent of alcohol by weight. [§ 564.01.] Castlewood International Corp. v. Wynne, 305 So.2d 773, 776 (Fla.1974).

wire (wīr) a long, slender, flexible structure of metal, used in surgery and dentistry.

wire, arch wire applied around the dental arch; used in correcting irregularities of the teeth.

Dr. Bernard Bender, a dentist, examined Deep and ordered and installed for him orthodontic appliances. They consisted of eight bands and two **arch wires**. Four teeth in his upper jaw and four in his lower were banded; the **arch wires** were attached to and passed through loops in these bands. There were no small wires, which actually supply the tension to the appliances, available in Dr. Bender's office at that time. U.S. v. Deep, 497 F.2d 1316, 1318, 1320 (9th Cir. 1974).

wire, Kifa guide

The action arises from a medical procedure on Helena Frerker, one of the plaintiffs, in which a **Kifa guide wire** was inserted into her body. When the guide wire was removed it was found that the tip had broken off. A subsequent surgical operation to remove the tip was necessary....

... He testified that with the size of the needle used on Mrs. Frerker's body he only used **Kifa guide wire** and testified to the conclusion that the tip of the **Kifa guide wire** broke off and lodged in her vein.

Each guide wire is delivered in a separate envelope. The envelope shows the make of the wire. Dr. Koehler testified that he didn't have anything to do with removing the wires from the package or the marking of the cloths before they were sterilized. He testified that the wire is removed from the original package before it is sterilized and that it is wrapped in a towel, labeled, and then put in a sterilizer, and thereafter sent up to his department for use. He testified that they can keep them sterile a couple of days so that they always have a supply of them on hand. The guide wires are left in the sterilized cloth until the last minute before use. Picker X-Ray Corp. v. Frerker, 405 F.2d 916–19 (8th Cir. 1969).

wire, Kirschner a steel wire for skeletal transfixion of fractured bones and for obtaining skeletal traction in fractures; it is inserted through the soft parts and the bone and held tight in a clamp.

Mr. Harrelson required immediate surgery to clean his hand and repair the fractures described. This included a skin graft, the implanting of **K-wires** inside these tube like bones, and the application of a splint, all requiring three to four hours. Harrelson v. Louisiana Pacific Corp., 434 So.2d 479, 482 (Ct.App. La.1983).

"... dislocation of the index metacarpal ... [surgically] reduced by [inserting] a pin [and] **K-wire**...." Anderson v. Safeco Ins. Co., 396 So.2d 322, 324 (Ct.App.La.1981).

Briefly, this surgical procedure fuses the joints by removing bone and stabilizes the toes with a **Kirschner Wire** which goes through the center of the bone and connects the phalanges. Brown v. St. John's Hospital, 367 N.E.2d 155 (App.Ct.Ill. 1977).

wisdom tooth (impacted), extraction of See *extraction, tooth.* (Raza case)

withdrawal (with-draw'al) abstention from drugs to which one is habituated or addicted. Also, denoting the symptoms occasioned by such withdrawal. See also *symptoms, withdrawal.*

The following account,[49] based upon observation and experimentation with addicts under medical supervision, describes in detail the process of opiate **withdrawal**: [[49] A. Light, E. Torrance, W. Karr, E. Fry & W. Wolff, Opium Addiction 10–11 (1929).]

"As the time approaches for what would have been the addict's next administration of the drug, ... he begins to move about in a rather aimless way, failing to remain in one position

long.... With this restlessness, yawning soon appears, which becomes more and more violent.... He may then lie on the floor close to the radiator, trying to keep warm. Even here he is not contented, and he either resumes his pacing about, or again throws himself onto the bed wrapping himself under heavy blankets. At the same time he complains bitterly of suffering with cold and then hot flashes, but mostly chills. He breathes like a person who is cold, in short, jerky, powerful respirations. His skin shows the characteristic pilomotor activity well known ... as 'cold turkey.'... Coincident with this feeling of chilliness, he complains of being unable to breathe through his nose. Nasal secretion is excessive.

"Often at the end of this period the addict may become extremely drowsy and unable to keep his eyes open. If he falls asleep, which is often the case, he falls into a deep slumber well known as the 'yen' sleep.... The sleep may last for as long as eight or twelve hours. On awakening he is more restless than ever. Lacrimation, yawning, sneezing, and chilliness are extreme. A feeling of suffocation at the back of the throat is frequently mentioned. Usually at this stage, the addict complains of cramps, locating them most frequently in the abdomen.... Vomiting and diarrhea appear. He may vomit large quantities of bile-stained fluid. Perspiration is excessive.... Muscular twitchings are commonly present; they may occur anywhere, but are most violent in the lower extremities.... He refuses all food and water, and frequently sleep is unknown from this point. It is at this stage that he may one minute beg for a 'shot' and the next minute threaten physical violence.... He will beat his head against the wall, or throw himself violently on the floor.... Seminal emission in the male and orgasm in the female frequently occur."

The acute symptoms of **withdrawal** generally reach a peak between 48 and 72 hours after the last dose and subside gradually during the following week. Distress may continue for weeks, however, and it may be months before physiological stability is achieved. But as terrifying as the **withdrawal** experience may seem, it does not end the addiction, for the underlying psychological dependence of the addict remains uncured. As a result, "[a]ddiction to heroin and to other opiates, once established, has the characteristics of a chronic relapsing disease." [Footnotes omitted.] U.S. v. Moore, 486 F.2d 1139, 1232–33 (D.C.Cir.1973).

Early **withdrawal** symptoms include lacrimation, nasal discharge, yawning and perspiration. Later, dilated pupils, loss of appetite, gooseflesh, (thus, the expression "cold turkey") restlessness and increased irritability and tremor will appear. At its peak intensity, the syndrome includes high irritability, insomnia, violent yawning, severe sneezing and lacrimation. Nausea and vomiting are common, as are intestinal spasms and diarrhea. Increased heart beat and elevated blood pressure, as well as muscular spasms, abdominal cramps and pains in the bones and muscles of the back are common. Death due to cardiovascular collapse can result from **withdrawal**. The symptoms are caused by the drug-induced alterations at the cellular level, most prominently in the central nervous system. People v. McCabe, 275 N.E.2d 407, 410 (Ill.1971).

womb See *uterus.*

work, light

Light work is essentially defined as lifting up to 20 pounds and carrying up to 10 pounds, with considerable walking and standing. Alexander v. Weinberger, 536 F.2d 779, 783 (8th Cir. 1976).

work, sedentary See *sedentary*.

Sedentary work is essentially defined as tasks performed in a generally seated position with occasional walking and standing and lifting up to ten pounds. Alexander v. Weinberger, 536 F.2d 779, 783 (8th Cir. 1976).

wound (wōōnd) [L. *vulnus*] a bodily injury caused by physical means, with disruption of the normal continuity of structures.

... with "wound" being defined as a breaking of the skin. Zorn v. Aetna Life Insurance Co., 260 F.Supp. 730, 733 (E.D. Tex.1965).

wounding

This reading of "bodily injury" defeats as well plaintiff's suggested interpretation of "wounding" ("blessure") as comprehending "hurt", emotional or physical. Read in context, as it must be, "wounding" is limited by the subsequent phrase "or any other bodily injury" and in its ordinary meaning does not, we believe, connote more than solely physical wounds. Only by abandoning the ordinary and natural meaning of the language of article 17, could we arrive at a reading of the terms "wounding" or "bodily injury" which might comprehend purely mental suffering without physical manifestations. Such an abandonment would little serve the interests of promoting uniformity in the treaty's interpretation and application—interests which we must observe and further. Rosman v. Trans World Airlines, Inc., 314 N.E.2d 848, 855 (N.Y.1974).

wrinkle

[A] wrinkle is a topographical configuration of skin resembling a furrow or valley and surrounding ridges. As the film contracts, its adhesive qualities cause the valley of the wrinkle to be drawn up to the level of the normal surface of the skin. When, after a period of hours, the amount of unevaporated liquid in the film is reduced below the quantity required to maintain surface tension, the film breaks down into its component solids and liquid, permitting the skin to return to a wrinkled configuration. U.S. v. Article of Drug, etc., 331 F.Supp. 912, 915 (D.Md.1971).

wrist (rist) the region of the articulation between the forearm and hand, which is made up of eight bones. See also *ossa carpi* and names of specific bones. The term is also applied to the corresponding part in the thoracic limb of quadrupeds. Called also *carpus*. See also *deformity, silver fork* (Lieder case).

The fracture of the wrist was treated with closed reduction using temporary pins in the thumb and elbow incorporated into the plastic cast....

... It is possible she may suffer from degenerative traumatic arthritis in the future and may require surgical fusion or joint replacement of her right wrist, in which she has diminished mobility and use. Stewart v. West Bradford Corp., 453 N.Y.S.2d 255–6 (3d Dep't 1982).

Dr. Gleason said the hand "... was crushed so severely that we could not restore the [wrist] joint to a normal function," and noted Mrs. Anderson's "... predisposition to pain and arthritis." Anderson v. Safeco Ins. Co., 396 So.2d 322, 324 (Ct.App.La.1981).

His injury was initially diagnosed as a fracture of the right distal radius (wrist). State Compensation Fund v. Bannister, 476 P.2d 875–6 (Ct.App.Ariz.1970).

wrongful birth See *birth, wrongful*.

wrongful life See *life, wrongful*.

wrongful pregnancy See *pregnancy, wrongful*.

X

xanthochromia (zan″tho-kro′me-ah) [*xantho-* + Gr. *chrō-ma* color + *-ia*] any yellowish discoloration, as of the skin or of the spinal fluid.

In this case xanthrochromia [sic] a yellow tinge to the cerebral spinal fluid—was also detected. Xanthrochromia is a characteristic finding in HSE cases because it is evidence of the presence of red cells in the CSF which have released hemoglobin. This hemoglobin is then converted to bilirubin, giving the fluid a characteristic yellow tinge. Xanthrochromia was specifically noted in the December 2 spinal tap, suggesting earlier hemorrhage. Stich v. U.S., 565 F.Supp. 1096, 1118 (D.N.J.1983).

Xanthomonas (zan″tho-mo′nas) a genus of microorganisms of the family Pseudomonadaceae, suborder Pseudomonadineae, order Pseudomonadales, occurring as monotrichous cells producing a yellow pigment, the type species being *X. hyacin′thi*. Most of the 60 described species, as well as many of the 14 species provisionally included, are pathogenic for plants.

The method for combating infections in plants growing in soil infested with pathogenic micro-organisms including bacterial spot (xanthomonas vesicatoria) of peppers and tomatoes. Nationwide Chemical Corp. v. Wright, 458 F.Supp. 828, 831 (M.D.Fla.1976).

xanthopsia (zan-thop′se-ah) [*xantho-* + Gr. *opsis* vision + *-ia*] a form of chromatopsia in which objects looked at appear yellow.

xanthrochromia See *xanthochromia*.

xenograft (zen′o-graft) a graft of tissue transplanted between animals of different species. Called also *heterograft, heterologous graft*, and *heteroplastic graft*.

xiphoid (zif′oid) [*xipho-* + Gr. *eidos* form] the xiphoid process (processus xiphoideus [NA]). See also *processus xiphoideus*.

x-ray (eks′ra) roentgen ray. See also *radiation*; and *rays, X*.

x-ray reader See under *ray, roentgen reader*.

xylem (zi′lem) [Gr. *xylon* wood] the tissue in woody plants which conducts water and dissolved salts up from the roots, characterized by the presence of tracheids. In bulk it forms wood. Cf. *phloem.*

xylene (zi′lēn) dimethylbenzene; an antiseptic hydrocarbon, $C_6H_4(CH_3)_2$, from methyl alcohol or coal tar; used in microscopy as a solvent and clarifier.

Tank No. 17 contains traces of **xylene**, a chemical with a flash point of 80 degrees fahrenheit. Tank No. 18 contains xylene mixed with PCB in the level of 6,700 ppm. (See Defendants' Exhibit A). Anne Arundel Cty. v. Governor, 413 A.2d 281, 285 (Ct.Spec.App.Md.1980).

Xylocaine (zi′lo-kān) trademark for preparations of lidocaine. See also *lidocaine.*

xylose (zi′lōs) a pentose, $CH_2OH(CHOH)_3CHO$, in a pyranose form, occurring in mucopolysaccharides of con-nective tissue and sometimes in the urine (see *xylosuria*); also obtained from vegetable gums, beechwood, and jute. The official preparation is used as a diagnostic aid in determining intestinal function. See also *xylulose.*

xylose isomerase See *isomerase, xylose.*

xylosuria (zi′lo-su′re-ah) presence of xylose in the urine. A form of alimentary pentosuria reportedly occurring after ingestion of certain fruits, e.g., cherries, plums, and grapes; the identity of the urinary pentose(s) has not been crisply established. It is to be distinguished from essential pentosuria, which results from a genetic defect.

xylulose (zi′lu-lōs) a pentose sugar, $CH_2OH(CHOH)_2CO \cdot CH_2OH$, occurring in two forms: L-xylulose, one of the few L sugars found in nature and sometimes excreted in the urine and D-xylulose. See also *pentosuria.*

Y

yohimbine (yo-him′bēn) an alkaloid, $C_{21}H_{26}N_2O_3$, from *Corynanthe johimbe* K. Schum. (Rubiaceae) and from *Rauwolfia serpentina* L. Benth. (Apocynaceae). It possesses adrenergic blocking properties and is used in arteriosclerosis and angina pectoris, and formerly as a local anesthetic and mydriatic and for its purported aphrodisiac properties.

Yohimbine is an alkaloid used to stimulate the para-sympathetic nervous system in animals and allegedly capable of such use in man. . . .

. . . In fact, he found that the anxiety-producing effect of the ingredient **yohimbine** would only complicate the problems of treating impotence of a psychogenic origin. . . .

. . . Dr. Steinberger was of the opinion that **yohimbine** had some use as an hallucinogen, but he was not aware of any evidence of use of **yohimbine** or nux vomica for the treatment of impotence or neurasthenia. U.S. v. 1,048,000 Capsules More or Less, 347 F.Supp. 768, 772, 774 (S.D.Tex.1972).

Z

zagoma See *arcus zygomaticus.*

zeolite (ze′o-līt) a hydrated double silicate with ion-exchange properties; probably the active constituent in permutit.

Furthermore, knowledge of the properties of crystalline **zeolites** and examples of the wide varieties of utility are demonstrated in the opinions of this court [4] and in the following definition from The Condensed Chemical Dictionary, 759–60 (6th ed. 1961): [Q.V.]. . . . [[4] Parker v. Frilette, 462 F.2d 544, 59 CCPA 1311 (1972); In re Mattox, 461 F.2d 826, 59 CCPA 1272 (1972); In re Michel, 461 F.2d 1384, 59 CCPA 1088 (1972); In re Kamm, 452 F.2d 1052, 59 CCPA 753 (1972); In re Frilette, 436 F.2d 496, 58 CCPA 799 (1971); Frilette v. Kimberlin, 412 F.2d 1390, 56 CCPA 1242 (1969); and In re Gladrow, 406 F.2d 1376, 56 CCPA 927 (1969).]

One key property of known crystalline **zeolites** is their ability to undergo ion exchange. As noted above, appellant does not challenge the ion exchange tests showing that zeolites within the count undergo ion exchange with calcium, potassium, and ammonium ions. (The record shows a resulting mole percent exchange with the sodium ions of the sodium monoxide in the **zeolite** structure of 66%, 92%, and 91%, respectively.)

The adsorptive properties of known crystalline **zeolites** are also significant, particularly the reversible loss and gain of water. Again, appellant has not challenged the experiments on a sample of the **zeolites** of the count showing the reversible loss and gain of water. A similarity of adsorptive properties between the **zeolites** of the count and known crystalline **zeolites** is further demonstrated by appellees' test data showing adsorption of oxygen, carbon dioxide, nitrogen, isobutane, and n-butane. Ciric v. Flanigen, 511 F.2d 1182, 1184, 1186 (U.S.Ct.Cust. & Pat.App.1975).

Zephiran (zef′ĭ-ran) trademark for preparations of benzalkonium. See also *benzalkonium chloride.*

zephiran chloride See *benzalkonium chloride.*

Zollinger-Ellison syndrome See *syndrome, Zollinger-Ellison.*

Z-plasty (ze-plas′te) a plastic operation for the relaxation of contractures, in which a Z-shaped incision is made, the middle bar of the Z being over the contracted scar, and the triangular flaps rotated so that their apices cross the line of contracture.

"... a **Z-plasty** was done there which is a surgical procedure where we change the direction of a straight scar into a zig-zag scar." Hukill v. U.S. Fidelity and Guaranty Co., 386 So.2d 172, 174 (Ct.App.La.1980).

zwitterion (tsvit'er-i"on) a dipolar ion, i.e., an ion that has both positive and negative regions of charge; amino acids, for example, occur as zwitterions in neutral solution, and the pH value at which the zwitterion state is at a maximum is the isoelectric point.

Appellant defines **zwitterionic** compounds as:

... organic compounds which in solution and over a relatively broad pH range contain on the same molecule both a positively charged substituent group (cation) and a negatively charged substituent group (anion). . . .

... a **zwitterionic** detergent is a detergent which under the ordinary conditions of use in a built detergent system bears both a positively charged (cationic) and negatively charged portion (anionic) on the hydrophobic portion of the molecule giving the detergent molecule an "inner salt" (ring) structure. Application of Smith, 398 F.2d 849–50 (U.S.Ct.Cust. & Pat. App.1968).

zwitterionic See *zwitterion*.

zygoma (zi-go'mah) [Gr. *zygōma* bolt or bar] a term sometimes applied to os zygomaticum.

Bilateral fracture of **zygoma** (cheek bones). Titus v. Smith, 330 F.Supp. 1192–3 (E.D.Pa.1971).

Dr. Gordon Davenport, a plastic surgeon, examined the plaintiff and found the left cheekbone (**Zygoma**) had been knocked out of place in the accident and that surgery was required. He also found nerve damage, causing numbness to the left side of the face. Although immediate surgery could not be performed because of the chest injury, Dr. Davenport later put the cheekbone back into place by an operation which consisted of drilling various holes through the cheekbone and inserting wires to keep the fracture in place. Later x-rays showed it had healed in a "good" position. Krause v. Milwaukee Mutual Ins. Co., 172 N.W.2d 181, 191 (Wis.1969).

zygomatic arch See *arcus, zygomaticus*.

zygote (zi'gōt) [Gr. *zygōtos* yoked together] the cell resulting from union of a male and a female gamete, until it divides; the fertilized ovum. More precisely, the cell after synapsis at the completion of fertilization until first cleavage. Also, used loosely to refer to the fertilized ovum and derivatives for an indefinite period, extending even to birth. Cf. *conceptus*. Cited in YWCA of Princeton, N.J. v. Kugler, 342 F.Supp. 1048, 1083 (D.N.J.1972).